THE WRITERS DIRECTORY

THIRTIETH EDITION

THE WRITERS DIRECTORY

THIRTIETH EDITION
VOLUME 4: M-Q

Editor
Lisa Kumar

ST. JAMES PRESS
A part of Gale, Cengage Learning

Detroit • New York • San Francisco • New Haven, Conn • Waterville, Maine • London

Writers Directory, 30th Edition

Project Editor: Lisa Kumar

Editorial Support Services: Natasha Mikheyeva

Manufacturing: Rita Wimberley

For product information and technology assistance, contact us at
Gale Customer Support, 1-800-877-4253.
For permission to use material from this text or product,
submit all requests online at **www.cengage.com/permissions.**
Further permissions questions can be emailed to
permissionrequest@cengage.com

While every effort has been made to ensure the reliability of the information presented in this publication, Gale, a part of Cengage Learning, does not guarantee the accuracy of the data contained herein. Gale accepts no payment for listing; and inclusion in the publication of any organization, agency, institution, publication, service, or individual does not imply endorsement of the editors or publisher. Errors brought to the attention of the publisher and verified to the satisfaction of the publisher will be corrected in future editions.

EDITORIAL DATA PRIVACY POLICY: Does this product contain information about you as an individual? If so, for more information about our editorial data privacy policies, please see our Privacy Statement at www.gale.cengage.com.

Gale
27500 Drake Rd.
Farmington Hills, MI, 48331-3535

ISBN-13: 978-1-4144-8712-0 (set)
ISBN-13: 978-1-4144-8713-7 (vol. 1)
ISBN-13: 978-1-4144-8714-4 (vol. 2)
ISBN-13: 978-1-4144-9901-7 (vol. 3)
ISBN-13: 978-1-4144-9902-4 (vol. 4)
ISBN-13: 978-1-4144-9903-1 (vol. 5)
ISBN-13: 978-1-4144-9904-8 (vol. 6)

ISBN-10: 1-4144-8712-6 (set)
ISBN-10: 1-4144-8713-4 (vol. 1)
ISBN-10: 1-4144-8714-2 (vol. 2)
ISBN-10: 1-4144-9901-9 (vol. 3)
ISBN-10: 1-4144-9902-7 (vol. 4)
ISBN-10: 1-4144-9903-5 (vol. 5)
ISBN-10: 1-4144-9904-3 (vol. 6)

ISSN 0084-2699

Printed in the United States of America
1 2 3 4 5 16 15 14 13 12

FD156

Contents

Preface

The Writers Directory is the newly revised and expanded thirtieth edition of this acclaimed reference work. It lists 26,615 writers—writing under 29,776 names—from all countries of the world who have had at least one work published in English.

The Directory is published in 6 individual volumes, with content divided as follows:

Volume 1: Lists entries from A-C
Volume 2: Lists entries from D-G
Volume 3: Lists entries from H-L
Volume 4: Lists entries from M-Q
Volume 5: Lists entries from R-U
Volume 6: Lists entries from V-Z, Obituaries, Index to Writing Categories, and Country of Citizenship Index

The *Directory* lists approximately 26,526 living writers of fiction and non-fiction who have published at least one full-length work in English. Listees run the gamut from the best-known, best selling authors of fiction and the most prominent non-fiction writers to those writers just embarking on their literary careers. The thirtieth edition includes nearly 1,000 writers whose listings have not appeared in a previous edition of *The Writers Directory.*

The **Obituaries** Section contains the entries for approximately 89 writers whose listings have appeared in previous editions of *The Writers Directory* and whose passing was made known to us in preparing this edition.

Compilation Methods

Selection of writers to appear in *The Writers Directory* is based primarily on reference value. Biographical and career information is researched for each writer, then a copy of the entry is sent to the writer for his or her approval and updates. By this process, the editors can assure comprehensive, current information. At the same time, entries in the previous edition were rigorously reviewed with an eye toward their current research value. As a result, some writers' entries have been retired to make way for those of new writers.

How to Read a Citation

Entries in *The Writers Directory* contain some or all of the following elements (please note that this is a sample entry-for demonstration purposes only):

▮ 1 ▮ WILLIAMS, Mae. ▮ 2 ▮ (Allison May Williams) ▮ 3 ▮ Also writes as William Allison. ▮ 4 ▮ American (born Malta), ▮ 5 ▮ b. 1945. ▮ 6 ▮ **Genres:** Novels, Biography. ▮ 7 ▮ **Career:** Freelance writer. ▮ 8 ▮ **Publications:** Paris, L'amour, 1972; (ed.) Running through the Weeds, 1982; (as William Allison) Louis, My Love (biography), 1987; The Waves at My Back, 1997. ▮ 9 ▮ **Address:** 27500 Drake Rd., Farmington Hills, MI 48331U.S.A. ▮ 10 ▮ **Online address:** maewil@aol.com ▮ 11 ▮ Died 1997.

▮ 1 ▮ Name of writer with fuller name information in parentheses

▮ 2 ▮ Full name of writer if different from writing name or pseudonyms but not used for writing

▮ 3 ▮ Pseudonym information

▮ 4 ▮ Nationality—if birthplace is different from nationality, it will follow the nationality in parentheses

▮ 5 ▮ Birth year

▮ 6 ▮ Genres—corresponds to **Index to Writing Categories**

▮ 7 ▮ Brief career information

▮ 8 ▮ Publications: title, year of publication, pseudonym if used, special awards

▮ 9 ▮ Address

▮ 10 ▮ Online address and/or web site

▮ 11 ▮ Death notation and year (in **Obituaries** Section only)

Cross references appear in the following form:

To main entry in main section: **ALLISON, William**. See **WILLIAMS, Mae**.

From main section to main entry in **Obituaries** section: **WILLIAMS, Mae.** See Obituaries.

From pseudonym in main section to main entry in **Obituaries** section: **ALLISON, William**. See **WILLIAMS, Mae** in the Obituaries.

Writers (and cross references) are listed alphabetically by surname which are sorted letter-by-letter. In cases where surnames are identical, writers are listed first by surname, then by given and middle names, and finally by suffixes such as Jr., Sr., II, or III. Surnames beginning with a prefix (such as Du, Mac, or Van), however spaced, are listed alphabetically under the first letter of the prefix and treated as if there were no space. Other compound surnames, hyphenated names, and names with apostrophes are alphabetized as if there were no space or punctuation. Surnames beginning with Saint or St. appear after names beginning with Sains and before names beginning with Sainu.

Entries in the **Obituaries** Section follow the same style as those in the main entries with the addition of the notation *Died* and the death year (if known) at the end of the entry.

Features

The Writers Directory contains many features to enhance its usefulness:

Boldface Rubrics allow quick and easy scanning for specifics on genre, career, publication, and mailing and online addresses.

The Obituaries Section lists the entries for those writers whose listing appeared in previous editions of The Writers Directory and whose passing was made known to us in preparing this edition. Cross references have been provided in the main body of the Directory to those deceased writers.

Indexing

The Writers Directory includes two indexes. In the **Index to Writing Categories**, one can locate writers by the type of works they write. New categories are added to The Writers Directory as needed to reflect new topics of interest and to define a writer's body of work more accurately. The **Country of Citizenship Index** lists writers by their country of citizenship as provided by the writer. Users are advised that one writer with multiple citizenship may appear under one country grouping (e.g., Canada-England) while another with the same citizenships may appear under a different grouping (e.g., England-Canada) depending on how the writer submitted the information.

The **Index to Writing Categories and Country of Citizenship Index** can be found in Volume 6 of the Directory following the **Obituaries** Section.

Also Available in Electronic Formats

Licensing. *The Writers Directory* is available for licensing. The complete database is provided in a fielded format and is deliverable on such media as disk or CD-ROM. For more information, contact Gale's Business Development Group at 1-800-877-GALE, or visit us on our web site at gale. cengage. com.

Online. *The Writers Directory* is accessible as part of Gale's Biography in Context database, as well as through the Gale Biographies database (File GALBIO) through Lexis-Nexis. For more information on Biography in Context, visit us on our web site at gale.cengage.com. For more information on Gale Biographies, contact LexisNexis, P.O. Box 933, Dayton, OH 45401-0933; phone (937) 865-6800; toll- free: 800-227-4908.

Suggestions Welcome

Comments and suggestions from users of *The Writers Directory* on any aspect of the product as well as suggestions for writers to be included in a future edition are cordially invited. Please write:

The Editor

The Writers Directory

St. James Press

Gale, a part of Cengage Learning

27500 Drake Rd.

Farmington Hills, Michigan 48331-3535.

Entry in *The Writers Directory* is at the discretion of the editor.

Abbreviations Used In The Writers Directory

A

AB	Alberta
ABC	American Broadcasting Company
ACT	Australian Capital Territory
AK	Alaska
AL	Alabama
Apt.	Apartment
AR	Arkansas
Assn.	Association
Assoc.	Associate
Asst.	Assistant
Ave.	Avenue
AZ	Arizona

B

b.	born
BBC	British Broadcasting Corporation
BC	British Columbia
Beds.	Bedfordshire
Berks.	Berkshire
Bldg.	Building
Blvd.	Boulevard
Brig.	Brigadier
Bros.	Brothers
Bucks.	Buckinghamshire

C

CA	California
Cambs.	Cambridgeshire
Can.	Canada
Capt.	Captain
CBC	Canadian Broadcasting Company
CBS	Columbia Broadcasting System (US)
CIA	Central Intelligence Agency (US)
CO; co.	Colorado; Company; County
Co-ed.	Co-editor
Co-trans.	Co-translator
Col.	Colonel
Contrib.	Contributor; Contributing
Corp.	Corporation
CPA	Certified Public Accountant
Cres.	Crescent
CT; Ct.	Connecticut; Court

D

DC	District of Columbia
DE	Delaware
Dept.	Department
Derbys.	Derbyshire
Dir.	Director
Div.	Division
Dr.	Doctor; Drive

E

E.	East
Ed.	Editor; Edition
Exec.	Executive

F

FBI	Federal Bureau of Investigation (US)
FL	Florida
Ft.	Fort

G

GA	Georgia
Gen.	General
Glam.	Glamorgan
Glos.	Glouchestershire
Gov.	Governor
Govt.	Government

H

Hants.	Hampshire
HE	His Eminence; His/Her Excellency
Herts.	Hertfordshire
HI	Hawaii
HM	His/Her Majesty
HMS	His/Her Majesty's Ship; His/Her Majesty's Service
Hon.	Honorable; Honorary

I

IA	Iowa
ID	Idaho
IL	Illinois
IN	Indiana
Inc.	Incorporated
Inst.	Institute
Intl.	International

J

Jr.	Junior

K

KS	Kansas
KY	Kentucky

L

LA	Louisiana
Lab.	Laboratory
Lancs.	Lancashire
Leics.	Leicestershire
LI	Long Island
Lincs.	Lincolnshire
Lt.	Lieutenant
Ltd.	Limited

M

MA	Massachusetts
Mag.	Magazine
Maj.	Major
MB	Manitoba
MD	Maryland
ME	Maine
Mgr.	Manager
MI	Michigan
Middx.	Middlesex
MN	Minnesota
MO	Missouri
MP	Member of Parliament
MT; Mt.	Montana; Mount, Mountain

N

N.	North
NASA	National Aeronautics and Space Administration
NATO	North Atlantic Treaty Organization
NB	New Brunswick
NBC	National Broadcasting System (US)
NC	North Carolina
NE	North East
NF	Newfoundland
NH	New Hampshire
NJ	New Jersey
NL	Newfoundland and Labrador
NM	New Mexico
No.	Number

Northants. Northamptonshire
Notts. Nottinghamshire
nr. Near
NS Nova Scotia
NSW New South Wales
NT Northern Territory (Australia); Northwest Territories (Canada)
NU Nunavut
NV Nevada
NW North West
NWT Northwest Territories
NY New York
NYC New York City

O

OH Ohio
OK Oklahoma
ON Ontario
OR Oregon
Orch. Orchestra
Org. Organization
Oxon. Oxfordshire

P

PA Pennsylvania
PE, PEI Prince Edward Island
PEN Poets, Playwrights, Essayists, Editors, Novelists
Pl. Place
PO Post Office
Pres. President
Prof. Professor
Prog. Program
Publrs. Publishers
Publs. Publications

Q

QC Quebec
QLD Queensland

R

Rd. Road
Rep. Representative
Rev. ed. Revised edition
RI Rhode Island
RR Rural Route
Rte. Route

S

S. South
SA South Australia
Salop. Shropshire
SC South Carolina
Sch. School
SD South Dakota
SE South East
Sec Secretary
SK Saskatchewan
Soc. Society
Sq. Square
Sr. Senior
St. Saint; Street
Staffs. Staffordshire
Ste. Suite
Supt. Superintendent
SW South West

T

Tas. Tasmania
Terr. Terrace
TN Tennessee
Trans. Translator; Translation
Treas. Treasurer
TX Texas

U

UK United Kingdom
UN United Nations
Unesco United Nations Educational, Scientific and Cultural Organization
Unicef United Nations Children's Emergency Fund
Univ. University
US; USA United States, United States of America
USS United States Ship; United States Service
USSR Union of Soviet Socialist Republics
UT Utah

V

VA Virginia
VIC Victoria
Vol(s). Volume(s)
VT Vermont

W

W. West
WA Washington; Western Australia
Warks. Warwicks; Warwickshire
WHO World Health Organization
WI Wisconsin
Wilts. Wiltshire
Worcs. Worcestershire
WV West Virginia
WY Wyoming

Y

YM-YWHA Young Men's-Young Women's Hebrew Association
YMCA Young Men's Christian Association
Yorks. Yorkshire
YWCA Young Women's Christian Association
YT Yukon Territory

M

MA, Liping. American/Chinese (born China), b. 1951. **Genres:** Education. **Career:** Chunqian Elementary School, teacher, 1970-76, principal, 1974-76; Yongfeng County Bureau of Education, school superintendent, 1978-80; Shanghai Research Institute for Higher Education, assistant research professor, 1983-88; Michigan State University, National Center for Research on Teacher Education, research assistant, 1989-91, research consultant, 1991-96; Stanford University, Pedagogy and Substance Project, research assistant, 1991-92, Center for Research on the Context of Teaching, research assistant, 1993-95; University of California, School of Education, McDonnell postdoctoral fellow, 1996-98; Carnegie Foundation for the Advancement of Teaching, consultant, 1998-99. Writer. **Publications:** (Ed.) Research on Teachers (in Chinese), 1990; Knowing and Teaching Elementary Mathematics: Teachers' Understanding of Fundamental Mathematics in China and the United States, 1999; (with C. Kessel) Knowing Mathematics: Intervention Program, 2001. Contributor to journals. **Address:** Carnegie Foundation for the Advancement, of Teaching, 51 Vista Ln., Stanford, CA 94305, U.S.A. **Online address:** ma@carnegiefoundation.org

MAAS, Sharon. Guyanese (born Guyana), b. 1951. **Genres:** Novels. **Career:** Guyana Graphic, trainee reporter, journalist; Sunday Chronicle, journalist. Writer. **Publications:** NOVELS: Of Marriageable Age, 1999; Peacocks Dancing, 2001; The Speech of Angels, 2002. Works appear in anthologies. Contributor to journals. **Address:** c/o Author Mail, HarperCollins Publishers, 77-85 Fulham Palace Rd., Hammersmith, London, GL W6 8JB, England. **Online address:** sharon@sharonmaas.com

MAASS, Peter. American (born United States), b. 1960. **Genres:** International Relations/Current Affairs, Young Adult Non-fiction. **Career:** Wall Street Journal, copy editor; New York Times, writer, 1985; International Herald Tribune, writer, 1985; Washington Post, foreign correspondent-Seoul, 1987-, foreign correspondent-Eastern Europe and the Balkans, 1990-, foreign correspondent-Bosnia, 1992-93, staff writer. **Publications:** NONFICTION: Love Thy Neighbor: A Story of War, 1996; Crude World: The Violent Twilight of Oil, 2009. Contributor to periodicals. **Address:** U.S.A. **Online address:** peter@petermaass.com

MAAZEL, Fiona. American (born United States), b. 1975?. **Genres:** Novels. **Career:** Paris Review, managing editor. **Publications:** Last Last Chance (novel), 2008. Contributor to periodicals. **Address:** U.S.A. **Online address:** stuff@lastlastchance.com

MABBETT, Ian William. Australian/British (born England), b. 1939. **Genres:** Area Studies, History, Theology/Religion, Politics/Government, Social Sciences, Bibliography, Humanities. **Career:** Thanet Technical College, assistant lecturer in English, 1963-64; Monash University, lecturer, 1965-72, senior lecturer, 1972-83, reader in history, 1983-; Australian National University, Humanities Research Centre, visiting professor; Princeton University, Institute for Advanced Study, reader in history; Aichi Bunkyo University, Indian & Buddhist Studies, professor, 2000-02, professor emeritus, 2002-. Writer. **Publications:** A Short History of India, 1968; Truth, Myth and Politics in Ancient India, 1971; Displaced Intellectuals in Twentieth Century China, 1975; (ed.) Early Thai History: A Select Bibliography, 1978; Modern China: The Mirage of Modernity, 1985; (ed.) Patterns of Kingship and Authority in Traditional Asia, 1985; Kings and Emperors of Asia, 1985; (with D. Chandler) The Khmers, 1995; (contrib.) Angkor, 2002; (with G. Bailey) The Sociology of Early Buddhism, 2003; Writing History Essays: A Student's Guide, 2006; (ed. with J.B. Bapat) The Iconic Female: Goddesses of India, Nepal and Tibet, 2008. **Address:** School of Historical Studies, Monash University, 6th Fl., Menzies Bldg., Clayton, VI 3800, Australia. **Online address:** ian.mabbett@arts.monash.edu.au

MABEE, Carleton. American/Chinese (born China), b. 1914. **Genres:** History, Biography, Transportation, Biography, Autobiography/Memoirs. **Career:** Olivet College, tutor, 1947-49; Clarkson College of Technology, assistant professor to professor, 1949-61; Keio University, professor of American civilization, 1953-54; Delta College, University Center, director of social studies division, 1961-64; Rose Polytechnic Institute (now Rose-Hulman Institute of Technology), Department of Humanities and Social Sciences, chair, 1964-65; State University of New York College, professor of history, 1965-80, professor emeritus, 1980-. Historian and writer. **Publications:** The American Leonardo: A Life of Samuel F.B. Morse, 1943, rev. ed., 2000; The Seaway Story, 1961; Black Freedom: The Nonviolent Abolitionists from 1830 Through the Civil War, 1970; Black Education in New York State: From Colonial to Modern Times, 1979; (ed. with James A. Fletcher) A Quaker Speaks from the Black Experience: The Life and Selected Writings of Barrington Dunbar, 1979; (with S.M. Newhouse) Sojourner Truth: Slave, Prophet, Legend, 1993; Listen to The Whistle: An Anecdotal History of the Wallkill Valley Railroad in Ulster and Orange Counties, New York, 1995; Bridging the Hudson: The Poughkeepsie Railroad Bridge and Its Connecting Rail Lines: A Many-faceted History, 2001; Promised Land: Father Divine's Interracial Communities in Ulster County, New York, 2008. **Address:** 2121 Rte. 44-55, Gardiner, NY 12525, U.S.A. **Online address:** carletonmabee@juno.com

MABEY, Richard Thomas. British (born England), b. 1941. **Genres:** Education, Environmental Sciences/Ecology, Natural History, Sciences. **Career:** Dacorum College of Further Education, lecturer in liberal studies, 1963-65; Penguin Books Educational Division, senior editor, 1966-73; freelance writer and broadcaster, 1974-; St. Catherine's College, visiting associate, 1982-86; Common Ground, director, 1988-. **Publications:** Class, 1967; Behind the Scene, 1968; The Pop Process, 1969; Children in Primary School: The Learning Experience, 1972; Food, 1972; Food for Free, 1972, new ed., 2007; The Unofficial Countryside, 1973; The Pollution Handbook, 1974; The Roadside Wildlife Book, 1974; Street Flowers, 1976; Plants With a Purpose: A Guide to the Everyday Uses of Wild Plants, 1977; In Search of Food: Traditional Eating & Drinking in Britain, 1978; Plantcraft: A Guide to the Everyday Use of Wild Plants, 1978; The Flowering of Britain, 1980; The Common Ground: A Place for Nature in Britain's Future? 1980; Back to the Roots, 1983; Oak & Company, 1983; Cold Comforts, 1983; In a Green Shade: Essays on Landscape, 1970-1983, 1983; The Frampton Flora, 1986, rev. ed., 2007; Gilbert White: A Biography of the Author of The Natural History of Selborne, 1986; Flowers of Kew: 350 Years of Flower Paintings from the Royal Botanic Gardens, 1989; Home Country, 1990; Victorian Flora: The Flower Paintings of Caroline May, 1991; A Nature Journal, 1991; Whistling in the Dark: In Pursuit of the Nightingale, 1993; Wildwood: In Search of Britain's Ancient Forests, 1993; Landlocked, 1994; Flora Britannica Book of Spring Flowers, 1998; Flora Britannica Book of Wild Herbs, 1998; Collected Writings, 1999; Nature

Cure, 2005; (with M. Cocker) Birds Britannica, 2005; Bugs Britannica, 2010; Weeds, 2011. EDITOR: (and intro.) The Natural History of Selborne, 1977; (and intro.) Landscape with Figures: An Anthology of Prose, 1983; Second Nature, 1984; Journals of Gilbert White, 1986; (and intro.) Gardener's Labyrinth, 1987; New Age Herbalist: How to Use Herbs for Healing, Nutrition, Body Care and Relaxation, 1988; The Oxford Book of Nature Writing, 1995; Flora Britannica, 1996; Nature Cure, 2005. **Address:** Sheil Land Associates Ltd., 52 Doughty St., London, GL WC1N 2LS, England.

MAC. (Melissa A. Calderone). American (born United States), b. 1977?. **Genres:** Children's Fiction, Children's Non-fiction. **Career:** Freelance writer. **Publications:** Anna Smudge: Professional Shrink, 2008. Contributor to periodicals. **Address:** U.S.A. **Online address:** mac@whoismrwho.com

MAC, Carrie. Canadian (born Canada), b. 1976?. **Genres:** Novels, Young Adult Fiction, Social Work, Adult Non-fiction. **Career:** Writer. **Publications:** OTHERS: The Beckoners, 2004; Charmed, 2004; Crush, 2006; Pain & Wastings, 2008; Jacked, 2009, The Gryphon Project, 2009. THE TRISKELIA SERIES: The Droughtlanders, 2006; Retribution, 2007; Storm, 2008. Contributor to periodicals. **Address:** Orca Book Publishers, PO Box 5626, Sta. B, Victoria, BC V8R 6S4, Canada. **Online address:** carrie@carriemac.com

MACADAMS, William. American (born United States), b. 1944. **Genres:** Film, Trivia/Facts, Biography, Autobiography/Memoirs. **Career:** Writer. **Publications:** Ben Hecht: The Man Behind the Legend, 1990; Ben Hecht: A Biography, 1995; (with P. Nelson) 701 Toughest Movie Trivia Questions of All Time, 1995; The Life & Death of a Book, 2003; Thrills, forthcoming. Contributor of articles to periodicals. **Address:** c/o Doris Ashbrook, Ashbrook & Statzer Literary Agents, 625 S 8th St., Richmond, IN 47374, U.S.A. **Online address:** wmcadams@infocom.com

MACAINSH, Noel. *See* **MACAINSH, Noel Leslie.**

MACAINSH, Noel Leslie. (Noel Macainsh). Italian/Australian (born Australia), b. 1926. **Genres:** Poetry, Art/Art History, Literary Criticism And History. **Career:** Australia Post, communications engineer, 1948-60; James Cook University of North Queensland, reader-in-English, 1969-89, senior lecturer in English, 1975-; Goethe Society of Townsville, president, 1972-. Writer. **Publications:** Clifton Pugh, 1962; Eight by Eight, 1963; Nietzsche in Australia: A Literary Inquiry into a Nationalistic Ideology, 1975; The Penguin Book of Australian Verse, 1976; The Pathos of Distance, 1992. Work appears in anthologies. Contributor to magazines. **Address:** Department of English, James Cook University of North Queensland, Townsville, QL 4810, Australia.

MACALAN, Peter. *See* **ELLIS, Peter Berresford.**

MACALISTER, Katie. (Katie Maxwell). American (born United States), b. 1964. **Genres:** Romance/Historical, Young Adult Fiction, Horror, Paranormal, Novels. **Career:** Writer. **Publications:** LIGHT DRAGONS: Love in the Time of Dragons, 2010; The Unbearable Lightness of Dragons, 2011; Sparks Fly, 2012. SILVER DRAGONS: Playing With Fire, 2008; Up in Smoke, 2008; Me and My Shadow, 2009. AISLING GREY: You Slay Me, 2004; Fire Me Up, 2005; Light My Fire, 2006; Holy Smokes, 2007; Deaths's Excellent Vacation, 2010. PARANORMALS ROMANCE: A Girl's Guide to Vampires, 2003; Sex and the Single Vampire, 2004; Sex, Lies and Vampires, 2005; Even Vampires Get the Blues, 2006; Just One Sip, 2006; The Last of the Red Hot Vampires, 2007; Ain't Myth-behaving: Two Novellas, 2007; Zen and the Art of Vampires, 2008; Crouching Vampire, Hidden Fang, 2009; (co-author) My Zombie Valentine, 2009; Cupid Cars, 2010; Confessions of a Vampire's Girlfriend, 2010; In the Company of Vampires, 2010; Much Ado About Vampires, 2011; A Tale of Two Vampires, 2012. STEAMPUNK ROMANCE: Steamed, 2010. CONTEMPORARIES ROMANCE: Improper English, 2003; Bird of Paradise in the Heat Wave Anthology, 2003; Men in Kilts, 2003; The Corset Diaries, 2004; EyeLiner of Gods, 2004; Hard Day's Knight, 2005; Blow Me Down, 2005; Suffragette in the City, 2011; It's All Greek to Me, 2011. HISTORICAL ROMANCE: Noble Intentions, 2002; Noble Destiny, 2003; The Trouble With Harry, 2004. AS KATIE MAXWELL: The Year My Life Went Down the Loo, 2003; They Wear What Under Their Kilts, 2004; What's French For Ew?, 2004; Taming of the Dru, 2004; Life, Love, and the Pursuit of Hotties, 2005; Got Fangs, 2005; Circus of the Darned, 2006. OTHER: Ghost of a Chance, 2008. **Address:** c/o Michelle Grajkowski, Three Seas Literary Agency, PO Box 8571, Madison, WI 53708, U.S.A. **Online address:** katie@katiemacalister.com

MACARTHUR, John R. American (born United States), b. 1956. **Genres:** Politics/Government, Social Sciences. **Career:** Wall Street Journal, reporter, 1977; Washington Star, reporter, 1978; Bergen Record, reporter, 1978-79; Chicago Sun-Times, reporter, 1979-82; United Press Intl., assistant foreign editor, 1982; Harper's Magazine Foundation, president and publisher, 1983-; Globe & Mail, columnist; Providence Journal, columnist; Article 19 International Centre on Censorship, co-founder, 1986. **Publications:** Second Front: Censorship and Propaganda in the Gulf War, 1992, 3rd ed., 2004; The Selling of "Free Trade": NAFTA, Washington, and the Subversion of American Democracy, 2000; (contrib.) Architecture of Authority, 2007; You Can't Be President: The Outrageous Barriers to Democracy in America, 2008. Contributor of articles to newspapers and magazines. **Address:** Harper's Magazine, 666 Broadway, 11th Fl., New York, NY 10012, U.S.A.

MACAULAY, Ronald K. S. Scottish (born Scotland), b. 1927. **Genres:** Language/Linguistics. **Career:** British Institute, lecturer, 1955-60; British Council, lecturer, 1960-64; International Summer School for English Language Teachers, visiting lecturer, 1961; ICANA Summer School for English Teachers, visiting lecturer, 1962, 1964; Pitzer College, assistant professor, 1965-67, associate professor, 1967-73, professor, 1973-99, dean of faculty, 1980-86, vice president for academic affairs, 1984-86, emeritus professor of linguistics, 1999-; University of California, visiting instructor, 1968. Writer. **Publications:** Language, Social Class, and Education: A Glasgow Study, 1977; (co-author) Spanish-English Bilingual Education in the United States, 1977; Generally Speaking: How Children Learn Language, 1980; Locating Dialect in Discourse: The Language of Honest Men and Bonnie Lassies in Ayr, 1991; The Social Art: Language and Its Uses, 1994, 2nd ed., 2006; Standards and Variation in Urban Speech: Examples from Lowland Scots, 1997; Talk that Counts: Age, Gender, and Social Class Differences in Discourse, 2005; Quantitative Methods in Sociolinguistics, 2009; Seven Ways of Looking at Language, 2011. EDITOR: (with R.P. Stockwell) Linguistic Change and Generative Theory, 1972; (with R. Stockwell) Cambio lingüístico y teorîa generativa, 1977; (with D. Brenneis) The Matrix of Language: Contemporary Linguistic Anthropology, 1996; Sociolinguistic Variation, 2004. Contributor to periodicals. **Address:** Department of Linguistics, Pitzer College, Broad Hall 127, 1050 N Mills Ave., Claremont, CA 91711, U.S.A. **Online address:** ronald_macaulay@pitzer.edu

MACAULAY, Teresa DiNola. *See* **MACAULAY, Teresa (E.).**

MACAULAY, Teresa (E.). Also writes as Teresa DiNola Macaulay. American (born United States), b. 1947. **Genres:** Children's Fiction, Novellas/Short Stories, Poetry, Literary Criticism And History. **Career:** Writer. **Publications:** Non-Violent Stories and Poems for Children, 1996. Work appear in anthologies. **Address:** 614 Clymer Ave., Morrisville, PA 19067, U.S.A. **Online address:** teresa@nonviolentbooks.com

MACCARTHY, Fiona. British (born England), b. 1940. **Genres:** Design, Biography. **Career:** The Guardian, feature writer, 1963-69; Evening Standard, feature writer, 1969-72; freelance writer, 1972-; Times, reviewer of books, 1981-92; Observer, reviewer of books, 1992-; Royal College of Art, senior fellow; Order of the British Empire, officer. **Publications:** All Things Bright and Beautiful: Design in Britian, 1830 to today, 1972; A History of British Design: 1830 to Today, 1979; The Simple Life: C.R. Ashbee in the Cotswolds, 1981; The British Tradition in Design: From 1880, 1981; British Design since 1880: A Visual History, 1982; (intro.) The Omega Workshops, 1913-1919: Decorative Arts of Bloomsbury, 1984; (intro. with P. Nuttgens) Eye for Industry: Royal Designers for Industry, 1936-1986, 1986; Eric Gill: A Lover's Quest for Art and God, 1989; William Morris: A Life for Our Time, 1995; Telling the Tale of Topsy: William Morris's Biographers: The 1993 Kelmscott Lecture, 1996; Stanley Spencer: An English Vision, 1997; (intro.) The Wood Engravings of David Gentleman, 2000; Byron: Life and Legend, 2002; Last Curtsey: The End of the Debutantes, 2006; The Last Pre-Raphaelite, 2011. **Address:** David Mellor Design Ltd., The Round Bldg., Hathersage, Sheffield, SY S32 1BA, England.

MACCLANCY, Jeremy. British (born England), b. 1953. **Genres:** Anthropology/Ethnology, History, Politics/Government. **Career:** Oxford University, tutor, 1986-; Oxford Brookes University, lecturer, 1991-93, School of Social Sciences and Law, professor of anthropology; Leicester University, visiting lecturer, 1992-. Writer. **Publications:** To Kill a Bird with Two Stones: A History of Vannatu, 1981; Consuming Culture: Why You Eat What You Eat, 1992; The Decline of Carlism: History and Anthropology in Northern

Spain, 1939-1989, 1994; (ed.) Sport, Identity and Ethnicity, 1996; (ed. with C. McDonaugh) Popularizing Anthropology, 1996; (ed.) Contesting Art: Art, Politics and Identity in the Modern World, 1997; Decline of Carlism, 2000; (ed.) Exotic No More: Anthropology on the Front Lines, 2002; (ed. with H. Macbeth) Researching Food Habits: Methods and Problems, 2003; Expressing Identities in the Basque Arena, 2007; (ed. with J. Henry and H. Macbeth) Consuming the Inedible: Neglected Dimensions of Food Choice, 2007; (ed. with S. Leoné) Imaging the Basques: Foreign Views on the Basque Country, 2008; (ed. with X. Ezeizabarrena) Sub-State Entities and Co-Sovereignty within the EU, 2008; (ed. with A. Fuentes) Centralizing Fieldwork: Critical Perspectives From Primatology, Biological And Social Anthropology, 2010. Contributor to journals. **Address:** Department of Anthropology and Geography, School of Social Sciences and Law, Oxford Brookes University, Headington Campus, Gipsy Ln., Oxford, OX OX3 0BP, England. **Online address:** jmacclancy@brookes.ac.uk

MACCOBY, Michael. American (born United States), b. 1933. **Genres:** Administration/Management, Anthropology/Ethnology, Psychology, History. **Career:** University of Chicago, instructor in social science, 1955-56; Harvard University, secretary of committee on educational policy, 1956-60, teaching fellow, 1957-60, John F. Kennedy School of Government, Program on Technology, Public Policy and Human Development, director, 1978-90, Center for Science and International Affairs, adjunct research fellow, 1990-93; Universidad Nacional Autonoma de Mexico, visiting professor of social psychology, 1960-61; U.S. Public Health Service, research fellow, 1960-63; psychotherapist in private practice, 1962-88; Mexican Institute of Psychoanalysis, professor of clinical psychology, 1964-66, faculty, 1970-75; Cornell University, visiting professor, 1966; University of California, lecturer in psychology, 1967-68; Washington School of Psychiatry, faculty, 1975-87; The Maccoby Group, president, 1989-. Consultant and writer. **Publications:** Social Character and Social Change in Mexico and the United States, 1970; (with E. Fromm) Social Character in a Mexican Village, 1970; The Gamesman: The New Corporate Leaders, 1976; (with R.M. Kanter and M. Darrow) Perspectives on Leadership, 1979; The Leader: A New Face for American Management, 1981; Why Work: Leading the New Generation, 1988, 2nd ed., 1995; (ed.) Sweden at the Edge: Lessons for American and Swedish Managers, 1991; (ed. with M. Cortina) A Prophetic Analyst, 1996; The Productive Narcissist, the Promise and Peril of Visionary Leadership, 2003; (with C. Heckscher, R. Ramirez and P. Tixier) Agents of Change, 2003; Narcissistic Leaders: Who Succeeds and Who Fails, 2007; Leaders We Need: And What Makes Us Follow, 2007. Contributor to books. **Address:** The Maccoby Group, 4825 Linnean Ave. NW, Washington, DC 20008, U.S.A. **Online address:** michael@maccoby.com

MACCOTTER, Paul. Irish/British (born England), b. 1958. **Genres:** History, Politics/Government, Economics, Humanities. **Career:** Genealogy Consultancy, owner and consultant. Historian, genealogist and writer. **Publications:** (Ed. with K. Nicholls) The Pipe Roll of Cloyne, 1996; Colmán of Cloyne: A Study, 2004; Medieval Ireland: Territorial, Political, and Economic Divisions, 2008. Contributor to journals and periodicals. **Address:** Four Courts Press Ltd., 7 Malpas St., Dublin, DU 8, Ireland.

MACCREADY, Robin Merrow. American (born United States) **Genres:** Novels, Mystery/Crime/Suspense. **Career:** Novelist and educator. **Publications:** Buried, 2006. **Address:** c/o Wendy Schmalz, Wendy Schmalz Agency, PO Box 831, Hudson, NY 12534-0831, U.S.A. **Online address:** robin@robinmerrowmaccready.com

MACDONALD, Amy. (Del Tremens). American (born United States), b. 1951. **Genres:** Children's Fiction, Writing/Journalism. **Career:** Proposition Theatre, publicity director, 1975-76; Harvard Post, editor, 1976-82; Highwire Magazine, senior editor, 1983-84; Cambridge University Press, copy editor, 1984-88; Harvard University, writing instructor, 1988; Stonecoast Writers Conference, instructor, 1991-93; University of Maine, adjunct professor, 1995; John F. Kennedy Center for Performing Arts, teaching artist, 1998-; Teaching Artist Journal, associate editor. **Publications:** BOARD BOOKS: (as Del Tremens) A Very Young Housewife, 1979; Let's Make a Noise, 1991; Let's Play, 1991; Let's Try, 1991; Let's Do It, 1991; Let's Pretend, 1993; Let's Go, 1993. PICTURE BOOKS: Little Beaver and the Echo, 1990; Rachel Fister's Blister, 1990; Cousin Ruth's Tooth, 1996; The Spider Who Created the World, 1996; Quentin Fenton Herter III, 2002; Please, Malese!, 2002. CHAPTER BOOKS: No More Nice, 1996; No More Nasty, 2001; Too Much Flapdoodle, 2008. ANTHOLOGIES: The New Walker Bear, 1991; The Walker Baby Bear, 1995; The Walker Book of Animal Tales, 1996; Stories and Fun for the Very Young, 1998; Bedtime: First Words, Rhymes and Actions, 1999; Books From Maine: A Raising Readers Collection, 2008. **Address:** John F. Kennedy Center for Performing Arts, 2700 F St. NW, Washington, DC 20566, U.S.A. **Online address:** amymac@maine.rr.com

MACDONALD, Anne Louise. Canadian (born Canada), b. 1955?. **Genres:** Novels, Picture/Board Books, Illustrations, Animals/Pets. **Career:** Author. **Publications:** PICTURE BOOKS: Nanny-Mac's Cat, 1995; The Memory Stone, 1998; The Dog Wizard, 1999. JUVENILE NOVELS: The Ghost Horse of Meadow Green, 2005; Seeing Red, 2009. SELF-ILLUSTRATED: My Natural Horses, 2010. **Address:** NS , Canada. **Online address:** annelouise@hugahorsefarm.com

MACDONALD, Ann-Marie. (Susan Macdonald). Canadian/German (born Germany), b. 1958. **Genres:** Novels, Plays/Screenplays, Adult Non-fiction. **Career:** Writer. **Publications:** NOVELS: Fall on Your Knees, 1996; The Way the Crow Flies, 2003; Belle Moral: A Natural History, 2005. PLAYS: Goodnight Desdemona, (Good Morning Juliet), 1990; The Arab's Mouth, 1995; The Attic, the Pearls and Three Fine Girls, 2000. **Address:** c/o Tulin Valeri, 869 Davenport Rd., Toronto, ON M6G 2B4, Canada.

MACDONALD, Copthorne. Canadian/American (born United States), b. 1936. **Genres:** Environmental Sciences/Ecology, Philosophy, Technology, Social Commentary, E-books. **Career:** International Telegraph & Sign, engineer, 1958-59; Westinghouse Electric Corp., project manager of visual communication and display, 1959-65; Ball Brothers Research Corp., Department of Electronic Design, manager, 1965-68; Vidcom Electronics, director of research, 1968-70; CQ: Radio Amateur's Journal, columnist, 1972-75; New Directions Radio (network), founder, 1972; Mother Earth News, columnist, 1973-83, associate editor; Prince Edward Island Energy Conservation Program, coordinator, 1980-84; The Wisdom Page Website, founder, editor and webmaster, 1995-; writer, 1985-. **Publications:** Energy Technologies: Options for Prince Edward Island, 1990; (with D. Kessler) Energy Technologies Workbook, 1990; Toward Wisdom: Finding Our Way to Inner Peace, Love & Happiness, 1993; Getting a Life: Strategies for Joyful and Effective Living, 1995; Bridging the Strait: The Story of the Confederation Bridge Project, 1997; Matters of Consequence: Creating a Meaningful Life and a World That Works, 2004. **Address:** PO Box 2941, Charlottetown, PE C1A 8C5, Canada. **Online address:** cop@copmacdonald.com

MACDONALD, Douglas J. American (born United States), b. 1947. **Genres:** Politics/Government, Third World, International Relations/Current Affairs, History. **Career:** Oglethorpe University, assistant professor of political science, 1982-83; Wellesley College, visiting assistant professor of political science, 1986-87; Harvard University, Center for International Affairs, associate research fellow, 1986-87; Colgate University, assistant professor of political science, 1987-93, associate professor of political science, 1994-, International Relations Program, director, 1993-95; Nobel Institute, senior research fellow, 1998; U.S. Army War College, Strategic Studies Institute, National Security Affairs, visiting research professor, 2005-07; U.S. Navy Fleet RSEP, Naval Postgraduate School, consultant and lecturer, 2007-09. Writer. **Publications:** To Save the Philippine Republic: The Decision to Reform the Government of the Philippines, 1949-1953 (monograph), 1989; Adventures in Chaos: American Intervention for Reform in the Third World, 1992; The New Totalitarians: Social Identities and Radical Islamist Political Grand Strategy, 2007. Works appear in anthologies. Contributor to periodicals. **Address:** Department of Political Science, Colgate University, 119 Persson Hall, 13 Oak Dr., Hamilton, NY 13346, U.S.A. **Online address:** dmacdonald@colgate.edu

MACDONALD, Hope. American (born United States), b. 1928. **Genres:** Theology/Religion, Literary Criticism And History, Social Sciences. **Career:** Writer and public speaker. **Publications:** Discovering How to Pray, 1976; Discovering the Joy of Obedience, 1980; When Angels Appear, 1982; The Flip Side of Liberation: A Call to Traditional Values, 1990, reprinted as Traditional Values for Today's New Women, 1992; Letters from Heaven, 1998. Contributor to magazines. **Address:** 109 SW Normandy Rd., Seattle, WA 98166, U.S.A.

MACDONALD, James D. Also writes as Victor Appleton, Martin DelRio, Robyn Tallis, Douglas Morgan, Nicholas Adams. American (born United States), b. 1954?. **Genres:** Science Fiction/Fantasy, Novels, Young Adult Non-fiction, Mystery/Crime/Suspense, Horror, Young Adult Fiction. **Career:**

Journalist. **Publications:** WITH D. DOYLE: Timecrime Inc., 1991; Night of the Living Rat, 1992; Knight's Wyrd, 1992; Groogleman, 1996; Requiem for Boone, 2000; The Apocalypse Door, 2002, 2nd ed., 2009; (with D. Doyle) Land of Mist and Snow, 2006; Lincoln's Sword, 2010. CIRCLE OF MAGIC SERIES: The Prisoners of Bell Castle, 1989; School of Wizardry, 1990; Tournament and Tower, 1990; City by the Sea, 1990; The Prince's Players, 1990; The High King's Daughter, 1990. MAGE WORLDS SERIES: The Price of the Stars, 1992; Starpilot's Grave, 1993; By Honor Betray'd, 1994; The Gathering Flame, 1995; The Long Hunt, 1996; (with J. Doyle) The Stars Asunder, 1999; (with J. Doyle) A Working of Stars, 2002. BAD BLOOD SERIES: Bad Blood, 1993; Hunters' Moon, 1994; Judgment Night, 1995. NOVELS AS ROBYN TALLIS: Night of Ghosts and Lightning, 1989; Zero-Sum Games, 1989. NOVELS AS NICHOLAS ADAMS: Pep Rally, 1991; Santa Claws, 1991; Vampire's Kiss, 1994. HORROR HISH SERIES AS NICHOLAS ADAMS: Mr. Popularity, 1990; Resolved: You're Dead, 1990; Heartbreaker, 1990; New Kid on the Block, 1991; Hard Rock, 1991; Sudden Death, 1991; Pep Rally, 1991; Final Curtain, 1991; Blood Game, 1993; Deadly Secret, 1993; Voice of Evil, 1993; You're Dead, 1993. NIGHTMARES AS NICHOLAS ADAMS: Horrorscope, 1991; I.O.U., 1991. PLANET BUILDERS SERIES AS ROBYN TALLIS: Mountain of Stolen Dreams, 1988; Night of Ghosts and Lightning, 1988; Rebel From Alphorion, 1988; Horrorvid, 1988; Visions from the Sea, 1989; Zero-Sum Games, 1989; Night of Two New Moons, 1989; Children of the Storm, 1989; Giants of Elenna, 1989; Fire in the Sky, 1989. NOVELS AS VICTOR APPLETON: Monster Machine, 1991; Aquatech Warriors, 1991. NOVELS AS MARTIN DELRIO: Mortal Kombat, 1995; Spider-Man Super-Thriller: Midnight Justice, 1996; Spider-Man Super-Thriller: Global War, 1996; Prince Valiant, 1997; A Silence in the Heavens, 2003; Truth and Shadows, 2003; Service for the Dead, 2003; (with N. Case) Searching for the Loch Ness Monster, 2011. OTHER AS DOUGLAS MORGAN: Tiger Cruise, 2001; (ed.) What Do You Do With A Drunken Sailor: Unexpurgated Sea Chanties, 2002. JUVENILE NONFICTION AS MARTIN DELRIO: The Loch Ness Monster, 2002. AS NICHOLAS ADAMS: (with S. Pepper) Firearms & Fortifications, 1986; (ed.) The Architectural Drawings of Antonio da Sangallo the Younger and his Circle, 1994; (ed. with B.G. Smith) History and the Texture of Modern Life, 2001; Skidmore, Owings & Merrill, 2007. Works appear in anthologies. **Address:** Scovil Galen Ghosh Literary Agency Inc., 276 5th Ave., Ste. 708, New York, NY 10001, U.S.A. **Online address:** doylemacdonald@sff.net

MACDONALD, Jerry (Paul). American (born United States), b. 1953. **Genres:** Natural History, Animals/Pets, Social Sciences. **Career:** New Mexico Museum of Natural History, paleontological field researcher, 1985-87; University of Virginia, instructor in sociology, 1987; Paleozoic Trackways project, director, 1987-90; U.S. Department of the Interior, adjunct research scientist for Bureau of Land Management, 1987-94; New Mexico State University, teacher of sociology, through 1989; Smithsonian Institution, Natural History Museum, research collaborator in paleobiology, through 1989; New Mexico Museum of Natural History, adjunct curator of paleontology, through 1991. Writer. **Publications:** Earth's First Steps: Tracking Life before the Dinosaurs, 1994; Behold the Behemoth: The Quest that Solved the Mystery of the Dinosaurs of Job, 1999. Contributor to scientific bulletins, periodicals and journals. **Address:** PO Box 2864, Las Cruces, NM 88004, U.S.A. **Online address:** oldearth@zianet.com

MACDONALD, Kyle. Canadian/American (born United States), b. 1979. **Genres:** Business/Trade/Industry, Economics, Humor/Satire. **Career:** Writer. **Publications:** One Red Paperclip: Or How an Ordinary Man Achieved His Dreams with the Help of a Simple Office Supply, 2007. Contributor to periodicals. **Address:** Three Rivers Press, 1745 Broadway, 13th Fl., New York, NY 10019-4368, U.S.A. **Online address:** oneredpaperclip@gmail.com

MAC DONALD, Laura M. Canadian/American (born United States), b. 1963?. **Genres:** Adult Non-fiction, Novels, History. **Career:** Radio commentator and writer. **Publications:** (With A. Pugsley) Kay Darling, 1994; (co-author) Open Book: Little Thoughts from a Big Head, 1999; (with G. Eckler) Bull!: 144 Stupid Statements from the Market's Fallen Prophets, 2003; Curse of the Narrows: The Halifax Disaster of 1917, 2005. **Address:** c/o Peter Miller, Walker and Co., 104 5th Ave., 7th Fl., New York, NY 10011, U.S.A. **Online address:** lmm@laurammacdonald.com

MACDONALD, Lyn. British (born England) **Genres:** History, Novels, Military/Defense/Arms Control, Travel/Exploration. **Career:** British Broadcasting Co., radio producer. Writer and historian. **Publications:** Bordeaux and Aquitaine, 1976; How To Be A Supercook And Work As Well, 1976; They Called It Passchendaele: The Story of the Third Battle of Ypres and of the Men Who Fought in It, 1978; The Roses of No Man's Land, 1980; Somme, 1983; 1914, 1987; 1914-1918: Voices and Images of the Great War, 1990; 1915, The Death of Innocence, 1993; To the Last Man: Spring 1918, 1999. **Address:** Viking Publicity, 375 Hudson St., New York, NY 10014, U.S.A.

MACDONALD, Malcolm. *See* **ROSS-MACDONALD, Malcolm (John).**

MACDONALD, Marianne. British/Canadian (born Canada), b. 1934. **Genres:** Novels, Children's Fiction, Plays/Screenplays, Literary Criticism And History. **Career:** University of Toronto, lecturer in English, 1960-62; University of Keele, lecturer in American studies, 1964-69; Middlesex Polytechnic, principal lecturer in English, 1972-86; writer, 1986-. **Publications:** CHILDREN'S BOOKS: Black Bass Rock, 1952; Smugglers Cove, 1955; The Treasure of Ur, 1958; The Pirate Queen, 1991; The Eighty-Nine Pennies of Emma Jones, 1992; The Witch Repair, 1995; Dragon for Sale, 1998. NOVELS: Death's Autograph, 1996; Ghost Walk, 1997; Smoke Screen, 1999; Road Kill, 2000; Blood Lies, 2001; Die Once, 2002; Three Monkeys, 2005; Faking It, 2006. OTHER: Ezra Pound: Purpose/Form/Meaning, 1983. EDITOR: The State of Literary Theory Today, 1982; Ezra Pound and History, 1985. **Address:** David Higham Associates, 5-8 Lower Johns St., Golden Sq., London, GL W1F 9HA, England. **Online address:** marianne@marianne-macdonald.co.uk

MACDONALD, Marylee. American (born United States), b. 1945. **Genres:** Novellas/Short Stories, Architecture, Engineering, Homes/Gardens, How-to Books. **Career:** University of Illinois, Building Research Council, managing editor, 1986-92; APT Bulletin, editor, 1986-91; Journal of Light Construction, editor, 1988-90; River Oak Review, non-fiction editor. **Publications:** (With S. Konzo) The Quiet Indoor Revolution, 1992; Unpaid Labor: A Novel; The Vermillion Sea: A Novel. Contributor to River Oak Review. **Address:** 2211 Central St., Ste. 15, Evanston, IL 60201, U.S.A. **Online address:** maryleemac@mindspring.com

MACDONALD, Michael Patrick. American/Irish (born Ireland), b. 1966. **Genres:** History, Biography, Autobiography/Memoirs. **Career:** South Boston Vigil Group, founder; Boston Gun-buyback Program, co-founder; Northeastern University, author-in-residence. Lecturer and screenwriter. **Publications:** All Souls: A Family Story from Southie, 1999; Easter Rising: An Irish American Coming Up from Under, 2006. **Address:** c/o Author Mail, Beacon Press, 25 Beacon St., Boston, MA 02108-2824, U.S.A. **Online address:** mpatrickmacdonald@mac.com

MACDONALD, Norman Malcolm. *See* Obituaries.

MACDONALD, Patricia J. American (born United States), b. 1949?. **Genres:** Novels. **Career:** Writer. **Publications:** The Unforgiven, 1981; Stranger in the House, 1983; Little Sister, 1986; No Way Home, 1989; Mothers Day, 1994; Secret Admirer, 1995; Lost Innocents, 1998; Not Guilty, 2002; Suspicious Origin, 2003; The Girl Next Door, 2004; Married to a Stranger, 2006; Stolen in the Night, 2007; From Cradle to Grave, 2010; Cast into Doubt, 2011. **Address:** Atria Books, 1230 Ave. of the Americas, New York, NY 10020, U.S.A.

MACDONALD, Sam A. American (born United States), b. 1972. **Genres:** Autobiography/Memoirs, Young Adult Non-fiction. **Career:** University of Pittsburgh, instructor in creative writing. Writer. **Publications:** The Agony of an American Wilderness: Loggers, Environmentalists, and the Struggle for Control of a Forgotten Forest, 2005; The Urban Hermit: A Memoir, 2008. **Address:** Department of English, University of Pittsburgh, 526 Cathedral of Learning, 4200 5th Ave., Pittsburgh, PA 15260-0001, U.S.A.

MACDONALD, Sarah. Australian (born Australia), b. 1966?. **Genres:** Communications/Media, Biography, Autobiography/Memoirs, Travel/Exploration. **Career:** Australian Broadcasting Corp., radio and television journalist and program host, 1990-99, 2002-; 2BL, local and state political reporter and correspondent; ABC Radio, political reporter; 702 ABC, staff. **Publications:** Holy Cow!: An Indian Adventure, 2002. **Address:** Australian Broadcasting Corp., ABC Ultimo Ctr., 700 Harris St., Ultimo, PO Box 9994, Sydney, NW 2001, Australia. **Online address:** sarahmac@triplej.abc.net.au

MACDONALD, Sharman. British/Scottish (born Scotland), b. 1951.

Genres: Novels, Plays/Screenplays, Women's Studies And Issues, Young Adult Fiction. **Career:** 7:84 Theatre Co., actress; Royal Court Theatre, actress; Thames Television, actress; Bush Theatre, writer-in-residence, 1984-85. Dramatist. **Publications:** When I Was a Girl I Used to Scream and Shout, 1985; The Beast, 1986; Night Night, 1988; When I Was a Girl I Used to Scream and Shout, 1988; All Things Nice, 1991; Shades, 1992; The Winter Guest, 1993; Shaman MacDonald: Plays, 1995; The Winter Guest: Screenplay, 1997; Sea Urchins, 1998; After Juliet, 1999; The Girl with Red Hair, 2003; Broken Hallelujah, 2005. **Address:** 211 Piccadilly, London, GL W1J 9HF, England.

MACDONALD, Stuart. Canadian (born Canada), b. 1957?. **Genres:** History. **Career:** Ordained Presbyterian minister, 1985; University of Toronto, Knox College, associate professor, 1996-, professor of Church and Society, Centre for Clergy Care & Congregational Health, senior researcher. Writer. **Publications:** The History and Philosophy of Art Education, 1970; Back to Lochaber: A Search for Historical Events, Travels, Tales and Customs, 1994; The Witches of Fife: Witch-Hunting in a Scottish Shire, 1560-1710, 2002. **Address:** Knox College, University of Toronto, 59 St. Georges St., Toronto, ON M5S 2E6, Canada. **Online address:** s.macdonald@utoronto.ca

MACDONALD, Susan. *See* **MACDONALD, Ann-Marie.**

MACDONNELL, Kathleen. Canadian/American (born United States), b. 1947?. **Genres:** Social Sciences, Young Adult Fiction. **Career:** CBC Radio, contributor; Young People's Theater, playwright-in-residence, 1999-2000; editor. **Publications:** Not an Easy Choice: A Feminist Re-examines Abortion, 1984, rev. ed., 2002; (ed. with M. Valverde) The Healthsharing Book: Resources for Canadian Women, 1985; (ed.) Adverse Effects: Women and the Pharmaceutical Industry, 1986; Ezzie's Emerald, 1990; The Nordlings, 1999; Kid Culture: Children and Adults and Popular Culture, 2000; Honey, We Lost the Kids: Re-thinking Childhood in the Multimedia Age, 2001, rev. ed., 2005; The Shining World, 2003; Putting on a Show: Theater for Young People, 2004; 1212: Year of the Journey, 2006; The Songweavers, 2008; Emily Included, forthcoming. **Address:** Second Story Press, 20 Maud St., Ste. 401, Toronto, ON M5V 2M5, Canada. **Online address:** kathleen@kathleenmcdonnell.com

MACDONOGH, Giles. British (born England), b. 1955. **Genres:** Food And Wine, History. **Career:** University of Paris II, charge de travaux diriges for legal English, 1982-83; Schiller International University, lecturer in history, 1983-84; freelance writer and translator, 1985-; University of Gastronomic Arts and Sciences, lecturer, 2006. **Publications:** A Palate in Revolution: Grimod de La Reyniere and the Almanach des Gourmands, 1987; A Good German: Adam von Trott zu Solz, 1990; Brillat-Savarin: The Judge and His Stomach, 1992; The Wine and Food of Austria, 1992; Syrah, Grenache and Mourvedre, Viking Guides to Grape Varieties, 1992; Prussia: The Perversion of an Idea, 1994; The Wines of Austria, a Traveller's Guide, 1997; Berlin, 1997; Frederick the Great: A Life in Deed and Letters, 2000; Last Kaiser: William the Impetuous, 2000; Last Kaiser: The Life of Wilhelm II, 2001; Portuguese Table Wines, 2001; After the Reich: The Brutal History of the Allied Occupation, 2007; 1938: Hitler's Gamble, 2009; The Great Battles, 2010. **Address:** c/o Georgina Capel, Capel & Land, 29 Wardour St., London, GL W1, England. **Online address:** giles@macdonogh.co.uk

MACDOUGAL, Bonnie. American (born United States), b. 1953. **Genres:** Novels, Mystery/Crime/Suspense, Young Adult Fiction. **Career:** Hughes, Thorsness, Gantz, Powell & Brundin, associate, 1978-79; Wright, Lindsey & Jennings, associate, 1979-82; Schnader, Harrison, Segal & Lewis, associate, 1982-88, senior attorney, 1988-94; Pepper, Hamilton & Scheetz, consulting attorney, 1994-95; freelance writer, 1996-. **Publications:** NOVELS: Breach of Trust, 1996; Angle of Impact, 1998; Out of Order, 1999; (co-author) Natural Suspect, 2001; Common Pleas, 2002. **Address:** Jean V. Naggar Literary Agency Inc., 216 E 75th St., Ste. 1E, New York, NY 10021, U.S.A. **Online address:** bonnie@bonniekistler.com

MACDOUGALL, David. Australian/American (born United States), b. 1939. **Genres:** Film, Anthropology/Ethnology, Communications/Media. **Career:** Rice University, Media Center, co-director, 1970-75; Australian Institute of Aboriginal Studies, Film Unit, director, 1975-91; Fieldwork Films, director, 1987-; Australian National University, Centre for Cross-Cultural Research, senior research fellow, 1997-2001, Research School of Humanities and the Arts, professorial research fellow, 2002-. Writer and filmmaker. **Publications:** ESSAYS: Transcultural Cinema, 1998; The Corporeal Image: Film, Ethnography and the Senses, 2006. **Address:** Research School of Humanities & the Arts, Australian National University, Sir Roland Wilson Bldg., Canberra, AC 0200, Australia. **Online address:** david.macdougall@anu.edu.au

MACDOWELL, Heather. American (born United States) **Genres:** Novels, Food And Wine. **Career:** Writer. **Publications:** (With R. MacDowell) Turning Tables (novel), 2008. **Address:** Kim Witherspoon, Inkwell Management, 521 5th Ave., 26th Fl., New York, NY 10175, U.S.A. **Online address:** roseandheather@turning-tables.com

MACDOWELL, Rose. American (born United States) **Genres:** Novels. **Career:** Writer. **Publications:** (with H. MacDowell) Turning Tables, 2008. **Address:** Kim Witherspoon, Inkwell Management, 521 5th Ave., 26th Fl., New York, NY 10175, U.S.A. **Online address:** roseandheather@turning-tables.com

MACE, Gordon. Canadian (born Canada), b. 1947. **Genres:** Politics/Government, International Relations/Current Affairs, Social Sciences. **Career:** Laval University, professor of political science, 1979-, International Studies Center, director, 2002-; Etudes Internationales, director, 2000-. Writer. **Publications:** Guide d'elaboration d'un projet de recherche, 1991, 2nd ed., 2000; (with L. Balthazar and L. Belanger) Trente ans de politique exterieure du Quebec, 1993; (ed. with J.P. Therien) Foreign Policy and Regionalism in the Americas, 1996; (co-author) The Americas in Transition: The Contours of Hemispheric Regionalism, 1999; (ed. with J.P. Therien and P. Haslam) Governing the Americas: Assessing Multilateral Institutions, 2007; Regionalism and the State: NAFTA and Foreign Policy Convergence, 2007; (ed. with A.F. Cooper and T.M. Shaw) Inter-American Cooperation at a Crossroads, 2010. **Address:** Department of Political Science, Laval University, Quebec City, QC G1V 0A6, Canada. **Online address:** gordon.mace@pol.ulaval.ca

MACEACHERN, Diane. American (born United States), b. 1952. **Genres:** Environmental Sciences/Ecology, Self Help, Sociology. **Career:** Alaska Wilderness League, board director, vice-chair; Big Green Purse, founder and chief executive officer; writer. **Publications:** Save Our Planet: 750 Everyday Ways You Can Help Clean up the Earth, 1990; Enough Is Enough: The Hell-Raiser's Guide to Community Activism, 1994; Beat High Gas Prices Now!: The Fastest, Easiest Ways to Save $20-$50 Every Month on Gasoline, 2005; Big Green Purse: Use Your Spending Power to Create a Cleaner, Greener World, 2008. **Address:** c/o Gail Ross, 1666 Connecticut Ave. NW, Ste. 501, Washington, DC 20009, U.S.A. **Online address:** diane@biggreenpurse.com

MACEDO, Stephen. American (born United States), b. 1957. **Genres:** Politics/Government, Law, Ethics, Education, Gay And Lesbian Issues, International Relations/Current Affairs, Institutions/Organizations, Urban Studies, Urban Studies. **Career:** U.S. House of Representatives, legislative assistant, 1981-82; Harvard University, assistant professor, 1986-90, associate professor of government, 1990-94; Syracuse University, Maxwell School of Citizenship and Public Affairs, Michael O. Sawyer professor of constitutional law and politics, 1994-99; Princeton University, University Center for Human Values, Laurance S. Rockefeller professor, 1999-, Program in Law and Public Affairs, founding director, 1999-2001, University Center for Human Values, director, 2001-. Writer. **Publications:** The New Right vs. The Constitution, 1986, rev. ed., 1987; Liberal Virtues: Citizenship, Virtue, and Community in Liberal Constitutionalism, 1991; Diversity and Distrust: Civic Education in a Multicultural Democracy, 1999; (co-author) American Constitutional Interpretation, 3rd ed., 2003; (co-author) Democracy at Risk: How Political Choices Undermine Citizen Participation and What We Can Do About It, 2005. EDITOR: Reassessing the Sixties: Debating the Political and Cultural Legacy, 1997; Deliberative Politics, 1999; (with I. Shapiro) Designing Democratic Institutions, 2000; (with Y. Tamir) Moral and Political Education, 2002; (with A. Buchanan) Secession and Self-Determination, 2003; (with I.M. Young) Child, Family, and State, 2003; (co-ed.) Educating Citizens: International Perspectives on Civic Values and School Choice, 2004; Universal Jurisdiction: National Courts and The Prosecution of Serious Crimes Under International Law, 2004; (with M.S. Williams) Political Exclusion and Domination, 2004; (co-ed. and intro.) Primates and Philosophers: How Morality Evolved, 2006; (and intro.) Striking First: Preemption and Prevention in International Conflict, 2008; (with I. Creppell and R. Hardin) Toleration on Trial, 2008; (ed. with J.K. Tulis) Limits of Constitutional Democracy, 2010. **Address:** Department of Politics, Princeton University, Corwin Hall 248, Princeton, NJ 08544-1006, U.S.A. **Online address:** macedo@princeton.edu

MACENULTY, Pat. American (born United States) **Genres:** Novels, Novellas/Short Stories, Women's Studies And Issues, Young Adult Fiction, Plays/Screenplays, Autobiography/Memoirs. **Career:** Johnson & Wales University, associate professor; Winthrop University, adjunct professor. Writer. **Publications:** NOVELS: Sweet Fire, 2002; Time to Say Goodbye, 2006; From May to December, 2007; Picara, 2009. COLLECTION: The Language of Sharks, 2004. PLAYS: Puck and The Mushy, Gushy Love Potion, 2006. MEMOIR: Wait Until Tomorrow, 2011. Contributor to periodicals. **Address:** Johnson & Wales University, Charlotte, 801 W. Trade St., Charlotte, NC 28202, U.S.A. **Online address:** pat@patmacenulty.com

MACEOIN, Denis. Also writes as Daniel Easterman, Denis Martin MacEoin, Jonathan Aycliffe. British/Irish (born Ireland), b. 1949. **Genres:** Novels, Novellas/Short Stories, Mystery/Crime/Suspense, Theology/Religion, Plays/Screenplays, Area Studies, History, Medicine/Health, Politics/Government, Young Adult Fiction, Adult Non-fiction. **Career:** Mohammed ben Abdollah University, faculty, 1979-80; Newcastle University, lecturer in Arabic and Islamic Studies, 1981-86, Royal Literary Fund fellow, 2005-08; University of London, chief examiner in O-level Persian, 1985-88; Durham University, Centre for Islamic and Middle East Studies, honorary fellow, 1986; novelist, 1986-. **Publications:** (Ed. With A. Al-Shahi) Islam in the Modern World, 1983; (with C. Thomson) The Health Crisis, 1987; A People Apart: The Bahai Community of Iran in the Twentieth Century, 1989; The Sources for Early Bābī Doctrine and History, 1992; Rituals in Babism and Bahaism, 1994; The Hijacking of British Islam, 2007; Sharia Law or One Law for All?, 2009; (as Denis Martin MacEoin) Messiah of Shiraz: Studies in Early and Middle Babism, 2009; When Worlds Collide, forthcoming. AS DANIEL EASTERMAN: The Last Assassin, 1985; The Seventh Sanctuary, 1987; The Ninth Buddha, 1989; Brotherhood of the Tomb, 1990; Night of the Seventh Darkness, 1991; Name of the Beast, 1992; New Jerusalems: Reflections on Islam, Fundamentalism and the Rushdie Affair, 1992; Judas Testament, 1994; The Night of the Apocalypse, 1995 in UK as Day of Wrath, 1996; The Final Judgement, 1996; K, 1997; Incarnation, 1998; The Jaguar Mask, 2000; Midnight Comes at Noon, 2001; Maroc, 2002; The Sword, 2007; The Spear of Destiny, 2008. AS JONATHAN AYCLIFFE: Naomi's Room, 1991; Whispers in the Dark, 1992; Vanishment, 1993; The Matrix, 1995, The Lost, 1996; The Talisman, 1998; The Shadow on the Wall, 2000; A Garden Lost in Time, 2004. **Address:** Dursley West, Fencer Hill Pk., Gosforth, Newcastle upon Tyne, TW NE3 2EA, England. **Online address:** denis.maceoin@ncl.ac.uk

MACEOIN, Denis Martin. *See* **MACEOIN, Denis.**

MACESICH, George. American (born United States), b. 1927. **Genres:** Economics, Local History/Rural Topics, Social Commentary, Adult Non-fiction, Money/Finance. **Career:** Illinois Institute of Technology, instructor in economics, 1956-57; University of Chicago, research associate, 1956-58; Chamber of Commerce of the United States, research economist, 1958-59; Florida State University, assistant professor, 1959-61, associate professor, 1961-63, professor of economics, 1963-, now professor emeritus, Center for Slavic and East European Studies, director, 1965, Center for Yugoslav-American Studies, director, 1965-, Institute in Yugoslavia, director, 1969-; University of Montenegro, State Council on Economic Development, director, 1961-63; U.S. Department of Commerce, consultant, 1961-64; University of Belgrade, professor of economics, 1971-; Council of Graduate Schools, consultant. Writer. **Publications:** Statistical Abstract for Florida, 1963; (ed.) Essays on Floridas Economic Development, 1963; Yugoslavia: Theory and Practice of Development Planning, 1964; Commercial Banking and Regional Development in the U.S. 1950-1960, 1965; Money and the Canadian Economy, 1967; Money in a European Common Market Setting, 1972; Financial, Industrial and Regional Development, 1972; Monetary and Financial Organization for Growth and Stability, 1972; Geldpolitik in Einem Gemeinsamen Europäischen Markt, 1972; Economic Stability: A Comparative Analysis, 1973; Monetary Theory and Policy: Theoretical and Empirical Issues, 1973; (with D. Dimitrijevic) Money and Finance in Contemporary Yugoslavia, 1973; The Intermaterial Monetary Economy and the Third World, 1981; (with H. Tsai) Money in Economic Systems, 1982; (ed. with R. Lang and D. Vojnic) Essays on the Political Economy of Yugoslavia, 1982; (with D. Dimitrijević) Money and Finance in Yugoslavia: A Comparative Analysis, 1983; Monetarism: Theory and Policy, 1983; The Politics of Monetarism, 1984; World Banking and Finance, 1984; World Crises and Developing Countries, 1985; Economic Nationalism and Stability, 1985; Monetary Policy and Rational Expectations, 1987; Monetary Reform and Cooperation Theory, 1989; (ed. with R. Lang and D. Vojnić) Essays on the Yugoslav Economic Model, 1989; Money and Democracy, 1990; (with D. Dimitrijevic) Money Supply Process, 1991; World Debt and Stability, 1991; Reform and Market Democracy, 1991; Monetary Policy and Politics: Rules Versus Discretion, 1992; (ed.) Yugoslavia in the Age of Democracy, 1992; Successor States and Cooperation Theory, 1994; (with D. Dimitrijević) Monetary Reform in Former Socialist Economies, 1994; Transformation and Emerging Markets, 1996; Integration and Stabilization, 1996; The United States in the Changing Global Economy, 1997; The World Economy at the Crossroads, 1997; Political Economy of Money: Emerging Fiat Monetary Regime, 1999; Money, Systems, and Growth: A New Economic Order?, 1999; Issues in Money and Banking, 2000; Money and Monetary Regimes: Struggle for Monetary Supremacy, 2002. Contributor to books. **Address:** Department of Economics, Florida State University, Rm. Bel 275, 288 Bellamy Bldg., 113 Collegiate Loop, Tallahassee, FL 32306-2180, U.S.A. **Online address:** gmacesic@fsu.edu

MACFADDEN, Bruce J. American (born United States), b. 1949. **Genres:** Natural History, Zoology, Sciences, History, Animals/Pets. **Career:** Yale University, Gibbs Instructor, through 1977; University of Florida, Florida Museum of Natural History, curator of vertebrate paleontology, Department of Geological Sciences, Latin American studies and Zoology, professor. Writer. **Publications:** (With M.F. Skinner) Diversification and Biogeography of the One-Toed Horses, Onohippidium and Hippidion, 1979; (with J.S. Waldrop) Nannippus Phlegon (Mammalia, Equidae) from the Pliocene (Blancan) of Florida, 1980; (ed. with J.L. Kirschvink and D.S. Jones) Magnetite Biomineralization and Magnetoreception in Organisms: A New Biomagnetism, 1985; (ed. with J. Damuth) Body Size in Mammalian Paleobiology: Estimation and Biological Implications, 1990; Fossil Horses: Systematics, Paleobiology and Evolution of the Family Equidae, 1992; (ed. with J. Damuth) Body Size in Mammalian Paleobiology: Estimation and Biological Implications, 2005. **Address:** Florida Museum of Natural History, University of Florida, 218 Dickinson Hall, Museum Rd. & Newell Dr., PO Box 117800, Gainesville, FL 32611-2035, U.S.A. **Online address:** bmacfadd@flmnh.ufl.edu

MACFADYEN, Amyan. British (born England), b. 1920. **Genres:** Zoology, Environmental Sciences/Ecology. **Career:** Bureau of Animal Population, research officer, 1947-56; University College of Swansea, lecturer and reader, 1956-65; University of Aarhus, Jordbundsbiologisk Institut, professor, 1965-67; University of Ulster, professor of biology, dean and pro-vice chancellor, 1967-86, now emeritus; Advances in Ecological Research, editor, 1974-92. **Publications:** Animal Ecology: Aims and Methods, 1957, 2nd ed., 1963; (with K. Petrusewicz) Productivity of Terrestrial Animals, 1970; (with J.M. Anderson) The Role of Terrestrial and Aquatic Organisms in Decomposition Processes, 1976. **Address:** 21 Eastgrove Rd., Sheffield, SY S10 2NN, England. **Online address:** amyan@gn.apc.org

MACFADYEN, David. American (born United States), b. 1964?. **Genres:** Literary Criticism And History, History, Social Sciences. **Career:** Dalhousie University, assistant professor, 1995-99, associate professor of Russian studies, 1999-2001; University of California, Department of Slavic Languages and Literatures, associate professor of Russian studies, 2001-04, professor, 2004-, chair, 2006-10, Center for Digital Humanities, affiliate faculty; Russian Association of Atlantic Canada, founder, 1998-. Writer. **Publications:** Joseph Brodsky and the Baroque, 1998; Joseph Brodsky and the Soviet Muse, 2000; Red Stars: Personality and the Soviet Popular Song, 1955-1991, 2001; Estrada?!: Grand Narratives and the Philosophy of the Russian Popular Song Since Perestroika, 2002; Songs for Fat People: Affect, Emotion, and Celebrity in the Russian Popular Song, 1900-1955, 2002; The Sad Comedy of El'dat Riazanov, 2003; Yellow Crocodiles and Blue Oranges: Russian Animated Film since World War Two, 2005; Russian Culture in Uzbekistan: One Language in the Middle of Nowhere, 2006; Russian Television Today: Primetime Drama and Comedy, 2007; Bling àla Russe, 2009; (co-ed.) Directory of Russian Cinema, 2010. Contributor to periodicals. **Address:** Department of Slavic Languages and Literatures, University of California, 322 Humanities Bldg., PO Box 951502, Los Angeles, CA 90095-1502, U.S.A. **Online address:** dmacfady@humnet.ucla.edu

MACFARLANE, Alan (Donald James). British/Indian (born India), b. 1941. **Genres:** History, Anthropology/Ethnology. **Career:** University of Cambridge, King's College, senior research fellow in history, 1971-74, lecturer, 1975-81, fellow, 1981-2009, reader in social anthropology, 1981-91, professor of anthropological science, 1991-2009, chair of the Mongolian and Inner Asian studies unit, 1995-2003, director of studies in anthropology, director, 2002-03, now emeritus professor and life fellow, 2009-; University of Liverpool, lecturer, 1974; London School of Economics, lecturer, 1978; Oxford University, lecturer, 1980; School of Oriental and African Studies, external examiner, 1983-85, lecturer, 2000; British Academy, fellow, 1986; Academia Europaea, fellow, 1990; University of Wales, external examiner, 1996-97, 2000; Keio University, lecturer, 1999; Royal Anthropological Institute, honorary vice president, 2003-05. Writer. **Publications:** Witchcraft in Tudor and Stuart England, 1970; The Family Life of Ralph Josselin, A 17th-Century Clergyman, 1970; (ed.) The Diary of Ralph Josselin, 1616-1683, 1976; Resources and Population: A Study of the Gurungs of Nepal, 1976; (with S. Harrison and C. Jardine) Reconstructing Historical Communities, 1977; The Origins of English Individualism: The Family, Property and Social Transition, 1978; (with Harrison) The Justice and the Mare's Ale: Law and Disorder in Seventeenth-Century England, 1981; A Guide to English Historical Records, 1983; (ed. and foreword) Witchcraft and Religion: The Politics of Popular Belief, 1984; Marriage and Love in England: Modes of Reproduction, 1300-1840, 1986; The Culture of Capitalism (essays), 1987; (with I. Gurung) Gurungs of Nepal, 1990; The Savage Wars of Peace: England, Japan and the Malthusian Trap, 1997; The Riddle of the Modern World, 2000; The Making of the Modern World, 2002; (with G. Martin) The Glass Bathysaphe: How Glass Changed the World, 2002; (with I. Macfarlane) Green Gold: The Empire of Tea, 2003; Letters to Lily: On How the World Works, 2005; Japan Through the Looking Glass, 2007; Reflections on Cambridge, 2009. Contributor to periodicals. **Address:** Department of Social Anthropology, University of Cambridge, Free School Ln., Cambridge, CB CB2 3RF, England. **Online address:** am12@cam.ac.uk

MACFARLANE, Leslie John. British (born England), b. 1924. **Genres:** Politics/Government, Sociology, Humanities, Law. **Career:** College of Commerce, lecturer in politics, 1957-63; Oxford University, Ruskin College, lecturer in politics, tutor in politics, 1963-69, St. John's College, tutor, fellow in politics and university lecturer, 1969-91, now emeritus fellow. Writer. **Publications:** British Politics 1918-64, 1965; The British Communist Party: Origin and Development until 1929, 1966; Modern Political Theory, 1970; Political Disobedience, 1971; Violence and the State, 1974; Issues in British Politics since 1945, 1975, 3rd ed., 1986; (contrib.) The Concept of Socialism, 1975; (contrib.) Social Ends and Political Means, 1976; The Right to Strike, 1981; The Theory and Practice of Human Rights, 1985; William Elphinstone and The Kingdom of Scotland, 1431-1514: The Struggle for Order, 1985; Human Rights: Realities and Possibilities, Northern Ireland, the Republic of Iceland, Yugoslavia, and Hungary, 1990; Socialism, Social Ownership and Social Justice, 1998. Contributor to books and journals. **Address:** St. John's College, St. Giles, Oxford, OX OX1 3JP, England.

MACFARLANE, Malcolm R. British (born England), b. 1942. **Genres:** Biography, Art/Art History, Autobiography/Memoirs, Humor/Satire. **Career:** Birmingham Corp., junior clerk, 1959-60; Lloyds Bank, senior manager, 1960-99; writer, 1999-; Bing Magazine, editor. **Publications:** Bing Crosby: Day by Day (biography), 2001; (with K. Crossland) Perry Como: A Biography and Complete Career Record. 2009. Contributor to periodicals. **Address:** 3 Osborne Close, Wilmslow, Wilmslow, CH SK9 2EE, England. **Online address:** macwilmslo@aol.com

MACFARLANE, Robert. British/American (born United States), b. 1976. **Genres:** Cultural/Ethnic Topics, Travel/Exploration, Social Sciences. **Career:** Emmanuel College, fellow, 2002-, lecturer in English, 2006-; University in Beijing, faculty. Writer. **Publications:** Mountains of the Mind, 2003; The Wild Places, 2007; Original Copy: Plagiarism and Originality in Nineteenth-Century Literature, 2007. Contributor to magazines. **Address:** c/o Author Mail, Granta Books, 2/3 Hanover Yard, Noel Rd., London, GL N1 8BE, England.

MACGILLIVRAY, Deborah. American (born United States) **Genres:** Romance/Historical, Literary Criticism And History. **Career:** Hearts Through History, vice president, 2002-05. Book reviewer and writer. **Publications:** Cat o'Nine Tales, 2007; One Snowy Knight, 2009. DRAGONS OF CHALLON SERIES: A Restless Knight, 2006; In Her Bed, 2007; Redemption, 2010. SISTERS OF COLFORD HALL SERIES: The Invasion of Falgannon Isle, 2006; Riding the Thunder, 2007; A Wolf in Wolf's Clothing, 2009; To Bell the Vampire, forthcoming; Yo Ho Ho and a Bottle of Scotch, forthcoming. **Address:** Love Spell, 200 Madison Ave., Ste. 2000, New York, NY 10016, U.S.A. **Online address:** contact@deborahmacgillivray.co.uk

MACGOWAN, Christopher (John). American/British (born England), b. 1948. **Genres:** Literary Criticism And History, Poetry. **Career:** Princeton University, editorial assistant, 1981-83; College of William and Mary, Department of English, assistant professor, 1984-90, associate professor of English, 1990-96, associate chair, professor of English and chair, 1996-. **Publications:** William Carlos Williams's Early Poetry: The Visual Arts Background, 1984; Twentieth-Century American Poetry, 2004; The Twentieth-Century American Fiction Handbook, 2011. EDITOR: (with A.W. Litz) The Collected Poems of William Carlos Williams, vol. I: 1909-1939, 1986, vol.II: 1939-1962, 1988; Paterson, 1992; The Letters of Denise Levertov and William Carlos Williams, 1998; Poetry for Young People: William Carlos Williams, 2003; William Carlos Williams, 2004. Contributor to periodicals. **Address:** Department of English, College of William and Mary, 318C Tyler Hall, PO Box 8795, Williamsburg, VA 23187, U.S.A. **Online address:** cjmacg@wm.edu

MACGOYE, Marjorie Oludhe. Kenyan/British (born England), b. 1928. **Genres:** Novels, Young Adult Fiction, Novellas/Short Stories, Ethics, Poetry, Writing/Journalism, Children's Fiction, Literary Criticism And History, Literary Criticism And History. **Career:** University of Nairobi, External Degree Program, editor, 1986-88. **Publications:** Growing Up at Lina School (juvenile), 1971; Murder in Majengo (novel), 1972; Song of Nyarloka and Other Poems, 1977; Story of Kenya: A Nation in the Making, 1986; Coming to Birth (novel), 1986; The Present Moment (novel), 1987; Street Life (novella), 1987; Victoria and Murder in Majengo (novel), 1993; Homing In, 1994; Moral Issues in Kenya: A Personal View, 1996; Chira (novel), 1997; The Black Hand Gang (juvenile), 1998; Make It Sing and Other Poems, 1998; A Farm Called Kishinev, 2005; Further Adventures of the Black Hand Gang, 2005; The Black Hand Gang Grow Up, 2006; Composition of Poetry, 2009; Creative writing in Prose, 2009. Contributor to periodicals. **Address:** PO Box 70344, Nairobi, 00400, Kenya.

MACGREGOR, James Murdoch. (J. T. McIntosh). Scottish (born Scotland), b. 1925. **Genres:** Food And Wine, Photography, Science Fiction/Fantasy, Young Adult Fiction, Literary Criticism And History. **Career:** Writer, 1954-; Thomson Organization Ltd., sub-editor, 1964-86. **Publications:** AS J.T. McINTOSH: World Out of Mind, 1953; Born Leader, 1954; One in 300, 1954; The Fittest, 1955 as The Rule of the Pagbeasts, 1956; Two Hundred Years to Christmas, 1961; The Million Cities, 1963; The Noman Way, 1964; Out of Chaos, 1965; Six Gates from Limbo, 1968; Take a Pair of Private Eyes, 1968; A Coat of Blackmail, 1970; Transmigration, 1970; Flight from Rebirth, 1971; The Cosmic Spies, 1972; The Space Sorcerers in US as The Suiciders, 1972; Galactic Takeover Bid, 1973; This is the Way the World Begins, 1976; Norman Conquest 2066, 1977; A Planet Called Utopia, 1979. OTHERS: Glamour in Your Lens, 1958; When the Ship Sank, 1959; Incident Over the Pacific, 1960 in UK as A Cry to Heaven, 1960; The Iron Rain, 1962; Wine Making for All, 1966; Beer Making for All, 1967, 2nd ed., 1973. **Address:** 63 Abbotswell Dr., Aberdeen, AB12 5QP, Scotland.

MACGREGOR, Neil. British/Scottish (born Scotland), b. 1946. **Genres:** Adult Non-fiction, Theology/Religion. **Career:** University of Reading, lecturer in history of art and architecture, 1975-81; University of London, Courtauld Institute of Art, part-time lecturer, 1977-86; The Burlington Magazine, editor, 1981; The National Gallery, director, 1987-2002; The British Museum, director, 2002-. Writer. **Publications:** A Victim of Anonymity: The Master of the Saint Bartholomew Altarpiece, 1994; (co-author) Bridget Riley: Dialogues on Art, 1995; (with E. Langmuir) Seeing Salvation: Images of Christ in Art, 2000; (ed. with O. Bonfait) Il Dio nascosto: I Grandi maestri del Seicento e l immagine diDio, 2000; (co-author) Whose Muse?: Art Museums and the Public Trust, 2004; A History of the World in 100 Objects, 2010. Contributor to magazines and periodicals. **Address:** The British Museum, Great Russell St., London, GL WC1B 3DG, England.

MACGUIRE, James. American (born United States), b. 1952. **Genres:** Poetry, Education, Travel/Exploration, History. **Career:** Catholic Relief Services, program director, 1977-79; Time Inc., Video Division, producer, director of strategic planning, 1980-82; Macmillan Inc., executive producer, 1982-88; Williamstown Theatre Festival, playwright in residence, 1987; MacGuire Communications, president, 1988-; Center for Educational Innovation, senior fellow, 1990-92; Center for Social Thought, senior fellow, 1992-93; America's Health Network, vice-president, development, 1994-99; Asia Network, chief programming officer for communications, 2001-. Board Director. **Publications:** London and the English Countryside, 1990; (with C. Buckley) Campion, 1990; (with S. Fliegel) Miracle in East Harlem: The Fight for Choice in Public Education, 1993; Beyond Partisan Politics, 1993; Dusk on

Lake Tanganyka (poems) 1999. Contributor of articles. **Address:** 412 E 55th St., New York, NY 10022, U.S.A. **Online address:** jmacg52@aol.com

MACH, Elyse (Janet). American (born United States), b. 1941. **Genres:** Music. **Career:** Netherland Philharmonic Orchestra, recital and piano soloist, 1962, 1966, 1968; Northeastern Illinois University, assistant professor, 1964-69, associate professor, 1970-74, professor of piano, theory and music history, 1975-, associate chairperson of department, 1983-86, distinguished professor; NBC-TV Symphony, soloist, 1965; Clavier music magazine, columnist, contributing editor, consulting editor, 1996-. **Publications:** (Ed.) The Liszt Studies, 1973; Contemporary Class Piano, vol. I, 1976, vol. II, 1982, 7th ed., 2011; Great Pianists Speak for Themselves, vol. I, 1980, vol. II, 1988; (ed.) Rare and Familiar: 28 Pieces for Piano, 1982; (with S. Gordon and M. Uszler) The Well-Tempered Keyboard Teacher, 1991, 2nd ed., 2000; Great Contemporary Pianists Speak for Themselves, 1992; Learning Piano: Piece by Piece, 2006. Contributor to periodicals. **Address:** Department of Music, Northeastern Illinois University, Rm. FA 136, Salme Harju Fine Arts Ctr., 5500 N St. Louis Ave., Chicago, IL 60625-4699, U.S.A. **Online address:** e-mach@neiu.edu

MACH, Thomas S. American (born United States), b. 1966?. **Genres:** Politics/Government, History. **Career:** Mount Vernon Nazarene College, faculty; Cedarville University, Department of History and Government, professor of history, 2000-, chair, 2009-. Writer. **Publications:** Gentleman George Hunt Pendleton: Party Politics and Ideological Identity in Nineteenth-Century America, 2007. **Address:** Cedarville University, 251 N Main St., Cedarville, OH 45314, U.S.A. **Online address:** macht@cedarville.edu

MACHANN, Clinton (John). American (born United States), b. 1947. **Genres:** Literary Criticism And History, Novellas/Short Stories, Novels. **Career:** Teacher, 1969-71; University of Texas, assistant instructor in English, 1974-76; Texas A&M University, assistant professor, 1976-83, associate professor, 1983-94, professor of English, 1994-. Writer. **Publications:** (With J.W. Mendl) Krasna Amerika: A Study of the Texas Czechs, 1851-1939, 1983; The Essential Matthew Arnold: An Annotated Bibliography of Major Modern Studies, 1993; Jason Jackson, 1993; The Genre of Autobiography in Victorian Literature, 1994; Matthew Arnold: A Literary Life, 1998; (with L.H. Konecny) Perilous Voyages: Czech and English Immigrants to Texas in the 1870s, 2004; Masculinity in Four Victorian Epics, 2010. EDITOR: (with F.D. Burt) Matthew Arnold in His Time and Ours: Centenary Essays, 1988; (with W.B. Clark) Katherine Anne Porter and Texas: An Uneasy Relationship, 1990; (and trans. with J.W. Mendl) Czech Voices: Stories from Texas in the Amerikan Narodni Kalendar, 1991; (with F.D. Burt) Selected Letters of Matthew Arnold, 1993; Czech-Americans in Transition, 1999. Contributor to periodicals. **Address:** Department of English, Texas A&M University, Blocker 210C, PO Box 4227, College Station, TX 77843-4227, U.S.A. **Online address:** c-machann@tamu.edu

MACHEDON, Luminita. Romanian (born Romania), b. 1952. **Genres:** Architecture, History, Photography. **Career:** Institute of Design Timisoara, architect designer, 1977-80; Project Bucharest, principal architect, 1984-99; ScM Design com, architect general manager, 1999-; Institute of Architecture, associate professor. Writer. **Publications:** (With E. Scoffham) Romanian Modernism: The Architecture of Bucharest, 1920-1940, 1999. Contributor to books and periodicals. **Address:** Sc M Design com, Sos. Stefan cel Mare, Ste. 36, Bucharest, 72 158, Romania. **Online address:** machedon@fx.ro

MACHOIAN, Ronald Glenn. American (born United States), b. 1965?. **Genres:** Autobiography/Memoirs, Bibliography, Military/Defense/Arms Control, History. **Career:** University of Nebraska, adjunct professor. Writer. **Publications:** William Harding Carter and the American Army: A Soldier's Story, 2006. Contributor to periodicals. **Address:** Department of History, University of Nebraska, 287 Arts and Sciences Hall, 6001 Dodge St., Omaha, NE 68182-2000, U.S.A.

MACHOR, James L(awrence). American (born United States), b. 1950. **Genres:** Literary Criticism And History, Urban Studies, Women's Studies And Issues, Novels. **Career:** Ohio State University, assistant professor, 1980-86, associate professor of English, 1986-90; Kansas State University, associate professor of English, 1990-95, professor of English, 1995-. Writer. **Publications:** Pastoral Cities: Urban Ideals and the Symbolic Landscape of America, 1987. EDITOR: (and contrib.) Readers in History: Nineteenth-Century American Literature and the Contexts of Response, 1993; (with P. Goldstein) Reception Study: From Literary Theory to Cultural Studies, 2001; (and contrib. with P. Goldstein) New Directions in American Reception Study, 2008; Reading Fiction in Antebellum America: Informed Response and Reception Histories, 1820-1865, 2011. **Address:** Department of English, Kansas State University, 108 English/Counseling Services Bldg., Manhattan, KS 66506-6501, U.S.A. **Online address:** machor@ksu.edu

MACHOTKA, Pavel. American/Italian/Czech (born Czech Republic), b. 1936. **Genres:** Art/Art History, Psychology, Biography. **Career:** Harvard University, instructor in social relations, 1962-65; University of Colorado, Medical Center, assistant professor, associate professor of clinical psychology, 1965-70; University of California, associate professor, professor of psychology, 1970-, Porter College, provost of college, 1976-79, chairperson of academic senate, 1992-94, Department of Psychology of Aesthetics, founder, Department of Psychology, chair; Perm State Institute of Arts and Culture, honorary professor, 1997. Writer. **Publications:** (Co-author) The Treatment of Families in Crisis, 1968; (with J.P. Spiegel) Messages of the Body, 1974, rev. ed. as The Articulate Body, 1982; The Nude: Perception and Personality, 1979; Cezanne: Landscape into Art, 1996; (co-ed.) Emotion, Creativity and Art, 1997; Style and Psyche: The Art of Lundy Siegriest and Terry St. John, 1999; Pavel Machotka: Light, Form, and Sensuality, 2002; Painting and Our Inner World, 2003, Les Sites Cézanniens en Provence, 2006, Cézanne: The Eye and the Mind, 2008. Contributor to art periodicals. **Address:** Department of Psychology, Social Sciences II, University of California, 273 Social Sciences 2, Santa Cruz, CA 95064, U.S.A. **Online address:** pavel@machotka.com

MACHOWICZ, Richard J. American (born United States) **Genres:** Military/Defense/Arms Control, Medicine/Health, inspirational/Motivational Literature, Sports/Fitness. **Career:** Bukido Institute, director, chief instructor and founder; Warpath Entertainment, co-founder; Personal protection specialist and martial arts trainer. Writer. **Publications:** Unleashing the Warrior Within: Using the Seven Principles of Combat to Achieve Your Goals, 2000; Unleash the Warrior Within: Develop the Focus, Discipline, Confidence and Courage You Need to Achieve Unlimited Goals, 2008. Contributor to periods. **Address:** Bukido Institute, 1223 Wilshire Blvd., Ste. 581, Santa Monica, CA 90403, U.S.A. **Online address:** information@bukido.com

MACIARIELLO, Joseph A. American (born United States) **Genres:** Children's Non-fiction. **Career:** Claremont Graduate University, The Drucker Institute, Horton professor of management and director of research and education, academic director, Marie Rankin Clarke professor of social science and management; China Management Institute, consultant. Writer. **Publications:** NONFICTION: Dynamic Benefit-Cost Analysis: Evaluation of Public Policy in a Dynamic Urban Model, 1975; Program-Management Control Systems, 1978, 2nd ed., (with C.J. Kirby) as Management Control Systems: Using Adaptive Systems to Attain Control, 1994; (with L.D. Asay) Executive Leadership in Health Care, 1991; Lasting Value: Lessons from a Century of Agility at Lincoln Electric, 2000; (with P.F. Drucker) The Daily Drucker: 366 Days of Insight and Motivation for Getting the Right Things Done, 2004; (with P. Drucker) The Effective Executive in Action: A Step-by-Step Guide to Right Action, 2005; (with P. Drucker) The Effective Executive in Action: A Journal for Getting the Right Things Done, 2006; (with P.F. Drucker) Management, 2008; Management Cases, rev. ed., 2009; (ed. with C.L. Pearce and H. Yamawaki) The Drucker Difference: What the World's Greatest Management Thinker Means to Today's Business Leaders, 2009; (with K.E. Linkletter) Drucker's Lost Art of Management: Fulfilling Peter Drucker's Timeless Vision for a Building Effective Organizations, 2011. **Address:** Peter F. Drucker and Masatoshi Ito, Graduate School of Management, Claremont Graduate University, 1021 N Dartmouth Ave., Claremont, CA 91711-6160, U.S.A. **Online address:** joseph.maciariello@cgu.edu

MACINNES, Mairi. British/American (born United States), b. 1925?. **Genres:** Novels, Poetry, Autobiography/Memoirs, Ghost Writer. **Career:** Writer and teacher. **Publications:** POETRY: Splinters, 1953; Herring, Oatmeal, Milk, and Salt, 1982; The House on the Ridge Road, 1988; Elsewhere and Back, 1993; The Ghostwriter, 1999; The Pebble: Old and New Poems, 2000. OTHER: Admit One (novel), 1956; (ed. with J. McCormick) Versions of Censorship, 1962; (ed. with M. Keller) A Dictionary of Words About Alcohol, 1968, 2nd ed., 1982; The Quondam Wives (novel), 1993; Clearances (autobiography), 2002; The Girl I Left Behind Me: Poems of a Lifetime, 2003. **Address:** Pantheon Books, 212 E 50th St., New York, NY 10022, U.S.A. **Online address:** mairi@mcormick88.fsnet.co.uk

MACINNES, Patricia. American (born United States), b. 1954. **Genres:**

Novels, Young Adult Fiction, Literary Criticism And History. **Career:** Writer. **Publications:** The Last Night on Bikini: A Novel, 1995. Works appear in anthologies. Contributor to periodicals. **Address:** Mary Jack Wald Associates Inc., 111 E 14th St., PO Box 113, New York, NY 10003, U.S.A.

MACINTOSH, Brownie. Also writes as John Young. American (born United States), b. 1950. **Genres:** Children's Fiction, Songs/Lyrics And Libretti. **Career:** Actor and Writer. **Publications:** The Streamlined Double Decker Bus, 1995; (with J. Thompson) A Pirate's Life for Me!: A Day Aboard a Pirate Ship, 1996. **Address:** 47 Exeter St., Newmarket, NH 03857, U.S.A. **Online address:** grebrd@aol.com

MACINTOSH, Robert. Canadian (born Canada), b. 1923. **Genres:** Money/Finance, Sports/Fitness, Politics/Government. **Career:** Bishop's University, assistant professor, 1950-53; Bank of Nova Scotia, executive vice president, 1953-80; York University, chairman of the board, 1969-73; Canadian Bankers Association, president, 1980-90; writer, 1990-; Dominion-Anglo Investment Co., director; Quaker Oats of Canada, board director; Onex Corp., board director; United Corp., board director; Chemical Bank of Canada, board director; York University, board director. **Publications:** Different Drummers: Banking and Politics in Canada, 1991; Forty-Love, The Queen's Club, 1997. Contributor of articles to journals. **Address:** 5 Powell Ave., Toronto, ON M4W 2Y6, Canada.

MACINTYRE, Alasdair. British/Scottish (born Scotland), b. 1929. **Genres:** Philosophy, Essays, Humanities. **Career:** Victoria University of Manchester, lecturer in philosophy of religion, 1951-55; University of Leeds, lecturer in philosophy, 1957-61; Oxford University, Nuffield College, research fellow, 1961-62, Carlyle visiting lecturer, 1981-82; Princeton University, Council of the Humanities, senior fellow, 1962-63, fellow and preceptor in philosophy, 1963-66, visiting professor; University of Newcastle upon Tyne, Riddell lecturer, 1964; Columbia University, Bampton lecturer, 1966; University of Essex, professor of sociology, 1966-70; Brandeis University, professor of history of ideas, 1970-72; Boston University, University, professor in philosophy and political science, 1972-80, College of Liberal Arts, dean, 1972-73; Wellesley College, Luce professor, 1980-82; Vanderbilt University, W. Alton Jones professor of philosophy, 1982-88, professor of philosophy, 1985; University of Notre Dame, professor of darkness and despair, 1985, McMahon/Hank professor of philosophy, 1988-94, research professor of philosophy, Reverend John A. O'Brien senior research professor, 2000-, professor emeritus of philosophy, 2010-; Duke University, arts and sciences professor of philosophy, 1995-2000, professor emeritus, 2000-; London Metropolitan University, Centre for Contemporary Aristotelian Studies, senior research fellow, 2010. Writer. **Publications:** Marxism: An Interpretation, 1953, 2nd ed. as Marxism & Christianity, 1995; The Unconscious, 1958, rev. ed., 2004; Difficulties in Christian Belief, 1959; Short History of Ethics, 1966, 2nd ed., 1998; Secularization and Moral Change, 1967; Unbewusste. Eine Begriffs analyse, 1968; (with P. Ricoeur) The Religious Significance of Atheism, 1969; (with S. Toulmin and R.W. Hepburn) Metaphysical Beliefs: Three Essays, 1957, 2nd ed., 1970; Herbert Marcuse: An Exposition and a Polemic, 1970; Marcuse, 1970; Against the Self-Images of the Age, 1971; Unconscious: A Conceptual Analysis, 1976, rev. ed., 2004; After Virtue: A Study in Moral Theory, 1981, 3rd ed., 2007; Is Patriotism a Virtue?, 1984; Education and Values, 1987; Whose Justice? Which Rationality?, 1988; First Principles, Final Ends and Contemporary Philosophical Issues, 1990; Three Rival Versions of Moral Enquiry: Encyclopaedia, Genealogy and Tradition, 1990; MacIntyre Reader, 1998; Dependent Rational Animals: Why Human Beings Need the Virtues, 1999. (contrib.) Kierkgaard after MacIntyre, 2001; Animali razionale dipendenti, 2001; Edith Stein: A Philosophical Prologue, 1913-1922, 2006; The Tasks of Philosophy: Selected Essays, 2006; Ethics and Politics: Selected Essays, 2006; After Virtue: A Study in Moral Theory, 2007; God, Philosophy, Universities: A Selective History of the Catholic Philosophical Tradition, 2009. EDITOR: (with A.G.N. Flew) New Essays in Philosophical Theology, 1955; (intro.) Hume's Ethical Writings, 1965; (and intro. with D.M. Emmet) Sociological Theory and Philosophical Analysis, 1970; Hegel: A Collection of Critical Essays, 1972; (with S. Hauerwas) Revisions, Changing Perspectives in Moral Philosophy, 1983; Alasdair MacIntyre's Engagement with Marxism: Selected Writings 1953-1974, 2008. **Address:** Notre Dame Center for Ethics and Culture, University of Notre Dame, 1042 Flanner, 424 Geddes Hall, Notre Dame, IN 46556, U.S.A.

MACINTYRE, Linden. Canadian (born Canada), b. 1943. **Genres:** Novels. **Career:** Halifax Herald, parliamentary reporter, 1964-67; Financial Times of Canada, parliamentary reporter, 1967-70; Chronicle Herald, correspondent, 1970-76; Canadian Broadcasting Corp. (CBC), reporter and host, 1976-80, The Journal, producer and reporter, 1980-86, 1988-90, Sunday Morning, host, 1986-88, The Fifth Estate, co-host, 1990-. **Publications:** The Long Stretch (novel), 1999; (with T. Burke) Who Killed Ty Conn?, 2000; Causeway: A Passage from Innocence, 2006; The Bishop's Man, 2009. **Address:** Transatlantic Literary Agency Inc., 72 Glengowan Rd., Toronto, ON M4N 1G4, Canada.

MACINTYRE, Stuart (Forbes). Australian (born Australia), b. 1947. **Genres:** History, Politics/Government. **Career:** Murdoch University, tutor in history, 1976, lecturer in history, 1979; Cambridge University, St. John's College, research fellow, 1977-78; University of Melbourne, lecturer, 1980-84, senior lecturer, 1984-86, reader in history, 1987-90, Ernest Scott professor of history, 1991-, dean of faculty of arts, 1999-2006, Laureate professor, 2002-; Australian National University, research fellow, 1982-83; Australian Historical Association, president, 1996-98; Australian Research Council, Humanities and Creative Arts, chair, 2002-04, professorial research fellow, 2009-; Harvard University, visiting professor of Australian studies, 2007-08; Academy of the Social Sciences in Australia, president, 2007-09. Writer. **Publications:** A Proletarian Science: Marxism in Britain, 1917-1933, 1980; Little Moscows: Communism and Working-Class Militancy in Inter-War Britain, 1980; Militant: The Life and Times of Paddy Troy, 1983; Winners and Losers: The Pursuit of Social Justice in Australian History, 1985; The Oxford History of Australia, vol. IV, 1986; The Labour Experiment, 1989; A Colonial Liberalism: The Lost World of Three Victorian Visionaries, 1991; A History for a Nation: Ernest Scott and the Making of Australian History, 1994; (comp. with B. Symons and S. Macintyre) Communism in Australia: A Resource Bibliography, 1994; The Reds, 1998; Concise History of Australia, 1999, 3rd ed., 2009; (with R.J.W. Selleck) Short History of the University of Melbourne, 2004; Poor Relation, 2010. EDITOR: Ormond College, Centenary Essays, 1984; Making History, 1984; Foundations of Arbitration: The Origins and Effects of State Compulsory Arbitration, 1989; (with S. Janson) Through White Eyes, 1990; Old Bebb's Store & Other Poems, 1992; (with J. Thomas) The Discovery of Australian History, 1890-1939, 1995; (with G. Davison and J. Hirst) Oxford Companion to Australian History, 1999; (with H. Irving) No Ordinary Act: Essays on Federation and the Constitution, 2001; (with J. Faulkner) True Believers: The Story of the Federal Parliamentary Labor Party, 2001; (with J. Isaac) New Province for Law and Order: 100 Years of Australian Industrial Conciliation and Arbitration, 2004; Historians Conscience: Australian Historians on the Ethics of History, 2004; (with K. Darian-Smith and P. Grimshaw) Britishness Abroad: Transnational Movements and Imperial Cultures, 2007. **Address:** Department of History, University of Melbourne, Rm. 326B E, John Medley Bldg., Parkville, VI 3010, Australia. **Online address:** s.macintyre@unimelb.edu.au

MACINTYRE, Wendy. Canadian/Scottish (born Scotland), b. 1947?. **Genres:** Novels, Young Adult Fiction. **Career:** Writer. **Publications:** NOVELS: Mairi, 1992; The Applecross Spell, 2003; (with R.P. MacIntyre) Apart, 2007. Contributor to journals. **Address:** House of Anansi Press and Groundwood Books, 110 Spadina Ave., Ste. 801, Toronto, ON M5V 2K4, Canada. **Online address:** wmacinty@sympatico.ca

MACK, Arien. American (born United States), b. 1931?. **Genres:** Psychology, Social Sciences, Medicine/Health. **Career:** New School University, Albert and Monette Marrow professor of psychology, 1966-, chair of department, 1972-82; Social Research (journal), 1970-; Massachusetts Institute of Technology, research scientist, 1984; Journal Donation Project, founder and director, 1990-; Social Research Conference Series, organizer and director, 1988-. Writer. **Publications:** (With I. Rock) Inattentional Blindness, 1998. EDITOR: Death in American Experience, 1973; In Time of Plague: The History and Social Consequences of Lethal Epidemic Diseases, 1991; Home: A Place in the World, 1993; Humans and Other Animals, 1999; Technology and the Rest of Culture, 2001. Works appear in anthologies. Contributor to psychology journals. **Address:** Eugene Lang College, New School University, Rm. 712, 80 5th Ave., New York, NY 10011-8002, U.S.A. **Online address:** mackarie@newschool.edu

MACK, Beverly (B.). American (born United States), b. 1952. **Genres:** Area Studies, Cultural/Ethnic Topics, History, Poetry. **Career:** Bayero University, tutor, 1980, lecturer in African oral and written literature and African-American literature, 1982-83; Georgetown University, adjunct assistant professor of African history, 1984-85; Nigeria-U.S. Business Council, program assistant, 1984; South East Consortium for International Development, Center for

Women in Development, project assistant, 1984-86; Yale University, Hausa language and African literature, assistant professor, 1986-87; George Mason University, adjunct assistant professor, 1987-88, visiting assistant professor of English, 1988-93; American Medical Students Association, language instructor, 1989; University of Kansas, Department of African and African American Studies, assistant professor, 1993-96, associate professor, 1996-2006, professor, 2006-, Religious Studies, professor; U.S. Agency for International Development, Center for Applied Linguistics, consultant. Writer. **Publications:** (Ed. with C. Coles) Hausa Women in the Twentieth Century, 1991; (ed. with J. Boyd) The Collected Works of Nana Asma'u 1793-1864, 1997; (with J. Boyd) One Woman's Jihad: Nana Asma'u, Scholar and Scribe, 2000; Muslim Women Sing: Hausa Popular Song, 2004. Work appears in anthologies. Contributor of articles. **Address:** Department of African & African-American Studies, University of Kansas, Bailey Hall, Rm. 9, 1440 Jayhawk Blvd., Lawrence, KS 66045-7574, U.S.A. **Online address:** bmack@ku.edu

MACK, Carol K. American (born United States) **Genres:** Novels, Plays/Screenplays, Mythology/Folklore, Young Adult Fiction. **Career:** New York University, lecturer and fiction writer adjunct, 1985-96; Marymount College, faculty. Writer. **Publications:** (With D. Ehrenfeld) The Chameleon Variant (novel), 1980; Postcards and Other Short Plays, 1987; (with D. Mack) A Field Guide to Demons, Fairies, Fallen Angels and Other Subversive Spirits, 1998; (with D. Mack) A Field Guide to Demons, Vampires, Fallen Angels and Other Subversive Spirits, 2010. PLAYS: Postcards, 1983; Territorial Rites, 1983. Works appear in anthologies. **Address:** Robert Freedman Dramatic Agency, 1501 Broadway, New York, NY 10036, U.S.A. **Online address:** ckm115@aol.com

MACK, Dana. American (born United States), b. 1954?. **Genres:** Human Relations/Parenting, Humanities, Politics/Government, Social Commentary, Sociology, Social Sciences. **Career:** Institute for American Values, writer and social science researcher; Center for Education Studies, writer, social science researcher and senior fellow. **Publications:** The Assault on Parenthood: How Our Culture Undermines the Family, 1997; Hungry Hearts: Evaluating the New Curricula for Teens on Marriage and Relationships, 2000; (ed. with D. Blankenhorn) The Book of Marriage: The Wisest Answers to the Toughest Questions, 2001. Contributor of reviews to periodicals. **Address:** PO Box 7174, Wilton, CT 06897, U.S.A.

MACK, David (A.). American (born United States), b. 1969?. **Genres:** Science Fiction/Fantasy, Novels, Ghost Writer, Novellas/Short Stories, Plays/Screenplays, E-books, Humor/Satire. **Career:** Infinity Dog Inc., founder, chief executive officer and executive producer. Freelance writer. **Publications:** Star Trek: Deep Space Nine-Starship Down, 1995; Star Trek: New Frontier Minipedia, 1998; Star Trek: Deep Space Nine-It's Only a Paper Moon, 1999; Star Trek: Divided We Fall, 2001; Star Trek: S.C.E.-Invincible, 2001; Ashes, 2002; Star Trek: The Starfleet Survival Guide, 2002; Star Trek: S.C.E.-Wildfire, 2003; New Frontier: No Limits-Waiting for G'Doh; Star Trek: S.C.E.-Failsafe, 2004; A Time to Kill, 2004; A Time to Heal, 2004; Tales of the Dominion War-Twilight's Wrath, 2004; Star Trek: S.C.E.-Small World, 2005; Vanguard: Harbinger, 2005; Warpath, 2006; Road of Bones, 2006; Mirror Universe: Glass Empires, 2007; Vanguard: Reap the Whirlwind, 2007; Destiny: Gods of Night, 2008; Destiny: Mere Mortals, 2008; Destiny: Lost Souls, 2008; Mirror Universe: Shards and Shadows-For Want of a Nail, 2009; The Calling, 2009; Vanguard: Precipice, 2009; The Roast of Keith R.A. DeCandido, 2009; Mirror Universe: The Sorrows of Empire, 2010; Farscape: Scorpius, 2010; The Roast of Michael Jan Friedman, 2010; Typhon Pact: Zero Sum Game, 2010; No Turning Back, 2011; Mirror Universe: Rise Like Lions, 2011; Vanguard: Storming Heaven, 2012. **Address:** c/o Lucienne Diver, The Knight Agency, PO Box 2659, Land O Lakes, FL 34639, U.S.A. **Online address:** davidmack@sff.net

MACK, Raneta Lawson. American (born United States), b. 1963?. **Genres:** Law, Social Sciences. **Career:** Davis Graham and Stubbs, associate attorney, 1988-91; Creighton University School of Law, assistant professor, 1991-94, associate professor, 1994-97, professor of law, 1997-; University of Toledo College of Law, visiting professor, 2003; Nebraska Appleseed Center for Law, board directors, 2009-. Writer. **Publications:** A Layperson's Guide to Criminal Law, 1999; The Digital Divide: Standing at the Intersection of Race and Technology, 2001; (with M.J. Kelly) Equal Justice in the Balance: America's Legal Responses to the Emerging Terrorist Threat, 2004; Comparative Criminal Procedure: History, Processes and Case Studies, 2008. **Address:** Creighton University School of Law, 2500 California Plz., Omaha, NE 68178, U.S.A. **Online address:** rmack@creighton.edu

MACKAY, Claire (Bacchus). Canadian (born Canada), b. 1930. **Genres:** Children's Fiction, Young Adult Fiction, Children's Non-fiction, Young Adult Non-fiction. **Career:** Polysar Corp., library assistant, 1952-55; Wascana Hospital, medical social worker, 1969-71; Steelworkers' Union, research librarian, 1972-78; Steel Labor, feature columnist, 1975-78; Canadian Society of Children's Authors, Illustrators, and Performers, founding member, secretary, 1977-79, president, 1979-81; freelance researcher and writer, 1978-; editorial consultant, 1986-91; Kids Toronto, feature columnist, 1986-93. Contributor to periodicals. **Publications:** Mini-Bike Hero, 1974; Mini-Bike Racer, 1976; Exit Barney McGee, 1979; (with M. Hewitt) One Proud Summer, 1981; Mini-Bike Rescue, 1982; The Minerva Program, 1984; (with J. Little) Bats about Baseball, 1995; Laughs: Funny Stories, 1997. NONFICTION: Pay Cheques and Picket Lines: All about Unions in Canada, 1987; The Toronto Story, 1990, rev. ed., 2002; Touching All the Bases: Baseball for Kids of All Ages, 1994; Horrible Canadian Histories: First Folks and Vile Voyageurs, 2001. Contributor to books. **Address:** Transatlantic Literary Agency, 72 Glengowan Rd., Toronto, ON M4N 1G4, Canada. **Online address:** claire.mackay@sympatico.ca

MACKAY, Donald (Iain). British/Japanese (born Japan), b. 1937. **Genres:** Economics, Politics/Government, Business/Trade/Industry. **Career:** Systems analyst, 1959-62; University of Aberdeen, lecturer, 1962-66, professor of political economy, 1971-76; University of Glasgow, lecturer, 1966-68, senior lecturer in applied economics, 1968-71; Scottish Journal of Political Economy, editor, 1971-82; Pieda P.L.C., chairman, 1974; Heriot-Watt University, professor of economics, 1976-82, professorial fellow, 1982, honorary professor, 1992-91; Governor National Institute of Economic and Social Research, faculty, 1982-. Writer. **Publications:** Geographical Mobility and the Brain Drain: A Case Study of Aberdeen University Graduates, 1860-1960, 1969; (contrib.) Local Labor Markets and Wage Structures, 1970; (co-author) Labour Markets Under Different Employment Conditions, 1971; North Sea Oil Through Speculative Glasses, 1975; (with G.A. MacKay) Political Economy of North Sea Oil, 1975; (ed.) Scotland 1980: The Economics of Self-Government, 1977; (with N.K. Buxton) British Employment Statistics: A Guide to Sources and Methods, 1977; (co-author) The Economic Impact of North Sea Oil on Scotland: Final Report to the Scottish Economic Planning Department on a Study Conducted Within the Department of Political Economy, the University of Aberdeen, 1973-77, 1978; (ed.) Scotland: The Framework for Change, 1979. **Address:** Newfield, 14 Gamekeeper's Rd., Edinburgh, LT EH4 6LU, Scotland.

MACKAY, Harvey (B.). American (born United States), b. 1932. **Genres:** Business/Trade/Industry. **Career:** Quality Park Envelope Co., salesman, 1954-59; Mackay Envelope Co., founder, owner, chairman and chief executive officer, 1959-; Sundance Institute, director; University of Minnesota, Carlson School of Management, director; United Feature Syndicate, columnist. **Publications:** Swim with the Sharks without Being Eaten Alive: Outsell, Outmanage, Outmotivate and Outnegotiate Your Competition, 1988; Beware the Naked Man Who Offers You His Shirt: Do What You Love, Love What You Do and Deliver More Than You Promise, 1990; Sharkproof: Get the Job You Want, Keep the Job You Love in Today's Frenzied Job Market, 1993; Dig Your Well before You're Thirsty, 1997; (with J.W. Hartman) Maverick Management: An Unconventional Guide to Success, 1998; Pushing the Envelope: All the Way to the Top, 1999; We Got Fired!-and It's The Best Thing that Ever Happened To Us, 2004; Use Your Head to Get Your Foot in the Door: Job Search Secrets No One Else Will Tell You, 2010; Mackay MBA of Selling in the Real World, 2011. Contributor to periodicals. **Address:** MackayMitchell Envelope Co., 2100 Elm St. SE, Minneapolis, MN 55414, U.S.A. **Online address:** harvey@mackay.com

MACKEN, JoAnn Early. American (born United States), b. 1953?. **Genres:** Animals/Pets, Biography, Natural History. **Career:** Mount Mary College, adjunct professor. Writer. **Publications:** Cats on Judy, 1997; Zebras, 2002; African Animals, 2002; Bears, 2002; Camels, 2002; Elephants, 2002; Farm Animals, 2002; Giraffes, 2002; Hippos, 2002; Lions, 2002; Monkeys, 2002; Penguins, 2002; Polar Animals, 2002; Rain Forest Animals, 2002; Sea Lions, 2002; Snakes, 2002; Tigers, 2002; (ed.) Welcome to Sri Lanka, 2003; Crossing Guard, 2003; Mail Carrier, 2003; Nurse, 2003; Sanitation Worker, 2003; Teacher, 2003; Veterinarian, 2003; Goldfish, 2004; Guinea Pigs, 2004; Kittens, 2004; Parakeets, 2004; Puppies, 2004; Rabbits, 2004; Sing-Along Song, 2004; Moose, 2005; Music Lessons, 2005; Ocean Floors, 2005; Opossums,

2005; Owls, 2005; Pigs, 2005; Porcupines, 2005; Sheep, 2005; Swimming, 2005; Art Classes, 2005; Bike Riding, 2005; Black Bears, 2005; Chickens, 2005; Cows, 2005; Deer, 2005; Goats, 2005; Gymnastics, 2005; Horses, 2005; Karate, 2005; Spring, 2006; Summer, 2006; Vultures, 2006; Wetlands, 2006; Winter, 2006; (with L. Sabin) The Wright Brothers: The Flight to Adventure, 2006; (with L. Sabin) Thomas Edison: Incredible Inventor, 2006; The Life Cycle of a Hummingbird, 2006; The Life Cycle of a Moth, 2006; Seas, 2006; Mountain Goats, 2006; Mountains, 2006; Ocean Floors, 2006; Plains, 2006; Rattlesnakes, 2006; Rivers, 2006; Roadrunners, 2006; Elk, 2006; Gary Paulsen: Voice of Adventure and Survival, 2006; Gila Monsters, 2006; Golden Eagles, 2006; Jackrabbits, 2006; Lakes, 2006; The Life Cycle of a Bat, 2006; The Life Cycle of a Cicada, 2006; The Life Cycle of a Dragonfly, 2006; The Life Cycle of a Flamingo, 2006; Autumn, 2006; Beaches, 2006; Bighorn Sheep, 2006; Condors, 2006; Coral Reefs, 2006; Cougars, 2006; Coyotes, 2006; Deserts, 2006; (with K. Brandt) Abraham Lincoln: Road to the White House, 2007; (with K. Brandt) Paul Revere, Son of Liberty, 2007; (with F. Sabin) Abigail Adams: Young Patriot, 2007; (with F. Sabin) Elizabeth Blackwell, the First Woman Doctor, 2007; (with L. Santrey) Ben Franklin: Extraordinary Inventor, Brave Leader, 2007; (with L. Santrey) George Washington: Founding Father, 2007; (co-author) Daniel Boone, 2007; (co-author) Davy Crockett, 2007; (co-author) Babe Ruth, 2007; (co-author) Roberto Clemente, 2007; Building a Road, 2008; Building a Skyscraper, 2008; Construction Crews, 2008; Construction Tools, 2008; Demolition, 2008; Digging Tunnels, 2008; Flip, Float, Fly: Seeds on the Move, 2008; Building a Bridge, 2009; Building a House, 2009; Waiting Out the Storm, 2010; A Day on the Town, 2010; The Dinosaur Museum, 2010; Road Signs, 2010; Shopping at the Mall, 2010; Flags around the World, 2011; Landmarks around the World, 2011. Contributor to magazines. **Address:** Shorewood, WI , U.S.A. **Online address:** joann@joannmacken.com

MACKENNA, John. Irish (born Ireland), b. 1952. **Genres:** Poetry, Novels, Novellas/Short Stories, History. **Career:** County Kildare Vocational Education Co., teacher, 1974-80; RTE Radio 1, senior producer, 1980-; writer, 2002-. **Publications:** The Occasional Optimist (poems), 1977; The lost village: A diary of Castledermot in 1925, 1985; The Fallen (stories), 1992; Clare (novel), 1993; The Lost Village (social history), 1995; A Year of Our Lives (stories), 1995; The Last Fine Summer (novel), 1997; A Haunted Heart (novel), 1999; (with J. Shackleton) Shackleton: An Irishman in Antarctica, 2002; River Field, 2007; The Space Between Us, 2009; (contrib.) Annals of Ballitore, 2009. **Address:** RTE Radio 1, Dublin, 4, Ireland. **Online address:** macken@rte.ie

MACKENNEY, Richard. Scottish/British (born England), b. 1953. **Genres:** History, Cultural/Ethnic Topics. **Career:** Rotary Foundation of Rotary Intl., graduate fellow; University of Edinburgh, senior lecturer in history, Early Modern European History, reader, head of history subject, professor; St Catharine's College, visiting fellow, 1992; Colgate University, distinguished visiting professor, 2003. Historian and writer. **Publications:** Tradesmen and Traders: The World of the Guilds in Venice and Europe, 1250-1650, 1987; The City-State, 1500-1700: Republican Liberty in an Age of Princely Power, 1989; Sixteenth Century Europe: Expansion and Conflict, 1993; Renaissance Italians, 1300-1600, 1997; Renaissances: The Cultures of Italy, 1300-1600, 2005. Contributor to periodicals. **Address:** Department of History, University of Edinburgh, Rm. 300, William Robertson Bldg., 50 George Sq., Edinburgh, EH8 9JY, Scotland. **Online address:** richard.mackenney@ed.ac.uk

MACKENZIE, Anna. New Zealander (born New Zealand), b. 1963. **Genres:** Natural History. **Career:** Writer. **Publications:** High Tide, 2003; Out on the Edge, 2005; The Sea-Wreck Stranger, 2007; Shadow of the Mountain, 2009; Ebony Hill, 2010. Contributor to periodicals. **Address:** New Zealand. **Online address:** amack@airnet.net.nz

MACKENZIE, Cameron A. (Cameron Alexander MacKenzie). American (born United States), b. 1947. **Genres:** Theology/Religion, History. **Career:** St. Matthew Lutheran Church, teacher, 1970-72, headmaster, 1972-83, pastor, 1975-83; Ordained Lutheran Church, Missouri Synod minister, 1972; Concordia Theological Seminary, Department of Historical Theology, assistant professor, 1983-92, associate professor, 1992-97, professor, 1997-2007, department chair, 1999-, Ellis professor of historical theology, 2007-, Ellis professor of historical theology chair; Concordia University, adjunct faculty, 1990-2007; Indiana University-Purdue University, associate faculty, 1992-; College of St. Francis, adjunct faculty, 1992. Writer. **Publications:** The Battle for the Bible in England, 1557-1582, 2002; Contributor to books and journals. **Address:** Concordia Theological Seminary, 6600 N Clinton St., Fort Wayne, IN 46825-4916, U.S.A. **Online address:** cameron.mackenzie@ctsfw.edu

MACKENZIE, Cameron Alexander. *See* **MACKENZIE, Cameron A.**

MACKENZIE, Craig. South African (born South Africa), b. 1960. **Genres:** Philosophy, Young Adult Non-fiction. **Career:** Rand Afrikaans University, Faculty of Humanities, Department English, senior lecturer, associate professor, professor. Writer. **Publications:** Bessie Head: An Introduction, 1989; Between the Lines II: Interviews with Nadine Gordimer, Menan du Plessis, Zoe Wicomb, Lauretta Ngcobo, 1993; (comp.) Transitions: Half a Century of South African Short Stories, 1999; Starlight on the Veld: Best of Bosman, 2001; (with G. Cornwell and D. Klopper) Columbia Guide to South African Literature in English since 1945, 2010. EDITOR: (with C. Clayton) Between the Lines: Interviews with Bessie Head, Ellen Kuzwayo, Miriam Tlali, 1989; A Woman Alone: Autobiographical Writings, 1990; Bessie Head: A Bibliography, 1992; Nadine Gordimer: A Bibliography, 1993; Mafeking Road and Other Stories, 1998; Bessie Head, 1999; Idle Talk: Voorkamer Stories I, 1999; Seed-time and Harvest and Other Stories, 1999; The Oral-Style South African Short Story in English: A.W. Drayson to H.C. Bosman, 1999; Old Transvaal Stories, 2000; The Rooinek and Other Boer War Stories, 2000; Unto Dust and Other Stories, 2002; Young Bosman, 2003; Complete Oom Schalk Lourens Stories, 2006. **Address:** Faculty of Humanities, Department of English, Rand Afrikaans University, PO Box 524, Auckland Park, 2006, South Africa. **Online address:** craigm@uj.ac.za

MACKENZIE, Donald (Angus). Scottish/British (born England), b. 1950. **Genres:** Sociology, History, Sciences, Business/Trade/Industry, Economics, Technology. **Career:** University of Edinburgh, lecturer in sociology, 1975-88, Science Studies Unit, lecturer, 1983-84, reader in sociology, 1988-92, School of Social and Political Science, professor of sociology, 1992-; Harvard University, visiting professor of the history of the science, 1997-98. Writer. **Publications:** Scotland's First National Theatre, 1963; (co-author) In and against the State, 1980; Statistics in Britain, 1865-1930: The Social Construction of Scientific Knowledge, 1981; (ed. with J. Wajcman) The Social Shaping of Technology: How the Refrigerator Got its Hum, 1985, 2nd ed., 1999; Inventing Accuracy: A Historical Sociology of Nuclear Missile Guidance, 1990; Knowing Machines: Essays on Technical Change, 1996; Mechanizing Proof: Computing, Risk and Trust, 2001; An Engine, Not a Camera: How Financial Models Shape Markets, 2006; (ed. with F. Muniesa and L. Siu) Do Economists Make Markets?: On The Performativity of Economics, 2007; Material Markets: How Economic Agents are Constructed, 2009. Contributor to books, journals and newspapers. **Address:** School of Social and Political Studies, University of Edinburgh, 6.26 Chrystal Macmillan Bldg., 15a George Sq., Edinburgh, EH8 9LD, Scotland. **Online address:** d.mackenzie@ed.ac.uk

MACKENZIE, G. Calvin. American (born United States), b. 1945. **Genres:** Politics/Government, History. **Career:** Colby College, vice president for development and alumni relations, 1985-88, Goldfarb Family distinguished professor of government; University of London, Institute of United States Studies, John Adams fellow, 1999-2000; National Commission on the Public Service, senior advisor, 2002; Presidential Appointee Initiative, senior advisor; Brookings Institution, visiting fellow; National Academy of Public Administration, fellow; Brademas Center on the Congress, senior research associate; Beijing Foreign Studies University, Fulbright lecturer; U.S. House Commission on Administrative Review, senior research analyst. Writer. **Publications:** The Politics of Presidential Appointments, 1981; (ed. with J. Cooper) The House at Work, 1981; American Government: Politics and Public Policy, 1986; (ed.) The In-and-Outers: Presidential Appointees and Transient Government in Washington, 1987; Obstacle Course: The Report of the Twentieth Century Fund Task Force on the Presidential Appointment Process with Background Papers by G. Calvin Mackenzie and Robert Shogan, 1996; (with S. Thornton) Bucking the Deficit: Economic Policymaking in America, 1996; The Irony of Reform: Roots of American Political Disenchantment, 1996; Starting Over: The Presidential Appointment Process in 1997, 1998; (ed.) Innocent until Nominated: The Breakdown of the Presidential Appointments Process, 2001; (with M. Hafken) Scandal Proof: Do Ethics Laws Make Government Ethical?, 2002; (with S.J. Wayne and R.L. Cole) Conflict and Consensus in American Politics, 2007; (with S.J. Wayne and R.L. Cole) Conflict and Consensus in American Politics, 2007; (with R. Weisbrot) The Liberal Hour: Washington and the Politics of Change in the 1960s, 2008. **Address:** Department of Government, Colby College, Waterville, ME 04901, U.S.A. **Online address:** gcmacken@colby.edu

MACKENZIE, **Jassy.** South African/Zimbabwean (born Zimbabwe), b. 1971?. **Genres:** Literary Criticism And History. **Career:** Writer. **Publications:** Random Violence, 2010; Stolen Lives, 2011. Contributor to periodicals. **Address:** Johannesburg, South Africa. **Online address:** webmaster@jassymackenzie.com

MACKENZIE, **Sally.** American (born United States) **Genres:** Novels, Romance/Historical. **Career:** U.S. Department of Agriculture, staff. Writer. **Publications:** NAKED SERIES: The Naked Duke, 2005; The Naked Marquis, 2006; The Naked Earl, 2007; The Naked Gentleman, 2008; The Naked Baron, 2009; (with V. Henley, V. Dahl and K. Astor) The Naked Laird in Lords of Desire, 2009; The Naked Viscount, 2010; The Naked King, 2011. Works appear in anthologies. **Address:** PO Box 2453, Kensington, MD 20891, U.S.A. **Online address:** writesally@comcast.net

MACKERRAS, **Colin Patrick.** Australian (born Australia), b. 1939. **Genres:** History, Theatre, International Relations/Current Affairs, Race Relations, Music, Area Studies. **Career:** Beijing Institute of Foreign Languages, foreign expert, 1964-66, 1986, 1995-96; Australian National University, Department of Far Eastern history, research fellow, 1969-73, senior research fellow, 1973; Griffith University, School of International Business and Asian Studies (IBAS), foundation professor, 1974-2004, professor emeritus, 2004-, School of MAS, chairman, 1979-85, head, 1988-89, 1996-2000, Key Centre for Asian Languages and Studies, co-director, 1988-96; Asian Ethnicity, editor-in-chief, founding editor, 2000-07; Beijing Foreign Studies University, honorary professor, 2005-10. **Publications:** (With N. Hunter) China Observed 1964-67, 1967; The Uighur Empire According to the T'ang Dynastic Histories, 1968; The Uighur Empire According to the Tang Dynastic Histories, A Study in Sino-Uighur Relations 744-840, 1972; The Rise of the Peking Opera, 1770-1870: Social Aspects of the Theatre in Manchu China, 1972; Amateur Theatre in China, 1949-1966, 1973; The Chinese Theatre in Modern Times, from 1840 to the Present Day, 1975; Musical Cultures of Asia: China, 1980; The Performing Arts in Contemporary China, 1981; Modern China: A Chronology from 1842 to the Present, 1982; The Democratic People's Republic of Korea in World Affairs, 1984; (with E.S.K. Fung) From Fear to Friendship: Australia's Policies Towards the People's Republic of China, 1966-1982, 1985; Western Images of China, 1989, 2nd ed., 1999; (with L.H. Gill) Portraits of China, 1990; Chinese Drama, 1990; (with A. Yorke) The Cambridge Handbook of Contemporary China, 1991; China Since 1978: Reform, Modernisation and Socialism with Chinese Characteristics, 1993; China's Minorities: Integration and Modernization in the Twentieth Century, 1994; China's Minority Cultures: Identities and Integration Since 1912, 1995; Peking Opera, 1997; China in Transformation, 1900-1949, 1998, rev. ed., 2008; Sinophiles and Sinophobes, 2000; The New Cambridge Handbook of Contemporary China, 2001; China's Ethnic Minorities and Globalisation, 2003. EDITOR: (with D. Leslie and W. Gungwu) Essays on the Sources for Chinese History, 1973; China: The Impact of Revolution: A Survey of Twentieth Century China, 1976; Chinese Theater from Its Origins to the Present Day, 1983; (with N. Knight) Marxism in Asia, 1985; (with C. Tung) Drama in the People's Republic of China, 1987; (with R. Cribb and A. Healy) Contemporary Vietnam: Perspectives from Australia, 1988; Eastern Asia: An Introductory History, 1992; Eastern Asia, 1992, 3rd ed., 2000; Australia and China, 1996; (with D.H. McMillen and A. Watson) Dictionary of the Politics of the People's Republic of China, 1998; (with R. Maidment) Culture and Society in the Asia-Pacific, 1998; Ethnicity in Asia, 2003; (with M. Clarke) China, Xinjiang and Central Asia: History, Transition and Crossborder Interaction into the 21st Century, 2009. Contributor to periodicals. **Address:** Department of International Business and Asian, Studies, Griffith University, 170 Kessels Rd., Nathan, QL 4111, Australia. **Online address:** c.mackerras@griffith.edu.au

MACKESY, **Piers Gerald.** British/Scottish (born Scotland), b. 1924. **Genres:** History. **Career:** Harvard University, Harkness Fellow, 1953-54; Oxford University, Pembroke College, tutor, senior tutor, vicegerent, fellow, 1954-88, now emeritus fellow; Institute for Advanced Study, visiting fellow, 1961-62; California Institute of Technology, visiting professor, 1966; Cambridge University, Lees Knowles lecturer, 1972; Clark University, lecturer, Bland-Lee lecturer; Naval War College, lecturer; British Academy, fellow; U.S. Military Academy, lecturer; National War College, lecturer; Northeastern University, lecturer. Writer. **Publications:** The War in the Mediterranean, 1803-1810, 1957; The War for America, 1775-1783, 1964, 2nd ed., 1993; Statesmen at War: The Strategy of Overthrow, 1798-1799, 1974; Could the British have Won the War of Independence?: Bland-Lee Lecture, September 1975, 1976; The Coward of Minden: The Affair of Lord George Sackville, 1979; War without Victory: The Downfall of Pitt, 1799-1802, 1984; War for America: 1775-1783, 1992; British Victory in Egypt, 1801: The End of Napoleon's Conquest, 1995. **Address:** Pembroke College, Pembroke Sq., Oxford, OX OX1 1DW, England.

MACKEY, **Richard A.** American (born United States), b. 1935?. **Genres:** Psychology, Human Relations/Parenting, Social Sciences, Gay And Lesbian Issues, Medicine/Health. **Career:** Camp Wediko, waterfront director, counselor, head counselor, summers, 1956-58; Catholic Charities, social caseworker, 1959-60; National Institute of Mental Health, Mental Health Study Center, psychiatric social worker, 1960-66; National Institute of Mental Health, research social worker in biometrics branch, 1960-61; Boston College, assistant professor, 1966-69, director of psychiatric social work program in community mental health, 1966-75, associate professor, 1969-84, chairperson of doctoral program, 1979-82, professor of social work, 1984-, now professor emeritus; private practice of clinical social work, 1968-90. Writer. **Publications:** Ego Psychology and Clinical Practice, 1985; (with B.A. O'Brien) Lasting Marriages: Men and Women Growing Together, 1995; (with B.A. O'Brien and E.F. Mackey) Gay and Lesbian Couples: Voices from Lasting Relationships, 1997. Contributor of articles to periodicals. **Address:** Graduate School of Social Work, Boston College, McGuinn Hall, 140 Commonwealth Ave., Chestnut Hill, MA 02467-3804, U.S.A. **Online address:** richard.mackey@bc.edu

MACKEY, **Thomas.** (Thomas C. Mackey). American (born United States), b. 1956. **Genres:** History, Law, Politics/Government. **Career:** Michigan State University, visiting assistant professor, 1985-86; University of Nebraska, visiting assistant professor, 1986-88; Eastern Montana College, assistant professor, 1988-89; Kansas State University, assistant professor, 1989-91; University of Louisville, Department of History, assistant professor, associate professor of history, 1994-2004, chair, 1999-2004, professor of history, 2004-, Brandeis School of Law, adjunct professor of law, 2004, McConnell Center, fellow. Writer. **Publications:** AS THOMAS C. MACKEY: Red Lights Out: A Legal History of Prostitution, Disorderly Houses, and Vice Districts, 1870-1917, 1987; Pornography on Trial: A Handbook with Cases, Laws, and Documents, 2002; Pursuing Johns: Criminal Law Reform, Defending Character, and New York City's Committee of Fourteen, 1920-1930, 2005. Contributor to periodicals. **Address:** Department of History, University of Louisville, 201C Gottschalk Hall, 2301 S 3rd St., Louisville, KY 40292, U.S.A. **Online address:** thomasmackey@louisville.edu

MACKEY, **Thomas C.** *See* **MACKEY**, **Thomas.**

MACKIN, **Jeanne.** American (born United States), b. 1951. **Genres:** History, Novels, Food And Wine, Homes/Gardens, Young Adult Non-fiction, Graphic Novels, Young Adult Fiction, Anthropology/Ethnology, Anthropology/Ethnology. **Career:** Harvard Business School, Alumni and Minority Affairs, secretary, 1971-72; Ithaca College, text and trade book department manager at college bookstore, 1973-76, Ithaca Opportunity Program, instructor, tutor and academic consultant, 1990-, Higher Education Opportunity Program, instructor, tutor and academic consultant, 1990-, Department of Writing, writing faculty, 1997-2004; Cornell University, Consumer News Service, staff writer, 1978-93, Media Services, staff writer, 1979-99, science writer, 1997-, Department of Human Resources, staff, 1988, College of Architecture, Art, and Planning, consultant, 1993, 1996, editor, 1979-82, intern supervisor in media services, 1984; Bennington College, teaching assistant in creative writing, 1985; Tompkins Cortland Community College, adjunct instructor in journalism, 1986; Goddard College, MFA in Creative Writing Program, writing faculty, 2001-. **Publications:** HISTORICAL NOVELS: The Frenchwoman, 1989; Queen's War: A Novel of Eleanor of Aquitaine, 1991; Dreams of Empire, 1996; The Sweet By and By, 2001. NONFICTION: The Cornell Book of Herbs and Edible Flowers, 1993; (ed. with D. Ackerman) The Book of Love (anthology), 1998. AS ANNA MACLEAN: LOUISA MAY ALCOTT MYSTERY SERIES: Louisa and the Missing Heiress, 2004; Louisa and the Country Bachelor, 2005; Louisa and the Crystal Gazer, 2006. OTHER: (ed.) Energy and Technology: The Design Connection, 1979. Contributor to periodicals. **Address:** c/o Esmond Harmsworth, Zachary, Schuster, Harmsworth Agency, 535 Boylston St., 11th Fl., Boston, MA 02116-3720, U.S.A. **Online address:** annasmysteries@aol.com

MACKINNON, **Catharine A.** American (born United States), b. 1946. **Genres:** Law, Politics/Government, Women's Studies And Issues, Social Sciences. **Career:** University of Minnesota, assistant professor of law, 1982-84; York University, professor of law, 1988-89; University of Michigan Law

School, professor, 1990-, Elizabeth A. Long professor of law, 1989-; University of Chicago, visiting professor of law, 1997; International Criminal Court, special gender adviser, 2008-; Harvard Law School, James Barr Ames visiting professor of law; Yale University, visiting professor of law; Harvard University, visiting professor of law; University of Basel, visiting professor of law; Osgoode Hall Law School, visiting professor of law; Stanford University, visiting professor of law; University of California, visiting professor of law; Institute for Advanced Study in the Behavioral Sciences, instructor and researcher; Wissenschaftskolleg zu Berlin, instructor and researcher. Writer. **Publications:** Sexual Harassment of Working Women: A Case of Sex Discrimination, 1979; Feminism Unmodified: Discourses on Life and Law, 1987; (with A. Dworkin) Pornography and Civil Rights: A New Day for Women's Equality, 1988; Toward a Feminist Theory of the State, 1989; Only Words, 1993; (ed. with A. Dworkin) In Harm's Way: The Pornography Civil Right's Hearings, 1997; Sex Equality, 2001, 2nd ed., 2007; (ed. with R.B. Siegel) Directions in Sexual Harassment Law, 2004; Women's Lives, Men's Laws, 2005; Are Women Human?: And Other International Dialogues, 2006. Contributor to periodicals. **Address:** University of Michigan Law School, 924 Legal Research, Ann Arbor, MI 48109, U.S.A.

MACKINNON, J. B. Canadian (born Canada), b. 1970?. **Genres:** Food And Wine. **Career:** Adbusters, contributing editor; journalist. **Publications:** Dead Man in Paradise: Unraveling a Murder from a Time of Revolution, 2005; (with A. Smith) Plenty: One Man, One Woman and a Raucous Year of Eating Locally, 2007; (with Alisa) The 100 Mile Diet A Year of Local Eating, 2008. Contributor to periodicals. **Address:** Anne McDermid & Associates Ltd., 83 Willcocks St., Toronto, ON M5S 1C9, Canada.

MACKINNON, Mark. Canadian (born Canada), b. 1974?. **Genres:** Politics/Government. **Career:** Globe and Mail, reporter, 1998-, Middle East correspondent, 2005-; Edmonton Journal, staff; Province Herald, staff. Journalist and writer. **Publications:** The New Cold War: Revolutions, Rigged Elections and Pipeline Politics in the Former Soviet Union, 2007. **Online address:** mark@markmackinnon.ca

MACKINTOSH-SMITH, Tim. British (born England), b. 1961. **Genres:** Travel/Exploration, History. **Career:** Harvard University, Center for Middle Eastern Studies, lecturer. Writer. **Publications:** Yemen: The Unknown Arabia, 2000; Travels With a Tangerine: A Journey in the Footnotes of Ibn Battutah, 2001; (intro.) Travels of Ibn Battutah, 2002; Travels with a Tangerine: From Morocco to Turkey in the Footsteps of Islam's Greatest Traveler, 2004; The Hall of a Thousand Columns: Hindustan to Malabar with Ibn Battutah, 2005; Landfalls, 2010. **Address:** c/o Author Mail, Overlook Press, 1 Overlook Dr., Woodstock, NY 12498, U.S.A. **Online address:** tim@mackintosh-smith.com

MACKLER, Carolyn. American (born United States), b. 1973. **Genres:** Novels, Poetry, Novellas/Short Stories. **Career:** Novelist. **Publications:** (Comp.) 250 Ways to Make America Better, 1999; Love and Other Four-Letter Words, 2000; The Earth My Butt and Other Big Round Things, 2003; Vegan Virgin Valentine, 2004; Guyaholic: A Story of Finding, Flirting, Forgetting, 2007; Tangled, 2010. **Address:** HarperCollins Children's Books, 10 E 53rd St., New York, NY 10022, U.S.A. **Online address:** carolyn@carolynmackler.com

MACKLIN, Robert. Australian (born Australia), b. 1941?. **Genres:** Novels, Biography, Autobiography/Memoirs. **Career:** Armak Productions, owner; Brisbane Courier Mail, staff; Canberra Times, associate editor, 1990-2002. **Publications:** The Queenslander, 1975; The Paper Castle, 1977; Newsfront, 1978; The Journalist: A Novel, 1979; Juryman, 1982; 100 Great Australians, 1983; The Secret Life of Jesus, 1990; War Babies: A Memoir, 2004; Fire in the Blood, 2005; Jacka VC: Australian Hero, 2006; Backs to the Wall: A Larrikin on the Western Front, 2007; Kevin Rudd: The Biography, 2007; (with R. Maylor) Sniper Elite: The World of a Top Special Forces Marksman, 2011. WITH PETER THOMPSON: The Battle of Brisbane: Australians and the Yanks at War, 2000; The Man Who Died Twice: The Life and Adventures of Morrison of Peking, 2004; Keep Off the Skyline: The Story of Ron Cashman and the Diggers in Korea, 2004; Kill the Tiger: The Truth about Operation Rimau, 2005; The Life and Adventures of Morrison of China, 2007; Big Fella: The Rise and Rise of BHP Billiton, 2009. **Address:** 83 Alexander St., Crows Nest, QL 2065, Australia. **Online address:** robert@robertmacklin.com

MACKOWSKI, Maura Phillips. American (born United States), b. 1956?. **Genres:** Air/Space Topics, History, Medicine/Health. **Career:** Arizona State University, lecturer in history. Freelance writer and academic. **Publications:** Testing the Limits: Aviation Medicine and the Origins of Manned Space Flight, 2006. **Address:** Gilbert, AZ , U.S.A. **Online address:** maura.mackowski@asu.edu

MACK SMITH, Denis. British (born England), b. 1920. **Genres:** History, Politics/Government, Biography. **Career:** Clifton College, assistant master, 1941-42; War Cabinet officer, 1943-45; Cambridge University, fellow, 1947-62, tutor, 1948-58, lecturer, 1952-62; All Souls College, senior research fellow, 1962-87, emeritus fellow, 1987-; Wolfson College, extraordinary fellow, 1987-, honorary fellow. Writer. **Publications:** Cavour and Garibaldi 1860: A Study in Political Conflict, 1954; Garibaldi, a Great Life in Brief, 1956; Italy: A Modern History, 1958, rev. ed., 1969; Latifundia in Modern Sicilian History, 1965; History of Sicily, 1968; Medieval Sicily, 1968; Modern Sicily, 1968; Da Cavour a Mussolini, 1968; Victor Emanuel, Cavour, and the Risorgimento, 1971; Mussolini as a Military Leader, 1974; Vittorio Emanuele II: 1975; Mussolini's Roman Empire, 1976; Un Monumento al Duce, 1976; Cento Anni di Vita Italiana Attraverso il Corriere della Sera, 1978; L'Italia del Ventesimo Secolo, 1978; Mussolini, 1981; Garibaldi, a Great Life in Brief, 1982; Garibaldi, una vita a più immagini, 1982; Cavour, 1985; (co-author) A History of Sicily, 1986; Italy and Its Monarchy, 1989; Mazzini, 1994; Modern Italy: A Political History, 1997; La Storia Manipulata, 1998. EDITOR: The Making of Italy 1796-1870, 1968; Great Lives Observed: Garibaldi, 1969; Le Rivoluzioni d'Italia, 1970; Scritti Politici, 1972; I Mille: Da Genova a Capua, 1981; Un Viaggio Elettorale, 1983; Nelson History of England. **Address:** All Souls College, University of Oxford, Oxford, OX OX1 4AL, England.

MACLACHLAN, Colin M. American (born United States) **Genres:** History. **Career:** California State University-Long Beach, assistant professor, 1969-74, associate professor, 1974-75; Tulane University, Department of History, associate professor, 1975-88, professor of history, 1988-, chair, 1991-94, director of graduate studies, 1999-2001, John Christy Barr distinguished professor, 1999-; University of California-Los Angeles, visiting associate professor, 1983. Writer. **Publications:** Criminal Justice in Eighteenth Century Mexico: A Study of the Tribunal of the Acordada, 1974; (with J.E. Rodriguez) The Forging of the Cosmic Race: A Reinterpretation of Colonial Mexico, 1980; Spain's Empire in the New World: The Role of Ideas in Institutional and Social Change, 1988; Anarchism and the Mexican Revolution: The Political Trials of Ricardo Flores Magón in the United States, 1991; (with W.H. Beezley) El Gran Pueblo: A History of Greater Mexico, 1994; (ed.) Narcotráfico, 1995; (with W.H. Beezley) Latin America: The Peoples and Their History, 2000; (with J.E. Rodriguez) Hacia El Ser Histórico De México: Una Reinterpretación De La Nueva España, 2001; A History of Modern Brazil: The Past against the Future, 2003; Argentina: What Went Wrong, 2006; (with W.H. Beezley) Mexicans in Revolution, 1910-1946: An Introduction, 2009; (with W.H. Beezley) Mexico's Crucial Century, 1810-1910: An Introduction, 2010. **Address:** Department of History, Tulane University, 121 Hebert Hall, 6823 St. Charles Ave., New Orleans, LA 70118, U.S.A. **Online address:** cmaclac@tulane.edu

MACLACHLAN, Patricia. American (born United States), b. 1938. **Genres:** Children's Fiction, Picture/Board Books, Novels, Literary Criticism And History. **Career:** Bennett Junior High School, English teacher, 1963-79; Smith College, visiting lecturer, 1986-. Writer. **Publications:** The Sick Day, 1979; Through Grandpa's Eyes, 1980; Arthur, for the Very First Time, 1980; Moon, Stars, Frogs, and Friends, 1980; Mama One, Mama Two, 1982; Cassie Binegar, 1982; Tomorrow's Wizard, 1982; Seven Kisses in a Row, 1983; Unclaimed Treasures, 1984; Sarah, Plain and Tall, 1985; The Facts and Fictions of Minna Pratt, 1988; Journey, 1991; Three Names, 1991; Baby, 1993; All the Places to Love, 1994; Skylark, 1994; What You Know First, 1995; (co-author) It's Fine To Be Nine, 2000; (with J. Blume, A.M. Martin and R. Dahl) It's Heaven to Be Seven, 2000; Caleb's Story, 2001; (with E. MacLachlan) Painting the Wind, 2003; (with E. MacLachlan) Bittle, 2004; More Perfect than the Moon, 2004; Who Loves Me?, 2005; (with E.M. Charest) Once I Ate a Pie, 2006; Grandfather's Dance, 2006; (with E.M. Charest) Fiona Loves The Night, 2007; Two Novels: Baby, Journey, 2007; Edward's Eyes, 2007; (co-author) Acting Out, 2008; The True Gift: A Christmas Story, 2009; How was the Night?, 2009; Here and There, 2010; (with E.M. Charest) I Didn't Do It, 2010; Word After Word After Word, 2010; (with E.M. Charest) Before You Came, 2011; Waiting for the Magic, 2011; Your Moon, My Moon, 2011; Lala Salama: A Tanzanian Lullaby, 2011; Boxcar Children Beginning, 2012; Kindred Souls, 2012; White Fur Flying, 2013. Works appear in anthologies.

Contributor to books and periodicals. **Address:** HarperCollins Publishers, 10 E 53rd St., New York, NY 10022, U.S.A.

MACLAINE, Shirley. American (born United States), b. 1934. **Genres:** Autobiography/Memoirs, Biography, inspirational/Motivational Literature. **Career:** Actress and writer. **Publications:** Don't Fall off the Mountain, 1970; (ed.) McGovern: The Man and His Beliefs, 1972; (intro.) The New Celebrity Cookbook, 1973; You Can Get There from Here, 1975; Out on a Limb, 1983; Dancing in the Light, 1985; It's All in the Playing, 1987; Going Within: A Guide for Inner Transformation, 1989; Dance While You Can (memoir), 1991; My Lucky Stars: A Hollywood Memoir, 1995; The Camino: A Journey of the Spirit, 2000; Out on a Leash: Exploring the Nature of Reality and Love, 2003; Sage-ing While Age-ing, 2007; I'm Over all that, 2011. **Address:** c/o Brit Elders, ShirleyMacLaine.com, PO Box 25962, Munds Park, AZ 86017-5962, U.S.A. **Online address:** info@shirleymaclaine.com

MACLANE, Jack. *See* **CRIDER, (Allen) Bill(y).**

MACLEAN, Glynne. New Zealander (born New Zealand), b. 1964. **Genres:** Young Adult Fiction, Novels, Science Fiction/Fantasy, Children's Fiction, Novellas/Short Stories, History, Poetry. **Career:** Novelist. **Publications:** SELF-ILLUSTRATED: Roivan, 2003. OTHERS: Love in Shades of Grey (adult novel), 2004; Easter Island For The Gannet (short story) 2004; The Spiral Chrysalis (junior fiction), 2008; The Time Stealers, 2008; The Test, 2009; The Silent, 2009; Escape (junior historical novel), 2009; Viennese Meow (short story), 2009; Space Race (junior science fiction novel), 2011; The Camel and the Tiger Moth, 2012. Contributor to journals. **Address:** c/o Michael Gifkins, Michael Gifkins & Associates, PO Box 6496, Auckland, 1141, New Zealand. **Online address:** glynne@glynne.co.nz

MACLEAN, Jill. Canadian/British (born England), b. 1941?. **Genres:** Poetry. **Career:** Dalhousie University, faculty; Mount Allison University, faculty; Sydney City Hospital, staff. Writer. **Publications:** Jean Pierre Roma of the Company of the East of Isle St. Jean, 1977; The Brevity of Red (poetry), 2003; The Nine Lives of Travis Keating, 2008; The Present Tense of Prinny Murphy, 2010. **Address:** Writer's Federation of Nova Scotia, 1113 Marginal Rd., Halifax, NS B3H 4P7, Canada.

MACLEAN, Judy Ellen. American (born United States), b. 1946. **Genres:** Young Adult Fiction, Novels, Literary Criticism And History. **Career:** Writer. **Publications:** Rosemary and Juliet (novel), 2003. **Address:** Alice Street Editions, 10 Alice St., Binghamton, NY 13904-1580, U.S.A. **Online address:** judymac131313@yahoo.com

MACLEAN, Rory. Canadian/British (born England), b. 1954. **Genres:** Travel/Exploration, Adult Non-fiction, History, inspirational/Motivational Literature, Mythology/Folklore, Popular Culture. **Career:** Freelance filmmaker and writer, 1976-89; writer and broadcaster, 1989-; Royal Society of Literature, fellow. **Publications:** Stalin's Nose: Travels Around the Bloc, 1992; Stalin's Nose: Across the Face of Europe, 1992; The Oatmeal Ark: Across Canada by Water, 1996; Under the Dragon: Travels in a Betrayed Land, 1999; Next Exit Magic Kingdom, 2000; Falling for Icarus: A Journey Among the Cretans, 2004; Magic Bus: On the Hippie Trail from Istanbul to India, 2006; Under the Dragon: A Journey through Burma, 2008; The Oatmeal Ark: From the Scottish Isles to a Promised Land, 2008; Missing Lives, 2010; Gift of Time, 2011. Contributor of articles to periodicals. **Address:** c/o Peter Straus, Rogers, Coleridge & White Ltd., 20 Powis Mews, London, GL W11 1JN, England. **Online address:** wander@rorymaclean.com

MACLEAN, Sarah. American (born United States), b. 1978. **Genres:** Novels, Romance/Historical. **Career:** Writer. **Publications:** The Season (novel), 2009; Nine Rules to Break When Romancing a Rake, 2010; Ten Ways to be Adored When Landing a Lord, 2010. **Address:** Brooklyn, NY , U.S.A. **Online address:** sarah@macleanspace.com

MACLEAR, Kyo. Canadian/British (born England), b. 1970?. **Genres:** Art/Art History, History, Novels. **Career:** Mix, editor, 1996-97; Toronto Life, visual arts columnist, 1997-99. **Publications:** Beclouded Visions: Hiroshima-Nagasaki and the Art of Witness, 1999; (with K. Walters) Private Investigations: Undercover in Public Space, 1999; (ed. with B. Testa) Life Style, 2000; (ed.) Lepanto: Cy Twombly, 2001; (ed.) Mark di Suvero, 2001; (ed.) Pop Art: The John and Kimiko Powers Collection, 2001; (ed.) Tokyo Think Zone Life Style, 2002; (ed.) Aiko Suzuki: Selected Works 1973-2003, 2003; (ed.) Incomplete Manifesto for Growth, 2007; The Letter Opener, 2007; (ed.) Andrew Rucklidge Paintings 2005-2007, 2008. Contributor to periodicals. **Address:** c/o Jackie Kaiser, Westwood Creative Artists, 94 Harbord St., Toronto, ON M5S 1G6, Canada. **Online address:** kyo@ca.inter.net

MACLEOD, Alison. British (born England), b. 1920. **Genres:** Novels, Plays/Screenplays, Politics/Government, Children's Fiction. **Career:** Daily Worker, staff, 1944-56; London College of Printing, visiting tutor, 1970; freelance journalist. **Publications:** Dear Augustine (play), 1958; The Heretics, 1965, 2nd ed., 1966; The Hireling, 1968 in UK as The Trusted Servant, 1972; City of Light, 1969 in UK as No Need of the Sun, 1971; The Muscovite, 1971; The Jesuit, 1972 in US as Prisoner of the Queen, 1973; The Portingale, 1976; Servicing Social Services: Local Authority Legal Representation in Child Care Cases, 1993; The Death of Uncle Joe, 1997; (with J. Hunt) The Best-Laid Plans: Outcomes of Judicial Decisions in Child Protection Cases, 1999. **Address:** 63 Muswell Hill Pl., London, GL N10 3RP, England.

MACLEOD, Elizabeth. Canadian (born Canada), b. 1988. **Genres:** Children's Fiction, Children's Non-fiction, Biography. **Career:** OWL Magazine, editor; Kids Can Press, executive editor. **Publications:** Lions, 1988; Koalas, 1989; Puffins, 1990; Australia, 1990; The Puzzlers Book, 1991; The Recycling Book, 1991; Dinosaurs: The Fastest, the Fiercest, the Most Amazing, 1995; The Phone Book: Instant Communication from Smoke Signals to Satellites and Beyond, 1995; Get Started: Stamp Collecting for Canadian Kids, 1996; I Heard a Little Baa, 1998; Bake It and Build It, 1998; Grow It Again, 1999; Alexander Graham Bell: An Inventive Life, 1999; Bake and Make Amazing Cakes, 2001; Lucy Maud Montgomery: A Writer's Life, 2001; To the Top of Everest, 2001; Gifts to Make and Eat, 2001; What Did Dinosaurs Eat?: And Other Things You Want to Know about Dinosaurs, 2001; The Wright Brothers: A Flying Start, 2002; Albert Einstein: A Life of Genius, 2003; Helen Keller: A Determined Life, 2004; Marie Curie: A Brilliant Life, 2004; Bake and Make Amazing Cookies, 2004; The Kids Book of Great Canadians, 2004; Harry Houdini: A Magical Life, 2005; Chock Full of Chocolate, 2005; The Kids Book of Great Canadian Women, 2006; Eleanor Roosevelt: An Inspiring Life, 2006; George Washington Carver: An Innovative Life, 2007; Helen Keller (First Reader), 2007; Alexander Graham Bell, 2007; The Kid's Book of Canada at War, 2007; (with F. Wishinsky) Everything but the Kitchen Sink: Weird Stuff You Didn't Know about Food, 2008; The Wright Brothers, 2008; Lucy Maud Montgomery, 2008; Mark Twain: An American Star, 2008; Royal Murder, 2008; Samuel de Champlain, 2008; Thomas Edison, 2008; Making Money: Minting and Printing, 2009; Marie Curie, 2009; Why Do Horses Have Manes?, 2009; Harry Houdini, 2009; Monster Fliers, 2010; Canadian Money, 2011; Canada's Trees, 2011. Works appear in anthologies. **Address:** 23 Tullis Dr., Toronto, ON M4S 2E2, Canada. **Online address:** emacleod@writerinresidence.com

MACLEOD, Ian R. British (born England), b. 1956. **Genres:** Science Fiction/Fantasy, Novels, Novellas/Short Stories, Young Adult Fiction. **Career:** British Civil Service, executive officer, 1979-90; Birmingham City Council, Adult Literacy Program, tutor, 1996-. Writer. **Publications:** Voyages by Starlight (science fiction stories), 1996; The Great Wheel (science fiction novel), 1997; The Light Ages, 2003; Breathmoss and Other Exhalations, 2003; Summer Isles, 2005; House of Storms, 2005; Song of Time, 2008. Contributor to magazines. **Address:** Owlswick Literary Agency, 123 Crooked Ln., King of Prussia, PA 19406, U.S.A.

MACLEOD, Joan. Canadian (born Canada), b. 1954. **Genres:** Plays/Screenplays, Poetry, Novels, Reference. **Career:** Tarragon Theatre, playwright-in-residence, 1985-91; University of British Columbia, 1991-92; University of Victoria, Department of Writing, instructor, 1992-, assistant professor, 2004-, professor, department chair. Writer. **Publications:** Toronto, Mississippi, 1989; Amigo's Blue Guitar, 1991; The Hope Slide/Little Sister, 1994; 2000, 1997; The Shape of a Girl/Jewel, 2002; Homechild, 2008; Another Home Invasion, 2009. **Address:** c/o Pam Winter, Gary Goddard Agency, 10 St. Mary St., Ste. 305, Toronto, ON M4Y 1P9, Canada. **Online address:** macleodj@finearts.uvic.ca

MACLEOD, John. Scottish (born Scotland), b. 1966?. **Genres:** Local History/Rural Topics, History, Humanities. **Career:** Herald, columnist. **Publications:** No Great Mischief If You Fall: A Highland Experience, 1993; Highlanders: A History of the Gaels, 1996; Dynasty: The Stuarts, 1560-1807,

1999. Contributor to periodicals. **Address:** St. Martin's Press, 175 5th Ave., New York, NY 10010-7703, U.S.A.

MACLEOD, Ken. British/Scottish (born Scotland), b. 1954. **Genres:** Novels, Science Fiction/Fantasy, inspirational/Motivational Literature, Adult Non-fiction. **Career:** Computer programmer. Writer. **Publications:** SCIENCE-FICTION NOVELS: The Star Fraction, 1995; The Stone Canal, 1996; The Cassini Division, 1998; Cydonia, 1998; The Sky Road, 1999; The Human Front, 2001; Newton's Wake: A Space Opera, 2004; Learning the World: A Scientific Romance, 2005; Learning the World: A Novel of First Contact, 2006; Giant Lizards from Another Star, 2006; The Highway Men, 2006; The Execution Channel, 2007; The Night Sessions, 2008; Fractions, 2008; Divisions, 2009; The Restoration Game, 2010. ENGINES OF LIGHT TRILOGY: Cosmonaut Keep, 2000; Dark Light, 2002; Engine City, 2003. **Address:** 10 Greenhill St., Stratford-upon-Avon, WW CV37 6LG, England. **Online address:** ken@libertaria.demon.co.uk

MACLEOD, Wendy. American (born United States) **Genres:** Plays/Screenplays, Music. **Career:** Kenyon College, James E. Michael playwright-in-residence, 1990-, professor of drama. Writer. **Publications:** Apocalyptic Butterflies, 1990; The Lost Colony, 1993; The Shallow End and The Lost Colony, 1993; The House of Yes, 1996; Sin, 1998; The Water Children, 1999; How to Make an Apple Pie and See the World, 2000; Schoolgirl Figure, 2000; Juvenilia, 2003; Things Being What They Are, 2003; Small Packages: The Collected Short Plays of Wendy MacLeod, 2010; Find and Sign, 2011. **Address:** Department of Dance Drama and Film, Kenyon College, Hill Theater, Gambier, OH 43022, U.S.A. **Online address:** macleod@kenyon.edu

MACMILLAN, (John) Duncan. Scottish (born Scotland), b. 1939. **Genres:** Art/Art History. **Career:** University of Edinburgh, professor of history, now professor emeritus of history, Talbot Rice Gallery, curator; The Scotsman, art critic. Writer. **Publications:** (Contrib.) Miró in America, 1982; Gavin Scobie, 1984; Painting in Scotland: The Golden Age, 1986; Scottish Art, 1460-1990, 1990; Eugenio Carmi, 1992; Symbols of Survival: The Art of Will MacLean, 1992; (contrib.) Peter Brandes, 1993; The Paintings of Steven Campbell, 1993; Scottish Art in the 20th Century, 1994; (with U. Eco) Carmi, 1996; Elizabeth Blackadder, 1999; Scottish Art, 1460-2000, 2000; Phaidon: Peter Brandes: det antikke Grækenland, 2001; (contrib.) Odyseen, 2002; The Most Humane Way to Kill a Lobster, 2005; Monster, 2007. **Address:** Department of History of Art, The University of Edinburgh, Old College, South Bridge, Edinburgh, EH8 9YL, Scotland. **Online address:** duncan.macmillan@ed.ac.uk

MACMILLAN, Ken. Canadian (born Canada), b. 1969?. **Genres:** History. **Career:** Trent University, Julian Blackbourn College, lecturer, 2001; McMaster University, lecturer, 2002; University of Calgary, assistant professor, 2002-07, associate professor of history, 2007-. Writer. **Publications:** (ed. with J. Abeles) John Dee, John Dee: The Limits of the British Empire, 2004; Sovereignty and Possession in the English New World: The Legal Foundations of Empire, 1576-1640, 2006. Contributor to journals and books. **Address:** Department of History, University of Calgary, 2500 University Dr., NW, Calgary, AB T2N 1N4, Canada. **Online address:** macmillk@ucalgary.ca

MACMILLAN, Norma. British/American (born United States), b. 1947. **Genres:** Food And Wine, Medicine/Health, Homes/Gardens, Sports/Fitness. **Career:** Freelance writer and editor, 1976-. **Publications:** Supercook's Low Cholesterol Cookbook, 1977; The Women's Institutes' Book of Favourite Recipes, 1989; (with C. Clements) Traditional American Cooking, 1989; (with B. Loubet) Cuisine Courante, 1991; (ed. and contrib.) Anne Willan's Look & Cook, 1993; (with A. Edelmann) Creative Cuisine, 1993; (contrib.) Anton Edelmann Creative Cuisine: Chef's Secrets from the Savoy, 1993; The Cook's Kitchen Bible, 1994; A Little New Orleans Cookbook, 1995; In a Shaker Kitchen: 100 Recipes From the Shaker Tradition, 1995; (with B. Loubet) Bistrot Bruno, 1995; (ed.) The Essential Cookbook, 1997; (with R. Corrigan) The Richard Corrigan Cookbook: From the Waters and the Wild, 1999. **Address:** 17 Hillersdon Ave., Barnes, London, GL SW13 0EG, England.

MACNEILL, Alastair. British/Scottish (born Scotland), b. 1960. **Genres:** Novels, Mystery/Crime/Suspense. **Career:** Riverside Holiday Inn, assistant front office manager, 1981-83; Hilton Hotel, food and beverage manager, 1983-84; Milpark Holiday Inn, assistant front office manager, 1984; East London Holiday Inn, front office manager, 1984-85; writer, 1985-. **Publications:** Alistair MacLean's Death Train, 1989; Alistair MacLean's Night Watch, 1989; Alistair MacLean's Red Alert, 1990; Alistair MacLean's Time of the Assasins, 1991; Alistair MacLean's Dead Halt, 1992; Alistair MacLean's Code Breaker, 1993; The Devil's Door, 1994; Alistair MacLean's Rendezvous, 1995; Moonblood, 1996; Double Blind, 1997; Damage Control, 1998; Counterplot, 1999; Time of the Assassins, 2000. **Address:** Christopher Little Literary Agency, Eel Brook Studios, 125 Moore Park Rd., London, GL SW6 4PS, England.

MACNISH, Tracy. American (born United States), b. 1971. **Genres:** Young Adult Fiction, Novels, Romance/Historical. **Career:** Writer. **Publications:** ROMANCE NOVELS: Veiled Promises, 2005; Veiled Desires, 2006; Veiled Passions, 2008; Stealing Midnight, 2009. **Address:** c/o Author Mail, Kensington Publishing Corp., 119 W 40th St., New York, NY 10018, U.S.A.

MACNIVEN, Ian S. Greek/American (born United States) **Genres:** Biography, Literary Criticism And History, Essays, History. **Career:** State University of New York, Maritime College, professor of humanities, professor emeritus of humanities; Durrell School of Corfu, faculty. Writer. **Publications:** Lawrence Durrell: A Biography, 1998; James Laughlin: A Biography, forthcoming. EDITOR: (with H.T. Moore) Literary Lifelines: The Richard Aldington-Lawrence Durrell Correspondence, 1981; (with L.B. Gamache) The Modernists: Studies in a Literary Phenomenon: Essays in Honor of Harry T. Moore, 1987; The Durrell-Miller Letters, 1935-1980, 1988. Contributor to periodicals. **Address:** Durrell School of Corfu, 11 Filellinon, PO Box 94, Corfu, 49-100, Greece.

MACOMBER, Debbie. American (born United States), b. 1948. **Genres:** Science Fiction/Fantasy, Romance/Historical, Young Adult Fiction, Novels, Young Adult Non-fiction, Picture/Board Books. **Career:** Nancy Berland Public Relations Inc., founder. Freelance writer. **Publications:** NOVELS: Starlight, 1983; That Wintry Feeling, 1984; Heartsong, 1984; Undercover Dreamer, 1984; Girl Like Janet, 1984; Thanksgiving Prayer, 1984; Gift of Christmas, 1984; Love Thy Neighbor, 1985; Promise Me Forever, 1985; Adam's Image, 1985; Borrowed Dreams: Alaska, 1985; Laughter in the Rain, 1985; The Trouble with Caasi, 1985; A Friend or Two, 1985; Christmas Masquerade, 1985; Let It Snow, 1986; The Matchmakers, 1986; Shadow Chasing, 1986; Yesterday's Hero, 1986; Reflections of Yesterday, 1986; White Lace and Promises, 1986; Jury of His Peers, 1986; Yesterday Once More, 1986; Friends and Then Some, 1986; All Things Considered, 1987; Love by Degree, 1987; Sugar and Spice, 1987; Love 'N' Marriage, 1987; Husband Required, 1987; No Competition, 1987; Mail-Order Bride, 1987; Any Sunday, 1988; The Playboy and the Widow, 1988; Yours and Mine, 1989; Almost an Angel, 1989; For All My Tomorrows, 1989; The Way to a Man's Heart, 1989; Country Bride, 1990; A Little Bit Country, 1990; Rainy Day Kisses, 1990; Fallen Angel, 1990; The Courtship of Carol Sommars, 1990; Father's Day, 1991; First Comes Marriage, 1991; Here Comes Trouble, 1991; Stolen Kisses, 1991; The First Man You Meet, 1992; The Forgetful Bride, 1991; The Man You'll Marry, 1992; My Hero, 1992; Morning Comes Softly, 1993; Lone Star Lovin', 1993; Ready for Romance, 1993; Ready for Marriage, 1994; Baby Blessed, 1994; The Bachelor Prince, 1994; One Night, 1994; Wanted, Perfect Partner, 1995; Just Married, 1995; Mrs. Miracle, 1996; The Marrying Kind, 1996; Montana, 1997; This Matter of Marriage, 1997; Three Brides, No Groom, 1997; Can This Be Christmas?, 1998; Married in Montana, 1998; 'Tis the Season, 1999; Promise, 2000; Thursdays at Eight, 2001; An Ideal Marriage?, 2001; Between Friends, 2002; The Christmas Basket, 2002; A Gift to Last, 2002; This Time For Keeps, 2003; The Snow Bride, 2003; Changing Habits, 2003; On a Snowy Night, 2004; When Christmas Comes, 2004; Home for the Holidays, 2005; There's Something About Christmas, 2005; His Winter Bride, 2008; Be My Angel, 2009; The Perfect Christmas, 2009; Christmas in Seattle, 2009; (with J. Davis and J. Hohl) Her Kind of Man, 2009; Call Me Mrs. Miracle, 2010; Family Affair, 2011; The First Man You'll Ever Meet, 2011; (with M.L. Carney) Yippy, Yappy Yorkie in a Green Doggy Sweater, 2012; The Inn at Rose Harbor, 2012; A Mother's Wish, 2012. WYOMING SERIES: Denim and Diamonds, 1989; The Wyoming Kid, 2006. LEGENDARY LOVERS SERIES: Cindy and the Prince, 1987; Some Kind of Wonderful, 1988; Almost Paradise, 1988. NAVY SERIES: Navy Wife, 1988; Navy Blues, 1989; Navy Brat, 1991; Navy Woman, 1991; Navy Baby, 1991; Navy Husband, 2005. MANNING SISTERS SERIES: The Cowboy's Lady, 1990; The Sheriff Takes a Wife, 1990. THOSE MANNING MEN SERIES: Marriage of Inconvenience, 1992; Stand-in Wife, 1992; Bride on the Loose, 1992; Same Time, Next Year, 1995; Silver Bells, 2009. ORCHARD VALLEY SERIES: Valerie, 1992; Norah, 1992; Stephanie, 1992. FROM THIS DAY FORWARD SERIES: Groom Wanted, 1993; Bride Wanted, 1993; Marriage Wanted, 1993. ANGELS EVERYWHERE SERIES: A Season of Angels,

1993; The Trouble with Angels, 1994; Touched by Angels, 1995; Shirley, Goodness and Mercy, 1999; Those Christmas Angels, 2003; Where Angels Go, 2007. MIDNIGHT SONS SERIES: Brides for Brothers, 1995; The Marriage Risk, 1995; Daddy's Little Helper, 1995; Because of the Baby, 1996; Falling for Him, 1996; Ending in Marriage, 1996. DELIVERANCE COMPANY SERIES: Someday Soon, 1995; Sooner or Later, 1996; Moon over Water, 1998 as The Sooner the Better, 2010. HEART OF TEXAS SERIES: Lonesome Cowboy, 1998; Texas Two-step, 1998; Caroline's Child, 1998; Dr. Texas, 1998; Nell's Cowboy, 1998; Lone Star Baby, 1998; Promise, Texas, 1999; Return to Promise, 2000. DAKOTA SERIES: Dakota Born, 1999; Dakota Home, 2000; Always Dakota, 2000; Buffalo Valley, 2001. CEDAR COVE SERIES: 16 Lighthouse Road, 2001; 204 Rosewood Lane, 2002; 311 Pelican Court, 2003; 44 Cranberry Point, 2004; 50 Harbor Street, 2004; 6 Rainier Drive, 2006; 74 Seaside Avenue, 2007; Cedar Cove Christmas, 2008; 8 Sandpiper Way, 2008; 92 Pacific Boulevard, 2009; 1022 Evergreen Place, 2010. BLOSSOM STREET SERIES: The Shop on Blossom Street, 2004; A Good Yarn, 2005; Susannah's Garden, 2006; Christmas Letters, 2006; Back On Blossom Street, 2007; Twenty Wishes, 2008; Summer on Blossom Street, 2009; Hannah's List, 2010; A Turn in the Road, 2011. NON FICTION: Knit Along with Debbie Macomber, 2005; Knit Together, 2007; Debbie Macomber's Cedar Cove Cookbook, 2009; One Simple Act: Discovering the Power of Generosity, 2009; Knit Along with Debbie Macomber: Hannah's List, 2009; God's Guest List, 2010; Knit Along With Debbie Macomber: A Turn in the Road, 2011; One Perfect Word, 2012; Best of Knit Along With Debbie Macomber, 2012; Patterns of Grace: Devotions from the Heart, 2012. PICTURE BOOK: (with M.L. Carney) The Truly Terribly Horrible Sweater-That Grandma Knit, 2009. COLLECTION: Ready for Love, 1999. **Address:** Nancy Berland Public Relations Inc., 2816 NW 57th St., Ste. 101, Oklahoma City, OK 73112-7042, U.S.A. **Online address:** info@nancyberland.com

MACOMBER, James. American (born United States) **Genres:** Novels, Horror. **Career:** Attorney, 1980-96. Writer, 1996-. **Publications:** JOHN CANN SERIES: Bargained for Exchange, 1996; Art and Part, 2003; A Grave Breach, 2007. **Address:** Oceanview Publishing Inc., CEO Center at Mediterranean Plz., 595 Bay Isles Rd., Ste. 120-G, Longboat Key, FL 34228, U.S.A. **Online address:** jim@jamesmacomber.com

MACOMBER, Robert N. American (born United States), b. 1953. **Genres:** Novels, Military/Defense/Arms Control, History. **Career:** Author, educator and historian. **Publications:** HONOR SERIES: HISTORICAL NOVELS: At the Edge of Honor, 2002; Point of Honor: The Continuing Exploits of Lt. Peter Wake, United States Navy, 2003; Honorable Mention: The Continuing Exploits of Lt. Peter Wake, United States Navy, 2004; A Dishonorable Few: The Continuing Exploits of Lt. Peter Wake, United States Navy, 2005; An Affair of Honor, 2006; A Different Kind of Honor: Lt. Cmdr. Peter Wake, U.S.N. in the War of the Pacific, 1879, 2007; The Honored Dead: A Novel of Lt. Cmdr. Peter Wake, U.S.N. in French Indochina, 1883, 2009; The Darkest Shade of Honor: A Novel of Cmdr. Peter Wake, U.S.N., 2009. Contributor of articles to magazines. **Address:** Matlacha, FL , U.S.A. **Online address:** macomber@robertmacomber.com

MACPHAIL, Catherine. British/Scottish (born Scotland), b. 1946. **Genres:** Novels, Young Adult Fiction, Plays/Screenplays, Essays, Children's Fiction. **Career:** Writer. **Publications:** Kintyre's Daughter, 1989; Blue Lights and Bandages (nonfiction), 1990; Run, Zan, Run, 1998; Fugitive, 1999; Fighting Back, 1999; Picking on Percy, 2000; Missing Tribes, 2001; A Kind of Magic, 2001; Bad Company, 2001; Missing, 2002; Dark Waters, 2003; Wheels, 2003; Granny Nothing, 2003; Granny Nothing and the Shrunken Head, 2003; Granny Nothing and the Secret Weapon, 2004; Granny Nothing and the Rusty Key, 2004; Another Me, 2003; Get That Ghost to Go!, 2003; Catch Us If You Can, 2004; Tribes, 2004; Underworld, 2005; Roxy's Baby, 2005; Traitors' Gate, 2005; Sticks and Stones, 2005; Get that Ghost to Go!, 2006; Into the Shadows, 2006; Dead Man's Close, 2006; The Beast Within, 2007; Sinister Intent, 2007; Under the Skin, 2007; Worse Than Boys, 2007; Ride of Death, 2008; Hide and Seek, 2009; Grass, 2009; Out of the Depths, 2010; Secret of the Shadows, 2012. **Address:** Bloomsbury Publishing PLC, 36 Soho Sq., London, GL W1D 3QY, England. **Online address:** catherine@macphailc.fsnet.co.uk

MACPHEE, Ross D(ouglas) E(arle). American/Scottish (born Scotland), b. 1949. **Genres:** Zoology, Medicine/Health, History, Animals/Pets. **Career:** University of Winnipeg, visiting assistant professor of anthropology, 1977-78; University of Manitoba, visiting assistant professor of anthropology, 1978-79; Canadian Review of Physical Anthropology, managing editor, 1978-79; Duke University, assistant professor, 1979-85, associate professor of anatomy, 1985-88; American Museum of Natural History, curator in mammalogy, 1988-, head of department, 1993-, Richard Gilder Graduate School, professor; State University of New York, adjunct associate professor of anthropology, 1989-; City University of New York, Graduate Center, adjunct professor of anthropology, 1991-; Carnegie Museum of Natural History, research associate in vertebrate paleontology, 1994-; Columbia University, adjunct senior research scientist, 1995-; New York University Medical Center, visiting instructor of cell biology, 2005-08. Writer. **Publications:** Auditory Regions of Primates and Eutherian Insectivores, 1981; (ed. and contrib.) Primates and Their Relatives in Phylogenetic Perspective, 1993; (ed.) Extinctions in Near Time: Causes, Contexts, and Consequences, 1999; Race to the End: Amundsen, Scott, and the Attainment of the South Pole, 2010. Contributor to books, scientific journals and popular magazines. **Address:** Division of Vertebrate Zoology/Mammalogy, American Museum of Natural History, Central Park W, 79th St., New York, NY 10024, U.S.A. **Online address:** macphee@amnh.org

MACPHERSON, Andrea. Canadian (born Canada), b. 1976?. **Genres:** Poetry, Writing/Journalism, Novels. **Career:** Prism Intl., editor, 2000-01; University of the Fraser Valley, Department of English, instructor, 2005-; Event Magazine, reviews editor, 2006-10; Malaspina University College, teacher; Simon Fraser University, Writing and Publishing Program, teacher; Kwantlen Polytechnic University, faculty; University College, faculty; Douglas College, faculty. Writer. **Publications:** When She Was Electric: A Novel, 2003; Natural Disasters: A Collection of Poems, 2007; Beyond the Blue, 2007; Away: Poems, 2008. Contributor to magazines. **Address:** c/o Carolyn Swayze, Carolyn Swayze Literary Agency Ltd., PO Box 39588, White Rock, BC V4A 0A9, Canada. **Online address:** andrea@andreamacpherson.com

MACQUEEN, John. Scottish (born Scotland), b. 1929. **Genres:** History, Intellectual History, Language/Linguistics, Literary Criticism And History. **Career:** Washington University, assistant professor of English, 1956-59; University of Edinburgh, lecturer, 1959-63, Masson professor of medieval and renaissance literature, 1963-71, professor of Scottish literature and oral tradition, 1971-88, endowment fellow, 1988-92, now professor emeritus, School of Scottish Studies, director, 1969-88. Writer. **Publications:** St. Nynia, 1961; Robert Henryson, 1967; Allegory, 1970; Progress and Poetry, 1982; Enlightenment and Scottish Literature, 1982; Numerology: Theory and Outline History of a Literary Mode, 1985; The Rise of the Historical Novel, 1989; Place-names in the Rhinns of Galloway and Luce Valley, 2002; Complete and Full with Numbers, 2005. EDITOR: (with T. Scott) The Oxford Book of Scottish Verse, 1966; (and intro.) Ballattis of Luve, 1970; (and intro. with W. MacQueen) A Choice of Scottish Verse, 1470-1570, 1972; (with W. MacQueen) Scotichronicon vol. III-IV, 1989, vol. I-II, 1993, (with W. MacQueen and D.E.R. Watt) vol. V-VI, 1995; Humanism in Renaissance Scotland, 1990; (trans. with W. MacQueen) A. Pitcairne, The Latin Poems, 2009. Contributor to journals. **Address:** University of Edinburgh, Old College, South Bridge, Edinburgh, EH8 9YL, Scotland. **Online address:** john.macqueen1@btinternet.com

MACQUEEN, Winifred (Wallace). Scottish (born Scotland), b. 1928. **Genres:** Classics, History, Translations, Poetry. **Career:** University of Glasgow, assistant lecturer in classics, 1952-55; University of Edinburgh, lecturer in classics, 1959-60; St. Hilary's School, teacher of classics, 1973-84. Writer. **Publications:** (With J. MacQueen) A Choice of Scottish Verse, 1470-1570, 1972; (ed. and trans. with J. MacQueen) Scotichronicon in Latin and English, vol. I, 1989, vol. II, 1993, vol. III, 1995; St Nynia, 2005; (ed. and trans. with J. MacQueen) Archibald Pitcairne: The Latin Poems, 2009. Contributor to journals. **Address:** Faber and Faber Ltd., Burnt Mill, Elizabeth Way, Harlow, EX CM20 2HX, England. **Online address:** jackmacqueen@aol.com

MACQUET, Dominique. American (born United States), b. 1966. **Genres:** Food And Wine. **Career:** Bistro Maison de Ville, executive chef, 1995-97; Dominique's Restaurant, executive chef, 1997-; Maison Dupuy Hotel, chef. Writer. **Publications:** Dominique's Fresh Flavors: Cooking with Latitude in New Orleans, 2000; (with J. DeMers) Dominique's Tropical Latitudes, 2007. **Address:** Dominique's Restaurant, 1001 Toulouse St., New Orleans, LA 70112, U.S.A. **Online address:** dominique@maisondupuy.com

MACRAE, Molly. American (born United States) **Genres:** Novels, Adult Non-fiction, Mystery/Crime/Suspense, Young Adult Fiction. **Career:** Children's Department of the Public Library, staff; History Museum in Jonesborough, curator. Writer. **Publications:** (Ed.) Humor, Rumor and Romance in Old Jonesborough, 1991; Wilder Rumors: A Lewis Wilder Mystery, 2007; Lawn Order: A Margaret and Bitsy Mystery, 2010. Contributor to periodicals. **Address:** Five Star Publishing, 1517 3rd Ave. NW, PO Box 998, Fort Dodge, IA 50501, U.S.A. **Online address:** molly@mollymacrae.com

MACSAI, Gwen. American (born United States) **Genres:** Plays/Screenplays, Humor/Satire, Essays. **Career:** WBEZ, assistant producer, 1984-87, producer, staff, 2003-; Radio Smithsonian, producer, 1987-; National Public Radio, freelance associate producer, through 2003. Television series writer. **Publications:** Lipshtick: Life as a Girl, 2000. **Address:** c/o Author Mail, HarperCollins, 10 E 53rd St., 7th Fl., New York, NY 10022, U.S.A.

MACTHÒMAIS, Ruaraidh. *See* **THOMSON, Derick S(mith).**

MACWEENEY, Alen. Irish (born Ireland), b. 1939?. **Genres:** Photography. **Career:** Photographer. **Publications:** The Traveling People of Ireland: Irish Tinker Music Sound Recording, 1981; (with R. Conniff) Irish Walls, 1986; (with M. le Bris) Dublin, un Guide Intime, 1986; (with S. Allison) Bloomsbury Reflections, 1990; (with Q. Bell and V. Nicholson) Charleston: A Bloomsbury House and Garden, 1997; (with R. Conniff) Ireland: Stone Walls & Fabled Landscapes, 1998; (with A. Penrose) The Home of the Surrealists: Lee Miller, Roland Penrose and Their Circle at Farley Farm, 2001; (with C. Ness) Spaces for Silence, 2002; Irish Travellers, Tinkers No More, 2007; (with M. Ennis) Once Upon a Time in Tallaght, 2011. Contributor of to periodicals. **Address:** 59 E 72 St., New York, NY 10021, U.S.A. **Online address:** a@alenmacweeney.com

MACY, Sue. American (born United States), b. 1954. **Genres:** Children's Non-fiction, History, Sports/Fitness, Women's Studies And Issues, Biography, Young Adult Non-fiction. **Career:** Scholastic Inc., research coordinator, 1976-78, Scholastic Newstime, assistant editor, associate editor, 1978-80, Math Magazines, editor and associate editorial director, 1983-88, Science and Math Magazines, editorial director, 1991-94, scholastic reference, project editor, 1994-96; freelance writer, 1980-83, 1999-; Fukutake Publishing Ltd., Challenge Plus, editor-in-chief, 1988-90; Careers & Colleges Magazine, editor-in-chief, 1997-99. **Publications:** A Whole New Ball Game: The Story of the All-American Girls Professional Baseball League, 1993; Winning Ways: A Photohistory of American Women in Sports, 1996; Barbie: Shooting Hoops, 1999; Bull's-Eye: A Photobiography of Annie Oakley, 2001; Swifter, Higher, Stronger: A Photographic History of the Summer Olympics, 2004, rev. ed., 2008; Freeze Frame: A Photographic History of the Winter Olympics, 2006; Bylines: A Photobiography of Nellie Bly, 2009; Wheels of Change: How Women Rode the Bicycle to Freedom (with a Few Flat Tires Along the Way), 2011; Basketball Belles: How Two Teams and One Scrappy Player Put Women's Hoops on the Map, 2011. EDITOR: (with J. Gottesman) Play Like a Girl: A Celebration of Women in Sports, 1999; Girls Got Game: Sports Stories & Poems, 2001. **Address:** Henry Holt and Company Inc., 175 5th Ave., New York, NY 10010, U.S.A. **Online address:** mail@suemacy.com

MADDEN, Chris (Casson). American (born United States), b. 1948. **Genres:** Design, Homes/Gardens. **Career:** Sports Illustrated, designer; Simon and Schuster Inc., designer; Farrar, Straus & Giroux, public relations director; Chris Madden Inc., founder, chief executive officer; Home and Garden Television (HGTV), host. Writer. **Publications:** The Summer House Cookbook, 1979; The Photographed Cat, 1980; Manhattan, 1981; Baby's First Helpings: Super-Healthy Meals for Super-Healthy Kids, 1983; Interior Visions: Great American Designers and the Showcase House, 1988; Rooms with a View: Two Decades of Outstanding American Interior Design from Kips Bay Decorator Show Houses, 1992; Kitchens, 1993; Bathrooms, 1996; A Room of Her Own: Women's Personal Spaces, 1997; (with K. Clark) Chris Madden's Guide to Personalizing Your Home: Simple, Beautiful Ideas for Every Room, 1997; Getaways: Carefree Retreats for All Seasons, 2000; Bedrooms: Creating the Stylish, Comfortable Room of Your Dreams, 2001; (with C. Schultz) Chris Casson Madden's New American Living Rooms, 2003; (with C. Schultz) Haven: Finding the Keys to Your Personal Decorating Style, 2004; At Home with Chris Madden, 2005; (with S.E. Palomba) The Soul of a House: Decorating with Warmth, Style, and Comfort, 2010. **Address:** Chris Madden Inc., 181 Westchester Ave., Ste. 408, Port Chester, NY 10573-4562, U.S.A.

MADDEN, David. American (born United States), b. 1933. **Genres:** Novels, Plays/Screenplays, Poetry, Literary Criticism And History, Novellas/Short Stories, History, Autobiography/Memoirs, Bibliography, Essays, Military/Defense/Arms Control, Adult Non-fiction. **Career:** Appalachian State Teachers College, instructor, 1958-59; Center College, instructor in English, 1960-62; University of Louisville, instructor in creative writing, 1962-64; Kenyon College, instructor in creative writing, 1964-66; Ohio University, instructor in creative writing, 1966-68; Louisiana State University, writer-in-residence, 1968-92, Creative Writing Program, director, 1992-94, United States Civil War Center, founding director, 1992-99, professor, 1996-2006, Donald and Velvia Crumbley professor of creative writing, 1999-, now Robert Penn Warren professor emeritus of creative writing. **Publications:** The Beautiful Greed, 1961; Wright Morris, 1965; Cassandra Singing: A Novel, 1969; The Poetic Image in Six Genres, 1969; The Shadow Knows, 1970; James M. Cain, 1970; (with R.B. Browne) The Popular Culture Explosion, 1972; Brothers in Confidence, 1972; Bijou: A Novel, 1974; Harlequin's Stick, Charlie's Cane: A Comparative Study of Commedia Dell'arte and Silent Slapstick Comedy, 1975; The Suicide's Wife: A Novel, 1978; Pleasure-Dome, 1979; A Primer of the Novel: For Readers and Writers, 1979, (with S.M. Flory and C. Bane) rev. ed., 2006; On the Big Wind, 1980; (with R. Powers) Writer's Revisions: An Annotated Bibliography of Articles and Books about Writers Revisions and Their Comments on the Creative Process, 1981; The New Orleans of Possibilities: Stories, 1982; Cain's Craft, 1985; Revising Fiction: A Handbook for Writers, 1988; (comp.) Eight Classic American Novels, 1989; The Fiction Tutor, 1990; Sharpshooter: A Novel of the Civil War, 1996; (comp.) A Pocketful of Poems, Vintage Verse, 1996; Touching The Web of Southern Novelists, 2006; Abducted by Circumstance: A Novel, 2010; James M. Cain: Hard-boiled Mythmaker, 2011; Civil War and Reconstruction Throughout History: Their Nature and Conduct Myriadmindedness: A Revolutionary Theory of Emotion, Imagination, and Thinking, forthcoming; London Bridge Nocturnes, forthcoming. EDITOR: Tough Guy Writers of the Thirties, 1968; Proletarian Writers of the Thirties, 1968; American Dreams, American Nightmares, 1970; (and intro.) Rediscoveries: Informal Essays in Which Well-known Novelists Rediscover Neglected Works of Fiction by One of Their Favorite Authors, 1971; Nathanael West: The Cheaters and the Cheated: A Collection of Critical Essays, 1973; (with F.N. Magil) The Contemporary Literary Scene, 1973, 1974; (with J.J. Folks) Remembering James Agee, 1974, (with J.J. Folks) 2nd ed., 1997; Creative Choices: A Spectrum of Quality and Technique in Fiction, 1975; (with V. Scott) Studies in the Short Story, 6th ed., 1984; (with P. Bach) Rediscoveries II: Important Writers Select Their Favorite Works of Neglected Fiction, 1988; The World of Fiction, 1990; (with P. Bach) Classics of Civil War Fiction, 1991; Nineteen Ninety-One, 1991; A Pocketful of Prose: Contemporary Short Fiction, 1992; A Pocketful of Prose: Vintage Short Fiction, 1992; A Pocketful of Plays: Vintage Drama, 1996; Beyond the Battlefield: The Ordinary Life and Extraordinary Times of The Civil War Soldier, 2000; The Legacy of Robert Penn Warren, 2000; (and intro.) Thomas Wolfe's Civil War, 2004; A Pocketful of Essays, 2006; (with A. Christensen) Wright Morris Territory, 2011; Absalom, Absalom!, 2012. Works appear in anthologies. Contributor of articles to journals and periodicals. **Address:** 118 Church St., Black Mountain, NC 28711, U.S.A. **Online address:** dmadden@lsu.edu

MADDEN, Deirdre. French/Irish (born Ireland), b. 1960. **Genres:** Novels, Young Adult Fiction. **Career:** National University of Ireland, University College, writer-in-residence, 1994-95; Trinity College, writing fellow, 1996-97. **Publications:** NOVELS: Hidden Symptoms, 1986; The Birds of the Innocent Wood, 1988; Remembering Light and Stone, 1992; Nothing is Black, 1994; One by One in the Darkness, 1996; Authenticity, 2002; Snakes' Elbows, 2005; Thanks for Telling Me, Emily, 2007; Molly Fox's Birthday, 2008; Jasper and the Green Marvel, 2011. Contributor to periodicals. **Address:** A. P. Watt Ltd., 20 John St., London, GL WC1N 2DR, England.

MADDEN, Patrick. American (born United States), b. 1971?. **Genres:** Essays. **Career:** Brigham University, assistant professor of English. Writer. **Publications:** Quotidiana, 2010. Contributor to journals and periodicals. **Address:** 815 South 1580 West, Lehi, UT 84043, U.S.A. **Online address:** madden@byu.edu

MADDEN, W. C. American (born United States), b. 1947?. **Genres:** Sports/Fitness, History. **Career:** Topics Newspapers, editor, 1987-90; U.S.A Group, technical writer, 1992-94; United Pentek, technical writer, 1997-98. **Publications:** The Hoosiers of Summer, 1994; P.S. Remembering Bush Stadium, 1995; The Dutiful Dozen, 1997; The Women of the All-American Girls Professional Baseball League, 1997; The All-American Girls Professional Baseball League Record Book, 1998; (co-author) Baseball Stories for the Soul: 50 Stories, Poems & Other Soulful Inspirations about America's Favorite Pastime, 2000; Baseball's First-Year Player Draft, 2001; The Western League: A Baseball History, 1885 through 1999, 2002; (with R. Kemmerer) Ted Williams: Hey, Kid, Just Get It Over The Plate!: A Book about Baseball's Golden Age, Its Great Players and Twinkling Stars, 2002; Indianapolis Then and Now, 2003; Indianapolis in Vintage Postcards, 2003; Baseball in Indianapolis, 2003; Haynes-Apperson and America's First Practical Automobile: A History, 2003; The Indy 500 (1956-1965), 2004; Crown Hill Cemetery, 2004; The College World Series: A Baseball History, 1947-2003, 2004; Monticello, 2007; White County in Vintage Postcards, 2007; Old Monticello Cemetery, 2008; White County Recipes and Restaurants, 2008; 175th Anniversary of White County, 2009; Haunted Lafayette, 2009; Lafayette, Murder and Mayhem, 2010. **Address:** WC Madden Enterprises L.L.C., 673 E Lakeside Dr., Monticello, IN 47960, U.S.A. **Online address:** maddenmddg@aol.com

MADDIGAN, Beth. Canadian (born Canada), b. 1967. **Genres:** Education, Children's Fiction. **Career:** A.C. Hunter Children's Library, library assistant, 1990-94, branch head, 1994-96; Cambridge Libraries and Galleries, children's services librarian, 1997-99, children's services coordinator, 1999-; Memorial University of Newfoundland, instructor, 1997-2003; University of Western Ontario, instructor, 2005. Writer. **Publications:** (With S. Drennan) The Big Book of Stories, Songs and Sing-Alongs: Programs for Babies, Toddlers and Families, 2003; (with S. Drennan) The Big Book of Reading, Rhyming and Resources: Programs for Children, Ages 4-8, 2005. **Address:** Cambridge Libraries and Galleries, 1 North Sq., Cambridge, ON N1S 2K6, Canada. **Online address:** bmaddigan@library.cambridge.on.ca

MADDISON, Carol. *See* **KIDWELL, Carol (Evelyn Beryl).**

MADDISON, Sarah. Australian (born Australia), b. 1968. **Genres:** Politics/Government, Administration/Management. **Career:** New South Wales Department of Juvenile Justice, juvenile justice officer, 1990-94; National Women's Media Center, policy advocate, 1997-98; New South Wales Department for Women, research and policy officer, 1999-2003; University of Sydney, casual tutor and casual lecturer, 1999-2000, lecturer level A, 2003, associate lecturer, 2003; University of New South Wales, lecturer, 2004-07, senior lecturer, 2007-; Indigenous Policy and Dialogue Research Unit, research director, Faculty of Arts and Social Sciences, senior associate dean; The Australia Institute, chair. Writer. **Publications:** (With S. Scalmer) Activist Wisdom: Practical Knowledge and Creative Tension in Social Movements, 2006; (ed. with C. Hamilton) Silencing Dissent: How the Australian Government Is Controlling Public Opinion and Stifling Debate, 2007; (with E. Partridge) How Well Does Australian Democracy Serve Australian Women?, 2007; Collective Identity and Australian Feminist Activism: Conceptualising a Third Wave, 2008; Black Politics: Inside the Complexity of Aboriginal Political Culture, 2009; (with R. Denniss) Introduction to Australian Public Policy: Theory and Practice, 2009; (ed. with M. Brigg) Unsettling the Settler State: Creativity and Resistance in Indigenous Settler-state Governance, 2011; Beyond White Guilt: The Real Challenge for Black-White Relations in Australia, 2011. **Address:** School of Politics and International Relations, University of New South Wales, Morven Brown Bldg., Sydney, NW 2052, Australia. **Online address:** sarah.maddison@unsw.edu.au

MADDOX, Bronwen. British/American (born United States), b. 1963. **Genres:** Politics/Government, Social Sciences. **Career:** Kleinwort Benson Securities (media investment team), director, 1986-91; Financial Times, investigative reporter; Times, bureau chief of Washington, DC, and U.S. editor, chief foreign commentator; Ditchley Foundation for transatlantic debate, governor. Journalist. **Publications:** In Defense of America, 2008. **Address:** London, GL , England. **Online address:** bronwen.maddox@thetimes.co.uk

MADDOX, Michelle. *See* **ROWEN, Michelle.**

MADDOX, Robert James. American (born United States), b. 1931. **Genres:** History, International Relations/Current Affairs, Politics/Government, Military/Defense/Arms Control. **Career:** Paterson State College, instructor of history, 1962-64; Michigan State University, assistant professor, 1964-66; Pennsylvania State University, College of Liberal Arts, assistant professor, 1966-68, associate professor, 1968-73, professor of history, 1973-, professor emeritus of American history. Writer. **Publications:** William E. Borah and American Foreign Policy, 1970; The New Left and American Foreign Policy 1973; The Unknown War with Russia: Wilson's Siberian Intervention, 1977; From War to Cold War: The Education of Harry S. Truman, 1988; The United States in World War II, 1992; Weapons for Victory: The Hiroshima Decision Fifty Years Later, 1995; Weapons for Victory: The Hiroshima Decision, 2004; (ed. and intro.) Hiroshima in History: The Myths of Revisionism, 2007. Contributor of articles to journals. **Address:** Department of History, Pennsylvania State University, 108 Weaver Bldg., University Park, PA 16802, U.S.A. **Online address:** rjm5@psu.edu

MADENSKI, Melissa (Ann). American (born United States), b. 1949. **Genres:** Adult Non-fiction, Children's Fiction. **Career:** Clackamas and Oceanlake Elementary Schools, teacher, 1972-77; Neskowin Valley School, language arts instructor, 1984-85; Northwest Writing Institute, intern, Lewis and Clark College, 1994-. Freelance writer and editor. **Publications:** Some of the Pieces, 1991; In My Mother's Garden, 1995. Contributor of non-fiction articles and essays to periodicals. **Address:** Lewis & Clark College, 615 SW Palatine Hill Rd., PO Box 712, Neotsu, OR 97364, U.S.A. **Online address:** madenski@lclark.edu

MADGETT, Naomi Cornelia Long. *See* **MADGETT, Naomi Long.**

MADGETT, Naomi Long. (Naomi Cornelia Long Madgett). American (born United States), b. 1923. **Genres:** Poetry, Race Relations, Literary Criticism And History, Young Adult Fiction. **Career:** Michigan Chronicle, reporter and copy reader, 1945-46, staff writer, 1946-47; Michigan Bell Telephone Co., service representative, 1948-54; Oakland University, research associate, 1965-66; Eastern Michigan University, associate professor, 1968-73, professor, 1973-84, professor emeritus of English, 1984-; University of Michigan, lecturer, 1970, visiting lecturer, 1970-71; Lotus Press Inc., founder, publisher, editor, 1972-; Michigan State University Press, senior poetry editor, 1993-98. **Publications:** (As Naomi Cornelia Long) Songs to a Phantom Nightingale, 1941; One and the Many, 1956; Star by Star, 1965, rev. ed., 1970; (with E. Tincher and H.B. Maloney) Success in Language and Literature (textbook), 1967; Pink Ladies in the Afternoon, 1972, 2nd ed., 1990; Deep Rivers, A Portfolio: Twenty Contemporary Black American Poets (teachers' guide), 1974; Exits and Entrances, 1978; A Student's Guide to Creative Writing, 1980; Phantom Nightingale: Juvenilia, 1981; (ed.) A Milestone Sampler: 15th Anniversary Anthology, 1988; Octavia and Other Poems, 1988; (ed.) Adam of Ifè: Black Women in Praise of Black Men, 1992; Remembrances of Spring: Collected Early Poems, 1993; Hymns Are My Prayers, 1997; Octavia: Guthrie and Beyond, 2002; Connected Islands: New and Selected Poems, 2004; Pilgrim Journey: An Autobiography, 2006. Contributor to books and periodicals. Works appear in anthologies. **Address:** Lotus Press Inc., PO Box 21607, Detroit, MI 48221-2531, U.S.A. **Online address:** nlmadgett@aol.com

MADHUBUTI, Haki R. (Donald L(uther) Lee). American (born United States), b. 1942. **Genres:** Poetry, Literary Criticism And History, Autobiography/Memoirs, Race Relations, Social Sciences, Essays. **Career:** DuSable Museum of African American History, apprentice curator, 1963-67; Montgomery Ward, stock department clerk, 1963-64; post office clerk in Chicago, 1964-65; Spiegels, junior executive, 1965-66; Third World Press, founder, editor and publisher, 1967-; Columbia College, teacher, 1968; Cornell University, writer-in-residence, 1968-69; Northeastern Illinois State College, poet-in-residence, 1969-70; Institute of Positive Education, director, 1969-91; University of Illinois, lecturer, 1969-71; Howard University, writer-in-residence, 1970-78; New Concept Development Center, co-founder, 1971; Morgan State College, staff, 1972-73; Central State University, faculty, 1979-80; Chicago State University, professor of English, 1984-, distinguished university professor, Gwendolyn Brooks Center, founder and director emeritus. **Publications:** POETRY: Book of Life, 1973; Earthquakes and Sunrise Missions, 1984; Killing Memory, Seeking Ancestors, 1987; Ground Work: New and Selected Poems of Haki R. Madhubuti/Don L. Lee (1966-1996), 1996; Heartlove: Wedding and Love Poems, 1998. AS DON L. LEE. POETRY: Think Black, 1967, rev. ed., 1969; Black Pride, 1968; Back Again, Home, 1968; One Sided Shoot-Out, 1968; For Black People (and Negroes Too), 1968; Don't Cry, Scream, 1969; We Walk the Way of the New World, 1970; (intro.) To Blackness: A Definition in Thought, 1970; Dynamite Voices I: Black Poets of the 1960s (essays), 1971; (ed. with P.L. Brown and F. Ward) To Gwen with Love, 1971; Direction Score: Selected and New Poems, 1971; (intro.) Marion Nicholas, Life Styles, 1971; From Plan to Planet: Life Studies: The Need for Afrikan Minds and Institutions, 1973. EDITOR: Confusion by Any Other Name, 1992; Children of Africa, 1993; (with M. Karenga) Million Man March/Day of Absence: A Commemorative Anthology: Speeches, Commentary, Photography, Poetry, Illustrations, Documents, 1996; (with G. Mitchell) Releasing the Spirit, 1998. OTHER: Kwanzaa: A Progressive and Uplifting African American Holiday, 1972; (intro.) Horizons East, by J.

Shiver Jr., 1974; (co-author) A Capsule Course in Black Poetry Writing, 1975; Enemies: The Clash of Races, 1978; Say That the River Turns: The Impact of Gwendolyn Brooks, 1987; Black Men: Obsolete, Single, Dangerous? Afrikan American Families in Transition: Essays in Discovery, Solution, and Hope, 1990; (intro.) So Far, So Good, by G. Scott-Heron, 1990; Claiming Earth: Race, Rage, Rape, Redemption: Blacks Seeking a Culture of Enlightened Empowerment, 1994; (with S. Madhubuti) African-Centered Education: Its Value, Importance, and Necessity in the Development of Black Children, 1994; Tough Notes: A Healing Call for Creating Exceptional Black Men: Affirmations, Meditations, Readings, and Strategies, 2002; Run Toward Fear: New Poems and a Poet's Handbook, 2004; Yellow Black: The First Twenty-One Years of a Poet's Life: A Memoir, 2005; Liberation Narratives: New and Collected Poems 1966-2009, 2009. Contributor to periodicals. **Address:** Department of English, Chicago State University, 9501 S King Dr., LIB 210A, Chicago, IL 60628-1598, U.S.A. **Online address:** h-madhubuti@csu.edu

MADIGAN, Brian (Christoper). American (born United States), b. 1949. **Genres:** Adult Non-fiction, Art/Art History. **Career:** Santa Clara University, lecturer in art history, 1982-83; University of Notre Dame, visiting assistant professor of art history, 1984-86; St. Mary's College, visiting assistant professor, 1986-97; Wayne State University, assistant professor, associate professor of art history, 1988-. Writer. **Publications:** (With F.A. Cooper) The Temple of Apollo Bassitas, 1992; Corinthian and Attic Vases in the Detroit Institute of Arts: Geometric, Black-figure and Red-figure, 2008. Contributor to books on Greek, Roman, and Byzantine Studies. **Address:** James Pearson Duffy, Department of Art and Art History, Wayne State University, 2153 Faculty/Administration Bldg., 5229 Cass Ave., Detroit, MI 48202, U.S.A. **Online address:** aa1708@wayne.edu

MADIGAN, Charles M. American (born United States), b. 1949. **Genres:** History. **Career:** Mirror, reporter and feature writer, 1966-68; Patriot, reporter, 1968-70; UPI, reporter, writer, editor, 1970-76, foreign correspondent, 1976-79; Chicago Tribune, staff writer, national correspondent, deputy national editor, Washington news editor, national editor, senior national correspondent, senior writer in politics and national affairs, 1979-2000, senior writer and op-ed columnist, 2000-07, Sunday Perspective, editor, 2001-06; Britannica.com, executive editor, 2000; Northwestern University, Medill School of Journalism, instructor in global studies, 2003-04; Roosevelt University, presidential writer-in-residence, 2007-; News21 Project, Northwestern University, editor and instructor; Carnegie-Knight Foundation, editor and instructor. **Publications:** (With J. O'Shea) Dangerous Company: The Consulting Powerhouses and the Businesses They Save and Ruin, 1997; (with G. Greenwald) Lessons from the Heart of American Business: A Roadmap for Managers in the 21st Century, 2001; (with A. Martinez) The Hard Road to the Softer Side: Lessons from the Transformation of Sears, 2001; (ed.) Global Chicago, 2004; Robert R. McCormick: A Celebration of His Life and Legacy: The History of the McCormick Tribune Foundation, 2005; (ed. and intro.) 30: The Collapse of the Great American Newspaper, 2007; Destiny Calling: How the People Elected Barack Obama, 2009. **Address:** Department of Communications, Roosevelt University, Rm. 505A, Gage Bldg., Chicago, IL 60605, U.S.A. **Online address:** cmadigan@roosevelt.edu

MADIGAN, Mark J. American (born United States), b. 1961. **Genres:** Literary Criticism And History. **Career:** University of Vermont, lecturer in English, 1991-96; Nazareth College of Rochester, assistant professor, 1996-2002, associate professor of English, 2002-, professor of English. Writer. **Publications:** (Contrib.) Youth and the Bright Medusa, 2009. EDITOR: (and intro.) Keeping Fires Night and Day: Selected Letters of Dorothy Canfield Fisher, 1993; (and intro.) The Bedquilt and Other Stories by Dorothy Canfield Fisher, 1996; Seasoned Timber, 1996. Contributor to books and periodicals. **Address:** Department of English, Nazareth College of Rochester, 4245 East Ave., Golisano 479, Rochester, NY 14618-3790, U.S.A. **Online address:** mmadiga2@naz.edu

MADIGAN, Patrick. American (born United States), b. 1945. **Genres:** Philosophy, Theology/Religion, Translations, Politics/Government. **Career:** Arrupe College, Jesuit School of Philosophy and Humanities, lecturer and founding librarian. Writer and priest. **Publications:** The Modern Project to Rigor: Descartes to Nietzsche, 1986; Christian Revelation and the Completion of the Aristotelian Revolution, 1988; Aristotle and His Modern Critics: The Uses of Tragedy in the Nontragic Vision, 1992; (trans.) S. Hildegard, Holistic Healing, 1994; (trans.) M.M. Garijo-Guembe, Communion of the Saints: Foundation, Nature, and Structure of the Church, 1994; Penance, Contemplation, and Service: Pivotal Experiences of Christian Spirituality, 1994; (trans.) L.M. Chauvet, Symbol and Sacrament: A Sacramental Reinterpretation of Christian Existence, 1995; The Completion of the Project of the West, and Its Romantic Sequel, 2003; (with P. Ojara) Marcel, Girard, Bakhtin: The Return of Conversion, 2004. Contributor to periodicals. **Address:** Jesuit Provincial Office, 500 S Jefferson Davis Pkwy., New Orleans, LA 70119-7182, U.S.A.

MADISON, Bennett. American (born United States), b. 1981. **Genres:** Novels, Social Commentary, Mystery/Crime/Suspense. **Career:** Writer. **Publications:** I Hate Valentine's Day, 2005; Lulu Dark Can See through Walls, 2005; Lulu Dark and the Summer of the Fox, 2006; The Blonde of the Joke, 2009. **Address:** New York, NY 10010, U.S.A. **Online address:** bennett.madison@gmail.com

MADISON, Gary (Brent). Canadian (born Canada), b. 1940. **Genres:** Sciences. **Career:** Universite de Nantes, Ecole Nationale Superieure de Mecanique, lecturer in English, 1965-67; Universite de Paris X, assistant in philosophy, 1968-70; McMaster University, assistant professor, 1970-75, associate professor, 1975-80, professor of philosophy, 1981-96, professor emeritus, 1996-; St. Joseph's College, visiting professor, 1972; Brock University, lecturer, 1972; York University, lecturer, 1977; University of Guelph, lecturer, 1980; University of Ottawa, lecturer, 1980; University of Toronto, Centre for Comparative Literature, affiliated professor, 1980-85, lecturer, 1985, professor of philosophy in graduate program, 1986-; Canadian Society for Hermeneutics and Postmodern Thought, director, 1984-89; Queen's University, lecturer, 1985; Redeemer College, lecturer, 1985, 1986, 1988; Laval University, lecturer, 1987. Writer. **Publications:** 7La phenoménologie de Merleau-Ponty: Une recherche des limites de la conscience, 1973; (ed.) Sens et existence, 1975; Understanding: A Phenomenological-Pragmatic Analysis, 1981; The Logic of Liberty, 1986; The Hermeneutics of Postmodernity: Figures and Themes, 1988; (with P. Fairfield and I. Harris) Is There a Canadian Philosophy?: Reflections on the Canadian Identity, 2000; The Political Economy of Civil Society and Human Rights, 1998; The Politics of Postmodernity, 2001. EDITOR: Sens et existence, 1975; Working through Derria, 1993; (with M. Fairbairn) Ethics of Postmodernity: Current Trends in Continental Thought, 1999. Contributor to books. **Address:** Department of Philosophy, McMaster University, University Hall 209, 1280 Main St. W, Hamilton, ON L8S 4K1, Canada. **Online address:** madison@mcmaster.ca

MADISON, James H. American (born United States), b. 1944. **Genres:** History, Art/Art History, Military/Defense/Arms Control. **Career:** Harvard University, Newcomen fellow, 1972-73; Indiana University, Department of History, visiting assistant professor of history, 1973-76, assistant professor 1976-81, associate professor, 1982-, professor, chair, Thomas and Kathryn Miller professor, now Thomas and Kathryn Miller professor emeritus, Liberal Arts and Management Program, director; Hiroshima University, Fulbright professor, 1997-98; Huntington Library, Hayens Fellow; University of Kent, instructor; Governor's Hoosier Heritage Foundation, president. Writer. **Publications:** Indiana through Tradition and Change: A History of the Hoosier State and its People, 1920-1945, 1982; (with H.F. Bedford and T. Colbourn) Americans, 1985; The American Constitution and the Old Federalism: Views from the Hoosier State, 1985; The Indiana Way: A State History, 1986; (ed.) Heartland: Comparative Histories of the Midwestern States, 1988; Eli Lilly: A Life, 1885-1977, 1989; (ed.) Wendell Willkie: Hoosier Internationalist, 1992; A Lynching in the Heartland: Race and Memory in America, 2001; (with W. Counts and S.R. Sanders) Bloomington Past and Present, 2002; Slinging Doughnuts for the Boys: An American Woman in World War II, 2007; World War II: A History in Documents, 2010. Contributor to journals. **Address:** Department of History, Indiana University, 742 Ballantine Hall, 1020 E Kirkwood Ave., Bloomington, IN 47405-7103, U.S.A. **Online address:** madison@indiana.edu

MADLEY, Thom. *See* **RICKMAN, Philip.**

MADRONA, Lewis Mehl. American (born United States), b. 1954. **Genres:** Medicine/Health. **Career:** University of Wisconsin, resident in family medicine, 1975-76, resident in psychiatry, 1976-77; Saint Mary's Hospital, resident in psychiatry, 1982; University of Texas, resident in family practice, 1991-92; University of Vermont, resident in family practice, 1992-94, resident in psychiatry, 1994-96; University of Hawaii, associate professor of family practice, 1996-97; University of Pittsburgh Medical Center, medical director, 1997-2000; Beth Israel Medical Center, special projects and clinical programs director, 2000-02; University of Arizona College of Medicine, assistant professor of clinical psychiatry, 2002-05; University of Saskatchewan, associate professor of family medicine and psychiatry, 2005-. Writer. **Publications:** (with G.H. Peterson) Pregnancy as Healing: Holistic Philosophy for Prenatal Care, 1984; (with G.H. Peterson) Cesarean Birth: Risk and Culture, 1985; Mind and Matter: Healing Approaches to Chronic Disease, 2nd ed., 1986; Coyote Medicine: Lessons from Native American Healing, 1997; Coyote Healing: Miracles in Native Medicine, 2003; Coyote Wisdom: The Power of Story in Healing, 2005; Narrative Medicine: The Use of History and Story in the Healing Process, 2007. Contributor to books and journals. **Address:** Department of Family Medicine, West Winds Primary Health Centre, University of Saskatchewan College of Medicine, 3311 Fairmont Dr., Saskatoon, SK S7M 3Y5, Canada. **Online address:** mehlmadrona@aol.com

MADSEN, Ross Martin. American (born United States), b. 1946. **Genres:** Children's Fiction, Humor/Satire. **Career:** Granite School District, social studies teacher, 1970-; Granger Community School, teacher, 1976-; Church of Jesus Christ, lay minister. Writer. **Publications:** Perrywinkle and the Book of Magic Spells, 1986; Stewart Stork, 1993; Perrywinkle's Magic Match, 1997. **Address:** 3136 Mark Ave., West Valley City, UT 84119, U.S.A.

MADSEN, Susan A(rrington). American (born United States), b. 1954. **Genres:** Children's Non-fiction, Theology/Religion, Theology/Religion. **Career:** Hyde Park Board of Adjustments, chairman, 1985-94; Logan Latter-day Saints Institute of Religion, adjunct faculty, 1991-95. Writer. **Publications:** (Comp. and ed.) Christmas: A Joyful Heritage, 1984; (with L.J. Arrington) Sunbonnet Sisters: True Stories of Mormon Women and Frontier Life, 1984; (with L.J. Arrington) Mothers of the Prophets, 1987, rev. ed. (with L.J. Arrington and E.M. Jones), 2009; The Lord Needed a Prophet, 1990, 2nd ed., 1996; I Walked to Zion: True Stories of Young Pioneers On the Mormon Trail, 1994; (ed.) Growing Up in Zion: True Stories of Young Pioneers Building the Kingdom, 1996; Second Rescue: The Story of the Spiritual Rescue of the Willie and Martin Handcart Pioneers, 1998; (with F.E. Woods) I Sailed to Zion: True Stories of Young Pioneers Who Crossed the Ocean, 2000; (ed. with R.H. Swaner) Hard-won Wisdom: Advice for a Richer Life From the Greatest Generation, 2007; Pioneer Christmas: Excerpts From Personal Journals, 2008. **Address:** 401 N 400 E, Hyde Park, UT 84318-3307, U.S.A.

MADSEN, Svend åge. Danish (born Denmark), b. 1939. **Genres:** Novels, Plays/Screenplays, Novellas/Short Stories, Literary Criticism And History, Poetry. **Career:** Writer. **Publications:** IN ENGLISH TRANSLATION: Dage med Diam ell: Livet om natten (novel), 1972; Tugt og utugt i mellemtiden (novel), 1976; Det sidste suk: skuespil i to akter (play), 1986. OTHERS: Besoeget; roman (novel), 1963; Lystbilleder, uroman, 1964; Otte gange Orphan (fiction), 1965; Tilfoejelser (novel), 1967; Modsatterne og Omvendterne (children's book), 1967; Et livstykke og andre stykker (plays), 1967; Liget og lysten (novel), 1968; Tredje gang saa tar vi ham (crime novel), 1969; Maskeballet (stories), 1970; Besøget, 1970; Saet verden er til (novel), 1971; (as Marianne Kainsdatter, with L. Madsen) Blodet paa minehaender (crime novel), 1973; Jakkels vandring (novel), 1974; Hadets baand (novel), 1978; Se dagens lys (novel), 1980; Den stø rste gå de (juvenile novel), 1982; Vi? Vi, Vi! (children's book), 1982; Af sporet erdu kommet (novel), 1984; Svejk i 3: Verdenskrig (play), 1984; Dr. Strangula: et melodrama i fem akter (play), 1985; Lad tiden gå: Roman (novel), 1986; Madsens kongespil: To spil af Svend åge Madsen (plays), 1986; Nøgne masker: skuespil i to akter (play), 1987; Svar udbedes (play), 1987; Slaegten Laveran (novel), 1988; At fortaelle menneskene (novel), 1989; Mellem himmel og jord (stories), 1990; Jagten på et menneske: Roman (juvenile novel), 1991; (as Marianne Kainsdatter, with L. Madsen) Et ved jeg som aldrig doer (crime novel), 1991; Edens gave (novel), 1993; Syv aldres galskab (novel), 1994; Den usynlige myre (children's book), 1995; Kvinden uden kroj (novel), 1996; Finder sted (novel), 1998; Genspejlet (novel), 1999; Naervr og Naesten, 2000; Ugudelige Farce, 2001; Gode Mennesker i århus: Laeselysten, 2003; Levemåder, 2004; Ude af Sit Gode Skindog Andre Noveller, 2004; Syvende Bånd: Roman, 2006; Manden Der Opdagede at Han Ikke Eksisterede, 2007; Mange Saere Ting For, 2009; Når Man Mailer, 2009. **Address:** Vestre Strandalle 154 B, Risskov, DK-8240, Denmark. **Online address:** sa.madsen@mail.tele.dk

MADUBUIKE, Ihechukwu (Chiedozie). Nigerian (born Nigeria), b. 1943. **Genres:** Language/Linguistics, Literary Criticism And History, Young Adult Fiction, History. **Career:** State University of New York, assistant professor, 1972-74; Ohio State University, assistant professor of African and Afro-American literature, 1975-76; Alvan Ikoku College of Education, principal lecturer in African and Afro-American literature, 1977-79; Federal Government of Nigeria, minister of education, 1979-81, federal minister of health, 1995-97; Imo State Government, commissioner for economic planning and finance, 1981-83; Champion Newspapers Ltd., executive director, 1992-95; Skyrock Nigeria Ltd., managing director; Pestfree Nigeria Ltd., managing director. Writer. **Publications:** A Handbook of African Names, 1976, 2nd ed., 1994; Ighota abu Igbo (title means: 'Understanding Igbo Poetry'), 1980; (with O. Jemie and Chinweizu) Toward the Decolonization of African Literature, vol. I, 1980; The Senegalese Novel: A Sociological Study of the Impact of the Politics of Assimilation, 1983; Sequences: A Collection of Poems Written During and After the Nigerian Civil War, 2004; Nigeria: Another Salvo From the Stable of a Critical Pathologist, 2008. **Address:** Skyrock Nigeria Ltd., PO Box 3538, Owerri, IM 00176, Nigeria.

MAECHLER, Stefan. Swiss (born Switzerland), b. 1957. **Genres:** Film, Young Adult Fiction, Literary Criticism And History. **Career:** Canton of Aargau, Department of Education, teacher, 1977-82, 1990-95, project coordinator for educational reform, 1995-2003; Foundation ECAP, teacher of German, 1985-88; Asylkoordination Zurich, assistant manager, 1987-89. Writer. **Publications:** (With K. Kasics) Closed Country, 1999; The Wilkomirski Affair: A Study in Biographical Truth, 2001; (with F. Daengeli) Wahre Szenen, 2003; Hilfe und Ohnmacht: der Schweizerische Israelitische Gemeindebund und die Nationalsozialistische Verfolgung 1933-1945, 2005. Contributor to books and periodicals. **Address:** c/o Eva Koralnik, Liepman AG, Maienburgweg 23, Zurich, CH-8044, Switzerland.

MAEDER, Thomas. American (born United States), b. 1951. **Genres:** Criminology/True Crime, Medicine/Health, Sciences, Humor/Satire, Law, Technology. **Career:** Freelance medical and technical writing, 1981-; Science Museum, exhibit developer, 1993-. Writer. **Publications:** Antonin Artaud, 1978; The Unspeakable Crimes of Dr. Petiot, 1980; Crime and Madness: The Origins and Evolution of the Insanity Defense, 1985; Children of Psychiatrists and Other Psychotherapists, 1989; Docteur Petiot, 1992; Adverse Reactions, 1994. WITH C. CRIMMINS: The Private Diary of Scarlett O'Hara, 1996; The 7 Habits of Highly Defective People: And Other Bestsellers That Won't Go Away: A Parody, 1996; Revenge of the Christmas Box: A Parody, 1996; Primary Whites: A Novel Look at Right-Wing Politics, 1996; Tamagotchi Egg: The Unofficial Guide, Intentionally Useless Advice for the Shell-Shocked Parent, 1997. **Address:** Witherspoon Associates, 235 E 31st St., New York, NY 10016, U.S.A.

MAES, Yvonne (M.). Canadian (born Canada), b. 1940?. **Genres:** Autobiography/Memoirs, Biography. **Career:** Sisters of the Holy Names, nun, 1959-96; St. Mary's Academy, teacher; Mabathoana High School, headmistress; Labrador Correctional Center, sexual abuse counselor. Writer. **Publications:** (With B. Slunder) The Cannibal's Wife: A Memoir, 1999. **Address:** Herodias Inc., 1603 79th St., Brooklyn, NY 11214, U.S.A.

MAES-JELINEK, Hena. Belgian (born Belgium), b. 1929. **Genres:** Literary Criticism And History. **Career:** University of Liege, professor; Rodopi (publishers), general editor. **Publications:** Criticism of Society in the English Novel between the Wars, 1970; The Naked Design: A Reading of Palace of the Peacock, 1976; Heart of Darkness, 1982; Wilson Harris, 1982. EDITOR: Commonwealth Literature and the Modern World, 1975; (intro.) Explorations: Essays by Wilson Harris, 1980; Multiple Worlds, Multiple Words, 1987; (with K.H. Petersen and A. Rutherford) A Shaping of Connections: Commonwealth Literature Then and Now, 1989; (with G.V. Davis) Crisis and Creativity in the New Literatures in English, 1990; Wilson Harris: The Uncompromising Imagination, 1991; (with G. Colliner and G.V. Davis) Talent(ed) Digger: Creations, Cameos and Essays in Honour of Anna Rutherford, 1996; (with B. Ledent) Contact and the Culmination, 1997. Contributor to periodicals. **Address:** University of Liege, 24 Place du Vingt Aout, Liege, 4000, Belgium. **Online address:** hmaes@ulg.ae.be

MAESTRIPIERI, Dario. American/Italian (born Italy), b. 1964. **Genres:** Psychology. **Career:** Istituto Superiore di Sanità (National Institute of Health), Section of Toxicology and Behavior, research assistant, 1985-89, Section of Behavioral Pathophysiology, research assistant, 1985-89; National Research Council, Institute of Psychobiology and Psychopharmacology, graduate research fellow, 1989-90; University of Cambridge, Sub-department of Animal Behaviour, visiting scientist, 1990-91; Emory University, Yerkes National Primate Research Center, Division of Psychobiology, research associate and affiliate scientist, 1992-2007, adjunct professor, Department of

Psychology, adjunct professor, 1994-2007; University of Chicago, Department of Comparative Human Development, faculty, 1999-, assistant professor, 1999-2003, associate professor, 2003-08, professor, 2008-, Institute for Mind and Biology, faculty, 2000, Center for Cognitive and Social Neuroscience, faculty, 2007, Center for Human Potential and Public Policy, faculty, 2007, Center for Health and the Social Sciences, faculty, 2009, Department of Psychiatry and Behavioral Neuroscience, faculty, 2010-; University of Puerto Rico, Medical School, adjunct professor, 2008-. Writer. **Publications:** (Ed.) Primate Psychology, 2003; Macachiavellian Intelligence: How Rhesus Macaques and Humans Have Conquered the World, 2007; (ed. with J.M. Mateo) Maternal Effects in Mammals, 2009; (with C. Carere) Animal Personalities: Behavior, Physiology, and Evolution, 2011; Games Primates Play: An Undercover Investigation of the Evolution and Economics of Human Relationships, 2012. Contributor to books and journals. **Address:** Department of Comparitive Human Development, University of Chicago, 5730 S Woodlawn Ave., Chicago, IL 60637, U.S.A. **Online address:** dario@uchicago.edu

MAESTRO, Giulio. American (born United States), b. 1942. **Genres:** Children's Fiction, Children's Non-fiction, Illustrations, History, Young Adult Fiction. **Career:** Design Organization Inc., assistant art director, 1965-66; Warren A. Kass Graphics Inc., assistant art director, 1966-69; freelance writer, designer and illustrator, 1969-. **Publications:** The Tortoise's Tug of War, 1971; The Remarkable Plant in Apartment 4, 1973 in UK as The Remarkable Plant in Flat No. 4, 1974; One More and One Less: Pictures, 1974; Leopard Is Sick, 1978; Leopard and the Noisy Monkeys, 1979; A Raft of Riddles, 1982; Halloween Howls: Riddles That Are A Scream, 1983; Just Enough Rosie, 1983; Riddle Romp, 1983; Tasty Homograph Riddles, 1984; What's a Frank Frank?: Razzle-Dazzle Riddles, 1985; What's Mite Might?: Homophone Riddles To Boost Your Word Power!, 1986; Riddle Roundup: A Wild Bunch to Beef Up Your Word Power!, 1989; More Halloween Howls: Riddles That Come Back To Haunt You, 1992; Macho Nacho and Other Rhyming Riddles, 1994; (with M. Maestro) Riddle City, USA!: A Book of Geography Riddles, 1994; (with M. Maestro) What Do You Hear When Cows Sing?: And Other Silly Riddles, 1996; (with M. Maestro) Geese Find the Missing Piece: School Time Riddle Rhymes, 1999. WITH B. MAESTRO: A Wise Monkey Tale, 1975; Where is My Friend?, 1976; Harriet Goes to the Circus, 1977; Busy Day: A Book of Action Words, 1978; Lambs for Dinner, 1978; On the Go: A Book of Adjectives, 1979; Harriet Reads Signs and More Signs: A Word Concept Book, 1981; Traffic: A Book of Opposites, 1981; The Key to the Kingdom, 1981; The Guessing Game, 1983; On the Town: A Book of Clothing Words, 1983; Around the Clock with Harriet: A Book About Telling Time, 1984; Harriet At Home, 1984; Harriet at Play, 1984; Harriet at School, 1984; Harriet at Work, 1984; Camping Out: A Book Of Action Words, 1985; Through the Year with Harriet: A Time Concept Book, 1985; Ferryboat, 1986; The Story of the Statue of Liberty, 1986; A More Perfect Union: The Story of Our Constitution, 1987; Dollars and Cents for Harriet: A Money Concept Book, 1988; Taxi: A Book of City Words, 1989; Delivery Van: Words For Town And Country, 1990; Temperature and You, 1990; The Discovery of the Americas, 1991; All Aboard Overnight: A Book Of Compound Words, 1992; Bike Trip, 1992; Exploration And Conquest: The Americas After Columbus, 1500-1620, 1994; A New Nation: The United States: 1783-1815, 2009. Illustrator of books by others. **Address:** HarperCollins Publishers, 1350 Ave. of the Americas, New York, NY 10019-4702, U.S.A. **Online address:** bcmaes@aol.com

MAFFI, Mario. Italian (born Italy), b. 1947. **Genres:** Urban Studies, Humanities, Literary Criticism And History, Geography, Popular Culture, Travel/Exploration, Documentaries/Reportage, Cultural/Ethnic Topics, Translations, History. **Career:** State University of Milan, assistant professor, 1975-98, associate professor of American studies, 1998-2004, professor of American studies, 2004-. Writer. **Publications:** La cultura underground, 1972, 3rd ed., 1980; Le origini della sinistra extraparlamentare, 1976; La giungla e il grattacielo: Gli scrittori e il sogno americano, 1965-1920, 1981; (with G. Fink, F. Minganti and B. Tarozzi) Storia della letteratura americana, 1991; Nel mosaico della citta'. Differenze etniche e nuove culture in un quartiere di New York, 1992, trans. as Gateway to the Promised Land: Ethnic Cultures in New York's Lower East Side, 1994; New York: L'isola delle colline, 1995; Sotto le Torri di Manhattan, 1998; Londra, Mappe, Storie, Labirinti, 2000; New York City, An Outsider's Inside View, 2004; Mississippi Il Grande Fiume Un viaggio alle sorgenti dell'America, 2004; Mississippi Voyage aux sources d'Amérique, 2008; Tamigi Storie di fiume, 2008. EDITOR: Nuovo teatro d'America, 1987; Voci dal silenzio, 1996; Voci di Frontiera, 1997. Contributor to journals. **Address:** Department of Language Sciences, State University of Milan, Piazza S. Alessandro 1, Milan, 20123, Italy. **Online address:** mario.maffi@unimi.it

MAGALONI, Beatriz. American (born United States), b. 1966. **Genres:** Politics/Government, History. **Career:** Center for Research and Development, professional associate, 1989-95; Social Science Research Council for Latin America and the Caribbean, staff, 1993-94; Instituto Tecnológico Autónomo de México, professor of political science, 1995-99, director of political science, 1997-99; Harvard University, visiting fellow, 1996-97; University of California, visiting assistant professor, 2000-01; Stanford University, Department of Political Science, assistant professor, 2001-09, associate professor, 2009-. Writer. **Publications:** (Ed. with L. Rubio and E. Jaime) A la puerta de la ley: El estado de derecho en México, 1993; Voting for Autocracy: Hegemonic Party Survival and Its Demise in Mexico, 2006. Contributor to books and periodicals. **Address:** Department of Political Science, Stanford University, Rm. 406, Encina Hall W, Stanford, CA 94305-6044, U.S.A. **Online address:** magaloni@stanford.edu

MAGAN, ManchAn. Irish (born Ireland), b. 1970?. **Genres:** Travel/Exploration, Transportation. **Career:** Telefis na Gaeilge TG4 (Irish-language travel channel), writer and coproducer. Writer. **Publications:** Manchán Ar Seachran: O Bhaile Atha Cliath Go Nairobi I Seanleorai Airm, 1998; Baba-ji Agus TNaG: Seachran San India, 2005; Angels and Rabies: A Journey through the Americas, 2006; Manchán's Travels: A Journey through India, 2007; Truck Fever: A Journey through Africa, 2008. Contributor to periodicals. **Address:** Westmeath, Ireland. **Online address:** manchan@ireland.com

MAGAS, Branka. British/Croatian (born Croatia) **Genres:** History, Social Sciences. **Career:** Bosnia Report, joint founding editor; Bosnian Institute, consultant. Historian. **Publications:** The Destruction of Yugoslavia: Tracing the Break-up, 1980-92, 1993; (ed.) Question of Survival: A Common Education System for Bosnia-Herzegovina, 1998; (ed. with I. Žanić) Rat u Hrvatskoj i Bosni i Hercegovini, 1991-1995, 2001; Croatia Through History, 2008. Contributor to newspapers and periodicals. **Address:** The Bosnian Institute, Hannibal House, Elephant and Castle, SAVO, 8th Fl., London, GL SE1 6TE, England.

MAGEE, Bryan. British (born England), b. 1930. **Genres:** Novels, Poetry, Music, Philosophy, Politics/Government, Social Commentary, Autobiography/Memoirs, Biography, Biography. **Career:** BBC, music critic, 1959-, theatre critic, 1966-; ITV Television, arts critic, 1966-; The Times, columnist, 1974-76; M.P. (U.K.) for Leyton, labour, 1974-82, S.D.P., 1982-83, King's College, visiting professor; University of London, visiting professor; Queen Mary College, fellow; Keble College, fellow. **Publications:** Crucifixion and Other Poems, 1951; Go West Young Man, 1958; To Live in Danger, 1960; The New Radicalism, 1962; The Democratic Revolution, 1964; The World We Make, 1965; One in Twenty; A Study of Homosexuality in Men and Women, 1966, new ed., 1968; The Television Interviewer, 1966; Aspects of Wagner, 1968; (ed.) Modern British Philosophy, 1971; The Philosophy of Karl Popper, 1973; Facing Death: A Novel, 1977; Men of Ideas 1978 as Talking Philosophy: Dialogues with Fifteen Leading Philosophers, 2001; The Philosophy of Schopenhauer, 1983; The Great Philosophers: An Introduction to Western Philosophy, 1987; Misunderstanding Schopenhauer, 1990; On Blindness: Letters Between Bryan Magee and Martin Milligan, 1995 as Sight Unseen: Letters Between Bryan Magee and Martin Milligan, 1998; Confessions of a Philosopher, 1997; The Story of Philosophy, 1998; Towards 2000; Wagner and Philosophy, 2000 as The Tristan Chord: Wagner and Philosophy, 2001; Clouds of Glory: A Hoxton Childhood, 2003. Contributor to periodicals. **Address:** 8 Ockham Ct., Bardwell Rd., Oxford, OX OX2 6SR, England.

MAGEE, David. American (born United States), b. 1965. **Genres:** Biography, Young Adult Non-fiction, Social Sciences. **Career:** Associated Press, staff; Jackson Clarion-Ledger, staff; Oxford Eagle, staff; Jefferson Press, founder and president; Rock Point Books, co-owner; journalist. **Publications:** Turnaround: How Carlos Ghosn Rescued Nissan, 2003; They Write Among Us: New Stories and Essays from the Best of Oxford Writers, 2003; Endurance: Winning Lifes Majors the Phil Mickelson Way, 2005; Ford Tough: Bill Ford and the Battle to Rebuild Americas Automaker, 2005; The John Deere Way: Performance That Endures, 2005; Getting Published: How to Learn and Master the Business of Writing, 2006; MoonPie: Biography of an Out-of-this-World Snack, 2007; How Toyota became 1: Leadership Lessons from the World's Greatest Car Company, 2007; The South Is Round: Contemplations of a 21st Century Redneck, 2007; Playing to Win: Jerry Jones and the Dallas Cowboys, 2008; Jeff Immelt and the New GE Way: Innovation, Transformation and Winning in the 21st Century, 2009; The Education of Mr. Mayfield: An Unusual Story of Social Change at Ole Miss, 2009. **Address:** Wiley Sons, 111 River St., 5th Fl., Hoboken, NJ 07030-5774, U.S.A. **Online address:** info@david-magee.com

MAGEE, Doug. American (born United States), b. 1947. **Genres:** Children's Fiction, Criminology/True Crime, Novels, Mystery/Crime/Suspense. **Career:** Writer, freelance photojournalist and filmmaker. **Publications:** Michael Jackson, 1985; (contrib.) Trucks You Can Count On, 1985. WITH R. NEWMAN: All Aboard ABC, 1990; Let's Fly From A to Z, 1992. NONFICTION: Slow Coming Dark: Interviews on Death Row, 1980; What Murder Leaves Behind: The Victim's Family, 1983; Never Wave Goodbye: A Novel of Suspense, 2010; Darkness All Around, 2011. **Address:** 1659 Lexington Ave., New York, NY 10029, U.S.A.

MAGER, Hugo. British (born England), b. 1967. **Genres:** Biography, Autobiography/Memoirs, History. **Career:** Writer. **Publications:** Elizabeth: Grand Duchess of Russia, 1998. **Address:** c/o Frances Kuffel, Jean V. Naggar Literary Agency Inc., 216 E 75th St., New York, NY 10021, U.S.A.

MAGGI, Armando. American/Italian (born Italy), b. 1959. **Genres:** Literary Criticism And History, Translations, History, Social Sciences. **Career:** Purdue University, visiting assistant professor, 1995-96; University of Pennsylvania, assistant professor, 1996-99; University of Chicago, associate professor, 1999-, professor. Writer. **Publications:** Uttering the Word: The Mystical Performances of Maria Maddalena de' Pazzi, a Renaissance Visionary, 1998; Identita e Impresa Rinascimentale, 1998; (trans. and intro.) Maria Maddalena de' Pazzi, 2000; Satan's Rhetoric: A Study of Renaissance Demonology, 2001; (ed.) Della Magia d'Amore, 2003; In the Company of Demons: Unnatural Beings, Love, and Identity in the Italian Renaissance, 2006; The Resurrection of the Body: Pier Paolo Pasolini from Saint Paul to Sade, 2009; (ed. with V. Kirkham) Petrarch: A Critical Guide to the Complete Works, 2009. Contributor to journals. **Address:** Department of Romance Languages and Literatures, University of Chicago, 1115 E 58th St., Chicago, IL 60637-1511, U.S.A. **Online address:** amaggi@uchicago.edu

MAGGIO, Frank P. American (born United States), b. 1937. **Genres:** Sports/Fitness, History, Biography. **Career:** Hinshaw & Culbertson, partner, 2002-; E.I. Dupont Nemours & Co., staff. Writer. **Publications:** Notre Dame and the Game That Changed Football: How Jesse Harper Made the Forward Pass a Weapon and Knute Rockne a Legend, 2007. **Address:** Hinshaw & Culbertson L.L.P., 100 Park Ave., PO Box 1389, Rockford, IL 61105-1389, U.S.A. **Online address:** fmaggio@hinshawlaw.com

MAGGIO, Mike. American (born United States), b. 1952. **Genres:** Novels, Poetry, Children's Fiction, Travel/Exploration, Literary Criticism And History, Novellas/Short Stories. **Career:** Bechtel, student advisor; Nextel, systems support analyst; ELS Amman, academic director; International Airports Projects, scholarship coordinator; Teligent, I.T. trainer; Buereau of Indian Affairs, systems administrator; Northern Virginia Community College, assistant professor of English. Writer. **Publications:** POETRY: Your Secret is Safe with Me, 1988; Oranges from Palestine: And Other Poems, 1996; Demockracy, 2007. FICTION: Sifting through the Madness, 1999; The Keepers, forthcoming; Haunted Garden, forthcoming. **Address:** Educate International L.L.C., 1549 Coomber Ct., Herndon, VA 20170, U.S.A. **Online address:** mikemaggio@mikemaggio.net

MAGGIO, Theresa (Marion). American (born United States), b. 1952. **Genres:** Travel/Exploration, Sports/Fitness, Recreation, Natural History, Reference. **Career:** Los Alamos National Laboratory, laser optics technician, 1979-83, science reporter, 1983-85; Brattleboro Reformer, reporter, night editor, photographer, 1987-91; freelance writer, 1991-. **Publications:** (With R. Muccigrosso and R. Blazek) Term Paper Resource Guide to Twentieth-Century United States History, 1999; (with T. Maggio) Mattanza: Love and Death in the Sea of Sicily, 2000; The Stone Boudoir: Travels through the Hidden Villages of Sicily, 2002. Contributor to periodicals. **Address:** c/o Author Mail, Perseus Books Group, 387 Park Ave. S, 12th Fl., New York, NY 10016, U.S.A. **Online address:** theresamaggio@hotmail.com

MAGGS, Colin Gordon. British (born England), b. 1932?. **Genres:** Transportation, Technology, Engineering, Reference. **Career:** Batheaston Church of England School, deputy headmaster, 1967-86. Writer. **Publications:** Weston Clevedon and Portishead Railway, 1964; Midland and South Western Junction Railway, 1967; Bristol and Gloucester/Avon and Gloucestershire Railways, 1969; Bath Tramways, 1971; Highbridge in Its Heyday, 1973; Weston Super Mare Tramways, 1974; Bristol Port Railway and Pier and the Clifton Extension Railway, 1975; Newport Tramways, 1977; East Somerset Railway, 1977; Sidmouth, Seaton and Lyme Regis Branches, 1977; Wrington Vale Light Railway, 1978; Barnstaple and Ilfracombe Railway, 1978, Railways to Exmouth, 1980; Taunton to Barnstaple Line: Devon and Somerset Railway, 1980; Rail Centres: Bristol, 1981; Railways of the Cotswolds, 1981; Bath to Weymouth Line, 1982; Rail Centres: Swindon, 1983; The Honeybourne Line: The Continuing Story of the Cheltenham to Honey Bourne and Stratford upon Avon Railway, 1985; The Camerton Branch, 1985; Rail Centres: Exeter, 1985; The Birmingham-Gloucester Line, 1986; The Clevedon Branch, 1987; GWR Principal Stations, 1987; Bristol Railway Panorama, 1990; Calne Branch, 1990; Last Days of the Somerset and Dorset, 1991; Mangotsfield to Bath Branch, 1991; Taunton Steam, 1991; Branch Lines of Gloucestershire, 1991; Swindon to Gloucester, 1991; Last Days of Steam in Bristol and Somerset, 1991; Branch Lines of Wiltshire, 1992; The Seaton Branch, 1992; The Best of the Last Days of Steam, 1993; Branch Lines of Berkshire, 1993; Branch Lines of Warwickshire, 1994; Branch Lines of Worcestershire, 1994; Branch Lines of Devon: Exeter Area, 1995; Branch Lines of Devon: Plymouth and Barnstaple Area, 1995; Branch Lines of Oxfordshire, 1995; Branch Lines of Dorset, 1996; The Sidmouth and Budleigh Salterton Branches, 1996; Branch Lines of Hampshire, 1997; The Exeter and Exmouth Railway, 1997; The Minehead Branch and the West Somerset Railway, 1998, 2nd ed., 2011; Colin Maggs' West of England, 1998; The East Somerset Railway, 1998; Steam: Tales from the Footplate, 1999; Branch Lines of Buckinghamshire, 2000; The Nailsworth and Stroud Branch, 2000; The GWR Bristol to Bath Line, 2001; The Yate to Thornbury Branch, 2000; Double-Headed, 2002; The GWR Swindon to Bath Line, 2003; The Wrington Vale Light Railway, 2004; The Culm Valley Light Railway: Tiverton Junction to Hemyock, 2006; Britain's Railways in Colour: BR Steam in the 1950s and 60s, 2009; Britain's Railways in Colour: BR Diesels in the 1960s and 1970s, 2010. **Address:** 8 Old Newbridge Hill, Bath, SM BA1 3LX, England.

MAGHRAOUI, Abdeslam M. American (born United States) **Genres:** Social Sciences, History, Sociology, Politics/Government. **Career:** Duke University, associate professor of political science; Muslim World Initiative, director, 2004-; United States Institute of Peace, director, 2004-; Al-Madina (nonprofit program to promote accountability of governance in the Arab world), director; Princeton University, Institute for the Transregional Study, visiting lecturer. Writer. **Publications:** Liberalism without Democracy: Nationhood and Citizenship in Egypt, 1922-1936, 2006. Contributor to journals. **Address:** Duke University, 339 Perkins Library, 104 Chapel Dr., Durham, NC 27708, U.S.A. **Online address:** abdeslam.maghraoui@duke.edu

MAGIDA, Arthur J. American (born United States), b. 1945. **Genres:** Theology/Religion, History, Paranormal, Social Commentary, Writing/Journalism, Communications/Media. **Career:** Patriot, reporter, 1967-68; Gazette and Daily, reporter, 1968-70; Ralph Nader's Congress Project, writer, editor and speechwriter, 1972-74; National Journal, environmental reporter, 1974-76; National Parks and Recreation Association, director of publications for energy conservation project, 1977-79; freelance writer and editor, 1979-83; Baltimore Jewish Times, senior editor, 1983-95; Jewish Lights Publishing, editorial director; University of Baltimore, School of Communications Design, writer-in-residence; Georgetown University, faculty. **Publications:** The Environment Committees, 1975; (ed.) How to Be a Perfect Stranger: A Guide to Etiquette in Other People's Religious Ceremonies, 2 vols., 1996, (ed. with S.M. Matlins) 5th ed. as How to be a Perfect Stranger: The Essential Religious Etiquette Handbook, 2011; Prophet of Rage: A Life of Louis Farrakhan and His Nation, 1996; Rabbi and the Hitman: A True Tale of Murder, Passion, and the Shattered Faith of a Congregation, 2003; Opening the Doors of Wonder: Reflections on Religious Rites of Passage, 2006; The Devil's Prophet: The Story of Hitler's Jewish Clairvoyant, 2011; The Nazi Séance: The Strange Story of the Jewish Psychic in Hitler's circle, 2011. Works appear in anthologies. Contributor to magazines and newspapers. **Address:** University of Baltimore, 1420 N Charles St., Baltimore, MD 21201, U.S.A. **Online address:** amagida@ubalt.edu

MAGILL, R. Jay. German (born Germany), b. 1972. **Genres:** History. **Career:** American Academy, web editor/writer, general editor; National Public Radio, Program, writer, host; Berlin Journal, editor, 2007. Illustrator. **Publi-**

cations: Chic Ironic Bitterness, 2007. Contributor to periodicals. **Address:** Berlin, Germany. **Online address:** rjaymagill@yahoo.com

MAGINN, Simon. (Simon Nolan). British (born England), b. 1961. **Genres:** Horror, Novels. **Career:** Songwriter, 1981-90; music teacher, 1990-. Novelist. **Publications:** NOVELS: Sheep, 1994; Virgins and Martyrs, 1995; A Sickness of the Soul, 1995; Methods of Confinement, 1996; Rattus, 2010. AS SIMON NOLAN: As Good as it Gets, 1999; The Vending Machine of Justice, 2001; Whitehawk, 2010. Contributor to magazines. **Address:** c/o Carole Blake, Blake Friedmann Literary Agency Ltd., 37-41 Gower St., London, GL WC1E 6HH, England.

MAGISTRALE, Anthony. *See* **MAGISTRALE, Tony.**

MAGISTRALE, Tony. (Anthony Magistrale). American (born United States), b. 1952. **Genres:** Literary Criticism And History, Writing/Journalism, Poetry, Essays, Novels, Psychology, Social Sciences. **Career:** Erie Community College, lecturer, 1974-76; University of Pittsburgh, Mellon pre-doctoral fellow, 1979-80; University of Vermont, visiting lecturer, 1981-82, Department of English, assistant professor of English, 1983-89, associate professor of English, 1989-97, professor of English, 1997-, Freshman Composition Program, director, 1988-91, Undergraduate Advising, director, 1999-2004, associate chair, 2005-09, chair, 2009-; University of Milan, Fulbright postdoctoral fellow, 1982-83; University of Stockholm, Swedish Program, director; University of Augsburg, visiting professor, 2004. Writer. **Publications:** Salvation on the Installment Plan: Poems, 1982; (with L.A. Bond and A.S. Magistrale) Writer's Guide: Psychology, 1987; Landscape of Fear: Stephen King's American Gothic, 1988; Moral Voyages of Stephen King, 1989; Stephen King: The Second Decade, 1992; (with K. Wagner) Writing across Culture: Study Abroad and The Writing Process, 1995; (with F.S. Frank) The Poe Encyclopedia, 1997; (with S. Poger) Poe's Children: Intersections between Tales of Horror and Detection, 1999; Student Companion to Edgar Allan Poe, 2001; Hollywood's Stephen King, 2003; Abject Terrors: Surveying the Modern and Postmodern Horror Film, 2005; (with L. Bonaffini) What She Says about Love: quello che lei dice sull'amore, 2008; Stephen King: America's Storyteller, 2010. EDITOR: Literature, 1989; Shining Reader, 1991; Dark Descent: Essays Defining Stephen King's Horrorscape, 1992; Casebook on The Stand, 1992; Angles of Vision: Reading, Writing, and the Study of Literature, 1992; Understanding Contemporary American Gothicism, 1996; (with M.A. Morrison) Dark Night's Dreaming: Contemporary American Horror Fiction, 1996; Discovering Stephen King's The Shining: Essays on the Bestselling Novel by America's Premier Horror Writer, 1998; (with J.A. Weinstock) Approaches to Teaching Poe's Prose and Poetry, 2008. Contributor to periodicals. **Address:** Department of English, University of Vermont, 400 Old Mill, Burlington, VT 05405-0114, U.S.A. **Online address:** anthony.magistrale@uvm.edu

MAGLIATO, Kathy. American (born United States), b. 1964?. **Genres:** Autobiography/Memoirs. **Career:** Wadsworth Research Center, resident, 1985-86; Albany Medical Center, resident, 1986-87; Akron General Medical Center, resident, 1991-93, 1994-96; University of Michigan, Medical Center, fellow, 1993-94; Loyola University, Medical Center, resident and fellow, 1997-99; University of Pittsburgh, Medical Center, fellow and clinical instructor, 1999-2000; Cedars-Sinai Medical Center, Mechanical Assist Device Program, transplant surgeon and director; Saint John's Medical Center, Women's Cardiac Services, staff surgeon and director. Writer. **Publications:** Healing Hearts: A Memoir of a Female Heart Surgeon, 2010. Contributor to books and journals. **Address:** U.S.A. **Online address:** info@kathymagliato.com

MAGLIOCCO, Sabina. American (born United States), b. 1959. **Genres:** Anthropology/Ethnology. **Career:** Monroe County Animal Control Commission, director, 1983-89; University of Wisconsin, visiting assistant professor, 1990-94; University of California-Los Angeles, visiting assistant professor, 1994; University of California-Santa Barbara, visiting assistant professor, 1995; University of California-Berkeley, visiting assistant professor, 1995-96, Guggenhein fellow, 1996-97; California State University, Department of Anthropology, assistant professor, professor and chair, 1997-, CSUN Cat People, faculty advisor; Western Folklore, editor, 2004-09. **Publications:** The Two Madonnas: The Politics of Festival in a Sardinian Community, 1993, 2nd ed., 2006; Neo-pagan Sacred Art and Altars: Making Things Whole, 2001; Witching Culture: Folklore and Neo-paganism in America, 2004. Contributor of articles to books and periodicals. **Address:** Department of Anthropology, California State University, Rm. 240-G, Sierra Hall, Northridge, CA 91330-8244, U.S.A. **Online address:** sabina.magliocco@csun.edu

MAGNARELLI, Sharon. American (born United States) **Genres:** Literary Criticism And History, Women's Studies And Issues. **Career:** High school Spanish teacher, 1968-71; Albertus Magnus College, professor of Spanish, 1976-94, department head, 1980-82, 1984-86, 1989-90, 1992-94; Yale University, visiting lecturer, 1977-78; Quinnipiac University, professor of Spanish, 1994-, professor of modern languages, chairperson of modern languages. Writer. **Publications:** The Lost Rib: Female Characters in the Spanish-American Novel, 1985; Reflections/Refractions: Reading Luisa Valenzuela, 1988; Understanding Joś Donoso, 1993; Home is Where the Heart Is: The Family Romance in Late Twentieth-Century Mexican and Argentine Theater, 2008. Works appear in anthologies. Contributor of articles to journals. **Address:** Department Modern Languages, College of Arts & Sciences, Quinnipiac University, Rm. 3 315, 275 Mt. Carmel Ave., Hamden, CT 06518, U.S.A. **Online address:** magnarelli@quinnipiac.edu

MAGNER, Lois N. American (born United States), b. 1943. **Genres:** Biology, Sciences, History, Women's Studies And Issues, Medicine/Health. **Career:** Purdue University, postdoctoral research associate in biochemistry, 1968-72, assistant professor, 1973-78, associate professor, 1978-93, professor of history, 1993-, now professor emeritus, School of Humanities, Social Science, and Education, assistant dean, 1979-80, Women's Resource Office, director, 1985-87. Writer. **Publications:** A History of the Life Sciences, 1979, 3rd ed., 2002; A History of Medicine, 1992, 2nd ed., 2005; (ed.) Doctors, Nurses and Medical Practitioners: A Bio-bibliographical Sourcebook, 1997; A History of Infectious Diseases and the Microbial World, 2009. **Address:** 4137 Bay Beach Ln., Ste. 551, Fort Myers Beach, FL 33931, U.S.A. **Online address:** magnerln@aol.com

MAGNET, Myron. American (born United States), b. 1944. **Genres:** Social Sciences, Politics/Government, Sociology. **Career:** Columbia University, preceptor, 1970-72, instructor, 1972-73, fellow in humanities, 1977-79, assistant professor, 1979-80; Middlebury College, lecturer, 1975-77; Fortune Magazine, writer, 1980-82, associate editor, 1982-83; Manhattan Institute for Policy Research, senior fellow, 1989; City Journal, editor, 1994-2006, editor-at-large, 2006-. **Publications:** NONFICTION: Dickens and the Social Order, 1985; The Dream and the Nightmare: The Sixties' Legacy to the Underclass, 1993; (ed. and intro.) The Millennial City: A New Urban Paradigm for 21st-Century America, 2000; (ed. and intro.) What Makes Charity Work?: A Century of Public and Private Philanthropy, 2000; (ed. and intro.) Modern Sex: Liberation and Its Discontents, 2001. Contributor of articles to periodicals. **Address:** Manhattan Institute, 52 Vanderbilt Ave., New York, NY 10017, U.S.A.

MAGNUS, Erica. American (born United States), b. 1946. **Genres:** Children's Fiction, Film, Illustrations, Science Fiction/Fantasy. **Career:** Great River Review, contributing artist, 1976-77, art director, 1977-79. Writer. **Publications:** Around me, 1992; My Secret Place, 1994. AUTHOR AND ILLUSTRATOR: Old Lars, 1984; The Boy and the Devil, 1986; The Crossing, 1996. **Address:** 15 Ondis Ave., Athens, OH 45701, U.S.A.

MAGOCSI, Paul Robert. Also writes as Ma-go-chee Michaels. Canadian/American (born United States), b. 1945. **Genres:** Area Studies, History, Language/Linguistics, Social Sciences. **Career:** Harvard University, senior research fellow, 1971-80, managing editor, 1975-82, lecturer, 1979-80; Carpatho-Rusyn Research Center, president, 1978-; University of Toronto, professor of history, 1980-, chair of Ukrainian studies; Hebrew University of Jerusalem, visiting professor, 1989; Multicultural History Society of Ontario, chief executive officer and director, 1990-97. **Publications:** Historiographical Guide to Subcarpathian Rus, 1975; Let's Speak Rusyn-Bisidujme po-rus'ky, 1976; Ukrainian Heritage Notes, 1977; The Shaping of a National Identity, 1978; Ukrainian Heritage Notes: The Language Question in Galicia, 1978; Let's Speak Rusyn-Hovorim po-rus'ky: 1979; National Cultures and University Chairs: An Inaugural Lecture, October 22, 1980, 1980; Wooden Churches in the Carpathians/Holzkirchen in der Karpaten, 1982; The Rusyn-Ukrainians of Czechoslovakia: An Historical Survey, 1983; Galicia: A Historical Survey and Bibliographic Guide, 1983; Our People: Carpatho-Rusyns and Their Descendants in North America, 1984, 4th ed., 2005; Ukraine: A Historical Atlas, 1985; Ucrainica in the University of Toronto Library, 2 vols., 1985; End of the Nation-State?: The Revolution of 1989 and the Future of Europe; Carpatho-Rusyn Studies: An Annotated Bibliography, vol. I: 1975-1984, 1988, vol. II: 1985-1994, 1998; The Russian Americans, 1989, 2nd ed., 1996; The Carpatho-Rusyn Americans, 1989, 2nd ed., 2000; The Rusyns of Slovakia, 1993; Historical Atlas of East Central Europe, 1993, 2nd ed., 2002; A History of Ukraine, 1996, 2nd ed. as A History of Ukraine: The Land and Its Peoples, 2010; Mapping Stateless Peoples: The East Slavs of the Carpathians, 1998; Of the Making of Nationalities There is No End, 2 vols., 1999; The Roots of Ukrainian Nationalism, 2002; Iarusin byl, iesm I budu-: vystupy na Svitovykh kongresakh rusinüv, 2005; Nasha ottsiuznyna, 2005; Ukraine: An Illustrated History, 2007. EDITOR: The Ukrainian Experience in the United States, 1979; Morality and Reality: The Life and Times of Andrei Sheptyts'kyi, 1989; The Persistence of Regional Cultures, 1993; A New Slavic Language is Born, 1996; (intro.) Rusyns of Hungary: Political and Social Developments, 1860-1910, 1997; (intro.) Medieval Carpathian Rus, 1998; Encyclopedia of Canada's Peoples, 1999; Canada's Aboriginal Peoples, 2002; Encyclopedia of Rusyn History and Culture, 2002, 2nd ed., 2005; Aboriginal Peoples of Canada: A Short Introduction, 2002; (with C. Hann) Galicia: A Multicultured Land, 2005. Contributor to scholarly journals. **Address:** Department of History, University of Toronto, Rm. 201, Medical Arts, St. George Campus, Toronto, ON M5S 1A1, Canada.

MAGONA, Sindiwe. American/South African (born South Africa), b. 1943. **Genres:** Novels, Young Adult Fiction. **Career:** School teacher, 1967-81; United Nations, press officer, 1984-2003, presenter, through 1994, Public Information Department, staff, through 2003, retired 2003. Writer. **Publications:** To My Children's Children, 1990; Living, Loving and Lying Awake at Night (fiction), 1991; Push-Push! and Other Stories, 1996; Forced to Grow, 1998; The Best Meal Ever!, 1998; Mother to Mother (fiction), 1998; (with B. Kirsch and S. Skorge) Clicking with Xhosa: A Xhosa, 2001; Life is a Hard But Beautiful Thing, 2005; Mud Chic: Lifestyle and Inspiration from the Xhosa People of the Old Transkei, 2006; Esona-sona sidlo!, 2006; Die heel, héél lekkerste kos!, 2006; Beauty's Gift, 2008; Please, Take Photographs, 2009. **Address:** Aaron M. Priest Literary Agency Inc., 708 3rd Ave., 23 Fl., New York, NY 10017-4201, U.S.A. **Online address:** magona-gobado@un.org

MAGORIAN, Michelle. British (born England), b. 1947. **Genres:** Novels, Songs/Lyrics And Libretti, Novellas/Short Stories, Poetry. **Career:** Writer and actress. **Publications:** Goodnight Mister Tom, 1981; Back Home, 1984; Waiting for My Shorts to Dry (poetry), 1989; Who's Going to Take Care of Me?, 1990; A Little Love Song (novel), 1991; Orange Paw Marks (poetry), 1991; Jump!, 1992; Not a Swan, 1992; In Deep Water (short stories), 1994; Cuckoo in the Nest, 1994; A Spoonful of Jam (novel), 1998; Be Yourself (short stories), 2003; Just Henry, 2008. Contributor to periodicals. **Address:** c/o Patricia White, Rogers, Coleridge and White Literary Agency, 20 Powis Mews, London, GL W11 1JN, England.

MAGRATH, Allan J. Canadian (born Canada), b. 1949. **Genres:** Marketing, Business/Trade/Industry, Industrial Relations. **Career:** University of Western Ontario, finance faculty, 1975-77, adjunct professor; 3M Canada Inc., director of corporate marketing services and new business ventures, 1978-. Writer. **Publications:** (With K.G. Hardy) Marketing Channel Management: Strategic Planning and Tactics, 1988; Market Smarts: Proven Strategies to Outfox and Outflank Your Competition, 1988; The Revolution in Sales and Marketing, 1990; The Six Imperatives of Marketing: Lessons From the World's Best Companies, 1992; How to Achieve Zero-Deficit Marketing, 1993; Deflationary Marketing, 1994; Marketing Strategies for Growth in Uncertain Times, 1995. Contributor to periodicals. **Address:** 3M Canada Inc., PO Box 5757, London, ON N6A 4T1, Canada. **Online address:** ajmagrath@mm.com

MAGUIRE, Gregory (Peter). American (born United States), b. 1954. **Genres:** Children's Fiction, Novels. **Career:** Vincentian Grade School, teacher of English, 1976-77; freelance writer, 1977-; Simmons College Center for the Study of Children's Literature, faculty and associate director, 1979-87; Children's Literature New England, founder, co-director and consultant, 1987-; Isabella Stewart Gardner Museum, artist-in-residence, 1994; Hambidge Center, artist-in-residence, 1998; Virginia Center for the Creative Arts, artist-in-residence, 1999. **Publications:** FOR CHILDREN AND YOUNG ADULTS: The Lightning Time, 1978; The Daughter of the Moon, 1980; Lights on the Lake, 1981; The Dream Stealer, 1983; The Peace and Quiet Diner (picture book), 1988, rev. ed., 1994; I Feel like the Morning Star, 1989; Lucas Fishbone (picture book), 1990; Missing Sisters, 1994; The Good Liar, 1995; Oasis, 1996; Crabby Cratchitt, 2000; Leaping Beauty: And Other Animal Fairy Tales, 2004; Matchless: A Christmas Story, 2009; Making Mischief: A Maurice Sendak Appreciation, 2009. OTHERS: (ed. with B.Harrison) Innocence and Experience: Essays and Conversations on Children's Literature, 1987; (ed. with B.Harrison) Origins of Story: On Writing for Children, 1999; (intro.) Wonderful Welcome to Oz: The Marvelous Land of Oz, Osma of Oz & The Emerald City of Oz, 2005; Next Queen of Heaven: A Novel, 2010. HAMLET CHRONICLES: Seven Spiders Spinning, 1994, rev. ed., 2005; Six Haunted Hairdos, 1997; Five Alien Elves, 1998; Four Stupid Cupids, 2000; Three Rotten Eggs, 2002; A Couple of April Fools, 2004; One Final Firecracker, 2005. FOR ADULTS: Wicked: The Life and Times of the Wicked Witch of the West, 1995; Confessions of an Ugly Stepsister, 1999; Lost: A Novel, 2001; Mirror Mirror, 2003; Couple of April Fools, 2005; Son of a Witch: A Novel, 2005; What-the-Dickens: The Story of a Rogue Tooth Fairy, 2007; (co-author) Click, 2007; Lion among Men, 2008; Out of Oz, 2011. Contributor to periodicals. **Address:** William Reiss, John Hawkins and Associates, 71 W 23rd St., Ste. 1600, New York, NY 10010, U.S.A. **Online address:** gm@gregorymaguire.com

MAGUIRE, Laurie E. British (born England), b. 1959. **Genres:** Literary Criticism And History, Essays. **Career:** University of Ottawa, faculty, 1988-99; University of Oxford, Magdalen College, professor of English, 1999-. Writer. **Publications:** Shakespearean Suspect Texts: The Bad Quartos and Their Contexts, 1996; (ed. with T.L. Berger) Textual Formations and Reformations, 1998; Studying Shakespeare: A Guide to the Plays, 2003; Where There's a Will There's a Way: Or, All I Really Need to Know I Learned from Shakespeare, 2006; Shakespeare's Names, 2007; (ed.) How to Do Things with Shakespeare: New Approaches, New Essays, 2008; Helen of Troy: From Homer to Hollywood, 2009. Works appear in anthologies. Contributor to periodicals. **Address:** Magdalen College, University of Oxford, Oxford, OX OX1 4AU, England. **Online address:** laurie.maguire@magd.ox.ac.uk

MAGUN, Carol. American (born United States), b. 1949. **Genres:** Novels, Young Adult Fiction. **Career:** Keter Publishing Co., editorial assistant, 1973-75; Historical Abstracts, staff, 1978-80; Van Leer Institute, assistant to the director, 1980-81; Harvard University, resident affiliate at Winthrop House, 1981-84; freelance abstract writer, 1984-86; Bentley College, assistant professor of English, 1987-, adjunct assistant professor of English, 1988-98, lecturer, 1998-2002; California Institute of Technology, lecturer in creative writing, 2003. **Publications:** Circling Eden: A Novel of Israel in Stories, 1995. Works appear in anthologies. Contributor to periodicals. **Address:** Division of Humanities & Social Sciences, California Institute of Technology, 201D Dabney Hall, PO Box 101-40, Pasadena, CA 91125, U.S.A. **Online address:** magun@hss.caltech.edu

MAHAJAN, Karan. American (born United States), b. 1984. **Genres:** Novels. **Career:** Writer. **Publications:** Family Planning: A Novel, 2008. Works appear in anthologies. Contributor to periodicals. **Address:** Brooklyn, NY , U.S.A. **Online address:** kmahajan@gmail.com

MAHARAJ, Rabindranath. Canadian/Trinidadian (born Trinidad and Tobago), b. 1955. **Genres:** Adult Non-fiction. **Career:** Teacher, 1980-2005; Lichen, co-founder, founding editor, 1998-2001; Trinidad Guardian, columnist, journalist; Toronto Reference Library, writer-in-residence, 2006; Diaspora Dialogues, mentor, 2006; University of Toronto, School of Continuing Studies, instructor, 2007-; Humber School for Writers, mentor, 2007. **Publications:** SHORT STORIES: The Interloper, 1995; The Writer and his Wife and Other Stories, 1996; The Book of Ifs and Buts, 2002. NOVELS: Homer in Flight, 1997; The Lagahoo's Apprentice, 2000; The Book of Ifs and Buts: Stories, 2002; A Perfect Pledge, 2005 OTHERS: The Picture of Nobody, 2010; The Amazing Absorbing Boy, 2010. Contributor of articles to books and periodicals. **Address:** c/o Hilary McMahon, Westwood Creative Artists, 94 Harbord St., Toronto, ON M5S 1G6, Canada. **Online address:** robinmah@hotmail.com

MAHARIDGE, Dale (Dimitro). American (born United States), b. 1956. **Genres:** History, Biography, Young Adult Non-fiction, Adult Non-fiction, Travel/Exploration, Social Sciences, Politics/Government. **Career:** Freelance writer, 1977, 1978-80; Gazette, staff writer, 1977-78; Cleveland Plain Dealer, writer; Sacramento Bee, special projects reporter, 1980-91; Columbia University, Graduate School of Journalism, assistant professor, 1991-92, associate professor, 2001-; Stanford University, Department of Communication, Lokey visiting professor, 1992-2002; Harvard University, 1988 Nieman fellow. **Publications:** NONFICTION: Journey to Nowhere: The Saga of the New Underclass, 1985; (with M. Williamson) And Their Children after Them: The Legacy of Let Us Now Praise Famous Men, James Agee, Walker

Evans, and the Rise and Fall of Cotton in the South, 1989; The Last Great American Hobo, 1993; The Coming White Minority: California's Eruptions and the Nation's Future, 1996; The Coming White Minority: California, Multiculturalism, and America's Future, 1999. OTHERS: (contrib.) Yosemite: A Landscape of Life, 1990; Homeland, 2004; Denison, Iowa: Searching for the Soul of America Through the Secrets of a Midwest Town, 2005; Someplace like America: Tales from the New Great Depression, 2011. Contributor to periodicals. **Address:** Graduate School of Journalism, Columbia University, 2950 Broadway, 116th St., New York, NY 10027-6902, U.S.A. **Online address:** dm2021@columbia.edu

MAHDAVI, Pardis. American (born United States), b. 1978?. **Genres:** Psychology. **Career:** Pomona College, assistant professor, 2006-. Anthropologist and journalist. **Publications:** Passionate Uprisings: Iran's Sexual Revolution, 2009. Contributor to books, periodicals and journals. **Address:** Department of Anthropology, Pomona College, Hahn Bldg., 420 N Harvard Ave., Claremont, CA 91711, U.S.A. **Online address:** pardis_mahdavi@pomona.edu

MAHER, Eamon. Irish/British (born England) **Genres:** Theology/Religion, Literary Criticism And History, Translations, Novels. **Career:** Association of Lecturers of French in the Institutes of Technology, president, 2003-04; Institute of Technology Tallaght, lecturer in French, National Centre for Franco-Irish Studies, director, 2004-; Liffey Press, associate editor, 2005-08; Association of Franco-Irish Studies, president. Writer and translator. **Publications:** Crosscurrents and Confluences: Echoes of Religion in Twentieth-Century Fiction, 2000; (trans.) Anticipate Every Goodbye, 2000; (with N. Cazaux) Faisons Affaires, 2002; John McGahern: From the Local to the Universal, 2003; (ed. with M. Böss and contrib.) Engaging Modernity: Readings of Irish Politics, Culture and Literature at the Turn of the Century, 2003; (ed. with G. Neville) France-Ireland: Anatomy of a Relationship: Studies in History, Literature and Politics, 2004; Un Regard En Arrière VersLa Littérature D'expression Française Du XXe Siècle: Questions D'identité Et De Marginalité: Actes Du Colloque De Tallaght, 2005; (ed. with L. Fuller and J. Littleton) Irish and Catholic?: Towards An Understanding of Identity, 2006; (ed. with E. O'Brien) La France Face a La Mondialisation: France and the Struggle Against Globalization: Bilingual Essays on the Role of France in the World, 2007; (ed. with E. O'Brien and G. Neville) Reinventing Ireland through a French Prism, 2007; (ed. with J. Littleton) Contemporary Catholicism in Ireland: A Critical Appraisal, 2008; Jean Sulivan, 1913-1980: La marginalité dans la vie et l'euvre, 2008; (ed. witth G. Neville and E. O'Brein) Modernity and Postmodernity in a Franco-Irish Context, 2008; Cultural Perspectives on Globalisation and Ireland, 2009; (ed. with J. Littleton) What being Catholic Means to Me, 2009; (ed. with J. Littleton) The Dublin/Murphy Report: A Watershed for Irish Catholicism, 2010; (ed. with E. O'Brien) War of the Words: Literary Rebellion in France and Ireland, 2010; The Church and Its Spire, 2011; (ed. with E. O'Brien) Breaking the Mould: Literary Representations of Irish Catholicism, 2011. Contributor to magazines. **Address:** National Centre for Franco-Irish Studies, Institute of Technology Tallaght, Tallaght, Dublin, 24, Ireland. **Online address:** eamon.maher@ittdublin.ie

MAHER, Mary. Irish (born Ireland), b. 1940?. **Genres:** Adult Non-fiction, Medicine/Health, Young Adult Fiction, Literary Criticism And History. **Career:** Chicago Tribune, feature writer, 1962-65; Irish Times, feature writer, reporter, assistant news editor, women's editor and assistant chief sub-editor, 1965-2001. **Publications:** You and Your Baby, 1973; The Devil's Card, 1992; If Only, 1997; (ed. with K.C. O'Brien) In Sunshine or in Shadow, 1998; (ed.) How Far We Have Travelled: The Voice of Mary Holland, 2004. **Address:** Irish Times Ltd., 10-16 D'Olier St., Dublin, DU 2, Ireland.

MAHER, Mary Z. American (born United States), b. 1941. **Genres:** Theatre, Film, Communications/Media. **Career:** Hofstra University, assistant professor of speech arts and sciences, 1972-2000; University of Arizona, now professor emeritus; Arizona State University, Arizona Center for Medieval and Renaissance Studies, visiting distinguished professor, 1992. Writer. **Publications:** Modern Hamlets and Their Soliloquies, 1992; Actor Nicholas Pennell: Risking Enchantment, 2005; Actors Talk About Shakespeare, 2009. Contributor to journals. **Address:** 2133 Birchwood Ln., Ashland, OR 97520, U.S.A. **Online address:** maherm@actorstalkingaboutshakespeare.com

MAHESHWARI, Shriram. Indian (born India), b. 1931. **Genres:** Public/Social Administration, Administration/Management, Politics/Government, Money/Finance. **Career:** Agra University, lecturer, 1955-61; St. Stephen's College, lecturer, 1962; University of Rajasthan, lecturer, 1964; University of Delhi, Indian School of Public Administration, reader in public administration, 1965-73, professor of political science and public administration, 1973-91; Centre for Political and Administrative Studies, director; Indian Public Administration Association, president, 1988-90; Maison des Sciences l'Hourire, visiting fellow. Writer. **Publications:** The General Election in India, 1963; The Evolution of Indian Administration, 1970; Local Government in India, 1971; Government through Consultation, 1972; Administrative Reforms Commission, 1972; (co-author) Public Administration, 1973, 16th ed., 1990; Indian Administration, 1973, 4th ed., 1990; The Civil Service in Great Britain, 1976; President's Rule in India, 1977; State Governments in India, 1979; Administrative Reform in India, 1981; Open Government in India, 1981; Indian Parliamentary System, 1981; Electoral Politics in the National Metropolis, 1982; Comparative Government and Politics, 1983; Political Development in India, 1984; Rural Development in India, 1985, 2nd ed., 1995; The Higher Civil Service in Japan, 1987; The Mandal Commission and Mandalisation, 1991; The Higher Civil Service in France, 1991; Problems and Issues in Administrative Federalism, 1992; Theories and Concepts in Public Administration, 1992; Administrative Reform in India, 1993; Indian Administration: An Historical Account, 1993; Indian Administrative System, 1994; (co-author) Public Service in Canada and India, 1994; Mandal Commission Revisited, 1995; The Census Administration Under the Raj and After, 1996; Major Civil Service Systems in the World, 1997; Administrative Theory, 1998; Administrative Thinkers, 1999; Administrative Reforms in India, 2002; A Dictionary of Public Administration, 2002; Public Administration in India: The Higher Civil Service, 2005. EDITOR: The Study of Public Administration in India, 1974; G.T. Chesney, Indian Polity, 1976; Teaching of Public Administration in India, 1979; Education in Public Administration in India, 1992. **Address:** 156 Golf Links, New Delhi, DH 10003, India. **Online address:** esarem@vsnl.com

MAHINDRA, Indira. Indian/Pakistani (born Pakistan), b. 1926. **Genres:** Novels, Sociology, Adult Non-fiction, Literary Criticism And History. **Career:** Isabella Thoburn College, professor of Indian history, 1948-50; Welham Girls High School, chair. Writer. **Publications:** The Rebellious Home Makers, 1980; The Club, 1984; The End Play, 1995; Man and His-Story, 1995. Contributor to periodicals. **Address:** c/o Caroline Dawnay, Peter Fraser & Dunlop Ltd., Chelsea Harbour, Lots Rd., London, GL SW 100 XF, England. **Online address:** indiramahindra@hotmail.com

MAHLER, Jonathan. American (born United States), b. 1969. **Genres:** Politics/Government, Law, History, Autobiography/Memoirs, Business/Trade/Industry. **Career:** Talk, senior editor; ForWard, editorial page editor; New York Times Magazine, writer. **Publications:** The Lexus Story, 2003; Ladies and Gentlemen the Bronx is Burning: 1977 Baseball Politics and the Battle for the Soul of a City, 2005; Hamden V. Rumsfeld: A Historic Challenge to the President, 2008. Contributor to periodicals. **Address:** The Forward, 45 E 33rd St., New York, NY 10016, U.S.A.

MAHMOOD, Saba. American (born United States), b. 1962?. **Genres:** Theology/Religion, Politics/Government, History. **Career:** Architect and housing developer, 1988-92; University of California, chancellor's postdoctoral fellow, 1998-99; University of Chicago, Divinity School, assistant professor, 1999-2003; Leiden University, International Institute for the Study of Islam, visiting professor, 2003; University of California, Department of Anthropology, assistant professor, 2004-07, associate professor, 2007-. Writer. **Publications:** Politics of Piety: The Islamic Revival and the Feminist Subject, 2005. Contributor to journals. **Address:** Department of Anthropology, University of California, 232 Kroeber Hall, Berkeley, CA 94720-3710, U.S.A. **Online address:** smahmood@berkeley.edu

MAHMUD, Shabana. British (born England), b. 1949?. **Genres:** Literary Criticism And History, Bibliography, Women's Studies And Issues, Language/Linguistics, Librarianship. **Career:** British Library, responsible for acquisitions in Urdu and Persia for the Oriental and India Office Collections, 1982-, business marketing executive; BBC World Service, Islamic Collection of the British Library, researcher and presenter of programs, 1983, 1992-93. Writer. **Publications:** Angare, ek jaiza, (facsimile edition of Urdu fiction), 1988; Urdu Language and Literature: A Bibliography of Sources in European Languages, 1992; Catalogue of Political Publications in Urdu (1900-1947) in the British Library, 1993; Anthology of Women's Poetry in Urdu from 1800 to the Present, forthcoming. Contributor to periodicals. **Address:** Oriental and India Office Collections, British Library, 96 Euston Rd., London, GL NW1 2DB, England. **Online address:** shabana.mahmud@bl.uk

MAHOKO. *See* **YOSHIMOTO, Banana.**

MAHON, Basil. British/Maltese (born Malta), b. 1937. **Genres:** Biography, Autobiography/Memoirs, Sciences. **Career:** Government Statistical Office, civil servant, 1974-96. Writer. **Publications:** (With M. Chapman) Plain Figures, 1986; Counting Heads II: A Practical Guide to Census Management, 1998; The Man Who Changed Everything: The Life of James Clerk Maxwell, 2003; Oliver Heaviside: Maverick Mastermind of Electricity, 2009. **Address:** John Wiley & Sons Inc., 111 River St., Hoboken, NJ 07030-5774, U.S.A. **Online address:** basil.mahon@tiscali.co.uk

MAHONEY, Richard D. American (born United States), b. 1952?. **Genres:** History, Politics/Government, Biography, Autobiography/Memoirs. **Career:** Oxford University, Templeton College, visiting professor; Harvard University, JFK School of Government, visiting professor; Beijing Institute of Foreign Trade, visiting professor; Universidad del Pacifico, visiting professor; The American Graduate School of International Management, professor emeritus; Thunderbird, professor emeritus; United States Senate, governor, 2002; Arizona State University, professor of international studies. Writer and historian. **Publications:** JFK: Ordeal in Africa, 1983; Pétalos, 1995; Sons and Brothers: The Days of Jack and Bobby Kennedy, 1999; (Richard Mahoney) Getting Away with Murder: The Real Story behind American Taliban John Walker Lindh and What the U.S. Government Had to Hide, 2004; The Kennedy Brothers: The Rise and Fall of Jack and Bobby, 2011. Contributor of articles to periodicals. **Address:** c/o Author Mail, Arcade Publishing, 141 5th Ave., 8th Fl., New York, NY 10010, U.S.A. **Online address:** richardmahoney@hotmail.com

MAHONEY, Rosemary. American (born United States), b. 1961. **Genres:** Sociology, Young Adult Non-fiction, Travel/Exploration, Essays, History, Literary Criticism And History. **Career:** Johns Hopkins University, instructor in writing, 1984-86; Hangzhou University, instructor in writing, 1987-88. Writer. **Publications:** The Early Arrival of Dreams: A Year in China, 1990; Whoredom in Kimmage: Irish Women Coming of Age, 1993; A Likely Story: One Summer with Lillian Hellman, 1998; The Singular Pilgrim: Travels on Sacred Ground, 2003; Down the Nile: Alone in a Fisherman's Skiff, 2007. Contributor to periodicals. **Address:** c/o Author Mail, Little Brown & Co., 1271 Ave. of the Americas, New York, NY 10020, U.S.A. **Online address:** mail@rosemarymahoney.org

MAHONY, Patrick J(oseph). Canadian/American/Irish (born Ireland), b. 1932. **Genres:** Literary Criticism And History, Psychology, Art/Art History, Sciences, Medicine/Health. **Career:** Universite de Montreal, professor of literature, 1963-, now professor emeritus; psychoanalyst, 1977-; Canadian Society of Psychoanalysts, diplomate and supervising and training psychoanalyst. Writer. **Publications:** Freud as a Writer, 1982; Freud and the Wolf Man, 1982; Cries of the Wolfman, 1984; Freud and the Rat Man, 1986; Psychoanalysis and Discourse, 1987; On Defining Freud's Discourses, 1987; Freud's Dora, 1996; (ed.) Freud Behind the Scenes, 1997; Honorary Festschrift: Penser Freud avec Mahony, 2004. Contributor to journals. **Address:** University of Montreal, PO Box 6128, Sta. Downtown, Montreal, QC H3C 3J7, Canada.

MAHOWALD, Mary Briody. American (born United States), b. 1935. **Genres:** Medicine/Health, Philosophy, Women's Studies And Issues. **Career:** Schoolteacher, 1955-65; St. Joseph's College, instructor in philosophy, 1969-70; Villanova University, assistant professor of philosophy, 1970-72; Indiana University-Purdue University, assistant and associate professor of philosophy, 1972-82; Case Western Reserve University, associate professor, 1982-89, professor of philosophy and biomedical ethics, 1989-90, Center for Biomedical Ethics, co-director, 1985-88; University of Chicago, professor, 1990-2000, now professor emeritus, 2000-. Writer. **Publications:** An Idealistic Pragmatism, 1972; Women and Children in Health Care: An Unequal Majority, 1993; (with A. Silvers and D. Wasserman) Disability, Difference Discrimination: Perspectives on Justice in Bioethics and Public Policy, 1998; Genes, Women, Equality, 2000; Bioethics and Women: Across the Life Span, 2006. EDITOR: Philosophy of Woman: Classical to Current Concepts, 1978, 3rd ed., 1994; (with V. McKusick, A. Scheuerle and T. Aspinwall) Genetics in the Clinic: Clinical, Ethical and Social Issues for Primary Care, 2001. Contributor to books and articles. **Address:** University of Chicago, MC 2050, 5841 S Maryland Ave., Chicago, IL 60637-1470, U.S.A. **Online address:** mm46@uchicago.edu

MAHY, Margaret. New Zealander (born New Zealand), b. 1936. **Genres:** Novellas/Short Stories, Children's Fiction, Young Adult Fiction, Poetry, History, Picture/Board Books, Young Adult Non-fiction. **Career:** Petone Public Library, assistant librarian, 1958-59; School Library Service, librarian-in-charge, 1967-76; Canterbury Public Library, children's librarian, 1976-80; Canterbury University, writer-in-residence, 1984; Western Australian College of Advanced Education, writer-in-residence, 1985. **Publications:** The Dragon of an Ordinary Family, 1969; A Lion in the Meadow, 1969; Mrs. Discombobulous, 1969; Pillycock's Shop, 1969; The Procession, 1969; The Little Witch, 1970; Sailor Jack and the 20 Orphans, 1970; The Princess and the Clown, 1970; The Boy with Two Shadows, 1971; Seventeen Kings and Forty Two Elephants (verse), 1972; The First Second, Third Margaret Mahy Storybook: Stories and Poems, 3 vols., 1972-75; The Man Whose Mother Was a Pirate, 1972; The Railway Engine and the Hairy Brigands, 1973; The Third Margaret Mahy Storybook, 1973 as Watch Me!, 2004; Rooms for Rent in UK as Rooms to Let, 1974; The Witch in the Cherry Tree, 1974; Clancy's Cabin, 1974; The Rare Spotted Birthday Party, 1974; Stepmother, 1974; New Zealand: Yesterday and Today, 1975; The Bus under the Leaves, 1975; The Ultra-Violet Catastrophe! Or, The Unexpected Walk with Great-Uncle Magnus Pringle, 1975; The Great Millionaire Kidnap, 1975; Leaf Magic, 1975; The Boy Who Was Followed Home, 1975; The Wind between the Stars, 1976; David's Witch Doctor, 1976; The Pirate Uncle, 1977; Nonstop Nonsense, 1977; The Great Piratical Rumbustification, 1979; Fearsome Robots and Frightened Uncles, 1980; Raging Robots and Unruly Uncles, 1981; The Chewing-Gum Rescue, 1982; The Haunting, 1983; The Pirate's Mixed-Up Voyage, 1983; The Changeover, 1984; Leaf Magic and Five Other Favourites, 1984; The Catalogue of the Universe, 1985; Jam, 1985; Aliens in the Family, 1986; The Tricksters, 1986; The Downhill Crocodile Whizz and Other Stories, 1986; Memory, 1987; The Horrible Story and Others, 1987; The Door in the Air, 1988; The Birthday Burglar and a Very Wicked Headmistress, 1988; The Blood and Thunder, 1989; Adventures on Hurricane Peak, 1989; The Pumpkin Man and the Crafty Creeper, 1990; Making Friends, 1990; Keeping House, 1991; Dangerous Spaces, 1991; The Queen's Goat, 1991; A Tall Story and Other Tales, 1992; Seven Chinese Brothers, 1992; Bubble Trouble: And Other Poems, 1992; The Horrendous Hullaballo, 1992; The Girl with the Green Ear, 1992; Underrunners, 1992; The Good Fortunes Gang, 1993; The Cousins Quartet, Books 1-4 (junior novels), 1994; When the King Rides By, 1995; Tick Tock Tales, 1994; My Mysterious World, 1995; Tingleberries, Tuckertubs and Telephones, 1995; A Busy Day for a Good Grandmother, 1995; The Other Side of Silence, 1995; The Five Sisters, 1996; Boom, Baby, Boom, Boom, 1997; Horribly Haunted School, 1997; (co-author) Don't Read This, 1998; Beaten by a Balloon, 1998; Summery Saturday Morning, 1998; Simply Delicious, 1999; 24 Hours, 2000; A Dissolving Ghost, 2000; Down the Dragon's Tongue, 2000; Dashing Dog, 2002; Alchemy (young adult novel), 2002; The Gargling Gorilla and Other Stories, 2003; Notes of a Bag Lady, 2003; Shock Forest and Other Stories, 2004; Maddigan's Fantasia, 2005; Kaitangata Twitch, 2005; Zerelda's Horses, 2005; Portable Ghosts, 2006; Down the Back of the Chair, 2006; Family Surprises, 2006; Magician of Hoad, 2009; Portable Ghosts, 2009; Heriot, 2009; (contrib.) The Word Witch: The Magical Verse of Margaret Mahy, 2009; Awesome Aotearoa: Margaret Mahy's History of New Zealand, 2009; Stop That Stew!, 2009; Organ Music, 2010; (with D. Elliot) The Moon & Farmer McPhee, 2010; The Man From the Land of Fandango, 2012. **Address:** Rd. 1, Lyttelton, 8082, New Zealand.

MAI, Francois Martin. Canadian (born Canada) **Genres:** Music, Biography, History. **Career:** University of Ottawa, professor of psychiatry; Ottawa Hospital, psychiatric consultant; Canadian Government, medical advisor for human resources and social development. **Publications:** Diagnosing Genius: The Life and Death of Beethoven, 2007. **Address:** University of Ottawa, 550 Cumberland St., Ottawa, ON K1N 6N5, Canada.

MAIER, Anne McDonald. American (born United States), b. 1954. **Genres:** Documentaries/Reportage, Adult Non-fiction, Mystery/Crime/Suspense, Criminology/True Crime. **Career:** People, Houston Bureau, research assistant, 1981-83, staff correspondent, 1983-92, bureau chief, 1992-; legal and public relationship consultant. Writer. **Publications:** Mother Love, Deadly Love: The Texas Cheerleader Murder Plot, 1992. **Address:** People, Houston Bureau, 2500 E T. C. Jester Blvd., Ste. 643, Houston, TX 77008, U.S.A.

MAIER, Karl. American (born United States), b. 1957?. **Genres:** Area Studies, Social Sciences, History. **Career:** Independent, Africa correspondent, 1986-96; Khartoum, journalist. Writer. **Publications:** (With K. Mustafa and A. Vines) Conspicuous Destruction: War, Famine, and the Reform Process in Mozambique, 1992; Angola: Promises and Lies, 1996; Into the House of the Ancestors: Inside the New Africa, 1998; This House Has Fallen: Midnight in Nigeria, 2000; This House Has Fallen: Nigeria in Crisis, 2002. Contributor to periodicals. **Address:** c/o Author Mail, Public Affairs, 250 W 57th St., Ste. 1321, New York, NY 10107, U.S.A.

MAIER, Paul Luther. American (born United States), b. 1930. **Genres:** Mystery/Crime/Suspense, Romance/Historical, Theology/Religion, Biography, Translations. **Career:** Western Michigan University, professor of ancient history, 1960-, Russell H. Seibert professor of ancient history; Christianity Today, Christian History, corresponding editor, 1992-. **Publications:** A Man Spoke, a World Listened: The Story of Walter A. Maier, 1963; First Christmas, 1971; First Easter, 1973; In the Fullness of Time, 1991; (with H. Hanegraaff) The Da Vinci Code-Fact or Fiction?, 2004. NOVELS: Pontius Pilate, 1968; The Flames of Rome, 1981; A Skeleton in God's Closet, 1994; More Than a Skeleton, 2003; The Real Story of the Creation, 2007; The Real Story of the Flood, 2008; The Real Story of the Exodus, 2009; The Constantine Codex, 2011. EDITOR: The Best of Walter A. Maier, 1980; Josephus: The Essential Writings, 1988; Josephus: The Essential Works, 1995; (and trans.) Eusebius-The Church History, 1999. **Address:** Department of History, Western Michigan University, 4356 Friedmann Hall, Kalamazoo, MI 49008, U.S.A. **Online address:** paul.maier@wmich.edu

MAIER, Thomas. American (born United States), b. 1956. **Genres:** Biography, Autobiography/Memoirs. **Career:** New York Newsday, reporter; Chicago Sun-Times, reporter. Journalist. **Publications:** Newhouse: All the Glitter, Power, and Glory of America's Richest Media Empire and the Secretive Man behind It, 1994; Dr. Spock: An American Life, 1998; The Kennedys: America's Emerald Kings, 2003; Masters of Sex: The Life and Times of William Masters and Virginia Johnson, the Couple Who Taught America How to Love, 2009. Contributor to periodicals. **Address:** Newsday, 235 Pinelawn Rd., Melville, NY 11747, U.S.A. **Online address:** thomasmaierbooks@gmail.com

MAIER-KATKIN, Daniel. American (born United States), b. 1945. **Genres:** Law. **Career:** Wel-Met Inc., unit director, program assistant, 1963-70; State University of New York, assistant professor, 1969-72, Student Health Center, therapist, 1971-72; Smith College, School of Social Work, lecturer, 1970-75, 1978; Pennsylvania State University, assistant professor, 1972-79, associate professor and program head, 1979-82, professor and department head, 1982-94; Florida State University, professor, 1994-, Center for the Advancement of Human Rights, fellow, 1994-, School of Criminology and Criminal Justice, dean, 1994-2003. Writer. **Publications:** (With D. Hyman and J. Kramer) Juvenile Delinquency and the Juvenile Justice System, 1976; The Nature of Criminal Law: Essays, Cases, and Other Materials, 1982; Stranger from Abroad: Hannah Arendt, Martin Heidegger, Friendship, and Forgiveness, 2010. Contributor to books and journals. **Address:** School of Criminology and Criminal Justice, Florida State University, 634 W Call St., Tallahassee, FL 32306-1127, U.S.A. **Online address:** dmaierkatkin@fsu.edu

MAIFAIR, Linda Lee. American (born United States), b. 1947. **Genres:** Children's Fiction, Children's Non-fiction, Mystery/Crime/Suspense, Literary Criticism And History. **Career:** Freelance writer, 1986-; Wilson College, senior lecturer in creative writing and adolescent literature, 1987-; Harrisburg Area Community College, adjunct faculty in composition, literature and theater, 1989-. **Publications:** The Day Snuffy Had the Sniffles, 1988; I Can't Wait Until Christmas: Featuring Jim Henson's Sesame Street Muppets, 1989; 18-Wheelers, 1991; I Want to Be a Firefighter, 1991; (with J.E. Tada and J. Musser) Joni's Story, 1992; (ed. with L. Walburg) Colin Powell, 1993; Batter Up, Bailey Benson!, 1997; Go Figure, Gabriella Grant!, 1997; Use Your Head, Molly Malone!, 1997; Whoa There, Wanda Wilson!, 1997. READY, SET, READ! SERIES: Brothers Don't Know Everything, 1993; No Girls Allowed, 1993; The Grump at the End of the Lane, 1995. DARCY DOYLE MYSTERY SERIES: The Case of the Mixed-Up Monsters, 1992; The Case of the Pampered Poodles, 1993; The Case of the Giggling Ghost, 1993; The Case of the Choosey Cheater, 1993; The Case of the Bashful Bully, 1994; The Case of the Missing Max, 1994; The Case of the Angry Actress, 1994; The Case of the Creepy Camp out, 1994; The Case of the Bashed-Up Bicycle, 1996; The Case of the Nearsighted Neighbor, 1996; The Case of the Sweet-Toothed Shoplifter, 1996; The Case of the Troublesome Treasure, 1996. Contributor of stories and articles to periodicals. **Address:** Zondervan, 5300 Patterson Ave. SE, Grand Rapids, MI 49530, U.S.A.

MAIL, Audrey Maureen. New Zealander (born New Zealand), b. 1924?. **Genres:** Education. **Career:** Hawera Main School, senior mistress, 1959-61; Turu-Turu School, junior classes supervisor, 1962-66; Hawera High School, career adviser, 1970-72, senior mistress, 1973-86. Writer. **Publications:** Springboard Series, 12 books, 1966; Little Reader, 5 books, 1967. **Address:** 36 Mawhitiwhiti Rd., Normanby, Taranaki, 4614, New Zealand.

MAILMAN, Erika. American (born United States) **Genres:** Novels, Young Adult Non-fiction, Mystery/Crime/Suspense. **Career:** Novelist. **Publications:** NON-FICTION: Oakland Hills, 2004. NOVELS: Woman of Ill Fame, 2006; The Witch's Trinity, 2007. Contributor to books. **Address:** Marly Rusoff & Associates Inc., PO Box 524, Bronxville, NY 10708-0524, U.S.A. **Online address:** witchstrinity@yahoo.com

MAINE, David. American/Pakistani (born Pakistan), b. 1963. **Genres:** Novels. **Career:** English teacher, 1995-; University of Phoenix, faculty, 2008-; Hawai'i-Pacific University, faculty, 2008-; University of Hawai'i, faculty, 2008-. Writer. **Publications:** The Preservationist, 2004 in UK as The Flood, 2005; Fallen, 2005; The Book of Samson, 2006; Monster, 1959, 2008; An Age of Madness, 2012. **Address:** Department of English, College of Languages, Linguistics and Literature, University of Hawai'i, Kuykendall 725, 1733 Donaghho Rd., Honolulu, HI 96822, U.S.A. **Online address:** dmaine@hawaii.edu

MAINGOT, Anthony P. American/Trinidadian (born Trinidad and Tobago), b. 1937. **Genres:** Area Studies, Sociology. **Career:** Yale University, faculty, 1966-72, Antilles Research Program, director; University of the West Indies, faculty, 1972-74; Florida International University, professor of sociology, 1974-95, professor emeritus of sociology, 1995-; Institute of Developing Economics, faculty, 1978-79; Rand Corp., staff, 1987-88; University of Miami, faculty, 1994-95; Silversea, staff. Writer. **Publications:** Caribbean Migration As a Structural Reality, 1983; Security Perspectives of Governing Elites in the English-Speaking Caribbean, 1985; (with J.H. Parry and P.M. Sherlock) A Short History of the West Indies, 4th ed., 1987; The Haitian Crisis: Two Perspectives, 1988; (ed.) Small Country Development and International Labor Flows: Experiences in the Caribbean, 1991; The United States and the Caribbean: Challenges of an Asymetrical Relationship, 1994; (with W. Lozano) United States and the Caribbean: Transforming Hegemony and Sovereignty, 2004; Estados Unidos y el Caribe, 2005; (ed. and intro.) Gordon K. Lewis on Race, Class and Ideology in the Caribbean, 2010; (ed. with R.S. Clem) Venezuela's Petro-Diplomacy: Hugo Chávez's Foreign Policy, 2011. Contributor to books and journals. **Address:** Department of Global & Sociocultural Studies, Florida International University, 334 DM, Modesto A. Maidique Campus, 11200 SW 8th St., Miami, FL 33199, U.S.A. **Online address:** anthony.maingot@fiu.edu

MAINIERO, Lisa A. American (born United States), b. 1957. **Genres:** Business/Trade/Industry, Economics, Psychology, Ethics, Medicine/Health, Social Sciences. **Career:** Fairfield University, Charles F. Dolan School of Business, professor of management. Writer. **Publications:** (With C.L. Tromley) Developing Managerial Skills in Organizational Behavior: Exercises, Cases & Readings, 1989, 2nd ed., 1994; Office Romance: Love, Power and Sex in the Workplace, 1989; (with D.D. Palmer) Managing Our Future, 1994; (with M. Brindle) Managing Power through Lateral Networking, 2000; (with S.E. Sullivan) The Opt-Out Revolt: Why People are Leaving Companies to Create Kaleidoscope Careers, 2006. **Address:** Charles F. Dolan School of Business, Fairfield University, Rm. 1119, 1073 N Benson Rd., Fairfield, CT 06824, U.S.A. **Online address:** lmainiero@fairfield.edu

MAINONE, Robert Franklin. American (born United States), b. 1929?. **Genres:** Poetry, Natural History, inspirational/Motivational Literature. **Career:** Michigan State University, Kellogg Bird Sanctuary, naturalist, 1967-91. Writer. **Publications:** An American Naturalist's Haiku Poems, 1964; Parnassus Flowers, 1965; Where Waves Were, 1966; This Boundless Mist, 1968; Shadows, 1971; Young Leaves, 1974; High on the Wind, 1975; Moonlight, 1979; The Journey North, 1984; The Spring Within, 1989; Seven Acres of Sky: Poems from a Haiku Diary, 1997. **Address:** 7431 Pine Lake Rd., Detroit, MI 49046-8458, U.S.A.

MAINS, Randolph P. American (born United States), b. 1946. **Genres:** Novels, Air/Space Topics. **Career:** Cairns, helicopter pilot, 1974-76; Bell Helicopter Intl., senior instructor pilot, 1976-79; Hermann Hospital, aeromedical pilot, 1979-80; University of California, San Diego Medical Center, chief life flight pilot, 1980-85; Royal Oman Police, Sultanate of Oman, flight examiner and helicopter pilot, 1985-. Writer. **Publications:** Life and Death, an EMS Pilot's Viewpoint, 1984; The Golden Hour: A Novel, 1989; Dear Mom, I'm Alive: Letters Home from Blackwidow 25, 1992. **Address:** PO Box 41, Seeb Airport, 111, Oman.

MAINWARING, Scott. American (born United States), b. 1954. **Genres:** Politics/Government. **Career:** University of Notre Dame, Kellogg Institute for International Studies, assistant professor of government and international studies, 1983-88, associate professor, 1988-93, professor, 1993-96, chairman, 1996-97, Eugene P. and Helen Conley professor of political science, 1996-, Department of Government, head, 1996-97, director, 1997-2002, 2003-08, 2009-. Writer. **Publications:** (Co-author) Igreja nas bases em tempo de transição (1974-1985), 1986; The Catholic Church and Politics in Brazil, 1916-1985, 1986; Consolidation of Democracy in Latin America: A Rapporteur's Report, 1986; (ed. with A. Wilde) The Progressive Church in Latin America, 1989; A IgrejaCatólica e a Política no Brasil 1916-1985, 1989; (ed. with G. O'Donnell and J.S. Valenzuela) Issues in Democratic Consolidation: The New South American Democracies in Comparative Perspective, 1992; (ed. with T.R. Sculty) Building Democratic Institutions: Party Systems in Latin America, 1995; (ed.) La Construcción de Instituciones Democráticas: Sistemas de Partidos en América Latina, 1996; (ed. with M.S. Shugart) Presidentialism and Democracy in Latin America, 1997; (ed. with A. Valenzuela) Politics, Society and Democracy: Latin American, 1998; Rethinking Party Systems in the Third Wave of Democratization: The Case of Brazil, 1999; (with R. Meneguello and T.J. Power) Os Partidos Conservadores no Brasil Contemporâneo, 2000; (ed.) Democracia: Discusiones y nuevas aproximaciones, 2000; Sistemas Partidários em Novas Democracias: O Caso do Brasil, 2001; (ed. with C. Welna) Democratic Accountability in Latin America, 2003; (ed. with T. Scully) Christian Democracy in Latin America: Electoral Competition and Regime Conflicts, 2003; (ed. with F. Hagopian) Third Wave of Democratization in Latin America: Advances and Setbacks, 2005; (ed. with A.M. Bejarano and E.P. Leongómez) The Crisis of Democratic Representation in the Andes, 2006; (ed. with T.R. Scully) Democratic Governance in Latin America, 2010; The Rise and Fall of Democracies and Dictatorships, forthcoming. **Address:** Kellogg Institute for International Studies, University of Notre Dame, 130E Hesburgh Ctr., Notre Dame, IN 46556, U.S.A. **Online address:** smainwar@nd.edu

MAIO, Samuel (Joseph). American (born United States), b. 1955. **Genres:** Novellas/Short Stories, Poetry, Literary Criticism And History. **Career:** University of Utah, teaching assistant, 1978-79; Trinidad State Junior College, instructor, 1979-81; University of Southern California, assistant lecturer, 1981-85; University of California, lecturer, 1985-90; San Jose State University, assistant professor, 1990-93, associate professor, 1993-98, professor, 1998-, San Jose Area Writing Project, director, English education coordinator. Writer. **Publications:** Creating Another Self: Voice in Modern American Personal Poetry, 1995, 2nd ed., 2005; Burning of Los Angeles: Poems, 1997; Counter-Measures: Metrical Poetry in the Modern Age, 1999; Meeting Cal, 2002; (ed.) Dramatic Monologues: A Contemporary Anthology, 2009. Contributor of essays to journals. **Address:** Department of English, San Jose State University, Rm. 223, 1 Washington Sq., San Jose, CA 95192-0090, U.S.A. **Online address:** smaio@email.sjsu.edu

MAIROWITZ, David Zane. French/American (born United States), b. 1943. **Genres:** Novels, Novellas/Short Stories, Plays/Screenplays, Politics/Government, Translations, Literary Criticism And History, Graphic Novels. **Career:** University of California, visiting professor in documentary theatre, 1967; Running Man magazine, editor, 1968-69; Village Voice, drama critic, 1968-76; Stanford University, visiting professor of political theatre, 1975; Plays and Players, drama critic, 1975-80; University of Avignon, teacher, 1982-. Writer. **Publications:** The Law Circus, 1969; The Radical Soap Opera: An Impression of the American Left from 1917 to the Present, 1974; Radical Soap Opera: Roots of Failure in the American Left, 1976; That Was Laura, But She's Only a Dream, 1976; In the Slipstream: Stories, 1977; Landscape of Exile, 1979; (contrib.) Parisian life, or, Fair Helen: An Operetta from the Second Empire, in Rehearsal and Performance One Year After Its Fall, 1980; Reic for Beginners, 1984; Kafka for Beginners, 1993; (with R. Crumb) Introducing Kafka, 1994; (with A. Korkos) Introducing Camus, 1998; (trans.) The Trial: A Graphic Adaptation of Franz Kafka's Novel, 2008; (trans.) Crime and Punishment, 2008; A Tale of Two Cities, 2010; Heart of Darkness, 2010. EDITOR: Some of IT, 1969; (with P. Stansill) BAMN: Outlaw Manifestos and Ephemera 1965-1970, 1971; (intro.) Inside German Communism, 1976. **Address:** 84 rue de la Bonneterie, Avignon, 84000, France. **Online address:** dzane@free.fr

MAIRS, Nancy (Pedrick). American (born United States), b. 1943. **Genres:** Poetry, Autobiography/Memoirs, Essays. **Career:** Smithsonian Astrophysical Observatory, junior editor, 1966-69; Harvard Law School, editorial assistant, 1970-72; University of Arizona, teaching assistant, 1972-75, 1977-83, 1985-86; Salpointe Catholic High School, teacher, 1975-77; Southwest Institute for Research on Women, project director, 1983-85; University of California, lecturer, 1986-87. **Publications:** POETRY: Instead It Is Winter, 1977; In All the Rooms of the Yellow House, 1984. ESSAYS: Plaintext: Deciphering a Woman's Life, 1986; An Erotics of Place and Space, 1989; Carnal Acts, 1990; Ordinary Time, 1993; Voice Lessons, 1994; Waist-High in the World, 1997; A Troubled Guest: Life and Death Stories, 2001. OTHERS: Remembering the Bone House: An Erotics of Place and Space, 1989; Dynamic God: Living an Unconventional Catholic Faith, 2007. **Address:** 579 S 3rd Ave., Tucson, AZ 85701-2463, U.S.A. **Online address:** nancymairs@msn.com

MAISEL, Eric. American (born United States), b. 1947. **Genres:** Novels. **Career:** Callboard Magazine, founder and writer; St. Marys College, adjunct faculty. Psychotherapist. **Publications:** Dismay, 1982; The Blackbirds of Mulhouse, 1984; The Fretful Dancer, 1986; Staying Sane in the Arts: A Guide for Creative and Performing Artists, 1992; Artists Speak: A Sketchbook, 1993; A Life in the Arts: Practical Guidance and Inspiration for Creative and Performing Artists, 1994; Fearless Creating: A Step-by-Step Guide to Starting and Completing Your Work of Art, 1995; Affirmations for Artists, 1996; Fearless Presenting: A Self-Help Workbook for Anyone Who Speaks Sells or Performs in Public, 1997; Living the Writers Life, 1999; Deep Writing: Seven Principles That Bring Ideas to Life, 1999; 20 Communication Tips for Families: A 30-Minute Guide to a Better Family Relationship, 2000; The Creativity Book: A Years Worth of Inspiration and Guidance, 2000; (with N. Maisel) Sleep Thinking: The Revolutionary Program That Helps You Solve Problems Reduce Stress and Increase Creativity while You Sleep, 2000; Twenty Communication Tips at Work: A Quick and Easy Guide to Better Business Relationships, 2001; Write Mind: 299 Things Writers Should Never Say to Themselves (and What They Should Say Instead), 2002; The Van Gogh Blues: The Creative Persons Path through Depression, 2002; Everyday Calm: 30 Ways to Soothe Your Inner Beast, 2004; The Art of the Book Proposal: From Focused Idea to Finished Proposal, 2004; Everyday Smart: 30 Ways to Spark Your Inner Genius, 2004; Coaching the Artist Within: Advice for Writers Actors Visual Artists and Musicians from Americas Foremost Creativity Coach, 2005; A Writers Paris: A Guided Journey for the Creative Soul, 2005; (with A. Maisel) What would Your Character Do?: Personality Quizzes for Analyzing Your Characters, 2006; Writer's San Fransisco: A Guided Journey for the Creative Soul, 2006; Ten Zen Seconds: Twelve Incantations for Purpose, Power and Calm, 2007; Creativity for Life: Practical Advice on the Artist's Personality and Career from America's Foremost Creativity Coach, 2007; Toxic Criticism: Break the Cycle with Friends, Family, Coworkers and Yourself, 2007; Everyday You: Create Your Day with Joy and Mindfulness, 2007; (with S. Raeburn) Creative Recovery: A Complete Addiction Treatment Program That Uses Your Natural Creativity, 2008; A Writer's Space: Make Room to Dream, to Work, to Write, 2008; Atheist's Way: Living Well Without Gods, 2009; (with A. Maisel) Brainstorm: Harnessing the Power of Productive Obsessions, 2010; Mastering Creative Anxiety: Twenty-Four Lessons for Writers, Painters, Musicians and Actors from America's Foremost Creativity Coach, 2011; Rethinking Depression, 2012. Contributor to periodicals. **Address:** New World Library, 14 Pamaron Way, Novato, CA 94949, U.S.A. **Online address:** ericmaisel@hotmail.com

MAISEL, Ivan. American (born United States), b. 1960. **Genres:** Sports/Fitness, History. **Career:** Sporting News, writer; Dallas Morning News, writer, 1987-94; Newsday, writer, 1994-97; Sports Illustrated, writer, 1997-2002; CNNSI.com, writer, 1997-2002; ESPN.com, columnist, 2002-, senior writer. **Publications:** (With K. Whiteside) A War in Dixie: Alabama v. Auburn: Inside College Football's Fiercest Rivalry, 2002; The Maisel Report: College Football's Most Overrated and Underrated Players, 2008. Contributor of articles to periodicals and journals. **Address:** HarperCollins Publishers, 10 E 53rd St., New York, NY 10022, U.S.A. **Online address:** ivan.maisel@espn3.com

MAISON, Della. *See* **KATZ, Bobbi.**

MAISTROS, Louis. American (born United States), b. 1962. **Genres:** Music. **Career:** Louie's Juke Joint (record, memorabilia, art shop and Vodou botanica), owner. Writer and musician. **Publications:** The Big Punch, 2000; The Sound of Building Coffins, 2009. **Address:** New Orleans, LA , U.S.A. **Online address:** louie@thejukejoint.com

MAITAL, Sharone L(evow). American/Israeli (born Israel), b. 1947. **Genres:** Human Relations/Parenting, Economics, Psychology. **Career:** School Psychological Services, psychologist, director, 1988-90; Haifa School Psychological Services, psychologist, 1988-; University of Haifa, Department of Education, adjunct senior lecturer, 1993-, research fellow; Israel Ministry of Education, Department of Educational Psychology and Counseling, deputy chief psychologist. Writer. **Publications:** (With S. Maital) Economic Games People Play, 1984; (ed. with S. Maital) Economics and Psychology, 1993. Contributor to periodicals. **Address:** Department of Counseling & Human Development, University of Haifa, Education and Sciences Bldg., Rm. 250, Mount Carmel, Haifa, 31905, Israel. **Online address:** maitals@construct.haifa.ac.il

MAITLAND, Barbara. British (born England) **Genres:** Children's Fiction, Young Adult Fiction, Animals/Pets, Horror. **Career:** Writer. **Publications:** The Bear Who Didn't Like Honey, 1997; The Bookstore Ghost, 1998; My Bear and Me, 1999; Moo in the Morning, 2000; The Bookstore Burglar, 2001; The Bookstore Valentine, 2002. **Address:** Dutton Children's Books, 345 Hudson St., New York, NY 10014-4502, U.S.A. **Online address:** barbaramaitland@cox.net

MAITLAND, Barry. Australian/Scottish (born Scotland), b. 1941?. **Genres:** Mystery/Crime/Suspense, Urban Studies, Novels. **Career:** University of Newcastle, professor of architecture, head, 1984-2000; University of Sheffield, faculty; writer, 2000-. Architect. **Publications:** (With D. Gosling) Design and Planning of Retail Systems, 1976; (with D. Gosling) Concepts of Urban Design, 1984; Shopping Malls: Planning and Design, 1985; The Pender Index: A Guide to the Architectural Work of the Pender Practice of Maitland, NSW, 1863-1988, 1999; Chelsea Mansions, 2011. BROCK AND KOLLA MYSTERY SERIES: The Marx Sisters, 1994; The Malcontenta, 1995; All My Enemies, 1996; The Chalon Heads, 1999; Silvermeadow, 2000; Babel, 2002; The Verge Practice, 2003; No Trace, 2006; Spider Trap, 2007; Bright Air, 2008; The Dark Mirror, 2009. **Address:** c/o Author Mail, Arcade Publishing, 307 W 57th St., 11th Fl., New York, NY 10018, U.S.A.

MAITLAND, Karen. British (born England), b. 1956?. **Genres:** Novels. **Career:** Writer, 1996-. **Publications:** The White Room, 1996; Company of Liars: A Novel of the Plague, 2008; The Owl Killers: A Novel, 2009. **Address:** c/o Victoria Hobbs, A.M. Heath & Company Ltd., 6 Warwick Ct., Holborn, London, GL WC1R 5DJ, England. **Online address:** karen@karenmaitland.com

MAITRA, Priyatosh. New Zealander/Indian (born India), b. 1930. **Genres:** Economics, Business/Trade/Industry, Politics/Government. **Career:** Indian Statistical Institute, research technician and lecturer, 1956-58; Makerere University, East African Institute of Social Research, research fellow, 1964-66; University of Tokyo, visiting professor, 1973-74; University of Edinburgh, visiting professor, 1980-81; Cambridge University, Economics Faculty, visiting senior research associate, 1987-88; University of Otago, senior lecturer in economics. Writer. **Publications:** Import-Substitution Potential in East Africa, 1967; Underdevelopment Revisited, 1977; The Mainspring of Economic Development, 1980; Population, Technology and Development: A Critical Analysis, 1986; (ed. with C. Tisdell) Technological Change, Development and Environment: Socio-Economic Perspectives, 1988; The Globalization of Capitalism in Third World Countries, 1995. **Address:** Department of Economics, University of Otago, Dunedin, 9010, New Zealand.

MAIZELS, John. British (born England), b. 1945. **Genres:** Art/Art History, Photography. **Career:** Freelance artist, 1967-77; art teacher, 1977-89; Raw Vision, editor, publisher and founder, 1989-. **Publications:** (Ed.) Raw Vision Magazine 1989; Raw Creation: Outsider Art and Beyond, 1996; (co-author) Fantasy Worlds, 1999; (ed.) Outsider Art Sourcebook I, 2002; (with L. Peiry and P. Lespinasse) Nek Chand's Outsider Art: The Rock Garden of Chandigarh, 2006; (ed.) Outsider Art Sourcebook II, 2009. **Address:** Raw Vision, PO Box 44, Watford, HF WD25 8LN, England. **Online address:** john@rawvision.com

MAJAJ, Lisa Suhair. Cypriot/American (born United States), b. 1960. **Genres:** Adult Non-fiction, Poetry, Women's Studies And Issues, History. **Career:** Beirut Language Institute, instructor in English, 1979-80; American University of Beirut, English tutor, 1980; University of Michigan, faculty of English, 1983, 1985-87; College of the Holy Cross, teacher of interdisciplinary and special studies, 1991-93; Amherst College, lecturer in women's and gender studies, 1992; Forkroads, contributing editor, 1995-96; Radius of Arab American Writers Inc., director, 1995-96; Arab-American University Graduates, secretary and newsletter editor, 1996-97; Boston Adult Education, teacher, 1996-97; Highgate Primary School, teacher in creative writing, 2002-03. **Publications:** (Ed. with A. Amireh) Going Global: The Transnational Reception of Third World Women Writers, 2000; (ed. with P.W. Sunderman and T. Saliba and contrib.) Intersections: Gender, Nation and Community in Arab Women's Novels, 2002; (ed. with A. Amireh) Etel Adnan: Critical Essays on the Arab-American Writer and Artist, 2002; These Words (poetry chapbook), 2003; What She Said, 2005; Geographies of Light, 2009; Wildfire, forthcoming. Contributor of articals to books and periodicals. **Address:** 4 Michael Koutsofta St., Engomi, Nicosia, 2407, Cyprus. **Online address:** lmajaj@cytanet.com.cy

MAJD, Hooman. American/Iranian (born Iran), b. 1957?. **Genres:** History. **Career:** Island Records, executive vice president, 1986-98; Polygram Records, co-founder and head of film and music; Palm Pictures, co-founder and head of film and music; Interview, contributing editor. Journalist. **Publications:** The Ayatollah Begs to Differ: The Paradox of Modern Iran, 2008. Contributor to periodicals and journals. **Address:** c/o Lindsay Edgecome, Levine Greenberg Literary Agency, 307 7th Ave., Ste. 2407, New York, NY 10001-6062, U.S.A. **Online address:** hm@hoomanmajd.com

MAJD, Kam. American/Iranian (born Iran) **Genres:** Technology, Young Adult Fiction, Air/Space Topics, Mystery/Crime/Suspense. **Career:** Writer and pilot. **Publications:** Highwire, 2002; High Impact, 2003. **Address:** c/o Author Mail, Bantam Doubleday Dell Publishing Group Inc., 1540 Broadway, New York, NY 10036, U.S.A. **Online address:** kam@kammajd.com

MAJID, Anouar. American/Moroccan (born Morocco), b. 1960. **Genres:** Novels, Theology/Religion, Cultural/Ethnic Topics, Humanities, Intellectual History, International Relations/Current Affairs. **Career:** City College of New York, instructor, 1986-87; Syracuse University, teaching assistant, 1987-91; Auburn Correctional Facility, instructor, 1988-91; University of New England, assistant professor, associate professor, professor of humanities and English, 1991-, founding chair and professor of English, 2000-09, Center for Global Humanities, founding director, 2009-, associate provost for global initiatives, 2010-. Writer. **Publications:** Si Yussef (novel), 1992; Unveiling Traditions: Postcolonial Islam in a Polycentric World, 2000; Freedom and Orthodoxy: Islam and Difference in the Post-Andalusian Age, 2004; A Call for Heresy: Why Dissent Is Vital to Islam and America, 2007; We Are All Moors: Ending Centuries of Crusades Against Muslims and Other Minorities, 2009. Contributor to periodicals. **Address:** University of New England, 716 Stevens Ave., Portland, ME 04103, U.S.A. **Online address:** amajid@une.edu

MAJOR, Andre. (André Major). Canadian (born Canada), b. 1942. **Genres:** Novels, Novellas/Short Stories, Plays/Screenplays, Essays, Translations, History. **Career:** Radio Canada, producer, 1973-, writer. **Publications:** POETRY: Le froid semeurt, 1961; Holocauste a 2 voix, 1961; Poemes pour durer, 1969. SHORT STORY COLLECTIONS: (with J. Brault and A. Brochu) Nouvelles, 1963; La chair de poule: Nouvelles, 1965; La folle d'Elvis: Nouvelles, 1981, trans. as Hooked on Elvis, 1983. NOVELS: Le Cabochon: Roman, 1964; Le Vent du diable: Roman, 1968; L'hiver au coeur, 1987, trans. as The Winter of the Heart, 1989; La vie provisoire: Roman, 1995, trans. as A Provisional Life, 1997. HISTOIRES DE DESERTEURS TRILOGY: L'Epouvantail, 1974, trans. as The Scarecrows of Saint-Emmanuel, 1977; L'épidémie: Histoiresde déserteurs, 1975, trans. as Inspector Therrien, 1980; Les Rescapés: Roman, 1976, trans. as Man on the Run, 1984; Histoires dedeserteurs, 1991. OTHERS: Félix-Antoine Savard, 1968; Le vent du diable, 1968; Poèmes pour durer, 1969; Ledesir. Suivi de Le Perdant, 1973; Une soirée en octobre, 1975; Cabochon, 1980; (ed.) L'ecriture en question, 1997; Le sourire d'Anton oul'adieu au roman (essays), 2001. **Address:** Radio-Canada, 1400 blvd., René-Lévesque E, Montreal, QC H2L 2M2, Canada. **Online address:** andremajor@ca.inter.net

MAJOR, André. *See* **MAJOR, Andre.**

MAJOR, Clarence. American (born United States), b. 1936. **Genres:** Novels, Novellas/Short Stories, Poetry, Language/Linguistics, Literary Criticism And History. **Career:** Proof Magazine, associate editor, 1959-60; Coercion Review, editor, 1958-65; Caw Magazine, associate editor, 1967-68; Journal of Black Poetry, associate editor, 1967-70; Harlem Education Program Writers Workshop, editor, 1967; Teachers and Writers Collaborative, editor, 1967-72; City University of New York, Brooklyn College, SEEK Program, lecturer, 1968-69, lecturer, 1973-75; Sarah Lawrence College, faculty, 1972-74; Howard University, faculty, 1974-75; University of Washington, assistant professor, 1976-77; University of Colorado, associate professor, 1977-81, professor of English, 1981-90; University of Nice, American Civilization, visiting professor, 1981-82; University of California, Department of English, professor of English, 1989-2007, professor emeritus, 2007-, director of creative writing, 1990-92. **Publications:** The New Black Poetry, 1969; Swallow the Lake, 1970; Dictionary of Afro-American Slang, 1970 in UK as Black Slang: A Dictionary of Afro-American Talk, 1971; Symptoms and Madness, 1971; Private Line, 1971; The Cotton Club: New Poems, 1972; The Syncopated Cakewalk, 1974; The Dark and Feeling; Black American Writers and Their Work, 1974; Reflexe et ossature (France), 1982; Inside Diameter: The France Poems, 1985; Surfaces and Masks (poetry), 1988; Fun and Games (stories), 1990; Parking Lots, 1992; Calling the Winds, 1993; Juba to Jive, 1994; Dirty Bird Blues, 1996; The Garden Thrives, 1996; Configurations: New and Selected Poems 1958-1998, 1998; Necessary Distance: Essays and Criticism, 2001; (ed.) Conversations with Clarence Major, 2002; Waiting for Sweet Betty (poems), 2002; Come by Here: My Mother's Life (nonfiction), 2002; One Flesh, 2003; Myself Painting: Poems, 2009. NOVELS: All-Night Visitors, 1969, rev. ed., 1998; NO, 1973; Reflex and Bone Structure, 1975; Emergency Exit, 1979; My Amputations, 1986; Such Was the Season, 1987; Painted Turtle: Woman with Guitar, 1988; Dirty Bird Blues 1996; One Flesh 2003. **Address:** Department of English, University of California, 351 Voorhies Hall, 1 Shields Ave., Davis, CA 95616, U.S.A. **Online address:** cmajor@ucdavis.edu

MAJOR, devorah. American (born United States), b. 1952?. **Genres:** Novels, Novellas/Short Stories, Poetry, Essays, Literary Criticism And History. **Career:** African-American Historical Society, librarian; Koncepts Cultural Gallery, editor of community arts magazine and web site; California College for the Arts, adjunct professor of diversity studies; San Francisco Fine Arts Museum, poet-in-residence. Novelist and writer. **Publications:** (With O.P. Adisa) Traveling Women, 1989. NOVELS: An Open Weave, 1995; Brown Glass Windows, 2002. POETRY: Street Smarts, 1996; With More Than Tongue, 2003; Where River Meets Ocean, 2003; Ice Journeys, 2009. EDITOR: Ascension II, 1983; Other Side of the Postcard, 2004. Contributor to periodicals. **Address:** c/o Janell Walden Agyeman, 636 NE 72nd St., Miami, FL 33138, U.S.A. **Online address:** devmajor@pacbell.net

MAJOR, John. British (born England), b. 1936?. **Genres:** History, Geography, Social Sciences. **Career:** University of Hull, lecturer in history, reader in modern history, senior lecturer. Author and historian. **Publications:** (With A. Preston) Send a Gunboat! A Story of the Gunboat and Its Role in British Policy, 1854-1904, 1967; The New Deal, 1967; The Contemporary World: A Historical Introduction, 1970; The Oppenheimer Hearing, 1971; Cementing the China Vase: David Hartley and America, 1774-1784, 1983; Prize Possession: The United States and the Panama Canal, 1903-1979, 1993; (ed. with R. Love, Jr.) The Year of D-Day: The 1944 Diary of Admiral Sir Bertram Ramsay, 1994; (with M.J. Cohen) History in Quotations, 2004. **Address:** Weidenfeld & Nicolson, The Orion Publishing Group Ltd., Wellington House, 125-130 Strand, London, GL WC2R 0BB, England.

MAJORS, Richard G. British/American (born United States), b. 1925?. **Genres:** Psychology, Sociology, Sciences, Adult Non-fiction. **Career:** University of Wisconsin System, assistant professor, 1990-93; The Urban Institute, senior research associate, 1993-; Journal of African American Men, founder, deputy editor, 1992. Public speaker and consultant. **Publications:** (With J.M. Billson) Cool Pose: The Dilemmas of Black Manhood in America, 1992; (ed. with J.U. Gordon) The American Black Male: His Present Status and His Future, 1994; Programs that Serve Black Male Youth, 1995; (ed.) Educating our Black Children: New Directions and Radical Approaches, 2001. Works appear in anthologies. Contributor to books. **Address:** 17 Regency Wharf, Hooten Ln., Leigh, LC WN7 3BF, England.

MAJUMDAR, Boria. Australian/Indian (born India), b. 1976. **Genres:** Sports/Fitness, History. **Career:** University of Chicago, visiting lecturer, 2003-; La Trobe University, Institute of Advanced Study, distinguished visiting fellow, 2005, senior research fellow, 2006-; University of Central Lancashire, senior research fellow; University of Calcutta, visiting fellow in history; International Olympic Museum, fellow; De Montfort University, International Research Centre for Sport, Socialisation and Society, deputy director, 2004; Cricket Association of Bengal, Centre for Academic Excellence, director; Ten Sports, media commentator; ESPN, media commentator; NDTV, media commentator; Headlines Today, media commentator; Channel 7, media commentator; Sport in Society, executive editor; Soccer and Society, executive editor; Sport in the Global Society, general editor. Historian. **Publications:** Cricket in Colonial India: 1850-1947, 2003; Once upon a Furore: Lost Pages of Indian Cricket, 2004; Twenty-two Yards to Freedom: A Social History of Indian Cricket, 2004; (ed. with J.A. Mangan) Cricketing Cultures in Conflict: World Cup 2003, 2004; (ed.) An Indian Cricket Reader: 1737-2003 in UK as Indian Cricket through the Ages: A Reader, 2005; (with K. Bandyopadhyay) A Social History of Indian Football: Striving to Score, 2006; (with K. Bandyopadhyay) Goalless: The Story of a Unique Footballing Nation, 2006; The Illustrated History of Indian Cricket, 2006; Lost Histories of Indian Cricket: Battles off the Pitch, 2006; Essays on Indian Cricket, 2006; Corridors of Uncertainty: World Cup 2007 & Beyond, 2007; Revisiting 1857: Myth, Memory, History, 2007; (ed. with H. Fan) Modern Sport: The Global Obsession; Politics, Religion, Class, Gender: Essays in Honour of J.A. Mangan, 2007; (ed. with J. Gemmell) Cricket, Race, and the 2007 World Cup, 2008; (with N. Mehta) Olympics: The India Story, 2008; Cricket in Colonial India, 1780-1947, 2008; (ed. with S. Collins) Olympism, the Global Vision: From Nationalism to Internationalism, 2008; Television in India: Satellites, Politics, and Cultural Change, 2008; Popular Culture in a Globalised India, 2009; (with N. Mehta) India and the Olympics, 2009. Contributor to periodicals. **Address:** Institute for Advanced Study, La Trobe University, Melbourne, VI 3086, Australia.

MAJURE, Janet. American (born United States), b. 1954. **Genres:** Novels, Medicine/Health, Documentaries/Reportage, Essays. **Career:** Arizona Daily Star, copy editor, 1976; The Denver Post, copy editor, 1976-78; the Arizona Republic, copy editor, 1978-79; W.R. Grace, financial analyst, 1981-82; Kansas City Star, copy editor, bureau chief, assistant city editor and business writer, 1983-89; Lawrence Observer, owner, publisher and editor, 1989; Microsoft White Papers, copy editor; Healthy Kansas Women, copy editor, 2000; University of Kansas School of Architecture, editor. Freelance writer. **Publications:** Elections, 1996; Recipes Worth Sharing, 1997; AIDS, 1998; Breast Cancer, 2000; Farm-Fresh Recipes, 2003; Not By Bread Alone: A Sampling of Kansas Food, Art and Culture, 2007; Teach Yourself Visually WordPress, 2010; Without Ceremony, 2010. FORTHCOMING: Return to Main Street; Incidents; Broken Vessel. Contributor to books. **Address:** 16 E 13th St., Lawrence, KS 66044, U.S.A. **Online address:** jmajure@sbcglobal.net

MAKARI, George Jack. American (born United States), b. 1960. **Genres:** History. **Career:** New York Hospital, resident psychiatrist, 1987-91, Reader's Digest research fellow, 1991-94, assistant professor, 1994-99, associate professor of psychiatry, 1999-; Cornell University, director of Institute for the History of Psychiatry; Columbia University, Center for Psychoanalytic Teaching and Research, faculty member, 1998; Rockefeller University, visiting associate professor, 2002. Writer. **Publications:** Revolution in Mind: The Creation of Psychoanalysis, 2008. Contributor of articles to journals. **Address:** Weill Medical College, Cornell University, 525 E 68th St., PO Box 140, New York, NY 10065, U.S.A. **Online address:** gjmakari@med.cornell.edu

MAKDISI, Saree. Lebanese/American (born United States), b. 1965?. **Genres:** History. **Career:** University of Chicago, assistant professor of English, 1993-2003; University of California, professor of English and comparative literature, 2003-. Educator and writer. **Publications:** (ed. with C. Casarino and R.E. Karl) Marxism beyond Marxism, 1996; Romantic Imperialism: Universal Empire and the Culture of Modernity, 1998; William Blake and the Impossible History of the 1790s, 2003; Palestine Inside Out: An Everyday Occupation, 2008. Contributor to periodicals. **Address:** Department of English, University of California, 149 Humanities Bldg., PO Box 951530, Los Angeles, CA 90095-1530, U.S.A. **Online address:** makdisi@humnet.ucla.edu

MÄKELÄ, Janne. Finnish (born Finland), b. 1955. **Genres:** Biography. **Career:** University of Turku, assistant, 1997, 2003-04, Graduate School on Cultural Interaction and Integration, research fellow, 1997-98, 2000, Department of Cultural History, docent of history of popular culture, 2007-; University of Helsinki, Renvall Institute, researcher, 2004-07, Academy of Finland, post-doctoral researcher. Writer. **Publications:** John Lennon Imagined: Cultural History of a Rock Star, 2004. **Address:** Renvall Institute for Area & Cultural Studies, University of Helsinki, PO Box 59, Helsinki, 00014, Finland. **Online address:** janne.makela@helsinki.fi

MAKEPEACE, Anne. American (born United States), b. 1947. **Genres:** Plays/Screenplays, Film, Anthropology/Ethnology, Art/Art History, Biography, Documentaries/Reportage. **Career:** Makepeace Productions Inc., president and director, 1982-; Sundance Institute, writer/director fellow. Producer and director. **Publications:** Edward S. Curtis: Coming to Light, 2001, 2nd ed., 2002. **Address:** Makepeace Productions, PO Box 6, Lakeville, CT 06039, U.S.A. **Online address:** amakepeace@aol.com

MAKINE, Andreï. French/Russian (born Russia), b. 1957?. **Genres:** Novels, Young Adult Fiction. **Career:** Writer. **Publications:** Au Temps du Fleuve Amour: Roman, 1994; Le Testament Français: Roman, 1995; The Crime of Olga Arbélina: Roman, 1999; Requiem pour l'Est: Roman, 2000; Confessions of a Fallen Standard-Bearer, 2000; Musique d'une vie: Roman, 2001; Requiem for a Lost Empire, 2001; Music of a Life, 2002; Terre et le ciel de Jacques Dorme: Roman, 2003; A Hero's Daughter, 2004; Femme qui attendait: Roman, 2004; The Earth and Sky of Jacques Dorme, 2005; Cette France qu'on oublie d'aimer, 2006; Amour Humain: Roman, 2006; The Woman Who Waited, 2006; Monde selon Gabriel: Mystère de Noël, 2007; Human Love, 2008; La vie d'un Homme Inconnu, 2009; Life of an Unknown Man, 2010; Livre des breèves amours éternelles, 2011; Dreams of My Russian Summers, 2011. **Address:** c/o Arcade Publishing, 141 5th Ave., 8th Fl., New York, NY 10010, U.S.A. **Online address:** info@andreimakine.com

MAKINEN, Merja. British (born England), b. 1953. **Genres:** Literary Criticism And History, Women's Studies And Issues, Young Adult Fiction. **Career:** Middlesex University, School of Arts and Education, principal lecturer in English Literature, 1985-, programme tutor, English Studies, director of programmes. Writer. **Publications:** (With K. Harris) Joyce Cary: A Descriptive Bibliography, 1989; (with L. Gamman) Female Fetishism: A New Look, 1994; (with L. Gamman) Female Fetishism, 1995; Feminist Popular Fiction, 2001; (ed. with N. Tredell) The Novels of Jeanette Winterson, 2005; Agatha Christie: Investigating Femininity, 2006. Contributor to books and periodicals. **Address:** English Literature Studies, Middlesex University, Bramley Rd., Trent Park Campus, London, GL N14 4YZ, England. **Online address:** m.makinen@mdx.ac.uk

MAKLER, Irris. Israeli/Australian (born Australia) **Genres:** Women's Studies And Issues. **Career:** British Broadcasting Corp., BBC-TV, researcher and producer, 1988-92; Channel 9 (television network), producer, 1992; Australian Broadcasting Corp., ABC-TV, producer and reporter, 1993-2000, Moscow correspondent, 2000-01; freelance correspondent, 2001-. **Publications:** Our Woman in Kabul, 2003; Guns and Roses, forthcoming. **Address:** International Creative Management, Marlborough House, 10 Earlham St., 3rd Fl., London, GL WC2H 9LN, England. **Online address:** irris@bigfoot.com

MAKOVSKY, Michael. American (born United States), b. 1963. **Genres:** History. **Career:** MSM Consulting, president, 2006-; Bipartisan Policy Center, foreign policy director, 2006-. Writer. **Publications:** Churchill's Promised Land: Zionism and Statecraft, 2007. **Address:** Washington, DC , U.S.A. **Online address:** mmakovsky@bipartisanpolicy.org

MAKOWSKI, Silky. (Silky Sullivan). American (born United States), b. 1940. **Genres:** Bibliography, Young Adult Fiction, Sports/Fitness. **Career:** White Lake Township Library, director, 1996-. Writer, lecturer and librarian. **Publications:** AS SILK MAKOWSKI: Serious About Series: Evaluations and Annotations of Teen Fiction in Paperback Series, 1998. AS SILKY SULLIVAN: HENRY AND MELINDA SPORTS STORIES: Henry and Melinda, 1982; Henry and Melinda Team Up, 1982; The B Street 5, 1982; Kings on Court, 1982; Mystery at the Basketball Game, 1982; Roller Skates, 1982; Grandpa was a Cowboy, 1996. Contributor to periodicals. **Address:** White Lake Township Library, 7527 E Highland Rd., White Lake, MI 48383, U.S.A.

MALAK, Amin. Canadian (born Canada), b. 1946?. **Genres:** Literary Criticism And History, Theology/Religion, History. **Career:** Grant MacEwan College, faculty. Writer. **Publications:** Muslim Narratives and the Discourse of English, 2005. Contributor to periodicals. **Address:** Department of English, Grant MacEwan College, PO Box 1796, Edmonton, AB T5J 2P2, Canada.

MALAM, John. British (born England) **Genres:** History, Children's Non-fiction, Animals/Pets, inspirational/Motivational Literature. **Career:** Ironbridge Gorge Museum, museum archaeologist, 1980-82; writer of children's books, 1989-. **Publications:** JUVENILES: I Can Learn... Counting 0 to 5, 1989; I Can Learn ... Counting 6 to 10, 1989; I Can Learn ... Writing Fun, 1990; Dinosaurs (pop-up book), 1990, (with D. Dixon) rev. ed. as Dinosaur, 2006; Machines (pop-up book), 1990; Stick and Color Fun: Planes, 1990; Stick and Color Fun: Birds, 1991; Stick and Color Fun: Endangered Animals, 1991; Dinosaur Skeletons (pop-up book), 1991; Children's Atlas of Endangered Animals, 1991; Dinosaurs and Other Prehistoric Animals (sticker book), 1991; Animals in Danger (sticker book), 1991; (ed. with H. van Lemmen) Fired Earth: 1, 000 Years of Tiles in Europe, 1991; My First Dinosaurs: With Lift-the-Flap Surprises, 1994; My First Questions and Answers: With Lift-the-Flap Surprises, 1995; Early Learning Center: Sticker Atlas of Europe, 1995; Little Red Riding Hood (story sticker book), 1995; Goldilocks and the Three Bears (story stickerbook), 1995; The Three Little Pigs (story sticker book), 1995; Jack and the Beanstalk (story sticker book), 1995; In the Town (jigsaw sticker book), 1995; On the Farm (jigsaw sticker book), 1995; Extraordinary World: Highest, Longest, Deepest (fold-out book), 1996; Guide to the World's Record Breakers, 1996; Loopy River and Other Mazes (sticker book), 1996; Bendyu Road and Other Mazes (sticker book), 1996; Flags of the World Sticker Atlas, 1996; Highest, Longest, Deepest: An Exploration of the World's Most Fantastic Features, 1997; Exploring Ancient Egypt, 1997, 2nd ed., 2004; The Traveller's Guide to Ancient Rome, 1998 as The Traveler's Guide to Ancient Rome, 1999; Soccer, 1998 as Fantastic Football, 2001; Ancient Greeks at a Glance 1998; Wacky Weather, 1998; Big Rigs, 1998; The Victorians, 1999; The Ancient Greeks, 1999; Gods and Goddesses, 1999; Greek Town, 1999; Myths and Civilization of the Ancient Romans, 1999; Mesopotamia and the Near East from 10, 000 B.C. to 539 B.C., 1999, 2nd ed., 2005; Queen Victoria, 1999; So You Want to Be a Pirate, 1999; The Ultimate Dinosaur Book, 2000; The Amazing A to Z of Dinosaurs, 2000; Earth, 2000; Song and Dance, 2000; Cleaning the House, 2000; Super Structures, 2000; You Wouldn't Want to Be a Roman Gladiator!: Gory Things You'd Rather Not Know, 2000; You Wouldn't Want to Be a Victorian Schoolchild!: Lessons You'd Rather Not Learn, 2001; The 1940s House (activity book; televisiontie-in), 2001; Dinosaurs, 2001, 2nd ed., 2006; Cars, 2001; Aircraft, 2001; Henry Ford, 2001; Florence Nightingale, 2001; Exploring Ancient Rome, 2001; An Ancient Greek Temple in US as An Ancient Greek Temple: The Story of the Building of the Temples of Ancient Greece, 2001; The Victorians, 2002; Encyclopedia of Dinosaurs and Other Prehistoric Creatures, 2002; You Wouldn't Want to Be a Victorian Miner!: A Job You'd Rather Not Do, 2002; The Mummy: Myths and Legends of the Desert, 2002; Ancient Egyptian Jobs, 2003; Exploring Ancient Greece, 2003; Exploring the Vikings, 2003; Exploring the Aztecs, 2003; Mummies, 2003; Prehistoric Life, 2003; Our Earth, 2003; Ancient Greece, 2004; The Gladiator's Secret, 2004; The Wooden Horse of Troy, 2005; Jason and the Argonauts, 2005; How to be a Pirate, 2006; (with J. Woodward) Dinosaur Atlas, 2006; Ancient Rome, 2007; Buried Treasure, 2007; You Wouldn't Want to Sail in the Spanish Armada!, 2007; You Wouldn't Want to Live in Pompeii!: A Volcanic Eruption You'd Rather Avoid, 2008; You Wouldn't Want to be a Victorian Mill Worker!: A Grueling Job You'd Rather Not Have, 2008; You Wouldn't Want to be a Worker on the Statue of Liberty!: A Monument You'd Rather not Build, 2009; You Wouldn't Want to be a Skyscraper Builder!: A Hazardous Job You'd Rather not Take, 2009. DATES INDIANA JONES EXPLORES SERIES: Indiana Jones Explores Ancient Egypt, 1991; Indiana Jones Explores Ancient Rome, 1992; Indiana Jones Explores Ancient Greece, 1993; Indiana Jones Explores the Incas, 1993; Indiana Jones Explores the Aztecs, 1994; Indiana Jones Explores the Vikings, 1994. MR. MEN SERIES: Mr. Bump and His Bumpy Day, 1996; Mr. Happy and His Best Smile Ever, 1996; Mr. Tickle, 1996; Mr. Bump, 1996; Mr. Greedy, 1996; Mr. Happy, 1996; Mr. Messy, 1996; Mr. Nosey, 1996; Mr. Funny, 1996; Everyone's Happy with Mr. Happy, 1997. TELL ME ABOUT SERIES: Tell Me about Isambard Kingdom Brunel, 1996; Tell Me about Vincent Van Gogh, 1996; Tell Me about Wolfgang Amadeus Mozart, 1996; Tell Me about Claude Monet, 1997; Tell Me about Beatrix Potter, 1997; Tell Me about Thor Heyerdahl, 1997; Tell Me about John Cabot, 1997; Tell Me about Roger Hargreaves, 1997; Tell Me about Pieter Brueghel, 1998; Tell Me about Leonardo da Vinci, 1998; Tell Me about Martin Luther King, 1999; Tell Me about Sojourner Truth, 2000; Tell Me about Robert Louis Stevenson, 2001; Tell Me about Florence Nightingale, 2003; Tell Me about Queen Elizabeth I, 2003; Tell Me about Queen Elizabeth II, 2003. BUILDING WORKS SERIES: Airport: Behind the

Scenes, Check-in to Take-off, 1999; Hospital: From Accident and Emergency to X-Ray, 1999; Library: From Ancient Scrolls to the World Wide Web, 2000; Theatre: From First Rehearsal to Opening Night in US as Theater: From First Rehearsal to Opening Night, 2000. MEGABITES SERIES: Mummies and the Secrets of Ancient Egypt, 2001; Gladiator: Life and Death in Ancient Rome, 2002; Titanic: Shipwrecks and Sunken Treasure, 2003. DANGER ZONE SERIES: Avoid Becoming a Pirate's Prisoner!, 2002; Avoid Sailing in the Spanish Armada, 2003; Avoid Being a Mammoth Hunter, 2004. WITH HISTORY SERIES: 11 February 1990: The Release of Nelson Mandela, 2002 in US as The Release of Nelson Mandela: February 11, 1990, 2003; 6 August 1945: The Bombing of Hiroshima in US as The Bombing of Hiroshima, 2002; 1 September 1939: Hitler Invades Poland in US as Hitler Invades Poland: 1 September 1939, 2003; 21 July 1969: Man Lands on the Moon in US as Man Walks on the Moon, 2003; 11 November 1918: The World War I Armistice in US as World War I, Armistice Day, 2003; 5 November 1605: The Gunpowder Plot, 2003; 14 October 1492: The Gunpowder Plot, 2003; 14 April 1912: The Titanic Hits and Iceberg, 2004; 13 October 1066: The Battle of Hastings, 2004. OTHERS: Ancient Mesopotamia, 2005; You Wouldn't Want to be a 19th-Century Coal Miner in England!, 2006; Killer Whales, 2008; Scary Creatures of the Night, 2008; Francis Drake and the Sea Rovers of the Spanish Main, 2008; Blackbeard and the Pirates of the Caribbean, 2008; Gulliver's Travels, 2009; Guglielmo Marconi, 2009; Leonardo da Vinci, 2009; Extreme exploration, 2009; Early Medieval Times, 2009; (with N. Morris) Beyond Europe, 2009; Birth of Modern Times, 2009; Barbarossa Brothers and Pirates of the Mediterranean, 2009; William Kidd and the Pirates of the Indian Ocean, 2009; Birth of Modern Nations, 2009; 100 Things You Should Know about Pyramids, 2009; Giants, 2010; (with I. Scurman) Ancient Roman Civilization, 2010; Werewolves, 2010; Witches, 2010; Vampires, 2010; Pinnipeds, 2010; Pyramids, 2010; Dragons, 2010; Fairies, 2010; Monsters, 2010; Ghosts, 2010; Egyptians, 2011; Life in Ancient Rome, 2011; How the Ancient Greeks Lived, 2011; Romans, 2011; Greeks, 2011; 100 Things You Should Know about Warriors, 2011; Vikings, 2011; 100 Things You Should Know about Samurai, 2011; 100 Things You Should Know about Mummies, 2011; Grow Your Own Butterfly Farm, 2012; Grow Your Own Cat Toy, 2012; Grow Your Own Sandwich, 2012; Grow Your Own Smoothie, 2012; Grow Your Own Snack, 2012; Grow Your Own Soup, 2012. **Address:** GL , England. **Online address:** john@johnmalam.co.uk

MALAMUD, Randy. American (born United States), b. 1962. **Genres:** Literary Criticism And History, Animals/Pets. **Career:** Columbia University, preceptor, 1984-89; Barnard College, instructor, 1988; Georgia State University, assistant professor of English, 1989-95, associate professor, 1995-2000, professor, 2000-, University Senate, president, 1994-95, 1996-97, Provost's Strategic Initiative Academic Advisory Group, faculty, 1995-96, South Atlantic Modern Language Association, executive director, 2001-02, College of Arts and Sciences, vice-chair of the faculty, 2001-04, 2010-, Department of English, associate chair, 2002-, acting chair, 2004-05, Writer. **Publications:** The Language of Modernism, 1989; T. S. Eliot's Drama: A Research and Production Sourcebook, 1992; Where the Words Are Valid: T.S. Eliot's Communities of Drama, 1994; Reading Zoos: Presentations of Animals and Captivity, 1998; Poetic Animals and Animal Souls, 2003; A Cultural History of Animals in the Modern Age, 2007. **Address:** Department of English, Georgia State University, 33 Gilmer St. SE, Ste. 8, PO Box 3970, Atlanta, GA 30302-3970, U.S.A. **Online address:** rmalamud@gsu.edu

MALAMUD-GOTI, Jaime. American/Argentine (born Argentina), b. 1943. **Genres:** Sociology, Anthropology/Ethnology. **Career:** Universidad de Buenos Aires, chair in criminal law, 1983-99; Argentine Supreme Court, solicitor, 1987-88; Supreme Court of Justice of the Nation, district attroney, 1987-88; Universidad de Palermo, professor, 1994-; University of Arkansas, instructor of sociology and anthropology, 1995-, Program on Applied Ethics, coordinator; University of San Andres, professor of law; Suaya, Bilbao, Memelsdorff & Asociados, consultant. Writer. **Publications:** (As Jaime E. Malamud Goti) Delito Imprudente, 1972; (as Jaime E. Malamud Goti) Persona Jurídica y Penalidad, 1981; Política Criminal de la Empresa: Cuestiones, Alternativas, 1983; Derecho Penal De La Competencia: Abastecimiento, Monopolios, 1984; Smoke and Mirrors: The Paradox of the Drug Wars, 1992; Punta del Este, 1995; The Game Without End: The Legacy of Terror and the Politics of Justice, 1996; Terror Y Justicia en la Argentina, 2000; Humo Y Espejos, 2004; Los Dilemas Morales de la Justicia Internacional, 2005; Political Trials: The Modern Challenge to the Authority of the Courts, forthcoming. **Address:** Department of Sociology and Anthropology, University of Arkansas at Little Rock, 2801 S University Ave., Little Rock, AR 72204-1099, U.S.A.

MALCOLM, Elizabeth. Australian (born Australia), b. 1948?. **Genres:** History, Biography, Autobiography/Memoirs. **Career:** University of New South Wales, faculty; University of Trondheim, faculty; University of Tromsø, faculty; Queen's University, faculty; University of Liverpool, faculty; University of Melbourne, Gerry Higgins Professor of Irish Studies, 2000-. Writer. **Publications:** Ireland Sober, Ireland Free: Drink and Temperance in Nineteenth-Century Ireland, 1986; Swift's Hospital: A History of St. Patrick's Hospital, Dublin, 1746-1989, 1989; (ed. with G. Jones) Medicine, Disease, and the State in Ireland, 1650- 1940, 1999; The Irish Policeman, 1822- 1922: A Life, 2006; (co-ed.) The Future of Irish Studies: Report of the Irish Forum, 2006. Contributor to books and journals. **Address:** Department of History, University of Melbourne, Rm. 539 E, John Medley Bldg., Melbourne, VI 3010, Australia. **Online address:** e.malcolm@unimelb.edu.au

MALCOLM, John. *See* **ANDREWS, John (Malcolm).**

MALCOLM, Joyce Lee. American (born United States), b. 1942. **Genres:** History, Law. **Career:** Boston University, assistant professor of history, 1978-79; Northeastern University, part-time assistant professor of history, 1979; Radcliffe College, fellow in history, 1979-80; National Endowment for the Humanities, fellow, 1979-80, Division of Research Programs, director, 2005-06; Harvard University, Law School, visiting fellow in legal history, 1980-82; American Bar Foundation, fellow, 1980-81; Institute for Humane Studies and Liberty Fund, fellow in law, 1981; National Park Service, consultant, 1982-83; Department of Interior, legal consultant, historical research, 1982-; New England Heritage Center, founder and director, 1986-2001; Bentley College, associate professor, 1988-92, professor of history, 1992-2006, department chair, 1992-94; Cambridge University, Robinson College, Bye fellow, 1989-; Massachusetts Institute of Technology, Security Studies Program, senior advisor, 1997-; Princeton University, James Madison fellow and visiting professor of politics, 2003-04; George Mason University School of Law, professor of legal history, 2006-; The Historical Society, board director. Writer. **Publications:** Caesar's Due: Loyalty and King Charles, 1642-1646, 1983; The Scene of the Battle, 1775, 1985; To Keep and Bear Arms: The Origins of an Anglo-American Right, 1994; (ed.) The Struggle for Sovereignty: Seventeenth-Century English Political Tracts, 2 vols., 1999; Guns and Violence: The English Experience, 2002; Peter's War: A New England Slave Boy and the American Revolution, 2009; Null and Void: The Origins of American Judicial Review, forthcoming; Stepchild of the Revolution: A Slave Child in Revolutionary America, forthcoming. Contributor of articles to journals. **Address:** School of Law, George Mason University, Rm. 418, Arlington Campus, 3301 Fairfax Dr., Arlington, VA 22201, U.S.A. **Online address:** jmalcolm@gmu.edu

MALCOLM, Noel. British (born England), b. 1956. **Genres:** History, Literary Criticism And History. **Career:** University of Cambridge, Gonville and Caius College, fellow, 1981-88, Peterhouse, honorary fellow, 2010-; The Spectator, political columnist, 1987-91, foreign editor, 1991-92; Daily Telegraph, political columnist, 1992-95; University of Oxford, All Souls College, senior research fellow, 2002-, Faculty of History, faculty. Historian. **Publications:** De Dominis, 1560-1624: Venetian, Anglican, Ecumenist, and Relapsed Heretic, 1984; George Enescu: His Life and Music, 1990; Bosnia: A Short History, 1994; (ed.) The Correspondence, 1994; The Origins of English Nonsense, 1997; Kosovo: A Short History, 1998; (ed. with Q. Hoare) Books on Bosnia: A Critical Bibliography of Works Relating to Bosnia-Herzegovina Published Since 1990 in West European Languages, 1999; Aspects of Hobbes, 2002; John Pell (1611-1685) and His Correspondence with Sir Charles Cavendish: The Mental World of an Early Modern Mathematician, 2005; Reason of State, Propaganda, and the Thirty Years' War: An Unknown Translation by Thomas Hobbes, 2007. **Address:** All Souls College, University of Oxford, Oxford, OX OX1 4AL, England. **Online address:** noel.malcolm@all-souls.ox.ac.uk

MALEFAKIS, Edward. American (born United States), b. 1932. **Genres:** History. **Career:** Northwestern University, instructor in history, 1962-63, associate professor, 1968-71; Wayne State University, assistant professor of history, 1963-64; Columbia University, assistant professor of history, 1964-68, professor of history, 1974-, now professor emeritus of history; University of Michigan, professor of history, 1971-74. Writer. **Publications:** Agrarian Reform and Peasant Revolution in Spain, 1970; Reforma agraria y revolución campesina en la España del siglo XX, 1976; Southern Europe in the 19th and 20th Centuries: An Historical Overview, 1992; Franquismo: El Juicio de la Historia, 2000; Guerra Civil española, 2006. EDITOR: Indalecio Prieto Discursos Fundamentales, 1975; La Guerra de Espana 1936-1939, 1986. **Address:** Department of History, Columbia University, 413 Fayerweather Hall,

1180 Amsterdam Ave., PO Box 2527, New York, NY 10027, U.S.A. **Online address:** eem1@columbia.edu

MALEY, Willy. Scottish (born Scotland), b. 1960. **Genres:** Plays/Screenplays, Young Adult Non-fiction, Cultural/Ethnic Topics, History. **Career:** University of London, Goldsmiths College, lecturer, 1992-94, Queen Mary College, lecturer, 1992-94; University of Glasgow, faculty, 1994-, professor of renaissance studies, 1999-, Creative Writing Postgraduate Programme, co-founder, 1995; Dartmouth College, visiting professor, 1997; University of Sunderland, visiting professor, 2006. Writer. **Publications:** NONFICTION: (ed. with B. Bradshaw and A. Hadfield) Representing Ireland: Literature and the Origins of Conflict 1534-1660, 1993; A Spenser Chronology, 1994; (ed. and intro. with B. Moore-Gilbert and G. Stanton) Postcolonial Criticism, 1997; (ed. with A. Hadfield) A View of the State of Ireland: From the First Printed Edition (1633), 1997; Salvaging Spenser: Colonialism, Culture, and Identity, 1997; (ed. with D.J. Baker) British Identities and English Renaissance Literature, 2002; Nation, State, and Empire in English Renaissance Literature: Shakespeare to Milton, 2003; (ed. with A. Murphy) Shakespeare and Scotland, 2004; (ed. with A. Benchimol) Spheres of Influence: Intellectual and Cultural Publics from Shakespeare to Habermas, 2007; Muriel Spark for Starters, 2008; (with P. Schwyzer) Shakespeare and Wales: From the Marches to the Assembly, 2010; (ed. with M. Tudeau-Clayton) This England, that Shakespeare, 2010; (ed. with M. Gardiner) Edinburgh Companion to Muriel Spark, 2010. PLAYS: (with J. Maley) From the Calton to Catalonia, 1990. Contributor to periodicals. **Address:** Department of English Literature, University of Glasgow, 5 University Gardens, Glasgow, G12 8QQ, Scotland. **Online address:** w.maley@englit.arts.gla.ac.uk

MALFI, Ronald Damien. American (born United States), b. 1977. **Genres:** Young Adult Fiction. **Career:** Writer. **Publications:** FICTION: The Space Between, 2000; The Fall of Never, 2004; The Nature of Monsters, 2006; Via Dolorosa, 2007; Passenger, 2008; Shamrock Alley, 2009; Snow, 2010; The Ascent: A Novel of Survival, 2010. **Address:** MD , U.S.A. **Online address:** ron@ronmalfi.com

MALIN, Irving. American (born United States), b. 1934. **Genres:** Literary Criticism And History, Biography, Criminology/True Crime, Autobiography/Memoirs. **Career:** Stanford University, acting instructor in English, 1955-56, 1957-58; Indiana University, instructor in English, 1958-60; City College of New York, instructor, assistant professor, 1960-69, associate professor, 1969-72, professor of English, 1972-96, professor emeritus, 1996-. Writer. **Publications:** William Faulkner: An Interpretation, 1957; New American Gothic, 1962; Jews and Americans, 1965; Saul Bellow's Fiction, 1969; Nathanael West's Novels, 1972; Isaac Bashevis Singer, 1972. EDITOR: (with I. Stark) Breakthrough: A Treasury of Contemporary American Jewish Literature, 1964; Psychoanalysis and American Fiction, 1965; Saul Bellow and the Critics, 1967; Truman Capote's In Cold Blood: A Critical Handbook, 1968; Critical Views of Isaac Bashevis Singer, 1969; (with M.J. Friedman) William Styron's The Confessions of Nat Turner: A Critical Handbook, 1970; Contemporary American-Jewish Literature: Critical Essays, 1973; (with R.K. Morris) The Achievement of William Styron, 1975; Conrad Aiken's Prose, 1982; Paul Bowles, 1986; James Dickey, 1994; Southern Novelists on Stage and Screen, 1995; William Goyen, 1997; A Goyan Companion: Appreciations of a Writer's Writer, 1997; (with B. Horvath and P. Ruffin) A Goyen Companion, 1997; (with S.G. Kellman) Into the Tunnel, 1998; (with B. Horvath) George Garrett: The Elizabethan Trilogy, 1998; (with S.G. Kellman) Leslie Fiedler and American Culture, 1999; (with B. Horvath) Pynchon and Mason and Dixon, 2000; (with J. Dewey and S.G. Kellman) Underwords: Perspectives on Don Delillo's Underworld, 2002. **Address:** City College of New York, 160 Convent Ave., New York, NY 10031, U.S.A.

MALKI, David. American (born United States) **Genres:** Humor/Satire. **Career:** TopatoCo (an artist-direct merchandise Web site), director of publicity and promotions. Writer, filmmaker, film editor and cartoonist. **Publications:** WONDERMARK COMIC STRIP COLLECTIONS: Beards of Our Forefathers, 2008; Clever Tricks to Stave Off Death, 2009; Dapper Caps and Pedal-Copters, 2010. Contributor to periodicals. **Address:** Wondermark, 2554 Lincoln Blvd., Ste. 214, Venice, CA 90291, U.S.A. **Online address:** davidmalki@gmail.com

MALKIN, Michelle. American (born United States), b. 1970. **Genres:** Criminology/True Crime. **Career:** Los Angeles Daily News, editorial writer and columnist, 1992-94; Seattle Times, editorial writer, 1996-99; Creators Syndicate, syndicated columnist, 1999-; Fox News Channel, contributor and commentator; Jazz Mustache L.L.C., founder, chairman, chief executive officer and owner. **Publications:** Invasion: How America Still Welcomes Terrorists, Criminals, and Other Foreign Menaces to Our Shores, 2002; In Defense of Internment: The Case for Racial Profiling in World War II and the War on Terror, 2004; Unhinged: Exposing Liberals Gone Wild, 2005; Culture of Corruption: Obama and His Team of Tax Cheats, Crooks, and Cronies, 2009. Contributor to periodicals. **Address:** Creators Syndicate, 5777 W Century Blvd., Ste. 700, Los Angeles, CA 90045, U.S.A. **Online address:** writemalkin@gmail.com

MALLETT, Daryl F(urumi). American (born United States), b. 1969. **Genres:** Novellas/Short Stories, Mystery/Crime/Suspense, Horror, Science Fiction/Fantasy, Literary Criticism And History, Bibliography, Language/Linguistics, Essays, Essays. **Career:** University of California, library assistant, 1988-91; Waymark, editor, 1988-89; Angel Enterprises, founder, editor and publisher, 1988-; Dragon's Lair Bookstore, special projects coordinator, 1988-94; Borgo Press, stock manager, editorial assistant, editor, senior editor, contributing editor, 1989-99; FFP Publishing, editor and publisher, 1990-91; America West Airlines, reservations agent, 1993-94; SFRA Review, editor, 1993-94; Todd Publishing, editor, 1993-94; Sirius Publishing Inc., technical writer, 1994-95; Housing Inspection Foundation, director, 1994; International Real Estate Institute, director, 1994; Appraisers Information Group, director, 1994; Central American Times, editor, 1994; Environmental Times, associate editor, 1994; Other Worlds, editor, 1994, associate editor, 1995-; Motion Pixels, technical writer, 1995; Xenos Books, assistant editor, 1995-; Gryphon Publications, associate editor, 1995-; Blue Fire Technologies Inc., founder, 1998, chief evangelical officer; M&V Magazine, contributing writer; Water Conditioning & Purification Magazine, contributing writer; Copper Basin News, reporter; Pinal Nugget, reporter; San Manuel Miner, reporter; Superior Sun, reporter; International Research Center, senior outside research associate; Prismic Publishing, founder; Arizona's Scottsdale Network at the Airpark, co-founder. **Publications:** (With M. Burgess and M.A. Burgess) The State and Province Vital Records Guide, 1993; (with A.Y. Mallett) The Work of Elizabeth Chater: An Annotated Bibliography & Guide, 1994; (with J. Hewett) The Work of Jack Vance: An Annotated Bibliography & Guide, 1994; The Environmental Inspector's Guide to... The National Environmental Policy Act, 1995; The Clean Air Act, 1995; The Clean Water Act, 1995; The Comprehensive Environmental Response, Compensation, and Liability Act, 1995; The Resource Conservation and Recovery Act, 1995; The Occupational Safety and Health Act, 1995; The Environmental Protection and Community Right-to-Know Act, 1995; Comprehensive Guidelines, 1995. EDITOR: (with C. Hakim and F. McConnel) Full Frontal Poetry, 1991; One Day with God: Guide to Retreats and the Contemplative Life, rev. ed., 1991; (with R. Reginald) Reginald's Science Fiction and Fantasy Awards, 1991, 3rd ed., 1993; (co-ed.) Science Fiction & Fantasy Literature, 1975-1991: A Bibliography of Science Fiction, Fantasy, and Horror Fiction Books and Nonfiction Monographs, 1992; Inside Science Fiction: Essays on Fantastic Literature, 1992; Vultures of the Void: A History of British Science Fiction Publishing, 1946-1956, 1992; (with R. Ewald and J. Gordon) Science Fiction Research Association Annual Directory 1993, 1993; (with K. Pruter and P. Seldis) The Russian Orthodox Church Outside Russia, 1993; The Transylvanian Library: A Consumer's Guide to Vampire Fiction, 1993; (with S. Burgess) Adventures of a Freelancer, 1993; (with M. Burgess) Geo. Alec Effinger: From Entropy to Budayeen, 1993; (with D. Salwak) Mary Roberts Rinehart, 1993; Wilderness Visions: The Western Theme in Science Fiction Literature, 2nd ed., 1993; (with D. Salwak and P. Seldis) Dragons & Martinis, 1993; Libido into Literature: The primera época of Benito Pérez Galdós, 1993; (P. Seldis and J. Gurley) The Price of Paradise, 1993; (with N. Kravetz) A Wayfarer in a World in Upheaval, 1993; International Society of Meeting Planners 1993 Directory of Members & Industry Professionals, 1993; Association of Construction Inspectors 1993-1994 Director of Members & Industry Professionals, 1993; 1994 Directory of Designated Members, 1994; Federal and State Environmental Agencies Directory, 1994; The Complete Guide of Environmental Inspection Forms, 1994; Environmental Assessment Association Directory of Members, 1994; (with M. Burgess) British Science Fiction Paperbacks and Magazines, 1949-1956: An Annotated Bibliography, 1994, rev. ed., 1995; Speaking of Horror: Interviews with Writers of the Supernatural, 1994; (with B. Clarke) The Work of William Eastlake: An Annotated Bibliography & Guide, 1994; Firefly, 1994; (with D. Salwak) Christopher Isherwood, 1994; W.E.B. DuBois: His Contribution to Pan-Africanism, 1994; (with D. Salwak) Roald Dahl: From the Gremlins to the Chocolate Factory, 2nd ed., 1994; (with M. Wolf) Imaginative Futures: Proceedings of the 1993 Science Fiction Research Association Conference, 1994; Christopher Hampton, 1994; (with H.

Hall) Pilgrims and Pioneers: The History and Speeches of the Science Fiction Research Association Award Winners, 1995; Street Kids & Other Plays, 1995; Street Kids and other Plays, 1995; (with M.A. Burgess and X. Zhang) The Chinese Economy: A Bibliography of Works in English, 1995; (with B. Clarke) The Work of Gary Brandner: An Annotated Bibliography & Guide, 1995; (with G. Lovisi) Other Worlds No. 6, 1996; Pandora's Box, 1996; (with P. Sargent) Beneath the Red Star, 1996; Islands in the Sky, 1996; Seven by Seven, 1996; Shroud Me Not, 1996; Amazing Pulp Heroes, 1996; (with G. Lovisi) Hardboiled No. 22, 1996; Sarasha, 1997; Murder Wears a Halo, 1997; Mitzi, 1997; The Brothers Challis, 1997; Letters from Dwight, 1998; Alien Life, 1998; The Fortress of Utopia, 1998; (with G. Lovisi) Hardboiled No. 24, 1998; The Whispering Gorilla, 1999; The Slitherers, 1999; Lord of Atlantis, 1999; Hero-Lore No.1, 1999; The Gargoyle, 2000; (ed.) Wail!, 2002; (ed.) Pulp Crime Classics, 2002; Sherlock Holmes, 2008. FORTHCOMING: (ed.) Things in Revolt!; (ed.) Polygraph; Arpartments; (ed.) After Dwight. Works appear in anthologies. Contributor to periodicals. **Address:** c/o Ricia Mainhardt, Ricia Mainhardt Agency, 612 Argyle Rd., Ste. L5, Brooklyn, NY 11230-1682, U.S.A. **Online address:** sfwriter00@ad.com

MALLICK, Ross. Canadian (born Canada), b. 1948?. **Genres:** Area Studies, Politics/Government, Third World, Social Sciences, Economics. **Career:** Development consultant and writer. **Publications:** Development Policy of a Communist Government: West Bengal since 1977, 1993; Indian Communism: Opposition, Collaboration and Institutionalization, 1994; Development, Ethnicity and Human Rights in South Asia, 1998. **Address:** 3 Banchory Cres., Ottawa, ON K2K 2V4, Canada. **Online address:** burdo1234@aol.com

MALLIN, Jay. American (born United States), b. 1927. **Genres:** International Relations/Current Affairs, Biography, Documentaries/Reportage, Autobiography/Memoirs, History. **Career:** Havana Herald, news editor, 1950-53; Time Magazine, stringer correspondent, 1956-80; Miami News, correspondent, 1957-63; Miami for Time, stringer correspondent, 1961-80; University of Miami, Center for Advanced International Studies, research scientist, 1967-70; Copley News Service, columnist, 1972-74; The Net, editor, 1974-82; Washington Times, Latin American correspondent, 1982-85; Radio Marti, news director, 1985-90; TV Marti, editor, 1990; International Research 2000, deputy director, 1994-95; Ancient Mariners Press, vice president, 2000-. Writer and consultant, 2000-. **Publications:** Crise au Saint-Domingue, 1965; Fortress Cuba: Russia's American Base, 1965; Caribbean Crisis, 1965; Terror in Viet Nam, 1966; Ernesto Che Guevara, Modern Revolutionary, Guerilla Theorist, 1973; General Vo Nguyen Giap, 1973; Fulgencio Batista, 1974; The Great Managua Earthquake, 1974; Merc: American Soldiers of Fortune, 1979; Cuba in Angola, 1987; Covering Castro: Rise and Decline of Cuba's Communist Dictator, 1994; Adventures in Journalism: A Memoir, 1998; Cuba's Armed Forces: From Colony to Castro, 2000; The Taking of Miami, 2005. EDITOR: Che Guevara on Revolution, 1969; Strategy for Conquest; Communist Documents on Guerrilla Warfare, 1970; (intro.) Terror and Urban Guerrillas: A Study of Tactics and Documents, 1971. Contributor to periodicals. **Address:** 4515 Willard Ave., Apt. 817, Chevy Chase, MD 20815, U.S.A. **Online address:** jaymallin2@aol.com

MALLIOS, Seth. American (born United States), b. 1971. **Genres:** Politics/Government, Young Adult Non-fiction. **Career:** University of Virginia, lecturer, 1998-99, instructor, 1996-2001; Journal of the Jamestown Rediscovery Center, founding editor, 2000-; San Diego State University, assistant professor, 2001-04, undergraduate advisor, 2004-06, chair of department, 2006-, professor of anthropology, 2007-, South Coastal Information Center, principal investigator, director and coordinator, 2001-06, principal investigator and director 2006-. **Publications:** NONFICTION: The Deadly Politics of Giving: Exchange and Violence at Ajacan, Roanoke, and Jamestown, 2006; (with D.M. Caterino) Cemeteries of San Diego, 2007. Contributor to books, journals and periodicals. **Address:** Department of Anthropology, College of Arts and Letters, San Diego State University, 5500 Campanile Dr., San Diego, CA 92182-6040, U.S.A. **Online address:** smallios@mail.sdsu.edu

MALLOCH, Theodore Roosevelt. American (born United States), b. 1952. **Genres:** Politics/Government, Business/Trade/Industry, Theology/Religion. **Career:** Roosevelt Group, chair and chief executive officer; Cable News Network, 1992 World Economic Development Congress, president; Spiritual Enterprise Institute, founder and chairman, 2005-; Yale University, research professor; CEO Learning Partnership, co-founder and director; PricewaterhouseCoopers LLP, co-founder and director; United Nations, ambassador; Wharton-Chase Econometrics, head of consulting; Salomon Brothers, staff; U.S. State Department, policy advisor. **Publications:** (Ed. with W.A. Harper) Where Are We Now? The State of Christian Political Reflection, 1981; Beyond Reductionism: Ideology and the Science of Politics, 1983; Issues in International Trade and Development Policy, 1987; (with D.M. Norris) Unleashing the Power of Perpetual Learning, 1997; (with S.T. Massey) Renewing American Culture: The Pursuit of Happiness, 2006; Spiritual Enterprise: Doing Virtuous Business, 2008; Thrift: Rebirth of a Forgotten Virtue, 2009; Being Generous, 2009. **Address:** 614 Blackbeard Rd., Queenstown, MD 21658, U.S.A. **Online address:** trmalloch@comcast.net

MALLON, Florencia E. American/Chilean (born Chile), b. 1951. **Genres:** History, Social Sciences, Translations, Humanities, Education, Reference. **Career:** Social Science Research Council and American Council of Learned Societies Intl., doctoral research fellow, 1976-78; Marquette University, instructor, 1980-81, assistant professor, 1981-82; University of Wisconsin, assistant professor, 1982-84, associate professor, 1984-88, professor, 1988-2006, Julieta Kirkwood professor of history, 2006-, Institute for Research in the Humanities, fellow, 1987-88, resident fellow, 1999-2000, senior resident, 2000-05; Yale University, visiting assistant professor, 1982; Stanford University, Center for Advanced Studies, fellow, 1990-91; National Endowment for the Humanities, fellow, 1990-91; John Simon Guggenheim Memorial, fellow, 1996; Research Institute for the Study of Man Ruth Landes, senior fellow, 1996; Universidad de la Frontera, Instituto de Estudios Indígenas, research associate, 1996-97; Universidad Católica de Temuco, Centro de Estudios Socio-culturales, research associate, 1997-99. Writer. **Publications:** The Defense of Community in Peru's Central Highlands: Peasant Struggle and Capitalist Transition, 1860-1940, 1983; (ed. with F. Cooper and A.F. Isaacman) Confronting Historical Paradigms: Peasants, Labor, and the Capitalist World System in Africa and Latin America, 1993; Peasant and Nation: The Making of Postcolonial Mexico and Peru, 1995; (ed., trans. and intro.) R.I.R. Paillalef, When a Flower Is Reborn: The Life and Times of a Mapuche Feminist, 2002; La Sangre Del Copihue: La Comunidad Mapuche de Nicolas Ailio y el Estado Chileno, 1906-2001, 2004; Courage Tastes of Blood: The Mapuche Community of Nicolas Ailio and the Chilean State, 1906-2001, 2005; (ed.) Decolonizing Native Histories: Collaboration, Knowledge, and Language in the Americas, 2012. Contributor to journals and periodicals. **Address:** Department of History, University of Wisconsin, 5125 Mosse Humanities Bldg., 455 N Park St., PO Box 5027, Madison, WI 53706-1483, U.S.A. **Online address:** femallon@wisc.edu

MALLON, Thomas. American (born United States), b. 1951. **Genres:** Novels, Literary Criticism And History. **Career:** Harvard University, teaching fellow in English and expository writing, 1974-78; Texas Tech University, visiting assistant professor of English, 1978-79; Vassar College, assistant professor, 1979-85, associate professor of English, 1985-89, professor of English, 1989-91; Gentlemen's Quarterly, literary editor, 1991-95, writer-at-large, 1995-2000; National Endowment for the Humanities, director, 2004, deputy chairman; George Washington University, professor, Creative Writing Program, director. **Publications:** NOVELS: Art and Sciences: A Seventies Seduction, 1988; Aurora 7, 1991; Henry and Clara, 1994; Dewey Defeats Truman, 1997; Two Moons: A Novel, 2000; Bandbox, 2004. OTHERS: Edmund Blunden (literary criticism), 1983; A Book of One's Own: People and Their Diaries, 1984; Arts and Sciences, 1988; Stolen Words: Forays into the Origins and Ravages of Plagiarism, 1989; Rockets and Rodeos and Other American Spectacles (essays), 1993; In Fact: Essays on Writers and Writing, 2001; Mrs. Paine's Garage and the Murder of John F. Kennedy (history), 2002; Fellow Travelers, 2007; Yours Ever: People and Their Letters, 2009; Watergate, 2012. **Address:** Department of English, George Washington University, 674 Rome Hall, 801 22nd St. NW, Ste. 760, Washington, DC 20052, U.S.A. **Online address:** tvmallon@gwu.edu

MALLORY, Drew. *See* **GARFIELD, Brian (F. W.).**

MALLORY, J(ames) P(atrick). Irish/American (born United States), b. 1945. **Genres:** Archaeology/Antiquities, Social Sciences. **Career:** University of California Extension, staff, 1975-77; Institute of Irish Studies, senior research fellow, 1978-79; Queen's University, senior lecturer in archaeology, 1981-, professor of prehistoric archaeology, 1998-, director of research, coordinator; Journal of Indo-European Studies, editor; Emania: Bulletin of the Navan Research Group, editor. **Publications:** (Ed.) Dereivka, a Settlement and Cemetery of Copper Age Horse Keepers on the Middle Dnieper, 1986; (ed.) Neolithic Cemeteries and Populations in the Dnieper Basin, 1987; In Search of the Indo-Europeans: Language, Archaeology and Myth, 1989; (with T.E.

McNeill) The Archaeology of Ulster from Colonization to Plantation, 1991; (ed.) Aspects of the Táin, 1992; (with D.Y. Telegin) The Anthropomorphic Stelae of the Ukraine, 1994; (ed. with G. Stockman) Ulidia, 1994; (with D.Q. Adams) Encyclopedia of Indo-European Studies, 1997; (with V.H. Mair) The Tarim Mummies: Ancient China and the Mystery of the Earliest Peoples from the West, 2000; (with D.Q. Adams) The Oxford Introduction to Proto-Indo-Europeans and the Proto-Indo-European World, 2006; (ed.) Origin of the Indo-Iranians, 2007; (with B. Hartwell and E. Nelis) Excavations on Donegore Hill, forthcoming. Contributor to periodicals. **Address:** School of Geography, Archaeology and Palaeoecology, Queen's University Belfast, Belfast, AT BT7 1NN, Northern Ireland. **Online address:** j.mallory@qub.ac.uk

MALLOW, Judy M(ofield). American (born United States), b. 1949. **Genres:** Crafts. **Career:** North Carolina Museum of History, featured artist, 1994; John C. Campbell Folk School, instructor, 1998-; Bay School of the Arts, instructor, 2001-. Writer. **Publications:** Pine Needle and Nut Crafting, 1984; Pine Needle Basketry: From Forest Floor to Finished Project, 1996. **Address:** Prim Pines Co., PO Box 148, Carthage, NC 28327, U.S.A. **Online address:** judymallow@embarqmail.com

MALLOY, Sean L. American (born United States), b. 1972. **Genres:** History. **Career:** University of California, assistant professor. Writer and historian. **Publications:** Atomic Tragedy: Henry L. Stimson and the Decision to Use the Bomb against Japan, 2008. **Address:** School of Social Sciences, Humanities and Art, University of California, 5200 N Lake Rd., Merced, CA 95343, U.S.A. **Online address:** smalloy@ucmerced.edu

MALMGREN, Dallin. American (born United States), b. 1949. **Genres:** Novels, Education, Humor/Satire, Young Adult Fiction, Technology, Administration/Management. **Career:** Ste. Genevieve High School, English teacher, 1981-84; Judson High School, journalism teacher, 1984-86; Samuel Clemens High School, English teacher and tennis coach, 1986-. Writer. **Publications:** The Whole Nine Yards, 1986; The Ninth Issue, 1989; Is This for a Grade?: A Survival Guide for Teaching in the '90s, 1994. **Address:** 107 Green Valley Loop Rd., Cibolo, TX 78108, U.S.A.

MALMONT, Valerie S(kuse). American (born United States), b. 1937. **Genres:** Mystery/Crime/Suspense, Novels. **Career:** Arlington County Public Library, children's librarian, 1965-66; U.S. Air Force, head librarian-special services, 1971-72; U.S. Navy, head librarian-special services, 1972-74; Chambersburg Area School District, librarian, 1978-84; Letterkenny Federal Credit Union, marketing assistant, 1986-88; Cumberland Valley Links, co-founder and treasurer, 1992-95. Writer. **Publications:** TORI MIRACLE SERIES OF MYSTERY NOVELS: Death Pays the Rose Rent, 1994; Death, Lies, and Apple Pies, 1997; Death, Guns, and Sticky Buns, 2000; Death, Snow, and Mistletoe, 2000; Death, Bones, and Stately Homes, 2003. **Address:** 33 Woodland Way, Chambersburg, PA 17202-3167, U.S.A. **Online address:** valmalmont@aol.com

MALOKA, Eddy Tshidiso. South African (born South Africa), b. 1965. **Genres:** History, Politics/Government, Industrial Relations. **Career:** Mpumalanga and Gauteng, adviser; Cape Town University, Mellon research fellow, 1992-95; University of Cape Town, lecturer, 1992, 1997; University of London, Ernest Oppenheimer fellow, 1994; University of the Western Cape, lecturer, 1995; Princeton University, visiting research fellow, 1996; Brown University, visiting research associate, 1996; Africa Institute of South Africa (AISA), chief executive officer, 1999-; Sowetan, columnist. Historian. **Publications:** (Ed. with E.l. Roux) Africa in the New Millennium: Challenges and Prospects, 1999; (ed.) A United States of Africa?, 1999; (ed. with E.l. Roux) Problematising the African Renaissance, 2000; The South African Communist Party, 1963-1990, 2002; (ed. with K.G. Adar and J.G.N. Yoh) Sudan Peace Process: Challenges and Future Prospects, 2004; (as Eddy Tshidiso Maloka) Basotho and the Mines: A Social History of Labour Migrancy in Lesotho and South Africa, c. 1890-1940, 2004; (ed. with P. Hugo) State of Africa, 2004. **Address:** Africa Institute of South Africa, PO Box 630, Pretoria, 0001, South Africa.

MALONE, Hank. (Henry Malone). American (born United States), b. 1940. **Genres:** Poetry, Psychology, Social Sciences, Urban Studies, Reference. **Career:** Writer, 1962-; Wayne State University, Graduate School, Social Work and Urban Studies, part-time faculty, 1967-71; American Broadcasting Co., talk-radio host, 1970-74; Department of Mental Health, director, 1976-85; Metrotag, clinical psychotherapist, 1985-95. **Publications:** Survival, Evasion, and Escape: Poems, 1985; Footstrikes and Spondees: Poems, 1993; New Mexico Haiku, 1995; Experiencing New Mexico (essays), 1998; James Dickey-On the Eve of the Millennium (long poem), 1999; Knife-Edged Urban Millennium Haiku: Poems, 2001; Time Spent in Albuquerque: Poems, 2006; The Greenlife: Poems, 2010. **Address:** 1220-J Nakomis Dr. NE, Albuquerque, NM 87112, U.S.A. **Online address:** hanksharon@aol.com

MALONE, Henry. *See* **MALONE, Hank.**

MALONE, James Hiram. American (born United States), b. 1930. **Genres:** Novels, Children's Fiction, Poetry, Songs/Lyrics And Libretti, How-to Books, Local History/Rural Topics, Cartoons, Essays, Essays. **Career:** U.S. Army Training Manuals, creator, 1950-59; K-Mart International Headquarters, Troy, MI, senior graphics designer, 1980-83; Atlanta Journal and Constitution, ad promotions creative director, 1983-90; Crowley's, Federal's, Chatham, Farmer Jack's, Montgomery Wards and Kmart International Headquarters' Stores, staff, 1960-83; Highland Park Junior College, arts instructor, 1970; Atlanta Journal Constitution Newspapers, ad promotions creative writer director, graphic designer; Bianco Art Collections of Atlanta, fine art producer, painter, 1990-92; Atlanta News Leader newspaper, 1992-; Detroit Collaborative Design Center, staff, 1999; Metropolitan College of Art, arts instructor, 2002; Contemporary Art Institute, vice-president, 2002-07; Studio Architech, co-founder, 2004; Laughing Trees Inc., founder, director; Grove Park Arts Alliance, chief executive officer; International Black Writers Association, president; United States Army Special Services Division Activities Publicity coordinator, chief illustrator, writer; Jackson Journal, contributor, U.S. Army Times Tabloids, contributor; U.S. Army Propaganda for Leaflets for Army Intelligence Department, writer, designer; G-2, G-3 Office Team, faculty. **Publications:** SELF-ILLUSTRATED: Here and There, 1954; Blues, 1954; Grandma Sarah's Closet, 1960; Brother, 1970; Malone's Atlanta, 1986; Simply Apply Yourself (Say) Literacy Guide, 1986; Y'All Come Back, 1988; Atlanta, the Democrats Are Coming, 1988; Street Beat News Leader Newspaper Column, 1990; No-Job Dad, 1992; Urban History: Buttermilk Bottom Repo History Art Markers, 1995; Black Movie Theaters Art Markers, 1996; Jone's Family Cart, 1997; April Mae Jones Coloring Book, 1998; If I Live, 1999; Artistic Trees Craftsmanship Guide, 2000. **Address:** 1796 North Ave. NW, Atlanta, GA 30318-6441, U.S.A. **Online address:** j.l.t.malone@att.net

MALONE, Mary T. Irish (born Ireland), b. 1938. **Genres:** Women's Studies And Issues, Theology/Religion, Humanities. **Career:** University of Waterloo, faculty, Graduate Department of Religious Studies, chair; Toronto School of Theology, assistant professor of church history, 1974-87; St. Jerome's University, associate professor of religious studies, 1987-98, now retired. Writer. **Publications:** Women Christian: New Vision, 1985; Women and Christianity, vol. I: The First Thousand Years, vol. II: From 1000 to the Reformation, vol. III: From the Reformation to the Twenty-first Century, 2001-2003. **Address:** Villamoyra, Killeens, WX 1, Ireland. **Online address:** mtmalone@indigo.il

MALONE, Susan (Mary). American (born United States), b. 1957. **Genres:** Novels, Biography, Young Adult Fiction, Medicine/Health, Human Relations/Parenting, Marketing. **Career:** Malone Farms, farm manager, 1987-94; Malone Editorial Services, editor and proofreader. **Publications:** By the Book (fiction), 1993; (with C. Weisbeck) Body Sculpting: The Weisbeck Way, 1993; (with K. Waldrep) Fourth and Long: The Kent Waldrep Story, 1996; (with G.L. Malone) The Five Keys for Understanding Men: A Woman's Guide, 1999; (ed.) The Fifth Sun: Aztec Mythology, 2004; (ed.) Stories That Sell: Turn Satisfied Customers into Your Most Powerful Sales & Marketing Asset, 2009; By the Book, 2009. **Address:** c/o Evan Fogelman, Fogelman Literary Agency, 7515 Greenville Ave., Ste. 712, Dallas, TX 75231, U.S.A. **Online address:** maloneeditorial@hotmail.com

MALOUF, David. Australian (born Australia), b. 1934. **Genres:** Songs/Lyrics And Libretti, Novels, Poetry, Novellas/Short Stories, Plays/Screenplays. **Career:** University of Queensland, assistant lecturer in English, 1955-57; Saint Anselm's College, school master, 1962-68; University of Sydney, lecturer, 1968-77. Writer. **Publications:** POETRY: Bicycle and Other Poems, 1970 in US as The Year of the Foxes and Other Poems, 1979; Poems, 1975-76, 1976; Wild Lemons, 1980; First Things Last, 1981; Poems 1959-89, 1992; Selected Poems, 1959-89, 1994. NOVELS: Johnno, 1975; The Edge of the World, 1978; An Imaginary Life, 1978; Child's Play, 1981; Fly Away Peter in US as The Bread of Time to Come, 1982; Harland's Half Acre, 1984; The

Great World, 1990; Remembering Babylon, 1993; Baa Baa Black Sheep: A Jungle Tale, 1993; The Conversations at Curlow Creek, 1996. STORIES: Antipodes, 1985; Dream Stuff: Stories, 2000; Every Move You Make, 2006; The Complete Stories, 2007; Typewriter Music, 2007. OPERA LIBRETTI: Voss, 1986; La Mer de Glace, 1991, Baa Baa Black Sheep, 1993. OTHER: (co-author) Four Poets, 1962; Neighbours in a Thicket, 1974; (with K. Brisbane and R.F. Brissenden) New Currents in Australian Writing, 1978; 12 Edmondstone Street, 1985; Blood Relations (drama), 1987; A Spirit of Play: The Making of Australian Consciousness, 1998; Untold Tales, 1999; (intro.) James Eyre, 1999; Typewriter Music, 2007; Every Move you Make, The Complete Stories, 2007; (intro.) The Family Mashber, 2008; Revolving Days: Selected Poems, 2008; On Experience, 2008; (co-author) The On-nibus, 2009; Ransom, 2009; The Happy Life, 2011. EDITOR: (co-ed.) We Took Their Orders and Are Dead: An Anti-War Anthology, 1971; Gesture of Hand (anthology of Australian poetry), 1975. **Address:** Rogers, Coleridge & White Ltd., 20 Powis Mews, London, GL W11 1JN, England.

MALPAS, J(effery) E(dward). Australian/British (born England), b. 1958. **Genres:** Philosophy. **Career:** University of Auckland, assistant lecturer in philosophy, 1982; University of New England, tutor in philosophy, 1985-89; Murdoch University, lecturer, 1989-93, senior lecturer in philosophy, 1993-97, associate professor in philosophy, 1997-99; University of Tasmania, professor of philosophy, 1999-, Centre for Applied Philosophy and Ethics, director, 2000-06, Australian Research Council, Australian professorial research fellow 2007-11. Writer. **Publications:** Donald Davidson and the Mirror of Meaning, 1992; Place and Experience, 1999; Heidegger's Topology, 2006. EDITOR: Philosophical Papers of Alan Donagan, 1994; (with R. Solomon) Death and Philosophy, 1999; (with M. Wrathall) Essays in Honor of Hubert Dreyfus, 2000; (with J. Kertscher and U. Arnswald) Gadamer's Century, 2002; From Kant to Davidson, 2003; (with S. Crowell) Transcendental Heidegger, 2007; (with N. Lickiss) Perspectives on Human Dignity, 2007; (with S. Zabala) Consequences of Hermeneutics: Fifty Years After Gadamer's Truth and Method, 2010; Dialogues with Davidson, 2011; The Place of Landscape, 2011. **Address:** School of Philosophy, University of Tasmania, Humanities Bldg. 357, PO Box 41, Hobart, TA 7001, Australia. **Online address:** jeff.malpas@utas.edu.au

MALPEZZI PRICE, Paola. American/Italian (born Italy), b. 1948?. **Genres:** Women's Studies And Issues, Biography, Social Sciences, History. **Career:** Université de Grenoble, instructor, 1975; Lewis and Clark College, instructor, 1972, 1978; University of Oregon, graduate teaching fellow, 1972, 1975-77, 1978; American Heritage Association, European Studies Tour for High School Students, co-leader, 1974; Massachusetts Night School, instructor, 1979-80; Boston University, lecturer, 1982-83; Colorado State University, Department of Foreign Languages and Literatures, assistant professor, 1983-89, associate professor, 1989-2004, professor of French and Italian, 2004-, chair, 2007-; Experience Plus! Touring Co. (biking and walking tour company), vice president. Writer. **Publications:** Moderata Fonte: Women and Life in Sixteenth-Century Venice, 2003; (with C. Ristaino) Lucrezia Marinella and the Querelle Des Femmes in Seventeenth-Century Italy, 2008. Contributor to journals. **Address:** Department of Foreign Languages & Literatures, Colorado State University, C105 Andrew G. Clark Bldg., 1774 Campus Delivery, Fort Collins, CO 80523-1774, U.S.A. **Online address:** paola.malpezzi_price@colostate.edu

MALSEED, Mark. American (born United States), b. 1975?. **Genres:** Business/Trade/Industry, Economics, Technology, Engineering, Information Science/Computers. **Career:** Lehigh University, Young Alumni Council, founding member; OhMyGov.com, co-founder. Writer and consultant. **Publications:** (With D.A. Vise) The Google Story, 2005. **Address:** Alexandria, VA , U.S.A. **Online address:** editor@truthdig.com

MALTBY, William S(aunders). American (born United States), b. 1940. **Genres:** History, Politics/Government, Biography, Autobiography/Memoirs, Social Sciences, Humanities. **Career:** Ohio University, assistant professor of history, 1966-68; University of Missouri, St. Louis, Department of History, assistant professor, 1968-70, associate professor, 1970-82, professor, 1982-97, professor emeritus, 1997-. Writer. **Publications:** The Black Legend in England: The Development of Anti-Spanish Sentiment, 1558-1660, 1971; Alba: A Biography of Fernando Alvarez de Toledo, Third Duke of Alba, 1507-1582, 1983; (with S.C. Hause) Western Civilization: A History of European Society, 1999, 2nd ed., 2005; (with S.C. Hause) Essentials of Western Civilization: A History of European Society, 2000; The Reign of Charles V, 2002; Rise and Fall of the Spanish Empire, 2009. **Address:** Department of History, University of Missouri, 484 Lucas Hall, 1 University Blvd., St. Louis, MO 63121-4499, U.S.A. **Online address:** wsmncb@cs.com

MALTESE, John Anthony. American (born United States), b. 1960. **Genres:** Music, Politics/Government, Law, Social Sciences. **Career:** Duke University, instructor in political science, 1982; Johns Hopkins University, instructor in political science, 1987; University of Georgia, Department of Political Science, assistant professor of political science, 1989-96, associate professor, 1996-2006, professor, 2006-, Josiah Meigs distinguished teaching professor of political science, 2004-, Albert Berry Saye professor, department head. Writer. **Publications:** (Ed. and contrib.) The Accompanist: An Autobiography of Andre Benoist, 1978; Spin Control: The White House Office of Communications and the Management of Presidential News, 1992, rev. ed., 1994; (with C.C. Euchner) Selecting the President: From Washington to Bush, 1992; The Selling of Supreme Court Nominees, 1995; (with J.A. Pika) The Politics of the Presidency, 2002, rev. ed., 2010. Work represented in anthologies. Contributor of articles and reviews to journals. **Address:** Department of Political Science, University of Georgia, 101G and 102C Baldwin Hall, Athens, GA 30602, U.S.A. **Online address:** jmaltese@uga.edu

MALTI-DOUGLAS, Fedwa. American/Lebanese (born Lebanon), b. 1946. **Genres:** Literary Criticism And History. **Career:** Centre National de la Recherche Scientifique, chercheur, 1974-76; San Diego State University, lecturer, 1976-77; University of Virginia, assistant professor of Arabic, 1977-; University of California, Von Grunebaum Center, consultant, 1976-77; University of Southern California, Von Grunebaum Center, consultant, 1976-77; University of Texas, Program in Comparative Literature, director; Rockefeller Foundation Humanities Residency Institute, director; Indiana University, College of Arts and Sciences, Department of Gender Studies, chair, professor of gender studies and comparative literature, Martha C. Kraft professor of humanities, School of Law, adjunct professor, Middle Eastern Studies Program, director; American Research Center-Egypt, fellow, 1977-78; Cornell University, senior fellow, annual distinguished James H. Becker alumna lecturer, 1992-93. Writer. **Publications:** (With G. Fourcade) The Treatment by Computer of Medieval Arabic Biographical Data: An Introduction and Guide to the Onomasticum [i.e., Onomasticon] Arabicum, 1976; Binā al-Naṣ ṣ al-Turāthī: Dirāsāt fī al-Adab Wa-al-Tarājim, 1985; Structures of Avarice: The Bukhalā in Medieval Arabic Literature, 1985; (with A. Douglas) L'idéologie par la Bande: Héros Politiques de France et d'Egypte au Miroir de la BD, 1987; Blindness and Autobiography: Al-Ayyām of Ṭāhā Ḥusayn, 1988; Woman's Body, Woman's Word: Gender and Discourse in Arabo-Islamic Writing, 1991; (with A. Douglas) Arab Comic Strips: Politics of an Emerging Mass Culture, 1994; (intro.) The Innocence of the Devil, 1994; A Woman and Her Sûfîs, 1995; Men, Women, and God(s): Nawal El Saadawi and Arab Feminist Poetics, 1995; Hisland: Adventures in Ac-Ac-Ademe, 1998; The Starr Report Disrobed, 2000; Medicines of the Soul: Female Bodies and Sacred Geographies in a Transnational Islam, 2001; Power, Marginality, and the Body in Medieval Islam, 2001; (ed.) Encyclopedia of Sex and Gender, 2007; Partisan Sex: Bodies, Politics, and the Law in the Clinton Era, 2009. **Address:** School of Law, Indiana University, 341 Law Bldg., 211 S Indiana Ave., Bloomington, IN 47405-7001, U.S.A. **Online address:** gender@indiana.edu

MALTZ, Diana. American (born United States), b. 1965. **Genres:** Art/Art History. **Career:** Stanford University, lecturer, 1997-98; Southern Oregon University, associate professor of English, 1999-, Department Language, Literature and Philosophy, chair. Writer. **Publications:** British aestheticism and the Urban Working Classes, 1870-1900: Beauty for the People, 2006. Contributor to journals. **Address:** Department of English and Writing, Southern Oregon University, CE 261, 1250 Siskiyou Blvd., Ashland, OR 97520, U.S.A. **Online address:** maltzd@sou.edu

MALTZ, Earl M. American (born United States), b. 1950. **Genres:** Law, Politics/Government, Civil Liberties/Human Rights. **Career:** Rutgers School of Law, distinguished professor of law. Writer. **Publications:** NONFICTION: Civil Rights, the Constitution, and Congress, 1863-1869, 1990; Rethinking Constitutional Law: Originalism, Interventionism, and the Politics of Judicial Review, 1994; The Chief Justiceship of Warren Burger, 1969-1986, 2000; Rehnquist Justice: Understanding the Court Dynamic, 2003; The Fourteenth Amendment and the Law of the Constitution, 2003; Dred Scott and the Politics of Slavery, 2007; Slavery and the Supreme Court, 1825-1861, 2009, Fugitive Slave on Trial: The Anthony Burns Case and Abolitionist Outrage, 2010. Contributor of articles to books and journals. **Address:** Rutgers School of Law, 621, 217 N 5th St., Camden, NJ 08102, U.S.A. **Online address:** emaltz@camden.rutgers.edu

MALUSA, Jim. American (born United States), b. 1957. **Genres:** Travel/Exploration, Air/Space Topics. **Career:** Botanist and freelance writer. **Publications:** Into Thick Air: Biking to the Bellybutton of Six Continents, 2008. Contributor to periodicals and journals. **Address:** Tucson, AZ , U.S.A. **Online address:** intothickair@yahoo.com

MALVASI, Mark G. American (born United States), b. 1957. **Genres:** History, Intellectual History, Literary Criticism And History, Novels, inspirational/Motivational Literature, Young Adult Fiction. **Career:** University of Puget Sound, assistant professor of American history, 1989-90; University of South Carolina, National Historical Publications and Records Commission, fellow; John C. Calhoun Papers, staff, 1990-91; University of Rochester, faculty; University of Alabama, assistant professor of American history, 1991-92; Yorktown University, Randolph-Macon College, associate professor of American history, 1992-. Writer. **Publications:** The Unregenerate South: The Agrarian Thought of John Crowe Ransom, Allen Tate and Donald Davidson, 1997; Andrew Lytle: The Last Agrarian, 2003; (ed.) Slavery in the Western Hemisphere, 1500-1888, 2003; (ed. with J.O. Nelson) Remembered Past: John Lukacs on History, Historians and Historical Knowledge: A Reader, 2004; Merigam: A Novel, 2006. CONTRIBUTOR: Slavery and Southern History, 1999; Lost Causes Regained: The Work of M.E. Bradford, 1999. Contributor to books and periodicals. **Address:** Department of History, Randolph-Macon College, Yorktown University, 4340 E Kentucky Ave., Ste. 457, Denver, CO 80246, U.S.A. **Online address:** malvasi@home.com

MALVASI, Meg Greene. (Meg Greene). American (born United States) **Genres:** Biography, History, Adult Non-fiction, Archaeology/Antiquities. **Career:** Freelance writer, 1994-; Center for Archaeological Research, College of William and Mary, architectural historian, 1997-99, 2004-. **Publications:** AS MEG GREENE: Pope John Paul II: A Biography, 2003; Jane Goodall: A Biography, 2005; Japan: A Primary Source Cultural Guide, 2005; The Hunt for Osama Bin Laden; Ancient Technology of Japan, 2006; William Henry Harrison, 2006; Transcontinental Treaty, 1819: A Primary Source Examination Of The Treaty Between The United States And Spain Over The American West, 2006; Billie Holiday: A Biography, 2007; William H. Harrison, 2007; Obesity, 2007; Rest in Peace: A History of American Cemeteries, 2008. IMMIGRANTS IN AMERICA SERIES: Legends of Ice Hockey: Peter Forsberg, 1998; Slave Young, Slave Long: A History of American Slavery, 1999; Your Government and How It Works: The DEA, 2001; Revolutionary War Heroes: Nathaniel Greene, 2001; Buttons, Bones, and the Organ Grinder's Monkey: Tales of Historical Archeology, 2001; Famous Figures of the Civil War: Jeb Stuart, 2002; Revolutionary War Heroes: Thaddeus Kosciuzko, 2002; The Russian Americans, 2002; Jacques Cartier, 2003; Careers in the National Guards' Search and Rescue Units, 2003; U.S. Warplanes: The B-52 Strato fortress, 2003; Louis Sachar, 2003; Into the Land of Freedom: A History of Reconstruction, 2004; The Greek Americans, 2004; Polish Americans, 2004. GALAXY OF SUPERSTARS SERIES: Lauryn Hill, 1999; Matt Damon, 2000; Will Smith, 2002. BUILDING HISTORY SERIES: The Kremlin, 2001; The Eiffel Tower, 2001. Contributor to periodicals. **Address:** 13803 Sterlings Bridge Rd., Midlothian, VA 23112, U.S.A. **Online address:** malvasi@comcast.net

MALVERN, Sue. British (born England), b. 1951. **Genres:** Art/Art History. **Career:** University of Reading, Department of Art History, senior lecturer, 1989-; Concordia University, commonwealth visiting fellow, 1991-92; Yale University, visiting research fellow, 2002; Bulmershe College, faculty. Writer. **Publications:** Modern Art, Britain and the Great War: Witnessing, Testimony and Remembrance, 2004. **Address:** England. **Online address:** s.b.malvern@reading.ac.uk

MALY, Michael T. American (born United States), b. 1968?. **Genres:** Social Sciences, Cultural/Ethnic Topics. **Career:** Roosevelt University, associate professor of sociology and chair of department. Writer. **Publications:** Beyond Segregation: Multiracial and Multiethnic Neighborhoods in the United States, 2005. Contributor to periodicals. **Address:** Department of Sociology, Roosevelt University, Rm. 870, Auditorium Bldg., 430 S Michigan Ave., Chicago, IL 60605, U.S.A. **Online address:** mmaly@roosevelt.edu

MALZAHN, Manfred. German (born Germany), b. 1955. **Genres:** Novellas/Short Stories, Poetry, Songs/Lyrics And Libretti, History, Literary Criticism And History. **Career:** Goethe Institute Iserlohn, teaching assistant and student counselor, 1983-85; University of Edinburgh, foreign language assistant, 1985-88; University of Monastir, senior lecturer, 1988-89; University of Setif, senior lecturer, 1990; University of Malawi, senior lecturer, 1991-92; National Chung Cheng University, professor, 1993-98; United Arab Emirates University, professor, 1998-. Writer. **Publications:** Aspects of Identity: The Contemporary Scottish Novel (1978-1981) as National Self-Expression, 1984; (co-author) Instant Lessons: Materialien fuer den Konversationsunterricht, 1987; Germany 1945-1949: A Source Book, 1991; (ed.) Chancellor College First Year Literature Anthology, 1992; (trans.) Albrecht Dihle, Greek and Latin Literature of the Roman Empire, 1994; Scots: Das Englisch der Schotten, 1994, 5th ed., 2009; Al-Arab wa-al-Almān: Abhòāth Mutamar Almāniyā wa-al-ālam al-Arabī alladhī uqidabi-Jāmiat al-Imārāt al-Arabīyah al-Muttahòidah, 30 Sibtambir-2 Uktūbir 2001, 2004. Contributor to books and periodicals. **Address:** Department of English Literature, Faculty of Humanities and Social Sciences, United Arab Emirates University, PO Box 17771, Al-Ain, 00000, United Arab Emirates. **Online address:** mmalzahn@uaeu.ac.ae

MAMET, David. American (born United States), b. 1947. **Genres:** Children's Fiction, Plays/Screenplays, Poetry, Film, Essays, Novels, Art/Art History, Humor/Satire, Picture/Board Books. **Career:** Marlboro College, lecturer-in-drama, 1970; Goddard College, artist-in-residence, 1971-73; St. Nicholas Theater Co., founder, 1973-, artistic director, 1973-76; Illinois Arts Council, faculty, 1974; University of Chicago, visiting lecturer in drama, 1975-76, 1979; Oui Magazine, contributing editor, 1975-76; Yale University, School of Drama, teaching fellow, 1976-77; Goodman Theater, associate artistic director, 1978-79; New Theater Co., associate director, 1985-; Columbia University, associate professor of film, 1988; Atlantic Theater Co., founding member. **Publications:** A Life in the Theatre, 1978; American Buffalo, Sexual Perversity in Chicago, Duck Variations: Three Plays, 1978; Sexual Perversity in Chicago and Duck Variations: Two Plays, 1978; The Water Engine: An American Fable and Mr. Happiness: Two Plays, 1978; Dark Pony and Reunion, 1979; The Woods, 1979; Lakeboat, 1981; Edmond, 1983; Warm and Cold (for children), 1984; Glengarry Glen Ross, 1984; Short Plays and Monologues, 1985; Goldberg Street (collection), 1985, The Cherry Orchard (adaptation), 1985; Dramatic Sketches and Monologues, 1985; Three Children's Plays, 1986; The Owl (for children), 1986; Writing in Restaurants (essays), 1986; Three Jewish Plays, 1987; Speed-the-Plow, 1988; (with S. Silverstein) Things Change: Uncle Vanya (adaptation), 1988; (with D. Sultan and R. Jay) Donald Sultan: Playing Cards, 1989; Some Freaks (essays), 1989; The Hero Pony (poetry), 1990; On Directing Film, 1991; Oh, Hell! (plays), 1991; The Cabin: Reminiscence and Diversions, 1992; Oleanna, 1992; The Village (novel), 1994; A Whore's Profession: Notes and Essays, 1994; The Cryptogram, 1995; Passover, 1995; Make-Believe Town: Essays and Remembrances, 1996; The Duck and the Goat, 1996; Three Uses of the Knife: On the Nature and Purpose of Drama, 1996; True and False: Heresy and Common Sense for the Actor, 1997; The Old Religion, 1997; The Old Neighborhood, 1997; On Acting, 1999; Chinaman (poems), 1999; Bar Mitzvah, 1999; Henrietta, 1999; Jafsie and John Henry, 1999; Homicide, 2000; Boston Marriage, 2000; Wilson: A Consideration of the Sources, 2000; (foreword) River Run Cookbook: Southern Comfort from Vermont, 2001; David Mamet in Conversation, 2001; South of the Northeast Kingdom, 2002; (with L. Kushner) Five Cities of Refuge, 2003; Faustus, 2004; Romance, 2005; (adapted) Voysey Inheritance, 2005; Wicked Son: Anti-Semitism, Self-Hatred and the Jews, 2006; Bambi vs. Godzilla: On the Nature, Purpose and Practice of the Movie Business, 2007; November, 2008; Keep Your Pantheon, 2009; (with W. Allen) Death Defying Acts, 2010; School, 2010; Race, 2010; The Trials of Roderick Spode: The Human Ant, 2010; Theatre, 2010; The Secret Knowledge: On the Dismantling of American Culture, 2011; (with E.L. Doctorow and A. Ginsberg) Poems for Life: A Special Collection of Poetry, 2011; The Anarchist, 2012. Contributor to periodicals. **Address:** c/o Howard Rosenstone, Rosenstone/Wender Associates, 3 E 48th St., 4th Fl., New York, NY 10017-1027, U.S.A.

MAN, Alfred Young. Canadian/American (born United States), b. 1948. **Genres:** Art/Art History, Humanities. **Career:** Rocky Boy Elementary School District, art instructor, 1973-74; K.W. Bergan Elementary School, art instructor, 1975; Flathead Valley Community College, media specialist and instructor in educational television, 1976-77; University of Lethbridge, assistant professor, 1977-92, associate professor of Native American studies, 1992-2000, acting chair, 1998, 1999, chair, 1999-2007, professor of Native American studies, 2000-07, professor emeritus, 2007-; First Nations University of Canada, Department of Indian Fine Arts, department head, 2007-10, now professor emeritus; University of Regina, professor, now professor emeritus. Writer, painter and musician. **Publications:** (With B. Kanbara and I. Jessel) Visions of Power, 1991; (with G. McMaster and L.A. Martin) Indigena: Contemporary Native Perspectives, 1992; Jeff Funnell: Notes From the Inquest, 1992; (contrib.) Kiskayetum: Allen Sapp, a Retrospective, 1994; The Socialization and Art-Politics of Native Art, 1997, rev. ed. as You Are In Indian Country: A Native Perspective on Native Art, 2007; North American Indian Art: It's a Question of Integrity, 1998; (contrib.) Begegnungen: indianische Künstler aus Nordamerika: Visionen-Positionen-Traditionen=Indian Reality Today: Contemporary: Indian Art of North America, 1999; The Socialization and Art-Politics of Native Art, rev. ed. as The Buckskin Ceiling: A Native Perspective on Native Art/Politics, 2009. EDITOR: Networking: National Native Indian Artists Symposium IV, 1988; A Dominican Experience: Three Aboriginal Artists of Canada in the Dominican Republic, 1989. **Address:** Department of Indian Fine Arts, First Nations University of Canada, 1 1st Nations Way, Regina, SK S4S 7K2, Canada. **Online address:** ayoungman@firstnationsuniversity.ca

MANASTER, Benjamin. American (born United States), b. 1938. **Genres:** Novels, Young Adult Fiction, Mystery/Crime/Suspense. **Career:** Writer and director. **Publications:** Skyla (novel), 1995. **Address:** 10335 Rossbury Pl., Los Angeles, CA 90064, U.S.A.

MANCALL, Peter C. (Peter Cooper Mancall). American (born United States), b. 1959. **Genres:** History, Economics, Cultural/Ethnic Topics. **Career:** Connecticut College, visiting assistant professor of history, 1986-87; Harvard University, lecturer on history and literature, 1987-89; University of Kansas, professor, 1989-2001; University of Southern California, professor of history, 2001-, professor of history and anthropology, 2005-, associate vice provost for research advancement, 2007-08, Huntington Early Modern Studies Institute, director, 2008-09. Writer. **Publications:** Valley of Opportunity: Economic Culture along the Upper Susquehanna, 1700-1800, 1991; Deadly Medicine: Indians and Alcohol in Early America, 1995; (with E. Hinderaker) At the Edge of Empire: The Backcountry in British North America, 2003; Hakluyt's Promise: An Elizabethan's Obsession for an English America, 2007; Fatal Journey: The Final Expedition of Henry Hudson-a Tale of Mutiny and Murder in the Arctic, 2009. EDITOR: Roll On, River: Rivers in the Lives of the American People, 1990; (intro.) Envisioning America: English Plans for the Colonization of North America, 1580-1640, 1995; Land of Rivers: America in Word and Image, foreword by Edward Hoagland, 1996; American Eras: Westward Expansion, 1800-1860, 1999; (with J.H. Merrell) American Encounters: Natives and Newcomers from European Contact to Indian Removal, 1500-1850, 2000; (with F.E. Hoxie and J.H. Merrell) American Nations: Encounters in Indian Country, 1850 to the Present, 2001; (with G.B. Nash) Encyclopedia of American History, vol. I: Three Worlds Meet Beginnings to 1607, 2002; Travel Narratives from the Age of Discovery: An Anthology, 2006; Bringing the World to Early Modern Europe: Travel Accounts and Their Audiences, 2007; The Atlantic World and Virginia, 1550-1624, 2007; (with J.H. Merrell) American Encounters: Natives and Newcomers from European Contact to Indian Removal, 1500-1850, 2007; (with B.H. Johnson) Making of the American West: People and Perspectives, 2007; (with J.A. Grigg) British Colonial America: People and Perspectives, 2008. Contributor to journals. **Address:** University of Southern California, College of Letters Arts & Sciences, 3520 Trousdale Pkwy., SOS 153, Los Angeles, CA 90089, U.S.A. **Online address:** mancall@usc.edu

MANCALL, Peter Cooper. *See* **MANCALL, Peter C.**

MANCHEL, Frank. American (born United States), b. 1935. **Genres:** Communications/Media, Film, History, Bibliography. **Career:** University of Vermont, professor of English and film studies. Writer, film historian and critic-at-large. **Publications:** Movies and How They are Made, 1968; When Pictures Began to Move, 1968; The La Mancha Project, 1968; La Mancha Plus One, 1969; When Movies Began to Speak, 1969; Terrors of the Screen, 1970; La Mancha Plus Two, 1970; Cameras West, 1971; Yesterday's Clown: The Rise of Film Comedy, 1973; Film Study: A Resource Guide, 1973; An Album of Great Science Fiction Films, 1976; Women on the Hollywood Screen, 1977; The Talking Clowns, 1978; Gangsters on the Screen, 1978; The Box-Office Clowns, 1979; An Album of Great Sports Movies, 1980; An Album of Great Science Fiction Movies, 1982; An Album of Modern Horror Films, 1983; Film Studies: An Analytical Bibliography, 4 vols., 1990; Every Step a Struggle: Interviews with Seven Who Shaped the African-American Image in Movies, 2007. **Address:** 682 Forest Rd., St. George, VT 05495-8046, U.S.A. **Online address:** fmanchel@uvm.edu

MANCUSI, Mari. (Marianne Mancusi). American (born United States), b. 1974?. **Genres:** Novels. **Career:** Writer and television producer. **Publications:** YOUNG ADULT NOVELS: Sk8er Boy, 2005; Boys That Bite, 2006; Stake That!, 2006; Girls That Growl, 2007; Gamer Girl, 2008; Bad Blood, 2010. NOVELS AS MARIANNE MANCUSI: A Connecticut Fashionista in King Arthur's Court, 2005; What, No Roses?, 2006; A Hoboken Hipster in Sherwood Forest, 2007; Moongazer, 2007; Razor Girl, 2008; News Blues, 2008; (with J. Kenner and J. Lee) These Boots Were Made for Stomping, 2008. **Address:** New York, NY , U.S.A. **Online address:** mari@marimancusi.com

MANCUSI, Marianne. *See* **MANCUSI, Mari.**

MANDANIPOUR, Shahriar. Iranian (born Iran), b. 1957. **Genres:** Novels. **Career:** Sarv, co-founder; Asr-e Pandjshanbeh, editor-in-chief; Brown University, international writing fellow. **Publications:** Hashtumi-n ru-z-i zami-n, 1992; Ma-h-i ni-mru-z, 1997; Dil-i dildadagi, 1998; Sharq-i Banafshah 1999; Mu-miya-va 'asal 2001; Abi-e Mavaray-e Bahar 2003; Kita-b-i arva-h-i Shahr'zäd: säzah'hä, shirgird'hä va furm'hä-yi Da-sta-n-i naw, 2004; Censoring an Iranian Love Story: A Novel, 2009. Contributor to books and magazines. **Address:** 1745 Broadway, New York, NY 10019, U.S.A. **Online address:** shahryarman@gmail.com

MANDEL, Brett H. American (born United States), b. 1969. **Genres:** Sports/Fitness, Urban Studies. **Career:** Philadelphia Independent Charter Commission, assistant policy director, 1992-94; Pennsylvania Economy League, associate, 1994-96, policy analyst and project manager, 1994-96; City of Philadelphia, assistant city controller, 1996-, Financial and Policy Analysis Unit, director, 1996-; Philadelphia Forward, executive director; National Education Technology Funding Corp., executive director; Center City Residents Association, vice president; Greater Philadelphia Men's Adult Baseball League, commissioner; Smith Memorial Playground and Playhouse, treasurer. Writer. **Publications:** Minor Players, Major Dreams, 1997; (co-author) Philadelphia: A New Urban Direction, 1999; Is This Heaven? The Magic of the Field of Dreams, 2002. Contributor to periodicals. **Address:** National Education Technology Funding Corp., 1201 16th St. NW, Ste. 610, Washington, DC 20036-3290, U.S.A. **Online address:** brett@libertynet.org

MANDEL, Charlotte. American (born United States), b. 1925. **Genres:** Poetry, Novellas/Short Stories. **Career:** Saturday Press Inc., Eileen W. Barnes Award Competition, editor and founder, 1981-92; Barnard College, Center for Research on Women, teacher of poetry writing, 1997-; Adult School of Montclair, teacher of poetry courses. **Publications:** POEMS: A Disc of Clear Water, 1981; Doll, 1986; The Life of Mary (poem-novella), 1988; Keeping Him Alive, 1990; The Marriages of Jacob (poem-novella), 1991; Sight Lines, 1998; Rock Vein Sky, 2008; Garden Dialogues, forthcoming. EDITOR: (with R. Hadas and M. Silverman) Saturday's Women: Eileen W. Barnes Award Anthology, 1982. Works appear in anthologies. Contributor of articles to periodicals. **Address:** Saturday Press Inc., PO Box 43534, Upper Montclair, NJ 07043, U.S.A. **Online address:** charmandel@aol.com

MANDEL, Emily St. John. American/Canadian (born Canada), b. 1979?. **Genres:** Novels. **Career:** Administrator and writer. **Publications:** NOVELS: Last Night in Montreal, 2009; The Singer's Gun, 2010. **Address:** c/o Katherine Fausset, Curtis Brown Ltd., 10 Astor Pl., New York, NY 10003, U.S.A. **Online address:** emilymandel@gmail.com

MANDEL, Miriam B. Israeli/Puerto Rican (born Puerto Rico), b. 1942. **Genres:** Literary Criticism And History. **Career:** Rutgers University, Graduate School of Education, editorial assistant, 1968-71; Douglass College, faculty; Clemson University, faculty; Tel Aviv University, senior lecturer in English. Writer. **Publications:** Reading Hemingway: The Facts in the Fictions, 1995, rev. ed., 2001; Hemingway's Death in the Afternoon: The Complete Annotations, 2002; (ed.) Companion to Hemingway's Death in the Afternoon, 2004; Madrid: Espasa-Calpe, 2005; Hemingway's The Dangerous Summer: The Complete Annotations, 2008; (ed.) Hemingway and Africa, 2011. Contributor to books and periodicals. **Address:** Department of English and American Studies, Tel Aviv University, 118 Rosenberg Bldg., PO Box 39040, Tel Aviv, 69978, Israel. **Online address:** mbmandel@post.tau.ac.il

MANDEL, Naomi. American (born United States), b. 1969. **Genres:** Young Adult Fiction. **Career:** University of Rhode Island, assistant professor of English, 2000-, associate professor of English and comparative literature, 2006-, teaching assistant program administrator and supervisor of literature TAs,

2001-05, Comparative Literature Program, interim director, 2008, director of graduate studies, 2010-; Journal for Mundane Behavior, co-founder; University of Rhode Island-Feinstein Campus, coordinator of English, 2007-09; Hebrew University, Halbert Centre for Canadian Studies, visiting professor, 2010. Writer. **Publications:** (Ed. with A.P. Durand) Novels of the Contemporary Extreme, 2006; Against the Unspeakable: Complicity, the Holocaust, and Slavery in America, 2006; (ed.) Bret Easton Ellis: American Psycho, Glamorama, and Lunar Park, 2011. **Address:** Department of English, University of Rhode Island, 185D Swan Hall, 60 Upper College Rd., Kingston, RI 02881, U.S.A. **Online address:** mandel@uri.edu

MANDEL, Oscar. American/Belgian (born Belgium), b. 1926. **Genres:** Novellas/Short Stories, Plays/Screenplays, Poetry, Art/Art History, Literary Criticism And History, Essays, Translations, Social Sciences, Social Sciences. **Career:** University of Amsterdam, Fulbright lecturer, 1960-61; California Institute of Technology, visiting associate professor of English, 1961-62, associate professor, 1962-68, professor, 1968-80, professor of literature, 1980-2003, professor emeritus, 2003-. Writer. **Publications:** A Definition of Tragedy, 1961; Chi Po and The Sorcerer, 1964; The Gobble-Up Stories, 1967; The Collected Plays, 2 vols., 1970-72; Simplicities (poetry), 1974; The Patriots of Nantucket: A Romantic Comedy of the American Revolution, 1975; Molière's Amphitryon, in a Licentious Translation, 1976; Philoctetes and the Fall of Troy: Plays, Documents, Iconography, Interpretations: Including Versions by Sophocles, André Gide, Oscar Mandel, and Heiner Müller, 1981; Annotations to Vanity Fair, 1981; Collected Lyrics and Epigrams, 1981; Definition of Tragedy, 1982; Ariadne and French Classical Tragedy, 1982; The Book of Elaborations: Essays, 1985; The Kukkurrik Fables: 43 Mini-Plays for all Media, 1987, 2nd rev. ed., 2004; Sigismund, Prince of Poland: A Baroque Entertainment, 1988; August von Kotzebue: The Comedy, the Man: Including The Good Citizens of Piffelheim, translated from Die deutscher Kleinstädter, 1990; The Virgin and the Unicorn: Four Plays, 1993; The Art of Alessandro Magnasco: An Essay in the Recovery of Meaning, 1994; The Cheerfulness of Dutch Art, 1996; Two Romantic Comedies: The Spaniards in Denmark and The Rebels of Nantucket, 1996; Fundamentals of the Art of Poetry, 1997; Prosper Merimee: Plays on Hispanic Themes, 2003; Le Pigeon qui etait fou (fables), 2003; Chi Po et le Sorcier (novel); Where is the Light?: Poems, 1955-2005, 2006. EDITOR AND TRANSLATOR: The Theatre of Don Juan: A Collection of Plays and Views (1630-1963), 1963; Seven Comedies of Marivaux, 1968; Five Comedies of Medieval France, 1970; Three Classic Don Juan Plays, 1971; The Land of Upside Down, 1978. Contributor to periodicals. **Address:** Division of Humanities & Social Sciences, California Institute of Technology, MC 228-77, 1200 E California Blvd., Pasadena, CA 91125, U.S.A. **Online address:** om@hss.caltech.edu

MANDEL, Peter (Bevan). American (born United States), b. 1957. **Genres:** Children's Fiction, Young Adult Fiction, Animals/Pets, Sports/Fitness, Travel/Exploration, Humor/Satire, Picture/Board Books. **Career:** Bryant College, assistant to president; Providence Journal-Bulletin, children's book review columnist. **Publications:** PICTURE BOOKS: Red Cat, White Cat, 1994; Say Hey! A Song of Willie Mays, 2000; Planes at the Airport, 2004; Boats on the River, 2004; Bun, Onion, Burger, 2009. NOVELS FOR YOUNG PEOPLE: Haunted House Mystery, 1986; Revenge of the Ghosts, 1986; Cry of the Wolf, 1987; Whisper's Secret Dream, 1987; My Ocean Liner: Across the North Atlantic on the Great Ship Normandie, 2000; Zoo Ah-choooo, 2011. HUMOR FOR ADULTS: The Official Cat I.Q. Test, 1991; The Cat Dictionary, 1994; The Official Dog I.Q. Test, 1995. OTHER: If One Lived on the Equator (poetry), 1993. Contributor to periodicals. **Address:** 239 Transit St., Providence, RI 02906, U.S.A. **Online address:** pbmandel@cox.net

MANDEL, Robert. American (born United States), b. 1949. **Genres:** International Relations/Current Affairs, Military/Defense/Arms Control, Civil Liberties/Human Rights, Social Sciences. **Career:** Central Intelligence Agency, intern, 1974-75; Lewis & Clark College, College of Arts and Sciences, Department of International Affairs, assistant professor of international affairs, 1976-82, associate professor of international affairs, 1982-88, professor of international affairs, 1988-, chair of international affairs, 1994-, Social Sciences Division, dean, 1990-92; Atlantic Council, academic associate, 1985. Writer and social scientist. **Publications:** Irrationality in International Confrontation, 1987; Conflict over the World's Resources: Background, Trends, Case Studies, and Considerations for the Future, 1988; The Changing Face of National Security: A Conceptual Analysis, 1994; Deadly Transfers and the Global Playground: Transnational Security Threats in a Disorderly World, 1999; Armies without States: The Privatization of Security, 2002; Security, Strategy, and the Quest for Bloodless War, 2004; The Meaning of Military Victory, 2006; Global Threat: Target-centered Assessment and Management, 2008; Dark Logic: Transnational Criminal Tactics and Global Security, 2011. **Address:** Department of International Affairs, Lewis & Clark College, Rm. 304, John R. Howard Hall, 0615 SW Palatine Hill Rd., Portland, OR 97219-7879, U.S.A. **Online address:** mandel@lclark.edu

MANDEL, Ruth Ellen. British (born England), b. 1955?. **Genres:** Politics/Government, Anthropology/Ethnology. **Career:** University College London, lecturer in anthropology. Writer. **Publications:** We Called for Manpower, but People Came Instead: The Foreign Problem and Turkish Guestworkers, 1988. (ed. with C. Humphrey) Markets and Moralities: Ethnographies of Postsocialism, 2002; Cosmopolitan Anxieties: Turkish Challenges to Citizenship and Belonging in Germany, 2008. Contributor to periodicals. **Address:** England. **Online address:** r.mandel@ucl.ac.uk

MANDELA, Nelson (Rolihlahla). South African (born South Africa), b. 1918. **Genres:** Civil Liberties/Human Rights, Race Relations, Autobiography/Memoirs, Biography. **Career:** African National Congress, deputy president, 1944-; Mandela and Tambo (law firm), partner, 1952-60; ANCs armed wing, leader, 1961; Congress Youth League, secretary and president; Umkonto we Sizwe African National Congress, elected president, 1991-; president of South Africa, 1994-99; Johannesburg law firm, clerk; Umkhonto we Sizwe, co-founder; Sabotage Campaigns, coordinator; SOS Children's Villages, vocal supporter. Writer. **Publications:** We Accuse: The Trial of Nelson Mandela, 1963; No Easy Walk to Freedom: Articles, Speeches, and Trial Addresses, 1965, rev. ed., 1973; Net legkogoputi k svobode, 1968; I Am Prepared to Die, 3rd ed., 1970; Nelson Mandela Speaks: Speeches, Statements, and Articles, 1970; Struggle is My Life, 1978, rev. ed. as Struggle is My Life: His Speeches and Writings Brought Together with Historical Documents and Accounts of Mandela in Prison by Fellow Prisoners, 1986, 3rd ed., 1990; Apartheid, 1985; Pour Nelson Mandela, 1986; Nelson Mandela: Biographisches Portrait mitSelbstzeugnissen, 1986; For Nelson Mandela, 1987; In the Prison of His Days, 1988, 3rd ed., 1990; Nelson Mandela, Symbol of Resistance and Hope for a Free South Africa: Selected Speeches Since His Release, 1990; Unser Weg in die Freiheit: Reden and Schriften, 1990; Walk the Last Mile with Us, 1990; Année Mandela, 1990; Mandela Through the Eyes of Harlem, 1990; Wij denken niet in kleur: Het Zuid-Afrika Van Nelson Mandela, 1990; Intensifiquemos la lucha: discursos en Africa, Europa y Norteamérica, 1990; Nelson Mandela, Speeches 1990: Intensify the Struggle to Abolish Apartheid, 1990; Mandela Document: The Full Text of the Document Presented by Nelson Mandela to PW Botha in July, 1989, 1990; Moyers-Beyond Hate, 1991; (with F. Castro) How Far We Slaves Have Come!: South Africa and Cuba in Today's World, 1991; (with F. Castro) Qué lejos hemos llegado losesclavos!, 1991; (contrib.) India's Message of Peace, 1992; Nelson Mandela Speaks: Forging a Democratic, Nonracial South Africa, 1993; Voices from Robben Island, 1994; Better Life for All: Working Together for Jobs, Peace, and Freedom, 1994; Long Walk to Freedom: The Autobiography of Nelson Mandela, 1994; Time to Build, 1994; Building a New South Africa, 1995; Address by President Nelson Mandela to the 49th ANC National Conference, 17 December 1994, Bloemfontein, 1995; (foreword) United Nations and Apartheid, 1996; Mandela: An Illustrated Autobiography, 1996; Robben Island-the Reunion, 1996; Truth and Reconciliation Special Reports, 1996-1998, 1997; Essential Nelson Mandela, 1997; South and Southern Africa into the Next Century, 1997; In the Words of Nelson Mandela, 1998; Building has Begun!: Government's Report to the Nation, 1998; Long Walk to Freedom with Connections: The Autobiography of Nelson Mandela, 2000; Nelson Mandela: Words of Wisdom: Selected Quotes, 2000; Letters to Madiba: Voices of South African Children, 2002; Madiba Magic: Nelson Mandela's Favorite Stories for Children, 2002; Nelson Mandela's Favorite African Folktales, 2002; Reflections in Prison: Voices from the South African Liberation Struggle, 2002; In His Own Words, 2003; Nelson Mandela: From Freedom to the Future, 2003; (ed.) Favorite African Folktales, 2004; Our History is Still Being Written: The Story of Three Chinese-Cuban Generals in the Cuban Revolution, 2005; (preface) Prisoner in the Garden: The Nelson Mandela Foundation, 2006; Mandela's Way: Fifteen Lessons On Life, Love and Courage, 2009; (contrib.) Nelson Mandela: A Life In Photographs, 2009; Selected Speeches and Writings of Nelson Mandela: The End of Apartheid in South Africa, 2010; (contrib.) Let Freedom Reign: The Words of Nelson Mandela, 2010; (contrib.) In the Words of Nelson Mandela: A Little Pocketbook, 2010; Conversations With Myself, 2010. **Address:** Houghton, PO Box 70000, Gauteng, 8000, South Africa.

MANDELBAUM, W. (W. Adam Mandelbaum). American (born United States) **Genres:** Military/Defense/Arms Control. **Career:** Stevenson Academy, writing instructor; Suffolk Community College, faculty; New York Institute of Technology, lecturer; attorney, information security consultant, U.S. intelligence agent and author. **Publications:** (As W. Adam Mandelbaum) The Psychic Battlefield: A History of the Military-Occult Complex, 2000. Contributor to periodicals. **Address:** 62 South St., Ste. 203, Oyster Bay, NY 11771, U.S.A. **Online address:** nylawman@justice.com

MANDELBAUM, W. Adam. *See* **MANDELBAUM, W.**

MANDELES, Mark D. American (born United States), b. 1950. **Genres:** Military/Defense/Arms Control, Air/Space Topics, History. **Career:** United States Air Force, dissertation fellow, 1982; Office of the Secretary of Defense, Office of Net Assessment, director; J. de Bloch Group, president, 1993-; American Military University, professor of security studies; Air Force's Gulf War Air Power Survey, secretary; Institute for Defense Analyses, secretary; Center for Naval Analyses, secretary; U.S. General Accounting Office, secretary; Office of Chief of Engineers, secretary; Center for Air Force History, secretary; Science Applications International Corp., secretary; OC Inc., secretary; ANSER Institute, secretary; Delex Systems, secretary. Writer and consultant. **Publications:** (With T.C. Hone and S.S. Terry) Managing Command and Control in the Persian Gulf War, 1996; The Development of the B- 52 and Jet Propulsion: A Case Study in Organizational Innovation, 1998; (with T.C. Hone and N. Friedman) American & British Aircraft Carrier Development, 1919-1941, 1999; The Future of War: Organizations as Weapons, 2005; Military Transformation Past and Present: Historical Lessons for the 21st Century, 2007. Contributor to periodicals and journals. **Address:** J. de Bloch Group, 8910 Autumn Leaf Ct., Fairfax, VA 22031-3218, U.S.A.

MANDELKER, Amy. American (born United States), b. 1953. **Genres:** Literary Criticism And History, Essays, Humanities. **Career:** University of California, visiting assistant professor of Russian, 1983-84; University of Southern California, visiting assistant professor of Russian, 1986-87; City University of New York, Hunter College, visiting assistant professor of Russian, 1986-87, Graduate Center, assistant professor and deputy executive officer, 1987-93, associate professor of comparative literature, 1993-. Writer. **Publications:** (Ed. with R. Reeder) The Supernatural in Slavic and Baltic Literature: Essays in Honor of Victor Terras, 1988; Framing Anna Karenina: Tolstoy, the Woman Question, and the Victorian Novel, 1993; (ed.) Bakhtin in Contexts: Across the Disciplines, 1995; (ed.) Tolstoy's Kreutzer Sonata: An AATSEEL Study Guide, 1996; (ed. with E. Powers) Pilgrim Souls: An Anthology of Spiritual Autobiographies, 1999; (ed. with L. Knapp) Approaches to Teaching Tolstoy's Anna Karenina, 2003; (ed. and intro.) War and Peace, 2010. Contributor of articles to books and journals. **Address:** Department of Comparative Literature, Graduate Ctr., City University of New York, 365 5th Ave., New York, NY 10016-4309, U.S.A. **Online address:** amandelker@aol.com

MANDELMAN, Avner. Canadian/Israeli (born Israel), b. 1947. **Genres:** Novellas/Short Stories, Young Adult Fiction, Novels. **Career:** Giraffe Capital Corp., president and chief executive officer, 1999-. Writer. **Publications:** Talking to the Enemy (Short Stories), 1998; Cuckoo, 2003; The Sleuth Investor: Uncover the Best Stocks Before They Make Their Move, 2007; Debba: A Novel, 2010; The Undertaker, forthcoming. Works appear in anthologies. Contributor to periodicals. **Address:** Giraffe Capital Corp., 4100 Yonge St., Ste. 504, Toronto, ON M2P 2G2, Canada. **Online address:** amandelman@giraffecapital.com

MANDLE, Jay R. American (born United States), b. 1941. **Genres:** Economics, Politics/Government. **Career:** Temple University, instructor; University of the West Indies, instructor; Nankai University (People's Republic of China), instructor; University of California, instructor; Bryn Mawr College, instructor; Swarthmore College, instructor; Lincoln University, instructor; University of Guyana, instructor; Colgate University, W. Bradford Wiley professor of economics. Writer. **Publications:** The Plantation Economy: Population and Economic Change in Guyana, 1838-1960, 1973; The Roots of Black Poverty: The Southern Plantation Economy after the Civil War, 1978; Patterns of Caribbean Development: An Interpretive Essay on Economic Change, 1982; Big Revolution, Small Country: The Rise and Fall of the Grenada Revolution, 1985; (with J.D. Mandle) Grass Roots Commitment: Basketball and Society in Trinidad and Tobago, 1988; (with L.A. Ferleger) No Pain, No Gain: Taxes, Productivity, and Economic Growth, 1992; Not Slave, Not Free: The African American Economic Experience since the Civil War, 1992; (with J.D. Mandle) Caribbean Hoops: The Development of West Indian Basketball, 1994; (with L.A. Ferleger) A New Mandate: Democratic Choices for a Prosperous Economy, 1994; Persistent Underdevelopment: Change and Economic Modernization in the West Indies, 1996; Globalization and the Poor, 2003; Democracy, America, and the Age of Globalization, 2008; Creating Political Equality: American Elections as a Public Good, 2010. Contributor of articles to books and journals. **Address:** Hamilton, NY , U.S.A. **Online address:** jmandle@colgate.edu

MANDLER, Peter. American (born United States), b. 1958. **Genres:** Adult Non-fiction, History, Politics/Government, Essays. **Career:** Princeton University, assistant professor of history, 1984-91; London Guildhall University, senior lecturer, 1991-95, reader, 1995-97, professor of modern history, 1997-; University of Cambridge, lecturer in modern British history, Gonville and Caius College, reader in modern British history, 2004-, Bailey College lecturer in history, academic staff, fellow, professor of modern cultural history. Writer. **Publications:** Aristocratic Government in the Age of Reform: Whigs and Liberals, 1830-1852, 1990; (ed.) The Uses of Charity: The Poor on Relief in the Nineteenth Century Metropolis, 1990; (ed. with S. Pedersen) After the Victorians: Private Conscience and Public Duty in Modern Britain: Essays in Memory of John Clive, 1994; The Fall and Rise of the Stately Home, 1997; History and National Life, 2002; (ed.) Liberty and Authority in Victorian Britain, 2006; The English National Character: The History of an Idea From Edmund Burke to Tony Blair, 2006. **Address:** Gonville and Caius College, University of Cambridge, Trinity St., Old Castle St., Cambridge, CB CB2 1TA, England. **Online address:** pm297@cam.ac.uk

MANEA, Norman. American/Romanian (born Romania), b. 1936. **Genres:** Novels, Novellas/Short Stories, Essays. **Career:** Institute for the Management and Conservation of Water, engineer, 1969-74; Bard College, international academy fellow, 1989-92, Frances Flournoy Professor of European Studies and Culture, writer-in-residence, 1992-. **Publications:** Noaptea pe latura lunga, 1969; Captivi, 1970; Atrium (novel), 1974; Primele porti, 1975; Cartea Fiului, 1976; Zilele si jocul, 1977; Anii de ucenicie ai lui August Prostul, 1979, 2nd ed., 2005; Octombrie, ora opt (fiction), 1981; Pe contur (title means: 'On the Contour'), 1984; Plicul Negru (novel), 1986; Roboterbiographie, 1987; Leergeld, 1989; Fericirea obligatorie, 1989; Fenster zur Arbeiterklasse, 1989; Le the de Proust, 1990; Der Trenchcoat, 1990; Training fur's Paradies, 1990; Le bonheur obligatoire (stories), 1991; El impermeable, 1991; On Clowns: The Dictator and the Artist (essays), 1992; October, Eight o'clock, 1992; Trennwand, 1992; Het verhoor, 1992; Compulsory Happiness, 1993, 2nd. ed. as Obligatory Happiness, 2005; The Black Envelope, 1995, 4th ed., 2004; Despre Clovni: Dictatorul Si Artistul, 1997; Den svarte konvoluten, 1999; Casa Melcului: Dialoguri, 1999; La busta nera, 2000; El Sobre nero, 2001; Întoarcerea huliganului, 2003; The Hooligan's Return (memoir), 2003, 2nd ed. 2006; Envelopes and Portraits, 2004; Anii de ucenicie ai lui August Prostul, 2005; Vizuina: Roman, 2009; Curierul de Est: dialog cu Edward Kanterian, 2010; (ed. with Sanda Cordoş) Romanian Writers on Writing, 2011. Contributor to periodicals. **Address:** Bard College, 30 Campus Rd., PO Box 5000, Annandale on Hudson, NY 12504-5000, U.S.A. **Online address:** manea@bard.edu

MANENT, Pierre. French (born France), b. 1949. **Genres:** Politics/Government. **Career:** Commentaire (political journal), editor, 1978-; Ecole des Hautes Etudes en Sciences Sociales, Centre de recherches politiques raymond aron, director; Boston College, Department of Political Science, visiting professor, associate professor. Writer. **Publications:** NONFICTION: Naissances de La Politique Moderne, 1977; Tocqueville et Lanature de la Democratie, 1982, trans. as Tocqueville and the Nature of Democracy, 1996; (co-author) European Liberty: Four Essays on Occasion of the 25th Anniversary of the Erasmus Prize Foundation, 1983; (ed.) Les Libéraux, 1986; Histoire Intellectuelle du Liberalisme: Dixlecons, 1987, trans. as An Intellectual History of Liberalism, 1994; La Cité de L'homme, 1994, trans. as The City of Man, 1998; De Gaulle: Statesmanship, Grandeur and Modern Democracy, 1996; Modern Liberty and Its Discontents, 1998; (foreword) Privilege and Liberty and Other Essays in Political Philosophy, 1999; Cours Familier de Philosophie Politique, 2001, trans. as World Beyond Politics?: A Defense of the Nation-State, 2006; (with A. Jacquard) Une Education Sans Autorite ni Sanction, 2003; La Raison Des Nations: Réflexions Sur La Démocratie En Europe, 2006; Democracy Without Nations?: The Fate of Self-Government in Europe, 2007; Le Regard Politique, 2010; Les Métamorphoses de la cité, 2010. Contributor to periodicals. **Address:** école des hautes études en sciences, sociales,

Centre de Recherches Politiques Raymond Aron, 105 Blvd. Raspail, 190-198 Ave. de France, Paris, 75244, France. **Online address:** crpra@ehess.fr

MANER, Martin. American (born United States), b. 1946. **Genres:** Literary Criticism And History, Music, Humor/Satire. **Career:** University of Virginia, lecturer in English, 1975-76; Wright State University, Department of English Language and Literatures, assistant professor, 1976-81, associate professor, 1981-89, professor, 1989-, now professor emeritus of English literature. Writer. **Publications:** The Philosophical Biographer: Doubt and Dialectic in Johnson's Lives of the Poets, 1988; The Spiral Guide to Research Writing, 1996; The Research Process, 2000. Contributor of journals. **Address:** Department of English Language & Literatures, Wright State University, 470 Millett Hall, Dayton, OH 45435, U.S.A. **Online address:** martin.maner@wright.edu

MANETTI, Larry. American (born United States), b. 1947. **Genres:** Autobiography/Memoirs, Biography, Essays. **Career:** Writer, actor and producer. **Publications:** (With C. Silverman) Aloha Magnum: Larry Manetti's Magnum, P.I. Memories, 1999. **Address:** c/o Richard Sindell, Waters & Nicolosi Inc., 9301 Wilshire Blvd., Ste. 300, Beverly Hills, CA 90210-6119, U.S.A. **Online address:** info@larrymanetti.com

MANGAN, Jane E. (Jane Erin Mangan). American (born United States), b. 1969. **Genres:** Natural History, Economics, Business/Trade/Industry. **Career:** Harvard University, assistant professor of history, 2000-03, associate professor of history, 2004; Davidson College, assistant professor of history, 2004-07, Malcolm Overstreet Partin Assistant Professor, 2007-. Writer and academic. **Publications:** (ed.) Natural and Moral History of the Indies, 2002; Trading Roles: Gender, Ethnicity, and the Urban Economy in Colonial Potosi, 2005. Contributor to periodicals and journals. **Address:** Department of History, Davidson College, PO Box 6990, Davidson, NC 28035-6990, U.S.A. **Online address:** jamangan@davidson.edu

MANGAN, Jane Erin. *See* **MANGAN, Jane E.**

MANGINI (GONZALEZ), Shirley. American (born United States), b. 1946. **Genres:** Literary Criticism And History. **Career:** University of New Mexico, instructor in Spanish, 1978-79, co-director of summer program in Madrid, 1979; Yale University, assistant professor, 1979-84, associate professor of Spanish, 1984-87, Davenport College, resident fellow, 1983-84; California State University, Department of Spanish and Portuguese, head, 1987-92, professor of Spanish, 1987-2004, graduate advisor, College of Liberal Arts, associate dean, 1992-93, Center for the Humanities, director, 1992-, professor emeritus, 2004-; Middlebury College, visiting professor, 1987; Rutgers University, Rutgers Center for Historical Analysis, visiting fellow, 1993. Writer. **Publications:** Gil de Biedma (in Spanish), 1979, 3rd ed., 1993; Rojos y rebeldes: La cultura de la disidencia durante el franquismo, 1987; Memories of Resistance: Women's Voices From the Spanish Civil War, 1995; Las Modernas de Madrid: Las Grandes Intelectuales Españolas de la Vanguardia, 2001; Maruja Mallo and the Spanish Avant-garde, 2010. EDITOR: Jaime Gil de Biedma, 1980; Antologia Poetica, 1981; Estacion: Ida y vuelta (critical edition), 1989. Contributor of articles to books and journals. **Address:** Department of Romance German & Russian Language, California State University, 1250 Bellflower Blvd., Long Beach, CA 90840, U.S.A. **Online address:** samg@csulb.edu

MANGO, Karin N. Lithuanian (born Lithuania), b. 1936. **Genres:** Children's Fiction, Young Adult Fiction, Children's Non-fiction, Local History/Rural Topics, Medicine/Health, Biography, Regional/Urban Planning, Young Adult Non-fiction, Young Adult Non-fiction. **Career:** George G. Harrap and Company Ltd., Education Department, assistant head, 1958-60; McGraw-Hill Book Co., education correspondent, 1960; Long Island Historical Society, part-time librarian, researcher, 1975-79; R.R. Bowker Co., freelance copy editor, proofreader, 1979-82; Suzanne Pathy Speak-Up Institute, staff writer, 1981-86; freelance writer, 1986-; League for the Hard of Hearing, librarian, 1990-96; Advocates for Better Communication, librarian, 1996-. **Publications:** Cantering Through, 1951; The Children's Book of Russian Folktales, 1961; The Children's St. Francis, 1963; New York Holiday, 1971; Armor: Yesterday and Today, 1980; A Various Journey, 1983; Map Making, 1984; Somewhere Green, 1987; Codes, Ciphers and Other Secrets, 1988; Just for the Summer, 1990; Hearing Loss, 1991; Portrait of Miranda, 1993. EDITOR: Long Island Printing, 1791-1830: A Checklist of Imprints, 1979; Calendar of Manuscripts of the Revolutionary Period, 1980; (with P.B. Glick) Communication Access: Everyone's Right, 1995; A. Romoff, Hear Again: Return to Life with a Cochlear Implant, 2000; C.N. Roth, Coping with Emergencies When You Have a Hearing Loss, 2003. Contributor to books and anthologies. **Address:** 83 Hillside Ave., Mount Kisco, NY 10549-1328, U.S.A. **Online address:** kmango@earthlink.net

MANGOLD, James. American (born United States), b. 1963. **Genres:** Plays/Screenplays, Film. **Career:** Walt Disney Productions, writer and director, 1985-89; screenwriter and director, 1989-. **Publications:** Heavy, 1996; Cop Land, 1997; (with L. Loomer and A.H. Phelan) Girl, Interrupted, 2000. **Address:** c/o Joanne Roberts, Susan Smith & Associates, 121-A N San Vicente Blvd., Beverly Hills, CA 90211, U.S.A.

MANHEIM, Jarol B(ruce). American (born United States), b. 1946. **Genres:** Politics/Government, Communications/Media, Organized Labor. **Career:** City College, assistant professor of political science, 1971-75; Virginia Polytechnic Institute and State University, associate professor of political science, 1975-87; George Washington University, professor of media and public affairs and political science, 1987-; School of Media and Public Affairs, founding director, 1990-96. Writer. **Publications:** (Ed.) Annual Editions Readings in American Government 1974; (with M. Wallace) Political Violence in the United States 1875-1974: A Bibliography, 1975; Deja Vu: American Political Problems in Historical Perspective, 1976; (with R.C. Rich, L. Willnat and C.L. Brians) Empirical Political Analysis, 1980, 8th ed., 2011; American Politics Yearbook, 1982; (with A. Ondrasik) Data Map: Index of Published Tables of Statistical Data, 1983, 4th ed., 1988; All of the People, All the Time, 1991; Strategic Public Diplomacy and American Foreign Policy: The Evolution of Influence, 1994; The Death of a Thousand Cuts: Corporate Campaigns and the Attack on the Corporation, 2000; Biz-War and the Out-of-Power Elite: The Progressive-Left Attack on the Corporation, 2004; Strategy in Information and Influence Campaigns, 2011. **Address:** School of Media & Public Affairs, George Washington University, Media & Public Affairs, Ste. 400, 805 21st St. NW, Washington, DC 20052, U.S.A. **Online address:** jarolb@gwu.edu

MANHEIN, Mary H(uffman). American (born United States) **Genres:** Autobiography/Memoirs, Medicine/Health, Social Sciences, Biography, Anthropology/Ethnology. **Career:** Louisiana State University, instructor in anthropology, forensic anthropologist, Forensic Anthropology and Computer Enhancement Services (FACES), director, Louisiana Repository for Unidentified and Missing Persons Information Database, director; City of Baton Rouge, deputy coroner for East Baton Rouge Parish. Writer. **Publications:** The Bone Lady: Life as a Forensic Anthropologist (memoir), 1999; Trail of Bones: More Cases From the Files of a Forensic Anthropologist, 2005. Contributor to books. **Address:** Department of Geography and Anthropology, Louisiana State University, 227 Howe-Russell Geoscience Complex, Baton Rouge, LA 70803-0001, U.S.A. **Online address:** gaman@lsu.edu

MANHIRE, Bill. New Zealander (born New Zealand), b. 1946. **Genres:** Novels, Novellas/Short Stories, Poetry, Literary Criticism And History. **Career:** Amphedesma Press, editor, 1971-75; Victoria University, lecturer, 1973-78, senior lecturer in English, 1978-88, reader in English, 1988-97, professor of english and creative writing, 1997-, International Institute of Modern Letters, director, Victoria University Press, fiction editor. **Publications:** Malady, 1970; The Elaboration, 1972; Song Circle, 1975; How to Take Off Your Clothes at the Picnic, 1977; Dawn/Water, 1979; Zoetropes, 1981; Good Looks, 1982; Locating the Beloved and Other Stories, 1983; Zoetropes: Poems 1972-82, 1984; Maurice Gee, 1986; The Brain of Katherine Mansfield, 1988; The New Land: A Picture Book, 1990; The Old Man's Example, 1990; Milky Way Bar, 1991; An Amazing Week in New Zealand, 1993; South Pacific, 1994; Fault, 1995; Hoosh, 1995; My Sunshine, 1996; Sheet Music, 1996; Songs of My Life, 1996; What to Call Your Child, 1999; Doubtful Sounds Essays and Interviews, 2000; Collected Poems, 2001; Under the Influence, 2003; Lifted, 2007; The Victims of Lightning, 2010. EDITOR: New Zealand Universities Arts Festival Yearbook 1969, 1969; New Zealand Listener Short Stories, 1977, vol. II, 1978; (with M. McLeod) Some Other Country: New Zealand's Best Short Stories, 1984; 3rd ed., 1997; Six by Six, 1989; Soho Square IV, 1992; 100 New Zealand Poems, 1993; Denis Glover: Selected Poems, 1995; Mutes & Earthquakes, 1997; (with M. McLeod) The New Zealand Short Story Collection, 1997; (with K. Anderson) Spectacular Babies, 2001; Wide White Page: Writers Imagine Antarctica, 2004; 121 New Zealand Poems, 2005; (with P. Callaghan) Are Angels OK?: The Parallel Universes of New Zealand Writers and Scientists, 2006; (with D. Wilkins) The Best of Best New Zealand Poems, 2011; (with K. Duncum, C. Price and D. Wilkins)

The Exercise Book, 2011. Contributor to periodicals. **Address:** International Institute of Modern Letters, Victoria University, Rm. 302, 16 Waiteata Rd., Kelburn Campus, PO Box 600, Wellington, 6012, New Zealand. **Online address:** bill.manhire@vuw.ac.nz

MANIA, Cathy. American (born United States), b. 1950. **Genres:** Environmental Sciences/Ecology, Children's Fiction. **Career:** Mathematics teacher, 1971-78; Alice Lloyd College, instructor in mathematics, 1979-86; Lexington Community College, adjunct professor of mathematics; Kentucky State University, instructor of mathematics, 2003, adjunct professor of mathematics, assistant professor of mathematics. Writer. **Publications:** (With R. Mania) A Forest's Life: From Meadow to Mature Woodland, 1997; (with R.C. Mania Jr.) Woodpecker in the Backyard, 2000. **Address:** Department of Mathematics, Kentucky State University, Rm. 109 Carver Hall, 400 E Main St., Frankfort, KY 40601, U.S.A. **Online address:** cathy.mania@kysu.edu

MANIA, Robert (C.). American (born United States), b. 1952. **Genres:** Environmental Sciences/Ecology, Animals/Pets. **Career:** Alice Lloyd College, associate professor of physics, 1980-86; Kentucky State University, professor of physics, 1986-. Writer. **Publications:** (With C. Mania) A Forest's Life: From Meadow to Mature Woodland, 1997; (with C. Mania) Woodpecker in the Backyard, 2000. **Address:** Kentucky State University, 109 Carver Hall, 400 E Main St., Frankfort, KY 40601, U.S.A. **Online address:** robert.mania@kysu.edu

MANICKA, Rani. American/Malaysian (born Malaysia) **Genres:** Novels, Literary Criticism And History, Young Adult Fiction. **Career:** Businessperson and writer. **Publications:** The Rice Mother, 2002; Touching Earth, 2004; The Japanese Lover, 2010. Contributor to periodicals. **Address:** c/o Author Mail, Viking, 375 Hudson St., New York, NY 10014, U.S.A.

MANJOO, Farhad. American (born United States), b. 1978. **Genres:** History. **Career:** Cornell Daily Sun, editor in chief; Wired News, writer; Salon.com, writer; Slate, staff writer, 2008-. **Publications:** True Enough: Learning to Live in a Post-Fact Society, 2008. **Address:** San Francisco, CA , U.S.A. **Online address:** farhad.manjoo@gmail.com

MANLOVE, Colin (Nicholas). British (born England), b. 1942. **Genres:** Literary Criticism And History, History. **Career:** Edinburgh University, lecturer, 1967-84, reader in English literature, 1984-93, retired, 1993. Writer. **Publications:** Modern Fantasy: Five Studies, 1975; Literature and Reality 1600-1800, 1978; The Gap in Shakespeare: The Motif of Division from Richard II to The Tempest, 1981; The Impulse of Fantasy Literature, 1983; Science Fiction: Ten Explorations, 1986; C.S. Lewis: His Literary Achievement, 1987; Critical Thinking: A Guide to Interpreting Literary Texts, 1989; Christian Fantasy: From 1200 to the Present, 1992; The Chronicles of Narnia: The Patterning of a Fantastic World, 1993; Scottish Fantasy Literature: A Critical Survey, 1994; (ed.) An Anthology of Scottish Fantasy Literature, 1996; The Fantasy Literature of England, 1999; From Alice to Harry Potter: Children's Fantasy in England, 2003. **Address:** 92 Polwarth Terr., Edinburgh, EH11 1NN, Scotland. **Online address:** colin@manlove.fsnet.co.uk

MANN, (Anthony) Phillip. New Zealander/British (born England), b. 1942. **Genres:** Novels, Science Fiction/Fantasy, Plays/Screenplays, Novellas/Short Stories, Poetry, Young Adult Fiction. **Career:** Humboldt State University, lecturer in drama, 1967-69; Victoria University, lecturer, 1969-75, senior lecturer, 1975-84, associate professor in drama, 1981-, reader in drama, 1984-, personal chair of drama, 1997-, professor, now retired; Xin Hua News Agency, English editor, 1978-80; Downstage Theatre, associate director, 1984-86; New Zealand Drama School, chairperson, 1991-93; University of Central England, visiting fellow in drama, 1995; Instituto Pedagogico Arubana, lecturer in drama, 2005-06. **Publications:** (Contrib.) Eight days a week, 1972; The Magic Hand, 1973; Il Suffit d'un Baton 1976; The Eye of the Queen, 1982; Mozart and Salieri Live on Stage, 1982; The Gospel According to Mickey Mouse 1984; Master of Paxwax, 1986; The Fall of the Families, 1987; Lux in Tenebris, 1987; Pioneers, 1988; An Old Fashioned Story, 1989; The Architect, 1989; Wulfsyarn: A Mosiac, 1990; Tragic Patterns in Shuriken 1991; Confronting History in N.Z. Drama, 1991; The Poverty Trap, 1992; Escape to the Wild Wood, 1993; Stand Alone Stan, 1994; Maestro, The Calendula Melody, 1991, Tales from the Borderland (stories), 1994; The Paradise Notebook (stories), 1994; The Disestablishment of Paradise (stories), 1994; (ed.) Tales from the Out of Time Café, 1995. LAND FIT FOR HEROES SERIES: vol. I: Into the Wild Wood, 1993, vol. II: Stand Alone Stan, 1993, vol. III: The Dragon Wakes, 1995, vol. IV: The Burning Forest, 1995. **Address:** 22 Bruce Ave., Brooklyn, Wellington, 6021, New Zealand. **Online address:** phillip.mann@gmail.com

MANN, Barbara E. American (born United States) **Genres:** Poetry, Popular Culture, History, Politics/Government. **Career:** Princeton University, Center for the Study of Religion, faculty fellow, 1997-2004; Jewish Theological Seminary, associate professor, Simon H. Fabian chairman in Hebrew literature. Writer. **Publications:** Redemption Street (poetry), 1992; A Place in History: Modernism, Tel Aviv and the Creation of Jewish Urban Space, 2006; Space and Place in Jewish Studies, 2011. Contributor to periodicals. **Address:** Jewish Theological Seminary, 602 Unterberg, 3080 Broadway, New York, NY 10027-4650, U.S.A. **Online address:** bamann@jtsa.edu

MANN, Brian. American (born United States), b. 1965?. **Genres:** Politics/Government, Social Sciences. **Career:** Alaska Public Radio, reporter; Paul Smith's College, North Country Public Radio, Adirondack Radio News Bureau, news reporter and bureau chief, 1999-. **Publications:** Welcome to the Homeland: A Journey to the Rural Heart of America's Conservative Revolution, 2006. **Address:** North Country Public Radio, St. Lawrence University, Rm. 201, EJ Noble Medical Bldg., 80 E Main St., Canton, NY 13617, U.S.A. **Online address:** brian@ncpr.org

MANN, Catherine. American (born United States), b. 1943. **Genres:** Novels. **Career:** TEEN, editor to editor-in-chief, 1970-72; KCBS-TV, news reporter, 1973-75; KMSP-TV, co-anchor, 1976; WDIV-TV, co-host of daily shows and television news field reporter, 1977-79; David Sheehan's Hollywood Show, segment producer, 1980-81; P.M. Magazine, Hollywood reporter, 1980-81; Entertainment Tonight, reporter. **Publications:** Tinsel Town, 1985; Rumors, 1988; Capitol Hill, 1992; Renegade, 2010. Contributor to periodicals. **Address:** c/o Pam Bernstein, William Morris Agency, 1350 Ave. of the Americas, New York, NY 10019, U.S.A.

MANN, Charles F. (Charles Frederick Mann). American (born United States), b. 1946. **Genres:** Poetry, Theology/Religion, Autobiography/Memoirs, Biography, Translations, Theology/Religion. **Career:** University of Ottawa, admissions officer, 1966-68; Boston School of Modern Languages, teacher of English and French, 1969-73; Claude Davy Media, television and video translator and interpreter, 1974-80; San Francisco Tutoring Service, director, principal, head teacher, 1981-90; San Francisco Elections Committee, officer, 1985-95; University of California, foreign language tutor, 1991-. Writer. **Publications:** Madeleine Delbrêl: A Life Beyond Boundaries, 1996, 2nd ed., 1998. TRANSLATOR: A World Without Hunger, 1977; J. Jugan, Universe-Media, 1978; P. Raphael, God Behind Bars, 1999; (with D.L. Schindler) M. Delbrel, We, the Ordinary People of the Streets, 2000. Contributor to periodicals. **Address:** 954 Geary St., Apt. 55, San Francisco, CA 94109-7036, U.S.A.

MANN, Charles Frederick. *See* **MANN, Charles F.**

MANN, Emily. (Emily Betsy Mann). American (born United States), b. 1952. **Genres:** Plays/Screenplays, Women's Studies And Issues, Young Adult Fiction. **Career:** Guthrie Theatre, associate director, 1978-79; BAM Theatre Co., resident director, 1981-82; McCarter Theatre Centre for the Performing Arts, artistic director, 1990-. Writer. **Publications:** Still Life: A Documentary, 1982; Nights and Days, 1984; Annulla: An Autobiography, 1985; Execution of Justice, 1986; Having Our Say: The Delany Sisters' First 100 Years, 1996; Testimonies: Four Plays, 1997; The House of Bernarda Alba: A Drama About Women in Villages of Spain, 1999; (adapted) Vishnevyĭ sad, 2000; (ed. with D. Roessel) Political Stages: Plays that Shaped a Century, 2002; Meshugah: A Comic Tragedy, 2004; Mrs. Packard: Inspired by a True Story, 2009. **Address:** McCarter Theatre,, Center for the Performing Arts, 91 University Pl., Princeton, NJ 08540, U.S.A.

MANN, Emily Betsy. *See* **MANN, Emily.**

MANN, James. *See* **HARVEY, John.**

MANN, Jeff(rey A.). American (born United States), b. 1959. **Genres:** Novellas/Short Stories, Poetry, Autobiography/Memoirs, Essays. **Career:** Guitarist and dulcimer player, 1979-83; Pipestem State Park, Recreation Department, staff, 1980, assistant naturalist, 1981; Lambda Environmental Technologies, contract botanist, 1987; West Virginia University, instructor of English, 1987-

89; Virginia Polytechnic Institute and State University, instructor of English, 1989-2003, assistant professor of creative writing, 2003-07, associate professor of creative writing, 2007-. Writer. **Publications:** POETRY: Bliss, 1998; Mountain Fireflies, 2000; Flint Shards from Sussex, 2000; Bones Washed with Wine, 2003; On the Tongue, 2006; Ash: Poems from Norse Mythology, 2011. OTHERS: Edge (essays), 2003; Loving Mountains, Loving Men (memoir and poetry), 2005; A History of Barbed Wire (short fiction), 2006; Binding the God: Ursine Essays from the Mountain South (essays), 2010. Works appear in anthologies. Contributor of articles to journals. **Address:** Department of English, Virginia Polytechnic Institute and State Universit, 210 Shanks Hall, Blacksburg, VA 24061-0112, U.S.A. **Online address:** jeffmann@vt.edu

MANN, Jessica. British (born England), b. 1937?. **Genres:** Mystery/Crime/Suspense, Literary Criticism And History, Adult Non-fiction. **Career:** Journalist, broadcaster and writer. **Publications:** THEA CRAWFORD: The Only Security, 1973; Captive Audience, 1975. TAMARA HOYLAND: Funeral Sites, 1981; No Man's Island, 1983; Grave Goods, 1984; Kind of Healthy Grave, 1986; Death beyond the Nile, 1988; A Faith, Hope and Homicide, 1991. NOVELS: A Charitable End, 1971; Mrs. Knox's Profession, 1972; The Sticking Place, 1974; The Eighth Deadly Sin, 1976; The Sting of Death, 1978; Faith Hope And Homicide, 1991; Telling Only Lies, 1992; A Private Inquiry, 1996; Death by the Mistletoe, 1997; Hanging Fire, 1997; The Survivor's Revenge, 1998; The Survivor's Revenge, 1999; Under a Dark Sun, 2000; Voice from the Grave, 2005; The Mystery Writer, 2006; Godrevy Light, 2009. NON FICTION: Deadlier Than The Male: Crime Writing-The Feminine Touch, 1981; The Out of Harm's Way: The Wartime Evacuation of Children from Britain, 2005. OTHER: Troublecross, 1973. **Address:** c/o Lavinia Trevor, The Glasshouse, 49a Goldhawk Rd., London, GL W12 8QP, England. **Online address:** jessicademann@gmail.com

MANN, John David. American (born United States), b. 1954?. **Genres:** inspirational/Motivational Literature, Business/Trade/Industry. **Career:** Changes Inc., co-founder and teacher, 1971-; East West Journal, editor; Solstice, founder, publisher and editor, 1986-89; Cell Tech, independent contractor, 1986-96; Upline, co-founder and editor, 1990-96; Network Marketing Lifestyles, editor-in-chief, 1999-2001; Networking Times, editor-in-chief, 2002-06; Kushi Institute, teacher. Musician. **Publications:** (Ed.) Energetics of Food, 1990; The Zen of MLM: Legacy, Leadership and the Network Marketing Experience: Essays and Editorials, 1991-2007, 2007; (with B. Burg) The Go-giver: A Little Story about a Powerful Business Idea, 2007; (with C. Johnson) You Call the Shots: Succeed Your Way and Live the Life You Want with the 19 Essential Secrets of Entrepreneurship, 2007; (with M.D. Siljander) A Deadly Misunderstanding: A Congressman's Quest to Bridge the Muslim-Christian Divide, 2008; (with J. Olson and A. Desetta) Success for Teens: Real Teens Talk about Using the Slight Edge, 2008; (with D. Krueger) The Secret Language of Money: How to Make Smarter Financial Decisions and Live a Richer Life, 2009. **Address:** U.S.A. **Online address:** jdm@johndavidmann.com

MANN, Judith (W.). (Judith Walker Mann). American (born United States), b. 1950. **Genres:** Art/Art History, Social Commentary, Adult Non-fiction, Business/Trade/Industry. **Career:** Old Dominion University, adjunct professor, 1986-87; Webster University, adjunct professor of art history, 1987-88; St. Louis Art Museum, curatorial assistant, 1988-91, assistant curator, 1991-97, curator of early European art, 1997-; Washington University, adjunct professor, 1989; University of Missouri in St. Louis, assistant professor, 1991-97; College of William and Mary, lecturer; American University in Paris, lecturer; University of Tulsa, lecturer; Southeast Missouri State University, lecturer. Writer. **Publications:** AS JUDITH WALKER MANN: Guide to Great Inexpensive Asian Restaurants in Portland, San Francisco & Seattle, 1988; Guide to Great Inexpensive Asian Restaurants in Seattle & Puget Sound, 1989; Mann for All Seasons: Wit and Wisdom from the Washington Post's Judy Mann, 1990; Medieval Art in the Collection of the Saint Louis Art Museum, 1992; Difference: Discovering the Hidden Ways We Silence Girls: Finding Alternatives that Can Give Them a Voice, 1994; Baroque into Rococo: Seventeenthand Eighteenth-Century Italian Paintings, 1997; (with K. Christiansen) Orazio and Artemisia Gentileschi: Father and Daughter Painters in Baroque Italy, 2001; (ed.) Artemisia Gentileschi: Taking Stock, 2005; (with. B. Bohn and C. Plazzotta) Federico Barocci: Renaissance Master of Color and Line, 2012. Contributor to books and periodicals. **Address:** St. Louis Art Museum, 1 Fine Arts Dr., Forest Pk., St. Louis, MO 63110-1380, U.S.A. **Online address:** jmann@slam.org

MANN, Judith Walker. *See* **MANN, Judith (W.).**

MANN, Kenny. British/American (born United States), b. 1946. **Genres:** History, Area Studies, Poetry, Children's Non-fiction, Novels. **Career:** Polydor records, public relations manager, 1972-74; Bank Street Publications, editor and writer, 1990-92; Simon and Schuster/Dillon Press, author and picture researcher, 1993-; Marshall-Cavendish Benchmark Books, author, 1998-; Long Island University, professor of writing, Friends World Program, writing program coordinator; Friends World College, writing program, coordinator. Filmmaker and writer. **Publications:** AFRICAN KINGDOMS OF THE PAST SERIES: The Western Sudan: Ghana, Mali, Songhay, 1996; The Guinea Coast: Oyo, Benin, Ashanti, 1996; Kongo Ndongo: West Central Africa, 1996; Zenj, Buganda: East Africa, 1996; Monomotapa, Zululand, Lesotho: Southern Africa, 1996; Egypt, Kush, Aksum: Northeast Africa, 1997. OTHER: I Am Not Afraid! Based on a Masai Folktale, 1993; Yellow Dog Dreaming (fiction), 1995; The Ancient Hebrews, 1998; Isabel and Ferdinand and Fifteenth-Century Spain, 2001. Contributor of articals to periodicals. **Address:** Rafiki Productions, 29 Henry St., PO Box 2789, Sag Harbor, NY 11963, U.S.A. **Online address:** ikimann@earthlink.net

MANN, Pamela. British (born England), b. 1946. **Genres:** Adult Non-fiction, Administration/Management, Law. **Career:** Nottinghamshire County Council Leisure Services/Libraries, senior library assistant, 1983-. Writer. **Publications:** Current Issues in Advising Nonprofit Organizations, 1998. **Address:** 149 Galway Cres., Retford, NH DN22 7YR, England. **Online address:** pamela.mann1@mypostoffice.co.uk

MANN, Paul. *See* **MANN, Paul (James).**

MANN, Paul (James). (Paul Mann). American/British (born England), b. 1947. **Genres:** Novels, Race Relations, Social Sciences, History. **Career:** Freelance journalist, 1963-87; novelist, 1987-. **Publications:** GEORGE SANSI SERIES: Season of the Monsoon: A Novel, 1993; The Ganja Coast, 1995; The Burning Ghats, 1996. NOVELS: The Libyan Contract, 1988; The Beirut Contract, 1989; The Traitor's Contract, 1991; The Britannia Contract, 1993; Great Stories from Mormon History, 1994; The Burning Tide, 1998. Contributor to journals and periodicals. **Address:** c/o Arnold Goodman, Goodman Associates, 500 West End Ave., New York, NY 10024, U.S.A.

MANN, Reva. Israeli/British (born England), b. 1957?. **Genres:** Social Sciences, Autobiography/Memoirs, Sex, Biography. **Career:** Writer and educator. **Publications:** The Rabbi's Daughter (memoir), 2007 as The Rabbi's Daughter: A True Story of Sex, Drugs and Orthodoxy, 2007. Contributor to periodicals. **Address:** c/o Jonny Geller, Curtis Brown Group Ltd., Haymarket House, 28-29 Haymarket, London, GL SW1Y 4SP, England.

MANN, Thomas E. American (born United States), b. 1944. **Genres:** Politics/Government, Social Sciences, Adult Non-fiction. **Career:** University of Michigan Survey Research Center, assistant study director, 1968-69; James G. O'Hara and Senator Philip A. Hart, legislative assistant, 1969-70; Brookings Institution, director of governmental studies, 1987-99, W. Averell Harriman chair, senior fellow in governance studies, 1991-; American Enterprise Institute for Public Policy Research, visiting fellow, co-director, 1979-81; Congressional Quarterly Elections Seminars, lecturer, 1980-; Princeton University, faculty; Johns Hopkins University, faculty; Georgetown University, faculty; University of Virginia, faculty; American University, faculty; International Business Machines, consultant; Public Broadcasting Service, consultant; American Political Science Association, executive director. Writer. **Publications:** Unsafe at Any Margin: Interpreting Congressional Elections, 1978; (ed. with N.J. Ornstein) The New Congress, 1981; (ed. with N.J. Ornstein) The American Elections of 1982, 1983; (ed.) A Question of Balance: The President, the Congress and Foreign Policy, 1990; (with N.J. Ornstein) A First Report of the Renewing Congress Project, 1992; (ed. with G.R. Orren) Media Polls in American Politics, 1992; (with N.J. Ornstein) A Second Report of the Renewing Congress Project, 1993; (ed. with M.K. Jennings) Elections at Home and Abroad, 1994; (ed. with N.J. Ornstein) Congress, the Press and the Public, 1994; (ed. with H.J. Aaron and T. Taylor) Values and Public Policy, 1994; (ed. with N.J. Ornstein) Intensive Care: How Congress Shapes Health Policy, 1995; (ed. with N.J. Ornstein) The Permanent Campaign and Its Future, 2000; (ed. with S. Takeshi) Governance for a New Century: Japanese Challenges, American Experience, 2002; (ed. with A. Corrado and T. Potter) Inside the Campaign Finance Battle: Court Testimony on the New Reforms, 2003; (ed. with B.E. Cain) Party Lines: Competition, Partisanship and Congressional Redistricting, 2005; (with P. Potter, A. Corrado and D.R. Ortiz) The New Campaign Finance Sourcebook, 2005; (with N.J. Ornstein) The Broken Branch: How Congress is Failing America and How to Get It Back on Track, 2006, 2nd ed., 2008; (with N. Ornstein and M. Malbin) Vital Statistics on Congress 2008, 2008. **Address:** Brookings Institution, 1775 Massachusetts Ave. NW, Washington, DC 20036, U.S.A. **Online address:** tmann@brookings.edu

MANN, William J. American (born United States), b. 1972. **Genres:** Film, Novels, Gay And Lesbian Issues, History, Social Commentary, Theatre. **Career:** Writer. **Publications:** NONFICTION: Wisecracker: The Life and Times of William Haines, 1998; Behind the Screen: How Gays and Lesbians Shaped Hollywood, 1910-1969, 2001; Edge of Midnight: The Life of John Schlesinger, 2003; Kate: The Woman Who Was Hepburn, 2006; How To Be a Movie Star: Elizabeth Taylor in Hollywood, 2009. NOVELS: The Men from the Boys, 1997; The Biograph Girl, 2000; Where the Boys Are, 2003; All American Boy, 2005; Object of Desire, 2009. Works appear in anthologies. Contributor to periodicals. **Address:** PO Box 505, Provincetown, MA 02657, U.S.A. **Online address:** williammannauthor@gmail.com

MANNA, Paul. American (born United States) **Genres:** Politics/Government, Social Sciences. **Career:** College of William & Mary, assistant professor, 2003-. Writer. **Publications:** School's In: Federalism and the National Education Agenda, 2006. **Address:** Government Department, College of William & Mary, PO Box 8795, Williamsburg, VA 23187-8795, U.S.A. **Online address:** pmanna@wm.edu

MANNE, Henry G. (Henry Girard Manne). American (born United States), b. 1928. **Genres:** Economics, Law. **Career:** Corporate law practice, 1953-54; St. Louis University, assistant professor of law, 1956-57, associate professor of law, 1959-62; University of Wisconsin, visiting assistant professor of law, 1957-59; George Washington University, associate professor, 1962-64, professor of law, 1964-68; University of Rochester, Kenan professor of law, 1968-74; Stanford University, visiting professor, 1971-72; University of Miami, distinguished professor of law, Law and Economics Center, director, 1974-80; Emory University, professor of law, Law and Economics Center, director, 1980-86; George Mason University School of Law, university professor, 1986-2000, dean, 1986-96, director of development and planning, 1996-2000, professor emeritus and dean emeritus, 2000-; University of Chicago, faculty; Northwestern University, faculty; Ave Maria Law School, distinguished visiting professor; University of Chicago Law Review, associate editor; University of Rome, lecturer; University of Pisa, lecturer; University of Strasbourg, lecturer. **Publications:** Insider Trading and the Stock Market, 1966; Supplementary Cases and Material for Business Association II, 1967; (ed.) Economic Policy and the Regulation of Corporate Securities, 1969; (with H.C. Wallich) The Modern Corporation and Social Responsibility, 1973; (with E. Solomon) Wall Street in Transition: The Emerging System and Its Impact on the Economy, 1974; The Economics of Legal Relationships, 1975; (co-ed.) Gold, Money, and the Law, 1975; (co-ed.) Auto Safety Regulation: The Cure or The Problem, 1976; (ed.) Corporate Governance, Past and Future, 1982; (ed. with J. Dorn) Economic Liberties and the Judiciary, 1987; An Intellectual History of the School of Law, 1993; Collected Works of Henry G. Manne, 2009. Contributor to periodicals. **Address:** George Mason University School of Law, 3301 Fairfax Dr., Arlington, VA 22201, U.S.A.

MANNE, Henry Girard. *See* **MANNE, Henry G.**

MANNERS *See* **Martin, Judith.**

MANNING, Christel (J.). American (born United States), b. 1961. **Genres:** Theology/Religion, Social Sciences, Sex, Sociology. **Career:** Hollins College, Department of Philosophy and Religion, instructor, 1994-95; Sacred Heart University, Department of Philosophy and Religious Studies, assistant professor, associate professor, director of MARS program, department chair, 1995-, professor. Writer. **Publications:** (Ed.) The Churches Speak On-Euthanasia: Official Statements from Religious Bodies and Ecumenical Organizations, 1991; God Gave Us the Right: Conservative Catholic, Evangelical Protestant and Orthodox Jewish Women Grapple with Feminism, 1999; (ed. with P. Zuckerman) Sex and Religion, 2005. Contributor to books and periodicals. **Address:** Department of Philosophy and Religious Studies, Sacred Heart University, Rm. 202, Administration Bldg., 5151 Park Ave., Fairfield, CT 06825-1000, U.S.A. **Online address:** manningc@sacredheart.edu

MANNING, Joe. American (born United States), b. 1941. **Genres:** Local History/Rural Topics, Poetry, Literary Criticism And History. **Career:** Connecticut Department of Social Services, caseworker, 1970-99; North Adams Public Schools, advisor for oral history programs; Massachusetts College of Liberal Arts, visiting lecturer. Author and photographer. **Publications:** Steeples: Sketches of North Adams, 1997, 3rd ed., 2001; Disappearing into North Adams, 2001; Gig at the Amtrak, 2005. **Address:** c/o Author Mail, Flatiron Press, 575 Bridge Rd., Ste. 9-1, Florence, MA 01062, U.S.A. **Online address:** joe@sevensteeples.com

MANNING, Martha M. (Martha Mary Manning). American (born United States), b. 1952. **Genres:** Medicine/Health, Psychiatry. **Career:** McLean Hospital, Harvard Medical School, postdoctoral fellow, 1981-83; George Mason University, assistant professor of psychology, 1983-88, 1989-93, professor of psychology. Writer. **Publications:** A Season of Mercy, 1988; Undercurrents: A Therapist's Reckoning with Her Own Depression, 1994; Chasing Grace: Reflections of a Catholic Girl, Grown Up, 1996; Male All'anima: Come Ho Vinto La Depressione, 1997; All Seasons Pass: Grieving a Miscarriage, 2000; The Common Thread: Mothers, Daughters, and the Power of Empathy, 2002; Place to Land: Lost and Found in an Unlikely Friendship, 2003. Contributor to periodicals. **Address:** c/o Anelle Eckstut, Levine Greenberg Literary Agency Inc., 307 7th Ave., Ste. 2407, New York, NY 10001, U.S.A.

MANNING, Martha Mary. *See* **MANNING, Martha M.**

MANNING, Richard Dale. American (born United States), b. 1951. **Genres:** Local History/Rural Topics, Writing/Journalism, Social Sciences. **Career:** Station WATZ, news director, 1975-79; Alpena News, reporter, 1977-79; Post-Register, city editor, 1979-81; Wood River Journal, editor, columnist, 1981-82; Times-News, columnist, 1982-85; Missoulian, reporter, columnist, 1985-89; freelance writer, 1989-; Stanford University, John S. Knight fellow in journalism, 1994-95; University of Montana, Institute for Educational Research and Service, senior research associate; Good Works in Trauma, founder, 2009-. **Publications:** Last Stand: Logging, Journalism, and the Case for Humility, 1991 as Last Stand: A Riveting Expose of Environmental Pillage and a Lone Journalist's Struggle to Keep Faith, 1992; A Good House: Building a Life on the Land, 1993; Grassland: The History, Biology, Politics and Promise of the American Prairie, 1995; One Round River: The Curse of Gold and the Fight for the Big Blackfoot, 1998; Food's Frontier: The Next Green Revolution, 2000; Inside Passage: A Journey beyond Borders, 2001; Against the Grain: How Agriculture has Hijacked Civilization, 2004; Rewilding the West: Restoration in a Prairie Landscape, 2009. **Address:** Institute for Educational Research and Service, The University of Montana, McGill Hall 026, Missoula, MT 59812-6376, U.S.A. **Online address:** richard.manning@umontana.edu

MANNING, Roberta Thompson. American (born United States), b. 1940. **Genres:** Cultural/Ethnic Topics, History. **Career:** Columbia University, Russian Institute, President's fellow, 1968-69, senior fellow, 1977-78; Leningrad State University, International Research and Exchanges, fellow, 1970-71; University of California, acting assistant professor of history, 1975; Boston College, assistant professor, 1975-81, associate professor of Russian and Soviet history, 1981-2001, professor of history, 2002-; Harvard University, Davis Center for Russian Studies, research associate, 1976-, fellow, 1982-83. Writer. **Publications:** The Crisis of the Old Order in Russia: Gentry and Government, 1982; Government in the Soviet Countryside in the Stalinist Thirties: The Case of Belyi Raion in 1937, 1984; (ed. with J.A. Getty) Stalinist Terror: New Perspectives, 1993; Belskii raion, 1937 God, 1998; (co-author) Tragediia Sovetskoi Derevni, 1999; Rise and Fall of The Extraordinary Measures, January-June, 1928: Toward a Reexamination of the Onset of the Stalin Revolution, 2001. **Address:** Department of History, Boston College, Rm. 417, 21 Campanella Way, 140 Commonwealth Ave., 885 Centre St., Chestnut Hill, MA 02467, U.S.A. **Online address:** manning@bc.edu

MANNING, Robert D. American (born United States), b. 1957. **Genres:** Novels, Civil Liberties/Human Rights, Economics, Politics/Government, Sociology, Documentaries/Reportage, Money/Finance. **Career:** University of Yucatan, senior Fulbright lecturer, 1986-87; University of Oaxaca, senior Fulbright lecturer, 1987; Smithsonian Institution, senior social science research analyst, 1988-94; American University, assistant professor of sociology, 1989-97; Georgetown University, visiting professor of sociology and Latin American studies, 1997-2000; Rochester Institute of Technology, E. Philip Saunders College of Business, Caroline Werner Gannett professor of the humanities, 2001-03, university professor and special assistant, 2003-05, Center for Consumer Financial Services, research professor and director, 2005-09; Filene Research Institute, research fellow, 2007-; Consumer Financial Services Institute, president, 2009-; Responsible Debt Relief Institute Inc., founder, president and chief executive officer. Writer. **Publications:** Credit Card Nation: The Consequences of America's Addiction to Credit, 2000; Living with Debt, 2005. EDITOR: (ed.) Globalization, Human Rights and Citizenship, 2002; In Debt We Trust: America Before the Bubble Burst Documentary, 2006; Responsible Debt Relief: An Algorithmic Assessment of Consumer Debt Capacity, 2007; Keeping People in Their Homes: Policy Recommendations for the Foreclosure Crisis, 2008; Using Shared Equity Agreements to Reduce Foreclosure: Policy and Analysis, 2009. Contributor of articles to books and periodicals. **Address:** Responsible Debt Relief Institute Inc., 1100 University Ave., Ste. 212, Rochester, NY 14607-1655, U.S.A. **Online address:** r.manning@responsibledebtrelief.org

MANOTTI, Dominique. French (born France), b. 1942. **Genres:** Novels. **Career:** Economic historian and writer. **Publications:** Kop, 1998; Nos fantastiques annees fric, 2001; Sombre sentier, 2001; Le corps noir, 2004; A nos chevaux!, 2007; Lorraine Connection, 2008. **Address:** England. **Online address:** romanoir@dominiquemanotti.com

MANRIQUE (ARDILA), Jaime. American/Colombian (born Colombia), b. 1949. **Genres:** Novels, Poetry, Biography, Young Adult Fiction, Novellas/Short Stories, Autobiography/Memoirs. **Career:** Eugene Lang College, part-time faculty, 1988-92; New School for Social Research, writer-in-residence, 1989-91; Goddard College, associate professor, 1992-94; Mt. Holyoke College, visiting professor, 1995; Columbia University, School of the Arts, adjunct faculty, 1998-99, associate professor, 2002-. Writer. **Publications:** Los adoradores de la luna, 1976; El cadaver de papa, 1978; Cadáver De Papá: Y, Versiones Poéticas, 1978; Notas de cine: Confesiones de un critico amateur, 1979; (trans. with J. Larkin) Sor Juana's Love Poems: Poemas de Amor: A Bilingual Edition, 1997; Eminent Maricones: Arena, Lorca, Puig, and Mc, 1999; Mi Cuerpo y otros poemas, 1999; (ed. with J. Dorris) Besame Mucho (short story collection), 1999; Autobiography of Bill Sullivan, 2006. POETRY: Adoradores De La Luna, 1976; Scarecrow, 1990; My Night with Federico García Lorca: Mi Noche Con Federico García Lorca, 1995; Tarzan, My Body, Christopher Columbus, 2001. NOVELS: Colombian Gold: A Novel of Power and Corruption, 1983, rev. ed., 1998; Latin Moon in Manhattan, 1993; Twilight at the Equator, 1997; Our Lives Are the Rivers, 2006. Contributor to periodicals. **Address:** School of the Arts, Columbia University, 305 Dodge Hall, 2960 Broadway, PO Box 1808, New York, NY 10027, U.S.A. **Online address:** jmardila@aol.com

MANSBRIDGE, Francis. Canadian/British (born England), b. 1943. **Genres:** History, Literary Criticism And History, Biography, Travel/Exploration, Theology/Religion. **Career:** East Kootenay Community College, instructor in English, 1975-91; Foreign Affairs College, instructor, 1981; Amnesty Intl., documentation officer, 1990; North Vancouver Museum and Archives, archivist, 1994-2006, staff; University of British Columbia, part-time faculty; University of Saskatchewan, part-time faculty; University of Regina, part-time faculty; University of Ottawa, part-time faculty. Writer. **Publications:** (Ed.) Wild Gooseberries: The Selected Letters of Irving Layton, 1989; Irving Layton: God's Recording Angel, 1995; Launching History: The Saga of Burrard Dry Dock, 2002; Hollyburn: The Mountain & the City, 2008; Vancouver Then & Now, 2009. Contributor to periodicals. **Address:** North Vancouver Museum and Archives, 3203 Institute Rd., North Vancouver, BC V7K 3E5, Canada.

MANSELL, Darrel. American (born United States), b. 1934. **Genres:** Literary Criticism And History, Autobiography/Memoirs, Essays. **Career:** Dartmouth College, instructor, 1962-64, assistant professor, 1964-68, associate professor, 1968-74, professor of English, 1974-99, professor emeritus, 1999-, advisor. Writer. **Publications:** The Novels of Jane Austen: An Interpretation, 1973. Contributor to journals. **Address:** Department of English, Dartmouth College, 6032 Sanborn House, Hanover, NH 03755, U.S.A.

MANSFIELD, Bruce Edgar. Australian (born Australia), b. 1926. **Genres:** History, Biography. **Career:** University of Sydney, temporary lecturer, 1949-51, lecturer, 1951-58, senior lecturer, 1958-64, associate professor of history, 1964-65, visiting professor, 1986-91, honorary associate, 1992-, emeritus professor; Journal of Religious History, editor, 1959-87; Macquarie University, professor of history, 1965-75, deputy vice-chancellor, 1976-85; Australian Historical Association, president, 1977-78. **Publications:** Australian Democrat: The Career of Edward William O'Sullivan 1846-1910, 1965; Knox: A History of Knox Grammar School 1924-1974, 1974; Phoenix of His Age: Interpretations of Erasmus 1550-1750, 1979; Man on His Own: Interpretations of Erasmus 1750-1920, 1992; (with M. Hutchinson) Liberality of Opportunity: A History of Macquarie University 1964-1989, 1992; Has Church History a Future? The Thatcher Lecture 1994, 1994; Erasmus in the Twentieth Century: Interpretations 1920-2000, 2003. **Address:** The University of Sydney, University Rd., Sydney, NW 2006, Australia.

MANSFIELD, Edward D. American (born United States), b. 1962. **Genres:** Politics/Government, Economics, Social Sciences. **Career:** University of Pennsylvania, Department of Political Science, teaching assistant, 1986-88, instructor, 1989, assistant professor, 1989-94, visiting lecturer, 1992-93, Hum Rosen professor, 2001-, chair, 2009-, Christopher H. Browne Center for International Politics, director, 2001-; Columbia University, Department of Political Science, assistant professor, 1989-94, associate professor, 1994-96; Ohio State University, Department of Political Science, associate professor, 1996-2000, professor, 2000-01. Writer and educator. **Publications:** Power, Trade, and War, 1994; (ed. with F. Kratochwil) International Organization: A Reader, 1994; (ed. with H.V. Milner) The Political Economy of Regionalism, 1997; (ed. with J.F. Blanchard and N.M. Ripsman) Power and the Purse: Economic Statecraft, Interdependence, and National Security, 2000; (ed. with B.M. Pollins) Economic Interdependence and International Conflict: New Perspectives on an Enduring Debate, 2003; (ed.) International Conflict and the Global Economy, 2004; (ed. with R. Sisson) The Evolution of Political Knowledge: Theory and Inquiry in American Politics, 2004; (with J. Snyder) Electing to Fight: Why Emerging Democracies Go to War, 2005; (ed. with F. Kratochwil) International Organization and Global Governance: A Reader, 2nd ed., 2006; (ed. with M.L. Bush) The WTO, Economic Interdependence, and Conflict, 2007. CONTRIBUTOR: Regional Integration and the Global Trading System, 1993; Perspectives on American Foreign Policy: Readings and Cases, 2000; International Political Economy: Perspectives on Global Power and Wealth, 4th ed., 2000; Routledge Encyclopedia of International Political Economy, 2001; Turbulent Peace: The Challenges of Managing International Conflict, 2001; Models, Numbers, and Cases: Methods for Studying International Relations, 2004; The Impact of International Law on International Cooperation: Theoretical Perspectives, 2004. Contributor to periodicals. **Address:** Department of Political Science, University of Pennsylvania, 223 Stiteler Hall, 208 S 37th St., Philadelphia, PA 19104-6215, U.S.A. **Online address:** emansfie@sas.upenn.edu

MANSFIELD, Howard. American (born United States), b. 1957. **Genres:** Air/Space Topics, Architecture, History, Essays, Sciences. **Career:** Writer. **Publications:** Cosmopolis: Yesterday's Cities of the Future, 1990; In the Memory House, 1993; Skylark: The Life, Lies and Inventions of Harry Atwood, 1999; The Same Ax, Twice: Restoration and Renewal in a Throwaway Age, 2000; The Bones of the Earth, 2004; (ed.) Where the Mountain Stands Alone: Stories of Place in the Monadnock Region, 2006; Hogwood Steps Out, 2008; (contrib.) Ruin: Photographs of a Vanishing America, 2009; Turn and Jump: How Time and Place Fell Apart, 2010. Contributor to periodicals. **Address:** PO Box 127, Hancock, NH 03449, U.S.A.

MANSFIELD, Nick. Australian (born Australia), b. 1959. **Genres:** Poetry, Humanities, inspirational/Motivational Literature, Philosophy, Theology/Religion, Cultural/Ethnic Topics. **Career:** Macquarie University, associate lecturer in English, 1985-89, Department of Critical and Cultural Studies, senior lecturer, 1992-, head of the department, Higher Degree Research, dean; Flinders University of South Australia, associate lecturer in English, 1991. Writer. **Publications:** To Die of Desire (poems), 1993; Masochism: The Art of Power, 1997; (with P. Fuery) Cultural Studies and the New Humanities: Concepts and Controversies, 1997; (with P. Fuery) Cultural Studies and Critical Theory, 2000; Subjectivity: Theories of Self from Freud to Haraway, 2000; Oznellik: Freud'dan Harawy'e Kendilik Kuramlari, 2006; Theorizing War: From Hobbes to Badiou, 2008; The God Who Deconstructs Himself: Subjectivity and Sovereignty Between Freud, Bataille and Derrida, 2010. **Address:** Department of Cultural Studies, Macquarie University, Rm. 250, Y3A Bldg., Balaclava Rd., North Ryde, NW 2109, Australia. **Online address:** nmansfield@scmp.mq.edu.au

MANSKI, Charles F. American (born United States), b. 1948. **Genres:** Economics, Mathematics/Statistics, Social Sciences. **Career:** Carnegie-Mellon University, assistant professor, 1973-77, associate professor of urban and public affairs, 1977-80; Cambridge Systematics Inc., senior associate, 1978-83; Transportation Science, associate editor, 1978-84; Hebrew University of Jerusalem, associate professor of economics, 1979-83, fellow, 2003-; Bank of Israel, consultant, 1980-82; Falk Institute for Economic Research-Israel, research associate, 1980-95; Econometrica, associate editor, 1980-88; National Bureau of Economic Research, research associate, 1983-; Journal of the American Statistical Association, associate editor, 1983-85, 2002-04; University of Wisconsin, professor of economics, 1983-89, Wolfowitz professor, 1989-93, Hilldale professor, 1993-98, Institute for Research on Poverty, director, 1988-91; Journal of Economic Perspectives, associate editor, 1986-89; Journal of Human Resources, editor, 1991-94; Stanford University, Center for Advanced Study in the Behavioral Sciences, fellow, 1992-93; Northwestern University, board of trustees professor in economics, 1997-, professor of economics, chair, 2007-10, Institute for Policy Research, faculty fellow; Santa Fe Institute, external faculty, 1997-2003; Institute of Mathematical Statistics, Annals of Applied Statistics, associate editor, 2006-10; University College London, Department of Economics, Leverhulme visiting professor, 2011. **Publications:** (With M.G. Kohn and D.S. Mundel) Empirical Investigation of Factors which Influence College, 1974; (with D.A. Wise) College Choice in America, 1983; Analog Estimation Methods in Econometrics, 1988; Identification Problems in the Social Sciences, 1995; Partial Identification of Probability Distributions, 2003; Social Choice with Partial Knowledge of Treatment Response, 2005; Identification for Prediction and Decision, 2007. EDITOR: (with D. McFadden) Structural Analysis of Discrete Data with Econometric Applications, 1981; (with I. Garfinkel) Evaluating Welfare and Training Programs, 1992; (with C.F. Citro and J. Pepper) Providing National Statistics on Health and Social Welfare Programs in an Era of Change, 1998; (with J.V. Pepper and Y.F. Thomas) Assessment of two Cost-Effectiveness Studies on Cocaine Control Policy, 1999; (with E. Evanson and T.M. Scanlan) Evaluating Food Assistance Programs in an Era of Welfare Reform, 1999; (with B. Fischhoff) Elicitation of Preferences, 2000; (with J.V. Pepper and C.V. Petrie) Informing America's Policy on Illegal Drugs, 2001. Works appear in anthologies. Contributor of articles to journals. **Address:** Department of Economics, Northwestern University, Rm. 3216, Arthur Andersen Hall, 2001 Sheridan Rd., Evanston, IL 60208-2600, U.S.A. **Online address:** cfmanski@northwestern.edu

MANSOOR, Peter R. American (born United States), b. 1960. **Genres:** Military/Defense/Arms Control, History. **Career:** U.S. Army/Marine Corps Counterinsurgency Center, founding director, 2006, Multi-National Force-Iraq, executive officer, 2007-08; Council on Foreign Relations, fellow, 2005-06; Ohio State University, Department of History, associate professor, Raymond E. Mason Jr. chair of military history. Writer. **Publications:** The GI Offensive in Europe: The Triumph of American Infantry Divisions, 1941-1945, 1999; Baghdad at Sunrise: A Brigade Commander's War in Iraq, 2008; (ed. with W. Murray) Hybrid Warfare: Fighting Complex Opponents From the Ancient World to the Present, 2012. Contributor to periodicals. **Address:** Department of History, Ohio State University, 214 Dulles Hall, 230 W 17th Ave., Columbus, OH 43210, U.S.A. **Online address:** mansoor.1@osu.edu

MANTEL, Hilary (Mary). British (born England), b. 1952. **Genres:** Novels. **Career:** The Spectator, film critic, 1987-91; Order of the British Empire, commander. Educator and novelist. **Publications:** Every Day Is Mother's Day, 1985; Vacant Possession, 1986; Eight Months on Ghazzah Street, 1988; Fludd, 1989; A Place of Greater Safety, 1992; A Change of Climate, 1994; An Experiment in Love, 1995; The Giant, O'Brien, 1998; Vacant Possession, 2000; Giving Up the Ghost: A Memoir, 2003; Learning to Talk: Short Stories, 2003; The Woman Who Died of Robespierre, 2003; Beyond Black, 2005; Wolf Hall, 2009. **Address:** A. M. Heath & Company Ltd., 6 Warwick Ct., Holborn, London, GL WC1R 5DJ, England.

MANTEL, Samuel J(oseph). American (born United States), b. 1921. **Genres:** Administration/Management, Medicine/Health. **Career:** Georgia Institute of Technology, assistant professor of social science, 1953-56; Case Institute of Technology (now Case Western Reserve University), assistant professor of economics, 1956-59, director of economics-in-action program, 1956-68, associate professor, 1959-69; University of Cincinnati, College of Business, professor of management and quantitative analysis, 1969-89, Joseph S. Stern professor of management, 1973-89, Joseph S. Stern professor emeritus of operations management, 1989-. Writer. **Publications:** Cases in Managerial Decisions, 1964; (with J.R. Meredith) Project Management: A Managerial Approach, 1985, 8th ed. as Project Managere, 2012; Operations Management for Pharmacists, 1991; (co-author) Project Management in Practice, 2001, 4th ed., 2011; (co-author) Core Concepts of Project Management in Practice, 2003, 2nd ed., 2005. CONTRIBUTOR: Principles of Economics, 1959; Analysis and Program Planning Budgetting, 1968; Systems Approach and the City, 1972; Quantitative Decision Aiding Techniques for Research and Development Management, 1972; Health Care Delivery Planning, 1973. Contributor to journals and periodicals. **Address:** University of Cincinnati, 501 Carl H. Lindner Hall, 2925 Campus Green Dr., PO Box 210130, Cincinnati, OH 45221-0130, U.S.A.

MANZ, Charles C. American (born United States) **Genres:** Administration/Management, Business/Trade/Industry, Economics, Money/Finance, Institutions/Organizations. **Career:** Pennsylvania State University, faculty, 1977-80; Auburn University, faculty, 1980-82; University of Minnesota, faculty, 1982-88; Arizona State University, faculty, researcher, 1989-97; University of Massachusetts-Amherst, Nirenberg chaired professor of business leadership, 1997-. Writer. **Publications:** The Art of Self-Leadership: Strategies for Personal Effectiveness in Your Life and Work, 1983; (with H.P. Sims, Jr.) Super Leadership: Leading Others to Lead Themselves, 1989, rev. ed. as The New Superleadership: Leading Others to Lead Themselves, 2001; Mastering Self-Leadership: Empowering Yourself for Personal Excellence, 1992, (with C.P. Neck) 5th ed., 2010; (with H.P. Sims, Jr.) Business without Bosses: How Self-Managing Teams are Building High-Performing Companies, 1993; (with H.P. Sims, Jr.) Company of Heroes: Unleashing the Power of Self-Leadership, 1996; For Team Members Only: Making Your Workplace Team Productive and Hassle-Free, 1997; The Leadership Wisdom of Jesus: Practical Lessons for Today, 1998, 2nd ed., 2005; (with G.L. Stewart and H.P. Sims, Jr.) Team Work and Group Dynamics, 1999; (co-author) The Wisdom of Solomon at Work: Ancient Virtues for Living and Leading Today, 2001; The Power of Failure: 27 Ways to Turn Life's Setbacks into Success, 2002; Emotional Discipline: The Power to Choose How You Feel, 2003; (with C. Neck, T. Mitchell and E. Thompson) Fit to Lead: The Proven 8-Week Solution for Shaping Up Your Body, Your Mind and Your Career, 2004; Temporary Sanity: Instant Self-leadership Strategies for Turbulent Times, 2004; The Greatest Leader Who Wasn't: A Leadership Fable, 2005; (with R.C. Edelman and T.R. Hiltabiddle) Nice Guys Can get the Corner Office: Eight Strategies for Winning in Business Without being a Jerk, 2008; (co-ed.) Virtuous Organization: Insights from Some of the World's Leading Management Thinkers, 2008. **Address:** Department of Management, Isenberg School of Management, University of Massachusetts, 121 Presidents Dr., SOM 307A, PO Box 34940, Amherst, MA 01003-4940, U.S.A. **Online address:** cmanz@som.umass.edu

MANZONI, Jean-François. Singaporean/Canadian/French (born France) **Genres:** Administration/Management, Engineering, Adult Non-fiction. **Career:** Ecole des Hautes Etudes Commerciales de Montréal, research assistant and teaching fellow, 1981-82, faculty lecturer, 1984-86; Ernst & Young, auditor and consultant, 1982-84; Harvard Business School, research assistant, 1987; Insead, visiting lecturer, 1989-92, assistant professor, associate professor, 1992-2004, professor of management practice and Shell chaired professor of human resources and organisational development, 2011-, PwC Research Initiative on High Performance Organisations, founder and director, 2001-04, Global Leadership Centre, director, 2011-; IMD, professor of leadership and organizational development, 2004-10. Writer. **Publications:** (With S. Dutta) Process Re-engineering, Organizational Change, and Performance Improvement, 1999; (ed. with M.J. Epstein) Performance Measurement and Management Control: A Compendium of Research, 2002; (with J. Barsoux) The Set-up-to-Fail Syndrome: How Good Managers Cause Great People to Fail, 2002; (ed. with M.J. Epstein) Performance Measurement and Management Control: Superior Organizational Performance, 2004; (co-author) Relations Difficiles Au Travail: Rompre Le Cercle Vicieux, 2004; (ed. with M.J. Epstein) Performance Measurement and Management Control: Improving Organizations and Society, 2006; (ed. with M.J. Epstein) Performance Measurement and Management Control: Measuring and Rewarding Performance, 2008; (ed. with M.J. Epstein and A. Davila) Performance Measurement and Management Control: Innovative Concepts and Practices, 2010. Contributor to periodicals. **Address:** Insead, 1 Ayer Rajah Ave., Singapore, 138676, Singapore. **Online address:** jean-francois.manzoni@insead.edu

MANZOOR, Sarfraz. British/Pakistani (born Pakistan), b. 1971?. **Genres:** Autobiography/Memoirs. **Career:** Guardian, journalist; Channel 4 News, producer and reporter; Channel 4, deputy commissioning editor. Journalist, television writer, columnist, documentary producer, broadcaster, commentator and memoirist. **Publications:** Greetings from Bury Park: Race, Religion, and Rock 'n' Roll (memoir), 2007. Contributor to periodicals. **Address:** England. **Online address:** sarfraz.manzoor@guardian.co.uk

MAOZ, Dan. Israeli (born Israel), b. 1960. **Genres:** Sciences, Astronomy, Physics. **Career:** Institute for Advanced Study, faculty, 1990-93; Tel-Aviv University, Raymond and Beverly Sackler School of Physics and Astronomy, Department of Astrophysics, professor, 1993-, chairman. Writer. **Publications:** (Ed. with A. Sternberg and E.M. Leibowitz) Astronomical Time Series: Proceedings of the Florence and George Wise Observatory, 25th Anniversary Symposium, Held in Tel-Aviv, Israel, 30 December, 1996-1 January, 1997, 1997; Astrophysics in a Nutshell, 2007. **Address:** Raymond and Beverly Sackler School of Physics, and Astronomy, Tel-Aviv University, Rm. 107, Kaplun-Physics Bldg., Tel-Aviv, 69978, Israel. **Online address:** maoz@wise.tau.ac.il

MAPP, Edward. (Edward Charles Mapp). American (born United States), b. 1929. **Genres:** Film, Reference. **Career:** New York Public Library, library assistant, 1948-53; educator, 1957-64; New York City Technical College, Library Learning Resources Center, director, 1964-77; United Nations Association of New York, director, 1975-78; City University of New York, Borough of Manhattan Community College, dean of faculty, 1977-82, professor of speech and communication, 1983-99, professor of library and learning resources and chair of department, 1964-, retired 1998; NYC Human Rights Commission, commissioner, 1988-94; City Colleges of Chicago, vice chancellor; The Friends of Thirteen Inc., director, 2000-, vice chairman, 2003, chairman, 2005; Thirteen's Legacy Society, co-chairman. Writer. **Publications:** (Comp.) Books for Occupational Education Programs: A List for Community Colleges, Technical Institutes and Vocational Schools, 1971; Blacks in American Films: Today and Yesterday, 1972; (ed. and intro.) Puerto Rican Perspectives, 1974; (comp.) Directory of Blacks in the Performing Arts, 1978, 2nd ed., 1990; (with J. Kisch) A Separate Cinema: Fifty Years of Black Cast Posters, 1992; African Americans and the Oscar: Seven Decades of Struggle and Achievement, 2003, 2nd ed., 2008. **Address:** The Scarecrow Press Inc., 4501 Forbes Blvd., Ste. 200, Lanham, MD 20706, U.S.A.

MAPP, Edward Charles. *See* **MAPP, Edward.**

MARA, Rachna. *See* **GILMORE, Rachna.**

MARACLE, Lee. American/Canadian (born Canada), b. 1950. **Genres:** Novels, Novellas/Short Stories, Young Adult Fiction, Autobiography/Memoirs, Adult Non-fiction. **Career:** Author, 1975-; University of Toronto, professor; University of Waterloo, lecturer; Southern Oregon University, lecturer; En'owkin International School of Writing, co-founder, teacher; Western Washington University, distinguished visiting professor of Canadian culture, 2001-, professor; University of Guelph, writer-in-residence; Centre for Indigenous Theatre, cultural director. **Publications:** Bobbi Lee: Indian Rebel (autobiography), 1975, new. ed., 1990; Sojourner's Truth and Other Storeis (stories), 1990; (co-ed.) Telling It: Women and Language across Cultures, 1990; Oratory: Coming to Theory, 1990. NOVELS: Sundogs, 1992; Ravensong, 1993; I Am Woman: A Native Perspective on Sociology and Feminism, 1996; Bent Box, 2000; (ed. with S. Laronde) My Home as I Remember, 2000; Daughters Are Forever, 2001; Will's Garden (young adult), 2002; First Wives Club: Coast Salish Style, 2010. Works appear in anthologies. Contributor to periodicals. **Address:** Center for Canadian-American Studies, Western Washington University, Canada House 201, 516 High St., Bellingham, WA 98225-9110, U.S.A. **Online address:** lee.maracle@wwu.edu

MARANDA, Pierre. Canadian (born Canada), b. 1930. **Genres:** Anthropology/Ethnology, Information Science/Computers, Language/Linguistics, Mythology/Folklore, Young Adult Fiction. **Career:** Harvard University, research fellow, 1964-68; Ecole Pratique des Hautes Etudes, research director, 1968-69; University of British Columbia, professor of anthropology, 1969-74; College de France, visiting professor, 1975; University Laval, research professor, 1975-, now professor emeritus; Universidade Federal Rio de Janeiro, visiting professor, 1983. Writer. **Publications:** (With E.K. Maranda) Structural Models in Folklore and Transformational Essays, 1962, 2nd ed., 1971; (with E.K. Maranda) Structural Analysis of Oral Tradition, 1971; Introduction to Anthropology: A Self-Guide, 1972; French Kinship: Structure and History, 1974; Dialogue conjugal, 1985; Discan: A Computer System for Content and Discourse Analysis, 1987; (with F. Nze-Nguema) L'Unite dans la diversite culturelle: Une Geste bantu. Tome1: Le Sens des symboles fang, mbede et eshira, 1993. EDITOR: (with J. Pouillion) Echanges et Communications, 2 vols., 1970; Mythology, 1972; Soviet Structural Folkloristics, vol. I, 1974; Symbolic Production Symbolique, 1977; The Social Appropriation of Logic, 1978; The Double Twist: From Ethnography to Morphodynamics, 2001. CONTRIBUTOR: Essays on the Verbal and Visual Arts, 1967; Calcul et formalisation dans lessciences de l'homme, 1968; Anthropologie et calcul, 1971; Structures etgenres de la litterature ethnique, 1972. Contributor to journals. **Address:** 1080 Ave. Des Braves, Quebec City, QC G1K 7P4, Canada. **Online address:** pmaranda@videotron.ca

MARANGONI, Alejandro G. Canadian/Spanish (born Spain), b. 1965. **Genres:** Sciences, Technology, Engineering, Medicine/Health, Environmental Sciences/Ecology. **Career:** University of Guelph, department of biochemistry, postdoctoral fellow, 1990-91, department of food science, assistant professor of food science, 1991-97, associate professor, 1997-2001, professor, 2001-, Graduate Program, coordinator, 1996-97, Department of Food Science, Canada research chair, 2001-11; Food Research Intl., editor-in-chief, 1998-; Centre National de la Recherche Scientifique, directeur de recherche, 2005-06; Journal of The American Oil Chemists Society, associate editor, 2005-; Ontario Ministry of Agriculture and Food, Product Development and Enhancement of Value Chains, research program director, 2008-. Writer. **Publications:** (Ed. with S.S. Narine) Physical Properties of Lipids, 2002; Enzyme Kinetics: A Modern Approach, 2003; (ed. with J.R. Dutcher) Soft Materials: Structure and Dynamics, 2005; Fat Crystal Networks, 2005; (ed. with N. Garti) Edible Oleogels: Structure and Health Implications, 2012; Food Chemistry Essentials, forthcoming. **Address:** Department of Food Science, University of Guelph, 50 Stone Rd. E, Guelph, ON N1G 2W1, Canada. **Online address:** amarango@uoguelph.ca

MARANISS, David. American (born United States), b. 1949. **Genres:** Biography, Novels, History, Young Adult Fiction, Literary Criticism And History. **Career:** WIBA Radio, reporter, 1972-75; Trenton Times, reporter, 1975-77; Washington Post, journalist, 1977-, associate editor; Madison Capital Times, staff. **Publications:** First in his Class: A Biography of Bill Clinton, 1995; (with M. Weisskopf) Tell Newt to Shut Up!: Prizewinning Washington Post Journalists Reveal how Reality Gagged the Gingrich Revolution, 1996; The Clinton Enigma, 1998; When Pride Still Mattered: A Life of Vince Lombardi, 1999; (with E. Nakashima) The Prince of Tennessee: The Rise of Al Gore, 2000; They Marched into Sunlight: War and Peace, Vietnam and America, October 1967, 2003; Clemente: The Passion and Grace of Baseball's Last Hero, 2006; (ed. and intro.) Best American Sports Writing 2007, 2007; Rome 1960: The Olympics that Changed the World, 2008; Into the Story: A Writer's Journey through Life, Politics, Sports and Loss, 2010. Contributor to periodicals. **Address:** Washington Post, 1150 15th St. NW, Washington, DC 20071, U.S.A. **Online address:** david@davidmaraniss.com

MARANTO, Gina (Lisa). American (born United States), b. 1955. **Genres:** Biology, Sciences. **Career:** Alumni Magazine Consortium, contributing editor, 1981-82; PC Tech Journal, copy editor, 1983; Discover Magazine Time Inc, staff writer, 1983-87; Time Inc., staff writer for discover, 1983-87; Time-Life Books, special contributor, 1987-93; freelance writer, 1993-; The Wolfsonian-FIU, consulting writer, 1997-2000; University of Miami, semester lecturer, 1998, fulltime lecturer, 1998-2005, senior lecturer, 2005-, acting director, 2005-06, interim director, 2006-07, director, 2007-. **Publications:** Quest for Perfection: The Drive to Breed Better Human Beings, 1996; (ed. with J.H. Dirckx) Designer Baby's, 1998; Stedman's Pocket Medical Dictionary, 1999. Contributor to books, articles, magazines and newspapers. **Address:** c/o Barney Karpfinger, Karpfinger Agency Literary, 357 W 20th St., New York, NY 10011, U.S.A. **Online address:** glmaranto@gmail.com

MARANTZ, Kenneth A. American (born United States), b. 1927. **Genres:** Art/Art History, Education, Bibliography. **Career:** Art teacher and adult education instructor, 1952-61; Pratt Institute, assistant professor of art education, 1961-63; University of Chicago, art teacher at Laboratory Schools and co-director of Art Center, 1963-67, assistant professor of education in arts, 1967-71; Ohio State University, associate professor, 1971-73, professor of art education, 1973-92, head of department, 1971-87, professor emeritus, 1992-; Columbus Gallery of Fine Arts, member of art advisory board, 1974-77; Columbus College of Art and Design, honorary professor of visual communications, 2000-; J. Paul Getty Foundation, consultant; Kent State University, adjunct professor of library science. Writer. **Publications:** (With S. Marantz) The Art of Children's Picture Books (bibliography): A Selective Reference Guide, 1988, 2nd ed., 1995; Dream Makers, 1990; (with S. Marantz) Artists of the Page: Interviews with Picture Book Illustrators, 1992; (ed.) Picturebooks: Art Source and Resource, 1993; (with S. Marantz) Multicultural Picture Books: Art for Understanding Others, 1994, 2nd ed., 2005; (with S. Marantz) Creating Picturebooks: Interviews with Editors, Art Directors, Reviewers, Booksellers, Professors, Librarians, and Showcasers, 1997. Work represented in anthologies. Contributor to periodicals. **Address:** Department of Art Education, Ohio State University, 258 Hopkins Hall, 128 N Oval Mall, Columbus, OH 43210, U.S.A. **Online address:** marantz.1@osu.edu

MARANTZ, Sylvia S. American (born United States), b. 1929. **Genres:** Communications/Media, Librarianship, Bibliography, Picture/Board Books, Art/Art History, Photography. **Career:** Candor Central School, foreign languages teacher, 1951-52; Plainedge School, Spanish teacher, 1958, librarian, 1960; Plainedge Free Community Library, 1960-62; University of Chicago, Laboratory Schools, librarian and media specialist, 1964-71; Ohio Arts Council, information officer and editor, 1971-72; head librarian, 1972-91; Ohio State University, lecturer, 1984, 1988; St. Michael School, head librarian, 1991-92. **Publications:** Picture Books for Looking and Learning: Awakening Visual Perceptions Through the Art of Children's Books, 1992. WITH K.A. MARANTZ: The Art of Children's Picture Books: A Selective Reference Guide, 1988, 2nd ed., 1995; Artists of the Page: Interviews with Children's Book Illustrators, 1992; Multicultural Picture Books: Art for Understanding Others, 1994, 2nd ed. as Multicultural Picturebooks: Art for Illuminating Our World, 2005; Creating Picture books: Interviews with Editors, Art Directors, Reviewers, Booksellers, Professors, Librarians, and Showcasers, 1997. Contributor to periodicals. **Address:** 2056 Middlesex Rd., Columbus, OH 43220-4642, U.S.A.

MARBER, Patrick. British (born England), b. 1964. **Genres:** Plays/Screenplays, Literary Criticism And History, Young Adult Fiction. **Career:** Playwright and director, 1990-. **Publications:** PLAYS: Dealer's Choice, 1995; Closer, 1997; After Miss Julie (television adaptation), 1998; Howard Katz, 2001; Plays One, 2003; Alan Partridge: Every Ruddy Word, 2003; Musicians: A Play, 2005; Don Juan in Soho: After Molière, 2007. Contributor to periodicals. **Address:** Judy Daish Associates, 2 St. Charles Pl., London, GL W10 63G, England.

MARBLE, Allan Everett. Canadian (born Canada), b. 1939. **Genres:** History, Local History/Rural Topics, Biography, Social Sciences, Medicine/Health. **Career:** St. Francis Xavier University, assistant professor, 1967-69; Technical University of Nova Scotia, professor, 1970-; Dalhousie University, associate professor, 1970, chairman, professor emeritus of electrical engineering, 2000-. Writer. **Publications:** The Hingley Family of Nova Scotia, 1966; Nova Scotians at Home and Abroad: Including Biographical Sketches of Over Six Hundred Native Born Nova Scotians, 1977; Catalogue of Published Genealogies of Nova Scotia Families, 1984; The Descendants of James McCabe and Ann Pettigrew, 1986; Deaths, Burials, and Probate of Nova Scotians, 1749-1799: From Primary Sources, 1990; Surgeons, Smallpox, and the Poor: A History of Medicine and Social Condition in Nova Scotia, 1749-1799, 1993; The House that Sexton Built: A Century of Outstanding Graduates, 2007; Archibald Family of Nova Scotia, 2008. **Address:** Department of Electrical and Computer Engineering, Dalhousie University, 1459 Oxford St., Halifax, NS B3H 4R2, Canada. **Online address:** allen.marble@dal.ca

MARCANTEL, Pamela. American (born United States), b. 1949. **Genres:** Romance/Historical, Novels. **Career:** University of Virginia, undergraduate administrator. Writer. **Publications:** An Army of Angels: A Novel of Joan of Arc, 1997; Johanna von Orléans, 2002. **Address:** Department of English, University of Virginia, Bryan Hall 236-C, PO Box 400121, Charlottesville, VA 22904, U.S.A. **Online address:** mpm3a@virginia.edu

MARCELL, Jacqueline. American (born United States), b. 1950?. **Genres:** Gerontology/Senior Issues, Medicine/Health, Psychiatry, Psychology, Adult Non-fiction, How-to Books, Human Relations/Parenting, Self Help, Social Work, Women's Studies And Issues, Autobiography/Memoirs. **Career:** Writer, publisher, radio host and speaker. **Publications:** Elder Rage, or Take My Father... Please!: How to Survive Caring for Aging Parents, 2nd ed., 2001. **Address:** Impressive Press, 3141 Michelson Dr., Ste. 606, Irvine, CA 92612-5670, U.S.A. **Online address:** jmarcell@elderrage.com

MARCELLO, Patricia Cronin. American (born United States), b. 1952. **Genres:** Biography, Autobiography/Memoirs. **Career:** Freelance writer, 1989-; Successful Women, associate editor, 1994-97; Institute of Children's Literature, instructor, 1997-2002. **Publications:** Pope John Paul II, 1998; Matt Damon, 1998; Diana: The Life of a Princess, 1998; The Titanic, 1999; Jerry Garcia, 1999; The Navajo, 2000; The Dalai Lama: A Biography, 2003; Ralph Nader: A Biography, 2004; Gloria Steinem: A Biography, 2004; Mohandas K. Gandhi: A Biography, 2006; Ai yu zi you de zhui xun: Dala Lama zhuan, 2006. **Address:** c/o Author Mail, Greenwood Press, 88 Post Rd. W, Westport, CT 06881, U.S.A. **Online address:** patm@patmarcello.com

MARCH, Hilary. *See* **PULVERTAFT, (Isobel) Lalage.**

MARCH, Kathryn S. American (born United States), b. 1949. **Genres:** Women's Studies And Issues, Social Sciences, Anthropology/Ethnology, History. **Career:** University of Washington, lecturer in general and interdisciplinary studies, 1972; Cornell University, lecturer, 1978-79, Mellon Postdoctoral Fellow, 1979-81, assistant professor, 1981-91, associate professor, 1991-2004, professor of anthropology, feminist studies, gender studies, sexuality studies and Asian studies, 2004-, Society for the Humanities, faculty fellow, 1992, Cornell-Nepal Joint Study Program, founder and chair, academic supervisor of Nepali language; Himalayan Research Bulletin, co-editor, 1981-87; Tribhuvan University, Padma Kanya College, visiting lecturer, 1997, Fulbright lecturer, 2005; Ice Hockey Big Sister Program, founder, 2002-. **Publications:** (With R. Taqqu) Women's Informal Associations in Developing Countries: Catalysts for Change?, 1985; (with D. Holmberg, B.B. Tamang and S.M. Tamang) Mutual Regards: America and Nepal Seen through Each Other's Eyes, 1994; If Each Comes Halfway: Meeting Tamang Women in Nepal, 2002; (ed. with K. Pyakuryal and B. Acharya) Nepal in Conflict: Theoretical Underpinnings, Conflict Resolution, Conflict Transformation, and Peace-Building, 2007; Gender and Geld, Textile and Tribute, forthcoming. **Address:** Department of Anthropology, Cornell University, 224 McGraw Hall, Ithaca, NY 14853, U.S.A. **Online address:** ksm8@cornell.edu

MARCH, N(orman) H(enry). British (born England), b. 1927. **Genres:** Chemistry, Physics, Sciences, Engineering. **Career:** University of Sheffield, professor of physics, 1961-71; Atomic Energy Research Establishment, Theoretical Physics Division, consultant, 1968-90; Imperial College, Blackett Laboratory, professor of theoretical solid-state physics, 1972-77; Oxford University, Coulson professor of theoretical chemistry, head of the department, 1977-94, fellow, 1977-, professor emeritus, 1994-; International Centre for Theoretical Physics, trieste. Writer. **Publications:** (With W.H. Young and S. Sampanthar) The Many-Body Problem in Quantum Mechanics, 1967; Liquid Metals, 1968; (with W. Jones) Theoretical Solid State Physics, vol. II, 1973; (with W. Jones) Perfect Lattices in Equilibrium, 1973; (with W. Jones) Non-Equilibrium and Disorder, 1973; (ed.) Orbital Theories of Molecules and Solids, 1974; Self-Consistent Fields in Atoms, 1975; (with M.P. Tosi) Atomic Dynamics in Liquids, 1976; (with M. Parrinello) Collective Effects in Solids and Liquids, 1982; (ed. with S. Lundqvist) The Theory of Inhomogeneous Electron Gas, 1983; (with M.P. Tosi) Coulomb Liquids, 1984; (ed. with M.P. Tosi) Polymers, Liquid Crystals, and Low Dimensional Solids, 1984; (ed. with R.A. Street and M.P. Tosi) Amorphous Solids and the Liquid State, 1985; Chemical Bonds Outside Metal Surfaces, 1986; (ed. with P.N. Butcher and M.P. Tosi) Crystalline Semiconducting Materials and Devices, 1986; (ed. with B.M. Deb) The Single-Particle Density in Physics and Chemistry, 1987; (ed. with S. Lundqvist and M.P. Tosi) Order and Chaos in Nonlinear Physical Systems, 1988; (with J.A. Alonso) Electrons in Metals and Alloys, 1989; (ed. with V. Bortolani and M.P. Tosi) Interaction of Atoms and Molecules with Solid Surfaces, 1990; Chemical Physics of Liquids, 1990; Liquid Metals: Concepts and Theory, 1991; Electron Density Theory of Atoms and Molecules, 1992; (with J.F. Mucci) Chemical Physics of Free Molecules, 1993; (ed. with P.N. Butcher and M.P. Tosi) Physics of Low-Dimensional Semiconductor Structures, 1993; (ed. with S.K. Srivastava) Condensed Matter: Disordered Solids, 1995; (with L.S. Cederbaum and K.C. Kulander) Atoms and Molecules in Intense Fields, 1996; Electron Correlation in Molecules and Condensed Phases, 1996; (with C.W. Lung) Mechanical Properties of Metals, 1999; (with M.P. Tosi) Introduction to Liquid State Physics, 2002; (ed. with G.G.N. Angilella) Many-Body Theory of Molecules, Clusters, and Condensed Phases, 2010. **Address:** Department of Chemistry, University of Oxford, 12 Mansfield Rd., Oxford, GL OX1 3TA, England.

MARCH, Wallace Eugene. American (born United States), b. 1935. **Genres:** Theology/Religion, Reference. **Career:** Ordained Presbyterian minister, 1964; Austin Presbyterian Theological Seminary, assistant professor, 1966-70, associate professor, 1970-74, professor, 1974-82; Presbyterian Church Council on Theology and Culture, chair, 1979-88; Louisville Presbyterian

Theological Seminary, Arnold Black Rhodes professor of Old Testament and professor of Bible studies, 1982-, dean of faculty, 1993-, now A.B. Rhodes professor emeritus of Old Testament; Appalachian Ministry Educational Resources Center, secretary and vice chairperson, 1992-97. Writer. **Publications:** (Ed.) Texts and Testaments: Critical Essays on the Bible and Early Church Fathers: A Volume in Honor of Stuart Dickson Currie, 1980; Basic Bible Study: Interpreting the Word, 1984; Israel and the Politics of Land: A Theological Case Study, 1994; The Mighty Acts of God, 2000; The Wide Wide Circle of Divine Love: A Biblical Case for Religious Diversity, 2005; Great Themes of the Bible, 2007; God's Land on Loan: Israel, Palestine and the World, 2007; God's Tapestry: Reading the Bible in a World of Religious Diversity, 2009; (with D.L. Griggs) Genesis from Scratch: The Old Testament for Beginners, 2010. **Address:** Louisville Presbyterian Theological Seminary, 1044 Alta Vista Rd., Louisville, KY 40205, U.S.A.

MARCHAND, Philip (Edward). Canadian/American (born United States), b. 1946. **Genres:** Novels, Mystery/Crime/Suspense, Criminology/True Crime. **Career:** Freelance journalist, 1974-; Toronto Star, books columnist, 1989-2008, retired, 2008. **Publications:** Just Looking, Thank You: An Amused Observer's View of Canadian Lifestyles, 1976; Marshall McLuhan: The Medium and the Messenger, 1989; Deadly Spirits (crime novel), 1994; Ripostes: Reflections on Canadian Literature, 1998; Ghost Empire: How the French Almost Conquered North America, 2005. Contributor to magazines. **Address:** Anne McDermid & Associates, 64 Bloem Ave., Toronto, ON M5E 1S1, Canada. **Online address:** pmarchand@thestar.ca

MARCHANT, Ian. British (born England), b. 1958?. **Genres:** Novels, Travel/Exploration, Plays/Screenplays. **Career:** Arvon Foundation, co-centre director, 2002-06; Birmingham City University, Royal Literary Fund Fellow, 2006-09, School of English, lecturer in creative writing. Writer. **Publications:** Juggling for a Degree: Mature Students Experience of University Life, 1994; In Southern Waters, 1999; The Battle for Dole Acre, 2001; Crypts, Caves and Tunnels of London, 2002; Parallel Lines, 2003; Men and Models, 2003, (co-author) White Open Spaces, 2006; The Longest Crawl: Being an Account of a Journey Through an Intoxicated Landscape or A Child's Treasury of Booze, 2007; Something of the Night, 2012. **Address:** Birmingham City University, The School of English, Rm. B616, City N Campus, Perry Barr, B42 2SU, England. **Online address:** ian.marchant@bcu.ac.uk

MARCHESSAULT, Jovette. Canadian (born Canada), b. 1938. **Genres:** Novels, Plays/Screenplays, Poetry, Biography, Literary Criticism And History. **Career:** Writer. **Publications:** NOVELS: AUTOBIOGRAPHICAL TRILOGY: Crachat solaire: Roman, 1974; Comme une enfant de la terre/I: Le crachat solitaire, 1974; Le Mere des herbes, 1980; Cailloux blancs pour les forets obscures. PERFORMANCE WORKS: Les vaches de nuit, 1979; Tryptique lesbien (monologues), 1980; Les Faiseuse d'anges, 1981; La Saga des poules mouillées, 1981; La Terre est trop courte, 1981; Alice and Gertrude, Natalie and Renee et ce cher Ernest, 1984; Anäis, dans la queue de la comète, 1984; Demande de travail sur les nebuléuses, 1988; Le voyage magnifique d'Emily Carr, 1990; Le lion de Bangor, 1993. OTHERS: Lettre de Californie (poem and biographies), 1982; Saga of the Wet Hens, 1983; Lesbian Triptych, 1985; Like a Child of the Earth, 1988; Mother of the Grass, 1989; White Pebbles in the Dark Forests, 1990; La péré grin ché rubinique: Confessions, 2001. Contributor to periodicals. **Address:** Etang aux Oies, Kingsbury, QC J0B 1X0, Canada.

MARCIANO, Francesca. Italian (born Italy), b. 1955. **Genres:** Novels, Film. **Career:** RAI, producer and director. Writer. **Publications:** (With P. Lapponi, A. Leoni and G. Mancini) La mia generazione, 1996; Rules of the Wild (novel), 1998; Casa Rossa, 2002; I'm Not Scared (film scripts), 2003; Casa Rossa: Romanzo, 2003; The End of Manners, 2008. Contributor to periodicals. **Address:** c/o Author Mail, Random House, 299 Park Ave., 3rd Fl., New York, NY 10171, U.S.A.

MARCOM, Micheline Aharonian. American/Saudi (born Saudi Arabia), b. 1968?. **Genres:** Adult Non-fiction, Novels, History. **Career:** Mills College, upward bound counselor and instructor in English, Graduate English Program, visiting assistant professor. Writer. **Publications:** Three Apples Fell from Heaven, 2001; The Daydreaming Boy, 2004; The Mirror in the Well, 2008; Draining the Sea, 2008. **Address:** Graduate English Program, Mills College, Rm. 310, Mills Hall, 5000 MacArthur Blvd., Oakland, CA 94613-1301, U.S.A. **Online address:** micheline@lmi.net

MARCOMBE, David. British (born England), b. 1947. **Genres:** History. **Career:** University of Nottingham, professor, M.A. in Local and Regional History Program, co-founder, 1983-2009, Centre for Local History, director, retired, 2009; Centre for Applied Research in Teacher Education, Curriculum and Pedagogy (CARTECP), staff. Writer. **Publications:** (Ed.) The Last Principality: Politics, Religion, and Society in the Bishopric of Durham, 1494-1660, 1987; (ed. with C.S. Knighton) Close Encounters: English Cathedrals and Society since 1540, 1991; English Small Town Life: Retford, 1520-1642, 1993; Sounding Boards: Oral Testimony and the Local Historian, 1995; (with A. Borrill) Newark's Riverside Heritage: Millgate, a Guided Walk, 1997; Leper Knights: The Order of St. Lazarus of Jerusalem in England, c. 1150-1544, 2003. Contributor to books and journals. **Address:** Boydell & Brewer Ltd., Whitwell House, St. Audry's Park Rd., Melton, Woodbridge, SU IP12 1SY, England.

MARCONI, Joe. American (born United States), b. 1945. **Genres:** Advertising/Public Relations, Business/Trade/Industry, Marketing. **Career:** Chicago Board Options Exchange, vice-president, 1974-82; Doremus and Co. Advertising, vice-president, 1984-87; Weber, Cohn & Riley Advertising, executive vice-president, 1987-93; S&S Public Relations, president, 1993-94; Marketing Communications, principal, 1994-, consultant; DePaul University, adjunct professor. Lecturer and writer. **Publications:** Getting the Best from Your Advertising, 1991; Crisis Marketing: When Bad Things Happen to Good Companies, 1992, 3rd ed., 2008; Beyond Branding: How Savvy Marketers Build Brand Equity to Create Products and Open New Markets, 1993; Image Marketing: Using Public Perceptions to Attain Business Objectives, 1996; Shock Marketing, 1997; A Complete Guide to Publicity, 1999; The Brand Marketing Book: Creating, Managing and Extending the Value of Your Brand, 2000; Future Marketing: Targeting Seniors, Boomers and Generations X and Y, 2001; Cause Marketing: Build Your Image and Bottom Line through Socially Responsible Partnerships, Programs and Events, 2002; Reputation Marketing: Building and Sustaining Your Organization's Greatest Asset, 2002; Public Relations: The Complete Guide, 2004; Creating the Marketing Experience: New Strategies for Building Relationships with Your Target Market, 2005; The Writing Book, 2008. Contributor to books. **Address:** Marketing Communications, 4235 Howard Ave., Western Springs, IL 60558, U.S.A. **Online address:** jamarconi@aol.com

MARCOT, Bruce G. American (born United States), b. 1953. **Genres:** Zoology, Environmental Sciences/Ecology, Sciences. **Career:** U.S. Department of Agriculture, Forest Service, contract ecologist, 1977-78, Six Rivers National Forest, biological technician, 1978-79, ecological consultant, 1983-84, Pacific Northwest Regional Office, wildlife ecologist, 1985-88, area wildlife ecologist, 1988-90, wildlife ecologist and ecosystem management technical coordinator, 1990-96, Wildlife Ecology Team, Ecosystems Processes Research Program, Portland Forestry Sciences Laboratory, research wildlife ecologist, 1996-; Oregon State University, doctoral study, graduate research assistant, 1979-84; Humboldt State University, instructor in wildlife management, 1980-81; Perkin-Elmer Corp., Biomedical Division, computer programmer, 1984-86; World Forestry Center, scientific adviser. Writer. **Publications:** (With M.L. Morrison and R.W. Mannan) Wildlife-Habitat Relationships: Concepts and Applications, 1992, 3rd ed., 2006; Conservation of Forests of India: An Ecologist's Tour, 1993; Owls of Old Forests of the World, 1995; (with J.W. Thomas) Of Spotted Owls, Old Growth and New Policies: A History Since the Interagency Scientific Committee Report, 1997; (with B.C. Wales and R. Demmer) Range Maps of Terrestrial Species in the Interior Columbia River Basin and Northern Portions of the Klamath and Great Basins, 2003; (ed. with O. Pourret and P. Naim) Bayesian Networks: A Practical Guide to Applications, 2008. Works appear in anthologies. Contributor of articles to journals. **Address:** Portland Forestry Sciences Laboratory, U.S. Department of Agriculture, 620 SW Main St., Ste. 400, PO Box 3890, Portland, OR 97205, U.S.A. **Online address:** bmarcot@fs.fed.us

MARCOTTE, Gilles. Canadian (born Canada), b. 1925. **Genres:** Literary Criticism And History, Intellectual History. **Career:** La Tribune, journalist, 1948-55; Duty, director of literary and artistic sections, 1948-55; NFB, writer-researcher, 1957-61; La Presse, literary editor, journalist, 1961-66; Universite of Montreal, professor of French, 1965-95, professor emeritus, 1997-; The News, literary critic; Le Devoir, literary critic. **Publications:** NONFICTION: Une litterature qui se fait: Essais critiques sur la litterature canadienne-francaise, 1962, rev. ed., 1968; Presence de la critique: Critique et litterature contemporaines au Canada francais, 1966; Les temps des poetes: description critique de la poesie actuelle au Canada francais, 1970; Les bonnes rencontres:

Chroniques litteraires, 1971; Le Roman a l'imparfait: Essais sur le roman quebecois d'aujourd'hui, 1976; (with A. Brochu) La litterature et la reste: Livre de Lettres, 1981; La Prose de Rimbaud, 1983; Litterature et circonstances: Essaies, 1989. FICTION: Le poids de Dieu, 1962; Retour a Coolbrook, 1965; Un Voyage, 1973; La Vie reelle: Histoires, 1989; (with P. Nepveu) Montreál imaginaire: Ville et littérature, 1989; (with J. Larose and D. Noguez) Rimbaud, 1993; Anthologie de la littérature qúbécoise, 1994; Une mission difficile: roman, 1997; Ecrire à Montréal, 1997; Jean Le Moyne, 1998; La mort de Maurice Duplessis: et autres récits, 1999; Le lecteur de poèmes; pré cé dé de Autobiographie d'un non-poète, 2000; Les livres et les jours: 1983-2001, 2002; Le manuscrit Phaneuf: roman, 2005; Petite anthologie péremptoire de la littérature québéoise, 2006; François Mauriac, le chrétien, le romancier, le journaliste: choix de textes, 2006. EDITOR: (with F. Hebert) Vaisseau d'or et croix du chemin: 1895-1935 (anthology), 1979; Montreal imaginaire: Ville et litterature, 1992. Contributor of articles to books and periodicals. **Address:** Department of French, Universite Montreal, C.P. 6128 Succ. Centreville, Montreal, QC H3C 3J7, Canada.

MARCOU, **David J.** (David Joseph Marcou). American (born United States), b. 1950. **Genres:** History, Politics/Government, Photography, Autobiography/Memoirs. **Career:** Yonhap News Agency, copy editor at international desk, 1984-85; Adams County Times, editor of friendship reporter, 1990; Western Wisconsin Technical College, instructor in writing and photography, 1991-2002; University of Wisconsin, clerk at textbook rental store, 1993-; photographer and writer, 2002-; People's Food Co-Op, clerk, 2006-. **Publications:** SELF-ILLUSTRATED: (as David Joseph Marcou) Vital Washington: A Jubilee Year 2000 Photo-Essay, 2000. OTHERS: If I Do the Research, the Lord Brings Me Luck: The Plain-Spoken Autobiography of David J. Marcou, 1992; Korea 2050: An American Journalist's View of How an Age-old Land is Coping with Rapid Change just West of the Rising Sun, 1993; My London Autumn: The Episodic Adventures of an Itinerant American Journalist in 1981 Britain, 1993; A Quintessential Picture Post Crisis Recalled, 1998; (ed.) Spirit of La Crosse: A Grassroots History, 2000; (ed. with L. Gerber) Spirit of America: Heartland Voices, World Views, 2001; (ed. with B.A. Pauls) America's Heartland Remembers: Words and Pictures before, during and after September 11th, 2001, 2002; (ed. with S. Kiedrowski) Light, Shadow & Spirit: On the Path of a Picture-Family of Life-Reflections, 2003; (ed.) The People Book: Photo-Essays and Montages in Monochrome, 2004; (ed.) Spirit of Wisconsin: A Historical Photo-Essay of the Badger State, 2005; (ed. and comp.) Spirit of the World: A Group Photographic Portrayal of Nature, People, Stories and Miracles, 2006; Pictures of Human Life, 2006. **Address:** 3M Communications, 1720 Prospect St., La Crosse, WI 54603, U.S.A. **Online address:** wordpic@hotmail.com

MARCOU, **David Joseph.** *See* **MARCOU**, **David J.**

MARCUM, **David.** American (born United States), b. 1960. **Genres:** Adult Non-fiction, Business/Trade/Industry, Psychology. **Career:** Marcum Smith LC (business consulting firm), co-founder, 2002-. Consultant and writer. **Publications:** (With S. Smith and M. Khalsa) Business Think: Rules for Getting It Right-Now, and No Matter What!, 2002; (with S. Smith) Egonomics: What Makes Ego Our Greatest Asset (or Most Expensive Liability), 2007. Contributor to periodicals. **Address:** Marcum Smith, 100 W Canyon Crest, Alpine, UT 84004, U.S.A. **Online address:** info@marcumsmith.com

MARCUS, **Alan I.** American (born United States), b. 1949. **Genres:** History, Agriculture/Forestry, Sciences, Medicine/Health, Politics/Government, Regional/Urban Planning, Technology. **Career:** University of Cincinnati, Special Collections Department, Archives for Medical History, archivist, 1974, Cincinnati Historical Society, Allen Temple AME Church History Project, principal investigator, 1979; University of Cincinnati Medical Center, Environmental Protection Agency Project, Department of Medicine, principal investigator, 1979-80, adjunct assistant professor, 1979-80, assistant professor, 1980-85, associate professor, 1985-88, professor of history, 1988-2005; Iowa State University, International Training School, assistant professor, 1979-80, Center for Historical Studies of Technology and Science, director, 1986-2005, History of Technology and Science Series, acting editor, 1988-90, Graduate Program in the History of Technology and Science, director, 1991-2005; The Jewish Hospital of Cincinnati History Project, director, 1980; AAUW Women and Medicine Project, consultant, 1982; National Endowment for the Humanities Summer Institute, associate director, 1984; Mississippi State University, professor of history and head of department, 2005-. **Publications:** Agricultural Science and the Quest for Legitimacy, 1985; (contrib.) Disease and Distinctiveness in the American South, 1988; (with H.P. Segal) Technology in America: A Brief History, 1989, 2nd ed., 1999; (contrib.) Beyond History of Science: Essays in Honor of Robert E. Schofield, 1990; Plague of Strangers: Social Groups and the Origins of City Services in Cincinnati, 1819-1870, 1991; (ed. with R. Lowitt) The United States Department of Agriculture in Historical Perspective, 1991; Cancer from Beef, 1994; (contrib.) The Rise of Big Business and the Beginnings of Antitrust and Railroad Regulation, 1994; (ed. with H. Cravens and D.M. Katzman) Technical Knowledge in American Culture, 1996; (ed. with H. Cravens) Health Care Policy in Contemporary America, 1997; Building Western Civilization: From the Advent of Writing to the Age of Steam, 1998; (ed.) Engineering in a Land-Grant Context: The Past, Present, and Future of an Idea, 2005; (with A.S. Bix) The Future is Now: Science and Technology Policy in America since 1950, 2006. Contributor to journals. **Address:** Department of History, Mississippi State University, 242 Allen Hall, PO Box H, Mississippi State, MS 39762, U.S.A. **Online address:** aimarcus@history.msstate.edu

MARCUS, **Ben.** American (born United States), b. 1967?. **Genres:** Novellas/Short Stories, Adult Non-fiction, Novels. **Career:** Brown University, lecturer in creative writing; Conjunctions, senior editor; Columbia University's School of the Arts, assistant professor of creative writing; Fence, fiction editor. **Publications:** The Age of Wire and String: Stories, 1995; Notable American Women: A Novel, 2002; Scotlandfuturebog, 2002; The Father Costume, 2002; (ed.) The Anchor Book of New American Short Stories, 2004; The Flame Alphabet, 2012. Contributor of book reviews to periodicals. **Address:** Denise Shannon Literary Agency, 20 W 22nd St., Ste. 1603, New York, NY 10010, U.S.A.

MARCUS, **Dave.** *See* **MARCUS**, **David L.**

MARCUS, **David L.** (Dave Marcus). American (born United States) **Genres:** Novels. **Career:** Miami Herald, reporter, 1982-2000; Dallas Morning News, South America bureau chief; Boston Globe, diplomatic correspondent; U.S. News and World Report, education writer, 1999-2006; Deerfield Academy, Wilson fellow, 2003-04; Newsday, education, writer, 2006-. **Publications:** What It Takes to Pull Me Through: Why Teenagers Get in Trouble and How Four of Them Got Out, 2005; Acceptance: A Legendary Guidance Counselor Helps Seven Kids Find the Right Colleges-and Find Themselves, 2009. **Address:** Jodi Solomon Speakers Bureau, 325 Huntington Ave., Ste. 112, Boston, MA 02115-4401, U.S.A. **Online address:** bookdave@gmail.com

MARCUS, **James.** American (born United States), b. 1959?. **Genres:** Literary Criticism And History, Novels, History, Travel/Exploration. **Career:** Amazon.com, senior editor, 1996-2001; Netscape/Propeller/AOL News, senior editor, 2006-09; Columbia Journalism Review, editor-at-large, 2007-10; Harper's Magazine, deputy editor, 2010-. Translator and writer. **Publications:** (Trans.) G. Parise, Abecedary, 1990; Amazonia: Five Years at the Epicenter of the Dot.com Juggernaut, 2004; Dino: The Life and Films of Dino di Laurentiis, 2004; (trans.) C. Bonini and G. D'Avanzo, Collusion: International Espionage and the War on Terror, 2007; (trans.) G. Casanova, The Duel, or, An Incident from the Life of G.C., A Venetian, 2011. **Address:** c/o Author Mail, New Press, 38 Greene St., 4th Fl., New York, NY 10013-2505, U.S.A. **Online address:** marcusja@earthlink.net

MARCUS, **Jana.** American (born United States), b. 1962. **Genres:** Photography, Popular Culture, Writing/Journalism, Popular Culture, Literary Criticism And History. **Career:** Writer. **Publications:** In the Shadow of the Vampire: Reflections from the World of Anne Rice, 1997. Contributor to periodicals. **Address:** c/o Stuart Bernstein, 63 Carmine St., Ste. 3D, New York, NY 10012, U.S.A. **Online address:** jana@janamarcus.com

MARCUS, **K(aren) Melissa.** American/Canadian (born Canada), b. 1956. **Genres:** Literary Criticism And History, Translations, History, Young Adult Fiction. **Career:** U.S. Department of State, Office of Western European Affairs, intern, 1979; freelance translator and French tutor, 1987-; Stanford University, lecturer in French, 1989-90; Northern Arizona University, assistant professor, 1990-96, associate professor of French, 1996-, Literary Translators Consortium, co-founder, 1996, professor, now professor emeritus of modern languages. Writer. **Publications:** (Trans.) Forbidden Vision, 1995; The Representation of Mesmerism in Honoré de Balzac's La Comedie Humaine, 1995; (trans.) M. Mokeddem, Forbidden woman-L'Interdite, 1998; (trans. and intro.) M. Mokeddem, Of Dreams and Assassins, 2000; (trans.) Layla, An Egyptian Woman, 2004. **Address:** Department of Modern Languages, Northern Arizona University, PO Box 6004, Flagstaff, AZ 86011, U.S.A. **Online address:** melissa.marcus@nau.edu

MARCUS, Leonard S. American (born United States), b. 1950. **Genres:** Children's Fiction, Art/Art History, Literary Criticism And History, Young Adult Non-fiction, Biography, Humor/Satire. **Career:** Parenting, contributing editor, 1988-; The Night Kitchen Radio Theater, literary director, 2006. **Publications:** (Ed. and intro.) New York Street Cries in Rhyme, 1977; The American Store Window, 1978; (with J.F. Kendall) Petrouchka: A Ballet Cut-Out Book, 1983; (ed.) Lion and the Unicorn, Picture Books, 1983; Lion and the Unicorn, Picture Books, 1984; An Epinal Album: Popular Prints from Nineteenth-Century France, 1984; (ed.) The Picture Book, 1985; (ed.) Humor and Play in Children's Literature, 1990; (ed. with A. Schwartz and intro.) Mother Goose's Little Misfortunes, 1990; Margaret Wise Brown: Awakened by the Moon, 1992, rev. ed., 1999; (comp.) Lifelines: A Poetry Anthology Patterned on the Stages of Life, 1994; 75 Years of Children's Book Week Posters: Celebrating Great Illustrators of American Children's Books, 1994; Morrow Junior Books: The First Fifty Years, 1996; Goodnight Moon, 1997; Making of Goodnight Moon, 1997; Caldecott Celebration: Six Artists and their Paths to the Caldecott Medal, 1998; Dear Genius: The Letters of Ursula Nordstrom, 1998; (comp. and ed.) Author Talk: Conversations with Judy Blume, 2000; Side by Side: Five Favorite Picture-Book Teams Go to Work, 2001; Ways of Telling: Conversations on the Art of the Picture Book, 2002; Storied City: A Children's Book, Walking-Tour Guide to New York City, 2003; (with A. Schwartz) Oscar: The Big Adventures of a Little Sock Monkey, 2006; (ed. and comp.) Wand in the Word: Conversations with Writers of Fantasy, 2006; Pass It Down: Five Picture Book Families Make Their Mark, 2007; Golden Legacy: How Golden Books Won Children's Hearts, Changed Publishing Forever and Became An American Icon Along the Way, 2007; A Caldecott Celebration: Seven Artists and Their Paths to the Caldecott Medal, 2008; (comp.and ed.) Show Me a Story!: Why Picture Books Matter: Conversations with 21 of the World's Most Celebrated Illustrators, 2012. AUTHOR OF INTRODUCTION: New York Street Cries in Rhyme, 1977; The Wind in the Willows, 1994; A Little Princess, 1994; The Complete Works of Lewis Carroll, 1994; Peter Pan, 1994; The Wonderful Wizard of Oz, 1994; The Art of Eric Carle, 1996; Penguin Book of Classic Children's Characters, 1997; The Original Curious George, 1998; Alice's Adventures in Wonderland, 1998; A Family Treasury of Little Golden Books, 1998; The Golden Books Family Treasury of Poetry, 1998; Century of Picture Books, 1999; Corduroy & Company: A Don Freeman Treasury, 2001; Garth Williams Treasury of Best Loved Golden Books, 2001; Nursery Classics: A Galdone Treasury, 2001; Mouse of My Heart, 2001; The Complete Adventures of Curious George, 2001; The Picture Book World of Garth Williams, 2002; The Borrowers Fiftieth Anniversary Edition, 2003; Make Way for McCloskey: A Robert McCloskey Treasury, 2004; The Art of Reading: Forty Illustrators Celebrate RIF's 40th Anniversary, 2005; Mary Engelbreit's Mother Goose, 2005; Minders of Make-believe: Idealists, Entrepreneurs and the Shaping of American Children's Literature, 2008; (comp. and ed.) Don't Make Me: Laugh: Conversations with Writers of Comedy, 2009; (ed.) Funny Business: Conversations with Writers of Comedy, 2009; Annotated Phantom Tollbooth, 2011. Contributor to periodicals. **Address:** Walker & Company, 175 5th Ave., New York, NY 10010, U.S.A. **Online address:** leonardsma@aol.com

MARCUS, Millicent. American (born United States), b. 1946. **Genres:** Film, Literary Criticism And History. **Career:** University of Texas, instructor, 1973-74, assistant professor, 1974-80, associate professor, 1980-87, professor of Italian, 1987-2000; University of Colorado, Study Abroad Program, assistant director, 1979; Syracuse University, visiting professor, 1986-87; University of Pennsylvania, visiting professor, 1987-89, 1991, 1993, Department of Romance Languages, Mariano Di Vito professor of Italian studies, director, undergraduate chair; Yale University, professor and director of graduate studies. Writer. **Publications:** Allegory of Form: Literary Self-Consciousness in the Decameron, 1979; Italian Film in the Light of Neorealism, 1986; Filmmaking by the Book: Italian Cinema and Literary Adaptation, 1993; After Fellini: National Cinema in the Postmodern Age, 2002; Italian Film in the Shadow of Auschwitz, 2007; (ed. with R. Sodi) New Reflections on Primo Levi: Before and After Auschwitz, 2011. Works appear in anthologies. Contributor to journals. **Address:** Film Studies Program, Yale University, Rm. 216, 53 Wall St., PO Box 208363, New Haven, CT 06511, U.S.A. **Online address:** mjmarcus@sas.upenn.edu

MARCUS, Paul. American (born United States), b. 1953. **Genres:** Psychology, History, Social Sciences. **Career:** University of London, staff; City University of New York, staff; New York University, staff. Writer. **Publications:** (Ed. with S.A. Luel) Psychoanalytic Reflections on the Holocaust, 1984; (ed. with A. Rosenberg) Healing Their Wounds: Psychotherapy with Holocaust Survivors and Their Families, 1989; (with I.W. Marcus) Scary Night Visitors: A Story for Children with Bedtime Fears, 1990; (with I.W. Marcus) Into the Great Forest: A Story for Children Away from Parents for the First Time, 1992; (with Rosenberg) Autonomy in the Nazi Concentration Camps and Mass Society, 1995; (ed. with A. Rosenberg) Psychoanalytic Versions of the Human Condition and Clinical Practice, 1998; Entrapment Defense, 1995; (with J.G. Cook) M. Bender, 1997; (ed. with A. Helmreich) Blacks and Jews on the Couch: Psychoanalytic Reflections on Black-Jewish Conflict, 1998; Autonomy in the Extreme Situation: Bruno Bettelheim, The Nazi Concentration Camp and The Mass Society, 1999; Ancient Religious Wisdom, Spirituality and Psychoanalysis, 2003; (with J. Helmreich) Warring Parents, Wounded Children and the Wretched World of Child Custody: Cautionary Tales, 2008; Being for the Other: Emmanuel Levinas, Ethical Living and Psychoanalysis, 2008; In Search of the Good Life: Emmanuel Levinas, Psychoanalysis and the Art of Living, 2010. Contributor to periodicals. **Address:** 114-06 Queens Blvd., Ste. A9, Forest Hills, NY 11375, U.S.A.

MARCUS, Sharon. American (born United States), b. 1966. **Genres:** Young Adult Fiction, Women's Studies And Issues, Gay And Lesbian Issues, Education, History, Literary Criticism And History. **Career:** University of California, associate professor of English; Columbia University, Department of English and Comparative Literature, Orlando Harriman professor of English and comparative literature. Writer. **Publications:** Apartment Stories: City and Home in Nineteenth-Century Paris and London, 1999; Between Women: Friendship, Desire, and Marriage in Victorian England, 2007. **Address:** Department of English and Comparative Literature, Columbia University, 308 Philosophy Hall, 1150 Amsterdam Ave., PO Box 4927, New York, NY 10027-7051, U.S.A. **Online address:** sm2247@columbia.edu

MARCUSE, Aída E. American/Uraguayian (born Uruguay), b. 1934. **Genres:** Children's Fiction, Young Adult Fiction, Plays/Screenplays, Education, Poetry, Children's Non-fiction, Mythology/Folklore, Translations, Translations. **Career:** Writer and translator, 1973-; Psychological Corporation (Harcourt Brace), writer of literary pieces, 1983-; Children's Press, translator, copyeditor, editor, consultant for books in Spanish, 1991-94; Scott, Foresman, video and reading program consultant, 1991. Educator. **Publications:** Habia Una Vez un Cuerpo... (Once upon a Time...a Body), 1972, new ed. 2010; Marcelo Casi-Casi... (Watch Out, Mark!), 1976; Muneca de Trapo (Raggedy Doll; poems), 1977; Pasos de Arena (Steps in the Sand, poetry for adults), 1982; Un Caballo a Motor (A Mechanical Horse), 1982; Un Barrilete para Grompón (A Kite for Grompon), 1985; La Cocina Viajera (The Traveling Kitchen), 1987; Cuentos de Antes de Ayer (Yesteryear's Stories), 1987; The Jaguar and the Deer, 1991; (adaptor) Aladino, 1992; (adaptor) Tomás Pulgar, 1992; (adaptor) Hansel y Gretel, 1992; (adaptor) Simbad el marino, 1992; (adaptor) Hermano Conejo, 1992; (adaptor) Alí Babá y los cuarenta ladrones, 1992; (adaptor) Caperucita y la luna de papel, 1993; (trans.) Tapiz de abuela, 1993; Me lo Dijo un Indio Viejo (An Old Indian Told Me), 1994; Mi diccionario de juguete (My Playing Dictionary), 1996; (trans.) Gran granero rojo, 1996; (trans.) Sonidos a mi alrededor, 1996; (trans.) Frida María: un cuento del Sudoeste de antes, 1997; (trans.) Willie no quiere que lo abracen, 1997; Prudencio el prudente, (limericks) 1997; Yo y los demas (I and the Others), 1998, new ed. 2010; Lo que cuentan los incas (folktales), 1998; Dona Pata y Don Canguro (poems); Más viejo que refrán: diccionario de refranes y expresiones idiomática, 2000; Tiempo de ser (poems for adults), 2001; Ese dia en la selva (verse), 2002; El gato Rafonero, poesias, 2003; Del Tio Jaguar y otros animales (folktales), 2004; Un trozo de pan (A Piece of Bread), 2005; El león y la araña, 2007; (trans.) Nuestro autobús, 2008; Quién hizo los mundos?, 2008. **Address:** 626 Coral Way, Ste. 1103, Coral Gables, FL 33134, U.S.A. **Online address:** amarcuse@bellsouth.net

MARCUSE, Gary. Canadian/American (born United States), b. 1949. **Genres:** Politics/Government, Military/Defense/Arms Control, Administration/Management. **Career:** Canadian Broadcasting Corp., writer, broadcaster and executive producer, CBC-Radio, presenter, 1975-91, CBC Television, programming executive, 2004-08; Face to Face Media Ltd., producer and director of television documentary; Documentary Organization of Canada, president. **Publications:** (With R. Whitaker) Cold War Canada: The Making of a National Insecurity State, 1945-1957, 1994. Contributor of articles to periodicals. **Address:** Face to Face Media Ltd., 1818 Grant St., Vancouver, BC V5L 2Y8, Canada.

MARDER, Norma. American (born United States), b. 1934. **Genres:** Novels, Autobiography/Memoirs, Literary Criticism And History. **Career:** Judson Dance Workshop, singer, 1960-65; New Verbal Workshop, co-director, 1970-80; Parkland College, Program for the Long Living, teacher, 1975-78; National Academy of Arts, head of voice department, 1975-79; Art Institute of Chicago, teacher of verbal improvisation workshop, 1977; Dartington College, teacher of verbal improvisation workshop, 1981; Champaign County Adult Day Care, writing teacher, 1983; freelance writer, 1984-; University of Illinois, editor, 1990-92; Monhegan Museum Association, trustee, 1991-96. **Publications:** An Eye for Dark Places, 1993. Contributor to periodicals. **Address:** 1009 W Church St., Champaign, IL 61821-3329, U.S.A.

MARDON, Austin Albert. Canadian (born Canada), b. 1962. **Genres:** History, Biography, Translations, Politics/Government, Novellas/Short Stories. **Career:** Antarctic Institute of Canada, president, 1985-, director, 1991-, researcher, 1992-; NASA/NSF, research scientist, 1986-87; Alberta Culture and Multiculturalism, historical researcher, 1989-90; RTAJ Fry Press, editor, 1990-97; Shoestring Press, editor, 1990-97; freelance writer, 1991-; Golden Meteorite Press, editor, 1997-; Stargate Research Laboratory, geophysical consultant, 1999-2007; Alberta Mental Health Self Help Network, assistant program manager, 1999-2005, staff; Greenwich University-Australia, adjunct faculty, 2000-03; Greenwich University-Hawaii, adjunct faculty, 2003-04; Stargate Research Laboratory-Idaho, geophysical consultant, 2003-04; Penza State Pedagogical University, honorary professor, 2003-; International Noble Academy, senior research fellow, 2003; Akamai University, adjunct faculty, 2004-; American Military University (AMU-APUS), adjunct instructor, 2005-06. **Publications:** (Trans. with E. Mardon) D. Munro, A Description of the Western Isles of Scotland, 1990; (with E. Mardon) The Alberta Judicial Biographical Dictionary, 1990; (with E. Mardon) Alberta Ethnic Mormon Politicians, 1991; A Conspectus of the Contribution of Herodotus to the Development of Geographical Thought, 1990; International Law and Space Rescue Systems, 1991; Kensington Stone and Other Essays, 1991; A Transient in Whirl, 1991; (co-author) Alberta Ethnic German Politicians, 1991; (co-author) When Kitty Met the Ghost, 1991; (co-author) The Girl Who Could Walk Through Walls, 1991; (with E. Mardon) The Men of the Dawn: Alberta Politicians from the North West Territories of the District of Alberta and Candidates for the First Alberta General Election, 1882-1905, 1991; (with J. Williams and E. Mardon) Down and Out and On the Run in Moscow, 1991; (with E. Mardon) Alberta Mormon Politicians, 1992; (with E. Mardon) Alberta Election Results, 1882-1992, 1993; (with E. Mardon) Edmonton Political Biographical Dictionary, 1882-1990: A Work in Progress, 1993; (with E. Mardon) Biographical Dictionary of Alberta Politicians, 1993; (with E. Mardon) Alberta General Election Returns & Subsequent Byelections 1882-1992, 1993; (co-author) Alberta Political Biographical Dictionary, 1994; (co-author) Alberta Executive Council 1905-1990, 1994; (with M.F. Korn) Alone against the Revolution, 1996; (co-author) Many Christian Saints for Children, 1997; (co-author) Early Saints, 1997; (co-author) Later Christian Saints for Children, 1997; (co-author) Childhood Memories and Legends of Christmas Past, 1998; (with E.G. Mardon) Community Names of Alberta, 1998; (co-author) United Farmers of Alberta, 1999; (with E. Mardon) Alberta Catholic Politicians, 2000; (with E.G. Mardon) Alberta Anglican Politicians: Historical and Biographical Profiles, 2001; (with E. Mardon) Liberals in Power in Alberta, 1905-1921, 2001; Political Networks in Alberta, 1905-1992, 2001; (with E. Mardon) What's is in a Name?: The History of Alberta Federal Riding Names, 2002; (co-author) Political Networks in Alberta 1905-1992, 2002; (co-author) Liberal Politicians in Alberta 1905-1921 2002; (co-author) Edmonton Members of the Legislature, 2004; (co-author) Senators and Members of the House of Commons from Edmonton, 2004; Alberta Politicians 1993-2004, 2004; (co-author) Edmonton Municipal Politicians, 2005; (with E. Mardon and M. Pickering) Edmonton Civic Politicians: Historical, Biographical and Contemporary, 2005; 7 Days in Moscow, 2005; The Contribution of Geography to the Recovery of Antarctic Meteorites, 2005; (with E. Mardon) Alberta Francophone Politicians, 2007; Scandinavian Politicians in Alberta, 2008; Alberta Politicians 2004, 2008; (comp. with E.G. Mardon) Lethbridge Politicians, 2008; English Medieval Comets, 2008; (with E.G. Mardon) Alberta Election Returns, 1887-1994, 2010; Alberta French Politicians, forthcoming; Alberta Election Statistics, forthcoming; Who's Who in Federal Politics in Alberta, forthcoming; Alberta Scandinavian Politicians, forthcoming. EDITOR: Stygian Relics of the Lachrymose, 1998; The Spectral Carnival Show and Other Stories, 1998; A Wake of Evil, 1999; Lady Juanita, 2002; The Avengers Trilogy, 2003; Samson's Return, 2004; A Novella of Short Stories, 2004; Journals of a Chronic Schizophrenic, 2004; Spirit in Poetry, 2004; Little Lady, 2004; A Full Glass of Reality, 2004; Room for Change, 2007; Dark Age Avengers, 2009. Contributor to periodicals. **Address:** Antarctic Institute of Canada, Main Post Office, PO Box 1223, Edmonton, AB T5J 2M4, Canada. **Online address:** aamardon@yahoo.ca

MAREK, Nancy. *See* **COTE, Nancy.**

MARENBON, John (Alexander). British (born England), b. 1955. **Genres:** Philosophy. **Career:** Cambridge University, Trinity College, research fellow, 1978, assistant college lecturer in English, 1979-83, college lecturer in English, 1983-97, Faculty of History, lecturer, 1986-, fellow and director of studies, 1979-2004, British Academy, research reader, 1991-93, lecturer in history of philosophy, 1997-2004, Trinity Hall, external director of studies in philosophy, 2001-04, senior research fellow, 2005-. Writer. **Publications:** From the Circle of Alcuin to the School of Auxerre: Logic, Theology, and Philosophy in the Early Middle Ages, 1981; Early Medieval Philosophy, 480-1150: An Introduction, 1983; Later Medieval Philosophy, 1150-1350: An Introduction, 1987; The Philosophy of Peter Abelard, 1997; Aristotelian Logic, Platonism and The Context of Early Medieval Philosophy in the West, 2000; Boethius, 2003; Le temps, la prescience et les futurs contingents, 2005; Medieval Philosophy: An Historical and Philosophical Introduction, 2006. EDITOR: Aristotle in Britain During the Middle Ages, 1996; Medieval Philosophy, 1998; Poetry and Philosophy in the Middle Ages, 2001; (with G. Orlandi and trans.) Collationes, 2001; Many Roots of Medieval Logic, 2007; Cambridge companion to Boethius, 2009; Methods and Methodologies: Aristotelian Logic East and West, 500-1500, 2011; Oxford Handbook of Medieval Philosophy, 2012. **Address:** Trinity College, Cambridge University, Saint John's St., Cambridge, CB2 1TQ, England. **Online address:** jm258@cam.ac.uk

MARES, Michael A. American (born United States), b. 1945. **Genres:** Natural History. **Career:** Universidad Nacional de Cordoba, adjunct professor of zoology, 1971; Universidad Nacional du Tucuman, adjunct professor of zoology, 1972, visiting professor, 1974; University of Pittsburgh, assistant professor, associate professor, 1973-81; University of Oklahoma, associate professor, 1981-85, professor of zoology, 1985-, Joeseph Brandt professor of zoology; Sam Noble Oklahoma Museum of Natural History, curator of mammals, 1981-, director of museum, 1983-2003, research curator, 2003-08, director of museum, 2008-, Stovall Museum, curator of mammals, 1981-85; University of Arizona, visiting scientist, 1980-81; Council for the International Exchange of Scholars, member of board of directors, 1988-91; American Society of Mammalogists, vice president, 2001-02. Writer. **Publications:** (With D.F. Williams) A New Genus and Species of Phyllotine Rodent (Mammalia, Muridae) From Northwestern Argentina, 1978; Convergent Evolution Among Desert Rodent, 1980; (ed. with H.M. Genoways) Mammalian Biology in South America, 1982; (with R.A. Ojeda and R.M. Barquez) Guide to the Mammals of Salta Province, 1989; The Mammals of Oklahoma, 1989; (with R.A. Ojeda) A Biogeographic Analysis of the Mammals of Salta Province, Argentina, 1989; (ed. with D.J. Schmidly) Latin American Mammalogy: History, Biodiversity, and Conservation, 1991; The Mammals of Tucuman, 1991; Guide to the Bats of Argentina, 1993; (ed.) Encyclopedia of Deserts, 1999; (with J.K. Braun and R.M. Barquez) The Bats of Argentina, 1999; A University Natural History Museum for the New Millennium, 2001; A Desert Calling: Life in a Forbidding Landscape, 2002. Contributor to periodicals. **Address:** Sam Noble Oklahoma Museum of Natural History, University of Oklahoma, 2401 Chautauqua Ave., Norman, OK 73072-7029, U.S.A. **Online address:** mamares@ou.edu

MARES, Theun. South African/Zimbabwean (born Zimbabwe), b. 1952. **Genres:** Novellas/Short Stories, Self Help. **Career:** Writer, 1994-; South Africa's Department of Education, adviser. **Publications:** Return of the Warriors, 1995; Cry of the Eagle, 1997; The Mists of Dragon Lore: The Toltec Teachings, vol. III, 1998; Quest for Maleness, 1999; This Darned Elusive Happiness, 1999; Unveil the Mysteries of the Female, 1999; Shadows of Wolf Fire, 2002; Book of Aphorisms, 2006. **Address:** c/o Lionheart Publishing, PO Box X5, Constantia, Cape Town, 7848, South Africa. **Online address:** cajm@iafrica.com

MARGALIT, Gilad. Israeli (born Israel), b. 1959?. **Genres:** Adult Nonfiction, Administration/Management, Politics/Government. **Career:** University of Haifa, lecturer, 1999-, senior lecturer, Department of General History, faculty, Haifa Center for German and European Studies, historian and deputy director. Writer. **Publications:** Yahas Ha hievrah Ha-Germanit U-mosdoteha

Shele-ahiar 1945 La-Tsoanim ule-redifatam Ba-Raikh Ha-Shelishi, 1995; Antigypsyism in the Political Culture of the Federal Republic of Germany: A Parallel with Antisemitism?, 1996; Germanyah ha-aheret veha-Tsoanim: Yehasam shel Ha-Germanim ahare 1945 li-redifat ha-Tsoanim ba-Raikh ha-shelishi, 1998; Die Nachkriegsdeutschen und ihre Zigeuner. Die Behandlung der Sinti und Roma Im Schatten von Auschwitz, 2001; Germany and its Gypsies, 2002; (with Y. Weiss) Zikaron ve-Shikhhah: Germanyah veha-Shoah, 2005; Ashmah, Sevel ve-zikaron: Germanyah Zokheret Et Meteha Be-Milhemet Ha-olam Ha-sheniyah, 2007; Guilt, Suffering, and Memory, 2010. CONTRIBUTOR: Challenging Ethnic Citizenship: German and Israeli Perspectives on Immigration, 2002; Remembering the Holocaust in Germany 1945-2000: German Strategies and Jewish Responses, 2002; Narrative der Shoah: Representationen der Vergangenheit in Historiographie, 2002; Sinti, Roma, Gypsies. Sprache-Geschichte-Gegenwart, 2003; Les habits neufs de l'antisemitisme en Europe, 2004; Les diasporas: 2000 ans d'histoire, by Lisa Anteby, William Berthomiere, Gabriel Sheffer, 2005. Contributor to journals. **Address:** Department of General History, University of Haifa, Mount Carmel, Haifa, 31905, Israel. **Online address:** margalit@research.haifa.ac.il

MARGAM, Kate. British (born England) **Genres:** Novels, Literary Criticism And History. **Career:** Writer and actor. **Publications:** NOVELS: Poor Kevin, 1999; Milch Cow, 2000. Contributor to periodicals. **Address:** c/o Author Mail, Serpents Tail Publishing, 3A Exmouth House, Pine St., London, GL EC1R 0JH, England.

MARGARITI, Roxani Eleni. American/Greek (born Greece), b. 1969. **Genres:** History, Business/Trade/Industry, Young Adult Non-fiction, Theology/Religion, Social Sciences. **Career:** American Numismatic Society, assistant curator of Islamic and East Asian coins and medals, 1997-2001; Princeton University, S.D. Goitein Laboratory for Geniza Research, editor of Judaeo-Arabic Cairo Geniza documents, 1999-2002, research and teaching assistant, 2001-02, Researcher and coordinator of Judeo-Arabic documents transcription pilot project, 2008-; Emory University, Department of Middle Eastern and South Asian Studies, assistant professor, 2002-08, associate professor, 2008-. Archaeologist. **Publications:** Aden & the Indian Ocean Trade: 150 Years in the Life of a Medieval Arabian Port (nonfiction), 2007; (ed. with A. Sabra and P.M. Sijpesteijn) Histories of the Middle East: Studies in Middle Eastern Society, Economy and Law in Honor of A.L. Udovitch, 2011. Contributor to books and journals. **Address:** Department of Middle Eastern and South Asian, Studies, Emory University, S-308 Callaway Ctr., 537 Kilgo Cir., Atlanta, GA 30322, U.S.A. **Online address:** rmargar@emory.edu

MARGOLF, Diane C. American (born United States), b. 1960. **Genres:** Theology/Religion, Law. **Career:** Colorado State University, professor. Writer. **Publications:** Religion and Royal Justice in Early Modern France: The Paris Chambre de L'Edit, 1598- 1665, 2003; (contrib.) Distant Lands and Diverse Cultures: The French Experience in Asia, 1600-1700, 2003. Contributor to books and periodicals. **Address:** Department of History, Colorado State University, B356 Clark, Fort Collins, CO 80523-1776, U.S.A. **Online address:** diane.margoolf@colostate.edu

MARGOLIAN, Howard T. Canadian (born Canada), b. 1957. **Genres:** Military/Defense/Arms Control, History, Law. **Career:** Department of Justice of Canada, Crimes against Humanity and War Crimes Section, investigator, senior war crimes investigator, consultant, 1990-98. Writer. **Publications:** Conduct Unbecoming: The Story of the Murder of Canadian Prisoners of War in Normandy, 1998; Unauthorized Entry: The Truth about Nazi War Criminals in Canada, 1946-1956, 2000; Beware the False Prophet: The Life and Legacy of Louis Riel, 2006. **Address:** University of Toronto Press, 10 Saint Mary St., Ste. 700, Toronto, ON M4Y 2W8, Canada.

MARGOLICK, David. American (born United States) **Genres:** Documentaries/Reportage, Social Sciences. **Career:** New York Times, legal reporter, 1981-86, national legal affairs editor and law columnist, 1987-96; Vanity Fair, contributing editor, 1995; Portfolio, contributing editor. **Publications:** Undue Influence: The Epic Battle for the Johnson and Johnson Fortune, 1993; At the Bar: The Passions and Peccadilloes of American Lawyers, 1995; Strange Fruit: Billie Holiday, Café Society, and an Early Cry for Civil Rights, 2000; Beyond Glory: Joe Louis vs Max Schmeling and A World On the Brink, 2005; Elizabeth and Hazel: Two Women of Little Rock, 2011. **Address:** c/o Author Mail, Alfred A Knopf Inc., 1745 Broadway, New York, NY 10019, U.S.A.

MARGOLIES, Daniel S. American (born United States), b. 1969. **Genres:** Politics/Government, Law, International Relations/Current Affairs. **Career:** Virginia Wesleyan College, Batten associate professor of history. Writer and historian. **Publications:** Henry Watterson and the New South: The Politics of Empire, Free Trade and Globalization, 2006; Spaces of Law in American Foreign Relations: Extradition and Extraterritoriality in the Borderlands and Beyond, 1877-1898, 2011. Contributor to book and periodicals. **Address:** Virginia Wesleyan College, Blocker 15, 1584 Wesleyan Dr., Norfolk, VA 23502, U.S.A. **Online address:** dmargolies@vwc.edu

MARGOLIN, Leslie. American (born United States), b. 1945?. **Genres:** Women's Studies And Issues, Mystery/Crime/Suspense, Social Sciences. **Career:** University of Iowa, College of Education, Department of Rehabilitation and Counselor Education, professor, Project on the Rhetoric of Inquiry, professor. Writer. **Publications:** Goodness Personified: The Emergence of Gifted Children, 1994; Under the Cover of Kindness: The Invention of Social Work, 1997; Murderess! The Chilling True Story of the Most Infamous Woman Ever Electocuted, 1999. MYSTERY NOVELS: Damaged, 2004; The Adulteress, 2006. **Address:** Rehabilitation and Counselor Education, College of Education, University of Iowa, 224 Bowman House, N459 Lindquist Ctr., Iowa City, IA 52242-1529, U.S.A. **Online address:** leslie-margolin@uiowa.edu

MARGOLIN, Phillip (Michael). American (born United States), b. 1944. **Genres:** Novels, Criminology/True Crime. **Career:** New York City, teacher at public schools, 1968-70; Oregon Court of Appeals, law clerk to chief judge, 1970-71; Multnomah County, deputy district attorney and special agent, 1971-72; private practice, 1972-96, 1980-86; Nash and Margolin, partner, 1974-80; Margolin and Margolin, staff, 1986-96; full-time writer, 1996-. **Publications:** The Girl in the Yellow Bikini, 1974; Heartstone, 1978; The Last Innocent Man, 1981; Gone, But Not Forgotten, 1993; After Dark, 1995; The Burning Man, 1996, 2nd ed. 1997; The Undertaker's Widow, 1998; Angie's Delight, 1998; The Jailhouse Lawyer, 1998; Wild Justice, 2000; (co-author) Natural Suspect, 2001; The Associate, 2001; Ties That Bind: A Novel, 2003; Sleeping Beauty, 2004; Lost Lake, 2005; Proof Positive, 2006; Executive Privilege, 2008; Fugitive: A Novel, 2009; Supreme Justice, 2010; The House on Pine Terrace, 2010; (with A.M. Rome) Vanishing Acts, 2011; (co-author) No Rest for the Dead, 2011; Capitol Murder, 2012. Contributor to periodicals and journals. **Address:** 621 SW Morrison St., Ste. 1025, Portland, OR 97205, U.S.A.

MARGOLIS, Jeffrey A. American (born United States), b. 1948. **Genres:** Documentaries/Reportage, Criminology/True Crime. **Career:** Richard Stockton College of New Jersey, adjunct faculty member, 1986-95; Lower Cape May Regional School District, guidance counselor, 1987-2002; Rowan University, College of Education, professional staff, 2002-; Bethel Investment Club, vice president. Writer. **Publications:** On Your Own, 1991; Teen Crime Wave: A Growing Problem, 1997; Violence in Sports: Victory at What Price?, 1999; Everything You Need to Know about Teens Who Kill, 2000. **Address:** University of Rowan, 2028 Education Hall, 201 Mullica Hill Rd., Glassboro, NJ 08028, U.S.A. **Online address:** margolis@rowan.edu

MARGOLIS, Jonathan. British (born England), b. 1955. **Genres:** Novels, Novellas/Short Stories, Adult Non-fiction, Young Adult Fiction, History, Biography. **Career:** Writer. **Publications:** Hothouse People, 1987; Cleese Encounters, 1992; (with G.Morris) The Commuter's Tale, 1992; The Big Yin: The Life and Times of Billy Connolly, 1994; Freddie Star Ate My Hamster, 1994; Lenny Henry, 1996; Bernard Manning, 1997; Michael Palin: A Biography, 1998; Uri Geller: Magician or Mystic?, 1999; A Brief History of Tomorrow: The Future, Past and Present, 2000; O: The Intimate History of the Orgasm, 2004; Guerrilla Marketing for Dummies, 2008. **Address:** c/o Jane Gelfman, Gelfman Schneider Literary Agents Inc., 250 W 57th St., New York, NY 10107, U.S.A.

MARGOLIS, Leslie. American (born United States) **Genres:** Novels. **Career:** 826NYC, Young-adult Writers' Colony, teacher. Writer. **Publications:** NOVELS: Fix, 2006; Price of Admission, 2007. ANNABELLE UNLEASHED SERIES: Boys Are Dogs, 2008; Girls Acting Catty, 2009; Everybody Bugs Out, 2011; One Tough Chick, forthcoming. MAGGIE BROOKLYN MYSTERY SERIES: Girl's Best Friend, 2010; Vanishing Acts, 2012. **Address:** Bloomsbury Publishing, 175 5th Ave., New York, NY 10010-7703, U.S.A. **Online address:** leslie@lesliemargolis.com

MARGOLIS, Seth J(acob). American (born United States) **Genres:** Mystery/Crime/Suspense, Novels, Psychology. **Career:** Writer. **Publications:** False Faces, 1991; (ed.) Selected from the Mambo Kings Play Songs of Love,

1992; (ed.) Selected from Lonesome Dove, 1992; Losing Isaiah, 1993; Vanishing Act, 1993; The Other Mother, 1993; Perfect Angel: A Novel of Psychological Suspense, 1997; The Hypnotist, 1997; Closing Costs, 2006. **Address:** St. Martin's Press, 175 5th Ave., New York, NY 10010-7703, U.S.A. **Online address:** seth@sethmargolis.com

MARGULIES, **Donald.** American (born United States), b. 1954. **Genres:** Plays/Screenplays, inspirational/Motivational Literature. **Career:** Freelance graphic designer, 1977-80; Yale University, instructor in playwriting, 1990-91, 1999-2004, Yale Drama School, faculty, 1992-99, adjunct professor of English and theatre studies, 2004-, professor of English and theater studies; Playwright's Lab, Sundance Institute, playwright-in-residence. Writer. **Publications:** PLAYS: Luna Park, 1982; Found a Peanut, 1984; What's Wrong with This Picture?, 1985; The Model Apartment, 1988; The Loman Family Picnic, 1989; Sight Unseen, 1991; Pitching to the Star and Other Short Plays, 1993; Sight Unseen and Other Plays, 1995; July 7, 1994: Short Plays and Monologues, 1997; Collected Stories, 1998; Dinner with Friends, 2000; (with S. Asch) God of Vengeance, 2000; Misadventure, 2001; Luna Park: Short Plays and Monologues, 2002; Two Days: Two Short Plays, 2004; Brooklyn Boy, 2005; Shipwrecked! An Entertainment-The Amazing Adventures of Louis de Rougemont (as told by himself), 2007; Time Stands Still, 2009. **Address:** Department of English, Yale University, Rm. 109, LC 304, 63 High St., PO Box 208302, New Haven, CT 06520-8302, U.S.A. **Online address:** donald.margulies@yale.edu

MARGULIES, **Jimmy.** American (born United States), b. 1951. **Genres:** Humor/Satire, Cartoons, Picture/Board Books, Graphic Novels. **Career:** Rothco Cartoons, cartoonist, 1973-85; CETA, artist, 1978-80; Army Times Journal Newspapers, cartoonist, 1980-84; Houston Post, editorial cartoonist, 1984-90; self-syndicated cartoonist, 1986-; The Record, editorial cartoonist, 1990-; King Features/North America Syndicate, syndicated cartoons and caricatures, 1991-. Writer. **Publications:** (Ed.) 100 Watts: The James Watt Memorial Cartoon Collection, 1983; Reagan Comics, 1984; My Husband Is Not a Wimp! Margulies Cartoons from the Houston Post, 1988; Hitting below the Beltway: The Best of Margulies, 1998. Contributor to periodicals. Works appear in anthologies. **Address:** The Record, 150 River St., Hackensack, NJ 07601-7152, U.S.A. **Online address:** jimmarg@aol.com

MARIANO, **Connie Concepcion.** American/Filipino (born Philippines), b. 1955?. **Genres:** Autobiography/Memoirs. **Career:** Naval Hospital, intern and resident in internal medicine, 1981-86, general internal medicine division head, 1990-92; National Board of Medical Examiners, diplomate, 1982-; USS Prairie, general medical officer and head of medical department division, 1982-84; Naval Medical Clinic, specialty clinic and urgent care facility director, 1986-90; White House, physician, 1992-, medical unit director and personal physician to President Bill Clinton, 1994-2001; Mayo Clinic, physician and assistant professor of medicine; Center for Executive Medicine, president and founder, 2005-; University School of Health Sciences, Uniformed Services, assistant professor of medicine. Speaker and writer. **Publications:** The White House Doctor (memoir), 2010. **Address:** Center for Executive Medicine, 33777 N Scottsdale Rd., Ste. 120, Scottsdale, AZ 85266-1570, U.S.A.

MARIAS, **Javier.** Spanish (born Spain), b. 1951. **Genres:** Novels, Novellas/Short Stories, Translations, Literary Criticism And History, Biography, Autobiography/Memoirs. **Career:** Oxford University, lecturer in Spanish literature. Writer and translator. **Publications:** Los Dominios del Lobo, 1971; Travesia del Horizonte, 1973; (with F. de Azua and V. Molina-Foix) Tres Cuentos Didacticos (short stories), 1975; El Monarca del Tiempo, 1978; El Siglo, 1983; El Hombre Sentimental, 1986; Travesía del horizonte, 1988; Todas las Almas, 1989; Mientras Ellas Duermen, 1990; Pasiones Pasadas, 1991; Corazón Tan Blanco, 1992; Vidas Escritas, 1992; Literatura y Fantasma, 1993; Mañana en la batalla piensa en mi, 1994; Vida del Fantasma: Entusiasmos, Bromas, Reminiscencias y Canones Recortados, 1995; Hombre que parecía no querer nada, 1996; Cuando fui mortal, 1996; Miramientos, 1997; Mano de sombra, 1997; Negra espalda del tiempo, 1998; Seré amado cuando falte, 1999; Dark Back of Time, 2001; A veces un caballero, 2001; Fiebre: y Lanza, 2002; Tu rostro mañana, 2002; Harán de mí un criminal, 2003; El monarca del tiempo, 2003; Donde todo ha sucedido, 2005; Oficio de oír llover, 2005; Your Face Tomorrow, vol. I: Fever and Spear, 2005, vol. II: Dance and Dream, 2006; Corazón tan blanco, 2006; Veneno y sombra y adiós, 2007; Demasiada nieve alrededor, 2007; Tu rostro mañana.1, 2008; Aquella mitad de mi tiempo, 2008; Lo que no vengo a decir, 2009; Los villanos de la nación, 2010; While the Women are Sleeping, 2010; Los Enamoramientos, 2011. **Address:** Harcourt Brace & Co., 525 B St., Ste. 1900, San Diego, CA 92101-4495, U.S.A.

MARIN, **Dalia.** German/Austrian (born Austria) **Genres:** Business/Trade/Industry, Economics. **Career:** Institute for Advanced Studies, Wissenschaftlicher assistant professor, 1984-94; European University Institute, Jean Monnet fellow, 1987-88, visiting fellow; Institute for Advanced Studies, assistant professor of economics, 1992-94; Harvard University, Department of Economics, visiting professor, 2001-02; Humboldt University, Institute for Advanced Studies in Vienna, assistant professor, through 1994, associate professor of economics, 1994-98; University of Munich, professor of economics, 1998-, Institute for International Economic Relations, chair; Russian European Centre for Economic Policy, team leader, 1998-2000; New York University, Stern School of Business, visiting professor, 2006-07; CES Ifo, research fellow; University of Michigan, The William Davidson Institute, research fellow; World Bank, consultant; European Bank for Reconstruction and Development, consultant; Stanford University, visiting professor. Writer. **Publications:** Wechselkurs und Industriegewinne: Eine empirische Studie zu den Verteilungswirkungen der Währungspolitik in österreich, 1983; Überleben durch Innovationsimport: Strukturdynamik in der Textilwirtschaft, 1987; (with M. Schnitzer) Contracts in Trade and Transition: The Resurgence of Barter, 2002; (ed. with E. Helpman and T. Verdier) The Organization of Firms in a Global Economy, 2008. **Address:** Department of Economics, University of Munich, Schackstrabe 4, Munich, D-80539, Germany. **Online address:** dalia.marin@lrz.uni-muenchen.de

MARIN, **Mindy.** American (born United States), b. 1960. **Genres:** Novels, Food And Wine. **Career:** Paramount Pictures, Television Division, casting assistant, 1978-; Warner Bros. Television, casting director, manager of talent and casting, through 1989; Casting Artists Inc., founder, 1989, casting director, 1989-; Bluewater Ranch Entertainment (production company), founder, 1991, developer of feature films and associate producer, 1992-, Bluewater Books, creator. Writer. **Publications:** The Secret to Tender Pie: America's Grandmothers Share Their Favorite Recipies, 1997. **Address:** Bluewater Ranch Entertainment, Casting Artists Inc., Bluewater Ranch Books, 1433 6th St., Santa Monica, CA 90401, U.S.A. **Online address:** oceanranch@aol.com

MARIN, **Rosario.** American/Mexican (born Mexico), b. 1958. **Genres:** Adult Non-fiction, Autobiography/Memoirs. **Career:** City National Bank, staff, 1981-86; California Department of Developmental Services, chief of legislative affairs, 1992-93; California State Council for Developmental Disabilities, chair, 1994-96; City of Huntington Park, mayor, 1999-2000; California State Department of Social Services, assistant deputy director, 1996-97; Governor's Office of Community Relations, deputy director, 1997-98; U.S. Department of Treasury, Washington, U.S. treasurer, 2001-03; AT&T, public relations manager for Hispanic market, public relations manager; California Integrated Waste Management Board, chair, 2004. Writer. **Publications:** Leading Between Two Worlds, 2007. **Address:** State and Consumer Services Agency, 915 Capitol Mall, Ste. 200, Sacramento, CA 95814, U.S.A. **Online address:** rosario-marin@sbcglobal.net

MARINEAU, **Michele.** Canadian (born Canada), b. 1955. **Genres:** Young Adult Fiction, Translations. **Career:** Translator and writer. **Publications:** YOUNG ADULT NOVELS: Cassiopee ou l'ete polonais, 1988; L'ete des baleines, 1989; L'Homme du Cheshire, 1990; La route de Chlifa, 1992, trans. as The Road to Chlifa, 1996; Lean Mean Machines, 2002; Histoire d'une barbouillette. TRANSLATOR: S. Ellis, Baby Project, Quelque temps dans la vie de Jessica, 1990; L.M. Montgomery, Along the Shore: Tales by the Sea, (title means: 'Sur le ravage'), 1991; Montgomery, Magic for Marigold, (title means: 'Le Monde merveilleux de Marigold'), 1991; Montgomery, Among the Shadows, (title means: 'Kilmeny du vieux verger'), 1992; Y. Tsuchiya, Faithful Elephants: A True Story of Animals, People and War, (title means: 'Fideles Elephants'), 2000. **Address:** 4666 Ave. de Lorimier, Montreal, QC H2H 2B5, Canada.

MARINICK, **Richard.** American (born United States), b. 1951. **Genres:** Novels, Mystery/Crime/Suspense, Young Adult Fiction. **Career:** Norfolk County, administrative assistant and district attorney. Writer. **Publications:** Boyos, 2004; In For a Pound, 2007. **Address:** Kates Mystery Books, 2211 Massachusetts Ave., Cambridge, MA 02140, U.S.A.

MARINO, Anne (N.). American (born United States) **Genres:** Adult Nonfiction. **Career:** California College of the Arts, adjunct professor of writing and literature. Writer. **Publications:** The Collapsible World, 2000. **Address:** c/o Christy Fletcher, Carlisle & Co., 24 E 64th St., New York, NY 10021, U.S.A. **Online address:** amarino@cca.edu

MARION, Jean-Luc. (Jean-Luc P. Marion). American/French (born France), b. 1946. **Genres:** Physics, Theology/Religion. **Career:** Poitiers University, professor, 1981-88; University of Paris X-Nanterre, professor, 1988-94; University of Paris, professor, 1995, director of philosophy, 1996, chair of école Doctorale Concepts et Langages, 1999; University of Chicago, Divinity School, John Nuveen professor of the philosophy of religion and theology, Andrew Thomas Greeley and Grace McNichols Greeley professor of Catholic studies and professor of the philosophy of religions and theology. Writer and philosopher. **Publications:** (With A. Benoit) Avec ou sans Dieu? Débat entre, 1970; (with J.R. Armogathe) Index des regulae ad directionem ingenii de René Descartes, 1976; Régles utiles et claires pour la direction de l'esprit en la recherche de la vérité, 1977; Sur la théologie blanche de Descartes: Analogie, création des vérités éternelles et fondement, 1981; (co-author) Analogie et dialectique: Essais de théologie fondamentale, 1982; (ed. with J. Deprun) La passion de la raison: Hommage Ferdinand Alquié, 1983; (ed. with G. Planty-Bonjour) Phénoménologie et métaphysique, 1984; (with A. Bonfand and G. Labrot) Trois essais sur la perspective, 1985; Jean-Francois Lacalmontie: Ce que cela donne, 1986; (ed. with N. Grimaldi) Le discours et sa méthode: Colloque pour le 350e anniversaire du Discours de la méthode, 1987; (ed. with J. Beyssade and L. Levy) Descartes, objecter et répondre: Actes du colloque Objecter et répondre, 1994; (co-author) Index des meditationes de prima philosophia de R. Descartes, 1996; (with A. Bonfand) Hergé: Tintin le Terrible, ou, l'alphabet des richesses, 1996; (ed.) Positivité et transcendance: suivi de, Lévinas et la phénoménologie, 2000; (co-ed.) Montaigne: Scepticisme, métaphysique, théologie, 2004; Certitudes négatives, 2010; Au lieu de soi, 2012. IN ENGLISH TRANSLATION: Sur l'ontologie grise de Descartes: Science cartésienne et savoir aristotélicien dans les Regulae, 1975, trans. as Descartes's Grey Ontology: Cartesian Science and Aristotelian Thought in the Regulae, 2004; L'Idole et la distance: Cinq études, 1977; Dieu sans l' être: Hors-texte, 1982; Théologiques, 1982; Sur le prisme métaphysique de Descartes: Constitution et limites de l'onto-théologie dans la pensée cartésienne, 1986; Prolégomènes la charité, 1986; Réduction et donation: Recherches sur Husserl, Heidegger et la phénoménologie, 1989; Questions cartésiennes, 1991, trans. as Cartesian Questions: Method and Metaphysics, 1999; La croisée du visible, 1991; étant donné: Essai d'une phénoménologie de la donation, 1997; De surcroît: études sur les phénomènes saturés, 2001; Le phénomène érotique: Six méditations, 2003; Le visible et le révélé, 2005; On the Ego and on God: Further Cartesian Questions, 2007. **Address:** Divinity School, University of Chicago, 300A Swift Hall, 1025 E 58th St., Chicago, IL 60637-1509, U.S.A. **Online address:** jmarion@uchicago.edu

MARION, Jean-Luc P. *See* **MARION, Jean-Luc.**

MARION, Robert W. American (born United States), b. 1952. **Genres:** Medicine/Health, Translations. **Career:** Montefiore Medical Center, pediatric geneticist, 1984-; Yeshiva University, Albert Einstein College of Medicine, Department of Pediatrics, professor, 1984-, Division of Development Medicine, chief, Division of Genetics, chief, Department of Obstetrics and Gynecology and Women's Health, Ruth L. Gottesman professor in developmental pediatrics, children's evaluation and rehabilitation center, executive director, Center for Congenital Disorders, director, Pediatric Component of Residency Program in Medical Genetics, director. Writer. **Publications:** Born Too Soon, 1985; Intern Blues: The Private Ordeals of Three Young Doctors, 1989; The Boy Who Felt No Pain, 1990; Learning to Play God: The Coming of Age of a Young Doctor, 1991; (trans.) Des Mots, des Images, 1992; Was George Washington Really the Father of Our Country?: A Clinical Geneticist Looks at World History, 1994; Rotations: The Twelve Months of Intern Life, 1997; Intern Blues: The Timeless Classic about the Making of a Doctor, 2001; Genetic Rounds: A Doctor's Encounters in the Field that Revolutionized Medicine, 2009. Contributor to journals and periodicals. **Address:** c/o Diana Finch, Diana Finch Literary Agency, 116 W 23rd St., Ste. 500, New York, NY 10011-2599, U.S.A. **Online address:** robert.marion@einstein.yu.edu

MARISTED, Kai. French/American (born United States) **Genres:** Novels, Young Adult Fiction. **Career:** The Los Angeles Times, book reviewer; Harvard university, faculty; Emerson College, Warren Wilson MFA Program, faculty. Journalist and writer. **Publications:** Out after Dark: A Novel, 1993; Fall, 1996; Belong to Me: Stories, 1997; Broken Ground: A Novel, 2003. Contributor to periodicals. **Address:** c/o Author Mail, Shoemaker & Hoard, 3704 Macomb St. NW, Ste. 4, Washington, DC 20016, U.S.A. **Online address:** cor@kaimaristed.net

MARIZ, Linda. *See* **FRENCH, Linda.**

MARK, David. American (born United States) **Genres:** Social Sciences, Politics/Government, History. **Career:** Congressional Quarterly, reporter; Associated Press, reporter; Campaigns & Elections, editor-in-chief; Politico, senior editor, 2006-. **Publications:** Going Dirty: The Art of Negative Campaigning, 2006. Contributor to periodicals and journals. **Address:** Politico, 1100 Wilson Blvd., Ste. 601, Arlington, VA 22209-2249, U.S.A. **Online address:** dmark@davidmark.org

MARK, Rebecca. Norwegian (born Norway), b. 1955. **Genres:** Literary Criticism And History, Young Adult Fiction, History. **Career:** St. Olaf College, assistant professor of English, 1986-89; Tulane University, Deep South Regional Humanities Center, founding member, director of special projects, associate professor of English, 1989-; Newcomb College Institute, interim executive director. Writer. **Publications:** The Dragon's Blood: Feminist Intertextuality in Eudora Welty's The Golden Apples, 1994. (ed. with R. Vaughan) The South, 2004; A Private Address, forthcoming; Ersatz America, forthcoming. **Address:** Department of English, Tulane University, Norman Mayer Rm. 229, 6823 St. Charles Ave., New Orleans, LA 70118-5665, U.S.A. **Online address:** rebecca@tulane.edu

MARKARIS, Petros. Greek/Turkish (born Turkey), b. 1937. **Genres:** Novels, Young Adult Fiction, Business/Trade/Industry. **Career:** Writer. **Publications:** Ho Brecht kai ho dialektikos logos, 1982; Amyna zmonmes: astynomiko mythistormema, 1998; Ho Tse autoktonmese, 2003; Deadline in Athens: An Inspector Costas Haritos Mystery, 2004; Moth, 2006; Vasikos Metochos, 2006; Palia, poly palia, 2008; Lõxantra, 2009; Che Committed Suicide, 2009; Basic Shareholder, 2009. **Address:** c/o Author Mail, Grove Press, 841 Broadway, New York, NY 10003, U.S.A.

MARKEL, Howard. American (born United States), b. 1960. **Genres:** History, Literary Criticism And History, Medicine/Health. **Career:** Johns Hopkins Hospital and School of Medicine, Department of Pediatrics, intern, 1986-87, resident in pediatrics, junior assistant resident, 1987-88, senior assistant resident, 1988-89, clinical fellow, 1986-89, senior clinical fellow, 1989-91, Harriet Lane research fellow, 1991-93; Johns Hopkins University, Institute of the History of Medicine, Owsei Temkin fellow in the history of medicine, 1989-93; University of Michigan, Medical School, assistant professor of pediatrics, 1993-98, attending physician, 1993-, Center for the History of Medicine, director, 1996-, associate professor of pediatrics and communicable diseases, 1998-2002, associate professor of history, 1999-2002, George E. Wantz professor of the history of medicine, 2000-06, George E. Wantz distinguished professor of the history of medicine, 2006-, professor of pediatrics and communicable diseases, 2002-, professor of history, 2002-, professor of health management and policy (public health), 2004-, professor of psychiatry, 2004-, Institute for the Humanities, John Rich professor, 2006-07; United States Department of Defense, Pandemic Influenza Preparedness Planning, historical consultant, 2005-06; U.S. Department of Health and Human Services, Centers for Disease Control and Prevention, principal historical consultant, 2006-. Writer. **Publications:** (With F.A. Oski) The H.L. Mencken Baby Book: Comprising the Contents of H.L. Mencken's What you Ought to Know about Your Baby, 1990; (co-author) The Portable Pediatrician: A Textbook for Medical Students and Physicians, 1992; (with F.A. Oski) The Practical Pediatrician: The A to Z Guide to Your Child's Health, Behavior, and Safety, 1996; Quarantine!: East European Jewish Immigrants and the New York City Epidemics of 1892, 1997; (ed. with J. Tarolli) Caring for Children: A Celebration of the Department of Pediatrics and Communicable Diseases at the University of Michigan, 1998; (ed. with A.M. Stern) Formative Years: Children's Health in the United States, 1880-2000, 2002; When Germs Travel: Six Major Epidemics that have Invaded America since 1900 and the Fears They have Unleashed, 2004; An Anatomy of Addiction: Sigmund Freud, William Halsted and the Miracle Drug, Cocaine, 2011; William and Sigmund: How the Brilliant Drs. Halsted and Freud Discovered Cocaine, Struggled to Break Free of Its Addictive Grip and Changed the World, forthcoming. Contributor to journals and newspapers. **Address:** Center for the History of Medicine, Medical School, University of Michigan, 102 Observatory St., Ann Arbor, MI 48109-0725, U.S.A. **Online address:** howard@umich.edu

MARKELL, David L. American (born United States), b. 1953. **Genres:** Law, Environmental Sciences/Ecology, Civil Liberties/Human Rights. **Career:** Delaware Supreme Court, law clerk, 1979-80; Sidley & Austin, associate, 1980-82; Pierson, Ball & Dowd, associate, 1982-84; U.S. Environmental Protection Agency, assistant regional counsel, 1984-87; U.S. Department of Justice, trial attorney for Environmental Enforcement Section, Land and Natural Resources Division, staff, 1987-88; New York Department of Environmental Conservation, Division of Environmental Enforcement, director, 1988-92, Office of Environmental Remediation, acting deputy commissioner, 1992; Albany Law School, assistant professor, 1992-95, associate professor, 1995-97, professor of law, 1997-2002, Fulbright senior specialist, 2001-06, academic coordinator, 2003-04; Lewis and Clark College, Northwestern School of Law, visiting professor, 1994; North American Commission for Environmental Cooperation, director of submissions on enforcement matters, 1998-2000, consultant, 2000-03; Tulane University, lecturer, 2001; designated Fulbright senior specialist, 2001-; Florida State University, Steven M. Goldstein professor of Law, 2002-, associate dean for academic affairs, 2007-08; University of Virginia, School of Law, visiting professor, 2009; University of New York, public service professor. Writer. **Publications:** (With P. Borchers) New York State Administrative Procedure and Practice, 1994, 2nd ed., 1998; (ed. with J. Knox and contrib.) Greening NAFTA: The North American Commission for Environmental Cooperation, 2003; (with C. Rechtschaffen) Reinventing Environmental Enforcement and the State/Federal Relationship, 2003; (co-author) Environmental Protection: Law and Policy, 6th ed., 2010; (co-ed.) Compliance & Enforcement in Environmental Law: Towards More Effective Implementation, 2010. **Address:** College of Law, Florida State University, Rm. A227E, Advocacy Ctr., 425 W Jefferson St., Tallahassee, FL 32306-1601, U.S.A. **Online address:** dmarkell@law.fsu.edu

MARKEN, Bill. *See* **MARKEN, William Riley.**

MARKEN, William Riley. (Bill Marken). American (born United States), b. 1942. **Genres:** Homes/Gardens, Reference. **Career:** Sunset, editor-in-chief, 1981-96; eHow.com, editor-in-chief, 1999; garden.com, columnist; Garden Escape, editor; Rebecca's Garden, editor; Taste, consultant; Garden Design, editor-in-chief. **Publications:** AS BILL MARKEN: (co-author) Container Gardening for Dummies, 1998, 2nd ed., 2010; (co-author) Annuals for Dummies, 1998; (co-author) Gardening for Dummies, 2nd ed., 1999; How to Fix (Just about) Everything, 2002. **Address:** c/o Author Mail, IDG Books Worldwide, 919 E Hillsdale Blvd., Ste. 400, Foster City, CA 94404, U.S.A.

MARKER, Sherry. (Alice Whitman). American (born United States), b. 1941. **Genres:** Travel/Exploration, Biography, History, Autobiography/Memoirs. **Career:** Smith College, lecturer in writing seminar, 1992-. Writer. **Publications:** FOR YOUNG ADULTS: London, 1990; Cooperation, 1991. TRAVEL BOOKS: The Meteora, 1984; The Peloponnese, 1984; Athens, Attica and the Islands of the Argo-Saronic Gulf, 1985; Macedonia, Thessaly and Epirus, 1987; Athens, 1988; Philip of Macedon and the Royal Sites of Macedonia, 1989; Athens and Attica, 1990; (with J. Bowman) Frommer's Greek Islands, 2000; (with J. Pettifer) Blue Guide Greece: The Mainland, 7th ed., 2006. BIOGRAPHIES AND AMERICAN HISTORY: Illustrated History of the United States, 1988; Norman Rockwell, 1989; Edward Hopper, 1990; America Then and Now, 1993; The Plains Indian Wars, 1996, rev. ed., 2010. Contributor to periodicals. **Address:** Smith College, 7 Elm St., Northampton, MA 01063, U.S.A.

MARKHAM, Ian Stephen. British (born England), b. 1962. **Genres:** Ethics, Theology/Religion, Cultural/Ethnic Topics. **Career:** University of Exeter, lecturer in theology, 1989-96; Liverpool Hope University College, Liverpool professor of theology and public life, 1996-98, Foundation dean, 1998-2001; Hartford Seminary, Center for Faith in Practice, dean, professor of theology and ethics, 2001-07; Leeds Metropolitan University, visiting professor, 2005-08; Virginia Theological Seminary, dean, president, 2007-. Writer. **Publications:** Plurality and Christian Ethics, 1994, rev. ed., 1999; (ed.) A World Religions Reader, 1996, 3rd ed., (ed. with C. Lohr), 2009; Truth and the Reality of God: A Godparent's Handbook, 1999; (ed. with T. Ruparell) Encountering Religion: An Introduction to the Religions of the World, 2001; A Theology of Engagement, 2003; (with G. Legood) Christian Hope, Christian Practice: A Funeral Guide, 2004; (ed. with I. Ozdemir) Globalization, Ethics and Islam: The Case of Bediuzzaman Said Nursi, 2005; (ed. with M. Percy) Why Liberal Churches are Growing, 2006; Why Bother With Ethics?, 2007; Do Morals Matter?: A Guide to Contemporary Religious Ethics, 2007; Understanding Christian Doctrine, 2007; Engaging with Beduizzaman Said Nursi: A Model of Interfaith Dialogue, 2009; (ed.) Blackwell Companion to the Theologians, 2009; Liturgical Life Principles: How Episcopal Worship can Lead to Healthy and Authentic Living, 2009; Against Atheism: Why Dawkins, Hitchens and Harris are Fundamentally Wrong, 2010; (ed. with M. Percy, M. Chapman and B. Hawkins) Christ and Culture, 2010; (with S. Birinci) An Introduction to Said Nursi: Life, Thought and Writings on Non-violent and Engaged Islam, 2010. **Address:** Virginia Theological Seminary, 3737 Seminary Rd., Alexandria, VA 22304, U.S.A. **Online address:** imarkham@vts.edu

MARKHAM, J. David. American (born United States), b. 1945. **Genres:** History, Translations. **Career:** Lake Worth Community High School, teacher. Writer and historian. **Publications:** (ed. with A. Shmuelevitz, M. Gichon and D. Mendelson) Napoleon and the French in Egypt and the Holy Land, 1789-1801: Articles Presented at the 2nd International Congress of Napoleonic Studies, Israel, July 4-11, 1999, 2002; (trans.) Imperial Glory: The Bulletins of Napoleon's Grande Armée, 1805-1814, with Additional Supporting Documents, 2003; Napoleon's Road to Glory: Triumphs, Defeats and Immortality, 2003; (intro.) To Befriend an Emperor: Betsy Balcombe's Memoirs of Napoleon on St Helena, 2005; Napoleon for Dummies, 2005; Napoleon and Doctor Verling on St. Helena, 2005; The Road to St Helena: Napoleon after Waterloo, 2008; (ed. with M. Resnick) History Revisited: The Great Battles: Eminent Historians Take on the Great Works of Alternative History, 2008. **Address:** Olympia, WA , U.S.A. **Online address:** imperialglory@comcast.net

MARKHAM, Lynne. British (born England), b. 1947. **Genres:** Children's Fiction, Novels, Young Adult Fiction. **Career:** Nottingham City Libraries, librarian, 1969-72; Botswana National Library Service, librarian, 1972-75; Nottinghamshire County Libraries, librarian, 1975-86; Arnold & Carlton College of Further Education, lecturer, 1993-. Writer. **Publications:** Now You See Me, 1991; Getting it Right, 1993; The Closing March, 1997; Finding Billy, 1998; Lionheart, 1998; Winter Wolf, 1999; Deep Trouble, 2000; Barney's Headcase, 2001; Blazing Star, 2002; Cinderalf, 2002; Ghost Sister, 2003. Contributor to periodicals. Works appear in anthologies. **Address:** David Higham Associates, 5-8 Lower John St., Golden Sq., London, GL W1F 9HA, England.

MARKHAM, Wendy. *See* **STAUB, Wendy Corsi.**

MARKIDES, Constantinos C. Cypriot (born Cyprus), b. 1960. **Genres:** Economics, Administration/Management. **Career:** Cyprus National Guard, officer, 1979-81; Boston University, tutor, 1982-83; Cyprus Development Bank, intern, 1985; Harvard Business School, research associate, 1985-88; Harvard College, non-resident tutor, 1987-89; London Business School, assistant professor, 1990-94, associate professor, 1994-98, professor, 1998-, Department of Strategic and International Management (SIM), chairman, 1999-2002, 2006-09, Robert P. Bauman chair in strategic leadership, 2001-. Writer. **Publications:** Diversification, Refocusing, and Economic Performance, 1995; All the Right Moves: A Guide to Crafting Breakthrough Strategy, 1999; (ed. with M.A. Cusumano) Strategic Thinking for the Next Economy, 2001; (with P. Geroski) Fast Second: How Smart Companies Bypass Radical Innovation to Enter and Dominate New Markets, 2005; Game-Changing Strategies: How to Create New Market Space in Established Industries by Breaking the Rules, 2008. Contributor to books and journals. **Address:** London Business School, Sussex Pl., Regent's Pk., London, GL NW1 4SA, England. **Online address:** cmarkides@london.edu

MARKO, Katherine McGlade. American (born United States), b. 1913?. **Genres:** Children's Fiction, Children's Non-fiction, Air/Space Topics. **Career:** Freelance writer. **Publications:** The Sod Turners, 1970; God, When Will I Ever Belong?, 1979; Whales, Giants of the Sea, 1980; How the Wind Blows, 1981; God, Why Did Dad Lose His Job?, 1982; Away to Fundy Bay, 1985; Animals in Orbit: Monkeynauts and Other Pioneers in Space, 1991; Hang out the Flag, 1992; Pocket Babies, 1995; Time Goes on Forever, 1997. **Address:** 471 Franklin Blvd., Elgin, IL 60120-4438, U.S.A.

MARKOE, Glenn E. American (born United States), b. 1951. **Genres:** Archaeology/Antiquities, Architecture. **Career:** University of California, Lowie Museum of Anthropology, research assistant, 1976-78; Los Angeles County Museum of Art, research associate, 1979-80, assistant curator of ancient art, 1980-81; Metropolitan Museum of Art, assistant in ancient Near Eastern art, 1981-82; Glencairn Museum, research consultant, 1983; University of Vermont, Robert Hull Fleming Museum, curator of collections, 1984-88; Cyprus

American Archaeological Research Institute, Fulbright fellow, 1986-87; Cincinnati Art Museum, Department of Classical and Near Eastern Art and Arts of Africa and the Americas, curator, administrative head, 1988-. Writer. **Publications:** (Co-ed.) Ancient Bronzes, Ceramics and Seals, 1981; Phoenician Bronze and Silver Bowls from Cyprus and the Mediterranean, 1985; (with N.J. Serwint) Animal Style on Greek and Etruscan Vases, 1985; (ed. with R.J. DeMallie and R.B. Hassrick) Vestiges of a Proud Nation: The Ogden B. Read Northern Plains Indian Collection, 1986; (ed. with A.K. Capel) Mistress of the House, Mistress of Heaven: Women in Ancient Egypt, 1996; Phoenicians, 2000; Petra Rediscovered: The Lost City of the Nabataeans, 2003. Contributor of articles to periodicals. **Address:** Department of Classical & Near Eastern Art, Cincinnati Art Museum, 953 Eden Park Dr., Cincinnati, OH 45202, U.S.A. **Online address:** gmarkoe@cincyart.org

MARKOE, Merrill. American (born United States), b. 1951?. **Genres:** Humor/Satire, Novels. **Career:** University of Southern California, art teacher, assistant professor; Buzz (magazine), humor columnist. **Publications:** (Ed.) Late Night with David Letterman: The Book, 1985; What the Dogs Have Taught Me and Other Amazing Things I've Learned, 1992; How to Be Hap-Hap-Happy like Me, 1994; Merrill Markoe's Guide to Love, 1997; The Day My Dogs Became Guys (juvenile), 1999; It's My F-ing Birthday (novel), 2002; (with A. Prieboy) Psycho Ex Game, 2004; Walking in Circles Before Lying Down: A Novel, 2006; Nose down, Eyes Up: A Novel, 2009; Cool, Calm and Contentious, 2011. Contributor to periodicals. **Address:** c/o Author Mail, Random House, 1540 Broadway, New York, NY 10036, U.S.A. **Online address:** merrill@merrillmarkoe.com

MARKOFF, John. American (born United States), b. 1949. **Genres:** Documentaries/Reportage, Information Science/Computers, Technology, Engineering, Sciences, Economics, Business/Trade/Industry. **Career:** Infoworld, reporter, editor, 1981-83; San Jose Mercury, columnist, 1983-84; Byte Magazine, editor, 1984-85; San Francisco Examiner, staff, 1985-88; New York Times, business reporter, 1988-, senior writer; Stanford University, Department of Communications, visiting lecturer. Writer. **Publications:** (With L. Siegel) The High Cost of High Tech: The Dark Side of the Chip, 1985; (with K. Hafner) Cyberpunk: Outlaws and Hackers on the Computer Frontier, 1991; (with T. Shimomura) Take-Down: The Pursuit and Capture of Kevin Mitnick, America's Most Wanted Computer Outlaw-by the Man Who Did it, 1996; What the Dormouse Said: How the Sixties Counterculture Shaped the Personal Computer Industry, 2005. **Address:** Hyperion Books for Children, 114 5th Ave., New York, NY 10011, U.S.A. **Online address:** jmarkoff@yahoo.com

MARKOOSIE. Canadian (born Canada), b. 1942. **Genres:** Children's Fiction, Young Adult Fiction, Adult Non-fiction, Social Sciences, Novels. **Career:** Atlas Aviation, pilot, 1969-75; Northern Quebec Innuit Association, translator, 1975-76; Community Council, manager, 1976-; Government of Quebec, administrator of public services, 1978-. Writer. **Publications:** Harpoon of the Hunter (novel), 1970. **Address:** Government of Quebec, Inukjuak, QC J0M 1M0, Canada. **Online address:** patsaug@hotmail.com

MARKOVITS, Andrei S. American/Romanian (born Romania), b. 1948. **Genres:** Novels. **Career:** Institute for Advanced Studies, research associate, 1973-74; New York University, faculty, 1974; John Jay College of Criminal Justice, City University of New York, faculty, 1974; Columbia University, faculty, 1975; Central European Studies, Harvard University, senior research associate, 1975-99, visiting professor, 2002-03; Wesleyan University, assistant professor of government, 1977-83; Wirtschafts und Sozialwissenschaftliches Institute, German Trade University Federation, research associate, 1979; International Institute for Comparative Social Research, Science Center, research associate, 1980; Boston University, associate professor of political science, 1983-92; Tel Aviv University, visiting professor, 1986; Osnabruck University, visiting professor, 1987; Bochum University, visiting professor, 1991; University of California at Santa Cruz, Department of Politics, professor, 1992-99, chair, 1992-95; University of Innsbruck, Fulbright professor, 1996; University of Michigan, Department Of Germanic Languages and Literature, Department of Political Science, Department of Sociology, professor, 19992003, Karl W. Deutsch Collegiate professor of comparative politics and German studies, 2003, Arthur F. Thurnau professor; St. Gallen University, visiting professor, 2004; Hebrew University, visiting professor, 2005; Dortmund University, visiting professor, 2006; Webster University, visiting professor, 2008. Writer. **Publications:** (Ed. with K.W. Deutsch) Fear of Science, Trust in Science: Conditions for Change in the Climate of Opinion, 1980; (ed.) The Political Economy of West Germany: Modell Deutschland, 1982; (ed. with F.E. Sysyn) Nationbuilding and the Politics of Nationalism: Essays on Austrian Galicia, 1982; (ed. with K.W. Deutsch and J. Platt) Advances in the Social Sciences, 1900-1980: What, Who, Where, How?, 1986; The Politics of the West German Trade Unions: Strategies of Class and Interest Representation in Growth and Crisis, 1986; (ed. with M. Silverstein) The Politics of Scandal: Power and Process in Liberal Democracies, Holmes & Meier, 1988; The West German Left, 1993; (with P.S. Gorski) The German Left: Red, Green and Beyond, 1993; (ed. with M.G. Huelshoff and S. Reich) From Bundesrepublik to Deutschland: German Politics after Unification, 1993; (with S. Reich) The German Predicament: Memory and Power in the New Europe, 1997; Breakdown, Breakup, Breakthrough: Germany's Difficult Passage to Modernity, 1999; (with J. Elsasser) Die Fratze Der Eigenen Geschichte: Von Der Goldhagen-Debatte Zum Jugoslawien-Krieg, 1999; (with S.L. Hellerman) Offside: Soccer and American Exceptionalism, 2001; (with Sieglinde K. Rosenberger) Demokratie: Mudus Und Telos, Bohlau Verlag, 2001; Amerika, Dich Hasst Sich's Besser: Antiamerikanismus Und Antisemitismus in Europa, 2007; Uncouth Nation: Why Europe Dislikes America, 2007; Querpass: Sport Und Politik in Europa Und Den USA, 2007. Contributor of articles. **Address:** University of Michigan, 3110 Modern Lang Bldg., 812 E Washington St., Ann Arbor, MI 48109-1275, U.S.A. **Online address:** andymark@umich.edu

MARKOWITZ, Harry M. American (born United States), b. 1927. **Genres:** Economics. **Career:** RAND Corp., research staff, 1952-60, 1961-63; CACI Intl., co-founder, 1962; Consolidated Analysis Centers Ltd., technical director, 1963-68; University of California, professor, 1968-69, professor, 1994-, Rady School of Management, adjunct professor of finance, professor of finance; Arbitrage Management Co., president, 1969-72; International Business Machines Corp., T.J. Watson Research Center, researcher, 1974-83; City University of New York, Baruch College, Marvin Speiser distinguished professor of finance and economics, 1983-94, now distinguished professor emeritus; Harry Markowitz Co., president, 1984-; Daiwa Securities Trust Co., director of research, 1990-2000; Riverview International Group Inc., director. Writer. **Publications:** Portfolio Selection, 1952; The Optimization of a Quadratic Function Subject to Linear Constraints, 1956; Portfolio Selection: Efficient Diversification of Investments, 1959, 2nd ed., 1991; (with B. Hausner and H.W. Karr) Simscript: A Simulation Programming Language, 1962, 2nd ed., 1963; (with M.A. Geisler) A Brief Review of Simscript as a Simulating Technique, 1963; (co-ed.) Process Analysis of Economic Capabilities, 1963; (ed.) Studies in Process Analysis: Economy-Wide Production Capabilities, 1963; (with P.M. Oldfather and A.S. Ginsberg) Programming by Questionnaire, 1966; (with P.J. Kiviat and R. Villanueva) The Simscript II Programming Language, 1968; Mean Variance Analysis in Portfolio Choice and Capital Markets, 1987; (contrib.) The Founders of Modern Finance, 1991; (with F.J. Fabozzi) The Theory and Practice of Investment Management, 2000, 2nd ed., 2011; (with F.J. Fabozzi and L. Kostovetsky) Theory and Practice of Investment Management Workbook, 2004; (ed.) Harry Markowitz: Selected Works, 2008. **Address:** Harry Markowitz Co., 1010 Turquoise St., Ste. 245, San Diego, CA 92109-1266, U.S.A. **Online address:** hmarkowitz@ucsd.edu

MARKS, Alan. British (born England), b. 1957. **Genres:** Children's Fiction, Illustrations, Mythology/Folklore. **Career:** Bath Academy of Art, faculty; Southampton Art College, faculty; Neugebauer Press, illustrator, 1988-; Oxford University Press, illustrator. Writer. **Publications:** SELF-ILLUSTRATED: (Adaptor) Childe Roland: An English Folk Tale, 1988; Nowhere to Be Found, 1988; (compiler) Ring-a-Ring O'Roses and a Ding, Dong, Bell: A Book of Nursery Rhymes, 1991; Over the Hills and Far Away, 1993; The Thief's Daughter, 1994; (with S. Pirotta) The Giant Oak Tree, 2007; (with S. Pirotta) Lonely Princess, 2007; (with S. Pirotta) Enchanted Gazelle, 2007; (with S. Pirotta) Glass Palace, 2007. Illustrator of books by others. Contributor to periodicals. **Address:** Padbrook, Mill Ln., Elmstone, Canterbury, KT CT3 1HE, England. **Online address:** alan@marksonpaper.co.uk

MARKS, (Amelia) Lee. American (born United States), b. 1948. **Genres:** Photography, Art/Art History, Photography. **Career:** Gilman Paper Co., Art Collection, consultant, 1980-91; Lee Marks Fine Art, founder, owner and director, 1981-. Writer. **Publications:** (With G. Lang and E.A. Lawrence) The Horse: Photographic Images, 1839 to the Present, 1991; New Realities: Hand-Colored Photographs, 1839 to the Present, 1997; (with A.R. George) Hope Photographs, 1998. **Address:** Lee Marks Fine Art, 2208 E 350 N, Shelbyville, IN 46176, U.S.A. **Online address:** lee@leemarksfineart.com

MARKS, Corey. American (born United States), b. 1970?. **Genres:** Poetry. **Career:** American Literary Review, poetry editor; University of Houston, instructor of English, 1994-2000; University of North Texas, Department of English, assistant professor of English, 2000-06, director of creative writing, 2005-, associate professor of English, 2006-. **Publications:** Renunciation: Poems, 2000; Radio Tree, forthcoming. Contributor to journals. **Address:** c/o Author Mail, University of Illinois Press, 1325 S Oak St., PO Box 566, Champaign, IL 61820-6903, U.S.A. **Online address:** corey.marks@unt.edu

MARKS, David (Francis). British (born England), b. 1945. **Genres:** Medicine/Health, Paranormal, Psychology, Self Help. **Career:** University of Otago, lecturer in psychology, 1970-74, senior lecturer in psychology, 1974-86; Middlesex University, School of psychology, professor and head, 1986-94, Health Research Center, head, 1989-2000; Special Group on Health Psychology, chair, 1992-94; Leicester University, School of Medicine, external examiner, 1995-99; City University of London, professor of psychology, 2000-, head of the department, 2002-05; Health Psychology Consultancy L.L.P., owner; British Psychological Society, fellow. Writer. **Publications:** (With P. Sulzberger and I. Hodgson) The Isis Smoking Cessation Programme, 1978, 3rd ed., 1980; (with R. Kammann) The Psychology of the Psychic, 1980, 2nd ed., 2000; The Quit for Life Programme, 1993; (with C. Francome) Improving the Health of the Nation, 1996; (co-author) Health Psychology, 2000, (with M. Murray and B. Evans) 3rd ed., Health Psychology: Theory, Research and Practice, 2010; (with C.M. Sykes) Dealing with Dementia, 2000. EDITOR: Theories of Image Formation, 1985; (with D.G. Russell) Imagery One, 1985; (with J.T.E. Richardson and D.G. Russell) Imagery Two, 1986; (with P. Hampson and J.T.E. Richardson) Imagery: Current Developments, 1990; The Health Psychology Reader, 2002; (with L. Yardley) Research Methods for Health Psychology, 2004. Contributor to periodicals. **Address:** Department of Psychology, City University, D508, Social Science Bldg., Northampton Sq., Walmsley W414, London, GL EC1V 0HB, England. **Online address:** d.marks.1@city.ac.uk

MARKS, Gil(bert S.). American (born United States), b. 1952?. **Genres:** Food And Wine, Medicine/Health, Medicine/Health. **Career:** Rabbi and writer. Kosher Gourmet magazine, founding editor; cooking class instructor, 1992-. **Publications:** The World of Jewish Cooking: More Than 500 Traditional Recipes from Alsace to Yemen, 1996; The World of Jewish Entertaining: Menus and Recipes for the Sabbath, Holidays and Other Family Celebrations, 1998; The World of Jewish Desserts: More than 400 Delectable Recipes from Jewish Communities from Alsace to India, 2000; Olive Trees and Honey: A Treasury of Vegetarian Recipes from Jewish Communities Around the World, 2004; Meals in Science and Practice: Interdisciplinary Research and Business Applications, 2009; The Encyclopedia of Jewish Food, 2010. **Address:** 208 W 80th St., New York, NY 10024, U.S.A. **Online address:** gilmarks@gilmarks.com

MARKS, Graham. British (born England), b. 1949?. **Genres:** Science Fiction/Fantasy, Novels, Poetry, Young Adult Fiction, Children's Fiction. **Career:** Stuff and Nonsense, freelance design consultant and publisher; Owl Magazine, freelance design consultant and publisher; Publishing News, freelance children's editor, 1993-. **Publications:** (Ed.) Bomber Bats and Flying Frogs, 1986; (ed.) Beat the Record, 1986; (ed.) Apple Peelers and Coin Stackers, 1986; Fire at Rig Fifteen, 1993; Inferno, 1993; Red Alert, 1993; Race of Truth, 1993; Renegade Rocket, 1993; Mysteron Trap, 1993; Place of the Angels, 1993; Rescue from the Skies, 1993; Spectrum Strikes Back, 1993; Solar Flare, 1993; Playing with Fire, 1993; Countdown to Disaster, 1993; Thunderbirds to the Rescue, 1993; Thunderbirds: The Ultimate Pop-up Fact Book, 1993; Radio, Radio: It'd be a Crime not to Listen, 2007; I Spy, 2009; Mean Streets, 2010; I Spy, 2012. CAPTAIN SCARLET SERIES: Seeing Is Touching: Ten Poems, 1970; The Finding of Stoby Binder, 1982; The Big Surprise, 1983; Bullet Trains and Underwater Tricycles, 1986; Webster and the Witch, 1986; Sheep Ahoy!, and Other Wacky Stories from the Newspapers, 1987; Gilbert's Best Jokes on Earth, 1988; Odd Pets, 1988; Pocket Book of London, 1988; Baseball! A Guide to the Ultimate American Game, 1988; A Shriek of Spooks, 1988; Misspronts: A Collection of Silly Misprints, 1988; A Barrel of Laughs, 1989; Wall's Jolly Lolly Joke Book, 1989; Charlene's Tail, 1992; Endangered Species, 1992; When Food Goes Bad, 1992; Subterranean Sea, 1992; Undersea Hijack, 1992; Tree Troubles, 1992; The Ghost Ship, 1992; Under Fire, 1992; Golden Child, 1992; Club Fred, 1992; Flight 104, 1993; The King's Complex, 1994; The Cocoa Mission, 1994; Hard Drive, 1995; Judge Dredd: The Junior Novelization, 1995; System Crash, 1995; The Spider Slayer, 1995; Download, 1995; Haden's Quest, 1996; Fault Line, 1996; The Mask: It's Not Easy Being Green, 1995; Wallace and Gromit in Nick Park's A Close Shave, 1996; Wallace and Gromit in the Wrong Trousers, 1996; Skitzo, 1997; Roger and the Rottentrolls in Reigning Sheep and Trolls, 1998; The Rottentrolls II: With a Vengeance (Sort Of), 1998; Farmyard Adventures, 1999; Toybox Tales, 1999; Teddy Bear Adventures, 1999; Bedtime Tales, 1999; Radio Radio, 2003; How It Works: Everyone Gets the Angel They Deserve, 2004; Zoo, 2005; Missing in Tokyo: A Novel, 2006; Snatched!, 2006; Omega Place, 2007; Kai-ro, 2007. **Address:** c/o Author Mail, Bloomsbury Publishing, 38 Soho Sq., London, GL W1D 3HB, England. **Online address:** mail@marksworks.co.uk

MARKS, Jonathan. American (born United States), b. 1955. **Genres:** Sciences. **Career:** Yale University, professor; University of California, professor; University of North Carolina at Charlotte, professor. Biological anthropologist and writer. **Publications:** Human Biodiversity: Genes, Race, and History, 1995; What It Means to Be 98% Chimpanzee: Apes, People, and Their Genes, 2002; Why I Am Not a Scientist: Anthropology and Modern Knowledge, 2009; The Alternative Introduction to Biological Anthropology, 2011. Contributor of articles to journals. **Address:** Department of Anthropology, University of North Carolina at Charlotte, Charlotte, NC 28223-0001, U.S.A. **Online address:** jmarks@uncc.edu

MARKS, Kathy (L.). Australian/British (born England), b. 1953. **Genres:** Adult Non-fiction, Social Sciences, Law, Criminology/True Crime. **Career:** West Virginia Department of Welfare, child abuse investigator, 1973-80; Franklin-Williamson Human Services, community worker, 1984-86; Jackson County Probation Office, adult probation officer, 1988-90; Illinois Department of Children and Family Services, child protective investigator, 1990-; Mobile Unit 15, police training instructor. **Publications:** Faces of Right Wing Extremism, 1996; Pitcairn: Paradise Lost, 2008; Lost Paradise: From Mutiny on the Bounty to a Modern-day Legacy of Sexual Mayhem, the Dark Secrets of Pitcairn Island Revealed, 2009; Trouble In Paradise: Uncovering The Dark, 2009. **Address:** 11570 Reservoir Rd., PO Box 305, Marion, IL 62959, U.S.A. **Online address:** kmarks@midwest.com

MARKS, Lara Vivienne. British (born England), b. 1963. **Genres:** Women's Studies And Issues, Medicine/Health, Politics/Government, Social Sciences. **Career:** Queen Mary and Westfield College, research fellow, 1990-93; Tropical Medicine, research fellow, 1993-94; Imperial College, lecturer, 1994; London School of Hygiene, research fellow; Cambridge University, visiting professor; Silico Research Ltd., senior research director; Open University, associate lecturer, King's College, senior research fellow. Writer. **Publications:** (Ed. with V. Fildes and H. Marland) Women and Children First: International Maternal and Infant Welfare, 1870-1945, 1992; Model Mothers: Jewish Mothers and Maternity Provision in East London, 1970-1939, 1994; Metropolitan Maternity: Maternal and Infant Welfare Services in Early Twentieth Century London, 1996; (ed. with M. Worboys) Migrants, Minorities and Health: Historical and Contemporary Studies, 1997; Sexual Chemistry: A History of the Contraceptive Pill, 2001; (ed. with J. Goodman and A. McElligott) Useful Bodies: Humans in the Service of Medical Science in the Twentieth Century, 2003; Assessing the Risk and Safety of the Pill: Maternal Mortality and the Pill, 2006. Contibutor to periodicals. **Address:** Open University, PO Box 197, Milton Keynes, BK MK7 6BJ, England. **Online address:** l.marks@open.ac.uk

MARKS, Mitchell Lee. American (born United States), b. 1955. **Genres:** Adult Non-fiction, Business/Trade/Industry, Administration/Management. **Career:** American Association for the Advancement of Science, mass media fellow, 1980; California State University, assistant professor of business administration, 1981-83; California School of Professional Psychology, associate professor and director of organizational psychology program, director, 1985-88; William M. Mercer Inc., principal, 1988-93; Delta Consulting Group Inc., senior director, 1993-96; San Francisco State University, assistant professor of business management, associate professor. Writer. **Publications:** (With P.H. Mirvis) Managing the Merger: Making It Work, 1992; From Turmoil to Triumph: New Life after Corporate Mergers, Acquisitions and Downsizings, 1994; (with P.H. Mirvis) Joining Forces: Making One Plus One Equal Three in Mergers, Acquisitions and Alliances, 1998, rev. ed., 2010; Charging Back up the Hill: Workplace Recovery after Mergers, Acquisitions and Downsizings, 2003; (ed. with K.P. De Meuse) Resizing the Organization: Managing Layoffs, Divestitures and Closings: Maximizing Gain While Minimizing Pain, 2003. Contributor to books. **Address:** Department of Management, San Francisco State University, BUS 311, 1600 Holloway Ave., San Francisco, CA 94132-4156, U.S.A. **Online address:** marks@sfsu.edu

MARKS, Paula Mitchell. American (born United States), b. 1951. **Genres:** Adult Non-fiction, Local History/Rural Topics, Education. **Career:** St. Edward's University, Department of American Studies, associate professor, 1988-, professor; Boards of Western Writers of America, staff; Texas Institute of Letters, staff. Writer. **Publications:** Turn Your Eyes Toward Texas: Pioneers Sam and Mary Maverick, 1989; And Die in the West: The Story of the O.K. Corral Gunfight, 1989; Precious Dust: The American Gold Rush Era, 1848-1900, 1994; Precious Dust: The Saga of the Western Gold Rushes, 1995; (intro.) Surviving on the Texas Frontier: The Journal of an Orphan Girl in San Saba County, 1996; Die in the West: The Story of O.K. Corral Gunfight, 1996; Hands to the Spindle: Texas Women and Home Textile Production, 1822-1880, 1996; In a Barren Land: American Indian Dispossession and Survival, 1998; (with J.F. de la Teja and R.Tyler) Texas: Crossroads of North America, 2004. Works appear in anthologies.Contributor to journals and periodicals. **Address:** Department of American Studies, St. Edward's University, Rm. 303 Holy Cross Hall, 3001 S Congress Ave., Austin, TX 78704, U.S.A. **Online address:** paulam@admin.stedwards.edu

MARKS, Richard. British (born England), b. 1945. **Genres:** Art/Art History, Theology/Religion. **Career:** University of York, Vanbrugh College, Department of History of Art, professor, now professor emeritus. Writer, art historian and art curator. **Publications:** (Comp. and ed. with A. Payne) British Heraldry from Its Origins to c. 1800, 1978; (with B.J.R. Blench) The Warwick Vase, 1979; (with N. Morgan) The Golden Age of English Manuscript Painting, 1200-1500, 1981; (co-author) The Burrell Collection, 1983; Burrell: A Portrait of a Collector: Sir William Burrell, 1861-1958, 1983, rev. ed., 1988; The Stained Glass of the Collegiate Church of the Holy Trinity, Tattershall (Lincs.), 1984; Wing as It Was: The Village, Its Hamlets and Its People in Victorian and Edwardian Times, 1984, vol. II, 1990; The Souvenir Guide to the Burrell Collection, 1985; Sir William Burrell, 1861-1958, 1985; (with R. Marks) Wavendon as It Was: The Village and Its People in Victorian and Edwardian Times, 1986; (with D. Beevers and J. Roles) Sussex Churches and Chapels, 1989; (with R. Marks) Ivinghoe as It Was: The Village, Its Hamlets and Its People in Victorian and Edwardian Times, 1990; Stained Glass in England during the Middle Ages, 1993; The Medieval Stained Glass of Northamptonshire, 1998; The County of Northamptonshire: A Summary Catalogue of Medieval Stained Glass, 1998; (ed. with S.R. Jones and A.J. Minnis) Courts and Regions in Medieval Europe, 2000; (ed. with P. Williamson and contrib.) Gothic: Art for England 1400-1547 (exhibition catalogue), 2003; Image and Devotion in Late Medieval England, 2004; (ed.) Late Gothic England: Art and Display, 2007. Contributor to books and journals. **Address:** Department of History of Art, Vanbrugh College, University of York, Heslington, NY YO10 5DD, England. **Online address:** richard.marks@york.ac.uk

MARKS, Stan(ley). Australian/British (born England), b. 1929. **Genres:** Novels, Children's Fiction, Plays/Screenplays, Cultural/Ethnic Topics, Local History/Rural Topics, Race Relations, Cartoons, Humor/Satire, Humor/Satire. **Career:** A.B.C., supervisor of publicity, 1958-64; Trans Australian Airlines, public relations officer, 1965-67; Australian Tourist Commission, public relations manager, 1969-85; Jewish Holocaust Museum and Research Centre, Centre News Magazine, editor. Journalist. **Publications:** God Gave You One Face (novel), 1964; Is She Fair Dinkum?, 1967; Graham Is an Aboriginal Boy, 4th ed., 1969; Mouse Who Sailed with Captain Cook, 1970; Animal Olympics, 1972; Rarua Lives in Papua New Guinea, 1973; Fifty Years of Achievement, 1974; Katut Lives in Bali, 1977; St. Kilda Sketchbook, 1980; Malvern Sketchbook, 1980; Welcome to Australia, 1985; Out and About in Melbourne, 1988; 10 Years: Jewish Holocaust Museum and Research Centre, 1994; St. Kilda Heritage Sketchbook, 1995; Reflections, 2004. Work appears in anthologies. Contributor to journals. **Address:** 348 Bambra Rd., South Caulfield, Melbourne, VI 3162, Australia. **Online address:** smar4858@bigpond.net.au

MARKS, Thomas A. American (born United States), b. 1950. **Genres:** History, Politics/Government, Social Sciences. **Career:** National Defense University, School for National Security Executive Education, professor of insurgency, terrorism and counter terrorism, 1995-, Department of Irregular Warfare, chair; Marine Corps University, Oppenheimer chair, 2002; U.S. Joint Special Operations University, adjunct professor; United States Army War College, Strategic Studies Institute, researcher. Writer. **Publications:** United Front in Thailand since October 1976, 1979; Thailand, the Threatened Kingdom, 1980; Making Revolution: The Insurgency of the Communist Party of Thailand in Structural Perspective, 1994; Maoist Insurgency since Vietnam, 1996; Counterrevolution in China: Wang Sheng and the Kuomintang, 1996, rev. ed. as Wang Sheng yu Guo ming dang: Fan ge mingyun dong zai Zhongguo, 2003; (as Tom Marks) The British Acquisition of Siamese Malaya (1896-1909), 1997; Sustainability of Colombian Military-Strategic Support for Democratic Security, 2005; Maoist People's War in Post-Vietnamese Asia, 2007. Contributor to periodicals and journals. **Address:** Foreign Policy Research Institute, 1528 Walnut St., Ste. 610, Philadelphia, PA 19102, U.S.A. **Online address:** markst@ndu.edu

MARKS-WHITE, Judith. American (born United States) **Genres:** Novels, Young Adult Fiction, Literary Criticism And History. **Career:** Time Inc., staff; Doubleday and Co., staff; Westport News, writer; Norwalk Community College, Department of English, adjunct professor. **Publications:** Seducing Harry: An Epicurean Affair, 2006; Bachelor Degree: A Novel, 2008. Contributor to periodicals. **Address:** c/o Wendy Sherman, Wendy Sherman Literary Associates Inc., 450 7th Ave., Ste. 2307, New York, NY 10123, U.S.A. **Online address:** author@judithmarks-white.com

MARKUS, Julia. American (born United States), b. 1939. **Genres:** Novels, Novellas/Short Stories, Adult Non-fiction, Biography. **Career:** Concordia College, instructor in English, 1961-63; Southern Connecticut State College, instructor in English, 1966-71; University of Maryland, instructor in English, 1973-75; Bay College of Baltimore, instructor in English, 1976-77; Decatur House Press, co-founder, 1976, vice president and editor, 1976-80; Hofstra University, professor of English, director of creative writers, 1981-. **Publications:** La Mora: A Novel, 1976; (ed. and intro.) Casa Guidi Windows, 1977; A Patron of the Arts (novella), 1977; Uncle: A Novel, 1978; American Rose: A Novel, 1980; Two Novellas, 2nd ed., 1981; Friends along the Way, 1985; A Change of Luck (novel), 1991; Dared and Done: The Marriage of Elizabeth Barrett and Robert Browning (biography), 1995; (ed. with W.S. Peterson) Sonnets from the Portuguese: Illuminated by the Brownings' Love Letters, 1996; Across an Untried Sea (biography): Discovering Lives Hidden in the Shadow of Convention and Time, 2000; J. Anthony Froude: The Last Undiscovered Great Victorian: A Biography, 2005. **Address:** Department of English, Hofstra University, 110 Mason Hall, 1000 Fulton Ave., Hempstead, NY 11549-1000, U.S.A. **Online address:** julia.y.markus@hofstra.edu

MARLAND, Hilary. British (born England), b. 1958. **Genres:** Art/Art History, Cultural/Ethnic Topics, Human Relations/Parenting, Young Adult Nonfiction, Medicine/Health. **Career:** Oxford University, Wellcome Unit for the History of Medicine, postdoctoral research fellow, 1985-87; Free University Amsterdam, Institute of Medical History, research lecturer, 1987-90; Erasmus University Rotterdam, research lecturer in medical history, 1987-96; Wellcome Research Fellow, 1993-96; University of Warwick, professor of history and director of the Centre for the History of Medicine, 1999-; Descartes Centre, visiting professor, 2008-09. Writer. **Publications:** NONFICTION: Medicine and Society in Wakefield and Huddersfield, 1780-1870, 1987; (ed. with V. Fildes and L. Marks) Women and Children First: International Maternal and Infant Welfare, 1870-1945, 1992; (ed.) The Art of Midwifery: Early Modern Midwives in Europe, 1993; (ed. with M. Pelling) The Task of Healing: Medicine, Religion, and Gender in England and the Netherlands, 1450-1800, 1996; (ed. with A.M. Rafferty) Midwives, Society, and Childbirth: Debates and Controversies in the Modern Period, 1997; (ed. with M. Gijswijt-Hofstra and H. de Waardt) Illness and Healing Alternatives in Western Europe, 1997; (ed. with M. Gijswijt-Hofstra) Cultures of Child Health in Britain and the Netherlands in the Twentieth Century, 2003; Dangerous Motherhood: Insanity and Childbirth in Victorian Britain, 2004. Contributor to books and journals. **Address:** University of Warwick, Coventry, WM CV4 7AL, England. **Online address:** hilary.marland@warwick.ac.uk

MARLETT, Jeffrey D. American (born United States) **Genres:** History, Theology/Religion. **Career:** Saint Louis University, Department of Theology, graduate assistant and adjunct faculty, 1993-97; Lyon College, faculty, 1997-98; College of Saint Rose, assistant professor of religious studies, 1998-2004, associate professor of religious studies, 2004-. Writer and historian. **Publications:** Saving the Heartland: Catholic Missionaries in Rural America, 1920-1960, 2002. Contributor to periodicals. **Address:** Department of Religious Studies, College of St. Rose, 432 Western Ave., Albany, NY 12203, U.S.A. **Online address:** marlettj@mail.strose.edu

MARLEY, Rita. Jamaican/Cuban (born Cuba), b. 1947. **Genres:** Biography, Autobiography/Memoirs, Music. **Career:** Bob Marley Museum, curator; Legalize It, performer, 1976; Adrian Boot and Chris Saliewzik, executive editor; Rita Marley Foundation, founder. Singer, reggae musician, record producer and writer. **Publications:** Bob Marley: Légende Rasta, 1995; (ed.) Bob Marley: Songs of Freedom, 1995; No Woman, No Cry: My Life with Bob Marley, 2004. **Address:** c/o Lorna Wainwright, Rita Marley Music, 220 Marcus Garvey Dr., Kingston, 11, Jamaica.

MARLIN, Henry. *See* **ROSS, Angus.**

MARLING, Karal Ann. American (born United States), b. 1943. **Genres:** Art/Art History, History, Politics/Government. **Career:** Case Western Reserve University, assistant professor, 1971-74; Vassar College, assistant professor, 1974-77; University of Minnesota, professor of art history and American studies, 1977-. Carleton College, visiting faculty; Buffalo Bill Center, visiting faculty; Cornell University, visiting faculty; University of Wyoming, visiting faculty; Harvard University, visiting faculty; University of Kansas, visiting faculty; Catholic University, visiting faculty. Writer. **Publications:** (With D.M. Gormley) Federal Art in Cleveland, 1933-1943: An Exhibition, September 16 to November 1, 1974, The Cleveland Public Library, 1974; Wall-to-Wall America: A Cultural History of Post-Office Murals in the Great Depression, 1982; The Colossus of Roads: Myth and Symbol Along the American Highway, 1984; Tom Benton and His Drawings: A Biographical Essay and a Collection of His Sketches, Studies, and Mural Cartoons, 1985; Joe Jones & J.B. Turnbull: Visions of the Midwest in the 1930s, 1987; Frederic C. Knight (1898-1979): Everhart Museum, Scranton, Pennsylvania, October25, 1987-January 17, 1988, 1987; George Washington Slept Here: Colonial Revivals and American Culture, 1876-1986, 1988; Looking Back: A Perspective on the 1913 Inaugural Exhibition, October 8-November 20, 1988, Memorial Art Gallery of the University of Rochester, 1988; Blue Ribbon: A Social and Pictorial History of the Minnesota State Fair, 1990; (with J. Wetenhall) Iwo Jima: Monuments, Memories, and the American Hero, 1991; (with M.A. Foresta and S.J. Gould) Between Home and Heaven: Contemporary American Landscape Photography from the Consolidated Natural Gas Company Collection of the National Museum of American Art, Smithsonian Institution, 1992; Edward Hopper, 1992; (ed. with J.H. Foy) The Arts and the American Home, 1890-1930, 1994; As Seen on TV: The Visual Culture of Everyday Life in the 1950s, 1994; In Search of the Corn Queen, 1994; Going Home with Elvis, 1995; Graceland: Going Home with Elvis, 1996; Designing Disneys Theme Parks: The Architecture of Reassurance, 1997; Civil Rights in Oz: Images of Kansas in American Popular Art, 1997; Norman Rockwell, 1997; Larchitecture Du Récomfort, 1997; Merry Christmas! Celebrating Americas Greatest Holiday, 2000; Looking North: Royal Canadian Mounted Police Illustrations: The Potlach Collection, Tweed Museum of Art, University of Minnesota Duluth, 2003; Debutante: Rites and Regalia of American Debdom, 2004; Old Glory, 2004; Designs on the Heart: The Homemade Art of Grandma Moses, 2006; (with C. Wegener) Money in the Bank: The Katherine Kierland Herberger Collection, 2006; (with C. Wegener) Wind & Whimsy: Weathervanes and Whirlygigs from Twin Cities Collections, 2007; Minnesota, Hail to Thee!: A Sesquicentennial History, 2008; Ice: Great Moments in the History of Hard, Cold Water, 2008. Contributor to periodicals. **Address:** Department of History, University of Minnesota, 352 Heller Hall, 271 19th Ave. S, Minneapolis, MN 55454, U.S.A. **Online address:** marli001@umn.edu

MARLIS, Stefanie. American (born United States), b. 1951. **Genres:** Poetry, Novels, Young Adult Fiction. **Career:** Community College of Marin, instructor; San Francisco State University, instructor, 1989-90; University of San Francisco, instructor, 1991; freelance copywriter, 1991-. **Publications:** Red Tools (chapbook), 1984; Slow Joy, 1989; Sheet of Glass, 1994; Rife, 1998; Fine, 2000; (with W. Arnold) Illuminations: Living by Candlelight, 2000; Cloudlife, 2004; Cloud Life, 2005; Love Knot, 2009. Contributor to periodicals. **Address:** 1224 Escalante St., Santa Fe, NM 87505, U.S.A. **Online address:** stafanie@stefaniemarlis.com

MARLOR, Clark Strang. American (born United States), b. 1922. **Genres:** Art/Art History, Speech/Rhetoric, Photography. **Career:** Kalamazoo College, instructor, 1946-47; Miami University, instructor, 1947-50; City University of New York, Queens College, instructor, 1950-55; Adelphi University, associate professor, professor, 1956-84, professor emeritus, 1984-. Writer. **Publications:** (Co-author) Bibliography of Speech and Allied Areas, 1962; A History of the Brooklyn Art Association with an Index of Exhibitions, 1970; The Society of Independent Artists: The Exhibition Record, 1917-1944, 1984; The Salons of America: 1922-1936, 1991; Brooklyn Artists Index, 1993. **Address:** 35 Prospect Pk. W, Apt. 6-C, Brooklyn, NY 11215, U.S.A.

MARLOW, Joyce. British (born England), b. 1929. **Genres:** Novels, Children's Fiction, History. **Career:** Actress, 1949-66; writer, 1966-; Copyright Licensing Agency, director. **Publications:** The Man with the Glove, 1964; A Time to Die, 1966; Billy Goes to War, 1967; The House on the Cliffs, 1968; The Peterloo Massacre, 1969; The Tolpuddle Martyrs, 1971; Captain Boycott and the Irish, 1973; The Life and Times of George I, 1973; The Uncrowned Queen of Ireland, 1975; Mr. and Mrs. Gladstone, 1977; Oak and the Ivy: An Intimate Biography of William and Catherine Gladstone, 1977; Kings and Queens of Britain, 1977; Kessie, 1985; Sarah, 1987; Anne, 1989; Industrial Tribunals and Appeals, 1991; Country Ways: Secrets for Finding and Keeping a Country Man, 1999; Making Memories: Celebrating Mothers and Daughters through Traditions, Crafts and Lore, 2001. EDITOR: The Virago Book of Women & the Great War, 1998; Votes for Women: The Virago Book of Suffragettes, 2000. **Address:** 3 Spring Bank, New Mills, High Peak, SK22 4AS, England. **Online address:** joyce.marlow@firenet.uk.net

MARLOWE, Katharine. *See* **VALE-ALLEN, Charlotte.**

MARMOT, Michael (Gideon). British (born England), b. 1945. **Genres:** Medicine/Health, Sciences. **Career:** Royal Prince Alfred Hospital, resident and fellow, 1969-70; University of California, Department of Biomedical and Environmental Health Sciences, lecturer, 1975-76; London School of Hygiene and Tropical Medicine (LSHTM), senior lecturer, 1976-85; University College of London, consultant in medical division, 1980-84, professor of epidemiology and public health, 1985-, International Centre for Health and Society, director, 1994-; Middlesex School of Medicine, consultant in medical division, 1980-84; Harvard University, School of Public Health, adjunct professor, 2004. Writer. **Publications:** Immigrant Mortality in England and Wales, 1970-78: Causes of Death by Country of Birth, 1984; (ed.) Coronary Heart Disease Epidemiology: From Aetiology to Public Health, 1992, 2nd ed., 2005; (ed. with R.G. Wilkinson) Social Determinants of Health, 1999, 2nd ed., 2006; (ed. with S. Stansfeld) Stress and the Heart: Psychosocial Pathways to Coronary Heart Disease, 2002; The Status Syndrome: How Social Standing Affects Our Health and Longevity, 2004; (ed. with R.G. Wilkinson) Social Determinants of Health, 2006; (ed. with J. Siegrist) Social Inequalities in Health: New Evidence and Policy Implications, 2006; (contrib.) Rose's Strategy of Preventive Medicine: The Complete Original Text, 2008. Contributor to journals. **Address:** Department of Epidemiology & Public Health, University College London, Gower St. Campus, 1-19 Torrington Pl., London, GL WC1E 6BT, England. **Online address:** m.marmot@ucl.ac.uk

MAROLDA, Edward J. American (born United States) **Genres:** Novels, Business/Trade/Industry, Economics, History, Military/Defense/Arms Control, Bibliography. **Career:** Unites States Navy, Naval Historical Center, acting director, officer, 1969, 1970, Histories and Archives Division, senior historian and chief, staff historian, 1971-87, contemporary history branch head, 1987-96, senior historian, 1996-; Georgetown University, Department of Liberal Studies, adjunct faculty. Writer. **Publications:** (Comp. with W.C. Heimdahl) Guide to United States Naval Administrative Histories of World War II, 1976; (comp. with G.W. Pryce, III) A Select Bibliography of the United States Navy and the Southeast Asian Conflict, 1950-1975, 1982, vol. II: From Military Assistance to Combat, 1959-1965, 1989; (with G.W. Pryce, III) A Short History of the United States Navy and the Southeast Asian Conflict, 1950-1975, 1984; Carrier Operations, 1987; The United States Navy and the Vietnam Conflict, 1989; (ed.) Operation End Sweep: A History of Minesweeping Operations in North Vietnam, 1993; By Sea, Air and Land: An Illustrated History of the U.S. Navy and the War in Southeast Asia, 1994; (ed.) FDR and the U.S. Navy, 1998; (with R.J. Schneller, Jr.) Shield and Sword: The United States Navy and the Persian Gulf War, 1998; The Washington Navy Yard: An Illustrated History, 1999; (ed.) Theodore Roosevelt, the U.S. Navy and the Spanish-American War, 2001; U.S. Navy in the Vietnam War: An Illustrated History, 2002; (ed.) U.S. Navy in the Korean War, 2007; Approaching Storm: Conflict in Asia, 1945-1965, 2009; Ready Seapower: A History of the U.S. Seventh Fleet, 2011. **Address:** The Naval Historical Center, Georgetown University, 3307 M St. NW, Ste. 202, Washington, DC 20007, U.S.A. **Online address:** edward.marolda@navy.mil

MARON, Margaret. American (born United States) **Genres:** Novels, Mystery/Crime/Suspense, Novellas/Short Stories. **Career:** Mystery Writers of America, director on the national board. Writer. **Publications:** DEBORAH KNOTT SERIES: Bootlegger's Daughter, 1992; Southern Discomfort, 1993; Shooting at Loons, 1994; Up Jumps the Devil, 1996; Killer Market, 1997; Home Fires, 1998; Storm Track, 2000; Uncommon Clay, 2001; Slow Dollar, 2002; High Country Fall, 2004; Rituals of the Season, 2005; Winter's Child,

2006; Hard Row, 2007; Death's Half Acre, 2008; Sand Sharks, 2009. SIGRID HARALD SERIES: One Coffee With, 1981; Death of a Butterfly, 1984; Death in Blue Folders, 1985; The Right Jack, 1987; Baby Doll Games, 1988; Corpus Christmas, 1989; Past Imperfect, 1991; Fugitive Colors, 1995. NON-SERIES: Bloody Kin, 1985; Shoveling Smoke: Selected Mystery Stories, 1997; Last Lessons of Summer, 2003; Suitable for Hanging: Selected Stories, 2004. OTHERS: Christmas Mourning, 2010; Three-day Town, 2011; The Buzzard Table, 2012; Deborah's Judgment, 2012; With This Ring, 2012. Works appear in anthologies. **Address:** Vicky Bijur Literary Agency, 333 W End Ave., New York, NY 10023, U.S.A. **Online address:** margaretmaron@nc.rr.com

MARON, Monika. German (born Germany), b. 1941. **Genres:** Novels, Novellas/Short Stories, Plays/Screenplays. **Career:** Für Dich, journalist; Wochenpost, journalist. **Publications:** Flugasche: Roman, 1981; Das Missverständnis, 1982; Die überläuferin: Roman, 1986; (with J. von Westphalen) Trotzdem herzlicheGrüsse, 1988; Stille Zeile Sechs: Roman, 1991; Nach Massgabe meiner Begreifungskraft, 1993; Animal Triste: Roman, 1996; Pawels Briefe: Eine Familiengeschichte, 1999; Quer über die Gleise, 2000; Endmoränen: Roman, 2002; (contrib.) Was weiss die Katze vom Sonntag?: Fotografien, 2002; Geburtsort Berlin, 2003; Wie ich ein Buch nicht schreiben kann undes trotzdem versuche, 2005; Ach Glück: Roman, 2007; Bitterfelder Bogen: ein Bericht, 2009; Zwei Brüder: Gedanken zur Einheit 1989-2009, 2010. **Address:** South Fischer Verlag GmbH, Hedderichstr. 114, PO Box 700 355, Frankfurt am Main, D-60553, Germany.

MAROTTI, Arthur F(rancis). American (born United States), b. 1940. **Genres:** Literary Criticism And History, Theology/Religion, History, Cultural/Ethnic Topics, Poetry. **Career:** Washington University, assistant professor, 1965-70; Wayne State University, associate professor, 1970, professor, 1985-2008, distinguished professor, 2008-10, distinguished professor emeritus, 2010-, College of Liberal Arts, associate dean, 1985-86, Charles Gershenson distinguished faculty fellow, 1995-97, director of religious studies, 2001-05, vice president, 2004-05, Department of English, interim chair, 2008; Johns Hopkins University, visiting associate professor, 1983; Universidade Federal de Santa Catarina, visiting professor, 2000; University of Michigan, visiting professor, 2004; Universidade Federal de Minas Gerais, visiting professor, 2005. Writer. **Publications:** John Donne, Coterie Poet, 1986; Manuscript, Print and the English Renaissance Lyric, 1995; Religious Ideology and Cultural Fantasy: Catholic and Anti-Catholic Discourses in Early Modern England, 2005. EDITOR: (with R. Wasserman, J. Dulan and S. Mathur) Reading with a Difference: Gender, Race and Cultural Identity, 1993; Critical Essays on John Donne, 1994; (with C.C. Brown) Texts and Cultural Change in Early Modern England, 1997; Catholicism and Anti-Catholicism in Early Modern English Texts, 1999; (with M.D. Bristol) Print, Manuscript and Performance: The Changing Relations of the Media in Early Modern England, 2000; (and intro. with R. Corthell, F. Dolan and C. Highley) Catholic Culture in Early Modern England, 2007; The Early Modern Englishwoman: A Facsimile Library of Essential Works Series II, Printed Writings, 1641-1700: Part 4, vol. III: Gertrude More, 2009; (with K. Jackson) Shakespeare and Religion: Early Modern and Postmodern Perspectives, 2011. Contributor to journals. **Address:** Department of English, Wayne State University, Rm. 9203.1, 5057 Woodward Ave., Detroit, MI 48202, U.S.A. **Online address:** a.marotti@wayne.edu

MAROUANE, Leila. French/Tunisian (born Tunisia), b. 1960?. **Genres:** Novels, Young Adult Fiction. **Career:** Horizons, journalist; El Watan, journalist; Politis, journalist; Jeune Afrique, journalist; Le Monde, journalist, 1990; writer, 1996-. **Publications:** La fille de la Casbah, 1996; Ravisseur, 1998; Le chatiment des hypocrites, 2001; The Abductor, 2001; Le châtiment des Hypocrites: Roman, 2001; La jeune fille et la mère, 2005; La vie sexuelle d'un islamiste à Paris, 2007; The Sexual Life of an Islamist in Paris, 2010. Contributor to periodicals. **Address:** c/o Author Mail, Quartet Books, 27 Goodge St., London, GL W1P 2LD, England.

MAROWITZ, Charles. American (born United States), b. 1934. **Genres:** Plays/Screenplays, Theatre. **Career:** Encore Magazine, co-founder, 1954-65, co-editor; Open Space Theatre, artistic director, 1968-81; Malibu Stage Co., artistic director, 1990-; Royal Shakespeare Co., founder and director; Swans Commentary, columnist, 2004-. **Publications:** The Method as Means, 1961; Stanislavsky and the Method, 1964; A Macbeth, 1971; Confessions of a Counterfeit Critic, 1973; The Shrew, 1975; Artaud at Rodex, 1977; Hedda, 1978; The Act of Being, 1978; The Marowitz Shakespeare, 1978; New Theatre Voices of the 50s and 60s, 1981; Sex Wars, 1982; Sherlock's Last Case, 1984; Potboilers: Three Black Comedies, 1986; Prospero's Staff: Acting and Directing in the Contemporary Theatre, 1986; Directing the Action: Acting and Directing in the Contemporary Theatre, 1986; Disciples, 1987; Wilde West, 1988; Clever Dick, 1989; Burnt Bridges: A Souvenir of the Swinging Sixties and Beyond, 1990; Recycling Shakespeare (criticism), 1991; Directing the Action (acting book), 1992; Edmond Rostand's Cyrano de Bergerac, 1995; Alarums & Excursions: Our Theatres in the Nineties, 1996; Bashville in Love: A Musical Comedy, 1998; The Other Way: An Alternative Approach to Acting and Directing, 1999; Stage Fright, 1999; Boulevard Comedies, 2000; Stage Dust: A Critic's Cultural Scrapbook from the 1990s, 2001; (with J. Kotl) Roar of the Canon, 2001; Quack, 2002; Murdering Marlowe, 2002; The Other Chekhov, (biography), 2004; How to Stage a Play, Make a Fortune, Win a Tony, and Become a Theatrical Icon, 2005; Silent Partners, 2008. ADAPTER: The Marowitz Hamlet, 1965; Marlowe: Dr. Faustus, 1965. EDITOR AND CONTRIBUTOR: Encore Reader, 1966; Theatre at Work, 1968; Open Space Plays, 1974; (with T. Milne and O. Hale) New Theatre Voices of the Fifties and Sixties: Selections from Encore Magazine 1956-1963, 1981. Contributor of journals. **Address:** Swans, PO Box 267, Boonville, CA 95415, U.S.A. **Online address:** winoman@aol.com

MARQUARDT, Elizabeth. American (born United States), b. 1970?. **Genres:** Sociology, Human Relations/Parenting. **Career:** University of Washington, School of Public Health, International Health Program, project coordinator, 1994-95; University of Chicago, MacLean Center for Clinical Medical Ethics, Project on Ethical Issues in Home Health Care, managing editor, 1996-97; Chicago Temple, First United Methodist Church, assistant pastor, 1997-99; Bates College, assistant chaplain, 1999-2000; FamilyScholars.org, editor, Institute for American Values, Center for Marriage and Families, director and vice president for family studies, 2000-. **Publications:** (Contrib.) Hooking Up, Hanging Out, and Hoping for Mr. Right, 2001; Between Two Worlds: The Inner Lives of Children of Divorce, 2005; (contrib.) The Revolution in Parenthood: The Emerging Global Clash between Adult Rights and Children's Needs, 2006. Contributor to periodicals. **Address:** Center for Marriage and Families, Institute for American Values, 1841 Broadway, Ste. 211, New York, NY 10023-7697, U.S.A. **Online address:** elizabeth@familyscholars.org

MARQUARDT, Virginia C. Hagelstein. American (born United States), b. 1945. **Genres:** Art/Art History, Cultural/Ethnic Topics, Politics/Government. **Career:** University of Wisconsin-Whitewater, instructor in art history, 1969-71; University of Denver, lecturer in art history, 1971-74; Metropolitan State College, instructor, 1971, 1973; University of Colorado, instructor, 1973, 1975; University of Colorado, Denver, instructor, 1973, 1974; University of Colorado, Colorado Springs, instructor, 1974; Colorado Women's College, instructor, 1974; University of Northern Colorado, instructor in art history, 1974-75; Pratt Institute, visiting instructor, 1981-83, visiting assistant professor of art history, 1984-85; Mercy College, adjunct instructor, 1983-85; Bernard M. Baruch College of the City University of New York, adjunct assistant professor, 1984-85; Marist College, assistant professor, 1985-88, associate professor, 1989-98, professor of art history, 1998-, coordinator of art history and core fine arts programs, 1989-95, Core/Liberal Studies Program, director. **Publications:** EDITOR AND CONTRIBUTOR: (with G.H. Roman) The Avant-Garde Frontier: Russia Meets the West, 1910-1930, 1992; Survivor from a Dead Age: The Memoirs of Louis Lozowick, 1997; Art and Journals on the Political Front, 1910-1940, 1997; Modern Art, 1900-1945: The Age of Avant-Gardes, 2007; American Culture and the Political Left, 1913-1939, forthcoming. OTHER: Modern Art, 1900-1945, forthcoming. Contributor of articles to journals. **Address:** Department of Art and Art History, Marist College, Steel Plant 05B, Poughkeepsie, NY 12601, U.S.A. **Online address:** virginia.marquardt@marist.edu

MARQUART, Debra. American (born United States), b. 1956?. **Genres:** Novellas/Short Stories, Poetry, Autobiography/Memoirs, Young Adult Nonfiction, Young Adult Fiction. **Career:** Iowa Woman, assistant poetry editor, 1994-95; Drake University, visiting professor of English, 1994-95; Iowa State University, assistant professor, 1995-2001, Center for Teaching Excellence, faculty fellow, 2000-01, Department of English, associate professor, 2001-, professor, MFA Program in Creative Writing & Environment, coordinator; University of Southern Maine, Stonecoast Low-Residency MFA program, professor. Writer. **Publications:** Everything's a Verb: Poems, 1995; Hunger in the Bones: Stories from the Road, 1998; The Hunger Bone: Rock and Roll Stories (short stories), 2001; From Sweetness: Poems, 2002; The Horizontal World: Growing Up Wild in the Middle of Nowhere (memoir), 2006. Contributor to periodicals. **Address:** Department of English, Iowa

State University, 206 Ross Hall, Ames, IA 50011, U.S.A. **Online address:** marquart@iastate.edu

MARQUIS, Max. Also writes as Michael Meath, Edward F. Barnes. British (born England), b. 1925?. **Genres:** Novels, Mystery/Crime/Suspense, Sports/Fitness, Young Adult Non-fiction, Young Adult Fiction, Biography. **Career:** French Radio English Service, broadcaster, 1952. Television writer; script editor; columnist and storyline writer. **Publications:** (Ed.) Mistress of Many, 1960; Sir Alf Ramsey: Anatomy of a Football Manager, 1970; The Care Takers, 1975; General Hospital, 1976; A Matter of Life, 1977; The Shadowed Heart, 1978; The Traitor Machine, 1980; Bodyguard to Charles, 1989; Vengeance, 1990; Deadly Doctors, 1992; The Twelfth Man, 1992; Elimination, 1993; Undignified Death, 1994; Written in Blood, 1995; Death of a Good Woman, 1998. Contributor to periodicals. **Address:** Rupert Crew Ltd., 1A King's Mews, London, GL WC1N 2JA, England. **Online address:** maxmhrqu@aol.com

MARQUIT, Amanda. American (born United States), b. 1986?. **Genres:** Novels, Young Adult Fiction, Literary Criticism And History. **Career:** Writer. **Publications:** Shut the Door, 2005. **Address:** c/o Arthur Klebanoff, Scott Meredith Literary Agency, 200 W 57th St., Ste. 904, New York, NY 10019, U.S.A.

MARQUSEE, Mike. British/American (born United States), b. 1953. **Genres:** Novels, Sports/Fitness, History, Humanities, Intellectual History, Social Commentary, Literary Criticism And History, Popular Culture, Race Relations, Politics/Government, Music, International Relations/Current Affairs, Biography, Social Sciences. **Career:** Labour Briefing, editor and contributor, 1986-92, political correspondent, 1992-95; freelance writer and broadcaster, 1992-; Labour Left Briefing, editor; University of Brighton, honorary faculty fellow, 2005. **Publications:** Slow Turn (novel), 1986; (with R. Heffernan) Defeat from the Jaws of Victory: Inside Kinnock's Labour Party, 1992; Anyone But England: Cricket and the National Malaise, 1994, as Anyone But Engand: An Outsider Looks at English Cricket, 2005; War Minus the Shooting: A Journey through South Asia during Cricket's World Cup, 1996; Redemption Song: Muhammad Ali and the Spirit of the Sixties, 1999, 2nd ed., 2005; Chimes of Freedom: The Politics of Bob Dylan's Art, 2003, rev. ed. as Wicked Messenger: Bob Dylan and the 1960s, 2005; If I Am not for Myself: Journey of an Anti-Zionist Jew, 2008. Contributor to periodicals. **Address:** 45 Chesholm Rd., London, GL N16 0DS, England. **Online address:** chimesoffreedom@blueyonder.co.uk

MARR, Andrew. Scottish (born Scotland), b. 1959. **Genres:** History, Politics/Government. **Career:** Scotsman, general reporter and business reporter, 1981-84, parliamentary correspondent, 1984-86, political editor, 1988; Economist, political editor, 1988-92; Independent, political correspondent, 1986-88, chief commentator, 1992-96, editor, 1996-98, editor-in-chief, 1998; British Broadcasting Corp., political editor, 2000-05. Journalist. **Publications:** The Battle for Scotland, 1992; Ruling Britannia: The Failure and Future of British Democracy, 1995; The Day Britain Died, 2000; My Trade: A Short History of British Journalism, 2004; History of Modern Britain, 2007; Making of Modern Britain: From Queen Victoria to VE Day, 2010. **Address:** c/o Profile Books, 58A Hatton Garden, London, GL EC1N 8LX, England.

MARR, David. Australian (born Australia), b. 1947. **Genres:** Art/Art History, Photography. **Career:** Bulletin (Australia), reporter; National Times (Australia), reporter and editor; Sydney Morning Herald, investigative reporter; Australian Broadcasting Corporation (ABC-TV), program presenter; ABC-TV, television reporter. **Publications:** Barwick, 1980; Society and the Writer, 1981; The Ivanov Trail, 1984; Patrick White: A Life, 1991; (ed.) Letters: Patrick White, 1994; (with M. Wilkinson) Dark Victory, 2003; The Henson case, 2008; One Hundred: A Tribute to the Mitchell Library, 2010. **Address:** Sydney Morning Herald, PO Box 506, Sydney, NW 2001, Australia.

MARR, David G(eorge). Australian/American (born United States), b. 1937. **Genres:** History, International Relations/Current Affairs, Politics/Government, Bibliography. **Career:** University of California, lecturer in history, 1968-69, assistant professor of Vietnamese studies, 1969-72, Center for South and Southeast Asian Studies, research associate, 1971-75; Cornell University, assistant professor, Indochina Resource Center, co-director, 1971-76; Australian National University, School of Pacific and Asian Studies, research fellow, 1975-, professor, 1975-2002, senior fellow, now professor emeritus, School of Culture, History and Language, visiting fellow; Vietnam Today, editor. **Publications:** Vietnamese Anticolonialism, 1885-1925, 1971; Tradition and Revolution in Vietnam, 1974; (ed.) Tradition and Revolution in Vietnam, 1974; (ed.) Reflections from Captivity: Phan Boi Chau's Prison Notes and Ho Chi Minh's Prison Diary, 1977; (ed. with A. Reid) Perceptions of the Past in Southeast Asia, 1979; Barwick, 1980; Vietnamese Tradition on Trial 1920-1945, 1981; Society and the Writer: Essays on Literature in Modern Asia, 1981; (with C.A. Thayer) Vietnam Since 1975: Two Views from Australia, 1982; Ivanov Trail, 1984; Independence of Death, 1984; (ed.) The Red Earth: A Vietnamese Memoir of Life on a Colonial Rubber Plantation, 1985; (ed. with A.C. Milner) Southeast Asia in the 9th to 14th Centuries, 1986; (ed. with C.P . White) Postwar Vietnam: Dilemmas in Socialist Development, 1988; Patrick White: A Life, 1991; (comp.) Vietnam Annotated Bibliography, 1992; Vietnam, 1992; (co-ed.) Vietnam and the Rule of Law, 1993; (ed.) Letters / Patrick White, 1994; Vietnam 1945: The Quest for Power, 1995; Vietnam Strives to Catch Up, 1995; Mass Media in Vietnam, 1998; Concepts of Statecraft in Vietnam, 2000; (with M. Wilkinson) Dark Victory, 2003; (ed. with B.J.T. Kerkvliet) Beyond Hanoi, 2004. CONTRIBUTOR: Students and Politics in Emerging Nations, 1969; Critical Essays on the Pentagon Papers, 1972; The World Military Order, 1979; Southeast Asia Under Japanese Occupation, 1980; Asia: The Winning of Independence, Macmillan, 1981; Burchett: Reporting the Other Side of the World, 1986; Death and Disease in Southeast Asia, 1987. **Address:** Research School of Pacific and Asian Studies, Division of Pacific and Asian History, Australian National University, Canberra, AC 0200, Australia. **Online address:** david.marr@anu.edu.au

MARR, Maggie. American (born United States), b. 1969?. **Genres:** Women's Studies And Issues, Novels. **Career:** ICM Agency, staff, 2001, agent. Attorney, film producer and writer. **Publications:** Hollywood Girls Club, 2007; Secrets of the Hollywood Girls Club, 2008. **Address:** c/o Kristin Nelson, Nelson Literary Agency, 1732 Wazee St., Ste. 207, Denver, CO 80202, U.S.A. **Online address:** maggiemarr@mac.com

MARR, Melissa. American (born United States), b. 1972. **Genres:** Young Adult Fiction, Novels, Novellas/Short Stories. **Career:** Writer and educator. **Publications:** Wicked Lovely, 2007; (co-author) Love Is Hell, 2008; Ink Exchange, 2008; Sanctuary, 2009; Fragile Eternity, 2009; Challenge, 2010; Radiant Shadows, 2010; Stopping Time, 2010; Darkest Mercy, 2011; Old Habits, 2011; Resolve, 2011; Love Struck, 2011; Graveminder, 2011; Faery Tales & Nightmares, 2012. Works appear in anthologies. **Address:** c/o Rachel Vater, Folio Literary Management L.L.C., 505 8th Ave., Ste. 603, New York, NY 10018-4629, U.S.A. **Online address:** info@melissa-marr.com

MARR, Timothy. American (born United States), b. 1960. **Genres:** History, Literary Criticism And History. **Career:** University of North Carolina, associate professor of American studies. Writer. **Publications:** (ed. with J. Bryan and M.K.B. Edwards) Ungraspable Phantom: Essays on Moby-Dick, 2006; The Cultural Roots of American Islamicism, 2006. **Address:** Department of American Studies, 227 Greenlaw Hall, CB3520, Chapel Hill, NC 27599-3520, U.S.A. **Online address:** marr@email.unc.edu

MARRINER TOMEY, Ann. American (born United States), b. 1943. **Genres:** Administration/Management, Medicine/Health, Sciences, Humanities. **Career:** Indiana State University, professor of nursing, now professor emeritus, Office of Sponsored Programs, research fellow; Midwest Alliance in Nursing, vice-chair, chair; Indiana State Nurses' Association, vice president, president; Sigma Theta Tau Intl., distinguished lecturer. Consultant and writer. **Publications:** AS ANN MARRINER: Guide to Nursing Management, 1980, 8th ed. as Guide to Nursing Management and Leadership, 2009. EDITOR AS ANN MARRINER: Current Perspective in Nursing Management, 1979; Contemporary Nursing Management, 1982; Nursing Theorists and Their Work, 1986, (as A.M. Tomey with M.R. Alligood) 7th ed., 2010. EDITOR AS ANN MARRINER-TOMEY: Nursing at Indiana University, 75 Years at the Heart of Healthcare, 1989; (with B. Henry, C. Arndt and M. DiVincenti) Dimensions of Nursing Administration, 1989; Case Studies in Nursing Management, 1990; Transformational Leadership in Nursing, 1993; (with M.R. Alligood) Nursing Theory: Utilization and Application, 1997, 3rd ed., 2006. Contributor of books to journals. **Address:** College of Nursing, Indiana State University, 749 Chestnut St., Terre Haute, IN 47809-1937, U.S.A. **Online address:** atomey@indstate.edu

MARRIOTT, Edward. British (born England), b. 1966?. **Genres:** Travel/Exploration, Sciences, Romance/Historical. **Career:** Evening Standard, reviewer. Journalist and broadcaster. **Publications:** The Lost Tribe: A Harrowing Passage into New Guinea's Heart of Darkness, 1997; Savage Shore: Life and Death with Nicaragua's Last Shark Hunters, 2000; Plague: A Story of Science, Rivalry, and the Scourge That Won't Go Away, 2003; Claude and Madeleine: A True Story, 2005. **Address:** Evening Standard Ltd., Northcliffe House, Rm. 203B, 2 Derry St., London, GL W8 5TT, England.

MARRIOTT, Kim. Australian (born Australia), b. 1961. **Genres:** Information Science/Computers, Mathematics/Statistics. **Career:** University of Melbourne, Machine Intelligence Project, research fellow, 1988-89; International Business Machines Co., Thomas J. Watson Research Center, research staff, 1989-92; Monash University, senior lecturer, 1993-98, associate professor of computer science and software engineering, 1998-, professor, Clayton School of Information Technology, head of school. Writer. **Publications:** (Ed. with B. Meyer) Visual Language Theory, 1998; (with P.J. Stuckey) Programming with Constraints: An Introduction, 1998; (ed. with B. Meyer and contrib.) Theory of Visual Languages, 1998; (ed. with A. Blackwell and A. Shimojima) Diagrammatic Representation and Inference, 2004. Contributor to books. **Address:** Clayton School of IT, Monash University, Clayton, VI 3800, Australia. **Online address:** kim.marriott@infotech.monash.edu.au

MARRIOTT, Michel. American (born United States), b. 1954. **Genres:** Novels, Mystery/Crime/Suspense, Science Fiction/Fantasy. **Career:** Marion Chronicle Tribune, reporter, 1977; Courier-Journal, reporter; Philadelphia Daily News, reporter; Washington Post, reporter; New York Times, reporter, 1987-94, Style Department, reporter, 1995-98, Circuits Section, reporter, 1998-; Newsweek, general editor, 1994-95; Columbia University, Graduate School of Journalism, professor; City College of New York, Department of Communications, Film and Video, professor; Antioch Writer's Workshop, professor; City University of New York, Bernard M Baruch College, professor of journalism. **Publications:** The Skull Cage Key, 2008. Contributor to newspapers and magazines. **Address:** Weissman School of Arts & Sciences, Baruch College, CUNY, Rm. 7-257, Newman Vertical Campus, 55 Lexington Ave., New York, NY 10010, U.S.A. **Online address:** michel_marriott@baruch.cuny.edu

MARRIOTT, Zoë. (Zoë Davina Marriott). American (born United States), b. 1982. **Genres:** Novels. **Career:** Writer. **Publications:** The Swan Kingdom, 2007; Daughter of the Flames, 2009. **Address:** U.S.A. **Online address:** zoe.marriott@ntlworld.com

MARRIOTT, Zoë Davina. *See* **MARRIOTT, Zoë.**

MARRONE, Steven P(hillip). American (born United States), b. 1947. **Genres:** History, Philosophy, Theology/Religion, Young Adult Non-fiction, Humanities. **Career:** Teacher, 1969-70; Tufts University, instructor, 1977-78, assistant professor, 1978-84, associate professor of history, 1984-96, professor of history, 1996-. Writer. **Publications:** William of Auvergne and Robert Grosseteste: New Ideas of Truth in the Early Thirteenth Century, 1983; Truth and Scientific Knowledge in the Thought of Henry of Ghent, 1985; The Light of Thy Countenance: Science and Knowledge of God in the Thirteenth Century, 2001. **Address:** Department of History, Tufts University, Rm. 01, East Hall, Upper Campus Rd., Medford, MA 02155, U.S.A. **Online address:** steven.marrone@tufts.edu

MARRS, Jim. American (born United States), b. 1943. **Genres:** Politics/Government, Plays/Screenplays, Adult Non-fiction, Air/Space Topics, Archaeology/Antiquities, History, International Relations/Current Affairs, Paranormal, Paranormal. **Career:** Magpie Magazine, editor and owner, 1963-64; reporter, cartoonist and photographer for Texas periodicals, 1965-80; freelance writer, 1970-; Jerre R. Todd & Associates, copywriter, public relations director and cartoonist, 1972-74, director of special projects, account executive, public relations director, copywriter and cartoonist, 1980-81; University of Texas-Arlington, teacher in office of continuing education, 1976-; The Marketing Group, public relations consultant and copywriter, 1982-83; The Springtown Current, publisher and co-owner, 1983-84; Cowtown Trails Magazine, editor, publisher and co-owner, 1983-84; Innotech Energy Corp., communications director, 1985-86; Northeast Health Care Center, communications director, 1985-86; First Bank and Trust, communications director, 1985-98. **Publications:** Crossfire: The Plot That Killed Kennedy, 1989; Enigma Files: The True Story of America's Psychic Warfare Program, 1995; Alien Agenda: Investigating the Extraterrestrial Presence Among Us, 1997; PSI Spies, 2000; Rule by Secrecy: The Hidden History That Connects the Trilateral Commission, the Freemasons and the Great Pyramids, 2000; Inside Job: Unmasking the 9-11 Conspiracies, 2004, 2nd ed. as Inside Job: The Shocking Case for a 9/11 Conspiracy, 2005; The Terror Conspiracy: Provocation, Deception and 9/11, 2006; PSI Spies: The True Story of America's Psychic Warfare Program, 2007; Rise of the Fourth Reich: The Secret Societies that Threaten to Take Over America, 2008; Above Top Secret: Uncover the Mysteries of the Digital Age, 2008; Sisterhood of the Rose, 2009; The Trillion-Dollar Conspiracy: How the New World Order, Man-Made Diseases and Zombie Banks Are Destroying America, 2010; Me & Lee: How I Came to Know, Love and Lose Lee Harvey Oswald, 2010; The Terror Conspiracy Revisited: What Really Happened on 9/11, and Why We're Still Paying the Price, 2011. **Address:** HarperCollins Publishers, 10 E 53rd St., New York, NY 10022, U.S.A. **Online address:** jim@jimmarrs.com

MARS, Julie. American (born United States), b. 1951?. **Genres:** Novels, Autobiography/Memoirs, Young Adult Fiction, Adult Non-fiction. **Career:** Writer. **Publications:** The Secret Keepers (novel), 2000; A Month of Sundays: Searching for the Spirit and My Sister (memoir), 2005; Anybody Any Minute (novel), 2008; Rust, 2012. **Address:** The Permanent Press, 4170 Noyac Rd., Sag Harbor, NY 11963, U.S.A. **Online address:** julie@juliemars.com

MARS, Perry. Guyanese (born Guyana), b. 1941. **Genres:** Area Studies, Local History/Rural Topics, Social Commentary, Politics/Government, Adult Non-fiction, History, Social Sciences. **Career:** University of Guyana, senior lecturer, 1976-87, Department of Political Science and Law, head, 1976-78, 1986-87, dean of faculty of social science, 1979-82, professor of political science and development studies, 1987-94, coordinator of research and international communications at Institute of Development Studies, 1987-92, acting director of the institute, 1988-89; California State University, visiting professor, 1983-84; New School for Social Research, Center for Studies of Social Change, visiting fellow, 1990-91; Wayne State University, visiting professor, 1991-92, associate professor, 1992-2000, professor of Africana studies, 2000-. Writer. **Publications:** Structural Inequalities and Political Violence in a Multi-Racial State, the Guyana Example, 1973; (ed. with H. Lutchman and H. Addo) Selected Issues in Guyanese Politics, 1976; (contrib.) Studies in Development and Change in the Modern World, 1989; Ideology and Change: The Transformation of the Caribbean Left, 1998; (ed. with A.H. Young) Caribbean Labor and Politics: Legacies of Cheddi Jagan and Michael Manley, 2004; (contrib.) Privatization and Industrial Welfare: Lessons from the South, forthcoming. Contributor to books and periodicals. **Address:** Department of Africana Studies, Wayne State University, 1 Maccabee Bldg., Ste. 11203, 11th Fl., Detroit, MI 48202, U.S.A. **Online address:** ad5965@wayne.edu

MARSA, Linda J. American (born United States), b. 1948. **Genres:** Medicine/Health, Industrial Relations, Adult Non-fiction. **Career:** Journalist, 1979-; University of California Extension, Writer's Program, senior instructor, 1988-; Los Angeles Times, staff writer; Omni and Ladies' Home Journal, contributing editor. **Publications:** Prescription for Profits: How the Pharmaceutical Industry Bankrolled the Unholy Marriage between Science and Business, 1997. Contributor to journals. **Address:** c/o Alice F. Martell, The Martell Literary Agency, 545 Madison Ave. 7th Fl., New York, NY 10022, U.S.A. **Online address:** lmarsa@earthlink.net

MARSALIS, Wynton. American (born United States), b. 1961. **Genres:** Music, Young Adult Fiction. **Career:** Writer, educator and musician. **Publications:** Sweet Swing Blues on the Road: A Year with Wynton Marsalis and His Septet, 1994; Marsalis on Music, 1995; (with C. Vigeland) Jazz in the Bittersweet Blues of Life, 2001; Jazz, 2002; (with S.S. Hinds) To a Young Jazz Musician: Letters from the Road, 2004; (intro.) Understanding Jazz: Ways to Listen, 2005; (with P. Schaap) Jazz ABZ: An A to Z Collection of Jazz Portraits (juvenile), 2005; (with G. Ward) Moving to Higher Ground: How Jazz Can Change Your Life, 2008. **Address:** Sony Music Entertainment Inc., Trumpeter 550 Madison Ave., New York, NY 10022, U.S.A. **Online address:** info@wyntonmarsalis.org

MARSDEN, Carolyn. American/Mexican (born Mexico), b. 1950. **Genres:** Novels, Novellas/Short Stories, Poetry, Children's Fiction, Sports/Fitness. **Career:** Bilingual (Spanish-English) teacher; Arizona Commission on the Arts, writer-in-residence, 1978-85. **Publications:** The Gold-threaded Dress, 2002; Mama Had to Work on Christmas, 2003; Silk Umbrellas, 2004; Moon Runner, 2005; The Quail Club, 2006; (with V.S. Loh) The Jade Dragon, 2006; When Heaven Fell, 2007; Bird Springs, 2007; (with T.P. Niem) Buddha's Diamonds, 2008; (with P. Matzigkeit) Sahwira: An African Friendship, 2009; Take Me with You, 2010; Starfields, 2011; The White Zone, 2012; My

Own Revolution, 2012. **Address:** c/o Kelly Sonnack, Andrea Brown Literary Agency, 1076 Eagle Dr., Salinas, CA 93905, U.S.A. **Online address:** carolynmarsden@gmail.com

MARSDEN, John. Australian (born Australia), b. 1950. **Genres:** Children's Fiction, Young Adult Fiction, Novels, Picture/Board Books, Children's Nonfiction. **Career:** Geelong Grammar School, English teacher, 1982-90; Writer, 1991-. **Publications:** The Journey, 1988; The Great Gatenby, 1988; So Much to Tell You, 1989, as So Much to Tell You: The Play, 1994; Staying Alive in Year Five, 1989; Out of Time, 1990; Letters from the Inside, 1992; Take My Word for It, 1993; Everything I Know about Writing, 1993; Looking for Trouble, 1993; Cool School, 1995; Creep Street: You Make It Happen, 1996; Checkers, 1996; Dear Miffy, 1997; Dead of Night, 1997; Prayer for the 21st Century, 1998; Killing Frost, 1998; Secret Men's Business, 1998; Norton's Hut, 1998; The Rabbits, 1999; Marsden on Marsden, 2000; The Head Book, 2001; Winter, 2002; A Day in the Life of Me, 2002; Millie, 2002; The Boy You Brought Home, 2002; The Magic Rainforest, 2002; Hamlet, 2008; (with M. Ottley) Home and Away, 2008. EDITOR: This I Believe, 1996; Four Weddings and a Funeral, 1996; I Believe This: 100 Eminent Australians Face Life's Biggest Question, 2004. TOMORROW, WHEN THE WAR BEGAN SERIES: The Dead of the Night, 1994; Tomorrow, When the War Began, 1995; The Third Day, the Frost, 1996; Darkness Be My Friend, 1997; Burning for Revenge, 1997; The Other Side of Dawn, 1999; The Night Is for Hunting, 2001; While I Live, 2003; Incurable, 2005; Circle of Flight, 2006. **Address:** Pan Macmillan, 31 Market St., Sydney, NW 2000, Australia.

MARSELLA, Anne (Francesca). American (born United States), b. 1964. **Genres:** Novellas/Short Stories, Novels. **Career:** University of Paris, professor of English, 1992-93; University of Paris II, professor of English, 1993-94; University of Cergy, lecturer in English, 1994-. Writer. **Publications:** The Lost and Found and Other Stories (short stories), 1994; Remedy, 2007; Patsy Boone, 2008. Contributor to periodicals. **Address:** c/o Charlotte Sheedy, Charlotte Sheedy Literary Agency Inc., 65 Bleecker St., New York, NY 10012, U.S.A.

MARSH, Charles R. American (born United States), b. 1958?. **Genres:** Photography, Theology/Religion. **Career:** University of Zurich, fellow, 1986-87; Free University of Amsterdam, fellow, 1989; Loyola College, professor of theology and ethics, 1990-99, Project on Theology and Community, director; University of Heidelberg, fellow, 1992; University of Virginia, associate professor of religious studies, 2000-, professor of religious studies, Project on Lived Theology, director. **Publications:** (Ed. with W.W. Floyd, Jr.) Theology and the Practice of Responsibility: Essays on Dietrich Bonhoeffer, 1994; Reclaiming Dietrich Bonhoeffer: The Promise of His Theology, 1994; God's Long Summer: Stories of Faith and Civil Rights, 1997; The Last Days: A Son's Story of Segregation at the Dawn of the New South, 2001; Beloved Community: How Faith Shapes Social Justice, from The Civil Rights Movement to Today, 2005; Wayward Christian Soldiers: Freeing the Gospel from Political Captivity, 2007; Welcoming Justice: God's Movement Toward Beloved Community, 2009; Strange Glory: A Life of Dietrich Bonhoeffer, 2012. **Address:** Department of Religious Studies, University of Virginia, 033 Halsey Hall, 1540 Jefferson Park Ave., PO Box 400126, Charlottesville, VA 22903, U.S.A. **Online address:** cmarsh@virginia.edu

MARSH, Derick Rupert Clement. Australian/South African (born South Africa), b. 1928?. **Genres:** Literary Criticism And History, Plays/Screenplays. **Career:** University of Natal, lecturer, senior lecturer in English, 1954-60; University of Sydney, senior lecturer in English, 1961-66; Queen's University, visiting professor of English, 1964-65; La Trobe University, foundation professor, 1966-76, 1980-89, foundation professor emeritus of English, 1989-; University of Western Australia, professor and head of the department of English, 1976-80. Writer. **Publications:** The Recurring Miracle: A Study of Cymbeline and the Last Plays, 1962, 3rd ed., 1980; Macbet: A lecture before the Sydney Branch of the English Association, 1964; (with K.G.W. Cross) Poetry: Reading and Understanding, 1966; A Critical Commentary on Shakespeare's Henry IV-Part I, 1967; Shakespeare's Hamlet, 1970; Creativity and Control, 1970; Passion Lends Them Power: A Study of Shakespeare's Love Tragedies, 1976. **Address:** La Trobe University, PO Box 821, Wodonga, VI 3689, Australia.

MARSH, Fabienne. American (born United States), b. 1957. **Genres:** Novels, Young Adult Non-fiction, Humor/Satire. **Career:** American Broadcasting Co., documentary film unit, researcher, 1980-84; consultant, writer and field producer for documentary films, 1984-; Johns Hopkins University, lecturer in creative writing, 1997-2000; University of Minnesota, lecturer, 2001; Chadwick School journalism advisor, 2006-09. **Publications:** NOVELS: Long Distances, 1988; The Moralist of the Alphabet Streets, 1991; Single, White, Cave Man, 2002. NONFICTION: (with M. Cader) Dave's World (humor), 1995; (ed. and contrib.) Saturday Night Live: The First Twenty Years, 1994. Contributor to magazines and newspapers. **Address:** c/o Richard Pine, Inkwell Management, 521 5th Ave., Ste. 26, New York, NY 10175, U.S.A.

MARSH, Jan. British (born England), b. 1942. **Genres:** Literary Criticism And History, Poetry, Biography, Autobiography/Memoirs, History. **Career:** Writer. **Publications:** Welfare State, 1975; Edward Thomas: A Poet for His Country, 1978; Back to the Land: The Pastoral Impulse in England, from 1880 to 1914, 1982; Pre-Raphaelite Sisterhood, 1985; Jane and May Morris: A Biographical Story, 1839-1938, 1986; Pre-Raphaelite Women: Images of Femininity, 1988; (with P.G. Nunn) Women Artists and the Pre-Raphaelite Movement, 1989; The Legend of Elizabeth Siddal, 1989; (with T. Lummis) The Woman's Domain: Women and the English Country House, 1990; Christina Rossetti: A Literary Biography, 1994 in US as Christina Rossetti: A Writer's Life, 1995; Bloomsbury Women: Distinct Figures in Life and Art, 1995; The Pre-Raphaelites: Their Lives in Letters and Diaries, 1996; Pre-Raphaelites, 1998; (with P.G. Nunn) Pre-Raphaelite Women Artists, 1999; Dante Gabriel Rossetti: Painter and Poet, 1999; (ed.) Collected Writings of Dante Gabriel Rossetti, 1999; Christina Rossetti, 2002; Art & Androgyny: The Life of Sculptor Fiore de Henriquez, 2004; (ed.) Black Victorians: Black People in British Art, 1800-1900, 2005; William Morris & Red House, 2005; (contrib.) Holman Hunt and the Pre-Raphaelite Vision, 2008. Contributor to periodicals. **Address:** c/o Jennifer Kavanagh, 39 Camden Park Rd., London, GL NW1 9AX, England.

MARSH, Joan F. American (born United States), b. 1923. **Genres:** Biography, History. **Career:** British Admiralty Delegation, staff, 1943-44; Foreign Economic Administration, staff, 1944-45; Video Ed Productions Inc., research editor, 1983-85. **Publications:** Martha Washington, 1993. Contributor to periodicals. **Address:** 101 E Kirke St., Chevy Chase, MD 20815, U.S.A.

MARSH, Nigel. Australian/British (born England), b. 1964?. **Genres:** Young Adult Non-fiction. **Career:** DArcy Australia, chief executive officer, 2001-02; Leo Burnett Australia, chief executive officer, chairman; Young & Rubicam Brands, group chief executive officer; Environmental Initiative Earth Hour, founder. Writer. **Publications:** Fat, Forty and Fired: One Man's Frank, Funny and Inspiring Account of Losing His Job and Finding His Life, 2007; Observations of a Very Short Man, 2007; Overworked and Underlaid: A Seriously Funny Guide to Life, 2009. **Address:** ICMI Melbourne, PO Box 2311, Prahran, VI 3181, Australia.

MARSH, Peter T. American/Canadian (born Canada), b. 1935. **Genres:** History, Politics/Government. **Career:** University of Saskatchewan, instructor, 1962-63, assistant professor of history, 1963-67; University of Sussex, visiting tutor, 1966; Oxford University, All Souls College, visiting fellow, 1966-67; Syracuse University, Department of History, associate professor, 1967-78, chair, 1968-70, professor of history, 1978-, now emeritus, University Honors Program, director, 1978-86, resident chair, 1987, 1988, professor of international relations, 1992-; University of Leicester, visiting professor of Victorian studies, 1970, Andrew W. Mellon Foundation Project, designer and director, 1984-86; Cambridge University, Emmanuel College, visiting fellow, 1974; University of Birmingham, Journal of British Studies, associate editor, 1978-84, Leverhulme fellow, 1996-97, honorary professor, 1997-. **Publications:** The Victorian Church in Decline: Archbishop Tait and the Church of England 1868-1882, 1969; The Discipline of Popular Government, 1978; Joseph Chamberlain: Entrepreneur in Politics, 1994; Bargaining on Europe: Britain and the First Common Market, 1860-1892, 1999; The Cutting Edge: Matthew Boulton College 1890-2005, 2006; The Chamberlain Litany: Letters witihin a Governing Family from Empire to Appeasement, 2010. EDITOR: The Conscience of the Victorian State, 1978; Contesting the Boundaries of Liberal and Professional Education: The Syracuse Experiment, 1988. Contributor to periodicals. **Address:** Maxwell School, Syracuse University, 145 Eggers Hall, Syracuse, NY 13244-1020, U.S.A. **Online address:** ptmarsh@powernet.co.uk

MARSH, Robert Mortimer. American (born United States), b. 1921. **Genres:** Business/Trade/Industry, Institutions/Organizations, Military/Defense/Arms Control, Sociology, Third World, History. **Career:** Columbia University, lecturer, 1957; University of Michigan, instructor, assistant professor, 1958-61; Cornell University, assistant professor of sociology and Asian studies, 1961-65; Duke University, associate professor of sociology, 1965-67; Brown University, professor of sociology, 1967-69, chairman of department, 1971-75, now professor emeritus; Harvard University, honorary research associate in East Asian studies, 1977-78. Writer. **Publications:** The Mandarins: The Circulation of Elites in China, 1600-1900, 1961; Comparative Sociology: A Codification of Cross-Societal Analysis, 1967; (with H. Mannari) Modernization and the Japanese Factory, 1976; (ed. with J.M. Armer) Comparative Sociological Research in the 1960's and 1970's, 1982; (with H. Mannari) Organizational Change in Japanese Factories, 1988; The Great Transformation: Social Change in Taipei, Taiwan since the 1960s, 1996; (ed. with M. Sasaki) Trust: Comparative Perpectives, 2011. **Address:** Department of Sociology, Brown University, Maxcy Hall, 112 George St., PO Box 1916, Providence, RI 02912, U.S.A. **Online address:** rmarsh@brown.edu

MARSH, Susan H. American/Chinese (born China), b. 1926. **Genres:** History, Politics/Government. **Career:** Brown University, part-time lecturer, 1968-77; Providence College, professor of political science, 1977-94, professor emeritus, 1994-; World Affairs Council of Rhode Island, director. Writer. **Publications:** Years of Upheaval, 1975; (ed. with M.Y. Kau) China in the Era of Deng Xiaoping: A Decade of Reform, 1993. **Address:** Department of Political Science, Providence College, 318 Howley Hall, 549 River Ave., 1 Cunningham Sq., Providence, RI 02918-0001, U.S.A.

MARSHAL, Nell. American (born United States), b. 1933. **Genres:** Novels, Money/Finance, Young Adult Fiction. **Career:** Bank Mortgage and Loan Co., vice-president, 1962-67; Union Mortgage Co., First Trust Deed Department, manager, 1968-72; Marshal Plan Inc., chief executive officer, 1973-91, newsletter writer, 1975-91; Ardevel Publishing Co., owner and writer, 1993-. **Publications:** An Investment in Time: What Happens to Your Money When an Investment Company Folds (novel), 1998. **Address:** CSS Publishing Co., 5450 N Dixie Hwy., Lima, OH 45807, U.S.A. **Online address:** taze@ipa.net

MARSHALL, Adré. South African (born South Africa), b. 1942. **Genres:** Literary Criticism And History, Business/Trade/Industry, Money/Finance. **Career:** University of Stellenbosch, lecturer in English, 1965-67; University of Port Elizabeth, lecturer in French, 1968, 1970, lecturer in English, 1983-86; University of Cape Town, lecturer in English, 1988-95, honorable research associate. Writer. **Publications:** The Turn of the Mind: Constituting Consciousness in Henry James, 1998. Contributor to books. **Address:** 3 Glenthorne Ln., Rondebosch, 7700, South Africa. **Online address:** adrod@mweb.co.za

MARSHALL, Alex. American (born United States), b. 1959?. **Genres:** Architecture, Economics. **Career:** Virginian-Pilot, staff writer, 1988-97; Harvard University, Graduate School of Design, Loeb fellow, 1999-2000; Governing Magazine, columnist; New Jersey Institute of Technology, New Jersey School of Architecture, instructor. Journalist. **Publications:** How Cities Work: Suburbs, Sprawl, and the Roads Not Taken, 2000; Beneath the Metropolis: The Secret Lives of Cities, 2006; The Surprising Design of Market Economies, 2012. Contributor to periodicals. **Address:** Regional Plan Association, 4 Irving Pl., 7th Fl., New York, NY 10003, U.S.A. **Online address:** alex@rpa.org

MARSHALL, Bridget M(ary). American (born United States), b. 1974. **Genres:** Adult Non-fiction. **Career:** Lehigh University, violinist, 1992-94, Writing Center, writing tutor, 1995-96, assistant professor of English; Payment Technologies Inc., technical and business writer, 1994-97; Kerouac Players, performer, 1994-96; University of Massachusetts-Amherst, teaching associate, 1997-; University of Massachusetts-Lowell, assistant professor of English. Writer. **Publications:** Animal Crackers: A Tender Book About Death and Funerals and Love, 1998; The Transatlantic Gothic Novel and the Law, 1790-1860, 2010. Contributor to newspapers and periodicals. **Address:** Department of English, University of Massachusetts, O'Leary Library, 61 Wilder St., Lowell, PA 01854-3049, U.S.A. **Online address:** bridget_marshall@uml.edu

MARSHALL, Christopher D(avid). New Zealander (born New Zealand), b. 1953. **Genres:** Theology/Religion, Education, Law. **Career:** Teacher, 1977-78; Mennonite Centre, tutor, 1985; Bible College of New Zealand, lecturer, 1986-99, Tyndale Graduate School of Theology, reader in New Testament, 1999-, head of New Testament, through 2004; Victoria University of Wellington, School of Art History, Classics and Religious Studies, associate professor, professor, 2004-, head. Writer. **Publications:** Faith as a Theme in Mark's Narrative, 1989; Kingdom Come: The Kingdom of God in the Teaching of Jesus, 1993; Beyond Retribution: A New Testament Vision for Justice, Crime, and Punishment, 2001; Crowned with Glory & Honor: Human Rights in the Biblical Tradition, 2001; Little Book of Biblical Justice: A Fresh Approach to the Bible's Teachings on Justice, 2005. Contributor to books and periodicals. **Address:** School of Art History, Classics & Religious, Studies, Victoria University of Wellington, 115 Hunter Bldg., PO Box 600, Wellington, 6012, New Zealand. **Online address:** chris.marshall@vuw.ac.nz

MARSHALL, Donald G. American (born United States), b. 1943. **Genres:** Literary Criticism And History, Philosophy. **Career:** University of California, assistant professor of English, 1969-75; University of Iowa, associate professor, 1975-79, professor of English, 1980-90; University of Illinois, Department of English, professor of English and head, 1990-2000, professor emeritus, 2000-; Illinois Humanities Council, board director, 1994-99; Council of Christian Scholarly Societies, president, 1998-2000; The Poetry Foundation, secretary, 1998-99, president, 1999-2001, chair, 2009-; Pepperdine University, Seaver College, Fletcher Jones chair of great books, 2003-. Writer. **Publications:** (Ed.) Literature as Philosophy: Philosophy as Literature, 1987; (trans. with J. Weinsheimer) H. Gadamer, Truth and Method, 1989, 2nd ed., 2004; Contemporary Critical Theory: A Selective Bibliography, 1993; (ed.) Force of Tradition: Response and Resistance in Literature, Religion, and Cultural Studies, 2005. Contributor to journals. **Address:** Seaver College, Pepperdine University, Rm. 206, Cultural Arts Ctr., 24255 Pacific Coast Hwy., Malibu, CA 90263, U.S.A. **Online address:** donald.marshall@pepperdine.edu

MARSHALL, Elizabeth Margaret. (Elizabeth Sutherland). Scottish (born Scotland), b. 1926. **Genres:** Novels, Romance/Historical, History, Young Adult Fiction, Social Sciences, Reference. **Career:** Scottish Episcopal Church, Social Service Board, assistant social worker, 1974-80; Groam Museum, curator, 1982-93. Writer. **Publications:** AS ELIZABETH SUTHERLAND: Lent Term, 1973; Black Isle: Portrait of the Past, 1973; Seer of Kintail, 1974; Hannah Hereafter, 1976; (ed.) The Prophecies of Brahan Seer, 1977; The Eye of God, 1977; The Weeping Tree, 1980; Ravens and Black Rain: The Story of Highland Second Sight, Including a New Collection of the Prophecies of the Brahan Seer, 1985; (ed.) The Gold Key and the Green Life: Some Fantasies and Celtic Tales, 1986; In Search of the Picts: A Celtic Dark Age Nation, 1994; Guide to the Pictish Stones, 1997; Five Euphemias: Women in Medieval Scotland 1200-1420, 1999; (with M.M. Johnston) Lydia: Wife of Hugh Miller of Cromarty, 2002. Contributor to journals. **Address:** 21 Swinton Rd., Baillieston, Fortrose, Glasgow, HI 69, Scotland.

MARSHALL, Ian. American/British (born England), b. 1954. **Genres:** Literary Criticism And History. **Career:** Temple University, instructor, 1986-88; Pennsylvania State University, Department of English, assistant professor, 1988-94, associate professor, 1994-2000, professor, 2000-. Writer. **Publications:** Story Line: Exploring the Literature of the Appalachian Trail, 1998; Peak Experiences: Walking Meditations on Literature, Nature, and Need, 2003; Walden by Haiku, 2009. Contributor to journals. **Address:** Department of English, Pennsylvania State University, 133 Misciagna Family Ctr., Ivyside Pk., Altoona, PA 16601-3760, U.S.A. **Online address:** ism2@psu.edu

MARSHALL, James Vance. *See* **PAYNE, Donald Gordon.**

MARSHALL, Janet (Perry). American (born United States), b. 1938. **Genres:** Children's Fiction, Illustrations, Education. **Career:** Author and illustrator. **Publications:** SELF-ILLUSTRATED PICTURE BOOKS: My Camera: At the Zoo, 1989; My Camera: At the Aquarium, 1989; Ohmygosh, My Pocket, 1992; Look Once, Look Twice, 1995; Banana Moon, 1998; A Honey of a Day, 2001. **Address:** 36 Bradley Hill Rd., Hingham, MA 02043, U.S.A. **Online address:** janetmarshall@attbi.com

MARSHALL, John. *See* Obituaries.

MARSHALL, John Douglas. American (born United States), b. 1947. **Genres:** Documentaries/Reportage, Autobiography/Memoirs, History. **Career:** Gazette-Times, columnist and reporter, 1973-78; Journal-American, columnist, 1978-81; Seattle Post-Intelligencer, columnist, feature writer and book editor, 1981-. **Publications:** (Co-author) Volcano: The Eruption of Mount St. Helens, 1981; Reconciliation Road: A Family Odyssey of War and Honor (memoir), 1993; (ed. and contrib.) Home Field: Nine Writers at Bat, 1997; Place of Learning, Place of Dreams: A History of the Seattle Public Library, 2004. **Address:** Seattle Post-Intelligencer, 2601 Elliott Ave., Ste. 300A, Seattle, WA 98121, U.S.A. **Online address:** johnmarshall@seattlepi.com

MARSHALL, Julie. *See* **SMITH, Bobbi.**

MARSHALL, Nancy Rose. American (born United States) **Genres:** Art/Art History. **Career:** Yale University, Department of Art History, lecturer, 1997-2000; Connecticut College, Department of Art History, visiting assistant professor, 1999; University of Wisconsin, Department of Art History, assistant professor of art history, 2000-06, associate professor, 2006-. Writer. **Publications:** (With M. Warner) James Tissot: Victorian Life/Modern Love (exhibition catalogue), 1999. Contributor to books. **Address:** Department of Art History, University of Wisconsin, 224 Elvehjem Bldg., 800 University Ave., Madison, WI 53706-1414, U.S.A. **Online address:** nrmarshall@wisc.edu

MARSHALL, Oshley Roy. *See* **MARSHALL, Roy.**

MARSHALL, Owen. New Zealander (born New Zealand), b. 1941. **Genres:** Novels, Novellas/Short Stories, Plays/Screenplays. **Career:** Waitaki Boys High School, deputy director, 1983-85; Craighead Diocesan School, deputy principal, 1986-91; Aoraki Polytechnic, teacher of fiction writing, 1993-; New Zealand Order of Merit, officer, 2000-; Canterbury University, University's Ursula Bethell writer-in-residence, 1981, lecturer, adjunct professor, 2005-. Writer. **Publications:** SHORT STORIES: Supper Waltz Wilson and Other New Zealand Stories, 1979; The Master of Big Jingles and Other Stories, 1982; The Day Hemingway Died and Other Stories, 1984; The Lynx Hunter and Other Stories, 1987; The Divided World: Selected Stories, 1989; Tomorrow We Save the Orphans: Fiction, 1993; The Ace of Diamonds Gang, 1993; Coming Home in the Dark, 1995; The Best of Owen Marshall's Short Stories, 1997; (ed.) Essential New Zealand Short Stories, 2002; When Gravity Snaps: Short Stories, 2002; Occasional: 50 Poems, 2004; Watch of Gryphons: And Other Stories, 2005; Drybread, 2007; Timeless Land, 2010; Sleepwalking in Antarctica and Other Poems, 2010; Larnarchs, 2011. NOVELS: A Many Coated Man, 1995; Harlequin Rex, 1999. EDITOR: Burning Boats: Seventeen New Zealand Short Stories, 1994; Letter from Heaven: Sixteen New Zealand Poets, 1995; Beethoven's Ears: Eighteen New Zealand Short Stories, 1996; Spinning a Line: New Zealnd Writing about Fishing, 2001; Authors' Choice: Letting New Zealand Writers Choose Their Favourite Stories and Explain Why, 2001; (contrib.) Best New Zealand Fiction, 2004. Contributor to books and periodicals. Works appear in anthologies. **Address:** Canterbury University Press, University of Canterbury, PO Box 4800, Christchurch, 8140, New Zealand. **Online address:** owen-marshall@timaru.com

MARSHALL, Paul A. American/British (born England), b. 1948. **Genres:** Adult Non-fiction, Politics/Government, Theology/Religion, Essays. **Career:** University of Western Ontario, instructor in geology, 1969-71; exploration geologist, 1970-75; Citizens for Public Justice, researcher in public policy, 1974-81; Fuller Theological Seminary, adjunct faculty; York University, lecturer, 1977-81, 1983; Institute for Christian Studies, professor of political theory, 1981-98, academic vice president, 1985-87; Rutgers University, adjunct faculty of graduate program in philosophy, 1983-84; University of Toronto, adjunct faculty in theology, 1986-89, 1993; Ontario Theological Seminary, adjunct faculty, 1987-95; London Institute of Contemporary Christianity, Third Way lecturer, 1987; Free University of Amsterdam, visiting professor, 1989, adjunct faculty of law, 1989-91; Satya Wacana University, visiting professor, 1989; University of Potchefstroom, Stoker lecturer, 1990; Juniata College, J. Omar Good distinguished visiting professor, 1991-92; Regent College, adjunct faculty, 1991-95; Dordt College, Thomas F. Staley distinguished lecturer, 1991; Redeemer College, Thomas F. Staley distinguished lecturer, 1992; Canadian Bible College, Thomas F. Staley distinguished lecturer, 1992; Trinity Western University, Thomas F. Staley distinguished lecturer, 1992; Queen's University, lecturer, 1993; European University for the Humanities, visiting professor, 1994; Catholic University of America, visiting professor, 1996; Institute on Religion and Democracy, senior fellow, 1996; Claremont Institute, visiting fellow, 1996-, senior fellow; Freedom House, senior fellow in religious freedom, 1998-; Hudson Institute, Center for Religious Freedom, senior fellow, 2006-. Writer. **Publications:** (Co-author) Labour of Love: Essays on Work, 1980; Thine Is the Kingdom: A Biblical Perspective on the Nature of Government and Politics Today, 1984; (ed. with R.V. Vennen) Social Science in Christian Perspective, 1988; (ed. with R.J. Mouw and S. Griffioen) Stained Glass: Worldviews and Social Science, 1989; (contrib.) The Basic Ideas of Calvinism, 1990; (ed. with J. Chaplin) Political Theory and Christian Vision: Essays in Memory of Bernard Zylstra, 1994; A Kind of Life Imposed on Man: Vocation and Social Order from Tyndale to Locke, 1996; (with L. Gilbert) Their Blood Cries Out: The Untold Story of Persecution Against Christians in the Modern World, 1997; Just Politics: A Christian Framework for Getting Behind the Issues, 1997; (with L. Gilbert) Heaven is Not My Home: Learning to Live in God's Creation, 1998; Egypt's Endangered Christians, 1999; (ed.) Religious Freedom in the World, 2000; Massacre of the Millennium, 2001; The Talibanization of Nigeria, 2002; (with L. Gilbert and R. Green) Islam at the Crossroads, 2002; God and the Constitution: Christianity and American Politics, 2002; (ed.) Radical Islam's Rules: The Worldwide Spread of Extreme Shari'a Law, 2005; (ed. with L. Gilbert and R.G. Ahmanson) Blind Spot: When Journalists Don't Get Religion, 2009. Contributor to books and periodicals. **Address:** Hudson Institute, 1015 15th St. NW, 6th Fl., Washington, DC 20005, U.S.A.

MARSHALL, Peter. British/Scottish (born Scotland), b. 1964?. **Genres:** Novels, Horror, Mystery/Crime/Suspense. **Career:** Ampleforth College, history master, 1990-94; University of Warwick, lecturer in history, 1994-2001, senior lecturer in history, 2001-04, director of undergraduate studies in history, 2003-, reader in history, 2004-, professor, 2006-; Toussaint Louverture Theatre Co. chairman. Historian and writer. **Publications:** The Catholic Priesthood and the English Reformation, 1994; (ed.) The Impact of the English Reformation 1500-1640, 1997; (ed. with B. Gordon) The Place of the Dead: Death and Remembrance in Late Medieval and Early Modern Europe, 2000; Beliefs and the Dead in Reformation England, 2002; (ed. with A. Ryrie) The Beginnings of English Protestantism, 2002; Reformation England, 1480-1642, 2003; (ed. with A. Walsham) Angels in the Early Modern World, 2006; Religious Identities in Henry VIII's England, 2006; Mother Leakey and The Bishop: A Ghost Story, 2007; (ed. with G. Scott) Catholic Gentry in English Society: Throckmortons of Coughton from Reformation to Emancipation, 2009; The Reformation: A Very Short Introduction, 2009. Contributor to books and periodicals. **Address:** Department of History, University of Warwick, Rm. 317, University House, Coventry, CV4 7AL, United Kingdom. **Online address:** p.marshall@warwick.ac.uk

MARSHALL, Peter (H.). British (born England), b. 1946. **Genres:** History, Philosophy, Archaeology/Antiquities, Astronomy, Civil Liberties/Human Rights, Cultural/Ethnic Topics, Environmental Sciences/Ecology, Ethics, Geography, History, Humanities, Intellectual History, Literary Criticism And History, Mythology/Folklore, Philosophy, Politics/Government, Sciences, Social Commentary. **Career:** St. Michel College, English teacher, 1966-67; University of London, Extramural Department, tutor in philosophy and literature, 1974-80; University College of North Wales, Extramural Department, tutor in philosophy, 1981-90. Writer. **Publications:** William Godwin, 1984; (with M. Amin and D. Willetts) Journey through Tanzania, 1984; (with B. Lewis) Into Cuba, 1985; Cuba Libre: Breaking the Chains?, 1987; William Blake: Visionary Anarchist, 1988; Demanding the Impossible: A History of Anarchism, 1992; Nature's Web: Rethinking Our Place on Earth, 1992; Journey through Maldives, 1992; Around Africa: From the Pillars of Hercules to the Strait of Gibraltar, 1994; Celtic Gold: A Voyage around Ireland, 1997; Riding the Wind: A New Philosophy for a New Era, 1998; The Philosopher's Stone: A Quest for the Secrets of Alchemy, 2001; World Astrology: The Astrologer's Quest to Understand the Human Character, 2004; Europe's Lost Civilization: Uncovering the Mysteries of the Megaliths, 2004; Theatre of the World: Alchemy, Astrology and Magic in Renaissance Prague, 2006; The Magic Circle of Rudolf II: Alchemy and Astrology in Renaissance Prague, 2006. EDITOR AND AUTHOR OF INTRODUCTION: The Anarchist Writings of William Godwin, 1986; Damon and Delia, 1988. Contributor of articles to books and periodicals. **Address:** A M Heath & Company Ltd., 6 Warwick Ct., Holborn, London, GL WC1R 5DJ, England. **Online address:** petermarshall7@beeb.net

MARSHALL, Rosalind Kay. Scottish (born Scotland), b. 1939. **Genres:** History, Biography, Women's Studies And Issues. **Career:** Dictionary of the Older Scottish Tongue, assistant editor, 1970-71; Scottish Record Office, outside editor, 1971-73; Scottish National Portrait Gallery, assistant keeper, 1973-99; Oxford Dictionary of National Biography, research associate. **Publications:** The Days of Duchess Anne: Life In The Household Of The Duchess Of Hamilton, 1656-1716, 1973; Childhood in Seventeenth Century Scotland: The Scottish National Portrait Gallery, 1976; Mary of Guise, 1977; Women in Scotland, 1660-1780, 1979; Virgins and Viragos: A History of Women in Scotland from 1080-1980, 1983; Costume in Scottish Portraits 1080-1980,

1986; Sir John Medina, 1986; Mary, Queen of Scots, 1987; Bonnie Prince Charlie, 1988; (ed.) Dynasty: The Royal House of Stewart, 1990; (ed. with G.R. Dalgleish) Art of Jewellery in Scotland, 1991; Elizabeth I, 1991; Henrietta Maria: The Intrepid Queen, 1991; Mary I, 1993; The Winter Queen, 1998; John Knox, 2000; Ruin and Restoration: St Mary's Church, Haddington, 2001; Scottish Queens, 1034-1714, 2003; Queen Mary's Women: Female Relatives, Servants, Friends and Enemies of Mary, Queen of Scots, 2006; St Giles': The Dramatic Story of a Great Church and its People, 2009. Contributor to periodicals. **Address:** National Galleries of Scotland, The Mound, Edinburgh, BR EH2 2EL, Scotland.

MARSHALL, Rose Parkman. *See* **DAVIS, Rose Parkman.**

MARSHALL, Roy. (Oshley Roy Marshall). Barbadian/British (born England), b. 1920. **Genres:** Law, Education. **Career:** University of Sheffield, professor of law, 1956-69; University of West Indies, vice-chancellor, 1969-74; Committee of Vice Chancellors and Principals of British Universities, secretary-general, 1974-79; University of Hull, vice-chancellor, 1979-85. Writer. **Publications:** (Ed. as O.R. Marshall) The Jubilee Lectures of the Faculty of Law, University of Sheffield, 1961. AS OSHLEY ROY MARSHALL: The Assignment of Choses in Action, 1950; (ed.) Theobald: On Wills, 12th ed., 1963; (with J.A. Nathan) A Casebook on Trusts, 5th ed., 1967; Commonwealth Legal Co-operation, 1979; Cases and Commentary on the Law of Trusts, 8th ed., 1986; (with Hayton) Commentary and Cases on the Law of Trusts and Equitable Remedies, 2001. **Address:** 2 St. Ann Sq., Netherhong, HD7 2YH, England.

MARSHALL, W. Gerald. American (born United States), b. 1948. **Genres:** Literary Criticism And History, Young Adult Fiction. **Career:** University of Hawaii, associate professor of English, 1977-. Writer. **Publications:** A Great Stage of Fools: Theatricality and Madness in the Plays of William Wycherley, 1993; (ed. and intro.) The Restoration Mind, 1997. **Address:** Department of English, University of Hawaii, 1733 Donaghho Rd., Honolulu, HI 96822, U.S.A.

MARSTON, Cam. American (born United States) **Genres:** Novels, Business/Trade/Industry, Economics, Marketing. **Career:** Nestle Brands Foodservice Co., salesperson; Generational Insight (formerly Marston Communications), founder and president, 1996-. Writer. **Publications:** Motivating the What's in It For Me? Workforce: Managing across the Generational Divide, 2005; Motivating the What's in iI For Me? Workforce: Manage across the Generational Divide and Increase Profits, 2007; Generational Selling Tactics that Work: Quick and Dirty Secrets for Selling to Any Age Group, 2011. **Address:** Generational Insight, PO Box 81118, Mobile, AL 36689, U.S.A. **Online address:** cam@generationalinsight.com

MARSTON, Edward. *See* **MILES, Keith.**

MARSZALEK, John F. American (born United States), b. 1939. **Genres:** History, Race Relations, Biography, Reference, Law, Politics/Government, Essays. **Career:** Canisius College, instructor, 1967-68; Gannon University, assistant professor, 1968-72, associate professor of history, 1972-73; Mississippi State University, associate professor, 1973-80, professor, 1980-94, W.L. Giles distinguished professor of history, 1994-2002, W.L. Giles distinguished professor emeritus, 2002-, director and mentor of distinguished scholars, 2004-07, Ulysses S. Grant Association, executive director and managing editor, 2008-. **Publications:** Court Martial: A Black Man in America, 1972, rev. ed. as Assault at West Point, 1994; (with S.H. Wier) A Black Businessman in White Mississippi 1886-1974, 1977; Sherman's Other War: The General and the Civil War Press, 1981, rev. ed., 1999; (with D.L. Conner) A Black Physician's Story: Bringing Hope in Mississippi, 1985; Grover Cleveland: A Bibliography, 1988; Sherman: A Soldier's Passion for Order, 1993, 2nd ed., 1994; The Petticoat Affair: Manners, Mutiny and Sex in the White House, 1997, 2nd ed., 1999; The Civil War in the Western Theater, 2001; (intro.) Simple Story of a Soldier, 2004; Commander of Lincoln's Armies: A Life of Henry Wager Halleck, 2004; Sherman's March to the Sea, 2005; A Black Congressman in the Age of Jim Crow: South Carolina's George Washington Murray, 2006. EDITOR: (and intro.) The Diary of Miss Emma Holmes 1861-1866, 1979; (with C.D. Lowery) Encyclopedia of African-American Civil-Rights, from Emancipation to the Present, 1992, rev. ed. as The Greenwood Encyclopedia of African-American Civil Rights: From Emancipation to the Twenty-first Century, 2 vols., 2003; (with W.D. Miscamble) American Political History: Essays on the State of the Discipline, 1997. Works appear in anthologies. Contributor to books, journals and magazines. **Address:** Mitchell Memorial Library, Mississippi State University, PO Box 5408, Mississippi State, MS 39762, U.S.A. **Online address:** johnmarsz@yahoo.com

MARTCHENKO, Michael. Canadian/French (born France), b. 1942. **Genres:** Children's Fiction, Illustrations, Humor/Satire. **Career:** Spitzer, Mills & Bates, art director, 1966-69; Needham, Harper & Steers, art director, 1969-70; Art Associates, designer/illustrator, 1970-72; TDF Artists Ltd., creative art director, 1972-93. Writer. **Publications:** SELF-ILLUSTRATED FOR CHILDREN: Birdfeeder Banquet, 1990; Ma, I'm a Farmer, 2003. Illustrator of books by others. **Address:** 100 Airdrie Rd., Toronto, ON M4G 1M3, Canada.

MARTEL, Aimee. *See* **THURLO, Aimee.**

MARTEL, Gordon. Canadian (born Canada) **Genres:** History, Military/Defense/Arms Control, Essays. **Career:** Trent University, assistant professor, 1977-81; Royal Roads Military College, assistant professor, 1981-83, associate professor, 1983-87, professor, 1987-95; De Montfort University, senior research fellow, 1995-2000, visiting faculty; Simon Fraser University, adjunct professor of history, 1995-; University of Northern British Columbia, History Program, professor of history, 1995-, now professor emeritus, chair of the history program, 1996-2004, CASHS, acting dean; University of Toronto, faculty; University of Oxford, St Antony's College, visiting faculty, Nuffield College, visiting faculty; University of Ulster, visiting faculty; University of Western Australia, visiting faculty; University of Victoria, Department of History, adjunct faculty. Writer. **Publications:** Imperial Diplomacy: Rosebery and the Failure of Foreign Policy, 1986; The Origins of the First World War, 1987, rev. ed., 2008; After Armageddon: The World after the First World War, 2011; Political Intelligence in Britain, 1900-1939, forthcoming. EDITOR: The Origins of the Second World War Reconsidered: The A.J.P. Taylor Debate after Twenty-five Years, 1986, 2nd ed. as The Origins of the Second World War Reconsidered: A.J.P. Taylor and the Historians, 1999; Studies in British Imperial History: Essays in Honour of A.P. Thornton, 1986; Modern Germany Reconsidered, 1870-1945, 1992; American Foreign Relations Reconsidered, 1890-1993, 1994; The Times and Appeasement: The Journals of A.L. Kennedy, 1932-1939, 2000; World War Two Reader, 2004; Companion to Europe: 1900-1945, 2006, 2nd ed., 2011; A Companion to International History 1900-2001, 2007; Encyclopedia of War, 2012. **Address:** History Program, University of Northern British Columbia, 3333 University Way, Prince George, BC V2N 4Z9, Canada. **Online address:** gmartel@uvic.ca

MARTEL, William C. American (born United States), b. 1955. **Genres:** Information Science/Computers, Military/Defense/Arms Control, Technology. **Career:** Harvard University, postdoctoral fellow, 1991-93; Maxwell Air Force Base, Center for Strategy and Technology (CSAT), founder and director, 1993-99, Air War College, associate professor of international relations, 1993-99; Naval War College, professor of national security affairs, 1999-2005, Space Technology and Policy Studies, chair, 1999-2005; Tufts University, Fletcher School of Law and Diplomacy, associate professor of international security studies, 2006-, Fletcher Summer Institute for the Advanced Study of Nonviolent Conflict, academic director, 2006, 2007, International Security Studies Program, faculty. Writer. **Publications:** (With P.L. Savage) Strategic Nuclear War: What the Superpowers Target and Why, 1986; (with J.F. Dunnigan) How to Stop a War: The Lessons of Two Hundred Years of War and Peace, 1987; (with D.P. Henry and C.R. Neu) Improving the USAF Technology Transfer Process: Prepared for the United States Air Force, 1991; (with W.T. Pendley) Nuclear Coexistence: Rethinking U.S. Policy to Promote Stability in an Era of Proliferation, 1994; (ed. with T.C. Hailes) Russia's Democratic Moment?: Defining US Policy to Promote Democratic Opportunities in Russia, 1995; (contrib.) The Absolute Weapon Revisited, 1998; (contrib.) Pulling Back from the Nuclear Brink: Slowing, Stopping, Reversing and Countering Nuclear Threats, 1998; (ed.) The Technological Arsenal: Emerging Defense Capabilities, 2001; Victory in War: Foundations of Modern Military Policy, 2007, rev. ed. as Victory in War: Foundations of Modern Strategy, 2011. Contributor to periodicals. **Address:** Fletcher School of Law and Diplomacy, Tufts University, 602 Cabot Intercultural Ctr., 160 Packard Ave., Medford, MA 02155, U.S.A. **Online address:** william.martel@tufts.edu

MARTELL, Christopher R. American (born United States), b. 1956. **Genres:** Psychiatry, Medicine/Health, Sciences. **Career:** United Cerebral Palsy of Greater Suffolk, applied behavioral science specialist, 1985; B.O.C.E.S. III Alternate Learning Center, school psychology intern, 1985-

86; Helen Keller Services for the Blind, applied behavioral science specialist, 1985-86; State University of New York Technical College, clinical psychology intern, 1986-87; Valley Stream Public Schools, school psychologist, 1986-87; Working Organization for Retarded Children, applied behavioral science specialist, 1986-88; New Medic-Community Re-entry Services, staff psychologist, 1989-90; Highline Public Schools, psychologist, 1990-92; University of Washington, Department of Psychology, clinical instructor, 1996-2000, research therapist, 1997-2001, clinical assistant professor, 2000-03, clinical associate professor, 2003-, Children's Hospital Medical Center, clinical research and clinical consultant, 2002-05, School of Medicine, Department of Psychiatry and Behavioral Sciences, clinical associate professor, 2006-; Washington State Psychological Association, president, 2000-01; American Board of Professional Psychology, secretary and treasurer, 2003-, work sample coordinator, 2004-; American Board of Cognitive-Behavioral Psychology, president; Children's Hospital and Regional Medical Center, clinical research and clinical consultant, 2004-; American Psychological Association, fellow. Writer. **Publications:** (With M.E. Addis and N.S. Jacobson) Depression in Context: Strategies for Guided Action, 2001; (with S.A. Safren and S.E. Prince) Cognitive-Behavioral Therapies with Lesbian, Gay and Bisexual Clients, 2004; (with M.E. Addis) Overcoming Depression One Step at a Time: The New Behavioral Activation Approach to Getting Your Life Back, 2004; (with A.M. Leventhal) Myth of Depression as Disease: Limitations and Alternatives to Drug Treatment, 2006; (with R. Herman-Dunn and S. Dimidjian) Behavioral Activation for Depression: A Clinician's Guide, 2010. Contributor to books and periodicals. **Address:** American Board of Professional Psychology, 600 Market St., Ste. 300, Chapel Hill, NC 27516, U.S.A. **Online address:** c.martell@comcast.net

MARTELL, Mike. *See* **SASSER, Charles W(ayne).**

MARTEN, Michael. British (born England), b. 1947. **Genres:** Air/Space Topics, Astronomy, Physics, Sciences, Travel/Exploration. **Career:** Photographer, author and journalist, 1968-79; Science Photo Library Ltd., founder, managing director and chairman, 1981-. **Publications:** (Co-author) An Index of Possibilities, 1975; (with J. Chesterman, J. May and J. Trux) Worlds within Worlds: A Journey into the Unknown, 1977; (with J. Chesterman) Man to Man, 1978; (with J. Chesterman) The Radiant Universe: Electronic Images from Space, 1980; (with J. May and R. Taylor) Weird and Wonderful Wildlife, 1982; (with J. May) The Book of Beasts, 1982; (with N. Henbest) The New Astronomy, 1983, 2nd ed., 1996; (with F. Close and C. Sutton) The Particle Explosion, 1986; (with J. Burgess and R. Taylor) Microcosmos, 1987 as Under the Microscope: A Hidden World Revealed, 1990; (with F. Close and C. Sutton) The Particle Odyssey, 2002. **Address:** Science Photo Library Ltd., 327-329 Harrow Rd., London, GL W9 3RB, England. **Online address:** michael@michaelmarten.com

MARTENS, Lorna. (Lorna Cutts Martens). American (born United States), b. 1946. **Genres:** Literary Criticism And History. **Career:** Yale University, instructor, 1973, acting instructor, 1973-74, 1976, assistant professor, 1976-83, associate professor of Germanic languages and literatures, 1983-87; University of Virginia, associate professor of Germanic languages and literatures, 1988-98, professor, 1998-. Writer. **Publications:** The Diary Novel, 1985; Shadow Lines: Austrian Literature from Freud to Kafka, 1996; The Promised Land? Feminist Writing in the German Democratic Republic, 2001; The Promise of Memory: Childhood Recollection and Its Objects in Literary Modernism, 2011. Contributor of articles to periodicals. **Address:** Department of Germanic Languages and Literatures, University of Virginia, 517 New Cabell Hall, PO Box 400125, Charlottesville, VA 22903, U.S.A. **Online address:** lm2e@virginia.edu

MARTENS, Lorna Cutts. *See* **MARTENS, Lorna.**

MARTENSEN, Robert L. American (born United States), b. 1947. **Genres:** History, Medicine/Health. **Career:** National Institutes of Health, director, 2007-; University of Kansas Medical Center, professor and chair of the history and philosophy of medicine. Writer, physician and historian. **Publications:** The Brain Takes Shape: An Early History, 2004; A Life Worth Living: A Doctor's Reflections on Illness in a High-tech Era, 2008. Contributor to journals. **Address:** Office of History, National Institutes of Health, Bldg. 45, 3AN38, PO Box 6330, Bethesda, MD 20892-6330, U.S.A. **Online address:** martensenr@mail.nih.gov

MARTIEN, Jerry. Also writes as Loon. American (born United States), b. 1939. **Genres:** Poetry, Money/Finance, History, Young Adult Non-fiction. **Career:** Humboldt State University, lecturer, 1992-, professor, through 2007; California Poets in the Schools, teacher. Writer. **Publications:** Journey Work (poems), 1989; Shell Game: A True Account of Beads and Money in North America, 1996; Pieces in Place (poems), 1999; Losing California, forthcoming. **Address:** PO Box 1051, Arcata, CA 95518, U.S.A. **Online address:** martien@humboldt1.com

MARTIN, Adrian R. American (born United States), b. 1944. **Genres:** History. **Career:** Educator and writer. **Publications:** (With G. Charlesworth) I Remember It as Though It Were Yesterday, 1982; Brothers from Bataan: POWs, 1942-1945, 1992; (with L.W. Stephenson) Operation Plum: The Ill-fated 27th Bombardment Group and the Fight for the Western Pacific, 2008. **Address:** New London, WI , U.S.A. **Online address:** adrianmartin@sbcglobal.net

MARTIN, Alex. British/American (born United States), b. 1953. **Genres:** Novels, Children's Fiction, Plays/Screenplays, Education, Food And Wine. **Career:** Monty Python Comedy Troupe, film producer and secretary, 1976-78; Crown and Manor Boys' Club, drama tutor, 1976-78; Sevenoaks School, teacher of English and French literature, 1978-80, head of drama department, 1979-80; freelance translator, 1980-82; Verona University, lecturer in English language and literature, 1983-87; freelance broadcaster and researcher, 1987-2003; BBC World Service, radio presenter, 1989-96; Abingdon College, teacher of translation, 1991-93; Oxford Brookes University, lecturer, 1998-2001, fellow, 2005-07; Oxford College of Further Education, lecturer, 2000-02; Westminster Institute of Education, writer-in-residence and RLF fellow, 2001-03. Writer. **Publications:** (Co-author) A Liar's Autobiography, 1980; The General Interruptor (novel), 1989; (with J. Fletcher) The Decadent Cookbook, 1995; Modern Plays: Introduction to Modern English Literature for Students of English, 1995; Modern Novels: Introduction to Modern English Literature for Students of English, 1995; Greece, 1995; The Decadent Gardener, 1996; The Decadent Traveller, 2000; (with J. Collie) What's It Like?, 2000; The Hell-Fire Touring Club, 2002. FOR CHILDREN: Boris the Tomato, 1984; Snow on the Stinker, 1988; Boris the Return, 1994; ZPTV, 1996; Zeus Perkins, Time Traveller, 1998. EDITOR WITH R. HILL: Modern Short Stories, 1991. **Address:** c/o Dedalus, Langford Lodge, St. Judith, Sawtry, CB PE17 5XE, England. **Online address:** medlarlucan@yahoo.co.uk

MARTIN, Allana. American (born United States) **Genres:** Novels, Mystery/Crime/Suspense, Literary Criticism And History, Young Adult Fiction. **Career:** Writer. **Publications:** TEXANA JONES MYSTERY SERIES: Death of a Healing Woman, 1996; Death of a Saint Maker, 1998; Death of an Evangelista, 1999; Death of a Myth Maker, 2000; Death of the Last Villista, 2001; Death of the River Master, 2003. Contributor to periodicals. **Address:** c/o Author Mail, St. Martins Press, 175 5th Ave., Rm. 1715, New York, NY 10010, U.S.A.

MARTIN, Andrew. *See* **MARTIN, Andy.**

MARTIN, Andy. (Andrew Martin). British (born England), b. 1952. **Genres:** Literary Criticism And History, Adult Non-fiction, Intellectual History, Popular Culture, Philosophy. **Career:** Cambridge University, assistant lecturer in French, 1986-90, lecturer of French, 1990-; New York Public Library, Cullman Center for Writers and Scholars, fellow, 2009-10. Writer. **Publications:** (As Andrew Martin) The Knowledge of Ignorance: From Genesis to Jules Verne, 1985; (as Andrew Martin) The Mask of the Prophet: The Extraordinary Fictions of Jules Verne, 1990; Walking on Water, 1991; Waiting for Bardot, 1996; Napoleon the Novelist, 2000; Stealing the Wave: The Epic Struggle between Ken Bradshaw and Mark Foo, 2007; Beware Invisible Cows: My Search for the Soul of the Universe, 2009; What It Feels Like To Be Alive: Sartre and Camus remix, forthcoming. Contributor to periodicals. **Address:** DGA Associates, 55 Monmouth St., London, GL WC2H 9DG, England. **Online address:** am260@cam.ac.uk

MARTIN, Ann Smart. American (born United States), b. 1960. **Genres:** Art/Art History, Cultural/Ethnic Topics. **Career:** St. Mary's City Commission, research assistant, laboratory assistant, excavator/field director; Thomas Jefferson Memorial Foundation (Monticello), staff; Virginia Commonwealth University, faculty; North Carolina Division of Cultural Resources, staff, 1980-83; Colonial Williamsburg Foundation, Department of Archaelogical Research, laboratory technician, 1983-86, Research Division, historian, 1994-98; College of William and Mary, instructor in history, 1989, Program in American Studies, instructor, 1990, adjunct assistant professor of American studies, 1995; Old Dominion University, instructor in history, 1989; University of Delaware, Winterthur Program in Early American Culture, assistant professor, 1992-94, Winterthur Museum, Office of Advanced Studies, acting director, 1993-94; Commonwealth Center in Early American Culture, visiting research associate, 1994-95; University of Wisconsin, assistant professor, 1998-2005, Stanley and Polly Stone associate professor, 2005-, Material Culture Program, director, 2004-; Warwick University, Institute of Advanced Studies (IAS) Fellowship, visiting fellow, visiting professor, 2008; Victoria and Albert Museum, visiting research fellow, 2008. Writer and art historian. **Publications:** (Ed. with J.R. Garrison) American Material Culture: The Shape of the Field, 1997; Makers and Users: American Decorative Arts, 1630-1820, from the Chipstone Collection, 1999; Buying into the World of Goods: Early Consumers in Backcountry Virginia, 2008. Contributor of articles to periodicals. **Address:** Department of Art History, University of Wisconsin, 800 University Ave., Madison, WI 53706, U.S.A. **Online address:** asmartin@wisc.edu

MARTIN, Carol A. American (born United States), b. 1941. **Genres:** Literary Criticism And History, Young Adult Fiction. **Career:** Boise State University, assistant professor, associate professor, 1972-80, professor of English, 1980-, department head, 1988-93, associate vice president for academic affairs, 1994-96; Idaho Humanities Council, vice chair, 1978-82. Writer. **Publications:** George Eliot's Serial Fiction, 1994; (ed.) Adam Bede, 2001, (intro.) new ed., 2008. Contributor to books. **Address:** Department of English, Boise State University, Rm. 222, Liberal Arts Bldg., 1910 University Dr., Boise, ID 83725-1525, U.S.A. **Online address:** cmartin@boisestate.edu

MARTIN, Claire. American (born United States), b. 1933. **Genres:** Children's Fiction, Children's Non-fiction, Novellas/Short Stories, Sciences. **Career:** Los Angeles Public Library, children's librarian, 1971-83; County College of Morris, reference librarian, 1986-88. Writer. **Publications:** I Can Be a Weather Forecaster, 1987; The Race of the Golden Apples, 1991; (reteller) Boots and the Glass Mountain, 1992. **Address:** Dial Books, 375 Hudson St., New York, NY 10014-3657, U.S.A.

MARTIN, Clancy M. American/Canadian (born Canada), b. 1967?. **Genres:** Ethics, Novels, Translations. **Career:** Southwestern University, adjunct professor, 2001-02; St. Edward's University, adjunct professor, 2001-03; University of Missouri, assistant professor, 2003-08, associate faculty member in creative writing, 2006-, associate professor, 2008-; Martin's Custom Jewelers, vice president, 1995-99; Quikset Companies, CDO, 1995-99; Cork: A Wine Bar, founder and president, 1999-2000; Swest Acquisition Co., founder and president, 1999-2000. Writer. **Publications:** (With R.C. Solomon) Above the Bottom Line: An Introduction to Business Ethics, 2003; (with R.C. Solomon) Morality and the Good Life: An Introduction to Ethics through Classical Sources, 2004, 5th ed. (with R.C. Solomon and W. Vaught) 2009; (with J.B. Ciulla and R.C. Solomon) Honest Work: A Business Ethics Reader, 2005; (with R.C. Solomon) Since Socrates: A Concise Sourcebook of Classic Readings, 2005; (trans.) Friedrich Nietzsche, Thus Spoke Zarathustra, 2007; (ed.) The Philosophy of Deception, 2009; How to Sell (novel), 2009; (ed. with R.C. Solomon and W. Vaught) Ethics across the Professions: A Reader for Professional Ethics, 2011. Contributor of short stories to magazines. Work appears in anthology. **Address:** University of Missouri, 220 Cockefair Hall, 5121 Rockhill Rd., Kansas City, MO 64110, U.S.A.

MARTIN, Courtney E. American (born United States) **Genres:** Novels, Women's Studies And Issues. **Career:** Secret Society for Creative Philanthropy, founder; Women's Media Center and Progressive Women's Voices Project, member; Girls Write Now, advisory board member; Bartos Institute for the Constructive Engagement of Conflict, advisory board member. Writer. **Publications:** Perfect Girls, Starving Daughters: The Frightening New Normalcy of Hating Your Body, 2008. **Address:** Brooklyn, NY , U.S.A. **Online address:** courtney@courtneymartin.com

MARTIN, Dale B. American (born United States), b. 1954?. **Genres:** Theology/Religion, History. **Career:** Yale University, Yale College, teaching fellow, 1983-87, Yale Divinity School, teaching fellow, 1983-87, professor of religious studies, 1999-2005, Woolsey professor of religious studies, 2005-, chair of religious studies, 2002-05, director of undergraduate studies, 2006-07, director of graduate studies, 2008-, Whitney Humanities Center, fellow, 2003-07; Rhodes College, Department of Religion, instructor, 1987-88; Duke University, assistant professor of religion, 1988-95, associate professor of religion, 1995-99. Writer. **Publications:** Slavery as Salvation: The Metaphor of Slavery in Pauline Christianity, 1990; The Corinthian Body, 1995; (ed. with H. Lapin) Jews, Antiquity, and the Nineteenth-Century Imagination, 2003; Inventing Superstition: From the Hippocratics to the Christians, 2004; (ed. with P.C. Miller) The Cultural Turn in Late Ancient Studies: Gender, Asceticism, and Historiography, 2005; Sex and The Single Savior: Gender and Sexuality in Biblical Interpretation, 2006; (ed. with J. Zangenberg and H.W. Attridge) Religion, Ethnicity, and Identity in Ancient Galilee: A Region in Transition, 2007; Pedagogy of the Bible: An Analysis and Proposal, 2008; New Testament History and Literature, 2012. Contributor to books and journals. **Address:** Department of Religious Studies, Yale University, PO Box 208287, New Haven, CT 06520-8287, U.S.A. **Online address:** dale.martin@yale.edu

MARTIN, David Alfred. British (born England), b. 1929. **Genres:** Sociology, Theology/Religion. **Career:** University of London, lecturer 1962-67, reader, 1967-71, professor of sociology, 1971-88, now professor emeritus of sociology; Southern Methodist University, Elizabeth Scurlock professor of human values, university professor of human values, 1986-90; Oxford University, Sarum lecturer, 1994-95; Lancaster University, Department of Religious Studies, professor; King's College, visiting professor; Boston University, visiting professor; Princeton Theological Seminary, visiting professor; Science and Religion Forum, president; Religion Section of the British Sociological Association, president. Writer. **Publications:** Pacifism, 1965; A Sociology of English Religion, 1967; The Religious and the Secular; Studies in Secularization, 1969; A Wilderness of Monkeys: The Case for Christianity in a Scientific Age, 1970; Tracts Against the Times, 1973; A General Theory of Secularization, 1978; The Dilemmas of Contemporary Religion, 1978; The Breaking of the Image: A Sociology of Christian Theory and Practice, 1978; (co-author) Estudios de sociología de la religión, 1979; Divinity in a Grain of Bread, 1989; Tongues of Fire: The Explosion of Protestantism in Latin America, 1990; Does Christianity Cause War?, 1997; Reflections on Sociology and Theology, 1997; Pentecostalism: The World Their Parish, 2001; Christian Language in the Secular City, 2002; Christian Language and Its Mutations: Essays in Sociological Understanding, 2002; On Secularization: Towards a Revised General Theory, 2005; Sacred History and Sacred Geography: Spiritual Journeys in Time and Space, 2008; Future of Christianity: Reflections on Violence and Democracy, Religion and Secularisation, 2011. EDITOR: Anarchy and Culture: The Crisis in the Universities, 1969; Fifty Key Words in Sociology, 1970; Crisis for Cranmer and King James, 1979, (with J.O. Mills and W.S.F. Pickering) Sociology and Theology, Alliance and Conflict, 1980; No Alternative: The Prayer Book Controversy, 1981; (with P. Mullen) Unholy Warfare: The Church and The Bomb, 1983; (with P. Mullen) Strange Gifts?: A Guide to Charismatic Renewal, 1984; (with P. Heelas and P. Morris) Religion, Modernity, and Postmodernity, 1998; (with L. Woodhead and P. Heelas) Peter Berger and the Study of Religion, 2001; (co-ed.) Rights and Duties of Dual Nationals: Evolution and Prospects, 2003; (co-ed.) Sociology and Theology: Alliance and Conflict, 2004. **Address:** Department of Sociology, London School of Economics, Houghton St., London, GL WC2A 2AE, England.

MARTIN, David S. American (born United States), b. 1937. **Genres:** Education, Genealogy/Heraldry, Sciences. **Career:** Elementary school teacher in Newton, 1961-67, assistant principal, 1969-70; Education Development Center, curriculum developer, 1965-68; Public schools in Beverly, curriculum coordinator, 1970-73; Elementary School in Mill Valley, supervising principal, 1973-75, director of curriculum and instruction for the school district, 1975-80; Dominican College, Education Department, chairperson, 1978-80; Gallaudet University, associate professor, 1980-85, School of Education and Human Services, dean, 1985-95, professor, 1995-2001, professor and dean emeritus of education, 2002-; Suffolk University, adjunct professor, 2001-; Lesley University, adjunct professor, 2001-; University of Massachusetts, adjunct professor, 2002-; The Open University, visiting research professor, 2003-. Writer. **Publications:** (With A. Glatthorn, M. Winters and P. Saif) Curriculum Leadership: Case Studies for Program Practitioners, 1989. EDITOR: Cognition, Education, and Deafness: Directions for Research and Instruction, 1985; Advances in Cognition, Education, and Deafness, 1991; Assessing Deaf Adults: Critical Issues in Testing and Evaluation, 2005; Deaf Learners: Developments in Curriculum and Instruction, 2006. Works appear in anthologies. Contributor of articles to journals and periodicals. **Address:** Department of Education, Gallaudet University, 800 Florida Ave. NE, Washington, DC 20002, U.S.A. **Online address:** davidmartindr@aol.com

MARTIN, Deana. American (born United States), b. 1948. **Genres:** Biography, Autobiography/Memoirs, Art/Art History. **Career:** Deana Martin Foundation, director, producer; Bodies by Deana, founder and owner. Writer, philanthropist and singer. **Publications:** (With W. Holden) Memories Are Made of This: Dean Martin through His Daughter's Eyes, 2004. Contributor to periodicals. **Address:** 3000 Green Mountain Dr., Branson, MO 65616, U.S.A.

MARTIN, Deborah. *See* **JEFFRIES, Sabrina.**

MARTIN, Deborah L. American (born United States), b. 1962. **Genres:** Homes/Gardens, Young Adult Non-fiction. **Career:** Writer. **Publications:** NONFICTION: (ed. with G. Gershuny) The Rodale Book of Composting, 1992; (with B.W. Ellis and J. Benjamin) Rodale's Low-Maintenance Gardening Techniques: Shortcuts and Time-Saving Hints for Your Greatest Garden Ever, 1995; (ed.) 1,001 Ingenious Gardening Ideas: New, Fun, and Fabulous Tips That Will Change the Way You Garden-Forever!, 1999; (with B.W. Ellis and J. Benjamin) Rodale's Low-Maintenance Landscaping Techniques: Shortcuts and Timesaving Hints for Your Greatest Garden Ever, 1999; (ed. with J. Benjamin) Great Garden Formulas: The Ultimate Book of Mix-It-Yourself Concoctions for Gardeners, 2000; (ed. with J.J. Cebenko) Insect, Disease & Weed I.D. Guide: Find-It-Fast Organic Solutions for Your Garden, 2001; Natural Stain Removal Secrets: Powerful, Safe Techniques for Removing Stubborn Stains from Anything, 2007; Best-Ever Backyard Birding Tips: Hundreds of Easy Ways to Attract the Birds You Love to Watch, 2008; (with B. Pleasant) The Complete Compost Gardening Guide: Banner Batches, Grow Heaps, Comforter Compost, and Other Amazing Techniques for Saving Time and Money, and Producing the Most Flavorful, Nutritious Vegetables Ever, 2008; (with B. Pleasant) Compost Gardening: A New Time-Saving System for More Flavorful Vegetables, Bountiful Blooms, and the Richest Soil You've Ever Seen, 2008. **Address:** PA , U.S.A. **Online address:** deb@compostgardening.com

MARTIN, E. A. *See* **MARTIN, Elizabeth A(nn).**

MARTIN, Elizabeth A(nn). (E. A. Martin). British (born England), b. 1945. **Genres:** Biology, Medicine/Health, Bibliography. **Career:** London Hospital Medical School, research assistant, 1967-68; Derwent Publications, editorial assistant, 1969-70; Market House Books Co., managing editor, 1970-. Writer. **Publications:** Trees, 1978; Trees: Identification Through the Year, 1984. EDITOR: (as E.A. Martin) Dictionary of Life Sciences, 1976, 2nd ed., 1983; The Penguin Book of the Natural World, 1976; (ed.) Collins English Dictionary, 1979, 6th ed., 2003; Concise Medical Dictionary, 1980, 8th ed., 2010; (ed.) The Macmillan Encyclopedia, 1981, 17th ed., 2002; (with A. Isaacs) Dictionary of Music, 1982; A Concise Dictionary of Law, 1984, 7th ed., 2010; (with R. Fergusson) Pocket Dictionary for Nurses, 1984, 6th ed. as Minidictionary for Nurses, 2008; Trees through the Year, 1984; (with A. Isaacs and J. Daintith) Concise Science Dictionary, 1984, 6th ed. as A Dictionary of Science, 2010; (with A. Isaacs) Longman Dictionary of 20th Century Biography, 1985, 3rd ed. as Who's Who in the 20th Century, 1999; Concise Dictionary of Biology, 1985, 4th ed. as A Dictionary of Biology, 2000; (with A. Isaacs and J. Daintith) The Oxford Dictionary for Scientific Writers and Editors, 1991; (with A. Isaacs and F. Alexander) Multilingual Dictionary of Publishing, Printing and Bookselling, 1992; (co-author) The Oxford Dictionary of Abbreviations, 1992, 2nd ed., 1998; A Dictionary of Medicines, 2000; Concise Colour Medical Dictionary, 2002; A-Z of Medicinal Drugs, 2003, 2nd ed., 2010; New Oxford Dictionary for Scientific Writers and Editors, 2009. Contributor to periodicals. **Address:** Market House Books Ltd., 1 Market House, Market Sq., Aylesbury, BK HP20 1TN, England. **Online address:** mhb_aylesbury@compuserve.com

MARTIN, Eric B. American (born United States), b. 1969?. **Genres:** Novels. **Career:** Educator and writer. **Publications:** (Ed.) The Campfire Collection: Spine-Tingling Tales to Tell in the Dark, 2000; Luck, 2000; Winners, 2004; The Virgin's Guide to Mexico, 2007; (with S. Elliott) Donald, 2011. **Address:** 1325 Ave. of the Americas, New York, NY 10019, U.S.A. **Online address:** redcoatmartin@hotmail.com

MARTIN, F. David. American (born United States), b. 1920. **Genres:** Art/Art History, Humanities. **Career:** University of Chicago, instructor in humanities, 1947-49; Bucknell University, assistant professor, 1949-50, associate professor, 1950-56, professor, 1956-83, John Howard Harris professor of philosophy and chairman, 1968-83, John Howard Harris professor emeritus of philosophy, 1983-. Writer. **Publications:** Art and the Religious Experience: The Language of the Sacred, 1972; (with L.A. Jacobus) The Humanities through the Arts, 1974, 8th ed., 2011; Sculpture and Enlivened Space, 1980; Facing Death: Theme and Variations, 2006. Contributor of articles to journals. **Address:** Department of Philosophy, Bucknell University, 1 Dent Dr., Lewisburg, PA 17837, U.S.A. **Online address:** martindfd@riverwoods.org

MARTIN, Fenton S(trickland). American (born United States), b. 1943. **Genres:** Bibliography, Reference, Politics/Government. **Career:** Massachusetts Institute of Technology Libraries, Acquisitions Department, Project Intrex Section, head, 1966-67, Order Section, head, 1967-68; Indiana University, Workshop in Political Theory and Policy Analysis, head librarian and archivist, 1971-86, head librarian, 1984-86, Research Collection Section, head librarian and archivist, 1986-2008, librarian emeritus, 2008-. Writer. **Publications:** The Parliament of Great Britain: A Bibliography, 1983; Political Science Journal Information, 1984, 4th ed., 1997; The Presidency: A Research Guide, 1985; (with R.U. Goehlert) Policy Analysis and Management: A Bibliography, 1985; (with R.U. Goehlert) The American Presidents: A Bibliography, 1987; The American Presidency: A Bibliography, 1987; (with R.U. Goehlert) Congress and Lawmaking: A Research Guide, 2nd ed., 1989; (with R.U. Goehlert) The U.S. Supreme Court: A Bibliography, 1990; (with R.U. Goehlert) How to Research the Supreme Court, 1992; (with R.U. Goehlert) The United States Congress, 1980-1990: An Annotated Bibliography, 1994; (with J.R. Sayre and R.U. Goehlert) Members of Congress: A Bibliography, 1996; How to Research the Presidency, 1996; (with R.U. Goehlert) How to Research Congress, 1996; Bibliography of American Government, 1997; (with R.U. Goehlert) American Government and Politics: A Guide to Books for Teachers, Librarians and Students, 1997; (with R.U. Goehlert) How to Research Elections, 2000; (with R.U. Goehlert) CQ's Resource Guide to Modern Elections: An Annotated Bibliography, 1960-1996, 2000. **Address:** Department of Political Science, Indiana University, 200 Woodburn Hall, Bloomington, IN 47405, U.S.A. **Online address:** martinf@indiana.edu

MARTIN, Francesca. British (born England), b. 1947. **Genres:** Children's Fiction, Illustrations, Social Sciences, Mythology/Folklore. **Career:** Writer, freelance designer and illustrator. **Publications:** SELF-ILLUSTRATED: The Honey Hunters: A Traditional African Tale, 1992; Clever Tortoise: A Traditional African Tale, 2000. **Address:** 124 Goldhurst Terr., London, GL NW6 3HR, England.

MARTIN, Geoffrey John. American/British (born England), b. 1934. **Genres:** Geography, Intellectual History, History. **Career:** Eastern Michigan University, assistant professor, 1959-65; Wisconsin State University, associate professor, 1965-66; Southern Connecticut State University, professor of geography, 1966-96, chairperson of department, 1976-79, professor emeritus, 1996-; Association of American Geographers, archivist, 1986-; Connecticut State University, distinguished professor, 1991-97, professor emeritus, 1997-. Writer. **Publications:** Africa in Maps, 1962; Mark Jefferson: Geographer, 1968; Ellsworth Huntington: His Life and Thought, 1973; (with P.E. James) The Association of American Geographers: The First Seventy-Five Years, 1978; The Life and Thought of Isaiah Bowman, 1980; (with P.E. James) All Possible Worlds: A History of Geographical Ideas, 1981, 4th ed., 2005. **Address:** Department of Geography, Southern Connecticut State University, 118 Morrill Hall, 501 Crescent St., New Haven, CT 06515-1355, U.S.A.

MARTIN, George E. American (born United States), b. 1932. **Genres:** Mathematics/Statistics. **Career:** University of Rhode Island, assistant professor of mathematics, 1964-66; State University of New York at Albany, assistant professor, professor of mathematics, 1966-, now professor emeritus. Writer. **Publications:** Foundations of Geometry and the Non-Euclidean Plane, 1975; Transformation Geometry: An Introduction to Symmetry, 1982; Polyominoes: A Guide to Puzzles and Problems in Tiling, 1991; Geometric Constructions, 1998; Counting: The Art of Enumerative Combinatorics, 2001. **Address:** Department of Mathematics & Statistics, State University of New York, Earth Science 110, 1400 Washington Ave., Albany, NY 12222, U.S.A. **Online address:** martin@math.albany.edu

MARTIN, George R.R. American (born United States), b. 1948. **Genres:** Novels, Novellas/Short Stories, Children's Fiction, Young Adult Fiction. **Career:** Medill News Service, journalism intern, 1971; New Jersey Department of Parks, sportswriter and public relations officer, 1971; Volunteers in Service to America (VISTA), Cook County Legal Assistance Foundation, communications coordinator, 1972-74; Windy City Science Fiction Writers' Workshop, founder and chairman, 1972-76; Clarke College, instructor in journalism, 1976-78, writer-in-residence, 1978-79; freelance writer, 1979-. **Publications:** NOVELS: Dying of the Light, 1978; (with L. Tuttle) Windhaven, 1981; Fevre Dream, 1982; The Armageddon Rag, 1983; The Ice Dragon, 2006; Dreamsongs, 2007. SONG OF ICE AND FIRE FANTASY SERIES: A Game of Thrones, 1996; A Clash of Kings, 1999; A Storm of Swords, 2000; A Feast for Crows, 2005; A Dance with Dragons, 2011. SHORT STORY COLLECTIONS: A Song for Lya and Other Stories, 1976; Songs of Stars and Shadows, 1977; The Sandkings, 1981; Songs the Dead Men Sing, 1983; Nightflyers, 1985; Tuf Voyaging, 1986; Portraits of His Children, 1987; The Pear-Shaped Man, 1991. EDITOR: New Voices in Science Fiction: Stories by Campbell Award Nominees, 1977; New Voices: Spellbinding Original Stories by the Next Generation of Science Fiction Greats, vol. I, 1978, vol. II, 1979, vol. III, 1980, vol. IV, 1981; (with I. Asimov and M.H. Greenberg) The Science Fiction Weight-loss Book, 1983; The John W. Campbell Awards, vol. V, 1984; (with P. Mikol) Night Visions 3, 1986 in UK as Night Visions: All Original Stories, 1987 as Night Visions: The Hellbound Heart, 1988; (with G. Dozois) Warriors, 2010; (with G. Dozois) Songs of Love and Death: Tales of Star-crossed Love, 2010. WILD CARDS SERIES: EDITOR: Wild Cards: A Mosaic Novel, 1986; Aces High, 1987; Jokers Wild: A Wild Cards Mosaic Novel, 1987; Aces Abroad: A Wild Cards Mosaic Novel, 1988; Down and Dirty: A Wild Cards Mosaic Novel, 1988; (with M.M. Snodgrass) Ace in the Hole: A Wild Cards Mosaic Novel, 1990; (with M.M. Snodgrass) Dead Man's Hand: A Wild Cards Mosaic Novel, 1990; (with M.M. Snodgrass) One-Eyed Jacks: A Wild Cards Mosaic Novel, 1991; (with M.M. Snodgrass) Jokertown Shuffle: A Wild Cards Mosaic Novel, 1991; (with M.M. Snodgrass) Double Solitaire: A Wild Cards Mosaic Novel, 1992; (with M.M. Snodgrass) Dealer's Choice: A Wild Cards Mosaic Novel, 1992; (with M.M. Snodgrass) Card Sharks: A Wild Cards Mosaic Novel, 1993; (with M.M. Snodgrass) Marked Cards: A Wild Cards Mosaic Novel, 1994; (with M.M. Snodgrass) Inside Straights: A Wild Cards Mosaic Novel, 2008; (with M.M. Snodgrass) Busted Flush: A Wild Cards Mosaic Novel, 2008; (with M.M. Snodgrass) Suicide King: A Wild Cards Mosaic Novel, 2009. OTHERS: Quartet: Four Tales from the Crossroads, 2001; (ed. with G. Dozois) Songs of the Dying Earth, 2010; (ed. with G. Dozois) Down These Strange Streets, 2011; (ed. with G. Dozois) Dangerous Women, forthcoming; (ed. with G. Dozois) Old Venus, forthcoming; (ed. with G. Dozois) Old Mars, forthcoming. Contributor to magazines. **Address:** Pimlico Literary Agency, 155 E 77th St., Ste. 1A, New York, NY 10021, U.S.A. **Online address:** georr@aol.com

MARTIN, George Whitney. American (born United States), b. 1926. **Genres:** Institutions/Organizations, Music, Biography. **Career:** Emmet, Marvin & Martin, Attorneys at Law, associate, 1955-58, partner, 1958-59; The Opera Quarterly, book editor, 1983-92; Metropolitan Opera Guild, director, 1958-70; Leake & Watts Children's Home Inc., director, 1959-67; Associated Independent Recording Studios, founder and chairman. **Publications:** The Opera Companion: A Guide for the Casual Operagoer, 1961, 5th ed., 1997; Battle of the Frogs and the Mice: An Homeric Fable, 1962, 2nd ed., 1987; Verdi, His Music, Life and Times, 1963, 5th ed., 2001; The Red Shirt and the Cross of Savoy: The Story of Italy's Risorgimento, 1748-1871, 1969; Causes and Conflicts: The Centennial History of the Association of the Bar of the City of New York, 1870-1970, 1970; Madam Secretary: Frances Perkins, 1976; (contrib.) The Verdi Companion, 1979; Opera Companion to Twentieth-century Opera, 1979; Opera Companion, 1982; The Damrosch Dynasty: America's First Family of Music, 1983; Aspects of Verdi, 1988; Verdi at the Golden Gate: Opera and San Francisco in the Gold Rush Years, 1993; (contrib.) Making Sure We are True to Our Founders: The Association of the Bar of the City of New York, 1970-95, 1997; Twentieth Century Opera: A Guide, 1999; CCB: The Life and Century of Chalres C. Burlingham, New York's First Citizen, 1858-1959, 2005; Verdi in America: Oberto through Rigoletto, 2011. **Address:** 53 Crosslands Dr., Kennett Square, PA 19348-2010, U.S.A. **Online address:** gwmartin@georgewmartin.com

MARTIN, Gerald Michael. American (born United States), b. 1944. **Genres:** Translations, History, Travel/Exploration. **Career:** University of Pittsburgh, Department of Hispanic Studies, Andrew W. Mellon professor of modern languages, professor emeritus; London Metropolitan University, senior research professor in Caribbean studies. Writer. **Publications:** (Ed. and trans.) M.A. Asturias, Hombres de Maiz: Edicíon Critica, 1981 trans. as Men of Maize, 1993; Journeys through the Labyrinth: Latin American Fiction in the Twentieth Century, 1989; Writers from Latin America, 1990; (trans.) Rafael Chirbes, Mimoun, 1992; Gabriel García Márquez: A Life, 2008; Cambridge Introduction to Gabriel García Márquez, 2012. **Address:** Caribbean Studies Centre, London Metropolitan University, 166-220 Holloway Rd., London, GL N7 8DB, England. **Online address:** gmmgmm@pitt.edu

MARTIN, Jack. Canadian (born Canada), b. 1950?. **Genres:** Education, Psychology, Young Adult Non-fiction. **Career:** Simon Fraser University, Burnaby Mountain endowed professor in the psychology; Deakin University, Gordon distinguished visiting professor, 1981-82; Ball State University, Emens distinguished visiting professor, 1989. Writer. **Publications:** Mastering Instruction, 1983; (with B.A. Heibert) Instructional Counseling: A Method for Counselors, 1985; The Construction and Understanding of Psychotherapeutic Change: Conversations, Memories, and Theories, 1994; (ed. with L.T. Hoshmand) Research as Praxis: Lessons from Programmatic Research in Therapeutic Psychology, 1995; (with J. Sugarman) The Psychology of Human Possibility and Constraint, 1999; Models of Classroom Management: Principles, Practices, and Critical Considerations, 3rd ed., 2000; (with J. Sugarman and J. Thompson) Psychology and the Question of Agency, 2003; (with J.H. Sugarman and S. Hickinbottom) Persons: Understanding Psychological Selfhood and Agency, 2009; (ed. with S.R. Kirschner) Sociocultural Turn in Psychology, 2010. **Address:** Faculty of Education, Simon Fraser University, Rm. RCB 8304, 8888 University Dr., Burnaby, BC V5A 1S6, Canada. **Online address:** jack_martin@sfu.ca

MARTIN, Jacqueline Briggs. American (born United States), b. 1945. **Genres:** Children's Fiction, Travel/Exploration. **Career:** University of Iowa, Cornell College, instructor in creative writing. Writer. **Publications:** Bizzy Bones and Uncle Ezra, 1984; Bizzy Bones and Moosemouse, 1986; Bizzy Bones and the Lost Quilt, 1988; Good Times on Grandfather Mountain, 1992; The Finest Horse in Town, 1992; Washing the Willow Tree Loon, 1995; The Second Street Gardens and Green Truck Almanac, 1995, as The Green Truck Garden Giveaway: A Neighborhood Story and Almanac, 1997; Grandmother Bryant's Pocket, 1996; Higgins Bend Song and Dance, 1997; Button, Bucket, Sky, 1998; Snowflake Bentley, 1998; The Lamp, the Ice, and the Boat Called Fish, 2001; The Water Gift and the Pig of the Pig, 2003; On Sand Island, 2003; Jacqueline Briggs Martin and You, 2006; Banjo Granny, 2006; Chicken Joy on Redbean Road, 2007; Chiru of High Tibet, 2010. **Address:** MCBookWords, Sharron L. McElmeel, 3000 N Center Point Rd., Cedar Rapids, IA 52411-9548, U.S.A. **Online address:** jacqueline@jacquelinebriggsmartin.com

MARTIN, Joanna. British (born England), b. 1951. **Genres:** History, Women's Studies And Issues. **Career:** Genealogist, historical researcher and lecturer, 1977-. Writer. **Publications:** Henry and the Fairy Palace: Fox Talbot and Glamorgan, 1993; Wives and Daughters: Women and Children in the Georgian Country House, 2004. EDITOR: The Penrice Letters, 1768-1795, 1993; (ed.) Governess in the Age of Jane Austen: The Journals and Letters of Agnes Porter, 1998; (with M.J. Edmunds) The Pennard Manor Court Book, 1673-1701, 2000. **Address:** Oak Tree Farm, Finborough Rd., Hitcham, Ipswich, SU IP7 7LS, England.

MARTIN, Josef. *See* **BAUER, Henry H.**

MARTIN, Judith. Also writes as Miss Manners, Manners. American (born United States), b. 1938. **Genres:** Novels, Human Relations/Parenting, Humor/Satire, Novellas/Short Stories, How-to Books. **Career:** United Feature Syndicate, syndicated columnist; Microsoft Network, columnist; The Washington Post, reporter and critic, 1960-83; George Washington University, faculty, 1978; Financial Times, contributor. **Publications:** (With R. Charlip) The Tree Angel, 1962; The Name on the White House Floor (essays), 1972; Miss Manners' Guide to Excruciatingly Correct Behavior, 1982, rev. ed., 2005; Gilbert: A Comedy of Manners (novel), 1982; Miss Manners' Guide to Rearing Perfect Children, 1984; Common Courtesy, 1985; Style and Substance (novel), 1986; Miss Manners' Guide for the Turn-of-the-Millennium, 1989; Miss Manners' on Painfully Proper Weddings, 1995; Miss Manners Rescues Civilization, 1996; Miss Manners' Basic Training: Communication, 1997; Miss Manners' Basic Training: Eating, 1997; Miss Manners' Basic Training: The Right Thing to Say, 1998; Miss Manners on Weddings, 1999; Miss Manners: A Citizen's Guide to Civility, 1999; Miss Manners' Guide to Domestic Tranquility, 1999; Star-Spangled Manners, 2002; No Vulgar Hotel: The Desire and Pursuit of Venice, 2007; (with J. Martin) Miss Manners' Guide to a Surprisingly Dignified Wedding, 2010. **Address:** United Feature Syndicate, 200 Madison Ave., New York, NY 10016-3903, U.S.A. **Online address:** missmanners@unitedmedia.com

MARTIN, J(ulia) Wallis. British (born England) **Genres:** Mystery/Crime/

Suspense, Biography. **Career:** Hodder and Stoughton, editor. **Publications:** A Likeness in Stone, 1997; The Bird Yard, 1998; The Long Close Call, 2000; Dancing with the Uninvited Guest, 2002. **Address:** c/o Author Mail, St. Martin Minotaur, 175 5th Ave., New York, NY 10010, U.S.A. **Online address:** jwallismartin@yahoo.co.uk

MARTIN, Julie (Breyer). American (born United States), b. 1938. **Genres:** Art/Art History, History, Young Adult Non-fiction, Theology/Religion. **Career:** Canadian Broadcasting Co., researcher and associate producer, 1966-67; Experiments in Art and Technology, editor, 1968-. **Publications:** WITH B. KLUVER: Kiki's Paris: Artists and Lovers 1900-1930, 1989; Robert Breer: A Painter in Paris, 1990. EDITOR WITH KLUVER: (and B. Rose) Pavilion, 1972; Kiki's Memoirs, 1996. OTHERS: (comp. with B. Headrick) Alabama Obituaries and Death Notices from the Gadsden Times, 1900-1905, 1999; (trans.) And the Wolves Howled, Fragments of Two Lifetimes, 2000; Whatever Happened to Right and Wrong?, 2005. Contributor to periodicals. **Address:** Experiments in Art and Technology Inc., 69 Appletree Row, Berkeley Heights, NJ 07922, U.S.A.

MARTIN, Justin. American (born United States), b. 1964?. **Genres:** Biography, Sports/Fitness. **Career:** Fortune Small Business, contributing editor; Fortune Magazine, staff writer. **Publications:** The Fantastic Baseball Quiz Book, 1996; The Fantastic Football Quiz Book, 1996; Greenspan: The Man Behind Money, 2000; Nader: Crusader, Spoiler, Icon, 2002; Genius of Place, 2011; Olmsted: A Life: The Life of Frederick Law Olmsted, 2011. Contributor to periodicals. **Address:** c/o Lisa Swayne, Swayne Agency Literary Management & Consulting, 56 W 45th St., Ste. 1202, New York, NY 10036-4216, U.S.A.

MARTIN, Larry Jay. American (born United States), b. 1943?. **Genres:** Westerns/Adventure, Novels, Mystery/Crime/Suspense, Autobiography/Memoirs. **Career:** Writer, 1991-. **Publications:** WESTERNS: Mojave Showdown, 1988; El Lazo, 1991; Against the 7th Flag, 1991; The Devil's Bounty, 1992; Rush to Destiny, 1992; The Benicia Belle, 1993; Shadow of the Grizzly, 1993; Buckshot, 1994; Sounding Drum, 1999; Last Stand, 1999; Condor Canyon, 2000; Blood Mountain, 2003; Stranahan, 2003; McKeag's Mountain, 2004; Wolf Mountain, 2004; O'Rourke's Revenge, 2005; Tenkiller, 2006; McCreed's Law, 2006. OTHERS: Life and Ministry of William J. Seymour, 1999; Windfall, 2008; Shadow of the Mast, 2008; Nemesis, 2011. Contributor to perioidcals. **Address:** Kensington Publishing Corp., 850 3rd Ave., New York, NY 10022, U.S.A. **Online address:** ljmartin@ljmartin.com

MARTIN, Lisa L. American (born United States), b. 1961?. **Genres:** International Relations/Current Affairs, Economics, Civil Liberties/Human Rights, Politics/Government. **Career:** University of California, Department of Political Science, assistant professor, 1989-92, Graduate School of International Relations and Pacific Studies, adjunct assistant professor, 1989-92; Harvard University, Department of Government, John L. Loeb associate professor of the social sciences, 1992-96, Clarence Dillon professor of international affairs, 1996-2008; Harvard Magazine, director, 1999-2005; Economics and Politics, associate editor, 1999-; International Organization, editor-in-chief, 2002-06; University of Wisconsin, Department of Political Science, professor. **Publications:** Coercive Cooperation: Explaining Multilateral Economic Sanctions, 1992; Democratic Commitments: Legislatures and International Cooperation, 2000; (ed. with B.A. Simmons) International Institutions: An International Organization Reader, 2001; (ed.) International Institutions in the New Global Economy, 2005; (ed.) Global Governance, 2008. Contributor of articles to books and periodicals. **Address:** Department of Political Science, University of Wisconsin, 416 North Hall, 1050 Bascom Mall, Madison, WI 53706-7389, U.S.A. **Online address:** llmartin3@wisc.edu

MARTIN, Lorna. Scottish (born Scotland), b. 1970?. **Genres:** Autobiography/Memoirs. **Career:** Herald, reporter; Observer, reporter; Grazia magazine, columnist, contributing editor. Writer and teacher. **Publications:** Girl on the Couch: Life, Love and Confessions of a Normal Neurotic, 2008. Contributor to periodicals. **Address:** Rupert Heath Literary Agency, 50 Albemarle St., London, GL W1S 4BD, England. **Online address:** lorna@lornamartin.com

MARTIN, Man. American (born United States), b. 1959. **Genres:** Novels. **Career:** Stephenson High School, English teacher and debate coach. Author and illustrator. **Publications:** Days of the Endless Corvette, 2007; Paradise Dogs: A Novel, 2011. **Address:** Carroll & Graf Publishers, 245 W 17th St., 11th Fl., New York, NY 10011-5379, U.S.A. **Online address:** manmartin@manmartin.net

MARTIN, Nora. American (born United States) **Genres:** Young Adult Fiction, Children's Fiction. **Career:** University of the Witwatersrand, Teachers Continuing Education Program, faculty, 1984-85; Lincoln County School District, teacher, 1988-91; Human Resources Development Council, teacher, 1993-94; writer and consultant, 1995-; Very Special Arts Montana, writing instructor, 1997-98; Montana State University, Department of Education, adjunct professor, 1997-; Gallatin Gateway School, Teacher Mentor Program, teacher, GATE coordinator and library media specialist, 1998-, director, 2006-; Montana Office of Public Instruction, Teacher Mentor Program, coordinator and trainer, 2006-. Writer. **Publications:** The Stone Dancers, 1995; The Eagles Shadow, 1997; A Perfect Snow, 2002; Flight of the Fisherbird, 2003. **Address:** c/o Author Mail, Bloomsbury Publishing, 175 5th Ave., Ste. 712, New York, NY 10010, U.S.A. **Online address:** hermitwanabe@hotmail.com

MARTIN, Patricia Preciado. American (born United States), b. 1939. **Genres:** Cultural/Ethnic Topics, History, Romance/Historical, Young Adult Fiction. **Career:** Writer and educator. **Publications:** (Ed.) La Frontera Perspective: Providing Mental Health Services to Mexican Americans, 1979; The Legend of the Bellringer of San Agustín: A Bilingual Children's Story, 1980; Images and Conversations: Mexican Americans Recall a Southwestern Past, 1983; Days of Plenty, Days of Want, 1988; Songs My Mother Sang to Me: An Oral History of Mexican-American Women, 1992; Milagro and Other Stories, 1996; Amor Eterno: Eleven Lessons in Love, 2000; (ed.) Beloved Land: An Oral History of Mexican Americans in Southern Arizona, 2004. Contributor to periodicals. **Address:** 1735 E Entrada Nueve, Tucson, AZ 85718-4819, U.S.A.

MARTIN, Philip R. American/Chinese (born China), b. 1943. **Genres:** Adult Non-fiction, Children's Non-fiction, History. **Career:** Automotive instructor, 1976-99; flight instructor, 1990-; volleyball instructor, 1998-. Writer. **Publications:** Auto Mechanics for the Complete Dummy, 1974, 2nd ed., 1982; Pilot's Wings of the United States: Civilian and Commercial, 1913-1995, 1996. **Address:** c/o Author Mail, Beach Cities Enterprises, 3640 E 10th St., PO Box 91051, Long Beach, CA 90804, U.S.A. **Online address:** wingman@earthlink.net

MARTIN, Phyllis R(odgers). American (born United States), b. 1955?. **Genres:** How-to Books, Language/Linguistics, Art/Art History, Literary Criticism And History, Children's Fiction. **Career:** Procter and Gamble, employment counselor; WKRC-TV, job expert, 1981-; Cincinnati Post, Columnist; Indianapolis Star, columnist. **Publications:** The Word Watcher's Handbook: A Deletionary of the Most Abused and Misused Words, 1977, 3rd ed., 1991; Martin's Magic Formula for Getting the Right Job, 1981, rev. ed. as Martin's Magic Formula for Getting the Right Job: 1-5+10+15+20 = The Right Job, 1987; Martin's Magic Motivation Book: How to Become an Anointed One in Your Organization, 1984; Moving Time for Kelly, 1988; New Blanket for Josh, 1988; Return to Chipping Sodbury, 1997; Katie's Mild Animal Hunt, 2000. Contributor to magazines. **Address:** 644 Doepke Ln., Cincinnati, OH 45231, U.S.A.

MARTIN, Rhona. British (born England), b. 1922. **Genres:** Novels, Romance/Historical, How-to Books, Writing/Journalism, Young Adult Non-fiction, Young Adult Fiction, Reference. **Career:** Willsons Ltd., fashion artist, 1940-41; Fire Guard Office, clerk, 1942-45; freelance theatrical designer, 1946-48; Club Labamba, catering manager, 1963-68; Odeon, assistant manager, 1968-72; Crown Chemical Co., secretary and accounts office manager, 1972-79; full-time writer, 1979-; Three Arts Workshops, founder and chairman. **Publications:** Gallows Wedding (novel), 1978; Mango Walk (novel), 1981; The Unicorn Summer (novel), 1984; Goodbye, Sally (novel), 1987; Writing Historical Fiction, 1988. Contributor of articles to magazines and newspapers. **Address:** c/o John McLaughlin, Campbell Thomson and McLaughlin Ltd., 1 Kings Mews, London, GL WC1N 2JA, England.

MARTIN, Robert M. Canadian (born Canada), b. 1942. **Genres:** Philosophy, Language/Linguistics, Young Adult Non-fiction. **Career:** Dalhousie University, assistant professor, 1968-75, associate professor, 1975-88, professor of philosophy, 1988-, now retired, The Dalhousie Review, editor. **Publications:** The Meaning of Language, 1987; The Philosopher's Dictionary, 1991, 3rd ed., 2002; There Are Two Errors in the Title of This Book, 1992, rev. ed., 2002; Scientific Thinking, 1997; On Ayer, 2001; (with S.M. Kaye) On Ockham, 2001; Introducing Symbolic Logic, 2004; Philosophical Conversations,

2006. **Address:** Department of Philosophy, Dalhousie University, McCain FASS Bldg., 6135 University Ave., Halifax, NS B3H 4P9, Canada. **Online address:** martin@dal.ca

MARTIN, Roderick. Hungarian/British (born England), b. 1940. **Genres:** Administration/Management, Industrial Relations, Sociology, Business/Trade/Industry. **Career:** University of York, lecturer in modern history, 1964-66; Oxford University, Jesus College, lecturer, 1966-69, Trinity College, University lecturer in politics and sociology, 1966-84, official fellow in politics and sociology, 1969-84; Monash University, visiting senior lecturer, 1975; University of London, Imperial College, professor of industrial sociology, 1984-88; University of Oxford, Templeton College, fellow in information management, 1988-91; University of Glasgow, Business School, professor of organizational behaviour, 1992-99, director, 1992-96; University of Southampton, professor of organizational behaviour, 1999-2005, School of Management, director, 2000-04; Central European University, Business School, professor of management, 2005-09, Center for Policy Studies, faculty, 2010-. Writer. **Publications:** (Ed. with D.E.H. Whiteley) Sociology, Theology and Conflict, 1969; Communism and the British Trade Unions, 1924-1933, 1969; (with R.H. Fryer) Redundancy and Paternalist Capitalism, 1973; The Sociology of Power, 1977; Sociologia do Podor, 1977; New Technology and Industrial Relations in Fleet Street, 1981; (with R. Undy, R. Blackwell and J. Hutton) Ballots and Trade Union Democracy, 1984; (with J. Wallace) Working Women in Recession: Employment, Redundancy, and Unemployment, 1984; (with B. Moores) Management Structures and Techniques, 1985; Beyond the Workplace: Industrial Relations in the Multi-plant Enterprise, 1988; Bargaining Power, 1992; (with R. Undy) Managing the Unions: The Impact of Legislation on Trade Union's Behaviour, 1996; (co-ed.) Workers, Firms, and Unions, vol. I: Industrial Relations in Transition, 1998, vol. II: Workers, Firms and Unions: The Development of Dual Commitment, 2000; Transforming Management in Central and Eastern Europe, 1999; (with P.D. Casson and T.M. Nisar) Investor Engagement: Investors and Management Practice Under Shareholder Value, 2007. **Address:** Center for Policy Studies, Central European University, Rm. 3014, 11 Bldg., 9 Nador St., Budapest, H-1051, Hungary.

MARTIN, Roger H(arry). American (born United States), b. 1943. **Genres:** Theology/Religion, History. **Career:** Middlebury College, assistant professor of history and assistant to president, 1976-80; Harvard University, lecturer in church history, 1980-86, Harvard Divinity School, associate dean, 1980-86; Moravian College, professor of church history and president, 1986-97; Randolph-Macon College, professor of history and president, 1997-2006, professor of history emeritus and president emeritus, 2006-. Writer. **Publications:** Evangelicals United: Ecumenical Stirrings in Pre-Victorian Britain, 1795-1830, 1983; Racing Odysseus: A College President Becomes a Freshman Again, 2008. Contributor to magazines. **Address:** 1321 Crown Ct., Mamaroneck, NY 10543, U.S.A. **Online address:** rmartin@rmc.edu

MARTIN, (Roy) Peter. Also writes as Hampton Charles, James Melville. British (born England), b. 1931. **Genres:** Mystery/Crime/Suspense, Food And Wine, Novels, Young Adult Fiction, Literary Criticism And History, Horror. **Career:** London County Council, local government officer, 1948-49, 1951-54; Royal Festival Hall, deputy publicity officer, 1956-60; British Cultural Institute, director, 1963-70; British Embassy, cultural attache, 1972-73, cultural counselor, 1979-83. Writer. **Publications:** (With J. Martin) Japanese Cooking, 1970; Modern Japan, 1989; The Chrysanthemum Throne, 1997. AS HAMPTON CHARLES: Miss Seeton, By Appointment, 1990; Advantage, Miss Seeton, 1990, rev. Ed., 1999; Miss Seeton at the Helm, 1990. AS JAMES MELVILLE: The Wages of Zen, 1979; The Chrysanthemum Chain, 1980; A Sort of Samurai, 1981; The Ninth Netsuke, 1982; Sayonara, Sweet Amaryllis, 1983; Death of a Daimyo, 1984; The Death Ceremony, 1985; Go Gently, Gaijin, 1986; The Imperial Way, 1986; Kimono for a Corpse, 1987; The Reluctant Ronin, 1988; A Haiku for Hanae, 1989; A Tarnished Phoenix, 1990; The Bogus Buddha: A Superintendent Otani Mystery, 1991; The Body Wore Brocade, 1992; Diplomatic Baggage, 1995; The Reluctant Spy, 1995. **Address:** Curtis Brown Ltd., Haymarket House, 28-29 Haymarket, London, GL SW1Y 4SP, England.

MARTIN, Russell. American (born United States), b. 1952. **Genres:** Novels, Novellas/Short Stories, Language/Linguistics, Sports/Fitness, Biography, Documentaries/Reportage, Mystery/Crime/Suspense, Young Adult Fiction, Adult Non-fiction. **Career:** Telluride Times, reporter, 1975-78, managing editor, 1978-79; Full-time writer, 1979-; Colorado College, visiting assistant professor of English, 1985, 1987, 1989, 1992. Writer. **Publications:** NON-FICTION: Cowboy: The Enduring Myth of the Wild West, 1983; (with J.P. Allen) Entering Space: An Astronaut's Odyssey, 1984; Matters Gray and White: A Neurologist, His Patients and the Mysteries of the Brain, 1986; The Color Orange: A Super Bowl Season with the Denver Broncos, 1987; A Story That Stands Like a Dam: Glen Canyon and the Struggle for the Soul of the West, 1990; Out of Silence: A Journey into Language, 1994; Disney's Goofy & Mickey's Growing ABC, 1994; Flipper: The Movie Storybook, 1996; Beethoven's Hair: An Extraordinary Historical Odyssey and a Scientific Mystery Solved, 2000; Picasso's War: The Destruction of Guernica and the Masterpiece That Changed the World, 2002; Sorrow of Archaeology: A Novel, 2005; Understanding Local Autonomy in Judaea between 6 and 66 CE, 2006; (with L. Nibley) The Mysteries of Beethoven's Hair, 2009. FICTION: Beautiful Islands, 1988; Piecing (stories). EDITOR AND INTRO.: (with M. Barasch) Writers of the Purple Sage: An Anthology of Recent Western Writing, 1984; New Writers of the Purple Sage: An Anthology of Contemporary Western Writers, 1992. Contributor to books and periodicals. **Address:** c/o Peter Matson, Sterling Lord Literistic Inc., 65 Bleecker St., New York, NY 10012, U.S.A. **Online address:** russell@syqproductions.net

MARTIN, Stephen-Paul. American (born United States), b. 1949. **Genres:** Poetry, Novels, Novellas/Short Stories, Young Adult Fiction, Young Adult Non-fiction. **Career:** Euterpe, poetry editor, 1976-78; Journal of the Arts and Social Theory, editor, 1980-; City University of New York, LaGuardia Community College, faculty, 1980-; Pace University, faculty, 1980-; New York Institute of Technology, faculty, 1983-; New School for Social Research, faculty, 1983-. **Publications:** POETRY: Edges, 1978; Poems, 1983; Until It Changes, 1988; Open Form and the Feminine Imagination: The Politics of Reading in Twentieth-Century Innovative Writing, 1988; Corona 2500, 1989; Advancing/Receding, 1989; Invading Reagan, 1990; Things, 1991. STORIES: Tales, 1989. FICTION: The Flood, 1992; Crisis of Representation, 1992; The Gothic Twilight, 1992; Fear and Philosophy, 1993; Undeserved Reputations, 1994; Not Quite Fiction, 1997. OTHER: Instead of Confusion, 2002; Possibility of Music, 2007; Changing the Subject, 2010. Work appears in anthologies. Contributor of articles. **Address:** California State University, 333 S Twin Oaks Valley Rd., San Marcos, CA 92096-0001, U.S.A.

MARTIN, Timothy (Peter). American (born United States), b. 1950. **Genres:** Literary Criticism And History. **Career:** University of Pennsylvania, lecturer in English, 1978-79, 1980-84; Chestnut Hill College, instructor of English, 1979-80; Rutgers University, Camden Campus, assistant professor, 1984-90, director of writing program, 1984-96, associate professor of English, 1990-, chair of English department, 1996-, Honors College, Academic Programs, associate dean/director. Writer. **Publications:** Joyce and Wagner: A Study of Influence, 1991; (ed. with V.J. Cheng) Joyce in Context, 1992; (ed. with A. Fogarty) Joyce on the Threshold, 2005. Works appear in anthologies. Contributor of articles to literature journals. **Address:** Department of English, Rutgers University, Camden Campus, M-F 7-5, 430 Armitage Hall, Camden, NJ 08102, U.S.A. **Online address:** timartin@camden.rutgers.edu

MARTIN, Troy. Also writes as Troy Wayne Martin. American (born United States), b. 1953. **Genres:** Theology/Religion. **Career:** First Church of the Nazarene, pastor, 1979-81; Church of the Nazarene, associate pastor, 1982-88; Olivet Nazarene University, assistant professor, 1988-91; Saint Xavier University, assistant professor, 1991-94, associate professor, 1994-2001, professor of religious studies, 2001-. Writer. **Publications:** Metaphor and Composition in First Peter, 1992; By Philosophy and Empty Deceit: Colossians as Response to a Cynic Critique, 1996; (with A. Clendenen) Forgiveness: Finding Freedom through Reconciliation, 2002; (with A.V. Oelger) I Promise to Hate, Despise, and Abuse You until Death Do Us Part: Marriage in a Narcissistic Age, 2010. **Address:** Department of Religious Studies, St. Xavier University, Rm. N-311, 3700 W 103rd St., Chicago, IL 60655, U.S.A. **Online address:** martin@sxu.edu

MARTIN, Troy Wayne. *See* **MARTIN, Troy.**

MARTIN, Vicky. *See* **MARTIN, Victoria Carolyn.**

MARTIN, Victoria Carolyn. Also writes as Vicky Martin. British (born England), b. 1945. **Genres:** Novels, Romance/Historical, Young Adult Fiction. **Career:** Writer. **Publications:** AS VICKY MARTIN: September Song, 1971; The Windmill Years, 1978; Changing Partners, 1979; Tigers of the Night, 1985; Obey the Moon, 1988. OTHERS: Seeds of the Sun, 1979; The

Boy Next Door, 1984; The Opposite House, 1985. **Address:** John Farquharson Ltd., 8 Bell Yard, Bellhouse, GL WC2A 2JR, England.

MARTIN, Wendy. *See* **MARTINI, Teri.**

MARTIN, William. (Frederick James). American (born United States), b. 1950. **Genres:** Novels, Plays/Screenplays. **Career:** Paul Revere Memorial Association, trustee; U.S.S. Constitution Museum, trustee; Associates of the Boston Public Library, board director. Writer. **Publications:** NOVELS: Back Bay, 1979; Nerve Endings, 1984; The Rising of the Moon, 1987; Cape Cod, 1991; Annapolis, 1996; Citizen Washington: A Novel, 1999; Harvard Yard, 2003; The Lost Constitution, 2007; City of Dreams, 2010. **Address:** c/o Robert Gottlieb, Trident Media Group L.L.C., 41 Madison Ave., Fl. 36, New York, NY 10010-2257, U.S.A. **Online address:** mail@williammartinbooks.com

MARTINAC, Paula. American (born United States), b. 1954. **Genres:** Novels, Gay And Lesbian Issues, Biography, Technology. **Career:** West Virginia State Museum, assistant curator, 1979-82; Prentice-Hall Inc., production editor, 1982-85; City University of New York, Feminist Press, production director, 1985-94; Conditions Magazine, editor, 1988-90; freelance writer, 1994-; Q Syndicate, editor-in-chief. **Publications:** (Ed.) One You Call Sister, 1989; (with C. Tomaso) Lesbian Short Fiction, 1989; Out of Time, 1990; Home Movies, 1993; Chicken: A Novel, 1997; K.D. Lang, 1997; The Queerest Places: A National Guide to Gay and Lesbian Historic Sites, 1997; The Lesbian and Gay Book of Love and Marriage: Creating the Stories of our Lives, 1998; (with S. Bittencourt) My Road To Microsoft: One Woman's Success Story, 2003. Contributor to periodicals. **Address:** c/o Mitchell Waters, Curtis Brown Ltd., 10 Astor Pl., New York, NY 10003, U.S.A.

MARTIN(-BERG), Laurey K(ramer). American (born United States), b. 1950. **Genres:** Literary Criticism And History, Language/Linguistics. **Career:** University of Wisconsin-Madison, Department of French and Italian, lecturer, 1982-83, visiting assistant professor, 1983-86, lecturer, 1986-92, senior lecturer in French, 1992-99, distinguished lecturer in French, 1999-; Amnesty Intl., translator, 1988-. Writer. **Publications:** (With W.J. Berg) Images, 1990; (with W.J. Berg) Emile Zola Revisited, 1992; (with W.J. Berg) Gustave Flaubert, 1997; (co-author) Paroles, 1999, rev. eds., 2002, 2006. Works appear in anthologies. Contributor to journals. **Address:** Department of French and Italian, University of Wisconsin Madison, 6th Fl. Van Hise, 618 Van Hise Hall, 1220 Linden Dr., Madison, WI 53706, U.S.A. **Online address:** lmartinb@facstaff.wisc.edu

MARTINES, Julia. *See* **O'FAOLAIN, Julia.**

MARTINET, Jeanne. American (born United States), b. 1958. **Genres:** Adult Non-fiction, How-to Books, Humor/Satire, Self Help, Social Commentary, Romance/Historical. **Career:** Workman Publishing Company Inc., publicity assistant, 1984-85; St. Martin's/Marek, editorial assistant, 1985; E.P. Dutton, assistant editor, 1985-87, associate editor, 1987-89, editor, 1989; freelance writer, 1989-. **Publications:** The Art of Mingling: Easy, Fun, and Proven Techniques for Mastering Any Room, 1992; Getting Beyond Hello: Miss Mingle's Guide to Navigating the Nineties, 1996; The Faux Pas Survival Guide: The Fine Art of Removing Your Foot from Your Mouth, 1996; Come-ons, Comebacks, and Kiss-Offs: Date Lines Every Woman Needs to Survive her Search for the Holy Male, 1997; Artful Dodging: Painless Techniques for Avoiding Anyone Anytime, 2000; Truer Than True Romance: Classic Love Comics Retold, 2001; Art of Mingling: Proven Techniques for Mastering Any Room, 2006; Life is Friends: A Complete Guide to the Lost Art of Connecting in Person, 2009. **Address:** 241 W 97th St., Ste. 5L, New York, NY 10025, U.S.A. **Online address:** jeanne@jeannemartinet.com

MARTINEZ, A. Lee. American (born United States), b. 1973. **Genres:** Young Adult Fiction. **Career:** Writer. **Publications:** Gil's All Fright Diner, 2005; In the Company of Ogres, 2006; A Nameless Witch, 2007; The Automatic Detective, 2008; Too Many Curses, 2008; Monster, 2009; Divine Misfortune, 2010. **Address:** The Cooke Agency, 278 Bloor St. E, Ste. 305, Toronto, ON M4W 3M4, Canada.

MARTINEZ, Andrés. American/Mexican (born Mexico), b. 1966?. **Genres:** Adult Non-fiction. **Career:** Pittsburgh Post-Gazette, business reporter, 1991-95; Post-Gazette, editorial writer, 1995-97; Wall Street Journal, business reporter, 1997-98; New York Times, staff, 2000-04, editorial writer, assistant editorial page editor; Los Angeles Times, editorial page editor, 2004-07; New America Foundation, Bernard L. Schwartz Fellows Program, director, 2008-. **Publications:** 24/7: Living It Up and Doubling Down in the New Las Vegas, 1999. **Address:** Bernard L. Schwartz Fellows Program, New America Foundation, 1899 L St. NW, Ste. 400, Washington, DC 20036-3868, U.S.A. **Online address:** martinez@newamerica.net

MARTÍNEZ, Dionisio D. American/Cuban (born Cuba), b. 1956. **Genres:** Adult Non-fiction, Poetry, Education. **Career:** Writer, critic and educator. **Publications:** Dancing at the Chelsea, 1992; History as a Second Language, 1993; Bad Alchemy: Poems, 1995; Climbing Back: Poems, 2001. Contributor to periodicals. Works appear in anthologies. **Address:** 4509 N Lincoln Ave., Tampa, FL 33614-6631, U.S.A. **Online address:** ddmartinez@aol.com

MARTINEZ, Dolores P. *See* **MARTINEZ, D. P.**

MARTINEZ, D. P. (Dolores P. Martinez). British (born England), b. 1957. **Genres:** Popular Culture, History, Cultural/Ethnic Topics, Theology/Religion, Film. **Career:** University of London, School of Oriental and African Studies, Department of Anthropology and Sociology, reader, senior lecturer in anthropology, associate dean of research, faculty of arts and humanities. Writer. **Publications:** (Ed. with J. van Bremen) Ceremony and Ritual in Japan: Religious Practices in an Industrialized Society, 1995; (ed.) The Worlds of Japanese Popular Culture: Gender, Shifting Boundaries and Global Cultures, 1998; Identity and Ritual in a Japanese Diving Village: The Making and Becoming of Person and Place, 2004; (ed.) Modern Japanese Culture and Society, 4 vols., 2007; (ed. with M.R. del Alisal and P. Ackermann as Dolores P. Martinez) Pilgrimages and Spiritual Quests in Japan, 2007; Remaking Kurosawa: Translations and Permutations in Global Cinema, 2009. **Address:** School of Oriental and African Studies, University of London, Rm. 567, College Bldgs., Thornhaugh St., Russell Sq., London, GL WC1H 0XG, England. **Online address:** dm6@soas.ac.uk

MARTINEZ, Elizabeth Coonrod. American (born United States), b. 1954. **Genres:** Literary Criticism And History, Young Adult Non-fiction, Biography, Translations, Humanities. **Career:** Woodburn Independent, reporter and photographer, 1983-84; Portland Oregonian, general assignment reporter, 1984-86; New Haven Independent, reporter and assistant editor, 1986-88; Albuquerque Monthly Magazine, managing editor, 1989; KLUZ-TV (Univision), news director and anchor, 1989-91; University of New Mexico, journalism instructor and workshop coordinator, 1990-94, teaching associate, 1991-93, journalism instructor and workshop coordinator, 1992-94, instructor in Spanish, 1993-95, Xalapa study abroad program, assistant director and instructor, 1993; Sonoma State University, Department of Modern Languages and Literatures, assistant professor, 1995-2000, associate professor of Spanish and Latin American literature, 2000-, chair, 2000-03, professor of Latin American literature, chair of Chicano and Latino studies, 2004-. **Publications:** HISPANIC HERITAGE SERIES: Henry Cisneros: Mexican-American Leader, 1993; Edward James Olmos: Mexican-American Actor, 1994; Sor Juana: A Trailblazing Thinker, 1994. COMING TO AMERICA SERIES: The Mexican American Experience, 1995; Before the Boom: Latin American Revolutionary Novels of the 1920s, 2001. OTHERS: (trans.) Clipper, Bolivar, and Soliman (three plays by I. Chocron), 1992; Lilus Kikus and Other Stories, 2005; Elena Poniatowska: Lilus Kikus and Other Stories, 2005; Josefina Niggli, Mexican American Writer: A Critical Biography, 2007. Contributor to periodicals and journals. **Address:** Department of Modern Languages and Literatures, Sonoma State University, 1810 E Cotati St., Rohnert Park, CA 94928, U.S.A. **Online address:** elizabeth.martinez@sonoma.edu

MARTINEZ, Guillermo. Argentine (born Argentina), b. 1962. **Genres:** Novels. **Career:** Writer and mathematician. **Publications:** FICTION: Infierno grande, 1989, new ed., 2006; Acerca de Roderer, 1992; La mujer del maestro (novel), 1998; Crimenes imperceptibles (novel), 2003; La muerte lenta de Luciana B., 2007; Yo tambien tuve una novia bisexual (novel), 2011. NONFICTION: Borges y la matematica (essays), 2003, new ed., 2005; La formula de la inmortalidad (essays), 2005; Godel (essay), 2009. Contributor to periodicals. **Address:** Carmen Balcells Agency, Diagonal 580, Barcelona, 08021, Spain. **Online address:** infogmartinez@yahoo.com.ar

MARTINEZ, Joseph G. R. American (born United States), b. 1946?. **Genres:** Literary Criticism And History, Education, Writing/Journalism, Mathematics/Statistics, Children's Fiction. **Career:** National College, Albuquerque Extension, instructor, 1976-82; University of Albuquerque, Reading Laboratory, director, 1978-79, assistant professor of mathematics, education and psychology, 1982-85; Bread of Life Bookstore, partner, 1978; University of New Mexico, lecturer in psychology and educational foundations, 1979-82, Valencia Campus, instructor, faculty, 1985-86, assistant professor, 1986-88, associate professor, 1989-96, professor, 1996-, Educational Foundations, presidential lecturer, 1988-89, 1989-90, Department of Educational Foundations, head, 1990-92; Santa Fe Indian School, consultant. Writer. **Publications:** (With N.C. Martinez) The Holt Workbook, 1986, 2nd ed., 1989; (with N.C. Martinez) Basic College Writing: A Text With Readings, 1991; Teaching Basic College Writing: A Guide, 1991; (with N.C. Martinez) Guide to British Poetry Explication, 1991, vol. II: Renaissance, 1992, vol. III: Restoration Through Romantic Period, 1993, vol. IV: Victorian to Contemporary, 1993; (with N.C. Martinez) Math Without Fear: A Guide to Preventing Math Anxiety in Children, 1996; Guide to British Prose Explication, vol. IV, 1994; (with N.C. Martinez) Reading and Writing in Mathematics: A Guide and a Resource Book, 2001; (with N.C. Martinez) Activities for Developing Mathematical Thinking: Exploring, Inventing and Discovering Mathematics, 2007; (with N.C. Martinez) Teaching Mathematics in Elementary and Middle School: Developing Mathematical Thinking, 2007. Contributor of articles to journals. **Address:** Mathematics, Science, Technology Programs, College of Education, University of New Mexico, MSC05 3040, Nokona Hall 144, Albuquerque, NM 87131, U.S.A. **Online address:** jomart@unm.edu

MARTÍNEZ, Manuel Luis. American (born United States), b. 1966. **Genres:** Novels, Novellas/Short Stories, Young Adult Non-fiction. **Career:** Indiana University, assistant professor, 1997-, visiting professor; Ohio State University, Department of English, associate professor, director of undergraduate studies, Latino and Latin American Space for Enrichment and Research, affiliate faculty. Writer. **Publications:** Crossing, 1998; Mis 4 Puntos Cardinales, 1999; The Migrating Text: Movement Discourse and the Counterculture, 2002; Countering the Counterculture: Rereading Postwar American Dissent from Jack Kerouac to Tomás Rivera, 2003; Drift: A Novel, 2003; Day of the Dead, 2010; Lomos, forthcoming; Tougher Than Us, forthcoming. **Address:** Department of English, Ohio State University, 453 Denney Hall, 164 W 17th Ave., Columbus, OH 43210, U.S.A. **Online address:** martinez.202@osu.edu

MARTINEZ, Nancy C. (Jean Conrad). American (born United States), b. 1921?. **Genres:** Novels, Education, Architecture, Information Science/ Computers, Literary Criticism And History, Mathematics/Statistics, Writing/ Journalism, Reference, Reference. **Career:** L.E. Ager Office, civil engineer, technical writer and office assistant, 1960-68; KRVC-Radio, traffic manager and copy writer, 1967-68; Community Action Center, instructor, 1971; National College of Business, instructor, 1975-80, 1982; University of Albuquerque, adjunct assistant professor, 1977-79, assistant professor of English, 1980 85, supervisor of reading laboratory, 1980-82, vice president for academic affairs, 1982-83, College of General Studies, dean, 1982-84; Bread of Life Bookstore, partner, 1979-; G.K. Hall and Co., field editor, 1985-97; University of New Mexico, Valencia Campus, Skills Development Center, coordinator and director of adult basic education and handicapped programs, 1985-86, lecturer, 1986, 1989-91, 2000-03, part-time instructor, adjunct assistant professor, 2003-04; Central New Mexico Community College, part-time instructor. **Publications:** (With J.M. Kuntz) Poetry Explication, 3rd ed., 1980; (with J.F. Parker and G. Piepenbrink) Independent Writer, 1986. NOVELS AS JEAN CONRAD: Applegate Landing, 1985; Golden Gates, 1987. WITH J.G.R. MARTINEZ: The Holt Workbook, 1986, 2nd ed., 1989; Basic College Writing: A Text with Readings, 1991; Teaching Basic College Writing, 1991; Guide to British Poetry Explication, vol. I: Old English through Medieval, 1991, vol. II: Renaissance, 1992, (and E. Anderson) vol. III: Restoration through Romantic Period, 1993, (and E. Anderson) vol. IV: Victorian to Contemporary, 1995; Math without Fear: A Guide for Preventing Math Anxiety in Children, 1996; Reading and Writing to Learn Mathematics: A Guide and a Resource Book, 2001; Teaching Mathematics in Elementary and Middle School: Developing Mathematical Thinking, 2007; Activities for Developing Mathematical Thinking: Exploring, Inventing, and Discovering Mathematics, 2007. **Address:** Department of English Language & Literature, University of New Mexico, 1 University of New Mexico, PO Box 03 2170, Albuquerque, NM 87131-0001, U.S.A. **Online address:** nanmart@unm.edu

MARTING, Diane E. American (born United States), b. 1952. **Genres:** Poetry, Area Studies, Humanities, Literary Criticism And History, Theatre, Women's Studies And Issues, Bibliography, Essays, Translations, Reference, Sex. **Career:** University of California, visiting assistant professor, 1985-86; University of Nebraska, assistant professor, 1986-88; Columbia University, assistant professor of Spanish and Portuguese, 1988-95; Senior Fulbright lecturer, 1988, 1989; University of Florida, assistant professor, 1995-2001; University of Michigan, visiting assistant professor, 2001-02; University of Mississippi, associate professor of Spanish, 2002-; Mississippi Foreign Language Association, president, 2004-06. Writer. **Publications:** (Ed.) Women Writers of Spanish America: An Annotated Bio-Bibliographical Guide, 1987; (ed.) Spanish American Women Writers: A Bio-Bibliographical Source Book, 1990; (ed.) Clarice Lispector: An Annotated Bio-Bibliography, 1993; The Sexual Woman in Latin American Literature, 2001. Contributor of articles, translations, and poems to periodicals. **Address:** Department of Modern Languages, University of Mississippi, E-104 Bondurant Hall, 1848 University Cir., PO Box 1848, University, MS 38677-1848, U.S.A. **Online address:** dmarting@olemiss.edu

MARTINI, Steven (Paul). American (born United States), b. 1946. **Genres:** Mystery/Crime/Suspense, Novels, Law, Young Adult Fiction. **Career:** Los Angeles Daily Journal, journalist, 1970-75; full-time writer, 1991-; California State Capitol, correspondent. **Publications:** PAUL MADRIANI MYSTERY SERIES: Compelling Evidence, 1992; Prime Witness, 1993; Undue Influence, 1994; The Judge, 1995; The Attorney, 1999; The Jury, 2001; The Arraignment, 2003; Double Tap, 2005; Shadow of Power, 2008; Guardian of Lies, 2009; The Rule of Nine, 2010. OTHERS: The Simeon Chamber, 1988, 2nd ed., 1998; The List, 1997; Critical Mass, 1998; Trader of Secrets, 2011. **Address:** 1050 Larrabee Ave., Ste. 104-303, Bellingham, WA 98225, U.S.A. **Online address:** contact@stevemartini.com

MARTINI, Teri. Also writes as Wendy Martin, Thérèse Martini, Alison King. American (born United States), b. 1930?. **Genres:** Novels, Children's Fiction, Children's Non-fiction, Mystery/Crime/Suspense, Romance/Historical, History, Young Adult Fiction. **Career:** Teacher, 1952-77; Institute of Children's Literature, instructor, 1977-. Writer. **Publications:** CHILDREN'S BOOKS: The Fisherman's Ring, 1954; True Book of Indians, 1954, rev. ed., 1970; True Book of Cowboys, 1955; Treasure of the Mohawk, 1956; Sandals on the Golden Highway: A Life of Junipero Serra, 1959; What a Frog Can Do, 1962; Mystery of the Hard Luck House, 1965; The Lucky Ghost Shirt, 1971; Patrick Henry, Patriot, 1972; Mystery of the Woman in the Mirror, 1973; John Marshall, 1974; Mystery Waters of Tonbridge Wells, 1975; All Because of Jill, 1976; Cowboys, 1981; The New True Book of Indians, 1982; Indians, 1982; Junípero Serra, God's Pioneer, 1989; The Secret Is Out: True Spy Stories, 1990; Feliz Navidad, Pablo, 1990; Christmas for Andy, 1991; Christopher Columbus: The Man Who Unlocked the Secrets of the World, 1992. ADULT BOOKS: AS WENDY MARTIN: Love's Journey, 1976; Two Hearts Adrift, 1976; Island Magic, 1988; Love on Trial, 1990; Tune in for Murder, 1993. AS THéRèSE MARTINI: To Love and Beyond, 1977; Dreams to Give, 1979; The Arrundel Touch, 1980; Love's Lost Melody, 1984. AS ALISON KING: The Dreamer Lost in Terror, 1976. Contributor to journals. **Address:** c/o Julie Fallowfield, McIntosh & Otis Inc., 353 Lexington Ave., New York, NY 10016-0941, U.S.A.

MARTINI, Thérèse. *See* **MARTINI, Teri.**

MARTIN-JONES, David. Scottish (born Scotland) **Genres:** Adult Non-fiction, Film. **Career:** University of St. Andrews, Department of Film Studies, lecturer, senior lecturer. Writer. **Publications:** Deleuze, Cinema and National Identity: Narrative Time in National Contexts, 2006; (contrib.) The Sociological Review, Monograph: Against Automobility, 2006; (contrib.) Made in Newcastle, 2007; (with D.Sutton) Deleuze Reframed, 2008; Scotland: Global Cinema: Genres, Modes and Identities, 2009; (ed.) Cinema at the Periphery, 2010; Deleuze and World Cinemas, 2011. **Address:** Film Studies, University of St. Andrews, 99 North St., St. Andrews, FF KY16 9AD, Scotland. **Online address:** dm70@st-andrews.ac.uk

MARTINO, Rick. American (born United States), b. 1947. **Genres:** Sports/ Fitness, Psychology. **Career:** University of Pittsburgh, Golf Swing Research Development Lab, director; Turner Network Television (TNT), golf commentator; Motion Golf Performance Institute, leader. Writer. **Publications:** (With D. Wade) The PGA Manual of Golf: The Professional's Way to Learn and Play Better Golf, 2002. Contributor to magazines and periodicals. **Address:** 100 Ave. of the Champions, Palm Beach Gardens, FL 33410, U.S.A. **Online address:** rmartino@pgahq.com

MARTINSEN, Martin. *See* **FOLLETT, Ken(neth Martin).**

MARTINSON, Deborah. American (born United States), b. 1946. **Genres:**

Autobiography/Memoirs, Biography. **Career:** Occidental College, associate professor of English writing, chair of English writing. Writer. **Publications:** In the Presence of Audience: The Self in Diaries and Fiction, 2003; Lillian Hellman: A Life with Foxes and Scoundrels, 2005. **Address:** Department of English Writing, Occidental College, 1600 Campus Rd., Ground Fl., Los Angeles, CA 90041, U.S.A. **Online address:** dmartin@oxy.edu

MARTINSON, Ida M(arie). American (born United States), b. 1936. **Genres:** Medicine/Health, Women's Studies And Issues. **Career:** Hong Kong Polytechnic University, professor of health sciences and head of department, chair; Foo Yin Junior College of Nursing and Midwifery, visiting professor, 1987; University of California, professor of nursing, now professor emeritus; Taiwan's National Defense Medical Center School of Nursing, consultant; National Cheng Kung University, consultant; Childhood Cancer Foundation, founder. Writer. **Publications:** (With G.R. Kepner) Mathematics for Health Professionals, 1977. EDITOR: Home Care for the Dying Child: Professional and Family Perspectives, 1976; (with D.K. Kjervik) Women in Stress: A Nursing Perspective, 1979; (with D.G. Moldow) Home Care for Seriously Ill Children: A Manual for Parents, 1984; (with D. Kjervik) Women in Health and Illness: Life Experiences and Crises, 1986; (with T. Krulik and B. Holaday) The Child and Family Facing Life Threatening Illness: A Tribute to Eugenia Waechter, 1987; (co-ed.) Toward a Science of Family Nursing, 1989; (with A. Widmer) Home Health Care Nursing, 1989, 2nd ed., 2002; (with J. Fitzpatrick) Selected Writings of Rosemary Ellis: In Search of the Meaning of Nursing Science, 1996. Contributor to books and journals. **Address:** Department of Health Care & Nursing, University of California, 2 Koret Way, PO Box 0606, San Francisco, CA 94143-0606, U.S.A. **Online address:** ida.martinson@ucsf.edu

MARTON, Jirina. Canadian/French/Czech (born Czech Republic), b. 1946. **Genres:** Children's Fiction, Illustrations. **Career:** Atelier Y. Agam, painter, 1979-80; Librairie Larousse, layout artist and designer, 1980-85. Writer and illustrator. **Publications:** SELF-ILLUSTRATED: L'eau, 1986; La ville grise (in Japanese), 1986; Midnight Visit at Molly's House, 1988; I'll Do It Myself, 1989; Mitzy (in Japanese), 1990; Flowers for Mom, 1991; Amelia's Celebration, 1992; You Can Go Home Again, 1994; Lady Kaguya's Secret, 1997. Illustrator of books by others. Contributor to periodicals. **Address:** 3 King St. W, Colborne, ON K0K 1S0, Canada. **Online address:** jmarton1@sympatico.ca

MARTON, Kati (Ilona). American/Hungarian (born Hungary), b. 1949. **Genres:** Novels, Biography, Documentaries/Reportage. **Career:** National Public Radio, reporter, 1971-72, America and the World, program host; WCAU-TV, news writer and reporter, 1973-77; ABC News, foreign correspondent and bureau chief, 1977-79; Sunday Times, columnist, 1983-85. Journalist and human rights activist. **Publications:** Wallenberg, 1982; An American Woman, 1987; The Polk Conspiracy: Murder and Cover-up in the Case of CBS News Correspondent George Polk, 1990; A Death in Jerusalem, 1994; Hidden Power: Presidential Marriages that Shaped Our Recent History, 2001; The Great Escape: Nine Jews Who Fled Hitler and Changed the World, 2006; Kilenc magyar aki világgá ment és megváltoztatta a világot, 2008; Enemies of the People: My Family's Journey to America, 2009; Nép ellenségei: Családom regénye, 2010. Contributor of articles to periodicals. **Address:** c/o Amanda Urban, International Creative Management, 730 5th Ave., New York, NY 10019, U.S.A. **Online address:** katimarton@earthlink.net

MARTY, Martin E. American (born United States), b. 1928. **Genres:** History, Theology/Religion. **Career:** Lutheran pastor, 1952-63; Christian Century, senior editor, 1956-98; Church History, co-editor, 1963-98; University of Chicago Divinity School, Fairfax M. Cone professor of divinity, 1963-98, Fairfax M. Cone distinguished service professor emeritus of the history of modern Christianity, 1998-; Public Religion Project, director, 1990-2000; Saint Olaf College, regent, interim president, 2000, senior regent. **Publications:** The New Shape of American Religion, 1959; A Short History of Christianity, 1959; New Directions in Biblical Thought, 1960; The Infidel: Free-Thought and American Religion, 1961; The Improper Opinion, 1961; Baptism, 1962; The Hidden Discipline, 1962; Pen-Ultimates: Comment on the Folk Religions of America, 1963; The Religious Press in America, 1963; Second Chance for American Protestants, 1963; Varieties of Unbelief, 1964; Church Unity and Church Mission, 1964; Death and Birth of Parish, 1964; (ed. with D.G. Peerman) Handbook of Christian Theologians, 1965; Youth Considers Do-It-Yourself Religion, 1965; Babylon by Choice; New Environment for Mission, 1965; The Modern Schism, 1969; The Search for a Usable Future, 1969; Righteous Empire, 1970; Protestantism, 1972; You Are Promise, 1973; The Fire We Can Light, 1973; You are Promise, 1974; The Pro & Con Book of Religious America: A Bicentennial Argument, 1975; A Nation of Behavers, 1977; Religion, Awakening and Revolution, 1977; Baptism, 1977; Religion in America, 1950 to the present, 1979; Short History of Christianity, 1980; Lord's Supper, 1980; Friendship, 1980; By Way of Response, 1981; The Public Church, 1981; A Cry of Absence, 1983; Pilgrims in Their Own Land, 1984; Being Good and Doing Good, 1984; An Invitation to American Catholic History, 1985; Modern American Religion, vol. I: The Irony of it All, 1893-1919, 1986, vol. II: The Noise of Conflict, 1919-1941, 1991, vol. III: Under God, Indivisible, 1996; Religion and Republic: The American Circumstance, 1987; Christian Churches in the United States, 1987; (ed. with F.E. Greenspahn) Pushing the Faith: Proselytism and Civility in a Pluralistic World, 1988; (ed.) Fundamentalisms Observed, 1991; The Glory and the Power, 1992; (ed.) Writing of American Religious History, 1992; (ed.) Varieties of Protestantism, 1992; (ed.) Trends in American Religion and the Protestant World, 1992; (ed.) Theological Themes in the American Protestant World, 1992; (ed.) Protestantism and Social Christianity, 1992; (ed.) Protestantism and Regionalism, 1992; (ed.) Civil Religion, Church and State, 1993; Cry of Absence: Reflections for the Winter of the Heart, 1993; (ed.) Women and Women's Issues, 1993; (ed.) Varieties of Religious Expression, 1993; (ed.) New and Intense Movements, 1993; (ed.) Missions and Ecumenical Expressions, 1993; (ed.) Native American Religion and Black Protestantism, 1993; (co-ed.) Fundamentalisms and the State: Remaking Polities, Economies and Militance, 1993; (co-ed.) Fundamentalisms and Society: Reclaiming the Sciences, the Family and Education, 1993; (ed.) Fundamentalism and Evangelicalism, 1993; (ed.) Ethnic and Non-Protestant Themes, 1993; Places Along the Way, 1994; Our Hope for Years to Come, 1995; Short History of American Catholicism, 1995; (with M. Marty) Our Hope for Years to Come: The Search for Spiritual Sanctuary, 1995; (ed. with R.S. Appleby) Fundamentalisms Comprehended, 1995; The One and the Many, 1997; (with M. Marty) 1928: Promise of Winter: Quickening the Spirit on Ordinary Days and in Fallow Seasons, 1997; When True Simplicity is Gained, 1998; (with J. Moore) Politics, Religion and the Common Good: Advancing A Distinctly American Conversation About Religion's Role in Our Shared Life, 2000; (with J. Moore) Education, Religion and the Common Good, 2000; (co-author) Festivals of the World: The Illustrated Guide to Celebrations, Customs, Events and Holidays, 2002; (co-author) Visions of Utopia, 2003; Speaking of Trust: Conversing with Luther about the Sermon on the Mount, 2003; Protestant Voice in American Pluralism, 2004; Martin Luther, 2004; When Faiths Collide, 2005; Righteous Empire Revisited, 2007; Mystery of the Child, 2007; Lutheran Questions, Lutheran Answers: Exploring Christian Faith, 2007; Christian World: A Global History, 2007; Baptism: A User's Guide, 2008; (intro.) Confessions of St. Augustine, 2009; Building Cultures of Trust, 2010; Dietrich Bonhoeffer's Letters and Papers from Prison: A Biography, 2011. **Address:** 175 E Delaware Pl., Ste. 8508, Chicago, IL 60611-7750, U.S.A. **Online address:** memarty@aol.com

MARTY, Sid. Canadian/British (born England), b. 1944. **Genres:** Poetry, Adult Non-fiction, Environmental Sciences/Ecology, Natural History, Autobiography/Memoirs. **Career:** Canadian Government National Parks Service, park warden, 1966-68, 1970-72, 1973-78; writer, 1978-. Singer and guitarist. **Publications:** Headwaters, 1973; Tumbleweed Harvest, 1973; Men for the Mountains, 1978; Nobody Danced with Miss Rodeo, 1981; The Warrior's Bow, 1983; A Grand and Fabulous Notion: The First Century of Canada's Parks, 1984; The Canadian Mountaineering Anthology, 1994; Leaning on the Wind: Under The Spell of The Great Chinook, 1995; Switchbacks: True Stories of the Canadian Rockies, 1999; Sky Humour, 1999; Black Grizzly of Whiskey Creek, 2008; Rider with Good Hands, 2011. **Address:** Black Moss Press, 2450 Byng Rd., Windsor, AB N8W 3E8, Canada. **Online address:** sid@sidmarty.com

MARTZ, Linda. American (born United States), b. 1939. **Genres:** History, Sociology, Economics. **Career:** Freelance writer, researcher, historian and editor, 1974-. **Publications:** (With J.P. Martín-Cleto) Toledo Y Los Toledanos En 1561, 1974; Poverty and Welfare in Habsburg Spain: The Example of Toledo, 1983; Ohio Records Finder: How to Use Public Documents to Uncover Information, 1998; A Network of Converso Families in Early Modern Toledo: Assimilating a Minority, 2003; (ed. with A. Higgie) Questions of Identity in Detective Fiction, 2007. Contributor to periodicals. **Address:** 6227 Madawaska Rd., Bethesda, MD 20816-3114, U.S.A. **Online address:** lmmartzl@aol.com

MARUSEK, David. American (born United States), b. 1951?. **Genres:** Novels. **Career:** University of Alaska, instructor. Writer and graphic designer.

Publications: Counting Heads, 2005; Getting to Know You: Stories, 2007; Mind Over Ship, 2009. Works appear in anthologies. **Address:** Fairbanks, AK , U.S.A. **Online address:** david@marusek.com

MARVEL, Thomas S. American (born United States), b. 1935. **Genres:** Architecture, History, Adult Non-fiction. **Career:** Marvel-Flores-Cobian, architect, 1960-; University of Puerto Rico, assistant professor of architecture, 1967-89; Puerto Rico Housing Finance Corp., design consultant, 1979-81; Comision Pro-sede Olimpiadas, Commissioner, 1987-97, 2004; Thomas S. Marvel Architects, principal, 1997-. Writer. **Publications:** (With M.L. Moreno) La arquitectura de templos parroquiales de Puerto Rico/Architecture of Parish Churches in Puerto Rico, 1984, 2nd ed., 1994; Antonin Nechodoma, Architect 1877-1928: The Prairie School in the Caribbean, 1994. **Address:** Marvel-Flores-Cobian & Asociados, 1555 Francia St., Santurce, PR 00911, U.S.A. **Online address:** marvelts@aol.com

MARVIN, Cate. (Catherine C. Marvin). American (born United States), b. 1969. **Genres:** Poetry, History, Literary Criticism And History. **Career:** City University of New York, College of Staten Island, assistant professor, associate professor of English, professor in creative writing, 2003-; Lesley University, low-residency M.F.A. program poetry writing, instructor; New York Foundation for the Arts Gregory Millard, fellow, 2007. Writer and poet. **Publications:** World's Tallest Disaster (poems), 2001; (ed. with M. Dumanis) Legitimate Dangers: American Poets of the New Century, 2006; Fragment of the Head of a Queen: Poems, 2007; (with W. Johns) Machine of Love and Grace: Selected Poems, 2011. Contributor to periodicals. **Address:** c/o Nickole Brown, Sarabande Books Inc., 2234 Dundee Rd., Ste. 200, Louisville, KY 40205, U.S.A. **Online address:** marvin@mail.csi.cuny.edu

MARVIN, Catherine C. *See* **MARVIN, Cate.**

MARVIN, Jay. American (born United States), b. 1953?. **Genres:** Novels. **Career:** KWMC, staff, 1971-; WWOD Lynchburg, staff; K102 FM, staff; WJEZ, staff; WJJD, staff; KKAT, staff; KIXZ, staff; WLS, staff; KHOW, staff; KKZN, staff. Writer. **Publications:** Punk Blood, 1998; The White Trash Chronicles, 2001. Contributor to books and journals. **Address:** c/o Author Mail, Department of English, Florida State University, 405 Williams Bldg., Tallahassee, FL 32306-1580, U.S.A. **Online address:** jmarvin@well.com

MARX, Anthony W. American (born United States), b. 1959. **Genres:** Politics/Government, Language/Linguistics. **Career:** University of Pennsylvania, administrative aide to the president, 1981-84; South African Committee for Higher Education Trust, consultant, 1984, 1986; CASE, visiting fellow, 1988, 1990; Columbia University, assistant professor of political science, 1990-96, associate professor, 1996-, professor, director of undergraduate studies of political science, Gates Foundation, director, Center for Historical Social Science, co-director, Columbia Urban Educators Program, founder, Columbia's Masters in International Affairs Program, director, 2001-02; Khanya College, co-founder; Amherst College, professor of political science, faculty of European studies, president, 2003-; New York Public Library, president and chief executive officer, 2011-. Writer. **Publications:** Lessons of Struggle: South African Internal Opposition, 1960-1990, 1992; Making Race and Nation: A Comparison of South Africa, the United States and Brazil, 1998; Faith in Nation: Exclusionary Origins of Nationalism, 2003. Contributor to periodicals and scholarly journals. **Address:** The New York Public Library, 455 5th Ave., New York, NY 10016, U.S.A. **Online address:** marx@amherst.edu

MARX, Elisabeth. American/British (born England) **Genres:** Business/Trade/Industry, Economics. **Career:** Norman Broadbent Intl. (executive search company), director; Hanover Fox Intl. (executive search company), leadership specialist; National University of Singapore, lecturer in psychology. Psychologist, management expert and writer. **Publications:** Breaking through Culture Shock: What You Need to Succeed in International Business, 1999, new ed., 2001. Contributor to periodicals. **Address:** c/o Author Mail, 374 US Rte. 1, PO Box 700, Yarmouth, ME 04096, U.S.A.

MARX, Eva. American (born United States) **Genres:** Medicine/Health, Education, Social Sciences, Young Adult Fiction. **Career:** Joint Center for Urban Studies, research assistant and assistant field supervisor, 1973-76; Judge Baker Guidance Center, administrative coordinator, 1976-79, New England Resource Center for Children and Families, coordinator, 1981-84; Massachusetts Department of Social Services, senior program analyst, 1980-81; Education Development Center Inc., consultant, 1984-86, Center for School Health Programs, associate director, 1994-. Writer. **Publications:** (Ed. with S. Wooley and D. Northrop) Health Is Academic: A Guide to Coordinated School Health Programs, 1998; (with V. Harrison and K.S. Riggs) Promoting Sexual Responsibility: A Teen Pregnancy Prevention Resource for School Employees, 2005. **Address:** Education Development Center Inc., 55 Chapel St., Newton, MA 02458-1060, U.S.A. **Online address:** emarx@edc.org

MARX, Gary T. American (born United States), b. 1938. **Genres:** Civil Liberties/Human Rights, Communications/Media, Criminology/True Crime, Information Science/Computers, Race Relations, Social Commentary, Sociology. **Career:** University of California, Survey Research Center, research associate, 1965-67, lecturer in sociology, 1966-67, chancellor's distinguished fellow; Harvard University, assistant professor of social relations, 1967-69, Harvard-Massachusetts Institute of Technology Joint Center for Urban Studies, research associate, 1967-73, lecturer, 1969-73; Massachusetts Institute of Technology, professor of sociology, 1973-92, professor emeritus, 1994-; Boston College, visiting associate professor, 1973-74; University of California, visiting associate professor, 1974; Wellesley College, visiting associate professor, 1975; Boston University, visiting associate professor, 1976; University of California, visiting associate professor, 1977-78; State University of New York, visiting associate professor, 1980-81; Center for Advanced Study in the Behavioral Sciences, fellow, 1987-88; American Sociological Association, Jensen Lecturer, 1988-89; University of Colorado, professor of sociology, 1992-99; Harvey Mudd College, Hixon-Riggs Professor of Science, Technology and Society; Harvard Law School, Criminal Justice Center, research associate; University of Washington, Stice memorial Lecturer-in-residence; West Virginia University, A.D. Carlson Visiting Distinguished Professor in the Social Sciences. Writer. **Publications:** The Social Basis of the Support of a Depression Era Extremist: Father Coughlin, 1962; Protest and Prejudice, 1967; (co-author) Inquiries in Sociology, 1972; (with N. Goodman) Society Today, 4th ed., 1982; Undercover Police: Surveillance in America, 1988; (with D. McAdam) Collective Behavior and Social Movements, 1993; River through Illinois, 2007. EDITOR/CO-EDITOR: Confrontation: Psychology and the Problems of Today, 1970; Racial Conflict: Tension and Change in American Society, 1971; Muckraking Sociology: Research as Social Criticism, 1972; Sociology: Classic and Popular Approaches, 1979; Undercover: Police Surveillance in Comparative Perspective, 1995; (with J.C. Alexander and C.L. Williams) Self, Social Structure, and Beliefs: Explorations in Sociology, 2005. CONTRIBUTOR: Readings in Negro Life and History, 1967; Is Anybody Listening to Black America?, 1968; Sociological Perspectives: Readings in Deviant Behavior and Social Problems, 1968; Law and Order: A Panacea?, 1968; Blacks in America: An Anthology, 1969; Power, Participation and Ideology, 1969; The Negro American and White Racism, 1970; Sociological Essays and Research: Introductory Readings, 1970; Black Americans: A Second Look, 1970; Study of Society, 1970; The Black Church in America, 1971; Society as It Is, 1971; Cities under Siege, 1971; Black Revolt: Strategies of Protest, 1972; Issues in Social Inequality, 1972; Black Political Power: A Reader, 1972; Collective Violence, 1972; The Personality Patterns of Black Americans, 1972; Black Psyche, 1972; Religion in Sociological Perspective, 1973; The Sociological Perspective, 1973; Social Psychology and Everyday Life, 1973; American Government and Politics, 1973; Research in Religious Behavior, 1974; The Social Meanings of Religion, 1974; Privacy in a Free Society, 1974; Criminology: A Radical Perspective, 1974; Social Movements, 1974; Vigilantism, 1975; Criminal Justice Research, 1976; Issues in Race and Ethnic Relations, 1977; Official Deviance, 1977; Performance Measures and Analytical Tools, 1978; The Dynamics of Social Movements, 1979; Social Theory and Research: A Critical Appraisal, 1981; Social Movements, 1982; An Introduction to Social Research, 1982; Legal Processes and Corrections, 1982; Encyclopedia of Crime and Justice, 1983; Police Issues, 1983; Studies in the Sociology of Social Problems, 1984; Deviant Behavior: Readings in the Sociology of Deviance, 1984; Police Ethics: Hard Choices in Law Enforcement, 1985; The Social Fabric, 1986; Policy Studies Review Annual, 1986; Essays in the Sociology of Social Control, 1988; New Directions in the Study of Law and Social Control, 1989; Authors of Their Own Lives: Intellectual Autobiographies by Twenty American Sociologists, 1990. **Address:** Massachusetts Institute of Technology, 77 Massachusetts Ave., Cambridge, MA 02139, U.S.A. **Online address:** gtmarx@bainbridge.net

MARX, Jeffrey. American (born United States), b. 1962. **Genres:** Sports/Fitness, Biography. **Career:** Wendy Marx Foundation for Organ Donor Awareness, co-founder and director, 1990-; Lexington Herald-Leader, staff. Journalist and public speaker. **Publications:** (With C. Lewis) Inside

Track: My Professional Life in Amateur Track and Field, 1990; (with C. Lewis) One More Victory Lap, 1996; It Gets Dark Sometimes, 2000; Season of Life: A Football Star, a Boy, a Journey to Manhood, 2004; The Long Snapper: A Second Chance, a Super Bowl, a Lesson for Life, 2009. Contributor to periodicals. **Address:** Baton Rouge, LA , U.S.A. **Online address:** jeffrey@jeffreymarx.org

MARX, Robert (Frank). American (born United States), b. 1933. **Genres:** Archaeology/Antiquities, Children's Non-fiction, History, Travel/Exploration. **Career:** USMC Diving School, director, 1955-56; International Minerals & Chemicals, oceanographic consultant, 1959-60; Saturday Evening Post, adventure editor, 1960-63; Dive Magazine, contributing editor, 1965-74; Jamaican Government, underwater archaeologist, 1965-68; Argosy Magazine, archaeology editor, 1967-78; Real Eight Co., underwater archaeological consultant and director of research and salvage, 1968-71; Ocean Industry Insurers, Ltd., consultant, 1971-97; Seafinders Inc., director and vice-president, 1971-74; Aquarius Magazine, contributing editor, 1972-76; University of California, president, faculty, 1974, 1975; Sea World Enterprises Inc., president, 1974-76; LOST Inc., expedition leader, 1978; Phoenician Explorations, operations director, 1979-2002; Phoenician South Seas Exploration, director of operations, 1979-, managing director, 1986-95; Tanit Corp., president, 1982-; Circle Bar Salvage of Louisiana Inc., president, 1984-98; Seahawk Deep Ocean Technology, archaeological consultant, 1988-2002; Port Royal Museum of Sunken Treasure, curator and director, 1993-96; Princess Cruise Lines, lecturer, 1993-95; Last Galleon Inc., archaeological consultant, 1997-; Africub Ltd., archaeological consultant, 1997-2005; Simex Entertainment, Maritime Historical Consultant, 1998-2003; Maritime Archaeological Partners Inc., managing director, 1999-2004; Double Anchor Salvage Inc., president, 1999-2005; Neptune's Bounty, archaeological consultant, 1999-2005; Sea Research Society, founding member; Spanish Government, Order of Isabella the Catholic, knight-commander; Oceanic Cruise Lines, lecturer, 2005-06; Cunard Cruise Lines, lecturer, 2006-. **Publications:** Historia de Isla de Cozumel, 1959; The Voyage of the Niña II, 1963; Following Columbus (children's), 1964; The Battle of the Spanish Armada 1588 (children's), 1965; The Battle of Lepanto 1571 (children's), 1966; They Dared the Deep, 1967; Pirate Port: The Story of the Sunken City of Port Royal, 1967; Always Another Adventure, 1967; Treasure Fleets of the Spanish Main, 1968; Brass and Copper Items Recovered from the Sunken City of Port Royal: May 1, 1966-March 31, 1968, 1968; Clay Smoking Pipes Recovered from the Sunken City of Port Royal October 1, 1967-March 31, 1968, 1968; Shipwrecks in Florida Waters, 1969; Shipwrecks in Mexican Waters, 1971; Shipwrecks of the Western Hemisphere, 1971; Naufragios en aguas mexicanas, 1971; Sea Fever: Famous Underwater Explorers, 1972; Port Royal Rediscovered, 1973; The Lure of Sunken Treasure, 1973; Secrets Beneath the Sea, 1975; The Underwater Dig, 1975, rev. ed., 1989; Still More Adventures, 1976; Capture of the Spanish Plate Fleet: 1628, 1976; Capture of the Treasure Fleet: The Story of Piet Heyn, 1977; Spanish Treasures in Florida Waters, 1978; Buried Treasures of the United States, 1978, rev. ed., 1987; Into the Deep, 1978; Spanish Treasure in Florida Waters, 1979; Diving for Adventure, 1979; Buried Treasure of the United States: How and Where to Locate Hidden Wealth, 1980; Quest for Treasure, 1982; The True Story of Robert Marx's Unrelenting Struggle against Storms, Sharks, Political Intrigue and Modern-day Pirates in his Effort to Recover this Lost 1656 King's Treasure, 1982; Shipwrecks in Florida Waters, 1985; Shipwrecks in the Americas, 1987; The History of Underwater Explorations, 1990; Sunken Treasure: How to Find It, 1990; (with J. Marx) In Quest of the Great White Gods, 1991; (with J. Marx) The Search for Sunken Treasure, 1993; Buried Treasures You Can Find, 1993; (with J. Marx) New World Shipwrecks, 1994; Deep, Deeper, Deepest, 1998; In the Wake of Galleons, 2001; (with V. Sandz) Encyclopedia of Western Atlantic Shipwrecks and Sunken Treasure, 2001; (co-author) Treasures from the Sea, 2003; Port Royal: The Sunken City, 2003; (with J.G. Marx) Treasure Lost at Sea: Diving to the World's Great Shipwrecks, 2004; (with J. Marx) World's Richest Wrecks: A Wreck Diver's Guide to Gold and Silver Treasures of the Seas, 2009; My Name's not Joe, forthcoming. **Address:** RS Operations L.L.C., 909 Mossville Rd., PO Box 3074, Peoria, IL 61615, U.S.A. **Online address:** rmarx@cfl.rr.com

MARX, Steven. American (born United States), b. 1942. **Genres:** Literary Criticism And History, Poetry. **Career:** California Polytechnic University, professor of English, 1988-. Writer. **Publications:** Youth against Age: Generational Strife in Renaissance Poetry, 1985; Shakespeare and the Bible, 2000; (ed.) Cal Poly Land: A Field Guide, 2002. Contributor to books and periodicals. **Address:** Department of English, California Polytechnic University, 47-25E Bldg., San Luis Obispo, CA 93407, U.S.A. **Online address:** smarx@calpoly.edu

MARY GILBERT *See* **DeFrees, Madeline.**

MARZLUFF, John M. American (born United States) **Genres:** Environmental Sciences/Ecology, Biology, Animals/Pets, Adult Non-fiction. **Career:** University of Washington, College of Forest Resources, associate professor of ecosystem sciences, Denman professor of sustainable resource science, professor of wildlife science, Denman chair, Urban Ecology Program, director; U.S. Fish and Wildlife Service's Recovery Team, leader. Writer. **Publications:** NONFICTION: (with R.P. Balda) The Pinyon Jay: Behavioral Ecology of a Colonial Cooperative Corvid, 1992; (ed. with R. Sallabanks) Avian Conservation: Research and Management, 1998; (ed.) Radiotelemetry and Animal Populations, 2001; (ed. with R. Bowman and R. Donnelly) Avian Ecology and Conservation in an Urbanizing World, 2001; (with T. Angell) In the Company of Crows and Ravens, 2005. **Address:** College of Forest Resources, University of Washington, 123E Anderson Hall, 4000 15th Ave. NE, PO Box 352100, Seattle, WA 98195-2100, U.S.A. **Online address:** corvid@u.washington.edu

MASALHA, Nur. British/Palestinian (born Palestine), b. 1957. **Genres:** International Relations/Current Affairs, Politics/Government, Area Studies, History, Philosophy, Theology/Religion, Reference, Translations, Translations. **Career:** Hebrew University, teaching and research assistant, 1979-82; Neve Shalom School for Peace, director, 1982-83; University of London, part-time lecturer, 1985-86; Institute for Palestine Studies, Constantine Zurayk research fellow, 1989-92; University of Bristol, part-time lecturer in development, administration and planning with special reference to the Middle East, 1991; University of Durham, Centre for Middle Eastern and Islamic Studies, honorary fellow, 1993-; London College, lecturer, 1994; Birzeit University, assistant professor, 1994-95, Richmond International University in London, Middle East Politics, 1997-2000; School of Oriental and African Studies, University of London, research associate, 2000-04; St. Mary's College, University of Surrey, research fellow, director of Holy Land Research Project and senior lecturer, 2001-, Centre for Religion and History, director, 2007-, professor, 2009. Writer. **Publications:** Tard al-Filastīnīyīn: Mafhūm al-trānsfīr fīal-fikr wa-al-takhtīt al-Suhyūnīyyan, 1882-1948 in US as Expulsion of the Palestinians: The Concept of Transfer in Zionist Political Thought, 1882-1948, 1992; (ed. and trans.) The Palestinians in Israel: Is Israel the State of all Its Citizens and Absentees?, 1993; An Israeli Plan to Transfer Galilee's Christians to South America: Yosef Weitz and Operation Yohanan, 1949-53, 1996; Ard akthar wa-Arab aqall: Siyāsat al-Trānsfīr al-Isrāīlīyah fīal-tatbīq, 1949-1996, 1997; A Land Without a People, 1997; Imperial Israel and the Palestinians: The Politics of Expansion, 1967-2000, 2000; Israeel al-Kubra wal-Filistiniyyun: Siyasat al-Tawasu', 2001; Teorias De La Expansion Territorial, 2002; The Politics of Denial: Israel and the Palestinian Refugee Problem, 2003; Israeel wa-Siyasat al-Nafi, 2003; (ed.) Catastrophe Remembered: Palestine, Israel and the Internal Refugees: Papers in Memory of Edward W. Said, 1935-2003, 2005; Politicas De La Negación: Israel Y Los Refugiados Palestininos, 2005; (ed.) The Nakba, Memory and Identity, 2006; Religion and the State in Israel and Palestine, 2006; Bible and Zionism: Invented Traditions, Archaeology and Post-Colonialism in Palestine-Israel, 2007. Contributor to journals. **Address:** School of Theology, Philosophy and History, St. Mary's College, Strawberry Hill, Waldegrave Rd., Twickenham, SR TW1 4SX, England. **Online address:** masalhan@smuc.ac.uk

MASCO, Joseph P. American (born United States), b. 1964?. **Genres:** Military/Defense/Arms Control, Adult Non-fiction, History, Humanities. **Career:** University of Oregon, Department of Anthropology, assistant professor, 2000-01; University of Chicago, Department of Anthropology, assistant professor, 2001-08, associate professor, 2008-, Chicago Center for Contemporary Theory, associated faculty, 2008-. Writer. **Publications:** The Nuclear Borderlands: The Manhattan Project in Post-Cold War New Mexico, 2006. Contributor to journals. **Address:** Department of Anthropology, University of Chicago, 1126 E 59th St., Chicago, IL 60637, U.S.A. **Online address:** jmasco@uchicago.edu

MASEKELA, Hugh. South African (born South Africa), b. 1939. **Genres:** Music, Autobiography/Memoirs, Biography. **Career:** Writer. **Publications:** (With D.M. Cheers) Still Grazing: The Musical Journey of Hugh Masekela, 2004. **Address:** c/o Author Mail, Random House Inc., 1745 Broadway, New York, NY 10019, U.S.A. **Online address:** hrm@starafrica.co.za

MASELLO, Robert. American (born United States), b. 1952. **Genres:** Novels, Young Adult Non-fiction. **Career:** Claremont McKenna College, visiting lecturer in literature, 2002-08. Writer. **Publications:** The Spirit Wood, 1987; Black Horizon, 1989; Private Demons, 1992; Papa-tudes, 1992; (comp.) Of Course I Love You, 1993; (comp.) Proverbial Wisdom: A Treasury of the World's Greatest Proverbs, 1993; Fallen Angels: And Spirits of the Dark, 1994; Vigil (novel), 2005; Bestiary (novel), 2006; Blood and Ice (novel), 2009. NON-FICTION: What Do Men Want from Women?, 1983; The Things Your Father Never Taught You, 1995; Raising Hell: A Concise History of the Black Arts--And Those Who Dared to Practice Them, 1996; A Friend in the Business: Honest Advice for Anyone Trying to Break into Television Writing, 2000; Writer Tells All: Insider Secrets to Getting Your Book Published, 2001; Robert's Rules of Writing: 101 Unconventional Lessons Every Writer Needs to Know, 2005. Contributor to periodicals and journals. **Address:** Santa Monica, CA , U.S.A. **Online address:** rmasello4@aol.com

MASER, Chris. American (born United States), b. 1938. **Genres:** Agriculture/Forestry, Area Studies, Zoology. **Career:** Yale University, vertebrate zoologist with prehistoric expedition, 1963-64; University of Puget Sound, Puget Sound Museum of Natural History, field associate, 1965-71, Oregon Coast Ecological Survey, principal investigator, 1970-72, assistant curator of mammals, 1971-73, associate curator, 1973-81, lecturer in natural history and ecology, 1973-74; U.S. Naval Medical Research Unit, mammalogist, 1966-67; U.S. Forest Service, scientific collaborator, 1971-87, Federal Research Natural Area System, senior summer scientist, 1974; Eastern Oregon State College, adjunct professor, 1975-80; U.S. Department of the Interior's Bureau of Land Management, District Office, research zoologist, 1975-77; Oregon State Office, wildlife biologist and research liaison, 1977-81, research wildlife biologist, 1981-87; Oregon State University, assistant professor of forestry, 1981-88; University of Washington, Burke Museum, museum research associate in zoology, 1986-; private consultant, 1988-90; U.S. Environmental Protection Agency, Environmental Monitoring Systems Laboratory, landscape ecologist, 1990-91; writer and private consultant, 1991-; UNESCO, International Biosphere Reserves, consultant; Washington Park Zoo, International Biosphere Reserves, consultant. **Publications:** (With R.M. Storm) A Key to Microtinae of the Pacific Northwest: Oregon, Washington, Idaho, 1970; (co-author) Federal Research Natural Areas in Oregon and Washington: A Guidebook for Scientists and Educators, 1972; (co-author) Research Natural Area Needs in the Pacific Northwest: A Contribution to Land-Use Planning, 1975; (ed. with J.W. Thomas and contrib.) Wildlife Habitats in Managed Rangelands: The Great Basin of Southeastern Oregon, 1979; (contrib.) Wildlife Habitats in Managed Forests: The Blue Mountains of Oregon and Washington, 1979; (co-author) Natural History of Oregon Coast Mammals, 1981; (contrib.) Elk of North America: Ecology and Management, 1982; (contrib.) The Fragmented Forest: Island Biogeography Theory and the Preservation of Biotic Diversity, 1984; (co-ed. and contrib.) From the Forest to the Sea: A Story of Fallen Trees, 1988; (with R.E. Lewis and J.H. Lewis) Fleas of the Pacific Northwest, 1988; The Redesigned Forest, 1988; The Forest Primeval: The Natural History of an Ancient Forest, 1989; (co-author) Synoptic Spore Key to Genera of Hypogeous Fungi in Northern Temperate Forests, with Special Reference to Animal Mycophagy, 1989; (with J.R. Sedell) Driftwood, 1991; The Crucible of Change, 1991; Global Imperative: Harmonizing Culture and Nature, 1992; (with J.R. Sedell) From the Forest to the Sea: The Ecology of Wood in Streams, Rivers, Estuaries and Oceans, 1994; Sustainable Forestry: Philosophy, Science and Economics, 1994; (with C.A. Pollio) Resolving Environmental Conflicts, 1996, 2nd ed., 2012; Sustainable Community Development, 1997; Mammals of the Pacific Northwest: From the Coast to the High Cascades, 1998; (with R. Beaton and K. Smith) Setting the Stage for Sustainability: Citizen's Handbook, 1998; Vision and Leadership in Sustainable Development, 1998; (with R. Beaton) Reuniting Economics and Ecology in Sustainable Development, 1999; (with R. Beaton) Reuniting Economy and Ecology in Sustainable Development, 1999; Ecological Diversity in Sustainable Development: The Vital and Forgotten Dimension, 1999; (with W. Smith) Forest Certification in Sustainable Development: Healing the Landscape, 2000; (with J. Silberstein) Land-Use Planning for Sustainable Development, 2000; (with Z. Maser) World is in My Garden: A Journey of Consciousness, 2001; The Perpetual Consequences of Fear and Violence: Rethinking the Future, 2004; Evaluating Sustainable Development: Giving People a Voice in their Destiny, 2004; Our Forest Legacy: Today's Decisions, Tomorrow's Consequences, 2005; (with J.G. Wiesner) Teaching Kids to Change the World: Lessons to Inspire Social Responsibility for Grades 6-12, 2008; (with A.W. Claridge and J.M. Trappe) Trees, Truffles, and Beasts: How Forests Function, 2008; (ed. with O. Ukaga and M. Reichenbach) Sustainable Development: Principles, Frameworks, And Case Studies, 2009; Earth in Our Care: Ecology, Economy and Sustainability, 2009; (ed. with O. Ukaga and M. Reichenbach) Sustainable Development: Principles, Frameworks, and Case Studies, 2010; Social-Environmental Planning: The Design Interface Between Everyforest and Everycity, 2010; (with C.R. Beaton) Economics and Ecology, 2012. Contributor of articles to books and journals. **Address:** Stillpoint Publishing, Meetinghouse Rd., PO Box 640, Walpole, NH 03608-0640, U.S.A. **Online address:** information@chrismaser.com

MASER, Shari. American (born United States), b. 1967. **Genres:** Human Relations/Parenting, Young Adult Fiction, Social Sciences. **Career:** Writer. **Publications:** Blessingways: A Guide to Mother-Centered Baby Showers-Celebrating Pregnancy, Birth, and Motherhood, 2004. Contributor to periodicals. **Address:** c/o Author Mail, Moondance Press, 4830 Dawson Dr., Ann Arbor, MI 48103-9484, U.S.A.

MASINI, Donna. American (born United States), b. 1954. **Genres:** Novels, Poetry, Young Adult Non-fiction. **Career:** The Writer's Voice, educator and novelist; West Side YMCA, teacher, 1992-; freelance author, 1994-; City University of New York, Hunter College, associate professor of English, 1995-, MFA Creative Writing Program, faculty, 1995-; New York University, faculty; Columbia University, faculty. **Publications:** That Kind of Danger, 1994; About Yvonne, 1997; Turning to Fiction: Poems, 2004; The Good Enough Mother, forthcoming. Contributor to periodicals. **Address:** c/o Gail Hochman, Brandt and Hochman Literary Agents Inc., 1501 Broadway, Ste. 2310, New York, NY 10036-5600, U.S.A. **Online address:** dmasini@hunter.cuny.edu

MASINI, Eleonora Barbieri. Italian/Guatemalan (born Guatemala), b. 1928. **Genres:** Social Sciences, Young Adult Fiction. **Career:** Center for Istituto Ricerche Applicate Documentazione E Studi, director of social forecasting, 1970-75; United Nations Educational, Scientific and Cultural Organization, Childrens Images of the Future, director of research, 1972-78, Women's International Network, co-ordinator, 1995-2005; World Futures Studies Federation, secretary, 1975-80; Pontifical Commission Justice and Peace, consultant, 1976-81; Gregorian University, Faculty of Social Sciences, professor of futures studies, 1976-2004, director of a course in social forecasting, 1977, professor of human ecology, 1991-2004, professor emeritus of futures studies and human ecology, 2004-; United Nations University, Visions of Desirable Societies, director of research, 1978-, coordinator of project on household, gender and age, 1984-90; World Futures Studies Federation, president, 1980-90, chair, 1990-93; St. Cloud University, Futures Studies and Women and Development, Fullbright professor, 1985-86; European Division of the World Academy of Art and Science, president, 1991-94; Writer. **Publications:** Space for Man, 1973; Social and Human Forecasting, 1973; Social Indicators and Forecasting: Forecasting Methods, 1977; (ed.) Visiones de sociedades deseables, 1979; Società e futuro: crisi dell'Occidente, esaurimento del suo modello di sviluppo e le possibili alternative, 1981; (co-author) Sociedad y Utopía, 1983; A Vision of Desirable Societies, 1983; (co-ed.) Questione etica: una sfida dalla memoria, 1990; (ed. with S. Stratigos) Women, Households and Change, 1991; Why Futures Studies?, 1993; Futures of Cultures, 1994; Penser le futur, 2000. Contributor to periodicals. **Address:** Faculty of Social Sciences, Gregorian University, Via Antonio Bertoloni 23, Rome, 00197, Italy. **Online address:** e.masini@mclink.it

MASKALYK, James. Canadian (born Canada), b. 1973?. **Genres:** Biography. **Career:** University of Toronto, Division of Emergency Medicine, Department of Medicine, assistant professor, St. Michael's Hospital, doctor; Open Medicine Journal, editor. **Publications:** Six Months in Sudan: A Young Doctor in a War-torn Village, 2009. **Address:** St. Michael's Hospital, University of Toronto, EPA, Rm. 1-008E Shuter Wing, 30 Bond St., Toronto, ON M5B 1W8, Canada. **Online address:** james.maskalyk@utoronto.ca

MASKARINEC, Gregory G. American (born United States), b. 1951?. **Genres:** Anthropology/Ethnology, Medicine/Health, Mythology/Folklore, Language/Linguistics, Social Sciences, Translations. **Career:** University of Hawaii, John A. Burns School of Medicine, associate professor, Department of Family Practice and Community Health, research director, director of cross-cultural curriculum 1999-; University of Zurich, visiting professor, 2000; University of Paris, faculty, 2003. Writer. **Publications:** The Rulings of the Night: An Ethnographic Study of Nepalese Shaman Oral Texts, 1995; Nepalese Shaman Oral Texts, 1998; Nepalese Shaman Oral Texts II, 2008. Contributor to books and journals. **Address:** Department of Family Medicine and Community Health, John A Burns School of Medicine, Physician

Center Mililani, 95-390 Kualielani Ave., Mililani, HI 96789, U.S.A. **Online address:** gregorym@hawaii.edu

MASLON, Laurence. American (born United States), b. 1959. **Genres:** Music, Business/Trade/Industry. **Career:** Arena Stage, associate artistic director; New York University, Tisch School of the Arts, Graduate Acting Program, associate arts professor, associate chair, Graduate Musical Theatre Writing Program, faculty; Public Broadcasting Service senior consultant. Writer. **Publications:** (Adapter) Conquest of the South Pole, 1990; (and ed.) The Arena Adventure: The First 40 Years, 1990; Broadway: The American Musical, 2004; (ed.) Kaufman & Co.: Broadway Comedies by George S. Kaufman, Edna Ferber, Moss Hart, Ring Lardner, and Morrie Ryskind, 2004; The Sound of Music Companion, 2007; The South Pacific Companion, 2007; Make 'Em Laugh: The Funny Business of America, 2008; The Some Like It Hot Companion, 2009. **Address:** Graduate Acting Program, Tisch School of the Arts, 721 Broadway, 5th Fl., New York, NY 10003, U.S.A.

MASO, Carole. American (born United States), b. 1956. **Genres:** Novels, Photography. **Career:** Illinois State University, writer-in-residence, 1991-92; George Washington University, writer-in-residence, 1992-93; Columbia University, associate professor, 1993-95; Brown University, Creative Writing Program, visiting writer-in-residence, 1994, director, 1995-98, associate professor of English, 1995-98, professor of literary arts, 1995-. Writer. **Publications:** NOVELS: The Art Lover: A Novel, 1990; Ava: A Novel, 1993; The American Woman in the Chinese Hat, 1994; Ghost Dance, 1995; Defiance, 1998. OTHERS: Aureole, 1996; Break Every Rule: Essays on Language, Longing and Moments of Desire, 2000; Room Lit by Roses: A Journal of Pregnancy and Birth, 2000; Beauty is Convulsive: The Passion of Frida Kahlo, 2002. Contributor to books and periodicals. Works appear in anthologies. **Address:** Georges Borchardt Inc., 136 E 57th St., New York, NY 10022, U.S.A. **Online address:** carole_maso@brown.edu

MASON, Adrienne. Canadian (born Canada), b. 1962. **Genres:** Young Adult Fiction, Children's Fiction, Adult Non-fiction, Earth Sciences, Geography, Animals/Pets. **Career:** Freelance writer and editor, 1991-; Raincoast Communications, hiking guide and biologist; Bamfield Marine Science Center, public education coordinator; Jasper National Park, teacher; Bluewater Adventures, teacher; West Island College, teacher. **Publications:** NONFICTION: The Green Classroom: 101 Practical Ways to Involve Students in Environmental Issues, 1991; Oceans: Looking at Beaches and Coral Reefs Tides and Currents Sea Mammals and Fish Seaweeds and Other Ocean Wonders, 1995; Living Things, 1997; Mealworms: Raise Them, Watch Them, See Them Change, 1998; The Nature of Spiders: Consummate Killers, 1999, rev. ed. as The World of the Spider, 1999; Whales, Dolphins and Porpoises, 1999; The World of Marine Mammals, 1999; Bats, 2003; Otters, 2003; West Coast Adventures: Shipwrecks, Lighthouses, and Rescues along Canada's West Coast, 2003; Tales from the West Coast: Smugglers, Sea Monsters, and Other Stories, 2003; Owls, 2004; Snakes, 2005; Move It!: Forces, Motion, and You, 2005; Touch It!: Materials, Matter, and You, 2005; Build It!: Structures, Systems, and You, and Change It!: Solids, Liquids, Gases, and You, 2006; Skunks, 2006; Robots, 2008. LU AND CLANCY SERIES FICTION: Lu and Clancy's Secret Codes, 1999; Lu and Clancy's Spy Stuff, 2000; Lu and Clancy's Carnival Caper, 2002; Lu and Clancy Sound Off, 2002; The Drop of Doom, 2007; (with D. Suzuki and A. McConell) The Sacred Balance: Rediscovering Our Place in Nature, 2008; Lost and Found, 2008; Secret Spies, 2008; 18 Meditations on Chesterman Beach, 2011. Contributor to periodicals. **Address:** PO Box 386, Tofino, BC V0R 2Z0, Canada. **Online address:** ak_mason@telus.net

MASON, Alane Salierno. American (born United States), b. 1964. **Genres:** Writing/Journalism, Young Adult Fiction, Biography. **Career:** W.W. Norton, senior editor. Translator. **Publications:** (Trans.) E. Vittorini, Conversations in Sicily, 2000; (ed. with S. Schnee and D. Felman) Words without Borders: The World through the Eyes of Writers, 2007. Contributor to periodicals. **Address:** W.W. Norton & Co., 500 5th Ave., New York, NY 10110, U.S.A.

MASON, Anita. British (born England), b. 1942. **Genres:** Novels, Young Adult Fiction, Education. **Career:** Trinity and All Saints College, writer-in-residence, 1983-84; Bath Spa University, fellow, 1999-2002; University of Warwick, fellow, 2003-09, Warwick Writing Programme, honorary teaching fellow. **Publications:** (Ed.) The Spastic School Child and the Outside World: Based on the Proceedings of a Study Group at St. Edmund Hall, 1966. NOVELS: Illustrated Dictionary of Jewellery, 1973; Bethany, 1981; The Illusionist, 1984; The War against Chaos, 1988; The Racket, 1990, 2nd ed., 2002; Reich Angel, 1994 as Angel in England, 1994; The Yellow Cathedral, 2002; Perfection, 2003; The Right Hand of the Sun, 2008; Stranded, 2009; Hummingbird, forthcoming. **Address:** c/o Jennifer Kavanagh, 44 Langham St., London, GL W1N 5RG, England. **Online address:** anita.mason@warwick.ac.uk

MASON, Bobbie Ann. American (born United States), b. 1940. **Genres:** Novels, Novellas/Short Stories, Literary Criticism And History, Autobiography/Memoirs, Young Adult Non-fiction, Young Adult Fiction, Biography. **Career:** Mayfield Messenger, writer, 1960; Mansfield State College, assistant professor of English, 1972-79; University of Kentucky, writer-in-residence, 2001-. **Publications:** Nabokov's Garden: A Nature Guide to Ada, 1974; The Girl Sleuth: A Feminist Guide to the Bobbsey Twins, Nancy Drew and Their Sisters, 1975; Shiloh and Other Stories, 1982; Landscapes, 1984; In Country: A Novel, 1985; Spence and Lila, 1988; Love Life: Stories, 1989; (co-author) Late Harvest: Rural American Writing, 1992; Feather Crowns: A Novel, 1993; (ed. and intro.) Midnight Magic: Selected Stories of Bobbie Ann Mason, 1998; Clear Springs: A Memoir, 1999; Zigzagging Down a Wild Trail, 2001; Elvis Presley, 2003; An Atomic Romance: A Novel, 2005; (ed. with K. Johannsen and M.A. Taylor-Hall) Missing Mountains, 2005; Nancy Culpepper: Stories, 2006; The Girl in the Blue Beret: A Novel, 2011. Works appear in anthologies. Contributor to periodicals. **Address:** Department of English, University of Kentucky, 1239 Patterson Office Twr., Lexington, KY 40506-0027, U.S.A. **Online address:** bamaso2@uky.edu

MASON, Christopher. British (born England), b. 1960. **Genres:** Social Commentary, Songs/Lyrics And Libretti, Criminology/True Crime, Design, Homes/Gardens, Travel/Exploration, Writing/Journalism. **Career:** Writer, journalist and photographer. **Publications:** Christopher Mason's Songs for the Rich and Famous, 1990; The Art of the Steal: Inside the Sothebys-Christies Auction House Scandal, 2004; Corruption in High Places, forthcoming. Contributor to journals. **Address:** 135 W 12th St., Ste. 3R, New York, NY 10011, U.S.A. **Online address:** christopher@christopher-mason.com

MASON, Connie. American (born United States), b. 1930. **Genres:** Romance/Historical. **Career:** Writer, 1983-. **Publications:** HISTORICAL ROMANCE NOVELS: Tender Fury, 1984; Caress and Conquer, 1985; For Honor's Sake, 1985; Promised Splendor, 1986; My Lady Vixen, 1986; Desert Ecstasy, 1987; Wild Is My Heart, 1987; Bold Land, Bold Love, 1988; Tempt the Devil, 1988; Beyond the Horizon, 1989; Love Me with Fury, 1989; Wild Love, Wild Land (NYC), 1989; Promise Me Forever, 1990; Brave Land, Brave Love, 1990; Surrender to the Fury, 1990; The Greatest Gift of All, 1990; Ice and Rapture, 1991; Lord of the Night, 1991; Treasures of the Heart, 1993; Christmas Star, 1992; Tears Like Rain, 1993; Wind Rider, 1993; A Promise of Thunder, 1993; A Child Is Born, 1993; Sierra, 1994; A Christmas Miracle, 1994; The Lion's Bride, 1994; Pure Temptation, 1996; A Love to Cherish, 1996; Flame, 1997; Shadow Walker, 1997; To Love a Stranger, 1997; Sheik, 1997; Viking!, 1998; To Tame a Renegade, 1998; Pirate, 1998, rev. ed., 2003; To Tempt a Rogue, 1999; Gunslinger, 1999; The Black Knight, 1999; The Outlaws: Jess, 2000; A Taste of Sin, 2000; The Outlaws: Rafe, 2000; A Breath of Scandal, 2001; The Outlaws: Sam, 2001; The Dragon Lord, 2001; A Touch So Wicked, 2002; The Rogue and the Hellion, 2002; Taken by You, 2002; Lionheart, 2002; Seduced by a Rogue, 2003; Laird of Stonehaven, 2003; The Last Rogue, 2004; Pirate Prince, 2004; Gypsy Lover, 2005; A Knights Honor, 2005; A Taste of Paradise, 2006; The Price Of Pleasure, 2007; Highland Warrior, 2007; Viking Warrior, 2008. SHORT STORIES: (with M. Baker, N. Hess and E. Chadwick) A Wilderness Christmas, 1993; (with T. Devine, M. Caudill and M. Campbell) Swept Away, 1998; (with L. Greenwood, B. Hutchinson and T. Scott) Their First Noel, 1998; (with L. Greenwood, N. McFather and S. Tanner) An Old-Fashioned Southern Christmas, 1999; (with N. Hess, R.L. Hatcher and M. Baker) A Frontier Christmas, 1999. OTHERS: To Tame Renegade, 1998; Sins of the Highlander, 2010; Lord of Devil Isle, 2010; (with M. Marlowe) Lord of Fire and Ice, 2012. Contributor to periodicals. **Address:** PO Box 3471, Holiday, FL 34690, U.S.A.

MASON, Daniel. (Daniel Philippe). American (born United States), b. 1976?. **Genres:** Novels, Young Adult Fiction, Literary Criticism And History. **Career:** Writer. **Publications:** The Piano Tuner, 2002; A Far Country, 2007. Contributor to periodicals. **Address:** c/o Author Mail, Knopf Publishing, 1745 Broadway, 4th Fl., New York, NY 10019, U.S.A.

MASON, David. American (born United States), b. 1954. **Genres:** Poetry, Literary Criticism And History, Music. **Career:** Moorhead State University, assistant professor, associate professor of English, 1989-98; Colorado College, assistant professor, 1998-2000, associate professor of English, 2000-09, professor, 2009-. Writer. **Publications:** (With M. Jarman) Rebel Angels: Twenty-Five Poets of the New Formalism, 1996; The Poetry of Life and the Life of Poetry: Essays and Reviews, 2000; (with J.F. Nims) Western Wind: An Introduction to Poetry, 2000, 5th ed., 2006; (co-ed.) Twentieth-Century American Poetry, 2004; (co-ed.) Twentieth-Century American Poetics: Poets on the Art of Poetry, 2004; Poems from the Baca Grande: A Tenth Anniversary Celebration of Poetry West at the Baca, 2004; Swimmers on the Shore: For Baritone Voice and Piano, 2004; Vedem, an Oratorio, with Lori Laitman, 2010. POETRY: The Buried Houses, 1991; The Country I Remember, 1996; Arrivals, 2004; Ludlow: A Verse Novel, 2007. MEMOIR: News from the Village, 2010. ESSAYS: Two Minds of a Western Poet, 2011. LIBRETTO: The Scarlet Libretto, 2012. Contributor to journals. **Address:** Department of English, Colorado College, 237 Armstrong, 14 E Cache la Poudre St., Colorado Springs, CO 80903-3298, U.S.A. **Online address:** dmason@coloradocollege.edu

MASON, David. (David Peter Mason). American (born United States), b. 1951. **Genres:** Novels, Mystery/Crime/Suspense. **Career:** Writer. **Publications:** Shadow over Babylon (novel), 1993. **Address:** c/o Dutton Publishers, 375 Hudson St., New York, NY 10014-3658, U.S.A.

MASON, David Peter. *See* **MASON, David.**

MASON, Felicia. American (born United States), b. 1962. **Genres:** Romance/Historical, Novels. **Career:** Journalist, novelist, college professor, motivational speaker. **Publications:** For the Love of You, 1995; Body and Soul, 1995; Seduction, 1996; Rhapsody, 1997; Foolish Heart, 1998; (with A. Byrd and D. Johnson) Man of the house, 1998; Forbidden Heart, 2000; (contrib.) Della's House of Style, 2000; Testimony, 2002; (contrib.) The Best Man, 2003; Sweet Accord, 2003; Gabriel's Discovery, 2004; Enchanted Heart, 2004; Sweet Devotion, 2004; Sweet Harmony, 2004; (with J. Thomas and F. Ray) How Sweet the Sound, 2005; Seductive Hearts, 2005; What Ana Mae Left Behind, 2005. **Address:** PO Box 1438, Yorktown, VA 23692, U.S.A.

MASON, Fran. British (born England), b. 1962?. **Genres:** Literary Criticism And History, Art/Art History, Film. **Career:** University of Winchester, lecturer in humanities. Writer. **Publications:** American Gangster Cinema: From Little Caesar to Pulp Fiction, 2002; Historical Dictionary of Postmodernist Literature and Theater, 2007. **Address:** Department of English, Creative Writing & American, Studies, University of Winchester, Sparkford Rd., Winchester, HM SO22 4NR, England. **Online address:** fran.mason@winchester.ac.uk

MASON, Haydn Trevor. British/Welsh (born Wales), b. 1929. **Genres:** Literary Criticism And History, Novellas/Short Stories, Young Adult Nonfiction. **Career:** Princeton University, instructor in French, 1954-57; University of Newcastle, lecturer, 1960-63; University of Reading, lecturer, 1964-65, reader, 1965-67; University of East Anglia, professor of European literature, 1967-79; Universite de Paris III, professor, 1979-81; University of Bristol, Department of French, professor, 1981-94, senior research fellow, 1994-, head, professor emeritus, 1994-; Voltaire Complete Works, general editor, 1998-2001. **Publications:** Pierre Bayle and Voltaire, 1963; Voltaire, 1974; Voltaire: A Biography, 1981; Studies on Voltaire and the Eighteenth Century, 1981; The Writer and His Society: France 1715-1800, 1981; Cyrano de Bergerac, L'autre Monde, 1984; Candide: Optimism Demolished, 1992. EDITOR: Marivaux: Les Fausses Confidences, 1964; (and trans.) Leibniz-Arnauld Correspondence, 1967; Voltaire: Zadig and Other Stories, 1971; Voltaire and His World, 1985; Myth and Its Making in the French Theatre, 1988; Pour Encourager les Autres, 1994; Voltaire: Candide, 1995; The Darnton Debate, 1998; Voltaire: Micromégas and Other Short Fictions, 2002. **Address:** Department of French, University of Bristol, 17 Woodland Rd., Bristol, BS8 1TE, England. **Online address:** haydnadrienne@yahoo.co.uk

MASON, J. D. American (born United States) **Genres:** Young Adult Fiction, Novels. **Career:** Writer. **Publications:** NOVELS: And on the Eighth Day She Rested, 2001; One Day I Saw a Black King, 2003; Don't Want No Sugar, 2004; This Fire Down in My Soul, 2007; You Gotta Sin to Get Saved, 2008; That Devil's No Friend of Mine, 2009; Take Your Pleasure Where You Find It, 2010; Somebody Pick Up My Pieces, 2011; Beautiful, Dirty, Rich, 2012; Confessions of the Other Woman, forthcoming. OTHERS: (co-author) Have a Little Faith, 2006; (with V. McGlothin) Sleep Don't Come Easy, 2008. **Address:** c/o Author Mail, St. Martin's Press, 175 5th Ave., New York, NY 10010, U.S.A. **Online address:** j_d_mason2002@yahoo.com

MASON, Jeffrey D(aniel). American (born United States), b. 1952. **Genres:** Plays/Screenplays, Theatre, Novels. **Career:** Drama teacher, 1975-79; University of California, associate instructor in dramatic art, 1980-82; Diablo Valley College, instructor in performing arts, 1982; San Francisco State University, lecturer in theater arts, 1983-84; Kern Art Theatre, founder; California State University, lecturer, 1984-85, assistant professor, 1985-87, associate professor, 1987-92, professor of theater and dance, 1992-2001, Department of Fine Arts, chair, 1991-97, College of Arts and Letters, dean, 2006-10; University of Oregon, professor, Department of Theatre Arts, head, 2001-05, Robert F. and Evelyn Nelson Wulf professor of the humanities, 2003-04, chair; Theatre Survey, book review editor, 2001-04. **Publications:** Wisecracks: The Farces of George S. Kaufman, 1988; Melodrama and the Myth of America, 1993; Cousin Jack (novel), 1996; (ed. with J.E. Gainor) Performing America: Cultural Nationalism in American Theater, 1999; Stone Tower: The Political Theater of Arthur Miller, 2008. Contributor to books and periodicals. **Address:** University of Oregon, Oregon Hall, Eugene, OR 97403, U.S.A. **Online address:** mason@csus.edu

MASON, Jim. American (born United States), b. 1940. **Genres:** Agriculture/Forestry, Animals/Pets, Anthropology/Ethnology, Environmental Sciences/Ecology, Ethics, Race Relations, Theology/Religion, Women's Studies And Issues, Women's Studies And Issues. **Career:** Bridgeport Legal Services, staff attorney, 1969-73; attorney in private family law practice, 1973-80; Friends of Animals, vice president, 1976-80; Animal's Agenda (monthly magazine), founder and editor, 1979-86. **Publications:** (With P. Singer) Animal Factories, 1980, rev. ed., 1990: What Agribusiness Is Doing to the Family Farm, the Environment and Your Health, 1990; Intensive Husbandry Systems, Animal Food Products and Human Health, American Society for the Prevention of Cruelty to Animals, 1990; An Unnatural Order: Uncovering the Roots of Our Domination of Nature and Each Other, 1993; An Unnatural Order: Why We Are Destroying the Planet and Each Other, 1997; (with P. Singer) Way We Eat: Why Our Food Choices Matter, 2006; No Holding Back, 2011. Contributor to periodicals. **Address:** PO Box 381, Mt. Vernon, MO 65712, U.S.A. **Online address:** jbmason@mo-net.com

MASON, Linda. American (born United States), b. 1954?. **Genres:** Administration/Management. **Career:** Booz-Allen, consultant, 1984; Save the Children Federation, Emergency Program, co-director, 1985; Bright Horizons Family Solutions L.L.C., co-founder, 1986-, president, 1986-98, chairman, 1998-; Horizons for Homeless Children, co-founder and board director; Massachusetts State Department of Early Education and Care, founding member; Mercy Corps, chair. Writer. **Publications:** (With R. Brown) Rice, Rivalry, and Politics: Managing Cambodian Relief, 1983; The Working Mother's Guide to Life: Strategies, Secrets, and Solutions, 2002. **Address:** Bright Horizons Family Solutions L.L.C., 200 Talcott Ave. S, Watertown, MA 02472-5705, U.S.A. **Online address:** welcome@brighthorizons.com

MASON, Matthew. (Matthew E. Mason). American (born United States), b. 1968. **Genres:** Politics/Government, Social Sciences, History, Literary Criticism And History. **Career:** University of Maryland, Department of History, graduate assistant, 1995-2002; Eastern Michigan University, Department of History and Philosophy, assistant professor, 2002-03; Brigham Young University, Department of History, assistant professor, 2003-09. Writer. **Publications:** Slavery and Politics in the Early American Republic, 2006; (ed. with N. Mason) The History of the Life and Adventures of Mr. Anderson, 2009; (ed. with J.C. Hammond) Contesting Slavery: The Politics of Bondage and Freedom in the New American Nation, 2011. Contributor of articles to books and journals. **Address:** Department of History, Brigham Young University, 2130 JFSB, Provo, UT 84602, U.S.A. **Online address:** matthew_mason@byu.edu

MASON, Matthew E. *See* **MASON, Matthew.**

MASON, Michael Paul. American (born United States), b. 1971. **Genres:** Medicine/Health, Psychology. **Career:** This Land Press, founder and editor, 2010; Discover Magazine, editor. **Publications:** Head Cases: Stories of Brain Injury and Its Aftermath, 2008. Contributor to periodicals. **Address:** James Fitzgerald Agency, 80 E 11th St., Ste. 301, New York, NY 10003-6000, U.S.A. **Online address:** michaelpmason@gmail.com

MASON, Prue. Australian (born Australia) **Genres:** Young Adult Non-fiction. **Career:** Writer. **Publications:** Camel Rider (young- adult novel), 2007. Contributor to an Australian magazine. **Address:** Maleny, QL , Australia. **Online address:** pruemason@bigpond.com

MASON, Robert. British (born England), b. 1970?. **Genres:** History, Politics/Government. **Career:** University of Edinburgh, lecturer, 1998-2007, senior lecturer in history, 2007-; Library of Congress, John W. Kluge Center, fellow, 2004-05. Writer. **Publications:** Richard Nixon and the Quest for a New Majority, 2004; The Republican Party and American Politics from Hoover to Reagan, 2011. **Address:** School of History, Classics and Archaeology, University of Edinburgh, Doorway 4, Teviot Pl., Edinburgh, EH8 9AG, Scotland. **Online address:** robert.mason@ed.ac.uk

MASON, Robert C(averly). American (born United States), b. 1942. **Genres:** Science Fiction/Fantasy, Autobiography/Memoirs, Biography, History. **Career:** Mirage Design, executive, 1975-77. Writer. **Publications:** Chickenhawk (memoir), 1983; Weapon (science fiction), 1989; (ed. with W.H. Young) Challenge and Change: Creating a New Era of Collaboration in Adult Continuing Education, 1992; Solo, 1992; Chickenhawk: Back in the World, 1993; The Burning, 2000; Dragonfly. Contributor to periodicals. **Address:** c/o Knox Burger, Harold Ober Associates, 425 Madison Ave., 10th Fl., New York, NY 10017, U.S.A.

MASON, Sarah J. (Hamilton Crane). British (born England), b. 1949. **Genres:** Mystery/Crime/Suspense, Novels, Young Adult Fiction, Literary Criticism And History. **Career:** Mystery writer, 1983-. **Publications:** MYSTERY NOVELS: Let's Talk of Wills, 1985; Death on Her Doorstep, 2003. AS HAMILTON CRANE: MISS SEETON MYSTERY NOVELS: Miss Seeton Cracks the Case, 1991; Miss Seeton Paints the Town, 1991; Hands Up, Miss Seeton, 1992; Miss Seeton by Moonlight, 1992; Miss Seeton Rocks the Cradle, 1992; Miss Seeton Goes to Bat, 1993; Miss Seeton Plants Suspicion, 1993; Starring Miss Seeton, 1994; Miss Seeton Undercover, 1994; Miss Seeton Rules, 1994; Sold to Miss Seeton, 1995; Sweet Miss Seeton, 1996; Bonjour Miss Seeton, 1997; Miss Seeton's Finest Hour, 1999. TREWLEY AND STONE MYSTERY NOVELS: Murder in the Maze, 1993; Frozen Stiff, 1993 as Deep-Frozen Death, 1999; Corpse in the Kitchen, 1993 as Corpse in the Case, 1999; Dying Breath, 1994 as Murder from Memory, 1999; Sew Easy to Kill, 1996; Seeing is Deceiving, 1997. **Address:** Curtis Brown, 28/29 Haymarket, London, GL SW1 4SP, England. **Online address:** 101336.2336@compuserve.com

MASON, Timothy. American (born United States), b. 1950. **Genres:** Plays/Screenplays, Novels. **Career:** Circle Repertory Co., playwright. **Publications:** The Last Synapsid (novel), 2009. PLAYS: Levitation, 1984; In a Northern Landscape, 1985; Only You, 1988, rev. ed., 1995; Ascension Day (one-act play), 1991; Babylon Gardens, 1993; The Fiery Furnace, 1994; Ten Plays for Children: From the Repertory of the Children's Theatre Company of Minneapolis, 1998; Six, 2005; Mullen's Alley, 2007; The Less Than Human Club: A Drama, 2007; Beauty and the Beast, 2007. **Address:** Delacorte Press, 1745 Broadway, New York, NY 10019, U.S.A. **Online address:** tim@thelastsynapsid.com

MASOOD, Maliha. American/Pakistani (born Pakistan), b. 1972?. **Genres:** History, Autobiography/Memoirs, Education, Travel/Exploration. **Career:** International Crisis Group, specialist in conflict resolution; The Diwaan Project, founder and president. Writer and research analyst. **Publications:** In the Middle of the East: A Muslim-American Woman's Odyssey from Cairo to Istanbul (memoir), 2005; Zaatar Days, Henna Nights: Adventures, Dreams and Destinations Across the Middle East, 2006. Works appear in anthologies. **Address:** Seal Press, 1700 4th St., Berkeley, CA 94710, U.S.A. **Online address:** zaatardays@gmail.com

MASS, Wendy. American (born United States), b. 1967. **Genres:** Novellas/Short Stories, Young Adult Fiction, Adult Non-fiction, Children's Fiction, Novels. **Career:** Writes of Passage (literary journal for teenagers), co-founder. Writer. **Publications:** Stonehenge, 1998; Teen Drug Abuse, 1998; Women's Rights, 1998; (ed.) Readings on Night, 2000; Great Authors of Children's Literature, 2000; (ed.) A Guide to Children's Literature, 2001; (ed. with S.P. Levine) Fantasy, 2002; Gods and Goddesses, 2002; John Cabot: Early Explorer, 2004; Ray Bradbury: Master of Science Fiction and Fantasy, 2004; Celebrate Halloween, 2006. OTHERS: Getting a Clue: Tammy, 1996; The Bad Hair Day, 1996; A Mango-shaped Space, 2003; Leap Day, 2004; Rapunzel: The One with All the Hair, 2005; Sleeping Beauty: The One Who Took the Really Long Nap, 2006; Jeremy Fink and the Meaning of Life, 2006; Heaven Looks a Lot like A Mall, 2007; Every Soul a Star: A Novel, 2008; 11 Birthdays, 2009; Finally, 2010; Candymakers, 2010; 13 Gifts, 2011; Beauty and the Beast: The Only One Who Didn't Run Away, 2012. Contributor to periodicals. **Address:** Curtis Brown Ltd., 10 Astor Pl., Fl. 3, New York, NY 10003-6935, U.S.A. **Online address:** wendy@wendymass.com

MASSA, Mark S(tephen). American (born United States) **Genres:** Theology/Religion, History. **Career:** Fordham University, professor of theology, distinguished professor of theology, Curran Center for American Catholic Studies, director, co-director, Karl Rahner Professor of Theology; Boston College, School of Theology and Ministry, dean. Writer. **Publications:** Charles Augustus Briggs and the Crisis of Historical Criticism, 1990; (ed. with R. Viladesau) Foundations of Theological Study: A Sourcebook, 1991; (ed. with R. Viladesau) World Religions: A Sourcebook for Students of Christian Theology, 1994; Charles Augustus Briggs, Union Theological Seminary and Twentieth-Century American Protestantism: A Centennial Address to the Friends of the Burke Library of Union Theological Seminary in the City of New York, 1994; Catholics and American Culture: Fulton Sheen, Dorothy Day, and the Notre Dame Football Team, 1999; Anti-Catholicism in America: The Last Acceptable Prejudice, 2003; (ed. with C. Osborne) American Catholic History: A Documentary Reader, 2008; The American Catholic Revolution: How the Sixties Changed the Church Forever, 2010. **Address:** Fordham University, Rm. 260, Duane Library, Rose Hill Campus. 441 E Fordham Rd., Bronx, NY 10458-5149, U.S.A. **Online address:** massasj@fordham.edu

MASSAD, Joseph A. American (born United States), b. 1963?. **Genres:** Young Adult Non-fiction, Sciences. **Career:** Columbia University, Department of Middle East and Asian Languages and Cultures, associate professor of modern Arab politics and intellectual history, 1999-. Writer. **Publications:** NONFICTION: Colonial Effects: The Making of National Identity in Jordan, 2001; (contrib.) Complications in Cardiothoracic Surgery: Avoidance and Treatment, 2004; The Persistence of the Palestinian Question: Essays on Zionism and the Palestinians, 2006; Desiring Arabs, 2007; (contrib.) Teaching World Literature, 2009; (contrib.) Edward Said: A Legacy of Emancipation and Representation, 2010. Contributor of articles to periodicals and journals. **Address:** Columbia University, 602 Kent Hall, 1140 Amsterdam Ave., PO Box 3928, New York, NY 10027, U.S.A. **Online address:** jam25@columbia.edu

MASSEY, Calvin R(andolph). American (born United States), b. 1949. **Genres:** Law, History, Novels, Young Adult Fiction. **Career:** University of California, associate professor of law, 1987-92, professor of law, 1992-, Harry and Lillian Hastings research professor of law, 1998-99; Boston College, visiting professor, 2000-02, 2003-04; Boston University School of Law, visiting professor of law, 2000-02, 2003-04; Washington and Lee University, School of Law, visiting professor of law, 2005-06; University of California-Berkeley, visiting professor. Writer. **Publications:** (With J. Grodin and R. Cunningham) The California State Constitution, 1993; Silent Rights: The Ninth Amendment and the Constitution's Unenumerated Rights, 1995; Constitutional Law, 1997, 2nd ed., 2001; Property, 1998, 7th ed., 2010; The Ursine Isles, 1998; American Constitutional Law: Powers and Liberties, 2001, 3rd ed., 2009; Horseshoes, Hand Grenades and the Constitution, forthcoming. Contributor to books and periodicals. **Address:** Hastings College of the Law, University of California, 200 McAllister St., San Francisco, CA 94102, U.S.A. **Online address:** masseyc@uchastings.edu

MASSEY, Doreen Barbara. British (born England), b. 1944. **Genres:** History, Social Sciences. **Career:** Centre for Environmental Studies, staff; Open University, professor of geography, through 2009, professor emeritus, 2009-; Oxford University, Saint Hugh's College, honorary fellow, 2001. Writer and geographer. **Publications:** (Ed. with M.C. Hayes) An Operational Urban Development Model of Cheshire, 1970; The Basic: Service Categorisation in Planning, 1971; Towards a Critique of Industrial Location Theory, 1974; (ed. with P.W.J. Batey) Alternative Frameworks for Analysis, 1977; (with A. Catalano) Capital and Land: Landownership by Capital in Great Britain, 1978; (with R.A. Meegan) The Geography of Industrial Reorganisation: The Spatial Effects of the Restructuring of the Electrical Engineering Sector under the Industrial Reorganisation Corporation, 1979; (with R. Meegan) The Anatomy of Job Loss: The How, Why and Where of Employment Decline, 1982; (ed. with J. Allen and J. Anderson) Geography Matters! A Reader, 1984; Spatial Divisions of Labor: Social Structures and the Geography of Production, 1984;

(ed. with R. Meegan) Politics and Method: Contrasting Studies in Industrial Geography, 1985; Nicaragua, 1987; (ed. with J. Allen) Uneven Redevelopment: Cities and Regions in Transition: A Reader, 1988; (ed. with J. Allen) The Economy in Question, 1988; Global Restructuring, Local Responses, 1988; (with F. Ginwala and M. Mackintosh) Gender and Economic Policy in a Democratic South Africa, 1991; (with P. Quintas and D. Wield) High-tech Fantasies: Science Parks in Society, Science and Space, 1992; Space, Place and Gender, 1994; Spatial Divisions of Labor: Social Structures and the Geography of Production, 1995; (ed. with S. Hall and M. Rustin) The Next Ten Years, 1997; (with J. Allen, A. Cochrane and J. Charlesworth) Rethinking the Region, 1998; (ed. with J. Allen and S. Pile) City Worlds, 1999; (ed. with J. Allen and M. Pryke) Unsettling Cities, 1999; (ed. with J. Allen and P. Sarre) Human Geography Today, 1999; For Space, 2005; World City, 2007; (ed. with N. Clark and P. Sarre) Material Geographies, 2008. Contributor to periodicals and journals. **Address:** Faculty of Social Sciences, Open University, Walton Hall, Milton Keynes, BK MK7 6AA, England. **Online address:** d.b.massey@open.ac.uk

MASSEY, James Earl. American (born United States), b. 1930. **Genres:** History, Theology/Religion, Biography. **Career:** Church of God of Detroit, associate pastor, 1953-54; Metropolitan Church of God, founder and senior pastor, 1954-76, honorary pastor-at-large, 1976-; National Association of the Church of God, historian, 1957-; Vital Christianity magazine, feature writer, 1960-82; Gospel Trumpet magazine, contributing editor, 1960-69; Publisher Board of the Church of God, vice chairman, 1962-78; Jamaica School of Theology, president, 1963-66; Tyndale House Publishers, editorial adviser, 1968-69; Anderson College, professor of religious studies, campus minister, 1969-77; Tuskegee University, dean of the chapel and university professor, 1984-89, dean emeritus, 1989-; Anderson University School of Theology, dean emeritus, 1989-95, distinguished professor-at-large, 1995-; Preaching magazine, contributing editor; Christianity Today, senior editor. **Publications:** The Growth of the Soul, 1955; An Introduction to the Negro Churches in the Church of God Reformation Movement, 1957; When Thou Prayest, 1960; The Worshipping Church: A Guide to the Experience of Worship, 1961; Raymond S. Jackson: A Portrait, 1967; The Soul under Seige, 1970; The Hidden Disciplines, 1972; The Responsible Pulpit, 1974; Howard Thurman: Preacher, The Sermon in Perspective: A Study of Communication and Charisma, 1976; Concerning Christian Unity, 1979; Designing the Sermon: Order and Movement in Preaching, 1980; (ed.) Christian Brotherhood Hour Study Bible, 1980; (ed. with W. McCown) Interpreting God's Word for Today: An Inquiry into Hermeneutics from a Biblical Theological Perspective, 1982; Educating for Service: Essays Presented to Robert H. Reardon, 1984; Spiritual Disciplines, 1985 as Spiritual Disciplines: A Believer's Openings to the Grace of God, 2009; A Bridge Between, 1988; Preaching from Hebrews, 1991; (contrib.) Sharing Heaven's Music: The Heart of Christian Preaching: Essays in Honor of James Earl Massey, 1995; The Burdensome Joy of Preaching, 1998; Sundays in the Tuskegee Chapel: Selected Sermons, 2000; Aspects of My Pilgrimage: An Autobiography, 2002; African Americans and the Church of God, Anderson, Indiana: Aspects of a Social History, 2005; Stewards of the Story: The Task of Preaching, 2006; (foreword) Doctrine that Dances: Bringing Doctrinal Preaching and Teaching to Life, 2008; (ed. with T. George and R. Smith) Our Sufficiency is of God: Essays on Preaching in Honor of Gardner C. Taylor, 2010. **Address:** Mass Communications Board of the Church of God, 1303 E 5th St., Anderson, IN 46011, U.S.A.

MASSEY, Jessica. *See* **GREENE, Jennifer.**

MASSEY, Victoria. British (born England) **Genres:** Young Adult Non-fiction, Biography, Autobiography/Memoirs. **Career:** Writer. **Publications:** One Child's War (audio book), 1978; The First Lady Diana: The Life of Lady Diana Spencer, 1710-1735, 1999. **Address:** Random House, Jonathan Cape, 20 Vauxhall Bridge Rd., London, GL SW1V 2SA, England. **Online address:** massey_victoria@hotmail.com

MASSIE, Elizabeth. (Chris Blaine). American (born United States), b. 1953?. **Genres:** Horror, Children's Fiction, Young Adult Fiction, Novels, Medicine/Health. **Career:** Teacher, 1975-94. Writer. **Publications:** HORROR: Sineater (novel), 1994; Southern Discomfort: The Selected Works (short stories), 1994; American Chills: Maryland-Ghost Harbor (young adult), 1995; Welcome Back to the Night, 1999; (with S.M. Rainey) Dark Shadows: Dreams of the Dark, 1999; Buffy the Vampire Slayer: Power of Persuasion, 1999; Wire Mesh Mothers, 2001; Shadow Dreams (short stories), 2002; (as Chris Blaine) Twisted Branch: A Novel of the Abbadon Inn, 2005; (as Homeplace, 2007; Brazen Bull, 2007. DAUGHTERS OF LIBERTY TRILOGY FOR CHILDREN: Patsy and the Declaration, 1997; Patsy's Discovery, 1997; Barbara's Escape, 1997. OTHERS: (contrib.) Jambo, Watoto!, 1997; Great Chicago Fire, 1871, 1999; A Forest Community, 2000; 1870: Not with Our Blood, 2000; 1863: A House Divided: A Novel of the Civil War, 2000; 1776: Son of Liberty: A Novel of the American Revolution, 2000; 1609: Winter of the Dead: A Novel About the Founding of Jamestown, 2000; Why Me?, 2003; King Takes Queen, 2007; Tudors: Thy Will be Done: A Novelization of Season Three of the Tudors, 2009; Images of America: Waynesboro, 2009; Writers Workshop of Horror, 2009; (with A.M. Clark) D.D. Murphry, Secret Policeman, 2009; (with L.J. Favor) Weighing In: Nutrition and Weight Management, 2010; Julie Walker is The Phantom in Race Against Death!, 2010; Homegrown, 2011; African American Educators, 2012. **Address:** Pocket Books, 1230 Ave. of the Americas, New York, NY 10020, U.S.A. **Online address:** beth@elizabethmassie.com

MASSIE, Joseph Logan. American (born United States), b. 1921. **Genres:** Administration/Management, Business/Trade/Industry, History, Biography, Economics. **Career:** Property Insurance Agency, owner, 1940-47; University of Chicago, assistant professor, 1955-57; University of Kentucky, faculty, 1957, professor of business administration, 1959-80, associate dean, 1966-69, acting dean, 1969-70, director of graduate studies, 1971-78, chairman of business administration, alumni professor of business administration, 1980-86, alumni professor emeritus and professor emeritus of business administration. Writer and visiting lecturer. **Publications:** Blazer and Ashland Oil: A Study in Management, 1960; (with W.W. Haynes) Management: Analysis, Concepts and Cases, 1961, (with W.W. Haynes and J.L. Massie) 3rd ed., 1975; Essentials of Management, 1964, 4th ed., 1987; (ed. with J. Luytjes) Management in an International Concept, 1972; (with J. Douglas) Managing: A Contemporary Introduction, 1973, 5th ed., 1992; Anderson's Way: The Story of an Entrepreneur, 1995; Studies in Comparative International Management, forthcoming. **Address:** Gatton College of Business and Economics, University of Kentucky, Lexington, KY 40506, U.S.A.

MASSIE, Sonja. (G. A. McKevett). American (born United States), b. 1952?. **Genres:** Mystery/Crime/Suspense, Novels, Young Adult Non-fiction. **Career:** Singile Living, managing editor. **Publications:** Legacy of the Wolf, 1986; Dream Carver, 1989; Moon Song, 1990; Carousel, 1990; (with M. Schneider) Especially for Girls Presents What Every Girl Should Know about Boys, 1992; Far and Away, 1992; Betrayal, 1996; The Dark Mirror, 1996; (with M.H. Greenberg) The Janet Dailey Companion: A Comprehensive Guide to Her Life and Her Novels, 1996; (contrib.) Unmasked, 1997; A Friend in Need, 1997; Irish Pride: 101 Reasons to Be Proud You're Irish, 1999; The Complete Idiot's Guide to Irish History and Culture, 1999; Daughter of Ireland, 2000. SAVANNAH REID MYSTERY SERIES: AS G.A. McKEVETT: Just Desserts, 1995; Bitter Sweets, 1996; Killer Calories, 1997; Cooked Goose, 1998; Sugar and Spite, 2000; Sour Grapes, 2001; Peaches and Screams, 2002; Death by Chocolate, 2003; Cereal Killer, 2004; Murder a la Mode, 2004; Corpse Suzette, 2006; Fat Free and Fatal, 2007; Poisoned Tarts 2008; A Body to Die For, 2009; Wicked Craving, 2010; A Decadent Way To Die, 2011. **Address:** Richard Curtis Associates Inc., 171 E 74th St., 2nd Fl., New York, NY 10021-3221, U.S.A. **Online address:** sonja@sonjamassie.com

MASSIE, Suzanne. American (born United States), b. 1931. **Genres:** History. **Career:** Time and Life magazines, researcher and reporter, 1952-53; Time/Life Books, researcher, 1965-67; Gourmet, managing editor, 1967; freelance writer, 1967-; Davis Center, fellow, 1985-97; President's U.S.-Soviet Exchange Initiative, special advisor, 1986-87; Harvard University Russian Research Center, fellow, 1987-; General Theological Seminary, professor of Anglican studies, 1993; International League for Human Rights, board director. **Publications:** (Ed.) Nicholas and Alexandra, 1967; (trans. with M. Hayward and G.L. Kline and comp.) Living Mirror: Five Young Poets Leningrad, 1972; (with R.K. Massie) Journey, 1975; Land of the Firebird: The Beauty of Old Russia, 1980; Pavlovsk: The Life of a Russian Palace, 1990. Contributor to magazines. **Address:** HeartTree Press, PO Box 1417, Blue Hill, ME 04614, U.S.A. **Online address:** crw@midmaine.com

MASSINGHAM, Harold (William). *See* Obituaries.

MASSON, Paul R(obert). American/Canadian (born Canada), b. 1946. **Genres:** Economics, Travel/Exploration, E-books, Business/Trade/Industry, Money/Finance. **Career:** Bank of Canada, economist, 1973-76, adviser and deputy chief, 1979-83; Organization for Economic Cooperation and Development, administrator, 1976-79, principal adviser administrator, 1983-84; International Monetary Fund, economist, adviser, division chief, and senior adviser, 1984-. Writer. **Publications:** (With D.E. Rose and J.G. Selody) Building a Small Macro-Model for Simulation: Some Issues, 1980; Asset Stocks and the Use of Monetary and Fiscal Policies to Reduce Inflation, 1983; (with S. Symansky and G. Meredith) MULTIMOD Mark II: A Revised and Extended Model, 1990; Characteristics of a Successful Exchange Rate System, 1991; (with A. Ghosh) Economic Cooperation in an Uncertain World, 1994; (with M. Mussa) The Role of the IMF: Financing and Its Interactions with Adjustment and Surveillance, 1995; (co-author) Exit Strategies: Policy Options for Countries Seeking Greater Exchange Rate Flexibility, 1998; Monetary and Exchange Rate Policy of Transition Economies of Central and Eastern Europe After the Launch of EMU, 1999; (with C. Pattillo) Monetary Union in West Africa (ECOWAS): Is It Desirable and How Could it be Achieved?, 2001; Globalization: Facts and Figures, 2001; (with C. Pattillo) Monetary Geography of Africa, 2005; (with M. Dailami and J.J. Padou) Global Monetary Conditions Versus Country-Specific Factors in the Determination of Emerging Market Debt Spreads, 2005; Lectures in International Finance: Crisis, Coordination, Currency, Unions, and Debt, 2007. EDITOR: (co-ed.) Macroeconomic Policies in an Interdependent World, 1989; (with M.B. Canzoneri and V. Grilli) Establishing a Central Bank: Issues in Europe and Lessons from the United States, 1992; (with M.P. Taylor) Policy Issues in the Operation of Currency Unions, 1993; France, Financial and Real Sector Issues, 1995; (with T.H. Krueger and B.G. Turtelboom) EMU and the International Monetary System: Proceedings of a Conference Held in Washington D.C. on March 17-18, 1997, 1997. **Address:** World Scientific Publishing Company, 27 Warren St., Ste. 401-402, Hackensack, NJ 07601, U.S.A. **Online address:** pmasson@imf.org

MASSON, Sophie. Australian/French/Indonesian (born Indonesia), b. 1959. **Genres:** Children's Fiction, Young Adult Fiction, Novels, inspirational/Motivational Literature. **Career:** Literature Board of the Australia Council, staff, 2004-08; New England Writers' Centre, deputy chair, 2011-. Writer and journalist. **Publications:** YOUNG-ADULT NOVELS: Sooner or Later, 1991; A Blaze of Summer, 1992; The Sun is Rising, 1996; The Tiger, 1996; Red City, 1998; Clementine, 1999; The Green Prince, 2000; The King of Greenwood, 2000; The Firebird, 2001; The Hand of Glory, 2002; The Lost Island, 2003; Dame Ragnell, 2003; The Tempestuous Voyage of Hopewell Shakespeare, 2003; In Hollow Lands, 2004; Malvolio's Revenge, 2005; The Curse of Zohreh, 2005; The Tyrant's Nephew, 2006; Snow, Fire, Sword, 2006; The Maharajah's Ghost, 2007; The Secret Army: Operation Loki, 2008; The Case of the Diamond Shadow, 2008. FOR CHILDREN: Fire in the Sky, 1990; Birds of a Feather, 1996; The Troublemaker, 1997; Small World, 2000; (ed.) The Road to Camelot, 2002. SEYRAC NOVEL SERIES: FOR CHILDREN: The Opera Club, 1993; The Cousin from France, 1994; Winter in France, 1994; The Secret, 1996; Family Business, 2000. STARMAKER NOVEL SERIES: FOR YOUNG ADULTS: Carabas, 1996 in US as Serafin, 2000; Cold Iron, 1998 in US as Malkin, 2000; The First Day, 2000. THOMAS TREW NOVEL SERIES: FOR YOUNG ADULTS: Thomas Trew and the Horns of Pan, 2006; Thomas Trew and the Hidden People, 2006; Thomas Trew and the Flying Huntsman, 2007; Thomas Trew and the Island of Ghosts, 2007; Thomas Trew and the Klint Kings Gold, 2007; Thomas Trew and the Selkie's Curse, 2007. LAYLINES ADULT FANTASY SERIES: The Knight by the Pool, 1998; The Lady of the Flowers, 1999; The Stone of Oakenfast, 2000; Forest of Dreams: The Laylines Trilogy, 2001. OTHERS: The House in the Rainforest, 1990; The Hoax, 1997; Walking in the Garden of the Mind, 2005; The Madman of Venice, 2008; The Hunt for Ned Kelly, 2010; The Phar Lap Mystery, 2010; The Understudy's Revenge, 2011; Life, Literature, Legends, 2011; Boggle Hunters, 2012; Ned Kelly's Secret, 2012; Moonlight and Ashes, 2012. **Address:** c/o Margaret Connolly, PO Box 945, Wahroonga, NW 2076, Australia. **Online address:** smasson@northnet.com.au

MASSUMI, Brian. Canadian/American (born United States), b. 1956. **Genres:** Literary Criticism And History. **Career:** University of Queensland, researcher; State University of New York, associate professor; McGill University, professor of English; University of California, instructor, 2000; University of London, instructor, 2008; University of Helsinki, instructor, 2009; Cornell University, instructor, 2010; European Graduate School, professor of critical empiricism, 2010; Universite de Montreal, professor of communication sciences. Writer. **Publications:** A User's Guide to Capitalism and Schizophrenia: Deviations from Deleuze and Guattari, 1992; (ed.) The Politics of Everyday Fear, 1993; (with K. Dean) First and Last Emperors: The Absolute State and the Body of the Despot, 1993; (ed.) A Shock to Thought: Expressions after Deleuze and Guattari, 2002; Parables for the Virtual: Movement, Affect, Sensation, 2002; Semblance and Event, 2011. **Online address:** brian.massumi@umontreal.ca

MAST, Gerald J. (Gerald Biesecker-Mast). American (born United States), b. 1965. **Genres:** Theology/Religion. **Career:** University of Pittsburgh, graduate teaching assistant, 1988-91, graduate teaching fellow, 1991-95; Community College of Allegheny County, Boyce Campus, part-time instructor, 1992-94; University of Iowa, assistant in instruction, 1995; Bluffton University, assistant professor of communication, 1996-2000, associate professor of communication, 2000-06, professor of communication, 2006-; East Canton Press-News, news writer, 1987; Graphic Publications, news & features editor, 1987-88; World Federalist Association of Pittsburgh, board of director, 1992-93; WQED Pittsburgh, public relations writer, 1995; Mennonite magazine, vice-chair of governance board, 2007-. **Publications:** AS GERALD BIESECKER-MAST: (ed. and contrib. with S.B. Mast) Anabaptists & Postmodernity, 2000; (ed. and contrib. with J.D. Weaver) Teaching Peace: Nonviolence and the Liberal Arts, 2003; Separation and the Sword in Anabaptist Persuasion: Radical Confessional Rhetoric from Schleitheim to Dordrecht, 2006. OTHER: (ed. with A.E. Weaver) The Work of Jesus Christ in Anabaptist Perspective: Essays in Honor of J. Denny Weaver, 2008. Contributor to books and journals. **Address:** Department of Communication & Theatre, Bluffton University, Bluffton, OH 45817, U.S.A. **Online address:** mastg@bluffton.edu

MASTERS, Alexander. (Rachel Swift). British/American (born United States) **Genres:** Biography, Medicine/Health. **Career:** Wintercomfort, staff; The Cambridge Two Campaign, chair. Writer. **Publications:** Stuart: A Life Backwards (biography), 2005. AS RACHEL SWIFT: (with D. Davies) Women's Pleasure, 1994; (with D. Davies) Fabulous Figures, 1995; (with D. Davies) Satisfaction Guaranteed, forthcoming. Contributor to periodicals. **Address:** c/o Author Mail, HarperCollins Publishers Ltd., 77-85 Fulham Palace Rd., London, GL W6 8JB, England.

MASTERS, Alexis. American (born United States), b. 1949. **Genres:** Novels, Travel/Exploration. **Career:** University of California, student administration and adviser, 1985-95; freelance internet web site designer, 1989-; freelance writer, 1990-. **Publications:** The Giuliana Legacy: A Novel, 2000; Giuliana's Challenge, forthcoming. **Address:** 6438 Arlington Blvd., Richmond, CA 94805-1606, U.S.A. **Online address:** alexis@giulianalegacy.com

MASTERS, J. D. *See* **HAWKE, Simon.**

MASTERS, Joan. *See* **MURPHEY, Cecil B(laine).**

MASTERS, Roger D. American (born United States), b. 1933. **Genres:** Biology, Philosophy, Politics/Government. **Career:** Yale University, Department of Political Science, instructor, 1961-62, assistant professor, 1962-67, Law School, visiting lecturer, 1988; Dartmouth College, Department of Government, associate professor, 1967-73, professor, 1973-98, chair, 1986-89, Nelson A. Rockefeller professor of government, 1991-98, Nelson A. Rockefeller professor emeritus of government and research professor of government, 1998-; U.S. Embassy, cultural attaché, 1969-71; Institute of Society, Ethics, and the Life Sciences, fellow, 1974-78; Association for Politics and the Life Sciences, vice chairman, 1991-93; Gruter Institute for Law and Behavioral Research, research associate, 1992-98; Foundation for Neuroscience and Society, president, 1998-. Writer. **Publications:** The Nation is Burdened, 1967; Political Philosophy of Rousseau, 1968; The Nature of Politics, 1989; Beyond Relativism, 1993; Machiavelli, Leonardo and the Science of Power, 1996; Fortune is a River: Leonardo da Vinci and Niccolò Machiavelli's Magnificent Dream to Change the Course of Florentine History, 1998; Philosophie politique de Rousseau, 2002. EDITOR: On the Social Contract, 1978; (with M. Gruter) Ostracism, 1984; (with C. Kelly) Collected Writings of Rousseau, 1990; (with G. Schubert) Primate Politics, 1991; (with M. Gruter) The Sense of Justice: Biological Foundations of Law, 1991; (with M.T. McGuire) The Neurotransmitter Revolution: Serotonin, Social Behavior, and the Law, 1993; (with C. Kelly and P.G. Stillman) The Confessions; and Correspondence, Including the Letters to Malesherbes, 1995. OTHERS: (trans. with J.R. Masters and ed. and intro.) J. Rousseau, First and Second Discourses, 1964; (ed. with C. Kelly and trans. with J.R. Bush and C. Kelly) Rousseau, Judge of Jean-Jacques: Dialogues, 1990; (ed. with C. Kelly and trans. with J.R. Bush and C. Kelly) J. Rousseau, Discourse on the Sciences and Arts (First Discourse), 1992; (ed. with C. Kelly) J. Rousseau, Discourse on the Origins of

Inequality (Second Discourse): Polemics and Political Economy, 1992; (ed. with C. Kelly and trans. with J.R. Bush and C. Kelly) J. Rousseau, Social Contract, 1994. **Address:** Department of Government, Dartmouth College, HB 6108, 09A Silsby Hall, Hanover, NH 03755, U.S.A. **Online address:** roger.d.masters@dartmouth.edu

MASTERS, Susan Rowan. American (born United States), b. 1943. **Genres:** Children's Fiction, Novels, History. **Career:** Chautauqua Institution, visiting roster. Writer. **Publications:** The Secret Life of Hubie Hartzel, 1990; Libby Bloom, 1995; Summer Song, 1995; Night Journey to Vicksburg, 2003. **Address:** Clarion Books, 215 Park Ave. S, New York, NY 10003, U.S.A. **Online address:** susan@srmasters.com

MASTERSON, Daniel M. American (born United States), b. 1945. **Genres:** History, Military/Defense/Arms Control. **Career:** Teacher, 1968-71; Michigan State University, instructor in history, 1970-75; North Carolina State University, visiting assistant professor of history, 1975; Marietta College, visiting professor, 1976-77; State University of New York College, visiting professor, 1977-78; Stanford University, National Endowment for the Humanities, fellow, 1978; Cornell University, fellow, 1978; Ohio Commission on Allied Health Education, program coordinator, 1979; U.S. Naval Academy, assistant professor, 1979-83, associate professor of history, 1983-, professor. Writer. **Publications:** (Ed. with J.F. Bratzel) The Underside of Latin American History, 1977; (ed.) Naval History: The Sixth Symposium of the U.S. Naval Academy, 1987; Militarism and Politics in Latin America: Peru from Sanchez Cerro to Sendero Luminoso, 1991; (with J. Dunnigan) The Way of the Warrior: Business Tactics and Techniques from History's Twelve Greatest Generals, 1997; Fuerza Armada y Sociedad en el Peru Moderno: un estudio sobre relaciones civiles militares, 1930-2000, 2001; The Japanese in Latin America, 2004; History of Peru, 2009; The Black and Tans in Irish Memory, forthcoming. **Address:** Department of History, United States Naval Academy, 107 Maryland Ave., Annapolis, MD 21402, U.S.A. **Online address:** masterso@usna.edu

MASTHAY, Carl (David). American (born United States), b. 1941. **Genres:** Anthropology/Ethnology, Astronomy, Biology, Chemistry, Earth Sciences, Language/Linguistics, Sciences, Translations, Translations. **Career:** Mosby Inc., medical editor and senior manuscript editor, 1968-2002; Stonehenge Viewpoint, copyeditor, 1982-88. **Publications:** History of the Masthay Family, 1972, 2nd ed., 1982; Personal Reflections from a China Trip, 1979; Mahican-Language Hymns, Biblical Prose, and Vocabularies from Moravian Sources, with 11 Mohawk Hymns (transcription and translation), 1980; Schmick's Mahican Dictionary, 1991; Kaskaskia Illinois-to-French Dictionary, 2002. Contributor to periodicals. **Address:** 838 Larkin Ave., St. Louis, MO 63141-7758, U.S.A. **Online address:** cmasthay@juno.com

MASTNY, Vojtech. American/Czech (born Czech Republic), b. 1936. **Genres:** History, International Relations/Current Affairs, Politics/Government, Military/Defense/Arms Control, Humanities. **Career:** California State College, assistant professor of history, 1967-68; Columbia University, assistant professor of history, 1968-74; Institute of East Central Europe, acting director, 1970-71; University of Illinois, professor of history, 1974-80; Johns Hopkins School of Advanced International Studies, visiting professor of soviet studies, 1977-82; Johns Hopkins University, visiting professor of Soviet studies, 1977-88; Institute for the Study of World Politics, Guggenheim fellow, 1977-78; U.S. Naval War College, professor of strategy, 1982-83; Boston University, professor of international relations, 1983-90; Harvard University, fellow, 1983; Netherlands Institute for Advanced Study, fellow, 1988-89; Federal Institute of Soviet, international fellow, 1988-90; University of Bonn, Fulbright senior professor, 1989-90; Johns Hopkins School of Advanced International Studies Bologna Center, professor of international relations, 1990-95; Woodrow Wilson International Center for Scholars, project coordinator, 1996-, research associate; National Security Archive, Parallel History Project on NATO and the Warsaw Pact, coordinator, 1999-. Writer. **Publications:** The Czechs under Nazi Rule: The Failure of National Resistance, 1939-1942, 1971; Russia's Road to the Cold War: Diplomacy, Warfare, and the Politics of Communism, 1941-1945, 1979; Helsinki, Human Rights, and European Security: Analysis and Documentation, 1986; The Helsinki Process and the Reintegration of Europe, 1986-1991, 1992; The Cold War and Soviet Insecurity: The Stalin Years, 1996; Learning from the Enemy: NATO as a Model for the Warsaw Pact, 2001; Konfrontationsmuster des Kalten Krieges 1946 bis 1956, 2003; China and Eastern Europe, 1960s-1980s: Proceedings of the International Symposium: Reviewing the History of Chinese-East European Relations from the 1960s to the 1980s, Beijing, 24-26 March 2004, 2004. EDITOR: Disarmament and Nuclear Tests, 1964-69, 1971; (intro.) East European Dissent, vol. I: 1953-1964, 1972, vol. II: 1965-1970, 1972; (intro.) Czechoslovakia: Crisis in World Communism, 1972; Power and Policy in Transition: Essays Presented on the Tenth Anniversary of the National Committee on American Foreign Policy in Honor of Its Founder, Hans J. Morgenthau, 1984; Soviet-East European Survey, 5 vols., 1985-88; Soviet Troop Withdrawals from Eastern Europe as a Political Problem: Past, Present, and Future, 1989; (with J. Zielonka) Human Rights and Security: Europe on the Eve of a New Era, 1991; Italy and East Central Europe: Dimensions of the Regional Relationship, 1995; (with R.C. Nation) Turkey between East and West: New Challenges for a Rising Regional Power, 1996; (with S. Ortino and M. Zagar) Changing Faces of Federalism: Institutional Reconfiguration in Europe from East to West, 2005; (with M. Byrne) Cardboard Castle?: An Inside History of the Warsaw Pact, 1955-1991, 2005; (with S.G. Holtsmark and A. Wenger) War Plans and Alliances in the Cold War: Threat Perceptions in the East and West, 2006; (with A. Wenger and C. Nuenlist) Origins of the European Security System: The Helsinki Process Revisited, 1965-75, 2008. **Address:** Woodrow Wilson International Center for Scholars, 1 Woodrow Wilson Plz., 1300 Pennsylvania Ave. NW, Washington, DC 20004-3027, U.S.A. **Online address:** vmastny@aol.com

MASTRAS, George. American (born United States), b. 1966. **Genres:** Novels. **Career:** Writer. **Publications:** Fidali's Way (novel), 2009. **Address:** Simon & Schuster Inc., 1230 Ave. of Americas, New York, NY 10020, U.S.A. **Online address:** george@fidalisway.com

MASUD, Naiyer. Indian (born India), b. 1936. **Genres:** Novels. **Career:** Islamia College, lecturer in Urdu and Persian studies, 1965; Lucknow University, lecturer in Persian, 1965-78, reader in Persian, 1978-91, professor of Persian, 1990-97, head of Persian department, through 1997. Writer. **Publications:** RTa'bīr-i Ghālib, 1973; ajab Ali Beg Surur, 1967; (trans.) F. Kafka, Kafka Ke Afsaney, 1979; Dūlha Ṣāḥib Urūj (biographies), 1980; Khutut-i mashāhīr bah nām Sayyid Mas'ūd ḥasan Rizvī, 1985; Sīmiyā: afsāne (short stories), 1987; Intikāb-i Bustān-i ḥikmat, 1988; Marsiyah khvānī kā fan (history criticism), 1989; Bazm-i Anīs, 1990; Itri kāfūr, afsāne (short stories), 1990; Yaganah, ahval o asar (criticism), 1991; Tāūs caman kī mainā: afsāne (short stories), 1998; Essence of Camphor, 1998; Itr-i kāfūr, 1999; Marikah-yi Anis va Dabīr (criticism), 2000; Anīs: savānih (biography), 2002; (ed.) Shifā'uddaulah kī sarguzasht (biography), 2004; Baccaun se bāten, 2004; Myna from Peacock Garden, 2005; Snake Catcher, 2005; Adābistān, 2006; Ganjifah, 2008; Muntakhab MazaMCNmīn, 2009; Mīr Anīs, 2011. **Address:** c/o Katha Sarvodaya, A3 Sarvodaya Enclave, New Delhi, DH 110017, India.

MATALIN, Mary. American (born United States), b. 1953. **Genres:** Politics/Government, Cultural/Ethnic Topics, Education. **Career:** Writer, political strategist and consultant. **Publications:** (Foreword) Unbridled Power: Inside the Secret Culture of the IRS, 1998; (with J. Carville and P. Knobler) All's Fair: Love, War, and Running for President, 1994; Letters to My Daughters, 2004; (intro.) Hatchet Jobs and Hardball: The Oxford Dictionary of American Political Slang, 2004; (intro.) The Oxford Dictionary of American Political Slang, 2006. Contributor to periodicals. **Address:** Gaslight Inc., 917 Prince St., Alexandria, VA 22314-3008, U.S.A.

MATALON, Ronit. Israeli (born Israel), b. 1959?. **Genres:** Novels, Plays/Screenplays. **Career:** Israeli Television, journalist; Daily Haaretz, journalist, critic and book reviewer; Camera Obscura School of the Arts, staff, literature professor, 1993; Haifa University, senior lecturer in Hebrew and comparative literature, professor of creative writing; Sam Spiegel Film School, faculty creative writing. **Publications:** (With R. Tsarefati) Sipur she-mathil be-levayah shel nahash (juvenile fiction, title means; 'A Story that Begins With a Snake's Funeral'), 1989; Zarim ba-bayit: sipurim, 1992; Dreams of Innocence, 1993; Zeh 'imha-panim elenu, 1995; Osher me-ahore ha-'etsim, 1997; One Facing Us: A Novel, 1998; śarah, śarah, 2000; Kero u-khetov, 2001; Bliss: A Novel, 2003; Uncover Her Face, 2005; Galu et paneha, 2006; Kol tś adenu, 2008; The Sound of Our Steps: A Novel, 2008. Contributor to periodicals. **Address:** c/o Author Mail, Henry Holt and Co., 175 5th Ave., 115 W 18th St., New York, NY 10011, U.S.A.

MATARESE, Susan M. American (born United States), b. 1950?. **Genres:** International Relations/Current Affairs. **Career:** University of Minnesota, teaching associate, 1974-78, instructor, 1978-79; University of Louisville, professor of political science, 1979-, honors program director, honors advisor; Communal Societies, associate editor; Kenyon College, fellow, 1982. **Publications:** American Foreign Policy and the Utopian Imagination, 2001. **Address:** Department of Political Science, University of Louisville, Rm. 210, Ford Hall, Belknap Campus, 2nd Fl., Louisville, KY 40292, U.S.A. **Online address:** smmata01@louisville.edu

MATAS, Carol. Canadian (born Canada), b. 1949. **Genres:** Children's Fiction, Young Adult Fiction, Theatre, Plays/Screenplays, Novels. **Career:** Writer, 1981-; University of Winnipeg, Continuing Education Division, instructor of creative writing; Bemidji State University, visiting professor; Manitoba Arts Council, artist-in-the-schools; Centennial Library, writer-in-residence. **Publications:** FOR CHILDREN: The DNA Dimension, 1982; The Fusion Factor, 1986, as It's Up to Us, 1991; Zanu, 1986; Me, Myself and I, 1987; Lisa in US as Lisa's War, 1987; Jesper in US as Code Name Kris, 1989; The Race, 1991; Adventure in Legoland, 1991; Kris's War, 1992; Safari Adventure in Legoland, 1993; Daniel's Story, 1993; Sworn Enemies, 1993; The Lost Locket, 1994; The Burning Time, 1994; The Primrose Path, 1995; After the War, 1996; The Garden, 1997; The Freak, 1997; Greater than Angels, 1998; Telling, 1998; In My Enemy's House, 1999; Cloning Miranda, 1999; Rebecca, 2000; The War Within, 2001; Sparks Fly Upward, 2002; Footprints in the Snow, 2002. WITH P. NODELMAN: Of Two Minds, 1994; More Minds, 1996; Out of Their Minds, 1998; Meeting of Minds, 1999. OTHERS: The Second Clone, 2001; Footsteps In The Snow, 2002; Rosie in New York City: Gotcha!, 2003; Rosie in Chicago: Play Ball!, 2003; Rosie in Los Angeles: Action!, 2004; The Dark Clone, 2005; Turned Away, 2005; Past Crimes, 2007; The Whirlwind, 2007; Visions, The Freak 2007; (with P. Nodelman) The Proof That Ghosts Exist, 2008; Far, The Freak, 2008; (with P. Nodelman) The Curse Of The Evening Eye, 2009; (with P. Nodelman) The Hunt For The Haunted Elephant, 2010; Tales Of A Reluctant Psychic, 2010; The Edge of When, 2012. **Address:** Transatlantic Literary Agency Inc., 2 Bloor St. E, Ste. 3500, Toronto, ON M4W 1A8, Canada. **Online address:** carol@carolmatas.com

MATAS, David. Canadian (born Canada), b. 1943. **Genres:** Law, Civil Liberties/Human Rights. **Career:** Thompson, Dorfman and Sweatman, barrister, 1970-71; Office of the Solicitor General of Canada, special assistant, 1971-72; McGill University, lecturer in constitutional law, 1972-73; Schwartz, McJannet, associate, 1973-79; University of Manitoba, lecturer in introductory economics, Canadian economic problems, 1982, lecturer in international law, 1985, lecturer in civil liberties, 1986-88, lecturer in immigration and refugee law, 1989-; B'nai Brith Canada, senior honorary counsel, 1989-, vice president, 1996-98, senior legal counsel; International Defence and Aid Fund for South Africa in Canada, director, 1990-91; Canada-South Africa Cooperation, director, 1991-93; International Commission of Jurists, vice president, 1994-2003; International Centre for Human Rights and Democratic Development, director, 1997-2003; Barrister & Solicitor, staff. Writer. **Publications:** Human Rights in Canada: A Status Report, 1985; (with S. Charendoff) Justice Delayed: Nazi War Criminals in Canada, 1987; Canadian Immigration Law 1986: The Sanctuary Trial, 1989; (with I. Simon) Closing the Doors: The Failure of Refugee Protection, 1989; No More: The Battle against Human Rights Violations, 1994; (ed. with E. Harlow and J. Rocamora) The Machinery of Death: A Shocking Indictment of Capital Punishment in the United States, 1995; Bloody Words: Hate and Free Speech, 2000; Aftershock: Anti-Zionism and Anti-Semitism, 2005; (with D. Kilgour) Bloody Harvest: The Killing of Falun Gong for Their Organs, 2009. **Address:** B'nai Brith Canada, 15 Hove St., Toronto, ON M3H 4Y8, Canada. **Online address:** dmatas@mts.net

MATCHETT, William H(enry). American (born United States), b. 1923. **Genres:** Poetry, Literary Criticism And History, Young Adult Fiction. **Career:** Harvard University, teaching fellow, 1953-54; University of Washington, instructor, 1954-56, assistant professor, 1956-60, associate professor, 1960-66, professor, 1966-83, professor emeritus of English, 1983-; American Friends Service Committee, chair, 1959-62; Modern Language Quarterly, editor, 1963-82. **Publications:** Water Ouzel and Other Poems, 1955; (with J. Beaty) Poetry: From Statement to Meaning, 1965; The Phoenix and the Turtle: Shakespeare's Poem and Chester's Loues Martyr, 1965; (ed.) The Life and Death of King John, 1966; Fireweed and Other Poems, 1980, 2nd ed. 2004; Shakespeare and Forgiveness, 2002. **Address:** Department of English, University of Washington, PO Box 351272, Seattle, WA 98104, U.S.A.

MATELSKI, Marilyn J. American (born United States), b. 1950. **Genres:** Communications/Media, Social Sciences, History. **Career:** Austin College, instructor, 1973-75; University of Colorado, instructor, 1975-78; Boston College, Department of Communication, assistant professor, 1978-81, assistant chair, 1980-95, 1998-2000, associate professor, 1982-91, professor, 1992-, chair, 1995-98. Writer. **Publications:** The Soap Opera Evolution: America's Enduring Romance with Daytime Drama, 1988; Broadcast Programming and Promotions Worktext, 1989; (co-author) Variety Sourcebook, vol. I: Broadcast-Video, 1990, vol. II: Film-Theater-Music, 1991; (ed.) Variety Yearbook, 1991; TV News Ethics, 1991; Daytime Television Programming, 1991; Variety: The Year in Review, 1992; Vatican Radio: Propagation by the Airwaves, 1995; (and ed. with N.L. Street) Messages from the Underground: Transnational Radio in Resistance and in Solidarity, 1997; Soap Operas Worldwide: Cultural and Serial Realities, 1999; (with N.L. Street) American Businesses in China: Balancing Culture and Communication, 2003, 2nd ed., 2008; (ed. with N.L. Street) War and Film in America: Historical and Critical Essays, 2003. **Address:** Department of Communication, Boston College, 542 Maloney Hall, 21 Campanella Way, Chestnut Hill, MA 02467-3859, U.S.A. **Online address:** marilyn.matelski@bc.edu

MATERA, Dary M. American (born United States), b. 1955?. **Genres:** Art/Art History, Novels, Children's Fiction, Young Adult Non-fiction, Music. **Career:** Arizona Republic, columnist; Miami News, reporter, 1977-82; Prevention Magazine, Rodale Press, editor; Spector/Anker Associates, staff. **Publications:** (With L. de Barbin) Are You Lonesome Tonight?: The Untold Story of Elvis Presley's One True Love and the Child He Never Knew, 1987; (with E. Rubin) Get Me Ellis Rubin!: The Life, Times, and Cases of a Maverick Lawyer, 1989; (with M. Franzese) Quitting the Mob: How the Yuppie Don Left the Mafia and Lived to Tell His Story, 1992, rev. ed. as Blood Covenant, 2003; (with J. Stedino) What's in It for Me?: How an Ex-Wiseguy Exposed the Greed, Jealousy and Lust That Drive American Politics, 1992; Strike Midnight, 1994; (with D. Theisen) Angels of Emergency: Rescue Stories from Americas Paramedics and EMTs, 1996; (with O.G. Peña and B.C. McKenna) The Peña Files: One Man's War against Federal Corruption and the Abuse of Power, 1996; (with E. George) Taming the Beast: Charles Manson's Life behind Bars, 1998; (with D. Theisen) Childlight: How Children Reach out to Their Parents from the Beyond, 2001; A Cry for Character: How a Group of Students Cleaned up Their Rowdy School and Spawned a Wildfire Antidote to the Columbine Effect, 2001; FBI's Ten Most Wanted, 2003; John Dillinger: The Life and Death of America's First Celebrity Criminal, 2004; (with T. McShane) The Stolen Masterpiece Tracker: Memoirs of the FBI's Leading Undercover Art Sleuth, 2006. Contributor to periodicals. **Address:** 1628 S Villas Ln., Chandler, AZ 85248-1804, U.S.A. **Online address:** dary@darymatera.com

MATERA, Lia. American/Canadian (born Canada), b. 1952?. **Genres:** Mystery/Crime/Suspense, Novellas/Short Stories. **Career:** Hastings Constitutional Law Quarterly, editor-in-chief, through 1981; Stanford University, Law School, teaching fellow, 1981-82; writer, 1987-. **Publications:** MYSTERY NOVELS: WILLA JANSSON SERIES: Where Lawyers Fear to Tread, 1986; A Radical Departure, 1987; Hidden Agenda, 1988; Prior Convictions, 1991; Last Chants, 1996; Star Witness, 1997; Havana Twist, 1998. LAURA DI PALMA SERIES: The Smart Money, 1988; The Good Fight, 1990; A Hard Bargain, 1992; Face Value, 1993; Designer Crimes, 1995. OTHERS: (ed.) Irreconcilable Differences, 1999; Counsel for the Defense and Other Stories, 2000. Works appear in anthologies. **Address:** Simon & Schuster Inc., 1230 Ave. of the Americas, New York, NY 10020, U.S.A. **Online address:** liamatera@aol.com

MATERSON, Ray. American (born United States), b. 1954?. **Genres:** Art/Art History. **Career:** University of Michigan, Residential College, artist-in-residence. Drug counselor, speaker and author. **Publications:** (With M. Materson) Sins and Needles: A Story of Spiritual Mending, 2002. Contributor to periodicals. **Address:** Workman Publishing Co., 225 Varick St., New York, NY 10014-4381, U.S.A. **Online address:** materson@aol.com

MATES, Susan Onthank. American (born United States), b. 1950. **Genres:** Novellas/Short Stories, Medicine/Health, Young Adult Fiction. **Career:** Lab technician, 1969-72, 1976; Brown University Medical School, assistant professor of medicine, 1982-84, assistant professor of biochemistry, 1984-86, clinical assistant professor of medicine, 1986-93, clinical associate professor of medicine, 1993-; Rhode Island State Tuberculosis Clinic, staff physician, 1986-. Writer. **Publications:** The Good Doctor (short stories), 1994. Contributor to books. **Address:** Roger Williams Medical Center, Rhode Island State Tuberculosis Clinic, 877 Chalkstone Ave., Providence, RI 02901, U.S.A.

MATHABANE, Mark. American/South African (born South Africa), b.

1960. **Genres:** Human Relations/Parenting, Race Relations, Third World, Women's Studies And Issues, Autobiography/Memoirs, Biography. **Career:** Catlin Gabel School, director of multicultural education. Writer and educator, 1985-. **Publications:** Kaffir Boy: The True Story of a Black Youth's Coming of Age in Apartheid South Africa, 1986 in UK as Kaffir Boy: Growing out of Apartheid, 1987; Kaffir Boy in America: An Encounter with Apartheid, 1989; (with G. Mathabane) Love in Black and White: The Triumph of Love over Prejudice and Taboo, 1992; African Women: Three Generations, 1994; Ubuntu: A Novel, 1999; (reteller) Miriam's Song: A Memoir, 2000; Deadly Memory, forthcoming; The Last Liberal, forthcoming. **Address:** 1320 NW Frazier Ct., Portland, OR 97229, U.S.A. **Online address:** mark@mathabane.com

MATHENY, Albert R(alston). American (born United States), b. 1950. **Genres:** Politics/Government, Natural History, Environmental Sciences/Ecology. **Career:** University of Florida, College of Liberal Arts and Sciences, Department of Political Science, associate professor, professor of political science, 1978-, associate chair, graduate coordinator, undergraduate coordinator, associate dean of student affairs, 1998-, Academic Advising Center, director. Writer. **Publications:** (With B.A. Williams) Democracy, Dialogue, and Environmental Disputes: The Contested Languages of Social Regulation, 1995; (contrib.) Democracy Imposed: U.S. Occupation Policy and the German Public, 1945-1949, 1995. **Address:** Department of Political Science, University of Florida, 234 Anderson Hall, PO Box 117325, Gainesville, FL 32611, U.S.A. **Online address:** matheny@polisci.ufl.edu

MATHER, Anne. Also writes as Caroline Fleming, Cardine Fleming. British (born England), b. 1946. **Genres:** Romance/Historical, Novels. **Career:** Writer. **Publications:** Caroline, 1965; Masquerade, 1966; Beloved Stranger, 1966; Design for Loving, 1966; Arrogance of Love, 1968; Dangerous Rhapsody, 1969; Enchanted Island, 1969; (as Caroline Fleming) Dark Venetian, 1969; Tangled Tapestry, 1969; Legend of Lexandros, 1969; Dangerous Enchantment, 1969; Charlottes Hurricane, 1970; The Arrogant Duke, 1970; Who Rides the Tiger, 1970; Moon Witch, 1970; Master of Falcons Head, 1970; Sweet Revenge, 1970; Lord of Zaracus, 1970; The Reluctant Governess, 1971; The Pleasure and the Pain, 1971; The Sanchez Tradition, 1971; Storm in a Rain Barrel, 1971; Dark Enemy, 1971; All the Fire, 1971; The High Valley, 1971; The Autumn of the Witch, 1972; The Night of the Bulls, 1972; Prelude to Enchantment, 1972; Monkshood, 1972; Living with Adam, 1972; A Distant Sound of Thunder, 1972; Jake Howard's Wife, 1973; A Savage Beauty, 1973; Chase a Green Shadow, 1973; White Rose of Winter, 1973; Mask of Scars, 1973; The Waterfalls of the Moon, 1973; The Shrouded Web, 1973; Seen by Candlelight, 1974; Leopard in the Snow, 1974; The Japanese Screen, 1974; Rachel Trevellyan, 1974; Silver Fruit upon Silver Trees, 1974; Dark Moonless Night, 1974; Witchstone, 1974; No Gentle Possession, 1975; For the Love of Sara, 1975; Country of the Falcon, 1975; Dark Castle, 1975; Take What You Want, 1975; Come the Vintage, 1975; Beware the Beast, 1976; Devils Mount, 1976; Forbidden, 1976; Valley Deep Mountain High, 1976; The Smouldering Flame, 1976; Wild Enchantress, 1976; Come Running, 1976; Devil in Velvet, 1977; Pale Dawn Dark Sunset, 1977; Alien Wife, 1977; The Medici Lover, 1977; Born out of Love, 1977; Charade in Winter, 1977; A Trial Marriage, 1977; Fallen Angel, 1978; Captive Destiny, 1978; Scorpions Dance, 1978; Follow Thy Desire, 1978; Proud Harvest, 1978; Lorens Baby, 1978; Rooted in Dishonour, 1978; Apollos Seed, 1979; Lure of Eagles, 1979; Melting Fire, 1979; Spirit of Atlantis, 1980; Whisper of Darkness, 1980; Images of Love, 1980; Sandstorm, 1980; A Haunting Compulsion, 1981; Duelling Fire, 1981; Forbidden Flame, 1981; Castles of Sand, 1981; Innocent Obsession, 1981; The Judas Trap, 1981; Hell or High Water, 1981; Stormspell, 1982; Impetuous Masquerade, 1982; A Passionate Affair, 1982; Smokescreen, 1982; Season of Mist, 1982; Edge of Temptation, 1982; Sirocco, 1983; Wild Concerto, 1983; Green Lightning, 1983; Cage of Shadows, 1983; An Elusive Desire, 1983; Moondrift, 1984; Pale Orchid, 1985; Act of Possession, 1985; An All-Consuming Passion, 1985; Stolen Summer, 1985; Hidden in the Flame, 1985; The Longest Pleasure, 1986; Burning Inheritance, 1987; Night Heat, 1987; A Fever in the Blood, 1989; Dark Mosaic, 1989; A Relative Betrayal, 1990; Diamond Fire, 1991; Betrayed, 1991; Blind Passion, 1991; Such Sweet Poison, 1991; Tidewater Seduction, 1992; Dangerous Sanctuary, 1992; Snowfire, 1993; Tender Assault, 1993; Rich as Sin, 1993; Anne Mather Duet, 1994; Strange Intimacy, 1994; Raw Silk, 1994; Treacherous Longings, 1995; A Woman of Passion, 1995; Relative Sins, 1996; Wicket Caprice, 1996; Lorens Baby, 1997; Dangerous Temptation, 1997; Dishonorable Intent, 1997; Long Nights Loving, 1997; Scorpions Dance, 1997; A Trial Marriage, 1997; Shattered Illusions, 1997; Pacific Heat, 1998; Sinful Pleasures, 1998; The Baby Gambit, 1999; Her Guilty Secret, 1999; Morgans Child, 1999; Wild Concerto, 1999; Seduction Guaranteed, 2000; All Night Long, 2000; Innocent Sins, 2000; The Millionaires Virgin, 2000; Savage Innocence, 2001; A Rich Man's Touch, 2001; His Virgin Mistress, 2002; Pacific Passions, 2002; Hot Pursuit, 2002; Sinful Truths, 2003; Stay Through the Night, 2003; Alejandro's Revenge, 2003; Forbidden Mistress, 2004; The Rodrigues Pregnancy, 2004; In the Italian's Bed, 2004; Savage Awakening, 2005; Jack Riordan's Baby, 2006; The Greek Tycoon's Pregnant Wife, 2007; Bedded for the Italian's Pleasure, 2007; The Pregnancy Affair, 2007; Mendez's Mistress, 2008; The Brazilian Millionaire's Love-Child, 2009; His Forbidden Passion, 2009; (with J. James and C. Marinelli) Passion & Pleasure, 2009; Innocent Virgin, Wild Surrender, 2010; (with S. Craven and M. Cox) Passionate Protectors?, 2010; (with C. Spencer and C. Marinelli) Tall, Dark and Italian, 2010; (with T. Morey and C. Mortimer) Virgin: Wedded by a Billionaire, 2010; Nights of Passion, 2011. **Address:** Harlequin Mills & Boon Ltd., Eton House, 18-24 Paradise Rd., Richmond, SR TW9 1SR, England. **Online address:** mystic-am@msn.com

MATHES, Charles (Elliott). American (born United States), b. 1949. **Genres:** Mystery/Crime/Suspense, Novels, Art/Art History, Poetry, Literary Criticism And History. **Career:** The Loretto Hilto Repertory Co., L.O.R.T. Theatre, script reader, 1971-72; St. Louisan Magazine, editor, 1972-73; Rodgers and Hammerstein, director, 1975-86; Visibles Inc., appraiser of fine and decorative arts, 1986-93; Jane Kahan Gallery, director, 1993-; Manhattan Gallery, director, 1993. **Publications:** Spirit of America: A State by State Celebration, 1990; Treasures of American Museums, 1991; In Every Moon There Is a Face: Poem (children's book), 2003. NOVELS: The Girl with the Phony Name, 1992; The Girl Who Remembered Snow, 1996; The Girl at the End of the Line, 1999; The Girl in the Face of the Clock, 2001. **Address:** Jane Kahan Gallery, 922 Madison Ave., 73rd St., Mezzanine Level, New York, NY 10021, U.S.A. **Online address:** charlesmathes@charlesmathes.com

MATHESON, Ann. Scottish (born Scotland), b. 1940. **Genres:** Librarianship, Language/Linguistics, Literary Criticism And History. **Career:** National Library of Scotland, assistant keeper, 1975-82, keeper, 1983-2000; Scottish Arts Council, Literature Committee, chairman, 1987-2003; Consortium of European Research Libraries, chairman, 2000-06; NEWSPLAN, chairman, 2000-08; LIBER, secretary-general, 2007-; University of Edinburgh, secretary of the general council, honorary editor, 2001-; Sabhal Mor Ostaig Library, chairman of the advisory committee, 2008-. Writer. **Publications:** (With M. Ferguson) The Scottish Gaelic Union Catalogue, vol. I, 1984; (ed. with P. Cadell) For the Encouragement of Learning, 1989; Theories of Rhetoric in the Eighteenth-Century Sermon, 1995; Old Tinto Villages, 1998. **Address:** National Library of Scotland, George IV Bridge, Edinburgh, EH1 1EW, Scotland. **Online address:** a.matheson@nls.uk

MATHESON, Richard (Burton). Also writes as Josh Rogan, Logan Swanson. American (born United States), b. 1926. **Genres:** Novellas/Short Stories, Mystery/Crime/Suspense, Romance/Historical, Science Fiction/Fantasy, Westerns/Adventure, Novels, Young Adult Non-fiction. **Career:** Writer. **Publications:** Someone Is Bleeding, 1953; Fury on Sunday, 1953; I Am Legend (SF novel), 1954; Born of Man and Woman (short stories), 1954 as Third from the Sun, 1954; Woman, 1954; The Shrinking Man (SF novel), 1956; The Shores of Space (short stories), 1957; A Stir of Echoes, 1958; Ride the Nightmare, 1959; The Beardless Warriors, 1960; Shock! (short stories), 1961; (with E. Lee) Comedy of Terrors, 1964; Shock 2 (short stories), 1964; Shock 3 (short stories), 1966; Shockwaves (short stories), 1970; Shock 4 (short stories), 1970; Hell House, 1971; (with J. Rice) The Night Stalker, 1972; The Night Strangler, 1973; Bid Time Return, 1975 as Somewhere in Time, 1999; What Dreams May Come: A Novel, 1978; (as Logan Swanson) Earthbound, 1982; (ed. with M.H. Greenberg and C.G. Waugh) Twilight Zone: The Original Stories, 1985; Darker, 1988; Richard Matheson: The Collected Stories, 1989; Journal of the Gun Years, 1991; The Gun Fight, 1993; 7 Steps to Midnight, 1993; The Path: A New Look at Reality, 1993; By the Gun, 1993; Shadow on the Sun, 1994; Now You See It, 1995; (ed. with R. Mainhardt) Robert Bloch: Appreciations of the Master, 1995; The Memoirs of Wild Bill Hickok, 1996; Hunger and Thirst, 2000; Medium's Rare, 2000; Nightmare at 20,000 Feet: Horror Stories, 2000; Hunted Past Reason, 2002; Abu and the Seven Marvels, 2002; Duel: Terror Stories, 2002; A Primer of Reality, 2002; Offbeat, 2002; (contrib.) Dogs of War, 2002; (with R.C. Matheson) Pride, 2002; Come Fygures, Come Shadowes, 2003; Darker Places, 2004; Richard Matheson's Hell House, 2004; Richard Matheson's Kolchak Scripts, 2004; Unrealized Dreams, 2004; (co-author) Kiss the Whip, 2005; Noir: Three Novels of Suspense, 2005; Unrealized Dreams: Three Scripts, 2005; The Link, 2006; Visions of Death: Richard Matheson's Edgar Allan Poe Scripts, vol. I, 2007; The Richard Matheson Companion, 2007; (with R. Bloch, D.J. Schow and F.P. Wilson) Completely Doomed, 2007; Matheson Uncollected, vol. I, 2007, vol. II, 2010; Button, Button: Uncanny Stories, 2008; Visions Deferred, 2009; (with J. Hill and S. King) Road Rage, 2009; Legends of the Gun Years, 2010; (contrib.) He is Legend, 2010; The Box, 2010; Other Kingdoms, 2011; Steel and other Stories, 2011. **Address:** PO Box 81, Woodland Hills, CA 91365-0081, U.S.A.

MATHEWS, Aidan (Carl). Irish (born Ireland), b. 1956?. **Genres:** Novels, Novellas/Short Stories, Poetry, Young Adult Fiction. **Career:** Raidió Teilifís Éireann, drama producer; St. Louis High School, teacher in English; Belvedere College, faculty in English. Writer. **Publications:** Windfalls (poetry), 1977; Minding Ruth (poetry), 1983; (ed.) Immediate Man: Cuimhni ar Chearbhall O Dalaigh, 1983; Adventures in a Bathyscope (short stories), 1988; Muesli at Midnight (novel), 1990; Exit/Entrance, 1990; Lipstick on the Host (short stories), 1992; According to the Small Hours, 1998; Communion, 2002; In the Poorer Quarters, 2007. **Address:** c/o Harcourt Brace, Harcourt Brace & Company, 6277 Sea Harbor Dr., Orlando, FL 32887, U.S.A. **Online address:** aidan.mathews@rte.ie

MATHEWS, Dan. American (born United States), b. 1964. **Genres:** Animals/Pets, Humor/Satire. **Career:** People for the Ethical Treatment of Animals, senior vice president. Writer. **Publications:** Committed: A Rabble-Rouser's Memoir, 2007. Contributor to periodicals. **Address:** People for the Ethical Treatment of Animals, 501 Front St., Norfolk, VA 23510, U.S.A. **Online address:** danm@peta.org

MATHEWS, Eleanor. *See* **MATHEWS, Ellie.**

MATHEWS, Ellie. (Eleanor Mathews). American (born United States), b. 1945?. **Genres:** Novels. **Career:** Writer. **Publications:** (as Eleanor Mathews) Ambassador to the Penguins: A Naturalist's Year aboard a Yankee Whaleship, 2003; The Linden Tree (novel), 2007; The Ungarnished Truth: A Cooking Contest Memoir, 2008. **Address:** Seattle, WA , U.S.A. **Online address:** ellie@elliemathews.com

MATHEWS, Lou. American (born United States), b. 1946. **Genres:** Novels, Young Adult Fiction, Literary Criticism And History. **Career:** Glendale College, editor, 1968-70; Glendale New Press, sportswriter, 1968-70; Bob's Big Boy Family Restaurants, editor of national and local corporate house organs, 1968-70; Sundaze, fiction editor, 1971-73; University of California-Santa Cruz, Quarry West, editor, 1977-80; L.A. Style, contributing editor, 1988-94, restaurant reviewer, 1992-94; University of California-Los Angeles, Westword, fiction editor, 1992-96, Writers' Program, instructor, 1989-. **Publications:** Valley Light, 1978; Portales (Spanish language text), 1987; Just Like James, 1996; L.A. Breakdown, 1999; The Muse in the Bottle: Great Writers Celebrate Drinking, 2002; Shaky Town; Quotations from Chairman Lou, forthcoming; Heal, forthcoming. **Address:** Extension Writers' Program, University of California, 10995 Le Conte Ave., Rm. 440, Los Angeles, CA 90024, U.S.A.

MATHEWS, (Thomas) Jay. American (born United States), b. 1945. **Genres:** Documentaries/Reportage, Social Sciences. **Career:** Washington Post, education reporter, 1971-; Newsweek, correspondent, 1992. **Publications:** (With L. Mathews) One Billion: A China Chronicle, 1983; (with S.M. Goldstein) Sino-American Relations After Normalization: Toward the Second Decade, 1986; Escalante: The Best Teacher in America, 1988; A Mother's Touch: The Tiffany Callo Story, 1992; Class Struggle: What's Wrong (and right) with America's Best Public High Schools, 1998; Harvard, Schmarvard: Getting Beyond the Ivy League to the College that is Best for You, 2003; (with I. Hill) Supertest: How the International Baccalaureate Can Strengthen Our Schools, 2005; Work Hard, Be Nice: How Two Inspired Teachers Created America's Best Schools, 2009. Contributor to periodicals. **Address:** Washington Post, 1150 15th St. NW, Washington, DC 20071, U.S.A. **Online address:** mathewsj@washpost.com

MATHEWSON, Casey C. M. German/American (born United States), b. 1961?. **Genres:** Architecture. **Career:** Haug & Mathewson Architekten, partner, 1992-2002; Mathewson Architektur Berlin (architectural research firm), founder, 2003-. Architect and writer. **Publications:** (Contri.) The New German Architecture, 1993; Architecture Today, 2004; XX Small Houses, 2005; Beach Houses, 2005; Architecture Directory, 2005; Frank O. Gehry: 1969-Heute, 21 Werke=Frank O. Gehry: 1969-Today, 21 Works in US as Frank O. Gehry: Selected Works, 1969 to Today, 2007; International Houses Atlas, 2007; (ed.) Residential Designs for the 21st Century: An International Collection, 2007. **Address:** Mathewson Architektur Berlin, Albrechtstrasse 122, Berlin, D-12099, Germany. **Online address:** info@mathewson-architektur.de

MATHEZ, Edmond A. American (born United States) **Genres:** Sciences, Earth Sciences. **Career:** University of Washington, geologist, 1973-83, Department of geological sciences, research assistant professor, 1983-87; Universite de Paris, associate, 1986-87; American Museum of Natural History, assistant curator, 1987-91, associate curator, 1991-96, curator, 1996-, Department of Earth and Planetary Sciences, chairman, 1993-99, Senate of the Scientific Staff, chairman, 1994-96, Gottesman Hall of Planet Earth, chief curator, 1999-; University of Copenhagen, Geologic Museum, visiting professor, 2000-01; City University of New York, Department of Earth and Environmental Sciences, adjunct professor; Columbia University, Lamont Doherty Earth Observatory, senior research scientist. Writer. **Publications:** (Ed.) Earth: Inside Out, 2001; (with J.D. Webster) The Earth Machine: The Science of a Dynamic Planet, 2004; Climate Change: The Science of Global Warming and Our Energy Future, 2009. Contributor to periodicals. **Address:** Department of Earth and Planetary Sciences, American Museum of Natural History, Central Park W 79th St., New York, NY 10024-5192, U.S.A. **Online address:** mathez@amnh.org

MATHIAS, Peter. British (born England), b. 1928. **Genres:** History, Business/Trade/Industry, Economics. **Career:** Cambridge University, Jesus College, research fellow, 1952-55, Queens College, fellow and director of studies in history, 1955-68, assistant lecturer on history, 1955-60, tutor, 1957-65, lecturer, 1960-68; University of Toronto, visiting professor, 1961; School of Advanced Studies, visiting professor, 1966; Solihill School, governor, 1966-72; Cambridge Economic History of Europe, general editor, 1967-84; Debates in Economic History, general editor, 1967-84; Oxford University, All Souls College, Chichele Professor of Economic History and fellow, 1969-87, emeritus fellow, 1987-; Abbey School, governor, 1969-; University of Pennsylvania, visiting professor, 1972; Barnard College, Virginia Gildersleeve Professor, 1972; Downing College, master and honorary fellow, 1987-95. **Publications:** The Brewing Industry in England, 1700-1830, 1959; English Trade Tokens: The Industrial Revolution Illustrated, 1962; Retailing Revolution: A History of Multiple Retailing in the Food Trades Based Upon the Allied Suppliers Group of Companies, 1967; The First Industrial Nation: An Economic History of Britain, 1700-1914, 1969, 2nd ed., 1988; (with T.C. Barker and R.H. Campbell) Business History, 2nd ed., 1971; Living with the Neighbours: The Role of Economic History: An Inaugural Lecture Delivered Before the University in the Hall of All Souls College, Oxford, on 24 November 1970, 1971; The Transformation of England: Essays in the Economic and Social History of England in the Eighteenth Century, 1979; (intro.) Accountancy and the British Economy, 1840-1980: The Evolution of Ernst & Whinney, 1981; (co-author) Rivoluzione industriale tra il Settecento e l'Ottocento, 1984; L'Economia Britannica dal 1815 al 1914, 1994; (contrib.) From Family Firms to Corporate Capitalism: Essays in Business and Industrial History in Honour of Peter Mathias, 1998; Cinque lezioni deteoria e storia, 2003. EDITOR: (with A.W.H. Pearsall) Shipping: A Survey of Historical Records, 1971; Science and Society 1600-1900, 1972; (with D.C. Coleman) Enterprise and History: Essays in Honour of Charles Wilson, 1984; (with J. Mason and J.H. Westcott) Predictability in Science and Society: A Joint Symposium of the Royal Society and the British Academy Held on 20 and 21 March 1986, 1986; (with J.A. Davis) The First Industrial Revolutions, 1990; (with J.A. Davis) Innovation and Technology in Europe: From the Eighteenth Century to the Present Day, 1991; (with T. Thompson) Standards & Mental Handicap: Keys to Competence, 1992; (with J.A. Davis) Enterprise and Labour: From the Eighteenth Century to the Present, 1996; (with J.A. Davis) Agriculture and Industrialization: From the Eighteenth Century to the Present Day, 1996; (with J.A. Davis) International Trade and British Economic Growth: From the Eighteenth Century to the Present Day, 1996. **Address:** All Souls College, Oxford University, 27 High St., Oxford, OX OX1 4AL, England.

MATHIESON, Donald Lindsay. New Zealander (born New Zealand), b. 1936?. **Genres:** Law, Theology/Religion. **Career:** Barrister, 1959-; Victoria University, lecturer, 1961-71, professor of law, 1977-81; Crown Law Office, crown counsel, 1971-76; Hogg Gillespie Carter and Oakley, senior partner, 1981-85; Queen's counsel, 1986. Writer. **Publications:** (Ed.) Cross on Evidence, 1963, 8th ed., 2005; Industrial Law in New Zealand, vol. I, 1970; (ed.) Faith at Work, 2001. **Address:** 33 Marsden Ave., Karori, Wellington, 6012, New Zealand.

MATHIS, Sharon Bell. American (born United States), b. 1937. **Genres:** Novels, Poetry, Biography, Children's Fiction. **Career:** Holy Redeemer Elementary School, teacher, 1959-65; Stuart Junior High School, teacher, 1965-75; News Explorer, D.C. Black Writers Workshop, writer-in-charge, 1970-73, director; Howard University, writer-in-residence, 1972-74; Ebony Junior! magazine, columnist, 1973-; Benning Elementary School, librarian, 1975-76; Friendship Educational Center, librarian, 1976-. **Publications:** Brooklyn Story, 1970; Sidewalk Story, 1971; Teacup Full of Roses, 1972; Ray Charles (biography), 1973; Listen for the Fig Tree, 1974; The Hundred Penny Box, 1975; Cartwheels (novel), 1978; Red Dog, Blue Fly, 1991; Running Girl: The Diary of Ebonee Rise, 1997. **Address:** Harcourt Trade Division, 525 B St., Ste. 1900, San Diego, CA 92101, U.S.A.

MATHISON, Melissa. Also writes as Melissa Mathison Ford. American (born United States), b. 1950. **Genres:** Plays/Screenplays, Film, Communications/Media, Biography. **Career:** Screenwriter and journalist. **Publications:** (As Melissa Mathison Ford) (forward) My Land and My People: The Original Autobiography of His Holiness the Dalai Lama of Tibet, 1997. Contributor to periodicals. **Address:** ICM, 40 W 57th St., New York, NY 10019, U.S.A.

MATILSKY, Sarah. *See* **RUTHCHILD, Rochelle Goldberg.**

MATLIN, David. American (born United States), b. 1944. **Genres:** Novels, Poetry, Humanities, Literary Criticism And History, Politics/Government, Young Adult Non-fiction. **Career:** State University of New York, Undergraduate and Graduate Prison Education Program, teacher, 1985-93; writer, 1993-97; San Diego State University, associate professor of creative writing, 1997-; Golden Handcuffs Review, contributing editor. **Publications:** Fontana's Mirror (poetry), 1982; Album, 1988; China Beach (poetry and prose), 1989; Dressed in Protective Fashion (poetry and prose), 1990; How the Night Is Divided (novel), 1993; Vernooykill Creek: The Crisis of Prisons in America (non-fiction), 1997; Halfman Dreamer, 1999; Prisons: Inside the New America: From Vernooykill Creek to Abu Ghraib, 2005; It Might Do Well with Strawberries, 2009. **Address:** Department of English & Comparative Literature, San Diego State University, 5500 Campanile Dr., San Diego, CA 92182-6020, U.S.A. **Online address:** dmatlin@mail.sdsu.edu

MATLOCK, Jack F. American (born United States), b. 1929. **Genres:** International Relations/Current Affairs, Area Studies. **Career:** Dartmouth College, instructor of Russian literature and culture, 1953-56; American Embassy-Soviet Union, vice consul and third secretary, 1961-63, minister counselor and deputy chief of mission, 1974-78, chargé d'Affaires ad interim, 1981; Vanderbilt University, visiting professor of political science, 1978-79; ambassador-Czechoslovakia, 1981-83; National Security Council, special assistant and senior director for European and Soviet affairs, 1983-86; ambassador-USSR, 1987-91; Columbia University, senior research fellow, 1991-93, Kathryn and Shelby Cullom Davis professor in the practice of international diplomacy, 1993-96, School of International and Public Affairs, adjunct professor of international and public affairs; Institute for Advanced Study, School of Historical Studies, George F. Kennan professor, 1996-2001; Princeton University, Joseph Weinberg visiting professor, 2001-02, Public and International Affairs, lecturer in public and international affairs, 2001-04; Hamilton College, Sol Linowitz professor of international relations, 2006. Writer. **Publications:** An Index to the Collected Works of J. V. Stalin, 1955; Autopsy on an Empire: The American Ambassador's Account of the Collapse of the Soviet Union, 1995; (intro.) Russia's Fate through Russian Eyes, 2001; Smert imperii, 2003; Reagan and Gorbachev: How the Cold War Ended, 2004; Superpower Illusions: How Myths and False Ideologies Led America Astray-And How to Return to Reality, 2010. Contributor to periodicals. **Address:** School of International and Public Affairs, Columbia University, International Affairs Bldg., 13th Fl., 420 W 118th St., New York, NY 10027-7235, U.S.A. **Online address:** jfm10@columbia.edu

MATOTT, Justin. American (born United States), b. 1961. **Genres:** Children's Fiction, Adult Non-fiction, Picture/Board Books, Young Adult Fiction. **Career:** Skoob Books, owner. Writer. **Publications:** ADULT NON FICTION: My Garden Visits, 1996; A Harvest of Reflections: Wisdom for the Soul through the Seasons, 1998; Independence Days: Still Just Boys and Other Stories, 2000; The Milestones Project: Celebrating Childhood Around the World, 2004; Aliens-All Mixed Up, 2008; The World According to Gabe, 2009. FOR CHILDREN: Ol' Lady Grizelda, 1998; When Did I Meet You Grandma?, 2000; When Did I Meet You Grandpa?, 2000; Drinking Fountain Joe, 2000; A Rabbit's Tale, 2000; Oliver Kringle, 2002; I Am A Poet!, 2003; I Am A Writer!, 2003; I Am An Artist!, 2003; I Can Write a Picturebook, 2003; The Milestones Project: Celebrating Childhood Around the World, 2004; The Sky is Falling, 2004; When I was a Boy-I Dreamed, 2004; When I Was a Girl-I Dreamed, 2005; The Tales of Mr. Murphy, 2005; There's a Fly on My Toast!, 2005; Chocolate Covered Frog Legs, 2005; Benjamin Bailey Goes to the Zoo, 2005; Go Ask Mom, 2006; Gabriel Book Of World Records, 2010. Contributor to periodicals. **Address:** Skoob Books, PO Box 631183, Littleton, CO 80163, U.S.A. **Online address:** justin@justinmatott.com

MATOUSEK, Mark. American (born United States), b. 1957. **Genres:** Young Adult Non-fiction. **Career:** Writer. V-Men, creative director, 2009-. Writer. **Publications:** NONFICTION: A Day in the Life of Hollywood: As Seen by 75 of the World's Leading Photographers on One Day, May 20, 1992, 1992; (ed.) Dialogues with a Modern Mystic, 1994; Sex, Death, Enlightenment: A True Story, 1996; The Boy He Left Behind: A Man's Search for His Lost Father, 2000; (ed.) Still Here: Embracing Aging, Changing and Dying, 2000; When You're Falling, Dive: Lessons in the Art of Living, 2008; Ethical Wisdom: What Makes Us Good, 2010. Contributor to books and periodicals. **Address:** c/o Joy Harris, 156 5th Ave., Ste. 617, New York, NY 10010, U.S.A.

MATOVINA, Timoteo. *See* **MATOVINA, Timothy M.**

MATOVINA, Timothy M. (Timoteo Matovina). American (born United States), b. 1955. **Genres:** Theology/Religion, Cultural/Ethnic Topics, History, Young Adult Non-fiction. **Career:** Loyola Marymount University, assistant professor, 1995-2000; University of Notre Dame, College of Arts and Letters, Department of Theology, associate professor, 2000-, professor, Cushwa Center for the Study of American Catholicism, William and Anna Jean Cushwa director, 2002-. Writer. **Publications:** NONFICTION: The Alamo Remembered: Tejano Accounts and Perspectives, 1995; Tejano Religion and Ethnicity: San Antonio, 1821-1860, 1995; (with V.P. Elizondo) San Fernando Cathedral: Soul of the City, 1998; (with V.P. Elizondo) Mestizo Worship: A Pastoral Approach to Liturgical Ministry, 1998; Guadalupe and Her Faithful: Latino Catholics in San Antonio, from Colonial Origins to the Present, 2005; Latino Catholicism: Transformation in America's Largest Church, 2012. EDITOR: (with A.F. Deck and Y. Tarango) Perspectivas: Hispanic Ministry, 1995; (with D.R. McDonald) Defending Mexican Valor in Texas: José Antonio Navarro's Historical Writings, 1853-1857, 1995; Beyond Borders: Writings of Virgilio Elizondo and Friends, 2000; (with G.E. Poyo) Presente!: U.S. Latino Catholics from Colonial Origins to the Present, 2000; (with G. Riebe-Estrella) Horizons of the Sacred: Mexican Traditions in U.S. Catholicism, 2002; (as Timoteo Matovina with A.M. Isasi-Díaz and N.M. Torres-Vidal) Camino a Emaús: compartiendo el ministerio de Jesús, 2002; (with V. Elizondo and A.F. Deck) The Treasure of Guadalupe, 2006; (and intro.) Virgilio Elizondo: Spiritual Writings, 2010. Contributor to journals. **Address:** Department of Theology, College of Arts and Letters, University of Notre Dame, 403 Geddes Hall, Notre Dame, IN 46556, U.S.A. **Online address:** matovina.1@nd.edu

MATRAY, James I(rving). American (born United States), b. 1948. **Genres:** History, Politics/Government, International Relations/Current Affairs. **Career:** University of Warsaw, Fulbright lecturer, 1988-89; University of Southern California, visiting associate professor of history, 1988-89; New Mexico State University, visiting assistant professor, 1980-82, assistant professor, 1982-87, associate professor, 1987-92, professor of history, 1992-2002, emeritus professor, 2002-; California State University, professor of history and chair of department, 2002-. Writer. **Publications:** The Reluctant Crusade: American Foreign Policy in Korea, 1941-1950, 1985; (ed.) A Historical Dictionary of the Korean War, 1991; (with K.C. Baum) Korea and the Cold War: Division, Destruction, and Disarmament, 1991; The Emergence of Japan as a Global Power, 2001; Encyclopedia of U.S.-East Asian Relations, 2002; (ed.) East Asia and the United States: An Encyclopedia of Relations since 1784, 2002; Korea Divided: The 38th Parallel and the Demilitarized Zone, 2005; (ed. with J. Kim and X. Li) The Encyclopedia of the Korean War: A Political, Social and Military History, 2nd ed., 2010. **Address:** Department of History, California State University, Rm. 223B, Trinity Hall, Chico, CA 95929-0761, U.S.A. **Online address:** jmatray@csuchico.edu

MATSEN, Bradford (Conway). American (born United States), b. 1944. **Genres:** Natural History, Plays/Screenplays, Sciences, Business/Trade/Industry. **Career:** Freelance journalist, photographer, 1970-; Matsen/Schnaper and Associates, consultant, 1976-77; Film Seattle Cinema Guide, publisher, 1978-79, editor, 1978-80; Alaska Fisherman's Journal, editor, 1980-84; National Fisherman Magazine, editor, 1985-; Mediation Institute and National Public

Radio, consultant; Public Broadcasting Service (PBS), producer of television documentary, 2002. **Publications:** Deep Sea Fishing, 1990; Northwest Coast: Essays and Images from the Columbia River to the Cook Inlet, 1991; Ray Troll's Shocking Fish Tales: Fish, Romance and Death in Pictures, 1991; Planet Ocean: A Story of Life, the Sea, and Dancing to the Fossil Record, 1994; (with T. Jay) Reaching Home: Pacific Salmon, Pacific People, 1994; Raptors, Fossils, Fins & Fangs: A Prehistoric Creature Feature, 1996; Fishing Up North: Stories of Luck and Loss in Alaskan Waters, 1998; Faces of Fishing: People, Food and the Sea at the Beginning of the Twenty-First Century, 1998; (with N. Burnett) Shape of Life, 2002; Incredible Submersible Alvin Discovers a Strange Deep-Sea World, 2003; Incredible Record-Setting Deep-Sea Dive of the Bathysphere, 2003; Incredible Search for the Treasure Ship Atocha, 2003; Extreme Dive Under the Antarctic Ice, 2003; Incredible Hunt for the Giant Squid, 2003; Incredible Quest to Find the Titanic, 2003; Descent: The Heroic Discovery of the Abyss, 2005; Go Wild in New York City, 2005; Titanic's Last Secrets: The Further Adventures of Shadow Divers John Chatterton and Richie Kohler, 2008; Jacques Cousteau: The Sea King, 2009; Death and Oil, 2011. **Address:** 7554 26th Ave. NW, Seattle, WA 98117-4423, U.S.A. **Online address:** bradocean@earthlink.net

MATSON, Cathy. American (born United States), b. 1951?. **Genres:** History, Business/Trade/Industry, Economics, Industrial Relations, Reference. **Career:** United Automotive, Aerospace, and Agricultural Implement Workers of America, instructor in Spanish, 1974-77; Cambridge University, tutor in U.S. history, 1981; Columbia University, instructor in history, 1982; State University of New York, Center for Labor Studies, adjunct teacher of history and labor studies, 1982-84; University of Tennessee, assistant professor of history, 1985-90; Trinity College, lecturer, 1985; University of Delaware, associate professor of history, 1990-, now professor; Johns Hopkins University, lecturer, 1994; University of Pennsylvania, lecturer, 1998. Writer. **Publications:** (Contrib.) New York and the Rise of American Capitalism, 1988; (with P. Onuf) A Union of Interests: Politics and Economy in the Revolutionary Era, 1990; (contrib.) New York and the Union: Contributions to the American Constitutional Experience, 1990; (contrib.) New York in the Age of the Constitution, 1992; (contrib.) Wages of Independence: Capitalism in the Early American Republic, 1997; Merchants and Empire: Trading in Colonial New York, 1998; (with S.M. Gillon) The American Experiment: A History of the United States, 2001, 3rd ed., 2009; (ed.) Economy of Early America: Historical Perspectives & New Directions, 2006. Contributor of articles to journals and books. **Address:** Department of History, University of Delaware, 121 John Munroe Hall, Newark, DE 19716, U.S.A. **Online address:** cmatson@udel.edu

MATSON, Suzanne. American (born United States), b. 1959. **Genres:** Poetry, Novels. **Career:** University of Washington, lecturer in English, 1987-88; Boston College, Department of English, assistant professor, 1988-94, associate professor, 1994-2002, professor, 2002-, chair. Writer. **Publications:** Sea Level: Poems, 1990; Durable Goods: Poems, 1993; The Hunger Moon: A Novel, 1997; A Trick of Nature: A Novel, 2000; Tree-Sitter: A Novel, 2006. Contributor to magazines. Works appear in anthologies. **Address:** Department of English, Boston College, 450 Carney Hall, 140 Commonwealth Ave., Chestnut Hill, MA 02467, U.S.A. **Online address:** suzanne.matson@bc.edu

MATSON, Wallace I. (Wallace Irving Matson). American (born United States), b. 1921. **Genres:** Philosophy, History, Theology/Religion, Young Adult Fiction. **Career:** Pomona College, visiting assistant professor of philosophy, 1949-50; University of Washington, assistant professor of philosophy, 1950-55; University of California, assistant professor, 1955-58, associate professor, 1958-65, professor of philosophy, 1965-91, chair of department, 1968-71, professor emeritus, 1991-. Writer. **Publications:** The Existence of God, 1965; A History of Philosophy, 1968; Sentience, 1976; (with T.B. Warren) The Warren-Matson Debate on the Existence of God, 1978; A New History of Philosophy, 1987, 2nd ed., 2000; Uncorrected Papers: Diverse Philosophical Dissents, 2006; Grand Theories and Everyday Beliefs, 2011. Contributor to journals. **Address:** Department of Philosophy, University of California, 244 Moses Hall, Ste. 2390, Berkeley, CA 94720-2390, U.S.A.

MATSON, Wallace Irving. *See* **MATSON, Wallace I.**

MATSUDA, Mari J. American (born United States), b. 1934?. **Genres:** History, Law. **Career:** Honorable Herbert Y.C. Choy of the Ninth Circuit Court of Appeals, law clerk; King & Nakamura, associate; training consultant; University of Hiroshima, lecturer; Stanford Law School, professor; University of Hawaii School of Law, professor; University of California, professor of law; Georgetown University Law Center, professor of law. Writer. **Publications:** (Ed.) Called from Within: Early Women Lawyers of Hawaii, 1992; Words that Wound: Critical Race Theory, Assaultive Speech, and the First Amendment, 1993; Where is Your Body?: And Other Essays on Race, Gender and the Law, 1996; (with C.R. Lawrence) We Won't Go Back: Making the Case for Affirmative Action, 1997. **Address:** Georgetown University Law Center, 600 New Jersey Ave. NW, McDonough 516, Washington, DC 20001, U.S.A. **Online address:** matsuda@law.georgetown.edu

MATSUMURA, Takao. Japanese (born Japan), b. 1942. **Genres:** Economics, History, Business/Trade/Industry, Industrial Relations. **Career:** Keio University, associate professor, 1972-81, professor of social history, 1982-. Writer. **Publications:** The Labour Aristocracy Revisited: The Victorian Flint Glass Makers, 1850-1880, 1983; (contrib.) 731 Butai sakusei shiryo, 1991; The Debates on the Unit 731, 1995; (ed. with K. Gakushi and E.K. Hencho) Mantetsu rōdōshi no kenkyū, 2002; (contrib.) Man tie yu Zhongguo lao gong, 2003; (ed. with M.S. hen kaisetsu) Kantōgun Kagakubu dokugasusen kyōiku enshū kankei shiryō, 2006; Nihon teikoku shugika no shokuminchi rōdōshi, 2007; Nihon teikoku shugika no shokuminchi rōodōshi, 2007; Saiban to rekishigaku: 731 Saikinsen Butai o hōtei kara miru, 2007; (with Y. Asobu and E.K. Hen) Mantetsu no chōsa to kenkyū: sono shinwa to jitsuzō, 2008. Contributor to periodicals. **Address:** Department of Economics, Keio University, 2-15-45 Mita, Minato-ku, Tokyo, 108-8345, Japan.

MATSUSAKA, John G. American (born United States), b. 1964?. **Genres:** Politics/Government, Economics, Adult Non-fiction. **Career:** University of Chicago, Department of Economics, lecturer in economics, 1987-89, George J. Stigler Center for the Study of the Economy and the State, John M. Olin visiting professor of economics, 2001; University of Southern California, Marshall School of Business, faculty, 1991-2000, assistant professor, 2001-, associate professor, professor of finance and business economics and Charles F. Sexton chair in American enterprise, vice-dean for faculty and academic affairs, 2007-, Gould School of Law, professor of business and law, 2004-, Department of Political Science, professor, 2005-, Dornsife College of Letters, Arts and Sciences, professor; Initiative and Referendum Institute, senior research fellow and board director, 1998-2003, president, 2004-; Stanford University, Hoover Institution, National fellow, 1994-95; White House Council of Economic Advisors, consultant. Writer. **Publications:** For the Many or the Few: The Initiative, Public Policy and American Democracy, 2004. Contributor to journals. **Address:** Office of the Vice Dean, Marshall School of Business, University of Southern California, 101L Bridge, 3670 Trousdale Pkwy., Los Angeles, CA 90089-0802, U.S.A. **Online address:** matsusak@usc.edu

MATTAWA, Khaled. American (born United States), b. 1964. **Genres:** Poetry, Translations. **Career:** California State University, professor; University of Michigan, associate professor; Banipal, contributing editor. Translator. **Publications:** POETRY: Ismalia Eclipse, 1995; Zodiac of Echoes, 2003; Amorisco, 2008; Tocqueville, 2010. TRANSLATOR FROM ARABIC: H. Janabi, Questions and Their Retinue, 1996; S. Youssef, Without an Alphabet, Without a Face: Selected Poems, 2002; F. Al-Azzawi, Miracle Maker: Selected Poems of Fadhil Al-Azzawi, 2003; M. Al-Massri, A Red Cherry on a White-Tiled Floor: Selected Poems, 2004; I. Mersal, These Are Not Oranges, My Love: Selected Poems, 2008; Adonis, Adonis: Selected Poems, 2010. OTHERS: (ed. with M. Akash) Post-Gibran Anthology of New Arab American Writing, 1999; (ed. with P. Kaldas) Dinarzad's Children: An Anthology of Contemporary Arab American Fiction, 2004; (ed. and intro.) Invitation to a Secret Feast: Selected Poems, 2008. Works appear in anthologies. Contributor to journals. **Address:** Department of English Language and Literature, University of Michigan, 3187 Angell Hall, 435 S State St., Ann Arbor, MI 48109, U.S.A. **Online address:** kmattawa@umich.edu

MATTEO, Sherri. American (born United States), b. 1951?. **Genres:** Medicine/Health, Communications/Media, Business/Trade/Industry, Information Science/Computers, Women's Studies And Issues, Politics/Government. **Career:** San Diego State University, assistant professor of women's studies, 1984-85; Stanford University, lecturer in human biology and feminist studies, 1987-96, Institute for Research on Women and Gender, associate director, 1987-92, deputy director, 1992-96; Insights into Information Technology in the Pacific Rim, managing editor, 1996; MWA Consulting, writer and editor, 1996 . **Publications:** (Co-ed.) Proceedings of the 1989 Conference of the Society for Menstrual Cycle Research, 1989; (ed. and intro.) American Women in the Nineties: Today's Critical Issues, 1993. **Address:** MWA Consulting, 261 Hamilton Ave., Ste. 421, Palo Alto, CA 94301-2536, U.S.A.

MATTESON, John. American (born United States), b. 1961. **Genres:** Novels, Biography. **Career:** U.S. District Court for the Eastern District of North Carolina, law clerk, 1986-87; Titchell, Maltzman (law firm), associate attorney, 1987-88; Maupin, Taylor, Ellis & Adams, associate attorney, 1988-91; Columbia University, researcher and instructor in composition, 1991-2001; City University of New York, John Jay College of Criminal Justice, Department of English, professor, 1997-, Honors Program, faculty director, Graduate Center, Leon Levy Center for Biography, fellow. Writer. **Publications:** Eden's Outcasts: The Story of Louisa May Alcott and Her Father, 2007; The Lives of Margaret Fuller: A Biography, 2012. Contributor to journals. **Address:** Department of English, John Jay College of Criminal Justice, City University of New York, Rm. 734A, 619 W 54th St., New York, NY 10019-3545, U.S.A. **Online address:** matteson151@earthlink.net

MATTESON, Stefanie (Newton). American (born United States), b. 1946. **Genres:** Mystery/Crime/Suspense. **Career:** The (Bergen) Record, reporter of science and medical stories, consumer writer and assistant lifestyle editor, 1977-82; Mystery Writers of America, director; Beckerman Public Relations, vice-president. **Publications:** MYSTERIES: Murder at the Spa, 1990; Murder at Teatime, 1991; Murder on the Cliff, 1991; Murder on the Silk Road, 1992; Murder at the Falls, 1993; Murder on High, 1994; Murder among the Angels, 1996; Murder under the Palms, 1997. **Address:** Beckerman Public Relations, 1 University Plz., Ste. 507, Hackensack, NJ 07601, U.S.A. **Online address:** smatteson@beckermanpr.com

MATTHEE, Rudi. (Rudolph P. Matthee). American/Dutch (born Netherlands), b. 1953. **Genres:** History, Business/Trade/Industry, Essays. **Career:** University of Delaware, Unidel distinguished professor of history. Writer. **Publications:** (As Rudolph P. Matthee) The Politics of Trade in Safavid Iran: Silk for Silver, 1600-1730, 1999; (ed. with B. Baron) Iran and Beyond: Essays in Middle Eastern History in Honor of Nikki R. Keddie, 2000; (ed. with N.R. Keddie) Iran and the Surrounding World: Interactions in Culture and Cultural Politics, 2002; The Pursuit of Pleasure: Drugs and Stimulants in Iranian History, 1500-1900, 2005. **Address:** Department of History, University of Delaware, 236 John Munroe Hall, 46 W Delaware Ave., Newark, NE 19716-2547, U.S.A. **Online address:** matthee@udel.edu

MATTHEE, Rudolph P. *See* **MATTHEE, Rudi.**

MATTHEW, Christopher. *See* **MATTHEW, Christopher C. F.**

MATTHEW, Christopher C. F. (Christopher Matthew). British (born England), b. 1939. **Genres:** Novels, Novellas/Short Stories, Travel/Exploration, Humor/Satire, History, Young Adult Fiction. **Career:** La Colline School of Languages, lecturer in English, 1963-64; London Press Exchange Ltd., advertising copywriter, 1964-66; J. Walter Thompson Company Ltd., copywriter, 1966-68; Masius, copywriter, 1968-70; Thomson Group Marketing, copywriter, 1970; freelance writer, broadcaster, 1970; The Times Travel Guide, editor, 1973-75. **Publications:** (As Christopher Matthew) A Different World: Stories of Great Hotels, 1976; (as Christopher Matthew) Diary of a Somebody, 1978; (as Christopher Matthew) The Long-Haired Boy, 1980; Loosely Engaged, 1980; The Crisp Report, 1981; (intro.) Three Men in a Boat, 1982; How to Survive Middle Age, 1983; The Junket Man, 1983; Family Matters, 1987; The Simon Crisp Diaries, 1988; The Amber Room, 1995; A Nightingale Sang in Fernhurst Road: A Schoolboy's Journal of 1945, 1998; (as Christopher Matthew) Now We Are Sixty, 1999; Knocking On, 2001; Now We Are Sixty (and a Bit), 2003; Madonna's Plumber, 2003, Summoned by Betjeman, forthcoming. Contributor to magazines and newspapers. **Address:** Eel Brook Studios, 125 Moore Park Rd., London, GL SW6 4PS, England. **Online address:** cmatt@ouetel.net.uk

MATTHEWS, Alex. American (born United States) **Genres:** Science Fiction/Fantasy, Mystery/Crime/Suspense, Cartoons, Novels, Young Adult Fiction. **Career:** Alex Matthews & Association, owner. Writer. **Publications:** Secret's Shadow, 1996; Satan's Silence, 1997; Vendetta's Victim, 1998; Wanton's Web, 1999; Cat's Caw, 2000; Death's Domain, 2001; Wedding's Widow, 2003; Blood's Burden, 2006; Murder's Madness, 2008; Healer's Heresy, 2011. **Address:** Alex Matthews & Association, 546 N Humphrey Ave., Oak Park, IN 60302, U.S.A. **Online address:** msalexm@aol.com

MATTHEWS, Brad. *See* **DEMILLE, Nelson (Richard).**

MATTHEWS, Carole. British (born England) **Genres:** Novels, Novellas/Short Stories, Young Adult Fiction. **Career:** Bedfordshire Adult Education, teacher; BBC Three Counties Radio, reviewer; holistic clinic, staff. Writer. **Publications:** Let's Meet on Platform Eight, 1997; More to Life than This, 2000; For Better, for Worse, 2000; A Minor Indiscretion, 2002; A Compromising Position, 2002; Bare Necessity, 2003; A Whiff of Scandal, 2004; The Sweetest Taboo, 2004; With or Without You, 2005; The Scent of Scandal, 2005; You Drive Me Crazy, 2005; (ed. with C. Manby and S. Mlynowski) Girls' Night Out, 2006; More to Life Than This, 2006; Welcome to the Real World, 2006; Chocolate Lovers' Club, 2007; The Chocolate Lovers' Diet, 2007; It's a Kind of Magic, 2008; All You Need Is Love, 2008; The Difference a Day Makes, 2009; That Loving Feeling, 2009; It's Now or Never, 2010; The Only Way is Up, 2010; Could This Be Love?, 2011. **Address:** c/o Hatchette Livre, Headline Book Publishing, 338 Euston Rd., London, GL NW1 3BH, England. **Online address:** cmatthewsmail@aol.com

MATTHEWS, Chris John. American (born United States), b. 1945. **Genres:** Politics/Government, Young Adult Non-fiction. **Career:** U.S. Peace Corps, trade development advisor, 1968-70; U.S. Senate Budget Committee, staff assistant, 1974-77; CBS This Morning (television program), political analyst, 1987; San Francisco Examiner, Washington bureau chief, 1987-2000, nationally syndicated columnist, 2000-02; MSNBC, host, 1999-; The Chris Matthews Show (syndicated program), host, 2002-. Journalist and political commentator. **Publications:** NONFICTION: Hardball: How Politics Is Played, Told by One Who Knows the Game, 1988; Kennedy and Nixon: The Rivalry That Shaped Postwar America, 1996; Now, Let Me Tell You What I Really Think, 2001; American: Beyond Our Grandest Notions, 2002; Life's a Campaign: What Politics Has Taught Me about Friendship, Rivalry, Reputation, and Success, 2007; The Hardball Handbook: How to Win at Life, 2009. Contributor to periodicals. **Address:** MSNBC, 30 Rockefeller Plz., New York, NY 10012, U.S.A.

MATTHEWS, Elizabeth W(oodfin). American (born United States), b. 1927. **Genres:** Librarianship, Bibliography, Reference, Biography. **Career:** Virginia State Library, library assistant, 1948-49; University of North Carolina, assistant in browsing room, 1949-50; Virginia Polytechnic Institute and State University, library assistant, 1950-51; Ohio State University, cataloger at university library, 1952-59; Battelle Memorial Institute, librarian, 1956; University of Illinois, cataloger and instructor in library science, 1962-63, lecturer in library science, 1964; Virginia Military Institute, cataloger, 1963-64; Southern Illinois University, catalog librarian, 1964-67, instructor, 1967-70, assistant professor, 1972-79, associate professor, 1979-85, professor, 1985-92, professor emeritus, 1992-; Morris Library, medical librarian, 1972-74, law librarian, 1974-92. Writer. **Publications:** Access Points to the Law Library Card Catalog Interpretation, 1982; Pages and Missing Pages in Virginia Courthouse Records with Reference to Woodfin, Howlett, Pantier, Luck, King, Duke, and Page, 1983, 2nd ed., 1989; Virginia Vignettes, 1984; Seventeenth Century English Law Reports in Folio: Description of Selected Imprints, 1986; The Law Library Reference Shelf: Annotated Subject Guide, 1988, 5th ed., 2003; Lincoln as a Lawyer: An Annotated Bibliography, 1991. Contributor of articles and reviews to periodicals. **Address:** Southern Illinois University, 900 S Normal Ave., Woody Hall, PO Box 4716, Carbondale, IL 62901, U.S.A.

MATTHEWS, Greg. American (born United States), b. 1949. **Genres:** Novels, Mystery/Crime/Suspense. **Career:** Writer. **Publications:** NOVELS: The Further Adventures of Huckleberry Finn, 1983; Heart of the Country, 1985; Little Red Rooster, 1987; The Gold Flake Hydrant, 1988; One True Thing, 1990; Power in the Blood, 1993; The Wisdom of Stones, 1994; Far from Heaven, 1997; Come to Dust, 1998; Red Earth, 2000. **Address:** c/o Tom Wallace, Wallace Literary Agency Inc., 177 E 17th St., New York, NY 10021, U.S.A.

MATTHEWS, Hugh. *See* **HUGHES, Matthew.**

MATTHEWS, Jack. Also writes as Matt Hughes, John Harold Matthews. American (born United States), b. 1925. **Genres:** Novels, Novellas/Short Stories, Plays/Screenplays, Poetry, Essays. **Career:** Urbana College, associate professor, 1959-62, professor of English, 1962-64; Ohio University, lecturer, 1964-70, professor, 1971-76, distinguished professor of English, 1976-2003, emeritus distinguished professor, 2003-; Wichita State University, distinguished writer-in-residence, 1970-71. **Publications:** SHORT STORIES: Bitter Knowledge, 1964; Tales of the Ohio Land, 1979; Dubious Persuasions, 1981; Crazy Women, 1985; Ghostly Populations, 1986; Dirty Tricks (short stories), 1990; Storyhood as We Know It, 1993; Booking Pleasures, 1996; Reading Matter, 2000; Schopenhauer's Will, 2002. NOVELS: Hanger Stout, Awake!, 1967; Beyond the Bridge, 1970; The Tale of Asa Bean, 1971; The Charisma Campaigns, 1972; Pictures of the Journey Back, 1973; Sassafras, 1983. ESSAYS: Booking in the Heartland, 1986; Memoirs of a Bookman, 1989; Booking Pleasures, 1995; Reading Matter, 2000. EDITOR: (with E.G. Hemley) The Writer's Signature: Idea in Story and Essay, 1972; Archetypal Themes in the Modern Story, 1973; Rare Book Lore: Selections From The Letters Of Ernest J. Wessen, 1992. OTHERS: An Almanac for Twilight (poetry), 1966; Collecting Rare Books for Pleasure and Profit, 1977; Sassafras, 1983; The Emeritus Professor, 1990; On the Shore of That Beautiful Shore, 1991; Interview with the Sphinx, 1992; Storyhood As We Know It: And Other Tales, 1993; Gambler's Nephew, 2011. **Address:** Department of English, Ohio University, 328 Ellis Hall, Athens, OH 45701-9333, U.S.A. **Online address:** matthej1@ohio.edu

MATTHEWS, John Harold. *See* **MATTHEWS, Jack.**

MATTHEWS, Joseph R(onald). American (born United States), b. 1942. **Genres:** Librarianship, Information Science/Computers, Education. **Career:** J. Matthews & Associates Inc., president, 1974-86; Inlex Inc., vice president of operations, 1986-88; Geac Computer Corporation Ltd., vice president of operations, 1988-; Data Research Associates Inc., staff; MAR Corporation Inc., staff; Electronic Online Systems Intl., vice president of sales. Writer and consultant. **Publications:** (Co-author) The County Information Systems Directory, 1975, 1976; Choosing an Automated Library System: A Planning Guide, 1980; Automated Circulation: Planning for a Region, 1981; Public Access to Online Catalogs: A Planning Guide for Managers, 1982, 2nd ed., 1985; (ed. with G.S. Lawrence and D.K. Ferguson) Using Online Catalogs: A Nationwide Survey: A Report of a Study Sponsored by the Council on Library Resources, 1983; (ed.) A Reader on Choosing an Automated Library System, 1983; (ed. with K. Hegarty) Automated Circulation: An Examination of Choices, 1984; Directory of Automated Library Systems, 1985, (contrib.) 2nd ed., 1989; (ed.) The Impact of Online Catalogs, 1986; Guidelines for Selecting Automated Systems, 1986; Internet Outsourcing Using an Application Service Provider: A How-to-do-it Manual For Librarians, 2002; The Bottom Line: Determining and Communicating the Value of the Special Library, 2002; (with T.R. Kochtanek) Library Information Systems: From Library Automation to Distributed Information Access Solutions, 2002; (with M.H. Gillespie) Service Providers: ASPs, ISPs, MSPs, and WSPs, 2002; Measuring for Results: The Dimension of Public Library Effectiveness, 2004; Technology Planning: Preparing and Updating a Library Technology Plan, 2004; Strategic Planning and Management for Library Managers, 2005; Library Assessment in Higher Education, 2007; Evaluation and Measurement of Library Services, 2007; Scorecards for Results: A Guide for Developing a Library Balanced Scorecard, 2008; Customer-focused Library: Re-inventing the Public Library from the Outside-in, 2009; (with P. Hernon) Listening to the Customer, 2011. **Address:** Electronic Online Systems International, 5838 Edison Pl, Carlsbad, CA 92008-6596, U.S.A.

MATTHEWS, Lloyd J. American (born United States), b. 1929?. **Genres:** Military/Defense/Arms Control, History. **Career:** South Vietnamese Forces, combat adviser, 1964-65, battalion commander, 1965, now retired; United States Military Academy, professor of English, 1971-78, associate dean, 1981-84; United States Army War College, Parameters Quarterly, editor, 1979-81, 1986-93, 1999, Strategic Studies Institute, external researcher; National Education Corp., project manager, 1984-85, project manager, 1993. **Publications:** The Political-Military Rivalry for Operational Control in U.S. Military Actions: A Soldier's Perspective, 1998. EDITED WITH D.E. BROWN: Assessing the Vietnam War: A Collection From the Journal of the U.S. Army War College, 1987; Parameters of War: Military History from the Journal of the U.S. Army War College, 1987; The Challenge of Military Leadership, 1989; The Parameters of Military Ethics, 1989. EDITOR: Newsmen and National Defense: Is Conflict Inevitable?, 1991; Challenging the United States Symmetrically and Asymmetrically: Can America be Defeated?, 1998; (with T. Pavri) Population Diversity and the U.S. Army, 1999; The Future of the American Military Presence in Europe, 2000; (with D.M. Snider and G.L. Watkins) The Future of the Army Profession, 2002. **Address:** Strategic Studies Institute, United States Army War College, 632 Wright Ave., Carlisle, PA 17013-5244, U.S.A. **Online address:** pmatthews@pa.net

MATTHEWS, L. S. British (born England), b. 1964. **Genres:** Novels, Children's Fiction. **Career:** Writer, artist and educator. **Publications:** NOVELS: Fish, 2003; The Outcasts, 2004; A Dog for Life, 2006; Deadly Night, 2006; The Game, 2006; Trapped, 2006; UFOs!, 2006; Lexi, 2007; After the Flood, 2008. **Address:** Delacorte Press, 1745 Broadway, New York, NY 10019, U.S.A. **Online address:** connect@lsmatthewsonline.co.uk

MATTHEWS, Mark. American (born United States) **Genres:** History, Politics/Government, International Relations/Current Affairs. **Career:** Baltimore Sun, Middle East reporter and correspondent, 1992-2007. **Publications:** Lost Years: Bush, Sharon and Failure in the Middle East, 2007. **Address:** Washington, DC , U.S.A. **Online address:** mmatth2112@aol.com

MATTHEWS, Peter (Hugoe). British (born England), b. 1934. **Genres:** Language/Linguistics. **Career:** University College of North Wales, lecturer, 1961-65; University of Reading, lecturer, 1965-69, reader, 1969-75, professor, 1975-80; University of Cambridge, Saint John's College, fellow, Department of Linguistics, professor and head, 1980-2000, now emeritus professor. Writer. **Publications:** (With D. Alexander) Adjectives before That-Clauses in English, 1964; Inflectional Morphology, 1972; Morphology: An Introduction to the Theory of Word-structure, 1974, 2nd ed., 1991; Generative Grammar and Linguistic Competence, 1979; Syntax, 1981; Do Languages Obey General Laws?, 1982; Grammatical Theory in the United States from Bloomfield to Chomsky, 1993; The Concise Oxford Dictionary of Linguistics, 1997, 2nd ed., 2007; A Short History of Structural Linguistics, 2001; Linguistics: A Very Short Introduction, 2003; Syntactic Relations: A Critical Survey, 2007. **Address:** Department of Linguistics, St John's College, University of Cambridge, St John's St., Cambridge, CB2 1TP, England.

MATTHEWS, Steven. British (born England), b. 1961?. **Genres:** Literary Criticism And History, Poetry. **Career:** Oxford Brookes University, Department of English and Modern Languages, professor, School of Arts and Humanities, joint director of research and assistant dean for research. Writer. **Publications:** (Ed. with K. Williams) Rewriting the Thirties: Modernism and After, 1997; Irish Poetry: Politics, History, Negotiation: The Evolving Debate, 1969 to the Present, 1997; Yeats as Precursor: Readings in Irish, British, and American Poetry, 2000; Les Murray, 2001; Modernism: Contexts in Literature, 2004; (ed.) Modernism: A Sourcebook, 2008. **Address:** Department of English and Modern Languages, Oxford Brookes University, Tonge Bldg., Gipsy Ln., Headington, Oxford, OX OX3 0BP, England. **Online address:** sjmatthews@brookes.ac.uk

MATTHEWS, Tom L. *See* **LALICKI, Tom.**

MATTHEWS, Victor H. American (born United States), b. 1950. **Genres:** History. **Career:** Clemson University, visiting assistant professor of history and religion, 1978-80; Anderson College, assistant professor of history, 1980-84; Missouri State University, associate professor, 1984-88, professor of religious studies, 1988-, Religious Studies Department, acting head, 1992, 2000, coordinator antiquities program, 1992-2004, acting head, 2000-01, College of Humanities and Public Affairs, associate dean, 2001-08, interim dean, 2008-09, dean, 2009-; Episcopal Church of America, reader of general ordination exams, 2006-08. Writer. **Publications:** NONFICTION: Pastoral Nomadism in the Mari Kingdom (ca. 1830-1760 B.C.), 1978; Manners and Customs in the Bible, 1988, 3rd ed., 2006; (with D.C. Benjamin, Jr.) Old Testament Parallels: Laws and Stories from the Ancient Near East, 1991, 3rd ed., 2006; (with D.C. Benjamin, Jr.) Social World of Ancient Israel, 1250-587 BCE, 1993; (ed. with J.E. Coleson) Go to the Land I Will Show You: Studies in Honor of Dwight W. Young, 1996. (with J.H. Walton) The IVP Bible Background Commentary: Genesis-Deuteronomy, 1997; (with J.C. Moyer) The Old Testament: Text and Context, 1997; (ed. with B.M. Levinson and T. Frymer-Kensky) Gender and Law in the Hebrew Bible and the Ancient Near East, 1998; (with D.A. deSilva) Untold Stories of the Bible, 1998; Old Testament, 2000; Social World of the Hebrew Prophets, 2001; A Brief History of Ancient Israel, 2002; (ed. with D. Clark) One Hundred, Years of American Archaeology in the Levant, 2003; Judges and Ruth, 2004; Old Testament Turning Points: The Narratives That Shaped a Nation, 2005; Manners & Customs in the Bible, 2006; Studying the Ancient Israelites: A Guide to Sources and Methods, 2007; 101 Questions and Answers on the Prophets of Israel, 2007; More Than Meets the Ear: Discovering the Hidden Contexts of Old Testament Conversations, 2008; 101 Questions and Answers on the Historical Books of the Bible, 2009. Contributor to periodicals. **Address:** U.S.A. **Online address:** victormatthews@missouristate.edu

MATTHEWS, Victoria (Ann). American/British (born England), b. 1941.

Genres: Horticulture, Homes/Gardens, Photography. **Career:** Royal Botanic Garden, Herbarium of Cultivated Plants, curator, 1974-86; Royal Horticultural Society, international narcissus registrar, 1986, international clematis registrar, 1994-; Kew, deputy editor, editor, 1986-93; New Plantsman, founder, 1993, editor, 1993-94. **Publications:** (With C. Grey-Wilson) Gardening on Walls, 1983; (contrib.) The European Garden Flora, 5 vol., 1984-1997; Kew Gardening Guide: Lilies, Collingridge, 1989; (ed.) Contemporary Botanical Artists: The Shirley Sherwood Collection, 1996; (with C. Grey-Wilson) Gardening with Climbers, 1997; The Healing Plants of Ida Hrubesky Pemberton: Catalogue of an Exhibition 25 September 2003-29 February 2004, 2003. Contributor of articles to journals and magazines. **Address:** 7350 SW 173rd St., Miami, FL 33157-4835, U.S.A.

MATTHIAS, John (Edward). American (born United States), b. 1941. **Genres:** Poetry, Literary Criticism And History. **Career:** University of Notre Dame, assistant professor, 1967-73, associate professor, 1973-81, professor of English, 1981-, now professor emeritus, Lilly Endowment Fellow; Notre Dame Review, poetry editor. **Publications:** Bucyrus, 1970; 23 Modern British Poets, 1971; (ed.) TriQuarterly 21: Contemporary British Poetry, 1971; (ed.) Twenty-three Modern British Poets, 1971; Other Poems, 1971; Hermans Poems, 1973; Turns, 1975; Double Derivation Association and Cliche, 1975; Two Poems, 1977; Crossing, 1979; Rostropovich at Aldeburgh, 1979; (ed.) Introducing David Jones: A Selection of His Writings, 1979; (ed. and trans. with G. Printz-Påhlson) Contemporary Swedish Poetry, 1979; (ed.) Five American Poets, 1979; Bathory and Lermontov, 1980; (trans. with G. Printz-Påhlson) J. Ostergren, Rainmaker, 1983; Northern Summer: New Selected Poems 1963-83, 1984; (trans. with V. Vučković) The Battle of Kosovo, 1987, rev. ed., 1999; Tva Dikter, 1989; Place Poems: An East Anglian Diptych, 1989; (ed. and intro.) David Jones: Man and Poet, 1989; A Gathering of Ways, 1991; Reading Old Friends: Essays, Reviews, and Poems on Poetics, 1975-1990, 1992; (ed.) Selected Works of David Jones, 1993; Swimming at Midnight, 1995; Beltane at Aphelion, 1995; Pages: New Poem and Cuttings, 2000; Pages, 2000; Working Progress, Working Title, 2002; (trans. with L.H. Svensson) J. Svenbro, Three-Toed Gull, 2003; New Selected Poems, 2004; Kedging: New Poems, 2007; (ed. and intro. with W. ORourke) Notre Dame Review: The First Ten Years, 2009; Trigons, 2010. Works appear in anthologies. **Address:** Department of English, University of Notre Dame, 356 O'Shaughnessy, 201 Decio Faculty Hall, Notre Dame, IN 46556-5639, U.S.A. **Online address:** john.e.matthias.1@nd.edu

MATTHIESSEN, Peter. American (born United States), b. 1927. **Genres:** Novels, Novellas/Short Stories, Anthropology/Ethnology, Natural History, Young Adult Non-fiction, Writing/Journalism. **Career:** Writer, 1950-; Paris Review, co-founder and founding fiction editor, 1953-. **Publications:** FICTION: Race Rock, 1954; Partisans, 1955; The Year of the Tempest, 1957; Raditzer, 1961; At Play in the Fields of the Lord, 1965; Far Tortuga, 1975; Mid Night Turning Gray, 1984; On the River Styx and Other Stories, 1989; Killing Mister Watson, 1990, rev. ed. as Black Autumn, 2008; Lost Man's River, 1997; Bone by Bone, 1999; Shadow Country: A New Rendering of the Watson Legend, 2008. NONFICTION: Wildlife in America, 1959, rev. ed., 1987; The Cloud Forest: A Chronicle of the South American Wilderness, 1961; Under the Mountain Wall: A Chronicle of Two Seasons in the Stone Age, 1962; The Atlantic Coast, a Chapter in The American Heritage Book of Natural Wonders, 1963; The Shorebirds of North America, 1967; Oomingmak: The Expedition to the Musk Ox Island in the Bering Sea, 1967; Profile, Cesar Chavez, 1969; Sal Si Puedes: Cesar Chavez and the New American Revolution, 1969; Blue Meridian, The Search for the Great White Shark, 1971; (contrib.) The Tree Where Man Was Born, 1972; Seal Pool, 1972; The Snow Leopard, 1978; Sand Rivers, 1981; In the Spirit of Crazy Horse, 1983; (co-author) 1000 Adventures: With Tales of Discovery, 1983; Indian Country, 1984; Men's Lives: The Surfmen and Baymen of the South Fork, 1986; Nine-headed Dragon River: Zen Journals, 1969-1985, 1986; (ed. and intro.) North American Indians, 1989; African Silences, 1991; Baikal: Sacred Sea of Siberia, 1992; Indian Country, 1992; Shadows of Africa, 1992; East of Lo Monthang: In the Land of the Mustang, 1995; Tigers in the Snow, 2000; The Birds of Heaven: Travels With Cranes, 2001; (co-author) Arctic National Wildlife Refuge: Seasons of Life and Land: A Photographic Journey, 2003; End of the Earth: Voyages to Antarctica, 2003; (ed. and intro.) North American Indians, 2004; (ed.) Courage for the Earth: Writers, Scientists, and Activists Celebrate the Life and Writing of Rachel Carson, 2007. OTHER: The Wind Birds: Shorebirds Of North America, 1967. Contributor of articles to periodicals and magazines. **Address:** c/o Neil Olson, Donadio & Olson Inc., 121 W 27th St., Ste. 704, New York, NY 10001, U.S.A.

MATTINGLEY, Christobel (Rosemary). Australian (born Australia), b. 1931. **Genres:** Novellas/Short Stories, Children's Fiction, Young Adult Fiction, Poetry, Children's Non-fiction, History, Race Relations, Biography, Picture/Board Books, Young Adult Non-fiction, Animals/Pets, Social Sciences. **Career:** Department of Immigration, librarian, 1951; Latrobe Valley Libraries, regional librarian, 1953; teacher and librarian, 1954-55; Prince Alfred College, librarian, 1956-57; South Australian section of Community Aid Abroad, co-founder, 1964; St. Peter's Girls' School, librarian, 1966-70; Wattle Park Teachers College, acquisitions librarian, 1971, reader services librarian, 1972; Murray Park College of Advanced Education, lecturer and reader education librarian, 1973-74; West Australian College of Advanced Education, Churchlands Campus, writer-in-residence, 1981. **Publications:** The Picnic Dog, 1970; Windmill at Magpie Creek, 1971; Worm Weather, 1971; Emu Kite, 1972; Queen of the Wheat Castles, 1973; The Battle of the Galah Trees, 1974; Show and Tell, 1974; Tiger's Milk, 1974; The Surprise Mouse, 1974; Lizard Log, 1975; The Great Ballagundi Damper Bake, 1975; The Long Walk, 1976; The Special Present and Other Stories, 1977; New Patches for Old, 1977; The Big Swim, 1977; Budgerigar Blue, 1978; The Jetty, 1978; Black Dog, 1979; Rummage, 1981; Brave with Ben, 1982; Lexl and the Lion Party, 1982; Duck Boy, 1983; (with P. Mullins) The Magic Saddle, 1983; Southerly Buster, 1983; The Angel with a Mouth-organ, 1984; Ghost Sitter, 1984; The Miracle Tree, 1985; McGruer and the Goat, 1986; (ed. with K. Hampton) Survival in Our Own Land: Aboriginal Experiences in South Australiasince 1836, 1988, rev. ed., 1992; The Butcher, the Beagle and the Dog Catcher, 1990; Tucker's Mob, 1992; The Sack, 1993; No Gun for Asmir, 1993; Asmir in Vienna, 1995; Poppy Peeker, 1995; Escape from Sarajevo, 1996; The Race, 1996; Daniel's Secret, 1997; Ginger, 1997; Work Wanted, 1998; Hurry up, Alice, 1998; Cockawun and Cockatoo, 1999; First Friend, 2000; King of the Wilderness: The Life of Deny King, 2001; Ruby of Trowutta, 2003; Nest Egg: A Clutch of Poems, 2005; Battle Order 204: A Bomber Pilot's Story, 2007; Chelonia Green: Champion of Turtles, 2009; For the Love of Nature: E.E. Gostelow's Birds & Flowers, 2010; A Brilliant Touch: Adam Forster's Wildflower Paintings, 2010. Contributor to books and periodicals. **Address:** A. P. Watt Ltd., 20 John St., London, GL WC1N 2DR, England. **Online address:** cmattingley@ozemail.com.au

MATTSON, Kevin. American (born United States), b. 1966. **Genres:** History, Politics/Government, Social Commentary. **Career:** University of Rochester, Institute of Technology, professor, 1994-95, professor of humanities, 1995-2001, Walt Whitman Center for the Culture and Politics of Democracy, research director, associate director, 1995-2001; Ohio University, Department of History, professor of history, 2001-04, Connor study professor of contemporary history, 2004-, Contemporary History Institute, faculty associate. Writer. **Publications:** Creating a Democratic Public: The Struggle for Urban Participatory Democracy During the Progressive Era, 1998; (intro.) The New State, 1999; Intellectuals in Action: The Origins of the New Left and Radical Liberalism, 1945-1970, 2002; (ed. with R. Hayduk) Democracy's Moment: Reforming the American Political System for the 21st Century, 2002; Engaging Youth: Combating the Apathy of Young Americans Toward Politics, 2003; (ed. with B. Johnson and P. Kavanagh) Steal This University: The Rise of the Corporate University and the Academic Labor Movement, 2003; When America Was Great: The Fighting Faith of Postwar Liberalism, 2004; Upton Sinclair and the Other American Century, 2006; (ed. with N. Jumonville) Liberalism for A New Century, 2007; Rebels All!: A Short History of the Conservative Mind in Postwar America, 2008; What the Heck are You Up To, Mr. President?: Jimmy Carter, America's Malaise, and the Speech that Should have Changed the Country, 2009; (with E. Alterman) Cause: The Fight for American Liberalism from Franklin Roosevelt to Barack Obama, 2012. Contributor to periodicals. **Address:** Department of History, Ohio University, 425 Bentley Annex, 4th Fl., Athens, OH 45701-2979, U.S.A. **Online address:** mattson@ohio.edu

MATTUSCH, Carol C. American/German (born Germany), b. 1947. **Genres:** Archaeology/Antiquities. **Career:** George Mason University, assistant professor, 1977-82, associate professor, 1982-90, professor of art and art history, 1990-98, department head of art and art history, 1982-92, Mathy professor of art history, 1998-; Smithsonian Institution, Associates Program, lecturer in resident, 1979-85; Archaeological Institute of America, traveling lecturer, 1979-85, 1998-99; University of Virginia, visiting professor, 1993; Yale University, lecturer; Harvard University, lecturer; Oberlin College, lecturer; Bryn Mawr College, lecturer; Smith College, lecturer; University of Iowa, lecturer; Association Internationale d'Archäologie Classique, co-chair, 2003; Pompeii and the Roman Villa, Art and Culture around the Bay of Naples, visiting curator, 2008-09; Harvard University, Art Museums, Toledo Museum of Art, curator. Writer. **Publications:** Bronzeworkers in the Athenian Agora, 1982; Greek Bronze Statuary: From the Beginnings through the Fifth Century B.C., 1988; Classical Bronzes: The Art and Craft of Greek and Roman Statuary, 1996; The Fire of Hephaistos: Large Classical Bronzes from North American Collections, 1996; The Victorious Youth, 1997; The Villa dei Papiri at Herculaneum: Life and Afterlife of a Sculpture Collection, 2005; Pompeii and the Roman Villa: Art and Culture around the Bay of Naples, 2008; (ed. and trans.) Johann Joachim Winckelmann, 2011. Contributor of articles to journals. **Address:** Department of History and Art History, George Mason University, Rm. 373A, Robinson Hall B, 4400 University Dr., Fairfax, VA 22030, U.S.A. **Online address:** mattusch@gmu.edu

MATUR, Bejan. Turkish (born Turkey), b. 1968. **Genres:** Theology/Religion. **Career:** Poet. **Publications:** Rüzgar Dolu Konaklar, 1996; Tanri Görmesin Harflerimi, 1999; Ayin Büyüttügü Ogullar, 2002; Onun Cölünde, 2002; Ibrahim'in Beni Terketmesi, 2008. **Address:** Istanbul, Turkey. **Online address:** b.matur@zaman.com.tr

MATUSOW, Allen J(oseph). American (born United States), b. 1937. **Genres:** History, Economics. **Career:** Rice University, Department of History, assistant professor, 1963-65, associate professor, 1966-70, professor of American history, 1970-83, William Gaines Twyman professor of history, 1983-, School of Humanities, dean, 1981-95, interim dean, 2009-10, James A. Baker III Institute for Public Policy, associate director for academic programs, 2002-, director; Stanford University, visiting associate professor of history, 1967-68. Writer. **Publications:** Farm Policies and Politics in the Truman Years, 1967; The Unraveling of America: A History of Liberalism in the 1960s, 1984; Nixon's Economy: Booms, Busts, Dollars, and Votes, 1998; Jimmy Carter and the Cold War, forthcoming. EDITOR: (with B.J. Bernstein) The Truman Administration: A Documentary History, 1966; (with B.J. Bernstein) Twentieth-century America: Recent Interpretations, 1969, 2nd ed., 1972; Joseph R. McCarthy, 1970. Contributor of articles to journals and periodicals. **Address:** Department of History, Rice University, 332 Humanities, MS-42, 6100 Main St., PO Box 1892, Houston, TX 77005-1827, U.S.A. **Online address:** matusow@rice.edu

MAUCERI, Philip. American (born United States), b. 1961. **Genres:** International Relations/Current Affairs, Anthropology/Ethnology, History, Politics/Government. **Career:** University of Pennsylvania, visiting lecturer in political science, 1990-91; University of Connecticut, visiting assistant professor of Latin American studies, 1991-94; University of Massachusetts, Center of Latin American Studies, visiting assistant professor, 1991-94; Universidad Simon Bolivar, visiting lecturer, 1993; University of Northern Iowa, College of Social and Behavioral Sciences, assistant professor of political science, 1994-98, associate professor, 1998-2005, Center for International Peace and Security Studies, founding director, 2003-05, Department of Political Science, interim head, 2003-05, professor and head, 2005-, dean, 2009-; Pontificia Universidad Católica Madre y Maestra, School of Social Sciences and Humanities, visiting professor, 2002. Writer. **Publications:** (Contrib.) Democracy in the Americas: Stopping the Pendulum, 1989; Militares: Insurgencia y democratización en el Perú, 1980-1988, 1989; State Under Siege: Development and Policy Making in Peru, 1996; (ed. with M.A. Cameron) The Peruvian Labyrinth: Polity, Society, Economy, 1997; (contrib.) The Counter-Insurgent State, 1997; (ed. with J. Burt) Politics in the Andes: Identity, Conflict, Reform, 2004; (ed. with S.E. Lobell) Ethnic Conflict and International Politics: Explaining Diffusion and Escalation, 2004. Contributor to books and periodicals. **Address:** Department of Political Science, College of Social and Behavioral Sciences, University of Northern Iowa, 319 Sabin Hall, Cedar Falls, IA 50614-0404, U.S.A. **Online address:** philip.mauceri@uni.edu

MAUCH, Christof. German (born Germany), b. 1960. **Genres:** History, Environmental Sciences/Ecology, Humanities, Biography. **Career:** University of Tuebingen, lecturer, 1990-94; University of Bonn, Department of English, assistant professor, 1994-96; University of Cologne, adjunct professor, 1994-96, professor, 1998-2007; American University, professorial lecturer, 1996; Georgetown University, OSS Oral History Project, director, 1997-98; German Historical Institute, deputy director, 1998-99, director, 1999-2007, director, 1999-2007; Ludwig-Maximilians-Universitaet Muenchen, chair of American cultural history and transatlantic relations, 2007-, research professor, 2010-; Lasky Center for Transatlantic Studies, director; Rachel Carson Center for Environment and Society, director. Writer. **Publications:** IN ENGLISH: (with E. Mauch) Horologisches Lexikon/Horological Dictionary, 2 vols., 1984; The Shadow War against Hitler, 2003. IN GERMAN: (with T. Brenner) Fuer eine Welt ohne Krieg, 1987, 2nd ed., 2003; (with U. Karbowiak) Unsere Geldkoepfe: Portraits der neuen Banknoten, 1990, 3rd ed., 1995; Poesie-Theologie-Politik, 1991; Techtel-Mechtel (limericks), 1993; Schattenkrieg gegen Hitler, 1999; Mrs. President: Von Martha Washington bis Hillary Clinton, 2000. EDITOR: Nicht aufs Kreuz gefallen, 1986; Texte-Daten-Bilder, 1990; (with J. Heideking) Geheimdienstkrieg gegen Deutschland, 1993; (with J. Heideking) USA und deutscher Widerstand, 1993; (with J. Heideking) American Intelligence and the German Resistance to Hitler, 1996; (with B. Zischke) Research and Funding: A German-American Guide for Historians and Social Scientists, 1999; (with P. Gassert) Mrs. President: von Martha Washington bis Hillary Clinton, 2000; (with T. Reuther) Americana in German Archives: A Guide to Primary Sources concerning the History of the United States and Canada, 2001; (with J. Heideking) Die Praesidenten der USA, 4th ed., 2005; (with H. Bungert and M. Frey) Verfassung-Demokratie-Politische Kultur, 2002; (with J. Salmons) German-Jewish Identities in America, 2003; (with J. Salmons) German Jewish Identities in America, 2003; (with J. Heideking) Geschichte der USA, 2003, 6th ed., 2008; Nature in German History, 2004; (with A. Lessoff) Adolf Cluss, Architect: From Germany to America, 2005; (with A.W. Daum) Berlin, Washington, 1800-2000: Capital Cities, Cultural Representation, and National Identities, 2005; (ed. with N. Stoltzfus and D. Weiner) Shades of Green: Global Environmentalism in Historical Perspective, 2006; (with T. Zeller) World beyond the Windshield: Roads and Landscapes in the United States and Europe, 2008; (with T. Zeller) Rivers in History: Perspectives on Waterways in Europe and North America, 2008; Wettlauf Um Die Moderne: Die USA Und Deutschland 1890 Bis Heute, 2008; Natural Disasters, Cultural Responses: Case Studies Toward a Global Environmental History, 2009; United States and Germany During the Twentieth Century: Competition and Convergence, 2010; Uncertain Environments, 2011. Contributor to books. **Address:** Rachel Carson Center, Leopoldstr. 11a, 4. OG, 406, Munich, D-80802, Germany. **Online address:** mauch@lmu.de

MAUER, Marc. American (born United States) **Genres:** Essays, Law, Social Sciences. **Career:** The Sentencing Project, assistant director, 1987-2005, executive director, 2005-. Writer. **Publications:** (Co-author) Bail Out: The Community Bail Fund Organizing Manual, 1980; Young Black Men and the Criminal Justice System: A Growing National Problem, 1990; Americans Behind Bars: A Comparison of International Rates of Incarceration, 1991; (with C. Shine) Does the Punishment Fit the Crime?: Drug Users and Drunk Drivers, Questions of Race and Class, 1993; Americans Behind Bars: The International Use of Incarceration, 1992-1993, 1994; (with T. Huling) Young Black Americans and the Criminal Justice System: Five Years Later, 1995; Americans Behind Bars: U.S. and International Use of Incarceration, 1995, 1997; (with C. Potler and R. Wolf) Gender and Justice: Women, Drugs and Sentencing Policy, 1999; The Race to Incarcerate, 1999, rev. ed., 2006; (with P.E. Allard) Regaining the Vote: An Assessment of Activity Relating to Felon Disenfranchisement Laws, 1999; (with J. Gainsborough) Diminishing Returns: Crime and Incarceration in the 1990s, 2000; (with M. Chesney-Lind) Invisible Punishment: The Collateral Consequences of Mass Imprisonment, 2002. **Address:** The Sentencing Project, 1705 DeSales St. NW, 8th Fl., Washington, DC 20036, U.S.A. **Online address:** mauer@sentencingproject.org

MAUGHAM, Frances. *See* **PARISH, James Robert.**

MAUGHAN, Jackie Johnson. American (born United States), b. 1948. **Genres:** Travel/Exploration, Sports/Fitness, Technology, Engineering. **Career:** San Francisco Newsreel, staff, 1969-72; Lewiston Morning Tribune, stringer, 1973-74; Greater Renton News, managing editor, 1975; Idaho State University, Office of University Relations, writer, producer and scriptwriter, 1976-87, instructor of English and philosophy, 1986, associate lecturer; Morning News, stringer, 1977. **Publications:** (With A. Puddicombe) Hiking the Backcountry: A Do-It-Yourself Guide for the Adventurous Woman, 1981; (with K. Collins) The Outdoor Woman's Guide to Sports, Fitness, and Nutrition, 1983; Hiker's Guide to Idaho, 1984; (with R. Maughan) Hiking Idaho, 1995, 2nd ed., 2001; (ed. and comp.) Go Tell It on the Mountain: Writings by Fire Lookouts, 1996. Contributor to periodicals. **Address:** Department of English, Idaho State University, LA 119, 921 S 8th Ave., Pocatello, ID 83209, U.S.A. **Online address:** maugjacq@isu.edu

MAUK, David C. Norwegian/American (born United States), b. 1945. **Genres:** History, Area Studies, Essays. **Career:** University of Trondheim, adjunct professor of English, 1980-85, 1986-91; Norwegian University of Science and Technology, adjunct professor of English, 1980-91, associate professor of American civilization, 1991-2004; New York University, instructor in American history, 1985-86; University of Oslo, associate professor of American civilization, 1995-, Nordic Association for American Studies, president; Norwegian Emigrant Museum, representative, 1995-; Minnesota Historical Society, Twin Cities Project, director of research, 1998-2000. Writer. **Publications:** (With J. Oakland) American Civilization: An Introduction, 1995, 5th ed., 2009; The Colony That Rose from the Sea: Norwegian Maritime Migration and Community in Brooklyn, 1850-1910, 1997. EDITOR: (with D. Tolfsby and O.T. Gulliksen) Norwegian-American Essays, 1996. Contributor to history journals. **Address:** Department of Literature, Area Studies & European Language, University of Oslo, NT 1112, Blindern, PO Box 1003, Oslo, N-0315, Norway. **Online address:** d.c.mauk@ilos.uio.no

MAUPIN, Armistead. American (born United States), b. 1944. **Genres:** Novels. **Career:** Charleston News and Courier, reporter, 1970-71; Associated Press, reporter, 1971-72; Lowry Russom and Leeper, public-relations account executive, 1973; Pacific Sun, columnist, 1974; San Francisco Opera, publicist, 1975; San Francisco Chronicle, Tales of the City column, author, 1976-77; KRON-TV, commentator, 1979; San Francisco Examiner, serialist, 1986; Channel Four/PBS miniseries Armistead Maupin's Tales of the City, executive producer, 1993. Writer. **Publications:** Tales of the City, 1978; More Tales of the City, 1980; Further Tales of the City, 1982; Babycakes, 1984; Significant Others, 1987; Sure of You, 1989; Heart's Desire, 1990; 28 Barbary Lane: The Tales of the City Omnibus in US as Back to Barbary Lane: The Final Tales of the City Omnibus, 1991; Maybe the Moon, 1992; Tales of the City, 1994; (intro.) The Question of Equality: Lesbian and Gay Politics in America Since Stonewall, 1995; Night Listener, 2000; (foreword) The Isherwood Century: Essays on the Life and Work of Christopher Isherwood, 2000; Michael Tolliver Lives, 2007; Mary Ann in Autumn: A Tales of the City Novel, 2010. **Address:** HarperCollins Publishers, 10 E 53rd St., New York, CA 10022, U.S.A.

MAURENSIG, Paolo. Italian (born Italy), b. 1943. **Genres:** Novels, Mystery/Crime/Suspense, Young Adult Fiction. **Career:** Freelance writer, 1993-. **Publications:** NOVELS: La Variante di Lüneburg, 1993; L'ombra e la meridiana, 1998; Venere Lesa: Romanzo, 1998; Uomo scarlatto: Romanzo, 2001; Guardiano dei sogni: Romanzo, 2003; (with R. Illy) Polietica: Una Promessa, 2003; Vukovlad: il Signore Dei Lupi, 2006; Gli Amanti Fiamminghi: Romanzo, 2008; Tempesta: il mistero di Giorgione: romanzo, 2009; Oro degli immortali, 2010. **Address:** Henry Holt and Company Inc., 175 5th Ave., New York, NY 10010, U.S.A.

MAURER, Diane Philippoff. *See* **MAURER-MATHISON, Diane V(ogel).**

MAURER, Warren R(ichard). American (born United States), b. 1929. **Genres:** Literary Criticism And History, Language/Linguistics, History. **Career:** University of California, acting instructor, 1964-65; Indiana University, assistant professor, 1965-68; University of Kansas, associate professor, 1968-73, professor of Germanic languages and literature, 1973-, department chair, 1969-72, now professor emeritus; Radio Free Europe, staff. **Publications:** The Naturalist Image of German Literature: A Study of the German Naturalists' Appraisal of Their Literary Heritage, 1972; (ed. with F. Baron and E.S. Dick) Rilke: The Alchemy of Alienation, 1980; Gerhart Hauptmann, 1982; Understanding Gerhart Hauptmann, 1992; Gerhart Hauptmann: A Century of Criticism (monograph), 1994. Contributor of articles to journals. **Address:** Department of Germanic Languages and Literatures, University of Kansas, Rm. 2080, 1445 Jayhawk Blvd., Lawrence, KS 66045-7590, U.S.A. **Online address:** german@ku.edu

MAURER-MATHISON, Diane V(ogel). (Diane Philippoff Maurer). American (born United States), b. 1944. **Genres:** Poetry, Crafts, How-to Books, Young Adult Non-fiction, Children's Non-fiction, Photography. **Career:** Writer and teacher. **Publications:** FOR CHILDREN: Dinosaurs Dining (poems), 1986; Make Your Own Spectacular Valentines, 1995. FOR ADULTS: (with J. Philippoff) Decorative Paper, 1993, rev. ed. as Papercraft: Making and Decorating Paper, 1995; (with J. Philippoff) Paper Art: The Complete Guide to Papercraft Techniques, 1997; The Ultimate Marbling Handbook: A Guide to Basic and Advanced Techniques for Marbling Paper and Fabric, 1999; Art of the Scrapbook: A Guide to Handbinding and Decorating Memory Books, Albums, and Art Journals, 2000; The Handcrafted Letter, 2001; The Art of Making Paste Papers, 2002; The Art and Craft of Handmade Cards, 2003; Artful Greetings, 2003; Paper in Three Dimensions: Origami, Pop-ups, Sculpture, Baskets, Boxes, and More, 2006; Collage, Assemblage, and Altered Art: Create Unique Images and Objects, 2007. FOR ADULTS (AS DIANE PHILIPPOFF MAURER): Fiber Arts: Macrame, Crochet, Wrapping, Coiling, Weaving, 1978; (with P. Maurer) An Introduction to Carrageenan & Watercolor Marbling, 1984. FOR ADULTS (AS DIANE VOGEL MAURER): (with P. Maurer) Marbling: A Complete Guide to Creating Beautiful Patterned Papers and Fabrics, 1991. OTHERS: One Froggy Day; The Amazing Tumbling Cow. **Address:** Diane Maurer Hand Marbled Papers, PO Box 78, Spring Mills, PA 16875, U.S.A. **Online address:** dkmaurer1@aol.com

MAURO, Nancy. American (born United States), b. 1973. **Genres:** Novels. **Career:** Writer and director. **Publications:** New World Monkeys: A Novel, 2009. Contributor to periodicals. Works appear in anthologies. **Address:** New York, NY , U.S.A. **Online address:** nancy@nancymauro.com

MAUTNER, Thomas. Swedish (born Sweden), b. 1935. **Genres:** Philosophy, Intellectual History, Ethics. **Career:** Australian National University, Department of Philosophy, faculty, 1965-98, College of Arts and Social Sciences, visiting fellow, 1998-. Writer. **Publications:** Vagledning till Hagerstromstudiet, 1994; A Dictionary of Philosophy, 1996, rev. ed. as The Penguin Dictionary of Philosophy, 1997, 2nd ed., 2005. EDITOR: Moralfilosofins grundlaggning, 1987; Two Texts on Human Nature, 1993. Contributions to journals. **Address:** School of Philosophy, Australian National University, 9 Coombs Bldg., Canberra, AC 0200, Australia. **Online address:** thomas.mautner@anu.edu.au

MAWDSLEY, Evan. Scottish (born Scotland), b. 1945. **Genres:** Politics/Government, Social Sciences. **Career:** University of Glasgow, professor of international history; Royal Historical Society fellow. Academic, historian and writer. **Publications:** The Russian Revolution and the Baltic Fleet: War and Politics, February 1917-April 1918, 1978; (with M.P. Mawdsley) Moscow and Leningrad: Blue Guide, 1980; The Russian Civil War, 2007; (co-ed.) History and Computing III: Historians, Computers and Data: Applications in Research and Teaching, 1990; A Directory of CPSU Central Committee Members, 1917-1990, 1991; (with T. Munck) Computing for Historians: An Introductory Guide, 1993; The Stalin Years: The Soviet Union, 1929-1953, 1998; (with S. White) The Soviet Elite from Lenin to Gorbachev: The Central Committee and Its Members, 1917-1991, 2000; Thunder in the East: The Nazi-Soviet War, 1941-1945, 2007. **Address:** University of Glasgow, Department of History, 1 University Gardens, Ste. 205, Glasgow, G12 8QQ, Scotland. **Online address:** e.mawdsley@history.arts.gla.ac.uk

MAWHINEY, Anne Marie. Canadian (born Canada), b. 1953. **Genres:** Sociology. **Career:** Canadian Ministry of Education, staff, 1974-75, Youth Horizons, staff, 1979-80; Sudbury Algoma Sanitorium, staff, 1975-79; Laurentian University, adjunct professor of social service, 1980-, School of Social Work, director, 1983-85, Native Social Work Program, coordinator, 1988-90, Faculty of Professional Schools, dean, 2002, special advisor to the president; Children's Services Advisory Group, vice chair, 1983-84; Native Child and Family Services, director, 1987-88; University of Kent, senior research associate, 1990; University of Bristol, visiting professor, 1991; Institute of Northern Ontario Research and Development, director, 1991-94, 1995-97; Laurentian Rowing Club, coach, 1992. Writer. **Publications:** (With T. Alcoze) Returning Home: A Report on a Native Human Services Project, 1988; (ed.) Rebirth: Political, Economic and Social Development in First Nations, 1993; Towards Aboriginal Self-Government: Relations between Status Indian Peoples and the Government of Canada, 1969-1984, 1994; (ed. with J. Pitblado) Boom Town Blues: Elliot Lake, Collapse and Revival in a Single-industry Community, 1999; Cardinal Virtues, forthcoming. Contributor to books. **Address:** School of Social Work, Laurentian University, Green Miller Ctr., Ramsey Lake Rd., 8th Fl., Willet, Sudbury, ON P3E 2C6, Canada. **Online address:** mawhiney@nickel.laurentian.ca

MAXFORD, Howard. British (born England), b. 1964. **Genres:** Film, Adult Non-fiction, Trivia/Facts, Horror, Humor/Satire. **Career:** Croydon, stage manager, 1983-. Writer and broadcaster. **Publications:** Hammer, House of Horror: Behind the Screams, 1996; The A-Z of Horror Films, 1997; The A-Z of Science Fiction & Fantasy Films, 1997; A-Z of Hitchcock, 2002. **Address:** B. T. Batsford Ltd., 583 Fulham Rd., London, GL SW6 5BY, England.

MAXIMOVICH, Stanley P. American (born United States), b. 1957. **Genres:** Medicine/Health, Self Help. **Career:** Loyola University, fellow in general surgery and plastic surgery, 1983-89; Edward Hospital, physician; Hinsdale Hospital, physician. Writer. **Publications:** 101 Ways to Feel and Look Great!

A Plastic Surgeon's Guide to Improve Your Life from the Inside Out, 1999. Contributor to medical journals. **Address:** W 40 S Clay St., Ste. 237, Hinsdale, IL 60521-3257, U.S.A. **Online address:** airmax999@msn.com

MAXTON, Hugh. *See* **MCCORMACK, W(illiam) J(ohn).**

MAXWELL, Catherine (Fern). *See* **MAXWELL, Cathy.**

MAXWELL, Cathy. (Catherine (Fern) Maxwell). American (born United States), b. 1953. **Genres:** Science Fiction/Fantasy, Novels, Romance/Historical, Young Adult Fiction. **Career:** KUPK-TV, newscaster, 1975-77; writer, 1991-. **Publications:** HISTORICAL ROMANCE NOVELS: All Things Beautiful, 1994; Treasured Vows, 1996; You and No Other, 1996; Falling in Love Again, 1997; When Dreams Come True, 1998; Because of You, 1999; Married in Haste, 1999; A Scandalous Marriage, 2000; The Marriage Contract, 2001; Flanna and the Lawman, 2001; The Wedding Wager, 2001; (with R. Langan and C. Davidson) Wild West Brides, 2002; (with L. Carlyle) Tea for Two: Two Novellas, 2002; The Lady is Tempted, 2002; Adventures of a Scottish Heiress, 2003; (with V. Alexander, L. Carlyle and E. James) One that Got Away, 2004; Seduction of an English Lady, 2004; Temptation of a Proper Governess, 2004; Price of Indiscretion, 2005; (foreword) Unknown Ajax, 2005; In the Bed of a Duke, 2006; Bedding the Heiress, 2007; In the Highlander's Bed, 2008; A Seduction at Christmas, 2008; The Earl Claims His Wife, 2009; Four Dukes and a Devil, 2009; The Marriage Ring, 2010; His Christmas Pleasure, 2010; The Seduction of Scandal, 2011; Lyon's Bride, 2012. **Address:** c/o Damaris Rowland, Rowland/Axelrod, 510 E 23rd St., Ste. 8-G, New York, NY 10010-5020, U.S.A. **Online address:** cathy@cathymaxwell.com

MAXWELL, Jaclyn L. American (born United States), b. 1973. **Genres:** Theology/Religion, History. **Career:** Ohio University, Department of History, assistant professor, Department of Classics and World Religions, assistant professor. Writer. **Publications:** Christianization and Communication in Late Antiquity: John Chrysostom and His Congregation in Antioch, 2006. Contributor to books. **Address:** Department of History, Ohio University, 413 Bentley Annex, Athens, OH 45701-2979, U.S.A. **Online address:** maxwelj1@ohio.edu

MAXWELL, Jessica. American (born United States), b. 1955?. **Genres:** Travel/Exploration. **Career:** Travel writer and journalist. **Publications:** Femme d'Adventure: Travel Tales from Inner Montana to Outer Mongolia, 1997; I Don't Know Why I Swallowed the Fly: My Fly Fishing Rookie Season, 1997; Driving Myself Crazy: Misadventures of a Novice Golfer, 2000; Roll around Heaven: An All-True Accidental Spiritual Adventure, 2009. Works appear in anthologies. Contributor to periodicals. **Address:** Vida, OR , U.S.A. **Online address:** jessica@rollaroundheaven.com

MAXWELL, John. *See* **FREEMANTLE, Brian (Harry).**

MAXWELL, John C. American (born United States), b. 1947. **Genres:** How-to Books, inspirational/Motivational Literature, Self Help, Sports/Fitness. **Career:** INJOY Inc., founder and president, 1985-2007; Skyline Wesleyan Church, senior pastor, 1995; full-time writer, speaker and consultant, 1995-; EQUIP, founder, 1996-. **Publications:** Your Attitude: Key to Success, 1984; Tough Questions-Honest Answers, 1985; Be All You Can Be!, 1987, 3rd ed. as Be All You Can Be: A Challenge to Stretch Your God-given Potential, 2007; The Communicator's Commentary: Deuteronomy, 1987; Be a People Person, 1989, 2nd ed. as Be a People Person: Effective Leadership through Effective Relationships, 2007; The Winning Attitude, 1991; Developing the Leader within You, 1993; Developing the Leaders around You, 1995; You Can't Be a Smart Cookie, If You Have a Crummy Attitude, 1995; (with B. Lewis) Your Family Time with God: A Weekly Plan for Family Devotions, 1995; Breakthrough Parenting, 1996; It's Just a Thought-But It Could Change Your Life: Life's Little Lessons on Leadership, 1996; Living at the Next Level: Insights for Reaching Your Dreams, 1996; Partners in Prayer, 1996; (comp.) People Power: Life's Little Lessons on Relationships, 1996; (with J. Dornan) Becoming a Person of Influence: How to Positively Impact the Lives of Others, 1997; The Success Journey, 1997; Your Bridge to a Better Future, 1997; The 21 Irrefutable Laws of Leadership: Follow Them and People Will Follow You, 1998, 10th ed., 2007; Think on These Things: Meditations for Leaders, 1999; The 21 Indispensable Qualities of a Leader: Becoming the Person that People Will Want to Follow, 1999; (with D. Reiland) The Treasure of a Friend, 1999; Failing Forward: Turning Mistakes into Stepping-Stones for Success, 2000; The 21 Most Powerful Minutes in a Leader's Day: Revitalize Your Spirit and Empower Your Leadership, 2000; Success: One Day at a Time, 2000; John Developing the Leader within You Workbook, 2001; (with M. Littleton) Leading as a Friend, 2001; (with J. Fischer) Leading from the Lockers, 2001; (with M. Littleton) Leading Your Sports Team, 2001; (with M. Littleton) Leading in Your Youth Group, 2001; (with M. Hall) Leading at School, 2001; The Power of Attitude, 2001; (comp.) The Power of Influence, 2001; The Power of Leadership, 2001; The Power of Thinking Big, 2001; The Right to Lead: A Study in Character and Courage, 2001; The 17 Indisputable Laws of Teamwork: Embrace Them and Empower Your Team, 2001; Leadership 101, 2002; The 17 Essential Qualities of a Team Player: Becoming the Kind of Person Every Team Wants, 2002; Running with the Giants: What Old Testament Heroes Want You to Know about Life and Leadership, 2002; Your Road Map for Success, 2002; Teamwork Makes the Dream Work, 2002; Thinking for a Change: 11 Ways Highly Successful People Approach Life and Work, 2003; Developing the Leaders Around You Workbook, 2003; Attitude 101: What Every Leader Needs to Know, 2003; Equipping 101: What Every Leader Needs to Know, 2003; Ethics 101: What Every Leader Needs to Know, 2003; Leadership: Promises for Every Day, a Daily Devotional, 2003; Relationships 101: What Every Leader Needs to Know, 2003; There's No Such Thing as Business Ethics: There's Only One Rule for Making Decisions, 2003; The Journey from Success to Significance, 2004; Today Matters: 12 Daily Practices to Guarantee Tomorrow's Success, 2004; Winning with People: Discover the People Principles that Work for You Every Time, 2004; (with L. Parrott) 25 Ways to Win with People: How to Make Others Feel like a Million Bucks, 2005; The 360-Degree Leader: Developing Your Influence from Anywhere in the Organization, 2005; Choice is Yours: Today's Decisions for the Rest of Your Life, 2005; (with S.R. Graves and T.G. Addington) Life@work: Marketplace Success for People of Faith, 2005; (with S.R. Graves and T.G. Addington) Life@work, 2005; Dare to Dream, then Do It: What Successful People Know and Do, 2006; Difference Maker: Making Your Attitude Your Greatest Asset, 2006; Leadership Promises for Your Week, 2007; Talent is Never Enough: Discover the Choices That Will take You beyond Your Talent, 2007; Leadership Principles for Graduates: Create Success in Life One Day at a Time, 2007; (with T. Elmore) Maxwell Leadership Bible, 2007; Make Today Count: The Secret of Your Success is Determined by Your Daily Agenda, 2008; Leadership Gold: Lessons I've Learned from a Lifetime of Leading, 2008; Go for Gold: Inspiration to Increase Your Leadership Impact, 2008; Mentoring 101: What Every Leader Needs to Know, 2008; Success 101: What Every Leader Needs to Know, 2008; Maxwell Daily Reader: 365 Days of Insight to Develop the Leader Within You and Influence Those Around You, 2008; Put Your Dream to the Test: 10 Questions that will Help You See it and Seize it, 2009; My Dream Map, 2009; Teamwork 101: What Every Leader Needs to Know, 2009; Self-improvement 101: What Every Leader Needs to Know, 2009; How Successful People Think: Change Your Thinking, Change Your Life, 2009; Everyone Communicates, Few Connect, 2010; How Successful People Think Workbook, 2011. **Address:** EQUIP Leadership Inc., 5400 Laurel Springs Pkwy., Ste. 301, PO Box 1808, Suwanee, GA 30024-6063, U.S.A.

MAXWELL, Kathleen. *See* **PTACEK, Kathryn.**

MAXWELL, Katie. *See* **MACALISTER, Katie.**

MAXWELL, Kenneth Robert. American/British (born England), b. 1941. **Genres:** History, International Relations/Current Affairs. **Career:** Newberry Library, fellow, 1968-69; University of Kansas, assistant professor, 1969-72, associate professor of history, 1972-73; Columbia University, School of International Affairs, associate professor of history, 1976-84, Research Institute of International Change, senior research fellow, 1978-92, senior research associate, 1992-2000; New York University, adjunct associate professor of Latin American and Caribbean studies, 1978-79; Tinker Foundation, program director, 1979-85; Princeton University, professor of history and Latin American studies, 1985-86; Camoes Center, director, 1988-89; Council on Foreign Relations, senior fellow for Latin America, 1989-2004, director of studies and vice president, 1996; Yale University, professor of history, 1991-92; Foreign Affairs, Americas editor, 1992-2004; Folha de Sao Paulo, op-ed columnist, 2003-; Harvard University, professor of history, 2004-08, David Rockefeller Center for Latin American Studies, senior fellow, 2004-08, Brazil Studies Program, director, 2006-08. **Publications:** Conflicts and Conspiracies: Brazil and Portugal 1750-1808, 1973, new ed., 2004; (ed.) The Press and the Rebirth of Iberian Democracy, 1983; (ed.) Portugal: Ten Years after the Revolution, 1984; Spain's Prospects, 1985; (ed.) Portugal in the 1980's: The Dilemmas of Democratic Consolidation, 1986; (ed. with M.H. Haltzel) Portugal: Ancient Country, New Democracy, 1989; (ed. with S.C. Monje) Portugal, the Constitution and the Consolidation of Democracy, 1976-1989, 1991; (ed.) Portuguese Defense and Foreign Policy Since Democratization, 1991; Spanish Foreign and Defense Policy, 1991; The New Spain: From Isolation to Influence, 1994; Pombal: A Paradox of the Enlightenment, 1995; The Making of Portuguese Democracy, 1995; Chocolate, Piratas e Outros Malandros: Ensaios Tropicais, 1999; Mais malandros: Ensaios tropicais e outros, 2002; Naked Tropics: Essays on Empire and Other Rogues, 2003; Conflicts and Conspiracies: Brazil and Portugal, 1750-1808, 2004. Contributor to books, newspapers and journals. **Address:** Department of History, Harvard University, Rm. S425, CGIS S Bldg., 1730 Cambridge St., Cambridge, MA 02138-4317, U.S.A. **Online address:** kmaxwell@fas.harvard.edu

MAXWELL, Nicholas. British (born England), b. 1937. **Genres:** Education, Ethics, Humanities, Philosophy, Physics, Sciences, Social Sciences, Institutions/Organizations, Intellectual History, International Relations/Current Affairs, Politics/Government, Technology. **Career:** Victoria University of Manchester, lecturer in philosophy of science, 1965-66; University of London, lecturer in philosophy of science, 1966-94, emeritus reader in history and philosophy of science, 1994-, now honorary senior research fellow; University of Pittsburgh, visiting lecturer, 1972-73, 1999. Writer. **Publications:** What's Wrong with Science? Towards a People's Rational Science of Delight and Compassion, 1976, 2nd ed., 2009; From Knowledge to Wisdom: A Revolution in the Aims and Methods of Science, 1984. 2nd ed., 2007; The Comprehensibility of the Universe: A New Conception of Science, 1998; The Human World in the Physical Universe: Consciousness, Free Will and Evolution, 2001; Is Science Neurotic?, 2004; (ed. with R. Barnett) Wisdom in the University, 2008; (ed. with L. McHenry) Science and the Pursuit of Wisdom: Studies in the Philosophy of Nicholas Maxwell, 2009; Cutting God in Half - And Putting the Pieces Together Again: A New Approach to Philosophy, 2010. **Address:** Pentire Press, 13 Tavistock Terrace, London, GL N19 4BZ, England. **Online address:** nicholas.maxwell@ucl.ac.uk

MAXWELL, Patricia Anne. Also writes as Elizabeth Trehearne, Maxine Patrick, Patricia Ponder, Jennifer Blake. American (born United States), b. 1942. **Genres:** Mystery/Crime/Suspense, Romance/Historical, Novels, Young Adult Non-fiction, Literary Criticism And History. **Career:** University of Northeastern Louisiana, writer-in-residence. **Publications:** NOVELS: Secret of Mirror House, 1969; Stranger at Plantation Inn, 1970; The Court of the Thorn Tree, 1973; The Bewitching Grace, 1973; Dark Masquerade, 1974; Bride of a Stranger, 1974; The Notorious Angel, 1977; Sweet Piracy, 1978; Night of the Candles, 1978. AS JENNIFER BLAKE: Love's Wild Desire, 1977; Tender Betrayal, 1979; The Storm and the Splendor, 1979; Golden Fancy, 1980; Embrace and Conquer, 1981; Royal Seduction, 1983; Surrender in Moonlight, 1984; Midnight Waltz, 1984; My First Real Romance, 1985; Fierce Eden, 1985; Royal Passion, 1986; Prisoner of Desire, 1986; Southern Rapture, 1987; Spanish Serenade, 1987; Louisiana Dawn, 1987; Perfume of Paradise, 1988; Love and Smoke: A Novel, 1989; Joy and Anger, 1991; Wildest Dreams, 1992; Arrow to the Heart, 1993; Shameless, 1994; Silver Tongued Devil, 1996; Tigress, 1996; Garden of Scandal, 1997; Kane, 1998; Luke, 1999; Roan, 2000, Clay, 2001; Wade, 2002; (with K. Hannah and L.L. Miller) With Love, 2002; (with H. Graham and D. Palmer) With a Southern Touch, 2002; Challenge to Honor, 2005; Dawn Encounter, 2006; Rogue's Salute, 2007; Guarded Heart, 2008, Gallant Match, 2009; Triumph in Arms, 2010. AS MAXINE PATRICK: The Abducted Heart, 1978; The Hired Wife, 1978; Bayou Bride, 1979; Snowbound Heart, 1979; Love at Sea, 1980; Captive Kisses, 1980; April of Enchantment, 1980. AS PATRICIA PONDER: Haven of Fear, 1974; Murder for Charity, 1974. AS ELIZABETH TREHEARNE: (with C. Albritton) Storm at Midnight, 1973. Contributor to periodicals. **Address:** Richard Curtis Associates Inc., 171 E 74th St., 2nd Fl., New York, NY 10021-3221, U.S.A.

MAXWELL, Robert A. American (born United States), b. 1968. **Genres:** History. **Career:** University of Pennsylvania, associate professor of art history. Writer and art historian. **Publications:** The Art of Medieval Urbanism: Parthenay in Romanesque Aquitaine, 2007; (ed.) Representing History, 900-1300: Art, Music, History, 2010. Contributor to periodicals and journals. **Address:** Department of the History of Art, University of Pennsylvania, 204 Elliot and Roslyn Jaffe History of Art Bldg., 3405 Woodland Walk, Philadelphia, PA 19104-6208, U.S.A. **Online address:** maxwellr@sas.upenn.edu

MAXWELL, Robin. American (born United States), b. 1948. **Genres:** Novels, Plays/Screenplays. **Career:** State Psychiatric Hospital, occupational therapist and unit supervisor, 1970-72; Hollywood, screenwriter, 1981-. **Publications:** NOVELS: The Secret Diary of Anne Boleyn, 1997; The Queen's Bastard, 1999; Virgin: Prelude to the Throne, 2001; The Wild Irish, 2003; To the Tower Born, 2005; Mademoiselle Boleyn, 2007; Signora da Vinci, 2009; O, Juliet, 2010. **Address:** High Desert, CA 92268-0302, U.S.A. **Online address:** robin@robinmaxwell.com

MAXWELL, Vicky. *See* **WORBOYS, Anne.**

MAY, Brian. American (born United States), b. 1959. **Genres:** Adult Non-fiction, Literary Criticism And History. **Career:** University of North Texas, assistant professor of English, 1991-97, associate professor of English, 1997-; Illinois State University, visiting professor of English, 1997-98; Northern Illinois University, Department of English, associate professor. Writer. **Publications:** The Modernist as Pragmatist: E. M. Forster and the Fate of Liberalism, 1997. Contributor to journals. **Address:** Department of English, Northern Illinois University, RH 321, 1425 W Lincoln Hwy., DeKalb, IL 60115-2828, U.S.A. **Online address:** bmay1@niu.edu

MAY, Daryl (Alden). American (born United States), b. 1936. **Genres:** Children's Non-fiction, Plays/Screenplays, Songs/Lyrics And Libretti, Travel/Exploration. **Career:** Pinellas County Sheriff Office, uniform deputy and vice-detective, 1962-71; writer, 1971-. **Publications:** FOR CHILDREN: (with R. Bansemer) Rachael's Splendifilous Adventure, 1991. **Address:** 920 S Hillcrest Ave., Clearwater, FL 33756-6151, U.S.A. **Online address:** bkildoo@aol.com

MAY, Derwent (James). British (born England), b. 1930. **Genres:** Novels, History. **Career:** Continental Daily Mail, drama critic, 1952-53; University of Indonesia, lecturer in English, 1955-58; University of Lodz, lecturer in English, 1959-63; University of Warsaw in Poland, lecturer in English, 1959-63; Times Literary Supplement, leader-writer and poetry editor, 1963-65; Listener, literary editor, 1965-86; The Sunday Telegraph, literary and arts editor, 1986-90; The European, literary and arts editor, 1990-92; The Times, European arts editor, 1992-. **Publications:** The Professionals, 1964; Dear Parson, 1969; (ed.) British and Commonwealth Novels of the Sixties, 1970; (ed.) European Novels of the Sixties, 1972; The Laughter in Djakarta, 1973; A Revenger's Comedy, 1979; (ed.) The Music of What Happens: Poems From the Listener 1965-1980, 1981; Proust, 1983; The Times Nature Diary, 1983; Hannah Arendt, 1986; The New Times Nature Diary, 1993; Feather Reports, 1996; Critical Times: The History of the Times Literary Supplement, 2001; How to Attract Birds to Your Garden, 2001; A Year in Nature Notes, 2004. Contributor to periodicals. **Address:** The Times, 3 Thomas More Sq., London, GL E98 1XY, England.

MAY, Gary. American (born United States), b. 1944. **Genres:** History, Biography. **Career:** Colgate University, instructor in history, 1974-75; University of Delaware, Department of History, associate professor, professor, 1975, Master of Arts in Liberal Studies Program, director. Writer and historian. **Publications:** China Scapegoat: The Diplomatic Ordeal of John Carter Vincent, 1979; Un-American Activities: The Trials of William Remington, 1994; The Informant: The FBI, the Ku Klux Klan and the Murder of Viola Liuzzo, 2005; John Tyler: American Presidents Series, 2008. **Address:** Department of History, University of Delaware, 119 John Munroe Hall, 46 W Delaware Ave., Newark, DE 19716-2547, U.S.A. **Online address:** garymay@udel.edu

MAY, Gita. American/Belgian (born Belgium), b. 1929. **Genres:** Biography, Essays, Humanities, Art/Art History. **Career:** Columbia University, lecturer, 1953-56, instructor, 1956-58, assistant professor, 1958-61, associate professor, 1961-68, professor of French, 1968-83, professor emeritus, 1983-, department chairman, 1983-93; U.S. Education Commission, lecturer, 1965; American Society for 18th-Century Studies, chair of the department and president, 1985; Age of Revolution and Romanticism, general editor, 1990-. **Publications:** Diderot et Baudelaire: critiques d Art, 1957, 3rd ed., 1973; (ed. with O. Fellows) Diderot Studies III, 1961; De Jean-Jacques Rousseau a Madame Roland: Essai sur la sensibilite preromantique et Revolutionnaire, 1964; Madame Roland and the Age of Revolution, 1970; Stendhal and the Age of Napoleon, 1977; Encyclopedia of Aesthetics, 1998; The Social Contract and The First and Second Discourses, 2002; Candide, or, Optimism, 2003; Voltaire's Candide, 2003; Elisabeth Vigée Le Brun: The Odyssey of an Artist in an Age of Revolution, 2005. Contributor to books. **Address:** Department of French and Romance Philology, Columbia University, 516 Philosophy Hall, PO Box 4902, New York, NY 10027, U.S.A. **Online address:** gm9@columbia.edu

MAY, Henry F(arnham). American (born United States), b. 1915. **Genres:** History, Theology/Religion. **Career:** Lawrence College (now Lawrence University), instructor in history, 1941-42; United States Navy Reserve, lieutenant, 1942-45; Scripps College, assistant professor, 1947-48, associate professor of history, 1948-49; Bowdoin College, visiting associate professor, 1950-51; University of California, associate professor, 1952-56, professor of history, 1956-63, Margaret Byrne professor of history, 1963-, chair of department, 1964-66, now professor emeritus; Belgian universities, Fulbright lecturer, 1959-60; Cambridge University, Pitt professor of American history and institutions, 1971-. Writer. **Publications:** Protestant Churches and Industrial America, 1949, 1967; The End of American Innocence: A Study of the First Years of Our Own Time 1912-1917, 1959; (with C.G. Sellers, Jr.) A Synopsis of American History, 1963, (with C.G. Sellers, Jr. and N.R. McMillen) 7th ed., 1992; The Discontent of the Intellectuals, a Problem of the Twenties, 1963; (ed.) Oldtown Folks, 1966; The Enlightenment in America, 1976; Ideas, Faiths and Feelings: Essays on American Intellectual and Religious History, 1952-1982, 1983; Coming to Terms: A Study in Memory and History, 1987; The Divided Heart: Essays on Protestantism and the Enlightenment in America, 1991; Three Faces of Berkeley: Competing Ideologies in the Wheeler Era, 1899-1919, 1993; (with G.A. Brucker and D.A. Hollinger) History at Berkeley: A Dialog in Three Parts, 1998. **Address:** Department of History, University of California, 3229 Dwinelle Hall, Berkeley, CA 94720-2550, U.S.A.

MAY, Jesse. American (born United States), b. 1970?. **Genres:** Sports/Fitness, Social Commentary, How-to Books, Young Adult Fiction, Literary Criticism And History. **Career:** Poker player. Writer. **Publications:** Shut Up and Deal, 1998; The Gambler's Guide to the World: The Inside Scoop from a Professional Player on Finding the Action, Beating the Odds, and Living It Up around the Globe, 2000; English Constitution: A Commentary on its Nature and Growth, 2002. Contributor to periodicals. **Address:** c/o Author Mail, Random House, 1745 Broadway, New York, NY 10019, U.S.A.

MAY, John. American (born United States), b. 1942?. **Genres:** Novels. **Career:** Bonaventure Co., managing partner; University of North Carolina-Greensboro Friends of the Library, chair of board of directors. Writer. **Publications:** Poe and Fanny: A Novel, 2004. Contributor to periodicals. **Address:** University of North Carolina, 1400 Spring Garden St., PO Box 26170, Greensboro, NC 27412, U.S.A. **Online address:** john.may@poeandfanny.com

MAY, Julian. Also writes as John Feilen, Jean Wright Thorne, Lee N. Falconer, Ian Thorne, Matthew G. Grant. American (born United States), b. 1931. **Genres:** Science Fiction/Fantasy, Novels, Adult Non-fiction, Young Adult Fiction, Mystery/Crime/Suspense, Young Adult Non-fiction, Novellas/Short Stories. **Career:** Booz Allen Hamilton, editor, 1953; Consolidated Book Publishers, editor, 1954-57; Publication Associates, editor and co-owner, 1957-68, editor, 1968-92. **Publications:** Lewis and Clark: Western Trailblazers, 1974; Kit Carson: Trailblazer of the West, 1974; Lafayette: Freedom's General, 1974; Osceola and the Seminole War, 1974; Paul Revere: Patriot and Craftsman, 1974; Pontiac: Indian General and Statesman, 1974; Robert E. Lee: The South's Great General, 1974; Squanto: The Indian Who Saved the Pilgrims, 1974; Sam Houston of Texas, 1974; Susan B. Anthony: Crusader for Women's Rights, 1974; Ulysses S. Grant: General and President, 1974; Development Planning in Transkei, 1985; (with J. Nattrass) Migration and Dependency: Sources and Levels of Income in Kwazulu, 1986; (with S.E. Stavrou) Informal Sector: Socio-Economic Dynamics and Growth in the Greater Durban Metropolitan Region, 1989; (contrib.) Rural Poverty and Institutions, 1994; (with M. Carter and D. Posel) The Composition and Persistence of Poverty in Rural South Africa: An Entitlements Approach, 1995; (contrib.) Experience and Perceptions of Poverty in South Africa, 1998; (with M.R. Carter) Poverty, Livelihood, and Class in Rural South Africa, 1998; (ed.) Poverty and Inequality in South Africa, 1998; (with J. Maluccio and L. Haddad) Social Capital and Income Generation in South Africa, 1993-98, 1999; (with T. Stevens and A. Stors) Monitoring the Impact of Land Reform on Quality of Life, 2000; (with K. Deininger) Is There Scope for Growth with Equity?: The Case of Land Reform in South Africa, 2000. RAMPART WORLDS SERIES: Perseus Spur, 1998; Orion Arm, 1999; The Sagittarius Whorl, 2001. THE SAGA OF PLIOCENE EXILE SERIES: The Many-Colored Land, 1981; The Golden Torc, 1981; Brede's Tale (short story), 1982; The Nonborn King, 1983; The Adversary, 1984; A Pliocene Companion: A Reader's Guide to The Many-Colored Land, The Golden Torc, The Nonborn King, The Adversary, 1984. INTERVENTION SERIES: Intervention, 1987; The Surveillance, 1988; Metaconcert, 1988. GALACTIC MILIEU SERIES: Jack the Bodiless, 1992; Diamond Mask, 1994; Magnificat, 1996. FANTASY FICTION: (with M.Z. Bradley and A. Norton) Black Trillium, 1990; Blood Trillium, 1992; Sky Trillium, 1997; Conqueror's Moon, 2004; Ironcrown Moon, 2005; Sorcerer's Moon, 2006. JUVENILE NONFICTION: There's Adventure in Atomic Energy, 1957; There's Adventure in Chemistry, 1957; There's Adventure in Electronics, 1957; There's Adventure in Geology, 1958; There's Adventure in Rockets, 1958; You and the Earth beneath Us, 1958; There's Adventure in Jet Aircraft, 1959; There's Adventure in Marine Science, 1959; Show Me the World of Astronomy, 1959; Show Me the World of Electronics, 1959; Show Me the World of Modern Airplanes, 1959; Show Me the World of Space Travel, 1959; Robots and Thinking Machines, 1961; There's Adventure in Astronautics, 1961; There's Adventure in Automobiles, 1961; Motion, 1962; (with T.E. Dikty) Every Boy's Book of American Heroes, 1963; They Turned to Stone, 1965; Weather, 1966; Rockets, 1967; They Lived in the Ice Age, 1968; Astronautics, 1968; The Big Island, 1968; The First Men, 1968; Horses: How They Came to Be, 1968; Alligator Hole, 1969; Before the Indians, 1969; Climate, 1969; How We Are Born, 1969; Living Things and Their Young, 1969; Man and Woman, 1969; Moving Hills of Sand, 1969; Why the Earth Quakes, 1969; Do You Have Your Father's Nose?, 1970; Dodos and Dinosaurs Are Extinct, 1970; (co-author) The Ecology of North America, 1970; The First Living Things, 1970; How to Build a Body, 1970; Millions of Years of Eggs, 1970; A New Baby Comes, 1970; Tiger Stripes and Zebra Stripes, 1970; Why Birds Migrate, 1970; Why Plants Are Green Instead of Pink, 1970; Wildlife in the City, 1970; Blue River: The Land beneath the Sea, 1971; Cactus Fox, 1971; These Islands Are Alive, 1971; Why People Are Different Colors, 1971; The Antarctic: Bottom of the World, 1972; The Arctic: Top of the World, 1972; Cascade Cougar, 1972; The Cloud Book, 1972; Deserts: Hot and Cold, 1972; Eagles of the Valley, 1972; Forests That Change Color, 1972; Giant Condor of California, 1972; Glacier Grizzly, 1972; Islands of the Tiny Deer, 1972; The Land Is Disappearing, 1972; Living Blanket on the Land, 1972; The Mysterious Evergreen Forest, 1972; Plankton: Drifting Life of the Waters, 1972; The Prairie has an Endless Sky, 1972; Prairie Pronghorn, 1972; Rainbows, Clouds, and Foggy Dew, 1972; Sea Lion Island, 1972; Sea Otter, 1972; Snowfall!, 1972; What Will the Weather Be?, 1972; Birds We Know, 1973; Fishes We Know, 1973; Insects We Know, 1973; The Life Cycle of a Bullfrog, 1973; The Life Cycle of a Cottontail Rabbit, 1973; The Life Cycle of a Monarch Butterfly, 1973; The Life Cycle of an Opossum, 1973; The Life Cycle of a Polyphemus Moth, 1973; The Life Cycle of a Raccoon, 1973; The Life Cycle of a Red Fox, 1973; The Life Cycle of a Snapping Turtle, 1973; Mammals We Know, 1973; Reptiles We Know, 1973; Wild Turkeys, 1973; How the Animals Came to North America, 1974; Cars and Cycles, 1978; The Warm-Blooded Dinosaurs, 1978. JUVENILE BIOGRAPHIES: Captain Cousteau: Undersea Explorer, 1972; Hank Aaron Clinches the Pennant, 1972; Jim Brown Runs with the Ball, 1972; Johnny Unitas and the Long Pass, 1972; Matthew Henson: Co-Discoverer of the North Pole, 1972; Mickey Mantle Slugs It Out, 1972; Sitting Bull: Chief of the Sioux, 1972; Sojourner Truth: Freedom Fighter, 1972; Willie Mays: Most Valuable Player, 1972; Amelia Earhart: Pioneer of Aviation, 1973; Bobby Orr: Star on Ice, 1973; Ernie Banks: Home Run Slugger, 1973; Fran Tarkenton: Scrambling Quarterback, 1973; Gale Sayers: Star Running Back, 1973; Hillary and Tenzing: Conquerors of Mount Everest, 1973; Kareem Abdul Jabbar: Cage Superstar, 1973; Quanah: Leader of the Comanche, 1973; Thor Heyerdahl: Modern Viking Adventurer, 1973; Roberto Clemente and the World Series Upset, 1973; Billie Jean King: Tennis Champion, 1974; Bobby Hull: Hockey's Golden Jet, 1974; Lee Trevino: The Golf Explosion, 1974; O.J. Simpson: Juice on the Gridiron, 1974; Roy Campanella: Brave Man of Baseball, 1974; A.J. Foyt: Championship Auto Racer, 1975; Arthur Ashe: Dark Star of Tennis, 1975; Bobby Clarke: Hockey with a Grin, 1975; Chris Evert: Princess of Tennis, 1975; Evel Knievel: Daredevil Stuntman, 1975; Evonne Goolalgong: Smasher from Australia, 1975; Frank Robinson: Slugging toward Glory, 1975; Janet Lynn: Figure Skating Star, 1975; Pele: World Soccer Star, 1975; Joe Namath: High Flying Quarterback, 1975; Muhammad Ali: Boxing Superstar, 1975; Vince Lombardi: The Immortal Coach, 1975; Phil Esposito: The Big Bruin, 1975. SPORTS NONFICTION: The Baltimore Colts, 1974; The Dallas Cowboys, 1974; The Green Bay Packers, 1974; The Kansas City Chiefs, 1974; The Miami Dolphins, 1974; The New York Jets, 1974; The Stanley Cup, 1975; The Super Bowl, 1975; The Indianapolis 500, 1975; The Kentucky Derby, 1975; The Masters Tournament of Golf, 1975; The U.S.

Open Golf Championship, 1975; Wimbledon: World Tennis Focus, 1975; The World Series, 1975; The NBA Playoffs: Basketball's Classic, 1975; The Olympic Games, 1975; The PGA Championship, 1976; The Pittsburgh Steelers, 1976, 3rd ed., 1980; The Winter Olympics, 1976; America's Cup Yacht Race, 1976; Boxing's Heavyweight Championship Fight, 1976; Daytona 500, 1976; Forest Hills and the American Tennis Championship, 1976; The Grand Prix, 1976; The Triple Crown, 1976; The Rose Bowl, 1976; The Washington Redskins, 1977; The Los Angeles Rams, 1977; The Minnesota Vikings, 1977; The New York Giants, 1977; The Oakland Raiders, 1977; The San Francisco 49ers, 1977; The Oakland Raiders: Super Bowl Champions, 1977; The Cincinnati Bengals, 1980; The Denver Broncos, 1980; The San Diego Chargers, 1980. NONFICTION AS JOHN FEILEN: Air, 1965; Deer, 1967; Squirrels, 1967; Dirt Track Speedsters, 1976; Racing on the Water, 1976; Winter Sports, 1976; Four-Wheel Racing, 1978; Motocross Racing, 1978. NONFICTION AS MATTHEW G. GRANT: A Walk in the Mountains, 1971; Jim Bridger the Mountain Man, 1973; Buffalo Bill of the Wild West, 1974; Champlain: Explorer of New France, 1974; Dolley Madison, 1974; Chief Joseph of the Nez Perce, 1974; Clara Barton: Red Cross Pioneer, 1974; Columbus: Discoverer of the New World, 1974; Coronado: Explorer of the Southwest, 1974; Crazy Horse: War Chief of the Oglala, 1974; Daniel Boone in the Wilderness, 1974; Davy Crockett: Frontier Adventurer, 1974; De Soto: Explorer of the Southeast, 1974; Dolly Madison: First Lady of the Land, 1974; Elizabeth Blackwell: Pioneer Doctor, 1974; Francis Marion: Swamp Fox, 1974; Geronimo: Apache Warrior, 1974; Harriet Tubman: Black Liberator, 1974; Jane Addams: Helper of the Poor, 1974; Jim Bridger: The Mountain Man, 1974; John Paul Jones: Naval Hero, 1974; Leif Ericson: Explorer of Vinland, 1974. NONFICTION AS IAN THORNE: Meet the Coaches, 1975; Meet the Defensive Linemen, 1975; Meet the Linebackers, 1975; Meet the Quarterbacks, 1975; Meet the Receivers, 1975; Meet the Running Backs, 1975; The Great Centers, 1976; Meet the Defensive Linemen, 1976; The Great Defenseman, 1976; The Great Goalies, 1976; The Great Wingmen, 1976; King Kong, 1976; Mad Scientists, 1977; Godzilla, 1977; Ancient Astronauts, 1977; Dracula, 1977; Frankenstein, 1977; Monster Tales of Native Americans, 1978; The Bermuda Triangle, 1978; Bigfoot, 1978; The Loch Ness Monster, 1978; UFOs, 1978. NONFICTION AS GEORGE ZANDERBERGEN: The Beatles, 1976; Made for Music: Elton John, Stevie Wonder, John Denver, 1976; Laugh It Up: Carol Burnett, Bill Cosby, Mary Tyler Moore, 1976; Nashville Music: Loretta Lynn, Mac Davis, Charley Pride, 1976; Stay Tuned: Henry Winkler, Lee Majors, Valerie Harper, 1976; Sweetly Singing: Cher, Roberta Flack, Olivia Newton John, 1976. NONFICTION AS BOB CUNNINGHAM: Ten-Five: Alaska Skip, 1977; Ten-Seven for Good Sam, 1977; Ten-Seventy: Range Fire, 1977; Ten-Thirty-Three: Emergency, 1977; Ten-Two Hundred: Come on Smokey!, 1977. FILM NOVELIZATIONS AS IAN THORNE: The Wolf Man, 1977; The Creature from the Black Lagoon, 1981; Frankenstein Meets the Wolfman, 1981; The Mummy, 1981; The Blob, 1982; The Deadly Mantis, 1982; It Came from Outer Space, 1982. OTHERS: (as Jean Wright Thorne) Horse and Rider, 1976; (as Jean Wright Thorne) Rodeo, 1976; (as Lee N. Falconer) A Gazetteer of the Hyborian World of Conan, 1977; Migrant Labour in Transkei, 1985. **Address:** Ralph M. Vicinanza Ltd., 303 W 18th St., New York, NY 10011-4440, U.S.A.

MAY, Larry. American (born United States), b. 1952. **Genres:** Philosophy, Social Sciences. **Career:** University of Connecticut, assistant professor, 1977-79; Purdue University, 1979-91, assistant professor, professor of philosophy; Washington University, professor of philosophy, 1991-; University of Wisconsin, visiting assistant professor of philosophy, 1979; Charles Sturt and Australian National Universities, Centre for Applied Philosophy and Public Ethics, research professor of social justice, 2007-11; Indiana State Senate, consultant, 1981; St. Louis Children's Hospital, Member of ethics committee, 1991. Writer. **Publications:** (with M. Curd) Professional Responsibility for Harmful Actions, 1984; The Morality of Groups: Collective Responsibility, Group-based Harm and Corporate Rights, 1987; Sharing Responsibility, 1992; The Socially Responsive Self: Social Theory and Professional Ethics, 1996; Masculinity and Morality, 1998; (with P. DesAutels and M.P. Battin) Praying for a Cure: When Medical and Religious Practices Conflict, 1999; Crimes against Humanity: A Normative Account, 2005; War Crimes and Just Wars, 2007; Aggression and Crimes against Peace, 2008. EDITOR: (with S. Hoffman) Collective Responsibility: Five Decades of Debate in Theoretical and Applied Ethics, 1991; (with R. Strikwerda) Rethinking Masculinity: Philosophical Explorations in Light of Feminism, 1992, 2nd ed. (ed. with R. Strikwerda and P. Hopkins), 1996; (with S. Sharratt) Applied Ethics: A Multicultural Approach, 1994, 4th ed., 2006; (with M. Friedman and A. Clark) Mind and Morals: Essays on Cognitive Science and Ethics, 1996; (with J. Kohn) Hannah Arendt: Twenty Years Later, 1996; (with C. Sistare and J. Schonsheck) Liberty, Equality and Plurality, 1997; (with N. Snow and A. Bolte) Legal Philosophy: Multiple Perspectives, 2000; (with M. Friedman, K. Parsons and J. Stiff) Rights and Reason: Essays in Honor of Carl Wellman, 2000; (with C. Sistare and L. Francis) Groups and Group Rights, 2001; (with E. Rovie and S. Viner) The Morality of War, 2006; (with E. Crookston) War: Essays in Political Philosophy, 2008; (with J. Brown) Philosophy of Law: Classical and Contemporary Readings, 2009. Contributor of articles to books. **Address:** Department of Philosophy, Washington University, 1 Brookings Dr., PO Box 1073, St. Louis, MO 63130, U.S.A. **Online address:** larrymay@artsci.wustl.edu

MAY, Lary L. American (born United States), b. 1944. **Genres:** Communications/Media, History, Politics/Government. **Career:** Princeton University, instructor in history, 1977-80; University of Minnesota, assistant professor of American studies, 1980-, professor. Writer. **Publications:** Screening Out the Past: The Birth of Mass Culture and the Motion Picture Industry, 1896-1929, 1980; (ed.) Recasting America: Culture and Politics in the Age of Cold War, 1989; The Big Tomorrow: Hollywood and the Politics of the American Way, 2000. **Address:** Department of American Studies, University of Minnesota, 211 Scott Hall, H 72 Pleasant St. SE, Minneapolis, MN 55455-0293, U.S.A. **Online address:** mayxx001@umn.edu

MAY, Steven W. American (born United States), b. 1941. **Genres:** Literary Criticism And History, Poetry, Bibliography, Biography, Language/Linguistics, History. **Career:** Augustana College, instructor, 1964-65; Indiana Central College, instructor, 1966-67; Northern Illinois University, assistant professor, 1968-69; Georgetown College, Department of English, lecturer, 1969, associate professor, 1974-80, professor, 1980-, now professor emeritus. Writer. **Publications:** Henry Stanford's Anthology: An Edition of Cambridge University Library Manuscript Dd. 5.75, 1988; Sir Walter Ralegh, 1989; The Elizabethan Courtier Poets: The Poems and Their Contexts, 1991; (with W.A. Ringler, Jr.) Elizabethan Poetry: A Bibliography and First-Line Index of English Verse, 1559-1603, 2004; (ed.) Queen Elizabeth I: Selected Works, 2004. Works appear in anthologies. **Address:** Department of English, Georgetown College, 400 E College St., Georgetown, KY 40324-1628, U.S.A. **Online address:** smay@georgetowncollege.edu

MAY, Todd Gifford. American (born United States), b. 1955. **Genres:** Literary Criticism And History, Psychology, Philosophy, Politics/Government. **Career:** Pennsylvania State University, graduate instructor, 1987; Indiana University of Pennsylvania, visiting assistant professor, 1989-91; Clemson University, Department of Philosophy and Religion, assistant professor, 1991-94, associate professor of philosophy and religion, 1994-98, professor, 1998-2007, Kathryn and Calhoun Lemon Professor of Philosophy, 2007-09, Class of 1941 Memorial Professor of the Humanities, 2009-. Writer. **Publications:** Between Genealogy and Epistemology: Psychology, Politics, and Knowledge in the Thought of Michel Foucault, 1993; The Political Philosophy of Poststructuralist Anarchism, 1994; Moral Theory of Poststructuralism, 1995; (ed. and intro.) Twentieth Century Continental Philosophy, 1997; Reconsidering Difference: Nancy, Derrida, Levinas, and Deleuze, 1997; Our Practices, Our Selves, Or, What It Means To Be Human, 2001; (ed. with M. Hamzeh) Operation Defensive Shield: Witnesses to Israeli War Crimes, 2003; Gilles Deleuze: An Introduction, 2005; The Philosophy of Foucault, 2006; Political Thought of Jacques Rancière: Creating Equality, 2008; Death, 2009; Contemporary Political Movements and the Thought of Jacques Rancière: Equality in Action, 2010. Works appear in anthologies. Contributor to journals. **Address:** Department of Philosophy and Religion, Clemson University, 224 Hardin Hall, 101 Strode Twr., Clemson, SC 29634, U.S.A. **Online address:** mayt@clemson.edu

MAY, Wynne. South African/Scottish (born Scotland) **Genres:** Novels, Romance/Historical, Young Adult Fiction. **Career:** African Explosives and Chemical Industries Ltd., staff; African Consolidated Films Ltd., staff; South African Broadcasting Corp., staff. Author. **Publications:** ROMANCE AND HISTORICAL NOVELS: A Cluster of Palms, 1967; The Highest Peak, 1967; The Valley of Aloes, 1967; When the Sun Sets, 1967; Tawny are the Leaves, 1968; Tamboti Moon, 1969; Where Breezes Falter, 1970; Sun, Sea and Sand, 1970; A Grain of Gold, 1971; The Tide at Full, 1971; A Slither of Silk, 1972; A Bowl of Stars, 1973; Pink Sands, 1974; The Sky at Night, 1975; Plume of Dust, 1975; The Bonds of Matrimony, 1975; A Plantation of Vines, 1977; Island of Cyclones, 1979; A Scarf of Flame, 1979; Wayside Flower, 1982; Peacock in the Jungle, 1982; Iceberg in the Tropics, 1983; Fire in the Ash, 1984;

The Leopard's Lair, 1984; Boma in the Bush, 1985; Peak of the Furnace, 1985; A Flaunting Cactus, 1986; Diamonds and Daisies, 1989; Tomorrow's Sun, 1989; Filigree of Fancy, 1990; Moon over Mombasa, 1991; Desert Rose, 1993; A Circle of Opals, 1995. **Address:** Shalimar, 40 Cotham Rd., Moseley, Natal, 4093, South Africa.

MAYALL, Beth. American (born United States) **Genres:** Novels, Adult Non-fiction, Sports/Fitness, Psychology, Young Adult Fiction. **Career:** Novelist, journalist and editor. **Publications:** All About You: Who Knew? Find Your Secret Self, 1999; Friends Rule!: How to be a Great Pal and Have Great Buds Too!, 2000; Get Over It!: How to Survive Breakups, Back-Stabbing Friends, and Bad Haircuts, 2000; What's Your Guy-Q? And Other Quizzes to Help Discover the Real You, 2000; (with J. Farrell) Middle School: The Real Deal: From Cafeteria Food to Combination Locks, 2001, rev. ed., 2007; Glamour Girl, 2002; Galaxy Girl, 2002; Mermaid Park, 2005. Contributor to periodicals. **Address:** c/o Author Mail, Razorbill/Penguin Putnam, 375 Hudson St., New York, NY 10014, U.S.A. **Online address:** beth@bethmayall.com

MAYBURY, Richard J. American (born United States), b. 1946. **Genres:** Novels, Money/Finance, How-to Books, Business/Trade/Industry. **Career:** Henry Madison Research Inc., president, 1982-; Moneyworld, global affairs editor. **Publications:** Precious Metals, Politics and Paper Money, 1978; Common Sense for the 1980's, 1981; Investment Frauds, Cons, and Rip-Offs: Secrets of the Trade, 1984; How You Can Strengthen Your Sales and Profits, 1986; Strengthen Your Sales Fast with the BCM Strategy, 1990; The Coming Soviet Civil War, 1990; How You Can Find the Best Investment Advice, 1992; You Can Profit from the Injection Effect, 1992; The Clipper Ship Strategy: For Success in Your Career, Business, and Investments, 1997, rev. ed., 2003; The Money Mystery: The Hidden Force Affecting Your Career, Business, and Investments, 1997, 3rd ed., 2004; The Thousand Year War in the Mideast: How It Affects You Today, 1999. UNCLE ERIC SERIES: FOR YOUNG ADULTS: Whatever Happened to Penny Candy?: For Students, Business People, and Investors: A Fast, Clear, and Fun Explanation of the Economics You Need for Success in Your Career, Business, and Investments, 1989, 6th ed., 2010; Whatever Happened to Justice?, 1993, rev. ed., 2004; Evaluating Books: What Would Thomas Jefferson Think about This?: Guidelines for Selecting Books Consistent with the Principles of America's Founders, 1994, 2nd ed., 2004; Uncle Eric Talks about-Personal, Career and Financial Security, 1994, 2nd ed., 2004; Are You Liberal? Conservative? or Confused?, 1995, 2nd ed., 2004; Ancient Rome: How It Affects You Today, 1995, 2nd ed., 2004; World War I: The Rest of the Story and How It Affects You Today, 1870 to 1935, 2002, rev. ed., 2003; World War II: The Rest of the Story and How It Affects You Today, 1930 to September 11, 2001, 2002, rev. ed., 2003. **Address:** Henry Madison Research Inc., PO Box 84908, Phoenix, AZ 85071, U.S.A.

MAYER, Barbara. American (born United States), b. 1939. **Genres:** How-to Books, Young Adult Non-fiction, Reference. **Career:** Journalism teacher and public relations director; Mayer Public Relations, owner. Writer. **Publications:** The College Survival Guide: An Insider's Guide to Success, 1981; The High School Survival Guide: An Insider's Guide to Success, 1981; How to Succeed in College, 1992; How to Succeed in High School, 1992, 2nd ed., 1999; Succeed in High School, 1997. **Address:** Highland High School, 9135 Erie St., Highland, IN 46322, U.S.A.

MAYER, Bob. Also writes as Bob McGuire, Robert Doherty, Greg Donegan, Robert Doherty. American (born United States), b. 1959. **Genres:** Novels, Science Fiction/Fantasy, Westerns/Adventure, Human Relations/Parenting, Writing/Journalism. **Career:** Writer, speaker and publisher. **Publications:** Eyes of the Hammer, 1991; Dragon Sim-13, 1992; Synbat, 1994; Cut Out, 1995; Z: A Dave Riley Novel, 1997; The Novel Writers Toolkit: A Guide to Writing Novels and Getting Published, 2003; (with J. Crusie) Don't Look Down, 2006; (with J. Crusie) Agnes & the Hitman, 2007; Who Dares Wins: the Green Beret Way to Conquer Fear and Succeed, 2009; (with J. Cruise) Wild Ride, 2010; Chasing the Ghost, 2010; Warrior Writer, 2010. AS ROBERT DOHERTY: The Rock, 1995; Psychic Warrior, 2000; Psychic Warrior: Project Aura, 2001. AREA 51 SERIES: Area 51, 1997; The Reply, 1998; The Mission, 1999; The Sphinx, 2000; The Grail, 2001; Excalibur, 2002; The Truth, 2003; Bodyguard of Lies, 2005; Section 8, 2005; Lost Girls, 2007; Citadel, 2007. AS BOB McGUIRE: The Line, 1996; The Gate, 1997. AS JOE DALTON: The Omega Missile, 1998; The Omega Operation, 2000. AS GREG DONEGAN, ATLANTIS SERIES: Atlantis, 1999; Bermuda Triangle, 2000; Devil's Sea, 2001. **Address:** PO Box 392, Langley, WA 98260, U.S.A. **Online address:** bob@bobmayer.org

MAYER, Gerda (Kamilla). British/Czech (born Czech Republic), b. 1927. **Genres:** Poetry, Literary Criticism And History. **Career:** Secretary, 1946-52. Writer. **Publications:** Oddments, 1970; Gerda Mayer's Library Folder, 1972; (ed.) Poet Tree Centaur: A Walthamstow Group Anthology, 1973; (with F. Elon and D. Halpern) Florence Elon, Daniel Halpern, Gerda Mayer, 1975; The Knockabout Show (for children), 1978; Monkey on the Analyst's Couch, 1980; (with N. Nicholson and F. Flynn) The Candy-Floss Tree (for children), 1984; March Postman, 1985; A Heartache of Grass, 1988; Time Watching, 1995; Bernini's Cat: New and Selected Poems, 1999; Hop-Pickers' Holiday, 2003. Contributor to periodicals. **Address:** 12 Margaret Ave., Chingford, London, GL E4 7NP, England.

MAYER, Jane. American (born United States), b. 1955?. **Genres:** Politics/Government. **Career:** Washington Star, metropolitan reporter; Wall Street Journal, staff, 1982, reporter, senior writer, 1983-95, front page editor, war correspondent, foreign correspondent; New Yorker, staff writer, 1995-; Time, stringer. **Publications:** (With D. McManus) Landslide: The Unmaking of the President, 1984-1988, 1988; (with J. Abramson) Strange Justice: The Selling of Clarence Thomas, 1994; The Dark Side: The Inside Story of How the War on Terror Turned into a War on American Ideals, 2008. **Address:** New Yorker, 4 Times Sq., New York, NY 10036-6592, U.S.A.

MAYER, Mercer. American (born United States), b. 1943. **Genres:** Children's Fiction, Illustrations, Picture/Board Books. **Career:** International Brotherhood of Teamsters, political cartoonist; Kahala Hilton Hotel, painter; children's book author and illustrator, 1967-. **Publications:** SELF-ILLUSTRATED FICTION FOR CHILDREN: A Boy, a Dog, and a Frog, 1967, 2nd ed., 2003; If I Had..., as If I Had a Gorilla, 1968; The Terrible Troll, 1968; There's a Nightmare in My Closet, 1968 in US as There's a Nightmare in My Cupboard, 1976, 2nd ed., 1990; Frog, Where Are You?, 1969, 2nd ed., 2003; I Am a Hunter, 1969; A Special Trick, 1970; (with M. Mayer) Mine, 1970; The Queen Always Wanted to Dance, 1971; (with M. Mayer) A Boy, a Dog, a Frog, and a Friend, 1971, 2nd ed., 2003; (with M. Mayer) Me and My Flying Machine, 1971; A Silly Story, 1972, 3rd ed., 2003; Bubble, Bubble, 1973, 3rd ed., 2003; Frog on His Own, 1973, 2nd ed., 2003; Mrs. Beggs and the Wizard, 1973, 2nd ed., 1980; Wizard Comes to Town, 1973, 2nd ed., 2003; A Frog and a Friend, 1974; Frog Goes to Dinner, 1974, 2nd ed., 2003; One Monster After Another, 1974; Two Moral Tales, 1974; Two More Moral Tales, 1974; What Do You Do with a Kangaroo?, 1974; You're the Scaredy-Cat, 1974, 2nd ed., 1980; Walk, Robot, Walk, 1974; The Great Cat Chase, 1975, 2nd ed., 2003; Just for You, 1975; (with M. Mayer) One Frog Too Many, 1975; Figure in the Shadows, 1975, 2nd ed., 2004; Ah-Choo, 1976; Four Frogs in a Box, 1976; Hiccup, 1976; Zipperump-a-Zoo, 1976; Liza Lou and the Great Yeller Belly Swamp, 1976, 2nd ed., 1980; Just Me and My Dad, 1977; Little Monster's Word Book, 1977; Mercer's Monsters, 1977; Oops, 1977; Professor Wormbog in Search for the Professor Wormbog's Gloomy Kerploppus: A Book of Great Smells, 1977; (ed.) The Poison Tree and Other Poems, 1977; Little Monster at Home, 1978; Little Monster at School, 1978; Little Monster at Work, 1978; Little Monster's Alphabet Book, 1978; Little Monster's Bedtime Book, 1978; Little Monster's Counting Book, 1978; Little Monster's Neighborhood, 1978; Little Monster's You-Can-Make-It Book, 1978; Appelard and Liverwurst, 1978; How the Trollusk Got His Hat, 1979; Little Monster's Library, 1978; Little Monster's Mother Goose, 1979; East of the Sun & West of the Moon, 1980; Herbert, the Timid Dragon, 1980; Little Monster's Scratch and Sniff Mystery, 1980; Professor Wormbog's Cut It, Glue It, Tape It, Do-It Books, 1980; Professor Wormbog's Crazy Cut-Ups, 1980; Liverwurst Is Missing, 1981, 2nd ed., 1990; Merry Christmas, Mom and Dad, 1982; Play with Me, 1982; Just a Snowy Day, 1983; Malcolm's Race, 1983; Gator Cleans House, 1983; Too's Bracelet, 1983; Sweetmeat's Birthday, 1983; Possum Child Goes Shopping, 1983; When I Get Bigger, 1983; Bat Child's Haunted House, 1983; All by Myself, 1983; I Was So Mad, 1983; Just Grandma and Me, 1983; Me Too!, 1983; The New Baby, 1983; Tonk in the Land of the Buddy-Bots, 1984; Tink's Subtraction Fair, 1984; Tink's Adventure, 1984; Tuk Goes to Town, 1984; Tuk Takes a Trip, 1984; Teep and Beep, Go to Sleep, 1984; Tink Goes Fishing, 1984; Little Critter's Day at the Farm, 1984; Little Critter's Holiday Fun Sticker Book, 1984; Little Monster's Moving Day, 1984; Little Monster's Sports Fun, 1984; The Sleeping Beatuy, 1984; Tinka Bakes a Cake, 1985; Trouble in Tinktonk Land, 1985; The Tinktonks Find a Home, 1985; Just Me and My Puppy, 1985; Tonk Gives a Magic Show, 1985; Zoomer Builds a Racing Car, 1985; Just Grandpa and Me, 1985; Just Go to Bed, 1985; Policeman Critter, 1986; Fireman Critter, 1986; Cowboy Critter, 1986; Astronaut Critter, 1986; Just Me and My Little Sister, 1986; Just Me and My Babysitter, 1986; Whinnie the Lovesick Dragon, 1986; (reteller) A

Christmas Carol: Being a Ghost Story of Christmas, 1986; There's an Alligator under My Bed, 1987; Construction Critter, 1987; Dr. Critter, 1987; Mail Critter, 1987; Sailor Critter, 1987; Just a Mess, 1987; Baby Sister Says No!, 1987; The Pied Piper of Hamlin, 1987; (with M. Mayer) There's an Alligator under My Bed, 1987; Happy Easter, Little Critter, 1988; Little Critter's Staying Overnight, 1988; Little Critter's This Is My House, 1988; Little Critter's These Are My Pets, 1988; Little Critter's The Trip, 1988; Little Critter's Picnic, 1988; Little Critter's Little Sister's Birthday, 1988 as Little Critter's The Best Present, 2000, 2nd ed., 2003; I Just Forgot, 1988; Just My Friend and Me, 1988; Little Critter's The Fussy Princess, 1989; Just a Daydream, 1989; Just Shopping with Mom, 1989; Just Camping Out, 1989; Little Critter's Christmas Book, 1989, new ed., 2001; Little Critter's this is My Friend, 1989; Just a Nap, 1989; Little Critter at Play, 1989; Little Critter's Day, 1989; There's Something Spooky in My Attic, 1989; Little Critter's This is My School, 1990; Just Going to the Dentist, 1990; Just Me and My Mom, 1990; Just a Rainy Day, 1990; Unicorn and the Lake, 1990; Two-Minute Little Critter Stories, 1990; Just Me and My Little Brother, 1991; Little Critter's Jack and the Beanstalk, 1991; Little Critter's Little Red Riding Hood, 1991; When I Grow Up, 1991; Little Critter at Scout Camp, 1991; Mercer Mayer's Herbert the Timid Dragon, 1991; Little Critter's Hansel and Gretel, 1991; Little Critter's Where Is My Frog?, 1991; Little Critter's Where's Kitty?, 1991; Where's My Sneaker?, 1991; Thrills and Spills, 1991; A Monster Followed, 1991; Dog and a Frog, 1992; What a Bad Dream, 1992; Very Speical Critter, 1992; Super Critter to the Rescue, 1992; Little Critter Colors, 1992; Little Critter Shapes, 1992; Little Critter Numbers, 1992; Little Critter's The Night before Christmas, 1992; I Am Helping, 1992; I Am Hiding, 1992; I Am Playing, 1992; I Am Sharing, 1992; (with G. Mayer) Just Me and My Cousin, 1992; (with G. Mayer) The New Potty, 1992; (with G. Mayer) This Is My Family, 1992; (with G. Mayer) Rosie's Mouse, 1992; Little Critter's Camp Out, 1993; Little Critter's Joke Book, 1993; Little Critter's Read-It-Yourself Storybook: Six Funny Easy-to-Read Stories, 1993; This Is My Town, 1993; (with G. Mayer) This Is My Body, 1993; (with G. Mayer) Going to the Races, 1993; (with G. Mayer) It's Mine, 1993; (with G. Mayer) Just a Gum Wrapper, 1993; (with G. Mayer) Just a Thunderstorm, 1993; (with G. Mayer) Just like Dad, 1993; (with G. Mayer) Just Me and My Bicycle, 1993; (with G. Mayer) Just Say Please, 1993; (with G. Mayer) Just Too Little, 1993; (with G. Mayer) Taking Care of Mom, 1993; (with G. Mayer) That's Not Fair, 1993; (with G. Mayer) Trick or Threat, Little Critter, 1993; (with G. Mayer) Just Me in the Tub, 1994; (with E. Farber and J.R. Sansevere) Surf's Up, 1994; (with E. Farber and J.R. Sansevere) The Secret Code, 1994; (with E. Farber and J.R. Sansevere) Top Dog, 1994; (with E. Farber and J.R. Sansevere) Ghost of Goose Island, 1994; (with E. Farber and J.R. Sansevere) Backstage Pass, 1994; (with E. Farber and J.R. Sansevere) The Mummy's Curse, 1994; (with E. Farber and J.R. Sansevere) Showdown at the Arcade, 1994; (with E. Farber and J.R. Sansevere) Circus of the Ghouls, 1994; (with E. Farber and J.R. Sansevere) The Cat's Meow, 1994; (with E. Farber and J.R. Sansevere) The Purple Kiss, 1994; (with E. Farber and J.R. Sansevere) My Teacher Is a Vampire, 1994; (with G. Mayer) I Didn't Know That, 1995; (with G. Mayer) I Didn't Mean To, 1995; (with G. Mayer) I Was so Sick, 1995; (with G. Mayer) I'm Sorry, 1995; (with G.Mayer) Just a Bad Day, 1995; (with G. Mayer) Just a Little Different, 1995; (with G. Mayer) Just an Airplane, 1995; (with G. Mayer) Just Leave Me Alone, 1995; (with G. Mayer) The Loose Tooth, 1995; (with G. Mayer) My Big Sister, 1995; (with G. Mayer) The School Play, 1995; Little Critter's Day at the Farm Sticker Book, 1995; Little Monster's Moving Day, 1995; Little Monster's Sports Fun, 1995; I Said I Was Sorry, 1995; Little Critter's ABC, 1995; Little Critter in Search of the Beautiful Princess, 1995; (with E. Farber and J.R. Sansevere) The E-Mail Mystery, 1995; (with E. Farber and J.R. Sansevere) The Little Shop of Magic, 1995; (with E. Farber and J.R. Sansevere) The Haunted House, 1995; (with E. Farber and J.R. Sansevere) Pizza War, 1995; (with E. Farber and J.R. Sansevere) Swamp Thing, 1995; (with E. Farber and J.R. Sansevere) The Alien, 1995; (with E. Farber and J.R. Sansevere) Golden Eagle, 1995; (with E. Farber and J.R. Sansevere) Jaguar Paw, 1995; (with E. Farber and J.R. Sansevere) The Prince, 1995; (with E. Farber and J.R. Sansevere) Octopus Island: An Advneture under the Sea, 1995; To Catch a Little Fishy, 1996; Bun Bun's Birthday, 1996; Little Sister's Bracelet, 1996; (with E. Farber and J.R. Sansevere) Blue Ribbon Mystery, 1996; (with E. Farber and J.R. Sansevere) Kiss the Vampire, 1996; (with E. Farber and J.R. Sansevere) Old How I Hall, 1996; (with E. Farber and J.R. Sansevere) No Howling in the House, 1996; (with E. Farber and J.R. Sansevere) The Goblin's Birthday Party, 1996; (with E. Farber and J.R. Sansevere) If You Dream a Dragon, 1996; (with E. Farber and J.R. Sansevere) Kiss of the Mermaid, 1996; (with E. Farber and J.R. Sansevere) Purple Pickle Juice, 1996, 2nd ed., 2003; (with E. Farberand J.R. Sansevere) Pirate Soup, 1996; (with E. Farber and J.R. Sansevere) Zombies Don't Do Windows, 1996; (with E. Farber and J.R. Sansevere) Werewolves for Lunch, 1996; (with E. Farber and J.R. Sansevere) Vampire Brides, 1996; Smell Christmas: A Little Critter Scratch-and-Sniff Book, 1997; Just a Bubble Bath, 1997; (with E. Farber and J.R. Sansevere) Midnight Snack, 1997; (with E. Farber and J.R. Sansevere) Night of the Walking Dead, 1997; (with E. Farber and J.R. Sansevere) No Flying in the Hall, 1997; (with E. Farber and J.R. Sansevere) The Roast and Toast, 1997; (with E. Farber and J.R. Sansevere) Mummy Pancakes, 1997; (with E. Farberand J.R. Sansevere) Love You to Pieces, 1997; (with J.R. Sansevere) How the Zebra Lost Its Stripes, 1998; Little Monster Private Eye Goes on Safari, 1998; Just a Magic Trick, 1998; (with G. Mayer) At the Beach with Dad, 1998; (with E. Farber and J.R. Sansevere) The Lost Wish, 1998; (with E. Farber and J.R. Sansevere) Oeey Gooey, 1998; (with E. Farber and J.R. Sansevere) Zoom on My Broom, 1998; (with E. Farber and J.R. Sansevere) Chomp, Chomp, 1998; (with E. Farber and J.R. Sansevere) Critters of the-Night Glow-in-the-Dark, 1998; The Golden Animal Book, 1999; Shibumi and the Kitemaker, 1999; Little Critter Sleeps Over, 1999; (with G. Mayer) Just a New Neighbor, 1999; (with G. Mayer) Just a Bully, 1999; The Rocking Horse Angel, 2000; (with G. Mayer) Just a Toy, 2000; Just Secret, 2001; A Yummy Lunch, 2001; Our Friend Sam, 2001; Snow Day, 2001; Surprise, 2001; Camping Out, 2001; (with G. Mayer) Just a Snowy Vacation, 2001; (with G. Mayer) Just a Piggy Bank, 2001; No One Can Play, 2002; Field Day, 2002; Our Park, 2002; My Trip to the Farm, 2002; My Trip to the Zoo, 2002; Helping Mom, 2002; The Mixed-up Morning, 2002; Play Ball, 2002; Just Not Invited, 2002; Class Trip, 2002; Grandma's Garden, 2002; Just Fishing with Grandma, 2003; Beach Day, 2003; Country Fair, 2003; Day at Camp, 2003; Goodnight, Little Critter, 2003; New Fire Truck, 2003; New Kid in Town, 2003; Our Tree House, 2003; Show and Tell, 2003; Tigers Birthday, 2003; (with G. Mayer) Just a Baseball Game, 2003; Little Critter's Picture dictionary, 2004; Bye-bye, Mom and Dad, 2004; Just a Snowman, 2004; Christmas for Miss Kitty, 2004; Happy Halloween, Little Critter!, 2004; Just a Dump Truck, 2004; Harvest Time, 2004; Just a Science Project, 2004; Just Big Enough, 2004; Little Christmas Tree, 2004; Good for Me and You, 2004; Merry Christmas, Little Critter!, 2004; (with G. Mayer) Just a Little Homework, 2004; Just a Little Critter Collection, 2005; Little Critter Storybook Collection, 2005; My Trip to the Hospital, 2005; Just a tugboat, 2005; There are Monsters Everywhere, 2005; Little Drummer Mouse: A Christmas Story, 2006; Muy Agradecido, 2006; Just so Thankful, 2006; It's Easter, Little Critter!, 2006; Happy Valentine's Day, Little Critter!, 2006; Just Me and the Dinosaurs, 2007; Happy Father's Day, 2007; Grandma, Grandpa, and Me, 2007; The Bravest Knight, 2007; Snowball Soup, 2008; My Earth Day Surprise, 2008; It's Earth Day!, 2008; To the Rescue!, 2008; First Day of School, 2008; Going to the Firehouse, 2008; Best Teacher Ever, 2008; Little Critter's the Night before Christmas, 2009; This is M Town, 2009; Going to the Sea Park, 2009; The Fall Festival, 2009; Bubble Bubble, 2009; Just a Little Sick, 2009; Little Critter's Where's my Sneaker?, 2010; Little Critter's where is My Frog?, 2010; Just a Little Music, 2010; Little Critter's where's Kitty?, 2010; Just Saving My Money, 2010; The Best Yard Sale, 2010; Just Critters Who Care, 2010; (with T. Becker) Scholastic 2011 Almanac for Kids, 2010; (with T. Becker) A Zombie's Guide To The Human Body, 2010; Little Monster's Fun, 2011; Little Monster's Fun and Learn Book, 2011; Little Critter Bedtime Storybook, 2011; Octopus Soup, 2011; Too Many Dinosaurs, 2011; The Best Show and Share, 2011; Busy Day, 2011; A Green, Green Garden, 2011; Just a Little Luck, 2011; Just Helping My Dad, 2011; Little Critter ABCs, 2011; Professor Wormbog in Search for the Zipperump-a-Zoo, 2011; Just a Little Too Little, 2012; Little Monster's Home, School, and Work Book, 2012; Little Critter's Bedtime Storybook, 2012; What a Good Kitty, 2012. BIG LITTLE CRITTER: Fair Play, 2012; Helping Out, 2012; My Family, 2012; On The Go, 2012; Staying Well, 2012. **Address:** Golden Books, 850 3rd Ave., New York, NY 10022-6222, U.S.A. **Online address:** tunamoon@aol.com

MAYER, Musa. American (born United States), b. 1943. **Genres:** Biography, Autobiography/Memoirs, Adult Non-fiction. **Career:** Ohio Community Mental Health system, counselor; MAMM Magazine, contributing editor; Food and Drug Administration, FDA Cancer Drug Development Program, patient representative/consultant, 2001. Advocate. **Publications:** (Afterword) Night Studio: A Memoir of Philip Guston, 1988; Examining Myself: One Woman's Story of Breast Cancer Treatment and Recovery, 1993; Holding Tight, Letting Go: Living with Metastatic Breast Cancer, 1997; Advanced Breast Cancer: A Guide to Living with Metastatic Disease, 1998; After Breast Cancer: Answers to the Questions You're Afraid to Ask, 2003. **Address:** MAMM, 54 W 22nd St., 4th Fl., New York, NY 10010, U.S.A. **Online address:** musa@echonyc.com

MAYER, Robert. American (born United States), b. 1939. **Genres:** Novels, Photography, Writing/Journalism, Autobiography/Memoirs, Young Adult Non-fiction. **Career:** Washington Post, copy editor, 1960; New York Newsday, reporter, 1961-67; Ford Foundation, consultant, 1973-74; Santa Fe Reporter, board director, 1974-88, managing editor, 1988-90, editor, 1993-97. **Publications:** NOVELS: Superfolks, 1977; The Execution, 1979; Midge and Decker, 1982; Sweet Salt, 1984; The Grace of Shortstops, 1984; The Search, 1986; I, JFK, 1989. NONFICTION: The Dreams of Ada: A True Story of Murder, Obsession, and a Small Town, 1987; Baseball and Men's Lives (memoir), 1994; Notes of a Baseball Dreamer, 2003; The Ferret's Tale, 2010; The Origin of Sorrow, 2010; Dance Macabre, 2011. Contributor to periodicals. **Address:** c/o Philip G. Spitzer, Philip G. Spitzer Literary Agency Inc., 50 Talmage Farm Ln., East Hampton, NY 11937, U.S.A. **Online address:** siringo@earthlink.net

MAYERS, David (Allan). American (born United States), b. 1951. **Genres:** Politics/Government. **Career:** Kenyon College, faculty, 1979-80; University of California, faculty, 1980-88; Boston University, Department of Political Science, professor of politics, 1989-, Department of History, faculty. Writer. **Publications:** American Policy Toward the Sino-Soviet Alliance, 1949-1955, 1979; Cracking the Monolith: U.S. Policy against the Sino-Soviet Alliance, 1949-1955, 1986; (ed. with R.A. Melanson) Reevaluating Eisenhower: American Foreign Policy in the 1950s, 1987; George Kennan and the Dilemmas of U.S. Foreign Policy, 1988; The Ambassadors and America's Soviet Policy, 1995; Wars and Peace: The Future Americans Envisioned, 1861-1991, 1998; Dissenting Voices in America's Rise to Power, 2007; FDR's Ambassadors and the Diplomacy of Crisis, forthcoming; Nuremberg and United States Agonistes, forthcoming. **Address:** Department of Political Science, Boston University, 201 PLS, 232 Bay State Rd., Boston, MA 02215, U.S.A. **Online address:** dmayers@bu.edu

MAYES, Linda C(arol). American (born United States), b. 1951. **Genres:** Medicine/Health, Psychiatry, Psychology, Human Relations/Parenting. **Career:** Vanderbilt University, intern, 1977-78, resident in pediatrics, 1978-80, postdoctoral fellow in neonatology, 1980-82; Yale University, Robert Wood Johnson general pediatrics fellow, 1982-84, Yale Child Study Center, postdoctoral research fellow in pediatrics, 1984-85, assistant professor, 1985-89, Elizabeth Mears And House Jameson assistant professor of child development, 1989-90, Elizabeth Mears And House Jameson associate professor of child development, 1990, Arnold Gesell associate professor of child psychiatry, pediatrics and psychology, 1991-, Arnold Gesell associate professor, 1995-2002, Arnold Gesell professor, 2002-, Morse College, fellow, 1990-, Bush Center on Social Policy, fellow, 1994-, Yale Child Study Center, coordinator of early childhood section, 1996-, Early Childhood Education Consortium, co-director, 1997-; National Center for Clinical Infant Programs, fellow, 1984-85, Yale School of Medicine, special advisor to the dean; National Institute of Child Health and Human Development, adjunct scientist, 1990-; Western New England Institute for Psychoanalysis, faculty, 2001-; University of London, visiting professor, 2001; Anna Freud Centre, Directorial Team, chairman. Writer. **Publications:** (Ed. with W.S. Gilliam and contrib.) Comprehensive Psychiatric Assessment of Young Children, 1999; (with D.J. Cohen, J.E. Schowalter and R.H. Granger) The Yale Child Study Center Guide to Understanding Your Child: Healthy Development from Birth to Adolescence, 2002; (ed. with P. Fonagy and M. Target) Developmental Science and Psychoanalysis: Integration and Innovation, 2007. Contributor to periodicals. **Address:** Yale Child Study Center, Yale School of Medicine, 230 S Frontage Rd., PO Box 207900, New Haven, CT 06520-7900, U.S.A. **Online address:** linda.mayes@yale.edu

MAYFIELD, Sue. British (born England), b. 1963. **Genres:** Children's Fiction, History, Theology/Religion. **Career:** Teacher and writer. **Publications:** FICTION: I Carried You on Eagles' Wings, 1991 as On Eagles Wings, 2004; Shoot! (for children), 2000; Blue (for children), 2001; Reckless, 2002; Drowning Anna (young adult novel), 2002; Voices, 2003; Poisoned, 2004; Patterns in the Sand, 2004; Our Wonderful World, 2004; Molly Muddle's Cake, 2004; Damage, 2006; (with R. Padua) I Can, You Can, Toucan! (for children), 2006; The Four Franks (for children), 2006. OTHER: Women and Power (history), 1988 as Timeline: Women and Power, 1989; Youth Emmaus, 2003; Life Attitudes, 2004; Life Balance, 2005, First Steps Through Bereavement, 2011. Contributor to periodicals. **Address:** c/o Author Mail, Hodder Headline, 338 Euston Rd., London, GL NW1 3BH, England. **Online address:** mail@suemayfield.com

MAYFIELD, Terry L. American (born United States), b. 1953. **Genres:** inspirational/Motivational Literature, Administration/Management, Business/Trade/Industry, Marketing. **Career:** Kent H. Landsberg Co., vice president of sales, 1981-; Mayfield Training & Development Inc., founder, 1993. Writer. **Publications:** How to Control Your Destiny: Creating Your Future Through Self Discovery, 1994; The Customer Connection: A Business Novel That Reveals the Link to Profit and Success, 2002. **Address:** Mayfield Training & Development Inc., 25852 McBean Pkwy., Ste. 100, Valencia, CA 91355-2129, U.S.A. **Online address:** mayfieldtd@aol.com

MAYHAR, Ardath (Hurst). Also writes as Frances Hurst, John Killdeer, Frank Cannon. American (born United States), b. 1930. **Genres:** Science Fiction/Fantasy, Westerns/Adventure, Children's Fiction, Young Adult Fiction, Novels. **Career:** East Texas Bookstore, operator, 1957-62; Capital Journal, proofreader, 1968-75; Daily Sentinel, proofreader, 1979-82; Full-time writer, 1982-; View from Orbit Bookstore, co-operator, 1984-99; Writer's Digest School, instructor, 1984-; self employed instructor/critic, 1999-. **Publications:** How the Gods Wove in Kyrannon, 1979; The Seekers of Shar Nuhn, 1980; Soul-Singer of Tyrnos, 1981; Warlock's Gift, 1982; Khi to Freedom, 1982; Runes of the Lyre, 1982; Golden Dream, 1983; Lords of the Triple Moons, 1983; (with M. Dunn) The Absolutely Perfect Horse, 1983; Exile on Vlahil, 1984; The Saga of Grittel Sundotha, 1985; The World Ends in Hickory Hollow, 1985; Medicine Walk (for children), 1985; Carrots and Miggle (for children), 1986; The Wall, 1987; Makra Choria, 1987; (with R. Fortier) Trail of the Seahawks, 1987; A Place of Silver Silence, 1988; (with R. Fortier) Monkey Station, 1989; People of the Mesa, 1992; Island in the Swamp, 1993; An Island in the Lake, 1993; Towers of the Earth, 1994; Hunters of the Plains, 1995; Slewfoot Sally and the Flying Mule, 1995; Through a Stone Wall: A Writer's Handbook and Literacy Autobiography, 1995; (with M. Dunn) Timber Pirates, 1997; A Road of Stars: A Tale of Art and Death, 1998; Polarities, 2000; The Snowlost/Exile on Vlahil: Being a Tale of Man and Moohl, Who Found Themselves Compatible, 2000; Riddles and Dreams, 2003; Prescription for Danger, 2007; (with R. Fortier) Witchfire, 2007; The Heirs of Three Oaks, 2007; The Body in the Swamp, 2009; Death in the Square, 2009; Messengers in White, 2009; A Planet Called Heaven, 2009; Lone Runner: A Novel of the Old West, 2009; A World of Weirdities, 2009; Strange Doin's in the Pine Hills, 2009; Crazy Quilt: The Best Short Stories of Ardath Mayhar, 2009; The Exiles of Damaria, 2009; Vendetta, 2009; Shock Treatment, 2009; The Clarrington Heritage, 2009; The Fugitives: A Tale of Prehistoric Times, 2009; The Door in the Hill: A Tale of the Turnipins, 2009; The Lintons of Skillet Bend: A Novel of East Texas, 2009; Strange View from a Skewed Orbit, 2009; The Methodist Bobcat: 27 Classic Science Fiction and Fantasy Stories, 2010; The Loquat Eyes: More Tall Tales from Cotton County, Texas, 2010; Slaughterhouse World/Knack' Attack, 2010. AS FRANK CANNON: Feud at Sweetwater Creek, 1987; Bloody Texas Trail, 1988; Texas Gunsmoke, 1988. AS JOHN KILLDEER: Wild Country, 1991; The Untamed, 1992; Wilderness Rendezvous, 1992; Blood Kin, 1993; Passage West, 1993; The Far Horizon, 1994; Fire on the Prairie, 1995; The Savage Land, 1995; (as Frances Hurst) High Mountain Winter, 1996. Contributor to periodicals. **Address:** 533 County Rd., Ste. 486, Chireno, TX 75937-5101, U.S.A. **Online address:** ardathm@netdot.com

MAYHEW, David Raymond. American (born United States), b. 1937. **Genres:** Politics/Government, History. **Career:** University of Massachusetts, instructor, 1963-64, assistant professor of government, 1964-67; Amherst College, visiting assistant professor of political science, 1965-66; Yale University, assistant professor, 1968-72, associate professor, 1972-77, professor, 1977-, Alfred Cowles professor of government, 1982-98, Sterling professor of political science, 1998-; Oxford University, John M. Olin visiting professor in American government, 2000-01; Harvard University, visiting professor of government, 2008. Writer. **Publications:** Party Loyalty Among Congressmen: The Difference Between Democrats and Republicans, 1947-1962, 1966; (ed. with W.C. Havard) Institutions & Practices of American Government, 1967; Two-Party Competition in the New England States, 1967; Congress: The Electoral Connection, 1974, 2nd ed., 2004; Placing Parties in American Politics: Organization, Electoral Settings, and Government Activity in the Twentieth Century, 1986; Divided We Govern: Party Control, Lawmaking, and Investigations, 1946-1990, 1991, 2nd ed., 2005; America's Congress: Actions in the Public Sphere, James Madison Through Newt Gingrich, 2000; Electoral Realignments: A Critique of an American Genre, 2002; Parties and Policies: How the American Government Works, 2008; Partisan Balance: Why Political Parties Don't Kill the U.S. Constitution System, 2011. **Address:** Department of Political Science, Yale University, 77 Prospect St.,

PO Box 208301, New Haven, CT 06520-8301, U.S.A. **Online address:** david.mayhew@yale.edu

MAYHEW, Margaret. British (born England), b. 1936. **Genres:** Novels, Young Adult Fiction, Romance/Historical. **Career:** Writer. **Publications:** The Master of Aysgarth, 1976; These Black Cormorants, 1976; The Owlers, 1977; The Cry of the Owl, 1977; The Railway King, 1979; The Flame and the Furnace, 1981; Regency Charade, 1986; Bluebirds, 1993; The Crew, 1997; The Little Ship, 1999; Old Soldiers Never Die, 1999; Our Yanks, 2001; The Pathfinder, 2002; Those in Peril, 2003; Rosebuds, 2004; A Foreign Field, 2004; I'll Be Seeing You, 2004; Quadrille, 2005; The Boat Girls, 2007; Three Silent Things, 2008; The Other Side of Paradise, 2009. **Address:** c/o Author Mail, Severn House Publishers, 9-15 High St., Sutton, SR SMI IDF, England.

MAYHEW, Robert. American (born United States), b. 1960. **Genres:** Literary Criticism And History. **Career:** Seton Hall University, professor of philosophy. Writer. **Publications:** (Ed.) Ayn Rand's Marginalia: Her Critical Comments on the Writings of over 20 Authors, 1995; (ed. and trans.) Aristophanes, Assembly of Women, 1997; Aristotle's Criticism of Plato's Republic, 1997; (ed.) The Art of Nonfiction: A Guide for Writers and Readers, 2001; The Female in Aristotle's Biology: Reason or Rationalization, 2004; (ed.) Essays on Ayn Rand's We the Living, 2004, 2nd ed., 2012; (ed.) Essays on Ayn Rands Anthem, 2005; Ayn Rand and Song of Russia: Communism and Anti-Communism in 1940s Hollywood, 2005; (ed.) Ayn Rand Answers: The Best of Her Q & A, 2005; (ed.) Essays on Ayn Rand's The Fountainhead, 2007; (trans.) Laws 10, 2007; (ed.) Essays on Ayn Rands Atlas Shrugged, 2009; Prodicus the Sophist, 2011. Contributor to periodicals. **Address:** Department of Philosophy, Seton Hall University, Rm. 311, Fahy Hall, 400 S Orange Ave., South Orange, NJ 07079, U.S.A. **Online address:** mayhewro@shu.edu

MAYNARD, Christopher. British/Canadian (born Canada), b. 1949?. **Genres:** Children's Non-fiction, Sciences, Reference, Children's Fiction, Air/Space Topics. **Career:** Macdonald Educational Ltd., editor, 1972; Intercontinental Book Productions, editor, 1976-77; Oasis Press and Maynard and How Publishing, director. **Publications:** NONFICTION FOR CHILDREN: Planet Earth, 1974; Prehistoric World, 1974; (with E. Holmes) Great Men of Science, 1975; The Real Cowboy, 1976; The Amazing World of Money, 1977; Economy Guide to Europe, 1978; Indians and Palefaces, 1978; The Razzmataz Gang, 1978; All about Ghosts, 1978; The Great Ice Age, 1978, rev. ed., 1987; Father Christmas and His Friends, 1979; (with E. Holmes) Great Men of Science, 1979; War Vehicles, 1980; (with J. Paton) Aircraft, 1982; (with J. Marks) Apple Peelers and Coin Stackers, 1986; (ed.) Richard Forsyth, Machines That Think, 1986; (with D. Jefferis) The Aces, 1987; (with D. Jefferis) Air Battles, 1987; The First Great Kids Catalog, 1987; Airplanes, 1993; Amazing Animal Babies, 1993; Jungle Animals, 1993; Amazing Animal Facts, 1993; Ballet, 1993; Castles, 1993; Dinosaurs, 1993; Helicopters, 1993; Horses, 1993; I Wonder Why Planes Have Wings and Other Questions About Transport, 1993; Space, 1993; Incredible Dinosaurs, 1994; Incredible Flying Machines, 1994; Incredible Little Monsters, 1994; Incredible Minibeasts, 1994; Space Shuttle, 1994; Submarines, 1994, rev. ed., 1995; Gymnastics, 1994; Los Submarinos, 1994; Questions and Answers about Explorers, 1995; Airplane, 1995; Why Are All Families Different?: Questions Children Ask about Families, 1997; Why are Pineapples Prickly?, 1997; Why Do Volcanoes Erupt?: Questions Children Ask About the Earth, 1997; Jobs People Do, 1997; Sharks, 1997; The Best Book of Dinosaurs, 1998; Pirates!: Raiders of the High Seas, 1998; Days of the Knights: A Tale of Castles and Battles, 1998; Aircraft, 1999; Racing Cars, 1999; Micro Monsters: Life under the Microscope, 1999; Ghosts, 1999; Extreme Machines, 2000; Kitchen Science, 2001; (with C. Pellant) My Book of Prehistoric Times, 2001; I Wonder Why Planes Have Wings and Other Questions About Transportation, 2003; Science Fun at Home, 2006. OTHERS: Revolution, 1999; Weapons and Warfare, 1981; Kids' New York, 2000; Bugs: A Close-up View of the Insect World, 2001; Backyard Science, 2001; (with S. Fuller) 1001 Facts about Rocks and Minerals, 2003. **Address:** c/o Author Mail, 9 Henrietta St., Covent Gardens, London, GL WC2E 8PS, England.

MAYNARD, Geoffrey (Walter). British (born England), b. 1921. **Genres:** Economics, Business/Trade/Industry. **Career:** University College of South Wales, lecturer in economics; Johns Hopkins University, research fellow, 1957-58; Economic Consultant, Her Majesty's Treasury, staff, 1962-65; Harvard University Advisory Group, economic adviser, 1965-66; Ministry of Overseas Development, consultant, 1966-; Reading University, reader in economics, 1966-, professor of economics, 1968-76, visiting professor of economics, 1976-; Bankers Magazine, editor, 1968-72; H.M. Treasury, deputy chief economic advisor, 1976-77; Chase Manhattan Bank, director of economics, 1977-86; Investcorp International Ltd., economic advisor, 1986-. **Publications:** The Control of Inflation, 1957; Economic Development and the Price Level, 1962; International Monetary Reform and Latin America, 1966; Special Drawing Rights and Development Aid, 1972; (with W. van Ryckeghem) A World of Inflation, 1976; The Economy under Mrs. Thatcher, 1988. **Address:** Flat 219, Queens Quay, 58 Upper Thames St., London, GL EC4, England. **Online address:** gwmaynard@hotmail.com

MAYNE, Kenny. American (born United States), b. 1959. **Genres:** Sports/Fitness, Humor/Satire. **Career:** KLVX (television station), reporter, 1982; KSTW (television station), production assistant, 1982-83, news writer, 1983-86, news reporter and weekend sports anchor, 1986-89; ESPN, SportsCenter, freelance reporter and field producer, 1990-94, SportSmash, anchor, 1994, SportsNight, reporter, 1994, feature reporter, 2007-. **Publications:** An Incomplete and Inaccurate History of Sport, 2008. Contributor to periodicals. **Address:** ESPN, ESPN Plz., Bristol, CT 06010, U.S.A.

MAYNE, Seymour. Canadian (born Canada), b. 1944. **Genres:** Novellas/Short Stories, Poetry, Translations, Young Adult Fiction. **Career:** Jewish Institute, lecturer in Jewish Canadian literature, 1964; Very Stone House, co-founder and managing editor, 1966-69; Ingluvin Publications, co-founder and literary editor, 1970-73; University of British Columbia, lecturer in English, 1972; University of Ottawa, assistant professor, 1973-78, associate professor, 1978-85, professor of English, 1985-, Institute of Canadian Studies, faculty, Vered Jewish Canadian Studies Program, coordinator; Mosaic Press/Valley Editions, co-founder and editor, 1974-83; Hebrew University of Jerusalem, visiting professor, 1979-80, 1983-84, writer-in-residence, 1987-88; Concordia University, visiting professor, 1982-83; Vered Jewish Canadian Studies Program, coordinator; Bywords, co-founder. **Publications:** That Monocycle the Moon, 1964; Tiptoeing on the Mount, 1965; From the Portals of Mouseholes, 1966; Manimals, 1969; Mutetations, 1969; Mouth, 1970; Face, 1971; For Stems of Light, 1974; Name, 1975, 2nd ed., 1976; Diasporas (poetry), 1977; The Impossible Promised Land: Poems New and Selected, 1981; Vanguard of Dreams: New and Selected Poems, 1984; Children of Abel, 1986; Diversions, 1987; Last Chance, 1989; Two Poems, 1989; Simple Ceremony (poetry), 1990; (co-author) Six Ottawa Poets, 1990; Killing Time (Poetry), 1992; Locust of Silence: New and Selected Poems, 1993; The Song of Moses and Other Poems, 1995; (co-author) Five O' Clock Shadows, 1996; Dragon Trees, 1997; City of the Hidden, 1998; 'Ir ha-nistar, 1998; Carbon Filter: Poems in Dedication, 1999; Light Industry, 2000; Five Word Sonnets, 2001; Hail: Word Sonnets, 2002; (co-author) Cinquefoil, 2003. Ricochet: Word Sonnets, 2004; September Rain, 2005; Hail/Granizo: Word Sonnets/sonetos de una palabra, 2006; (with B.G. Rotchin) Dream of Birds: Word Sonnets, 2007; Reflejos: sonetos de una palabra, 2008; Les pluies de septembre: poèmes choisis 1980-2005, 2008; Leensok letoch haor hachi chazak: Mevchar shirim, 2009. EDITOR/CO-EDITOR: Collected Poems of Red Lane, 1968; 40 Women Poets of Canada, 1971; Engagements: The Prose of Irving Layton, 1972; Cutting the Keys, 1974; (and intro.) The A.M. Klein Symposium, 1975; Splices, 1975; (and intro.) Choice Parts, 1976; (and intro.) Irving Layton: The Poet and His Critics, 1978; (and co-trans.) Generations: Selected Poems of Rachel Korn, 1982; (and intro.) Essential Words: An Anthology of Jewish Canadian Poetry, 1985; Crossing the River: Selected Poems of Moshe Dor, 1989; At the Edge, 1995; (with B.G. Rotchin) Jerusalem, 1996; (with U. Caplan) A.M. Klein, Selected Poems, 1997; (with B.G. Rotchin) A Rich Garland, 1999; (with J. Fiamengo and R. Thornton) Visible Living: Poems, 2006. TRANSLATOR: (with C. Leach) J. Harasymowicz, Genealogy of Instruments, 1974; Burnt Pearls: Ghetto Poems of Abraham Sutzkever, 1981; (with L. Firestone-Seghi and H. Schwartz) Jerusalem as She Is: New and Selected Poems of Shlomo Vinner, 1991; M. Ravitch, Night Prayer and Other Poems, 1993; J. Harasymowicz, I Live on a Raft, 1994. **Address:** Department of English, University of Ottawa, ARTS 354, 70 Laurier Ave. E, Ottawa, ON K1N 6N5, Canada. **Online address:** mayne@uottawa.ca

MAYO, C(atherine) M(ansell). (Catherine Mansell Carstens). American (born United States), b. 1961. **Genres:** Novels, Novellas/Short Stories, Economics, Money/Finance, Travel/Exploration, Translations, inspirational/Motivational Literature. **Career:** Euro American Capital Corporation Ltd., economist, 1988-90; Instituto Tecnologico Autonomo de Mexico, professor of economics, 1990-95; Tameme (bilingual literary magazine), founding editor, 1994-; Dancing Chiva Literary Arts, founding editor; The Writers Center, faculty. **Publications:** Sky over El Nido: Stories, 1995; Miraculous Air: Journey of a Thousand Miles through Baja California, 2002; (ed.) Mexico: A Traveler's Literary Companion, 2006; The Last Prince of the Mexican Empire, 2009. AS CATHERINE MANSELL CARSTENS: Las Nuevas Finanzas en Mexico, 1992; Las Finanzas Populares en Mexico, 1995; Liberalizacion e Innovacion Financiera en los Paises Desarrollados y en America Latina, 1996. Works appear in anthologies. Contributor to periodicals. **Address:** c/o Christina Ward, Christina Ward Literary Agency, PO Box 515, North Scituate, MA 02060, U.S.A. **Online address:** cmmayo@cmmayo.com

MAYO, Gretchen Will. American (born United States), b. 1936. **Genres:** Children's Fiction, Biography, Illustrations. **Career:** Teacher, 1958-63; Community Newspapers, reporter, 1966-70; artist, 1970-88. **Publications:** SELF-ILLUSTRATED AND RETELLER: More Star Tales, 1990; Meet Tricky Coyote!, 1993; That Tricky Coyote!, 1993; Big Trouble for Tricky Rabbit!, 1994; Here Comes Tricky Rabbit, 1994. OTHERS: (reteller) Star Tales: North American Indian Stories about the Stars, 1987; Earthmaker's Tales: North American Indian Stories about Earth Happenings, 1989; Frank Lloyd Wright, 2004; Orange Juice, 2004; Milk, 2004; Pasta, 2004; Cereal, 2004; Applesauce, 2004; Frozen Vegetables, 2004; The Wright Brothers, 2004; (with K. O'Hern) Los Hermanos Wright, 2006. Illustrator of books by others. **Address:** 5213 Lakefield Rd., Cedarburg, WI 53012-2146, U.S.A. **Online address:** gwmayo@hotmail.com

MAYO, Wendell. American (born United States), b. 1953. **Genres:** Novels, Novellas/Short Stories, Young Adult Fiction, Horror, Cultural/Ethnic Topics, Mythology/Folklore, Popular Culture, International Relations/Current Affairs, International Relations/Current Affairs. **Career:** British Petroleum, engineering supervisor, 1975-85; Indiana University, assistant professor of English, 1991-94; Purdue University, assistant professor of English, 1991-94; University of Southwestern Louisiana, assistant professor of creative writing and literature, 1994-96, Creative Writing Program, director, 1994-96; Bowling Green State University, professor of creative writing and literature, 1996-, Creative Writing Program, director, 1996-. Writer. **Publications:** Centaur of the North: Stories, 1996, 2nd ed., 1999; In Lithuanian Wood (novel), 1999; B. Horror: And Other Stories, 1999; Vilko Valanda (stories), 2003. Contributor to magazines. **Address:** Creative Writing Program, Department of English, Bowling Green State University, 226 East Hall, Bowling Green, OH 43403, U.S.A. **Online address:** wmayo@bgsu.edu

MAYOR, Adrienne. American (born United States), b. 1946. **Genres:** History, Natural History, Mythology/Folklore, Popular Culture, Sciences, Earth Sciences, Classics, Archaeology/Antiquities, Biography, Anthropology/Ethnology. **Career:** Peale Museum, consultant, 2008-. Writer. **Publications:** The First Fossil Hunters: Paleontology in Greek and Roman Times, 2000, rev. ed., 2010; Greek Fire, Poison Arrows, and Scorpion Bombs: Biological and Chemical Warfare in the Ancient World, 2003, rev. ed., 2008; Fossil Legends of the First Americans, 2005; The Poison King: The Life and Legend of Mithradates, Rome's Deadliest Enemy, 2009. Contributor to journals and periodicals. **Address:** Department of Classics, Stanford University, Bldg. 110, Main Quad, 450 Serra Mall, PO Box 2145, Stanford, CA 94305-2145, U.S.A. **Online address:** mayor@stanford.edu

MAYOR, Federico. (Federico Mayor Zaragoza). Spanish (born Spain), b. 1934. **Genres:** Medicine/Health, Essays. **Career:** University of Granada, professor of biochemistry, 1963-72, Department of Pharmacy, director, 1967-68, rector, 1968-72, honorary rector, 1972-; Oxford University, Trinity College, visiting professor and senior fellow, 1966-67; Spanish Society of Biochemistry, chairperson, 1970-74; Autonomous University of Madrid, professor of biochemistry, 1973, Severo Ochoa Molecular Biology Center, co-founder and director, 1974-78, scientific chair person, 1983-87; Spanish Ministry for Education, under-secretary, 1974-75; Culture of Peace Foundation, president; Spanish Parliament, Parliamentary Commission for Education and Science, member of parliament, deputy and chair person, 1977-78; United Nations University, representative of the director-general, 1980-81; Spanish minister for education and science, 1981-82; Institute of the Sciences of Man, director, 1983-87; Issyk-Kul Forum (Frunze, Kirghiz Republic), founding member, 1986-; UNESCO, European Center for Higher Education, director-general, 1987-99; European Parliament, member, 1987; European Research Council Expert Group, president, 2003-04; European Academy of Arts, Sciences, and Literature, founding member. Writer. **Publications:** (Trans.) Strohecker and Henning, Vitamin Assay, 1967; Manana siempre es tarde (essay), 1987, as Tomorrow Is Always Too Late, 1992; Mañana siempre es tarde, 1987; (ed. with S. Ochoa and M. Barbacid) Oncogenes y Patologia Molecular, 1987; Aguafuertes (poems), 1991; Patterns, 1994; (co-author) The New Page (essay), 1994; Nova Pàgina, 1994; La memoire de l'avenir (essay), 1994, trans. as Memory of the Future, 1995; Science and Power, 1995; La Paix, Demain? (essay), 1995; UNESCO an Ideal in Action: The Continuing Relevance of a Visionary Text, 1997; Terral: 1990-1997, 1997; (comp. with R. Droit) Taking Action for Human Rights in the Twenty-First Century, 1998; Nudos gordianos, 1999; (with S. Tanguiane) Enseignement supérieur au XXIe siècle, 2000; (trans.) Monde nouveau, (title means: 'The World Ahead: Our Future in the Making'), 2001; Fuerza de la palabra, 2005; Diálogo ibérico en el marco europeo y mundial, 2006. EDITOR: (with S. Grisolia and R. Baguena) The Urea Cycle, 1976; Scientific Research and Goals: Towards a New Development Model, 1982; La lucha contra la enfermedad, 1986. Contributor to book and journals. **Address:** Fundación Cultura de Paz, Calle Velázquez 14, 3o dcha, Madrid, 28001, Spain.

MAYS, John Bentley. Canadian/American (born United States), b. 1941?. **Genres:** Documentaries/Reportage. **Career:** York University, Calumet College, teacher, 1971-; Open Letter, contributing editor, 1975-80; Toronto Globe and Mail, architecture columnist, 1979-, visual arts critic, 1980-98; full-time writer, 1980-; National Post, international cultural correspondent, 1998-2001, freelance journalist, through 2001, columnist; The Catholic Register, current affairs columnist. **Publications:** The Spiral Stair, 1977; Emerald City: Toronto Visited, 1994; Power in the Blood: Land, Memory and a Southern Family, 1997; In The Jaws of the Black Dogs: A Memoir of Depression, 1999; Arrivals: Stories from the History of Ontario, 2002; Eminence: Toronto's Elite, 2015. **Address:** 692 St. Clarens Ave., Apt. 2, Toronto, ON M6H 3X1, Canada. **Online address:** johnbentleymays@rogers.com

MAYSE, Susan. Australian/Canadian (born Canada), b. 1948?. **Genres:** Novels, History. **Career:** Writer and consultant. **Publications:** Arrivals, 1983; Deep Seams, 1986; Merlin's Web, 1987; Jade Spirit, 1988; The Shooting of Ginger Goodwin, 1989; Ginger: The Life and Death of Albert Goodwin, 1990; Earthquake: Surviving the Big One, 1992; My Father, My Friend, 1993; Yours in Revolt, 1995; Awen, 1997; Victoria: Crown Jewel of British Columbia, Including Esquimalt, Oak Bay, Saanich and the Peninsula, 2010. Contributor to periodicals. **Address:** 20033-9769 5th St., Sydney, BC V8L 5C9, Canada.

MAYSEH- LAHGO, Carmelo. *See* **MESA-LAGO, Carmelo.**

MAZER, Anne. American (born United States), b. 1953. **Genres:** Children's Fiction, Young Adult Fiction, Picture/Board Books, Children's Non-fiction, Young Adult Non-fiction. **Career:** Freelance writer, 1982-. **Publications:** CHILDREN'S FICTION: Watch Me, 1990; The Yellow Button 1990; The Salamander Room, 1991; The Fixits, 1998; (with R. Collins) The No-Nothings and Their Baby, 2000. MIDDLE GRADE NOVELS: Moose Street, 1992; The Oxboy, 1993; The Accidental Witch, 1995; Goldfish Charlie and the Case of the Missing Planet, 1996. THE AMAZING DAYS OF ABBY HAYES SERIES: Every Cloud Has a Silver Lining, 2000; The Declaration of Independence, 2000; Reach for the Stars, 2000; Have Wheels, Will Travel, 2001; Look before You Leap, 2001; The Pen is Mightier Than the Sword, 2001; Two Heads Are Better Than One, 2002; The More, the Merrier, 2002; Out of Sight, Out of Mind, 2002; Everything New under the Sun, 2003; Too Close for Comfort, 2003; Good Things Come in Small Packages, 2003; Some Things Never Change, 2004; The Best is Yet to Come, 2004; Knowledge Is Power, 2004. EDITOR: America Street: A Multicultural Anthology of Stories, 1993; Going Where I'm Coming From: Memoirs of American Youth, 1995; Working Days: Stories of Teens and Work, 1997; (intro.) A Walk in My World: International Short Stories about Youth, 1998. OTHERS: Gordy, 1995; Kid in King Arthur's Court, 1995; Disney's 101 Dalmatians: Special Collector's Edition, 1996; Sliver of Glass and Other Uncommon Tales (short stories), 1997; Now You See It, Now You Don't, 2005; That's the Way the Cookie Crumbles, 2005; Home Is Where the Heart Is, 2006; Violet Makes a Splash, 2007; The Trouble with Violet, 2007; What Goes Up Must Come Down, 2008; Violet Takes the Cake, 2008; All That Glitters Isn't Gold, 2009; Sealed with a Kiss 2009; Mabel on The Move 2009. NON-FICTION: (with E. Potter) Spilling Ink: A Young Writer's Handbook, 2010. Contributor to periodicals. **Address:** c/o Alice Tasman, Jean V. Naggar Literary Agency Inc., 216 E 75th St., Ste. 1E, New York, NY 10021, U.S.A. **Online address:** annemazer@yahoo.com

MAZER, Harry. American (born United States), b. 1925. **Genres:** Young Adult Fiction, Novels, Children's Fiction. **Career:** New York Central, railroad brake man and switchtender, 1950-55; New York Construction, sheet metal worker, 1957-59; Central Square School, teacher of English, 1959-60; Aerofin Corp., welder, 1960-63; full-time writer, 1963-. **Publications:** YOUNG ADULTS NOVELS: Guy Lenny, 1971; Snow Bound, 1973; The Dollar Man, 1974; (with N.F. Mazer) The Solid Gold Kid, 1977; The War on Villa Street, 1978; The Last Mission, 1979; The Island Keeper: A Tale of Courage and Survival, 1981; I Love You, Stupid!, 1981; Hey Kid! Does She Love Me?, 1984; When the Phone Rang, 1985; Cave under the City, 1986; The Girl of His Dreams, 1987; City Light, 1988; (with N.F. Mazer) Heartbeat, 1989; Someone's Mother Is Missing, 1990; (with N.F. Mazer) Bright Days, Stupid Nights, 1992; Who Is Eddie Leonard?, 1993; The Dog in the Freezer, 1997; The Wild Kid, 1999; A Boy at War, 2002; A Boy No More, 2004. OTHER: (ed.) Twelve Shots: Outstanding Short Stories about Guns, 1997; Heroes Don't Run, 2005; My Brother Abe: Sally Lincoln's Story, 2009; (with P. Lerangis) Somebody Please Tell Me Who I Am, 2012. **Address:** c/o Marilyn Marlow, Curtis Brown Ltd., 10 Astor Pl., New York, NY 10003, U.S.A. **Online address:** harry@foxmazer.com

MAZETTI, Katarina. Swedish (born Sweden), b. 1944. **Genres:** Novellas/Short Stories. **Career:** Journalist and educator. **Publications:** Krigshjältar och Konduktörer: Berättelser, 2000. **Address:** Lund, Sweden. **Online address:** katarina.mazetti@mac.com

MAZOWER, Mark. American/British (born England), b. 1958. **Genres:** Area Studies, History, Adult Non-fiction, Humanities. **Career:** Princeton University, assistant professor of history; Sussex University, reader in history; Birkbeck College, professor; Columbia University, professor, Ira D. Wallach professor of world order studies, Center for International History, director, chair. Writer. **Publications:** Greece and the Inter-War Economic Crisis, 1991; Inside Hitler's Greece: The Experience of Occupation, 1941-44, 1993; (ed.) The Policing of Politics in the Twentieth Century: Historical Perspectives, 1997; Dark Continent: Europe's Twentieth Century, 1998; (ed.) After the War was Over: Reconstructing the Family, Nation and State in Greece, 1943-1960, 2000; Balkans: A Short History, 2000; (ed. with J.R. Lampe) Ideologies and National Identities: Tthe Case of Twentieth-Century Southeastern Europe, 2004; Salonica, City of Ghosts: Christians, Muslims and Jews, 1430-1950, 2005; (ed.) Networks of Power in Modern Greece: Essays in Honour of John Campbell, 2008; Hitler's Empire: How the Nazis Ruled Europe, 2008; Hitler's Empire: Nazi Rule in Occupied Europe, 2008; No Enchanted Palace: The End of Empire and the Ideological Origins of the United Nations, 2009. Contributor to periodicals. **Address:** Department of History, Columbia University, 503 Fayerweatner Hall, 1180 Amsterdam Ave., PO Box 2514, New York, NY 10027, U.S.A. **Online address:** mm2669@columbia.edu

MAZOYER, Deborah. (Deborah Shelley). American (born United States), b. 1960?. **Genres:** Novels, Romance/Historical. **Career:** Writer. **Publications:** AS DEBORAH SHELLEY WITH S. MOSLEY: Talk about Love, 1999; It's in His Kiss, 1999; My Favorite Flavor, 2000; One Starry Night, 2000; Marriage 101, 2008. Works appear in anthologies. **Online address:** deborahshelley@mindspring.com

MAZRUI, Ali Al('Amin). American/Kenyan (born Kenya), b. 1933. **Genres:** Novels, History, International Relations/Current Affairs, Politics/Government, Race Relations, Military/Defense/Arms Control, Theology/Religion. **Career:** Makere University, lecturer, 1963-65, Department of Political Science, professor, 1965-69, head, 1965-73, Faculty of Social Sciences, dean, 1967-69; International Congress of Africanists, vice-president, 1967-73; World Order Models Project, director of African section, 1968-; International Political Science Association, vice-president, 1970-73; University of Michigan, professor of political science, 1974-91, Center for Afro-American and African Studies, director, 1978-81, International Congress of African Studies, vice president, 1978-85; African Studies Association, president, 1978-79; University of Jos, research professor of political science, 1981-86, Albert Luthuli professor-at-large; Cornell University, Andrew D. White professor-at-large, 1986-92, Andrew D. White professor-at-large emeritus; World Congress of Black Intellectuals, vice-president, 1988-; State University of New York, Binghamton University, Allbert Schweitzer professor in the humanities, 1989-, professor of political science, African studies and philosophy, interpretation and culture, Institute of Global Cultural Studies, director, 1991-; School of Islamic and Social Sciences, Ibn-Khaldun professor-at-large, 1996-2001; University of Guyana, Walter Rodney professor of history and governance, 1997-98; Jomo Kenyatta University of Agriculture and Technology, chancellor; International African Institute, vice president; World Bank, advisor; American Muslim Council, board director; Association of Muslim Social Scientists, presdient. Writer. **Publications:** Towards a Pax Africana: A Study of Ideology and Ambition, 1967; The Anglo-African Commonwealth, 1967; Språkproblem i Östafrika, 1967; On Heroes and Uhuru-worship, 1967; Ancient Greece in African Political Thought, 1967; Post Imperial Fragmentation: The Legacy of Ethnic and Racial Conflict, 1969; Violence and Thought: Essays on Social Tensions in Black Africa, 1969; The Trial of Christopher Okigbo (novel), 1971; Cultural Engineering and Nation Building in East Africa, 1972; World Culture and Black Experience, 1974; African University as a Multinational Corporation: Comparative Problems of Penetration and Dependency, 1975; The Political Sociology of the English Language: An African Perspective, 1975; Soldiers and Kinsmen in Uganda: The Making of a Military Ethnocracy, 1975; A World Federation of Cultures: An African Perspective, 1976; Africa's International Relations: The Diplomacy of Dependency and Change, 1977; Political Values and the Educated Class in Africa, 1978; The Barrel of the Gun and the Barrel of Oil in the North-South Equation, 1978; Sex in Politics and Modern History, 1979; The African Condition: A Political Analysis, 1980; Archives and the Common Man: Towards an Indigenous Theoretical Framework, 1980; Niger-saki: Does Nigeria have a Nuclear Option?, 1980; Kilio Cha Haki, 1981; The Moving Cultural Frontier of World Order: From Monotheism to North-South Relations, 1982; (with M. Tidy) Nationalism and New States in Africa: From about 1935 to the Present, 1984; Africans: A Reader, 1986; The Africans: A Triple Heritage, 1986; The Culture of World Politics: North-South Relations in Global Perspective, 1988; Banking, Finance, and Development, 1988; Cultural Forces in World Politics, 1990; Satanic Verses or a Satanic Novel?: The Moral Dilemas of the Rushdie Affair, 1990; Erosion of the State and the Decline of Race: Bismarck to Boutros, Othello to O.J. Simpson, 1995; (with A.M. Mazrui) Swahili State and Society: The Political Economy of an African Language, 1995; Christianity and Islam in Africa's Political Experience: Piety, Passion and Power, 1996; (with A.M. Mazuri) The Political Culture of Language, 1996; (with A.M. Mazuri) The Power of Babel, 1998; Afro-Arab Crossfire: Between the Flames of Terrorism and the Force of Pax-Americana, 2002; Black Reparations in the Era of Globalization, 2002; African Predicament and the American Experience: A Tale of Two Edens, 2004; Nkrumah's Legacy and Africa's Triple Heritage Between Globalization and Counter Terrorism, 2004; Islam: Between Globalization & Counter-Terrorism, 2006; Euro-Jews and Afro-Arabs: The Great Semitic Divergence in World History, 2008; Politics of War and the Culture of Violence: North-South Essays, 2008; Africa in the Shadow of Clash of Civilizations, 2008; Comparative Democracy and Cultural Wisdom: Africanity, Islam, and the West, 2008. EDITOR: (with R.I. Rotberg) Protest and Power in Black Africa, 1970; (with H.H. Patel) Africa in World Affairs, 1973; (with H.H. Patel) Africa: The Next Thirty Years, 1974; The Warrior Tradition in Modern Africa, 1977; (with T.K. Levine, T.B. Carrier and F.L. Werden) The Africans: A Reader, 1986; (with C. Wondji) Africa Since 1935: Volume VIII of UNESCO General History of Africa, 1993; (with I. Okpewho and C.B. Davies) African Diaspora: African Origins and New World Identities, 1999; (with S. Kafrawi and P.M. Dikirr) Globalization and Civilization: Are They Forces in Conflict?, 2008. Contributor of articles to journals. **Address:** The Institute of Global Cultural Studies, Binghamton University, State University of New York, LNG-100, PO Box 6000, Binghamton, NY 13902-6000, U.S.A. **Online address:** amazrui@binghamton.edu

MAZUR, Joseph. American (born United States), b. 1942?. **Genres:** Mathematics/Statistics. **Career:** Marlboro College, professor, now professor emeritus of mathematics; University of Warwick, The Mathematics Institute, visiting professor. Writer. **Publications:** How to Study Calculus, 1994; Euclid in the Rainforest: Discovering Universal Truth in Logic and Math, 2005; (ed.) Number: The Language of Science, 4th ed., 2005; The Motion Paradox: The 2500-Year-Old Puzzle behind All the Mysteries of Time and Space, 2007; What's Luck Got to Do With It?, 2010; Meaning? The Origins of Modern Icons, Signs and Symbols in Mathematics, Poetry and Life, forthcoming; Zola Takes The A-Train, forthcoming; The Amazing Light Bulb Change, forthcoming. **Address:** Marlboro College, 2582 South Rd., PO Box A, Marlboro, VT 05344, U.S.A. **Online address:** joe@marlboro.edu

MAZUR, Laurie Ann. American (born United States), b. 1961. **Genres:** Administration/Management, Marketing, Social Sciences. **Career:** New York Public Interest Research Group, publications director, 1983-88; freelance writer, 1988-94; Pew Global Stewardship Initiative, writer, 1992-. **Publications:** (Ed.) Beyond the Numbers: A Reader on Population, Consumption, and the Environment, 1994; (with M.F. Jacobson) Marketing Madness: A Survival Guide for a Consumer Society, 1995; (with S.E. Sechler) Global Interdependence and the Need for Social Stewardship, 1997; (ed.) A Pivotal Moment: Population, Justice, and the Environmental Challenge, 2010. **Address:** 6905 Woodland Ave., Takoma Park, MD 20912, U.S.A.

MAZURANA, Dyan E. American (born United States) **Genres:** Women's Studies And Issues, Social Sciences, History, Politics/Government. **Career:** Harvard University, Kennedy School of Government, research fellow, 2001-02; Tufts University, Alan Shawn Feinstein International Famine Center, senior research fellow and research director of gender, youth and community program, 2002-, Fletcher School of Law and Diplomacy, associate professor. Writer. **Publications:** NONFICTION: (with S.R. McKay) Women and Peacebuilding, 1999; Women, Peace and Security: Study of the United Nations Secretary-General As Pursuant Security Council Resolution 1325, 2002; (with E. Stites and N. Nojumi) Human Security and Livelihoods of Rural Afghans, 2002-2003, 2004; (with K. Carlson) From Combat to Community: Women and Girls of Sierra Leone, 2004; (with S. McKay) Where Are the Girls? Girls in Fighting Forces in Northern Uganda, Sierra Leone and Mozambique; Their Lives during and after the War, 2004; (ed. with A. ven-Roberts and J. Parpart) Gender, Conflict and Peacekeeping, 2005; (with N. Nojumi and E. Stites) After the Taliban: Life and Security in Rural Afghanistan, 2009. Contributor to books. **Address:** Alan Shawn Feinstein International Famine Center, Friedman School of Nutrition Science and Policy, Tufts University, 200 Boston Ave., Ste. 4800, Medford, MA 02155, U.S.A. **Online address:** dyan.mazurana@tufts.edu

MAZZA, Cris. American (born United States), b. 1956. **Genres:** Novels, Novellas/Short Stories, Sex, Women's Studies And Issues, Literary Criticism And History, Young Adult Fiction. **Career:** Brooklyn College, lecturer, 1981-83; San Diego Mesa College, lecturer, 1985-88; Miramar College, lecturer, 1987-88; University of San Diego, lecturer in English, 1987-90; University of California, visiting professor, 1988-91; Allegheny College, writer-in-residence, 1990-92; FC2, director, 1992-2005; University of Illinois, assistant professor, 1993-96, associate professor, 1996-2000, professor, 2000-, Program for Writers, director. **Publications:** STORIES: Animal Acts, 1988; Is It Sexual Harassment Yet?, 1991; Revelation Countdown, 1993; Former Virgin, 1997. NOVELS: How to Leave a Country, 1992; Exposed, 1994; Your Name Here, 1995; Dog People, 1997; Girl Beside Him, 2001; Homeland, 2004; Disability, 2005; Many Ways to Get It, Many Ways to Say It, 2005; Waterbaby, 2007. OTHER: (ed. with T. Orland) In a Quiet Voice, 1990; (co-ed.) Chick-Lit: Postfeminist Fiction, 1995, vol. II, 1996; Indigenous: Growing up Californian, 2003; Trickle-Down Timeline, 2009; Various Men Who Knew Us as Girls, 2010. **Address:** University of Illinois, 601 S Morgan St., PO Box 162, Chicago, IL 60601, U.S.A. **Online address:** cmazza@uic.edu

MAZZARELLA, William T. S. American (born United States), b. 1969. **Genres:** Social Sciences, Business/Trade/Industry, Economics, Sociology. **Career:** University of Chicago, Department of Anthropology and Social Sciences, assistant professor, 2001-08, associate professor, 2008-. Writer. **Publications:** Shoveling Smoke: Advertising and Globalization in Contemporary India, 2003; (ed. with R. Kaur) Censorship in South Asia: Cultural Regulation from Sedition to Seduction. Contributor of articles to books and journals. **Address:** Department of Anthropology, University of Chicago, 1126 E 59th St., Chicago, IL 60637, U.S.A. **Online address:** mazzarel@uchicago.edu

MAZZARO, Jerome. American (born United States), b. 1934. **Genres:** Poetry, Literary Criticism And History, Translations, Adult Non-fiction, Biography, Reference. **Career:** General Motors Corp., technical and procedures writer, 1955-56; University of Detroit, instructor of English, 1958-61; Fresco, editor, 1960-61; State University of New York, Cortland, assistant professor of English, 1962-64; North American Review, assistant editor, 1963-65; Noetics, assistant editor, 1964-65; University at Buffalow, State University of New York, professor of Italian and comparative literature, 1964-96; Salmagundi, contributor editor, 1968-98; Modern Poetry Studies, editor, 1970-79; The Poetry Review, editor, 1985-86. **Publications:** POETRY: Six Poems, 1959; Changing the Windows, 1966; The Caves of Love, 1985; Rubbings, 1985; Weathering the Changes, 2002. EDITOR: Modern American Poetry, 1970; Profile of Robert Lowell, 1971; Profile of William Carlos Williams, 1971; (co-ed.) John Logan: The Collected Poems, 1989; John Logan: The Collected Fiction, 1991. OTHERS: The Achievement of Robert Lowell: 1939-1959, 1960; (trans.) Juvenal's Satires, 1965; The Poetic Themes of Robert Lowell, 1965; Transformations in the Renaissance English Lyric, 1970; Of Love, Abiding Love, 1970; William Carlos Williams: The Later Poems, 1973; Postmodern American Poetry, 1980; The Figure of Dante: An Essay on the Vita Nuova, 1981; Mind Plays: Essays on Luigi Pirandello's Theater, 2000; Robert Lowell and Ovid, 2001; War Games (fiction), 2001; Robert Lowell and America, 2002; Memory and Making, 2003; Unlocking the Heart: Sincerity and the English Sonnet, 2004. **Address:** 392 Central Pk. W, Apt. 11J, New York, NY 10025-5819, U.S.A. **Online address:** jerrymazzaro@aol.com

MAZZENO, Laurence W. American (born United States), b. 1946. **Genres:** Literary Criticism And History, inspirational/Motivational Literature, History, Military/Defense/Arms Control, Business/Trade/Industry. **Career:** U.S. Military Academy, instructor, assistant professor, 1974-77; U.S. Military Personnel Service Co., executive officer, data processing systems officer, 1977-78, commander, 1978-79, personnel staff officer for the deputy chief of staff, U.S. Army-Europe, personnel, 1979-80; U.S. Naval Academy, assistant professor of English, 1980-82, Division of English History, executive assistant, 1982-84, chair of English department, 1986-89; Office of the Chief of Public Affairs, deputy director of internal public relations, 1984-86; Mesa State College, Humanities Fine Arts, dean, 1989-92, Social Behavioral Sciences, dean, 1990-91, dean of business, 1991-92, acting associate vice president for academic affairs, 1991-92; Ursuline College, vice president for academic affairs, 1992-95, chief operating officer, 1995-96, interim president, 1996-97; Alvernia College, president, 1997-2005, president emeritus, 2005-. Writer. **Publications:** The Victorian Novel: An Annotated Bibliography, 1989; Herman Wouk, 1994; Victorian Poetry: An Annotated Bibliography, 1995; (ed.) Masterplots: 1,801 Plot Stories and Critical Evaluations of the World's Finest Literature, 2nd ed., 1996, rev. ed. as Masterplots: About A Boy-The Big Rock Candy Mountain, 2010; The British Novel, 1680-1832: An Annotated Bibliography, 1997; Matthew Arnold: The Critical Legacy, 1999; Alfred Tennyson: The Critical Legacy, 2004; The Dickens Industry: Critical Perspectives 1835-2005, 2008; Omi: Mother Courage, 2008; Jane Austen: Two Centuries of Criticism, 2011; (ed.) Critical Insights: Jane Austen, Pride and Prejudice, 2011. **Address:** PO Box 319, Weems, VA 22576-0319, U.S.A. **Online address:** mazzmedia@aol.com

MAZZONIS, Querciolo Odoardo. Italian (born Italy), b. 1965. **Genres:** Theology/Religion. **Career:** International House, Italian Department, director, 1991-97; University of Westminster, lecturer, 1993-98; University of London-Thornley, Institute of Historical Research, research fellow, 1998-99; University of London-London, Goldsmiths College, lecturer, 1999-2000; University of Birmingham, lecturer, 2000-01; National University of Ireland, lecturer, 2001-03; Università degli Studi di Siena, senior lecturer, 2004-08; Università degli Studi de Teramo, senior lecturer, 2010-. Writer. **Publications:** Anthropology and Gender in the Spirituality of Angela Merici as Gender and Society in the Spirituality of Angela Merici, 2000; Spirituality, Gender, and the Self in Renaissance Italy: Angela Merici and the Company of St. Ursula (1474-1540), 2007. Contributor to periodicals and journals. **Address:** Dipartimento di Studi Storicosocialie, Università degli Studi di Siena, Filosofici, V. Cittadini 33, Arezzo, 52100, Italy. **Online address:** qmazzonis@hotmail.com

MAZZUCA TOOPS, Laura. American (born United States), b. 1955. **Genres:** Travel/Exploration, Novels. **Career:** Crain Communications, assistant editor, 1987-92; National Association of Independent Insurers (NAII), senior public affairs specialist, 1998-; Columbia College, journalism teacher; American Agent and Broker, editor. Journalist and reporter. **Publications:** The Best Guide to Women's Health, 1998; A Native's Guide to Chicago's Western Suburbs, 1999; Hudson Lake, 2006. NOVELS: Slapstick (historical), 2000. Contributor of articles to periodicals. **Address:** NAII Headquarters, 2600 River Rd., Des Plaines, IL 60018-3286, U.S.A. **Online address:** lmazztoops@aol.com

MBAYE, Marietou (Bileoma). (Ken Bugul). Senegalese/Beninese (born Benin), b. 1947. **Genres:** Novels, Biography. **Career:** ASBEF, program coordinator, 1982-86; IPPF, program officer, 1986-93; Africans Intl., administrator; University of Western Australia, faculty. Writer. **Publications:** AS KEN BUGUL: Le Baobab Fou, 1982, trans. as The Abandoned Baobab: The Autobiography of a Senegalese Woman, 1991; Cendres et braises, 1994; Riwan ou le chemin de sable, 1999; La Folie et la Mort (novel), 2000; De l'Autre Cote du Regard, 2002; Rue Félix Faure, 2005; La Pièce d'Or, 2006; Confessions de Zinc, 2008; Mes hommes à moi, 2008. **Address:** The University of Western Australia, 35 Stirling Hwy., Crawley, WA 6009, Australia. **Online address:** ken_bugul@yahoo.fr

MBUENDE, Kaire (Munionganda). American (born United States), b. 1953. **Genres:** Area Studies, History, Politics/Government, Social Sciences. **Career:** Statesman and diplomat. SWAPO External Headquarters, information officer, 1974-75; University of Aarhus, assistant lecturer, 1981; University of Lund, assistant lecturer, 1984-86, Development Studies, lecturer, 1986-87; Institute for Future Studies, reader, 1987-89; Government of Namibia, Constituent Assembly, deputy minister of agriculture, water and rural development, 1990-93, deputy minister of foreign affairs, 2002-04; Southern African Development Community (SADC), executive secretary, 1994-; United Nations Organization, ambassador, 2006; Republic of Namibia, vice-chair. Writer. **Publications:** Namibia the Broken Shield: Anatomy of Imperialism and Revolution, 1986; (ed. with P. Katjavivi and P. Frostin) Church and Liberation in Namibia, 1989; Social Movements and the Demise of Apartheid Colonialism in Namibia, forthcoming. Contributor to periodicals. **Address:** Southern African Development Community, Plot No. 54385, Central Business District, PO Box 0095, Gaborone, 0095, Botswana.

MCADAM, Colin. Canadian/Hong Kong (born Hong Kong), b. 1971?. **Genres:** Novels. **Career:** Novelist and writer. **Publications:** Some Great Thing, 2004; Fall, 2009; Black Bugs, forthcoming. **Address:** c/o Douglas Stewart, 65 Bleecker St., New York, NY 10012, U.S.A. **Online address:** info@colinmcadam.com

MCADAM, Ian. Canadian (born Canada), b. 1960. **Genres:** Literary Criticism And History, Psychology. **Career:** University of Lethbridge, assistant professor of Renaissance literature, 1995-2000, associate professor, 2000-, professor, chair. Writer. **Publications:** The Irony of Identity: Self and Imagination in the Drama of Christopher Marlowe, 1999; Magic and Masculinity in Early Modern English Drama, 2009. **Address:** Department of English, University of Lethbridge, A840B University Hall, 4401 University Dr., Lethbridge, AB T1K 3M4, Canada. **Online address:** mcadam@uleth.ca

MCADAMS, Dan P. American (born United States), b. 1954. **Genres:** Psychology. **Career:** Harvard University, Department of Psychology and Social Relations, teaching fellow and tutor, 1977-79; University of Minnesota, Institute of Child Development, visiting lecturer, 1979-80; St. Olaf College, visiting lecturer, 1979-80; Pepperdine University, honorary visiting lecturer, 1980; Loyola University of Chicago, Department of psychology, assistant professor, 1980-85, associate professor, 1985-89; Michigan State University, Henry A. Murray lecturer, 1988; Journal of Personality and Social Psychology, consulting editor, 1988-92, 2003-04; Northwestern University, professor of psychology and human development and social policy, 1989-, chair of psychology department, Program in Human Development and Social Policy, chair, 1992-94, 2005-08, Program in Counseling Psychology, chair, 1995-97, Charles Deering McCormick professor of teaching excellence, 1995-98, Foley Center for the Study of Lives, director, Center on Aging, fellow; Journal of Personality, associate editor, 1986-91; Contemporary Psychology, advisory editor, 1991-98; Sigma Xi, national lecturer, 1992-93; Personality and Social Psychology Review, consulting editor, 1995-2005; Motivation and Emotion, consulting editor, 2005-. **Publications:** Power, Intimacy and the Life Story: Personological Inquiries into Identity, 1985; Intimacy: The Need to Be Close, 1989; The Person: An Introduction to Personality Psychology, 1990, 4th ed., 2006; The Stories We Live By: Personal Myths and the Making of the Self, 1993; Redemptive Self: Stories Americans Live by, 2006; George W. Bush and the Redemptive Dream: A Psychological Portrait, 2011. EDITOR: (with R.L. Ochberg) Psychobiography and Life Narratives, 1988; (with E.D. St. Aubin) Generativity and Adult Development: How and Why We Care for the Next Generation, 1998; (with R. Josselson and A. Lieblich) Turns in the Road: Narrative Studies of Lives in Transition, 2001; (with E. Aubin and T. Kim) Generative Society: Caring for Future Generations, 2003; (with R. Josselson and A. Lieblich) Up Close and Personal: The Teaching and Learning of Narrative Research, 2003; (with R. Josselson and A. Lieblich) Healing Plots: The Narrative Basis of Psychotherapy, 2004; (with R. Josselson and A. Lieblich) Identity and Story: Creating Self in Narrative, 2006; (with R. Josselson and A. Lieblich) Meaning of Others: Narrative Studies of Relationships, 2007. Contributor to books and periodicals. **Address:** School of Education and Social Policy, Northwestern University, 102 Swift, 209 Annenberg Hall, 2120 Campus Dr., Evanston, IL 60208, U.S.A. **Online address:** dmca@northwestern.edu

MCADAMS, Janet. American (born United States), b. 1957?. **Genres:** Poetry, Novels, Literary Criticism And History, Anthropology/Ethnology. **Career:** University of Oklahoma, Native American Literature and Creative Writing, teacher; University of Alabama, Literature and Creative Writing, teacher; American School of El Salvador, teacher; Kenyon College, faculty, Robert P. Hubbard professor of poetry and associate professor of English. **Publications:** The Island of Lost Luggage (poetry), 2000; (ed. with G. Hobson and K. Walkiewicz) The People Who Stayed: Southeastern Indian Writing after the Removal, 2010; Disappearing to the New World, forthcoming; The Children of Animals, forthcoming; Earthwork, forthcoming; Red Weather(novel), forthcoming; Not too Sane: Art and the Romance of Suffering, forthcoming. Works appear in anthologies. Contributor of poetry to journals. **Address:** Department of English, Lentz House and Sunset Cottage, Kenyon College, Sunset Cottage 206, Gambier, OH 43022-9623, U.S.A. **Online address:** mcadamsj@kenyon.edu

MCAFEE, Carol. American (born United States), b. 1955. **Genres:** Novels, Young Adult Non-fiction, Literary Criticism And History. **Career:** State Bar of California, attorney, 1981. Writer. **Publications:** The Climbing Tree (adult), 1989; Who's the Kid Around Here, Anyway? (young adult), 1991; Walk Among Birches: A Novel, 2002. FORTHCOMING: Letters to My Father, Mistrial and the Finder, Perfect. **Address:** c/o Ralph Arnsdorf, 337 Rosebank Ave., Baltimore, MD 21212-3536, U.S.A. **Online address:** carol@carolmcafee.com

MCAFEE, John P. American (born United States), b. 1947?. **Genres:** Novels, Poetry, Literary Criticism And History. **Career:** Christ School for Boys, English teacher and coach of varsity soccer and wrestling, 1972-74; T.C. Roberson High School, drama director, varsity soccer and wrestling coach, 1974-80; A.C. Reynolds High School, director of drama, varsity soccer and wrestling coach, 1987-. Writer. **Publications:** Slow Walk in a Sad Rain, 1993; On Rims of Empty Moons, 1997. Works appear in anthologies. **Address:** Texas Tech University Press, PO Box 41037, Lubbock, TX 79409-1037, U.S.A.

MCALINDON, Thomas. (Tom McAlindon). British (born England), b. 1932. **Genres:** Literary Criticism And History. **Career:** National University of Ireland, University College, assistant lecturer in English, 1960-61; University of Hull, lecturer in English, 1961-78, senior lecturer in English, 1979-, professor, now professor emeritus; University of Ottawa, faculty, 1978-79. Writer. **Publications:** Shakespeare and Decorum, 1974; English Renaissance Tragedy, 1986; Shakespeare's Tragic Cosmos, 1991; Doctor Faustus: Divine in Show, 1994; Shakespeare's Tudor History, 2001; Shakespeare Minus Theory, 2004; Bloodstains in Ulster: The Notorious Case of Robert the Painter, 2006; Two Brothers, Two Wars: From the Western Front to the Burmese Jungle, 2008. **Address:** 39 Elms Dr., Hull, HU10 7QH, England. **Online address:** t.e.mcalindon@hull.ac.uk

MCALINDON, Tom. *See* **MCALINDON, Thomas.**

MCALL, Christopher. Canadian/British (born England), b. 1948. **Genres:** Sociology, Race Relations, Language/Linguistics, Social Sciences, Young Adult Non-fiction, Politics/Government. **Career:** McGill University, research fellow, 1981-83; Concordia University, faculty lecturer, 1984-88; University of Montreal, professor of sociology, 1988-. Writer. **Publications:** Class, Ethnicity, and Social Inequality, 1990; (with F. Le Goff and L. Tremblay) Proximité et distance: Les défis de communicationentre intervenants et clientéle multiethnique en CLSC, 1997; (with F.L. Goff and C. Montgomery) Transformation du communautaire: Expériences d'intervention auprés de jeunes sans-emploi, 2005. Contributor of articles to journals. **Address:** Departement of Sociology, University of Montreal, PO Box 6128, Sta. Centre-ville, Montreal, QC H3C 3J7, Canada. **Online address:** christopher.mcall@umontreal.ca

MCALLEN, Jack. American (born United States), b. 1929. **Genres:** Business/Trade/Industry, Women's Studies And Issues, Social Sciences, Adult Non-fiction. **Career:** Printz Co. (retail apparel company), clerk, department manager, 1945-50, 1956-62; H.J. Heinz (retail food store), special salesperson, 1955-56; Harding Business College, lecturer; Kent State University, lecturer. Writer. **Publications:** The Boss Should Be a Woman: How Women Can Manage Their Way to the Top and Compromise Nothing; How to Succeed Because You Are a Woman, 1993. **Address:** 7858 Castle Rock Dr. NE, Warren, OH 44484-2058, U.S.A.

MCALPINE, Alistair. (Robert Alistair McAlpine). British (born England), b. 1942. **Genres:** Novels, Art/Art History, Psychology, Biography. **Career:** Sir Robert McAlpine's and Sons, director, 1958-80; George Weidenfeld Holdings, director, 1975-83; Conservative and Unionist Party, vice-president,

1975-90, deputy chairperson, 1979-83. Writer. **Publications:** The Servant (fiction), 1992; Journal of a Collector, 1994; Letters to a Young Politician: From his Uncle, 1996; The New Machiavelli: The Art of Politics in Business (fiction), 1997; Once a Jolly Bagman: Memoirs, 1997; New Machiavelli: The Art of Politics in Business, 1998; (with C. Giangrande) Collecting and Displaying Conran Octopus, 1998; Bagman to Swagman: Tales of Broome, the North-West and Other Australian Adventures, 1999; (ed.) The Ruthless Leader: Three Classics of Strategy and Power, 2000; (with C. Giangrande) The Essential Guide to Collectibles: A Source Book of Public Collections in Europe and the U.S.A, 2001; (with K. Dixey) Triumph From Failure: Lessons from Life for Business Success, 2003. **Address:** c/o Sir Robert McAlpine, Yorkshire House, Grosvenor Cres., London, GL SW1X 7EP, England.

MCALPINE, Rachel (Taylor). New Zealander (born New Zealand), b. 1940. **Genres:** Novels, Children's Fiction, Plays/Screenplays, Poetry, Adult Non-fiction, Information Science/Computers, Language/Linguistics, How-to Books, Writing/Journalism, Children's Non-fiction, Young Adult Fiction. **Career:** High school teacher, 1960, 1979-83; British Consulate General, consular clerk, 1961-63; Macquarie University, writer-in-residence, 1982; freelance writer, 1984-92; Canterbury University, writer-in-residence, 1986; Doshisha Women's College, lecturer, 1993-95; Contented Enterprises Ltd., founder and director, 2007. **Publications:** POETRY: Lament for Ariadne, 1975; Stay at the Dinner Party, 1977; Fancy Dress, 1979; House Poems, 1980; Recording Angel, 1983; Thirteen Waves, 1986; Selected Poems, 1988; Tourist in Kyoto, 1993; (ed.) Another 100 New Zealand Poems for Children, 2001; A for Blog, 2005. FICTION: The Limits of Green, 1985; Running Away from Home, 1987; Farewell Speech, 1990; Humming, 2005; Scarlet Heels: 21 Stories About Sex, 2010. OTHER: Masako in New Zealand, 1994; The Secret Life of New Zealand, 1995; Katherine Mansfield in New Zealand, 1995. FOR CHILDREN: Maria in the Middle, 1993; Maria and the Lady Next Door, 1994. NON-FICTION: Song in the Satchel: Poetry in the High School, 1980; Real Writing, 1992; Global English for Global Business, 1997; The Passionate Pen, 1998; Web Word Wizardry, 1999, 2nd ed., 2002; Crash Course in Corporate Communications, 1999; Nine Winning Habits of Successful Authors, 2000; Better Business Writing on the Web, 2007; Write me a Web Page, Elsie! 2009. **Address:** Contented Enterprises Ltd., PO Box 19244, Wellington, 6149, New Zealand. **Online address:** rachel@writing.co.nz

MCALPINE, Robert Alistair. *See* **MCALPINE, Alistair.**

MCARTHUR, Judith N. American (born United States), b. 1951. **Genres:** Women's Studies And Issues, Cultural/Ethnic Topics, Military/Defense/Arms Control, Politics/Government, History. **Career:** University of Houston, lecturer in history, adjunct professor. Writer. **Publications:** (Ed. with R. Winegarten) Citizens at Last: The Woman Suffrage Movement in Texas: Essays, 1987; (with O.V. Burton) A Gentleman and an Officer: A Military and Social History of James B. Griffin's Civil War, 1996; Creating the New Woman: The Rise of Southern Women's Progressive Culture in Texas, 1893- 1918, 1998; (with H.L. Smith) Minnie Fisher Cunningham: A Suffragist's Life in Politics, 2003; (ed. with A. Boswell) Women Shaping the South: Creating and Confronting Change, 2006; (with H.L. Smith) Texas Through Women's Eyes: The Twentieth-century Experience, 2010. **Address:** University of Houston, 3007 N Ben Wilson St., Victoria, TX 77901-5731, U.S.A. **Online address:** mcarthurj@uhv.edu

MCARTHUR, Nancy. American (born United States) **Genres:** Children's Fiction, Children's Non-fiction, Novels. **Career:** Baldwin-Wallace College, part-time journalism lecturer, part-time journalism professor. Freelance writer. **Publications:** How to Do Theatre Publicity, 1978; Megan Gets a Dollhouse, 1988; Pickled Peppers, 1988; The Plant that Ate Dirty Socks, 1988; The Return of the Plant that Ate Dirty Socks, 1990; The Adventure of the Buried Treasure, 1990; The Adventure of the Backyard Sleepout, 1992; The Escape of the Plant that Ate Dirty Socks, 1992; The Secret of the Plant that Ate Dirty Socks, 1993; More Adventures of the Plant that Ate Dirty Socks, 1994; The Plant that Ate Dirty Socks Goes Up in Space, 1995; Mystery of the Plant that Ate Dirty Socks, 1996; The Plant that Ate Dirty Socks Gets a Girlfriend, 1997; The Adventure of the Big Snow, 1998; The Plant that Ate Dirty Socks Goes Hollywood, 1999. Contributor to books and periodicals. **Address:** PO Box 296, Berea, OH 44017, U.S.A. **Online address:** mcarthur@apk.net

MCAULAY, Alex. American/British (born England), b. 1977. **Genres:** Young Adult Fiction, Children's Fiction, Novels. **Career:** Writer and musician. **Publications:** Bad Girls, 2005; Lost Summer, 2006; Oblivion Road, 2007; Shelter Me, 2009; Octonions a Development of Clifford's Bi-Quaterninons, 2009. **Address:** c/o Dave Dunton, Harvey Klinger Inc., 300 W 55th St., Ste. 11V, New York, NY 10019, U.S.A. **Online address:** info@alexmcaulay.com

MCAULEY, James J. Irish (born Ireland), b. 1936. **Genres:** Poetry. **Career:** Electricity Supply Board, journalist, 1954-66; Kilkenny Magazine, art critic, 1960-66; Dolmen Press, editor, 1960-66; Poetry Ireland, associate editor, 1962-66; Dublin's Municipal Gallery of Modern Art, lecturer, 1965-66; University of Arkansas, English Department, teaching assistant, 1966-68; Lycoming College, assistant professor, director of creative writing, 1968-70; Eastern Washington University, assistant professor, 1970-73, associate professor, 1973-78, professor of English, 1978-98, professor emeritus of English, 1998-, Eastern Washington University Press, director, 1993-98; University of Victoria, visiting lecturer, 1975. **Publications:** Observations, 1960; A New Address, 1965; The Revolution (libretto), 1966; Draft Balance Sheet, 1970; After the Blizzard, 1975; The Exile's Recurring Nightmare, 1975; An Irish Bull, and Praise (libretto), 1981; Recital: Poems 1975-80, 1982; The Exile's Book of Hours, 1982; Coming and Going: New and Selected Poems 1968-88, 1989; Meditations with Distractions: Poems, 1988-1998, 2000; New and Selected Poems, 2005. **Address:** Department of English, Eastern Washington University, 526 5th St., Cheney, WA 99004, U.S.A. **Online address:** jjmca@tinet.ie

MCAULEY, Paul J. Scottish/British (born England), b. 1955. **Genres:** Novels, Novellas/Short Stories, Science Fiction/Fantasy. **Career:** Oxford University, cell biologist, 1980-96; University of California, Department of Cardiovascular Medicine, visiting researcher, 1980-96; University of St. Andrews, lecturer, 1980-96; writer, 1996-. **Publications:** NOVELS: Four Hundred Billion Stars, 1988; Secret Harmonies in US as Of the Fall, 1989; Eternal Light, 1993; Red Dust, 1993; Pasquale's Angel, 1995; Fairyland, 1995; Child of the River, 1998; Ancients of Days, 1999; Shrine of Stars, 2000; The Secret of Life, 2001; Whole Wide World, 2002; White Devils, 2004; Mind's Eye, 2004; Cowboy Angels, 2007; Players, 2007; The Quiet War, 2008; Gardens of the Sun, 2009; City of the Dead, 2011; In the Mouth of the Whale, 2012. SHORT STORIES: The King of the Hill, and Other Stories, 1991; The Invisible Country, 1996; Little Machines, 2004. OTHERS: (ed. with K. Newman) In Dreams (anthology), 1992. NOVELLAS: (co-author) Futures: Four Novellas, 2001; The Eye of the Tyger, 2003; Stories From The Quiet War, 2011. Contributor to magazines. **Address:** MBA Literary Agents, 45 Fitzroy St., London, GL W1P 5HR, England. **Online address:** mcauley@omegacom.demon.co.uk

MCAULEY, Roisin. British/Irish (born Ireland) **Genres:** Novels, History, Travel/Exploration. **Career:** British Broadcasting Corp. (BBC), newsreader, announcer and reporter; BBC Radio, presenter. Television producer and director. **Publications:** Emerald Greens: The Essential Guide to Holiday Golf in Ireland, 2000; Singing Bird, 2004; Meeting Point, 2005; Finding Home, 2008; French Secrets, 2011. **Address:** c/o Author Mail, William Morrow & Co., 10 E 53rd St., 7th Fl., New York, NY 10022, U.S.A.

MCBEATH, Gerald (Jerry) A. American (born United States), b. 1942. **Genres:** Area Studies, Local History/Rural Topics, Politics/Government. **Career:** Rutgers College, visiting assistant professor, 1970-72; City University of New York, John Jay College, Department of Government, assistant professor, 1972-76, Richmond College, Social Studies Division, adjunct assistant professor, 1972-74, Graduate School of Political Science, Fulbright Hays lecturer, visiting associate professor, 1974-75; National Chengchi University, visiting associate professor, 1974-75; Soochow University, visiting associate professor, 1974-75; American Studies Institute, visiting associate professor, 1974-75; Tamkang College of Arts, visiting associate professor, 1974-75; University of Alaska, assistant professor, 1976-77, associate professor, 1977-82, professor of political science, 1982-, director of faculty development, 1990-92, College of Liberal Arts, acting dean, 1991-93, department chair, Institute of Social and Economic Research, research staff, 1977-78, 1980; China Foreign Affairs University, Fulbright professor, 2004. Writer. **Publications:** Political Integration of the Philippine Chinese, 1973; (with T.A. Morehouse) The Dynamics of Alaska Native Self-Government, 1980; (with P.H. Chang and R.N. Clough) Taiwan, Pawn or Pivot?, 1980; (with T.A. Morehouse and L. Leask) Alaska Urban and Rural Governments, 1984; (with T.A. Morehouse) Alaska Politics and Government, 1994; The Alaska State Constitution: A Reference Guide, 1997; Wealth and Freedom: Taiwan's New Political Economy, 1998; (with J. Rosenberg) Comparative Environmental Politics, 2006; (with T.K. Leng) Governance of Biodiversity Conservation in China and Taiwan, 2006; (with M.E. Reyes and M.F. Ehrlander) Education Reform in the American States, 2008; The Political Economy of Oil in Alaska: Multinationals versus the State, 2008; (with J.H. McBeath) Environmental Change and Food Security in China, 2010. EDITOR: (with P.G. Cornwall) Alaska's Rural Development, 1982; (with T.A. Morehouse) Alaska State Government and Politics, 1987. Contributor to books and journals. **Address:** Department of Political Science, University of Alaska, 601B Gruening, PO Box 756420, Fairbanks, AK 99775, U.S.A. **Online address:** gamcbeath@alaska.edu

MCBRATNEY, Sam. Irish/British (born England), b. 1943. **Genres:** Novellas/Short Stories, Children's Fiction, Children's Non-fiction, Young Adult Fiction, Self Help. **Career:** Teacher, 1970-90; writer, 1990-. **Publications:** FOR CHILDREN: Mark Time, 1976; A Dip of the Antlers, 1977; The Final Correction, 1978; Boy Blue, 1979; From the Thorenson Dykes, 1980; The Hanging Man, 1980; The Man Who Tried to Fly, 1980; The Pigeon Killer, 1980; The Stolen Honda, 1980; Lagan Valley Details: Short Stories, 1980; Jimmy Zest, 1982; Zesty, 1984; Colvin and the Snake Basket, 1985; Jimmy Zest Is Best, 1985; The Missing Lollipop, 1986; Uncle Charlie Weasel and the Cuckoo Bird, 1986; Claudius Bald Eagle, 1987; The Ghosts of Hungryhouse Lane, 1988; The Jimmy Zest All-Stars, 1988; Uncle Charlie Weasel's Winter, 1988; Funny, How the Magic Starts, 1989; The Secret of Bone Island, 1989; Zesty Goes Cooking, 1989 as Jimmy Zest, Super Pest, 2002; Bones and the Beast, 1990; Bones and the Monster, 1990; Bones at the Pet Show, 1990; Busy Street, 1990; Cyclops and the Greenbeans, 1990; How We Travelled Long Ago, 1990; Jill Has Three Pets, 1990; Noah Sorts the Animals, 1990; Pip Goes to Africa, 1990; The Thursday Creature, 1990; School Trip to the Stars, 1990; Jealous Jools and Dominique, 1991; Who Likes Work?, 1991; Animals at Work, 1991; Something Big, 1992; Put a Saddle on the Pig, 1992 as You Just Don't Listen!, 1994; The Green Kids, 1992; Art, You're Magic!, 1992; Bananas, 1993; Breakfast with Ublob, 1993; A Case of Blue Murder, 1993; The Chieftain's Daughter, 1993; Flash Eddie and the Big Bad Wolf, 1994; Guess How Much I Love You, 1994; Henry Seamouse, 1994; Hurray for Monty Ray!, 1994; The Lough Neagh Monster, 1994; The Stranger from Somewhere in Time, 1994; The Ghastly Gerty Swindle, with the Ghosts of Hungryhouse Lane, 1994; The Dark at the Top of the Stairs, 1995; Wonderful Oliver Sundew, 1995; In Crack Willow Wood, 1995; Firetail Cat, 1995; Francis Fry Private Eye, 1995; Suzuki Goodbye, 1995; Francis Fry and the OTG, 1996; Just One!, 1996; The Caterpillow Fight, 1996; Little Red Riding Hood, 1996; Long Tall Short & Hairy Poems, 1996; Celtic Myths, 1997; Just You & Me, 1998; Kristel Dimond, Timecop, 1998; Bert's Wonderful News, 1998; Fishy Business for Francis Fry, 1999; Once There Was a Hoodie, 1999; One Grand Sweet Song, 1999; I'm Sorry, 2000; I'll Always Be Your Friend, 2001; Elemono P, 2001; In the Light of the Moon, 2001; Stranger from Somewhere in Time, 2002; The Kingfisher Mini Treasury of Bedtime Stories, 2004; You're All My Favorites, 2004; I Love It When You Smile, 2005; (with C. Fuge) Yes We Can!, 2007; Guess How Much I Love You in the Summer, 2007; Colors Everywhere, 2008; When I'm Big, 2008; One Voice, Please, 2008; A Nutbrown Hare Storybook Pair, 2008; Guess How Much I Love You in the Winter, 2008; Guess How Much I Love You in the Autumn, 2008; (with A. Jeram) Let's Play in the Snow, 2008; (with A. Jeram) A Surprise for the Nutbrown Hares, 2009; Guess How Much I Love You All Year Round, 2009; Guess How Much I Love You in the Spring, 2009; Guess How Much I Love You Sweetheart Edition, 2009. EDITOR: Today and Yesterday (stories), 1992; People, Places and Ideas (stories), 1993. OTHER: (contrib.) Alien Adventures, 2008. **Address:** 17 Ballymote Rd., Glenavy, Crumlin, AT BT29 4NS, Northern Ireland.

MCBRIDE, Genevieve G. American (born United States), b. 1949. **Genres:** History, Women's Studies And Issues. **Career:** Milwaukee Journal, freelance writer, 1970-71; Milwaukee Star and Courier, production editor, 1971-72; Waukesha Freeman, assistant news editor, 1972-74; Carroll College, director of public relations, 1974-83, lecturer in communication, 1983-84; Marquette University, instructor in journalism, 1980-84; University of Wisconsin-Waukesha County Center, lecturer, 1980-81; University of Wisconsin-Madison, lecturer in mass communication, 1987-88, teaching assistant in mass communication, 1984-86; University of Wisconsin-Milwaukee, lecturer in mass communication, 1988, instructor, 1988-89, assistant professor of mass communication, 1989-94, associate professor of mass communication, 1994-2001, associate professor of history, 2001-, director of women studies, 2005-06; National Museum of Womens History, founding member. **Publications:** On Wisconsin Women: Working for Their Rights From Settlement to Suffrage, 1993; (ed.) Women's Wisconsin: From Native Matriarchies to the New Millennium, 2005. Contributor to books. **Address:** Department of History, University of Wisconsin, 347 Holton Hall, 2200 E Kenwood Blvd., PO Box 413, Milwaukee, WI 53201, U.S.A. **Online address:** gmcbride@uwm.edu

MCBRIDE, Jule. (Julianne Randolph Moore). American (born United States), b. 1959. **Genres:** Romance/Historical, Novels. **Career:** Writer. **Publications:** ROMANCE NOVELS: Wild Card Wedding, 1993; Baby Trap, 1993; The Wrong Wife?, 1994; The Baby and the Bodyguard, 1994; Bride of the Badlands, 1995; The Baby Maker, 1995; The Bounty Hunter's Baby, 1996; Baby Romeo: P. I., 1996; Cole in My Stocking, 1996; Mission: Motherhood, 1997; Verdict: Parenthood, 1997; Wed to a Stranger, 1997; Who's Been Sleeping in My Bed? 1997; Diagnosis: Daddy, 1998; How the West was Wed, 1998; AKA: Marriage, 1998; Smoochin' Santa, 1998; Santa Slept Over, 1999; The Strong, Silent Type, 1999; Hitched by Christmas (Heart of the West, 6), 1999; Prescription-Baby (Maitland Maternity), 2000; A Baby for the Boss, 2000; Secret Baby Spencer, 2000; (co-author) Wild to Wed: The Wedding Gamble/Wild Card Wedding, 2000; Naughty by Nature, 2002; Night Pleasures, 2001; A Way with Women, 2002; The Protector, 2002; The Sex Files, 2002; The Seducer, 2002; The Hotshot, 2002; (with M. Way and S. Fox) With This Ring, 2003; (with S. Wiggs and N. Warren) It Happened One Christmas, 2003; All Tucked in, 2003; Bedspell, 2004; I Thee Bed-, 2005; Nights in White Satin, 2005; Something Borrowed, 2005; Pleasure Chest, 2006; Something in the Water-, 2006; Cold Case, Hot Bodies, 2007; Naked Ambition, 2009; Naked Attraction, 2009. Works appear in anthologies. **Address:** c/o Karen Solem, Writers House Inc., 21 W 26th St., New York, NY 10010, U.S.A.

MCBRIDE, Mandy. *See* **LANAGAN, Margo.**

MCBRIDE, Mary. American/British (born England), b. 1946?. **Genres:** Romance/Historical, Novels, Young Adult Fiction, Literary Criticism And History. **Career:** Writer and educator. **Publications:** ROMANCE NOVELS: Riverbend, 1993; Fly away Home, 1993; The Fourth of Forever, 1994; The Sugarman, 1994; The Gunslinger, 1995; Forever and a Day, 1995; Darling Jack, 1996; The Ballad of Josie Dove in Outlaw Brides, 1996; Quicksilver's Catch, 1997; Storming Paradise, 1998; The Marriage Knot, 1999; Just One Look, 1999; Bluer than Velvet, 2000; Bandera's Bride, 2000; Baby, Baby, Baby, 2001; Season of Bounty in A Western Family Christmas, 2001; Moonglow, Texas, 2001; Sarah's Knight, 2002; Still Mr. & Mrs., 2002; My Hero, 2003; Ms. Simon Says, 2004; Say it Again, Sam, 2004; The Magnate's Takeover, 2008. OMNIBUS: (with E. Coffman and R. Langan) Outlaw Brides, 1996; (with M. Criswell and L. Ireland) A Western Family Christmas, 2001. Works appear in anthologies. **Address:** c/o Author Mail, Silhouette Books, 233 Broadway, Ste. 101, New York, NY 10279, U.S.A. **Online address:** mary@marymcbride.net

MCBRIDE, Robert. Irish (born Ireland), b. 1941. **Genres:** Literary Criticism And History, Art/Art History. **Career:** Queen's University, assistant lecturer, 1965-68, lecturer, 1968-73, instructor in French, 1973, senior lecturer in French, 1973-81; University of Ulster, professor of French, 1982-, now professor emeritus. Writer. **Publications:** The Sceptical Vision of Molière: A Study in Paradox, 1977; Aspects of Seventeenth-Century French Drama and Thought, 1979; The Triumph of Ballet in Moliere's Theatre, 1992; L'Imposteur, precurseur du Tartuffe, 1999; Molière et son premier Tartuffe: genèse et évolution d'une pièce á scandale, 2011. EDITOR: (with R.L. Davis and J.H. Gillespie) Humanities, 1984; Lettre sur la comedie de L'Imposteur, 1994. **Address:** Department of French, University of Ulster, Cromore Rd., Coleraine, BT52 1SA, Northern Ireland. **Online address:** r.mcbride@ulster.ac.uk

MCBRIDE, Simon. British (born England) **Genres:** Photography, Crafts, Design. **Career:** Simon McBride Photography, owner. **Publications:** Spirit of England, 1989; (with K. Howes) Private Ireland: Irish Living, 2000; (with A. Black) Ski Style: Alpine Interiors, Architecture and Living Style, 2000; (with D. Glenn) Under Sail: Aboard the World's Finest Boats, 2001; (with E.H. Minchilli) Restoring a Home in Italy: Twenty Two Home Owners Realize Their Dream, 2001; Tuscan Elements, 2002; (with E.H. Minchilli) Villas on the Italian Lakes: Orta Maggiore Como Garda, 2004; (with S. Griffiths) The English House: English Country Houses and Interiors, 2004. **Address:** Simon McBride Photography, 4 Cleveland Pl. W, Bath, SM BA1 5DG, England. **Online address:** simon@simon-mcbride.co.uk

MCBRIDE, Stephen. Canadian/British (born England), b. 1947. **Genres:** Economics, Politics/Government, Industrial Relations. **Career:** Lakehead

University, assistant professor, 1982-87, associate professor of political studies, 1987-93, head of department, 1983-88; Simon Fraser University, associate professor, 1993-95, professor of political science, 1995-, head of department, 1993-2002, Center for Global Political Economy, director, 2003-. Writer. **Publications:** Not Working: State Unemployment and Neo-Conservatism in Canada, 1992; (with J. Shields) Dismantling a Nation: Canada and the New World Order, 1993, 2nd ed. as Dismantling a Nation: The Transition to Corporate Rule in Canada, 1997; Paradigm Shift: Globalization and the Canadian State, 2001, 2nd ed., 2005; (with H. Whiteside) Private Affluence, Public Austerity: Economic Crisis & Democratic Malaise in Canada, 2011. EDITOR/CO-EDITOR: Regulating Labour: The State, Neo-Conservatism and Industrial Relations, 1990; Continuities and Discontinuities: The Political Economy of Social Welfare and Labour Market Policy in Canada, 1994; The Training Trap, 1996; Globalization and Its Discontents, 2000; Power in the Global Era: Grounding Globalization, 2000; Global Instability, 2002; (with M.G. Cohen) Global Turbulence: Social Activists' and State Responses to Globalization, 2003; (with G. Teeple) Relations of Global Power: Neoliberal Order and Disorder, 2011. **Address:** Department of Political Science, Simon Fraser University, Rm. AQ-6071, 8888 University Dr., Burnaby, BC V5A 1S6, Canada. **Online address:** mcbride@sfu.ca

MCBRIDE, Susan. American (born United States), b. 1964?. **Genres:** Novels, Mystery/Crime/Suspense, Young Adult Fiction. **Career:** Novelist. **Publications:** NOVELS: And Then She was Gone, 1999; Overkill, 2001; Blue Blood, 2004; The Good Girl's Guide to Murder, 2005; The Lone Star Lonely Hearts Club, 2006; Night of the Living Deb, 2007; Too Pretty to Die, 2008; The Debs, 2008; Love, Lies and Texas Dips, 2009; The Cougar Club, 2010; Little Black Dress, 2011. **Address:** The Jane Rotrosen Agency, 318 E 51st St., New York, NY 10022, U.S.A. **Online address:** sueauthor@aol.com

MCBRIEN, Richard P(eter). American (born United States), b. 1936. **Genres:** Theology/Religion, inspirational/Motivational Literature, Cultural/Ethnic Topics. **Career:** Southern Connecticut State College, Newman chaplain, 1962-63; Loyola University of Chicago, lecturer in theology, 1964-65; Pope John XXIII National Seminary, theology faculty, 1965-74, professor of theology and dean of studies, 1965-70; Boston College, visiting professor, 1966-70, associate professor, 1970-72, professor of theology, 1972-80, Institute of Religious Education and Pastoral Ministry, director, 1975-80; Catholic Theological Society of America, president, 1973-74; Harvard University, John Fitzgerald Kennedy School of Government, visiting fellow, 1975-76; University of Notre Dame, Crowley-O'Brien professor of Roman Catholic theology, 1980-, chairman of the department, 1980-91; ABC News, consultant. Writer. **Publications:** The Church in the Thought of Bishop John Robinson, 1966; What Do We Really Believe?, 1969; Do We Need the Church?, 1969; Church: The Continuing Quest, 1970; Who Is a Catholic?, 1971; For the Inquiring Catholic, 1973; The Remaking of the Church: An Agenda for Reform, 1973; Has the Church Surrendered?, 1974; Roman Catholicism, 1975; In Search of God, 1977; Basic Questions for Christian Educators, 1977; Catholicism, 1980, rev. ed., 1994; Caesar's Coin: Religion and Politics in America, 1987; Ministry: A Theological, Pastoral Handbook, 1987; (ed.) American Catholics, 1989; Report on the Church: Catholicism after Vatican II, 1992; Inside Catholicism: Rituals and Symbols Revealed, 1995; (ed.) Harper Collins Encyclopedia of Catholicism, 1995; Responses to 101 Questions on the Church, 1996; Lives of the Popes: The Pontiffs from St. Peter to John Paul II, 1997; Lives of the Saints: From Mary and St. Francis of Assisi to John XXIII and Mother Teresa, 2001; Pocket Guide to the Saints, 2006; Pocket Guide to the Popes, 2006; Church: The Evolution of Catholicism, 2008. Contributor to journals. **Address:** Department of Theology, University of Notre Dame, 281 Decio Hall, Notre Dame, IN 46556-4619, U.S.A. **Online address:** rmcbrien@nd.edu

MCCABE, Angela. *See* **HALPERN, Daniel.**

MCCAFFERTY, Barbara Taylor. *See* **REUSCHE, Taylor McCafferty.**

MCCAFFERTY, Jane. American (born United States), b. 1960?. **Genres:** Novellas/Short Stories. **Career:** University of Pittsburgh, instructor in English, 1987-91; Allegheny College, writer-in-residence, 1991-93; Carnegie Mellon University, assistant professor of creative writing, associate professor of English. Writer. **Publications:** Director of the World and Other Stories, 1992; One Heart: A Novel, 1999; Thank You for the Music: Stories, 2004; (with J. Daniels) From Milltown to Malltown, 2010; First You Try Everything, 2012. **Address:** Departmentof English, Carnegie Mellon University, 245 N Baker Hall, 5000 Forbes Ave., Pittsburgh, PA 15213-3890, U.S.A. **Online address:** janem@andrew.cmu.edu

MCCAFFERTY, Jim. American (born United States), b. 1954. **Genres:** Children's Fiction. **Career:** University of Mississippi Wesley Foundation, chair of board of director, 1986-89; Newspaper columnist, 1986-93; Friends of the Jackson Zoo, board director, 1991-, secretary, 1993-; Books for the World, board director, 1992-; freelance writer and photographer for magazines and newspapers; lawyer and writer. **Publications:** Holt and the Teddy Bear, 1991; Holt and the Cowboys, 1993. **Address:** PO Box 5092, Jackson, MS 39296, U.S.A. **Online address:** jtm@netdoor.com

MCCAFFERTY, Maureen. American (born United States), b. 1954. **Genres:** Novels, Novellas/Short Stories, Literary Criticism And History, Children's Fiction. **Career:** City University of New York, Law School, department of faculty support, secretary, 1984-, Admission and Requirement Search, associate director, coordinator of faculty recruitment. Writer. **Publications:** Patchwork of Dreams, 1996; Let Go the Glass Voice, 1997. Contributor to periodicals. Works appear in anthologies. **Address:** School of Law, City University of New York, 65-21 Main St., Flushing, NY 11367-1358, U.S.A. **Online address:** mk@maclaw.law.cuny.edu

MCCAFFERTY, Taylor. *See* **REUSCHE, Taylor McCafferty.**

MCCAFFERY, Margo. (Margo Smith McCaffery). American (born United States), b. 1938. **Genres:** Medicine/Health, Young Adult Fiction. **Career:** Texas Women's University, instructor in surgical nursing, 1958-59; Navarro Co. Memorial Hospital, Surgical Unit, assistant head nurse, 1958-59; Vanderbilt University, assistant professor of nursing of children and chairman, 1961-62; University of California, instructor in pediatric nursing, 1962-65, assistant professor in pediatric nursing, 1965-70, junior research nurse, 1962-63, postgraduate research nurse, 1963; Nursing Care of Patients with Pain, consultant, 1970-; World Health Organization, Expert Committee on Cancer Pain Relief, staff. Writer. **Publications:** Clinical Nursing: Nursing Practice Theories Related to Cognition, Bodily Pain, and Man-Environment Interactions, 1968; Nursing Management of the Patient with Pain, 1972, 2nd ed., 1979; (with N.T. Meinhart) Pain: A Nursing Approach to Assessment and Analysis, 1983; Pain: Clinical Manual for Nursing Practice, 1989, (with C. Pasero) 2nd ed., 1999; (with C. Pasero) Pain Assessment and Pharmacologic Management, 2011. Contributor of articals to journals. **Address:** 8347 Kenyon Ave., Los Angeles, CA 90045-2740, U.S.A.

MCCAFFERY, Margo Smith. *See* **MCCAFFERY, Margo.**

MCCAFFERY, Steve. American/British (born England), b. 1947. **Genres:** Poetry, Novels, Literary Criticism And History. **Career:** York University, Department of English, teaching assistant, 1968-69, assistant professor, 1998-2000, associate professor, 2000-03, professor, 2003-04, Graduate Studies, faculty, 1998-; University of Toronto, New College, Summer Creative Writing Workshops, faculty, 1976-78; Blue Mountain College, faculty, 1976-83; Humber College of Applied Arts, Third Age Centre, faculty, 1978-81; University of California-San Diego, Department of Literature, lecturer, 1989; Queen's University, Department of English, lecturer, 1993-95; California Institute of the Arts, School of Critical Studies, visiting professor, 1997; North American Centre for Interdisciplinary Poetics, associate professor, 2001-, director and coordinator, 2001-; University of Cape Town, visiting professor, 2002; State University of New York-Buffalo, David Gray professor of poetry and letters, 2004-, David Gray chair of poetry and letters. Writer. **Publications:** POETRY: Transitions to the Beast: Post Semiotic Poems, 1970; Carnival: The First Panel, 1967-70, 1973; Dr. Sadhu's Muffins, 1974; 'Ow's Waif: And Other Poems, 1975; Carnival: The Second Panel, 1970-75, 1978; Intimate Distortions: A Displacement of Sappho, 1979; (with B.P. Nichol) In England Now That Spring: Polaroid Poems, Found Texts, Visions & Collaborations, Records of a Journey Thru Scotland & England May 1978, 1979; Evoba: The Investigations Meditations, 1976-78, 1987; The Black Debt, 1989; Theory of Sediment, 1991; The Cheat of Words, 1996; Seven Pages Missing, 2000; Bouma Shapes, 2002; Seven Pages Missing, 2002; Dark Ladies, 2006; (with A. Halsey) Paradigm of the Tinctures, 2007; The Basho Variations, 2007; Slightly Left of Thinking, 2008. NOVEL: Panopticon, 1984. OTHERS: Book of Written Readings, 1974; (ed. with B.P. Nichol) Story So Four, 1976; Six Fillious, 1978; (with B.P. Nichol) Sound Poetry: A Catalogue for the Eleventh International Sound Poetry Festival, Toronto,

Canada, October 14 to 21, 1978, 1979; Knowledge Never Knew, 1983; North of Intention: Critical Writings, 1973-1986, 1986, 2nd ed., 2000; (ed. and intro. with B.P. Nichol) Rational Geomancy: The Kids of the Book-Machine: The Collected Research Reports of the Toronto Research Group, 1973-1982, 1992; (ed. with J. Rasula) Imagining Language, 1998; Prior to Meaning: The Protosemantic and Poetics, 2001; Every Way Oakly: Homolinguistic Translations of Gertrude Stein's Tender Buttons, 2008; (ed. with S. Fredman) Form, Power, and Person in Robert Creeley's Life and Work, 2010. **Address:** The Poetics Program, State University of New York, 438 Clemens Hall, Buffalo, NY 14260-4610, U.S.A. **Online address:** stevemcc@buffalo.edu

MCCAFFREY, Anne (Inez). *See* Obituaries.

MCCAFFREY, James M. American (born United States), b. 1946. **Genres:** History, Military/Defense/Arms Control, Autobiography/Memoirs, Military/Defense/Arms Control. **Career:** University of Houston, Department of History, associate professor, professor, 1989-. Writer. **Publications:** This Band of Heroes: Granbury's Texas Brigade, C.S.A., 1985; Army of Manifest Destiny: The American Soldier in the Mexican War, 1846-1848, 1992; (with J.F. Kinney) Wake Island Pilot: A World War II Memoir, 1995; Surrounded by Dangers of All Kinds: The Mexican War Letters of Lieutenant Theodore Laidley, 1997; (ed.) Only a Private: A Texan Remembers the Civil War, 2004; Army in Transformation, 1790-1860, 2006; Inside the Spanish-American War: A History Based on First-Person Accounts, 2009. **Address:** Department of Social Sciences, University of Houston, Rm. N-1018, 1 Main St., Houston, TX 77002, U.S.A. **Online address:** mccaffreyj@uhd.edu

MCCAFFREY, K. T. Irish (born Ireland), b. 1947?. **Genres:** Mystery/Crime/Suspense, Illustrations, Novels. **Career:** Irish Tourist Board, design consultant. Illustrator of children's books, 1989-. Writer. **Publications:** Revenge, 1999; Killing Time, 1999; The Body Rock, 2001; End of the Line: A Novel, 2004; Bishop's Pawn, 2007; The Cat Trap, 2008; No Curtain Call, 2010. **Address:** Robert Hale Ltd., 45-47 Clerkenwell Grn., 16 The Woodlands, London, GL EC1R 0HT, England. **Online address:** ktmccaffrey@webmac.ie

MCCAIN, Charles. American (born United States), b. 1955. **Genres:** History, Novels. **Career:** Novelist. **Publications:** An Honorable German: A Novel of World War II, 2009. Contributor to periodicals. **Address:** Washington, DC , U.S.A. **Online address:** charles@charlesmccain.com

MCCAIN, Gillian. American/Canadian (born Canada), b. 1966. **Genres:** Poetry. **Career:** St. Mark's Church, The Poetry Project, programme coordinator, 1991-94, newsletter editor, 1994-95, president and board director. **Publications:** Tilt (poetry), 1996; (with L. McNeil) Please Kill Me: The Uncensored Oral History of Punk, 1996; Religion (poetry), 1999. Works appear in anthologies. Contributor to periodicals. **Address:** The Poetry Project, St. Mark's Church, 131 E 10th St., New York, NY 10003-7504, U.S.A. **Online address:** gmcfries@aol.com

MCCALL, Dan (Elliott). American (born United States), b. 1940. **Genres:** Novels, Literary Criticism And History, Young Adult Fiction. **Career:** Tokyo Language Institute, teacher, 1961; Columbia University, preceptor, 1964-66; Cornell University, assistant professor, 1966-71, associate professor of English, 1971-74, professor of English, 1974-2006, professor emeritus, 2006-; University of California, visiting professor, 1969; Allenwood Prison, discussion leader, 1969-70; University of Nice, visiting professor, 1972; The Claremont Colleges, visiting professor, 1977. Writer. **Publications:** The Man Says Yes, 1969; The Example of Richard Wright, 1969; Jack the Bear, 1974; Beecher: A Novel, 1979; Bluebird Canyon, 1983; Queen of Hearts, 1985; The Silence of Bartleby, 1989; Triphammer, 1990; Messenger Bird, 1993; Citizens of Somewhere Else: Nathaniel Hawthorne and Henry James, 1999; (ed.) Melville's Short Novels: Authoritative Texts, Contexts, Criticism, 2002. **Address:** Department of English, Cornell University, 250 Goldwin Smith Hall, Ithaca, NY 14853-3201, U.S.A. **Online address:** dem15@cornell.edu

MCCALL, Jeffrey. American (born United States), b. 1954. **Genres:** Adult Non-fiction, Communications/Media. **Career:** DePauw University, Department of Communication and Theatre, professor, John D. Hughes professor of communication and theatre, 1985-, WGRE Radio station, director. Writer. **Publications:** Viewer Discretion Advised: Taking Control of Mass Media Influences, 2007. **Address:** Department of Communication and Theatre, DePauw University, PCCM WGRE, PO Box 37, Greencastle, IN 46135-0037, U.S.A. **Online address:** jeffmccall@depauw.edu

MCCALL, Marsh Howard. American (born United States), b. 1939. **Genres:** Classics. **Career:** Harvard University, instructor in classics, 1965-68; Center for Hellenic Studies, fellow, 1968-69; Johns Hopkins University, assistant professor, 1969-70, associate professor of classics, 1970-75, chair of department, 1971-73; University of London, visiting professor, 1973-74; University of California, visiting associate professor of classics, 1975-76; Stanford University, associate professor of classics, 1976-, chair of department, 1977-, associate dean of undergraduate studies, dean of continuing studies, professor of classics and dean, now professor emeritus. Writer. **Publications:** Ancient Rhetorical Theories of Simile and Comparison, 1969; (ed.) Aeschylus: A Collection of Critical Essays, 1972. Contributor to journals. **Address:** Departmentt of Classics, Stanford University, Rm. 205, Bldg. 110, 450 Serra Mall, PO Box 2145, Stanford, CA 94305-2145, U.S.A. **Online address:** mmccall@stanford.edu

MCCALL, Richard D. American (born United States), b. 1947?. **Genres:** Theology/Religion, History, Education. **Career:** Episcopal Divinity School, associate professor of liturgy and church music, 1999-; St. John's Memorial Chapel, provost, 1999-; General Board of Examining Chaplains of the Episcopal Church, chaplain; Indiana University, English/Theatre Program, director; Adelphi University, adjunct faculty in acting and directing; Cathedral of the Incarnation, canon residentiary and director of educational ministries; St. Paul's Church, rector; Church Divinity School of the Pacific, dean of the chapel and lecturer in liturgics. Writer. **Publications:** Do This: Liturgy as Performance, 2007. Contributor to books and periodicals. **Address:** Episcopal Divinity School, 99 Brattle St., Cambridge, MA 02138-3402, U.S.A. **Online address:** rmccall@eds.edu

MCCALL, Robert B. (Robert Booth McCall). American (born United States), b. 1940. **Genres:** Psychology, Human Relations/Parenting, Mathematics/Statistics, Communications/Media, Medicine/Health. **Career:** University of Illinois, Department of Psychology, teaching assistant, 1963-64, NIH Predoctoral fellow; Harvard University, Department of Social Relations, National Science Foundation fellow, 1965-66; University of North Carolina, assistant professor of psychology, 1966-68; Antioch College, associate professor, 1968-77; Fels Research Institute, Department of Psychology, senior scientist and chief, 1968-77, Section on Perceptual Cognitive Development, chief, 1971-77; University of Kansas, Department of Human Development and Family Life, adjunct professor, 1977-86; Father Flanagan's Boys Town, senior scientist and science writer, 1977-86, Program Planning and Evaluation, executive assistant to the director, 1985-86; University of Nebraska, Department of Psychology, graduate faculty fellow, 1978-86; Parents Magazine, contributing editor and monthly columnist, 1980-89; University of Pittsburgh, Office of Child Development, professor of psychology and co-director, 1986-. **Publications:** Fundamental Statistics for Psychology, 1970, 8th ed., 2001; (with M.I. Appelbaum and P.S. Hogarty) Developmental Changes in Mental Performance, 1973; Exploratory Manipulation and Play in the Human Infant, 1974; (with D.H. Eichorn and P.S. Hogarty) Transitions in Early Mental Development, 1977; (with R.D. Parke and R.D. Kavanaugh) Imitation of Live and Televised Models by Children One to Three Years of Age, 1977; Infants, 1979; (with V.E. Pomeranz) Your Child's First Year, 1986; (with C. Evahn and L. Kratzer) High School Underachievers, 1992; Contributor of articles. **Address:** Office of Child Development, University of Pittsburgh, 400 N Lexington Ave., Pittsburgh, PA 15208, U.S.A. **Online address:** mccall2@pitt.edu

MCCALL, Robert Booth. *See* **MCCALL, Robert B.**

MCCALL, Storrs. Canadian (born Canada), b. 1930. **Genres:** Philosophy, Earth Sciences, Mathematics/Statistics, Sciences, Social Sciences, Politics/Government. **Career:** McGill University, assistant professor of philosophy, 1955-63, professor of philosophy, 1975-; University of Pittsburgh, associate professor of philosophy, 1963-71; Makerere University, visiting professor of philosophy, 1965-71. Writer. **Publications:** Aristotle's Modal Syllogisms, 1963; Polish Logic, 1920-39, 1967; A Model of the Universe: Space-time, Probability and Decision, 1994. **Address:** Department of Philosophy, McGill University, Rm. 915, Leacock Bldg., 845 Sherbrooke St. W, Montreal, QC H3A 2T5, Canada. **Online address:** storrs.mccall@mcgill.ca

MCCALL, Wendell. *See* **PEARSON, Ridley.**

MCCALLUM, Shara. American/Jamaican (born Jamaica), b. 1972. **Genres:** Poetry, Literary Criticism And History. **Career:** University of Memphis, assistant professor of English. Writer. **Publications:** The Water Between Us,

1999; Song of Thieves, 2003. Contributor of articles to journals. Works appear in anthologies. **Address:** Department of English, University of Memphis, Patterson 431, Memphis, TN 38152, U.S.A. **Online address:** smmccllm@memphis.edu

MCCALLUM, Taffy Gould. American (born United States), b. 1942. **Genres:** Cultural/Ethnic Topics, Young Adult Non-fiction, Social Sciences, Politics/Government. **Career:** Camp Seneca, head counselor, 1962-63; Wometco Enterprises, computer programmer, 1963-64; Everglades School for Girls, teacher of French and mathematics, 1964-66; De Barros & Beber Interior Designs, business manager, 1973-74; Economic Research Analysts, financial planner, 1973-75; WPBT-TV, director of public information and special projects, 1975-76, director of program underwriting, 1976-77, on-air interviewer, 1976-79; Housing Engineers of Florida Inc., director of leasing, 1978-83, executive vice president, 1992-97, president, 1998-; National Benefit Auction, director of promotion and advertising, 1979-80. Writer. **Publications:** South Africa: Land of Hope, 1989; (comp.) White Woman Witchdoctor: Tales of the African Life of Rae Graham, 1994; (with L. Georgian) Create Your Own Future: A Practical Guide to Developing Your Psychic and Spiritual Powers, 1996. **Address:** 10 Edgewater Dr., Ste. 14F, Coral Gables, FL 33133-6968, U.S.A. **Online address:** taffyg@bellsouth.net

MCCALLY, David. American (born United States), b. 1949. **Genres:** Environmental Sciences/Ecology, Natural History. **Career:** Eckerd College, visiting assistant professor, 1995-99; University of South Florida, visiting professor of history, 1998-99, 2000-01; Bethune-Cookman College, visiting professor of history, 1999-2000; University of Florida, adjunct professor of history, 2001-02. Writer. **Publications:** The Everglades: An Environmental History, 1999; Ecology of Dreams: Americans in South Florida, forthcoming. **Address:** 2519 NW 4th Terr., Gainesville, FL 32609-2975, U.S.A. **Online address:** davidmccally@aol.com

MCCALMAN, Iain. Australian (born Australia), b. 1947. **Genres:** History. **Career:** Australian National University, professor, Centre for Cross-Cultural Research, deputy director, Humanities Research Centre, director; University of Sydney, research professor; Manchester University, visiting fellow; Oxford University, visiting fellow; Edinburgh University, Institute for Advanced Studies in the Humanities, visiting fellow; Washington University, visiting fellow; Research School for Social Sciences, visiting fellow. Writer and historian. **Publications:** Radical Underworld: Prophets, Revolutionaries, and Pornographers in London, 1795-1840, 1988; (ed. and intro.) The Horrors of Slavery and Other Writings, 1991; (ed.) An Oxford Companion to the Romantic Age: British Culture 1776-1832, 1999; (ed. with A. Cook and A. Reeves) Gold: Forgotten Histories and Lost Objects of Australia, 2001; The Seven Ordeals of Count Cagliostro: The Greatest Enchanter of the Eighteenth Century in US as The Last Alchemist: Count Cagliostro, Master of Magic in the Age of Reason, 2003; (ed. with A. McGrath) Proof and Truth: The Humanist as Expert, 2003; (ed. with M.T. Davis and C. Parolin) Newgate in Revolution: An Anthology of Radical Prison Literature in the Age of Revolution, 2005; (ed. with N. Erskine) In the Wake of the Beagle: Science in the Southern Oceans from the Age of Darwin in US as Darwin's Armada: Four Voyages and the Battle for the Theory of Evolution, 2009. **Address:** Department of History, School of Philosophical and Historical Inquiry, University of Sydney, Sydney, NW 2006, Australia. **Online address:** iain.mccalman@arts.usyd.edu.au

MCCAMANT, Jim. American (born United States), b. 1933. **Genres:** Money/Finance, Sciences, Business/Trade/Industry. **Career:** Medical Technology Stock Letter (MTSL), editor, 1984-2001, editor-at-large, 2001-; Shaefer, Lowe & McCamant and San Francisco Investment Corp. (brokerage firms), founder and principal. **Publications:** Biotech Investing: Every Investor's Guide, 2002. Contributor of periodicals. **Address:** Medical Technology Stock Letter, 2748 Adeline St., Ste. A, PO Box 40460, Berkeley, CA 94703-2251, U.S.A. **Online address:** mtsl@bioinvest.com

MCCANN, Colum. American/Irish (born Ireland), b. 1965. **Genres:** Novellas/Short Stories, Novels, Young Adult Fiction. **Career:** European Graduate School, professor, writer-in-residence; Hunter College's Master of Fine Arts Program in Creative Writing, professor; The Irish Press, journalist; Herald, staff; Connaught Telegraph, staff; United Press, staff; Evening Press, youth correspondent, 1984-85, Hunter College, faculty of creative writing. **Publications:** Fishing the Sloe-Black River (short stories), 1993; Songdogs (novel), 1995; This Side of Brightness, 1998; Everything in This Country Must (stories), 2000; Dancer: A Novel, 2003; Zoli: A Novel, 2006; (contrib.) The World Unfurled, 2008; Let the Great World Spin, 2009; Thirteen Ways of Looking, 2013. Contributor to books and periodicals. **Address:** c/o Sarah Chalfant, Wylie Agency, 250 W 57th St., Ste. 2114, New York, NY 10107, U.S.A.

MCCANN, Graham. British (born England), b. 1961. **Genres:** Biography, Film, Autobiography/Memoirs. **Career:** Cambridge University, King's College, lecturer in social and political theory, 1986-. Writer. **Publications:** Marilyn Monroe: The Body in the Library, 1988; Woody Allen: New Yorker, 1990; Rebel Males: Clift, Brando, and Dean, 1993; Cary Grant: A Class Apart, 1996; Morecambe and Wise, 1998; Dad's Army: The Story of a Classic Television Show, 2001; Frankie Howerd: Stand-Up Comic, 2004; Spike & Co: Inside the House of Fun with Milligan, Sykes, Galton & Simpson, 2006; (intro.) Composing for the Films, 2007; Fawlty Towers: The Story of the Sitcom, 2007; Do You Think That's Wise: The Life of John Le Mesurier, 2010. **Address:** Faculty of Social & Political Sciences, Cambridge University, The Old Schools, Trinity Ln., Cambridge, CB2 1TN, England.

MCCANN, James C. American (born United States), b. 1950. **Genres:** History, Area Studies. **Career:** Addis Ababa University, Institute of Ethiopian Studies, research associate, 1982, 1985; Boston University, faculty, 1984, African Studies Center, director, 1992-95; professor of history and associate director for development; International Livestock Commission for Africa (ILCA), staff, 1985-86; Oxfam, consultant on Ethiopia, 1987; American Jewish World Service/Save the Children, consultant on social context of food storage, 1990; International Center for the Improvement of Maize and Wheat (CIMMYT), visiting scientist, 2000, Mother-Baby Maize Breeding Program, visiting scientist, 2004; University of Oslo, Norwegian Centre for Human Rights, consultant, 2005. Writer. **Publications:** Household Economy, Demography, and the Push Factor in Northern Ethiopian History, 1916-1935, 1983; Plows, Oxen, and Household Managers: A Reconsideration of the Land Paradigm and the Production Equation in Northeast Ethiopia, 1984; The Political Economy of Rural Rebellion in Ethiopia: Northern Resistance to Imperial Expansion, 1928-1935, 1984; From Poverty to Famine in Northeast Ethiopia: A Rural History, 1900-1935, 1987; A Great Agrarian Cycle? A History of Agricultural Productivity and Demographic Change in Highland Ethiopia, 1900-1987, 1988; Frontier Agriculture, Food Supply, and Conjuncture: A Revolution in Dura on Ethiopia's Mazega, 1898- 1930, 1989; People of the Plow: An Agricultural History of Ethiopia, 1800-1990, 1995; Green Land, Brown Land, Black Land: An Environmental History of Africa, 1800-1990, 1999; Maize and Grace: Africa's Encounter with a New World Crop, 1500-2000, 2005; Stirring the Pot: African Cuisine and Global Change, 1500-2000, 2009. CONTRIBUTOR: Drought and Hunger in Africa: Denying Famine a Future, 1987; Ecology and Stress in Northeast Africa: Historical and Anthropological Perspectives, 1987; The End of Slavery in Africa, 1988; The Political Economy of Ethiopia, 1990; Drought Follows the Plow: Marginal Land Agriculture in Seven Countries, 1993; African Studies and the Undergraduate Curriculum: New Directions for the 21st Century, 1994; Creeping Environmental Phenomena, 1994; Personality and Political Culture in African History, 1998; The Ethiopian Elections: Democracy Advanced or Restricted, 2000; Transatlantic Rebels: Agrarianism in Comparative Context, 2004; The City and the Country: New Themes in Environmental History, 2005. Contributor to journals. **Address:** African Studies Ctr., Boston University, 270 Bay State Rd., Boston, MA 02215, U.S.A. **Online address:** mccann@bu.edu

MCCANN, Maria. British (born England), b. 1956?. **Genres:** Novels, Adult Non-fiction, Young Adult Fiction, Romance/Historical. **Career:** Strode College, lecturer in English, 1985-. Novelist. **Publications:** As Meat Loves Salt, 2001; The Wilding, 2010. **Address:** Strode College, Church Road St., Tunbridge Wells, Somerset, SM BA16 0AB, England.

MCCANN, Michelle R. (Michelle Roehm McCann). American (born United States), b. 1968. **Genres:** Children's Fiction, Biography. **Career:** Beyond Words Publishing, Children's Division, founder and director, 1991-2001; Graphic Arts Publishing Center, children's book editor, 2001-; Portland State University, adjunct professor, 2002-. **Publications:** CHILDREN'S BOOKS: Girls Know Best, 1997; Boys Know It All, 1998; Girls Who Rocked the World 2, 2000; Boys Who Rocked the World, 2001; Luba: The Angel of Bergen- Belsen (biography of L.Tryszynska-Frederick), 2003. AS MICHELLE ROEHM McCANN: Going Places: True Tales from Young Travelers, 2003; (with M. Monson-Burton) Finding Fairies: Secrets for Attracting Little People from Around the World, 2004. **Address:** 1025 SE Lexington St., Portland, OR 97202, U.S.A. **Online address:** mrmccann@easystreet.com

MCCANN, Michelle Roehm. *See* **MCCANN, Michelle R.**

MCCANN, Philip. *See* **FELSTEIN, Ivor.**

MCCANN, Richard. American (born United States), b. 1949. **Genres:** Novellas/Short Stories, Poetry, Medicine/Health, Essays. **Career:** University of Maryland, European Division, lecturer in film history, 1978-82; Goteborgs Universite, Fulbright lecturer in American studies, 1982-83; Mary Washington College, assistant professor of English, 1983-86; George Washington University, Jenny McKean Moore writer-in-Washington, 1987-88; American University, professor of literature, 1988-; PEN/Faulkner Foundation, director; Provincetown Arts, advisory editor. **Publications:** FICTION: Mother of Sorrows, 2005. POETRY: Dream of the Traveler, 1976; Nights of 1990, 1994; Nights of 1990, 1994; Ghost Letters, 1994. EDITOR: Through Parable Streets, 1971; (with M. Gibson) Landscape and Distance: Contemporary Poets from Virginia, 1975; (with M. Klein) Things Shaped in Passing: More Poets for Life Writing from the AIDS Pandemic, 1997. Contributor to magazines. **Address:** Department of Literature, American University, 229 Battelle-Tompkins, 4400 Massachusetts Ave. NW, Washington, DC 20016, U.S.A. **Online address:** rmccann@american.edu

MCCANNON, John. American (born United States), b. 1967. **Genres:** History, Art/Art History. **Career:** University of Chicago, teaching fellow, 1993; Northeast Louisiana University, assistant professor of history, 1994-96; Norwich University, assistant professor of history, 1996-99; Long Island University, assistant professor of history, 1999-2001; University of Saskatchewan, associate professor of history, 2001-11, director of undergraduate studies; Canadian Journal of History, editor; Southern New Hampshire University, professor of history, 2011-. **Publications:** Red Arctic: Polar Exploration and the Myth of the North in the Soviet Union, 1932-1939, 1998; How To Prepare for the AP Examination in World History, 2002; The Arctic: A Brief Global History, 2012. Contributor of articles to journals. **Address:** School of Arts and Sciences, Southern New Hampshire University, 2500 N River Rd., Nashua, NH 03106, U.S.A. **Online address:** j.mccannon@snhu.edu

MCCANTS, Clyde T. American (born United States), b. 1933. **Genres:** Music, Art/Art History, Biography, Autobiography/Memoirs. **Career:** Elon University, assistant professor of English, 1955-60; Erskine College, assistant professor and associate professor of English, 1960-65; Gaston Community College, faculty and department chair, 1965-67; Lauderdale Associate Reformed Presbyterian Church, pastor, 1970-73; Associate Reformed Presbyterian Church, director of church extension, 1974-77; Associate Reformed Presbyterian Church, pastor, 1977-78; Erskine Theological Seminary, faculty, 1978-82; Associate Reformed Presbyterian Church, pastor, 1982-93; Bethel Associate Reformed Presbyterian Church, pastor, 1993-98; Friends of South Carolina Libraries, chairman, 1998-2000; County Library Commission, chairman, 1998-2002. Writer. **Publications:** Opera for Libraries: A Guide to Core Works Audio and Video Recordings Books and Serials, 2003; American Opera Singers and Their Recordings: Critical Commentaries and Discographies, 2004; Verdi's Aida: A Record of the Life of the Opera on and Off the Stage, 2006; Rigoletto, Trovatore and Traviata: Verdi's Middle Period Masterpieces On and Off The Stage, 2009. **Address:** White Oak ARP Church, 284 Patrick Rd., Winnsboro, SC 29180-6630, U.S.A.

MCCANTS, William D. American (born United States), b. 1961. **Genres:** Education, Humor/Satire, Young Adult Fiction, Romance/Historical. **Career:** South Gate Middle School, Los Angeles Unified School District, teacher of history and English, 1987-91; Massachusetts Institute of Technology, associate housemaster, 1992-; Lexington High School, psychology instructor, 1993-. Writer. **Publications:** Anything Can Happen in High School (and It Usually Does), 1993; Much Ado about Prom Night, 1995. **Address:** Green Hall, Ste. 115, 350 Memorial Dr., Cambridge, MA 02139, U.S.A.

MCCAREY, Peter. Swiss/Scottish (born Scotland), b. 1956. **Genres:** Poetry, Philosophy, Literary Criticism And History. **Career:** World Health Organization, translator, 1988-, Language Services, head; United Nations One Percent for Development Fund, project manager, 1988-97; Southfields, associate editor. 1997-99. **Publications:** Hugh MacDiarmid and the Russians, 1987; (with A. Riach) For What It Is, 1988; Town Shanties, 1990; The Devil in the Driving Mirror, 1995; Tantris; Double Click, 1997; Translator Trattoria, 1998; In the Metaforest, 2000; The Syllabary, 2002; Collected Contraptions, 2011. **Address:** World Health Organization, 20 Appia Ave., Geneva, 1211, Switzerland.

MCCARGO, Duncan. British (born England), b. 1963. **Genres:** History, Autobiography/Memoirs, Biography, Communications/Media, Politics/Government. **Career:** Queen's University of Belfast, faculty; Kobe Gakuin University, faculty; National University of Singapore, Asia Research Institute, visiting senior research fellow, 2006-07; University of Leeds, School of Politics and International Studies, professor of Southeast Asian politics. Writer and political scientist. **Publications:** (With R. Bowra) Policy Advocacy and the Media in Thailand, 1997; Chamlong Srimuang and the New Thai Politics, 1997; Contemporary Japan, 2000, 2nd ed., 2004; Politics and the Press in Thailand: Media Machinations, 2000; (ed.) Reforming Thai Politics, 2002; Media and Politics in Pacific Asia, 2003; (ed.) Rethinking Vietnam, 2004; (with U. Pathmanand) The Thaksinization of Thailand, 2005; (ed.) Rethinking Thailand's Southern Violence, 2007; Tearing Apart the Land: Islam and Legitimacy in Southern Thailand, 2008. Contributor to books and periodicals. **Address:** School of Politics and International Studies, University of Leeds, Social Sciences Bldg., Leeds, WY LS2 9JT, England. **Online address:** d.j.mccargo@leeds.ac.uk

MCCARRY, Charles. American (born United States), b. 1930. **Genres:** Novels, Biography, Literary Criticism And History. **Career:** Lisbon Evening Journal, editor and reporter, 1952-55; Youngstown Vindicator, reporter and columnist, 1955-56; confidential assistant to the secretary of labor, 1956-58; Central Intelligence Agency, staff, 1958-67; freelance journalist, 1967-83; National Geographic Magazine, editor-at-large, 1983-90. **Publications:** Citizen Nader (biography), 1972; The Miernik Dossier, 1973; The Tears of Autumn, 1975; The Secret Lovers, 1977; Double Eagle, 1979; The Better Angels, 1979; The Great Southwest, 1980; (co-author) Isles of the Caribbean, 1980; The Last Supper, 1983; (with A.M. Haig) Caveat: Realism, Reagan and Foreign Policy, 1983; The Bride of the Wilderness, 1988; (with D.T. Regan) For the Record: From Wall Street to Washington, 1988; Paths of Resistance: The Art and Craft of the Political Novel, 1989; Second Sight, 1991; (with A.M. Haig) Inner Circles: How America Changed the World: A Memoir, 1992; Shelley's Heart, 1995; (ed.) From the Field, 1997; From the Field: A Collection of Writings from National Geographic, 1997; Lucky Bastard, 1998; Old Boys, 2004; Tears of Autumn, 2005; Christopher's Ghosts, 2007. Contributor to periodicals. **Address:** c/o Owen Laster, William Morris Agency, 1350 Ave. of the Americas, New York, NY 10019, U.S.A.

MCCARTHY, Colin (John). British (born England), b. 1951. **Genres:** Natural History, Animals/Pets, Children's Fiction. **Career:** Natural History Museum, curator in reptile and amphibian group, 1970-90, assistant scientific officer, 1970-75, scientific officer, 1975-79, higher scientific officer, 1979-89, senior scientific officer, 1989, collections manager, 1990-. Writer. **Publications:** Poisonous Snakes, 1987; (with P. Perry) The Concise Illustrated Book of Reptiles, 1990; Reptile, 1991. Contributor of articles to journals. **Address:** Natural History Museum, Cromwell Rd., London, GL SW7 5BD, England. **Online address:** cjm@nhm.ac.uk

MCCARTHY, Cormac. American (born United States), b. 1933. **Genres:** Novels, Plays/Screenplays. **Career:** Tennessee Valley Authority, legal staff 1934-67, chief counsel 1958-67; principal attorney, 1967-, now retired; Random House, editorial advisement. Writer. **Publications:** NOVELS: The Orchard Keeper, 1965; Outer Dark, 1968; Child of God, 1974; Suttree, 1979; Blood Meridian, or, The Evening Redness in the West, 1985; All the Pretty Horses, 1992; The Crossing, 1994; Cities of the Plain, 1998; Border Trilogy, 1999; No Country for Old Men, 2005; Road, 2006; Sunset Limited: A Novel in Dramatic Form, 2006. PLAYS: The Gardener's Son (teleplay), 1977; The Stonemason: A Play in Five Acts, 1994. **Address:** c/o Amanda Urban, International Creative Management, 40 W 57th St., New York, NY 10019, U.S.A.

MCCARTHY, Gary. American (born United States), b. 1943. **Genres:** Romance/Historical, Westerns/Adventure, Novels. **Career:** State of Nevada, occupational specialist, 1970-76, labor economist, 1970-77, rehabilitation program evaluator, 1977-; Copley International Corp., economist, 1977-79; writer, 1979-. **Publications:** The Derby Man, 1976; Showdown at Snakegrass Junction, 1978; The First Sheriff, 1979; Mustang Fever, 1980; The Pony Express War, 1980; Winds of Gold, 1980; Silver Shot, 1981; Explosion at Donner Pass, 1981; The Legend of the Lone Ranger (novelization of screenplay), 1981; North Chase, 1982; Rebel of Bodie, 1982; The Rail Warriors, 1983; Silver Winds, 1983; Wind River, 1984; Powder River, 1985; The Last Buffalo Hunt, 1985; Mando, 1986; Protecting The President, 1986; The Mustangers, 1987; Transcontinental, 1987; Sodbuster, 1988; Apache Gold, 1988; Blood Brothers, 1989; The Colorado, 1989; The Russian River, 1990; Gringo

Amigo, 1990; Whiskey Creek, 1992; The American River, 1992; The Horsemen, 1992; Cherokee Lighthorse, 1992; Blue Bullet, 1993; Comstock Camels, 1993; The Gila River, 1993; Ambushers, 1994; Yosemite, 1995; Grand Canyon, 1996; The Humboldt River, 1996; Mesa Verde, 1997; Stallion Valley, 1994; Los Angeles Lakers Facts and Trivia, 1996; Yellowstone, 1998; The Cimarron River, 1998; Gunsmoke vol. I, 1998, vol. II, 1999, vol. III, 1999; Dead Man's Witness: A Novel, 1999; Marshal Festus: A Novel, 1999; Bordertown Justice, 2000; The Buffalo Hunters, 2001; Restitution, 2003; Maddie O'Brien's Christmas Donkeys, 2010; Yosemite, 2010; Grand Canyon Thunder, 2011; Yellowstone Thunder, 2011; Mesa Verde Thunder, 2011; Yosemite Thunder, 2011; River Thunder, 2011. **Address:** PO Box 161, Williams, AZ 86046, U.S.A. **Online address:** gary@canyoncountrybooks.com

MCCARTHY, John F. Australian (born Australia), b. 1964. **Genres:** Politics/Government, Environmental Sciences/Ecology. **Career:** Murdoch University, Asia Research Centre, research fellow; Australian National University, Crawford School of Economics and Government, Environmental Management and Development Programme, senior lecturer. Writer, political scientist, anthropologist and researcher. **Publications:** The Fourth Circle: A Political Ecology of Sumatra's Rainforest Frontier, 2006; (ed. with C. Warren) Community, Environment and Local Governance in Indonesia: Locating the Commonweal, 2009. Contributor to books and periodicals. **Address:** Australia. **Online address:** john.mccarthy@anu.edu.au

MCCARTHY, Justin. (Justin A. McCarthy). American (born United States), b. 1945. **Genres:** History, Area Studies, Cultural/Ethnic Topics. **Career:** Middle East Technical University and Ankara University, Peace Corps, staff, 1967-69; University of California, computer programmer, 1973-77; University of Louisville, professor of history, 1978-, department head, 1986-92, Institute for the Social Studies and Humanities, director, 1995-97, distinguished professor of arts and sciences, 1996; Princeton University, Office of Population Research, visiting research fellow, 1979-80; University of London, London School of Oriental and African Studies, visiting fellow, 1984-85; Bogazici University, visiting professor, 1985. Writer. **Publications:** The Arab World, Turkey and the Balkans (1878-1914), 1982; Muslims and Minorities: The Population of Ottoman Anatolia and the End of the Empire, 1983; (with C. McCarthy) Turks and Armenians: A Manual on the Armenian Question, 1989; The Population of Palestine: Population History and Statistics of the Late Ottoman Period and the Mandate, 1990; (with T. Halman and U. Bates) Focus on Turkey, 1991; The Muslims of Bosnia-Herzegovina, 1994; The Jews of the Ottoman Empire, 1995; Death and Exile: Ethnic Cleansing of the Ottoman Muslims, 1821-1922, 1995; The Ottoman Turks: An Introductory History to 1923, 1997; Ottoman Peoples and the End of Empire, 2001; Population History of the Middle East and the Balkans, 2002; (with J. McCarthy) Who are the Turks?: A Manual For Teachers, 2003; (co-author) The Armenian Rebellion at Van, 2006; The Turk in America: Creation of an Enduring Prejudice, 2010; (with McCarthy) A Teachers' Manual on the Ottoman Turks, forthcoming. Contributor to books and journals. **Address:** Department of History, University of Louisville, Gottschalk Hall, 2301 S 3rd St, Louisville, KY 40292, U.S.A. **Online address:** jmc@louisville.edu

MCCARTHY, Justin A. *See* **MCCARTHY, Justin.**

MCCARTHY, Mignon. American (born United States), b. 1911?. **Genres:** Adult Non-fiction, Women's Studies And Issues, Autobiography/Memoirs, Biography. **Career:** California Campaign for Economic Democracy, executive director, 1980-82; Jane Fonda's Workout Inc., officer and director, 1980-83; writer, 1982-. **Publications:** (With J. Fonda) Women Coming of Age (nonfiction), 1984; (with K. Abdul-Jabbar) Kareem (memoir), 1990. Contributor to periodicals. **Address:** c/o Esther Newberg, International Creative Management Inc., 40 W 57th St., New York, NY 10019-4001, U.S.A.

MCCARTHY, Nan. (Nancy J. McCarthy). American (born United States), b. 1961. **Genres:** Novels, Writing/Journalism, Autobiography/Memoirs, Popular Culture, Technology, Information Science/Computers, Marketing, Communications/Media, E-books, Reference. **Career:** This Week on Okinawa Magazine, editor, 1983-85; Personal Publishing Magazine, managing editor, 1987-91; Quark Inc., Creative Services Department, editorial director, 1991-92; Rainwater Press, founder, 1992-; The Kansas City Star, Midwest Voices, columnist, 2005. Author, publisher and public speaker. **Publications:** (As Nancy J. McCarthy) Quark Design: A Step-by-Step Approach to Page Layout Software, 1995; Chat, 1998; Connect, 1998; Crash, 1998; Live 'til I Die: A Memoir of My Father's Life, 2002. **Address:** Rainwater Press, 9414 W 141st St., Overland Park, KS 66221-2156, U.S.A. **Online address:** nan@rainwater.com

MCCARTHY, Nancy J. *See* **MCCARTHY, Nan.**

MCCARTHY, Patrick A. American (born United States), b. 1945. **Genres:** Literary Criticism And History. **Career:** Murray State University, instructor in English, 1968-69; William Paterson College of New Jersey, instructor in English, 1973-74; State University of New York at Binghamton, visiting assistant professor of English, 1974-75; Broome Community College, instructor in English, 1975-76; University of Miami, Department of English, assistant professor, 1976-81, associate professor, 1981-84, professor, 1984-, interim chair, 2003-04, chair, 2005-, director of graduate studies, 1986-95, director of undergraduate studies, 1998-99, acting chair of history department, 2002-03. Writer. **Publications:** The Riddles of Finnegans Wake, 1980; Olaf Stapledon, 1982; Ulysses: Portals of Discovery, 1990; Forests of Symbols: World, Text and Self in Malcolm Lowry's Fiction, 1994. EDITOR: Critical Essays on Samuel Beckett, 1986; (with C. Elkins and M.H. Greenberg) The Legacy of Olaf Stapledon: Critical Essays and an Unpublished Manuscript, 1989; Critical Essays on James Joyce's Finnegans Wake, 1992; Malcolm Lowry's La Mordida: A Scholarly Edition, 1996; (with P. Tiessen) Joyce/Lowry: Critical Perspectives, 1997; Star Maker, 2004. **Address:** Department of English, University of Miami, Rm. 321, Ashe Bldg., 1252 Memorial Dr., Coral Gables, FL 33124, U.S.A. **Online address:** p.mccarthy@miami.edu

MCCARTHY, Sherri N. (Sherri Nevada McCarthy-Tucker). American (born United States), b. 1958. **Genres:** Psychology, Human Relations/Parenting, Education, Romance/Historical, Poetry, Social Sciences. **Career:** Journalist, 1976-84; Johns Hopkins University, Center for Talented Youth, Young Students Program, instructor, 1985-86; Arizona State University, instructor, 1985-86, teaching assistant, 1991-93, faculty associate, 1993-96; Fountain Hills School District, coordinator and instructor, 1985-87; Knox Elementary, instructor, 1987-90; Maricopa County Community Colleges, faculty associate in liberal arts, 1988-96; Kohala High School, special education instructor and psychologist, 1990-91; Parker School, Community Education Program, faculty, 1990-91; Northern Arizona University, Statewide Programs, faculty associate, 1993-94, Department of Educational Psychology, assistant professor, 1996-, associate professor of educational psychology, professor; Chandler-Gilbert Community College, psychology faculty and department chair, 1994-96; Vologda State Pedagogical University, professor of psychology, 2003-04; Leningrad State Regional University, professor of psychology, 2003-04; Universidade Federal do Rio Grande do Sul, professor, 2004-06; International Council of Psychologists, board director, 2005-; Asian Psychological Association, board director, 2006-; Engaging Peace, board director, 2010-. **Publications:** Metamorphosis-A Book of Poems, 1974; A Comparison of Three Methods of Teaching Reading, 1987; A Death in the Family, 1988; Personal Filing Systems: Creating Information Retrieval Systems on Microcomputers, 1988; (as Sherri N. McCarthy-Tucker) Coping with Special-Needs Classmates, 1993; Teaching Reality-Based Formal Logic to Adolescents to Improve Critical Thinking Skills, 1995; (ed. with C.S. Hutz) Preventing Teen Violence, 2006; (with V. Karandashev) International Practices in the Teaching of Psychology, 2006; Teaching Psychology Around the World, vol. I, 2007, vol. II, 2009, vol. III, forthcoming; (ed. with J.L.S. Jaafar) Building Asian Families and Communities in the 21st Century, 2009; East Meets West: Parenting in a Changing World, 2010; (with K. Malley-Morrison) International Handbook of Peace and Reconciliation, forthcoming; (with K. Malley-Morrison and D. Hines) International Handbook of Government Aggression, forthcoming; (with K. Moore) Asian Psychology, forthcoming. Contributor to journals. **Address:** Department of Educational Psychology, Northern Arizona University, Rm. 219, AC Bldg., 2020 S Ave. 8E, PO Box 6236, Yuma, AZ 85365, U.S.A. **Online address:** sherri.mccarthy@nau.edu

MCCARTHY, Susan. American (born United States) **Genres:** Agriculture/Forestry, Animals/Pets, Environmental Sciences/Ecology, Zoology. **Career:** Writer. **Publications:** (With J.M. Masson) When Elephants Weep: The Emotional Lives of Animals, 1995; Becoming a Tiger: How Baby Animals Learn to Live in the Wild, 2004. Contributor to periodicals. **Address:** c/o Author Mail, HarperCollins Publishers Inc., 10 E 53rd St., New York, NY 10022, U.S.A.

MCCARTHY, Thomas. Irish (born Ireland), b. 1954?. **Genres:** Poetry, Novels, Young Adult Fiction, Young Adult Non-fiction. **Career:** Writer and poet,

1978-; Cork City Libraries, librarian and assistant director, 1978-; Macalester College, visiting international professor, 1994-95. **Publications:** POETRY: The First Convention, 1978; The Sorrow Garden, 1981; The Non-Aligned Storyteller, 1984; Seven Winters in Paris, 1989; The Lost Province, 1996; Mr. Dineen's Careful Parade: New and Selected Poems, 1999; Merchant Prince, 2005. OTHERS: Without Power (novel), 1991; Asya and Christine (novel), 1992; Gardens of Remembrance, 1998; (ed.) Turning Tide: New Writing from County Waterford, 2002; Last Geraldine Officer, 2009. Contributor to periodicals. **Address:** Cork City Libraries, 57-61 Grand Parade, Grand Parade, CK 2, Ireland.

MCCARTHY, Wil. American (born United States), b. 1966. **Genres:** Science Fiction/Fantasy, Novels, Children's Fiction, Young Adult Fiction, Literary Criticism And History. **Career:** Lockheed-Martin Corp., space launch systems engineer, 1988-97, flight systems engineer, 1997-98; Omnitech Robotics, systems engineering manager, 1998-2000, senior research and development engineer, 1999-; Colorado Free University, creative writing instructor; Jefferson County Adult/Continuing Education Program, creative writing instructor. Writer. **Publications:** SERIES: Aggressor Six, 1994; Flies from the Amber, 1995; Fall of Sirius, 1996. NOVELS: Murder in the Solid State, 1996; Bloom, 1998; The Collapsium, 2000; The Wellstone, 2003; Lost in Transmission, 2004; To Crush the Moon, 2005. NON-FICTION: Hacking Matter: Levitating Chairs, Quantum Mirages, and the Infinite; Weirdness of Programmable Atoms, 2003; To Crush The Moon, 2005. SHORT STORIES: Dirtyside Down, 1991; (with G.R. Hyde) A Midnight Clear, 1994; Jarvik Hearts, 1996. EDITOR: (with M.H. Greenberg and J. Helfers) Once upon a Galaxy, 2002. Contributor to periodicals. **Address:** Omnitech Robotics International L.L.C., 2630 S Raritan Cir., Englewood, CO 80110, U.S.A. **Online address:** wmccarth@sff.net

MCCARTHY-TUCKER, Sherri Nevada. *See* **MCCARTHY, Sherri N.**

MCCARTNEY, Alistair. American/Australian (born Australia), b. 1971?. **Genres:** Novels. **Career:** Antioch University-Los Angeles, teacher of creative writing and literature; Antioch University-Santa Barbara, teacher of creative writing and literature. Writer. **Publications:** The End of the World Book: A Novel, 2008. Works appear in anthologies. Contributor to periodicals. **Address:** Los Angeles, CA , U.S.A. **Online address:** amccartney@antioch.edu

MCCARTNEY, Scott. American (born United States), b. 1960. **Genres:** Adult Non-fiction, Information Science/Computers, History, Politics/Government. **Career:** Associated Press, southwest regional reporter, 1985-92; The Wall Street Journal, columnist and travel editor, 1993-. **Publications:** (With T. Bartimus) Trinity's Children: Living along America's Nuclear Highway, 1991; Defying the Gods: Inside the New Frontiers of Organ Transplants, 1994; ENIAC, the Triumphs and Tragedies of the World's First Computer, 1999; The Wall Street Journal Guide to Power Travel: How to Arrive with Your Dignity, Sanity, and Wallet Intact, 2009. **Address:** The Wall Street Journal, 1211 Ave. of the Americas, New York, NY 10036, U.S.A.

MCCARTY, Hanoch. American (born United States), b. 1940. **Genres:** Human Relations/Parenting, inspirational/Motivational Literature, Food And Wine, Education. **Career:** Southern Illinois University, instructor, 1967-69; University of Hartford, assistant professor of education, 1971-72; Cleveland State University, associate professor of education, 1972-90. Writer. **Publications:** Acts of Kindness: How to Create a Kindness Revolution, 1994; (with S.B. Simon) Weekends: Great Ideas for Memorable Adventures, 1994; A Year of Kindness, 1995; The Daily Journal of Kindness, 1996; The Fourth Course of Chicken Soup for the Soul, 1997; Motivating Your Audience: Speaking from the Heart, 1999; (with F. Siccone) Motivating Your Students: Before You Can Teach Them, You Have to Reach Them, 2001. **Address:** 12970 Self-Esteem Ln., Galt, CA 95632-0066, U.S.A. **Online address:** hanoch@bestspeaker.com

MCCARTY, John. American (born United States), b. 1944?. **Genres:** Film, History, Literary Criticism And History, Social Sciences. **Career:** WTEN-TV, promotions assistant, 1970-71; WAAB-FM, copy director, 1971-72; WAAF-FM, copy director, 1971-72; WRGB-TV, creative director, 1972-78; WGY-AM, creative director, 1972-78; WGFM-FM, creative director, 1972-78; State of New York, media specialist, 1978-80; General Electric Corporation Marketing, senior writer, 1980-83; freelance writer, 1983-; State University of New York, adjunct professor of cinema. **Publications:** NONFICTION: You're on Open Line!: Inside the Wacky World of Late-night Talk Radio, 1978; Splatter Movies: Breaking the Last Taboo: A Critical Survey of the Wildly Demented Sub-genre of the Horror Film That Is Changing the Face of Film Realism Forever, 1981; Video Screams, 1983; Alfred Hitchcock Presents: An Illustrated Guide to the Ten-Year Television Career of the Master of Suspense, 1985; Psychos: Eighty Years of Mad Movies, Maniacs and Murderous Deeds, 1986; The Films of John Huston, 1987; The Little Shop of Horrors Book, 1988; The Official Splatter Movie Guide, 1989; The Modern Horror Film: Fifty Contemporary Classics from The Curse of Frankenstein to The Lair of the White Worm, 1990; Deadly Resurrection, 1990; Thrillers: Seven Decades of Classic Film Suspense, 1992; Movie Psychos and Madmen: Film Psychopaths from Jekyll and Hyde to Hannibal Lecter, 1993; Hollywood Gangland: The Movies' Love Affair with the Mob, 1993; (ed.) The Fearmakers: The Screen's Directorial Masters of Suspense and Terror, 1994; The Sleaze Merchants: Adventures in Exploitation Filmmaking, 1995; The Films of Mel Gibson, 1997; Atavar Speaks, 2000; Hammer Films, 2002; Bullets over Hollywood: The American Gangster Picture from the Silents to The Sopranos, 2004. **Address:** 3 Fairview Terr., East Greenbush, NY 12061-2601, U.S.A. **Online address:** jmccart6@nycap.rr.com

MCCASLIN, Richard B(ryan). American (born United States), b. 1961. **Genres:** History. **Career:** Louisiana State University, teaching assistant, 1982-83; University of Texas, teaching assistant and research associate, 1984-87; The History Co., associate historian, 1987-89; Pellissippi State Community College, instructor in history, 1988-89; University of Tennessee, research assistant professor, 1988-90; Roane State Community College, instructor in history, 1989; Corpus Christi State University, adjunct professor, 1989; High Point University, assistant professor, 1990-94, associate professor, 1994-2000, professor, 2000-04; Hawaii Pacific University, visiting professor, 2003-; University of North Texas, associate professor, professor, 2004-. Writer. **Publications:** (With E.F. Gloyna) Commitment to Excellence: One Hundred Years of Engineering Education at the University of Texas at Austin, 1986, (contrib.) One Hundred Years of Science and Technology in Texas: A Sigma Xi Centennial Volume, 1986; (ed.) The Papers of Andrew Johnson, vol. VIII, 1989, vol. IX, 1991; (contrib.) The Texas Senate: Republic to Civil War, 1991; Andrew Johnson: A Bibliography, 1992; Tainted Breeze: The Great Hanging at Gainesville, Texas, October, 1862, 1994; Portraits of Conflict: A Photographic History of South Carolina in the Civil War, 1994; Remembered Be Thy Blessings: High Point University-The College Years, 1924-1991, 1994; Portraits of Conflict: A Photographic History of North Carolina in the Civil War, 1997; (contrib.) The Texas Senate: Civil War to the Eve of Reform, 1999; Lee in the Shadow of Washington, 2001; The Last Stronghold: The Fort Fisher Campaign, 2003; Portraits of Conflict: A Photographic History of Tennessee in the Civil War, 2007; At the Heart of Texas: One Hundred Years of the Texas State Historical Association, 2007; (ed.) Soldier's Letters to Charming Nellie, 2008; Fighting Stock: John S. Rip Ford of Texas, 2011. FORTHCOMING: Embattled Republic: Texas Fights for Independence, 1835-1845; A Distant Thunder: Civil War in the Trans-Mississippi. Contributor of articles to periodicals. **Address:** Department of History, University of North Texas, 1155 Union Cir., Ste. 310650, Denton, TX 76203, U.S.A. **Online address:** mccaslin@unt.edu

MCCAUGHREAN, Geraldine (Jones). Also writes as Geraldine Jones, Felix Culper. British (born England), b. 1951. **Genres:** Novels, Children's Fiction, Children's Non-fiction, Education, Translations, Plays/Screenplays, Young Adult Fiction, Young Adult Non-fiction, Picture/Board Books, Novellas/Short Stories. **Career:** Thames Television, secretary, 1970-73; Marshall Cavendish Ltd., assistant editor, 1977-80, sub-editor, 1978-79, staff writer, 1982-88; Carreras-Rothman Ltd., editorial assistant, 1980-81. Writer, 1981-. **Publications:** FOR CHILDREN: Who's That Knocking on My Door?, 1986; My First Space Book, 1989; My First Earth Book, 1989; The Snow Country Princess, 1991; The Princess and the Moon; 1992; Over the Deep Blue Sea, 1992; On the Day the World Began, 1994; The Quest of Isis, 1994; Cowboy Jess, 1995; The Pirate's Son, 1998; My First Oxford Book of Stories, 1999; Six Storey House, 2002; Gilgamesh the Hero, 2002; The Jesse Tree, 2003; Doctor Quack, 2003; Dog Days, 2003; Jalopy: A Car's Story in Five Drivers, 2003; Smile!, 2004; Sky Ship, 2004; The Longest Story in the World, 2006; Tamburlaine's Elephants, 2007; Greek Heroes, 2007; King Arthur and the Round Table, 2007; Death-defying Pepper Roux, 2009; Pull Out All the Stops!, 2010 in US as The Glorious Adventures of the Sunshine Queen, 2011. RETELLINGS SERIES: One Thousand and One Arabian Nights, 1982; The Canterbury Tales, 1984; El Cid, 1989; The Odyssey, 1993; Moby Dick, or the White Whale, 1996; John Bunyan's a Pilgrim's Progress, 1999; The Questing

Knights of the Faerie Queen, 2004. AS FELIX CULPER: Seaside Adventure, 1986; Tell the Time, 1986; Orville and Cuddles (8 titles), 1986; In the Town, Having Fun, On the Move, 1986; The Infinite Beyond, 1989; The Mighty Deep, 1989. AS GERALDINE JONES: Adventure in New York, 1979; Raise the Titanic, 1980; Sabre Tooth, 1980; Modesty Blaise, 1981. FOR YOUNG ADULTS: A Little Lower Than the Angels, 1987; A Pack of Lies, 1988; Gold Dust (novel), 1993; Plundering Paradise (novel), 1996; Forever X, 1998; The Stones are Hatching, 1999; The Kite Rider: A Novel, 2001; Stop the Train!: A Novel, 2001; Showstopper!, 2003; Not the End of the World, 2004; The White Darkness, 2005; Mo, 2006; (with S.M. Fischer) Peter Pan in Scarlet, 2006. NOVELS FOR ADULTS: The Maypole, 1989; Fires' Astonishment, 1990; Vainglory, 1991; Lovesong, 1996; The Ideal Wife, 1997. PICTURE BOOKS: Saint George and the Dragon, 1989; The Story of Christmas, 1989; The Story of Noah and the Ark, 1989; The Cherry Tree, 1991; Blue Moon Mountain, 1994; Baabra Lamb, 1994; Blue Moo, 1994; Good Dog, 1994; Gregorie Peck, 1994; The Little Angel, 1995; Unicorns! Unicorns!, 1997; Hope on a Rope, 1998; Noah and Nelly, 1998; Never Let Go, 1998; The Story of the Nativity, 1998; Pageant of the Past, 1999; Aesop's Fables, 1999; Grandma Chickenlegs, 2000; How the Reindeer Got Their Antlers, 2000; My Grandmother's Clock, 2002; Bright Penny, 2002; The Beauty and the Beast, 2000; One Bright Penny, 2002; Fig's Giant, 2005; Father and Son, 2006; The Nativity Story, 2007; Wenceslas, 2007; welve Dancing Princesses, 2011; Pittipat's Saucer of Moon, 2012. BRAMBLEDOWN TALES SERIES: Blackberry Bunny, 1989; Henry Hedgehog's Hat, 1989; Hoppity Hare's Adventures, 1989; Little Brown Mouse, 1989; Piggy Goes to Market, 1989; The Rabbits' New Home, 1989; Tiny Chick's Tail, 1989; Yellow Duckling's Story, 1989. WIZZIWIG SERIES: Wizziwig and the Crazy Cooker, 1995; Wizziwig and the Singing Car, 1995; Wizziwig and the Sweet Machine, 1995; Wizziwig and the Wacky Weather Machine, 1995. MYTHS AND LEGENDS OF THE WORLD SERIES: The Golden Hoard: Myths and Legends of the World, 1996; The Silver Treasure, 1996; The Bronze Cauldron, 1997; The Crystal Pool: Myths and Legends of the World, 1998. GREEK MYTHS SERIES: Adventures of Odysseus, 1997; The Perils of Perseus, 1997; Perseus and the Gorgon Medusa, 1997; Theseus and the Minotaur, Orpheus and Eurydice, Apollo and Daphne, 1997; Jason and the Golden Fleece, 1997; Persephone and the Pomegranite Seeds, 1997; The Twelve Labours of Heracles, 1997; Daedalus and Icarus, 1997; The Wooden Horse, 1997; Hermes Tricks the Gods, 2000; Phaeton and the Sun Chariot, 2000; Zeus Conquers the Titans, 2000; Athena and the Olive Tree, 2001. ROMAN MYTHS SERIES: City of Dreams, 2000; Burning the Books, 2000; Romulus and Remus, 2000; A Shot in the Dark, 2000. HEROES SERIES: Hercules, 2003; Perseus, 2003; Odysseus, 2003; Theseus, 2005. OTHERS: A Pack of Lies, 1990; Good-Dog, 1994; King Arthur, 1996; The Doubleday Book of Princess Stores, 1997; Too Big!, 1998; Britannia, 100 Stories form British History, 1999; The Nutcracker, 1999; The Hay Cart, 1999; What Am I For?, 1999; A Sheepless Night, 1999; Starry Tales, 2000; The Orchard Book of Love and Friendship, 2000; Brave Magic, 2000; The Great Chase, 2000; Britannia on Stage: 25 Plays from British History, 2000; The Pioneers of Piano Ridge, 2000; Stories of Robin Hood, 2001; Cat and Rat Fall Out, 2001; The Greeks On Stage: 25 Plays from Greek Myths, 2002; Dancing the Night Away, 2003; Cyrano, 2006; (with R. Impey, M. Mayo and A. Matthews) Magical Princess Stories, 2009; Robin Hood and the Golden Arrow: And a World of Other Stories, 2011; King Arthur And a World of Other Stories, 2011; George and the Dragon: And a World of Other Stories, 2011; The Little Monk, 2011; The Wish-Bringer, 2012. **Address:** c/o Jacqueline Korn, David Higham Associates Ltd., 5-8 Lower John St., Golden Sq., London, GL W1F 9HA, England. **Online address:** mccaughrean@btinternet.com

MCCAUGHREN, Tom. Irish (born Ireland), b. 1936. **Genres:** Children's Fiction, Young Adult Fiction, Documentaries/Reportage, History, Natural History, Mystery/Crime/Suspense. **Career:** Irish Times, reporter/defense correspondent, 1955-68, RTE Radio and Television, reporter, 1968-75, assistant news editor, 1976-78, security correspondent, 1978-2000; Garda College, visiting lecturer in media and dommunications skills; The Courier and News, journalist; Ballymena/Belfast Telegraph, journalist; The Irish Times, journalist. **Publications:** The Peacemakers of Niemba, 1966; The Legend of the Golden Key, 1983; The Legend of the Phantom Highwayman, 1983; Run with the Wind, 1983; The Legend of the Corrib King, 1984; Run to Earth, 1984; The Children of the Forge, 1985; Run Swift, Run Free, 1986; The Silent Sea, 1987; Rainbows of the Moon, 1989; Run to the Ark, 1991; In Search of the Liberty Tree, 1994; Run to the Wild Wood, 1996; Ride a Pale Horse, 1998; Run for Cover, 1999. **Address:** 137 Whitehall Rd., Terenure, Dublin, 6, Ireland. **Online address:** tommccaughren@hotmail.com

MCCAULEY, Martin. British/Irish (born Ireland), b. 1934. **Genres:** History, Politics/Government, Biography, Autobiography/Memoirs. **Career:** Engaged in building industry, 1955-61; University of London, School of Slavonic and East European Studies, senior lecturer, 1968-78, 1985-91, senior lecturer in politics, 1992-98, Department of Social Sciences, chairman, 1993-95. Writer. **Publications:** Khrushchev and the Development of Soviet Agriculture: The Virgin Land Programme, 1953-1964, 1976; Marxism-Leninism in the German Democratic Republic, 1979; The Stalin File, 1979; East Germany, The Dilemmas of Division, 1980; Lenin: Life and Works, 1980; Power and Authority in East Germany, 1981; The Soviet Union since 1917, 1981; East-West German Relations, 1983; Stalin and Stalinism, 1983, 3rd ed., 2008; The Origins of the Cold War, 1983, 3rd ed. as Origins of the Cold War, 1941-1949, 2008; East Germany since 1945, 1983 as The German Democratic Republic since 1945, 1983; Octobrists to Bolsheviks: Imperial Russia 1905-1917, 1984; (with P. Waldron) The Origins of the Modern Russian State 1855-81, 1987; (comp. with P. Waldron) The Emergence of the Modern Russian State, 1855-81, 1988; (ed.) Gorbachev and Perestroika, 1990; Nikita Sergeevich Khrushchev, 1991; The Soviet Union 1917-1991, 1993; Longman Biographical Directory of Decision Makers in Russia and the Successor States, 1993; The Khrushchev Era, 1953-1964, 1995; The Longman Companion to Russia Since 1914, 1997; Who's Who in Russia Since 1900, 1997; Russia since 1914, 1998; Who's Who in Russia since 1900, 1998; Russia, America and the Cold War 1945-1991, 1998, 2nd ed., 2008; Gorbachev, 1998; The Rise and Fall of the Soviet Union, 2007. EDITOR: The Russian Revolution and the Soviet State 1917-1921, 1975, rev. ed., 1979; (ed.) Communist Power in Europe 1944-1949, 1977; (ed.) The Soviet Union after Brezhnev, 1983; (contrib.) The Soviet Union in the 1980s, 1983; (ed. with S. Carter) Leadership and Succession in the Soviet Union, Eastern Europe and China, 1985; Trade and Transport in Russia and Eastern Europe, 1985; (ed.) Khrushchev and Khrushchevism, 1987; (ed.) The Soviet Union under Gorbachev, 1987; The Soviet Union under Gorbachev, 1987; Gorbachev and Perestroika, 1990; (ed.) Directory of Russian MPS: People's Deputies of the Supreme Soviet of Russia-Russian Federation, 1992; (contrib.) Longman Biographical Dictionary of Decision Makers in Russia and the Successor States, 1993; (ed.) Russia's Leading Commercial Banks, 1994; Bandits, Gangsters and the Mafia: Russia, the Baltic States, and the CIS since 1992, 2001; Afghanistan and Central Asia, 2002. **Address:** London School of Slavonic and East European Studies, University of London, Senate House, Malet St., London, GL WC1E 7HU, England. **Online address:** mccauley.m@limehousegroup.net

MCCAULEY, Sue. New Zealander (born New Zealand), b. 1941. **Genres:** Novels, Plays/Screenplays, Adult Non-fiction. **Career:** New Zealand Broadcasting Service, copywriter, 1959-60; Listener, journalist, 1960-62; Taranaki Herald, reporter, 1963-64; Christchurch Press, reporter, 1964-65; University of Auckland, writer-in-residence, 1986; University of Canterbury, writer-in-residence, 1993; Thursday magazine, columnist. **Publications:** NOVELS: Other Halves, 1982; Then Again, 1986; Bad Music, 1990; It Could Be You, 1997. OTHERS: (ed. with R. McLachlan) Erotic Writing, 1992; A Fancy Man, 1996; Escape from Bosnia: Aza's Story, 1996; Life on Earth, 2003. Contributor to periodicals. **Address:** c/o Ray Richards, Richards Literary Agency, PO Box 31-240, Auckland, 0741, New Zealand. **Online address:** suemccauley@paradise.net.nz

MCCHESNEY, Robert Waterman. American (born United States), b. 1952?. **Genres:** Business/Trade/Industry, Economics, Communications/Media, Adult Non-fiction, Writing/Journalism. **Career:** The Evergreen State College, teaching instructor, 1975-77; University of Washington, teaching assistant, 1983-87, teaching instructor, 1985-88; University of Wisconsin, School of Journalism and Mass Communication, assistant professor, 1988-94, associate professor, 1994-98; University of Illinois, National Center for Supercomputer Applications, senior research scientist, 1999-, Graduate School of Library and Information Science, Institute of Communications Research, research associate professor, 1999-2000, research professor, 2000-07, Department of Communication, Gutgsell endowed professor, 2007-; Free Press, president and co-founder; WILL-AM Radio, show host. Writer. **Publications:** (Ed. with W.S. Solomon) Ruthless Criticism: New Perspectives in U.S. Communication History, 1993; Telecommunications, Mass Media, and Democracy: The Battle for the Control of U.S. Broadcasting, 1928-1935, 1993; (with E.S. Herman) The Global Media: The New Missionaries of Corporate Capitalism, 1997; Corporate Media and the Threat to Democracy, 1997; (ed. with E.M. Wood and J.B. Foster) Capitalism and the Information Age: The Political Economy of the Global Communication Revolution, 1998; Rich Media, Poor Democracy: Communication Politics in Dubious Times, 1999;

(with J. Nichols) It's the Media, Stupid, 2000; (with D. Schiller) The Political Economy of International Communications: Foundation for the Emerging Global Debate about Media Ownership and Regulation, 2003; (ed. with B. Scott) Our Unfree Press: 100 Years of Radical Media Criticism, 2004; (ed. with J.B. Foster) Pox Americana: Exposing the American Empire, 2004; The Problem of the Media: U.S. Communication Politics in the Twenty-first Century, 2004; (ed. with R. Newman and B. Scott) The Future of Media: Resistance and Reform in the 21st Century, 2005; (with J. Nichols) Tragedy and Farce: How the American Media Sell Wars, Spin Elections, and Destroy Democracy, 2005; Communication Revolution: Critical Junctures and the Future of Media, 2007; Political Economy of Media: Enduring Issues, Emerging Dilemmas, 2008; (with J. Nichols) Death and Life of American Journalism, 2010; (intro.) Liberty and the News, 2010; (ed. with V. Pickard) Will the Last Reporter Please Turn Out the Lights, 2011. Contributor to periodicals. **Address:** Department of Communication, University of Illinois at Urbana-Champaign, 316 Communication, Rm. 103, 1207 W Oregon St., Urbana, IL 61801-3716, U.S.A. **Online address:** rwmcches@illinois.edu

MCCLAIN, Lisa. American (born United States), b. 1965. **Genres:** History, Theology/Religion. **Career:** Boise State University, faculty member, 2001-, director of the Gender Studies program, 2002-; University of Texas, lecturer in history. Historian, educator and writer. **Publications:** Lest We Be Damned: Practical Innovation and Lived Experience among Catholics in Protestant England, 1559-1642, 2004. Contributor to periodicals. **Address:** Boise State University, 1910 University Dr., Boise, ID 83725, U.S.A. **Online address:** lmcclain@boisestate.edu

MCCLANAHAN, Jeffery. Also writes as Anna Jeffrey, Sadie Callahan, Dixie Cash. American (born United States), b. 1941. **Genres:** Novels, Young Adult Fiction, Romance/Historical. **Career:** Writer. **Publications:** WITH PAMELA CUMBIE, UNDER JOINT PSEUDONYM DIXIE CASH: Since You're Leaving Anyway, Take Out the Trash, 2004; My Heart May Be Broken, but My Hair Still Looks Great, 2005; I Gave You My Heart, but You Sold It Online, 2006; Don't Make Me Choose between You and My Shoes, 2008; Curing the Blues with a New Pair of Shoes, 2009; Our Red Hot Romance is Leaving Me Blue, 2010; I Can't Make You Love Me, But I Can Make You Leave, 2011. UNDER PSEUDONYM ANNA JEFFREY: The Love of a Cowboy, 2003; The Love of a Stranger, 2004; The Love of a Lawman, 2005; Sweet Water, 2006; Salvation, Texas, 2007; Sweet Return, 2007. UNDER PSEUDONYM SADIE CALLAHAN: Lone Star Woman, 2009. **Address:** c/o Author Mail, HarperCollins Publishers, 10 E 53rd St., 7th Fl., New York, NY 10022, U.S.A. **Online address:** annajeffrey76048@yahoo.com

MCCLANAN, Anne L. American (born United States), b. 1966. **Genres:** Sex, History, Humanities. **Career:** University of North Carolina, assistant professor of art history, 1998-99; Portland State University, Department of Art, assistant professor of art history, 1999-2004, associate professor, 2004-08, professor, 2008-, Middle East Studies Center, faculty. Writer. **Publications:** (Ed. with K.R. Encarnación) The Material Culture of Sex, Procreation, and Marriage in Premodern Europe, 2002; Representations of Early Byzantine Empresses: Image and Empire, 2002; (ed. with J. Johnson) Negating the Image: Case Studies in Iconoclasm, 2006; Invisible Landscapes: Medieval Italian Representation of the Natural World, forthcoming. Contributor to periodicals. **Address:** Department of Art, Portland State University, Rm. 123, Art Bldg., 2000 SW 5th Ave., PO Box 751, Portland, OR 97201, U.S.A. **Online address:** anne@pdx.edu

MCCLARY, Susan. American (born United States), b. 1946. **Genres:** Music, Women's Studies And Issues. **Career:** Trinity University, lecturer, 1977; University of Minnesota, associate professor, 1977-91, Center for Humanistic Studies, acting director, 1984-85; McGill University, professor, 1991-94; University of California Los Angeles, Department of Musicology, professor, 1994-2009, Department of Music, Clark professor, 2005-, professor, 2009-11, International Institute, associate vice-provost, 2007-10; University of Oslo, professor II, 2007-; Case Western Reserve University, professor, 2011-; Writer. **Publications:** (Ed. with R. Leppert) Music and Society: The Politics of Composition, Performance and Reception, 1987; Feminine Endings: Music, Gender and Sexuality, 1991; Georges Bizet, Carmen, 1992; Conventional Wisdom: The Content of Musical Form, 2000; Modal Subjectivities: Self-Fashioning in the Italian Madrigal, 2004; Reading Music: Selected Essays, 2007; Desire and Pleasure in Seventeenth-Century Music, 2012; Structures of Feeling in Seventeenth-Century Cultural Expression, 2012. **Address:** Department of Music, Case Western Reserve University, 10900 Euclid Ave., Cleveland, OH 44106, U.S.A. **Online address:** mcclary@me.com

MCCLATCHY, J(oseph) D(onald). American (born United States), b. 1945. **Genres:** Poetry, Songs/Lyrics And Libretti. **Career:** LaSalle College, instructor in English, 1968-71; Four Quarters, associate editor, 1968-72; Yale University, assistant professor of English, 1974-81, adjunct professor, professor of English, 1991-, Yale Review, editor, 1991-; Princeton University, lecturer in creative writing, 1981-91; University of California, faculty; Academy of American Poets, chancellor, 1996-2003, board director, through 2006; Columbia University, faculty; Rutgers University, faculty; Johns Hopkins University, faculty, 1999; American Poetry Review, contributing editor; The American Academy of Arts and Letters, president. **Publications:** Scenes from Another Life, 1981; Stars Principal: Poems, 1986; Kilim, 1987; White Paper on Contemporary American Poetry, 1989; The Rest of the Way: Poems, 1990; 10 Commandments: Poems, 1998; Twenty Questions: Posed by Poems, 1998; Hazmat: Poems, 2002; Division of Spoils: Selected Poems, 2003; American Writers at Home, 2004; Mercury Dressing: Poems, 2009; Seven Mozart Librettos, 2011. LIBRETTOS FOR OPERAS: A Question of Taste: Opera in one Act, 1989; Mario the Magician, 1994; Orpheus Decending, 1995; Emmeline, 1996. EDITOR: Anne Sexton: The Artist and Her Critics, 1978; (intro.) Recitative: Prose by James Merrill, 1986; Poets on Painters: Essays on the Art of Painting by Twentieth-Century Poets, 1988; (and intro.) The Vintage Book of Contemporary American Poetry, 1990; (with G.R. Minkoff) Poetry of Song: Five Tributes to Stephen Sondheim, 1992; Woman in White: Selected Poems of Emily Dickinson, 1991; The Vintage Book of Contemporary World Poetry, 1996; (intro. with J. Hollander) Christmas Poems, 1999; On Wings of Song: Poems about Birds, 2000; (with S. Yenser) Collected Poems, 2001; (and intro.) Bright Pages: Yale Writers, 1701-2001, 2001; Love Speaks Its Name: Gay and Lesbian Love Poems, 2001; Poems of the Sea, 2001; Horace, the Odes, 2002; (with S. Yenser) James Merrill: Collected Novels and Plays, 2002; Selected Poems, 2003; Poets of the Civil War, 2005; (with S. Yenser) The Changing Light at Sandover, 2006; (foreword) Field Knowledge, 2006; (and contrib.) Thornton Wilder, 2007; Four Seasons: Poems, 2008; Whole Difference: Selected Writings of Hugo von Hofmannsthal, 2008; James Merrill, 2008. Works appears in anthologies. **Address:** Department of English, Yale University, 314 Prospect, 63 High St., PO Box 208302, New Haven, CT 06520-8302, U.S.A. **Online address:** j.d.mcclatchy@yale.edu

MCCLAY, Wilfred M(ark). American (born United States), b. 1951. **Genres:** Intellectual History, Humanities, Politics/Government, History. **Career:** Towson State University, instructor in history, 1985-86; University of Dallas, assistant professor of history, 1986-87; Tulane University, assistant professor of history, 1987-93, associate professor of history, 1993-99; Georgetown University, Royden B. Davis chair in interdisciplinary studies, 1998-99; University of Tennessee, SunTrust Bank, chair of excellence in humanities, professor of history, 1999-; Princeton University, James Madison Society of Scholars, fellow, 2002-; Ethics and Public Policy Center, senior fellow, 2004; University of Rome, Fulbright senior lecturer in American history, 2007; Pepperdine University, School of Public Policy, William E. Simon distinguished visiting professor, 2009-10. Writer. **Publications:** (Ed.) Walter Lippmann, The Phantom Public, 1993; The Masterless: Self and Society in Modern America, 1994; (ed.) Lippmann, The Foundations of Political Science, 1994; The Masterless: Self and Society in Modern America, 1994; Student's Guide to U.S. History, 2000; (ed. with H. Heclo) Religion Returns to the Public Square: Faith and Policy in America, 2003; (ed.) Figures in The Carpet: Finding the Human Person in the American Past, 2007. Contributor to journals. **Address:** SunTrust Bank Chair of Excellence in Humanities, University of Tennessee at Chattanooga, Dept. 6256, 615 McCallie Ave., Chattanooga, TN 37403-2598, U.S.A. **Online address:** bill-mcclay@utc.edu

MCCLEARY, Kathleen. American (born United States), b. 1959. **Genres:** Novels, Young Adult Non-fiction. **Career:** Freelance writer. **Publications:** House and Home (novel), 2008. Contributor to journals. **Address:** c/o Ann Rittenberg, Rittenberg Literary Agency, 30 Bond St., New York, NY 10012, U.S.A. **Online address:** kam@kathleenmccleary.com

MCCLELLAN, B(ernard) Edward. American (born United States), b. 1939. **Genres:** Education, Cultural/Ethnic Topics. **Career:** Ohio State University, instructor of history, 1966-70; Indiana University, lecturer on history of education, 1970-72, assistant professor, 1972, associate professor, 1977-91, chair of department of educational leadership and policy studies, 1988-90, 1998-2000, executive associate dean, 1990-91, professor, 1991-2003, professor emeritus, 2003-. Writer. **Publications:** (Intro.) The Hoosier School-Master: A Novel, 1984; Schools and the Shaping of Character: Moral Education in America, 1607-Present, 1992; Moral Education in America: Schools and the Shaping of Character from Colonial Times to the Present, 1999. EDITOR: (with E. Steiner and R. Arnove) Education and American Culture, 1980; (with W.J. Reese) The Social History of American Education, 1988. **Address:** School of Education, Indiana University, Rm. EDU4244, W.W. Wright Education Bldg., 107 S Indiana Ave., Bloomington, IN 47405-7000, U.S.A.

MCCLELLAN, Stephen T. American (born United States), b. 1942. **Genres:** Information Science/Computers, Economics. **Career:** U.S. Department of Commerce, office equipment industry analyst, 1968-71; Spencer Trask and Co., vice president, 1971-77; Salomon Brothers, vice president, securities analyst covering computer industry, 1977-85; Merrill Lynch Capital Markets, vice president, 1985-2003, All-American Research Team, institutional investor, 1985-2004; Software/Services Analyst Group, president and founder; New York Computer Industry Analyst Group, president; Wall Street, securities analyst; Financial Analysis Federation, chartered financial analyst. Writer. **Publications:** The Coming Computer Industry Shakeout: Winners, Losers, and Survivors, 1984; Full of Bull: Do What Wall Street Does, Not What It Says, To Make Money in the Market, 2007, rev. ed. as Full of Bull: Unscramble Wall Street Doubletalk to Protect and Build Your Portfolio, 2010. Contributor to magazines and newspapers. **Address:** c/o Julie Phifer, FT Press, 1 Lake St., Upper Saddle River, NJ 07458-1813, U.S.A. **Online address:** info@stephentmcclellan.com

MCCLELLAN, Tierney. *See* **REUSCHE, Taylor McCafferty.**

MCCLELLAND, Charles Edgar. American (born United States), b. 1940. **Genres:** History, Intellectual History, Economics, Medicine/Health. **Career:** Princeton University, instructor of history, 1966-68; University of Pennsylvania, assistant professor of history, 1968-74; University of New Mexico, professor of history, 1974-, now professor emeritus. Writer. **Publications:** The German Historians and England: A Study in Nineteenth-Century Views, 1971; (ed. with S.P. Scher) Postwar German Culture: An Anthology, 1974; State, Society and University in Germany 1700-1914, 1980; The German Experience of Professionalization: Modern Learned Professions and Their Organizations from the Early Nineteenth Century to the Hitler Era, 1991; (with L. Rice) Up against It: Photographs of the Berlin Wall, 1991; Professionen im modernen Osteuropa, 1995; Prophets, Paupers, or Professionals?: A Social History of Everyday Visual Artists in Modern Germany, 1850 to Present, 2003. **Address:** Institute for the Medical Humanities, University of Texas, 301 University Blvd., Galveston, TX 77555-1311, U.S.A. **Online address:** cemcc@unm.edu

MCCLELLAND, Diane Margaret. *See* **PEARSON, Diane (Margaret).**

MCCLELLAND, Vincent Alan. British (born England), b. 1933. **Genres:** History, Theology/Religion, Essays. **Career:** Teacher, 1958-62; Mount Pleasant College of Education, lecturer in English and history, 1962-64; University of Liverpool, lecturer in Education, 1964-69; National University of Ireland, professor of education, 1969-77; Hull College of Higher Education, board governor; Hull College of Further Education, board governor; Scarborough College, board governor; University of Hull, professor of educational studies and director of the Institute of Education, 1978, now professor emeritus. Writer. **Publications:** Cardinal Manning: His Public Life and Influence, 1865-92, 1962; English Roman Catholics and Higher Education 1830-1903, 1973; (contrib.) The Church Now, 1980; (contrib.) Victorian Churches and Churchmen: Essays Presented to Vincent Alan McClelland, 2005. EDITOR: Educational Theory in a Changing World, 1980; Christian Education in a Pluralist Society, 1988; (with V.P. Varma) Advances in Teacher Education, 1989; (with V.P. Varma) The Needs of Teachers, 1996; By Whose Authority?, 1996; (with M. Hodgetts) From Without the Flaminian Gate: 150 Years of Roman Catholicism in England and Wales, 1850-2000, 2000. Contributor of articles to journals and periodicals. **Address:** School of Education, University of Hull, Cottingham Rd., Hull, HB HU6 7RX, England.

MCCLENDON, Charles B. (Charles Bixby McClendon). American (born United States) **Genres:** History, Archaeology/Antiquities. **Career:** Brandeis University, Department of Fine Arts, Sidney and Ellen Wien professor and chair, Religious Studies Program, faculty. Writer. **Publications:** (Ed.) Rome and the Provinces: Studies in the Transformation of Art and Architecture in the Mediterranean World, 1986; The Imperial Abbey of Farfa: Architectural Currents of the Early Middle Ages, 1987; The Origins of Medieval Architecture: Building in Europe, A.D. 600-900, 2005. **Address:** Department of Fine Arts, Brandeis University, 209 Mandel Ctr., 415 S St., PO Box 028, Waltham, MA 02454, U.S.A. **Online address:** mcclendon@brandeis.edu

MCCLENDON, Charles Bixby. *See* **MCCLENDON, Charles B.**

MCCLENDON, Lise (Webb). American (born United States), b. 1952. **Genres:** Novels, Young Adult Fiction. **Career:** Creighton University, educational media producer, 1974-76; Film Critic, writer, 1977-78; Central Wyo. (Riverton) Collge, instructor radio-TV, 1981-83; Mountain Media, owner, 1983-87; Billings Mont., writer, 1987. **Publications:** Sharp Horns Rising, 1989; ALIX THORSSEN SERIES: The Bluejay Shaman, 1994; Painted Truth: An Alix Thorssen Mystery, 1995; Nordic Nights: An Alix Thorssen Mystery, 1999; Blue Wolf: An Alix Thorssen Mystery, 2001. DORIE LENNOX SERIES: One O'Clock Jump, 2001; Sweet and Lowdown: A Dorie Lennox Mystery, 2002. NOVEL: Blackbird Fly, 2009. Contributor to periodicals. **Address:** c/o Kimberley Cameron, Reece Halsey Agency, 8733 Sunset Blvd., Ste. 101, Los Angeles, CA 90069, U.S.A. **Online address:** info@lisemcclendon.com

MCCLENDON, Thomas V. American (born United States), b. 1954. **Genres:** Young Adult Non-fiction. **Career:** U.S. District Court, law clerk, 1980-81; McCutchen, Doyle, Brown & Enersen (law firm), law clerk, 1981-84; AT&T Communications, attorney, 1984-86; Farella, Braun & Martel (law firm), attorney, 1987-88; University of California-Los Angeles, visiting assistant professor of history, 1995-96; University of California-Berkeley, visiting lecturer in history, 1997-98; Southwestern University, assistant professor, 1998-2003, associate professor, 2003-07, professor of history, 2007-. Writer. **Publications:** Genders and Generations Apart: Labor Tenants and Customary Law in Segregation-Era South Africa, 1920s to 1940s (nonfiction), 2002. Contributor of articles and book to professional journals. **Address:** Department of History, Southwestern University, PO Box 7396, Georgetown, TX 78626-6144, U.S.A. **Online address:** mcclendt@southwestern.edu

MCCLINTICK, David. American (born United States), b. 1940. **Genres:** Documentaries/Reportage, Biography, Autobiography/Memoirs, Law, Film, Business/Trade/Industry. **Career:** Wall Street Journal, staff writer and investigative reporter, 1968-79; writer, 1979-. **Publications:** Stealing from the Rich: The Home-Stake Oil Swindle, 1977; Indecent Exposure: A True Story of Hollywood and Wall Street, 1982; Swordfish: A True Story of Ambition, Savagery, and Betrayal, 1993. Contributor to periodicals. **Address:** c/o Amanda Urban, International Creative Management, 40 W 57th St., New York, NY 10019, U.S.A.

MCCLOUD, Sean. American (born United States) **Genres:** Theology/Religion, History. **Career:** University of North Carolina, Department of Religious Studies, associate professor. Writer. **Publications:** Making the American Religious Fringe: Exotics, Subversives, and Journalists, 1955-1993, 2004; Divine Hierarchies: Class in American Religion and Religious Studies, 2007; (ed. with W.A. Mirola) Religion and Class in America: Culture, History, and Politics, 2009. Contributor to books and periodicals. **Address:** Department of Religious Studies, University of North Carolina, 215 Macy, 9201 University City Blvd., Charlotte, NC 28223, U.S.A. **Online address:** spmcclou@uncc.edu

MCCLURE, Ellen M. American (born United States), b. 1968. **Genres:** History, Politics/Government. **Career:** University of Illinois, College of Liberal Arts and Sciences, assistant professor of French, associate professor, director of undergraduate studies for French. Writer. **Publications:** Sunspots and the Sun King: Sovereignty and Mediation in Seventeenth-Century France, 2006. Contributor of articles to periodicals and journals. **Address:** College of Liberal Arts and Sciences, University of Illinois, 1722 University Hall, 601 S Morgan St., Chicago, IL 60607, U.S.A. **Online address:** ellenmc@uic.edu

MCCLURE, George W. American (born United States), b. 1951. **Genres:** History, Self Help. **Career:** University of Michigan, visiting assistant professor, 1983-84; University of Michigan, lecturer, 1984-85; University of Dallas, visiting assistant professor, 1985-86; University of Alabama, assistant professor, professor of history, 1986-. Writer. **Publications:** Sorrow and Consolation in Italian Humanism, 1991; The Culture of Profession in Late Renaissance Italy, 2004. Contributor to periodicals. **Address:** Department of History, University of Alabama, 4616 27th St. E, PO Box 870212, Tuscaloosa, AL 35404, U.S.A. **Online address:** gmmcclure@tenhoor.as.ua.edu

MCCLURE, Gillian Mary. British (born England), b. 1948. **Genres:** Children's Fiction, Illustrations. **Career:** Illustrator and writer. **Publications:** The Emperor's Singing Bird, 1974; Prickly Pig, 1976; Fly Home McDoo, 1979; What's the Time Rory Wolf, 1982; Tog the Ribber, or, Granny's Tale, 1985; Witch Watch, 1989; What Happened to the Picnic?, 1987; Cat Flap, 1989; Tinker Jim, 1992; The Christmas Donkey, 1993; Poems That Go Bump in the Night, 1994; PLR and the Problem of International English, 1998; Selkie, 1999; Tom Finger, 2002; Mario's Angels, 2006; The Land of the Dragon King and Other Korean Stories, 2008; The Little White Sprite 2011. Illustrator of books by others. **Address:** 9 Trafalgar St., Cambridge, CB4 1ET, England. **Online address:** gillianmcclure@ntlworld.com

MCCLURE, Ken. British/Scottish (born Scotland), b. 1942?. **Genres:** Mystery/Crime/Suspense, Novels. **Career:** City Hospital, junior lab technician; writer, 2000-; Medical Research Council of Great Britain, researcher and consultant. **Publications:** NOVELS: Fenton's Winter, 1989; Pestilence, 1991; Requiem, 1992; Crisis, 1993; Chameleon, 1995; Trauma, 1995; Donor, 1998; Pandora's Helix, 1998; The Scorpion's Advance, 1998; Resurrection, 1999; Tangled Web, 2000; Deception, 2001; Wildcard, 2002; The Gulf Conspiracy, 2004; Eye of the Raven, 2005; Past Lives, 2006; The Lazarus Strain, 2007; Hypocrites' Isle, 2008; White Death, 2009; Dust to Dust, 2010; Lost Causes, 2011. **Address:** c/o Author Mail, Allison & Busby, 13 Charlotte Mews, London, GL W1T 4EJ, England. **Online address:** info@kenmcclure.com

MCCLURE, Laura (Kathleen). American (born United States), b. 1959. **Genres:** Literary Criticism And History, Women's Studies And Issues, Classics, Sex, Cultural/Ethnic Topics. **Career:** University of Chicago, lecturer, 1987-90, Basic Program of Liberal Education, instructor, 1988-91; University of Wisconsin, Department of Classics, assistant professor, 1991-99, associate professor, 1999-2003, professor, 2003-, Jane Ellen Harrison professor of classics, 2005-10, chair, Department of Women's Studies, affiliate faculty, 1991-99, Integrated Liberal Studies, affiliate faculty, 1991-99, Department of Theater and Drama, affiliate faculty, 1991-99, Integrated Liberal Studies Program, chair, 2002-. Writer. **Publications:** Rhetoric and Gender in Euripides: A Study of Sacrifice Actions, 1991; Spoken like a Woman: Speech and Gender in Athenian Drama, 1999; Courtesans at Table: Gender and Greek Literary Culture in Athenaeus, 2003. EDITOR: (with A. Lardinois) Making Silence Speak: Women's Voices in Greek Literature and Society, 2001; Sexuality and Gender in the Classical World: Readings and Sources, 2002; (with C.A. Faraone) Prostitutes and Courtesans in the Ancient World, 2006. Contributor of articles to journals. **Address:** Department of Classics, University of Wisconsin, 902 Van Hise Hall, 1220 Linden Dr., Madison, WI 53706, U.S.A. **Online address:** lmcclure@facstaff.wisc.edu

MCCLURE, Sandy. American (born United States), b. 1948. **Genres:** Documentaries/Reportage, History, Politics/Government. **Career:** Town and Country, part-time sports reporter, 1979-81; Free Press, borough and environmental reporter, 1982-85; Globe-Times, city hall reporter, 1985-87; Mercury, borough, police and courthouse reporter, 1987-89; Trentonian, statehouse and investigative reporter, 1989-95, statehouse reporter, 2000-01; Intelligencer, reporter, 1995-2000; Gannett New Jersey State Bureau, political writer, 2001- . **Publications:** Christie Whitman for the People: A Political Biography, 1996; (with B. Ingle) Soprano State: New Jersey's Culture of Corruption, 2008. **Address:** c/o Elizabeth Frost Knappman, New England Publishing, PO Box 5, Chester, CT 06412, U.S.A. **Online address:** sbensinger@yahoo.com

MCCLURE, Tori Murden. American (born United States), b. 1963. **Genres:** Autobiography/Memoirs. **Career:** Spalding University, vice president for external relations, enrollment management, and student affairs. Boston City Hospital, chaplain. Writer. **Publications:** A Pearl in the Storm: How I Found My Heart in the Middle of the Ocean, 2009. **Address:** Louisville, KY , U.S.A. **Online address:** americanpearl@bellsouth.net

MCCOLE, John. American (born United States), b. 1954. **Genres:** History. **Career:** Harvard University, assistant professor, associate professor, 1987-94, visiting associate professor, 1998-99; University of Oregon, Department of History, associate professor, 1994-, professor, department head. **Publications:** Walter Benjamin and the Antinomies of Tradition, 1993; (ed. with S. Benhabib and W. Bonss) On Max Horkheimer: New Perceptives, 1993. **Address:** Department of History, University of Oregon, 275C McKenzie Hall, Eugene, OR 97403-1288, U.S.A. **Online address:** mccole@uoregon.edu

MCCOLGAN, John Joseph. American (born United States), b. 1946. **Genres:** Politics/Government, History, Administration/Management, Social Sciences. **Career:** City of Boston, deputy archivist. Historian and writer. **Publications:** British Policy and the Irish Administration, 1920-22, 1983. Contributor to journals. **Address:** City of Boston, Boston City Hall, 1 City Hall Sq., Boston, MA 02201-1020, U.S.A.

MCCOLLEY, Diane Kelsey. American (born United States), b. 1934. **Genres:** Literary Criticism And History, Music, Art/Art History, Poetry. **Career:** Rutgers University, Department of English, assistant professor, 1979-84, associate professor, 1984-93, professor, 1993-, distinguished professor, now emeritus. Writer. **Publications:** Milton's Eve, 1983; A Gust for Paradise: Milton's Eden and the Visual Arts, 1993; Poetry and Music in Seventeenth-Century England, 1997; Poetry and Ecology in the Age of Milton and Marvell, 2007. **Address:** Department of English, Rutgers University, Camden Campus, Armitage Hall, 4th Fl., Camden, NJ 08102, U.S.A. **Online address:** mccolley@crab.rutgers.edu

MCCOLLUM, Michael (Allen). American (born United States), b. 1946. **Genres:** Science Fiction/Fantasy, Novels. **Career:** Pratt and Whitney Aircraft, Florida Research and Development Center, experimental engineer, 1969-72; Allied Signal Aerospace (formerly Garrett Fluid Systems Co.), Fluid Systems Division, senior project engineer, 1972-, senior engineering manager; writer, 1979-; Sci Fi-Arizona, proprietor, chief executive officer; Honeywell, chief engineer; Third Millennium Publishing, operator. Writer. **Publications:** SCIENCE FICTION: A Greater Infinity, 1982; Life Probe, 1983; Procyon's Promise, 1985; Antares Dawn, 1986; Antares Passage, 1987; Thunder Strike!, 1989; The Clouds of Saturn, 1991; The Sails of Tau Ceti, 1992; Gibraltar Earth, 2000; The Art of Science Fiction, vol. I, 2000, vol. II, 2000; The Art of Writing, vol. I, 2000, vol. II, 2000; The Astrogator's Handbook, 2000; Antares Victory, 2002; Gibraltar Sun, 2006; Gibraltar Stars, 2009. OTHER: Gridlock and Other Stories, 1996. Contributor to periodicals. **Address:** Sci Fi - Arizona Inc., PO Box 14026, Tempe, AZ 85284-0068, U.S.A.

MCCONDUIT, Denise Walter. (Denise Frances Walter). American (born United States), b. 1950. **Genres:** Children's Fiction, Education. **Career:** Shell Offshore Inc., exploration technician, 1971-. Writer. **Publications:** D.J. and the Zulu Parade, 1995; D.J. and the Jazz Fest, 1997; D.J. and the Debutante Ball, 2004. Contributor of articles to magazines. **Address:** One Shell Sq., PO Box 61933, New Orleans, LA 70161, U.S.A.

MCCONICA, James Kelsey. Canadian (born Canada), b. 1930. **Genres:** History, Biography, Autobiography/Memoirs. **Career:** University of Saskatchewan, instructor, 1956-57, assistant professor of history, 1957-62; Pontifical Institute of Medieval Studies, associate professor, 1967-70, professor of history, 1971-, president, 1996-; All Souls College, visiting fellow, 1969-71, 1977, James Ford special lecturer, 1977, research fellow, 1978-84, research fellow, 1990-97, academic dean, 1990-92; Princeton University, Davis Center for Historical Studies, fellow, 1971; University of Toronto, Centre of Medieval Studies, professor, 1972-, associate director and academic secretary, 1973-76, now professor emeritus; University of St. Michael's College, president and vice-chancellor, 1984-90. Writer. **Publications:** English Humanists and Reformation Politics Under Henry VIII and Edward VI, 1965; (ed.) The Correspondence of Erasmus, vol. III: Letters 298-445, 1514-1516, 1976, vol. IV: Letters 446-593, 1516-1517, 1977; Collected Works of Erasmus, 1976, 1977; Thomas More: A Short Biography, 1977; (ed.) The History of the University of Oxford, vol. III: The Collegiate University, 1986; Erasmus, 1991; A History of All Souls College, forthcoming. Contributor to perioidcals. **Address:** Centre for Medieval Studies, University of Toronto, 125 Queen's Pk., 3rd Fl., Toronto, ON M5S 2C7, Canada. **Online address:** james.mcconica@utoronto.ca

MCCONKEY, James (Rodney). American (born United States), b. 1921. **Genres:** Novels, Novellas/Short Stories, Literary Criticism And History, Autobiography/Memoirs. **Career:** Morehead State College, assistant professor, associate professor of English, 1950-56; Cornell University, Department of English, assistant professor, 1956-62, associate professor, 1962-65, professor, 1965-87, Goldwin Smith professor of English literature, 1987-92, professor emeritus, 1992-. Writer. **Publications:** The Novels of E.M. Forster, 1957; Night Stand (short stories), 1965; Crossroads, 1968; A Journey to Sahalin (novel), 1971; The Tree House Confessions (novel), 1979; Court of Memory (autobiography), 1983; To a Distant Island (novel), 1984; Kayo: The Authentic and Annotated Autobiographical Novel from Outer Space (novel), 1987; Rowan's Progress (history and biography), 1992; Stories from My Life with the Other Animals(autobiography), 1993; The Telescope in the Parlor (essays), 2004. EDITOR: The Structure of Prose, 1962; Chekhov and Our Age, 1985; The Anatomy of Memory, 1996. **Address:** 402 Aiken Rd., Trumansburg, NY 14886, U.S.A. **Online address:** jrm9@cornell.edu

MCCONNELL, Michael N. American (born United States), b. 1949. **Genres:** History. **Career:** University of Alabama, associate professor; Fort Ligonier Association, consultant; The College of William & Mary, faculty. Historian and writer. **Publications:** A Country Between: The Upper Ohio Valley and Its Peoples, 1724-1774, 1992; Army and Empire: British Soldiers on the American Frontier, 1758-1775, 2004. **Address:** The College of William & Mary, PO Box 8795, Williamsburg, VA 23187-8795, U.S.A. **Online address:** mcconnel@uab.edu

MCCONNOCHIE, Mardi. Australian (born Australia), b. 1971. **Genres:** Novels, Plays/Screenplays, Sports/Fitness, Children's Fiction. **Career:** Novelist. **Publications:** Coldwater: A Novel, 2001; The Snow Queen, 2003; Fivestar, 2005; Melissa, Queen of Evil, 2006; Dangerous Games, 2007. Contributor to periodicals. **Address:** c/o Author Mail, HarperCollins Publishers, 25 Ryde Rd., PO Boax 321, Pymble, NW 2073, Australia.

MCCOOL, Daniel C. American (born United States), b. 1950. **Genres:** History, Law, Young Adult Non-fiction. **Career:** Southwest Indian Youth Center, research assistant, 1973-74; University of Arizona, Department of Political Science, research assistant, 1976-78, research and teaching associate, 1978-82, American Indian Education Program, lecturer, 1981; Texas A&M University, visiting lecturer, 1982-83, assistant professor, 1983-87; University of Utah, assistant professor, 1987-89, associate professor, 1989-96, professor of political science, 1996-, Center for Public Policy and Administration, director of public administration education, 1987-90, College of Social and Behavioral Science, associate dean, 1990-93, American West Center, director, 1998-2007, Environmental Studies Program, director, 2003-, Sustainability Curriculum Development, co-director, 2011-; National Oceanic and Atmospheric Administration, consultant, 1999-2002; U.S. Department of Justice, consultant, 2000-01; ACLU's Voting Rights Project, consultant, 2003-05; Southwest Center for Environmental Research and Policy, consultant; Rocky Mountain American Indian Economic and Education Foundation, advisor, 2003-06; Guadalupe Schools, volunteer tutor, 2007-08. Writer. **Publications:** (With J.N. Clarke) Staking Out the Terrain: Power Differentials among Natural Resource Management Agencies, 1985, 2nd ed., 1996; Command of the Waters: Iron Triangles, Federal Water Development and Indian Water, 1987; Native Waters: Contemporary Indian Water Settlements and the Second Treaty Era, 2002; (with S.M. Olson and J.L. Robinson) Native Vote: American Indians, the Voting Rights Act and the Right to Vote, 2007. EDITOR: Public Policy Theories, Models and Concepts: An Anthology, 1995; (contrib.) Waters of Zion: The Politics of Water in Utah, 1995; (with D. Goodman) Contested Landscape: The Politics of Wilderness in Utah and the West, 1999. Contributor of articles and book to professional journals. **Address:** Environmental Studies Program, University of Utah, Rm. 252, 260 S Central Campus Dr., Salt Lake City, UT 84112, U.S.A. **Online address:** dan.mccool@geog.utah.edu

MCCOOLE, Sinéad. Irish/American (born United States), b. 1968?. **Genres:** Adult Non-fiction, Biography, History, Autobiography/Memoirs. **Career:** Kilmainham Gaol Historical Museum, researcher and lecturer. Historian and writer. **Publications:** Hazel: A Life of Lady Lavery, 1880-1935, 1996; Guns and Chiffon: Women Revolutionaries and Kilmainham Gaol 1916-1923, 1997; Mary Herbert of Muckross House, 1817-1893, 1999; Researcher's Handbook: Sources for Twentieth-Century Irish History: Limerick City Library Historian-in-Residence Millennium Project, 2000; Hard Lessons: The Child Prisoners of Kilmainham Gaol, 2001; Cross-Border Reflections on 1916: Drogheda-Shankill Partnership, Dublin Conference, 27th-29th April 2001, 2001; No Ordinary Women: Irish Female Activists in the Revolutionary Years, 1900-1923, 2003; Mollie Gill, 2006; (foreword) Every Dark Hour: A History of Kilmainham Jail, 2007; 60 Years of the Cuala Press, 2008; Easter Widows, forthcoming. **Address:** 3 The Nurseries, Ballybrack, DU 1, Ireland. **Online address:** sineadmccoole@eircom.net

MCCORD, Patricia. American (born United States), b. 1943. **Genres:** Children's Fiction, Young Adult Fiction. **Career:** Boeing Co., public relations staff. Writer. **Publications:** How I Found Myself at the Fair, 1980; A Bundle of Sticks, 1983; Rip-Off, 1985; Pattis Pet Gorilla, 1987; Love Is for the Dogs, 1989; Pictures in the Dark, 2004. Works appear in anthology. **Address:** Bloomsbury Childrens Books, 175 5th Ave., Ste. 712, New York, NY 10010, U.S.A. **Online address:** pmccord@patriciamccord.com

MCCORKINDALE, Susan. American (born United States), b. 1962?. **Genres:** Autobiography/Memoirs. **Career:** Family Circle Magazine, marketing director; Popular Science, marketing director. Writer and educator. **Publications:** Confessions of a Counterfeit Farm Girl (autobiographical), 2008. **Address:** Upperville, VA , U.S.A. **Online address:** susanmccorkindale@counterfeitfarmgirl.com

MCCORKLE, Jill (Collins). American (born United States), b. 1958. **Genres:** Novels, Novellas/Short Stories, Young Adult Fiction. **Career:** Teacher, 1982-83; Florida Institute of Technology Library, Melbourne, acquisitions librarian, 1983-84; University of North Carolina, Medical School, secretary, 1984, lecturer, 1986-, 1989-92; Duke University, instructor in creative writing, 1986; Tufts University, lecturer, 1987-89; Harvard University, Briggs-Copeland lecturer in creative writing, 1992-; Brandeis University, faculty, Fannie Hurst visiting writer; Bennington College, MFA Program, faculty, 1994-; North Carolina State University, faculty, professor of creative writing. Writer. **Publications:** The Cheerleader: A Novel, 1984; July 7th: A Novel, 1984; Cheer Leader, 1985; Tending to Virginia: A Novel, 1987; Ferris Beach: A Novel, 1990; Crash Diet: Stories, 1992; Carolina Moon: A Novel, 1996; Final Vinyl Days and Other Stories, 1998; Creatures of Habit: Stories, 2001; Going Away Shoes: Stories, 2009. **Address:** Department of English, North Carolina State University, NCSU Campus, 221 Tompkins Hall, PO Box 8105, Raleigh, NC 27695, U.S.A. **Online address:** jill_mccorkle@ncsu.edu

MCCORMACK, Derek. Canadian (born Canada) **Genres:** Novellas/Short Stories. **Career:** Writer. **Publications:** Dark Rides: A Novel in Stories, 1996; Halloween Suite, 1998; Wild Mouse, 1998; Wish Book: A Catalogue of Stories, 1999; Western Suit, 2001; The Journey Prize Anthology: Short Fiction from the Best of Canadas New Writers, 2002; The Haunted Hillbilly, 2003; Grab Bag, 2004; Christmas Days, 2005; The Show that Smells, 2008. **Address:** Gutter Press, 56 The Esplanade, Ste. 503, Toronto, ON M5E 1A7, Canada.

MCCORMACK, Mike. Irish (born Ireland), b. 1965?. **Genres:** Novels, Novellas/Short Stories, Young Adult Fiction. **Career:** National University of Ireland, lecturer of creative writing, writer-in-residence. **Publications:** Getting It in the Head (short stories), 1996; Crowe's Requiem (novel), 1998; Notes from a Coma (novel), 2005. **Address:** c/o Jonathan Cape, Random House Group Ltd., 20 Vauxhall Bridge Rd., London, GL SW1V 2SA, England.

MCCORMACK, W(illiam) J(ohn). (Hugh Maxton). Irish (born Ireland), b. 1947. **Genres:** Poetry, Literary Criticism And History, Novels, Young Adult Non-fiction, Young Adult Fiction, Humanities. **Career:** University of London, professor of literary history, Goldsmith's College, professor of English and department head, senior research fellow. Writer. **Publications:** AS HUGH MAXTON: Stones, 1970; The Noise of the Fields: Poems, 1970-1975, 1976; Jubilee for Renegades: Poems, 1976-1980, 1982; The Enlightened Cave: Inscriptions, 1983; Passage, with Surviving Poems, 1985; Six Snapdragons, 1985; At the Protestant Museum: Poems, 1986; The Puzzle Tree Ascendant, 1988; (trans.) A.N. Nagy, Between: Selected Poems of Ágnes Nemes Nagy, 1988; (ed.) Selected Poems, 1991; The Engraved Passion: New & Selected Poems, 1970-1991, 1991; Swift Mail: Thirty Postcards to a Friend, 1992; Waking: An Irish Protestant Upbringing, 1997; Gubu Roi: Poems & Satires, 1991-1999, 2000; Poems 2000-2005, 2005; Twenty 16 Vision: A Novel, 2009. NONFICTION: (ed. and comp.) A Festschrift for Francis Stuart on His Seventieth Birthday, 28 April 1972, 1972; Sheridan Le Fanu and Victorian Ireland, 1980, 2nd ed., 1991; (ed. with A. Stead) James Joyce and Modern Literature, 1982; Ascendancy and Tradition in Anglo-Irish Literary History from 1789 to 1939, 1985; The Battle of the Books: Two Decades of Irish Cultural Debate, 1986; Dissolute Characters: Irish Literary History Through Balzac, Sheridan Le Fanu, Yeats and Bowen, 1993; The Dublin Paper War of 1786-1788: A Bibliographical and Critical Inquiry: Including an Account of the Origins of Protestant Ascendancy and its 'Baptism' in 1792, 1993; From Burke to Beckett: Ascendancy, Tradition and Betrayal in Literary History, 1994; The Pamphlet Debate on the Union Between Great Britain and Ireland, 1797-1800, 1996; (ed. with C. Carville and M. Butler) Patronage, 1997; (ed.) The Blackwell Companion to Modern Irish Culture, 1999; Ferocious Humanism: An Anthology of Irish Poetry From Before Swift to Yeats and After, 2000; Fool of the Family: A Life of J.M. Synge, 2000. OTHERS: (ed.

and intro.) Uncle Silas, 1981; (ed.) Kellys and the O'Kellys, or, Landlords and Tenants, 1982; (ed. and intro.) The Eustace Diamonds, 1983; (ed.) In the Prison of his Days, 1988; (ed. and intro. with K. Walker) The Absentee, 1988; Sheridan Le Fanu, 1997; (ed. with M. Butler and M. Myers) Novels and Selected Works of Maria Edgeworth, 1999; Parliamentary Register, or, History of the Proceedings and Debates of the House of Commons in Ireland, 9th October, 1781-15th July, 1797, 1999; Roger Casement in Death, or, Haunting the Free State, 2002; Silence of Barbara Synge, 2003; (ed. and intro.) Memories of West Wicklow, 1813-1939, 2005; (ed. with C. King) Michael Davitt: From the Gaelic American, 2008; 'We Irish' in Europe: Yeats, Berkeley and Joseph Hone, 2010. **Address:** c/o Aosdana, The Arts Council, 70 Merrion Sq., Dublin, DU 2, Ireland.

MCCORMICK, Anita Louise. American (born United States), b. 1957. **Genres:** Air/Space Topics, Communications/Media, Environmental Sciences/Ecology, History, How-to Books, Sciences, Young Adult Non-fiction, Technology, Reference. **Career:** Freelance writer and editor, 1987-; TAB/McGraw-Hill, freelance copy editor, 1992-. **Publications:** Shortwave Radio Listening for Beginners, 1993; Space Exploration, 1994; The Shortwave Listener's Q and A Book, 1994; Vanishing Wetlands, 1995; Native Americans and the Reservation in American History, 1996; Access to the Airwave: My Fight for Free Radio, 1997; The Industrial Revolution in American History, 1998; The Internet: Surfing the Issues, 1998; The Vietnam Antiwar Movement in American History, 2000; The Pony Express in American History, 2001; The Invention of the Telegraph and Telephone in American History, 2004. Contributor to periodicals. **Address:** Enslow Publishers Inc., Dept F61, 40 Industrial Rd., PO Box 398, Berkeley Heights, NJ 07922-0398, U.S.A. **Online address:** anitamccormick@msn.com

MCCORMICK, Blaine. American (born United States) **Genres:** Adult Non-fiction, History, Autobiography/Memoirs. **Career:** ARCO Oil & Gas Co., human resource management professional, 1990-92; Pepperdine University, assistant professor, 1996-98; Baylor University, Hankamer School of Business, associate professor, professor of management and associate dean for undergraduate programs. Writer. **Publications:** Ben Franklin's 12 Rules of Management, 2000; At Work with Thomas Edison: 10 Business Lessons from America's Greatest Innovator, 2001; (with D. Davenport) Shepherd Leadership: Wisdom for Leaders from Psalm 23, 2003; Ben Franklin: America's Original Entrepreneur: Franklin's Autobiography Adapted for Modern Times, 2005; (with T. Edison) Innumerable Machines in My Mind, 2005; (co-author) Electrifying New York and Abroad, 2007. Contributor to periodicals. **Address:** Hankamer School of Business, Baylor University, HSB 319, 1 Bear Pl., Ste. 98006, Waco, TX 76798-8006, U.S.A. **Online address:** blaine_mccormick@baylor.edu

MCCORMICK, Charles H(oward). American (born United States), b. 1932. **Genres:** History. **Career:** National Aeronautic and Space Administration, contract assistant and specialist, 1961-63; U.S. National Park Service, historian, 1964-68; Fairmont State College, assistant professor, professor of history, 1970-95. Writer. **Publications:** Leisler's Rebellion, 1689-1691, 1989; This Nest of Vipers: McCarthyism and Higher Education in the Mundel Affair, 1951-1952, 1989; Seeing Reds: Federal Surveillance of Radicals in the Pittsburgh Mill District, 1917-1921, 1997; Hopeless Cases: The Hunt for the Red Scare Terrorist Bombers, 2005. Contributor of articles to journals. **Address:** 18700 Walkers Choice Rd., Apt. 402, Gaithersburg, MD 20886, U.S.A. **Online address:** chmccor.grd.hist@aya.yale.edu

MCCORMICK, Ken. (Ken J. McCormick). American (born United States), b. 1952. **Genres:** Economics, Business/Trade/Industry. **Career:** University of Northern Iowa, assistant professor, 1982-86, associate professor, 1986-91, professor of economics, 1991-. Writer. **Publications:** Veblen in Plain English: A Complete Introduction to Thorstein Veblen's Economics, 2006. Contributor to periodicals and journals. **Address:** Department of Economics, University of Northern Iowa, 1227 W 27th St., Cedar Falls, IA 50614-0129, U.S.A. **Online address:** kenneth.mccormick@uni.edu

MCCORMICK, Ken J. *See* **MCCORMICK, Ken.**

MCCORMICK, Sabrina. American (born United States), b. 1974?. **Genres:** Sciences, Medicine/Health. **Career:** Michigan State University, Department of Sociology, faculty, Environmental Science and Policy Program, faculty; George Washington University, School of Public Health and Health Services, research faculty. Writer and sociologist. **Publications:** Mobilizing Science: Movements, Participation, and the Remaking of Knowledge, 2009; No Family History: The Environmental Links to Breast Cancer, 2009. Contributor to journals. **Address:** Department of Sociology, Michigan State University, 316 Berkey Hall, East Lansing, MI 48824-1111, U.S.A. **Online address:** sabrina.mccormick@gmail.com

MCCORMICK, Theresa Mickey (E.). American (born United States), b. 1939. **Genres:** Education, Social Sciences. **Career:** Monongalia County Schools, teacher of art and multicultural education, 1968-78; Emporia State University, lecturer in multicultural education, 1981-84; Iowa State University, professor of multicultural and nonsexist teacher education, 1984-2007, professor emeritus, 2007-, Women's Studies Program, affiliate faculty; Kenyatta University, Curriculum Development Department, visiting professor, 1999; National Taiwan Normal University, visiting professor, 2002. Writer. **Publications:** Creating the Nonsexist Classroom: A Multicultural Approach, 1994; (with L.A. Sommerville) Multicultural Education: Awareness & Activities, 1998. Contributor to books. **Address:** Department of Curriculum and Instruction, Iowa State University, N165E Lagomarcino Hall, University Relations, Ames, IA 50011, U.S.A. **Online address:** theresmc@iastate.edu

MCCOUCH, Hannah. American (born United States) **Genres:** Novels, Romance/Historical, Literary Criticism And History. **Career:** Writer. **Publications:** Girl Cook: A Novel, 2003; Mountain Betty: A Novel, 2005. Contributor to periodicals. **Address:** c/o Author Mail, Villard, 1745 Broadway, New York, NY 10019, U.S.A.

MCCOY, Glenn. American (born United States), b. 1965?. **Genres:** Children's Fiction, Illustrations. **Career:** Belleville News-Democrat, editorial cartoonist, 1988-. Writer and designer. **Publications:** FOR CHILDREN; SELF-ILLUSTRATED: Penny Lee and Her TV, 2002; I See Santa Everywhere, 2008. COMICS COLLECTIONS: The Duplex, 1998; Bad Habits: A Duplex Collection, 2006; (with G. McCoy) The Flying McCoys: Comics for a Bold New World, 2006; (with G. McCoy) Monkey Business: Another Cartoon Collection by the Flying McCoys, 2007. Contributor to magazines. **Address:** Belleville News-Democrat, 120 S Illinois, PO Box 427, Belleville, IL 62220, U.S.A.

MCCOY, Max. Also writes as Rheuben Buckner. American (born United States), b. 1958. **Genres:** Novels, Westerns/Adventure, Writing/Journalism, Adult Non-fiction. **Career:** The Wilson Quarterly, writer; Fortean Times, writer; Front Page Detective, writer; American Photographer, writer; Pittsburg Morning Sun, reporter, 1980-83, reporter and photographer, 1983-89, Joplin Globe, reporter and photographer, 1982-83, investigative writer, 2001-06; Pittsburg State University, instructor, 1989-90; Parsons Sun, county government reporter, 1992; Emporia State University, instructor in creative and professional writing, 1994, assistant professor of journalism, 2006-. **Publications:** NOVELS: The Sixth Rider, 1991; Sons of Fire, 1993; The Wild Rider, 1995; Home to Texas, 1995; Indiana Jones and the Philosopher's Stone, 1995; Indiana Jones and the Dinosaur Eggs, 1996; Indiana Jones and the Hollow Earth, 1997; Indiana Jones and the Secret of the Sphinx, 1999; Jesse: A Novel of the Outlaw Jesse James, 1999; The Moon Pool, 2004; Into the West, 2005; Hinterland, 2005; A Breed Apart: A Novel of Wild Bill Hickok, 2006; Hellfire Canyon, 2007; I, Quantrill, 2008; Canyon Diablo, 2010; Damnation Road, 2010. Works appear in anthologies. Contributor to periodicals. **Address:** Department of English, Emporia State University, Rm. 404C, Plumb Hall, PO Box 4019, 1200 Commercial St., Emporia, KS 66801, U.S.A. **Online address:** max@maxmccoy.com

MCCOY, Sarah. American (born United States), b. 1980. **Genres:** Novels. **Career:** Old Dominion University, faculty; University of Texas, faculty. Writer. **Publications:** The Time It Snowed in Puerto Rico: A Novel, 2009. **Address:** c/o Doris S. Michaels, DSM Agency, 1841 Broadway, Ste. 903, New York, NY 10023, U.S.A. **Online address:** sarah@sarahmccoy.com

MCCOY, William C. American (born United States), b. 1945. **Genres:** Adult Non-fiction, Poetry, Education. **Career:** Teacher, 1967-; Spring Independent School District, teacher, 1989-2000. Writer, 2000-. **Publications:** What We Work With: Troubling Times for Educators, 2002; Life in Context, 2006; Shadowbytes, 2009. **Address:** 811 Hilltop Dr., Leander, TX 78641, U.S.A. **Online address:** wcvmccoy@cox-internet.com

MCCRACKEN, Elizabeth. American (born United States), b. 1966?. **Genres:** Novels, Novellas/Short Stories, Autobiography/Memoirs. **Career:**

Drexel University, adjunct assistant lecturer, 1991-92; Sommerville Public Library, circulation desk chief, 1993-95, audiovisual department, first assistant, 1997; Sommerville Arts Council, community writing instructor, 1995, 1996; Provincetown Fine Arts Work Center Summer Program, instructor, 1996-98; Iowa Summer Writing Festival, writing instructor, 1997-98; Western Michigan University, writer-in-residence, 1998; Skidmore College, writer-in-residence; University of Texas-Austin, resident faculty, James Michener chair of fiction. **Publications:** Here's Your Hat What's Your Hurry: Stories, 1993; The Giant's House (novel): A Romance, 1996; Niagara Falls All Over Again, 2001; An Exact Replica of a Figment of My Imagination: A Memoir, 2008. Contributor to periodicals. Works appear in anthologies. **Address:** Skidmore College, 815 N Broadway, Saratoga Springs, NY 12866, U.S.A. **Online address:** elizabeth.mccracken@rocketmail.com

MCCRAW, Thomas K. American (born United States), b. 1940. **Genres:** History, Business/Trade/Industry, Politics/Government, Biography. **Career:** University of Texas, assistant professor, 1970-74, associate professor, 1974-78; Harvard Business School, Newcomen research fellow, 1973-74, visiting associate professor, 1976-78, professor of business administration, 1978-89, course head, 1981-84, 1996-2002, director of research, 1984-86, chair and co-chair of the Business, Government and the International Economy Unit, 1986-97, Isidor Straus professor of business history, 1989-2006, Isidor Straus professor of business history emeritus, 2006-; Business History Review, editor and co-editor, 1994-2004. **Publications:** Morgan vs. Lilienthal: The Feud within the TVA, 1970; TVA and the Power Fight 1933-1939, 1971; Prophets of Regulation, 1984; (co-author) Management Past and Present, 1996; American Business, 1920-2000, 2000; Prophet of Innovation: Joseph Schumpeter and Creative Destruction, 2007; American Business Since 1920: How it Worked, 2009. EDITOR: (and contrib.) Regulation in Perspective: Historical Essays, 1981; (and contrib.) America vs. Japan, 1986; The Essential Alfred Chandler: Essays Toward a Historical Theory of Big Business, 1988; (and contrib.) Creating Modern Capitalism: How Entrepreneurs, Companies and Countries Triumphed in Three Industrial Revolutions, 1997; (co-ed. and contrib.) The Intellectual Venture Capitalist: John H. McArthur and the Work of the Harvard Business School, 1980-1995, 1999. **Address:** Harvard Business School, Soldiers Field, Boston, MA 02163, U.S.A. **Online address:** tmccraw@hbs.edu

MCCRAY, W. Patrick. American (born United States), b. 1967. **Genres:** Novels. **Career:** University of California, associate professor of the history of modern physical sciences and technology, Center for Nanotechnology in Society, co-director, faculty, 2003, professor, 2005-. Writer. **Publications:** Glassmaking in Renaissance Venice: The Fragile Craft, 1999; Giant Telescopes: Astronomical Ambition and the Promise of Technology, 2004; Keep Watching the Skies!: The Story of Operation Moonwatch and the Dawn of the Space Age, 2008. Contributor to journals. **Address:** Department of History, University of California, HSSB 4224, Santa Barbara, CA 93106-9410, U.S.A. **Online address:** pmccray@history.ucsb.edu

MCCREA, Scott. American (born United States) **Genres:** Plays/Screenplays, Biography, Literary Criticism And History, Language/Linguistics. **Career:** State University of New York, Purchase College, Conservatory of Theater Arts and Film, part-time faculty. Playwright. **Publications:** The Case for Shakespeare: The End of the Authorship Question, 2004. **Address:** Conservatory of Theater Arts and Film, Purchase College, Rm. 1017, Dance Bldg., 735 Anderson Hill Rd., Purchase, NY 10577-1402, U.S.A. **Online address:** scott.mccrea@purchase.edu

MCCREERY, Charles Anthony Selby. British (born England), b. 1942. **Genres:** Philosophy, Psychology, Sciences. **Career:** Institute of Psychophysical Research, research officer, 1964-; Magdalen College, lecturer in experimental psychology, 1996-2000. Writer. **Publications:** Science, Philosophy and ESP, 1967; Psychical Phenomena and the Physical World, 1973; (with C. Green) Apparitions, 1975; (with C. Green) Lucid Dreaming: The Paradox of Consciousness During Sleep, 1994. **Address:** Institute of Psychophysical Research, 118 Banbury Rd., Oxford, OX OX2 7, England. **Online address:** charles.mccreery@eidosnet.co.uk

MCCRONE, John (Robert). British (born England), b. 1957. **Genres:** Intellectual History, Language/Linguistics, Philosophy, Psychology, Biology. **Career:** Writer. **Publications:** The Ape That Spoke: Language and the Evolution of the Human Mind, 1990; The Myth of Irrationality: The Science of the Mind from Plato to Star Trek, 1993; Going Inside, 1999; How the Brain Works, 2002. **Address:** 10 Sterry Dr., Thames Ditton, SR KT7 0YN, England. **Online address:** mccrone@dichotomistic.com

MCCRONE, Kathleen E. Canadian (born Canada), b. 1941. **Genres:** History, Young Adult Non-fiction, Sports/Fitness, Women's Studies And Issues. **Career:** University of Windsor, lecturer, 1968-72, assistant professor, 1972-76, associate professor, 1976-84, professor of history, 1984-, dean of arts and social sciences, 1990-2002, faculty of history, 2004, now professor emeritus, University Humanities Research Group, director, 2004-06. Writer. **Publications:** Playing the Game: Sport and the Physical Emancipation of English Women, 1870-1914 in UK as Sport and the Physical Emancipation of English Women, 1870-1914, 1988. **Address:** Department of History, University of Windsor, Rm. 1157, Chrysler Hall N, 401 Sunset Ave., Windsor, ON N9B 3P4, Canada. **Online address:** kem@uwindsor.ca

MCCRORIE, Edward (P.). American (born United States), b. 1936. **Genres:** Poetry, Translations. **Career:** Providence College, professor of English, 1964-, now professor emeritus. Writer. **Publications:** After a Cremation (poems), 1974; (trans.) Virgil, The Aeneid of Virgil, 1991; Needle Man (poems), 1999; (trans.) Homer, The Odyssey, 2004. **Address:** Department of English, Providence College, Phillips Memorial Library LL10, 1 Cunningham Sq., Providence, RI 02918, U.S.A.

MCCRORY, Donald P(eter). British/Irish (born Ireland), b. 1943. **Genres:** Literary Criticism And History, Poetry, Human Relations/Parenting. **Career:** North East Surrey College of Technology, lecturer in modern languages, 1974-84; American International University, head of Spanish and German, 1984-2001; Royal Society of Geographers, fellow, 1997, now retired. Writer. **Publications:** (With P. McWilliams) Ordnance Survey Memoirs of Ireland, vol. III: Co Down I: South Down, 1990; (intro.) Siddhartha, 1998; No Ordinary Man: The Life and Times of Miguel de Cervantes, 2002; The Checklist, 2005. POETRY: The Conscious Light: A Sonnet Sequence, 1978; Another World, 1980; Wind on the Skin, 1983; The Sweet Taste of Goodness, 1986; A Piece of Glass, 1990; New Beginnings (collected poetry), 1993. Contributor to periodicals. **Address:** 42 Lea Rd., Preston, Preston, LC PR2 1TP, England. **Online address:** donald_mccrory@yahoo.co.uk

MCCRUMB, Sharyn. American (born United States), b. 1948. **Genres:** Novels, Novellas/Short Stories, Mythology/Folklore. **Career:** Newspaper reporter; 1976-81; Virginia Tech, teacher of journalism and Appalachian studies; 1982-88; novelist, 1983-. **Publications:** BALLAD SERIES: If Ever I Return, Pretty Peggy-O, 1990; The Hangman's Beautiful Daughter, 1992; She Walks These Hills, 1994; The Rosewood Casket, 1996; The Ballad of Frankie Silver, 1998; Songcatcher, 2001; Ghost Riders, 2003; The Devil Amongst the Lawyers, 2010; The Ballad of Tom Dooley, 2011. OTHERS: ST. DALE, 2005; Once Around the Track, 2007; (with A. Edwards) Faster Pastor, 2010. JAY OMEGA SERIES: Bimbos of the Death Sun, 1987; Zombies of the Gene Pool, 1992. SHORT STORIES: Our Separate Days, 1989; Foggy Mountain Breakdown and Other Stories, 1997. **Address:** PO Box 220, Catawba, VA 24070, U.S.A. **Online address:** sharyn@sharynmccrumb.com

MCCUE, Lisa (Emiline). American (born United States), b. 1959. **Genres:** Children's Fiction, Animals/Pets. **Career:** Writer. **Publications:** WITH D. McCUE SELF-ILLUSTRATED: Ducky's Seasons, 1983; Froggie's Treasure, 1983; Teddy Dresses, 1983; Kitty's Colors, 1983; Puppy's Day School, 1984; Bunny's Numbers, 1984; Kitten's Christmas, 1985; Baby Elephant's Bedtime, 1985; Panda's Playtime, 1985; Raccoon's Hide and Seek, 1985. SELF-ILLUSTRATED: Fun and Games in Fraggle Rock, 1984; Corduroy's Day: A Counting Book, 1985; Corduroy's Party, 1985; Corduroy's Toys, 1985; The Little Chick, 1986; 10 Little Puppy Dogs, 1987; Corduroy Goes to the Doctor, 1987; Corduroy on the Go, 1987; Corduroy's Busy Street, 1987; Puppy Peek-a-Boo, 1989; Kittens Love, 1990, rev. ed., 1998; Puppies Love, 1990, rev. ed., 1998; Whose Little Baby Says?, 1990; Bunnies Love, 1991; Ducklings Love, 1991; Fuzzy Teddy, 1992; Fuzzy Kitten, 1992; Spike & Mike, 1992; Fuzzytail Lamb, 1992; Fuzzytail Bunny, 1992; The Animal Christmas, 1993; Please Take This Puppy/Kitten Home, 1993; Professor Pipsqueak Chunky Flap, 1994; Fuzzytail Farm, 1994; Christmas Stories and Poems, 1994; Animal ABCs, 1994; Corduroy's Birthday, 1995; Professor Pipsqueak's Please Touch and Feel Backyard Tour, 1995; Corduroy's Halloween, 1995; Little Fuzzytail, 1995; Kitty's Carrier, 1995; Great Big Flap Book, 1996; Quick, Quack, Quick, 1996; The Lion and the Mouse, 1996; Fuzzytail Friends' Lift-and-Look Animal Book, 1997; Jingle Bell Mice, 1997; Fuzzytail World, 1998; Corduroy's Easter, 1998; First Mother Goose, 1999; Corduroy's Sleepover,

2007; Quiet Bunny's Many Colors, 2011; Little Bunny, 2012. OTHERS: Lisa McCue's Animals' Advent, 1994; Quiet Bunny, 2009; Fuzzytails 123: A Touch-and-feel Counting Book, 2010; Little Chimp's Big Day, 2010; Animal's Christmas Countdown, 2010; Play Ball, Corduroy, 2010; Fuzzytails ABC: A Foldout Counting Book, 2011; Quiet Bunny & Noisy Puppy, 2011; Cork and Fuzz: Finders Keepers, 2011. Illustrator of books by others. **Address:** c/o Ronnie Ann Herman, Herman Agency, 350 Central Park W, New York, NY 10025, U.S.A.

MCCULLIN, Don(ald). British (born England), b. 1935. **Genres:** Adult Non-fiction, Photography, Travel/Exploration. **Career:** The Observer Newspaper, freelance photo journalist, 1961-64; The Sunday Times Newspaper, staff photographer, 1964-84, overseas correspondent, 1966-84; freelance photographer, 1984-. **Publications:** Destruction Business, 1971, rev. ed. as Is Anyone Taking Any Notice? A Book of Photographs and Comments. With Phrases Drawn from the 1970 Nobel Lecture by Alexander Solzhenitsyn, 1973; The Homecoming, 1979; (contrib.) The Palestinians, 1979; Donald McCullin, 1982; Beirut: A City in Crisis, 1983; McCullin, 1983; Perspectives, 1987; (with M. Shand) Skulduggery, 1987; Open Skies, 1989; (with L. Cherster) Unreasonable Behaviour: An Autobiography, 1990; An Empire of the East: Travels in Indonesia, 1993; Don McCullin, A Retrospective, 1994, rev. ed., 2003; Sleeping with Ghosts: A Life's Work in Photography, 1996; India, 1999; Cold Heaven, 2001; Life Interrupted, 2004; Don McCullin in Africa, 2005; In England, 2007; (with P. McCartney) A Day in the Life of The Beatles, 2010; Southern Frontiers: A Journey Across the Roman Empire, 2010. **Address:** Abner Stein Agency, 10 Roland Gardens, London, GL SW7 3PH, England.

MCCULLOCH, Sara. *See* **URE, Jean.**

MCCULLOUGH, Bob. *See* **MCCULLOUGH, Robert.**

MCCULLOUGH, Colleen. Australian (born Australia), b. 1937. **Genres:** Novels, Food And Wine, Biography, Criminology/True Crime, Mystery/Crime/Suspense, Horror, Young Adult Fiction. **Career:** Royal North Shore Hospital of Sydney, Department of Neurophysiology, founder and neurophysicist, 1958-63; Yale University, School of Internal Medicine, Department of Neurology, associate in research, 1967-77; writer, 1976-. **Publications:** MASTERS OF ROME SERIES: The First Man in Rome, 1990; The Grass Crown, 1991; Fortune's Favorites, 1993; Caesar's Women, 1995; Caesar: Let The Dice Fly, 1999; The October Horse: A Novel Of Caesar And Cleopatra, 2002; Antony and Cleopatra, 2007. NOVELS: Tim, 1977; The Thorn Birds, 1977; An Indecent Obsession, 1981; A Creed for the Third Millennium, 1985; The Ladies of Missalonghi, 1987; The Song of Troy, 1998; Morgan's Run, 2000; The Touch, 2003; Angel, 2005; The Independence of Miss Mary Bennet, 2008; Sex, Greed, and Murder, 2010. OTHERS: An Australian Cookbook, 1982; Cooking with Colleen McCullough and Jean Easthope, 1982; Roden Cutler, V.C.: The Biography, 1998; On, Off, 2006; Too Many Murders, 2009; Naked Cruelty, 2010; The Prodigal Son, 2012. Contributor to magazines. **Address:** PO Box 333, Norfolk Island, Oceania, AC 2899, Australia.

MCCULLOUGH, David Willis. American (born United States), b. 1937. **Genres:** Mystery/Crime/Suspense, History, Young Adult Non-fiction, Novels, Humanities. **Career:** Book-of-the-Month Club, Editorial Department, staff, 1964-95. Writer. **Publications:** The Path Between the Seas, 1977; McCullough's Brief Lives: Selected Eye on Books Interviews, 1980, rev. ed. as People, Books & Book People, 1981; Brooklyn-And How It Got that Way, 1983; (ed.) Great Detectives: A Century of the Best Mysteries from England and America, 1984; (ed.) American Childhoods: An Anthology, 1987; (ed.) City Sleuths and Tough Guys: Crime Stories from Poe to the Present, 1989; Think on Death: A Hudson Valley Mystery, 1991; Truman, 1992; Point No-Point: A Ziza Todd Mystery, 1992; Three Score and Ten: A History of Christ School, Arden, North Carolina, 1900-1970, 1996; (ed.) Chronicles of the Barbarians: Eyewitness Accounts of Pillage and Conquest from the Ancient World to the Fall of Constantinople, 1998; (ed.) Wars of the Irish Kings: A Thousand Years of Struggle from the Age of Myth Through the Reign of Queen Elizabeth I, 2000; John Adams, 2002; The Unending Mystery: A Journey Through Labyrinths and Mazes, 2004; 1776, 2005. **Address:** 117 Villard Ave., Hastings on Hudson, NY 10706-1802, U.S.A.

MCCULLOUGH, Donald W. American (born United States), b. 1949. **Genres:** Human Relations/Parenting, Self Help, Theology/Religion, Education. **Career:** Ordained Presbyterian minister, 1974; Presbyterian church, pastor, 1974-78; Solana Beach Presbyterian Church, pastor, 1980-94; Fuller Theological Seminary, adjunct professor, 1981-; San Francisco Theological Seminary, president and professor of theology and preaching, 1994-2000; Salt Lake Theological Seminary, president, 2004-06; Mendocino Presbyterian Church, pastor, 2007-. Writer. **Publications:** Waking from the American Dream: Growing through Your Disappointments, 1988 as The Power of Realistic Thinking: How to Cope When How-to Books Fail, 1992; Finding Happiness in the Most Unlikely Places, 1990; (with M. Dunham and G. MacDonald) Mastering Personal Growth, 1992; The Trivialization of God: The Dangerous Illusion of a Manageable Deity, 1995; Say Please, Say Thank You: The Respect We Owe One Another, 1998; The Wisdom of Pelicans: A Search for Healing at the Water's Edge: 2002; The Consolations of Imperfection: Learning to Appreciate Life's Limitations, 2004; If Grace is So Amazing, Why Don't We Like It?, 2005. Contributor to periodicals. **Address:** c/o Auhtor Mail, Brazos Press, Baker Book House, PO Box 6287, Grand Rapids, MI 49516-6287, U.S.A. **Online address:** don@mendopres.org

MCCULLOUGH, James P. American (born United States), b. 1936. **Genres:** Psychology. **Career:** Virginia Commonwealth University, professor of clinical psychology, distinguished professor of psychology and psychiatry. Writer. **Publications:** Treatment for Chronic Depression: Cognitive Behavioral Analysis System of Psychotherapy, 2000; Skills Training Manual for Diagnosing and Treating Chronic Depression: Cognitive Behavioral Analysis System of Psychotherapy, 2001; Patient's Manual for CBASP, 2003; Treating Chronic Depression with Disciplined Personal Involvement: Cognitive Behavioral Analysis System of Psychotherapy (CBASP), 2006; Using Disciplined Personal Involvement to Treat Chronic Depression: CBASP, 2006; Preparing the Pre-Therapy Patient for Psychotherapy, forthcoming. **Address:** Department of Psychology, Virginia Commonwealth University, Rm. 207, 806 W Franklin St., PO Box 842018, Richmond, VA 23284-2018, U.S.A. **Online address:** jmccull@vcu.edu

MCCULLOUGH, Kate. American (born United States), b. 1961?. **Genres:** Adult Non-fiction. **Career:** University of California, lecturer in women's studies, 1991; Miami University, assistant professor of English and women's studies, 1992-98, associate professor of English and women's studies, 1998-2001; Cornell University, visiting professor, 1999-2001, associate professor of English and feminist gender and sexuality studies, 2001-. Writer. **Publications:** Regions of Identity: The Construction of America in Women's Fiction, 1885-1914, 1999; Displacement as Narrative Structure, forthcoming. Contributor to periodicals. **Address:** Department of English, Cornell University, 250 Goldwin Smith Hall, Ithaca, NY 14853-3201, U.S.A. **Online address:** mkm23@cornell.edu

MCCULLOUGH, Michael E. American (born United States), b. 1969. **Genres:** Theology/Religion, Medicine/Health, Psychology. **Career:** Louisiana Tech University, assistant professor of psychology, 1995-96; National Institute for Healthcare Research, director of research, 1996-2000; Southern Methodist University, associate professor of psychology, 2000-02; University of Miami, Department of Psychology, associate professor, 2002-06, professor, 2006-, Evolution and Human Behavior Laboratory, director, Evolution and Behavior Emphasis, coordinator. Writer. **Publications:** (With S.J. Sandage and E.L. Worthington) To Forgive Is Human: How to Put Your Past in the Past, 1997; (with H.G. Koenig and D.B. Larson) Handbook of Religion and Health, 2001; Beyond Revenge: The Evolution of the Forgiveness Instinct, 2008. EDITOR: (with D.B. Larson and J.P. Swyers) Scientific Research on Spirituality and Health: A Report Based on the Scientific Progress in Spirituality Conferences, 1998; (with K.I. Pargament and C.E. Thoresen) Forgiveness: Theory, Research, and Practice, 2000; (with S.G. Post, B. Johnson and J.P. Schloss) Research on Altruism and Love: An Annotated Bibliography of Major Studies in Psychology, Sociology, Evolutionary Biology, and Theology, 2003; (with R.A. Emmons) The Psychology of Gratitude, 2004. Works appear in anthologies. Contributor to books and journals. **Address:** Department of Psychology, University of Miami, PO Box 248185, Coral Gables, FL 33124-0751, U.S.A. **Online address:** mikem@miami.edu

MCCULLOUGH, Robert. (Bob Mccullough). American (born United States), b. 1956?. **Genres:** Sports/Fitness, Recreation, Travel/Exploration. **Career:** Freelance writer. **Publications:** AS BOB MCCULLOUGH: (with M. Jaffe) New York Running Guide, 1998; (reteller) My Greatest Day in Baseball, 1946-1997, 1998; (with D. Carter) Washington, D.C., Running

Guide, 1999; My Greatest Day in NASCAR, 2000; (reteller) My Greatest Day in Golf: The Legends of Golf Recount Their Greatest Moments, 2001; (reteller) My Greatest Day in Football: The Legends of Football Recount Their Greatest Moments, 2001. **Address:** c/o Author Mail, St. Martin's Press, 175 5th Ave., New York, NY 10010, U.S.A. **Online address:** salaryguy@aol.com

MCCULLOUGH, **Sharon Pierce.** (Sharon Pierce). American (born United States), b. 1943. **Genres:** Crafts, Illustrations, Picture/Board Books, Children's Fiction, Young Adult Fiction, Animals/Pets. **Career:** Alligator Artworks, owner, designer, 1988-2009; Ziggity Zoom L.L.C., co-creator, producer, chief compliance officer, 2008-. Writer and illustrator. **Publications:** AS SHARON PIERCE: Making Folk Toys and Weather Vanes, 1984; Making Whirligigs and Other Wind Toys, 1985; Making Old-time Folk Toys, 1986; Making Holiday Folk Toys and Figures, 1987; (with H. Surman) Making Miniature Country Houses, 1990. AS SHARON PIERCE MCCULLOUGH SELF-ILLUSTRATED: Bunbun, the Middle One, 2001; Bunbun: Artists' Cards, 2001; Bunbun at Bedtime, 2001, 2nd ed., 2006; Bunbun at the Fair, 2002, 2nd ed., 2006. **Address:** ZiggityZoom L.L.C., 5305 Proteus Ct., Virginia Beach, VA 23464-2421, U.S.A. **Online address:** sharon@sharonpiercemccullough.com

MCCULLY, **Betsy.** American (born United States), b. 1950?. **Genres:** Natural History. **Career:** City University of New York, Kingsborough Community College, adjunct assistant professor, 1995-2000, associate professor of English, 2001-. Writer, academic, public speaker and environmental educator. **Publications:** City at the Water's Edge: A Natural History of New York, 2007. Contributor to books, periodicals and journals. **Address:** Department of English, Kingsborough Community College, City University of New York, 2001 Oriental Blvd., Brooklyn, NY 11235, U.S.A. **Online address:** betsymccully@yahoo.com

MCCULLY, **Emily Arnold.** American (born United States), b. 1939. **Genres:** Novels, Children's Fiction, Illustrations, Biography, Picture/Board Books, Young Adult Fiction. **Career:** Freelance magazine and advertising artist, 1961-67; illustrator of books for children, 1966-; writer, 1975-. Brown University, teacher; Boston University, teacher; Cummington Community of the Arts, teacher; Rockland Center for the Arts, teacher. **Publications:** SELF-ILLUSTRATED FOR CHILDREN: The Playground, 1983; Picnic, 1985; First Snow, 1985; The Show Must Go On, 1987; School, 1987; New Baby, 1988; Christmas Gift, 1988; You Lucky Duck!, 1988; The Grandma Mix Up, 1988; Zaza's Big Break, 1989; The Evil Spell, 1990; Grandmas at the Lake, 1990; Speak Up, Blanche!, 1991; Mirette on the High Wire, 1992; Grandmas at Bat, 1993; Crossing the New Bridge, 1994; My Real Family, 1994; Little Kit, or The Industrious Flea Circus Girl, 1995; The Pirate Queen, 1995; The Ballot Box Battle, 1996; The Bobbin Girl, 1996; Starring Mirette & Bellini, 1997; Popcorn at the Palace, 1997; Beautiful Warrior, 1998; Kung Fu Nun, 1998; An Outlaw Thanksgiving, 1998; Mouse Practice, 1999; Hurry!: Before It's Too Late, 2000; Monk Camps Out, 2000; Mirette & Bellini Cross Niagara Falls, 2000; The Orphan Singer, 2001; Four Hungry Kittens, Dial Books for Young Readers, 2001; Grandmas Trick-or-Treat, 2001; The Battle for St. Michael's, 2002; Picnic, 2003; Squirrel and John Muir, 2004; Marvelous Mattie: How Margaret E. Knight Became an Inventor, 2006; Escape of Oney Judge, 2007; Manjiro: The Boy Who Risked His Life for Two Countries, 2008; Wonder Horse: The True Story of the World's Smartest Horse, 2010; The Secret Cave: Discovering Lascaux, 2010. FOR ADULTS: A Craving, 1984; Life Drawing, 1987. OTHERS: Play & Sing -It's Christmas!, 1980; The Amazing Felix, 1993; Late Nate in a Race, 2012; Sam and the Big Kids, 2013. Illustrator of books by others. **Address:** Harriet Wasserman Literary Agency Inc., 137 E 36th St., New York, NY 10016, U.S.A.

MCCULLY, **Marilyn.** British (born England) **Genres:** Art/Art History, History, Biography. **Career:** Art historian and writer. **Publications:** Els Quatre Gats: Art in Barcelona around 1900, 1978; (ed.) A Picasso Anthology: Documents, Criticism, Reminiscences, 1981; Der Junge Picasso: Frühwerk und Blaue Periode, 1984; Homage to Barcelona, the City and Its Art, 1888-1936, 1987; (intro.) Picasso, Works on Paper: Barcelona, Blue and Pink Periods, 1988; (with J. Richardson) A Life of Picasso, 1991; (ed.) Picasso: The Early Years, 1892-1906, 1997; (ed.) Picasso: Painter and Sculptor in Clay, 1998; Paul Wunderlich, 1999, (ed.) Picasso: Scolpire e Dipingere la Ceramica, 2000; (ed.) Loving Picasso: The Private Journal of Fernande Olivier, 2002; Il Cubismo: Rivoluzione E Tradizione, 2004; Picasso Ceramics: The Attenborough Collection, 2007; Picasso in Paris, 1900-1907, 2011; (with S.G. Galassi) Picasso's Drawings, 1890-1921: Reinventing Tradition, 2011. **Address:** c/o Author Mail, Harry N. Abrams Inc., 100 5th Ave., New York, NY 10011, U.S.A.

MCCUSKER, **Paul.** American (born United States), b. 1958. **Genres:** Novels, Plays/Screenplays, Humor/Satire. **Career:** Focus on the Family Radio Theater, founder, writer and director; Continental Ministries, playwright. **Publications:** The Meaning of Life and Other Vanities, 1986; Youth Ministry Drama and Comedy, 1987; Family Outings: A Play about Relationships in Three Acts, a Prologue, and an Epilogue, 1988; The Revised Standard Version of Jack Hill, 1988; Snapshots & Portraits: A Two-Act Play about the Family, 1989; Void Where Prohibited, 1989; 60-Second Skits, 1991; Short Skits for Youth Ministry, 1993; Pap's Place: A Two-Act Play about Family and Change, 1993; Playwriting: A Study in Choices and Challenges, 1995; (with A. Plass) You Say Tomato: The Transatlantic Correspondence of George and Brad, 1995; Season Tickets: The Christmas Edition, With Three Scripts, 1996; Catacombs, 1997; Dear Diary, 1997; Epiphany: A Novella, 1998; The Faded Flower: A Novella, 2001; The Mill House, 2004; A Season of Shadows, 2005. ADVENTURES IN ODYSSEY SERIES: FOR YOUNG READERS: High Flyer with a Flat Tire, 1992; The Secret Cave of Robinwood, 1992; Strange Journey Back, 1992; Behind the Locked Door, 1993; Lights Out at Camp What-a-Nut, 1993; The King's Quest, 1994; Danger Lies Ahead, 1995; Point of No Return, 1995; Dark Passage, 1996; Freedom Run, 1996; A Carnival of Secrets, 1997; The Stranger's Message, 1997; Adventures in Odyssey Radio Scripts, 1998. TIME TWIST SERIES: FOR YOUNG READERS: Sudden Switch, 1996; Stranger in the Mist, 1996; Memory's Gate, 1996. PASSAGES SERIES: FOR YOUNG READERS: Annison's Risk, 1999; Arin's Judgment, 1999; Darien's Rise, 1999; Draven's Defiance, 2000; Fendar's Legacy, 2000; Glennall's Betrayal, 2000. TIME THRILLER TRILOGY SERIES: FOR YOUNG READERS: Ripple Effect, 2008; Out of Time, 2009; Memory's Gate, 2009. TIME SCENE INVESTIGATORS (TSI) SERIES: (with W. Larimore) TSI: The Gabon Virus, 2009. **Address:** Colorado Springs, CO , U.S.A. **Online address:** pemccusker@aol.com

MCCUTCHEON, **Elsie (Mary Jackson).** British/Scottish (born Scotland), b. 1937. **Genres:** Children's Fiction, History, Young Adult Fiction, Military/Defense/Arms Control, Literary Criticism And History. **Career:** Teacher, 1961-63; freelance journalist, 1965-80; Norfolk Archaeological Rescue Group, publicity officer, 1976-78; Friends of the Suffolk Record Office, editor, 1984-. **Publications:** CHILDREN'S NOVELS: The Moonlight Paupers, 1978; Summer of the Zeppelin, 1983; The Rat War, 1985; Smokescreen, 1986; Storm Bird, 1987; Twisted Truth, 1988; OTHER: Bury St. Edmunds: Historic Town, 1987; Norwich through the Ages, 1989. Works appear in anthology. Contributor to magazines and newspapers. **Address:** Wendover, Sharpes Lane, Horringer, Bury St., Edmunds, SU 1P29 5PS, England.

MCCUTCHEON, **John.** American (born United States), b. 1952. **Genres:** Songs/Lyrics And Libretti, Music, Children's Fiction. **Career:** Writer, musician and composer. **Publications:** Water from Another Time, 1989; Stone by Stone, 1995; Happy Adoption Day! (songs), 1996; Christmas in the Trenches, 2006. **Address:** Appalsongs Records, PO Box 156, Charlottesville, VA 22902-0156, U.S.A.

MCCUTCHEON, **Sandy.** Australian/New Zealander (born New Zealand), b. 1947?. **Genres:** Mystery/Crime/Suspense, Novels, Autobiography/Memoirs, Plays/Screenplays, Children's Fiction. **Career:** Illusion Farm Community, founder; Illusion Circus Theatre Co., playwriter; ABC Radio, host. Writer, broadcaster and public speaker. **Publications:** In Wolfs Clothing, 1997; Peace Crimes, 1998; Poison Tree, 1999; Safe Haven, 2000; Quirky Questions, 2000; Blik, 2004; The Magician's Son, 2001; Delicate Indecencies, 2002; The Haha Man, 2003; Black Widow, 2006; The Cobbler's Apprentice, 2006; The Hill of Mice, 2008. **Address:** c/o Author Mail, HarperCollins Australia, 25 Ryde Rd., PO Box 321, Pymble, NW 2073, Australia. **Online address:** sampo.kalevala@gmail.com

MCCUTCHEON, **W. A.** *See* **MCCUTCHEON**, **William Alan.**

MCCUTCHEON, **William Alan.** (W. A. McCutcheon). British (born England), b. 1934. **Genres:** Archaeology/Antiquities, Engineering, Geography, History, Technology, Transportation, Social Sciences, Adult Non-fiction, Adult Non-fiction. **Career:** Royal Belfast Academical Institution, teacher of geography and French, 1956-62; Government of Northern Ireland, Ministry of Finance, Survey of Industrial Archaeology, director, 1962-68; Ulster Museum, staff, 1968-, director, 1977-82; Ditcham Park School, teacher of geography, 1986-93; Queen's University of Belfast, School of Geosciences, honorary senior research fellow, 1999-2002. Writer. **Publications:** The Canals of the North of Ireland, 1965; Railway History in Pictures: Ireland, vol. I, 1969, vol. II, 1971; Wheel and Spindle: Aspects of Irish Industrial History, 1977; The Industrial Archaeology of Northern Ireland, 1980. **Address:** 25 Moira Dr., Ardmilne, Bangor, DN BT20 4RW, Northern Ireland.

MCDANIEL, Bruce A. American (born United States), b. 1946. **Genres:** Adult Non-fiction, Business/Trade/Industry, Economics. **Career:** Triton High School, teacher, 1968-70; La-Ville High School, teacher, 1970-71; Anderson College, instructor, 1971-72; State University of New York, Genesee Community College, assistant professor, 1972-75; Colorado State University, instructor and teaching assistant, 1975-79; Indiana University-Purdue University, assistant professor of economics, 1979-81; Marquette University, assistant professor and graduate faculty, 1981-84, adjunct assistant professor of economics, 1984-86; University of Northern Colorado, graduate faculty, 1992-, assistant professor of economics, 1992-98, associate professor, 1998-2004, chair, 1999-2001, professor, 2004-, teacher education faculty and Sam Walton fellow, 1999-; Prairieland Inc., president, 1994-. Writer. **Publications:** Entrepreneurship and Innovation: An Economic Approach, 2002. **Address:** Department of Economics, University od Northern Colorado, Candelaria 1281G, PO Box 101, Greeley, CO 80632-0101, U.S.A. **Online address:** bruce.mcdaniel@unco.edu

MCDANIEL, Charles. American (born United States), b. 1958?. **Genres:** Economics, Theology/Religion. **Career:** Baylor University, visiting professor, 2002-, J.M. Dawson Institute of Church-State Studies, associate director, 2002-08, faculty. Writer. **Publications:** God and Money: The Moral Challenge of Capitalism, 2007. **Address:** Institute of Church-State Studies, Baylor University, 1 Bear Pl., Ste. 97308, Waco, TX 76798-7308, U.S.A.

MCDANIEL, Lurlene. American (born United States), b. 1944. **Genres:** Children's Fiction, Young Adult Fiction, Novels. **Career:** Writer. **Publications:** JUVENILE NOVELS: A Horse for Mandy, 1981; The Pony Nobody Wanted, 1982; The Battle of Zorn, 1983; Peanut Butter for Supper Again, 1985. YOUNG ADULT NOVELS: What's It Like to Be a Star?, 1982; I'm a Cover Girl Now, 1982; Will I Ever Dance Again?, 1982; Head over Heels, 1983; If I Should Die Before I Wake, 1983; Sometimes Love Just Isn't Enough, 1984; Three's a Crowd, 1984; The Secret Life of Steffie Martin, 1985; Eternal Flame (Serenade/Serenata, No. 13), 1985; Hold Fast the Dream (Serenade/Serenata, No. 20), 1985; Love's Full Circle (Serenade/Serenata, No. 33), 1986; Why Did She Have to Die?, 1986; More Than Just a Smart Girl, 1987; Mother, Please Don't Die, 1988; My Secret Boyfriend, 1988; When Dreams Shatter (Lifelines), 1988; Goodbye Doesn't Mean Forever, 1989; Somewhere Between Life and Death, 1991; Time to Let Go, 1991; Now I Lay Me Down to Sleep, 1991; When Happily Ever After Ends, 1992; Baby Alicia Is Dying, 1993; Don't Die, My Love, 1995; Too Young to Die, 1995; Angels Watching Over Me, 1996; Saving Jessica, 1996; I'll Be Seeing You, 1996; Lifted up by Angels, 1997; Till Death Do Us Part, 1997; For Better, for Worse, Forever, 1997; Starry, Starry Night, 1998; Until Angels Close My Eyes, 1998; Angel of Mercy, 1999; The Girl Death Left Behind, 1999; Angel of Hope, 2000; How Do I Love Thee?: Three Stories, 2001; To Live Again, 2001; Telling Christina Goodbye, 2002; A Rose for Melinda, 2002; The Angels Trilogy, 2002; Garden of Angels, 2003; The Time Capsule, 2003; As Long As We Both Shall Live, 2003; Journey of Hope, 2004; Hit and Run, 2007; Prey, 2008; Briana's Gift, 2008; Breathless, 2009; Heart to Heart, 2010; Keep Me in Your Heart: Three Novels, 2011; Red Heart Tattoo, 2012. DAWN ROCHELLE BOOKS: YOUNG ADULT SERIES: Six Months to Live, 1985; I Want to Live, 1987; So Much to Live For, 1991; No Time to Cry, 1993. ONE LAST WISH: YOUNG ADULT SERIES: A Time to Die, 1992; Mourning Song, 1992; Mother, Help Me Live, 1992; Someone Dies, Someone Lives, 1992; Sixteen and Dying, 1992; Let Him Live, 1992; The Legacy: Making Wishes Come True, 1993; Please Don't Die, 1993; She Died Too Young, 1994; All the Days of Her Life, 1994; A Season for Goodbye, 1995; Reach for Tomorrow, 1999. ANGELS IN PINK SERIES: Garden of Angels, 2003; Kathleen's Story, 2004; Raina's Story, 2005; Holly's Story, 2005; Briana's Gift, 2006; Letting go of Lisa, 2006. OTHERS: A Gift of Love, 1996; True Love: Three Novels, 2009; Reaching through Time: Three Novellas, 2011. Contributor to books and periodicals. **Address:** c/o Meg Ruley, Jane Rotrosen Agency, 318 E 51st St., New York, NY 10022, U.S.A.

MCDANIEL, Sylvia (J.). American (born United States), b. 1956. **Genres:** Romance/Historical. **Career:** J.A. Majors, marketing manager, 1976-98; North Texas Romance Writers of America, president, 1995; Verizon, engineer; Citizens Telecommunications, engineer, 2001. Writer. **Publications:** ROMANCE NOVELS: Before The Violets Bloom, 1967; In His Arms Again, 1999; A Hero's Heart, 1999; The Rancher Takes a Wife, 2000; A Scarlet Bride, 2000; The Outlaw Takes a Wife, 2001; The Marshall Takes a Wife, 2001; Sunlight on Josephine Street, 2002; The Price of Moonlight, 2002; Starlight Surrender, 2004. **Address:** c/o Maureen Walters, Curtis Brown Ltd., 10 Astor Pl., New York, NY 10003, U.S.A. **Online address:** sylvia.mcdaniel@gte.net

MCDANNELL, Colleen. American (born United States), b. 1954?. **Genres:** Theology/Religion, Popular Culture. **Career:** University of Colorado, History of Christianity, visiting assistant professor, 1984; University of Maryland, European division, lecturer, 1985-88; Universität Mannheim, lecturer, 1988-89; University of Utah, Sterling M. McMurrin professor of religious studies, 1989-, professor of history, 1996-; Dartmouth College, Dickinson distinguished professor, 2003; UC Santa Barbara, Walter Capps visiting professor of religious studies, 2004. Writer. **Publications:** The Christian Home in Victorian America, 1840-1900, 1986; (with B. Lang) Heaven: A History, 1988, 2nd ed., 2001; Material Christianity: Religion and Popular Culture in America, 1995; (ed.) Religions of the United States in Practice, 2001; Picturing Faith: Photography and the Great Depression, 2004; (ed.) Catholics in the Movies, 2008; Spirit of Vatican II: A History of Catholic Reform in America, 2011. **Address:** Department of History, University of Utah, Rm. 211, 380 South 1400 East, Salt Lake City, UT 84112, U.S.A. **Online address:** colleen.mcd@utah.edu

MCDERMOTT, Alice. American (born United States), b. 1953. **Genres:** Novels, Young Adult Fiction, Humor/Satire. **Career:** University of New Hampshire, lecturer in English, 1978-79; Redbook, fiction reader, 1979-80; Esquire, fiction reader, 1979-80; Virginia Center for the Creative Arts, writer-in-residence, 1995, 1997; Redbook's Young Writers Contest, consulting editor; University of California, lecturer in writing, instructor; Johns Hopkins University, writer-in-residence, Richard A. Macksey professor of the humanities; Hollins College, writer-in-residence; Lynchburg College, writer-in-residence; American University, teacher. **Publications:** NOVELS: A Bigamist's Daughter, 1982; That Night, 1987; At Weddings and Wakes, 1991; Charming Billy, 1998; Child of My Heart, 2002; After This, 2006. Contributor to periodicals. **Address:** Harriet Wasserman Literary Agency, 137 E 36th St., New York, NY 10016, U.S.A.

MCDERMOTT, Jeanne. American (born United States), b. 1955?. **Genres:** Sciences, Children's Fiction, Adult Non-fiction. **Career:** Science journalist, 1980-; Massachusetts Institute of Technology, Public Understanding of Technology and Science, Vannevar Bush fellow, 1984-85; Shady Hill School, science teacher, 1999-. **Publications:** The Killing Winds: The Menace of Biological Warfare, 1987; Faces, 1993; Babyface: A Story of Heart and Bones, 2000. Contributor to publications. **Address:** Shady Hill School, 178 Coolidge Hill, Cambridge, MA 02138, U.S.A. **Online address:** jmcdermott10@rcn.com

MCDEVITT, Jack. American (born United States), b. 1935. **Genres:** Science Fiction/Fantasy. **Career:** Woodrow Wilson High School, instructor in English, history, theatre director, 1963-68; Mount St. Charles Academy, instructor in English, history and theatre, 1968-71; Newfound Memorial High School, Department of English, chair, 1971-73; U.S. Customs Service, customs inspector, 1975-82, regional training officer, 1982-85, Federal Law Enforcement Training Center, supervisor and management trainer, 1985-95; full-time writer, 1995-. **Publications:** SCIENCE-FICTION NOVELS: The Hercules Text, 1986; A Talent for War, 1989; The Engines of God, 1994; Ancient Shores, 1996; Standard Candles (short story collection), 1996; Eternity Road, 1997; Moonfall, 1998; Infinity Beach, 2000; Deepsix, 2001; Chindi, 2002; Omega, 2003; Polaris, 2004; Seeker, 2005; Outbound (short story collection), 2006; Odyssey, 2006; Cauldron, 2007; The Devil's Eye, 2008; Cryptic: The Best Short Stories of Jack McDevitt, 2009; Time Travelers Never Die, 2009; Echo, 2010; Firebird, 2011. Contributor to magazines. Works appear in anthologies. **Address:** Cryptic Inc., 540 Sunset Blvd., Brunswick, GA 31525, U.S.A. **Online address:** cryptic@gate.net

MCDONAGH, Martin. British (born England), b. 1970. **Genres:** Plays/Screenplays. **Career:** Royal National Theatre, resident playwright. **Publications:** The Beauty Queen of Leenane, 1996; A Skull in Connemara, 1997; The Lonesome West, 1997; The Cripple of Inishmaan, 1997; Beauty Queen of Leenane and Other Plays, 1998; Martin McDonagh Plays 1, 2000; Ualach an uaignis, 2002; The Pillowman, 2003; The Lieutenant of Inishmore, 2003; In Bruges, 2008; A Behanding In Spokane, 2010. Contributor to periodicals. **Address:** Knight Hall Agency Ltd., 7 Mallow St., Lower Ground Fl., London, GL EC1Y 8RQ, England.

MCDONALD, **Brian.** American (born United States) **Genres:** Adult Nonfiction, Travel/Exploration. **Career:** Gotham Writers' Workshop, writing instructor; Kingsborough Community College, faculty; Fordham University, faculty; City University of New York, School of Professional Studies, associate director for faculty and staff resources. Writer. **Publications:** My Father's Gun: One Family, Three Badges, One Hundred Years in the NYPD, 1999; Safe Harbor: A Murder in Nantucket, 2006; Last Call at Elaine's: A Journey from One Side of the Bar to the Other, 2008; In the Middle of the Night, 2009. Contributor to periodicals. **Address:** School of Professional Studies, City University of New York, 101 W 31st St., New York, NY 10001-3507, U.S.A. **Online address:** brian.mcdonald@mail.cuny.edu

MCDONALD, **Brix.** American (born United States), b. 1952. **Genres:** Children's Fiction, Young Adult Fiction, Romance/Historical. **Career:** Writer. **Publications:** Riding on the Wind, 1998; Outlaws, 1999. **Address:** Avenue Publishing, 2110 Artesia Blvd., Ste. 196, 603 Seagaze Dr., PO Box 531, Redondo Beach, CA 90278, U.S.A. **Online address:** nvlwriter13@aol.com

MCDONALD, **Christie.** American (born United States), b. 1942. **Genres:** Language/Linguistics, Literary Criticism And History, History. **Career:** University of Montreal, professor of French, 1969-83, 1986-93; Emory University, professor of French, 1984-86; Harvard University, Department of Romance Languages and Literatures, professor, 1994-, department chair, 2000-, Smith professor of the French language and literature, Mather House, co-master. Writer. **Publications:** The Extravagant Shepherd: A Study of the Pastoral Vision in Rousseau's Nouvelle Héloïse, 1973; The Dialogue of Writing: Essays in the Eighteenth-Century French Literature, 1984; Dispositions: Quatre Essaissur les écrits de Jean-Jacques Rousseau, Stéphane Mallarmé, Marcel Proust et Jacques Derrida, 1986; The Proustian Fabric: Associations of Memory, 1991. EDITOR: The Ear of the Other: Otobiography, Transference, Translation, 1985, rev. ed., 1988; (with G. Wihl) Transformations in Personhood and Culture after Theory: The Languages, Aesthetics, and Ethics, 1994; (with S.R. Suleiman) French Global: A New Approach to Literary History, 2010; (with S. Hoffmann) Rousseau and Freedom, 2010. OTHERS: (contrib.) Oreille de l'autre: Otobiographies, Transferts, Traductions, 1982. **Address:** Department of Romance Languages and Literatures, Harvard University, 518 Boylston Hall, Cambridge, MA 02138, U.S.A. **Online address:** cmcdonal@fas.harvard.edu

MCDONALD, **Collin.** American (born United States), b. 1943. **Genres:** Children's Fiction, Young Adult Fiction, Ghost Writer, Horror, Novellas/Short Stories, Mystery/Crime/Suspense. **Career:** Pioneer Press-Dispatch, reporter, 1967; University of Minnesota, Department of Information and Agricultural Journalism, editor, 1969-70; Modern Medicine Publications, journal editor, 1970-77; 3M Co., writer and publicist, 1977-83; freelance magazine writer and children's author, 1983-. **Publications:** Nightwaves: Scary Tales for After Dark, 1990; The Chilling Hour: Tales of the Real and Unreal, 1992; Shadows and Whispers: Tales from the Other Side, 1994; The Ghosts of Summer (young adult novel), forthcoming. Contributor to magazines. **Address:** c/o Florence Feiler, 1524 Sunset Plaza Dr., Los Angeles, CA 90069, U.S.A. **Online address:** colmac@earthlink.net

MCDONALD, **Craig.**, b. 1962?. **Genres:** Art/Art History. **Career:** Writer, journalist and editor. **Publications:** Art in the Blood, 2006; Head Games, 2007; Toros & Torsos, 2008. Contributor of articles to book and magazines. **Online address:** craig@craigmcdonaldbooks.com

MCDONALD, **Forrest.** American (born United States), b. 1927. **Genres:** Business/Trade/Industry, Economics, History, Biography, Children's Fiction, Politics/Government, Autobiography/Memoirs. **Career:** Wisconsin Historical Society, utility research director, 1953-56; American History Research Center, executive secretary, 1956-58, director, distinguished senior fellow; Brown University, associate professor, 1959-64, professor of history, 1964-67; Columbia University, visiting professor, 1962; Duke University, visiting professor, 1963; New York University, visiting professor, 1966; Wayne State University, professor of history, 1967-76; University of West Florida, visiting professor, 1975; University of Alabama, professor of history, 1976-87, distinguished university professor, 1987-2002, distinguished university professor emeritus, 2002-; College of William and Mary, James Pinckney Harrison professor, 1986-87. Writer. **Publications:** Let There Be Light: The Electric Utility Industry in Wisconsin 1881-1955, 1957; We the People: The Economic Origins of the Constitution, 1958, rev. ed., 1992; Insull, 1962; The Anti-Federalists, 1781-1789, 1963; E Pluribus Unum: The Formation of the American Republic, 1776-1790, 1965, 2nd ed., 1979; The Torch Is Passed: The United States in the 20th Century, 1968; Confederation and Constitution, 1781-1789, 1968; Enough Wise Men: The Story of Our Constitution, 1970; United States in the Twentieth Century, 1970; The Boys Were Men: The American Navy in the Age of Fighting Sail, 1971; (with L.E. Decker and T.P. Govan) The Last Best Hope: A History of the United States, 1972; Phaeton Ride: The Crisis of American Success, 1974; The Presidency of George Washington, 1974; The Presidency of Thomas Jefferson, 1976; Alexander Hamilton: ABiography, 1979; (with E.D. Genovese and D. Burner) American People, 1980; (with E.S. McDonald) A Constitutional History of the United States, 1982; Novus Ordo Seclorum: The Intellectual Origins of the Constitution, 1985; (with E.S. McDonald) Requiem: Variations on Eighteenth-Century Themes, 1988; (co-author) First Hand America, 1990; The American Presidency: An Intellectual History, 1994; States' Rights and the Union: Imperium in Imperio, 1776-1876, 2000; Recovering the Past: A Historian's Memoir, 2004. EDITOR: Empire and Nation, 1962, 2nd ed., 1999; (with E.S. McDonald) Confederation and Constitution, 1781-1789, 1968. **Address:** Department of History, University of Alabama, PO Box 870212, Tuscaloosa, AL 35487-0212, U.S.A.

MCDONALD, **Ian.** British/Irish (born Ireland), b. 1960?. **Genres:** Science Fiction/Fantasy, Novels, Novellas/Short Stories, inspirational/Motivational Literature, Young Adult Fiction. **Career:** Network of East-West Women, executive director, 1994-95; International Museum of Women, program director; U.S. Holocaust Memorial Museum, media relations director. Writer. **Publications:** Empire Dreams, 1988; Desolation Road, 1988; Out on Blue Six, 1989; King of Morning, Queen of Day, 1991; Hearts, Hands and Voices, 1992; The Broken Land, 1992; Speaking in Tongues, 1992; Kling Klang Klatch, 1992; Terminal Café, 1994; Scissors Cut Paper Wrap Stone, 1994; Necroville, 1994; Evolutions Shore, 1995; Sacrifice of Fools, 1996; Kirinya, 1998; Tendeleo's Story, 2000; (contrib.) Futures: Four Novellas, 2001; Ares Express, 2001; River of Gods, 2004; The Djinn's Wife, 2006; Brasyl, 2007; Cyberabad Days, 2009; Desolation Road, 2009; The Dervish House, 2010; Planesrunner, 2011. **Address:** 1 Church View, Hollywood, County Down, AV BT18 9DP, England. **Online address:** ianmc@extremeproduction.com

MCDONALD, **Ian (A.).** Guyanese/Trinidadian (born Trinidad and Tobago), b. 1933. **Genres:** Novels, Plays/Screenplays, Poetry, Writing/Journalism, Essays, Young Adult Fiction. **Career:** Bookers Sugar Estates Ltd., secretary, 1959-64, administrative secretary, 1964-70; Guyana Sugar Corp., director of marketing and administration, 1976-99; Theatre Co. of Guyana, director, 1981-; Demerara Publishers, chair, 1988-; Sugar Association of the Caribbean, chief executive officer, 2000-, now retired. Writer. **Publications:** The Humming-Bird Tree (novel), 1969; The Tramping Man (play), 1976. POETRY: Selected Poems, 1983; Mercy Ward, 1988; Essequibo, 1992; Jaffo the Calypsonian, 1994; Between Silence and Silence, 2003. EDITOR: AJS at 70: A Celebration on His 70th Birthday of the Life, Work and Art of A.J. Seymour, 1984; (with S. Brown) Heinemann Book of Caribbean Poetry, 1992; (with J. de Weever and intro.) Collected Poems, 1937-1989, 2000. Contributor to magazines. **Address:** Demerara Sugar Terminal, Sugar Corporation of the Caribbean, Riverview Ruimveldt, Georgetown, 592, Guyana. **Online address:** dstgsc@guyana.net.gy

MCDONALD, **J. I(an) H.** Scottish (born Scotland), b. 1933. **Genres:** Theology/Religion, Race Relations, Psychiatry, Education, Cultural/Ethnic Topics. **Career:** Church of Scotland, parish minister, 1958-63; Moray House College, lecturer, 1964-80; University of Edinburgh, lecturer, 1980-87, senior lecturer, 1987-92, reader, 1992-98, honorary fellow, 1998-; Educational Institute of Scotland, fellow, 1986; Expository Times, editor, 2001-. **Publications:** (Ed.) Church Nursery Group: A Guide and Practical Programme, 1974; Kerygma and Didache: The Articulation and Structure of the Earliest Christian Message, 1980; (with D.B. Forrester and G. Tellini) Encounter with God, 1983, 2nd ed. as Encounter with God: An Introduction to Christian Worship and Practice, 2004; (with I.C.M. Fairweather) The Quest for Christian Ethics: An Inquiry into Ethics and Christian Ethics, 1984; (with B. Chilton) Jesus and the Ethics of the Kingdom, 1988; The Resurrection: Narrative and Belief, 1989, Biblical Interpretation and Christian Ethics, 1993; Christian Values, 1995; The Crucible of Christian Morality, 1998. **Address:** New College, University of Edinburgh, Mound Pl., Edinburgh, BR EH1 2LU, Scotland. **Online address:** extim@div.ed.ac.uk

MCDONALD, Joyce. American (born United States), b. 1946. **Genres:** Children's Fiction, Young Adult Fiction, Literary Criticism And History, Novels, History. **Career:** Charles Scribners Sons, production assistant, 1976-78; Springer-Verlag, production editor, 1978-80; freelance editor, copyeditor, 1980-84; McDonald Publishing Company Inc./Shoe Tree Press, publisher and editor, 1984-89; Betterway Publications Inc., editor, 1989-90; Drew University, adjunct lecturer, 1989-2000; East Stroudsburg University, assistant professor of English, 1990-96; Spalding University, instructor in writing program, 2004. **Publications:** Mail-Order Kid, 1988; Homebody (picture book), 1991; Comfort Creek, 1996; The Stuff of Our Forebears: Willa Cather's Southern Heritage, 1998; Don't Cramp My Style: Stories about that Time of the Month, 2004. YOUNG ADULT NOVELS: Swallowing Stones, 1997; Shadow People, 2000; Shades of Simon Gray, 2001; Devil on My Heels, 2004. **Address:** Random House Books for Children, 1745 Broadway, 9th Fl., New York, NY 10019-4305, U.S.A. **Online address:** joycemcdonald.net@nac.net

MCDONALD, Patricia M. British (born England), b. 1946. **Genres:** Theology/Religion, Literary Criticism And History, Social Sciences. **Career:** Catholic University of America, assistant professor, 1989-90; Mount Saint Mary's College, assistant professor, 1990-, associate professor, 1996-2002; Ushaw College, lecturer in New Testament and director of teaching and learning, 2002-. Writer and theologian. **Publications:** God and Violence: Biblical Resources for Living in a Small World, 2004. Contributor to books and periodicals. **Online address:** p.mcdonald@ushaw.ac.uk

MCDONALD, Ronan Daniel. British/Irish (born Ireland), b. 1970. **Genres:** History, Literary Criticism And History. **Career:** University of Reading, School of English and American Literature, lecturer, 2000-. Writer. **Publications:** Tragedy and Irish Literature: Synge, O'Casey, B2002; Samuel Beckett: The Life and the Work, 2005; The Cambridge Introduction to Samuel Beckett, 2006; The Death of the Critic, 2007. **Address:** School of English, University of Reading, Whiteknights, Reading, RG6 6AA, England. **Online address:** r.d.a.mcdonald@reading.ac.uk

MCDONALD, Sandra. American (born United States), b. 1966. **Genres:** Young Adult Fiction, Science Fiction/Fantasy. **Career:** Writer, educator and speaker. **Publications:** The Outback Stars, 2007; Stars Down Under, 2008; Stars Blue Yonder, 2009; Diana Comet and other improbable stories, 2010. Contributor of stories to periodicals. **Address:** Lethe Press, 118 Heritage Ave., Maple Shade, NJ 08052-3018, U.S.A. **Online address:** sandra@sandramcdonald.com

MCDONELL, Chris. Canadian (born Canada), b. 1960. **Genres:** Sports/Fitness, Biography, Young Adult Fiction. **Career:** Writer. **Publications:** COMPILER: For the Love of Hockey: Hockey Stars' Personal Stories, 1997, rev. ed., 2001; The Game I'll Never Forget: 100 Hockey Stars' Stories, 2002; The Football Game I'll Never Forget: 100 NFL Stars? Stories, 2004; Shooting from the Lip: Hockey's Best Quotes and Quips, 2004; (with E. Zweig) Big Book of Sports Quotes, 2010. OTHERS: Hockey's Greatest Stars: Legends and Young Lions, 1999, rev. ed., 2005; Hockey All-Stars: The NHL Honor Roll, 2000. Contributor to periodicals. **Address:** 41 Gunn St., London, ON M6G 1C6, Canada.

MCDONNELL, Kevin Lee. South African/Australian (born Australia), b. 1932. **Genres:** Education, Sciences, Theology/Religion, History. **Career:** Macquarie University, tutor, 1973-77; Mount St. Mary Teachers College, lecturer, 1974-79; Christian Brothers, provincial staff, 1984-90; C.B. International Renewal Program, director, 1991; Adult Faith Education Team, director, 1993-98; Catholic Bible College, founding principal, 1998-2006, rector emeritus, 2006-. Writer. **Publications:** (With R.G. Cull and G.R. Meyer) Science and the Environment of Man, 1966; (with R.G. Cull and G.R. Meyer) Objective Tests in Science, 1967; (with K.R. Glasson) Graded Exercises in Geological Mapping, 1968; (with D.G. Massey and J.H.S. Tebbutt) Enquiring into the Earth, 1968; (ed. with J.J. Veevers) Phanerozoic Earth History of Australia, 1985; (ed. with J.J. Veevers and C.M. Powell) Permian-Triassic Pangean Basins and Foldbelts along the Panthalassan Margins of Gondwanaland, 1994. **Address:** Catholic Bible College, 13 5th St., PO Box 1954, Rosettenville, 2130, South Africa. **Online address:** klmcdonnell@edmundrice.org

MCDONNELL, Patrick. American (born United States), b. 1956. **Genres:** Cartoons, Illustrations, Picture/Board Books, Animals/Pets, Children's Fiction. **Career:** Steel Tips, drummer, 1970-81; New York Times, Sunday Magazine, columnist, 1978-93; Parents Magazine, Bad Baby, creator; Sports Illustrated, contributor; Reader's Digest, contributor; Forbes, contributor; Time, contributor; The Humane Society, director; Fund for Animals, director. **Publications:** MUTTS COLLECTIONS: Mutts, 1996; Cats and Dogs, 1997; More Shtuff, 1998; Yesh!, 1999; Mutts Sundays, 1999; Our Mutts, 2000; Mutts: Sunday Mornings, 2001; A Little Look-See, 2001; What Now?, 2002; I Want To Be the Kitty, 2003; Mutts: The Comic Art of Patrick McDonnell, 2003; Mutts, Sunday Afternoons, 2004; Dog-Eared: Mutts Nine, 2004; Mutts: Sunday Afternoon, 2004; Mutts comics: Who Let the Cat Out?, 2005; Mutts: Sunday Evenings, 2005; Everyday Mutts, 2006; Animal Friendly, 2007; The Best of Mutts, 1994-2004, 2007; Mutts Shelter Stories: Love, Guaranteed, 2008; Earl & Mooch: A Mutts Treasury, 2010. OTHER: (with K. O'Connell and G.R. De Havenon) Krazy Kat: The Comic Art of George Herriman, 1986; Bad Baby (collection), 1988; The Gift of Nothing, 2005; Art, 2006; Just Like Heaven, 2006; Hug Time, 2007; South, 2008; Wag!, 2009; Stop and Smell the Roses: A Mutts Treasury, 2009; (foreword) Sergio Aragonés: Five Decades of his Finest works, 2010; Me Jane, 2011. Illustrator of books by others. **Address:** c/o Author Mail, Andrews McMeel Universal, 4520 Main St., Kansas City, MO 64111, U.S.A. **Online address:** dailystrip@emails.muttscomics.com

MCDONOUGH, Peter. American (born United States), b. 1939. **Genres:** History, Politics/Government, Social Sciences. **Career:** Instituto Universitario de Pesquisas do Rio de Janeiro, graduate program director; University of Michigan, professor of political science, 1971-89; Vanderbilt University, professor of political science, 1989-90; Arizona State University, professor of political science, 1990, now professor emeritus. Writer. **Publications:** Power and Ideology in Brazil, 1981; (with A. DeSouza) The Politics of Population in Brazil: Elite Ambivalence and Public Demand, 1981; Men Astutely Trained: A History of the Jesuits in the American Century, 1992; (co-author) The Cultural Dynamics of Democratization in Spain, 1998; (with E.C. Bianchi) Passionate Uncertainty: Inside the American Jesuits, 2002; The Catholic Labyrinth: Ideas, Images and Institutions in the Remaking of the American Church, forthcoming. **Address:** School of Politics and Global Studies, Arizona State University, PO Box 873902, Tempe, AZ 85287-3902, U.S.A. **Online address:** peter.mcdonough@asu.edu

MCDONOUGH, Tom. American (born United States), b. 1969. **Genres:** Art/Art History, Philosophy, Literary Criticism And History. **Career:** State University of New York, Binghamton University, Department of Art History, assistant professor, 1999-2006, associate professor, 2006-, chair, faculty of philosophy, interpretation and culture and faculty of comparative literature; University of California, Department of Art History, visiting associate professor, 2008-09. Writer. **Publications:** (Ed.) Guy Debord and the Situationist International: Texts and Documents, 2002; (co-ed.) The Invisible Flaneuse?: Gender, Public Space, and Visual Culture in Nineteenth-Century Paris, 2006; The Beautiful Language of My Century: Reinventing the Language of Contestation in Postwar France, 1945-1968, 2007; (ed.) The Situationists and the City, 2009; (contrib.) Deconstructive Impulse: Women Artists Reconfigure the Signs of Power, 1973-1991, 2011. **Address:** Department of Art History, Binghamton University, 4400 Vestal Pkwy. E, PO Box 6000, Binghamton, NY 13902, U.S.A. **Online address:** tmcdonou@binghamton.edu

MCDOUGAL, Dennis. (Dennis Edward McDougal). American (born United States), b. 1949. **Genres:** Mystery/Crime/Suspense, Biography, Documentaries/Reportage, Novels. **Career:** Universal Studios, head; Riverside Press-Enterprise, staff writer, 1973-77; Long Beach Press-Telegram, staff writer, 1977-81; Los Angeles Times, staff writer, 1978-93; full-time writer, 1993-; TV Guide, contributing writer, 1994-2003; Cable News Network, producer, 1994; New York Times, contributing writer, 2004-; Premiere, writer. **Publications:** Angel of Darkness: The True Story of Randy Kraft and the Most Heinous Murder Spree of the Century, 1991; (with P. O'Donnell) Fatal Subtraction: The Inside Story of Buchwald v. Paramount, 1992, 2nd ed., 1996; In the Best of Families: The Anatomy of a True Tragedy, 1994; Mother's Day, 1995; The Last Mogul: Lew Wasserman and the Hidden History of Hollywood, 1998; The Yosemite Murders, 2000; Privileged Son: Otis Chandler and the Rise and Fall of the L.A. Times Dynasty, 2001; (with M. Murphy) Blood Cold: Fame, Sex and Murder in Hollywood, 2002; Five Easy Decades: How Jack Nicholson Became the Biggest Movie Star in Modern Times, 2008; Things Have Changed: The Lives of Bob Dylan, 2011. **Address:** 2571 Belmont Ave., PO Box 7725, Long Beach, CA 90815, U.S.A. **Online address:** dennis@littoral.net

MCDOUGAL, Dennis Edward. *See* **MCDOUGAL, Dennis.**

MCDOUGALL, Gay J. American (born United States), b. 1947. **Genres:** Civil Liberties/Human Rights. **Career:** Debevoise, Plimpton, Lyons & Gates, legal aide, associate, 1972-74; Minimum Standards Unit, staff attorney, 1976-77; Office of the Deputy Mayor for Criminal Justice, associate counsel, 1979-80; Commission of Independence for Namibia, founder, 1989; Global Rights, executive director, 1994-2006; United Nations Human Rights Bodies, independent expert, 1997-2001; International Convention on the Elimination of All Forms of Racial Discrimination (CERD), independent expert, 1998; UN, independent expert on minority issues, 2005-; Africare, director. Writer and civil rights activist. **Publications:** Deaths in Detention and South Africa's Security Laws, 1983; (with N.B. Pityana and G. McDougall) Namibia: UN Resolution 435 and the Independence of Namibia, 1989; South Africa's Death Squads: A Report, 1990. **Address:** Global Rights, 1200 18th St. NW, Ste. 602, Washington, DC 20036, U.S.A.

MCDOUGALL, James. British (born England), b. 1974. **Genres:** History, Cultural/Ethnic Topics. **Career:** St. Antony's College, Middle East Centre, junior research fellow, 2002-04; Princeton University, assistant professor, 2004-; University of London, School of Oriental and African Studies, lecturer in the history of Africa. Writer and academic. **Publications:** (ed.) Nation, Society, and Culture in North Africa, 2003; History and the Culture of Nationalism in Algeria, 2006. **Address:** School of Oriental and African Studies, University of London, Thornhaugh St., Russell Sq., London, GL WC1H 0XG, England. **Online address:** jm56@soas.ac.uk

MCDOWELL, Gary L. American (born United States), b. 1949. **Genres:** History, Law, Politics/Government, Economics. **Career:** Social studies teacher at public schools, 1972-73; Dickinson College, assistant professor of political science, 1979-83; Harvard Law School, fellow in law and political science, 1981-82; Tulane University, Newcomb College, assistant professor, 1983-85, associate professor of political science, 1985-86; National Endowment for the Humanities, Office of the Bicentennial of the Constitution, director, 1984-85; U.S. Department of Justice, Office of Public Affairs, associate director, 1985-87; Smithsonian Institution, Woodrow Wilson International Center for Scholars, fellow, 1987-88; National Legal Center for the Public Interest, vice-president for legal and public affairs, 1988-89; University of London, Institute of United States Studies, director, 1992-2003, professor of American studies, 1993-; University of Richmond, Jepson School of Leadership Studies, Tyler Haynes interdisciplinary professor of leadership studies and political science, 2003-05; Tyler Haynes interdisciplinary professor of leadership studies, political science and law, 2005-. Writer. **Publications:** Taking the Constitution Seriously: Essays on the Constitution and Constitutional Law, 1981; Equity and the Constitution: The Supreme Court, Equitable Relief, and Public Policy, 1982; The Constitution and Contemporary Constitutional Theory, 1985; (with K.R. Feinberg and J.M. Kress) Legal System Assault on the Economy, 1986; Curbing the Courts: The Constitution and the Limits of Judicial Power, 1988; (with E.W. Hickok) Justice vs. Law: Courts and Politics in American Society, 1993; Language of Law and the Foundations of American Constitutionalism, 2010. EDITOR: (with R.A. Rossum) The American Founding: Politics, Statesmanship, and the Constitution, 1981; (with E.W. Hickok, Jr. and P.J. Costopoulos) Our Peculiar Security: The Written Constitution and Limited Government, 1993; (with C.A. Sheehan) Friends of the Constitution: Writings of the Federalists, 1787-1788, 1994; (with S.L. Noble) Reason and Republicanism: Thomas Jefferson's Legacy of Liberty, 1997; (with C.A. Sheehan) Friends of the Constitution: Writings of the Other Federalists, 1787-1788, 1998; (with J.S. Smith) Juvenile Delinquency in the United States and the United Kingdom, 1999; (with J. O'Neill) America and Enlightenment Constitutionalism, 2006; (with H. Liebert and T.L. Price) Executive Power in Theory and Practice, 2012. Contributor of articles to journals. **Address:** Jepson School of Leadership Studies, University of Richmond, 242 Jepson Hall, 28 Westhampton Way, Richmond, VA 23173-0001, U.S.A. **Online address:** gmcdowel@richmond.edu

MCDOWELL, John (Henry). American/South African (born South Africa), b. 1942. **Genres:** Classics, Philosophy, Essays. **Career:** University College of Rhodesia, temporary assistant lecturer in classics, 1963; Lincoln College, junior research fellow, 1966; University College, fellow and praelector in philosophy, 1966-86, emeritus fellow, 1988-; Oxford University, university lecturer in philosophy, 1967-86, special lecturer, 1978-81, John Locke lecturer, 1991; Harvard University, James C. Loeb fellow in classical philosophy, 1969; University of Michigan, visiting associate professor of philosophy, 1975; University of California, visiting associate professor of philosophy, 1977; University of Minnesota, visiting professor of philosophy, 1982; Jadavpur University, visiting professor of philosophy, 1983; Princeton University, Council of the Humanities, senior fellow and Old Dominion fellow in philosophy, 1984; University of Pittsburgh, professor of philosophy, 1986-88, distinguished university professor, 1988-. Writer. **Publications:** (Trans. and contrib.) Plato, Theaetetus, 1973; (ed. with G. Evans) Truth and Meaning: Essays in Semantics, 1976; (ed.) Varieties of Reference, 1982; (ed. with G. Evans) The Varieties of Reference, 1982; (ed. with P. Pettit) Subject, Thought, and Context, 1986; Mind and World, 1994; Meaning, Knowledge, and Reality, 1998; Mind, Value, and Reality, 1998; Engaged Intellect: Philosophical Essays, 2009; Having the World in View: Essays on Kant, Hegel, and Sellars, 2009; Perception as a Capacity for Knowledge, 2011. Contributor to journals. **Address:** Department of Philosophy, University of Pittsburgh, CL 1009-H, Pittsburgh, PA 15260, U.S.A. **Online address:** jmcdowel@pitt.edu

MCDOWELL, Lesley. Scottish (born Scotland), b. 1967?. **Genres:** Literary Criticism And History. **Career:** Journalist. **Publications:** The Picnic, 2007; Between the Sheets: The Literary Liaisons of Nine 20th-Century Women Writers, 2010. Contributor to journals and periodicals. **Address:** Glasgow, Scotland. **Online address:** lesley@lesleymcdowell.orangehome.co.uk

MCDOWELL, Linda. British (born England), b. 1949?. **Genres:** Social Sciences. **Career:** Oxford University, School of Geography and the Environment, professor of human geography, professorial fellow of Saint John's College, director of the International Graduate School, Transformations: Economy, Society and Place research cluster, joint co-ordinator; Open University, faculty; Cambridge University, faculty; University of California, London School of Economics, faculty; University College London, faculty; ESRC Gender Equality Network, researcher. Writer. **Publications:** (with D. Morgan) Patterns of Residence: Costs and Options in Student Housing, 1979; (with M. Ball and F. Gray) The Transformation of Britain: Contemporary Social and Economic Change, 1989; (with J. Allen) Landlords and Property: Social Relations in the Private Rented Sector, 1989; Capital Culture: Gender at Work in the City, 1997; Gender, Identity and Place: Understanding Feminist Geographies, 1999; Redundant Masculinities? Employment Change and White Working Class Youth, 2003; Hard Labour: The Forgotten Voices of Latvian Migrant Volunteer Workers, 2005; (contrib.) Gender Divisions and Working Time in the New Economy: Changing Patterns of Work, Care and Public Policy in Europe and North America, 2006. EDITOR: (with C. Hamnett and P. Sarre) The Changing Social Structure, 1989; Undoing Place? A Geographical Reader, 1997; (with J.P. Sharp) Space, Gender, Knowledge: Feminist Readings, 1997; (with J.P. Sharp) A Feminist Glossary of Human Geography, 1999. **Address:** School of Geography, South Parks Rd., Oxford, OX OX1 3QY, England. **Online address:** linda.mcdowell@geog.ox.ac.uk

MCDUFF, Margaret Dusa. British/American (born United States), b. 1945. **Genres:** Mathematics/Statistics. **Career:** University of Cambridge, Scientific Research Council fellow in mathematics, 1970-72; University of York, lecturer, 1972-76; Massachusetts Institute of Technology, visiting assistant professor, 1974-75; Institute for Advanced Study, faculty, 1976-77; University of Warwick, 1976-78; Mathematical Sciences Research Institute, faculty, 1978; State University of New York, assistant professor of mathematics, 1978-80, associate professor, 1980-84, professor, 1984-98, head of mathematics department, 1991-93, distinguished professor, 1998-, now distinguished professor emeritus; Harvard University, visiting professor, 2000; Courant Institute, visiting professor, 2001; Columbia University, Barnard College, Department of Mathematics, professor, Helen Lyttle Kimmel chair. **Publications:** (With D. Salamon) J-Holomorphic Curves and Quantum Cohomology, 1994; (with D. Salamon) Introduction to Symplectic Topology, 1995, 2nd ed., 1998; J-holomorphic Curves and Symplectic Topology, 2004. Contributor to journals. **Address:** Department of Mathematics, Columbia University, Rm. 612, 333 Milbank Hall, MC4410, 3009 Broadway, New York, NY 10027-6598, U.S.A. **Online address:** dmcduff@barnard.edu

MCELDOWNEY, Eugene. Irish (born Ireland), b. 1943. **Genres:** Novels, Young Adult Fiction, Literary Criticism And History. **Career:** Irish Times, journalist and editor, 1972-2002; full-time writer, 1994-. **Publications:** CECIL MEGARRY SERIES: A Kind of Homecoming, 1994; A Stone of the Heart, 1995; The Sad Case of Harpo Higgins, 1996; Murder at Piper's Gut, 1997. NOVELS: The Faloorie Man, 1999, Stella's Story, 2002. **Address:** Imrie & Dervis Literary Agency, 7 Carlton Mansions, Holmleigh Rd., London, GL N16 5PX, England. **Online address:** emceld@hotmail.com

MCELMEEL, Sharron L. American (born United States), b. 1942. **Genres:** Writing/Journalism, Biography, Autobiography/Memoirs. **Career:** College Hill Grocery Store, checkout clerk, 1960-63; Cedar Rapids Community School District, classroom teacher to library media specialist, 1964-98; Verturbo University, Drake College, Grant Wood Area Education Agency, instructor of professional development courses and courses carrying graduate credit through Marycrest College, 1976-2005; KCCK-FM Radio, book reviewer and commentator, 1979-84; Frank N. Magid Associates (media consulting firm), researcher, 1980-81; U.S. Postal Service, operator of a postal route, 1981; Grant Wood Area Education Agency, staff development instructor, 1982-; Mount Mercy College, children's literature, educational technology and young adult literature, adjunct instructor, 1988-2005; Linworth Publishing, associate reviews editor, 1998-; Building a Community of Readers, project director, 2001; University of Northern Iowa, children's literature, adjunct instructor, 2003; University of Wisconsin, Teaching Childrens Literature in the Classroom, instructor, 2004-, Young Adult Literature in the Reading Program, instructor, 2005-; Library Sparks, columnist; McBookwords, director. Educational consultant. **Publications:** Author a Month: For Pennies, 1988; My Bag of Book Tricks, 1989; Bookpeople: A First Album, 1990; Author a Month (For Nickels), 1990; Bookpeople: A Second Album, 1990; (ed.) Iowa, A Place to Read, 1990; Adventures with Social Studies, 1991; Bookpeople: A Multicultural Album, 1992; Authors for Children, 1992; Celebrating Authors: Meet Jacqueline Briggs Martin, 1992; Celebrating Authors: Meet Carol Gorman, 1992; Author a Month (For Dimes), 1993; McElmeel Booknotes, 1993; The Poet Tree, 1993; (contrib.) The Fine Art of Murder: The Mystery Reader's Indispensable Companion, 1993; ABCs of an Author/Illustrator Visit, 1994, 2nd ed., 2001; Latest and Greatest Read-alouds, 1994; Great New Nonfiction Reads, 1995; Educator's Companion to Children's Literature, 1995; Internet for Schools, 1997, (with C. Simpson) 3rd ed., 2000; Research Strategies for Moving Beyond Reporting, 1997; Literature Frameworks: From Apples to Zoos, 1997, 2nd ed., 2002; (with C. Smallwood) WWW Almanac: Making Curriculum Connections to Special Days, Weeks, Months, 1999; (ed.) Shoptalk, Ideas For Elementary School Librarians & Technology Specialists, 1999; 100 Most Popular Children's Authors: Biographical Sketches and Bibliographies, 1999; 100 Most Popular Picture Book Authors and Illustrators, 2000; (ed.) Tips, Ideas For Secondary School Librarians & Technology Specialists, 2000; Character Education: A Book Guide For Teachers, Librarians and Parents, 2002; Children's Authors and Illustrators Too Good to Miss: Biographical Sketches and Bibliographies, 2004; (with D.L. McElmeel) Authors in the Kitchen: Recipes, Stories and More, 2005; Best Teen Reads: 2005, 2005; (with J.B. Martin) Jacqueline Briggs Martin and You, 2006; Authors in the Pantry: Recipes, Stories and More, 2007; The Best Teen Reads, 2007; Picture That! from Mendel to Normandy: Picture Books and Ideas, Curriculum and Connections for Tweens and Teens, 2009; (with M.A. Harlan and D. Loertscher) Young Adult Literature and Multimedia: A Quick Guide 2010, 2010; Best Teen Reads: 2010, 2010. Contributor of articles to magazines. **Address:** University of Wisconsin, 140 Voc Rehab Bldg, 712 S Broadway St., Menomonie, IA 54751, U.S.A. **Online address:** mcelmeel@mcelmeel.com

MCELMURRAY, Karen Salyer. American (born United States), b. 1956. **Genres:** Adult Non-fiction, Novels, Young Adult Fiction, History, Literary Criticism And History. **Career:** University of Virginia, graduate instructor, 1984-86, adjunct faculty, 1986-87; Virginia Polytechnic Institute, instructor, 1988-89; University of North Carolina, instructor, 1989-92; University of Georgia, teaching associate, 1992-96, instructor, 1996-97; Lynchburg College, assistant professor of creative writing, 1997-2001; Berry College, writer-in-residence, 2001-02, visiting professor, 2002-03; Georgia College and State University, Department of English, Speech and Journalism, assistant professor tenure-track, 2003-; Sewanee Young Writers' Conference, faculty. Writer. **Publications:** Strange Bird in the Tree of Heaven: A Novel, 1999; Mother of the Disappeared: An Appalachian Birth Mother's Journey, 2001; Surrendered Child: A Birth Mother's Journey, 2004; Black Dog, 2008; The Motel of the Stars, 2008; Wanting Inez, forthcoming. Contributor to periodicals. **Address:** Creative Writing Program, Georgia College & State University, PO Box 44, Milledgeville, GA 31061, U.S.A. **Online address:** karen.mcelmurray@gcsu.edu

MCELROY, Colleen J. American (born United States), b. 1935. **Genres:** Novels, Plays/Screenplays, Poetry, Adult Non-fiction, Young Adult Fiction, Travel/Exploration, Autobiography/Memoirs. **Career:** Rehabilitation Institute, chief speech clinician, 1963-66; University of Missouri, affiliate faculty of speech, 1965-66; Western Washington University, assistant professor of English, 1966-73, director of speech and hearing services; University of Washington, predoctoral lecturer, 1972-73, assistant professor, 1973-79, associate professor, 1979-82, director of creative writing, 1983-86, professor of English, 1983, now professor emeritus of English and creative writing; Dark Waters Literary Magazine, editor-in-chief, 1973-78; Seattle Review, poetry editor, 1991-, editor-in-chief, 1995-2006. **Publications:** Speech and Language of the Preschool Child: A Survey, 1972; The Mules Done Long Since Gone, 1973; Music from Home: Selected Poems, 1976; (contrib.) Iron Country, 1978; Winters Without Snow, 1979; (contrib.) The Third Woman, 1980; (contrib.) Backbone 2, 1980; Winters without Snow (poems), 1980; Lie and Say You Love Me, 1981; Looking for a Country under Its Original Name, 1984; Queen of the Ebony Isles, 1984; Jesus and Fat Tuesday and Other Short Stories, 1987; Bone Flames: Poems, 1987; Lie and Say You Love Me (poems), 1988; Blue Flames (poems), 1989; What Madness Brought Me Here: New and Selected Poems, 1968-88, 1990; Driving under the Cardboard Pines (fiction), 1990; A Long Way from St. Louie: Travel Memoirs, 1997; Travelling Music, 1998; Over the Lip of the World: Among the Storytellers of Madagascar, 1999; (ed.) Page to Page: Retrospective of Writers from The Seattle Review, 2006; Sleeping With the Moon: Poems, 2007. **Address:** Department of English, University of Washington, PO Box 354330, Seattle, WA 98105, U.S.A. **Online address:** dragnldy@u.washington.edu

MCELROY, John Harmon. American (born United States), b. 1934. **Genres:** Area Studies, History, Social Sciences, Politics/Government, Romance/Historical. **Career:** Punahou School, English instructor, 1958-60; Clemson University, visiting English instructor, 1964-65; University of Wisconsin, assistant professor of American literature, 1966-70, associate professor, 1970-76; University of Salamanca, Fulbright professor of American studies, 1968-69; University of Arizona, professor of American literature, through 1976, professor emeritus, 1976-; Federal University of Santa Catarina, Fulbright professor of American studies, 1986. Writer and historian. **Publications:** Finding Freedom: America's Distinctive Cultural Formation, 1989; American Beliefs: What Keeps a Big Country and a Diverse People United, 1999; Divided We Stand: The Rejection of American Culture Since the 1960s, 2006; (ed.) The Life and Voyages of Christopher Columbus, 1981; (ed. and intro.) The Sacrificial Years: A Chronicle of Walt Whitman's Experiences in the Civil War, 1999. **Address:** Department of English, University of Arizona, Rm. 445, 1423 E University Blvd., Modern Languages Bldg., PO Box 210067, Tucson, AZ 85721, U.S.A. **Online address:** jmcelroy@u.arizona.edu

MCELROY, Joseph (Prince). American (born United States), b. 1930. **Genres:** Novels. **Career:** University of New Hampshire, instructor and assistant professor of English, 1956-62; City University of New York, Queens College, professor of English, 1964-95; Johns Hopkins University, visiting professor, 1976; Northwestern University, writer-in-residence, 1977; Columbia University, visiting professor, 1978; Washington University, Hurst professor, 1979; University of Paris, visiting professor, 1981; New York University, visiting professor, 1984. Writer. **Publications:** A Smuggler's Bible, 1966; Hind's Kidnap, 1969; Ancient History, 1971; Lookout Cartridge, 1974; Plus, 1977; Ship Rock, 1980; Women and Men, 1987; The Letter Left to Me, 1988; Actress in the House: A Novel, 2003; Night Soul and Other Stories, 2010. Contributor to periodicals. **Address:** Georges Borchardt Literary Agency, 136 E 57th St., New York, NY 10022, U.S.A. **Online address:** jmcelrol@earthlink.net

MCELROY, Susan Chernak. American (born United States), b. 1952. **Genres:** Animals/Pets, Natural History, Homes/Gardens. **Career:** Marin Humane Society, technical editor; Humane Society of Sonoma County, technical editor; Humane Society of Utah, technical editor; Marin Wildlife Center, technical editor; Knowland State Park Baby Zoo, technical editor. **Publications:** Animals as Teachers and Healers: True Stories and Reflections, 1995; Animals as Guides for the Soul: Stories of Life-Changing Encounters, 1998; Unforgettable Mutts: Pure of Heart Not of Breed, 1999; Heart in the Wild: A Journey of Self-Discovery with Animals of the Wilderness, 2002; All My Relations: Living with Animals as Teachers and Healers, 2004; Why Buffalo Dance: Animal and Wilderness Meditations through the Seasons, 2006. Contributor to periodicals. **Address:** c/o Elaine Markson, Elaine Markson Literary, 44 Greenwich Ave., New York, NY 10011, U.S.A.

MCELYA, Micki. American (born United States), b. 1972. **Genres:** History. **Career:** University of Alabama, assistant professor of American studies, 2003-08; University of Connecticut, assistant professor of history, 2008-; New York University, prize teaching fellow, 2002-03. Writer and historian. **Publications:** Clinging to Mammy: The Faithful Slave in Twentieth-Century

America, 2007. Contributor to books. **Address:** Department of History, University of Connecticut, 241 Glenbrook Rd., Storrs, CT 06269-2103, U.S.A. **Online address:** micki.mcelya@uconn.edu

MCENERY, John H. British/Scottish (born Scotland), b. 1925. **Genres:** Economics, History, Military/Defense/Arms Control, Sociology, Social Sciences. **Career:** British Government, 1949-81, Cabinet Secretariat, member, 1957-59, British delegation to North Atlantic Treaty Organization (NATO), staff, 1964-66, British embassy in Bonn, staff, 1966-69, Yorkshire and Humberside, regional director, 1972-76, under secretary for Concorde, 1977-81; freelance consultant, 1981-. Writer. **Publications:** Manufacturing Two Nations, 1981; (with C. Russak) Towards a New Concept of Conflict Evaluation, 1985; Epilogue in Burma, 1945-48: The Military Dimension of British Withdrawal, 1990; Fortress Ireland: The Story of the Irish Coastal Forts and the River Shannon Defence Line, 2006. Contributor to periodicals. **Address:** Royal Bank of Scotland, 48 Haymarket, London, GL SW1Y 4SE, England.

MCENTYRE, Marilyn Chandler. (Marilyn R(uth) Chandler). American/Indian (born India), b. 1949. **Genres:** Literary Criticism And History, Humanities, Medicine/Health, inspirational/Motivational Literature. **Career:** Mills College, assistant professor, 1984-90, associate professor of English, 1990-93, chair of department; Trenton State College, associate professor of English, 1993-96; Westmont College, associate professor, 1996-2004, professor of English, 2004-08, Gaede Institute for the Liberal Arts, fellow, 2008-; University of California, professor of medical humanities, 2010-. Writer. **Publications:** A Healing Art: Regeneration through Autobiography, 1990; Dwelling in the Text, 1991; Where Icarus Falls, 1998; (ed. with A.H. Hawkins) Approaches to Teaching Literature and Medicine, 2000; In Quiet Light: Poems on Vermeer's Women, 2000; Drawn to the Light: Poems on Rembrandt's Religious Paintings, 2003; The Light at the Edge: Poems, 2006; The Color of Light: Poems on Van Gogh's Late Paintings, 2007; Christ, My Companion: Meditations on the Prayer of St. Patrick, 2008; Caring for Words in a Culture of Lies, 2009. **Address:** Gaede Institute for the Liberal Arts, Westmont College, 106 Reynolds Hall, 955 La Paz Rd., Santa Barbara, CA 93108-1099, U.S.A. **Online address:** mcentyre@westmont.edu

MCEVILLEY, Thomas. American (born United States), b. 1939. **Genres:** Novels, Art/Art History, Literary Criticism And History, Poetry. **Career:** Rice University, associate professor, 1969-, distinguished lecturer in art history, through 2005, distinguished lecturer emeritus, 2005-; School of the Art Institute of Chicago, visiting professor, 1985-86; Yale University, School of Art, visiting professor, 1991-92; City University of New York, Graduate Center, visiting professor, 1995. Art critic, poet and novelist. **Publications:** The Impregnation of the Guggenheim Museum, 1982; 44 Four-Line Poems, 1982; Pat Steir: The Breughel Series, A Vanitas of Style, 1985; Ulay and Marina Abramović: Modus Vivendi, 1985; Les Levine: Billboard Projects: Blamegod, 1985; Focus on the Image: Selections from the Rivendell Collection, 1986; Janis Kounellis, 1986; Julian Schnabel, 1986, rev. ed., 1987; (with D. Kuspit and R. Smith) Lucas Samaras: Objects and Subjects 1969-1986, 1988; (with U. and M. Abramovic) The Lovers, 1989; (with E. Orr and J.L. Byars) Zero Mass, 1989; William Anastasi, 1989; Georg Baselitz: Sculpture Forty-Five, 1990; Women of Dresden, 1990; Art & Discontent: Theory at the Millennium, 1991; Dennis Oppenheim: Selected Works, 1967-90: And the Mind Grew Fingers, 1992; Art & Otherness: Crisis of Cultural Identity, 1992; (with J. Durham) Elaine Reichek: Native Intelligence, 1992; The Exile's Return: Towards a Redefining Painting for the Post-Modern Era, 1993; Fusion: West African Artists at the Venice Biennale, 1993; Yves Klein: Conquistador of the Void, 1993; (with A. Baraka) Thornton Dial: Image of The Tiger, 1993; Ulay: Der Erste Akt: The First Act, 1994; Leon Golub, 1994; Diogenes: Definition, 1994; Ingeborg Lüscher: Brightless/Stillness: Goldie Paley Gallery, Moore College of Art and Design, 1995; Fictivespace: Judith Schwarz/Arlene Stamp, 1995; (contrib.) Marina Abramoviac: Objects, Performance, Video Sounds, 1995; Pat Steir: The Water Paintings, 1995; (with R. Denson) Capacity: History, the World and the Self in Contemporary Art and Criticism, 1996; (with J. Helfenstein and N. Spector) Meret Oppenheim: Beyond the Teacup, 1996; (co-author) James Croak, 1998; (co-author) Kounelles: M/S Ionion Peiraias, 1998; Sculpture in the Age of Doubt, 1999; The Shape of Ancient Thought: Comparative Studies in Greek and Indian Philosophies, 2002; Bernar Venet, 2002; The Triumph of Anti-Art: Conceptual and Performance Art in the Formation of Post Modernism, 2003; Art of Dove Bradshaw: Nature, Change and Indeterminacy, 2003; Sappho, 2008; Yves the Provocateur: Yves Klein and Twentieth-Century Art, 2010; Art, Love, Friendship: Marina Abramovic and Ulay, Together & Apart, 2010. NOVELS: Partygoing, 1964; Wakerobin, 1965; North of Yesterday, or, Flowers of Warz, 1987; The Arimaspea, 1993. Contributor to books. **Address:** Rice University, MS 549, 6100 Main St., PO Box 1892, Houston, TX 77005-1827, U.S.A. **Online address:** mcevilley@mindspring.com

MCEWAN, Barbara. American (born United States), b. 1926. **Genres:** Agriculture/Forestry, Horticulture, History, Social Sciences. **Career:** High school biology teacher, 1950-51; Milwaukee Audubon Society, affiliate, 1955-60; Quail Hollow Nursery, owner and operator, 1974-88; Quail Hollow Landscape Design, secretary and treasurer, 1992-. Writer. **Publications:** Thomas Jefferson's Poplar Forest, 1987; Thomas Jefferson: Farmer, 1991; White House Landscapes, 1992; The Agriculture Crisis, 1993. Works appear in anthologies. Contributor to periodicals. **Address:** 104 Haines Point Terr., Forest, VA 24551-1854, U.S.A.

MCEWAN, Ian. British (born England), b. 1948. **Genres:** Novels, Novellas/Short Stories, Plays/Screenplays, Literary Criticism And History, Young Adult Non-fiction, Theatre, Photography, Picture/Board Books, Picture/Board Books. **Career:** Sussex University, reader of English. Writer. **Publications:** NOVELS: The Cement Garden, 1978; The Comfort of Strangers, 1981; The Imitation Game, 1981; Rose Blanche, 1985; The Child in Time, 1987; The Innocent, 1990; Black Dogs, 1992; The Good Son, 1993; The Daydreamer, 1994; Enduring Love, 1997; Amsterdam, 1998; Atonement, 2002; Saturday, 2005; On Chesil Beach, 2007; For You, 2008; Solar, 2010. OTHERS: First Love, Last Rites, 1975; In Between the Sheets, and Other Stories, 1978; Or Shall We Die?, 1983; The Ploughman's Lunch 1985; Soursweet, 1988; A Move Abroad: Or Shall We Die?, 1989; The Short Stories, 1995. Contributor to periodicals and journals. **Address:** Jonathan Cape Publicity Department, Random House, 20 Vauxhall Bridge Rd., London, GL SW1V 2SA, England.

MCEWEN, Helena. British/Scottish (born Scotland), b. 1961. **Genres:** Novels. **Career:** Kensington and Chelsea College, painting teacher, 1998-2000, 2003; writer and artist, 2000-; Trinity Hospice, facilitator, 2001; University College Falmouth, part-time lecturer, 2005-06. **Publications:** The Big House, 1999; Ghost Girl, 2004; Invisible River, 2011. Contributor to periodicals. **Address:** c/o Author Mail, Bloomsbury Publishing, 38 Soho Sq., London, GL W1V 5DF, England.

MCEWEN, Indra Kagis. Canadian (born Canada), b. 1945. **Genres:** Architecture, Intellectual History, Philosophy, Art/Art History, Politics/Government. **Career:** Anderson Architects, architect, 1986-87; Paulin & Lariviere, architectes, 1988-89; National Theatre School of Canada, Scenography Division, lecturer, 1992-2005; McGill University School of Architecture, visiting lecturer, 1994-98; Concordia University, adjunct professor of art history, 2003-. Writer. **Publications:** Ordonnance for the Five Kinds of Columns after the Method of the Ancients, 1993; Socrates Ancestor: An Essay on Architectural Beginnings, 1993; Vitruvius: Writing the Body of Architecture, 2003; The Horseman on the Hill, forthcoming. **Address:** Department of Art History, Concordia University, 3.809 EV Complex, Catherine St. W, Ste. 1515, 1455, de Maisonneuve Blvd. W, Montreal, QC H3G 2W1, Canada. **Online address:** indra.mcewen@sympatico.ca

MCEWEN, Todd. British/Scottish/American (born United States), b. 1953?. **Genres:** Novels, Young Adult Fiction. **Career:** Granta Magazine, editor; University of Kent, faculty of creative writing; The Guardian, reviewer. **Publications:** Fisher's Hornpipe, 1983; McX: A Romance of the Dour, 1990; Arithmetic, 1998; Who Sleeps with Katz, 2003. **Address:** School of English, University of Kent, NC20, Canterbury, KT CT2 7NX, England. **Online address:** t.w.mcewen@kent.ac.uk

MCFADDEN, David W. Canadian (born Canada), b. 1940. **Genres:** Novels, Poetry, Novellas/Short Stories, Young Adult Non-fiction. **Career:** Hamilton Spectator, proofreader, 1962-70, reporter, 1970-76; Simon Fraser University, writer-in-residence, 1979; Kootenay School of Writing, David Thompson University Centre, teacher of creative writing, 1979-; Coach House Press, editor; SwiftCurrent, contributing editor; Canadian Art Magazine, contributing editor; Quill and Quire, contributing editor; Hamilton This Month, contributing editor; David Thompson University, faculty. **Publications:** The Poem Poem, 1967; The Saladmaker, 1968; Letters from the Earth to the Earth, 1968; The Great Canadian Sonnet (novel), 1970; Poems Worth Knowing, 1971; Intense Pleasure, 1972; The Ova Yogas, 1972; A Knight in Dried Plums, 1975; The Poet's Progress, 1977; On the Road Again, 1978; I Don't Know, 1978; A New Romance, 1978; A Trip around Lake Erie (novel), 1980; A Trip around

Lake Huron (novel), 1980; (ed.) My Body Was Eaten by Dogs: Selected Poems, 1981; Three Stories and Ten Poems, 1982; Country of the Open Heart, 1982; Animal Spirits: Stories to Live By, 1983; A Pair of Baby Lambs, 1983; The Art of Darkness, 1984; Canadian Sunset (novel), 1986; Gypsy Guitar: One Hundred Poems of Romance and Betrayal, 1987; A Trip around Lake Ontario (novel), 1988; Anonymity Suite, 1992; An Innocent in Ireland (nonfiction), 1995; There'll Be Another (poetry), 1995; Great Lakes Suite (nonfiction), 1997; An Innocent in Scotland (nonfiction), 1999; Five Star Planet, 2002; Innocent in Newfoundland: Even More Curious Rambles and Singular Encounters, 2003; Cow Swims Lake Ontario, or, The Case of the Waterloggen Quadruped, 2003; Innocent in Cuba: Further Curious Rambles and Singular Encounters, 2005; Why are You so Sad?, 2007; Be Calm, Honey: 129 Sonnets, 2008; Why are You So Long and Sweet?: Collected Long Poems, 2010. **Address:** c/o Writers, 40 Wellington St. East, 3rd Fl., Toronto, ON M5E 1C7, Canada. **Online address:** david_mcfadden@wier.ca

MCFADDEN, Johnjoe. British/Irish (born Ireland), b. 1956. **Genres:** Sciences, Natural History, Young Adult Fiction. **Career:** St. Mary's Hospital Medical School, Department of Biochemistry, research fellow, 1982-84; St. George's Hospital Medical School, Department of Surgery, research fellow, 1984-88; University of Surrey, School of Biological Sciences, lecturer, 1988-94, reader, 1994-2001, deputy head, 2001-, professor of molecular genetics, 2002-, head of microbial sciences group. Writer. **Publications:** (And ed.) Molecular Biology of the Mycobacteria, 1990; Quantum Evolution: The New Science of Life, 2001; (ed. with R.H. Wells) Human Nature: Fact and Fiction, 2006; Ockham's Razor, forthcoming. Contributor to books. **Address:** School of Biological Sciences, University of Surrey, Rm. 07 AX 01, Guildford, SR GU2 7XH, England. **Online address:** j.mcfadden@surrey.ac.uk

MCFADDEN, Steven. American (born United States), b. 1948. **Genres:** Agriculture/Forestry, Cultural/Ethnic Topics, Environmental Sciences/Ecology, Local History/Rural Topics, Mythology/Folklore, Philosophy, Race Relations, Biography, Biography, Medicine/Health. **Career:** Watertown Sun (newspaper), editor, 1975-78; SPS Communications Inc., communications director, 1977-79; John Mercer Associates (writing consultants), senior associate, 1978-92; Social Planning Services Inc., executive director, 1979-82; Chiron Communications, founder and director, 1985-91, director, 2000-; Wisdom Conservancy at Merriam Hill Education Center, director, 1991-95; Sunbow Walk for the Earth, coordinator, 1995-96; Chiron Communications, director, 1996-2008; Cultural Centers Coalition of Lincoln, NE, development coordinator, 2009-11; Good Medicine Consulting, director, 2010. **Publications:** Know Thyself, Heal Thyself, 1982; (with T. Groh) Farms of Tomorrow, 1990; Profiles in Wisdom: Native Elders Speak about the Earth, 1991, rev. ed., 2000; Ancient Voices, Current Affairs, 1992, rev. ed. as Legend of the Rainbow Warriors, 2001; (with T. Groh) Farms of Tomorrow Revisited, 1998; (co-author) Hand to Hand: The Longest-Practicing Reiki Master Tells His Story, 2002; Odyssey of the 8th Fire, 2007; The Call of the Land: An Agrarian Primer for the 21st Century, 2009; Native Knowings: Wisdom Keys for 2012 and Beyond, 2010; The Call of the Land, 2nd ed., 2011. Work represented in anthologies. Contributor to magazines and newspapers. **Address:** Chiron Communications, 1519 F St., Lincoln, NE 68508, U.S.A. **Online address:** chiron@chiron-communications.com

MCFALL, Gardner. American (born United States), b. 1952. **Genres:** Poetry, Children's Fiction, Photography. **Career:** Cooper Union for the Advancement of Science and Art, assistant professor of humanities, 1990-98; State University of New York, Purchase College, lecturer in creative writing, 1993; City University of New York, Hunter College, adjunct associate professor of children's literature, 2003-. Writer. **Publications:** Jonathan's Cloud (children's book), 1986; Naming the Animals, 1994; The Pilot's Daughter (poetry), 1996; (ed.) Made with Words, 1998; (intro.) The Wind in the Willows, 2005; Russian Tortoise (poetry), 2009; Amelia: The Libretto, 2009. **Address:** Department of English, Hunter College, City University of New York, Rm. 1238 HW, 695 Park Ave., New York, NY 10065-5024, U.S.A. **Online address:** cathgm@nyc.rr.com

MCFARLAND, Barkinglips. *See* **FRANKLIN, Linda Campbell.**

MCFARLAND, Dennis. American (born United States), b. 1950?. **Genres:** Novels, Literary Criticism And History. **Career:** Stanford University, teacher of creative writing, 1981-86; Emerson College, teacher or creative writing, 1987-89. Writer. **Publications:** The Music Room, 1990; School for the Blind, 1994; A Face at the Window, 1997; Singing Boy, 2001; Prince Edward, 2004; Letter from Point Clear, 2007. Contributor to periodicals. **Address:** Brandt & Hochman, 1501 Broadway, New York, NY 10036, U.S.A. **Online address:** dennis@dennismcfarland.com

MCFARLAND, Henry Hammer. *See* **MCFARLAND, Henry O.**

MCFARLAND, Henry O. (Henry Hammer McFarland). American (born United States), b. 1934. **Genres:** Children's Fiction. **Career:** McFarland Ford Sales Inc., co-founder, 1957-, president, 1957-2002, treasurer; Hampton Ford-Hyundai Inc., treasurer. Writer. **Publications:** FOR CHILDREN AS HENRY HAMMER McFARLAND: Ralph's World, 2002; Ralph and Jimbo's Great Golf Adventure, 2002; It's a Dog's World, 2003. **Address:** McFarland Ford Sales Inc., 151 Portsmouth Ave., Exeter, NH 03833, U.S.A. **Online address:** hankrye@aol.com

MCFARLAND, Martha. *See* **SMITH-ANKROM, M. E.**

MCFARLAND, Stephen L. American (born United States), b. 1950. **Genres:** History, Military/Defense/Arms Control, Engineering. **Career:** University of Texas, graduate research assistant, 1977-78, graduate teaching assistant, 1979-80; St. Edwards University, adjunct professor of history, 1980; Auburn University, assistant professor, 1981-87, associate professor, 1987-95, professor of history, 1995-, associate dean, 1997-2000, acting associate provost, dean, 2001-; United States Air Force Air War College, visiting professor of military history, 1992-93. Writer. **Publications:** (With W.P. Newton) To Command the Sky: The Battle for Air Superiority over Germany, 1942-1944, 1991; America's Pursuit of Precision Bombing, 1910-1945, 1995; A Concise History of the U.S. Air Force, 1997; Conquering the Night: Army Air Forces Night Fighters at War (U.S. Army Air Forces in World War II), 1998. **Address:** Department of History, Auburn University, 310 Thach Hall, Auburn, AL 36849-5207, U.S.A. **Online address:** mcfarsl@auburn.edu

MCFARLANE, Peter (William). Australian (born Australia), b. 1940. **Genres:** Novels, Novellas/Short Stories, Poetry, Education, Writing/Journalism, Autobiography/Memoirs, Literary Criticism And History. **Career:** Department of Education and Children's Services, teacher and co-ordinator, 1962-69, advisor, 1971-94; English teacher and assistant department head, 1969-71; Troupe Theatre, director, 1978. Writer. **Publications:** POETRY: (with G. Boomer) Orange Moon, 1975; (with R. Harris) A Book to Write Poems By, 1983; My Grandfather's Horses, 1983; (with R. Harris) A Book to Perform Poems By, 1985; (with R. Harris) Making the Magic, 1988; (with L. Temple) Blue Light, Clear Atoms, 1996; (with R. Harris) Doing Bombers Off the Jetty, 1997; Among Ants Between Bees, 1998. NOVELS: The Tin House, 1989, rev. ed., 1992; Rebecca the Wrecker, 1995, rev. ed., 1997; The Enemy You Killed, 1996, rev. ed., 1997; Bruce the Goose, 1996; Betty the Balloon Buster, 1996; Soula the Ruler, 1997; Max the Man Mountain, 1997; Barnaby the Barbarian, 1998; Michaela the Whaler, 1999; More Than a Game, 1999; Goat Boy, 2001; Bomber Boy, 2002; Kart Girl, 2003. STORIES: The Flea and Other Stories, 1992, rev. ed., 1994; Lovebird, 1993, rev. ed., 1995. OTHER: Exploring the Writer's Craft, 2000. EDITOR: The Projected Muse: Extracts from Six Australian Film Scripts, 1977; (with T. Duder and contrib.) The New Zealand/Australian Anthology of Short Stories, 1997; (with L. Temple) Among Ants between Bees, 1998. Works appear in anthologies. **Address:** 8 Carlton St., Highgate, SA 5063, Australia.

MCFEELY, Eliza. American (born United States), b. 1956. **Genres:** Anthropology/Ethnology, History, Theology/Religion. **Career:** Princeton University, lecturer in history, 1996-99, teacher preparation program, program administrator, 1999-2000; College of New Jersey, instructor in history, 2000-, assistant professor of history. Writer. **Publications:** Zuni and the American Imagination, 2001. **Address:** Department of History, College of New Jersey, 2000 Pennington Rd., Social Sciences Bldg., PO Box 7718, Ewing, NJ 08628-0718, U.S.A. **Online address:** mcfeely@tcnj.edu

MCFETRIDGE, John. Canadian (born Canada), b. 1959. **Genres:** Novels. **Career:** Writer. **Publications:** (with S. Albert) Below the Line, 2003; Dirty Sweet (novel), 2006; Everybody Knows This Is Nowhere (novel), 2008. **Address:** c/o Sarah Cooper, The Saint Agency, 18 Gloucester Ln., Ste. 200, Toronto, ON M4Y 1L5, Canada. **Online address:** john@johnmcfetridge.ca

MCGAHAN, Andrew. Australian (born Australia), b. 1966?. **Genres:** Novels, Plays/Screenplays, Young Adult Fiction. **Career:** Writer. **Publications:** FICTION: Praise, 1992; 1988, 1997. OTHERS: Last Drinks, 2000; The White

Earth, 2004; Underground, 2006; Wonders of a Godless World, 2010. **Address:** St. Martin's Press, 175 5th Ave., Ste. 1500, New York, NY 10010-7703, U.S.A.

MCGANN, Michael. *See* **NAHA, Ed.**

MCGARRITY, Michael. American (born United States), b. 1939?. **Genres:** Mystery/Crime/Suspense, Novels. **Career:** New Mexico Law Enforcement Academy, deputy sheriff and instructor; New Mexico Public Defender's Office, investigator; New Mexico Prison System, teacher of psychology. Writer. **Publications:** KEVIN KERNEY MYSTERY SERIES: Tularosa, 1996; Mexican Hat, 1997; Serpent Gate, 1998; Hermit's Peak, 1999; The Judas Judge, 2000; Under the Color of Law, 2001; The Big Gamble, 2002; Everyone Dies, 2003; Slow Kill, 2004; Nothing But Trouble, 2005; Death Song, 2007; Dead or Alive, 2008. NOVEL: Hard Country, 2012. Contributor to periodicals and journals. **Address:** Penguin Group Inc., 375 Hudson St., New York, NY 10014, U.S.A. **Online address:** mcgarrity@michaelmcgarrity.com

MCGAUGHY, J. Kent. American (born United States), b. 1964. **Genres:** History, Biography, Autobiography/Memoirs. **Career:** University of Houston, Department of History, teaching assistant, 1991-96; Alvin Community College, adjunct instructor, 1992-96; Houston Community College, Northwest College, adjunct instructor, 1996-97, professor of history, 1997-, director of honors program, 1999-2007, associate chair, 2009-. Writer. **Publications:** Richard Henry Lee of Virginia: A Portrait of an American Revolutionary, 2004. **Address:** Northwest College, Houston Community College, 1550 Foxlake Dr., Katy Campus, Houston, TX 77084-6029, U.S.A. **Online address:** kent.mcgaughy@hccs.edu

MCGEE, Garry. American (born United States), b. 1966?. **Genres:** Music, Art/Art History. **Career:** Writer. **Publications:** Band on the Run: A History of Paul McCartney and Wings, 2003; Doris Day: Sentimental Journey, 2005; (with D. Day) Que Sera, Sera: The Magic of Doris Day Through Television, 2006; Jean Seberg-Breathless, 2008. **Address:** c/o Author Mail, Rowman & Littlefield Publishing Group, 4501 Forbes Blvd., Ste. 200, Lanham, MD 20706, U.S.A.

MCGEE, Glenn. American (born United States), b. 1967?. **Genres:** Philosophy, Ethics. **Career:** Vanderbilt University, coordinator of program in ethics and genetics, 1993-94; University of Massachusetts, Center for Applied and Professional Ethics, assistant professor of philosophy and founding director, 1994-95; University of Iowa, post doctoral fellow, 1994-95; University of Pennsylvania, assistant professor, 1995-2005, Bioethics Education Network, assistant professor, associate director for education, head, 1998-, John B. Francis endowed chair, 2009-; Villanova University, distinguished visiting professor, 1997-98; Albany Medical College, Alden March Bioethics Institute, founding director, 2005-, professor; The American Journal of Bioethics, founder and editor-in-chief, 2008-. **Publications:** The Perfect Baby: A Pragmatic Approach to Genetics, 1997, 2nd ed. as The Perfect Baby: Parenthood in the New World of Cloning and Genetics, 2000; Being Genomic, 2002; Beyond Genetics: Putting the Power of DNA to Work in Your Life, 2003. EDITOR: The Human Cloning Debate, 1998, (with A. Caplan) 4th ed., 2004; Pragmatic Bioethics, 1999, 2nd ed., 2003; (with K. Saito) The New Immortality: Science and Speculation about Extending Life Forever, 2001; (with D. Magnus and A. Caplan) Who Owns Life?, 2002. **Address:** Alden March Bioethics Institute, MC 153, 47 New Scotland Ave., Albany, NY 12208-3478, U.S.A. **Online address:** glenn.mcgee@bioethics.net

MCGEE, Marni. American (born United States) **Genres:** Archaeology/Antiquities, Animals/Pets, History. **Career:** American School, teacher, 1967-69; freelance writer and editor, 1974-94; full-time writer, 1994-; StoryFaire, founder, 2007. **Publications:** The Quiet Farmer, 1991; Diego Columbus Adventures on the High Seas, 1992; Forest Child, 1994; Jack Takes the Cake, 1998; Sleepy Me, 2001; The Colt and the King, 2001; Wake up Me!, 2002; The Ancient Roman World, 2004; The Noisy Farm: Lots of Animal Noises to Enjoy!, 2004; The Ancient Near Eastern World, 2005; Winston the Book Wolf, 2006; While Angels Watch, 2006; Song in Bethlehem, 2007; National Geographic Investigates Ancient Greece: Archaeology Unlocks the Secrets of Greece's Past, 2007; Silly Goose, 2008; Bumble, the Little Bear With Big Ideas, 2010; The Best Christmas Ever, 2010; Millicent's Christmas, 2010; Messy Me, 2011; Surferella, 2011. Works appear in anthologies. **Address:** c/o Nancy Gallt, Nancy Gallt Literary Agency, 273 Charlton Ave., South Orange, NJ 07079, U.S.A.

MCGEE, Spike. *See* **MOODY, Fred.**

MCGEE, Terence Gary. Canadian/New Zealander (born New Zealand), b. 1936. **Genres:** Geography, Regional/Urban Planning, Economics, Theology/Religion. **Career:** University of Wellington, assistant lecturer, 1960, lecturer in geography, 1965-68; University of Malaya, lecturer in geography, 1961-64; University of Hong Kong, professor of geography, 1968-73; Australian National University, senior fellow, 1973-77; University of British Columbia, Department of Geography, professor, through 2001, Institute of Asian Research, director, 1978-, professor emeritus of Asian research, 2001-. Writer. **Publications:** (Contrib.) Wang Gungwu, 1964; The Southeast Asian City: A Social Geography of the Primate Cities of Southeast Asia, 1967; (with D.W. McTaggart) Petaling Jaya: A Socio-Economic Survey of a New Town in Selangor, Malaysia, 1967; (contrib.) Social Process in New Zealand, 1969; The Urbanization Process: Western Theory and Southeast Asian Experience, 1969; Hawkers in Selected Asian Cities: A Preliminary Investigation, 1970; The Urbanization Process in the Third World: Explorations in Search of a Theory, 1971; Hawkers in Hong Kong, 1973; Food Dependency in the Pacific: A Preliminary Statement, 1975; Hawkers in Southeast Asian Cities: Planning for the Bazaar Economy, 1977; (with P.J. Rimmer and D.W. Drakakis-smith) Food, Shelter and Transport in Southeast Asia and the Pacific, 1978; (co-author.) Food Distribution in the New Hebrides, 1980; Labor Markets, Urban Systems and the Urbanisation Process in Southeast Asian Countries, 1982; Proletarianization, Industrialization and Urbanization in Asia: A Case Study of Malaysia, 1982; (with W.R. Armstrong) Theatres of Accumulation: Studies in Asian and Latin American Urbanization, 1985; (ed. with Y.M. Yeung) Community Participation in Delivering Urban Services in Asia, 1986; (with N. Ginsburg and B. Koppell) The Extended Metropolis in Asia: A New Phase of the Settlement Transition in Asia, 1991; (ed. with Y.M. Fung and K.S. Pun) Ling Kee New School Atlas for Hong Kong, 1986; (co-author) Industrialisation and Labour Force Processes: A Case Study of Peninsular Malaysia, 1986; (ed. with K. Eliot and B. Lee) Canadian Perspectives on Modern Japan, 1990; (ed. with N. Ginsburg and B. Koppel) The Extended Metropolis: Settlement Transition in Asia, 1991; (ed. with I.M. Robinson) The Mega-Urban Regions of Southeast Asia, 1995; (ed. with I. Robinson) The Mega Urban Regions of Southeast Asia, 1995; (ed. with R.F. Walters) Asia-Pacific: New Geographies of the Pacific Rim, 1997; Five Decades of Urbanization in Southeast Asia: A Personal Encounter, 1997; (ed. with A. Kumssa) New Regional Development Paradigms, vol. I, 2001; China's Urban Space: Development Under Market Socialism, 2007. Contributor to journals. **Address:** Institute of Asian Research, University of British Columbia, 1855 W Mall, Ste. 254, Vancouver, BC V6T 1Z2, Canada. **Online address:** tmcgee@interchange.ubc.ca

MCGEE, Toni. (Toni McGee Causey). American (born United States) **Genres:** Young Adult Fiction, Romance/Historical. **Career:** Writer. **Publications:** AS TONI MCGEE CAUSEY: Bobbie Faye's Very (Very, Very, Very) Bad Day, 2007; Bobbie Faye's (Kinda, Sorta, not Exactly) Family Jewels, 2008; Charmed and Dangerous, 2009; Girls Just Wanna Have Guns, 2009; When a Man Loves a Weapon, 2009. **Address:** c/o Stephanie Kip Rostan, Levine Greenberg Literary Agency Inc., 307 7th Ave., Ste. 2407, New York, NY 10001, U.S.A. **Online address:** toni@tonimcgeecausey.com

MCGHEE, Hallie M. American (born United States), b. 1964?. **Genres:** Children's Fiction. **Career:** Harper Collins Publishers, associate publisher for Michael di Capua imprint, 1991-; Pippin Properties (literary agency), founder, 1998. Writer and literary agent. **Publications:** Dessert First, 2009; Just Desserts, 2010; No Room for Dessert, 2011; Mitchell's License, 2011. Contributor to periodicals. **Address:** Pippin Properties, 155 E 38th St., Ste. 2H, New York, NY 10016, U.S.A.

MCGILL, Alice. American (born United States) **Genres:** Children's Fiction, Young Adult Fiction. **Career:** Writer and educator. **Publications:** (With M.C. Smith and E. Washington) Griots' Cookbook: Rare and Well-done, 1985; Molly Bannaky, 1999; Miles' Song, 2000; In the Hollow of Your Hand: Slave Lullabies, 2000; Here We Go Round, 2002; Sure as Sunrise: Stories of Bruh Rabbit and His Walkin' Talkin' Friends, 2004; (contrib.) Don't Cramp My Style: Stories about that Time of the Month, 2004; Way Up and Over Everything, 2008. **Address:** Houghton Mifflin Co., 222 Berkley St., Boston, MA 02116, U.S.A. **Online address:** amcgill@erols.com

MCGILL, Angus. British (born England), b. 1934?. **Genres:** Humor/Satire, Children's Fiction, Travel/Exploration. **Career:** The Evening Standard Newspaper, columnist, 1962-92, feature writer and scriptwriter for a comic strip.

Publications: Yea Yea Yea, 1963; (with D. Poelsma) Clive, 1968; Pub: A Celebration, 1969; (with D. Poelsma) Clive in Love, 1970; (with D. Poelsma) Clive and Augusta, 1972; (with D. Poelsma) Augusta the Great, 1977; (with D. Poelsma) I, Augusta, 1978; (with K. Thomson) Live Wires, 1982; London Pub Guide, 1995, 3rd ed., 1997; (with D. Poelsma) Augusta No: 1, 1996. **Address:** 83 Winchester Ct., Vicarage Gate, London, GL W8 4AF, England. **Online address:** mcgatoz@aol.com

MCGILL, Dan M(ays). American (born United States), b. 1919. **Genres:** Money/Finance, Economics. **Career:** University of Tennessee, associate professor of finance, 1947-48; University of North Carolina, Julian Rice associate professor of life insurance, 1948-51; University of Pennsylvania, Wharton School, associate professor, 1952-56, professor, 1956-59, Frederick H. Ecker professor of life insurance, 1959-90, professor emeritus of insurance and risk management, 1990-, chair, Pension Research Center, research director, 1952-90, chair, 1965-; S.S. Huebner Foundation, executive director, 1954-65, 1967-74, 1978-; International Foundation of Health, Welfare, and Pension Plans Inc., director, 1969-72; INA Investment Securities, director, 1972-; NRG Life Reassurance Corp., director, 1984-; National Health and Welfare Retirement Association Inc., director. Writer. **Publications:** An Analysis of Government Life Insurance, 1949; (ed.) Pensions: Problems and Trends, 1955; Fundamentals of Private Pensions, 1955, (co-author) 8th ed., 2005; (ed.) The Beneficiary in Life Insurance, 1956; Life Insurance Sales Management, 1957; The Legal Aspects of Life Insurance, 1959, 2nd ed., 1997; Life Insurance, 1959, rev. ed., 1967; (ed.) All Lines Insurance, 1960; Fulfilling Pension Expectations, 1962; The Guaranty Fund for Private Pension Obligations, 1970; The Preservation of Pension Benefit Rights, 1972; Employer Guarantee of Pension Benefits, 1974; (ed.) Social Security and Private Pension Plans: Competitive or Complementary?, 1977; (with H.E. Winklevoss, R.S. Neff and G.D. Allison) Public Pension Plans: Standards of Design, Funding, and Reporting, 1979; (ed.) Financing the Civil Service Retirement System: A Threat to Fiscal Integrity, 1979; (ed.) Social Investing, 1984; (ed.) Proxy Voting of Pension Plan Equity Securities, 1989. Contributor to journals. **Address:** Wharton School, University of Pennsylvania, 3000 Steinberg-Dietrich Hall, 3620 Locust Walk, Philadelphia, PA 19104-6302, U.S.A.

MCGILLOWAY, Brian. British/Irish (born Ireland), b. 1974?. **Genres:** Mystery/Crime/Suspense. **Career:** St. Columb's College, teacher and head of English. Writer. **Publications:** INSPECTOR DEVLIN MYSTERY SERIES: Borderlands, 2008; Gallows Lane, 2008; Bleed a River Deep, 2009. Contributor of short stories to journals. Works appear in anthologies. **Address:** St. Columb's College, Buncrana Rd., County Derry, Derry, ND BT48 8NH, Northern Ireland.

MCGINN, Daniel. American (born United States) **Genres:** Business/Trade/Industry, Economics. **Career:** National business correspondent in Boston, 1999-; Correspondent in New York, 1992-96; Business correspondent & bureau chief in Detroit, 1996-99; Newsweek's Kaplan University, Newsweek M.B.A. program, moderator of online video discussions, 2006-. Journalist. **Publications:** House Lust: America's Obsession with Our Homes, 2008. Contributor to periodicals. **Online address:** dan@houselustthebook.com

MCGINNISS, Joe. American (born United States), b. 1942. **Genres:** Politics/Government, Social Commentary, Biography, Adult Non-fiction, Novels. **Career:** Port Chester Daily Item, reporter, 1964; Worcester Telegram, reporter, 1965; Philadelphia Bulletin, sportswriter, 1966; Philadelphia Inquirer, columnist, 1967-68; freelance writer, 1968-; Bennington College, lecturer in writing. **Publications:** The Selling of the President, 1968, 1969; The Dream Team, 1972; Heroes, 1976; Going to Extremes, 1980, 2nd ed., 2010; Fatal Vision, 1983; Blind Faith, 1989; Heroes, 1990; Cruel Doubt, 1991; Last Brother: The Rise and Fall of Teddy Kennedy, 1993; Miracle of Castel di Sangro, 1999; Big Horse, 2004; Never Enough, 2007; The Rogue, 2011. Contributor of articles to periodicals. **Address:** Janklow and Nesbit Associates, 445 Park Ave., New York, NY 10022, U.S.A.

MCGINNISS, Joe. American (born United States), b. 1970?. **Genres:** Novels. **Career:** Writer, 2008-. **Publications:** The Delivery Man, 2008. **Address:** c/o Katharine Cluverius, International Creative Management, 40 W 57th St., New York, NY 10019, U.S.A. **Online address:** joemcginnissjr@aol.com

MCGLOTHIN, Victor. American (born United States) **Genres:** Young Adult Fiction, Novels. **Career:** Writer. **Publications:** In Spite Of, 1998; Autumn Leaves: Love So Deep, 1999; Autumn Leaves: A Novel, 2002; What's a Woman to Do?, 2003; Every Sistah Wants It, 2004; (with E. Sewell and P.T. Duck) Whispers between the Sheets, 2005; (with C. Green and T. Price-Thompson) Indecent Exposure, 2006; (with M. Monroe) Borrow Trouble, 2006; Down on My Knees, 2006; Sinful, 2007; Ms. Etta's Fast House, 2007; Sinful Too, 2008; (with V. McGlothin) Sleep Don't Come Easy, 2008; The Secrets of Newberry, 2010. **Address:** PO Box 864198, Plano, TX 75086-4198, U.S.A. **Online address:** thewritebrother@hotmail.com

MCGOOGAN, Ken. Canadian (born Canada), b. 1947. **Genres:** Literary Criticism And History, Novels, Biography, Documentaries/Reportage, Autobiography/Memoirs. **Career:** Calgary Herald, journalist, literary editor; Montreal Star, journalist; Toronto Star, journalist; Toronto Public Library, writer-in-residence; University of Toronto, School of Continuing Studies, instructor. **Publications:** Canada's Undeclared War: Fighting Words from the Literary Trenches, 1991; Visions of Kerouac: A Novel, 1993, rev. ed. as Kerouac's Ghost, 1996; Calypso Warrior: A Novel, 1995; Chasing Safiya, 1999; Fatal Passage: The Untold Story of John Rae, The Arctic Adventurer Who Discovered the Fate of Franklin, 2001; (with C.L. Doan) Going for Gold, 2002; Ancient Mariner: The Arctic Adventures of Samuel Hearne, The Sailor Who Walked to the Arctic Ocean, 2003; Ancient Mariner: The Arctic Adventures of Samuel Hearne, The Sailor Who Inspired Coleridge's Masterpiece, 2004; Lady Franklin's Revenge: A True Story of Ambition, Obsession and the Remaking of Arctic History, 2005; Race to the Polar Sea: The Heroic Adventures of Elisha Kent Kane, 2008. **Address:** School of Continuing Studies, University of Toronto, 158 St. George St., Toronto, ON M5S 2V8, Canada. **Online address:** ken.mcgoogan@gmail.com

MCGOUGH, Roger. British (born England), b. 1937. **Genres:** Children's Fiction, Plays/Screenplays, Poetry, Children's Non-fiction, Young Adult Fiction. **Career:** Teacher, 1960-62; Technical College, assistant lecturer, 1962-64; Liverpool College of Art, lecturer in liberal studies, 1969-70; Loughborough University of Technology, fellow in poetry, 1973-75; Thames Valley University, honorary professor, 1993-; University of Hamburg, writer-in-residence, 1994-; John Moores University, fellow, 1999-; Poetry Society, vice-president. **Publications:** Birds, Marriages and Deaths, 1964; The Chauffeur-Driven Rolls, 1966; The Commission, 1967; (with A. Henri and B. Patten) The Mersey Sound: Penguin Modern Poets Ten, 1967, rev. ed., 1983; Frinck, a Life in the Day of, 1967; Summer with Monika: Poems, 1967, 2nd ed., 1978; Watchwords, 1969; The Puny Little Life Show, 1969; Zones, 1969; Stuff, 1970; After the Merrymaking, 1971; Out of Sequence, 1972; Gig, 1973; Sporting Relations, 1974, rev. ed., 1996; In the Glassroom, 1976; The Lifeswappers, 1977; Mr. Noselighter, 1977; Holiday on Death Row, 1979; Golden Nights and Golden Days, 1979; All the Trimmings, 1980; Unlucky for Some, 1980; You Tell Me, 1981; Waving at Trains, 1982; The Great Smile Robbery, 1982; (with B. Patten) Behind the Lines, 1982; (with A. Henri and B. Patten) New Volume, 1983; Sky in the Pie, 1983; Crocodile Puddles, 1984; Wind in the Willows, 1984; Melting into the Foreground, 1986; The Stowaways, 1986; Noah's Ark, 1986; Nailing the Shadow, 1987; An Imaginary Menagerie, 1988; A Matter of Chance, 1988; Helen Highwater: A Shropshire Lass, 1989; Selected Poems, 1967-1987, 1989; Counting by Numbers, 1989; Pillow Talk, 1990; The Lighthouse that Ran Away, 1991; You at the Back: Selected Poems, vol. II, 1991; Defying Gravity, 1992; My Dad's a Fire Eater, 1992; Lucky, 1993; Another Custard Pie, 1993; Stinkers Ahoy, 1995; The Magic Fountain, 1995; The Kite and Caitlin, 1996; Until I Met Dudley: How Everyday Things Really Work, 1997; The Spotted Unicorn, 1998; Bad Bad Cats, 1998; (ed.) Ring of Words, 1998; The Way Things Are, 1999; (ed.) The Kingfisher Book of Funny Poems, 2002; Everyday Eclipses, 2002; What on Earth can It Be?, 2002; Good Enough to Eat, 2002; My Oxford ABC and 123 Picture Rhyme Book, 2002; Moonthief, 2003; The Bee's Knees, 2003; (ed.) Wicked Poems, 2003; (ed.) More Funny Stories, 2003; All The Best, 2004; The Monsters' Guide to Choosing a Pet, 2005; Dotty Inventions, 2005; Said and Done: The Autobiography, 2005; Poems for Bootle, 2007; Slapstick, 2008; (contrib.) The Book of Liverpool: A City in Short Fiction, 2008; (adapter) The Hypocondriac, 2009; That Awkward Age, 2009. Contributor to periodicals. **Address:** c/o Charles Walker, United Agents, 12-26 Lexington St., London, GL W1F OLE, England.

MCGOWAN, Anthony. British (born England), b. 1965?. **Genres:** Novels, Young Adult Fiction. **Career:** Open University, tutor in philosophy. Journalist. **Publications:** NOVELS: Stag Hunt, 2004; Mortal Coil, 2005; Hellbent, 2005; Henry Tumour, 2006; The Knife That killed Me, 2008; Jack Tumor,

2009; Einstein's Underpants, 2010; The Fall, 2011. BARE BUM GANG SERIES: The Football Face-Off, 2009; The Holy Grail, 2009; The Valley of Doom, 2009; Battle the Dogsnatchers, 2010. WILLARD PRICE SERIES: Leopard Adventure, 2012. OTHER: The Donut Diaries, 2011. **Address:** Delacorte Press, 1745 Broadway, New York, NY 10019-4368, U.S.A. **Online address:** hellbentmcgowan@mac.com

MCGOWAN, Christopher. Canadian/British (born England), b. 1942. **Genres:** Zoology, Children's Non-fiction. **Career:** Royal Ontario Museum, Department of Vertebrate Palaeontology, curatorial assistant, 1969-70, assistant curator, 1970-74, associate curator, 1974-80, curator, 1980-, Department of Palaeobiology, senior curator, 1994-2002; University of Toronto, Department of Zoology, associate professor, 1972-89, professor, 1990-. Writer. **Publications:** In the Beginning: A Scientist Shows Why the Creationists Are Wrong, 1983; The Successful Dragons: A Natural History of Extinct Reptiles, 1983; Dinosaurs, Spitfires, and Sea Dragons, 1991; Discover Dinosaurs: Become a Dinosaur Detective, 1992; Diatoms to Dinosaurs: The Size and Scale of Living Things, 1994; Make Your Own Dinosaur out of Chicken Bones, 1997; The Raptor and the Lamb, 1997; A Practical Guide to Vertebrate Mechanics, 1999; T. Rex to Go: Build Your Own from Chicken Bones, 1999; Dinosaur: Digging up a Giant, 1999; The Dragon Seekers: How an Extraordinary Circle of Fossilists Discovered the Dinosaurs and Paved the Way for Darwin, 2001; Ichthyopterygia, 2003; Rail, Steam, and Speed: The Rocket and the Birth of Steam Locomotion, 2004; Abacus, 2010; Dinosaur Discovery: Everything You Need to be a Paleontologist, 2010. Contributor to periodicals. **Address:** ON , Canada. **Online address:** scripta1@aol.com

MCGOWAN, John P. American (born United States), b. 1953. **Genres:** Intellectual History, Literary Criticism And History, Cartoons. **Career:** University of San Francisco, lecturer, 1978-79; University of Michigan, assistant professor, 1979-83; Stanford University, lecturer, 1983; University of California Press, editorial assistant, 1983-84; Eastman School of Music, assistant professor of English, 1984-91, associate professor of English, 1987-91; University of Rochester, assistant professor, 1984-87, associate professor of English, 1987-92, Department of Humanities, chair, 1991-92; University of North Carolina, professor, 1992-2006, Ruel W. Tyson Jr. distinguished professor of the humanities, 2006-, Department of English, director of placement for graduate students, 1992-95, 2003-05, Program in Social Theory and Cross-Cultural Studies, co-director, 1994-96, Program in Social Theory and Cross-Cultural Studies, director, 1996-98, Royster Society of Fellows, director, 1996-99, University Program in Cultural Studies, associate director, 1997-99, University Program in Cultural Studies, director of undergraduate studies, 2004-05, Institute for the Arts and Humanities, director; University of California, Departments of English and Comparative Literature, visiting professor, 2001. **Publications:** Representation and Revelation: Victorian Realism from Carlyle to Yeats, 1986; Postmodernism and Its Critics, 1991; Hannah Arendt: An Introduction, 1997; Democracy's Children: Intellectuals and the Rise of Cultural Politics, 2002. Contributor to periodicals. **Address:** Department English & Comparative Literature, University of North Carolina, Greenlaw Hall CB, Ste. 3520, Chapel Hill, NC 27599-3520, U.S.A. **Online address:** jpm@email.unc.edu

MCGOWAN, Mark George. Canadian (born Canada), b. 1959?. **Genres:** History, Theology/Religion, Essays. **Career:** Saint Michael's College, University of Toronto, principal and professor. Writer. **Publications:** (ed. with B.P. Clarke) Catholics at the Gathering Place: Historical Essays on the Archdiocese of Toronto, 1841-1991, 1993; The Waning of the Green: Catholics, the Irish and Identity in Toronto, 1887-1922, 1999; Michael Power: The Struggle to Build the Catholic Church on the Canadian Frontier, 2005. **Address:** University of St. Michael's College, 81 St. Mary St., Toronto, ON M5S 1J4, Canada. **Online address:** mark.mcgowan@utoronto.ca

MCGOWAN, Todd. American (born United States), b. 1967. **Genres:** Young Adult Non-fiction. **Career:** University of Vermont, Department of Film and Television Studies, director of film and television studies, associate professor. Writer. **Publications:** The Feminine No!: Psychoanalysis and the New Canon, 2001; The End of Dissatisfaction?: Jacques Lacan and the Emerging Society of Enjoyment, 2004; Lacan and Contemporary Film, 2004; The Impossible David Lynch, 2007; The Real Gaze: Film Theory after Lacan, 2007; Out of Time: Desire in Atemporal Cinema, 2011; The Fictional Christopher Nolan, 2012; (with P. Eisentstein) Rupture: On the Emergence of the Political, 2012; Enjoying What We Don't Have: A Psychoanalytic Politics, 2012. **Address:** Department of Film & Television Studies, University of Vermont, 431 Old Mill, Burlington, VT 05405-4030, U.S.A. **Online address:** todd.mcgowan@uvm.edu

MCGRANE, Bernard. American (born United States), b. 1947. **Genres:** Communications/Media, Sociology, Advertising/Public Relations, Anthropology/Ethnology, Education, Intellectual History, Humanities, Philosophy, Philosophy, Politics/Government. **Career:** Vermont College, assistant professor, 1977-80; Norwich University, assistant professor, 1977-80; Colby College, visiting assistant professor, 1980-82; Cuesta College, visiting assistant professor, 1982-83; University of California, visiting lecturer in sociology, 1983-85; Loyola Marymont College, visiting professor of sociology, 1984-85; Pitzer College, visiting assistant professor of sociology, 1985-86; University of California-Irvine, lecturer in sociology, 1985-89, part-time lecturer, 1994-2001; Chapman University, Department of Sociology, assistant professor, 1989-95, associate professor, 1995-, department chair, 1993-95; University of California-Los Angles, part-time visiting lecturer, 2002-04. Writer. **Publications:** Beyond Anthropology: Society and the Other, 1989; The UN-TV and the 10 mph Car: Experiments in Personal Freedom and Everyday Life, 1994; (with I. Bell) This Book Is Not Required: An Emotional Survival Manual for Students, 1998, 3rd ed., 2005; (with J. Gunderson) Watching TV is Not Required: Thinking About Media and Thinking about Thinking, 2010. Contributor to periodicals. **Address:** Department of Sociology, Chapman University, Roosevelth Hall 216, 1 University Dr., Orange, CA 92866, U.S.A. **Online address:** mcgrane@chapman.edu

MCGRATH, Barbara B(arbieri). American (born United States), b. 1954. **Genres:** Children's Non-fiction, Children's Fiction, Picture/Board Books. **Career:** Educator and writer. **Publications:** The M&M's Brand Counting Book, 1994; The M&M's Brand Chocolate Candies Counting Book, 1994; More M&M's Brand Chocolate Candies Math, 1998; The Cheerios Counting Book, 1998; The Goldfish Fun Book, 1998; The Baseball Counting Book, 1999; The M&M's Christmas Gift Book, 2000; Necco Sweethearts Be My Valentine Book, 2000; The M&M's Brand Halloween Treat Book, 2000; Skittles Bite Size Candies Riddles Math, 2000; Kellogg's Froot Loops! Counting Fun Book, 2000; Goldfish Counting Fun Book, 2000; Kellogg's Froot Loops Color Fun Book, 2001; The M&M's Brand Valentine Book, 2001; The M&M's Brand Easter Egg Hunt, 2001; The M&M's Brand Birthday Book, 2001; Mas Matematicas Con los Chocolates de Marca M&M, 2001; The M&M's Brand Color Pattern Book, 2002; The M&M's Brand All-American Parade Book, 2003; I Love Words, 2003; (with P. Alderman) Soccer Counts!, 2003; The M&M's Count to One Hundred Book, 2003; Count Around the Circle, 2004; The M&M's Brand Addition Book, 2004; The M&M'S Brand Subtraction Book, 2005; The Little Green Witch, 2005; (comp.) The Storm, 2006; Little Red Elf, 2009; Teddy Bear Counting, 2010; Teddy Bear Math, 2011; Teddy Bear, Teddy Bear, School Day Math, 2012. Contributor to journals. **Address:** c/o Sharon Kelleher, Sharon Kelleher Agency, 5 Wyoming Ave. N, North Reading, MA 01864, U.S.A. **Online address:** bbmcgrath@aol.com

MCGRATH, Carmelita. Canadian (born Canada), b. 1960?. **Genres:** Poetry, Novels, Young Adult Fiction, Picture/Board Books, Natural History, Essays, Politics/Government. **Career:** Tickle Ace Magazine, editor. Poet and freelance writer. **Publications:** (With D. Anger and S. Pottle) Women and Work in Newfoundland, 1986; Poems on Land and on Water, 1992; Walking to Shenak, 1994; To the New World (poems), 1997; Stranger Things Have Happened, 1999; Hearts Larry Broke: New Fiction from the Burning Rock, 2000; The Dog Next Year (picture book), 2001; Ghost Poems (poetry chapbook), 2001. EDITOR: No Place for Fools: The Political Memoirs of Don Jamieson, vol. I, 1989; (with B. Neis and M. Porter) Their Lives and Times: Women of Newfoundland and Labrador: A Collage, 1995; (with L. Cullum and M. Porter) Weather's Edge: A Compendium, 2006. Contributor to books and periodicals. **Address:** 10 Bannerman St., St. John's, NL A1C 3M3, Canada. **Online address:** cmcgrath@avint.net

MCGRATH, Kristina. American (born United States), b. 1950. **Genres:** Novels. **Career:** New York Poets in the Schools, teacher, 1973-84; California Poets in the Schools, teacher, 1986-90; University of Louisville, lecturer, 1996-; Sarabande Books, editorial associate, 1996-. **Publications:** House Work: A Novel, 1994. Contributor of stories to anthologies and periodicals. **Address:** Malaga Baldi Literary Agency, 204 W 84th St., New York, NY 10024-4600, U.S.A.

MCGRATH, Melanie. British (born England), b. 1964?. **Genres:** Adult

Non-fiction, Autobiography/Memoirs, Travel/Exploration, Social Sciences. **Career:** North Carolina University, Department of Creative Writing, visiting professor; Roehampton University, faculty. Journalist. **Publications:** Motel Nirvana: Dreaming of the New Age in the American Desert (travelbook), 1996; Hard, Soft & Wet: The Digital Generation Comes of Age (nonfiction), 1998; Silvertown: An East End Family Memoir, 2002; The Long Exile: A Tale of Inuit Betrayal and Survival in the High Arctic, 2007; Hopping: The Hidden Lives of an East End Hop Picking Family, 2009; White Heat, 2011. **Address:** David Godwin Associates, 55 Monmouth St., London, GL WC2H 9DC, England.

MCGRATH, Patrick. American/British (born England), b. 1950. **Genres:** Novels, Horror, Plays/Screenplays, Literary Criticism And History, Mystery/Crime/Suspense, Young Adult Non-fiction. **Career:** Media Dimensions, Speech Technology Magazine, managing editor, 1982-87; New York Times Book Review, reviewer; Washington Post Book World, reviewer. **Publications:** NOVELS: The Grotesque: A Novel, 1989; Spider, 1990; Dr. Haggard's Disease, 1993; The Angel and Other Stories, 1995; Asylum, 1997; Martha Peake: A Novel of the Revolution, 2000; Port Mungo: A Novel, 2004; Trauma, 2008. OTHER: The Lewis and Clark Expedition (non-fiction), 1985; Blood and Water and Other Tales, 1988; (ed. with B. Morrow) The New Gothic: A Collection of Contemporary Gothic Fiction, 1991 in UK as The Picador Book of the New Gothic, 1992; (intro.) Moby Dick, 1999; Ghost Town: Tales of Manhattan Then and Now, 2005; (intro.) Don't Look Now: Stories, 2008. Contributor to magazines and periodicals. **Address:** 21 E 2nd St., Ste. 10, 231 W 22nd St., New York, NY 10003-8912, U.S.A.

MCGRATH, Sean. *See* **DOUGLAS, John (Frederick James).**

MCGRAW, Erin. American (born United States), b. 1957. **Genres:** Novellas/Short Stories, Novels. **Career:** DePauw University, instructor, 1985-86, assistant professor of English, 1986-91; Yaddo Colony, fellow, 1988; Stanford University, Wallace Stegner fellow in creative writing, 1989-90; University of Cincinnati, assistant professor of English, 1991-97, associate professor of English, 1997-2001; Ohio State University, associate professor of English, 2001-05, professor or English, 2005-; MacDowell Colony, fellow. Writer. **Publications:** SHORT STORIES: Bodies at Sea, 1989; Lies of the Saints, 1996; The Good Life, 2004. NOVELS: The Baby Tree, 2002; Seamstress of Hollywood Boulevard, 2008. Works appear in anthologies. Contributor to periodicals. **Address:** Department of English, Ohio State University, 160 Denney Hall, 164 W 17th Ave., Columbus, OH 43210, U.S.A. **Online address:** mcgraw.46@osu.edu

MCGRAW, Milena. American/Czech (born Czech Republic), b. 1944. **Genres:** Novels, History, Literary Criticism And History, Young Adult Fiction. **Career:** Freelance writer. **Publications:** After Dunkirk (novel), 1998. **Address:** Houghton Mifflin Harcourt, 222 Berkeley St., Boston, MA 02116, U.S.A. **Online address:** pmmcgraw7@cs.com

MCGRAW, Phillip C. American (born United States), b. 1950. **Genres:** Human Relations/Parenting, Self Help. **Career:** Courtroom Sciences Inc., cofounder. Television host, writer, psychologist and litigation consultant. **Publications:** Life Strategies: Doing What Works, Doing What Matters, 1999; Life Strategies Workbook, 2000; Relationship Rescue: A Seven Step Strategy for Reconnecting with Your Partner, 2000; Relationship Rescue Workbook, 2000; Self Matters: Creating Your Life from the Inside Out, 2001; Self Matters Companion, 2002; Philisms, 2002; The Ultimate Weight Solution: The 7 Keys to Weight Loss Freedom, 2003; Ultimate Weight Solution Cookbook: Recipes for Weight Loss Freedom, 2004; Ultimate Weight Solution Food Guide, 2004; Family First: Your Step-by-Step Plan for Creating a Phenomenal Family, 2004; Love Smart: Find the One You Want, Fix the One You Got, 2005; Family First: Specific Tools, Strategies and Skills for Creating a Phenomenal Family, 2005; Real Life: Preparing for the 7 Most Challenging Days of Your Life, 2008. Contributor to periodicals. **Address:** 1 Corporate Plz., 4950 N O'Connor Rd., 1st Fl., Irving, TX 75062-2718, U.S.A.

MCGREEVY, John T. American (born United States) **Genres:** History, Theology/Religion, Race Relations. **Career:** Stanford University, instructor, 1987, Coe Workshop in American History, assistant director, 1988; The Menlo School, instructor, 1988; Hales Franciscan High School, instrutor, 1989-90; Valparaiso University, Lilly postdoctoral fellow in humanities and the arts, 1992-93; Harvard University, assistant professor of history and literature, 1993-96, Dunwalke associate professor of American history and associate professor of history and literature, 1996-97; University of Notre Dame, Department of History, associate professor of history, 1997-99, placement director, 1998-99, 2000-01, John A. O'Brien associate professor of history, 1999-2004, chair, 2002-08, professor of history, 2004-, College of Arts and Letters, I.A. O'Shaughnessy dean, 2008-; Organization of American Historians, distinguished lecturer, 2004-. Writer. **Publications:** Parish Boundaries: The Catholic Encounter with Race in the Twentieth-Century Urban North, 1996; Catholicism and American Freedom: A History, 2003; (intro.) La Pensée Catholique en Amérique du Nord: Réseaux Intellectuels et échanges Culturels Entre L'Europe, Le Canada et Les Etats-Unis (années 1920-1960), 2010; Martyrs and Miracles: Nineteenth Century Jesuits and the American Catholic World They Made, forthcoming. Contributor to books and periodicals. **Address:** Office of the Dean, College of Arts and Letters, University of Notre Dame, 100 O'Shaughnessy Hall, Notre Dame, IN 46556-0368, U.S.A. **Online address:** mcgreevy.5@nd.edu

MCGREGOR, Andrew. New Zealander (born New Zealand), b. 1971. **Genres:** Economics. **Career:** UNICEF Australia, on staff; University of Otago, lecturer; Victoria University of Wellington, senior lecturer. Writer. **Publications:** Southeast Asian Development, 2008. **Address:** School of Geography, Environment, and Earth Sciences, Victoria University of Wellington, PO Box 600, Wellington, 6012, New Zealand. **Online address:** andrew.mcgregor@vuw.ac.nz

MCGREGOR, James H. S. American (born United States), b. 1946. **Genres:** Literary Criticism And History, Urban Studies, Archaeology/Antiquities, Environmental Sciences/Ecology, Poetry. **Career:** Syracuse University, instructor in classics, 1975-79; Colgate University, visiting assistant professor of English, 1979-80; University of Georgia, Department of Comparative Literature, assistant professor, 1981-, associate professor, 1988-, professor, 2001-, co-head, 2002-10, head, 2010-; University of California, Berkeley, visiting professor of Italian, 1984-85. Writer. **Publications:** The Image of Antiquity in Boccaccio's Filocolo, Filostrato and Teseida, 1991; The Shades of Aeneas: The Imitation of Vergil and the History of Paganism in Boccaccio's Filostrato, Filocolo and Teseida, 1991; (trans. and intro.) Luigi Guicciardini, The Sack of Rome, 1993; (ed.) Approaches to Teaching Boccaccio's Decameron, 2000; Rome from the Ground Up, 2005; Venice from the Ground Up, 2006; Washington from the Ground Up, 2007; Paris from the Ground Up, 2009; The Mediterranean: Inhabiting the Landscape, Imagining a World, forthcoming. **Address:** Department of Comparative Literature, University of Georgia, 129 Joseph E Brown Hall, Athens, GA 30602, U.S.A. **Online address:** mcgregor@uga.edu

MCGREGOR, Jon. British (born Bermuda), b. 1976?. **Genres:** Novels, Young Adult Fiction, Psychology, Literary Criticism And History, Young Adult Fiction. **Career:** Nottingham Writer's Studio, founding member. Writer. **Publications:** If Nobody Speaks of Remarkable Things (novel), 2002; So Many Ways To Begin: A Novel, 2006; Even the Dogs: A Novel, 2010. Work represented in anthologies. Contributor to periodicals. **Address:** Bloomsbury Publishing, 38 Soho Sq., London, GL W1D 3HB, England.

MCGREGOR, Tom. *See* **GRANT, Graeme.**

MCGREW, W. C. (William Clement McGrew). American (born United States), b. 1944?. **Genres:** Biology, Animals/Pets, Politics/Government. **Career:** Miami University, professor. Writer. **Publications:** An Ethological Study of Children's Behavior, 1972; Chimpanzee Material Culture: Implications for Human Evolution, 1992; (ed. with R.W. Wrangham, F.B.M. de Waal and P.G. Heltne) Chimpanzee Cultures, 1994; (ed. as William C. McGrew with L.F. Marchant and T. Nishida) Great Ape Societies, 1996; The Cultured Chimpanzee: Reflections on Cultural Primatology, 2004. Contributor to periodicals. **Address:** Department of Zoology, Miami University, 501 E High St., Oxford, OH 45056, U.S.A. **Online address:** mcgrewwc@muohio.edu

MCGREW, William Clement. *See* **MCGREW, W. C.**

MCGRORY, Brian. American (born United States), b. 1962?. **Genres:** Novels. **Career:** Patriot Ledger, reporter; New Haven Register, reporter; Boston Globe, suburban reporter, national reporter, bureau political correspondent, 1989-98, metro columnist, 1998-2007, 2009-, metro editor, 2007-09, White House correspondent, general assignment reporter, associate editor.

Journalist. **Publications:** JACK FLYNN SERIES: The Incumbent, 2000; The Nominee, 2002; Dead Line, 2004; Strangled, 2007. **Address:** Boston Globe, PO Box 55819, Boston, MA 02205-5819, U.S.A. **Online address:** mcgrory@globe.com

MCGRUDER, Aaron. American (born United States), b. 1974. **Genres:** Cartoons, Humor/Satire. **Career:** Cartoonist; screenwriter. **Publications:** The Boondocks: Because I Know You Dont Read the Newspapers, 2000; Fresh for 01-You Suckas!: A Boondocks Collection, 2001; A Right to Be Hostile: The Boondocks Treasury, 2003; Birth of a Nation: A Comic Novel, 2004; Public Enemy Number 2: An All-New Boondocks Collection, 2005; All the Rage: The Boondocks Past and Present, 2007. **Address:** Universal Press Syndicate, 4520 Main St., Kansas City, MO 64111-7701, U.S.A.

MCGUANE, Thomas. American (born United States), b. 1939. **Genres:** Novels, Novellas/Short Stories, Westerns/Adventure, Plays/Screenplays, Young Adult Non-fiction, Adult Non-fiction, Biography, Autobiography/Memoirs, Autobiography/Memoirs. **Career:** Freelance writer, 1968-. **Publications:** The Sporting Club: A Novel, 1968; The Bushwhacked Piano, 1971; Ninety-Two in the Shade, 1973; Missouri Breaks: An Original Screenplay, 1976; Panama, 1978; An Outside Chance: Essays on Sports, 1980; Nobody's Angel, 1981; Something to Be Desired, 1984; In the Crazies: Book and Portfolio, 1984; To Skin a Cat: Stories, 1986; (co-author) Silent Seasons: Twenty-one Fishing Stories, 1988; Keep the Change, 1989; Outside Chance: Classic & New Essays on Sport, 1990; Nothing but Blue Skies, 1992; (ed. with G. Stout) Best American Sports Writing 1992, 1992; Sons, 1993; Live Water, 1996; The Longest Silence: A Life in Fishing, 1999; Some Horses, 1999; Upstream: Fly Fishing in the American Northwest, 2000; The Cadence of Grass, 2002; (with D. Jay) Horses, 2005; Gallatin Canyon: Stories, 2006; Driving on the Rim: A Novel, 2010. **Address:** c/o Amanda Urban, International Creative Management, 730 5th Ave., New York, NY 10019, U.S.A.

MCGUCKIAN, Maeve Therese Philomena. *See* **MCGUCKIAN, Medbh (McCaughan).**

MCGUCKIAN, Medbh (McCaughan). Also writes as Maeve Therese Philomena McGuckian. Irish (born Ireland), b. 1950. **Genres:** Poetry, Novellas/Short Stories. **Career:** Educator, 1975-; Saint Patrick's College, instructor, 1975-; Queen's University, writer-in-residence, editor, 1985-88; University of California, visiting poet and instructor in creative writing, 1991; University of Ulster, writer-in-residence; Trinity College, writer-in-residence. **Publications:** Single Ladies: Sixteen Poems, 1980; Portrait of Joanna, 1980; (with D. Gorman and D. Marshall) Trio Poetry, 1981; The Flower Master, 1982; Venus and the Rain, 1984, rev. ed., 1994; (ed.) The Big Striped Golfing Umbrella: Poems by Young People from Northern Ireland, 1985; On Ballycastle Beach, 1988, rev. ed., 1995; (with N. Archer) Two Women, Two Shores, 1989; Marconi's Cottage, 1991; Captain Lavender, 1995; Selected Poems, 1978-1994, 1997; Shelmalier, 1998; Horsepower Pass By!: A Study of the Car in the Poetry of Seamus Heaney, 1999; Drawing Ballerinas, 2001; The Face of the Earth, 2002; Had I a Thousand Lives, 2003; Book of the Angel, 2004; The Currach Requires No Harbours, 2006; My Love has Fared Inland, 2008. **Address:** Gallery Press, Loughcrew, Old Castle, ME 1, Ireland.

MCGUIGAN, Mary Ann. American (born United States), b. 1949. **Genres:** Young Adult Fiction, Novels, Novellas/Short Stories. **Career:** Teacher, 1972-81; Moody's Investors Service, editor of financial publications, 1981-84; Vantage Press Inc., editor of fiction and nonfiction, 1981-84; A. Foster Higgins Inc., communications consultant, 1984-93; Bloomberg Financial Markets, Wealth Manager, managing editor, 1993-, Bloomberg Press, executive developmental editor. **Publications:** YOUNG ADULT NOVELS: Cloud Dancer, 1994; Where You Belong, 1997; Morning in a Different Place, 2009. Contributor of articles to magazines and newspapers. **Address:** Bloomberg Financial Markets, 100 Business Park Dr., PO Box 888, Skillman, NJ 08558-2601, U.S.A. **Online address:** maryann@maryannmcguigan.com

MCGUIRE, Bob. *See* **MAYER, Bob.**

MCGUIRE, Brian Patrick. American (born United States), b. 1946. **Genres:** Novels. **Career:** St. John's College, tutor, 1970-71; Bruel and Kjaer, translator, 1971; Vesterbros Studenterkursus, adjunct, 1971-72; Copenhagen Institute of History, Postdoctoral fellow, 1972-74; Copenhagen University Institute for Greek and Latin, lecturer, 1975-96, medieval center chair, 1988-96; Roskilde University Institute of History and Social Theory, professor, 1996-. Writer. **Publications:** Conflict and Continuity at am Abbey: A Cistercian Experience in Medieval Denmark, 1976; Kulturblomstring og samfundskrise i 1300-tallet, 1979; The Cistercians in Denmark: Their Attitudes, Roles, and Functions in Medieval Society, 1982; (with K. Grubb Jensen and K.V. Jensen) Mennesker i Danmarks og Europas middelalder, 1986; War and Peace in the Middle Ages, 1987; Friendship & Community: The Monastic Experience, 350-1250, 1988; The Difficult Saint: Bernard of Clairvaux and His Tradition, 1991; Brother and Lover: Aelred of Rievaulx, 1994; The Birth of Identities: Denmark and Europe in the Middle Ages, 1996; (trans. and intro.) Jean Gerson: Early Works, 1998; Fjernt fra menneskers farden: sider af Esrum klosters 850-alsrige Historie, 2000; Friendship and Faith: Cistercian Men, Women, and Their Stories, 1100-1250, 2002; Jean Gerson and the Last Medieval Reformation, 2005; Den levende middelalder: fortallinger om dansk og europaisk identitet, 2005; (ed.) A Companion to Jean Gerson, 2006; A Companion to Bernard of Clairvaux, 2011. Contributor to periodicals and journals. **Address:** Roskilde UniversitetsCtr., Bldg, 03 2 1, Universitetsvej 1, PO Box 260, Roskilde, DK-4000, Denmark.

MCGUIRK, Carol. American (born United States) **Genres:** Literary Criticism And History. **Career:** Bennington College, instructor in literature and languages, 1975; Williams College, assistant professor of English, 1976-78; Rutgers University, assistant professor of English, 1978-85; Florida Atlantic University, associate professor of English, 1985-90, professor of English, 1990-; Florida State University, London Study Center, visiting professor, 1990; Scotlands, editorial director, 1993-; DePauw University, Science Fiction Studies, co-editor, 1997-. **Publications:** Robert Burns and the Sentimental Era, 1985; Benjamin Disraeli, 1987; Encyclopedia of the Enlightenment, 2000. EDITOR: Robert Burns: Selected Poems, 1993; Critical Essays on Robert Burns, 1998. Contributor to journals. **Address:** Department of English, Florida Atlantic University, 777 Glades Rd., CU 313, PO Box 3091, Boca Raton, FL 33431, U.S.A. **Online address:** cmcguirk@fau.edu

MCGURL, Mark J. American (born United States), b. 1966. **Genres:** Literary Criticism And History, Art/Art History. **Career:** New York Times, journalist; New York Review of Books, journalist; University of California, Department of English, professor. **Publications:** The Novel Art: Elevations of American Fiction after Henry James, 2001; The Program Era: Postwar Fiction and the Rise of Creative Writing, 2009. Contributor to periodicals. **Address:** Department of English, University of California, PO Box 951530, Los Angeles, CA 90095-1530, U.S.A. **Online address:** mcgurl@humnet.ucla.edu

MCGURN, James (Edward). British (born England), b. 1953. **Genres:** Language/Linguistics, Sports/Fitness, History. **Career:** New Cyclist, editor and publisher; Bike Culture Quarterly, co-publisher. **Publications:** Tolles Theater, 1983; Vous etes en Scene, 1986. On Your Bicycle: An Illustrated History of Cycling, 1987; Comparing Languages: English and Its European Relatives, 1989; Cross-country Cycling, 1993; (with A. Davidson) Encyclopedia: An Alternative Guide to Cycling, 1998; (with A. Davidson) Encyclopedia 2001: The International Guide to Alternatives in Cycling, 2000. Contributor to periodicals. **Address:** The Raylor Ctr., James St., Open Rd., York, YO2 3DW, England.

MCHENRY, Leemon B. American (born United States), b. 1956. **Genres:** Philosophy. **Career:** University of Edinburgh, instructor, 1982-84, Institute for Advanced Studies in the Humanities, visiting researcher, fellow, 2009; Old Dominion University, adjunct assistant professor, 1985-86; Davidson College, visiting assistant professor, 1986-88; Central Michigan University, visiting assistant professor, 1988-90; Wittenberg University, assistant professor, 1990-95; Loyola Marymount University, faculty; Johns Hopkins University, visiting researcher; University of California, visiting researcher; California State University, Department of Philosophy, lecturer, 1997-; Center for Process Studies, philosophy review editor, 1997-2007. **Publications:** Whitehead and Bradley: A Comparative Analysis, 1992. (ed. with F. Adams) Reflections on Philosophy: Introductory Essays, 1993, 3rd ed., 2010; (ed. with P. Dematteis and P.S. Fosl) British Philosophers: 1800-2000, 2002; (ed. with P. Dematteis) American Philosophers Before 1950, 2003; (ed. with P. Dematteis) American Philosophers, 1950-2000, 2003; (with P. Basile) Consciousness, Reality and Value, 2007; Science and the Pursuit of Wisdom, 2009; Philosophy: The Classic Readings, 2010; (ed.) Importance of Subjectivity: Selected Essays in Metaphysics and Ethics, 2011. Contributor of articles to journals. **Address:** Department of Philosophy, California State University, Sierra Twr. 516, 18111 Nordhoff St., Northridge, CA 91330-8253, U.S.A. **Online address:** leemon.mchenry@csun.edu

MCHUGH, Heather. American (born United States), b. 1948. **Genres:** Poetry, Translations. **Career:** State University of New York, assistant professor, associate professor of English, 1976-82; Warren Wilson College, M.F.A. Program for Writers, core faculty, 1980-; University of Washington, professor of English and Milliman distinguished writer-in-residence, 1983-; University of California, Holloway lecturer, 1987; Columbia University, visiting faculty, 1987; Academy of American Poets, chancellor, 1999-2005; American Academy of Arts and Sciences, fellow, 2001. **Publications:** Dangers, 1977; World of Difference, 1981; (trans.) J. Follain, D'après tout: Poems, 1981; (ed.) The Matter with Stairs, 1986; To the Quick, 1987; Shades, 1988; (trans. with N. Boris) Because the Sea is Black: Poems by Blaga Dimitrova, 1989; (with T. Phillips) Where are They Now?, 1990; Broken English: Poetry and Partiality (essays), 1993; Hinge & Sign: Poems, 1968-1993, 1994; The Father of the Predicaments, 1999; (trans. with N. Popov) P. Celan, Glottal Stop: 101 Poems, 2000; (trans.) Euripides, Cyclops, 2001; (ed. with E.B. Voigt) Hammer and Blaze: A Gathering of Contemporary American Poets, 2002; Eyeshot, 2003; Upgraded to Serious, 2009. Works appear in anthologies. **Address:** Department of English, University of Washington, PDL A-506, PO Box 354330, Seattle, WA 98195-4330, U.S.A. **Online address:** postcocious@gmail.com

MCHUGH, John (Francis). *See* Obituaries.

MCHUGH, Maureen F. American (born United States), b. 1959. **Genres:** Novellas/Short Stories, Science Fiction/Fantasy. **Career:** City University of New York, College of Staten Island, administrator and teacher, 1985-86; Ethicon, technical writer, 1991-; Cincinnati Writers Project, workshop instructor; 42 Entertainment, writer and managing editor; No Mimes Media, founding partner. **Publications:** SCIENCE FICTION: China Mountain Zhang, 1992; Missionary's Child, 1992; Half the Day is Night, 1994; Nekropolis, 2001. OTHERS: Mission Child, 1998; Nekropolis, 2001; Mothers & Other Monsters, 2005; After the Apocalypse, 2011. Contributor to magazines. Works appear in anthologies. **Address:** No Mimes Media, 213 40th St., Manhattan Beach, CA 90266, U.S.A. **Online address:** mcq@en.com

MCILROY, Brian. Canadian/Irish (born Ireland), b. 1959. **Genres:** Film. **Career:** Lewes Technical College, lecturer in video production, film studies, and drama, 1982-84; University of Manitoba, lecturer, 1988-89; University of British Columbia, instructor, 1989-91, assistant professor, 1991-96, associate professor, 1996-2001, professor of film studies, 2001-, Film Studies Program, chair, 1997-99, 2004-07, Arts One Program, faculty, 2007-08, director, through 2010. Writer. **Publications:** World Cinema 2: Sweden, 1986; Irish Cinema: An Illustrated History, 1988; (ed. with A. Loiselle) Auteur/Provocateur: The Films of Denys Arcand, 1995; Shooting to Kill: Filmmaking and the Troubles in Northern Ireland, 1998; (ed.) Genre and Cinema: Ireland and Transnationalism, 2007. Contributor of articles to books and periodicals. **Address:** Department of Theatre and Film, University of British Columbia, 2329 West Mall, 6354 Crescent Rd., Vancouver, BC V6T 1Z2, Canada. **Online address:** bmcilroy@interchange.ubc.ca

MCILVOY, Kevin. American (born United States), b. 1953. **Genres:** Novels, History, Young Adult Fiction, inspirational/Motivational Literature. **Career:** New Mexico State University, professor, MFA Program in Creative Writing, teacher; Warren Wilson College, faculty, MFA Program for Writers, teacher; Puerto del Sol Magazine, editor-in-chief. **Publications:** NOVELS: A Waltz, 1981; The Fifth Station, 1988; Little Peg, 1990; Hyssop, 1998; Complete History of New Mexico: Stories, 2005. Contributor to magazines. **Address:** Department of English, New Mexico State University, MSC 3E, PO Box 30001, Las Cruces, NM 88003, U.S.A. **Online address:** kmcilvoy@nmsu.edu

MCILWAINE, John. British (born England), b. 1937. **Genres:** Adult Nonfiction, Bibliography, Reference. **Career:** India Office Library and Records, Foreign and Commonwealth Office, assistant librarian, 1962-65; University College London, lecturer, 1965-94, senior lecturer, 1994-2000, personal chair and professor of the bibliography of Asia and Africa, 2000-01, honorary research fellow and professor emeritus, 2001-; Standing Conference on Library Materials on Africa (SCOLMA), chair; National Council on Orientalist Library Resources (NCOLR), chair; African Research and Documentation, editor. **Publications:** (With R. Staveley and I.C. McIlwaine) Introduction to Subject Study, 1967; (ed.) Theses on Africa Submitted to Universities in the United Kingdom, 1963-1975, 1978; (ed. with I.C. McIlwaine and P.G. New) Bibliography and Reading: A Festschrift in Honour of Ronald Staveley, 1983; Africa: A Guide to Reference Material, 1993, 2nd ed., 2007; Writings on African Archives, 1996; Maps and Mapping of Africa: A Resource Guide, 1997; (ed. with J. Whiffin) Collecting and Safeguarding the Oral Traditions: An International Conference, Khon Kaen, Thailand, 16-19 August 1999, 2001; Do No Harm: A Register of Standards, Codes of Practice, Etc., Relating to Preservation and Conservation, 2005; Disaster Preparedness and Planning: A Brief Manual, 2006; Prevenção de desastres e planos de emergência, 2008. **Address:** University College London, Gower St., London, GL WC1E 6BT, England. **Online address:** uczcw06@ucl.ac.uk

MCINERNEY, Jay. American (born United States), b. 1955. **Genres:** Novels, Novellas/Short Stories. **Career:** Hunterdon County, reporter, 1977; Time-Life Inc., text book editor, 1978-79; Random House Publishers, reader, editorial staff, 1980-81; New Yorker Magazine, fact checker, 1980-; Syracuse University, instructor in English, 1983; writer, 1983-; House & Garden Magazine, wine columnist; The Wall Street Journal, wine columnist. **Publications:** Bright Lights, Big City, 1984; Ransom, 1985; Story of My Life, 1988; Brightness Falls, 1992; Last of the Savages, 1996; Model Behavior: A Novel and Stories, 1998; Bacchus & Me, 2000; Good Life, 2006; Hedonist in the Cellar: Adventures in Wine, 2006; How it Ended: New and Collected Stories, 2009. Contributor to books and periodicals. **Address:** Amanda Urban, International Creative Management, 40 W 57th St., New York, NY 10019, U.S.A.

MCINTIRE, C(arl) T(homas). (Thomas McIntire). Canadian/American (born United States), b. 1939. **Genres:** History, Theology/Religion, Philosophy, Essays, Biography. **Career:** Shelton College, instructor in history, 1965-67; Trinity Christian College, assistant professor of history, 1967-71; University of Toronto, Trinity College, lecturer, 1982-84, associate professor of history, 1984-88, professor of history, 1988-99, Centre for the Study of Religion, director of graduate studies, 1992-2003, professor of history and religion, 1999-; Victoria College, fellow, 1999-; Universite canadienne en France, visiting professor, 1988-92. Writer. **Publications:** The Ongoing Task of Christian Historiography, 1974; The Renewal of Christian Views of History in an Age of Catastrophe, 1977; Herbert Butterfield on Christianity and History, 1979; England against the Papacy, 1858-1861, 1983; Historical Study and the Historical Dimension of Our World, 1984; Dooyeweerd's Philosophy of History, 1985; Christian Views of History, 1987; Approaches and Themes in the History of Missions, 1987; Toynbee's Achievement, 1989; Toynbee's Philosophy of History: His Christian Period, 1989; Paris Walks on Art and Society, 1770s-1920s, 1992; Changing Religious Establishments and Religious Liberty in France: part I: 1787-1879, Changing Religious Establishments and Religious Liberty in France: part II: 1879-1908, 1997; (co-author) The Parish and Cathedral of St. James, Toronto, 1797-1997, 1998; Women in the Life of St. James Cathedral, 1935-1998, 1998; Secularization, Secular Religions, and Religious Pluralism in European and North American Societies, 1998; From Church and State to Religions as Public Life in Modern Europe, 2002; Hegemony in the Historiography of Universities: The Toronto Case, 2003; Herbert Butterfield: Historian as Dissenter, 2004; Transcending Dichotomies in History and Religion, 2006; How Religious Studies Misunderstands Religion, 2007; Historical Study of Religion, 2009; The Formation of the United Church of Canada, 1899-1929, 2011; Protestants of Canada, 2011. EDITOR/CO-EDITOR: God, History, and Historians, 1977; Herbert Butterfield, Writings on Christianity and History, 1979; History and Historical Understanding, 1984; The Legacy of Herman Dooyeweerd, 1985; Canadian Protestant and Catholic Missions, 1820s-1960s, 1987; Toynbee: Reappraisals, 1989; Historiography, 1992, rev. ed., 1998; The History of Modern Christianity, 1998; Anglican History and Theology, 1998; The World Christian Religious Tradition, 2005, rev. ed., 2011. **Address:** Department for the Study of Religion, University of Toronto, 170 Saint George St., Toronto, ON M5R 2M8, Canada. **Online address:** ct.mcintire@utoronto.ca

MCINTIRE, Thomas. *See* **MCINTIRE, C(arl) T(homas).**

MCINTOSH, Fiona. (Lauren Crow). Australian/British (born England), b. 1960?. **Genres:** Novels, Mystery/Crime/Suspense. **Career:** Travelnews Australia, co-founder. Writer. **Publications:** TRINITY SERIES: Betrayal, 2001; Destiny, 2002; Revenge, 2002. THE QUICKENING SERIES: Myrren's Gift, 2003; Bridge of Souls, 2005; Blood and Memory, 2005. PERCHERON SERIES: Odalisque, 2005; Emissary, 2006; Goddess, 2007. NOVEL: (as Lauren Crow) Bye Bye Baby, 2007. VALISAR TRILOGY: Royal Exile, 2008; Tyrant's Blood, 2009; King's Wrath, 2010. OTHER: The Whisperer, 2009; Beautiful Death, 2009; Fields of Gold, 2010. **Address:** HarperCollins, 10 E 53rd St., 7th Fl., New York, NY 10022, U.S.A.

MCINTOSH, J. T. *See* **MACGREGOR, James Murdoch.**

MCINTOSH, **Kinn Hamilton.** *See* **AIRD**, **Catherine.**

MCINTOSH, **Marjorie Keniston.** American (born United States), b. 1940. **Genres:** History. **Career:** Radcliffe Institute, research associate, 1967-68; Simmons College, instructor in history, 1968-70; University of Colorado, lecturer in history, 1971-72, assistant professor, 1979-86, associate professor, 1986-92, Center for British Studies, founder and executive director, 1988-90, professor of history, 1992-2000, distinguished professor of history, 2000-06, distinguished professor of history emeritus, 2006-; Makerere University, visiting lecturer; Islamic University in Uganda, visiting lecturer, 2008. Writer. **Publications:** Autonomy and Community: The Royal Manor of Havering, 1200-1500, 1986; A Community Transformed: The Manor and Liberty of Havering, 1500-1620, 1991; Controlling Misbehavior in England, 1370-1600, 1997; Working Women in English Society, 1300-1620, 2005; (with G.B. Kyomuhendo) Women, Work & Domestic Virtue in Uganda, 1900-2003, 2006; Yoruba Women, Work, and Social Change, 2009; Poor Relief in England, 1350-1600, 2011. **Address:** Department of History, University of Colorado, Hellems Hall 204, UCB 234, Boulder, CO 80309-0234, U.S.A. **Online address:** marjorie.mcIntosh@colorado.edu

MCINTYRE, **Ian (James).** British/Scottish (born Scotland), b. 1931. **Genres:** Art/Art History, History, International Relations/Current Affairs, Literary Criticism And History, Military/Defense/Arms Control, Politics/Government, Theatre, Biography, Biography. **Career:** British Broadcasting Corp., current affairs talks producer, 1957, At Home and Abroad, editor, 1959, writer and broadcaster, 1970-76, British Broadcasting Corporation Radio 4, controller, 1976-78, British Broadcasting Corporation Radio 3, controller, 1978-87; Independent Television Authority, program services officer, 1961; Conservative Party, staff, 1962-70; Times (newspaper), associate editor, 1989-90. **Publications:** NONFICTION: The Proud Doers: Israel after Twenty Years, 1968; (ed. and contrib.) Words: Reflections on the Uses of Language, 1975; Dogfight: The Transatlantic Battle over Airbus, 1992; The Expense of Glory: A Life of John Reith, 1993; Dirt & Deity: A Life of Robert Burns, 1996; Garrick, 1999; Joshua Reynolds: The Life and Times of the First President of the Royal Academy, 2003; Hester: The Remarkable Life of Dr Johnson's 'Dear Mistress', 2008; Robert Burns: A Life, 2008. Contributor of articles to periodicals. **Address:** Spylaw House, Newlands Ave., Radlett, HF WD7 8EL, England. **Online address:** mcintyre@dircon.co.uk

MCINTYRE, **Lee C(ameron).** American (born United States), b. 1962. **Genres:** Philosophy, Chemistry, Sciences. **Career:** Boston University, Center for Philosophy and History of Science, research associate, 1991-93, research fellow and visiting researcher; Tufts University, Tufts Experimental College, visiting lecturer, 1992; Colgate University, assistant professor of philosophy, 1993-99; Harvard University, Faculty of Arts and Sciences, policy advisor, 2000-, Institute for Quantitative Social Science, executive director; Simmons College, lecturer of philosophy; Federal Reserve Bank of Boston, Department of Research, associate editor. **Publications:** (Ed. with M. Martin) Readings in the Philosophy of Social Science, 1994; Laws and Explanation in the Social Sciences: Defending a Science of Human Behavior, 1996; Dark Ages: The Case for a Science of Human Behavior, 2006; (ed. with D. Baird and E. Scerri) Philosophy of Chemistry: Synthesis of a New Discipline, 2006. Contributor of articles to journals. **Address:** Center for Philosophy and History of Science, Boston University, 745 Commonwealth Ave., Boston, MA 02215, U.S.A. **Online address:** lee@leemcintyrebooks.com

MCINTYRE, **Vonda N(eel).** American (born United States), b. 1948. **Genres:** Science Fiction/Fantasy, Novellas/Short Stories, Novels, Sciences, Mystery/Crime/Suspense, Horror, Natural History. **Career:** Writer, 1969-. **Publications:** Of Mist and Grass and Sand, 1973; The Exile Waiting, 1975; (with M. Randall and J.D. Vinge) The Crystal Ship: Three Original Novellas of Science Fiction, 1976; (ed. with S.J. Anderson) Aurora: Beyond Equality, 1976; Dreamsnake, 1978; Fireflood and Other Stories, 1979; (contrib.) Interfaces, 1980; The Entropy Effect, 1981; Star Trek II: The Wrath of Khan, 1982; Superluminal, 1983; Star Trek III: The Search for Spock, 1984; The Bride, 1985; Star Trek IV: The Voyage Home, 1986; Barbary, 1986; Enterprise: The First Adventure, 1988; Starfarers, 1989; Screwtop, 1989; Transition 1991; Metaphase, 1992; The Crystal Star, 1994; Nautilus, 1994; The Moon and the Sun, 1997; Star Trek: Duty, Honor, Redemption, 2004. Contributor to magazines. **Address:** c/o Frances Collin, Frances Collin Literary Agency, PO Box 33, Wayne, PA 19087-0033, U.S.A. **Online address:** vonda@vondanmcintyre.com

MCINTYRE, **W(illiam) David.** New Zealander/British (born England), b. 1932. **Genres:** History, International Relations/Current Affairs, Social Sciences. **Career:** University of Nottingham, assistant lecturer, 1959-61, lecturer in history, 1961-65; University of Canterbury, professor of history, 1966-98, head of department, 1986-96, professor emeritus of history, 1998-, research associate. Writer. **Publications:** Colonies into Commonwealth, 1966, 3rd ed., 1974; The Imperial Frontier in the Tropics 1865-1875, 1967; Britain, New Zealand and the Security of Southeast Asia in the 1970s, 1969; Neutralism, Non-Alignment and New Zealand, 1969; Britain and the Commonwealth since 1907, 1970; (ed. with W.J. Gardner) Speeches and Documents on New Zealand History, 1971; (with A. Ross and A.D. Mcintosh) Commonwealth: Its Past, Present and Future, 1973; The Commonwealth of Nations, 1869-1971: Origins and Impact, 1977; The Rise and Fall of the Singapore Naval Base 1919-1942, 1979; (ed. and intro.) The Journal of Henry Sewell 1853-1857, 2 vols., 1980; (with L. Richardson) Provincial Perspectives, 1981; New Zealand Prepares for War 1919-39, 1988; The Significance of the Commonwealth 1965-1990, 1991; Background to the Anzus Pact, 1945-55, 1994; British Decolonization, 1946-1997: When, Why, and How did the British Empire Fall?, 1998; (with M. McIntyre) Tour of Duty: Midshipman Comber's Journal, 1838-42, 1999; A Guide to the Contemporary Commonwealth, 2001; Shifting Starr: A Presbyterian Drama: St. Andrew's at Rangi Ruru, 1956-2006, 2006; Dominion of New Zealand: Statesmen and Status, 1907-1945, 2007; The Britannic Vision: Historians and the Making of the British Commonwealth of Nations, 1907-48, 2009. Contributor to books. **Address:** Macmillan Brown Center for Pacific Studies, University of Canterbury, Rm. 203, Te Ao Marama, Arts Rd., PO Box 4800, Christchurch, 1, New Zealand. **Online address:** david.mcintyre@canterbury.ac.nz

MCIVOR, **James.** American (born United States), b. 1957?. **Genres:** Novels, History. **Career:** Freelance writer. **Publications:** God Rest Ye Merry, Soldiers: A True Civil War Christmas Story, 2005. Contributor to periodicals. **Address:** c/o Author Mail, Penguin Group, Viking Publicity, 375 Hudson St., New York, NY 10014, U.S.A.

MCKANAN, **Dan Patrick.** American (born United States), b. 1967. **Genres:** Theology/Religion, History. **Career:** Saint John's University, College of Saint Benedict, department chair and associate professor of theology, 1998-2008; Harvard Divinity School, Ralph Waldo Emerson Unitarian Universalist Association Senior Lecturer in Divinity, 2008-. Writer. **Publications:** AS DAN MCKANAN: Identifying the Image of God: Radical Christians and Nonviolent Power in the Antebellum United States, 2002; Touching the World: Christian Communities Transforming Society, 2007; The Catholic Worker after Dorothy: Practicing the Works of Mercy in a New Generation, 2008; Prophetic Encounters: Religion and the American Radical Tradition, 2011. **Address:** Harvard Divinity School, 45 Francis Ave., Cambridge, MA 02138, U.S.A. **Online address:** dmckanan@hds.harvard.edu

MCKAUGHAN, **Larry (Scott).** American (born United States), b. 1941. **Genres:** Children's Fiction, Psychology, Children's Non-fiction. **Career:** Adolph Meyer Zone Center, psychologist, 1967-68; University of Oregon, teaching assistant, 1970-71; St. Meinrad College, assistant professor of psychology, 1971-72; Alderson-Broaddus College, associate professor of psychology, 1972-79; University of California at Berkeley, research associate, 1979-80; Lane Community College, instructor, 1981-84; Institute for the Study of Human Action and Responsibility, research associate and director, 1981-86; freelance writer, 1985-. **Publications:** Why Are Your Fingers Cold?, 1992. Contributor to periodicals. **Address:** 2985 Ellen Ave., Eugene, OR 97405-1315, U.S.A.

MCKAY, **Claudia.** American (born United States), b. 1934. **Genres:** Mystery/Crime/Suspense, Science Fiction/Fantasy, Technology, Novels. **Career:** New Victoria Publishers, editor and publisher, 1976-. **Publications:** SCIENCE FICTION: Womanspace, 1980; Promise of the Rose Stone, 1986; Forever Pearl, 2003. MYSTERIES: The Kali Connection, 1994; Twist of Lime: A Lynn Evans Mystery, 1997. **Address:** New Victoria Publishers, PO Box 27, Norwich, VT 05055, U.S.A.

MCKAY, **Don.** Canadian (born Canada), b. 1942. **Genres:** Poetry, Physics. **Career:** Brick Books, co-founder, publisher and editor, 1975-; University of Western Ontario, professor; Fiddlehead Magazine, editor, 1991-96; University of Victoria, adjunct professor; University of New Brunswick, faculty; The Banff Centre, creative writing teacher and associate director for poetry; Sage Hill Writing Experience, faculty. **Publications:** Moccasins on Concrete:

Poems, 1972; Air Occupies Space, 1973; Long Sault, 1975; Lependu, 1978; Lightning Ball Bait, 1980; Birding, or Desire: Poems, 1983; Sanding Down this Rocking Chair on a Windy Night, 1987; Night Field: Poems, 1991; Apparatus, 1997; Another Gravity, 2000; Mr. Haeusler's Amazing Bicycles, 2000; Aria: A Suite for Voice, 2000; Book of Moonlight: Poems, 2000; Vis à Vis: Fieldnotes on Poetry & Wilderness, 2001; Camber: Selected Poems, 1983-2000, 2004; (contrib.) Five Ways to Lose Your Way, 2004; Deactivated West 100, 2005; Strike/Slip, 2006; Field Marks: The Poetry of Don McKay, 2006; Nerve Language, 2007; Shell of the Tortoise, 2011. **Address:** c/o Author Mail, McClelland & Stewart Ltd., 75 Sherbourne St., 5th Fl., Toronto, ON M5A 2P9, Canada.

MCKAY, Hilary. British (born England), b. 1959. **Genres:** Novels, Picture/Board Books, Children's Fiction, Young Adult Fiction. **Career:** Writer. **Publications:** The Exiles, 1991; The Exiles at Home, 1993; Dog Friday, 1994; The Amber Cat, 1995; Happy and Glorious, 1996; Practically Perfect, 1996; Why Didn't You Tell Me?, 1996; The Exiles in Love, 1996; Dolphin Luck, 1998; Strange Bear, 1998; Where's Bear?, 1998; The Birthday Wish, 1998; Cold Enough for Snow, 1998; Pirates Ahoy!, 1999; The Surprise Party, 2000; Keeping Cottontail, 2000; Keeping Cotton Tail, 2000; Saffy's Angel, 2001; Was That Christmas?, 2001; (with R. Cheminais) Inclusion and School Improvement, 2002; There's a Dragon Downstairs, 2003; Indigo's Star, 2004; Permanent Rose, 2005; Rose's Flying Feeling, 2005; Swop!, 2005; Dragon!, 2006; Caddy Ever After, 2006; The Story of Bear, 2007; Forever Rose, 2007; Amazing!, 2008; The Surprise Party: Paradise House, 2009; The Chickenpox Club, 2009; Rescuing Robin, 2009. PARADISE HOUSE SERIES: The Zoo in the Attic, 1995; The Treasure in the Garden, 1995; The Echo in the Chimney, 1996; The Magic in the Mirror, 1996; Strong Smell of Magic, 1999; Birthday Party, 2000; Keeping Cottontail, 2000. BEETLE AND FRIENDS SERIES: Beetle and the Hamster, 2002; Beetle and the Bear, 2002; Beetle and Lulu, 2002; Cedar Tree, 2002; Beetle and the Big Tree, 2002; Beetle and the Bear, 2002. CHARLIE SERIES: Charlie and the Big Snow, 2007; Charlie and the Cat-flap, 2007; Charlie and the Great Escape, 2007; Charlie and the Cheese and Onion Crisps, 2008; Charlie and the Haunted Tent, 2008; Charlie and the Rocket Boy, 2008; Hello Charlie, 2009; Charlie and the Tooth Fairy, 2009; Charlie and the Big Birthday Bash, 2009; Wishing for Tomorrow: The Sequel to the Little Princess, 2010; Caddy's World, 2011; The Duck in the Park, 2011; Lulu and the Cat in the Bag, 2011; Lulu and the Dog from the Sea, 2011. **Address:** Jennifer Luithlen Agency, 88 Holmfield Rd., Leicester, LE2 1SB, England. **Online address:** ashleyclose@beeb.net

MCKAY, Ian. Canadian (born Canada), b. 1953?. **Genres:** History, Cultural/Ethnic Topics. **Career:** Queen's University, professor of history, 1988-, graduate supervisor. Writer. **Publications:** NONFICTION: The Craft Transformed: An Essay on the Carpenters of Halifax, 1885-1985, 1985; (ed. with G. Burrill) People, Resources, and Power, 1987; (ed. with S. Milsom) Toward a New Maritimes: A Selection from Ten Years of New Maritimes, 1992; (ed. with L. Jackson) Windjammers and Bluenose Sailors: Stories of the Sea, 1993; The Quest of the Folk: Antimodernism and Cultural Selection in Twentieth-Century Nova Scotia, 1994; (ed.) For a Working-class Culture in Canada: A Selection of Colin McKay's Writings on Sociology and Political Economy, 1897-1939, 1996; Rebels, Reds, Radicals: Rethinking Canada's Left History, 2005; Reasoning Otherwise: Leftists and the People's Enlightenment in Canada, 1890-1920, 2008; (with R. Bates) In the Province of History: The Making of the Public Past in Twentieth-Century Nova Scotia, 2010. Contributor of articles to books and journals. **Address:** Canada. **Online address:** imckay@magma.ca

MCKAY, Ron. Scottish (born Scotland), b. 1949. **Genres:** Novels. **Career:** Sunday Times, stringer; Scotland on Sunday, reporter, 1992-, weekly columnist; East, editorial director; Arab TV, founder. **Publications:** NONFICTION: (with B. Barr) The Story of the Scottish Daily News, 1976. FICTION: The Catalyst, 1991; The Prophet, 1992; Mean City, 1995; The Leper Colony, 1997. **Address:** Scotland on Sunday, 70 W Regent St., Regent Ct., Glasgow, HI G2 2QZ, Scotland.

MCKAY, Sharon E. Canadian (born Canada), b. 1954?. **Genres:** Children's Fiction, Children's Non-fiction, Young Adult Fiction. **Career:** Writer. **Publications:** The New Child Safety Handbook, 1988; The New Parent Survival Handbook, 1990; (with J. Rubin and I. Mansoor) English Works!, 1995; (with K. Zarzour) Good to Go, 2008; Whispers from the Ghettos, 2009; (with K. Kacer) Whispers in Hiding, 2009; (with K. Kacer) Whispers from the Camps, 2009; Thunder Over Kandahar, 2010. FOR CHILDREN: (with D. MacLeod) Chalk around the Block, 1993; The Picky Eater: Recipes and Survival Tips for Parents of Fussy Eaters, 1993; The Official Kick-the-Can Games Book, 1994; The Halloween Book, 1994; Take a Hike, 1995; Pat-a-Cake Dough Book, 1996; Make-a-Face: Book and Body Painting Kit for Kids of All Ages, 1996; Time Capsule for the Twenty-first Century, 1998; Timothy Tweedle the First Christmas Elf, 2000; Charlie Wilcox, 2000; Harleys Blue Day, 2001; A Bee in Karleys Bonnet, 2001; What Are Friends For?, 2001; Rodneys Race, 2001; Charlie Wilcoxs Great War, 2002; Esther, 2004; War Brothers, 2008. OUR CANADIAN GIRL SERIES: Penelope: Terror in the Harbour, 2002; Penelope: The Glass Castle, 2002; Penelope: An Irish Penny, 2003; Penelope: Christmas Reunion, 2004. **Address:** PO Box 729, Kilbride, ON L0P 1G0, Canada. **Online address:** dmcmac111@aol.com

MCKAY, Susan. American (born United States), b. 1942. **Genres:** Social Commentary, Women's Studies And Issues, Social Sciences. **Career:** University of Wyoming, professor of women's studies and nursing. Writer. **Publications:** Assertive Childbirth: The Future Parents' Guide to a Positive Pregnancy, 1983; (with C.R. Phillips) Family-Centered Maternity Care: Implementation Strategies, 1984; (with D.E. Mazurana) Women and Peace Building, 1999; (with D.E. Mazurana) Raising Women's Voices for Peace Building: Vision, Impact, and Limitations of Media Technologies, 2001; Courage Our Stories Tell: The Daily Lives and Maternal Child Health Care of Japanese American Women at Heart Mountain, 2002; Northern Protestants: An Unsettled People, 2003; (with D.E. Mazurana) Where Are the Girls?: Girls in Fighting Forces in Northern Uganda, Sierra Leone, and Mozambique: Their Lives during and after the War, 2004; Bear in Mind These Dead, 2008. **Address:** Women's Studies Program, University of Wyoming, Ross Hall 119, Dept. 4297, 1000 E University Ave., Laramie, WY 82071, U.S.A. **Online address:** mckay@uwyo.edu

MCKEACHIE, Wilbert J. American (born United States), b. 1921. **Genres:** Education, Psychology. **Career:** University of Michigan, instructor, 1948-50, assistant professor, 1950-55, associate professor, 1955-58, professor of psychology, 1959-75, chairman of department, 1961, U.S. Office of Education, consultant, 1964, now professor emeritus. Writer. **Publications:** (Co-author) Readings in Introductory Psychology: With a Set of Principles of Elementary Psychology, 1951; Teaching Tips, 1951, (with M. Svinicki) 13th ed. as McKeachie's Teaching Tips: Strategies, Research, and Theory for College and University Teachers, 2011; (co-author) Improving Undergraduate Education in Psychology, 1952; (ed.) Review Outline of Psychology, 1955, 3rd ed., 1962; (ed.) The Appraisal of Teaching in Large Universities, 1959; (co-author) Undergraduate Curriculum in Psychology, 1961; Man in His World: Human Behavior, 1962; (R.L. Isaacson and J.E. Milholland) Research on the Characteristics of Effective College Teaching, 1964; (with C.L. Doyle) Psychology, 1966, 3rd ed. 1976; (with C.L. Doyle) Some Thoughts about Teaching the Beginning Course in Psychology, 1967; (co-author) The Importance of Teaching, 1968; Research on College Teaching, A Review, 1970; Psychology: The Short Course, 1970; XIP Readings in Psychology, 1972; (ed.) Learning, Cognition and College Teaching, 1980; (with K.E. Eble) Improving Undergraduate Education through Faculty Development, 1985; Teaching Psychology: A Handbook: Readings from Teaching of Psychology, 1990. **Address:** Department of Psychology, University of Michigan, 1346A E Hall, 530 Church St., Ann Arbor, MI 48109-1043, U.S.A. **Online address:** billmck@umich.edu

MCKEAN, Charles (Alexander). Scottish (born Scotland), b. 1946. **Genres:** Architecture, History, Urban Studies. **Career:** Royal Institute of British Architects, regional secretary and projects officer, 1968-79; The Times of London, architectural critic, 1977-84; Royal Incorporation of Architects in Scotland, chief executive, secretary and treasurer, 1979-94, RIAS Services Ltd., secretary, 1984-88; McKean Investments, director, 1986-2009; University of Dundee, Duncan of Jordanstone School of Architecture, head, 1995-97, professor of Scottish architectural history, 1997-. Writer. **Publications:** (With T. Jestico) Modern Buildings in London: A Guide, 1976; Fight Blight: A Practical Guide to the Causes of Urban Dereliction and What People Can Do about It, 1977; Architectural Guide to Cambridge and East Anglia since 1920, 1980; Edinburgh: An Illustrated Architectural Guide, 1982; (with D. Walker) Dundee: An Illustrated Introduction, 1984; Stirling and the Trossachs: An Illustrated Architectural Guide, 1985; The District of Moray: An Illustrated Architectural Guide, 1987; The Scottish Thirties, 1987; (with D. Walker and F. Walker) Central Glasgow: An Illustrated Architectural Guide, 1989; Banff and Buchan: An Illustrated Architectural Guide, 1990; Architectural Contributions to Scottish Society Since 1840, 1990; Edinburgh: Portrait of a City, 1991; (with R. Jacques) West Lothian: An Illustrated Architectural

Guide, 1994; (ed.) Perth and Kinross: The Making of the Museum of Scotland, 2000; The Scottish Chateau: The Country House of Reniassance Scotland, 2001; (ed.) Battle for the North: The Tay and Forth Bridges and the 19th-century Railway Wars, 2006; (with P. Whatley and K. Baxter) Lost Dundee, 2008; (with R. Oram and P. Martin) Tain: A Burgh Survey, 2009; (ed. with C.A. Whatley and B. Harris) Dundee: Renaissance to Enlightenment 1500-1820, 2009; (with R. Oram, P. Martin and T. Neighbour) Whithorn: A Burgh Survey, 2010; (co-author) Fraserburgh: A Burgh Survey, 2011. Works appear in anthologies. Contributor to journals and newspapers. **Address:** Department of History, Dundee University, Nethergate, Dundee, DD1 4HN, Scotland. **Online address:** c.a.mckean@dundee.ac.uk

MCKEAN, J(ohn) M(aule). British/Scottish (born Scotland), b. 1943. **Genres:** Architecture, Design, History. **Career:** Fielden & Mawson, architect, 1965-66; University of Ceylon (now Sri Lanka), lecturer, 1968-69; Greater London Council, architect, 1969-70; Architects Journal, staff of technical editors, 1971-73, staff of news and features editors, 1973-75; Architecture, British correspondent, 1975-77; London College of Printing, design history tutor, 1975-77; Architectural Association, tutor, 1975-79; North East London Polytechnic, architectural tutor, 1976-80; Polytechnic of North London, design tutor, 1979-, senior subject tutor in history, ideas, and theory of design, 1980-, History of Design Unit, head, 1981-85, architecture course leader, 1985-89; University of Brighton, head of interior architecture, 1990-96, professor of architecture, 1996-; Middlesex University, faculty. **Publications:** (Co-author) Architecture of the Western World, 1980; (co-author) Masterpieces of Architectural Drawing, 1982; (co-author) The Principles of Architecture, 1983; The World Crystal, 1984; Archetypal Dwelling, 1986; Learning from Segal/ Von Segal Lernen, 1988; Places for Peace: A Handbook on Peace Gardens, 1989; The Royal Festival Hall, 1992, 2nd ed., 2001; Crystal Palace, 1993; Jim Stirling at Leicester, 1994; (co-author) Greek Thomson, 1995; (co-author) Charles Rennie Mackintosh, 1996; C.R. Mackintosh Pocket Guide, 1998; (contrib.) Charles Rennie Mackintosh: Architect, Artist, Icon, 2000; (with C. Baxter) Charles Rennie Mackintosh: Gift Book, 2002; Giancarlo De Carlo: Layered Places, 2004; C.R. Mackintosh-Interior Architect, 2005; (with C. Baxter) Charles Rennie Mackintosh, 2009. Contributor to journals. **Address:** University of Brighton, Mithras House, Lewes Rd., Brighton, ES BN2 4AT, England. **Online address:** john.mckean7@ntlworld.com

MCKEAN, Robert B. Scottish (born Scotland), b. 1943. **Genres:** History, Politics/Government, Social Sciences, Essays. **Career:** University of Stirling, lecturer in history, 1968-92, senior lecturer in history, 1992-97, reader in history, 1997-, dean of the faculty of arts, 2003-, professor, 2005-. Writer. **Publications:** The Russian Constitutional Monarchy, 1907-1917, 1977; St. Petersburg between the Revolutions: Workers and Revolutionaries, June 1907-February 1917, 1990; (ed.) New Perspectives in Modern Russian History: Selected Papers from the Fourth World Congress for Soviet and East European Studies, Harrogate, 1990, 1992; Between the Revolutions, Russia 1905 to 1917, 1998; Late Imperial Russia: Problems and Prospects: Essays in Honour of R.B. McKean, 2005. **Address:** Department of History, University of Stirling, Rm. A4, Pathfoot Bldg., Stirling, FK9 4LA, Scotland. **Online address:** r.b.mckean@stir.ac.uk

MCKECHNIE, Paul (Richard). Australian/British (born England), b. 1957. **Genres:** Classics, Translations, History, Social Sciences. **Career:** The Perse School, classics teacher, 1984-87, assistant master in classics and religious education, 1987-91; Kamuzu Academy, Department of Classics, head, 1987-91; University of Malawi, Department of Classics, external examiner, 1990-91; University of Auckland, senior lecturer, 1998-2007; Macquarie University, Department of Ancient History, associate professor, 2007-. Writer. **Publications:** (Ed. and trans. with S.J. Kern) Hellenica Oxyrhynchia, 1988; Outsiders in the Greek Cities in the Fourth Century B.C., 1989; The First Christian Centuries: Perspectives on the Early Church, 2001; (ed.) Thinking Like a Lawyer: Essays on Legal History and General History for John Crook on His Eighteenth Birthday, 2002; (with G. Ferrero) Characters and Events of Roman History: From Caesar to Nero, 2005; (ed. with P. Guillaume) Ptolemy II Philadelphus and his World, 2008. **Address:** Department of Ancient History, Ancient Cultures Research Ctr., Macquarie University, W6A500, Balaclava Rd., North Ryde, NW 2109, Australia. **Online address:** paul.mckechnie@mq.edu.au

MCKEE, Annie. American/British (born England), b. 1955?. **Genres:** Novels. **Career:** Peace Education Program, administrator, 1982-87; Waianae High School, teacher, 1982-87; Kamehameha Schools, consultant, 1986-87; Case Western Reserve University, graduate research assistant, 1987-90, instructor, 1988-90; Cleveland State University, graduate teaching assistant, 1988-89; University of Hartford, assistant professor of management, 1990-93; Jagiellonian University, instructor, 1992; University of Pennsylvania, The Wharton School, associate director of leadership program, 1993-96, Aresty Institute of Executive Education, lecturer, 1995-, associate director of program development, 1996-98, Center for Professional Development, managing director, 1997-99, Graduate School of Education, faculty, adjunct professor, 1999-; The Hay Group, director of management development services, 1999-2001; Teleos Leadership Institute, founder, co-chair and managing director, 2001-. Writer. **Publications:** (With D. Goleman and R. Boyatzis) Primal Leadership: Realizing the Power of Emotional Intelligence, 2002; (with R. Boyatzis) Resonant Leadership: Renewing Yourself and Connecting with Others through Mindfulness, Hope, and Compassion, 2005; (with R. Boyatzis and F. Johnston) Becoming a Resonant Leader: Develop your Emotional Intelligence, Renew Your Relationships, Sustain Your Effectiveness, 2008; Management: A Focus on Leaders, 2011. Contributor to books and periodicals. **Address:** Teleos Leadership Institute, 7837 Old York Rd., Elkins Park, PA 19027, U.S.A. **Online address:** amckee@teleosleaders.com

MCKEE, David (John). British (born England), b. 1935. **Genres:** Novellas/ Short Stories, Children's Fiction, Plays/Screenplays, Poetry, Picture/Board Books, Animals/Pets. **Career:** King Rollo Films, founder. Writer. **Publications:** OTHERS: Bronto's Wings, 1964; Two Can Toucan, 1964; Hans in Luck, 1967; Mark and the Monocycle, 1968; The Magician Who Lost His Magic, 1970; Six Men, 1971; (reteller) The Man Who Was Going to Mind the House: A Norwegian Folk-tale, 1973; Lord Rex: The Lion Who Wished, 1973; The Magician and the Sorcerer, 1974 in UK as Melric and the Sorcerer, 1987; The Day the Tide Went Out and Out and Out, 1975; Elmer Again and Again, 1975; The Magician and the Petnapping, 1976; Two Admirals, 1977; The Magician and the Balloon in US as Melric and the Balloon, 1978; Tusk-Tusk, 1978; The Magician and the Dragon, 1979 in UK as Melric and the Dragon, 1987; King Rollo and the Birthday, 1979; King Rollo and the Bread, 1979; King Rollo and the New Shoes, 1979; Not Now Bernard, 1980; King Rollo and the Dishes, 1980; The Magicians and Double Trouble, 1981; King Rollo and the Search, 1981; King Rollo and the Bath, 1981; King Rollo and King Frank, 1981; I Hate My Teddy Bear, 1982; King Rollo and the Breakfast, 1982; King Rollo and the Dog, 1982; King Rollo and the Masks, 1982; King Rollo and the Balloons, 1982; King Rollo and the Tree, 1982; King Rollo's and the Playroom, 1983; The Adventures of King Rollo, 1983; Further Adventures of King Rollo, 1983; King Rollo's Playroom and Other Stories, 1983; The Hill and the Rock, 1984; King Rollo and the Letter, 1984; King Rollo's Letter and Other Stories, 1984; Two Monsters, 1985; King Rollo's Spring, 1987; King Rollo's Summer, 1987; King Rollo's Autumn, 1987; King Rollo's Winter, 1987; The Sad Story of Veronica Who Played the Violin: Being an Explanation of Why the Streets Are Not Full of Happy, Dancing People, 1987; The Magician's Apprentice, 1987 in UK as Melric's Apprentice, 1988; Snow Woman, 1987; Who's a Clever Baby, Then? in US as Who's a Clever Baby?, 1988; The Magician and the Crown, 1988; The Monster and the Teddy Bear, 1989; King Rollo and Santa's Beard, 1990; The Mystery of the Blue Arrows, 1990; Annabelle Pig and the Travellers and Benjamin Pig and the Apple Thiefs, 1990; Tales of Melric the Magician, 1991; Elmer Again, 1991; Zebra's Hiccups, 1991; Tales of Merlic the Magician, 1991; King Rollo's Christmas, 1992; The School Bus Comes at Eight O' Clock, 1993; Elmer's Day, 1994; Elmer's Friends, 1994; Elmer in the Snow, 1995; Elmer on Stilts, 1995; Isabel's Noisy Tummy, 1995; Elmer the Pop-Up Book, 1996; Charlotte's Piggy Bank, 1996; I Can Too!, 1997; Elmer Takes Off, 1997; Prince Peter and the Teddy Bear, 1997; Elmer Plays Hide and Seek, 1998; Macaroni, 1998; Elmer and the Lost Teddy, 1999; Mary's Secret, 1999; Elmer the Lost Teddy, 1999; Elmer and the Stranger, 2000; Look There's Elmer, 2000; Elmer's First Joke Book, 2000; Elmer and the Kangaroo, 2000; King Rollo and the New Stockings, 2001; Elmer and Grandpa, 2001; Elmer's Concert, 2001; Elmer and Butterfly, 2002; Elmer's New Friend, 2002; The Adventures of Charmin the Bear, 2003; Who is Mrs. Green?, 2003; Charmin the Bear, 2003; The Conquerors, 2004; Elmer and Snake, 2004; Three Monsters, 2004; Elmer and Rose, 2005; Elmer's Special Day, 2009; Elmer and the Wind, 2009; Denver, 2012; Elmer and Super El, 2012; Elmer and the Big Bird, 2012; Elmer's First Counting Book, 2012; Elmer's Opposites, 2012. SELF-ILLUSTRATED: Mr. Benn, Red Knight, 1968; Elmer: The Story of a Patchwork Elephant, 1968; 123456789 Benn, 1970; Elmer and Wilbur, 1994; Elmer and the Hippos, 2009; Elmer's Christmas, 2011; Elmer and the Rainbow, 2011. EXTRAORDINARY ADVENTURES OF MR. BENN SERIES: Mr. Benn Annual, 1972; Big Game Benn, 1979; Big Top Benn, 1980; Mr.

Benn: Caveman, 1993; Mr. Benn: Diver, 1993; Mr. Benn: Spaceman, 1993; Mr. Benn, Gladiator, 2001; Mr. Benn: Clown, 2011. Illustrator of books by others. **Address:** c/o Author Mail, Andersen Press Ltd., 20 Vauxhall Bridge Rd., London, GL SW1V 2SA, England.

MCKEE, Steve. American (born United States), b. 1952. **Genres:** Human Relations/Parenting, Biography, Social Sciences. **Career:** Journals Friday, editor; Daily Fix, writer, 2001-02; Wall Street Journal, global copy desk editor. **Publications:** The Call of the Game, 1987; Coach, 1994; My Father's Heart: A Son's Journey, 2008. Contributor to journals. **Address:** Da Capo Press, Perseus Books Group, 387 Park Ave. S, 12th Fl., New York, NY 10016, U.S.A. **Online address:** steve@steve-mckee.com

MCKEEN, William. American (born United States), b. 1954. **Genres:** Biography, Autobiography/Memoirs, Essays, Literary Criticism And History, Music. **Career:** The Courier-Tribune, reporter, weekend editor and copy editor, 1971-73; The Palm Beach Post, copy editor and columnist, 1974; The American Spectator, production editor, 1974; The Saturday Evening Post, staff editor, 1975-76; Western Kentucky University, Department of Journalism, instructor, 1977-81, assistant professor, 1981-82; University of Oklahoma, H.H. Herbert School of Journalism and Mass Communication, assistant professor, 1982-86, assistant director, 1984-86; The Norman, reporter, 1983; University of Florida, College of Journalism and Communications, Department of Journalism, assistant professor, 1986-90, associate professor, 1990-94, professor, 1994-2010, chair, 1998-2010; The Gainesville, copy editor, 1987, 1991, 1992-93; The Courier-Journal, copy editor, 1990; The St. Petersburg Times, copy editor, 1991-92; Boston University, College of Communication, Department of Journalism, professor and chair, 2010-. **Publications:** The Beatles: A Bio-Bibliography, 1989; Hunter S. Thompson, 1991; Bob Dylan: A Bio-Bibliography, 1993; Tom Wolfe, 1995; (ed.) Rock and Roll Is Here to Stay: An Anthology, 2000; (ed. with J. Chance) Literary Journalism: A Reader, 2001; Highway 61: A Father-and-Son Journey Through the Middle of America, 2003; Outlaw Journalist: The Life and Times of Hunter S. Thompson, 2008; Mile Marker Zero: The Moveable Feast of Key West, 2011; Homegrown: Stories of Childhood in Florida, 2012. Contributor to books and periodicals. **Address:** Department of Journalism, College of Communication, Boston University, 640 Commonwealth Ave., Boston, MA 02215-2422, U.S.A. **Online address:** wmckeen@bu.edu

MCKELLAR, Danica. American (born United States), b. 1975. **Genres:** Mathematics/Statistics. **Career:** Actress and writer. **Publications:** Math Doesn't Suck: How to Survive Middle-School Math without Losing Your Mind or Breaking a Nail, 2007; Kiss My Math: Showing Pre-Algebra Who's Boss, 2008. **Address:** Don Buchwald & Associates, 6500 Wilshire Blvd., Ste. 2200, Los Angeles, CA 90048, U.S.A. **Online address:** email@mathdoesntsuck.com

MCKELVEY, Tara. American (born United States), b. 1963?. **Genres:** History, Military/Defense/Arms Control. **Career:** The New York Times, clerk; The American Prospect, senior editor; New York University School of Laws Center on Law and Security, research fellow, 2006; Dart Center for Journalism and Trauma, Ochberg fellow, 2007; Stanford University, Hoover Media fellow, 2008; University of Cambridge, Templeton-Cambridge Journalism fellow in science and religion. **Publications:** (Ed.) One of the Guys: Women as Aggressors and Torturers, 2007; Monstering: Inside America's Policy of Secret Interrogations and Torture in the Terror War, 2007. **Address:** Carroll & Graf Publishers, 245 W 17th St., 11th Fl., New York, NY 10011, U.S.A. **Online address:** contact@taramckelvey.com

MCKELVY, William R. American (born United States), b. 1967. **Genres:** Literary Criticism And History. **Career:** University of Virginia, graduate instructor, 1993-95; Boston University, lecturer, 1995; Wellesley College, instructor, 1997; Washington University, Department of English, visiting assistant professor, 1998-99, assistant professor, 1999-2007, associate professor, 2007-. Writer. **Publications:** The English Cult of Literature: Devoted Readers, 1774-1880, 2007. Contributor of articles to journals and periodicals. **Address:** Department of English, Washington University, PO Box 1122, Saint Louis, MO 63130-4899, U.S.A. **Online address:** wmckelvy@wustl.edu

MCKENDRICK, James (Stewart). (Jamie McKendrick). British (born England), b. 1955. **Genres:** Poetry. **Career:** University of Salerno, lecturer, 1984-88; Wadham College, part-time instructor in Sarah Lawrence Program, 1991-; Hertford College, poet-in-residence, 1999-; University of Oxford, Department of Continuing Education, tutor; Masaryk University, poet-in-residence; University of Gothenburg, poet-in-residence; University College, writer-in-residence. Writer. **Publications:** POETRY AS JAMIE McKENDRICK: The Sirocco Room, 1991; The Kiosk on the Brink, 1993; The Marble Fly, 1997; Sky Nails: Poems 1979-1997, 2001; Ink Stone, 2003; The Faber Book of Twentieth-Century Italian Poems, 2004; (ed.) Faber Book of 20th-century Italian Poems, 2004; Crocodiles & Obelisks, 2007; (trans.) G. Bassani, Giardino dei Finzi-Contini (title means: 'The Garden of the Finzi-Continis'), 2007; (trans.) Vanishing Points: Poems, 2010; (trans.) Fabrication=Affabulazione, 2010. **Address:** Department for Continuing Education, University of Oxford, Rewley House, 1 Wellington Sq., Oxford, OX1 2JA, England.

MCKENDRICK, Jamie. *See* **MCKENDRICK, James (Stewart).**

MCKENDRY, Joe. American (born United States), b. 1972. **Genres:** Young Adult Fiction, Illustrations. **Career:** Rhode Island School of Design, teacher; Massachusetts College of Art, teacher. Freelance artist and author. **Publications:** SELF-ILLUSTRATED: Beneath the Streets of Boston: Building America's First Subway, 2005; One Times Square, 2011. **Address:** c/o Author Mail, David R. Godine Publishing Inc., 15 Court Sq., Ste. 320, Boston, MA 02108-4715, U.S.A. **Online address:** jsmckendry1@verizon.net

MCKENNA, Colleen O'Shaughnessy. American (born United States), b. 1948. **Genres:** Children's Fiction, Young Adult Fiction, Novels, Literary Criticism And History. **Career:** Teacher, 1970-73. Writer. **Publications:** MURPHY SERIES: Too Many Murphys, 1988; Fourth Grade Is a Jinx, 1989; Fifth Grade, Here Comes Trouble, 1989; Eenie, Meanie, Murphy, No, 1990; Murphy's Island, 1990; The Truth About Sixth Grade, 1991; Mother Murphy, 1992; Camp Murphy, 1993. GORDIE BARR SERIES: Third Grade Ghouls!, 2001; Third Grade Stinks!, 2001; Doggone-Third Grade!, 2002; Third Grade Wedding Bells?, 2006; Scout's Honor, forthcoming. FOR CHILDREN: Merry Christmas, Miss McConnell!, 1990; The Brightest Light, 1992; Not Quite Sisters, 1993; Stuck in the Middle, 1993; Good Grief, Third Grade, 1993; Live from the Fifth Grade, 1994; New Friends, 1995; Queen of the May, 1996; Valentine's Day Can Be Murder, 1995. **Address:** 101 Fox Ridge Farms, Pittsburgh, PA 15215, U.S.A.

MCKENNA, Elizabeth Perle. *See* **PERLE, Liz.**

MCKENNA, Lindsay Gvhdi. Also writes as Eileen Gvhdi Nauman, Eileen Nauman, Beth Brookes. American (born United States), b. 1946. **Genres:** Romance/Historical, Novels, Medicine/Health. **Career:** Akron University, creative writing teacher, 1975-80; Kent State University, creative writing, Uranian and medical astrology teacher, 1975-79; West Point Volunteer Fire Department, firefighter, 1980-83; Union Institute, adjunct faculty, 1992; Desert Institute of Classical Homeopathy, member of faculty. Writer, educator and astrologer. **Publications:** Interpreting Your Novien Moon, 1978; Too Near the Fire, 1984; Texas Wildcat, 1985; Red Tail, 1985; Heart of the Eagle, 1986; Solitaire, 1987; A Measure of Love, 1987; Heart of the Tiger, 1988; Return of a Hero, 1989; No Surrender, 1989; A Question of Honor, 1989; Come Gentle the Dawn, 1989; Colored Stones and Healing, 1990; (with R. Rainville, A. Major and K. Creighton) Silhouette Christmas Stories 1990, 1990; Under Fire, 1991; The Gauntlet, 1991; No Quarter Given, 1991; Dawn of Valor, 1991; Sun Woman, 1991; Ride the Tiger, 1992; Soul Recovery and Extraction, 1992; King of Swords, 1992; Lord of Shadowhawk, 1992; Off Limits, 1992; One Mans War, 1992; Heart of the Wolf, 1993; Brave Heart, 1993; The Rogue, 1993; Point of Departure, 1993; Commando, 1993; Lovers: Dark and Dangerous, 1994; Count Down, 1994; Dangerous Alliance, 1994; Shadows Light, 1994; Hangar 13, 1994; Morgan's Wife, 1995; Morgan's Son, 1995; Morgan's Rescue, 1995; Poisons That Heal, 1995; Morgan's Marriage, 1996; Heart of the Hunter, 1998; Wild Mustang Woman, 1998; Stallion Tamer, 1998; The Cougar, 1998; Hunters Woman, 1999; Hunters Pride, 1999; Heart of the Jaguar, 1999; Beauty in Bloom: Homeopathy to Support Menopause, 2000; Heart of the Warrior, 2000; A Man Alone, 2000; Man of Passion, 2000; The Untamed Hunter, 2000; Heart of Stone, 2001; Man with a Mission, 2001; Woman of Innocence, 2002; Destiny's Woman, 2002; Her Healing Touch, 2002; The Heart Beneath, 2002; The Will to Love, 2002; Ride the Thunder, 2002; (co-author) Snowy Nights, 2003; An Honorable Woman, 2003; Protecting His Own, 2003; Firstborn, 2004; Morgan's Legacy, 2004; First Born, 2004; Sister of Fortune, 2004; Daughter of Destiny, 2004; Morgan's Honor, 2004; Enemy Mine, 2005; Silent Witness, 2005; Wild Woman, 2005; Code of Silence, 2005; Beyond the Limit, 2006; Unforgiven, 2006; Dark Truth, 2007; Passionate Partners, 2007; Heart of the Storm, 2007; Quest,

2007; Dangerous Prey, 2008; Mission: Christmas, 2008; Shadows from the Past, 2009; His Woman in Command, 2010; The Adversary, 2010; Deadly Identity, 2010; Guardian, 2010; Reunion, 2010; Deadly Silence, 2011; Operation: Forbidden, 2011; The Last Cowboy, 2011. AS BETH BROOKES: Untamed Desire, 1982; Hold Fast 'til Morning, 1982; On Wings of Passion, 1983; Torrid Nights, 1984; Where Enchantment Lies, 1986. AS EILEEN NAUMAN: The American Book of Nutrition and Medical Astrology, 1982; Captive of Fate, 1983; Chase the Clouds, 1983; Love Me before Dawn, 1984; Wilderness Passion, 1984; Touch the Heavens, 1985; Dare to Love, 1985; The Right Touch, 1986; Hostage Heart, 1987; Colored Stones and Their Meaning, 1988; Beginnings, 1989; Night Flight, 1990; My Only One, 1991; Medical Astrology, 1993; HELP! and Homeopathy, 1998; 21st Century Epidemics and Homeopathy, 1999; (with G. Derin-Kellogg) Homeopathy 911, 2000; Homeopathy for Epidemics, 2004. **Address:** PO Box 2513, Cottonwood, AZ 86326-2513, U.S.A. **Online address:** docbones@gotsky.com

MCKENNA, Marian Cecilia. American (born United States), b. 1926. **Genres:** History, Urban Studies. **Career:** Hunter College, City University of New York, member of faculty, 1953-59; Manhattanville College, faculty, 1959-66; University of Calgary, Department of History, professor of history, 1966-93, professor emeritus, 1993-. Writer. **Publications:** Borah, 1961; Pictorial History of Catholicism, 1962; Myra Hess: A Portrait, 1976; Tapping Reeve and the Litchfield Law School, 1986; (ed.) The Canadian and American Constitutions in Comparative Perspective, 1993; Franklin Roosevelt and the Great Constitutional War: The Court-Packing Crisis of 1937, 2002; The Vikings Return, 2010. **Address:** Department of History, University of Calgary, 2500 University Dr. NW, Calgary, AB T2N 1N4, Canada. **Online address:** mmckenna@ucalgary.ca

MCKENNA, Maryn. American (born United States), b. 1959. **Genres:** Medicine/Health. **Career:** Atlanta Journal-Constitution, reporter; Boston Herald, staff; East-West Center, associate and teacher, 2006-. **Publications:** Beating Back the Devil: On the Front Lines with the Disease Detectives of the Epidemic Intelligence Service, 2004; Superbug: The Fatal Menace of MRSA, 2010. Contributor to periodicals. **Address:** Minneapolis, MN , U.S.A. **Online address:** mmckenna@mindspring.com

MCKENNA, Patrick J. Canadian (born Canada), b. 1951. **Genres:** Business/Trade/Industry, Law, Marketing, Administration/Management, E-books, Adult Non-fiction, Institutions/Organizations, inspirational/Motivational Literature, Self Help. **Career:** Hudson's Bay Co., assistant division manager, 1973-75; Alberta Office of Canadian Chamber of Commerce, general manager, 1976-79; OCTV Ltd., vice-president and director, 1979-82; Achieve Enterprises Ltd., vice president, 1981-83; Edge International Inc., founder and partner, 1982-2007; McKenna Associates Inc., principal, 2008-. Writer. **Publications:** Building Business Abroad, 1985; (with G.A. Riskin) Practice Development: Creating the Marketing Mindset, 1989; Herding Cats: A Handbook for Managing Partners and Practice Leaders, 1995; Beyond Knowing: Sixteen Cage-Rattling Questions to Jump-Start Your Practice Team, 2000; (with D.H. Maister) First among Equals: How to Manage a Group of Professionals, 2002: First 100 Days: Transitioning A New Managing Partner, 2006; Passing The Baton: The Last 100 Days, 2008. **Address:** Ashridge House, 11226 60th St., Edmonton, AB T5W 3Y8, Canada. **Online address:** patrick@patrickmckenna.com

MCKENZIE, Andrea Katherine. Canadian (born Canada), b. 1967?. **Genres:** Literary Criticism And History. **Career:** University of Victoria, professor of history. Writer and historian. **Publications:** A Mother's String, 2005; Tyburn's Martyrs: Execution in England, 1675-1775, 2007. Contributor to books, periodicals and journals. **Address:** University of Victoria, Clearihue B211, PO Box 1700, Sta. CSC, Victoria, BC V8W 2Y2, Canada. **Online address:** mckenzie@uvic.ca

MCKENZIE, Barbara. American (born United States), b. 1934. **Genres:** Literary Criticism And History, Novellas/Short Stories. **Career:** University of Miami, instructor in English, 1958-59; Dade County Junior College (now Miami-Dade Junior College), instructor in English, 1960-61; Florida State University, Extension Program at the Strategic Air Command Base, instructor in English, 1963-64; Drew University, assistant professor of English, 1964-68; University of Georgia, assistant professor, 1968-72, associate professor of radio, television and film, 1972-86; freelance photographer and writer, 1986-. **Publications:** Mary McCarthy, 1967; (ed.) The Process of Fiction: Contemporary Stories and Criticism, 1969; (comp.) Fiction's Journey: Fifty Stories, 1978; Flannery O'Connor's Georgia, 1980; Your First Cavalier, 1984; Colour and Light, Illness and Death: A New Interpretation of Kafka's der Prozess, 2011. **Address:** 60 Springdale St., Athens, GA 30601, U.S.A.

MCKENZIE, Evan. American (born United States), b. 1951. **Genres:** Politics/Government, Children's Fiction, Social Sciences. **Career:** Alaska Federation of Natives, field representative, 1975-77; Delta Institute, project director, 1979-81; San Diego County, deputy district attorney, 1981-85; National University, department of criminal justice administration, adjunct instructor, 1982-85; attorney in civil litigation practice, 1985-90; San Diego State University, School of Public Administration and Urban Studies, adjunct instructor, 1985-89; Albright College, assistant professor of political science, 1990-94; University of Illinois, assistant professor of political science, 1994-97, associate professor of political science, 1997-; The John Marshall Law School, adjunct instructor, 1999-. Writer and consultant. **Publications:** (With R.A. Roos) The Kids Nobody Wants: Treating The Seriously Delinquent Youth, 1982; Privatopia: Homeowner Associations and The Rise of Residential Private Government, 1994; Beyond Privatopia, 2011. **Address:** Department of Political Science, University of Illinois, 1007 W Harrison St., PO Box 276, Chicago, IL 60607-7137, U.S.A. **Online address:** mckenzie@uic.edu

MCKENZIE, John D. American (born United States), b. 1924. **Genres:** Novels, History, Autobiography/Memoirs, Biography, Military/Defense/Arms Control. **Career:** International Minerals and Chemical Corp., director of administration, 1950-72; Industrial Minerals Ventures Inc., vice-president for research, development and marketing, 1973-76; International Medical Corp., executive vice-president, 1976-79; Marketing Communications Inc., co-owner and president, 1980-89; writer and independent consultant, 1989-95. **Publications:** Uncertain Glory: Lee's Generalship Re-Examined, 1997; On Time on Target: The World War II Memoir of a Paratrooper in the 82 Airborne, 2000. Contributor to magazines and periodicals. **Address:** 332 S Paradise Rd., Golden, CO 80401-9455, U.S.A.

MCKENZIE, Judith (Sheila). Australian (born Australia), b. 1957?. **Genres:** Architecture, Archaeology/Antiquities, History, Humanities. **Career:** Oxford University, sub-faculty of archaeology, faculty of oriental studies and classics, St. Hugh's College, Rhys-Davids Junior Research Fellow, 1987-90, British Academy postdoctoral research fellow, 1990-93. **Publications:** The Architecture of Petra, 1990, rev. ed., 2005; (contrib. with S. Dalley) From Nineveh to New York: The Strange Story of the Assyrian Reliefs in the Metropolitan Museum and the Hidden Masterpiece at Canford School, 1997; Architecture of Alexandria and Egypt, c. 300 B.C. to A.D. 700, 2007. Contributor to books and publications. **Address:** St. Hughs College, Oxford University, St Margaret's Rd., Oxford, OX OX2 6LE, England. **Online address:** judith.mckenzie@arch.ox.ac.uk

MCKENZIE, Nancy Affleck. American (born United States), b. 1948. **Genres:** History, Young Adult Fiction, Young Adult Non-fiction, Children's Non-fiction, Novels. **Career:** Thorobrook Farm, stable manager, 1986-90; Desktop Publishing Co. president and owner, 1989-2000; Childbirth Instructor Magazine, senior editor, 1994-99. **Publications:** GUINEVERE AND KING ARTHUR SERIES: The Child Queen, 1994; The High Queen, 1995. NOVEL: Grail Prince, 2003. TRISTAN AND ESYLLTE SERIES: Prince of Dreams: A Tale of Tristan and Essylte, 2003. CHRYSALIS QUEEN QUARTET: Guinevere's Gift, 2008; Guinevere's Gamble, 2009. Contributor to periodicals. **Address:** c/o Jean Naggar, Jean V. Naggar Literary Agency Inc., 216 E 75th St., Ste. 1E, New York, NY 10021, U.S.A. **Online address:** mckenzien@worldnet.att.net

MCKENZIE, Robert Tracy. American (born United States), b. 1960. **Genres:** History, Military/Defense/Arms Control. **Career:** University of Washington, professor of history. Writer. **Publications:** One South or Many? Plantation Belt and Upcountry in Civil War-Era Tennessee, 1994; Lincolnites and Rebels: A Divided Town in the American Civil War, 2006. Contributor to books and journals. **Address:** Department of History, University of Washington, 315 Smith, PO Box 353560, Seattle, WA 98195-3560, U.S.A. **Online address:** r7t14@u.washington.edu

MCKEON, Michael. American (born United States), b. 1943?. **Genres:** Politics/Government, Poetry, Novels, History, Literary Criticism And History. **Career:** Boston University, assistant professor, associate professor, 1971-88; Brandeis University, visiting professor, 1986-87; State University of New Jersey, Rutgers University, professor of English, 1988-90, distinguished professor, 1990-95, board of governors professor of literature, 1995-. Writer. **Publications:** Politics and Poetry in Restoration England: The Case of Dryden's Annus Mirabilis, 1975; The Origins of the English Novel, 1600-1740, 1987; (ed.) Theory of the Novel: A Historical Approach, 2000; The Secret History of Domesticity: Public, Private, and the Division of Knowledge, 2005. Contributor to periodicals and journals. **Address:** Department of English, Rutgers University, Murray Hall, 510 George St., New Brunswick, NJ 08901-1167, U.S.A. **Online address:** michael.mckeon@rutgers.edu

MCKEOWN, Tom. American (born United States), b. 1937. **Genres:** Poetry. **Career:** Alpena College, instructor in English, 1962-64; University of Wisconsin-Oshkosh, instructor in English, 1964-68, professor of English, 1983-87, 1989-94; Stephens College, instructor in English, 1968-74; University of Wisconsin-Stevens Point, instructor in English and creative writing, 1976-81, professor of English, 1983-; Savannah College of Art and Design, professor of English, 1982-83; Poetry Tutorials, staff, 1994-. Writer. **Publications:** Alewife Summer, 1967; Last Thoughts, 1969; The Winds of the Calendar, 1969; Drunk All Afternoon, 1969; The Milk of the Wolf, 1970; The Cloud Keeper, 1972; The Luminous Revolver, 1973; Driving to New Mexico, 1974; The House of Water, 1974; Maya Dreams, 1977; Certain Minutes: Poems, 1978; (contrib.) Circle of the Eye: Eleven Poems by Tom McKeown for Medium Voice and Piano, 1982; Invitation of the Mirrors, 1985; Three Hundred Tigers, 1994. Contributor to periodicals. **Address:** 1130 Timothy Trl., Oshkosh, WI 54904-7431, U.S.A.

MCKEVETT, G. A. *See* **MASSIE, Sonja.**

MCKIBBEN, Bill. (William Ernest). American (born United States), b. 1960. **Genres:** Environmental Sciences/Ecology, Communications/Media, Theology/Religion. **Career:** New Yorker, staff writer, 1982-87; editor, 1983-87. **Publications:** The End of Nature, 1989; The Age of Missing Information, 1992; (ed. and intro.) Birch Browsings, 1992; (with T.T. Williams and W.L. Heat-Moon) Three Essays, 1993; The Comforting Whirlwind: God, Job, and the Scale of Creation, 1994; Hope Human and Wild: True Stories of Living Lightly on the Earth, 1995; 25 Bicycle Tours in the Adirondacks, 1995; Hundred Dollar Holiday: The Case for a More Joyful Christmas, 1998; Maybe One: A Case for Smaller Families, 1998; Long Distance: A Year of Living Strenuously, 2000; The Return of the Wolf, 2000; (contrib.) Hamish Fulton, 2002; Enough: Staying Human in an Engineered Age, 2003; Enough: Genetic Engineering and the End of Human Nature, 2003; Wandering Home: A Long Walk Across America's Most Hopeful Landscape, Vermont's Champlain Valley and New York's Adirondacks, 2005; Live Well, Live Wild, 2006; Deep Economy: The Wealth of Communities and the Durable Future, 2007; Fight Global Warming Now: The Handbook for Taking Action in Your Community, 2007; Earth Under Fire, 2007; The Bill Mckibben Reader: Pieces from an Active Life, 2008; (ed.) American Earth: Environmental Writing Since Thoreau, 2008; Eaarth: Making a Life on a Tough New Planet, 2010; Long Distance. Testing the Limits of Body and Spirit in a Year of Living Strenuously, 2010. **Address:** c/o Times Books, 175 5th Ave., New York, NY 10010, U.S.A. **Online address:** bill@billmckibben.com

MCKIE, Robin. British (born England), b. 1950. **Genres:** Adult Non-fiction, Children's Non-fiction, History, Biology, Sciences. **Career:** Scotsman Publications, journalist, 1973-78; Times Newspaper, journalist, 1978-82; The Observer, science and technology editor, 1982-. **Publications:** Panic: The Story of AIDS, 1986; (co-author) Chernobyl: The End of the Nuclear Dream, 1987; The Genetic Jigsaw: The Story of the New Genetics, 1988; (with W. Bodmer) The Book of Man: The Human Genome Project and the Quest to Discover Our Genetic Heritage, 1994; (with C. Stringer) African Exodus: The Origins of Modern Humanity, 1997; Dawn of Man: The Story of Human Evolution, 2000; Face of Britain, 2006. NONFICTION FOR CHILDREN: Lasers, 1983; Technology: Science at Work, 1984; Nuclear Power, 1985; Solar Power, 1985; Robots, 1986; Energy, 1989. Contributor to periodicals. **Address:** The Observer, King's Pl., 90 York Way, London, GL NI 9GU, England. **Online address:** robin.mckie@observer.co.uk

MCKILLEN, Elizabeth. American (born United States), b. 1957. **Genres:** History, Organized Labor, Economics. **Career:** Kirkland & Ellis (law firm), historical researcher, 1981-82; Newberry Library, researcher for Pullman project, 1982-83; Northwestern University, lecturer in history, 1986-87; Colgate University, visiting assistant professor of history, 1987-88; Clarkson University, visiting assistant professor of history, 1989-90; Ohio State University, visiting assistant professor of history, 1990-91; University of Maine, Department of history, assistant professor, 1992, professor; Cleveland Labor History Museum, exhibit coordinator, 1992. Writer. **Publications:** Chicago Labor and the Quest for a Democratic Diplomacy, 1914-1924, 1995; Beyond Gompers: The AFL, the Creation of the ILO, and U.S. Labor Dissent, forthcoming. Contributor of articles to periodicals. **Address:** Department of History, University of Maine, 140 Stevens Hall, Orono, ME 04469, U.S.A. **Online address:** elizabeth.mckillen@umit.maine.edu

MCKINLAY, Brian John. Australian (born Australia), b. 1933. **Genres:** History, Mathematics/Statistics, Local History/Rural Topics, Poetry, Politics/Government, Social Sciences. **Career:** Teacher, 1955-70; Melbourne Teachers College, tutor in librarianship, 1970-75; State College of Melbourne, lecturer; Jacaranda Press, consultant, 1970-74; Education Department of Victoria, regional history editor for Corangamite region, 1973-84; Ministry of Education, chief education history officer, 1984-. **Publications:** Primary Mathematics, 1965; The First Royal Tour 1867-1868, 1970; Western District Sketchbook, 1971; Diamond Valley Sketchbook, 1973; Carlton Sketchbook, 1974; (ed. with J. Braithwaite and C. Deer) Migration Unit: Teacher's Guide, 1975; Collingwood and Fitzroy Sketchbook, 1978; A Documentary History of the Australian Labour Movement 1850-1975, 1979; History at Your Fingertips, 1979; Growing Things, 1979; ALP: A Short History of the Australian Labor Party, 1981; Australia, 1942: End of Innocence, 1985; Schooldays, 1985; Outdoors for Kids, 1987; Australia for Kids, 1988; Sweet and Simple Pleasure, 1988; A Century of Struggle, 1988; Young Anzacs, 1990; Australian Labor History in Documents, 1990; By Heart, 1993. **Address:** Ministry of Education, Rialto Twr., 525 Collins St., Melbourne, VI 3000, Australia. **Online address:** brianmckinlay@bigpond.com

MCKINLEY, (Jennifer Carolyn) Robin. British/American (born United States), b. 1952. **Genres:** Novels, Novellas/Short Stories, Science Fiction/Fantasy, Children's Fiction, Young Adult Fiction, Social Sciences. **Career:** Ward & Paul, editor and transcriber, 1972-73; writer, 1975-; Research Associates, research assistant, 1976-77; teacher and counselor, 1978-79; Little, Brown Inc., editorial assistant, 1979-81; freelance reader and editor, 1983-91. **Publications:** Beauty: A Retelling of the Story of Beauty and the Beast, 1978; The Door in the Hedge, 1981; The Blue Sword, 1982; (ed.) Imaginary Lands, 1985; (adapter) Tales from The Jungle Book, 1985; The Hero and the Crown, 1985, 2nd ed., 2007; (adapter) Black Beauty, 1986; The Outlaws of Sherwood, 1988; (adapter) Light Princess, 1988; Rowan, 1992; My Father is in the Navy, 1992; Deerskin, 1993; A Knot in the Grain and Other Stories, 1994; Rose Daughter, 1997; The Stone Fey, 1998; Spindle's End, 2000; (with P. Dickinson) Water: Tales of Elemental Spirits, 2002; Sunshine, 2003; Dragonhaven, 2007; Chalice, 2008; (with P. Dickinson) Fire: Tales of Elemental Spirits, 2009; Pegasus, 2010. Works appear in anthologies. Contributor to periodicals. **Address:** c/o Merrilee Heifetz, Writers House Inc., 21 W 26th St., New York, NY 10010-1003, U.S.A. **Online address:** nuraddin@robinmckinley.com

MCKINNEY, Meagan. American (born United States), b. 1961. **Genres:** Novels, Novellas/Short Stories, Romance/Historical, Young Adult Fiction. **Career:** Writer and biologist. **Publications:** No Choice But Surrender, 1987; My Wicked Enchantress, 1988; When Angels Fall, 1990; Till Dawn Tames the Night, 1991; Ground She Walks Upon, 1994; Gentle From the Night, 1995; A Man to Slay Dragons, 1996; A Dance with the Devil, 1997; My Wicked Enchantress, 1997; No Choice But Surrender, 1998; The Fortune Hunter, 1998; In the Dark, 1998; One Small Secret, 1999; The Merry Widow, 1999; Still of the Night, 2001; Moonlight Becomes Her, 2001. VAN ALEN SISTERS SERIES: Lions and Lace, 1992; Fair is the Rose, 1993. MATCHED IN MONTANA SERIES: The Cowboy Meets His Match, 2000; The Lawman Meets His Bride, 2000; The M.D. Courts His Nurse, 2001; Plain Jane and the Hotshot, 2003; Cowboy Claims His Lady, 2003; Billionaire Boss, 2003. **Address:** The Ahearn Agency, 2021 Pine St., New Orleans, LA 70118, U.S.A.

MCKINNEY, Nadine. American (born United States), b. 1938. **Genres:** Mystery/Crime/Suspense, Young Adult Non-fiction. **Career:** Boone County Board of Education, elementary teacher, 1970-85. Writer. **Publications:** Eyes in the Attic, 1994. Works appear in anthologies. Contributor to newspapers. **Address:** PO Box 248, Peytona, WV 25154, U.S.A.

MCKINNEY, Sally (Brown). American (born United States), b. 1933. **Genres:** Communications/Media, Travel/Exploration, Writing/Journalism,

Autobiography/Memoirs, Education, Sports/Fitness, Recreation, History, History. **Career:** Evergreen Street Word and Picture Co., owner, 1980-85; Syndicated Travel Features, owner, 1985-; Society of American, travel writer. Travel consultant. **Publications:** Country Roads of Indiana: Drives, Day Trips, and Weekend Excursions, 1993, 2nd ed., 1999; Fairs and Festivals: Illinois, Indiana, and Ohio, 1996; Hiking Indiana, 2000; New Zealand: Adventures in Nature, 2000; Great Indiana Weekend Adventures, 2001; The Indiana University Experience, 2001. Contributor to periodicals. **Address:** Syndicated Travel Features, 122 N Jefferson St., PO Box 1225, Bloomington, IN 47408, U.S.A. **Online address:** sallymckinney@hotmail.com

MCKINNEY, Tina Brooks. American (born United States) **Genres:** Novels, Women's Studies And Issues. **Career:** Writer. **Publications:** All That Drama, 2004; Lawd, Mo' Drama, 2007; Fool, Stop Trippin', 2008; Dubious, 2008; Deep Deception, 2009; Snapped, 2010; Around The Way Girls 8, 2011. **Address:** Covington, GA , U.S.A. **Online address:** tybrooks2@yahoo.com

MCKINNON, K. C. *See* **PELLETIER, Cathie.**

MCKINNON, Ronald I(an). American/Canadian (born Canada), b. 1935. **Genres:** Economics, Money/Finance, Politics/Government. **Career:** Royal Roads Military College, faculty, 1952-54; Royal Canadian Air Force, staff, 1952-56; University of Alberta, faculty, 1954-56; University of Minnesota, instructor in business administration, 1957-59; Syracuse University, lecturer in economics, 1960-61; Stanford University, assistant professor, 1961-66, associate professor, 1966-69, professor, 1969-84, William D. Eberle Professor of International Economics, 1984-2008, emeritus professor of economics, 2005-; Center for Advanced Study in the Behavioral Sciences, fellow, 1974-75; Brookings Institution, Rockefeller Visiting Research Professor of International Economics, 1970-71; Princeton University, Frank D. Graham Memorial Lecturer, 1977; University of Malaya, Tun Ismail Ali Chair in Monetary and Financial Economics, 2002. Writer. **Publications:** (With W.E. Oates) The Implications of International Economic Integration for Monetary, Fiscal and Exchange-Rate Policy, 1966; Money and Capital in Economic Development, 1973; (ed. and contrib.) Money and Finance in Economic Growth and Development: Essays in Honor of Edward S. Shaw, 1976; Money in International Exchange: The Convertible Currency System, 1979; An International Standard for Monetary Stabilization, 1984; The Order of Economic Liberalization: Financial Control in the Transition to a Market Economy, 1991; The Rules of the Game: International Money and Exchange Rates, 1996; (with K. Ohno) Dollar and Yen: Resolving Economic Conflict Between the United States and Japan, 1997; Exchange Rates under the East Asian Dollar Standard: Living with Conflicted Virtue, 2005; China's Exchange Rate Trap: Japan Redux? American Economic Review, 2006; (with G. Schnabl) The Case for Stabilizing China's Exchange Rate: Setting the Stage for Fiscal Expansion, China & the World Economy, 2009. **Address:** Department of Economics, Stanford University, Rm. 321, Landau Economics Bldg., Stanford, CA 94305-6072, U.S.A. **Online address:** mckinnon@stanford.edu

MCKINSEY, Beth. *See* **MCKINSEY, Elizabeth.**

MCKINSEY, Elizabeth. (Beth McKinsey). American (born United States), b. 1947. **Genres:** Education, Literary Criticism And History, Young Adult Fiction. **Career:** Bryn Mawr College, assistant professor, 1975-77; Harvard University, assistant professor, 1977-82, associate professor of English, 1982-86, senior lecturer, 1986-89; Radcliffe College, Bunting Institute, director, 1985-89; Carleton College, dean, 1989-2002, professor of English and American studies, 1989-. Writer. **Publications:** The Western Experiment: New England Transcendentalists in the Ohio Valley, 1973; Niagara Falls: Icon of the American Sublime, 1985; (co-author) Niagara: Two Centuries of Changing Attitudes, 1697-1901, 1985. Contributor to periodicals. **Address:** Department Of American Studies, Carleton College, 211 Language & Dining Ctr., 1 N College St., Northfield, MN 55057, U.S.A. **Online address:** emckinse@carleton.edu

MCKISSACK, Fredrick L(emuel). American (born United States), b. 1939. **Genres:** Children's Fiction, Biography, History. **Career:** Civil engineer, 1964-74; writer, 1982-; All-Writing Services, co-owner. **Publications:** WITH P.C. McCKISSACK: Look What You've Done Now, Moses, 1984; Abram, Abram, Where Are We Going?, 1984, Cinderella, 1985; Country Mouse and City Mouse, 1985; The Little Red Hen, 1985; The Three Bears, 1985; The Ugly Little Duck, 1986; Fredrick Douglas: A Biography, 1986; When Do You Talk to God? Prayers for Small Children, 1986; King Midas and His Gold, 1986; A Real Winner, 1987; The King's New Clothes, 1987; Tall Phil and Small Bill, 1987; Three Billy Goats Gruff, 1987; My Bible ABC Book, 1987; All Paths Lead to Bethlehem, 1987; Messy Bessey, 1987; Frederick Douglass: The Black Lion, 1987; The Big Bug Book of Counting, 1987; The Big Bug Book of Opposites, 1987; The Big Bug Book of Places to Go, 1987; The Big Bug Book of Things to Do, 1987; The Big Bug Book of the Alphabet, 1987; The Civil Rights Movement in America from 1865 to the Present, 1987, 2nd ed., 1991; Bugs!, 1988, rev. ed., 2000; The Children's ABC Christmas, 1988; Constance Stumbles, 1988; Oh, Happy, Happy Day! A Child's Easter in Story, Song and Prayer, 1989; God Made Something Wonderful, 1989; Messy Bessey's Closet, 1989; James Weldon Johnson: Lift Every Voice and Sing, 1990; A Long Hard Journey: The Story of the Pullman Porter, 1990; History of the Civil Rights Movement, 1990; Taking a Stand against Racism and Racial Discrimination, 1990; W.E.B. DuBois, 1990; Messy Bessey's Garden, 1991; The Story of Booker T. Washington, 1991; Carter G. Woodson: The Father of Black History, 1991, rev. ed., 2002; Frederick Douglass: Leader Against Slavery, 1991, rev. ed., 2002; George Washington Carver: The Peanut Scientist, 1991, rev. ed., 2002; Ida B. Wells-Barnett: A Voice Against Violence, 1991, rev. ed., 2001; Louis Armstrong: Jazz Musician, 1991, rev. ed., 2001; Marian Anderson: A Great Singer, 1991, rev. ed., 2001; Martin Luther King, Jr.: Man of Peace, 1991, rev. ed., 2001; Mary Church Terrell: Leader for Equality, 1991, rev. ed., 2001; Mary McLeod Bethune: A Great Teacher, 1991, rev. ed., 2001; Ralph J. Bunche: Peacemaker, 1991, rev. ed., 2002; From Heaven Above: The Story of Christmas Proclaimed by the Angels, 1992; Jesse Owens, 1992, rev. ed., 2001; From Heaven Above, 1992; Langston Hughes: Great American Poet, 1992, rev. ed., 2002; Sojourner Truth: A Voice for Freedom, 1992, rev. ed., 2002; Zora Neale Hurston: Writer and Storyteller, 1992, rev. ed., 2002; Satchel Paige: The Best Arm in Baseball, 1992, rev. ed., 2002; Sojourner Truth: Ain't I a Woman? 1992; Madam C.J. Walker: Self-Made Millionaire, 1992, rev. ed., 2001; Paul Robeson: A Voice to Remember, 1992, rev. ed., 2001; Booker T. Washington: Leader and Educator, 1992, rev. ed., 2001; God Makes All Things New, 1993; Christmas in the Big House, Christmas in the Quarters, 1994; The Royal Kingdoms of Ghana, Mali, and Songhay: Life in Medieval Africa, 1994; African-American Scientists, 1994; African-American Inventors, 1994; Red-tail Angels: The Story of the Tuskegee Airmen of World War II, 1995; Rebels Against Slavery, 1996; Messy Bessey's School Desk, 1998; Let My People Go: Bible Stories of Faith, Hope, and Love as told by Price Jefferies, A Free Man of Color to His Daughter, Charlotte, in Charleston, South Carolina, 1806-1816, 1998; Messy Bessey and the Birthday Overnight, 1998; Let My People Go: Bible Stories Told by a Freeman of Color to his Daughter, Charlotte, in Charleston, South Carolina, 1806-16, 1998; Young, Black and Determined: A Biography of Lorraine Hansberry, 1998; Messy Bessey's Holidays, 1999; Messy Bessey, 1999; Black Hands, White Sails: The Story of African-American Whalers, 1999; Black Hoops: The History of African-Americans in Basketball, 1999; Miami Gets It Straight, 2000; Messy Bessey's Family Reunion, 2000; Miami Makes the Play, 2001; Jesse Owens: Olympic Star, 2001; Miami Sees It Through, 2002; Carter G. Woodson: The Father of Black History, 2002; Days of Jubilee: The End of Slavery in the United States, 2003; (and with J.P. McKissack) Clone Codes, 2010; (and with J.P. McKissack) Cyborg: A Clone Codes Novel, 2011. **Address:** All-Writing Services, 225 S Meramec, Ste. 206, Clayton, MO 63105-3511, U.S.A.

MCKISSACK, Patricia C(arwell). (L'Ann Carwell). American (born United States), b. 1944. **Genres:** Children's Fiction, Young Adult Fiction, Novels, Children's Non-fiction. **Career:** Junior High School, English teacher, 1968-75; Forest Park College, part-time instructor in English, 1975-85; Concordia Publishing House, children's book editor, 1976-81; University of Missouri, instructor, 1978-; All-Writing Services, co-owner, 1981-; Institute of Children's Literature, children's book editor, 1984-. Educational consultant. **Publications:** FOR CHILDREN: (as L'Ann Carwell) Good Shepherd Prayer, 1978; (as L'Ann Carwell) God Gives New Life, 1979; Ask the Kids, 1979; Who Is Who?, 1983; Martin Luther King, Jr.: A Man to Remember, 1984; Paul Lawrence Dunbar: A Poet to Remember, 1984; Michael Jackson, Superstar, 1984; The Apache, 1984; It's the Truth, Christopher, 1984; Lights Out, Christopher, 1984; Mary McLeod Bethune: A Great American Educator, 1985; Aztec Indians, 1985; The Inca, 1985; The Maya, 1985; Our Martin Luther King Book, 1986; Flossie and the Fox, 1986; Who Is Coming?, 1986; Give It with Love, Christopher: Christopher Learns about Gifts and Giving, 1988; Speak Up, Christopher: Christopher Learns the Difference between Right and Wrong, 1988; A Troll in a Hole, 1988; Nettie Jo's Friends, 1988; Mirandy and Brother Wind, 1988; Jesse Jackson: A Biography, 1989; Monkey-Monkey's Trick: Based on an African Folk-Tale, 1989; (with R.

Kronberg) A Piece of the Wind and Other Stories to Tell, 1990; No Need for Alarm, 1990; A Million Fish-More or Less, 1992; History of Haiti, 1996; (with R.L. Duyff) All Our Fruits and Vegetables, 1996; (with R.L. Duyff) It's a Sandwich!, 1996; Ma Dear's Aprons, 1997; Run away Home, 1997; A Picture of Freedom: The Diary of Clottee, 1998; Color Me Dark: The Diary of Nellie Lee Love, the Great Migration North, 2000; Goin' Someplace Special, 2000; The Honest-to-Goodness Truth, 2000; Miami Gets It Straight, 2000; Tippy Lemmey, 2003; Look to the Hills: The Diary of Lozette Moreau, a French Slave Girl, 2004; (with J. Carville) Lu and the Swamp Ghost, 2004; (with A. Zarembka) To Establish Justice, 2004; (with O.J. Moss) Precious and the Boo Hag, 2005; Where Crocodiles Have Wings, 2005; Amistad: The Story of a Slave Ship, 2005; Abby Takes a Stand, 2005; Loved Best, 2005; Away West, 2006; A Song for Harlem, 2007; A Friendship for Today, 2007; Stitchin' and Pullin': A Gee's Bend Quilt, 2008; The Home-run King, 2008; (with F.L. McKissack and J.P. McKissack) Clone Codes, 2010; (with F.L. McKissack and J.P. McKissack) Cyborg: A Clone Codes Novel, 2011; Ol' Clip-Clop: A Ghost Story, 2011; Never Forgotten, 2011; (with F.L. McKissack, Jr.) The Visitor, 2012; (with F.L. McKissack, Jr.) Best Shot in the West, 2012. CHILDREN'S FICTION WITH F.L. McKISSACK, JR.: Look What You've Done Now, Moses, 1984; Abram, Abram, Where Are We Going?, 1984; Cinderella, 1985; Country Mouse and City Mouse, 1985; The Little Red Hen, 1985; The Three Bears, 1985; The Ugly Little Duck, 1986; When Do You Talk to God?: Prayers for Small Children, 1986; King Midas and His Gold, 1986; Frederick Douglass: The Black Lion, 1987; A Real Winner, 1987; The King's New Clothes, 1987; Tall Phil and Small Bill, 1987; Three Billy Goats Gruff, 1987; My Bible ABC Book, 1987; All Paths Lead to Bethlehem, 1987; Messy Bessey, 1987; The Big Bug Book of Counting, 1987; The Big Bug Book of Opposites, 1987; The Big Bug Book of Places to Go, 1987; The Big Bug Book of the Alphabet, 1987; Bugs!, 1988, rev. ed., 2000; The Big Bug Book of Things to Do, 1987; The Children's ABC Christmas, 1988; Constance Stumbles, 1988; Oh, Happy, Happy Day!: A Child's Easter in Story, Song, and Prayer, 1989; God Made Something Wonderful, 1989; Messy Bessey's Closet, 1990, rev. ed., 2001; Messy Bessey's Garden, 1991, rev. ed., 2002; From Heaven Above, 1992; God Makes All Things New, 1993; Sports, 1994; Messy Bessey's School Desk, 1998; Let My People Go: Bible Stories of Faith, Hope and Love as Told by Price Jefferies, a Free Man of Color, to His Daughter, Charlotte, in Charleston, South Carolina, 1806-1816, 1998; Messy Bessey and the Birthday Overnight, 1998; Messy Bessey's Holidays, 1998; Black Hands, White Sails: The Story of African-American Whalers, 1999; Messy Bessey's Family Reunion, 2000; Miami Makes the Play, 2001; Miami Sees It Through, 2002; Days of Jubilee: The End of Slavery in the United States, 2003; (adaptors) Itching and Twitching: A Nigerian Folktale, 2003; Hard Labor: The First African Americans, 1619, 2004; The Adventures of Deadwood Dick, 2009. NONFICTION WITH F. McKISSACK: Frederick Douglass: A Biography, 1986; The Civil Rights Movement in America from 1865 to the Present, 1987, 2nd ed., 1991; James Weldon Johnson: Lift Every Voice and Sing, 1990; A Long Hard Journey: The Story of the Pullman Porter, 1990; History of the Civil Rights Movement, 1990; Taking a Stand against Racism and Racial Discrimination, 1990; W.E.B. DuBois, 1990; The Story of Booker T. Washington, 1991; Carter G. Woodson: The Father of Black History, 1991, rev. ed., 2002; Frederick Douglass: Leader against Slavery, 1991, rev. ed., 2002; George Washington Carver: The Peanut Scientist, 1991, rev. ed., 2002; Ida B. Wells-Barnett: A Voice against Violence, 1991, rev. ed., 2001; Louis Armstrong: Jazz Musician, 1991, rev. ed., 2001; Marian Anderson: A Great Singer, 1991, rev. ed., 2001; Martin Luther King, Jr.: Man of Peace, 1991, rev. ed., 2001; Mary Church Terrell: Leader for Equality, 1991, rev. ed., 2002; Mary McLeod Bethune: A Great Teacher, 1991, rev. ed., 2001; Ralph J. Bunche: Peacemaker, 1991, rev. ed., 2002; Jesse Owens: Olympic Star, 1992, rev. ed., 2001; From Heaven Above, 1992; Langston Hughes: Great American Poet, 1992, rev. ed., 2002; Sojourner Truth: Ain't I a Woman?, 1992; Zora Neale Hurston: Writer and Storyteller, 1992, rev. ed., 2002; Satchel Paige: The Best Arm in Baseball, 1992, rev. ed., 2002; Sojourner Truth: Voice for Freedom, 1992, rev. ed., 2002; Madam C.J. Walker: Self-Made Millionaire, 1992, rev. ed., 2001; Paul Robeson: A Voice to Remember, 1992, rev. ed., 2001; Booker T. Washington: Leader and Educator, 1992, rev. ed., 2001; Christmas in the Big House, Christmas in the Quarters, 1994; The Royal Kingdoms of Ghana, Mali and Songhay: Life in Medieval Africa, 1994; African-American Scientists, 1994; Black Diamond: The Story of the Negro Baseball Leagues, 1994; African Americans, 1994; African-American Inventors, 1994; Red-Tail Angels: The Story of the Tuskegee Airmen of World War II, 1995; Rebels against Slavery: American Slave Revolts, 1996; Young, Black and Determined: A Biography of Lorraine Hansberry, 1998. PICTURE BOOK: The All-I'll-Ever-Want Christmas Doll, 2007. COLLECTIONS: (co-author) The World in 1492, 1992; The Dark-thirty: Southern Tales of the Supernatural, 1992; Porch Lies: Tales of Slicksters, Tricksters, and Other Wily Characters, 2006. Contributor of articles to magazines. **Address:** All-Writing Services, 225 S Meramec Ave., Ste. 206, Clayton, MO 63105-3511, U.S.A.

MCKITTERICK, David John. British (born England), b. 1948. **Genres:** Librarianship, Literary Criticism And History. **Career:** Darwin College, fellow, 1978-86; Trinity College, fellow and librarian, 1986-; Cambridge University, honorary professor of historical bibliography, 2006-. Writer. **Publications:** (Comp.) Aspects of French Eighteenth Century Typography, 1982; The Sandars and Lyell Lectures: A Checklist with an Introduction, 1983; Four Hundred Years of University Printing and Publishing in Cambridge, 1584-1984: Catalogue of the Exhibition in the University Library, 1984; Cambridge University Library: A History: The Eighteenth and Nineteenth Centuries, 1986; (with J.P. Feather) The History of Books and Libraries: Two Views, 1986; A New Specimen Book of Curwen Pattern Papers, 1987; Wallpapers by Edward Bawden Printed at the Curwen Press, 1988; A History of Cambridge University Press, vol. I: Printing and the Book Trade in Cambridge, 1534-1698, 1992, vol. II: Scholarship and Commerce, 1698-1872, 1998; (with D. Vaisey) The Foundations of Scholarship: Libraries and Collecting, 1650-1750, 1992; (intro.) An Introduction to Bibliography for Literary Students, 1994; The Cambridge History of the Book in Britain, vol. II-VI, 1998-2009; Print, Manuscript and the Search for Order, 1450-1830, 2003; (intro.) A Stickful of Nonpareil, 2009. EDITOR: The Library of Sir Thomas Knyvett of Ashwellthorpe, 1978; Stanley Morison and D.B. Updike: Selected Correspondence, 1979; Selected Essays on the History of Letter-Forms in Manuscript and Print, 1980; Andrew Perne: Quatercentenary Studies, 1991; Concordance to the Complete Poems and Plays of T.S. Eliot, 1995; Making of the Wren Library, Trinity College, Cambridge, 1995; Trinity Apocalypse, 2005. **Address:** Trinity College, A4b New Ct., Cambridge, CB2 1TQ, England. **Online address:** djm1008@cus.cam.ac.uk

MCKITTERICK, Rosamond Deborah. British (born England), b. 1949. **Genres:** History. **Career:** Cambridge University, assistant lecturer, 1979-85, lecturer, 1985-91, reader in early medieval European history, 1991-97, professor in early medieval European history, 1997-; Newnham College, research fellow, 1974-77, fellow, 1977- 97, professorial fellow, 1997-, vice principal, 1996-98; Cambridge University, Lady Margaret preacher, 1999; Rome British Academy, British School, Balsdon fellow, 2001-02; Netherlands Institute of Advanced Studies, fellow-in-residence, 2005-06. Academic, historian and writer. **Publications:** The Frankish Church and the Carolingian Reforms, 789-895, 1977; (ed. with D. Whitelock and D. Dumville) Ireland in Early Mediaeval Europe: Studies in Memory of Kathleen Hughes, 1982; The Frankish Kingdoms under the Carolingians, 751-987, 1983; The Carolingians and the Written Word, 1989; The Uses of Literacy in Early Mediaeval Europe, 1990; Books, Scribes and Learning in the Frankish Kingdoms, 6th-9th Centuries, 1994; Carolingian Culture: Emulation and Innovation, 1994; The New Cambridge Medieval History, 7 vols., 1995; The Frankish Kings and Culture in the Early Middle Ages, 1995; (ed. with R. Quinault) Edward Gibbon and Empire, 1997; History and Its Audiences: Inaugural Lecture, 2000; (ed.) The Early Middle Ages: Europe 400-1000, 2001; Atlas of the Medieval World, 2004; History and Memory in the Carolingian World, 2004; Perceptions of the Past in the Early Middle Ages, 2006; Charlemagne: The Formation of Carolingian Political Identity, 2008. **Address:** Cambridge University, Faculty of History, West Rd., Cambridge, CB3 9EF, England. **Online address:** rdm21@cam.ac.uk

MCKITTRICK, David. British/Irish (born Ireland), b. 1949. **Genres:** Novels, Adult Non-fiction, Military/Defense/Arms Control, Young Adult Fiction. **Career:** East Antrim Times, reporter, 1971-73; Irish Times, reporter, 1973-76, Northern Edition, reporter, 1976-81, London Edition, reporter, 1981-85; British Broadcasting Corp. (BBC), journalist, 1985-86; Independent, Ireland correspondent, 1986-. **Publications:** Despatches from Belfast, 1989; Endgame: The Search for Peace in Northern Ireland, 1994; (with E. Mallie) The Fight for Peace: The Secret Story behind the Irish Peace Process, 1996; The Nervous Peace, 1996; (co-author) Lost Lives: The Stories of the Men, Women and Children Who Died as a Result of the Northern Ireland Troubles, 1999; Through the Minefield, 1999; (with D. McVea) Making Sense of the Troubles, 2000 in US as Making Sense of the Troubles: The Story of the Conflict in Northern Ireland, 2002; (with E. Mallie) Endgame in Ireland, 2001. Contributor to periodicals. **Address:** Ireland Correspondent, The Independent, Independent House, 191 Marsh Wall, London, GL E14 9RS, England.

MCKNIGHT, David. Australian (born Australia), b. 1951?. **Genres:** Military/Defense/Arms Control, Social Commentary, Politics/Government, Social Sciences, Young Adult Non-fiction. **Career:** Sydney Morning Herald, journalist; ABC TV, journalist; Tribune, journalist; University of Technology, associate professor of journalism; Centre for Policy Development, fellow; University of New South Wales, associate professor of arts faculty, Journalism and Media Research Centre, senior research fellow. **Publications:** (Ed.) Moving Left: The Future of Socialism in Australia, 1986; Australia's Spies and Their Secrets, 1994; Espionage and the Roots of the Cold War: The Conspiratorial Heritage, 2002; Beyond Right and Left: New Politics and the Culture Wars, 2005; Goodbye to All That?, 2010. Contributor to journals. **Address:** University of New South Wales, Rm. 108, Level 1, 1-3 Eurimbla Ave., Sydney, NW 2052, Australia. **Online address:** d.mcknight@unsw.edu.au

MCKNIGHT, Stephen A. American (born United States), b. 1944. **Genres:** Intellectual History, Theology/Religion, Philosophy, Politics/Government. **Career:** Emory University, instructor in humanities, 1970-72; University of Florida, assistant professor, 1972-77, associate professor of humanities and affiliate associate professor of philosophy, 1977-80, Department of Humanities, chair, 1977-80, associate professor, 1979, 1980-91, special adviser to the vice president for research, 1983-86, professor of European intellectual and cultural history, 1991-, now professor emeritus of European intellectual and cultural history; University of North Carolina, Carol Belk distinguished professor of humanities, 1993; St. Peter's College, Will and Ariel Durant professor of humanities, 1994-95; U.S. Information Agency, Office of Academic Programs, Educational and Cultural Affairs, director, 1981-83. Writer and consultant. **Publications:** Sacralizing the Secular: The Renaissance Origins of Modernity, 1989; The Modern Age and the Recovery of Ancient Wisdom: A Reconsideration of Historical Consciousness, 1450-1650, 1991; Religious Foundations of Francis Bacon's Thought, 2006. EDITOR AND CONTRIBUTOR: Eric Voegelin's Search for Order in History, 1978; Science, Pseudo-Science, and Utopianism in Early Modern Thought, 1992; (with G.L. Price) International and Interdisciplinary Perspectives on Eric Voegelin, 1997; (with G. Hughes and G.L. Price) Politics, Order, and History: Essays on the Work of Eric Voegelin, 2001. Contributor to journals. **Address:** Department of History, University of Florida, 207 Keene-Flint Hall, PO Box 117320, Gainesville, FL 32611-7320, U.S.A. **Online address:** smcknigh@history.ufl.edu

MCKOWN, Delos B. (Delos Banning McKown). American (born United States), b. 1930?. **Genres:** Philosophy, Novels, Theology/Religion, Social Sciences. **Career:** Berea College, instructor in philosophy and religion, 1958-59; University of Idaho, visiting instructor in philosophy, 1960-61; Little Rock University (now University of Arkansas), assistant professor of philosophy, 1961-62; Auburn University, Department of Philosophy, assistant professor, 1962-72, associate professor, 1972-79, professor of philosophy, 1979-99, professor emeritus, 1999-, head of department, 1972-99; Center for Inquiry Institute, adjunct professor, 1990-. Writer. **Publications:** The Classical Marxist Critiques of Religion: Marx, Engels, Lenin, Kautsky, 1975; With Faith and Fury (novel), 1985; The Mythmaker's Magic: Behind the Illusion of Creation Science, 1993; Behold the Antichrist: Bentham on Religion, 2004. Works appear in anthologies. Contributor of articles to journals. **Address:** Department of Philosophy, Auburn University, 6080 Haley Ctr., Auburn, AL 36849, U.S.A. **Online address:** dbmckown@charter.net

MCKOWN, Delos Banning. *See* **MCKOWN, Delos B.**

MCKY, Katie. American (born United States), b. 1956. **Genres:** Social Work, Sports/Fitness. **Career:** Writer and educator. **Publications:** It all Began with a Bean, 2004; Tough Kids, Tough Classrooms, 2004; Pumpkin Town! or, Nothing is Better and Worse than Pumpkins, 2006; Wolf Camp, 2009. Contributor to periodicals. **Address:** c/o Peggy Tierney, Tanglewood Press, PO Box 3009, Terre Haute, IN 47803-0009, U.S.A. **Online address:** katemcky@hotmail.com

MCLAGAN, Jennifer. Australian (born Australia) **Genres:** Food And Wine. **Career:** Food writer, food stylist and chef. **Publications:** Bones: Recipes, History, and Lore, 2005; Cooking on the Bone: Recipes, History and Lore, 2007; Fat: An Appreciation of a Misunderstood Ingredient, with Recipes, 2008; Oddbits: What to Do With the Rest, 2011. Contributor to periodicals. **Address:** The Blumer Literary Agency, 350 7th Ave., Ste. 2003, New York, NY 10001-1930, U.S.A.

MCLAGLEN, John J. *See* **HARVEY, John.**

MCLAIN, Paula. American (born United States), b. 1965. **Genres:** Novels, Human Relations/Parenting. **Career:** Novelist. **Publications:** Less of Her (poems), 1999; Like Family: Growing Up in Other People's Houses (memoir), 2003; Stumble, Gorgeous (poems), 2005; A Ticket to Ride (novel), 2008. **Address:** Julie Barer, Barer Literary, LLC, 270 Lafayette St., Ste. 1504, New York, NY 10012, U.S.A. **Online address:** paulamclain@paulamclain.net

MCLANE, Maureen N. American (born United States), b. 1967. **Genres:** Poetry. **Career:** Boston Review, contributing editor; Chicago Tribune, chief poetry critic; New York University, associate professor; Harvard University, faculty; University of Chicago, faculty; Massachusetts Institute of Technology, faculty; East Harlem Poetry Project, faculty. **Publications:** Romanticism and the Human Sciences: Poetry, Population, and the Discourse of the Species, 2000; Same Life, 2008; Balladeering, Minstrelsy, and the Making of British Romantic Poetry, 2008; (with J. Chandler) The Cambridge Companion to British Romantic Poetry, 2008; World Enough, 2010. **Address:** Department of English, New York University, Rm. 528, 13 University Pl., New York, NY 10003, U.S.A. **Online address:** maureen.mclane@nyu.edu

MCLAREN, Anne E. Australian (born Australia), b. 1955?. **Genres:** History. **Career:** Royal Melbourne Institute of Technology, lecturer, 1986; University of Melbourne, Department of History, lecturer, 1986, Faculty of Arts Asia Institute, senior lecturer, 2000-05, associate professor, 2006-; Victoria College, project officer, 1988, Chinese Program, lecturer, 1989-90; La Trobe University, Department of Asian Languages, Chinese Program, director, 1991-2000. Writer. **Publications:** (Ed. and contrib.) The Chinese Femme Fatale: Stories from the Ming Period, 1994; Chinese Popular Culture and Ming Chantefables, 1998; (ed. and contrib. with A. Finnane) Dress, Sex and Text in Chinese Culture, 1999; (ed. and contrib.) Chinese Women: Living and Working, 2004; Performing Grief: Bridal Laments in Rural China, 2008. Contributor to books and periodicals. **Address:** Asia Institute, University of Melbourne, Melbourne, VI 3010, Australia. **Online address:** mclaae@unimelb.edu.au

MCLAREN, Clemence. American (born United States), b. 1938. **Genres:** Young Adult Fiction, Novels. **Career:** Pan American Airlines, flight attendant, 1960-61; teacher, 1962-84; Johns Hopkins University, Summer Program, dean, 1987-; University of Hawaii, adjunct professor and researcher, 1987-95; Kamehameha Secondary Schools, teacher of senior English, 1993-, administrator. Writer. **Publications:** Inside the Walls of Troy, 1996; Dance for the Land, 1999; Waiting for Odysseus, 2000; Aphrodite's Blessing, 2002; Dance for the Āina, 2003; Achilles' War, forthcoming. **Address:** Linda Allen Literary Agency, 949 Green St., Ste. 5, San Francisco, CA 94123-4829, U.S.A. **Online address:** clemi@clemencemclaren.com

MCLAREN, John. Australian (born Australia), b. 1932. **Genres:** Education, Literary Criticism And History, Politics/Government, History, Essays, Cultural/Ethnic Topics. **Career:** Overland Magazine, associate editor, 1966-93, editor, 1993-97, now consulting editor; Darling Down Institute of Advanced Education, head of department of humanities, 1972-76; Footscray Institute of Technology, department of humanities, head, principal lecturer, 1976-; Victoria University of Technology, professor, through 1991, now professor emeritus. **Publications:** Our Troubled Schools, 1968; Libraries for the Public, 1969; A Dictionary of Australian Education, 1974; (with E.R. Treyvaud) Equal but Cheaper: The Development of Australian Colleges of Advanced Education, 1976; Culture, Literature and the Humanities (microform): A Study of the Development of the Ideas of Literary and Humanities Studies in the Western World from the Renaissance, with Special Attention to the Writings of F.R. Leavis, 1985; Australian Literature: An Historical Introduction, 1989; New Pacific Literatures: Culture and Environment in the European Pacific, 1993; Writing in Hope and Fear: Literature as Politics in Postwar Australia, 1996; States of Imagination: Nationalism and Multiculturalism in Australian and Southern Asian Literature, 2001; Free Radicals of the Left in Postwar Melbourne, 2003; Dialect of the Diaspora-Sourceland, Empire and Homelands, 2003; Not in Tranquillity: A Memoir, 2005; Alan Marshall: Trapped in his Own Image, 2005; Unfnished Journey: The Life and Work of Vincent Buckley, 2009. EDITOR: Towards a New Australia, 1972; A Nation Apart: Essays in Honour of Andrew Fabinyi: Personal Views of Australia in the Eighties, 1983. **Address:** Victoria University of Technology, Footscray Park Campus, Rm. E 207, PO Box 14428, Melbourne, VI 8001, Australia. **Online address:** john.mclaren@vu.edu.au

MCLAREN, Joseph. American (born United States), b. 1948. **Genres:** Adult Non-fiction. **Career:** Mercy College, professor of English, 1976-90; Hofstra University, professor of English, 1990-. Writer. **Publications:** Langston Hughes: Folk Dramatist in the Protest Tradition, 1921-1943, 1997; (ed. with E.A. Hurley and R. Larrier) Migrating Words and Worlds: Pan-Africanism Updated, 1999; (ed. with C.B. Mwaria and S. Federici) African Visions: Literary Images, Political Change, and Social Struggle in Contemporary Africa, 2000; (with J. Heath) I Walked with Giants: The Autobiography of Jimmy Heath, 2010. Contributor to books. **Address:** Department of English, Hofstra University, 120 Mason Hall, Hempstead, NY 11549, U.S.A. **Online address:** joseph.mclaren@hofstra.edu

MCLAREN, Philip. Australian (born Australia), b. 1943?. **Genres:** Novels, Young Adult Fiction. **Career:** Writer. **Publications:** Sweet Water-Stolen Land, 1993, rev. ed., 2001; Scream Black Murder, 1995; Lightning Mine, 1999; There'll Be New Dreams, 2001; Utopia, 2007. **Address:** PO Box 1, Newport Beach, NW 2106, Australia. **Online address:** pmclaren@bigpond.net.au

MCLAREY, Myra. (M. L. Rose). American (born United States), b. 1942. **Genres:** Novels, Biography, Children's Fiction. **Career:** Centerville Community College, teacher of western civilization, 1966-67; Florida Memorial College, assistant professor of history and humanities, 1969-70; Tennessee Governor's Academy for Teachers, faculty member, 1987-95; University of Arkansas, instructor in western civilization, 1988; Harvard University, faculty of writing, 1991-2000; Bard College, faculty associate, 1993-; Ensworth High School, Department of English, chair. Writer. **Publications:** (With S. Moncrief) Moncrief: My Journey to the NBA, 1990; Water from the Well (novel), 1995; (with K.T. McLarey) When You Take a Pig to a Party, 2000. AS M.L. ROSE: The Road to Eden's Ridge, 2002. Contributor to periodicals. **Address:** c/o Leigh Feldman, Darhansoff & Verrill, Rm. 802, 236 W 26th St., New York, NY 10001-6736, U.S.A.

MCLARIN, Kim. American (born United States), b. 1964?. **Genres:** Novels, Young Adult Fiction, Biography. **Career:** Emerson College, writer-in-residence, assistant professor, 2003-; Northwestern University, faculty; The Associated Press, journalist; The Philadelphia Inquirer, journalist, staff writer; The New York Times, journalist, staff writer; WGBH, host. **Publications:** Taming It Down, 1998; Meeting of the Waters, 2001; (with I. Shabazz) Growing up X, 2002; Jump at the Sun, 2006. **Address:** Department of Writing, Literature and Publishing, Emerson College, 120 Boylston St., Boston, MA 02116-4624, U.S.A. **Online address:** kim@kimmclarin.com

MCLAUGHLIN, Andrée Nicola. Also writes as Andrée Nicola. American (born United States), b. 1948. **Genres:** Poetry, Area Studies, Women's Studies And Issues, Essays. **Career:** City University of New York, Medgar Evers College, professor of humanities, 1974-92, chair of special programs, 1977-79, dean of administration, 1979-82, Department of Interdisciplinary Studies, professor of languages, literature and philosophy and professor of interdisciplinary studies, 1992-, chair; Cross-Cultural Black Women's Studies Summer Institute, international coordinator, 1987-; Hamilton College, distinguished visiting professor of women's studies, 1989-91; Office of International Women's Affairs, director, 1997-2001, Dr. Betty Shabazz distinguished chair in social justice, 2001-. Writer. **Publications:** (Ed. with J.M. Braxton) Wild Women in the Whirlwind: Afra-American Culture and the Contemporary Literary Renaissance (essays), 1990; Through the Barrel of Her Consciousness: Contemporary Black Women's Literature and Activism in Cross-Cultural Perspective, 1993; Double Dutch! (poetry), 1993. **Address:** Department of Interdisciplinary Studies, Medgar Evers College, Rm. B1032P, 1650 Bedford Ave., Brooklyn, NY 11225-2201, U.S.A. **Online address:** mclaughlin@mec.cuny.edu

MCLAUGHLIN, Andrew. American (born United States), b. 1941?. **Genres:** Environmental Sciences/Ecology, Adult Non-fiction, Earth Sciences. **Career:** City University of New York, Lehman College, professor of philosophy, now professor emeritus. Writer. **Publications:** Regarding Nature: Industrialism and Deep Ecology, 1993. **Address:** Lehman College, City University of New York, 250 Bedford Park Blvd. W, Bronx, NY 10468, U.S.A. **Online address:** amcl@warwick.net

MCLAUGHLIN, Ann L. American (born United States), b. 1928. **Genres:** Novels, Literary Criticism And History, Novellas/Short Stories. **Career:** American University, instructor, 1984-89; Writer's Center, instructor, 1989-. Writer. **Publications:** NOVELS: Lightning in July, 1989; The Balancing Pole, 1991; Sunset at Rosalie, 1996; Maiden Voyage, 1999; The House on Q Street, 2002; Leaving Bayberry House: A Novel, 2010; Trial in Summer, 2011. Contributor of articles to periodicals. **Address:** 6702 Maple Ave., Chevy Chase, MD 20815, U.S.A. **Online address:** annlmcl@aol.com

MCLAUGHLIN, Corinne. American (born United States), b. 1947. **Genres:** Sociology, Politics/Government, Theology/Religion. **Career:** U.S. Social Security Administration, claims representative, 1968; Ramparts, editorial assistant, 1970-71; Rolling Stone, editorial assistant, 1972; Marianne Frostig School for the Educationally Handicapped, educational therapist, 1974; Findhorn Foundation, adjunct professor, 1975-77; Sirius Inc., co-founder, 1978, director of public relations, 1978-90, director of educational programs, publishing and the book store, 1978-85, Sirius School of Spiritual Science, co-founder; Boston College, adjunct professor, 1979-80; American University, adjunct professor, 1982, 1991-93; New Synthesis Institute, co-director, 1986-88; University of Massachusetts, adjunct professor, 1987-95; President Clinton's Council on Sustainable Development, Sustainable Communities Task Force, coordinator, 1994; The Center for Visionary Leadership, co-founder, executive director and board secretary. Writer. **Publications:** (With G. Davidson) Builders of the Dawn: Community Lifestyles in a Changing World, 1985; The New Synthesis, 1987; (with G. Davidson) Spiritual Politics: Changing the World From the Inside Out, 1994; (with G. Davidson) Practical Visionary: A New World Guide for Spiritual Growth and Social Change, 2010. Contributor of articles to journals and magazines. **Address:** The Center for Visionary Leadership, 369 3rd St., Ste. 563, San Rafael, CA 94901, U.S.A.

MCLAUGHLIN, Martin L. British (born England), b. 1950. **Genres:** Adult Non-fiction, Literary Criticism And History, Humanities, Translations. **Career:** University of Oxford, Magdalen College, academic staff, Agnelli-Serena professor of Italian Studies. Writer and translator. **Publications:** Literary Imitation in the Italian Renaissance: The Theory and Practice of Literary Imitation in Italy from Dante to Bembo, 1995; Italo Calvino, 1998. TRANSLATOR: Italo Calvino, The Path to the Spiders' Nests, 1998, rev. ed., 2000; Why Read the Classics?, 1999; Hermit in Paris: Autobiographical Writings, 2003; Sergio Ghione, Turtle Island: A Journey to Britain's Oddest Colony, 2003; Umberto Eco, On Literature, 2004; (co-trans.) The Complete Cosmicomics, 2009; Into the War, 2011. EDITOR: (co-ed.) Leopardi: A Scottis Quair, 1987; Britain and Italy From Romanticism to Modernism: A Festschrift for Peter Brand, 2000; (with P. Hainsworth) Biographies and Autobiographies in Modern Italy: A Festschrift for John Woodhouse, 2007; (co-ed.) Image, Eye and Art in Calvino: Writing Visibility, 2007; (with Z. Baranski) Italy's Three Crowns: Reading Dante, Petrarch and Boccaccio, 2007; (with L. Panizza) Petrarch in Britain: Interpreters, Imitators and Translators over 700 Years, 2007; (co-ed.) Sinergie narrative: Cinema e letteratura nell'Italia contemporanea, 2008; (with Z. Baranski) Dante the Lyric and Ethical Poet; Dante lirico e etico, 2010; (co-ed.) Dante in Oxford: The Paget Toynbee Lectures, 2011. **Address:** Magdalen College, Oxford University, Oxford, OX OX1 4AU, England. **Online address:** martin.mclaughlin@magd.ox.ac.uk

MCLAUGHLIN, Ritta. American (born United States) **Genres:** Novels, Humor/Satire. **Career:** Investment banker and writer. **Publications:** Every Friday Night: My Year of Dating Misadventures, 2003. Contributor to periodicals. **Address:** Doubleday, 1745 Broadway, New York, NY 10019, U.S.A.

MCLEAN, Duncan. Scottish (born Scotland), b. 1964. **Genres:** Novels, Novellas/Short Stories, Plays/Screenplays, Music, Young Adult Fiction. **Career:** Clocktower Press, editor and publisher, 1990-. **Publications:** Bucket of Tongues, 1992; Bunker Man (novel), 1995; (contrib.) Made in Scotland: An Anthology of New Scottish Plays, 1995; (ed.) Ahead of Its Time: A Clocktower Press Anthology, 1997; Lone Star Swing: On the Trail of Bob Wills and His Texas Playboys, 1998; Blackden, 1999; Aalst: A New Version, 2007. **Address:** W. W. Norton & Company Inc., 500 5th Ave., New York, NY 10110, U.S.A.

MCLEAN, Iain (S.). British/Scottish (born Scotland), b. 1946. **Genres:** Politics/Government. **Career:** University of Oxford, Nuffield College, research fellow, 1969-71, official fellow in politics, 1993-, investment bursar, 2002-06, Department of Politics and International Relations, lecturer in politics, 1978-91, professor of politics, 1993-, Public Policy Unit, director, 2005-08, University College, fellow and praelector in politics, 1978-91; University of Newcastle upon Tyne, lecturer in politics, 1971-78, visiting professor, 1993-96; Economic Development Committee, chairman, 1976-78; Washington University, visiting professor, 1980; Lee University, visiting professor, 1980; Stanford University, visiting professor, 1990-91; University of Warwick, professor of politics, 1991-93, visiting professor, 1993-96; Welshpool & Llanfair Light Railway Preservation Company Ltd., vice chairman. Writer. **Publications:** Keir Hardie, 1975; Elections, 1976, 2nd ed., 1980; Dealing in Votes, 1982; The Legend of Red Clydeside, 1983; Public Choice: An Introduction, 1987; Democracy and New Technology, 1989; (with M. Johnes) Aberfan: Government and Disasters, 2000; Rational Choice and British Politics, 2001; (with F. McGillivray, R. Pahre and C. Schonhardt-Bailey) International Trade and Political Institutions Instituting Trade in the Long 19th Century, 2001; (with A. McMillan) State of the Union: Unionism and the Alternatives in the United Kingdom Since 1707, 2005; Fiscal Crisis of the United Kingdom, 2005; Adam Smith: Radical and Egalitarian: An Interpretation for the 21st Century, 2006; What's Wrong with the British Constitution?, 2010. EDITOR: (and trans. and intro. with F. Hewitt) Condorcet: Foundations of Social Choice and Political Theory, 1994; (and trans. and intro. with A.B. Urken) Classics of Social Choice, 1995; (with A. McMillan and B. Monroe) A Mathematical Approach to Proportional Representation: Duncan Black on Lewis Carroll, 1996; Concise Oxford Dictionary of Politics, 1996, (with A. McMillan) 3rd ed., 2009; (with D. Butler) Fixing the Boundary: Defining and Redefining Single-member Electoral Districts, 1996; The Theory of Committees and Elections, 1998; (with C. Jennings) Applying the Dismal Science: When Economists Give Advice to Governments, 2006. **Address:** Nuffield College, University of Oxford, New Rd., Oxford, OX OX1 1NF, England. **Online address:** iain.mclean@nuffield.ox.ac.uk

MCLEAN, Jacqueline. *See* **KOLOSOV, Jacqueline.**

MCLEAN, J. W. American (born United States), b. 1922. **Genres:** Administration/Management, Money/Finance, Self Help, Business/Trade/Industry. **Career:** Merrill, Lynch, Fenner & Bean, account executive, 1946-48; First National Bank of Tulsa, trainee, vice-president and commercial loan officer, 1949-58; Texas National Bank, senior vice-president, president and chief executive officer, 1958-64; Bank of America, senior vice-president and director of marketing, 1964-67; Liberty National Bank and Trust Co., president, chairman and chief executive officer, 1967-87, retired, 1987; Federal Reserve System, director to president of Federal Advisory Council, 1979; writer and consultant, 1987-; Allied Bank Intl., chair; Banks of Mid-America, chair and chief executive officer; Reading & Bates Corp., founding director; Devon Energy Corp., board director; University of Oklahoma, adjunct professor; Center for Creative Leadership, senior adviser. **Publications:** Say Yes or Say Why: Fundamental Principles of Sound Bank Credit, 1964; Cross-Selling Banking Services to Business, 1965; So You Want to Be the Boss?: A CEO's Lessons in Leadership, 1990; (with W. Weitzel) Leadership: Magic, Myth or Method?, 1991; Conquering Quandaries, 1992; There Ain't No Straight Putts, 1992; So You Want to Chip It Close, 2003. Works appear in anthologies. Contributor to books. **Address:** 5 Cypress Point Ct., Frisco, TX 75034-6826, U.S.A.

MCLEAN, Paul D. American (born United States), b. 1962. **Genres:** History. **Career:** University of Chicago, Social Sciences Collegiate Division, quarterly lecturer, 1992-95, William Rainey Harper instructor, 1996-99; Rutgers University, assistant professor, 1999-2006, associate professor of sociology, 2006-; Santa Fe Institute, Working Group on Networks and Markets, visiting researcher, 2001-06. Sociologist and writer. **Publications:** The Art of the Network: Strategic Interaction and Patronage in Renaissance Florence, 2007. Contributor to books and periodicals. **Address:** Department of Sociology, Rutgers, State University of New Jersey, 26 Nichol Ave., New Brunswick, NJ 08901, U.S.A. **Online address:** pmclean@rci.rutgers.edu

MCLEAN, Russel D. Scottish (born Scotland), b. 1980. **Genres:** Mystery/Crime/Suspense. **Career:** Writer. **Publications:** J. McNEE CRIME SERIES: The Good Son, 2009; The Lost Sister, 2011. Contributor to periodicals. Works appear in anthologies. **Address:** Dundee, Scotland. **Online address:** crimescenescotland@yahoo.co.uk

MCLEAN, Sammy. (Sammy Kay McLean). American (born United States), b. 1929. **Genres:** Poetry, Language/Linguistics, Literary Criticism And History, Young Adult Fiction. **Career:** Dartmouth College, instructor, 1961-63, assistant professor of German language and literature, 1963-65; University of Maryland Overseas Program, lecturer in German, 1965-67; University of Washington, assistant professor, 1967-73, associate professor of germanics and comparative literature, 1973-90, associate professor emeritus of comparative literature and germanics. Writer. **Publications:** The Bänkelsang and the Work of Bertolt Brecht, 1972. **Address:** Department of Germanic Languages & Literature, University of Washington, 340-C Denny Hall, PO Box 353130, Seattle, WA 98195, U.S.A. **Online address:** smclean@u.washington.edu

MCLEAN, Sammy Kay. *See* **MCLEAN, Sammy.**

MCLEAN, Stuart. Canadian (born Canada), b. 1948. **Genres:** Adult Non-fiction. **Career:** Dawson College, administrator, 1971-74; Canadian Broadcasting Corp., Radio, staff, 1978-82, executive producer, 1982-84, weekly contributor, 1984-94, host, 1994-; Ryerson Polytechnic University, director of broadcast journalism, 1984, professor of broadcast journalism, 1987-2004, professor emeritus, 2004-. Writer. **Publications:** The Morningside World of Stuart McLean, 1989; Welcome Home: Travels in Small town Canada, 1992; Stories from the Vinyl Cafe, 1995; (ed.) When We Were Young: A Collection of Canadian Stories, 1996; Home from the Vinyl Cafe: A Year of Stories, 1998; Vinyl Cafe Unplugged, 2000; Vinyl Cafe Diaries, 2003; Dave Cooks the Turkey, 2005; Secrets from the Vinyl Cafe, 2006; Extreme Vinyl Café, 2009; Vinyl Cafe Notebooks, 2010. **Address:** CBC Radio, PO Box 500, Sta. A, Toronto, ON M5W 1E6, Canada. **Online address:** vinylcafe@toronto.cbc.ca

MCLEAN, Virginia Overton. American (born United States), b. 1946. **Genres:** Travel/Exploration, Children's Fiction. **Career:** Commercial Appeal, journalist; Newsday, journalist. **Publications:** The Memphis Guide, 1982; Chasing the Moon to China, 1987; (with K.P. Klyce) Kenya, Jambo!, 1989; Pastatively Italy, 1995. Contributor to periodicals. **Address:** 3838 Poplar Ave., PO Box 11441, Memphis, TN 38111-7614, U.S.A.

MCLELLAN, David. British (born England), b. 1940. **Genres:** Intellectual History, Biography, Translations. **Career:** University of Kent, lecturer, 1966-71, senior lecturer in politics, 1971, reader, 1972-76, professor of political theory, 1976-, now professor emeritus; University of London, Goldsmiths' College, visiting professor of political theory; State University of New York, visiting professor. Writer. **Publications:** The Young Hegelians and Karl Marx, 1969; Marx Before Marxism, 1970; The Thought of Karl Marx, 1971; Karl Marx: His Life and Thought, 1973; Engels, 1977; Karl Marx, 1978, 4th ed., 2006; Marxism after Marx, 1979; Karl Marx: The Legacy, 1983; Ideology, 1985; Marxism and Religion, 1987; Simone Weil: Utopian Pessimist, 1990; Religion and Public Life, 1992; Unto Caesar: The Political Relevance of Christianity, 1993; Political Christianity, 1997. EDITOR: Karl Marx: The Early Texts, 1971; (and trans.) The Grundrisse, 1971; Karl Marx: Selected Writings, 1975; Karl Marx: Interviews and Recollections, 1981; Marx, The First Hundred Years, 1983; The Essential left, 2nd ed., 1986; Marxism, 1988; (with S. Sayers) Socialism and Morality, 1990; (with S. Sayers) Socialism and Democracy, 1991; (with D. Cohn-Sherbok) Religion in Public Life, 1992; (and intro.) The Condition of the Working Class in England, 1993; Capital: An Abridged Edition, 1995; (and intro.) The Communist Manifesto, 1998; Selected Writings, 2000. **Address:** Department of Politics and International Relations, Rutherford College, University of Kent, Canterbury, KT CT2 7NS, England. **Online address:** david@mclellankent.com

MCLENDON, Jacquelyn Y. American (born United States), b. 1943. **Genres:** Children's Non-fiction, Literary Criticism And History, Biography, Autobiography/Memoirs, Autobiography/Memoirs. **Career:** Hofstra University, assistant professor, 1986-89; Amherst College, assistant professor, 1989-92; College of William and Mary, associate professor of English, 1992-, associate chairperson of department, 1995-2001, Black Studies Program, co-founder and director, 1997-, professor. Writer. **Publications:** The Politics of Color in the Fiction of Jessie Fauset and Nella Larsen, 1995; (intro.) Sarah Lee Brown Fleming, Hope's Highway, Clouds and Sunshine: Clouds and Sunshine, 1995; Phillis Wheatley: A Revolutionary Poet (juvenile), 2003. Contributor of articles to periodicals. **Address:** Department of English, College of William and Mary, Tyler Hall 230, PO Box 8795, Williamsburg, VA 23187-8795, U.S.A. **Online address:** jymcle@wm.edu

MCLENNAN, Rebecca M. American/Canadian (born Canada), b. 1967. **Genres:** Politics/Government. **Career:** Harvard University, assistant professor of history and social studies, 1999-2003, Dunwalke associate professor of history and associate professor of social studies, 2003-04; University of California, assistant professor of history, 2003-06, associate professor of history, 2006-. Writer. **Publications:** The Crisis of Imprisonment: Protest, Politics, and the Making of the American Penal State, 1776-1941, 2008. Contributor to books and periodicals. **Address:** Department of History, University of California, 3229 Dwinelle Hall, Berkeley, CA 94720-2550, U.S.A.

MCLEOD, Carolyn. Canadian (born Canada), b. 1969. **Genres:** Sciences, Women's Studies And Issues. **Career:** University of Tennessee, assistant professor of philosophy, 2001-02; University of Western Ontario, Department of Philosophy, assistant professor, 2002-06, associate professor, 2006-, graduate chair, 2008-10, 2011-; University of Toronto, Munk Centre for International Studies, Comparative Program on Health and Society, new faculty fellow, 2004-05. Writer. **Publications:** Self-Trust and Reproductive Autonomy, 2002. Contributor of articles to books and periodicals. **Address:** Department of Philosophy, University of Western Ontario, Rm. 3142, Stevenson Hall, London, ON N6A 5B8, Canada. **Online address:** cmcleod2@uwo.ca

MCLEOD, Grover S(tephen). American (born United States), b. 1923. **Genres:** Novels, Novellas/Short Stories, Law, Social Sciences, Young Adult Fiction. **Career:** Lawyer and Writer. **Publications:** Neal McLeod: Emigrant from the Isle of Skye, Scotland, 1774-1961, 1962; Sub Sailor, 1964; Sketches from the Bar, 1966; Teodoro, 1969; About Women, 1974; Submarine Stories, 1977; Civil Actions at Law in Alabama, 1980, 2nd ed., 1987; Trial Practice and Procedure in Alabama, 1983, 2nd ed., 1991; Equitable Remedies and Extraordinary Writs in Alabama, 1983, 2nd ed., 1994; Sub Duty, 1986; The Ghost of Chimera, 1988; The Sultan's Gold, 1988; The Trials of FAT, 1989; Worker's Compensation in Alabama for On-the-Job Injuries, 1990; The Legal Circus, 1992; Drake Captain of the South Seas, 1994. **Address:** 1204 17th St. S, Birmingham, AL 35205, U.S.A.

MCLEOD, Joseph (Bertram). Canadian (born Canada), b. 1929. **Genres:** Poetry, Plays/Screenplays, History. **Career:** Peterborough Summer Theatre, artistic director; Seneca College, Minkler Theatre, artistic director; Maslak McLeod Gallery, curator and director. Writer. **Publications:** POETRY: Conversations with Maria, 1974; Collected Citizen, 1976; And the Rivers Our Blood, 1977; Cleaning the Bones, 1977; Protect My House, 1977; Greendream: Collected and New Poems, 1982; Shorter Chinese Lyrics, 1984; Rim Poems, 1990; Leario my Deario ... is Dead, 2005. PLAYS: Sam Slick, 1973. Work appears in anthologies. Contributor to periodicals. **Address:** Maslak McLeod Gallery, 118 Scollard St., Toronto, ON M5R 1G2, Canada. **Online address:** curator@maslakmcleod.com

MCLEOD, Scott Willard. American (born United States), b. 1960. **Genres:** Art/Art History, Illustrations, Cartoons. **Career:** DC Comics, Production Department, staff, 1982-83; freelance comic book artist and writer, 1983-; freelance journalist and reviewer, 1985-; teacher, 1993-. **Publications:** Zot!, 1984; Destroy!! (comic book), 1986; Understanding Comics: The Invisible Art (nonfiction comic), 1993; Reinventing Comics (nonfiction comic), 2000; Making Comics: Storytelling Secrets Of Comics, Manga and Graphic Novels (nonfiction comic), 2006; Google Chrome Comic (nonfiction comic), 2008. Contributor of articles to periodicals. **Address:** PO Box 115, Newbury Park, CA 91319, U.S.A. **Online address:** scott@scottmccloud.com

MCLEOD, Wallace. Canadian (born Canada), b. 1931. **Genres:** Archaeology/Antiquities, Classics, History, Social Sciences. **Career:** Trinity College, instructor in classical languages, 1955-56; University of British Columbia, instructor in classics, 1959-61; University of Western Ontario, lecturer classics, 1961-62; University of Toronto, Victoria College, Department of Classics, assistant professor, 1962-66, associate professor, 1966-74, professor, 1974-96, professor emeritus, 1996-, associate chair, 1975-78, acting chair, 1978-79; Phoenix Magazine, associate editor, 1965-70, acting editor, 1973, acting associate editor, 1985, 1989, 1993. **Publications:** (Comp.) Family of Richard Vanderburgh of Richmond Hill, 1962; Composite Bows from the Tomb of Tutankhamun, 1970; Meeting the Challenge: The Lodge Officer at Work, 1976; The Sufferings of John Coustos: A Facsimile Reprint, 1979; Whence Come We?: Freemasonry in Ontario, 1764-1980, 1980; Self Bows and Other Archery Tackle from the Tomb of Tutankhamun, 1982; The Old Gothic Constitutions: Facsimile Reprints, 1985; The Old Charges: Prestonian Lecture, 1986; Calcott's Candid Disquisition: A Facsimile Reprint, 1989; For the Cause of Good: The First 25 Years of the Masonic Foundation, 1990; The Grand Design: Selected Masonic Addresses and Papers of Wallace McLeod, 1991; The Quest for Light: Selected Masonic Addresses, 1997, rev. ed., 2004; A Daily Advancement in Masonic Knowledge: The Collected Blue Friar Lectures, 2003. EDITOR: Beyond the Pillars: More Light on Freemasonry, 1973; (with R.W. Weisberger and S.B. Morris) Freemasonry on Both Sides of the Atlantic: Essays Concerning the Craft in the British Isles, Europe, the United State, and Mexico, 2002. **Address:** Victoria College, University of Toronto, 73 Queen's Park Crescent, Northrop Frye Hall 106, Toronto, ON M5S 1K7, Canada. **Online address:** w.mcleod@utoronto.ca

MCLERRAN, Alice. American (born United States), b. 1933. **Genres:** Children's Fiction, Adult Non-fiction, Picture/Board Books. **Career:** State University, assistant professor of anthropology, 1969-72; Nursing Home Ombudsman Project, research analyst, 1974-75; Massachusetts Mental Health Center, evaluator of children's services, 1975-77, chief of evaluation, 1978; Harvard University, School of Medicine, lecturer in anthropology, 1977-78, School of Public Health, lecturer in health services, 1978. Writer. **Publications:** PICTURE BOOKS: The Mountain That Loved a Bird, 1985, new ed., 2000; Roxaboxen, 1991; I Want to Go Home, 1992; Dreamsong, 1992; Hugs, 1993; Kisses, 1993; The Ghost Dance, 1995; The Year of the Ranch, 1996. NOVELS: Secrets, 1990; Dragonfly, 2000. OTHER: The Legacy of Roxaboxer: A Collection of Voices (biography/memoir), 1998. **Address:** 70 S Country Rd., Bellport, NY 11713, U.S.A. **Online address:** alicemclerran@mac.com

MCLOUGHLIN, Leslie John. British (born England), b. 1935. **Genres:** History, Language/Linguistics, Translations. **Career:** Teacher, 1964-75; Middle East Centre for Arab Studies, principal instructor and director of studies, 1965-68, 1970-75; University of Pennsylvania, visiting professor, 1969; University of Edinburgh, faculty, 1969-70; Columbia University, visiting professor, 1970; National Guard of Saudi Arabia, consultant, 1981-82; School of Oriental and African Studies, faculty, 1984-86; The British Association of Teachers of Arabic, co-founder, 1987; Middle East Centre for Arab Studies Association, founder, 1987; independent consultant, 1987-2005; McLoughlin Associates, consultant, 1993-; London Center for Arab Studies, co-founder, 1994-97; Exeter University, faculty, 2000-07, Institute of Arab and Islamic Studies, fellow, 2000-09, honorary research fellow, 2009-, senior research fellow. Writer. **Publications:** Course in Colloquial Arabic, 1974; Further Course in Colloquial Arabic, 1979; Colloquial Arabic (Levantine), 1982, 2nd ed., 2009; Qāmūs al-muta'allim-lil-ta'ābir al-āmmīyah: Arabī-Inkilīzī, 1988; Qāmūs al-mutáallim lil-táābir al-'āmmīyah, 1988; Ibn Saud: Founder of a Kingdom, 1993; A Nest of Spies? A History of M.E.C.A.S., 1994; (trans.) G. Algosaibi, Apartment Freedom, 1994; In A Sea of Knowledge: British Arabists in the Twentieth Century, 2002; Confessions of an Arabic Interpreter, 2009. **Address:** Institute of Arab and Islamic Studies, University of Exeter, Stocker Rd., Exeter, AV EX4 4ND, England. **Online address:** l.j.mcloughlin@ex.ac.uk

MCLUHAN, (Thomas) Eric (Marshall). Canadian/American (born United States), b. 1942. **Genres:** Communications/Media, Literary Criticism And History. **Career:** Monday Morning Magazine, contributing editor, 1965-68; Evelyn Wood Institutes of Reading, instructor, chief of instructional staff, 1965-68; Una Voce-Canada, board director; Fordham University, faculty, 1968-69; Human Development Corp., Editor, 1968-70; Fanshawe College, faculty, 1972-73; Ontario College of Art, faculty, 1973-75, 1978-79; Dawson College, faculty, 1978-80; McLuhan and Davies Communications Inc., partner and president, 1980-95; Harris Institute for the Arts, faculty, 1996-, instructor director of media studies; University of Wisconsin, instructor; York University, faculty, 1981-90, instructor, course director, 1989-90; Catholic Children's Aid Society, board director; Toronto Area Right to Life Association, board director; Journal of Social and Biological Structures, associate editor, 1990-; University of Toronto, instructor, Faculty of Information Studies, faculty, 1997-99, McLuhan Program Intl., founder and associate director, director, 1997-99. **Publications:** (With M. McLuhan and K. Hutchon) City as Classroom: Understanding Language and Media, 1977; (with K. Hutchon and M. McLuhan) Media, Messages & Language: The World as Your Classroom, 1980; (with M. McLuhan) Laws of Media: The New Science, 1988; (ed. with F. Zingrone and W. Constantineau) Who Was Marshall McLuhan?, 1995; (ed. with F. Zingrone) Essential McLuhan, 1995; The Role of Thunder at Finnegans Wake, 1997; Electric Language, 1998; (ed. with J. Szlarek) Medium and the Light: Reflections on Religion, 1999; (intro.) Trek, 2003; (contrib.) The Book of Probes, 2003; The Human Equation (five vols.), 2010-2011; Media and Formal Cause, 2009; Theories of Communication, 2009. **Address:** 3538 Scoharie Rd., RR 1, Bloomfield, ON K0K 1G0, Canada. **Online address:** mcluhane@sympatico.ca

MCMAHAN, Alison. American (born United States), b. 1960. **Genres:** Young Adult Non-fiction, Film. **Career:** Manhattan Day School, manager, 1984-85; freelance writer, 1986-; Interactive Media Communications, production coordinator, 1986-87; Guadalupe Productions, film producer, 1987-88; University of Amsterdam, associate professor, 1997-2001; Homunculus Productions L.L.C., president, 2003-, Homunculus Music, president, 2003-; Emerson College, faculty. Director and producer. **Publications:** Alice Guy Blaché: Lost Visionary of the Cinema (nonfiction), 2002; The Films of Tim

Burton: Animating Live Action in Contemporary Hollywood (nonfiction), 2005. Contributor to journals and periodicals. **Address:** Continuum International Publishing Group, 80 Maiden Ln., Ste. 704, New York, NY 10038, U.S.A. **Online address:** alison@homunculusprods.com

MCMAHAN, Ian (D.). American (born United States) **Genres:** Novels, History. **Career:** City University of New York, Brooklyn College, Department of Psychology, associate professor, professor, now professor emeritus. Writer. **Publications:** For Young Readers: Highlights of American History, 1968; The Fox's Lair, 1983; McGee and the Ghost Ship, 1984; Lake Fear, 1985; The Lost Forest, 1985; Footwork, 1986; Get It Done! A Guide to Motivation, Determination and Achievement, 1996; Secrets of the Pharaohs, 1998; Think Yourself Rich: Use the Power of Your Subconscious Mind to Find True Wealth, 2001; Amazing Laws of Cosmic Mind Power, 2001. **Address:** Department of Psychology, Brooklyn College, City University of New York, 5401 James Hall, 2900 Bedford Ave., Brooklyn, NY 11210, U.S.A. **Online address:** imcmahan@brooklyn.cuny.edu

MCMAHAN, Janna. American (born United States) **Genres:** Novels. **Career:** Post No Bills (entertainment marketing firm), head writer and media relations director. **Publications:** Undertow, 2001; Calling Home, 2008; (with F. Michaels, M. Bostwick and R. Noonan) Snow Angels, 2009; The Ocean Inside, 2009. Works appear in anthologies. Contributor to journals. **Address:** Columbia, SC , U.S.A. **Online address:** info@jannamcmahan.com

MCMAHON, Darrin. (Darrin M. McMahon). American (born United States) **Genres:** History, Humanities, Intellectual History. **Career:** Columbia University, Society of Fellows in the Humanities, Mellon fellow, 1997-99; New York University, Remarque Institute, postdoctoral fellow, 2000-01; Yale University, postdoctoral fellow, 2001-; Institute für die Wissenschaften von Menschen, Rockefeller junior visiting fellow, 2001; Florida State University, associate professor, 2004-07, Ben Weider professor of history, 2007-; University of Rouen, faculty; Keythought L.L.C., director. Writer. **Publications:** (As Darrin M. McMahon) Enemies of the Enlightenment: The French Counter-Enlightenment and the Making of Modernity, 2001; (contrib. as Darrin M. McMahon) Reflections on the Revolution in France, 2003; (as Darrin M. McMahon) Happiness: A History, 2006; (ed. with P. Hanley) Enlightenment: Critical Concepts in Historical Studies, 2009. Contributor to periodicals. **Address:** Department of History, Florida State University, 452 Bellamy Bldg., PO Box 3062200, Tallahassee, FL 32306-2200, U.S.A. **Online address:** dmcmahon@fsu.edu

MCMAHON, Darrin M. *See* **MCMAHON, Darrin.**

MCMAHON, Eileen M. American (born United States), b. 1957. **Genres:** Local History/Rural Topics, Earth Sciences. **Career:** Loyola University of Chicago, staff; St. Xavier University, staff; Columbia University, staff; Lewis University, assistant professor. Writer. **Publications:** What Parish Are You From? The Chicago Irish Parish Community Relations, 1916-1970, 1995; Time and the River-A History of the Saint Croix: A Historic Resource Study of the Saint Croix National Scenic Riverway, 2002; (with T. Karamanski) Woods River: The St. Croix River in Upper Midwest History, 2009. **Address:** 40 Commons Dr., Palos Park, IL 60464, U.S.A.

MCMAHON, Jennifer. American (born United States), b. 1968. **Genres:** Young Adult Fiction, Psychiatry. **Career:** Writer, 2000-. Counselor. **Publications:** (Ed. with M.L. Tompkins) Illuminations: Expressions of the Personal Spiritual Experience, 2006; (ed.) Aesthetics and Material Beauty: Aesthetics Naturalized, 2007; Promise Not to Tell: A Novel, 2007; My Tiki Girl, 2008; Island of Lost Girls: A Novel, 2008; Dismantled: A Novel, 2009; Don't Breathe a Word, 2011. **Address:** c/o Dan Lazar, Writers House Inc., 21 W 26th St., New York, NY 10010, U.S.A. **Online address:** jennifer@jennifer-mcmahon.com

MCMAHON, Katharine. British (born England) **Genres:** Novels. **Career:** University of Hertfordshire, Royal Literary Fund Fellow and advisory fellow; University of Warwick, Royal Literary Fund fellow and advisory fellow. Writer, educator and lyricist. **Publications:** NOVELS: A Way through the Woods, 1990; Footsteps, 1997; Confinement, 1998; After Mary, 2000; The Alchemist's Daughter, 2006; Rose of Sebastopol, 2007; The Crimson Rooms, 2009; Season of Light, 2011. **Address:** c/o Author Mail, Orion Publishing Group, Orion House, 5 Upper St Martin's Ln., London, GL WC2H 9EA, England. **Online address:** katharine.mcmahon1@googlemail.com

MCMAHON, Maureen M. (Ainsley Abbott). Australian/American (born United States), b. 1952. **Genres:** Novellas/Short Stories, Mystery/Crime/Suspense, Romance/Historical. **Career:** Western Michigan University, clerical supervisor; St. Philips Elementary School, teacher; Michigan Mutual Insurance Co., supervisor; Australian Runner (magazine), staff writer; Writers Digest (magazine), creative writing instructor; Ocean Grove Neighborhood Centre, creative writing instructor; Electronically Published Professionals, founder and director; Books We Love, co-founder and administrator. **Publications:** Shadows in the Mist, 2000; A Nightingale in the Sycamore (short fiction), 2001; Return of the Gulls, 2004 as Haunting Passions, 2011; One Touch Beyond, 2008; Enchanted Holidays, 2004. AS AINSLEY ABBOTT: Catey's Capture, 2008; Jemimah's Genie, 2009. **Address:** PO Box 442, Ocean Grove, VI 3226, Australia. **Online address:** maureen@maureenmcmahon.com

MCMANN, Lisa. American (born United States), b. 1968. **Genres:** Novels. **Career:** Writer. **Publications:** Wake (novel), 2008; Fade (novel), 2009; Gone, 2010. **Address:** Mesa, AZ , U.S.A. **Online address:** lisa@lisamcmann.com

MCMANUS, Antonia. Irish (born Ireland), b. 1952. **Genres:** History, Education. **Career:** Convent of Mercy, teacher, 1985-86; Roman Catholic High School, teacher, 1986-93; Trinity College, lecturer in education, 1993-2003; Froebel College of Education, lecturer, 2002-; Hibernia College, academic director. Writer. **Publications:** The Irish Hedge School and Its Books, 1695-1831, 2002. **Address:** 139 Kirwin Ave., Avondale, Trim, ME 26376, Ireland. **Online address:** ktmcmanus@lircom.net

MCMANUS, John C. American (born United States), b. 1965. **Genres:** Military/Defense/Arms Control, History, Adult Non-fiction. **Career:** University of Tennessee, instructor and research associate, 1992-98; St. Louis Community College, instructor in history, 1998-2000; Missouri University of Science and Technology, instructor, 2000, assistant professor of U.S. military history, 2003-07, associate professor of history, 2007-, professor of history; University of Tennessee, Center for the Study of War and Society, assistant director. Writer. **Publications:** A History of Oregon's State Solo Contest for High School Students: A Compilation of Champions and Their Literature from 1924 to 1995, 1995; The Deadly Brotherhood: The American Combat Soldier in World War II, 1998; Deadly Sky: American Combat Airmen in World War II, 2000; Americans at Normandy: The Summer of 1944 the American War from the Normandy Beaches to Falaise, 2004; Americans at D-Day: The American Experience at the Normandy Invasion, 2004; Alamo in the Ardennes: The Untold Story of the American Soldiers Who Made the Defense of Bastogne Possible, 2007; U.S Military History For Dummies, 2007; 7th Infantry Regiment: Combat in an Age of Terror: The Korean War through the Present, 2008; Grunts: The American Infantry Combat Experience, World War II through the Present, 2009; American Courage, American Carnage: The 7th Infantry Regiment's Combat Experience, 1812 through World War II, 2009; Grunts: Inside the American Infantry Combat Experience, World War II through Iraq, 2010; September Hope, 2012. **Address:** Missouri University of Science and Technology, 1870 Miner Cir., 117 Humanities and Social Sciences Bldg., Rolla, MO 65409-1260, U.S.A. **Online address:** mcmanusj@mst.edu

MCMANUS, Michael. British (born England), b. 1967?. **Genres:** Novels, Law, Adult Non-fiction. **Career:** Sir Edward Heath Private Office, head, 1995-2000; Bell Pottinger Public Affairs, director. Writer. **Publications:** Jo Grimond: Towards the Sound of Gunfire, 2001; Tory Pride and Prejudice, 2011. **Address:** Biteback Publishing, Westminster Twr., 3 Albert Embankment, 10th Fl., London, GL SE1 7SP, England. **Online address:** soundofgunfire@yahoo.co.uk

MCMANUS, Michael J. American (born United States), b. 1941. **Genres:** Novels, Homes/Gardens. **Career:** Time Magazine, correspondent, 1963-68; syndicated columnist, 1977; Marriage Savers Inc., co-founder, 1996-. **Publications:** How to Save Urban America: Key Issues Confronting Cities and Suburbs, 1973; 50 Practical Ways to Take Our Kids Back from the World, 1993; Marriage Savers: Helping Your Friends and Family Stay Married, 1993, rev. ed. as Marriage Savers: Helping Your Friends and Family Avoid Divorce, 1995; Insuring Marriage: 25 Proven Ways to Prevent Divorce, 1994; Manual to Create a Marriage Savers Congregation, 1999; (with H. McManus) Living Together: Myths, Risks and Answers, 2008. **Address:** Marriage Savers Inc., 9311 Harrington Dr., Potomac, MD 20854, U.S.A. **Online address:** michaeljmcmanus@cs.com

MCMANUS, Ruth. Irish (born Ireland), b. 1971. **Genres:** Geography, History,

Reference. **Career:** Dublin City University, St. Patrick's College, Department of Geography, professor and head; Geographical Viewpoint Journal, editor; AGTI, editor. **Publications:** Dublin, 1910-1940: Shaping the City and Suburbs, 2002. **Address:** Department of Geography, St. Patricks College, E227, Drumcondra, DU 9, Ireland. **Online address:** ruth.mcmanus@spd.dcu.ie

MCMASTER, Gerald. Canadian (born Canada), b. 1953. **Genres:** Art/Art History, Illustrations. **Career:** University of Regina, head of Indian art program, 1977-81; Canadian Museum of Civilization, curator of contemporary Indian art, 1981-; Native Art Studies Association of Canada Newsletter, general editor, 1988-89; Carleton University, adjunct research professor, 1992-98; National Museum of the American Indian, board director, 1995-98; Canadian Museum of Civilization, curator; Smithsonian Institute, deputy assistant director; Canadian Art at the Art Gallery Ontario, curator. **Publications:** Challenges, 1985; (ed. with L.Martin) Indigena: Contemporary Native Perspectives, 1992; (contrib.) Sharing the Circle: Contemporary Work by First Nation Artists, 1992; Edward Poitras: Canada XLVI Biennale di Venezia, 1995; Jeffrey Thomas: Portraits from the Dancing Grounds, 1996; Mary Longman: Traces, 1996; (ed.) Reservation X: The Power of Place in Aboriginal Contemporary Art, 1998; Unbury My Heart: An Exhibition of the Art of Shelley Niro: February 25-April 8, 2001; (ed. with B. Bernstein) First American Art: The Charles and Valerie Diker Collection of American Indian Art, 2004; (ed. with C.E. Trafzer) Native Universe: Voices of Indian America, 2004; (ed.) New Tribe, New York: The Urban Vision Quest, 2005; (ed. with J. Baker) Remix: New Modernities in a Post-Indian World, 2007; (contrib.) Carl Beam: The Poetics of Being, 2010; (ed.) Inuit Modern: The Samuel and Esther Sarick Collection, 2010. Contributor to periodicals. Illustrator of books by D.May. **Address:** Canadian Museum of Civilization, 100 Laurier St., PO Box 3100, Sta. B, Hull, QC J8X 4H2, Canada. **Online address:** gerald_mcmaster@ago.net

MCMASTER, Juliet (Sylvia). Canadian/British/Kenyan (born Kenya), b. 1937. **Genres:** Children's Fiction, Literary Criticism And History, Illustrations, Young Adult Fiction, Art/Art History, Biography, Novels, Young Adult Fiction, Young Adult Fiction. **Career:** University of Alberta, assistant professor, 1965-70, associate professor, 1970-76, professor, 1976-86, university professor of English, 1986-2000, distinguished university professor emeritus, 2000-; Juvenilia Press, general editor, 1994-. **Publications:** Thackeray: The Major Novels, 1971; Jane Austen on Love, 1978; Trollope's Palliser Novels: Theme and Pattern, 1978; (with R.D. McMaster) The Novel from Sterne to James: Essays on the Relation of Literature to Life, 1981; Dickens the Designer, 1987; Index of the Mind: Physiognomy in the Novel, 1990; Jane Austen the Novelist: Essays Past and Present, 1996; Reading the Body in the Eighteenth-Century Novel, 2004. EDITOR: Jane Austen's Achievement: Papers Delivered at the Jane Austen Bicentennial Conference at the University of Alberta, 1976; (with B. Stovel) Jane Austen's Business: Her World and Her Profession, 1996; (with E. Copeland) The Cambridge Companion to Jane Austen, 1997, 2nd ed., 2011; (ed. with C. Alexander) Child Writer from Austen to Woolf, 2005; Woman Behind the Painter: The Diaries of Rosalie, Mrs. James Clarke Hook, 2006. Illustrator of books by J. Austen. **Address:** Department of English, University of Alberta, 3-5 Humanities Ctr., Edmonton, AB T6G 2E5, Canada. **Online address:** juliet.mcmaster@ualberta.ca

MCMASTER, Lindsey. Canadian (born Canada), b. 1972?. **Genres:** History. **Career:** Nipissing University, Department of English Studies, faculty. Writer. **Publications:** Working Girls in the West: Representations of Wage-Earning Women, 2008. Contributor to journals. **Address:** Nipissing University, 100 College Dr., PO Box 5002, North Bay, ON P1B 8L7, Canada. **Online address:** lindseym@nipissingu.ca

MCMASTER, Rhyll. Australian (born Australia), b. 1947. **Genres:** Novels, Poetry, Young Adult Fiction. **Career:** University of Queensland, secretary, 1966-71; Canberra Hospital, nurse, 1976-78; The Canberra Times, poetry editor; Sydney Morning Herald, reviewer. **Publications:** POETRY: The Brineshrimp, 1972; Washing the Money, 1986; On My Empty Feet, 1993; Flying the Coop, 1994; Chemical Bodies, 1997; The Evolutionary History of Edward Kelly in Primary Colours (based on paintings of Sidney Nolan's Ned Kelly series), 1999; Feather Man, 2007; Pure Fiction (novel), forthcoming. Contributor to books. **Address:** Marion Boyars Publishers, 26 Parke Rd., London, GL SW13 9NG, England. **Online address:** rhyllm@bigpond.com

MCMASTER, Susan. Canadian (born Canada), b. 1950. **Genres:** Poetry, Songs/Lyrics And Libretti, Autobiography/Memoirs, Plays/Screenplays, Women's Studies And Issues, Gerontology/Senior Issues. **Career:** Edmonton public schools, teacher, 1971-73; Access Magazine (Access Alberta), editor, 1973-75; Branching Out Magazine, founding editor, 1973-75, associate, 1975-80; freelance editor and writer, 1975-89; First Draft Intermedia Group, co-founder, 1980-90; National Gallery of Canada, senior book editor, 1989-2008; Vernissage Magazine, founding editor, editor-in-chief, 1989-2008; Geode Music and Poetry (aka SugarBeat), wordsmith, 1995-2005. **Publications:** POETRY: Seven Poems (broadside), 1983; Dark Galaxies, 1986; The Hummingbird Murders, 1992; Learning to Ride, 1994; Uncommon Prayer: A Book of Dedications, 1997; La Deriva del Pianeta/World Shift, 2003; Until the Light Bends, 2004; Ygdrasil: A Journal of the Poetic Arts: Susan McMaster-Selected Poems 1981-2007, 2008; Crossing Arcs: Alzheimer's, My Mother, and Me, 2009; Paper Affair: Poems Selected and New, 2010. WORDMUSIC: (with A. McClure and C. Dupuis) Pass This Way Again: A Collection of Performance Poetry, 1983; (with A. McClure and C. Morton) North/South: Performance Scores for One to Seven Speakers, 1987. MEMOIR: The Gargoyle's Left Ear: Writing in Ottawa, 2007. EDITOR: Dangerous Graces: Women's Poetry on Stage from Fire Works!: A Celebration of Women's Theatre, Canadian Theatre Company (poetry script anthology), 1987; (with C. Ford) Illegitimate Positions: Women and Language, 1992; Two Women Talking: Correspondence 1985-87, Erin Moure and Bronwen Wallace, 1993; (with C. Morton) Bookware: Ottawa Valley Poets, 1994; Siolence: Poets on Women, Violence, and Silence, 1998; Convergence: Poems for Peace, 2001-02, 2003; Waging Peace: Poetry and Political Action, 2002; Sugar Mule: A Literary Magazine-The Canadian Issue, 2009; Pith & Wry: Canadian Poetry, 2010. Works appear in anthologies. Contributor to magazines. **Address:** 43 Belmont Ave., Ottawa, ON K1S 0T9, Canada. **Online address:** smcmaster@ncf.ca

MCMASTERS, Kelly. American (born United States), b. 1976?. **Genres:** Autobiography/Memoirs, Biography, History. **Career:** Mediabistro.com, writing teacher; Columbia University, Graduate School, writing teacher; KGB Nonfiction Reading Series, director. Journalist. **Publications:** Welcome to Shirley: A Memoir from an Atomic Town, 2008. Contributor to periodicals and journals. **Address:** New York, NY , U.S.A. **Online address:** kelly@kellymcmasters.com

MCMICHAEL, Andrew Francis. American (born United States), b. 1966. **Genres:** Information Science/Computers, History. **Career:** American Historical Association, webmaster, 1995-96, internet and web consultant, 1996-98; Vanderbilt Oral History Project, web consultant, 1999; Princeton University, Papers of Thomas Jefferson, assistant editor, 2000-02; George Mason University, Center for History and New Media, Echo Project, consultant, 2000-03; Western Kentucky University, assistant professor of history, 2002-07, associate professor of history, 2007-. Historian. **Publications:** History on the Web: Using and Evaluating the Internet, 2005; Atlantic Loyalties: Americans in Spanish West Florida, 1785-1810, 2008. Contributor to books and periodicals. **Address:** Western Kentucky University, Bldg. 21086, 1906 College Heights Blvd., Bowling Green, KY 42101, U.S.A. **Online address:** andrew.mcmichael@wku.edu

MCMILLAN, Alan D. Canadian (born Canada), b. 1945. **Genres:** Anthropology/Ethnology, Archaeology/Antiquities, Sciences, History. **Career:** Archaeological Survey of Canada, field supervisor, 1969; Douglas College, instructor in anthropology, 1970-, Department of Anthropology and Sociology, chairman, 1979-81, 1999-; Toquaht Archaeological Project, co-director, 1991-96; Simon Fraser University, adjunct professor of archaeology. Writer. **Publications:** (With D.E. St. Claire) Alberni Prehistory: Archaeological and Ethnographic Investigations on Western Vancouver Island, 1982; Native Peoples and Cultures of Canada: An Anthropological Overview, 1988, 2nd ed., 1995; Since the Time of the Transformers: The Ancient Heritage of the Nuu-chah-nulth, Ditidaht and Makah, 1999; (with E. Yellowhorn) First Peoples in Canada, 2004; (with D.E. St. Claire) Ts'ishaa: Archaeology and Ethnography of a Nuu-chah-nulth Origin Site in Barkley Sound, 2005. **Address:** Department of Archaeology, Simon Fraser University, 8888 University Dr., Burnaby, BC V5A 1S6, Canada. **Online address:** mcmillan@sfu.ca

MCMILLAN, James. (Coriolanus). American (born United States), b. 1925. **Genres:** Economics, Politics/Government, Social Commentary. **Career:** Bennett College, Art Department, chair, 1947, staff, 1956; Glasgow Evening Citizen, industrial writer, 1952-53, assistant editor, 1953-57; Daily Express London, leader writer, 1957-69, chief leader writer, 1969-76; Express Newspapers, policy adviser, 1976-86; North Carolina A&T State University,

Guilford College, Art Department, professor of art and chair, 1969-88, professor emeritus, 1988-; African American Atelier, co-founder and president, 1991. **Publications:** (As Coriolanus) The Glass Lie, 1965; (with B. Harris) The American Take-Over of Britain, 1967; The Honours Game, 1969; Anatomy of Scotland, 1969; The Roots of Corruption: The Erosion of Traditional Values in Britain from 1960 to the Present Day, 1972; (with P. Grosvenor) The British Genius, 1973; The Way We Were, 1900-1914, 1978; The Way It Was, 1914-1934: Based on the Files of Express Newspapers, 1979; The Way It Happened, 1935-1950: Based on the Files of Express Newspapers, 1980; (with J. Kersten) The Secret of Torgau: Why the Plot to Kill Hitler Failed, 1982; Five Men at Nuremberg, 1984; The Way It Changed 1950-1975, 1987; The Dunlop Story: The Life, Death and Re-birth of a Multi-National, 1989; Margaret Thatcher: From Finchley to the World, 1990. **Address:** Art Department, Guilford College, North Carolina A&T State University, 5800 W Friendly Ave., Greensboro, NC 27410-4108, U.S.A.

MCMILLAN, Rosalyn A. American (born United States), b. 1953. **Genres:** Novels. **Career:** Ford Motor Co., seamstress, 1976-96. Writer. **Publications:** NOVELS: Knowing, 1996; One Better, 1997; Blue Collar Blues, 1998; The Flip Side of Sin, 2000; This Side of Eternity, 2001; We Ain't the Brontës, 2011. Contributor to periodicals. **Address:** Detroit, MI , U.S.A.

MCMILLAN, Terry. American (born United States), b. 1951. **Genres:** Novels, Literary Criticism And History, Young Adult Fiction. **Career:** University of Wyoming, instructor, 1987-90; University of Arizona, professor, 1990-92. Writer. **Publications:** Mama (novel), 1987; Disappearing Acts (novel), 1989; (ed.) Breaking Ice: An Anthology of Contemporary American Black Fiction, 1990; Waiting to Exhale (novel), 1992; How Stella Got Her Groove Back, 1996; A Day Late and a Dollar Short, 2001; The Interruption of Everything, 2005; It's Ok If You're Clueless: and 23 More Tips for the College Bound, 2006; Getting to Happy, 2010. **Address:** Free At Last Inc., PO Box 2408, Danville, CA 94526, U.S.A. **Online address:** fanmail@terrymcmillan.com

MCMILLEN, Christian W. American (born United States), b. 1969?. **Genres:** Young Adult Non-fiction, Law, History. **Career:** University of Virginia, College and Graduate School of Arts & Sciences, assistant professor of history and American studies, associate professor. Writer. **Publications:** Making Indian Law: The Hualapai Land Case and the Birth of Ethnohistory (nonfiction), 2007. **Address:** Department of History, University of Virginia, 282 Nau Hall, PO Box 400180, Charlottesville, VA 22904-4180, U.S.A. **Online address:** cwm6w@virginia.edu

MCMILLEN, Neil Raymond. American (born United States), b. 1939. **Genres:** History, Economics, Politics/Government, Social Sciences. **Career:** Vanderbilt University, faculty; University of Missouri, faculty; Ball State University, assistant professor of history, 1967-69; University of Southern Mississippi, assistant professor, 1969-70, Basic College, dean, 1970-71, associate professor of history, 1971-78, professor, 1978-, Charles W. Moorman distinguished alumni professor, now professor emeritus of history. Writer. **Publications:** The Citizens' Council; Organized Resistance to the Second Reconstruction, 1954-64, 1971; Thomas Jefferson: Philosopher of Freedom, 1973; (co-author) Synopsis of American History, 1974, 8th ed., 1997; Dark Journey: Black Mississippians in the Age of Jim Crow, 1989; (ed.) Remaking Dixie: The Impact of World War II on the American South, 1997. Contributor to journals. **Address:** Depart of History, The University of Southern Mississippi, 118 College Dr., Ste. 5047, Hattiesburg, MS 39406-0001, U.S.A.

MCMILLEN, Sally G(regory). American (born United States), b. 1944. **Genres:** History, Women's Studies And Issues, Social Sciences, Human Relations/Parenting. **Career:** Brooklyn Public Library, reference librarian, 1966-68; Boston Atheneum, reference librarian, 1968-70; University High School, librarian, 1975-78; University of North Carolina, instructor in history, 1983-84; Duke University, instructor, 1983-84; Middle Tennessee State University, assistant professor of history, 1985-88; Davidson College, Department of History, assistant professor, 1988-91, associate professor, 1991-98, professor, 1998-, Mary Reynolds Babcock professor of history, 2003-, department chair, 2002-; National Endowment for the Humanities, fellow, 1991-92. Writer. **Publications:** Motherhood in the Old South: Pregnancy, Childbirth, and Infant Rearing, 1990; Southern Women: Black and White in the Old South, 1992, 2nd ed., 2002; To Raise up the South: Sunday Schools in Black and White Churches, 1865-1915, 2001; Seneca Falls and The Origins of The Women's Rights Movement, 2008; (co-ed.) Major Problems in the History of the American South: Documents and Essays, 2012. Contributor to periodicals. **Address:** Department of History, Davidson College, 2254 Chambers, PO Box 6994, Davidson, NC 28035-6994, U.S.A. **Online address:** samcmillen@davidson.edu

MCMULLAN, Gordon. British (born England), b. 1962. **Genres:** Literary Criticism And History, Theatre, Politics/Government. **Career:** University of Newcastle, lecturer, 1989-95; University of London, King's College, lecturer in English, 1995-2001, reader, 2001-07, professor of English, 2007-; Huntington Library, visiting fellow, 1995. Writer. **Publications:** The Politics of Unease in the Plays of John Fletcher, 1994; Shakespeare and the Idea of Late Writing: Authorship in the Proximity of Death, 2007; Shakespeare and the Cultures of Performance, forthcoming. EDITOR: (with J. Hope) The Politics of Tragicomedy: Shakespeare and After, 1992; Renaissance Configurations: Voices/Bodies/Spaces, 1580-1690, 1995; 1 Henry IV, 2003; (with A.Thompson) In Arden: Editing Shakespeare Essays in Honour of Richard Proudfoot, 2003; (with D. Matthews) Reading the Medieval in Early Modern England, 2007. **Address:** Department of English, King's College, University of London, S2.16, Strand, London, GL WC2R 2LS, England. **Online address:** gordon.mcmullan@kcl.ac.uk

MCMULLAN, Margaret. American (born United States), b. 1960. **Genres:** Novels, Novellas/Short Stories, Young Adult Fiction, Plays/Screenplays, Adult Non-fiction, Humanities, History, Human Relations/Parenting, Race Relations, Photography, Social Sciences, Urban Studies, Women's Studies And Issues, Autobiography/Memoirs, Ethics, Civil Liberties/Human Rights, Cultural/Ethnic Topics, Popular Culture. **Career:** Glamour, associate entertainment editor, 1982-85; University of Arkansas, Fayetteville, assistant professor of English, 1989-90; University of Evansville, associate professor, 1990-2003, Department of English, chair, 2002-, professor, 2003-; Southampton Literature and Writing Conference, Stony Brook Southampton, faculty, 2009, 2010; Eastern Kentucky University, Low-Residency MFA Program, winter residency visiting writer, 2010; University of Pecs, Fulbright professor of the American south, contemporary American novel and creative writing, 2010. **Publications:** NOVELS: When Warhol was Still Alive, 1994; In My Mother's House, 2003; How I Found the Strong, 2004; When I Crossed No-Bob, 2007; Cashay, 2009; Sources of Light, 2010. Works appear in anthologies. Contributor to books. **Address:** Department of English, University of Evansville, Rm. 328 Olmsted Administration Hall, 1800 Lincoln Ave., Evansville, IN 47720, U.S.A. **Online address:** mm44@evansville.edu

MCMULLEN, Jeremy. British (born England), b. 1948?. **Genres:** Civil Liberties/Human Rights, Industrial Relations, Law, Economics. **Career:** Queen's counsel; Kelley Drye & Warren, attorney, 1972-73; GMB Union Legal and Regional Officer, 1973-84; Employment Appeal Tribunal, judge; Southwark Crown Court, judge. Writer. **Publications:** Rights at Work: A Worker's Guide to Employment Law, 1978, 2nd ed., 1983; Employment Law under the Tories, 1981; Policing the Miner's Strike, 1985; Rights Guide, 1989; (co-author) Employment Tribunal Procedure, 1996, 3rd ed., 2004; Employment Precedents, 1996. **Address:** Employment Appeal Tribunal, 58 Victoria Embankment, London, GL EC4Y 0DS, England. **Online address:** jmcmullen@lix.compulink.co.uk

MCMULLEN, Sean (Christopher). Australian (born Australia), b. 1948. **Genres:** Novels, Novellas/Short Stories, Science Fiction/Fantasy, Young Adult Fiction, Literary Criticism And History, Music. **Career:** Walter and Eliga Hall Institute, laboratory assistant, 1969-70; Woolworths, driver, 1970-71; Department of Works, technical clerk, 1972-75; librarian, 1975-80; Bureau of Meteorology, computer systems analyst, 1981-. Writer. **Publications:** SHORT STORIES: Call to the Edge, 1992. NOVELS: The Centurion's Empire, 1998; The Ancient Hero (young adult), 2004; Before the Storm (Young Adult), 2007; The Iron Warlock, 2010. GREATWINTER SERIES (NOVELS): Voices in the Light, 1994; Mirrorsun Rising, 1995; Souls in the Great Machine, 1999; The Miocene Arrow, 2000; Eyes of the Calculor, 2001. MOONWORLDS SERIES (NOVELS): Voyage of the Shadowmoon, 2002; Glass Dragons, 2004; Voidfarer, 2005; The Time Engine, 2008. OTHER: (ed. with P. Collins and S. Paulsen) The Melbourne University Press Encyclopedia of Australian Science Fiction and Fantasy, 1998; (with R. Blackford and V. Ikin) Strange Constellations: A Critical History of Australian Science Fiction, 1999. Contributor to periodicals. **Address:** PO Box 2653, Melbourne, VI 3001, Australia. **Online address:** scm@unite.com.au

MCMULLEN, William Wallace. American (born United States), b. 1952. **Genres:** Music, Literary Criticism And History, History. **Career:** Middle

School, band director, 1974-77; Juilliard School, teaching fellow, 1981-83; City University of New York, College of Staten Island, adjunct lecturer of music theory, 1983-86; University of Nebraska-Lincoln, School of Music, assistant professor of oboe, 1986-93, associate professor, 1993-2004, professor, 2004-; Lincoln Symphony, principal oboe, 1986-. Writer. **Publications:** Soloistic English Horn Literature from 1736-1984, 1994. **Address:** School of Music, University of Nebraska, 228 Westbrook Music Bldg., Lincoln, NE 68588-0100, U.S.A. **Online address:** wmcmullen1@unl.edu

MCMURRY, Richard M. American (born United States), b. 1939. **Genres:** History, Essays, Military/Defense/Arms Control. **Career:** Emory University, lecturer in history, 1966-67; Valdosta State College, assistant professor, 1967-70, associate professor, 1970-75, professor of history, 1975-81; North Carolina State University, professor, adjunct professor of history, 1981-88. Writer. **Publications:** The Road Past Kennesaw: The Atlanta Campaign of 1864, 1972; (ed. with J.I. Robertson, Jr.) Rank and File: Civil War Essays in Honor of Bell Irvin Wiley, 1976; John Bell Hood and the War for Southern Independence, 1982; Two Great Rebel Armies: An Essay in Confederate Military History, 1989; John Bell Hood And The War For Southern Independence, 1992; (ed. with J.A. Doyle and J.D. Smith) This Wilderness of War, 1998; Virginia Military Institute Alumni in the Civil War, 1999; Atlanta 1864: Last Chance for the Confederacy, 2000; The Fourth Battle of Winchester: Toward a New Civil War Paradigm, 2002; (ed.) An Uncompromising Secessionist: The Civil War of George Knox Miller, Eighth (Wade's) Confederate Cavalry, 2007. **Address:** 2405 Tillett Rd. SW, PO Box 4303, Roanoke, VA 24015-0303, U.S.A.

MCMURTRY, Larry (Jeff). American (born United States), b. 1936. **Genres:** Novels, Westerns/Adventure, Plays/Screenplays, Essays, Young Adult Non-fiction, History, Novellas/Short Stories. **Career:** Writer, 1961-; Houston Post, reviewer; Texas Christian University, instructor, 1961-62; Rice University, lecturer in English and creative writing, 1963-69; Washington Post, reviewer; Booked Up Book Store, co-owner, 1970-; George Mason College, visiting professor, 1970; American University, visiting professor, 1970-71; American Film, contributing editor, 1975-. **Publications:** LAST PICTURE SHOW SERIES: The Last Picture Show, 1966; Texasville, 1987; Duane's Depressed, 1999; When the Light Goes, 2007; Rhino Ranch, 2009. TERMS OF ENDEARMENT SERIES: Terms of Endearment, 1975; The Evening Star, 1992. DESERT ROSE SERIES: The Desert Rose, 1983; The Late Child, 1995. LONESOME DOVE SERIES: Lonesome Dove, 1985; Streets of Laredo, 1993; Dead Man's Walk, 1995; Comanche Moon, 1997. BERRYBENDER NARRATIVE SERIES: Sin Killer, 2002; The Wandering Hill, 2003; By Sorrow's River, 2003; Folly and Glory, 2004. NOVELS: Horseman, Pass By, 1961 as Hud, 1971; Leaving Cheyenne, 1963; Moving On, 1970; All My Friends Are Going to Be Strangers, 1972; Cadillac Jack, 1982; Somebody's Darling, 1978; Anything for Billy, 1989; Some Can Whistle, 1989; Buffalo Girls, 1990; (with D. Ossana) Pretty Boy Floyd, 1994; (with D. Ossana) Zeke and Ned, 1997; Boone's Lick, 2000; Loop Group, 2004; Telegraph Days, 2006. COLLECTIONS: (with D. Ossana and A. Proulx) Brokeback Mountain: Story to Screenplay, 2006. NONFICTION: In a Narrow Grave: Essays on Texas, 1968; Film Flam: Essays On Hollywood, 1987; Walter Benjamin at the Dairy Queen, 1999; Crazy Horse, 1999; Roads: A Millennial Journey Along America's Great Interstate Highways, 2000; Paradise, 2001; Sacagawea's Nickname: Essays On the American West, 2001; Oh What a Slaughter: Massacres in the American West 1846-1890, 2005; The Colonel and Little Missie: Buffalo Bill, Annie Oakley, and the Beginnings of Superstardom in America, 2006; Missouri River, 2006; Books: A Memoir, 2008; Literary Life: A Second Memoir, 2009; Hollywood: A Third Memoir, 2010; Custer, 2012. OTHERS: (ed.) Still Wild: Short Fiction of the American West, 1950 to the Present, 2000; (foreword) A Book of Photographs from Lonesome Dove, 2007. Contributor of articles to magazines and newspapers. **Address:** Simon & Schuster Inc., 1230 Ave. of the Americas, New York, NY 10020-1513, U.S.A.

MCNAB, Claire. (Clair Carmichael). American/Australian (born Australia), b. 1940. **Genres:** Mystery/Crime/Suspense, Children's Fiction, Young Adult Non-fiction, Novels. **Career:** Writer. **Publications:** NOVELS: Under the Southern Cross, 1992; Off Key, 1992; Silent Heart, 1993; Writing My Love, 2006; Aspects of the Heart, 2009. MYSTERY NOVELS CAROL ASHTON SERIES: Lessons in Murder, 1988; Fatal Reunion, 1989; Death down Under, 1990; Cop Out, 1991; Dead Certain, 1992; Body Guard, 1994; Double Bluff: A Carol Ashton Mystery, 1995; Inner Circle, 1996; Chain Letter, 1997; Past Due, 1998; Set Up, 1999; Under Suspicion, 2000; Death Club, 2001; Blood Link: The 15th Detective Inspector Carol Ashton Mystery, 2003; Fall Guy: The 16th Detective Inspector Carol Ashton Mystery, 2004; Lethal Care, 2012. DENISE CLEEVER SERIES: Murder Undercover: A Denise Cleever Thriller, 1999; Death Understood: A Denise Cleever Thriller, 2000; Out of Sight: A Denise Cleever Thriller, 2001; Recognition Factor: A Denise Cleever Thriller, 2002; Death by Death: A Denise Cleever Thriller, 2003. FOR CHILDREN AS CLAIR CARMICHAEL: The Mystery of the Haunted Dog, 1991; The Mystery of the Alien Spacecraft, 1992; Virtual Realities, 1992; Cybersaur, 1993; Worldwarp, 1994; Minimal Farm (picture book), 1994; Trouble at Minimal Farm (picture book), 1994; Sideswipe, 1995; Dr. Death, 1997; Deadly Friends, 1997; Virtual Realities Trilogy, 1997; Originator, 1998; Dear Jamie, 1998; Fabricant, 1999; Incognito, 2000; Saving Aunt Alice, 2001. NONFICTION: (as Claire Carmichael) Really Relating, 1989, 2nd ed., 1997; (as Clair Carmichael) Getting It Right, 1996; (with S. Gedan) The Loving Lesbian, 1997. AS KYLIE KENDALL MYSTERIES: The Wombat Strategy, 2004; Quokka Question, 2005; Kookaburra Gambit, 2005; Dingo Dilemma, 2006; The Platypus Ploy, 2007. OTHER: Accidental Murder, 2002; Writing My Love, 2006; Murder at Random, 2006. Contributor of articles and short fiction to periodicals. **Address:** Margaret Connolly & Associates, PO Box 945, Wahroonga, NW 2096, Australia. **Online address:** clairemcnab@aol.com

MCNAIR, Harold M. American (born United States), b. 1933. **Genres:** Chemistry, Sciences. **Career:** Eindhoven Technical University, Fulbright postdoctoral fellow, 1960, Phillips Fellow and visiting professor, 1981; Esso Research and Engineering, research chemist, 1960-61; F&M Scientific Corp., technical director, general manager, 1961-64; Varian Aerograph, director of international operations, director of marketing worldwide, 1964-68; Virginia Polytechnic Institute and State University, associate professor, 1968-71, professor of chemistry, 1971, department head, 1990, now professor emeritus; University of Neuchatel, visiting professor, 1975. Writer. **Publications:** (With E.J. Bonelli) Basic Gas Chromatography, 5th ed., 1969; (with E.H. Benjamin) Cromatograf ía Líquida de Alta Presión, 1973; Cromatografía de Gases, 1981; Gas Chromatography in Analytical Methods for Good Laboratory Practice, 2000. Contributor to journals. **Address:** Department of Chemistry, Virginia Polytech Institute and State University, 205 Engel Hall, PO Box 0212, Blacksburg, VA 24061, U.S.A. **Online address:** hmcnair@vt.edu

MCNAIR, Wesley C. American (born United States), b. 1941. **Genres:** Poetry, Essays, Novellas/Short Stories. **Career:** Hillsboro-Deering School, English teacher, 1963-64; New London Central School, English teacher, 1964-68; Colby-Sawyer College, instructor, assistant professor, associate professor of English, 1968-87; Catholic University of Chile, senior Fulbright professor of American literature and civilization, 1977-78; Marietta College, poet-in-residence, 1977; Dartmouth College, visiting associate professor, 1984; University of Maine, associate professor, professor of English, 1987-, director of the BFA program in creative writing, Libra Professor, 1995, professor emeritus and writer-in-residence, 2005-; Tyrone Guthrie Centre for the Arts, Robert Frost Poet-in-residence, 1987; Colby College, visiting professor, 2000-04; University of Southern Maine, faculty, 2002-03. Writer. **Publications:** POETRY: The Faces of Americans in 1853, 1984; The Town of No, 1989; My Brother Running, 1993; The Dissonant Heart, 1995; The Town of No & My Brother Running, 1997; Talking in the Dark, 1998; Fire, 2002; The Ghosts of You and Me, 2005; Lovers of the Lost: New & Selected Poems, 2010. OTHERS: 12 Journeys in Maine (chapbook), 1992; Mapping the Heart: Reflections on Place and Poetry, 2003; (with B. Roorbach and R. Kimber) A Place on Water: Essays, 2004; Words I Chose, 2012. EDITOR: (and contrib.) Pushcart Prize Anthology: Best of the Small Presses, 1986; The Quotable Moose: A Contemporary Maine Reader (anthology), 1994; The Maine Poets: An Anthology of Verse, 2003; The Maine Poets (anthology), 2003; Contemporary Maine Fiction: An Anthology of Short Stories, 2005; Place called Maine: 24 Authors on the Maine Experience, 2008; Today's Best Maine Fiction, 2008; Maine in Four Seasons: 20 Poets Celebrate the Turning Year, 2010; First Person Maine, forthcoming. Works appear in anthologies. Contributor to periodicals. **Address:** Roberts Learning Center, University of Maine, 246 Main St., Farmington, ME 04938-1994, U.S.A. **Online address:** wesley.mcnair@maine.edu

MCNALLY, Patrick S. American (born United States) **Genres:** Adult Non-fiction, Travel/Exploration, Social Sciences. **Career:** Writer and historian. **Publications:** From Chappaquiddick to New York and Washington: Through Oklahoma City, 2004. **Address:** c/o Author Mail, Author Solutions Inc., 1663 S Liberty Dr., Bloomington, IN 47403-5161, U.S.A. **Online address:** patricksmcnally@aol.com

MCNALLY, Terrence. American (born United States), b. 1939. **Genres:** Plays/Screenplays, Music, Songs/Lyrics And Libretti, Natural History, Theatre. **Career:** Actors Studio, stage manager, 1961, tutor, 1961-62; The Seventh Art, film critic, 1963-65; Columbia College Today, assistant editor, 1965-66. Playwright. **Publications:** PLAYS: (adapter) The Lady of the Camellias, 1963; And Things That Go Bump in the Night, 1964; Apple Pie: Three One-Act Plays, 1967; Here's Where I Belong, 1968; Cuba Si!, Bringing It All Back Home, Last Gasps: Three Plays, 1969; The Golden Age, 1975. OTHERS: Sweet Eros, Next and Other Plays, 1969; Noon, 1969; Sweet Eros and Witness: Two One-Act Plays, 1969; Where Has Tommy Flowers Gone?: A Play, 1972; Whiskey: A One-Act Play, 1973; Bad Habits, 1974, rev. ed., 1990; The Ritz and Other Plays, 1976; The Rink: A New Musical, 1985; The Lisbon Traviata, 1986, rev. ed., 1992; It's Only a Play: A Comedy, 1986; Frankie and Johnny in the Claire de Lune, 1988; (with I. Horovitz and L. Melfi) Faith, Hope and Charity, 1989; Three Plays, 1990; Lips Together, Teeth Apart, 1992; Terrence McNally: 15 Short Plays, 1994; A Perfect Ganesh, 1994; Love! Valour! Compassion!, 1995; Andre's Mother and Other Short Plays, 1995, rev. ed., 2005; Master Class, 1996; (with J. Pintauro and L. Wilson) By the Sea by the Sea by the Beautiful Sea, 1996; Kiss of the Spider Woman, 1997; Corpus Christi: A Play, 1998; The Full Monty: The Complete Book and Lyrics of the Hit Broadway Musical, 2002; A Man of No Importance, 2002; The Stendhal Syndrome, 2005; At the Statue of Venus, 2005; Dedication, or, The Stuff of Dreams, 2006; Some Men: And Deuce, 2007; Deuce, 2009; (intro. with T. Kirdahy) Gay in America, 2011. Contributor to books and periodicals. **Address:** c/o Peter Franklin, William Morris Agency, 1325 Ave. of the Americas, New York, NY 10019, U.S.A.

MCNAMARA, Dennis L. American (born United States), b. 1945. **Genres:** Business/Trade/Industry, Sociology, International Relations/Current Affairs, Area Studies. **Career:** Sogang University, lecturer, 1971-72, assistant professor, Student Counselling Center, director, 1977-78, 1982; Foreign Service Institute, U.S. State Department, lecturer, 1984-; Georgetown University, assistant professor, 1984-90, associate professor of sociology, 1990-95, Park professor of sociology and Korean studies, 1995-, professor of sociology, 1996-, Department of Sociology & Anthropology, chair, 2007-08; American University, Business Council for International Understanding, lecturer, 1987; Thammasat University, adjunct professor, 2006. Writer. **Publications:** The Colonial Origins of Korean Enterprise, 1910-1945, 1990; Bridging State and Society, East and West, 1994; Textiles and Industrial Transition in Japan, 1995; Trade and Transformation in Korea 1876 to 1945, 1995; (ed.) Corporatism and Korean Capitalism, 1999; Market and Society in Korea: Interest, Institution, and The Textile Industry, 2002; Business Innovation in Asia: Knowledge and Technology Networks from Japan, 2009. **Address:** Department of Sociology, Georgetown University, 209-03 CB, 3700 O Sts. NW, Washington, DC 20057-1037, U.S.A. **Online address:** mcnamard@georgetown.edu

MCNAMARA, Eugene Joseph. Canadian/American (born United States), b. 1930. **Genres:** Novels, Poetry, Literary Criticism And History, Novellas/Short Stories. **Career:** Fenwick High School, English teacher, 1953-55; University of Illinois, instructor in English, 1955-59; University of Windsor, associate professor, professor, 1959-95, University of Windsor Review, founder, editor, 1965-87, director of graduate program in creative writing, 1967-, professor emeritus, 1996-; Mainline, editor, 1967-74. **Publications:** Discovery: Voyage of Exploration, 1962; For The Mean Time, 1965; (ed. and comp.) The Interior Landscape: Literary Criticism of Marshall McLuhan, 1943-1962, 1969; Outerings, 1970; Love Scenes, 1970; Dillinger Poems, 1971; Hard Words, 1972; Passages and Other Poems, 1972; Diving for the Body, 1974; In Transit, 1975; Salt (stories), 1975; Screens, 1977; The Search for Sarah Grace (stories), 1977; Forcing the Field (poems), 1982; Call It a Day, 1984; Spectral Evidence (short stories), 1985; The Moving Light (poems), 1986; Laura as Novel Film and Myth, 1992; Fox Trot (stories), 1994; Mary Celestino: The Forces of Nature, 1996; Keeping in Touch: New and Selected Poems, 1998; Waterfalls: New and Selected Stories, 2000; Grace Notes: Poems, 2001; Irving's Coat: Windsor's Literary Renaissance, 2006; Orphan's Waltz: A Novel, 2008; Spindrift: Poems, 2009. **Address:** Department of English, University of Windsor, 401 Sunset Ave., Windsor, ON N9B 3P4, Canada.

MCNAMARA, Kathleen R. American (born United States), b. 1962?. **Genres:** Money/Finance. **Career:** Princeton University, lecturer, 1994-95, assistant professor of politics and international affairs, 1995-2003, Georgetown University, associate professor of government, 2003-, Edmund A. Walsh School of Foreign Service, associate professor, 2003-, Mortara Center for International Studies, director, 2010-. Writer. **Publications:** The Currency of Ideas: Monetary Politics in the European Union, 1998; (ed. with S. Meunier) Making History: European Integration and Institutional Change at Fifty, 2007. **Address:** Mortara Center for International Studies, Georgetown University, 101 3600 N St. NW, Washington, DC 20057, U.S.A. **Online address:** krm32@georgetown.edu

MCNAMARA, Mary. American (born United States), b. 1963?. **Genres:** Novels, Mystery/Crime/Suspense, Humor/Satire. **Career:** Los Angeles Times, entertainment writer, 1991-. **Publications:** Oscar Season (novel), 2008; Starlet: A Novel, 2010. **Address:** Los Angeles, CA , U.S.A. **Online address:** mary.mcnamara@latimes.com

MCNAMEE, Eoin. (John Creed). Irish (born Ireland), b. 1961?. **Genres:** Novels, Biography, Novellas/Short Stories. **Career:** Writer. **Publications:** The Last of Deeds, 1989; Resurrection Man, 1994; The Language of Birds, 1995; The Last of Deeds And Love in History, 1995; The Blue Tango, 2001; (as John Creed) The Sirius Crossing, 2002; (as John Creed) The Day of the Dead, 2003; The Ultras, 2004; (as John Creed) Black Cat Black Dog, 2006; The Navigator, 2006; 12: 23: Paris. 31st August 1997, 2007; City of Time, 2008; The Frost Child, 2009; Ring of Five, 2010; Orchid Blue, 2010; The Unknown Spy, 2011. **Address:** Picador, St. Martin Press, 175 5th Ave., New York, NY 10010-7703, U.S.A.

MCNAMEE, Gregory. American (born United States), b. 1957. **Genres:** Geography, Food And Wine, History, Classics, Environmental Sciences/Ecology, Local History/Rural Topics, Mythology/Folklore, Music, Social Commentary, Sciences. **Career:** Encyclopedia Britannica, consultant in world geography, contributing editor; University of Arizona, professor; Southwest Center, research associate. Journalist. Resist Much Obey Little: Some Notes on Edward Abbey, 1985; Philoktetes/Sophokles, 1986; Living in Words: Interviews from The Bloomsbury Review 1981-1988, 1988; Inconstant History, 1990; Return of Richard Nixon and Other Essays, 1990; Christ on the Mount of Olives and Other Stories, 1991; Gila: The Life and Death of an American River, 1994; The Sierra Club Desert Reader: A Literary Companion, 1995; In the Presence of Wolves, 1995; A Desert Bestiary: Folklore Literature and Ecological Thought from the Worlds Dry Places, 1996; A World of Turtles: A Literary Celebration, 1997; Grand Canyon Place Names, 1997; Open Range and Parking Lots, 1999; Blue Mountains Far Away: Journeys Into the American Wilderness, 2000; The Mountain World: A Literary Journey, 2000; The Serpents Tale: Snakes in Folklore and Literature, 2000; The Girl Who Made Stars, 2001; American Byzantium, 2001; The Bearskin Quiver, 2002; The North Wind and the Sun, 2004; Comeback Wolves, 2005; Moveable Feasts: The History, Science, and Lore of Food, 2006; Monumental Arizona, 2007; Careers in Renewable Energy, 2007; Saguaro, 2007; Otero Mesa: Preserving America's Wildest Grassland, 2008; Aelian's On the Nature of Animals, 2011; The Only Living One to Tell: The Life of a Kwevkepaya Indian, 2012. **Publications:** Resist Much Obey Little: Some Notes on Edward Abbey, 1985; Philoktetes/Sophokles, 1986; Living in Words: Interviews from The Bloomsbury Review 1981-1988, 1988; Inconstant History, 1990; Return of Richard Nixon and Other Essays, 1990; Christ on the Mount of Olives and Other Stories, 1991; Gila: The Life and Death of an American River, 1994; The Sierra Club Desert Reader: A Literary Companion, 1995; In the Presence of Wolves, 1995; A Desert Bestiary: Folklore Literature and Ecological Thought from the Worlds Dry Places, 1996; A World of Turtles: A Literary Celebration, 1997; Grand Canyon Place Names, 1997; Open Range and Parking Lots, 1999; Blue Mountains Far Away: Journeys Into the American Wilderness, 2000; The Mountain World: A Literary Journey, 2000; The Serpents Tale: Snakes in Folklore and Literature, 2000; The Girl Who Made Stars, 2001; American Byzantium, 2001; The Bearskin Quiver, 2002; The North Wind and the Sun, 2004; Comeback Wolves, 2005; Moveable Feasts: The History, Science, and Lore of Food, 2006; Monumental Arizona, 2007; Careers in Renewable Energy, 2007; Saguaro, 2007; Otero Mesa: Preserving America's Wildest Grassland, 2008. **Address:** AZ , U.S.A. **Online address:** gm@gregorymcnamee.com

MCNARON, Toni (A. H.). (Toni Ann Hurley Mcnaron). American (born United States), b. 1937. **Genres:** Literary Criticism And History, Women's Studies And Issues, Autobiography/Memoirs. **Career:** All Saints' College, instructor, 1959-61; University of Wisconsin, teaching assistant, 1961-63; University of Minnesota, assistant professor, 1964-67, associate professor, 1967-82, professor of English, 1982-2001, professor emeritus, 2001-. Writer. **Publications:** (Ed. with Y. Morgan) Voices in the Night: Women Speaking about Incest, 1982; (ed.) The Sister Bond: A Feminist View of a Timeless

Connection, 1983; I Dwell in Possibility: A Memoir, 1992, 2nd ed., 2001; (ed. with B. Zimmerman) New Lesbian Studies: Into the 21st Century, 1996; Poisoned Ivy: Lesbian and Gay Academics Confronting Homophobia, 1996. **Address:** Department of English, University of Minnesota, 207 Church St. SE, 207 Lind Hall, Minneapolis, MN 55455, U.S.A. **Online address:** mcnar001@maroon.fc.umn.edu

MCNARON, Toni Ann Hurley. *See* **MCNARON, Toni (A. H.).**

MCNAUGHT, Judith. American (born United States), b. 1944. **Genres:** Romance/Historical. **Career:** United Airlines, personnel interviewer and flight attendant, 1966-67; KMOX-CBS Radio, executive producer, 1970-73; Communico, assistant director, 1973-75; Moritz Inc., assistant director and motion picture director, 1973-76; Sommers Schwartz Inc., legal administrator, 1976-78; U.S. Transportation Co., controller, 1978; Pro-Temps Inc., president, 1979-85; Eagle Syndication, president, 1987-. Writer. **Publications:** Tender Triumph, 1983; Double Standards, 1984; Whitney, My Love, 1985; Once and Always, 1987; Something Wonderful, 1988; A Kingdom of Dreams, 1989; Almost Heaven, 1990; Paradise, 1991; Perfect, 1993; Until You, 1994; Remember When, 1996; Night Whispers, 1998; (with J. Deveraux and A. Kane) A Gift of love, 2001; Paradise: Tender Triumph, 2001; Someone To Watch Over Me, 2003; Every Breath You Take, 2005; Can't Take My Eyes Off of You, 2011. Contributor to periodicals. **Address:** c/o Perry Knowlton, Curtis Brown Ltd., 10 Astor Pl., New York, NY 10003, U.S.A.

MCNAUGHTON, Deborah (L.). American (born United States), b. 1950. **Genres:** Money/Finance, Economics. **Career:** Professional Credit Counselors Inc., founder and president, 1984-. Writer. **Publications:** (With J.F. Avanzini) Have a Good Report: Christian Credit Repair, 1991; Everything You Need to Know about Credit, 1993; The Insider's Guide to Managing Your Credit: How to Establish, Maintain, Repair, and Protect Your Credit, 1998; All about Credit: Questions (and Answers) about the Most Common Credit Problems, 1999; Destroy Your Debt! Your Guide to Total Financial Freedom: Strategies for Personal and Entrepreneurial Debt Elimination, 2001; Yes You Can!, 2001; Financially Secure: An Easy-to-Follow Money Program for Women, 2002; The Get out of Debt Kit: Your Roadmap to Total Financial Freedom, 2002; Ms. Entrepreneur, 2003; (with M. Weinstein) Rich and Thin: Slim Down, Shrink Debt, and Turn Calories into Cash, 2007; (with M. Weinstein) Money Trouble: Surviving Your Financial Crisis, 2009; The Essential Credit Repair Handbook: A Quick and Handy Guide for Anyone Who Wants to Get and Stay Out of Debt, 2011. **Address:** Professional Credit Counselors Inc., 711 W Kimberly Ave., Ste. 155, Placentia, CA 92870, U.S.A. **Online address:** tcmdeb@aol.com

MCNAUGHTON, Janet. Canadian (born Canada), b. 1953. **Genres:** Young Adult Fiction. **Career:** Quill and Quire, book reviewer. Writer. **Publications:** Catch Me Once, Catch Me Twice, 1994; To Dance at the Palais Royale, 1996; Make or Break Spring, 1998; The Secret under My Skin, 2000; The Saltbox Sweater, 2001; An Earthly Knight, 2003; Brave Jack and the Unicorn, 2005; The Raintree Rebellion, 2006; Dragon Seer, 2009; Dragon Seer's Gift, 2011. Contributor to books. **Address:** c/o Author Mail, Quill & Quire, 70 The Esplanade, Ste. 210, Toronto, ON M5E 1R2, Canada. **Online address:** janet@janetmcnaughton.ca

MCNEAL, Patricia. American (born United States), b. 1942. **Genres:** Administration/Management, History, Theology/Religion, Women's Studies And Issues, Politics/Government, Humanities. **Career:** Good Shepherd School, grade school teacher, 1964-65; Our Lady of Perpetual Help Academy, high school teacher, 1965-67; Saint Hubert's High School, teacher, 1967-69; Philadelphia Chapter of the Catholic Peace Fellowship, president, 1970-71; College of Notre Dame of Maryland, assistant professor, 1972-73; Indiana University South Bend, part-time assistant professor, 1974-87, part-time associate professor, 1987-93, acting director of women's studies program, 1993-2003, professor of women's studies, 1999-, now professor emeritus; University of Notre Dame, visiting professor, 1989. Writer. **Publications:** The American Catholic Peace Movement, 1928-1972, 1978; Harder than War: Catholic Peacemaking in Twentieth-Century America, 1991. Contributor of articles to periodicals. **Address:** Women's Studies Program, Indiana University-South Bend, 2259 Wiekamp Hall, 1700 Mishawaka Ave., PO Box 7111, South Bend, IN 46634-7111, U.S.A. **Online address:** pmcneal@iusb.edu

MCNEELY, Ian F. American (born United States), b. 1971. **Genres:** Young Adult Non-fiction, Medicine/Health, History. **Career:** University of Oregon, assistant professor, 2002-06, associate professor of history, 2006-. Writer. **Publications:** NONFICTION: Medicine on a Grand Scale: Rudolf Virchow, Liberalism and the Public Health, Wellcome Trust Centre for the History of Medicine, 2002; The Emancipation of Writing: German Civil Society in the Making, 1790s-1820s, 2003; (with L. Wolverton) Reinventing Knowledge: From Alexandria to the Internet, 2008. Contributor of articles to books and journals. **Address:** University of Oregon, 319 McKenzie Hall, Eugene, OR 97403-1288, U.S.A. **Online address:** imcneely@uoregon.edu

MCNEES, Kelly O'Connor. American (born United States), b. 1980?. **Genres:** Novels. **Career:** HarperCollins Publishers, editorial assistant, 2002-03; University of Michigan Press, editorial assistant, 2003-04; Deering Middle School, English teacher, 2006-07; Word Bird Editorial Services, editor, 2007-. **Publications:** The Lost Summer of Louisa May Alcott (novel), 2010. **Address:** Chicago, IL , U.S.A. **Online address:** thelostsummeroflma@gmail.com

MCNEIL, Legs. *See* **MCNEIL, Roderick Edward.**

MCNEIL, Linda L. American (born United States), b. 1946. **Genres:** Self Help. **Career:** Porter Memorial Hospital, staff physical therapist, 1969-71; Westland Manor Nursing Home, staff physical therapist, 1972-74; Rehab Therapy Inc., owner and president, 1974-87; Western Home Health, owner and president, 1981-85; Best Home Health Care, owner and president, 1981-85; InSpeech Inc., manager, 1987-89; Choices and Changes Ltd., trainer and writer, 1989-. **Publications:** 7 Keys to Changing Any Attitude or Circumstance in Your Life, 1997; 7 Keys to Changing your Life, Health and Wealth, 1998. Contributor to periodicals. **Address:** PO Box 280234, Lakewood, CO 80228, U.S.A. **Online address:** linmcneil@aol.com

MCNEIL, Roderick Edward. (Legs McNeil). American (born United States), b. 1956. **Genres:** Sex. **Career:** Punk Magazine, co-founder, 1975-79, writer; Spin Magazine, senior editor, 1985-91; Nerve magazine, editor-in-chief, 1993-, founder and editor. **Publications:** AS LEGS MCNEIL: (ed. with G. McCain) Please Kill Me: The Uncensored Oral History of Punk, 1996; Pop Culture: One Hundred Stories from Pepsi-Cola's First One Hundred Years, 1998; (co-author) Lobotomy: Surviving the Ramones, 2000; (with J. Osborne and P. Pavia) The Other Hollywood: The Uncensored Oral History of the Porn Film Industry, 2005; (with M. Leigh) I Slept with Joey Ramone: A Family Memoir, 2009. **Address:** Riverside Literary Agency, 41 Simon Keets, Leyden, MA 01337, U.S.A.

MCNEIL, William F. American (born United States), b. 1932. **Genres:** Sports/Fitness, Biography, Social Sciences, Geography, History. **Career:** E.U. du Pont de Nemours Inc., chemical engineer, 1960-67; Rhone Poulenc Inc., director of manufacturing, 1968-86. Writer. **Publications:** Dodger Diary, 1985; Mike Tyson, the Boy Who Would Be King, 1987; Dodger Chronicles, 1993; The King of Swat, 1997; Dodgers Encyclopedia, 1997; Ruth, Maris, McGwire and Sosa: Baseball's Single-Season Home Run Champions, 1999; The Secret of Ancient America, 2nd ed., 1999; Baseball's Other All-Stars, 2000; California Winter League: America's First Integrated Professional Baseball League, 2002; The Single Season Home Run Kings, 2003; Cool Papas and Double Duties, 2001; Gabby Hartnett, 2004; Visitors to Ancient American, 2004; Backstop: A History of the Catcher and A Sabermetric Ranking of 50 All-Time Greats, 2006; Evolution of Pitching in Major League Baseball, 2006; Black Baseball Out of Season: Pay for Play Outside of the Negro Leagues, 2007; Miracle in Chavez Ravine: The Los Angeles Dodgers in 1988, 2008; Red Sox Nation Guide to the Players, 2008; All-Stars for All Time: A Sabermetric Ranking of the Major League Best, 1876-2007, 2009. **Address:** 5 Woodland Dr., Pittsfield, MA 01201, U.S.A. **Online address:** wmcneil68@hotmail.com

MCNEILL, Christine. British/Austrian (born Austria), b. 1953. **Genres:** Poetry, inspirational/Motivational Literature, Translations. **Career:** Linguaphone Institute, tutor of German and TEFL, 1976-78; Inner London Education Authority, tutor, 1976-81; North Norfolk District Council, tutor of German, 1989-. Writer. **Publications:** Kissing the Night (poetry), 1993; (trans.) R.R. Rilke, Marienleben (title means: 'The Life of the Virgin Mary: A Cycle of Poems'), 2003. Contributor to periodicals. **Address:** 31 Burnt Hills, Cromer, Cromer, NF NR27 9LW, England.

MCNEILL, J(ohn) R(obert). American (born United States), b. 1954. **Genres:** History. **Career:** Athens College, instructor in world geography,

1975-76; Duke University, instructor, 1980-81, visiting assistant professor of history, 1982-83; Marine Biological Laboratory, Ecosystems Center, researcher, 1982-83; Goucher College, assistant professor of history, 1983-85; Georgetown University, assistant professor, 1985-90, associate professor, 1990-93, professor of history, 1993-, Cinco Hermanos chair in environmental and international affairs, 2003-06, university professor, 2006-. Writer. **Publications:** The Atlantic Empires of France and Spain: Louisbourg and Havana, 1700-1763, 1985; (ed. with A. Karras) Atlantic American Societies: From Columbus to Abolition, 1992; The Mountains of the Mediterranean World: An Environmental History, 1992; Something New Under the Sun: An Environmental History of the 20th Century World, 2000; (ed.) Environmental History in the Pacific, 2001; (with W.H. McNeil) The Human Web: A Bird's-Eye View of World History, 2003; (ed. with S. Krech III and C. Merchant) Encyclopedia of World Environmental History, 2004; (ed. with V. Winiwarter) Soils and Societies: Perspectives from Environmental History, 2006; (ed. with J. Martinez-Alier and A. Hornborg) Rethinking Environmental History, 2007; (with W.H. McNeil) Wen ming zhi wang: wu guo jie de ren lei jin hua shi, 2007; Epidemics and Geopolitics in the American Tropics, 1640-1920, 2008. Mosquito Empires: Ecology and War in the Greater Caribbean, 1620 - 1914, 2010; (ed. with C.R. Unger) Environmental Histories of the Cold War, 2010; (ed. with J.A. Pádua and M. Rangarajan) Environmental History: As if Nature Existed, 2010. Contributor of articles to journals. **Address:** Department of History, Georgetown University, 614 ICC, PO Box 571035, Washington, DC 20057, U.S.A. **Online address:** mcneillj@georgetown.edu

MCNEILL, William Hardy. American/Canadian (born Canada), b. 1917. **Genres:** History, Cultural/Ethnic Topics, Military/Defense/Arms Control, Environmental Sciences/Ecology. **Career:** University of Chicago, instructor, professor, 1947-69, chair of department, 1961-69, Robert A. Millikan distinguished service professor of history, 1969-87, Robert A. Millikan distinguished professor emeritus of history, 1987-; University of Frankfurt, exchange professor, 1956; University of Hawaii, John H. Burns distinguished visiting professor, 1980; Oxford University, George Eastman professor, 1980-81. Writer. **Publications:** The Greek Dilemma, War and Aftermath, 1947; (with F. Smothers and E.D. McNeill) Report on the Greeks: Findings of a Twentieth Century Fund Team which Surveyed Conditions in Greece in 1947, 1948; History Handbook, 1949, rev. ed. as History Handbook of Western Civilization, 1953; America, Britain and Russia: Their Cooperation and Conflict 1941-46, 1953; Past and Future, 1954; Greece: American Aid in Action 1947-1956, 1957; (with M.R. Buske and W. Roehm) The World: Its History in Maps, 1963; The Rise of the West, 1963; Europe's Steppe Frontier 1500-1800, 1964; A World History, 1967; The Contemporary World, 1967; Sir Herbert Butterfield, Cho Yun Hsu and William H. McNeill on Chinese and World History, 1970; Venice, the Hinge of Europe 1081-1797, 1974; The Shape of European History, 1974; Plagues and People, 1976; Metamorphosis of Greece since World War II, 1978; The Human Condition: An Historical and Ecological View, 1980; Pursuit of Power: Technology, Armed Force and Society since 1000 A.D., 1982; The Great Frontier: Freedom and Hierarchy in Modern Times, 1983; Mythistory and Other Essays, 1986; Polyethnicity and National Unity in World History, 1986; A History of the Human Community, 1987; Arnold J. Toynbee, A Life, 1989; Population and Politics, 1990; Hutchins' University: The University of Chicago 1929-1950, a Memoir, 1991; The Global Condition, 1992; Keeping Together in Time, 1995; Disruption of Traditional Forms of Nurture, 1998; La Civilización De Occidente: Manual De Historia, 2000; (with J.R. McNeill) The Human Web: A Bird's-eye View of World History, 2003; The Pursuit of Truth: A Historian's Memoir, 2005; (contrib.) Transatlantic History, 2006; (co-author) The Human Web, 2007; (with R.J. McNeil) Summers Long Ago: On Grandfather's Farm and in Grandmother's Kitchen, 2009. EDITOR/CO-EDITOR: (intro.) Lord Action, Essays in the Liberal Interpretation of History, 1967; Readings in World History, 10 vols., 1968-73; Human Migration: Patterns and Policies, 1978; The Cold War, 1949 to 1973, 1980; (with M.R. Waldman) The Islâmic World, 1983; Berkshire Encyclopedia of World History, 2005, 2nd ed., 2010; Africa in World History, 2011; World Environmental History, 2011; Religion and Belief Systems in World History, 2011. Contributor to periodicals. **Address:** University of Chicago, 5801 S Ellis Ave., Chicago, IL 60637, U.S.A.

MCNEILLIE, Andrew. British/Welsh (born Wales), b. 1946. **Genres:** Biography, Poetry. **Career:** Clutag Press, Archipelago, founder, 2000; Archipelago, founder and editor, 2007-, University of Exeter, faculty, 2000, professor; University of Aberystwyth, honorary professor of English; Oxford University Press, senior editor, literature editor; English Association, fellow; British Broadcasting Corp., radio newsroom, news journalist. **Publications:** Nevermore, 2000; An Aran Keening, 2001; Now, Then, 2002; Slower, 2006; Ian Niall: Part of His Life (biography), 2007; Once, 2009; In Mortal Memory, 2010. **Address:** Department of English, University of Exeter, Queen's Bldg., Queen's Dr., Exeter, DN EX4 4QH, England. **Online address:** a.mcneillie@exeter.ac.uk

MCNEISH, James. New Zealander (born New Zealand), b. 1931. **Genres:** Novels, Plays/Screenplays, Autobiography/Memoirs, Biography. **Career:** New Zealand Herald, journalist and arts editor, 1950-58; teacher, 1960-62; BBC, staff; freelance radio broadcaster and radio documentary producer, 1962-; Bridge in New Zealand (private educational travel trust), co-founder and director, 1974-82; Berlin Kunstler program, writer-in-residence, 1983; National Library of New Zealand, research fellow, 1999. **Publications:** Tavern in the Town, 1957; Fire Under the Ashes: A Life of Danilo Dolci, 1965; Mackenzie, 1970; The Mackenzie Affair, 1972; Larks in a Paradise, 1974; The Glass Zoo, 1976; As for the Godwits (autobiography), 1977; Art of the Pacific, 1980; Belonging: Conversations in Israel, 1980; Joy: A Novel, 1982; (with H. McNeish) Walking on My Feet, 1983; Ahnunglos in Berlin: A Berlin Diary, 1985; Lovelock, 1986; Penelope's Island, 1990; The Man from Nowhere and Other Prose, 1991; My Name Is Paradiso, 1995; Mr. Halliday and the Circus Master, 1996; The Mask of Sanity: The Bain Murders, 1997; An Albatross Too Many, 1998; Dance of the Peacocks: New Zealanders in Exile at the Time of Hitler and Mao Tse-tung, 2003; Sixth Man: The Extraordinary Life of Paddy Costello, 2007; The Crime of Huey Dunstan, 2010. **Address:** c/o Michael Gifkins, PO Box 6496, Auckland, 1, New Zealand. **Online address:** godwits@xtra.co.nz

MCNERNEY, Gerald. (Jerry McNerney). American (born United States), b. 1951. **Genres:** Military/Defense/Arms Control, Engineering, Economics. **Career:** Kirtland Air Force Base, Sandia National Laboratories, contractor; U.S.Windpower, senior engineer, 1984-94; PG&E, energy consultant, 1994-; FloWind, energy consultant, 1994-; Electric Power Research Institute, energy consultant, 1994-; California's 11th Congressional District, representative, 2007. Writer. **Publications:** Terrorism and Fear, Enter the Third Level, 1993; (as Jerry McNerney) Enter the Third Level, 1994; (with M. Cheek) Clean Energy Nation: Freeing America from the Tyranny of Fossil Fuels, 2009. **Address:** 1210 Longworth House Office Bldg., Washington, DC 20515, U.S.A.

MCNERNEY, Jerry. *See* **MCNERNEY, Gerald.**

MCNETT, Molly. American (born United States), b. 1966. **Genres:** Novellas/Short Stories. **Career:** Northern Illinois University, Department of English, instructor, 2001-. Writer. **Publications:** One Dog Happy (short stories), 2008. **Address:** Department of English, Northern Illinois University, Reavis 215, RH 310, Dekalb, IL 60115, U.S.A. **Online address:** mmcnett@niu.edu

MCNICOLL, Sylvia (Marilyn). Canadian (born Canada), b. 1954. **Genres:** Children's Fiction, Young Adult Fiction, Literary Criticism And History. **Career:** Canadian International Paper Co., senior cash management clerk, 1973-80; freelance writer, 1980-88; full-time writer, 1988-; Sheridan College, creative writing instructor, 1989-96; York University, Faculty of Education and the Writers' Development Trust, writer-in-electronic-residence program, writer-in-electronic-residence, 1994-97, 2002. Today's Parent Toronto, features editor. **Publications:** JUNIOR FICTION: The Tiger Catcher's Kid, 1989; Project Disaster, 1990; The Big Race!, 1996; Dan Clowning Around, 1998; Matt Heartbreak Hero, 1998; Lauren Dream Dating, 1998; Jenna Standing Tall, 1999; Abbi Secret Stranger, 1999; Dan Double Drama, 1999; Slam Dunk Robot, 2006. YOUNG ADULT FICTION: Blueberries and Whipped Cream, 1988; Jump Start, 1989; More Than Money, 1990; Facing the Enemy, 1992; Bringing up Beauty, 1994; Walking a Thin Line, 1997; Grave Secrets, 1999; Caught in a Lie, 2000; A Different Kind of Beauty, 2003; Beauty Returns 2006; Last Chance for Paris 2008. Contributor to periodicals. **Address:** 2646 Cavendish Dr., Burlington, ON L7P 3R7, Canada. **Online address:** sylvia.mcnicoll@cogeco.ca

MCNULTY, Bridget. South African (born South Africa), b. 1982?. **Genres:** Literary Criticism And History. **Career:** Freelance journalist, 2006-; Real Simple, features writer, 2007; Blue Sky Publications, writer, 2007-08; Just the Planet, contributing writer, 2009-; John Brown Media Group, online editor, 2010-11; A Sweet Life, editor, 2011-. **Publications:** Strange Nervous Laughter, 2007. **Address:** Thomas Dunne Books, 175 5th Ave., New York, NY 10010, U.S.A. **Online address:** hello@bridgetmcnulty.com

MCNUTT, Patrick A. Irish (born Ireland), b. 1957. **Genres:** Economics, Politics/Government, Law. **Career:** Economic and Social Research Institute, research assistant, 1978-80; National University of Ireland, University College, Department of Economics, lecturer, 1982-83, junior lecturer, 1983-90, senior lecturer, 1990-94, Centre for Research in Economics and Law, founding director, 1991-94, Social Sciences Research Centre, chairman, 1992-94; University of Limerick, Department of Business Studies, visiting lecturer, 1985-92; University of Ulster, professor of political economy, 1994-96, Centre for Research in Economics and Law, founding director, 1994-96; Competition Authority, chairperson and chief executive officer, 1996-2000; Trinity College, Department of Political Science, research associate, 1998-2000; Indecon London Economics Consultancy Group, consultant, director and partner, 2000-03; Jersey Competition Regulatory Authority, consultant, 2001-04; University of Wales, School of Accountancy, Banking & Economics, visiting professor, 2001-05; Patrick McNutt & Associates, partner, founder and consultant, 2003-; Manchester Business School, visiting fellow, 2004-; Patrick McNutt Consulting, chief executive officer. Writer. **Publications:** Understanding Economic Issues, 1986; The Economics of Public Choice, 1996, 2nd ed., 2002; Law, Economics, and Antitrust: Towards a New Perspective, 2005; Political Economy of Law, 2010. **Address:** Patrick McNutt & Associates, 14 Temple Park Ave., Dublin, DU 1, Ireland. **Online address:** peanutt@indigo.ie

MCNUTT, Randy. American (born United States), b. 1948. **Genres:** Documentaries/Reportage, Adult Non-fiction, Biography, Photography. **Career:** Cincinnati Enquirer, feature writer and reporter, 1976-2000; Hamilton Hobby Press, editor and publisher, 1981-2000; Ohio (magazine), contributing editor, 1985-99; Miami University, visiting assistant professor of journalism, 1990-91. **Publications:** NONFICTION: Cal Stewart, Your Uncle Josh, 1981; (with C. Bauer) Talking Machine Madness, 1985; (ed. and comp.) No Left Turns: A Handbook for Conservatives Based on the Writings of John M. Ashbrook, 1986; We Wanna Boogie: An Illustrated History of the American Rockabilly Movement, 1988; Ghosts: An Eccentric Ohio Travel Journal, 1995; Ghosts: Ohio's Haunted Landscapes, Lost Arts and Forgotten Places, 1996, 2nd ed., 2008; (with R. Kennedy) Little Labels-Big Sound: Small Record Companies and the Rise of American Music, 1999; Guitar Towns: A Journey to the Crossroads of Rock 'n' Roll, 2002; Still too Hot to Handle: More Historic American Recording Studios and the Hits of the 20th Century, 2003; (with C. Bauer) Hamilton, 2005; Lost Ohio: More Travels into Haunted Landscapes, Ghost Towns and Forgotten Lives, 2006; (with C. Bauer) Butler County, 2006; The Cincinnati Sound, 2007; (with C. Bauer) Ohio Civil War Tales: A Primer of Copperheads, Hotheads, Tinclads, Abolitionists, Train Thieves and Quantrill's Missing Skull, 2009; King Records of Cincinnati, 2009. Contributor to periodicals. **Address:** HHP Books, PO Box 18455, Fairfield, OH 45018, U.S.A. **Online address:** randy@randymcnutt.com

MCPHEE, Jenny. American (born United States), b. 1962. **Genres:** Adult Non-fiction, Translations, History, Social Sciences. **Career:** Writer and translator. **Publications:** (With L. McPhee and M. McPhee) Girls: Ordinary Girls and Their Extraordinary Pursuits, 2000; The Center of Things, 2001; No Ordinary Matter, 2004; A Man of No Moon, 2007. TRANSLATOR: (with M. McPhee) Pope J. Paul II, Crossing the Threshold of Hope, 1994; P. Maurensig, Canone Inverso, 1998; (with R. Fremantle) F. Quadri, Robert Wilson, 1998. **Address:** c/o Kimberly Witherspoon, InkWell Management, 521 5th Ave., 26th Fl., New York, NY 10175, U.S.A. **Online address:** jenny.mcphee@hotmail.com

MCPHEE, John (Angus). American (born United States), b. 1931. **Genres:** Documentaries/Reportage, Essays, Air/Space Topics, Earth Sciences, Education, Environmental Sciences/Ecology, Food And Wine, Natural History, Sports/Fitness, Young Adult Non-fiction, Adult Non-fiction, Literary Criticism And History, Writing/Journalism. **Career:** Time Magazine, associate editor, 1957-64; New Yorker Magazine, staff writer, 1964-; Princeton University, faculty, 1964-, Ferris professor of journalism, 1975-2010. **Publications:** A Sense of Where You Are: A Profile of William Warren Bradley, 1965, 2nd ed., 1995; The Headmaster: Frank L. Boyden of Deerfield, 1966; Oranges, 1967; The Pine Barrens, 1968; A Roomful of Hovings and Other Profiles, 1968; Levels of the Game, 1969; The Crofter and the Laird, 1970; Encounters with the Archdruid, 1971; Wimbledon: A Celebration, 1972; The Deltoid Pumpkin Seed, 1973; The Curve of Binding Energy, 1974; Pieces of the Frame, 1975; The Survival of the Bark Canoe, 1975; The John McPhee Reader, 1976; Coming into the Country, 1977; Giving Good Weight, 1979; Alaska: Images of the Country, 1981; Basin and Range, 1981; In Suspect Terrain, 1983; Heirs of General Practice, 1984; Annals of the Former World, 1984; La Place de la Concorde Suisse, 1984; Table of Contents, 1985; Rising from the Plains, 1986; Outcroppings, 1988; The Control of Nature, 1989; Looking for a Ship, 1990; Assembling California, 1993; The Ransom of Russian Art, 1994; The Second John McPhee Reader, 1996; Irons in the Fire, 1997; Annals of the Former World, 1998; The Founding Fish, 2002; (intro.) A Week on the Concord and Merrimack Rivers, 2004; Uncommon Carriers, 2006; Silk Parachute, 2010; (ed. with C. Rigolot) The Princeton Reader: Contemporary Essays by Writers and Journalists at Princeton University, 2010. **Address:** Farrar, Straus and Giroux, 19 Union Sq. W, New York, NY 10003-3304, U.S.A. **Online address:** angus@princeton.edu

MCPHEE, Martha (A.). American (born United States), b. 1964. **Genres:** Novels, Adult Non-fiction, Theology/Religion, inspirational/Motivational Literature. **Career:** Hofstra University, assistant professor, 1997-, associate professor of English. Writer and translator. **Publications:** (Trans with J. McPhee) Crossing the Threshold of Hope, 1994; Bright Angel Time, 1997; (with J. McPhee and L. McPhee) Girls: Ordinary Girls and Their Extraordinary Pursuits, 2000; Gorgeous Lies (novel), 2002; L'America, 2006; Dear Money, 2010. Contributor to periodicals. **Address:** Department of English, Hofstra University, 106 Mason Hall, Hempstead, NY 11549-1000, U.S.A. **Online address:** martha.s.mcphee@hofstra.edu

MCPHEE, Norma H. American (born United States), b. 1928. **Genres:** Children's Non-fiction, Adult Non-fiction, Education, Young Adult Non-fiction. **Career:** Freelance writer, 1964; Jason and Nordic Publishers, founder, chief executive officer, 1988-. **Publications:** FOR ADULTS: Programs for Church Year, 1971; Discussion Programs for Junior Highs, 1974; Programs and Skits for Young Teens, 1978; More Programs and Skits for Young Teens, 1980; The Narrow Gate, 1982; Fun Stuff for Kids: Childrens Bible Related Activities, 1984; Sensitivity and Awareness Guide, 1994, 3rd ed. as Sensitivity and Awareness: A Guide for Developing Understanding Among Children, 1996. FOR CHILDREN AS NAN HOLCOMB: How About a Hug, 1983; Danny and the Merry-Go-Round, 1984; Andy Finds a Turtle, 1987; Patrick and Emma Lou, 1989; A Smile from Andy, 1989; Andy Opens Wide, 1990; Sarahs Surprise, 1990; Fair and Square, 1992; Leahs Night of Wonder, 1999; Of Easter Eggs and Things, 2000. Contributor to books. **Address:** Jason & Nordic Publishers, PO Box 441, Hollidaysburg, PA 16648, U.S.A. **Online address:** turtlbks@nb.net

MCPHEE, Peter. Scottish (born Scotland), b. 1957?. **Genres:** Novels. **Career:** Winnipeg Sun, editor and film critic; Tag Advertising, staff; West Canadian Printing, production manager. Sculptor and artist. **Publications:** NOVELS: A Way with Horses, 1996; Runner, 1999; Out of Time, 2003; Every Move, 2004; New Blood, 2007. **Address:** Langdon, AB , Canada. **Online address:** author@prmcphee.com

MCPHEE, Sarah (Collyer). American (born United States), b. 1960?. **Genres:** Architecture. **Career:** Metropolitan Museum of Art, assistant editor and writer, 1984-86; Emory University, Department of Art History, lecturer, 1995-97, assistant professor, 1997-2001, associate professor, 2001-11, professor, 2011-; Columbia University, Department of Art History and Archaeology, visiting associate professor, 2003-04. Author. **Publications:** (Co-author) Filippo Juvarra: Drawings from the Roman Period 1704-1714, vol. II, 1999; Bernini and the Bell Towers: Architecture and Politics at the Vatican, 2002; Bernini's Mistress: A Portrait of Costanza Piccolomini, forthcoming. Contributor to books and periodicals. **Address:** Department of Art History, Emory University, M35 Carlos Hall, 581 S Kilgo Cir., Atlanta, GA 30322, U.S.A. **Online address:** smcphee@emory.edu

MCPHERSON, James A(lan). American (born United States), b. 1943. **Genres:** Novels, Transportation, Novellas/Short Stories, Literary Criticism And History, Young Adult Fiction. **Career:** University of Iowa, Law School, instructor in writing, 1968-69, instructor in Afro-American literature, 1969-, Writers Workshop, professor of creative writing, 1981-, F. Wendell Miller Professor of Creative Writing, 1998-, professor of English, 1981-; University of California, lecturer in English, 1969-70; Morgan State University, faculty, 1975-76; University of Virginia, faculty, 1976-81; Double Take Magazine, editor, 1995-; Stanford University, behavioral studies fellow, 1997-; Harvard University, visiting professor; Yale University, English faculty; Meiji University, visiting professor; Chiba University, visiting professor. **Publications:** Hue and Cry: Short Stories, 1969; (ed. with M. Williams) Railroad: Trains and Train People in American Culture, 1976; Elbow Room: Stories, 1977; A

World Unsuspected, 1987; The Prevailing South, 1988; Crabcakes, 1998; (ed. with D. Henry) Fathering Daughters: Reflections by Men, 1998; A Region Not Home: Reflections from Exile, 2000; (foreword) The Stories of Breece D'J Pancake, 2002. Works appear in anthologies. Contributor to periodicals. **Address:** Graduate Program in Creative Writing, University of Iowa, 102 Dey House, Iowa City, IA 52242-1408, U.S.A.

MCPHERSON, James Munro. American (born United States), b. 1936. **Genres:** History, Race Relations, Military/Defense/Arms Control, Social Sciences, Essays. **Career:** Princeton University, instructor, 1962-65, assistant professor, 1965-68, associate professor, 1968-72, professor, 1972-82, Edwards professor of American history, 1982-91, George Henry Davis 1886 Professor of American History, 1991-2004, George Henry Davis 1886 Professor Emeritus of American History, 2004-; University College of London, Commonwealth Fund lecturer, 1982; Stanford University, Behavioral Sciences Center, fellow, 1982-83. Writer and consultant. **Publications:** The Struggle for Equality: Abolitionists and the Negro in the Civil War and Reconstruction, 1964, 2nd ed., 1995; The Negro's Civil War: How American Negroes Felt and Acted in the War for the Union, 1965; Marching toward Freedom: The Negro in the Civil War, 1860-1865, 1968; (contrib.) Blacks in America: Bibliographical Essays, 1971; The Abolitionist Legacy: From Reconstruction to the NAACP, 1975, 2nd ed., 1995; Ordeal by Fire: The Civil War and Reconstruction, 1982, (with J.K. Hogue) 4th ed., 2009; Images of the Civil War, 1982; (with J.M. Kousser) Region, Race and Reconstruction: Essays In Honor Of C. Vann Woodward, 1982; Lincoln and the Strategy of Unconditional Surrender, 1984; How Lincoln Won the War with Metaphor, 1985; Battle Cry of Freedom: The Era of the Civil War, 1988; (ed.) Battle Chronicles of the Civil War, 1989; Abraham Lincoln and the Second American Revolution, 1990; (ed.) American Political Leaders: From Colonial Times to the Present, 1991; Why the Confederacy Lost, 1992; Gettysburg, 1993; What They Fought For, 1861-65, 1994; (ed.) The Atlas of the Civil War, 1994; We Cannot Escape History: Lincoln and the Last Best Hope on Earth, 1995; Drawn with the Sword: Reflections on the American Civil War, 1996; (ed.) The American Heritage New History of the Civil War, 1996; For Cause and Comrades: Why Men Fought in the Civil War, 1997; (with P.R. McPherson) Lamson of the Gettysburg: The Civil War Letters Of Lieutenant Roswell H. Lamson, U.S. Navy, 1997; Gettysburg The Painting of Mort Kunstler, 1998; (with W.J. Cooper) Writing the Civil War: The Quest to Understand, 1998; (with J.O. Appleby and A. Brinkley) The American Journey, 1998; Is Blood Thicker Than Water?: Crises of Nationalism in the Modern World, 1998; (with D.J. Wilson) Accepting the Prize: Two Historians Speak, 2000; For a Vast Future Also, 2000; (ed.) To the Best of My Ability: The American Presidents, 2000, rev. ed., 2001; (ed.) Encyclopedia of Civil War Biographies, 2000; (ed. with A. Brinkley and D. Rubel) Days of Destiny: Crossroads In American History: America's Greatest Historians Examine Thirty-One Uncelebrated Days That Changed The Course Of History, 2001; Crossroads of Freedom: Antietam, the Battle that Changed the Course of the Civil War, 2002; (ed.) The Civil War Reader, 1862, 2002; Fields of Fury: The American Civil War, 2002; The American Vision, 2003; Hallowed Ground: A Walk at Gettysburg, 2003; The Illustrated Battle Cry of Freedom, 2003; (intro.) The Most Fearful Ordeal: Original Coverage of the Civil War, 2004; (intro.) Civil War, 2005; Into The West, 2006; This Mighty Scourge: Perspectives On The Civil War, 2007; Tried by War: Abraham Lincoln as Commander in Chief, 2008; Abraham Lincoln, 2009; (contrib.) Hearts Touched by Fire, 2011; War on the Waters, 2012. Contributor to periodicals. **Address:** Department of History, Princeton University, 106 41 William St., 129 Dickinson Hall, Princeton, NJ 08544-1017, U.S.A. **Online address:** jmcphers@princeton.edu

MCPHERSON, Sandra. American (born United States), b. 1943. **Genres:** Poetry, Civil Liberties/Human Rights, History, Language/Linguistics. **Career:** Honeywell Inc., technical writer, 1966; University of Iowa, Writers Workshop, faculty, 1974-76, 1978-80; Antioch Review, poetry editor, 1979-81; University of California-Berkeley, Writers Workshop, Holloway lecturer, 1981; Pacific Northwest College of Art, Oregon Writers Workshop, faculty, 1981-85; California Quarterly, poetry editor, 1985-87; University of California-Davis, professor of English, 1985-2008, professor emeritus, 2008-; Swan Scythe Press, founding publisher and editor, 1999-. **Publications:** Elegies for the Hot Season, 1970; Radiation, 1973; The Year of Our Birth, 1978; Sensing, 1979; Patron Happiness, 1983; Pheasant Flower, 1985; Floralia, 1985; Streamers, 1988; Designating Duet, 1989; The God of Indeterminacy, 1993; The Spaces between Birds: Mother/Daughter Poems, 1967-1995, 1996; Edge Effect: Trails and Portrayals, 1996; A Visit to Civilization, 2002; Expectation Days, 2007. Contributor to periodicals. Works appear in anthologies. **Address:** Swan Scythe Press, 515 P St., Ste. 804, Sacramento, CA 95814, U.S.A. **Online address:** sandyjmc@mindspring.com

MCQUAIN, Jeffrey Hunter. American (born United States), b. 1955. **Genres:** Language/Linguistics, Sciences, Education, History, Theology/Religion. **Career:** New York Times, researcher, 1983-; United Media, writer and columnist, 1988-94. **Publications:** (With S. Malless) Handlist to English: Basic Terms for Literature, Composition and Grammar, 1986; (with S. Malless) Elements of English: A Glossary of Basic Terms for Literature, Composition and Grammar, 1988; (ed. with M.H. Manser) The World Almanac Guide to Good Word Usage, 1989; Power Language: Getting the Most Out of Your Words, 1996; (with S. Malless) Coined by Shakespeare: Words and Meanings First Used by The Bard, 1998; Never Enough Words: How Americans Invented Expressions as Ingenious, Ornery and Colorful as Themselves, 1999; Home-grown English: How Americans Invented Themselves and Their Language, 2002; (with S. Malless) Coined by God: Words and Phrases That First Appear in the English Translations of the Bible, 2003; (with P.M. Matthews) The Bard on the Brain: Understanding the Mind through the Art of Shakespeare and the Science of Brain Imaging, 2003. **Address:** The Word Doctor, PO Box 4008, Rockville, MD 20849-4008, U.S.A.

MCQUAY, Peri Phillips. Canadian (born Canada), b. 1945?. **Genres:** Documentaries/Reportage, Natural History, Crafts, Homes/Gardens, Writing/Journalism, Environmental Sciences/Ecology, Education, Cultural/Ethnic Topics, Cultural/Ethnic Topics. **Career:** Writer, 1979-. **Publications:** The View from Foley Mountain, 1987, rev. ed., 1995; A Wing in the Door: Life with a Red-Tailed Hawk, 2001; Towards Home, forthcoming; Singing Meadow, forthcoming. Contributor to books and periodicals. **Address:** RR 1, Crozier Rd., Westport, ON K0G 1X0, Canada. **Online address:** peri@kingston.net

MCQUEEN, Rod. Canadian (born Canada) **Genres:** Novels, History. **Career:** Canadian Business, contributing senior editor; Financial Post, senior writer. **Publications:** The Money-Spinners: An Intimate Portrait of the Men Who Run Canadas Banks, 1983; Leap of Faith: The MacDonald Report, 1985; Risky Business: Inside Canadas $86-Billion Insurance Industry, 1985; Blind Trust: Inside the Sinclair Stevens Affair, 1987; The Last Best Hope: How to Start and Grow Your Own Business, 1995; Who Killed Confederation Life?: The Inside Story, 1996; The Eatons: The Rise and Fall of Canadas Royal Family, 1998, rev. ed., 1999; Cant Buy Me Love: How Martha Billes Made Canadian Tire Hers, 2001; The Icarus Factor: The Rise and Fall of Edgar Bronfman Jr., 2004; Fantasy in Florence: Leaving Home and Loving It, 2007; Manulife: How Dominic D'Alessandro Built a Global Giant and Fought to Save It, 2009; BlackBerry: From Cult Object to Cultural Revolution, 2009; BlackBerry: The Inside Story of Research in Motion, 2010. **Address:** c/o Author Mail, Random House of Canada, 1 Toronto St., Ste. 300, Toronto, ON M5C 2V6, Canada.

MCQUOWN, Judith H. American (born United States), b. 1941. **Genres:** Business/Trade/Industry, Money/Finance, Medicine/Health. **Career:** McQuown's Designer Markdowns weekly newsletter, editor; Municipal Securities, Underwriting Division, chief, 1972-73; Judith H. McQuown and Company Inc., president, 1973-; Boardroom Reports, contributing editor, 1978-79; Macmillan Publishing Co., senior editor, 1981. **Publications:** Inc. Yourself: How to Profit by Setting Up Your Own Corporation, 1977, 10th ed., 2001; Tax Shelters That Work for Everyone: A Common Sense Guide to Keeping More Of The Money You Earn, 1979; (with O. Laugier) The Fashion Survival Manual: How to Find It, Fix It, Fake It, and Make It on a Budget, 1981; Playing the Takeover Market: How to Profit from Corporate Mergers, Spin offs, Tender Offers and Liquidations, 1982; How to Profit after You Inc. Yourself, 1985; Keep One Suitcase Empty: The Bargain Shopper's Guide to Best Factory Outlets in England, Ireland, and Wales, 1987; Use Your Own Corporation to Get Rich: How to Start Your Own Business and Achieve Maximum Profits, How to Build Your Existing Business and Increase Your Profits!, 1991; 1001 Tips for Living Well with Diabetes: Firsthand Advice that Really Works, 2004. **Address:** 1 Gracie Ter., New York, NY 10028-7955, U.S.A.

MCRAE, Barry (Donald). British (born England), b. 1935. **Genres:** Music, Biography, Art/Art History. **Career:** United Distillers, junior, 1951-58, assistant purchasing manager, 1958-68, purchasing manager, 1968-92; writer, 1960-. **Publications:** The Jazz Cataclysm, 1967; The Jazz Handbook, 1987; Miles Davis, 1988; Ornette Coleman, 1988; Dizzy Gillespie: His Life and Times, 1988. Contributor to journals. **Address:** 24 Bearwood Close, Potters Bar, HF EN6 5HJ, England.

MCRAE, Cricket. American (born United States), b. 1964. **Genres:** Mystery/Crime/Suspense. **Career:** Microsoft, program manager. Writer. **Publications:** HOME CRAFTING MYSTERY SERIES: Lye in Wait, 2007; Heaven Preserve Us, 2008; Spin a Wicked Web, 2009; Something Borrowed, Something Bleu, 2010; Wined and Died, 2011. **Address:** c/o Midnight Ink, 2143 Wooddale Dr., Woodbury, MT 55125-2989, U.S.A. **Online address:** cricketmcrae@gmail.com

MCRAE, Kenneth Douglas. Canadian (born Canada), b. 1925. **Genres:** History, Language/Linguistics, Politics/Government. **Career:** University of Toronto, lecturer, 1950-52; Carleton University, Department of Political Science, assistant professor, 1955-57, associate professor, 1957-64, professor of political science, 1964-95, professor emeritus of political science, 1996-; Royal Commission on Bilingualism and Biculturalism, research supervisor, 1964-69; Canadian Political Science Association, president, 1978-79; Royal Society of Canada, honorary secretary, 1980-83. Writer. **Publications:** (Contrib.) The Six Bookes of a Commonweale, 1962; (co-author) The Founding of New Societies: Studies in the History of the United States, Latin America, South Africa, Canada and Australia, 1964; Switzerland: Example of Cultural Coexistence, 1964; Conflict and Compromise in Multilingual Societies, vol. I: Switzerland, 1983, vol. II: Belgium, 1986, vol. III: Finland, 1997. EDITOR: The Six Bookes of a Commonweale, 1962; The Federal Capital: Governmental Institutions, 1969; La Capitale fédérale, 1969; Consociational Democracy: Political Accomodation in Segmented Societies, 1974. **Address:** Department of Political Science, Carleton University, Rm. B640, Loeb Bldg., 1125 Colonel By Dr., Ottawa, ON K1S 5B6, Canada.

MCREYNOLDS, Glenna Jean. (Tara Janzen). American (born United States), b. 1953. **Genres:** Young Adult Non-fiction, Romance/Historical, Novels, Science Fiction/Fantasy. **Career:** Writer. **Publications:** South's Honor, 1987; Thieves in the Night, 1987; Stevie Lee, 1989; Dateline: Kydd and Rios, 1990; Blue Dalton, 1990; Outlaw Carson, 1991; Moonlight and Shadows, 1991; A Piece of Heaven, 1992; Shameless, 1992; The Courting Cowboy, 1993; Avenging Angel, 1993; River of Eden, 2002. DRAGON DANIEL SERIES: The Dragon and the Dove, 1994; Dragon's Eden, 1995. CELTIC SAGA SERIES: The Chalice and the Blade, 1997; Dream Stone, 1998; Prince of Time, 2000. AS TARA JANZEN: Crazy Hot, 2005; Crazy Cool, 2005; Crazy Wild, 2006; Crazy Kisses, 2006; Crazy Sweet, 2006; Crazy Love, 2006; Cutting Loose, 2007; On the Loose, 2007; Loose and Easy, 2008; Breaking Loose, 2009; Loose Ends, 2010. **Address:** Random House Inc., 1745 Broadway, 10th Fl., New York, NY 10019, U.S.A. **Online address:** tara@tarajanzen.com

MCSHANE, Mark. (Marc Lovell). British/Australian (born Australia), b. 1929. **Genres:** Novels, Mystery/Crime/Suspense, Humor/Satire, Literary Criticism And History. **Career:** Writer. **Publications:** The Straight and Crooked, 1960; The Passing of Evil, 1961; Séance on a Wet Afternoon, 1961 in US as Séance, 1962; Untimely Ripped, 1962, new ed. 1965, The Girl Nobody Knows, 1965; Night's Evil, 1966; Crimson Madness of Little Doom, 1966; Way to Nowhere, 1967; Ill Met by a Fish Shop on George Street, 1968; Singular Case of the Multiple Dead, 1969; The Man Who Left Well Enough, 1971; Séance for Two, 1972; The Othello Complex, 1974; The Headless Snowman, 1974; Lashed but not Leashed, 1976; Lifetime, 1977; The Hostage Game, 1979; The Halcyon Way, 1982; Just a Face in the Dark, 1987; Once upon a Fairy Tale, 1990; Mourning Becomes the Hangman, 1991. AS MARC LOVELL: Ghost of Megan, 1968 in US as Memory of Megan, 1970; Imitation Thieves, 1971; A Presence in the House, 1972; An Enquiry into the Existence of Vampires, 1974, as Vampires in the Shadows, 1976; Dreamers in a Haunted House, 1975; The Blind Hypnotist, 1976; The Second Vanetti Affair, 1977; The Guardian Spector, 1977; Fog Sinister, 1977; A Voice from the Living, 1978; And They Say You Can't Buy Happiness, 1979; Hand over Mind, 1979; Shadows and Dark Places, 1980; The Spy Game, 1980; The Spy with His Head in the Clouds, 1982; The Last Séance, 1982; Spy on the Run, 1982; Apple Spy in the Sky, 1983; Apple to the Core, 1983; Looking for Kingford, 1983; How Green Was My Apple, 1984; The Only Good Apple in a Barrel of Spies, 1984; The Spy Who Got His Feet Wet, 1985; The Spy Who Barked in the Night, 1985; Good Spies Don't Grow on Trees, 1986; That Great Big Trenchcoat in the Sky, 1988; The Spy Who Fell off the Back of the Bus, 1988; Ethel and the Naked Spy, 1989; Comfort Me with Spies, 1990; The Fourth Nail, 2002; The Man Who Made Love, 2003. **Address:** Collier Associates, 2000 Flat Run Rd., Seaman, OH 45679, U.S.A.

MCTAVISH, Lianne. Canadian (born Canada), b. 1967. **Genres:** Novels. **Career:** University of Alberta, professor of history of art, design & visual culture; University of New Brunswick, faculty member, 1996-; Beaverbrook Art Gallery, associate curator, 2003-07. Writer. **Publications:** Vision: The Marion McCain Atlantic Art Exhibition 2004 = Vision: L'Exposition d'art Atlantique Marion McCain 2004, 2004; Childbirth and the Display of Authority in Early Modern France, 2005. Contributor to books. **Address:** University of Alberta, Edmonton, AB T6G 2R3, Canada. **Online address:** imctavis@ualberta.ca

MCVAUGH, Michael R(ogers). American (born United States), b. 1938. **Genres:** History, Translations. **Career:** University of North Carolina, Department of History, assistant professor, 1964-70, associate professor, 1970-76, professor, 1976-96, William Smith Wells professor, 1996-, now William Smith Wells professor emeritus; Cambridge University, Clare Hall, visiting fellow, 1994; Wellcome Institute for the History of Medicine, research associate, 1999-2000; Oxford University, Magdalen College, visiting fellow, 2000; University of Paris, Ecole Pratique des Hautes Etudes, directeur d'etudes invite, 2001. Writer. **Publications:** (Ed. with L. García-Ballester and J.A. Paniagua) Arnaldi de Villanova Opera Medica Omnia, 1975; (with S.H. Mauskopf) The Elusive Science: Origins of Experimental Psychical Research, 1980; (with L.E. Voigts) A Latin Technical Phlebotomy and Its Middle English Translation, 1984; (with L. García-Ballester and A. Rubio-Vela) Medical Licensing and Learning in 14th-Century Valencia, 1989; Medicine before the Plague: Practitioners and Their Patients in the Crown of Aragon, 1285-1345, 1993; (with R. McVaugh and M. Ayers) Chapel Hill and Elisha Mitchell, the Botanist, 1996; Inventarium sive Chirurgia magna Guigonis de Caulhiaco (Guy de Chauliac), 2 vols., 1997; (ed. with E. Sylla) Texts and Contexts in Ancient and Medieval Science: Studies on the Occasion of John E. Murdoch's Seventieth Birthday, 1997; (ed. and trans. With L. Ferre) Tabula Antidotarii of Armengaud Blaise and Its Hebrew Translation, 2000; (trans. with G. Bos) Maimonides, On Asthma: Critical Editions of Hebrew and Latin Medieval Translations, 2008; (trans.) On Poisons and the Protection against Lethal Drugs, 2009. Works appear in anthologies. Contributor of articles to journals. **Address:** Department of History, University of North Carolina, Hamilton Hall, PO Box 3195, Chapel Hill, NC 27599-3195, U.S.A. **Online address:** mcvaugh@email.unc.edu

MCVEY, Vicki. (Vicki Dow). American (born United States), b. 1946. **Genres:** Environmental Sciences/Ecology, Geography, Children's Non-fiction, Education. **Career:** Institute of Arctic and Alpine Research, cartographer and technical illustrator, 1975-79; Mountain Environmental Atlas: The Indian Peaks Area, Front Range, coordinator and chief cartographer, 1979-82; University of Colorado, Department of Geography, research and teaching assistant, 1982-84; freelance writer, 1987-; Arvada Center, presenter of hands-on workshops for children on maps and mapping, 1991-92; University of Colorado, Center for Geographic Education, Department of Geography, consultant in geographic education, 1991-92; WovenWord Press, head editor/book designer. **Publications:** The Sierra Club Wayfinding Book, 1989; (co-author) Spaceship Earth: Flight Instructor's Log Book, 1991; The Sierra Club Book of Weatherwisdom, 1991; The Sierra Club Kid's Guide to Planet Care & Repair, 1993; Las Companeras: Women in the Nicaraguan Revolution, 1994; (with D.L. Brook) Shifting Focus: A Handbook for ITV Educators, 2000. AS VICKI DOW: (contrib.) Mountain Research and Development and Geobotanical Atlas of the Prudhoe Bay Region. **Address:** WovenWord Press, 811 Mapleton Ave., Boulder, CO 80304, U.S.A.

MCWHIRTER, George. Canadian/Irish (born Ireland), b. 1939. **Genres:** Novels, Novellas/Short Stories, Poetry, Translations. **Career:** Kilkeel Secondary School, assistant master, 1962-64; Bangor Grammar School, assistant master, 1964-65; University of Barcelona, English teacher, 1965-66; Alberni Secondary School, English teacher, 1966-68; Prism Intl., managing editor, 1968-69, poetry editor, 1970-76, co-editor, 1976-77, advisory editor, 1977-2005; University of British Columbia, assistant professor, 1970-76, associate professor, 1976-82, professor of creative writing, 1982-2005, chairman of department, 1983-93, professor emeritus, 2005-; Words from Inside, editor, 1974-75; Vancouver Pacific Dolphins, treasurer, 1992-93. **Publications:** SHORT STORIES: Bodyworks, 1974; God's Eye, 1981; Coming to Grips with Lucy, 1982; A Bad Day to Be Winning, 1991; Musical Dogs, 1996. POETRY: Catalan Poems, 1971; Bloodlight for Malachi McNair, 1974; Queen of the Sea, 1976; Twenty-Five, 1978; The Island Man, 1981; Fire before Dark, 1983; A Staircase for All Souls, 1992; Incubus, 1995; Fab and Other Poems, 1997; Ovid in Saskatchewan, 1998; The Book of Contradictions, 2002; Incorrection, 2007; (trans.) H. Aridjis, Poemas Solares (title means: 'Solar Poems'), 2010. NOVELS: Paula Lake, 1984; Cage, 1987; The Listeners, 1991.

OTHER: Columbuscade, 1974; Anachronicles, 2008. EDITOR: (and trans.) The Selected Poems of Jose Emilio Pacheco, 1987; (and contrib.) Where Words Like Monarchs Fly (anthology of Mexican poets), 1998; (and trans.) Eyes to See Otherwise: The Selected Poems of Homero Aridjis, 1960-2000, 2000; A Verse Map of Vancouver, 2009; Too Tall for You, forthcoming. Contributor to periodicals. **Address:** Department of Creative Writing, University of British Columbia, Buchanan, Rm. E462, 1866 Main Mall, Vancouver, BC V6T 1Z1, Canada. **Online address:** mcwhirte@unixg.ubc.ca

MCWHORTER, John H. American (born United States), b. 1965. **Genres:** Language/Linguistics, Sociology, Social Sciences. **Career:** University of California, faculty in linguistics, 1993-94, associate professor of linguistics, 1995-; Cornell University, assistant professor of linguistics, 1994-95; Manhattan Institute for Policy Research, senior fellow, City Journal, contributing editor; Stanford University, Stanford Humanities Center, fellow. **Publications:** LINGUISTICS: Towards a New Model of Creole Genesis, 1997; The Word on the Street: Fact and Fable about American English, 1998; (ed.) Language Change and Language Contact in Pidgins and Creoles, 1999; The Missing Spanish Creoles: Recovering the Birth of Plantation Contact Languages, 2000; Spreading the Word: Language and Dialect in America, 2000; The Power of Babel: A Natural History of Language, 2001; Defining Creole, 2005; Language Interrupted: Signs of Non-Native Acquisition in Standard Language Grammars, 2007; Our Magnificent Bastard Tongue: The Untold Story of English, 2008. SOCIOLOGY: Losing the Race: Self-Sabotage in Black America, 2000; Authentically Black: Essays for the Black Silent Majority, 2002; Doing Our Own Thing: The Degradation of Language and Music and Why We Should, Like, Care, 2003; Winning the Race: Beyond the Crisis in Black America, 2005; All About the Beat: Why Hip-Hop Can't Save Black America, 2008; What Language Is: And What It Isn't And What It Could Be, 2011; Linguistic Simplicity and Complexity: Why Do Languages Undress?, 2011. Contributor of articles to journals. **Address:** Manhattan Institute for Policy Research Inc., 1203 Dwinelle Hall, 52 Vanderbilt Ave., New York, NY 10017, U.S.A. **Online address:** johnmcw@socrates.berkeley.edu

MCWILLIAM, Candia. British/Scottish (born Scotland), b. 1955. **Genres:** Novels, Writing/Journalism. **Career:** Vogue Magazine, staff, 1976-79; Slade, Bluff and Bigg (advertising agency), staff, 1979-81. Writer. **Publications:** A Case of Knives (novel), 1988; Soho Square II, 1989; A Little Stranger (novel), 1989; Revenge, 1990; Storia 4, 1990; A Roomful of Birds, 1991; The Devil and Dr. Tuberose, 1992; Femmes de Siecle, 1992; The Pleasure of Reading, 1992; Looking for the Spark, 1994, Debatable Land (novel), 1994; Change of Use, 1996; Wait til I Tell You, 1997; Shorts 2: The Macallan, Scotland on Sunday Short Story Collection, 1999; What to Look for in Winter: A Memoir in Blindness, 2010. Works appear in anthologies. Contributor to periodicals. **Address:** c/o Lynn Nesbit, Janklow & Nesbit Associates, 598 Madison Ave., New York, NY 10022, U.S.A.

MCWILLIAMS, Karen. (K. J. McWilliams). American (born United States), b. 1943. **Genres:** Children's Fiction, Young Adult Fiction, Adult Nonfiction, Children's Non-fiction, Novels. **Career:** Placerville and Redlands, grade-school teacher, 1966-69; Department of Defense Overseas Schools, staff, 1969-77; St. Croix, school librarian, 1977-83; writer, 1983-. **Publications:** Pirates, 1989; Writer's Handbook, 1994; Once upon a Time, 1997. MIDDLE-GRADE NOVELS AS K.J. McWILLIAMS: The Journal of Leroy Jeremiah Jones, a Fugitive Slave, 2001; The Diary of a Slave Girl, Ruby Jo, 2002; The Journal of Darien Dexter Duff, An Emancipated Slave, 2002. **Address:** 4345 27th Ct. SW, Ste. 104, Naples, FL 34116-7977, U.S.A. **Online address:** ksophiedog@aol.com

MCWILLIAMS, K. J. *See* **MCWILLIAMS, Karen.**

MCWILLIAMS, Margaret (Ann Edgar). American (born United States), b. 1929. **Genres:** Food And Wine, Medicine/Health, Cultural/Ethnic Topics, Travel/Exploration. **Career:** California State University, assistant professor, 1961-66, associate professor, 1966-68, professor of home economics, 1968-92, chairman of department, 1968-76, professor emeritus of food and nutrition, 1992-. Writer. **Publications:** Food Fundamentals, 1966, 10th ed., 2012; Nutrition for the Growing Years, 1967, 5th ed., 1995; (with L. Kotschevar) Understanding Food, 1969; (with L. Davis) Food for You, 1971, 2nd ed., 1972; (with F.J. Stare) Living Nutrition, 1973, 4th ed., 1984; Meatless Cookbook, 1973; (with F.J. Stare) Nutrition for Good Health: Eating Less and Living Longer!, 1974, 2nd ed., 1982; Reflections, 1976; Illustrated Guide to Food Preparation, 3rd ed., 1976, 11th ed., 2012; Experimental Foods Laboratory Manual, 1977, 7th ed., 2011; (with H. Paine) Modern Food Preservation, 1977; Fundamentals of Meal Management, 1978, 5th ed., 2009; (with H. Heller) World of Nutrition, 1984; Parents' Nutrition Book, 1986; Foods: Experimental Perspectives, 1989, 7th ed., 2011; Lifelong Nutrition, 2001; Food Around the World: A Cultural Perspective, 2003, 3rd ed., 2010; Foreign Food Adventures, 2012. **Address:** PO Box 220, Redondo Beach, CA 90277, U.S.A. **Online address:** mmcwredondo@aol.com

MCWILLIE, Judith M. American (born United States), b. 1946. **Genres:** History. **Career:** University of Georgia, Lamar Dodd School of Art, professor of drawing and painting, 1974-, now professor emeritus; INTAR Latin American Gallery, curator of exhibitions, 1989-92; Exhibitions Intl., consultant. Writer. **Publications:** (Contrib.) Another Face of the Diamond: Pathways Through the Black Atlantic South: January 23-March 3, 1989, 1988; (contrib.) The Migrations of Meaning: A Source Book, 1992; (with G. Gundaker) No Space Hidden: The Spirit of African American Yard Work, 2005. Works appear in anthologies. Contributor of articles to periodicals. **Address:** Lamar Dodd School of Art, University of Georgia, Rm. S382, 270 River Rd., Athens, GA 30602-7676, U.S.A. **Online address:** mcwillie@uga.edu

MDA, Zakes. American/South African (born South Africa), b. 1948. **Genres:** Novels, Plays/Screenplays, Poetry. **Career:** Radio Lesotho, program director, 1984-85; National University of Lesotho, Department of English, lecturer in English, 1985-, professor and head, 1991-; University of Lesotho, director and Marotholi Travelling Theatre, founder, 1985-92; University of Durham, writer-in-residence, 1991; Yale University, Southern African Research Program, visiting research fellow, 1992-93, visiting professor; University of Vermont, professor of English, 1993-94, visiting professor; University Witwatersrand, School of Dramatic Art, visiting professor, 1994, professor, 1994-95; Market Theatre, dramaturg, 1995; Thapama Productions, director, 1996-; Awunanga, director, 1998-; SingingAfrica.com, director and editor, 2000-; Ohio University, professor of creative writing. **Publications:** PLAYS: We Shall Sing for the Fatherland and other Plays, 1980; And the Girls in Their Sunday Dresses: Four Works, 1993. NOVELS: She Plays with the Darkness, 1995; Ways of Dying, 1995; Melville 67: A Novella for Youth, 1997; The Heart of Redness, 2000; The Madonna of Excelsior, 2004; The Whale Caller, 2005; Cion, 2007; Black Diamond, 2009. POETRY: Bits of Debris: The Poetry of Zakes Mda, 1986. OTHERS: New South African Writing, 1977; We Shall Sing for the Fatherland, 1979; Dead End, 1979; Dark Voices Ring, 1979; The Hill, 1980; Banned: A Play for Radio, 1982; Summer Fires, 1982; Bits of Debris: The Poetry of Zakes Mda, 1986; Joys of War, 1988; The Nun's Romantic Story, 1991; Soho Square, 1992; When People Play People: Development Communication through Theatre, 1993; (comp. and intro.) Four Plays, 1996; (comp. and intro.) Let us Play, 1998; Mintlangu ya Zakes Mda, 2002; Imidlalo yaZakes Mda: SiSwati, 2002; Ditiragatso tsa Zakes Mda: Sesotho sa Leboa, 2002; (with K. Moropa and AALRDISA) Imidlalo kaZakes Mda: isiXhosa, 2002; (with D.B.Z. Ntuli and AALRDISA) Imidlalo kaZakes Mda: isiZulu, 2002; Fools, Bells and the Habit of Eating, 2002; Imidlalo Kazakes Mda, Dzidirama dza, 2003; Sometimes there is a Void, 2011. **Address:** Department of English, Ohio University, 365 Ellis, 120 Chubb Hall, Athens, OH 45701-2979, U.S.A. **Online address:** mda@ohio.edu

MEACOCK, Heather. British (born England), b. 1949. **Genres:** Anthropology/Ethnology, Theology/Religion, Philosophy. **Career:** St. Bernard's Preparatory School, teacher and coordinator of history curriculum, 1986-95, 1997-; Brunel University, senior lecturer in religious studies and religious education, 1995-96; La Sainte Union College of Higher Education, senior lecturer in religious education, 1995-97; Birbeck College, part-time lecturer, 2000-06; Anglia Ruskin University, senior lecturer, pathway leader for BA learning and teaching. Writer. **Publications:** An Anthropological Approach to Theology: A Study of John Hick's Theology of Religious Pluralism toward Ethical Criteria for a Global Theology of Religions, 2000. Contributor to periodicals. **Address:** Anglia Ruskin University, East Rd., Cambridge, CB1 1PT, England. **Online address:** heather.meacock@anglia.ac.uk

MEAD, Chris. American (born United States), b. 1959. **Genres:** Biography, Sports/Fitness, Autobiography/Memoirs. **Career:** Honorable Joseph H. Young, law clerk, 1985-86; Williams & Connolly, associate, 1986-89; District of Maryland, assistant U.S. attorney, 1989-94; District of Columbia, special assistant U.S. attorney, 1994; London & Mead, partner, 1994-. Writer. **Publications:** Champion: Joe Louis, Black Hero in White America, 1985; Joe

Louis: Black Champion in White America, 2009. **Address:** London & Mead, 1225 19th St. NW, Ste. 320, Washington, DC 20009, U.S.A. **Online address:** cmead@londonandmead.com

MEAD, Christopher Curtis. American (born United States), b. 1953. **Genres:** Architecture, Art/Art History, History, Urban Studies. **Career:** University of New Mexico, Department of Art and Art History, lecturer, 1980-86, assistant professor, 1986-89, associate chair, 1988-90, associate professor of art and art history, 1989-96, chair, 1992-95, professor of art history and architecture, 1996-, Regents' professor of architecture, special assistant, 2004, School of Architecture and Planning, Architecture Program, joint faculty, 1995-2003, Department of Art and Art History, professor, 2004-, College of Fine Arts, interim dean, 2001-02, dean, 2004-09, University Art Museum, adjunct curator, 1986-2001. Writer. **Publications:** Space for the Continuous Present in the Residential Architecture of Bart Prince, 1989; (ed. and intro.) The Architecture of Robert Venturi, 1989; Houses by Bart Prince: An American Architecture for the Continuous Present, 1991; Charles Garnier's Paris Opera: Architectural Empathy and the Renaissance of French Classicism, 1991; The Architecture of Bart Prince: A Pragmatics of Place, 1999, rev. ed., 2010; Roadcut: The Architecture of Antoine Predock, 2011; Making Modern Paris: Victor Baltard's Central Markets and the Urban Practice of Architecture, 2012. Contributor of articles to books and periodicals. **Address:** School of Architecture and Planning, University of New Mexico, George Pearl Hall, MSC04 2530, 1 University of New Mexico, Albuquerque, NM 87131-0001, U.S.A. **Online address:** ccmead@unm.edu

MEAD, Jane. American (born United States), b. 1958. **Genres:** Poetry. **Career:** Wake Forest University, poet-in-residence and associate professor of English, 1996-; New England College, faculty; Colby College, faculty; Drew University, Caspersen School of Graduate Studies, faculty. **Publications:** The Lord and the General Din of the World, 1996; House of Poured-Out Waters, 2001; The Usable Field, 2008; Liminal, forthcoming. **Address:** Caspersen School of Graduate Studies, Drew University, 115 Samuel W. Bowne Hall, 36 Madison Ave., Madison, NJ 07940, U.S.A.

MEAD, Philip (Stirling). Australian (born Australia), b. 1953. **Genres:** Poetry, Literary Criticism And History. **Career:** University of Melbourne, Lockie lecturer in Australian Writing, 1987-95; Meanjin Quarterly Magazine, poetry editor, 1987-94; University of Tasmania, senior lecturer in English, 1995-, associate professor and coordinator of English; University of Western Australia, Winthrop Professor of Australian literature, Humanities and Social Sciences Research Committee, chair, 2009-10, Ludwig Hirschfeld-Mack visiting chair. **Publications:** POETRY: Songs from Another Country, 1975; Be Faithful to Go: Poems, 1980; The Spring-Mire: Poems, 1982; This River Is in the South, 1984. EDITOR: (with G. Murnane and J. Lee) The Temperament of Generations: Fifty Years of Writing in Meanjin, 1990; (with J. Tranter) The Penguin Book of Modern Australian Poetry, 1991; (with J. Tranter) Bloodaxe Book of Modern Australian Poetry, 1994; Kenneth Slessor: Critical Readings, 1997; (intro.) Hardening of the Light: Selected Poems, 2006. **Address:** English and Cultural Studies, The University of Western Australia, 35 Stirling Hwy., Crawley, WA 6009, Australia. **Online address:** philip.mead@uwa.edu.au

MEAD, Rebecca. American/British (born England), b. 1966. **Genres:** Young Adult Non-fiction, Cultural/Ethnic Topics, Social Sciences. **Career:** New York (magazine), fact-checker, contributing editor; New Yorker (magazine), staff writer, 1997-. **Publications:** One Perfect Day: The Selling of the American Wedding (nonfiction), 2007. **Address:** The New Yorker, 4 Times Sq., New York, NY 10036, U.S.A. **Online address:** rebecca@rebeccamead.com

MEADE, Glenn. Irish (born Ireland), b. 1957?. **Genres:** Novels, Criminology/True Crime, Westerns/Adventure. **Career:** Irish Times, journalist; Irish Independent, journalist. **Publications:** NOVELS: Brandenburg, 1994; Snow Wolf, 1995; The Sands of Sakkara, 1999; Resurrection Day, 2002; Web of Deceit, 2004; The Devil's Disciple, 2006; The Second Messiah, 2011; Anatomy of a Story: The Romanov Conspiracy, 2012. Contributor to periodicals. **Address:** St. Martin's Press, 175 5th Ave., New York, NY 10010-7703, U.S.A. **Online address:** info@glennmeadeauthor.com

MEADER, Jonathan. American (born United States), b. 1943. **Genres:** Art/Art History, Travel/Exploration. **Career:** Artist and print maker, 1969-; writer, 1995-. **Publications:** The Wordless Travel Book, 1995; (ed.) In Praise of Women, 1997. **Address:** PO Box 97, Mill Valley, CA 94942, U.S.A. **Online address:** art@jmeader.com

MEADOWS, Mark Stephen. American (born United States), b. 1968. **Genres:** History. **Career:** Writer. **Publications:** Pause & Effect: The Art of Interactive Narrative, 2003; I, Avatar: The Culture and Consequences of Having a Second Life, 2008; Tea Time with Terrorists: A Motorcycle Journey into the Heart of Sri Lanka's Civil War, 2010; We, Robot: Skywalker's Hand, Blade Runners, Iron Man, Slutbots, and How Fiction Became Fact, 2011. Contributor to periodicals. **Address:** Los Angeles, CA , U.S.A. **Online address:** mail@markmeadows.com

MEAGHER, Timothy J. American (born United States), b. 1949. **Genres:** History, Theology/Religion, Cultural/Ethnic Topics. **Career:** Archives of the Archdiocese of Boston, assistant archivist; Catholic University of America, associate professor and university archivist. Writer. **Publications:** NONFICTION: From Paddy to Studs: Irish-American Communities in the Turn of the Century Era, 1880 to 1920, 1986; (ed. and intro.) Urban American Catholicism: The Culture and Identity of the American Catholic People, 1988; (ed. with R.H. Bayor) The New York Irish, 1996; Inventing Irish America: Generation, Class, and Ethnic Identity in a New England City, 1880-1928, 2001; The Columbia Guide to Irish American History, 2005. **Address:** Department of History, Catholic University of America, 101 Cardinal Hall W, Washington, DC 20064, U.S.A. **Online address:** meagher@cua.edu

MEAKER, Marijane (Agnes). Also writes as Ann Aldrich, Mary James, Vin Packer, M. E. Kerr. American (born United States), b. 1927. **Genres:** Novels, Young Adult Fiction, Gay And Lesbian Issues, Young Adult Non-fiction, Children's Fiction, Children's Non-fiction, Adult Non-fiction. **Career:** E.P. Dutton, assistant file clerk, 1949-50; freelance writer, 1949-; Commercial Manhattan Central High School, writing teacher, 1968; Ashawagh Hall Writers' Workshop, founding member, 1982. **Publications:** FICTION FOR YOUNG ADULTS AS M.E. KERR: Dinky Hocker Shoots Smack!, 1972; If I Love You, Am I Trapped Forever?, 1973; The Son of Someone Famous, 1974; Is That You, Miss Blue?, 1975; Love Is a Missing Person, 1975; I'll Love You When You're More Like Me, 1977; Gentlehands, 1978; Little Little, 1981; What I Really Think of You, 1982; Me, Me, Me, Me, Me: Not A Novel, 1983; Him She Loves?, 1984; I Stay Near You: 1 Story in 3, 1985; Night Kites, 1986; Fell, 1987; Fell Back, 1989; Fell Down, 1991; Linger, 1993; Deliver Us from Evie, 1995; Hello, I Lied: A Novel, 1997; Blood on the Forehead: What I Know about Writing, 1998; What Became of Her: A Novel, 2000; The Books of Fell, 2001; Slap Your Sides: A Novel, 2001; Snakes Don't Miss Their Mothers: A Novel, 2003; Your Eyes in Stars: A Novel, 2006; Someone Like Summer, 2007. AS ANN ALDRICH: We Walk Alone, 1955; We, Too, Must Love, 1958; Carol in a Thousand Cities, 1960; We Two Won't Last, 1963; Take a Lesbian to Lunch, 1972. FICTION AS MARY JAMES: Shoebag, 1990; The Shuteyes, 1993; Frankenlouse, 1994; Shoebag Returns, 1996. NOVELS AS M.J. MEAKER: Sudden Endings, 1964; Hometown, 1967. AS MARIJANE MEAKER: Game of Survival, 1968; Shockproof Sydney Skate, 1972; Highsmith: A Romance of the 1950s, 2003. NOVELS AS VIN PACKER: Dark Intruder, 1952; Spring Fire, 1952; Look Back to Love, 1953; Come Destroy Me, 1954; Whisper His Sin, 1954; The Thrill Kids, 1955; Dark Don't Catch Me, 1956; The Young and Violent, 1956; 3 Day Terror, 1957; The Evil Friendship, 1958; 5:45 to Suburbia, 1958; The Twisted Ones, 1959; The Damnation of Adam Blessing, 1961; The Girl on the Best Seller List, 1961; Something in the Shadows, 1961; Intimate Victims, 1962; Alone at Night, 1963; The Hare in March, 1967; Don't Rely on Gemini, 1969; Scott Free, 2007. **Address:** c/o Eugene Winick, McIntosh & Otis Inc., 475 5th Ave., New York, NY 10017-6220, U.S.A. **Online address:** mekerr13@aol.com

MEANEY, John. (Thomas Blackthorne). British (born England), b. 1957?. **Genres:** Young Adult Fiction, Novels, Science Fiction/Fantasy. **Career:** Educator and writer. **Publications:** NULAPEIRON SEQUENCE: Context, 2005; Paradox, 2005; To Hold Infinity, 2006; Resolution, 2006. TRISTOPOLIS: Bone Song, 2008; Dark Blood, 2008 in US as Black Blood, 2009; Absorption, 2010; (as Thomas Blackthorne) Edge, 2010; (as Thomas Blackthorne) Point, 2011; Transmission, 2012. **Address:** Bantam Books, 20 Vauxhall Bridge Rd., London, GL SW1V 2SA, England. **Online address:** johnmeaney@johnmeaney.com

MEANS, D. Bruce. American (born United States), b. 1941. **Genres:** Natural History, Sciences, Adult Non-fiction. **Career:** Tall Timbers Research Station, research biologist, 1970-74, assistant director, 1974-77, director, 1978-84, executive director, 1984; Florida State University, adjunct assistant professor, 1976-82, adjunct associate professor, 1982-89, adjunct professor of biology, 1989; Florida State Museum, adjunct curator of herpetology, 1984-87; Smithsonian Institution, research associate in zoology, 1989-92; Coastal Plains Institute and Land Conservancy, founder, president and executive director, 1984-. Writer. **Publications:** NONFICTION: The Status of Desmognathus Brimleyorum Stejneger and an Analysis of the Genus Desmognathus (Amphibia, Urodela) in Florida, 1974; (with S.H. Wolfe and J.A. Reidenauer) An Ecological Characterization of the Florida Panhandle, 1988; (with E. Whitney and A. Rudloe) Priceless Florida: Natural Ecosystems and Native Species, 2004; (with J. Valentine) Florida Magnificent Wilderness: State Lands, Parks and Natural Areas, 2006; Stalking the Plumed Serpent and Other Adventures in Herpetology, 2008. Contributor of articles to periodicals. **Address:** Coastal Plains Institute and Land Conservancy, 1313 North Duval St., Tallahassee, FL 32303, U.S.A. **Online address:** means@bio.fsu.edu

MEANS, Howard. (Howard Bursk Means). American (born United States), b. 1944. **Genres:** Military/Defense/Arms Control, Politics/Government, Novels. **Career:** Chronicle of Higher Education, special projects editor, 1975-77; Washingtonian, senior writer, 1977-82, senior editor, 1989-2000; Orlando Sentinel, columnist, 1982-89, critic-at-large; King Features Syndicate, columnist. **Publications:** (Ed. with P.W. Semas) Faculty Collective Bargaining, 1976; (contrib.) Washington, the District and Beyond, 1987; Colin Powell: Soldier/Statesman-Statesman/Soldier, 1992; (with J. Taylor and W. Wacker) 500-Year Delta: What Happens after What Comes Next, 1997; (with J. Taylor and W. Wacker) Visionary's Handbook: Nine Paradoxes That Will Shape the Future of Your Business, 2000; Money & Power: The History of Business, 2001; (with S. Sheehan) The Banana Sculptor, the Purple Lady, and the All-Night Swimmer: Hobbies, Collecting, and Other Passionate Pursuits, 2002; (with L.J. Freeh) My FBI: Bringing Down the Mafia, Investigating Bill Clinton, and Fighting the War on Terror, 2006; Avenger Takes His Place: Andrew Johnson and the 45 Days That Changed the Nation, 2006; Johnny Appleseed: The Man, the Myth, the American Story, 2011. NOVELS: CSA-Confederate States of America: A Novel, 1998. **Address:** c/o Brian Ulicky, Simon & Schuster Inc., 1230 Ave. of the Americas, New York, NY 10020-1513, U.S.A. **Online address:** howardmeans@yahoo.com

MEANS, Howard Bursk. *See* **MEANS, Howard.**

MEARES, Leonard F. *See* **WHITEHEAD, David (Henry).**

MEARNS, Barbara (Crawford). British/Scottish (born Scotland), b. 1955. **Genres:** History, Sciences, Biography, Homes/Gardens, Autobiography/Memoirs. **Career:** Crichton Royal Hospital, Child Psychiatry Department, occupational therapist, 1976-80, 1984-85, biohistorical researcher and writer, 1985-; Carnsalloch Cheshire Home, occupational therapist, 1982-83; A Rocha (Christians in Conservation), international administrator, 1997-. **Publications:** WITH R. MEARNS: Biographies for Birdwatchers: The Lives of Those Commemorated in Western Palearctic Bird Names, 1988; Audubon to Xantus: The Lives of Those Commemorated in North American Bird Names, 1992; The Bird Collectors, 1998; John Kirk Townsend-Collector of Audubon's Birds and Mammals, 2007. Contributor to periodicals. **Address:** A Rocha, 3 Hooper St., Cambridge, CB CB1 2NZ, England. **Online address:** international@arocha.org

MEARNS, Richard (James). Scottish/Malaysian (born Malaysia), b. 1950. **Genres:** Biology, History, Travel/Exploration, Biography, Sports/Fitness. **Career:** Royal Society for the Protection of Birds and Nature Conservancy Council, staff, 1982-85; Dumfries and Galloway Council, countryside ranger, 1986-. Writer. **Publications:** (With B. Mearns) Biographies for Birdwatchers: The Lives of Those Commemorated in Western Palearctic Bird Names, 1988; (with H. Brown and R. McOwan) Great Walks: Scotland, 1989; (with B. Mearns) Audubon to Xantus: The Lives of Those Commemorated in North American Bird Names, 1992; (with B. Mearns) The Bird Collectors, 1998; (with B. Mearns) John Kirk Townsend: Collector of Audubon's Western Birds and Mammals, 2007. Contributor to periodicals. **Address:** Connansknowe, Kirkton, DG DG1 1SX, Scotland.

MEARS, Emira. Canadian (born Canada), b. 1976?. **Genres:** Business/Trade/Industry, Administration/Management. **Career:** Raised Eyebrow Web Studio Inc., founder and web strategist, 2000-. Writer. **Publications:** The Boss of You: Everything a Woman Needs to Know to Start, Run, and Maintain Her Own Business, 2008. **Address:** Raised Eyebrow Web Studio Inc., 209-163 W Hastings St., Vancouver, BC V6B 1H5, Canada. **Online address:** thebosses@laurenandemira.com

MEARS, Gillian. Australian (born Australia), b. 1964. **Genres:** Novels, Novellas/Short Stories, Romance/Historical, Theatre, Essays, Literary Criticism And History. **Career:** Writer. **Publications:** Ride a Cock Horse, 1989; Fineflour, 1990; The Mint Lawn (novel), 1991; The Grass Sister (novel), 1995; Collected Stories, 1997; Paradise Is a Place, 1997; A Map of the Gardens: Stories, 2002; Foal's Bread, 2011; The Cat with the Coloured Tail, forthcoming; Remenant, forthcoming. Contributor to periodicals. **Address:** c/o Gaby Naher, The Naher Agency, PO Box 249, Paddington, NW 2021, Australia.

MEASHAM, Donald Charles. American/British (born England), b. 1932. **Genres:** Poetry, Literary Criticism And History, inspirational/Motivational Literature, Autobiography/Memoirs. **Career:** Teacher, 1956-63; Hockley County Secondary School, head of English department, 1960-63; Matlock College of Higher Education, principal lecturer in English, 1963-69, head of department, 1969-83; Derbyshire College of Higher Education, head of school of humanities, 1983-90; Staple magazine, founder and editor, 1983-. **Publications:** EDITOR: Fourteen: Autobiography of an Age Group, 1965; English Now and Then, 1965; The Personal Element in Prose and Poetry, 1968; Sentiment and Sentimental Psychology in Jane Austen, 1971; Lawrence and the Real England, 1985; John Ruskin: The Last Chapter, 1989. COMPILER: Leaving: An Anthology for the Last Year at School, 1965; Larger than Life, 1966. **Address:** Staple Magazine, 114 - 116 St., Stephen's Rd., Sneinton, SM NG2 4JS, England.

MEATH, Michael. *See* **MARQUIS, Max.**

MEBUS, Scott. American (born United States), b. 1974. **Genres:** Novels, Romance/Historical, Literary Criticism And History, Young Adult Fiction. **Career:** Music Television, producer; Video Hits One, producer, freelance music producer, editor; RPI University, artist in residency. **Publications:** Booty Nomad, 2003; The Big Happy: A Novel, 2006; Gods of Manhattan, 2008; Gods of Manhattan: Spirits in the Park, 2009; Gods of Manhattan: The Sorcerer's Secret, 2010. **Address:** c/o David Dunton, Harvey Klinger Agency, 301 W 53rd St., Ste. 11V, New York, NY 10019-4532, U.S.A.

MECHLING, Lauren. American (born United States), b. 1978?. **Genres:** Novels. **Career:** Writer. **Publications:** YOUNG-ADULT NOVELS: (with Laura Moser) The Rise and Fall of a 10th-Grade Social Climber, 2005; All Q, No A: More Tales of a 10th-Grade Social Climber, 2006; Foreign Exposure: The Social Climber Abroad, 2007; Dream Girl, 2008. Contributor to periodicals. **Address:** Brooklyn, NY , U.S.A. **Online address:** authors@socialclimberbooks.com

MECKEL, Richard A(lan). American (born United States), b. 1948. **Genres:** History, Medicine/Health. **Career:** Brown University, lecturer, 1979-82, assistant professor, 1982-88, associate professor of American civilization, 1989-. Writer. **Publications:** Save the Babies: American Public Health Reform and the Prevention of Infant Mortality, 1850-1929, 1990; (ed. with J. Golden and H.M. Prescott) Children and Youth in Sickness and in Health: A Historical Handbook and Guide, 2004; Conserving the Young: Child Health Policy in 20th Century America, forthcoming; Classrooms and Clinics: The American School Hygiene Movement, forthcoming. Contributor to journals. **Address:** Department of American Civilization, Brown University, 82 Waterman St., PO Box 1892, Providence, RI 02912, U.S.A. **Online address:** richard_meckel@brown.edu

MECKELSON, Doug. American (born United States), b. 1962?. **Genres:** Self Help, Philosophy. **Career:** Elder Wisdom Circle, founder, 2001, president. Writer. **Publications:** (With D. Haithman) The Elder Wisdom Circle Guide for a Meaningful Life: Seniors Across America Offer Advice to the Next Generations, 2007. **Address:** Elder Wisdom Circle, 734 Tampico, Walnut Creek, CA 94598-2929, U.S.A.

MEDDEB, Abdelwahab. French (born France), b. 1946?. **Genres:** Novels, Poetry. **Career:** Sinbad Editions, literary consultant, director and advisor, 1974-87; University of Geneva, visiting professor, 1989-90; European University, Institute of Florence, visiting researcher, 1991; Transcultura Foundation, director of research, 1991; SUPELEC, associate professor, 1991-93; Intersignes, co-editor, 1992-94; UNESCO, consultant, 1993; Yale University, visiting professor, 1993; University of Paris V Rene Descartes, research professor, 1993-94; University of Paris X at Nanterre, professor of comparative literature, 1995-. Educator and writer. **Publications:** Talismano: A Roman, 1979; Phantasia: A Roman, 1986; Tombeau d'Ibn Arabi, 1987; Les Dits de Bistami, 1989; La Gazelle et L'enfant, 1992; Méditerranées, Portraits de Lieux Avec Mémoire, 1995; (contrib.) En Tunisie, 1997; Aya Dans les Villes, 1999; La Maladie de l'Islam, 2002; Zloupotreba islama, 2003; Face Á l'Islam, 2004; Islam and Its Discontents, 2004; SaigyO, Vers Le Vide: Poèmes, 2004; Occident Vist Des d'Orient, 2005; Contre-prêches: Chroniques, 2006; La conférence de Ratisbonne: Enjeux et Controverses, 2007; Sortir De La Malédiction: L'Islam Entre Civilisation Et Barbarie, 2008; Pari De Civilisation, 2009; (with A. Glucksmann and N. Bacharan) Plus belle histoire de la liberté, 2009; Tombeau of Ibn Arabi and White Traverses, 2010; Jour d'après: dédicaces à Abdelkébir Khatibi, 2010; Talismano, 2011; Printemps de Tunis: la mèi tamorphose de l'histoire, 2011. **Address:** University of Paris X at Nanterre, 200 Ave. de la Republique, Nanterre, 92001, France.

MEDEARIS, John. American (born United States), b. 1963. **Genres:** Politics/Government. **Career:** Boston Phoenix, staff writer, 1986-89; Los Angeles Times, staff writer, 1989-91; California State University, assistant professor of political science, 1999-2001; University of California, assistant professor of political science, 2001-05, associate professor of political science, 2005-. **Publications:** Joseph Schumpeter's Two Theories of Democracy, 2001; Joseph A. Schumpeter, 2009; Democracy Where It's Difficult, forthcoming. Contributor to journals. **Address:** Department of Political Science, University of California, Watkins Hall 2226, 900 University Ave., Riverside, CA 92521, U.S.A. **Online address:** john.medearis@ucr.edu

MEDEIROS, Teresa. American/German (born Germany), b. 1962. **Genres:** Romance/Historical. **Career:** Full-time writer, 1992-; Western State Psychiatric Hospital, nurse. **Publications:** ROMANCE NOVELS: Lady of Conquest, 1989; Shadows and Lace, 1990; Heather and Velvet, 1992; Once an Angel, 1993; A Whisper of Roses, 1993; Thief of Hearts, 1994; Fairest of Them All, 1995; Breath of Magic, 1996; Touch of Enchantment, 1997; Nobody's Darling, 1998; Charming the Prince, 1999; The Bride and the Beast, 2000; A Kiss to Remember, 2001; One Night of Scandal, 2003; Yours until Dawn, 2004, After Midnight, 2005; The Vampire Who Loved Me, 2006; Some Like It Wicked, 2008; Some Like It Wild, 2009; The Devil Wears Plaid, 2010; Goodnight Tweetheart, 2010; The Pleasure of Your Kiss, 2011; Coming Attractions, 2012. **Address:** c/o Andrea Cirillo, Jane Rotrosen Agency, 318 E 51st St., New York, NY 10022, U.S.A. **Online address:** teresa@teresamedeiros.com

MEDHURST, Martin J. American (born United States), b. 1952. **Genres:** Communications/Media, Politics/Government, Speech/Rhetoric, Reference. **Career:** University of California, assistant professor of rhetoric, 1979-85, associate professor, 1985-88; M.J. Medhurst and Associates, president and chief executive officer, 1981-87; Texas A&M University, associate professor of speech communication, 1988-91, professor, 1991-2003, Speech Communication Department, associate head, 1991-98; George Bush School of Government and Public Service, Center for Presidential Studies, Program in Presidential Rhetoric, coordinator, 1993-2003; Rhetoric and Public Affairs Journal, editor, 1998-; Baylor University, distinguished professor of rhetoric and communication, professor of political science, 2003-. **Publications:** Dwight D. Eisenhower: Strategic Communicator, 1993; (co-author) Cold War Rhetoric: Strategy, Metaphor, and Ideology, 1990. EDITOR AND CONTRIBUTOR: (with T.W. Benson) Rhetorical Dimensions in Media: A Critical Casebook, 1984, 2nd ed., 1991; (with A. Gonzalez and T.R. Peterson) Communication and the Culture of Technology, 1990; Landmark Essays on American Public Address, 1993; Eisenhower's War of Words: Rhetoric and Leadership, 1994; Beyond the Rhetorical Presidency, 1996; (with H.W. Brands) Critical Reflections on the Cold War: Linking Rhetoric and History, 2000; (with K. Ritter) Presidential Speechwriting: From the New Deal to the Reagan Revolution and Beyond, 2003; Rhetorical Presidency of George H.W. Bush, 2006; (with J.A. Aune) The Prospect of Presidential Rhetoric, 2008; Before the Rhetorical Presidency, 2008; (with S.E. Lucas) Words of a Century: The Top 100 American Speeches, 1900-1999, 2009. Contributor to journals. **Address:** Department of Communication, Baylor University, 213 Marrs McLean, 1 Bear Pl., Ste. 97368, PO Box 97000, Waco, TX 76798-7368, U.S.A. **Online address:** martin_medhurst@baylor.edu

MEDICINE-EAGLE, Brooke. American (born United States), b. 1943. **Genres:** Autobiography/Memoirs. **Career:** Teacher, 1965-68; San Francisco State University, professor of Native American studies, 1975-76; teacher and consultant, 1978-. Writer. **Publications:** Buffalo Woman Comes Singing: The Spirit Song of a Rainbow Medicine Woman, 1991; The Last Ghost Dance: A Guide for Earth Mages, 2000. Works appear in anthologies. Contributor to periodicals. **Address:** Singing Eagle Enterprises, 1 2nd Ave. E, PO Box C401, Polson, MT 59860-2156, U.S.A. **Online address:** bme@medicineeagle.com

MEDINA, Nico. American (born United States), b. 1982. **Genres:** Novels. **Career:** Gleim Publications, proofreader, 2001-04; Viking Children's Books, associate production editor, 2004-, writer, 2005-. **Publications:** The Straight Road to Kylie, 2007; Fat Hoochie Prom Queen, 2008. **Address:** New York, NY , U.S.A. **Online address:** nico@nicomedina.com

MEDINA, Tony. American (born United States), b. 1966. **Genres:** Poetry, Literary Criticism And History. **Career:** Howard University, associate professor. Poet and activist. **Publications:** POETRY: Emerge and See, 1991; No Noose Is Good Noose, 1996; Sermons from the Smell of a Carcass Condemned to Begging, 1998; Committed to Breathing, 2003; Poets against the Killing Fields, 2008; My Old Man Was Always on the Lam, 2009. YOUNG ADULT AND CHILDREN'S LITERATURE: Christmas Makes Me Think, 2001; DeShawn Days, 2001; Love to Langston, 2002; Follow-Up Letters to Santa from Kids Who Never Got a Response, 2003; I and I: Bob Marley, 2009. EDITOR: (with S.E. Anderson) In Defense of Mumia, 1996; Jessica Care Moore, The Words Don't Fit in My Mouth, 1997; (with D.I.M. Gilbert) Catch the Fire!!! A Cross-Generational Anthology of Contemporary African-American Poetry, 1998; Fast Cities and Objects That Burn, 1999; (with L.R. Rivera) Bum Rush the Page: A Def Poetry Jam, 2001; (with S.A. Bashir and Q.A. Lansana) Role Call: A Generational Anthology of Social and Political Black Art and Literature, 2002; The Subtle Art of Breathing, 2005; (with N. Giovanni, W. Perdomo and M. Scott) Hip Hop Speaks to Children: A Celebration of Poetry with a Beat, 2008. Works appear in anthologies. Contributor to books and journals. **Address:** Department of English, College of Arts and Sciences, Howard University, Washington, DC 20059, U.S.A.

MEDNICK, Kevin. American (born United States), b. 1953?. **Genres:** Novels, Literary Criticism And History, Law. **Career:** Bendall and Mednick, partner. Writer and attorney. **Publications:** An Almost Life, 2007. **Address:** Mike Fila, Himmelrich PR, 3600 Clipper Mill Rd., Ste. 245, Baltimore, MD 21211, U.S.A. **Online address:** kevinsmednick@broadviewnet.net

MEDOFF, Jillian. American (born United States), b. 1963. **Genres:** Novels. **Career:** Novelist. **Publications:** Hunger Point, 1997; Good Girls Gone Bad, 2002; I Couldn't Love You More, 2012. **Address:** Zachary Shuster Harmsworth L.L.C., 1776 Broadway, Ste. 1405, New York, NY 10019, U.S.A. **Online address:** jillianmedoff@gmail.com

MEDOFF, Mark (Howard). American (born United States), b. 1940. **Genres:** Novels, Young Adult Fiction, Plays/Screenplays. **Career:** Capitol Radio Engineering Institute, supervisor of publications, 1962-64; New Mexico State University, instructor, 1966-71, assistant professor, 1971-74, associate professor, 1974-79, professor of English, 1979-93, writer-in-residence, 1966-, dramatist-in-residence, 1975-, head of drama department, 1978-87, head of English department; American Southwest Theatre Co., co-founder, artistic director, 1984-87; University of Houston, professor, 2007-. **Publications:** Doing a Good One for the Red Man, 1969; The Froegle Dictum, 1971; The Waron Tatem, 1972; Four Short Plays (includes Doing a Good One for the Red Man, The Froegle Dictum, The War on Tatem, and The Ultimate Grammar of Life), 1974; (with C. Johnson) The Odyssey of Jeremy Jack, 1974; When You Comin Back, Red Ryder?: A Play in Two Acts, 1974; The Wager: A Play in Three Acts: With Two Short Plays, Doing a Good One for the Red Man, The War on Tatem, 1975; The Kramer, 1976; The Halloween Bandit, 1978; Children of a Lesser God: A Play in Two Acts, 1980; Hands of its Enemy: A Play in Two Acts, 1987; Big Mary: A Play, 1989; Majestic Kid, 1989; Hero Trilogy, 1989; Heart Outright: A Play, 1990; City of Joy, 1992; Dreams of Long Lasting, 1992; Kringle's Window, 1994; Stefanie Hero, 1994; Les Enfants Dusilence, 1994; Homage that Follows, 1995; Stumps, 1995; (with R. Marks) Showdown on Rio Road, 1998; (with P. Treon) Crunch Time, 1998; Gunfighter: A Gulf War Chronicle, 2003; (foreword) Dramaturgy of Mark Medoff: Five Plays Dealing with Deafness and Social Issues, 2004; Tommy J & Sally, 2005; Prymate, 2005. **Address:** c/o Gilbert Parker, William Morris Agency, 1325 Ave. of the Americas, New York, NY 10019, U.S.A. **Online address:** markmedoff@comcast.net

MEDVED, Diane. (Diane C. Elvenstar). American (born United States), b. 1951. **Genres:** Self Help, Human Relations/Parenting, Sociology, Psychology, Politics/Government. **Career:** Writer. **Publications:** (As Diane C. Elvenstar) Children, to Have or Have Not? A Guide to Making and Living with Your Decision, 1982; (as Diane C. Elvenstar) First Comes Love: Deciding

Whether or Not to Get Married, 1983; The Case against Divorce, 1989; (with D. Quayle) American Family: Discovering the Values that Make Us Strong, 1996; (with D. Quayle) Saving Childhood: Protecting Our Children From the National Assault on Innocence, 1998. **Address:** HarperCollins Publishers, 10 E 53rd St., New York, NY 10022-5299, U.S.A.

MEDVEDEV, Grigori. (Grigorii Medvedev). Russian (born Russia), b. 1933?. **Genres:** Novels, Novellas/Short Stories, Technology, Documentaries/ Reportage, Poetry, Engineering. **Career:** Associate with atomic submarines, 1957-63; affiliate with a nuclear power plant, 1964-71; Nuclear Power Plant in Chernobyl, deputy chief engineer, 1971-75; Moscow Institute of Atomic Stations, chief technologist, 1976-78; Soviet Ministry of Energy, deputy director of nuclear power plant construction, 1979-87; writer, 1988-. **Publications:** Impulses (stories), 1986; Operatory: Povest, Rasskazy, 1987; The Moment of a Lifetime (stories), 1988; Mig zhizni: Povesti, Rasskazy, 1988; Nuclear Trouble (stories), 1990; IAdernyĭ Zagar, 1990, rev. ed., 2002; The Truth about Chernobyl, 1991; Energoblok: Povesti, 1991; The Devil of Civilization (stories), 1992; No Breathing Room: The Aftermath of Chernobyl, 1993; Atomnaia Rus: Stikhi, 1996; Tunnel (novel), 1997; Vnutri ia zyka, 2004; Lozîa besmen: roman-trilogiîa, veros, 2006. **Address:** Basic Books, 387 Park Ave. S, New York, NY 10016, U.S.A.

MEDVEDEV, Grigorii. *See* **MEDVEDEV, Grigori.**

MEDVEDEV, Roy (Alexandrovich). Russian (born Russia), b. 1925. **Genres:** History, Literary Criticism And History. **Career:** Teacher, 1951-54; director, 1955-56; Prosveshchenie Publishing House, deputy to editor-in-chief, 1957-61; Research Institute of Vocational Education, Department of Vocational Education, head, 1961-71; freelance writer, 1971-. **Publications:** Let History Judge: The Origins and Consequences, 1971; (with Z.A. Medvedev) Questions of Madness, 1971; (ed.) Politicheskiĭ dnevnik, 1972; On Socialist Democracy, 1975; (with Z.A. Medvedev) Khrushchev: The Years in Power, 1976; Political Essays, 1976; Problems in the Literary Biography of Mikhail Sholokhov, 1977; (ed.) Samizdat Register, 2 vols., 1977-80; The October Revolution, 1979; On Stalin and Stalinism, 1979; On Soviet Dissent, 1980; Nikolai Bukharin: The Last Years, 1980; Leninism and Western Socialism, 1981; All Stalin's Men, 1983; Khrushchev, 1983; An End to Silence: Uncensored Opinion in the Soviet Union; 1984; China and the Superpowers, 1986; (with G. Chiesa) Time of Change, 1990; Brezhnev: A Political Biography, 1991; Lichnost i epokha: politicheskiĭ portret L.I. Brezhneva, 1991; Sviazv remen, 1992; Gensek s Lubianki: Politicheskaia Biografiia IUV Andropova, 1993; Chubaĭs i vaucher: iz istorii rossiĭskoĭ privatizatsii, 1997; Kapitalizm v Rossii, 1998; Politiki i politika Rossii: Vremia i bremia vybora, 1999; Post-Soviet Russia: A Journey Through the Yeltsin Era, 2000; Zagadka Putina, 2000; (with Z.A. Medvedev) The Unknown Stalin, 2001; Vremia Putina?: Rossiia na rubezhe vekov, 2001; (with Z. Medvedev) Neizvestnyĭ Stalin, 2001; (with Z. Medvedev) Izbrannye proizvedeniia, 2002; Vladimir Putin-deĭstvuiushchiĭ president, 2002; Putin, 2002; Sovetskiĭ Soiuz: posledniĭ god zhizni, 2003; Desiat politikov novoĭ Rossii, 2003; (with Z. Medvedev) Solzhenitsyn i Sakharov: dva proroka, 2004; (with Z. Medvedev) The Unknown Stalin: His Life, Death and Legacy, 2004; IUriĭ Andropov: neizvestnoe ob izvestnom, 2004; Putin: Four Years in the Kremlin, 2004; Moskovskaia model IUriia Luzhkova, 2005; Chto chital Stalin?: liudi i knigi: pisatel i kniga v totalitarnom obshchestve, 2005; Blizhniĭ krug Stalina: soratniki vozhdia, 2005; Vladimir Putin: vtoroĭ srok, 2006; Nikita Khrushchev: otets, ili, otchim sovetskoĭ ottepeli?, 2006; Andropov, 2006; Vladimir Putin: tretego sroka ne budet?, 2007; Moskva: Institut ekonomicheskikh strategiĭ: Mezhdunarodnaia akademiia issledovaniĭ budushchego, 2007; Moskva: Institut ekonomicheskikh strategiĭ, 2007; Raskolotaia Ukraina, 2007; Kazakhstanskii proryv, 2007; Politicheskie portrety, 2008; I Urii Luzhkov i Moskva, 2008; Dmitrii Medvedev-Prezident Rossiiskoi Federatsii, 2008; Vladimir Putin: Prodolzhenie Sleduet, 2009; Dmitrii Medvedev: dvoinaia prochnost vlasti, 2009; Sovetskii Soiuz: Poslednie gody zhizni, konets sovetskoi imperii, 2010; Aleksandr Lukashenko: Kontury belorusskoĭ modeli, 2010; Boris El'tsin, 2011. **Address:** PO Box 258, Moscow, 125475, Russia.

MEDVEDEV, Zhores (Alexandrovich). British/Russian (born Russia), b. 1925. **Genres:** Biology, History, Politics/Government, Sociology. **Career:** Moscow Agricultural Academy, senior research scientist, 1951-62; Institute of Medical Radiology, head of laboratory of molecular radiobiology, 1963-69; Institute of Physiology and Biochemistry of Farm Animals, senior research scientist, 1970-72; National Institute for Medical Research, Division of Genetics, senior research scientist, 1973-91, retired, 1991, Experimental Gerontology, associate editor. **Publications:** Protein Biosynthesis and Problem of Heredity, Development, and ageing, 1966; Molekuliarno-geneticheskie mekhanizmy razvitiia, 1968; The Rise and Fall of T.D. Lysenko, 1969; Mezhdunarodnoe sotrudnichestvo uchenykh i natsional'nye granitsy i Taĭna perepiski okhraniaetsia zakonom, 1970; Kto sumasshedshiĭ?, 1971; (with R.A. Medvedev) Question of Madness, 1971; Medvedev Papers: Fruitful Meetings Between Scientists of the World; And, Secrecy of Correspondence is Guaranteed by Law, 1971; Ten Years after Ivan Denisovich, 1973; Desiat let posle Odnogo dnia Ivana Denisovicha, 1973; Secrecy of Correspondence is Guaranteed by Law, 1975; (with R.A. Medvedev) Khrushchev: The Years in Power, 1976; (with A. Roberts) (with A. Roberts) Hazards of Nuclear Power, 1977; Soviet Science, 1978; Nuclear Disaster in the Urals, 1979; Andropov, 1983; Gorbachev, 1986; Soviet Agriculture, 1987; The Legacy of Chernobyl, 1990; Vzlet i padenie Lysenko: Istoriia biologicheskoi diskussii v SSSR, 1929-1966, 1993; (with R. Medvedev) Rossiia i Zapad v kontse XX veka: Glavy iz knigi Putti Rossii, 1997; (with R.A. Medvedev) The Unknown Stalin, 2001; (with R. Medvedev) Neizvestnyĭ Stalin, 2001; (with R. Medvedev) Izbrannye proizvedeniia, 2002; Stalin i evreĭskaia problema: novyĭ analiz, 2003; (with R. Medvedev) Solzhenitsyn i Sakharov: dva proroka, 2004; (with R. Medvedev) The Unknown Stalin: His Life, Death, and Legacy, 2005; (with N. Chomsky) Legacies of Harm, 2007; Poloniĭ v Londone: po sledam rassledovaniia Skotlend-IArda, 2008. **Address:** 4 Osborn Gardens, Mill Hill, London, GL NW7 1DY, England.

MEDWAY, Gareth J. American (born United States) **Genres:** Paranormal, Theology/Religion, History. **Career:** The Fellowship of Isis, priest. Writer. **Publications:** Lure of the Sinister: The Unnatural History of Satanism, 2001. Contributor to periodicals. **Address:** New York University Press, 838 Broadway, 3rd Fl., New York, NY 10003-4812, U.S.A.

MEDWED, Mameve. American (born United States) **Genres:** Novels. **Career:** The Celebrity Register, researcher and writer, 1963; Cambridge Center for Adult Education, instructor for fiction writing workshops, 1979-; Lesley University, Lesley College, mentor for master's degree in fine arts program, 1986-88; Simmons College, Robert M. Gay memorial lecturer, 1996. Writer. **Publications:** NOVELS: Mail, 1997; Host Family, 2000; The End of an Error, 2003; How Elizabeth Barrett Browning Saved my Life, 2006; Of Men and their Mothers, 2008. Contributor of articles to periodicals and newspapers. **Address:** c/o Lisa Bankoff, International Creative Management, 40 W 57th St., New York, NY 10019, U.S.A. **Online address:** mameve@comcast.net

MEE, Susie (B.). American (born United States), b. 1938. **Genres:** Poetry, Novels, Biography. **Career:** Literary Cavalcade, associate editor, 1985-89; Voice, associate editor, 1985-89; New York University, School of Continuing and Professional Studies, part-time assistant professor of creative writing, 1987-; Staten Island College, teacher of poetry workshop, 1995-; Learning Leaders Inc., Authors Read Aloud Program, program specialist, 1999-, director; West 22nd Street Block Association, vice president. Writer and consultant. **Publications:** Stories of the Poets (biographical essays), 1989; The Undertaker's Daughter (poems), 1992; The Girl Who Loved Elvis (novel), 1993; (ed.) Downhome: An Anthology of Southern Women Writers, 1995. **Address:** Authors Read Aloud Program, Learning Leaders Inc., 80 Maiden Ln., 11th Fl., New York, NY 10038, U.S.A.

MEEHAN, Paula. Irish (born Ireland), b. 1955. **Genres:** Plays/Screenplays, Poetry, Music, Novellas/Short Stories. **Career:** South Inner City, literacy organizer, 1984-88; Eastern Washington University, Irish co-coordinator of poetry master classes, 1985-; Arts Council Writers in the Prison Scheme, teacher of writing workshops in prisons, 1986-; Frost Place, poet-in-residence, 1987; Trinity College, writer-in-residence, 1992; National University of Ireland, University College, writer by association, 1992; Verbal Arts Centre, outreach resident for Derry and Antrim counties, 1993; TEAM Theatre in Education, writer-in-residence, 1994. **Publications:** POETRY: Return and No Blame, 1984; Reading the Sky, 1986; The Man Who Was Marked by Winter, 1991; Pillow Talk, 1994; Mysteries of the Home: A Selection of Poems, 1996; Dharmakaya, 2000; Cell: A Play in Two Parts for Four Actors and a Voice, 2000; Three Irish Poets: An Anthology, 2003; Dublin Stories: The Fifth Collection, 2003; Six Sycamores, 2004; Music for Dogs: Work for Radio, 2008; Painting Rain, 2009. **Address:** 7 Moyclare Pk., Baldoyle, Dublin, 13, Ireland. **Online address:** ithaca@eircom.net

MEEINK, Frank. American (born United States), b. 1975?. **Genres:** Autobiography/Memoirs. **Career:** Harmony through Hockey, co-founder; Iowa

Chops, director of fan development. Writer. **Publications:** (With J.M. Roy) Autobiography of a Recovering Skinhead: The Frank Meeink's Story, 2010. **Address:** Admire Entertainment, PO Box 152, Palisades, NY 10964, U.S.A.

MEEKER, Clare Hodgson. American (born United States), b. 1952. **Genres:** Children's Fiction, Children's Non-fiction, Mythology/Folklore. **Career:** KCTS/9, manager of planned giving, 1982-85; Washington Volunteer Lawyers for the Arts, director, 1986-88; Seattle University, grant writer, 1988-90; K-12 Schools, teacher of creative writing workshops. Lawyer. **Publications:** A Tale of Two Rice Birds: A Folktale from Thailand, 1994; Who Wakes Rooster?, 1996; Partner in Revolution: Abigail Adams, 1998; Lootas Little Wave Eater: An Orphaned Sea Otter's Story, 1999; Arctic Journey, 2001; I Could Not Keep Silent: The Life of Rachel Carson, 2001; Hansa, the True Story of an Asian Elephant Baby, 2002; Manorah The Bird Princess, 2007; Soccer Dreams: Playing The Seattle Sounders FC Way, 2011. **Address:** 8035 SE 33rd Pl., Mercer Island, WA 98040, U.S.A. **Online address:** clare@claremeeker.com

MEEKS, Christopher (Nelson). American (born United States), b. 1953. **Genres:** Documentaries/Reportage, Plays/Screenplays, Novels, Children's Fiction. **Career:** Prelude Press, senior editor, 1983-87; California Institute of the Arts, writer and editor, 1987-2000, adjunct professor of critical studies, 1994-2000; Inherit the Earth Technologies, owner, 1990-95; Santa Monica College, adjunct professor of English, 1998-; School of Film Video, adjunct professor, 2000-08; Art Center College of Design, instructor, 2002-; University of California, instructor; Santa Monica College, instructor. **Publications:** On Being a Writer, 1989; Japan: World Partner, 1990; Skydiving, 1991; Roald Dahl: Kids Love His Stories, 1993; Arnold Schwarzenegger: Hard Work Brought Success, 1993; The Middle-Aged Man & The Sea: Stories, 2005; Who Lives? (play), 2006; Months and Seasons (stories), 2008; The Brightest Moon of the Century (novel), 2009; Love At Absolute Zero, 2011; Falling Down Mt. Washington, forthcoming. Contributor to books and periodicals. Works appear in anthologies. **Address:** Department of English, Santa Monica College, 1900 Pico Blvd., Santa Monica, CA 90405, U.S.A. **Online address:** cmeeks@artcenter.edu

MEEKS, Esther MacBain. American (born United States), b. 1921?. **Genres:** Children's Fiction, Songs/Lyrics And Libretti. **Career:** American Society of Composers, script writer; National Broadcasting Co., Recording Division, script writer. **Publications:** Jeff and Mr. James Pond, 1962; Web of Winter, 1967, 5th ed., 1989; Canticles for Christmas, 1969. **Address:** 2911 Oak St., Terre Haute, IN 47803, U.S.A.

MEEKS, Wayne A. American (born United States), b. 1932. **Genres:** Theology/Religion, History, Sociology. **Career:** Ordained Presbyterian minister, 1956; University of Tuebingen, Fulbright fellow, 1956-57; Dartmouth College, instructor in religion, 1964-65; Yale University, United Ministry, university pastor, 1965-66, associate professor, 1969-73, chair of department, 1972-75, professor of religious studies, 1973-, Woolsey professor of biblical studies, 1985-, Woolsey professor emeritus, 1999-, Division of the Humanities, director, 1988-91; Indiana University, assistant professor, 1966-68, associate professor, 1968-69. Writer. **Publications:** Go from Your Fathers House: A College Students Introduction to the Christian Faith, 1964; The Prophet-King: Moses Traditions and the Johannine Christology, 1967; (with R.L. Wilken) Jews and Christians in Antioch in the First Four Centuries of the Common Era, 1978; The First Urban Christians: The Social World of the Apostle Paul, 1983, 2nd ed., 2003; The Moral World of the First Christians, 1986; The Origins of Christian Morality: The First Two Centuries, 1993; In Search of the Early Christians: Selected Essays, 2002; Christ is the Question, 2006. EDITOR: The Writings of St. Paul, 1972, (with J.T. Fitzgerald) 2nd ed., 2007; (with F.O. Francis) Conflict at Colossae, 1972; (with J. Jervell) God's Christ and His People, 1977; Zur Soziologie des Urchristentums, 1979; Gods and the One God, 1986; The New Testament in Its Social Environment, 1988; (with D.L. Balch and E. Ferguson) Greeks, Romans and Christians: Essays in Honor of Abraham J. Malherbe, 1990; (with A.J. Malherbe) The Future of Christology: Essays in Honor of Leander E. Keck, 1993; (co-ed.) The Harper Collins Study Bible, New Revised Standard Version, With the Apocryphal, 1993, rev. ed., 2006. Contributor to periodicals. **Address:** 6 Brookhaven Rd., Hamden, CT 06517, U.S.A. **Online address:** wayne.meeks@yale.edu

MEER, Sarah. British (born England), b. 1969. **Genres:** History, Popular Culture, Social Sciences. **Career:** Cambridge University, Selwyn College, American Studies, Keasbey research fellow, 1995-98, lecturer, senior lecturer, director of studies in English; Nottingham Trent University, lecturer, 1998-2003. Editor. **Publications:** Uncle Tom Mania: Slavery, Minstrelsy, and Transatlantic Culture in the 1850s, 2005; (ed. with D. Kohn and E.B. Todd) Transatlantic Stowe: Harriet Beecher Stowe and European Culture, 2006. Contributor to periodicals. **Address:** Selwyn College, Grange Rd., Cambridge, CB CB3 9DQ, England. **Online address:** sm10003@cam.ac.uk

MEGARRY, Tim. British (born England), b. 1941. **Genres:** Anthropology/Ethnology, Archaeology/Antiquities, History, Humanities, Sex, Sociology, Young Adult Non-fiction, Social Sciences, Social Sciences. **Career:** University of Greenwich, School of Social Sciences, senior lecturer in sociology and anthropology, 1972-. Writer. **Publications:** Society in Prehistory: The Origins of Human Culture, 1995; (ed.) From the Caves to Capital: Readings in Historical and Comparative Sociology, 1995; (ed. and intro.) The Making of Modern Japan, 1995. **Address:** School of Social Sciences Bronte Hall, University of Greenwich, Avery Hill Campus, 201 Avery Hill Rd., London, GL SE9 2HB, England. **Online address:** t.w.megarry@greenwich.ac.uk

MEGGED, Aharon. Israeli/Polish (born Poland), b. 1920. **Genres:** Novels, Plays/Screenplays, Essays, Translations, History. **Career:** Massa bi-weekly, editor, 1952-55; Lamerchav daily newspaper, literary editor, 1955-68; Israel Embassy, cultural attaché, 1968-71; Davar Daily, journalist, 1971-85; Haifa University, author-in-residence, 1974; Oxford University, author-in-residence, 1978; Israeli P.E.N. Centre, president, 1980-88. Writer. **Publications:** El ha-yeladim be-Teman (title means: 'To the Children in Yemen'), 1948; Ruah yamim (title means: 'Spirit of the Seas'), 1950; Hedvah va-ani: u-farashat korotenu ba- ir Tel-Aviv, 1955, rev. ed., 1975; Hedva and I, 1955; Yisrael haverim (title means: 'Israeli Folk'), 1955; Mikrehha-kcsil, tsiyurim: Aryeh Navon, 1959; Fortunes of a Fool, 1962; Ha-Berihah: sheloshah masa òt (title means: 'The Escape'), 1962; The First Sin (play), 1962, rev. ed., 1982; (contrib.) Ha-Kibuts, 1963; Mi-sipure Ha-yom Ha-sheni: Geshem Nedavot, 1965; ha-Hai àl ha-met (novel), 1965, trans. as Living on the Dead, 1970; àvel (title means: 'Iniquity'), 1966; ha-Yom ha-Sheni (title means: 'The Second Day'), 1967; The Short Life: A Novel, 1972, rev. ed., 1980; Hayim ha-Ketsarim: Roman, 1972; Sheloshah sipurim, 1972; Mahberot Evyatar: Roman, (title means: 'Evyatar's Notebooks'), 1973; 'Al Etsim Va-avanim (title means: 'Of Trees and Stones'), 1973; Hatsot ha-yom (title means: 'Midday'), 1973; ha-Atalef (title means: 'The Bat'), 1975; Haints u-veno veha-ruah ha-ra àh (title means: 'Heinz, His Son and the Evil Spirit'), 1976; Asahel: A Novel, 1978, trans., 1982; Ahavat ne ùrim (title means: 'Young Love'), 1979; Massa be-av (title means: 'Journey in the Month of Av'), 1981; Gamalha-me òfef ve-dabeshet ha-zahav (title means: 'The Flying Camel and the Golden Hump'), 1982; Masaha-yeladim el ha-Arets ha-Muvtahat: parshatyalde Selvino, 1984, trans. as The Story of the Selvino Children: Journey to the Promised Land, 2002; Ezor ha-ra àsh (title means: 'The Turbulent Zone'), 1985; Maaseh me-guneh: sheloshah sipurim (title means: 'Indecent Act'), 1986; Foigelman, 1987; Shulhan ha-ketivah: kovets maamarim be-inyene sifrut (title means: 'The Writing Desk'), 1989; Nadav ve-imo: sipur li-vene-ha-neurim(title means: 'Nadav and His Mother'), 1989; Mivhar Sipurim, 1989; Yom ha-or shel Anat, (title means: 'Anat's Day of Illumination'), 1992; Gaguìm le-Olgah, (title means: 'Longing for Olga'), 1994; Dudaim min ha-arets ha-kedoshah (title means: 'Mandrakes from the Holy Land'), 1998; Persefoneh zokheret, (title means: 'Persephone Remembers'), 2000; àd ha-èrev (title means: 'Till Evening Falls'), 2001; Nikmat Yotam (title means: 'Yotam's Vengeance'), 2003; Yarhe ha-devash shel Profesor Lunts, 2005; Zevuvim: Roman, 2008; Aśeret ha-yamim ha-nora im, 2010. PLAYS: Harhek ba-aravah: Mahazeh be-shalosh (title means: 'Far in the Wasteland'), 1951; Sheloshah me-hem, 2006. **Address:** Gloris Stern Literary Agency, 1230 Park Ave., New York, NY 10028, U.S.A.

MEGGERS, Betty J. American (born United States), b. 1921. **Genres:** Archaeology/Antiquities, Environmental Sciences/Ecology. **Career:** American University, instructor in anthropology, 1950-51; Smithsonian Institution, research associate, 1954-, National Museum of Natural History, Latin American Archaeology Program, head, director; American Anthropological Association, executive secretary, 1959-61; Programa Nacional de Pesquisas Arqueologicas na Bacia Amazonica (PRONAPABA), principal investigator; Battelle Memorial Foundation, consultant. Writer. **Publications:** The Beal-Steere Collection of pottery from Marajó, 1947; (with C. Evans) Uma interpretacão das culturas da Ilha Marajó, 1954; (with C. Evans) Archaeological Investigations at the Mouth of the Amazon, 1957; (with C. Evans) O emprêgo do método comparativo na interpretac ão arqueológica, 1958; (with C. Evans and E. Estrada) Cultura Valdivia, 1959; (contrib.) Aboriginal Cultural Development in Latin America, 1963; (with C. Evans) Guia para prospecção arqueológica no Brasil, 1965; (with C. Evans and E. Estrada) Early Formative Period of Coastal Ecuador: The Valdivia and Machalilla Phases, 1965; (with C. Evans) Archeological Investigations in British Guiana, 1960; Ecuador, 1966; (with C. Evans) Archeological Investigations on the Rio Napo, Eastern Ecuador, 1968; Amazonia: Man and Culture in a Counterfeit Paradise, 1971, rev. ed., 1996; Prehistoric America, 1972, 3rd ed., 2010; (co-author) Estudios arqueológicos: Antillas y tierras bajas de Sudamérica, Ecuador, 1977; Aspectos arqueológicos de las tierras bajas de Suramérica y las Antillas, 1978; (contrib.) Umi no kodaishi, 1996; Enfoques teóricos para la investigación arqueológica, 1998; Ecología y biogeografía de la Amazonía, 1999. TRANSLATOR: Darcy Ribeiro, The Civilizational Process, 1968; Luis G. Lumbreras, People and Cultures of Ancient Peru, 1974. EDITOR: (with E.S. Ayensu and W.D. Duckworth) Tropical Forest Ecosystems in Africa and South America: A Comparative Review, 1973; (with L. Nunez) Investigaciones Paleoindias al Sur de la Linea Ecuatorial, 1987; Prehistoria Sudamericana, 1992. **Address:** National Museum of Natural History, Smithsonian Institution, MRC-112, PO Box 37012, Washington, DC 20560, U.S.A.

MEGIVERN, James J(oseph). American (born United States), b. 1931. **Genres:** Theology/Religion, Adult Non-fiction, History, Social Commentary. **Career:** Mary Immaculate Seminary and College, instructor in biblical languages and literature, 1962-64; St. John's University, assistant professor of theology and head of department, 1966-70; New York City Board of Education, South Bronx Paraprofessional Training Program, director, 1970-74; University of North Carolina, Department of Philosophy and Religion, associate professor, 1974-77, head of department, 1975-92, chairperson of faculty, 1976-77, professor of philosophy and religion, 1977-2001, professor emeritus, 2001-; City University of New York, Queensborough Community College, lecturer, 1970-73; Manhattan College, lecturer, 1971-73; Fordham University, lecturer, 1971-74; Emory University, visiting professor, 1981. Writer. **Publications:** Concomitance and Communion: A Study in Eucharistic Doctrine and Practice, 1963; (comp.) Bible Interpretation, 1978; (comp.) Worship and Liturgy, 1978; The Death Penalty: An Historical and Theological Survey, 1997; (with M.L. Megivern) People of Vision: A History of the American Council of the Blind, 2003. EDITOR: (with C.J. Dollen and J.K. McGowan) The Church, 1979; (with C.J. Dollen and J.K. McGowan) Spirituality, 1979; (with C.J. Dollen and J.K. McGowan) Mass and the Sacraments, 1979; (with C.J. Dollen and J.K. McGowan) Personal Ethics, 1979; (with C.J. Dollen and J.K. McGowan) Sacred Scripture, 1979; (with C.J. Dollen and J.K. McGowan) The Saviour, 1979; (with C.J. Dollen and J.K. McGowan) Social Thought, 1979; (and contrib.) The Catholic Tradition, 1980. CONTRIBUTOR: The Paradox of Religious Secularity, 1967; Perspectives in Philosophy, 1975. Contributor to magazines. **Address:** Department of Philosophy and Religion, University of North Carolina, 269 Bear Hall, 601 S College Rd., Wilmington, NC 28403-3297, U.S.A. **Online address:** jimmeg2@aol.com

MEHAFFEY, Karen Rae. American/Scottish (born Scotland), b. 1959. **Genres:** History, Women's Studies And Issues, Bibliography, Librarianship. **Career:** Gale Research Co., research assistant for literary criticism, 1982-83, research coordinator, 1983-84; University of Michigan, library assistant in archives, 1985; high school music teacher, 1986-88; Sacred Heart Major Seminary, Edmund Cardinal Szoka Library, assistant librarian in cataloging and technical services, 1988-, library director, 1992-2004; University of Detroit Mercy, reference librarian, 2007-08; Cengage, customer service librarian, 2008. Writer. **Publications:** Victorian American Women, 1840-1880: An Annotated Bibliography, 1992; The Afterlife: Mourning Rituals and the Mid-Victorians, 1993; Rachel Weeping: Mourning in Nineteenth Century America, 2006, 2nd ed., 2009; American Etiquette in the 19th Century, forthcoming; They Called Her Captain: Emily Virginia Mason, forthcoming. Contributor of articles to books and journals. **Address:** 17350 Hidden Lake Way, Northville, MI 48168-2290, U.S.A. **Online address:** krmehaffey@yahoo.com

MEHO, Lokman I. Lebanese/American (born United States), b. 1968?. **Genres:** Information Science/Computers, Librarianship, Bibliography, Reference. **Career:** American University of Beirut, librarty assistant, 1986-95, Department of Political Studies and Public Administration, graduate and research assistant, 1990-95, Middle East for Research and Studies, bibliographer, 1991-95; North Carolina Central University, librarty assistant, 1996-97, adjunct lecturer in library and information science, 1997-98; University of North Carolina, School of Information and Library Science, research assistant, 1997-2001, teaching fellow, 1998-2001; State University of New York, University at Albany, School of Information Science and Policy, assistant professor, 2002-04; Indiana University, School of Library and Information Science, assistant professor, 2004-08, associate professor, 2008-09, Master of Library Science Program, co-director, 2005-08, director, 2008-09; American University, Department of Political Studies and Public Administration, associate professor, 2009-, Center for Arab and Middle Eastern Studies, associate faculty, 2009-, University Libraries, director, 2009-. Writer. **Publications:** The Kurds and Kurdistan: A Selective and Annotated Bibliography, 1997; (with M.A. Nsouli) Libraries and Information in the Arab World: An Annotated Bibliography, 1999; (with K. Maglaughlin) Kurdish Culture and Society: An Annotated Bibliography, 2001; The Kurdish Question in U.S. Foreign Policy: A Documentary Sourcebook, 2004; (with M.A. Nsouli) Censorship in the Arab World: An Annotated Bibliography, 2006. Contributor to journals. **Address:** University Libraries, American University of Beirut, PO Box 11-236, Riad El-Solh, 1107 2020, Lebanon. **Online address:** lmeho@aub.edu.lb

MEHRABIAN, Albert. American (born United States), b. 1939?. **Genres:** Psychology, Money/Finance, Writing/Journalism. **Career:** University of California, assistant professor, associate professor, 1964-76, professor of psychology, through 1996, professor emeritus of psychology, 1996-. Writer. **Publications:** (With M. Wiener) Language within Languages: Immediacy, A Channel in Verbal Communication, 1968; An Analysis of Personality Theories, 1968; Tactics of Social Influence, 1970; Silent Messages: Implicit Communication of Emotions and Attitudes, 1971, 2nd ed., 1981; Nonverbal Communication, 1972; (with J.A. Russell) Approach to Environmental Psychology, 1974; (with S. Ksionzky) A Theory of Affiliation, 1974; Public Places and Private Spaces: The Psychology of Work, Play, and Living Environments, 1976; Basic Behavior Modification, 1978; Raume des Alltags Oder Wie die Umwelt Unser Verhalten Bestimm, 1978; Basic Dimensions for a General Psychological Theory: Implications for Personality, Social, Environmental, and Developmental Studies, 1980; Eating Characteristics and Temperament: General Measures and Interrelationships, 1987; The Name Game: The Decision that Lasts a Lifetime, 1990; Your Inner Path to Investment Success: Insights into the Psychology of Investing, 1991; Supseek Teuksungkwa Keegil, 1999; Baby Name Report Card: Beneficial and Harmful Baby Names, 2002; Nonverbal Communication, 2007. **Address:** Department of Psychology, University of California, 1285 Franz Hall, PO Box 951563, Los Angeles, CA 90095-1563, U.S.A. **Online address:** am@kaaj.com

MEHROTRA, Arvind Krishna. Indian/Pakistani (born Pakistan), b. 1947. **Genres:** Poetry, Translations. **Career:** Ezra-Fakir Press, founder, 1966; University of Allahabad, Department of English and Modern Europian Languages, lecturer in English, 1968-77, reader in English, 1978-, professor and head; University of Iowa, visiting writer, 1971-73; University of Hyderabad, lecturer in English, 1977-78. Writer. **Publications:** Bharatmata: A Prayer, 1966; Woodcuts on Paper, 1967; Pomes/Poemes/Poemas, 1971; Nine Enclosures, 1976; Distance in Statute Miles, 1982; Middle Earth, 1984; The Oxford India Anthology of Twelve Modern India Poets, 1992; The Transfiguring Places, 1998. TRANSLATOR: B. Gjuzel, Three Poems, 1973; The Absent Traveller, 1991; (and intro.) Kabir, Songs of Kabir, 2011. EDITOR: Twenty Indian Poems, 1990; The Oxford India Anthology of Twelve Modern Indian Poets, 1992; (co-ed.) Periplus: Poetry in Translation, 1993; Illustrated History of Indian Literature in English, 2003; History of Indian Literature in English, 2003; Last Bungalow: Writings on Allahabad, 2007; Concise History of Indian Literature in English, 2009; (and intro.) Boatride & Other Poems, 2009; Arun Kolatkar: Collected Poems in English, 2010. **Address:** Department of English and Modern Europian, Languages, University of Allahabad, Anand Bhawan, Allahabad, UP 211 002, India. **Online address:** arvindmehrotra@rediffmail.com

MEHROTRA, Sri Ram. Indian (born India), b. 1931. **Genres:** History, Politics/Government. **Career:** Saugor University, lecturer in history, 1950-58; University of London, Institute of Commonwealth Studies, research fellow, 1960-61, School of Oriental and African Studies, research fellow, 1961-62, lecturer in South Asian Politics, 1962-71; Indian Institute of Advanced Study, fellow, 1971-79; Himachal Pradesh University, professor of history, 1972-91; Maharshi Dayanand University, Jawaharlal Nehru professor, 1992-96; St John's College, visiting fellow; University of Wisconsin, visiting professor; University of Rajasthan, now professor emeritus. Writer. **Publications:** India and the Commonwealth, 1885-1929, 1965; The Emergence of the Indian National Congress, 1971; The Commonwealth and the Nation, 1978; Towards

India's Freedom and Partition, 1978; A History of the Indian National Congress, 1995; (ed. with E.C. Moulton) Selected Writings of Allan Octavian Hume, 2004. Contributor to journals. **Address:** University of Rajasthan, JLN Marg, Jaipur, RJ 302004, India.

MEHTA, Gita. American/Indian (born India), b. 1943?. **Genres:** Novellas/Short Stories, Novels, Theology/Religion, Young Adult Fiction, Biography, Autobiography/Memoirs. **Career:** British Broadcasting Corp., director of documentary films; National Broadcasting Co., director of documentary films. Writer. **Publications:** Karma Cola: Marketing the Mystic East, 1979; Raj: A Novel, 1989; śrīmad Bhāgavatī Ya Tattvajñā Na: śrīmad Bhā Gavatapurā Noanumo Talasparśī Vivecana, 1989; A River Sutra (stories), 1993; Snakes and Ladders: Glimpses of India, 1997; Vāsanā d Vā sudevah: eka vimarśa, 1998; (contrib.) Clemente, 1999; (contrib.) Eternal Ganesha, 2006. Contributor to periodicals. **Address:** c/o Nan A. Talese, Doubleday Broadway Group, Random House, 1745 Broadway, New York, NY 10019, U.S.A.

MEHTA, Suketu. American/Indian (born India), b. 1963?. **Genres:** Young Adult Fiction. **Career:** New York University, faculty, 2008, associate professor of Journalism, professor. Writer. **Publications:** Maximum City: Bombay Lost and Found, 2004. **Address:** c/o Author Mail, Alfred A. Knopf Inc., 1745 Broadway, New York, NY 10019, U.S.A. **Online address:** suketu@suketu.com

MEHTA, Ved (Parkash). American/Indian (born India), b. 1934. **Genres:** Novels, Novellas/Short Stories, Area Studies, History, Autobiography/Memoirs, Biography, Young Adult Fiction. **Career:** New Yorker Magazine, staff writer, 1961-94; Bard College, visiting professor, 1985, 1986; Sarah Lawrence College, visiting professor, 1988; Balliol College, visiting fellow, 1988-89, honorary fellow, 1999; New York University, New York Institute for the Humanities, fellow, 1988-92, visiting professor, 1989-90; Yale University, Berkeley College, associate fellow, 1988-, Rosenkranz Chair in Writing and residential fellow, 1990-93, lecturer in history, 1990, 1991, 1992, lecturer in English, 1991-93; Williams College, Arnold Bernhard visiting professor of English and history, 1994; Vassar College, Randolph visiting distinguished professor, 1994-96; Columbia University, Media Studies Center, Freedom Forum, senior fellow, 1996-97; Center for Advanced Study in the Behavioral Sciences, fellow, 1997-98. **Publications:** Face to Face, 1957, 2nd ed., 1997; Walking the Indian Streets, 1960, rev. ed., 1971; Fly and the Fly-Bottle, 1963; The New Theologian, 1966; Delinquent Chacha, 1967; Portrait of India, 1970, 2nd ed., 1993; John is Easy to Please, 1971; Mahatma Gandhi and His Apostles, 1977; The New India, 1978; Photographs of Chachaji, 1980; A Family Affair: India under Three Prime Ministers, 1982; Three Stories of the Raj, 1986; Rajiv Gandhi and Rama's Kingdom, 1994; A Ved Mehta Reader, 1998. CONTINENTS OF EXILE (autobiographical series): Daddyji, 1972; Mamaji, 1979; Vedi, 1982; The Ledge between the Streams, 1984; Sound-Shadows of the New World, 1986; The Stolen Light, 1989; Up at Oxford, 1993; Remembering Mr. Shawn's New Yorker, 1998; All for Love, 2001; Dark Harbor, 2003; The Red Letters, 2004; Veritas, forthcoming. **Address:** 139 E 79th St., New York, NY 10021, U.S.A. **Online address:** mehta.ved@gmail.com

MEIER, Diane. (Diane Meier Delaney). American (born United States), b. 1950. **Genres:** Novels, Cultural/Ethnic Topics. **Career:** Meier Advertising, founder and president, 1979-. Writer. **Publications:** (As Diane Meier Delaney) The New American Wedding: Ritual and Style in a Changing Culture, 2005; The Season of Second Chances: A Novel, 2010. **Address:** Meier Advertising, 907 Broadway, New York, NY 10010-7107, U.S.A. **Online address:** dmeier@meierbrand.com

MEIER, Paul D. American (born United States), b. 1912?. **Genres:** Self Help, Psychiatry, Psychology. **Career:** University of Arkansas, College of Medicine, resident in psychiatry, 1972-74; Duke University, resident in psychiatry, 1974-75; Trinity Evangelical Divinity School, assistant professor of pastoral psychology and counseling, 1976-87; Minirth-Meier Clinics (now Meier Clinics), co-founder and executive vice president, 1976-, psychiatrist, 1976-2000; Memorial Hospital of Garland, chief of psychiatric services, 1982; Mountain Climbing Expedition, team physician, 1985; Southwestern Seminary, lecturer; The Baptist Seminary, lecturer; The Greek Bible Institute and Seminary, lecturer. Writer. **Publications:** The Fakers, 1980; Don't Let Jerks Get the Best of You, 1993. NOVELS: The Third Millennium, 1993; (with R.L. Wise) Fourth Millennium, 1996; (with R.L. Wise) Beyond the Millennium, 1998; (with R.L. Wise) Secret Code, 1999. OTHERS: Christian Child-Rearing and Personality Development, 1977, (with D.E. Ratcliff and F.L. Rowe) 2nd ed., 1995; (with F.B. Minirth) Happiness Is a Choice: A Manual on the Symptoms, Causes, and Cures of Depression, 1978, 2nd ed. as Happiness is a Choice: The Symptoms, Causes, and Cures of Depression, 1994; 100 Ways to Overcome Depression, 1979; The Unwanted Generation: A Guide to Responsible Parenting, 1981; The Workaholic and His Family: An Inside Look, 1981; (with R. Meier) Family Foundations: How to Have a Happy Home, 1981; (with F.B. Minirth and F.B. Wichern) Introduction to Psychology and Counseling: Christian Perspectives and Applications, 1982, (co-author) 2nd ed., 1991; Counseling and the Nature of Man, 1982; (with W.L. Carter and F.B. Minirth) Why Be Lonely?, 1982; (co-author) The Monster Within: Overcoming Bulimia, 1984; (with D. Houmes) Growing in Step: A Christian Guide to Stepparenting, 1985; (with R. Case and F.B. Minirth) The Money Diet, 1985; Sweet Dreams: A Guide to Productive Sleep, 1985; Beating the Clock, 1985; Meditating for Success, 1985; How to Beat Burnout, 1986; 100 Ways to Live a Happy and Successful Life: Overcoming Depression, 1986; Taking Control: New Hope for Substance Abusers and Their Families, 1988; The Healthy Christian Life, 1988; Sex in the Christian Marriage, 1988; (with F.B. Minirth and D. Hawkins) Worry-Free Living, 1989; (with R. Hemfelt and F.B. Minirth) Love Is a Choice: Recovery for Codependent Relationships, 1989; A Mother's Choice: Day Care or Home Care?, 1989; Before Burnout, 1990; Love Hunger, 1990; (with F.B. Minirth and D. Hawkins) Happy holidays, 1990; (with R. Hemfelt and F.B. Minirth) We Are Driven: The Compulsive Behaviors America Applauds, 1991; (co-author) Walk With the Serenity Prayer: Daily Devotions for People in Recovery, 1991; (with F.B. Minirth and K. Kinback) Ask the Doctors, 1991; The Path to Serenity, 1991; (with F.B. Minirth) Free to Forgive, 1991; (with F.B. Minirth and D.E. Ratcliff) Bruised and Broken: Understanding and Healing Psychological Problems, 1992; (co-author) Filling the Holes in Our Souls, 1992; Don't Let the Jerks Get the Best of You, 1993; What They Didn't Teach You in Seminary, 1993; (with D.E. Ratcliff and F.L. Rowe) Child-Rearing and Personality Development, 2nd ed., 1993; (with F.B. Minirth and S. Arterburn) Miracle Drugs, 1995; (with R.L. Wise) Windows of the Soul, 1995; (with F.B. Minirth and S. Arterburn) Complete Life Encyclopedia, 1995; (with S. Arterburn and F.B. Minirth) Safe Places, 1997; Beating Burnout, 1997; (co-author) Happiness Is a Choice for Teens, 1997; (with B. Courrege and H. Gardiner) WWJD?, 1998; (with S. Arterburn and F.B. Minirth) Mastering Your Moods, 1999; (with W.L. Carter and F.B. Minirth) Overcoming Loneliness, 2000; Mood Swings, 2000; (with F.B. Minirth and S. Arterburn) Spiritual Life Guide: Biblically Based, Medically Sound Solutions to All of Life's Challenges and Passages-Physical, Emotional, Spiritual, 2001; (with C. Meier) Unbreakable Bonds: Practicing the Art of Loving and Being Loved, 2002; (with S. Arterburn and R.L. Wise) Fear Less for Life: Break Free to Living with Hope and Confidence, 2002; Compelled to Achieve: Finding Balance Between Success and Excess, 2003; (with R.L. Wise) Crazy Makers: Getting Along with the Difficult People in your Life, 2003; (co-author) Blue Genes: Breaking Free of the Chemical Imbalances that Affect Your Mood, Your Mind, Your Life, and Your Loved Ones, 2005; (co-author) Blue Genes: Breaking Free from the Chemical Imbalances that Affect Your Moods, Your Mind, Your Life, and Your Love Ones, 2005; (with J. Hiskey) Winning is a Choice: How the Champions Do it, and How We Can Too, 2007; (with T. Clements) What I've Learned Since I knew it All: 12 Secrets to Living a Satisfied Life, 2008; (with D.L. Henderson) Finding Purpose Beyond Our Pain: Uncover the Hidden Potential in Life's Most Common Struggles, 2009; (with T. Clements and L. Johnson) Postpartum Survival Guide: Everything You Need to Know About Postpartum Depression, 2009. **Address:** Meier Clinics, 2099 N Collins Blvd., Ste. 100, Richardson, TX 75080, U.S.A.

MEIER, Richard (Alan). American (born United States), b. 1934. **Genres:** Architecture, Autobiography/Memoirs. **Career:** Architect, 1957-63; Cooper Union, professor of architecture, 1962-73; Richard Meier & Associates, principal architect, 1963-80; American Academy-Rome, resident architect, 1973-74; Yale University, William Henry Bishop visiting professor of architecture, 1975-77; Harvard University, visiting professor of architecture, 1977; Richard Meier & Partners Architects LLP, principal architect, 1980-; Pratt Institute, faculty; Princeton University, faculty; University of California, faculty. Writer. **Publications:** Smith House, Darien, Connecticut, 1967; (contrib.) Villa Savoye, Poissy, France, 1929-31, 1972; House in Old Westbury, Long Island, New York, 1971, 1973; Smith House, Darien, Connecticut, 1967, House in Old Westbury, Long Island, New York, 1971, 1973; Douglas House, Harbor Springs, Michigan, U.S.A., 1974, 1975; Richard Meier, Architect: Buildings and Projects, 1966-1976, 1976; On Architecture: Lecture, 1981; (contrib.) Shards, 1983; Richard Meier, Architect, 1964/1984, 1984; (foreword) Richard Meier: Architectural Drawings 1971-1984, 1985; Richard Meier:

Stadthaus Ulm, 1993; (intro.) Ackerberg House & Addition: Richard Meier, 1996; Building the Getty, 1997; (contrib.) Stamberg Aferiat, 1997; (contrib.) Richard Meier, Barcelona Museum of Contemporary Art, 1997; (contrib.) American Dream, 2003; (foreword) Hariri & Hariri Houses, 2005; (intro.) Richard Meier: Museums: 1973/2006, 2006; (intro.) Richard Meier: Houses and Apartments, 2007; (foreword) Grotta House by Richard Meier, 2007. **Address:** Richard Meier & Partners Architects L.L.P., 475 10th Ave., 6th Fl., New York, NY 10018, U.S.A. **Online address:** mail@richardmeier.com

MEIJER, Fik. Dutch (born Netherlands), b. 1942?. **Genres:** History, Antiques/Furnishings. **Career:** University of Amsterdam, professor of naval history and maritime archaeology of classical antiquity, 1992-99, professor of ancient history, 1999-2007, professor emeritus of ancient history, 2007-. Writer. **Publications:** Wrakken, ankers en amforen: Archeologisch onderzoek in de Middellandse Zee, 1976; A History of Seafaring in the Classical World, 1986; (ed.) Clio and Antiquity: History and Historiography of the Greek and Roman World, 1987; Schipper, zeil de haven binnen, alles is al verkocht: Handel en transport in de oudheid, 1990; (with O. van Nijf) Trade, Transport, and Society in the Ancient World: A Sourcebook, 1992; De Oudheid van opzij: Oudhistorische notities, 1997; Paulus' zeereis naar Rome: Een reconstructie, 2000; Keizers sterven niet in bed: Van Caesar tot Romulus Augustulus, 44 v.Chr.-476 n.Chr., 2002; Gladiatoren: Volksvermaak in het Colosseum, 2003; Vercingetorix: De mythe van Frankrijks oudste held, 2004; Macht zonder grenzen: Rome en zijn imperium, 2006; Oudheid is nog niet voorbij, 2007; Bejubeld en verguisd: helden en heldinnen in de oudheid, 2008; Hond van Odysseus: het dier in de oudheid, 2009; De Middellandse Zee, 2010; (with M. Driessen) Sail Rome!, 2010. **Address:** c/o Author Mail, Uitgeverij Verloren, PO Box 1741, Hilversum, 1200 BS, Netherlands.

MEIKLE, William. Scottish (born Scotland), b. 1958. **Genres:** Science Fiction/Fantasy, Horror, Mystery/Crime/Suspense, Novels, Novellas/Short Stories. **Career:** SEMA, team leader and analyst programmer, 1982, trainer, 1986-90, project leader, 1987-88, staff manager, 1988-89, customer support services manager, 1989-90, project manager, 1990-91; Grampian Health Board, project manager, 1991-96; North of Scotland Water Authority, systems manager, 1996; Scottish Hydro Electric PLC, project manager, 1997-98, technical author and analyst, 1998-99; National Australia Group, technical author and designer, 1999; Scottish and Southern Energy PLC, project manager, 1999-2000; Agilent Technologies, technical author and analyst, 2000-01; writer, 2001-. **Publications:** Island Life (horror novel), 2001; The Johnson Amulet and Other Scottish Terrors (short stories), 2001. WATCHERS TRILOGY: The Coming of the King, 2003; The Battle for the Throne, 2003; The Midnight Eye Files: The Amulet, 2005; Culloden, 2006; Eldren: The Book of the Dark, 2007; Generations, 2007; Berserker, 2010; The Valley, 2010; The Midnight Eye Files: The Skin Game, 2011; The Creeping Kelp, 2011; Sherlock Holmes: Revenant, 2011; The Invasion/The Valley, 2011. **Address:** PO Box 319, Catalina, NL A0C 1J0, Canada. **Online address:** meiklewilliam@yahoo.com

MEILMAN, Philip W(arren). American (born United States), b. 1951. **Genres:** Education, Psychology. **Career:** College of William and Mary, Counseling Center, staff psychologist, 1977-80, director, 1990-96; University of Nebraska Medical Center, Pain Management Center, administrative director, 1980-85; Dartmouth College, assistant director of counseling and human development, 1986-90; Cornell University, Counseling and Psychological Services, senior research and clinical psychologist, 1996-2005, director, 1996-2003; Georgetown University, director of counseling and psychiatric service, 2005-, professor of psychiatry 2006-; Southern Illinois University, Core Institute, Center for Alcohol and Other Drug Studies, co-director. Writer. **Publications:** (With P.A. Grayson) Beating the College Blues, 1992; (with C.A. Presley and R. Lyerla) Alcohol and Drugs on American College Campuses: Use, Consequences, and Perceptions of the Campus Environment, vol. I-IV; (with P.A. Grayson) College Mental Health Practice, 2006. Contributor to periodicals. **Address:** Counseling & Psychiatric Service, Georgetown University, 1 Darnall Hall, 37th & O St. NW, Washington, DC 20057, U.S.A. **Online address:** pwm9@georgetown.edu

MEINESZ, Alexandre. French (born France), b. 1946. **Genres:** Environmental Sciences/Ecology. **Career:** University of Nice-Sophia Antipolis, assistant, 1970-80, assistant professor, 1980-89, director of Laboratoire Environnement Marin Littoral, 1989-, professor II, 1989-2002, professor of biology I, 2002-; Regional Agency for the Environment, director, 1989-; Agency for the Environment, administrator. Writer. **Publications:** Le Roman Noir de l'algue Tueuse: Caulerpa Taxifolia Contre la Mediterranée, 1997; Killer Algae, 2001; Comment la vie a Commencé: Les Trois Genèses du Vivant, 2008; How Life Began: Evolution's Three Geneses, 2008. **Address:** Faculté des Sciences, Laboratoire Environnement Marin Littoral, Universite de Nice-Sophia Antipolis, EA 4228 ECOMERS, Parc Valrose, Nice, 06108, France. **Online address:** meinesz@unice.fr

MEINKE, Peter. American (born United States), b. 1932. **Genres:** Essays, Poetry, Novellas/Short Stories. **Career:** Teacher, 1958-60; Hamline University, instructor, 1961-65, assistant professor of English, 1965-66, poet-in-residence, 1973; Eckerd College, assistant professor, 1966-68, associate professor, 1968-72, professor of literature and director of writing workshop, 1972-93, now professor emeritus; University of Neuchatel, Overseas Program, director, 1971-72; University of Warsaw, Fulbright senior lecturer, 1978-79; Davidson College, McGee writer-in-residence, 1989; University of North Carolina, distinguished writer-in-residence, 1996; Old Dominion University, Darden chair in creative writing, 2003-05; poet laureate of St. Petersburg, 2009-; Converse College, distinguished visiting writers, 2010. **Publications:** Howard Nemerov, 1968; The Legend of Larry the Lizard, 1968; Very Seldom Animals, 1969; The Night Train and the Golden Bird, 1977; The Piano Tuner, 1986; The Shape of Poetry, 1999, 2nd ed., 2008; Unheard Music: Stories, 2007. POETRY: Lines from Neuchâtel, 1974; Rat Poems: or, Rats Live on No Evil Star, 1978; Trying to Surprise God, 1981; Underneath the Lantern, 1986; Night Watch on the Chesapeake, 1987; Far from Home, 1988; Liquid Paper: New and Selected Poems, 1991; Campocorto, 1996; Scars, 1996; Zinc Fingers: Poems A to Z, 2000; Maples and Orange Trees (bilingual), 2004; Contracted World: New & More Selected Poems, 2006; Unheard Music (fiction), 2007; Lines from Neuchatel, 35th Anniversary Edition, 2009. **Address:** 147 Wildwood Ln. SE, St. Petersburg, FL 33705, U.S.A. **Online address:** meinkep@eckerd.edu

MEINTJES, Louise. American/South African (born South Africa), b. 1960?. **Genres:** Music. **Career:** Duke University, assistant professor of ethnomusicology, 1996-, director of graduate studies in music and associated faculty in department of cultural anthropology, associate professor of music. Writer. **Publications:** Sound of Africa!: Making Music Zulu in a South African Studio, 2003. Contributor to Ethnomusicology. **Address:** Department of Music, Duke University, 072 Mary Duke Biddle, PO Box 90665, Durham, NC 27708-0666, U.S.A. **Online address:** meintjes@duke.edu

MEIR, Avinoam. Israeli (born Israel), b. 1946. **Genres:** Area Studies, Geography. **Career:** Yavneh Publishing House, cartographic editorial assistant, 1970-72; Tel Aviv University, teaching assistant, 1971-72; University of Cincinnati, teaching assistant, 1974-77; Ben-Gurion University of the Negev, Department of Geography, lecturer, 1977-81, senior lecturer, 1981-87, associate professor, 1987-96, professor, 1996-, chairperson, 1982-84, Blaustein Institute for Desert Research, research fellow, 1979-82, 1987-88, Urban Studies Division, chairperson, 1986-88, Department for General B.A. Studies, chairperson, 1997-2002, vice dean for regional colleges affairs, 1989-97; Ha Negev College, lecturer, 1977-78, associate professor, 1989-, academic coordinator of faculty of social sciences and humanities, 1989-97; University of California, visiting professor, 1984-85; Sapir College, associate professor, 1989-96; Achva College, associate professor, 1984-, professor. Writer. **Publications:** (Contrib.) Geography Research Forum, 1984; Hitnahagut Demografit-Piryonit shel ha-Bedyim Ha-nayadim-le-meḥetsah ba-Negev, 1990; (co-author) Regional Development: The Challenge of the Frontier, 1993; (with G. Me'ir) Ha-Yishuv ha-Arvi be-Yiśráel: Tahalikhim Ge'ografiyim, 1994; Neyar 'Avodah, 1996; As Nomadism Ends: The Israeli Bedouin of the Negev, 1996; Ha-Metaḥ ben Bedye ha-Negev la-medinah: Mediniyut u-metsi'ut, 1999; (with A. Me'ir and S. El-A'sam) Temurot be-ma'amad ha-zaḳen ba-ḥevrah ha-Bedyit ha-mit'ayeret u-mashma'uyotehen ha-tsiburiyot, 2000; Kalkalah ve-kark'a bi-kerev Bedye ha-Negev: tahalikhim ḥadashim, ḥadashot, 2006; (with Z. Donis) Univerisiṭah, ir, ye-yeḥasim ba-merḥav: Mikhlelet Sapir yeha-ir Sederot, 2006. EDITOR: (with E. Stern) Contemporary and Future Geography, 1979; (with E. Stern and Y. Gradus) The Negev Atlas, 1987; (with E. Stern) International Aspects of Rural and Urban Metropolitan Systems, 1989; (with D. Grossman) The Arabs in Israel: Geographical Processes, 1993; (with O. Yiftachel) Ethnic Frontiers and Peripheries: Landscapes of Development and Inequality in Israel, 1996. Contributor to books and journals. **Address:** Department of Geography and Environmental Development, Ben-Gurion University of the Negev, Rm. 236, Ben Gurion Blvd., PO Box 653, Beer Sheva, 84105, Israel. **Online address:** ameir@bgu.ac.il

MEISEL, Joseph S. American (born United States), b. 1965. **Genres:** Social Work, History. **Career:** Columbia University, Office of Management and Budget, financial operations analyst, 1989-90, budget officer, 1989-92, senior analyst, 1990-92, 1994-97, consultant, 1997-99, 1994-99, adjunct faculty, 2001-02; St. Deiniol's Library, residential fellow, 1998; Andrew W. Mellon Foundation, Research Universities and Humanistic Scholarship, program officer, 1999-2010; City University of New York, Bernard M. Baruch College, adjunct faculty, 2004; Brown University, deputy provost, 2010-. Writer. **Publications:** Public Speech and the Culture of Public Life in the Age of Gladstone, 2001; Knowledge and Power: The Parliamentary Representation of Universities in Britain and the Empire, 2011. Contributor of articles to periodicals. **Address:** Andrew W. Mellon Foundation, 140 E 62nd St., New York, NY 10021, U.S.A. **Online address:** jsm@mellon.org

MEKLER, Eva. (Yetta Emmis). American/Polish (born Poland), b. 1945. **Genres:** Theatre, Education, Novels, Mystery/Crime/Suspense, Plays/Screenplays, Film, Literary Criticism And History. **Career:** Usdan Center for the Creative and Performing Arts, teacher and production director, 1985-; Board of Education, school psychologist. Writer and actress. **Publications:** (Ed. with M. Schulman) Contemporary Scenes for Student Actors, 1980; (with M. Schulman) Bringing Up a Moral Child: A New Approach for Teaching Your Child to Be Kind, Just and Responsible, 1985; (ed. with M. Schulman) The Actor's Scenebook: Scenes and Monologues from Contemporary Plays, 1987; The New Generation of Acting Teachers, 1987; Masters of the Stage: British Acting Teachers Talk about Their Craft, 1989; (with M. Schulman) Bringing up a Moral Child: Teaching Your Child to be Kind, Just and Responsible, 1994; Sunrise Shows Late: A Novel, 1997; (comp. with M. Schulman) Great Scenes and Monologues for Actors, 1998; (as Yetta Emmis) Drek: The Real Yiddish Your Bubba Never Taught You, 1998; (comp. with M. Schulman) Play the Scene: The Ultimate Collection of Contemporary and Classic Scenes and Monologues, 2004; The Polish Woman: A Novel, 2007. **Address:** c/o Al Zuckerman, Writers House, 21 W 26th St., New York, NY 10010, U.S.A. **Online address:** evamekler45@yahoo.com

MELADY, Thomas (Patrick). American (born United States), b. 1927. **Genres:** International Relations/Current Affairs, Third World, Race Relations, History, Adult Non-fiction, Race Relations. **Career:** Addis Ababa University, lecturer, 1955-56; Duquesne University, director of development, 1956-59, Institute of African Affairs, founder, 1956-59; St. John's University, lecturer, 1960-67, Rome Graduate Center, distinguished visiting professor, 1998, 1999; Fordham University, adjunct professor of African history, 1966-69; Seton Hall University, Department of Asian and Non-Western Studies, professor and chairman, Africa Service Institute, president, 1967-69; U.S. ambassador to Burundi, 1969-72; UN General Assembly, senior advisor, 1970; Sacred Heart University, president, 1976-86, president emeritus, 1986-; U.S. ambassador to Uganda, 1972-73; Office of International Studies, professor of Afro-Asian affairs and director, 1973-74; St. Joseph's University, executive vice-president, 1974-76; U.S. Department of Education, assistant secretary, 1981-82; Connecticut Public Expenditures Council, president and chief executive officer, 1986-89; U.S. ambassador to Vatican, 1989-93; George Washington University, distinguished visiting professor, 1993-94; Institute of World Politics, professor and senior diplomat in residence, 2001-. Writer. **Publications:** Profiles of African Leaders, 1961; White Man's Future in Black Africa, 1962; Faces of Africa, 1964; (ed.) Kenneth Kaunda of Zambia: Selections from His Writings, 1964; Revolution of Color, 1965; Western Policy and the Third World, 1967; (with M. Melady) House Divided: Poverty, Race, Religion and the Family of Man, 1969; Development: Lessons for the Future, 1973; Burundi: The Tragic Years, 1974; (co-author) Uganda: The Asian Exiles, 1975; Idi Amin Dada: Hitler in Africa, 1977; The Ambassador's Story: The United States and the Vatican in World Affairs, 1994; (ed.) Catholics in the Public Square: The Role of Catholics in American Life, Culture and Politics, 1995; (ed.) Public Catholicism: The Challenge of Living the Faith in a Secular American Culture, 1996; Shine the Light: Believe, Witness and Evangelize, 1997; Faith Family Friends: Memoirs of Thomas Patrick Melady-Diplomat-Educator-Soldier, 2003; (with M.B. Melady) Ten African Heroes: The Sweep of Independence in Black Africa, 2011; (with R.B. Subartono) Developing Societies, forthcoming. MONOGRAPHS: Taxation as a Factor in the Development of Underdeveloped Countries, 1954; The Economic Future of Ethiopia, 1959; An Evaluation of the United States' Position in Guinea, Liberia and Ghana, 1960; Race Relations and Harmony among Men, 1966. Contributor of articles to journals. **Address:** Orbis Books, PO Box 302, Maryknoll, NY 10545-0302, U.S.A. **Online address:** ambmelady@aol.com

MELAMED, Leo. American/Polish (born Poland), b. 1932. **Genres:** Science Fiction/Fantasy, Economics, Autobiography/Memoirs. **Career:** Dellsher Investment Company Inc., founder, chairman and chief executive officer, 1965-93; Chicago Mercantile Exchange, chairperson, 1969-72, 1976-77, chairman emeritus, 1991-, senior policy adviser, 1997-, CME Group Foundation, chairman; GLOBEX, chairperson, 1987-93; Sakura Dellsher Inc., chairperson and chief executive officer, 1993-2000; Melamed & Associates Inc., chairman and chief executive officer, 1993-; Hua Mei Capital Co., vice chairman; Chicago Tribune, editor; One Chicago L.L.C., board director. **Publications:** The Tenth Planet (science fiction novel), 1987; (ed.) The Merits of Flexible Exchange Rates: An Anthology, 1988; Leo Melamed on the Markets: Twenty Years of Financial History as Seen by the Man Who Revolutionized the Markets, 1992; (B. Tamarkin) Leo Melamed: Escape to the Futures (memoir), 1996; For Crying Out Loud: From Open Outcry to the Electronic Screen, 2009. **Address:** Melamed & Associates Inc., 10 S Wacker Dr., Ste. 3275, Chicago, IL 60606-7415, U.S.A. **Online address:** lmelamed@melamedassoc.com

MELANCON, Michael. (Michael S. Melancon). American (born United States), b. 1940. **Genres:** Sociology, History. **Career:** International Research & Exchanges Board, research fellow, 1977-78, 1990-91; New Mexico State University, visiting assistant professor; Harvard University, visiting assistant professor, 1983-84; Auburn University, assistant professor, 1984-90, associate professor, 1990. Writer and academic. **Publications:** Stormy Petrels: The Socialist Revolutionaries in Russia's Labor Organizations, 1905-1914, 1988; The Socialist Revolutionaries and the Russian Anti-War Movement, 1914-1917, 1990; Rethinking Russia's February Revolution: Anonymous Spontaneity or Socialist Agency?, 2000; (ed. with A.K. Pate) New Labor History: Worker Identity and Experience in Russia, 1840-1918, 2002; (ed. as Michael S. Melancon with John C. Swanson) Modern Europe: Sources and Perspectives from History, 2003; (ed. with S.P. McCaffray) Russia in the European Context, 1789-1914: A Member of the Family, 2005; The Lena Goldfields Massacre and the Crisis of the Late Tsarist State, 2006; (ed. with J. Swanson) Nineteenth Century Europe: Sources and Perspectives from History, 2007. **Address:** Department of History, Auburn University, 310 Thach Hall, Auburn, AL 36849, U.S.A. **Online address:** melanms@mail.auburn.edu

MELANCON, Michael S. *See* **MELANCON, Michael.**

MELANÇON, Robert. Canadian (born Canada), b. 1947. **Genres:** Poetry, Literary Criticism And History. **Career:** Université de Montréal, Department of French Studies, professor, 1972-; Le Devoir, poetry reviewer, 1977-80; En Toutes Lettres, poetry reviewer, 1986-. Writer. **Publications:** POETRY: Inscriptions, 1978; Peinture aveugle, 1979, rev. ed., trans. as Blind Painting, 1985; Territoire, 1981; (with J. Brault) Au petit matin, 1993; L'avant-printemps à Montréal: Poésie, 1994; Notes sur unjour d'hiver, 1997; Air (in French and English), 1997; Le dessinateur, 2001; Paradis des apparences: essai de poèmes réalistes. 2004. OTHERS: Lieu commun, 1977; (ed.) Paul-Marie Lapointe, 1987; (trans.) A.M. Klein, The Second Scroll, 1990; Qu'est-ce qu'un classiquequé bécois?, 2004. **Address:** Départment d'etudes francaises, Universityersité de Montréal, C-8038, PO Box 6128, Sta. Downtown, Montreal, QC H3C 3J7, Canada. **Online address:** robert.melancon@umontreal.ca

MELCHIOR, Ib (Jorgen). (Ib Mel-key-or). American/Danish (born Denmark), b. 1917. **Genres:** Novels, Novellas/Short Stories, Plays/Screenplays, Autobiography/Memoirs, Translations, Art/Art History. **Career:** Radio City Music Hall and Center Theatre, stage manager, 1941-42; G-L Enterprises, associate producer, 1952-53. Freelance writer, director and producer, 1957-. **Publications:** Order of Battle, 1972; Sleeper Agent, 1975; The Haigerloch Project, 1977; The Watchdogs of Abaddon, 1979; The Marcus Device, 1980; The Tombstone Cipher, 1983; Eva, 1984; V-3, 1985; Code Name: Grand Guignol, 1987; (with C. Baldon) Steps and Stairways, 1989; (with F. Brandenburg) Quest (non-fiction), 1990; Order of Battle: Hitler's Werewolves, 1991; Case By Case: A U.S. Army Counterintelligence Agent in World War II, 1993; (with C. Baldon) Reflections on the Pool, 1997; Lauritz Melchior: The Golden Years of Bayreuth, 2003. **Address:** 8228 Marmont Ln., Los Angeles, CA 90001, U.S.A. **Online address:** ijmelchior@aol.com

MELCHIORI, Barbara Arnett. Italian/British (born England), b. 1926. **Genres:** Poetry, Literary Criticism And History, Young Adult Fiction, Romance/Historical, Novels. **Career:** Turin University, assistant lecturer in English; Rome University, lecturer, professor of English, 1976-2000. Writer. **Publications:** Browning's Poetry of Reticence, 1968; Feelings about Aspects: Henry James on Pierre Loti, 1969; (with G. Melchiori) Gusto di

Henry James, 1974; Terrorism in the Late Victorian Novel, 1985; Grant Allen: The Downward Path Which Leads to Fiction, 2000. Contributor to periodicals. **Address:** via Capodistria 9, Rome, 00198, Italy. **Online address:** arnett_m@uniroma3.it

MELDAHL, Keith Heyer. American (born United States) **Genres:** History. **Career:** Mira Costa College, professor of geology and oceanography, 1997-; University of Arizona, faculty; Oberlin College, faculty. Writer. **Publications:** Hard Road West: History and Geology along the Gold Rush Trail, 2007. **Address:** Mira Costa College, 1 Barnard Dr., Oceanside, CA 92056, U.S.A. **Online address:** kmeldahl@miracosta.edu

MELE, Alfred R. American (born United States), b. 1951. **Genres:** Philosophy, Essays, Business/Trade/Industry, Economics, Psychology. **Career:** Davidson College, visiting professor, 1979, assistant professor, 1979-85, associate professor, 1985-91, professor of philosophy, 1991-2000, Vail professor of philosophy, 1995-2000; Florida State University, William H. and Lucyle T. Werkmeister professor of philosophy, 2000-, Big Questions in Free Will Project, director, 2010-. Writer. **Publications:** Irrationality: An Essay on Akrasia, Self-Deception, and Self-Control, 1987; Springs of Action: Understanding Intentional Behavior, 1992; (ed. with J. Heil) Mental Causation, 1993; Autonomous Agents: From Self-Control to Autonomy, 1995; (ed.) The Philosophy of Action, 1997; Self-Deception Unmasked, 2001; Motivation and Agency, 2003; (ed. with P. Rawling) The Oxford Handbook of Rationality, 2004; Free Will and Luck, 2006; (ed. with M. Timmons and J. Greco) Rationality and the Good, 2007; Effective Intentions: The Power of Conscious Will, 2009; (ed. with R.F. Baumeister and K.D. Vohs) Free Will and Consciousness: How Might They Work?, 2010; Backsliding, 2012. Works appear in anthologies. Contributor to journals. **Address:** Department of Philosophy, Florida State University, 288 Dodd Hall, Tallahassee, FL 32306-1500, U.S.A. **Online address:** amele@fsu.edu

MELE, Christopher. American (born United States) **Genres:** Sociology, Politics/Government, History. **Career:** Pace University, lecturer, 1989-90; New School for Social Research, Eugene Lang College, lecturer, 1989-93; University of North Carolina, Department of Sociology and Anthropology, lecturer, 1993-94, assistant professor of sociology and anthropology, 1994-96; State University of New York, University at Buffalo, Department of Sociology, assistant professor of sociology, 1996-2000, associate professor of sociology, 2000-, adjunct associate professor, 2010-, director of undergraduate studies. Writer. **Publications:** Selling the Lower East Side: Culture, Real Estate, and Resistance in New York City, 2000; (ed. with J. Eade) Understanding the City: Contemporary and Future Perspectives, 2002; (ed. with T.A. Miller) Civil Penalties, Social Consequences, 2005; (ed. with J. Lin) Urban Sociology Reader, 2005, 2nd ed., forthcoming. Contributor of articles to books and periodicals. **Address:** Department of Sociology, University at Buffalo, State University of New York, 407 Park Hall, Buffalo, NY 14260-4140, U.S.A. **Online address:** cmele@acsu.buffalo.edu

MELIA, Fulvio. American/Italian (born Italy), b. 1956. **Genres:** Physics. **Career:** Northwestern University, assistant professor, 1987-91; University of Arizona, presidential young investigator, 1988-95, associate professor, 1991-93, professor, 1993-; Astrophysical Journal Letters, associate editor. **Publications:** Electrodynamics, 2001; The Black Hole at the Center of Our Galaxy, 2003; The Edge of Infinity: Supermassive Black Holes in the Universe, 2003; The Galactic Supermassive Black Hole, 2007; Cracking the Einstein Code: Relativity and the Birth of Black Hole Physics, 2009; High-Energy Astrophysics, 2009. **Address:** Department of Astronomy, University of Arizona, Tucson, AZ 85721-0001, U.S.A. **Online address:** melia@physics.arizona.edu

MELICH, Tanya. American (born United States), b. 1936. **Genres:** Communications/Media, Politics/Government, Women's Studies And Issues, Adult Non-fiction. **Career:** Salt Lake Tribune, reporter, 1957; Foreign Policy Association, researcher and writer, 1962; American Broadcasting Co., director of national election research for ABC News, 1963-64; Mitchell Melich for Governor, state campaign deputy director, 1964; Lindsay for Mayor Campaign, research director, 1965; Rockefeller for Governor Campaign, scheduler, 1966; editorial assistant to Thomas E. Dewey, 1967-68; Allen-van Slyck Group, public affairs writer, 1969; Philip van Slyck Inc., public affairs writer, 1971-72, CBS Inc., Corporate Affairs Division, editor of corporate information, 1975-76, Public Policy Unit, associate director, 1976-78, director of civic affairs, 1978-81; Political Issues Management, president and consultant in public policy analysis and strategy, 1983-. **Publications:** The Republican War against Women: An Insider's Report from behind the Lines, 1996, rev. ed., 1998. Contributor to books. **Address:** Political Issues Management, 115 E 9th St., New York, NY 10003-5422, U.S.A. **Online address:** tannoe@earthlink.net

MELION, Walter S. American/Filipino (born Philippines), b. 1952. **Genres:** Art/Art History, Biography, Autobiography/Memoirs. **Career:** Duke University, instructor, 1983-86; Johns Hopkins University, Department of History of Art, instructor, 1986-88, assistant professor, 1988-92, associate professor, 1992-94, professor, 1994-2004, chairman, 2001-04; Emory University, Department of Art History, associate professor, 1992-94, Lovis Corinth visiting professor, 2000-01, Asa Griggs Candler professor of art history, 2004-, chair, 2011-, Department of German, affiliate, 2007-, affiliate of studies in sexualities, 2007-. Writer. **Publications:** (Ed. with S.J. Barnes) Cultural Differentiation and Cultural Identity in the Visual Arts, 1989; Shaping the Netherlandish Canon: Karel van Mander's Schilder-Boeck, 1991; (ed. with S. Küchler) Images of Memory: On Remembering and Representation, 1991; (intro.) Annotations and Meditations on the Gospels, 2003; (ed. with R. Falkenburg and T.M. Richardson) Image and Imagination of the Religious Self in Late Medieval and Early Modern Europe, 2007; (ed. with J. Clifton and contrib.) Scripture for the Eyes (essay), 2009; The Meditative Art: Studies in the Northern Devotional Print, 1550-1625, 2009; (ed. with L.P. Wandel) Early Modern Eyes, 2010; (ed. with K. Enenkel) Meditatio: Refashioning the Self: Theory and Practice in Late Medieval and Early Modern Intellectual Culture, 2011; (ed. with C. Brusati and K. Enenkel) Authority of the Word, 2012. **Address:** Department of Art History, Emory University, 139 Carlos Hall, 581 S Kilgo Cir., Atlanta, GA 30322, U.S.A. **Online address:** walter.melion@emory.edu

MEL-KEY-OR, Ib. *See* **MELCHIOR, Ib (Jorgen).**

MELKO, Paul. American (born United States), b. 1968. **Genres:** Sciences. **Career:** Writer. **Publications:** The Walls of the Universe, 2006; Singularity's Ring, 2008; Ten Sigmas and Other Unlikelihoods, 2008; The Walls of the Universe, 2009. Contributor to periodicals. **Address:** Columbus, OH , U.S.A. **Online address:** melko@sff.net

MELLAN, Olivia. American (born United States), b. 1946. **Genres:** Money/Finance, Business/Trade/Industry. **Career:** Washington Therapy Guild, affiliate; Investment Adviser magazine, columnist. Consultant. **Publications:** Money Harmony: Resolving Money Conflicts in Your Life and Relationships, 1994; (with S. Christie) Overcoming Overspending: A Winning Plan for Spenders and Their Partners, 1995, rev. ed., 2004; Your Money Style, 2001; (with S. Christie) Money-Shy to Money-Sure: A Woman's Road Map to Financial Well-Being, 2001; (with S. Christie) The Advisor's Guide to Money Psychology, 2nd ed. 2004; (with S. Christie) The Client Connection, 2009. Contributor to periodicals and journals. **Address:** Olivia Mellan & Associates Inc., 2607 Connecticut Ave. NW, Washington, DC 20008-1522, U.S.A. **Online address:** om@moneyharmony.com

MELLEN, Joan. American (born United States), b. 1941. **Genres:** Novels, Film, History, Biography, Law. **Career:** Temple University, College of Liberal Arts, assistant professor, 1967-73, associate professor, 1973-76, professor of English, 1977-, teacher of fiction in graduate program in creative writing; Oxford University Press, consultant; Pantheon Books, consultant. Writer. **Publications:** A Filmguide to the Battle of Algiers, 1973; Marilyn Monroe, 1973; Women and Their Sexuality in the New Film, 1974; Voices from the Japanese Cinema, 1975; The Waves at Genji's Door: Japan Through Its Cinema, 1976; Big Bad Wolves: Masculinity in the American Film, 1977; (ed.) The World of Luis Buñuel: Essays in Criticism, 1978; Natural Tendencies, 1981; Privilege: The Enigma of Sasha Bruce, 1982; (with D. Richie) Films of Akira Kurosawa, 1984; Bob Knight: His Own Man, 1988; His Own Man, 1989; Kay Boyle: Author of Herself, 1994; Hellman and Hammett: The Legendary Passion of Lillian Hellman and Dashiell Hammett, 1996; Gabriel García Márquez, 2000; Magic Realism, 2000; One Hundred Years of Solitude, 2001; Seven Samurai, 2002; In the Realm of the Senses, 2004; A Farewell to Justice: Jim Garrison, JFK's Assassination, and the Case that Should have Changed History, 2005; Jim Garrison: His Life and Times, the Early Years, 2008. **Address:** Department of English, Temple University, 1147 Anderson Hall, 10th Fl., 1114 Polett Walk, Philadelphia, PA 19122-6090, U.S.A. **Online address:** joanmellen@aol.com

MELLIN, Robert. Canadian (born Canada), b. 1950?. **Genres:** Architecture, Homes/Gardens. **Career:** McGill University, School of Architecture, associate professor of architecture; Heritage Foundation of Newfoundland and Labrador, chairman. Writer and architect. **Publications:** A City of Towns, 1995; Tilting: House Launching, Slide Hauling, Potato Trenching and Other Tales from a Newfoundland Fishing Village, 2003; Residential Heritage Conservation in St. John's, 2005; Newfoundland Modern: Architecture in the Smallwood Years, 1949-1972, 2011. **Address:** School of Architecture, McGill University, Rm. 313, Macdonald-Harrington Bldg., 815 Sherbrooke St. W, Montreal, QC H3A 2K6, Canada. **Online address:** robert.mellin@mcgill.ca

MELLING, O. Irish (born Ireland), b. 1952. **Genres:** Novels, Young Adult Fiction, Science Fiction/Fantasy. **Career:** Writer and editor. **Publications:** AS O.R. MELLING: The Druid's Tune, 1983; The Singing Stone, 1986; Falling Out of Time, 1990; The Light-Bearer's Daughter, 2001; The Hunter's Moon, 2005; The Summer King, 2006; Book of Dreams, 2009. OTHERS: My Blue Country, 1996. CHRONICLES OF FAERIE SERIES: The Book of Dreams, 2003; Golden Book of Faerie, 2004; People of the Great Journey, forthcoming. **Address:** Penguin Group Canada, 90 Eglinton Ave. E, Ste. 700, Toronto, ON M4P 2Y3, Canada. **Online address:** info@ormelling.com

MELLIZO (CUADRADO), Carlos. American/Spanish (born Spain), b. 1942. **Genres:** Novels, Novellas/Short Stories, Philosophy, Essays, Translations. **Career:** Teacher, 1966; Universidad Complutense de Madrid, lecturer in philosophy, 1967-68; University of Wyoming, assistant professor, 1970-74, associate professor, 1974-77, professor of modern and classical languages, 1977-, general editor of publications of the department, 1974-82, Department of Philosophy, adjunct professor, 1998-, now professor emeritus; Phi Sigma Iota, vice president, 1984-86; Alianza Editorial, translator, 1985-. **Publications:** Romero (novel), 1975; En torno a David Hume, 1978; Carmela (novella), 1978; Nueva Introduccion a Francisco Sanchez El Esceptico, 1982; Una cuestión de tiempo, 1991; La Vida Privada De John Stuart Mill y Harriet Taylor, 1994. STORIES: Los Cocodrilos, 1970; Historia de Sonia y otras historias, 1987; Un americano en Madrid, 1997; La lingua de Buka (Buka's Language), 2000; Antes del Descenso (Before the Descent), 2004. EDITOR: Homenaje a Azorín (essays), 1974; (with R. Landeira) Ignacio Aldecoa (essays), 1977; (with L. Salstad) Blas de Otero: Study of a Poet, 1979; Escritos Epistolares, 1998; España, Estados Unidos y la crisis de 1898, 1998; Nacer, vivir, morir, 1998; Antes del descenso y otras palabras finales, 2004. TRANSLATOR: D. Hume, Dialogues Concerning Natural Religion, 1976; D. Hume, Abstract, 1976; F. Sanchez, That Nothing is Known, 1977; F. Sanchez, Of the Duration and Brevity of Life, 1982; D. Hume, My Life: A Letter from a Gentleman to His Friend in Edinburgh, 1985; J.S. Mill, Autobiografia, 1986; J.S. Mill, The Utility of Religion, 1986; D. Hume, Suicide and Other Essays, 1988; T. Hobbes, Leviatan, 1989; J. Locke, Second Treatise on Civil Government, 1992; D. Hume, An Inquiry Concerning the Principles of Morals, 1994; J.S. Mill, Nature, 1998; J. Locke, An Essay and a Letter on Toleration, 1999; E. Burke, Reflections on the Revolution in France, 2003; T. Veblen, Theory of the Leisure Class, 2004; D. Hume, Of Love and Marriage, 2006. **Address:** Department of Modern & Classical Languages, University of Wyoming, Rm. 232, Hoyt Hall, Dept. 3603, 1000 E University Ave., Laramie, WY 82071-2000, U.S.A.

MELLOR, D. H. British (born England), b. 1938. **Genres:** Mathematics/Statistics, Sciences, Philosophy, Essays. **Career:** Pembroke College, fellow, 1964-70; University of Cambridge, assistant lecturer, 1965, lecturer, 1970, reader, 1983, professor, 1986-99, professor emeritus of philosophy, 1999-, pro-vice-chancellor, 2000-01; Darwin College, fellow, 1971-2005. Writer. **Publications:** The Matter of Chance, 1971; Real Time, 1981; Matters of Metaphysics, 1991; The Facts of Causation, 1995; Real Time II, 1998; (contrib.) Real Metaphysics: Essays in Honour of D.H. Mellor, 2002; Probability: A Philosophical Introduction, 2005. EDITOR: (and intro.) Foundations: Essays in Philosophy, Logic, Mathematics and Economics, 1978; Science, Belief and Behavior: Essays in Honour of R.B. Braithwaite, 1980; Prospects for Pragmatism: Essays in Memory of F.P. Ramsey, 1980; Philosophical Papers, 1990; Ways of Communicating: The Darwin College Lectures, 1990; (with A. Oliver) Properties, 1997; (with H. Lillehammer) Ramsey's Legacy, 2005. **Address:** Faculty of Philosophy, University of Cambridge, Sidgwick Ave., Cambridge, CB CB3 9DA, England. **Online address:** dhm11@cam.ac.uk

MELLOR, Jodie. *See* **OLDFIELD, Jenny.**

MELLOR, John W(illiams). American/French (born France), b. 1928. **Genres:** Economics, Adult Non-fiction, Marketing, Business/Trade/Industry, Agriculture/Forestry, Essays. **Career:** Cornell University, lecturer, 1952-54, assistant professor, 1954-58, associate professor, 1958-61, professor of agricultural economics, 1961-77, Center for International Studies, associate director, 1961-64, director, 1964-65, Program on Comparative Economic Development, director, 1973-77; Balwant Rajput College, Council of Economic and Cultural Affairs, fellow and visiting professor, 1959-60; Rockefeller Foundation, Indian Agricultural Research Institute, visiting professor, 1964-65; United States Agency for International Development, chief economist and associate assistant administrator for policy development and analysis, 1976-77; International Food Policy Research Institute, director, 1977-91; John Mellor Associates Inc., president, 1991-98, 2007-; Abt Associates Inc., vice president, 1998-2006. Writer. **Publications:** The Economics of Agricultural Development, 1966; Notes on Foodgrains Prices, India, 1967-68 and 1968-69, 1967; Note on Agricultural Price Policy, 1968 India Wheat Price Support, 1968; (co-author) Developing Rural India: Plan and Practice, 1968; Agricultural Prices in Economic Development: Their Role, Function, and Operation, 1970; (with U.J. Lele) Political Economy of Employment Oriented Development, 1971; (with U.J. Lele) A Labor Supply Theory of Economic Development, 1971; (with U.J. Lele) Technological Change and Distributive Bias in a Dual Economy, 1972; Accelerated Growth in Agricultural Production and the Intersectoral Transfer of Resources, 1972; (with U.J. Lele) Growth Linkages of the New Foodgrain Technologies, 1972; Interaction of Growth Strategy, Agriculture, and Foreign Trade: The Case of India, 1974; (with M.S. Mudahar) Simulating a Developing Economy with Modernizing Agricultural Sector: Implications For Employment And Economic Growth, 1974; Modernizing Agriculture, Employment, and Economic Growth: A Simulation Model, 1974; (with J.M. Cohen and A.A. Goldsmith) Revolution and Land Reform in Ethiopia: Peasant Associations, Local Government, and Rural Development, 1976; The New Economics of Growth: A Strategy for India and the Developing World, 1976; (ed.) India, a Rising Middle Power, 1979; International Monetary Economy and the Third World, 1981; (with H. Tsai) Money in Economic Systems, 1982; (ed. with R. Lang and D. Vojnic) Essays on the Political Economy of Yugoslavia, 1982; Monetarism, Theory and Policy, 1983; World Banking and Finance: Cooperation Versus Conflict, 1984; Politics of Monetarism: Its Historical and Institutional Development, 1984; Economic Nationalism and Stability, 1976; (ed. with G.M. Desai) Agricultural Change and Rural Poverty: Variations on a Theme by Dharm Narain, 1985; Economic Nationalism and Stability, 1985; (ed. with C.L. Delgado and M.J. Blackie) Accelerating Food Production in Sub-Saharan Africa, 1987; Monetary Policy and Rational Expectations, 1987; (ed. with R. Ahmed) Agricultural Price Policy for Developing Countries, 1988; Lectures on Agricultural Growth and Employment: An Equitable Growth Strategy and Its Knowledge Needs, 1988; (ed. with R. Lang and D. Vojnic) Essays on the Yugoslav Economic Model: Money and Democracy, 1990; World Debt and Stability, 1991; Monetary Policy and Politics: Rules Versus Discretion, 1992; (co-ed.) Yugoslavia in the Age of Democracy: Essays on Economic and Political Reform, 1992; (with B.M. Desai) Institutional Finance for Agricultural Development: An Analytical Survey of Critical Issues, 1993; Successor States and Cooperation Theory: A Model for Eastern Europe, 1994; Monetary Reform in Former Socialist Economies, 1994; (ed.) Agriculture on the Road to Industrialization, 1995; Integration and Stabilization: A Monetary View, 1996; Transformation and Emerging Markets, 1996; United States in the Changing Global Economy: Policy Implications and Issues, 1997; World Economy at the Crossroads, 1997; Political Economy of Money: Emerging Fiat Monetary Regime, 1999; Money, Systems, and Growth: A New Economic Order?, 1999; Issues in Money and Banking, 2000; Money and Monetary Regimes: Struggle for Monetary Supremacy, 2002. CONTRIBUTOR: Food: A Tool in International Development, 1962; The Professional Education of Students from Other Lands, 1963; Agricultural Development and Economic Growth, 1967; Agricultural Cooperatives and Markets in Developing Countries, 1969; Subsistence Agriculture and Economic Development, 1969; A.E.A. Readings in the Economics of Agriculture, 1969; Some Issues Emerging from Recent Breakthroughs in Food Production, 1971. Contributor of articles to journals. **Address:** John Mellor Associates Inc., 801 Pennsylvania Ave. NW, Ste. PH 18, Washington, DC 20004-2615, U.S.A. **Online address:** jmellor@jmassocinc.com

MELLOWS, Anthony (Roger). British (born England), b. 1936. **Genres:** Law, History. **Career:** Alexanders Easton Kinch, senior partner, 1962-96; University of London, King's College, School of Law, assistant lecturer in law, 1962-64, lecturer, 1964-71, reader, 1971-74, professor, 1974-90, professor emeritus, 1990-; chancellor order of St. John, 1991-99; vice-lord prior, 2005-08, lord prior, 2008. Writer. **Publications:** Local Searches and Enquiries, 1964, 2nd ed. 1967; Conveyancing Searches, 1964; The Preservation and Felling of Trees, 1964; The Trustee's Handbook, 1965, 3rd ed. 1975; Land

Charges, 1966; (co-author) The Modern Law of Trusts, 1966, 9th ed. 2008; Taxation for Executors and Trustees, 1967, 6th ed. 1984; The Law of Succession, 1970, 4th ed. 1983; Taxation of Land Transactions, 1973, 3rd ed. 1982; (contrib.) Parker and Mellows: The Modern Law of Trusts, 9th ed., 2008. **Address:** King's College, University of London, Rm. K0.30, Strand, GL WC2R 2LS, England.

MELMAN, Billie. Israeli (born Israel), b. 1952?. **Genres:** Women's Studies And Issues, Cultural/Ethnic Topics. **Career:** Tel Aviv University, teaching assistant in history, 1978-79, teaching and research assistant in history, 1979-80, visiting lecturer in history, 1984-86, Allon fellow and lecturer in modern history, 1986-91, senior lecturer in modern history, 1991-97, associate professor of history, 1998-2005, professor of history, 2005-, School of Historical Studies, director, 2008-, Henri Glasberg chair of European studies; Harvard University, Minda de Gunzburg Center for European Studies, visiting fellow, 1990-91; University of Michigan, Institute for the Humanities, Norman Freehling visiting professor, 1993-94. Writer. **Publications:** Women and the Popular Imagination in the Twenties: Flappers and Nymphs, 1988; Women's Orients: English Women and the Middle East, 1718-1918: Sexuality, Religion and Work, 1992; (ed.) Borderlines: Genders and Identities in War and Peace, 1870-1930, 1997; The Culture of History: English Uses of the Past, 1800-1953, 2006; London: Makom, Anashim Ve-Imperyah (1800-1960), 2009; Popularizing National Pasts: 1800 to the Present, 2011. **Address:** Department of History, Tel Aviv University, PO Box 39040, Ramat, 69978, Israel. **Online address:** bmelman@post.tau.ac.il

MELMAN, Peter Charles. American (born United States), b. 1971. **Genres:** Novels. **Career:** English teacher, 1993-95; Zagat Restaurant Survey, restaurant critic and editorial assistant, 1995; Barnes & Noble, clerk, 1996; Elliott Bay Book Co., clerk, 2001; Book Court, clerk, 2002; Hunter College High School, teacher, 2002-. Writer. **Publications:** Landsman: A Novel, 2007. Contributor to periodicals. **Address:** Department of English & Theatre Arts, Hunter College High School, 71 E 94th St., New York, NY 10128, U.S.A. **Online address:** pmelman@hccs.hunter.cuny.edu

MELMAN, Yossi. (Yossi Bili Melman). Israeli/Polish (born Poland), b. 1950. **Genres:** Politics/Government, Area Studies, Young Adult Fiction. **Career:** Kol Israel, economic correspondent, 1975-80; Ha'aretz (daily newspaper), European correspondent, 1980-84, special correspondent, 1989-, feature writer and columnist; Davar (daily newspaper), chief diplomatic correspondent, 1984-89; Jane's Defence Weekly, Israeli correspondent, 1984-87; Glasgow Herald, Israeli correspondent, 1984-89. **Publications:** The CIA Report on Israel's Intelligence Community (in Hebrew), 1982; The Master Terrorist: The True Story of Abu Nidal, Adama, 1986; (with D. Raviv) Behind the Uprising: Israelis, Jordanians, and Palestinians, 1989; (with Raviv) The Imperfect Spies, 1989; (with D. Raviv) Meraglim lo mushlamim: sipuro shel ha-modiin ha-Yiśre'eli, 1990; (with D. Raviv) Every Spy a Prince: The Complete History of Israel's Intelligence Community, 1990; The New Israelis: An Intimate View of a Changing People, 1992; (with D. Raviv) Friends in Deed: Inside the U.S.-Israel Alliance, 1994; (with D. Raviv) Shutafim li-devar ma'aśeh: be-tokhekhe ha-berit ha-Yiśreelit-Ameriḳanit, 1994; (with E. Haber) Hameraglim, 2002; (with M. Javedanfar) Nuclear Sphinx of Tehran: Mahmoud Ahmadinejad and the State of Iran, 2007; (with M. Javedanfar) Ha-Sefinḳs: Aḥmadineg'ad ṿeha-mafteaḥ la-petsatsah ha-Iranit, 2007. **Address:** Ha'aretz Daily Newspaper, Schocken 21 St., Tel Aviv, 61001, Israel.

MELMAN, Yossi Bili. *See* **MELMAN, Yossi.**

MELNICK, Jeffrey Paul. American (born United States) **Genres:** Race Relations, Music, Literary Criticism And History. **Career:** Babson College, associate professor of American studies; Trinity College, visiting professor; Harvard University, visiting professor. Writer. **Publications:** A Right to Sing the Blues: African Americans, Jews, and American Popular Song, 1999; Black-Jewish Relations on Trial: Leo Frank and Jim Conley in the New South, 2000; (ed. with R. Rubin) American Popular Music: New Approaches to the Twentieth Century, 2001; (ed. with H. Hathaway and J. Jarab) Race and the Modern Artist, 2003; (with R. Rubin) Immigration and American Popular Culture: An Introduction, 2007; 9/11 Culture: America Under Construction, 2009. **Address:** History and Society Division, Babson College, 231 Forest St., Babson Park, MA 02457-0310, U.S.A. **Online address:** melnick@babson.edu

MELNICK, Ralph. American (born United States), b. 1946. **Genres:** History, Literary Criticism And History, Theology/Religion. **Career:** NYC Department of Social Services, caseworker, 1970-71; Atlantic Counseling Center, Drug Rehabilitation Program, supervisor and counselor, 1971; American Jewish Historical Society, archivist and librarian, 1971-72, freelance archivist, 1985-89; Zionist Archives and Library, archivist and librarian, 1975-77; College of Charleston, head of special collections at library, associate professor and lecturer in religion and history, 1977-84; Avery Institute for African-American History and Culture, founding board director and curator of collections, 1980-84; Williston Northampton School, library director and teacher of religion, 1984-2003; University of Massachusetts, visiting professor of Judaic studies, 2002-03, lecturer; Convent of the Sacred Heart, library director and teacher of English, 2003-05; The Child School, library director, 2005-06; Sierra Canyon School, library consultant and development officer, 2006-08; Westfield Athenaeum, assistant library director, 2006-. Writer. **Publications:** (Comp.) The Wendell Mitchell Levi Library and Archives-A Catalog of its Holdings, 1979; (co-author) Guide for America: Holy Land Studies, vol. I, 1980, vol. II, 1982, vol. III, 1984; (ed.) Catalog of the Scientific Apparatus at the College of Charleston, 1800-1940, 1980; From Polemics to Apologetics: Jewish-Christian Rapprochement in 17th Century Amsterdam, 1981; The Stolen Legacy of Anne Frank: Lillian Hellman, Meyer Levin and the Staging of the Diary, 1997; The Life and Work of Ludwig Lewisohn, vol. I: A Touch of Wildness, 1998, vol. II: This Dark and Desperate Age, 1998; Justice Betrayed: A Double Killing in Old Santa Fe, 2002; Senda Berenson: The Unlikely Founder of Women's Basketball, 2007. Contributor to magazines. **Address:** Department of Judaic and Near Eastern Studies, University of Massachusetts, 744 Herter Hall, 161 Presidents Dr., Amherst, MA 01003-9312, U.S.A. **Online address:** rmelnick@judnea.umass.edu

MELNIKOFF, Pamela (Rita). British (born England) **Genres:** Children's Fiction, Poetry, History, Science Fiction/Fantasy, Young Adult Fiction. **Career:** Jewish Chronicle, reporter and feature writer, 1960-70; film critic, 1970-96. **Publications:** The Star and the Sword, 1965; Plots and Players: The Lopez Conspiracy (young adult novel), 1988; Prisoner in Time: A Child of the Holocaust (young adult novel), 1992. **Address:** Jewish Chronicle, 25 Furnival St., London, GL EC4A 1JT, England. **Online address:** pamela@somethingjewish.co.uk

MELNYCZUK, Askold. American (born United States), b. 1954. **Genres:** Adult Non-fiction, Novels, Translations. **Career:** AGNI Magazine, founding editor, 1972-; Boston University, preceptor and editor, 1982-2001; Harvard University, preceptor, 1990-92; Bennington Graduate Writing Seminars, lecturer, 1995; University of Massachusetts, director of creative writing, 2002-, associate professor. Writer. **Publications:** What Is Told (novel), 1995; (co-ed.) From Three Worlds: New Ukrainian Writing, 1996; (foreword) Peltse and Pentameron, 1996; (trans.) Yuri Vynnychuk, The Windows of Time Frozen: And Other Stories, 2000; Ambassador of the Dead: A Novel, 2001; The House of Widows: An Oral History, 2008; Smedley's Secret Guide to World Literature, forthcoming. Contributor to periodicals. **Address:** Department of English, University of Massachusetts, Wheatley Bldg., 6th Fl., 100 Morrissey Blvd., 100 Morrissey Blvd., Boston, MA 02125-3393, U.S.A. **Online address:** askold.melnyczuk@umb.edu

MELNYK, Andrew. American (born United States), b. 1962. **Genres:** Adult Non-fiction, Humanities. **Career:** University of Oxford, Magdalen College, junior lecturer, 1988-89; University of Virginia, visiting assistant professor, 1989-90; College of William and Mary, visiting assistant professor, 1990-91; University of Missouri, Philosophy Department, assistant professor, 1991-97, associate professor, 1997-2005, professor, 2005-, department chair, 2006-. Writer. **Publications:** A Physicalist Manifesto: Thoroughly Modern Materialism, 2003. Contributor to journals. **Address:** Department of Philosophy, University of Missouri, 439 Strickland Hall, Columbia, MO 65211-4160, U.S.A. **Online address:** melnyka@missouri.edu

MELNYK, Steven A. American/Canadian (born Canada), b. 1953. **Genres:** Business/Trade/Industry, Administration/Management, Economics. **Career:** University of Western Ontario, Department of Economics, research assistant, 1975-76, School of Business Administration, research assistant, 1977, 1978; Michigan State University, Graduate School of Business Administration, Department of Management, assistant professor of production and operations management, 1980-85, associate professor of production and operations management, 1985-90, professor of production and operations management, 1990-, Eli Broad College of Business, Department of Marketing and Supply Chain Management, professor; American Red Cross, consultant. Writer.

Publications: (Co-author) Shop Floor Control, 1985; (with P.L. Carter) Shop Floor Control Principles and Practices and Case Studies, 1987; (with P.L. Carter) Production Activity Control: A Practical Guide, 1987; (ed.) Tool Management and Control, 1990; (with R. Narasimhan) Computer Integrated Manufacturing: A Source Book, 1990; (with R. Narasimhan) Computer Integrated Manufacturing: Guidelines and Applications from Industrial Leaders, 1992; (with D.R. Denzler) Operations Management: A Value-Driven Approach, 1996; (with R.T. Smith) Green Manufacturing, 1996; (co-author) ISO 14000: Assessing its Impact on Corporate Effectiveness and Efficiency, 1999; Supply Chain Management: Redefining the Transformation Process, 1999; Measurements, Metrics and the Value-Driven Operations Management System, 1999; (with R.T. Christensen) Back to Basics: Your Guide to Manufacturing Excellence, 2000; (with M. Swink) Value-Driven Operations Management: An Integrated Modular Approach, 2002; (with M. Swink, M.B. Cooper and J.L. Hartley) Managing Operations Across the Supply Chain, 2010; (with D.L. Stewart, R.J. Calantone and C. Speier) Metrics and the Supply Chain: An Exploratory Study, forthcoming. **Address:** Eli Broad College of Business, Michigan State University, 327 N Business Complex, 632 Bogue St., Ste. N370, East Lansing, MI 48824-1121, U.S.A. **Online address:** melnyk@bus.msu.edu

MELONIO, Francoise. French (born France), b. 1951. **Genres:** Literary Criticism And History, History. **Career:** Univeristy of Paris, associate professor in secondary education, 1976-80; National Center for Scientific Research, historical researcher, 1980-92; Universite Paris X-Nanterre, professor of French literature, 1992-98; Universite Paris IV, professor of French literature, 1998-2004, 2005-, director, 2004; Middlebury College, visiting professor, 2000, 2001; University of Sydney, visiting professor, 2004; Institute of Political Studies of Paris, lecturer in history and history of political representation, 2006-. Writer. **Publications:** Tocqueville and the French, 1993; (ed. with F. Furet) L'Entreprise encyclopédique: études réunies et présentées, 1997; Histoire culturelle de la France, 1998; (ed. with F. Gerbod) L'égalité au tournant du siècle: Péguy et ses contemporains: Actes, 1998; (ed. and intro. with F. Furet) The Old Regime and the Revolution, 1998; Nainarce et affirmation d'une culture nationale, la France de 1815 á 1880, 2001. **Address:** Universite Paris IV, 1 rue Victor Cousin, Paris, 75230, France. **Online address:** francoise.melonio@paris-sorbonne.fr

MELOSH, Barbara. American (born United States), b. 1950. **Genres:** History, Women's Studies And Issues, Autobiography/Memoirs, Theology/Religion, Literary Criticism And History. **Career:** Brown University, visiting lecturer in American civilization, 1978-79; University of Wisconsin, assistant professor of history and women's studies, 1979-83; George Mason University, assistant professor, 1983-86, associate professor of English and American studies, 1986-92, professor of English, American studies, history, 1992-2005, professor emeritus, 2005-; National Museum of American History, associate curator of medical sciences 1983-90; Salem Lutheran Church, pastor. Writer. **Publications:** The Physician's Hand: Work Culture and Conflict in American Nursing, 1982; Engendering Culture: Manhood and Womanhood in New Deal Public Art and Theater, 1991; Strangers and Kin: The American Way of Adoption, 2002. EDITOR: (intro.) American Nurses in Fiction: An Anthology of Short Stories, 1984; Gender and American History since 1890, 1993. Contributor to periodicals. **Address:** 7 Deer Run Dr., Wilmington, DE 19807-2403, U.S.A. **Online address:** pastorbarbara@salemsouthbaltimore.org

MELTON, Brian C. (Brian Christopher Melton). American (born United States), b. 1976. **Genres:** Novels, Biography, Science Fiction/Fantasy, Novellas/Short Stories, History. **Career:** Liberty University, Department of History, associate professor of history; Lantern Hollow Press, co-founder and editor. **Publications:** Sherman's Forgotten General: Henry W. Slocum, 2007; Waverly Hall: Relois, 2011; Robert E. Lee: A Life, 2012. Contributor to various articles to journals. **Address:** Department of History, Liberty University, 1971 University Blvd., Lynchburg, VA 24502-2269, U.S.A. **Online address:** 221b_baker_st@live.com

MELTON, Brian Christopher. *See* **MELTON, Brian C.**

MELTON, Buckner F. American (born United States) **Genres:** Novels, History. **Career:** Duke University, history instructor, 1989; Georgia Southern University, visiting assistant professor of history, 1990-91; Elon College, assistant professor of history, 1991-96; University of North Carolina, clinical associate professor of law, 1996-2003; Mercer University, part-time faculty, distinguished writer-in-residence, press fellow, 2003-; National Public Radio, commentator; NewsHour, co-commentator; MSNBC, commentator. **Publications:** The First Impeachment: The Constitution's Framers and the Case of Senator William Blount, 1998; Aaron Burr: Conspiracy to Treason, 2001; A Hanging Offense: The Strange Affair of the Warship Somers, 2003; Aaron Burr: The Rise and Fall of an American Politician, 2004; (ed.) The Quotable Founding Fathers: A Treasury of 2, 500 Wise and Witty Quotations from the Men and Women Who Created America, 2004; Sea Cobra: Admiral Halsey's Task Force and the Great Pacific Typhoon, 2007; Law, 2010. **Address:** Mercer University, 1400 Coleman Ave., Macon, GA 31207, U.S.A. **Online address:** melton@bucknermelton.com

MELTON, Judith. American (born United States), b. 1941?. **Genres:** Writing/Journalism, Biography, Autobiography/Memoirs. **Career:** University of Tulsa, professor, 1969-72; Clemson University, professor of German and women studies, 1972-, coordinator of women studies program, interim associate dean of architecture, arts and humanities; Association of the Departments of Foreign Languages, president. Writer. **Publications:** (Trans.) Rewriting History: The Original and Revised World War II Diaries of Curt Prufer, Nazi Diplomat, 1988; The Face of Exile: Autobiographical Journeys, 1998. **Address:** Department of Languages, Clemson University, 511 Strode, Clemson, SC 29634, U.S.A. **Online address:** jmlton@mail.clemson.edu

MELTON, Marliss. Also writes as Marliss Melton Arruda. American (born United States) **Genres:** Young Adult Fiction, Children's Fiction, Romance/Historical. **Career:** Deep Creek Junior High School, English teacher, 1988-89; Moorestown High School, English and Spanish teacher, 1989-92; James Blair Middle School, Spanish teacher, 1992-93; Lafayette High School, Spanish teacher, 1992-93; York High School, Spanish teacher, 1993-98; Virginia Commonwealth University, ESL teacher, 2000; Christopher Newport University, ESL teacher, 2000; College of William and Mary, faculty, 2000-05. Writer. **Publications:** (As Marliss Moon) Danger's Promise, 2002; (as Marliss Melton Arruda) Sofi's Blessing, 2002; (as Marliss Moon) By Starlight (sequel to Danger's Promise), 2003. NAVY SEAL SERIES: Forget Me Not, 2004; In the Dark, 2005; Time to Run, 2006; Next to Die, 2007; Too Far Gone, 2008; Don't Let Go, 2008. BLACK OPS SERIES: Show No Fear, 2009; The Protector, 2011. **Address:** c/o Author Mail, Warner Forever, 1271 Ave. of the Americas, New York, NY 10020-1393, U.S.A. **Online address:** marlissmelton@cox.net

MELTZER, Brad. American (born United States), b. 1970. **Genres:** Mystery/Crime/Suspense, Novels, Graphic Novels, Young Adult Non-fiction, Young Adult Fiction, Humor/Satire. **Career:** Writer and attorney. **Publications:** The Tenth Justice, 1997; Dead Even, 1998; The First Counsel, 2001; The Millionaires, 2002; Archer's Quest: Green Arrow, 2003; The Zero Game, 2004; Identity Crisis, 2005; The Book of Fate, 2006; The Book of Lies, 2008; (with G. Johns) Justice League of America (comics), 2008; Heroes for My Son, 2010; Inner Circle, 2011. Contributes to periodicals. **Address:** 20533 Biscayne Blvd., Ste. 371, Aventura, FL 33180, U.S.A.

MELTZER, David. American (born United States), b. 1937. **Genres:** Novels, Novellas/Short Stories, Science Fiction/Fantasy, Children's Fiction, Poetry, Songs/Lyrics And Libretti, Cultural/Ethnic Topics, Literary Criticism And History, Music, Theology/Religion. **Career:** Discovery Bookshop, manager, 1959-67; Maya, editor, 1966-71; Tree Magazine, editor, 1970-; Tree Books, editor, 1970-; Urban School, teacher, 1975-76; New College of California, Graduate Poetics Program, faculty, 1980-. **Publications:** (With D. Schenker) Poems, 1957; Ragas, 1959; The Clown: A Poem, 1960; We All Have Something to Say to Each Other, 1962; Introduction to the Outsiders (essay), 1962; Bazascope Mother (essay), 1964; The Process, 1965; In Hope I Offer a Fire Wheel, 1965; Journal of the Birth, 1967; Nature Poem, 1967; Dark Continent, 1967; Round the Lunch Box, 1969; Yesod, 1969; Glue Factory, 1969; Abulafia Song, 1969; Lovely, 1969; From Eden Book, 1969; Isla Vista Notes, 1970; Greenspeech, 1970; Luna, 1970; Letter and Numbers, 1970; Bronx Lil-Head of Lillin S.A.C., 1970; 32 Beams of Light, 1970; (co-author) The Thirteenth Quarto: Poems & Drawings, 1971; Bark: A Polemic, 1973; Hero/Lil, 1973; Tens: Selected Poems 1961-1971, 1973; The Eyes, the Blood, 1973; French Broom, 1973; Blue Rags, 1974; Harps, 1975; The Secret Garden: An Anthology of Texts from the Jewish Mystical Tradition, 1976; Six, 1976; Abra (for children), 1976; Two-Way Mirror: A Poetry Notebook (prose), 1977; The Art, the Veil (poetry), 1981; The Name: Selected Poems, 1973-1983, 1984; The Book within the Book, 1988; Arrows: Selected Poetry 1957-1992, 1994; No Eyes: Lester Young, 2000; Beat Thing, 2004; When I Was a Poet, 2011. NOVELS: Orf, 1968; The Agency Trilogy, 1968; The Brain-Plant Tetralogy, 1970;

Star, 1970; Under, 1995. EDITOR: (with M. McClure and L. Ferlinghetti) Journal for the Protection of All Beings, 1961, No. 4, 1978; The San Francisco Poets, 1971; Knots, 1971; Birth: An Anthology, 1973; Death, 1984; Reading Jazz, 1993; Writing Jazz (anthology), 1999; San Francisco Beat (interviews), 2001. **Address:** PO Box 9005, Berkeley, CA 94709, U.S.A. **Online address:** dmelt@earthlink.net

MELUCH, R(ebecca) M. (Rebecca Ashe). American (born United States), b. 1956. **Genres:** Romance/Historical, Science Fiction/Fantasy, Novels. **Career:** Writer, 1978-; human resources information system analyst, 1999-. **Publications:** Sovereign, 1979; Wind Child, 1982; Jerusalem Fire, 1985; War Birds, 1989; Wind Dancers, 1990; Chicago Red, 1990; The Queen's Squadron, 1992; (as Rebecca Ashe) Masque of the Swan, 1996. TOUR OF THE MERRIMACK: The Myriad, 2005; Wolf Star, 2006; The Sagittarius Command, 2007; Strength and Honor, 2008; The Ninth Circle, 2011. **Address:** 1127 Chapman Ln., Medina, OH 44256-7081, U.S.A. **Online address:** rmmeluch@yahoo.com

MELUSKY, Joseph A. American (born United States), b. 1952. **Genres:** Politics/Government, Civil Liberties/Human Rights. **Career:** West Chester State College, instructor, 1979; University of Delaware, lecturer, 1979-80; Saint Francis University, political science faculty, 1980-, president of faculty senate, 1985-87, department chair, 1992-2005, 2007-10, dean of general education, 1993-94, interim vice-president for academic affairs, 2005-06. Writer. **Publications:** To Preserve These Rights: The Bill of Rights, 1791-1991, 1991; The Constitution: Our Written Legacy, 1991; (comp. with W.H. Ridgway) The Bill of Rights: Our Written Legacy, 1993; The American Political System: An Owner's Manual, 2000; (with K.A. Pesto) Cruel and Unusual Punishment: Rights and Liberties under the Law, 2003; The Contemporary Constitution: Modern Interpretations, 2006. **Address:** Saint Francis University, 316B Scotus Hall, PO Box 600, Loretto, PA 15940, U.S.A. **Online address:** jmelusky@francis.edu

MELVILLE, Arabella. British (born England), b. 1948. **Genres:** Sports/Fitness, Medicine/Health, Human Relations/Parenting, Sciences. **Career:** McGill University, research assistant, 1973-74; Libertine Magazine, freelance writer and editor, 1974-77; University of Wales, University College of Swansea, research fellow in psychology, 1978-80; University of York, NHS Centre for Reviews and Dissemination, research fellow, 1995-; Life Profile Ltd., director. **Publications:** (With C. Johnson) Cured to Death: The Effects of Prescription Drugs, 1983; (with C. Johnson) The Long-Life Heart: How to Avoid Heart Disease and Live a Longer Life, 1985; (with C. Johnson) Hay Fever: No Need to Suffer, 1985; (with C. Johnson) Persistent Fat and How to Lose It, 1986 in US as Fat Free Forever, 1987; Alternatives to Drugs, 1987 in US as Health without Drugs, 1990; (with C. Johnson) Immunity Plus: How to Be Healthy in the Age of New Infections, 1988; (with C. Johnson) The Complete Diet Book, 1989; (with C. Johnson) Eat Yourself Thin: Lose Weight, Gain Energy, 1990; Natural Hormone Health, 1990; Light My Fire, 1994; Improving Outcomes in Breast Cancer, 1996; Difficult Men: Strategies for Women Who Choose not to Leave, 1999. Contributor of articles to magazines and newspapers. **Address:** David Grossman Literary Agency Ltd., 110-114 Clerkenwell Rd., London, GL EC1M 5SA, England. **Online address:** arabella_melville@port35.freeserve.co.uk

MELVILLE, Charles (Peter). British (born England), b. 1951. **Genres:** History. **Career:** University of London, Imperial College of Science and Technology, research assistant, 1974-82; Cambridge University, assistant lecturer, 1984-88, lecturer in Islamic studies, 1988-2001, reader in Persian history, 2001-, professor of Persian history, 2008; Disasters (journal), editor, 1982-89; Pembroke College, fellow; Shahnama Project, director, 1999-; The Islamic Manuscript Association, president, 2006-; Central Electricity Generating Board, consultant. **Publications:** (With N.N. Ambraseys) A History of Persian Earthquakes, 1982; (with A. Ubaydli) Christians and Moors in Spain, vol. I-III, 1988-92; (with N.N. Ambraseys and R.D. Adams) The Seismicity of Egypt, Arabia and the Red Sea: A Historical Review, 1994. EDITOR: (with P.W. Avery and G. Hambly) The Cambridge History of Iran, vol. VII, 1991; Safavid Persia, 1996; (with B. Brend) Epic of the Persian Kings: The Art of Ferdowsi's Shahnameh, 2010; Proceedings of the Third European Conference of Iranian Studies: Held in Cambridge, 11th to 15th September 1995. Contributor to journals. **Address:** Pembroke College, Cambridge University, Cambridge, CB2 1RF, England. **Online address:** cpm1000@cam.ac.uk

MELVILLE, James. *See* **MARTIN, (Roy) Peter.**

MELVILLE, Jennie. *See* **BUTLER, Gwendoline (Williams).**

MELVILLE, Pauline. British/Guyanese (born Guyana), b. 1948?. **Genres:** Novellas/Short Stories, Novels, Young Adult Fiction. **Career:** Writer. **Publications:** Shape-Shifter: Stories, 1990; The Ventriloquist's Tale, 1997; The Migration of Ghosts, 1998; (ed.) Words in the Snow: A Filandón, 2007; Eating Air, 2009. **Address:** St. Martin's Press, 175 5th Ave., New York, NY 10010-7703, U.S.A.

MELZACK, Ronald. Canadian (born Canada), b. 1929. **Genres:** Psychology, Children's Fiction. **Career:** University College, lecturer, 1957-58; University of Pisa, research fellow, 1958-59; Massachusetts Institute of Technology, associate professor, 1959-63; McGill University, associate professor, 1963-67, professor of psychology, 1967-, now professor emeritus. Writer. **Publications:** The Day Tuk Became a Hunter and Other Eskimo Stories, 1967; Raven, Creator of the World, 1970; The Puzzle of Pain, 1973; Why the Man in the Moon is Happy and Other Eskimo Creation Stories, 1977; (with P.D. Wall) The Challenge of Pain, 1982, new ed., 2008. EDITOR: Pain Measurement and Assessment, 1983; (with P.D. Wall) Textbook of Pain, 1984, 4th ed., 1999; (with D.C. Turk) Handbook of Pain Assessment, 1992, 3rd ed., 2011; (with P.D. Wall) Handbook of Pain Management, 2003. **Address:** Department of Psychology, McGill University, 1205 Dr. Penfield Ave., Montreal, QC H3A 1B1, Canada. **Online address:** ronald.melzack@mcgill.ca

MEMMOTT, David R. American (born United States), b. 1948. **Genres:** Poetry, Novels, Novellas/Short Stories, Essays. **Career:** State of Oregon, office specialist; Wordcraft of Oregon L.L.C., editor and publisher, managing editor; Ice River Magazine, managing editor, 1987-90; Digital artist and book designer. **Publications:** NOVEL: House on Fire: Poetry and Collage, 1992; Shadow Bones: Stories, 1999; Primetime: A Post Cyberpunk Novel, 2007; POETRY: (ed.) Alpha Gallery: Selections from the Fantastic Small Press, 1991; The Larger Earth: Descending Notes of a Grounded Astronaut (poems), 1996; Within the Walls of Jericho (poems), 1998; Giving It Away (poems), 2009. OTHERS: (co-ed.) Angel Body and Other Magic for the Soul (anthology), 2002. **Address:** Wordcraft of Oregon L.L.C., PO Box 3235, La Grande, OR 97850, U.S.A. **Online address:** dsmemmott@verizon.net

MENACHE, Sophia. Israeli/Argentine (born Argentina) **Genres:** History, Communications/Media, Theology/Religion, Social Commentary, inspirational/Motivational Literature. **Career:** University of Haifa, academic staff, 1973, Department of General History, lecturer, professor of history, 2000-, head, dean of graduate studies, Pre-academic Unit, academic head; Fordham University, visiting research associate, 1984; Cambridge University, visiting fellow, 1995-96. Writer. **Publications:** The Vox Dei: Communication in the Middle Ages, 1990; (with J. Horowitz) L'Humour en Chaire: Le rire dans l'église médiévale, 1994; Clement V, 1998; The Birth of Parliaments in the Middle Ages, 2005; The Catholic Church in the Middle Ages: Ideology and Politics, 2006; Hithavutam shel parlamenṭim bi-Yeme ha-Benayim, 2006; Ha-Kenesiyah ha-ḳatolit bi-Yeme ha-Benayim: ide'ologyah u-poliṭiḳah, 2006; Peraḳim be-toldot ha-ra'ayon ha-medini bi-Yeme ha-Benayim, 2007; (with B. Arbel and Y. ṭerḳel) Bene-adam ṿe-ḥayot aḥerot be-aspaḳlaryah hisṭorit, 2007. EDITOR: (with M. Goodich and S. Schein) Cross Cultural Convergences in the Crusader Period: Essays Presented to Aryeh Grabois on His Sixty-fifth Birthday, 1995; Communication in the Jewish Diaspora: The Pre-Modern World, 1996. Contributor to periodicals. **Address:** Department of General History, University of Haifa, Mt. Carmel, Haifa, 31905, Israel. **Online address:** menache@research.haifa.ac.il

MENAND, Louis. American (born United States), b. 1952. **Genres:** Philosophy, History. **Career:** Columbia University, Preceptor, 1977-78; Princeton University, assistant professor of English, 1980-87; City University of New York, The Graduate Center, associate professor of English, 1988-93, 1993-94, professor, 1994-2001, distinguished professor of English, 2001-03, Queens College, associate professor, 1988-93, 1987-88; Harvard University, professor of English and American literature and language, 2003-04, Anne T. and Robert M. Bass professor, 2004-; The New Republic, staff; The New Yorker, staff. Writer. **Publications:** Discovering Modernism: T.S. Eliot and His Context, 1987, 2nd ed., 2007; The Metaphysical Club: A Story of Ideas in America, 2001; Marketplace of Ideas, 2001; American Studies, 2002; Story of the Soup Cans, 2006. EDITOR: (with L. Berlowitz and D. Donoghue) America in Theory, 1988; The Future of Academic Freedom, 1996; (intro.) Pragmatism:

A Reader, 1997; (with A.W. Litz and L. Rainey) The Cambridge History of Literary Criticism, vol. VII: Modernism and the New Criticism, 2001. Contributor to periodicals. **Address:** Department of English, Harvard University, 155 Barker Ctr., 12 Quincy St., Cambridge, MA 02138, U.S.A. **Online address:** menand@fas.harvard.edu

MENARD, Orville D. American (born United States), b. 1933. **Genres:** Politics/Government, Social Sciences. **Career:** Texas Arts and Industries University, instructor in political science, 1963-64; University of Nebraska, assistant professor, 1964-68, associate professor, 1968-73, College of Arts and Sciences, assistant dean, 1974-75, professor of political science, 1974-90, Ralph Wardle Diamond professor of political science, 1990-96, chairman of department, 1992-95, now professor emeritus; U.S. Department of State, senior faculty fellow, 1967. Writer. **Publications:** The Army and the Fifth Republic, 1967; Political Bossism in Mid-America: Tom Dennison's Omaha, 1900-1933, 1989. Contributor to periodicals. **Address:** Department of Political Science, University of Nebraska, Rm. 275, Arts and Sciences Hall, Omaha, NE 68182-0271, U.S.A. **Online address:** omenard@cox.net

MENCIMER, Stephanie. American (born United States), b. 1969. **Genres:** Politics/Government, International Relations/Current Affairs, Law. **Career:** Washington City Paper, senior writer; Washington Post, investigative reporter; Legal Times, staff writer; Mother Jones, legal affairs and domestic policy correspondent; Washington Monthly, contributing editor. **Publications:** Blocking the Courthouse Door: How the Republican Party and Its Corporate Allies Are Taking Away Your Right to Sue, 2006. Contributor of articles to periodicals. **Address:** Mother Jones, 222 Sutter St., Ste. 600, San Francisco, CA 94108, U.S.A. **Online address:** thetortellini@earthlink.net

MENDELSOHN, Martin. British (born England), b. 1935?. **Genres:** Business/Trade/Industry, Law, Marketing. **Career:** Adlers, partner and consultant, 1959-92; City University Business School, visiting professor of franchising, 1988-89; Eversheds, partner and chairman, 1992-; Franchise Group, chairman; Middlesex University Business School, visiting professor of franchise marketing; Encyclopedia of International Franchising Law, editor; University Business School, visiting professor of franchise management; Horwath Franchise Services Ltd., chairman; British Franchise Association, legal consultant. **Publications:** The Guide to Franchising, 1970, 7th ed., 2004; How to Evaluate a Franchise, 1981, 7th ed., 2001; How to Franchise Your Business, 1981, 6th ed., 2003; International Franchising: An Overview, 1984; Franchisor's Manual, 1988; The Ethics of Franchising, 1988, 3rd ed., 2004; How to Franchise Internationally, 1989, 4th ed., 2004; Franchising and Business Development, 1991; (B. Harris) Franchising and the Block Exemption Regulation, 1991; (ed.) Franchising in Europe, 1993; (ed.) Franchising Law, 1995, 2nd ed., 2004; Franchising, 1996; (with L. Rudnick) Negotiating an International Master Franchising Agreement, 2001; (S. Rose) Guide to the EC Block Exemption for Vertical Agreements, 2001; (ed.) International Encyclopedia of Franchising, 2003. **Address:** 9 Sandown Ct., Marsh Ln., Stanmore, Middlesex, HA7 4HZ, England. **Online address:** romebrand@btclick.com

MENDELSON, Cheryl. American (born United States), b. 1946. **Genres:** Homes/Gardens, Novels. **Career:** Purdue University, professor of philosophy; Columbia University, professor of philosophy; Barnard College, visiting professor, professor of philosophy; Debevoise & Plimpton, lawyer; Skadden, Arps, Slate, Meagher & Flom, lawyer. Writer. **Publications:** Home Comforts: The Art and Science of Keeping House, 1999; Morningside Heights: A Novel, 2003; Laundry: The Home Comforts Book of Caring for Clothes and Linens, 2005; Love, Work, Children: A Novel, 2005; Anything for Jane: A Novel, 2007; Good Life: The Moral Individual in an Antimoral World, 2012. **Address:** c/o Author Mail, Simon & Schuster, 1230 Ave. of the Americas, New York, NY 10020, U.S.A.

MENDENHALL, George Emery. American (born United States), b. 1916. **Genres:** History, Language/Linguistics, Theology/Religion. **Career:** Trinity Lutheran Church, pastor, 1942-43; Hamma Divinity School, assistant professor, 1947-50, associate professor of old testament, 1950-52; American Oriental Society, president, 1951; University of Michigan, associate professor, 1952-58, Lutheran Student Foundation, president, 1962-65, Henry Russell lecturer, 1972-73, professor, 1958-86, professor emeritus of near eastern studies, 1986-; Journal of the American Oriental Society, associate editor, 1954-59; American Center of Oriental Research, annual professor, 1955-56, director, 1965-66, 1975; British School of Archaeology in Jerusalem, field supervisor, 1956; Society of Biblical Literature, president, 1960; Archaeological Institute of America, president, 1963-65; American Schools of Oriental Research, president, 1963-65; Biblical Colloquium, president, 1963-65; Hopkins University, A.O. Lovejoy lecturer, 1967; American Center of Oriental Research, director, 1975; Yarmouk University, Institute of Archaeology and Anthropology, Epigraphy Section, visiting professor, 1987-93. Writer. **Publications:** Law and Covenant in Israel and the Ancient Near East, 1955; The Tenth Generation: The Origins of the Biblical Tradition, 1973; The Syllabic Inscriptions from Byblos, 1985; (with F. al-Khraysheh) A Comparative Glossary of Pre-Islamic Arabic; Ancient Israel's Faith and History: An Introduction to the Bible in Context, 2001; Our Misunderstood Bible, 2006. **Address:** Department of Near Eastern Studies, University of Michigan, 4111 Thayer Academic Bldg., 202 S Thayer St., Ann Arbor, MI 48109, U.S.A. **Online address:** gmendy@umich.edu

MENDER, Mona (Siegler). American (born United States), b. 1926. **Genres:** Mystery/Crime/Suspense, Women's Studies And Issues, Music, Biography, Information Science/Computers, Reference, Social Sciences. **Career:** Teacher of piano and music theory, 1947-75; New Jersey Symphony Orchestra League, state education chairperson, 1980-82; New Jersey Symphony Orchestra, state chairperson of board of regents, 1983-84, board of directors, 1983-92. Writer. **Publications:** Music Manuscript Preparation: A Concise Guide, 1991; Extraordinary Women in Support of Music, 1997; The Cock Crows No More, 2000. **Address:** PO Box 327, Basking Ridge, NJ 07920, U.S.A.

MENDES, Irene Vilar. (Irene Vilar). Puerto Rican (born Puerto Rico), b. 1969. **Genres:** Adult Non-fiction, Women's Studies And Issues. **Career:** Que Pasa magazine, managing editor, 1985-87; Syracuse University, public relations director, 1986-88, Syracuse University Press, acquisitions editor, 2000-02; Point of Contact, assistant to the editor, 1990-92, managing editor, 1993-98; University of Wisconsin Press, editor of The Americas book series, 2002-. **Publications:** (As Irene Vilar) A Message from God in the Atomic Age, 1996; Sea Journal, 1997; Ladies' Gallery: A Memoir of Family Secrets, 2009; Impossible Motherhood: Testimony of an Abortion Addict, 2009; Truman's Affair, forthcoming; The Critical Relation, forthcoming. **Address:** c/o Lisa Bankoff, International Creative Management Inc., 825 8th Ave., 26 Fl, New York, NY 10019, U.S.A. **Online address:** irvilarc@syr.edu

MENDES, Pedro Rosa. Portuguese (born Portugal), b. 1968. **Genres:** Travel/Exploration, Animals/Pets, Novels. **Career:** Público, war correspondent. **Publications:** O Melhor café, 1996; Baía dos tigres, 1998; Peregrinação de Enmanuel Jhesus, 2010. Contributor to periodicals. **Address:** c/o Author Mail, Harcourt International Education Group, 6277 Sea Harbor Dr., Orlando, FL 32887-0001, U.S.A.

MENDILOW, Jonathan. American/British (born England), b. 1950. **Genres:** Politics/Government, History, Humanities. **Career:** City of Jerusalem, manager of Office of Public Relations, 1974-77; Hebrew University of Jerusalem, instructor, 1978-80, assistant professor, 1980-85, Joseph Saltiel College, Division of Social Sciences and Liberal Arts, chair, 1981-85; University of Tel Aviv, assistant professor, 1979-85; University of the Witwatersrand, senior lecturer, 1985-86; University of Southern California, visiting professor, 1985-87; Rider University, Department of Political Science, associate professor, 1987-93, professor, 1993-, chairman, 2005-. Writer. **Publications:** (Ed.) From the French Revolution to the Rise of Fascism: Readings in the History of Political Thought, 1982; The Romantic Tradition in British Political Thought, 1986; Ideology, Party Change and Electoral Campaigns in Israel, 1965-2001, 2003. **Address:** Rider University, 277 Fine Arts, 2083 Lawrence Rd., Lawrenceville, NJ 08648, U.S.A. **Online address:** jmendilow@rider.edu

MENDOZA, Lisa. American (born United States), b. 1958. **Genres:** Humor/Satire, Animals/Pets. **Career:** KSEE-TV, news reporter and producer, 1981-95; KFSN-TV, news producer, 1995-97; Borders Books, community relations coordinator, 1997-; Community Food Bank, board director; Fresno Communications Network, officer. **Publications:** Hi! It's Me, Your Dog!, 2000; Matthew and Max, forthcoming. Works appear in anthologies. Contributor to periodicals. **Address:** Quill Driver Books, 2006 S Mary, Fresno, CA 93721, U.S.A. **Online address:** lmendoza@prodigy.net

MENDYK, Stan A. E. Canadian (born Canada), b. 1953. **Genres:** History,

Social Sciences. **Career:** Teacher, 1983-85; University of New Brunswick, assistant professor of history, 1985-86; Municipality of Metropolitan Toronto, Management Services Department, librarian and researcher, 1988-89; Ontario Hydro, International Marketing Department, librarian and researcher, 1988; Camelot Press, humanities and social science editor and marketing director, 1988-; Brock University, instructor, 1989; Trent University, instructor, 1989-90; University of Manitoba, assistant professor of history, 1990-91; University of Winnipeg, assistant professor of history, 1991; University of Toronto, Department of history, lecturer, 1995-96; University of Saskatchewan, lecturer, 1997; Oxford University Press, New Dictionary of National Biography, researcher and writer, 1998-; Toronto District School Board, teacher and librarian, 2000-. **Publications:** Speculum Britanniae: Regional Study, Antiquarianism, and Science in Britain to 1700, 1989. Contributor to journals. **Address:** 216 Chadburn St., Oshawa, ON L1H 5V6, Canada.

MENÉNDEZ, Ana (Maria). American (born United States), b. 1970. **Genres:** Children's Fiction, Young Adult Fiction, Novels, Film. **Career:** The Miami Herald, journalist, 1991-, columnist, 2005-; Southern Bell, intern management assistant; Orange County Register, journalist; University of Texas, visiting writer. **Publications:** COLLECTION: In Cuba I Was a German Shepherd, 2001. NOVELS: Loving Che, 2003; The Last War, 2009; Adios, Happy Homeland, 2011. Contributor to magazines. **Address:** The Miami Herald, 1 Herald Plz., Miami, FL 33132-1609, U.S.A. **Online address:** anamariamenendez@hotmail.com

MENES, Orlando Ricardo. American (born United States), b. 1958. **Genres:** Psychology, Poetry, Translations. **Career:** Computer Power Inc., technical writer, 1987-88; University of Illinois, lecturer, 1998-99; University of Dayton, assistant professor, 1999-2000; University of Notre Dame, Department of English, assistant professor, 2000-07, associate professor, 2007-. **Publications:** Borderlands with Angels, 1994; Rumba atop the Stones, 2001; (ed. and intro.) Renaming Ecstasy: Latino Writings on the Sacred, 2004; Furia, 2005; (trans.) A. Storni, My Heart Flooded with Water, 2009; The Open Light: Poets from Notre Dame, 1991-2008, 2010. Contributor to magazines. **Address:** Department of English, University of Notre Dame, 356 O'Shaughnessy Hall, Notre Dame, IN 46556-5639, U.S.A. **Online address:** orlando.menes.1@nd.edu

MENNINGHAUS, Winfried. German (born Germany), b. 1952. **Genres:** Philosophy, Ethics, Humanities, Poetry. **Career:** Suhrkamp (publishing house), Frankfurt am Main, editor, 1979-85; FreeUniversity of Berlin, associate professor, 1985-89, Institut fuer Allgemeine und Vergleichende Literaturwissenschaft, professor, 1989-; Hebrew University of Jerusalem, visiting professor, 1987-88; University of California, visiting professor, 1992; Yale University, visiting professor, 1994, 2002. **Publications:** Walter Benjamins Theorie der Sprachmagie, 1980; Paul Celan: Magie der Form, 1980; Artistische Schrift. Studien zur Kompositionskunst Gottfried Kellers, 1982; Schwellenkunde: Walter Benjamins Passage des Mythos, 1986; Unendliche Verdopplung. Die fruehromantische Grundlegung der Kunsttheorie im Begriff absoluter Selbstreflexion, 1987; ueber Paul Celan, 1988; Lob des Unsinns. Ueber Kant, Tieck und Blaubart, 1995; Ekel: Theorie und Geschichte einer starken Empfindung, 1999; Literaturwissenschaft und politische Kultur. Eberhard Lämmert zum 75. Geburtstag, 1999; (ed. with K. Scherpe) Das Versprechen der Schoenheit, 2003; Haelfte des Lebens: Versuch ueber Hoellderlins Poetik, 2005; Kunst als Befoerderung des Lebens: Perspektiven transzendentaler und evolutionaerer Asthetik, 2008; Wozu Kunst? Aesthetik nach Darwin, 2011. **Address:** Peter Szondi-Institut fuer Allgemeine und, Vergleichende Literaturwissenscahft (AVL), Habelschwerdter Allee 45, Rm. JK 28/225, Berlin, D-14195, Germany. **Online address:** winfried.menninghaus@fu-berlin.de

MENO, Joe. American (born United States), b. 1974?. **Genres:** Novels, Novellas/Short Stories, Young Adult Fiction. **Career:** Columbia College, associate professor of fiction writing, professor; Punk Planet Magazine, contributing editor. Novelist. **Publications:** NOVELS: Tender as Hellfire, 1999; How the Hula Girl Sings, 2001; Hairstyles of the Damned, 2004; Bluebirds Used to Croon in the Choir, 2005; The Boy Detective Fails, 2006; Demons in the Spring: Stories, 2008; Great Perhaps, 2009; (with J. Baichtal) The Cult of LEGO, 2011. Contributor to books and magazines. **Address:** Columbia College Chicago, Rm. 1200 O, 624 S Michigan Ave., Chicago, IL 60605, U.S.A. **Online address:** jmeno@colum.edu

MENOCAL, Narciso G(arcia). American/Cuban (born Cuba), b. 1936. **Genres:** Architecture, Biography. **Career:** University of Florida, instructor, 1964-70; University of Illinois, instructor, 1971-72; University of Wisconsin, instructor, 1972-74, Department of Art History, assistant professor, 1974-80, associate professor, 1980-86, professor, 1986-, now professor emeritus, chairman, 1984-87; Columbia University, Temple Hoyne Buell Center for the Study of American Architecture, senior fellow, 1989-90; Guggenheim fellow, 1990-91. Writer. **Publications:** (Intro.) Keck & Keck, Architects, 1980; Architecture as Nature: The Transcendentalist Idea of Louis Sullivan, 1981; (with R. Twombly) Louis Sullivan: The Poetry of Architecture, 2000; Postcolonial Nationalist Myths in Cuban Literature, Art, and Architecture, 1825-1964, forthcoming. EDITOR: Wright Studies, vol. I: Taliesin 1911-1914, 1992, vol. II; My Father Who Is On Earth, 1994; Fallingwater and Pittsburgh, 2000. Contributor to books and periodicals. **Address:** Department of Art History, University of Wisconsin, 203 Elvehjem, Museum of Art, 800 University Ave., Madison, WI 53706, U.S.A. **Online address:** nmenocal@wisc.edu

MENON, Dilip M(adhav). Indian (born India), b. 1962. **Genres:** History, Politics/Government. **Career:** Cambridge University, visiting fellow in commonwealth studies, Magdalene College, fellow, 1989-92; Centre for Development Studies, visiting fellow, 1992-94; Nehru Memorial Museum and Library, Centre for Contemporary Studies, fellow, 1994-; University of Delhi, Department of History, professor; University of Witwatersrand, Mellon chair in Indian studies, professor of history, 2009-11; Yale University, Agrarian Studies Program, fellow. Writer. **Publications:** Caste, Nationalism, and Communism in South India: Malabar, 1900-1948, 1994; (trans.) P. Kunhambu, Saraswativijayam, 2002; Blindness of Insight: Essays on Caste in Modern India, 2006; (ed.) Cultural History of Modern India, 2006. **Address:** Department of History, University of Delhi, Teen Murti House, New Delhi, DH 110007, India. **Online address:** dilip.menon@wits.ac.za

MENON, Rajan. American (born United States), b. 1953. **Genres:** Military/Defense/Arms Control, Politics/Government, History. **Career:** Vanderbilt University, adjunct professor of political science, 1978-85; Lehigh University, assistant professor, 1985-87, associate professor, 1987-91, professor, 1991, Monroe J. Rathbone professor of international relations, 1991-; Columbia University, adjunct professor of political science, 1997-98; Carnegie Corporation of New York, International Peace and Security Program, academic fellow and senior advisor, 1999-2000; National Bureau for Asian Research, Eurasia Policy Studies, director, 1999-2002; Council on Foreign Relations, senior fellow. Writer and consultant. **Publications:** NONFICTION: Soviet Power and the Third World, 1986; (ed. with D.N. Nelson) Limits to Soviet Power, 1989; Treacherous Terrain: The Political and Security Dimensions of Energy Development in the Caspian Sea Zone, 1998; (ed. with Y.E. Federov and G. Nodia) Russia, the Caucasus and Central Asia: The 21st Century Security Environment, 1999; (ed. with R. Ebel) Energy and Conflict in Central Asia and the Caucasus, 2000; The End of Alliances, 2007. Contributor to books and periodicals. **Address:** New America Foundation, 1899 L St. NW, Ste. 400, Washington, DC 20036, U.S.A. **Online address:** menon@newamerica.net

MENON, Ritu. Indian (born India), b. 1948. **Genres:** Women's Studies And Issues, Literary Criticism And History, Theology/Religion. **Career:** Kali for Women, co-founder, 1984-, editor-in-chief, trustee, Women Unlimited, founder; Women's Feature Service (international agency), chairperson, secretary; Women's World, vice president. **Publications:** (Ed. with U. Butalia) In Other Words: New Writing by Women in India, 1992; (ed. with K. Bhasin and N.S. Khan) Against All Odds: Essays on Women, Religion, and Development from India and Pakistan, 1994; (with U. Butalia) Making a Difference: Feminist Publishing in the South, 1995; (with K. Bhasin) Borders and Boundaries: Women in India's Partition, 1998; (ed.) Women Who Dared, 2002; (ed.) Say No to Gender Based Violence: Responses from South Asia, 2003; (ed.) No Woman's Land: Women from Pakistan, India & Bangladesh Write on the Partition of India, 2004; (with Z. Hasan) Unequal Citizens: A Study of Muslim Women in India, 2004; (ed. with Z. Hasan) The Diversity of Muslim Women's Lives in India, 2005; (with Z. Hasan) Educating Muslim Girls: A Comparison of Five Indian Cities, 2005; (ed.) Women Writes on Partition of Pakistan and India, 2006; (with K. Kannabiran) From Mathura to Manorama: Resisting Violence against Women in India, 2007. **Address:** Kali for Women, K-92 1st Fl., B 1/8 Hauz Khas, New Delhi, DH 110016, India. **Online address:** kaliw@del2.vsn.net.in

MENTZ, Steve. (Steven R. Mentz). American (born United States), b. 1966. **Genres:** History, Romance/Historical. **Career:** Iona College, assistant professor, 2000-03; St. John's University, associate professor, 2003-. Writer.

Publications: (ed. with C. Dionne) Rogues and Early Modern English Culture, 2004; Romance for Sale in Early Modern England: The Rise of Prose Fiction, 2006. **Address:** St. John's University, 8000 Utopia Pkwy., Jamaica, NY 11439-9000, U.S.A. **Online address:** mentzs@stjohns.edu

MENTZ, Steven R. *See* **MENTZ, Steve.**

MENTZER, Raymond A. American (born United States), b. 1945. **Genres:** History, Theology/Religion, Language/Linguistics. **Career:** University of Wisconsin, assistant professor, 1973-74; Montana State University, professor of history, 1973-2001; Sixteenth Century Essays and Studies, editor, 1996-2006; Université Paul Valéry, Centre d'Histoire moderne et contemporaine de l'Europe, associate, 1998-; University of Iowa, Department of Religious Studies, Daniel J. Krumm Family chair in reformation studies, 2001-, Daniel J. Krumm Family professor of reformation studies. **Publications:** Heresy Proceedings in Languedoc, 1500-1560, 1984; Blood and Belief: Family Survival and Confessional Identity among the Provincial Huguenot Nobility, 1994; La construction de l'identité Réformée aux 16e et 17e siècles: Le rôle des Consistoires, 2006. EDITOR: Sin and the Calvinists: Morals Control and the Consistory in the Reformed Tradition, 1994; (with A. Spicer) Society and Culture in the Huguenot World, 1559-1685, 2002; (with F. Moreil and P. Chareyre) Dire l'interdit: The Vocabulary of Censure and Exclusion in the Early Modern Reformed Tradition, 2010. Contributor to periodicals. **Address:** Department of Religious Studies, University of Iowa, 316 Gilmore Hall, Iowa City, IA 52242-1320, U.S.A. **Online address:** raymond-mentzer@uiowa.edu

MENZ, Deb. American (born United States), b. 1954. **Genres:** Crafts, Art/Art History. **Career:** Weaving Workshop Inc., co-owner, 1984-89; Mount Mary College, lecturer and workshop presenter; Sievers School of Fiber Arts, lecturer and workshop presenter; Black Swamp Spinners, lecturer and workshop presenter; Contemporary Hand weavers of Houston, lecturer and workshop presenter. Writer. **Publications:** Color in Spinning, 1998; Color Works: The Crafter's Guide to Color, 2004. Contributor of articles to periodicals. **Address:** 2205 Mayflower Dr., Middleton, WI 53562, U.S.A. **Online address:** debmenz@tds.net

MENZEL, Peter. American (born United States), b. 1948. **Genres:** Photography, Social Sciences. **Career:** Peter Menzel Photography, founder. Photojournalist. **Publications:** Material World, 1994; (With F. D'Aluisio) Women in the Material World, 1996; (with F. D'Aluisio) Man Eating Bugs: The Art and Science of Eating Insects, 1998; (with F. D'Aluisio) Robo Sapiens: Evolution of a New Species, 2000; (with F. D'Aluisio) Hungry Planet: What the World Eats, 2005; (with F. D'Aluisio) What the World Eats: Around the World in Eighty Diets, 2010; (with F. D'Aluisio) What I Eat: Around the World in 80 Diets, 2010. Contributor to periodicals. **Address:** 199 Kreuzer Ln., Napa, CA 94559, U.S.A. **Online address:** peter@menzelphoto.com

MERCANTINI, Jonathan. American (born United States), b. 1973. **Genres:** History. **Career:** Canisius College, assistant professor; University of Miami, faculty; Kean University, assistant professor, 2007-. Writer. **Publications:** Who Shall Rule at Home? The Evolution of South Carolina Political Culture, 1748-1776, 2007. Contributor of articles and book. **Address:** Kean University, 1000 Morris Ave., Union, NJ 07083, U.S.A. **Online address:** jmercant@kean.edu

MERCATI, Cynthia. American (born United States) **Genres:** Plays/Screenplays, Novels, Novellas/Short Stories, History, Humor/Satire. **Career:** Des Moines Playhouse, playwright-in-residence. Author and playwright. **Publications:** When the Nerds Bit Beverly Hills, 1987; Makin It, 1988; Facing Up, 1989; Winners!, 1989; Cinderella: Or Its Okay to Be Different, 1994; The Baseball Show: An American Tale of Pine Tar Bleacher Seats and Hometown Heroes, 1995; The Strength of Our Spirit: The Vision of Anne Frank, 1998; The Chisholm Trail, 2000; Wagons Ho!: A Diary of the Oregon Trail, 2000; The Secret Room, 2000; The Pony Express, 2000; A Light in the Sky, 2000; The King Christian Club, 2000; Remember the Alamo!, 2000; To See the Stars, 2000; Kit Carson: A Life of Adventure, 2000; A Trip through Time, 2000; You Gotta Have Goop, 2001; Square Against the World: The Story of a Sod House, 2001; Schoolhouse on the Prairie, 2001; Shakespeare and Me, 2001; Star Searches, 2001; The Great Race: The Building of the Transcontinental Railroad, 2002; The Freedom Tree, 2002; Faces of Freedom, 2003; New Clothes for the Emperor, 2004. **Address:** 721 20th St., Des Moines, IA 50314, U.S.A. **Online address:** mercatiwriter@aol.com

MERCATI, Maria (B.). British/Zimbabwean (born Zimbabwe), b. 1951. **Genres:** Medicine/Health. **Career:** Hale Clinic, oriental body work therapist and acupuncturist, 1995-98; Bodyharmonics Centre, founder, 1992-; The Chinese Medicine Academy, faculty. Writer. **Publications:** The Handbook of Chinese Massage: Tui Na Techniques to Awaken Body and Mind, 1997; Thai Massage Manual: Natural Therapy for Flexibility, Relaxation, and Energy Balance, 1998; Tui Na: Massage for a Healthier, Brighter Child, 1999; (with N.L. Dính) Kỹ thuạt & thụ c hành massage y học phụ c hòi súc khoe & thu giãn, 2003. **Address:** Bodyharmonics Centre, 54 Fleckers Dr., Cheltenham, GC GL51 3BD, England. **Online address:** mariamercati@bodyharmonics.co.uk

MERCER, Derrik. British (born England), b. 1944. **Genres:** Travel/Exploration, History, Military/Defense/Arms Control, Art/Art History. **Career:** Sunday Times, reporter, news editor, deputy magazine editor, managing news editor, 1969-82; Independent Television News, editor of Channel Four News, 1982-83; freelance author and journalist, 1983-87; London Borough of Richmond, school governor, 1984-92; Chronicle Communications Ltd., editor-in-chief and managing director, 1987-92. Writer. **Publications:** (Ed. with O. Gillie) The Sunday Times Book of Body Maintenance, 1978 in US as The Complete Book of Body Maintenance, 1979, rev. ed. as The Sunday Times New Book of Body Maintenance, 1982; (ed. with P. Clarke and B. Jackman) The Sunday Times Book of the Countryside: Including One Thousand Days out in the Great Britain and Ireland, 1980; (ed. with P. Clarke and B. Jackman) One Thousand Days Out, 1981; The National Trust: Exploring Unspoilt Britain, 1985; (with G. Mercer) Children First and Always: A Portrait of Great Ormond Street, 1986; The Fog of War: The Media on the Battlefield, 1987; (with D. Puttnam) Rural England: The Countryside at the Crossroads, 1988; (ed.) Chronicle of the Twentieth Century, 1988; (ed.) Chronicle of the Year 1988, 1989; (ed.) Chronicle of the Second World War, 1990; (ed.) Chronicle of the Royal Family, 1991; (ed. with J. Burne) Chronicle of the World, 1996; World War II Day by Day: Witness the Tumultuous, Tragic and Triumphant Days That Shook the World, 2004. **Address:** c/o Richard Simon, 43 Doughty St., London, GL WC1N 2LH, England.

MERCER, Jeremy. French/Canadian (born Canada), b. 1971?. **Genres:** Novels, Translations, Mystery/Crime/Suspense, Autobiography/Memoirs, Adult Non-fiction, Criminology/True Crime, History, Young Adult Fiction, Young Adult Fiction. **Career:** Ottowa Citizen, crime reporter, 1995-99; Kilometer Zero (magazine), founder and editor, 2000-. **Publications:** The Champagne Gang: High Times and Sweet Crimes, 1998; Money for Nothing: Ten Great Ways to Make Money Illegally, 1999; Time Was Soft There: A Paris Sojourn at Shakespeare & Co. in UK as Books, Baguettes and Bedbugs, 2005; (trans.) R. Badinter, Abolition: One Man's Battle Against the Death Penalty, 2008; When the Guillotine Fell: The Bloody Beginning and Horrifying End to France's River of Blood, 1791-1977, 2008. **Address:** c/o Kristin Lindstrom, Lindstrom Literary Management, 871 N Greenbriar St., Arlington, VA 22205, U.S.A. **Online address:** jeremy@kilometerzero.org

MERCER, Joyce. *See* **MERCER, Joyce Ann.**

MERCER, Joyce Ann. (Joyce Mercer). American (born United States), b. 1957. **Genres:** Women's Studies And Issues. **Career:** Fairview Deaconess Hospital, chaplain in adolescent chemical dependency program, 1985-89; Emory University, Egleston Children's Hospital, part-time medical social worker, 1991-94; Youth Theology Institute, Candler School of Theology, research coordinator, 1992-95; Macalester College, staff, 1994-97; United Theological Seminary, adjunct faculty, 1995-97; Union Theological Seminary-Philippines, practical theology, faculty, M. Theol. Program of Southeast Asia Graduate School of Theology, faculty, 1997-2000; San Francisco Theological Seminary (SFTS) and The Graduate Theological Union (GTU), associate professor of practical theology and Christian education; Interdisciplinary studies, GTU core doctoral faculty, 2000-06; University of California, Women's Studies, faculty; Virginia Theological Seminary-Alexandria, associate professor of pastoral theology, 2006-08, professor of practical theology, 2008-. Writer and pastor. **Publications:** (As Joyce Mercer) Behind the Mask of Adolescent Satanism, 1991; Welcoming Children: A Practical Theology of Childhood, 2005; (with D.G. Baker) Lives to Offer: Accompanying Youth on Their Vocational Quests, 2007; Girl Talk, God Talk: Why Faith Matters to Teenage Girls and Their Parents, 2008. Contributor to books. **Address:** Virginia Theological Seminary, 3737 Seminary Rd., Alexandria, VA 22304, U.S.A. **Online address:** jmercer@vts.edu

MERCER, Judy. American (born United States) **Genres:** Mystery/Crime/Suspense, Young Adult Non-fiction, Literary Criticism And History, Young Adult Fiction. **Career:** News reporter, advertising copywriter, advertising director, television correspondent and freelance writer. **Publications:** Fast Forward, 1995; Double Take, 1997; Split Image, 1998; Blind Spot, 2000. **Address:** c/o Author Mail, Pocket Books, 1230 Ave. of the Americas, New York, NY 10020-1513, U.S.A.

MERCHANT, Paul. *See* **ELLISON, Harlan (Jay).**

MEREDITH, Martin. American (born United States), b. 1942?. **Genres:** History, Biography, Autobiography/Memoirs, Military/Defense/Arms Control. **Career:** London Observer and Sunday Times, foreign correspondent; St. Antony's College, research fellow. Writer. **Publications:** The Past Is Another Country: Rhodesia, 1890-1979, 1979, rev. ed., 1980; The First Dance of Freedom: Black Africa in the Postwar Era, 1984; In the Name of Apartheid: South Africa in the Postwar Period, 1988; A Guide to South Africa's 1994 Election, 1994; Nelson Mandela: A Biography, 1998; Coming to Terms: South Africa's Search for Truth, 1999; Africa's Elephant: A Biography, 2001; Fischer's Choice: A Life of Bram Fischer, 2002; Our Votes, Our Guns: Robert Mugabe and the Tragedy of Zimbabwe, 2002; Mugabe: Power and Plunder in Zimbabwe, 2002; Elephant Destiny: Biography of an Endangered Species in Africa, 2003; Fate of Africa: From The Hopes of Freedom to the Heart of Despair: A History of Fifty Years of Independence, 2005; Diamonds, Gold, and War: The British, the Boers, and the Making of South Africa, 2007; Mandela, 2010; Born in Africa: The Quest for the Origins of Human Life, 2011. Contributor to periodicals. **Address:** c/o Author Mail, Public Affairs, 250 W 57th St., Ste. 1312, New York, NY 10107, U.S.A.

MEREDITH, Richard A. British (born England), b. 1948. **Genres:** Travel/Exploration. **Career:** Daily Express, journalist; Post Newspaper Group, co-founder and director; Holcot Press, founder and director, through 2000. **Publications:** One Way or Another: A Travelogue of True Adventure (and Misadventure) Stories, 2002; Which Way Next: Story of the Daewoo Challenge, 2004; Historic First Crossing of Asia's New Highway to the West, 2007. **Address:** MercuryBooks, 1 Frederica Cottages, Newport Pagnell, BK MK16 0DD, England. **Online address:** ricmeredith@hotmail.com

MEREDITH, Ted Jordan. American (born United States), b. 1950. **Genres:** Food And Wine, Homes/Gardens. **Career:** Writer. **Publications:** Northwest Wine: The Vinifera Wines of Oregon, Washington, and Idaho, 1980, 4th ed. as Northwest Wine: Wine Growing Alchemy along the Pacific Ring of Fire, 1990; (ed.) Mrs. Rorer's Famous Nineteenth-Century Recipes, 1981; (with R. Hutchinson and R. Figiel) A Dictionary of American Wines, 1985; Wines and Wineries of America's Northwest: The Premium Wines of Oregon, Washington, and Idaho, 1986; Northwest Wine Companion, 1988; Bamboo for Gardens, 2001; The Complete Book of Garlic: A Guide for Gardeners, Growers, and Serious Cooks, 2008; Timber Press Pocket Guide to Bamboos, 2009. **Address:** Timber Press Inc., 133 SW 2nd Ave., Ste. 450, Portland, OR 97204, U.S.A.

MERIANS, Linda E. American (born United States), b. 1955. **Genres:** History. **Career:** University of Maryland at College Park, instructor in English, 1983; Bucknell University, assistant professor of English, 1984-87; La Salle University, assistant professor, 1987-91, director of women's studies program, 1989-91, associate professor of English, 1991-; Stony Brook University, assistant vice president for advancement, Corporate and Foundation Affairs, director, faculty, chief of staff to the president; Columbia University, lecturer; University of Ottawa, lecturer; City University of New York, Graduate Center, lecturer; East-Central/American Society for Eighteenth-Century Studies, executive secretary, 1995-. Writer. **Publications:** (Contrib.) Dictionary of Literary Biography, 1989; (ed. and contrib.) The Secret Malady: Venereal Disease in Eighteenth-Century Britain and France, 1996; Envisioning the Worst: Representations of Hottentots in Early-Modern England, 2001. Contributor of articles to periodicals. **Address:** Stony Brook University, 401 Park Ave. S, 2nd Fl., New York, NY 10016, U.S.A. **Online address:** linda.merians@stonybrook.edu

MERKHOFER, Miley W(esson Lee). American (born United States), b. 1947. **Genres:** Administration/Management, Environmental Sciences/Ecology. **Career:** SRI Intl., Decision Analysis Group, manager of research programs, 1975-83; Applied Decision Analysis Inc., vice president, 1984-98; PricewaterhouseCoopers L.L.C., partner, 1998-2001; University of California, lecturer; Lee Merkhofer Consulting, president; Folio Technologies L.L.C., partner. Writer. **Publications:** Decision Science and Social Risk Management: A Comparative Evaluation of Cost-Benefit Analysis, Decision Analysis, and Other Formal Decision-Aiding Approaches, 1987; (with V.T. Covello) Risk Assessment Methods: Approaches for Assessing Health and Environmental Risks, 1993. Contributor of books to journals. **Address:** Lee Merkhofer Consulting, 22706 Medina Ct., Cupertino, CA 95014-2670, U.S.A. **Online address:** lmerkhofer@prioritysystem.com

MERLIN, David. *See* **MOREAU, David Merlin.**

MERNE, Oscar James. Irish (born Ireland), b. 1943. **Genres:** Environmental Sciences/Ecology, Natural History, Zoology, Marine Sciences/Oceanography, Travel/Exploration, Photography, History. **Career:** RTE Television, Weekly Wildlife Program, assistant producer, 1966-68; Wexford Wildfowl Reserve, head warden, 1968-77; Department of Fisheries and Forestry, Forest and Wildlife Service, animal ecology, wildlife research and conservation officer, 1977-. Writer. **Publications:** Ducks, Geese and Swans, 1974; The Birds of Wexford, 1974; (with R. Roche) Saltees: Islands of Birds and Legends, 1977; Irish Wading Birds, 1980. Contributor to journals. **Address:** Deparment of Arts, Heritage, Gaeltacht, the Islands Dúchas the Heritage Service, National Parks & Wildlife, 7 Ely Pl., Dublin, 2, Ireland. **Online address:** omerne@ealga.ie

MERNISSI, Fatima. Moroccan (born Morocco), b. 1940?. **Genres:** Sociology, History, Cultural/Ethnic Topics, Theology/Religion. **Career:** Universite Mohammed V, professor of sociology. Writer. **Publications:** Beyond the Veil: Male-Female Dynamics in a Modern Muslim Society, 1975, rev. ed., 1987; Country Reports on Women in North Africa, Libya, Morocco, Tunisia, 1978; Sulūk al-jinsī fī mujtama Islāmī resmālī taba ī, 1982; (contrib.) Kayd al-nisā? Kaydal-rijāl?: ḥikāyah sha bīyah Maghribīyah, 1983; Doing Daily Battle, 1983; (trans.) Al Hubb Fi Hadaratina Al-Islamiya, 1983; L'amour dans les pays musulmans, 1984; ḥbb fi ḥaḍ āratinā al-Islāmīyah, 1984; (co-author) Nisāal-Sharb: Dirāsah maydānīyah, 1985; Women in Moslem Paradise, 1986; Chahrazad n'est pas Marocaine: Autrement, elle serait salariee!, 1988; (ed.) Le Maroc raconté par ses femmes, 1984, rev. ed. as Le Monde n'est pas un harem: Paroles de femmes du Maroc, 1991; Le Harem politique: Le Prophète et les femmes, 1987; (contrib.) Femmes partagées, famille-travail: Collection, 1988; The Veil and the Male Elite, 1988; (trans.) Shahrazad n'est Pas Marocaine, Autrement Elle Serait Salariée!, 1988; Sultanes oubliées: femmes chefs d'Etat en Islam, 1990; (contrib.) Femme et pouvoirs: Collection, 1990; Can We Women Head a Muslim State, 1991; Peur-modernité: confit Islam démocratie, 1992; (contrib.) Marocaines et sécurité sociale, 1992; The Forgotten Queens of Islam, 1993; Dreams of Trespass: Tales of a Harem Girlhood in UK as The Harem Within: Tales of a Moroccan Girlhood, 1994; Women's Rebellion & Islamic Memory, 1996; (contrib.) Suwar nisā īyah, 1996; NGOs of the High Atlas, 1997; Ai t-Débrouille du Haut-Atlas, 1997; (co-author) Nisāalá ajniḥat al-ḥulm, 1998; êtes-vous vacciné contre leharem?: Teste-test pour les messieurs qui adorent les dames, 1998; Sultānāt mansīyah: nisā ḥākimāt fībilād al-Islām, 2000; (co-author) Hal antummuḥaṣ ṣ anūn ḍ idda al-ḥarīm: naṣ ṣ ikhtibā lil-rijāl alladhīna ya shaqūna al-nisā, 2000; Scheherazade Goes West: Different Cultures, Different Harems, 2001; Islam and Democracy: Fear of the Modern World, 2002; ONG rurales du Haut-Atlas: les Aït-Débrouille, 2003; Sindbads marocains: Voyage dans le Maroccivique, 2004; (trans.) Un Libro Para La Paz, 2004; (intro.) A Quoi Rêvent Les Jeunes, 2007. **Address:** c/o Edite Kroll, Edite Kroll Literary Agency Inc., 20 Cross St., Saco, ME 04072-2702, U.S.A. **Online address:** fatema@mernissi.net

MERON, Theodor. American (born United States), b. 1930. **Genres:** Civil Liberties/Human Rights, Law. **Career:** New York University, professor of international law, 1977-2006, Charles L. Denison Chair, 1994-, professor emeritus, 2006-; Institute of International Studies, professor, 1991-; International Law in the U.S. Department of State, counselor, 2000-01; UN War Crimes Tribunal, appeals judge, 2001-, president, 2003-05; American Journal of International Law, co-editor-in-chief. **Publications:** Investment Insurance in International Law, 1976; The United Nations Secretariat: The Rules and the Practice, 1977; (ed.) Human Rights in International Law: Legal and Policy Issues, 2 vols., 1984; Human Rights Law-Making in the United Nations: A

Critique of Instruments and Process, 1986; Human Rights in Internal Strife: Their International Protection, 1987; Human Rights and Humanitarian Norms as Customary Law, 1989; Henry's Wars and Shakespeare's Laws, 1993; Bloody Constraint: Law and Chivalry in Shakespeare, 1998; War Crimes Law Comes of Age: Essays, 1998; The Humanization of International Law, 2006; The Making of International Criminal Justice: A View from the Bench 2011. Contributor to law journals. **Address:** 40 Washington Sq. S, Ste. 304, New York, NY 10012, U.S.A. **Online address:** meront@un.org

MERRELL, Susan Scarf. American (born United States) **Genres:** Human Relations/Parenting, Social Sciences. **Career:** Journalist, 1990-. **Publications:** The Accidental Bond: The Power of Sibling Relationships, 1995; A Member of the Family, 2000. **Address:** c/o Author Mail, HarperCollins Inc., 10 E 53rd St., 7th Fl., New York, NY 10022, U.S.A. **Online address:** susanmerrell@me.com

MERRETT, Christopher. British (born England), b. 1951. **Genres:** Librarianship, Politics/Government, Sports/Fitness, Social Sciences. **Career:** University of London, London School of Oriental and African Studies, library assistant, 1973-74; Natal Society Library, assistant librarian, 1975-77; University of Cape Town, Architecture Library, assistant librarian, 1978-79; University of Natal, deputy university librarian, 1979-96, university librarian, 1996-2002, director of administration, 2002-; Maritzburg District Cricket Union, secretary, 1982-85, 1986-87. Writer. **Publications:** Map Cataloguing and Classification: A Comparison of Approaches, 1976; A Selected Bibliography of Natal Maps, 1800-1977, 1979; Map Classification: A Comparison of Schemes with Special Reference to the Continent of Africa, 1982; Thesaurus of South African Socio-Political and Economic Terms fro man Anti-Apartheid Perspective, 1990; State Censorship and the Academic Process in South Africa, 1991; A Culture of Censorship: Secrecy and Intellectual Repression in South Africa, 1994; A Selected Chronological Bibliography on Censorship and the Freedoms of Information and Expression in South Africa, 2001; (with B. Murray) Caught behind: Race and Politics in Springbok Cricket, 2004; Sport, Space and Segregation: Politics and Society in Pietermaritzburg, 2009. **Address:** University Library, University of KwaZulu-Natal, Rabie Saunders Bldg., Fl. 2, PO Box X014, Scottsville, 3209, South Africa. **Online address:** mmerrett@nu.ac.za

MERRIDALE, Catherine. British/American (born United States), b. 1959?. **Genres:** Politics/Government, History, Social Sciences. **Career:** Bristol University, reader in European history; University of London, Queen Mary, professor of contemporary history, 2005-. Writer. **Publications:** Moscow Politics and the Rise of Stalin: The Communist Party in the Capital, 1925-32, 1990; Night of Stone: Death and Memory in Russia, 2000; Night of Stone: Death and Memory in Twentieth-Century Russia, 2001. EDITOR: (co-author) Soviet Government Officials, 1922-1941, 1989; (with C. Ward) Perestroika: The Historical Perspective, 1991; Ivan's War: Life and Death in the Red Army, 1939-1945, 2005. Contributor to books and journals. **Address:** Department of History, Queen Mary, University of London, Arts 2 3.04, Mile End Rd., London, GL E1 4NS, England. **Online address:** c.merridale@bristol.ac.uk

MERRILL, Ellen C. American (born United States), b. 1935. **Genres:** History, Anthropology/Ethnology, Social Sciences. **Career:** Loyola University New Orleans, instructor, 1965-67; University of New Orleans, instructor, 1967-69; Historic New Orleans Collection, curator of education and director of German archive, 1977-85; Nicholls State University, adjunct professor, 1984-85; Dillard University, Department of World Languages, associate professor and chair, 1986-2001. Writer. **Publications:** Self-Affirmation and Self-Abnegation in the Prose Works of Hermann Hesse, 1975; (trans. and ed.) H. Blume, The German Coast during the Colonial Era, 1722-1803, 1990; Germans of Louisiana, 2005. Contributor to periodicals. **Address:** Pelican Publishing Company, 1000 Burmaster St., Gretna, LA 70053-2246, U.S.A. **Online address:** ecmerrill@earthlink.net

MERRILL, Hugh (Davis). American (born United States), b. 1942. **Genres:** Music, Writing/Journalism, Communications/Media, Plays/Screenplays, Language/Linguistics, Art/Art History, Social Sciences. **Career:** Huntsville Times, political and civil rights reporter, 1964-66, 1968-69; Birmingham News, political and civil rights reporter, 1966-68; Atlanta Journal, feature writer and reporter, 1969-72; North Fulton Today, political editor and columnist, 1974-75; WAGG-Radio, news writer and announcer, 1976-78; Harpeth Herald, editor, 1978-80; Louisville Today, editor, 1980-81; Atlanta Weekly, staff writer, 1982-85; Gwinnett Daily News, daily columnist, 1985-88; Emory University, teacher of American studies, 1991, 1992; University of West Florida, assistant professor of communications, 1992; Atlanta Children's Theater, actor, resident playwright; Third Masque Theater, founder, actor, playwright; Anniston Community Theater, resident director; Public Broadcasting System, chief researcher. Campaign staff member, press liaison, press secretary and writer. **Publications:** The Blues Route, 1990; Esky: The Early Years at Esquire, 1995; The Red Hot Typewriter: The Life and Times of John D. MacDonald, 2000. Contributor to magazines. **Address:** Department of Communication Arts, University of West Florida, 11000 University Pkwy., Pensacola, FL 32514, U.S.A.

MERRILL, Jean (Fairbanks). American (born United States), b. 1923. **Genres:** Children's Fiction, Humor/Satire, Young Adult Fiction, History, Travel/Exploration, Military/Defense/Arms Control. **Career:** Scholastic Magazines Inc., assistant feature editor, 1945-46, feature editor, 1946-49; Literary Cavalcade, associate editor, 1950-51, editor, 1956-57; Bank Street College of Education, Publications Division, associate editor, 1965-66, consultant, 1967-71, editor. **Publications:** (With R. Solbert) Henry, The Hand Painted Mouse, 1951; The Woover, 1952; Boxes, 1953; (with R. Solbert) The Tree House of Jimmy Domino, 1955; The Travels of Marco, 1955; A Song for Gar, 1957; (with R. Solbert) The Very Nice Things, 1959; (with R. Solbert) Blue's Broken Heart, 1960; (reteller) Shan's Lucky Knife: A Burmese Folk Tale, 1960; (with R. Solbert) Emily Emerson's Moon, 1960; The Superlative Horse: A Tale of Ancient China, 1961; Tell about the Cowbarn, Daddy, 1963; The Pushcart War, 1964; (with R. Solbert) High, Wide, and Handsome and Their Three Tall Tales, 1964; (with R. Solbert) The Elephant Who Liked to Smash Small Cars, 1967; (with R. Solbert) Red Riding: A Story of How Katy Tells Tony a Story Because it is Raining, 1968; (ed. with R. Solbert) A Few Flies and I, 1969; The Black Sheep, 1969; (with F.G. Scott) Here I Come-Ready or Not!, 1970; (with R. Solbert) Mary, Come Running, 1970; (with F.G. Scott) How Many Kids Are Hiding on My Block?, 1970; Please, Don't Eat My Cabin, 1971; The Second Greatest Clown in the World, 1971; The Jackpot, 1971; The Toothpaste Millionaire, 1972; (with F.G. Scott) The Bumper Sticker Book, 1973; Maria's House, 1974; Marah, 1981; (adapter) The Girl Who Loved Caterpillars: A Twelfth-Century Tale from Japan, 1992. Contributor to periodicals. **Address:** Angel's Ark, 29 S Main St., Randolph, VT 05060-1371, U.S.A.

MERRILL, Wendy. American (born United States) **Genres:** Autobiography/Memoirs, Biography, Essays. **Career:** Writer. **Publications:** Falling into Manholes: The Memoir of a Bad/Good Girl (essays), 2008; (ed.) Fit for love, 2010. Works appear in anthologies. **Address:** Penguin Group Inc., 375 Hudson St., New York, NY 10014, U.S.A. **Online address:** wendy@fallingintomanholes.com

MERRIMAN, Catherine. British (born England), b. 1949. **Genres:** Novels, Novellas/Short Stories, Young Adult Fiction, Children's Fiction, Self Help. **Career:** University of Glamorgan, Faculty of Humanities and Social Sciences, lecturer, 1995-, senior lecturer in creative and professional writing. Writer. **Publications:** NOVELS: Leaving the Light On, 1992; Fatal Observations, 1993; State of Desire, 1996; Broken Glass, 1998; Brotherhood, 2003. STORIES: Silly Mothers, 1991; Of Sons and Stars, 1997; Getting a Life: Short Stories, 2001. OTHER: (ed.) Laughing, Not Laughing: Women Writing on My Experience of Sex, 2004. **Address:** Faculty of Humanities and Social Sciences, University of Glamorgan, Treforest Campus, FH104, Pontypridd, GW CF37 1DL, Wales. **Online address:** cmerrima@glam.ac.uk

MERRIMAN, John M. American (born United States), b. 1946. **Genres:** Young Adult Fiction. **Career:** Yale University, assistant professor, 1973-78, associate professor, 1978-83, professor of history, 1983-97, Charles Seymour professor of history, 1996-, Calhoun College, resident fellow, 1974-75, 1976-81. Writer and historian. **Publications:** NON-FICTION: The Agony of the Republic: The Repression of the Left in Revolutionary France, 1848-1851, 1978; The Red City: Limoges and the French Nineteenth Century, 1985; (with E.K. Kenney) The Pear: French Graphic Arts in the Golden Age of Caricature, 1991; The Margins of City Life: Explorations on the French Urban Frontier, 1815-1851, 1991; A History of Modern Europe: From the Renaissance to the Present, 1996, 3rd ed., 2009; The Stones of Balazuc: A French Village in Time, 2002; Police Stories: Making the French State, 1815-1851, 2006; Dynamite Club: How a Bombing in fin-de-siecle Paris Ignited the Age of Terror, 2009. EDITOR: (and intro.) 1830 in France, 1975; Consciousness and Class

Experience in Nineteenth-century Europe, 1979; French Cities in the Nineteenth Century, 1981; For Want of a Horse: Choice and Chance in History, 1985; (with J.L. McClain and U. Kaoru) Edo and Paris: Urban Life and the State in the Early Modern Era, 1994; (with J. Winter) Europe 1789 to 1914: Encyclopedia of the Age of Industry and Empire, 2006; (with J. Winter) Europe since 1914: Encyclopedia of the Age of War and Reconstruction, 2006. **Address:** Department of History, Yale University, PO Box 208324, New Haven, CT 06520-8324, U.S.A. **Online address:** john.merriman@yale.edu

MERRIN, Jeredith. American (born United States), b. 1944. **Genres:** Poetry, Literary Criticism And History, Women's Studies And Issues. **Career:** University of California, instructor in gifted program, 1983-85; Ohio State University, assistant professor to associate professor, 1987-97, professor of English, 1997-, professor emeritus. Writer. **Publications:** An Enabling Humility: Marianne Moore, Elizabeth Bishop and The Uses of Tradition, 1990; Shift (poems), 1996; Bat Ode (poems), 2001; Mon Age, forthcoming; Of Two Minds, forthcoming. Contributor to books and periodicals. Works appear in anthologies. **Address:** Department of English, College of Humanities, Ohio State University, 421 Denney Hall, 164 W 17th Ave., Columbus, OH 43210, U.S.A. **Online address:** merrin.1@osu.edu

MERRITT, Constance. American (born United States), b. 1966. **Genres:** Poetry. **Career:** Sweet Briar College, Margaret Banister writer-in-residence, 2003-05. Poet. **Publications:** A Protocol for Touch, 2000; Blessings and Inclemencies: Poems, 2007; Two Rooms: Poems, 2009. **Address:** University of North Texas Press, PO Box 311336, Denton, OH 76203, U.S.A.

MERRY, Robert William. American (born United States), b. 1946. **Genres:** Biography, History. **Career:** Denver Post, reporter and copy editor, 1972-74; National Observer (DowJones Inc.), reporter, 1974-77; Wall Street Journal, reporter, 1977-86, Washington correspondent; Roll Call (newspaper of Capitol Hill), editor, 1986-87; Congressional Quarterly Inc., managing editor, 1987-89, executive editor, 1990-97, editor-in-chief, chief executive officer, president and publisher, 1997-2010; STRATFOR, publisher, 2010-. **Publications:** Taking on the World: Joseph and Stewart Alsop-Guardians of the American Century (biography), 1996; Sands of Empire: Missionary Zeal, American Foreign Policy, and the Hazards of Global Ambition, 2005; A Country of Vast Designs: James K. Polk, the Mexican War, and the Conquest of the American Continent, 2009; Sands of Empire, 2010; Where they Stand: The American Presidents in the Eyes of Voters and Historians, 2012. Contributor to books. **Address:** Stratfor, 221 W 6th St., Ste. 400, Austin, TX 78701, U.S.A. **Online address:** rmerry@cq.com

MERRY, Sally Engle. American (born United States), b. 1944. **Genres:** Sociology, Environmental Sciences/Ecology. **Career:** Wellesley College, assistant professor, 1977-83, associate professor, 1983-90, professor of anthropology, 1990-, Class of 1949 professor in ethics, 1994-99, Marion Butler McLean professor in history of ideas, 2003; New York University, professor of anthropology and law and society, research associate in anthropology, 1969-70; Arizona State University, distinguished visiting scholar, 1987; Amherst College, visiting professor, 1993; Bunting Institute, Radcliffe College, fellow, 1994-95; American Bar Foundation, visiting research fellow, 1999; Harvard University, Kennedy School, Carr Center for Human Rights Policy, fellow, 2001-02; Renmin University, Sociology of Law in China, visiting scholar, 2001. Writer. **Publications:** Urban Danger: Life in a Neighborhood of Strangers, 1981; Getting Justice and Getting Even: Legal Consciousness among Working-class Americans, 1990; (ed. with N. Milner) The Possibility of Popular Justice: A Case Study of Community Mediation in the United States, 1993; Colonizing Hawaii: The Cultural Power of Law, 2000; (ed. with D. Brenneis) Law and Empire in the Pacific: Fiji and Hawaii, 2004; Human Rights and Gender Violence: Translating International Law into Local Justice, 2006; The Practice of Human Rights: Tracking Law between the Global and the Local, 2007; Gender Violence: A Cultural Perspective, 2009. **Address:** New York University, Rufus D. Smith Hall, 25 Waverly Pl., New York, NY 10003, U.S.A. **Online address:** sally.merry@nyu.edu

MERSER, Cheryl. American (born United States), b. 1951?. **Genres:** Adult Non-fiction, Homes/Gardens, Horticulture. **Career:** Random House, publicity manager, 1976-85. Writer. **Publications:** Honorable Intentions: The Manners of Courtship in the '80s, 1983; (with M. Andrews) How To Sell More Cookies, Condos, Cadillacs, Computers-and Everything Else, 1986; Grown-Ups: A Generation in Search of Adulthood, 1987; Guild Hall of East Hampton: An Adventure in the Arts, the First 60 Years, 1993; A Starter Garden: The Guide for the Horticulturally Hapless, 1994; Relax! It's Only Dinner: Eat Spendidly Anytime Without Losing Your Mind, 1995; (with K.J. Gross and J. Stone) Cooking Tools, 1996; The Garden Design Book, 1997. **Address:** PO Box 2393, Sag Harbor, NY 11963, U.S.A.

MERTHA, Andrew C. American (born United States), b. 1965. **Genres:** Business/Trade/Industry, Economics. **Career:** English teacher, 1988-89; Washington University, assistant professor, 2001-08; Cornell University, professor, 2008-. Writer. **Publications:** The Politics of Piracy: Intellectual Property in Contemporary China, 2005; China's Water Warriors: Citizen Action and Policy Change, 2008. Contributor of articles to journals. **Address:** Department of Government, Cornell University, 316 White Hall, Ithaca, NY 14853, U.S.A. **Online address:** am847@cornell.edu

MERTUS, Julie A. American (born United States), b. 1963?. **Genres:** Law, Social Sciences. **Career:** Southern District of New York, clerk, 1988-89; American Civil Liberties Union, attorney, 1990-91; New York University, adjunct professor, 1991-94; State of New York, Affirmative Litigation Division, assistant corporation counsel, 1992-93; Center for Reproductive Law and Policy, consultant, 1992-93; Helsinki Watch/Human Rights Watch, attorney, 1993-94; Harvard University, Center for International Affairs, program affiliate, 1995-97, Harvard Law School, human rights fellow, visiting fellow, 1996-97; Emory University, School of Law, visiting professor, 1997-98; Ohio Northern University, assistant professor, 1998-2000; American University, School of International Service, associate professor, 2000-, co-director of the MA program in ethics, peace and global affairs, professor; U.S. Institute of Peace, senior fellow; MacArthur Foundation, fellow; United Nations High Commissioner for Refugees, Human Rights and Humanitarian, consultant; Writer. **Publications:** Open Wounds: Human Rights Abuses in Kosovo, 1994; Ženska ljudska prava: praktična primena, 1995; Step-by-Step: Enforcing Human Rights of Women and Girls, 1997; Women's Ruman Rights, 1997; The Suitcase: Refugee Voices from Bosnia and Croatia, with Contributions from over Seventy-five Refugees and Displaced People, 1997; Local Action/Global Change: Learning about the Human Rights of Women and Girls, 1999; The Gender Connection: Humanitarian Law and Policy, 1999; Kosovo: How Myths and Truths Started a War, 1999; From Legal Transplants to Transformative Justice: Human Rights and the Promise of Transnational Civil Society, 1999; War's Offensive on Women: The Humanitarian Challenge in Bosnia, Kosovo, and Afghanistan, 2000; (co-author) Kanants' Iravunk' Nere, K'ayl ar K'ayl, 2002; Bait and Switch: Human Rights and U.S. Foreign Policy, 2004, 2nd ed., 2008; Women's Participation in the International Criminal Tribunal for the Former Yugoslavia, 2004; The United Nations and Human Rights: A Guide for a New Era, 2005, 2nd ed., 2009; (ed. with J.W. Helsing) Human Rights and Conflict: Exploring the Links between Rights, Law, and Peacebuilding, 2006; (with N. Flowers) Local Action, Global Change: A Handbook on Women''s Human Rights, 2008; Human Rights Matters: Local Politics and National Human Rights Institutions, 2009. **Address:** School of International Service, American University, Clark Hall 203, 4400 Massachusetts Ave. NW, Washington, DC 20016-8017, U.S.A. **Online address:** mertus@american.edu

MERTZ, Barbara (Louise) G(ross). Also writes as Elizabeth Peters, Barbara Michaels. American (born United States), b. 1927. **Genres:** Mystery/Crime/Suspense, Romance/Historical, Archaeology/Antiquities, History. **Career:** Writer. **Publications:** Temples, Tombs and Hieroglyphs: The Story of Egyptology, 1964, 2nd ed., 2007; Red Land, Black Land: The World of the Ancient Egyptians, 1966, 2nd ed., 2008; (with R. Mertz) Two Thousand Years in Rome, 1968. AS BARBARA MICHAELS: The Master of Blacktower, 1966; Sons of the Wolf, 1967; Ammie, Come Home, 1968; Prince of Darkness, 1969; The Dark on the Other Side, 1970; Greygallows, 1972; The Crying Child, 1973; Witch, 1973; House of Many Shadows, 1974; The Sea King's Daughter, 1975; Patriot's Dream, 1976; Wings of the Falcon, 1977; Wait for What Will Come, 1978; The Walker in Shadows, 1979; The Wizard's Daughter, 1980; Someone in the House, 1981; Black Rainbow, 1982; Dark Duet, 1983; Here I Stay, 1983; The Grey Beginning, 1984; Be Buried in the Rain, 1985; Shattered Silk, 1986; Search the Shadows, 1987; Smoke and Mirrors, 1989; Into the Darkness, 1990; Vanish with the Rose, 1992; Houses of Stone, 1993; Stitches in Time, 1995; The Dancing Floor, 1997; Other Worlds, 1999. MYSTERY-ROMANCES AS ELIZABETH PETERS: The Jackal's Head, 1968; The Camelot Caper, 1969; The Dead Sea Cipher, 1970, The Night of Four Hundred Rabbits, 1971 in UK as Shadows in the Moonlight, 1975; The Seventh Sinner, 1972; Borrower of the Night, 1973; The Murders of Richard III, 1974; Crocodile on the Sandbank, 1975; Legend in Green Velvet, 1976, as Ghost in Green Velvet, 1977; Devil-May-Care, 1977; Street of the Five Moons, 1978; Summer of the Dragon, 1979; The Love Talker, 1980; The Curse of the Pharaohs, 1981; The Copenhagen Connection, 1982; Silhouette in Scarlet, 1983; Die for Love, 1984; The Mummy Case, 1985; Lion in the Valley, 1986; Trojan Gold, 1987; Deeds of the Disturber, 1988; Naked Once More, 1989; The Last Camel Died at Noon, 1991; The Snake, the Crocodile and the Dog, 1992; Night Train to Memphis, 1994; The Hippopotamus Pool, 1996; Seeing a Large Cat, 1997; The Ape Who Guards the Balance: An Amelia Peabody Mystery, 1998; The Falcon at the Portal, 1999; He Shall Thunder in the Sky, 2000; Lord of the Silent, 2001; The Golden One, 2002; Children of the Storm, 2003; (with K. Whitbread) Amelia Peabody's Egypt, 2003; Guardian of the Horizon, 2004; The Serpent on the Crown, 2005; Tomb of the Golden Bird, 2006; The Laughter of Dead Kings, 2008; A River in the Sky: A Novel, 2010. Contributor to books and periodicals. **Address:** Dominick Abel Literary Agency, 146 W 82nd St., Ste. 1B, New York, NY 10024, U.S.A.

MERULLO, Roland. American (born United States), b. 1953. **Genres:** Novels, Travel/Exploration, Romance/Historical. **Career:** United States Information Agency, staff; Bennington College, teacher of creative writing and literature, 1993-2000; Amherst College, visiting lecturer of creative writing, 1993. Writer. **Publications:** NOVELS: Leaving Losapas, 1991; A Russian Requiem: A Novel, 1993: Revere Beach Boulevard, 1998; In Revere, in Those Days: A Novel, 2003; Golfing with God: A Novel, 2005; Little Love Story: A Novel, 2005; Breakfast With Buddha: A Novel, 2007; Fidel's Last Days: A Novel, 2008; American Savior: A Novel of Divine Politics, 2008; The Talk Funny Girl: A Novel, 2011. OTHER: Passion for Golf: In Pursuit of the Innermost Game, 2000; Revere Beach Elegy: A Memoir of Home and Beyond, 2002; Italian Summer: Golf, Food, and Family at Lake Como, 2009. Contributor to periodicals. **Address:** Marly Rusoff & Associates Inc., PO Box 524, Bronxville, NY 10708, U.S.A.

MERWIN, W(illiam) S(tanley). American (born United States), b. 1927. **Genres:** Plays/Screenplays, Poetry, Translations, Reference, Essays. **Career:** Poet's Theatre, playwright-in-residence, 1956, 1961-63; Roger Planchon's Theatre de la Cite, associate, 1964-65; Library of Congress, poetry consultant, 1999-. **Publications:** A Mask for Janus, 1952; The Dancing Bears (poems), 1954; Green with Beasts (poems), 1956; Favor Island, 1957; The Poem of the Cid, 1956; The Drunk in the Furnace, 1960; Some Spanish Ballads, 1961; (ed.) West Wind: Supplement of American Poetry, 1961; The Gilded West, 1961; The Moving Target, 1963; Collected Poems, 1966; The Lice, 1967; Three Poems, 1968; Selected Translations 1948-1968, 1968; Animae, 1969; The Carrier of Ladders, 1970; The Miner's Pale Children, 1970; Signs, 1971; Chinese Figures: Second Series, 1971; Japanese Figures, 1971; Asian Figures, 1973; Writings to an Unfinished Accompaniment, 1973; The First Four Books of Poems, 1975; Mary, 1976; The Compass Flower, 1977; Houses and Travellers, 1977; Selected Translations, 1968-1978, 1978; Feathers from the Hill, 1978; Unframed Originals: Recollections, 1982; Finding the Islands, 1982; Opening the Hand, 1983; Regions of Memory: Uncollected Prose 1949-1982, 1987; The Rain in the Trees: Poems, 1988; Selected Poems, 1988; (ed. and intro.) The Essential Wyatt, 1989; The Lost Upland, 1992; Travels: Poems, 1993; The Second Four Books of Poems, 1993; The Vixen: Poems, 1996; (comp.) Lament for the Makers: A Memorial Anthology, 1996; Flower and Hand: Poems 1977-1983, 1996; Medieval Epics, 1998; The Folding Cliffs: A Narrative, 1998; East Window: The Asian Translations, 1999; The River Sound: Poems, 1999; The Pupil, 2001; The Mays of Ventadorn, 2002; Sir Gawain and the Green Knight: A New Verse Translation, 2002; The Ends of the Earth: Essays, 2004; Migration: New and Selected Poems, 2005; Present Company, 2005; Summer Doorways: A Memoir, 2005; (with L. Hicks and S. O'Connor) Retracing the Day, 2006; Book of Fables, 2007; (contrib.) Bloodaxe Poetry Introductions 3, 2007; The Shadow of Sirius, 2008; Cuatro Salmos, 2010. TRANSLATOR: El poema del mio Cid (title means: 'The Poem of the Cid'), 1959; Satires, 1961 as The Satires of Persius, 1973; The Life of Lazarillo de Tormes His Fortunes and Adversities, 1962; (and intro.) Products of the Perfected Civilization: Selected Writings of Chamfort, 1969; (and ed.) J. Follain, Transparence of the World, 1969; P. Neruda, Twenty Love Poems and a Song of Despair, 1969; A. Porchia, Voices, 1969, rev. ed. as Voices: Aphorisms, 1988; The Song of Roland, 1970; (with C. Brown) O. Mandelstam, Selected Poems, 1973; (with J.M. Masson) Sanskrit Love Poetry, 1977; (with G.E. Dimock, Jr.) Iphigeneia at Aulis, 1978; (with J.M. Masson) The Peacock's Egg: Love Poems from Ancient India, 1981; Robert the Devil, 1982; (and intro.) Products of the Perfected Civilization: Selected Writings of Chamfort, 1984; Four French Plays, 1985; From the Spanish Morning, 1985; (with S. Shigematsu) M. Soseki, Sun at Midnight: 23 Poems, 1985; R. Juarroz, Vertical Poetry, 1988; (with L. Hughes) F.G. Lorca, Blood Wedding and Yerma, 1994; D. Alighieri, Purgatorio, 2000; J. Sabines, Pieces of Shadow, 2007; (and foreword) Spanish Ballads, 2008. Works appear in anthologies. Contributor to magazines. **Address:** Random House Inc., 1745 Broadway, New York, NY 10019, U.S.A.

MERZ, Jon F. American (born United States), b. 1956. **Genres:** Sciences, Biology, Medicine/Health. **Career:** EDS Nuclear/Impell Corp., engineer; Westinghouse Corp., engineer, 1981-85, contracts specialist, 1985-87, attorney, 1987-88; Carnegie Mellon University, research fellow, 1991-92; RAND Corp., policy analyst, 1992-95; University of Pennsylvania, associate professor of medical ethics, 1995-, School of Medicine, Department of Medical Ethics, associate chair, Center for Bioethics, senior fellow; IRB Forum online, manager, 2003-; CPTech, fellow, 2006-; Penn School of Medicine curriculum, faculty; Penn School of Engineering and Applied Science, faculty; International IP Law, Trade and Policy, senior fellow. Writer. **Publications:** (With K.F. Greif) Current Controversies in the Biological Sciences: Case Studies of Policy Challenges from New Technologies, 2007. Contributor to periodicals and journals. **Address:** Center for Bioethics, University of Pennsylvania, 3401 Market St., Ste. 320, Philadelphia, PA 19104-3318, U.S.A. **Online address:** merz@mail.med.upenn.edu

MERZ, Jon F. American (born United States), b. 1969?. **Genres:** Novels. **Career:** New Ronin Entertainment, co-founder; Planet Pulp Online, founder. Writer and advertising copywriter. **Publications:** LAWSON VAMPIRE SERIES: The Fixer, 2002; The Invoker, 2002; The Destructor, 2003; The Syndicate, 2003. OTHERS: Danger-Close: A Jake Thunder Adventure, 2004; (with N.M. Nordstrom) Learning Later, Living Greater: The Secret for Making the Most of Your After-50 Years, 2006; (with R. Franklin) The Complete Idiot's Guide to Ultimate Fighting, 2007; The Kensei, 2011. Contributor to periodicals. **Address:** c/o Joe Monti, Barry Goldblatt Literary, 320 7th Ave., Ste. 266, Brooklyn, NY 11215, U.S.A. **Online address:** jon@jonfmerz.com

MESA-LAGO, Carmelo. (Carmelo Mayseh- Lahgo). American (born United States), b. 1934. **Genres:** Economics, Medicine/Health, Area Studies, Public/Social Administration, Social Sciences. **Career:** University of Madrid, School of Law, assistant professor, 1961-62; University of Miami, research associate, 1962-65; University of Pittsburgh, assistant professor, 1967-70, associate professor, 1970-76, Center for Latin American Studies, director, 1974-86, professor of economics, 1976-80, distinguished service professor of economics and Latin American studies, 1996-99, distinguished service professor emeritus of economics and Latin American studies, 1999-; Florida International University, professor, 1999-2002; Universidad de Salamanca, visiting professor, 2008; Tulane University visiting professor, 2009. Writer. **Publications:** The Labor Sector and Socialist Distribution in Cuba, 1968; The Labor Force, Employment, Unemployment and Underemployment in Cuba 1898-1970, 1972; Cuba in the 1970's, 1974; Social Security in Latin America, 1978; The Economy of Socialist Cuba, 1981; Ascent to Bankruptcy, Social Security Financing in Latin America, 1989; La Seguridad Social y el Sector Informal, 1990; Health Care for the Poor in Latin America and the Caribbean, 1992; Changing Social Security in Latin America, 1994; Are Economic Reforms Propelling Cuba to the Market?, 1994; Breve Historia Economica de Cuba Socialista, 1994; Manual de Economia de la Seguridad Social Latinoamericana, 1998; Market, Socialist and Mixed Economies: Comparative Policy and Performance, 2000; La Economia y el Bienestar Social en Cuba a Comienzos del Siglo XXI, 2003; Las Reformas de Pensiones en America Latina y su Impacto en los Principios de la Seguridad Social, 2004; The Cuban Economy Today, 2005; Cuba's Aborted Reform, 2005; Las Reformas de Salud en America Latina y el Caribe y su Impacto en los Principios de la Seguridad Social, 2006; Reassembling Social Security: A Survey of Pension and Healthcare Reforms in Latin America, 2008; World Crisis Effects on Social Security in Latin America and the Caribbean, 2010; Social Protection in Central America, 2010. EDITOR AND CONTRIBUTOR: Revolutionary Change in Cuba, 1971; Comparative Socialist Systems, 1975; Cuba in the World, 1979; Cuba in Africa, 1982; The Crisis of Social Security and Health Care, 1985; Cuba after the Cold War, 1993; Do Options Exist?: The Reform of Pension and Health-Care Systems in Latin America, 1998. **Address:** Department of Economics, University of Pittsburgh, 4529 Posvar Hall, Pittsburgh, PA 15260, U.S.A. **Online address:** cmesa@usa.net

MESERVE, Walter Joseph. American (born United States), b. 1923.

Genres: Plays/Screenplays, History, Literary Criticism And History, Theatre, Biography, Art/Art History, Humanities. **Career:** University of Kansas, instructor, 1951-53, assistant professor to associate professor, 1953-63, professor of English, 1963-67; University of Manchester, lecturer, 1959-60; University of California, visiting professor, 1967-68; Indiana University at Bloomington, professor of theater and drama, 1968-88; Feedback Theatre books/Prospero Press, vice president and editor-in-chief, 1983-; Graduate School of the City University of New York, Institute for American Theatre Studies, director, 1983-88, distinguished professor of theater and English, 1988-93, distinguished professor emeritus, 1993-. Writer. **Publications:** The Complete Plays of W.D. Howells, 1960; Outline History of American Drama, 1965, rev. ed., 1994; Robert E. Sherwood: Reluctant Moralist, 1970; An Emerging Entertainment: The Drama of the American People to 1828, 1977; (co-author) The Revels History of Drama in English VIII: American Drama, 1977; American Drama to 1900: A Guide to Information Sources, 1980; Heralds of Promise: The Drama of the American People During the Age of Jackson 1829-1849, 1986; Playhouse America!, 1991; (with M.A. Meserve) The Theatre Lover's Cookbook: Recipes from 60 Favorite Plays, 1992; (with M.A. Meserve) A Chronological Outline of World Theatre, 1992; (with M.A. Meserve) The Musical Theatre Cookbook: Recipes from Best Loved Musicals, 1993; (with M.A. Meserve) Prospero's Almanac, vol. I, 1997. EDITOR/ CO-EDITOR: (and intro.) Discussions of Modern American Drama, 1966; (and intro.) Discussions of American Drama, 1966; (with W.R. Reardon) American Satiric Comedies, 1969; Modern Drama from Communist China, 1970; The Rise of Silas Lapham, 1971; Merrill Studies in Death of a Salesman, 1972; (and intro. with R.I. Meserve) Modern Literature from China, 1974; (with M.A. Meserve) Who's Who in the American Theatre, 1990; (and intro.) On Stage, America!: A Selection of Distinctly American Plays, 1996; (and intro. with M.A. Meserve) When Conscience Trod the Stage: American Plays of Social Awareness, 1998; (and intro. with M.A. Meserve) Fateful Lightning: American Civil War Plays, 2000. **Address:** Feedback Theatrebooks & Prospero Press, PO Box 174, Brooklin, ME 04616, U.S.A.

MESHEL, Jeffrey W. American (born United States), b. 1957?. **Genres:** Young Adult Fiction. **Career:** Mast Capital Investors, vice president and director, 1980-84; Mercury Capital Corp., co-founder and president, 1985-; Mercury Properties, co-founder and president, 1985-; Mercury Equity Group, co-founder, 1985-, president, 2000-; Paradigm Capital Group, co-founder, chief executive officer/president, 1989-; The Strategic Forum, founder and chairman, 2000-; Signature Bank, director, 2005-; Bintro.com, chairman/founder, 2006-. Writer. **Publications:** (With D. Garr) One Phone Call Away: Secrets of a Master Networker, 2005; The Opportunity Magnet: Attract Success in Every Aspect of Your Life, 2010. **Address:** Signature Bank, 565 5th Ave., New York, NY 10017-2413, U.S.A. **Online address:** jeffm@mercurycap.com

MESIBOV, Gary B. American (born United States), b. 1945. **Genres:** Medicine/Health. **Career:** University of Guam, instructor, assistant professor of psychology, 1968-71, department head, 1969-71; University of North Carolina, postdoctoral fellow in clinical child psychology, 1974-75, Division for Disorders of Development and Learning, psychologist, 1975-79, Department of Psychiatry, assistant professor, 1975-81, associate professor, 1981-87, professor of psychology, 1987-, Department of Psychology, clinical professor, Treatment and Education of Autistic and related Communication Division (TEACCH), co-ordinator of adolescent and adult services, 1979-82, associate director of the division, 1983-87, co-director, 1988-92, director, 1992-2010; Journal of Pediatric Psychology, associate editor, 1976-82; Journal of Autism and Developmental Disorders, associate editor, 1983-, acting editor, 1988-89; Residential Services Inc., president, 1980-81. **Publications:** (Contrib.) Individualized Assessment and Treatment for Autistic and Developmentally Disabled Children, 1979; (with L.W. Adams and L.G. Klinger) Autism: Understanding the Disorder, 1997; (with V. Shea and L.W. Adams) Understanding Asperger Syndrome and High Functioning Autism, 2001; (co-author) TEACCH Approach to Autism Spectrum Disorders, 2005; (foreword) Asperger's... What Does it Mean to Me?, 2006. EDITOR WITH E. SCHOPLER: Autism in Adolescents and Adults, 1983; The Effects of Autism on the Family, 1984; Communication Problems in Autism, 1985; Social Behavior in Autism, 1986; Neurobiological Issues in Autism, 1987; Diagnosis and Assessment in Autism, 1988; High-Functioning Individuals with Autism, 1992; Behavioral Issues in Autism, 1994; Learning and Cognition in Autism, 1995; (and with L.J. Kunce) Asperger Syndrome or High-Functioning Autism?, 1998. Contributor to books and journals. **Address:** University of North Carolina, 210 Pittsboro St., Chapel Hill, NC 27599, U.S.A. **Online address:** gary_mesibov@med.unc.edu

MESLE, C. Robert. American (born United States), b. 1949. **Genres:** Philosophy, Theology/Religion, Humanities. **Career:** Graceland University, Department of Philosophy and Religion, professor, head and director of honors program, 1980-; University of Kansas, Center for Humanistic Studies, Andrew Mellon fellow, 1985; University of Santa Clara, NEH fellow, 1986; Davis & Elkins College, William E. Phipps religion and philosophy interdisciplinary lecturer, 2000; East China School of Science and Technology, Whitehead Academy, lead professor, 2009. Writer. **Publications:** Fire in My Bones: A Study in Faith and Belief, 1984; The Bible as Story and Struggle, 1989; (with J. Hick) John Hick's Theodicy: A Process Humanist Critique, 1991; (with J.B. Cobb, Jr.) Process Theology: A Basic Introduction, 1993; (ed.) Theology V: The Jesus Seminar, 1998; (ed. with J. Wilson) Theology 9: Process Theology and Religious Pluralism, 2002; Process-relational Philosophy: An Introduction to Alfred North Whitehead, 2008. Contributor to books, journals, periodicals and magazines. **Address:** Department of Philosophy and Religion, Graceland University, 1 University Pl., Lamoni, IA 50140-1699, U.S.A. **Online address:** bobmesle@graceland.edu

MESSEL, Harry. Australian/Canadian (born Canada), b. 1922. **Genres:** Education, Environmental Sciences/Ecology, Physics, Sciences. **Career:** University of Adelaide, lecturer of mathematical physics, 1951-52; University of Sydney, professor, 1952-87, professor emeritus of physics, 1987-, School of Physics, head, Science Foundation for Physics, director; Australian Atomic Energy Commission, member, 1974-81; Bond University, chancellor, 1992-97, executive chancellor, 1993-96. Writer. **Publications:** Selected Lectures in Modern Physics for School Science Teachers, 1958; Lecture Notes on an Introductory Course in Modern Physics, 1958; (co-author) A Modern Introduction to Physics, 3 vols., 1960-61; (with S. Butler) Space and the Atom, 1961; (with S. Butler) A Journey through Space and the Atom, 1962; (with S. Butler) The Universe of Time and Space, 1962; (with S. Butler) Light and Life in the Universe, 1964; (co-author) Science for High School Students, 1964; (with S. Butler) An Introduction to Modern Physics, 1964; (co-author) Time, 1965; (co-author) Abridged Science for High School Students, 2 vols., 1965; (co-author) Senior Science for High School Students, 1965; (with D. Crawford) Electron-Photon Shower Distribution Function, 1970; (co-author) Multistrand Senior Science for High School Students, 1975; (co-author) Tidal Rivers in Northern Australia and Their Crocodile Populations, 20 monographs, 1979-87; Science Update, 1983; (co-author) Highlights in Sciences, 1987. EDITOR: Energy for Survival, 1979; The Biological Manipulation of Life, 1981; The Study of Populations, 1985. EDITOR WITH S. BUTLER: From Nucleus to Universe, 1960; Space Physics and Radio Astronomy, 1964; The Universe and Its Origin, 1964; Atoms to Andromeda, 1965; Apollo and the Universe, 1967; Man in Inner and Outer Space, 1968; Nuclear Energy Today and Tomorrow, 1969; Pioneering in Space, 1970; Molecules to Man, 1971; Brain Mechanisms and the Control of Behaviour, 1972; Focus on the Stars, 1973; Solar Energy, 1974; Our Earth, 1975; Australian Animals and Their Environment, 1977; (with L.R.B. Elton) Time and Man, 1978; (with A.A. Burbidge) The Status of the Salt-water Crocodile in the Glenelg, Prince Regent, and Ord River Systems, Kimberley, Western Australia, 1979; Victoria and Fitzmaurice River Systems, 1979; (with A.G. Wells and W.J. Green) Alligator Region River Systems, 1979; Survey of tidal Waterways in Northern Australia and their Crocodile Populations, 20 Monographs, 1979-87; (co-ed.) Tidal Waterways of the Kimberley Surveyed during 1977, 1978, and 1986, 1987; (ed.) Crocodiles: An Action Plan for their Conservation, 1992. **Address:** Science Foundation for Physics, School of Physics, University of Sydney, Sydney, NW 2006, Australia. **Online address:** messel@bigpond.net.au

MESSENGER, Christian K(arl). American (born United States), b. 1943. **Genres:** Literary Criticism And History, Social Sciences. **Career:** Wittenberg University, assistant professor of English, 1973-76; University of Illinois, assistant professor, 1976-82, associate professor, 1982-90, professor of English, 1990-. Writer. **Publications:** Sport and the Spirit of Play in American Fiction: Hawthorne to Faulkner, 1981; Sport and the Spirit of Play in Contemporary American Fiction, 1990; (with C. Walker) Long Time Coming: A Black Athlete's Coming-of-Age in America, 1995; The Godfather and American Culture: How the Corleones Became Our Gang, 2002. **Address:** Department of English, University of Illinois, MC 162, University Hall, 601 S Morgan St., Ste. 1920, Chicago, IL 60607, U.S.A. **Online address:** chrism1@uic.edu

MESSER, Donald E(dward). American (born United States), b. 1941. **Genres:** Theology/Religion, Social Sciences. **Career:** United Methodist church, associate pastor, 1969-71, delegate to jurisdictional conference, 1984, 1988, 1992, 1996; Augustana College, assistant professor of sociology, 1969-71; Dakota Wesleyan University, president, 1971-81, Stark lecturer, 1991; South Dakota Foundation of Private Colleges, president, 1973-75, director; Iliff School of Theology, president, 1981-2000, Practical Theology, president emeritus and professor emeritus, Henry White Warren professor emeritus; Global AIDS, executive director, 2007-. Writer. **Publications:** Christian Ethics and Political Action, 1984; Contemporary Images of Christian Ministry, 1989; A Conspiracy of Goodness: Contemporary Images of Christian Mission, 1992; Calling Church and Seminary into the 21st Century, 1995; Breaking the Conspiracy of Silence: Christian Churches and the Global AIDS Crisis, 2004; (with G. McGovern and B. Dole) Ending Hunger Now: A Challenge to Persons of Faith, 2005; Names, Not Just Numbers: Facing Global Aids and World Hunger, 2010. EDITOR: Send Me? The Itineracy in Crisis, 1991; (with S.B. Geis) Caught in the Crossfire: Helping Christians Debate Homosexuality, 1994; (with B. Abraham) Unity, Liberty and Charity: Building Bridges under Icy Waters, 1996; (with S.B. Geis) How Shall We Die? Helping Christians Debate Assisted Suicide, 1997; (with S.B. Geis) The Befuddled Stork: Helping Persons of Faith Debate Beginning-of-Life Issues, 2000; (with A.J. Weaver) Connected Spirits: Friends and Spiritual Journeys, 2007; 52 Ways to Create an AIDS-Free World, 2009; Cherishing Life & Love: Reflections of Paul Murphy, 2009. Contributor of articles to journals. **Address:** Iliff School of Theology, 2201 S University Blvd., Denver, CO 80210, U.S.A.

MESSER, Richard. British (born England), b. 1965. **Genres:** Theology/Religion, Adult Non-fiction. **Career:** University of Reading, faculty administrator, 1991-93, examinations officer, 1993-98, director of planning support, 1998-2008, director of academic services, 2008-. Writer. **Publications:** Does God's Existence Need Proof?, 1993. **Address:** Academic Services, University of Reading, PO Box 217, Whiteknights, BR RG6 6AH, England. **Online address:** r.j.messer@reading.ac.uk

MESSER, Sarah. American (born United States), b. 1966?. **Genres:** Poetry. **Career:** University of Wisconsin, Institute for Creative Writing, Diane Middlebrook poetry fellow, 1997-98; University of North Carolina, assistant professor of creative writing, associate professor of creative writing. Writer. **Publications:** Bandit Letters, 2001; Red House: Being a Mostly Accurate Account of New England's Oldest Continuously Lived-in House, 2004. **Address:** Department of Creative Writing, University of North Carolina, Kenan Hall, 601 S College Rd., Wilmington, NC 28403, U.S.A. **Online address:** messers@uncw.edu

MESSER, Thomas M. American/Czech (born Czech Republic), b. 1920. **Genres:** Art/Art History, Biography, Literary Criticism And History. **Career:** Office of War Information, staff, 1942-43; Roswell Museum of History and Art (now Roswell Museum and Art Center), director, 1949-52; American Federation of Arts, assistant director, 1952-53, director of exhibitions, 1953-55, director, 1955-56; Time Inc., consultant and director, 1956; Institute of Contemporary Art, director, 1957-61; Harvard University, adjunct professor of modern art, 1960; Solomon R. Guggenheim Museum, director, 1961-88, trustee, 1980-88; Barnard College, adjunct professor, 1966, 1971; Wesleyan University, senior fellow of center for advanced study, 1966; Center for Inter-American Relations, trustee, 1974-; MacDowell Colony Inc., president, 1977-80; Peggy Guggenheim Collection, director emeritus, 1980; Wooster School, trustee. Writer. **Publications:** (With A.L. Jenks) Contemporary Painters of Japanese Origin in America, 1958; Elements of Modern Painting, 1961; Modern Art: An Introductory Commentary, 1962; The Emergent Decade: Latin American Painters and Painting in the 1960's, 1966; Paul Klee Exhibition At The Guggenheim Museum: A Post Scriptum, 1968; Julius Bissier, 1893-1965, 1968; A Retrospective Exhibition, 1968; Edvard Munch, 1971; (intro.) 100 Works By Modern Masters From the Guggenheim Museum, 1984; (ed.) I Maestri del Guggenheim: Milano, 12 Maggio-26 Luglio 1985, Padiglione d'arte contemporanea, 1985; (ed.) A Half-Century of European Painting, 1910-1960, from the Guggenheim Museum, New York: Venice, Spring 1986, 1986; (ed.) Handbook: The Peggy Guggenheim Collection, 1986; Fifty Years of Collecting: An Anniversary Selection, 1987; (with G. Adriani) Joseph Beuys: Drawings, Objects, and Prints, 1989; Jean Dubuffet, 1901-1985, 1990; Antoni Tapies: Eine Retrospektive, 1993; (ed.) Eduardo Chillida: Eine retrospektive, 1993; Nicolas de Stael: Retrospektive, 1994; Asger Jorn, 1994; Asger Jorn: Retrospektive, 1994; (with E. Chillida and A. Tapies) Photographien Emanuel Raab: Zu den Retrospektiven Eduardo Chillida und Antoni Tapies: Schirn Kunsthalle Frankfurt, 1993, 1994; Lucio Fontana: Retrospektive, 1996; Vasily Kandinsky, 1997; Between Art and Life: Vom Abstrakten Expressionismus zur Pop Art, 1999; (preface) Charles Seliger: Redefining Abstract Expressionism, 2002. Contributor of article to journals. **Address:** Solomon R. Guggenheim Museum, 1071 5 Ave., New York, NY 10021, U.S.A. **Online address:** tmmesser@aol.com

MESSNER, Michael A. American (born United States), b. 1952. **Genres:** Sociology, Sports/Fitness, Children's Fiction. **Career:** California State University, instructor in sociology, 1976, teaching assistant, 1979-83, lecturer in sociology and social services, 1983-87; Sacramento City College, Interdisciplinary Experimental College, instructor, 1976-77, instructor in sociology, 1976-78; Canada College, instructor in sociology, 1980; Solano Community College, instructor in sociology, 1980-82; Chabot College, instructor, 1980-83; University of Southern California, assistant professor of Sociology and gender studies, 1987-94, associate professor of sociology and gender studies, 1994-2002, Gender Studies Program, coordinator of graduate certificate program, 1993-99; Sociology Department, director of graduate studies, 1997-2001, sociology department chair, 2001-07, professor of sociology and gender studies, 2002-, director of faculty development, 2008-, Gender Studies Program, interim director, 2010-11. Writer. **Publications:** (Comp. with M.S. Kimmel) Men's Lives, 1989, 8th ed., 2010; (ed. with D.F. Sabo) Sport, Men and the Gender Order: Critical Feminist Perspectives, 1990; Power at Play: Sports and the Problem of Masculinity, 1992; (co-ed. and contrib.) Exercising Power: The Making and Remaking of the Body, 1993; (with D.F. Sabo) Sex, Violence & Power in Sports: Rethinking Masculinity, 1994; (contrib.) Gender Stereotyping in Televised Sports: A Follow-Up to the 1989 Study, 1994; (ed. with P. Hondagneu-Sotelo and M.B. Zinn) Through the Prism of Difference: Readings on Sex and Gender, 1997; The Politics of Masculinities: Men in Movements, 1997; (ed. with J. McKay and D. Sabo) Masculinities, Gender Relations and Sport, 2000; (ed. with P. Hondagneu-Sotelo and B. Zinn) Gender Through the Prism of Difference, 2000, 4th ed., 2010; Taking the Field: Women, Men and Sports, 2002; (ed. with M. Gatz and S.J. Ball-Rokeach) Paradoxes of Youth and Sport, 2002; Out of Play: Critical Essays on Gender and Sport, 2007; It's all for the Kids: Gender, Families and Youth Sports, 2009; King of the Wild Suburb: A Memoir of Fathers, Sons and Guns, 2011. Works appear in anthologies. Contributor to periodicals. **Address:** Department of Sociology, University of Southern California, KAP 352, 3620 S Vermont Ave., Los Angeles, CA 90089-2539, U.S.A. **Online address:** messner@usc.edu

MESSNER, Patricia A. American (born United States), b. 1954. **Genres:** Education, Picture/Board Books. **Career:** Christian School, teacher, 1976-78; Countryside Young Mens Christian Association, teacher, 1985-87; Lebanon City Schools, media specialist, 1989. Writer. **Publications:** (With B.S. Copeland) Linking Picture Books to Standards, 2003; (with B.S. Copeland) Collaborative Library Lessons for the Primary Grades: Linking Research Skills to Curriculum Standards, 2004; Collaborative Library Lessons for Primary Grades, 2005; Using Picture Books to Teach Language Arts, 2006; (with B.S. Copeland) Year in Picture Books: Linking to the Information Literacy Standards, 2007; (with B.S. Copeland) Every Day Reading Incentives, 2009; (with B.S. Copeland) School Library Spaces: Just the Basics, 2011; School Library Management: Just the Basics, 2012. **Address:** Lebanon City Schools, Donovan Elementary School, 401 Justice Ave., Lebanon, OH 45036, U.S.A. **Online address:** messnerpat@yahoo.com

MESSORI, Vittorio. Italian (born Italy), b. 1941?. **Genres:** Theology/Religion, Novels, Essays. **Career:** TuttiLibri, editor. **Publications:** Ipotesi su Gesù, 1976, trans. as Jesus Hypotheses, 1977, trans. in US as Faith's Answer: The Mystery of Jesus, 1986; Scommessa sulla morte: la prosposta cristiana, illusione o speranza?, 1982; (with J. Ratzinger) Rapporto sulla fede, 1985, trans. as The Ratzinger Report: An Exclusive Interview on the State of the Church, 1985; Inchiesta sul cristianesimo: Sei tu il Messia che deve venire? (interviews), 1987; (with E. Cuoghi) Attorno a casa tua, 1988; Un italiano serio, 1990; Il beato serio: il beato Francesco Faà di Bruno, 1990, as Il beato Faà di Bruno: un cristiano in un mondo ostile, 1998; Pati sotto Ponzio pilato?: un'indagine sulla passione e morte di Gesù, 1992; (with P. Gheddo) Nel nome del padre: la conquista cristiana; sopruso omissione?, 1992; (with G. Biffi) Pensare la storia: une letture cattolica dell'avventura umana, 1992; La sfida della fede: fuori e dentro la Chiesa: l'attualità in una prospettiva cristiana, 1993; (ed.) Varcare la soglia della speranza, 1994, trans. as Crossing the Threshold of Hope, 1994; (with G. Romano) Opus Dei: un'indagine, 1994, trans. as Opus Dei: Leadership and Vision in Today's Catholic Church, 1997;

Przekrocyć próg Nadziei: Jan Pawel II odopwiada na Pytania, 1994; (ed.) Cruzando el umbral de la esperanza, 1995; Le cose della vita (essays), 1995; (with M. Brambilla) Qualche ragione per credere, 1997; Il miracolo: Spagna 1640: idagine sul più sconvolgente prodigio mariano, 1998; Dicono che è risorto: un'indagine sul Sepolcro vuoto, 2000; Uomini, Storia, fede, 2001; (with R. Cammilleri) Occhi di Maria, 2001; (with L. Mondadori) Conversione: una Storia Personale, 2002; Io, il Bambino Ebreo Rapito da Pio IX: Il Memoriale inedito del Protagonista del Caso Mortara, 2005; Ipotesi su Maria: Fatti, Indizi, Enigmi, 2005; Emporio cattolico: uno sguardo diverso sulla storia e l'attualità, 2006; Qualche ragione per credere: un catechismo postmoderno, 2008. **Address:** Societa Editrice Internazionale SPA, Corso Regina Margherita 176, Torino, 10152, Italy. **Online address:** malliasebastiano@tin.it

MESSUD, Claire. American (born United States), b. 1966. **Genres:** Novellas/Short Stories, Young Adult Fiction, Novels. **Career:** Warren Wilson College, instructor in writing; Johns Hopkins University, Graduate Writing Program, instructor in writing; University of the South, writer-in-residence, 2000-; Amherst College, visiting writer, 2000-02; Kenyon College, Thomas professor of creative writing, 2003; Harvard University, Radcliffe Institute for Advanced Study, fellow, 2004-05; Tulane University, writer-in-residence. **Publications:** When the World Was Steady, 1994; The Last Life, 1999; The Hunters: Two Short Novels, 2001; The Emperor's Children, 2006; The Professor's History, 2006; (intro.) David Golder, The Ball, Snow in Autumn, The CourilofAffair, 2008; The Woman Upstairs, 2012. Contributor to periodicals. **Address:** Harcourt Inc., 15 E 26th St., New York, NY 10010-1505, U.S.A.

MESTA, Gabriel. *See* **ANDERSON, Kevin J(ames).**

MESTER, Terri A. American (born United States), b. 1948. **Genres:** Adult Non-fiction, Literary Criticism And History. **Career:** Northern Ohio Live Magazine, contributing editor, 1980-86; The History of the Cleveland Commission on Higher Education, project editor, 1985; Hiram College, teacher of English, 1993-94; Cuyahoga Community College, teacher, 1993-95; Kent State University, part-time instructor in English, 1994-, College of Business Administration, faculty; Ursuline College, teacher, 1994-, 1998; University of Akron, teacher, 1995-97; Workplace Writing (consulting service), director, 1996-; Cleveland State University, staff, 1998; consultant, 1998-; Case Western Reserve University, instructor, 2002-, prelaw advisor in undergraduate studies, Case School of Engineering, faculty. **Publications:** Movement and Modernism: Yeats, Eliot, Lawrence, Williams, and Early Twentieth-Century Dance, 1997. Contributor to magazines and newspapers. **Address:** Weatherhead School of Management, Case Western Reserve University, 10900 Euclid Ave., Cleveland, OH 44106-7235, U.S.A. **Online address:** terri.mester@case.edu

MESTROVIC, Stjepan G. American/Croatian (born Croatia), b. 1955. **Genres:** International Relations/Current Affairs, Sociology. **Career:** Lander College, assistant professor, associate professor of sociology, 1981-90; Texas A&M University, faculty, 1989-, professor of sociology, 1990-. Writer. **Publications:** Emile Durkheim and the Reformation of Sociology, 1988; The Coming Fin de Siecle: An Application of Durkheim's Sociology to Modernity and Postmodernity, 1991; Durkheim and Postmodern Culture, 1992; The Road from Paradise: The Possibility of Democracy in Eastern Europe, 1993; Habits of the Balkan Heart: Social Character and the Fall of Communism, 1993; The Barbarian Temperament: Towards a Postmodern Critical Theory, 1993; The Balkanization of the West: The Confluence of Postmodernism with Postcommunism, 1994; Genocide after Emotion: The Postemotional Balkan War, 1996; (ed. with T. Cushman) This Time We Knew: Western Responses to Genocide in Bosnia, 1996; The Conceit of Innocence: How the Conscience of the West Was Lost in the War against Bosnia, 1997; Postemotional Society, 1997; Anthony Giddens: The Last Modernist, 1998; Thorstein Veblen on Theory, Culture and Society, 2004; The Trials of Abu Ghraib: An Expert Witness Account of Shame and Honor, 2007; Heart of Stone: My Grandfather, Ivan Mestrovic, 2007; Srce od kamena: moj djed Ivan Meštrović, 2007; Rules of Engagement? A Social Anatomy of an American War Crime-Operation Iron Triangle, 2008; The Good Soldier on Trial, 2009. **Address:** Department of Sociology, Texas A & M University, 435 Academic Bldg., College Station, TX 77843, U.S.A. **Online address:** mestrovic@neo.tamu.edu

METCALF, Allan (Albert). American (born United States), b. 1940. **Genres:** Language/Linguistics, Reference, History, Writing/Journalism, Politics/Government. **Career:** University of California-Riverside, assistant professor of English, 1966-73; University of California-Santa Cruz, California Summer Program in Linguistics, co-director, 1973; MacMurray College, Jacksonville Correctional Center, instructor, 1989, 1995-2003, Department of English, associate professor, 1973-81, professor, 1981-, chair, 1973-83, 1997-2000, Program in Journalism, director, 1975-2003, registrar and assistant vice president for academic affairs and registrar, 2003-. Writer. **Publications:** (With T.E. Armbruster, E.C. Howell IV and S. Prasad) Riverside English: The Spoken Language of a Southern California Community, 1971; Poetic Diction in the Old English Meters of Boethius, 1973; Chicano English, 1979; (with W.J. Kerrigan) Writing to the point, 1987; Research to the Point, 1991, 2nd ed., 1995; Essentials of Writing to The Point, 1995; (with D.K. Barnhart) America in So Many Words: Words That Have Shaped America, 1997; The World in So Many Words: A Country-by-Country Tour of Words That Have Shaped Our Language, 1999; How We Talk: American Regional English Today, 2000; Predicting New Words: The Secrets of Their Success, 2002; Presidential Voices: Speaking Styles from George Washington to George W. Bush, 2004; OK: The Improbable Story of America's Greatest Word, 2010. Contributor of articles to journals. **Address:** Department of English, MacMurray College, 477 E College Ave., Jacksonville, IL 62650-2510, U.S.A. **Online address:** allan.metcalf@mac.edu

METCALF, Donald. Australian (born Australia), b. 1929. **Genres:** Medicine/Health, Sports/Fitness, Sciences, Biology. **Career:** Walter and Eliza Hall Institute, Cancer Research Unit, Carden fellow, 1954-56, head, 1958-96, assistant director, 1965-96, Institute of Medical Research, professor; University of Melbourne, research professor of cancer biology, 1986-96, professor emeritus, 1996-. Writer. **Publications:** (With M.A.S. Moore) Haemopoietic Cells, 1971; Nature of Myeloid Leukaemia, 1973; Hemopoietic Colonies: In Vitro Cloning of Normal and Leukemic Cells, 1977; (ed. with N.L. Warner) Leukemia, 1981; Clonal Culture of Hemopoietic Cells: Techniques and Applications, 1984; The Hemopoietic Colony Stimulating Factors, 1984; The Molecular Control of Blood Cells, 1988; (with N.A. Nicola) Hemopoietic Colony-Stimulating Factors: From Biology to Clinical Applications, 1995; (ed. and E, Mihich) Normal and Malignant Hematopoiesis: New Advances, 1995; Summon Up the Blood: In Dogged Pursuit of the Blood Cell Regulators, 2001; Blood Lines: An Introduction to Characterizing Blood Diseases of the Post-Genomic Mouse, 2004. **Address:** The Walter & Eliza Hall Institute, 1G Royal Parade, Parkville, VI 3050, Australia. **Online address:** metcalf@wehi.edu.au

METCALF, John (Wesley). Canadian/British (born England), b. 1938. **Genres:** Novels, Literary Criticism And History, Essays, Novellas/Short Stories, Young Adult Fiction, Autobiography/Memoirs. **Career:** Teacher, 1961-69; Loyola College, lecturer in English, 1969-71, 1973-75, writer-in-residence, 1976; McGill University, lecturer in English, 1969-71; University of New Brunswick, writer-in-residence, 1972-73; Loyola of Montreal, writer-in-residence, 1976; University of Ottawa, writer-in-residence, 1977; writer, 1977-; Concordia University, writer-in-residence, 1980-81; University of Bologna, writer-in-residence, 1985. **Publications:** EDITOR: The Razor's Edge, 1967; The Flight of the Phoenix, 1968; Daughter of Time, 1968; (contrib.) New Canadian Writing, 1969; (with G. Callaghan) Salutation, 1970; (intro.) The Narrative Voice: Short Stories and Reflections by Canadian Authors, 1972; (with J. Harcourt) Best Canadian Stories, 2 vols., 1976-77; (with C. Blaise) Here and Now, 1977; (with C. Blaise) Best Canadian Stories, 3 vols., 1978-80; Stories Plus: Canadian Short Stories with Authors Commentaries, 1979; New Worlds, 1980; (ed.) First Impressions, 1980; (contrib.) Second Impressions, 1981; (contrib.) Third Impressions, 1982; (with L. Rooke) Best Canadian Stories, 2 vols., 1981-82; Making It New: Contemporary Canadian Stories, 1982; (with L. Rooke) The New Press Anthology: Best Canadian Short Fiction, 1984; The Bumper Book, 1986; Carry On Bumping, 1988; (ed.) Writers in Aspic, 1988; (with L. Rooke) The Macmillan Anthology, vol. I-II, 1988-89, vol. III (with K. Thompson), 1990; (with J.R. Struthers) How Stories Mean, 1993; (with C. Wilkshire) Writers Talking, 2003; (ed.) Alden Nowlan: Essays on His Works, 2006; (with J.R. Struthers) Selected Essays, 2008. COMPILER: (with G. Callaghan) Rhyme and Reason, 1969; Sixteen by Twelve, 1970; Kaleidoscope, 1972; The Speaking Earth: Canadian Poetry, 1973; The Teeth of My Father, 1975. OTHERS: The Lady Who Sold Furniture, 1970; Going Down Slow, 1972; (with J. Newlove) Dreams Surround Us: Fiction and Poetry, 1977; (co-author) Wordcraft, 1977; Girl in Gingham, 1978; Private Parts: A Memoir, 1980; General Ludd, 1980; Selected Stories, 1982; Kicking Against the Pricks, 1982; Adult Entertainment: Short Fiction, 1986; What Is a Canadian Literature?, 1988; (with S. Solecki and W.J. Keith) Volleys, 1990; Shooting the Stars(novellas), 1993; Canadian Classics: An Anthology of Short Stories, 1993; Freedom from Culture: Selected Essays

1982-92, 1994; Kayhut: A Warrior's Odyssey, 1998; Forde Abroad: A Novella, 2003; Aesthetic Underground: A Literary Memoir, 2003; Standing Stones: The Best Stories of John Metcalf, 2004; Shut Up He Explained: A Literary Memoir, 2007. Works appear in anthologies. **Address:** University of Toronto Press, 10 St. Mary St., Ste. 700, Toronto, ON M4Y 2W8, Canada.

METGE, (Alice) Joan. New Zealander (born New Zealand), b. 1930. **Genres:** Anthropology/Ethnology, Cultural/Ethnic Topics. **Career:** University of Auckland, Department of University Extension, lecturer, 1961-64; Victoria University, senior lecturer, 1965-68, associate professor of anthropology, 1968-88. Writer. **Publications:** A New Maori Migration; Rural and Urban Relations in Northern New Zealand, 1964; The Maoris of New Zealand, 1967, rev. ed. as The Maoris of New Zealand: Rautahi, 1976; (with P. Kinloch) Talking Past Each Other: Problems of Cross-cultural Communication, 1978; In and Out of Touch: Whakamaa in Cross Cultural Context, 1986; Te Kohao o Te Ngira, 1990; New Growth from Old: The Whānau in the Modern World, 1995; Kōrero tahi, 2001; Tuamaka: The Challenge of Difference in Aotearoa New Zealand, 2010. **Address:** 3 Mariri Rd., Onehunga, Auckland, 1006, New Zealand.

METRES, Philip. American (born United States), b. 1970. **Genres:** Poetry, Translations. **Career:** John Carroll University, associate professor of English. Writer, poet and academic. **Publications:** (trans. and intro.) S. Gandlevsky, A Kindred Orphanhood, 2003; (trans. with T. Tulchinsky) L. Rubenstein, Catalogue of Comedic Novelties: Selected Poems of Lev Rubenstein, 2004; Primer for Non-Native Speakers, 2004; Instants, 2006; Behind the Lines: War Resistance Poetry on the American Homefront since 1941, 2007; To See the Earth (poems), 2008; (ed. with A. Smith and L. Smith) Come Together: Imagine Peace, An Anthology of Peace Poems, 2008. Contributor to books and journals. **Address:** Department of English, John Carroll University, 20700 N Park Blvd., University Heights, OH 44118-4520, U.S.A. **Online address:** pmetres@jcu.edu

METTAM, Roger C. British (born England), b. 1939?. **Genres:** History, Novels, Sociology, Social Sciences. **Career:** Queen Mary and Westfield College, reader in history. Writer. **Publications:** (With D. Johnson) French History and Society: The Wars of Religion to the Fifth Republic, 1974; (ed.) Government and Society in Louis XIV's France, 1977; Power and Faction in Louis XIV's France, 1988; (ed. with C. Giry-Deloison) Patronages et clientélismes, 1550-1750: France, Angleterre, Espagne, Italie, 1995. **Address:** Department of History, Queen Mary and Westfield College, Mile End Rd., London, GL E1 4NS, England.

METZ, Allan (Sheldon). American (born United States), b. 1950. **Genres:** Biography, Politics/Government, Popular Culture, Bibliography, Autobiography/Memoirs. **Career:** Drury University, F.W. Olin Library, reference collection librarian, 1992-, online instructor, 2003-; Ozarks Technical Community College, teacher of workshops on using internet software, 1996-; Southwest Missouri State University, reference librarian, 1997-2000. Writer. **Publications:** (Comp.) Bill Clinton's Pre-Presidential Career: An Annotated Bibliography, 1994; (comp.) A NAFTA Bibliography, 1996; (comp.) National Service and AmeriCorps: An Annotated Bibliography, 1997; (ed. with C. Benson) The Madonna Companion: Two Decades of Commentary, 1999; (comp.) Bill Clinton: A Bibliography, 2002; (comp.) Blondie, from Punk to the Present: A Pictorial History, 2002; (ed.) Ronald Reagan: A Bibliography, 2008; (comp. with J.R. Greene) Richard Nixon: A Bibliography, forthcoming. Contributor to books and periodicals. **Address:** F.W. Olin Library, Drury University, 900 N Benton Ave., Springfield, MO 65802, U.S.A. **Online address:** ametz@drury.edu

METZ, Don. American (born United States), b. 1940. **Genres:** Novels, Architecture, Biography, Young Adult Fiction, Humor/Satire. **Career:** Metz & Thornton, principal and partner, 1980-; Lyme Planning Board, chair, 1986-89. Writer. **Publications:** New Architecture in New Haven, 1966, rev. ed., 1973; Super House, 1978; (ed.) Compact House Book, 1983; Catamount Bridge: A Novel, 1988; King of the Mountain: A Novel, 1990; (ed.) New Compact House Designs: 27 Award-Winning Plans, 1250 Square Feet or Less, 1991; The Confessions of a Country Architect, 2007. **Address:** 114 Franklin Hill Rd., Lyme, NH 03768, U.S.A. **Online address:** donmetz@valley.net

METZ, Julie. American (born United States), b. 1959?. **Genres:** Autobiography/Memoirs. **Career:** Freelance graphic designer, 1988-; Harper & Row Publishers, junior staff designer. Writer and artist. **Publications:** Perfection: A Memoir of Betrayal and Renewal, 2009. Contributor to books. **Address:** Brooklyn, NY , U.S.A. **Online address:** julie@perfectionbook.com

METZENTHEN, David. Australian (born Australia), b. 1958. **Genres:** Children's Fiction, Young Adult Fiction. **Career:** Radio 3DB, copywriter. **Publications:** Danger Wave, 1990; Lee Spain, 1991; Brocky's Bananagram, 1994; Roadie, 1995; Johnny Hart's Heroes, 1996; Animal Instinct, 1996; Cody and Zero, 1997; Lefty Lemon Kicks Goals, 1997; Finn and the Big Guy, 1997; The Diary of Fat Robby Pile, 1997; Rodney the Surfing Duck, 1997; Falling Forward, 1998; Fort Island, 1998; Mick the Mimic, 1998; Gilbert's Ghost Train, 1998; The Red Hot Footy Fiasco, 1998; Stony Heart Country, 1999; Rodney, the Surfing Duck, 1999; The Hand-Knitted Hero, 1999; Tiff and the Trout, 2004; The Rainbirds, 2007; Black Water, 2007; Jarvis 24, 2009. **Address:** Penguin Books Australia Ltd., 250 Camberwell Rd., PO Box 701, Camberwell, VI 3124, Australia.

METZGER, Deena P. American (born United States), b. 1936. **Genres:** Novels, Plays/Screenplays, Poetry, Writing/Journalism, Essays, Autobiography/Memoirs, Environmental Sciences/Ecology, Psychology, Third World, Theatre. **Career:** Los Angeles Valley College, professor of English, 1966-69, 1972-77; Woman's Building, founder and director of writing program, 1973-77; writer and therapist, 1977-; National Endowment for the Arts, fellow, 1978; Eleusinian Mysteries, co-leader, 1980, 1990; Meyerhoff Institute, co-director, 1995; Non Govermental Organizations, Everyday Gandhis, senior advisor; Hand to Hand Press, co-director. Writer. **Publications:** Skin: Shadows/Silence (novel), 1976; Not as Sleepwalkers (play), 1977; Dark Milk (poetry), 1978; The Axis Mundi Poems, 1981; Woman Who Slept with Men to Take the War Out of Them and Tree, 1981; Dreams Against the State (play), 1981; What Dinah Thought (novel), 1989; Looking for the Faces of God (poetry), 1989; Writing for Your Life: A Guide and Companion to the Inner World, 1992; A Sabbath among the Ruins (poetry), 1992; Tree: Essays and Pieces, 1997; (ed. with B. Peterson and L. Hogan) Intimate Nature: The Bond Between Women and Animals, 1998; The Other Hand: A Novel, 2000; Entering the Ghost River, 2002; Doors: A Fiction for Jazz Horn, 2004; From Grief into Vision: A Council, 2007; Ruin and Beauty: New and Selected Poems, 2009; Tanzania Safari: Future Guardians of Peace, 2009; Feral, a Novel. 2011; La Negra y Blanca, a Novel, 2011. Contributor of articles to magazines. Works appear in anthologies. **Address:** PO Box 186, Topanga, CA 90290, U.S.A. **Online address:** deenametzger@verizon.net

METZGER, Michael M(oses). American/German (born Germany), b. 1935. **Genres:** Literary Criticism And History, Autobiography/Memoirs, Biography. **Career:** University of Illinois, instructor in German, 1961-63; State University of New York, University at Buffalo, assistant professor, 1963-67; associate professor of German, 1967-71, professor of German, 1971-, now professor emeritus. Writer. **Publications:** Lessing and the Language of Comedy, 1966; (with G.F. Schmidt) Der Hofmeister und die Gouvernante, 1969; (ed. with K. Mommsen) Fairy Tales As Ways of Knowing: Essays on Märchen in Psychology, Society and Literature, 1981. WITH E.A. METZGER: Clara und Robert Schumann, 1967; Paul Klee, 1967; Stefan George, 1972; (ed. and intro.) Institutiones Vitae Aulicæ: Oder, Hofschul, 1978; (ed.) Benjamin Neukirchs Anthologie Herrn von Hoffmannswaldau und Anderer Deutschen Gedichte, vol. V, 1981, vol. VI, 1988, vol. VII, 1991; (ed.) Herrn von Hoffmannswaldau und andrer deutschen auserlesener und bissher ungedruckter Gedichte: Siebender Theil: Nach dem Druck vom Jahre 1727 mit einer kritischen Einleitung und Lesarten, sowie einem Anhang, Poetischer Staar-Stecher (1730), 1991; Reading Andreas Gryphius: Critical Trends 1664-1993, 1994; (ed.) A Companion to the Works of Rainer Maria Rilke, 2001. **Address:** University at Buffalo, State University of New York, 910 Clemens Hall, North Campus, Buffalo, NY 14260-4620, U.S.A. **Online address:** mmetzger@acsu.buffalo.edu

METZGER, Robert A(lan). American (born United States), b. 1956. **Genres:** Science Fiction/Fantasy, Novels, Young Adult Fiction, Young Adult Non-fiction. **Career:** Hughes Research Laboratories, research scientist and electrical engineer, 1980-; Georgia Institute of Technology, research scientist and electrical engineer, 1990-; Compound Semiconductor Magazine, co-founder. Writer. **Publications:** NOVELS: Quad World, 1991; Picoverse, 2002; Cusp, 2005. Contributor to periodicals. **Address:** c/o Author Mail, Ace Books, Penguin Group Inc., 375 Hudson St., New York, NY 10014-3657, U.S.A. **Online address:** ram@rametzger.com

METZINGER, Thomas. German (born Germany), b. 1958. **Genres:** Sciences, Psychology, Young Adult Non-fiction. **Career:** Association for the Scientific Study of Consciousness, co-founder; Johannes Gutenberg-Universität, professor of philosophy, Theoretical Philosophy Group, director. Writer and philosopher. **Publications:** NONFICTION: Neuere Beiträge zur Diskussion des Leib-Seele-Problems, 1985; Subjekt und Selbstmodell: Die Perspektivität Phänomenalen Bewusstseins vor dem Hintergrund einer Naturalistischen Theorie Mentaler Repräsentation, 1993; (ed.) Conscious Experience, 1995; (ed.) Neural Correlates of Consciousness: Empirical and Conceptual Questions, 2000; Being No One: The Self-model Theory of Subjectivity, 2003; The Ego Tunnel: The Science of the Mind and the Myth of the Self, 2009. **Address:** Philosophisches Seminar, Johannes Gutenberg-Universität, Mainz, 55099, Germany. **Online address:** metzinger@uni-mainz.de

METZL, Jonathan M. American (born United States), b. 1965. **Genres:** Medicine/Health. **Career:** University of Michigan, associate professor and senior attending physician, Program in Culture, Health, and Medicine, director, Institute for Research on Women and Gender, assistant research scientist. Writer and psychiatrist. **Publications:** Prozac on the Couch: Prescribing Gender in the Era of Wonder Drugs, 2003; (ed. with S. Poirier) Difference and Identity: A Special Issue of Literature and Medicine, 2005; The Protest Psychosis: How Schizophrenia Became a Black Disease, 2010; (ed. with A. Kirkland) Against Health: How Health Became the New Morality, 2010. Contributor to periodicals and journals. **Address:** University of Michigan, 2203 Lane Hall, 204 S State St., Ann Arbor, MI 48109-1209, U.S.A. **Online address:** jmetzl@umich.edu

MEUNIER, Lisa. *See* **FRAUSTINO, Lisa Rowe.**

MEURN, Robert J. American (born United States), b. 1937. **Genres:** Marine Sciences/Oceanography, Natural History. **Career:** Stanwick Corp., senior maritime consultant, 1974-78; Texas Maritime Academy, assistant professor, commandant of cadets and executive officer of Texas Clipper, 1977-78; U.S. Merchant Marine Academy, professor of maritime studies, 1978-, now emeritus, head of nautical science division. Writer. **Publications:** (With C.L. Sauerbier) Marine Cargo Operations, 1985, 4th ed., 2011; Watchstanding Guide for the Merchant Officer, 1990, rev. ed., 2007; Survival Guide for the Mariner, 1993, 2nd ed., 2006. **Address:** U.S. Merchant Marine Academy, 3000 Steamboat Rd., Kings Point, NY 11024, U.S.A. **Online address:** meurnr@usmma.edu

MEYER, Carolyn. American (born United States), b. 1935. **Genres:** Young Adult Fiction, Travel/Exploration, Children's Fiction, Young Adult Non-fiction, Novels. **Career:** McCall's Magazine, columnist, 1967-72; Institute of Children's Literature, instructor, 1973-79; Bucknell University, Alpha Lambda Delta lecturer, 1974; Los Angeles Times, children and young adult book reviewer, 1989-90. Writer and speaker. **Publications:** Miss Patch's Learn-to-Sew Book, 1969; Stitch by Stitch: Needlework for Beginners, 1970; The Bread Book; All about Bread and How to Make It, 1971; Yarn: The Things It Makes and How to Make Them, 1972; Saw, Hammer, and Paint: Woodworking and Finishing for Beginners, 1973; Christmas Crafts: Things to Make the 24 Days before Christmas, 1974; Milk, Butter, and Cheese: The Story of Dairy Products, 1974; Needlework Book of Bible Stories, 1975; People Who Make Things: American Craftsmen and How They Live and Work, 1975; (with J. Wexler) Rock Tumbling: From Stones to Gems to Jewelry, 1975; Amish People: Plain Living in a Complex World, 1976; Coconut, the Tree of Life, 1976; Lots and Lots of Candy, 1976; Being Beautiful: The Story of Cosmetics from Ancient Art to Modern Science, 1977; Eskimos: Growing Up in a Changing Culture, 1977; C.C. Poindexter, 1978; Mask Magic, 1978; The Center: From a Troubled Past to a New Life, 1979; Rock Band: Big Men in a Great Big Town, 1980; Eulalia's Island, 1982; The Summer I Learned about Life, 1983; The Luck of Texas McCoy, 1984; (with C. Gallenkamp) Mystery of the Ancient Maya, 1985, rev. ed., 1995; Elliott & Win, 1986; Voices of South Africa: Growing Up in a Troubled Land, 1986; Denny's Tapes, 1987; Voices of Northern Ireland: Growing Up in a Troubled Land, 1987; A Voice from Japan: An Outsider Looks In, 1988; Wild Rover, 1989; Killing the Kudu, 1990; Where the Broken Heart Still Beats: The Story of Cynthia Ann Parker, 1992; White Lilacs, 1993; Rio Grande Stories, 1994; Drummers of Jericho, 1995; Gideon's People, 1996; In a Different Light: Growing Up in a Yup'ik Eskimo Village in Alaska, 1996; Jubilee Journey, 1997; Mary, Bloody Mary, 1999; Anastasia: The Last Grand Duchess, 2000; Isabel: Jewel of Castilla, 2000; Beware, Princess Elizabeth, 2001; Doomed Queen Anne, 2002; Brown Eyes Blue, 2003; Kristina, the Girl King, 2003; Patience, Princess Catherine, 2004; Marie, Dancing, 2005; Loving Will Shakespeare, 2006; Duchessina, a Novel of Catherine de Medici, 2007; In Mozart's Shadow: His Sister's Story, 2008; The True Adventures of Charley Darwin, 2009; The Bad Queen: Rules and Instructions for Marie-Antoinette, 2010; Cleopatra Confesses, 2011; The Wild Queen: The Days and Nights of Mary, Queen of Scots, 2012. **Address:** c/o Jodi Reamer, Writers House Inc., 21 W 26th St., New York, NY 10010, U.S.A. **Online address:** meyerwrite@comcast.net

MEYER, Charles Robert. American (born United States), b. 1920. **Genres:** History, Theology/Religion, Cultural/Ethnic Topics. **Career:** University of Saint Mary of the Lake Mundelein Seminary, assistant professor, 1949-67, dean of theologians, 1954-66, librarian, 1966-67, associate professor, 1967-69, professor of systematic theology, 1968, School of Theology, dean, 1977-81, Departments of Systematic Theology and Church History, professor emeritus, 1991-. Writer. **Publications:** The Thomistic Concept of Justifying Contrition, 1949; A Contemporary Theology of Grace, 1971; The Touch of God: A Theological Analysis of Religious Experience, 1972; Man of God: A Study of the Priesthood, 1974; What a Modern Catholic Believes about the Holy Spirit, 1974; Religious Belief in a Scientific Age, 1983. Contributor to journals. **Address:** Department of Systematic Theology, Lake Mundelein Seminary, University of Saint Mary, 1000 E Maple Ave., Mundelein, IL 60060, U.S.A. **Online address:** cmeyer@usml.edu

MEYER, Deon. South African (born South Africa), b. 1958. **Genres:** Novels, Horror, Criminology/True Crime. **Career:** Die Volksblad, reporter. Crime writer, consultant and journalist. **Publications:** Wie met vuur speel, 1994; Feniks, 1996; Bottervisse in die jêm 13 kortverhale, 1997; Dead Before Dying, 1999; Dead at Daybreak, 2000; Heart of the Hunter, 2003; Devil's Peak, 2007; Blood Safari, 2009; Thirteen Hours, 2010; Trackers, 2011. **Address:** c/o Isobel Dixon, Blake Friedmann Literary, Film & TV Agency, 122 Arlington Rd., London, GL NW1 7HP, England. **Online address:** info@deonmeyer.com

MEYER, Dick. American (born United States), b. 1958. **Genres:** Social Sciences, Young Adult Non-fiction, Medicine/Health. **Career:** Freelance writer, 1983-84; New York Times, staff, 1983-84; Public Citizen, staff writer, 1984-85; CBS News, researcher, 1985, producer and off-air reporter, 1987-93, The CBS Evening News, co-producer, 1993-99, CBSNews.com, editorial director; National Public Radio (NPR), staff, through 2008, executive editor, Digital Media, editorial director, 2008-. **Publications:** Why We Hate Us: American Discontent in the New Millennium, 2008. **Address:** National Public Radio, 635 Massachusetts Ave. NW, Washington, DC 20001, U.S.A.

MEYER, Donald J. American (born United States), b. 1951. **Genres:** Human Relations/Parenting, Psychology. **Career:** Sibling Support Project, director; University of Washington, Supporting Extended Family Members Program, founder. Writer. **Publications:** (With P.F. Vadasy and R.R. Fewell) Living with a Brother or Sister with Special Needs: A Book for Sibs, 1985, (with P.F. Vadasy) rev. ed., 1996; (with P.F. Vadasy) Sibshops: Workshops for Siblings of Children with Special Needs, 1994, rev. ed., 2008; (ed.) Uncommon Fathers: Reflections on Raising a Child with a Disability, 1995; (ed.) Views from Our Shoes: Growing Up with a Brother or Sister with Special Needs, 1997; (ed.) The Sibling Slam Book: What It's Really Like to Have a Brother or Sister with Special Needs, 2005; (ed.) Thicker Than Water: Essays by Adult Siblings of People with Disabilities, 2009. **Address:** Sibling Support Project, 6512 23rd Ave. NW, Ste. 213, Seattle, WA 98117, U.S.A. **Online address:** donmeyer@siblingsupport.org

MEYER, Eugene L. American (born United States), b. 1942. **Genres:** History, Local History/Rural Topics, Travel/Exploration, Urban Studies, Money/Finance, Education. **Career:** New York Herald Tribune, Washington bureau, librarian and freelance, 1964-65; Philadelphia Bulletin, reporter, 1965-70; Washington Post, reporter, bureau chief and editor, 1970-2004; Ohio State University, James Thurber journalist-in-residence and teacher of non-fiction writing, 1990-91; Nieman Watchdog, contributor, 2004-. **Publications:** Maryland Lost and Found: People and Places from Chesapeake to Appalachia, 1986; Chesapeake Country, 1990; Maryland Lost and Found...Again, 2000. Work appears in anthologies. **Address:** Silver Spring, MD , U.S.A. **Online address:** meyergene@aol.com

MEYER, Gabriel Ray Henry. Argentine (born Argentina), b. 1947. **Genres:** Military/Defense/Arms Control, Young Adult Fiction. **Career:** National Catholic Register, correspondent, 1990-; Metatron: Ritual Theater Collective, co-founder, 1994; Sulha Peace Project, co-founder and director, 2001-. Writer. **Publications:** The Gospel of Joseph, 1994; In the Shade of the Terebinth: Tales of a Night Journey, 1994; (with E. Snyder) A Ride on the Political Merry-go-round, 1996; War and Faith in Sudan, 2005. Contributor to periodicals. **Address:** Eerdmans Publishing Company, 2140 Oak Industrial Dr. NE, Grand Rapids, MI 49505, U.S.A. **Online address:** amen.sulha@gmail.com

MEYER, Leisa D. American (born United States), b. 1962. **Genres:** Military/Defense/Arms Control, History, Women's Studies And Issues, Cultural/Ethnic Topics, Social Sciences, Gay And Lesbian Issues. **Career:** College of William and Mary, assistant professor, associate professor of history, 1999-, distinguished associate professor of American studies and history, chair and director of women's studies. Writer. **Publications:** Creating GI Jane: Sexuality and Power in the Women's Army Corps during World War II, 1996. **Address:** Department of History, College of William & Mary, 352 James Blair Hall, PO Box 8795, Williamsburg, VA 23187-8795, U.S.A. **Online address:** ldmeye@wm.edu

MEYER, Lysle E(dward). American (born United States), b. 1932. **Genres:** History, Social Sciences. **Career:** Ohio State University, instructor in history, 1966; Moorhead State University, assistant professor, professor of history, 1966-73, head of history department, 1970-73, 1985-90, now professor emeritus; University of Zululand, visiting professor, 1972-73; University of the North (South Africa), visiting professor, 1973; Concordia College, adjunct lecturer, 1979, 1984, 1992; North Dakota State University, adjunct lecturer, 1986, 1987, 1989, 1990. Writer. **Publications:** (Ed.) Historical Papers, 1971; The Farther Frontier: Six Case Studies of Americans and Africa, 1848-1936, 1992. Contributor to journals. **Address:** Department of History, Moorhead State University, Rm. 374, MacLean Hall, 1104 7th Ave. S, Moorhead, MN 56563-0001, U.S.A.

MEYER, Michael. Also writes as Mike Meyer, Michael J. Meyer. American (born United States), b. 1972. **Genres:** Travel/Exploration. **Career:** National Geographic Society Center for Sustainable Destinations, representative. Writer. **Publications:** The Last Days of Old Beijing: Life in the Vanishing Backstreets of a City Transformed, 2008. Contributor to periodicals. **Address:** U.S.A. **Online address:** meyer@lastdaysofoldbeijing.com

MEYER, Michael J. *See* **MEYER, Michael.**

MEYER, Mike. *See* **MEYER, Michael.**

MEYER, Philipp. American (born United States), b. 1974. **Genres:** Young Adult Fiction. **Career:** Writer. **Publications:** American Rust, 2009. Contributor to periodicals. **Address:** c/o Esther Newberg, International Creative Management, 825 8th Ave., New York, NY 10019, U.S.A. **Online address:** reader@philippmeyer.net

MEYER, Richard E. American (born United States), b. 1939. **Genres:** Architecture, Art/Art History, Cultural/Ethnic Topics, History, Social Sciences. **Career:** University of Washington, assistant, 1965-69, director of residential seminars, 1968-69; Oregon College of Education, instructor, 1969-72, assistant professor of English, 1972-81; Monmouth Public Library Board, chairman, 1978-80; Bulmershe College of Higher Education, Reading University, Fulbright exchange professor, 1980-81; Western Oregon State College, assistant professor, 1981-82, associate professor, 1982-95, professor of English, 1995, now professor emeritus. Writer and consultant. **Publications:** (Ed. and contrib.) Cemeteries and Gravemarkers: Voices of American Culture, 1989, (ed. and contrib.) Ethnicity and the American Cemetery, 1993; (with P. McDowell) The Revival Styles in American Memorial Art, 1994. FORTHCOMING: Form and Function in the Contemporary Gravemarker: The Renaissance of the American Gangster Movie, 1972-1992. Contributor to periodicals and journals. **Address:** Department of English, Western Oregon University, 345 N Monmouth Ave., Monmouth, OR 97361, U.S.A.

MEYERHOFF, Jenny. American (born United States), b. 1972. **Genres:** Children's Fiction, Humor/Satire. **Career:** Author and teacher. **Publications:** Third Grade Baby, 2008; Queen of Secrets, 2010. **Address:** Deerfield, IL , U.S.A. **Online address:** mail@jennymeyerhoff.com

MEYERING, Sheryl L. American (born United States), b. 1948. **Genres:** Literary Criticism And History, Young Adult Fiction, Women's Studies And Issues. **Career:** High school English teacher, 1971-82; Michigan State University, assistant professor of American thought and language, 1986-88; Southern Illinois University, associate professor of English, 1988-, director of graduate studies, 1995-96, professor of English, now professor emeritus; Papers on Language and Literature, associate editor. **Publications:** (Ed.) Charlotte Perkins Gilman: The Woman and Her Work, 1989; Sylvia Plath: A Reference Guide, 1973-1988, 1990; (ed.) Toward a New Synthesis: John Fowles, John Gardner, Norman Mailer, 1991; A Reader's Guide to the Short Stories of Willa Cather, 1994; Understanding O Pioneers! and My Antonia: A Student Casebook to Issues, Sources and Historical Documents, 2002. Contributor to books and periodicals. **Address:** Department of English Language and Literature, Southern Illinois University, Peck Hall 3206, PO Box 1431, Edwardsville, IL 62026-1431, U.S.A. **Online address:** meyering@aol.com

MEYEROWITZ, Joanne. American (born United States), b. 1954. **Genres:** History, Women's Studies And Issues. **Career:** University of Cincinnati, assistant professor, 1985-90, associate professor of history, 1990-99; Indiana University, professor of history, 1999-2004; Journal of American History, editor, 1999-2004; Yale University, professor of history and American studies, 2004-, Yale Research Initiative on the History of Sexualities, co-director. **Publications:** Women Adrift: Independent Wage Earners in Chicago, 1880-1930, 1988; (ed.) Not June Cleaver: Women and Gender in Postwar America, 1945-1960, 1994; How Sex Changed: A History of Transsexuality in the United States, 2002; (ed.) History and September 11th, 2003. **Address:** Department of History, Yale University, HGS 101, PO Box 208324, New Haven, CT 06520-8324, U.S.A. **Online address:** joanne.meyerowitz@yale.edu

MEYEROWITZ, Patricia. American/British (born England), b. 1933. **Genres:** Novels, Art/Art History, Literary Criticism And History, Novellas/Short Stories, Writing/Journalism, Homes/Gardens. **Career:** Artist and writer. **Publications:** Jewelry and Sculpture through Unit Construction, 1967, 2nd ed. as Making Jewelry and Sculpture Through Unit Construction, 1978; (ed.) Writings and Lectures 1911-1945, 1967; (intro.) How to Write, 1975; And a Little Child: Stories of Anyone: A Monologue, 1982; (ed.) Look at Me Now and Here I Am: Writings and Lectures, 1911-1945, 2004. Works appear in anthologies. **Address:** PO Box 8, Easton, PA 18044-0008, U.S.A.

MEYERS, Annette (Brafman). (Maan Meyers). American (born United States), b. 1934. **Genres:** Mystery/Crime/Suspense, Novels, History. **Career:** Teacher, 1955-60; Harold Prince, assistant, 1960-76; ICRF, administrative director, 1977-78; Society of Stage Directors and Choreographers, regional administrator, 1979; New York University, teacher and producer of commercial theater, 1980; Michael King Associates, senior vice-president and executive recruiter, 1980-96; Sisters in Crime, president, 1996-97. Writer. **Publications:** NOVELS: The Big Killing, 1989; Tender Death, 1990; The Deadliest Option, 1991; Blood on the Street, 1992; Murder: The Musical, 1993; These Bones Were Made for Dancin', 1995; The Groaning Board, 1997; Free Love, 1999; Murder Me Now, 2001; Repentances, 2004; Hedging: A Smith and Wetzon Mystery, 2005. DUTCHMAN SERIES WITH M. MEYERS AS MAAN MEYERS: The Dutchman, 1992; The Kingsbridge Plot, 1993; The High Constable, 1994; The Dutchman's Dilemma, 1995; The House on Mulberry Street, 1996; The Lucifer Contract, 1997; The Organ Grinder, 2008. Works appear in anthologies. **Address:** Stuart Krichevsky Literary Agency Inc., 381 Park Ave. S, Ste. 428, New York, NY 10016, U.S.A. **Online address:** annette@meyersmysteries.com

MEYERS, Jeffrey. American (born United States), b. 1939. **Genres:** Art/Art History, Literary Criticism And History, Bibliography, Biography. **Career:** University of California, assistant professor of English, 1963-65; University of Maryland, Far East Division, lecturer in English, 1965-66; Tufts University, assistant professor of English, 1967-71; writer, 1971-74, 1992-; University of Colorado, professor of English, 1975-92; University of Kent, visiting professor, 1979-80; University of Massachusetts, visiting professor, 1982-83; University of Alabama, Jemison professor, 1992. **Publications:** Fiction and the Colonial Experience, 1973; The Wounded Spirit, 1973; T.E. Lawrence: A Bibliography, 1974; A Reader's Guide to George Orwell, 1975; Painting and the Novel, 1975; Catalogue of the Library of the Late Siegfried Sassoon, 1975; A Fever at the Core, 1976; George Orwell: An Annotated Bibliography of Criticism, 1977; Homosexuality and Literature 1890-1930, 1977; Married to Genius, 1977; Katherine Mansfield: A Biography, 1980; The Enemy: A Biography of Wyndham Lewis, 1980; Wyndham Lewis: A Revaluation, 1980; D.H. Lawrence and the Experience of Italy, 1982; Disease and the Novel 1860-1960, 1985; The Craft of Literary Biography, 1985; D.H. Lawrence and Tradition, 1985; Hemingway: A Biography, 1985; The Legacy of D.H. Lawrence, 1987; Manic Power: Robert Lowell and His Circle, 1987; Robert Lowell: Interviews and Memoirs, 1988; T.E. Lawrence: Soldier, Writer, Legend, 1989; The Biographer's Art, 1989; The Spirit of Biography, 1989; D.H. Lawrence: A Biography, 1990; Joseph Conrad: A Biography, 1991; Edgar Allan Poe: His Life and Legacy, 1992; Scott Fitzgerald: A Biography, 1994; (intro.) The Moon and Sixpence, 1995; Edmund Wilson: A Biography, 1995; Robert Frost: A Biography, 1996; Bogart: A Life in Hollywood, 1997; Gary Cooper: An American Hero, 1998; Privileged Moments: Encounters with Writers, 2000; (intro.) Double Indemnity, 2000; (intro.) The Lost Weekend, 2000; Orwell: Wintry Conscience of a Generation, 2000; Hemingway: Life into Art, 2000; Inherited Risk: Errol and Sean Flynn in Hollywood and Vietnam, 2002; (intro.) The House of Mirth, 2003; Somerset Maugham: A Life Repressed, 2004; Impressionist Quartet: The Intimate Genius of Manet and Matisse, Degas and Cassatt, 2005; Modigliani: A Life, 2006; Samuel Johnson: The Struggle, 2008; (afterword) The Return of the Native, 2008; Orwell, 2010; The Genius and the Goddess, 2010; John Huston, 2011. EDITOR: George Orwell: The Critical Heritage, 1975; Hemingway: The Critical Heritage, 1982; Graham Greene: A Revaluation, 1990; Wyndham Lewis 1985; Early Frost, 1996; (with V. Meyers) The Sir Arthur Conan Doyle Reader: From Sherlock Holmes to Spiritualism, 2002; W. Somerset Maugham Reader, 2004. **Address:** 84 Stratford Rd., Kensington, CA 94707, U.S.A. **Online address:** vjmeyers@nothingbutnet.net

MEYERS, Kent. American (born United States), b. 1956?. **Genres:** Novels, Novellas/Short Stories, Young Adult Fiction. **Career:** Black Hills State University, faculty, 1986-, associate professor, 1991-, writer-in-residence, 2006-, professor of English; University of Northern Iowa, writing center director; Pacific Lutheran University, Rainier Writers Workshop, instructor. **Publications:** The Witness of Combines, 1998; Light in the Crossing: Stories, 1999. NOVELS: The River Warren, 1998; The Work of Wolves, 2004; Twisted Tree, 2009. Contributed to periodicals and anthologies. **Address:** Department of English, Black Hills State University, MH318, 1200 University St., Ste. 9096, Spearfish, SD 57799, U.S.A. **Online address:** kent.meyers@bhsu.edu

MEYERS, Maan. *See* **MEYERS, Martin.**

MEYERS, Maan. *See* **MEYERS, Annette (Brafman).**

MEYERS, Martin. (Maan Meyers). American (born United States), b. 1934. **Genres:** Mystery/Crime/Suspense, Romance/Historical, Novels, Novellas/Short Stories. **Career:** Writer and actor. **Publications:** A Federal Case, 1978; Suspect (novel based on film), 1987; (with R. Esser) Western Canada's Oil Sands: An Investment Boom Increases the Marketing Challenge, 2002; (with R.J. Goodman) The Refining Parable: Will Power Generation Take Its Cue from Downstream Oil?, 2002. PATRICK HARDY SERIES: Kiss and Kill, 1975; Hung up to Die, 1976; Red Is for Murder, 1976; Reunion for Death, 1976; Spy and Die, 1976. DUTCHMAN SERIES WITH A. MEYERS AS MAAN MEYERS: The Dutchman, 1992; The Kingsbridge Plot: An Historical Mystery, 1993; The High Constable: An History Mystery, 1994; The Dutchman's Dilemma, 1995; The House on Mullberry Street, 1996; The Lucifer Contract: A Civil War Thriller, 1998; Facing Structural Change: the Global Refining Industry Responds to Demand, 2003. **Address:** c/o Chris Tomasino, RLR 7 W 51st St., New York, NY 10019, U.S.A. **Online address:** marty@meyersmysteries.com

MEYERSON, Debra E. American (born United States), b. 1957. **Genres:** Adult Non-fiction, Race Relations. **Career:** University of Michigan, Business School, assistant professor of organizational behavior, 1990-95; University of California, Haas School of Business, visiting assistant professor of organizational behavior, 1994; Stanford University, Graduate School of Business, visiting assistant professor of organizational behavior, 1994-96, visiting professor of organizational behavior, 1999-2002, associate professor of education, 2003-, associate professor of organizational behavior, School of Engineering, Center for Work, Technology, and Organization, visiting professor of organizational behavior, 1998-2002, Stanford Center on Philanthropy and Civil Society, faculty co-director, Stanford Educational Leadership Institute, co-director; Envision Schools, director, Center for Social Innovation, affiliate faculty, Center for Comparative Studies on Race and Ethnicity, affiliate faculty, Center for Poverty and Inequality, affiliate faculty, Institute for Research on Women and Gender, affiliate faculty; Simmons College, Graduate School of Management, Center for Gender in Organizations, professor, 1997-2002. Writer. **Publications:** Tempered Radicals: How People Use Difference to Inspire Change at Work, 2001; Tempered Radicals: How Everyday Leaders Inspire Change at Work, 2003; Rocking the Boat: How to Effect Change Without Making Trouble, 2008. Contributor to periodicals. **Address:** School of Education, Stanford University, CE 427, 485 Lasuen Mall, Stanford, CA 94305-3096, U.S.A. **Online address:** debram@stanford.edu

MEYERSON, Mark D. Canadian (born Canada), b. 1957. **Genres:** Politics/Government, Cultural/Ethnic Topics, History. **Career:** University of Toronto, Department of History, associate professor, professor. Writer. **Publications:** The Muslims of Valencia in the Age of Fernando and Isabel: Between Coexistence and Crusade, 1991; A Jewish Renaissance in Fifteenth-Century Spain, 2004; Jews in an Iberian Frontier Kingdom: Society, Economy and Politics in Morvedre, 1248-1391, 2004. EDITOR: (with E.D. English) Christians, Muslims and Jews in Medieval and Early Modern Spain: Interaction and Cultural Change, 1999; (with T.E. Burman and L. Shopkow) Religion, Text and Society in Medieval Spain and Northern Europe: Essays in Honor of J.N. Hillgarth, 2002; (with D. Thiery and O. Falk) A Great Effusion of Blood?: Interpreting Medieval Violence, 2004. **Address:** Department of History, University of Toronto, 3071 Sidney Smith Hall, Rm. 2074, 100 St. George St., Toronto, ON M5S 3G3, Canada. **Online address:** meyerson@chass.utoronto.ca

MEYERSON, Michael I. American (born United States), b. 1955. **Genres:** Law, Politics/Government, Mathematics/Statistics. **Career:** Brooklyn Law School, instructor, 1982-85; University of Baltimore, School of Law, professor of law and Piper and Marbury faculty fellow, 1985-, Baltimore Scholars Program, director; New York Law School, adjunct assistant professor; Cardozo Law School, adjunct assistant professor. Writer. **Publications:** (With D.L. Brenner and M.E. Price) Cable Television and Other Nonbroadcast Video: Law and Policy, 1986; Political Numeracy: Mathematical Perspectives on Our Chaotic Constitution, 2002; Liberty's Blueprint: How Madison And Hamilton Wrote The Federalist Papers, Defined The Constitution, And Made Democracy Safe For The World, 2008; Endowed By Our Creator: How The Framers Invented An American Vision of Freedom of Religion, 2012. Contributor to journals. **Address:** School of Law, University of Baltimore, Rm. LC 409, 1415 Maryland Ave., Baltimore, MD 21201-5779, U.S.A. **Online address:** mmeyerson@ubalt.edu

MEYNELL, Hugo A(nthony). Canadian/British (born England), b. 1936. **Genres:** Philosophy, Theology/Religion. **Career:** University of Leeds, lecturer, 1963-73, senior lecturer in philosophy and theology, 1973-81; Emory University, visiting professor, 1978; University of Calgary, FRSC professor of religious studies, 1981-2001, now professor emeritus. Writer. **Publications:** Sense, Nonsense and Christianity: An Essay on the Logical Analysis of Religious Statements, 1964; Grace versus Nature: Studies in Karl Barth's Church Dogmatics, 1966; The New Theology and Modern Theologians, 1967; God and the World: The Coherence of Christian Theism, 1971; Introduction to the Philosophy of Bernard Lonergan, 1976; Freud, Marx and Morals, 1981; The Intelligible Universe: A Cosmological Argument, 1982; The Theology of Bernard Lonergan, 1986; The Nature of Aesthetic Value, 1986; The Art of Handel's Operas, 1986; Is Christianity True?, 1994; Redirecting Philosophy: Reflections of the Nature of Knowledge from Plato to Lonergan, 1998; Postmodernism and the New Enlightenment, 1999; Detenuring of an Eminent Professor: A Personal Story, 2008; The Epistemological Argument against Atheism, 2011. EDITOR: Religion and Irreligion, 1985; (with G.F. McLean) Person and Nature, 1988; (with G.F. McLean) Person and God, 1988; (with G.F. McClean) Person and Society, 1988; (with G.F. McClean) The Nature of Metaphysical Knowledge, 1988; Grace, Politics and Desire: Essays on Augustine, 1990; (with J.J. MacIntosh) Faith, Scepticism and Personal Identity, 1994; (with M. Stoeber) Critical Reflections on the Paranormal, 1996. Contributor to journals. **Address:** Department of Religious Studies, University of Calgary, Rm. 1301, Social Sciences Bldg., 527 Campus Pl. NW, Calgary, AB T2N 1N4, Canada.

MEZEY, Robert. American (born United States), b. 1935. **Genres:** Poetry, Translations, Autobiography/Memoirs. **Career:** Western Reserve University, instructor, 1963-64; Franklin and Marshall College, poet-in-residence, 1965-66; California State University, assistant professor of English, 1966-68; University of Utah, associate professor of English, 1973-76; Pomona College, associate professor of English, professor of English, 1976-99, professor emeritus, 1999-, poet-in-residence; Kenyon College, visiting professor; Claremont Graduate School, teacher. **Publications:** POETRY: Berg Goodman Mezey: Poems, 1957; The Wandering Jew, 1960; The Lovemaker: Poems, 1961; White Blossoms: Poems, 1965; Favors, 1968; The Book of Dying: Poems, 1970; Last Words for John Lawrence Simpson 1896-1969, 1970; The Door Standing Open: New and Selected Poems 1954-1969, 1970; Couplets, 1976; Small Song, 1979; Selected Translations, 1981; Evening Wind (poems), 1987; Natural Selection, 1995; Selected Poems, 1995; Collected Poems, 1952-1999, 2000. TRANSLATOR: The Mercy of Sorrow, 1965; Tungsten, 1982. EDITOR: (with S. Berg) Naked Poetry: Recent American Poetry in Open Forms, 1969; (trans.) Poems from the Hebrew, 1973; (and intro. with D. Justice) The Collected Poems of Henri Coulette, 1990; (and intro.) Selected Poems: Thomas Hardy, 1998; (and intro.) Poetry of E.A. Robinson, 1999; Poems of the American West, 2002; (and foreword) A Word like Fire: Selected Poems, 2005. **Address:** Department of English, Pomona College, Crookshank Hall, 140 W 6th St., Claremont, CA 91711-6335, U.S.A. **Online address:** mezteadancer@aol.com

MEZLEKIA, Nega. Canadian/Ethiopian (born Ethiopia), b. 1958?. **Genres:** Autobiography/Memoirs, Novels, Social Sciences, History, Biography. **Career:** Civil engineer and author. **Publications:** Notes from the Hyena's Belly: Memories of My Ethiopian Boyhood, 2000; The God Who Begat a Jackal, 2001; The Unfortunate Marriage of Azeb Yitades, 2006; Media Blitz: A Personal Battle, 2009. **Address:** c/o Author Mail, 10 Alcorn Ave., Ste. 300, Toronto, ON M4V 3B2, Canada.

MICALE, Mark S. American (born United States), b. 1957. **Genres:** Psychiatry, History, Essays, Translations. **Career:** University of Illinois, associate professor of history and the history of medicine. Writer. **Publications:** (Ed., intro. and trans. with F. Dubor) H.F. Ellenberger, Beyond the Unconscious: Essays of Henri F. Ellenberger in the History of Psychiatry, 1993; (ed. with R. Porter) Discovering the History of Psychiatry, 1994; Approaching Hysteria: Disease and Its Interpretations, 1995; (ed. with R.L. Dietle and intro.) Enlightenment, Passion, Modernity: Historical Essays in European Thought and Culture, 2000; (ed. with P. Lerner) Traumatic Pasts: History, Psychiatry, and Trauma in the Modern Age, 1870-1930, 2001; (ed. and intro.) The Mind of Modernism: Medicine, Psychology, and the Cultural Arts in Europe and America, 1880-1940, 2004; Hysterical Men: The Hidden History of Male Nervous Illness, 2008. **Address:** University of Illinois, MC-466, 444 Gregory Hall, 810 S Wright St., Urbana, IL 61801, U.S.A. **Online address:** msmicale@illinois.edu

MICHAEL, Colette V(erger). American/French (born France), b. 1937. **Genres:** Poetry, Film, Intellectual History, Literary Criticism And History, Philosophy, Bibliography, History, Translations, Translations, Social Sciences. **Career:** University of Wisconsin-Madison, extension lecturer and lecturer in French, 1974; Shimer College, professor of humanities, 1975-77; Northern Illinois University, assistant professor, 1977-84, associate professor, 1984-90, professor of foreign languages and literatures, 1990-. Writer and host. **Publications:** Choderlos de Laclos: The Man, His Works and His Critics: An Annotated Bibliography, 1982; Intemperies (poems), 1982; Sens dessus dessous, 1984; Laclos: les milieux philosophiques et le mal, 1985; (ed. and intro.) Les tracts feministes au XVIII eme siecle, 1986; The Marquis de Sade: The Man, His Works and His Critics: An Annotated Bibliography, 1986; Essai sur le caractere, les moeurs et l'esprit des femmes dans les differens siecles, 1987; Negritude: An Annotated Bibliography, 1988; Sade: His Ethics and Rhetoric, 1989; (trans.) H. Metzger, Chemistry, 1991; Sur Le Divorce en France: vu par les ecrits du dix-huitieme siecle, 1989; Grounds of Natural Philosophy, 1996; Le Marquis de Sade: Critics & Revolution, 1998; Sur les femmes en France au dix-huitième siècle: un âge de tenèbre, 2006; Holy Academia, 2010. Contributor of articles to journals. **Address:** Department of Foreign Languages and Literatures, Northern Illinois University, 111 Watson Hall, DeKalb, IL 60115-1862, U.S.A. **Online address:** cmichael@niu.edu

MICHAEL, George J. American (born United States), b. 1961. **Genres:** Theology/Religion. **Career:** University of Virginia, College at Wise, assistant professor, associate professor of political science and administration of justice. Writer. **Publications:** Confronting Right Wing Extremism and Terrorism in the USA, 2003; The Enemy of My Enemy: The Alarming Convergence of Militant Islam and the Extreme Right, 2006; Willis Carto and the American Far Right, 2008; Theology of Hate: A History of the World Church of the Creator, 2009; Lone Wolf Terror and The Rise of Leaderless Resistance, 2012. **Address:** University of Virginia's College at Wise, Department of Social and Behavioral Sciences, 1 College Ave., Wise, VA 24293, U.S.A. **Online address:** gjm3a@uvawise.edu

MICHAEL, Judith. *See* **FAIN, Michael.**

MICHAEL, Judith. *See* **BARNARD, Judith.**

MICHAEL, Livi. British (born England), b. 1960. **Genres:** Novels. **Career:** Manchester Metropolitan University, instructor in English literature and creative writing, 1993-98; Sheffield Hallam University, instructor in English literature and creative writing, 1998-, senior lecturer in creative writing; freelance writer, 2004-; University of Leeds, fellow, 2010-. **Publications:** ADULT FICTION: Under a Thin Moon, 1992; Their Angel Reach, 1994; All the Dark Air, 1997; Inheritance, 2000. FOR CHILDREN: Frank and the Black Hamster of Narkiz, 2002; Frank and the Chamber of Fear, 2003; Frank and the Flames of Truth, 2004; Frank and the New Narkiz, 2005; 43 Bin Street, 2005; Frank and the New Narkiz, 2005; Seventeen Times As High As the Moon, 2006. YOUNG ADULT NOVELS: The Whispering Road, 2005; The Angel Stone, 2006; City of Dogs, 2007; Sky Wolves, 2008; Faerie Heart, 2009. Woks appear in anthologies. **Address:** c/o Author Mail, Viking, Penguin Group, 80 Strand, London, GL WC2R 0RL, England. **Online address:** mail@livimichael.com

MICHAELOWA, Axel. Swiss/German (born Germany), b. 1968. **Genres:** Economics, Business/Trade/Industry, Economics, Technology, Engineering, Natural History. **Career:** Hamburg Institute of International Economics, researcher, 1994-97, representative, 1995-, teleworker, 1997-99, head of research program on international climate policy, 1999-2006; Perspectives GmbH, senior founding partner, 2003-; University of Zurich's, Institute of Political Science, head of research, 2007-. Writer. **Publications:** Joint Implementation of Greenhouse Gas Reductions Under Consideration of Fiscal and Regulatory Incentives, 1995; Internationale Kompensationsmöglichkeiten zur CO2-Reduktion unter Berücksichtigung steuerlicher Anreize und ordnungsrechtlicher Massnahmen, 1995; (with M. Dutschke) Handel mit Emissionsrechten für Treibhausgase: Empfehlungen aus ökonomischer Sicht auf der Grundlage des Kyoto-Protokolls, 1998; (with C. Rolfe and M. Dutschke) Closing the Gap?: A Comparison of Approaches to Encourage Early Greenhouse Gas Emission Reductions, 1999; (with T. Koch) Critical Issues in Current Climate Policy: Hot Air, Multi-Level Emission Trading Registries and Changes in Emission Commitments due to International Conflicts, 1999; (ed. with M. Dutschke) Climate Policy and Development Flexible Instruments and Developing Countries, 2000; (with T. Koch) Glossary of International Climate Policy Terms, 2001; (with S.E. Lütken) Corporate Strategies and the Clean Development Mechanism: Developing Country Financing for Developed Country Commitments?, 2008; (ed.) Carbon Markets or Climate Finance: Low Carbon and Adaptation Investment Choices For the Developing World, 2012. Contributor to journals and newspapers. **Address:** Department for Political Science, University of Zurich's, Affolternstrasse 56, Zurich, 8050, Switzerland. **Online address:** axel.michaelowa@pw.uzh.ch

MICHAELS, Anne. Canadian (born Canada), b. 1958. **Genres:** Novels, Poetry, Literary Criticism And History. **Career:** University of Toronto, Department of English, adjunct faculty. Writer. **Publications:** The Weight of Oranges, 1985; Miner's Pond: Poems, 1991; Fugitive Pieces, 1996, 2nd ed., 1997; Peçem fuga. 1.a edicCDLao, 1997; Flygtigestykker: roman, 1997; Verborgen verleden. 4. druk Amserdam: Anthos, 1997; Fluchtstücke: Roman. 4. Aufl Berlin: Berlin Verlag, 1997; Skin Divers, 1999; Winter Vault, 2009. Works appear in anthologies. Contributor to periodicals. **Address:** McClelland & Stewart Ltd., 481 University Ave., Ste. 900, Toronto, ON M5G 2E9, Canada.

MICHAELS, Barbara. *See* **MERTZ, Barbara (Louise) G(ross).**

MICHAELS, Fern. *See* **KUCZKIR, Mary.**

MICHAELS, Jamie. American (born United States) **Genres:** Mystery/Crime/Suspense. **Career:** Novelist. **Publications:** Kiss My Book, 2007. **Address:** c/o Michael Bourret, Dystel & Goderich Literary Management, 1 Union Sq. W, Ste. 904, New York, NY 10003, U.S.A.

MICHAELS, Kristin. *See* **WILLIAMS, Jeanne.**

MICHAELS, Lisa. American (born United States), b. 1966. **Genres:** Autobiography/Memoirs, Novels. **Career:** Threepenny Review, senior editor, 1992-97, contributing editor, 1997-; Antioch University, associate faculty, 1998-, faculty, 1998-. **Publications:** Split: A Counterculture Childhood, 1998; Grand Ambition: A Novel, 2001; Natural Rhythms: Connect the Creational Dance of Your Life to the Pulse of the Universe, 2008. Contributor to periodicals. **Address:** W.W. Norton and Company Inc., 500 5th Ave., New York, NY 10110, U.S.A. **Online address:** lisa@lisamichaelsbooks.com

MICHAELS, Ma-go-chee. *See* **MAGOCSI, Paul Robert.**

MICHAELS, Rune. Icelander (born Iceland) **Genres:** Novels. **Career:** Writer. **Publications:** Genesis Alpha, 2007; The Reminder, 2008. **Address:** Reykjavik, Iceland. **Online address:** rune@runemichaels.com

MICHAELS, Walter Benn. American (born United States), b. 1948?. **Genres:** Race Relations, Adult Non-fiction, History, Social Sciences. **Career:** Johns Hopkins University, assistant professor of English, 1974-77, Centennial fellow, 1976, professor of English and humanities, 1987-2001, Department of English, chair, 1998-2001; University of California, assistant professor of English, 1977-80, Regents junior faculty fellow, 1978, associate professor of English, 1980-86, professor of English, 1986-87; University of Minnesota, Joseph Warren Beach lecturer, 1987; University of Michigan Law School, Sunderland fellow, 1987; Princeton University, Whitney J. Oates fellow in the humanities, 1989; Harvard University Museums, Leventritt lecturer in the arts, 1994; National Endowment for the Humanities Summer Seminar, director, 1995; Tel Aviv University, distinguished professor of american literature, 1996, Vardi lecturer, 1999; Cornell University, School of Criticism and Theory, professor, 1997; Stanford University, Ian Watt lecturer, 2001; University of Illinois, Department of English, professor, 2001-, head, 2002-; University of Wisconsin, Inaugural American Studies lecturer, 2002; Concordia University, Lahey lecturer, 2005; University of Victoria, Landsdowne visitor, 2005. Writer. **Publications:** (Ed. with D.E. Pease) The American Renaissance Reconsidered, 1985; The Gold Standard and the Logic of Naturalism: American Literature at the Turn of the Century, 1987; James Welling: Photographs 1977-90, 1990; Our America: Nativism Modernism and Pluralism, 1995; (with S. Knapp) Against Theory 2: Sentence Meaning, Hermeneutics: Protocol of the Fifty-Second Colloquy, 8 December 1985, 1996; The Shape of the Signifier: 1967 to the End of History, 2004; The Trouble with Diversity: How We Learned to Love Identity and Ignore Inequality, 2006; The Beauty of a Social Problem, forthcoming. Contributor to books and periodicals. **Address:** Department of English, University of Illinois, University Hall, Ste. 1901, 601 S Morgan St., PO Box 162, Chicago, IL 60607-7120, U.S.A. **Online address:** wbm@uic.edu

MICHALAK, Stanley J. American (born United States), b. 1938. **Genres:** Military/Defense/Arms Control, Politics/Government, Social Sciences. **Career:** Ohio State University, visiting lecturer in political science, 1964-66; Franklin & Marshall College, assistant professor, 1966-71, associate professor, 1971-80, professor of government, 1980-2004, department chair, 1973-76, 1980-82, Center for Liberal Arts and Society, director, 1999-2002, Learn and Serve Program, director, 2000-02, now Honorable John C. and Mrs. Kunkel professor of government emeritus; University of Montana, visiting assistant professor, 1968; Indiana University, visiting assistant professor, 1969-70; Foreign Policy Research Institute, visiting research fellow, 1979-81. Writer. **Publications:** United States National Security Issues, 1978; United Nations Conference on Trade and Development: An Organization Betraying Its Mission, 1983; (ed. with R.C. Gray) American Foreign Policy: From the Seventies to the Eighties, 1984; (ed.) Competing Conceptions of American Foreign Policy: Worldviews in Conflict, 1992; A Primer in Power Politics: Five Easy Lessons, 2001. Contributor to books. **Address:** Franklin and Marshall College, PO Box 3003, Lancaster, PA 17604-3003, U.S.A. **Online address:** stanley.michalak@fandm.edu

MICHEELS, Peter A. American (born United States), b. 1945. **Genres:** Adult Non-fiction, Mystery/Crime/Suspense. **Career:** Bellevue Hospital Center, psychiatric case worker, 1970-83, staff psychologist, 1983-; Fire Department of New York (FDNY), fire marshall, deputy chief, honorary fire marshall, honorary deputy chief. Writer. **Publications:** Braving the Flames, 1989; Arson: The Story of the Bureau of Fire Investigation, 1991; Heat: The Fire Investigators and their War on Arson and Murder, 1991; The Detectives: 1994, 2nd ed., 2003. **Address:** Bellevue Hospital Center, 462 1st Ave., New York, NY 10016, U.S.A.

MICHELMAN, Kate. American (born United States), b. 1942. **Genres:** Law, Politics/Government, Biography, Autobiography/Memoirs. **Career:** Pennsylvania State University, School of Medicine, Department of Psychiatry, clinical assistant professor, 1978-80; Adams County Early Childhood Services, executive director, 1978; Planned Parenthood of the Capitol Region, executive director, 1980-85; National Abortion and Reproductive Rights Action League, staff, president, 1985-2004, executive director, 1985-, now retired. Writer. **Publications:** With Liberty and Justice for All: A Life Spent Protecting the Right to Choose, 2005. **Address:** Hudson Street Press, 375 Hudson St., New York, NY 10014, U.S.A.

MICHELS, Christine. *See* **MICHELS, Sharry C.**

MICHELS, Sharry C. Also writes as Christine Michels, Sharice Kendyl. American/Canadian (born Canada), b. 1957. **Genres:** Novels, Romance/Historical, Young Adult Fiction, Mystery/Crime/Suspense. **Career:** Novelist. **Publications:** NOVELS AS CHRISTINE MICHELS: Ascent to the Stars, 1994; Danger's Kiss, 1994; In Fugitive Arms, 1995; In Destiny's Arms, 1996; Beneath a Crimson Moon, 1997; Beyond Betrayal, 1998; A Season of Miracles: Try to Remember, 1998; Undercover with the Enemy, 2000. AS SHARICE KENDYL: (with B. Carstensen) To Share a Sunset, 1990. **Address:** c/o Ethan Ellenberg, Ethan Ellenberg Agency, 548 Broadway, Ste. 5E, New York, NY 10012, U.S.A. **Online address:** smichels@fastmail.fm

MICHELSEN, G. F. *See* **FOY, George Michelsen.**

MICHELSON, Bruce (F.). (Bruce Frederic Michelson). American (born United States), b. 1948. **Genres:** Literary Criticism And History, Education, Writing/Journalism. **Career:** University of Illinois, Department of English, assistant professor, 1976-82, associate professor, 1982-95, professor, 1995-, Campus Honors Program, director, 1996-; Mark Twain Circle of America, director. Writer. **Publications:** Wilbur's Poetry: Music in a Scattering Time, 1991; Mark Twain on the Loose: A Comic Writer and American Self, 1995; Literary Wit, 2000; Teaching with the Norton Anthology of American Literature, 2001, 7th ed., 2008; Printer's Devil: Mark Twain and the American Publishing Revolution, 2006. Contributor to books and journals. **Address:** Campus Honors Program, University of Illinois, MC-134, 1205 W Oregon, Urbana, IL 61801, U.S.A. **Online address:** brucem@uiuc.edu

MICHELSON, Bruce Frederic. *See* **MICHELSON, Bruce (F.).**

MICHELSON, Karin. Canadian (born Canada), b. 1953. **Genres:** Adult Non-fiction. **Career:** University of Western Ontario, faculty, 1979-83, Centre for the Research and Teaching of Canadian Native Languages, director; Harvard University, faculty, 1982-89; State University of New York, University of Buffalo, faculty, 1989-, Department of Linguistics, associate professor, professor, chair, 2005-; McGill University, faculty. Writer. **Publications:** (Ed.) Three Stories in Oneida, 1981; A Comparative Study of Lake-Iroquoian Accent, 1988; (ed. with D.B. Gerdts) Theoretical Perspectives on Native American Languages, 1989; (with M. Doxtator) Oneida-English/English-Oneida Dictionary, 2002. **Address:** Department of Linguistics, University of Buffalo, 614 Baldy Hall, Buffalo, NY 14260, U.S.A. **Online address:** kmich@buffalo.edu

MICHELSON, Richard. American (born United States), b. 1953. **Genres:** Graphic Novels, Novels, Picture/Board Books. **Career:** R. Michelson Galleries, owner; National Yiddish Book Center, curator of exhibitions. Writer. **Publications:** SELF-ILLUSTRATED: Did You Say Ghosts?, 1993; Animals That Ought to Be: Poems about Imaginary Pets, 1996; A Book of Flies Real or Otherwise, 1999; Ten Times Better, 2000. OTHERS: Grandpa's Gamble (picture book), 1999; Too Young for Yiddish (picture book), 2002; Happy Feet: The Savoy Ballroom Lindy Hoppers and Me (picture book), 2005; Across the Alley (picture book), 2006; Oh No, Not Ghosts!, 2006; Tuttle's Red Barn, 2007; A is for Abraham: A Jewish Family Alphabet, 2008; As Good as Anybody: Martin Luther King Jr. and Abraham Joshua Heschel's Amazing March Toward Freedom, 2008; Busing Brewster, 2010; Twice as Good, 2011; Lipman Pike, 2011. POEMS: Tap Dancing for the Relatives, 1985; (contrib.) Masks, 1999; Battles and Lullabies, 2006. Contributor to books. **Address:** R. Michelson Galleries, 132 Main St., Northampton, MA 01060, U.S.A. **Online address:** rich@richardmichelson.com

MICHELSON, William. Canadian/American (born United States), b. 1940. **Genres:** Architecture, Environmental Sciences/Ecology, Geography, Sociology, Urban Studies, Social Sciences, Education. **Career:** Princeton University, instructor, 1964-65, assistant professor of sociology, 1965-66; Ontario Institute for Studies in Education, assistant professor, 1966-68, associate professor of sociology and educational planning, 1968-69; University of Toronto, assistant professor, 1966-68, associate professor of sociology, 1968-69, associate professor of sociology and urban studies, 1969-72, professor of sociology, 1972-, Center for Urban and Community Studies, acting director, 1972-73, associate director, 1973-, The Child in the City Programme, director, 1976-, S.D. Clark Professor of Sociology, now professor emeritus; Canadian Ministry of State for Urban Affairs, senior researcher, 1971-72; University of California, visiting professor, 1966; University of Lund, visiting professor,

1975-76. Writer. **Publications:** Space as a Variable in Sociological Enquiry: Serendipitous Findings on Macroenvironment, 1969; (with P. Reed) Theoretical Status and Operational Usage of Life Style in Environmental Research, 1970; Selected Aspects of Environmental Research in Scandinavia, 1970; Man and His Urban Environment: A Sociological Approach, 1970, 2nd. ed., 1976; Environmental Change: An Interim Report on Results from the Project, The Physical Environment as Attraction and Determinant, Social Effects in Housing, 1973; Place of Time in the Longitudinal Evaluation of Spatial Structures by Women, 1973; (with K. Garland) Differential Role of Crowded Homes and Dense Residential Areas in the Incidence of Selected Symptoms of Human Pathology, 1974; (ed.) Behavioral Research Methods in Environmental Design, 1975; Time-Budgets and Social Activity: Proceedings of the Meeting of the Working Group on Time-Budgets and Social Activity in Toronto, Canada, August, 1974, 1975; Reversing the Inevitable Trend: High-Rise Housing in Sweden and Denmark, 1976; Man and His Urban Environment: A Sociological Approach, with Revisions, 1976; Environmental Choice, Human Behavior and Residential Satisfaction, 1977; (co-author) Contemporary Topics in Urban Sociology, 1977; (ed.) Public Policy in Temporal Perspective: Report on the Workshop on the Application of Time-Budget Research to Policy Questions in Urban and Regional Settings (7-9 October 1975, Laxenburg, Austria), 1979; (ed. with S.V. Levine and E. Michelson) Child in the City, 1979; From Sun to Sun: Daily Obligations and Community Structure in the Lives of Employed Women and Their Families, 1985; (ed. with R.B. Bechtel and R.W. Marans) Methods in Environmental and Behavioral Research, 1987; (with T. Wikstrom and K.P. Linden) Hub of Events or Splendid Isolation: The Home as a Context for Teleworking, 1998; (ed. with D.W. Magill) Images of Change, 1999; (ed. with R. Dunlap) Handbook of Environmental Sociology, 2002; Time Use: Expanding Explanation in the Social Sciences, 2005. CONTRIBUTOR: The Form of Cities in Central Canada, 1973; The Community, 1974; Sociology Canada: Readings, 1974; Science for Better Environment, 1976; Perspectives on Environment and Behavior: Theory, Research and Application, 1976. Contributor to journals. **Address:** Department of Sociology, University of Toronto, Rm. 242, 725 Spadina Ave., Toronto, ON M5S 2J4, Canada. **Online address:** william.michelson@utoronto.ca

MICHIE, Jonathan. British (born England), b. 1957. **Genres:** Economics, Business/Trade/Industry. **Career:** Oxford Polytechnic, lecturer, 1983; Oxford University, Balliol College, lecturer in economics, 1983, Magdalen Colleges, lecturer in economics, 1983, professor of innovation and knowledge exchange, Department of Education, Kellogg College, SKOPE, senior research fellow and president, Department for Continuing Education, director; Trades Union Congress, economist, 1983-88; Commission of the European Communities, expert, 1988-90; Open University, tutor in economics, 1989-90; Brunel University, research fellow and lecturer in economics, 1989-90; Cambridge University, St. Catharine's College, fellow and lecturer in economics, Newnham College, lecturer in economics, 1990-92, Judge Business School, university lecturer in accounting and finance, 1992-97, Robinson College, fellow and director of studies in economics, 1992-97, ESRC Centre for Business Research, research associate; University of London, Birkbeck College, Sainsbury professor of management, 1997-2004, Sainsbury chair of management, School of Management and Organisational Psychology, head, 1997-2004; University of Birmingham, professor, 2004-, Birmingham Business School, director, 2004-08; MUST, (Manchester United Supporters Trust), founder; Sandwell & West Birmingam Hospitals NHS Trust, non-executive director; Analysys Ltd., consultant. Writer. **Publications:** Wages in the Business Cycle: An Empirical and Methodological Analysis, 1987; (with N. Costello and S. Milne) Beyond the Casino Economy: Planning for the 1990s, 1989; (with S. Deakin) Theory and Practice of Contracting, 1997; (with M. Kitson) The Political Economy of Competitiveness, 2000. EDITOR: The Economics of Restructuring and Intervention, 1991; The Economic Legacy: 1979-1992, 1992; (with J.G. Smith) Unemployment in Europe, 1994; (with J.G. Smith) Managing the Global Economy, 1995; (with J.G. Smith) Creating Industrial Capacity, 1996; (with P.J. Buckley) Firms, Organizations and Contracts: A Reader in Industrial Organizations, 1996; (with S. Deakin) Contracts, Co-operation, and Competition: Studies in Economics, Management, and Law, 1997; (with J.G. Smith) Employment and Economic Performance: Jobs, Inflation, and Growth, 1997; (with V. Padayachee) The Political Economy of South Africa's Transition: Policy Perspectives in the Late 1990s, 1997; (with D. Archibugi) Technological Globalisation: The End of the Nation State, 1997; (with J. Howells) Technology, Innovation, and Competitiveness, 1997; (with A. Reati) Employment, Technology, and Economic Needs: Theory, Evidence, and Public Policy, 1998; (with J.G. Smith) Globalization, Growth, and Governance: Creating an Innovative Economy, 1998; (with B.H. Moss) The Single European Currency in National Perspective: A Community in Crisis, 1998; (with D. Archibugi) Trade, Growth, and Technical Change, 1998; (with S. Hamil and C. Oughton) A Game of Two Halves: The Business of Football, 1999; (with M. Kitson) The Political Economy of Competitiveness: Essays on Employment, Public Policy, and Corporate Performance, 1999; (with J.G. Smith) Global Instability: The Political Economy of World Economic Governance, 1999; (with D. Archibugi and J. Howells) Innovation Policy in a Global Economy, 1999; A Reader's Guide to the Social Sciences, 2001; Systems of Production, 2003; Handbook of Globalisation, 2003; Political Economy of the Environment, 2010. **Address:** Department of Education, University of Birmingham, 15 Norham Gardens, Oxford, OX OX2 6PY, England. **Online address:** j.michie@bbk.ac.uk

MICHOD, Richard E. (Richard Earl Michod). American (born United States), b. 1951. **Genres:** Sex, Biology, Sciences. **Career:** University of Arizona, Department of Ecology and Evolutionary Biology, assistant professor, 1978-82, associate professor, 1982-87, professor, 1987-, department head, 2000-; Rockefeller University, Neurosciences Institute, research fellow, 1984; Czechoslovak Academy of Sciences, lecturer, 1987; Georgetown University, Bicentennial Lecturer, 1989; University of Paris-Sud, visiting research professor, 1990-91; lecturer. Writer. **Publications:** Eros and Evolution: A Natural Philosophy of Sex, 1995; Darwinian Dynamics: Evolutionary Transitions in Fitness and Individuality, 1999. EDITOR: (with B.R. Levin) The Evolution of Sex: An Examination of Current Ideas, 1988; (with M. Hechtor and L. Nadel) The Origin of Values, 1993. Works appear in anthologies. Contributor to journals. **Address:** Department of Ecology and Evolutionary Biology, University of Arizona, Rm. 310 Biosciences W, PO Box 210088, Tucson, AZ 85721, U.S.A. **Online address:** michod@u.arizona.edu

MICHOD, Richard Earl. *See* **MICHOD, Richard E.**

MICKEL, Emanuel J. American (born United States), b. 1937. **Genres:** Literary Criticism And History. **Career:** University of Nebraska, assistant professor, 1965-67, associate professor, 1967-68; Indiana University, Department of French and Italian associate professor, 1968-73, professor, 1973-, head, 1984-95, chair, Medieval Studies Institute, director, 1976-91, associate dean, 1976-78. Writer. **Publications:** The Artificial Paradises in French Literature, vol. I, 1969; (ed. with R.T. Cargo) Studies in Honor of Alfred G. Engstrom, 1972; Marie de France, 1974; Naissance du Chevalier au cygne, 1977; (with J.A. Nelson) The Old French Crusade Cycle, vol. I, 1977; Eugène Fromentin, 1981; Ganelon, Treason and the Chanson de Roland, 1989; (intro.) Complete Twenty Thousand Leagues under the Sea: A New Translation of Jules Verne's Science Fiction Classic, 1991; (ed.) Shaping of Text: Style, Imagery, and Structure in French Literature: Essays in Honor of John Porter Houston, 1993; (ed.) Les enfances Godefroi: and, Le retour de Cornumarant, 1999. **Address:** Department of French and Italian, Indiana University, Ballantine Hall 147, 1020 E Kirkwood Ave., Bloomington, IN 47405-7103, U.S.A. **Online address:** mickel@indiana.edu

MICKELBURY, Penny. American (born United States), b. 1948. **Genres:** Plays/Screenplays, Mystery/Crime/Suspense, Novels, Novellas/Short Stories. **Career:** Atlanta Voice, staff, 1968-69; Athens Banner-Herald, reporter, 1970-71; Washington Post, reporter, 1971-72; ABC-TV, political reporter; National Center on Black Aged, public relations director, 1972-75; WHUR-FM, news reporter, 1975-78; WJLA-TV, news reporter, 1978-84, assistant news director, 1984-87; City Kids Repertory Co., teacher, 1988-89; Alchemy: Theatre of Change, co-founder and managing director, 1990-93; teacher, 1994-; Los Angeles Leadership Academy, teacher; Los Angeles Public Library, Adult Literacy Program, literacy coordinator. **Publications:** MYSTERY NOVELS: Keeping Secrets, 1994; Night Songs, 1995; One Must Wait, 1998; Where to Choose, 1998; Paradise Interrupted, 2001; Darkness Descending, 2005. OTHERS: The Step Between, 2000; Love Notes, 2002; Two Graves Dug, 2005; Murder Too Close: A Phil Rodriquez Book, 2008. Contributor of short stories to books. Works appear in anthologies. **Address:** Charlotte Sheedy Literary Agency, 65 Bleecker St., New York, NY 10010, U.S.A. **Online address:** pmickel@bellsouth.net

MICKENBERG, Julia L. American (born United States) **Genres:** Politics/Government. **Career:** Pitzer College, visiting assistant professor of history, 2000-01; University of Texas at Austin, assistant professor, 2001-07, associate professor of American studies, 2007-. Writer. **Publications:** Learning from the Left: Children's Literature, the Cold War and Radical Politics in the United States, 2005; (ed. with P. Nel) Tales for Little Rebels: A Collection of Radical Children's Literature, 2008. Contributor to books and journals. **Address:** University of Texas at Austin, American Studies, 1 University Sta., Austin, TX 78712, U.S.A. **Online address:** mickenberg@mail.utexas.edu

MICKLE, Shelley Fraser. American (born United States), b. 1944. **Genres:** Novels, Novellas/Short Stories, Young Adult Fiction, Children's Non-fiction. **Career:** Wild Onion Press L.L.C., president. Writer. **Publications:** The Queen of October: A Novel, 1989; Replacing Dad: A Novel, 1993; The Kids Are Gone, the Dog is Depressed & Mom's on the Loose, 2000; The Turning Hour: A Novel, 2001; The Assigned Visit, 2006; Barbaro: America's Horse, 2007; The Polio Hole: The Story of the Illness That Changed America, 2009; Jason and Elihu: A Fisherman's Story, 2010; Old Wives Tales Told by a Half-dozen Old Wives, forthcoming. **Address:** Wild Onion Press L.L.C., 12808 NW 56th Ave., Gainesville, FL 32653, U.S.A. **Online address:** shelleyfm@aol.com

MICKLEM, Sarah. American (born United States), b. 1955?. **Genres:** Novels, Romance/Historical. **Career:** Time Warner, graphic designer. Cave Canem, co-founder, 1996; Girl Scouts of the USA, graphic designer. Writer. **Publications:** Firethorn: A Novel, 2004; Wildfire: A Novel, 2009. Contributor to periodicals. **Address:** c/o Author Mail, Simon & Schuster, 1230 Ave. of the Americas, New York, NY 10020, U.S.A.

MICKLEWHITE, Maurice Joseph. *See* **CAINE, Michael.**

MICKOLUS, Edward (Francis). American (born United States), b. 1950. **Genres:** Mystery/Crime/Suspense, International Relations/Current Affairs, Politics/Government, Bibliography, Film. **Career:** US Central Intelligence Agency, intelligence officer, 1975-2008; Vinyard Software, founder & president, 1984-. Writer. **Publications:** (Co-author) Preparing a Delegation for a High School Model United Nations: A Bibliography, 1974; ITERATE: International Terrorism: Attributes of Terrorist Events, 1976, rev. ed., 1981; Annotated Bibliography on Transnational and International Terrorism, 1976; The Literature of Terrorism: A Selectively Annotated Bibliography, 1980; Transnational Terrorism: A Chronology of Events 1968-1979, 1980; Combatting International Terrorism: A Quantitative Analysis, 1981; (comp. with P.A. Flemming) Terrorism 1980-1987: A Selectively Annotated Bibliography, 1988; (co-author) International Terrorism in the 1980's: A Chronology of Events, vol. I, 1988, vol. II, 1989; Terrorism, 1988-1991: A Chronology of Events and a Selectively Annotated Bibliography, 1993; (with S.L. Simmons) Terrorism, 1992-1995: A Chronology of Events and a Selectively Annotated Bibliography, 1997; Terrorism, 1996-2001: A Chronology, 2002; Terrorism, 2002-2004: A Chronology, 2006; Terrorism, 2005-2007, 2008; (with S.L. Simmons) The Terrorist List: Asia, Pacific, and Sub-Saharan Africa, 2011; (with S.L. Simmons) The Terrorist List: Europe-Eurasia, 2011; (with S.L. Simmons) The Terrorist List: North America, 2011; The Terrorist List: The Middle East, 5 vols., 2011; (with S.L. Simmons) The Terrorist List: South America, 2011; Two Spies Walk Into a Bar: Espionage Humor, 2011; Terrorism, 2008-2010, 2011; Secret Book of CIA Humor, 2011. CONTRIBUTOR: Terrorism: Interdisciplinary Perspectives, 1977; Contemporary Terrorism: Selected Readings, 1978; Terrorism in the Contemporary World, 1978; Quantitative Approaches to Political Intelligence: The CIA Experience, 1978; Political Terrorism and Business: The Threat and Response, 1979; The Politics of Terrorism, 1979, rev. ed., 1982; Responding to the Terrorist Threat: Security and Crisis Management, 1980; Behavioral Approaches to the Study of Terrorism, 1981; Managing Terrorism: Strategies for the Corporate Executive, 1982. FORTHCOMING: The Counterespionage Calendar; (with J.T. Brannan) Coaching Winning Model United Nations Teams; First Tour; Prez-Ex-Prez (novel); His Words; WIMZEE: Personalized License Plates in America; The Ties That Blind; Wit and Wisdom of Fortune Cookies; That's Not Quite All, Folks: Movie Easter Eggs; Speaking Truth to Power: Memoirs of Intelligence Analysts; My 33 Years in the CIA. Contributor of articles to journals. **Address:** Vinyard Software Inc., 2305 Sandburg St., Dunn Loring, VA 22027-1124, U.S.A. **Online address:** edmickolus@hotmail.com

MICOU, Paul. French/American (born United States), b. 1959. **Genres:** Novels, Mystery/Crime/Suspense, Literary Criticism And History, Young Adult Fiction. **Career:** Writer. **Publications:** The Music Programme, 1989; The Cover Artist, 1990; The Death of David Debrizzi, 1991; Rotten Times, 1992; The Last Word, 1993; Adam's Wish, 1994; The Leper's Bell, 1999; Confessions of a Map Dealer, 2008. **Address:** Transworld Publishers Ltd., 61-63 Uxbridge Rd., Ealing, London, GL W5 55A, England.

MIDDA, Sara. British (born England), b. 1951. **Genres:** Children's Fiction, Homes/Gardens, Illustrations, Photography. **Career:** Mitsukoshi (department store), product designer. Illustrator and writer. **Publications:** In and Out of the Garden, 1981; Sara Midda's South of France: A Sketch Book, 1990; Growing Up and Other Vices, 1994; Sara Midda Baby Stationery/Thank You Notes, 1999; Sara Midda Baby Book, 1999; Sara Midda Baby Stationery/Shower Invitations, 1999; A is for Adultery, Angst and Adults Only, 2002; How to Build an A, 2008. Contributor of articles to periodicals. **Address:** 19 Steele Rd., London, GL NW3 4SH, England.

MIDDLEBROOK, Martin. British (born England), b. 1932. **Genres:** History, Military/Defense/Arms Control. **Career:** Historian and writer. **Publications:** The First Day on the Somme, 1971; The Nuremberg Raid, 1973; Convoy, 1976; Convoy: The Battle for Convoys SC.122 and HX.229, 1976; Battleship: The Loss of the Prince of Wales and the Repulse, 1977 in US as Battleship: The Sinking of the Prince of Wales and the Repulse, 1979; The Kaiser's Battle, 1978; (ed. and intro.) The Diaries of Private Horace Bruckshaw, 1915-1916, 1979; The Battle of Hamburg, 1980; The Peenemunde Raid, 1982; The Schweinflunt-Regensburg Mission, 1983; The Bomber Command War Diaries, 1985; Operation Corporate: The Falklands War, 1982, 1985, rev. ed., 1987; Convoy, 1986; Task Force: The Falklands, 1987; The Berlin Raids, 1988; The Fight for the Malvinas, 1989; The Somme Battlefields, 1991; Arnhem 1944, 1994; Your Country Needs You, 2000; First day on the Somme: 1 July 1916, 2002; Convoy: The Greatest U-boat Battle of the War, 2003; Argentine Fight for the Falklands, 2003; Captain Staniland's Journey: The North Midland Territorials Go to War, 2003; (with M. Middlebrook) The Middlebrook Guide to the Somme Battlefields, 2007. EDITOR: The Bruckshaw Diaries, 1979; The Everlasting Arms, 1988; Captain Staniland's Journey-The North Midlands Territorials Go to War, 2003; Convoy: The Greatest U-Boat Battle of the War, 2003; The Argentine Fight for the Falklands, 2003. Contributor to periodicals. **Address:** 48 Linden Way, Boston, LI PE21 9DS, England.

MIDDLEMAS, Keith. *See* **MIDDLEMAS, (Robert) Keith.**

MIDDLEMAS, (Robert) Keith. (Keith Middlemas). British (born England), b. 1935. **Genres:** Design, History, Politics/Government, Biography, Autobiography/Memoirs. **Career:** House of Commons, clerk, 1958-66; University of Sussex, lecturer, 1966-76, reader, 1976-86, professor, 1986-98, professor emeritus, 1998-; Findon Conservation Association, chairman, 1969-72; Stanford University, visiting professor, 1984; University of Beijing, visiting professor, 1989. Writer. **Publications:** Command the Far Seas: A Naval Campaign of the First World War, 1961; The Master Builders: Thomas Brassey, Sir John Aird, Lord Cowdray and Sir John Norton-Griffiths, 1963; The Clydesiders: A Left Wing Struggle for Parliamentary Power, 1965; (intro.) British Furniture Through the Ages, 1966; Continental Coloured Glass, 1971; Antique Glass in Color, 1971; Cabora Bassa: Engineering and Politics in Southern Africa, 1975; Power and the Party: Changing Faces of Communism in Western Europe Since 1968, 1980; Industry, Unions and Government: Twenty-One Years of NEDC, 1983; Power, Competition and the State, vol. I, 1986, vol. II, 1990, vol. III, 1991; Orchestrating Europe: The Informal Politics of European Union 1973-95, 1995; The Changing Nature of the Modern State: Britain 1940-1980, forthcoming. AS KEITH MIDDLEMAS: (with D.C. Davis) Colored Glass, 1968; (with J. Barnes) Baldwin: A Biography, 1969, rev. ed., 1970 in US as Life of Baldwin, 1970; (ed.) Whitehall Diary, 1969; Life and times of Edward VII, 1972, rev. ed., 1975; The Strategy of Appeasement: The British Government and Germany, 1937-39 in UK as Diplomacy of illusion: The British Government and Germany, 1937-39, 1972; Life and Times of George VI, 1974; Double Market: Art Theft and Art Thieves, 1975; Pursuit of Pleasure: High Society in the 1900s, 1977; Politics in Industrial Society: The Experience of the British System Since 1911, 1979. Contributor to periodicals. **Address:** W Burton House, W Burton, Pulborough, WS RH20 1HD, England.

MIDDLETON, Haydn. British (born England), b. 1955. **Genres:** Science Fiction/Fantasy, History, Mythology/Folklore, Young Adult Fiction, Novels. **Career:** Leo Burnett Ltd., advertising executive, 1976-77; tutor, 1977-79, 1980-85; Oxford University Press, history editor, 1979-80; writer, 1980-; D'Overbroeck's Tutorial College, head of history, 1980-85; Oxford University, Department of External Studies, lecturer, 1987-88; Writers in Oxford, vice chairman, 1995-97. **Publications:** Sixteenth Century, 1982; Euro 96, 1995; The Queen's Captive, 1996; Thomas Edison: The Wizard Inventor, 1997; Cleopatra, 1997; Henry Ford: The People's Carmaker, 1997; The Knight's Vengeance, 1997; Sport in Britain, 1998; Captain Cook: The Great Ocean Explorer, 1998; William Shakespeare: The Master Playwright, 1998;

Roald Dahl: An Unauthorized Biography, 1999; Modern Olympic Games, 2000, rev. ed., 2008; Great Olympic Moments, 2000, rev. ed., 2008; Crises at the Olympics, 2000, rev. ed., 2008; Ancient Olympic Games, 2000, rev. ed., 2008; Mother Teresa: An Unauthorized Biography, 2001; Frank Lloyd Wright, 2001; Pyramids, 2002; Mark Twain, 2002; Ancient Greek Jobs, 2003; Ancient Greek Homes, 2003; Ancient Greek Women, 2003; Ancient Greek War and Weapons, 2003; World-class Marathon Runner, 2004. JUVENILE: Britain and the World since 1750, 1982; Everyday Life in 16th Century Europe, 1983; Britons and Romans, 1983; Tudor Times, 1984; The Dark Ages, 1984; (with H. Leyser) Invasion and Integration, 1986; Island of the Mighty, 1987; Rulers and Rebels, 1987; The Age of Chivalry, 1988; (ed. with D. Heater) Twentieth Century World History Atlas, 1989; The United Kingdom: Ten Centuries in the Making, 1994; Britain's Links with the World, 1998; Diana Princess of Wales Life and Times, 1998. ADULT FICTION: The People in the Picture, 1987; (with A. Toorchen) Son of Two Worlds: A Retelling of the Timeless Celtic Saga of Pryderi, 1989; The Lie of the Land, 1989; The Collapsing Castle, 1991; the King's Evil, 1995; Grimm's Last Fairytale, 1999. Contributor to periodicals. **Address:** Christopher Little Literary Agency, 125 Moore Park Rd., London, GL SW6 4PS, England. **Online address:** thetunisians@hotmail.com

MIDDLETON, (John) Christopher. British (born England), b. 1926. **Genres:** Novellas/Short Stories, Poetry, Essays, Translations. **Career:** University of Zurich, lecturer in English, 1952-55; University of London, King's College, senior lecturer in German, 1955-56; University of Texas, visiting professor, 1961-62, professor of German literature, 1966-98. Writer. **Publications:** Torse 3: Poems 1949-1961, 1962; (with D. Holbrook and D. Wevill) Penguin Modern Poets 4, 1963; The Metropolitans (libretto), 1964; Nonsequences: Selfpoems, 1965; Our Flowers and Nice Bones, 1969; The Fossil Fish: 15 Micro-poems, 1970; Briefcase History: 9 Poems, 1972; Fractions for Another Telemachus, 1974; The Lonely Suppers of W.V. Balloon, 1975; Eight Elementary Inventions, 1976; Pataxanadu and Other Prose, 1977; Bolshevism in Art and Other Expository Writings, 1978; Carminalenia (poetry), 1980; The Pursuit of the Kingfisher (essays), 1983; III Poems, 1983; Serpentine, 1985; Two Horse Wagon Going By, 1986; Selected Writings, 1989; The Balcony Tree, 1992; (trans.) Andalusian Poems, 1993; Intimate Chronicles, 1996; Jackdaw Jiving: Essays on Poetry and Translation, 1998; In the Mirror of the Eighth King (prose), 1999; Faint Harps and Silver Voices: Selected Translations, 2000; (ed. and trans.) Elegies and Other Poems, 2000; Twenty Tropes for Doctor Dark, 2000; The Word Pavilion and Selected Poems, 2001; (trans. with H. Mathews and R. Waldrop) Many Glove Compartments, 2001; CryptoTopgraphia: Stories of Secret Places, 2002; Of the Mortal Fire: Poems 1999-2003, 2003; Tankard Cat, 2004; (trans.) Speaking to the Rose: Writings, 1912-1932, 2005; Anti-basilisk, 2005; Tenor on Horseback: Poems, 2007; If from the Distance: Two Essays, 2007; (trans.) 130 Poems, 2010; Poems 2006-2009, 2010; Company of Ghosts, 2010. EDITOR: (and trans. with M. Hamburger) Modern German Poetry 1910-1960, 1962; (and trans. with W. Burford) The Poet's Vocation, 1967; German Writing Today, 1967; Selected Poems, by G. Trakl, 1968; (and trans.) R. Walser: Selected Stories, 1982; (and trans.) Goethe, Selected Poems, 1983. **Address:** Carcanet Press, Alliance House, 30 Cross St., 4th Fl., Manchester, LC M2 7AQ, England.

MIDKIFF, Mary D. American (born United States), b. 1955?. **Genres:** Medicine/Health, Recreation, Natural History, Animals/Pets. **Career:** American Horse Council, executive secretary of showing and state horse councils, 1986-91; Animal Welfare Task Force, executive secretary, 1986-91; Equestrian Resources Inc., president, 1991-; Women & Horses Fitness and Performance Program, founder and developer, 1991-. Writer and equestrian marketing specialist. **Publications:** Fitness, Performance, and the Female Equestrian, 1996; She Flies without Wings: How Horses Touch a Woman's Soul, 2001. **Address:** Equestrian Resources Inc., PO Box 20187, Boulder, CO 80308, U.S.A. **Online address:** mmidkiff@womenandhorses.com

MIDWINTER, Eric (Clare). British (born England), b. 1932. **Genres:** Education, Gerontology/Senior Issues, History, Sports/Fitness, Biography, Illustrations, Literary Criticism And History. **Career:** Home Office Community Development Projects, educational consultant; teacher, 1956-68; Liverpool Educational Priority Area Project, director, 1968-72; Center for Urban Community Education, director of priority, 1972-75; National Consumer Council, head of the public affairs unit, 1975-80; Center for Policy on Ageing, director, 1980-91; University of Exeter, visiting professor of education, 1992-2001; Community Education Development Center, chair, 1994-2000. Writer. **Publications:** Law and Order in Early Victorian Lancashire, 1968; Victorian Social Reform, 1968; Social Administration in Lancashire, 1830-1860, 1969; Nineteenth Century Education, 1970; Old Liverpool, 1971; (ed.) Projections: An Education Priority Project at Work, 1972; Social Environment and the Urban School, 1972; Priority Education, 1972; Patterns of Community Education, 1973; (ed.) Preschool Priorities, 1974; Education and the Community, 1975; Education for Sale, 1977; Make 'em Laugh: Famous Comedians and Their Worlds, 1979; Schools in Society, 1980; W.G. Grace: His Life and Times, 1981; Age Is Opportunity, 1982; (ed.) Mutual Aid Universities, 1984; The Wage of Retirement, 1985; Fair Game, 1986; Caring for Cash: The Issue of Private Domiciliary Care, 1986; Polls Apart, 1987; Retired Leisure, 1987; The Lost Seasons, 1987; Redefining Old Age: A Review of CPA's Recent Contributions to Social Policy, 1987; New Design for Old, 1988; Red Roses Crest the Caps, 1989; Creating Chances: Arts by Older People, 1990; The Old Order: Crime and Older People, 1990; Out of Focus: Old Age, the Press and Broadcasting, 1991; Brylcreem Summer, 1991; Illustrated History of Country Cricket, 1992; Lifelines, 1993; First Knock, 1994; The Development of Social Welfare in Britain, 1994; Darling Old Oval, 1995; State Educator: The Life and Enduring Importance of W.E. Forster, 1996; Pensioned Off: Retirement and Income Examined, 1997; The Billy Bunter Syndrome, 1998; Yesterdays: The Way We Were, 1998; From Meadowland to Multinational, 1999; Yesterdays: Our Finest Hours, 2001; Quill on Willow: Cricket in Literature, 2001; As One Stage Door Closes... The John Wade Story, 2002; Novel Approaches: A Guide to the Popular Classic Novel, 2003; The People's Jesters: British Comedians in the 20th Century, 2006; Salisbury, 2006. **Address:** c/o Murray Pollinger, 4 Garrick St., London, GL WC2 9BH, England.

MIDWOOD, Bart(on A.). American (born United States), b. 1938. **Genres:** Novellas/Short Stories, Novels, Literary Criticism And History. **Career:** Real estate agent, writer; Esquire magazine, reviewer, 1969-71; New York Studio for Writers, co-director and teacher, 1989-95; Prudential/L.I. Realty, licensed sales agent, 1997-98; National Homefinders, licensed sales agent, 1998-. **Publications:** Bodkin, 1967; Phantoms: A Collection of Stories, 1970; The Nativity, 1981; Bennett's Angel: A Novel, 1989; The World in Pieces, 1998. Contributor to periodicals. **Address:** 32-A Hicks St., Brooklyn, NY 11201-1327, U.S.A. **Online address:** bmidwood@aol.com

MIELE, Angelo. American/Italian (born Italy), b. 1922. **Genres:** Air/Space Topics, Sciences, Engineering. **Career:** Polytechnic Institute of Brooklyn, research assistant professor of aeronautical engineering, 1952-55; Purdue University, professor of aeronautical engineering, 1955-59; Boeing Scientific Research Labs, Astrodynamics and Flight Mechanics, director, 1959-64; University of Washington, visiting professor of aeronautics and astronautics, 1961-64; Rice University, A.J. Foyt Family professor in engineering and professor of aerospace sciences and mathematical sciences, 1964-93, A.J. Foyt Family professor emeritus in mechanical engineering, 1993-, research professor, 2000-. Writer. **Publications:** Flight Mechanics, 1962; (contrib.) Mechanics and Control, 1994. EDITOR: Theory of Optimum Aerodynamic Shapes: Extremal Problems in the Aerodynamics of Supersonic, Hypersonic, and Free-Molecular Flows, 1965; (with A. Salvetti) Applied Mathematics in Aerospace Science and Engineering, 1994; (with A. Frediani) Advanced Design Problems in Aerospace Engineering, 2003; (contrib.) Advances in Mechanics: Dynamics and Control: Proceedings of the 14th International Workshop on Dynamics and Control: Moscow-Zvenigorod, Russia May 28-June 2, 2007, 2008. Contributions to books. **Address:** Rice University, Rm. 216 RL, 101 Mechanical Engineering Bldg., 6100 Main St., PO Box 1892, Houston, TX 77251-1892, U.S.A. **Online address:** miele@rice.edu

MIELE, Frank. American (born United States), b. 1948?. **Genres:** Race Relations, Social Sciences, Adult Non-fiction. **Career:** Skeptic Magazine, columnist, advertising director, senior editor, 1994. Researcher and consultant. **Publications:** Intelligence, Race and Genetics: Conversations with Arthur R. Jensen, 2002; (with W. Kistler) Reflections on Life: Science, Religion, Truth, Ethics, Success, Society, 2003; (with V. Sarich) Race: The Reality of Human Differences, 2004. Contributor to magazines and periodicals. **Address:** Skeptic Magazine, PO Box 338, Altadena, CA 91001, U.S.A. **Online address:** skepticmag@aol.com

MIESCHER, Stephan F. American (born United States), b. 1961. **Genres:** History. **Career:** University of California, professor. Writer. **Publications:** (With K. Trüeb) Maännergeschichten: Schwule in Basel Seit 1930, 1988; (ed. with L. White and D.W. Cohen) African Words, African Voices: Critical Practices in Oral History, 2001; (ed. with L.A. Lindsay) Men and Masculinities in Modern Africa, 2003; Making Men in Ghana, 2005; (ed. with C.M. Cole and T. Manuh) Africa after Gender?, 2007. **Address:** Department of History, University of California, Santa Barbara, CA 93106-9410, U.S.A. **Online address:** miescher@history.ucsb.edu

MIETH, Dietmar. German (born Germany), b. 1940. **Genres:** Medicine/Health, Ethics, Theology/Religion. **Career:** University of Tuebingen, assistant in theology, 1967-74, Academic Reform Commission, chairman, 1970-72, chair, 1974, professor of theological ethics, 1981-, dean, 1984-85, 1996-98, 2007-08, faculty, 1985-90, Center for Ethics in the Sciences and the Humanities, director, 1990-2001; University of Fribourg, visiting professor, 1974, professor of theological ethics and director, 1974-81; International Association of Moral Theology and Social Ethics, manging director, 1975-77; International Congress, president, 1975-77; Six Language International Journal Concilium, director, 1978-2001; European Society for Catholic Theology, inititator, 1989-95; International Theological Journal Concilium, editor and co-editor, 1995-2001; Ethics Network Baden Württemberg, founder and chairman, 2000-08; Interdisciplinary Human Ethics Institute and Sciences, chairman, 2002-; Institute for Christian Ethics and Policy Advice, chairman, 2004-; University of Vienna, Catholic Theological Faculty, chairman, 2005-; Meister Eckhart Gesellschaft, president, 2008-; University of Erfurt, fellow, 2009-. **Publications:** IN ENGLISH: In Vitro Fertilisation in the 1990s, 1998. EDITOR: (ed.) Meister Eckhart, 1979, 3rd ed., 1991; (with M. Vidal) Outside the Market No Salvation?, 1997; (with C. Theobald) Unanswered Questions, 1999; (with H. Haring, M. Junker-Kenny) Creating Identity, 2000; (with K. Kuschel) On the Search of Universal Values, 2001; (with M.P. Aquino) Return of the Just War, 2001. EDITOR WITH J. POHIER: The Dignity of the Despised of the Earth, 1979; Christian Ethics and Economics, 1980; Christian Ethics, 1980; Unemployment and the Right to Work, 1982; The Ethics of Liberation, the Liberation of Ethics, 1984; Suicide and the Right to Die, 1985; Changing Values and Virtues, 1987; Ethics in the Natural Sciences, 1989. EDITOR WITH L.S. CAHILL: Aging, 1991; Migrants and Refugees, 1993; Family, 1995. OTHERS: Towards a Dynamic Morality, 1970; Epics and Ethics: e. theolog -eth. Interpretation d. Joseph Novels of Thomas Mann, 1976; Dichtung, Glaube und Moral: Studien zur Begründung e. narrativen Ethik: mit e. Interpretation zum Tristanroman Gottfrieds von Strassburg, 1976; Moral und Erfahrung: Beiträge zur theologisch-ethischen Hermeneutik, 1977; Ethisch handeln lernen: zu Konzeption und Inhalt ethischer Erziehung, 1978, (with G. Sting) Ethically Learn to Act: To Design and Content of Ethical Education, 1978; Gotteserfahrung und Weltverantwortung: über die christliche Spiritualität des Handelns, 1982; (with H. Jonas) Was für morgen lebenswichtig ist: unentdeckte Zukunftswerte, 1983; (with H. Jonas) What is for Tomorrow Vital: Undiscovered Future Value, 1983; Ehe als Entwurf: zur Lebensform der Liebe, 1984; Neuen Tugenden: ein ethischer Entwurf, 1984; New Virtues: An Ethical Design, 1984; Marriage as a Draft for the Life of Love, 1984; Arbeit und Menschenwürde, 1985; Work and Menschenwürde, 1985; Spannungseinheit von Theorie und Praxis: theologische Profile, 1986; (with K. Barewell) Migration and Menschenwürde: Facts, Analysis and Ethical Criteria, 1987; (with J.P. Wils) Ethics Without a Chance?: Explorations in the Technological Age, 1989; Geburtenregelung: ein Konflikt in der katholischen Kirche, 1990; (with K. Steigleder) Ethics in the Sciences: Ariadne's Thread in the Technical Maze?: Fifth Blaubeurer Symposium of 8 -12. October 1989, 1990; (with H.K. Steigleder) Ethik in den Wissenschaften: Ariadnefaden im technischen Labyrinth?: Fünftes Blaubeurer Symposium vom 8.-12. Oktober 1989, 1990; Birth Control: A Conflict in the Catholic Church, 1990; (with I. Meith) Abortion: The Challenge and the Alternatives, 1991; (with J. Wils) Ethik ohne Chance?, 1991; (ed. with J.P. Wils) Ethics Without a Chance?: Explorations in the Technological Age, 1991; (ed. with P. Hünermann) Streitgespräch to Theology and Teaching: The Instruction about the Ecclesial Vocation of the Theologian in the Debate, 1991; (with I. Mieth) Schwangerschaftsabbruch: die Herausforderung und die Alternativen, 1991; (ed. with J.P. Wils) Basic Concepts of Christian Ethics, 1992; (with J. Wils) Grundbegriffe der christlichen Ethik, 1992; (with W. Haug) Religiöse Erfahrung: historische Modelle in christlicher Tradition, 1992; Moraltheologie im Abseits?: Antwort auf die Enzyklika Veritatis splendor, 1994; (with K. Wojtyla) Wer Gott dient, wird nicht krumm, 1997; (ed. with E. Hildst) In Vitro Fertilisation in the 1990's: Towards a Medical, Social and Ethical Evaluation, 1998; (ed. with C. Theobald) Unanswered Questions, 1999; Erzählen und Moral: Narrativität im Spannungsfeld von Ethik und ästhetik, 2000; Ethik und Wissenschaft in Europa: die gesellschaftliche, rechtliche und philosophische Debatte, 2000; (ed. with H. Häringand M.J. Kenny) Creating Identity, 2000, (with H. Snijdewind) Religion Zwischen Gewalt und Beliebigkeit, 2001; Diktatur der Gene: Biotechnik zwischen Machbarkeit und Menschenwürde, 2001; Was wollen wir können?: Ethik im Zeitalter der Biotechnik, 2002; (with C. Baumgartner) Patente am Leben?: ethische, rechtliche und politische Aspekte der Biopatentierung, 2003; Meister Eckhart: Mystik und Lebenskunst, 2004; (ed. with C. Rehmann-Sutter and M. Düwell) Bioethics in Cultural Contexts: Reflections on Methods and Finitude, 2006; (with U. Konnertz and H. Haker) Ethik, Geschlecht, Wissenschaft, 2006; (ed. with K. Hilbert) Criteria of Biomedical Ethics: Theological Contribution to the Social Discourse, 2006; (ed. with U. Konnertz and H.Haker) Ethics, Gender, Science: The Ethical Turn as a Challenge for Interdisziplinären Gender Studies, 2006; (with K. Hilpert) Kriterien biomedizinischer Ethik, 2006; Grenzenlose Selbstbestimmung?: der Wille und die Würde Sterbender, 2008; (ed. with C. Rehmann-Sutter and M. Düwell) Contingent Nature of Life: Bioethics and Limits of Human Existence, 2008. Author of books in German; (with N. Müller and C. Hübenthal) Sport und Christentum: eine anthropologische, theologische und pastorale Herausforderung, 2008. Contributor to periodicals. **Address:** Theologicum, University of Tuebingen, Liebermeisterstr 12, Tuebingen, 72076, Germany. **Online address:** dietmar.mieth@uni-tuebingen.de

MIGHETTO, Lisa. American (born United States), b. 1955?. **Genres:** Environmental Sciences/Ecology, History. **Career:** Pacific Lutheran University, lecturer in history, 1983; University of Puget Sound, assistant professor of history, 1987-91; Historical Research Associates Inc., History Division, director, 1991-, senior historian and vice president; University of Washington, affiliate faculty; American Society for Environmental History, executive director. Writer and researcher. **Publications:** (Ed.) Muir among the Animals: The Wildlife Writings of John Muir, 1986; Wild Animals and American Environmental Ethics, 1991; (with C. Homstad) Engineering in the Far North: A History of the U.S. Army Engineer District in Alaska, 1867-1992, 1997; (with M. Montgomery) Hard Drive to the Klondike: Promoting Seattle during the Gold Rush, 2002; (co-author) Currents of Change: A History of the Portland District, U.S. Army Corps of Engineers, 1980-2000, 2003. Contributor to periodicals. **Address:** Interdisciplinary Arts and Sciences Program, University of Washington, 1900 Commerce St., PO Box 358436, Tacoma, WA 98402-3112, U.S.A. **Online address:** director@aseh.net

MIGHTON, John. Canadian (born Canada), b. 1957. **Genres:** Plays/Screenplays, Reference. **Career:** Junior Undiscovered Math Prodigies (JUMP), founder and developer, 1998-; University of Toronto, adjunct professor of mathematics, 2000-; Theatre Passe Muraille, writer-in-residence; Caribbean American Repertory Theatre, writer-in-residence; Fields Institute for Research in Mathematical Sciences, fellow; Order of Canada, officer, 2010. Dramatist. **Publications:** Scientific Americans, 1990; Possible Worlds, 1992; A Short History of Night, 1992; Body and Soul, 1994; The Little Years, 1996; The Myth of Ability: Nurturing Mathematical Talent in Every Child, 2004; Half Life, 2005; The End of Ignorance: Multiplying Our Human Potential, 2007. Contributor to periodicals. **Address:** JUMP, 1 Yonge St., Ste. 1006, Toronto, ON M5E 1E5, Canada.

MIGLIAZZO, Arlin C. American (born United States), b. 1951. **Genres:** History, Cultural/Ethnic Topics. **Career:** Biola University, instructor in European and American history, 1977-78; Washington State University, lecturer in American history, 1979-81; Pacific Lutheran University, instructor, 1981; Judson Baptist College, assistant professor of history and political science, 1982-83; Whitworth University, assistant, professor of history, 1983-, department chair, 1987-88, 1991-97, 1998-99, 2002-03, 2005-06, 2009-10, director of faculty development, 2000-03; Spokane Community College, adjunct professor, 1988; Keimyung University, Fulbright professor of American history, 1990. **Publications:** (Ed.) Career Opportunities for Historians, 2nd ed., 1981; (ed. and intro.) Land of True and Certain Bounty: The Geographical Theories and Colonization Strategies of Jean Pierre Purry, 2002; (ed.) Teaching as an Act of Faith: Theory and Practice in Church-Related Higher Education, 2002; To Make This Land Our Own: Community, Identity, and Cultural Adaptation in Purrysburg Township, South Carolina, 1732-1865, 2007. **Address:** Department of History, Whitworth University, 300 W Hawthorne Rd., Weyerhaeuser Hall 210 L, Spokane, WA 99251, U.S.A. **Online address:** amigliazzo@whitworth.edu

MIGNOLO, Walter D. American (born United States), b. 1941. **Genres:** History. **Career:** University of Michigan, Department of Romance Studies, assistant professor, associate professor, full professor, 1975-92; Duke University, Department of Romance Studies, William H. Wannamaker distinguished professor, 1993-; University of Indiana, visiting assistant professor, 1973-74, University of Michigan, visiting assistant professor, 1974-75. Writer. **Publications:** Elementos para una teoria del texto literario, 1978; Teoria del texto e interpretaciOn de textos, 1986; (co-author) Teorias literarias en la actualidad, 1989; (ed. with E.H. Boone) Writing without Words: Alternative Literacies in Mesoamerica and the Andes, 1994; The Darker Side of the Renaissance: Literacy, Territoriality and Colonization, 1995, 2nd ed., 2003; Local Histories/Global Designs: Coloniality, Subaltern Knowledges and Border Thinking, 2000; Capitalismo y geopolitica del conocimiento: el eurocentrismo y la filosofia de la liberaciOn en el debate intelectual contemporAneo, 2001; (intro.) Natural and Moral History of the Indies, 2002; The Idea of Latin America, 2005; (co-author) Interculturalidad, descolonizaciOn del estado y del conocimiento, 2006; Rereading the Black Legend: The Discourses of Religious and Racial Difference in the Renaissance Empires, 2007. **Address:** Franklin Ctr., Duke University, 2204 Erwin Rd., Durham, NC 27708-0402, U.S.A. **Online address:** wmignolo@acpub.duke.edu

MIHAILOVIĆ, Dragoslav. Yugoslav (born), b. 1930. **Genres:** Novels, Novellas/Short Stories, Plays/Screenplays. **Career:** University of Poitiers, Department of Serbo-Croatian language, lecturer, 1974. Writer. **Publications:** Frede, laku noc, 1967; Kad su cvetale tikve (novel), 1968; Petrijinvenac, 1975; Cizmasi, 1983; Uhvati zvezdupadalicu, 1983; Uvodjenje u posao: Drame, 1983; Dela Dragoslava Mihailovica, 6 vols., 1984; Goli otok, vol. I, 1990, vol. II-III, 1995; Vijetnamci, 1990; Lovna stenice, 1993; Gori Morava, 1994; Dela Dragoslava Mihailovica, 7 vols., 1990; Odlomci a zlotvori, 1996; Zlotvori, 1997; Barabe, konji I gegule, 1997; Jalova jesen, 2000; Czveno I plavo, 2001; Tzeis prolece (novel), 2002; Trece prolece, 2002; Najlepše priče Dragoslava Mihailovía, 2003; Kad su cvetale tikve; Petrijin venac; Zlotvori, 2003; Kratka istorija satiranja, 2005; Majstorsko pismo, 2007; Dijalekti i srpska književnost: tema Borine nedelje 2007, 2007; Preživljavanje, 2010. Works appear in anthologies. Contributor to periodicals. **Address:** Serbian Academy of Arts and Sciences, 35 Knez Mihailova, PO Box 366, Beograd, 11001, Yugoslavia.

MIHESUAH, Devon Abbott. American (born United States), b. 1957. **Genres:** Anthropology/Ethnology, Criminology/True Crime. **Career:** American Indian Center, secretary, 1977-78; Texas Christian University, School of Education, graduate assistant, 1981-82, Upward Bound, computer instructor, 1980, 1985-86, departmental assistant, 1984-85, teaching assistant in history, 1985-88; Grants High School, teacher, coach, 1982-84; Western Hills High School, teacher, coach, 1984; Northern Arizona University, assistant professor, associate professor, 1989-99, professor of history, 1999, professor of applied indigenous studies and history, 2000; University of Kansas, Cora Lee Beers Price teaching professor in international cultural understanding; American Indian Quarterly, editor. **Publications:** Cultivating the Rosebuds: The Education of Women at the Cherokee Female Seminary, 1851-1909, 1993; American Indians: Stereotypes and Realities, 1996; (ed.) Natives and Academics: Researching and Writing about American Indians, 1998; Repatriation: Social and Political Dialogues, 2000; (ed.) Repatriation Reader: Who Owns Indian Remains?, 2000; (ed.) The Roads of My Relations, 2000; (ed.) First to Fight, 2002; Indigenous American Women: Decolonization, Empowerment, Activism, 2003; (ed. with A.C. Wilson) Indigenizing the Academy: Transforming Scholarship and Empowering Communities, 2004; Lightning Shrikes, 2004; Grand Canyon Rescue: A Tuli Black Wolf Adventure, 2004; Recovering Our Ancestors' Gardens: Indigenous Recipes and Guide to Diet and Fitness, 2005; So You Want to Write About American Indians?: A Guide for Writers, Students and Scholars, 2005; Chronicles of Oklahoma, 2008; Choctaw Crime and Punishment, 1884-1907, 2009; Big Bend Luck, 2009; Document of Expectations, 2011. Contributor of articles to books and journals. **Address:** Center for Indigenous Nations Studies, University of Kansas, 203D Bailey Hall, 1410 Jayhawk Blvd., Lawrence, KS 66045, U.S.A. **Online address:** mihesuah@ku.edu

MIHM, Stephen. American (born United States), b. 1968. **Genres:** Economics, History. **Career:** New York Times, project editor, 1998-2001; Freelance writer, 1999-; New York Times Digital, producer, 2000-01; Harvard Business School, Newcomen postdoctoral research fellow in business history, 2003-04; University of Georgia, assistant professor, 2004-09, associate professor, 2009-. **Publications:** (Ed. with K. Ott and D. Serlin) Artificial Parts, Practical Lives: Modern Histories of Prosthetics, 2002; A Nation of Counterfeiters: Capitalists, Con Men and the Making of the United States, 2007; (with N. Roubini) Crisis Economics: A Crash Course in the Future of Finance, 2010; The Countrys Currency: A History of the Dollar from the American Revolution to the American Century , 2012. **Address:** Department of History, University of Georgia, 302 LeConte, Athens, GA 30602, U.S.A. **Online address:** mihm@uga.edu

MIJARES, Sharon G. American (born United States), b. 1942. **Genres:** Psychology. **Career:** Women's Resource Center, sexual abuse counselor, 1993-95; National University, adjunct faculty, 1995-2005; Chapman University (now Brandman University), faculty, 1999-2005; California Institute for Human Science, faculty, 2006-; Del Mar Integrative Health Center, psychotherapist; Vermont College, adjunct faculty; Union Institute and University, adjunct faculty. Writer. **Publications:** The Babysitter's Manual: A Manual On How to be Successful and Quite Professional When Taking Care Of Other People's Children, 1983; (ed.) Modern Psychology and Ancient Wisdom: Psychological Healing Practices from the World's Religious Traditions, 2003; (ed. with G.S. Khalsa) The Psychospiritual Clinician's Handbook: Alternative Methods For Understanding and Treating Mental Disorders, 2005; The Blossom and the Rose Stem: The Relationship Between Spirituality and Religion, 2006; (co-author) Root of all Evil: An Exposition of Prejudice, Fundamentalism, and Gender Imbalance, 2007; (ed.) Revelation of the Breath: A Tribute to Its Wisdom, Power, and Beauty, 2009. **Address:** California Institute for Human Science, 701 Garden View Ct., Encinitas, CA 92024, U.S.A. **Online address:** sharon.mijares12@gmail.com

MIKAELSEN, Ben (John). American (born United States), b. 1952. **Genres:** Novels, Westerns/Adventure, Children's Fiction, Young Adult Fiction, Mystery/Crime/Suspense. **Career:** Writer. **Publications:** Rescue Josh McGuire, 1991; Sparrow Hawk Red, 1993; Stranded, 1995; Countdown, 1996; Petey, 1998; Touching Spirit Bear, 2001; Red Midnight, 2002; Tree Girl, 2004; Ghost of Spirit Bear, 2008. **Address:** 233 Quinn Creek Rd., Bozeman, MT 59715-8213, U.S.A. **Online address:** ben@benmikaelsen.com

MIKALSON, Jon D. American (born United States), b. 1943. **Genres:** Classics, Philosophy, Theology/Religion, Essays. **Career:** University of Virginia, Department of Classics, assistant professor, 1970-77, associate professor, 1977-84, chair, 1978-90, William R. Kenan, Jr. professor of classics, 1984-, director of undergraduate studies, Echols Scholars Program, director; American School in Athens, Whitehead professor. Writer. **Publications:** The Sacred and Civil Calendar of the Athenian Year, 1975; Athenian Popular Religion, 1983; Honor Thy Gods: Popular Religion in Greek Tragedy, 1991; Religion in Hellenistic Athens, 1998; (ed. with G. Schmeling) Qui Miscuit Utile Dulci: Festschrift Essays for Paul Lachlan MacKendrick, 1998; Herodotus and Religion in the Persian Wars, 2003; Ancient Greek Religion, 2005, 2nd ed., 2010; Greek Popular Religion in Greek Philosophy, 2010. **Address:** Department of Classics, University of Virginia, B002 Cocke Hall, PO Box 400788, Charlottesville, VA 22904-4788, U.S.A. **Online address:** jdm9x@virginia.edu

MIKHAIL-ASHRAWI, Hanan. *See* **ASHRAWI, Hanan (Mikhail).**

MIKLOWITZ, Gloria D. American (born United States), b. 1927. **Genres:** Children's Fiction, Adult Non-fiction, Children's Non-fiction, Autobiography/Memoirs, Biography, Novels, Novellas/Short Stories, Young Adult Fiction, Young Adult Fiction. **Career:** U.S. Naval Ordnance Test Station, scriptwriter, 1952-57; Pasadena City College, instructor, 1971-80; Writers Digest School, instructor. Writer. **Publications:** FICTION FOR CHILDREN: Barefoot Boy, 1964; The Zoo That Moved, 1968; The Parade Starts at Noon, 1970; The Marshmallow Caper, 1971; Sad Song, Happy Song, 1973; Ghastly Ghostly Riddles, 1977; (with P. Desberg) Win, Lose, or Wear a Tie: Sports Riddles, 1980. FICTION FOR YOUNG ADULTS: Turning Off, 1973; A Time to Hurt, a Time to Heal, 1974; Runaway, 1977; Unwed Mother, 1977; (with P. Desberg) Riddles for Scary Nights, 1977; Did You Hear What Happened to Andrea?, 1979; The Love Bombers, 1980; Before Love, 1982; Close to the Edge, 1983; Carrie Loves Superman, 1983; The Day the Senior Class Got Married: A Novel, 1983; The War Between the Classes, 1985; After the Bomb, 1985; Love Story, Take Three, 1986; Week One, 1987; Secrets Not Meant to Be Kept, 1987; Good-bye Tomorrow, 1987; The Emerson High Vigilantes, 1988; Anything to Win, 1989; Suddenly Super Rich, 1989; Standing Tall, Looking Good, 1991; Desperate Pursuit, 1992; The Killing Boy, 1993; Past Forgiving, 1995; Masada: The Last Fortress, 1998; Camouflage, 1998; Secrets in the House of Delgado, 2001; The Enemy has a Face, 2003. NON-FICTION: (with W.A. Young) The Zoo was My World, 1969; Harry Truman, 1975; Paramedics, 1977; Nadia Comăneci, 1977; Earthquake!, 1977; Save that Raccoon!, 1978; Tracy Austin, 1978; Martin Luther King, Jr., 1978, new. ed., 2004; Steve Cauthen, 1978; Natalie Dunn, World Roller Skating Champion (biography), 1979; Roller Skating, 1979; Movie Stunts and the People Who do Them, 1980; (with M. Yates) The Young Tycoons: Ten Success Stories, 1981; Jane Goodall, 2002; Ray Kroc, 2002; Sacajawea, 2002; Shirley Temple Black, 2002; Venus & Serena Williams, 2002; Albert Einstein, 2002; Amelia Earhart, 2002; Bill Gates, 2002; César Chávez, 2002; Charles Schulz, 2002; Dr. Seuss, 2002. Works appear in anthologies. Contributor to periodicals. **Address:** Curtis Brown Ltd., 10 Astor Pl., New York, NY 10003, U.S.A. **Online address:** glow7@aol.com

MIKOLYZK, Thomas A. American (born United States), b. 1953. **Genres:** Essays, Literary Criticism And History, Poetry, Bibliography, Education, Biography, Reference. **Career:** New England boarding school, teacher, 1982-; Lake Forest College, librarian, 1986-89; William Rainey Harper College, librarian, 1989-93; Nite-Owl Reference, librarian, 1989-; District 62 Library, librarian, 1989-93; Avery Coonley School, librarian, 1993-97, assistant director of education consultants, 1993-; Science & Arts Academy, headmaster. Writer. **Publications:** Langston Hughes: A Bio-Bibliography, 1990; (comp.) Oscar Wilde: An Annotated Bibliography, 1993. Contributor to periodicals. **Address:** Science & Arts Academy, 1825 Miner St., Des Plaines, IL 60016, U.S.A. **Online address:** tmikolyzk@scienceandartsacademy.org

MILANOVIC, Branko. American/French (born France), b. 1953. **Genres:** Social Sciences. **Career:** World Bank, country economist, 1988-91, Department of Research, lead economist; Institute of Economic Sciences, research fellow, 1980-83, 1986-88; Johns Hopkins University, School for Advanced International Studies, adjunct professor of economics, 1996-2007, visiting professor, 1997-; University of Maryland, senior lecturer, visiting professor, School for Public Policy, adjunct professor, 2007-; Carnegie Endowment for International Peace Global Policy Program, senior associate. Writer. **Publications:** Export Incentives and Turkish Manufactured Exports, 1980-1984, 1986; Jugoslovenska privreda izmdu stagnacije i razvoja, 1986; Liberalization and Entrepreneurship: Dynamics of Reform in Socialism and Capitalism, 1989; Ekonomska nejednakost u Jugoslaviji, 1990; (with F. Dhanji) Privatization in Eastern and Central Europe, 1991; Poverty in Poland, 1978-88, 1991; The Transition from Socialism in Eastern Europe: Domestic Restructuring and Foreign Trade, 1992; Distributional Impact of Cash and In-Kind Social Transfers in Eastern Europe and Russia, 1992; Cash Social Transfers, Direct Taxes and Income Distribution in Late Socialism, 1993; Social Costs of the Transition to Capitalism: Poland, 1990-91, Transition and Macro- Adjustment, 1993; Transfers and the Transition from Socialism: Key Tradeoffs, 1994; Protiv nacizma, 1994; Determinants of Cross-Country Income Inequality: An Augmented Kuznets' Hypothesis, 1994; Poverty, Inequality and Social Policy in Transition Economies, 1995; Nations, Conglomerates and Empires: Trade-Off between Income and Sovereignty, 1996; Explaining the Increase in Inequality during the Transition, 1998; Poverty and Economic Transition: How Do Changes in Economies of Scale Affect Poverty Rates of Different Households?, 1998; Income, Inequality and Poverty during the Transition from Planned to Market Economy, 1998; Change in the Perception of the Poverty Line during the Times of Depression: Russia, 1993-96, 1999; Poverty and Social Assistance in Transition Countries, 2000; Dividing the Spoils Pensions, Privatization and Reform in Russia's Transition, 2000; Democracy and Income Inequality: An Empirical Analysis, 2001; Decomposing World Income Distribution: Does the World Have a Middle Class?, 2001; Can We Discern the Effect of Globalization on Income Distribution? Evidence from Household Budget Surveys, 2002; Does Liberte-eegalite? A Survey of the Empirical Links between Democracy and Inequality, 2002; When Markets Fail: Social Policy and Economic Reform, 2002; Income Convergence during the Disintegration of the World Economy, 1919-39, 2002; Income and Influence: Social Policy in Emerging Market Economies, 2003; Is Inequality in Africa Really Different?, 2003; Half a World: Regional Inequality in Five Great Federations, 2005; Dataset Racial Tension, 6 vols., 2005; Worlds Apart: Measuring International and Global Inequality, 2005; Does Tariff Liberalization Increase Wage Inequality? Some Empirical Evidence, 2005; Global Income Inequality: What It Is and Why It Matters, 2006; Measuring Ancient Inequality, 2007; Dva lica globalizacije, 2007; The Haves and the Have-Nots, 2011. **Address:** Basic Books, Perseus Books Group, 1094 Flex Dr., Jackson, TN 38301, U.S.A. **Online address:** bmilanovic@worldbank.org

MILBANK, (Alasdair) John. British (born England), b. 1952?. **Genres:** Theology/Religion, Social Sciences, Philosophy. **Career:** University of Virginia, Department of Religious Studies, Frances Ball professor; Lancaster University, teaching fellow; Cambridge University, lecturer in ethics, reader in philosophical theology; University of Nottingham, professor of religion, politics and ethics, 2004-. Writer. **Publications:** Theology and Social Theory: Beyond Secular Reason, 1991, 2nd ed., 2006; The Religious Dimension in the Thought of Giambattista Vico, 1668-1744, 1991, vol. II, 1992; The Word Made Strange: Theology, Language, Culture, 1997; The Mercurial Wood: Sites, Tales, Qualities, 1997; (ed. with C. Pickstock and G. Ward) Radical Orthodoxy: A New Theology, 1999; (with C. Pickstock) Truth in Aquinas, 2001; Being Reconciled: Ontology and Pardon, 2002; (with E. Wyschogood and G. Ward) Theological Perspectives on God and Beauty, 2003; Suspended Middle: Henri de Lubac and the Debate Concerning the Supernatural, 2005; Theology and the Political, 2005; The Legend of Death: Two Poetic Sequences, 2008; The Future of Love: Essays in Political Theology. 2009; (ed. with S. Oliver) Radical Orthodoxy Reader, 2009; (with S. zizek) Monstrosity of Christ: Paradox or Dialectic?, 2009; (with C. Pickstock, S. zizek and C. Davis) Paul's New Moment: Continental Philosophy and the Future of Christian Theology, 2010. **Address:** Department of Theology and Religious Studies, University of Nottingham, University Pk., Nottingham, NT NG7 2RD, England. **Online address:** john.milbank@nottingham.ac.uk

MILES, Barry. British (born England), b. 1943. **Genres:** Literary Criticism And History, Music, Bibliography, Biography. **Career:** Better Books (bookshop), manager, 1965; Indica Books and Gallery, owner and manager, 1966-70; International Times, founder and editor, 1966-70; Zapple Records, label manager, 1969; New Musical Express, journalist, 1976-78; Omnibus Press, editor-in-chief, 1976-78, 1980-83; Time Out (magazine), editor, 1979. **Publications:** A Catalogue of the William S. Burroughs Archive, 1973; (with P. Marchbank) The Illustrated Rock Almanac, 1977; (comp.) The Beatles in Their Own Words, 1978; (comp.) Bob Dylan in His Own Words, 1978; (comp. with J. Maynard) William S. Burroughs: A Bibliography, 1953-1973: Unlocking Inspector Lee's Word Hoard, 1978; Pink Floyd, 1980, 3rd ed., 1994; (comp.) David Bowie in His Own Words, 1980; The Rolling Stones: An Illustrated Discography, 1980; (comp.) John Lennon in His Own Words, 1981, 2nd ed., 1994; Pink Floyd: The Illustrated Discography, 1981; David Bowie: The Black Book, 1981, 2nd ed., 1984; The Pretenders, 1981; The Ramones, 1981; The Jam, 1981; Talking Heads, 1981; (comp.) Mick Jagger in His Own Words, 1982; The Clash, 1983; (ed.) Howl: Original Draft Facsimile, Transcript and Variant Versions, Fully Annotated by Author, With Contemporaneous Correspondence, Account of First Public Reading, Legal Skirmishes, Precursor Texts and Bibliography, 1986; Ginsberg: A Biography, 1989; The Work of William S. Burroughs, 1991; Two Lectures on the Work of Allen Ginsberg, 1993; (ed.) Selected Letters of Allen Ginsberg, in press; (comp.) Zappa in His Own Words, 1992; William Burroughs: El hombre invisible: A Portrait, 1993; Frank Zappa: A Visual Documentary, 1993; Rolling Stones: A Visual Documentary, 1994; Two Essays on the Work of Allen Ginsberg, 1994; (with C. Perry) I Want to Take You Higher: The Psychedelic Era, 1965-69, 1997; Paul McCartney: Many Years from Now, 1997; Jack Kerouac, King of the Beats: A Portrait, 1998; The Beat Hotel: Ginsberg, Burroughs and Corso in Paris, 2000; (ed. with J. Grauerholz) Naked Lunch, 2001; Zappa, 2004; Hippie, 2004; (contrib.) 4973, 2008; Peace: 50 Years of Protest, 2008; British invasion, 2009; London Calling: A Countercultural History of London Since 1945, 2010; Allen Ginsberg, 2010; In the Seventies: Adventures in the Counter-culture, 2011. Contributor to periodicals. **Address:** c/o Andrew Wylie, The Wylie Agency, 250 W 57th St., Ste. 2114, New York, NY 10107, U.S.A.

MILES, Betty. American (born United States), b. 1928. **Genres:** Children's Fiction, Children's Non-fiction, Environmental Sciences/Ecology, Food And Wine, Young Adult Fiction. **Career:** New Lincoln School, secretary, assistant kindergarten teacher, 1950-51; Bank Street College of Education, publications associate, 1958-65; freelance writer, 1965-; instructor in children's language and literature, 1971-; Random House Beginner Books, consultant. **Publications:** A House for Everyone, 1958; What Is the World?, 1958; The Cooking Book, 1959; Having a Friend, 1959; A Day of Summer, 1960; Mr. Turtle's Mystery, 1961; A Day of Winter, 1962; The Feast on Sullivan Street, 1963; (ed.) The Bank Street Readers, 1965; A Day of Autumn, 1967; Joe Finds a Way, 1969; A Day of Spring, 1970; (with J. Blos) Just Think!, 1971; Save the Earth!, 1974, rev. ed as Save the Earth: An Action Handbook for Kids, 1991; The Real Me, 1974; Channeling Children: Sex Stereotyping in Prime Time TV, 1975; Around and Around - Love, 1975; Just the Beginning, 1975; All It Takes Is Practice, 1976; Looking On, 1978; The Trouble with Thirteen, 1979; Maudie and Me and the Dirty Book, 1980; The Secret Life of the Underwear Champ, 1981; I Would If I Could, 1982; Sink or Swim, 1986; Hey! I'm Reading!, 1995; Goldilocks and the Three Bears, 1998; The Sky Is Falling, 1998; The Tortoise and the Hare, 1998; The Three Little Pigs, 1998. **Address:** 94 Sparkill Ave., Tappan, NY 10983, U.S.A.

MILES, Christopher (John). British (born England), b. 1939. **Genres:** Plays/Screenplays. **Career:** Milesian Film Productions, director and screenwriter, 1962-; Royal College of Art, professor of film and television, 1989-93; Georgia Institute of Technology, lecturer; Balliol College, lecturer. **Publications:** (With J.J. Norwich) Love in the Ancient World, 1997. Contributor of articles to books and periodicals. **Address:** c/o Conrad Williams, Blake Friedmann Agency, 122 Arlington Rd., London, GL NW1 7HP, England. **Online address:** conrad@blakefriedmann.co.uk

MILES, Dudley (Robert Alexander). British (born England), b. 1947. **Genres:** Biography, History. **Career:** British Post Office, executive officer, 1970-75; writer, 1976-86; Dudley Miles Company Services Ltd., director, 1989-. **Publications:** Francis Place, 1771-1854: The Life of a Remarkable Radical, 1988. **Address:** Dudley Miles Company Services Ltd., 210D Ballards Ln., London, GL N3 2NA, England. **Online address:** dudley.miles@blueyonder.co.uk

MILES, Jack. Also writes as John Alvin Miles, John Russiano Miles. American (born United States), b. 1942. **Genres:** Theology/Religion, Biography. **Career:** Jesuit seminarian, 1960-70; Loyola University, assistant professor, 1970-74; University of Montana, instructor in religious studies, 1974-75; Scholars Press, assistant director, 1974-75; University of Chicago, postdoctoral fellow, 1975-76; Doubleday & Co., associate editor, editor, 1976-78; University of California Press, editor, executive editor, 1978-85; Los Angeles Times, book editor, 1985-91, Book Prize Program, director, 1985-95; Claremont Graduate University, Humanities Center, director, 1995-97; Atlantic Monthly, contributing editor, 1995-2007; California Institute of Technology, Mellon visiting professor of humanities, 1997-98; J. Paul Getty Trust, senior advisor to the president, 1999-2006; Beliefnet.com, columnist, 2000-; Arts-Journal.com, columnist, 2001-02; Pacific Council on International Policy, senior fellow for religious affairs, 2004-; University of California-Irvine, distinguished professor of English and religious studies, 2007-; University of California-Santa Barbara, regents lecturer. **Publications:** Retroversion and Text Criticism, 1984; God: A Biography, 1995; Christ: A Crisis in the Life of God, 2001; (with P. Fogelman and N. Fujinami) Robert Graham: The Great Bronze Doors for the Cathedral of Our Lady of the Angels, 2002; (ed.) Norton Anthology of World Religions, forthcoming. Contributor to books. **Address:** Department of English, University of California-Irvine, 472 Krieger Hall, PO Box 2650, Irvine, CA 92697, U.S.A. **Online address:** milesj@uci.edu

MILES, John Alvin. *See* **MILES, Jack.**

MILES, John Russiano. *See* **MILES, Jack.**

MILES, Keith. Also writes as Edward Marston, Christopher T. Mountjoy, Kenneth Harper, Martin Inigo, David Garland. British/Welsh (born Wales), b. 1940. **Genres:** Novels, Novellas/Short Stories, Mystery/Crime/Suspense, Children's Fiction, Plays/Screenplays, Theatre, Biography. **Career:** Wulfrun College, lecturer in modern history, 1962-65; Winson Green Prison, drama lecturer, 1962-64; playwright and author, 1965-; Theater Co., founder, 1978; Crime Writers Association, chairman, 1997-98. **Publications:** (With J. Jones) Dragon's Teeth, 1972; Günter Grass (critical study), 1975; The Warrior Kings, 1978; We'll Meet Again, 1981; (with D. Butler) Marco Polo, 1981; The Finest Swordsman in All France, 1983; Breaks, 1983; Russian Masters, 1984; Not for Glory, Not for Gold, 1985; Bullet Hole, 1986; Double Eagle, 1987; Jahangir and the Khan Dynasty (biography), 1988; Green Murder, 1990; Flagstick, 1991; (ed.) The Handbook of Rugby, 1995; Murder in Perspective, 1997; Saint's Rest, 1998; Bermuda Grass, 2002; Honolulu Play-Off, 2004; (as David Garland) Saratoga: A Novel of the American Revolution, 2005; (as David Garland) Valley Forge, 2006. FOR CHILDREN: Skydive, 1987; Seabird, 1987; Bushranger, 1988; Snowstorm, 1988; Frontier, 1988; Iggy, 1988; Melanie, 1988; Tariq, 1989; Bev, 1989; Death Vault, 1990; Fast Wheels, 1990; New Blood, 1995; Flanes, 1995; Fever, 1995; Emergency, 1995; Coma, 1995; Target, 1995; Stress, 1996; X-Ray, 1996; High Rise, 1996. AS CONRAD ALLEN: Murder on the Lusitania, 1999; Murder on the Mauretania, 2000; Murder on the Minnesota, 2002; Murder on the Caronia, 2003; Murder on the Marmora, 2004; Murder on the Salsette, 2005; Murder on the Oceanic, 2006; Murder on the Celtic, 2007. AS MARTIN INIGO: Stone Dead, 1991; Touch Play, 1991. AS EDWARD MARSTON: The Queen's Head, 1988; The Merry Devils, 1989; The Trip to Jerusalem, 1990; The Nine Giants, 1991; The Mad Courtesan, 1992; The Wolves of Savernake, 1993; The Silent Woman, 1994; The Ravens of Blackwater, 1994; The Roaring Boy, 1995; The Dragons of Archenfield, 1995; Lions of the North, 1996; The Laughing Hangman, 1996; The Serpents of Harbledown, 1996; The Fair Maid of Bohemia, 1997; The Stallions of Woodstock, 1997; The Hawks of Delamere, 1998; The Wanton Angel, 1998; The Wildcats of Exeter, 1998; The Foxes of Warwick, 1999; The King's Evil, 1999; The Owls of Gloucester, 1999; The Amorous Nightingale, 2000; The Elephants of Norwich, 2000; The Devil's Apprentice, 2001; The Repentant Rake, 2001; The Bawdy Basket, 2002; The Frost Fair, 2002; The Vagabond Clown, 2003; The Counterfeit Crank, 2004; The Railway Detective, 2004; The Malevolent Comedy, 2005; The Excursion Train, 2005; The Princess of Denmark, 2006; The Parliament House, 2006; The Railway Viaduct, 2006; The Iron Horse, 2007; The Painted Lady, 2007; Murder on the Brighton Express, 2008; Soldier of Fortune, 2008; Drums of War, 2008; Prisons-Five Hundred Years of Life Behind Bars, 2009; The Silver Locomotive Mystery, 2009; Fire and Sword, 2009; Railway to the Grave, 2010; Under Siege, 2010. AS CHRISTOPHER T. MOUNTJOY: Coming of Age, 1984; Queen and Country, 1985; The Honourable Member, 1986. AS KENNETH HARPER: Falling in Love, 1985; Dance with a Stranger 1985; The Deathstone, 1986; Peril under Paris, 1986; Book of Power, 1986; Venice Menace, 1986; The Everglades Oddity, 1987; Panda Power, 1987; The Plunder of the Glow-Worm Grotto, 1987; Dragonfire, 1987; Janine's Genie, 1988; Slimer, Come Home, 1988; Ghosts-R-Us, 1988; Demob, 1993. Contributor to periodicals. **Address:** 11 Quarry View, Ashford, Kent, TN23 5WD, England. **Online address:** milomarston@aol.com

MILES, Leland. American (born United States), b. 1924. **Genres:** Language/Linguistics, Literary Criticism And History, Philosophy, Theology/Religion. **Career:** Hanover College, associate professor of English, 1949-50, professor and chair of department of English, 1950-60; University of Cincinnati, director of English programs, associate professor of English, 1960-63; professor of English, 1963-64; Bridgeport Area Cultural Counci, vice-president, 1964; University of Bridgeport, dean, College of Arts and Sciences, 1964-67, president, 1974-87, president emeritus, 1987-; Alfred University, president, 1967-74; Western New York Nuclear Research Center, trustee, 1967-73, College Center of Finger Lakes, chair, 1968-71; Empire State Foundation, Board of Directors, vice-chair, 1969-71, chair, 1971-73; International Association of University Presidents, president, 1981-84, chief of UN mission, 1988-96, IAUP/UN Commission on Disarmament Education, chairman, 1991-96. Writer. **Publications:** Americans Are People, and Other Assertions, 1956; John Colet and the Platonic Tradition, 1961; Where Do You Stand on Linguistics?, 1964; (ed.) St. Thomas More's Dialogue of Comfort against Tribulation, 1965; Provoking Thought: What Colleges Should Do for Students, 2001. Contributor to books and articles. **Address:** Office of the President, University of Bridgeport, 126 Park Ave., Bridgeport, CT 06604, U.S.A.

MILES, Rosalind. British (born England), b. 1943. **Genres:** Novels, Young Adult Fiction, Young Adult Non-fiction. **Career:** Writer. **Publications:** The Fiction of Sex: Themes and Functions of Sex Difference in the Modern Novel, 1974; The Problem of Measure for Measure: A Historical Investigation, 1976; Danger!: Men at Work, 1983; Modest Proposals; or May I Call You Mine?, 1984; Women and Power, 1985; Bitter Legacy, 1986; Ben Jonson: His Life and Work, 1986; The Female Form: Women Writers and the Conquest of the Novel, 1987; The Womens History of the World, 1989; Ben Jonson: His Craft and Art, 1990; Prodigal Sins, 1991; Rites of Man: Love, Sex, Death, and the Making of the Male, 1991; Act of Passion, 1993; I Elizabeth, 1994; Guenevere: Queen of the Summer Country, 1998; Queen of the Summer Country, 1999; The Child of the Holy Grail, 2000; Knight of the Sacred Lake, 2000; Who Cooked the Last Supper?: The Women's History of the World, 2001; Isolde, Queen of the Western Isle: The First of the Tristan and Isolde Novels, 2002; Isolde Novels, 2003; The Lady of the Sea: The Third of the Tristan and Isolde Novels, 2004; The Maid of the White Hands, 2005; (with R. Cross) Hell Hath No Fury: True Profiles of Women at War from Antiquity to Iraq, 2008; (with R. Cross) Warrior Women: Great War Leaders from Boudicca to Catherine the Great, 2011. **Address:** Crown Publishers, 1745 Broadway, New York, NY 10019, U.S.A. **Online address:** reader@rosalind.net

MILES, Steven H. American (born United States), b. 1950. **Genres:** Medicine/Health, Sciences, Sports/Fitness. **Career:** Hennepin County Medical Center, chief medical resident and internal medicine resident, 1976-81, Division of Geriatric Medicine, staff, 1990-95, chief, 1993-94; University of Minnesota, Department of Internal Medicine, assistant professor, 1982-86, Medical School, associate professor of medicine, 1990-99, professor of medicine, 1999-, Center for Bioethics, professor of medicine, 1990-99, Maas Family endowed chair, Center for Advanced Feminist Studies, affiliate faculty, 1991-99, Graduate School, faculty, 1992-, Center on Aging, faculty, 1994-99, Law

School Concentration in Health Law and Bioethics, affiliate faculty, 2005-, faculty of bioethics, 2008-, Center for Genocide and Holocaust Studies, affiliate faculty, 2008-; University of Chicago, Pritzker School of Medicine, Department of Medicine, assistant professor of medicine and associate director of center for clinical medical ethics, 1986-89; Regions Medical Center, Department of Geriatric Medicine, staff, 1995-99. Writer and consultant. **Publications:** (With C.F. Gomez) Protocols for Elective Use of Life-Sustaining Treatments: A Design Guide, 1989; The Hippocratic Oath and the Ethics of Medicine, 2004; Oath Betrayed: Torture, Medical Complicity, and the War on Terror, 2006, 2nd ed. as Oath Betrayed: America's Torture Doctors, 2009; (contrib.) The Power of Pills: Social, Ethical and Legal Issues in Drug Development, Marketing and Pricing Policies, 2006; (contrib.) One of the Guys, 2007. Contributor to journals. **Address:** Medical School, University of Minnesota, 410 Church St. SE, Ste. N504 Boynton, Minneapolis, MN 55455-0346, U.S.A. **Online address:** miles001@umn.edu

MILES, Tiya. (Tiya Alicia Miles). American (born United States), b. 1970. **Genres:** Social Sciences. **Career:** Dartmouth College, co-ordinator of Shabazz African American Center, 1998-2000; University of California, assistant professor of ethnic studies, 2000-02; University of Michigan, assistant professor of American culture, American Culture, History, Afroamerican and African Studies and Native American Studies, associate professor, 2002-. Writer. **Publications:** Ties That Bind: The Story of an Afro-Cherokee Family in Slavery and Freedom, 2005; (ed. with S.P. Holland) Crossing Waters, Crossing Worlds: The African Diaspora in Indian Country, 2006; House On Diamond Hill: A Cherokee Plantation Story, 2010. Contributor to books and periodicals. **Address:** Center for Afroamerican and African Studies, University of Michigan, 4700 Haven Hall, Ann Arbor, MI 48109-1045, U.S.A. **Online address:** tiya@umich.edu

MILES, Tiya Alicia. *See* **MILES, Tiya.**

MILES, Victoria. Canadian (born Canada), b. 1966?. **Genres:** Children's Fiction. **Career:** Children's author. **Publications:** Sea Otter Pups, 1993; Bald Eaglets, 1993; Spotted Owlets, 1993; Cougar Kittens, 1993; Pup's Supper, 1998; Wild Science: Amazing Encounters between Animals and the People Who Study Them, 2004; City Bat, Country Bat, 2004; Magnifico, 2006; The Chocolatier's Apprentice, 2006; Old Mother Bear, 2007. Contributor to periodicals. **Address:** Curtis Brown Ltd., 10 Astor Pl., New York, NY 10003, U.S.A. **Online address:** victorianunuk@telus.net

MILES, William F. S. American (born United States), b. 1955. **Genres:** Area Studies, Politics/Government, Cultural/Ethnic Topics. **Career:** U.S. State Department, personal services contractor, 1980; Bayero University, research associate, 1983-84; Northeastern University, International Development Concentration, chair, 1984-2003, assistant professor, 1984-91, associate professor, 1991-96, professor of political science, 1996-, Stotsky professor of Jewish historical and cultural studies, 1998-2002; Annamalai University, research associate, 1987-88; University of Mauritius, faculty of social studies and humanities, 1996-97; Brown University, Watson Institute for International Studies, adjunct professor, 2004-09; U.S. Agency for International Development, consultant. Writer. **Publications:** Elections and Ethnicity in French Martinique: A Paradox in Paradise, 1986; Elections in Nigeria: A Grassroots Perspective, 1988; Hausaland Divided: Colonialism and Independence in Nigeria and Niger, 1994; International and Minoritarian Francophonie: Convergence and Contradiction, 1995; Imperial Burdens: Countercolonialism in Former French India, 1995; Bridging Mental Boundaries in a Postcolonial Microcosm: Identity and Development in Vanuatu, 1998; (ed.) Third World Views of the Holocaust: Summary of the International Symposium, 2002; (ed.) Political Islam in West Africa: State-society Relations Transformed, 2007; Zion in the Desert: American Jews in Israel's Reform Kibbutzim, 2007; (with S.B. Miles) My African Horse Problem, 2008. **Address:** Department of Political Science, Northeastern University, 323 Meserve Hall, Boston, MA 02115, U.S.A. **Online address:** b.miles@neu.edu

MILGRAM, Gail Gleason. American (born United States), b. 1942. **Genres:** Education, Bibliography, Reference. **Career:** Teacher, 1963-69; Rutgers University, Douglass College, supervisor, 1970-71, associate professor, 1971-76, director of education and training, 1976-, School of Alcohol and Drug Studies, executive director and professor, now professor emeritus, New Jersey Department of Health, consultant. Writer. **Publications:** (With A.L. Ayars) The Teenager and Alcohol, 1970; The Teenager and Smoking, 1972; The Teenager and Sex, 1974; A Discussion Leader's Guide for Hollywood Squares: Beverage Alcohol Use and Misuse, 1975; Alcohol Education Materials: An Annotated Bibliography, 1975; Your Future in Education, 1976; Alcohol Education Materials, 1973-1978: An Annotated Bibliography, 1980; Coping with Alcohol, 1980; What, When and How to Talk to Children about Alcohol and Other Drugs: A Guide for Parents, 1983; (with T. Griffin) What, When, and How to Talk to Students about Alcohol and Other Drugs: A Guide for Teachers, 1986; Facts about Drinking: Coping with Alcohol Use, Abuse, and Alcoholism, 1990; (with D.S. Anderson) Action Planner, 2000. Contributor to journals. **Address:** Center of Alcohol Studies, Rutgers University, Rm. 211 BAS, 607 Allison Rd., Piscataway, NJ 08854-8001, U.S.A. **Online address:** gmilgram@rci.rutgers.edu

MILHAUPT, Curtis J. American (born United States), b. 1962?. **Genres:** Economics. **Career:** Shearman & Sterling, attorney, 1989-94; Washington University Law School, faculty, 1994-98; Columbia University School of Law, professor of comparative corporate law and Japanese law, 1999-, Center for Japanese Legal Studies, director, vice dean for intellectual life, 2010-; Tsinghua University, visiting professor of law, 2006; Hong Kong University, visiting professor in corporate and financial law, 2007. Writer. **Publications:** (Ed. with J.M. Ramseyer and M.K. Young) Japanese Law in Context: Readings in Society, the Economy, and Politics, 2001; Global Markets, Domestic Institutions: Corporate Law and Governance in a New Era of Cross-Border Deals, 2003; (with M.D. West) Economic Organizations and Corporate Governance in Japan: The Impact of Formal and Informal Rules, 2004; (with J.M. Ramseyer and M.D. West) The Japanese Legal System: Cases, Codes, and Commentary, 2006; (ed. with H. Kanda and K. Kim) Transforming Corporate Governance in East Asia, 2008; (with K. Pistor) Law and Capitalism: What Corporate Crises Reveal about Legal Systems and Economic Development around the World, 2008. Contributor of articles to periodicals. **Address:** New York, NY , U.S.A. **Online address:** milhaupt@law.columbia.edu

MILHORN, Howard Thomas. *See* **MILHORN, H. Thomas.**

MILHORN, H. Thomas. (Howard Thomas Milhorn). American (born United States), b. 1936. **Genres:** Novels, Medicine/Health, Self Help, Writing/Journalism, Sciences. **Career:** Pressure Vessel Manufacturing Co., mechanical drafter, 1956-57; Sandford Process Co., junior engineer, 1958-59; Eastman Kodak Co., mechanical drafter, 1964; National Institutes of Health, fellow, 1964-65; University of Mississippi, School of Medicine, professor of family medicine, professor of physiology and biophysics and associate professor of psychiatry and human behavior, 1964-92, retired, 1992; Mississippi Academy of Family Physicians, board director, 1983-89; Mississippi Baptist Chemical Dependency Center, faculty, 1987-91; Laurel Wood Center, Chemical Dependency Services, medical director, 1992-96; East Mississippi State Hospital, staff physician, 1996-2000. Writer. **Publications:** (As Howard T. Milhorn, Jr.) The Application of Control Theory to Physiological Systems, 1966; Fluid and Electrolyte Balance, 1982; Chemical Dependence: Diagnosis, Treatment, and Prevention, 1990; Drug and Alcohol Abuse: The Authoritative Guide for Parents, Teachers, and Counselors, 1994; Caduceus Awry (novel), 2000; Crime: Computer Viruses to Twin Towers, 2004; Electrocardiography for the Family Physician: The Essentials, 2005; Writing Genre Fiction: A Guide to the Craft, 2006; Cybercrime: How to Avoid Becoming a Victim, 2007; The History of Astronomy and Astrophysics: A Biographical Approach, 2008; History of Physics, 2008. Contributor to journals. **Address:** 1900 45th Ct., Meridian, MS 39305-2700, U.S.A. **Online address:** milhorn1@comcast.net

MILIS, Ludo(vicus) J. R. Belgian (born Belgium), b. 1940. **Genres:** History, Social Commentary, Adult Non-fiction, Essays, Theology/Religion. **Career:** University of Ghent, professor of medieval history, 1974-; Belgian Historical Institute (Rome), president, 1986-2001. Writer. **Publications:** Ordre Des Chanoines Réguliers D'Arrouaise: Son Histoire Et Son Organisation, De La Fondation De L'abbaye-mère (vers 1090) à lafind Des Chapitres Annuels (1471), 1969; (ed.) Constitutiones Canonicorum Regularium Ordinis Arroasiensis, 1970; (ed.) Liber ordinis Sancti Victoris Parisiensis, 1984; (ed.) De Heidense Middeleeuwen, 1991, 2nd ed., 1992; Angelic Monks and Earthly Men: Monasticism and Its Meaning to Medieval Society, 1992, 3rd ed., 2008; De indiscrete charme van Jan Schuermans, pastoor van Ename, 1645-1655, 1994; (co-ed.) Law, History, the Low Countries and Europe, 1994; (ed.) La chretiente del'Antiquite au Moyen-Age, 1998; (ed.) The Pagan Middle Ages, 1998; Religion, Culture and Mentalities in the Medieval Low Countries: Selected Essays, 2005; (ed. with W. Verbeke and J. Goossens) Medieval Narrative Sources: A Gateway Into the Medieval Mind, 2005; Van waarheden en werkelijkheid: de opvattingen van de middeleeuwers in het blikveld van nu,

2011. **Address:** Department of Medieval History, University of Ghent, Blandijnberg 2, Ghent, B-9000, Belgium. **Online address:** ludo.milis@rug.ac.be

MILLAR, Cormac. *See* **O CUILLEANAIN, Cormac.**

MILLARD, Alan Ralph. British (born England), b. 1937. **Genres:** Archaeology/Antiquities, Language/Linguistics, Theology/Religion. **Career:** Tyndale Library for Biblical Research, librarian, 1963-70; Tyndale Bulletin, advisory editor, 1980-; Journal of Semitic Studies, advisory editor, 1991-; Palestine Exploration Quarterly, advisory editor, 1992-; University of Liverpool, Hebrew and Ancient Semitic Languages, Rankin professor, 1992-2003, Rankin emeritus professor 2003-. **Publications:** (With W.G. Lambert) Cuneiform Texts from Babylonian Tablets, vol. XLVI, 1965; (with W.G. Lambert) Catalogue of the Cuneiform Tablets in the Kouyunijk Collection, 1968; (with W.G. Lambert) Atrahasis: The Babylonian Story of the Flood, 1969; The Bible B.C.: What Can Archaeology Prove?, 1977; (with A.A. Assaf and P. Bordreuil) La Statue de Tell Fekherye et son Inscription Bilingue assyro-araméenne, 1983; Treasures from Bible Times, 1985; Discoveries from the Time of Jesus, 1990; The Eponyms of the Assyrian Empire, 910-649 BC, 1994; Discoveries from Bible Times, 1997; Reading and Writing in the Time of Jesus, 1999. EDITOR: The Lion Handbook to the Bible, 1973; The Lion Encyclopaedia of the Bible, 1978; (with D.J. Wiseman) Essays on the Patriarchal Narratives, 1980; (with J.K. Hoffmeier and D.W. Baker) Faith, Tradition and History, 1994; (with P. Bienkowski) British Museum Dictionary of the Ancient Near East, 1999; (with J. K. Hoffmeier) The Future of Biblical Archaeology, 2004. **Address:** School of Archaeology & Oriental Studies, University of Liverpool, 12-14 Abercromby Sq., PO Box 147, Liverpool, L69 7WZ, England. **Online address:** amillard@liverpool.ac.uk

MILLARD, Candice. American (born United States) **Genres:** Travel/Exploration, Westerns/Adventure, History. **Career:** National Geographic magazine, writer and editor. **Publications:** River of Doubt: Theodore Roosevelt's Darkest Journey, 2005; The Destiny of the Republic: A Tale of Medicine, Madness and the Murder of a President, 2011. Contributor to periodicals. **Address:** c/o Author Mail, Doubleday, 1745 Broadway, New York, NY 10019, U.S.A.

MILLEN, R. L. *See* **MILLEN, Rochelle L.**

MILLEN, Rochelle L. (R. L. Millen). American (born United States), b. 1943. **Genres:** Novels. **Career:** McMaster University, Departments of Philosophy and Religion, instructor, 1972-74, 1972-76; Shalom Hartman Institute, resident associate, 1976-77; Pardes Graduate Institute, lecturer, 1977-79; United Hebrew School of Detroit, educational consultant, 1978-83; Yeshiva University High School, faculty Jewish studies, 1983-86; Stern College for Women, adjunct assistant professor of jewish studies, 1985-86; University of Nebraska, assistant professor, 1987-89; Wexner Heritage Foundation, faculty, 1987-89; Wittenberg University, Department of religion, assistant professor, 1988-94, associate professor, 1994-2001, professor, 2001-. Writer. **Publications:** (Co.ed) New Perspectives on the Holocaust: A Guide for Teachers and Scholars, 1996; Women, Birth, and Death in Jewish Law and Practice, 2004; (ed. and intro. with M. Goldenberg) Testimony, Tensions, and Tikkun: Teaching the Holocaust in Colleges and Universities, 2007; Sambor: A Tale of Interwar Poland, forthcoming. **Address:** Department of Religion, Wittenberg University, PO Box 720, Springfield, OH 45501, U.S.A. **Online address:** rmillen@wittenberg.edu

MILLER, Aaron David. American (born United States), b. 1949?. **Genres:** Autobiography/Memoirs, Politics/Government. **Career:** U.S. State Department Bureau of Intelligence and Research, staff; Office of the Historian, staff; U.S. Department of State, advisor, 1978-2003; American Embassy, staff member, 1984; United States Holocaust Memorial Council, staff member, 1998-2000; Seeds of Peace (a nonprofit peace organization), president, 2003-06; Woodrow Wilson International Center for Scholars, public policy fellow, 2006-. Writer, advisor, negotiator and diplomat. **Publications:** Search for Security: Saudi Arabian Oil and American Foreign Policy, 1939-1949, 1980; The PLO and the Politics of Survival, 1983; The Arab States and the Palestine Question: Between Ideology and Self-Interest, 1986; The Pursuit of Arab- Israel Peace: Have We Reached the Point of No Return?, 1998; The Much Too Promised Land: America's Elusive Search for Arab-Israeli Peace (memoir), 2008. Contributor to newspapers and periodicals. **Address:** Scholar Administration Office, Woodrow Wilson Ctr., 1 Woodrow Wilson Plz., 1300 Pennsylvania Ave. NW, Washington, DC 20004-3027, U.S.A. **Online address:** aaron.miller@wilsoncenter.org

MILLER, Abraham (H.). American (born United States), b. 1940. **Genres:** Law, Politics/Government, Sociology. **Career:** University of Michigan, Institute for Social Research, assistant study director, 1964-66; University of Illinois, assistant professor of political science, 1966-68; University of California, assistant professor of sociology, 1968-71; University of Cincinnati, associate professor, 1971-76, professor of political science, 1976, now professor emeritus; National Institute of Justice, visiting fellow, 1976-77; U.S. Department of Justice, visiting fellow, 1976-77; International Studies Association, Intelligence Studies Section, head. Writer. **Publications:** (Ed. with J. McEvoy) Black Power and Student Rebellion, 1969; Information and Change: Requirements for Urban Decision Making, 1970; 1968 Election in Illinois: A Descriptive and Theoretical Analysis, 1971; Terrorism and Hostage Negotiations, 1980; (ed.) Terrorism, the Media, and the Law, 1982. **Address:** Department of Political Science, University of Cincinnati, 7148 Edwards One, PO Box 210375, Cincinnati, OH 45221-0375, U.S.A. **Online address:** abraham.miller@uc.edu

MILLER, Alyce. (Alyce L. Miller). American/Swiss (born Switzerland), b. 1953. **Genres:** Novels, Natural History, Novellas/Short Stories. **Career:** Santa Clara University, adjunct faculty, 1993-94; Ohio University, Athens, visiting assistant professor, 1994-95; Indiana University, associate professor, professor, 1995-. Writer. **Publications:** The Nature of Longing: Stories, 1994; Stopping for Green Lights (novel), 1999; Water: Nine Stories, 2008. Works appear in anthologies. **Address:** Department of English, Indiana University, 442 Ballantine Hall, 1020 E Kirkwood Ave., Bloomington, IN 47405-7103, U.S.A. **Online address:** animallawyer2003@yahoo.com

MILLER, Alyce L. *See* **MILLER, Alyce.**

MILLER, Amie Klempnauer. American (born United States), b. 1965. **Genres:** Autobiography/Memoirs. **Career:** Public Radio Intl., senior development officer, 1997-2003; freelance writer and consultant, 2003-; DEI Foundation, development advisor; Planned Parenthood, staff; Environmental Defense Fund, staff; Minnesota International Center, staff. **Publications:** She Looks Just Like You: A Memoir of (Nonbiological Lesbian) Motherhood, 2010. Works appear in anthologies. Contributor to periodicals. **Address:** St. Paul, MN , U.S.A. **Online address:** amie@amiekmiller.com

MILLER, Anesa. (Anesa Miller-Pogacar). American (born United States), b. 1954. **Genres:** Literary Criticism And History, Poetry, Cultural/Ethnic Topics. **Career:** University of Kansas, instructor in Russian language and literature, 1979-83; Bowling Green State University, assistant professor of Russian, 1986-94; Memorial Foundation for Lost Children, Bowling Green, editor, 1994-. **Publications:** AS ANESA MILLER-POGACAR: (trans. and intro.) After the Future: Paradoxes of Postmodernism and Contemporary Russian Culture, 1995; (ed. with E.E. Berry) Re-Entering the Sign: Articulating New Russian Culture, 1995. OTHER: A Road Beyond Loss: Three Cycles of Poems and an Epilogue, 1995. Contributor to periodicals. **Address:** Memorial Foundation for Lost Children, 708 East Wooster, Bowling Green, OH 43402, U.S.A. **Online address:** jpankse@bgnet.bgsu.edu

MILLER, Arthur R(aphael). American (born United States), b. 1934. **Genres:** Law, Civil Liberties/Human Rights. **Career:** Cleary, Gottlieb, Steen and Hamilton, attorney, 1958-61; Columbia University Law School, instructor and associate director of Project International Procedure, 1961-62; University of Minnesota Law School, associate professor of law, 1962-65; University of Michigan Law School, professor of law, 1965-72; Mental Health Research Institute, research associate, 1966-68; Harvard University Law School, visiting professor, 1971-72, professor of law, 1972-86, Bruce Bromley professor, 1986-; Federal Judicial Center, faculty. Writer. **Publications:** (With H. Smit) International Co-Operation in Civil Litigation: A Report on Practices and Procedures Prevailing in the United States, 1961; (with J.B. Weinstein and H.L. Korn) New York Civil Practice, vol. VIII, 1963; (with J.B. Weinstein and H.L. Korn) CPLR, 1963; Materials on Equitable Remedies, 1966; The Computer and Individual Privacy, 1967; (with J.B. Weinstein and H.L. Korn) Weinstein-Korn-Miller Manual: Civil Practice Law and Review, 1967, 2nd rev. ed., 1980; (with J.J. Cound and J.H. Friedenthal) Pleading, Joinder and Discovery: Cases and Materials, 1968; (with Cound and Friedenthal) Civil Procedure Cases and Materials, 1968; (with J.J. Cound and J.H. Friedenthal) Civil Procedure Supplement: Containing Selected Federal and State Statutes, Rules, Problems, Forms and Recent Decisions, 1968; Personal Privacy in the Computer Age: The Challenge of a New Technology in an Information Age, 1969; The Assault on Privacy: Computers, Data Banks and Dossiers, 1971; (with J.H. Friedenthal) Friedenthal and Miller on Civil Procedure, 1975; Manual for Complex Litigation: With Amendments to June 3, 1977, including Rules of Procedure of the Judicial Panel on Multidistrict Litigation (for use with Federal Practice and Procedure), 1977; An Overview of Federal Class Actions: Past, Present and Future, 1977; Attorneys' Fees in Class Actions: A Report to the Federal Judicial Center, 1980; Miller's Court, 1982; Josephson's Essential Principles of Civil Procedure, 1982; (with Friedenthal) Sum and Substance of Civil Procedure, 1983; (with M.H. Davis) Intellectual Property: Patents, Trademarks and Copyright in a Nutshell, 1983, 4th ed., 2007; The August 1983 Amendments to the Federal Rules of Civil Procedure: Promoting Effective Case Management and Lawyer Responsibility: Revision of Remarks at a Federal Judicial Center Workshop, January 20, 1984, 1984; Software Protection: The U.S. Copyright Office Speaks on the Computer/Copyright Interface, 1984; (with J.H. Friedenthal and M.K. Kane) Civil Procedure, 1985, 4th ed., 2005; (with T.L. Gossman) Business Law, 1990. Contributor to periodicals. **Address:** Harvard University Law School, Areeda Hall, 1545 Massachusetts Ave., Cambridge, MA 02138, U.S.A.

MILLER, Blair. American (born United States), b. 1955. **Genres:** Film, Autobiography/Memoirs, Biography, Humor/Satire. **Career:** Citibank Student Loan Corp., promissory note clerk, 1991-. Writer. **Publications:** American Silent Film Comedies: An Illustrated Encyclopedia of Persons, Studios, and Terminology (nonfiction), 1995. **Address:** Blair Miller & Associates, 1809 Central St., Ste. 2E, Evanston, IL 60201, U.S.A.

MILLER, Brenda. American (born United States), b. 1959?. **Genres:** Essays. **Career:** Western Washington University, assistant professor, associate professor of English; Bellingham Review, editor-in-chief. **Publications:** Season of the Body: Essays, 2002; (with S. Paola) Tell It Slant: Writing and Shaping Creative Nonfiction, 2004; Blessing of the Animals, 2009. Listening Against the Stone: Selected Essays, 2011. Works appear in anthologies. Contributor to periodicals. **Address:** Department of English, Western Washington University, Humanities 303, 516 High St., PO Box 9055, Bellingham, WA 98225, U.S.A. **Online address:** brenda.miller@wwu.edu

MILLER, Charles A. American (born United States), b. 1937. **Genres:** Intellectual History, Essays, Adult Non-fiction, Politics/Government. **Career:** Clark College, Department of Social Science, assistant professor, 1967-70; Princeton University, Department of Politics, assistant professor, 1970-74; Lake Forest College, Department of Politics and American Studies, associate professor, 1974-85, professor, 1985-98, professor emeritus, 1998-. Writer. **Publications:** The Supreme Court and the Uses of History, 1969; (comp. with W.L. Howarth) Nature in American Life: A Preliminary Bibliographical Guide; With Supplement, 1971 and 1972, 1972; A Catawba Assembly, 1973; The Official and Political Manual of the State of Tennessee, 1974; (comp.) Isn't that Lewis Carroll?: A Guide to the Most Mimsy Words and Frabjous Quotations of Lewis Carroll's Alice's Adventures in Wonderland, Through the Looking-Glass, and The Hunting of the Snark, 1984; Jefferson and Nature: An Interpretation, 1988; Ship of State: The Nautical Metaphors of Thomas Jefferson, with Numerous Examples by Other Writers from Classical Antiquity to the Present, 2003; (ed., intro. and contrib.) Homer's Sun Still Shines: Ancient Greece In Essays, Poems and Translations, 2004. **Address:** Department of Politics, Lake Forest College, 555 N Sheridan Rd., Lake Forest, IL 60045-2338, U.S.A.

MILLER, Christian. *See* **BOWMAN, Christian.**

MILLER, Christopher. American (born United States), b. 1961. **Genres:** Novels. **Career:** Bennington College, instructor, 2002-. Writer. **Publications:** Simon Silber: Works for Solo Piano, 2002; Sudden Noises from Inanimate Objects: A Novel in Liner Notes, 2004; Cardboard Universe: A Guide to the World of Phoebus K. Dank, 2009; Eat, forthcoming. Contributor to periodicals. **Address:** Bennington College, 1 College Dr., Bennington, VT 05201-6003, U.S.A. **Online address:** cmiller@bennington.edu

MILLER, Daniel. British (born England), b. 1954. **Genres:** Anthropology/Ethnology, Communications/Media. **Career:** University College London, lecturer, 1981-90, reader, 1990-95, professor, 1995-. Writer. **Publications:** (Ed. with C. Tilley) Ideology, Power and Prehistory, 1984; Artefacts as Categories: A Study of Ceramic Variability in Central India, 1985; Material Culture and Mass Consumption, 1987; (ed. with M. Rowlands and C. Tilley) Domination and Resistance, 1989; (ed.) Unwrapping Christmas, 1993; Modernity: An Ethnographic Approach: Dualism and Mass Consumption in Trinidad, 1994; Acknowledging Consumption: A Review of New Studies, 1995; (ed.) Worlds Apart: Modernity through the Prism of the Local, 1995; Capitalism: An Ethnographic Approach, 1997; A Theory of Shopping, 1998; (ed.) Material Cultures: Why Some Things Matter, 1998; (ed. with J.G. Carrier) Virtualism: A New Political Economy, 1998; (with P. Jackson and M. Rowlands) Shopping, Place and Identity, 1998; (ed. with P. Jackson, M. Lowe and F. Mort) Commercial Cultures: Economies, Practices, Spaces, 2000; (with D. Slater) The Internet: An Ethnographic Approach, 2001; The Dialectics of Shopping, 2001; (ed.) Car Cultures, 2001; Consumption: Critical Concepts in the Social Sciences, 2001; Home Possessions: Material Culture behind Closed Doors, 2001; (with M. Banerjee) The Sari, 2003; (ed. with S. Kuchler) Clothing as Material Culture, 2005; (ed.) Materiality, 2005; (with H. Horst) The Cell Phone: An Anthropology of Communication, 2006; The Comfort of Things, 2008. Contributor of articles to journals. **Address:** University College London, Gower St., London, GL WC1E 6BT, England. **Online address:** d.miller@ucl.ac.uk

MILLER, David C. American (born United States), b. 1951. **Genres:** Literary Criticism And History. **Career:** Brown University, teaching assistant, 1977-79; Bennington College, instructor in literature and languages, 1981-82; Harvard University, tutor in history and literature, 1982-84; Reed College, assistant professor of English, 1984-85; Allegheny College, Department of English, assistant professor, 1985-86, associate professor of English, 1986-2005, professor of English, chair, 2006-09; Stanford University, Department of English, Mellon postdoctoral fellow, 1986-88. Writer. **Publications:** Dark Eden: The Swamp in Nineteenth-Century American Culture, 1989; (ed.) American Iconology: New Approaches to Nineteenth-Century Art and Literature, 1993. Contributor of articles to journals. **Address:** Department of English, Allegheny College, Rm. 209 OddFellows, 520 N Main St., PO Box 95, Meadville, PA 16335, U.S.A. **Online address:** dmiller@allegheny.edu

MILLER, David (Leslie). British (born England), b. 1946. **Genres:** Politics/Government, Social Commentary, Adult Non-fiction, Essays. **Career:** University of Lancaster, lecturer in politics, 1969-76; University of Ibadan, visiting lecturer in political science, 1976; University of East Anglia, School of Social Studies, lecturer in politics, 1976-79; Oxford University, Nuffield College, senior tutor, 1980-86, 1990-91, official fellow in social and political theory, 1979-, junior proctor, 1988-89, Politics Group, chairman, 1991-93, 1999-2001, department of politics, director of graduate studies, 2001, 2006-08, professor of political theory, 2002-; University of Melbourne, visiting fellow in political science, 1986; Uppsala University, department of government, visiting fellow, 1994. Writer. **Publications:** Social Justice, 1976, 2nd ed., 1979; Philosophy and Ideology in Hume's Political Thought, 1981; Anarchism, 1984; Market, State and Community: Theoretical Foundations of Market Socialism, 1989; On Nationality, 1995; Principles of Social Justice, 1999; Citizenship and National Identity, 2000; Political Philosophy: A Very Short Introduction, 2003; National Responsibility and Global Justice, 2007. EDITOR: (with L. Siedentop) The Nature of Political Theory, 1984; (co-ed.) The Blackwell Encyclopaedia of Political Thought, 1987; Liberty 1991; (with M. Walzer) Pluralism, Justice and Equality, 1995; Politikai filozófiák enciklopédiája, 1995; (with S.H. Hashmi) Boundaries and Justice: Diverse Ethical Perspectives, 2001; (intro.) Liberty Reader, 2006; (intro.) Thinking Politically: Essays in Political Theory, 2007. **Address:** Politics Group, Nuffield College, Oxford University, 1 New Rd., Oxford, OX OX1 1NF, England. **Online address:** david.miller@nuf.ox.ac.uk

MILLER, David W. American (born United States), b. 1957. **Genres:** Novels. **Career:** International Business Machines (IBM), marketing representative, 1979-82, advisory regional marketing representative, 1983-84, marketing manager, large accounts, 1985-86, regional marketing manager, 1987; State Street Bank and Trust Co., managing director; State Street London Ltd., 1987-89; HSBC Holdings (formerly Midland Bank, PLC), head of client relations and trust services, Midland Securities Services (MSS), 1989-90, director, MSS, 1991-92; Peter Wostke and Partners, LP, London, partner, investment banking, corporate finance and investment management, 1993-95; Avodah Institute, co-founder, 1999, president; Yale Divinity School and Yale Business School, Yale Center for Faith and Culture, executive director, adjunct professor of business ethics, 2003-; Princeton University, director of faith and work initiative, lecturer; HSBC Group, Securities Services and Global Custody Division, senior executive and director. Consultant, Presbyterian minister; writer. **Publications:** God at Work: The History and Promise of the Faith at Work Movement, 2007. Contributor to periodicals. **Address:**

The Avodah Institute, 240 Greenwood Dr., Key Biscayne, FL 33149, U.S.A. **Online address:** david.w.miller@yale.edu

MILLER, Deborah. Australian (born Australia), b. 1957?. **Genres:** Novels, Science Fiction/Fantasy, Poetry. **Career:** Foreign correspondent in Israel, 1981-91. Writer. **Publications:** (Ed.) Expanding the Boundaries: Continuing Education in the Community Mental Health System, 1980; The Company of Words (fiction), 1998; (ed.) Sacred Fire: Torah From the Years of Fury 1939-42, 2000; The Maisonettes, 2004. **Address:** Papyrus Publishing, PO Box 7144, Upper Ferntree Gully, VI 3156, Australia.

MILLER, Donald L. American (born United States), b. 1944?. **Genres:** History, Biography, Autobiography/Memoirs, Military/Defense/Arms Control. **Career:** Lafayette College, John Henry McCracken professor of history; Public Broadcasting Service, A Biography of America, host; documentary film maker. Writer. **Publications:** The New American Radicalism: Alfred M. Bingham and Non-Marxian Insurgency in the New Deal Era, 1979; (with R.E. Sharpless) The Kingdom of Coal: Work, Enterprise, and Ethnic Communities in the Mine Fields, 1985; (ed.) The Lewis Mumford Reader, 1986; Lewis Mumford: A Life, 1989; City of the Century: The Epic of Chicago and the Making of America, 1996; The Story of World War II, 2001; D-Days in the Pacific, 2005; Masters of the Air: America's Bomber Boys Who Fought the Air War Against Nazi Germany, 2006. Contributor to newspapers and periodicals. **Address:** Lafayette College, 302 Ramer History House, Easton, PA 18042, U.S.A. **Online address:** millerd@lafayette.edu

MILLER, Donalyn. American (born United States), b. 1967. **Genres:** Young Adult Non-fiction, Reference. **Career:** North Star of Texas, Writing Project, consultant. Writer. **Publications:** The Book Whisperer: Awakening the Inner Reader in Every Child, 2009. **Address:** TX , U.S.A. **Online address:** thebookwhisperer@gmail.com

MILLER, Donna P. American (born United States), b. 1948. **Genres:** Librarianship, Language/Linguistics, Art/Art History. **Career:** Educator, 1971-; Mesa County Valley School District 51, library media co-ordinator, 1998-2001, 2004-07; Linworth Publishing Inc., editor, 2001-04. **Publications:** (With J. Anderson) Developing an Integrated Library Program, 1996; (with K. Larsen) Day by Day: Professional Journaling for Library Media Specialists, 2003; The Standards-Based Integrated Library: A Collaborative Approach for Aligning the Library Program with the Classroom Curriculum, 2004; Crash Course in Teen Services, 2008; Great Day for a Dog!, forthcoming. Contributor to periodicals. **Address:** Mesa County Valley School District 51, 123 W Orchard Ave., Grand Junction, CO 81505, U.S.A. **Online address:** donnapmiller@yahoo.com

MILLER, Douglas T. American (born United States), b. 1937. **Genres:** History, Biography, Civil Liberties/Human Rights. **Career:** University of Maine, instructor, 1963-65, assistant professor of history, 1965-66; Michigan State University, assistant professor, 1966-68, associate professor, 1968-75, professor of history, 1975-97, now distinguished professor emeritus; University of Amsterdam, John Adams chair in American civilization, 1987-88. Writer. **Publications:** Jacksonian Aristocracy: Class and Democracy in New York, 1830-1860, 1967; The Birth of Modern America, 1820-1850, 1970; (ed.) The Nature of Jacksonian America, 1972; Then Was the Future: The North in the Age of Jackson, 1815-1850, 1973; (with M. Nowak) The Fifties: A Social and Cultural History, 1976; (with M. Nowak) The Fifties: The Way We Really Were, 1977; Visions of America: Second World War to the Present, 1988; Frederick Douglass And the Fight for Freedom, 1988; Henry David Thoreau: A Man for All Seasons, 1991; On Our Own: Americans in the Sixties, 1996; Thomas Jefferson and the Creation of America, 1997. **Address:** Department of History, Michigan State University, 410 Abbot Rd., East Lansing, MI 48824, U.S.A. **Online address:** millerdo@adelphia.net

MILLER, Edward A. American (born United States), b. 1927?. **Genres:** History, Biography, Young Adult Non-fiction, Autobiography/Memoirs. **Career:** Henningson, Durham & Richardson, director of operation, vice-president and national program director; Amperif Corp., divisional vice-president and general manager. Writer. **Publications:** Gullah Statesman: Robert Smalls from Slavery to Congress, 1839-1915, 1995; Lincoln's Abolitionist General: The Biography of David Hunter, 1997; The Black Civil War Soldiers of Illinois: The Story of the Twenty-ninth U.S. Colored Infantry, 1998. Contributor to journals. **Address:** 304 Aspen Pl., Alexandria, VA 22305, U.S.A. **Online address:** eamiller1@earthlink.net

MILLER, E. Ethelbert. American (born United States), b. 1950. **Genres:** Poetry, Literary Criticism And History, Autobiography/Memoirs. **Career:** Howard University, Afro-American Studies Resource Center, director, 1974-; Bennington College, Writing Seminars, member of the core faculty; Ascension Poetry Reading Series, founder and organizer, 1974-2000; Harpeth Hall School, Carell writer-in-residence; University of Nevada, visiting professor of English, 1993; Institute for Policy Studies, chair; Poet Lore Magazine, co-editor; Provisions Learning Library, board chair; The Humanities Council of Washington, DC, chair; American University, adjunct professor; Emory & Henry College, faculty; Saint Louis University, African American Review, advisory editor; WDCU-FM, host; WPFW, host. **Publications:** (With A. Khalil) Interface, 1972; Andromeda (poetry), 1974; The Land of Smiles and the Land of No Smiles (poetry), 1974; The Migrant Worker, 1978; Season of Hunger, Cry of Rain: Poems, 1975-1980, 1982; Where Are the Love Poems for Dictators?, 1986, 2nd ed., 2001; First Light, 1994; Whispers, Secrets and Promises, 1998; Fathering Words: The Making of an African American Writer, 2000; How We Sleep on the Nights We Don't Make Love, 2004; The 5th Inning, 2009. EDITOR: (with A. Zu-Bolton II) Synergy D.C. Anthology, 1975; Women Surviving Massacres and Men, 1977; In Search of Color Everywhere, 1994; Beyond the Frontier, 2002. Contributor to books and periodicals. **Address:** Afro-American Studies Resource Center, Howard University, MSC 590 514, 2400 6th St. NW, Washington, DC 20059, U.S.A. **Online address:** emiller698@aol.com

MILLER, Elmer S(chaffner). American (born United States), b. 1931. **Genres:** Anthropology/Ethnology, Sociology, Social Sciences. **Career:** Mennonite Board of Missions, missionary, 1958-63; Temple University, instructor, 1966-67, assistant professor, 1967-71, department head, 1970-77, 1981-82, associate professor, 1971-80, professor of anthropology, 1980-96, director of University Abroad, 1982-85, College of Arts and Sciences, associate dean, 1986-89, Institute for Languages and International Studies, acting director, 1988, professor emeritus of anthropology, 1996-; Universidade de Brasilia, visiting professor, 1975; Goddard College, field faculty, 1975-. Writer. **Publications:** Introduction to Cultural Anthropology, 1979; (with C.A. Weitz) Introduction to Anthropology, 1979; Los tobas argentinos: Armonia y disonancia en una sociedad, 1979, trans. as Harmony and Dissonance in Argentine Toba Society, 1980; A Critically Annotated Bibliography of the Gran Chaco Toba, 2 vols., 1980; Nurturing Doubt: From Mennonite Missionary to Anthropologist in the Argentine Chaco, 1995; (ed. and contrib.) Peoples of the Gran Chaco, 1999. Contributor to books and journals. **Address:** Department of Anthropology, Temple University, Gladfelter Hall, 2nd Fl., 1115 W Berks St., Philadelphia, PA 19122, U.S.A. **Online address:** esmiller@temple.edu

MILLER, Geoffrey F. American (born United States), b. 1965?. **Genres:** Psychology, Sciences, Business/Trade/Industry. **Career:** University of Nottingham, psychology department, lecturer, 1995; Max Planck Institute for Psychological Research, Center for Adaptive Behavior and Cognition, research scientist, 1995-96; University College London, Centre for Economic Learning and Social Evolution, senior research fellow, 1996-2000; London School of Economics, Centre for the Philosophy of the Natural and Social Sciences, research associate, 2001; University of New Mexico, psychology department, assistant professor, 2001-08, associate professor, 2008-. **Publications:** (Ed. with C.T.H. Baker) Treatment of Integral Equations by Numerical Methods, 1997; The Mating Mind: How Sexual Choice Shaped the Evolution of Human Nature, 2000; Mating Intelligence: Sex, Relationships and the Mind's Reproductive System, 2008; Spent: Sex, Evolution and Consumer Behavior, 2009; All-consuming Instincts: Why We Buy Fake Cues of Evolutionary Success, forthcoming. **Address:** Department of Psychology, University of New Mexico, 160 Logan Hall, MSC03 2220, Gower St., Albuquerque, NM 87131-1161, U.S.A. **Online address:** gfmiller@unm.edu

MILLER, Glenn T(homas). American (born United States), b. 1942. **Genres:** History. **Career:** Union Seminary, instructor of philosophy of religion, 1971-72; St. Mary's Seminary, assistant professor of theology, 1972-74, assistant professor of history of Christianity, 1972-; Hamilton College, visiting assistant professor of religion, 1974-76; Southeastern Baptist Theological Seminary, professor, 1976-91; Bangor Theological Seminary, professor, 1992-, director, dean, 1992-96, Waldo professor of ecclesiastical history, 1994-. Writer. **Publications:** Religious Liberty in America: History and Prospects, 1976; Piety and Intellect: The Aims and Purpose of Ante-Bellum Theological Education, 1990; The Modern Church: From the Dawn of the

Reformation to the Eve of the Third Millennium, 1997; Piety and Profession: American Protestant Theological Education, 1870-1970, 2007. Contributor to books and periodicals. **Address:** Bangor Theological Seminary, Peabody Hall, 300 Union St., 2 College Cir., PO Box 411, Bangor, ME 04402-0411, U.S.A. **Online address:** gmiller@bts.edu

MILLER, Glenn (W.). Australian (born Australia), b. 1956. **Genres:** Novels, E-books, Horror, Young Adult Fiction. **Career:** Novelist. **Publications:** Cry the Night, 2002; Kiss to Kill, forthcoming. **Address:** Atlantic Bridge Publishing, N Crittenden Ave., Indianapolis, IN 46220, U.S.A. **Online address:** glennmiller@dodo.com.au

MILLER, James Edward. American (born United States), b. 1945. **Genres:** History, Politics/Government. **Career:** National Archives, specialist in contemporary affairs records, 1973-80; U.S. Department of State, historian specializing in southern Europe, 1980-, Bureau of Intelligence and Research, country analyst, 1983; Georgetown University, Master of Science in Foreign Service, adjunct professor; Foreign Service Institute, U.S. Diplomatic History and Foreign Service, instructor, 1985-, Western European Studies, chair; University of Sassari, visiting professor, 1989; University of Cagliari, visiting professor, 1991. Writer. **Publications:** (With D. Ellwood) Guide to American Documentation of the European Resistance Movement in World War II, 1975; Italian Foreign Policy: The Regional Politics of an Intermediate State, 1985; The United States and Italy, 1940-1950: The Politics and Diplomacy of Stabilization, 1986; (ed. with J. Tropea and C. Beattie-Repetti) Support and Struggle: Italians and Italian-Americans in a Comparative Perspective, 1986; From Elite to Mass Politics: Italian Socialism in the Giolittian Era, 1900-1914, 1990; The Baseball Business: Pursuing Pennants and Profits in Baltimore, 1990; La Politica Estura di una Media Potinza, 1993; Politics in a Museum: Governing Postwar Florence, 2002; Democracy in Education, Education for Democracy: An Oral History of the American Federation of Teachers Local 1931, 2006; The United States and the Making of Modern Greece: History and Power, 1950-1974, 2009. **Address:** U.S. Department of State, Bureau of Public Affairs, 2201 C St. NW, Washington, DC 20520, U.S.A. **Online address:** millerje@georgetown.edu

MILLER, James M. American (born United States), b. 1933. **Genres:** Chemistry. **Career:** Drew University, assistant professor of chemistry, 1959-64, associate professor of chemistry, 1964-69, professor of chemistry, 1969-95, chairman of the department, 1971-83, 1988-91, 1994-95, professor emeritus, 1995-. Writer. **Publications:** Separation Methods in Chemical Analysis, 1975; Chromatography: Concepts and Contrasts, 1988, 2nd ed., 2005; (with H.M. McNair) Basic Gas Chromatography, 1998, 2nd ed., 2009; (ed. and contrib.) Chemical Analysis in a GMP Environment, 2000. **Address:** Department of Chemistry, Drew University, 36 Madison Ave., Madison, NJ 07940, U.S.A. **Online address:** jmiller@drew.edu

MILLER, Jane. American (born United States), b. 1949. **Genres:** Novels, Essays, Novellas/Short Stories, Young Adult Fiction, Poetry. **Career:** University of Arizona, professor of English, instructor in creative writing. Writer. **Publications:** Many Junipers, Heartbeats, 1980; The Greater Leisures, 1983; (with O. Broumas) Black Holes, Black Stockings, 1985; American Odalisque, 1987; Working Time: Essays on Poetry, Culture and Travel, 1992; August Zero, 1993; Memory at These Speeds: New and Selected Poems, 1996; Wherever You Lay Your Head, 1999; A Palace of Pearls, 2005; Midnights, 2008. **Address:** Department of English, University of Arizona, Rm. 445, Modern Languages Bldg., 1423 E University Blvd., PO Box 210067, Tucson, AZ 85721, U.S.A. **Online address:** houston@email.arizona.edu

MILLER, Jeffrey. Canadian (born Canada), b. 1950?. **Genres:** Mystery/Crime/Suspense, Novels. **Career:** Lawyers Weekly, columnist, 1983. **Publications:** (comp.) Street Talk: The Language of Coronation Street, 1986; Naked Promises: A Chronicle of Everyday Wheeling & Dealing, 1989; The Law of Contempt in Canada, 1997; Ardor in the Court! Sex and the Law, 2002; Where There's Life, There's Lawsuits: Not Altogether Serious Ruminations on Law and Life, 2003; (trans.) The Psychology of Criminal Investigation: The Search for the Truth, 2008; AMICUS CURIOUS MYSTERY SERIES: Murder at Osgoode Hall, 2004; Murder's Out of Tune, 2005; Murder on the Rebound, 2007. **Address:** Anne McDermid & Associates Ltd., 83 Willcocks St., Toronto, ON M5S 1C9, Canada.

MILLER, Jeffrey G. American (born United States), b. 1941. **Genres:** Business/Trade/Industry, Law. **Career:** Harvard University, Law School, research associate, 1967-68, business faculty, 1973-81; United States Environmental Protection Agency, Enforcement Branch, chief, 1971-73, Enforcement Division, director, 1973-75, deputy assistant administrator for water enforcement, 1975-79, acting assistant administrator for enforcement, 1979-81, Water Pollution Permitting and Enforcement Program, head; Boston University, professor of operations management, 1981-, Manufacturing Roundtable, founder, director of roundtable, 1989, director of manufacturing futures project, 1981-; Pace University, Law School, professor of law, 1987-, James D. Hopkins chair in law, 1991-2001, associate dean for graduate studies, 2000-02, associate dean for environmental law programs, 2002-03, vice dean for academic affairs, 2006-. Writer. **Publications:** Operations Management: Texts and Cases, 1974; Production Inventory Systems, 1979; Citizen Suits: Private Enforcement of Federal Pollution Control Laws, 1987; (with T.R. Colosi) Fundamentals of Negotiation: A Guide for Environmental Professionals, 1989; (with J. Nakane and A. De Meyer) Benchmarking Global Manufacturing, 1992; (ed. with J.A. Klein) The American Edge: Leveraging the Nation's Unique Core Competencies, 1993; Crime Victims Compensation: The Impact of the Community Protection Act, 1994; (with C.N. Johnston) Law of Hazardous Waste Disposal and Remediation: Cases, Legislation, Regulations, Policies, 1996, 2nd ed., 2005; (with A. Powers and N.L. Elder) Introduction to Environmental Law: Cases and Materials On Water Pollution Control, 2008. Contributor to journals. **Address:** Law School, Pace University, Rm. P211, 78 N Broadway, White Plains, NY 10603, U.S.A. **Online address:** jmiller@law.pace.edu

MILLER, Jim. American (born United States), b. 1965?. **Genres:** History. **Career:** San Diego City College, professor of English and Labor Studies, political action vice president, San Diego City College Literary Center, founding director, 2006-08, San Diego City College International Book Fair, founding director, 2006-08; San Diego City Works Press, co-founder. Writer. **Publications:** (With K. Mayhew and M. Davis) Under the Perfect Sun: The San Diego Tourists Never See, 2003; (ed.) Sunshine/Noir: Writing from San Diego and Tijuana, 2005; (with K. Mayhew) Better to Reign in Hell: Inside the Raiders Fan Empire, 2005; Democracy in Education; Education for Democracy: An Oral History of the American Federation of Teachers, Local 1931, 1969-2006, 2006; Drift (novel), 2007; Flash, 2010. **Address:** San Diego City College, Rm. C207, 1313 Park Blvd., San Diego, CA 92101, U.S.A. **Online address:** miller229@earthlink.net

MILLER, John. British (born England), b. 1937?. **Genres:** Biography, Autobiography/Memoirs, Art/Art History. **Career:** British Broadcasting Corporation (BBC), writer and producer, 1962-81; UNESCO, producer, 1971-72; TVS Television, producer, 1981-92. **Publications:** (With J. Powell and J. Gielgud) An Actor and His Time, 1979; Gielgud: An Actor and His Time, 1980; (with S. Waddell) Roots of England, 1980; An Englishman's Home: Goodwood House, Broadlands, Arundel Castle, Breamore House, Stratfield Saye, Penshurst Place, Wilton House, Uppark, Sutton Place, Chartwell, 1985; Broadcasting: Getting in and Getting On, 1990; (with J. Gielgud) Shakespeare: Hit or Miss?, 1991; (with J. Gielgud) Acting Shakespeare, 1992; Ralph Richardson: The Authorized Biography, 1995; (with J.D. Young) London Theatre Walks: Thirteen Dramatic Tours through Four Centuries of History and Legend, 1998, 2nd ed., 2003; Judi Dench: With a Crack in Her Voice, 2000; Up in the Clouds Gentlemen Please, 2001; Peter Ustinov: The Gift of Laughter, 2003. Contributor to periodicals. **Address:** Orion House, 5 Upper St., Martin's Ln., London, GL WC2H 9EA, England.

MILLER, J(ohn) D(onald) Bruce. *See* Obituaries.

MILLER, John G. American (born United States), b. 1958?. **Genres:** Psychology, Business/Trade/Industry, Economics, Reference. **Career:** Cargill Inc., staff, 1986-; QBQ Inc., founder, chief executive officer. Writer. **Publications:** QBQ!: The Question behind the Question, 2001 as QBQ!: The Question behind the Question: Practicing Personal Accountability in Work and in Life, 2004; Flipping the Switch: Unleash the Power of Personal Accountability Using the QBQ!, 2006; Outstanding!: 47 Ways to Make your Organization Exceptional, 2010. Contributor to periodicals. **Address:** QBQ Inc., 11368 Nucla St., Denver, CO 80022, U.S.A. **Online address:** john@qbq.com

MILLER, Jonathan (Wolfe). British (born England), b. 1934. **Genres:** Medicine/Health, Biography, Theatre, Plays/Screenplays, Art/Art History, Photography. **Career:** Maggio Musicale, staff; La Scala, staff; Metropolitan Opera, staff; Deutsche Staatsoper, staff; Bayerische Staatsopera, staff; Vienna Staatsoper, staff; Royal Opera House, staff; University of Sussex, research fellow in neuropsychology; University College, research fellow in history of medicine, 1970-73; National Theatre, associate director, 1973-75; BBC Shakespeare Series, executive producer, 1979-80; Maggio Musicale, director, 1986-; Old Vic Theatre, artistic director, 1988-90; English National Opera, staff, 2009-. Author and television producer. **Publications:** (Co-author) Beyond the Fringe (revue), 1961; Benito Cereno, 1964; Old Glory, 1964; My Kinsman, Major Molineux, 1964; Prometheus Bound, 1967; Harvey and the Circulation of the Blood, 1968; Hamlet, 1970; Marshall McLuhan in UK as McLuhan, 1971; Julius Caesar, 1971; (ed.) Freud: The Man, His World, His Influence, 1972; Richard II, 1972; Shakespeare & Co., 1974; Pygmalion, 1974; The Body in Question (for TV), 1978; Darwin for Beginners, 1982; (with B. van Loon) Charles Darwin, 1982; States of Mind, 1983; The Human Body, 1983; (with D. Pelham) The Facts of Life: Three-Dimensional, Movable Illustrations Show the Development of a Baby from Conception to Birth, 1984; Subsequent Performances, 1986; (ed. with J. Durant) Laughing Matters: A Serious Look at Humour, 1988; (ed.) Don Giovanni: Myths of Seduction and Betrayal, 1990; Afterlife of Plays, 1992; On Reflection, 1998; Nowhere in Particular, 1999. **Address:** IMG Artists, Media House, 3 Burlington Ln., London, GL W4 2TH, England.

MILLER, Judith. (Judith P. Miller). American (born United States), b. 1948. **Genres:** International Relations/Current Affairs, History. **Career:** Freelance journalist, 1976; The New York Times, reporter, editor and correspondent, 1977-2005, bureau chief, 1983-87, Paris correspondent, 1986, Washington bureau news editor and deputy bureau chief, 1987-88, Securities and Exchange Commission, reporter, bureau chief, 1983, Sunday Magazine, special correspondent, Washington bureau chief; Manhattan Institute for Policy Research, adjunct fellow, 2007; City Journal, contributing editor, 2008; Fox News, staff, commentator, 2008-; The Wall Street Journal, contributor; The Progressive, correspondent; National Public Radio, correspondent; Newsmax, contributing writer. **Publications:** (With L. Mylroie) Saddam Hussein and the Crisis in the Gulf, 1990; One, by One, by One: Facing the Holocaust, 1990; (with L. Mylroie) Saddam Hussein and the Crisis in the Gulf, 1990; God Has Ninety-Nine Names, 1996; (with S. Engelberg and W. Broad) Germs: Biological Weapons and America's Secret War, 2001; (intro.) Silent Places: Landscapes of Jewish Life and Loss in Eastern Europe, 2003. Contributor to journals. **Address:** Fox News Channel, 1211 Ave. of the Americas, New York, NY 10036, U.S.A.

MILLER, Judith P. *See* **MILLER, Judith.**

MILLER, Karl (Fergus Connor). British/Scottish (born Scotland), b. 1931. **Genres:** Marine Sciences/Oceanography, Biography. **Career:** Royal Treasury, assistant principal, 1956-57; British Broadcasting Corp. (BBC-TV), television producer, 1957-58; The Spectator, literary editor, 1958-61; New Statesman, literary editor, 1961-67; University College London, Lord Northcliffe professor of modern English literature and head of the department of English language and literature, 1974-92, professor emeritus, 1992-; London Review of Books, founder and editor, 1979-89, co-editor, 1989-92; Times Higher Education, honorary fellow. **Publications:** Writing in England Today: The Last Fifteen Years, 1968; Memoirs of a Modern Scotland, 1970; A Listener Anthology: August 1967-June 1970, 1970; A Second Listener Anthology, 1973; Cockburn's Millennium (biography), 1975; (and intro.) London Review of Books: Anthology One, 1981; Landscape Poets: Robert Burns, 1981; Doubles: Studies in Literary History, 1985; Authors, 1989; Rebecca's Vest: A Memoir, 1993; (ed. and intro.) Three Hostages, 1995; (ed. and intro.) Weir of Hermiston, 1996; Dark Horses (memoir): An Experience of Literary Journalism, 1998; Electric Shepherd: A Likeness of James Hogg, 2003; Tretower to Clyro: Essays, 2011. Contributor to journals and periodicals. **Address:** Department of English Language and Literature, University College London, Gower St., London, GL WC1E 6BT, England.

MILLER, K(eith) Bruce. American (born United States), b. 1927. **Genres:** Philosophy. **Career:** Los Angeles Music and Art School, teacher of violin, 1955-60; University of Southern California, American Baptist campus chaplain, 1958-76, part-time instructor, 1959-62, part-time lecturer in philosophy, 1964-71; Yale University, post-doctoral research fellow, 1970-71; Luther Rice College, president, 1976-78; Averett College, professor of philosophy, 1986, now retired. Writer. **Publications:** Ideology and Moral Philosophy: The Relation of Moral Ideology to Dynamic Moral Philosophy, 1971. **Address:** 4525 Roberts Rd., Fairfax, VA 22032-3611, U.S.A.

MILLER, Keith G. *See* **GRABER MILLER, Keith Allen.**

MILLER, Kerby A. American (born United States), b. 1944. **Genres:** History. **Career:** University of California, lecturer in history, 1976-77; Queen's University, Institute of Irish Studies, senior fellow, 1977-78, visiting lecturer, 1985-86; University of Missouri, assistant professor, 1978-83, associate professor of history, 1983-88, professor of history, 1988-, Middlebush professor of history, 2000-03, Curators' professor of history, 2008-; New York University, Glucksman Ireland House, visiting lecturer, 2002. Writer. **Publications:** Emigrants and Exiles: Ireland and the Irish Exodus to North America, 1985; (with P. Wagner) Out of Ireland: The Story of Irish Emigration to America, 1994; (ed. with J. S. Donnelly, Jr.) Irish Popular Culture, 1650-1850, 1997; (with P. Miller) Journey of Hope: The Story of Irish Immigration to America, 2001; (with A. Schrier, B.D. Boling and D.N. Doyle) Irish Immigrants in the Land of Canaan: Letters and Memoirs from Colonial and Revolutionary America, 1675-1815, 2003; Ireland and Irish America: Culture, Class and Transatlantic Migration, 2008. Contributor to books and journals. **Address:** Department of History, University of Missouri, 8 Read Hall, Columbia, MO 65211, U.S.A. **Online address:** millerk@missouri.edu

MILLER, Kiri Mariah. American (born United States), b. 1979. **Genres:** Art/Art History. **Career:** Brown University, Manning Assistant Professor of Music, 2010-. Ethnologist and writer. **Publications:** (Ed.) The Chattahoochee Musical Convention, 1852-2002: A Sacred Harp Historical Sourcebook, 2002; Traveling Home: Sacred Harp Singing and American Pluralism, 2008. Contributor to books and periodicals. **Address:** Brown University, Orwig Music Bldg., 1 Young Orchard Ave., PO Box 1924, Providence, RI 02912, U.S.A. **Online address:** kiri_miller@brown.edu

MILLER, Kit. American (born United States), b. 1956?. **Genres:** Documentaries/Reportage, Art/Art History. **Career:** Writer. **Publications:** Inside the Glitter: Lives of Casino Workers, 2000. Contributor to periodicals. **Address:** c/o Author Mail, Great Basin Publishing, 6185 Franktown Rd., Carson City, NV 89704, U.S.A.

MILLER, Kristie. (Kristie Twaddell). American (born United States), b. 1944. **Genres:** Women's Studies And Issues, Biography, Education, Language/Linguistics, Social Sciences. **Career:** Brown Daily Herald, managing editor; teacher, 1969-84; Chicago Tribune Co., director, 1981-2001; News-Tribune, columnist, 1984-2009; Foreign Service Spouse Oral History Project, columnist, 1989-94. **Publications:** (Ed. as Kristie Twaddell with J.E. Alatis) English as a Second Language in Bilingual Education: Selected TESOL Papers, 1976; Ruth Hanna McCormick: A Life in Politics, 1880-1944, 1992; (ed. with M. Gustafson and E.I. Perry) We Have Come to Stay: American Women and Political Parties, 1880-1960, 1999; Isabella Greenway: An Enterprising Woman, 2004; (ed. with R.H. McGinnis) Volume of Friendship: The Letters of Eleanor Roosevelt and Isabella Greenway, 1904-1953, 2009; Ellen Axson Wilson and Edith Bolling Galt Wilson, 2010; Ellen and Edith: Woodrow Wilson's First Ladies, 2010. **Address:** University Press of Kansas, 2502 Westbrooke Cir., Lawrence, KS 66045-4444, U.S.A. **Online address:** krste@aol.com

MILLER, Laura. American (born United States), b. 1960. **Genres:** Children's Fiction, Autobiography/Memoirs, Science Fiction/Fantasy. **Career:** Salon.com, co-founder and staff writer, 1995-. **Publications:** (Ed. with A. Begley) The Salon.com Reader's Guide to Contemporary Authors, 2000; The Magician's Book: A Skeptic's Adventures in Narnia, 2008. Contributor to periodicals. **Address:** Little, Brown and Company, 237 Park Ave., New York, NY 10017, U.S.A. **Online address:** magiciansbook@yahoo.com

MILLER, Lee E. American (born United States), b. 1959. **Genres:** Psychology. **Career:** R.H. Macy & Company Inc., vice president for labor and employee relations; Barneys New York, senior vice president for human resources; Seton Hall University, adjunct professor of management, 1995-; USA Networks, senior vice president for human resources, 1998-99; TV Guide, senior vice president for human resources, 2000-01; NegotiationPlus.com, consultant, 2001-, managing director; The Cabot Advisory Group, senior consultant; International Association of Corporate and Professional Recruiters, chair; Union County Motion Picture Advisory Board, secretary. Writer. **Publications:** Employment Discrimination, 1984; Get More Money on Your Next Job, 1998; (with J. Miller) A Womans Guide to Successful Negotiating, 2002; (with B. Jackson) UP: Influence Power and the U Perspective: The Art of Getting What You Want, 2007; Get More Money on Your Next Job-In Any Economy, 2009; (with J. Miller) Woman's Guide to Successful Negotiating: How to Convince, Collaborate & Create Your Way to Agreement, 2011. **Ad-**

dress: NegotiationPlus.com, 45 Park Pl. S, Ste. 240, Morristown, NJ 07960, U.S.A. **Online address:** negotiate@earthlink.net

MILLER, Leslie Adrienne. American (born United States), b. 1956. **Genres:** Poetry. **Career:** University of Missouri, instructor in English, 1979-80, 1981-82; Catonsville Community College, instructor, 1982; University of Maryland, instructor, 1982-83; Goucher College, instructor, 1982-83; Johns Hopkins Center for Talented Youth, instructor, 1983; Stephens College, director of creative writing program, 1983-87; Washington College, instructor, 1984-85; Open Places, managing editor, 1985-87; University of Houston, instructor, 1987-90; University of Oregon, visiting writer, 1990; University of St. Thomas, assistant professor, associate professor, 1991-2002, professor of English, 2002-; University of Iowa, graduate instructor. Writer. **Publications:** (With M. Graham) Hanging on the Sunburned Arm of Some Homeboy (poetry chapbook), 1982; No River (poetry chapbook), 1987; Staying up for Love (poetry), 1990; Ungodliness (poetry), 1994; Yesterday Had a Man in It (poetry), 1998; Eat Quite Everything You See (poetry), 2002; The Resurrection Trade, 2007. **Address:** Department of English, University of St. Thomas, JRC 333, St. Paul, MN 55105-1096, U.S.A. **Online address:** lamiller@stthomas.edu

MILLER, Lynn H. American (born United States), b. 1937. **Genres:** Plays/Screenplays, Politics/Government, History, Social Sciences. **Career:** University of California, assistant professor of political science, 1965-69; Temple University, associate professor of political science, 1969-, professor of political science, associate dean of graduate school, 1973-, now professor emeritus of political science. Writer. **Publications:** (With J.C. Bollens) Organizing Mankind: An Analysis of Contemporary International Organization, 1972; (ed. with R.W. Pruessen) Reflections on the Cold War: A Quarter Century of American Foreign Policy, 1974; Global Order: Values and Power in International Politics, 1985, 4th ed., 1998; (with J.H. Schuster) Governing Tomorrow's Campus: Perspectives and Agendas, 1989; (with L. Jensen) Global Challenge: Change and Continuity in World Politics, 1997; (with A.H. Emgarth) French Philadelphia: The French Cultural and Historical Presence in the Delaware Valley, 2006; (with A.H. Emgarth) Philadelphie à la Française, 2007. **Address:** Department of Political Science, Temple University, Rm. 409, Gladfelter Hall, 1115 Polett Walk, Philadelphia, PA 19122-6089, U.S.A.

MILLER, Margaret. *See* **BAMBOLA, Sylvia.**

MILLER, Matthew. American (born United States), b. 1961. **Genres:** Economics, Politics/Government. **Career:** McKinsey & Co., consultant, 1989-; U.S. Office of Management and Budget, senior advisor, 1993-95; KCRW, Left, Right & Center, host. Writer. **Publications:** The Two Percent Solution: Fixing America's Problems in Ways Liberals and Conservatives Can Love, 2003; The Tyranny of Dead Ideas: Letting Go of the Old Ways of Thinking to Unleash a New Prosperity, 2009. Contributor of articles to periodicals. **Address:** KCRW, 1900 Pico Blvd., Santa Monica, CA 90405, U.S.A. **Online address:** matt@mattmilleronline.com

MILLER, Neil. American (born United States), b. 1945?. **Genres:** Gay And Lesbian Issues, Adult Non-fiction. **Career:** Gay Community News, editor, 1975-78; Boston Phoenix, staff writer, 1982-86; Tufts University, Department of English, lecturer, 1998-. **Publications:** In Search of Gay America: Women and Men in a Time of Change, 1989; Out in the World: Gay and Lesbian Life from Buenos Aires to Bangkok, 1992; Out of the Past: Gay and Lesbian History from 1869 to the Present, 1995, rev. ed., 2005; Sex Crime Panic: A Journey to the Paranoid Heart of the 1950s, 2002; Kartchner Caverns: How Two Cavers Discovered and Saved One of the Wonders of the Natural World, 2008; Banned in Boston: The Watch and Ward Society's Crusade against Books, Burlesque, and the Social Evil, 2010. Contributor to periodicals. **Address:** Department of English, Tufts University, 210 East Hall, Medford, MA 02155, U.S.A. **Online address:** neil.miller@tufts.edu

MILLER, Nina. American (born United States), b. 1958?. **Genres:** Adult Non-fiction. **Career:** Northwestern University, professor; Iowa State University, associate professor of English, teacher of American literature, African American literature, and women's studies; Rocky Mountain College of Art and Design, chair of liberal studies. Writer. **Publications:** Making Love Modern: The Intimate Public Worlds of New York's Literary Women, 1999. **Address:** Rocky Mountain College of Art and Design, 1600 Pierce St., Lakewood, CO 80214, U.S.A. **Online address:** nmiller@rmcad.edu

MILLER, Paul D. American (born United States), b. 1970?. **Genres:** History, Novels, Music, Literary Criticism And History, Young Adult Fiction. **Career:** A Gathering of the Tribes (magazine), advertising copy writer, co-publisher; 21 Magazine, editor; European Graduate School, Media and Communications Program, professor; C-Theory, editor, contributing editor; Origin Magazine, arts editor. **Publications:** (Contrib.) Pass the Mic: Beastie Boys, 1991-1996, 2001; Free Port (Sep 15 - Dec 9 2001), 2001; Rhythm Science, 2004; (contrib.) Truth, Technology and the Visual/Virtual World, 2006; (ed.) Sound Unbound: Sampling Digital Music and Culture, 2008; Book of Ice, 2011; Flow My Blood the DJ Said, forthcoming. **Address:** Media and Communications Program, European Graduate School, 151 1st Ave., Ste. 14, New York, NY 10003, U.S.A. **Online address:** djspooky@musicandart.net

MILLER, R. Craig. American (born United States), b. 1946. **Genres:** Design, Art/Art History. **Career:** Columbia University, Avery Architectural Library, curator of drawings, 1974-75; Metropolitan Museum of Art, associate curator of American decorative arts, 1978-86, associate curator of twentieth-century art, 1983-90; Musee des Arts Decoratifs de Montrealm, Le Chateau Dufresne, director, 1981-83; Denver Art Museum, curator of design and architecture, 1990-; Indianapolis Museum of Art, curator of design arts and director of design initiatives; The Miller Center for Esthetic Excellence, founder, 2007; Newark Beth Israel Medical Center, staff; Saint Barnabas Medical Center, staff. Writer. **Publications:** (Co-author) Design in America: The Cranbrook Vision, 1925-1950, 1983; Modern Design in The Metropolitan Museum of Art, 1890-1990, Abrams, 1990; (and intro.) Susan Grant Lewin, Counterculture: The Formica Story, Rizzoli International, 1991; Merchandising Interior Design: Methods of Furniture Fabrication in America Between The World Wars, 1991; (co-author) Design 1935-1965: What Modern Was, Martin Eidelberg, 1991; (and intro.) US Design, 1975-2000, 2002; (with P. Sparke and C. McDermott) European Design since 1985: Shaping the New Century, 2009. Works appears in anthology. **Address:** Department of Design & Architecture, Denver Art Museum, 100 W 14th Avenue Pkwy., Denver, CO 80218, U.S.A.

MILLER, Rebecca. (Rebecca Augusta Miller). American (born United States), b. 1962. **Genres:** Novels, Novellas/Short Stories, Plays/Screenplays. **Career:** Writer and director. **Publications:** SELF-ILLUSTRATED: A Woman Who ..., 2003. OTHERS: Personal Velocity (short stories), 2001; The Ballad of Jack and Rose, 2005; The Private Lives of Pippa Lee, 2008. **Address:** c/o Sarah Chalfant, Wylie Agency, 17 Bedford Sq., London, GL WC1B 3JA, England.

MILLER, Rebecca Augusta. *See* **MILLER, Rebecca.**

MILLER, Richard Lawrence. American (born United States), b. 1949. **Genres:** History, Politics/Government, Biography, Novels, Autobiography/Memoirs. **Career:** Hoover Presidential Library, photographer, 1970; KCCK-Radio, public affairs director, 1975; University of Iowa, College of Pharmacy, library assistant, 1976-79; KCUR-Radio, producer, 1981-82. Writer. **Publications:** Truman: The Rise to Power, 1986; Heritage of Fear: Illusion and Reality in the Cold War: A Review, 1988; The Case for Legalizing Drugs, 1991; Nazi Justiz: Law of the Holocaust, 1995; Drug Warriors and Their Prey: From Police Power to Police State, 1996; Drug of Abuse: A Reference Guide to Their History and Use, 2002; Whittaker: Struggles of a Supreme Court Justice, 2002; Encyclopedia of Addictive Drugs, 2002; Lincoln And His World, 2006. Contributor to periodicals. **Address:** PO Box 7038, Kansas City, MO 64113-0038, U.S.A.

MILLER, Robert H. American (born United States), b. 1944. **Genres:** Cultural/Ethnic Topics, History, Biography, History, Autobiography/Memoirs, Children's Fiction. **Career:** Temple University, Department of Religion, assistant professor, professor. Writer. **Publications:** Reflections of a Black Cowboy, 1991; A Pony for Jeremiah, 1996. STORIES OF THE FORGOTTEN WEST SERIES: The Story of Stagecoach Marcy Fields, 1994; Buffalo Soldiers: The Story of Emanuel Stance, 1995; The Story of Jean Baptiste Du Sable, 1995; The Story of Nat Love, 1995. Contributor to periodicals. **Address:** 503 S 6th St., Camden, NJ 08103, U.S.A. **Online address:** rmille05@temple.edu

MILLER, Roger G. (Roger Gene Miller). American (born United States), b. 1946. **Genres:** History, Air/Space Topics, Military/Defense/Arms Control. **Career:** North Texas State University, assistant instructor, 1965-70, Lowry Technical Training Center, Lowry Air Force Base (AFB), center historian, 1980-83, Headquarters Air Training Command, Randolph AFB, staff historian, 1983-87, Seventeenth Air Force, Sembach AFB, Federal Republic of Germany, command historian, 1987-89, Air Staff Branch, Office of Air Force History, staff historian, 1989-93, Air Force History and Museums Program, Bolling AFB, staff historian, 1993-2007, senior historian, 2007-09, deputy director, 2009-; Indiana University, American Studies Program, research assistant, 1976-77; U.S. Air Force Intern Program, director of the history of air power course, 1996-2003; Air Force Historical Studies Office, staff. Writer. **Publications:** Crime, Corrections and Quality Force: A History of the 3320th Correction and Rehabilitation Squadron, 1951-1985, 1987; (ed.) Seeing Off the Bear: Anglo-American Air Power Cooperation during the Cold War: Proceedings, Joint Meeting of the Royal Air Force Historical Society and the Air Force Historical Foundation, 1995; To Save a City: The Berlin Airlift, 1948-1949, 1998; (contrib.) Golden Legacy, Boundless Future: Essays on the United States Air Force and the Rise of Aerospace Power, 2000; A Prelude to War: The 1st Aero Squadron and the Mexican Punitive Expedition of 1916, 2003; (contrib.) The Diary of Old No. 1, edited by Meghan Cunningham, 2003; A preliminary to War: The 1st Aero Squadron and the Mexican Punitive Expedition of 1916, 2003; Billy Mitchell: Stormy Petrel of the Air, 2007; Like a Thunderbolt: The Lafayette Escadrille and the Advent of American Pursuit in World War I, 2007. Contributor to periodicals. **Address:** Air Force Historical Studies Office, 2822 Doherty Dr. SW, Ste. 404, Joint-Base Anacostia-Bolling, Washington, DC 20373-5899, U.S.A. **Online address:** roger.miller@pentagon.af.mil

MILLER, Roger Gene. *See* **MILLER, Roger G.**

MILLER, Russell. British (born England), b. 1938. **Genres:** History, Biography, Autobiography/Memoirs. **Career:** East London News Agency, apprentice reporter, 1955-57; Ilford Recorder, reporter, 1957-58, chief reporter and news editor, 1960-62; Daily Sketch and Sunday Dispatch, reporter, 1962-65. **Publications:** Click, 1974; (with R. Boar) The Incredible Music Machine, 1982; Bunny: The Real Story of Playboy, 1984; The House of Getty, 1985; Bare-Faced Messiah: The True Story of L. Ron Hubbard, 1987; Nothing Less than Victory, 1993; Ten Days in May, 1995; Magnum: Fifty Years at the Front Line of History, 1997; Behind the Lines: The Oral History of Special Operations in World War II, 2002; Adventures of Arthur Conan Doyle: A Biography, 2008. WITH THE EDITORS OF TIME-LIFE BOOKS: The Resistance, 1979; The East Indiamen, 1980; The Commandos, 1981; The Soviet Air Force at War, 1983; Continents in Collision, 1983. **Address:** Sterling Lord Literistic Inc., 65 Bleeker St., New York, NY 10012-2420, U.S.A.

MILLER, Seumas. Australian/Scottish (born Scotland), b. 1953?. **Genres:** Philosophy, Social Sciences, Business/Trade/Industry, Economics, Politics/Government. **Career:** University of Canberra, lecturer in communication studies, 1986-88; Rhodes University, senior lecturer in philosophy, 1988-89, associate professor of philosophy, 1990-91, 1992-93; Charles Sturt University, School of Humanities and Social Sciences, foundation professor of social philosophy, 1994-, head, 1994-99, ARC Commonwealth Special Research Centre in Applied Philosophy and Public Ethics, foundation director, 2000-07, Centre for Applied Philosophy and Public Ethics, professor of philosophy, 2003-; University of Melbourne, senior research fellow in philosophy and public issues, 1992-93, professional fellow, 1999-, professor of philosophy, 2006; Australian National University, professor of philosophy, 2003-, Division of Centre for Applied Philosophy and Public Ethics, director, 2003-; Delft University of Technology, senior research fellow, 2009-; Writer. **Publications:** (With R. Freadman) Re-Thinking Theory: A Critique of Contemporary Literary Theory and an Alternative Account, 1992; (with J. Blackler and A. Alexandra) Police Ethics, 1997, rev. ed., 2005; Social Action: A Teleological Account, 2001; (with A. Alexandra and S. Matthews) Reasons, Values and Institutions, 2002; (ed. with T. Campbell) Human Rights and the Moral Responsibilities of Corporate and Public Sector Organisations, 2004; (with P. Roberts and E. Spence) Corruption and Anti-Corruption: An Applied Philosophical Approach, 2005; (with J. Blackler) Ethical Issues in Policing, 2005; Ethical and Philosophical Consideration of the Dual-use Dilemma in the Biological Sciences, 2008; (with A. Alexandra) Ethics in Practice: Moral Theory and the Professions, 2009; Terrorism and Counter-Terrorism: Ethics and Liberal Democracy, 2009; (with A. Alexandra) Integrity Systems for Occupations, 2010; Moral Foundations of Social Institutions: A Philosophical Study, 2010; Institutional Corruption: A Study in Applied Philosophy, forthcoming; Ethics of the Dual Use Dilemma in Science and Technology, forthcoming; Investigative Ethics, forthcoming. Contributor to journals and periodicals. **Address:** Centre for Applied Philosophy and Public Ethics, Charles Sturt University, PO Box 8260, Canberra, AC 2602, Australia. **Online address:** smiller@csu.edu.au

MILLER, Shawn William. American (born United States), b. 1964?. **Genres:** History. **Career:** Brigham Young University, assistant professor, 1997-, professor of history, chair of department, 2007-10. Writer. **Publications:** Fruitless Trees: Portuguese Conservation and Brazil's Colonial Timber, 2000; An Environmental History of Latin America, 2007. Contributor to periodicals. **Address:** Department of History, Brigham Young University, JFSB 2113, Provo, UT 84602, U.S.A. **Online address:** shawn_miller@byu.edu

MILLER, Thomas W. American (born United States), b. 1943. **Genres:** Medicine/Health, Psychiatry. **Career:** Genesee Valley Rotary Camp Inc., program director, 1964-67; Veterans Administration Hospital, intern in counseling psychology, 1966-67; Buffalo State Hospital, senior clinical psychologist, 1967-69; Psychiatric Clinic, clinical intern in psychology, 1968-69, clinical psychologist, 1969-70; Buffalo Psychiatric Center, associate clinical psychologist, 1968-75; Daemen College, professor, 1970-81; Rosary Hill College, associate professor of psychology and director of psychological service, 1970-74, vice-president for student affairs, 1974-75; Veterans Administration Medical Center, clinical psychologist and coordinator of systematic internal review, 1975-81; State University of New York, clinical associate, 1975-81, clinical assistant professor of psychiatry, 1979-81; Veterans Administration Medical Center, chief of psychology service, 1981-96; University of Kentucky, professor of psychology and psychiatry, 1981-, now professor emeritus; University of London, Institute of Psychiatry, visiting professor, 1989; Murray State University, professor, through 1996. Writer. **Publications:** (Ed.) Stressful Life Events: Clinical Readings in Health Care Delivery, 1988; (ed.) Chronic Pain: Clinical Issues in Health Care Management, 1990; (contrib.) Torture and Its Consequences, 1992; (contrib.) Handbook of Stress, 1993; (with L.J. Veltkamp) Clinical Handbook of Child Abuse and Neglect, 1994; (contrib.) Handbook of Post-Traumatic Stress Disorder, 1994; (ed.) Theory and Assessment of Stressful Life Events, 1996; (ed. and intro.) Clinical Disorders and Stressful Life Events, 1997; (contrib.) Trauma and Memory, 1997; (ed.) Children of Trauma: Stressful Life Events and Their Effects on Children and Adolescents, 1998; (with L.J. Veltkamp) Clinical Handbook of Adult Exploitation and Abuse, 1998; (ed.) Handbook of Stressful Transitions Across the Lifespan, 2010. Contributor to books and periodicals. **Address:** Department of Educational and Counseling, Psychology, University of Kentucky, 237 Dickey Hall, Lexington, KY 40506-0017, U.S.A. **Online address:** tjmiller06@insightbb.com

MILLER, Tice L. American (born United States), b. 1938. **Genres:** Theatre, Photography, Art/Art History, Humanities. **Career:** Kansas City Junior College, instructor, 1961-62; University of West Florida, assistant professor, 1968-72; University of Nebraska-Lincoln, associate professor, 1972-80, professor of theater arts, 1980-2008, professor emeritus of theater arts, 2008-; Nebraska Repertory Theatre, executive director, 1988-97, department head, 1989-97; National Educational Theatre Convention, co-chairman, 1986. Writer. **Publications:** Bohemians and Critics: American Theatre Criticism in the Nineteenth Century, 1981; (intro.) A History of the American Theatre from its Origins to 1832, 2005; Entertaining the Nation: American Drama in the Eighteenth and Nineteenth Centuries, 2007. EDITOR: (contrib.) Shakespeare around the Globe: Notable Postwar International Revivals, 1986; (with D. Wilmeth) The Cambridge Guide to American Theatre, 1993; (with R. Engle) The American Stage: Social and Economic Issues from the Colonial Period to the Present, 1993. Contributor to books and journals. **Address:** Johnny Carson School of Theatre and Film, University of Nebraska-Lincoln, 215 Temple Bldg., 12th & R St., Lincoln, NE 68588-0201, U.S.A. **Online address:** tmiller1@unl.edu

MILLER, William Ian. American (born United States), b. 1946. **Genres:** Law. **Career:** Wesleyan University, assistant professor of English, 1975-80; University of Houston, associate professor of law, 1981-84; University of Michigan, visiting associate professor of law, 1984-85, professor of law, 1985-98, Thomas G. Long professor of law, 1998-; University of Bergen, visiting professor; University of St. Andrews, Carnegie centenary professor, 2007. Writer. **Publications:** (Trans. with T.M. Andersson) Law and Literature in Medieval Iceland: Ljaosvetninga Saga and Valla-Ljaots Saga/Ljaosvetninga Saga and Valla-Ljaots Saga, 1989; Bloodtaking and Peacemaking:

Feud, Law, and Society in Saga Iceland, 1990; Humiliation: And Other Essays on Honor, Social Discomfort, and Violence, 1993; The Anatomy of Disgust, 1997; The Mystery of Courage, 2000; Faking It, 2003; Eye for an Eye, 2006; Audun and the Polar Bear: Luck, Law, and Largesse in a Medieval Tale of Risky Business, 2008; Losing It: In Which An Aging Professor Laments His Shrinking Brain, 2011. Contributor to journals. **Address:** School of Law, University of Michigan, 411 Hutchins Hall, 625 S State St., Ann Arbor, MI 48109, U.S.A. **Online address:** wimiller@umich.edu

MILLER, William L. Scottish (born Scotland), b. 1943. **Genres:** Communications/Media, Politics/Government. **Career:** University of Strathclyde, lecturer, 1968-83, senior lecturer in politics, 1983-85; Virginia Polytechnic Institute and State University, visiting fellow, 1983-84; University of Glasgow, Edward Caird professor of politics, 1985-, now professor emeritus; British Broadcasting Corp., consultant; Scottish Television, consultant. Writer. **Publications:** Causal Modelling in Three-Party Systems: Trichotomous Regression Studies of Scotland, England and America, 1977; Electoral Dynamics in Britain since 1918, 1977; (with J. Brand and M. Jordan) Oil and the Scottish Voter, 1974-79, 1980; The End of British Politics?: Scots and English Political Behaviour in the Seventies, 1981; The Survey Method in the Social and Political Sciences, 1983; (with M. Harrop) Elections and Voters: A Comparative Introduction, 1987; Irrelevant Elections?: The Quality of Local Democracy in Britain, 1988; (co-author) How Voters Change: The 1987 British Election Campaign in Perspective, 1990; Media and Voters: The Audience, Content, and Influence of Press and Television at the 1987 General Election, 1991; (ed.) Alternatives to Freedom: Arguments and Opinions, 1995; (with A.M. Timpson and M. Lessnoff) Political Culture in Contemporary Britain: People and Politicians, Principles and Practice, 1996; (with S. White and P. Heywood) Values and Political Change in Postcommunist Europe, 1998; (M. Dickson and G. Stoker) Models of Local Governance: Public Opinion and Political Theory in Britain, 2000; (with A.B. Grødeland and T.Y. Koshechkina) A Culture of Corruption?: Coping with Government in Post-Communist Europe, 2001; (ed.) Anglo-Scottish Relations from 1900 to Devolution and Beyond, 2005; (with J. Duckett) Open Economy and its Enemies: Public Attitudes in East Asia and Eastern Europe, 2006; (with A. Hussain) Multicultural Nationalism: Islamophobia, Anglophobia, and Devolution, 2006. Contributor to journals and newspapers. **Address:** Department of Politics, University of Glasgow, Adam Smith Bldg., Glasgow, G12 8RT, Scotland. **Online address:** william.miller@glasgow.ac.uk

MILLER, Wilma Hildruth. American (born United States), b. 1936. **Genres:** Education. **Career:** Elementary school teacher, 1958-64; Wisconsin State University, assistant professor, 1965-68; Illinois State University, associate professor, 1968-72, professor of education, 1972-98, professor emeritus, 1998-; Western Washington State College, visiting professor, 1970. Writer. **Publications:** Identifying and Correcting Reading Difficulties in Children, 1971; The First R: Elementary Reading Today, 1972, 2nd ed., 1977; (ed.) Elementary Reading Today: Selected Articles, 1972; Diagnosis and Correction of Reading Difficulties in Secondary School Students, 1973; Teaching Reading in the Secondary School, 1974; Reading Diagnosis Kit, 1974, 3rd ed., 1986; Reading Correction Kit, 1975; Corrective Reading Skills Activity File, 1977; The Reading Activities Handbook, 1980; Teaching Elementary Reading Today, 1984; Reading Teacher's Complete Diagnosis and Correction Manual, 1988; Reading Comprehension Activities Kit, 1990; Complete Reading Disabilities Handbook, 1993; Alternative Assessment Techniques in Reading and Writing, 1995; Reading & Writing Remediation Kit, 1997; Ready-to-Use Activities & Materials for Improving Content Reading Skills, 1999; Strategies for Developing Emergent Literacy, 2000; The Reading Teacher's Survival Kit, 2001; Reading Skills Problem Solver, 2001; Survival Reading Skills for Secondary Students, 2003; Improving Early Literacy: Strategies and Activities for Struggling Students (K-3), 2005. **Address:** 302 N Coolidge St., Normal, IL 61761-2435, U.S.A. **Online address:** whmille@ilstu.edu

MILLER-LACHMANN, Lyn. American (born United States), b. 1956. **Genres:** Young Adult Fiction, Cultural/Ethnic Topics, Literary Criticism And History. **Career:** New York City Public Schools, teacher, 1981-83; Siena College, reference librarian, 1990-94; MultiCultural Review, editor-in-chief, 1994-2010; Congregation Gates of Heaven, Reform Jewish Religious School, teacher, 1999-. **Publications:** FICTION: Hiding Places, 1987; (ed.) Once upon a Cuento, 2003; Dirt Cheap: A Novel, 2006; Gringolandia, 2009. NONFICTION: (ed.) Our Family, Our Friends, Our World: An Annotated Guide to Significant Multicultural Books for Children and Teenagers, 1992; Global Voices, Global Visions: A Core Collection of Multicultural Books, 1995; (with L.S. Taylor) Schools for All: Educating Children in a Diverse Society, 1995; (with H. Quinn) Downsized but Not Defeated: The Family Guide to Living on Less, 1997. Contributor to books. **Address:** 194 Lenox Ave., Albany, NY 12208, U.S.A. **Online address:** lynml@me.com

MILLER-POGACAR, Anesa. *See* **MILLER, Anesa.**

MILLET, Lydia. American (born United States), b. 1968. **Genres:** Novels, Literary Criticism And History, Animals/Pets, Science Fiction/Fantasy, Young Adult Fiction. **Career:** Writer. **Publications:** NOVELS: Omnivores, 1996; George Bush, Dark Prince of Love: A Presidential Romance, 2000; My Happy Life, 2002; Oh Pure and Radiant Heart, 2005; Everyone's Pretty, 2005; How the Dead Dream, 2008; Ghost Lights, 2011; The Fires Beneath the Sea, 2011. STORY COLLECTION: Love in Infant Monkeys, 2009. **Address:** c/o Maria Massie, Lippincott Massie McQuilkin, 27 W 20th St., New York, NY 10011, U.S.A. **Online address:** lydiamillet@yahoo.com

MILLET, Richard. French (born France), b. 1953?. **Genres:** Novels, Travel/Exploration, Literary Criticism And History. **Career:** Gallimard, editor. **Publications:** L'invention du corps de Saint Marc: Roman, 1983; L'innocence: roman, 1984; Sept passions singulières: récits, 1985; Le sentiment de la langue: mélange, 1986; Le plus haut miroir, 1986; Beyrouth (travel), 1987; L'angélus: récit, 1988; La chamber d'ivoire: récit, 1989; (with J. Brault) Recueil, 1991; Accompagnement: lectures, 1991; Laura Mendoza: récit, 1991; L'écrivain Sirieix: récit, 1992; Le chant des adolescents: récits, 1993; Le sentiment de la langue: I, II, III, 1993; Coeur blanc: nouvelles (novellas), 1994; Un balcon à Beyrouth: récit, 1994; La gloire des Pythre: roman, 1995; (ed. and contrib., with G. Bocholier) Pour saluer Robert Marteau (criticism), 1996; L'amour mendiant: notes sur le désir, 1996; L'amour des trois soeurs Piale: roman, 1997; Cité perdue: Istanbul, 1967-1995, 1998; Lauve le pur: roman, 1999; La voix d'alto: roman, 2001; Ma vie parmi les ombres: roman (title means: 'My Life in the Shadows'), 2003; Le renard dans le nom: récit, 2003; Pour la musique contemporaine: chroniques discographiques, 2004; Musique secrète, 2004; Le dernier écrivain, 2004; Musique secrète, 2004; Fenêtre au crépuscule: conversation avec Chantal Lapeyre-Desmaison, 2004; Goût des femmes laides: roman, 2005; Harcèlement littéraire, 2005; Glory of the Pythres, 2005; Dévorations: roman, 2006; Sacrifice, 2006; Art du bref: récit, 2006; Tombés avec la nuit: thé âtre, 2007; Place des pensées: sur Maurice Blanchot, 2007; Désenchantement de la littérature, 2007; Orient désert, 2007; Opprobre: essai de démonologie, 2008; La confession négative, 2009; Le sommeil sur les cendres, 2010; Brumes de Cimmérie, 2010; L'enfer du roman, 2010; Tarnac, 2010; Fatigue du sens, 2011. **Address:** c/o Author Mail, Northwestern University Press, 629 Noyes St., Evanston, IL 60208-4210, U.S.A.

MILLET, Robert L. American (born United States), b. 1947. **Genres:** Theology/Religion, History. **Career:** Brigham Young University, faculty, 1983-, professor of religious education, outreach and interfaith relations, emeritus dean of religious education, Department of Ancient Scripture, chair; Latter-day Saints (LDS), manager of outreach and interfaith relations for church public affairs. Writer. **Publications:** Magnifying Priesthood Power, 1974; (with J.F. McConkie) Sustaining and Defending the Faith, 1985; (with J.F. McConkie) Doctrinal Commentary on the Book of Mormon, 1987; (with J.F. McConkie) In His Holy Name, 1988; (with J.F. McConkie) The Holy Ghost, 1989; By Grace are We Saved, 1989; Life in Christ, 1990; An Eye Single to the Glory of God: Reflections on the Cost of Discipleship, 1991; Steadfast and Immovable: Striving for Spiritual Maturity, 1992; (with J.F. McConkie) Our Destiny: The Call and Election of the House of Israel, 1993; Christ-Centered Living, 1994; The Power of the Word: Saving Doctrines from the Book of Mormon, 1994; Within Reach, 1995; (with J.F. McConkie) Joseph Smith: The Choice Seer, 1996; When a Child Wanders, 1996; Alive in Christ: The Miracle of Spiritual Rebirth, 1997; The Mormon Faith: A New Look at Christianity, 1998; Jesus Christ: The Only Sure Foundation, 1999; Life after Death: Insights from Latter-day Revelation, 1999; Parables and Other Teaching Stories, 1999; (co-author) The Redeemer: Reflections on the Life and Teachings of Jesus the Christ, 2000; Selected Writings of Robert L. Millet, 2000; Lost and Found: Reflections on the Prodigal Son, 2001; More Holiness Give Me, 2001; I Will Fear No Evil: How the Lord Sustains Us in Perilous Times, 2002; (with L.D. Newell) Jesus, the Very Thought of Thee: Daily Reflections on the New Testament, 2002; Grace Works, 2003; (with L.D. Newell) When Ye Shall Receive These Things: Daily Reflections on the Book of Mormon, 2003; (with L.D. Newell) Draw Near Unto Me: Daily Reflections on the Doctrine and Covenants, 2004; Getting at the Truth: Responding to Difficult Questions about LDS Beliefs, 2004; Are We There Yet?, 2005; A Different Jesus: The Christ of the Latter-day Saints, 2005; (with L.D. Newell) A Lamp unto My Feet: Daily Reflections on the Old Testament, 2005; (with G.C.V. Johnson) Bridging the Divide: The Continuing Conversation between a Mormon and an Evangelical, 2007; (with G.R. McDermott) Claiming Christ: A Mormon-Evangelical Debate, 2007; Men of Valor: The Powerful Impact of a Righteous Man, 2007; The Vision of Mormonism: Pressing the Boundaries of Christianity, 2007; What Happened to the Cross? Distinctive LDS Teachings, 2007; Holding Fast: Dealing with Doubt in the Latter Days, 2008; Men of Influence: The Potential of the Priesthood to Lift the World, 2009. EDITOR: (with K.P. Jackson) The Gospels, 1986; (with J.F. McConkie) The Life Beyond, 1986; Acts to Revelation, 1987; To Be Learned Is Good If-, 1987; (with L.E. Dahl) The Capstone of Our Religion: Insights into the Doctrine & Covenants, 1989; Joseph Smith: Selected Sermons & Writings, 1989; (with J.F. McConkie) The Man Adam, 1990; (with R.J. Matthews) Plain and Precious Truths Restored: The Doctrinal and Historical Significance of the Joseph Smith Translation: Papers Presented at the BYU Symposium As Translated Correctly Joseph Smith's Translation of the Bible: January 13 and 14, 1995, 1995; (with N.B. Reynolds) Latter-day Christianity: 10 Basic Issues, 1998; (with A.C. Skinner) C.S. Lewis: The Man and His Message, 1999. Contributor to periodicals. **Address:** Department of Religious Education, Brigham Young University, Provo, UT 84602, U.S.A.

MILLETT, **John.** Australian (born Australia), b. 1921. **Genres:** Poetry, Young Adult Fiction, History, Literary Criticism And History. **Career:** Solicitor, 1952-; Poetry Australia, staff, 1962, managing editor, 1970-86, editor, 1987-96; South Head Press, editor, 1970-; Antill Millett and Partners, partner; Terrace du Forum, featured poet, 1989. **Publications:** Calendar Adam, 1971; The Silences, 1973; Love Tree of the Coomera, 1975; West of the Cunderans, 1977; (with G. Perry) Last Bride at Longsleep, 1981; Tail Arse Charlie, 1982; Come Down Cunderang, 1985; Blue Dynamite, 1986; The Nine Lives of Big Meg O'Shannessy: Poems, 1989; The World Faces Johnny Tripod, 1992; View from the Turret, 1994; Clothe Yourself in Summer, 1996; Dragonfly Tie, 1997; Last Draft, 2002; The People Singers: The Surfers Paradise Poems, 2005. **Address:** Magistrates House, The Market Pl., Berrima, NW 2577, Australia.

MILLETT, **Kate.** American (born United States), b. 1934. **Genres:** Social Commentary, Women's Studies And Issues, Autobiography/Memoirs, Mystery/Crime/Suspense, Essays. **Career:** Writer, 1958-; sculptor, photographer and painter, 1959-; University of North Carolina, English professor, 1959; teacher, 1960-61; Waseda University, English teacher, 1961-63; Barnard College, professor of English and philosophy, 1964-69; Bryn Mawr College, sociology professor, 1971; California State University, distinguished visiting professor, 1973-; Women's Art Colony Farm, founder. **Publications:** Sexual Politics, 1970; Flying, 1974; (ed.) The Prostitution Papers: A Candid Dialogue, 1975; Sita, 1977, rev. ed., 1992; (intro.) Caterpillars: Journal Entries by 11 Women, 1977; The Basement: Meditations on Human Sacrifice, 1979, rev. ed., 1991; Elegy for Sita, 1979; Going to Iran, 1981; (contrib.) Denken over liefde en macht, 1982; The Loony-Bin Trip, 1990; Believe Me, you don't want a Picture of that!, 1991; The Politics of Cruelty: An Essay on the Literature of Political Imprisonment, 1994; A.D.: A Memoir, 1995; Kate Millett, Sculptor: The First Thirty-Eight Years, 1997; Mother Millett, 2001. Contributor to magazines. **Address:** Georges Borchardt Inc., 136 E 57th St., New York, NY 10022-2707, U.S.A.

MILLETT, **Martin J(ohn).** British (born England), b. 1955. **Genres:** Archaeology/Antiquities, Classics. **Career:** Hampshire County Museum Service, assistant keeper of archaeology, 1980-81; University of Durham, lecturer in archaeology, 1981-98; University of Southampton, professor of archaeology, 1999-2001; University of Cambridge, Laurence professor of classical archaeology, 2001-; Fitzwilliam, fellow, chair of the faculty, 2011-; British Academy, fellow; Society of Antiquaries of London, director. Writer. **Publications:** (With E.C. Hill and T.F.C. Blagg) The Roman Riverside Wall and Monumental Arch in London, 1980; Excavations on the Romano-British Small Town at Neatham Hampshire 1969-1986, 1986; The Romanization of Britain: An Essay in Archaeological Interpretation, 1990; The English Heritage Book of Roman Britain, 1995; (with J.M. Carvete and S.J. Keay) A Roman Provincial Capital and Its Hinterland, 1995; (with P. Halkon) Rural Settlement and Industry: Studies in the Iron Age and Roman Archaeology of Lowland East Yorkshire, 1999; (co-author) Portus: An Archaeological Survey of the Port of Imperial Rome, 2005; (with L.A. Jones and C. Barclay) Shiptonthorpe, East Yorkshire: Archaeological Studies of a Romano-British Roadside Settlement, 2006. EDITOR: Pottery and the Archaeologist, 1979; (with C. Haselgrove and I. Smith) Archaeology from the Ploughsoil, 1985; (with Blagg) The Early Roman Empire in the West, 1990; Integration in the Early Roman West, 1995; (with S. James) Britons and Romans: Advancing an Archaeological Agenda, 2001; (co-ed.) Burial Practice in the Roman World: Contextual Studies, 2001; (with J. Pearce and M. Struck) Burial, Society and Context in the Roman world, 2001. **Address:** Faculty of Classics, University of Cambridge, Sidgwick Ave., Cambridge, CB3 9DA, England. **Online address:** mjm62@cam.ac.uk

MILLETT, **Paul.** British (born England), b. 1954?. **Genres:** Classics, Literary Criticism And History, Politics/Government, Law, History, Essays. **Career:** Downing College, Collins Fellow and admissions tutor, director of studies in classics; University of Cambridge, senior lecturer in Classics. Writer. **Publications:** Lending and Borrowing in Ancient Athens, 1991; Theophrastus and His World, 2007. EDITOR: (with P. Cartledge and S. Todd) Nomos: Essays in Athenian Law, Politics and Society, 1990; (with P. Cartledge and S.V. Reden) Kosmos: Essays in Order, Conflict and Community in Classical Athens, 1998; (with S.P. Oakley and R.J.E. Thompson) Ratio Et Res Ipsa: Classical Essays Presented By Former Pupils To James Diggle On His Retirement, 2011. **Address:** Downing College, Cambridge University Press, 40 W 20th St., Cambridge, CB2 1DQ, United Kingdom. **Online address:** paul.millett@dow.cam.ac.uk

MILLHISER, **Marlys.** American (born United States), b. 1938. **Genres:** Novellas/Short Stories, Mystery/Crime/Suspense, Novels, Young Adult Fiction, Children's Fiction, Horror, Literary Criticism And History. **Career:** Writer, 1965-. **Publications:** NOVELS: Nella Waits, 1974; The Mirror, 1978; Nightmare Country, 1981; The Threshold, 1984; Murder at Moot Point, 1992; Death of the Office Witch, 1993. OTHERS: Michael's Wife, 1972; Willing Hostage, 1976; Murder in a Hot Flash, 1995; It's Murder Going Home, 1996; Nobody Dies in a Casino, 1999; Killer Commute, 2000; The Rampant Reaper, 2002; Voices in the Wardrobe, 2005. Contributor to periodicals. **Address:** c/o Deborah Schneider, Gelfman Schneider Literary Agents Inc., 250 W 57th St., Ste. 2122, New York, NY 10107, U.S.A. **Online address:** millhiser@aol.com

MILLIGAN, **Bryce.** American (born United States), b. 1953?. **Genres:** Poetry, Young Adult Fiction, Children's Fiction, Adult Non-fiction. **Career:** Pax: A Journal for Peace through Culture, editor, 1983-87; San Antonio Express News, book critic, 1983-87; Guadalupe Cultural Arts Center, director of literature program, 1985-86, 1994-2000; Vortex: A Critical Review, founding editor, 1986-90; San Antonio Light, book critic, 1987-90; Huehuetitlan, co-editor, 1989-96; Wings Press, owner, 1995-; North East School of Arts, director of creative writing program, 2000-02. **Publications:** FOR YOUNG ADULTS: With the Wind, Kevin Dolan, 1987; Battle of the Alamo: You Are There, 1990; Comanche Captive: You Are There, 1990; Lawmen: Stories of Men Who Tamed the West, 1994; The Mountain Men: Stories of Men Who Tamed the Wilderness, 1995. POETRY: FOR ADULTS: Daysleepers & Other Poems, 1984; Litany Sung at Hell's Gate, 1990; From inside the Tree, 1990; Working the Stone, 1993; Alms for Oblivion: A Poem in Seven Parts, 2002; Lost and Certain of It, 2006. FOR CHILDREN: Brigid's Cloak: An Ancient Irish Story, 2002; The Prince of Ireland and the Three Magic Stallions, 2003. OTHER: (ed. with A. de Hoyos and M.G. Milligan) Daughters of the Fifth Sun: A Collection of Latina Fiction and Poetry, 1995; (ed.) This Promiscuous Light: Young Women Poets of San Antonio, 1996; (ed.) Corazon del Norte: Writing by North Texas Latinos, 1996; (ed. with A. de Hoyos and M.G. Milligan) Floricanto Si!: A Collection of Latina Poetry, 1998; Princess, Priestess, Poet: Enheduanna of Ur, forthcoming. **Address:** Wings Press, 627 E Guenther, San Antonio, TX 78210, U.S.A. **Online address:** milligan@wingspress.com

MILLION, **Joelle.** American (born United States), b. 1946?. **Genres:** Women's Studies And Issues, Biography. **Career:** Minnesota State University, history professor. Author and historian. **Publications:** Woman's Voice, Woman's Place: Lucy Stone and the Birth of the Woman's Rights Movement, 2003. **Address:** c/o Author Mail, Greenwood Publishing Group, 88 Post Rd. W, PO Box 5007, Westport, CT 06880-4208, U.S.A.

MILLMAN, **Brock.** Canadian (born Canada), b. 1963?. **Genres:** History, International Relations/Current Affairs, Social Sciences, Politics/Government. **Career:** University of British Columbia, lecturer in history; University of Windsor, instructor; Royal Military College, instructor; University of Western Ontario, associate professor of history, graduate chair, coordinator for international relations program. Writer. **Publications:** The Ill-made Alliance: Anglo-Turkish Relations, 1934-1940, 1998; Managing Domestic Dissent in First World War Britain, 1914-1918, 2000; Pessimism and British War Policy, 1916-1918, 2001. Contributor to periodicals. **Address:** Department of History, University of Western Ontario, 2224 Lawson Hall, 1151 Richmond St., London, ON N6A 5B8, Canada. **Online address:** bmillman@uwo.ca

MILLMAN, Cynthia R. American (born United States), b. 1954. **Genres:** Biography, Autobiography/Memoirs, Dance/Ballet. **Career:** Isadora Duncan Commemorative Dance Co., dancer, 1976-80; Learning through an Expanded Arts Program, artist-in-residence, 1980-84; Hunter College Campus Elementary School, creative movement teacher, 1981-82; Dalton School, First Program, movement teacher, 1982-88, assistant librarian, 1987-88, head librarian, 1988-95; West Side Montessori School, creative movement and drama teacher, 1983-87; Big Apple Lindy Hoppers, dancer, 1990-95, co-director, 1992-95; New York Swing Dance Society, director, 1991-96; Fieldston Outdoors, movement teacher; Town School, head librarian, 1995-. Writer. **Publications:** (With F. Manning) Frankie Manning: Ambassador of Lindy Hop, 2007. Contributor to magazines. **Address:** Temple University Press, 1852 N 10th St., Philadelphia, PA 19122, U.S.A. **Online address:** info@frankiemanning.com

MILLMAN, Gregory J. American (born United States), b. 1951?. **Genres:** Business/Trade/Industry, Education, Economics. **Career:** Freelance journalist. **Publications:** The Floating Battlefield: Corporate Strategies in the Currency Wars, 1990; The Vandals' Crown: How Rebel Currency Traders Overthrew the World's Central Banks, 1995; The Day Traders: The Untold Story of the Extreme Investors and How They Changed Wall Street Forever, 1999; (with M. Millman) Homeschooling: A Family's Journey, 2008. **Address:** Tarcher Books, 375 Hudson St., New York, NY 10014-3657, U.S.A. **Online address:** gjmillman@yahoo.com

MILLMAN, Isaac. American/French (born France), b. 1933. **Genres:** Children's Fiction, History. **Career:** Illustrator and writer. **Publications:** SELF-ILLUSTRATED: Moses Goes to a Concert, 1998; Moses Goes to School, 2000; Moses Goes to the Circus, 2003; Moses Sees a Play, 2004; Hidden Child, 2005; (with J. Leslie) Arbeit Macht Frei: Work Sets You Free, vol. I, 2011. Illustrator of books by others. Contributor to periodicals. **Address:** 249 E 48th St., Ste. 16B, New York, NY 10017-1535, U.S.A.

MILLMAN, Joan (M.). American (born United States), b. 1931. **Genres:** Novels, Education, Novellas/Short Stories, Sciences, Business/Trade/Industry, Literary Criticism And History. **Career:** Elementary school teacher, 1951-70; Salem State College, teacher, 1998-2000; Emerson College, Department of Writing, Publishing and Literature, adjunct faculty; Framingham State University, faculty. Writer. **Publications:** (With P. Behrmann) Excel I, 1968; (with P. Behrmann) How Many Spoons Make a Family?: A Book of Primary Math Experiences for Children, 1971; Excel II, 1976; (with P. Behrmann) Parents as Playmates, 1979; Guide to Public Relations in Boston, 1983; The Effigy (story collection), 1990. **Address:** 30 Ackers Ave., Ste. 1, Brookline, MA 02445-4160, U.S.A. **Online address:** joanmillmn@aol.com

MILLNER, Cork. American (born United States), b. 1931. **Genres:** Novels, Plays/Screenplays, Food And Wine, Self Help. **Career:** University of California, Santa Barbara City College, writing instructor. Writer. **Publications:** NONFICTION: Vintage Valley: California Wines, 1983, rev. ed., 1985; Sherry: The Golden Wine of Spain, 1984; Wines and Wineries of Santa Barbara County, 1985; Cork Millner's Recipe of the Winemakers, 1986; Santa Barbara Celebrities: Conversations from the American Riviera, 1986; (with L. Millner) Looking Great without Diet or Exercise: How to Look Thin Instantly, 1987; The Art of Interviewing: How to Write and Sell the Personality Profile, 1987; Write from the Start, 1994; Portraits, 1994; (with C.W. Sperling and J. Warner) Hollywood Be Thy Name: The Warner Brothers Story, 1994; Vintage Cork (humor), 1997; The Q's and A's of Interviewing-For Writers, 2002; Christmas Ornament, 2006; Everything Shakespeare Book, 2008. NOVELS: Polo Wives, 2002; The Goddess Spot, 2004; She Jesus: The Secret Gospel of John, 2009. PLAYS: Beefcake Bazaar (comedy), 1982. OTHERS: (ed.) Ancient Memories, 1991; (ed.) Magic Makeover: Tricks for Looking Thinner, Younger, and More Confident - Instantly!, 1997. **Address:** 3375 Foothill Rd., Ste. 935, Carpinteria, CA 93013, U.S.A. **Online address:** vincork@aol.com

MILLNER, Denene. American (born United States), b. 1969?. **Genres:** Human Relations/Parenting, Novels, Young Adult Non-fiction. **Career:** Hofstra University, adjunct professor, 1988-; Associate Press-New Jersey, general assignment reporter, 1990-93; Associate Press-New York, political reporter, 1990-93; City Hall Bureau, political reporter; New York Daily News, political and entertainment reporter, 1993-2001; Honey Magazine, features editor, 1998-2001, senior editor, 2001-, executive editor; Parenting Magazine, articles editor, 2003-05, reality check columnist and contributing editor, advice columnist, 2005-; Legal Outreach Inc., writing instructor; Harlem Overhead, editorial director; Essence Magazine, contributing writer; Odyssey Couleur, associate editor. **Publications:** The Sistahs' Rules: Secrets for Meeting, Getting, and Keeping a Good Black Man, 1997. WITH N. CHILES: What Brothers Think, What Sistahs Know: The Real Deal on Love and Relationships, 1999; What Brothers Think, What Sistahs Know About Sex: The Real Deal on Passion, Loving, and Intimacy, 2000; Money, Power, Respect: What Brothers Think, What Sistahs Know About Commitmen, 2001; Love Don't Live Here Anymore, 2002; In Love and War, 2003; A Love Story, 2004. OTHERS: (with A. Burt-Murray and M. Miller) Angry Black Woman's Guide to Life, 2004; (with A. Burt-Murray and M. Miller) The Vow: A Novel, 2005; Dreamgirls: A Novelization, 2006; (with M. Miller) Hotlanta, 2008; (with M. Miller) If Only You Knew: A Hotlanta Novel, 2008; (with N. Leakes) Never Make the Same Mistake Twice: Lessons on Love and Life Learned the Hard Way, 2009; (with M. Miller) What Goes Around: A Hotlanta Novel, 2009; (with S. Harvey) Act Like a Lady, Think Like a Man, 2009; (with S. Harvey) Straight Talk, No Chaser, 2010; Miss You, Mina, 2010; (with H.R. Peete and R.E. Peete) My Brother Charlie, 2010. Contributor to periodicals. **Address:** c/o William Morrow, HarperCollins Publishers, 10 E 53rd St., New York, NY 10022-5244, U.S.A.

MILLS, A(nthony) D(avid). American/British (born England), b. 1935. **Genres:** Language/Linguistics, Travel/Exploration, Local History/Rural Topics, History. **Career:** University of Uppsala, lecturer in English, 1958-61; University of London, Queen Mary College, lecturer, 1961-77, senior lecturer, 1977-79, reader in English, 1979-87, reader emeritus, 1988-. Writer. **Publications:** (Ed.) The Dorset Lay Subsidy Roll of 1332, 1971; Dorset Place Names: Their Origins and Meanings, 1986; The Place Names of Dorset, 60 vols., 1989; A Dictionary of English Place Names, 1991; The Place Names of the Isle of Wight: Their Origins and Meanings, 1994; (co-author) Gordon, Gaffney & Graham's Questions in Company Accounting, 1994; A Dictionary of London Place Names, 2001; A Dictionary of British Place-Names, 2003. Contributor to scholarly journals. **Address:** Oxford University Press Publicity, 198 Madison Ave., New York, NY 10016, U.S.A.

MILLS, Dana. *See* **JACKSON, Jane.**

MILLS, Greg. South African (born South Africa), b. 1962. **Genres:** Military/Defense/Arms Control, Economics, History. **Career:** University of the Western Cape, lecturer, 1990-94; Centre for Defence and International Security Studies, research associate, 1991-; South African Institute of International Affairs, Western Cape Branch, chair, 1991-93, director, 1994-96, national director, 1996-2005; Brenthurst Foundation, director, 2005-; Prism Group of Ninth International Security Assistance Force, head, 2006-07; Cambridge University, Centre for African Studies, visiting fellow, 2009; NATO Higher Defence College, visiting faculty. Writer. **Publications:** South African Security after Apartheid: A Framework for Analysis, 1993; Plus ça change, plus c'est la même chose: South Africa and Southern African Security after Apartheid, 1993; The South African Armed Forces: Ethnicity and Integration, 1993; War and Peace in Southern Africa: Crime, Drugs, Armies, and Trade, 1996; South Africa and Security Building in the Indian Ocean Rim, 1998; The South African National Defence Force: Between Downsizing and New Capabilities?, 1998; (with M. Edmonds) Beyond the Horizon: Defence, Diplomacy and South Africa's Naval Opportunities, 1998; The Wired Model: South Africa, Foreign Policy, and Globalisation, 2000; Sudan: Complexity, Conflict and Co-operation, 2001; (with M. Edmonds) South Africa's Defence Industry: A Template for Middle Powers?, 2001; Poverty to Prosperity: Globalisation, Good Governance and African Recovery, 2002; (with J. Herbst) The Future of Africa: A New Order in Sight?, 2003; The Security Intersection: The Paradox of Power in an Age of Terror, 2005; (with D. Williams) Seven Battles That Shaped South Africa, 2006; From Africa to Afghanistan: With Richards and NATO to Kabul, 2007; Why Africa Is Poor: And What Africans Can Do About It, 2010. EDITOR: Action for Social Change, Whose Responsibility? Papers and Discussion Summaries from the Eighth National Conference of the Australian Council of Social Service, 1974; From Pariah to Participant: South Africa's Evolving Foreign Relations, 1990-1994, 1994; (with J. Cilliers) Peacekeeping in Africa, 1995; Maritime Policy for Developing Nations, 1995; (with A. Begg and A. van Nieuwkerk) South Africa in the Global Economy, 1995; (with A. Handley) From Isolation to Integration? The South African Economy in the 1990s, 1996; (with R.I. Rotberg) War and Peace in Southern Africa: Crime, Drugs, Armies, and Trade, 1998; Southern Africa into the Next Millennium, 1998; (with A. Handley) South Africa and Southern Africa: Regional Integration and Emerging Markets, 1998; South Africa and the Future of the Non-aligned Movement, 1998; (with C. Mutschler) Exploring South-South Dialogue: Mercosur in Latin America and SADC in Southern Africa, 1999; (with J. Cilliers) From Peacekeeping to Complex Emergencies: Peace Support Missions in Africa, 1999; (with J. Stremlau) The Privatisation of Security in Africa, 1999; (with J. Stremlau) The Commonwealth in the Twenty-First Century, 1999; (with P. Mathoma and J. Stremlau) Putting People First: African Priorities for the UN Millennium Assembly, 2000; (with J. Stremlau) The Reality behind the Rhetoric: The United States, South Africa, and Africa, 2000; (with T. Bertelsmann-Scott) The EU-SA Agreement: South Africa, Southern Africa and the European Union, 2000; (with M. Edmonds) South Africa and Naval Power at the Millennium, 2000; (with M. Glinzler and W. Mabena) Multilateral Organisations in the Asia-Pacific: Lessons and Experiences for Southern Africa, 2001; (with G. Shelton) Asia- Pacific and Africa: Realising Economic Potential, 2003; (with N. Skidmore) Towards China Inc? Assessing the Implications for Africa, 2004; (with R. Cobbold) Global Challenges and Africa: Bridging Divides, Dealing with Perceptions, Rebuilding Societies, 2004; (with M. Edmonds and C. Lee) Arms and Security in Asia, 2004; (with C. Clapham and J. Herbst) Big African States, 2006. Contributor to periodicals. **Address:** Brenthurst Foundation, PO Box 61631, Marshalltown, Johannesburg, 2107, South Africa.

MILLS, Judith Christine. British (born England), b. 1956. **Genres:** Art/Art History. **Career:** Painter, sculptor, illustrator and author. **Publications:** The Stonehook Schooner, 1997; Bridge 6, 1999; The Painted Chest, 2000; Wild Cameron Women, 2000; The Sacred Seal, 2001; Messenger, 2003; The Book of the Sage, 2004; The Strange Voyage of the Raconteur, 2005; Carew, 2006. Illustrator of books by others. **Address:** Case Goods Warehouse, 55 Mill St., Ste. 74, Toronto, ON M5A 3C4, Canada. **Online address:** info@jcmillsgallery.com

MILLS, Linda G. American (born United States), b. 1951. **Genres:** Law. **Career:** Hawkins Center of Law and Services for People with Disabilities, founder, 1984; University of California, faculty; New York University, Silver School of Social Work, professor of social work, public policy and law and senior vice provost for undergraduate education and university life, Center on Violence and Recovery, founder. Writer, lawyer and sociologist. **Publications:** The Heart of Intimate Abuse: New Interventions in Child Welfare, Criminal Justice, and Health Settings, 1998; A Penchant for Prejudice: Unraveling Bias in Judicial Decision Making, 1999; Insult to Injury: Rethinking Our Responses to Intimate Abuse, 2003; Violent Partners: A Breakthrough Plan for Ending the Cycle of Abuse, 2008. Contributor to journals. **Address:** Silver School of Social Work, New York University, Ehrenkranz Ctr., 1 Washington Sq. N, New York, NY 10003-6654, U.S.A. **Online address:** linda.mills@nyu.edu

MILLS, Margaret A(nn). American (born United States), b. 1946?. **Genres:** Mythology/Folklore, Anthropology/Ethnology. **Career:** Harvard University, teaching fellow, 1970-78; Harvard University, Radcliffe College, assistant senior tutor, 1976-78; University of Northern Iran, U.S. liaison officer for academic affairs, 1978-79; Skagit Valley College, adjunct lecturer, 1982; University of Washington, visiting lecturer, 1982; Pomona College, Claremont, associate dean of students and dean of women, 1982-83; University of Pennsylvania, assistant professor, 1983-89, associate professor of folklore and folk life, 1989-93, Department of Folklore and Folk Life, graduate chair, 1992-95, chair and undergraduate chair of folklore and folk life, 1995-98; Ohio State University, Department of Near Eastern Languages and Cultures, professor and chair, 1998-. Writer. **Publications:** Cupid and Psyche in Afghanistan: An International Tale in Cultural Context, 1978; Oral Narrative in Afghanistan: The Individual in Tradition, 1990; (ed. with A. Appadurai and F.J. Korom) Gender, Genre, and Power in South Asian Expressive Traditions, 1991; Rhetorics and Politics in Afghan Traditional Storytelling, 1991; (with R. Rahmoni) Conversations with Dauvlat Khâlâv, 2000; (ed. with P.J. Claus and S. Diamond) South Asian Folklore: An Encyclopedia, 2003. Works appear in anthologies. Contributor to professional journals. **Address:** Department of Near Eastern Languages & Cultures, The Ohio State University, Rm. 203, 1735 Neil Ave., 131 Mershon Ctr., Columbus, OH 43210-1293, U.S.A. **Online address:** mills.186@osu.edu

MILLS, Patricia J(agentowicz). American (born United States), b. 1944. **Genres:** Philosophy, Humanities. **Career:** York University, lecturer in humanities, 1976-78, lecturer in social sciences, 1978-81; University of Toronto, Department of Philosophy, postdoctoral fellow, 1984-86, lecturer in women's studies, 1984-85, assistant professor of philosophy, 1986-88; University of Massachusetts, assistant professor, 1988-91, associate professor of political science, 1991-, professor emeritus, 1988-2006; Smith College, lecturer, 1992; Manhattan, editor and consultant, 2007-. **Publications:** Woman, Nature and Psyche, 1987; (ed. and contrib.) Re-Reading the Canon: Feminist Interpretations of G.W.F. Hegel, 1996; Ecological Feminist Perspectives, 1996. Contributor of articles to books and periodicals. **Address:** 425 W End Ave., Apt. 7A, New York, NY 10024, U.S.A. **Online address:** pjmills@polsci.umass.edu

MILLS, Peter R. American (born United States), b. 1962. **Genres:** Adult Non-fiction, Anthropology/Ethnology, History. **Career:** Bureau of Land Management, survey archaeologist, 1984; University of Vermont, archaeologist, 1984-85, visiting assistant professor of archaeology, 1996-97; Washington State University, coordinator of lithic laboratory, 1985-87, Museum of Anthropology, assistant to curator, 1985-87; Crow Canyon Archaeological Center, staff archaeologist, 1986; University of Idaho, field archaeologist, 1986; Bureau of Indian Affairs, Alaska Native Claims Settlement Act Office, survey archaeologist and ethnologist, 1987; Massachusetts Historical Commission, preservation planner and assistant state archaeologist, 1988-90; University of Alaska, Arctic Environmental Information and Data Center, field archaeologist and lithic analyst, 1990; Bernice P. Bishop Museum, project co-director in applied research group, 1990-91; Biosystems Analysis Inc., field survey director, 1993; Earthwatch, assistant director of survey and excavation, 1995; University of Hawaii-Hilo, Department of Anthropology, assistant professor, 1997-2002, associate professor of anthropology, 2002-, professor, chair; John Young Homestead, Archaeological Field School, operator, 1999; Laupahoehoe Train Museum, board director, 2000. Writer. **Publications:** A Walk through History: Pedestrian Survey of the Old Government Beach Road, Honalo to Honua'ino, North Kona, Hawai'i Island, 2 vols., 2000; Hawai'i's Russian Adventure: A New Look at Old History, 2002. Contributor of articles and reviews to periodicals. **Address:** Department of Anthropology, University of Hawaii Hilo, 200 W Kawili St., Hilo, HI 96720, U.S.A. **Online address:** millsp@hawaii.edu

MILLS, Richard W. British (born England), b. 1945?. **Genres:** Education, Social Sciences, Cultural/Ethnic Topics, Psychology. **Career:** Institute of Community Studies, associate, 1967-73; sociologist and author. **Publications:** Young Outsiders: A Study of Alternative Communities, 1973; Classroom Observation of Primary School Children: All in a Day, 1980 as Observing Children in the Primary Classroom: All in a Day, 1988. EDITOR: Occasions (textbook series), 1976; Teaching English across the Ability Range, 1977; (with J. Mills) Bilingualism in the Primary School: A Handbook for Teachers, 1993; (with J. Mills) Childhood Studies: A Reader in Perspectives of Childhood, 2000. Contributor to periodicals. **Address:** 31 Pennethorne Close, London, GL E9, England.

MILLS, Robert. British (born England), b. 1973. **Genres:** History, Cultural/Ethnic Topics, Art/Art History. **Career:** King's College London, School of Arts and Humanities, Department of English, senior lecturer, director; University of Connecticut, Charles Owen, Jr. distinguished visiting professor in medieval studies, 2006. Writer. **Publications:** (Ed. with B. Bildhauer) The Monstrous Middle Ages, 2003; (ed. with E. Campbell) Troubled Vision: Gender, Sexuality, and Sight in Medieval Text and Image, 2004; Suspended Animation: Pain, Pleasure, and Punishment in Medieval Culture, 2005; (with H.G. Cocks, M. Cook and R. Trumbach) A Gay History of Britain: Love and Sex between Men since the Middle Ages, 2007. Contributor to periodicals and journals. **Address:** Department of English, King's College London, Rm. S2.05, Strand, London, GL WC2R 2LS, England. **Online address:** robert.mills@kcl.ac.uk

MILLS, Stephanie. American (born United States), b. 1948. **Genres:** Environmental Sciences/Ecology, Sciences, Technology. **Career:** Earth Times, editor-in-chief, 1970; Earth, story editor, 1971; Friends of the Earth, Outings Program, director, 1975-76, director of membership development, 1976-78, editor-in-chief, 1977-78; Farallones Institute, board director, 1976-78; Co-Evolution Quarterly, assistant editor, editor, 1980-82; California Tomorrow, editor-in-chief and research director, 1982-83; World College West, director of development, 1983-84; freelance writer and lecturer, 1984-; Oryana Natural Foods Cooperative, president of board directors, 1992-93. **Publications:**

(Ed. with R. Theobald) Failure of Success: Ecological Values vs. Economic Myths, 1973; Whatever Happened to Ecology? (memoir), 1989; (ed. and contrib.) In Praise of Nature, 1990; In Service of the Wild: Restoring and Reinhabiting Damaged Land, 1995; (ed.) Turning Away from Technology: A New Vision for the 21st Century, 1997; Epicurean Simplicity, 2002; (with B. McKibben) Live Well, Live Wild: A Community Concourse on Undomesticating and Rewilding, 2006; Tough Little Beauties: Selected Essays and Other Writings, 2007; On Gandhi's Path, 2010. Contributor to magazines. **Address:** c/o Katinka Matson, Brockman Inc., 5 E 59th St., New York, NY 10022, U.S.A.

MILLS, Stephen (Paul). British (born England), b. 1952. **Genres:** Natural History, Sciences. **Career:** Environmental Investigation Agency, chair and head of campaigns; The International Association of Wildlife Film-Makers, chairman and director. Writer and producer. **Publications:** Nature In Its Place, 1988; (with P. Riemer) Ford-based Kit Cars, 1988; (with M. Amsler and K. Kirsch) Improving It: Accountability by Design, 1991; Tiger, 2004. Contributor to periodicals. **Address:** BBC Wildlife Magazine, Broadcasting House, Whiteladies Rd., Bristol, GL BS8 2LR, England. **Online address:** s.p.mills@talk21.com

MILLS, Vicki A. American (born United States), b. 1948. **Genres:** Business/Trade/Industry, Information Science/Computers, Travel/Exploration. **Career:** Mills Custom Services Publishing, owner, 1971-2005. Writer. **Publications:** Fly Free Stay Cheap, 1997; (with K.P. Quintanilla) En 1, 2, 3 Puedes Usar Y Disfrutar La Computadora: Aprende Lo Basico De Forma Sencilla Y Clara, 2004; Any Body Can Enjoy Computers: The Clear and Simple Basics, 2004. Contributor to periodicals. **Address:** PO Box 2287, Cathedral City, CA 92235-2287, U.S.A. **Online address:** vamills@aol.com

MILLS, Wilmer. *See* Obituaries.

MILLSPAUGH, Ben P. American (born United States), b. 1936. **Genres:** Air/Space Topics, Sciences. **Career:** Julesburg High School, science teacher; Euclid Junior High School, science teacher, 1960-67; United Airlines, flight operations instructor, 1967-69; Littleton High School, director of aviation and aerospace, 1969-91; Civil Air Patrol's Rocky Mountain Region, director of aerospace education, now retired. Writer. **Publications:** Ultralight Airman's Information Manual, 1982; Private Pilot's License Program, 1985; Commercial Pilot's License Program, 1985; Z Car Enthusiast's Guide, 1986; Ultralight Airman's Manual, 1987; Z Car: A Legend in Its Own Time, 1991; Aviation and Space Science Projects, 1992; Aerospace Science Projects, 1994; (with B. Taylor) Let's Build Airplanes and Rockets!, 1996; Aerospace Education 2000 Activity Book, 1996. Contributor to books. **Address:** 6334 S Jay Way, Littleton, CO 80123, U.S.A.

MILLUM, Trevor. British (born England), b. 1945. **Genres:** Novels, Novellas/Short Stories, Poetry, Adult Non-fiction, Information Science/Computers, Illustrations, Young Adult Fiction. **Career:** Nchelenge Secondary School, teacher, 1971-74; Matthew Humberstone School, teacher of English, 1975-77; Baysgarth School, teacher of English and head of department, 1977-81; United World College of Southeast Asia, head of faculty of English, 1981-84; Longcroft School, head of faculty of languages, 1984-88, advisory teacher for information technology, 1988-90; Resource I.T. Centre, centre manager, 1990-; National Association for the Teaching of English, director, 1999-, consultant. Writer. **Publications:** SELF-ILLUSTRATED: Traffic Island and Other Stories, 1984. OTHERS: Images of Woman: Advertising in Women's Magazines, 1975; Exercises in African History, 1978; Warning: Too Much Schooling Can Damage Your Health, 1988; (ed. and intro.) Pigs is Pigs, 1988; Mixing It, 1989; (ed. and intro.) Funny Bones, 1989; Nimbus for the Nervous, 1990; (ed.) Farm, 1990; (ed.) The Importance of Being Earnest, 1991; The Mouse and the Muse, 1991; I.T. into Practice, 1992; Control for the Confused, 1992; Tramps and Their Excuses: A Study of the Writing of Travellers in Borneo in the 19th and 20th Centuries, 1994; Double Talk, 1994; (ed.) She Stoops to Conquer, 1994; (ed.) The Duchess of Malfi, 1996; Twenty Things to Do with a Word Processor, 2000; The Curious Case of Dr. Mann, 2002; On the Edge, 2003; Journey to Fear, 2003; ICT and Literacy, 2005; Interactive Literacy, 2005; (ed. with C. Warren) Sharing Not Staring, 2008; (with T. Rank and C. Warren) Teaching English using ICT: A Practical Guide for Secondary School Teachers, 2011; Flat World Jack, forthcoming. Contributor to journals. **Address:** Fern House, Barrow on Humber, North Lincolnshire, LI DN19 7AA, England.

MILLWARD, Robert. British (born England) **Genres:** Politics/Government, Biography. **Career:** University of Manchester, Department of Economics, lecturer, 1965-69, senior lecturer, 1973-74, professor, 1989-, now professor emeritus of economic history; University of Salford, professor of economics, 1975-89. Writer. **Publications:** (Co-author) Public Sector Economics, 1983; (with J.F. Peck) Public and Private Ownership of British Industry, 1820-1990, 1994; (ed. with J. Singleton) The Political Economy of Nationalisation in Britain, 1920- 1950, 1995; Private and Public Enterprise in Europe: Energy, Telecommunications and Transport, 1830- 1990, 2005; (ed. with F. Amatori and P. Toninelli) Reappraising State Owned Enterprise: A Comparison of The UK and Italy, 2011. Contributor of articles to journals. **Address:** History Subject Group, School of Arts, Histories & Cultures, University of Manchester, N2.16 Samuel Alexander Bldg. Oxford Rd., Manchester, M13 9PL, England. **Online address:** r.millward@manchester.ac.uk

MILNE, David. British (born England), b. 1976?. **Genres:** Biography, Autobiography/Memoirs. **Career:** University of Nottingham, lecturer; University of East Anglia, lecturer in American politics. Writer. **Publications:** America's Rasputin: Walt Rostow and the Vietnam War, 2008. **Address:** American & Canadian Studies, University of Nottingham, University Pk., Nottingham, NG7 2RD, England. **Online address:** david.milne@nottingham.ac.uk

MILNE, Kevin Alan. American (born United States), b. 1973. **Genres:** Novels, Literary Criticism And History. **Career:** Writer. **Publications:** The Paper Bag Christmas, 2006; The Nine Lessons: A Novel of Love, Fatherhood, and Second Chances, 2009; Sweet Misfortune: A Novel, 2010; Final Note: A Novel, 2011. **Address:** Center Street, 237 Park Ave., New York, NY 10017, U.S.A. **Online address:** kevin@kevinamilne.com

MILNE, Larry. *See* **HOYLE, Trevor.**

MILNE, Lorna. Scottish (born Scotland), b. 1959. **Genres:** Literary Criticism And History, Politics/Government, Cultural/Ethnic Topics. **Career:** Her Majesty's Diplomatic Service, political secretary, 1983-87; University of Auckland, lecturer, 1988-91; University of Aston in Birmingham, lecturer, 1991-95; University of Saint Andrews, senior lecturer in French, 1996-, professor and vice-principal. Writer. **Publications:** L'Evangile Selon Michel: La Trinité Initiatique dans l'Oeuvre de Tournier, 1994; (ed. with J. Gaffney) French Presidentialism and the Election of 1995, 1997; (ed.) Postcolonial Violence, Culture and Identity in Francophone Africa and the Antilles, 2007; (with M. Orr) Narratives of French Modernity: Themes, Forms and Metamorphoses: Essays in Honour of David Gascoigne, 2011. Contributor of articles to journals. **Address:** Department of French, School of Modern Languages French, University of St. Andrews, Buchanan Bldg., Rm. 406B, St. Andrews, FF KY16 9PH, Scotland. **Online address:** lcm2@st-andrews.ac.uk

MILNE, Seumas. British (born England), b. 1958. **Genres:** Economics, Essays, Organized Labor, Industrial Relations, Business/Trade/Industry, History, Young Adult Fiction. **Career:** The Economist, staff journalist, 1981-84; The Guardian, news reporter, staff journalist, 1984-, labour correspondent, 1990-95, labour editor, 1995-, comment editor, 2001-07, columnist, associate editor, 2007-. **Publications:** (With N. Costello and J. Michie) Beyond the Casino Economy: Planning for the 1990s, 1989; The Enemy Within: MI5, Maxwell and the Scargill Affair, 1994, rev. ed. as The Enemy Within: The Secret War against the Miners, 1995, 3rd ed., 2004. Works appear in anthologies. **Address:** The Guardian, 119 Farringdon Rd., London, GL EC1, England.

MILNOR, Kristina. American (born United States) **Genres:** Literary Criticism And History, Cultural/Ethnic Topics. **Career:** Columbia University, Barnard College, Tow Family Foundation, assistant professor of classics, 1998-2006, associate professor of classics, 2006-. Writer. **Publications:** Gender, Domesticity, and the Age of Augustus: Inventing Private Life, 2005. **Address:** Barnard College, Department of Classics & Ancient Studies, 219 Milbank, 3009 Broadway, New York, NY 10027, U.S.A. **Online address:** km384@columbia.edu

MILOFSKY, Carl. American (born United States), b. 1948. **Genres:** Sociology, Politics/Government. **Career:** Yale University, assistant professor of sociology, 1978-82; Bucknell University, Department of Sociology and Anthropology, assistant professor, 1982-84, associate professor, 1982-90, professor and chairperson, [illegible]; Nonprofit and Voluntary Sector quarterly, editor, 1992-. **Publications:** Special Education: A Sociological Study of California Programs, 1976; (ed.) Community Organizations: Studies in Resource Mobilization and Exchange, [illegible], Testers and Testing: The Sociology of School

Psychology, 1989; (ed.) Community Chest, 1989; (with A. Hunter) Pragmatic Liberalism: Constructing A Civil Society, 2007; (ed. with R.A. Cnaan) Handbook of Community Movements and Local Organizations, 2007; Smallville: Institutionalizing Community in Twenty-first-century America, 2008. **Address:** Department of Sociology and Anthropology, Bucknell University, 701 Moore Ave., 204 Coleman Hall, Lewisburg, PA 17837, U.S.A. **Online address:** carl.milofsky@bucknell.edu

MILOFSKY, David. American (born United States), b. 1946. **Genres:** Novels. **Career:** University of Denver, assistant professor of English, 1982-88, director of writing programs; Colorado State University, professor of English, 1988-, director of writing programs, University of Honors Program, faculty, Center for Literary Publishing, founder, director; Denver Quarterly, editor; Colorado Review, editor; Middlebury College, faculty; Iowa State University, faculty; University of Wisconsin, faculty. **Publications:** (Ed.) New Voices: Poetry and Fiction from Colorado State University, 1994. NOVELS: Playing from Memory, 1981; Eternal People, 1998; Color of Law, 2000; A Friend of Kissinger, 2003. **Address:** Department of English, Colorado State University, 1773 Campus Delivery Eddy Hall, Fort Collins, CO 80523-1773, U.S.A. **Online address:** david.milofsky@colostate.edu

MILSOM, Stroud Francis Charles. (Toby Milsom). British (born England), b. 1923. **Genres:** History, Law, Natural History, Humanities. **Career:** Trinity College, staff, 1941-44, fellow and lecturer, 1949-55; University Pennsylvania, commonwealth fund fellow, 1947-48; University of London, London School of Economics, lecturer, 1955-56, professor of legal history, 1964-76; New College, cuf lecturer, fellow and tutor, 1956-64, dean 1959-64; New York University, visiting lecturer, 1958-70; The Selden Society, literary director, 1964-80, president, 1985-88; British Academy, fellow, 1967, lecturer, 1980; Yale University, visiting professor, 1968-86; Royal Historical Society, fellow, 1970; American Society For Legal History, corresponding fellow, 1971; Cambridge University, Maitland memorial lecturer, 1972, Saint John's College, fellow, 1976-, professor of law, 1976-90, professor emeritus of law, 1990-, Faculty of Law, chairman, 2010-; Harvard University, visiting professor, 1973; Indiana University, Addison Harris lecturer, 1974; University of Colorado, Charles Inglis Thompson professor, 1977; Monash University, Wilfred Fullagar memorial lecturer and visiting professor, 1981; Oxford University, Ford's lecturer in English history, 1986; Columbia University, Carpentier lecturer, 1995. Writer. **Publications:** (Intro.) Novae Narrationes, 1963; (intro.) Pollock and Maitland's History of English Law, 1968; Historical Foundations of the Common Law, 1969, 2nd ed., 1981; The Legal Framework of English Feudalism: The Maitland Lectures Given in 1972, 1976; Studies in the History of the Common Law, 1985; (with J.H. Baker) Sources of English Legal History, 1986; A Natural History of the Common Law, 2003. Contributor to books. **Address:** St. John's College, Cambridge University, Cambridge, CB CB2 1TP, England.

MILSOM, Toby. *See* **MILSOM, Stroud Francis Charles.**

MILTNER, Robert. American (born United States), b. 1949. **Genres:** Novellas/Short Stories, Poetry, Essays, History, Humanities. **Career:** Holy Family High School, teacher of English, 1975-77; Padua Franciscan High School, English chair and teacher, 1977-87; Kent State University, Department of English, instructor, 1987-98, coordinator for developmental education, 1987-95, director of writing center, 1990-92, 1995-97, assistant professor, 1998-; Walsh University, instructor in English, 1993-94. **Publications:** POETRY: The Seamless Serial Hour, 1993; Against the Simple, 1995; On the Off Ramp, 1996; Ghost of a Chance, 2001; Four Crows on a Phone Line, 2002; A Box of Light, 2002; Jealous Light, 2003. OTHER: (ed. with S.L. Kleppe) New Paths to Raymond Carver: Critical Essays on His Life, Fiction and Poetry, 2008. Contributor to periodicals. **Address:** Department of English, KSU Stark Campus, 114 Fine Arts, 6000 Frank Ave., NW, North Canton, OH 44720, U.S.A. **Online address:** rmiltner@stark.kent.edu

MILTON, Giles. British (born England), b. 1966. **Genres:** Novels, Young Adult Fiction, Adult Non-fiction. **Career:** Freelance journalist and historian. **Publications:** The Riddle and the Knight: In Search of Sir John Mandeville, 1996; Nathaniel's Nutmeg; Or, the True and Incredible Adventures of the Spice Trader Who Changed the Course of History, 1999; Big Chief Elizabeth: The Adventures and Fate of the First English Colonists in America, 2000; Samurai William: The Englishman Who Opened Japan, 2002; White Gold: The Extraordinary Story of Thomas Pellow and Islam's One Million White Slaves, 2004; Paradise Lost: Smyrna, 1922, 2008. NOVELS: Edward Trencom's Nose: A Novel of History, Dark Intrigue and Cheese, 2007; According to Arnold: A Novel of Love and Mushrooms, 2009. Contributor to periodicals. **Address:** Pan Macmillan, 20 New Wharf Rd., London, GL N1 9RR, England. **Online address:** gilesmilton@gilesmilton.com

MILTON, Pat. American (born United States) **Genres:** International Relations/Current Affairs, Engineering. **Career:** Associated Press, journalist; CBS News Investigative Unit, producer. 2008-. **Publications:** In the Blink of an Eye: The Inside Story of the FBI's Investigation of TWA Flight 800, 1999. Contributor to periodicals. **Address:** c/o Author Mail, Random House Inc., 1745 Broadway, New York, NY 10019, U.S.A.

MIN, Anchee. American/Chinese (born China), b. 1957. **Genres:** Novels, Autobiography/Memoirs, Romance/Historical. **Career:** Writer and actor. **Publications:** Red Azalea: A True Story of Life and Love in China (memoir), 1994; Chinese Propoganda Posters, 2003; The Last Empress, 2007. NOVELS: Katherine, 1995; Becoming Madam Mao, 2000; Wild Ginger, 2002; Empress Orchid, 2004; Pearl of China, 2010. **Address:** The Steven Barclay Agency, 12 Western Ave., Petaluma, CA 94952, U.S.A.

MIN, Anselm K. (Anselm Kyongsuk Min). American (born United States), b. 1940. **Genres:** Theology/Religion, History, Humanities. **Career:** Claremont Graduate University, School of Religion, Philosophy of Religion and Theology Program, professor, 1992-, dean, 2009-, John D. and Lilian Maguire distinguished professor of religion, 2010-. Writer. **Publications:** (With W.E. Biernatzki and L.J. Im) Korean Catholicism in the 1970s: A Christian Community Comes of Age, 1975; (as Anselm Kyongsuk Min) Dialectic of Salvation: Issues in Theology of Liberation, 1989; The Solidarity of Others in a Divided World: A Postmodern Theology after Postmodernism, 2004; Paths to the Triune God: An Encounter between Aquinas and Recent Theologies, 2005. **Address:** School of Religion, Claremont Graduate University, 831 N Dartmouth Ave., Claremont, CA 91711-5909, U.S.A. **Online address:** anselm.min@cgu.edu

MIN, Anselm Kyongsuk. *See* **MIN, Anselm K.**

MINAHAN, John A. American (born United States), b. 1956. **Genres:** Literary Criticism And History, Music, Education, Novels, Children's Fiction. **Career:** Musician, 1978-81; University of Virginia, teacher of music, 1981; Rome School of Music, teacher of music, 1982-83; Northern Virginia Community College, teacher of music, 1983-86; Brown University, teacher of English, 1986-92; Stonehill College, teacher of English, 1992-; Lincoln School, assistant professor of English, 2009-10. Writer. **Publications:** Word Like a Bell: John Keats, Music, and the Romantic Poet, 1992; Teaching Democracy: A Professor's Journal, 1993; Abigail's Drum, 1995. **Address:** Department of English, Lincoln School, 301 Butler Ave., Providence, RI 02906, U.S.A. **Online address:** jminahan@lincolnschool.org

MINAR, Barbra (Goodyear). American (born United States), b. 1940. **Genres:** Children's Fiction, Human Relations/Parenting, Poetry, Medicine/Health, Theology/Religion, Novels, inspirational/Motivational Literature. **Career:** Teacher, 1960-76; Santa Barbara County Schools, art consultant, 1976-80; Santa Ynez Valley Presbyterian School, preschool director, 1980-85; Spiritual Christian Retreat Leader, inspirational speaker, 1990-2000; Direct Link for the Disabled, president, 1993-94. Writer and storyteller. **Publications:** FOR CHILDREN: Little Book Bear, 1989; Super Helping Hero: A Book about Helpfulness, 1990; Lamper's Meadow, 1992. OTHERS: Book Bear's Sleep-Over, 1989; Honey Cookies to Share, 1989; Surprise Present, 1989; Very Special Bear, 1989; Unrealistic Expectations: The Thief of Women's Joy, 1990; Close Connections: Creatively Loving Those Nearest You, 1992; Walking into the Wind: Being Healthy With a Chronic Disease, 2000. Contributor to books, newspapers, journals and magazines. **Address:** 2854 Quail Valley Rd., Solvang, CA 93463-9510, U.S.A. **Online address:** bminar@syv.com

MINARIK, Else H(olmelund). American/Danish (born Denmark), b. 1920. **Genres:** Children's Fiction, Poetry, Children's Non-fiction, Animals/Pets. **Career:** Daily Sentinel, reporter, 1940-50; Commack Public Schools, art teacher, 1950-54; Rome Daily Centennial, journalist. **Publications:** Little Bear, 1957; No Fighting, No Biting!, 1958; Father Bear Comes Home, 1959; Cat and Dog, 1960; Little Bear's Friend, 1960; Little Bear's Visit, 1961; Little Giant Girl and the Elf Boy, 1963; The Winds That Come from Far Away and Other Poems, 1964; A Kiss for Little Bear, 1968; (trans.) J. Loof, My

Grandpa is a Pirate, 1968; What If?, 1987; It's Spring!, 1989; Percy and the Five Houses, 1989; The Little Girl and the Dragon, 1991; Am I Beautiful?, 1992; Little Bear and the Missing Pie, 2002; Little Bear Makes a Scarecrow, 2002; The Search for Spring, 2002; Little Bear's Loose Tooth, 2002; Little Bear's Scary Night, 2002; Father's Flying Flapjacks, 2002; To Grandmother's House, 2002; I Miss You, Father Bear, 2002; A Present for Mother Bear, 2002; Little Bear's Egg, 2002; Little Bear's New Friend, 2002; Father Bear's Special Day, 2003; The Cricket Who Came to Dinner, 2003; Get Well Soon, Little Bear!, 2003; Through the Snowy Woods, 2003; Spring Cleaning, 2003; April Fools!, 2003; Little Bear Makes a Mask, 2003; The Snowball Fight, 2003; Little Bear's Bad Day, 2003; Little Bear's Picture, 2003; Little Bear's Valentine, 2003; Mother Bear's Picnic, 2003; Lost in Little Bear's Room, 2004; Lucky Little Bear, 2004; Asleep Under the Stars, 2004; The Butterfly Garden, 2004; Emily's Birthday, 2004; The Toys' Wedding, 2004; Professor Little Bear, 2005; Little Bear and the Marco Polo, 2010. **Address:** Greenwillow Books, 10 E 53rd St., New York, NY 10022, U.S.A.

MINC, Alain J. R. French (born France), b. 1949. **Genres:** History, Politics/Government, Social Sciences. **Career:** City of Paris, inspector of finances, 1975-79; St. Gobain, director of finance, 1979-86, chief financial officer, 1979; CIR Intl., vice-chairman, 1986-; Cerus, vice president and director general, 1986-91, general manager; A.M. Conseil, founder, president, 1991-; CaixaCorp., board director, 2007-. Writer. **Publications:** (With S. Nora) L'informatisation De La Société: Annexes, 1978; (with S. Nora) L'informatisation De La Société: Rapport à M. Le Président De La République, 1978; (with S. Nora) The Computerization of Society: A Report to the President of France, 1980; L'après-crise Est Commencé: Essai (title means: 'The After-Crisis Has Begun'), 1982; L'avenir En Face (title means: 'Facing the Future'), 1984; Le Syndrome Finlandais (title means: 'The Finland Syndrome'), 1986; La Machine égalitaire (title means: 'The Equality Machine'), 1987; La Grande Illusion, 1989; L'argent Fou (title means: 'Mad Money'), 1990; La Vengeance Des Nations (title means: 'The Vengeance of Nations'), 1990; Français, Si Vous Osiez (title means: 'French, If You Dare'), 1991; The Great European Illusion: Business in the Wider Community, 1992; Le Nouveau Moyen Age (title means: 'The New Middle Age'), 1993; Le Média-choc (title means: 'The Media Shock'), 1993; La France De L'an 2000: Rapport Au Premier Ministre De La Commission Présidée Par Alain Minc, 1994; (with P. Séguin) Deux France?, 1994; L'ivresse Démocratique, 1995; Antiportraits, 1996; Louis Napoléon Revisité, 1997; La Mondialisation Heureuse, 1997; Au Nom De La Loi, 1998; Spinoza, Un Roman Juif, 1999; www.capitalisme.fr, 2000; Epîtres à Nos Nouveaux Maîtres, 2002; Le Fracas Du Monde: Journal de L'année 2001, 2002; Les Prophètes Du Bonheur: Une Histoire Personnelle De La Pensée économique, 2004; Ce Monde Qui Vient, 2004; Le Crépuscule Des Petits Dieux, 2005; Sorte De Diable: Les Vies De John Maynard Keynes, 2006; Histoire De France, 2008; Dix Jours Qui ébranleront Le Monde, 2009; Une histoire politique des intellectuels, 2010; Un petit coin de paradis, 2011. Contributor of articles to journals. **Address:** A.M. Conseil, 10 Ave. George V, Paris, 75008, France.

MINCHIN, Timothy J. Australian/British (born England), b. 1969. **Genres:** History, Economics. **Career:** Cambridge University, Mellon research fellow, 1995-98; University of St. Andrews, lecturer in history, 1998-; La Trobe University, Department of Humanities and Social Sciences, senior lecturer, 2004-06, reader and associate professor, 2006-10, professor, 2010-, honors coordinator, School of Historical and European Studies, head. Writer. **Publications:** What Do We Need a Union For?: The TWUA in the South, 1945-1955, 1997; Hiring the Black Worker: The Racial Integration of the Southern Textile Industry, 1960-1980, 1999; The Color of Work: The Struggle for Civil Rights in the Southern Paper Industry, 1945-1980, 2001; Forging a Common Bond: Labor and Environmental Activism in the BASF Lockout, 2003; Don't Sleep with Stevens!: The J.P. Stevens Campaign and the Struggle to Organize the South, 1963-80, 2005; Fighting Against the Odds: A History of Southern Labor since World War II, 2005; From Rights To Economics: The Ongoing Struggle For Black Equality In The U.S. South, 2007; (with J.A. Salmond) After the Dream: Black and White Southerners Since 1965, 2011. Contributor to periodicals and journals. **Address:** Department of Humanities and Social Sciences, La Trobe University, E119, David Myers Bldg., 3086 Plenty Rd., Melbourne, VI 3086, Australia. **Online address:** t.minchin@latrobe.edu.au

MINCKLER *See* **Bull, Schuyler M.**

MINDELL, Amy (Kaplan). American (born United States), b. 1958. **Genres:** Medicine/Health, Psychology, Theology/Religion, Self Help. **Career:** Process Work Institute, co-founder, 1990. Writer, educator and psychologist. **Publications:** (With A. Mindell) Riding the Horse Backwards: Process Work in Theory and Practice, 1992; Metaskills: The Spiritual Art of Therapy, 1994; Coma: A Healing Journey: A Guide for Family, Friends and Helpers, 1999; Alternative to Therapy: A Few Basic Process Work Principles, 2002; Dreaming Source of Creativity: 30 Creative and Magical Ways to Work on Yourself, 2005; Alternative to Therapy: A Creative Lecture Series on Process Work, 2006; (with A. Mindell) Coma: The Dreambody near Death, 2010; (with A. Mindell) The Internal Holocausts: The Roots and Solution to Terrorism, forthcoming. Contributor to periodicals. **Address:** Process Work Institute, 2049 NW Hoyt St., Ste. 2, Portland, OR 97209-1260, U.S.A. **Online address:** amy@aamindell.net

MINDT, Alex. American (born United States) **Genres:** Young Adult Fiction, Novellas/Short Stories. **Career:** Gotham Writers Workshop, teacher. Writer. **Publications:** Male of the Species, 2007. **Address:** Kimberley Cameron Associates, 1550 Tiburon Blvd., Ste. 704, Tiburon, CA 94920, U.S.A. **Online address:** alex@alexmindt.com

MINEAR, Richard Hoffman. American (born United States), b. 1938. **Genres:** History, Cartoons, Translations, Social Sciences, Politics/Government. **Career:** Ohio State University, assistant professor, 1967-70; University of Massachusetts, Department of History, associate professor, 1970-75, professor of history, 1975-2008, associate chair, professor emeritus, 2008-. Writer. **Publications:** Japanese Tradition and Western Law: Emperor, State, And Law In The Thought Of Hozumi Yatsuka, 1970; Victors' Justice: Tokyo War Crimes Trial, 1971; Dr. Seuss Goes to War: The World War II Editorial Cartoons of Theodor Seuss Geisel, 1999; The Scars Of War: Tokyo During World War II: Writings Of Takeyama Michio, 2007; War and Conscience in Japan: Nambara Shigeru and the Asia-Pacific War 2010. EDITOR: Through Japanese Eyes, 1974, 4th rev. ed., 2007. TRANSLATOR: (intro.) Requiem for Battleship Yamato, 1985; (intro.) Japan's Past, Japan's Future: One Historian's Odyssey, 2001. EDITOR AND TRANSLATOR: Hiroshima: Three Witnesses, 1990; (intro.) Black Eggs: Poems, 1994; (intro.) When We Say Hiroshima: Selected Poems, 1999; Hiroshima: The Autobiography of Barefoot Gen, 2010; The Day the Sun Rose in the West: Bikini, the Lucky Dragon and I, 2011. **Address:** Department of History, College of Humanities and Fine Arts, University of Massachusetts, Herter 727, Amherst, MA 01003, U.S.A. **Online address:** rhminear@history.umass.edu

MINER, Ellis D(evere). American (born United States), b. 1937. **Genres:** Air/Space Topics, Astronomy. **Career:** Jet Propulsion Laboratory, technical staff, space scientist, 1965-2005, technical manager, 1991-98, National Aeronautics and Space Administration Cassini Mission to Saturn and Titan, science adviser, 1998-2002, Planetary and Life Detection Section, 2002-, deputy manager, now retired. Writer. **Publications:** Uranus: The Planet, Rings, and Satellites, 1990, 2nd ed., 1998; (ed. with J.T. Bergstralh and M.S. Matthews) Uranus, 1991; Neptune: The Planet, Rings, and Satellites, 2002; (co-author) Planetary Ring Systems, 2007. **Address:** 11335 Sunburst St., Lake View Terrace, CA 91342, U.S.A. **Online address:** ellis.d.miner@jpl.nasa.gov

MINETOR, Randi (S.). American (born United States), b. 1958. **Genres:** Travel/Exploration, Recreation, Natural History, History, Women's Studies And Issues, Technology, Advertising/Public Relations. **Career:** Dallas Morning News, staff, 1981; Freetime Magazine, assistant editor, 1982-84; Geva Theater, director of audience development, 1984-87; Saphar and Associates Inc., copywriter, 1988-98; Minetor and Company Inc., founder and president, 1998-. **Publications:** Breadwinner Wives and the Men they Marry: How to Have a Successful Marriage While Out Earning Your Husband, 2002; Acadia National Park Pocket Guide, 2008; Great Smoky Mountains National Park Pocket Guide, 2008; Passport to Your National Parks Companion Guide North Atlantic Region, 2008; Passport to Your National Parks Companion Guide Southeast Region, 2008; Passport to Your National Parks Companion Guide National Capital Region, 2008; Gulf Islands National Seashore Pocket Guide, 2009; Washington, D.C.: A Guided Tour Through History, 2009; Gettysburg: A Guided Tour Through History, 2009; Everglades National Park Pocket Guide, 2009; Best Easy Day Hikes Rochester, New York, 2009; Best Easy Day Hikes Buffalo, 2010; Best Easy Day Hikes Syracuse, 2010; Best Easy Day Hikes Albany, 2010; Fredericksburg: A Guided Tour Through History, 2010; New York Immigrant Experience: A Guided Tour Through History, 2010; New Orleans: A Guided Tour Through History, 2010; Backyard Birding: A Guide to Attracting and Identifying Birds, 2011; Best Easy Day Hikes: Hudson River Valley, 2011; How to Start a Home-based Public Relations Business, 2012. FORTHCOMING: Passport to Your National Parks Companion Guide Midwest Region; Passport to Your National Parks Companion Guide Mid-atlantic Region; Passport to Your National Parks Companion Guide Pacific Northwest & Alaska Regions; Passport to Your National Parks Companion Guide Rocky Mountain Region; Passport to Your National Parks Companion Guide Southwest Region; Passport to Your National Parks Companion Guide Western Region; National Park Quest Guide to Assateague Island National Seashore; National Park Quest Guide to Cape Cod National Seashore. Contributor to periodicals. **Address:** Minetor and Company Inc., 32 Bengal Terr., Rochester, NY 14610-2809, U.S.A. **Online address:** randi@minetor.com

MINGIONE, Enzo. Italian (born Italy), b. 1947. **Genres:** Social Sciences, Sociology, Urban Studies. **Career:** University of Milan, General Sociology and Urban Sociology, research and teaching fellow, 1970-73, associate professor of sociology of organization, 1989-90; University of Messina, associate professor of economic sociology, 1973-89, Department of Theory and Analysis of Social and Political Phenomena, director, full professor of urban sociology and director, 1990-93; University College, Centre for Urban Studies, Urban Sociology and Urban History, teaching fellow, 1974-75; University of California, Department of Sociology, visiting professor, 1994; University of Padova, full professor of sociology and director, 1994-99; University of Milano-Bicocca, full professor of sociology and deputy dean, 1999-2004, faculty of sociology, dean, 2004-10. Writer. **Publications:** La proletarizzazione dei ceti medi (title means: The Proletarianization of Middle Classes), 1971; (co-author) Citta e conflitto sociale (title means: The City and Social Conflict), 1972; Impiegati, sviluppo capitalistico e lotta di classe (title means: White Collars, Capitalist Development and Class Struggles), 1973; Mercato del lavoro e occupazionein Italia dal 1945 ad oggi (title means: Labor Market and Employment in Italy from 1945 On), 1974, rev. ed., 1981; Scuola e mercato del lavoro (title means: Education and Labor Market), 1975; Social Conflict and the City, 1981; Urbanizzazione, classi sociali, lavoro informale: saggi sulprocesso di urbanizzazione in relazione allo sviluppo economico, allacrisi attuale, alla ristrutturazione-decentramento industriale (title means: Urbanization, Social Classes and Informal Work), 1983; Fragmented Societies: A Sociology of Economic Life Beyond the Market Paradigm, 1991. EDITOR: L'uso del territorio in Cina (title means: The Use of Land in China), 1977; Classi sociali e agricoltura meridionale (title means: Social Classes and Southern Italian Agriculture), 1981; (with N. Redclift) Beyond Employment: Household, Gender, and Subsistence, 1985; Urban Poverty and the Under-Class, 1996. OTHERS: Sfide dell'esclusione: metodi, luoghi, soggetti, verso una riforma del welfare in Italia, 1999; Lavoro, 2002; (with F. Gambino and F. Pristinger) Distanze e legami: una ricerca su capitale sociale e diseguaglianze nel Veneto, 2003; Il Lavoro, with Enrico Pugliese, Roma: Carocci, 2010. Works appear in anthologies. Contributor of articles to periodicals. **Address:** Fondazione Bignaschi, 3 Via Olmetto, Milano, 20123, Italy. **Online address:** enzo.mingione@unimib.it

MINKLER, Meredith. American (born United States), b. 1946. **Genres:** Gerontology/Senior Issues, Medicine/Health. **Career:** Ford Foundation, family planning associate, 1970-71; Planned Parenthood, education associate, 1972-73; University of California, School of Public Health, professor of public health education, 1975-, professor of health and social behavior, Health and Social Behavior Program, director, Center on Aging, co-founder and founding director; Brookdale National Information Center on Grandparents Raising Grandchildren, founder. Writer. **Publications:** (With S.R. Blum) Community-based Home Health and Social Services for California's Elderly: Present Constraints and Future Alternatives, 1982; (ed. with C.L. Estes) Readings in the Political Economy of Aging, 1984; (ed. with C.L. Estes) Critical Perspectives on Aging: The Political and Moral Economy of Growing Old, 1991; (with K.M. Roe) Grandmothers as Caregivers: Raising Children of the Crack Cocaine Epidemic, 1993; (ed.) Community Organizing and Community Building for Health, 1997, 2nd ed., 2005; (ed. with C.L. Estes) Critical Gerontology: Perspectives From Political And Moral Economy, 1999; (ed. with N. Wallerstein) Community Based Participatory Research for Health, 2003, 2nd ed. as Community-based Participatory Research for Health: From Process to Outcomes, 2008; (ed.) Community Organizing and Community Building for Health and Welfare, 2012. **Address:** School of Public Health, University of California, 207-D University Hall, Berkeley, CA 94720-7360, U.S.A. **Online address:** mink@berkeley.edu

MINNICH, James M. Korean (born Korea (South)) **Genres:** Military/Defense/Arms Control. **Career:** U.S. Army Foreign Area Officer; Joint United States Military Affairs Group-Korea, Policy Operations, Training and Liaison, director. Writer. **Publications:** The Denuclearization of North Korea: The Agreed Framework and Alternative Options Analyzed, 2002; The North Korean People's Army: Origins and Current Tactics, 2005. Contributor of articles to periodicals. **Online address:** james.minnich@us.army.mil

MINOCK, Daniel. American (born United States), b. 1944. **Genres:** Essays, Literary Criticism And History. **Career:** Wayne State University, instructor, 1970-75, assistant professor of English, 1975-77; Washtenaw Community College, professor of English, through 1982, now professor emeritus. Writer. **Publications:** Thistle Journal: And Other Essays, 1998. **Address:** Washtenaw Community College, 300 LASB, 4800 E Huron River Dr., PO Box D-1, Ann Arbor, MI 48106, U.S.A. **Online address:** dminock@aol.com

MINOGUE, Kenneth Robert. British/Australian/New Zealander (born New Zealand), b. 1930. **Genres:** Philosophy, Politics/Government, Social Sciences. **Career:** University of Exeter, assistant lecturer in public administration, 1955-56; University of London, London School of Economics and Political Science, lecturer and senior lecturer, 1956-70, reader, 1971-84, professor of political science, 1984-95, professor emeritus, 1995-. Writer. **Publications:** The Liberal Mind, 1963; Nationalism, 1967; The Concept of a University, 1973; (with F.D. Rushworth and J. Wolfenden) Purposes in Education, 1974; Alien Powers: The Pure Theory of Ideology, 1985, 2nd ed., 2007; The Constitutional Mania, 1993; Politics: A Very Short Introduction, 1995; The Silencing of Society, 1997; Waitangi, Morality, Reality, 1998; Does Australia Have an Identity Problem?, 2003; Servile Mind: How Democracy Erodes the Moral Life, 2010. EDITOR: (with A. Crespigny) Contemporary Political Philosophers, 1975; (with M. Biddiss) Thatcherism: Personality and Politics, 1987; Conservative Realism, 1996. **Address:** London School of Economics and Political Science, University of London, Houghton St., London, GL WC2A 2AE, England. **Online address:** k.minogue@lse.ac.uk

MINOGUE, Valerie Pearson. Welsh/British (born England), b. 1931. **Genres:** Literary Criticism And History, Young Adult Fiction, Humanities. **Career:** University of Wales, University College, assistant lecturer in French, 1952-53; British Museum Library, staff, 1961; British Broadcasting Corp., staff; University of London, part-time faculty, Queen Mary College, lecturer, 1962-75, senior lecturer in French, 1975-81; Swansea University, Department of Romance, chair and head and part-time research professor of French, 1981-88, research professor, 1988-96, professor emeritus, 1996-; Romance Studies, founding co-editor, 1982-85, editor, 1986-95, general editor, 1995-2004. **Publications:** Proust-Du côté de chez Swann, 1973; Nathalie Sarraute and the War of the Words: A Study of Five Novels, 1981; Zola: L'Assommoir, 1991; (contrib.) Oeuvres Completes, 1996; (ed. with G. Evans and G. Jacobs) Narrative Voices in Modern French Fiction: Studies in Honour of Valerie Minogue on the Occasion of Her Retirement, 1997. Contributor of articles to books, journals and periodicals. **Address:** School of Arts, Swansea University, Singleton Pk., Swansea, WG SA2 8PP, Wales. **Online address:** valerie@valminogue.com

MINOR, Wendell G. American (born United States), b. 1944. **Genres:** Novels, Children's Fiction, Illustrations. **Career:** Hallmark Cards, illustrator, 1966-67; Paul Bacon, illustrator, 1968-70; freelance illustrator, 1970-. Writer. **Publications:** SELF-ILLUSTRATED FOR CHILDREN: Grand Canyon: Exploring a Natural Wonder, 1998; Pumpkin Heads, 2000; (with F. Minor) Christmas Tree!, 2005; Yankee Doodle America: The Spirit of 1776 from A-Z, 2006; FOR ADULTS: (with F.F. Minor) Art for the Written Word: Twenty-Five Years of Book Cover Art, 1995; (with F. Minor) If You Were A Penguin, 2009; My Farm Friends, 2011. **Address:** 15 Old N Rd., PO Box 1135, Washington, CT 06793, U.S.A. **Online address:** wendell@minorart.com

MINOT, Susan A. American (born United States), b. 1956. **Genres:** Novels, Novellas/Short Stories, Plays/Screenplays, Poetry, Young Adult Fiction. **Career:** New York Review of Books, editorial assistant, 1981; Grand Street, associate editor, 1982-86; New York University, Graduate Writing Program, adjunct professor, 1987; Columbia University, teacher of writing workshops, 1988-89, adjunct professor, 1989-90. Writer. **Publications:** NOVELS: Monkeys, 1986; Lust & Other Stories (short fiction), 1989; Folly, 1992; Evening, 1998; Rapture (novella), 2002. OTHER: Poems 4 A.M., 2002. Contributor to periodicals. **Address:** c/o Georges Borchardt, 136 E 57th St., New York, NY 10022, U.S.A.

MINOW, Newton N(orman). American (born United States), b. 1926.

Genres: Communications/Media, Politics/Government. **Career:** Federal Communications Commission, chairman, 1961-63; Encyclopaedia Britannica Inc., general counsel and director, 1963-65; Rand Corp., director, 1965-75, 1976-, chairman, 1970-72; Sidley Austin Brown and Wood, attorneys, partner, 1965-91, senior counsel, 1991-; Northwestern University, Annenberg Washington Program Communications Policy Studies, director, 1987-, Walter Annenberg professor of communications and policy, 1987-, now emeritus; Carnegie Corporation of New York, chairman, 1993-97; Carnegie Foundation, chairman; Public Broadcasting Service, chairman; Commission on Presidential Debates, vice chairman; Chicago Bar Foundation, fellow. Writer. **Publications:** (With C.M. Sloan) For Great Debates, 1987; How Vast the Wasteland Now?, 1991; Television's Values and the Values of Our Children, 1995; (with C. LaMay) Abandoned in the Wasteland: Children, Television and the First Amendment, 1995; (with J.B. Minow) As Our Parents Planted for Us, So Shall We Plant for Our Cildren, 1999; (co-author) Opening Salvos, 1999; (with C. LaMay) Inside the Presidential Debates: Their Improbable Past and Promising Future, 2008. Contributor to periodicals. **Address:** Sidney Austin L.L.P., 1 S Dearborn, Chicago, IL 60603, U.S.A. **Online address:** nminow@sidley.com

MINSHALL, Vera. British (born England), b. 1924. **Genres:** Novels, Young Adult Non-fiction, Literary Criticism And History. **Career:** Stenographer, 1939-46; Stock Port Central Reference Library, library clerk, 1975-82. Writer. **Publications:** I Was a Stranger, 1963; The Doctor's Secret, 1966; Call of the High Road, 1967; This Stony Ground, 1969. Contributor to periodicals. **Address:** 17 Fenton Ave., Stepping Hill, Stockport, CH SK7 4AN, England.

MINSKY, Betty Jane. American (born United States), b. 1932. **Genres:** Business/Trade/Industry, Economics. **Career:** Freelance writer, 1954-; Michigan Chamber of Commerce-Cheboygan, manager, 1961-65; Michigan Chamber of Commerce-St. Johns, manager, 1965-; Lansing State Journal Daily Newspaper, staff writer, 1967-88; Clinton Area New Development Organization, executive director, 1988-93; business consultant. **Publications:** Gimmicks Make Money in Retailing, 1963, 2nd ed., 1972. Contributor of articles to magazines. **Address:** St. Johns Chamber of Commerce, 201 1/2 N Clinton Ave., St. Johns, MI 48879, U.S.A. **Online address:** bjm@voyager.net

MINTER, David Lee. American (born United States), b. 1935. **Genres:** Literary Criticism And History, inspirational/Motivational Literature. **Career:** Yale University, Danforth Instructor in English, 1964-65, lecturer in English, 1966-67; University of Hamburg, lecturer, 1965-66; Rice University, assistant professor, 1967-69, associate professor, 1969-73, professor of English, 1973-80, Bruce and Elizabeth Dunlevie professor of English, 1990-, Libbie Shearn Moody professor of English, now professor emeritus, interim vice provost and university librarian, 1995-96, interim provost, 1999-; Columbia University, visiting associate professor, 1971; Washington University, visiting associate professor, 1972; Emory University, professor of English, dean of Emory College, vice president for arts and sciences, 1980-90. Writer. **Publications:** The Interpreted Design as a Structural Principle in American Prose, 1969; (ed.) Twentieth Century Interpretations of Light in August: A Collection of Critical Essays, 1970; William Faulkner: His Life and Work, 1980; (co-ed.) The Harper American Literature, 1986, 3rd ed., 1998; (ed.) The Sound and the Fury: An Authoritative Text, Backgrounds and Contexts, Criticism, 1987; (co-ed.) The Columbia Literary History of the United States, 1987; A Cultural History of the American Novel: Henry James to William Faulkner, 1994; Faulkner's Questioning Narratives: Fiction of His Major Phase, 1929-42, 2001. **Address:** Department of English, Rice University, 6100 Main St., Houston, TX 77001, U.S.A. **Online address:** dcmint@rice.edu

MINTZ, Alan L. American/New Zealander (born New Zealand) **Genres:** Cultural/Ethnic Topics, Literary Criticism And History, Theology/Religion, Autobiography/Memoirs, Novels. **Career:** Columbia University, assistant professor of Hebrew, 1977-81; University of Maryland, assistant professor, 1981-83, Meyerhoff Center for Jewish Studies, director, 1981-88, associate professor, 1983-88, Robert H. Smith professor of Hebrew literature, 1988-92; Brandeis University, Joseph H. and Belle R. Braun professor of modern Hebrew literature, 1992-2001; Jewish Theological Seminary, Department of Jewish Literature, Chana Kekst professor of Hebrew literature and chair, 2001-, [illegible] Program, director. Writer. **Publications:** George Eliot and the Novel of Vocation, 1978; Hurban: Responses to Catastrophe in Hebrew Literature, 1984; Banished from Their Father's Table: Loss of Faith and Hebrew Autobiography, 1989; Popular Culture and the Shaping of Holocaust Memory in America, 2001; Translating Israel: Contemporary Hebrew Literature and Its Reception in America, 2001; Sanctuary in the Wilderness: A Critical Introduction to American Hebrew Poetry, 2011. EDITOR: (with J.A. Sleeper) The New Jews, 1971; Hebrew in America: Perspectives and Prospects, 1993; (and intro. with A.G. Hoffman) A Book that Was Lost and other Stories, 1995; The Boom in Contemporary Israeli Fiction, 1997; Reading Hebrew Literature: Critical Discussions of Six Modern Texts, 2003. Works appear in anthologies. Contributor of articles to journals and magazines. **Address:** Department of Jewish Literature, Jewish Theological Seminary, Unterberg 507, 3080 Broadway, New York, NY 10027-4650, U.S.A. **Online address:** almintz@jtsa.edu

MINTZ, Joel A(lan). American (born United States), b. 1949. **Genres:** Law. **Career:** Williamson and Williamson, law clerk, 1972-73; Public Education Association, New York Lawyers Committee for Civil Rights under Law, law clerk, 1973; Natural Resources Defense Council, law clerk, 1974; U.S. Environmental Protection Agency, Air Enforcement Branch, enforcement attorney, 1975-76, Water and Hazardous Materials Enforcement Branch, Case Development Unit, chief attorney, 1977-78, Office of the Regional Administrator, state relations coordinator and policy adviser, 1979-80, Office of Hazardous Waste Enforcement, senior litigation attorney, 1980-81; Nova Southeastern University, assistant professor, 1982-85, associate professor, 1985-87, professor of law, 1987-, Clinical Program in Environmental and Land Use Law, founder and co-director, 1997-2006; Everglades Law Center, director. Writer. **Publications:** Enforcement at the EPA: High Stakes and Hard Choices, 1995; (with F.P. Grad) Environmental Law: Cases and Problems, 2000; (with M.D. Gelfand and P. Salsich) State and Local Taxation and Finance in a Nutshell, 2nd ed., 2000, 3rd ed., 2007; (with C. Rechtschaffen and R. Kuehn) Environmental Enforcement: Cases and Materials, 2007; (with R.H. Rosenberg and L.A. Bakken) Fundamentals of Municipal Finance, 2010; (ed. with J.C. Dernbach) Symposium on Law for Sustainability, 2011. Contributor to books and journals. **Address:** Shepard Broad Law Center, Nova Southeastern University, 3305 College Ave., Fort Lauderdale, FL 33314, U.S.A. **Online address:** mintzj@nova.edu

MINUCHIN, Salvador. American/Argentine (born Argentina), b. 1921. **Genres:** Psychology, Human Relations/Parenting, Biography. **Career:** Bellevue Hospital, part-time resident in psychiatry, 1950; University of Pennsylvania, professor of pediatrics and child psychology, 1965-83; Philadelphia Child Guidance Clinic, director, 1965-75, director emeritus, 1975-; Philadelphia Child and Family Therapy Training Center Inc., founder, 1975; Family Studies Inc., principal, 1981-96; New York University Medical Center, research professor of psychiatry, 1983-96; Wiltwyck School for Boys, family therapist. Writer. **Publications:** (Co-author) Families of the Slums: An Exploration of Their Structure and Treatment, 1967; Families & Family Therapy, 1974; (with B.L. Rosman and L. Baker) Psychosomatic Families: Anorexia Nervosa in Context, 1978; (with H.C. Fishman) Family Therapy Techniques, 1981; Family Kaleidoscope, 1984; (ed. with H.C. Fishman) Evolving Models for Family Change: A Volume in Honor of Salvador Minuchin, 1986; (with J. Elizur) Institutionalizing Madness: Families, Therapy and Society, 1989; (with M.P. Nichols) Family Healing: Tales of Hope and Renewal from Family Therapy, 1993. Family Healing: Strategies for Hope and Understanding, 1994; (with W. Lee and G.M. Simon) Mastering Family Therapy: Journeys of Growth and Transformation, 1996, 2nd ed., 2006; (P. Minuchin and J. Colapinto) Working with Families of the Poor, 1998, 2nd ed., 2007; (with M.P. Nichols and W.Y. Lee) Assessing Families and Couples: From Symptom to System, 2007. Contributor to books. **Address:** Philadelphia Child and, Family Therapy Training Center Inc., PO Box 4092, Philadelphia, PA 19118-8092, U.S.A.

MIRABELLI, Eugene. American (born United States), b. 1931. **Genres:** Novels, Young Adult Fiction. **Career:** Williams College, instructor, 1960-64; State University of New York, assistant professor, 1965-69, associate professor, 1969-94, professor, 1994-96, professor emeritus, 1996-; Alternative Literary Programs, founder, director, treasurer. Writer. **Publications:** The Burning Air, 1959; The Way In, 1968; No Resting Place, 1972; The World at Noon, 1994; The Language Nobody Speaks, 1999; The Passion of Terri Heart, 2004; Queen of the Rain was in Love With the Prince of the Sky, 2008; Goddess in Love With a Horse, 2008; Renato, The Painter: An Account of his Youth & His 70th Year in His Own Words, 2010. **Address:** Spring Harbor Press, PO Box 346, Delmar, NY 12054, U.S.A. **Online address:** mirabelli@global2000.net

MIRIKITANI, Janice. American (born United States), b. 1941. **Genres:** Poetry, Politics/Government. **Career:** Contra Costa Unified School District, teacher, 1964-65; Glide Church, administrative assistant, 1966-69; Glide

Church/Urban Center, program director, 1969-; San Francisco State University, lecturer in Japanese American literature and creative writing, 1972; Glide Dance Group, choreographer and artistic director, 1973-; Glide Foundation, founding president, 1983-; San Francisco Arts Commission, commissioner, 1996-; Asian American Publications, co-founder. Writer. **Publications:** POETRY AND PROSE: Awake in the River: Poetry, Prose, 1978; Shedding Silence: Poetry and Prose, 1987; We, the Dangerous: New and Selected Poems, 1995; Love Works, 2001. OTHERS: (with C. Williams) Breaking Free: A Glide Songbook, 1989. EDITOR: Third World Women, 1973; (co-ed.) Time to Greez!: Incantations from the Third World (poetry), 1975; Ayumi: A Japanese American Anthology, 1980; (with C. Williams) I Have Something to Say about This Big Trouble: Children of the Tenderloin Speak Out, 1989; Watch Out! We're Talking, 1993; What Matters: Young Writers and Artists Speak Out, 2004. Contributor to periodicals and journals. **Address:** Glide Foundation, 330 Ellis St., San Francisco, CA 94102, U.S.A. **Online address:** child_youth_family@glide.org

MIROFF, Bruce. American (born United States), b. 1945. **Genres:** Politics/Government. **Career:** University at Albany, State University of New York, Rockefeller College of Public Affairs & Policy, Department of Political Science, professor. Political scientist, educator, writer and editor. **Publications:** Pragmatic Illusions: The Presidential Politics of John F. Kennedy, 1976; Icons of Democracy: American Leaders as Heroes, Aristocrats, Dissenters and Democrats, 1993, new ed., 2000; (with R. Seidelman and T. Swanstrom) The Democratic Debate: An Introduction to American Politics, 1995, 4th ed., 2007; (ed. with R. Seidelman and T. Swanstrom) Debating Democracy: A Reader in American Politics, 1997, 6th ed., 2008; The Liberals Moment: The McGovern Insurgency and the Identity Crisis of the Democratic Party, 2007. Contributor to periodicals. **Address:** University at Albany, State University of New York, 1400 Washington Ave., Albany, NY 12222, U.S.A. **Online address:** miroff@albany.edu

MIROVITSKAYA, Natalia. American/Russian (born Russia), b. 1954. **Genres:** Sciences. **Career:** Russian Academy of Sciences, Institute of World Economy and International Relations, Department of Ocean Affairs, research associate, 1980-86, senior researcher; North Carolina State University, visiting associate professor of political science, 1992, 1997; Duke University, research fellow in public policy, 1995-, Sanford School of Public Policy, Center for International Development, lecturing fellow in public policy, 1996-. Writer and economist. **Publications:** (With I.V. Shishkov as N.S. Mirovitskaia) Mezhdunarodnye aspekty Prodovol' Stvennoĭ Problemy, 1983; (with V.A. Korzun as N.S. Mirovitskaia) Bioresursy Mirovogo Okeana: Mezhdunarodnye aspekty, 1991; (co-author) The Bering Sea Ecosystem, 1996; (ed. with W. Ascher) The Caspian Sea: A Quest for Environmental Security, 2000; (ed. with W. Ascher) A Guide to Sustainable Development and Environmental Policy, 2001. **Address:** Center for International Development, Duke University, 264 Rubenstein Hall, PO Box 90237, Durham, NC 27708-0237, U.S.A. **Online address:** nataliam@duke.edu

MIROWSKI, Philip. American (born United States), b. 1951. **Genres:** Economics, Sciences, Intellectual History. **Career:** University of Michigan, Institute of Labor and Industrial Relations, research associate, 1976-77; University of Santa Clara, assistant professor, 1978-81; Tufts University, assistant professor, 1981-84, associate professor of economics, 1985-90; University of Massachusetts, visiting associate professor, 1984-85; Yale University, visiting associate professor, 1987-88; University of Notre Dame, professor of economics, Carl Koch professor of economics and the history and philosophy of science, 1990-, John J. Reilly Center for Science, Technology, and Values, Technology and Values, faculty fellow. Writer. **Publications:** The Birth of the Business Cycle, 1985; (ed.) The Reconstruction of Economic Theory, 1986; Against Mechanism: Protecting Economics from Science, 1988; More Heat Than Light: Economics as Social Physics, Physics as Nature's Economics, 1989; (ed.) Edgeworth on Chance, Economic Hazard, and Statistics, 1994; (ed. and contrib.) Natural Images in Economic Thought: Markets Read in Tooth and Claw, 1994; (ed. with S. Tradewell) The Economic Writings of William Thornton, 1999; (ed. with E. Sent) Science Bought and Sold: Essays in the Economics of Science, 2002; Machine Dreams: Economics Becomes a Cyborg Science, 2002; The Effortless Economy of Science?, 2004; (ed. with D. Plehwe) The Road from Mont Pèlerin, 2009; Science-Mart, 2011; (ed. with R. van Horn and T.A. Stapleford) Building Chicago Economics, 2011. **Address:** John J. Reilly Center for Science, Technology, and, Values, University of Notre Dame, 400 Decio Faculty Hall, Notre Dame, IN 46556, U.S.A. **Online address:** philip.e.mirowski.1@nd.edu

MIRVISH, Dan. (Martin Eisenstadt). American (born United States), b. 1967. **Genres:** Autobiography/Memoirs. **Career:** University of California, extension class teacher; National Aeronautics and Space Administration, freelance graphic artist; Slamdance Film Festival, co-founder. Screenwriter, director and producer. **Publications:** (As Martin Eisenstadt with E. Gorlin) I Am Martin Eisenstadt: One Man's Wildly Inappropriate Adventures with the Last Republicans (fake memoir), 2009. Contributor to periodicals. **Address:** U.S.A. **Online address:** bugeater@slamdance.com

MISA, Thomas J. American (born United States), b. 1959. **Genres:** Technology, Engineering, Education. **Career:** Illinois Institute of Technology, associate professor, 1987-2005; University of Minnesota, Charles Babbage Institute, director, 2006-, History of Science and Technology, professor, 2006-, Department of Electrical and Computer Engineering, professor, 2006-. Writer. **Publications:** (Ed. with A. Rip and J. Schot) Managing Technology in Society, 1995; A Nation of Steel: The Making of Modern America, 1865-1925, 1995; (ed. with P. Brey and A. Feenberg) Modernity and Technology, 2003; Leonardo to the Internet: Technology and Culture from the Renaissance to the Present, 2004, 2nd ed., 2010; (ed. with M. Hård) Urban Machinery: Inside Modern European Cities, 2007; Gender Codes: (ed.) Why Women are Leaving Computing, 2010; (with R.W. Seidel) College of Science and Engineering: The Institute of Technology Years (1935-2010), 2010. **Address:** Charles Babbage Institute, University of Minnesota, 211 Andersen Library, 222 21st Ave. S, Minneapolis, MN 55455, U.S.A. **Online address:** tmisa@umn.edu

MISCAMBLE, Wilson D. American/Australian (born Australia), b. 1953. **Genres:** Theology/Religion, History, Politics/Government. **Career:** Office of National Assessments, Department of Prime Minister and Cabinet, North American analyst, 1980-82; University of Notre Dame, professor of history, 1988-, chair of department, 1993-98. Writer. **Publications:** George F. Kennan and the Making of American Foreign Policy, 1947-1950, 1992; American Political History: Essays on the State of the Discipline, 1997; Keeping the Faith, Making a Difference, 2000; Go Forth and Do Good: Memorable Notre Dame Commencement Addresses, 2003; From Roosevelt to Truman: Potsdam, Hiroshima and the Cold War, 2007. **Address:** Department of History, University of Notre Dame, 219 O'Shaughnessy, Notre Dame, IN 46556, U.S.A. **Online address:** wmiscamb.1@nd.edu

MISHAN, E. J. (Ezra J. Mishan). British (born England), b. 1917. **Genres:** Economics, Social Commentary, Sociology. **Career:** London School of Economics, lecturer, reader in economics, professor in economics, 1956-77; American University, visiting professor, 1970-72; Johns Hopkins University, lecturer, 1971; University of Maryland, visiting professor, 1974-75; writer, 1975-. **Publications:** Keizai seisaku no shomondai, 1963; Welfare Economics: Five Introductory Essays, 1964; The Cost of Economic Growth, 1967, rev. ed., 1993; Twenty-One Popular Economic Fallacies, 1969; Growth: The Price We Pay, 1969; Welfare Economics: An Assessment, 1969; Technology and Growth: The Price We Pay, 1970; Cost-Benefit Analysis, 1971 in UK as Elements of Cost-Benefit Analysis, 1972, 4th ed., 1988; Economics for social decisions; Elements of Cost-benefit Analysis, 1972; Making the World Safe for Pornography, 1973; The Economic Growth Debate, 1977; An Introduction to Normative Economics, 1980; Economic Efficiency and Social Welfare, 1980; Pornography, Psychedelics, and Technology, 1980; Introduction to Political Economy, 1982; What Political Economy is all About: An Exposition and Critique, 1982; Economic Myths and the Mythology of Economics, 1986; Thirteen Persistent Economic Fallacies, 2009; Eleven Popular Fallacies of the Liberal Establishment, forthcoming. Contributor to periodicals. **Address:** 22 Gainsborough Gardens, London, GL NW11 9BL, England.

MISHAN, Ezra J. *See* **MISHAN, E. J.**

MISHICA, Clare. American (born United States), b. 1960. **Genres:** Children's Fiction, Young Adult Fiction, Children's Non-fiction, Young Adult Non-fiction, Novellas/Short Stories, Education. **Career:** Teacher, 1982-85; Suomi College, Teaching and Learning Center, staff, 1993-. Writer. **Publications:** Billions of Bugs, 1993; The Penguin's Big Win, 1994; Charlie the Champ, 1994; Max's Answer, 1994; A Friend for Fraidy Cat, 1994; (with M. Keefer and C. Rogers) Surprising Stories: Three Fun-to-Read-Aloud Stories with a Message, 1999; Here Comes the Parade, 2005. Contributor of articles to periodicals. **Address:** Children's Book Press, 965 Mission St., Ste. 518, San Francisco, CA 94103, U.S.A. **Online address:** gmishica@ccisd.k12.mi.us

MISHKIN, Tracy. American (born United States) **Genres:** Poetry, Essays, Young Adult Fiction, History. **Career:** Georgia College, professor of English, 1993-2004; State University, professor of English, 1993-2004; Butler University, professor of English, 1993-2004; Bureau of Jewish Education Inc., program director, 2004-. Writer. **Publications:** (Ed.) Literary Influence and African-American Writers: Collected Essays, 1996; The Harlem and Irish Renaissances: Language, Identity and Representation, 1998. Contributor of articles to books. **Address:** Bureau of Jewish Education Inc., 6711 Hoover Rd., Indianapolis, IN 46260-4197, U.S.A. **Online address:** tmishkin@bjeindy.org

MISHRA, Pankaj. Indian (born India), b. 1969?. **Genres:** Novels, Travel/Exploration. **Career:** HarperCollins, India Division, chief editor; Wellesley College, visiting professor, 2001, 2004, 2006; University College London, Department of English, visiting fellow, 2007-08. **Publications:** Butter Chicken in Ludhiana: Travels in Small Town India (nonfiction), 1995; The Romantics (novel), 2000; (intro. and ed.) The Writer and the World: Essays, 2002; (intro. and ed.) Literary Occasions: Essays, 2003; An End to Suffering: The Buddha in the World, 2004; (intro.) Kim, 2004; (intro. and ed.) India in Mind: An Anthology, 2005; Temptations of the West: How to be Modern in India, Pakistan, Tibet and Beyond, 2006. Contributor of articles and reviews to periodicals. **Address:** c/o Author Mail, Vintage/Anchor Publicity, 1745 Broadway, 20th Fl., New York, NY 10019-4305, U.S.A.

MISHRA, Sudesh (Raj). Australian/Fijian (born Fiji), b. 1962. **Genres:** Plays/Screenplays, Poetry, Literary Criticism And History, Young Adult Fiction. **Career:** University of the South Pacific, lecturer in English, 1989-93, professor of literature, School of Language Arts and Media, head, Pacific Writing Forum, writer-in-residence; Fiji Writers' Association, president, 1991-; Flinders University of South Australia, Australian Research Council, postdoctoral research fellow, 1993; Stirling University, professor of literature; Deakin University, School of Communication and Creative Arts, senior lecturer in professional writing, associate professor in creative writing, honours course adviser; Fiji National University, visiting professor, 2010. **Publications:** POETRY: Rahu, 1987; Tandava, 1991; Memoirs of a Reluctant Traveller, 1994. OTHERS: (ed. with S. Smiles) Trapped: A Collection of Writing from Fiji, 1992; Preparing Faces: Modernism and Indian Poetry in English, 1995; Diaspora and the Difficult Art of Dying, 2002; Diaspora Criticism, 2006. **Address:** Deakin University, 221 Burwood Hwy., Burwood, VI 3125, Australia. **Online address:** sudesh.mishra@deakin.edu.au

MISSAMOU, Tchicaya. American/Congolese (born Congo), b. 1978?. **Genres:** Autobiography/Memoirs. **Career:** Warrior Fitness Camp, founder. Writer. **Publications:** (With T. Sentell) In the Shadow of Freedom: A Heroic Journey to Liberation, Manhood, and America (memoir), 2010. Contributor to periodicals. **Address:** Warrior Fitness Camp, 28065 Smyth Dr., Valencia, CA 91355, U.S.A.

MISS MANNERS *See* **Martin, Judith.**

MISURELLA, Fred. American (born United States), b. 1940. **Genres:** Adult Non-fiction, Novellas/Short Stories, Novels, Literary Criticism And History. **Career:** University of Iowa, instructor in English, 1972-74; University of Paris, Fulbright lecturer, 1975-76, lecturer in American civilization and literature, 1975-77; City University of New York, adjunct professor of English, 1978; East Stroudsburg University, professor of English, 1978-; Village Voice, copy editor, 1978. Writer. **Publications:** Understanding Milan Kundera: Public Events, Private Affairs, 1993; Short Time (novella), 1996; Lies to Live By: Stories, 2005. Contributor of articles to periodicals. **Address:** Department of English, East Stroudsburg University, Rm. 309, Stroud Hall, 200 Prospect St., East Stroudsburg, PA 18301, U.S.A. **Online address:** fmisurella@po-box.esu.edu

MITCHAM, Judson. American (born United States), b. 1948?. **Genres:** Novels, Poetry. **Career:** Fort Valley State University, associate professor of psychology, 1974-, now retired; University of Georgia, adjunct professor of creative writing; Emory University, Summer Writers' Institute, director, visiting associate professor in fiction; Mercer University, College of Liberal Arts, adjunct instructor of English. Writer. **Publications:** Somewhere in Ecclesiastes: Poems, 1991; The Sweet Everlasting: A Novel, 1996; This April Day, 2003; Sabbath Creek: A Novel, 2004; A Little Salvation: Poems Old and New, 2007. Contributor to magazines. **Address:** Creative Writing Program, Emory University, N111 Callaway Ctr., 537 Kilgo Cir., Atlanta, GA 30322-1120, U.S.A. **Online address:** jcmitcham@earthlink.net

MITCHARD, Jacquelyn. American (born United States), b. 1955. **Genres:** Novels, Novellas/Short Stories, Children's Fiction, Plays/Screenplays, Children's Non-fiction, Biography, Essays, Young Adult Fiction, Young Adult Fiction. **Career:** Milwaukee Journal Sentinel, columnist; High school English teacher, 1974-76; Pioneer Press, managing editor and reporter, 1976-79; The Capital Times, reporter, 1979-84; Milwaukee Journal, metro reporter and columnist, 1984-88; PARADE Magazine, contributing editor; Wondertime Magazine, contributing editor. **Publications:** NOVELS: The Deep End of the Ocean, 1996; The Most Wanted, 1998; Twelve Times Blessed, 2003; Christmas, Present, 2003; Breakdown Lane, 2005; Cage of Stars, 2006; Still Summer, 2007. NON-FICTION: Mother Less Child, 1985; The Rest of Us: Dispatches from the Mothership, 1997. CHILDREN'S NON-FICTION: Jane Addams: Pioneer in Social Reform and Activist for World Peace, 1991; (with B. Behm) Jane Addams: Peace Activist, 1992. CHILDREN'S FICTION: Baby Bat's Lullaby, 2004; Starring Prima!: The Mouse of the Ballet Jolie, 2004; Rosalie, My Rosalie: The Tail of a Duckling, 2005; Ready, Set, School!, 2007. OTHERS: A Theory of Relativity, 2001; Now You See Her, 2007; All We Know of Heaven, 2008; The Midnight Twins, 2008; Look Both Ways, 2009; No Time to Wave Goodbye, 2009; Watch for Me by Moonlight: A Midnight Twins Novel, 2010; Second Nature: A Love Story, 2011. Contributor to periodicals. **Address:** c/o Jane Gelfman, Gelfman Schneider Literary Agents Inc., 250 W 57th St., New York, NY 10107, U.S.A. **Online address:** jackie@jackiemitchard.com

MITCHEL, Patrick. Irish (born Ireland) **Genres:** Social Sciences. **Career:** Irish Bible Institute, director of studies, lecturer in theology. Writer. **Publications:** Evangelicalism and National Identity in Ulster, 1921-1998, 2003. **Address:** Irish Bible Institute, Ulysses House, 22-24 Foley St., Dublin, DU 1, Ireland.

MITCHELL *See* **Davies-Mitchell, Margaret (Constance).**

MITCHELL, (Charles) Julian. British (born England), b. 1935. **Genres:** Novels, Plays/Screenplays, Biography. **Career:** Freelance writer, 1962-; Colorado State University, writer-in-residence, 1965; Chelsea School of Art, governor. **Publications:** (Ed.) Light Blue, Dark Blue: An Anthology of Recent Writing from Oxford and Cambridge Universities, 1960; (co-author) Introduction, 1960; Imaginary Toys, 1961; A Disturbing Influence, 1962; As Far as You Can Go, 1963; The White Father, 1964; (adapter) A Heritage and Its History, 1965; A Circle of Friends, 1966; Arabesque, 1966; The Undiscovered Country, 1968; Shadow in the Sun, 1972; Truth and Fiction, 1972; (with P. Churchill) Jennie: Lady Randolph Churchill: A Portrait with Letters, 1974; (adapter) A Family and a Fortune: A Play, 1974; Half-Life: A Play, 1977; Henry IV, 1979; Another Country; After Aida, 1985; Adelina Patti, 1987; The Evils of Tobacco, 1987; Vincent and Theo, 1990; Falling over England, 1994; August, 1994; Wilde, 1997. **Address:** 47 Draylott Pl., London, GL SW3 3DB, England.

MITCHELL, Chris. American (born United States), b. 1964?. **Genres:** Criminology/True Crime, Mystery/Crime/Suspense, Theology/Religion, Sociology. **Career:** The Week, senior editor. **Publications:** (With J. Maple) The Crime Fighter: Putting the Bad Guys Out of Business, 1999; (with J. Miller) The Crime Fighter: How You Can Make Your Community Crime Free, 2000; (with J. Miller and M. Stone) The Cell: Inside the 9/11 Plot and Why the FBI and CIA Failed to Stop It, 2002; A Place for Skeptics: A Spiritual Journey for Those Who May Have Given Up on Church But Not on God, 2005; (ed.) Trusted Computing (Professional Applications of Computing), 2005. Contributor to periodicals. **Address:** c/o Author Mail, Hyperion Editorial Department, 77 W 66th St., 11th Fl., New York, NY 10023, U.S.A.

MITCHELL, David (John). British (born England), b. 1924. **Genres:** History, Biography, Travel/Exploration, Military/Defense/Arms Control. **Career:** Picture Post, staff writer, 1947-52; Pictorial Press Ltd., owner and editor, 1953-56; Central Office of Information, picture editor, 1957-65; freelance writer, 1965-. **Publications:** (Ed.) Flanders and Other Fields: Memoirs of Baroness de T'Serclaes, 1964; Women on the Warpath: Story of Women of the First World War in US as Monstrous Regiment, 1966; The Fighting Pankhursts, 1967; The Pankhursts, 1970; 1919 Red Mirage, 1970; The Missionary Impulse, 1973; Bernardo O'Higgins, 1975; Pirates, 1976; Queen Christabel: A Biography of Christabel Pankhurst, 1977; The Jesuits: A History, 1980; The Spanish Civil War, 1982; Travellers in Spain: An Illustrated Anthology, 1990; (ed.) The Spanish Attraction, 2004. Contributor of articles to periodicals. **Address:** 20 Mountacre Close, Sydenham Hill, London, GL SE26 6SX, England. **Online address:** tj.mitch@virgin.net

MITCHELL, Don. American (born United States), b. 1961. **Genres:** Geography, Politics/Government, Social Sciences. **Career:** University of Colorado, instructor, 1992-94, assistant professor, 1994-97; Cultural Geographies, North American editor, 1996-2003; Syracuse University, associate professor, 1997-2002, professor, 2002-, department chair, 2003-, People's Geography Project, director. Academic and geographer. **Publications:** The Lie of the Land: Migrant Workers and the California Landscape, 1996; Cultural Geography: A Critical Introduction, 2000; The Right to the City: Social Justice and the Fight for Public Space, 2003; (with L.A. Staeheli) The People's Property? Power, Politics, and the Public, 2007. Contributor to periodicals and journals. **Address:** Department of Geography, Syracuse University, 144 Eggers Hall, Syracuse, NY 13244-0001, U.S.A. **Online address:** dmmitc01@maxwell.syr.edu

MITCHELL, Ellinor R. American/Swiss (born Switzerland), b. 1930. **Genres:** Medicine/Health, Sciences, Self Help. **Career:** Cell Block Theatre, instructor, 1974-80. Writer. **Publications:** Plain Talk about Acupuncture, 1987; Fighting Drug Abuse with Acupuncture: The Treatment That Works, 1995; The Ch'i Factor, forthcoming; Morgan Island, forthcoming. **Address:** 277 W End Ave., Ste. 15-A, New York, NY 10023, U.S.A.

MITCHELL, Emily. American/British (born England), b. 1975. **Genres:** Biography, Young Adult Fiction, History. **Career:** City University of New York, Lehman College, faculty; Index Magazine, editor; West Virginia University, A.B. Middlebury College, assistant professor of creative writing; California College of the Arts, faculty. **Publications:** The Last Summer of the World (novel), 2007. Contributor to periodicals. **Address:** Department of English, West Virginia University, A.B. Middlebury College, 205 Colson Hall, 72 S Main St., Morgantown, WV 26506-6296, U.S.A. **Online address:** emily.mitchell@mail.wvu.edu

MITCHELL, Erica. *See* **POSNER, Richard.**

MITCHELL, Gillian. Scottish (born Scotland) **Genres:** Adult Non-fiction, Music. **Career:** University of Wales, faculty, 2004-; University of St. Andrews, faculty, lecturer. Writer and historian. **Publications:** The North American Folk Music Revival: Nation and Identity in the United States and Canada, 1945-1980, 2007. Contributor to periodicals. **Address:** School of History, University of St. Andrews, Rm. 2.24A St. Katharine's Lodge, 71 South St., St. Andrews, FF KY16 9QW, Scotland. **Online address:** gamm2@st-and.ac.uk

MITCHELL, Helen Buss. American (born United States), b. 1941. **Genres:** History, Philosophy, Adult Non-fiction, Military/Defense/Arms Control. **Career:** Freelance journalist, 1972-79; Howard Community College, associate dean for continuing education, 1979-93, professor of philosophy and director of women's studies, 1993-. **Publications:** Roots of Wisdom: Speaking the Language of Philosophy, 1996, 6th ed., 2010; (comp.) Roots of World Wisdom: A Multicultural Reader, 1997, 2nd ed., 1999; Readings from the Roots of Wisdom, 1997, 3rd ed., 2001; Taking Sides: Clashing Views in World History, 1998, 3rd ed., 2010; (with J.R. Mitchell) Taking Sides: Clashing Views in Western Civilization, 2000; (with J.R. Mitchell) The Holocaust: Readings & Interpretations, 2001. **Address:** Departmentt of Arts and Humanities, Howard Community College, 10901 Little Patuxent Pkwy., Columbia, MD 21044, U.S.A. **Online address:** hmitchell@howardcc.edu

MITCHELL, Janet. American (born United States), b. 1963. **Genres:** Science Fiction/Fantasy. **Career:** Writer and director. **Publications:** The Creepy Girl, and Other Stories, 2009. Contributor to periodicals. **Address:** U.S.A. **Online address:** janet.lorraine.mitchell@gmail.com

MITCHELL, Jay P. American (born United States), b. 1940. **Genres:** Novels, Romance/Historical, Young Adult Fiction. **Career:** Ordained United Methodist, minister, 1964; Southern New England Conference of United Methodist Church, staff, 1964-84. Writer. **Publications:** NOVELS: Runaway from Innocence, 1993; Hidden Strings, 1996. Works appear in anthologies. Contributor of stories and poems to periodicals. **Address:** 4 Statesman Terr., PO Box 791, Marshfield, MA 02050, U.S.A.

MITCHELL, Jerome. American (born United States), b. 1935. **Genres:** Literary Criticism And History, History, Biography, Reference. **Career:** University of Chattanooga, lecturer in English, 1959-61; University of Illinois, assistant professor of English, 1965-67; University of Georgia, associate professor, 1967-72, professor of English, 1972-97, now professor emeritus; South Atlantic Bulletin, associate editor, 1970-76. Writer. **Publications:** Thomas Hoccleve: A Study in Early Fifteenth Century English Poetic, 1968; The Walter Scott Operas: An Analysis of Operas Based on the Works of Sir Walter Scott, 1977; Scott, Chaucer and Medieval Romance, 1987; More Scott Operas, 1996. EDITOR: (with W. Provost) Chaucer the Love Poet, 1973; (with J. Helterman) Old and Middle English Literature, 1994. Contributor to journals. **Address:** Department of English, Franklin College of Arts & Sciences, University of Georgia, 254 Park Hall, Athens, GA 30602-6205, U.S.A.

MITCHELL, John C. American (born United States), b. 1955. **Genres:** Information Science/Computers, Engineering, Technology. **Career:** American Telephone and Telegraph, Bell Laboratories, technical staff, 1984-88; Stanford University, professor of computer science, 1988-, Mary and Gordon Crary Family professor of electrical engineering. Writer. **Publications:** (Ed. with C.A. Gunter) Theoretical Aspects of Object-Oriented Programming: Types, Semantics and Language Design, 1994; (ed. with M. Hagiya) Theoretical Aspects of Computer Software: International Symposium, 1994; Foundations for Programming Languages, 1996; Concepts in Programming Languages, 2002; (ed. with J. Levy and E.W. Mayr) Exploring New Frontiers of Theoretical Informatics, IFIP 18th World Computer Congress, TC1 3rd International Conference on Theoretical Computer Science (TCS2004), 22-27 August 2004, Toulouse, France, 2004. **Address:** Department of Computer Science, Stanford University, Gates 4B-476, 353 Serra Mall, PO Box 9045, Stanford, CA 94305-9045, U.S.A. **Online address:** mitchell@cs.stanford.edu

MITCHELL, John Hanson. American (born United States), b. 1940. **Genres:** Environmental Sciences/Ecology, Earth Sciences, Mythology/Folklore, Natural History, History, Biography. **Career:** Environmental Centers of Hartford, director, 1967-70; freelance writer, 1970-73; Massachusetts Audubon Society, assistant editor, 1973-80, Sanctuary Magazine, editor, 1980-. **Publications:** Hiking Cape Cod, 1975; (ed.) The Curious Naturalist, 1980; (ed. with W. Hanley) The Energy Book: A Look at the Death Throes Of One Energy Era and the Birth Pangs of Another, 1980; Ceremonial Time: Fifteen Thousand Years on One Square Mile, 1984; A Field Guide to Your Own Back Yard, 1985; Living at the End of Time, 1990; Walking towards Walden: A Pilgrimage in Search of Place, 1995; (with C. Leahy and T. Conuel) The Nature of Massachusetts, 1996; A Field Guide to your Own Backyard, 2nd ed., 1999; Trespassing: An Inquiry into the Private Ownership of Land, 1999; The Wildest Place on Earth: Italian Gardens and the Invention of Wilderness, 2001; Following the Sun: From Spain to the Hebrides, 2002; Looking for Mr. Gilbert: The Reimagined Life of an African American, 2005; The Rose Café: Love and War In Corsica, 2007; The Paradise of all These Parts: A Natural History of Boston, 2008. **Address:** Massachusetts Audubon Society, 208 S Great Rd., Lincoln, MA 01773, U.S.A. **Online address:** jmitchell@massaudubon.org

MITCHELL, Juliet. (Juliet Constance Wyatt Mitchell). British/New Zealander (born New Zealand), b. 1940. **Genres:** Literary Criticism And History, Psychiatry, Women's Studies And Issues. **Career:** University of Leeds, lecturer in English, 1962-63; University of Reading, lecturer in English, 1965-70; Cornell University, distinguished visiting professor, 1994; University of Cambridge, Jesus College, lecturer in gender and society, 1996-2000, fellow, 1996-, Department of Human Geography, research fellow, professor of psychoanalysis and gender studies, 2000-, Department of Social and Political Sciences, head, 2002-, convener of gender studies, Centre for Gender Studies, founding director, Jesus College, fellow emeritus; University College London, professor, Expanded Doctoral School in Psychoanalytic Studies, director, 2010-; British and International Psychoanalytical Societies, fellow. Broadcaster and writer. **Publications:** Women: The Longest Revolution, 1966; Woman's Estate, 1972; Psychoanalysis and Feminism, 1974; Women and Equality, 1975; Women: The Longest Revolution, 1984; Mad Men and Medusas, 2000; Siblings: Sex and Violence, 2003. EDITOR: Rights and Wrongs of Women, 1976; The Fortunes and Misfortunes of the Famous Moll Flanders, 1978; Feminine Sexuality: Jacques Lacan and the École Freudienne, 1982; (with A. Oakley) What is Feminism?, 1986; The Selected Melanie Klein, 1987; (with M. Parsons) Before I Was I, 1993; Who's Afraid of Feminism?, 1997. **Address:** c/o Deborah Rogers, Rogers, Coleridge & White Ltd., 20 Powis Mews, London, GL W11 1JN, England. **Online address:** juliet.mitchell@ucl.ac.uk

MITCHELL, Juliet Constance Wyatt. *See* **MITCHELL, Juliet.**

MITCHELL, Linda E. American (born United States), b. 1957. **Genres:** History, Women's Studies And Issues. **Career:** Alfred University, assistant professor, 1991-96, associate professor, 1996-2001, Hagar professor of humanities, 2003-07, Medieval/Renaissance Studies Minor, co-director, 2001-08; University of Missouri, Martha Jane Phillips Starr/ Missouri distinguished professor of women's and gender studies and professor of history, 2008-. Writer. **Publications:** (Ed.) Women in Medieval Western European Culture, 1999; Portraits of Medieval Women: Family, Marriage, and Politics in England, 1225-1350, 2003; Family Life in the Middle Ages, 2007; (comp. and ed. with K.L. French and D.L. Biggs) The Ties That Bind: Essays in Medieval British History in Honor of Barbara Hanawalt, 2010. Contributor to books, periodicals and journals. **Address:** Department of History, University of Missouri, 203 Cockefair Hall, Interdisciplinary Studies, 204B Haag Hall, Kansas, MO 64110, U.S.A. **Online address:** mitchellli@umkc.edu

MITCHELL, Margaree King. American (born United States), b. 1953. **Genres:** Children's Fiction, Plays/Screenplays, Young Adult Fiction, Literary Criticism And History. **Career:** Monumental Baptist Church, Department of Drama, director, 1987-90. Writer. **Publications:** Uncle Jed's Barbershop, 1993; Granddaddy's Gift, 1996; Susie Mae, 2000; Grandmama's Song, 2010. Contributor of short stories to magazines. **Address:** 6804 E Hwy. 6 S, Ste. 335, Houston, TX 77083, U.S.A. **Online address:** margareekm@aol.com

MITCHELL, Mark. (Mark Lindsey Mitchell). Italian/American (born United States), b. 1961. **Genres:** Gay And Lesbian Issues, Essays, Novels, Biography, Adult Non-fiction, Young Adult Fiction. **Career:** Writer. **Publications:** (With D. Leavitt) Italian Pleasures, 1996; Virtuosi: A Defense and a (Sometimes Erotic) Celebration of Great Pianists, 2000; (with D. Leavitt) In Maremma: Life and a House in Southern Tuscany, 2001; Vladamir de Pachmann: A Piano Viruoso's Life and Art, 2002. EDITOR: (with D. Leavitt) The Penguin Book of Gay Short Stories, 1994; The Penguin Book of International Gay Writing, 1995; (with D. Leavitt) Pages Passed from Hand to Hand: The Hidden Tradition of Homosexual Literature in English from 1748 to 1914, 1998; (and intro. with D. Leavitt) Selected Stories, 2001; (and intro. with A. Evans) Moriz Rosenthal in Word and Music: A Legacy of the Nineteenth Century, 2006. Contributor to periodicals. **Address:** c/o Jin Auh, The Wylie Agency, 250 W 57th St., Ste. 2114, New York, NY 10107, U.S.A.

MITCHELL, Mark Lindsey. *See* **MITCHELL, Mark.**

MITCHELL, Mark T. American (born United States) **Genres:** Adult Non-fiction. **Career:** Patrick Henry College, faculty, 2002, assistant professor of philosophy and political theory, Department of Government, associate professor, chairman; Princeton University, James Madison Program, visiting fellow. Writer. **Publications:** Michael Polanyi: The Art of Knowing, 2006; (ed. with N. Schlueter) The Humane Vision of Wendell Berry, 2011. **Address:** Department of Government, Patrick Henry College, 10 Patrick Henry Cir., PO Box 1776, Purcellville, VA 20132, U.S.A. **Online address:** mtmitchell@phc.edu

MITCHELL, Mary E. American (born United States), b. 1951. **Genres:** Novels. **Career:** Bethany Hill School, writing instructor. Writer. **Publications:** Starting Out Sideways (novel), 2007; Americans in Space (novel), 2009. Contributor to magazines and newspapers. **Address:** Boston, MA , U.S.A. **Online address:** mary@maryemitchell.com

MITCHELL, Memory F. American (born United States), b. 1924. **Genres:** History, Politics/Government. **Career:** Meredith College, instructor in history, 1949-50; North Carolina State Board of Public Welfare, administrative assistant, 1950-54; Cabarrus County Domestic Relations Court, judge, 1954-55; North Carolina Division of Archives and History, records management supervisor, 1956-61, historical publications administrator, 1961-; Olivia Raney Library, staff, 1961-69; Historical Publications, section chief, 1961-82, Raleigh Community Ambassador Project, director. Writer. **Publications:** North Carolina's Signers: Brief Sketches of the Men Who Signed the Declaration of Independence and the Constitution, 1964; Legal Aspects of Conscription and Exemption in North Carolina 1861-1865, 1965. EDITOR: Messages, Addresses and Public Papers of Terry Sanford: Governor of North Carolina 1961-1965, 1966; North Carolina Documents, 1584-1868, 1967; Messages, Addresses and Public Papers of Daniel Killian Moore, Governor of North Carolina 1965-69, 1971; Addresses and Public Papers of Robert Walter Scott: Governor of North Carolina 1969-1973, 1974; Addresses and Public Papers of James Eubert Holshouser, Jr., Governor of North Carolina 1973-77, 1978; Addresses and Public Papers of James Baxter Hunt, Jr., Governor of North Carolina 1977-1981, 1982. Contributor of articles to journals. **Address:** North Carolina Division of Archives and History, 4610 Mail Service Ctr., 109 E Jones St., Raleigh, NC 27601, U.S.A. **Online address:** fmmitch@mindspring.com

MITCHELL, Michele. American (born United States), b. 1965. **Genres:** History, Women's Studies And Issues. **Career:** New York University, associate professor of history, Gender & History, editor, 2005-08. **Publications:** (Ed. with S. Gunning and T.W. Hunter) Dialogues of Dispersal: Gender, Sexuality and African Diasporas, 2004; Righteous Propagation: African Americans and the Politics of Racial Destiny after Reconstruction, 2004. **Address:** Department of History, New York University, King Juan Carlos I of Spain Ctr., 53 Washington Square South, New York, NY 10012-1098, U.S.A. **Online address:** michele.mitchell@nyu.edu

MITCHELL, Nancy. American (born United States) **Genres:** Novels, Social Sciences, Mystery/Crime/Suspense. **Career:** Fremont Council PTA, secretary, president and treasurer; Peralta District PTA, treasurer; Lightstream Publications, founder. Writer. **Publications:** THE CHANGING EARTH TRILOGY: Earth Rising: Disaster Strikes the Bay Area, 1999; Raging Skies: Catastrophe in the East Bay, 1999; Global Warning: Attack on the Pacific Rim!, 1999; (with L. Mordaunt) Fit at 55-Plus: Weight Loss and Fitness for the Rest of Your Life, 2003. **Address:** 44999 Cree Ct., PO Box 3229, Fremont, CA 94539-6513, U.S.A. **Online address:** nancyr@thegrid.net

MITCHELL, Nathan. American (born United States), b. 1943. **Genres:** History, Theology/Religion, Social Sciences, Essays. **Career:** Saint Meinrad's School of Theology, professor of liturgy; University of Notre Dame, professor of liturgy. Writer. **Publications:** Cult and Controversy: The Worship of the Eucharist outside Mass, 1982; A Commentary on the General Instruction of the Roman Missal: Developed under the Auspices of the Catholic Cult and Controversy: The Worship of the Eucharist outside Mass, 1982; Mission and Ministry: History and Theology in the Sacrament of Order, 1990; The Postures of the Assembly during the Eucharistic Prayer, 1994; Eucharist as Sacrament of Initiation, 1994; Rule of Prayer, Rule of Faith: Essays in Honor of Aidan Kavanagh, 1996; Liturgy and the Social Sciences, 1999; Real Presence: The Work of Eucharist, 2001; Meeting Mystery: Liturgy, Worship, Sacraments, 2006; A Commentary on the General Instruction of the Roman Missal: Developed under the Auspices of the Catholic Academy of Liturgy and Cosponsored by the Federation of Diocesan Liturgical Commissions, 2007; Mystery of the Rosary: Marian Devotion and the Reinvention of Catholicism, 2009. **Address:** Department of Theology, University of Notre Dame, 130 Malloy Hall, Notre Dame, IN 46556, U.S.A. **Online address:** nathan.d.mitchell.2@nd.edu

MITCHELL, Peter. (Peter John Mitchell). British (born England), b. 1962. **Genres:** Social Sciences, History. **Career:** University of Oxford, St. Hugh's College, lecturer in African prehistory, dean, Department of Archaeology and Anthropology, tutor and fellow. Writer. **Publications:** (As P.J. Mitchell) The Early Microlithic Assemblages of Southern Africa, 1988; (with P.L. Carter and P. Vinnicombe as P.J. Mitchell) Sehonghong: The Middle and Later Stone Age Industrial Sequence at a Lesotho Rock-Shelter, 1988; Catalogue of Stone Age Artefacts from Southern Africa in the British Museum, 2002; The Archaeology of Southern Africa, 2002; (ed. with A. Haour and J. Hobart) Researching Africa's Past: New Contributions from British Archaeologists: Proceedings of a Meeting Held at St. Hugh's College, Oxford, Saturday, April 20th 2002, 2003; African Connections: An Archaeological Perspective on Africa and the Wider World, 2005; (with L. Barham) The First Africans: African Archaeology from the Earliest Tool Makers to Most Recent Foragers, 2008; (ed. with S. Badenhorst and J.C. Driver) Animals and People, 2008; (ed. with K. Ikeya and H. Ogawa) Interactions between Hunter-gatherers and Farmers, 2009; (ed. with D. Smith) Flood's People, 2009. EDITOR: PEOPLES AND CULTURES OF AFRICA SERIES: Peoples and Cultures of Africa, 2006; Peoples and Cultures of Central Africa, 2006; Peoples and Cultures of North Africa, 2006; Peoples and Cultures of West Africa, 2006; Peoples and Cultures of

East Africa, 2006; Peoples and Cultures of Southern Africa, 2006. **Address:** St. Hugh's College, University of Oxford, St. Margaret's Rd., Oxford, OX OX2 6LE, England. **Online address:** peter.mitchell@st-hughs.ox.ac.uk

MITCHELL, Peter John. *See* **MITCHELL, Peter.**

MITCHELL, Roger. American (born United States), b. 1935. **Genres:** Poetry, Biography, Essays, Literary Criticism And History, Young Adult Fiction. **Career:** University of Wisconsin, instructor, 1963-65, assistant professor of English, 1965-68; Jagiellonian University, Department of English, Fullbright lecturer, 1966-67; Marquette University, assistant professor, 1968-71, associate professor of English, 1971-75; Indiana University, Department of English, professor, 1975-99, emeritus professor, 1999-, Creative Writing Program, director, 1990-96, Ruth Lilly chair of poetry, 1990-95; The Minnesota Review, editor and publisher, 1973-81; Leicester University, Department of English, visiting lecturer, 1978-79; Colorado College, Department of English, visiting emeritus professor, 2002-04, 2007; Hamilton Stone Reviews, poetry editor, 2009-. **Publications:** (With S. Kahn) Another Time, 1968; Reading the News (poems), 1969; In a Meantime, 1971; Letters from Siberia, and Other Poems, 1971; Edges, 1973; Moving, 1976; Homage to Beatrix Potter, 1978; (ed. with S.R. Sanders) The Human Crowd: New Fiction From The Minnesota Review, 1981; To Recommend Renewal, 1984; Clear Space on a Cold Day, 1986; Adirondack: Poems, 1988; Clear Pond: The Reconstruction of a Life, 1991; The Word for Everything, 1996; Braid, 1997; Savage Baggage, 2001; Delicate Bait: Poems, 2003; Half/mask, 2007; Lemon Peeled the Moment Before: New and Selected Poems, 1967-2008, 2008. Contributor to journals. **Address:** Department of English, Indiana University, 442 Ballantine Hall, 1020 E Kirkwood Ave., Bloomington, IN 47405-7103, U.S.A. **Online address:** mitchclr@indiana.edu

MITCHELL, Sharon. American (born United States), b. 1962. **Genres:** Novels. **Career:** Boston University, instructor, adjunct professor, 1987-94, psychologist, 1989-94; University of Delaware, psychologist, Center for Counseling and Student Development, assistant director, assistant professor, 1994-2003, professor; University at Buffalo, director of counseling services, 2003-. Novelist. **Publications:** Nothing But the Rent (novel), 1998; Sheer Necessity, 1999; Near Perfect, 2001. Contributor to periodicals. **Address:** Counseling Services, University at Buffalo, 120 Richmond Quad, Buffalo, NY 14261-0053, U.S.A. **Online address:** smitch@buffalo.edu

MITCHELL, Siri L. American (born United States), b. 1969. **Genres:** Novels. **Career:** Writer. **Publications:** NOVELS: Chateau of Echoes, 2005; Kissing Adrien, 2005; The Cubicle Next Door, 2006; Something beyond the Sky, 2006; Moon over Tokyo, 2007; A Constant Heart, 2008; Love's Pursuit, 2009; She Walks in Beauty, 2010. **Address:** U.S.A. **Online address:** siri@sirimitchell.com

MITCHELL, Stephen. American (born United States), b. 1943?. **Genres:** Translations, Songs/Lyrics And Libretti, History. **Career:** Writer, poet and translator. **Publications:** Somebody like You: Poems, 1971; Poems, 1972; Parables and Portraits, 1990; The Gospel according to Jesus: A New Translation and Guide to His Essential Teachings for Believers and Unbelievers, 1991; (ed. and trans.) Duino Elegies, 1992; Meetings with the Archangel: A Comedy of the Spirit, 1998; The Frog Prince: A Fairy Tale for Consenting Adults, 1999; (with B. Katie) Loving What Is: Four Questions That Can Change Your Life, 2002; (with B. Katie) A Thousand Names for Joy: Living in Harmony with the Way Things Are, 2007; (ed.) Question Your Thinking, Change the World: Quotations from Byron Katie, 2007; Second Book of the Tao, 2009. EDITOR: Dropping Ashes on the Buddha: The Teaching of Zen Master Seung Sahn, 1976; The Enlightened Heart: An Anthology of Sacred Poetry, 1989; The Enlightened Mind: An Anthology of Sacred Prose, 1991; (with R. Hass) Into the Garden: A Wedding Anthology: Poetry and Prose on Love and Marriage, 1993; Book of Psalms, 1993; W. Whitman, Song of Myself, 1993; Bestiary: An Anthology of Poems about Animals, 1996; The Essence of Wisdom: Words from the Masters to Illuminate the Spiritual Path, 1998. TRANSLATOR AND ADAPTOR: Into the Whirlwind: A Translation of the Book of Job, 1979, as The Book of Job, 1987; D. Pagis, Points of Departure, 1981; (and ed.) R.M. Rilke, The Selected Poetry of Rainer Maria Rilke, 1982; R.M. Rilke, The Notebooks of Malte Laurids Brigge, 1983; R.M. Rilke, Die Weise von Liebe und Tod des Cornets Christoph Rilke, (title means: 'The Lay of the Love and Death of Cornet Christoph Rilke') (bilingual ed.), 1983; (and foreword) R.M. Rilke, Letters to a Young Poet, 1984; (and intro.) R.M. Rilke, The Sonnets to Orpheus, 1985; (and ed. with C. Bloch) Y. Amichai, The Selected Poetry of Yehuda Amichai, 1986; (and foreword) Lao-tzu, Tao Te Ching: A New English Version, 1988; R.M. Rilke, Duino Elegies, 1992; (and ed.) R.M. Rilke, Ahead of All Parting: The Selected Poetry and Prose of Rainer Maria Rilke, 1995; Genesis: A New Translation of the Classic Biblical Stories, 1996; D. Pagis, The Selected Poetry of Dan Pagis, 1996; P. Neruda, Full Woman, Fleshly Apple, Hot Moon: Selected Poems of Pablo Neruda, 1997; (with J.A. Autry) Real Power: Business Lessons from the Tao Te Ching, 1998; Bhagavad Gita: A New Translation, 2000; Gilgamesh: A New English Version, 2004; (ed.) Duino Elegies; and The Sonnets to Orpheus, 2009; (and intro.) Iliad, 2011. FOR CHILDREN: The Creation, 1990; Tao Te Ching: An Illustrated Journey, 1999; Jesus: What He Really Said and Did, 2002; The Wishing Bone and Other Poems, 2003; Aladdin's Magic Lamp and Other Tales from the 1001 Nights, forthcoming. Contributor to periodicals. **Address:** c/o Author Mail, HarperCollins Ltd,, 10 E 53rd St., New York, NY 10022, U.S.A.

MITCHELL, Stephen (G.). British (born England), b. 1948. **Genres:** History, Archaeology/Antiquities, Education, Reference. **Career:** University of Wales, University College of Swansea, lecturer, professor, 1976-2001; University of Exeter, professor, 2002, head of the department. Writer. **Publications:** Asvan Kale, Keban Resue Excavations, Eastern Anatolia, 1980; Regional Epigraphic Catalogues of Asia Minor II, The Ankara District, 1982; (ed.) Armies and Frontiers in Roman and Byzantine Anatolia: Proceedings of a Colloquium held at University College, Swansea, in April 1981, 1983; (ed. with B. Levick and M. Waelkens) Monumenta Asiae Minoris Antiqua IX. Inscriptions from Aezani and the Aezanitis, 1988; Anatolia: Land, Men, and Gods in Asia Minor, 1993, 2 vols., 1995; Cremna in Pisidia: An Ancient City in Peace and in War, 1995; (with M. Waelkens) Pisidian Antioch: The Site and Its Monuments, 1998; (with G.H.R. Horsley) The Inscriptions of Central Pisidia: Including Texts from Kremna, Ariassos, Keraia, Hyia, Panemoteichos, the Sanctuary of Apollo of the Perminoundeis, Sia, Kocaaliler, and the Döşeme Boğazi, 1999; (ed. with G. Greatrex) Ethnicity and Culture in Late Antiquity, 2000; (with C. Katsari) Patterns in the Economy of Roman Asia Minor Author of Monographs, 2005; A History of the Later Roman Empire, AD 284-641: The Transformation of the Ancient World, 2007; (ed. with G. Erkut) Black Sea: Past, Present and Future: Proceedings of the International, Interdisciplinary Conference, Istanbul, 14-16 October 2004, 2007; The Imperial Temple at Ankara and the Res Gestae of the Emperor Augustus: A Historical Guide, 2008; (ed. with P. Van Nuffelen) Monotheism between Pagans and Christians in Late Antiquity, 2009; (ed. with P. van Nuffelen) One God: Pagan Monotheism in the Roman Empire, 2010. Contributor to periodicals. **Address:** Department of Classics and Ancient History, College of Humanities, Exeter University, Amory Bldg., Exeter, DN EX4 4RJ, England. **Online address:** s.mitchell@ex.ac.uk

MITCHELL, Susanna. *See* **MITCHELL, Susanna (Ryland).**

MITCHELL, Susanna (Ryland). (Susanna Mitchell). British/Irish (born Ireland), b. 1941. **Genres:** Novels, Young Adult Fiction. **Career:** Ulster Television, sales executive, 1961-64. Novelist, Writer. **Publications:** The Token, 1984; The Christening, 1986; The Colour of His Hair, 1994. Contributor to periodicals. **Address:** Curtis Brown, Haymarket House, 4th Fl., 28-29, Haymarket, London, GL SW1Y 4SP, England. **Online address:** susanna.mitchell@neweconomics.org

MITCHELL, Thomas R. American (born United States), b. 1950. **Genres:** Literary Criticism And History, Mystery/Crime/Suspense, Biography, Autobiography/Memoirs, Young Adult Fiction. **Career:** Laredo Community College, instructor in English and department chair, 1973-98; Image Group (advertising agency), partner, 1976-79; Mitchell & Burdess Advertising, co-owner, 1979-81; Texas A&M International University, associate professor of English and department chair, 1998-, professor, College of Arts and Sciences, dean. Writer. **Publications:** Hawthorne's Fuller Mystery, 1998. Contributor to books and periodicals. **Address:** Department of Language and Literature, Texas A&M International University, 301A LBVSC, 5201 University Blvd., Laredo, TX 78041, U.S.A. **Online address:** tmitchell@tamiu.edu

MITCHELL, Todd. American (born United States), b. 1974. **Genres:** Novels, Young Adult Fiction. **Career:** Colorado State University, instructor in creative writing and literature. Writer. **Publications:** The Traitor King, 2007; The Secret to Lying, 2010; Flight of Angels, 2011. **Address:** Department of English, Colorado State University, 323B Eddy Hall, 1773 Campus Delivery, Ft. Collins, CO 80523-1773, U.S.A. **Online address:** toddmitchellbooks@hotmail.com

MITCHELL, William P. American (born United States), b. 1937. **Genres:** Anthropology/Ethnology, History. **Career:** New York Academy of Sciences, Anthropology Section, co-chair; City University of New York, Brooklyn College, lecturer in anthropology, 1963, 1968; Monmouth College, assistant professor, 1968-73, associate professor, 1973-78, professor of anthropology, 1978-, Freed professor of social sciences, 1986-, Freed Foundation endowed chair in social science, School of Humanities and Social Sciences, dean, Honors School, interim dean, 2009-10; Universidad Catolica de Lima, research associate, 1983, 1996, visiting professor, 1987-88; Global Studies Consortium of New Jersey Colleges and Universities, founding president, 1985-87. Writer. **Publications:** Peasants on the Edge: Crop, Cult and Crisis in the Andes, 1991; Voices from the Global Margin: Confronting Poverty and Inventing New Lives in the Andes, 2006. EDITOR: (with D. Guillet and contrib.) Irrigation at High Altitudes: The Social Organization of Water Control Systems in the Andes, 1993; (ed. with B. Jaye) Picturing Faith: A Facsimile Edition of the Pictographic Quechua Catechism in the Huntington Free Library, 1999. Works appear in anthropologies. Contributor of articles to journals and books. **Address:** Department of History & Anthropology, Monmouth University, Wilson Annex O-11, 400 Cedar Ave., West Long Branch, NJ 07764, U.S.A. **Online address:** mitchell@monmouth.edu

MITCHELSON, Mitch. (Peter Richard Mitchelson). British (born England), b. 1950. **Genres:** Plays/Screenplays, Theatre, Young Adult Non-fiction, Children's Non-fiction, Sports/Fitness, Art/Art History. **Career:** Actor, director, producer and writer. **Publications:** Circus Skills and Commedian Discovering the Self Through Drama and Movement, 1996; The Most Excellent Book of How to Be a Juggler, 1997, new ed. as How to Be a Juggler, 2007; Circus and Clown for Continuum: Companion to 20th Century Theatre, 2000. Contributor to books and periodicals. **Address:** 54 Wedgwood House, China Walk Estate, London, GL SE11 6LL, England. **Online address:** original@clara.net

MITCHELSON, Peter Richard. *See* **MITCHELSON, Mitch.**

MITCHELTREE, Tom. American (born United States), b. 1946. **Genres:** Novels, Mystery/Crime/Suspense, Young Adult Fiction. **Career:** Chemeketa Community College, part-time teacher, 1974-, adjunct faculty, now retired; World Berry Players, board director. Writer. **Publications:** Terror in Room 201, 1980; Katie's Will, 1997; Dataman, 1998; Katie's Gold, 2003; Blink of an Eye, 2004; Death of a Carpenter, 2006; Missing, Maybe Dead, 2006. Works appear in anthologies. **Address:** 448 4th St., Woodburn, OR 97071, U.S.A. **Online address:** tmitche7@cp.chemeketa.edu

MITHEN, Steven J. (Steven John Mithen). British (born England), b. 1960. **Genres:** Young Adult Non-fiction, Archaeology/Antiquities, Sciences, E-books. **Career:** Trinity Hall, research fellow, 1987-91; McDonald Institute for Archeological Research, research associate, 1990-92; University of Reading, lecturer, 1992-96, senior lecturer, 1996, reader, 1998-2000, professor of early history, 2000-, dean of archeology, head of department, 2002-, pro-vice-chancellor. Writer. **Publications:** Thoughtful Foragers: A Study of Prehistoric Decision Making, 1990; The Prehistory of the Mind: A Search for the Origins of Art, Religion, and Science, 1996; (ed.) Creativity in Human Evolution and Prehistory, 1998; Hunter-Gatherer Landscape Archaeology, 2000; After the Ice: A Global Human History, 20000-5000 B.C., 2004; The Singing Neanderthals: The Origins of Music, Language, Mind and Body, 2005; (ed. with B. Finlayson) Early prehistory of Wadi Faynan, Southern Jordan: Archaeological Survey of Wadis Faynan, Ghuwayr and al-Bustan and Evaluation of the Pre-pottery Neolithic A Site of WF16, 2007; (ed. with E. Black) Water, Life & Civilisation: Climate, Environment, and Society in the Jordan Valley, 2011. **Address:** Department of Archaeology, University of Reading, Whiteknights, PO Box 226, Reading, RG6 6AB, England. **Online address:** s.j.mithen@reading.ac.uk

MITHEN, Steven John. *See* **MITHEN, Steven J.**

MITMAN, Gregg. American (born United States), b. 1960. **Genres:** Natural History, Sports/Fitness. **Career:** University of Oklahoma, Department of History of Science, assistant professor, 1991-95, associate professor, 1995- 99, professor, 1999-2000; University of Wisconsin, professor of medical history, 2001-, Department of History of Science, interim chair, 2003-04, William Coleman professor of history of science, 2005-, Center for Culture, History and Environment, director, 2007-; University of Wisconsin, Department of the History of Science, visiting assistant professor, 1989-90, visiting associate professor, 1995-96; University of Minnesota, Program in the History of Science and Technology, visiting assistant professor, 1990-91, visiting professor, 2000-01; Max Planck Institute for the History of Science, visiting scholar, 1999-2000, 2008. Writer. **Publications:** The State of Nature: Ecology, Community and American Social Thought, 1900-1950, 1992; Reel Nature: America's Romance with Wildlife on Films, 1999; (ed. with L. Daston) Thinking with Animals: New Perspectives on Anthropomorphism, 2005; Breathing Space: How Allergies Shape Our Lives and Landscapes, 2007. Contributor of articles to journals. **Address:** University of Wisconsin, 1415 Medical Sciences Ctr., 1300 University Ave., Madison, WI 53706-1585, U.S.A. **Online address:** gmitman@med.wisc.edu

MITROFF, Ian I. American (born United States), b. 1938. **Genres:** Education. **Career:** University of California, Engineering Materials Laboratory, research assistant, 1960-62; Lockheed Missiles and Space Company Inc., graduate engineer, 1962-63, Extension Division, lecturer in mathematics and engineering, 1963-64, Space Sciences Lab, graduate economist and research assistant, 1964-67, adjunct professor; California State College, lecturer in management science, 1966-67; University of Pittsburgh, Graduate School of Business, assistant professor of business administration, 1967-70, Interdisciplinary Department of Information Science, associate professor of business administration, 1970-74, associate professor of business, information science and sociology, 1974-75, Interdisciplinary Department of Information Science and the Department of Sociology, professor, 1975-77, 1978-80; University of Pennsylvania, Wharton School, The Busch Center, Department of Management, visiting professor, 1977; University of Southern California, Marshall School of Business, Harold Quinton distinguished professor of business policy, 1980-, Center for Crisis Management, founder, 1986-96, Annenberg School for Communication, Department of Journalism, professor of journalism, 2001-, now professor emeritus; Alliant International University, Marshall Goldsmith School of Management, faculty. Writer. **Publications:** Subjective Side of Science: A Philosophical Inquiry into the Psychology of the Apollo Moon Scientists, 1974; (with R.H. Kilmann) Methodological Approaches to Social Science, 1978; (with R.O. Mason) Challenging Strategic Planning Assumptions: Theory, Cases, and Techniques, 1981; (with R.O. Mason) Creating a Dialectical Social Science: Concepts, Methods, and Models, 1981; (with R.O. Mason and V.P. Barabba) 1980: Census, Policy Making Amid Turbulence, 1983; Stakeholders of the Organizational Mind, 1983; (with R.H. Kilmann) Corporate Tragedies: Product Tampering, Sabotage, and Other Catastrophes, 1984; (with S.A. Mohrman and G. Little) Business Not as Usual: Rethinking Our Individual, Corporate, and Industrial Strategies for Global Competition, 1987; Break-Away Thinking: How to Challenge your Business Assumptions (and Why You Should), 1988; (with W. Bennis) Unreality Industry: The Deliberate Manufacturing of Falsehood and What it is Doing to Our Lives, 1989, rev. ed., 1993; (with T.C. Pauchant) We're So Big and Powerful Nothing Bad can Happen to Us: An Investigation of America's Crisis Prone Corporations, 1990; (with T.C. Pauchant) Transforming the Crisis-Prone Organization: Preventing Individual, Organizational, and Environmental Tragedies, 1992; Unbounded Mind: Breaking the Chains of Traditional Business Thinking, 1993; (with C.M. Pearson) Crisis Management: A Diagnostic Guide for Improving Your Organization's Crisis-Preparedness, 1993; (with H.A. Linstone) Challenge of the 21st Century: Managing Technology and Ourselves in a Shrinking World, 1994; (with R.O. Mason and C.M. Pearson) Framebreak: The Radical Redesign of American Business, 1994; Essential Guide to Managing Corporate Crises: A Step-by-Step Handbook for Surviving Major Catastrophes, 1996; Smart Thinking for Crazy Times: The Art of Solving the Right Problems, 1998; (with E.A. Denton) A Spiritual Audit of Corporate America: A Hard Look at Spirituality, Religion, and Values in the Workplace, 1999; Managing Crises Before They Happen: What Every Executive and Manager Needs to Know About Crisis Management, 2001; Crisis Leadership: Planning for the Unthinkable, 2004; Why Some Companies Emerge Stronger and Better From a Crisis: 7 Essential Lessons for Surviving Disaster, 2006; Dirty Rotten Strategies, 2009. **Address:** 510 Mountain Blvd., Oakland, CA 94611, U.S.A. **Online address:** ianmitroff@earthlink.net

MITSON, Eileen N(ora). British (born England), b. 1930. **Genres:** Novels, Autobiography/Memoirs, inspirational/Motivational Literature, Theology/Religion. **Career:** Woman Alive Magazine, columnist, 1982-94. Writer. **Publications:** Stairway of Surprises, 1964; The Door in the Wall, 1967; His Bright Designs, 1968; Beyond the Shadows, 1968; His Bright Designs, 1968; Amazon Adventure, 1969; House Full of Strangers: A Contemporary Novel, 1971; The Inside Room, 1973; A Kind of Freedom, 1976; The Innermost

Room, 1976; Reaching for God, 1978; (co-author) Creativity, 1985; Songs of Freedom: Stories of Lives Transformed by the Deep Power of Christ, 2005. **Address:** 39 Oaklands, Hamilton Rd., Reading, BR RG1 5RN, England.

MITTELMARK, Howard. American (born United States), b. 1957. **Genres:** Novels, Young Adult Non-fiction. **Career:** Writer. **Publications:** (With S. Newman) How Not to Write a Novel: 200 Classic Mistakes and How to Avoid Them: A Misstep-by-Misstep Guide (nonfiction), 2008. NOVELS: Age of Consent, 2007; The Lesser World, 2008. Contributor to books and magazines. **Address:** New York, NY , U.S.A. **Online address:** mittelmark@gmail.com

MITTELSTADT, Jennifer. American (born United States), b. 1970. **Genres:** Politics/Government. **Career:** Wesleyan University, Pew Foundation fellow, 1991; University of Minnesota, Clarke Chambers research fellow, Social Welfare History Archives, 1997; University of Michigan, Mellon Candidacy fellow, 1997-98, Institute for Research on Women and Gender, fellow, 1998, Rackham dissertation fellow, 1998, Mellon dissertation fellow, 1998-99, Rackham Graduate School, Rackham predoctoral fellow, 1999-2000; City University of New York, Brooklyn College, adjunct assistant professor, 2001-02; visiting assistant professor, 2002-03; Pennsylvania State University, assistant professor of history and women's studies, 2003-10, Rock Ethics Institute faculty fellow, 2007; Rutgers, The State University of New Jersey, School of Arts and Sciences, Department of History, associate professor, 2010-. Writer and producer. **Publications:** From Welfare to Workfare: The Unintended Consequences of Liberal Reform, 1945-1965, 2005; (with P. Nadasen and M. Chappell) Welfare in the United States: A History with Documents, 1935-1996, 2009. Contributor of articles to journals. **Address:** Department of History, School of Arts and Sciences, Rutgers, The State University of New Jersey, 223A Van Dyck Hall, 16 Seminary Pl., New Brunswick, NJ 08901, U.S.A. **Online address:** jmittel@rci.rutgers.edu

MITTMAN, Stephanie. (Stevi Mittman). American (born United States), b. 1950. **Genres:** Novels, Novellas/Short Stories, Romance/Historical. **Career:** Stained glass artist, 1976-91; novelist, 1991-. **Publications:** ROMANCE NOVELS: Bridge to Yesterday, 1995; A Taste of Honey, 1995; The Marriage Bed, 1996; Sweeter than Wine, 1997; A Kiss to Dream On, 1998; The Courtship, 1998; Head over Heels, 1999; Heart Full of Miracles, 2000. AS STEVI MITTMAN: (co-author) Holiday Wishes: If I Make It Through December/ Perfect Christmas, 2006; What Goes with Blood Red, Anyway?, 2006; Who Makes Up these Rules, Anyway?, 2006; (co-author) Summer Dreams: Summertime Blues/Kokomo/Who's That In The Itsy-Bitsy, Anyway?, 2007; Why is Murder on the Menu, Anyway?, 2007; Whose Number Is Up, Anyway?, 2007; Who Creamed Peaches, Anyway?, 2008. Works appear in anthologies. **Address:** Ithaca, NY , U.S.A. **Online address:** stevi@stevimittman.com

MITTMAN, Stevi. *See* **MITTMAN, Stephanie.**

MITTON, Tony. British (born England), b. 1951. **Genres:** Children's Fiction. **Career:** Cambs Lea, primary school teacher, 1975-98, primary and special needs teacher, 1986-. Freelance writer. **Publications:** FOR CHILDREN: Nobody Laughed, 1994; Mr. Marvel and the Cake, 1996; Mr. Marvel and the Car, 1996; Mr. Marvel and the Lemonade, 1996; Mr. Marvel and the Washing, 1996; Big Bad Raps, 1996; Playtime with Rosie Rabbit, 1996; Bedtime for Rosie Rabbit, 1996; Royal Raps, 1996; Dazzling Diggers, 1997; Rosie Rabbit's Birthday Party, 1997; Rosie Rabbit Goes to Preschool, 1997; Roaring Rockets, 1997; Monster Raps, 1998; Fantastic Raps, 1998; Where's My Egg?, 1998, 2nd ed., 1999; Spooky Hoo Hah!, 1998; Flashing Fire Engines, 1998; The Magic Pot, 1998; Plum (poems), 1998, rev. ed., 2003; A Door to Secrets: Riddles in Rhyme, 1998; The Seal Hunter, 1998; Terrific Trains, 1998; There's No Such Thing! A Flip-Flap Book, 1999; The Red & White Spotted Handkerchief, 2000; (ed.) Earth Changes, Human Destiny: Coping and Attuning with the Help of the Revelation of St. John, 2000; What's the Time Mr Wolf?, 2000; I Want to Shout and Stamp About, 2000; Pip, 2001; Fluff-and Other Stuff, 2001; Down by the Cool of the Pool, 2002; Amazing Aeroplanes, 2002; Busy Boats, 2002; Crazy Camelot Capers, 2002; Dinosaurumpus, 2003; Amazing Machines, 2003; Goodnight Me, Goodnight You, 2003; Brilliant Boats, 2003; Tough Trucks, 2003, rev. ed., 2005; Tremendous Tractors, 2003, rev. ed., 2005; Riddledy Piggledy, 2003; Spooky Hour, 2004; The Tale of Tales, 2004; Amazing Machines Jigsaw Book, 2004; Cool Cars, 2005; Once Upon a Tide, 2006; Super Submarines, 2006; All Afloat on Noah's Boat!, 2007; Christmas Wishes, 2007; Playful Little Penguins, 2007; (with A. Parker) The Amazing Machines: Truckload of Fun, 2007; Gnash, Gnaw, Dinosaur!: Prehistoric Poems with Lift-the-Flap Surprises!, 2009; Very Curious Bear, 2009; Farmer Joe and the Music Show, 2009; Rainforest Romp, 2009; Super Safari, 2009; Jolly Olly Octopus, 2010; Rumble, Roar, Dinosaur!: More Prehistoric Poems With Lift-the-Flap Surprises!, 2010; Storyteller's Secrets, 2010. RETELLER: Three Tales from Scotland, 1995; The Three Billy Goats, 1996; Goldilocks, 2000; Little Red Riding Hood, 2000. RAP RHYMES SERIES: Robin Hood Raps, 2000; Scary Raps, 2000; Groovy Greek Hero Raps, 2000; Mega Greek Myth Raps, 2000; Mighty Greek Myth Raps, 2001; Great Greek Myth Raps, 2001. Contributor to periodicals. **Address:** 41 Sturton St., Cambridge, CM CB1 2QG, England. **Online address:** tony@tonymitton.co.uk

MIURA, Hiroshi. Japanese (born Japan), b. 1944. **Genres:** History, Biography. **Career:** Peter Pan Seafoods Inc., quality controller, 1978-81; Consulate-General of Japan, clerk, 1982-84; NEC Semiconductors, Japanese/English interpreter and translator, 1988-92; Canon Manufacturing, Japanese/English interpreter and translator, 1993-97; Shikoku University, lecturer, 1998-; Anan National College of Technology, lecturer, 1999-. Writer. **Publications:** The Life and Thought of Kanzo Uchimura, 1861-1930, 1996. Contributor to books. **Address:** 4-32-11 Shomachi, Tokushima-shi, Tokushima-ken, 770-0044, Japan. **Online address:** tokushima272001@yahoo.co.jp

MIX, Elizabeth K. American (born United States), b. 1964. **Genres:** Women's Studies And Issues. **Career:** University of Minnesota, Continuing Education and Extension, instructor, 1994; Saint Olaf College, Department of Art, assistant professor, 1994-95; Minnesota State University, Department of Art, assistant professor, 1995-2000; Purdue University, Department of visual and Performing Arts, Division of Fine Arts, assistant professor, 2001-06; Butler University, Department of Media Arts, assistant art history professor. Writer. **Publications:** The Complete Mayeux: Use and Abuse of a French Icon, 1997; (with G.P. Weisberg) Art Nouveau: A Research Guide for Design Reform in France, Belgium, England and the United States, 1998; Evil by Design: The Creation and Marketing of the Femme-Fatale, 2006. Contributor of articles to books and journals. **Address:** IN , U.S.A. **Online address:** emix@butler.edu

MIXON, Laura J. American (born United States), b. 1957. **Genres:** Science Fiction/Fantasy, Sciences. **Career:** Dow Chemical, research engineer; General Electric, machine shop environmental manager; Salomon Inc., vice president for environmental affairs; Environmental Resources Management, environmental engineering consultant, 2001-. Freelance science fiction writer. **Publications:** Omni Astropilots, 1987; Glass Houses, 1992; (with S. Gould) Greenwar, 1997; Proxies, 1998; Burning the Ice, 2002. Work represented in anthologies. Contributor to magazines. **Address:** c/o Tor Books, 175 5th Ave., 14th Fl., New York, NY 10010-7703, U.S.A. **Online address:** ljm@thuntek.net

MIYARES, Coco Emilia Fusco. American (born United States), b. 1960. **Genres:** Film, Art/Art History. **Career:** Temple University, assistant professor of visual arts, 1995-98, associate professor, 1998-2001; Columbia University, associate professor of art, 2001-; Parsons The New School for Design, Department of Fine Art, chair. Writer, artist and filmmaker. **Publications:** AS COCO FUSCO: The Hybrid State Films, 1991; English Is Broken Here: Notes on Cultural Fusion in the Americas, 1995; (ed.) Corpus Delecti: Performance Art of the Americas, 2000; The Bodies That Were Not Ours: And Other Writings, 2001; (ed. with B. Wallis) Only Skin Deep: Changing Visions of the American Self, 2003; A Field Guide for Female Interrogators, 2008. **Address:** Parsons The New School for Design, 72 5th Ave., 2nd Fl., New York, NY 10011, U.S.A. **Online address:** coco.fusco@gmail.com

MIYAZAKI, Hirokazu. American (born United States) **Genres:** Anthropology/Ethnology, Philosophy, Sociology, Social Sciences. **Career:** Northwestern University, Department of Anthropology, postdoctoral fellow, 1997-99; University of Tokyo, Institute of Oriental Culture, visiting research fellow, 1999-2000; Yale University, Department of Anthropology, postdoctoral associate and lecturer, 2001-02; Cornell University, Department of Anthropology, associate professor, 2007-, director of graduate studies, Center for the Study of Economy and Society, fellow. Writer. **Publications:** The Method of Hope: Anthropology, Philosophy and Fijian Knowledge, 2004. Contributor of articles to books and periodicals. **Address:** Department of Anthropology, Cornell University, 261 McGraw Hall, Ithaca, NY 14853, U.S.A. **Online address:** hm67@cornell.edu

MIZEJEWSKI, Linda. American (born United States), b. 1952. **Genres:** Novels, Humor/Satire. **Career:** Ohio State University, associate professor of

English, 1991-, professor of English, Department of Women's Studies, chair. Writer. **Publications:** The Other Woman, 1983; Divine Decadence: Fascism, Female Spectacle and the Makings of Sally Bowles, 1992; The Ziegfeld Girl: Image and Icon in Culture and Cinema, 1999; Hardboiled & High Heeled: The Woman Detective in Popular Culture, 2004; It Happened One Night, 2010. Contributor of articles to periodicals and journals. **Address:** Department of Women's Studies, Ohio State University, 113D University Hall, 230 N Oval Mall, Columbus, OH 43210, U.S.A. **Online address:** mizejewski.1@osu.edu

MIZRAHI, Isaac. American (born United States), b. 1961. **Genres:** Fash Ion/Costume, Art/Art History, Reference. **Career:** Perry Ellis, designer, 1982-84; Jeffrey Banks, staff, 1984-85; Calvin Klein, staff, 1985-87; Isaac Mizrahi Firm, founder, 1987. Writer. **Publications:** Isaac Mizrahi Presents the Adventures of Sandee, The Supermodel, or, Yvesaac's Model Diaries, 1997; How to have Style, 2008. **Address:** Isaac Mizrahi Studio, 475 10th Ave., 4th Fl., New York, NY 10018, U.S.A. **Online address:** info@isaacmizrahiny.com

MIZUNO, Awa. *See* **AKAMATSU, Ken.**

MLODINOW, Leonard. American (born United States), b. 1954?. **Genres:** Air/Space Topics, Mathematics/Statistics, Physics, Psychology, Sciences. **Career:** Night Court, writer; MacGyver, writer; Hunter, writer; Star Trek: The Next Generation, story editor; Walt Disney Co., executive producer, computer games; Scholastic Inc., vice president for software development, vice president and publisher for math education, 1997-2003; California Institute of Technology, research fellow and lecturer, 2005-; Max Planck Institute for Physics and Astrophysik, Alexander von Humboldt fellow. **Publications:** Euclid's Window: The Story of Geometry from Parallel Lines to Hyperspace, 2001; Feynman's Rainbow: A Search for Beauty in Physics and in Life, 2003; Some Time with Feynman, 2003; (with M. Costello) The Last Dinosaur, 2004; Titanic Cat, 2004; (with S. Hawking) Briefer History of Time, 2005; The Drunkard's Walk: How Randomness Rules Our Lives, 2008; (with S. Hawking) The Grand Design, 2010; (with D. Chopra) War of the Worldviews: Science vs. Spirituality, 2011; Subliminal: How Your Unconscious Mind Rules Your Behavior, 2012. Contributor to periodicals. **Address:** California Institute of Technology, 1200 E California Blvd., PO Box 216-76, Pasadena, CA 91125, U.S.A. **Online address:** len@caltech.edu

MNOOKIN, Robert H(arris). American (born United States), b. 1942. **Genres:** Law, Social Sciences, History. **Career:** Howard, Rice, Nemerovski, Canady, Robertson and Falk, associate attorney, 1970-72, california of counsel, 1972-85; University of California, acting professor and director of childhood and government project at Earl Warren Legal Institute, 1972-74, Boalt Law School, professor of law, 1975-81; Oxford University, Wolfson College, visiting fellow, 1978; Stanford University, Stanford Law School, visiting professor of law, 1980-81, professor, 1981-89, Center for Advanced Study in the Behavioral Sciences, fellow, 1981-82, 2006-07, Jewish Community Federation, chair, 1984-86, Stanford Center on Conflict and Negotiation, director, 1988-93, Adelbert H. Sweet professor of law, 1989-93; Harvard University, Harvard Law School, visiting professor of law, 1990-91, Samuel Williston professor of law, 1993-, Harvard Negotiation Research Project, director, American Academy of Arts and Sciences, fellow, 1995-; Columbia Law School, visiting professor of law, 1998; University of Virginia, School of Law, John M. Olin visiting professor, 2000; Catholic University, Franquai international chair, 2006. Writer. **Publications:** Child, Family, and State: Problems and Materials on Children and the Law, 1978, 6th ed., 2008; In the Interests of Children: Advocacy, Law Reform and Public Policy, 1985; (with E.E. Maccoby) Dividing the Child: Social and Legal Dilemmas of Custody, 1992; (ed. with others) Barriers to Conflict Resolution, 1995; (co-author) Mediación: una respuestainterdisciplinaria, 1997; (ed. with L.E. Susskind and P.C. Foster) Negotiating on Behalf of Others: Advice to Lawyers, Business Executives, Sports Agents, Diplomats, Politicians, and Everybody Else, 1999; (with S. Pepper and A. Tulumello) Beyond Winning: Negotiating to Create Value in Deals and Disputes, 2000; Bargaining with the Devil: When to Negotiate, When to Fight, 2010. Contributor to books and journals. **Address:** Harvard Law School, 416 Hauser Hall, Cambridge, MA 02138, U.S.A. **Online address:** mnookin@law.harvard.edu

MNOOKIN, Seth. American (born United States) **Genres:** Medicine/Health, Sciences, Intellectual History, Writing/Journalism, Popular Culture, Sports/Fitness. **Career:** The Palm Beach Post, journalist; Forward, journalist; Brill's Content, journalist; Inside.com, journalist; Newsweek, senior writer, 2002-03; Vanity Fair, contributing editor, 2005-. **Publications:** Hard News: The Scandals at the New York Times and Their Meaning for American Media, 2004, rev. ed., 2005; Feeding the Monster: How Money, Smarts, and Nerve Took a Team to the Top, 2006, rev. ed., 2007; The Panic Virus: A True Story of Medicine, Science, and Fear, 2011. **Address:** Brooklyn, NY , U.S.A. **Online address:** monsterfeedback@gmail.com

MO, Timothy. British/Hong Kong (born Hong Kong), b. 1950. **Genres:** Novels, Children's Fiction, Young Adult Fiction, Animals/Pets, Psychology, Literary Criticism And History. **Career:** New Statesman, journalist; Boxing News, journalist. **Publications:** The Monkey King, 1978; Sour Sweet, 1982; An Insular Possession, 1986; The Redundancy of Courage, 1991; Brownout on Breadfruit Boulevard, 1995; Renegade or Halo2, 1999. Contributor to periodicals. **Address:** Paddleless Press, BCM Paddleless, London, GL WC1N 3XX, England. **Online address:** timothymo@eudoramail.com

MOALLEM, Minoo. American (born United States), b. 1954. **Genres:** Politics/Government, History. **Career:** San Francisco State University, Department of Women's Studies, chair, 2001-06; University of California, professor of gender and women's studies, 2006-, chair of department, 2008-10. Writer and sociologist. **Publications:** (With R. Krooth) The Middle East: A Geopolitical Study of the Region in the New Global Era, 1995; (ed. and intro. with C. Kaplan and N. Alarcón) Between Woman and Nation: Nationalisms, Transnational Feminisms, and the State, 1999; Between Warrior Brother and Veiled Sister: Islamic Fundamentalism and the Politics of Patriarchy in Iran, 2005. Contributor to journals. **Address:** Department of Gender & Women's Studies, University of California, 608 Barrows Hall, Berkeley, CA 94720-1070, U.S.A. **Online address:** mmoallem@berkeley.edu

MOAT, John. British/Indian (born India), b. 1936. **Genres:** Novels, Young Adult Fiction, Poetry. **Career:** Arvon Foundation, founder, 1968-; Tandem, founder, 1998. Writer. **Publications:** NOVELS: Heorot, 1968; Bartonwood, 1978; The Tugen and the Toot, 1973; Mai's Wedding, 1983; The Missing Moon, 1988; Rain, and Other Stories, 2000; A Fabrication of Gold, 2011; Blanche, 2012. NONFICTION: A Standard of Verse, 1969; (with J. Fairfax) The Way to Write: A Stimulating Guide to the Craft of Creative Writing, 1981. POETRY: 6d. per Annum: Poems, 1966; Thunder of Grass: Poems, 1970; The Ballad of the Leaf, 1974; Skeleton Key, 1982; Fiesta & The Fox Reviews His Prophecy, 1980; Welcombe Overtures, 1987, rev. ed., 2010; Firewater and The Miraculous Mandarin, 1989; Practice, 1994; Snow, and Other Stories, 1995; The Valley, 1998; 100 Poems, 1998; Hermes & Magdalen, 2004; The Founding of Arvon, 2006. **Address:** Crenham Mill, Hartland, Bideford, DN EX39 6HN, England. **Online address:** johnmoat43@gmail.com

MOATS, David. American (born United States), b. 1947?. **Genres:** Military/Defense/Arms Control. **Career:** Rutland Herald, wire editor, state editor, assistant managing editor, city editor, 1981-92, editorial page editor, 1992-. Journalist. **Publications:** Civil Wars: A Battle for Gay Marriage, 2004. Contributor to periodicals. **Address:** Rutland Herald, 27 Wales St., PO Box 668, Rutland, VT 05702-0668, U.S.A. **Online address:** david.moats@rutlandherald.com

MOBERG, David O. (David O(scar) Moberg). American (born United States), b. 1922. **Genres:** Sociology, Theology/Religion, Gerontology/Senior Issues. **Career:** Bethel College and Seminary, instructor, professor of sociology, chairman of department of social sciences, 1952-68; State University of Groningen, Fulbright professor, 1957-58; Eternity Magazine, consulting editor, 1960-86; Journal of the American Scientific Affiliation, editor, 1962-64, consulting editor, 1964-73; Sociological Quarterly, associate editor, 1963-69; University of Muenster, Fulbright professor, 1964-65; San Francisco Theological Seminary, S.T.D. Program, adjunct professor, 1964-73; The Other Side, contributing editor, 1967-76; Marquette University, professor of sociology, 1968-91, chairman of the department, 1968-77, professor emeritus of sociology, 1991-; Review of Religious Research, editor, 1969-73, contributing editor, 1973-77, associate editor, 1983-99; Adris Newsletter, editor, 1971-76; McCormick Theological Seminary, adjunct professor, 1975-79, 1981-82; Christian Sociological Society Newsletter, literature reviewer/book review editor, 1981-93; California Sociologist, consulting editor, 1982-86; Research in the Social Scientific Study of Religion, co-editor, 1986-2004; Perspectives on Science and Christian Faith, consulting editor, 1987-. **Publications:** The Church as a Social Institution, 1962, 2nd ed., 1984; (with R.M. Gray) The Church and the Older Person, 1962, rev. ed., 1977; Inasmuch: Christian Social Responsibility in the Twentieth Century, 1965, (ed.) International Directory of Religious Information Systems, 1971; Spiritual Well-Being: Background and Issues, White House Conference on Aging, 1971; The Great Reversal:

Evangelism Versus Social Concern, 1972, rev. ed. as The Great Reversal: Evangelism and Social Concern, 1977; (ed.) Spiritual Well-Being: Sociological Perspectives, 1979; Wholistic Christianity, 1985; (ed.) Aging and Spirituality: Spiritual Dimensions of Aging Theory, Research, Practice, and Policy, 2001. Contributor of articles to books and journals. **Address:** Department of Social and Cultural Sciences, Marquette University, 340 Lalumiere Hall, 1250 W Wisconsin Ave., PO Box 1881, Milwaukee, WI 53233-2225, U.S.A.

MOBERG, David O(scar). *See* **Moberg, David O.**

MOBLEY, Joe A. American (born United States), b. 1945. **Genres:** Local History/Rural Topics, History. **Career:** North Carolina Division of Archives and History, archivist, 1974-76, researcher, 1976-82, editor, 1983-2001, historian and administrator; North Carolina State University, Department of History, faculty. **Publications:** (Ed.) The Papers of Zebulon Baird Vance, vol. I-II, 1963-95, vol. III, 1999; James City: A Black Community in North Carolina, 1863-1900, 1981; The USS North Carolina: Symbol of a Vanished Age, 1985; Pamlico County: A Brief History, 1991; Ship Ashore!: The U.S. Lifesavers of Coastal North Carolina, 1994; North Carolina: The History of an American State, Competency Goals Resources, 1998; (ed.) The Way We Lived in North Carolina, 2003; War Governor of the South: North Carolina's Zeb Vance in the Confederacy, 2005; Weary of War: Life on the Confederate Home Front, 2008; Raleigh, North Carolina: A Brief History, 2009; Tar Heel Commanders: The Confederate Generals of North Carolina: Tar Heels in Command, 2011. Contributor to books and periodicals. **Address:** Department of History, North Carolina State University, 269 Withers Hall, PO Box 8108, Raleigh, NC 27695-8108, U.S.A. **Online address:** joemobley@att.net

MOCH, Leslie Page. American (born United States), b. 1944?. **Genres:** History. **Career:** University of Illinois, Department of Sociology, visiting research associate, 1978-79, visiting lecturer, 1979-80; University of Texas, Department of History, assistant professor, 1980-84; University of Michigan, Department of History, assistant professor, 1984-86, associate professor, 1986-93, professor and chair of department, 1993-96; Michigan State University, Department of History, professor, 1996-, director of graduate studies and associate chair, 1998-2001; école des Hautes études en Sciences Sociales, Centre de Recherches Historiques, enseignant-chercheur, 2005; Netherlands Institute for Advanced Study in the Humanities and Social Sciences, fellow-in-residence, 2007-08. Writer. **Publications:** (Ed. with G.D. Stark) Essays on the Family and Historical Change, 1983; Paths to the City: Regional Migration in Nineteenth-Century France, 1983; Moving Europeans: Migration in Western Europe since 1650, 1992, 2nd ed., 2003; (ed. with D. Hoerder) European Migrants: Global and Local Perspectives, 1996; (ed. with M.P. Hanagan and W.T. Brake) Challenging Authority: The Historical Study of Contentious Politics, 1998; (ed. with H.J. Graff and P. McMichael) Looking Forward and Looking Backward: Perspectives on Social Science History, 2005; The Pariahs of Yesterday: Bretons in Paris, 2012. Contributor of articles to journals. **Address:** Department of History, Michigan State University, 307 Morrill Hall, East Lansing, MI 48824-1036, U.S.A. **Online address:** leslie@msu.edu

MOCHIZUKI, Ken. American (born United States), b. 1954. **Genres:** Children's Fiction, Young Adult Fiction, Biography. **Career:** Actor, 1976-81; print journalist and freelance writer, 1985-96; International Examiner (newspaper), staff writer, 1985-89; Northwest Nikkei (newspaper), assistant editor, 1990-95, author and presenter, 1991-. **Publications:** Beacon Hill Boys, 2002. PICTURE BOOKS: Baseball Saved Us, 1993; Heroes, 1995; Passage to Freedom: The Sugihara Story, 1997; Be Water, My Friend: The Early Years of Bruce Lee, 2006. Contributor to periodicals. **Address:** 25426 213th Ave. SE, Ste. 51, Maple Valley, WA 98038, U.S.A. **Online address:** kenmoch@aol.com

MODAHL, Mary. American (born United States), b. 1962. **Genres:** Business/Trade/Industry. **Career:** Bank of Boston, loan officer, 1986-87; private practice consultant, 1987-88; Forrester Research Inc., industry analyst, director of network strategy research, vice-president of research, vice-president of marketing, 1988-2001; Yankee Group, board director, 2006-. Writer and consultant. **Publications:** Now or Never: How Companies Must Change Today to Win the Battle for Internet Consumers, 2000. Contributor to periodicals. **Address:** Yankee Group, 7th Fl., 1 Liberty Sq., Boston, MA 02109-4868, U.S.A.

MODINOS, Antonis. Cypriot (born Cyprus), b. 1938. **Genres:** Physics. **Career:** National Technical University of Athens, professor of physics, 1989-, now emeritus. Writer. **Publications:** Field, Thermionic, and Secondary Electron Emission Spectroscopy, 1984; Quantum Theory of Matter: A Novel Introduction, 1996; Cries and Whispers, 2000. **Address:** Department of Applied Mathematical, and Physical Science, National Technical University of Athens, Rm. 117, Zografou Campus, Zografou, 157 80, Greece. **Online address:** modinos@central.ntua.gr

MOE, Christian H(ollis). American (born United States), b. 1929. **Genres:** Plays/Screenplays, Theatre. **Career:** Southern Illinois University, assistant professor, 1958-63, associate professor, 1963-68, professor, 1968-96, professor emeritus, 1996-, Playwriting Program, director, 1969-96, Graduate Studies in Theatre, director, 1970-88, Department of Theatre, chair, 1988-96. Writer. **Publications:** (With G. McCalmon) Creating Historical Drama, 1965, rev. ed., 2005; (with S. Parker) Creating Historical Drama; A Guide for Communities, Theatre Groups and Playwrights, 2nd ed., 2005. PLAYS: (with D. Payne) The Strolling Players, 1971; (with C. Garbutt) How Santa Claus Came to Simpson's Crossing (play adaptation), 1975; (with C. Garbutt) Three Rabbits White, 1979. EDITOR: (with D. Payne) Six New Plays for Children, 1971; (with B. Butler and A. McLeod) America at the Confluence, 1973; (with R.E. Jackson) Eight Plays for Youth: Varied Theatrical Experiences for Stage and Study, 1992. **Address:** 603 S Curtis Pl., Carbondale, IL 62901, U.S.A. **Online address:** chrismoe@siu.edu

MOE, Richard. American (born United States), b. 1936. **Genres:** History. **Career:** Office of the Mayor, administrative assistant, 1961-62; Office of the Lieutenant Governor of Minnesota, administrative assistant, 1963-67; Minnesota Democratic-Farmer-Labor Party, finance director, 1967-69; Minnesota Democratic-Farmer-Labor Party-Washington, chairman, 1969-72; Office of Senator Walter F. Mondale, administrative assistant, 1972-76; Office of the Vice-President of the United States, chief of staff, 1977-81; Davis, Polk & Wardwell, partner, 1981-93; National Trust for Historic Preservation, president, 1993-2010, retired, 2010. Writer. **Publications:** The Last Full Measure: The Life and Death of the First Minnesota Volunteers, 1993; (with C. Wilkie) Changing Places: Rebuilding Community in the Age of Sprawl, 1997. **Address:** c/o Gerard McCauley, Gerard McCauley Agency Inc., PO Box 844, Katonah, NY 10536, U.S.A.

MOEN, Matthew C. American (born United States), b. 1958. **Genres:** Politics/Government, Theology/Religion. **Career:** University of Maine, Department of Political Science, assistant professor, 1986-91, associate professor, 1992-96, chair, 1994-, professor, 1996-, special assistant to the president, Congressional Internship Program, director; University of South Dakota, College of Arts and Sciences, dean, 2002-, professor of political science, Lohre distinguished professor, acting provost/vice president of academic affairs; Council of Colleges of Arts and Sciences, president, 2007-08. Writer. **Publications:** The Christian Right and Congress, 1989; The Transformation of the Christian Right, 1992; (ed. with L.S. Gustafson) The Religious Challenge to the State, 1992; (with G.W. Copeland) Contemporary Congress: A Bicameral Approach, 1999; (with K.T. Palmer and R.J. Powell) Changing Members: The Maine Legislature in the Era of Term Limits, 2005. **Address:** College of Arts & Sciences, University of South Dakota, Rm. 110, 414 E Clark St., Vermillion, SD 57069, U.S.A. **Online address:** matthew.moen@usd.edu

MOENSSENS, Andre A. American/Belgian (born Belgium), b. 1930. **Genres:** Criminology/True Crime, Education, Law, Sciences, Horror, Reference. **Career:** Institute of Applied Science, head instructor in criminalistics, 1960-66; Illinois Institute of Technology, Chicago-Kent College of Law, instructor, professor of law, 1966-73; University of Richmond, School of Law, professor of law, director of Institute for Criminal Justice, 1973-95, professor emeritus, 1996-; University of Missouri at Kansas City, Douglas Stripp professor of law, 1996-2002, professor emeritus, 2002-. Writer. **Publications:** Legal Status of Fingerprints, 1964; Fingerprints and the Law, 1969; Fingerprint Techniques, 1971; (with F.E. Inbau and L.R. Vitullo) Scientific Police Investigation, 1972; (with R.E. Moses and F.E. Inbau) Scientific Evidence in Criminal Cases, 1973, 3rd ed., 1986; (with F.E. Inbau and J.R. Thompson) Cases and Comments on Criminal Law, 1973, 6th ed. 1996; (ed.) Sources of Proof in Preparing a Lawsuit, 1976, 5th ed., 1995; Direct and Cross Examination of Experts, 1977; Cases and Comments on Criminal Procedure, 1979; Trial Practice And Advocacy, 1981; (with S. Singer and R.J. Bacigal) Criminal Procedure: Cases and Comments, 1987; (with C.E. Henderson and S.G. Portwood) Scientific Evidence in Civil and Criminal Cases, 1995, 5th ed., 2007; Criminal Law, 1998; (co-author) Cases and Comments, 2003, 8th ed., 2008; (ed. with A. Jamieson) Wiley Encyclopedia of Forensic Science,

2009. **Address:** University of Richmond, 28 Westhampton Way, Richmond, VA 23173, U.S.A. **Online address:** moenssensa@aol.com

MOERMAN, D. Max. American (born United States), b. 1964?. **Genres:** History, Theology/Religion, Geography. **Career:** Barnard College, Department of Asian and Middle Eastern Cultures, associate professor; Columbia University, Donald Keene Center for Japanese Culture, associate director, Columbia Center for Japanese Religions, associate director. Writer. **Publications:** Localizing Paradise: Kumano Pilgrimage and the Religious Landscape of Premodern Japan, 2005. Contributor to books and journals. **Address:** Department of Asian & Middle Eastern Cultures, Barnard College, 303 Milbank, New York, NY 10027, U.S.A. **Online address:** dmoerman@barnard.edu

MOEYAERT, Bart. Belgian (born Belgium), b. 1964. **Genres:** Children's Fiction, Young Adult Fiction, Novels, Plays/Screenplays, Poetry. **Career:** Writer. **Publications:** Duet Met Valse Noten, 1983; Blote Handen, 1996; Wespennest, 1997; Het Is De Liefde Die We Niet Begrijpen, 1999; Rover, Dronkeman (play), 2000; Broere: De Oudste, De Stilste, De Echtste, De Verste, De Liefste, De Snelste En Ik, 2001; Luna Van De Boom, 2001; Ongelikt, 2001; De Schepping, 2003; Gedichten Voor Gelukkige Mensen (poetry), 2008; Het Paradijs, 2010; De Melkweg, 2011. **Address:** Breydelstraat 5, Antwerpen, 2018, Belgium. **Online address:** mail@bartmoeyaert.com

MOFFAT, Gwen. British (born England), b. 1924. **Genres:** Novels, Mystery/Crime/Suspense, Westerns/Adventure, Environmental Sciences/Ecology, Recreation, Travel/Exploration, Autobiography/Memoirs, Young Adult Fiction, Literary Criticism And History. **Career:** Writer. **Publications:** MYSTERY NOVELS: Lady with a Cool Eye, 1973; Deviant Death: A Crime Novel, 1974; The Corpse Road, 1974; Miss Pink at the Edge of the World: A Crime Novel, 1975; Over the Sea to Death, 1976; A Short Time to Live, 1976; Persons Unknown, 1978; Die Like a Dog, 1982; Last Chance Country, 1983; Grizzly Trail, 1984; Snare, 1987; The Stone Hawk, 1989; Rage, 1990; The Raptor Zone, 1990; Pit Bull, 1991; Veronica's Sisters, 1992; The Outside Edge, 1993; Cue the Battered Wife, 1994; The Lost Girls, 1998; A Wreath of Dead Moths, 1998; Running Dogs, 1999; Private Sins, 1999; Quicksand, 2001; Retribution, 2002; Man Trap, 2003; Dying for Love, 2005. OTHER: Space below My Feet (autobiography), 1961; Two Star Red: A Book about R.A.F. Mountain Rescue, 1964; On My Home Ground (autobiography), 1968; Survival Count (on conservation), 1972; Hard Option: A Novel, 1975; Hard Road West: Alone on the California Trail, 1981; The Buckskin Girl (western), 1982; The Storm Seekers, 1989; Gone Feral, 2007. Contributor to periodicals. **Address:** Juliet Burton Literary Agency, 2 Clifton Ave., London, GL W12 9DR, England.

MOFFAT, Wendy. American (born United States), b. 1955. **Genres:** History. **Career:** Dickinson College, Department of English, instructor, 1984-86, assistant professor, 1986-94, chair, 1999-2002, associate professor, 1994-2010, professor, 2010-. Writer and consultant. **Publications:** A Great Unrecorded History: A New Life of E.M. Forster in UK as E.M. Forster: A New Life, 2010. Contributor to periodicals. **Address:** Department of English, Dickinson College, PO Box 1773, Carlisle, PA 17013, U.S.A. **Online address:** moffat@dickinson.edu

MOFFEIT, Tony A. (Tony Archie Moffeit). American (born United States), b. 1942. **Genres:** Poetry. **Career:** Oklahoma Department of Libraries, field librarian, 1965-67; Central State University, reference librarian, 1967-71; Oklahoma State University, archivist, 1971-74; Western Kentucky University, social sciences librarian, 1974-76; Colorado State University, Southern Colorado Library, department chair, library services and poet-in-residence, 1976-2003, professor of library science, professor emeritus of library science, 1976-2003. Writer. **Publications:** POETRY: I Got the Blues: An Introduction to Songpoetry, 1976; Pueblo Blues, 1986; Luminous Animal, 1989; Neon Peppers, 1992; Poetry Is Dangerous: The Poet Is an Outlaw, 1995; (with K. Laws) Tango, 1997; Midnight Knocking at the Door, 1998; Billy the Kid and Freida Kahlo, 2000. Contributor to periodicals. **Address:** Southern Colorado Library, Colorado State University, 2200 Bonforte Blvd., Pueblo, CO 81001-4901, U.S.A. **Online address:** tony.moffeit@colostate-pueblo.edu

MOFFEIT, Tony Archie. *See* **MOFFEIT, Tony A.**

MOFFETT, Samuel Hugh. American/Korean (born Korea (South)), b. 1916. **Genres:** History, Theology/Religion, Social Sciences. **Career:** Presbyterian Board of Foreign Missions, director of youth work, 1945-47; Presbyterian missionary in China, staff, 1947-51; Yenching University, faculty, 1948-49; Nanking Theological Seminary, faculty, 1949-50; Princeton Theological Seminary, visiting lecturer in ecumenics, 1953-55, professor, 1981-87, Henry Luce professor emeritus of missions and ecumenics, 1987-; Presbyterian Church, Missionary in Korea, staff, 1955-81, commission representative in Korea, 1960-64; Kyongan Higher Bible School, principal, 1957-59; Presbyterian College and Theological Seminary, professor of historical theology and church history, 1960-81, dean of graduate school, 1966-70, associate president, 1970-81; Asian Center for Theological Studies and Mission, director, 1974-81. Writer. **Publications:** The Christian Mission: Its Motive and Its Task, 1952; Christ Calls the Church to Mission and to Unity, 1953; Where'er the Sun, 1953; The Church Today: Obstacles and Opportunities, 1960; The Christians of Korea, 1962; (with E.F. Moffett) Joy for an Anxious Age: A Study Guide on Philippians, 1966; The Biblical Background of Evangelism, 1968; Asia and Missions (in Korean), 1976; (ed. with P.A. Underwood and N.R. Sibley) First Encounters: Korea 1880-1910, 1982; A History of Christianity in Asia: vol. I: Beginnings to 1500, 1992, rev. ed., 1998, vol. II: 1500 to 1900, 2005. Contributor to journals. **Address:** Princeton Theological Seminary, 64 Mercer St., PO Box 821, Princeton, NJ 08542-0803, U.S.A.

MOFFITT, Sharon McMahon. American (born United States), b. 1947. **Genres:** Poetry. **Career:** Charles Wright Academy, teacher of creative writing and English, 1994-2000; Tacoma School of the Arts, adjunct artist, 2002-03; University Place Presbyterian Church, poet, teacher and ordained elder. **Publications:** The Blessed: A Sinner Reflects on Living the Christian Life, 2002. Contributor to periodicals. **Address:** University Place Presbyterian Church, 8101 27th St. W, University Place, WA 98466-2716, U.S.A. **Online address:** sdmoffitt@hotmail.com

MOGELON, Ronna. Canadian (born Canada), b. 1960. **Genres:** Food And Wine, Cartoons, Animals/Pets, Humor/Satire. **Career:** Writer and illustrator. **Publications:** SELF-ILLUSTRATED: Wild in the Kitchen: Recipes for Wild Fruits, Weeds, and Seeds, 2001. OTHERS: Freda Pemberton Smith: Her Work in Honour of Her Eightieth Birthday (monograph), 1982; Famous People's Cats, 1995; (ed.) Zukes Galore, 2005. **Address:** M. Evans & Company Inc., 216 E 49th St., New York, NY 10017-1502, U.S.A. **Online address:** ronna@mogelon.com

MOGGACH, Deborah. British (born England), b. 1948. **Genres:** Novels, Plays/Screenplays, Mystery/Crime/Suspense, Humor/Satire, Sex, History. **Career:** Society of Authors, chairman; Oxford University Press, librarian, 1970-72; educator, 1972-74; writer, 1972-74, 1978-. **Publications:** You Must Be Sisters, 1978; Close to Home, 1979; The Quiet Drink, 1980; Hot Water Man, 1982; Porky, 1983; To Have and to Hold, 1986; Smile and Other Stories, 1987; Driving in the Dark, 1988; Stolen, 1990; The Stand-In, 1991; The Ex-Wives, 1993; Changing Babies and Other Stories, 1995; Seesaw, 1996; Close Relations, 1997; Tulip Fever, 1999; Final Demand, 2001; These Foolish Things, 2004; In the Dark, 2007; (co-author) Great Escapes, 2008; (co-author) Because I'm a Girl, 2009. Contributor to periodicals. **Address:** c/o Jonathan Lloyd, Curtis Brown Group Ltd., Haymarket House, 28-29 Haymarket, London, GL SW1Y 4SP, England. **Online address:** info@deborahmoggach.com

MOGHADDAM, Fathali M. American/Iranian (born Iran) **Genres:** Psychology, History, Social Sciences. **Career:** McGill University, faculty; Georgetown University, Department of Psychology, professor, Department of Government, Conflict Resolution Program, director. Writer. **Publications:** (With D.M. Taylor) Theories of Intergroup Relations: International Social Psychological Perspectives, 1987, 2nd ed., 1994; (with D.M. Taylor and S.C. Wright) Social Psychology in Cross-Cultural Perspective, 1993; The Specialized Society: The Plight of the Individual in an Age of Individualism, 1997; (with C. Studer) Illusions of Control: Striving for Control in Our Personal and Professional Lives, 1998; Social Psychology: Exploring Universals across Cultures, 1998; The Individual and Society: A Cultural Integration, 2002; (ed. with R. Harré) The Self and Others: Positioning Individuals and Groups in Personal, Political, and Cultural Contexts, 2003; (ed. with A.J. Marsella) Understanding Terrorism: Psychosocial Roots, Consequences, and Interventions, 2004; (ed. with N.J. Finkel) The Psychology of Rights and Duties: Empirical Contributions and Normative Commentaries, 2005; Great Ideas in Psychology: A Cultural and Historical Introduction, 2005; From the Terrorists' Point of View: What They Experience and Why They Come to Destroy, 2006; (with R. Harré and N. Lee) Conflict Resolution through Positioning Analysis, 2008; Multiculturalism and Intergroup Relations: Psychological Implications for Democracy in Global Context, 2008; How Globalization Spurs Terrorism,

2008; The New Global Inequality, 2009; (ed. with R.Harré) Words of Conflict, Words of War: How the Language We Use in Political Processes Sparks Fighting, 2010; New Global Insecurity: How Terrorism, Environmental Collapse, Economic Inequalities and Resource Shortages are Changing Our World, 2010. **Address:** Department of Psychology, Georgetown University, White-Gravenor Hall 306, PO Box 571001, Washington, DC 20057-1001, U.S.A. **Online address:** moghaddf@georgetown.edu

MOGIL, Cindy R. American (born United States), b. 1954. **Genres:** Trivia/Facts, Medicine/Health. **Career:** Emory University Heart Center, assistant manager and certified medical technician, 1993-98; American Red Cross, health and safety coordinator and instructor, 1993-; Ridgeview Institute, sponsor and facilitator of prescription support group, 1998-; Prescription Anonymous Inc. (nonprofit support organization), founder, president and chief executive officer, 1998-; National Foundation for Women Legislators, policy coordinator, 2002-. Writer. **Publications:** Swallowing a Bitter Pill: How Prescription and Over-the-Counter Drug Abuse Is Ruining Lives-My Story, 2001. Contributor to periodicals. **Address:** Prescriptions Anonymous Inc., PO Box 10534, Gaithersburg, MD 20898-0534, U.S.A. **Online address:** cindy@prescriptionanonymous.org

MOHAN, Rakesh. American/Indian (born India), b. 1948. **Genres:** Economics. **Career:** World Bank, economist in development economics department, 1976-80; Indian Planning Commission, Perspective Planning Division, senior consultant, 1980-83, Housing and Urban Development Division, senior consultant, 1980-83; World Bank, economist, 1983-85, Philippines Division, East Asia and Pacific Region, senior economist, 1985-86; Indian Planning Commission, Development Policy Division, economic adviser, 1986-88; Ministry of Industry, economic adviser, 1988-96, Expert Group on Petrochemicals, chairperson, 1992, Expert Group on Commercialization of Infrastructure Projects, chairperson, 1994-95; Ministry of Industry, economic adviser, 1988-; National Housing Bank, director, 1992-95; United Nations University, Institute for New Technologies, distinguished visiting fellow, 1993-94; Reserve Bank of India, deputy governor, 2005-09; Stanford University, Stanford Centre for International Development, distinguished consulting professor, 2009-, non-resident senior research fellow; Yale University, Jackson Institute of Global Affairs, senior fellow, School of Management, professor in the practice of international economics of finance, 2010-; Indian Institute of Human Settlements, vice-chairman; McKinsey and Co., global adviser; National Council of Applied Economic Research, director general; Indian Council for Research, director and chief executive; Infrastructure Development Finance Co., vice chairman; State Bank of India, director; National Housing Bank, director; Industrial Reconstruction Bank of India, director; Industrial Credit and Investment Corporation of India (ICICI), director; Small Industries Development Bank of India, director. Writer. **Publications:** Urban Economic and Planning Models: Assessing the Potential for Cities in Developing Countries, 1979; The People of Bogota: Who They Are, What They Earn, Where They Live, 1980; The Determinants of Labour Earnings in Developing Metropoli: Estimates from Bogota and Cali, 1981; (with M.W. Wagner and J. Garcia) Measuring Urban Malnutrition and Poverty: A Case Study of Bogota and Cali, Colombia, 1981; The Effects of Population Growth, of the Pattern of Demand, and of Technology on the Process of Urbanization: An Application to India, 1982; (with N. Hartline) The Poor of Bogota: Who They Are, What They Do, and Where They Live, 1984; An Anatomy of the Distribution of Urban Income: A Tale of Two Cities in Colombia, 1984; Labor Force Participation in a Developing Metropolis: Does Sex Matter?, 1985; Work, Wages and Welfare in a Developing Metropolis: Consequences of Growth in Bogota, Colombia, 1986; Understanding the Developing Metropolis: Lessons from the City Study of Bogota and Cali, Colombia, 1993; (with I.J. Ahluwalia and O. Goswami) Policy Reform in India, 1996, 2nd ed., 1997; (contrib.) Culture, Democracy, and Development, 1999; (ed.) Facets of the Indian Economy, 2002; Small Scale Industry Policy in India: A Critical Evaluation, 2002; On the Occasion of National Conference on Growth and Macroeconomic Issues and Challenges in India, 2008; Monetary Policy in a Globalized Economy: A Practitioners View, 2009; (ed. with S. Acharya) Indias Economy: Performances and Challenges: Essays in Honour of Montek Singh Ahluwalia, 2010; Growth with Financial Stability: Central Banking in an Emerging Market, 2011. **Address:** Stanford Center for International Development, John A. and Cynthia Fry Gunn Bldg., 366 Galvez St., Stanford, CA 94305-6015, U.S.A. **Online address:** rmohan1948@gmail.com

MOHANTI, Prafulla. British/Indian (born India), b. 1936. **Career:** Greater London Council, architect and planner, 1965-70; freelance writer and painter, 1970-. **Publications:** My Village, My Life: Nanpur-Portrait of An Indian Village, 1973; Through Brown Eyes, 1985; Changing Village, Changing Life, 1990; Village Voice, 2004; Death of an Indian Village, forthcoming. SELF-ILLUSTRATED: Indian Village Tales, 1975. Contributor to journals. **Address:** A. M. Heath & Company Ltd., 6 Warwick Ct., Holborn, London, GL WC1R 5DJ, England.

MOHAR, Bojan. Canadian/Slovenian (born Slovenia), b. 1956. **Genres:** Mathematics/Statistics. **Career:** University of Ljubljana, professor of mathematics, 1980-; Simon Fraser University, visiting professor, 1986-87, Department of Mathematics, professor. **Publications:** (Co-author) Problems in Programming: Experience through Practice, 1991; (with C. Thomassen) Graphs on Surfaces, 2001. **Address:** Department of Mathematics, Simon Fraser University, SC K10525, 8888 University Dr., Burnaby, BC V5A 1S6, Canada. **Online address:** mohar@math.sfu.ca

MOHER, Francis Anthony. *See* **MOHER, Frank.**

MOHER, Frank. (Francis Anthony Moher). Canadian (born Canada), b. 1955. **Genres:** Plays/Screenplays, Cultural/Ethnic Topics, Theatre, Writing/Journalism, Young Adult Fiction. **Career:** Alberta Report News Magazine, books reviewer, 1981-86; University of Alberta, sessional lecturer in drama, 1981-83, 1986; Alberta Playwriting Centre, co-founder, 1981-82; Workshop West Theatre, playwright-in-residence, 1984-86, associate director, 1987-88; Western Report Newsmagazine, book reviewer, 1986; Vancouver Island University, Department of Creative Writing and Journalism, instructor in dramatic writing and journalism, 1990-; E-script, executive director, 1996-; Saturday Night Magazine, senior editor, 1997-98, contributing editor, 1997-2000; ProPlay, publisher, 2001-; Western Edge Theatre, artistic producer, 2003-; Backofthebook.ca, publisher, editor, 2006-; University of British Columbia, faculty. **Publications:** PLAYS: Pause, 1975; Stage Falls, 1978; Down for the Weekend 1980; Odd Jobs, 1986, The Third Ascent, 1988; Prairie Report, 1988; (with G. Reid) Sliding for Home, 1990; At Sea, 1990; Kidnapping the Bride, 1991; Farewell, 1991; Blue Trumpeter, 1993; Supreme Dream, 1995; All I Ever Wanted, 1995; Tolstoy's Wife, 1997; Weather, 1999; Big Baby, 2004; Moonbound!, 2009. Contributor to periodicals. **Address:** Colbert Agency, 303 Davenport Rd., Toronto, ON M5R 1K5, Canada. **Online address:** frankmoher@shaw.ca

MOHIN, Ann. American (born United States), b. 1946. **Genres:** Novels, Novellas/Short Stories, Poetry, Young Adult Fiction. **Career:** Freelance editor, 1968-79. **Publications:** The Farm She Was: A Novel, 1998. Contributor of articles to periodicals. **Address:** 338 Pike Rd., McDonough, NY 13801, U.S.A. **Online address:** anchor@clarityconnect.com

MOHLE, Robert L. American (born United States), b. 1949. **Genres:** Travel/Exploration, Regional/Urban Planning. **Career:** Professional geologist and writer. **Publications:** Adventure Kayaking: Trips From Big Sur to San Diego includes Channel Islands, 1998. **Address:** Wilderness Press, Keen Communications, 2204 1st Ave. S, Ste. 102, Birmingham, AL 35233, U.S.A.

MOHR, Jay. American (born United States), b. 1970. **Genres:** Novels. **Career:** Saturday Night Live, performer and writer, 1993-95. Actor, television host and stand-up comedian. **Publications:** Gasping for Airtime: Two Years in the Trenches of Saturday Night Live, 2004; No Wonder My Parents Drank: Tales from a Stand-Up Dad, 2010. **Address:** c/o Author Mail, Hyperion Books, 114 5th Ave., New York, NY 10011, U.S.A. **Online address:** jay@jaymohr.com

MOHR, Merilyn. *See* **SIMONDS, Merilyn.**

MOHR, Nicholasa. American (born United States), b. 1938. **Genres:** Children's Fiction, Novels, Plays/Screenplays, Novellas/Short Stories, Young Adult Fiction, Women's Studies And Issues. **Career:** Art Center of Northern New Jersey, instructor, 1970-71; MacDowell Colony, writer-in-residence, 1972, 1974, 1976; State University of New York, lecturer in Puerto Rican studies, 1977; Rutgers University, lecturer, 1985, 1986; City University of New York, Queens College, distinguished visiting professor, 1988-91; American International University, Richmond College, writer-in-residence, 1994-95. **Publications:** YOUNG ADULT FICTION: Nilda, 1973, 2nd ed., 1986; El Bronx Remembered: A Novella and Stories, 1975, 2nd ed., 1986; In Nueva York, 1977; Felita, 1979; Going Home, 1986; All for the Better: A Story of el Barrio, 1993; Isabel's New Mom, 1993; The Magic Shell, 1995; (with

A. Martorell) The Song of ElCoqúi and Other Tales of Puerto Rico, 1995; I Never Even Seen My Father, 1995; Old Letivia and the Mountain of Sorrows, 1996; OTHERS: Rituals of Survival: A Women's Portfolio, 1985; Growing Up inside the Sanctuary of My Imagination, 1994; (with A. Martorell) The song of el coquí and other tales of Puerto Rico, 1995; Vieja Letivia y el Monte de los Pesares, 1996; A Matter of Pride and Other Stories, 1997. Works appear in anthologies. Contributor to books and magazines. **Address:** 727 President St., Brooklyn, NY 11215-1207, U.S.A.

MOHR, Richard D(rake). American (born United States), b. 1950. **Genres:** Gay And Lesbian Issues, Civil Liberties/Human Rights, Antiques/Furnishings, Philosophy, Classics, Law, Popular Culture, Sex, Social Commentary, Crafts, Ethics, Theology/Religion. **Career:** University of Illinois, professor, professor emeritus of philosophy and classics. Writer. **Publications:** The Platonic Cosmology, 1985; Gays/Justice: A Study of Ethics, Society and Law, 1988; Gay Ideas: Outing and Other Controversies, 1992; A More Perfect Union: Why Straight America Must Stand Up for Gay Rights, 1994; Pottery, Politics, Art: George Ohr and the Brothers Kirkpatrick, 2003; God and Forms in Plato: The Platonic Cosmology, 2nd ed., 2005; Long Arc of Justice: Lesbian and Gay Marriage, Equality, and Rights, 2005; (ed.) One Book, The Whole Universe: Plato's Timaeus Today, 2010. **Address:** University of Illinois, MC-468, 105 Gregory Hall, 810 S Wright St., Urbana, IL 61801, U.S.A. **Online address:** rdmohr@illinois.edu

MOHUN, Arwen. *See* **MOHUN, Arwen Palmer.**

MOHUN, Arwen Palmer. (Arwen Mohun). American (born United States), b. 1961?. **Genres:** History, Social Sciences. **Career:** University of Delaware, faculty in women's studies, 1997-99, Department of History, assistant professor, 1992-98, associate professor, 1998-, Hagley program, director; Hopewell Furnace National Historic Site, consultant; National Museum of American History, consultant. Writer. **Publications:** (Ed. as Arwen Mohun with R. Horowitz) His and Hers: Gender, Consumption and Technology, 1998; (as Arwen P. Mohun) Steam Laundries: Gender, Technology and Work in the United States and Great Britain, 1880-1940, 1999; (ed. with N.E. Lerman and R. Oldenziel as Arwen Mohun) Gender and Technology: A Reader, 2003; Better Safe than Sorry: How America became a Risk Society, forthcoming. Contributor to periodicals. **Address:** Department of History, University of Delaware, 211 John Munroe Hall, Newark, DE 19716, U.S.A. **Online address:** mohun@udel.edu

MOI, Toril. American/Norwegian (born Norway), b. 1953?. **Genres:** Literary Criticism And History, Women's Studies And Issues. **Career:** Teacher, 1974-79; University of Trondheim, university lecturer in French, 1981; Emmanuel College, college supervisor in French, 1982, 1983; Oxford University, faculty, 1982-85, Pembroke College, lecturer, 1983-84, Wadham College, lecturer, 1984, Lady Margaret Hall, lecturer, 1984, 1985, New College, visiting fellow, 2006; University of Umeå, visiting lecturer, 1982; University of Bergen, Centre for Feminist Research in the Humanities, director, 1985-88, adjunct professor of comparative literature, 1988-96; Duke University, Graduate Program in Literature, visiting professor, 1987, professor of literature and romance studies, 1989-99, James B. Duke professor of literature and romance studies, 1999-, professor of theater studies, 2006-, Center for Philosophy, Arts and Literature, director, 2009-, professor of English, 2007-, professor of philosophy; Bucknell University, Andrew W. Mellon lecturer, 1988; University of Victoria, Landsdowne visiting professor, 1989; Union College, Thomas Lamont visiting professor, 1989; Dartmouth College, The School of Criticism and Theory, lecturer, 1989; Yale University, visiting professor, 1990; University of Melbourne, Ormond College, Scott fellow, 1990; University of Virginia, Commonwealth Center for Cultural Change, external fellow, 1991-95; Universityof Alberta, Department of English, distinguished visiting professor, 1994; Cornell University, School of Criticism and Theory, professor, 1997, 2005; Johns Hopkins University, Humanities Center, associate, 2005-09. Writer. **Publications:** Sexual/Textual Politics: Feminist Literary Theory, 1985, 2nd ed., 2002; Feminist Theory and Simone de Beauvoir, 1990; Simone de Beauvoir: The Making of an Intellectual Woman, 1993, 2nd ed., 2008; What Is a Woman? and Other Essays, 1999; (intro.) Camille: The Lady of the Camellias, 2004; Sex, Gender, and the Body: The Student Edition of What is a Woman?, 2005; Henrik Ibsen and the Birth of Modernism: Art, Theater, Philosophy, 2006. EDITOR: The Kristeva Reader, 1986; French Feminist Thought: A Reader, 1987; (with J.A. Radway) Materialist Feminism, 1994. Contributor to books. **Address:** Center for Philosophy, Arts and Literature, Duke University, B184 Smith Warehouse, Bay 5, 114 S Buchanan Blvd., 1st Fl., PO Box 90403, Durham, NC 27708, U.S.A. **Online address:** toril@duke.edu

MOIRA, Kate. (Kate Moira Ryan). American (born United States), b. 1965. **Genres:** Plays/Screenplays, Novellas/Short Stories. **Career:** Three Dollar Bill, literary manager. Playwright. **Publications:** Cavedweller, 2004; (as Kate Moira Ryan) Otma: A Drama, 2006; (with J. Gold) 25 Questions for a Jewish Mother, 2007; (with L.S. Chapman) The Beebo Brinker Chronicles, 2009. **Address:** Dramatists Play Service Inc., 440 Park Ave., New York, NY 10016, U.S.A. **Online address:** katemoiraryan@aol.com

MOISE, Edwin E(variste). American (born United States), b. 1946. **Genres:** Area Studies, History, Military/Defense/Arms Control, Economics, Business/Trade/Industry. **Career:** Appalachian State University, instructor in history, 1976-77; University of Detroit, adjunct professor of history, 1978; Clemson University, History Department, visiting assistant professor, 1979-81, assistant professor, 1981-84, associate professor, 1984-88, professor, 1988-. Writer. **Publications:** Land Reform in China and North Vietnam: Consolidating the Revolution at the Village Level, 1983; Modern China: A History, 1986, 3rd ed., 2008; Tonkin Gulf and the Escalation of the Vietnam War, 1996; Historical Dictionary of the Vietnam War, 2001, rev. ed. as A to Z of the Vietnam War, 2005. **Address:** Department of History, Clemson University, 126 Hardin Hall, Clemson, SC 29634-0527, U.S.A. **Online address:** eemoise@clemson.edu

MOK, Esther. Malaysian (born Malaysia), b. 1953. **Genres:** Children's Nonfiction, Young Adult Fiction. **Career:** San Francisco Unified School District, science teacher at middle school and instructor at high school, 1984-; kindergarten teacher, 1995-. Writer. **Publications:** Sumo, the Wrestling Elephant, 1994. **Address:** Visitaction Valley Elementary School, 55 Schwerin St., San Francisco, CA 94134, U.S.A.

MOKYR, Joel. American (born United States), b. 1946. **Genres:** Industrial Relations, History. **Career:** Yale University, acting instructor, 1972-73; Northwestern University, assistant professor of economics and history, 1974-77, associate professor of economics, 1978-80, visiting associate professor of economics, 1979-80; professor of economics, 1980-81, professor of economics and history, 1981-94, Robert H. Strotz professor of arts and sciences and professor of economics and history, 1994-, Department of Economics, chair, 1998-2001; Stanford University, visiting associate professor of economics, 1979-80; University of Chicago, Graduate School of Business, visiting associate professor, 1981; Harvard University, visiting professor of economics, 1982-83; University College of Dublin, visiting professor of economics, 1986; Hebrew University of Jerusalem, visiting professor of economics, 1993; University of Manchester, visiting professor of history, 1996; University of Tel Aviv, Eitan Berglas School of Economics, Sackler professorial fellow; Center for Advanced Studies in the Behavioral Sciences, fellow, 2001-02. Writer. **Publications:** Industrialization in the Low Countries, 1795-1850, 1976; Why Ireland Starved: A Quantitative and Analytical History of the Irish Economy, 1800-1850, 1983, The Lever of Riches: Technological Creativity and Economic Progress, 1990; Twenty Five Centuries of Technological Change: An Historical Survey, 1990; The British Industrial Revolution: An Economic Perspective, 1993, 2nd ed., 1999; The Gifts of Athena: Historical Origins of the Knowledge Economy, 2002; Enlightened Economy: An Economic History of Britain, 1700-1850, 2009. EDITOR: The Economics of the Industrial Revolution, 1985; Oxford Encyclopedia of Economic History, 2003; (with D.S. Landes and W.J. Baumol) Invention of Enterprise: Entrepreneurship from Ancient Mesopotamia to Modern Times, 2010; (ed. with L. Cruz) Birth of Modern Europe: Culture and Economy, 1400-1800: Essays in Honor of Jan De Vries, 2010. **Address:** Department of Economics, Northwestern University, Rm. 3214 Andersen Hall, 2001 Sheridan Rd., Evanston, IL 60208, U.S.A. **Online address:** j-mokyr@northwestern.edu

MOL, Hans. *See* **MOL, Johannis (Hans) J(acob).**

MOL, J. J. *See* **MOL, Johannis (Hans) J(acob).**

MOL, Johannis (Hans) J(acob). Also writes as J. J. Mol, Hans Mol. Australian/Dutch (born Netherlands), b. 1922. **Genres:** Sociology, Theology/Religion. **Career:** Bethel Presbyterian Church, pastor, 1956-60; University of Canterbury, lecturer in sociology, 1961-63; Australian National University, Institute of Advanced Studies, fellow in sociology, 1963-70; Council of the International Sociological Association, secretary, 1970-74, president, 1974-

78; McMaster University, Department of Religion Studies, professor, 1970-87, emeritus professor, 1987-; University of Missouri, Paine lecturer, 1978. Writer. **Publications:** OTHER: Churches and Immigrants, 1961; The Relevance of a Shackled Vision: A Sociologist's Interpretation of the Churches' Dilemma in a Secular World, 1965; Changes in Religious Behavior of Dutch Immigrants, 1965; The Breaking of Traditions, 1968; How God Hoodwinked Hitler, 1987. AS HANS MOL: Church-Attendance in Christchurch, New Zealand, 1962; Religion and Race in New Zealand, 1966; Christianity in Chains, 1969; Religion in Australia, 1971; Identity and the Sacred: A Sketch for a New Social Scientific Theory of Religion, 1976; Wholeness and Breakdown: A Model for the Interpretation of Nature and Society, 1978; The Fixed and the Fickle: Religion and Identity in New Zealand, 1982; The Firm and the Formless: Religion and Identity in Aboriginal Australia, 1982; Meaning and Place: An Introduction to the Social Scientific Study of Religion, 1983; Faith and Fragility: Religion and Identity in Canada, 1985; The Faith of Australians, 1985; (with E.G. d'Aquili) The Regulation of Physical and Mental Systems: Systems Theory of the Philosophy of Science, 1990; Calvin for the Third Millennium, 2003; Tinpot Preacher (autobiography), 2003. EDITOR: (with M. Hetherton and M. Henty) Western Religion, 1972; Identity and Religion, 1978. Contributor of articles to books and journals. **Address:** 23 Mol Cres., Queanbeyan, NW 2620, Australia.

MOLDAW, Carol. American (born United States), b. 1956?. **Genres:** Poetry, Novels. **Career:** Poet and educator. **Publications:** POETRY: Taken from the River, 1993; Chalkmarks on Stone, 1998; Through the Window, 2001; The Lightning Field, 2003; So Late, So Soon: New and Selected Poems, 2010. NOVELS: The Widening, 2008. Contributor of stories and poems to periodicals and journals. **Address:** Pojoaque, NM , U.S.A. **Online address:** info@carolmoldaw.com

MOLDEA, Dan E. American/Romanian (born Romania), b. 1950. **Genres:** Criminology/True Crime, Politics/Government, History. **Career:** Portage County Community Action Council, deputy director, 1973-74; ACTION/Peace Corps, executive assistant, 1979-80; Washington Independent Writers, president, 1981-82; Institute for Policy Studies, associate fellow, 1981-86; National Writers Union, national vice president, 2002-03. Writer. **Publications:** The Hoffa Wars: Teamsters, Rebels, Politicians and the Mob, 1978; The Hunting of Cain: A True Story of Money, Greed and Fratricide, 1983; (contrib.) First Harvest: The Institute for Policy Studies, 1963-1983, 1983; Dark Victory: Ronald Reagan, MCA and the Mob, 1986; Interference: How Organized Crime Influences Professional Football, 1989; The Killing of Robert F. Kennedy: An Investigation of Motive, Means and Opportunity, 1995; (with T. Lange and P. Vannatter) Evidence Dismissed: The Inside Story of the Police Investigation of O.J. Simpson, 1997; A Washington Tragedy: How the Death of Vincent Foster Ignited a Political Firestorm, 1998; Confessions of a Guerrilla Writer: Adventures in the Jungles of Crime, Politics and Journalism, forthcoming. Contributor to books and periodicals. **Address:** PO Box 32274, Washington, DC 20007, U.S.A. **Online address:** moldea@moldea.com

MOLE, John. British (born England), b. 1941. **Genres:** Children's Fiction, Poetry, Literary Criticism And History. **Career:** Haberdashers' Aske's School, English teacher, 1964-73; Riverdale Country School, exchange teacher, 1969-70; Verulam School, Department of English, chairman, 1973-81; Saint Albans School, Department of English, chairman, 1981-98; University of Hertfordshire, visiting poet, 1998-; City of London, poet, 1999-; Mandeville Press, editor. **Publications:** A Feather for Memory, 1961; The Instruments, 1971; Something about Love, 1972; The Love Horse, 1973; (ed.) Poetry: A Selection, 1974; Scenarios, 1975; Landscapes, 1975; A Partial Light, 1975; Our Ship, 1977; The Mortal Room, 1977; The Tales of Rover, 1977; On the Set, 1978; From the House Opposite, 1979; (with A. Thwaite) British Poetry since 1945, 1981; Feeding the Lake, 1981; (with P. Scupham) Christmas Past, 1981; (with P. Scupham) Christmas Games, 1983; (ed. with A. Thwaite) Poetry 1945 to 1980, 1983; In and Out of the Apple, 1984; (with P. Scupham) Christmas Visits, 1985; Learning the Ropes, 1985; (with P. Scupham) Winter Emblems, 1986; (with P. Scupham) Christmas Fables, 1987; Homing, 1987; (with P. Scupham) Christmas Gifts, 1988; (with P. Scupham) Christmas Books, 1989; Passing Judgements (criticism), 1989; Depending on the Light, 1993; Selected Poems, 1995; For the Moment, 2000; Counting the Chimes: New and Selected Poems 1975-2003, 2004. JUVENILE: (with M. Norman) Once There Were Dragons, 1979; Boo to a Goose, 1987; The Mad Parrot's Countdown, 1990; Catching the Spider, 1990; The Conjuror's Rabbit, 1992; Back by Midnight, 1994; Hot Air, 1996; Copy Cat, 1997; The Dummy's Dilemma, 1999; My Dream Balloon, 1999; The Wonder Dish, 2002; Other Day, 2007; The Bone in Her Leg, 2009; All the Frogs, 2010; The Point of Loss, 2011. **Address:** 11 Hill St., St. Albans, HF AL3 4QS, England. **Online address:** jdmole@hotmail.com

MOLESWORTH, Carl. American (born United States), b. 1947. **Genres:** History, Biography, Documentaries/Reportage. **Career:** Daily World, journalist, 1977-83; Skagit Valley Herald, journalist, 1983-94; Vernon Publications Inc., journalist, 1994-. **Publications:** (With S. Moseley) Wing to Wing: Air Combat in China, 1943-45, 1990; (with F.S. Gabreski) Gabby: A Fighter Pilot's Life, 1991; Sharks Over China, 1994; P-40 Warhawk Aces of the C.B.I, 2000; Very Long Range P-51 Mustang Units of the Pacific War, 2006; P-40 Warhawk vs Ki-43 Oscar: China 1944-45, 2008; 23rd Fighter Group: Chennault's Sharks, 2009; 57th Fighter Group: First in the Blue, 2011; P-40 Warhawk vs Bf 109 Mto 1942-44, 2011. **Address:** 12675 C St-Bay View, Mt. Vernon, WA 98273, U.S.A. **Online address:** cmolesworth@reedbusiness.com

MOLESWORTH, Charles. American (born United States), b. 1941. **Genres:** Poetry, Literary Criticism And History, Biography, Essays, Humanities. **Career:** City University of New York, Queens College, assistant professor, 1967-71, associate professor, 1972-77, professor of English, 1978-2008; University of Paris, visiting professor, 1978, 1983, 2001; University of Toulouse, faculty, 1993; Salmagundi, art columnist, 1997-. **Publications:** (Contrib.) Contemporary Poetry in America: Essays and Interviews, 1974; Common Elegies (poetry), 1977; The Fierce Embrace: A Study of Contemporary American Poetry, 1979; Words to that Effect (poetry), 1981; The Ironist Saved from Drowning: The Short Stories of Donald Barthelme, 1982; Gary Synder's Vision: Poetry and the Real Work, 1983; Marianne Moore: A Literary Life, 1990, 2nd ed., 1991; (ed.) Heath Anthology of American Literature, 1999; Alain Locke: Biography of a Philosopher, 2008; And Bid Him Sing: A Biography of Countee Cullen, 2012; (ed.) Collected Essays of Alain Locke, 2012. **Address:** 109-23 71st Rd., Apt. 6G, Forest Hills, NY 11375, U.S.A. **Online address:** cmole@earthlink.net

MOLINA, Silvia. Mexican (born Mexico), b. 1946. **Genres:** Novels, Novellas/Short Stories, Children's Fiction, Essays, History, Young Adult Fiction. **Career:** Ediciones Corunda (a publishing house), manager. Writer. **Publications:** NOVELS: La mañana debe seguir gris, 1977, as Gray Skies Tomorrow, 1993; Ascensión Tun, 1981; La familia vino del norte, 2nd ed., 1987; Imagen de Hector, 1990; Muchacha en Azul, 2001. SHORT STORIES: Lides de estano, 1984; Dicen que me case yo, 1989; Un hombre cerca, 2nd ed., 1993. FOR CHILDREN: El papel, 1985; El algodon, 1987; Los cuatro hermanos, 1988; La creacion del hombre, 1989; La leyenda del sol y de la luna, 1991; Los tres corazones, 1992; Mi familia y la Bella Durmiente cien anos despues, 1993. OTHERS: Leyendo en la Tortuga: Recopilacion, 1981; (intro.) Campeche: Punta del ala del pais: poesia, narrativa y teatro, 1450-1990, 1991; Fundación de la Mamoria, 1993; Circuito Cerrado, 1995; Campeche Imagen de Eternidad, 1996; El amor que me juraste, 1998; Hortalizas: las tradiciones pueden enriquecerse, 1999; Diario de Sofia, 2003; En silencio, la lluvia, 2008; Matamoros: el resplandor en la batalla, 2010. **Address:** Oaxaca 1, San Jeronimo Aculco, DF 10700, Mexico.

MOLINARY, Rosie. American (born United States), b. 1973. **Genres:** Social Sciences, Sports/Fitness, Self Help. **Career:** Garinger High School, director of student activities. Writer. **Publications:** Hijas Americanas: Beauty, Body Image, and Growing Up Latina, 2007; Beautiful You: A Daily Guide to Radical Self-acceptance, 2010. Contributor to books. **Address:** Seal Press, 1700 4th St., Berkeley, CA 94710, U.S.A. **Online address:** latinabookproject@adelphia.net

MOLLENAUER, Lynn Wood. American (born United States), b. 1966?. **Genres:** History. **Career:** University of North Carolina, assistant professor of history, associate professor of history. Writer. **Publications:** Strange Revelations: Magic, Poison and Sacrilege in Louis XIV's France, 2007. **Address:** Department of History, University of North Carolina, 229 Morton Hall, 601 S College Rd., Wilmington, NC 28403, U.S.A. **Online address:** mollenauerl@uncw.edu

MOLLENKAMP, Carrick. American (born United States), b. 1969?. **Genres:** Documentaries/Reportage, Law, Business/Trade/Industry. **Career:** The Times, clerk; Daily Journal, staff; Triangle Business Journal, Staff; News and Observer, staff writer, 1994-96; The Wall Street Journal, reporter, 1997-, correspondent. **Publications:** (With A. Levy, J. Menn and J. Rothfeder) The People vs. Big Tobacco: How the States Took on the Cigarette Giants, 1998. Contributor to periodicals. **Address:** The Wall Street Journal, 200 Liberty St., New York, NY 10281, U.S.A. **Online address:** carrick.mollenkamp@wsj.com

MOLLENKOTT, Virginia Ramey. American (born United States), b. 1932. **Genres:** Education, Gay And Lesbian Issues, Literary Criticism And History, Philosophy, Theology/Religion, Women's Studies And Issues, Social Sciences. **Career:** Temple University, instructor in English, 1954-55; Shelton College, Department of English, instructor, 1955-56, associate professor of English and chairperson, 1956-63; Nyack Missionary College, Department of English, chairperson, 1963-67; Seventeenth-Century News, assistant editor, 1965-75; William Paterson University, Department of English, associate professor, 1967-74, chairperson, 1972-76, professor of English, 1974-97, professor emeritus, 1997-; The Witness, contributing editor, 1994-2000, 2002-; The Other Side, contributing editor, 2003-07. **Publications:** Adamant and Stone Chips: A Christian Humanist Approach to Knowledge, 1968; In Search of Balance, 1969; Women, Men, and the Bible, 1977, rev. ed., 1988; (with L. Scanzoni) Is the Homosexual My Neighbor?, 1978, rev. ed., 1994; Speech, Silence, Action!, 1980; The Divine Feminine, 1983; (contrib.) Views from the Intersection, 1984; Godding: Human Responsibility and the Bible, 1987; Sensuous Spirituality: Out from Fundamentalism, 1992, rev. ed., 2008; Omnigender: A Trans-Religious Approach, 2001, rev. ed., 2007; (with V. Sheridan) Transgender Journeys, 2003. EDITOR: Adam among the Television Trees: An Anthology of Verse by Contemporary Christian Poets, 1971; Women of Faith in Dialogue, 1987. Contributor to books and journals. **Address:** Department of English, William Paterson University, 300 Pompton Rd., Wayne, NJ 07470, U.S.A. **Online address:** jstvrm@warwick.net

MOLLICK, Ethan Reuben. American (born United States), b. 1975. **Genres:** Business/Trade/Industry. **Career:** Mercer Management Consulting, analyst; eMeta Corp., head of business development, through 2006, co-founder and chief operating officer; University of Pennsylvania, The Wharton School, Management Department, Edward B. and Shirley R. Shils assistant professor of management. Writer and consultant. **Publications:** (With D. Edery) Changing the Game: How Video Games Are Transforming the Future of Business, 2008. Contributor to periodicals. **Address:** The Wharton School, University of Pennsylvania, 2015 Steinberg-Deitrich Hall, 3620 Locust Walk, Philadelphia, PA 19104-6370, U.S.A. **Online address:** emollick@wharton.upenn.edu

MOLNAR, Michael. British (born England), b. 1946. **Genres:** Intellectual History, Psychology, Translations, Literary Criticism And History. **Career:** Freud Museum, research director, 1986-. Writer. **Publications:** Body of Words: Reading of Belyi's Kotik Letaev, 1987; (trans.) Paradise: Selected Poems of Elena Shvarts, 1993; (co-author) 20 Maresfield Gardens, 1998; (trans. and intro.) The Diary of Sigmund Freud 1929-1939: A Record of the Final Decade, 1929-1939, 1992; (co-ed.) Unser Herz zeigt nach dem Süden. Reisebriefe 1895-1923, 2002. Work appears in anthologies. **Address:** Freud Museum, 20 Maresfield Gardens, London, GL NW3 5SX, England. **Online address:** michael@freud.org.uk

MOLONEY, James. Australian (born Australia), b. 1954. **Genres:** Novels, Children's Fiction, Young Adult Fiction, Science Fiction/Fantasy. **Career:** Marist College, teacher and librarian at primary school, 1983-93, 1995-96; writer, 1994-. **Publications:** FOR YOUNG ADULTS: Crossfire, 1992; Dougy, 1993; Gracey, 1994; Swashbuckler, 1995; The House on River Terrace, 1995; A Bridge to Wiseman's Cove, 1996; The Pipe, 1996; The Snakeman, 1998; Buzzard Breath & Brains, 1998; Angela, 1998; Touch Me, 2000; Boys and Books: Building a Culture of Reading around Our Boys, 2000; David the Best Model Maker in the World, 2000; Blue Hair Day, 2001; Moving House, 2001; A Box of Chicks, 2002; Intergalactic Heroes, 2002; Grommet Saves the World, 2003; The Tunnels of Ferdinand, 2004; The Scorpion's Tail, 2005; Black Taxi, 2005; Lost Property, 2005; 68 Teeth, 2005; Malig Tumora, 2006; In the Lair of the Mountain Beast, 2006; The Book of Lies, 2007; Master of the Books, 2007; Duck Sounds, 2007; The Trolley Boys, 2007; Scream World, 2007; Quack! Quack!, 2007; Trapped, 2008; Kill the Possum, 2008; The Book from Baden Dark, 2009; The Mobile Phone Detective, 2010; How to Talk to a Frill Neck Lizard, 2010. **Address:** 142 Buena Vista Ave., Coorparoo, Brisbane, QL 4151, Australia. **Online address:** jamesmo@bigpond.net.au

MOLONEY, Susie. Canadian (born Canada), b. 1962. **Genres:** Novels, Mystery/Crime/Suspense, Young Adult Fiction. **Career:** Writer. **Publications:** NOVELS: Bastion Falls, 1995; A Dry Spell, 1997; 362 Belisle St, 2002; The Dwelling, 2003; The Thirteen, 2011. OTHER: Three Days of Darkness, forthcoming. **Address:** c/o Daniel Lazar, Writers House, 21 W 26th St., New York, NY 10010, U.S.A. **Online address:** susie@susiemoloney.com

MOMADAY, N(avarre) Scott. American (born United States), b. 1934. **Genres:** Novels, Novellas/Short Stories, Poetry, Autobiography/Memoirs, Travel/Exploration, Illustrations, Young Adult Non-fiction. **Career:** University of California-Santa Barbara, assistant professor, 1963-65, associate professor of English, 1968-69; University of California-Berkeley, associate professor of English and comparative literature, 1969-73; Stanford University, professor of English, 1973-82; University of Arizona, professor of English and comparative literature, 1982-, Regents' professor of English, Regents' professor of humanities, now professor emeritus of English; New Mexico State University, faculty; Columbia University, visiting professor; Princeton University, visiting professor. Writer. **Publications:** SELF-ILLUSTRATED: The Gourd Dancer (verse), 1976. OTHERS: Owl in the Cedar Tree, 1965; The Journey of Tai-Me: Retold Kiowa Indian Tales, 1967 as The Way to Rainy Mountain, 1969; House Made of Dawn (novel), 1968; The American Indian in an Unhappy Hunting Ground, 1969; Bringing on the Indians, 1971; Colorado: Summer/Fall/Winter/Spring, 1973; Angle of Geese and Other Poems, 1974; Before An Old Painting Of The Crucifixion, 1975; The Colors of Night, 1976; A First American Views His Land, 1976; The Names: A Memoir, 1976; A Poem, 1979; (intro.) With Eagle Glance: American Indian Photographic Images, 1868 To 1931: An Exhibition of Selected Photographs from The Collection Of Warren Adelson and Ira Spanierman, 1982; I A sviazan dobrom s zemleĭ: izsovremennoĭ literatury indeĭt s ev SShA: sbornik, 1983; Discovering the Land of Light, 1985; On Bavarian Byways, 1986; A Coyote in the Garden, 1988; The Ancient Child (novel), 1989; Ancestral Voice: Conversations with N. Scott Momaday, 1989; Enduring Culture: A Century of Photography of the Southwest Indians, 1991; In the Presence of the Sun: Stories and Poems, 1961-1991, 1992; Storyteller, 1992; Turtle Island Alphabet: A Lexicon of Native American Symbols and Culture, 1992; The Native Americans: Indian Country, 1993; Circle of Wonder: A Native American Christmas Story, 1994; Conversations with N. Scott Momaday, 1997; The Man Made of Words, 1997; In the Bear's House, 1999; (foreword) Sacred Legacy: Edward S Curtis And the North American Indian, 2000; Four Arrows & Magie: A Kiowa Story, 2006; Three Plays, 2007; (afterword) To Walk in Beauty: A Navajo Family's Journey Home, 2009; Again the Far Morning: New and Selected Poems, 2011. EDITOR: The Complete Poems of Frederick Goddard Tuckerman, 1965; American Indian Authors, 1972. Illustrator of books by L.V. Andrews. Contributor of articles to periodicals. **Address:** Department of English, University of Arizona, Rm. 445, 1423 E University Blvd., Modern Languages Bldg., PO Box 210067, Tucson, AZ 85721, U.S.A. **Online address:** natachee@aol.com

MOMMSEN, Hans. German (born Germany), b. 1930. **Genres:** History, Education. **Career:** University of Tübingen, assistant at historical seminar, 1958-60, professor, 1960-61; University of Heidelberg, assistant at historical seminar, 1963-67, professor, 1963-68; Ruhr University of Bochum, professor of modern European history, 1968-83, professor emeritus, 1983-, Institute for the History of the Labor Movement, director, 1977-83; Harvard University, visiting professor, 1974; University of California, visiting professor, 1978; Hebrew University of Jerusalem, visiting professor, 1980; Georgetown University, visiting professor, 1982; Institute for Advanced Study, fellow, 1983-84; Oxford University, St. Antony's College, fellow, 1996-97; Institute fuer die Wissenschaften vom Menschen, visiting fellow, 1998. Writer. **Publications:** Sozialdemokratie und die Nationalitatenfrage im habsburgischenVielvölkerstaat, 1963; (co-author) Bergarbeiter. Ausstellungzur-geschichte der organisierten Bergarbeiterbewegung in Deutschland, 1969; (ed. with D. Petzina and B. Weisbrod) Industrielles System und politische Entwicklung in der Weimarer Republik: Verhandlungen, 1974; Sozialdemokratie zwischen Klassenbewegung und Volkspartei: Verhandungen der Sekt. Geschichte d. Arbeiterbewegung d. Dt. Historikertages in Regensburg, Okt. 1972, 1974; Beamtentum im Dritten Reich. Mit ausgewählten Quellen zurnationalsozialistischen Beamtenpolitik, 1976; Klassenkampf oder Mitbestimmung: Zum Problem d. Kontrolle wirtschaftl. Macht in d. Weimarer Republik, 1978; Arbeiterbewegung und nationale Frage: Ausgew.Aufsätze, 1979; (with U. Borsdorf) Glück auf, Kameraden!: Die Bergarbeiter u. ihre Organisationen in Deutschland, 1979; Arbeiterbewegungund industrieller Wandel: Studien zu gewerkschaftl. Organisations problemenim Reich u. an d. Ruhr, 1980; (ed. with I. Ackerman and W.H. Berger) Politik und Gesellschaft im altenund neuen Österreich: Festschrift für Rudolf Neck zum 60. Geburtstag, 1981; (with W. Schultze) Vom Elend der Handarbeit: Problemehistorischer Unterschichtenforschung, 1981;

(contrib.) The Challenge of the Third Reich, 1986; The Policies of Genocide, 1986; Auf der Suche nachhistorischer Normalität: Beiträge zum Geschichtsbildstreit in der Bundesrepublik, 1987; (contrib.) Nazi-Kunst ins Museum?, 1988; (ed. with S. Willems) Herrschaftsalltag im Dritten Reich: Studien und Texte, 1988; Die Verspielte Freiheit: Der Weg der Republik von Weimar in den Untergang, 1918 bis 1933, 1989; Der Nationalsozialismus und die deutsche Gesellschaft: Ausgewählte Aufsätze, 1991; From Weimar to Auschwitz: Essays in German History, 1992; (ed. with W. Benz and H. Buchheim) Nationalsozialismus: Studien zur Ideologie und Herrschaft, 1993; (ed. with H. Grebing and K. Rudolph) Demokratie und Emanzipation zwischen Saale und Elbe: Beiträge zur Geschichte dersozialdemokratischen Arbeiterbewegung bis 1933, 1993; (ed. with J. Kořalka) Ungleiche Nachbarn; Demokratische und nationale Emanzipation bei Deutschen, Tschechen und Slowaken (1815-1914), 1993; Widerstand und politische Kulturin Deutschland und österreich, 1994; Von der Aufgabe der Freiheit: Politische Antwortung und bürgerliche Gesellschaft im 19. und 20. Jahrhundert: Festschrift für Hans Mommsen zum 5. November 1995, 1995; Volkswagenwerk und seine Arbeiter im Dritten Reich, 1996; The Rise and Fall of Weimar Democracy, 1996; Nationalsocialisme et la societe allemande, 1997; (contrib.) Stalinism and Nazism: Dictatorships in Comparison, 1997; Mythos von der Modernität: Zur Entwicklung derRütungsindustrie im Dritten Reich, 1999; (contrib.) 50 Jahre Bundesrepublik Deutschland: Daten und Diskussionen, 1999; Future Challenges to Holocaust Scholarship as an Integrated Part of the Study of Modern Dictatorship, 2000; Erste Weltkrieg und die europäischeNachkriegsordnung: Sozialer Wandel und Formveränderung der Politik, 2000; (contrib.) Alfred Toepfer, Stifter und Kaufmann: Bausteine einer Biographie kritische Bestandsaufnahme, 2000; (ed. with D. Kovac, J. Malir and M. Marek) Erste Weltkrieg und die Beziehungen zwischen Tschechen, Slowaken und Deutschen, 2001; (contrib.) Verbrechen der Wehrmacht: Dimensionen des Vernichtungskrieges 1941-1944: Ausstellungskatalog, 2002; (contrib.) Wüstweiler Hof, 2002; Auschwitz, 17. Juli 1942: Der Weg zureuropäischen Endlösung der Judenfrage, 2002; Alternatives to Hitler: German Resistance Under the Third Reich, 2003; Germans Against Hitler: The Stauffenberg Plot and Resistance Under theThird Reich, 2009; Zur Geschichte Deutschlands im 20. Jahrhundert: Demokratie, Diktatur, Widerstand, 2010. Contributor to books. **Address:** Department of History, Ruhr-Universitat Bochum, Universitaetsstrasse 150, Bochum, 44801, Germany. **Online address:** hans.mommsen@t-online.de

MONACO, James. American (born United States), b. 1942. **Genres:** Communications/Media, Film, Art/Art History. **Career:** City University of New York, lecturer in literature, film, drama and media, 1964-70; New School for Social Research, staff, 1967-85, Center Search for Education, Elevation and Knowledge (SEEK) Program, chairman, 1969; New York Zoetrope Inc., founder and publisher, 1975-, president, 1977-; New York University, adjunct professor of film and television, 1977; James Monaco Inc., founder, 1980; National Public Radio, media commentator, 1980-85; Baseline Inc., founder and president, 1982-92; UNET 2 Corp., founder and president, 1992-; Village Green Recycling Team, vice-president; Institute of Directors London, fellow; Copyright Clearance Center, director; Columbia University, faculty. Writer. **Publications:** A Standard Glossary for Film Criticism, 1970, 2nd ed., 1975; (with S. Schenker) Books about Film: A Bibliographical Checklist, 1970, 3rd ed., 1976; Recent British Films, 1972; (contrib.) American Film Directors: A Library of Film Criticism, 1974; Film: How and Where to Find Out What You Want to Know, 1975; The New Wave: Truffaut, Godard, Chabrol, Rohmer, Rivette, 1976, new ed., 2002; How to Read a Film: The Art, Technology, Language, History, and Theory of Film and Media, 1977, 4th ed. as How to Read a Film: Movies, Media, and Beyond: Art, Technology, Language, History, Theory, 2009; (comp.) Media Culture: Television, Radio, Records, Books, Magazines, Newspapers, Movies, 1978; Alain Resnais: The Role of Imagination, 1978; American Film Now: The People, The Power, The Money, The Movies, 1979, rev. ed., 1994; (contrib.) The Book of the Cinema, 1979; Who's Who in American Film Now, 1981, 2nd ed., 1987; The French Revolutionary Calendar, 1983; The Connoisseur's Guide to the Movies, 1985; The Encyclopedia of Film, 1991; (co-author) The Movie Guide, 1992, 2nd ed., 1995; The Dictionary of New Media: The New Digital World: Video, Audio, Print, 1999. EDITOR: Celebrity: The Media as Image Makers, 1978; Salt of the Earth: The Story of a Film, 2003. **Address:** UNET 2 Corp., 80 E 11th St., New York, NY 10003, U.S.A. **Online address:** jim@readfilm.com

MONAGHAN, David (Mark). Canadian/British (born England), b. 1944. **Genres:** Literary Criticism And History, Film, Popular Culture. **Career:** Mount St. Vincent University, staff, 1970-, professor of English, 1980-2009, professor emeritus, 2009-. Writer. **Publications:** Jane Austen: Structure and Social Vision, 1980; (ed.) Jane Austen in a Social Context, 1981; The Novels of John le Carre: The Art Survial, 1985; Smiley's Circus: A Guide to the Secret World of John le Carre, 1986; (ed.) Emma, Jane Austen, 1992; The Falklands War: Myth and Countermyth, 1998; (with A. Hudelet and J. Wiltshire) The Cinematic Jane Austen: Essays on the Filmic Sensibility of the Novels, 2009. Contributor to journals. **Address:** Department of English, Mount St. Vincent University, 166 Bedford Hwy., Halifax, NS B3M 2J6, Canada. **Online address:** david.monaghan@msvu.ca

MONAGHAN, Nicola. British (born England), b. 1971. **Genres:** Novels. **Career:** Birmingham City University, National Academy of Writing, fellow, through 2009; Nottingham University, lecturer and course leader, 2010-; First Story, writer-in-residence. Writer. **Publications:** The Killing Jar, 2006; The Okinawa Dragon, 2008; Starfishing, 2008. **Address:** Luigi Bonomi Associates, 91 Great Russell St., London, GL WC1B 3PS, England. **Online address:** nicola@nicolamonaghan.co.uk

MONAHAN, John. American (born United States), b. 1946. **Genres:** Law, Psychiatry, Social Sciences, Psychology. **Career:** University of Virginia, School of Law, Doherty professor of law, 1980-, John S. Shannon distinguished professor of law, Horace W. Goldsmith research professor of law, professor of psychology and psychiatric medicine and fellow; Stanford University, Law School, fellow; New York University, School of Law, fellow; University of Oxford, fellow, All Souls College, fellow. Writer. **Publications:** (Ed. with D. Chappell) Violence and Criminal Justice, 1975; (ed.) Community Mental Health and the Criminal Justice System, 1976; (with K. Heller) Psychology and Community Change, 1977; (ed.) Who is the Client?: The Ethics of Psychological Intervention in the Criminal Justice System, 1980; Predicting Violent Behavior: An Assessment of Clinical Techniques, 1981; Clinical Prediction of Violent Behavior, 1981; (ed. with H.J. Steadman) Mentally Disordered Offenders: Perspectives from Law and Social Science, 1983; Social Science in Law: Cases and Materials, 1985, (with L. Walker) 7th ed., 2010; (ed. with H.J. Steadman) Violence and Mental Disorder: Developments in Risk Assessment, 1994; Social Science in Law, 1994; (ed. with D.L. Dennis) Coercion and Aggressive Community Treatment: A New Frontier in Mental Health Law, 1996; (ed. with R.J. Bonnie) Mental Disorder, Work Disability, and The Law, 1997; (co-author) Rethinking Risk Assessment: The MacArthur Study of Mental Disorder and Violence, 2001; (with L. Walker) Introduction to Social Science in Law, 2006. **Address:** School of Law, University of Virginia, Rm. WB177D, 580 Massie Rd., Charlottesville, VA 22903, U.S.A. **Online address:** jmonahan@virginia.edu

MONAHAN, Patrick J. (Patrick John Monahan). Canadian (born Canada), b. 1954. **Genres:** Area Studies, Law, Politics/Government. **Career:** York University, faculty, 1982-, associate professor, 1986-95, professor of law, 1995-, Centre for Public Law and Public Policy, director, through 2002, Osgoode Hall Law School, dean, 2003-09, Academic and Provost, vice-president, 2009-; Government of Ontario, Office of the Attorney General, policy adviser, 1986-89, Office of the Premier, policy adviser, 1989-90. Writer. **Publications:** Politics and the Constitution, 1987; (with A. Hutchinson) The Rule of Law: Ideal or Ideology, 1987; After Meech Lake: An Insider's View, 1990; Meech Lake: The Inside Story, 1991; (ed. with K. McRoberts) The Charlottetown Accord, the Referendum and the Future of Canada, 1993; Storming the Pink Palace, 1995; (co-author) The Charter of Rights and the Public Policy Process in Canada; Constitutional Law, 1997, 3rd ed., 2006; (with P.W. Hogg) Liability of the Crown, 2000. Contributor to professional journals. **Address:** Osgoode Hall Law School, York University, Rm. 222A, 4700 Keele St., Toronto, ON M3J 1P3, Canada. **Online address:** provost@yorku.ca

MONAHAN, Patrick John. *See* **MONAHAN, Patrick J.**

MONAHAN, William G(regory). American (born United States), b. 1927. **Genres:** Education, History, Adult Non-fiction. **Career:** Public High School, teacher in social studies and athletic coach, 1951-56, principal, 1954-56; Kentucky State Department of Education, assistant superintendent, 1956-58; Michigan State University, instructor in education, 1958-60; University of Oklahoma, assistant professor, 1960-62, associate professor of education, 1962-65; University of Iowa, associate professor, 1965-67, professor of education, 1967-72; Iowa Center for Research in School Administration, associate director, 1966-72; West Virginia University, professor of education, 1972-92, professor emeritus, 1992-, College of Human Resources and Education, dean, 1972-92. Writer. **Publications:** (With R.E. Ohm) Educational Administration: Philosophy in Action, 1965; (with W.R. Lane and R.G. Corwin) Foundations of Educational Administration: A Behavioral Analysis, 1967; Theoretical Dimensions of Educational Administration, 1975; (with H.R. Hengst) Contemporary Educational Administration, 1982; (with E.R. Smith) Leading People: What School Leaders Can Learn from Military Leadership Development, 1995. Contributor to journals. **Address:** West Virginia University, PO Box 6201, Morgantown, WV 26506, U.S.A.

MONBIOT, George (Joshua). (George Mon-by-o). Welsh/British (born England), b. 1963. **Genres:** Travel/Exploration, Environmental Sciences/Ecology. **Career:** British Broadcasting Corp. (BBC) Radio 4, producer of natural history programs, 1985-87, current affairs producer for World Service, 1987-; East London University, visiting professor; University of Keele, honorary professor; Oxford Brookes University, visiting professor; Bristol University, visiting professor; ArrestBlair.org, founder; University of Oxford, visiting professor; The Guardian, columnist. **Publications:** Poisoned Arrows, 1989; Gifpijlen, 1990; Amazon Watershed: The New Environmental Investigation, 1991; No Man's Land: An Investigative Journey through Kenya and Tanzania, 1994; Captive State, 2000; Manifesto for a New World Order, 2004; The Age of Consent, 2004; Heat: How to Stop the Planet Burning, 2006; Bring on the Apocalypse, 2008. **Address:** The Guardian, Kings Pl., 90 York Way, London, GL N1 9GU, England. **Online address:** g.monbiot@zetnet.co.uk

MON-BY-O, George. *See* **MONBIOT, George (Joshua).**

MONCRIEFF, Elspeth. British (born England), b. 1959. **Genres:** Art/Art History. **Career:** Victoria and Albert Museum, curator, 1984-87; Antique Collector, deputy editor, 1987-90; Apollo, deputy editor, 1990-92; Art Newspaper, art market correspondent, 1996-2004; Masterpiece, deputy editor, 1999-; World of Antiques and Art, editor; 2006-; Moncrieff-Bray Gallery, owner. **Publications:** (With I. Joseph and S. Joseph) Farm Animal Portraits, 1996; (intro.) Edward Bawden: Editioned Prints, 2005; Andrew Gifford, 2006; Stephen Palmer, 2011. **Address:** Moncrieff-Bray Gallery, Woodruffs Farm, Woodruffs Ln., Egdean, Petworth, WS RH20 1JX, England. **Online address:** moncrieff.bray@btinternet.com

MONDA, Antonio. American/Italian (born Italy), b. 1962. **Genres:** Art/Art History, Theology/Religion, Essays. **Career:** New York University, Kanbar Institute of Film and Television, associate professor, Tisch School of the Arts, professor. Writer and director. **Publications:** (Ed.) Second Act: A Rediscovery of Italian Cinema, Second Season Is Presented at the Museum of Modern Art, New York, February 18-March 2, 1999, by Istituto Italiano Di Cultura, Cinecittà International, a Division of Ente Gestione Cinema, 1999; (ed. with M.L. Bandy) The Hidden God: Film and Faith, 2003; La magnifica illusione: Un viaggio nel cinema americano, 2003; Do You Believe? Conversations on God and Religion, 2007; (with E. Blumenthal and J. Taymor) Julie Taymor: Playing with Fire; Theater, Opera, Film, 3rd ed., 2007; Hanno preferito le tenebre: dodici storie del male, 2010. Contributor to periodicals. **Address:** Tisch School of the Arts, New York University, Rm. 1115, 721 Broadway, New York, NY 10003, U.S.A. **Online address:** antonio.monda@nyu.edu

MONE, Gregory. American (born United States) **Genres:** Novels, Humor/Satire. **Career:** Popular Science, associate editor. **Publications:** The Wages of Genius, 2003; The Truth About Santa: Wormholes, Robots, and What Really Happens on Christmas Eve, 2009; Fish, 2010. **Address:** Popular Science, 2 Park Ave., 9th Fl., New York, NY 10016-5614, U.S.A.

MONESSON, Harry S. American (born United States), b. 1935?. **Genres:** Novels, Novellas/Short Stories, Science Fiction/Fantasy, Children's Fiction, Young Adult Fiction, Poetry, Mythology/Folklore, Cartoons, Humor/Satire, Illustrations, Genealogy/Heraldry, Picture/Board Books. **Career:** McGuire Air Force Base, civilian aircraft jet engine technician, 1966-77; Cranberry and blueberry farm, owner and manager, 1977-; publisher, 1992-. Writer. **Publications:** Knibblers in the Sands, Sand Sharks in the Pines (novel), 1988; Up a Cranberry Tree (poems), 1990, vol. II, 1997; Cries on the Wind, 1991; Short Stories, 2001; (with M. Brawn) End Wife Abuse or Else..., 2002; Mega Moms, 2004; Muscle Gals, 2005. FOR CHILDREN: The World's Biggest Tummy (picture book), 1992; Berry Patch Tales (short stories), 1999, Buggenskrogin (novel), 2000; After the Bunker, 2000; Sand Sharks in the Pines (novel), 2001; The Duffel Bag, forthcoming. **Address:** 315 Magnolia Rd., Pemberton, NJ 08068-1807, U.S.A.

MONET, Jean. Canadian (born Canada), b. 1932. **Genres:** Law, Novels, How-to Books. **Career:** McGill University, lecturer; University of Sherbrooke, lecturer; Quebec Bar Association, lecturer; Universite de Montreal, lecturer; Laval Universite, lecturer; Canadian Bar Association, Continuing Education Program, lecturer; Canadian Institute of Certified Accountants, lecturer; Colby, Monet, Demers, Delage & Crevier LLP (law firm), counsel. Writer. **Publications:** Vos biens, Votre décès et les impôts, 5 vols., 1967-74; Your Assets, Death & Taxes, 1971; (with S.D. Hart) Estate Planning for Canadians, rev. ed., 1975; La Soutane et la Couronne, 1993; The Cassock and the Crown: Canada's Most Controversial Murder Trial, 1996. **Address:** Colby, Monet, Demers, Delage & Crevier L.L.P., Tour McGill College, 1501 McGill College Ave., Ste. 2900, Montreal, QC H3A 3M8, Canada. **Online address:** jmonet@colby-monet.com

MONFREDO, Miriam Grace. American (born United States) **Genres:** Romance/Historical. **Career:** New York State Council of the Arts, teacher. Newspaper writer, director, librarian and historian. **Publications:** HISTORICAL MYSTERIES. GLYNIS TRYON SERIES: Seneca Falls Inheritance, 1992; North Star Conspiracy, 1993; Blackwater Spirits, 1995; Through a Gold Eagle: A Glynis Tryon Mystery, 1996; The Stalking Horse, 1998; Must the Maiden Die, 1999; Sisters of Cain, 2000; Brothers of Cain, 2001; Children of Cain, 2002. EDITOR: (with S. Newman) Crime through Time, 1997; (with S. Newman) Crime through Time II, 1998. **Address:** Berkley Publishing Group, 200 Madison Ave., New York, NY 10016, U.S.A.

MONG-LAN. (Mong-lan). American/Vietnamese (born Vietnam), b. 1970?. **Genres:** Poetry, Art/Art History. **Career:** University of Arizona, instructor of poetry, English composition and business writing, 1998-2000; Le Chateau de Lavigny (writer's colony), writer-in-residence, 2000; Wallace E. Stegner fellow, 2000-02; Stanford University, teaching assistant, 2001; University of Maryland, University College, Asian Division, teacher. Writer and visual artist. **Publications:** POETRY: Song of the Cicadas, 2001; Why is the Edge Always Windy?, 2005; Love Poem to Tofu and Other Poems, 2007; Tango, Tangoing: Poems & Art, 2008; Tango, Tangueando: Poemas & Dibujos (bilingual Spanish-English edition), 2009. ARTWORK: Force of the Heart: Tango, Art, 2011. Contributor of articles to journals. Works appear in anthologies. **Address:** Sugar Land, TX 77478, U.S.A. **Online address:** monglan11@yahoo.com

MONG-LAN. *See* **MONG-LAN.**

MONHOLLON, Michael L. American (born United States), b. 1959. **Genres:** Novels, Mystery/Crime/Suspense. **Career:** Attorney, 1984-97; Hardin-Simmons University, Kelley College of Business, associate professor of business law, 1998-, professor of business law, associate dean and interim dean, 2003-04, dean, 2004-, faculty advisor, 2001-03; Connecting Caring Communities, board director; First Baptist Church of Abilene, R.A. leader, 2000-01, 2002-03, deacon, 2003; Abilene Philharmonic Foundation, board director, 2001-03, treasurer, 2001-02; Abilene Community Theater, actor, 2002, 2003. Writer. **Publications:** Criminal Intent, 1992; Divine Invasion, 1998. **Address:** Kelley College of Business, Hardin-Simmons University, 2200 Hickory St., PO Box 16220, Abilene, TX 79601-2345, U.S.A. **Online address:** mikeml@hsutx.edu

MONIÈRE, Denis. Canadian (born Canada), b. 1947. **Genres:** International Relations/Current Affairs, Politics/Government, Young Adult Non-fiction. **Career:** University of Montreal, Department of Political Science, director and professor. Writer. **Publications:** NONFICTION IN ENGLISH TRANSLATION: Le Development des ideologies au Quebec: Des Origines nos jours, 1977. IN FRENCH: Critique epistemologique de l'analyse systemique de David Easton: Essai sur lerapport entre théorie et idéologie, 1976; (with A. Vachet) Les Idéologies au Québec: Bibliographie, 1976, 3rd ed., 1980; Développement des idéologies au Québec: Des origines à nosjours, 1977; (with J. Gosselin) Le Trust de la foi, 1978; Les Enjeux dureferendum, 1979; Cause commune: Manifeste Pour Une Internationale despetites cultures, 1981; Pour la Suite de l'histoire: Essai sur laconjoncture politique au Québec, 1982; André Laurendeau et ledestin d'un peuple, 1983; Avez-vous lu Hirschman?: Essai sur ladéception politique, 1985; Ludger Duvernay et la révolution Intellectuelle au Bas-Canada, 1987; Le Discours électoral: Les Politiciens sot-ils fiables?, 1988; L'Indépendence: Essai, 1992; Le Combat des chefs: Analyse des débats télévisés au Canada, 1992; (with J.H. Guay) La Bataille du Québec, vol. I: Les Elections federales de 1993, 1994, vol. II: Les Elections Quebecoises de 1994, 1995; Votez Pour Moi: Une Histoire Politique du Québec

Moderne à Traversla Publicité électorale, 1998; Pour Comprendre le Nationalisme Au Québec et Ailleurs, 2001; Les Relations France-Québec, 2005; Histoire de la République du Québec: 25 ans de souveraineteACU: Essai de politique fiction, 2006; (ed. with R. Comeau and C. Courtois) Histoire intellectuelle de l'indépendantisme québécois, 2010. OTHERS: André Laurendeau et le destin d'un peuple, 1983; L'indépendance, 1992; Louis-Alexandre Taschereau vous parle, 2010. **Address:** Les Editions Quebec Amerique, 329 rue de la Commune St. W, Fl. 3, Montreal, QC H2Y 2E1, Canada. **Online address:** denis.moniere@umontreal.ca

MONING, Karen Marie. American (born United States), b. 1964. **Genres:** Novels, Romance/Historical, Paranormal, Science Fiction/Fantasy. **Career:** Writer, 1999-. **Publications:** HIGHLANDER SERIES: ROMANCE NOVELS: Beyond the Highland Mist, 1999; To Tame a Highland Warrior, 1999; The Highlander's Touch, 2000; Kiss of the Highlander, 2001; The Dark Highlander, 2002; The Immortal Highlander, 2004; Spell of the Highlander, 2005. FEVER SERIES: URBAN FANTASY: Darkfever, 2006; Bloodfever, 2007; Faefever, 2008; Dreamfever, 2009; Shadowfever 2011. OTHERS: (contrib.) Tapestry (anthology), 2002; Into the Dreaming, 2006. **Address:** Atlanta, GA , U.S.A. **Online address:** karen@karenmoning.com

MONK, Isabell. American (born United States), b. 1952. **Genres:** Plays/ Screenplays, Psychology, Young Adult Fiction, Literary Criticism And History. **Career:** Actor and writer. **Publications:** Hope, 1999; Family, 2001; Blackberry Stew, 2005; Come to Me, forthcoming. **Address:** 421 Upton Ave. S, Minneapolis, MN 55405, U.S.A.

MONK, Raymond. British (born England), b. 1925. **Genres:** Biography, Philosophy, Music. **Career:** University of Southampton, lecturer in philosophy, 1992-; Elgar Foundation, director. Writer. **Publications:** Elgar Studies, 1990; Ludwig Wittgenstein: The Duty of Genius, 1990; (ed.) Edward Elgar: Music and Literature, 1992; Bertrand Russell: The Spirit of Solitude 1872-1921, 1996; Bertrand Russell: The Ghost of Madness, 1921-1970, 2000; (ed. with F. Raphael) The Great Philosophers, 2000; How to Read Wittgenstein, 2005. Contributor to books. **Address:** Department of Law, Arts & Social Sciences, Humanities School, University of Southampton, Rm. 65/1035, Avenue Campus, Southampton, SO17 1BJ, England. **Online address:** r.monk@soton.ac.uk

MONK, Robert C. American (born United States), b. 1930. **Genres:** History, Theology/Religion, Biography, Autobiography/Memoirs. **Career:** Texas A&M University, Wesley Foundation, director, 1954-58; Texas Methodist Student Movement, associate director, 1961-64; McMurry University, professor of religion, 1964-95, professor emeritus, 1995-. Writer. **Publications:** John Wesley: His Puritan Heritage, A Study of the Christian Life, 1966, 2nd ed., 1999; (co-author) Exploring Religious Meaning, 1974, 6th ed., 2003; (with J.D. Stamey) Exploring Christianity: An Introduction, 1984, 2nd ed., 1990; (co-author) The Methodist Excitement in Texas, 1984. **Address:** McMurry University, S. 14th & Sayles, Abilene, TX 79697, U.S.A. **Online address:** monkr@campus.mcm.edu

MONMONIER, Mark. American (born United States), b. 1943. **Genres:** Design, Environmental Sciences/Ecology, Geography, Technology, Earth Sciences, History, Adult Non-fiction, Meteorology/Atmospheric Sciences, Meteorology/Atmospheric Sciences. **Career:** University of Rhode Island, assistant professor, 1969-70; State University of New York, assistant professor, 1970-73; Syracuse University, associate professor, 1973-79, professor, 1979-98, distinguished professor of geography, 1998-; U.S. Geological Survey, research geographer, 1979-84; American Cartographer, editor, 1982-84; Cartographica, contributing editor, 1984-2003; New York State Program in Geographic Information and Analysis, deputy director, 1989-90. **Publications:** Gipsy: A Geographic Incremental Plotting System, 1969; Plotter Mapping (GIPSY2 and SURGE2), 1971; Maps, Distortion and Meaning, 1977; Computer-Aided Map Design, Two Subroutines to Improve Cartographic Communication Through Data Selection, 1978; Computer-Assisted Cartography, 1982; (with G. Schnell) The Study of Population: Elements, Patterns and Processes, 1983; Technological Transition in Cartography, 1985; Maps with the News: The Development of American Journalistic Cartography, 1988; (with G. Schnell) Map Appreciation, 1989; How to Lie with Maps, 1991, 2nd ed., 1996; Mapping it Out: Expository Cartography for the Humanities and Social Sciences, 1993; Drawing the Line: Tales of Maps and Cartocontroversy, 1995; Cartographies of Danger: Mapping Hazards in America, 1997; Air Apparent: How Meteorologists Learned to Map, Predict and Dramatize Weather, 1999; Bushmanders and Bullwinkles: How Politicians Manipulate Electronic Maps and Census Data to Win Elections, 2001; Spying with Maps: Surveillance Technologies and the Future of Privacy, 2002; Rhumb Lines and Map Wars, 2004; From Squaw Tit to Whorehouse Meadow: How Maps Name, Claim, and Inflame, 2006; Coast Lines: How Mapmakers Frame the World and Chart Environmental Change, 2008; (ed. with G. Herb and D. Kaplan) Cambridge World Atlas, 2009; No Dig, No Fly, No Go: How Maps Restrict and Control, 2010. Contributor to periodicals and journals. **Address:** Department of Geography, Maxwell School of Citizenship and Public Affairs, Syracuse University, 144 Eggers Hall, Syracuse, NY 13244-1020, U.S.A. **Online address:** mon2ier@maxwell.syr.edu

MONOSON, S. Sara. American (born United States), b. 1960. **Genres:** Adult Non-fiction, Philosophy, Politics/Government. **Career:** Northwestern University, assistant professor, 1993-2000, associate professor of political science and classics, 2001-, Department of Classics, chair; Classical Traditions Initiative, director. Writer. **Publications:** Plato's Democratic Entanglements: Athenian Politics and the Practice of Philosophy, 2000. Contributor to periodicals. **Address:** Department of Political Science, Northwestern University, Scott Hall, 601 University Pl., Evanston, IL 60208, U.S.A. **Online address:** s-monoson@northwestern.edu

MONROE, Mary. American (born United States), b. 1951. **Genres:** inspirational/Motivational Literature. **Career:** Writer. **Publications:** The Upper Room, 1985; God Don't Like Ugly, 2000; Gonna Lay down My Burdens, 2002; God Still Don't Like Ugly, 2003; Red Light Wives, 2004; In Sheep's Clothing, 2005; Borrow Trouble, 2006; God Don't Play, 2006; Deliver Me from Evil, 2007; She had It Coming, 2008; The Company We Keep, 2009; God Ain't Blind, 2009; God Ain't Through Yet, 2010, Mama Ruby, 2011. **Address:** c/o Andrew Stuart, The Stuart Literary Agency, 260 W 52nd St., Ste. 24C, New York, NY 10019, U.S.A. **Online address:** marymonroe4401@aol.com

MONROE, Steve. American (born United States), b. 1961?. **Genres:** Novels, Mystery/Crime/Suspense. **Career:** Grubb & Ellis Co., retail real estate staff; Anixter center, teacher. Writer. **Publications:** NOVELS: '57, Chicago, 2001; '46, Chicago, 2002. **Address:** c/o Publicity Director, Hyperion Books, 77 W 66th St., 11th Fl., New York, NY 10023, U.S.A. **Online address:** steve@steve-monroe.net

MONSARRAT, Ann Whitelaw. Maltese/British (born England), b. 1937. **Genres:** Cultural/Ethnic Topics, Fash Ion/Costume, Biography. **Career:** West Kent Mercury, journalist, 1954-58; Daily Mail, journalist, 1958-61; Stationery Trade Review, assistant editor, 1961; freelance writer, 1962-. **Publications:** And the Bride Wore: The Story of the White Wedding, 1973; An uneasy Victorian: Thackeray the Man, 1811-1863, 1980. **Address:** Campbell Thomson & McLaughlin Ltd., 31 Newington Green, London, GL N16 9PU, England.

MONSHIPOURI, Mahmood. Iranian/American (born United States), b. 1952. **Genres:** Third World. **Career:** University of Georgia, instructor, 1985-86; Alma College, professor, 1986-98, acting department head, 1988-89, 1990-91; Central Michigan University, adjunct assistant professor, 1988-93; Quinnipiac University, Department of Political Science, professor and chairman, 1998-; Yale University, Center for International and Area Studies, visiting fellow, 2003-06; San Francisco State University, Department of International Relations, associate professor. Writer. **Publications:** Democratization, Liberalization and Human Rights in the Third World, 1995; Islamism, Secularism and Human Rights in the Middle East, 1998; (co-ed.) Constructing Human Rights in the Age of Globalization, 2003; Muslims in Global Politics: Identities, Interests and Human Rights, 2009; US-Iran Relations: Embracing a New Realism, 2009; Human Rights in the Middle East: Frameworks, Goals and Strategies, 2011; Terrorism, Security and Human Rights: Harnessing the Rule of Law, 2012. Contributor of articles to journals. **Address:** Department of Political Science, Quinnipiac University, 275 Mt. Carmel Ave., Hamden, CT 06518-1949, U.S.A. **Online address:** mahmood.monshipour@quinnipiac.edu

MONSON, Ingrid (T.). American (born United States), b. 1955. **Genres:** Music. **Career:** Trumpeter, 1980-85; Klezmer Conservatory Band, founding member, 1980, trumpeter, 1980-87; Klezmer Connection, co-leader, 1987-89; University of Chicago, assistant professor of music, 1991-95; Chicago Humanities Institute, fellow, 1992, 1993; New York University, lecturer, 1995; University of Michigan, visiting assistant professor of music, 1995-96; Washington University, assistant professor of music, 1996-99, Earle H.

and Suzanne S. Harbison faculty fellow, 1996-99, associate professor of music, 1999-2001; University of Wisconsin, lecturer, 1997; University of North Carolina, lecturer, 1998; Yale University, lecturer, 1998; Harvard University, Quincy Jones Visiting Assistant Professor, 1999, Quincy Jones Professor of African American Music, 2001-, Department of Music, chair, 2005-08, graduate advisor in ethnomusicology, director. Writer. **Publications:** Saying Something: Jazz Improvisation and Interaction, 1996; (ed.) African Diaspora: A Musical Perspective, 2000; Freedom Sounds: Civil Rights Call Out to Jazz and Africa, 2007. Contributor of articles to books and journals. **Address:** Department of African and African American Studies, Harvard University, 202S Music Bldg., University Hall, 1 Harvard Yard 2 N, Cambridge, MA 02138, U.S.A. **Online address:** imonson@fas.harvard.edu

MONSOUR, Theresa. American (born United States) **Genres:** Novels, Mystery/Crime/Suspense, Young Adult Fiction. **Career:** St. Paul Pioneer Press, reporter and staff writer, 1980-. Journalist. **Publications:** PARIS MURPHY SERIES: Clean Cut, 2003; Cold Blood, 2004; Dark House, 2005. Contributor to periodicals. **Address:** St. Paul Pioneer Press, 345 Cedar St., St. Paul, MN 55101-6000, U.S.A.

MONTAGNIER, Luc. American/French (born France), b. 1932. **Genres:** Biology, Medicine/Health. **Career:** University of Paris, assistant to science faculty, 1955-60; Medical Research Council, researcher, 1960-63; Institute of Virology, researcher, 1963-64; Institut de Radium, head of laboratory, 1965-72; Institut Pasteur, founder and head of viral oncology unit, 1972-2000, professor, 1985-2000, head of department of AIDS and retro viruses, 1990-96, now professor emeritus; Centre National de La Recherche Scientifique (CNRS), director, 1974-2000; City University of New York, Queens College, Center for Molecular and Cellular Biology, Salick professor and director, 1997-; Shanghai Jiao Tong University, university chair professor, 2010-. Writer. **Publications:** Vaincre le SIDA: Entretiens avec Pierre Bourget, 1986; AIDS and HIV Diseases, 1993; (coordinator) Le Sida et La Société Française: Rapport au Premier Ministre, 1994; Des Virus et Des Hommes, 1994; AIDS Research at Ec Level, Biomedical and Health Research, vol. VI., 1997; De los virus y de los hombres, 1997; AIDS, and Neurodegenerative Diseases, 1997; Virus: The Co-Discoverer of HIV Tracks Its Rampage and Charts the Future, 2000; Nobel et le moine: dialogues de notre temps, 2009. EDITOR: (with J. Allain and R.C. Gallo) Human Retroviruses and Diseases They Cause: Symposium Highlights, 1988; (with M. Gougeon and contrib.) New Concepts in AIDS Pathogenesis, 1993; (with R. Olivier and C. Pasquier) Oxidative Stress in Cancer, AIDS and Neurodegenerative Diseases, 1997. Contributor to journals and periodicals. **Address:** Center for Molecular & Cellular Biology, Queens College, City University of New York, 65-30 Kissena Blvd., Flushing, NY 11367, U.S.A.

MONTAGU, Jennifer (Iris Rachel). British (born England), b. 1931?. **Genres:** Art/Art History, Architecture. **Career:** Arts Council of Great Britain, assistant regional director, 1953-54; University of Reading, lecturer, 1958-64; Warburg Institute, assistant curator, 1964-71, curator of the photographic collection, 1971-91; Cambridge University, Slade professor of the history of fine art, 1980-81; Jesus College, fellow. Writer. **Publications:** Bronzes, 1963; (with J. Thuillier) Charles Le Brun, 1963; Alessandro Algardi, 1985; Index of Emblems of the Italian Academies: Based on Michele Maylender's Storie delle accademie d'Italia, 1988; Roman Baroque Sculpture: The Industry of Art, 1989; The Expression of the Passions: The Origin and Influence of Charles Le Brun's Conférence sur l'expression générale et particulière, 1994; Gold, Silver, and Bronze: Metal Sculpture of the Roman Baroque, 1996; Algardi: l'altra faccia del barocco: Roma, Palazzo delle esposizioni, 21 gennaio-30 aprile 1999, 1999; (intro.) François du Quesnoy, 1597-1643, 2005; (with G. Barucca) Ori e argenti: capolavori del '700 da Arrighi a Valadier, 2007; (ed. with A. Bacchi, C. Hess and A. Desmas) Bernini and the Birth of Baroque Portrait Sculpture, 2008; Antonio Arrighi: A Silversmith and Bronze Founder in Baroque Rome, 2009. **Address:** 10 Roland Way, London, GL SW7 3RE, England.

MONTAGUE, George T(homas). American (born United States), b. 1929. **Genres:** Theology/Religion. **Career:** Roman Catholic High School, Department of Religion, chaplain and chair, 1961-62; St. Mary's University, associate professor, 1962, professor of theology, 1971-, Graduate Program in Theology, director, 1963-72; Marianist Seminary, rector, 1972-74; St. Louis University, adjunct associate professor, 1973-74, visiting professor; University of St. Michael's College, professor of theology, 1974-79; Catholic Biblical Association of America, president, 1977-78; Brothers of the Beloved Disciple, founder, 1995-; Toronto School of Theology, visiting professor; Franciscan University of Steubenville, visiting professor; Catholic Biblical Quarterly, editor. **Publications:** Growth in Christ: A Study in Saint Paul's Theology of Progress, 1961; Maturing in Christ, 1964; The Living Thought of Saint Paul, 1966, 2nd ed., 1976; The Books of Zephaniah, Nahum, Habakkuk, Lamentations, Obadiah, 1967; The Biblical Theology of the Secular, 1968; The Books of Ruth and Tobit, 1973; The Books of Esther and Judith, 1973; The Spirit and His Gifts, 1974; Riding the Wind, 1974; Building Christ's Body: The Dynamics Of Christian Living According to St. Paul, 1975; The Holy Spirit: Growth of a Biblical Tradition, 1976; Mark, Good News for Hard Times: A Popular Commentary on the Earliest Gospel, 1981; Companion God: A Cross-Cultural Commentary on the Gospel of Matthew, 1989, rev. ed., 2010; Our Father, Our Mother: Mary and the Faces of God, 1990; (with K. McDonnell) Christian Initiation and Baptism in the Holy Spirit, 1991; (ed. with McDonnell) Fanning the Flame, 1991; The Apocalypse: Understanding the Book of Revelation and the End of the World, 1992; The Woman and the Way: A Marian Path to Jesus, 1994; Still Riding the Wind, 1994; Understanding the Bible: A Basic Introduction to Biblical Interpretation, 1997, rev. ed., 2007; Apocalypse and the Third Millennium, 1998; The Vision of the Beloved Disciple: Meeting Jesus in the Gospel of John, 2000; Holy Spirit, Make Your Home in Me: Biblical Meditations on Receiving the Gift of the Spirit, 2008; First and Second Timothy, Titus, 2008; Mary's Life In The Spirit, 2011; First Corinthians, 2011. **Address:** Brothers of the Beloved Disciple, 1701 Alametos, San Antonio, TX 78201-3500, U.S.A. **Online address:** gmontague@stmarytx.edu

MONTAGUE, John (Patrick). Irish/American (born United States), b. 1929. **Genres:** Novels, Novellas/Short Stories, Plays/Screenplays, Poetry, Essays, Translations, inspirational/Motivational Literature, Autobiography/Memoirs, Autobiography/Memoirs. **Career:** Standard (newspaper), film critic, 1949-52; Bord Failte, executive, 1956-59; Irish Times, Paris correspondent, 1961-64; University of California, visiting lecturer, 1964, 1965; University of Dublin, visiting lecturer, 1967, 1968, University College Cork, lecturer in poetry, 1972-88; University of Vincennes, visiting lecturer, 1968; State University of New York, University at Albany, writer-in-residence, 1990, Ireland chair of poetry. **Publications:** Forms of Exile: Poems, 1958; The Old People, 1960; Poisoned Lands and Other Poems, 1961, rev. ed., 1977; (with T. Kinsella and R. Murphy) Three Irish Poets, 1961; (ed. with T. Kinsella and contrib.) The Dolmen Miscellany of Irish Writing, 1962; Death of a Chieftain and Other Stories, 1964; Old Mythologies: A Poem, 1965; All Legendary Obstacles, 1966; Patriotic Suite, 1966; (ed. with L. Miller) A Tribute to Austin Clarke on His Seventieth Birthday, 9 May 1966, 1966; Home Again, 1967; A Chosen Light, 1967; Hymn to the New Omagh Road, 1968; The Bread God, 1968; A New Siege, 1969; (with J. Hewitt) The Planter and the Gael, 1970; Tides, 1971; Small Secrets, 1972; The Rough Field, 1972, 6th ed., 2005; Fair House: Versions of Irish Poetry, 1973; (ed. and trans.) The Faber Book of Irish Verse, 1974; (contrib.) Irish Poets in English, 1972; (trans.) A Fair House, 1973; The Cave of Night, 1974; (contrib.) Time Was Away: The World of Louis MacNeice, 1974; O'Riada's Farewell, 1974; A Slow Dance, 1975; The Book of Irish Verse, 1976, new ed., 1995; The Great Cloak, 1978; The Leap, 1979; Selected Poems, 1982; The Dead Kingdom, 1984; This Nutral Realm, 1984; The Lost Notebook (novella), 1987; Langue greffée, 1988; (with B. Kennelly and T. Kinsella) Myth, History, and Literary Tradition/Mount Eagle, 1989; (ed. and intro.) Bitter Harvest: An Anthology of Contemporary Irish Verse, 1989; The Figure in the Cave and Other Essays, 1989; New Selected Poems, 1989; Born in Brooklyn: John Montague's America, 1991; An Occasion of Sin, 1992; About Love, 1993; Time in Armagh, 1993; (trans. with C.K. Williams) Ponge, 1994; Collected Poems, 1995; A Love Present and Other Stories, 1997; Chain Letter, 1997; The Bag Apron, 1998; Smashing the Piano, 1999; (trans.) E. Guillevic, Carnac, 1999; Company: A Chosen Life, 2001; Drunken Sailor, 2004; Pear is Ripe: A Memoir, 2007; Ball of Fire, 2008; (with N.N. Dhomhnaill and P. Durcan) Poet's Chair: The First Nine Years of the Ireland Chair of Poetry, 2008; In My Grandfather's Mansion, 2010; Speech Lessons, 2011. Contributor to journals and newspapers. **Address:** Peters Fraser & Dunlop, The Rights House, 34-43 Russell St., London, GL WC2B 5HA, England.

MONTAGU OF BEAULIEU. British (born England), b. 1926. **Genres:** Recreation, Social Commentary, Art/Art History, Biography, Autobiography/Memoirs. **Career:** Voice and Vision Ltd., director, 1950-53; National Motor Museum, founder and director, 1952-; Veteran and Vintage Magazine, editor, 1956-79; Pioneer Publications Ltd., chairman, 1956-; National Motor Museum Trust, founder and chairman; Collector's Car, consulting editor, 1979-. **Publications:** The Motoring Montagus: The Story of the Montagu Motor Museum, 1959; Lost Causes of Motoring, 1960; Jaguar: A Biography, 1961; The Gordon Bennett Races, 1963; Rolls of Rolls Royce: A Biography of the Hon. C.S. Rolls, 1967; The Gilt and the Gingerbread, or, How to Live in a Stately Home and Make Money, 1967; Lost Causes of Motoring in Europe, vol. I, 1969, vol. II, 1971; More Equal Than Others: The Changing Fortunes of the British & European Aristocracies, 1970; (with A. Bird) Steam Cars, 1770-1970, 1971; The Horseless Carriage, 1975; (with G.N. Georgano) Early Days on the Road: An Illustrated History 1819-1941, 1976; Behind the Wheel: The Magic and Manners of Early Motoring, 1977; (with M. Frostick) Royalty on the Road, 1980; (with P. Macnaghten) Home, James, the Chauffeur in the Golden Age of Motoring, 1982; Early Days of Rolls-Royce and the Montagu Family, 1986; The British Motorist, 1987; English Heritage, 1987; Daimler Century, 1995; Wheels within Wheels: An Unconventional Life, 2000; (contrib.) The Beaulieu Encyclopedia of the Automobile. Coachbuilding, 2001. **Address:** The National Motor Museum, Beaulieu, Brockenhurst, HM SO42 7ZN, England.

MONTAIGNE, Fen. American (born United States), b. 1952. **Genres:** Environmental Sciences/Ecology, International Relations/Current Affairs, Natural History, Sciences, Travel/Exploration. **Career:** Philadelphia Inquirer, inquirers moscow correspondent, 1990-93, chief; freelance writer, 1996-; Yale Environment 360 Magazine, senior editor. **Publications:** (With O. Kalugin) The First Directorate: My 32 Years in Intelligence and Espionage against the West, 1994; Reeling in Russia, 1998; Hooked: Fly-Fishing Through Russia, 1998; (with S. Williams) Surviving Galeras, 2001; Broken Empire, 2001; Medicine by Design: The Practice and Promise of Biomedical Engineering, 2006; Fraser's Penguins: Warning Signs From Antarctica, 2010. Contributor to periodicals. **Address:** 121 Corlies Ave., Pelham, NY 10803-1901, U.S.A. **Online address:** fen.montaigne@gmail.com

MONTANDON, Mac. American (born United States), b. 1971. **Genres:** Young Adult Non-fiction, Sciences, Humor/Satire. **Career:** Writer. **Publications:** (Ed.) Innocent When You Dream: The Tom Waits Reader, 2005; Jetpack Dreams: One Man's Up and Down (but Mostly Down) Search for the Greatest Invention That Never Was, 2008; Proper Care and Feeding of Zombies, 2010; (with O. Munn) Suck it, Wonder Woman!: The Misadventures of a Hollywood Geek, 2010. Contributor to periodicals. **Address:** Wiley, 111 River St., Hoboken, NY 07030-5774, U.S.A. **Online address:** macmontandon@gmail.com

MONTAUREDES, Rita. American (born United States) **Genres:** Medicine/Health. **Career:** Writer. **Publications:** (With E. Marks) Coping with Glaucoma, 1997. **Address:** c/o Bonita K. Nelson, B. K. Nelson Literary Agency, 84 Woodland Rd., Pleasantville, NY 10570, U.S.A. **Online address:** mysticmw@worldnet.att.net

MONTEFIORE, Jan. *See* **MONTEFIORE, Janet.**

MONTEFIORE, Janet. (Jan Montefiore). British (born England), b. 1948. **Genres:** Essays, Literary Criticism And History, History. **Career:** University of Kent, Rutherford College, School of English, professor of 20th century English literature, director of learning and teaching, Centre for Gender, Sexuality and Writing, director. Writer. **Publications:** (As Jan Montefiore) Feminism and Poetry: Language, Experience, Identity in Women's Writing, 1987, 3rd ed., 2004; Men and Women Writers of the 1930s: The Dangerous Flood of History, 1996; Arguments of Heart and Mind: Selected Essays 1977-2000, 2002; Rudyard Kipling, 2007; (ed. and intro.) Rudyard Kipling: The Man Who Would be King and Other Stories, 2011. **Address:** School of English, Rutherford College, University of Kent, NC 2, Canterbury, KT CT2 7NX, England. **Online address:** j.e.montefiore@kent.ac.uk

MONTEJO, Victor (D.). American/Guatemalan (born Guatemala), b. 1951. **Genres:** Anthropology/Ethnology, Mythology/Folklore, Novellas/Short Stories, Humanities. **Career:** Bucknell University, consultant in Latin American studies, 1984-85, Department of Sociology/Anthropology, visiting assistant professor, 1993-94; University of California, assistant professor, 1996-98, associate professor, 1998-2010, Department of Native American Studies, professor and chair, 2000-03; University of Montana, assistant professor, 1996-99; Congressional Commission for Indigenous Affairs, congressman and minister of peace, 2004-08, president. Writer. **Publications:** Kanil, Man of Lightning: A Legend of Jacaltenango, 1984; Testimony: Death of a Guatemalan Village, 1987; The Bird Who Cleans the World and Other Mayan Fables, 1991; Brevísima Relación testimonial de la continua Destrucción del mayab', 1992; Sculptured Stones, 1995; Las Aventuras de mister Puttison entre los Mayas, 1998; Voices form Exile: Violence and Survival in Modern Mayan History, 1999; Q'anil, el hombre rayo: unaleyenda de jacaltenango= Komam q'anil, ya' k'uh winaj: Yik'ti' al xajla', 1999; Q'anil: Man of Lightning, 2001; Adventures of Mr. Puttison among the Maya, 2002; Oxlanh b'aqtun: recordando al sacerdote jaguar (chilam balam) en el portón del nuevo milenio, 2003; Maya Intellectual Renaissance: Identity, Representation, and Leadership, 2005. **Address:** Department of Native American Studies, University of California, 2407 Hart Hall, 1 Shields Ave., Davis, CA 95616, U.S.A. **Online address:** vmontejo@ucdavis.edu

MONTENEGRO, Laura Nyman. American (born United States), b. 1953. **Genres:** Children's Fiction, Illustrations, Picture/Board Books, Young Adult Fiction. **Career:** Zapato Puppet Theatre, co-founder, performer and musician, 1982-; New Mexico Arts Council, artist-in-residence, 1982-85; National Louis University, adjunct professor of poetry, illustration and bookmaking, 1987-88; Evanston Public Library-Evanston, children's services library assistant, graphic artist, storyteller, and muralist, 1988-95; Dr. Martin Luther King Experimental Laboratory School, art teacher, 1998-99; Children's Picture books, instructor of illustrations, design and writing, 2005-; Theatre Zarko, co-founder. Writer. **Publications:** SELF-ILLUSTRATED: A Bird about to Sing, 2003. OTHERS: One Stuck Drawer, 1991; Sweet Tooth, 1995; (with M.M. Nussbaum) My First Holy Communion: Sunday Mass and Daily Prayers, 2001; A Poet's Bird Garden, 2007. **Address:** Farrar, Straus & Giroux, 18 W 18th St., New York, NY 10011, U.S.A. **Online address:** lauramontenegro@earthlink.net

MONTES, Marisa. Puerto Rican (born Puerto Rico), b. 1951. **Genres:** Children's Fiction, Young Adult Fiction, Mystery/Crime/Suspense, Humor/Satire. **Career:** Lawyer, 1980-84; Matthew Bender and Company Inc., legal writer and editor-manager of publishing operations, 1984-94; Writer, 1987-. **Publications:** Something Wicked's in Those Woods (middle-grade suspense), 2000; Juan Bobo Goes to Work: A Puerto Rican Folktale, 2000; Egg-Napped! (picture book), 2002; A Circle of Time (young-adult mystery), 2002. GET READY FOR GABI SERIES: A Crazy Mixed-up Spanglish Day, 2003; Who's That Girl?, 2003; No More Spanish!, 2004; Please Don't Go, 2004; Gatos Black on Halloween, 2006. Contributor to periodicals. **Address:** Barbara S. Kouts Literary Agency, PO Box 560, Bellport, NY 11713, U.S.A.

MONTGOMERY, David. British (born England), b. 1928. **Genres:** Biography, Autobiography/Memoirs, History. **Career:** Shell Intl., trainee, manager, 1951-62; Yardley Intl., director, 1962-74; Terimar Services, chairperson and managing director, 1974-2000; Vision Interamericana, columnist, 1974-94; Antofagasta Railway, chairman, 1979-82; Brazilian Chamber of Commerce, chairman, 1982-84. **Publications:** (With A. Horne) Monty: The Lonely Leader, 1944-1945, 1994. **Address:** 54 Cadogan Sq., London, GL SW1X 0JW, England.

MONTGOMERY, David Bruce. American (born United States), b. 1938. **Genres:** Marketing, Administration/Management, Business/Trade/Industry, Mathematics/Statistics. **Career:** Massachusetts Institute of Technology, M.I.T. Operations Research Center, associated faculty, 1966-70, assistant professor, 1966-69, associate professor, 1969-70; TIMS Marketing College, co-founder, 1967; Journal of Marketing Research, computer applications subeditor, 1968-72, editorial consultant, 1972-75; Marketing Science Institute, senior research associate, 1969-70, executive director, 1995-97; Management Analysis Center, principal, 1969; Management Science, department editor for marketing, 1969-71; The MAC Group Inc., Principal, 1970-90; Journal of Marketing, associate editor, 1970-72; Stanford University, Graduate School of Business, associate professor, 1970-73, professor of management, 1976-78, Robert A. Magowan professor of marketing, 1978-92, Sebastian S. Kresge professor of marketing, 1992-99, emeritus, 1999-, School of Engineering, Industrial Engineering-Engineering Management Department, affiliated faculty, 1990, Graduate School of Business, area coordinator for marketing, 1972-76, 1978-79, trust faculty fellow, 1990-91; Singapore Management University, Lee Kong Chian School of Business, dean, 2003-05, dean emeritus, 2005, consultant, visiting professor of marketing and management, 2006-10; Hong Kong Polytechnic University, university distinguished chair professor of marketing, 2008. **Publications:** (With G.L. Urban) Management Science in Marketing, 1969; (with W.F. Massy and D.G. Morrison) Stochastic Models of Buying Behavior, 1970; (co-author) Consumer Behavior: Theoretical Sources, 1973; (with G.S. Day, G.J. Eskin and C.B. Weinberg) Cases in Computer and Model Assisted Marketing: Planning, 1973; (with G.J. Eskin) Cases in Computer and Model Assisted Marketing: Data Analysis, 1975. EDITOR:

(with G.L. Urban) Applications of Management Science in Marketing, 1970; Management Science: Marketing Management Models, 1971; (with D.R. Wittink) Proceedings of the First ORSA/TIMS Special Interest Conference on Market Measurement and Analysis, 1980; (with D.R. Wittink) Market Measurement and Analysis, 1980; (with G.S. Day) J. of Marketing: Fundamental Issues and Directions for Marketing, 1999; (with O.P. Heil) International Journal of Research in Marketing: Competition and Marketing, 2001. Contributor to periodicals. **Address:** Graduate School of Business, Stanford University, 518 Memorial Way, Stanford, CA 94305-5015, U.S.A. **Online address:** montgomery_david@gsb.stanford.edu

MONTGOMERY, Diane. British (born England), b. 1940. **Genres:** Education. **Career:** Gipsy Hill College of Teacher Education, senior lecturer, 1969-75; Kingston Polytechnic, principal lecturer and program director, 1975-89; Learning Difficulties Research Project, director, 1981-; Middlesex University, head of School of Teacher Education, professor of education and dean of faculty, 1989-94, professor emeritus, 1994-; NACE Journal Educating Able Children, editor-in-chief. Educator and writer. **Publications:** Study Skills: Teaching and Learning Strategies, 1983, rev. ed., 1991; (with A. Rawlings) Classroom Management, 1986; (co-author) Lifesavers, 1987; (with N. Hadfield) Practical Teacher Appraisal, 1989; (with N. Hadfield) Appraisal in the Primary Classroom, 1990; Managing Behaviour Problems, 1990; Children with Learning Difficulties, 1990; (contrib.) Improving Student Learning through Assessment and Evaluation, 1995; Educating the Able, 1996; Developmental Spelling: A Handbook, 1997; Spelling: Remedial Strategies, 1997; Reversing Lower Attainment: Developmental Curriculum Strategies for Overcoming Disaffection and Underachievement, 1998; (contrib.) Directions in Educational Psychology, 1998; Positive Teacher Appraisal through Classroom Observation, 1999; Spelling, Handwriting and Dyslexia: Overcoming the Barriers to Learning, 2006; The Smile, forthcoming. EDITOR: Able Underachievers, 2000; Helping Teachers Improve through Classroom Observation, 2001; Gifted Children with Special Educational Needs, 2003; Able, Gifted and Talented Underachievers, 2009; (ed.) Teaching Reading through Spelling, 1983-87. Contributor to books and periodicals. **Address:** Learning Difficulties Research Project, 21 Butt Ln., Maldon, Essex, EX CM9 5HD, England.

MONTGOMERY, Maureen E. New Zealander/British (born England) **Genres:** Social Work, Politics/Government, Literary Criticism And History, Social Sciences, History. **Career:** University of Sussex, School of American and English Studies, faculty; University of East Anglia, School of American and English Studies, faculty; West London Institute of Higher Education, lecturer in American studies, 1984-85; University of Canterbury, lecturer, 1986-92, senior lecturer, 1993-, head of department, 1996-99, associate professor. Writer. **Publications:** Civil Rights in the United States of America, 1986; Gilded Prostitution: Status, Money and Transatlantic Marriages, 1870-1914, 1989; Displaying Women: Spectacles of Leisure in Edith Wharton's New York, 1998; Whiteness and Politeness: The Racialization of Civilization, 1880-1930, forthcoming. Contributor to periodicals. **Address:** Department of American Studies, University of Canterbury, Rm. 503 History Bldg., PO Box 4800, Christchurch, 8140, New Zealand. **Online address:** maureen.montgomery@canterbury.ac.nz

MONTGOMERY, M(aurice) R(ichard). American (born United States), b. 1938. **Genres:** Natural History, Transportation, History. **Career:** Boston Globe, feature writer, 1973-; Harvard University, Nieman fellow, 1983-84. **Publications:** In Search of L.L. Bean, 1984, rev. ed., 1985; (with G.L. Foster) Field Guide to Airplanes of North America, 1984, 3rd ed., 2006; Saying Goodbye: A Memoir for Two Fathers, 1989; The Way of the Trout: An Essay on Anglers, Wild Fish, and Running Water, 1991; Many Rivers to Cross: Of Good Running Water, Native Trout, and the Remains of Wilderness, 1995; Jefferson and the Gun-Men: How the West was Almost Lost, 2000; Cow's Life: The Surprising History of Cattle and How the Black Angus Came to be Home on the Range, 2004. Contributor to periodicals. **Address:** Boston Globe, 135 Morrissey Blvd., PO Box 55819, Boston, MA 02205-5819, U.S.A.

MONTGOMERY, Scott L. American (born United States), b. 1951?. **Genres:** Sciences, Education. **Career:** University of Washington, Henry M. Jackson School of International Studies, task force instructor, energy consultant and adjunct faculty, Honors Program, adjunct faculty. Writer, geologist and technical translator. **Publications:** Minds for the Making: The Role of Science in American Education, 1750-1990, 1994; The Scientific Voice, 1996; The Moon and the Western Imagination, 1999; Science in Translation: Movements of Knowledge through Cultures and Time, 2000; The Chicago Guide to Communicating Science, 2003; Powers That Be: Global Energy for the Twenty-first Century and Beyond, 2010; Return to Babel: Does Science Need a Global Language?, forthcoming. **Address:** University of Chicago Press, 1427 E 60th St., Chicago, IL 60637-2902, U.S.A. **Online address:** scottlm@u.washington.edu

MONTGOMERY, Sy. American (born United States), b. 1958. **Genres:** Adult Non-fiction, Children's Non-fiction. **Career:** Courier-News, science writer, 1980-84; freelance writer, 1984-; Brookfield Conservation Park, research associate, 1984; Antioch University New England, Graduate School, Center for Tropical Ecology and Conservation, associate. **Publications:** Walking with the Great Apes: Jane Goodall, Dian Fossey, Biruté Galdikas, 1991; Nature's Everyday Mysteries: A Field Guide to the World in Your Backyard (essays), 1993 as The Curious Naturalist: Nature's Everyday Mysteries, 2000; Spell of the Tiger: The Man-Eaters of Sundarbans, 1995; Seasons of the Wild: A Year of Nature's Magic and Mysteries (essays), 1995; Journey of the Pink Dolphins: An Amazon Quest, 2000; Search for the Golden Moon Bear: Science and Adventure in Southeast Asia, 2002, The Wild Out Your Window: Exploring Nature Near At Hand, 2002; The Good Good Pig: The Extraordinary Life of Christopher Hogwood, 2006; Birdology: Adventures with A Pack of Hens, a Peck of Pigeons, Cantankerous Crows, Fierce Falcons, Hip Hop Parrots, Baby Hummingbirds and One Murderously Big Living Dinosaur, 2010. FOR CHILDREN: The Snake Scientist, 1999; The Man-Eating Tigers of Sundarbans, 2001; Encantado: Pink Dolphin of the Amazon, 2002; Golden Moon Bear: Science and Adventure in the Asian Tropics, 2004; The Tarantula Scientist, 2004; Quest for the Tree Kangaroo: An Expedition to the Cloud Forest of New Guinea, 2006; Saving the Ghost of the Mountain: An Expedition Among Snow Leopards in Mongolia, 2009; Kakapo Rescue: Saving the World's Strangest Parrot, 2010. Contributor to periodicals. **Address:** The Lavin Agency, 222 3rd St., Ste. 1130, Cambridge, MA 02142, U.S.A. **Online address:** sy@authorwire.com

MONTIER, Jean-Pierre. French (born France), b. 1956. **Genres:** Art/Art History, Photography, Literary Criticism And History. **Career:** Universite Rennes 2, teacher, 1989-, vice president in charge of cultural policy, professor. Writer. **Publications:** (Trans.) R. Taylor, L'art sans art d'Henri Cartier-Bresson (title means: 'Henri Cartier-Bresson and the Artless Art'), 1996; Josef Koudelka: L'epreuve Totalitaire, 2004; Revoir Henri Cartier-Bresson, 2009; Regarde!: Colette et Mathurin Meheut, 2010. Contributor to periodicals. **Address:** Universite Rennes 2-Haute Bretagne, Campus Villejean, Place du Recteur Le Moal, Rennes, 35043, France. **Online address:** jean-pierre.montier@uhb.fr

MONTOYA, Peter. American (born United States), b. 1968. **Genres:** Business/Trade/Industry, Marketing. **Career:** Peter Montoya Inc., president; Personal Branding Magazine, founder, president and publisher, 1997-; MarketingLibrary.net, creator, 1997-. Writer. **Publications:** (With T. Vandehey) Brand Called You: Personal Marketing for Financial Advisors, 1999; The Brand Called You: The Ultimate Brand-building and Business Development Handbook to Transform Anyone into an Indispensable Personal Brand, 1999; (with T. Vandehey) The Personal Branding Phenomenon: Realize Greater Influence, Explosive Income Growth and Rapid Career Advancement by Applying the Branding Techniques of Michael, Martha & Oprah, 2002; Brand Called You: The Step-by-step Guide to Branding and Business Development for Solopreneurs, 2003; (with T. Vandehey) Brand Called You: Create a Personal Brand that Wins Attention and Grows Your Business, 2009. **Address:** c/o Author Mail, Personal Branding Press, 1540 S Lyon St., Santa Ana, CA 92705-4613, U.S.A. **Online address:** petermontoya@petermontoya.com

MONTPARKER, Carol. American (born United States) **Genres:** Music, Biography. **Career:** Writer, 1976-; Concert pianist, piano teacher, Clavier and senior editor, musician. **Publications:** Anatomy of a New York Debut Recital: A Chronicle, 1981; A Pianist's Landscape, 1998; Polly and the Piano, 2004; The Blue Piano and Other Stories, 2004. **Address:** c/o Author Mail, Amadeus Press, 512 Newark Pompton Tpke., Pompton Plains, NJ 07444-1900, U.S.A. **Online address:** cmontparker@yahoo.com

MONTPETIT, Charles. Canadian (born Canada), b. 1958. **Genres:** Young Adult Fiction, Children's Fiction, Adult Non-fiction, Cartoons, Young Adult Non-fiction, Civil Liberties/Human Rights, Essays, Graphic Novels, Humor/Satire, Illustrations, Mystery/Crime/Suspense, Novellas/Short Stories, Novels, Sex. **Career:** Writer and art director. **Publications:** FOR CHILDREN

, coordinator; Landmarks ctions, board chair, 2011-. ducer. **Publications:** (With has Present and Past, 1998; w Yorkers: The Schomburg ergence of African-American d of Prayer: A Celebration of e) Fighting for America: Black l, 2005; (with H. Dodson and -American Journey, 2009. Con- g Center for Research in Black alcolm X Blvd., New York, NY e@fightingforamerica.org

Canada), b. 1952. **Genres:** Crimi- ersity of British Columbia, teacher. rdship's Arsenal, 1985; Enemies of Chairs, 2000; Waiting for the Lady, on Magic, 2005. LAND OF SMILES Bewitching Smile, 1993; A Haunting RIME NOVELS: Spirit House, 2008; fort Zone, 1995; The Big Weird, 1996; ttaya 24/7, 2004; The Risk of Infidelity alk, 1998. **Address:** Bangkok, Thailand. m

MOORE, Christopher.

orn United States), b. 1940. **Genres:** Poli- ersity of New Hampshire, Department of r, Institute for Policy and Social Science Re- y of New Hampshire Survey Center, founder lup Poll, vice president, managing editor, se- sity of New Hampshire Carey Institute, senior ntist. **Publications:** The Superpollsters: How te Public Opinion in America, 1992, 2nd ed., M.D. Larsen) Demand and Needs Assessment Drugs among Native American Indians Living akota, 1998; (with A. Bhardwaj and M.D. Larsen) e Abuse Indicator Study for Treatment Resource Steal an Election: The Inside Story of How George Network Miscalled the 2000 Election and Changed 006; The Opinion Makers: An Insider Exposes the 2008. Contributor to journals and periodicals. **Ad-** , 73 Main St., Durham, NH 03824, U.S.A. **Online** wmoore.us

American (born United States), b. 1955. **Genres:** No- Information Science/Computers, Theology/Religion, oirs, Humor/Satire. **Career:** United Press Intl., reporter, ings Films, filmmaker, 1979-81; Danceteller, dancer and iversity of Pennsylvania, Wharton School of Business, r Applied Research, editor, 1985-87; Pennsylvania State or of creative writing, 1990-2007; Ohio University, profes- r of creative writing; Brevitymag.com, founder and editor. e Emperor's Virtual Clothes: The Naked Truth about Inter- 5; The Accidental Buddhist: Mindfulness, Enlightenment, 1997; Toothpick Men: Short Stories, 1998; (ed.) Sudden nmoth Book of Miniscule Fiction, 2003; Truth of the Matter: Creative Nonfiction, 2007; Between Panic and Desire, 2008; sonal Essay: A Guide for Writing and Publishing Creative ; Lit from Within: Contemporary Masters on the Art and 2011; The Mindful Writer, 2012. **Address:** Department of iversity, 353 Ellis Hall, Athens, OH 45701, U.S.A. **Online** 4@ohio.edu

American (born United States), b. 1946. **Genres:** Novels, eer: Integrated Technology Research Corp., director, 1997-. ons: (With D. McClaran) Idaho Whitewater: The Complete 9; Price Guide to Rock & Roll Collectibles, 1993; Travel ing Agreements, 1997; Seduced by a Mile: How Frequent Exploited to Outflank Corporate America and Increase Air- (with J. Pizzo) Collector's Guide to Bubble Bath Contain- ers: Identification & Values, 1998; (with J. Hilton) Rock-n-Roll Treasures: Identification & Value Guide, 1999; The Wine Chronicles: Writing Your Own Fine Wine Book, 2002; (trans.) Nisioisin, Kubikiri Cycle, 2008; (trans.) T. Okazaki, Afro Samurai, 2 vols., 2008. **Address:** Integrated Technology Research Corp., 913 N Market St., Ste. 230, PO Box 1790, Wilmington, DE 19801-3019, U.S.A. **Online address:** moorege@aol.com

MOORE, Gwyneth. *See* **VERYAN, Patricia.**

MOORE, Hal G. American (born United States), b. 1929. **Genres:** Mathematics/Statistics. **Career:** Salt Lake City Public Schools, teacher, 1952-53; Carbon Jr. College, instructor, 1953-55; U.S. Naval Ordnance Test Station, mathematician, 1957; Purdue University, instructor, 1957-61; Brigham Young University, assistant professor, 1961-67, associate professor, 1967-71, associate department chair, 1986-89, professor of mathematics, 1971-95, professor emeritus, 1995-. Writer. **Publications:** Pre-Calculus Mathematics, 1973, 2nd ed., 1977; (with J. Higgins) University Calculus, 1969; (with A. Yaqub) Elementary Linear Algebra with Applications, 1980, 2nd ed. as A First Course in Linear Algebra, 1991, 3rd ed. as A First Course in Linear Algebra with Applications, 1998; College Algebra and Trigonometry, 1984; Linear Algebra: A First Course, 1992, 3rd ed., 1998. **Address:** Department of Mathematics, Brigham Young University, 276 TMCB, Provo, UT 84602, U.S.A. **Online address:** mooreh@math.byu.edu

MOORE, Harold G(regory). American (born United States), b. 1922. **Genres:** History, Military/Defense/Arms Control, Human Relations/Parenting. **Career:** Ski Resort, executive vice-president. Writer. **Publications:** (With J.M. Tuten) Building a Volunteer Army: The Fort Ord Contribution, 1975; (with J.L. Galloway) We Were Soldiers Once and Young: Ia Drang-The Battle That Changed the War in Vietnam, 1992, rev. ed., 2004; (foreword) To Fight with Intrepidity: The Complete History of the U.S. Army Rangers, 1622 to Present, 1998; (with J.L. Galloway) We Were Soldiers Once-- and Young: Ia Drang, the Battle that Changed the War in Vietnam, 2004; (with J.L. Galloway) We are Soldiers Still: A Journey Back to the Battlefields of Vietnam, 2008. Contributor to periodicals. **Address:** PO Box 118, Crested Butte, CO 81224, U.S.A.

MOORE, Ishbel (Lindsay). Canadian/Scottish (born Scotland), b. 1954. **Genres:** Young Adult Fiction, Children's Fiction, Romance/Historical, Science Fiction/Fantasy. **Career:** Writer. **Publications:** The Summer of the Hand, 1994; The Medal, 1994; Branch of Talking Teeth, 1995; Xanthe's Pyramid, 1998; Daughter, 1999; Annilea, 2000; Kitchen Sink Concert, 2002. DOLINA TRILOGY: Dolina May, 1997; Dolina's Grad, 1998; Dolina's Decision, 2000. OTHERS: Music for Its Own Sake, 1997; (with M. Branningan as Alexandra Duncan) Rock of Ages (adult romance), 2001. Contributor to periodicals. **Address:** 1086 Peel St., St. Andrews, MB R1A 3W5, Canada. **Online address:** ishbel@ilmoorebooks.ca

MOORE, James A. American (born United States), b. 1965?. **Genres:** Novels, Novellas/Short Stories, Ghost Writer, Horror. **Career:** Author. **Publications:** The Color of Her Eyes, 1995; Get of Genris Tribe book: Of Axe and Claw, 1995; (with K.A. Murphy) House of Secrets, 1995; Werewolf: Hell-Storm, 1996; The King's Folly, 1997; Blood Magic: Secrets of Thaumaturgy, 1999; (ed.) Animal, Agricultural and Food Processing Wastes: Proceedings of the Eighth International Symposium, October 9-11, 2000, Des Moines, Iowa, 2000; Under the Overtree, 2000; Fireworks, 2001; Serenity Falls, 2002; Buffy the Vampire Slayer: Chaos Bleeds, 2003; Possession, 2004; Newbies, 2004; Rabid Growth, 2005; Blood Red, 2005; (with C. Golden) Bloodstained Oz, 2006; Deeper, 2007; (with J. Strand) The Haunted Forest Tour, 2007; Vendetta, 2009; Harvest Moon, 2009; Cherry Hill, 2010; Smile No More, 2011; Subject Seven, 2011. SERENITY FALLS SERIES: Writ in Blood, 2005; The Pack, 2005; Dark Carnival, 2005. **Address:** c/o Author Mail, Dorchester Publishing Company Inc., 200 Madison Ave., Ste. 2000, New York, NY 10016, U.S.A. **Online address:** horrors@aol.com

MOORE, James T(almadge). American (born United States), b. 1936. **Genres:** History, Theology/Religion, Social Sciences, Biography, Autobiography/Memoirs, History, Natural History, Earth Sciences, Earth Sciences. **Career:** North Harris College South, history faculty, 1981-98; Our Lady of Walsingham Catholic Church, co-founder, pastor, 1996-; Roman Catholic church, pastor. Writer. **Publications:** Indian and Jesuit: A Seventeenth-Century Encounter, 1982; Through Fire and Flood: The Catholic Church in Frontier Texas, 1836-1900, 1992; Acts of Faith: The Catholic Church in Texas, AND YOUNG ADULTS: Moi ou la planete, 1973; Temps perdu, 1984, trans. as Lost Time, 1990; Temps mort, 1988; Copie carbone, 1993; (co-author) 6 decembre, 1995; (with H. Rathjen) December 6: From the Montreal Massacre to Gun Control: The Inside Story, 1999; La grande menace, 2005, trans. as The Great Menace, 2006 and La gran amenaza, 2008. OTHER: Guide de tarification 1991, 1990; Liberte d'expression: guide d'utilisation, 2003. EDITOR and CONTRIBUTOR: La premiere fois, 1991; The First Time, 1995. Contributes of articles to books. **Address:** 3013 rue Holt, Montreal, QC H1Y 1R2, Canada. **Online address:** cmontpetit@hotmail.com

MONZINI, Paola. Italian (born Italy), b. 1965?. **Genres:** Criminology/True Crime, Sex, Biography. **Career:** United National Interregional Crime and Justice Research Institute (UNICRI), associate researcher; Direzione Investigativa Antimafia, consultant. Writer. **Publications:** Gruppi criminali a napoli e marsiglia: la delinquenza organizzata nella storia di due città: 1820- 1990, 1999; Il mercato delle donne: prostituzione, tratta e sfruttamento, 2002. **Address:** Zed Books Ltd., 7 Cynthia St., London, N1 9JF, United Kingdom. **Online address:** pao.monz@libero.it

MONZÓ, Quim. Spanish (born Spain), b. 1952. **Genres:** Novels, Novellas/Short Stories, Essays, Plays/Screenplays, History. **Career:** Journalist and graphic artist. **Publications:** SHORT STORIES: (with B. Mesquida) Self Service, 1977; Uf, va dir ell, 1978; Olivetti, Moulinex, Chaffoteaux et Maury, 1980; L'illa de Maians, 1985; El perquè de tot plegat, 1993; Guadalajara, 1996; Vuitanta-sis contes, 1999; El millor dels mons, 2001; Tres Nadals, 2003. NOVELS: L'udol del griso al caire de les clavegueres, 1976; Benzina (Gasoline), 1983; La magnitud de la tragèdia, 1989. OTHER: El dia del senyor, 1984; (with R. Barnils and J. Vendrell) Lloro, el moro, el mico i el senyor de Puerto Rico, 1987; *Zzzzzzzz*, 1987; La maleta turca, 1990; Hotel Intercontinental, 1991; No plantaré cap arbre, 1994; Gasolina, 1995; Del tot indefens davant dels hostils imperis alienígenes, 1998; Tot és mentida, 2000; El tema del tema, 2003; (foreword) Contes, arguments i estirabots, 2003; Catorze ciutats comptant-hi Brooklyn, 2004; Mil cretins, 2007. OTHER: Esplendor i glòria de la Internacional Papanates, 2010. Contributor to books. **Address:** c/o Author Mail, Quaderns Crema, Muntaner, 462, Barcelona, E-08006, Spain. **Online address:** benavent@fastmail.fm

MOOD, Terry Ann. *See* **LEOPOLD, Terry Ann Mood.**

MOODIE, Craig. American (born United States), b. 1956. **Genres:** Novels, Children's Fiction, Novellas/Short Stories, Young Adult Fiction. **Career:** Children's book author. **Publications:** A Sailor's Valentine: Stories, 1994; Our Perfect Youth: Stories, 1998; A Man of Many Skies, 2000; The Sea Singer (for middle-grade readers), 2005; Salt Luck, 2005; Seaborn (for young adults), 2008; Into the Trap (for middle-grade readers), 2011. **Address:** c/o Andrea Cascardi, Transatlantic Literary Agency Inc., 2 Bloor St. E, Toronto, ON M4W 1A8, Canada. **Online address:** contact@moodiebooks.com

MOODY, Bill. American (born United States), b. 1941. **Genres:** Novellas/Short Stories, Mystery/Crime/Suspense, Music. **Career:** Jazz drummer, 1963-; freelance writer, 1968-; disc jockey, 1989-97; University of Nevada, English instructor; Sonoma State University, creative writing instructor. **Publications:** The Jazz Exiles: American Musicians Abroad (nonfiction), 1993. MYSTERIES: Solo Hand, 1994; Death of a Tenor Man, 1995; Sound of the Trumpet, 1997; Bird Lives!, 1999; Looking for Chet Baker: An Evan Horne Mystery, 2002; Shades of Blue, 2008. Contributor to periodicals. **Address:** c/o Philip Spitzer, Philip G. Spitzer Literary Agency, 50 Talmage Farm Ln., East Hampton, NY 11937-4300, U.S.A. **Online address:** solohand27ats@earthlink.net

MOODY, David. British (born England), b. 1970?. **Genres:** Horror, Novels. **Career:** Writer. **Publications:** Straight to You, 1996; Trust, 2005; Autumn: The Human Condition, 2005. THE HATER SERIES: Hater, 2006; Dog Blood, 2010; Them or Us, 2011. AUTUMN SERIES: Autumn, 2005; Autumn: The City, 2005, new ed. 2011; Autumn: Purification, 2005, new ed. 2011; Autumn: Disintegration, 2011; Autumn: Aftermath, 2012. **Address:** Thomas Dunne Books, 175 5th Ave., New York, NY 10010, U.S.A. **Online address:** davidmoody@djmoody.co.uk

MOODY, Fred. (Spike Mcgee). American (born United States), b. 1949. **Genres:** Adult Non-fiction, Bibliography, Information Science/Computers, Technology. **Career:** Ardis Publishers, editor, 1974-80; Melmoth Typesetting, owner, 1980-86; Seattle Weekly, staff writer, 1983-, managing editor; Bainbridge Foundation, secretary, 1988-90, University of Washington Extension, faculty, 1989-92; National Institute for Technology in Liberal Education, program officer for libraries and scholarly communications; Rice University Press, editor-in-chief, 2007-10; Pacific Northwest, reporter and writer; Seattle Weekly, freelance writer, staff writer, news editor, managing editor. **Publications:** Ten Russian Bibliographies of Twentieth-Century Literature, 1977; Fighting Chance: An NFL Season with the Seattle Sea Hawks, 1989; I Sing the Body Electronic: A Year with Microsoft on the Multimedia Frontier, 1995; The Visionary Position: The Inside Story of the Digital Dreamers Who Are Making Virtual Reality a Reality, 1999; Seattle And the Demons of Ambition: A Love Story, 2003. **Address:** c/o Nat Sobel, Sobel-Weber Associates, 146 E 19th St., New York, NY 10003-2404, U.S.A. **Online address:** fmoody@nitle.org

MOODY, Martha. (Martha Moody Jacobs). American (born United States), b. 1955. **Genres:** Novels. **Career:** Freelance author, 2001-. **Publications:** Best Friends (novel), 2001; The Office of Desire (novel), 2007; Sometimes Mine, 2009. Contributor to periodicals and journals. **Address:** c/o Elisabeth Weed, Weed Literary L.L.C., 27 W 20th St., New York, NY 10011, U.S.A. **Online address:** info@marthamoody.net

MOODY, Peter R(ichard). American (born United States), b. 1943. **Genres:** Area Studies, Politics/Government. **Career:** University of Notre Dame, Department of Government and International Studies, assistant professor, 1971-77, associate professor, 1977-83, director of graduate studies, 1978-85, professor, 1983-, Asian Studies Program, director, 1973-2000; Summer Studies Program in Korea, Institute for East Asian Studies, visiting fellow, 1987; San Francisco State University, Center for U.S.-China Policy Studies, research associate, 2006-. Writer. **Publications:** The Politics of the Eighth Central Committee of the Communist Party of China, 1973; Opposition and Dissent in Contemporary China, 1977; Chinese Politics after Mao: Development and Liberalization, 1976 to 1983, 1983; Political Opposition in Post-Confucian Society, 1988; Political Change on Taiwan: A Study of Ruling Party Adaptability, 1992; Tradition and Modernization in China and Japan, 1995; Conservative Thought in Contemporary China, 2007. **Address:** Department of Political Science, University of Notre Dame, 534 Flanner Hall, Notre Dame, IN 46556-0762, U.S.A. **Online address:** peter.r.moody.1@nd.edu

MOON, Jeremy. British (born England), b. 1955. **Genres:** Politics/Government, Business/Trade/Industry. **Career:** University of Keele, professor of political science, 1981-82; University of Strathclyde, postdoctoral research fellow in government, 1982-85; University of Western Australia, professor of political science, 1985-, chair; Ladbroke House, School of Law, Governance and Information Management, head; Nottingham University Business School, International Centre for Corporate Social Responsibility, director, professor of corporate social responsibility; McGill University, visiting professor in political science; Toronto University, visiting professor in political science; European University Institute, Jean Monnet research fellow. Writer. **Publications:** The Salience and Anatomy of Political Issues: Britain and Europe, 1945-1963, 1985; European Integration in British Politics, 1950-1963: A Study of Issue Change, 1985; (with J.J. Richardson) Unemployment in the United Kingdom: Politics and Policies, 1985; (with L. Bekemans and M. Glagow) Beyond Market and State: Alternative Approaches to Meeting Societal Demands, 1989; Innovative Leadership in Democracy: Policy Change Under Thatcher, 1993; (with A. Crane and D. Matten) Corporations and Citizenship, 2008. EDITOR: (with B. Stone) Power and Freedom in Modern Politics, 2002; (with C. Sharman) Australian Politics and Government: The Commonwealth, The States, and The Territories, 2003; (with M. Orlitzky and G. Whelan) Corporate Governance and Business Ethics, 2010; (with J.P. Gond) Corporate Social Responsibility: Critical Perspectives on Business and Management, 2011. **Address:** Nottingham University Business School, Jubilee Campus, Nottingham, NT NG8 1BB, England. **Online address:** jeremy.moon@nottingham.ac.uk

MOON, Nicola. British (born England), b. 1952. **Genres:** Children's Fiction, Animals/Pets. **Career:** Research assistant in cancer research, 1973-74; secondary schoolteacher, 1974-79. Writer. **Publications:** At the Beginning of a Pig, 1994; Jodie's Colours, 1994; Lucy's Picture, 1995; Penguins in the Fridge, 1995; Mouse Finds a Seed, 1996; Something Special, 1997; Billy's Sunflower, 1997; Happy Birthday Amelia, 1999; JJ Rabbit and the Monster, 2000; My Most Favourite Thing, 2000; Alligator Tails and Crocodile Cakes, 2000; (with C. Thompson) Peth gorau yn y byd, 2000; My Most Favorite Thing, 2001; Planets, 2002; Mouse Tells the Time, 2002; Noisy Neighbors, 2004; Tick-Tock, Drip-Drop!: A Bedtime Story, 2004; Margarine and Marbles, 2006. Contributor to periodicals. **Address:** David Higham Associates Ltd., 5-8 Lower John St., Golden Sq., London, GL W1F 9HA, England.

MOON, **Susan.** (Susan Ichi Su Moon). American (born United States), b. 1942. **Genres:** Novellas/Short Stories, Humor/Satire. **Career:** Open Books Press, founding editor, 1978-94; Western States Legal Foundation, board director, 1984-90; Ragdale Foundation, board director, 1988-98; St. Mary's College, writing instructor, 1988-95; Turning Wheel, editor, 1990-; National Endowment for the Arts, creative writing fellow, 1993; Blue Mountain Center, residency fellow, 1990, 1993, 1996. **Publications:** Risking Peace, 1984; (as Susan Ichi Su Moon) Life and Letters of Tofu Roshi, 1988; This is Getting Old: Zen Thoughts On Aging With Humor and Dignity, 2010. EDITOR: (with L. Friedman) Being Bodies: Buddhist Women on the Paradox of Embodiment, 1997; (foreword) Warm Smiles from Cold Mountain, 2nd ed., 1999; Not Turning Away: The Practice of Engaged Buddhism, 2004. Contributor of stories and articles to periodicals. **Address:** 1631 Grant St., Berkeley, CA 94703-1375, U.S.A. **Online address:** sue@bpf.org

MOON, **Susan Ichi Su.** *See* **MOON**, **Susan.**

MOONEN, **Rick.** American (born United States), b. 1956. **Genres:** Food And Wine. **Career:** La Cote Basque, saucier, 1980; RM and Branzini, owner and executive chef, 2002-05; RM Seafood, owner and executive chef, 2005-; Food & Wine Magazine, contributing editor. **Publications:** (With R. Finamore) Fish without a Doubt: The Cook's Essential Companion, 2008. **Address:** Mandalay Bay Resort and Casino, RM Seafood, 3950 Las Vegas Blvd. S, Las Vegas, NV 89119, U.S.A.

MOONEY, **Brian C.** American (born United States) **Genres:** Biography, Autobiography/Memoirs, Politics/Government, History, Adult Non-fiction. **Career:** Boston Globe, reporter, 1988-, columnist, globe staff; Boston Herald, reporter, Spotlight Team, political columnist; Lowell Sun, reporter; Medford Daily Mercury, reporter. **Publications:** (With M. Kranish and N.J. Easton) John F. Kerry: The Complete Biography by the Boston Globe Reporters Who Know him Best, 2004. **Address:** Boston Globe, 135 Morrissey Blvd., PO Box 52438, Boston, MA 02125, U.S.A. **Online address:** bmooney@globe.com

MOONEY, **Jonathan.** American (born United States) **Genres:** How-to Books, Psychology. **Career:** Project Eye-to-Eye (a mentoring and advocacy group for students with learning differences), co-founder and president. Writer, educator and public speaker. **Publications:** (With D. Cole) Learning Outside the Lines: Two Ivy League Students with Learning Disabilities and ADHD Give You the Tools for Academic Success and Educational Revolution, 2000; The Short Bus: A Journey Beyond Normal (memoir; travelogue), 2007. **Address:** Henry Holt and Company Inc., 175 5th Ave., New York, NY 10010, U.S.A. **Online address:** jonathanmooney@earthlink.net

MOONEY, **Robert.** American (born United States) **Genres:** Adult Non-fiction. **Career:** Washington College, assistant professor of English and creative writing, associate professor of English and creative writing; O'Neill Literary House, director. Novelist. **Publications:** Father of the Man, 2002. Contributor of short fiction to periodicals. **Address:** Department of English, Washington College, 228 Smith, 300 Washington Ave., Chestertown, MD 21620, U.S.A. **Online address:** rmooney2@washcoll.edu

MOONMAN, **Eric.** British (born England), b. 1929. **Genres:** Administration/Management, Politics/Government, Business/Trade/Industry. **Career:** Daily Mirror, journalist, 1954-56; British Institute of Management, human relations adviser, 1956-62; Victoria University of Manchester, senior research fellow in management sciences, 1962-66; British Parliament, parliamentary private secretary, 1968-70; Natural History Museum Development Trust, director, 1990-91; City University, visiting professor, health/marketing, 1990, honorary visiting professor, 2006-07, professor; International Red Cross, consultant, 1992-95; ERG Radio group of stations, chair, 1993-2001; Zionist Federation of Great Britain, president, 2001-; University of Liverpool, senior fellow; Stag FM, director; DMG Radio, chairman; Christian Friends of Israel, Geoffrey Smith Director; Radio Essex, director. **Publications:** The Manager and the Organization, 1960; Communication in an Expanding Organization: A Case Study in Action Research, 1969; Communication of Objectives in an Expanding Company, 19[illegible]; Reluctant Partnership: A Critical Study of the Relationship Between Government and Industry, 1970; (with D. Alexander) Business and the Arts, 1974; Alternative Government, 1984; Learning to Live in the Violent Society, 2005. EDITOR: Science and Technology in European, 1968; Press: A Case for Commitment, 1969; The British Computer Industry and Industrial Innovation: The Implications of the Parliamentary Select Committee, 1971; Violent Society, 1987. **Address:** Zionist Federation of Great Britain and Ireland, PO BOx 1948, London, GL WC1N 3XX, England. **Online address:** emoonman@soi.city.ac.uk

MOORCOCK, **Michael (John).** Also writes as Bill Barclay, Edward P. Bradbury, James Colvin. American/British (born England), b. 1939. **Genres:** Novels, Science Fiction/Fantasy, Novellas/Short Stories, Ghost Writer, Young Adult Non-fiction, Graphic Novels. **Career:** Tarzan Adventures, editor, 1956-58; Amalgamated Press, editor and writer, 1959-61; Liberal Party, editor and pamphleteer, 1962-63; New Worlds, editor, 1964-71, 1976-80. **Publications:** The Stealer of Souls and Other Stories, 1963; Stormbringer, 1965; The Fire Clown, 1965 as The Winds of Limbo, 1969; The Sundered Worlds, 1965 as The Blood Red Game, 1970; The LSD Dossier, 1966; (as Bill Barclay) Printer's Devil, 1966; (as Bill Barclay) Somewhere in the Night, 1966; (as James Colvin) The Deep Fix, 1966; The Twilight Man, 1966 as The Shores of Death, 1970; The Wrecks of Time, 1967 as The Rituals of Infinity, 1971; The Jewel in the Skull, 1967; Sorcerer's Amulet, 1968 as The Mad God's Amulet, 1969; Sword of the Dawn, 1968; The Ice Schooner, 1969; Behold the Man, 1969; The Final Programme, 1969; The Time Dweller (stories), 1969; The Secret of the Runestaff, 1969 as The Runestaff, 1969; The Singing Citadel (stories), 1970; The Eternal Champion, 1970; The Chinese Agent, 1970; Phoenix in Obsidian, 1970 as The Silver Warriors, 1973; A Cure for Cancer, 1971; The Warlord of the Air, 1971; (ed. with L. Jones) The Nature of the Castrophe, 1971; The Knight, Queen, King of the Swords (trilogy), 3 vols., 1971; The Sleeping Sorceress, 1971 as The Vanishing Tower, 1977; An Alien Heat, 1972; The Dancers at the End of Time, 1972; Breakfast in the Ruins: A Novel of Inhumanity, 1972; The English Assassin: A Romance of Entropy, 1972; Elric of Melniboné as The Dreaming City, 1972; The Jade Man's Eyes, 1973; The Bull and the Spear, 1973; Count Brass, 1973; The Chronicle of Prince Corum and the Silver Hand, 1973; The Champion of Garathorm, 1973; The Oak and the Ram, 1973; The Chronicles of Castle Brass, 1973 as Count Brass, 1993; (with P. Druillet) Elric: The Return to Melnibone, 1973; The Land Leviathan: A New Scientific Romance, 1974; The Hollow Lands, 1974; The Sword and the Stallion, 1974; (with P. James) The Distant Suns, 1975; The Quest for Tanelorn, 1975; The Adventures of Una Persson and Catherine Cornelius in the Twentieth Century, 1976; The End of All Songs, 1976; Moorcock's Book of Martyrs (stories), 1976 as Dying for Tomorrow, 1978; The Lives and Times of Jerry Cornelius, 1976; Legends from the End of Time, 1976; The Sailor on the Seas of Fate, 1976; (with M. Butterworth) The Time of the Hawklords, 1976; The Transformation of Miss Mavis Ming, 1977 as Messiah at the End of Time, 1978; The Weird of the White Wolf, 1977; (ed. and intro.) England Invaded: A Collection of Fantasy Fiction, 1977; The Bane of the Black Sword, 1977; Sojan (for children), 1977; The Condition of Muzak: A Jerry Cornelius Novel, 1977; Gloriana, or, the Unfulfill'd Queen: Being a Romance, 1978; The Real Life Mr. Newman, 1979; (with H.V. Chaykin) The Swords of Heaven, the Flowers of Hell, 1979; My Experiences in the Third World War, 1980; The Great Rock 'n' Roll Swindle, 1980; Byzantium Endures, 1981; The Entropy Tango: A Comic Romance, 1981; The War Hound and the World's Pain, 1981; The Steel Tsar, 1981; The Brothel in Rosenstrasse: An Extravagant Tale, 1982; The Golden Barge: A Fable, 1984; The Laughter of Carthage, 1984; The Opium General and Other Stories, 1984; Elric at the End of Time (stories), 1984; (co-author) Exploring Fantasy Worlds: Essays on Fantastic Literature, 1985; (ed. and trans.) The City in the Autumn Stars: Being a Continuation of the Story of the Von Bek Family and Its Association With Lucifer, Prince of Darkness, and the Cure for the World's Pain, 1986; The Dragon in the Sword: Being the Third and Final Story in the History of John Daker, the Eternal Champion, 1986; Wizardry and Wild Romance: A Study of Epic Fantasy, 1987; Mother London, 1989; (with J. Cawthorn) Fantasy: The 100 Best Books, 1988; The Fortress of the Pearl, 1989; Casablanca (stories), 1989; The Revenge of the Rose, 1991; New Worlds, 1991; Jerusalem Commands, 1992; Earl Aubec and Other Stories, 1993; (ed.) The Time Machine, 1993; Cornelius Quartet, 1993; A Cornelius Calendar, 1993; Lunching with the Anti-Christ: A Family History: 1925-2015, 1995; Blood: A Southern Fantasy, 1995; Queens of Deliria, 1995; Fabulous Harbours: A Sequel to Blood, 1995; War amongst the Angels: An Autobiographical Story, 1996; Michael Moorcock's Multiverse, 1999; (with S. Constantine) Silverheart, 2000; King of the City, 2000; The Dreamthief's Daughter: A Tale of the Albino, 2001; Firing the Cathedral, 2002; The History of the Runestaff, 2003; Skrayling Tree: The Albino in America, 2003; [illegible] A Memoir, 2004; New Worlds: An Anthology, 2004; (contrib.) Bug Jack Barron, 2004; (with S. Gabriel) Jerry Cornell's Comic Capers, 2005; The White Wolf's Son: The Albino Underground, 2005; The Vengeance [illegible]
Metatemporal Detective, 2007; Elric: The Making of a S[illegible]
the Beast, 2007; Elric: To Rescue Tanelorn, 200[illegible]
2008; Elric: The Sleeping Sorceress, 2008; Elri[illegible]
of Michael Moorcock, 2009; Elric: In the Dream[illegible]
The Jewel in the Skull, 2010; Hawkmoon: The [illegible]
Elric: Swords and Roses, 2010; Into the Media W[illegible]
fiction, 1956-2006, 2010; Doctor Who: Eleventh Do[illegible]
of the Terraphiles, 2010; Modem Times 2.0, 2011; Th[illegible]
(with C. Roberson) Elric: The Balance Lost, vol. I-II, [illegible]
Swarm, 2012; (with M. Hodder and P. Magrs) Zenith Li[illegible]
A. Kausch) London Peculiar and Other Nonfiction, 2012. [illegible]
SERIES AS EDWARD P. BRADBURY: Warriors of Mar[illegible]
Mars, 1965; Barbarians of Mars, 1965. Contributor to peric[illegible]
c/o Howard Morhaim, Howard Morhaim Literary Agency Inc[illegible]
St., Brooklyn, NY 11201-3371, U.S.A.

MOORE, **Alison.** American (born United States), b. 1951. **Gen**[illegible]
Novellas/Short Stories, Young Adult Fiction. **Career:** Arts Reac[illegible]
tions, director, 1991; University of Arizona, MFA Creative Writing [illegible]
assistant professor of English/creative writing. Writer. **Publication**[illegible]
Spaces between Emergencies: Stories, 1992; Synonym for Love [illegible]
1995; The Middle of Elsewhere, 2006; Almost Egypt, forthcoming[illegible]
dress: 351 Cowpoke Canyon, Driftwood, TX 78619, U.S.A. **Online add**[illegible]
alison@alisonmoorebooks.com

MOORE, **Allan F.** British (born England), b. 1954. **Genres:** Music. **Career** Thames Valley University, senior lecturer in music, 1985-99; University of Surrey, Department of Music and Sound Recording, professor of popular music, 2000-, head of music research, Postgraduate Research Programme, director; University of London, Royal Holloway, faculty; City University, faculty; Twentieth-Century Music, founding co-editor. **Publications:** Rock: The Primary Text, 1993, 2nd ed., 2001; Beatles: Sgt. Pepper's Lonely Hearts Club Band, 1997; (ed.) Cambridge Companion to Blues and Gospel Music, 2002; (ed.) Analyzing Popular Music, 2003; Aqualung, 2004; (ed.) Critical Essays in Popular Musicology, 2007; Library of Essays in Popular Music, 8 vols., 2011; Song Means: Analysing and Interpreting Recorded Popular Song, 2012; No Better than the Real Thing: An Encounter with the Music of U2, forthcoming; From Worcester City Beteg ar Douar: An Exploration of Anglo-Celtic Folk Song, forthcoming. Contributor to journals. **Address:** Department of Music and Sound Recording, University of Surrey, Rm. 42 PA, Guildford, SR GU2 7XH, England. **Online address:** allan.moore@surrey.ac.uk

MOORE, **Andrew S.** American (born United States), b. 1968. **Genres:** Theology/Religion, History, Race Relations. **Career:** St. Anselm College, Department of History, associate professor. Writer. **Publications:** The South's Tolerable Alien: Roman Catholics in Alabama and Georgia, 1945-1970, 2007. **Address:** St. Anselm College, 100 St. Anselm Dr., Manchester, NH 03102, U.S.A. **Online address:** amoore@anselm.edu

MOORE, **Anne Elizabeth.** American (born United States) **Genres:** Sociology. **Career:** School of the Art Institute of Chicago, instructor in visual critical studies, 2008-; Columbia College, journalism, faculty; University of Illinois, Chicago's graduate department, faculty; Zines, self-publisher, 1993-; Fantagraphics Books, staff, 1999-2004; Punk Planet, Independents Day Media, staff; Columbia College, Exhibitions: Book and Paper Center, staff; Museum of Contemporary Art, staff; Whitney Biennial, staff, 2008. Writer. **Publications:** Hey, Kidz! Buy This Book: A Radical Primer on Corporate and Governmental Propaganda and Artistic Activism for Short People, 2004; Stop Reading This: A Manifesto for Radical Literacy, 2004; (ed. with H. Pekar) The Best American Comics 2006, 2006; (ed. with C. Ware) The Best American Comics 2007, 2007; Unmarketable: Brandalism, Copyfighting, Mocketing and the Erosion of Integrity, 2007. **Address:** Chicago, IL , U.S.A. **Online address:** aem@anneelizabethmoore.com

MOORE, **Brenda L(ee).** American (born United States), b. 1950. **Genres:** History, Race Relations, Military/Defense/Arms Control. **Career:** U.S. Department of the Army, equal opportunity specialist, 1973-79; National Study of Internal Medicine Manpower, project assistant, 1983, field supervisor, 1984; Ameritech Corp., researcher consultant, 1985; University of Chicago, National Opinion Research Center, assistant survey director, 1985-86; Chicago Urban League, research assistant, [illegible]; Chicago [illegible] field evaluator consultant, 1987-88; Indiana University Northwest, visiting

M[illegible]
og[illegible]
visi[illegible]
Univ[illegible]
honor[illegible]
Writer. [illegible]
a Life, 1[illegible]
S. Moore[illegible]
Racism in [illegible]
Address: La[illegible]
chicago, IL 6[illegible]

MOORE, **Cass**[illegible]
Genres: Educatio[illegible]
ics. **Career:** Munc[illegible]
assistant professor, [illegible]
University of Virginia[illegible]
1981-82; Windsor Pro[illegible]
broker, 1983-85; Palo A[illegible]
Interagency Council on [illegible]
Publications: Haunted Ho[illegible]
Public Out of House and H[illegible]
1967-2005, 2007. Contribut[illegible]
dress: Cato Institute, 1000 Ma[illegible]
5403, U.S.A. **Online address:** [illegible]

MOORE, **Christine Palamidess**[illegible]
Genres: Novels, Plays/Screenplay[illegible]
cleo Ecletico Theater, stage manag[illegible]
New Woman magazine, columnist [illegible]
writer, 1988-; Boston University, ins[illegible]
Publications: Cocaine Claims the Wh[illegible]
Virgin Knows (novel), 1995. The Fiddle [illegible]
American Woman, Italian Style: Italian A[illegible]
en, 2011. Contributor to periodicals and jo[illegible]
Cambridge, MA 02140-2210, U.S.A. **Onlin**[illegible]

MOORE, **Christopher.** (Christopher Paul M[illegible]
States), b. 1952. **Genres:** Novels, Young A[illegible]
[illegible] National Black Network [illegible]
Library, Schomburg Center for Research in Black[illegible]

1900-1950, 2002. Contributor to journals. **Address:** Our Lady of Walsingham Catholic Church, 7809 Shadyvilla Ln., Houston, TX 77055, U.S.A.

MOORE, John Michael. British (born England), b. 1935. **Genres:** Classics, Philosophy, History. **Career:** Winchester College, assistant master, 1960-64; Radley College, Classics Department, head, 1964-83, director of sixth form studies, 1974-83; Harvard University, Center for Hellenic Studies, junior fellow, 1970-71; The King's School Worcester, headmaster, 1983-. Writer. **Publications:** The Manuscript Tradition of Polybius, 1965; (intro. with P.A. Brunt) Res Gestae Divi Augusti: The Achievements of the Divine Augustus, 1967; (with J.J. Evans) Variorum: A Greek Translation Book, 1969; Time Charts, 1969; (trans. and intro.) Aristotle and Xenophon on Democracy and Oligarchy, 1975. **Address:** 9 College Green, Worcester, HW WR1 2LH, England.

MOORE, John N(orton). American (born United States), b. 1937. **Genres:** Civil Liberties/Human Rights, International Relations/Current Affairs, Law, Marine Sciences/Oceanography, Military/Defense/Arms Control, Politics/Government. **Career:** University of Florida, assistant professor of law, 1963-65; University of Virginia, associate professor, 1965-68, professor of international law, 1968-76, Walter L. Brown professor of law, 1976-, Center for National Security Law, director, Center for Oceans Law and Policy, director, Center for Oceans Law and Policy, director; National Security Council Interagency Task Force, chair, 1973-76; Center for Law and National Security, director; U.S. Institute of Peace, chairman, board director, 1985-91; American Bar Association, chairman. Writer. **Publications:** Law and the Indo-China War, 1972; (co-author) Deep Seabed Mining in the Law of the Sea Negotiation: Toward a Balanced Development System, 1978; Law and the Grenada Mission, 1984; The Legal Structure of Defense Organization, 1986; The Secret War in Central America, 1987; (co-author) International Law and the Brezhnev Doctrine, 1987; The Secret War in Central America, 1987; The Struggle for Peace in Central America: Sandinista Assault on World Order, 1987; Crisis in the Gulf, 1992; Treaty Interpretation, the Constitution and the Rule of Law, 2001; The National Law of Treaty Implementation, 2001; Solving the War Puzzle, 2004; (with F. Pires) Ocean Law, 2 vols., forthcoming. EDITOR: The Arab Israeli Conflict, 1972, rev. ed., 1977; Law and Civil War in the Modern World, 1975; (with R.B. Lillich) Readings in International Law from the Naval War College Review, 1947-1977, 1980; International and United States Documents on Oceans Law and Policy, 5 vols., 1986; (with F.S. Tipson and R.F. Turner) National Security Law, 1990, 2nd ed., 2005; The Vietnam Debate, 1990; (co-ed.) Entry Into Forces of the Law of the Sea Convention, 1995; National Security Law Documents, 1995, 2nd ed., 2006; Deception and Deterrence in Wars of National Liberation, State-Sponsored Terrorism and Other Forms of Secret Warfare, 1997; (co-ed.) Security Flashpoints: Oil, Islands, Sea Access, and Military Confrontation, 1998; (with A. Morrison) Strengthening the United Nations and Enhancing War Prevention, 2000; Civil litigation Against Terrorism, 2004; (with R.A. Fisher and R.F. Turner) To Oppose any Foe, 2006; (with R.F. Turner) Legal Issues in the Struggle Against Terror, 2010. **Address:** University of Virginia School of Law, Rm. SL344, 580 Massie Rd., Charlottesville, VA 22903, U.S.A. **Online address:** jnm9s@virginia.edu

MOORE, J. Stuart. American (born United States), b. 1953. **Genres:** Medicine/Health, History, Literary Criticism And History. **Career:** Teacher, 1975-77; Virginia Polytechnic Institute and State University, visiting instructor in history, 1979, instructor in history, 1980, 1981; Radford University, visiting instructor in history, 1979-80, 1981-83, instructor, 1989-90, assistant professor of history, 1990-, associate professor of History; Hollins College, instructor in history, 1985-88; Virginia College, instructor, 1985; External Degree Services Inc., college recruiter, 1985. Writer. **Publications:** Chiropractic in America: The History of a Medical Alternative, 1993; Lone, 2004; Earthlight, 2006; Stuart Moore's Para, 2006. Contributor of articles to journals. **Address:** Department of History, Radford University, Cook Hall of International Education, PO Box 6491, Radford, VA 24142, U.S.A. **Online address:** jsmoore@radford.edu

MOORE, Julianne Randolph. *See* **MCBRIDE, Jule.**

MOORE, Kay. American (born United States), b. 1948. **Genres:** Human Relations/Parenting, Food And Wine, Novels, Sports/Fitness. **Career:** United Press Intl., writer, 1969-72; Houston Chronicle, feature writer, 1972-86; Plano Star Courier, city editor, 1986-88; freelance journalist, 1988-; Word Inc., manuscript editor; Lifeway Books, design editor, 1992-94; writer, editor and conference leader, 1994-; Hannibal Books, president, 1999-. **Publications:** WITH L. MOORE: When You Both Go to Work: How Two-Paycheck Families can Stay Active in the Church, 1982; (and D. Harris) Playing the Game: A Sports Novel, 1984; (and G. Teaff) Winning: It's How You Play the Game, 1985; Gathering the Missing Pieces in an Adopted Life, 1995; When the Heart Soars Free, 1999; Way Back in the Country: Recipes from Six Generations of East Texas Farm Cooking and the Stories Behind Them, 2002; (W. Byrd and P. Warren) Counseling with Adolescents, forthcoming; Counseling with Children, forthcoming. EDITOR: (with L. Moore and contrib.) The Guideposts Biblical Commentary on the General Epistles, 1986; Search for Significance Workbook, 1992. Contributor to periodicals. **Address:** Family Matters Seminars, PO Box 461592, Garland, TX 75046-1592, U.S.A. **Online address:** hannibalbooks@earthlink.net

MOORE, Laurie. American (born United States) **Genres:** Autobiography/Memoirs, Mystery/Crime/Suspense. **Career:** Police officer, sergeant, district attorney investigator and writer. **Publications:** FICTION: Creative Intimacy: A Practical Guide to Better Relationships, 2001; Constable's Run, 2002; The Lady Godiva Murder, 2002; Constable's Apprehension, 2003; The Wild Orchid Society: A Cezanne Martin Mystery, 2004; Constable's Wedding, 2005; Jury Rigged, 2008; Woman Strangled New at Ten, 2009; Deb on Arrival Live at Five: A Debutante Detective Mystery, 2010; Couple Gunned Down-News at Ten, 2011; Wanted Deb or Alive, 2011. **Address:** PO Box 10333, Fort Worth, TX 76147-2222, U.S.A. **Online address:** laurie@lauriemooremysteries.com

MOORE, Lisa Jean. American (born United States), b. 1967. **Genres:** Politics/Government. **Career:** City University of New York, College of Staten Island, associate professor of sociology, 1998-2006; City University of New York, Graduate Center, associate professor of sociology, 2002-06; State University of New York, Purchase College, associate professor of sociology and women's studies, 2006-08, coordinator of gender studies, 2006-10, professor of sociology and women's studies, 2008-. Writer. **Publications:** (With J. Lorber) Gender and the Social Construction of Illness, 2nd ed., 2002; (with J. Lorber) Gendered Bodies: Feminist Perspectives, 2007; Sperm Counts: Overcome by Man's Most Precious Fluid, 2007; (with M.J. Casper) Missing Bodies: The Politics of Visibility, 2009; (ed. with M. Kosut) The Body Reader: Essential Social and Cultural Readings, 2010. Contributor to periodicals. **Address:** Purchase College, 735 Anderson Hill Rd., Purchase, NY 10577, U.S.A. **Online address:** lisa-jean.moore@purchase.edu

MOORE, Lorrie. American (born United States), b. 1957. **Genres:** Novels, Novellas/Short Stories, Children's Fiction, Self Help. **Career:** Cornell University, lecturer in English, 1982-84; University of Wisconsin, assistant professor, 1984-87, associate professor, 1987-91, professor of English, 1991-2000, Delmore Schwartz professor in the humanities, 2000-. Writer. **Publications:** Self-Help: Stories, 1985; Anagrams: A Novel, 1986; The Forgotten Helper: A Story for Children, 1987; Like Life: Stories, 1990; Willing, 1991; Community Life, 1992; (ed.) I Know Some Things: Stories About Childhood by Contemporary Writers, 1992; Terrific Mother, 1993; Who Will Run the Frog Hospital?: A Novel, 1994; Birds of America: Stories, 1998; (ed.) The Faber Book of Contemporary Stories About Childhood, 1998; The Forgotten Helper: A Christmas Story, 2000; (ed. with K. Kenison) The Best American Short Stories 2004, 2004; Collected Stories, 2008; Gate at the Stairs: A Novel, 2009. Contributor to periodicals. **Address:** Department of English, University of Wisconsin, 7181 Helen C White Hall, Madison, WI 53706, U.S.A.

MOORE, Louis. American (born United States), b. 1946. **Genres:** Human Relations/Parenting, inspirational/Motivational Literature, Biography, Novels. **Career:** Houston Chronicle, religion editor, 1972-86; Plano Star Courier, editor, 1986-88; Collin County Community College, professor of journalism, 1988-89; Southern Baptist Christian Life Commission, director for publications, 1989-94; Belmont College, part-time journalism teacher, 1989; International Mission Board of the Southern Baptist Convention, associate vice president for communications, 1994-2000; Hannibal Books, co-owner, 1999-. **Publications:** (With K. Moore) When You Both Go to Work: How Two-Paycheck Families can Stay Active in the Church, 1982; (with K. Moore and D. Harris) Playing the Game: A Sports Novel, 1984; (with K. Moore and G. Teaff) Winning: It's How You Play the Game, 1985; Witness to the Truth: Lessons Learned by a Veteran Journalist through Four Decades of Watching the Church, 2008; (with H. Hovde) Families of the Bible: How They Coped with Today's Problems, 2009. EDITOR: (with K. Moore) The Guideposts Biblical Commentary on the General Epistles, 1986; Eating Problems for Breakfast, 1988; (with R.D. Land) The Earth Is the Lord's: Christians and the Environment, 1992; (with R.D. Land) Citizen Christians: The Rights and Responsibilities of Dual Citizenship, 1994; (with R.D. Land) Life at Risk: The Crises in Medical Ethics, 1995. **Address:** Hannibal Books, PO Box 461592, Garland, TX 75046, U.S.A. **Online address:** louismoore@hannibalbooks.com

MOORE, Lucy. British/American (born United States), b. 1970?. **Genres:** History, Novels, Adult Non-fiction, Biography. **Career:** The Observer, reviewer; The Sunday Times, reviewer. Historian and journalist. **Publications:** The Thieves Opera, 1997; (ed.) Con Men and Cutpurses: Scenes from the Hogarthian Underworld, 2000; Amphibious Thing: The Life of Lord Hervey, 2000; Maharanis: The Extraordinary Tale of Four Indian Queens and Their Journey from Purdah to Parliament, 2005; Maharanis: A Family Saga of Four Queens, 2006; Liberty: The Lives and Times of Six Women in Revolutionary France, 2007; Anything Goes: A Biography of the Roaring Twenties, 2008. **Address:** c/o Viking Publicity, Penguin Group, 375 Hudson St., New York, NY 10014, U.S.A.

MOORE, Maureen (Audrey). Canadian (born Canada), b. 1943. **Genres:** Novels, Young Adult Fiction, Romance/Historical. **Career:** Writer. **Publications:** The Illumination of Alice Mallory (novel), 1991. Works appear in anthologies. **Address:** c/o Iris Tupholme, HarperCollins Canada Ltd., 1995 Markham Rd., Scarborough, ON M1B 5M8, Canada.

MOORE, Michele. American (born United States), b. 1942?. **Genres:** Medicine/Health. **Career:** Writer. **Publications:** The Only Menopause Guide You'll Need, 2000; Dick: A Guide to the Penis for Men and Women, 2002; Cesarean Section: Understanding and Celebrating Your Baby's Birth, 2003; Dick: A Users Guide, 2004; Do You Really Need Surgery?: A Sensible Guide to Hysterectomy and Other Procedures for Women, 2004; A Woman's Concise Guide to Common Medical Tests, 2005; Pregnancy and Parenting After Thirty-five: Mid-Life New Life, 2006; Just the Facts: Abortion A-Z, 2007; Feed Your Family on $75 Per Week and Eat Well, 2009; Savory & Sweet and Mostly Local, 2010. **Address:** PO Box 248, Alstead, NH 03602, U.S.A. **Online address:** mcmooremd@earthlink.net

MOORE, Peggy Margaret. *See* **MOORE-HART, Margaret A.**

MOORE, Perry. American (born United States) **Genres:** Young Adult Nonfiction. **Career:** Writer. **Publications:** The Chronicles of Narnia: The Lion, the Witch, and the Wardrobe: The Official Illustrated Movie Companion, 2005; Hero, 2007. **Address:** Merrilee Heifetz, Writers House, 21 W 26th St., New York, NY 10010, U.S.A.

MOORE, Peter N. American (born United States), b. 1961. **Genres:** History, Theology/Religion, Social Sciences. **Career:** Georgia State University, visiting lecturer, 2002-05; University of Georgia, adjunct instructor, 2002-05; Texas A&M University, associate professor of history, 2005-. Writer. **Publications:** World of Toil and Strife: Community Transformation in Backcountry South Carolina, 1750-1805, 2007; (ed.) South Carolina Diary of Reverend Archibald Simpson, 2012. Contributor of articles to periodicals. **Address:** Texas A&M University, Rm. 279, 6300 Ocean Dr., Corpus Christi, TX 78412, U.S.A. **Online address:** peter.moore@tamucc.edu

MOORE, Philip N(icholas). American (born United States), b. 1957. **Genres:** Novels, Horror, Science Fiction/Fantasy, History, Intellectual History, International Relations/Current Affairs, Military/Defense/Arms Control, Paranormal, Philosophy, Politics/Government, Sex, Theology/Religion, Essays, Illustrations, Reference, Air/Space Topics. **Career:** Temple Mount excavation with archaeologists Elat and Binyamin Mazar, volunteer; Genesis Project film, staff, 1988-90. Writer. **Publications:** The End of History: Messiah Conspiracy, 1996; Nightmare of the Apocalypse: The Rabbi Conspiracy, 1997; Eternal Security for True Believers: The Rabin Assassination-Predicted: An Excerpt from the End of History, Messiah Conspiracy, vol. II, essays, 1997; A Liberal Interpretation of the Prophecy of Israel: Disproved, 1997; What If Hitler Won the War?, 1998; The End of Earth as We Know It, 1999; Israel and the Apocalypse Prophecies of Newton, forthcoming. **Address:** Ramshead Press Intl., PO Box 12-227, Atlanta, GA 30355-2227, U.S.A. **Online address:** theconine@aol.com

MOORE, Phyllis. American (born United States) **Genres:** Novels. **Career:** School of the Art Institute, teacher and co-chair of M.F.A. program; Kansas City Art Institute, associate professor, 2003-, creativing writing program, head, Paris Study Abroad Program, coordinator, School of Liberal Arts, associate professor and director, 2003-. Writer. **Publications:** A Compendium of Skirts, 2002. Contributor of articles to periodicals. **Address:** Kansas City Art Institute, 4415 Warwick Blvd., Kansas City, MO 64111-1820, U.S.A. **Online address:** pmoore@kcai.edu

MOORE, Rachel. *See* **SAUNDERS, Jean (Innes).**

MOORE, Randall Charles. *See* **MOORE, Randy Charles.**

MOORE, Randy Charles. (Randall Charles Moore). American (born United States), b. 1954. **Genres:** Biology, Botany, Sciences. **Career:** University of California, teaching assistant, 1975-77; Baylor University, assistant professor, 1980-83, associate professor, 1983-88; Pontificia Universidad Catolica de Chile, corresponding professor, 1986; Wright State University, professor and chair of biology department, 1988-93, College of Science and Mathematics, assistant dean, associate dean, 1990-93; Trotwood Madison School District, science teacher, 1990-; University of Akron, Buchtell College of Arts and Sciences, professor of biology and dean, 1993-; University of Minnesota, General College, professor, 2000-. Writer. **Publications:** OTHERS: (ed.) Vegetative Compatibility Responses in Plants, 1983; (with D.S. Vodopich) The Living Desert, 1991; Soil Survey of Pike National Forest Eastern Part, Colorado Parts of Douglas El Paso Jefferson and Teller Counties, 1992; Writing to Learn Biology, 1992; (with D. Vodopich) Biology Laboratory Manual, 1993, 8th ed., 2007; (co-author) Botany, 1995, 2nd ed., 1998; Classic and Modern Readings in Biology, 1996; Writing to Learn Science, 1997; (with R. Storey and G. Uno) Principles of Botany, 2000; Evolution in the Courtroom: A Reference Guide, 2002; (with J. Moore) Evolution 101, 2006; (with M.D. Decker) More than Darwin: An Encyclopedia of the People and Places of the Evolution-Creationism Controversy, 2008; (with M. Decker and S. Cotner) Chronology of the Evolution-creationism Controversy, 2010; (with S. Cotner) Arguing for Evolution, 2011. AS RANDALL C. MOORE: (contrib.) Life: Beginnings of Life, Animal Life, Plant Life, Evolution of Life, Behavior and Ecology of Life, 1992. Contributor to books. **Address:** Biology Program, University of Minnesota, MCB 3-104, 420 Washington Ave. SE, Minneapolis, MN 55455, U.S.A. **Online address:** rmoore@umn.edu

MOORE, Robin. American (born United States), b. 1950. **Genres:** Novels, Children's Fiction, History, Science Fiction/Fantasy, Novellas/Short Stories. **Career:** Author and storyteller, 1981-; Groundhog Press, owner. **Publications:** The Fifth Estate, 1973; The Treasure Hunter, 1974; A History of Coombe Abbey, 1983; The Bread Sister of Sinking Creek: Life on the Pennsylvania Frontier, 1984; Maggie among the Seneca, 1990; Awakening the Hidden Storyteller: How to Build a Storytelling Tradition in Your Family, 1991; Up the Frozen River, 1993; When the Moon Is Full: Supernatural Stories from the Old Pennsylvania Mountains, 1994; The Cherry Tree Buck and Other Stories, 1995; Remembering Maggie: A Guide to Living the Dream, 1995; (adapter) Hunchback of Notre Dame, 1996; Encounter on the Moon, 1996; Hercules, 1997; Tarzan of the Apes, 1999; Creating a Family Storytelling Tradition: Awakening the Hidden Storyteller, 1999; Fins, Furs and Feathers; (with R. Flynn) The Accidental Pope, 2000; The Man with the Silver Oar, 2002. **Address:** GroundHog Press, PO Box 1311, Doylestown, PA 18901, U.S.A. **Online address:** robin@robin-moore.com

MOORE, Rogan H. (Rogan Hart Moore). American/British (born England), b. 1955. **Genres:** Genealogy/Heraldry, History, Local History/Rural Topics, Young Adult Fiction, Military/Defense/Arms Control. **Career:** U.S. Naval Reserve, staff, 1974-80; Lackawanna College, adjunct professor of humanities and social science, 1986-; Lehigh Carbon Community College, adjunct professor, 1997-; Northampton Community College, adjunct professor, 2000-; University of St. Francis, adjunct professor, 2000-. Writer. **Publications:** (Comp. as Rogan Hart Moore) Josiah Moore of Hunterdon County, New Jersey: Some Ancestors and Descendants, 1986; (as Rogan Hart Moore) A History and Genealogy of the Moore Family of Fayette County, Pennsylvania, 1999; The Bloodstained Field: A History of the Sugarloaf Massacre, September 11, 1780, 2000. EDITOR: Directory of Genealogical and Local Historical Researchers in North America, 1989; The Civil War Memoirs of Sergeant George W. Darby, 1861-1865, 1999; Celebrate Conyngham: A Centennial History of Conyngham Borough, 1901-2001, 2001. **Address:** PO Box 704, Conyngham, PA 18219-0704, U.S.A. **Online address:** rhmoore@epix.net

MOORE, Rogan Hart. *See* **MOORE, Rogan H.**

MOORE, Roy L. American (born United States), b. 1947. **Genres:** Communications/Media, Law. **Career:** Virginia Polytechnic Institute and State University, assistant professor of communication, 1975-77; Georgia State University, assistant professor, 1977-82, associate professor, 1982-86, associate vice president of academic affairs, professor of mass communication, American council on education fellow, 2001-02; University of Kentucky, associate professor, 1986-88, director of graduate studies in communication, 1988-93, School of Journalism and Telecommunications, acting director, 1993-94, 2001, professor, 1994-, associate dean for graduate studies, 1995-, now professor emeritus; U.K. First Amendment Center, executive director; U.K. College of Communications and Information Studies, associate dean; Middle Tennessee State University, College of Mass Communication, dean, 2008-. Writer. **Publications:** Mass Communication Law and Ethics, 1994, 2nd ed., 1999; (with R.T. Farrar and E.L. Collins) Advertising and Public Relations Law, 1998, (with C. Maye and E.L. Collins) 2nd ed., 2011; (ed. with M.D. Murray) Mass Communication Education, 2003; (with M.D. Murray) Media Law and Ethics, 2008, 4th ed., 2011. **Address:** College of Mass Communications, Middle Tennessee State University, Rm. 247C Bragg Mass Communication Bldg., 1301 E Main St., Murfreesboro, TN 37132-0001, U.S.A. **Online address:** rmoore@mtsu.edu

MOORE, Sam. American (born United States), b. 1931?. **Genres:** Autobiography/Memoirs, Biography. **Career:** Thomas Nelson Publishers, CEO and chairman; National Book, founder. Writer. **Publications:** American by Choice: The Remarkable Fulfillment of an Immigrant's Dreams, 1998. **Address:** Thomas Nelson Inc., PO Box 141000, Nashville, TN 37214, U.S.A.

MOORE, Stephanie Perry. American (born United States), b. 1969?. **Genres:** Novels, Theology/Religion, inspirational/Motivational Literature, Young Adult Fiction, Children's Fiction. **Career:** Nia Publishing, general editor; Real (a Bible-based zine), co-editor. Motivational speaker and community activist. **Publications:** Flame, 2001; A Lova' like No Otha', 2003; Chasing Faith, 2007; Wearing My Halo Tilted, 2008; The Way we Roll, 2009; Work What You Got (young adult novel), 2009; Got it Going on, 2009; Act like You Know, 2009; Enjoying True Peace, 2010; Get What You Give, 2010; Right Thing, 2011; (with D.C. Moore) Making the Team, 2011; No Fear!, 2011; A+ Attitude, 2011; Speak Up!, 2011; Something Special, 2011; (with D.C. Moore) Learning the Rules, 2011; (with D.C. Moore) Taking the Lead, 2012; (with D.C. Moore) Going the Distance, 2012; (with D.C. Moore) Winning the Battle, 2012. PAYTON SKKY SERIES: YOUNG ADULT NOVELS: Staying Pure, 1997; Sober Faith, 2000; Saved Race, 2001; Sweetest Gift, 2001; Surrendered Heart, 2002. LAUREL SHADRACH SERIES: YOUNG ADULT NOVELS: Purity Reigns, 2002; Totally Free, 2002; Equally Yoked, 2003; Absolutely Worthy, 2003; Finally Sure, 2004. CARMEN BROWNE SERIES: CHILDREN'S NOVELS: True Friends, 2005; Sweet Honesty, 2005; Golden Spirit, 2006; Perfect Joy, 2006; Happy Princess, 2007. FAITH THOMAS SERIES: YOUNG ADULT NOVELZINES: God Can Work It Out, 2007; God Wants You to Shine, 2007. PERRY SKKY, JR. SERIES: YOUNG ADULT NOVELS: Prime Choice, 2007; Pressing Hard, 2007; Problem Solved, 2007; Prayed Up, 2008; Promise Kept, 2008. YASMIN PEACE SERIES: YOUNG ADULT NOVELS: Finding Your Faith, 2009; Believing in Hope, 2009; Experiencing the Joy, 2009; Learning to Love, 2009. **Address:** Moody Publishers, 820 N LaSalle Blvd., Chicago, IL 60610, U.S.A. **Online address:** dsssmoore@aol.com

MOORE, Terry Terrell. (Thomas Terrell Moore). American (born United States), b. 1954?. **Genres:** Novels. **Career:** Marvel Comics, script writer. Cartoonist. **Publications:** STRANGERS IN PARADISE SERIES: Immortal Enemies, 1996; I Dream of You, 1996; It's a Good Life, 1998; High School!, 1999; Sanctuary, 1999; My Other Life, 2000; Child of Rage, 2001; Tropic of Desire, 2001; Queen of Hearts, 2002; Love Me Tender, 2002; Brave New World, 2002; Heart in Hand, 2003; Flower to Flame, 2003; David's Story, 2004; Tomorrow Is Now, 2004; Strangers in Paradise, 2004; Strangers in Paradise, 6 vols., 2007. PARADISE TOO SERIES: Drunk Ducks, 2003; Checking for Weirdos, 2003. STRANGERS IN PARADISE SERIES COLLECTIONS: The Collected Strangers in Paradise, 3 vols., 2004. ECHO SERIES: Echo, 2008; Echo: Moon Lake, 2008. OTHER: (with D. Mack) Kabuki: Masks of the Noh TP, 1999; (with T. Millionaire and A. Watson) Star Wars: Tales, 2002; (with A. Benson and C. Golden) Buffy the Vampire Slayer: Willow and Tara, 2003; (with B.M. Bendis) Ultimate Marvel Team-up, 2004; (with M. Bourne and M. Alfred) Tales of Ordinary Madness, 2004. **Address:** Abstract Studio Inc., PO Box 271487, Houston, TX 77277, U.S.A. **Online address:** sipnet@strangersinparadise.com

MOORE, Thomas S(cott). American (born United States), b. 1945. **Genres:** Business/Trade/Industry, Sociology, Social Sciences, International Relations/Current Affairs, Anthropology/Ethnology. **Career:** Teacher, 1972-74; University of Wisconsin-Parkside, assistant professor, 1979-86; Denison University, assistant professor, 1986-88; University of Wisconsin-Milwaukee, visiting assistant professor, senior lecturer in sociology, 1988-. Writer. **Publications:** The Disposable Work Force: Worker Displacement and Employment Instability in America, 1996. Contributor of articles to journals. Works appear in anthologies. **Address:** Department of Sociology, University of Wisconsin-Milwaukee, Bolton Hall 704, PO Box 413, Milwaukee, WI 53201-0413, U.S.A. **Online address:** tsm@uwm.edu

MOORE, Thomas Terrell. *See* **MOORE, Terry Terrell.**

MOORE, Tim. British (born England), b. 1964. **Genres:** Travel/Exploration. **Career:** Writer. **Publications:** Frost on My Moustache: The Arctic Exploits of a Lord and a Loafer, 2000; The Grand Tour: The European Adventure of a Continental Drifter, 2001; Continental Drifter: Taking the Low Road with the First Grand Tourist, 2001; French Revolutions: Cycling the Tour de France, 2002; Do Not Pass Go: From the Old Kent Road to Mayfair, 2002; Spanish Steps: One Man and His Ass on the Pilgrimage Way to Santiago, 2004; Travels with My Donkey: One Man and His Ass on a Pilgrimage to Santiago, 2004; I Believe in Yesterday, 2008; (with P. Whitehead) Must Be Santa, 2011. Contributor to periodicals. **Address:** c/o Author Mail, St. Martins Press, 175 5th Ave., New York, NY 10010, U.S.A.

MOORE, T. M. American (born United States), b. 1949?. **Genres:** Theology/Religion. **Career:** The Fellowship of Ailbe, principal; Wilberforce Forum, fellow, Centurions Program, dean; Chesapeake Theological Seminary, president; Christian Worldview Fellowship and Resources, The Chuck Colson Center, content manager; The Worldview Church, general editor. Consultant, theologian and writer. **Publications:** (With D.J. Kennedy) Chain Reaction!: Changing the World from Where You Are, 1985; Celtic Flame: The Burden of Patrick, 2000; Disciplines of Grace: From Spiritual Routine to Spiritual Renewal, 2001; Ecclesiastes: Ancient Wisdom When All Else Fails, 2001; Preparing Your Church for Revival, 2001; The Psalms for Prayer, 2002; I Will Be Your God: How God's Covenant Enriches Our Lives, 2002; (ed.) Growing in God's Spirit, 2003; Redeeming Pop Culture: A Kingdom Approach, 2003; (ed.) Praying Together for True Revival, 2004; Consider the Lilies: A Plea for Creational Theology, 2005; (ed.) Pursuing Holiness in the Lord, 2005; Culture Matters: A Call for Consensus on Christian Cultural Engagement, 2007; The Ground for Christian Ethics, 2009; The Ailbe Psalter, 2011. **Address:** InterVarsity Press, 430 Plaza Dr., PO Box 1400, Westmont, IL 60559, U.S.A.

MOORE-COLYER, Richard. Welsh/British (born England), b. 1945. **Genres:** Geography, Area Studies, Human Relations/Parenting. **Career:** University of Wales, University College of Wales, professor, 1970-. Writer. **Publications:** The Welsh Cattle Drovers, 1976, rev. ed., 2002; Man's Proper Study, 1982; Roads and Trackways of Wales, 1984; The Teifi: Scenery and Antiquities of a Welsh River, 1987; (ed.) A Land of Pure Delight: Selections from the Letters of Thomas Johnes of Hafod, 1748-1816, 1992; Cherished Heartland: Future of the Uplands in Wales, 2005. Work represented in anthologies. Contributor to scholarly journals. **Address:** Institute of Rural Studies, University of Wales, Stapledon Bldg., Aberystwyth, SY23 3AL, Wales.

MOORE-GILBERT, Bart. (B. J. Moore-Gilbert). British/Tanzanian (born Tanzania, United Republic of), b. 1952. **Genres:** Literary Criticism And History, Cultural/Ethnic Topics. **Career:** Roehampton Institute, lecturer in English, 1980-89; University of London, Goldsmiths College, Postcolonial Studies and English, professor, 1989-; University of Mexico, visiting professor, 2004. Writer. **Publications:** Kipling and Orientalism, 1987; Postcolonial Theory: Contexts, Practices, Politics, 1997; Hanif Kureishi, 2001; Postcolonial Life-writing: Culture, Politics and Self-representation, 2009. EDITOR: (with J. Seed) Cultural Revolution?: The Challenge of the Arts in the 1960s, 1992; Cultural Closure? The Challenge of the Arts in the 1970s, 1994; Writing India, 1757-1990: The Literature of British India, 1787-1980, 1996; (intro.) Postcolonial Criticism, 1997; Between Colonialism and Postcolonialism: A Reader, 1998. **Address:** Department of English and Comparative Literature, Goldsmiths College, University of London, Rm. 512, 5th Fl., Warmington Twr., London, GL SE14 6NW, England. **Online address:** b.moore-gilbert@gold.ac.uk

MOORE-GILBERT, B. J. *See* **MOORE-GILBERT, Bart.**

MOORE-HART, Margaret A. (Peggy Margaret Moore). American (born United States), b. 1946. **Genres:** Education. **Career:** Teacher, 1969-72; Simmons Child World, teacher, 1975-84; Clemson University, assistant professor of elementary education, 1986-88; Eastern Michigan University, assistant professor of reading education, 1988-92, associate professor, 1998, professor of reading. Writer. **Publications:** (With B. Diamond) Multicultural Literacy: Mirroring the Reality of the Classroom, 1995; Teaching Writing in Diverse Classrooms, K-8: Shaping Writers' Development Through Literature, Real-Life Experiences and Technology, 2009. Contributor to journals. **Address:** Department of Teacher Education, Eastern Michigan University, Porter Bldg., Ste. 314Q, Ypsilanti, MI 48197, U.S.A. **Online address:** peggy.moore@emich.edu

MOORHEAD, John (Anthony). Australian (born Australia), b. 1948. **Genres:** History, Intellectual History, Theology/Religion. **Career:** University of Tasmania, tutor in history, 1975; University of Queensland, lecturer, 1976-82, senior lecturer in history, 1983-93, reader in history, 1994-99, McCaughey professor of history, 2000-10, professor emeritus, 2011-; University of Edinburgh, Institute for Advanced Studies in the Humanities, fellow, 1987; Cambridge University, Clare Hall, fellow, 1990; Australian Academy of the Humanities, fellow, 2003. Writer. **Publications:** (Trans. and intro.) Victor of Vita: History of the Vandal Persecution, 1992; (with R. Cusimano) Suger: The Deeds of Louis the Fat, 1992; Theoderic in Italy, 1992; Justinian, 1994; Ambrose: Church and Society in the Late Roman World, 1999; The Roman Empire Divided, 400-700, 2001, 2nd ed., 2012; Gregory the Great, 2005; (ed.) The Cambridge Companion to Boethius, 2009. Contributor to journals. **Address:** School of History, Philosophy, Religion & Classics, University of Queensland, Brisbane, QL 4072, Australia. **Online address:** j.moorhead@mailbox.uq.edu.au

MOOTE, A. Lloyd. American/Canadian (born Canada), b. 1931. **Genres:** History, Novels, Young Adult Fiction. **Career:** University of Toronto, lecturer, 1958-61; University of Cincinnati, assistant professor, 1961-62; University of Southern California, assistant professor, 1962-65, associate professor, 1965-71, professor of history, 1971-92, professor emeritus, 1993-; Queens University, visiting professor, 1965-66; Wellcome Institute for the History of Medicine, visiting fellow, 1993-94; University of Essex, visiting fellow, 1993-94; Rutgers University, affiliated professor, 1994-. Writer. **Publications:** The Seventeenth Century: Europe in Ferment, 1970; (contrib.) Louis XIV and the Craft of Kingship, 1970; The Revolt of the Judges: The Parlement of Paris and the Fronde 1643-1652, 1972; (co-author) The World of Europe, 1979; Louis XIII, The Just, 1989; (with D.C. Moote) The Great Plague: The Story of London's Most Deadly Year, 2004. Contributor to journals. **Address:** Department of History, University of Southern California, 3520 Trousdale Pkwy., Los Angeles, CA 90089-0034, U.S.A. **Online address:** dlmoote@verizon.net

MORALES, Aaron Michael. American (born United States), b. 1976?. **Genres:** Novellas/Short Stories, Novels. **Career:** Indiana Business College, noncredit instructor, 1999; Purdue University, graduate instructor in English, 2000-03; Robert Morris College, adjunct instructor in English and communications, 2002-04; Columbia College, adjunct instructor in English, 2003; Richard J. Daley College, City College of Chicago, assistant professor of English language and literature, 2004-05; Indiana State University, assistant professor of English, 2005-. Writer. **Publications:** From Here You Can Almost See the End of the Desert (short stories), 2008; Drowning Tucson (novel), 2010. Contributor to periodicals. **Address:** Indiana State University, Root Hall A-215, Terre Haute, IN 47809, U.S.A. **Online address:** aaron.morales@indstate.edu

MORALES, Edmundo. American (born United States), b. 1943. **Genres:** Sociology, Social Commentary, Politics/Government. **Career:** West Chester University, Department of Anthropology and Sociology, associate professor of sociology, 1989-, professor, chairperson. Writer. **Publications:** (Ed.) Drugs in Latin America, 1986; Cocaine: White Gold Rush in Peru, 1989; The Guinea Pig: Healing, Food and Ritual in the Andes, 1995. Contributor to periodicals. **Address:** Department of Anthropology & Sociology, West Chester University, 102 Old Library Bldg., West Chester, PA 19383, U.S.A. **Online address:** emorales@wcupa.edu

MORALES, Rebecca (Hope). American (born United States), b. 1925?. **Genres:** Area Studies, Business/Trade/Industry, Economics, Engineering. **Career:** University of Tennessee, Graduate School of Planning, part-time assistant professor, 1974-77; University of California-Los Angeles, Graduate School of Architecture and Urban Planning, adjunct lecturer and assistant researcher, 1980-82, assistant professor, 1982-90, Latin American Center, associate director, 1988-90; Universidad Autonoma de Baja California, Fulbright lecturer, 1985; The Tomas Rivera Center, director of policy research, 1992; The Claremont Graduate School, Center for Politics and Economics, visiting associate professor, 1992-94; United Nations Economic Commission for Latin America and the Caribbean, economics affairs officer, 1994; University of California-Santa Cruz, Latin American and Latino Studies, chancellors professor, 1995, Center for U.S. Mexican Studies, research associate, 1997-2005, Center for U.S. Mexican Studies, visiting research fellow, 1991-92; University of Illinois, Center for Urban Economic Development, director, 1995-97, Urban Planning and Public Affairs, associate professor, 1995-98; Morales and Associates, associate, 1998-2003; New Economics for Women Inc., co-founder; San Diego Automotive Museum, curator, 2007-08; San Diego Center for Algae Biotechnology, operations manager, 2009. Writer. **Publications:** (Ed. with F. Bonilla) Latinos in a Changing U.S. Economy: Comparative Perspectives on Growing Inequality, 1993; Flexible Production: The Restructuring of the International Automobile Industry, 1994; (co-author) Borderless Borders: U.S. Latinos, Latin Americans and the Paradox of Interdependence, 1998. Contributor to books and periodicals. **Address:** 7318 Draper Ave., La Jolla, CA 92037-5023, U.S.A. **Online address:** rebeccamorales@earthlink.net

MORALES, Waltraud Queiser. American (born United States), b. 1947. **Genres:** History, International Relations/Current Affairs, Politics/Government, Sociology, Third World. **Career:** Regis College, instructor in history, 1972; University of South Carolina, visiting assistant professor of government, 1978; East Carolina University, visiting assistant professor of political science, 1978-80; University of Central Florida, assistant professor, 1980-85, associate professor of political science, 1986-95, professor, 1995-, Office of International Studies, interim director, 1994-96, United Faculty of Florida, president, 2000-01; Journal of the Florida Political Science Association, Political Chronicle, editor, 1999-2001. **Publications:** Social Revolution: Theory and Historical Application (monograph), 1973; (with E.A. Duff and J.F. McCamant) Violence and Repression in Latin America: A Quantitative and Historical Analysis, 1976; Geopolítica dela politica exterior de Bolivia, 1984; (with H.A. Vanden) Lucha por lasoberanía: Nicaragua y los no alineados, 1986; (with J. Donnelly and R. Moore) Human Rights: A User's Guide, 1989; Bolivia: Land of Struggle, 1992; Brief History of Bolivia, 2003, 2nd ed., 2010. Works appear in anthologies. Contributor of articles to journals and newspapers. **Address:** Department of Political Science, University of Central Florida, 307F Phillips Hall, 4000 Central Florida Blvd., PO Box 161356, Orlando, FL 32816-1356, U.S.A. **Online address:** morales@mail.ucf.edu

MORAN, Bruce T. American (born United States), b. 1948. **Genres:** History. **Career:** University of Nevada, professor of history, 1976-, chair of history department, adjunct professor of philosophy; University of London, Welcome Trust Centre for the History of Medicine, honorary research associate. Writer and historian. **Publications:** The Alchemical World of the German Court: Occult Philosophy and Chemical Medicine in the Circle of Moritz of Hessen, 1572-1632, 1991; (ed.) Patronage and Institutions: Science, Technology, and Medicine at the European Court, 1500-1750, 1991; Chemical Pharmacy Enters the University: Johannes Hartmann and the Didactic Care of Chymiatria in the Early Seventeenth Century, 1991; (ed. with M.L. Hildreth) Disease and Medical Care in the Mountain West: Essays on Region, History, and Practice, 1998; Distilling Knowledge: Alchemy, Chemistry, and the Scientific Revolution, 2005; Andreas Libavius and the Transformation of Alchemy: Separating Chemical Cultures with Polemical Fire, 2007. **Address:** Department of History, University of Nevada, Mack Social Sciences Bldg., Ste. 243, PO Box 0308, Reno, NV 89557-0037, U.S.A. **Online address:** moran@unr.edu

MORAN, Charles. American (born United States), b. 1936. **Genres:** Literary Criticism And History, Education, History, How-to Books. **Career:** University of Massachusetts, faculty, 1967-, professor, 1983-, now professor emeritus, Western Massachusetts Writing Project, co-director; State University of New York, visiting lecturer, 1981. Writer. **Publications:** (Ed. with E.F. Penfield) Conversations: Contemporary Critical Theory and the Teaching of Literature, 1990; (ed. with A. Herrington) Writing, Teaching and Learning in the Disciplines, 1992; (with G.E. Hawisher, C.L. Selfe and P. LeBlanc) Computers and the Teaching of Writing in American Higher Education, 1979-1994. A History, 1996; (ed. with A. Herrington) Genre across the Curriculum, 2005; (ed. with A. Herrington and K. Hodgson) Teaching the New Writing: Technology, Change, and Assessment in the 21st-Century Classroom, 2009. Contributor to books and periodicals. **Address:** Department of English, University of Massachusetts, 170 Bartlett Hall, PO Box 30515, Amherst, MA 01003-0515, U.S.A. **Online address:** cmoran@english.umass.edu

MORAN, James P. American (born United States), b. 1958. **Genres:** Horticulture, Young Adult Fiction. **Career:** Judicial law clerk, 1987-88; assistant U.S. attorney, 1988-93; assistant federal public defender, 1993-; Florida A&M University, Institute on Urban Policy and Commerce, assistant professor, 1998-2001, College of Pharmacy and Pharmaceutical Sciences, development officer, 2001-, coordinator of advancement/alumni affairs. Writer. **Publications:** Public Garden, 1994. Contributor to periodicals. **Address:** College of Pharmacy and Pharmaceutical Sciences, Florida A&M University, 322 New Pharmacy Bldg., 1415 S Martin Luther King Jr. Blvd, Tallahassee, FL 32307, U.S.A. **Online address:** james.moran@famu.edu

MORAN, Johanna C. American (born United States), b. 1951. **Genres:** Novels. **Career:** Writer. **Publications:** The Wives of Henry Oades: A Novel, 2010. **Address:** Sarasota, FL , U.S.A. **Online address:** johanna@johannamoran.com

MORAN, Mary (Molly) Hurley. American (born United States), b. 1947. **Genres:** Literary Criticism And History, Autobiography/Memoirs. **Career:** Tri-County Technical College, instructor in English, 1980-82; Limestone College, instructor in English, 1980-82; Central Wesleyan College, instructor in English, 1980-82; Clemson University, assistant professor of English, 1982-86; Analysis and Technology Inc., technical editor, 1987-88; University of Georgia, instructor, 1988-91, assistant professor, 1991-96, associate professor of English, 1996-2005, professor, 2006-. Writer. **Publications:** Margaret Drabble: Existing within Structures, 1983; Penelope Lively, 1993; Finding Susan, 2003. Contributor to books and newspapers. **Address:** Division of Academic Enhancement, University of Georgia, 233 Milledge Hall, Athens, GA 30602-5554, U.S.A. **Online address:** mhmoran@uga.edu

MORAN, Maya. American/Dutch (born Netherlands), b. 1934. **Genres:** Architecture, Art/Art History. **Career:** Landmark (newspaper), staff. freelance writer, designer and educator. **Publications:** Down to Earth: An Insider's View of Frank Lloyd Wright's Tomek House, 1995. **Address:** 200 S Lake Ave., Michigan City, IN 46360, U.S.A. **Online address:** mayamanny@hotmail.com

MORAN, Michelle. American (born United States) **Genres:** Novels, Literary Criticism And History, Young Adult Fiction. **Career:** Writer and educator. **Publications:** Nefertiti: A Novel, 2007; The Heretic Queen: A Novel, 2008; Cleopatra's Daughter: A Novel, 2009; Madame Tussaud: A Novel, 2011. **Address:** c/o Russell Galen, Scovil Galen Ghosh, 276 5th Ave., Ste. 708, New York, NY 10001, U.S.A.

MORANVILLE, Sharelle Byars. American (born United States) **Genres:** Children's Fiction. **Career:** Writer and educator. **Publications:** Over the River, 2002; The Purple Ribbon, 2003; Higher Geometry, 2006; The Snows, 2007; The Hop, 2012. **Address:** 1530 S Deer Rd., West Des Moines, IA 50266, U.S.A. **Online address:** sharellemoranville@mac.com

MORASH, Chris. *See* **MORASH, Christopher.**

MORASH, Christopher. (Chris Morash). Irish/Canadian (born Canada), b. 1963. **Genres:** Literary Criticism And History, History. **Career:** National University, Department of English, lecturer, 1990-, head; St. Patrick's College, lecturer in English, 1990. Writer. **Publications:** Writing the Irish Famine, 1995; History of Irish Theater, 1601-2000, 2002; A History of the Media in Ireland, 2009. EDITED AS CHRIS MORASH: Hungry Voice: The Poetry of the Irish Famine, 1989; Creativity and its Contexts, 1995; (with R. Hayes) Fearful Realities: New Perspectives on the Famine, 1996; Irish Theater on Tour, 2005. **Address:** Centre for Media Studies, National University of Ireland, Maynooth, Rm. 0.19, Iontas Bldg., Ground Fl., Maynooth, KL 2, Ireland. **Online address:** chris.morash@nuim.ie

MORAVEC, Hans P(eter). American/Austrian (born Austria), b. 1948. **Genres:** Engineering, Social Commentary, Sociology, Technology. **Career:** Acadia University, part-time programmer, 1967-69; University of Western Ontario, Department of Computer Science, research assistant, 1969-71; Stanford University, Artificial Intelligence Lab, research assistant, 1971-80; Carnegie Mellon University, Robotics Institute, Computer Science Department, research scientist, 1980-85, senior research scientist, 1985-93, principal research scientist, 1993-95, research professor, 1995-2005, adjunct faculty, 2005-, Mobile Robot Laboratory, director, 1980-2005; Seegrid Corp., co-founder, chief scientist, 2003-. Writer. **Publications:** Robot Rover Visual Navigation, 1981; Mind Children: The Future of Robot and Human Intelligence, 1988; The Age of Mind: Transcending the Human Condition through Robots, 1994; Computer in classe: le nuove tecnologie nella scuola, 1997; Robot: Mere Machine to Transcendent Mind, 1999. Works appear in anthologies. Contributor to books and periodicals. **Address:** Robotics Institute, Carnegie Mellon University, NSH 4000B, 5000 Forbes Ave., Pittsburgh, PA 15213-3815, U.S.A. **Online address:** hpm@cmu.edu

MORAVEC, Ivo. Canadian/Czech (born Czech Republic), b. 1948?. **Genres:** Autobiography/Memoirs, Biography, Politics/Government. **Career:** Industrial economist and writer. **Publications:** Tightrope Passage: Along the Refugee Route to Canada, 1997. Contributor to periodicals. **Address:** 60 Byron Ave. E, Apt. B, London, ON N6C 1C5, Canada.

MORDECAI, Pamela (Claire). Canadian/Jamaican (born Jamaica), b. 1942. **Genres:** Novels, Children's Fiction, Young Adult Fiction, Poetry, Education, Language/Linguistics, Literary Criticism And History. **Career:** Mico Training College, assistant lecturer, 1968, 1969, lecturer in English, 1973-74; University of the West Indies, research fellow, 1971-72, publications officer, 1974-88; Jamaica Information Service, radio producer and presenter, 1968-71; Gaynstead Extension School, supervisor, 1970; freelance television interviewer and presenter, 1974-80; Caribbean Journal of Education, publications officer and editor, 1974-88; DeBrosse Redman Black and Co., managing director, 1988-94; Sandberry Press, publisher, 1988-. **Publications:** Journey Poem, 1989; Sun Rhymes First ABC Colouring Book (juvenile), 1989; De Man: A Performance Poem, 1995; Ezra's Goldfish and Other Storypoems, 1995; The Costume Parade, 2000; Rohan Goes to Big School, 2000; (with M. Mortecai) Culture and Customs of Jamaica, 2001; Certifiable, 2001; The True Blue of Islands, 2005; Pink Icing and Other Stories, 2006. EDITOR: (with M. Morris) Jamaica Woman: An Anthology of 15 Jamaican Women Poets, 1980; New Island Readers, Book 1, 1983; From Our Yard: Jamaican Poetry Since Independence, 1987; Jamaica 21 Anthology of Poetry, 1987; (with G.W. Gordon) Sunsong One, 1987; (with Walker-Gordon) Sunsong Two, 1987; (with Walker-Gordon) New Caribbean Introductory Reader, Books 1 and 2, 1987; (with B. Wilson) Her True True Name, 1989; Daughters of the Red Land, 1995; Calling Cards: New Poetry, 2005. Contributor to periodicals. **Address:** c/o Margaret Hart, HSW Literary Agency, 3199 Lakeshore Blvd. W, Toronto, ON M8V 1K8, Canada. **Online address:** marpam@sympatico.ca

MORDEN, Simon. British (born England), b. 1966?. **Genres:** Novellas/Short Stories. **Career:** Gateshead Primary School, part-time teaching assistant; British Science Fiction Association, Focus Magazine, editor, 2004. **Publications:** Thy Kingdom Come (short stories), 2002; Heart, 2002; Brilliant Things (short stories), 2004; Another War (novella), 2005; The Lost Art, 2008; Degrees of Freedom, 2011; Theories of Flight, 2011; Equations of Life, 2011. Contributor to periodicals. **Address:** Antony Harwood Literary Agency, 103 Walton St., Oxford, OX2 6EB, England. **Online address:** bookofmorden@blueyonder.co.uk

MORE, J. *See* **LEITCH, Will.**

MOREAU, David Merlin. (David Merlin). British/Egyptian (born Egypt), b. 1927. **Genres:** Novels, Administration/Management, Medicine/Health, Adult Non-fiction, Business/Trade/Industry, Biography, Literary Criticism And History. **Career:** John Wyeth & Brothers, export manager, 1952-56; Beecham Group, European market controller, 1956-65; Syntex Pharmaceutical Ltd., founder, managing director, 1965-70; Weddel Pharmaceutical Ltd., general manager, 1970-72, chairman, 1972-79; Aerial Photographer for publications, staff, 1970-; Elga Group, managing director, 1972-80; Dewplan Group, publicity director, 1981-. Writer. **Publications:** (As David Merlin) The Simple Life, 1962; (as David Merlin) That Built-In Urge, 1963; Summer's End, 1966; Look behind You: An Alphabetical Guide to Executive Survival, 1973; More Wrestling Than Dancing, 1990; Run or Submit, 1999. Contributor to magazines and newspapers. **Address:** Rowley Cottage, Langley Park, BK SL3 6DT, England. **Online address:** david@gibbet.demon.co.uk

MOREH, Shmuel. Israeli/Iraqi (born Iraq), b. 1932. **Genres:** Novellas/Short Stories, Poetry, History, Literary Criticism And History, Theatre, Bibliography, Translations. **Career:** Hebrew University of Jerusalem, Institute of Asian and African Studies, lecturer, 1966-, senior lecturer, 1970-, assoc professor,

1975-, professor of Arabic language and literature, 1983-2002, professor emeritus, 2002-; Bar-Ilan University, professor, 1983-2003, fellow; Israeli Television Literary Magazine, co-editor, 1985-90; University of California, Center for Near Eastern Studies, visiting professor. **Publications:** BOOKS IN ENGLISH: Jewish Poets And Writers of Modern Iraq, 1974; Al-Jabarti's Chronicle of the First Seven Months of the French Occupation of Egypt, June-December, 1798, 1975, 2nd ed., 1993; Modern Arabic Poetry, 1800-1970: The Development Of Its Forms And Themes Under The Influence Of Western Literature, 1976; Short Stories by Jewish Writers from Iraq, 1981; Studies in Modern Arabic Prose and Poetry, 1988; Live Theatre and Dramatic Literature in the Medieval Arab World, 1992; (with P. Sadgrove) Jewish Contributions to Nineteenth-Century Arabic Theatre, 1996; (trans. with P. Crone) The Book of Strangers: Mediaeval Arabic Graffiti on the Theme of Nostalgia, 2000. BOOKS IN HEBREW: (ed. and trans. with M. Milson) On the Other Shore: A Selection of Modern Egyptian Short Stories, 1980; (ed.) Studies on the History of the Iraqi Jewry and Their Culture, 1981; (ed. with Z. Yehuda) Hatred of Jews and the Farhud (Pogrom of 1941) in Iraq, 1993; (ed. with M. Milson) Bibliography for the Study of Modern Arabic Literature, 1800-1980, 1993; The Tree and the Branch: Studies in Modern Arabic Literature and Contributions of Iraqi-Jewish Writers, 1997. BOOKS IN ARABIC: Arabic Works by Jewish Writers, 1863-1973, 1973; Biographies and Bibliographies in Arabic Literature in Israel, 1948-86, 1987; Anthology of Modern Arabic Poetry, 1993; (ed. with M. Milson) Modern Arabic Literature A Research Bibliography, 1800-1980, 1993; (ed. with M. Shawarba) The Quik-Tempered Simpleton, 1997; Those Were the Days of Youth and Love (poetry anthology), 1998. OTHERS: Alwān min al-shir al-Arabī, 1967; Fihrisal-matbūāt al-Arabīyah allatī allafahā awnasharahā al-udabā wa-al-ulamā al-Yahū d, 1863-1973, 1973; Fihris al-matbūāt al-Arabīyah fī Isrāīl, 1948-1972, 1974; Tārīkh muddat al-Faransīs bi-Misor: Muharram-Rajab 1213 H, 15 Yūniyū-Dīsimbir 1798 M, 1975; Tarājim wa-āthār fī al-adab al-Arabī fīIsrāīl, 1948-1978, 1978; Meḥḳarim be-toldot Yehudelraḳ uve-tarbutam, 1981; Tarājim wa-āthār fī al-adabal-Arabī fī Isrāīl, 1948-1986, 1987; ṣ ayḥah minIrāq al-ahd al-bāid: shir, 1990; Sinat Yehudim u-feraotbe-Iraḳ: ḳovets meḥḳarim u-teudot, 1992; Maṣ ādirli-dirāsat al-adab al-Arabī al-ḥadīth wa-alāmihi, 1800-1980, 1993; Muntakhabāt min al-shir al-Arabīal-muāṣ ir, 1993; Nubūāt rajul majnūn fī madīnahmalūnah: majmūah qisoasoīyah, 1995; Ha-Ilan ṿehe-anaf: ha-sifrut ha-Arvit ha-ḥadashah ṿi-yetsiratam ha-sifrutit ha-Arvitshel yotse Iraḳ, 1997; Arab wa-Yahūd: dirāsāt fīal-mādoi wa-naẓrah ilá al-mustaqbal, 1998; Mūjaztārīkh Yahūd al-Irāq: min saby Bābil ilánuzūhoihim ām 1951, 1998; Yā Manal Yā Manālī: Ughniyāt Bi-al-lahjah Al-misrīyah Al-qāhirīyah, 2004; Ma'a Al-ghinā Al-Irāqī Mutribūn Wa-mutribāt Wa-aghānin Min Al-turāth Al-'Irāqī, 2005; Qūt Al-tuyūr: Dīwān Shi'r; 2006; Gaḥelet Rishonah: ṿe-livṭe Maḥshavah: Mivḥr Sipurim ṿ-shirim, 2006; Mi-gedot ha-ḥideḳel Li-gedot Ha-Yarḳon: Sipurim ṿe-zikhronot, 2006; (ed. with Z, Yehuda) Farhūd: The 1941 Pogrom in Iraq, 2010. **Address:** The Faculty of Humanities, Institute of Asian and African Studies, Hebrew University of Jerusalem, Hum. 5331, Mount Scopus, Jerusalem, 91905, Israel. **Online address:** moreh@h2.hum.huji.ac.il

MOREHOUSE, Lyda. American (born United States), b. 1967. **Genres:** Science Fiction/Fantasy, Novels, Young Adult Fiction. **Career:** Minnesota Historical Society, staff. Writer and educator. **Publications:** Archangel Protocol, 2000; Fallen Host, 2002; Messiah Node, 2003; Apocalypse Array, 2004; Resurrection Code, 2011. **Address:** c/o Author Mail, Roc Books, 375 Hudson St., New York, NY 10014-3658, U.S.A. **Online address:** l_morehouse@hotmail.com

MORELAND, Richard C. American (born United States), b. 1953. **Genres:** Literary Criticism And History, Biography, Education. **Career:** Louisiana State University, assistant professor, associate professor, professor of American literature, 1987-, associate chair, Graduate Studies in English, director, Department of English, professor and chair; University of Wales, Leverhulme fellow, 1991-92. Writer. **Publications:** Faulkner and Modernism: Rereading and Rewriting, 1990; Learning from Difference: Teaching Morrison, Twain, Ellison and Eliot, 1999; (ed.) Companion to William Faulkner, 2007. **Address:** Department of English, Louisiana State University, 260 Allen Hall, Baton Rouge, LA 70803-5001, U.S.A. **Online address:** enmore@lsu.edu

MORELL, James B. American (born United States), b. 1956. **Genres:** Law, History. **Career:** Attorney, 1988-; Los Angeles Daily Journal, consultant. Writer. **Publications:** The Law of the Sea: An Historical Analysis of the 1982 Treaty and Its Rejection by the United States, 1991. **Address:** c/o Superior Court of Orange County, 700 W Civic Center Dr., Santa Ana, CA 92701-4045, U.S.A.

MOREM, Susan. American (born United States) **Genres:** Education, Self Help. **Career:** Premier Presentation Inc., president. Writer, consultant and speaker. **Publications:** How to Gain the Professional Edge: Achieve the Personal and Professional Image You Want, 1997, 2nd ed., 2005; How to Get a Job and Keep It: Career and Life Skills You Need to Succeed, 2002, 2nd ed., 2007; 101 Tips for Graduates: A Code of Conduct for Success and Happiness in Your Professional Life, 2005, rev. ed., 2010. **Address:** Premier Presentation Inc., PO Box 41115, Minneapolis, MN 55441, U.S.A. **Online address:** sue@suemorem.com

MORENCY, Pierre. Canadian (born Canada), b. 1942. **Genres:** Poetry, Plays/Screenplays, Translations. **Career:** Université Laval, teacher of literature, 1960; Théâtre étudiant de Lévis, founder and director, 1961-64; Collège de Lévis, faculty, 1963-68; Inédits Journal, founder, director, 1969-71; Radio-Canada, broadcaster. Writer. **Publications:** Poèmes de la froide merveille de vivre, 1967; Poèmes de la vie déliée, 1968; (with P. Bertrand) Poèmes, 1970; Les Appels anonyms, 1971; Au nord constamment de l'amour, 1973; Lieu de naissance, 1973; (trans.) J.T. McDonough, Charbonneau et le chef (play), 1974; Marlot dans les merveilles, 1975; Le Temps des oiseaux, 1975; Les Passeuses, 1976; Tournebire et le Malin Frigo: les écoles de bon Bazou, 1978; Torrentiel, 1978; (contrib.) Ecrire l'amour, 1984; Effets personnels, 1986; Quand nous serons: poèmes 1967-1978, 1988; L'oeil américain: histories naturelles du nouveau monde, 1989; Lumiere des oiseaux: histories naturelles du nouveau monde, 1992; Les paroles qui marchent dans la nuit, 1994; Le regard infini: parcs, places et jardins publics de Québec, 1999; Words that Walk in the Night, 2001; A l'heure du loup, 2002; Poèmes, 1966-1986, 2004; Amouraska: poèmes, 2008. **Address:** c/o Author Mail, éditions Multi-Mondes, 930 Rue Pouliot, Sainte-Foy, QC G1V 3N9, Canada.

MORENO, Jonathan D. American (born United States), b. 1952. **Genres:** Ethics, Social Sciences, Politics/Government. **Career:** Washington University, fellow, Science Progress, editor; Hastings Center, staff, fellow, adjunct associate, 1984-85; George Washington University, faculty of philosophy and medicine, 1985-89; Children's National Medical Center, philosopher-in-residence, 1985-89; State University of New York, Health Science Center, professor of pediatrics and medicine, 1989-98, Division of Humanities in Medicine, founder and director, 1989-98; University of Pennsylvania, Center for Bioethics, faculty associate, 1995-97, professor, David and Lyn Silfen University professor; University of Virginia, Emily Davie and Joseph S. Kornfeld professor of biomedical ethics, Center for Biomedical Ethics, director, 1998-, Emily Davie and Joseph S. Kornfeld chair of biomedical ethics, 1998-2006, visiting professor of biomedical ethics; Swarthmore College, faculty; University of Texas, faculty; Center for American Progress, senior fellow. Writer. **Publications:** (With B.R. Glassner) Discourse in the Social Sciences: Strategies for Translating Models of Mental Illness, 1982; (with J.C. Ahronheim and C. Zuckerman) Ethics in Clinical Practice, 1994, 2nd ed., 2005; Deciding Together: Bioethics and Moral Consensus, 1995; Undue Risk: Secret State Experiments on Humans, 2000; Is There an Ethicist in the House?: On the Cutting Edge of Bioethics, 2005; Mind Wars: Brain Research and National Defense, 2006; The Body Politic: The Battle Over Science in America, 2011. EDITOR: (with B.R. Glassner) The Qualitative-Quantitative Distinction in the Social Sciences, 1989; Paying the Doctor: Health Policy and Physician Reimbursement, 1991; Arguing Euthanasia: The Controversy over Mercy Killing, Assisted Suicide and the Right to Die, 1995; In the Wake of Terror: Medicine and Morality in a Time of Crisis, 2003; (with R. Weiss) Science Next: Innovation for the Common Good from the Center for American Progress, 2009; (with S. Berger) Progress in Bioethics: Science, Policy and Politics, 2010. Contributor of book chapters to publications. **Address:** Center for Bioethics, University of Pennsylvania, 3401 Market St., Ste. 320, Philadelphia, PA 19104-3308, U.S.A. **Online address:** morenojd@mail.med.upenn.edu

MORENO, Paul D. American (born United States), b. 1965. **Genres:** Law, History, Race Relations. **Career:** State University of New York, graduate teaching assistant, 1987-88; University of Maryland, graduate teaching assistant, 1989-94; St. Thomas Aquinas College, assistant professor, 1994-98; Massachusetts News, editor-in-chief, 1998-99; Hillsdale College, William and Berniece Grewcock Chair in the Constitution of the United States and associate professor of history, 1999-, John M. Olin Junior Faculty Fellow, 2001-02. **Publications:** From Direct Action to Affirmative Action: Fair Employment Law and Policy in America, 1933-1972, 1997; Black Americans and Organized Labor: A New History, 2006. **Address:** Hillsdale College, 33 E College St., Hillsdale, MI 49242-1205, U.S.A. **Online address:** pmoreno@hillsdale.edu

MORETON, **John.** *See* **COHEN**, **Morton N(orton).**

MORETON, **N. Edwina.** British (born England), b. 1950. **Genres:** Military/Defense/Arms Control, International Relations/Current Affairs, Politics/Government, Writing/Journalism, History, Social Sciences. **Career:** Massachusetts Institute of Technology, Harkness fellow, 1976-78; University of Wales, lecturer in political science, 1978-80; Economist, editorial staff, 1980-, diplomatic editor, 1990-, deputy foreign editor, 1993-. **Publications:** East Germany and the Warsaw Alliance: The Politics of Détente, 1978; (co-author) Nuclear War and Nuclear Peace, 1983; (with G. Flynn and G. Treverton) Public Images of Western Security, 1985. EDITOR: (with G. Segal) Soviet Strategy Toward Western Europe, 1984; Germany between East and West, 1987. **Address:** Economist, 25 St. James, London, GL SW1A 1HG, England.

MOREY, **Ann Janine.** (Ann-Janine Morey-Gaines). American (born United States), b. 1951. **Genres:** Literary Criticism And History, Theology/Religion, Social Sciences, Criminology/True Crime. **Career:** University of Southern California, instructor in women's studies, 1978-79; California State University, instructor, 1978-79; Southern Illinois University, assistant professor, 1979-85, associate professor of religious studies, 1985-89, associate professor of English, 1989-94, professor, 1994-, director of general education, 1993-99; Whitman College, Johnston visiting professor of religion, 1985-; Grinnell College, Roberts lecturer, 1987-; Valparaiso University, lecturer, 1988-; University of Tennessee, lecturer, 1990-; James Madison University, College of Arts and Letters, associate dean for interdisciplinary programs, 1999-2005, director of the writing program, associate dean for cross disciplinary studies, associate vice provost for cross disciplinary studies. Writer. **Publications:** (As Ann-Janine Morey-Gaines) Apples and Ashes: Culture, Metaphor, and Morality in the American Dream, 1982; Religion and Sexuality in American Literature, 1992; What Happened to Christopher: An American Family's Story of Shaken Baby Syndrome, 1998. Works appear in anthologies. Contributor to periodicals and journals. **Address:** Department of English, James Madison University, Moody 102, 800 S Main Str., Harrisonburg, VA 22807-0001, U.S.A. **Online address:** moreyai@jmu.edu

MOREY, **Melanie M.** American (born United States) **Genres:** Popular Culture, Adult Non-fiction. **Career:** Palm Beach Academy, faculty and dean of women, 1971-73; White Mountain School, faculty and dean of women, 1973-76; Boston University, administrative director of residence life, 1977-79; Newton Country Day School of the Sacred Heart, faculty and director of studies, 1979-81; Newton-Wellesley Hospital, residency training program in medicine, medical education coordinator, 1981-87; Western New England College, MBA Program, adjunct faculty, 1983; St. Ignatius Parish, director of religious education, 1983-84; The Channel Program, educational methodology and field supervision, director of education program, 1988-90, director of development, 1990-91; Seattle University, Graduate School of Education, adjunct faculty, 1989; Roman Catholic Archdiocese of Seattle, Soundings Program for Ministerial Discernment, faculty, 1990; Regis College, Field Experience Internship, Revision of College By-Laws, assistant, 1993; Leadership and Legacy Associates Inc., founder and senior associate, 1995-2003; Villanova University, Education Department, adjunct faculty, 1998-2000; Boston College, Institute of Religious Education and Pastoral Ministry, special assistant for external relations and strategic planning, 1998-99, Summer Institute for Administrators in Catholic Higher Education, presenter, 2001-; Narrow Gate Consulting (division of the Catholic Education Institute), senior director for research and consulting, 2003-; Council for Independent College, Summer Seminar for Presidents and Potential Presidents on the Intersection of Personal Vocation and the Office of the Presidency, facilitator, 2005-; Integrating the Catholic Intellectual Tradition, co-founder and co-director, 2006-. Writer and consultant. **Publications:** WITH J.J. PIDERIT: Catholic Higher Education: A Culture in Crisis, 2006; Renewing Parish Culture: Building for a Catholic Future, 2008; (ed.) Teaching the Tradition, 2012. **Address:** Catholic Education Institute, St. Helena Hall, 925 Hutchinson River Pkwy., Ste. 202, Bronx, NY 10465, U.S.A. **Online address:** melaniemorey@gmail.com

MOREY-GAINES, **Ann-Janine.** *See* **MOREY**, **Ann Janine.**

MORGAN, **Alison M.** Also writes as Alison Mary Raikes. Welsh/British (born England), b. 1930. **Genres:** Children's Fiction, Young Adult Fiction. **Career:** Educator, 1953-59. Writer. **Publications:** Fish, 1971 in US as A Boy Called Fish, 1973; Pete, 1972; Ruth Crane, 1973; At Willie Tucker's Place, 1975; River Song, 1976; Leaving Home in US as All Kinds of Prickles, 1980; Paul's Kite, 1981; Brighteye, 1984; Christabel, 1984; The Eyes of the Blind, 1985; Staples for Amos, 1986; The Raft, 1988; The Wild Morgans, 1988; A Walk with Smudge, 1989; Smudge and the Danger Lion, 1989; The Biggest Birthday Card in the World, 1989; Caroline's Coat, 1991; Granny and the Hedgehog, 1995. **Address:** AP Watt Ltd., 20 John St., London, GL WC1N 2DR, England.

MORGAN, **Austen.** British/Irish (born Ireland), b. 1949. **Genres:** History, Biography, Law, Politics/Government, Social Sciences. **Career:** University of Warwick, Industrial Relations Research Unit, research associate, 1975-77; University of Dublin, Trinity College, visiting academic, 1980-81; freelance writer, 1981-; barrister at law, 1995-. **Publications:** (Ed. with B. Purdie) Ireland, Divided Nation, Divided Class, 1980; J. Ramsay MacDonald, 1987; James Connolly: A Political Biography, 1988; Labour and Partition: The Belfast Working Class, 1905-1923, 1991; Harold Wilson, 1992; The Belfast Agreement: A Practical Legal Analysis, 2000; The Hand Of History?, 2011. **Address:** 33 Bedford Row, London, GL WC1R 4JH, England. **Online address:** austen@austenmorgan.com

MORGAN, **Bernice.** Canadian (born Canada), b. 1935. **Genres:** Novels, Novellas/Short Stories, Women's Studies And Issues. **Career:** The Gazette, editor; The Bulletin, communications officer and editor. **Publications:** The Very Thought of Thee: Adventures of an Arctic Missionary, 1952; (ed. with H. Porter and G. Rubia) From This Place: A Selection of Writing by Women of Newfoundland and Labrador, 1978; Random Passage (novel), 1992; Waiting for Time (novel), 1995; The Topography of Love: Stores, 2000; Cape Random: A Novel, 2002; Cloud of Bone, 2007. **Address:** Breakwater Books, 100 Water St., PO Box 2188, St. Johns, NL A1C 6E6, Canada.

MORGAN, **Dan.** American (born United States), b. 1937. **Genres:** Adult Non-fiction, Business/Trade/Industry, Economics, History, Technology. **Career:** Washington Post, reporter and editor, 1963-, coresspondent, 1967-73, staff writer. **Publications:** Soviet Union and Eastern Europe: New Paths, Old Ruts, 1973; Merchants of Grain, 1979; (ed. and intro.) Patrick Welsh, Tales Out of School: A Teacher's Candid Account from the Front Lines of the American High School Today, 1986; Rising in the West: The True Story of an Okie Family from the Great Depression through the Reagan Years, 1992, as Rising in the West: The True Story of an Okie Family in Search of the American Dream, 1993. Contributor to periodicals. **Address:** International Creative Management, 40 W 57th St., New York, NY 10019, U.S.A.

MORGAN, **David.** American (born United States), b. 1960. **Genres:** Communications/Media, Art/Art History, Music. **Career:** Journalist. **Publications:** (Contrib.) Monty Python Speaks!: John Cleese, Terry Gilliam, Eric Idle, Terry Jones, and Michael Palin Recount an Amazing, and Silly, Thirty-Year Spree in Television and Film-In Their Own Words, Squire!, 1999; Knowing the Score: Film Composers Talk About the Art, Craft, Blood, Sweat, and Tears of Writing for Cinema, 2000. Contributor to books and periodicals. **Address:** c/o William Contardi, Brandt & Hochman Literary Agents Inc., 1501 Broadway, Ste. 2310, New York, NY 10036, U.S.A. **Online address:** morgands1@aol.com

MORGAN, **Diane.** American (born United States), b. 1947. **Genres:** Animals/Pets, Young Adult Fiction. **Career:** Wilson College, adjunct assistant professor, adjunct professor of religion and philosophy, 1998-, assistant professor of philosophy, professor; Frederick Community College, faculty. Writer. **Publications:** Understanding Your Horse's Lameness, rev. ed., 1992; The Basset Hound Owner's Survival Guide, 1998; The Complete Idiot's Guide to Siberian Huskies, 1999; The Best Guide to Eastern Philosophy and Religion, 2001; Siberian Huskies for Dummies, 2001; The Beagle: An Owner's Survival Guide, 2002; The Poodle: An Owner's Survival Guide, 2002; Feeding Your Dog for Life: The Real Facts about Proper Nutrition, 2002; The Simple Guide to Choosing a Dog, 2003; Magical Tarot, Mystical Tao: Unlocking the Hidden Power of the Tarot Using the Ancient Secrets of the Tao Te Ching, 2003; The Buddhist Experience in America, 2004; Feeding Your Horse for Life, 2004; Train the Wolf in Your Dog: Genetic Clues to Solving Behavior Problems, 2004; The Dachshund: An Owner's Survival Guide, 2004; The Charmed Garden: Sacred and Enchanting Plants for the Magically Inclined Herbalist, 2004; The Beagle, 2005; The Bulldog, 2005; Bird Care, 2005; The German Shepherd Dog, 2005; Good Dogkeeping: Today's Guide to Caring for Your Best Friend, 2005; The Labrador Retriever, 2005; The Dog Dictionary: Canine Lingo from A to Z, 2005; The Maltese, 2006; (with R. Miller) Chihuahuas, 2006; Sneeze-Free Dog Breeds, 2006; Quick & Easy the Well-Behaved Family Dog: Step-by-Step Techniques for Parenting a Happy

Dog, 2007; From Satan's Crown to the Holy Grail: Emeralds in Myth, Magic, and History, 2007; The Weimaraner, 2007; Fire and Blood: Rubies in Myth, Magic, and History, 2008; Parson & Jack Russell Terriers, 2007; (with W.L. Hunthausen) The Living Well Guide for Senior Dogs: Everything You Need to Know for a Happy & Healthy Companion, 2007; The Sneeze-Free Cat Owner: Allergy Management and Breed Selection for the Allergic Cat Lover, 2007; Snakes in Myth, Magic, and History: The Story of a Human Obsession, 2008; Gemlore: Ancient Secrets and Modern Myths from the Stone Age to the Rock Age, 2008; Your Inner Dog, 2008; Good Catkeeping, 2007; The Whole Horse Wellness Guide: Natural and Conventional Care for a Healthy Horse, 2008; Encyclopedia of Dog Sports and Activities: A Field Guide to 35 Fun Activities for You and Your Dog, 2009; Essential Islam: A Comprehensive Guide to Belief and Practice, 2010; Essential Buddhism, 2010; The Dog Care Handbook: The Complete Guide for a Healthy, Happy and Well-trained Dog, 2011; Complete Guide to Dog Care, 2011. **Address:** Wilson College, 1015 Philadelphia Ave., Chambersburg, PA 17201, U.S.A. **Online address:** dmorgan@wilson.edu

MORGAN, Douglas. *See* **MACDONALD, James D.**

MORGAN, Elizabeth Seydel. American (born United States), b. 1939. **Genres:** Poetry. **Career:** Saint Catherine's School, founder of creative writing program; University of Richmond, teacher of poetry writing; Lee University, teacher of poetry writing; Virginia Museum of Fine Arts, staff; Virginia Correctional Center for Women, staff; Hollins University, Louis D. Rubin Jr. writer-in-residence, 2007; Washington University, faculty; Lee University, faculty; Virginia Museum of Fine Arts, faculty. Poet. **Publications:** POEMS: Parties, 1988; The Governor of Desire, 1993; On Long Mountain, 1998; Without a Philosophy, 2007. Works appear in anthologies. Contributor to periodicals. **Address:** c/o Author Mail, Louisiana State University Press, PO Box 25053, Baton Rouge, LA 70894-5053, U.S.A.

MORGAN, Francesca. American (born United States) **Genres:** Adult Nonfiction, Women's Studies And Issues. **Career:** National Institutes of Health, archival technician, 1990-91; University of North Texas, Department of History, assistant professor of history, 1998-2002; Northwestern University, Department of History, departmental associate, 2002-06; Northeastern Illinois University, Department of History, visiting lecturer, 2003-06, secretary, 2006-10, assistant professor of history, 2006-10, associate professor, 2010-, Women's Studies Program, faculty, 2007-. Writer. **Publications:** Women and Patriotism in Jim Crow America, 2005. Contributor to journals. **Address:** Department of History, Northeastern Illinois University, 5500 N St. Louis Ave., Chicago, IL 60625-4699, U.S.A. **Online address:** f-morgan@neiu.edu

MORGAN, Glyn. American (born United States), b. 1958?. **Genres:** Politics/Government. **Career:** Harvard University, associate professor of government and social studies. Academic and writer. **Publications:** The Idea of a European Superstate: Public Justification and European Integration, 2005. Contributor to periodicals and journals. **Address:** Harvard University, Department of Government, 1737 Cambridge St., Cambridge, MA 02138, U.S.A. **Online address:** gmorgan@gov.harvard.edu

MORGAN, Hunter. *See* **FAULKNER, Colleen.**

MORGAN, Janet. British/Canadian (born Canada), b. 1945. **Genres:** Communications/Media, Politics/Government, Biography. **Career:** Exeter College, lecturer in politics, 1974-76; St. Hugh's College, director of studies, 1975-76, lecturer in politics, 1976-78; U.K. Cabinet Office, Central Policy Review, staff, 1978-81; British Broadcasting Corp., special adviser to director general, 1981-84; All Souls College, visiting fellow, 1983; Granada Group, adviser, 1984-87; Murray International Investment Trust, non-executive director; Albion Enterprise VCT P.L.C., non-executive director; Scottish Oriental Smaller Companies Investment Trust P.L.C., non-executive director. Writer. **Publications:** The House of Lords and the Labour Government, 1964-1970, 1975; Reinforcing Parliament: Services and Facilities for Members of Parliament: Some International Comparisons, 1976; (ed.) The Diaries of a Cabinet Minister 1964-70, vol. III, 1977; (ed.) Backbench Diaries of Richard Crossman, 1981; (ed. with R. Hoggart) Future of Broadcasting: Essays on Authority, Style and Choice, 1982; (with J. Spicer) Presse et l'Etat. laréglementation de la presse écrite dans douze pays occidentaux, 1982; Agatha Christie: A Biography, 1984, rev. ed., 1986; Edwina Mountbatten: A Life of Her Own, 1991; The Secrets of Rue St Roch, 2004. **Address:** Jenny Brown Associates, 33 Argyle Pl., Edinburgh, LT EH9 1JT, Scotland. **Online address:** jenny@jennybrownassociates.com

MORGAN, Jeanne. *See* **ZARUCCHI, Jeanne Morgan.**

MORGAN, Jennifer L. American (born United States) **Genres:** Social Sciences, Women's Studies And Issues. **Career:** New York University, Department of History, associate professor, professor of social and cultural analysis, Graduate Studies, director; Rutgers University, faculty. Writer. **Publications:** (Contrib.) Money, Trade, and Power: The Evolution of Colonial South Carolina's Plantation Society, 2000; (contrib.) A Companion to American Women's History, 2002; Laboring Women: Reproduction and Gender in New World Slavery, 2004; Accounting for the Women in Slavery, forthcoming. Contributor to journals. **Address:** Office of the Dean, Faculty of Arts and Science, New York University, 5 Washington Sq. N, 1st Fl., PO Box 5911, New York, NY 10003, U.S.A. **Online address:** jennifer.morgan@nyu.edu

MORGAN, Joseph G. American (born United States), b. 1953. **Genres:** History. **Career:** Teacher, 1975-78, 1985-93; Iona College, professed perpetual vows, 1980, associate professor of American history, 1989-, Department of History, chair, 1989-2008. Writer. **Publications:** The Vietnam Lobby: The American Friends of Vietnam, 1955-1975, 1997; Wesley Fishel and Vietnam: A Special Kind of Friend' in The Human Tradition in America Since 1945, 2003; A Change in Course: American Catholics, Anticommunism and the Vietnam War in US as Catholic Historian, 2004. **Address:** Department of History, Iona College, 715 North Ave., New Rochelle, NY 10801, U.S.A. **Online address:** jmorgan@iona.edu

MORGAN, Jude. *See* **WILSON, T. R.**

MORGAN, Kimberly J. American (born United States), b. 1970. **Genres:** Theology/Religion, Politics/Government. **Career:** George Washington University, associate professor, 2001-. Writer. **Publications:** Working Mothers and the Welfare State: Religion and the Politics of Work-Family Policies in Western Europe and the United States, 2006. Contributor to books. **Address:** Woodrow Wilson International Center for Scholars, Ronald Reagan Bldg. and International Trade Ctr., 1 Woodrow Wilson Plz., 1300 Pennsylvania Ave. NW, Washington, DC 20004-3027, U.S.A. **Online address:** kjmorgan@gwu.edu

MORGAN, Lael. American (born United States), b. 1936. **Genres:** History, How-to Books, Anthropology/Ethnology, Recreation, Social Commentary, Travel/Exploration. **Career:** Juneau Daily Empire, reporter, 1965-66; Fairbanks Daily News Miner, reporter, 1966-69; Los Angeles Times, reporter, 1969-74; Tundra Times, reporter, 1971-73; Alaska Northwest Publishing Co., editor, 1974-80; National Geographic, writer, 1982-87; Washington Post, writer, 1982-87; California State University, Office of Public Affairs, acting director, 1987-88; Chapman College, instructor, 1988; Epicenter Press, founding partner and acquisitions editor, 1988-; University of Alaska, Department of Journalism and Broadcasting, chair, 1995-97; Casco Bay Weekly, managing editor, 1999-2002; University of Texas, College of Liberal Arts, Department of Communication, lecturer, 2003-. **Publications:** The Woman's Guide to Boating & Cooking, 1968, 2nd ed., 1974; And the Land Provides: Alaskan Natives in a Year of Transition, 1975; Tatting: A New Look at the Old Art of Making Lace, 1977; Alaska Whales and Whaling, 1978; Alaska's Native People, 1979; The Aleutians, 1980, 2nd ed., 1981; Kotzebue Basin, 1981; (co-ed.) Alaska Southeast to McKinley: A Belt of Emeralds, 1986; Art and Eskimo Power: The Life and Times of Alaskan Howard Rock, 1989; Earthquake Survival Manual, 1993; Good Time Girls of the Alaska Gold Rush, 1998; Wanton West: Madams, Money, Murder and the Wild Women of Montana's Frontier, 2011; Eskimo Star: From Tundra to Tinseltown: The Ray Mala Story, 2011. **Address:** Department of Communication, University of Texas, 700 W Greek Row Dr., PO Box 19107, Arlington, TX 76019-0107, U.S.A. **Online address:** morgan03@uta.edu

MORGAN, Marjorie. *See* **CHIBNALL, Marjorie McCallum.**

MORGAN, Marlo. American (born United States), b. 1936. **Genres:** Science Fiction/Fantasy, Young Adult Fiction. **Career:** Physician, chiropractic and writer. **Publications:** Mutant Message Down Under, 1994, 2nd ed., 2004; Message from Forever, 1998. Contributor to periodicals. **Address:** HarperCollins Publishers, 10 E 53rd St., New York, NY 10022, U.S.A.

MORGAN, Mary. American (born United States), b. 1943. **Genres:** Adult

Non-fiction, Self Help, Autobiography/Memoirs, Biography. **Career:** Teacher, 1969-73; Arkansas State Health Department, educator, 1973; University of Arkansas Medical School, Continuing Education in Psychiatry, program coordinator, 1973-75; writer, 1976-; Dr. Spock Co., founder. **Publications:** Stepparenting, 1986; (with B. Spock) Spock on Spock: A Memoir of Growing Up With the Century, 1989. Contributor to magazines. **Address:** The Dr. Spock Co., 1075 Curtis St., Menlo Park, CA 94025, U.S.A.

MORGAN, M. Gwyn. American/British (born England), b. 1937. **Genres:** History, Military/Defense/Arms Control. **Career:** Victoria University of Wellington, Department of classics, lecturer, 1961-67; University of California, Department of History, assistant professor, 1968-70; University of Texas, departments of classics and history, associate professor, 1970-76, professor, 1976-, now professor emeritus. Writer. **Publications:** 69 A.D.: The Year of Four Emperors, 2006. **Address:** Department of Classics and History, University of Texas, 1 University Sta. B7000, WAG 109, Austin, TX 78712, U.S.A. **Online address:** mgm@mail.utexas.edu

MORGAN, Michael L. American (born United States), b. 1944. **Genres:** Theology/Religion, Philosophy, History. **Career:** Indiana University, instructor, 1975-78, assistant professor, 1978-83, associate professor, 1983-90, professor, 1990-2003, Chancellor's Professor Emeritus of Philosophy and Jewish Studies, 2004, Office of Academic Affairs, associate dean, 1994-96, director of graduate studies and scheduling officer of philosophy department; Kelley School of Business, director of undergraduate program. Writer, rabbi and academic. **Publications:** (ed.) The Jewish Thought of Emil Fackenheim: A Reader, 1987; Platonic Piety: Philosophy and Ritual in Fourth-Century Athens, 1990; (ed.) Classics of Moral and Political Theory, 1992, 4th ed., 2005; Dilemmas in Modern Jewish Thought: The Dialectics of Revelation and History, 1992; (ed.) Jewish Philosophers and Jewish Philosophy, 1996; (ed. and trans. with P.W. Franks) Philosophical and Theological Writings, 2000; (ed.) A Holocaust Reader: Responses to the Nazi Extermination, 2001; Beyond Auschwitz: PostHolocaust Jewish Thought in America, 2001; Interim Judaism: Jewish Thought in a Century of Crisis, 2001; (ed.) Spinoza: Complete Works, 2002; (ed.) The Essential Spinoza: Ethics and Related Writings, 2006; (ed. with P.E. Gordon) The Cambridge Companion to Modern Jewish Philosophy, 2007; Discovering Levinas, 2007; On Shame, 2008; (ed. with B. Pollock) The Philosopher as Witness: Fackenheim and Responses to the Holocaust, 2008. Contributor of articles to books, periodicals and journals. **Address:** Department of Philosophy, Indiana University, 26 Sycamore Hall, 1033 E 3rd St., Bloomington, IN 47405-7005, U.S.A. **Online address:** morganm@indiana.edu

MORGAN, Neil. American (born United States), b. 1924. **Genres:** Geography, History, Social Commentary, Travel/Exploration, Biography, Photography. **Career:** Raleigh News and Observer, reporter, 1942-43; San Diego Daily Journal, columnist, 1946-50; San Diego Evening Tribune, columnist, 1950-, travel editor, 1976-, associate editor, 1978-, editor, 1981-92; Copley News Service, assignment west, syndicated columnist, 1958-; NPR station KPBS, commentator, 2004; voiceofsandiego.org, co-founder and senior editor of the news website, 2005-. Journalist, author and lecturer. **Publications:** My San Diego, 1951; It Began with a Roar, 1953; (with L. Smollar) Know Your Doctor, 1954; Crosstown, 1955; My San Diego 1960, 1959; Westward Tilt: The American West Today, 1963; Neil Morgan's San Diego, 1964; The Pacific States: California, Oregon, Washington, 1967; Pancho Villa, 1967; The California Syndrome, 1969; (with R.M. Witty) Marines of the Margarita, 1970; San Diego: The Unconventional City, 1972; (with T. Blair) Yesterday's San Diego, 1976; Sam Ragan, 1981; (intro.) Best of San Diego: A Discriminating Guide, 1982; This Great Land, 1983; (contrib.) Above San Diego: A New Collection of Historical and Original Aerial Photographs of San Diego, 1990; (co-ed.) Managing and Marketing Services in the 1990s, 1990; (with J. Morgan) Dr. Seuss & Mr. Geisel: A Biography, 1995. Contributor of articles to magazines. **Address:** Voiceofsandiego.org, 2508 Historic Decatur Rd., Ste. 120, San Diego, CA 92106, U.S.A. **Online address:** nmorgan@san.rr.com

MORGAN, Nicholas H. (Nick Morgan). American (born United States), b. 1953. **Genres:** Plays/Screenplays, Communications/Media, Literary Criticism And History, Poetry. **Career:** University of Virginia, assistant dean of admissions, 1982-83, assistant vice-president and provost, 1983-84; chief speechwriter for Virginia Governor Charles S. Robb, 1984-86; Unisys Corp., senior speechwriter, 1986-87; Princeton University, director of development communications and lecturer in English, 1987-94; Gemini Consulting, writer and consultant, 1994-95; CSC Index, consultant, 1995-97; Public Words, communication consultant, 1997-. **Publications:** Secret Journeys: Theory and Practice in Reading Dickens, 1992; Working the Room: How to Move People to Action through Audience-Centered Speaking, 2003; Trust Me: Four Steps to Authenticity and Charisma, 2009. Works appear in anthologies. Contributor to periodicals. **Address:** Public Words, 470 Atlantic Ave., 4th Fl., Boston, MA 02210, U.S.A. **Online address:** nick@publicwords.com

MORGAN, Nick. *See* **MORGAN, Nicholas H.**

MORGAN, Philip. British (born England), b. 1948?. **Genres:** History. **Career:** University of Hull, senior lecturer in contemporary European history, 1977-. Writer. **Publications:** Italian Fascism, 1919-1945, 1995; Fascism in Europe, 1919-1945, 2003; The Fall of Mussolini: Italy, the Italians, and the Second World War, 2007. **Address:** University of Hull, Cottingham Rd., Hull, HU6 7RX, England. **Online address:** p.j.morgan@hull.ac.uk

MORGAN, Philip D. American (born United States), b. 1949?. **Genres:** History, Local History/Rural Topics, Social Sciences. **Career:** The Open University, tutor, 1975-77; University of Keele, lecturer in American history, 1976-77; The Flinders University of South Australia, research fellow, 1978; VPI & State University, assistant professor, 1982-83; Institute of Early American History, post-doctoral fellow, 1981-84, editor of publications, 1984-87; College of William and Mary, adjunct associate professor, 1984-87, William and Mary Quarterly, editor, 1997-2000, professor, 1997-2000, Harry C. Black professor of history; University of California, visiting assistant professor, 1985-86; Florida State University, associate professor, 1987-94, professor, 1995-97; Harvard University, Charles Warren Center, research fellow, 1987-88, visiting associate professor, 1994; Johns Hopkins University, professor, 2000-; Eighteenth-Century Studies, advisory editor, 2001-04. **Publications:** Slave Counterpoint: Black Culture in the Eighteenth-Century Chesapeake and Lowcountry, 1998. EDITOR: Don't Grieve after Me: The Black Experience in Virginia, 1619-1986, 1986; (with L.G. Carr and J.B. Russo) Colonial Chesapeake Society, 1988; (comp. with D.L. Ammerman) Books about Early America: 2001 Titles, 1989; (with I. Berlin) The Slaves' Economy: Independent Production by Slaves in the Americas, 1991; (with B. Bailyn) Strangers within the Realm: Cultural Margins of the First British Empire, 1991; Diversity and Unity in Early North America, 1993; (with I. Berlin) Cultivation and Culture: Labor and the Shaping of Slave Life in the Americas, 1993; (with S. Hawkins) Black Experience and the Empire, 2004; (with C.L. Brown) Arming Slaves: from Classical Times to the Modern Age, 2006; (with R.L. Kagan) Atlantic Diasporas: Jews, Conversos and Crypto-Jews in the Age of Mercantilism, 1500-1800, 2009; (with J.P. Greene) Atlantic History: A Critical Appraisal, 2009; African American Life in the Georgia Lowcountry: The Atlantic World and the Gullah Geechee Race in the Atlantic World 1700-1900, 2010; (ed. with N. Canny) The Oxford Handbook of the Atlantic World, 1450-1850, 2011. Contributor to periodicals. **Address:** Department of History, Johns Hopkins University, 370 Gilman Hall, 3400 N Charles St., Baltimore, MD 21218, U.S.A. **Online address:** pmorgan@jhu.edu

MORGAN, Robert C. American/Welsh (born Wales), b. 1943. **Genres:** Art/Art History, Essays. **Career:** Rochester Institute of Technology, professor of the history and theory of art, 1988-2001; Columbia University, Barnard College, visiting professor, 1991-92; New York City art gallery, director, 1989-90; Pratt Institute, Graduate School of Fine Arts, adjunct professor; School of Visual Arts, lecturer. Curator and writer. **Publications:** Robert Barry, 1986; Haim Steinbach, 1988; Duchamp, Androgyny, Etc..., 1990; Oskar De Mejo: The Naive Surrealist, 1991; New Media Arts, 1992; A Hans Bellmer Miscellany, 1993; After the Deluge: Essays on the Art of the Nineties, 1993; Conceptual Art: An American Perspective, 1994; Art into Ideas: Essays on Conceptual Art, 1995; Between Modernism and Conceptual Art, 1997; The End of the Art World, 1998; Bernar Venet, 1961-70, 1999; Gary Hill, 2000; Bruce Nauman, 2002; Alain Kirili, 2002; Clement Greenberg: Late Writings, 2003; Vasarely, 2004; Made Wianta: Wild Dogs in Bali, 2005; The Artist and Globalization, 2008; Will Barnet: A Sketchbook, 1932-1934, 2009. Contributor of articles to journals. **Address:** Department of Fine Arts, Pratt Institute, 200 Willoughby Ave., Brooklyn, NY 11205, U.S.A. **Online address:** rcmorgan12@aol.com

MORGAN, Robert (R.). American (born United States), b. 1944. **Genres:** Poetry, Essays, Biography. **Career:** University of North Carolina, Greensboro, teaching assistant, 1967-68; Salem College, instructor in English, 1968-69; farmer, housepainter and writer, 1969-71; Cornell University, Department of English, lecturer, 1971-73, assistant professor, 1973-78, associate professor, 1978-84, professor of English, 1984-92, acting chair, 1986-87,

1988, Kappa Alpha professor of English, 1992-, director of undergraduate studies, 1980-81, 1983-85, chair of creative writing, 1982-83, 1997; Davidson College, McGee visiting writer, 1998; Appalachian State University, distinguished visiting professor of writing, 2000, Rivers-Coffey distinguished visiting writer, 2007; Furman University, visiting writer, 2002; Duke University, distinguished visiting writer, 2003, writer-in-residence, 2004; East Carolina University, visiting writer, Whichard professor and chair, 2005. **Publications:** Zirconia Poems, 1969; The Voice in the Crosshairs, 1971; Red Owl: Poems, 1972; Land Diving: New Poems, 1976; Trunk and Thicket, 1978; Groundwork: Poems, 1979; Bronze Age, 1981; At the Edge of the Orchard Country, 1987; The Blue Valleys: A Collection of Stories, 1989; Sigodlin: Poems, 1990; Green River: New and Selected Poems, 1991; The Mountains Won't Remember Us, and Other Stories, 1992; Good Measure: Essays, Interviews, and Notes on Poetry, 1993; The Hinterlands: A Mountain Tale in Three Parts, 1994; The Truest Pleasure, 1995; Wild Peavines: New Poems, 1996; Gap Creek: A Novel, 1999; The Balm of Gilead Tree: New and Selected Stories, 1999; Topsoil Road: Poems, 2000; This Rock: A Novel, 2001; Brave Enemies: A Novel, 2003; The Strange Attractor: New and Selected Poems, 2004; Boone: A Biography, 2007; October Crossing, 2009; Terroir, 2011; Lions of the West: Heroes and Villains of the Westward Expansion, 2011. Works appear in anthologies. Contributor to periodicals. **Address:** Department of English, Cornell University, 363 Goldwin Smith Hall, Ithaca, NY 14853-3201, U.S.A. **Online address:** rrm4@cornell.edu

MORGAN, Robin. American (born United States), b. 1941. **Genres:** Novels, Children's Fiction, Plays/Screenplays, Poetry, International Relations/Current Affairs, Politics/Government, Women's Studies And Issues, Autobiography/Memoirs, Essays, Philosophy, Social Commentary, History, Communications/Media, Civil Liberties/Human Rights, Anthropology/Ethnology, Romance/Historical. **Career:** Curtis Brown Ltd., associate literary agent, 1960-62; freelance editor, 1964-70; Grove Press, consulting editor, 1968-70; writer, 1970-; Ms. Magazine, contributing editor, 1977-87, editor-in-chief, 1989-93, international consulting editor, 1993-. **Publications:** FICTION: Dry Your Smile, 1987; The Mer-Child: A Legend for Children and Other Adults, 1991; The Burning Time, 2006; The Yarner, 2012. NONFICTION: Going Too Far: The Personal Chronicle of a Feminist, 1977; The Anatomy of Freedom: Feminism, Physics and Global Politics, 1982 as Anatomy of Freedom: Feminism in Four Dimensions, 1994; The Demon Lover: On the Sexuality of Terrorism, 1989 as Demon Lover: The Roots of Terrorism, 2001; The Word of a Woman: Feminist Dispatches, 1968-1991, 1992; A Woman's Creed, 1994; Saturday's Child: A Memoir, 2001; Fighting Words: A Tool Kit for Combating the Religious Right, 2006. POETRY: Monster: Poems, 1972; Lady of the Beasts: Poems, 1976; Death Benefits, 1981; Depth Perception: New Poems and a Masque, 1982; Upstairs in the Garden: Poems Selected and New, 1968-1988, 1990; A Hot January: Poems 1996-1999, 1999. PLAYS: Their Own Country, 1961; The Duel (verse play), 1982. ANTHOLOGIES: Sisterhood is Powerful: An Anthology of Writings from the Women's Liberation Movement, 1970; (ed. with C. Bunch-Weeks and J. Cooke) The New Women: A Motive Anthology on Women's Liberation, 1970; Sisterhood is Global: The International Women's Movement Anthology, 1984, rev. ed., 1996; Sisterhood is Forever: The Women's Anthology for a New Millennium, 2003. Contributor to periodicals and journals. Works appear in anthologies. **Address:** New York, NY , U.S.A. **Online address:** info@robinmorgan.us

MORGAN, Rosemarie (Anne Louise). British/American (born United States), b. 1938?. **Genres:** Literary Criticism And History. **Career:** Yale University, lecturer in English, 1985-2002, research fellow, 2003-10; Post College, adjunct professor, 1986-88; Kansai University, distinguished visiting professor, 1994; University of British Columbia, distinguished visiting professor, 1989; The Thomas Hardy Association, president; The Thomas Hardy Society, vice president. Writer. **Publications:** Women and Sexuality in the Novels of Thomas Hardy, Routledge, 1988; Cancelled Words: Rediscovering Thomas Hardy, Routledge, 1992; Student Companion to Thomas Hardy, 2007; Orphanism, forthcoming. EDITOR: T.T.H.A. Occasional Series: Editing Hardy, 1999; Far from the Madding Crowd, 2000; (with R. Nemesvari) Human Shows: Essays in Honour of Michael Millgate, 2000; Days to Recollect: Essays in Honour of Robert Schweik, 2000; (with with W.W. Morgan) The Emma Poems, 2001; Ashgate Research Companion to Thomas Hardy, 2010; The Hardy Review, vol. XIII, 2011. **Address:** 124 Bishop St., New Haven, CT 06511, U.S.A. **Online address:** rm314@st-andrews.ac.uk

MORGAN, Roxanne. *See* **GENTLE, Mary.**

MORGAN, Stacy T(owle). American (born United States), b. 1959?. **Genres:** Children's Fiction, Young Adult Fiction, Transportation, Mystery/Crime/Suspense. **Career:** Park City Daily News, feature writer, 1983-84; Syracuse University, instructor in English, 1984-85; leader of home-school cooperatives, 1993-97; WRVG-FM Radio, staff, 1998. Writer. **Publications:** The Cuddlers, 1993. RUBY SLIPPERS SCHOOL SERIES: Adventures in the Caribbean, 1996; The British Bear Caper, 1996; Escape from Egypt, 1996; The Belgium Book Mystery, 1996; Journey to Japan, 1997; New Zealand Shake-up, 1997. **Address:** Bethany House, 11400 Hampshire Ave. South, Minneapolis, MN 55438-2852, U.S.A. **Online address:** rubyslip@in-motion.net

MORGAN, Stevie. *See* **DAVIES, Nicola.**

MORGAN, Virginia. *See* **MUNDIS, Hester (Jane).**

MORGAN, Wendy. *See* **STAUB, Wendy Corsi.**

MORGAN-WITTS, Max. British/American (born United States), b. 1931. **Genres:** History, International Relations/Current Affairs, Military/Defense/Arms Control, Documentaries/Reportage, Film. **Career:** Granada Television, director and producer, 1957-63; British Broadcasting Corp., producer, 1963-66, series executive editor, 1966-72, executive producer, director; writer, 1970-; MMW Productions Ltd., chairman, 1985-. **Publications:** The Golden Opportunity of a Thousand Years, 1986; The Creationists, 1991. WITH G. THOMAS: The Day The World Ended, 1969; The San Francisco Earthquake in UK as Earthquake: The Destruction of San Francisco, 1971; Shipwreck: The Strange Fate of the Morro Castle, 1972; Voyage of the Damned, 1974; Guernica, The Crucible of World War II, 1975 in UK as The Day Guernica Died, 1975; Día en Que Murió Guernica, 1976; Enola Gay in UK as Ruin from the Air: The Atomic Mission to Hiroshima, 1977; The Day the Bubble Burst: A Social History of the Wall Street Crash of 1929, 1979; Trauma: The Search for the Cause of Legionnaires Disease, 1981 in US as Anatomy of an Epidemic, 1982; Pontiff, 1983; Averting Armageddon in UK as The Year of Armageddon: The Pope and the Bomb, 1984; Ruin from the Air: The Enola Gay's Atomic Mission to Hiroshima, 1990. Contributor to periodicals. **Address:** A. M. Heath & Company Ltd., 6 Warwick Ct., Holborn, London, GL WC1R 5DJ, England.

MORGENSTERN, S. *See* **GOLDMAN, William.**

MORGENSTERN, Susie Hoch. French/American (born United States), b. 1945. **Genres:** Children's Fiction, Translations. **Career:** University of Nice, professor of English, 1971, now retired. Writer and literary critic. **Publications:** IN ENGLISH TRANSLATION: C'est pas juste, 1982, trans. as It's Not Fair!, 1983 in UK as Stacey the Unstoppable, 1987; Lettres d'amour de 0 à10, 1996; Trois jours sans, 1998; Même les princesses doivent aller a l'école, 1992. IN FRENCH: Alphabet hébreu, 1977; Oukélé latélé?, 1984; (with A. Morgenstern) Terminale, tout le monde descend, 1985; Musée blues, 1986; Premier amour, dernier amour, 1987; L'Amerloque, 1993; Une vieille histoire, 1997; Les deux moitiés de l'amitié, 2005; LaSixième, 2007. OTHERS: I Will Make Miracles, 2008. **Address:** 16 Rue du Grand Pin, Nice, 06100, France.

MORI, Kyoko. American/Japanese (born Japan), b. 1957. **Genres:** Young Adult Fiction, Poetry, Novels, Autobiography/Memoirs, Essays, Adult Non-fiction, Young Adult Non-fiction. **Career:** Saint Norbert College, associate professor of English and writer-in-residence, 1984-; Harvard University, Briggs-Copeland lecturer in creative writing; George Mason University, Department of English, associate professor, professor, MFA Creative Writing Program, faculty; Lesley University, Low-Residency MFA Program, faculty. **Publications:** YOUNG ADULT FICTION: Shizuko's Daughter, 1993; One Bird, 1995. ADULT POETRY: Fallout, 1994. OTHERS: The Dream of Water: A Memoir (autobiography), 1995; Polite Lies: On Being a Woman Caught between Cultures (essays), 1997; Stone Field, True Arrow (novel), 2000. Contributor to books, periodicals and journals. **Address:** Department of English, George Mason University, A 119 Robinson Hall, 4400 University Dr., Ste. 3E4, Fairfax, VA 22030, U.S.A. **Online address:** kmori@gmu.edu

MORIARTY, Karen. American (born United States), b. 1946. **Genres:** Young Adult Fiction, Biography. **Career:** High school teacher and counselor, 1970-72; Hoffman Estates, high school counselor, 1972-76; Lake County Area Vocational Center, coordinator, 1976-80; Consolidated High School District 230, director of pupil personnel services, 1980-83, assistant superintendent,

1983-95; Dr. Newsome and Associates, psychologist, 1992-93; Moriarty Associates, president and psychologist, 1993-98; Open Door Publishing Inc., president. William Rainey Harper College, instructor in psychology. Writer. **Publications:** Baby Richard: A Four Year Old Comes Home, 2003. Contributor to periodicals. **Address:** Open Door Publishing Inc., PO Box 353311, Palm Coast, FL 32135, U.S.A. **Online address:** r1kmor@bestnetpc.com

MORIARTY, Laura. American (born United States), b. 1970?. **Genres:** Novels. **Career:** University of Kansas, professor. Writer. **Publications:** The Center of Everything (novel), 2003; The Rest of Her Life (novel), 2007; While I'm Falling (novel), 2009. **Address:** Lawrence, KS , U.S.A. **Online address:** laura_moriarty@yahoo.com

MORIARTY, Marilyn F(rances). American (born United States), b. 1953. **Genres:** Writing/Journalism. **Career:** Pan-American Business College, instructor in English as a second language, 1976-77; Saddleback Community College, instructor in rhetoric and composition, 1985-86; University of California, Humanities Research Institute, fellow, 1991; Hollins University, assistant professor, 1992-98, associate professor of English, 1998-, professor of English; National Humanities Center, fellow, 1994. Writer. **Publications:** (Ed. with W. Lillyman and D. Neuman) Critical Architecture and Contemporary Culture, 1994; Writing Science through Critical Thinking, 1997; Moses Unchained, 1998. Contributor to periodicals. **Address:** Department of English, Hollins University, PO Box 9677, Roanoke, VA 24020, U.S.A. **Online address:** moriarty@hollins.edu

MORIARTY, Michael. Canadian/American (born United States), b. 1941. **Genres:** Plays/Screenplays, Mystery/Crime/Suspense, Novels, Literary Criticism And History. **Career:** Actor, playwright, musician, composer and novelist. **Publications:** NOVELS: The Voyeur: A J.C. Kaminer Mystery, 1997; The Gift of Stern Angels, 1997. Contributor of articles to magazines. **Address:** Lasher Management, PO Box 247, Flushing, NY 11367-0247, U.S.A.

MORILLO, Stephen (Reeder). American (born United States), b. 1958. **Genres:** History, Cartoons. **Career:** Gambit, cartoonist, assistant art director and production manager, 1983-87; Loyola University, assistant professor of history, 1987; University of Georgia, instructor in history, 1988-89; Wabash College, assistant professor, professor of history, 1989-; Hawaii Pacific University, NEH distinguished visiting professor of diplomacy and military studies, 2003-04. Writer. **Publications:** Warfare under the Anglo-Norman Kings, 1066-1135, 1994; (ed. and intro.) The Battle of Hastings: Sources and Interpretations, 1996; (Ed.) The Haskins Society Journal, 1999-2007; What is Military History?, 2006; (co-author) War in World History: Society, Technology and War from Ancient Times to the Present, 2007. **Address:** Department of History, Wabash College, PO Box 352, Crawfordsville, IN 47933-0352, U.S.A. **Online address:** morillos@wabash.edu

MORIMOTO, Anri. Japanese (born Japan), b. 1956. **Genres:** Theology/Religion, Humanities, Area Studies, Intellectual History, Philosophy. **Career:** Matsuyama-Joto Kyokai, pastor, 1982-86; International Christian University, pastor, 1991-2002, director of religious center, 1995-, associate professor, 1997-2001, Division of Humanities, professor, 2001-08, Princeton Theological Seminary, visiting professor, 2002-03, Department of Philosophy and Religion, professor, 2008-. Writer. **Publications:** Jonathan Edwards and the Catholic Vision of Salvation, 1995; Christian Ethics in Ecumenical Context: Theology, Culture, and Politics in Dialogue, 1995; Christian Responses to Asian Challenges: A Glocalization View on Christian Higher Education in East Asia, 2007; A Grand Design for Peace: Achieving Peace and Reconciliation for a Future World, 2009; Asian and Oceanic Christianities in Conversation: Exploring Theological Identities at Home and in Diaspora, 2011. **Address:** Rodopi, 248 E 44th St., 2nd fl., New York, NY 10017, U.S.A. **Online address:** morimoto@icu.ac.jp

MORIN, Paula. American (born United States), b. 1945. **Genres:** Young Adult Non-fiction, Animals/Pets. **Career:** Oregon Folk Arts, Oregon Art Community, field researcher, 1979; N.W. Exposure Photography Inc., founding director, 1979; Circle Sky Productions, photographer and oral historian, 1979-81; University of Montana, photographer, 1981-82; Heritage Photo Works L.L.C., owner and photographer, 1991-96; Prescott College, adjunct faculty, 1993; Paula Morin Photo Art and Looking Glass Images, artist and photographer, 1997; Montana Arts Council, arts consultant, 1999. Writer. **Publications:** Honest Horses: Wild Horses in the Great Basin, 2006. **Address:** University of Nevada Press, Morrill Hall, PO Box 0166, Reno, NV 89557-0166, U.S.A. **Online address:** info@paulamorin.com

MORINIS, Alan. (E. Alan Morinis). Canadian (born Canada), b. 1949. **Genres:** Theology/Religion, Travel/Exploration, Psychology. **Career:** Meta Communications, president, 1985-88; Ark Films Inc., president, 1989-97; The Mussar Institute, instructor. Writer, anthropologist and filmmaker. **Publications:** (As E. Alan Morinis) Pilgrimage in the Hindu Tradition: A Case Study of West Bengal, 1984; (ed. with N.R. Crumrine) Pilgrimage in Latin America, 1991; (ed.) Sacred Journeys: The Anthropology of Pilgrimage, 1992; (ed. with R.H. Stoddard) Sacred Places, Sacred Spaces: The Geography of Pilgrimages, 1997; Climbing Jacob's Ladder: One Man's Rediscovery of a Jewish Spiritual Tradition, 2002; Everyday Holiness: The Jewish Spiritual Path of Mussar, 2007; Climbing Jacob's Ladder: One Man's Journey to Rediscover a Jewish Spiritual Tradition, 2007; Every Day, Holy Day: 365 Days of Teachings and Practices from the Jewish Tradition of Mussar, 2010. **Address:** Mussar Institute, 133-12520 Horseshoe Way, Richmond, BC V7A 5K3, Canada. **Online address:** alan@mussarinstitute.org

MORINIS, E. Alan. *See* **MORINIS, Alan.**

MORISON, Robert F. American (born United States), b. 1950. **Genres:** Business/Trade/Industry, Marketing. **Career:** BSG Concours, executive vice president and director of research; Public Broadcasting Service, Nightly Business Report, commentator; General Electric Information Services Co. staff; CSC Index, staff. Writer and researcher. **Publications:** (With K. Dychtwald and T.J. Erickson) Workforce Crisis: How to Beat the Coming Shortage of Skills and Talent, 2006; (with T.H. Davenport and J.G. Harris) Analytics at Work: Smarter Decisions, Better Results, 2010. Contributor to journals. **Address:** Harvard Business Publishing, 60 Harvard Way, Boston, MA 02163, U.S.A. **Online address:** rfmorison@bsgconcours.com

MORLAND, Dick. *See* **HILL, Reginald (Charles).**

MORLEY, Margaret. British/American (born United States), b. 1941. **Genres:** Novels, Biography, Young Adult Fiction, Literary Criticism And History. **Career:** Writer. **Publications:** A Friend in Need, 1976; The Films and Faces of Laurence Olivier, 1978; Larger Than Life (biography of Robert Morley), 1979; Worry: How to Kick the Serenity Habit in 98 Easy Steps, 1981; Ten Days in China, 1986; Celia Eden, 1987; The Summer Woods, 1990; Wild Spirit: The Story of Percy Bysshe Shelley, 1992. Contributor to periodicals. **Address:** c/o Camilla Hornby, Curtis Brown, Haymarket House, 28-29 Haymarket, London, GL SW1Y 4SP, England.

MORMINO, Gary R. (Gary Ross Mormino). American (born United States), b. 1947. **Genres:** Social Sciences. **Career:** University of Southern Florida-Tampa, faculty, 1977-, Department of History, professor; University of Southern Florida-St. Petersburg, Frank E. Duckwall professor of history, Florida Studies Program, co-director. Writer and historian. **Publications:** (As Gary Ross Mormino) Immigrants on the Hill: Italian-Americans in St. Louis, 1882-1982, 1986; (with G.E. Pozzetta) The Immigrant World of Ybor City: Italians and Their Latin Neighbors in Tampa, 1885-1985, 1987; (with I. Serra) Italian Americans & Florida, 2003; Land of Sunshine, State of Dreams: A Social History of Modern Florida, 2005; Italians in Florida, 2008. **Address:** Florida Studies Program, University of Southern Florida, SNL 100, 140 7th Ave., S, St. Petersburg, FL 33701, U.S.A. **Online address:** gmormino@stpt.usf.edu

MORMINO, Gary Ross. *See* **MORMINO, Gary R.**

MORNELL, Pierre. *See* Obituaries.

MÖRNER, Magnus. Swedish (born Sweden), b. 1924. **Genres:** Cultural/Ethnic Topics, History, Bibliography. **Career:** Institute of Iberoamerican Studies, director, 1953-65; University of California, visiting professor, 1963-64; Cornell University, visiting professor, 1964-65; Colegio de Mexico, visiting professor, 1965-66; Columbia University, visiting professor, 1965-66; City University of New York, Queens College, Department of Latin American History, faculty, 1966-69; Institute of Latin American Studies, director, 1969-76; University of Texas, visiting professor, 1972, 1983; University of Pittsburgh, Andrew W. Mellon Professor of History, 1976-81; University of Goeteborg, Department of Modern History, faculty, 1982-90; Facultad Latinoamericana de Ciencias Sociales (FLACSO), visiting professor, 1984, 1987, 1990. Writer. **Publications:** The Political and Economic Activities of the Jesuits in the La

Plata Region: The Hapsburg Era, 1953, rev. ed., 1976; Latinamerika, 1957; Estudios y documentos suecos relativos al movimiento emancipador de Hispanoamerica, 1961; The Expulsion of the Jesuits from Latin America, 1965; Race Mixture in the History of Latin America, 1967; (ed.) Race and Class in Latin America, 1970; La Corona espanola y los foraneos en los pueblos de indios de America, 1970; El colonato en la America Meridional Andina desde el siglo XVIII Informe preliminar, 1970; Latinamerikas indianer, 1973; Estado, razas y cambio social en la Hispanoamérica colonial, 1974; Investigación en ciencias sociales e históricas sobre América Latina: enfoque preliminar para una guía, 1975; Síntese das atividades do Instituto desde 1969 até 1974, 1975; Distribución de ingresos en un distrito andino en los años 1830, 1977; Perfil de la sociedad rural del Cuzco a fines de la Colonia, 1978; Notas sobre el comercio y los comerciantes del Cusco desde fines de la colonia hasta 1930, 1979; Historia social latinoamericana: nuevos enfoques, 1979; Evolución demográfica de Hispanoamérica durante el período colonial, 1979; (co-author) El Sector agrario en América Latina: estructura económica y cambio social, 1979; European Travelogues as Sources to Latin American History from the Late Eighteenth Century Until 1870, 1981; The Andean Past: Land Societies and Conflicts, 1984; Compraventas de tierras en el Cuzco, 1825-1869, 1984; Adventurers and Proletarians: A Study of Migration in Latin America, 1985; Dos ensayos analíticos sobre la Rebelión de Túpac Amaru en el Cuzco, 1985; (ed. with T. Svensson) History of the Third World in Nordic Research, 1986; (ed. with T. Svensson) Classes, Strata, And Elites: Essays On Social Stratification in Nordic and Third World History, 1988; Bibliography of Magnus Mörner: 1947-1990, 1990; (ed. with T. Svensson) Transformation of Rural Society in the Third World, 1991; Doctorado honoris causa, 1991; Ensayos sobre historia latinoamericana: enfoques, conceptos y métodos, 1992; (ed. with P.C. Emmer) European Expansion and Migration: Essays on the Intercontinental Migration from Africa, Asia, and Europe, 1992; Aventureros y proletarios: los emigrantes en Hispanoamérica, 1992; Region and State in Latin America's Past, 1993; Local Communities and Actors in Latin America's Past, 1994; (ed. with M. Rosendahl) Threatened Peoples and Environments in the Americas, 1995; Comparative Approaches to the History of the Countries around the Baltic Sea, 1998; Corona Española y los for áneos en los pueblos de indios de América, 1999; Människor, landskap, varor & vägar: essäer från svenskt 1600- och 1700-tal, 2001; (with A.R. Mörner) Spanien i svenska arkiv, 2001. Contributor to journals. **Address:** Snoehoejdsstigen 10, Moelndal, S-431 39, Sweden. **Online address:** magnus.aare@swipnet.se

MORO, Javier. Spanish (born Spain), b. 1955?. **Genres:** Adult Non-fiction, History, Autobiography/Memoirs. **Career:** Writer. **Publications:** Senderos de Libertad, 1992; El Piandé: de Jaipur, 1995; La Mundializaciandón de la Pobreza, 1999; Las Montañas de Buda, 2000; (with D. Lapierre) Il andétait minuit cinq andà Bhopal, 2001; (with D. Lapierre) It was Five Past Midnight in Bhopal, 2001; Senderos de libertad, 2005; Pasión India, 2005; Passion India: the Story of the Spanish Princess of Kapurthala, 2006; Sari Rojo, 2008. **Address:** c/o Author Mail, Warner Books Inc., 1271 Ave. of the Americas, New York, NY 10020, U.S.A.

MOROZUMI, Atsuko. British/Japanese (born Japan), b. 1955?. **Genres:** Children's Fiction. **Career:** Writer and illustrator. **Publications:** FOR CHILDREN: One Gorilla: A Counting Book, 1990; My Friend Gorilla, 1998; Time for Bed, 2000; Helping Daddy, 2000; Playing: Lift-the-Flap Fun, 2000; In the Park, 2000. Illustrator of books by M. Price. Contributor to periodicals. **Address:** c/o Farrar, Straus & Giroux Inc., 19 Union Sq. W, New York, NY 10003, U.S.A.

MORPURGO, Michael. British (born England), b. 1943. **Genres:** Young Adult Fiction, Young Adult Non-fiction, Novels, Children's Fiction, Picture/Board Books, Animals/Pets, Novellas/Short Stories. **Career:** Teacher, 1967-75; Farms for City Children, joint founder and director, 1976-. Writer. **Publications:** YOUNG ADULT FICTION: It Never Rained, 1974; Thatcher Jones, 1975; (comp. with G. Barrett) The Story-Teller, 1976; Friend or Foe, 1977; Do All You Dare, 1978; The Ghost-Fish, 1979; That's How, 1979; Love at First Sight, 1979; The Day I Took the Bull by the Horn, 1979; All around the Year, 1979; The Nine Lives of Montezuma, 1980; The Marble Crusher, 1980; Miss Wirtles Revenge, 1981; War Horse, 1982; The White Horse of Zennor, and Other Stories from Below the Eagle's Nest, 1982; Twist of Gold, 1983; Little Foxes, 1984; Why the Whales Came, 1985; Tom's Sausage Lion, 1986; King of the Cloud Forests, 1987; Jo-Jo the Melon Donkey, 1987; Conker, 1987; Mossop's Last Chance, 1988; My Friend Walter, 1988; Mr. Nobody's Eyes, 1990; And Pigs Might Fly!, 1990; Albertine, Goose Queen, 1990; Waiting for Anya, 1991; Martians at Mudpuddle Farm, 1991; Colly's Barn, 1991; Jigger's Day Off, 1992; The King in the Forest, 1993; The Sandman and the Turtles, 1994; Snakes and Ladders, 1994; Arthur, High King of Britain, 1994; The War of Jenkins' Ear, 1995; Mum's the Word, 1995; Blodin the Beast, 1995; The Wreck of the Zanzibar, 1995; Mossop Losfigatto, 1996; Long Way Home, 1996; The Dancing Bear, 1996; The Ghost of Grania O'Malley, 1996; Robin of Sherwood, 1996; The Butterfly Lion, 1996; Sam's Duck, 1996; Red Eyes At Night, 1997; Gullivers Travels, 1997; Wartman, 1998; Escape from Shangri-La, 1998; Joan of Arc of Domremy, 1999; Wombat Goes Walkabout, 2000; Snakes and Ladders, 2000; The Silver Swan, 2000; Billy the Kid, 2000; Toro! Toro!, 2001; Out of the Ashes, 2001; Cool!, 2002; Mister Skip, 2002; The Last Wolf, 2002; The Sleeping Sword, 2002; Black Queen, 2002; Cool as a Cucumber, 2003; Dear Olly, 2000; Kensuke's Kingdom, 2003; Sir Gawain and the Green Knight, 2004; Private Peaceful, 2004; The McElderry Book of Aesop's Fables, 2005; I Believe in Unicorns, 2006; Beowulf, 2006; The Best Christmas Present in the World, 2006; Alone on a Wide Wide Sea, 2006; The Amazing Story of Adolphus Tips, 2006; Mairi's Mermaid, 2006; Born To Run, 2007; On Angel Wings, 2007; It's a Dog's Life, 2007; War Horse, 2007; The Mozart Question, 2008; This Morning I Met a Whale, 2008; Hansel and Gretel, 2008; Kaspar: Prince of Cats, 2008; Animal Tales: Three Stories in One, 2008; Running Wild, 2009; The Kites are Flying, 2009; The Best of Times, 2009; Singing for Mrs. Pettigrew: Stories and Essays from a Writing Life, 2009; Shadow, 2010; An Elephant in the Garden, 2010; Not Bad for a Bad Lad, 2010; Little Manfred, 2011; Outlaw: The Story of Robin Hood, 2012; Sparrow: The Story of Joan of Arc, 2012; Mr Skip, 2012. EDITOR: Ghostly Haunts, 1994; Muck and Magic: Tales from the Countryside, 1995; Beyond the Rainbow Warrior, 1996; Farm Boy, 1997; Animal Stories, 1999; The Kingfisher Book of Great Boy Stories: A Treasury of Classics from Children's Literature, 2000; The Kingfisher Treasury of Classic Stories, 2002; Ox-Tales: Water, 2009; (with A. Geras, P. Pullman and J. Wilson) Magic Beans: A Handful of Fairytales from the Storybag, 2011. OTHERS: (comp. with C. Simmons) Living Poets, 1974; Words of Songs, 1985; The Birthday Book, 2008; A Life in Stories, 2012. **Address:** David Higham Associates Ltd., 5-8 Lower John St., Golden Sq., London, GL W1R 4HA, England. **Online address:** morpurgoevents@harpercollins.co.uk

MORR, Kenyon. *See* **SUMNER, Mark (C.).**

MORREIM, E. Haavi. American (born United States), b. 1950. **Genres:** Ethics, Medicine/Health, Young Adult Non-fiction. **Career:** University of Virginia, School of Medicine, medical philosopher, 1980-82, assistant professor of philosophy in medicine, 1982-84; Virginia Commonwealth University, adjunct professor, 1980; University of Tennessee, College of Medicine, Department of Human Values and Ethics, assistant professor, 1984-88, associate professor, 1988-93, professor, 1993-, Department of Preventive Medicine, Division of Health Services and Policy Research, professor, 1998-2006. Writer. **Publications:** Balancing Act: The New Medical Ethics of Medicine's New Economics, 1991; Holding Health Care Accountable: Law and the New Medical Marketplace, 2001. Contributor to books, journals and periodicals. **Address:** Department of Human Values and Ethics, University of Tennessee, Coleman College Of Medicine Bldg., 956 Ct., Ste. G212, Memphis, TN 38163, U.S.A. **Online address:** hmorreim@uthsc.edu

MORREY, Douglas J. British/Scottish (born Scotland), b. 1974. **Genres:** Film, Adult Non-fiction, Biography, Humor/Satire. **Career:** University of Warwick, Department of French Studies, lecturer, associate professor. Writer. **Publications:** Jean-Luc Godard, 2005; (with A. Smith) Jacques Rivette, 2009. **Address:** Department of French Studies, University of Warwick, Gibbet Hill Rd., Coventry, WM CV4 7AL, England. **Online address:** d.j.morrey@warwick.ac.uk

MORRILL, John S(tephen). British (born England), b. 1946. **Genres:** History, Biography, Politics/Government, Language/Linguistics. **Career:** Oxford University, research fellow, 1971-74; University of Stirling, research fellow, 1970-74, lecturer in history, 1974-75; Cambridge University, professor of British and Irish history, lecturer in history, 1975, reader, fellow, Selwyn College, director of studies in history, 1975-92, tutor, 1975-, 1979-92, admissions tutor, 1982-87, senior tutor, 1987-92, fellow, vice master, 1992-2001, assistant master, professor of history; Trinity College Oxford, honorary fellow; Trinity College Dublin, honorary fellow. Historian and writer. **Publications:** Cheshire, 1630-1660; County Government and Society During the English Revolution, 1974; The Revolt of the Provinces: Conservatives and Radicals During the English Civil War, 1630-1650, 1976, 2nd ed. as Revolt in the Provinces: The People of England and the Tragedies of War, 1630-

1648, 1998; The Cheshire Grand Jury, 1625-1659: A Social and Administrative Study, 1976; (with G.E. Aylmer) The Civil Wars and Interregnum: Sources for Local Historians, 1979; Seventeenth-Century Britain, 1603-1714, 1980; Reactions to the English Civil War, 1642-1649, 1982; (ed. with G.E. Aylmer) Land, Men and Beliefs: Studies in Early-Modern History, 1983; (contrib.) The Oxford Illustrated History of Britain, 1984; (with C.W. Daniels) Charles I, 1989; (ed. with J.S.A. Adamson) Oliver Cromwell and the English Revolution, 1990; (ed.) The Scottish National Covenant in Its British Context, 1638-1661, 1990; (ed.) The Impact of the English Civil War, 1991; (ed.) Revolution and Restoration: England in the 1650s, 1992; The Nature of The English Revolution, 1993; (with P. Slack and D. Woolf) Public Duty and Private Conscience in Seventeenth-Century England: Essays Presented to G.E. Aylmer, 1993; The Nature of the English Revolution: Essays, 1993; (ed.) The Oxford Illustrated History of Tudor and Stuart Britain, 1996; (ed. with B. Bradshaw) The British Problem, 1534-1707: State Formation in the Atlantic Archipelago, 1996; (ed. with I. Gentles and B. Worden) Soldiers, Writers and Statesmen of the English Revolution, 1998; (ed. with J. Ohlmeyer) The Civil Wars: A Military History of England, Scotland and Ireland 1638-1660, 1998; Stuart Britain: A Very Short Introduction, 2000; The Promotion of Knowledge: Lectures to Mark the Centenary of the British Academy, 1902-2002, 2004; Oliver Cromwell, 2007; Firmly I Believe and Truly, 2011. Contributor of articles to journals. **Address:** Selwyn College, Cambridge University, Rm. 4.15, 4th Fl., Grange Rd., Cambridge, CM CB3 9DQ, England. **Online address:** jsm1000@hermes.cam.ac.uk

MORRIS, Alan. British (born England), b. 1955. **Genres:** Literary Criticism And History. **Career:** Universite de Paris IV, lecturer in English, 1982-83; University of Strathclyde, lecturer in French, 1983-85; Huddersfield Polytechnic, lecturer in French, 1986-88; University of Strathclyde, lecturer, 1989-93, senior lecturer in French, 1993-. Writer. **Publications:** Collaboration and Resistance Reviewed: Writers and the Mode Retro in Post-Gaullist France, 1992; Patrick Modiano, 1996; (co-ed.) Words & Things: Essays in Memory of Keith Foley, 2009. Contributor to books and periodicals. **Address:** School of Humanities (French), University of Strathclyde, 26 Richmond St., Glasgow, G1 1XH, Scotland. **Online address:** a.i.morris@strath.ac.uk

MORRIS, Bernard E. American (born United States), b. 1935. **Genres:** Biography, Poetry. **Career:** University of California, composition instructor, 1966-72; Modesto Junior College, literature and composition instructor, 1972-2003, professor emeritus, 2003-. Writer. **Publications:** Taking Measure: The Poetry and Prose of X.J. Kennedy, 2003. Contributor of articles to books and journals. **Address:** 108 Chabot Ct., Modesto, CA 95354, U.S.A. **Online address:** bemsil@pacbell.net

MORRIS, Bill. American (born United States), b. 1952?. **Genres:** Novels, Biography, Literary Criticism And History. **Career:** Greensboro News and Record, columnist; AOL News, contributor. **Publications:** Motor City in UK as Biography of a Buick, 1992; All Souls' Day (novel), 1997. Contributor to periodicals. **Address:** c/o Author Mail, Simon & Schuster Inc., 1230 Ave. of the Americas, 11th Fl., New York, NY 10020-1513, U.S.A.

MORRIS, Bob. American (born United States), b. 1950?. **Genres:** Novels. **Career:** Florida Key Free Press, editor; Fort Myers News-Press, reporter and columnist, through 1986; Orlando Sentinel, columnist, 1986-94; Aqua magazine, founder, 1997-; Caribbean Travel & Life, editor, 1999; Gulfshore Life, editor, through 2002; freelance writer, 2002-; Rollins College, teacher of creative writing; Story Farm Publishing Co., founder and president. **Publications:** True Floridians and Other Passing Attractions, 1981; Iron Nekkid and You'll Always Get Burned, 1992; Bahamarama, 2004; Jamaica Me Dead, 2005; Bermuda Schwartz, 2007; Deadly Silver Sea, 2008; Baja Florida, 2010. **Address:** c/o Job Veltre, Artists Literary Group, 27 W 20th St., Ste. 1003, New York, NY 10011, U.S.A. **Online address:** bobmorris@cfl.rr.com

MORRIS, Bob. American (born United States), b. 1958. **Genres:** Biography, Autobiography/Memoirs, Adult Non-fiction. **Career:** Writer and radio broadcaster. **Publications:** Crispin the Terrible, 2000; (with B. Widdicombe) The Blue Jean, 2002; Assisted Loving: True Tales of Double Dating with My Dad, 2008; (with D. Carroll) The Legs Are the Last to Go: Aging, Acting, Marrying and Other Things I Learned the Hard Way, 2008. Contributor to periodicals. **Address:** c/o Jay Mandel, William Morris Agency, 1325 Ave. of the Americas, New York, NY 10019-6026, U.S.A. **Online address:** bobmorris@assistedloving.com

MORRIS, Charles R. American (born United States) **Genres:** Economics, History, Military/Defense/Arms Control, Money/Finance. **Career:** Chase Manhattan Bank, executive; State of Washington, Health and Human Services, secretary. Lawyer and writer. **Publications:** The Cost of Good Intentions: New York City and the Liberal Experiment, 1960-1975, 1980; A Time of Passion: America, 1960-1980, 1984; Iron Destinies, Lost Opportunities: The Arms Race between the U.S.A. and the U.S.S.R., 1945-1987, 1988; The Coming Global Boom: How to Benefit Now from Tomorrow's Dynamic World Economy, 1990; (with C.H. Ferguson) Computer Wars: How the West Can Win in a Post-IBM World, 1993, rev. ed., 2002; (with C.H. Ferguson) Computer Wars: The Fall of IBM and the Future of Global Technology, 1994; AARP: America's Most Powerful Lobby and the Clash of Generations, 1996; American Catholic: The Saints and Sinners Who Built America's Most Powerful Church, 1997; Money, Greed, and Risk: Why Financial Crises and Crashes Happen, 1999; Too Much of a Good Thing?: Why Health Care Spending Won't Make Us Sick, 2000; Tycoons: How Andrew Carnegie, John D. Rockefeller, Jay Gould, and J.P. Morgan Invented the American Supereconomy, 2005; Apart at the Seams: The Collapse of Private Pension and Health Care Protections, 2006; Surgeons: Life and Death in a Top Heart Center, 2007; Trillion Dollar Meltdown: Easy Money, High Rollers, and the Great Credit Crash, 2008; Sages: Warren Buffett, George Soros, Paul Volcker, and the Maelstrom of Markets, 2009. Contributor to periodicals and journals. **Address:** Bantam Books Inc., 1540 Broadway, New York, NY 10036-4094, U.S.A.

MORRIS, Chris(topher Crosby). Also writes as Daniel Stryker, Casey Prescott. American (born United States), b. 1946. **Genres:** Military/Defense/Arms Control, Songs/Lyrics And Libretti, Ghost Writer, Science Fiction/Fantasy, Young Adult Fiction, Novels. **Career:** United States Global Strategy Council, research director. Writer and musician. **Publications:** (With J. Morris) 40 Minute War, 1984; (as Casey Prescott) Asset in Black, 1985; (with J. Morris) Medusa, 1986; (with J. Morris) Outpassage, 1988; (with J. Morris) City at the Edge of Time, 1988; (with J. Morris) The Little Helliad, 1988; (with J. Morris) Tempus Unbound, 1989; (with J. Morris) Threshold, 1990; Storm Seed, 1990; (as Daniel Stryker) Hawkeye, 1991; (as Daniel Stryker) Cobra, 1991; (with J. Morris) Trust Territory, 1992; (ed. with J.Morris) The Non Lethality Initiative: The American Warrior, 1992; (with J. Morris) The Stalk, 1993; (with J. Morris) The Sacred Band, 2010. **Address:** PO Box 438, Harrodsburg, KY 40330, U.S.A. **Online address:** ccmorris@capecod.net

MORRIS, Christopher Hugh. British (born England), b. 1938. **Genres:** International Relations/Current Affairs. **Career:** Daily Sketch, reporter, 1958-62; Daily Express, correspondent, 1962-67; Australian Broadcasting Corp., correspondent, 1967-72; Canadian Broadcasting Corp., correspondent, 1967-72; BBC News, reporter, 1972-80; BBC TV News, special correspondent, 1980-87; The Times, correspondent, 1988; Sky TV News, presenter and foreign correspondent, 1989-2000; Omnivision, Pinewood Studios, Iver Heath, managing director, 2000-11; Harrods, director of public affairs and television, 2002-03; Daily Mail, correspondent; BBC TV, correspondent; radio, correspondent; NBC, correspondent. **Publications:** The Day They Lost the H Bomb, 1966 in UK as The Big Catch, 1966. **Address:** Omnivision, Pinewood Studios, Iver Heath, BK SL0 0NH, England. **Online address:** c_morris@msn.com

MORRIS, Christopher W. American (born United States), b. 1949. **Genres:** Philosophy, Adult Non-fiction, Social Commentary. **Career:** University of Ottawa, assistant professor of philosophy, 1977-82; Universite du Quebec a Montreal, visiting assistant professor, 1981; University of Texas, visiting assistant professor, 1982; University of California, visiting assistant professor of philosophy, 1982-85; University of California, visiting lecturer in philosophy, 1985-86; Universite de Montreal, visiting assistant professor of philosophy, 1985; Bowling Green State University, associate professor, 1986-94, professor of philosophy, 1994-2001, Social Philosophy and Policy Center, senior research fellow, 1990-2001; University of North Carolina, visiting associate professor, 1988-89; Ecole Polytechnique, research associate, 1991-2000; CREA, research associate, 1991-; University of Maryland College Park, professor of philosophy, 2002-; University of Amsterdam, visiting research fellow. Writer. **Publications:** EDITOR AND CONTRIBUTOR: (with R.G. Frey) Liability and Responsibility: Essays in Law and Morals, 1991; (with R.G. Frey) Violence, Terrorism, and Justice, 1991; (with R.G. Frey) Value, Welfare, and Morality, 1993; (with J. Coleman) Rational Commitment and Social Justice: Essays of Gregory Kavka, 1998; The Social Contract Theorists: Critical Essays on Hobbes, Locke and Rousseau, 1999; (with A. Ripstein) Practical Rationality and Preference: Essays for David Gauthier,

2001; Amarthya Sen, 2009. OTHERS: An Essay on the Modern State, 1998; (comp.) Questions of Life and Death: Readings in Practical Ethics, 2012. **Address:** Department of Philosophy, University of Maryland, Skinner Bldg., College Park, MD 20742, U.S.A. **Online address:** cwmorris@umd.edu

MORRIS, (Clifford) Eric. British/Welsh (born Wales), b. 1940. **Genres:** Military/Defense/Arms Control, History. **Career:** Teacher, 1963-66; University of Liverpool, lecturer in international relations and military history, 1967-70; University of Wales, Aberystwyth, visiting lecturer, 1968-71; Royal Military Academy, Department of War Studies and International Affairs, lecturer and deputy head, 1970-84; Pacific International Ltd., Special Projects Division, military/defense director, 1984-86; political/defense analyst and consultant, 1986-; Eric Morris International Consulting Ltd., co-director. Writer. **Publications:** Blockade: Berlin and the Cold War, 1973; Tanks, 1975; Weapons & Warfare of the 20th Century: A Comprehensive and Historical Survey of Modern Military Methods and Machines, 1976; Blindés, 1976; The Russian Navy: Myth and Reality, 1977; War in Peace: An Illustrated History of Conflict since 1945, 1981; Corregidor: The End of the Line, 1981; Salerno: A Military Fiasco, 1983; Churchill's Private Armies, 1986; Terrorism: Threat and Response, 1987; Guerrillas in Uniform: Churchill's Private Armies in the Middle East and the War Against Japan, 1940-1945, 1989; Circles of Hell: The War in Italy, 1943-45, 1993; (with A. Hoe) Re-enter the SAS: The Special Air Service and the Malayan Emergency, 1994; Corregidor: The American Alamo of World War II, 2000. **Address:** Eric Morris International Consulting Ltd., Wassell Grove Business Ctr., Wassell Grove Ln., Stourbridge, WM DY9 9JH, England.

MORRIS, Dashaun Jiwe. *See* **MORRIS, Jiwe.**

MORRIS, David. American (born United States), b. 1967. **Genres:** Adult Non-fiction. **Career:** Trent University, Lady Eaton College, associate professor of philosophy; Concordia University, associate professor of philosophy, department chair. Writer. **Publications:** The Sense of Space, 2004. Contributor to various journals. **Address:** Department of Philosophy, Concordia University, Rm. 205, 2100 Mackay, 1455 Maisonneuve Blvd., Montreal, ON H3G 1M8, Canada. **Online address:** davimorr@alcor.concordia.ca

MORRIS, Deborah. American (born United States), b. 1956. **Genres:** Children's Non-fiction, Young Adult Non-fiction, Human Relations/Parenting. **Career:** Avon Products, assistant district manager, 1982-88; author and magazine freelancer, 1985-; Tejas Writer's Roundtable, co-founder and host, 1991-; Springcreek Community Church, youth leader, 1994-96; American Red Cross, disaster team leader. **Publications:** REAL KIDS, REAL ADVENTURES SERIES: Shark Attack!, 1994, rev. ed., 2002; Whirlpool, 1994; Real Kids, Real Adventures: True Stories, 1994, rev. ed. as Real Kids, Real Adventures in Texas, 2002; Bear Attack, 1995; Runaway Bus, 1995; Amy to the Rescue, 1995; Plane Crash on Christmas Day, 1995; Adrift, 1996; Apartment Fire, 1996; Lost, 1998; Glacier, 1998; Mountain Lion, 2000; Earthquake, 2005. OTHER: Trapped in a Cave!: A True Story, 1993; (with G.W. Sheldon) What Would Jesus Do?: A Contemporary Retelling of Charles M. Sheldon's Classic in his Steps, 1993; Teens 911: Snowbound, Helicopter Crash and Other True Survival Stories, 2002. Contributor to periodicals. **Address:** PO Box 461572, Garland, TX 75046, U.S.A. **Online address:** deb@realkids.com

MORRIS, Desmond. British (born England), b. 1928. **Genres:** Novels, Anthropology/Ethnology, Biology, Zoology, Human Relations/Parenting, Young Adult Fiction, Animals/Pets, Young Adult Fiction, Young Adult Fiction. **Career:** Oxford University, Department of Zoology, researcher in animal behavior, 1954-56, Wolfson College, research fellow, 1973-81; Zoological Society of London, head of Granada TV and Film Unit, 1956-59, curator of mammals, 1959-67; Institute of Contemporary Arts, director, 1967-68; full-time writer, 1968-98. **Publications:** International Zoo Yearbook, 1959; The Biology of Art: A Study of the Picture-Making Behaviour of the Great Apes and its Relationship to Human Art, 1962; The Mammals, Introducing Curious Creatures, 1965; Mammals: A Guide to the Living Species, 1965; Apes and Monkeys, 1965; Des Serpents et des Hommes, 1965; (with R. Morris) Men and Snakes, 1965; Zoo Time, 1966; (with R. Morris) Men and Apes, 1966; (with R. Morris) Men and Pandas, 1966; (ed.) Primate Ethology, 1967; The Naked Ape: A Zoologist's Study of the Human Animal, 1967; The Human Zoo, 1969, rev. ed., 1996; Patterns of Reproductive Behaviour: Collected Papers, 1970; Intimate Behaviour, 1971, rev. ed., 1997; Manwatching: A Field Guide to Human Behavior, 1977; (co-author) Gestures, Their Origins and Distribution, 1979; Animal Days, 1979; The Soccer Tribe, 1981; (with R. Morris) Giant Panda, 1981; Inrock (fiction), 1983; The Book of Ages, 1983; The Art of Ancient Cyprus: With A Check-List of the Author's Collection, 1985; Bodywatching: A Field Guide to the Human Species, 1985; The Illustrated Naked Ape: A Zoologist's Study of the Human Animal, 1986; Dogwatching, 1986; The Secret Surrealist: The Paintings of Desmond Morris, 1987; Cat Lore, 1987; Catwatching, 1987; The Animals Roadshow, 1988; The Human Nestbuilders, 1988; Catlore, 1988; Tribes, 1988; Horsewatching, 1988; The Animal Contract: Sharing the Planet, 1990; Animalwatching, 1990; Babywatching, 1991; Surrealist World of Desmond Morris, 1991; Christmas Watching, 1992; The World of Animals, 1993; The Naked Ape Trilogy, 1994; The Human Animal: A Personal View of the Human Species, 1994; Illustrated Catwatching, 1994; Bodytalk: A World Guide to Gestures, 1994; Illustrated Babywatching, 1995; Illustrated Dogwatching, 1996; Cat World: A Feline Encyclopedia, 1997; The Human Sexes: A Natural History of Man and Woman, 1997; Illustrated Horsewatching, 1998; Cool Cats, 1999; Body Guards, 1999; Cat Breeds of the World, 1999; The Naked Eye: My Travels in Search of the Human Species, 2000; Dogs: The Ultimate Dictionary of Over 1, 000 Dog Breeds, 2001; People watching, 2002; Naked Woman: A Study of the Female Body, 2005; Watching: Encounter with Humans and Other Animals, 2006, new ed., 2007; Fantastic Cats, 2007; Dark Inside My Head, 2007; Baby: A Portrait of the Amazing First Two Years of Life, 2008; Lines of Thought, 2008; Naked Man: A Study of the Male Body, 2008; Amazing Baby, 2008; Owl, 2009; Planet Ape, 2009. Contributor to books and periodicals. **Address:** c/o Jonathan Cape, Random House, 20 Vauxhall Bridge Rd., London, GL SW1V 2SA, England. **Online address:** dmorris@patrol.i-way.co.uk

MORRIS, Edmund. American/Kenyan (born Kenya), b. 1940. **Genres:** Biography, History, Music, Autobiography/Memoirs. **Career:** Advertising copywriter, 1964-71; writer and biographer, 1971-; New York Times, contributing editor, 1975-76. **Publications:** The Rise of Theodore Roosevelt (Pulitzer Prize), 1979; Dutch: A Memoir of Ronald Reagan, 1999; (intro.) The Education of Henry Adams, 1999; (intro.) America's Library: The Story of the Library of Congress, 1800-2000, 2000; The Rise of Theodore Roosevelt, 2001; Theodore Rex, 2001; Beethoven: The Universal Composer, 2005; Colonel Roosevelt, 2010. **Address:** The Wylie Agency, 250 W 57th St., Ste. 2114, New York, NY 10107-2199, U.S.A.

MORRIS, Frances. British (born England), b. 1959. **Genres:** Art/Art History, Novels, Philosophy. **Career:** Arnolfini Gallery, exhibition organizer, 1985-87; Tate Gallery, curator, 1987-. Writer. **Publications:** (With H. Clouzot) Painted and Printed Fabrics: The History of the Manufactory at Jouy and Other Ateliers in France, 1760-1815, 1972; No Pasaran!, 1986; Paris Post War: Art and Existentialism 1945-55, 1993; Yoko Teranchi, 1994; (with S. Morgan) Rites of Passage: Art for the End of the Century, 1995; Luciano Fabro, 1997; Chris Burden: When Robots Rule-The Two-Minute Airplane Factory, 1999; (with R. Flood) Zero to Infinity: Arte Povera, 1962-1972, 2001; (with S. Glennie, D. Thorp) Paul McCarthy at Tate Modern, 2003; Henri Rousseau, 2005; Tate Modern Handbook, 2006; (ed.) Henri Rousseau: Jungles in Paris, 2006; (ed.) Louise Bourgeois, 2007, 2nd ed., 2008; (ed.) Yayoi Kusama, 2012. **Address:** Tate Gallery, Millbank, London, GL SW1P 4RG, England.

MORRIS, G. Scott. (Scott Morris). American (born United States), b. 1954. **Genres:** Medicine/Health. **Career:** St. John's United Methodist Church, associate minister, 1986-; Church Health Center, founder and executive director, 1987-; Washington National Cathedral, preacher, 2001. Writer. **Publications:** (Ed.) Hope and Healing, 1995; Relief for the Body, Renewal for the Soul: A Doctor's True Stories of Healing and Hope, 2001; (ed.) I am the Lord Who Heals You: Reflections on Healing, Wholeness, and Restoration, 2004; (as Scott Morris with S.M. Miller) Health Care You Can Live With: Discover Wholeness in Body and Spirit, 2011. **Address:** Church Health Center, 1210 Peabody Ave., Memphis, TN 38104-4506, U.S.A. **Online address:** morriss@churchhealthcenter.org

MORRIS, James. *See* **MORRIS, Jan.**

MORRIS, James McGrath. American (born United States), b. 1954. **Genres:** Travel/Exploration. **Career:** KHFM, announcer, 1970; KRQE-AM, reporter, 1970; Missourinet (radio network), reporter, 1970; Seven Locks Press, publisher, 1980-91; Public Interest Publications, executive director, 1991-; West Springfield High School, social studies teacher, 1996-2005, advanced placement academic co-ordinator. **Publications:** Wineries of the Finger Lakes, 1985; (ed. with P. Weene) Thomas Jefferson's European Travel Diaries, 1987;

Wineries of the Northeast, 1989; (ed. with L. Adler) Grant Seekers Guide: Foundations That Support Social and Economic Justice, 4th ed., 1996, 6th ed., 2005; Jailhouse Journalism: The Fourth Estate Behind Bars, 1998; The Rose Man of Sing Sing: A True Tale of Life, Murder, and Redemption in the Age of Yellow Journalism, 2003; Pulitzer: A Life in Politics, Print, and Power, 2010. Contributor to books and periodicals. **Address:** c/o Alan Nevins, Renaissance Literary and Talent, PO Box 17379, Beverly Hills, CA 90209, U.S.A. **Online address:** mail@jamesmcgrathmorris.com

MORRIS, Jan. (James Morris). Welsh/British (born England), b. 1926. **Genres:** Novels, History, Travel/Exploration, Autobiography/Memoirs, Young Adult Non-fiction, Science Fiction/Fantasy, Adult Non-fiction. **Career:** Western Daily Press, editorial staff, 1944; Arab News Agency, editorial staff, 1947-48; The Times, editorial staff, correspondent, 1951-56; The Guardian, editorial staff, 1957-62; freelance writer, 1961-. **Publications:** AS JAMES MORRIS: As I Saw the USA as Coast to Coast, 1956; Islam Inflamed: A Middle East Picture as The Market of Seleukia, 1957; Sultan in Oman, 1957; Coronation Everest, 1958; South African Winter, 1958; The Hashemite Kings, 1959; Venice, 1960, rev. ed., 1974; The World of Venice, 1960, rev. ed., 1984; The Upstairs Donkey: And Other Stolen Stories, 1961; South America, 1961; Cities, 1963; The Road To Huddersfield: A Journey to Five Continents, 1963 as The World Bank: A Prospect, 1963; The Outriders: A Liberal View of Britain, 1963; The Presence of Spain, 1964; Oxford, 1965, rev. ed., 1978; Pax Britannica: The Climax of an Empire, 1968; The Great Port: A Passage Through New York, 1969; (intro.) Persia, 1969; Places, 1972; Heaven's Command: An Imperial Progress, 1973; Farewell the Trumpets: An Imperial Retreat, 1978. AS JAN MORRIS: The Preachers, 1973; Conundrum, 1974; Travels, 1976; The Oxford Book of Oxford, 1978; Spain, 1979; Destinations: Essays From Rolling Stone, 1980; My Favourite Stories of Wales, 1980; The Venetian Empire: A Sea Voyage, 1980; (comp.) Wales: An Anthology, 1982; The Spectacle of Empire: Style, Effect and The Pax Britannica, 1982; Wales, The First Place, 1982; A Venetian Bestiary, 1982; Stones of Empire: The Buildings of the Raj, 1983; Journeys, 1984; The Matter of Wales: Epic Views of a Small Country, 1984; Last Letters from Hav, 1985; Among the Cities, 1985; Architecture of the British Empire, 1986; Scotland, the Place of Visions, 1986; Manhattan '45, 1987; Hong Kong, 1988; Pleasures of a Tangled Life (autobiography), 1989; Ireland: Your Only Place, 1990; City to City, 1990; O Canada, 1990; Sydney, 1992; Locations, 1992; Travels with Virginia Woolf, 1993; A Machynlleth Triad, 1994; Fisher's Face, or, Getting To Know The Admiral, 1995; The Princeship of Wales, 1995; Fifty Years of Europe: An Album, 1997; Building Hong Kong, 2000; Lincoln: A Foreigner's Quest, 2000; Our First Leader: A Welsh Fable, 2000; Over Europe, 2001; Trieste and the Meaning of Nowhere, 2001; Coast to Coast: A Journey Across 1950s America, 2002; A Writer's House in Wales, 2002; World: Travels 1950-2000, 2003; A Writer's World, 2003; Hav: Comprising Last Letters from Hav of the Myrmidons, 2006; Contact!: A Book of Glimpses, 2009; Contact!: A Book of Encounters, 2010. Contributor to periodicals. **Address:** Trefan Morys, Llanystumdwy, GY LL5 2OLP, Wales. **Online address:** janmorris1@msn.com

MORRIS, Janine A. American (born United States) **Genres:** Novels, Romance/Historical. **Career:** Law Offices of Darryl Jones, legal secretary/paralegal, 1994-2001; Hot 97, Programming Department, music coordinator, 2000-06; New York State Bar Association, attorney, 2009-10; writer, 2005-; CBS Radio, staff writter, 2007-; Armand Group, attorney, 2010-; Morris Law P.L.L.C., owner and attorney, 2010-; Emmis Communications, staff; Jive Records, staff. Journalist. **Publications:** NOVELS: Diva Diaries, 2006; She's No Angel, 2007; Playthang, 2008; Drama 99 FM, 2009. **Address:** c/o Adeola Saul, Kensington Publishing Corp., 119 W 40th St., New York, NY 10018-2500, U.S.A. **Online address:** jam@janineamorris.com

MORRIS, Jeffrey B(randon). American (born United States), b. 1941. **Genres:** Adult Non-fiction, Children's Non-fiction, History, Law, Politics/Government, Young Adult Non-fiction, Biography, Autobiography/Memoirs, Autobiography/Memoirs. **Career:** Supreme Court of the U.S., lawyer; U.S. District Court for the District of Columbia, lawyer; City College of the City University of New York, instructor, lecturer, assistant professor of political science, 1968-72; Columbia University, special assistant and provost, 1974-76; Chief Justice, 1976-81; University of Pennsylvania, assistant professor of political science, 1981-88; Brooklyn Law School, visiting associate professor of law, 1988-90; Touro Law School, associate professor, professor of law, 1990-. Writer. **Publications:** GREAT PRESIDENTIAL DECISIONS SERIES (for children): The Washington Way, 1994; The Jefferson Way, 1994; The Truman Way, 1995; The Reagan Way, 1995; The Lincoln Way, 1996; The FDR Way, 1996. ADULT NONFICTION: Federal Justice in the Second Circuit: A History of the United States Courts in New York, Connecticut & Vermont, 1787 to 1987, 1988; To Administer Justice on Behalf of All the People: The U.S. District Court for the Eastern District of New York, 1992; (co-author) American Voices: A History of the United States, 1992; Making Sure We Are True to Our Founders: The Association of the Bar of the City of New York, 1970-95, 1997; Calmly to Poise the Scales of Justice: A History of the Courts of the District of Columbia Circuit, 2001; Brooklyn Law School: The First Hundred Years, 2001; Establishing Justice in Middle America: A History of the United States Court of Appeals for the Eighth Circuit, 2007. OTHER: (ed. with R.B. Morris) Encyclopedia of American History, 4th ed., 1970, 7th ed., 1996; (with H.S. Commager and A. Nevins) A Pocket History of the United States, 1986, 9th ed., 1992; (ed. with R.B. Morris) Great Presidential Decisions, 7th ed., 1988; Leadership on the Federal Bench: The Craft and Activism of Jack Weinstein, 2011. Contributor to books. **Address:** Touro College Jacob D. Fuchsberg Law Center, Touro Law School, Rm. 415D, 225 Eastview Dr., Central Islip, NY 11722, U.S.A. **Online address:** jmorris@tourolaw.edu

MORRIS, Jiwe. (Dashaun Jiwe Morris). American (born United States), b. 1981. **Genres:** Novels, Autobiography/Memoirs, Social Sciences, Politics/Government. **Career:** Writer. **Publications:** (With J. Davis) War of the Bloods in My Veins: A Street Soldier's March toward Redemption, 2008. **Address:** Newark, NJ 07101, U.S.A. **Online address:** warofthebloods@jiweera.com

MORRIS, J. M. *See* **MORRIS, Mark.**

MORRIS, Keith Lee. American (born United States), b. 1963. **Genres:** Young Adult Fiction. **Career:** Clemson University, associate professor of creative writing. Writer. **Publications:** The Greyhound God, 2003; The Best Seats in the House and Other Stories, 2004; The Dart League King, 2008; Call It What You Want, 2010. Contributor to periodicals. **Address:** Clemson, SC , U.S.A. **Online address:** km@clemson.edu

MORRIS, Kenneth M. American (born United States), b. 1945. **Genres:** Money/Finance, Business/Trade/Industry, Economics. **Career:** City University of New York, John Jay College of Criminal Justice, associate professor, 1967-79; Siegel and Gale, president, 1979-98; Lightbulb Press, chairperson and chief executive officer, 1998-; Electronic Document Systems Foundation, board director. Writer. **Publications:** (With M. Holzer and W. Ludwin) Literature in Bureaucracy: Readings in Administrative Fiction, 1979; The Wall Street Journal Guide to Understanding Money & Markets: Stocks, Bonds, Mutual Funds, Futures, Money, 1989; American Dreams: One Hundred Years of Business Ideas and Innovation from the Wall Street Journal, 1990; The Wall Street Journal Guide to Understanding Personal Finance, 1992, 4th ed., 2004; The Wall Street Journal Guide to Understanding Money and Investing, 1993, 3rd ed., 2004; The Wall Street Journal Guide to Understanding Your Taxes, 1994; The Wall Street Journal Guide to Planning Your Financial Future, 1995, (with V.B. Morris) 3rd ed., 2002; (with A.M. Siegel and V.B. Morris) Your Guide to Understanding Investing, 1996, (with V.B. Morris) rev. ed., 2002; A Woman's Guide to Investing, 1997, (with V.B. Morris) 3rd ed., 2003; (with A.M. Siegal and B. Larson) The Asian Wall Street Journal Asia Business News Guide to Understanding Money and Investing in Asia, 1998; Guide to the Information Age, 1999; (with V.B. Morris) Creating Retirement Income, 1999; User's Guide to the Information Age, 1999; (with V.B. Morris) Dictionary of Financial Terms, 2000, rev. ed., 2007; (with V.B. Morris) The Essential Guide to Your 401(k), 2001; (ed. with S. Armstrong) Mahāsi Sayadaw's Analysis of Today's Vipassana Techniques, 2002; (with V.B. Morris) Welcome to Your Financial Life: A Guide to Personal Finance in Your 20's and 30's, 2003; (with V.B. Morris) A Guide to Understanding Retirement Investing, 2004; (with V.B. Morris) Planning Your Retirement Income, 2004; (with V.B. Morris) Guide to Long Term Investing with Stocks and ETFs, 2004; (with V.B. Morris) Guide to Managing Retirement Income, 2005; (with V.B. Morris) Standard & Poor's Guide to Money and Investing, 2005; (with V.B. Morris) Standard & Poor's Guide to Saving for Retirement, 2006. **Address:** Lightbulb Press Inc., 112 Madison Ave., Ste. 5, New York, NY 10016, U.S.A. **Online address:** kmorris@lightbulbpress.com

MORRIS, Larry E. American (born United States), b. 1951. **Genres:** Biography, Autobiography/Memoirs, History, Humanities. **Career:** Ensign Magazine, assistant editor; Novella Magazine, senior editor; Brigham Young University, Institute for the Study and Preservation of Ancient Religious Texts, faculty; Young Mens Christians Association, president. **Publications:** (With

J.A. Parry) The Mormon Book of Lists, 1987; The Edge of the Reservoir (novel), 1988; (ed.) A Treasury of Latter-day Saint Letters, 2001; And Now You Know: The Rest of the Story from the Lives of Well-Known Latter-day Saints, 2002; Words to Live by: Life Strategies of the Latter-day Prophets, 2003; The Fate of the Corps: What Became of the Lewis and Clark Explorers after the Expedition, 2004; (ed. with J.W. Welch) Oliver Cowdery: Scribe, Elder, Witness; Essays from BYU Studies and FARMS, 2006. Contributor to periodicals. **Address:** Salt Lake City, UT , U.S.A. **Online address:** mlemorris@yahoo.com

MORRIS, Lois B. American (born United States), b. 1943. **Genres:** Psychiatry, Medicine/Health. **Career:** Frommer Publications, editor-in-chief; freelance writer and journalist, 1980-; Allure Magazine, columnist, 1991-. **Publications:** The Little Black Pill Book, 1983; Talking Sex with Your Kids, 1984; (with M.S. Gold) The Good News about Depression: Cures and Treatments in the New Age of Psychiatry, 1987, rev. ed., 1995; (with J.M. Oldham) The Personality Self-portrait: Why You Think, Work, Love, and Act the Way You Do, 1990, rev. ed. as The New Personality Self-portrait: Why You Think, Work, Love, and Act the Way You Do, 1995; (with G.P. Murphy and D. Lange) Informed Decisions: The Complete Book of Cancer Diagnosis, Treatment, and Recovery, 1997, 2nd ed., 2002; (with H.J. Tian) Along the Roaring River: My Wild Ride from Mao to the Met, 2008. Contributor to periodicals and magazines. **Address:** New York, NY , U.S.A. **Online address:** lolo@loisbmorris.com

MORRIS, Lynn. American (born United States), b. 1954?. **Genres:** Romance/Historical, Novels, Natural History, Theology/Religion. **Career:** Writer. **Publications:** CHENEY DUVALL M.D. SERIES WITH G. MORRIS: Shadow of the Mountains, 1994; The Stars for a Light, 1994; A City Not Forsaken, 1995; Secret Place of Thunder, 1996; Toward the Sunrising, 1996; In the Twilight, in the Evening, 1997; Island of the Innocent, 1998; Driven with the Wind, 2000. CHENEY AND SHILOH: THE INHERITANCE WITH G. MORRIS: Where Two Seas Met, 2001; The Moon by Night, 2004; There is a Season, 2005. CREOLE WITH G. MORRIS: The Immortelles (The Creoles Series, 2), 2004; The Alchemy, 2004; The Tapestry, 2005; The Exiles: Chantel, 2006. WITH G. MORRIS AND A. MORRIS: The Beginning of Sorrows, 1999; Fallen Stars, Bitter Waters: America has Fallen, The Antichrist Reigns - and God's Remnant is Sealed, 2000. OTHERS: The Balcony, 1997; Red and Lowering Sky, 2004. **Address:** Bethany House Publishers, 11400 Hampshire Ave., Bloomington, MN 55438-2852, U.S.A.

MORRIS, Marilyn (A.). American (born United States), b. 1957. **Genres:** History. **Career:** University of London, Royal Holloway College, research assistant for Jeremy Bentham; Yale University, assistant editor, 1988-91; University of North Texas, assistant professor, 1991-97, associate professor of history, 1997-, Study Of Sexualities Program, founder and director, 2003-09, LGBT Studies Program, co-director, 2009-; Huntington Library, fellow, 1999, 2001; Lewis Walpole Library, fellow; Yale Center for British Art, fellow, 2001; University of Texas, Harry Ransom Center, fellow, 2001. **Publications:** The British Monarchy and the French Revolution, 1998. Contributor of articles to books and periodicals. **Address:** Department of History, University of North Texas, 1155 Union Cir., Ste. 310650, Wooten Hall 265, Denton, TX 76203-5017, U.S.A. **Online address:** mmorris@unt.edu

MORRIS, Mark. (J. M. Morris). British (born England), b. 1963. **Genres:** Novels, Horror, Novellas/Short Stories, Young Adult Fiction, Young Adult Non-fiction. **Career:** Writer, 1988-. **Publications:** NOVELS: Toady, 1989 in US as The Horror Club, 1991; Stitch, 1991; The Immaculate, 1993; The Secret of Anatomy, 1994; Mr. Bad Face, 1996; Longbarrow, 1997; Genesis, 1999; (as J.M. Morris) Lonely Places, 2002; The Uglimen, 2002; (as J.M. Morris) Fiddleback, 2002; Nowhere Near an Angel, 2005; Dead Island, 2011. OTHERS: Close to the Bone (stories), 1995; Doctor Who: The Bodysnatchers, 1997; (with G. Joyce) Separate Skins, 1998; Doctor Who: Deep Blue, 1999; The Dogs (novella), 2001; (with P. Janczewski) Fatal Error, 2003; (with S. Clark, T. Lamsley and T. Lebbon) Fourbodings, 2005; The Deluge, 2007; Doctor Who: Forever Autumn, 2007; Doctor Who: Ghosts of India, 2008; Hellboy: The All-Seeing Eye, 2008; Torchwood: Bay of the Dead, 2009; Cinema Futura, 2010. Works appear in anthologies. Contributor of articles in periodicals. **Address:** c/o Robert Kirby, Peters Fraser and Dunlop, The Rights House, 34-43 Russell St., London, GL WC2B 5HA, England. **Online address:** mark@markmorriswriter.com

MORRIS, Mary. American (born United States), b. 1947. **Genres:** Novels, Novellas/Short Stories, Travel/Exploration, Young Adult Fiction, Literary Criticism And History, Biography. **Career:** Princeton University, lecturer in creative writing, 1981-87, 1991-93; University of California-Irvine, writer-in-residence, 1987; American University, writer-in-residence, 1988; New York University, lecturer in creative writing, 1989; Sarah Lawrence College, professor, 1993-. **Publications:** Vanishing Animals and Other Stories, 1979; Crossroads: A Novel, 1983; The Bus of Dreams, 1985; Nothing to Declare: Memoirs of a Woman Traveling Alone, 1988, rev. ed., 1999; The Waiting Room: A Novel, 1989; Wall-to-Wall: From Beijing to Berlin by Rail (travel memoir), 1991; A Mother's Love (novel), 1993; (ed. and intro. with L. O'Connor) Maiden Voyages: Writings of Women Travelers, 1993 in UK as The Virago Book of Women Travellers, 1994, as The Illustrated Virago Book of Women Travellers, 2000; House Arrest: A Novel, 1996; The Night Sky, 1997; The Lifeguard, 1997; Angel and Aliens: A Journey West (travel memoir), 1999; Acts of God: A Novel, 2000; The Revenge, 2004; The River Queen: A Memoir, 2007; The Jazz Palace, forthcoming. Contributor of articles to periodicals. **Address:** c/o Ellen Levine Literary Agency, Trident Media Group, 41 Madison Ave., 36th Fl., New York, NY 10010-2257, U.S.A. **Online address:** mmorris348@yahoo.com

MORRIS, Mary (Joan) McGarry. American (born United States), b. 1943. **Genres:** Novels, Young Adult Non-fiction, Young Adult Fiction. **Career:** Writer. **Publications:** Vanished, 1988; A Dangerous Woman, 1991; Songs in Ordinary Time, 1995; Fiona Range, 2000; A Hole in the Universe, 2004; The Lost Mother, 2005; The Last Secret: A Novel, 2009; Light From a Distant Star: A Novel, 2011. Contributor of book to periodicals. **Address:** c/o Jean V. Naggar, Jean V. Naggar Literary Agency Inc., 216 E 75th St., New York, NY 10021, U.S.A. **Online address:** mary@marymcgarrymorris.com

MORRIS, Michael. British (born England) **Genres:** Young Adult Fiction, Philosophy. **Career:** University of Sussex, professor of philosophy, 1985-. Writer. **Publications:** The Good and the True, 1992; An Introduction to the Philosophy of Language, 2007; Routledge Philosophy Guidebook to Wittgenstein and the Tractatus, 2008. Work represented in anthologies. Contributor to periodicals. **Address:** Department of Philosophy, University of Sussex, Arts B233, Falmer, Brighton, ES BN1 9QN, England. **Online address:** m.r.morris@sussex.ac.uk

MORRIS, Nigel. British (born England), b. 1955. **Genres:** Film, Communications/Media. **Career:** University of Lincoln, principal lecturer in media theory, 2000-. Writer. **Publications:** The Cinema of Steven Spielberg: Empire of Light, 2007. Contributor to books and periodicals. **Address:** Department of Media Production, University of Lincoln, Brayford Pool, Lincoln, LI LN6 7TS, England. **Online address:** nmorris@lincoln.ac.uk

MORRIS, Rachel. British (born England) **Genres:** Novels, History, Young Adult Fiction, Law. **Career:** Tavellers in Cardiff Law School, Telephone Legal Advisory Service, advice worker, 1996-98; Cardiff Law School, Traveller Law Research Unit, research associate; novelist. **Publications:** The Fringe Orphan, 1992; (ed. with L. Clements) Gaining Ground: Law Reform for Gypsies and Travellers, 1999; (with L. Clements) Disability, Social Care, Health and Travelling People: A Report Examining Existing Research and Literature Relating to the Social and Health Care Needs of Gypsies and Other Travellers, 2001. **Address:** Random House, 20 Vauxhall Bridge Rd., London, GL SW1V 2SA, England.

MORRIS, Roger. American (born United States), b. 1938. **Genres:** History, International Relations/Current Affairs, Politics/Government. **Career:** Harvard University, teaching fellow in government, 1965-66; U.S. Department of State, U.S. Foreign Service officer and executive secretariat of secretary of state, 1966-67; White House, staff, 1967; National Security Council, staff, 1968, senior staff, 1968-70; legislative assistant for U.S. Senator Walter Mondale, 1970-72; Carnegie Endowment for International Peace, director of policy studies, 1972-74; Oxfam America, director, 1975-78; U.S. Agency for International Development, consultant, 1978-79; New Mexico Project for Investigative Reporting, director, 1982-; KNME-TV, co-producer, 1989-; University of New Mexico, adjunct professor of political science and general honors, 1990-; Sunmount Syndicate, co-owner, editor and columnist, 1990-; Green Institute, senior fellow, 2004-08. **Publications:** (Co-author) Passing By: The U.S. and Genocide in Burundi, 1973; (with H. Sheets) Disaster in the Desert: Humanitarian Relief in the African Drought, 1974; Uncertain Greatness: Henry Kissinger and American Foreign Policy, 1977; Haig: The General's Progress, 1982; The Devil's Butcher Shop: The New Mexico Prison

Uprising, 1983; Richard Milhous Nixon: The Rise of an American Politician, 1990; Promises of Change: Image and Reality in the Clinton Presidency, 1993; (with R. Paine) Will You Manage?: The Needs of Local Authority Chief Executives, 1995; Partners in Power: The Clintons and Their America, 1996; (with S. Denton) The Money and the Power: The Making of Las Vegas and Its Hold on America, 1947-2000, 2001; Shadows of the Eagle, 2007; The Rise and Rise of Robert Gates: The Specialist, 2007; Richard Milhous Nixon: Crucible of Power, 1953-1960, forthcoming. FORTHCOMING: ROBERT GATES SERIES: The Rise and Rise of Robert Gates: The Gates Inheritance; The Rise and Rise of Robert Gates: The World That Made Bob. Contributor of articles to periodicals. **Address:** 181 9 Mile Rd., Santa Fe, NM 87508-8912, U.S.A.

MORRIS, Scott. *See* **MORRIS, G. Scott.**

MORRIS, Stephen. French/British (born England), b. 1935. **Genres:** Plays/Screenplays, Poetry. **Career:** Whitchurch Hospital, research worker, 1963-65; Mansfield Art College, assistant lecturer in art, 1966-67; Wolverhampton University, Faculty of Art, assistant lecturer, 1967-69, lecturer, 1969-72, senior lecturer, 1972-85. Full-time writer and artist. **Publications:** Alien Poets, 1965; Poems to Aberfan, 1966; (with P. Finch) Wanted for Writing Poetry, 1968; Penny Farthing Madness, 1969; Born Under Leo, 1972; The Revolutionary, and Other Poems, 1972; The Kingfisher Catcher, 1974; Death of a Clown, 1976; Widening Circles, 1977; The Moment of Truth, 1978; Too Long at the Circus, 1980; Barnegat Light, 1984; The Umbrellas of Mr. Parapluie, 1985; Rolling Dice, 1986; To Forgive the Unforgivable, 1997; Twelve, 1998; Limbus of the Moon, 2005. Works appear in anthologies. Contributor to magazines and newspapers. **Address:** 4 rue Las Cours, Aspiran, Herault, 34800, France. **Online address:** morris.stephen@wanadoo.fr

MORRIS, S(tephen) Brent. American (born United States), b. 1950. **Genres:** Adult Non-fiction, History, Social Sciences, Literary Criticism And History. **Career:** Duke University, instructor in mathematics, 1972-75; Trestleboard, founding editor, 1973-75; Johns Hopkins University, lecturer in electrical engineering and computer science, 1979-84; Furman University, IBM lecturer in computer science, 1992; Free State Freemason, editor, 1998-2001; Supreme Council, The Scottish Rite Journal, managing editor, 2005-; National Security Agency, Cryptologic Mathematician Program, executive; National Cryptologic School, teacher. **Publications:** The Folger Manuscript, 1993; Cornerstones of Freedom, 1993; Is It True What They Say about Freemasonry?, 1994, rev. ed., 1997; Masonic Philanthropies: A Tradition of Caring, 2nd ed., 1997; Magic Tricks, Card Shuffling and Dynamic Computer Memories, 1998; (ed. with R.W. Weisberger and W. McLeod) Freemasonry on Both Sides of the Atlantic: Essays Concerning the Craft in the British Isles, Europe, The United States, and Mexico, 2002; (with A. Hoyos) Is it True What they Say About Freemasonry?: The Methods of Anti-Masons, 2004; (ed. with A. de Hoyos) Freemasonry in Context: History, Ritual, Controversy, 2004; (ed.) International Masonic periodicals, 1738-2005: A Bibliography of the Library of the Supreme Council, 2006; Complete Idiot's Guide to Freemasonry, 2006. **Address:** 11251 Sitting Bull Cir., Lusby, MD 20657, U.S.A. **Online address:** sbrent@erols.com

MORRIS, Sylvia Jukes. American/British (born England) **Genres:** Biography, Autobiography/Memoirs. **Career:** Writer. **Publications:** Edith Kermit Roosevelt: Portrait of a First Lady, 1980; Rage for Fame: The Ascent of Clare Boothe Luce, 1997. **Address:** Random House Inc., 201 E 50th St., New York, NY 10022-7703, U.S.A.

MORRIS, Timothy. American (born United States), b. 1959. **Genres:** Literary Criticism And History, Children's Fiction. **Career:** Princeton University, assistant in instruction, 1981-83; Bryn Mawr College, instructor, 1983-84; Rutgers-New Brunswick, instructor, 1983-86; Fordham University, visiting assistant professor, 1987-88; University of Texas at Arlington, visiting assistant professor, 1988-90, assistant professor, 1990-95, associate professor, 1995-2001, professor, 2001-, graduate advisor, associate chair. Writer. **Publications:** Becoming Canonical in American Poetry, 1995; Making the Team: The Cultural Work of Baseball Fiction, 1997; You're Only Young Twice: Children's Literature and Film, 2000. Contributor to periodicals. **Address:** University of Texas at Arlington, 203 Carlisle Hall, PO Box 19035, Arlington, TX 76019, U.S.A. **Online address:** tmorris@uta.edu

MORRISON, Bill. American (born United States), b. 1935?. **Genres:** Children's Fiction, Children's Non-fiction, Illustrations. **Career:** Massachusetts College of Art, instructor in children's illustration. Writer. **Publications:** SELF-ILLUSTRATED FOR CHILDREN: Squeeze a Sneeze, 1977; Louis James Hates School, 1978; Simon Says, 1983; Roswell Walks Among Us, 1997. OTHERS: (contrib.) Futurama-o-rama, 2002; (ed.) The Homer Book, 2004; (ed.) The Bart Book, 2004; (contrib.) Futurama Adventures, 2004; (ed.) Ralph Wiggum Book, 2006; (ed.) The Lisa Book, 2006; (ed.) The Marge Book, 2009; (ed.) Chief Wiggum's Book of Crime and Punishment, 2009. Illustrator of books by others. **Address:** 68 Glandore Rd., Westwood, MA 02090-2239, U.S.A. **Online address:** humorimage@verizon.net

MORRISON, Bill. Irish (born Ireland), b. 1940. **Genres:** Plays/Screenplays, Young Adult Fiction. **Career:** Victoria Theatre, resident writer, Stoke-on-Trent, 1969-71; BBC radio, drama producer, 1975-76; Everyman Theatre, resident writer, 1977-79, artistic director, 1983-85; C.F. Mott College, lecturer, 1977-78; Radio City, drama producer, 1979-80; Playhouse Theatre, associate director, 1981-83, artistic director, 1983-85. Writer. **Publications:** Sam Slade is Missing, 1973; Flying Blind, 1978; Tess of the d'Urbervilles (adaptation), 1980; A Love Song for Ulster, 1994; What Every Parent Needs to Know About Children and Drugs, 1998. **Address:** Alan Brodie Representation, 211 Piccadilly, London, GL W1V 9LD, England.

MORRISON, Grant. Scottish (born Scotland), b. 1960. **Genres:** Graphic Novels, Cartoons, Novels. **Career:** Writer. **Publications:** Lovely Biscuits (includes prose stories and plays Depravity and Red King Rising), 1998. ZENITH SERIES: Zenith Phase 1: Tygers, 1988; Zenith Phase 2: The Hollow Land, 1989; Zenith Phase 3: War in Heaven, 1990; Zenith Phase 5, 1996; 2000 A.D. Presents Zenith Phase 1, 2003. ANIMAL MAN SERIES: Animal Man, 1991; Origin of Species, 2002; Deus ex Machina, 2003. INVISIBLES SERIES; Say You Want a Revolution, 1996; Bloody Hell in America, 1998; Counting to None, 1999; Kissing Mister Quimper, 2000; Apocalipstic, 2001; Entropy in the U.K., 2001; The Invisible Kingdom, 2002. JUSTICE LEAGUE OF AMERICA SERIES: JLA Wild C.A.T.S, Covert Action Teams, 1997; New World Order, 1997; American Dreams, 1997; Rock of Ages, 1998; (with M. Waid and C. Priest) Strength in Numbers, 1998; (with M. Millar) Justice for All, 1999; (with D. Jurgens) Secret Origins: Featuring the JLA, 1999; World War III, 2000; Earth 2, 1999. NEW X-MEN SERIES: vol. I, 2002; E Is for Extinction, 2002; Imperial, 2002; New Worlds, 2002. vol. II, 2003; Riot at Xavier's, 2003; Assault on Weapon Plus, 2003; Planet X, 2004; Here Comes Tomorrow, 2004. OTHER: Arkham Asylum: A Serious House on Serious Earth, 1989; Legends of the Dark Knight, 1989; Steed and Mrs. Peel, 1991; (creator of plot, with N. Gaiman and R. Curtis) The Totally Stonking, Surprisingly Educational and Utterly Mindboggling Comic Relief Comic, 1991; Dare, 1991; Batman Gothic, 1992; The Doom Patrol: Crawling from the Wreckage, 1992; The Mystery Play, 1994; (with M. Millar) Judge Dredd: Book of the Dead, 1995; Kill Your Boyfriend, 1995; Spawn 4: Escalation, 1997; Flex Mentallo: Man of Muscle Mystery, 1998; Marvel Boy, 2001; (with J. Michael Stracynski) Nuff Said, 2002; The Filth, 2002; Fantastic Four: 1 2 3 4, 2004; Sebastion O, 2004; DC Comics Presents: Mystery in Space, 2004; Sebastian O, 2004; The Doom Patrol: The Painting That Ate Paris, 2004; WE3, 2005; Vimanarama, 2005; Seaguy, 2005; Seaguy-The Slaves of Mickey Eye, 2005; Seven Soldiers of Victory, 2006; All-star Superman, 2007; Batman and Son, 2007; The Flash: Emergency Stop, 2008; Batman: The Black Glove, 2008; Batman R.I.P., 2009; Flash: The Human Race, 2009; Final Crisis Companion: Director's Cut, 2009; Batman and Robin: Batman Reborn, 2010; Absolute All-Star Superman, 2010; The Authority: The Lost Year Book 1, 2010; Supergods: Our World in the Age of the Superhero, 2011; Batman: Under the Cowl, 2010; Batman: The Return of Bruce Wayne, 2011; Joe the Barbarian Deluxe Edition, 2011; If, forthcoming. **Address:** c/o Jon Levin, Creative Artists Agency, 9830 Wilshire Blvd., Beverly Hills, CA 90212-1825, U.S.A.

MORRISON, Helen. American (born United States), b. 1942. **Genres:** Horror, Social Sciences. **Career:** Johnson and Johnson Research Foundation, research technician, 1962-65; AME Associate, lab personnel director, 1965-67; Biosearch Incorporate, associate director, 1967-70; University of Wisconsin Hospital, intern, 1972-73, resident in psychiatry, 1972-75, fellow in child psychiatry, 1975-76; Wisconsin Psychiatric Research Institute, research associate, 1976-77; Loyola University, Stritch School of Medicine, director of child psychiatry, 1978-80; Center for Health Sciences, University of Wisconsin, member of executive board, president of house staff association. Writer. **Publications:** My Life Among the Serial Killers: Inside the Minds of the World's Most Notorious Murderers, 2004. Contributor to periodicals. **Address:** c/o HarperCollins Publishers, 10 E 53rd St., New York, NY 10022, U.S.A.

MORRISON, Jeffry H. American (born United States), b. 1961. **Genres:** History. **Career:** Kallina & Associates, attorney, 1987-92; Georgetown University, lecturer & research fellow, 1995-99, adjunct professor of history, 2002-04; U.S. Air Force Academy, assistant professor of political science, 1999-2001; Regent University, assistant professor, 2001-03, associate professor of government, 2004-; Princeton University, visiting assistant professor of politics, 2003-04. Political scientist, historian, educator, lawyer, writer and editor. **Publications:** (ed. with D.L. Dreisbach and M.D. Hall) The Founders on God and Government, 2004; John Witherspoon and the Founding of the American Republic, 2005. Contributor to journals. **Address:** Robertson School of Government, Regent University, 1000 Regent University Dr., Virginia Beach, VA 23464, U.S.A. **Online address:** jeffmor@regent.edu

MORRISON, Keith. American/Jamaican (born Jamaica), b. 1942. **Genres:** Art/Art History. **Career:** Hyde Park Art Center, teacher of art, 1965-67; Fisk University, assistant professor of drawing, 1967-69; DePaul University, Department of Art, chair and associate professor, 1969-71; University of Illinois, College of Art and Architecture, associate professor of printmaking and department chair, 1971-79, associate dean, 1972-76; University of Maryland, Department of Art, professor, 1979-92, chair, 1987-92, College of Arts and Humanities, dean, 1996-97; San Francisco State University, San Francisco Art Institute, professor of art, 1992-93, dean of academic affairs, 1993-94, College of Creative Arts, dean, 1994-; Temple University, Tyler School of Arts, professor, dean, through 2008; Harlem Urban Development Corp., cultural-economic consultant. **Publications:** 200 Years of Afro-American Women in Art: A Critic's View, 1980; Art in Washington and Its Afro-American Presence: 1940-1970, 1985; Keith Morrison: Recent Painting, March 10-April 28, 1990, 1990; (with L. Cohen and L. Manion) A Guide to Teaching Practice, 1996. Contributor to articles and periodicals. **Address:** 887 DeHaro St., San Francisco, CA 94107-2705, U.S.A. **Online address:** keithamorrison@aol.com

MORRISON, Kristin Diane. American (born United States), b. 1934. **Genres:** Literary Criticism And History, Theatre, Art/Art History. **Career:** Immaculate Heart College, instructor in English, 1960-61; South Carolina State College, professor of English, 1966-67; New York University, Washington Square College of Arts and Sciences, assistant professor of English, 1967-69; Boston College, assistant professor of English, 1969-71, associate professor, 1971-84, professor of English, 1984-, now professor emeritus of English; Newton College, academic dean and professor of English, 1972-74. Writer. **Publications:** (Co-author) Crowell's Handbook of Contemporary Drama, 1971; Handbook of Contemporary Drama, 1972; In Black and White, 1972; Canters and Chronicles: The Use of Narrative in the Plays of Samuel Beckett and Harold Pinter, 1983; William Trevor, 1993. Contributor to journals. **Address:** Department of English, Boston College, Carney Hall, 140 Commonwealth Ave., Chestnut Hill, MA 02467, U.S.A. **Online address:** kristin.morrison@bc.edu

MORRISON, Martha A. American (born United States), b. 1948. **Genres:** Theology/Religion, Children's Fiction. **Career:** Harvard University, Harvard Semitic Museum, visiting specialist, 1974-76; Brandeis University, assistant professor, 1974-86; Ben Gurion University Land of Gerar Expedition, area director and director of education, 1982-85; Yale University, visiting lecturer, 1983; Boston College, lecturer, 1987-, part-time faculty; Wellesley College Class of 1970, president. Writer. **Publications:** FOR YOUNG READERS: (with S.F. Brown) Judaism, 1991, 4th ed., 2009. FOR ADULTS: (ed. with D.I. Owen and contrib.) Studies on the Civilization and Culture of Nuzi and the Hurrians, vol. I: In Honor of Ernest R. Lacheman on His Seventy-fifth Birthday, April 29, 1981, 1981, vol. II: Texts and Studies, 1985, vol. IV: The Eastern Archives of Nuzi, 1993. Contributor to journals. **Address:** Theology Department, Boston College, Maloney Hall 340L, 140 Commonwealth Ave., 21 Campanella Way, Ste. 340L, Chestnut Hill, MA 02467, U.S.A.

MORRISON, (Philip) Blake. British (born England), b. 1950. **Genres:** Novels, Children's Fiction, Plays/Screenplays, Poetry, Songs/Lyrics And Libretti, Literary Criticism And History, Autobiography/Memoirs. **Career:** Goldsmiths' College, part-time lecturer, 1976-80; Open University, part-time lecturer, 1976-80; Times Literary Supplement, poetry and fiction editor, 1978-81; The Observer, deputy literary editor, 1981-86, literary editor, 1987-89; Poetry Book Society, chair, 1984-87; Independent on Sunday, literary editor, 1989-95, staff writer, 1994-95; Goldsmiths College, professor of creative and life writing, 2003-. **Publications:** The Movement: English Poetry and Fiction of the 1950's, 1980; (co-author) Poetry Introduction 5, 1982; Seamus Heaney, 1982; (ed. with A. Motion) The Penguin Book of Contemporary British Poetry, 1982; Dark Glasses, 1984, rev. ed., 1989; The Ballad of the Yorkshire Ripper and Other Poems, 1987; The Yellow House, 1987; And When Did You Last See Your Father?: A Son's Memoir of Love and Loss, 1993, new ed., 2006; (adapter and trans.) The Cracked Pot: A Play, 1996; As If: A Crime, a Trial, a Question of Childhood, 1997; Too True, 1998; Dr Ox's Experiment, 1998; Selected Poems, 1999; The Justification of Johann Gutenberg, 2000; Things My Mother Never Told Me, 2002; Oedipus/Antigone, 2003; South of the River, 2007; We Are Three Sisters, 2011. Contributor to books and periodicals. **Address:** c/o Sarah Ballard, United Agents, 12-26 Lexington St., London, GL W1F 0LE, England. **Online address:** blakemorr@aol.com

MORRISON, Taylor. American (born United States), b. 1971. **Genres:** Art/Art History, Children's Non-fiction, Illustrations, Sciences. **Career:** Writer. **Publications:** Antonio's Apprenticeship: Painting a Fresco in Renaissance Italy, 1996; The Neptune Fountain: A Young Sculptor in Renaissance Italy, 1997; Cheetah, 1998; The Great Unknown, 2001; Buffalo Nickel, 2002; The Coast Mappers, 2004; Civil War Artist, 2004; Wildfire, 2006; Mastodon Mystery, 2006; Tsunami Warning, 2007; The Tides, forthcoming. Contributor of articles. **Address:** Taylor Morrison, 37280 SW Goddard Rd., Cornelius, OR 97113, U.S.A. **Online address:** taylor_morrison@yahoo.com

MORRISON, Toni. American (born United States), b. 1931. **Genres:** Novels, Poetry, Music, Picture/Board Books, Young Adult Non-fiction, Children's Non-fiction, Plays/Screenplays. **Career:** Texas Southern University, instructor in English, 1955-57; Howard University, instructor in English, 1957-64; Random House, senior editor, 1965-85; State University of New York-Purchase, Purchase College, associate professor of English, 1971-72; Yale University, visiting lecturer, 1976-77; State University of New York, Schweitzer professor of humanities, 1984-89; Bard College, visiting professor, 1986-88; University of Michigan, Obert C. Tanner lecturer, 1988; Syracuse University, Jeannette K. Watson distinguished professor, 1988; Princeton University, Robert F. Goheen professor of humanities, 1989-, now Robert F. Goheen professor emeritus of humanities; Trinity College, Clark lecturer, 1990; Harvard University, Massey lecturer, 1990; The Toni Morrison Society, founder, 1993-. **Publications:** The Bluest Eye: A Novel, 1970; Sula, 1974; (ed.) The Black Book, 1974; Song of Solomon, 1977; Tar Baby, 1981; Dreaming Emmett, 1986; Beloved: A Novel, 1987; Jazz, 1992; Playing in the Dark: Whiteness and the Literary Imagination, 1992; (ed. and intro.) Race-ing Justice, En-Gendering Power: Essays on Anita Hill, Clarence Thomas and the Construction of Social Reality, 1992; Conversations with Toni Morrison, 1994; (ed.) To Die for the People: The Writings of Huey P. Newton, 1995; Four Songs for Soprano, Cello and Piano, 1995; The Dancing Mind, 1996; (ed. and intro.) Deep Sightings and Rescue Missions: Fiction, Essays and Conversations, 1996; (ed. with C.B. Lacour) Birth of a Nation Hood: Gaze, Script and Spectacle in the O.J. Smipson Case, 1997; Paradise, 1998; Spirits in the Well: For Voice and Piano, 1998; The Big Box, 1999; The Book of Mean People, 2002; (with S. Morrison) The Book of Mean People, 2002; Love, 2003; (with S. Morrison) The Lion or the Mouse?, 2003; (with S. Morrison) The Ant or the Grasshopper?, 2003; Toni Morrison's Song of Solomon: A Casebook, 2003; (with S. Morrison) The Poppy or the Snake?, 2003; Remember: The Journey to School Integration, 2004; (with S. Morrison) Mirror or the Glass, 2004; Margaret Garner: Opera in Two Acts, 2005; Memoirs, 2005; (with S. Morrison) Who's Got Game?: Three Fables, 2007; Mercy: A Novel, 2008; What Moves at the Margin: Selected Nonfiction, 2008; Burn This Book, 2009; (with S. Morrison) Peeny Butter Fudge, 2009; (with S. Morrison) Little Cloud and Lady Wind, 2010; (with S. Morrison) Tortoise or the Hare, 2010; (contrib.) Inner Sanctum, 2010; Home, 2012. Contributor to magazines and periodicals. **Address:** Toni Morrison Society Inc., PO Box 54346, Atlanta, GA 30308, U.S.A. **Online address:** tonimorrisonsociety@gmail.com

MORRISS, Frank. American (born United States), b. 1923. **Genres:** Children's Fiction, Theology/Religion, Essays. **Career:** Register System of Newspapers, associate editor, 1949-60; Regis College, instructor, 1955-61, lecturer in English, 1960-61; Loretto Heights College, instructor in English and philosophy, 1956-61; St. Michael's College, assistant debate coach and instructor in English, 1961-63; The Wanderer, contributing editor and columnist; Vermont Catholic Tribune, associate editor, 1961-63; Register, editor of national edition, 1963-; writer, 1967-. **Publications:** Boy of Philadelphia: A Story About the Continental Congress, 1955; Adventures of Broken Hand, 1957; Alfred of Wessex, 1959; Submarine Pioneer: John Philip Holland, 1961; The Forgotten Revelation: Essays on God and Nature, 1964; Saints for the Small, 1964; The Conservative Imperative, 1970; The Divine Epic, 1974;

A Neglected Glory, 1976; (with J. Gawey) Catholic Perspectives: Abortion, 1979; (with J. Garvey) Abortion, 1979; The Catholic as Citizen: The Church's Social Teaching: Order, Justice, Freedom, Peace, 1979; A Christmas Celebration, 1983; Thinking Critically, 1991; A Little Life of Our Lord: The Story of the Christ, 1993; Saints in Verse, 2000; Two Chapels-John Henry Newman Modern Martyr, 2000; Francis Thompson, 2008. FORTHCOMING: The Rise of Uncatholicism; Chronicle of Disloyalty. **Address:** 3505 Owens St., Wheat Ridge, CO 80033, U.S.A.

MORRISSEY, Will. American (born United States), b. 1951. **Genres:** History, Politics/Government, Social Sciences. **Career:** Queens College, A Journal of Political Philosophy, associate editor, 1979-; Office of New Jersey State Senator S. Thomas Gagliano, legislative aide, 1981-89; New Jersey Transit Corp., assistant for communications in office of the executive director, 1989-90; The Jersey Shore Partnership, consultant, 1994-2000; Monmouth County Historical Commission, executive director, 1996-2000; New School University, Eugene Lang College, teaching assistant, 1998-99; Hillsdale College, assistant professor of political science, 2000-. Writer. **Publications:** Reflections on De Gaulle: Political Founding in Modernity, 1983, rev. ed., 2003; Reflections on Malraux: Cultural Founding in Modernity, 1984; (with P. Eidelberg) Our Culture Left or Right, 1992; Culture in the Commercial Republic, 1996; A Political Approach to Pacifism, 2 vol., 1996; Self-Government and the American Founding: Presidents of Founding and Civil War, 2004; Dilemma of Progressivism: How Roosevelt, Taft, and Wilson Reshaped the American Regime of Self-government, 2009. **Address:** Hillsdale College, 405 Delp Hall, PO Box 9, Hillsdale, MI 49242, U.S.A. **Online address:** will.morrissey@hillsdale.edu

MORRISSON, Mark S. American (born United States) **Genres:** Adult Non-fiction. **Career:** Chicago Review, associate nonfiction editor, 1989-91, nonfiction editor, 1991-94; University of Chicago, B.A. project supervisor, 1993-94, Center for Continuing Studies, instructor, 1995-96; Columbia College, instructor, 1994; Pennsylvania State University, University Park, assistant professor, 1996-2002, associate professor of English, 2002-08, professor of English and science, technology and society, 2008-, Undergraduate Studies, director and chair, 2001-03, associate department head, 2004-; Modernist Studies Association, founding member, 1998-2001, president, 2008-. **Publications:** The Public Face of Modernism: Little Magazines, Audiences, and Reception, 1905-1920, 2000; (ed. and intro. with J. Selzer) Tambour: A Snapshot of Modernism at a Crossroads, 2002; (contrib.) Joyce and the City, 2002; (contrib.) The Cambridge Companion to American Modernism, 2005; (contrib.) A Companion to Modernist Literature and Culture, 2006; (contrib.) Oxford Encyclopedia of British Literature, 2006; (contrib.) The Modernist Journals Project, 2007; Modern Alchemy: Occultism and the Emergence of Atomic Theory, 2007; (with R.G. Schulze) Monograph on Occult Modernism and Modernist Occultism, forthcoming. **Address:** Department of English, Pennsylvania State University, 136 Burrowes Bldg., University Park, PA 16802, U.S.A. **Online address:** mxm61@psu.edu

MORRITT, Hope. Also writes as Malvena Hope Morritt, Hope Cameron. Canadian (born Canada), b. 1930. **Genres:** Novels, History, Autobiography/Memoirs, Biography, Travel/Exploration. **Career:** Edmonton Journal, staff writer and editor, 1946; Edmonton Bulletin, staff writer and editor, 1947; CFWH Radio, announcer/programmer, 1947-49; Canadian Army, secretary, 1948-50; freelance writer, 1950-72; Sarnia Observer, reporter and editor, 1972-75; London Free Press, reporter, 1976-80; Lambton College of Applied Arts and Technology, teacher of English, 1980-, teacher of creative writing; Edmonton Bulletin, reporter and women's page editor. **Publications:** Sarah, 1974; (with N.W. Linder) Nahanni, 1975; (with N.W. Linder) Pauline (biography), 1979; Land of the Fireweed (memoir), 1985; Bohunk Road (novel), 1987; (contrib.) Pyramid, 1980; (contrib.) Flare-up, 1983; Soldier Come Home (poetry), 1989; Rivers of Oil, the Founding of North America's Petroleum Industry (history), 1993; Rendezvous with Death-The Jane Johnson Story (biography), 1995; Women and Computer Based Technologies: a Feminist Perspective, 1997; With Maisie's Love: A Pioneer Family's Survival through War & Peace (memoir), 2002. **Address:** c/o Alan Cohen, Davis-Cohen Associates, 182 Sullivan St., New York, NY 10012, U.S.A.

MORRITT, Malvena Hope. *See* **MORRITT, Hope.**

MORROW, Ann. British/Irish (born Ireland) **Genres:** Biography, Autobiography/Memoirs, History, Romance/Historical, Young Adult Fiction. **Career:** Daily Telegraph, royal correspondent, court correspondent, 1976-82; Daily Express Newspapers, journalist. Broadcaster and educator. **Publications:** The Queen, 1983; The Queen Mother, 1984; Highness: The Maharajahs of India, 1986; Picnic in a Foreign Land, 1989; Princess, 1991; The Maharajas of India, 1998; Without Equal: H.M. Queen Elizabeth, the Queen Mother, 2000, rev. ed., 2002; Cousins Divided: George V and Nicholas II, 2006. **Address:** c/o Curtis Brown, Haymarket House, 28/29 Haymarket, London, GL W1Y 4SP, England.

MORROW, John. New Zealander/British (born England), b. 1951. **Genres:** Politics/Government, Literary Criticism And History, History. **Career:** Victoria University of Wellington, School of History, Politics and Philosophy, professor of political theory, assistant vice-chancellor; University of Auckland, Department of Political Studies, professor of political studies, 2002-, dean of arts, 2003-09, academic deputy vice chancellor, 2009-; University of Cambridge, visiting lecturer of history, Robinson College, bye fellow; University of Edinburgh, Institute for Advanced Studies in the Humanities, visiting fellow; Folger Shakespeare Library, visiting fellow. Writer. **Publications:** (Ed. with P. Harris) T.H. Green: Lectures on the Principles of Political Obligation, and Other Writings, 1986; Coleridge's Political Thought: Property, Morality, and the Limits of Traditional Discourse, 1990; (ed.) Coleridge's Writings, 1991; (with M. Francis) A History of English Political Thought in the Nineteenth Century, 1994; A History of Political Thought: A Thematic Introduction, 1998, 2nd ed. as History of Western Political Thought: A Thematic Introduction, 2005; (ed.) Young England: The New Generation: A Selection of Primary Texts, 1999; Thomas Carlyle, 2006; (ed. with J. Scott) Liberty, Authority, Formality, 2008. **Address:** Department of Political Studies, University of Auckland, Auckland Mail Ctr., PO Box 92019, Auckland, 1142, New Zealand. **Online address:** j.morrow@auckland.ac.nz

MORROW, Skip. American (born United States), b. 1952. **Genres:** Animals/Pets, Illustrations, Humor/Satire. **Career:** Musician and singer, 1974-80; writer and illustrator, 1980-; Recycled Paper Greetings, designer, 1984-. **Publications:** The Official I Hate Cats Book, 1980; The Second Official I Hate Cats Book, 1981; For the Birds, 1982; The Official I Hate Love Book, 1982; (ed. with R. Wolin and N. Hollander) Drawn Together, 1983; The End, 1983; Don't Laugh, You're Next, 1983; (ed. with N. Hollander and R. Wolin) Drawn Together: Relationships Lampooned, Harpooned and Cartooned, 1983; The Joy of Smoking, 2000; I Still Hate Cats, 2000. **Address:** Not-A Rd., Ste. 30, PO Box 123, Wilmington, VT 05363, U.S.A. **Online address:** skip@skipmorrow.com

MORSE, Donald E. American (born United States), b. 1936. **Genres:** Literary Criticism And History, Translations, Essays. **Career:** University of Connecticut, instructor in English, 1960-62; Williamantic State College, instructor in English, 1962-63; Bobson College, assistant professor of literature, 1963-67; Oakland University, assistant professor, 1967-69, associate professor, 1969-74, professor of English, 1974-99, chairman and professor of rhetoric, communications and journalism, 1980-86, professor emeritus, 1999-; CEA Forum, editor, 1976-77; CEA Critic, editor, 1976-78; Lajos Kossuth University, Fulbright professor, 1987-89, 1991-93; University of Debrecen, Soros Pprofessor, 1990, 1994; Maasstrict (Netherlands) Centre for Transatlantic Studies, visiting professor; Partium University, visiting professor. **Publications:** The Choices of Fiction, 1974; (ed.) Fantastic in World Literature and the Arts: Selected Essays from the Fifth International Conference on the Fantastic in the Arts, 1987; Reader's Guide to Kurt Vonnegut, 1991; (ed.with C. Bertha) More Real than Reality: The Fantastic in Irish Literature and the Arts, 1991; (ed. with M.B. Tymn and C. Bertha) Celebration of the Fantastic: Selected Papers from the Tenth Anniversary International Conference on the Fantastic in the Arts, 1992; (ed. with C. Bertha and István Pálffy) Small Nation's Contribution to the World: Essays on Anglo-Irish Literature and Language, 1993; (with C. Bertha) Worlds Visible and Invisible: Essays on Irish Literature, 1994; (ed.) Delegated Intellect: Emersonian Essays on Literature, Science, and Art in Honor of Don Gifford, 1995; The Novels of Kurt Vonnegut: Imagining Being an American, 2003; (ed. with C. Bertha and M. Kurdi) Brian Friel's Dramatic Artistry: The Work Has Value, 2006; (ed.) Anatomy of Science Fiction, 2006; Kurt Vonnegut, 2007; (trans. with C. Bertha) Silenced Voices: Hungarian Plays from Transylvania, 2008; (ed.) Mythic Fantasy of Robert Holdstock: Critical Essays on the Fiction, 2011; (ed.) Zones of Remembering: Time, Memory and the (Un)conscious by Don Gifford, 2011. Contributor to periodicals and translator. **Address:** Institute of English and American Studies, University of Debrecen, 4010 Debrecen, Pf 73, Egyetem ter 1, Debrecen, H4010, Hungary. **Online address:** donaldemorse@gmail.com

MORSE, Melvin (L.). American (born United States), b. 1953. **Genres:** Psychology, Language/Linguistics, Children's Fiction, Social Sciences. **Career:** Indian Health Service, general pediatrics, 1982-83; Children's Orthopedic Hospital and Medical Center, resident in pediatrics, 1982-85; Medical Director. Pediatric Therapy Center, 1984-85; University of Washington, School of Medicine, associate professor of pediatrics, 1985-; pediatrician in private practice, 1985-; Valley General Hospital, creator of pediatric teaching program for residents in family practice; Pediatric Interim Care Center (therapeutic foster home), co-founder; University of California, intern in pediatrics. Writer. **Publications:** (With P. Perry) Closer to the Light: Learning from the Near-Death Experiences of Children, 1990; (with P. Perry) Transformed by the Light: The Powerful Effect of Near-Death Experiences on People's Lives, 1992; (with B. Eadie) Embraced by the Light, 1993; (with P. Perry) Parting Visions: Uses and Meanings of Pre-Death, Psychic and Spiritual Experiences, 1994; (with K. Kemper) The Holistic Pediatrician, 1996; (with P.M.H. Atwater) Beyond the Light: What Isn't Being Said about Near Death Experiences, 1996; (contrib.) The Near Death Experience: A Reader, 1996; (with P. Perry) Where God Lives: The Science of the Paranormal and How Our Brains Are Linked to the Universe, 2000. Contributor to journals and periodicals. **Address:** University of Washington Medical School, Seattle Children's Hospital, Seattle, WA 98195, U.S.A. **Online address:** neardeathdoc@melvinmorse.com

MORSI, Pamela. American (born United States), b. 1951. **Genres:** Romance/Historical, Novels, Literary Criticism And History. **Career:** Muskogee Public Library, library assistant, 1973-75; Ellis Library, library assistant, 1975-76; Oklahoma State University, School of Medicine, librarian, 1976-80; Roper Hospital, librarian, 1985-92; full-time writer, 1992-. **Publications:** ROMANCE NOVELS: Heaven Sent, 1990; Courting Miss Hattie, 1991; Garters, 1992; (with J.A. Caldwell, A. Carberry and K. Lockwood) Summer Magic, 1993; Wild Oats, 1993; Runabout, 1994; Marrying Stone, 1994; Something Shady, 1995; No Ordinary Princess, 1997; Sealed with a Kiss, 1998; Sweetwood Bride, 1999; Here Comes the Bride, 2000; Doing Good, 2002 as The Social Climber of Davenport Heights, 2010; Letting Go, 2003; Suburban Renewal, 2004; By Summer's End, 2005; Cotton Queen, 2006; Night We Met, 2006; Bitsy's Bait & BBQ, 2007; Last Dance at Jitterbug Lounge, 2008; Red's Hot Honky-Tonk Bar, 2009; The Bikini Car Wash, 2010. **Address:** PO Box 6249, San Antonio, TX 78209, U.S.A. **Online address:** pam@pamelamorsi.com

MORSON, Ian. (Medieval Murderers). British (born England) **Genres:** Mystery/Crime/Suspense, History, Novellas/Short Stories. **Career:** Freelance writer, 1995-. **Publications:** NOVELS: Falconer's Crusade, 1995; Falconer's Judgement, 1996; Falconer and the Face of God, 1996; A Psalm for Falconer, 1997; Falconer and the Great Beast, 1998; Falconer and the Ritual of Death, 2008; City of the Dead, 2008; Falconer's Trial, 2009; Falconer and the Death of Kings, 2011. AS MEDIEVAL MURDERERS: The Tainted Relic, 2005; Sword of Shame, 2006; House of Shadows, 2009; King Arthur's Bones, 2009; The Lost Prophecies, 2010; The Sacred Stone, 2010. **Address:** St. Martin's Press Inc., Rm. 1715, 175 5th Ave., New York, NY 10010, U.S.A. **Online address:** ian.morson@hotmail.co.uk

MORTIMER, Edward. Austrian/British (born England), b. 1943. **Genres:** History, Politics/Government, Social Commentary. **Career:** All Souls College, prize fellow, 1965-67, 1970-72; Times, assistant Paris correspondent, 1967-70, foreign specialist and lead writer, 1973-85; Carnegie Endowment, fellow, senior associate, 1980-81; Financial Times, assistant foreign editor, 1987-; United Nations, Speechwriting Unit, head, 1998-2001, director of communication, 2001-07, senior aide to secretary general; The Salzburg Global Seminar, senior vice president and chief program officer, 2007-; Warwick University, honorary professor; Oxford University, fellow. Journalist and political consultant. **Publications:** France and the Africans, 1944-1960: A Political History, 1969; Eurocommunism: Myth or Reality?, 1979; Faith and Power: The Politics of Islam, 1982; The Rise of the French Communist Party, 1920-1947, 1984; Roosevelt's Children: Tomorrow's World Leaders and Their World, 1987; World that FDR Built: Vision and Reality, 1989; Revolution and Change in Europe: Implications for the Atlantic Area Nations, 1993; People, Nation, and State: The Meaning of Ethnicity and Nationalism, 1999. Contributor to periodicals. **Address:** Salzburg Global Seminar, Leopoldskronstrabe 56, Salzburg, 5020, Austria.

MORTIMER, Gavin. French/British (born England) **Genres:** Novellas/Short Stories, History. **Career:** Full time writer, 1996-. **Publications:** The Best Book of Rugby Songs Ever!, 1998; Shackleton: The Story of Ernest Shackleton and the Antarctic Explorers, 1999; Fields of Glory, 2001; Stirling's Men: The Inside History of the SAS in World War II, 2005; The Longest Night: The Bombing of London on May 10, 1941, 2005; The Ultimate Guide to Cricket, 2006; (with D. Mortimer) Baa Baa Rainbow Sheep: PC Tales from the Unhinged Kingdom, 2007; The Story of Yellow Leaf: Journal of Sioux Girl, 2008; The Great Swim, 2008; Find Out about the United Kingdom, 2009; Blitz: An Illustrated History, 2010; Double Death, 2010; SAS in World War II, 2011; The Daring Dozen, 2012. Contributor to periodicals. **Address:** c/o Felicity Blunt, Curtis Brown Group Ltd., Haymarket House, 28-29 Haymarket, London, GL SW1Y 4SP, England. **Online address:** gavin@gavinmortimer.com

MORTIMER, James Edward. British (born England), b. 1921. **Genres:** Industrial Relations, Law, History. **Career:** TUC Economic Department, staff, 1946-48, 1948-68; Draughtsmen's and Allied Technician's Association, national official, 1948-68; London Cooperative Society, director, 1967-70; EDC Engineering Construction, chairman, 1974-81; Conciliation and Arbitration Service, chairman, 1974-81; Labour Party, general secretary, 1982-85. Writer. **Publications:** (Co-author) Russia Welcomed Us: The Report of the British & Irish Workers' Delegation to the USSR, May 1953, 1953; A History of the Association of Engineering and Shipbuilding Draughtsmen, 1960; (with C. Jenkins) British Trade Unions Today, 1965; (with C. Jenkins) The Kind of Laws the Unions Ought to Want, 1968; Industrial Relations, 1968; Trade Unions and Technological Change, 1971; History of the Boilermakers' Society, 1973; Job Status and Income, 1974; (with V.A.E. Mortimer) A Professional Union: The Evolution of the Institution of Professional Civil Servants, 1980; A Life on the Left, 1999. **Address:** 19 Northweald Ln., Kingston upon Thames, SR KT 2 5GL, England.

MORTON, Alexandra (Hubbard). Canadian/American (born United States), b. 1957. **Genres:** Children's Non-fiction, Zoology, Natural History, Animals/Pets, Photography. **Career:** Navel Oceans Systems Center, staff, 1978-79; Raincoast Research Society (originally named Lore Quest), director and co-founder, 1981-; Broughton Archipelago Stewardship Alliance, co-founder, 1999-. Writer. **Publications:** Siwiti: A Whale's Story (for children), 1993; In the Company of Whales: From the Diary of a Whale Watcher (for children), 1993; (with B. Proctor) Heart of the Raincoast: A Life Story (biography), 1998; Listening to Whales: What the Orcas Have Taught Us (essays), 2002; Beyond the Whales: The Photographs and Passions of Alexandra Morton, 2004; (co-author) A Stain Upon the Sea: West Coast Salmon Farming, 2004. Contributor of articles to periodicals. **Address:** Raincoast Research Society, Simoom Sound, BC V0P 1S0, Canada. **Online address:** wildorca@island.net

MORTON, Andrew. British (born England), b. 1953. **Genres:** Biography. **Career:** Daily Star, news reporter, 1980-81, royal correspondent, 1982-85; News of the World and Daily Mail, royal correspondent, 1985-88; freelance writer, 1988-. **Publications:** (With M. Seamark) Andrew, the Playboy Prince (biography), 1983; The Royal Yacht Britannia, 1984; Inside Kensington Palace, 1986; Fodor's Royalty Watching (guidebook), 1987; Theirs Is the Kingdom: The Wealth of the British Royal Family (nonfiction), 1989; Duchess: An Intimate Portrait of Sarah, Duchess of York (biography), 1989; Diana's Diary: An Intimate Portrait of the Princess of Wales (biography), 1990; Inside Buckingham Palace (nonfiction), 1991; Diana: Her True Story (biography), 1992, rev. ed., 1997; Diana: Her New Life, 1994; Moi: The Making of an African Statesman, 1998; Monica's Story, 1999; Madonna, 2001; Posh and Becks, 2000; Nine for Nine: The Pennsylvania Mine Rescue Miracle, 2002; Diana: In Pursuit of Love, 2004; Tom Cruise: An Unauthorized Biography, 2008; Angelina, 2010. **Address:** Michael O'Mara Books, 16 Lion Yard, Tremadoc Rd., London, GL SW4 7NQ, England.

MORTON, Brian. Hong Kong/British (born England), b. 1942. **Genres:** Biology, Zoology, Environmental Sciences/Ecology, Business/Trade/Industry. **Career:** Hong Kong University, Zoology Department, lecturer, 1970-75, reader in marine biology, 1975-82, chair in marine biology, 1981-2003, professor of zoology, 1982-2003, Swire Institute of Marine Science, founding director; Texas Christian University, chair, 1981; Swire Marine Laboratory, director, 1990-. Writer. **Publications:** EDITOR: The Future of the Hong Kong Seashore, 1979; The Malacofauna of Hong Kong and Southern China: Proceedings of the First International Workshop, 23 March-8 April 1977, 1980; (with C.K. Tseng) The Marine Flora and Fauna of Hong Kong and

Southern China: Proceedings of the First International Marine Biological Workshop, Hong Kong, 18 April-10 May 1980, 1982; (with D. Dudgeon) Malacofauna of Hong Kong and Southern China, II: Proceedings of the Second International Workshop on the Malacofauna of Hong Kong and Southern China, Hong Kong, 6-24 April 1983, 1985; Marine Flora and Fauna of Hong Kong and Southern China IV: Proceedings of the Eighth International Marine Biological Workshop, The Marine Flora and Fauna of Hong Kong and Southern China, Hong Kong, 2-20 April 1995, 1997; Marine Biology of the South China Sea III: Proceedings of the Third International Conference on the Marine Biology of the South China Sea: Hong Kong, 28 October-1 November 1996, 1998; Marine Flora and Fauna of Hong Kong and Southern China V: Proceedings of the Tenth International Marine Biological Workshop, the Marine Flora and Fauna of Hong Kong and Southern China, Hong Kong, 2-26 April 1998, 2000; Perspectives on Marine Environmental Change in Hong Kong and Southern China, 1977-2001: Proceedings of an International Workshop Reunion Conference, Hong Kong, 21-26 October 2001, 2003; Historical Ecology of the River Arun and Its Beaches at Littlehampton, West Sussex: 1, 000 Years of Change, 2007. OTHERS: (with J. Morton) The Sea Shore Ecology of Hong Kong, 1983; (with D.S. Melville) Mai Po Marshes, 1983; (with J.C. Britton) Shore Ecology of the Gulf of Mexico, 1989; (with E. Harper) An Introduction to the Caped Aguilar Marine Reserve, 1995. Contributor to periodicals. **Address:** Swire Institute of Marine Science, University of Hong Kong, Cape d'Aguilar, Shek O, Hong Kong, 852, Hong Kong.

MORTON, Brian. American (born United States), b. 1955. **Genres:** Novels, Literary Criticism And History. **Career:** Dissent, book review editor, 1988-2000, executive editor, 1995-2000; New York University, instructor, 1992-94, 1999-; 92nd Street YM-YWHA, instructor, 1993-98; New School for Social Research, instructor, 1995-97; Sarah Lawrence College, instructor, 1998-. **Publications:** The Dylanist, 1991; Starting Out in the Evening, 1998; Window Across the River, 2003; Breakable You, 2006. Contributor to periodicals. **Address:** Sarah Lawrence College, 1 Mead Way, Bronxville, NY 10708-5999, U.S.A. **Online address:** bmorton@slc.edu

MORTON, Bruce Rutherfurd. Australian/New Zealander (born New Zealand), b. 1926?. **Genres:** Mathematics/Statistics, Meteorology/Atmospheric Sciences, Adult Non-fiction, Documentaries/Reportage, History. **Career:** University College, assistant lecturer, 1955-56; University of Manchester, lecturer and senior lecturer, 1956-66; Monash University, chair and professor of applied mathematics, 1967-91, chairman of department of mathematics, 1974-76, professor emeritus, 1991-. Writer. **Publications:** Numerical Approximation, 1965; (with B. Morton) Two Surveys of the Crown of Thorns Starfish Over a Section of the Great Barrier Reef. A Report of the Steering Committee for the Crown of Thorns Survey, March 1976, 1976. **Address:** Department of Mathematics and Statistics, Monash University, PO Box 28M, Monash, VI 3800, Australia. **Online address:** bruce.morton@sci.monash.edu.au

MORTON, James (Severs). British (born England), b. 1938. **Genres:** Criminology/True Crime, Law, Biography, Autobiography/Memoirs, Criminology/True Crime. **Career:** New Law Journal, editor, 1989-, editor-in-chief. Writer and educator. **Publications:** Defending, 1980; Handling Criminal Cases, 1985; The Criminal Justice Act: A Commentary, 1988; Low Speak, 1989; Crown Court Practice, 1989; Taking Liberties: The Criminal Jury in the 1990s, 1989; Sentencing, 1990; Nipper, 1991; Lowspeak 2, 1991; Gangland, 1992; Bent Coppers, 1993; A Guide to the Criminal Justice and Public Order Act 1994, 1994; Gangland 2, 1994; Mad Frank, 1994; Supergrasses & Informers, 1995; A Calendar of Killing, 1997; Mad Frank and Friends, 1998; Gangland International, 1998; Sex, Crimes and Misdemeanours, 1999; Mad Frank's Diary, 2000; East End Gangland, 2000; Gangland Lawyers, 2001; Catching the Killers, 2001; Mad Frank's London, 2001; Gangland Today, 2002; Gang Slang, 2002; Mad Frank's Britain, 2002; First Detective: The Life and Revolutionary Times of Eugène François Vidocq: Criminal, Spy and Private Eye, 2004; (with S. Lobez) Gangland Australia: Colonial Criminals to the Carlton Crew, 2007; Lola Montez: Her Life & Conquests, 2007; (with S. Lobez) Dangerous to Know: An A-Z of Murder and Mayhem in Australasia, 2009. **Address:** c/o Barbara Levy, 21 Kelly St., London, GL NW1 8PG, England.

MORTON, Kate. Australian (born Australia), b. 1976. **Genres:** Novels. **Career:** Author. **Publications:** The Shifting Fog, 2006 in US as The House at Riverton: A Novel, 2008; The Forgotten Garden, 2008. Conttributor to periodicals. **Address:** Atria Books, 1230 Ave. of the Americas, New York, NY 10020, U.S.A. **Online address:** mail@katemorton.com

MORTON, Oliver. British (born England) **Genres:** Air/Space Topics, Natural History, Environmental Sciences/Ecology. **Career:** Economist, staff, 1987-95; Wired U.K., contributing editor, editor-in-chief, 1995-97; Daily Davos, managing editor, 1998-2001; World Health Organization, Commission on Macroeconomics and Health, writer and editor, 2001; Nature Publishing Group, chief news and features editor, 2005-09; Hybrid Vigor Institute, fellow. **Publications:** Mapping Mars: Science, Imagination, and the Birth of a World, 2002; Eating the Sun: How Plants Power the Planet, 2007. Contributor to periodicals and journals. **Address:** The Wylie Agency, 250 W 57th St., Ste. 2114, New York, NY 10107-2199, U.S.A.

MORTON, Patricia. Canadian (born Canada), b. 1945?. **Genres:** History, Social Sciences, Sociology, Adult Non-fiction. **Career:** Trent University, associate professor, professor of history, now professor emeritus. Writer. **Publications:** Disfigured Images: The Historical Assault on Afro-American Women, 1991; (ed. and intro.) Discovering the Women in Slavery: Emancipating Perspectives on the American Past, 1996. **Address:** Department of History, Trent University, 1600 W Bank Dr., Peterborough, ON K9J 7B8, Canada. **Online address:** dmort05@att.global.net

MORTON, Peter. (Peter Ralph Morton). Australian (born Australia), b. 1946. **Genres:** Sciences, Biography, History, Young Adult Non-fiction. **Career:** Flinders University, associate professor of English. Writer. **Publications:** NONFICTION: The Vital Science: Biology and the Literary Imagination, 1860-1900, 1984; Testing Blue Streak at Woomera: An Episode in Anglo-Australian Collaboration and Conflict, 1988; Fire across the Desert: Woomera and the Anglo-Australian Joint Project, 1946-1980, 1989; After Light: A History of the City of Adelaide and Its Council, 1878-1928, 1996; The Busiest Man in England: Grant Allen and the Writing Trade, 1875-1900, 2005. **Address:** School of Humanities, Flinders University, PO Box 2100, Adelaide, SA 5001, Australia. **Online address:** peter.morton@flinders.edu.au

MORTON, Peter Ralph. *See* **MORTON, Peter.**

MORTON, Ray. American (born United States), b. 1961?. **Genres:** History, Genealogy/Heraldry. **Career:** Script Magazine, senior writer and columnist; American Film Institute, screenwriting fellow. Script analyst. **Publications:** King Kong: The History of a Movie Icon from Fay Wray to Peter Jackson, 2005; Close Encounters of the Third Kind: The Making of Steven Spielberg's Classic Film, 2007; Amadeus, 2011; A Hard Day's Night, 2011. **Address:** c/o Author Mail, Applause Theater & Cinema Books, 19 W 21st St., New York, NY 10010-6805, U.S.A. **Online address:** ray@raymorton.com

MORTON, Richard Everett. British/Canadian (born Canada), b. 1930. **Genres:** Literary Criticism And History, Theatre. **Career:** University of the Witwatersrand, lecturer in English, 1955-59; Lake Erie College, assistant professor of English, 1960-62; McMaster University, Department of English, assistant professor, 1962-66, associate professor, 1966-70, professor, 1970-96, chairman, 1976-83, professor emeritus, 1983-; Canada Shakespeare Seminar, lecturer, 1963; University of Birmingham Shakespeare Seminar, lecturer, 1971. Writer. **Publications:** Outline of the Works of Dylan Thomas, 1970; Notes on the Poetry of William Butler Yeats, 1971; Anne Sexton's Poetry of Redemption: The Chronology of a Pilgrimage, 1988; John Dryden's Aeneas: A Hero in Enlightenment Mode, 2000; Examining Changes in the Eighteenth-Century French Translations of Homer's Iliad, 2003; The English Enlightenment Reads Ovid, 2009. EDITOR: (with W.M. Peterson) Three Hours after Marriage, 1961; Lutrin Made English, 1967; Poems by Anne Killigrew, 1967; (with P.S. Fritz) Woman in the 18th Century, 1976; Poems of Sir Aston Cokayne, 1977; (with J.D. Browning) Religion in the 18th Century, 1979. **Address:** Department of English, McMaster University, 321 Chester New Hall, 1280 Main St. W, Hamilton, ON L8S 4L9, Canada. **Online address:** mortonre@mcmaster.ca

MORTON, Timothy. American (born United States), b. 1968. **Genres:** Intellectual History, Politics/Government, Sciences. **Career:** Lincoln College, tutor, 1989-2000; Magdalen College, tutor, 1989-2000; Oxford University, Campion Hall, tutor, 1989-2000; Princeton University, visiting fellow, 1992-93; New York University, visiting assistant professor, 1993-95; University of Colorado, assistant professor, 1995-99, associate professor, 2000-03; University of California, professor of literature and environment, 2003-. Writer. **Publications:** Shelley and the Revolution in Taste: The Body and the Natural World, 1994; The Poetics of Spice: Romantic Consumerism and the Exotic, 2000; (ed. and intro.) Radical Food: The Culture and Politics of Eating and Drinking, 1790-1820, 2000; (ed. with N. Smith) Radicalism in British Literary Culture, 1650-1830: From Revolution to Revolution, 2002; (ed.) A Routledge Literary Sourcebook on Mary Shelley's Frankenstein, 2002; (ed.) Cultures of Taste/Theories of Appetite: Eating Romanticism, 2004; (contrib.) Romanticism: An Oxford Guide, 2005; (ed.) The Cambridge Companion to Shelley, 2006; Ecology without Nature: Rethinking Environmental Aesthetics, 2007; (contrib.) Palgrave Advances in Byron Studies, 2007; The Ecological Thought, 2010. Contributor to periodicals. **Address:** Department of English, University of California, Rm. 211 Voorhies, 1 Shields Ave., Davis, CA 95616, U.S.A. **Online address:** tbmorton@ucdavis.edu

MORUS, Iwan Rhys. Welsh/British (born England), b. 1964?. **Genres:** Sciences, Physics, Biography. **Career:** University of Wales, professor of history; Aberystwyth University, Department of History and Welsh History, staff. Writer. **Publications:** Frankenstein's Children: Electricity, Exhibition and Experiment in Early-Nineteenth-Century London, 1998; (ed.) Bodies/ Machines, 2002; Michael Faraday and the Electrical Century, 2004; (with P.J. Bowler) Making Modern Science: A Historical Survey, 2005; When Physics Became King, 2005; Shocking Bodies: Life, Death & Electricity in Victorian England, 2011. **Address:** Department of History & Welsh History, University of Wales, C46, Hugh Owens Bldg., Aberystwyth, DY SY23 3DY, Wales. **Online address:** irm@aber.ac.uk

MORWOOD, Mike. Australian/New Zealander (born New Zealand), b. 1950. **Genres:** Archaeology/Antiquities, Anthropology/Ethnology. **Career:** Queensland Government, researcher; University of New England in Armidale, professor, 1981-2004, professorial fellow, 2004-; University of Wollongong, professor, 2007-. Writer, anthropologist and archaeologist. **Publications:** (ed. with D.R. Hobbs) Rock Art and Ethnography: Proceedings of the Ethnography Symposium (H), Australian Rock Art Research Association Congress, Darwin 1988, 1992; Visions from the Past: The Archaeology of Australian Aboriginal Art, 2002; (with P. van Oosterzee) The Discovery of the Hobbit: The Scientific Breakthrough That Changed the Face of Human History, 2007; (with P. van Oosterzee) A New Human: The Startling Discovery and Strange Story of the "Hobbits" of Flores, Indonesia, 2007. **Address:** School of Earth & Environmental Sciences, University of Wollongong, Wollongong, NW 2522, Australia. **Online address:** mmorwood@une.edu.au

MOSCHELLA, David C. British/American (born United States), b. 1954. **Genres:** Adult Non-fiction, Technology, Business/Trade/Industry. **Career:** International Data Corp., senior vice president of worldwide research, 1980-95; writer and consultant, 1996-2003; Means Business Inc., vice president of content, 1999-2000; Computerworld, columnist; Computer Sciences Corp., Research and Advisory Services, global research director, 2005-. **Publications:** Waves of Power: Dynamics of Global Technology Leadership, 1964-2010, 1997; Customer-Driven IT: How Users Are Shaping Technology Industry Growth, 2003. **Address:** Research and Advisory Services, Computer Sciences, Corp., 3170 Fairview Park Dr., Falls Church, VA 22042, U.S.A. **Online address:** dmoschella@earthlink.net

MOSCHIS, George P. American (born United States), b. 1944. **Genres:** Marketing, Adult Non-fiction, Economics, Sociology, Business/Trade/Industry, Social Sciences. **Career:** Georgia State University, assistant professor and urban life faculty, 1977-81, associate professor, 1981-84, research professor, 1984-87, professor of marketing, 1987-, Alfred Bernhardt research professor, Center for Mature Consumer Studies, founding director, 1986-. Writer. **Publications:** (With G.G. Alexandrides) Export Marketing Management, 1977; Acquisition of the Consumer Role by Adolescents, 1978; (with T.J. Stanley and M. Sewell) Consumer Profiles by Payment Types, 1982; (with T.J. Stanley) The National Affluent Market Study, 1982; Consumer Socialization: A Life Cycle Perspective, 1987; Assessing Older Adults' Perceptions of Select Marketing Practices and New Technologies Capable of Enhancing Their Well-Being, 1989; (with B.B. Payne) Explanations of the Low Food Stamp Utilization Rates among Low-Income Elderly: Sociological and Psychological Perspectives, 1990; Older Consumer Orientations Toward Marketing Activities and Responses to New Products, 1990; (co-author) Changing Needs in a Changing Society, 1991; (with J.R. Lumpkin and K.M. Gibler) Retirement Housing and Long-Term Health Care: Attitudes and Perceptions of the Mature Consumer, 1992; Marketing to Older Consumers: A Handbook of Information for Strategy Development, 1992; Marketing Strategies for the Mature Market, 1994; Gerontographics: Life-Stage Segmentation for Marketing Strategy Development, 1996; (co-author) The Maturing Marketplace: Buying Habits of Baby Boomers and Their Parents, 2000. Contributor to journals. **Address:** Department of Marketing, J. Mack Robinson College of Business, Georgia State University, Rm. 1337, RCB Bldg., 35 Broad St. NW, PO Box 3989, Atlanta, GA 30303-0444, U.S.A. **Online address:** gmoschis@gsu.edu

MOSCHONAS, Andreas. Greek (born Greece), b. 1941. **Genres:** Sociology, Education, Economics, History. **Career:** Foundation of Mediterranean Studies, researcher, 1983-90; University of Crete, associate professor of political sociology, Department of Sociology, department head and professor of sociology, 1990-, Jean Monnet professor of European integration, Jean Monnet chair in political sociology of European integration, faculty of social sciences, Centre for European Studies and Research, director. Writer. **Publications:** Paradosiaka, Mikroastika Strōmata: He Periptōse tesHellados/ Traditional Petty Bourgeoisie: The Case of Greece, 1986; Koinōnikes Taxeis, Koinōnike allage Kai Oikonomike Anaptyxe Ste Mesogeio: Diethnes Synedrio Tou Hidrymatos Mesogeiakōn Meletōn, Athena 1984/Social Classes, Social Change and Economic Development in the Mediterranean: International Conference of the Foundation for Mediterranean Studies, Athens 1984, 1986; Taxikepale sten Hellada kai E.O.K.: Melete Gia Tis Koinōnikes Kai Politikes Epiptōseis Apo ten Entaxe Tes ChōrasSte Diadikasia tes Koinotikes Holoklerōses/ Class Struggle in Greece and the EEC, 1990; (ed. with G.A. Kourvetaris) The Impact of European Integration: Political, Sociological and Economic Changes, 1996; Education and Training in the European Union, 1998; Taxeis Kai Strōmata Stis Synchrones Koinōnies, 1998. **Address:** Department of Sociology, University of Crete, Rethymno, Crete, 74100, Greece. **Online address:** moschonas@social.soc.uoc.gr

MOSELEY, Marcus. American (born United States) **Genres:** Autobiography/Memoirs. **Career:** YIVO Institute for Jewish Research, assistant archivist, 1987-91, research associate, 1991-2002; New York University, Mellon Fellow & assistant professor, 1991-92, Dorot Fellow & assistant professor, 1993-95; Hebrew Union College-Jewish Institute of Religion, visiting assistant professor, 1992; Sarah Lawrence College, assistant professor, 1993-95; Harvard University, assistant professor, 1995-2001; Johns Hopkins University, visiting professor, 2003-05; Posen Library of Jewish Culture and Civilization, consultant editor, 2003; Northwestern University, associate professor, 2005-. Scholar and writer. **Publications:** Being for Myself Alone: Origins of Jewish Autobiography, 2006. Contributor to books and periodicals. **Address:** Northwestern University, 2-525 Kresge Hall, 1880 Campus Dr., Evanston, IL 60208-2203, U.S.A. **Online address:** m-moseley@northwestern.edu

MOSELEY, Michael E(dward). American (born United States), b. 1941. **Genres:** Anthropology/Ethnology, Humanities. **Career:** Harvard University, instructor and lecturer, 1968-70, assistant professor, associate professor, 1970-76, Peabody Museum, assistant curator, 1969-73, associate curator, 1973-75; Field Museum of Natural History, associate curator, 1976-83, curator, 1983-84; University of Chicago, research associate, 1980-84; University of Florida, Department of Anthropology, professor, 1984-, distinguished professor. Writer. **Publications:** (With C.J. Mackey) Twenty-Four Architectural Plans of Chan Chan, Peru: Structure and Form at the Capital of Chimor, 1974; Maritime Foundations of Andean Civilization, 1975; Pre-agricultural Coastal Civilizations in Peru, 1977; Peru's Golden Treasures: An Essay on Five Ancient Styles, 1978; (ed. with K.C. Day) Chan Chan, Andean Desert City, 1982; (comp.) Trabajos arqueológicos en Moquegua, Perú, 1990; (ed. with A. Cordy-Collins) Northern Dynasties: Kingship and Statecraft in Chimor: A Symposium at Dumbarton Oaks, 12th and 13th October 1985, 1991; The Incas and Their Ancestors: The Archaeology of Peru, 1992, rev. ed., 2001. **Address:** Department of Anthropology, University of Florida, Rm. B356, Turlington Hall, PO Box 117305, Gainesville, FL 32611-7305, U.S.A. **Online address:** moseley@ufl.edu

MOSER, Benjamin. Dutch/American (born United States), b. 1976. **Genres:** Biography, Translations. **Career:** Foreign Affairs Magazine, staff; Alfred A. Knopf, staff; Harvill Press, editor; Harper's Magazine, columnist. Translator and critic. **Publications:** Why This World: A Biography of Clarice Lispector, 2009. TRANSLATOR OF NOVELS BY L.A. GARCIA-ROZA: The Silence of the Rain, 2002; December Heat, 2003; Southwesterly Wind, 2004; A Window in Copacabana, 2005; Pursuit: An Inspector Espinosa Mystery, 2006; Blackout: An Inspector Espinosa Mystery, 2008; Alone in the Crowd, 2009. Contributor to books and magazines. **Address:** Utrecht, Netherlands. **Online address:** bfmoser@gmail.com

MOSER, Edward P. American (born United States), b. 1958. **Genres:** Biology, Information Science/Computers, Politics/Government, Humor/Satire. **Career:** Data General, editor, 1981-82; Dun and Bradstreet Software, senior editor, 1982-85; Computer Corporation of America, staff writer, 1985-88; U.S. Senate, intern, 1988; National Academy of Sciences, staff consultant, writer and researcher, 1989-91; Arist Corp., senior systems analyst and writer, 1992; Human Genome Sciences, senior writer, 2002-. **Publications:** Willy Nilly: Bill Clinton Speaks Out, 1994; The Politically Correct Guide to American History, 1996; The Politically Correct Guide to the Bible, 1997; The Politically Correct Guide to American History, 1999; Secure Internet Practices, 2000; The Age of Regenerative Medicine, 2002; A patriots A to Z of America: Things Every Good American Should Know, 2011. EDITOR: Finding Common Ground: U.S. Export Controls, 1991; The Government Role in Civilian Technology, 1992. **Address:** 2001 N Adams St., Ste. 814, Arlington, VA 22201, U.S.A. **Online address:** mosered@juno.com

MOSER, Laura. American (born United States), b. 1978?. **Genres:** Novels. **Career:** New York Sun, crime reporter, columnist. Writer. **Publications:** YOUNG-ADULT NOVELS: (with L. Mechling) The Rise and Fall of a 10th-Grade Social Climber, 2005; (with L. Mechling) All Q, No A: More Tales of a 10th-Grade Social Climber, 2006; (with L. Mechling) Foreign Exposure: The Social Climber Abroad, 2007; (with H. Pasternak) 5-Factor World Diet, 2009. Contributor to periodicals. **Address:** Ballantine Books, 1745 Broadway, New York, NY 10019, U.S.A. **Online address:** authors@socialclimberbooks.com

MOSER, Paul K. American (born United States), b. 1957. **Genres:** Philosophy. **Career:** Vanderbilt University, graduate teaching fellow, 1980-82; Loyola University Chicago, assistant professor of philosophy, 1983-85, associate professor of philosophy, 1986-89, professor of philosophy, 1989-, chairperson, 1997-, Loyola University Core Curriculum, faculty director, 2004-09; American Philosophical Quarterly, editor, 2007-. **Publications:** Empirical Justification, 1985; Knowledge and Evidence, 1989; Philosophy After Objectivity, 1993; (with D.H. Mulder) Contemporary Approaches to Philosophy, 1994; (with D.H. Mulder and J.D. Trout) The Theory of Knowledge: A Thematic Introduction, 1998, trans. as A Teoria Do Conhecimentio: Uma Introducao Tematica, 2004; The Elusive God: Reorienting Religious Epistemology, 2008; The Evidence for God, 2010. EDITOR: Empirical Knowledge: Readings in Contemporary Epistemology, 1986, 2nd ed., 1996; (with A.V. Nat) Human Knowledge: Classical and Contemporary Approaches, 1987, 3rd ed., 2003; A Priori Knowledge, 1987; Reality In Focus: Contemporary Readings on Metaphysics, 1990; Rationality In Action: Contemporary Approaches, 1990; (with J.D. Trout) Contemporary Materialism, 1995; (with T.L. Carson) Morality and the Good Life, 1997; (with T.L. Carson) Moral Relativism, 2001; (with D. Howard-Snyder) Divine Hiddenness: New Essays, 2002; Oxford Handbook of Epistemology, 2002; The Rationality of Theism, 2003; Jesus and Philosophy: New Essays, 2009. **Address:** Department of Philosophy, Loyola University Chicago, Crown Ctr. 333, 1032 W Sheridan Rd., Chicago, IL 60660-1537, U.S.A. **Online address:** pmoser@luc.edu

MOSES, Michael Valdez. American (born United States), b. 1957?. **Genres:** Literary Criticism And History, Young Adult Fiction. **Career:** Duke University, Department of English, associate professor, Gerst Program for Political, Economic and Humanistic Studies, founding member, National Humanities Center, fellow, director of graduate studies; Association of Literary Scholars and Critics, president. Writer. **Publications:** (Ed.) The Writings of J.M. Coetzee, 1994; The Novel and the Globalization of Culture, 1995; (ed. with R. Begam) Modernism and Colonialism: British and Irish Literature, 1899-1939, 2007; Nation of the Dead: The Politics of Irish Literature 1890-1990, forthcoming. **Address:** Department of English, Duke University, 319 Allen Bldg., PO Box 90015, Durham, NC 27708, U.S.A. **Online address:** mmoses@acpub.duke.edu

MOSES, Robert P(arris). American (born United States), b. 1935. **Genres:** Education, Mathematics/Statistics, Adult Non-fiction. **Career:** Horace Mann School, mathematics teacher, 1958-61; Mississippi Council of Federated Organizations, director, 1962-65; Tanzania Ministry of Education, mathematics teacher, 1969-76; Martin L. King Elementary, algebra teacher, 1982-87; The Algebra Project Inc., founder and president, 1982-, dean; Cornell University, Frank H.T. Rhodes Class of '56 professor. Writer. **Publications:** (With C.E. Cobb, Jr.) Radical Equations: Math Literacy and Civil Rights, 2001; Radical Equations: Civil Rights from Mississippi to the Algebra Project, 2002. **Address:** The Algebra Project Inc., 99 Bishop Allen Dr., Cambridge, MA 02139, U.S.A.

MOSES, (Russell) Greg(ory). American (born United States), b. 1954. **Genres:** Philosophy, Biography. **Career:** KTAM-Radio, news director, 1981-85; Texas A&M University, teaching assistant, 1984-85, visiting lecturer, 1988-95; Emory University, teaching assistant, 1985-86; University of Texas, teaching assistant, 1987-88; Marist College, assistant professor of philosophy, 1995-2002; New York Theological Seminary, coordinator of certificate program in human services, 1997-; Texas Civil Rights Review, editor. **Publications:** Revolution of Conscience: Martin Luther King, Jr. and the Philosophy of Nonviolence, 1997; (contrib.) Bricks without Straw: A Comprehensive History of African Americans in Texas, 1997; (ed. with J. Paris) Liberation between Selves, Sexualities and War, 2006. Contributor of articles to periodicals. **Address:** NY , U.S.A. **Online address:** gmosesx@gmail.com

MOSETTIG, Michael David. American (born United States), b. 1942. **Genres:** Politics/Government, Economics, Business/Trade/Industry. **Career:** Carpenter News Bureau, reporter, 1961-65; Newhouse National News Service, reporter, 1965-69; United Press Intl., reporter, 1969-70; NBC News, producer, 1971-79; Columbia University, associate professor, 1972-83, adjunct professor, 1983-; MacNeil-Lehrer News Hour, producer, 1983-85, senior producer, 1985-. **Publications:** (With R.E. Müller and D. Moore) Revitalizing America: Politics for Prosperity, 1980. Contributor to journals and magazines. **Address:** c/o Andrew Wylie, The Wylie Agency Inc., 250 W 57th St., Ste. 2114, New York, NY 10019, U.S.A.

MOSHER, Richard. American/Indian (born India) **Genres:** Novels, Children's Fiction. **Career:** Writer and teacher. **Publications:** NOVELS: The Taxi Navigator, 1996; Zazoo, 2001. **Address:** Putnam Publishing Group, 200 Madison Ave., New York, NY 10016, U.S.A.

MOSHIRI, Farnoosh. American/Iranian (born Iran), b. 1951. **Genres:** Novels, Novellas/Short Stories, Essays, Poetry. **Career:** University of Houston, professor of literature and creative writing; Houston Community College, professor of literature and creative writing; Montgomery College, professor of literature and creative writing; Syracuse University, professor of literature and creative writing; University of Houston-Downtown, professor of literature and creative writing. **Publications:** At the Wall of the Almighty (novel), 2000; The Bathhouse (novel), 2001; The Crazy Dervish and the Pomegranate Tree, 2004; Against Gravity, 2006; The Drum-Tower: A Novel, 2012. Works appear in anthologies. **Address:** Department of English, University of Houston-Downtown, 1 Main St., Houston, TX 77002, U.S.A. **Online address:** farnooshmoshiri@yahoo.com

MOSIER, John. American (born United States), b. 1944. **Genres:** History, Military/Defense/Arms Control, Translations, Communications/Media. **Career:** Loyola University, assistant professor, 1967-68, assistant dean, 1969-71, executive secretary of academic affairs, 1971-74, Film Institute, associate director, 1975-85, director, 1985-91, professor of English, 1985-, department chair, 1989-91; New Orleans Review, editor, 1980-92; film critic, 1985-. **Publications:** (With D. Gaillard) Women and Men Together: An Anthology of Short Fiction, 1978; The Myth of the Great War: A New Military History of World War I, 2001; The Blitzkrieg Myth, 2003; Grant, 2006; Cross of Iron, 2006; Deathride: Hitler vs. Stalin-Eastern Front 1941-1945, 2010. Contributor to books, journals and periodicals. **Address:** Department of English, Loyola University, PO Box 50, New Orleans, LA 70118, U.S.A. **Online address:** jmosier@loyno.edu

MOSKIN, Julia. American (born United States), b. 1967?. **Genres:** Food And Wine, How-to Books. **Career:** New York Times, Dining section, reporter, 2004-, staff writer. Restaurant critic and food writer. **Publications:** (With G. Gand and R. Tramonto) American Brasserie: 180 Simple, Robust Recipes Inspired by the Rustic Foods of France, Italy and America, 1997; (with R. Palomino) Bistro Latino: Home Cooking Fired Up with the Flavors of Latin America, 1998; (with G. Gand and R. Tramonto) Butter, Sugar, Flour, Eggs, 1999; (with G. Gand) Gale Gand's Just a Bite: 125 Luscious, Little Desserts, 2001; (with B. Flay) Bobby Flay Cooks American: Great Regional Recipes with Sizzling New Flavors, 2001; (with P. Yeo) Patricia Yeo: Cooking from A to Z, 2002; (with G. Gand) Gale Gand's Short and Sweet: Quick Desserts with Eight Ingredients or Less, 2003; (with B. Flay) Bobby Flay's Boy Gets Grill: 125 Reasons to Light Your Fire!, 2004. Contributor to periodicals. **Address:** c/o Author Mail, Hyperion Books, 77 W 66th St., New York, NY 10023, U.S.A.

MOSKOWITZ, Anita F(iderer). American (born United States), b. 1937?.

Genres: Art/Art History. **Career:** City University of New York, Brooklyn College, adjunct instructor in art, 1971-73; Union College, adjunct assistant professor of art, 1978-79; Cooper Union, adjunct assistant professor of art, 1981; State University of New York, assistant professor, 1981-86, associate professor, 1986-93, professor of art, 1993-, director of graduate studies, 1990-93, Department of Art, chairperson, 2007-10; National Gallery of Art, public lecturer, 1994. Writer. **Publications:** The Sculpture of Andrea and Nino Pisano, 1986; Nicola Pisano's Arca di San Domenico and Its Legacy (monograph), 1994; Italian Gothic Sculpture: c.1250-1400, 2001; Nicola and Giovanni Pisano: The Pulpits: Pious Devotion, Pious Diversion, 2005; The Façade Reliefs of Orvieto Cathedrao, 2009. Contributor of articles and journals. **Address:** Department of Art, State University of New York, Rm. 4223, 2224 Staller Center for the Arts, Stony Brook, NY 11794-5400, U.S.A. **Online address:** anita.moskowitz@stonybrook.edu

MOSKOWITZ, David V. American (born United States), b. 1969. **Genres:** Biography, Music, Social Sciences. **Career:** University of South Dakota, College of Fine Arts, Department of Music, associate professor. Writer. **Publications:** Caribbean Popular Music: An Encyclopedia of Reggae, Mento, Ska, Rock Steady and Dancehall, 2006; Bob Marley: A Biography, 2007; The Words and Music of Bob Marley, 2007. **Address:** Department of Music, University of South Dakota, 124 UFA Warren M. Lee Ctr. for the Fine Arts, 414 E Clark St., Vermillion, SD 57069, U.S.A. **Online address:** dave.moskowitz@usd.edu

MOSKOWITZ, Faye (Stollman). American (born United States), b. 1930. **Genres:** Novellas/Short Stories, Literary Criticism And History, Essays. **Career:** Edmund Burke College Preparatory School, middle school director, 1975-86; George Washington University, Department of English, lecturer, 1972-, associate professor, 1989-2002, chair, 1998-2006, professor, 2002-. Writer. **Publications:** A Leak in the Heart: Tales from a Woman's Life (essays), 1985; Whoever Finds This: I Love You (stories), 1988; And the Bridge Is Love: Life Stories (essays), 1991; Her Face in the Mirror: Jewish Women Writing on Mothers and Daughters, 1994; Peace in the House (memoir), 2002. Works appear in anthologies. Contributor of articles to periodicals. **Address:** Department of English, George Washington University, 658 Rome Hall, 2142 G St. NW, Washington, DC 20052, U.S.A. **Online address:** faymos@gwu.edu

MOSKOWITZ, Marina. Scottish (born Scotland), b. 1968?. **Genres:** Social Sciences, Money/Finance. **Career:** University of Glasgow, School of Humanities, senior lecturer in history and American studies, reader in history and American studies, Andrew Hook Centre for American Studies, associate director, director. Writer. **Publications:** (Contrib.) Middling Sorts: New Approaches to the American Middle Classes, 2001; Standard of Living: The Measure of the Middle Class in Modern America, 2004; (ed. with E.H. Brown and C. Gudis) Cultures of Commerce: Representation and American Business Culture, 1877-1960, 2006; (contrib.) Considering Class: Essays on the Discourse of the American Dream, 2007; (ed. with M. Schweitzer) Testimonial Advertising in the American Marketplace: Emulation, Identity, Community, 2009; Seed Money: The Economies of Horticulture in Nineteenth-Century America, forthcoming. Contributor to books and journals. **Address:** Department of History, School of Humanities, University of Glasgow, 1 University Gardens, Glasgow, G12 8QQ, Scotland. **Online address:** marina.moskowitz@glasgow.ac.uk

MOSKOWITZ, Robert A. American (born United States), b. 1946. **Genres:** Administration/Management, Business/Trade/Industry, Gerontology/Senior Issues, Information Science/Computers, Money/Finance. **Career:** Prentice-Hall Inc., editorial director, 1968-70; writer and publisher, 1970-75; Temple University, faculty, 1972-77; WUHY, writer, director, and producer, 1972-78; Public Interest Media Project, founder and President, 1973-79; Personal Productivity Center, president, 1975-81; Hill and Knowlton, senior consultant, 1981-84; Madison Fielding Public Relations, vice president and client services, 1984-87; Crown Communications Group, president, 1987-, founder, managing partner; Key Publications, president, 1991-; CNBC Television, commentator, 1992-98; America On Line, computer information service, faculty, 1993-98; American Telecommuting Association, president, 1993-, founder; The Internet, faculty, 1996-; InnerWorth.com, vice president and editor-in-chief, 2001-02; MoneyTours.com/.net, vice president, 2002-06; Real Estate Financial Planning Institute, managing editor, 2007-08. **Publications:** How to Organize Your Work and Your Life, 1981, rev. ed., 1993; (with F. Moskowitz) Parenting Your Aging Parents, 1991; Out on Your Own: Everything You Need to Know Before, During, and After Leaving the Nest, 1993; The Small Business Computer Book: A Guide in Plain English, 1993. **Address:** Crown Communications Group, 827 Second St., Ste. 104, PO Box 6375, Santa Monica, CA 90403, U.S.A. **Online address:** robertam@ix.netcom.com

MOSLEY, Nicholas. (Ravensdale). British (born England), b. 1923. **Genres:** Novels, History, Theology/Religion, Travel/Exploration, Autobiography/Memoirs, Literary Criticism And History, Young Adult Fiction. **Career:** Prism, joint editor, 1957-59, poetry editor, 1962-65. **Publications:** Spaces of the Dark, 1951; The Rainbearers, 1955; Corruption: A Novel, 1957; African Switchback, 1958; The Life of Raymond Raynes, 1961; Meeting Place, 1962; Accident: A Novel, 1965; Experience and Religion: A Lay Essayin Theology, 1965, rev. ed., 1967; Assassins, 1966; The Impossible Object: A Novel, 1968; Natalie, Natalia, 1971; The Assassination of Trotsky, 1972; Julian Grenfell: His Life and the Times of His Death 1888-1915, 1976; Catastrophe Practice: Plays for not Acting, and Cypher, A Novel, 1979, rev. ed., 1989; Imago Bird, 1980; Serpent, 1981; Rules of the Game: Sir Oswald and Lady Cynthia Mosley 1869-1933, 1982, rev. ed., 1990; Beyond the Pale: Sir Oswald Mosley and Family 1933-1980, 1983; Judith: A Novel, 1986, rev. ed., 1991; Hopeful Monsters: A Novel, 1990; Rules of the Game/Beyond the Pale: Memoirs of Sir Oswald Mosley And Family, 1991; (intro.) The Tide Is Right, 1992; Efforts At Truth: An Autobiography, 1994; Children of Darkness and Light, 1996; The Hesperides Tree, 2001; Inventing God, 2003; The Uses of Slime Mould: Essays of Four Decades, 2004; Look at the Dark, 2005; Time at War: A Memoir, 2006; Experience & Religion: A Lay Essay in Theology, 2006; Look at the Dark, 2006; God's Hazard: A Novel, 2009; Paradoxes of Peace, or, The Presence of Infinity, 2009; A Garden of Trees, 2011. **Address:** c/o Michael Sissons, PFD, Drury House, 34-43 Russell St., London, GL WC2B 5HA, England.

MOSLEY, Philip. American (born United States), b. 1947?. **Genres:** Novels, Plays/Screenplays, Poetry, Cultural/Ethnic Topics, Film, Literary Criticism And History, Local History/Rural Topics, Theatre, Documentaries/Reportage, Translations. **Career:** Teacher, 1968; Kolding Gymnasium, teacher of English, 1970-71; University of Wisconsin, lecturer in comparative literature, 1973-76; Griffith University, lecturer in comparative literature, 1977-79; University of East Anglia, part-time lecturer in literature, 1980-81; Glasgow College, lecturer in communication, 1981-88; Pennsylvania State University, Department of English and comparative literature, associate professor, professor, 1988-; Medical Humanities Review, advisory editor, 1988-95; University of Toulouse, visiting professor, 2000; Free University of Brussels, Fulbright professor, 2003-04. Writer. **Publications:** Ingmar Bergman: The Cinema as Mistress, 1981; (ed.) Georges Rodenbach: Critical Essays, 1996; Split Screen: Belgian Cinema and Cultural Identity, 2001; (ed. and intro.) Anthracite!: An Anthology of Pennsylvania Coal Region Plays, 2006. TRANSLATOR: (intro.) G. Vaes, October Long Sunday, 1997; W. Lambersy, Tea Masters, Teahouses (poems), 1982; W. Lambersy, Anchors of Ink (poems), 1982; (intro.) G. Rodenbach, Bruges-la-morte (novel), 1986, reprinted 2007; (intro.) M. Maeterlinck, The Intelligence of Flowers, 2007; F. Jacqmin, The Book of the Snow, 2010. **Address:** Pennsylvania State University, Worthington Scranton, 120 Ridge View Dr., 105 Gallagher Conference Ctr., Dunmore, PA 18512-1699, U.S.A. **Online address:** jpm11@psu.edu

MOSLEY, Shelley Elizabeth. American (born United States), b. 1950. **Genres:** Children's Fiction, Young Adult Fiction. **Career:** Glendale Community College Library Media Center, reference librarian. Writer. **Publications:** NONFICTION: (with J. Charles) The Suffragists in Literature for Youth: The Fight for the Vote, 2006; (ed. with J. Charles) Romance Today: An A-to-Z Guide to Contemporary American Romance Writers, 2006; (with J. Charles, J. Hamilton-Selway and S. VanWinkle) The Complete Idiot's Guide to the Ultimate Reading List, 2007; (with D.C. Tucker) Crash Course in Library Supervision: Meeting the Key Players, 2007. Contributor to Journal. **Address:** Glendale, AZ , U.S.A. **Online address:** deborahshelley@mindspring.com

MOSLEY, Steven. American (born United States), b. 1952. **Genres:** Theology/Religion, Biography. **Career:** Japan Union Mission, film producer, 1975-80; It Is Written (television series), assistant director of public relations, 1983-88. Writer. **Publications:** Take Five, 1987; God: A Biography, 1988 as Glimpses of God, 1990; A Tale of Three Virtues: Cures for Colorless Christianity, 1989; There I Go Again; How to Keep from Falling for the Same Old Sin, 1991; A Language for the Heart, 1992; If Only God Would Answer: What to Do When You Ask, Seek, and Knock- And Nothing Happens, 1992; Burned Out on Being Good: What to Do if Religion Is Wearing You Out, 1998; Deepen My Heart, 1998; Great Stories and How to Tell Them, 2000; Your Religion Is Too Small: Breaking out of a Small View of Faith, 2000; Secrets of the Mustard Seed, 2002; Secrets of Jesus' Touch, 2003. WITH M. FINLEY: Simply Salvation, 1993; To Hope Again, 1993; When Faith Crumbles: Hard Evidence for Rock-Solid Faith, 1993; Dark Tunnels with Bright Lights: The Real Truth about Life after Death, 1994; Hearts at Home: Building Solid Families in a Shaky World, 1994; Why so Many Denominations?: Revelation's Four Horseman Provide an Answer, 1994; Winning Your Biggest Battles, 1994; Growing through Life's Toughest Times, 1995; Looking for God in all the Wrong Places, 1995; Strong Medicine for a Sick Society, 1995; Jesus Face to Face, 1996; A Religion that Works, 1996; Unshakable Faith: How to Stand Fast in the Worst of Times, 1996; Things that Matter Most, 1997; Soul Care: Becoming Whole in a Broken World, 1998; What You Can Know-for Sure!, 1998; Which Way America?: What the Bible Says about Where We're Going, 1998; Hope for a New Century, 1999; More Seeing Is Believing: Dramatic Evidence of a Creator-God, 1999; Revelation's Three Greatest Mysteries, 1999; When Your Faith Is Shaken, 1999; Experience God: His Love, Compassion, Power, Strength, and Faithfulness, 2000; Still Standing True, 2000; God's Little Advice Book, 2001; Jerusalem Showdown, 2001; What My Parents Did Right, 2001; Breaking through Barriers to God, 2002; Disappearing Truths, 2002; The Ultimate Survivor, 2002; Letters from a Lonely Isle, 2002; Revelation's Three Most Wanted, 2003; I Want More, 2003; Unfinished Business with the Dead, 2003; The Safest Place on Earth, 2003; Faith Against the Odds, 2003; Faith Roots, 2003. **Address:** 15531 Placid Cir., Huntington Beach, CA 92647-2930, U.S.A. **Online address:** steven@stevenmosley.com

MOSLEY, Walter. American (born United States), b. 1952. **Genres:** Novels, Novellas/Short Stories. **Career:** New York University Africana Studies Institute, artist in residence, 1996. Novelist and computer programmer. **Publications:** Devil in a Blue Dress, 1990; A Red Death, 1991; White Butterfly, 1992; Black Betty, 1994; R.L.'s Dream, 1995; A Little Yellow Dog, 1996; Gone Fishin': An Easy Rawlins Novel, 1997; Always Outnumbered, Always Outgunned: The Socrates Fortlow Stories, 1998; Blue Light: A Novel, 1998; (ed.) Black Genius: African-American Solutions to African-American Problems, 1999; Walkin' the Dog, 1999; Workin' on the Chain Gang: Shaking off the Dead Hand of History, 2000; Fearless Jones: A Novel, 2001; Futureland, 2001; Bad Boy Brawley Brown, 2002; What Next: An African American Initiative Toward World Peace, 2002; Six Easy Pieces (novel): Easy Rawlins Stories, 2003; Fear Itself: A Novel, 2003; What Next: A Memoir toward World Peace, 2003; Little Scarlet, 2004; Man in My Basement: A Novel, 2004; The Man in My Basement: A Novel, 2004; Cinnamon Kiss, 2005; 47, 2005; Life Out of Context: Which Includes a Proposal for the Non-Violent Takeover of the House of Representatives, 2006; Fear of the Dark: A Novel, 2006; Fortunate Son, 2006; Wave, 2006; Blonde Faith, 2007; This Year You Write Your Novel, 2007; Killing Johnny Fry: A Sexistentialist Novel, 2007; Diablerie: A Novel, 2008; Right Miste, 2008; Tempest Tales, 2008; The Last Days of Ptolemy Grey, 2010; Known to Evil, 2011; Conversations with Walter Mosley, 2011; When the Thrill is Gone, 2011; Twelve Steps Toward Political Revelation, 2011; All I Did Was Shoot My Man, 2012. Contributor to periodicals. **Address:** c/o Author Mail, Little, Brown & Co., 1271 Ave. of the Americas, New York, NY 10020, U.S.A.

MOSS, Carolyn (J.). American (born United States), b. 1932. **Genres:** Literary Criticism And History, Biography, Language/Linguistics, History, Humanities. **Career:** Teacher, 1961-64; Paducah Community College, associate professor, 1964-73; Southern Illinois University, visiting assistant professor, 1976-87. Writer. **Publications:** Bibliographical Guide to Self-Disclosure Literature, 1956-76, 1977; (with S.P. Moss) The New Composition by Logic, rev. ed., 1978; (with S.P. Moss) Charles Dickens and His Chicago Relatives: A Documentary Narrative, 1994; (with S.P. Moss) Charles Dickens-Thomas Powell Vendetta: The Story in Documents, 1996; Kate Field: Pen Photographs of Charles Dickens's Readings Taken from Life, 1998; (with S.P. Moss) American Episodes Involving Charles Dickens, 1999; (with S.P. Moss) Dickens, Trollope, Jefferson: Three Anglo-American Encounters, 2000. EDITOR: (intro.) Kate Field: Selected Letters, 1996. Contributor to periodicals. **Address:** 400 N Oakland, Ste. F-33, Carbondale, IL 62901, U.S.A. **Online address:** mosses@siu.edu

MOSS, Cynthia F. American (born United States), b. 1940?. **Genres:** Psychology, Animals/Pets, Sciences. **Career:** University of Tuebingen, NATO postdoctoral fellow in animal physiology, 1985-87; Brown University, postdoctoral research associate in psychology and neurobiology, 1987-89; Harvard University, assistant professor, 1989-94, Morris Kahn associate professor of psychology, 1994-95; University of Maryland, associate professor of psychology, 1995-99, professor, 1999-, Neuroscience and Cognitive Science Program, director. Writer. **Publications:** Portraits in the Wild: Behavior Studies of East African Mammals, 1975, 2nd ed., 1982; Portraits in the Wild: Animal Behaviour in East Africa, 1976; Elephant Memories: Thirteen Years in the Life of an Elephant Family, 1988; Echo of the Elephants: The Story of an Elephant Family, 1992; (ed. with S. Shettleworth and contrib.) Neuroethological Studies of Cognitive and Perceptual Processes, 1996; Little Big Ears: The Story of Ely, 1997; Elephant Woman: Cynthia Moss Explores the World of Elephants, 1997; (contrib.) Neural Systems for Robotics, 1997; (ed. with J.A. Thomas and M. Vater) Echolocation in Bats and Dolphins, 2004; (ed. with H. Croze and P.C. Lee) Amboseli Elephants: A Long-Term Perspective on a Long-Lived Mammal, 2011. Contributor to books and journals. **Address:** Department of Psychology, University of Maryland, 2123M Biology/Psychology Bldg., College Park, MD 20742, U.S.A. **Online address:** cmoss@psyc.umd.edu

MOSS, Cynthia J(ane). Kenyan/American (born United States), b. 1940. **Genres:** Biology, Zoology, Animals/Pets, Sciences. **Career:** Newsweek, reporter and researcher, 1964-68, research assistant, 1968-70, 1972-75; Tsavo National Park, research assistant, 1970; freelance journalist, 1970-71; Wildlife News, editor, 1971-; research assistant in Amboseli, 1972-75; Amboseli Elephant Research Project, co-editor, 1979-, director; Cambridge University, Sub-Department of Animal Behavior, research associate. **Publications:** Portraits in the Wild: Behavior Studies of East African Mammals, 1975, 2nd ed., 1982; Portraits in the Wild: Animal Behaviour in East Africa, 1976; Elephant Memories: Thirteen Years in the Life of an Elephant Family, 1988; Echo of the Elephants: The Story of an Elephant Family, 1992; (ed. with S.J. Shettleworth) Neuroethological Studies of Cognitive and Perceptual Processes, 1996; Little Big Ears: The Story of Ely, 1997; (ed. with J.A. Thomas and M. Vater) Echolocation in Bats and Dolphins, 2004; (ed. with H. Croze and P.C. Lee) Amboseli Elephants: A Long-term Perspective on a Long-lived Mammal, 2011. Contributor to periodicals. **Address:** Amboseli Elephant Research Project, Amboseli National Pk., PO Box 48177, Namanga, 00100, Kenya.

MOSS, Eric Owen. American (born United States), b. 1943. **Genres:** Architecture. **Career:** Eric Owen Moss Architects, founder, 1973-; Southern California Institute of Architecture, professor of design, 1974-, director, 2002-; Harvard University, Eliot Noyes chair, 1990; Yale University, Eero Saarinen chair, 1991; University of Michigan, lecturer; Pratt Institute, lecturer; Rice University, lecturer; University of Applied Arts, lecturer; Columbia University, lecturer; Royal Danish Academy of Fine Arts, faculty. Writer. **Publications:** (With Morphosis) California Architecture, 1985; Lindblade Tower & Paramount Laundry: Reconversion à Culver City, Californie, USA, 1990; Eric Owen Moss: Buildings and Projects, vol. I, 1991, vol. II, 1996, vol. III, 2003; Eric Owen Moss, 1993, rev. ed., 2000; Lawson-Westen House, 1995; Eric Owen Moss: The Box, 1995; Gnostic Architecture, 1999; (contrib.) Sessions: George Yu, Marcelo Spina, Marta Malé-Alemany, Benjamin H. Bratton, Hernan Diaz-Alonso, 2004; The Uncertainty of Doing, 2006; Who Says What Architecture Is?, 2007; Eric Owen Moss: Construction Manual 1988-2008, 2009. **Address:** Eric Owen Moss Architects, 8557 Higuera St., Culver City, CA 90232-2535, U.S.A. **Online address:** mail@ericowenmoss.com

MOSS, Jenny. American (born United States), b. 1958. **Genres:** Children's Fiction. **Career:** National Aeronautics and Space Administration, engineer; University of Houston-Clear Lake, adjunct writing professor. Writer. **Publications:** Winnie's War, 2009; Look inside a Castle, 2010; Look inside a Pueblo, 2010; Shadow, 2010. **Address:** Houston, TX , U.S.A. **Online address:** jenny@jenny-moss.com

MOSS, Marissa. American (born United States), b. 1959. **Genres:** Children's Fiction, Picture/Board Books, Graphic Novels, Young Adult Nonfiction, Novels, Novellas/Short Stories. **Career:** Author and illustrator. **Publications:** SELF-ILLUSTRATED PICTURE BOOKS: True Heart, 1980; Who Was It?, 1989; Regina's Big Mistake, 1990; Want to Play?, 1990; After-School Monster, 1991; Knick Knack Paddywack, 1992; But Not Kate, 1992; In America, 1994; Mel's Diner, 1994; The Ugly Menorah, 1996. AMELIA'S NOTEBOOK SERIES: Amelia's Notebook, 1995; Amelia Writes Again, 1996; My Notebook: With Help from Amelia, 1997; Amelia Hits the Road, 1997; Amelia Takes Command, 1998; Amelia's Guide to Gossip: The Good, the Bad, and the Ugly, 1998; Dr. Amelia's Boredom Survival Guide, 1999; Luv, Amelia Luv, Nadia, 1999; The All-New Amelia, 1999; Amelia Works It Out, 2000; Amelia Creativity Kit, 2000; Amelia's Family Ties, 2000; Amelia's Easy-as-Pie Drawing Guide, 2000; Madame Amelia Tells All, 2001; Oh Boy, Amelia!, 2001; Amelia's Moving Pictures, 2001; Amelia Lends a Hand, 2002; Amelia's School Survival Guide with Sticker, 2002; Amelia's Best Year Ever: Favorite Amelia Stories from American Girl Magazine, 2003; Amelia's 6th-Grade Notebook, 2005; Amelia's Most Unforgettable Embarrassing Moments, 2005; Amelia's 5th-Grade Notebook, 2006; Amelia's Are-we-there-yet Longest Ever Car Trip, 2006; Amelia's Book of Notes & Note Passing, 2006; Amelia's Bully Survival Guide, 2006; Amelia's Longest, Biggest, Most-fights-ever Family Reunion, 2006; Amelia's Must-keep Resolutions for the Best Year Ever!, 2006; Amelia Tells All, 2007; Amelia's 7th-Grade Notebook, 2007; Vote 4 Amelia, 2007; Amelia's Guide to Babysitting, 2008; Amelia's Itchy-twitchy, Lovey-dovey Summer At Camp Mosquito, 2008; Amelia's Science Fair Disaster, 2008; Amelia's Middle School Survival Guide, 2009; Amelia's Cross-My-Heart, Hope-to-Die Guide to the Real, True You!, 2010; Amelia's BFF, 2011; Amelia's Boy Survival Guide, 2012. OTHER: Invasion Of Alien Eraser And Other Cool Stuff, 2004. SELF-ILLUSTRATED CHILDREN BOOKS: Rachel's Journal: The Story of a Pioneer Girl, 1998; Emma's Journal: The Story of a Colonial Girl, 1999; Hannah's Journal: The Story of an Immigrant Girl, 2000; Brave Harriet: The First Woman to Fly the English Channel, 2001; Rose's Journal: The Story of a Girl in the Great Depression, 2001; Galen: My Life in Imperial Rome: An Ancient World Journal, 2002; Max's Logbook, 2003; Mighty Jackie: The Strike-Out Queen, 2004; Max's Mystical Logbook, 2004; Sky High: The True Story of Maggie Gee, 2009; Alien Eraser to the Rescue, 2009; Alien Eraser Unravels the Mystery of the Pyramids, 2009; Alien Eraser Reveals the Secrets of Evolution, 2009; The Pharaoh's Secret, 2009; The Name Game!, 2010; The Vampire Dare!, 2011; The Bravest Woman in America, 2011; Amelia's Summer Survival Guide, 2011; Nurse, Soldier, Spy: The Story of Sarah Edmonds, a Civil War Hero, 2011. Illustrator of books by others. **Address:** c/o Author Mail, Scholastic Inc., 555 Broadway, New York, NY 10012-3919, U.S.A.

MOSS, Miriam. British (born England), b. 1955. **Genres:** Children's Fiction, Poetry, Children's Non-fiction. **Career:** King's School, teacher, 1977-82; Imani School, teacher, 1982-83; Windlesham House School, teacher, 1983-85. Writer. **Publications:** A Slave in Ancient Greece, 1986; The Victorians, 1986; The American West, 1986; Great Explorers, 1986; The Crusades, 1986; Ancient China, 1987; A Norman Baron, 1987; Language and Writing, 1987; Fairs and Circuses, 1987; Zoos, 1987; Uniforms, 1988; Working Clothes, 1988; Clothes in Hot Weather, 1988; Clothes in Cold Weather, 1988; Fashionable Clothes, 1988; Children's Clothes, 1988; Traditional Costumes, 1988; The Schools' Librarian, 1988; Easter, 1988; The School Nurse, 1988; A Schoolchild in World War II, 1988; In the Pond, 1988; (as Sue Crawford) How Clothes are Made, 1989; The Fashion Industry, 1989; Work Clothes, 1989; Women and Business, 1989; Fashion Model, 1990; Fashion Photographer, 1990; Fashion Designer, 1990; Street Fashion, 1990; Eggs, 1990; Fruit, 1990; Keep Fit, 1992; Eat Well, 1992; Be Positive, 1992; Castles, 1993; The Weather in Spring, 1994; The Weather in Summer, 1994; The Weather in Autumn, 1994; The Weather in Winter, 1994; Forts and Castles, 1994; Henry's Kite, 1995; Vitamins in Food, 1995; Fibre in Food, 1995; Caramel and Vanille: Their First Adventure, 1995; Caramel and Vanille: Their Adventures Down Under, 1995; Caramel & Vanille: Adventures on Their Magic Carpet, 1996; Jigsaw, 1997; Kim and the Computer Mouse, 1997; Kim and the Missing Paintpot, 1997; Kim and the Bin Giant, 1997; Kim and the Shape Dragon, 1997; Windswept, 1997; The Snoops, 1997; Arctic Song, 1999; The Sunshine Cat, 1999; One Day It Was Wet, 1999; Am I a Cat?, 1999; Take a Walk on a Rainbow, 1999; Can I Have Some?, 1999; Buzzy Bees 1 2 3, 1999; What's That Shape, 1999; (ed. with R.L. Rubinstein and M.H. Kleban) The Many Dimensions of Aging, 2000; This Is the Tree, 2000; The Snow Bear, 2000; Poetry In: Hello New!, 2000; Smudge Goes Fishing, 2001; Smudge's Grumpy Day, 2001; It's My Turn, Smudge!, 2001; A New House for Smudge, 2001; I'll Be Your Friend, Smudge, 2001; Wibble Wobble, 2001; Scritch Scratch, 2001; The Horse Girl, 2002; The Best Dog in the World, 2003; Bad Hare Day, 2003; I Forgot to Say I Love You, 2003; Wiley and Jasper, 2003; Come Back Soon, 2003; Jungle Song, 2004; Bare Bear, 2005; Spotty Dotty, 2005; This Is the Oasis, 2005; Don't Forget I Love You, 2006; Smudge's Grumpy Day, 2007; This is the Reef, 2007; Bedtime, Billy Bear!, 2007; Matty Takes Off!, 2008; Chiff Chaff & Chickpea, 2008; Babysitter for Billy Bear, 2008; Matty in a Mess!, 2009; Billy Bear's New Baby, 2009. **Address:** Bloomsbury Children's Books, 38 Soho Sq., London, GL WIV 6HB, England.

MOSS, Stanley. American (born United States), b. 1925. **Genres:** Poetry, Biography. **Career:** Halcyon, founding editor, 1947; Stanley Moss and Co., president, 1959-; Sheep Meadow Press, publisher, 1977-. **Publications:** The Wrong Angel, 1966; Skull of Adam, 1979; (ed.) The Art of Poetry: Interviews with Stanley Kunitz, 1989; The Intelligence of Clouds: Poems, 1989; Asleep in the Garden, 1997; (ed.) A Tribute to Stanley Kunitz on His Ninety-sixth Birthday, 2001; History of Color: New and Collected Poems, 2003; Songs of Imperfection, 2005; Grieving Shias: Poems, 2006; (ed. with P. Diamond) A Book for Daniel Stern: By Friends, 2006; New & Selected Poems 2006, 2006; Rejoicing: New and Collected Poems, 2009; God Breaketh Not All Men's Hearts Alike: New and Later Collected Poems, 2011. Contributor to newspapers and magazines. **Address:** Sheep Meadow Press, 145 Central Pk. W, PO Box 1345, New York, NY 10023, U.S.A. **Online address:** stmoss@gmail.com

MOSS, Stirling. British (born England), b. 1929. **Genres:** Novellas/Short Stories, Recreation, Sports/Fitness. **Career:** Racer, 1946-2011; Stirling Moss Ltd., managing director, 1954-; Phonix Travel Ltd., director; S.M. Fine Jewels, director; American Street Garage Ltd., director; Motor Racing Stables Ltd., director; Institute of Engineers, fellow. Writer. **Publications:** Book of Motor Sports, 1955; In the Track of Speed, 1957, 2nd ed., 1962; Le Mans '59, 1959; (ed.) My Favourite Car Stories, 1960; A Turn at the Wheel, 1961; (with K. Purdy) All But My Life, 1963, 2nd ed., 1973; (with L. Pomeroy) The Design and Behaviour of the Racing Car, 1964; How to Watch Motor Racing, 1975; (with M. Hailwood) Racing and All That, 1980; (with D. Nye) Stirling Moss: My Cars, My Career, 1987; (with D. Nye) Fangio, A Pirelli Album, 1991; (with C. Shelbourn) Great Drives in The Lakes and Dales, 1993; (with C. Hilton) Stirling Moss's Motor-Racing Masterpieces, 1994; (foreword) Shelsley Walsh Story: A Century of Motorsport, 2005; (with A. Henry) Stirling Moss: All My Races, 2009. **Address:** Stirling Moss Ltd., 44-46 Shepherd St., Mayfair, London, GL W1Y 8JN, England.

MOSS, Thylias (Rebecca). American (born United States), b. 1954. **Genres:** Poetry, Plays/Screenplays, Novels, Autobiography/Memoirs, Young Adult Fiction, Literary Criticism And History. **Career:** The May Co., order checker, 1973-74, junior executive auditor, 1975-79, data entry supervisor, 1974-75; University of New Hampshire, graduate assistant, 1981-83, lecturer, 1983-84; Phillips Academy, instructor, 1984-92; University of New Hampshire, visiting professor, 1991-92; Brandeis University, Fannie Hurst poet, 1992; University of Michigan, assistant professor, 1993-94, associate professor, 1994-98, professor of English, 1998-. Writer. **Publications:** POETRY: Hosiery Seams on a Bowlegged Woman, 1983; Pyramid of Bone, 1989; At Redbones, 1990; Rainbow Remnants in Rock Bottom Ghetto Sky, 1991; Small Congregations: New and Selected Poems, 1993; Last Chance for the Tarzan Holler: Poems, 1998; Tokyo Butter: A Search for Forms of Deirdre: Poems, 2006. OTHERS: I Want To Be, 1993; Tale of a Sky-Blue Dress (memoir), 1998; Slave Moth: A Narrative in Verse, 2004; Limited Fork Weblogs, 2007. **Address:** Department of English Language and Literature, The University of Michigan, 3247 Angell Hall, 435 S State St., Ann Arbor, MI 48109-1003, U.S.A. **Online address:** thyliasm@umich.edu

MOST, Kenneth S. American (born United States), b. 1924. **Genres:** Money/Finance. **Career:** Polytechnic of Central London, accounting faculty, 1960-64; University of Singapore, accounting faculty, 1964-67, department head; University of Florida, accounting faculty, 1967-70; Texas A&M University, accounting faculty, 1970-75, department head; Florida International University, professor of accounting, 1975-93, department head, now retired; University of Hawaii, visiting professor; University of Texas, visiting professor; Memphis State University, visiting professor; University of Marburg, visiting professor. Writer. **Publications:** How to Make Money on the Stock Exchange, 1969; Accounting Theory, 1977, 2nd ed., 1982; Cost Accounting, 1982; International Conflict of Accounting Standards (monograph), 1984; The Perceived Usefulness of Financial Statements for Investors' Decisions, 1985; (with L.S. Chang) International Auditing (monograph), 1988; The Future of the Accounting Profession: A Global Perspective, 1993; The Lucky Unborn, 1996; Peter Woods Abroad, 2005. Contributor to journals. **Address:** 2623 Holly Springs Dr., Germantown, TN 38138, U.S.A. **Online address:** topmost@aol.com

MOSTERT, P(aul) S(tallings). American (born United States), b. 1927. **Genres:** Mathematics/Statistics. **Career:** Tulane University, assistant professor, 1954-57, associate professor, 1957-62, professor, 1962-70, chairman of department, 1968-70; University of Tubingen, visiting professor, 1962-63; Semigroup Forum, managing editor, 1968-87, executive editor, 1970-85; University of Kansas, professor of mathematics, 1970-92, chairman of the department, 1970-73, professor emeritus, 1992-; Equix Inc., president, 1984-

85; Pennfield Biomechanics Corp., president, 1985-89; Equix Biomechanics Corp., president, 1989-97; Mostert Group L.L.C., owner, 1997-2003, director of research, 2003-; University of Kentucky, visiting professor; University of Tuebingen, visiting professor; Mostert Seales Research Co., manager. **Publications:** Analytic Trigonometry, 1960; (with K.H. Hoffmann) Splitting in Topological Groups, 1963; (with K.H. Hofmann) Elements of Compact Semigroups, 1967; (ed.) The Proceedings of the Conference on Transformation Groups, 1968; (with K.H. Hofmann) Cohomology Theories for Compact Abelian Groups, 1973. **Address:** 3298 Roxburg Dr., Lexington, KY 40503-3432, U.S.A. **Online address:** mostert.paul@gmail.com

MOTCHENBACHER, C(urt) D. American (born United States), b. 1931. **Genres:** Engineering, Technology, Sciences. **Career:** Honeywell Inc., engineer, 1956, Corporate Research Center, research engineer, 1957-67, Defense Systems Division, engineering fellow and meteorology instructor, 1967-82, Underseas Systems Division, senior engineering fellow in torpedo development, 1983-87. Writer. **Publications:** (With F.C. Fitchen) Low-Noise Electronic Design, 1973; (with J.A. Connelly) Low-Noise Electronic System Design, 1993. **Address:** PO Box 111778, Hialeah, FL 33011, U.S.A. **Online address:** curtnmaryjo@earthlink.net

MOTEW, Becky Willis. (Rebecca Willis Motew). American (born United States) **Genres:** Women's Studies And Issues, Young Adult Fiction. **Career:** Lit Brothers (department store), advertising copywriter. Writer. **Publications:** Peppers, Paul and Elizabeth: A Comedy in One Act, 1995; Coupon Girl, Making It Publishing, 2006. Contributor to books. **Address:** Love Spell Publisher, 200 Madison Ave., Ste. 2000, New York, NY 10016, U.S.A.

MOTEW, Rebecca Willis. *See* **MOTEW, Becky Willis.**

MOTION, Andrew (Peter). British (born England), b. 1952. **Genres:** Novels, Poetry, Literary Criticism And History, Essays, Young Adult Fiction, Biography, Autobiography/Memoirs. **Career:** University of Hull, lecturer in English, 1976-80; Poetry Review, editor, 1981-83; Chatto and Windus Publishers, poetry editor, 1983-84, editorial director, 1985-89; freelance writer, 1989-; Faber and Faber, editorial consultant, 1989-91; University of East Anglia, professor of creative writing, 1995-2003; University of London, Royal Holloway and Bedford New College, professor of creative writing, 2003-, MA in Creative Writing, director. **Publications:** Goodnestone: A Sequence, 1972; Inland, 1976; The Pleasure Steamers, 1978; The Poetry of Edward Thomas, 1980; Independence, 1981; Philip Larkin, 1982; (ed. with B. Morrison) The New Penguin Book of Contemporary British Poetry, 1982; Secret Narratives, 1983; Dangerous Play: Poems 1974-1984, 1984; The Lamberts: George, Constant & Kit, 1986; Natural Causes, 1987; Two Poems, 1989; The Pale Companion (novel), 1989; Love in a Life, 1990; Famous for the Creatures, 1992; Philip Larkin: A Writer's Life, 1993; The Price of Everything, 1994; Salt Water, 1997; Keats, 1998; Selected Poems, 1976-1997, 1998; Babel, 1999; Wainewright the Poisoner: The Confession of Thomas Griffiths Wainewright, 2000; Public Property, 2002; The Invention of Dr. Cake, 2003; (ed.) First World War Poems, 2003; In the Blood: A Memoir of My Childhood, 2006; (contrib.) Three Motion Settings: For Baritone and Piano, 2006; (ed.) William Barnes: Poems, 2007; Selected Poems, 2008; Cinder Path, 2009; Mower: New and Selected Poems, 2009; Ways of Life: On Places, Painters and Poets, 2009. **Address:** Department of English, Royal Holloway, University of London, Egham Hill, Bedford Sq., Egham, SR TW20 0EX, England. **Online address:** andrew.motion@rhul.ac.uk

MOTLEY, Annette. British (born England), b. 1938?. **Genres:** Novels, Novellas/Short Stories, Romance/Historical, Young Adult Fiction. **Career:** Educator and writer. **Publications:** My Lady's Crusade, 1977; The Sins of the Lion, 1979; The Quickenberry Tree, 1983; Green Dragon, White Tiger, 1986; Men on White Horses, 1988; The Oldest Obsession, 1997; Balancing Acts, 1998. **Address:** Little Brown & Company Ltd., 165 Great Dover St., London, GL SE1 4YA, England.

MOTOMURA, Hiroshi. American/Japanese (born Japan), b. 1953. **Genres:** History, Law, Politics/Government. **Career:** Hogan and Hartson, associate, 1979-82; University of Colorado, Law School, professor, 1982-; Hokkaido University, Fulbright lecturer, 1987-88; University of Michigan, Law School, visiting professor, 1989; University of North Carolina, visiting professor, 2001, Law School, professor, through 2007; University of California, Law School, visiting professor, 2007, Susan Westerberg Prager professor of law, 2007-. Writer. **Publications:** Americans in Waiting: The Lost Story of Immigration and Citizenship in the United States, 2006. WITH D.A. MARTIN: (with T. Alexander) Immigration, Process and Policy, 1995; (ed. with K. Hailbronner) Immigration Admissions: The Search for Workable Policies in Germany and the United States, 1997; (ed. with K. Hailbronner) Immigration Controls: The Search for Workable Policies in Germany and the United States, 1998; (with T.A. Aleinikoff) Immigration and Citizenship: Process and Policy, 4th ed., 1998, 5th ed., 2003. Contributor to periodicals. **Address:** School of Law, University of California, 385 Charles E. Young Dr., 1242 Law Bldg., PO Box 951476, Los Angeles, CA 90095-1476, U.S.A. **Online address:** motomura@law.ucla.edu

MOTT, Robert L. American (born United States), b. 1924?. **Genres:** Plays/Screenplays, Adult Non-fiction, Photography. **Career:** Columbia Broadcasting System, sound effects artist, 1951-69; National Broadcasting Co., sound effects artist, 1970-88; freelance writer, 1988-. **Publications:** Sound Effects: Radio, TV, and Film, 1990; Radio Sound Effects: Who Did It and How In the Era of Live Broadcasting, 1993; Radio Live! Television Live!: Those Golden Days When Horses Were Coconuts, 2000. **Address:** 396 Miller Way, Arroyo Grande, CA 93420, U.S.A.

MOTT, Wesley T. American (born United States), b. 1946. **Genres:** Literary Criticism And History. **Career:** Boston University, lecturer in English, 1972-74; Thomas College, assistant professor, 1974-77, associate professor of English, 1978, Division of Liberal Arts, director, 1976-78; University of Wisconsin, lecturer in English, editor and project director, 1978-87; Edgewood College, adjunct faculty; Worcester Polytechnic Institute, assistant professor, 1987-89, associate professor, 1989-94, professor of English, 1994-; Emerson Society Papers, managing editor, 1989-2005, editor, 2005-09; Ralph Waldo Emerson Society, secretary and treasurer, 1989-99, president, 2001-03, 2010-11. **Publications:** The Strains of Eloquence: Emerson and His Sermons, 1989. EDITOR: The Complete Sermons of Ralph Waldo Emerson, 1992; (and contrib.) Biographical Dictionary of Transcendentalism, 1996; (and contrib.) Encyclopedia of Transcendentalism, 1996; (with R.E. Burkholder) Emersonian Circles: Essays in Honor of Joel Myerson, 1997; (and contrib.) The American Renaissance in New England, 3 vols., 2000-01; Bonds of Affection: Thoreau on Dogs and Cats, 2005. Contributor of articles to books and periodicals. **Address:** Department of Humanities and Arts, Worcester Polytechnic Institute, 100 Institute Rd., Worcester, MA 01609-2280, U.S.A. **Online address:** wmott@wpi.edu

MOTYL, Alexander J(ohn). American/Ukranian (born Ukraine), b. 1953. **Genres:** Novels, Area Studies, Politics/Government. **Career:** Columbia University, assistant professor, 1985-90, associate professor, 1990-92, Harriman Institute, associate director, 1992-99; Rutgers University, professor, 1999-2011. Writer. **Publications:** The Turn to the Right: The Ideological Origins and Development of Ukrainian Nationalism, 1919-1929, 1980; Will the Non-Russians Rebel?: State, Ethnicity, and Stability in the U.S.S.R., 1987; Sovietology, Rationality, Nationality: Coming to Grips with Nationalism in the U.S.S.R., 1990; Dilemmas of Independence: Ukraine after Totalitarianism, 1993; Revolutions, Nations, Empires: Conceptual Limits and Theoretical Possibilities, 1999; Imperial Ends: The Decay, Collapse, and Revival of Empires, 2001; Whiskey Priest, 2005; Who Killed Andrei Warhol, 2007; Flippancy, 2009; The Jew Who Was Ukrainian, 2011. EDITOR: (with H. Kostiuk) Volodymyr Vynnychenko, Diary: 1921-1925, 1983; The Post-Soviet Nations: Perspectives on the Demise of the U.S.S.R., 1992; Thinking Theoretically about Soviet Nationalities: History and Comparison in the Study of the U.S.S.R., 1992; The Encyclopedia of Nationalism, 2000. **Address:** Department of Political Science, Rutgers University, Newark, NJ 07102-1895, U.S.A. **Online address:** ajmotyl@andromeda.rutgers.edu

MOUGIOS, Vassilis. Greek (born Greece), b. 1958. **Genres:** Sciences, Chemistry, Medicine/Health. **Career:** Eli Lilly, clinical research associate, 1988-89; Aristotle University of Thessaloniki, lecturer in exercise biochemistry, 1989-94, assistant professor, 1994-2000, associate professor, 2000-10, professor, 2010-. Writer. **Publications:** Exercise Biochemistry, 2006. Contributor to journals. **Address:** Department of Physical Education, Aristotle University of Thessaloniki, Thessaloniki, 541 24, Greece. **Online address:** mougios@phed.auth.gr

MOULAKIS, Athanasios. Afghani/American/Greek (born Greece), b. 1945. **Genres:** Literary Criticism And History, Education, History. **Career:** Ruhr University, assistant professor of political philosophy, 1969-77; University of London, London School of Economics and Political Science, lecturer in political philosophy, 1977-79; European University Institute, professor of political philosophy and department head, 1979-86; University of Colorado, Herbst professor of humanities, 1989-2000; University of Lugano, Institute for Mediterranean Studies, director, 2000-; Harvard University, distinguished lecturer; American University of Afghanistan, professor of government, acting president and chief academic officer, 2008-. Writer. **Publications:** Homanoia: Eintracht u. d. Entwicklung e. polit. Bewusstseins, 1973; Simone Weil: Die Politik der Askese, 1981; L'Art du possible, 1988; Beyond Utility: Liberal Education for a Technological Age, 1993; Realist Constitutionalism in Renaissance Florence, 1998; Simone Weil and the Politics of Self-Denial, 1998; Republican Realism in Renaissance Florence: Francesco Guicciardini's Discorso di Logrogno, 1998. EDITOR: Legitimacy, 1986; The Promise of History: Essays in Political Philosophy, 1986; History of Political Ideas, vol. I, 1998; Order and History, vol. II: The World of the Polis, 1999; Root Causes of Instability and Violence in the Balkans, 2005. **Address:** The American University of Afghanistan, Darulaman Rd., Kabul, 1, Afghanistan. **Online address:** athanasios.moulakis@lu.unisi.ch

MOULD, Daphne D. C. Pochin. Irish/British (born England), b. 1920. **Genres:** History, Theology/Religion, Travel/Exploration, Autobiography/Memoirs, Young Adult Fiction. **Career:** Author and freelance journalist, 1939-; Radio Eireann, broadcaster. **Publications:** The Roads from the Isles: A Study of the North-West Highland Tracks, 1950; Scotland of the Saints, 1952; West over Sea (Outer Hebrides), 1953; The Rock of Truth, 1953; Ireland of the Saints, 1953; The Mountains of Ireland, 1955, 2nd ed., 1976; Irish Pilgrimage, 1955; The Celtic Saints, 1956; The Irish Dominicans, 1957; Peter's Boat, 1959; The Angels of God, 1961; The Irish Saints, 1963; Saint Brigid, 1965; The Aran Islands, 1972; Ireland from the Air, 1972; Irish Monasteries, 1976; Valentia Island, 1978; Captain Roberts of the Sirius, 1988; Discovering Cork, 1991. **Address:** Aherla House, Aherla, CK 1, Ireland.

MOULESSEHOUL, Mohammed. (Yasmina Khadra). French (born France), b. 1955. **Genres:** Novels, Mystery/Crime/Suspense, Novellas/Short Stories. **Career:** Novelist. **Publications:** Amen!, 1984; Houria: Nouvelles, 1984; Fille du Pont, 1985; El-Kahira, Cellule de la Mort, 1986; De L'autre Côté de la Ville, 1988; Privilège du Phénix: Roman, 1989. AS YASMINA KHADRA: Morituri, 1997; Double Blanc, 1997; L'automne des Chimandères, 1998; Les Agneaux du Seigneur, 1998; Le Dingue Au Bistouri, 1999; A quoi Rêvent les Loups, 1999; L'automne des Chimères, 1999; L'écrivain: Roman, 2000; L'écrivain: Roman, 2001; Les Hirondelles de Kaboul: Roman, 2002; L'imposture des mots, 2002; Cousine K, 2003; Attentat: Roman, 2005; La part du mort, 2005; Sirènes de Bagdad: Roman, 2006; Ce que le Jour Doit à la Nuit: Roman, 2008; What the Day Owes the Night, 2009; L'Olympe des Infortunes, 2010. **Address:** c/o Author Mail, Doubleday Broadway, 1745 Broadway, New York, NY 10019, U.S.A. **Online address:** contact@yasmina-khadra.com

MOUNTFIELD, David. *See* **GRANT, Neil.**

MOUNTFIELD, Gail. *See* **GRANT, Neil.**

MOUNTFORD, Kent. American (born United States), b. 1938. **Genres:** History. **Career:** Environmental Protection Agency, Chesapeake Bay Program, senior scientist; Cove Corp., estuarine ecologist and environmental historian. Educator and writer. **Publications:** Closed Sea: From the Manasquan to the Mullica, a History of Barnegat Bay, 2002; (with H.C. Rountree and W.E. Clark) John Smith's Chesapeake Voyages, 1607-1609, 2007. **Address:** Cove Corp., 10200 Breeden Rd., Lusby, MD 20657, U.S.A. **Online address:** kentmountford@chesapeake.net

MOUNTJOY, Christopher T. *See* **MILES, Keith.**

MOUNTROSE, Phillip. American (born United States), b. 1950. **Genres:** Human Relations/Parenting. **Career:** Paradise Oaks Youth Services, special education teacher, 1990-99; Hollistic Communications, owner, director; International Association of Holistic Practitioners, founding director. Writer. **Publications:** Getting thru to Kids: Problem-Solving with Children Ages Six to Eighteen, 1997; Tips and Tools for Getting thru to Kids, 1999; (with J. Mountrose) Getting thru to Your Self with EFT, 2000; (with J. Mountrose) Getting thru to Your Soul, 2000; (with J. Mountrose) The Heart and Soul of EFT and Beyond: A Soulful Exploration of the Emotional Freedom Techniques and Holistic Healing, 2006. Contributor to periodicals. **Address:** Holistic Communications, PO Box 279, Arroyo Grande, CA 93421, U.S.A. **Online address:** phillip@gettingthru.org

MOURE, Kenneth. Canadian/American (born United States) **Genres:** Economics, History, Politics/Government. **Career:** University of California, Department of History, assistant professor of history, 1988-94, associate professor of history, 1994-2001, professor, 2001-, chair; University of Alberta, Department of History and Classics, professor and chair. Writer. **Publications:** Managing the Franc Poincaré: Economic Understanding and Political Constraint in French Monetary Policy, 1928-1936, 1991; La politique du franc Poincare (1926-1936), 1998; (ed. with M.S. Alexander) Crisis and Renewal in France 1918-1962, 2002; The Gold Standard Illusion: France the Bank of France and the International Gold Standard, 1914-1939, 2002. **Address:** Department of History and Classics, University of Alberta, 2-28 Tory Bldg., Edmonton, AB T6G 2H4, Canada. **Online address:** kenneth.moure@ualberta.ca

MOURLEVAT, Jean-Claude. French (born France), b. 1952. **Genres:** Young Adult Non-fiction, Autobiography/Memoirs. **Career:** Writer and teacher. **Publications:** Histoire de l'enfant et de l'oeuf, 1997; Kolos et les quatre voleurs, 1998; Le jeune loup qui n'avait pas de nom, 1998; La balafre, 1998; A comme voleur, 1998; L'enfant ocean, 1998; Le voyage de zoe, 1999; Les billes du diable, 2000; La riviere a l'envers: Tomek, 2000; Le petit royaume, 2000; La riviere a l'envers: Hannah, 2002; L'homme qui ne possedait rien, 2002; L'homme a l'oreille coupee, 2003; La troisieme vengeance de Robert Poutifard, 2003; L'homme qui levait les pierres, 2004; La balade de Cornebique, 2004; Sous le grand banian, 2005; Le combat d'hiver, 2006; Je voudrais rentrer a la maison (autobiography), 2006; La prodigieuse aventure de Tillmann Ostergrimm, 2007; Le chagrin du roi mort, 2009. TRANSLATOR: Jo Pestum, 1998; Klaus Gordon, Robinson et Juliette, 1998; Monica Dittrich, Bon voyage petit ours!, 2000; Rolf Fanger and Ulrike Moltgen, L'ours et la lune, Jeux d'Aujourd'hui, 2000; Michael Ende, Jim Bouton et Lucas, le chauffeur de locomotive, 2004. **Address:** Gallimard-Jeunesse, 5, rue Sébastien-Bottin, Paris, 75328, France. **Online address:** jcmourlevat@wanadoo.fr

MOUSSALLI, Ahmad S. Lebanese (born Lebanon), b. 1956. **Genres:** Theology/Religion, Politics/Government, History. **Career:** Georgetown University, Center for Christian-Muslim Understanding, visiting professor; University of Copenhagen, Carsten Niebuhr Institute for Near Eastern Studies, visiting professor; U.S. Institute of Peace Specialist, senior fellow, 1999-2000; American University of Beirut, associate professor, professor of political science, 2001-. Writer. **Publications:** Al-Fikr al-Islāmī al-muāsòir: dirāsātwa-shakhsòīyāt. Sayyid Qutòb: Bahòth muqāranli-mabādi al-usòūlīyīnwa-al-isòlāhòīyīn, 1990; Radical Islamic Fundamentalism: The Ideological and Political Discourse of Sayyid Qutb, 1992; World Order and Islamic Fundamentalism, 1992; Al-Usūlīyahal-Islāmīyah: Dirāsah fī al-khitābal-aydiyūlujī wa al-siyāsī inda Sayyid Qutb: bahòthmuqāran li-mabādī al-usòūlīyīnwa-al-isòlāhòīyīn, 1993; Islamic Fundamentalism: A Study in Sayyid Qutb's Ideological and Political Discourse, 1993; (ed.) Islamic Fundamentalism: Myths and Realities, 1998; Moderate and Radical Islamic Fundamentalism: The Quest for Modernity, Legitimacy and the Islamic State, 1999; Historical Dictionary of Islamic Fundamentalist Movements in the Arab World, Iran and Turkey, 1999; Understanding Islam: Basic Principles, 2000; The Islamic Quest Democracy, Pluralism and Human Rights, 2001; The Roots of Intellectual Crisis in the Arab Homeland, 2002; Judhūr Azmat al-muthaqqaf fī al-watan al-Arabī, 2002; The Images of Islam in the Western World, 2003; Al-Gharb wa-al-Wilāyātal-Muttahidah wa-al-Islām al-siyāsī: Hòaqīqatal-sòirā al-hòadòārī wa-al-siyāsī, 2003; Mawsuat al-harakat al-Islamiyah fi al-watan al-Arabi wa-Iran wa-Turkiya, 2004; Siyāsat Amrīkā al-khārijīyah wa-al-siyāsāt al-Islāmīyah, 2006; U.S. Foreign Policy and Islamist Politics, 2008. Contributor to journals. **Address:** Civilization Sequence Program, Department of Political Studies, American University of Beirut, 202 Jesup Hall, PO Box 11-0236, Beirut, 1107 2020, Lebanon. **Online address:** asmouss@aub.edu.lb

MOWAT, Claire (Angel Wheeler). Canadian (born Canada), b. 1933. **Genres:** Children's Fiction, Young Adult Fiction, Autobiography/Memoirs, Travel/Exploration, History. **Career:** Commercial artist, graphic designer and writer. **Publications:** The Outport People (memoir), 1983; Pomp and Circumstances (non fiction), 1989; The Girl From Away (juvenile fiction), 1992; The French Isles (young adult fiction), 1994; Last Summer in Louisbourg (young adult fiction), 1998; Travels with Farley, 2005. Contributor to periodicals. **Address:** 18 King St., Port Hope, ON L1A 2R4, Canada.

MOWAT, Farley (McGill). Canadian (born Canada), b. 1921. **Genres:** Children's Fiction, Animals/Pets, Anthropology/Ethnology, Children's Non-fiction, Environmental Sciences/Ecology, History, Military/Defense/Arms Control, Natural History, Travel/Exploration, Humor/Satire, Biography, Sports/Fitness, Literary Criticism And History. **Career:** Writer. **Publications:** People of the Deer, 1952; The Regiment, 1955, 2nd ed., 1973; Lost in the Barrens, 1956; The Dog Who Wouldn't Be, 1957; (ed.) Coppermine Journey: An Account of a Great Adventure, 1958; The Grey Seas Under: The Perilous Rescue Missions of a North Atlantic Salvage Tug, 1958; The Desperate People, 1959, rev. ed., 1975; (ed.) Ordeal by Ice: The Search for the Northwest Passage, 1960, rev. ed., 1973; The Serpent's Coil: An Incredible Story of Hurricane-Battered Ships and the Heroic Men Who Fought to Save Them, 1961; Owls in the Family, 1961, rev. ed., 1973; The Black Joke, 1962, rev. ed., 1973; Never Cry Wolf, 1963; Westviking: The Ancient Norse in Greenland and North America, 1965; West Viking, 1965; The Curse of the Viking Grave, 1966; (ed.) The Polar Passion: The Quest for the North Pole, 1967, rev. ed., 1973; Canada North, 1967; This Rock within the Sea: A Heritage Lost, 1968; The Boat Who Wouldn't Float, 1969; The Siberians, 1970 in Canada as Sibir: My Discovery of Siberia, 1970, rev. ed., 1973; A Whale for the Killing, 1972; Wake of the Great Sealers, 1973; (ed.) Tundra: Selections from the Great Accounts of Arctic Land Voyages, 1973; The Snow Walker, 1975; Death of a People-the Ihalmiut, 1975; The Great Betrayal: Arctic Canada Now, 1976; Canada North Now: The Great Betrayal, 1976; Top of the World Trilogy, 1976; Two Against the North, 1977; And No Birds Sang, 1979; (contrib.) The World of Farley Mowat, 1980; The World of Farely Mowat: A Selection from His Works, 1980; Sea of Slaughter, 1984; My Discovery of America, 1985; Woman in the Mists: The Story of Dian Fossey and the Mountain Gorillas of Africa, 1987 in Canada as Virunga: The Passion of Dian Fossey, 1987; The New Founde Land, 1989; Rescue the Earth: Conversations with the Green Crusaders, 1990; My Father's Son: Memories of War and Peace, 1992; Born Naked, 1993; Aftermath: Travels in a Post-War World, 1995; A Farley Mowat Reader, 1997; The Farfarers: Before the Norse, 1998 in UK as Alban Quest: The Search for a Lost Tribe, 1999; Walking on the Land, 2000; High Latitudes: A Northern Journey, 2002; High Latitudes: An Arctic Journey, 2003; No Man's River, 2004; Bay of Spirits: A Love Story, 2006; Otherwise, 2008; Eastern Passage, 2010; The Farfarers: A New History of North America, 2011. Works appear in anthologies. Contributor to magazines and periodicals. **Address:** Key Porter Books Ltd., 70 The Esplanade, Toronto, ON M5E 1R2, Canada.

MOWDAY, Bruce Edward. American (born United States), b. 1950. **Genres:** Criminology/True Crime, Novels. **Career:** Daily Local News, reporter and editor, 1974-97; Mowday Group Inc., founder, president, 1997-. **Publications:** (With D. Fetzer) Unlikely Allies: Fort Delaware's Prison Community in the Civil War, 2000; Along the Brandywine River, 2001; September 11, 1777: Washington's Defeat at Brandywine Dooms Philadelphia, 2002; Coatesville, 2003; Downingtown, 2004; The Selling of an Author: A Marketing Guide for Writers to Increase Book Sales, 2005; West Chester, 2005; West Chester: Six Walking Tours, 2006; Chester County Mushroom Farming, 2008; Parkesburg, 2009; Jailing the Johnston Gang: Bringing Serial Murderers to Justice, 2009; (with M.A. Mowday) Spanning the Centuries: The History of Caln Township in the American Landscape, 2009; (with S. Latta) The First 85 Years: A History of A. Duie Pyle, Inc, 2009; (with J. Donahue) Richie Ashburn-Why the Hall Not?, 2011. **Address:** Mowday Group Inc., PO Box 439, Downingtown, PA 19335, U.S.A. **Online address:** mowday@mowday.com

MOWLE, Thomas S. American (born United States), b. 1965. **Genres:** Politics/Government, Philosophy. **Career:** U.S. Air Force, manager of development of aircraft, missile, and information systems; U.S. Air Force Academy, associate professor of political science, 2002-, retired; El Paso County, public trustee, 2008-. Writer. **Publications:** NONFICTION: Allies at Odds? The United States and the European Union, 2004; (ed., intro. and contrib.) Hope Is Not a Plan: The War in Iraq from inside the Green Zone, 2007; (with D.H. Sacko) The Unipolar World: An Unbalanced Future, 2007. Contributor of articles to periodicals. **Address:** El Paso County Public Trustee Office, 105 E Vermijo Ave., Ste. 101, Colorado Springs, CO 80903, U.S.A.

MOXHAM, Roy. British (born England), b. 1939. **Genres:** History, Novels, Travel/Exploration. **Career:** University of London Library, preservation and conservation officer, 1995-, now retired; Institute of English Studies, associate fellow and teacher. Writer. **Publications:** The Freelander, 1990; The Great Hedge of India, 2001; Tea-Addiction, Exploitation and Empire, 2003; A Brief History of Tea, 2009; Outlaw-India's Bandit Queen and Me, 2010; Malabar Dreams, 2010; Tea: The British Connection, forthcoming. **Address:** c/o Carole Blake, Blake Friedman, 122 Arlington Rd., London, GL NW1 7HP, England.

MOXLEY, Gina. Irish (born Ireland), b. 1957?. **Genres:** Plays/Screenplays. **Career:** Actress and playwright. Writer. **Publications:** Danti-Dan, 1994. Contributor to periodicals. **Address:** c/o Author Mail, Faber & Faber, 3 Queen Sq., London, GL WC1N 3AU, England.

MOXLEY, Jennifer. American (born United States), b. 1964. **Genres:** Poetry, Translations. **Career:** Impercipient (magazine), editor, 1992-95; Baffler (magazine), poetry editor, 1997-; University of Maine, Honors College, assistant professor, 2001-07, associate professor of English, 2007-; Poker (magazine), contributing editor, 2003-. **Publications:** The First Division of Labour (chapbook), 1995; (trans.) Jacqueline Risset, The Translation Begins, 1996; Imagination Verses, 1996, 2nd ed., 2003; Enlightenment Evidence (chapbook), 1996; Ten Still Petals (chapbook), 1996; Wrong Life: Ten New Poems (chapbook), 1999; The Sense Record and Other Poems, 2002, 2nd ed., 2003; The Occasion (chapbook), 2002; (trans.) A. Portugal, Absolute bob, 2002; Often Capital, 2005; Fragments of a Broken Poetics (prose chapbook), 2006; The Line, 2007; The Middle Room (prose), 2007; (trans.) J. Risset, Sleep's Powers, 2008; Clampdown, 2009. Works appears in anthologies. **Address:** University of Maine, Rm. 213, 5752 Neville Hall, Orono, ME 04469, U.S.A. **Online address:** jennifer.moxley@umit.maine.edu

MOXLEY, Sheila. British (born England), b. 1966. **Genres:** Children's Fiction, Illustrations, Children's Non-fiction. **Career:** Sadie Fields Production Ltd., design work and construction of pop-up books, 1987-92; self-employed illustrator, 1989-; The Designers Guild, textile design work, 1995. Writer. **Publications:** Christmas Long Ago: Christmas Past with Changing Pictures, 1992; ABCD: An Alphabet Book of Cats and Dogs, 2001. Illustrator of books by others. **Address:** Unit 8B Huguenot Pl., 17A Heneagest St., London, GL E1 5LN, England. **Online address:** info@sheilamoxley.co.uk

MOY, James S. American (born United States), b. 1948. **Genres:** Communications/Media, Cultural/Ethnic Topics, Theatre, Literary Criticism And History, Social Sciences. **Career:** University of Texas, instructor in theater history, 1977-79; University of Oregon, assistant professor of theater, 1979-81; University of Wisconsin, assistant professor, 1981-84, associate professor, 1984-94, professor of theater and drama, 1994-2003, chair, 1998-2003; Theater Journal, co-editor, 1982-83, editor, 1984-85, associate editor, 1986-90; Routledge Press, manuscript reader, 1990-92; PMLA, reader, 1991-91; University of New Mexico, College of Fine Arts, dean, 2003-04; City University of Hong Kong, School of Creative Media, dean and chair professor, 2004-; theatrical performer and director. Writer. **Publications:** Marginal Sights: Staging the Chinese in America, 1993; (ed. with S.Y. Chin, W.L. Ng and G. Okihiro) Re-Visioning Asian America: Locating Diversity (essays), 1994. Contributor to books and periodicals. **Address:** City University Hong Kong, 83 Tat Chee Ave., Kowloon, 53703-3677, Hong Kong. **Online address:** jsmoy@cityu.edu.hk

MOYA, Jose C. Cuban/American (born United States), b. 1952. **Genres:** History, Young Adult Non-fiction, Social Sciences, Humanities. **Career:** Ellis Island Project, research associate, 1984-85; Lujan University, assistant professor, 1987; University of California, assistant professor, 1988-96, associate professor, 1996, professor, now professor emeritus; University of Paris, visiting professor, 2000; Barnard College, Department of History, professor, 2005-, Human Rights Studies Program, faculty. Writer. **Publications:** Cousins and Strangers: Spanish Immigrants in Buenos Aires, 1850-1930, 1998; (with A.E. Fernandez) La Inmigración española en la Argentina, 1999; (ed.) Oxford Handbook of Latin American History, 2010; (with A. McKeown) World Migration In The Long Twentieth Century, 2011. **Address:** Department of History, Barnard College, 413 Lehman Hall, 3009 Broadway, New York, NY 10027, U.S.A. **Online address:** jmoya@barnard.edu

MO YAN *See* **Moye, Guan.**

MOYE, Guan. (Mo Yan). Chinese (born China), b. 1955. **Genres:** Novels, Novellas/Short Stories, Young Adult Fiction. **Career:** Writer, 1980-; Beijing Procuratorial Daily, editor, 1997-. **Publications:** AS MO YAN: NOVELS: Hong gao liang jiazu, 1987; Bao zha, 1988; Tian tang suan tai zhi ge, 1989;

Huan le shi san zhang, 1989; Explosions and Other Stories; Jiu guo, 1992; Shifu, You'll Do Anything for a Laugh (short stories); Fengru feitun, 1996. IN CHINESE: Tou ming di hong luo bo, 1986; Shisan bu, 1989; Mingding guo, 1995; Hong erdou, 1998; Republic of Wine, 2000; Shifu, You'll Do Anything for a Laugh, 2001; (with Y. Lianke zh) Liang Xin Zuo Zheng, 2002; Red Sorghum, 2003; Big Breasts and Wide Hips, 2004. OTHERS: Tou ming de hong luo bo, 1986; Hong gao liang jia zu, 1987; Jin fa ying er, 1993; Shen liao, 1993; Fen nu de suan tai, 1993; Shi cao jia zu, 1993; Zai bao zha, 1994; Dao shen piao, 1995; Xian nü ren, 1995; Ming ding guo, 1995; Mo Yan wen ji, 1995; Hong gao liang, 1995; Hong er duo, 1998; Shi fu yue lai yue you mo, 2000; Tan xiang xing, 2001; Liang xin zuo zheng, 2002; Mu zhi kao, 2003; Mo Yan zhong pian xiao shuo xuan, 2004; Yu da shi yue hui, 2005. Contributor to periodicals. **Address:** c/o Author Mail, Arcade Publishing Co., 141 5th Ave., New York, NY 10010, U.S.A.

MOYE, J. Todd. American (born United States) **Genres:** History. **Career:** University of Texas, teaching assistant, 1994-98, assistant instructor, 1998-99, instructor, 2000; College of Charleston, Avery Research Center for African-American History and Culture, postdoctoral fellow and adjunct professor of history, 1999-2000; National Park Service, Tuskegee Airmen Oral History Project, director, 2000-05; University of North Texas, Oral History Program, director, 2005-, assistant professor of history, 2005-09, associate professor of history, 2009-. Writer. **Publications:** Let the People Decide: Black Freedom and White Resistance Movements in Sunflower County, Mississippi, 1945-1986, 2004; Freedom Flyers: The Tuskegee Airmen of World War II, 2010. Contributor to reference books. **Address:** Department of History, University of North Texas, Wooten Hall 257, 1155 Union Cir., Ste. 310650, PO Box 310650, Denton, TX 76203, U.S.A. **Online address:** moye@unt.edu

MOYÉ, Lemuel A. American (born United States) **Genres:** Medicine/Health, Sciences, Mathematics/Statistics. **Career:** Regenstrief Institute for Health Care, clinical biostatistician, 1979-84; Methodist Hospital Graduate Medical Center, physician, 1979-82; United States Steel, physician, 1982-83; Methodist Health Care Center, acting medical director, physician, 1982-84; MediClinic Physicians' Association, physician, 1984-, owner, 1986-87; Baylor College of Medicine, consulting clinical biostatistician, 1985; University of Texas Health Science Center at Houston, School of Public Health, research assistant professor, 1987-89, assistant professor of biometry, 1989-95, professor of biostatistics, 1995-, physician and biostatistician. Writer. **Publications:** (With A.S. Kapadia) Difference Equations with Public Health Applications, 2000; Statistical Reasoning in Medicine: The Intuitive P-value Primer, 2000, 2nd ed., 2006; Multiple Analyses in Clinical Trials: Fundamentals for Investigators, 2003; (with A.S. Kapadia and W. Chan) Mathematical Statistics with Applications, 2005; Face to Face with Katrina Survivors: A First Responder's Tribute, 2006; Statistical Monitoring of Clinical Trials: Fundamentals for Investigators, 2006; Finding Your Way in Science: How You Can Combine Character, Compassion and Productivity in Your Research Career, 2006; Elementary Bayesian Biostatistics, 2008. **Address:** School of Public Health, University of Texas Health Science Ctr., E815 RAS Bldg., 1200 Herman Pressler Dr., Houston, TX 77030-3900, U.S.A. **Online address:** lemuel.a.moye@uth.tmc.edu

MOYER, Ann E. American (born United States), b. 1955. **Genres:** History, Poetry. **Career:** Rhodes College, assistant professor, 1987-88; University of Chicago, Mellon postdoctoral instructor, 1988-91; University of Oregon, visiting assistant professor, 1991-92; University of California, assistant professor, 1992-95; University of Pennsylvania, Department of History, assistant professor, 1995-2002, associate professor of history, 2002-, undergraduate chair, University Press, Journal of the History of Ideas, co-editor, 2005-, executive editor. **Publications:** Musica Scientia: Musical Scholarship in the Italian Renaissance, 1992; The Philosophers' Game: Rithmomachia in Medieval and Renaissance Europe, 2001; (trans. and intro. with M. Laureys) R. Brandolini, On Music and Poetry, 2001. **Address:** Department of History, University of Pennsylvania, 215C College Hall, 3451 Walnut St., Philadelphia, PA 19104-6379, U.S.A. **Online address:** moyer@sas.upenn.edu

MOYER, Kermit. American (born United States), b. 1943. **Genres:** Novels. **Career:** American University, instructor, 1970-72, assistant professor, 1972-82, associate professor, 1982-88, professor of literature, 1988-, now professor emeritus. Writer. **Publications:** Tumbling (story collection), 1988; The Chester Chronicles, 2010. Contributor to periodicals. **Address:** Department of Literature, American University, Battelle 231, 4400 Massachusetts Ave. NW, Washington, DC 20016-8047, U.S.A. **Online address:** kermitmoyer@comcast.net

MOYNAHAN, Brian. British (born England), b. 1941?. **Genres:** History, Theology/Religion, Military/Defense/Arms Control. **Career:** Yorkshire Post, journalist; Town Magazine, journalist; Times Magazine, journalist; Sunday Times, foreign correspondent, European editor. **Publications:** Airport International, 1978 in US as Airport Confidential, 1980; Claws of the Bear: A History of the Soviet Armed Forces from 1917 to the Present, 1989; Comrades: 1917-Russia in Revolution, 1992; (contrib.) The Russian Century: A Photographic History of Russia's Hundred Years, 1994; The British Century: A Photographic History of the Last Hundred Years, 1997; Rasputin: The Saint Who Sinned, 1997; The Faith: A History of Christianity, 2002; If God Spare My Life: William Tyndale, The English Bible and Sir Thomas More-A Story of Martyrdom and Betrayal, 2002; God's Bestseller: William Tyndale, Thomas More, and the Writing of the English BibleA Story of Martyrdom and Betrayal, 2003; French Century: An Illustrated History of Modern France, 2007; Forgotten Soldiers, 2007; Jungle Soldier: The True Story of Freddy Spencer Chapman, 2009; Leningrad Symphony, 2012. Contributor to periodicals. **Address:** c/o Author Mail, Random House, 1745 Broadway, New York, NY 10019, U.S.A.

MOYNAHAN, Julian (Lane). American (born United States), b. 1925. **Genres:** Novels, Literary Criticism And History, Cultural/Ethnic Topics. **Career:** Amherst College, instructor in English, 1953-55; Princeton University, assistant professor of English, 1955-63; University College, Fulbright professor, 1963-64; State University of New Jersey, Rutgers University, Department of English, associate professor, 1964-66, professor of English, 1966-, now professor emeritus; University of Wyoming, visiting professor, 1965-; Harvard University, visiting professor, 1967-; Breadloaf Graduate School, visiting professor, 1969-; Manhattanville College, National Endowment for the Humanities, professor of humanities, 1972-; Princeton University, Christian Gauss lecturer, 1975-. Writer. **Publications:** Sisters and Brothers: A Novel, 1960; (contrib.) Dickens and the Twentieth Century, 1962; The Deed of Life: The Novels and Tales of D. H. Lawrence, 1963; Pairing Off, 1969; (intro.) A Modern Lover and Other Stories, 1969; Vladimir Nabokov, 1971; Garden State: A Novel, 1973; (contrib.) Seven American Literary Stylists from Poe to Mailer, 1973; Where the Land and Water Meet: A Novel, 1979; Anglo-Irish: The Literary Imagination in a Hyphenated Culture, 1995. EDITOR: Sons and Lovers: Text, Background, and Criticism, 1968; (and intro.) The Portable Thomas Hardy, 1977; (contrib.) Towards a Poetics of Fiction, 1978; (contrib.) Lawrence and Women, 1978; (intro.) Blue Evenings in Berlin: Nabokov's Short Stories of the 1920's, 1978. Contributor of articles to periodicals and magazines. **Address:** Department of English, School of Arts and Sciences, Rutgers University, Murray Hall, 510 George St., New Brunswick, NJ 08901-1167, U.S.A. **Online address:** moy@njj.com

MOYNIHAN, Michael. American (born United States), b. 1969. **Genres:** Music, Mythology/Folklore, Popular Culture, Theology/Religion, Documentaries/Reportage, Theology/Religion. **Career:** Musician and artist, 1984-; writer, 1993-. **Publications:** (With D. Soederlind) Lords of Chaos: The Bloody Rise of the Satanic Metal Underground, 1998; (ed.) Introduction to Magic: Rituals and Practical Techniques for the Magus, 2001; (ed.) Men Among the Ruins: Post-War Reflections of a Radical Traditionalist, 2002; Blood Brothers: The Inside Story of The Cork Hurlers, 1996-2008, 2008; Rebels: Cork GAA Since 1950, 2010; (trans. and ed.) Barbarian Rites: The Spiritual World of the Vikings and the Germanic Tribes, 2011. Contributor to periodicals. **Address:** Dominion Press, PO Box 129, Waterbury Center, VT 05677-0129, U.S.A. **Online address:** dominion@pshift.com

MOYO, Dambisa. Zambian (born Zambia), b. 1969. **Genres:** Economics, Politics/Government. **Career:** World Bank, economist, writer and consultant; Goldman Sachs, head of economic research and strategy for Sub-Saharan Africa. **Publications:** Dead Aid: Why Aid Is Not Working and How There Is a Better Way for Africa, 2009; How The West Was Lost: Fifty Years of Economic Folly and The Stark Choices Ahead, 2011. Contributor to periodicals. **Address:** Farrar, Straus and Giroux, 18 W 18th St., New York, NY 10011, U.S.A. **Online address:** helena@dambisamoyo.com

MOYSER, George H. British/American (born United States), b. 1945?. **Genres:** Politics/Government, Theology/Religion, Area Studies. **Career:** Victoria University of Manchester, lecturer, 1972-73, assistant professor, 1973-76, associate professor, 1976-87; University of Vermont, associate professor, 1987-92, professor, 1992-2010, chair, 1996-, professor emeritus, 1996-2010; McGill University, visiting professor, 1993-94; Writer. **Publications:** (With K.N. Medhurst) Church and Politics in a Secular Age, 1988; (with A. Mabileau, G. Parry and P. Quantin) Local Politics and Participation in Britain and France, 1990; Politics and Religion in the Modern World, 1991; (with G. Parry) Political Participation and Democracy in Britain, 1992. EDITOR: Church and Politics Today, 1985; Research Methods for Elite Studies, 1987. **Address:** Department of Political Science, University of Vermont, Rm. 538 Old Mill, 94 University Pl., Burlington, VT 05405-0114, U.S.A. **Online address:** george.moyser@uvm.edu

MOZETIČ, Brane. *See* **CARON, Brane Mozetic.**

MRAZ, John. American/Mexican (born Mexico), b. 1943. **Genres:** History, Cultural/Ethnic Topics. **Career:** Universidad Autónoma de Puebla, Institute of Social Sciences and Humanities, research professor, 1984-; Secretaría de Educación Pública, national researcher, 1990-; University of Barcelona, visiting professor, 1992-93; University of Connecticut, visiting professor/researcher, 1992-93; University of California, visiting professor/researcher, 1992-93; San Diego State University, visiting professor/researcher, 1992-93; Dartmouth College, visiting professor/researcher, 1996; Fototeca, Instituto Nacional de Antropología e Historia, visiting professor, 1993-94; Oxford University, visiting professor, 1997; Duke University, visiting professor, 2000-01; Universidade Federal Fluminense, visiting professor, 2004. Writer. **Publications:** Mexico, 1900-1960: Brehme, Casasola, Kahlo, Modotti, López, 1992; (with J.M. Storey) Uprooted: Braceros in the Hermanos Mayo Lens, 1996; La mirada inquieta: nuevo fotoperiodismo mexicano, 1976-1996, 1996; Nacho López y el fotoperiodismo mexicano en los años cincuenta, 1999; Nacho López, Mexican Photographer, 2003; (with J.V. Storey) Trasterrados: braceros vistos por los hermanos Mayo, 2005; Looking for Mexico: Modern Visual Culture and National Identity, 2009; (co-author) Walter Reuter: El Viento Limpia El Alma, 2009; Fotografiar La Revolución Mexicana: Compromisos e Iconos, 2010; Photographing the Mexican Revolution: Commitments, Testimonies, Icons, 2012. Contributor of articles to books and periodicals. **Address:** Institute of Social Sciences & Humanities, Independent University of Puebla, Puebla, PU 72810, Mexico. **Online address:** elijohn@infosel.net.mx

MRAZEK, Robert J. (Robert Jan Mrazek). American (born United States), b. 1945. **Genres:** Military/Defense/Arms Control, Novels, Young Adult Non-fiction, Art/Art History. **Career:** United States Navy, officer, 1967-68; author, 1993-; Alaska Wilderness League, co-founder and chairman, 1993-2006. **Publications:** Stonewall's Gold: A Novel, 1999; Unholy Fire: A Novel of the Civil War, 2003; Deadly Embrace: A Novel of World War Two, 2006; A Dawn Like Thunder: The True Story of Torpedo Squadron Eight, 2008; (with H.R. Mrazek) Art Pottery of Joseph Mrazek, 2009; To Kingdom Come: An Epic Saga of Survival in the Air War Over Germany, 2011. **Address:** CA , U.S.A. **Online address:** rjmrazek1942@gmail.com

MRAZEK, Robert Jan. *See* **MRAZEK, Robert J.**

MRKVICKA, Edward F(rancis). American (born United States), b. 1944. **Genres:** Money/Finance, Business/Trade/Industry, Economics, Social Sciences. **Career:** National Bank, marketing officer, 1964-72; Bank of Westmont, assistant vice president and marketing officer, 1972-73; First State Bank, vice president and cashier, 1973-76; First National Bank, president, 1976-81; Reliance Enterprises Inc. (Financial News Syndicate, Omni, Financial Group, Eagle Publishing), owner, chairman, president and chief executive officer, 1982-; Illinois National Bank, chairman, president and chief executive offier; National Enquirer "Money Expert", columnist. **Publications:** Battle Your Bank-and Win!, 1985; Moving Up: Proven Strategies for Career Success, 1985; The Bank Book, 1989, 3rd ed. as The Bank Book: How to Revoke Your Bank's License to Steal and Save up to $100000, 1994; 1037 Ways to Make or Save Up to $100000 This Year Alone, 1991; he Rational Investor: Common Sense Advice for Winning in the Stock Market, 1991; Your Bank is Ripping You Off, 1997, rev. ed., 1999; J.K. Lasser's Pick Winning Stocks, 2000; (with K.H. Mrkvicka) Be Not Deceived, 2007; The Prayer Promise of Christ, 2010; No Innocent Affair, 2011. **Address:** Reliance Enterprises Inc., PO Box 413, Marengo, IL 60152, U.S.A. **Online address:** edward.mrkvicka@be-not-deceived.com

MUCHA, Zak. American (born United States), b. 1971?. **Genres:** Novels. **Career:** Writer. **Publications:** The Beggars' Shore, 1999; The Speed of Mercy, forthcoming. **Address:** c/o Author Mail, Red 71 Press Inc., 1701 Broadway, Ste. 357, Vancouver, WA 98663-3436, U.S.A. **Online address:** zakmucha@aol.com

MUCHMORE, Jo Ann. American (born United States), b. 1937. **Genres:** Essays, Children's Fiction, Self Help, Human Relations/Parenting. **Career:** Actress, 1965-; Adobe Theatre, artistic director, 1970-77; Temple Civic Theatre, managing director, 1977-79, 1983-91; Dick Cavett Show, Public Broadcasting Service (PBS), production assistant, 1979-82; Poncan Theatre, executive director, 1991-97. Writer. **Publications:** A Forever Thing, My Dears (essays), 1991; Johnny Rides Again, 1995. **Address:** Holiday House Inc., 425 Madison Ave., New York, NY 10017, U.S.A.

MUCKENHOUPT, Margaret. American (born United States) **Genres:** Psychology, Biography. **Career:** Belmont Citizens Forum, editor, 1996-; Harvard@Home, editorial consultant, 1996-; McGraw-Hill, contract writer, 1996-; Booz Allen and Hamilton, writing instructor, writing tutor and trainer, 1996-; Newton Community Education, instructor, 1996-; Continental Unitarian Universalist Young Adult Network, chair, 1996-; Harvard University, teaching fellow, 1988-95; Massachusetts Institute of Technology, research assistant, 1988-95; Brown University, teaching assistant, 1988-95; SERV Centers of New Jersey, research assistant, 1988-95; Susan Yecies and Associates Inc., associate, 1988-95; Somerset Spectator, editorial assistant, 1988-95. **Publications:** Sigmund Freud: Explorer of the Unconscious, 1997; Mental Health on Campus: Best Practices, 2000; Dorothea Dix: Advocate for Mental Health Care, 2003. **Address:** c/o Author Mail, Oxford University Press, 198 Madison Ave., New York, NY 10016, U.S.A. **Online address:** megmuck@yahoo.com

MUDDIMAN, John. British (born England), b. 1947. **Genres:** Theology/Religion. **Career:** St. Stephen's House, vice-principal, 1976-83; University of Nottingham, lecturer, 1983-90; Oxford University, Mansfield College, tutorial fellow and lecturer of New Testament studies, 1990-, university assessor, 2009-10, Oxford Centre for Christianity and Culture, faculty of theology. Writer. **Publications:** The Bible: Fountain and Well of Truth, 1983; Ephesians (Blacks New Testament Commentary), 1999; (ed.) New Testament of the Oxford Bible Commentary, 2000; (ed. with J. Barton) Oxford Bible Commentary, 2001; (ed. with J. Barton) The Gospels, 2010; (ed. with J. Barton) The Pentateuch, 2010; (ed. with J. Barton) The Pauline Epistiles, 2010. Contributor to books. **Address:** Mansfield College, Oxford University, Mansfield Rd., Oxford, OX OX1 3TF, England. **Online address:** john_muddiman@mansfield.ox.ac.uk

MUDIMBE, V. Y. American/Congolese (born Congo), b. 1941. **Genres:** Poetry, Novels, Essays, Literary Criticism And History, Philosophy. **Career:** Lovanium University, Department of Romance Languages, assistant, 1966-68, assistant professor of Indo-European languages and historical linguistics of French, 1970-71; National School of Law and Public Administration, lecturer, 1967-68; University of Paris-Nanterre, lecturer, 1969-71; National University of Zaire, associate professor, 1971-74, professor, 1974-80, Center for Theoretical and Applied Linguistics, director, 1971-74, dean of the faculty of philosophy and letters, 1972-74, International Semiology Center, secretary general, 1974-78, Center for Theoretical and Applied Linguistics, research director, 1974-79; International Congress of African Studies, secretary general, 1973-78, vice-president, 1978-85; Haverford College, Margaret Gest professor of comparative religions, 1981-82, Ira Reid professor of history and sociology, 1982-83, professor of general programs, 1984-87; Society for African Philosophy in North America, general secretary, 1988-99; Duke University, professor, 1988-90, Ruth F. DeVamey professor of romance studies, 1991-94, professor of literature, 1995-2000, Trinity College of Arts and Science, Newman Ivey White professor of literature, 2000-, professor of comparative literature. Writer. **Publications:** Déchirures (poetry), 1971; Initiation au Francais, 2 vols., 1971; Autour de la Nation: Lecons de Civisme: Introduction (essay), 1972; Francais: Les Structure Fondamentales I, 1972; Francais: Les Structures Fondamentales II, 1972; Réflexions sur la vie quotidienne (essay), 1972; Entre les eaux: Dieu, un prêtre, la révolution (novel), 1973; Entretailles (and) Fulgurances d'une lezarde (poetry), 1973; L'Autre Face du royaume: Une introduction a la critique des languages en folie (essay), 1973; (with P. Detienne) Francais: Les Structures Fondamentales, 1973; (with A. Tashdjian, M. Le Boul and M. Pierre) Francais: Les Structures Fondamentales IV, 1974; (with J.L. Vincke) Le Prix du péché: Essaide phychanalyse existentielle des traditions Europeenes et Africaines, 1974; Les Fuseaux parfois (poetry), 1974; Carnets d'Amérique (essay), 1976; Contributions a l'etude des variations du genre grammaticaldes Mots francais d'Origine latine: I. Mots a initiale vocalique, 1976; (with M. Lutece, Kilanga M. and L. Wasamba) Procedes d'enrichissement etcreation de termes nouveaux dans un groupe de langues de l'Afrique Centrale, 1976; (co-author) LaVocabulaire Politique Zairois, 1976; Le Bel Immonde: récit (novel), 1976; Air: Etude semantique, Acta Ethnologica et Linguistica, 1979; L'Ecart, Presence Africaine, 1979; La Culture et la science au Zaire 1960-1975: Essai sur les sciences sociales et humaines (essay), 1980; Ladépendance de l'Afrique et les moyens d'y remédier: Actes de la 4esession du Congrès international des études africaines, Kinshasa, 12-15 décembre 1978/Africa's Dependence and the Remedies, 1980; (ed.) Africa's Dependence: La Dependance de l'Afrique, 1980; (co-author) Du Congo au Zaire 1960-1980: Essai de bilan, 1980; Visage de la philosophie et de latheologie comtemporaines au Zaire (essay), 1981; L'Odeur du pere: Essaisur des limites de la science et de la vie en Afrique noire, Presence Africaine, 1982; The Invention of Africa: Gnosis, Philosophy, and the Order of Knowledg, 1988; Shaba Deux: les carnets de Mere Marie-Gertrude (novel), 1989; Les Fuseaux (poetry), 1989; Parables and Fables: Exegesis, Textuality, and Politics in Central Africa, 1991; (ed.) The Surreptitious Speech: Présence Africaine and the Politics of Otherness, 1947-1987, 1992; (ed. with R.H. Bates and J. O'Barr) Africa and the Disciplines: The Contributions of Research in Africa to the Social Sciences and Humanities, 1993; The Idea of Africa, 1994; Les corps glorieux des mots et desêtres, 1994; (ed.) The Encyclopedia of African Religions and Philosophy; Tales of Faith: Religion as Political Performance in Central Africa, 1997; (ed.) Nations, Identities, Cultures, 1997; L'Afrique au miroir deslittératures, des sciences de l'homme et de la société: Mélanges offerts à V.Y. Mudimbe, 2003; Cheminements: Carnets de Berlin, 2006; Disagreement on African Faultlines, 2006; Sine Numine, 2006; (co-author) The Normal & Its Orders, 2007; In the House of Libya, 2009; (ed.) Encyclopedia of African Religions & Philosophy, 2009; Phenomenology of Madness, 2011; On African Fault Lines: Questions in Philosophy of Cultures, 2011. Contributor of articles to books, newspapers, periodicals and journals. **Address:** Program in Literature, Trinity College of Arts and Science, Duke University, 125D Friedl Bldg., PO Box 90670, Durham, NC 27708-0670, U.S.A. **Online address:** vmudimbe@duke.edu

MUEENUDDIN, Daniyal. Pakistani (born Pakistan), b. 1963?. **Genres:** Novellas/Short Stories. **Career:** Debevoise & Plimpton (law firm), lawyer, 1998-2001. Writer and farmer. **Publications:** In Other Rooms, Other Wonders, 2009. Contributor of short stories to periodicals. **Address:** Khanpur, Pakistan. **Online address:** inotherrooms@gmail.com

MUEHL, Lois Baker. American (born United States), b. 1920. **Genres:** Children's Fiction, Poetry, Education, History. **Career:** Teacher, 1941-42; J.M. Mathes Advertising Agency, copywriter, 1945; freelance writer and teacher of writing, 1955-65; Writer, 1957-; University of Iowa, Reading Laboratory, Rhetoric Program, director, 1965-85, associate professor of rhetoric, now associate professor emeritus; Johnson C. Smith University, reading specialist, 1967-69; Developmental Reading Lab, director. **Publications:** My Name Is, 1959; Worst Room in the School, 1961; One Very Happy Family (play), 1964; Hidden Year of Devlin Bates, 1967; Winter Holiday Brain Teasers, 1979; A Reading Approach to Rhetoric, 1983; (with S. Muehl) Hermann, Missouri 1852: News and Voices, 1987; (with S. Muehl) Trading Cultures in the Classroom: Two American Teachers in China, 1993; Talkable Tales: Read-a-Rebus Stories, 1993. Contributor of articles to books and periodicals. **Address:** Department of Rhetoric, University of Iowa, 169 English-Philosophy Bldg., Iowa City, IA 52242-1486, U.S.A.

MUEHLEN, Maria. *See* **VON FINCKENSTEIN, Maria.**

MUELLER, Andrew. British/Australian (born Australia), b. 1968?. **Genres:** History, Art/Art History, Photography. **Career:** Melody Maker, reviews editor, 1991-93; Time Out, columnist, 2002-04; Independent on Sunday Review, columnist, 2004-06; Financial Times Magazine, columnist, 2008. **Publications:** Rock and Hard Places: Travels to Backstages, Frontlines and Assorted Sideshows, 1999; I Wouldn't Start from Here: The 21st Century and Where It All Went Wrong, 2007; Rock and Hard Places: Travels to Backstages, Frontlines and Assorted Sideshows, 2010. Contributor of articles to periodicals. **Address:** Soft Skull Press, 1919 5th St., Berkeley, CA 94710, U.S.A. **Online address:** mail@andrewmueller.net

MUELLER, Daniel. American (born United States) **Genres:** Novellas/Short Stories, Autobiography/Memoirs. **Career:** Western Michigan University, visiting writer, 2000; Dartmouth College, visiting assistant professor, 2000-01; University of New Mexico, assistant professor of English, 2001-06, associate professor, 2006-; Queens University of Charlotte, Low-Residency MFA Program, faculty, 2005-. **Publications:** How Animals Mate: Short Stories, 1999. Contributor to magazines. **Address:** Department of English Language & Literature, University of New Mexico, MSCO3 2170, 1 University of New Mexico, Albuquerque, NM 87131-0001, U.S.A. **Online address:** danieljamesmueller@gmail.com

MUELLER, Joan. American (born United States), b. 1956. **Genres:** Theology/Religion. **Career:** Creighton University, associate professor. Franciscan Sisters of Joy, founder, 1995. Writer. **Publications:** Faithful Listening: Discernment in Everyday Life, 1996; Why Can't I Forgive You? A Christian Reflection, 1996; Is Forgiveness Possible?, 1998; Francis: The Saint of Assisi, 2000; Clare's Letters to Agnes: Texts and Sources, 2001; Clare of Assisi: The Letters to Agnes, 2003; The Privilege of Poverty: Clare of Assisi, Agnes of Prague and the Struggle for a Franciscan Rule for Women, 2006. **Address:** Department of Theology, Creighton University, Omaha, NE 68178, U.S.A. **Online address:** jmueller@creighton.edu

MUELLER, Lisel. American/German (born Germany), b. 1924. **Genres:** Poetry, Translations. **Career:** Goddard College, MFA Program, visiting faculty, 1977-80; Wichita State University, distinguished writer-in-residence, 1981; Warren Wilson College, MFA Program for Writers, visiting faculty, 1983-86; University of Chicago, visiting lecturer, 1984, now retired. **Publications:** POETRY: Dependencies, 1965; Life of a Queen (chapbook), 1970; The Private Life, 1976; Voices from the Forest (chapbook), 1977; The Need to Hold Still, 1980; Second Language, 1986; Bride's Complaint: 1987: For Soprano and Computer Generated Electronics: A Setting of a Poem, 1987; Waving from Shore, 1989; Learning to Play by Ear, 1990; Alive Together: New and Selected Poems, 1996; Grave Deposits, 2010. TRANSLATOR: The Selected Later Poems of Marie Luise Kaschnitz, 1980; M.L. Kaschnitz, Whether or Not, 1984; M.L. Kaschnitz, Circe's Mountain, 1990; White of Ships, 2008. **Address:** Louisiana State University Press, 3990 W Lakeshore Dr., PO Box 25053, Baton Rouge, LA 70808, U.S.A.

MUELLER, Robert Emmett. American (born United States), b. 1925. **Genres:** Novels, Science Fiction/Fantasy, Essays, Illustrations. **Career:** Philco Radio Research, researcher; Bell Labs, staff. Writer. **Publications:** Inventivity, 1963; Inventor's Notebook, 1964; Eyes in Space, 1965; The Science of Art: The Cybernetics of Creative Communication, 1967. **Address:** c/o Toni Strassman, 116 E 19th St., New York, NY 10003-2130, U.S.A.

MUGGESON, Margaret Elizabeth. Also writes as Everatt Jackson, Margaret Dickinson. British (born England), b. 1942. **Genres:** Novels, Mystery/Crime/Suspense, Young Adult Fiction. **Career:** Skegness District Education Office, local government officer, 1963-70; writer, 1970-. **Publications:** Pride of the Courtneys, 1968; Brackenbeck, 1969; Portrait of Jonathan, 1970; (as Everatt Jackson) The Road to Hell, 1975; Sarah, 1981; Adelina, 1981; Carrie, 1981; Lifeboat!, 1983; Beloved Enemy, 1984; Plough the Furrow, 1994; Sow the Seed, 1995; Reap the Harvest, 1996; The Miller's Daughter, 1997; Chaff upon the Wind, 1998; The Fisher Lass, 1999; The Tulip Girl, 2000; The River Folk, 2001; Tangled Threads, 2002; Twisted Strands, 2003; Red Sky in the Morning, 2004; Without Sin, 2005; Pauper's Gold, 2006; Wish Me Luck, 2007; (Margaret Dickinson) As Sing As We Go, 2008; Suffragette Girl, 2009; Sons and Daughters, 2010; Forgive and Forget, 2011. **Address:** Anthony Sheil Associates Ltd., 2-3 Morwell St., London, GL WC1B 3AR, England. **Online address:** authorfeedback@authortrek.com

MUGNY, Gabriel. Swiss (born Switzerland), b. 1949. **Genres:** Sociology, Psychology. **Career:** University of Geneva, professor of social psychology; Swiss Journal of Psychology, co-editor. **Publications:** (With W. Doise and J. Deschamps) Psychologie Sociale Expérimentale, 1978; (with W. Doise) Dévelopement social de l'intelligence, 1981; (with S. Papastamou) Meionotetes kai exousia, 1983; (with F. Carugati) Intelligence au pluriel: les representations sociales de l'intelligence et de son developpement, 1985; (with J.A. Pérez) Déni et la raison: psychologie de l'impact social des minorites, 1986; (with D. Oberlé and J. Beauvois) Relations Humaines, Groupes et Influence Sociale, 1995. EDITOR: (with S. Moscovici and E. Van Avermaet) Perspectives on Minority Influence, 1985; (with M. von Cranach and W. Doise) Social Representations and the Social Bases of Knowledge, 1992; (with F. Butera) Social Influence in Social Reality; Promoting Individual and Social Change, 2001. **Address:** Universite de Geneve, Section de Psychologie, Mail 0110 / Uni-Pignon 705, 40 Boulevard du Pont d'Arve, Geneva, 1211, Switzerland. **Online address:** gabriel.mugny@unige.ch

MUGO, Mĩcere Gĩthae. (M. M. G. Mugo). American/Kenyan (born Kenya), b. 1942?. **Genres:** Literary Criticism And History, Plays/Screenplays, Poetry. **Career:** Alliance Girls' High School, deputy headmistress, 1967-68; Kabare Girls' High School, headmistress, 1968-69; University of Nairobi, Department of Literature, lecturer, senior lecturer, 1973-80, associate professor, 1980-82, Faculty of Arts, dean, 1980-82; St. Lawrence University, visiting professor, 1982-84; University of Zimbabwe, associate professor, 1984-92, Literature Unit, head of English, 1986-92; Cornell University, Africana Studies and Research Centre, visiting professor, 1992-93; Syracuse University, Department of African American Studies, associate professor, 1993-97, professor of African American studies, 1997-, chair, 2005-08, Meredith professor for teaching excellence, co-chair of undergraduate studies, 1994-95; United Women of Africa Organization, founder and president, 2003-; Pan African Community of Central New York, founder and president. Writer. **Publications:** Daughter of My People, Sing! (poetry), 1976; The Long Illness of Ex-Chief Kiti, 1976; (with N. wa Thiong'o) The Trial of Dedan Kimathi, 1976; Visions of Africa: The Fiction of Chinua Achebe, Margaret Laurence, Elspeth Huxley, and Ngugi wa Thiong'o (criticism), 1978; Zimani and Sifiso, 1988; (ed.) Zimbabwe School Readers' Series, 1988; (as M.M.G. Mugo) African Orature and Human Rights, 1991; (intro.) Songs from the Temple: Poems, 1992; My Mother's Poem and Other Songs: Songs and Poems, 1994; Muthoni wa Kirima, Mau Mau Woman Field Marshal: Interrogation of Silencing, Erasure, and Manipulation of Female Combatants' Texts, 2004; African Orature and Human Rights in Gikuyu, Shona, and Ndebele Zamani Cultures, 2004; Writing and Speaking from the Heart of My Mind, 2011. Contributor of articles to journals. **Address:** Department of African American Studies, Syracuse University, 209 Sims Hall, Syracuse, NY 13244-1230, U.S.A. **Online address:** mmmugo@syr.edu

MUGO, M. M. G. *See* **MUGO, Mĩcere Gĩthae.**

MUHANJI, Cherry. (Jeannette Cherry Muhanji). American (born United States), b. 1939. **Genres:** Novels, Gay And Lesbian Issues, Young Adult Fiction, Sciences. **Career:** Women's Resource and Action Center, librarian, 1985-93; University of Iowa, research assistant, 1990-92, 1994-96, teaching assistant, 1991-97; Goddard College, assistant professor, 1996-99; University of Minnesota, visiting professor, 1997-99; University of Missouri, visiting professor of English, 1999, interim director of black studies, 1999-2000; Union Institute and University, Graduate School, adjunct faculty, 2001; Portland State University, assistant professor of university studies, 2001-06, 2007, adjunct professor of women's studies. Writer. **Publications:** (With K. Scott and E. High) Tight Spaces, 1987; Her: A Novel, 1990, 2nd ed., 2006. Works appear in anthologies. Contributor to periodicals. **Address:** Portland State University, 1825 SW Broadway, PO Box 751, Portland, OR 97201-3256, U.S.A. **Online address:** muhanji@pdx.edu

MUHANJI, Jeannette Cherry. *See* **MUHANJI, Cherry.**

MUHLHAHN, Cara. American (born United States), b. 1957?. **Genres:** Autobiography/Memoirs. **Career:** Cara Muhlhahn Midwifery, founder. Writer. **Publications:** Labor of Love: A Midwife's Memoir, 2009. **Address:** Cara Muhlhahn Midwifery, 646 E 11th St., Ste. C3, New York, NY 10009, U.S.A. **Online address:** info@cmmidwifery.com

MUI, Chunka. American/Hong Kong (born Hong Kong), b. 1962. **Genres:** Business/Trade/Industry, Administration/Management. **Career:** Computer Sciences Corp., CSC Index, vice president; Diamond Management and Technology Consultants network, partner and chair; Devil's Advocate Group, director. Writer. **Publications:** (With L. Downes) Unleashing the Killer App: Digital Strategies for Market Dominance, 1998, 2nd ed., 2000; (with P.B. Carroll) Billion Dollar Lessons: What You Can Learn from the Most Inexcusable Business Failures of the Last Twenty-five Years, 2008. **Address:** Devil's Advocate Group, 1521 W Adams St., Studio B, Chicago, IL 60607, U.S.A. **Online address:** chunka.mui@devilsadvocategroup.com

MUIR, Helen. British (born England), b. 1937. **Genres:** Novels, Children's Fiction, Science Fiction/Fantasy, Animals/Pets, Food And Wine, Adult Nonfiction, Young Adult Fiction. **Career:** Birkenhead News, reporter; The Hampstead Highgate Express, reporter; London Sunday Times, reporter, through 1980. Writer. **Publications:** NOVELS: Don't Call It Love, 1975; Noughts and Crosses: A Child's Game for Two Players, 1976; The Belles Lettres of Alexandea Bonaparte, 1980; Many Men and Talking Wives, 1981; Nothing for You, Love, 1988; Consequences, 1994; Celestial Seasonings, 1995. CHILDREN'S BOOKS: Jack Russell Jackson, 1983; Dan's Secret Pony, 1985; Lila the Edible Frog, 1986; Montagu Mountain Goat, 1987; Wonderwitch, 1988; The Racing Witch, 1988; Modge and Podge, 1988; Tiger Trouble, 1989; Magic Mark, 1990; Wonderwitch and The Rooftop Cats, 1991; The Twenty Ton Chocolate Mountain, 1994; Wonderwitch Goes to the Dogs, 1995; Wonderwitch and the Spooks, 1997. Contributor to periodicals. **Address:** MBA Literary Agents, 62 Grafton Way, London, GL W1T 5DW, England.

MUIR, Richard. British (born England), b. 1943. **Genres:** Geography, History, Photography, Natural History, Archaeology/Antiquities. **Career:** Trinity College Dublin, lecturer in geography, 1970-71; Cambridge College of Art and Technology, lecturer, senior lecturer in geography, 1971-80; freelance author and photographer, 1980-94; Landscapes Journal, co-founder and editor, 2000-; University of Ripon, lecturer in geography, 1994-2001; York St. John University, lecturer in geography, 1994-2001. **Publications:** Modern Political Geography, 1975; The English Village, 1980; Riddles in the British Landscape, 1981; The Shell Guide to Reading the Landscape, 1981; Politics, Geography and Behaviour, 1981; The Lost Villages of Britain, 1982; History From the Air, 1983; (with C. Taylor) Visions of the Past, 1983; (with H. Welfare) The National Trust Guide to Prehistoric and Roman Britain, 1983; A Traveller's History of Britain and Ireland, 1983; (with E. Duffey) The Shell Countryside Book, 1984; (with J. Ravensdale) East Anglian Landscapes: Past and Present, 1984; (with N. Muir) The National Trust Guide to Dark Age and Medieval Britain, 400-1350, 1985; Shell Guide to Reading the Celtic Landscapes, 1985; (with N. Muir) The National Trust Rivers of Britian, 1986; Landscape and Nature Photography, 1986; Stones of Britain, 1986; Old Yorkshire, 1987; (with N. Muir) Hedgerows: The History and Wildlife, 1987; The Countryside Encyclopedia, 1988; (with N. Muir) Fields, 1989; Portraits of the Past, 1989; Barely bridge, 1990; Castles & Strongholds, 1990; The Dales of Yorkshire, 1991; The Villages of England, 1992; Coastlines, 1993; Political Geography: A New Introduction, 1997; The Yorkshire Countryside: A Landscape History, 1997; Approaches to Landscape, 1999; New Reading the Landscape, 1999; Landscape Detective, 2001; Landscape Encyclopaedia: Reference Guide to the Historic Landscape, 2004; Ancient Trees, Living Landscapes, 2006; How to Read a Village, 2007; An Elegy for the Dales: Nidderdale, 2010. **Address:** Waterfall Close, Station Rd., Birstwith, Harrogate, NY HG3 3AG, England. **Online address:** richard.muir1@btinternet.com

MUIR, Star A. American (born United States), b. 1958. **Genres:** Communications/Media, Economics. **Career:** University of Massachusetts, lecturer, 1982-85; George Mason University, assistant professor, 1988-95, assistant director of debate, 1988-97, associate professor of communication, 1995-, director of scheduling and hiring, College Debate Institute, developer and director, 1989-95, editor of departmental student handbook and newsletters, 1991-, Division of Instructional and Technology Support Services, director of learning support services; American Express, consultant; Duracell Corp., consultant; Northern Virginia Justice Academy, consultant; Parcher Group, consultant. **Publications:** (With J.K. Muir) Foundations in Public Communication Handbook, 1992, 2nd ed., 1996; The Policy Debate Handbook, 1995; (ed. with T.L. Veenendall) Earthtalk: Communication Empowerment for Environmental Action, 1996; The College Policy Debate Handbook, 1998; The High School Policy Debate Handbook, 1998. Contributor to books and periodicals. **Address:** Department of Communication, George Mason University, Rm. 3D6, Thompson Hall 217, 4400 University Dr., Fairfax, VA 22030, U.S.A. **Online address:** smuir@gmu.edu

MUKHERJEE, Bharati. American/Indian (born India), b. 1940. **Genres:** Novels, Novellas/Short Stories, Autobiography/Memoirs, Cultural/Ethnic Topics, History, Politics/Government, Adult Non-fiction. **Career:** Marquette University, instructor in English, 1964-65; University of Wisconsin, instructor, 1965; McGill University, lecturer, 1966-69, assistant professor, 1969-73, associate professor, 1973-78, professor of English, 1978; Skidmore College, visiting associate professor of English, 1979-80, 1981-82; Emory University, visiting professor of English, 1983; Montclair State College, associate professor of English, 1984; City University of New York, professor of English, 1987-89; University of California, professor of English, 1987-. Writer. **Publications:** The Tiger's Daughter, 1972; Wife, 1975; Kautilya's Concept of Diplomacy: A New Interpretation, 1976; (with C. Blaise) Days and Nights in Calcutta, 1977; Darkness, 1985; (with C. Blaise) The Sorrow and the Terror: The Haunting Legacy of the Air India Tragedy, 1987; The Middleman and Other Stories, 1988; Jasmine, 1989; Political Culture and Leadership in India, 1991; Regionalism in Indian Perspective, 1992; The Holder of the World (novel), 1993; Leave It to Me, 1997; Desirable Daughters: A Novel, 2002;

The Tree Bride: A Novel, 2004; Miss New India, 2011; Bangalore by the Bay, forthcoming. Contributor to periodicals. **Address:** Department of English, University of California, 334 Wheeler Hall, Berkeley, CA 94720-1030, U.S.A. **Online address:** mukhster@aol.com

MUKHERJEE, Rabin. Canadian/Indian (born India), b. 1932. **Genres:** Urban Studies, Politics/Government. **Career:** Govern of West Bengal, executive director of developmental planning, 1965-77; Supreme Court of India, senior advocate, 1978-95; writer and consultant, 1995-; Habitat Developers Ltd., managing director; Happy Hope Ltd., director; United Nations, consultant; World Bank, consultant. **Publications:** Urbanisation for Human Settlement in Developing Countries, 1977; Urban Development and Planning: Calcutta Metropolis, 1978; Regional Development, 1975; Democracy-a Failure, Shefocracy-the Solution for Human Welfare, 2000. **Address:** 24 Mabelle Ave., Ste. 2807, Etobicoke, ON M9A 4X8, Canada. **Online address:** habitat@giaselol.vsnl.net.in

MUKHTAR, Mohamed Haji. American/Somali (born Somalia), b. 1947. **Genres:** Reference, Language/Linguistics. **Career:** Somali National University, associate professor of history, 1975-82; British Broadcasting Corp., producer and correspondent for programs, 1986-; National University of Malaysia, senior lecturer in African and Middle Eastern history, 1987-91; Savannah State University, professor of history and coordinator of history program, 2001-. Writer. **Publications:** Habka Cilmiga ee Baarista Taarikhda, 1978; (co-ed.) Somalia: World Bibliographical Series, 1989; Historical Dictionary of Somalia, 2003; Essential English-Maay Dictionary, 2006. Contributor to books and journals. **Address:** Department of Social and Behavioral Sciences, Savannah State University, 3219 College St., Savannah, GA 31404, U.S.A. **Online address:** mukhtarm@savstate.edu

MULCAHY, Greg. American (born United States), b. 1958?. **Genres:** Novels, Novellas/Short Stories. **Career:** Lakewood Community College (now Century Community College), part-time faculty in English, 1989-; Minnesota State College Faculty, president. Writer. **Publications:** Out of Work: Stories and Novella (stories), 1993; Constellation: A Novel, 1996; Drinking in Silence (stories), 2000; Carbine: Stories, 2010. Contributor to periodicals. **Address:** Minnesota State College, 55 Sherburne Ave., St. Paul, MN 55103, U.S.A. **Online address:** greg.mulcahy@edmn.org

MULCAHY, Lisa. American (born United States) **Genres:** Theatre, Plays/Screenplays, Writing/Journalism. **Career:** Writer, director and producer. **Publications:** Renegade Sluts on Bikes, 1995; Building the Successful Theater Company, 2002, 2nd ed., 2011; Bye Bye Boredom!: The Girl's Life Big Book of Fun, 2003; Theater Festivals: Best Worldwide Venues for New Works, 2005; The Actor's Other Career Book: Using Your Chops to Survive and Thrive, 2006. Contributor to books, periodicals and magazines. **Address:** c/o Author Mail, Allworth Press, 10 E 23rd St., Ste. 510, New York, NY 10010-4459, U.S.A. **Online address:** lmulcahy@mymailstation.com

MULCAHY, Matthew. American (born United States), b. 1968?. **Genres:** History. **Career:** Loyola College, assistant professor, 1999-2005, associate professor of history, 2005-. Writer. **Publications:** Hurricanes and Society in the British Greater Caribbean, 1624-1783, 2006. Contributor of articles to periodicals. **Address:** Department of History, Loyola College, 4501 N Charles St., Baltimore, MD 21210-2699, U.S.A. **Online address:** mmulcahy@loyola.edu

MULDOON, Paul. (Paul Benedict Muldoon). American/Irish (born Ireland), b. 1951. **Genres:** Poetry. **Career:** British Broadcasting Corp., radio producer, 1973-78; Columbia University, School of Arts, part-time teacher, 1987-88; Princeton University, lecturer in writing, 1987-, part-time teacher, 1987-88, director of creative writing program, 1993-, professor of creative writing, 1995-, Howard G.B. Clark 21 Professor, Peter B. Lewis Center for the Arts, chair; University of California, Roberta Holloway lecturer, 1989; University of Massachusetts, visiting professor, 1989-90; University of Oxford, professor of poetry, 1999-2004; Hertford College, honorary fellow. Writer. **Publications:** Knowing My Place, 1971; New Weather, 1973; Spirit of Dawn, 1975; Mules, 1977; Names and Addresses, 1978; Why Brownlee Left, 1980; Immram, 1980; Out of Siberia, 1982; Quoof, 1983; The Wishbone, 1984; Mules and Early Poems, 1985; Selected Poems, 1968-1983, 1986; Meeting the British, 1987; (with M. Valiante) Zero Discharge: A Strategy for the Regulation of Toxic Substances in the Great Lakes Ecosystem, 1988; Madoc: A Mystery, 1991; (trans.) Astrakhan Cloak, 1992; Shining Brow, 1993; Incantata, 1994; The Prince of the Quotidian, 1994; The Annals of Chile, 1994; Six Honest Serving Men, 1995; Kerry Slides, 1996; New Selected Poems: 1968-94, 1996; Hopewell Haiku, 1997; The Bangle, 1998; Hay, 1998; (trans. with R. Martin) Birds, 1999; To Ireland, I, 2000; Poems, 1968-1998, 2001; Vera of Las Vegas, 2001; Moy Sand and Gravel, 2002; Sixty Instant Messages to Tom Moore, 2005; Medley for Morin Khur, 2005; Horse Latitudes, 2006; General Admission, 2006; End of the Poem, 2006; When the Pie was Opened, 2008; Plan B, 2009; Wayside Shrines, 2009; Maggot, 2010. EDITOR: The Scrake of Dawn: Poems by Young People from Northern Ireland, 1979; The Faber Book of Contemporary Irish Poetry, 1986; (and intro.) The Essential Byron, 1988; The Faber Book of Beasts, 1997. **Address:** Faber & Faber, 3 Queen Sq., London, GL WC1N 3AU, England. **Online address:** muldoon@princeton.edu

MULDOON, Paul Benedict. *See* **MULDOON, Paul.**

MULGREW, Ian. Canadian/Scottish (born Scotland), b. 1957. **Genres:** Documentaries/Reportage, Medicine/Health, Sports/Fitness, Biography. **Career:** Thomson Newspapers Ltd., 1977-80; Globe and Mail, staff, 1980-, West Coast bureau chief, 1981-85; Province, city editor, 1985-89; Vancouver Sun, senior reporter, 1997-, senior feature writer, legal affairs columnist; Toronto Star, book critic; Kwantlen College, teacher of journalism. **Publications:** Unholy Terror: The Sikhs and International Terrorism, 1988; Final Payoff: The True Price of Convicting Clifford Robert Olson, 1990; (ghostwriter) Webster! An Autobiography of Jack Webster, 1991; Who Killed Cindy James, 1991; (with C. Angus) Amazon Extreme: Three Men, a Raft, and the World's Most Dangerous River, 2001 in US as Amazon Extreme: Three Ordinary Guys, One Rubber Raft, and the Most Dangerous River on Earth, 2002; (with C. Angus) Lost in Mongolia: Rafting the World's Last Unchallenged River, 2002; Bud Inc.: Inside Canada's Marijuana Industry, 2005; (with B. Ackles) Water Boy: From the Sidelines to the Owner's Box Inside the CFL, the XFL, and the NFL, 2007. **Address:** Vancouver Sun, 200 Granville St., Ste. 1, Vancouver, BC V6C 3N3, Canada. **Online address:** imulgrew@vancouversun.com

MULGREW, Jason. American (born United States), b. 1979. **Genres:** Autobiography/Memoirs. **Career:** Writer. **Publications:** Everything Is Wrong with Me: A Memoir of an American Childhood Gone, Well, Wrong, 2010. **Address:** Los Angeles, CA , U.S.A. **Online address:** teresa.brady@harpercollins.com

MULLAN, David George. Canadian/British (born England), b. 1951. **Genres:** History, Theology/Religion, Literary Criticism And History. **Career:** Brock University, ecumenical chaplain, 1980-81; Victoria Avenue Baptist Church, pastor, 1985-88; Cape Breton University, assistant professor, 1989-92, associate professor, 1992-2002, professor, 2002-. Writer. **Publications:** Episcopacy in Scotland: The History of an Idea, 1560-1638, 1986; (ed.) Religious Pluralism in the West: An Anthology, 1998; Scottish Puritanism, 1590-1638, 2000; Religious Controversy in Scotland, 1625-1639, 2002; Women's Life Writing in Early Modern Scotland: Writing the Evangelical Self, c. 1670-c. 1730, 2003; Protestant Piety in Early Modern Scotland: Letters, Lives and Covenants, 1650-1712, 2008; Edinburgh: Scottish History Society, 2008; (ed. with C. Gribben) Literature and the Scottish Reformation, 2009; Narratives of the Religious Self in Early-Modern Scotland, 2010. **Address:** Department of History, Cape Breton University, CC234, 1250 Grand Lake Rd., PO Box 5300, Sydney, NS B1P 6L2, Canada. **Online address:** david_mullan@cbu.ca

MULLANE, Richard Michael. *See* **MULLANE, (R.) Mike.**

MULLANE, (R.) Mike. (Richard Michael Mullane). American (born United States), b. 1945. **Genres:** Autobiography/Memoirs, Children's Non-fiction, Mystery/Crime/Suspense. **Career:** National Aeronautics and Space Administration (NASA), astronaut, 1978-90. Writer. **Publications:** Red Sky: A Novel of Love, Space, and War, 1993; Liftoff!: An Astronaut's Dream, 1995; Do Your Ears Pop in Space?: And 500 Surprising Questions about Space Travel, 1997; (as Mike Mullane) Riding Rockets: The Outrageous Tales of a Space Shuttle Astronaut, 2006. **Address:** Stories From Space L.L.C., 1301 Las Lomas Rd. NE, Albuquerque, NM 87106, U.S.A. **Online address:** mike@mikemullane.com

MULLANEY, James P. American (born United States) **Genres:** Novels, Young Adult Fiction. **Career:** Writer. **Publications:** The Ministry of Culture, 2007. **Address:** Thomas Dunne Books, 175 5th Ave., New York, NY 10010-7703, U.S.A.

MULLANY, Janet. (Jane Lockwood). American/British (born England)

Genres: Novels. Career: Writer and archaeologist. Publications: Dedication, 2005; The Rules of Gentility, 2007; (as Jane Lockwood) Forbidden Shores, 2007; A Most Lamentable Comedy, 2009; Improper Relations, 2010; Jane and the Damned, 2010; (with M. Balogh, C. Gleason and S. Krinard) Bespelling Jane Austen, 2010; Mr. Bishop and the Actress, 2011; Tell Me More, 2011; Jane Austen: Blood Persuasion, 2011. **Address:** c/o Author Mail, HarperCollins Publishers, 10 E 53rd St., New York, NY 10022, U.S.A. **Online address:** elailah@yahoo.com

MULLEN, Bill V. American (born United States), b. 1959?. **Genres:** Race Relations, Politics/Government. **Career:** Changsha Railway Institute, foreign teacher, 1985-86; Bryn Mawr College, visiting instructor, 1989-90; Youngstown State University, Center for Working-Class Studies, co-director, 1995-96; Youngstown State University, assistant professor of English, 1990-94, associate professor of English and Africana studies, 1994-2000, professor of English and Africana studies, 2000; Wuhan University, J. William Fulbright lecturer in American literature, 1998; University of Texas-San Antonio, associate professor of English, 2000-02, professor, 2002, American Studies Program, co-coordinator, 2002-03, assistant graduate advisor, 2003-04, graduate advisor, 2004-05; Purdue University, professor of English, 2005-, director of American Studies, 2005-10. Writer. **Publications:** (Ed.) Revolutionary Tales: African-American Women's Short Stories, from the First Story to the Present, 1995; (ed. with S.L. Linkon) Radical Revisions: Rereading 1930s Culture, 1996; Popular Fronts: Chicago and African-American Cultural Politics, 1935-46, 1999; Left of the Color Line: Race, Radicalism, and Twentieth-Century Literature of the United States, 2003; Afro-Orientalism, 2004; (ed. with C. Watson) W.E.B. Du Bois on Asia: Crossing the World Color Line, 2005; Afro Asia: Revolutionary Political and Cultural Connections Between African Americans and Asian Americans, 2008. Contributor to periodicals. **Address:** Department of English, College of Liberal Arts, Purdue University, 315 Heavilon Hall, 500 Oval Dr., West Lafayette, IN 47907-2038, U.S.A. **Online address:** bvmullen@purdue.edu

MULLEN, Michael. Irish (born Ireland), b. 1937. **Genres:** Children's Fiction, Novels, Young Adult Non-fiction, Young Adult Fiction, Travel/Exploration. **Career:** Teacher, 1962-85; St. Joseph's College, teacher of English, 1962-66. Writer. **Publications:** FOR CHILDREN: FICTION: Magus, the Lollipop Man, 1981; Sea Wolves from the North, 1982; Barney the Hedgehog, 1988; The Viking Princess, 1988; The Little Drummer Boy, 1989; The Caravan, 1990; The Long March, 1990; The Flight of the Earls, 1991; Glór na Mara (in Gaelic), 1991; The Four Masters, 1992; The First Christmas, 1993; Marcus the School Mouse, 1993; Na Saoithe Anoir (in Gaelic), 1993; An toileán órga (in Gaelic), 1994; To Hell or Connaught, 1994; Michaelangelo, 1994; The Last Days of the Romanovs, 1995; Flight from Toledo, 1996; Pillars of Fire, 1997; Scáth a Aingeal (in Gaelic), 1997. NONFICTION: The Darkest Years: A Famine Story, 1996. FOR ADULTS: NOVELS: Kelly, 1981; The Festival of Fools, 1984; The Hungry Land, 1986; Rites of Inheritance, 1990; The House of Mirrors, 1992; The Midnight Country, 1995; Mayo: The Waters and the Wild, 2004; Díoltas, 2005; Fear agus an luch, 2007; Seolta bána, 2007; The Road Taken: A Guide to the Roads and Scenery of Mayo, 2008; Scríbhneoir stuáilte, 2009. OTHER: Transna na machairi, 2010. **Address:** Rarhbawn Dr., Castlebar, MA 1, Ireland.

MULLEN, Patrick B. American (born United States), b. 1941. **Genres:** Cultural/Ethnic Topics, Mythology/Folklore. **Career:** State University of New York College, assistant professor of English and folklore, 1968-69; University of Wisconsin, visiting instructor, 1969-70; Ohio State University, assistant professor, 1969-72, associate professor, 1972-81, professor of folklore, 1981-2005, Center for Folklore Studies, director, 1993-96, Department of English, professor emeritus, 2005-; University of Rome, Fulbright lecturer, 1983; Cuyahoga Valley National Recreation Area, staff, 1983; Ohio Folklore Society, president; Utah State University, visiting professor, 1990. Writer. **Publications:** I Heard the Old Fishermen Say: Folklore of the Texas Gulf Coast, 1978; (with T.C. Lloyd) Lake Erie Fishermen: Work, Identity, and Tradition, 1990; Listening to Old Voices: Folklore, Life Stories, and the Elderly, 1992; (ed. with F.E. Abernethy and A.B. Govenar) Juneteenth Texas: Essays in African-American Folklore, 1996; Man Who Adores the Negro: Race and American Folklore, 2008. Work appears in anthologies. Contributor of articles to journals. **Address:** Ctr. for Folklore Studies, Ohio State University, 308 Dulles Hall, 230 W 17th Ave., Columbus, OH 43210-1340, U.S.A. **Online address:** mullen.4@osu.edu

MULLER, Eddie. American (born United States), b. 1958. **Genres:** Film, Novels, Mystery/Crime/Suspense. **Career:** Film Noir Foundation, founder and president. Journalist. **Publications:** (With D. Faris) Grindhouse: The Forbidden World of Adults Only Cinema, 1996; (with D. Faris) That's Sexploitation!: The Forbidden World of Adult Cinema, 1997; Dark City: The Lost World of Film Noir, 1998; Dark City Dames: The Wicked Women of Film Noir, 2001; The Distance: A Novel, 2002; The Art of Noir: The Posters and Graphics from the Classic Era of Film Noir, 2002; Shadow Boxer: A Billy Nichols Novel, 2003; (with T. Hunter) Tab Hunter Confidential: The Making of a Movie Star, 2005; San Francisco Noir, 2005. Contributor to periodicals. **Address:** c/o Author Mail, HarperCollins Publishers, 10 E 53rd St., New York, NY 10022, U.S.A. **Online address:** eddie@eddiemuller.com

MULLER, Herta. German/Romanian (born Romania), b. 1953. **Genres:** Novels, Translations, Novellas/Short Stories. **Career:** Translator, teacher and writer. **Publications:** Niederungen (stories), 1982, trans. as Nadirs, 1999; Druckender Tango, 1984; Der Mensch ist ein grosser Fasan auf der Welt, 1986, trans. as The Passport, 1989; Barfüssiger Februar: Prosa (title means: 'Barefoot February'), 1987; Reisende auf einem Bein, 1989, trans. as Traveling on One Leg, 1998; Der Teufel sitzt im Speigel: wie Wahrnehmung sich erfindet, 1991; Eine warme Kartoffle ist ein warmes Bett, 1992; Der Fuchs war damals schon der Jäger: Roman, 1992; Der Wachter nimmt seinen Kamm: Collagen, 1992; Herztier: Roman (novel), 1994, trans. as The Land of Green Plums, 1996; Hunger und Seide: Essays, 1995; In der Falle, 1996; Heute wär ich mir lieber nicht begegnet: Roman, 1997, trans. as The Appointment, 2001; Im Haarknoten wohnt eine Dame: Collagen, 2000; Heimat ist das, was gesprochen wird: Eine Rede, 2001; Handtasche: Prosa, Lyrik, Szenen and Essays, 2001; Children of Ceausescu, 2001; (with Y. Tawada and A. Walser) Wenn die Katze ein Pferd wäre, könnte man durch die Bäume reiten: Prosa, 2001; Lebensangst und Worthunger, 2001; König verneigt sich und tötet, 2003; Blassen Herren mit den Mokkatassen, 2005; Der Brahms-Klarinettist Richard Mühlfeld, 2007; Atemschaukel: Roman, 2009; Ich glaube nicht an die Sprache, 2009; Niederungen: Prosa, 2010; Immer derselbe Schnee und immer derselbe Onkel, 2011. **Address:** Henry Holt & Co., 115 W 18th St., New York, NY 10011, U.S.A.

MÜLLER, Ingo. German (born Germany), b. 1936. **Genres:** Sciences, Physics, Chemistry, History, Law, Engineering. **Career:** Johns Hopkins University, assistant professor, associate professor, 1970-75; University of Düsseldorf, professor of theoretical physics, 1975-76; University of Paderborn, professor of theoretical physics, 1976-79; Technical University of Berlin, professor of thermodynamics, 1979-85, emeritus professor, 1985-. Writer. **Publications:** Entropy, Absolute Temperature and Coldness in Thermodynamics: Boundary Conditions in Porous Materials, 1971; Thermodynamik: Die Grundlagen der Materialtheorie, 1973; Thermodynamics, 1985; (with J. Fehr) Moderne Kachelofen: Bewahrte Technik in neuer Form: Nutzungsvarianten, Energiesparkonzepte, 1987; (with T. Ruggeri) Extended Thermodynamics, 1993, 2nd ed., Rational Extended Thermodynamics, 1998; (with P. Strehlow) Rubber and Rubber Balloons: Paradigms of Thermodynamics, 2004; (with W. Weiss) Entropy and Energy: A Universal Competition, 2005; A History of Thermodynamics: The Doctrine of Energy and Entropy, 2007. Contributor to journals. **Address:** Technical University of Berlin, Strasse des 17 Juni 135, Berlin, 10623, Germany. **Online address:** ingo.mueller@alumni.tu-berlin.de

MULLER, Jan-Werner. American (born United States), b. 1970?. **Genres:** Politics/Government. **Career:** All Souls College, fellow, 1996-2003; St. Antony's College, European Studies Centre, research fellow, 2003-05; Princeton University, Department of Politics, assistant professor, 2005-, associate professor; Collegium Budapest Institute, Advanced Study, visiting fellow; New York University, Remarque Institute, visiting fellow; Harvard University, Center for European Studies, visiting fellow; European University Institute, Robert Schuman Centre for Advanced Studies, visiting fellow; Ecole des Hautes Etudes en Sciences Sociales, visiting professor; European College of Liberal Arts, co-founder; Germany's first private, English-speaking liberal arts college, founding research director. Writer. **Publications:** Another Country: German Intellectuals, Unification, and National Identity, 2000; (ed.) Memory and Power in Post-War Europe: Studies in the Presence of the Past, 2002; (ed.) German Ideologies since 1945: Studies in the Political Thought and Culture of the Bonn Republic, 2003; A Dangerous Mind: Carl Schmitt in Post-War European Thought, 2003; Constitutional Patriotism, 2007; Contesting Democracy: Political Thought in Twentieth-Century Europe, 2011. **Address:** Department of Politics, Princeton University, 234 Corwin Hall, Princeton, NJ 08544, U.S.A. **Online address:** jmueller@princeton.edu

MULLER, Jerry Z(ucker). American/Canadian (born Canada), b. 1954. **Genres:** Intellectual History, History, International Relations/Current Affairs, Economics. **Career:** Catholic University of America, Department of History, assistant professor, 1984-90, associate professor of history, 1990-96, professor of history, 1996-, chair, 2009-; Social Science and Modern Society, editor, 1997-. **Publications:** The Other God That Failed: Hans Freyer and the Deradicalization of German Conservatism, 1987; Adam Smith in His Time and Ours: Designing the Decent Society, 1993; (ed. with M.F. Deshmuckh) Fritz Stern at 70, 1997; (ed.) Conservatism: An Anthology of Social and Political Thought from David Hume to the Present, 1997; The Mind and the Market: Capitalism in Modern European Thought, 2002; Capitalism and the Jews, 2010. Contributor to periodicals. **Address:** Department of History, Catholic University of America, 620 Michigan Ave. NE, Washington, DC 20064, U.S.A. **Online address:** mullerj@cua.edu

MULLER, (Lester) Robin. Canadian (born Canada), b. 1953. **Genres:** Mythology/Folklore, Illustrations, Children's Fiction, Ghost Writer. **Career:** University of Toronto, Department of Fine Art, studio coordinator, 1977-83; Graph Em, art director, 1984; Sheridan College, Department of Animation, instructor. Writer and editorial illustrator. **Publications:** RETOLD FOLKTALES: SELF-ILLUSTRATED: Tatterhood, 1984; The Sorcerer's Apprentice, 1986; The Lucky Old Woman, 1987; Little Kay, 1988; The Magic Paintbrush, 1990; The Nightwood, 1991; (reteller) Mollie Whuppie and the Giant, 1993. SELF-ILLUSTRATED: Row, Row, Row Your Boat, 1993; (and contrib.) Little Wonder, 1994; Badger's New House, 2002; Moon and Star, 2005. OTHERS: Hickory, Dickory, Dock, 1992; The Angel Tree, 1997; 13 Ghosts of Halloween, 2007. **Address:** 46 Wolfrey Ave., Toronto, ON M4K 1K8, Canada.

MULLER, Marcia. American (born United States), b. 1944. **Genres:** Novellas/Short Stories, Mystery/Crime/Suspense, Young Adult Fiction. **Career:** Sunset Magazine, merchandising supervisor, 1967-69; University of Michigan, Institute for Social Research, interviewer, 1971-73; freelance writer and novelist, 1973-; Invisible Ink, partner, 1979-83. **Publications:** Edwin of the Iron Shoes: A Novel of Suspense, 1978; Ask the Cards a Question, 1982; The Cheshire Cat's Eye: A Sharon McCone Mystery, 1983; The Tree of Death, 1983; Games to Keep the Dark Away, 1984; Leave a Message for Willie, 1984; The Legend of the Slain Soldiers: An Elena Oliverez Mystery, 1985; There's Nothing to Be Afraid Of, 1985; The Cavalier in White, 1986; Eye of the Storm, 1988; There Hangs the Knife, 1988; There's Something in a Sunday: A Sharon McCone Mystery, 1989; Dark Star, 1989; The Shape of Dread, 1989; Trophies and Dead Things, 1990; Where Echoes Live, 1991; Deceptions, 1991; Pennies on a Dead Woman's Eyes, 1992; Wolf in the Shadows, 1993; Till the Butchers Cut Him Down: A Sharon McCone Mystery, 1994; The McCone Files, 1995; A Wild and Lonely Place, 1995; The Broken Promise Land, 1996; Both Ends of the Night, 1997; While Other People Sleep, 1998; A Walk through the Fire, 1999; McCone and Friends, 2000; Listen to the Silence, 2000; Point Deception, 2001; Dead Midnight, 2002; Time of the Wolves: Western Stories, 2003; Cyanide Wells, 2003; Dangerous Hour, 2004; Cape Perdido, 2005; Vanishing Point, 2006; Ever-Running Man, 2007; Burn Out, 2008; Locked In, 2009; Coming Back, 2010; City of Whispers, 2011. WITH B. PRONZINI: Double, 1984; Beyond the Grave, 1986; 1001 Midnights: The Aficionado's Guide to Mystery and Detective Fiction, 1986; The Lighthouse: A Novel of Terror, 1987; Duo, 1998; Season of Sharing: A Sharon McCone and Nameless Detective Story, 2001; Crucifixion River: Western Stories, 2007. EDITOR WITH B. PRONZINI: The Web She Weaves: An Anthology of Mystery and Suspense Stories by Women, 1983; Child's Ploy: An Anthology of Mystery and Suspense Stories, 1984; Witches' Brew: Horror and Supernatural Stories by Women, 1984; Dark Lessons: Crime and Detection on Campus, 1985; She Won the West: An Anthology of Western and Frontier Stories by Women, 1985; Chapter and Hearse: Suspense Stories about the World of Books, 1985; The Wickedest Show on Earth: A Carnival of Circus Suspense, 1985; The Deadly Arts, 1985; (and M.H. Greenberg) Lady on the Case, 1988; Kill or Cure: Suspense Stories about the World of Medicine, 1989; Detective Duos, 1997. **Address:** PO Box 2536, Petaluma, CA 94953-2536, U.S.A.

MULLETT, John St. Hilary. British (born England), b. 1925?. **Genres:** History, Music, Theology/Religion, Adult Non-fiction, History. **Career:** Que Que, rector, 1952-60; Church of England, rector of Ashwell, 1977-90; St. Catharine's College, fellow commoner, 1990, magazine editor, 1982-2000. **Publications:** One People, One Church, One Song, 1968; Oxton St. Saviour Guide, 1977; They Took Them to Church, 1979; To Love and to Cherish, 1982; A Church Service Following a Second Marriage, 1983; Eight Walks to the Bays of Lipsi, 1992; Gloria in Excelsis in CMQ, 1999; Sanctus in CMQ, 2000. **Address:** Hodder & Stoughton, 338 Euston Rd., London, GL NW1 3BH, England. **Online address:** jsm37@cam.ac.uk

MULLIGAN, William. Scottish/British (born England), b. 1975. **Genres:** History. **Career:** University College, lecturer; University of Glasgow, Department of History, lecturer. Writer. **Publications:** The Creation of the Modern German Army: General Walther Reinhardt and the Weimar Republic, 1914-1930, 2005; (ed. with B. Simms) The Primacy of Foreign Policy in British History, 1660-2000: How Strategic Concerns Shaped Modern Britain, 2010; Origins of the First World War, 2010. **Address:** Department of History, University of Glasgow, Rm. 301, 2 University Gardens, Glasgow, G12 8QQ, Scotland. **Online address:** w.mulligan@history.arts.gla.ac.uk

MULLIN, Caryl Cude. Canadian (born Canada), b. 1969. **Genres:** Novels. **Career:** Actress, 1989-90; Emmanuel School, English teacher. Writer. **Publications:** A Riddle of Roses, 2000; Rough Magic, 2009. **Address:** c/o Author Mail, Second Story Press, 20 Maud St., Ste. 401, Toronto, ON M5V 2M5, Canada. **Online address:** scoremaster@videotron.ca

MULLIN, Robert Bruce. American (born United States), b. 1953. **Genres:** Theology/Religion, Social Commentary, Adult Non-fiction, History. **Career:** Yale University, instructor, 1984-85; Wesleyan University, visiting assistant professor, 1984-85; North Carolina State University, assistant professor to professor, 1985-98; General Theological Seminary of the Episcopal Church, Society for the Promotion of Religion and Learning, professor of history and world mission and professor of modern Anglican studies, 1998-, subdean for academic affairs, 2000-05. Writer. **Publications:** Episcopal Vision/American Reality: High Church Theology and Social Thought in Evangelical America, 1986; (with S.E. Ahlstrom) The Scientific Theist: A Life of Francis Ellingwood, 1987; (ed.) Moneygripe's Apprentice: The Personal Narrative of Samuel Seabury III, 1989; (ed. with R.E. Richey) Reimagining Denominationalism: Interpretive Essays, 1994; Miracles And The Modern Religious Imagination, 1996; The Puritan As Yankee: A Life of Horace Bushnell, 2002; A Short World History of Christianity, 2008. **Address:** General Theological Seminary, Seabury Hall, 4th Fl., 440 W 21st St., New York, NY 10011, U.S.A. **Online address:** mullin@gts.edu

MULLINS, Edwin B(randt). British (born England), b. 1933. **Genres:** Novels, Art/Art History, History. **Career:** Medici Society, editorial assistant, 1957-58; Two Cities, co-editor, 1958-60; Illustrated London News, art correspondent, 1958-62; Financial Times, sale-room correspondent, 1962-67; Sunday Telegraph, art critic, 1962-69; Daily Telegraph Magazine, art correspondent and advisor, 1964-86; British Broadcasting Corp., television art presenter, 1973-. **Publications:** F.N. Souza; An Introduction, 1962; Henri Manguin 1874-1949, 1966; Alfred Wallis, 1967, rev. ed., 1994; Josef Herman, 1967; (intro.) Paintings & Drawings, 1967; Art of Georges Braque, 1968; Braque, 1968; The Art of Elisabeth Frink, 1972; The Pilgrimage to Santiago, 1974; Angels on the Point of a Pin, 1979; (ed.) Great Paintings, 1981; Sirens, 1983; (ed.) The Arts of Britain, 1983; The Painted Witch: How Western Artists Have Viewed the Sexuality of Women, 1985; A Love Affair with Nature, 1985; The Golden Bird, 1987; The Lands of the Sea, 1988; Master Painter, 1989; The Royal Collection, 1992; The Devil's Work, 1997; Cluny: In Search Of God's Lost Empire, 2006; Avignon of the Popes: City of Exiles, 2007; Popes of Avignon: A Century in Exile, 2008; Roman Provence: A History and Guide, 2011. Contributor to periodicals. **Address:** British Broadcasting Corp., PO Box 1922, Darlington, DU DL3 0UR, England.

MULLINS, Hilary. American (born United States), b. 1962. **Genres:** Gay And Lesbian Issues, Animals/Pets, Young Adult Non-fiction, Reference. **Career:** Pacific Research and Training Alliance, administrative assistant, 1991-93; freelance writer, 1993-; lay minister, 2000-; teacher, 2000-. **Publications:** Cats (and Their Dykes), 1991; The Cat Came Back (young adult), 1993; (co-author) The Romantic Naiad, 1993; Women on Women III, 1993; Sleeping with Dionysus, Women, Ecstasy and Addition, 1994; (co-author) The Mysterious Naiad, 1994; Tomboys!, 1995; Die Katzekam zurück, 1999. **Address:** c/o Publicity Director, Naiad Press Inc., PO Box 10543, Tallahassee, FL 32302, U.S.A. **Online address:** hmullins@earthlink.net

MULRONEY, Brian. Canadian (born Canada), b. 1939. **Genres:** Young Adult Non-fiction, Autobiography/Memoirs, Politics/Government, Social Sciences. **Career:** Ogilvy, Cope, Porteous, Montgomery, Renault, Clarke &

Kirkpatrick (law firm), partner, through 1976; Iron Ore Company of Canada, vice president of corporate affairs, 1976-77, president, 1977-83; Progressive Conservative Party, leader, 1983-84; prime minister of Canada, 1984-93; Youth for Diefenbaker, national vice president; Quebecor, chairman. Writer. **Publications:** NONFICTION: Where I Stand, 1983; The Mulroney Team, 1984; Trade Outlook: Globalization or Regionalization, 1990; Memoirs: 1939-1993, 2007. **Address:** c/o Ogilvy Renault, 1981 McGill College Ave., Ste. 1100, Montreal, QC H3A 3C1, Canada.

MULROY, Kevin. American (born United States), b. 1954. **Genres:** History. **Career:** University of California, bibliographer, 1992-93; Autry Museum of Western Heritage, director of research and publications, 1993-2001; University of Southern California, assistant dean of contracts and grants and associate executive director of research collections and services, 2001-08; University of California, associate university librarian for academic services, 2008-. Writer and historian. **Publications:** Freedom on the Border: The Seminole Maroons in Florida, the Indian Territory, Coahuila, and Texas, 1993; Western Amerykański: Polish Poster Art and the Western, 1999; (ed. with L.B. de Graaf and Q. Taylor) Seeking El Dorado: African Americans in California, 2001; The Seminole Freedmen: A History, 2007. Contributor to books and periodicals. **Address:** Los Angeles Library Administration, University of California, 11334 Charles E. Young Research Library, PO Box 951575, Los Angeles, CA 90095-1575, U.S.A. **Online address:** kmulroy@library.ucla.edu

MUN, Nami. American/Korean (born Korea (South)), b. 1968?. **Genres:** Novels. **Career:** Columbia College, assistant professor of creative writing, 2009-. Writer. **Publications:** Miles from Nowhere (novel), 2009. Contributor to books and periodicals. **Address:** Chicago, IL , U.S.A. **Online address:** milesfromnowherethenovel@gmail.com

MUNBY, Jonathan. British (born England) **Genres:** Film, Cultural/Ethnic Topics, History, Popular Culture. **Career:** University of Lancaster, professor of American studies, 1995-, Lancaster Institute for the Contemporary Arts, senior lecturer in film studies and American studies. Writer. **Publications:** Public Enemies, Public Heroes: Screening the Gangster from Little Caesar to Touch of Evil, 1999; Under a Bad Sign: Criminal Self-representation in African American Popular Culture, 2011. Works appear in anthologies. Contributor to journals. **Address:** Lancaster Institute for the Contemporary Arts, University of Lancaster, Rm. B160, County Main, LICA Bldg., Lancaster, LC LA1 4YW, England. **Online address:** j.munby@lancaster.ac.uk

MUNDIS, Hester (Jane). Also writes as Virginia Morgan, Ayn Westminster, Miriam Asher. American (born United States), b. 1938. **Genres:** Novels, Animals/Pets, Young Adult Fiction, Mystery/Crime/Suspense, Medicine/Health, Reference. **Career:** Fawcett Publications, editorial assistant, 1957-62; MacFadden Bartell Corp., associate editor, 1962-63; Dell Publishing Company Inc., associate editor, 1963-65, copy chief, 1965-67; Popular Library Inc., executive editor, 1967-70; Avon Books, senior editor, 1970-71. Freelance writer, 1971-; The New York Times, editor. **Publications:** Mercy at the Manor (gothic spoof), 1965; (as Aynn Westminster) Moon in Shadow, 1974; (as Aynn Westminster) Nightmare in Eden, 1974; Jessica's Wife, 1975; No He's Not a Monkey, He's an Ape and He's My Son, 1976; (as Miriam Asher) Black Wind, 1976; Separate Ways, 1978; (as Virginia Morgan) Tame the Rising Tide, 1979; Working Girl, 1981; Powermom, 1984, new ed. 1994; 101 Ways to Avoid Reincarnation, or, Getting it Right the First Time, 1989; (with J. Hanna) Jack Hanna's Ultimate Guide to Pets, 1996; (contrib.) Heart Songs for Animal Lovers: True Stories of Devotion, Courage and Love, 1999; My Chimp Friday: The Nana Banana Chronicles, 2002; (with E. Mindell) Dr. Earl Mindell's Unsafe At any Meal: How to Avoid Hidden Toxins in Your Food, 2002; (with E. Mindell) Earl Mindell's New Vitamin Bible, 2004. **Address:** c/o Phyllis Westberg, Harold Ober Associates, 425 Madison Ave., Ste. 1001, New York, NY 10017, U.S.A. **Online address:** hester@hestermundis.com

MUNDY, Liza. American (born United States), b. 1960?. **Genres:** Medicine/Health, Biography. **Career:** University of Virginia, teacher of writing; Washington Post Magazine, feature writer, staff writer, reporter. **Publications:** Everything Conceivable: How Assisted Reproduction is Changing Men, Women, and the World, 2007; Michelle: A Biography, 2008. **Address:** The Washington Post, 1150 15th St. NW, Washington, DC 20071, U.S.A. **Online address:** lm@lizamundy.com

MUNEVAR, Gonzalo. American (born United States), b. 1945?. **Genres:** Philosophy, Sciences, Novels, Novellas/Short Stories, Poetry, Biology, Air/Space Topics, Astronomy, Astronomy. **Career:** San Francisco State University, lecturer, 1975-76; University of Nebraska, assistant professor, 1976-85, professor, 1985-86, Nebraska Foundation, professor of philosophy, 1986-89; Stanford University, Stanford Humanities Center, faculty fellow, visiting associate professor of philosophy, 1983-84; Evergreen State College, professor of history and philosophy of science, 1989-97; Kobe University of Commerce, visiting professor, 1993; University of California, visiting professor of philosophy, 1997-99; Lawrence Technological University, Department of Humanities, Social Sciences and Communication, professor, 1999-, chair, 1999-2004. Writer. **Publications:** Radical Knowledge: A Philosophical Inquiry into the Nature and Limits of Science, 1981; (ed.) Beyond Reason: Essays on the Philosophy of Paul Feyerabend, 1991; (ed.) Spanish Studies in the Philosophy of Science, 1996; Evolution and the Naked Truth: A Darwinian Approach to Philosophy, 1998; The Master of Fate (novel), 1999; (ed. with J. Preston and D. Lamb) The Worst Enemy of Science?: Essays in Memory of Paul Feyerabend, 2000; Variaciones Sobre Temas de Feyerabend, 2006; El Amo del Destino, 2006; Evolucion y la Verdad Desnuda, 2008. Contributor to periodicals. **Address:** Department of Humanities, Lawrence Technological University, Rm. S229, 21000 W 10 Mile Rd., Southfield, MI 48075-1058, U.S.A. **Online address:** gmunevar@ltu.edu

MUNGOSHI, Charles L. Zimbabwean (born Zimbabwe), b. 1947. **Genres:** Novellas/Short Stories, Novels, Plays/Screenplays, Translations. **Career:** Rhodesian Forestry Commission, Forest Research Station, research assistant, 1967-69; Textbook Sales (booksellers), junior invoicing clerk, 1969-74; Highfield Drama Club, Highfield Community Centre, founder and chair, 1969-73; Ecumenical Arts Association, voluntary creative writing and drama instructor; actor in radio plays, 1971-; Zimbabwe Publishing House, literary editor, 1981-85, director/creative writing editor, 1987-; The Literature Bureau, editor, 1975-81; University of Zimbabwe, writer-in-residence, 1985-87; Zimbabwe Television's Local Drama Programme, actor, 1985. Novelist. **Publications:** IN SHONA: Ndiko Kupindana Kwamazuva (novel), 1975; Makunun'unu Maodzamwoyo (novel), 1977; Inongova Njakenjake (play), 1980; Kunyarara Hakusi Kutaura? (novel), 1983. IN ENGLISH: Coming of the Dry Season (short stories), 1972; Waiting for the Rain (novel), 1975; Some Kinds of Wounds and Other Short Stories (short stories), 1980; The Milkman Doesn't Only Deliver Milk: Poems (verse), 1981; The Setting Sun and the Rolling World: Selected Stories, 1989; Stories from a Shona Childhood, 1989; One Day, Long Ago: More Stories from a Shona Childhood, 1991; Walking Still, 1997. OTHER: (trans.) N. Thiongo, Tsanga Yembeu, as A Grain of Wheat, 1988. Works appear in anthologies. **Address:** 47/6156 Uta Cres., Zengeza 1, Chitungwiza, 6156, Zimbabwe.

MUNHALL, Edgar. American (born United States), b. 1933. **Genres:** Art/Art History. **Career:** Yale University, instructor, 1959-64, assistant professor, 1964-65; University Art Gallery, assistant curator of prints and drawings, 1959-64, assistant professor, 1964-65; Frick Collection, curator, 1965-99, curator emeritus, 2000-; Columbia University, adjunct professor, 1979-81; du, contributing editor, 1980-84; lecturer. **Publications:** Masterpieces of the Frick Collection, 1970; Ingres and the Comtesse d'Haussonville, 1985; Francois-Marius Granet: Watercolors from the Musée Granet at Aix-en-Provence, 1988; (with B. Davidson and N. Tscherny) Paintings from the Frick Collection, 1990; Little Notes Concerning Watteau's Portal of Valenciennes, 1992; Whistler and Montesquiou: The Butterfly and the Bat, 1995; The Frick Collection: A Tour, 1999; Greuze the Draftsman, 2002. Contributor to periodicals. **Address:** Frick Collection, 1 E 70th St., New York, NY 10021, U.S.A. **Online address:** munhall@frick.org

MUNIZ, Olga M. American/Puerto Rican (born Puerto Rico), b. 1954. **Genres:** Children's Fiction, Poetry, Education, inspirational/Motivational Literature, Language/Linguistics, Bibliography, E-books, Translations, Translations. **Career:** Barbara Ann Roessler Christian Academy, English and Italian teacher, 1978-79; Language Immersion School, teacher, 1979-80; Colegio Cristiano, teacher, 1980-81; Indiana University, associate instructor in Spanish, 1982-86, 1987-91, Spanish instructor, 1987; Indiana University, preceptor and coordinator of Spanish, 1985-86; Hillsdale College, assistant professor of Spanish and Italian, 1991-; Global Reach Language Services, co-owner, president, interpreter and translator, 1995-. Writer. **Publications:** La mujer en el contex to epistolar poetico del siglo de oro, 1996; The Sparrow/El canto del gorrion, 2000. **Address:** Department of Spanish, Hillsdale College, 33 E College St., Hillsdale, MI 49242, U.S.A. **Online address:** omuniz@hillsdale.edu

MUÑOZ, Manuel. American (born United States), b. 1972. **Genres:** Young Adult Non-fiction, Young Adult Fiction. **Career:** University of Arizona, Creative Writing Program, assistant professor. Writer. **Publications:** Zigzagger, 2003; The Faith Healer of Olive Avenue, 2007; What You See in the Dark, 2011. Contributor to periodicals. **Address:** c/o Stuart Bernstein, Representation for Artists, 63 Carmine St., Ste. 3D, New York, NY 10014, U.S.A. **Online address:** munozm@email.arizona.edu

MUNRO, Alice. Canadian (born Canada), b. 1931. **Genres:** Novels, Novellas/Short Stories, Young Adult Fiction, Romance/Historical. **Career:** Alice Munro Bookstore, founder, 1963; University of Western Ontario, writer-in-residence, 1974-75; University of British Columbia, writer-in-residence, 1980. **Publications:** Dance of the Happy Shades and Other Stories, 1968; Lives of Girls and Women, 1971; Something I've Been Meaning to Tell You: Thirteen Stories, 1974; Who Do You Think You Are?: Stories, 1978 in US as The Beggar Maid: Stories of Flo and Rose, 1979; The Moons of Jupiter: Stories, 1982; The Progress of Love, 1986; Friend of My Youth: Stories, 1990; Open Secrets: Stories, 1994; Selected Stories, 1996; The Love of a Good Woman: Stories, 1998; Queenie: A Story, 1999; Hateship, Friendship, Courtship, Loveship, Marriage: Stories, 2001; No Love Lost, 2003; Runaway: Stories, 2004; Vintage Munro, 2004; Carried Away: A Selection of Stories, 2006; The View from Castle Rock: Stories, 2006; Away From Her, 2007; Alice Munro's Best: Selected Stories, 2008; My Best Stories, 2009; (contrib.) Courting Johanna, 2009; Too Much Happiness: Stories, 2009; New Selected Stories, 2011; Dear Life, 2012. Contributor to books and periodicals. **Address:** Abner Stein Agency, 10 Roland Gardens, London, GL SW7 3PH, England.

MUNRO, Donald J(acques). American (born United States), b. 1931. **Genres:** Philosophy, Adult Non-fiction. **Career:** University of Michigan, assistant professor, 1964-68, Center for Chinese Studies, associate, 1964-, associate professor, 1968-73, professor of philosophy, 1973-96, professor of Chinese, 1991-96, distinguished senior lecturer, 1994-95, professor emeritus of philosophy and of Chinese, 1996-; University of California, Center for Chinese Studies, visiting research philosopher, 1969-70; Stanford University, Evans-Wentz lecturer, 1970; University of Washington, Fritz lecturer, 1980; Trent University, Gilbert Ryle lecturer, 1983; University of Vermont, John Dewey lecturer, 1988-89; Chinese University of Hong Kong, Ch'ien Mu professor, 2002-03. Writer. **Publications:** The Concept of Man in Early China, 1969; The Concept of Man in Contemporary China, 1977; (ed.) Individualism and Holism: The Confucian and Taoist Philosophical Perspectives, Center for Chinese Studies, 1985; Images of Human Nature: A Sung Portrait, 1988; The Imperial Style of Inquiry in Twentieth Century China: The Emergence of New Approaches, 1996; Chinese Ethics for the New Century, 2005; Ethics in Action: Workable Guidelines for Public and Private Choices, 2008. **Address:** International Institute, University of Michigan, 1080 S University Ave., Ste. 2660, Ann Arbor, MI 48109-1106, U.S.A. **Online address:** dmunro@umich.edu

MUNRO, John M(urchison). Cypriot/Lebanese/British (born England), b. 1932. **Genres:** History, Literary Criticism And History, Poetry, Social Sciences, Education, Young Adult Fiction. **Career:** Washington University, part-time instructor in English, 1956-60; University of North Carolina-Chapel Hill, instructor in English, 1960-63; University of Toronto, assistant professor of English, 1963-65; American University of Beirut, associate professor, 1965-68, professor of English, 1968-87, associate dean of arts and sciences, 1970-73, 1987-96; Lebanese University, professor, 1967-80; European Union, MEDA Team, media and culture consultant, 1997-; American University in Cairo, professor of mass communication; University of Malta, part-time visiting professor in human rights and democratisation. Freelance journalist. **Publications:** (With T.Y. Greet and C. Edge) The Worlds of Fiction, 1964; (ed.) English Poetry in Transition, 1880-1920, 1968; Arthur Symons, 1969; The Decadent Poetry of the Eighteen-Nineties, 1970; (with S.B. Bushrui) Images and Memories: A Pictorial Record of the Life and Work of W.B. Yeats, 1970; (ed. with S.B. Bushrui)Chant of Mystics and other Poems, 1970; The Royal Aquarium: Failure of a Victorian Compromise, 1971; Selected Poems of Theo. Marzials, 1974; James Elroy Flecker, 1976; A Mutual Concern: The Story of the American University of Beirut, 1977; The Nairn Way: Desert Bus to Baghdad, 1980; Adnan the Dreamer, 1981; The Road to Jerusalem, 1981; Theater of the Absurd: Lebanon, 1982-88; Cyprus: Between Venus and Mars, A History of the Island from Ancient Times until the Present, 1984; Giesen's Lebanon, 1984; Trade and Peace in the Middle East, 1985; Out on a Wing, 1986; Cotton, 1987; (ed. with K. Beckson) Arthur Symons, Selected Letters, 1880-1935, 1989; Beirut Giesen, 1995; Giesen, 1995. **Address:** Prastio-Evdhimou, Limassol, 1, Cyprus. **Online address:** munro@medateam-eg.org

MUNRO, Mary. *See* **HOWE, Muriel.**

MUNSCH, Robert. Canadian/American (born United States), b. 1945. **Genres:** Children's Fiction, Young Adult Fiction, Humor/Satire, Children's Non-fiction, Picture/Board Books, Literary Criticism And History. **Career:** Bay Area Childcare, teacher, 1973-75; University of Guelph, Family Studies Laboratory Preschool, head teacher and assistant professor, 1975-84; writer, 1984-. **Publications:** The Sandcastle Contest, 1970; I'm so Embarrassed!, 1970; The Mud Puddle, 1979, rev. ed., 1995; The Dark, 1979; The Paper Bag Princess, 1980, rev. ed., 2009; Jonathan Cleaned Up, Then He Heard a Sound or, Blackberry Subway Jam, 1981; The Boy in the Drawer, 1982; Murmel, Murmel, Murmel, 1982; Angela's Airplane, 1983; David's Father, 1983; The Fire Station, 1983; Mortimer, 1983; Millicent and the Wind, 1984; Thomas' Snowsuit, 1985, 2nd ed., 1998; 50 below Zero, 1985; I Have to Go!, 1986; A Promise is a Promise, 1988; Angela's Airplane, 1988; Giant or, Waiting for the Thursday Boat, 1989; Pigs!, 1989; Good Families Don't, 1990; Get Me Another One!, 1992; Moira's Birthday, 1992; Where is Gah-Ning?, 1994; (with S. Askar) From Far Away, 1995; Stephanie's Ponytail, 1996; Something Good, 1997; The Dark, 1997; Alligator Baby, 1998; Aaron's Hair, 1998; Andrew's Loose Tooth, 1998; Get out of Bed!, 1998; Munschworks: The First Munsch Collection, 1998; Love You Forever, 1998; Wait and See, 1998; The Boy in the Drawer, 1998; Show and Tell, 1998; Purple, Green, and Yellow, 1998; Ribbon Rescue, 1999; Munschworks 2: The Second Munsch Treasury, 1999; We Share Everything!, 1999; (with M. Kusugak) Munschworks 3: The Third Munsch Treasury, 2000; Mmm, Cookies!, 2000; Makeup Mess, 2001; (with M. Kusugak) The Munschworks Grand Treasury, 2001; Up, Up, Down!, 2001; Playhouse, 2002; More Pies!, 2002; Zoom!, 2003; Lighthouse: A Story of Remembrance, 2003; Boo!, 2004; Smelly Socks, 2004; Munsch More!, 2004; I'm So Embarrassed, 2006; No Clean Clothes, 2006; Class Clown, 2007; Kiss Me, I'm Perfect, 2008. Contributor of articles to periodicals. **Address:** Writers' Union of Canada, 90 Richmond St. E, Ste. 200, Toronto, ON M5C 1P1, Canada.

MUNSON, Carol Barr Swayze. (Noel Carroll). American (born United States), b. 1944. **Genres:** Mystery/Crime/Suspense. **Career:** Corporate executive, 1982-85. Writer. **Publications:** AS NOEL CAROLL: Accidental Encounter, 1999; Circle of Distrust, 1999; Never by Blood, 2002; Broken Odyssey, 2004; Starve the Devil, 2004; The Exclusion Zone, 2006; Art in Three Dimensions, 2010; Living in an Artworld: Reviews and Essays on Dance, Performance, Theater and the Fine Arts in the 1970s and 1980s, 2012; The Containment Group, forthcoming. **Address:** Allen-Ayers Books, 4621 S Atlantic Ave., Ste. 7603, Ponce Inlet, FL 32127, U.S.A. **Online address:** noelcarroll@worldnetatt.net

MUNSON, Noel J. Also writes as John Barr, Noel Carroll. American (born United States), b. 1938. **Genres:** Novels. **Career:** Pharmaceutical Data Services, vice president and general manager, 1977-78; Pharmaceutical Card Services Inc., chief executive officer, 1978-82; MEDAC Inc., chief executive officer, 1982-85; Allen-Ayers Books, publisher. Writer. **Publications:** AS NOEL CARROLL WITH C.S. MUNSON: Circle of Distrust, 1999; Accidental Encounter, 1999; Hey, God; Got A Minute?, 2002; Never By Blood, 2002; Broken Odyssey, 2004; Starve The Devil, 2004; Exclusion Zone, 2006; If You Can Keep It, 2008; The Containment Group, forthcoming. **Address:** Allen-Ayers Books, 4621 S Atlantic Ave., Ste. 7603, Ponce Inlet, FL 32127, U.S.A. **Online address:** noelcarroll@worldnet.att.net

MUNSON, Ronald. American (born United States), b. 1939. **Genres:** Novels, Philosophy, Medicine/Health. **Career:** Columbia University, preceptor in philosophy; University of California, visiting professor; Harvard Medical School, visiting professor; Johns Hopkins University, School of Medicine, visiting professor; National Institutes of Health, bioethicist; National Cancer Institute, bioethicist; Washington University, School of Medicine, bioethicist; University of Missouri, professor of philosophy of science and medicine; Japanese National Television, consultant. Writer. **Publications:** (Ed. and intro.) Man and Nature; Philosophical Issues in Biology, 1971; The Way of Words: An Informal Logic, 1976; Intervention and Reflection: Basic Issues in Medical Ethics, 1979, 8th ed., 2008; (with D.A. Albert and M.D. Resnik) Reasoning in Medicine: An Introduction to Clinical Inference, 1988; (with D.A. Conway) The Elements of Reasoning, 1990 as Basics of Reasoning, 2001; Nothing Human (novel), 1991; Fan Mail (novel), 1993; Night Vision (novel), 1995;

Raising the Dead: Organ Transplants, Ethics, and Society, 2002; Outcome Uncertain: Cases and Contexts in Bioethics, 2003; The Elements of Reasoning, 2007; The Woman Who Decided to Die: Challenges and Choices at the Edges of Medicine, 2009. Contributor to periodicals. **Address:** Department of Philosophy, University of Missouri, 565 Lucas Hall, 1 University Blvd., St. Louis, MO 63121-4499, U.S.A. **Online address:** munson@umsl.edu

MUNSON, Sam. American (born United States), b. 1981?. **Genres:** Novels. **Career:** Commentary Magazine, online editor. **Publications:** The November Criminals: A Novel, 2010. Contributor to periodicals. **Address:** New York, NY , U.S.A. **Online address:** sam.munson@gmail.com

MURAKAMI, Haruki. Japanese (born Japan), b. 1949. **Genres:** Novels, Novellas/Short Stories, Adult Non-fiction, Young Adult Non-fiction, Translations, Autobiography/Memoirs, Young Adult Fiction, Humanities, Humanities. **Career:** Jazz bar Peter Cat, co-owner and manager, 1974-81; full-time writer, 1981-; Princeton University, visiting fellow in East Asian studies, 1991, associate researcher, 1991-93; Tufts University, writer-in-residence, 1993-95; William Howard Taft University, teacher. **Publications:** NOVELS: Kaze no uta o kike, 1979 as Hear the Wind Sing, 1987; 1973-nen nopinboru, 1980 as Pinball, 1973, 1985; Hitsuji o megaru bōken, 1982, new ed., 1990; Kangarū-biyori, 1983; Sekai no owari to hādo-boirudo wandarando, 1985, new ed., 1990; Noruwei no mori, 1987; Dansu dansu dansu, 1988; Nejimakidorikuronikuru, 1994; South of the Border, West of the Sun, 1999; Supūtoniku no koibito, 1999, as Sputnik Sweetheart, 2002; Hard Boiled Wonderland and the End of the World, 2003. SHORT STORY COLLECTIONS: A Day in the Life: Stories, 1983. COLLECTIONS: Murakami Haruki zensakuhin, 1979-1989, 1991. OTHERS: Murakami Asahidō, 1984; Toshi no fūkeigaku, 1985; Kaiten mokuba nodeddo hīto, 1985; Kaze no uta o kike; 1973-nen no pinbōru, 1990; Tōi taiko, 1990; Murakami Haruki no uta, 1990; Andaguraundo, 1997, as Yakusoku Sareta Basho de, 1998; Kami no kodomotachi wa mina odoru, 2000; (ed.) Murakami Haruki zensakuhin, 1990-2000, 2002; (ed. and intro.) Birthday Stories, 2004; Afutā dāku, 2004; Vintage Murakami, 2004; Zou no shoumetsu, 2005; Tokyo Kitan-Shu, 2005; Blind Willdow, Sleeping Woman: 25 Stories, 2006; (intro.) Rashōmon and Seventeen Other Stories, 2006; (intro.) Ryunosuke Akutagawa, Rashomon and Seventeen Other Stories, 2006; Hashiru koto ni tsuite kataru toki ni boku no kataru koto, 2007; 1Q84: A Novel, 2009. Contributor of articles to books and periodicals. **Address:** Alfred E. Knopf Inc., 201 E 50th St., New York, NY 10022, U.S.A. **Online address:** yuane@lycos.com

MURARKA, Shyam P. American/Indian (born India), b. 1940. **Genres:** Engineering, Technology, Adult Non-fiction. **Career:** Bell Laboratories, supervisor in materials technology, 1972-84; Rensselaer Polytechnic Institute, professor of materials engineering, through 1984, Center for Integrated Electronics and Electronics Manufacturing, associate director, director, 1994-96, New York Sematech Center of Excellence, technical director, SRC Center for Advanced Interconnect Science and Technology, director, Department of Materials Science and Engineering, now professor emeritus. Writer. **Publications:** Silicides for VLSI Applications, 1983; (with M.C. Peckerar) Electronic Materials: Science and Technology, 1989; (ed. with A. Katz and A. Appelbaum) Advanced Metallizations in Microelectronics: Symposium held April 16-20, 1990, 1990; Metallization: Theory and Practice for VLSI and ULSI, 1993; (co-ed.) Advanced Metallization for Devices and Circuits-Science, Technology, and Manufacturability: Symposium held April 4-8, 1994, San Francisco, California, U.S.A., 1994; (co-ed.) Interface Control of Electrical, Chemical, and Mechanical Properties: Symposium held November 29-December3, 1993, Boston, Massachusetts, U.S.A., 1994; (ed. with F.E. Chen) Microelectronics Technology and Process Integration: 20-21 October 1994, 1994; (with J.M. Steigerwald and R.J. Gutmann) Chemical Mechanical Planarization of Microelectronic Materials, 1997; (co-ed.) Advanced Interconnects and Contact Materials and Processes for Future Integrated Circuits: Symposium held April 13-16, 1998, 1998; (with I.V. Verner and R.J. Gutmann) Copper-Fundamental Mechanisms for Microelectronic Applications, 2000. Contributor to scientific journals. **Address:** Low Center for Industrial Innovation, Rensselaer Polytechnic Institute, Rm. 6023, 110 8th St., Troy, NY 12180-3590, U.S.A. **Online address:** murars@rpi.edu

MURAVCHIK, Joshua. American (born United States), b. 1947. **Genres:** Civil Liberties/Human Rights, International Relations/Current Affairs, Politics/Government, History. **Career:** Young People's Socialist League (now Young Social Democrats), national chair, 1968-73; Coalition for a Democratic Majority, executive director, 1974-79, president; freelance writer, 1984-87; Institute of World Politics, adjunct professor, 1992-; Washington Institute for Near East Policy, fellow-in-residence, 1984-87; Johns Hopkins University, Paul H. Nitze School of Advanced International Studies, Foreign Policy Institute, fellow, 2009-. Writer. **Publications:** The Senate and National Security: A New Mood, 1980; Perceptions of Israel in the American Media: Summary of a Conference, 1985; The Uncertain Crusade: Jimmy Carter and Dilemmas of Human Rights Policy, 1986; Nicaragua's Slow March to Communism, 1986; News Coverage of the Sandinista Revolution, 1988; Exporting Democracy: Fulfilling America's Destiny, 1991; U.S. Foreign Policy Options and Australian Interests, 1992; (contrib.) Democracy in the Middle East: Defining the Challenge, 1993; The Imperative of American Leadership: A Challenge to Neo-Isolationism, 1996; Role of Think Tanks, NGOs, and Advocacy Groups in Influencing Public Policy, 1996; Heaven on Earth: The Rise and Fall of Socialism, 2002; Covering the Intifada: How the Media Reported the Palestinian Uprising, 2003; Future of the United Nations: Understanding the Past to Chart a Way Forward, 2005; Next Founders: Voices of Democracy in the Middle East, 2009; Obama's Radical Transformation of America: Year One, 2010. Contributor to newspapers and magazines. **Address:** Foreign Policy Institute, Nitze School of Advanced Intl Studies, Johns Hopkins University, 1619 Massachusetts Ave., NW, Washington, DC 20036, U.S.A. **Online address:** jmuravc1@jhu.edu

MURCHIE, Noël. American (born United States), b. 1935. **Genres:** Travel/Exploration, Autobiography/Memoirs. **Career:** Freelance writer, 1965-; Hawaii School for Girls, high school writing teacher, 1974-77; Seabury Hall, English teacher and running coach, 1983-90. **Publications:** (With P. Ryan) Hawaii: A Running Guide, 1981; The Accidental Hermit (memoir), 2000. Contributor to periodicals. Works appear in anthologies. **Address:** Nine Toes Press, PO Box 444, Orcas, WA 98280, U.S.A. **Online address:** murchie@rockisland.com

MURCHISON, William. American (born United States), b. 1942. **Genres:** Documentaries/Reportage, Politics/Government. **Career:** Dallas Times Herald, reporter and columnist, 1966-73; Dallas Morning News, columnist and associate editor of editorial page, 1973-2001; Texas Republic, editor, 1993-; Baylor University, Radford professor of journalism, 2002-, Radford distinguished professor in journalism; Chronicles, corresponding editor. **Publications:** (With H. Merklein) Those Gasoline Lines and How They Got There, 1980; Reclaiming Morality in America, 1994; (afterword) The Thirty Years War: The Politics of the Sixties Generation, 1995; (with W.F. Buckley) There's More to Life Than Politics, 1998; William Grant Still: A Study in Contradictions, 1999; Mortal Follies: Episcopalians and the Crisis of Mainline Christianity, 2009. **Address:** Department of Journalism, Baylor University, 1 Bear Pl., Ste. 97330, Waco, TX 76798-7330, U.S.A. **Online address:** bill@williammurchison.com

MURCOTT, Anne. British (born England), b. 1941?. **Genres:** History, Sociology, Medicine/Health. **Career:** University of Wales-Swansea, research assistant, 1966-69; University of Wales-Cardiff, lecturer, senior lecturer, 1971-91; Sociology of Health and Illness: A Journal of Medical Sociology, editor, 1983-87; University of London, School of Hygiene and Tropical Medicine, senior lecturer, 1991-94, honorary visiting professor; South Bank University, professor of the sociology of health, 1994-, now professor emeritus; University of Nottingham, Institute for Science and Society, Faculty of Social Sciences, special professor; Food Standards Agency, chair. Writer. **Publications:** (Co-author) Power, Persistence and Change: A Second Study of Banbury, 1975; (with S. Mennell and A.H. van Otterloo) The Sociology of Food: Eating, Diet, and Culture, 1992. EDITOR: (with P. Atkinson and R. Dingwall) Prospects for the National Health, 1979; The Sociology of Food and Eating: Essays on the Sociological Significance of Food, 1983; Nation's Diet: The Social Science of Food Choice, 1998; (with R.G. Burgess) Developments in Sociology, 2001; Sociology and Medicine: Selected Essays by P.M. Strong, 2006. Works appear in anthologies. **Address:** Institute for Science and Society, University of Nottingham, Rm. B115, Law and Social Sciences Bldg., University Pk., Nottingham, NT NG7 2RD, England. **Online address:** anne.murcott@nottingham.ac.uk

MURDERERS, Medieval. *See* **MORSON, Ian.**

MURDOCH, Brian (Oliver). British (born England), b. 1944. **Genres:** Literary Criticism And History, Theology/Religion. **Career:** University of Glasgow, lecturer in German, 1968-70; University of Illinois, assistant professor of German, 1970-72; University of Stirling, lecturer, 1972-, senior lecturer, through 1991, professor of German, 1991-, now professor emeritus; Cambridge University, visiting fellow, 1989; Oxford University, visiting fellow 1994, 2002. Writer. **Publications:** The Fall of Man in the Early Middle High German Biblical Epic, 1972; The Recapitulated Fall, 1974; The Irish Adam and Eve Story from Saltair na Rann, vol. II: Commentary, 1976; (with J.S. Groseclose) Diealthochdeutschen poetischen Denkmaeler, 1976; Hans Folz and the Adam Legends, 1977; (with M. Read) Siegfried Lenz, 1978; Old High German Literature, 1983; Kudrun: A New Translation, 1987; Fighting Songs and Warring Words, 1989; Walthari: A Verse Translation of the Medieval Latin Waltharius, 1989; Remarque: Im Westen nichts Neues, 1991, 2nd ed., 1995; Cornish Literature, 1993; The Germanic Hero, 1996; Adam's Grace, 2000; (with J. Tasioulas) The Apocryphal Lives of Adam and Eve, 2002; The Medieval Popular Bible, 2004; German Literature of the Early Middle Ages, 2004; Novels of Erich Maria Remarque: Sparks of Life, 2006; The Apocryphal Adam and Eve, 2009. EDITOR: (and contrib. with D. Wells and R. Wisbey) Concordances to the Early Middle High German Biblical Epic, 1976; (with L. Jillings) Martin Luther: Selections, 1977; (with M.G. Ward) Studies in Modern Austrian Literature, 1981; (with M.G. Ward) Studies in 19th Century Austrian Literature, 1983; E.M. Remarque, Im Westen nichts Neues, 1984, rev. ed., 1988; S. Zweig, Schachnovelle, 1986; (with W. Kidd) Memory and Memorials: The Commemorative Century, 2004; (with M. Read) Early Germanic Literature and Culture, 2004; Perspectives -All Quiet on the Western Front, 2010. TRANSLATOR: E.M. Remarque, All Quiet on the Western Front, 1993; (ed.) Dedalus Book of Medieval Literature: The Grin of the Gargoyle, 1995; M. Pressler, Shylock's Daughter, 2001; M. Pressler, Malka, 2002. Work appear in anthologies. Contributor to journals and magazines. **Address:** School of Arts, School of Languages, Cultures & Religions, University of Stirling, Stirling, CN FK9 4LA, Scotland. **Online address:** b.o.murdoch@stir.ac.uk

MURDOCH, David H. (David Hamilton Murdoch). British (born England), b. 1937. **Genres:** History, Film, Social Sciences. **Career:** University of Leeds, assistant lecturer, 1964-67, lecturer, 1967-91, senior lecturer in history, 1991-95, principal teaching fellow, 1995-; Northern Universities American Studies Group, staff, 1976-87; British Broadcasting Corporation Television, consultant, 1984, 1986, 2002; National Association of Foreign Study Advisers, 1987. Writer. **Publications:** (Ed.) Rebellion in America: A Contemporary British Viewpoint, 1765-1783, 1979; Cowboy, 1993; North American Indian, 1995; The American West: The Invention of a Myth, 2001. **Address:** Department of History, University of Leeds, Woodhouse Ln., Leeds, WY LS2 9JT, England.

MURDOCH, David Hamilton. *See* **MURDOCH, David H.**

MURDOCH, Lydia. American (born United States), b. 1970?. **Genres:** History, Social Sciences, Sociology. **Career:** Vassar College, associate professor of history. Writer. **Publications:** Imagined Orphans: Poor Families, Child Welfare, and Contested Citizenship in London, 2006. **Address:** Department of History, Vassar College, 124 Raymond Ave., PO Box 711, Poughkeepsie, NY 12604-0001, U.S.A.

MURDOCH, Norman H. American (born United States), b. 1939. **Genres:** History, Theology/Religion. **Career:** University of Cincinnati, instructor, 1968-92, assistant professor, 1972-86, professor of history, 1992-, professor emeritus, 2004-; University of Zimbabwe, research associate, 1998; Westmont College, lecturer, 1999. Writer. **Publications:** A Centennial History: The Salvation Army in Cincinnati, 1885-1985, 1985; (comp. and intro.) Bicentennial Addresses on the United States Constitution and the Northwest Ordinance, 1988; Origins of the Salvation Army, 1994; Frank Smith: Salvationist Socialist (1854-1940): Principal Ideologue of the Darkest England Scheme that Created Salvation Army Social Services, 2003; Soldiers of the Cross, Pioneers of Social Change: Susie Swift and David Lamb, 2006. Contributor to journals. **Address:** Department of Humanities & Social Sciences, University of Cincinnati, 5750 Sterling Creek Rd., Jacksonville, OR 97530, U.S.A. **Online address:** murdocnh@ucmail.uc.edu

MURDOCK, Linda. American (born United States) **Genres:** Food And Wine, Mystery/Crime/Suspense, Local History/Rural Topics. **Career:** Bond [illegible], 1986-88; Accuracy First Printing, owner, 1988-2009; Bellwether Books, writer, 2001-. **Publications:** A Busy Cook's Guide to Spices: How to Introduce New Flavors to Everyday Meals, 2001; Almost Native How to Pass as a Coloradan, 2004; Mystery Lover's Puzzle Book, Crosswords with Clues from Your Favorite Mystery Series, 2007; A Busy Cook's Guide to Flavor-Packed Cookies and Bars, 2010. **Address:** Bellwether Books, PO Box 9757, Denver, CO 80209, U.S.A. **Online address:** murd@bellwetherbooks.com

MURDY, Louise Baughan. American (born United States), b. 1935. **Genres:** Literary Criticism And History, Poetry. **Career:** Florida State University, instructor in humanities and English, 1962-63; Winthrop College, part-time assistant professor, 1963-70, part-time associate professor, 1970-74; Winthrop University, associate professor of English, 1974-, associate professor emeritus, 1997-. Writer. **Publications:** Sound and Sense in Dylan Thomas's Poetry, 1966. **Address:** Department Of English, Winthrop University, 250 Bancroft Hall, Rock Hill, SC 29733, U.S.A.

MURKOFF, Bruce. American (born United States), b. 1953?. **Genres:** Novels, Young Adult Non-fiction, History. **Career:** Screenwriter and novelist. **Publications:** (With L. Koenig) Lady against the Odds, 1992; Waterborne: A Novel, 2004; Red Rain, 2010. **Address:** c/o Author Mail, Alfred A. Knopf Inc., 1745 Broadway, New York, NY 10019, U.S.A.

MURKOFF, Heidi Eisenberg. American (born United States), b. 1958?. **Genres:** Human Relations/Parenting, Film. **Career:** The What to Expect Foundation, co-founder and president. Writer. **Publications:** WITH A. EISENBERG AND S.E. HATHAWAY: The Special Guest Cookbook: Elegant Menus and Recipes for Those Who Are Allergic to Certain Foods, Bland Dieters/Calorie Counters, Cholesterol Conscious, Diabetic/Hypoglycemic, Kosher/Milk Sensitive, Ovolacto Vegetarian, Pritikin Proselytes, Salt-Avoiding, Strictly Vegetarian, 1982; What to Expect when You're Expecting, 1984, (with S. Mazel) 4th ed., 2008; What to Eat When You're Expecting, 1986; What to Expect the First Year, 1989, 2nd. ed., 2003; What to Expect the Toddler Years, 1994. FOR CHILDREN: WHAT TO EXPECT KIDS SERIES: What to Expect at Bedtime, 2000; What to Expect When the Babysitter Comes, 2000; What to Expect when You Go to the Doctor, 2000; What to Expect when Mommy's Having an Baby, 2000; What to Expect when You Use the Potty, 2000; What to Expect when the New Baby Comes Home, 2001; What to Expect at Preschool, 2001; What to Expect at a Play Date, 2001; (with L. Rader) What to Expect when You Go to Kindergarten, 2002; What to Expect When You Go to the Dentist, 2002; OTHERS: (with S. Mazel) What to Expect Baby-Sitter's Handbook, 2003; (with S. Mazel) What to Expect: Eating Well When You're Expecting, 2005; (with S. Mazel) What to Expect Before You're Expecting, 2009; (with S. Mazel) What to Expect the Second Year: From 12 to 24 Months, 2011. **Address:** The What to Expect Foundation, 211 W 80th St., Lower Level, New York, NY 10024, U.S.A.

MURNANE, Gerald. Australian (born Australia), b. 1939. **Genres:** Novels, Novellas/Short Stories, Natural History, Young Adult Fiction. **Career:** Victorian Education Department, publications officer, through 1973; Deakin University, senior lecturer in fiction writing. Writer and educator. **Publications:** Tamarisk Row, 1974; A Lifetime on Clouds, 1976; The Plains, 1985, rev. ed., 2001 in US as The Plains, 2003 in Sweden as Slatterna, 2005; Landscape with Landscape, 1987; Inland, 1988; Velvet Waters, 1990; (ed. with J. Lee and P. Mead) Temperament of Generations: Fifty Years of Writing in Meanjin, 1990; Emerald Blue, 1995; Invisible Yet Enduring Lilacs, 2005; Barley Patch, 2009. **Address:** 2 Falcon St., Macleod, VI 3085, Australia.

MURPHEY, Cecil B(laine). Also writes as Celia Blaine, Joan Masters, Melanie Harwood. American (born United States), b. 1933. **Genres:** Novels, inspirational/Motivational Literature, Self Help, Autobiography/Memoirs, Ghost Writer. **Career:** Writer. **Publications:** INSPIRATIONAL AND SELF-HELP: Prayer: Pitfalls and Possibilities, 1975; Put On A Happy Faith!, 1976; But God Has Promised, 1976; Somebody Knows I'm Alive, 1977; How to Live a Christian Life, 1977; When in Doubt, Hug 'Em!: How To Develop A Caring Church, 1978; Prayerobics, Getting Started and Staying Going, 1979; Comforting Those Who Grieve, 1979; Getting There from Here: Helps On Divine Guidance, 1981; Seven Daily Sins (And What to Do About Them), 1981; Spaceship Earth, 1981; Devotions for Joggers, 1982; Devotions for Calorie Counters, 1982; Devotions for Lovers, 1982; Devotions for Travelers, 1982; Devotions for Worriers, 1982; Fitness: The Answer Book, 1983; (with J. Miller) Headaches: The Answer Book, 1983; Devotions for Winners, 1983; Devotions for Grandparents, 1983; (as Joan Masters) Devotions for Nurses, 1983; Press On: A Disciple's Guide to Spiritual Growth, 1983; (with A. D'Souza) Being a Leader, [illegible]; (with M. Youssef) The Leadership Style of Jesus, 1986; (with A. D'Souza) Leading Others, 1986; (with A. D'Souza) Leading Effectively Leader, 1986; (with P. Spitz) Good People Die on Sunday, 1986; Another Chance: Learning To Like Yourself, 1987; (with M. Youssef) He-ism versus Me-ism, 1987; Day to Day: Spiritual Help When Someone You Love Has Alzheimer's, 1988; Keeping My Balance: Spiritual Help When Someone I Love Abuses Drugs, 1988; Breaking the Silence: Spiritual Help When Someone You Love Is Mentally Ill, 1989; (with S. Billigmeier) Inner Eating: How to Free Yourself Forever from the Tyranny of Good, 1991; Man Talk: Resources for Exploring Male Issues, 1991; (with R. Breland) In Search of a Lovely Moment, 1991; (with L. Bueno) Fast Your Way to Health, 1991; (with B. Carson) Think Big: Unleashing Your Potential, 1992; (with J.C. Robertson) Help Yourself: A Revolutionary Alternative Recovery Program, 1992; (with J.C. Robertson) Kids Don't Want to Use Drugs: How You and Your Kids Can Avoid the Dangers, 1992; (with J.C. Robertson) The Help Yourself Love Yourself Non Diet Weight-Loss Plan, 1992; Invading the Privacy of God, 1997; (with J. Kuzma) Live 10 Healthy Years Longer, 2000; My Parents My Children: Spiritual Help For Caregivers, 2000; Simply Living: Modern Wisdom From The Ancient Book Of Proverbs, 2001; Seeking God's Hidden Face: When God Seems Absent, 2001; God: More than a Name, 2001; The God Who Pursues: Encountering A Relentless God, 2002; (with S. Chand) Futuring: Leading Your Church Into Tomorrow, 2002; The Relentless God, 2003; (with S. Chand) Who's Holding Your Ladder?: Selecting Your Leaders-Leadership's Most Critical Decision, 2003; Committed But Flawed: Finding Fresh Ways to Grow Spiritually, 2004; Aging Is An Attitude: Positive Ways To Look At Getting Older, 2005; When Someone You Love Has Alzheimer's, 2004; When Someone You Love Abuses Drugs or Alcohol, 2004; When Someone You Love Suffers from Depression or Mental Illness, 2004; (with S. Chand) Who Moved My Ladder?, 2004; (with J. Meyer) Battlefield of the Mind Daily Devotional: Insights That Will Change the Way You Think, 2005; (with S. Thomas) The Immortality of Influence, 2006; (with D. Piper) Daily Devotions Inspired By 90 Minutes In Heaven: 90 Readings For Hope And Healing, 2006; Heaven is Real: Lessons On Earthly Joy From The Man Who Spent 90 Minutes In Heaven, 2007; (with V. Garberding) Please Get to Know Me, 2008; When Someone You Love Has Cancer: Comfort and Encouragement for Caregivers and Loved Ones, 2009; When God Turned off the Lights: True Stories of Seeking God in the Darkness, 2009; (with M. Gibson) Christmas Miracles, 2009; Words of Comfort for Times of Loss, 2010; (with M. Loehr) Who's Got Your Back?, 2010; When a Man You Love was Abused: A Woman's Guide to Helping Him Overcome Childhood Sexual Molestation, 2010; Hope and Comfort for Every Season, 2010; Knowing God, Knowing Myself, 2010; (with D. Piper) Getting to Heaven: Departing Instructions for Your Life Now, 2011; When Someone You Love No Longer Remembers, 2011; (with M. Gibson) The Spirit of Christmas, 2011, Unleash the Writer Within, 2011; (with T. Belk) Because You Care: Spiritual Encouragement for Caregivers, 2012; Making Sense When Life Doesn't: The Secrets of Thriving in Tough Times, 2012. CO-AUTHOR: AUTOBIOGRAPHIES: (with B.J. Thomas) In Tune, 1982; (with S. Cottrell) No Mountain Too High, 1984; (with V. Barfield) Woman on Death Row, 1985; (with L. Vaschenko) Cry Freedom: The Story of Lida Vaschenko and Her Remarkable Escape from Soviet Russia, 1987; (with S.T. Cathy) It's Easier to Succeed than to Fail, 1989; (with N.D. Vaughan) With Byrd at the Bottom of the World: The South Pole Expedition of 1928-1930, 1990; (with B. Carson) Gifted Hands: The Ben Carson Story, 1990; (with D. Kartsonakis) Dino: Behind the Glitz and Glamour: An Autobiography, 1990; (with B. Carson and N. Aaseng) Ben Carson, 1992; (with U. McCullough-Innocent) Something Special: The Story of Ullanda Innocent, 1994; (with N.D. Vaughan) My Life of Adventure, 1995; (with F. Graham) Rebel with a Cause, 1995; (with S. Chand) Failure: The Womb of Success, 1999; (with B. Sanidad) Choosing to Live, 2001; (with S. Thomas-El) I Choose to Stay: A Black Teacher Refuses To Desert The Inner City, 2003; (with D.Wilkins) United by Tragedy: A Father's Story, 2003; (with L. Harris) It All Starts at Home: 15 Ways to Put Family First, 2004; (with D. Piper) 90 Minutes in Heaven: A True Story Of Death & Life, 2004; (with S. Alexander) Touchdown Alexander, 2006; (with E.L. Long) 60 Seconds to Greatness: Seize the Moment and Plan for Success, 2010. OTHERS: (ed.) Encyclopedia of Christian Marriage, 1984; (ed.) Encyclopedia for Today's Christian Woman, 1984; (comp.) The Dictionary of Biblical Literacy, 1989; 1001 Things You Need to Know About the Bible, 1991; (with J. Rogers) A Touch of Georgia: Where to Go and What to Do in the Peach State, 1996; (co-author) The Bible A to Z, 1998; 4,000 Questions, Answers, and Puzzles from the Bible, 1999; (with A. Ross) Beyond World Class: Transforming Companies Through Value-based Leadership, 2001; (with A. Ross) Unconditional Excellence: Answering God's Call To Be Your Professional Best, 2002. NOVELS: (as Melanie Haywood) One Day I'll Find You, 1985; (as Celia Blaine) Return to Maradadi, 1985; Star Crossed Love, 1985; (as Celia Blaine) Love's Broken Promises, 1985; (as Melanie Haywood) Rendezvous in Acapulco, 1985; Destined to Love, 1985; (as Celia Blaine) Forbidden Past, 1985; (as Melanie Haywood) Promises to Keep, 1985; Appointment in Zurich, 1985; Romance at Sunrise, 1985; (as Melanie Haywood) Sorrow, the Seed of Love, 1985; (with M. Youssef) Master Mind, 1989, rev. ed. as The Voice: A Novel of the New World Order, 1991; (with M. Youssef) Earth King, 1989, rev. ed. as Man of Peace: A Novel of the Antichrist, 1992; Happy Face (children's fiction), 1990; Happy Face Again (children's fiction), 1991; (with E. Bailey) Mr. Dream Merchant, 1998; Everybody Loved Roger Harden: An Everybody's a Suspect Mystery, 2008; Everybody Wanted Room 623: An Everybody's a Suspect Mystery, 2008; Everybody Called Her a Saint: An Everybody's a Suspect Mystery, 2008. Contributor to periodicals. **Address:** c/o Deidre Knight, PO Box 550648, Atlanta, GA 30355, U.S.A. **Online address:** cec_haraka@msn.com

MURPHEY, Rhoads. American (born United States), b. 1919. **Genres:** Geography, History, Social Sciences. **Career:** University of Washington, assistant professor, 1952-55, associate professor, 1955-60, professor of geography, 1960-64; University of Pennsylvania, visiting professor, 1957-58; Journal of Asian Studies, editor, 1959-65; Association for Asian Studies, board director, 1959-70, 1973, executive secretary, 1976-, president, 1987; Association of American Geographers, councillor, 1963-66; University of Michigan, professor of geography, 1964-, Center for Chinese Studies, director, 1969-76, professor of Asian studies and geography, professor of history, 1982-, professor emeritus of history, 1996-; Cambridge University, St. John's College, fellow, 1966-67; Citizens to Change U.S. China Policy, founder and director, 1970-72. **Publications:** Shanghai: Key to Modern China, 1953; An Introduction to Geography, 1961, 4th ed., 1978; (co-author) A New China Policy, 1965; The Scope of Geography, 1966, 3rd ed., 1982; (ed. with A. Feuerwerker and M.C. Wright) Approaches to Modern Chinese History, 1967; The Treaty Ports and China's Modernization: What Went Wrong?, 1970; (co-author) Experiment Without Precedent: The New China, 1972; (ed. with M. Meisner) The Mozartian Historian: Essays on the Works of Joseph R. Levenson, 1976; The Outsiders: The Western Experience in India and China, 1977; Patterns on the Earth: An Introduction to Geography, 1978; The Fading of the Maoist Vision: City and Country in China's Development, 1980; (co-author) The Chinese, 1986; China: In the Global Community, 1988; A History of Asia, 1992, 6th ed., 2009; Fifty Years of China to Me: Personal Recollections of 1942-1992, 1994; East Asia: A New History, 1997, 5th ed., 2010; Tale of the Curlew, 2001. **Address:** Department of History, University of Michigan, 1029 Tisch Hall, 435 S State St., Ann Arbor, MI 48109-1003, U.S.A.

MURPHY, Austin. American (born United States), b. 1961?. **Genres:** Novels, Adult Non-fiction, Sports/Fitness, Education. **Career:** Sports Illustrated, senior writer, 1984-; Bucks County Courier Times, sports reporter; Illinois Chronicle, sports reporter. **Publications:** (Ed. with P.C. Empie) Papal Primacy and the Universal Church, 1974; (co-ed.) Teaching Authority and Infallibility in the Church, 1980; Scientific Investment Analysis, 1994; The Super Bowl: Sport's Greatest Championship, 1998; The Sweet Season: A Sportswriter Rediscovers Football, Family, and a Bit of Faith at Minnesota's St. John's University, 2001; How Tough Could It Be?: The Trials and Errors of a Sportswriter Turned Stay-at-Home Dad, 2004; Saturday Rules: A Season with Trojans and Domers (and Gators and Buckeyes and Wolverines), 2007; Scientific Investment Analysis, 5th ed., 2008, 7th ed., 2010; (with D. Phinney) The Happiness of Pursuit, 2011. Contributor to magazines. **Address:** Sports Illustrated, 135 W 50th St., New York, NY 10020, U.S.A.

MURPHY, C. L. *See* **LAWRENCE, Steven C.**

MURPHY, Claire Rudolf. American (born United States), b. 1951. **Genres:** Children's Fiction, Young Adult Fiction, Children's Non-fiction, History, Mythology/Folklore, Novels, Literary Criticism And History, Social Commentary, Social Commentary. **Career:** St. Mary's Mission High School, teacher of English and drama, 1974-77; Fairbanks Borough School District, secondary school teacher of English and drama, 1977-83; Fairbanks Correctional Center, writing instructor, 1984-89; Alaska State Writing Consortium, teaching consultant, 1984-98; University of Alaska, instructor in composition, 1990-91; freelance writer, 1991-; Eastern Washington University, creative writing instructor, 1999-. **Publications:** Friendship Across Arctic Waters: Alaskan Cub Scouts Visit Their Soviet Neighbors, 1991; (reteller) The Prince and the Salmon People, 1993; (with C. Mason) A Child's Alaska (photo essay), 1994; Gold Star Sister (novel), 1994; Caribou Girl (picture book), 1997; (with J.G. Haigh) Gold Rush Women, 1997; (with J.G. Haigh) Children of the Gold Rush, 2000; (with J. Haigh) Gold Rush Dogs, 2001; Gold Rush Winter, 2002; (co-author) Daughters of the Desert: Stories of Remarkable Women from Christian, Jewish and Muslim Traditions, 2003; Children of Alcatraz: Growing Up on the Rock, 2006. YOUNG ADULT NOVELS: To the Summit, 1992; Free Radical, 2002. OTHERS: I Am Sacajawea, I Am York: Our Journey West with Lewis and Clark, 2005; Marching with Aunt Susan: Susan B. Anthony and the Fight for Women's Suffrage, 2011. Contributor to periodicals. **Address:** 1512 E 19th Ave., Spokane, WA 99203, U.S.A. **Online address:** info@clairerudolfmurphy.com

MURPHY, Cullen. (John Cullen Murphy). American (born United States), b. 1952. **Genres:** Essays, History, Law, Adult Non-fiction. **Career:** Wilson Quarterly, senior editor, 1977-84; Atlantic Monthly, managing editor, 1985-2002, editor, 2002-06; Vanity Fair, editor-at-large, 2006-. **Publications:** (With W. Rathje) Rubbish!: The Archaeology of Garbage, Harper, 1992; Just Curious, 1995; The Word According to Eve: Women and the Bible in Ancient Times and Our Own, 1999; Are We Rome?: The Fall of An Empire and the Fate of America, 2007. **Address:** Vanity Fair Magazine, 375 Faunce Corner Rd. N, Dartmouth, MA 02747, U.S.A.

MURPHY, Dervla Mary. American/Irish (born Ireland), b. 1931. **Genres:** Politics/Government, Travel/Exploration, History, Education. **Career:** Writer, 1952-. **Publications:** Full Tilt: Ireland to India With a Bicycle, 1965; Tibetan Foothold, 1966, rev. ed., 1969; The Waiting Land: A Spell in Nepal, 1967; In Ethiopia with a Mule, 1968; On a Shoestring to Coorg: An Experience of South India, 1976; Where the Indus Is Young: A Winter in Baltistan, 1977; A Place Apart, 1978; Wheels within Wheels: Autobiography, 1979, 2nd ed., 1980; Race to the Finish?: The Nuclear Stakes, 1981; Nuclear Stakes, Race to the Finish, 1982; Eight Feet in the Andes, 1983; Changing the Problem: Post-forum Reflections, 1984; Muddling through in Madagascar, 1985; Ireland, 1985; Tales from the Two Cities: Travels of Another Sort, 1987; Cameroon with Egbert, 1989; Transylvania and Beyond (travel), 1992; The Ukimwi Road: From Kenya to Zimbabwe, 1993; South from the Limpopo: Travels Through South Africa, 1997; Visiting Rwanda, 1998; One Foot in Laos, 2001; Through the Embers of Chaos: A Balkan Journey, 2002; Through Siberia by Accident: A Small Slice of Autobiography, 2005; (intro.) Turkestan Solo: A Journey Through Central Asia, 2005; Silverland: A Winter Journey Beyond the Urals, 2007; Island that Dared: Journeys in Cuba, 2008. Contributor to magazines and newspapers. **Address:** The Old Market, Lismore, WA 1111, Ireland.

MURPHY, Garth. American/Australian (born Australia) **Genres:** Novels, Romance/Historical. **Career:** Writer and historian. **Publications:** The Indian Lover, 2002. **Address:** c/o Author Mail, Simon Schuster, 1230 Ave. of the Americas, New York, NY 10020, U.S.A. **Online address:** garth@theindianlover.com

MURPHY, (Gavin) Martin (Hedd). British (born England), b. 1934. **Genres:** Classics, History, Theology/Religion, Biography, Translations, Philosophy. **Career:** Benedictine monk of Downside Abbey, 1955-61; teacher of classics, 1962-72; Pergamon Press, chief educational editor, 1972-75; freelance writer and teacher, 1975-; New Dictionary of National Biography, research associate, 1997-2004. **Publications:** (Trans.) From Constantine to Charlemagne, 1960; Stories from Ovid, 1971; The Roman Catholic Church, 1976; Blanco White: Self-Banished Spaniard, 1989; St. Gregory's College, Seville, 1592-1767, 1992. EDITOR: Metamorphoses XI, 1972; The Journey of Twelve Students from St. Omers to Seville, 1622, Camden Miscellany XXXII, 1994. Contributor of articles to journals. **Address:** Milton Manor, Abingdon, OX OX14 4EN, England.

MURPHY, Gordon J. American (born United States), b. 1927. **Genres:** Engineering, Information Science/Computers, Technology. **Career:** Milwaukee School of Engineering, assistant professor, 1949-51; General Motors Corp., AC Electronics Division, systems engineer, 1951-52; University of Minnesota, assistant professor, 1956-57; Northwestern University, associate professor, 1957-60, Department of Electrical Engineering and Computer Science, chairman, 1960-69, professor, 1960-97, professor emeritus, 1997-; IPC Systems Inc., president, 1973-2005, The Laboratory for the Design of Electronic Systems, director, 1987-97. Writer. **Publications:** Basic Automatic Control Theory, 1957, 2nd ed., 1966; Control Engineering, 1959. **Address:** Technological Institute, Northwestern University, Rm. M386, 2145 Sheridan Rd., Evanston, IL 60208-0834, U.S.A. **Online address:** murphy@ece.northwestern.edu

MURPHY, Gregory L(eo). American (born United States) **Genres:** Psychology, Writing/Journalism, Sciences, Medicine/Health. **Career:** Bell Laboratories, technical staff, 1984; Brown University, assistant professor, associate professor, 1982-91; University of Illinois, associate professor, professor, 1991-2001; New York University, professor of psychology, 2001-. Writer. **Publications:** The Big Book of Concepts, 2002. Contributor to periodicals and journals. **Address:** Department of Psychology, New York University, Rm. 550, 6 Washington Pl., New York, NY 10003-6603, U.S.A. **Online address:** gregory.murphy@nyu.edu

MURPHY, Haughton. *See* **DUFFY, James H(enry).**

MURPHY, James Bernard. American (born United States), b. 1958. **Genres:** Ethics, Philosophy, Politics/Government, Law, Social Sciences. **Career:** Dartmouth College, Department of Government, assistant professor, 1990-96, associate professor, 1996-2005, professor, 2005-, Master of Arts in Liberal Studies, adjunct professor, 1995-, Daniel Webster Program, faculty director, 2008-. Writer. **Publications:** The Moral Economy of Labor: Aristotelian Themes in Economic Theory, 1993; (ed. with R.O. Brooks) Aristotle and Modern Law, 2003; Philosophy of Positive Law: Foundations of Jurisprudence, 2005; (ed. with A. Perreau-Saussine) The Nature of Customary Law, 2007. **Address:** Department of Government, Dartmouth College, 206 Silsby Hall HB 6108, Hanover, NH 03755, U.S.A. **Online address:** james.b.murphy@dartmouth.edu

MURPHY, James H. American (born United States), b. 1960. **Genres:** Literary Criticism And History. **Career:** Castleknock College, English teacher, 1985-89; St Patrick's College, visiting lecturer in English, 1989-98; All Hallows College, director of adult education, 1984-85, Department of English, lecturer in English and head, 1991-2001, director of post-graduate research, 1991-2001; DePaul University, visiting associate professor of English, 2001-04, associate professor of English, 2004-06, professor of English, 2006-, director of Irish studies, 2005-08; University of Oxford, Greyfriars Hall, visiting fellow, 2007-08. Writer. **Publications:** Catholic Fiction and Social Reality in Ireland, 1873-1922, 1997; Abject Loyalty: Nationalism and Monarchy in Ireland during the Reign of Queen Victoria, 2001; Ireland, a Social, Cultural and Literary History, 1791-1891, 2003; The Red Earl in Ireland, forthcoming. EDITOR: (and intro.) No Bland Facility: Selected Writings on Literature, Religion and Censorship, 1991; New Beginnings in Ministry, 1992; Nos Autem: Castleknock College and Its Contribution, 1996; (with M. Kelleher) Gender Perspectives in Nineteenth-Century Ireland: Public and Private Spheres, 1997; (and intro.) Marcella Grace, 2001; (with E.A. Taylor-Fitz Simon) The Irish Revival Reappraised, 2003; Evangelicals and Catholics in Nineteenth-Century Ireland, 2005. **Address:** Department of English, College of Liberal Arts & Sciences, DePaul University, McGaw Hall, 802 W Belden Ave., Chicago, IL 60614, U.S.A.

MURPHY, James S. American (born United States), b. 1934. **Genres:** Economics, Self Help, Business/Trade/Industry. **Career:** Allied Chemical Inc., staff, 1962-70; Sperry & Hutchinson, assistant, 1970-71; W.R. Grace, manager of long range and economic planning, 1971-73; Bowater Inc., director of corporate development, 1973-83; Cogit Consulting Group, partner, 1983-86; London International U.S. Holdings, vice president, 1986-89; Technology Catalysts International Corp., director of U.S. marketing, 1989-91; Advanced Gas Technologies, director, 1991-, Little Ones Inc., director, 1991-, NGT Equipment, director, 1991-. Writer. **Publications:** The Condom Industry in the United States, 1990. Contributor to journals. **Address:** 3611 Mallow Dr., Ormond Beach, FL 32174, U.S.A.

MURPHY, Jill (Frances). British (born England), b. 1949. **Genres:** Children's Fiction, Illustrations, Novels, Picture/Board Books, Humor/Satire, Horror, Animals/Pets. **Career:** Freelance writer and illustrator, 1976-. **Publications:** WORST WITCH SERIES: The Worst Witch, 1974; The Worst Witch Strikes Again, 1980; A Bad Spell for the Worst Witch, 1982; The Worst Witch All at Sea, 1993; (with R. Griffiths) The Worst Witch's Spelling Book, 1995; Adventures of the Worst Witch, 1996; The Worst Witch Saves the Day, 2005; The Worst Witch to the Rescue, 2007; The Worst Witch Collection, 2007. LARGE FAMILY SERIES: Peace at Last, 1980; Five Minutes' Peace, 1986; A Piece of Cake, 1989; A Quiet Night In, 1993; Mr. Large in Charge, 2005; Lester Learns a Lesson, 2008; Lucy Meets Mr. Chilly, 2008; Grandpa in Trouble, 2009; Sebastian's Sleepover, 2009. NOVELS: Worlds Apart, 1988;

Geoffrey Strangeways, 1990 as Jeffrey Strangeways, 1992; Dear Hound, 2009. OTHERS: My Teddy, 1973; On the Way Home, 1982, rev. ed., 2007; Whatever Next!, 1983 as What Next, Baby Bear!, 1984; Mrs. Bear, 1985; Baby Bear, 1985; The Christmas Babies, 1992; The Last Noo-noo, 1995; All Aboard, 1996; The Large Family Collection, 2000; All for One, 2002; Mother Knows Best, 2011. SELF-ILLUSTRATED: All in One Piece, 1987; The Worst Witch at Sea, 1995; The Worst Witch in Trouble, 2007; The Worst Witch at School, 2007. **Address:** Penguin Books Ltd., 80 Strand, London, GL WC2R 0RL, England.

MURPHY, John C. American (born United States), b. 1947. **Genres:** Zoology. **Career:** Plainfield School District 202, teacher and head of science department, 1974-; Field Museum of Natural History, Division of Amphibians and Reptiles, research associate; Chicago Herpetological Society, president; Writer. **Publications:** Amphibians and Reptiles of Trinidad and Tobago, 1997; (with R.W. Henderson) Tales of Giant Snakes: A Historical Natural History of Anacondas and Pythons, 1997; Homalopsid Snakes: Evolution in the Mud, 2007. **Address:** 15824 Weather Vane Way, Plainfield, IL 60544, U.S.A. **Online address:** fordonia1@comcast.net

MURPHY, John Cullen. *See* **MURPHY, Cullen.**

MURPHY, Joseph E. American (born United States), b. 1930. **Genres:** Money/Finance, Travel/Exploration, Business/Trade/Industry. **Career:** Midwest Communications Inc., director, 1956-87, vice-chairman, 1986-89, chairman, 1990-92; Woodard Elwood & Co., Investment Research and Financial Analysis, director, corporate secretary, 1961-67; Northwestern National Bank, vice-president, 1967-83. Writer. **Publications:** Adventure beyond the Clouds: How We Climbed China's Highest Mountain-and Survived! (juvenile), 1986; With Interest: How to Profit from Interest Rate Fluctuations, 1987; Stock Market Probability: How to Improve the Odds of Making Better Investment Decisions, 1988, rev. ed. as Stock Market Probability: Using Statistics to Predict and Optimize Investment Outcomes, 1994; The Random Character of Interest Rates: Applying Statistical Probability to the Bond Markets, 1990, rev. ed., 2001; South to the Pole by Ski, 1990; To the Poles by Ski and Dogsled, 1996; Bond Tables of Probable Future Yields, 1996; (ed.) The Random Character of Corporate Earnings, 1997; Taklamakan, 1997; Corporate Compliance: After Caremark, 1997; Bond Tables of Probable Future Prices, 1997; Bond Tables of Probable Future Returns, 1997; Why the Stock Market Rises: A Statistical Study of Stock Prices, 1998; Corporate Compliance: Caremark and the Globalization of Good Corporate Conduct, 1998; Mauritania in Photographs, 1999; The Valuation of Options, 1999; Advanced Corporate Compliance Workshop, 1999. **Address:** 2116 W Lake Isles Pkwy., Minneapolis, MN 55405, U.S.A.

MURPHY, Justin D. American (born United States), b. 1964. **Genres:** Military/Defense/Arms Control, History. **Career:** Southeastern Oklahoma State University, Student Support Services, tutor, 1986-87, Tutorial Program, director, 1987; Texas Christian University, graduate assistant, 1987-89, teaching assistant, 1989-91; Tarrant County Junior College, adjunct instructor, 1989-91; Howard Payne University, instructor, 1991-, assistant professor of history, 1994-98, associate professor of history, 1998-2001, professor of history, 2001-, Brand professor of history, 2007-, Douglas MacArthur Academy of Freedom Honors Program, assistant director, 1993-95, director, 1997-, Brand resident chair of free enterprise and public policy, 1995-97, School of Humanities, acting dean, 2007-; Newsletter of the Douglas MacArthur Academy of Freedom, Academy Forum, editor, 1995-. **Publications:** (Ed. and contrib. with S.C. Tucker and L.M. Wood) The European Powers in the First World War: An Encyclopedia, 1996; (ed. and contrib. with S.C. Tucker) Encyclopedia of U.S. Military History, 3 vols., 2002; Military Aircraft, Origins to 1918: An Illustrated History of Their Impact, 2005; (ed.) Encyclopedia of North American Colonial Conflicts to 1775: A Political, Social, and Military History, 2008; (with M.A. McNiece) Military Aircraft, 1915-1945: An Illustrated History of Their Impact, 2008. Contributor to books and journals. **Address:** Howard Payne University, 1000 Fisk Ave., Brownwood, TX 76801-2794, U.S.A. **Online address:** jumurphy@hputx.edu

MURPHY, Mark A. American (born United States) **Genres:** Business/Trade/Industry, Economics. **Career:** VHA Inc., vice president; Murphy Leadership Institute, president and chief executive officer; Leadership IQ, founder and chief executive officer. Writer. **Publications:** (With E.C. Murphy) Leading on the Edge of Chaos: The Ten Critical Elements for Success in Volatile Times, 2002; The Deadly Sins of Employee Retention, 2006; Generation Y and the New Rules of Management, 2009; Hundred Percenters: Challenge Your Employees to Give It Their All, and They'll Give You Even More, 2010; Hard Goals: The Secrets to Getting from Where You Are to Where You Want to Be, 2011; Hiring for Attitude: A Revolutionary Approach to Recruiting and Selecting People with Both Tremendous Skills and Superb Attitude, 2012. **Address:** Leadership IQ, 1050 Connecticut Ave. NW, Ste. 1012, 10th Fl., Washington, DC 20036, U.S.A. **Online address:** info@leadershipiq.com

MURPHY, Martha W(atson). (Martha Wynne Murphy). American (born United States), b. 1951. **Genres:** Novellas/Short Stories, Food And Wine, History, Homes/Gardens, How-to Books, Medicine/Health, Self Help, Essays, Essays, Reference. **Career:** Murphy's Bed and Breakfast, founder, 1985-; Ocean State Business Institute, part-time teacher, 1986-. Freelance writer, 1987-. **Publications:** (Comp.) The Bed and Breakfast Cookbook: Great American B and B's and Their Recipes from All Fifty States, 1991; How to Start and Operate Your Own Bed and Breakfast: Down-to-earth Advice from an Award-Winning B&B Owner, 1994; A New England Fish Tale: Seafood Recipes and Observations of a Way of Life from a Fisherman's Wife, 1997; Don Bousquet's Rhode Island Cookbook, 1997. Contributor to periodicals. **Address:** Murphy's Bed & Breakfast, 43 S Pier Rd., Narragansett, RI 02882, U.S.A.

MURPHY, Martha Wynne. *See* **MURPHY, Martha W(atson).**

MURPHY, Mary Elizabeth. *See* **WILSON, F(rancis) Paul.**

MURPHY, Patricia J. American (born United States), b. 1963?. **Genres:** Children's Non-fiction, Medicine/Health, Area Studies, Politics/Government, Sciences, Young Adult Fiction, Young Adult Non-fiction. **Career:** Pattycake Productions, founder, writer and photographer, 1985-, chief creative director, 1997-; The Chicago Cubs, marketing assistant, 1985-86; The Davidson Marketing Group, copywriter, 1986-87; Pritchett Elementary, teacher, 1990-91; Everett Elementary, teacher, 1992-97. **Publications:** Everything You Need to Know about Staying in the Hospital, 2001; Think Twice, Be Nice, 2001; Sometimes We're Happy, Sometimes We're Sad, 2001; Eye Wonder, 2001; Simple Machines, 2001; How a Frog Gets Its Legs, 2001; A Visit to the Art Museum, 2002; Fun with Fractions, 2002; My Body, 2002; Everybody Works, 2002; Jobs in My Neighborhood, 2002. ROOKIE READ ABOUT HOLIDAYS SERIES: Canada Day, 2002; Election Day, 2002. COUNTRIES OF THE WORLD SERIES: Denmark, 2003; Tanzania, 2003; India, 2003; Ireland, 2003; South Africa, 2004; Canada, 2004; Nigeria, 2005. ROOKIE READER FICTION SERIES: I Need You, 2003. ROOKIE READ ABOUT SCIENCE SERIES: Around and Around, 2002; Back and Forth, 2002; Push and Pull, 2002; Up and Down, 2002. LET'S SEE LIBRARY: OUR NATION SERIES: The Presidency, 2001; Voting and Elections, 2001; Our National Holidays, 2002; The U.S. Supreme Court, 2002; The U.S. Congress, 2002. TRUE BOOK SERIES: Hearing, 2003; Sight, 2003; Smell, 2003; Taste, 2003; Touch, 2004. DISCOVERING CULTURES: India, 2003; Ireland, 2003; South Africa, 2004; Canada, 2005; Nigeria, 2005. GRASSLAND ANIMALS SERIES: Badgers, 2004; Coyotes, 2004; Prairie Dogs, 2004; Red Foxes, 2004. LIBRARY OF WHY SERIES: Why Are the North and South Poles So Cold?, 2004; Why Does the Moon Change Its Shape?, 2004; Why do Some Animals Shed their Skin?, 2004; Why Is the Earth Round?, 2004; Why Do Snakes and Other Animals Shed Their Skins?, 2004; Why Is the Sun So Hot?, 2004; Why Do Some Animals Hibernate?, 2004. FIRST LOOK: Moving, 2008; Separation and Divorce, 2008; Illness, 2008; Death, 2008. OTHERS: (contrib.) Teacher: Thought a Day Calendar, 2003; Peeking at Plants With a Scientist, 2004; Prairie Dogs, 2004; Red Foxes, 2004; Badgers, 2004; Coyotes, 2004; Exploring Space with an Astronaut, 2004; Garrett Morgan: Inventor of the Traffic Light and Gas Mask, 2004; Grace Hopper: Computer Whiz, 2004; Investigating Insects with a Scientist, 2004; The Abacus, 2004; Airport, 2004; Apple Orchard, 2004; Dentist's Office, 2004; Police Station, 2004; Get a Kick Out of Soccer!, 2005; Week, 2005; Year, 2005; Months, 2005; Day, 2005; Amazing American: Andrew Carnegie, 2006; Creative Minds, 2006; Staying Happy, 2006; Avoiding Drugs, 2006; Earning Money, 2006; Evitar las drogas, 2006; A Frog's Life: Learning Sequential Order Using a Timeline, 2006; Mantenerse Feliz, 2006; Telling Time, 2007; How Does the Wind Blow?, 2007; Subtracting Puppies and Kittens, 2008; Counting Puppies and Kittens, 2008; Adding Puppies and Kittens, 2008; Measuring Puppies and Kittens, 2008; Huerta de manzanas, 2008; Telling Time with Puppies and Kittens, 2007; Discovering Underwater Secrets With a Nature Photographer, 2008; Let's Play Soccer, 2008; Journey of a Pioneer, 2008; Never Eat Soggy Waffles: Fun Mnemonic Memory Tricks, 2008; Divorce and Separation, 2008; Mirando a las plantas con un cientifico, 2009. FORTHCOMING FICTION: At Grandma Jo's; Big, Bad Words; Baby Kisses; City Bunnies; A Fine Idea for Valentine's Day; Frog and Bunny; Grandma Jo's Garden; Grandma Jo's Backyard; Happy Nappy; The Kids From Spoiled-Rotten-Ville; Lucky Socks; Made with Love; Make Your Own Sunshine; Oh, Baby!; One Grandma, Two Grandmas, Three Grandmas, Four!; The Original Paige Turner; So Many Holes!; Three Toes for the Rainforest; When Gordo Came to School. FORTHCOMING NON-FICTION: A to Z Families: An Alphabet Album; My Body is Busy; My Face Wears a Smile; We All Fall Down!; Just a Few Words; One (a Math concept book); Santa's Twelve Days of Christmas; Waiting for a Miracle. BOOKS IN THE WORKS: The Adventures of Jack and Jack; Being a Baby is Hard Work; The Daffy Doodle Gossip Club; Clarence Goes to Camp; The Happy Scarf; If Mama Said YES All the Time; The Neighborhood Witch; Do You Know the Muffin Girl?. **Address:** Pattycake Productions, PO Box 494, Arlington Heights, IL 60006-0494, U.S.A. **Online address:** patricia@patriciajmurphy.com

MURPHY, Patrick J. American (born United States), b. 1973. **Genres:** Autobiography/Memoirs. **Career:** Murphy & O'Connor, associate; Mount St. Mary College, adjunct professor, 2000-03; U.S. Military Academy, military faculty, 2000, assistant professor, 2001-03; Widener University, School of Law Intensive Trial Advocacy Program, instructor, 2004-05; Cozen O'Connor, associate, 2005; U.S. Air Force Academy, lecturer; U.S. representative from Pennsylvania; U.S. District Court, Southern District of New York, judge advocate and special assistant; Fox Rothschild L.L.P., partner. Writer. **Publications:** (With A. Frankel) Taking the Hill: From Philly to Baghdad to the United States Congress, 2008. **Address:** 1007 Longworth HOB, Washington, DC 20515, U.S.A.

MURPHY, Peter. Australian (born Australia), b. 1956. **Genres:** Communications/Media, Philosophy, Politics/Government, Social Sciences, Geography. **Career:** La Trobe University, tutor, 1981-85, 1987, research fellow, 1997-98; New School for Social Research, visiting professor and research fellow, 1986; Swinburne Institute of Technology, lecturer in politics, 1987; University of Melbourne, tutor in politics, 1987; University of Ballarat, lecturer, 1988-93, senior lecturer in politics, 1994-97; Baylor University, visiting professor, 1996-97; Looksmart, senior editor, 1998-2001; Victoria University, senior lecturer, 2001-04, Master of Communications Programme, director, 2003-04; Ateneo de Manila University, visiting fellow, 2004; Monash University, associate professor of communications, 2004-, research coordinator, 2005, deputy assistant dean for research, 2006, School of English, Communications and Performance Studies, deputy head, 2007-, Social Aesthetics Research Unit, director, 2009-; Seoul National University, Department of Communications, visiting professor, 2007. **Publications:** (With S. Watson) Surface City: Sydney at the Millennium, 1997; Civic Justice, 2001; (with D. Roberts) Dialectic of Romanticism, 2004; (with M.A. Peters and S. Marginson) Creativity and the Global Knowledge Economy, 2009; (with S. Margison and M. Peters) Imagination: Three Models of Imagination in the Age of the Knowledge Economy, 2009. EDITOR: (with M. Crozier) The Left in Search of a Center, 1996; Friendship, 1998; (with J.P. Arnason) Agon, Logos, Polis, 2001; (with S. Margison and M. Peters) Global Creation: Space, Mobility and Synchrony in the Age of the Knowledge Economy, 2009; (with E. de la Fuente) Philosophical and Cultural Theories of Music, 2010. Contributor to books and journals. **Address:** School of English, Comm. & Performance Studies, Monash University, Clayton Campus, Rm. S721, Menzies Bldg., Wellington Rd., Clayton, VI 3800, Australia. **Online address:** peter.murphy@arts.monash.edu.au

MURPHY, Rae Allan. Canadian (born Canada), b. 1935. **Genres:** Novels, Politics/Government, Business/Trade/Industry, International Relations/Current Affairs, History. **Career:** Conestoga College, lecturer in journalism and Canadian studies, 1972-, professor, now retired. Writer. **Publications:** Vietnam: Impressions of a People's War, 1967; (with R. Chodos and P. Brown) Winners, Losers: The 1976 Tory Leadership Convention, 1976; (with R. Chodos and P. MacFadden) Your Place Or Mine (novel), 1979; (with R. Chodos and N. auf der Maur) Brian Mulroney, the Boy From Baie Comeau, 1984; (with R. Chodos and E. Hamovitch) Selling Out: Four Years of the Mulroney Government, 1988; (with R. Chodos and E. Hamovitch) The Unmaking of Canada: The Hidden Theme in Canadian History Since 1945, 1991; (with R. Chodos and E. Hamovitch) Canada in the Global Economy, 1993; (contrib.) The Essentials of Canadian History: Pre-Colonization to 1867-the Beginning of a Nation, 1993; (with R. Chodos and E. Hamovitch) Lost in Cyberspace?, 1997; (with R. Chodos and E. Hamovitch) Paul Martin: A Political Biography, 1998; (with C.M. Bain and T.A. Crowley) Canadian History, 2008. EDITOR: (with M. Starowicz) Corporate Canada: Fourteen Probes Into the Workings of a Branch-Plant Economy, 1972; (with R. Chodos) Let Us Prey, 1974. **Address:** 3650 Kaneff Cres., Ste. 903, Mississauga, ON L5A 4A1, Canada.

MURPHY, Robert. British (born England), b. 1947. **Genres:** Film, History, Humanities. **Career:** Sheffield Hallam University, School of Cultural Studies, lecturer in film studies, 1990-; De Montfort University, Department of Media, Film and Journalism, professor of film studies. Writer. **Publications:** (Ed. with S. Aspinall) Gainsborough Melodrama, 1983; Realism and Tinsel: Cinema and Society in Britain, 1939-1948, 1989; Realism and Tinsel: Cinema and Society in Britain, 1939-1949, 1992; Sixties British Cinema, 1992; Smash and Grab: Gangsters In The London Underworld 1920-60, 1993; (ed.) The British Cinema Book, 1997, 3rd ed., 2009; (ed. with S. Chibnall) British Crime Cinema, 1999; (ed.) British Cinema of the 90s, 2000; British Cinema and the Second World War, 2000. **Address:** Department of Media, Film and Journalism, De Montfort University, The Gateway, Leicester, LE LE1 9BH, England. **Online address:** rpmurphy@dmu.ac.uk

MURPHY, Shane M. Australian (born Australia), b. 1957. **Genres:** Sports/Fitness, Psychology, Medicine/Health. **Career:** Western Connecticut State University, assistant professor of psychology, professor of psychology; Capella University, clinical psychology faculty of the graduate program; USOC's Sport Psychology Department, head, Division of Sport Science and Technology, associate director, 1992-94; Gold Medal Psychological Consultants, co-founder, 1994, partner, 1994-. Writer. **Publications:** (Ed.) Sport Psychology Interventions, 1995; The Achievement Zone: 8 Skills for Winning All the Time from the Playing Field to the Boardroom, 1996; The Cheers and the Tears: A Healthy Alternative to the Dark Side of Youth Sports Today, 1999; (with D. Hirschhorn) Trading Athlete: Winning the Mental Game of Online Trading, 2001; (ed.) Sport Psych Handbook, 2005. **Address:** Department of Psychology, Western Connecticut State University, WA 311, 181 White St., Danbury, CT 06810, U.S.A. **Online address:** murphys@wcsu.edu

MURPHY, Shirley R(ousseau). American (born United States), b. 1928. **Genres:** Mystery/Crime/Suspense, Science Fiction/Fantasy, Children's Fiction, Young Adult Fiction, Novellas/Short Stories, Novels, Picture/Board Books, Literary Criticism And History, Young Adult Non-fiction. **Career:** Sam Kweller, packaging designer, 1952-53; Bullock's, interior decorator, 1953-55; San Bernardino Valley College, teacher of mosaics, 1957-59; Canal Zone Library-Museum, documents assistant, 1964-67. Writer. **Publications:** FOR JUVENILES: White Ghost Summer, 1967; The Sand Ponies, 1967; Elmo Doolan and The Search for the Golden Mouse, 1970; (with P.J. Murphy) Carlos Charles, 1971; Poor Jenny, Bright as a Penny, 1974; The Grass Tower, 1976; (contrib.) Anywhere, Anywhen, 1976; Silver Woven in My Hair, 1977; The Flight of the Fox, 1978; The Pig Who Could Conjure the Wind, 1978; Soonie and the Dragon, 1979; (with P.J. Murphy) Mrs. Tortino's Return to the Sun, 1980; Tattie's River Journey, 1983; Valentine for a Dragon, 1984; (with W. Suggs) Medallion of the Black Hound, 1989; The Song of the Christmas Mouse, 1990; Wind Child, 1999. CHILDREN OF YNELL SERIES: The Ring of Fire, 1977; The Wolf Bell, 1979; Caves of Fire and Ice, 1980; The Castle of Hape, 1980; The Joining of the Stone, 1981. DRAGONBARDS SERIES: Nightpool, 1985; The Ivory Lyre, 1987; The Dragonbards, 1988. JOE GREY SERIES: MYSTERIES: Cat on the Edge, 1996; Cat under Fire, 1997; Cat Raise the Dead, 1998; Cat in the Dark, 1999; Cat to the Dogs, 2000; Cat Spitting Mad, 2001; Cat Laughing Last, 2002; Cat Seeing Double, 2003; Cat Fear No Evil, 2004; Cat Cross Their Graves, 2005; Cat Breaking Free, 2005; Cat Pay the Devil, 2007; Cat Deck the Halls, 2007; Cat Striking Back, 2009; Cat Playing Cupid, 2009; Cat Coming Home, 2010; Cat Telling Tales, 2011. OTHERS: The Catswold Portal, 1992; (co-author) Motherhood Is Murder, 2003; (ed. and intro.) Christmas Cats: A Literary Companion, 2005. Works appear in anthologies. Contributor to periodicals. **Address:** Martha Millard Literary Agency, 50 W 67th St., Ste. 1G, New York, NY 10023-6227, U.S.A. **Online address:** murphy@joegrey.com

MURPHY, Sylvia. British/Palestinian (born Palestine), b. 1937. **Genres:** Novels, Education, Photography, Animals/Pets, Writing/Journalism, How-to Books, Poetry, Children's Fiction, Picture/Board Books, Young Adult Nonfiction, Novellas/Short Stories. **Career:** Inner London Education Authority, assistant teacher, 1969-74; deputy head teacher, 1974-77; Beaford Arts Centre, publicity officer, 1977-79; teacher, 1979-81; Sidmouth College, head of Careers and Social Education, 1981-87. Freelance journalist and photographer. **Publications:** The Complete Knowledge of Sally Fry (novel), 1983; Learning to Work Together: Journal of Moral Education, 1984; Cory Carnival, 1986; The Life and Times of Barly Beach (novel), 1987; Keeping Nyala in Style (non-fiction), 1995; Dealing with a Death in the Family (how to), 1997; Surviving Your Partner (how to), 1998; Candy's Children, 2007; Crocodiles, 2008; Echoes, 2008; Big Ginger: The Life of a Remarkable Cat, 2009; Tyfoon's Tale, 2009; Trust: What Would Your Family Do for a Fortune?, 2010; Shadow: The Story of a Wartime Cat, 2010; A Home for Jack: A Story for Every Child Who Has Wanted a Kitten to Look After, 2010, Henry the Sad Giant, Trinity: The Lifeboat Cat. Contributor to journals. **Address:** David Higham Associates Ltd., 5-8 Lower John St., Golden Sq., London, GL W1F 9HA, England. **Online address:** sylviag@burngullow.freeserve.co.uk

MURPHY, **Tom.** Irish (born Ireland), b. 1935. **Genres:** Novels, Plays/Screenplays, Business/Trade/Industry, Young Adult Fiction. **Career:** Vocational School, engineering teacher, 1957-62; Moli Productions, founding member, 1974; Druid Theatre Co., director and writer-in-association, 1983-85. Writer. **Publications:** A Whistle in the Dark, 1971; The Morning after Optimism, 1971; Famine, 1977; The Whitehouse, 1973; On the Inside, 1976; The Sanctuary Lamp, 1976; On the Outside, 1976; The J. Arthur Maginnis Story, 1976; Crucial Week in the Life of a Grocer's Assistant, 1978; The Informer, 1981; She Stoops to Conquer, 1982; The Gigli Concernt, 1983; Conversations on a Homecoming, 1985; Bailegangaire, 1985; A Thief of a Christmas, 1985; Too Late for Logic, 1989; The Patriot Game, 1991; The Seduction of Morality, 1995; Cup of Coffee, 1995; She Stoops to Folly, 1995; The Wake, 1997; The House, 2000; The Cherry Orchard, 2003; Drunkard, 2004; Alice Trilogy, 2005. **Address:** Alexandra Cann Representation, 12 Abingdon Rd., London, GL W8 6AF, England. **Online address:** murch1@eircom.net

MURR, **Naeem.** American/British (born England) **Genres:** Novels. **Career:** Stanford University, teaching assistant, 1993; Pembroke College, creative writing teacher, 1995; University of Houston, fiction instructor, 1996-97; freelance writer, 1997-; Lynchburg College, writer-in-residence, 1998; Northwestern University, visiting professor of creative writing, writer-in-residence; University of Missouri, writer-in-residence; Western Michigan University, writer-in-residence. **Publications:** The Boy (novel), 1998 in Spain as El Chico, 1999; Sohn der Dunkelheit, 2000; The Genius of the Sea, 2003; The Perfect Man, 2006, Nude, 2012. Contributor to journals. **Address:** Houghton Mifflin Co., 222 Berkeley St., Boston, MA 02116, U.S.A. **Online address:** info@naeemmurr.com

MURRAY, **Albert.** American (born United States), b. 1916. **Genres:** Novels, Art/Art History, Autobiography/Memoirs. **Career:** Tuskegee Institute, part-time instructor, instructor in literature, 1940-43, 1946-51; Columbia University, Graduate School of Journalism, instructor, 1968; Colgate University, O'Connor professor of literature, 1970, O'Connor lecturer, 1973, professor of humanities, 1982, Colgate professor of humanities; University of Massachusetts, visiting professor of literature, 1971; University of Missouri, Paul Anthony Brick lecturer, 1972; Emory University, writer-in-residence, 1978; Barnard College, adjunct professor of creative writing, 1981-83; Drew University, Woodrow Wilson fellow, 1983; Jazz at Lincoln Center, founder; Washington and Lee University, Du Pont Visiting Professor; The New School for Social Research, faculty. Writer. **Publications:** The Omni-Americans: New Perspectives on Black Experience and American Culture, 1970, rev. ed. as The Omni-Americans: Some Alternatives to the Folklore of White Supremacy, 1983; South to a Very Old Place, 1971; The Hero and the Blues, 1973; Train Whistle Guitar, 1974; Stomping the Blues, 1976; (contrib.) Good Morning Blues: The Autobiography of Count Basie, 1985; Reflections on Logic, Politics, and Reality: A Challenge to the Sacred Consensus of Contemporary American Thinking, 1989; The Spyglass Tree, 1991; The Seven League Boots: A Novel, 1995; The Blue Devils of Nada: A Contemporary American Approach to Aesthetic Statement, 1996; (with G. Gelburd and T. Golden) Romare Bearden in Black-and-White: Photomontage Projections, 1964, 1997; Conversations with Albert Murray, 1997; (intro. and ed. with J.F. Callahan) Trading Twelves: The Selected Letters of Ralph Ellison and Albert Murray, 2000; From the Briarpatch File: On Context, Procedure, and American Identity, 2001; Conjugations and Reiterations, 2001; The Magic Keys, 2005. **Address:** 45 W 132nd St., New York, NY 10037-3101, U.S.A.

MURRAY, **Bruce T.** American (born United States), b. 1964. **Genres:** Adult Non-fiction. **Career:** Orange County Register, city editor, 1998-99; Los Angeles Times, city editor and bureau chief, 1999-2000; Web Sage Content Development, president, 2006-; Daily Times-Republic, reporter and editor; Rolla Daily News, reporter and editor; Daily Advertiser, reporter and editor. Web developer. **Publications:** Religious Liberty in America: Navigating the First Amendment in the Newsroom and Beyond (nonfiction), 2005, rev. ed. as Religious Liberty in America: The First Amendment in Historical and Contemporary Perspective, 2008. **Address:** CA , U.S.A. **Online address:** murray@websage.us

MURRAY, **Charles (Alan).** American (born United States), b. 1943. **Genres:** Public/Social Administration. **Career:** American Institute for Research, research scientist, 1974-79, chief scientist, 1979-81; Manhattan Institute for Policy Research, senior fellow, 1982-90; American Enterprise Institute, resident fellow, 1990-2003, Bradley fellow, 1990; Organisation for Economic Cooperation and Development, 1991. Writer. **Publications:** (Co-author) The Link between Learning Disabilities and Juvenile Delinquency: Current Theory and Knowledge, 1976; (with R.E. Krug) National Evaluation of the Pilot Cities Program: A Team Approach To Improving Local Criminal Justice Systems, 1976; A Behavioral Study of Rural Modernization: Social and Economic Change in Thai Villages, 1977; (with D. Thomson and C.B. Israel) UDIS, Deinstitutionalizing The Chronic Juvenile Offender, 1977; (with L.A. Cox) Beyond Probation, 1979; Safety Nets And The Truly Needy: Rethinking The Social Welfare System, 1982; Losing Ground: American Social Policy 1950-80, 1984; In Pursuit: Of Happiness and Good Government, 1988; (with C.B. Cox) Apollo: The Race to the Moon, 1989; (with R.J. Herrnstein) The Bell Curve: Intelligence and Class Structure in American Life, 1994; Charles Murray And The Underclass: The Developing Debate/Charles Murray; Commentaries, Ruth Lister, 1996; What it Means To Be A Libertarian: A Personal Interpretation, 1997; Income Inequality and IQ, 1998; The Underclass Revisited, 1999; Human Accomplishment: The Pursuit of Excellence in the Arts and Sciences, 800 BC to 1950, 2003; In Our Hands: A Plan to Replace the Welfare State, 2006; Real Education: Four Simple Truths for Bringing America's Schools Back to Reality, 2008; (ed. with F.C. Harwood) Golden Constant: The American Institute For Economic Research: 75 years of Free Thinking On The Free Market (1933-2008), 2008; Happiness of The People, 2009. **Address:** American Enterprise Institute, 1150 17th St. NW, Washington, DC 20036, U.S.A. **Online address:** cmurray@aei.org

MURRAY, **Craig.** British (born England), b. 1958. **Genres:** Military/Defense/Arms Control. **Career:** Foreign and Commonwealth Office, staff, 1984; British High Commission, Second Secretary, 1986- 89; Foreign and Commonwealth Office, Maritime Section, head, 1989-92, Cyprus section, head, 1992-94; British Embassy, first secretary (political and economic), 1994-97; Foreign and Commonwealth Office, African Department, deputy head, 1997-98; British High Commission, West Africa Branch, deputy high commissioner, 1998-2002; British ambassador to Uzbekistan, 2002-04; Member of Parliament, 2005; University of Dundee, Scotland, rector, 2007-10. Writer. **Publications:** Murder in Samarkand: A British Ambassador's Controversial Defiance of Tyranny in the War on Terror, 2006; Dirty Diplomacy: The Rough-and-tumble Adventures of a Scotch-drinking, Skirt-chasing, Dictator-busting and Thoroughly Unrepentant Ambassador Stuck on the Frontline of the War against Terror, 2007. **Address:** Craig Murray Campaign, 31 Sinclair Gardens, West Kensington, London, GL W14 0AU, England. **Online address:** craigjmurray@tiscali.co.uk

MURRAY, **David (J.).** British (born England), b. 1945. **Genres:** Cultural/Ethnic Topics, Literary Criticism And History, Anthropology/Ethnology, Economics. **Career:** University of Kent, lecturer, 1969-70; University of Nottingham, lecturer in American studies, 1970-, professor of American literature and culture, 2002-, The Criss Cross Project, director, 2002-05, Faculty of Arts, now professor emeritus; California State University, assistant professor, 1974. Writer. **Publications:** Modern Indians, 1982; Forked Tongues: Speech, Writing, and Representation in North American Indian Texts, 1990; Indian Giving: Economies of Power in Early Indian-White Exchanges, 1999; Matter, Magic, and Spirit: Representing Indian and African American Belief, 2007. EDITOR: Literary Theory and Poetry: Extending the Canon, 1989; American Cultural Critics, 1995; (with G. Lock) Thriving on a Riff, 2009; (with G. Lock) The Hearing Eye, 2009. **Address:** Faculty of Arts, University of Nottingham, Rm. B60, Trent Bldg., University Pk., Nottingham, NG7 2RD, England. **Online address:** david.murray@nottingham.ac.uk

MURRAY, **Elaine.** Canadian (born Canada), b. 1941. **Genres:** Education, Paranormal, Theology/Religion. **Career:** Elementary school music teacher, 1975-88, now retired; Haldimand-Norfolk Realties Ltd., salesperson, 1980-88; Simcoe Little Theatre, actress. Writer. **Publications:** A Layman's Guide to New Age & Spiritual Terms, 1993. **Address:** RR 1, Vittoria, ON N0E 1W0, Canada. **Online address:** jaguare@kwic.com

MURRAY, George. *See* **MURRAY, G. T.**

MURRAY, G. T. (George Murray). American (born United States), b. 1927. **Genres:** Engineering, Technology. **Career:** Materials Research Corp., vice president, 1957-77; California Polytechnic State University, professor, 1978-92. Writer and consultant. **Publications:** (As George Murray) Introduction to Engineering Materials: Behavior, Properties and Selection, 1993, (with C.V. White and W. Weise) 2nd ed., 2008; (ed.) Handbook of Materials Selection for Engineering Applications, 1997. Contributor to journals. **Address:** 5728 Tamerisk Way, San Luis Obispo, CA 93401, U.S.A. **Online address:** gmurray2@charter.net

MURRAY, James M. American (born United States), b. 1954. **Genres:** History, Economics, Business/Trade/Industry. **Career:** University of Cincinnati, McMicken College of Arts and Sciences, professor of history, 1984-2007; Western Michigan University, Medieval Institute, director, 2007-, professor of history. Writer. **Publications:** Notarial Instruments in Flanders between 1280 and 1452, Commission Royale d'Histoire, 1995; (with E.S. Hunt) A History of Business in Medieval Europe, 1200-1550, 1999; Bruges, Cradle of Capitalism, 1280-1390, 2005. Contributor to periodicals and journals. **Address:** Department of History, Medieval Studies, Western Michigan University, Kalamazoo, MI 49008-5334, U.S.A. **Online address:** james.murray@wmich.edu

MURRAY, Janet Horowitz. American (born United States), b. 1946. **Genres:** Literary Criticism And History, Women's Studies And Issues, Technology, Social Sciences, Business/Trade/Industry, Information Science/Computers. **Career:** International Business Machines, systems programmer, 1967; Massachusetts Institute of Technology, teacher and researcher, 1971-99, Laboratory for Advanced Technology in the Humanities, founding director, 1992-96, Center for Educational Computing Initiatives, senior research scientist, 1996-99; Georgia Institute of Technology, School of Literature, Communication, and Culture, Graduate Program in Digital Media, professor, 1999-, director of graduate studies, 2000-10, Experimental Television Laboratory, director. Writer. **Publications:** (Ed.) Strong-Minded Women and Other Lost Voices from Nineteenth-century England, 1982; (ed. with M. Stark) Englishwoman's Review of Social and Industrial Questions, 1866-1910, 1984; (ed. with A.K. Clark) Englishwoman's Review of Social and Industrial Questions: An Index, 1985; Courtship and the English Novel: Feminist Readings in the Fiction of George Meredith, 1987; (intro.) Miss Miles, or, A Tale of Yorkshire Life 60 Years Ago, 1990; Hamlet on the Holodeck: The Future of Narrative in Cyberspace, 1997. Contributor to books and periodicals. **Address:** School of Literature, Communication, and Culture, Georgia Institute of Technology, Rm. 320A, Technology Square Research Bldg., 686 Cherry St., Atlanta, GA 30332-0165, U.S.A. **Online address:** jmurray@gatech.edu

MURRAY, John E. American (born United States), b. 1959?. **Genres:** History. **Career:** Ohio State University, Department of Economics, Anna M. Dice fellow, 1982, 1991, lecturer in economics, 1992-94; University of Toledo, assistant professor, 1994-2000, associate professor, 2000-06, professor of economics, 2006-; University of Michigan, Michigan Historical Demography Workshop, research associate, 2007-. Writer. **Publications:** Origins of American Health Insurance: A History of Industrial Sickness Funds, 2007; (ed. with R.W. Herndon) Children Bound to Labor: The Pauper Apprentice System in Early America, 2009. Contributor to books, journals and periodicals. **Address:** Department of Economics, University of Toledo, Toledo, OH 43606-3390, U.S.A. **Online address:** john.murray@utoledo.edu

MURRAY, Les(lie) (Allan). Australian (born Australia), b. 1938. **Genres:** Poetry, Novels, Young Adult Fiction. **Career:** Australian National University, scientific and technical translator, 1963-67; freelance writer, 1971-; Poetry Australia, co-editor, 1973-80; Angus & Robertson Publisher, poetry reader, 1977-91; Quadrant Magazine, literary editor, 1988-; University of New England, writer-in-residence; University of Stirling, writer-in-residence; University of Newcastle, writer-in-residence; University of Copenhagen, writer-in-residence; University of New South Wales, writer-in-residence; University of Sydney, writer-in-residence. **Publications:** (With G.J. Lehmann) TheIlex Tree, 1965; The Weatherboard Cathedral, 1969; Poems against Economics, 1972; Lunch and Counter Lunch, 1974; Selected Poems: The Vernacular Republic, 1975; The Peasant Mandarin, 1978; Ethnic Radio, 1978; The Boys Who Stole the Funeral: A Novel Sequence, 1980; Equanimities, 1982; The Vernacular Republic: Poems, 1961-81, 1982; The People's Otherworld, 1984; Persistence in Folly, 1984; The Australian Year, 1985; The Australian Seasons, 1985; Selected Poems, 1986; (ed.) The New Oxford Book of Australian Verse, 1986; (ed.) Anthology of Australian Religious Poetry, 1986, 2nd ed., 1991; The Daylight Moon, 1987; The Idyll Wheel: Cycle of a Year at Bunyah, 1987; Dog Fox Field: Poems, 1990; Blocks and Tackles: Articles and Essays 1982 to 1990, 1990; The Rabbiter's Bounty: Collected Poems, 1991; Collected Poems, 1991; Translations from the Natural World: Poems, 1992; The Paperbark Tree, 1992; (ed.) A. B. Paterson: Selected Poems, 1992, rev. Ed., 1996; (ed.) Five Fathers: Five Australian Poets of the Pre-academic Era, 1994; Subhuman Redneck Poems, 1996; A Working Forest: Selected Essays, 1996; A Working Forest: Selected Prose, 1997; New Selected Poems, 1998; Fredy Neptune: A Novel in Verse, 1998; The Quality of Sprawl, 1999; Learning Human and Conscious and Verbal, 1999; Conscious and Verbal, 1999; Learning Human: Selected Poems, 2000; Poems the Size of Photographs, 2002; New Collected Poems, 2003; Best Australian Poems 2004, 2004; Hell and After: Four Early English-Language Poets of Australia, 2005; Best Australian Poems 2005, 2005; (contrib.) Letters to Les, 2005; Biplane Houses, 2006; Taller when Prone: Poems, 2010; Killing the Black Dog: A Memoir of Depression, 2011. **Address:** Margaret Connolly and Associates, 16 Winton St., Warrawee, NW 2074, Australia.

MURRAY, Louise. American (born United States), b. 1966. **Genres:** Animals/Pets. **Career:** American Society for the Prevention of Cruelty to Animals (ASPCA), director of medicine, Bergh Memorial Animal Hospital, director of intern program. Writer and broadcaster. **Publications:** Vet Confidential: An Insider's Guide to Protecting Your Pet's Health, 2008. Contributor to journals and periodicals. **Address:** Vet Confidential, 9 East St., 3rd Fl., Boston, MA 02111, U.S.A.

MURRAY, Paul T(hom). American (born United States), b. 1944. **Genres:** Sociology, History, Civil Liberties/Human Rights. **Career:** Meharry Medical College, Center for Health Care Research, research associate, 1970-72; Millsaps College, assistant professor of sociology, 1972-78; University of Montevallo, assistant professor of sociology, 1978-79; Siena College, School of Liberal Arts, Department of Sociology, professor of sociology, 1979-, department chair; Albany Board of Education, vice-president, 1992-94, president, 1994; Fisk University, faculty; United States Department of Justice, consultant. Writer. **Publications:** The Civil Rights Movement: References and Resources, 1993. Contributor to books and periodicals. **Address:** Department of Sociology, School of Liberal Arts, Siena College, 515 Loudon Rd., Loudonville, NY 12211-1462, U.S.A. **Online address:** murray@siena.edu

MURRAY, Raymond C. American (born United States), b. 1929. **Genres:** Earth Sciences, Criminology/True Crime, Sciences. **Career:** Shell Development Co., manager of research, 1955-66; University of New Mexico, associate professor of geology, 1966-67; Rutgers University, professor of geology and chairman of department, 1967-77; University of Montana, vice president for research, 1977-96; forensic geologist, 1973-. Writer. **Publications:** (Ed. with L.C. Pray) Dolomitization and Limestone Diagenesis: A Symposium, 1965; (with H. Blatt and G.V. Middleton) The Origin of Sedimentary Rocks, 1972, 2nd ed., 1980; (with J.C.F. Tedrow) Forensic Geology: Earth Sciences and Criminal Investigation, 1975; (with L. Solebello) Forensic Examination of Soils, 2001; Evidence From the Earth: Forensic Geology and Criminal Investigation, 2004, 2nd ed., 2011; Earth Evidence, 2007. **Address:** 106 Ironwood Pl., Missoula, MT 59803, U.S.A. **Online address:** rmurray@bresnan.net

MURRAY, Stephen O. American (born United States), b. 1950. **Genres:** Sociology, Anthropology/Ethnology. **Career:** Social Network Congress, consultant, 1978-80; El Instituto Obregon, research director, 1982-. Writer. **Publications:** SOCIOLOGY AND ANTHROPOLOGY: Group Formation in Social Science, 1983; Oceanic Homosexualities, 1992; Theory Groups and the Study of Language in North America: A Social History, 1994; (with K. Hong) Taiwanese Culture, Taiwanese Society: A Critical Review of Social Science Research Done on Taiwan, 1994; Latin American Male Homosexualities, 1995; American Gay, 1996; Angkor Life, 1996; (ed. with W. Roscoe) Islamic Homosexualities: Culture, History and Literature, 1997; American Sociolinguistics: Theorists and Theory Groups, 1998; (ed. with W. Roscoe) Boy-Wives and Female Husbands: Studies in African Homosexualities, 1998; Homosexualities, 2000; (with K. Hong) Looking through Taiwan: American Anthropologists Collusion with Ethnic Domination, 2005. **Address:** El Instituto Obregon, 1360 De Haro, San Francisco, CA 94107-3239, U.S.A. **Online address:** keelung@itsa.ucsf.edu

MURRAY, Victoria. (Victoria Christopher Murray). American (born United States) **Genres:** Novels, Novellas/Short Stories. **Career:** Businesswoman and entrepreneur, 1979-97. Writer. **Publications:** AS VICTORIA CHRISTOPHER MURRAY: Temptation, 1997; Joy, 2001; (co-author) Blessed Assurance: Inspirational Short Stories Full of Hope and Strength for Life's Journey, 2003; Truth Be Told, 2004; Grown Folks Business, 2005; A Sin and a Shame, 2006; The Ex Files, 2007; Diamond, 2008; India, 2008; Too Little, Too Late, 2008; Aaliyah, 2009; Veronique, 2009; Lady Jasmine, 2009; Sins of the Mother, 2010; The Deal, the Dance, and the Devil, 2011; (with R.T. Billingsley) Sinners and Saints, 2012. Contributor to magazines. **Address:** c/o Author Mail, Walk Worthy Press, 33290 W 14 Mile Rd., Ste. 482, West Bloomfield, MI 48322-3549, U.S.A. **Online address:** vecm1@aol.com

MURRAY, Victoria Christopher. *See* **MURRAY, Victoria.**

MURRAY, William J(ames). Australian (born Australia), b. 1937?. **Genres:** Sports/Fitness, Politics/Government, Social Sciences. **Career:** La Trobe University, senior lecturer in history, professor of history, honorary research associate. Writer. **Publications:** (As Bill Murray) The Old Firm: Sectarianism, Sport and Society in Scotland, 1984, 2nd ed., 2001; The Right-Wing Press in the French Revolution, 1789-92, 1986; Unconditional Freedom: Social Revolution through Individual Empowerment, 1993; (as Bill Murray) Football: A History of the World Game, 1994; (as Bill Murray) The World's Game: A History of Soccer, 1996; The Old Firm in the New Age: Celtic and Rangers since the Souness Revolution, 1998, rev. ed. as Bhoys, Bears and Bigotry: the Old Firm in the New Age, 2003. EDITOR: (with J.T. Gilchrist) Eye-Witness: Selected Documents from Australia's Past, 1968; (with J.T. Gilchrist) The Press in the French Revolution: A Selection of Documents Taken from the Press of the Revolution for the Years 1789-1794, 1971; (as Bill Murray) Crisis, Conflict and Consensus: Selected Documents Illustrating 200 Years in the Making of Australia, 1984; (with A. Krüger) The Nazi Olympics: Sport, Politics and Appeasement in the 1930s, 2003; (with R. Hay as Bill Murray) World Game Downunder, 2006. **Address:** Department of History, La Trobe University, David Myers Bldg. E120, Plenty Rd., Brindoora, VI 3086, Australia. **Online address:** w.murray@latrobe.edu.au

MURRAY, Yxta Maya. American (born United States) **Genres:** Adult Non-fiction, Novels, Mystery/Crime/Suspense. **Career:** Loyola Marymount University, Loyola Law School, professor of Law, 1995-. Writer. **Publications:** Locas, 1997; What It Takes to Get to Vegas, 1999; The Conquest, 2002; Queen Jade: A Novel, 2005; King's Gold: An Old World Novel of Adventure, 2008; The Good Girl's Guide to Getting Kidnapped, 2010. Contributor of articles. **Address:** Loyola Law School, Loyola Marymount University, 919 Albany St., Los Angeles, CA 90015-1211, U.S.A. **Online address:** yxta.murray@lls.edu

MURRELL, John. American (born United States), b. 1945. **Genres:** Plays/Screenplays, Social Commentary. **Career:** Alberta Theatre Projects, playwright-in-residence, 1975; Stratford Festival, associate director, 1977-78; Banff Centre for the Arts, head of playwrights colony, 1985-89, artistic director and executive producer of theatre arts, 1999-2005, executive artistic director of performing arts, 2005-07; Canada Council, head of theatre section, 1988-92. **Publications:** Waiting for the Parade: Faces of Women in War, 1980; Farther West: New World, 1985; Democracy, 1991; The Faraway Nearby, 1995. TRANSLATOR: Uncle Vanya: Scenes from a Rural Life, 1978; Cyrano de Bergerac, 1995; Elisa's Skin, 2001; The Seven Days of Simon Labrosse, 2002; The Four Lives of Marie, 2002; Carole Fréchette: Two Plays, 2007; Cicero and the Roman Republic, 2008. **Address:** Susan Schulman Literary Agency, 454 W 44th St., New York, NY 10036, U.S.A.

MURRELL, Nathaniel S(amuel). American (born United States), b. 1945. **Genres:** Philosophy, Theology/Religion. **Career:** Constantine Methodist School, teacher, 1965-70; West Indies School of Theology, academic dean and lecturer, 1980-83; Caribbean Graduate School of Theology, visiting lecturer, 1986-96; West Presbyterian Church, pastor, 1987-91; College of Saint Elizabeth, tutor, 1987-88; College of Wooster, assistant professor of black studies and religion, 1991-95; Methodist Theological School, adjunct assistant professor of African American religion, 1994-95; Chestnut Street Presbyterian Church, interim pastor, 1996-99; University of North Carolina, assistant professor, associate professor. Writer. **Publications:** (Ed. with W.D. Spencer and A.A. McFarlane) Chanting Down Babylon: The Rastafari Reader, 1998; (ed. with H. Gossai) Religion, Culture, and Tradition In the Caribbean, 2000; Afro-Caribbean Religions: An Introduction to their Historical, Cultural, and Sacred Traditions, 2010. Contributor to books. **Address:** Department of Philosophy & Religion, University of North Carolina, 282 Bear Hall, 601 S College Rd., Wilmington, NC 28403-3297, U.S.A. **Online address:** murrells@uncw.edu

MURREN, Doug(las). American (born United States), b. 1951. **Genres:** Adult Non-fiction, Sociology, Theology/Religion. **Career:** Fuller Theological Seminary, lecturer; Asbury Seminary, lecturer; Regents College, lecturer; Leland Center, lecturer; Eastside Foursquare Church, senior pastor; Square 1 Ministries, director. Writer. **Publications:** (With R. Rearick) Iceman: A True Story (nonfiction), 1987; (with B. Shurin) Is It Real when It Doesn't Work?, 1990; Baby Boomerang, 1990; How to Keep Your Dreams Alive, 1993; Leadershift, 1994; Churches that Heal: Becoming a Church That Mends Broken Hearts and Restores Shattered Lives, 1999. Contributor to magazines. **Address:** Square 1 Ministries, 7734 10th Ave. NW, Seattle, WA 98117, U.S.A. **Online address:** dmurren@square1.org

MURRY, Katherine Middleton. British (born England), b. 1925. **Genres:** Biography, Autobiography/Memoirs, Literary Criticism And History. **Career:** Writer. **Publications:** Beloved Quixote: The Unknown Life of John Middleton Murry, 1986. Contributor to periodicals. **Address:** Church Cottage, Barrow, Bury St. Edmunds, SU IP29 5BA, England.

MUSACCHIO, George. American/Italian (born Italy), b. 1938. **Genres:** Intellectual History, Literary Criticism And History, Biography, Humanities, Philosophy, Theology/Religion. **Career:** California Baptist College, instructor, 1964-66, assistant professor, 1966-68, associate professor, 1968-71, professor of English and head of department, 1971-89; Lamp-Post, editor, 1977-80, contributing editor, 1991-; Baylor University, visiting professor, 1985; Golden Gate Baptist Theological Seminary, visiting professor, 1987; Calvin College, visiting professor, 1988; University of Mary Hardin-Baylor, College of Arts and Sciences, dean, 1990-94, Frank W. Mayborn chair of arts and sciences, professor of English, 1990-2004, professor emeritus of English, 2004-. **Publications:** Milton's Adam and Eve: Fallible Perfection, 1991; C.S. Lewis, Man and Writer: Essays and Reviews, 1994. Contributor of articles to journals and magazines. Works appear in anthologies. **Address:** University of Mary Hardin-Baylor, 900 College St., PO Box 8008, Belton, TX 76513-2599, U.S.A. **Online address:** gmusacchio@att.net

MUSGRAVE, Gerald L. American (born United States), b. 1942?. **Genres:** Economics, Medicine/Health, Administration/Management. **Career:** Stanford University, research professor; University of Michigan, professor; Economics America Inc., president; National Center for Policy Analysis, senior fellow. Writer. **Publications:** (Ed.) The Galbraith Viewpoint in Perspective: Critical Commentary on The Age of Uncertainty Television Series, 1977; Social Security in the United States: A Classified Bibliography, 1978; Social Security Worldwide: A Classified Bibliography, 1978; (with J.B. Ramsey) APL-STAT: A Do-It-Yourself Guide to Computational Statistics Using APL, 1981; (with W.S. Barnett) The Economic Impact of Mandated Family Leave on Small Businesses and their Employees, 1991. WITH J.C. GOODMAN: The Changing Market for Health Insurance: Opting Out of the Cost-Plus System, 1985; Health Care for the Elderly: The Nightmare in Our Future, 1987; Freedom of Choice in Health Insurance, 1988; Health Care After Retirement: Who Will Pay the Cost?, 1989; Controlling Health Care Costs with Medical Savings Accounts, 1992; Patient Power: Solving America's Health Care Crisis, 1992; (and D.M. Herrick) Lives at Risk: Single-Payer National Health Insurance Around the World, 2004. Contributor to periodicals. **Address:** Economics America Inc., 612 Church St., Ann Arbor, MI 48104-3002, U.S.A.

MUSGRAVE, Susan. Canadian/American (born United States), b. 1951. **Genres:** Novels, Children's Fiction, Poetry, Essays, Novellas/Short Stories, Young Adult Non-fiction, Young Adult Fiction. **Career:** Arvon Foundation, instructor, 1975, 1980; University of Waterloo, instructor and writer-in-residence, 1983-85; Vancouver Public Library, writer-in-residence, 1986; Kootenay School of Writing, instructor, 1986; Ganarska Writers Colony, Fiction Workshop, writer-in-residence, 1988; Camosun College, instructor, 1988-2006; York University, writer-in-electronic-residence, 1991-94; University of Western Ontario, writer-in-residence, 1992-93; University of Toronto, presidential writer-in-residence, 1995; Victoria School of Writing, writer-in-residence, 1996, 1998, 2006; University of British Columbia, adjunct professor, 2005-. Columnist. **Publications:** Songs of the Sea-Witch, 1970; Skuld, 1971; Mindscapes, 1971; Entrance of the Celebrant, 1972; Equinox, 1972; Grave-Dirt and Selected Strawberries, 1973; Gullband Thought Measles was a Happy Ending, 1974; Against, 1974; Two Poems, 1975; The Impstone, 1976; (with S. Virgo) Kistkatinaw Songs, 1977; Selected Strawberries and

Other Poems, 1977; Becky Swan's Book, 1977; For Charlie Beaulieu in Yellowknife Who Told Me Go Back to the South and Write Another Poem about Indians, 1977; Two Poems for the Blue Moon, 1977; A Man to Marry, A Man to Bury, 1979; Conversation During the Omelette Aux Fines Herbes, 1979; The Charcoal Burner (novel), 1980; Hag Head (for children), 1980; Tarts and Muggers: Poems New and Selected, 1982; Cocktails at the Mausoleum, 1985, rev. ed., 1992; The Dancing Chicken: A Novel, 1987; Great Musgrave (essays), 1989; Kestrel and Leonardo (children's poetry), 1990; The Embalmer's Art, 1991; In the Small Hours of the Rain, 1991; Musgrave Landing: Musings on the Writing Life, 1994; Forcing the Narcissus: Poems, 1994; (with M. Gay) Dreams are more Real than Bathtubs, 1998; Things that Keep and Do not Change, 1999; Cargo of Orchids, 2000; What the Small Day Cannot Hold: Collected Poems, 1970-1985, 2000; You're in Canada Now ... Motherfucker, 2005; Obituary of Light: The Sangan River Meditations, 2009; Origami Dove, 2011. EDITOR: (and comp.) Because You Loved Being a Stranger: 55 Poets Celebrate Patrick Lane, 1994; You Be Me: Friendship in the Lives of Teen Girls, 2002; Fed Anthology, 2003. Works appear in anthologies. Contributor to periodicals. **Address:** The Bukowski Agency, 14 Prince Arthur Ave., Ste. 202, Toronto, ON M5R 1A9, Canada. **Online address:** musgrave.susan@gmail.com

MUSGROVE, Frank. *See* Obituaries.

MUSHET, Cindy. American (born United States), b. 1960. **Genres:** Food And Wine. **Career:** Sur Le Table, cooking instructor; Le Cordon Bleu, cooking instructor. Writer and chef. **Publications:** Desserts: Mediterranean Flavors, California Style, 2000; The Art and Soul of Baking, 2008; Baking Kids Love, 2009. Contributor to book. **Address:** Los Angeles, CA , U.S.A. **Online address:** cindy@cindymushet.com

MUSK, Justine. (Justine Wilson). American/Canadian (born Canada), b. 1972?. **Genres:** Novels, Mystery/Crime/Suspense, Horror, Romance/Historical. **Career:** Writer and educator. **Publications:** Blood Angel (horror novel), 2005; Uninvited (young adult supernatural thriller novel), 2007; Lord of Bones, 2008; (co-author) Mammoth Book of Vampire Romance 2, 2009. **Address:** Running Press, 2300 Chestnut St., Ste. 200, Philadelphia, PA 19103, U.S.A. **Online address:** soulful@me.com

MUSSELMAN, Jennifer. American (born United States), b. 1973. **Genres:** Social Sciences. **Career:** MTV Networks, Nickelodeon Television Channel, senior director of communications. Writer. **Publications:** (With P. DeGregori) The Hip Girl's Handbook for Home, Car & Money Stuff, 2002; (with P. Fletcher) The Hip Girl's Handbook for the Working World, 2005; Own It! The Ups and Downs of Homebuying for Women Who Go It Alone, 2008. Contributor to periodicals. **Address:** c/o Jodee Krainik, 1700 4th St., Berkeley, CA 94710, U.S.A. **Online address:** jen@jennifermusselman.com

MUSTAZZA, Leonard. American (born United States), b. 1952. **Genres:** Literary Criticism And History, Art/Art History, Biography, Autobiography/Memoirs, Humanities. **Career:** Pennsylvania State University, Abington College, lecturer, 1983-84, assistant professor, 1984-89, associate professor, 1989-91, professor, 1991-99, associate dean, 1992-2002, distinguished professor of English and American studies, 1999-. Writer. **Publications:** Such Prompt Eloquence: Language as Agency and Character in Milton's Epics, 1988; Forever Pursuing Genesis: The Myth of Eden in the Novels of Kurt Vonnegut, 1990; (ed.) The Critical Response to Kurt Vonnegut, 1994; (ed. with S. Petkov) The Frank Sinatra Reader, 1995; (with V. Abt) Coming after Oprah: Cultural Fallout in the Age of the TV Talk Show, 1997; Ol' Blue Eyes: A Frank Sinatra Encyclopedia, 1998; (ed.) Frank Sinatra and Popular Culture: Essays on an American Icon, 1998; Frank Sinatra: An Annotated Bibliography, 1939-1998, 1999; Literary Filmography: 6, 200 Adaptations of Books, Short Stories and other Nondramatic Works, 2006; (ed.) Slaughterhouse-five, 2011. Contributor of articles to books and periodicals. **Address:** Department of English, Pennsylvania State University, Abington College, 418 Sutherland Bldg., Abington, PA 19001-3990, U.S.A. **Online address:** lxm7@psu.edu

MUSTO, Barry. (Robert Simon). British (born England), b. 1930. **Genres:** Novels, Mystery/Crime/Suspense, Children's Fiction, Young Adult Fiction. **Career:** Harper & Tunstall Ltd., export manager, 1974-; British Broadcasting Corp., writer. **Publications:** The Lawrence Barclay File, 1969; Storm Centre, 1970; The Fatal Flaw, 1970; (as Robert Simon) The Sunless Land, 1972; Codename-Bastille, 1972; No Way Out, 1973; The Weighted Scales, 1973; The Lebanese Partner, 1983. Contributor of stories to magazines. **Address:** c/o J. F. Gibson, PO Box 173, London, GL SE10 0RY, England.

MUSTO, Michael. American (born United States), b. 1955. **Genres:** Novels, Writing/Journalism, Young Adult Fiction. **Career:** Village Voice, columnist, 1984-. **Publications:** Downtown, 1986; Manhattan on the Rocks (novel), 1989; La Dolce Musto: Writings by the World's Most Outrageous Columnist, 2007; Fork on the Left, Knife in the Back, 2011. Contributor to journals and magazines. **Address:** The Village Voice, 36 Cooper Sq., New York, NY 10003, U.S.A.

MUSZYNSKI, Stuart. American (born United States) **Genres:** Autobiography/Memoirs, Self Help. **Career:** Project Love, Remember the Children Foundation, co-founder, president and chief executive officer. Writer. **Publications:** Searching for Values: A Grandmother, a Grandson and the Discovery of Goodness (memoir), 2005. **Address:** Project Love, 23611 Chagrin Blvd., Ste. 380, Beachwood, OH 44122, U.S.A. **Online address:** stuartm@projectlove.org

MUTH, Richard F(erris). American (born United States), b. 1927. **Genres:** Economics, Urban Studies. **Career:** University of Chicago, Graduate School of Business, associate professor, 1959-64; Institute for Defense Analyses, economist, 1964-66; Washington University, professor of economics, 1966-70; Stanford University, professor of economics, 1970-83; Emory University, Department of Economics, Fuller E. Callaway professor, 1983-2000, chair, 1983-90, Fuller E. Callaway professor emeritus, 2000-. Writer. **Publications:** (With H.S. Perloff, E.S. Dunn and E. Lampard) Regions, Resources and Economic Growth, 1960; Cities and Housing, 1969; Permanent Income, Instrumental Variables and the Income Elasticity of Housing Demand, 1970; Public Housing: An Economic Evaluation, 1973; Urban Economic Problems, 1974; (with A.C. Goodman) Economics of Housing Markets, 1989. **Address:** Department of Economics, Emory University, Atlanta, GA 30322, U.S.A. **Online address:** rmuth@emory.edu

MUTUA, Makau wa. American/Kenyan (born Kenya), b. 1958?. **Genres:** Civil Liberties/Human Rights, Economics. **Career:** State University of New York, Buffalo Law School, faculty, 1997-, dean, 2008-, distinguished professor; Kenya Human Rights Commission, co-founder and chair; Buffalo Human Rights Center, director; Government of Kenya, Task Force on the Establishment of a Truth, Justice, and Reconciliation Commission, chair; Harvard Law School, Human Rights Program, director; Harvard University, Law School, visiting professor; University of Iowa, College of Law, visiting professor; University of Puerto Rico, School of Law, visiting professor; United Nations University for Peace, visiting professor. Writer, attorney, human rights lawyer, activist, public speaker and administrator. **Publications:** Zaire: Repression as Policy: A Human Rights Report, 1990; (with R. Howse) Protecting Human Rights in a Global Economy: Challenges for the World Trade Organization, 2000; Human Rights: A Political and Cultural Critique, 2002; Eyes on the Prize, 2003; Report of the Task Force on the Establishment of a Truth, Justice, and Reconciliation Commission, 2003; Kenya's Quest for Democracy: Taming Leviathan, 2008; (ed.) Human Rights NGOs in East Africa: Political and Normative Tensions, 2009. Contributor to books, newspapers, periodicals and journals. **Address:** Buffalo Law School, State University of New York, 319 O'Brian Hall, North Campus, Buffalo, NY 14260-1100, U.S.A.

MUTZ, Diana C. American (born United States), b. 1962?. **Genres:** Politics/Government, Adult Non-fiction. **Career:** University of Wisconsin, assistant professor, 1988-94, associate professor of political science, 1994-99, associate chair, 1996-99; Political Behavior, editor, editor-in-chief, 1998-2003; Ohio State University, professor of political science, journalism and mass communications, 1999-2003; University of Pennsylvania, Samuel A. Stouffer professor of political science and communication, 2003-, Samuel A. Stouffer chair in political science and communication, Institute for the Study of Citizens and Politics, Annenberg Public Policy Center, director, 2003-; Brookings Institution, senior fellow in governance studies, 2007-. **Publications:** (Contrib.) Reasoning and Choice: Explorations in Political Psychology, 1992; (ed. with P.M. Sniderman and R.A. Brody) Political Persuasion and Attitude Change, 1996; Impersonal Influence: How Perceptions of Mass Collectives Affect Political Attitudes, 1998; Hearing the Other Side: Deliberative Versus Participatory Democracy, 2006; Population-based Survey Experiments, 2011. Contributor to journals. **Address:** Department of Political Science, University of Pennsylvania, Rm. 217, 235 Stiteler Hall, 3620 Walnut St., Philadelphia, PA 19104-6215, U.S.A. **Online address:** mutz@sas.upenn.edu

MUUSS, Rolf Eduard. American/German (born Germany), b. 1924. **Genres:** Education, Psychology, Young Adult Non-fiction, Human Relations/Parenting, Social Sciences. **Career:** School teacher, 1945-46, 1951-53; Child Study Center for Emotionally Disturbed Children, houseparent, 1953; State University of Iowa, Child Welfare Research Station, research assistant professor, 1957-59; Goucher College, associate professor of education and child development, 1959-64, professor of education, 1964-95, professor emeritus, 1995-, director of the special education program, 1977, Elizabeth C. Todd distinguished professor, 1980-84, Department of Sociology and Anthropology, chairman, 1980-83; Hopkins University, research associate in education, 1962-63; Sheppard and Enoch Pratt Hospital, teaching associate, 1969-80; State of Maryland, hearing officer of special education, 1980-95. Writer. **Publications:** First Aid for Classroom Discipline Problems, 1962; Theories of Adolescence, 1962, 6th ed., 1996; Adolescent Behavior and Society: A Book of Readings, 1971, 5th ed., 1998; Grundlagen der Jugendpsychologie, 1982. Contributor of articles to journals. **Address:** 800 Southerly Rd., Apt. 304, Towson, MD 21286, U.S.A. **Online address:** rmuuss@goucher.edu

MYCIO, Mary. Ukranian/American (born United States) **Genres:** Natural History, Earth Sciences. **Career:** IREX U-Media Legal Defense and Education Program, director, 1998-; International Research and Exchanges Board, head of Legal Defense and Education Project, 1999-; freelance journalist and lawyer. **Publications:** Wormwood Forest: A Natural History of Chernobyl, 2005. Contributor to periodicals. **Address:** IREX U-Media Legal Defense and Education Program, vul. Khreshchatyk 27A, Ste. 28, Kyiv, 01001, Ukraine. **Online address:** myciomary@yahoo.com

MYDDELTON BIDDULPH, Gualtiero Malde'. *See* **SERVADIO, Gaia (Cecilia Gemmalina).**

MYER, Neilma. *See* **SIDNEY, Neilma.**

MYERS, Alyse. American (born United States), b. 1956?. **Genres:** Autobiography/Memoirs. **Career:** New York Is Book Country, chair; New York Times, vice-president of brand programs. Writer. **Publications:** Who Do You Think You Are?: A Memoir, 2008. **Address:** c/o Robin Straus, Robin Straus Agency, 229 E 79th St., New York, NY 10075-0866, U.S.A. **Online address:** alyse@alysemyers.com

MYERS, Bill. American (born United States), b. 1953. **Genres:** Novels, Children's Fiction, Young Adult Fiction, Theology/Religion, Picture/Board Books, Young Adult Non-fiction. **Career:** Writer, actor and director. **Publications:** ADULT'S NON-FICTION: Dr. Luke Examines Jesus, 1979; Nikolai, Marshal, Scott, Pickering, 1979; Christ B.C., 1990; The Dark Side of the Supernatural, 1999; Then Comes Marriage, 2001. FICTION: Blood of Heaven, 1996; Threshold, 1997; Fire of Heaven, 1999; Eli, 2000; When the Last Leaf Falls, 2001; Fire of Heaven Trilogy, 2001; The Face of God, 2002; Wager, 2003; My Life as a Tarantula Toe Tickler, 2003; The Case of the Hiccupping Ears, 2003; The Case of the Drooling Dinosaurs, 2003; Bloodstone Chronicles: A Journey of Faith, 2003; Soul Tracker, 2004; Presence, 2005; The Case of the Yodeling Turtles, 2005; Seeing, 2007; Voice, 2008; Stink Bug Saves the Day!: The Parable of the Good Samaritan, 2008; (with D. Wimbish) Side of the Supernatural: What is of God and What Isn't, 2008; Invisible Terror Collection, 2008; House that Went Ker-splat!: The Parable of the Wise and Foolish Builders, 2008; Dark Power Collection, 2008; Trapped By Shadows, 2009; (with J. Riordan) On the Run, 2009; (with J. Riordan) The Enemy Closes In, 2009; The Chamber of Lies, 2009; Angel of Wrath, 2009; (with J. Riordan) Elijah Project, 2010. CHILDREN'S BOOKS: (with K.C. Johnson) McGee and Me!: The Big Lie, 1989; (with K.C. Johnson) A Star in the Breaking, 1989; (with K.C. Johnson) The Not So Great Escape, 1989; Skate Expectations, 1989; Twister and Shout, 1989; It was the Fight before Christmas, 1989; Back to the Drawing Board, 1990; Do the Bright Thing, 1990; Take Me Out of the Ball Game, 1990; Journey to Fayrah: The Portal, 1991; Journeys to Fayrah: The Experiment, 1991; Journeys to Fayrah: The Whirlwind, 1992; Journeys to Fayrah: The Tablet, 1992; In the Nick of Time, 1992; (with R. West) The Blunder Years, 1993; (with R. West) Beauty in the Least, 1993; My Life as a Smashed Burrito with Extra Hot Sauce, 1993; My Life as Alien Monster Bait, 1993; My Life as a Broken Bungie Cord, 1993; My Life as Crocodile Junk Food, 1993; My Life as Dinosaur Dental Floss, 1994; My Life as a Torpedo Test Target, 1994; My Life as a Human Hockey Puck, 1994; My Life as an Afterthought Astronaut, 1995; My Life as Reindeer Road Kill, 1995; My Life as a Toasted Time Traveler, 1996; My Life as Polluted Pond Scum, 1996; My Life as a Big Foot Breath Mint, 1997; My Life as a Blundering Ballerina, 1997; The Ghost of KRZY, 1997; The Curse, 1997; The Mystery of the Invisible Knight, 1997; Phantom of the Haunted Church, 1998; My Life as a Screaming Skydiver, 1998; The Scream, 1998; The Ancients, 1998; My Life as a Human Hairball, 1998; Invasion of the UFOs, 1998; My Life as a Walrus Whoopee Cushion, 1999; Fangs for the Memories, 1999; The Case of the Missing Minds, 1999; My Life as a Mixed Up Millennium Bug, 1999; My Life as a Beat up Basketball Backboard, 2000; Secret of the Ghostly Hot Rod, 2000; I Want My Mummy, 2000; My Life as a Cowboy Cowpie, 2001; My Life as Invisible Intestines, 2001; Curse of the Horrible Hair Day, 2001; Scam of the Screwball Wizards, 2001; The Undead, 2002; The Case of the Chewable Worms, 2002; The Case of the Giggling Geeks, 2002; The Case of the Flying Toenails, 2002; My Life as a Sky Surfing Skateboarder, 2002; The Mystery of the Melodies from Mars, 2002; (with D. Wimbish) Room with a Boo, 2002; My Life as a Prickly Porcupine from Pluto, 2004; My Life as a Splatted-flat Quarterback, 2005; My Life as a Belching Baboon with Bad Breath, 2005; My Life as a Stupendously Stomped Soccer Star, 2006; My Life as a Haunted Hamburger hold the Pickles, 2006; My Life as a Super-sized Superhero with Slobber, 2007; The God Hater, 2010; The Judas Gospel, 2011. PICTURE BOOKS: (with M.W. Hickman) My Friend William Moved Away, 1979; Baseball for Breakfast, 1999; Nervous Norman Hot on the Trail, 2009; Freddie's Fast-cash Getaway: The Parable of the Prodigal Son, 2009. TJ AND THE TIME STUMBLERS SERIES: New Kid Catastrophes, 2010; AAAARGH!!!, 2011; Ho-ho-nooo!, 2011; Oops!, 2011; Switched!, 2012; Yikes!!!, 2012. FOR TEENS: Faith Workout, 1986; Hot Topics, Tough Questions, 1987; Jesus: An Eyewitness Account, 1988; More Hot Topics, 1989; The Society, 1994; The Deceived, 1994; The Spell, 1995; The Haunting, 1995; The Guardian, 1995; The Encounter, 1995; Faith Encounter, 1999; Just Believe It, 2001; Millom, 2004. **Address:** c/o Author Mail, Zondervan, 5300 Patterson Ave. SE, Grand Rapids, MI 49530-0001, U.S.A. **Online address:** bill@billmyers.com

MYERS, Drew(fus Young). American (born United States), b. 1946. **Genres:** Chemistry, Sciences, Technology, Engineering. **Career:** Eastman Kodak Co., senior research associate, 1974-85; Alpha C.I.S.A., consultant, 1986-90, Emulsions Division, director of research and development, 1990-. Writer. **Publications:** Surfactant Science and Technology, 1988, 3rd ed., 2006; Surfaces, Interfaces and Colloids, 1991, 2nd ed., 1999. Contributor to books. **Address:** Alpha C.I.S.A., C.C., Ste. 66, Rio Tercero Cordoba, 5850, Argentina. **Online address:** drewmyers@arnet.com.ar

MYERS, Eric. American (born United States) **Genres:** Biography, Literary Criticism And History, Social Sciences, Biography, Humanities. **Career:** New York Times, contributor. Writer. **Publications:** (With H. Mandelbaum) Screen Deco: A Celebration of High Style in Hollywood, 1985; (with H. Mandelbaum) Forties Screen Style: A Celebration of High Pastiche in Hollywood, 1989; Uncle Mame: The Life of Patrick Dennis, 2000. Contributor to periodicals. **Address:** c/o Author Mail, St. Martins Press, 175 5th Ave., New York, NY 10010, U.S.A.

MYERS, Greg. British (born England), b. 1954. **Genres:** Sciences, Biology. **Career:** Lancaster University, Department of Linguistics and English Language, professor of rhetoric and communication, head of department, Centre for Language in Social Life, faculty, Centre for Science Studies, faculty. Writer. **Publications:** Writing Biology: Texts in the Social Construction of Scientific Knowledge, 1990; Words in Ads, 1994; (ed. with G.N. Leech and J. Thomas) Spoken English on Computer: Transcription, Mark-Up, and Application, 1995; Ad Worlds: Brands, Media, Audiences, 1998; Matters of Opinion: Talking about Public Issues, 2004; The Discourse of Blogs and Wikis, 2010. Contributor to periodicals. **Address:** Department of Linguistics and English Language, Lancaster University, Rm. C54, County S, Lancaster, LC LA1 4YL, England. **Online address:** g.myers@lancaster.ac.uk

MYERS, Helen. (Helen R. Myers). American (born United States), b. 1946?. **Genres:** Music, Romance/Historical, Novels. **Career:** American Wind Symphony Orchestra, clarinetist, 1966-67; Columbia University, Center for Studies in Ethnomusicology, research fellow, 1973-75, lecturer in music history, 1975-76, visiting associate professor, 1993; New Grove Dictionary of Music and Musicians, junior editor for ethnomusicology, 1976-77, resident ethnomusicologist, 1981-89; University of Mauritius, Mahatma Gandhi Institute, advisor, 1986; Trinity College, associate professor of music, 1989-, research fellow, St. Anthony Hall professor of music; University of London, Goldsmiths' College, lecturer, 1981-89; Columbia University, visiting associate professor, 1993; New Grove Dictionary of Music and Musicians, head consultant ethnomusicologist, 1994-99; Freelance, editor and writer, 2010-; Yale University, visiting research fellow. **Publications:** (With B. Nettl) Folk Music in the United States: An Introduction, 1976; Partners for Life, 1987; Donovan's Mermaid, 1988; Smooth Operator, 1988; That Fontaine Woman!, 1989; Someone to Watch over Me, 1989; The Pirate O'Keefe, 1989; Kiss Me Kate, 1990; Confidentially Yours, 1989; Invitation to a Wedding, 1990; After You, 1990; A Fine Arrangement, 1991; When Gabriel Called, 1991; Through My Eyes, 1991; Three Little Chaperones, 1992; Navarrone, 1992; Seawitch, 1992; Forbidden Passion, 1992; Night Mist, 2001; Jake, 1993; Whispers in the Woods, 1994; A Father's Promise, 1994; Once Upon a Full Moon, 1994; To Wed at Christmas, 1994; Watching for Willa, 1995; The Law is No Lady, 1995; The Rebel and the Hero, 1995; The Merry Matchmakers, 1995; Just a Memory Away, 1996; Baby In a Basket, 1996; After That Night, 1996; The Officer and The Renegade, 1997; Music of Hindu Trinidad: Songs from the India Diaspora, 1998; Come Sundown, 1998; Beloved Mercenary, 1998; More than You Know, 1999; Lost, 2000; Dead End, 2001; Final Stand, 2002; No Sanctuary, 2003; While Others Sleep, 2004; What Should Have Been, 2006; A Man to Count on, 2007; The Last Man She'd Marry, 2008; Daddy on Demand, 2009; Hope's Child, 2010; It's News to Her, 2011; Almost a Hometown Bride, 2012. EDITOR AND CONTRIBUTOR: Ethnomusicology: An Introduction, 1992; Ethnomusicology: Historical and Regional Studies, 1993; It Started with a House, 2010; Ethnomusicology: World Music Cultures, forthcoming. Works appear in anthologies. Contributor of articles. **Address:** Harlequin.com, PO Box 5190, Buffalo, NY 14240-5190, U.S.A.

MYERS, Helen R. *See* **MYERS, Helen.**

MYERS, Kevin. Irish/British (born England), b. 1947. **Genres:** Autobiography/Memoirs. **Career:** RTE (Radio Telefis Eireann), journalist, 1971-78; Sunday Telegraph, columnist; Irish Times, columnist. Writer. **Publications:** From the Irish Times Column An Irishman's Diary, 2000; Banks of Green Willow, 2001; Watching the Door: A Memoir, 1971-1978, 2006; More Myers: An Irishman's Diary, 1997-2006, 2007. Contributor of articles to periodicals. **Address:** Scribner, 1230 Ave. of the Americas, New York, NY 10020, U.S.A. **Online address:** kmyers@independent.ie

MYERS, Lois E. American (born United States), b. 1946. **Genres:** History. **Career:** Baylor University, Institute for Oral History, senior lecturer and associate director, 1986-92, Texas Oral History Association, secretary and treasurer, 1987, interim director. Writer. **Publications:** Letters by Lamplight: A Woman's View of Everyday Life in South Texas, 1873-1883, 1991; (contrib.) Rock beneath the Sand: Country Churches in Texas, 2003; (with T.L. Charlton and R. Sharpless) Handbook of Oral History, 2006; (with T.L. Charlton and R. Sharpless) History of Oral History: Foundations and Methodology, 2007; (with T.L. Charlton and R. Sharpless) Thinking About Oral History: Theories and Applications, 2008. **Address:** Institute for Oral History, Baylor University, 1 Bear Pl., Ste. 97271, 1311 S 5th St., Waco, TX 76798-7271, U.S.A. **Online address:** lois_myers@baylor.edu

MYERS, Robert Manson. American (born United States), b. 1921. **Genres:** Novels, Plays/Screenplays, History, Humanities, Language/Linguistics, Literary Criticism And History, Music, Theatre, Humor/Satire. **Career:** Yale University, instructor in English, 1945-47; College of William and Mary, assistant professor of English, 1947-48; Tulane University, assistant professor of English, 1948-54; Brearley School, English faculty, 1954-56; University of Maryland, assistant professor, 1959-63, associate professor, 1963-68, professor of English, 1968-86, professor emeritus of English, 1986; University of Rotterdam, Fulbright professor, 1958-59. Writer. **Publications:** Early Moral Criticism of Handelian Oratorio, 1947; Handel's Messiah: A Touchstone of Taste, 1948; From Beowulf to Virginia Woolf: An Astounding and Wholly Unauthorized History of English Literature, 1952; Handel, Dryden and Milton, 1956; Restoration Comedy, 1961; (ed.) The Children of Pride (novel), 1972; (ed.) A Georgian at Princeton (novel), 1976; Quintet: Five Plays Cycle Drawn from the Children of Pride, 1991; Sixes and Sevens: Three Plays, 2004; The Bostonians: A Play In Two Acts from the Novel by Henry James (play), 2005; Poynton Park (play): A Play In Three Acts from the Novel The Spoils Of Poynton By Henry James, 2005. **Address:** 3804 Deckford Pl., Charlotte, NC 28211, U.S.A.

MYERS, Tamar. American/Israeli (born Israel), b. 1948. **Genres:** Novellas/Short Stories, Mystery/Crime/Suspense, Novels. **Career:** Writer. **Publications:** MYSTERY NOVELS: Too Many Crooks Spoil the Broth, 1994; Parsley Sage, Rosemary, and Crime, 1995; No Use Dying over Spilled Milk, 1996; Larceny and Old Lace, 1996; Gilt by Association, 1996; Just Plain Pickled to Death, 1997; The Ming and I, 1997; So Faux, So Good, 1997; Between a Wok and a Hard Place, 1998; Eat, Drink and Be Wary, 1998; Baroque and Desperate, 1999; Play It Again, Spam, 1999; Estate of Mind, 1999; The Hand That Rocks the Ladle, 2000; A Penny Urned, 2000; The Crepes of Wrath, 2001; Nightmare in Shining Armor, 2001; Gruel and Unusual Punishment, 2002; Splendor in the Glass, 2002; Custard's Last Stand, 2003; Tiles and Tribulations, 2003; Statue of Limitations: A Den of Antiquity Mystery, 2004; Thou Shalt not Grill: A Pennsylvania Dutch Mystery with Recipes, 2004; Dark Side of Heaven, 2005; Assault and Pepper, 2005; Monet Talks: A Den of Antiquity Mystery, 2005; Grape Expectations: A Pennsylvania Dutch Mystery with Recipes, 2006; Cane Mutiny: A Den of Antiquity Mystery, 2006; Hell Hath No Curry: A Pennsylvania Dutch Mystery with Recipes, 2007; Death of a Rug Lord: A Den of Antiquity Mystery, 2008; As the World Churns: A Pennsylvania Dutch Mystery with Recipes, 2008; Batter Off Dead: A Pennsylvania Dutch Mystery, 2009; The Witch Doctor's Wife, 2009; Poison Ivory, 2009; Butter Safe Than Sorry, 2010; The Headhunter's Daughter, 2011; The Glass Is Always Greener, 2011. OTHER: Angels, Angels Everywhere (stories), 1995. **Address:** New American Library, 375 Hudson St., New York, NY 10014, U.S.A. **Online address:** tamar@tamarmyers.com

MYERS, Tim. Also writes as Chris Cavender, Elizabeth Bright, Melissa Glazer. American (born United States), b. 1958?. **Genres:** Novels, Mystery/Crime/Suspense. **Career:** Writer. **Publications:** LIGHTHOUSE INN SERIES: Innkeeping with Murder, 2001; Reservations for Murder, 2002; Murder Checks Inn, 2003; Room for Murder, 2003; Booked for Murder, 2004. CANDLESHOP SERIES: At Wick's End, 2004; Snuffed Out, 2004; Death Waxed Over, 2005; A Flicker of Doubt, 2006. SOAP BOUTIQUE MYSTERIES SERIES: Dead Men Don't Lye, 2006; A Pour Way to Dye, 2006; A Mold for Murder, 2007. CLAY AND CRIME MYSTERY SERIES AS MELISSA GLAZER: A Murderous Glaze, 2007; The Cracked Pot, 2008; A Fatal Slip, 2008. NOVELS AS ELIZABETH BRIGHT: Reap the Wild Harvest, 1979; Desire's Legacy, 1981; A Heritage of Passion, 1982. CARD-MAKING MYSTERY SERIES AS ELIZABETH BRIGHT: Invitation to Murder, 2005; Murder and Salutations, 2006; Deadly Greetings, 2006. PIZZA MYSTERIES SERIES AS CHRIS CAVENDER: A Slice of Murder, 2009; Pepperoni Pizza Can Be Murder, 2010. Works appear in anthologies. Contributor to magazines and periodicals. **Address:** GA , U.S.A. **Online address:** timothylmyers@hotmail.com

MYERS, Walter Dean. Also writes as Walter M. Myers. American (born United States), b. 1937. **Genres:** Children's Fiction, Young Adult Fiction, Business/Trade/Industry, Young Adult Non-fiction, Poetry, Novels, Autobiography/Memoirs, Picture/Board Books, Picture/Board Books. **Career:** New York State Department of Labor, employment supervisor, 1966-69; Bobbs-Merrill Company Inc., senior trade book editor, 1970-77; full-time writer, 1977-. **Publications:** FICTION FOR CHILDREN: (as Walter M. Myers) Where Does the Day Go?, 1969; The Dragon Takes a Wife, 1972; The Dancers, 1972; Fly, Jimmy, Fly!, 1974; The Story of the Three Kingdoms, 1995; How Mr. Monkey saw the Whole World, 1996; The Blues of Flats Brown, 2000. YOUNG ADULT FICTION: Fast Sam, Cool Clyde, and Stuff, 1975; Brainstorm, 1977; Mojo and the Russians, 1977; Victory for Jamie, 1977; It Ain't All for Nothin', 1978; The Young Landlords, 1979; The Black Pearl and the Ghost or One Mystery After Another, 1980; The Golden Serpent, 1980; Hoops, 1981; The Legend of Tarik, 1981; Won't Know till I Get There, 1982; The Nicholas Factor, 1983; Tales of a Dead King, 1983; Mr. Monkey and the Gotcha Bird: An Original Tale, 1984; Motown and Didi: A Love Story, 1984; The Outside Shot, 1984; Adventure in Granada, 1985; The Hidden Shrine, 1985; Duel in the Desert, 1986; Ambush in the Amazon, 1986; Sweet Illusions, 1987; Crystal, 1987; Fallen Angels, 1988; Scorpions, 1988; Me, Mop, and the Moondance Kid, 1988; The Mouse Rap, 1990; Somewhere in the Darkness, 1992; The Righteous Revenge of Artemis Bonner, 1992; Mop, Moondance, and the Nagasaki Knights, 1992; Darnell Rock Reporting, 1994; The Glory Field, 1994; Shadow of the Red Moon, 1995; Slam!, 1996; Smiffy Blue: Ace Crime Detective: The Case of the Missing Ruby and Other Stories, 1996; The Journal of Joshua Loper: A Black Cowboy, 1999; The Journal of Scott Pendleton Collins: A World War II Soldier, 1999; Monster, 1999, rev. ed., 2004; 145th Street (short stories), 2000; The Journal of Biddy Owens, the Negro Leagues, 2001; Patrol: An American Soldier in Vietnam, 2001; Handbook for Boys, 2002; Three Swords for Granada, 2002; The Dream Bearer, 2003; The Beast, 2003. YOUNG ADULT NON-FICTION: The World of Work: A Guide to Choosing a Career, 1975; Social Welfare, 1976; Now Is Your Time!, 1991; A Place Called Heartbreak: A Story of Vietnam,

1992; Young Martin's Promise, 1992; Malcolm X: By Any Means Necessary, 1993; Remember Us Well: An Album of Pictures and Verse, 1993; Toussaint L'Ouverture: The Fight for Haiti's Freedom, 1996; One More Riverto Cross: An African-American Photograph Album, 1996; Amistad: A Long Road to Freedom, 1998; At Her Majesty's Request: An African Princess in Victorian England, 1999; Malcolm X: A Fire Burning Brightly, 2000; Bad Boy (memoir), 2001; The Greatest: Muhammad Ali, 2001; A Time to Love: Stories from the Old Testament, 2003, Game, 2008; Lockdown, 2010; Carmen, 2010; (with R. Workman) Kick, 2011; All the Right Stuff, 2012. POETRY: The Great Migration, 1993; Brown Angels, 1993; Glorious Angels, 1995; Harlem, 1997; Angel to Angel: A Mother's Gift of Love, 1998; Blues Journey, 2003; New York Draft Riot Poetry, 2008. OTHERS: Antarctica: Journeys to the South Pole, 2004; Here in Harlem: Poems in Many Voices, 2004; USS Constellation: Pride of the American Navy, 2004; Shooter, 2004; I've Seen the Promised Land: The Life of Dr. Martin Luther King, Jr., 2004; Autobiography of My Dead Brother, 2005; Street Love, 2006; Jazz, 2006; (with W. Miles) Harlem Hellfighters: When Pride Met Courage, 2006; What They Found: Love on 145th Street, 2007; Harlem Summer, 2007; Ida B. Wells: Let the Truth be Told, 2008; We Are America: Tribute from the Heart, 2008; Sunrise over Fallujah, 2008; Dope Sick, 2009; Amiri and Odette: A Love Story, 2009; Looking like Me, 2009; Riot, 2009; The Easy Life, 2010; The Cruisers, 2010; Muhammad Ali: The People's Champion, 2010; Looking for the Easy Life, 2010; Checkmate, 2011; A Star Is Born, 2012; Just Write: Here's How, 2012; Tribute, 2014. Works appear in anthologies. Contributor of articles to periodicals. **Address:** Miriam Altshuler Literary Agency, 53 Old Post Rd. N, Red Hook, NY 12571-2262, U.S.A.

MYERS, Walter M. *See* **MYERS, Walter Dean.**

MYERS, W. David. American (born United States), b. 1956. **Genres:** History. **Career:** Yale College, Department of Religious Studies, teaching assistant, 1979-82; Yale Divinity School, teaching assistant, 1982-83; Woodrow Wilson Foundation, Charlotte W. Newcombe fellow, 1985; Georgetown University, instructor in history, adjunct lecturer in history, 1987-88; University of Maryland, visiting instructor, 1988-89; Catholic University of America, instructor in history, adjunct lecturer in history, 1990; Fordham University, instructor in history, 1990-91, assistant professor of history, 1991-96, associate professor, 1996-. Writer. **Publications:** Poor, Sinning Folk: Confession and Conscience in Counter-Reformation Germany, 1996; Death and a Maiden: The Tragical History of Margarethe Schmidt, Infanticide, 2011. **Address:** Department of History, Fordham University, Dealy Hall 631, Rose Hill Campus, Bronx, NY 10458-5159, U.S.A. **Online address:** dmyers@fordham.edu

MYERS, William. British/Irish (born Ireland), b. 1939. **Genres:** Literary Criticism And History, History, Sciences, Ethics. **Career:** University of Nottingham, teacher, 1964-72; University of Leicester, senior lecturer, Department of English, professor, 1972-. Writer. **Publications:** Dryden, 1973; The Teaching of George Eliot, 1984; (ed.) Restoration and Revolution, 1986; Milton and Free Will: An Essay in Criticism and Philosophy, 1987; Evelyn Waugh and the Problem of Evil, 1991; (ed. and intro.) The Constant Couple; The Twin Rivals; The Recruiting Officer; The Beaux' Stratagem, 1995; The Presence of Persons: Essays on Literature, Science and Philosophy in the Nineteenth Century, 1998. **Address:** Department of English, University of Leicester, University Rd., Leicester, LE1 7RH, England.

MYERSON, Daniel. American (born United States) **Genres:** Novels, History, Sports/Fitness, Politics/Government, Social Sciences. **Career:** Columbia University, faculty; New York University, faculty; Bennington College, faculty. Writer. **Publications:** (With R. Kaufman and D. Fujita) Yes You Can!: 22 Years as a Weight Watchers Group Leader, 1999; Shakespeare, 2000; Blood and Splendor: The Lives of Five Tyrants from Nero to Saddam Hussein, 2001; (with J. Clemen, B. Schell and D. Kirkwood) The Town That Lost a Ton: How One Town Used the Buddy System to Lose 3998 Pounds...and How You Can Too!, 2002; The Linguist And The Emperor: The Race To Decipher The Rosetta Stone, 2003; Untitled Book on The Tomb of Tutankhamun, 2006; In the Valley of the Kings: Howard Carter and the Discovery of Tutankhamen's Tomb, 2009. **Address:** Sourcebooks Inc., 1935 Brookdale Rd., Ste. 139, Naperville, IL 60563-7994, U.S.A.

MYINT-U, Thant. American (born United States), b. 1966. **Genres:** History, Trivia/Facts. **Career:** United Nation's Relief Fund, Transitional Authority for Cambodia in Phnom Penh, human rights officer, 1992-93, policy advisor, United Nation's Protection Force, chief spokesman, 1994, United Nation's Special Representative for Bosnia and Herzegovina, political advisor, 1996; United Nation Secretariat, Office for the Coordination of Humanitarian Affairs, policy analyst, 2000-, Department of Political Affairs, Policy Planning Unit, chief, 2004, Executive Office of the Secretary-General, senior officer, 2005-06; Trinity College, fellow, 1995-99; University of Cambridge, Magdalene College, Centre for History and Economics, research associate. Writer and historian. **Publications:** (With E. Sellwood) Knowledge and Multilateral Interventions: The UN's Experiences in Cambodia and Bosnia-Herzegovina, 2000; The Making of Modern Burma, 2001; The River of Lost Footsteps: Histories of Burma, 2006; Where China Meets India: Burma and The New Crossroads of Asia, 2011. Contributor to periodicals. **Address:** Farrar, Straus and Giroux, 18 W 18th St., New York, NY 10011, U.S.A. **Online address:** myint-u@ipacademy.org

MYLES, Eileen. American (born United States), b. 1949. **Genres:** Poetry, Novels, Plays/Screenplays, Gay And Lesbian Issues, Travel/Exploration, Art/Art History, Songs/Lyrics And Libretti, Young Adult Fiction, Young Adult Fiction. **Career:** St. Mark's Poetry Project, artistic director, 1984-86; University of California, professor of writing, 2002-07; University of Montana, Hugo writer, 2010. Poet, novelist and journalist. **Publications:** (Ed.) Dodgems, 1977-79; The Irony of the Leash, 1978; A Fresh Young Voice from the Plains, 1981; Sappho's Boat, 1982; Bread and Water (stories), 1987; Feeling Blue, (play) 1988; 1969 (story), 1989; Leaving New York (performance), 1989; Modern Art (play), 1990; Not Me (poems), 1991; Chelsea Girls (stories), 1994; (ed.) The New Fuck You/Adventures in Lesbian Reading, 1995; Maxfield Parrish Early and New Poems, 1995; School of Fish (poems), 1997; Cool for You (novel), 2000; Skies (poems), 2001; On My Way(poems), 2001; Hell (libretto), 2004; (ed.) Best Lesbian Erotica, 2006; Sorry, Tree (poems) 2007; The Importance of Being Iceland (essays), 2009; Inferno (a poet's novel), 2010. Contributor to periodicals. **Address:** 86 E 3rd St. 3C, New York, NY 10003, U.S.A. **Online address:** eileen.myles@gmail.com

MYLES, Simon. *See* **FOLLETT, Ken(neth Martin).**

MYLROIE, Laurie. American (born United States), b. 1953. **Genres:** Politics/Government, International Relations/Current Affairs, Military/Defense/Arms Control, History, Young Adult Non-fiction, Technology. **Career:** Harvard University, assistant professor, 1985-90, Center for Middle Eastern Studies, research fellow, 1990-91; U.S. Naval War College, associate professor, 1991-92; Washington Institute for Near East Policy, research fellow in arab politics, 1992-. Writer. **Publications:** Politics and the Soviet presence in the People's Democratic Republic of Yemen: Internal Vulnerabilities and Regional Challenges, 1983; (with J. Miller) Saddam Hussein and the Crisis in the Gulf, 1990; The Future of Iraq, 1991; Study of Revenge: Saddam Hussein's Unfinished War against America, 2000; Study of Revenge: The First World Trade Center Attack and Saddam Hussein's War against America, 2001; The War Against America: Saddam Hussein and the World Trade Center Attacks: A Study of Revenge, 2001; Bush vs. the Beltway: How the CIA and the State Department tried to Stop the War on Terror, 2003. **Address:** Washington Institute for Near East Policy, 1828 L St. NW, Ste. 1050, Washington, DC 20036-5128, U.S.A. **Online address:** mylroie2@yahoo.com

MYNTON, Henry. American (born United States) **Genres:** Novels, Young Adult Fiction, Mystery/Crime/Suspense. **Career:** Writer. **Publications:** The Pachinko Woman, 1999. **Address:** c/o Author Mail, William Morrow, 10 E 53rd St., 7th Fl., New York, NY 10022, U.S.A.

MYRICK, David F. American (born United States) **Genres:** History, Transportation, Young Adult Non-fiction. **Career:** Southern Pacific Transportation Co., Telegraph Hill Bulletin, staff, 1944-73, Treasury Department, editor and publisher, 1956-60, treasurer, 1962-73, assistant to the vice-president, 1973-77; The Dakota Farmer Co., vice-president and director, 1961-67. **Publications:** Reproduction of Thompson and West's History of Nevada, 1881, with Illustrations and Biographical Sketches of Its Prominent Men and Pioneers, 1958; Railroads of Nevada and Eastern California, vol. I: The Northern Roads, 1962, vol. II: The Southern Roads, 1963, vol. III: More on the Northern Roads; (ed.) Life and Times of the Central Pacific Railroad, 1969; New Mexico's Railroads: A Historical Survey, 1970, rev. ed., 1990; San Francisco's Telegraph Hill, 1972, rev. ed., 2001; Rails around the Bohemian Grove, 1973; Railroads of Arizona, vol. I, 1975, vol. II, 1980, vol. III, 1984, vol. IV: Santa Fe Route, 1998, vol. V: Santa Fe to Phoenix, 2001; Postosi: An Empire of Silver, 1980; Montecito and Santa Barbara, vol. I, 1988, vol. II, 1991; Santa Fe to Phoenix, 2001; Western Pacific Construction History, 2005; Southern

Pacific Water Lines: Marine, Bay and River Operations of the Southern Pacific System, 2007. **Address:** PO Box 5237, Santa Barbara, CA 93150, U.S.A.

MYSS, Caroline. American (born United States), b. 1952. **Genres:** Medicine/Health, Theology/Religion. **Career:** Journalist, 1974; Stillpoint Publishing Inc., co-founder, 1983-90; American Holistic Medical Association, co-founder, 1984; Professional Intuitive Training, co-founder and developer, 1992-2004; Institute for the Science of Medical Intuition, co-founder, 1996-; CMED Institute (Caroline Myss Education), founder, 2003-; San Francisco State University, lecturer; Southern Connecticut University, lecturer; University of Massachusetts, lecturer; Brandeis University, lecturer; Regent's College, lecturer; Cambridge University, lecturer; Oxford University, lecturer. **Publications:** WITH C.N. SHEALY: Aids: Passageway to Transformation, 1987; Creation of Health: The Emotional, Psychological and Spiritual Responses That Promote Health and Healing, 1998. OTHERS: Anatomy of the Spirit: The Seven Stages of Power and Healing, 1996; Why People Don't Heal and How They Can, 1997; Sacred Contracts: Awakening Your Divine Potential, 2001; Caroline Myss's Journal of Inner Dialogue: Working with Your Chakras, Archetypes, and Sacred Contract, 2003; Channeling Grace: Daily Acts of Service, 2004; Invisible Acts of Power: Personal Choices that Create Miracles, 2004; (foreword) An Autobiography of George Washington, 2006; Entering the Castle: An Inner Path to God and Your Soul, 2007; (foreword) On Life After Death, 2008; Defy Gravity: Healing Beyond the Bounds of Reason, 2009. Contributor to periodicals. **Address:** c/o Author Mail, Simon & Schuster Adult Publishing Group, 1230 Ave. of the Americas, 10th Fl., New York, NY 10020-1513, U.S.A.

N

NAAM, Ramez. American/Egyptian (born Egypt) **Genres:** Technology. **Career:** Microsoft Corp., computer engineer, Apex Nano Technologies, chief executive officer; Foresight Institute, senior associate; Institute for Ethics and Emerging Technologies, fellow. Writer. **Publications:** More than Human: Embracing the Promise of Biological Enhancement, 2005. **Address:** Ted Weinstein Literary Management, 35 Stillman St., Ste. 203, San Francisco, CA 94107, U.S.A. **Online address:** author@morethanhuman.org

NÄASLUND, Göorel Kristina. (Göorel Kristina Carheden). Swedish (born Sweden), b. 1940. **Genres:** Children's Fiction, Psychology, How-to Books. **Career:** Expressen (daily newspaper), journalist, 1970-. Psychologist, educator and freelance writer. **Publications:** AS GöOREL KRISTINA CARHEDEN: Foods and Festivals, Swedish Style, 1968; (trans. as Göorel Kristina Carheden) Swedish Cooking, 1971; Vår Skona Grona Mat (for children), 1977; Vår första svampbok, 1998; Lilla äppelboken (for children), 2002; 100 älskade äpplen, 2002; Lilla vinterboken (for children), 2005; Our Apple Tree, 2005; Vem var det där?: en bok om ansiktsblindhet, 2006. Contributor to periodicals. **Address:** c/o Author Mail, Karnhuset, Drottning Kristinas vag 19, Sigtuna, 193 35, Sweden.

NABHAN, Gary Paul. American (born United States), b. 1952. **Genres:** Cultural/Ethnic Topics, Technology, Engineering. **Career:** University of Arizona, Office of Arid Lands Studies and Plant Sciences, research associate, 1978-85, Department of Native American Studies and English, visiting lecturer, 1998-2000, Southwest Center, research social scientist, research professor, Department of Geography and Regional Development, adjunct professor; Native Seeds/SEARCH, founder and research director, 1982-93; Desert Botanical Garden, associate director for research and collections, 1986-90; Arizona State University, Department of Botany, adjunct assistant professor, 1987-90; Conservation Intl., research associate, 1990-93; Arizona-Sonora Desert Museum, director of conservation science, 1993-2000; Northern Arizona University, Center of Sustainable Environments, director, professor of applied indigenous studies and environmental sciences, 2000-08. Writer. **Publications:** The Desert Smells Like Rain: A Naturalist in Papago Indian Country, 1982; (with B. Burns and C. Miksic) Corn of Southwestern United States and Northern New Mexico, 1984; Gathering the Desert, 1985; Saguaro: A View of Saguaro National Monument & the Tucson Basin, 1986; (ed. with J. Cole) Arizona Highways Presents Desert Wildflowers, 1988; Enduring Seeds: Native American Agriculture and Wild Plant Conservation, 1989; Wild Phaseolus Ecogeography in the Sierra Madre Occidental, Mexico, 1990; (with K. Dahl) Conservation of Plant Genetic Resources: Grassroots Efforts in North America, 1992; (ed.) Counting Sheep: Twenty Ways of Seeing Desert Bighorn, 1993; Songbirds, Truffles, and Wolves: An American Naturalist in Italy, 1993; (ed. with J.L. Carr) Ironwood: An Ecological and Cultural Keystone of the Sonoran Desert, 1994; Desert Legends: Re-Storying the Sonoran Borderlands, 1994; (with S. Trimble) Geography of Childhood: Why Children Need Wild Places, 1994; (with C. Wilson) Canyons of Color, 1995; (with S.L. Buchmann) Forgotten Pollinators, 1996; Cultures of Habitat: On Nature, Culture and Story, 1997; (with T.E. Sheridan) La Vida Norteña, 1998; (with A. Astorga) Efraín of the Sonoran Desert: A Lizard's Life Among the Seri Indians, 2001; Coming Home to Eat: The Pleasures and Politics of Local Foods, 2002; The Desert Smells Like Rain: A Naturalist in O'Odham Country, 2002; Singing the Turtles to Sea: The Comcaác Art and Science of Reptiles, 2003; (with A.G. Valenzuela-Zapata) Tequila: A Natural and Cultural History, 2003; Cross-Pollinations: The Marriage of Science and Poetry, 2004; (ed.) Conserving Migratory Pollinators and Nectar Corridors in Western North America, 2004; Cross-Pollination: The Marriage of Science and Poetry, 2004; Why Some Like it Hot: Food, Genes, and Cultural Diversity, 2004; (foreword) Earth Notes: Exploring the Southwest's Canyon Country from the Airwaves: From the Popular KNAU Public Radio Show, 2005; Arab/American: Landscape, and Cuisine Culture in Two Great Deserts, 2008; (ed. and intro.) Renewing America's Food Traditions: Saving and Savoring the Continent's Most Endangered Foods, 2008; Where Our Food Comes From: Retracing Nikolay Vavilov's Quest to End Famine, 2009; Heritage Farming in the Southwest, 2010; (with K.M. Friese and K. Kraft) Chasing Chiles, 2011; Exploring the Unique Flavors and Sundry Places of the Borderlands, 2012. Contributor to periodicals. **Address:** Southwest Center, University of Arizona, 1052 N Highland Ave., Tucson, AZ 85721-0185, U.S.A. **Online address:** gpnabhan@email.arizona.edu

NACOS, Brigitte L. American (born United States) **Genres:** Politics/Government, History. **Career:** Columbia University, adjunct assistant, adjunct associate, 1988-2002, adjunct professor of political science, 2002-. Writer. **Publications:** Jimmy Carter: Der Präsident, 1977; The Press Presidents and Crises, 1990; Terrorism and the Media: From the Iran Hostage Crisis to the World Trade Center Bombing, 1994; From Bonn to Berlin: German Politics in Transition, 1998; Decisionmaking in a Glass House: Mass Media Public Opinion and American and European Foreign Policy in the Twenty-first Century, 2000; Mass-Mediated Terrorism: The Central Role of the Media in Terrorism and Counterterrorism, 2002, 2nd ed., 2007; Terrorism And Counterterrorism: Understanding Threats And Responses In The Post-9/11 World, 2006, 3rd ed., 2009; (with O. Torres-Reyna) Fueling Our Fears: Stereotyping, Media Coverage And Public Opinion of Muslim Americans, 2007; (with Y. Bloch-Elkon and R.Y. Shapiro) Selling Fear: Counterterrorism, the Media, and Public Opinion, 2011. Contributor to books and periodicals. **Address:** Department of Political Science, Columbia University, 730 International Affairs Bldg., 420 W 118th St., PO Box 3320, New York, NY 10027-6902, U.S.A. **Online address:** bn1@columbia.edu

NÁDAS, Péter. Hungarian (born Hungary), b. 1942. **Genres:** Novels, Novellas/Short Stories, Essays. **Career:** Budapest Magazine, journalist, 1965-69; freelance writer, 1969-. **Publications:** Családregény Vége: Regény, 1977; Leírás, 1979; Nézotér, 1983; Emlékiratok Könyvé, 1986; Játéktér, 1988; évkonyv, Ezerkilencszáznyolcvanhét-Ezerkilencszáznyolcvannyolc, 1989; Vonulás: Két Filmnovella, 1995; Esszék, 1995; Drámák, 1996; Talált Cetli: és Más Elegyes Irások, 1996; (with R. Swartz) Párbeszéd: Négy Napezerkilencszáznyolcvankilencben, 1997; Kritikák, 1999; (with E. Péter and K. Imre) Kalauz: Bojtár Endrekísèro írásaival, 2003; Saját Halál, 2004; Párhuzamos Tortènetek, 2005; Hátországi napló: újabb esszék, 2006; Fire and Knowledge: Fiction and Essays, 2007; Szirèînèînek: szatiîrjàîtèîk, 2010; Parallel Stories: A Novel, 2010. **Address:** Farrar Straus & Giroux Inc., 19 Union Sq. W, New York, NY 10003-3304, U.S.A.

NADEAU, Adel. American (born United States), b. 1940. **Genres:** Education. **Career:** Miller Elementary, vice principal, 1983-84; Longfellow Spanish Immersion Magnet School, principal, 1984-87; Linda Vista Elementary

School, principal, 1987-; San Diego County Office of Education, educator, principal, principal-in-residence, 1994-, chair. Writer. **Publications:** (With O.B. Miramontes and N.L. Commins) Restructuring Schools for Linguistic Diversity: Linking Decision Making to Effective Programs, 1997, 2nd ed., 2011. **Address:** San Diego County Office of Education, Rm. 612, 6401 Linda Vista Rd., San Diego, CA 92111-7399, U.S.A. **Online address:** anadeau@sdcoe.k12.ca.us

NADELMANN, Ethan A. American (born United States), b. 1957. **Genres:** Adult Non-fiction, Law, Psychology, Politics/Government, Social Sciences. **Career:** Stanley H. Kaplan Educational Center, instructor, 1980-81; U.S. Department of State, consultant to Bureau of International Narcotics Matters, 1984-85; Princeton University, assistant professor of politics and public affairs, 1987-94, Center of International Studies, faculty associate, 1987-94, Center of Domestic and Comparative Policy Studies, faculty associate, 1990-94; Rutgers University, Center for Historical Analysis, associate fellow, 1991-93; Lindesmith Center, founder and director, 1994-2000; Drug Policy Alliance Network, founder and executive director, 2000-. **Publications:** Cops across Borders: The Internationalization of U.S. Criminal Law Enforcement, 1993; (co-ed. and contrib.) Psychoactive Drugs and Harm Reduction: From Faith to Science, 1993; (with P. Andreas) Policing the Globe: Criminalization and Crime Control in International Relations, 2006. Contributor to periodicals. **Address:** Drug Policy Alliance Network, 70 W 36th St., Fl. 16, New York, NY 10018, U.S.A. **Online address:** enadelmann@drugpolicy.org

NADEN, Corinne J. American (born United States), b. 1930. **Genres:** Children's Fiction, Children's Non-fiction, Novels, Local History/Rural Topics, History, Biography, Adult Non-fiction, Literary Criticism And History, Autobiography/Memoirs. **Career:** Franklin Watts, children's book editor, 1970; R.R. Bowker, senior editor for reference and professional books, 1980. **Publications:** The First Book of Rivers, 1967; Frank Lloyd Wright, 1968; The Haymarket Affair, 1968; The Chicago Fire, 1969; Golf, 1970; Grasslands around the World, 1970; Let's Find out about Bears, 1971; The Triangle Shirtwaist Fire, 1971; Let's Find out About Frogs, 1972; The Nile River, 1972; Woodlands Around the World, 1973; The Colony of New Jersey, 1974; The Mississippi: America's Great River System, 1974; Driving Your Bike Safely, 1979; Cycle Chase: The Championship Season, 1980; High Gear: From Motorcycles to Superwheels, 1980; John Henry, Steel-Driving Man, 1980; (adaptor) L. Frank Baum's Dorothy and The Wicked Witch, 1980; (adaptor) L. Frank Baum's Off to See the Wizard, 1980; (adaptor) L. Frank Baum's Over the Rainbow, 1980; Motorcycle Challenge: Trials and Races, 1980; Rough Rider: The Challenge of Moto-Cross, 1980; Pegasus the Winged Horse, 1981; Perseus and Medusa, 1981; Theseus and the Minotaur, 1981; Ronald McNair, 1991; I Can Read about Sharks, 1996; The A-Z of Drugs, 2006; Patients' Rights, 2007; Abortion, 2008; Political Campaigns, 2009; Romeo and Juliet, 2009; Mao Zedong and the Chinese Revolution, 2009; Health Care: A Right or a Privilege?, 2010; The Taming of the Shrew, 2010; As You Like It, 2011; Benazir Bhutto, 2011; The Golden Age of American Musical Theatre: 1943-1965, 2011; Jeanette Rankin, 2012. WITH J.T. GILLESPIE: Juniorplots 3: A Book Talk Guide for Use with Readers Ages 12-16, 1987; Seniorplots: A Book Talk Guide for Use with Readers Ages 15-18, 1989; (ed.) Best Books for Children: Preschool Through Grade 6, 4th ed., 1990, 5th ed., 1994; Juniorplots 4: A Book Talk Guide for Use with Readers, Ages 12-16, 1993; Middleplots 4: A Book Talk Guide for Use with Readers Ages 8-12, 1994; The Newbery Companion: Booktalk and Related Materials for Newbery Medal and Honor Books, 1996, 3rd ed. as The Newbery/Printz companion: Booktalk and Related Materials for Award Winners and Honor Books, 2006; (comp.) Characters in Young Adult Literature, 1997; Teenplots: A Booktalk Guide to Use with Readers Ages 12-18, 2003; Classic Teenplots: A Booktalk Guide to Use with Readers Ages 12-18, 2006. NONFICTION WITH R. BLUE: Barbara Bush: First Lady, 1991; Christa McAuliffe: Teacher in Space, 1991; Colin Powell: Straight to the Top, 1991; Barbara Jordan, 1992; John Muir: Saving the Wilderness, 1992; U.S. Navy, 1993; U.S. Air Force, 1993; U.S. Coast Guard, 1993; People of Peace, 1994; Working Together against Hate Groups, 1994; Black Sea, 1995; Andes Mountains, 1995; The White House Kids, 1995; Whoopi Goldberg: A Entertainer, 1995; Jerry Rice, 1995; Heroes Don't Just Happen: Biographies of Overcoming Bias and Building Character in Politics, 1997; Staying Out of Trouble in a Troubled Family, 1998; Why Fight?: The Causes of the American Civil War, 2000; The Duty to Rescue, 2000; Belle Starr and the Wild West, 2000; Chris Rock, 2000; Jonas Salk: Polio Pioneer, 2001; Cleopatra, 2001; Punishment and Rehabilitation, 2001; The History of Gospel Music, 2001; Benjamin Banneker: Mathematician and Stargazer, 2001; Wesley Snipes, 2001; Halle Berry, 2002; Dian Fossey: At Home with the Giant Gorillas, 2002; New York, 2002; Monica Seles, 2002; Harriet Tubman: Riding the Freedom Train, 2003; Tony Blair, 2003; Nicolas Cage, 2003; Mississippi, 2003; Massachusetts, 2003; Mae Jemison: Out of This World, 2003; John Travolta, 2003; Wilma Rudolph, 2004; Lenin, 2004; George W. Bush, 2004; Mormonism, 2004; Muammar Qaddafi, 2005; Condoleezza Rice, 2006; Cornel West, 2006; Fidel Castro and the Cuban Revolution, 2006; Henry Louis Gates, Jr., 2006; Maya Angelou, 2006; Toni Morrison, 2006; James Monroe, 2009; Ron's Big Mission, 2009. WHO'S THAT IN THE WHITE HOUSE SERIES WITH R. BLUE: The Expansion Years: 1857-1901, 1998; The Formative Years: 1829 to 1857, 1998; The Founding Years: 1789 to 1829, 1998; The Modern Years: 1969 to 2001, 1998; The Progressive Years: 1901 to 1933, 1998; The Turbulent Years: 1933 to 1969, 1998. Madeleine Albright: U.S. Secretary of State, 1999; You're the Boss: Positive Attitude and Work Ethics, 1999. HOUSE DIVIDED SERIES WITH R. BLUE: The Bloodiest Days: The Battles of 1861 and 1862, 2000; Chancellorsville to Appomattox: The Battles of 1863 to 1865, 2000; Civil War Ends: Assassination, Reconstruction, and the Aftermath, 2000. GREAT PEOPLES AND THEIR CLAIM TO FAME SERIES WITH R. BLUE: Ancient Chinese and the Great Wall of China, 2003; The Aztecs and Tenochtitlan, 2003; Ancient Romans and the Colosseum, 2003; Ancient Maya and Tikal, 2003; Ancient Greeks and the Parthenon, 2003; Ancient Egyptians and the Pyramids, 2003. EXPLORING THE AMERICAS SERIES WITH R. BLUE: Exploring the Southeastern United States, 2003; Exploring the Pacific Northwest, 2003; Exploring the Mississippi River Valley, 2003; Exploring Northeastern America, 2003; Exploring the St. Lawrence River Region, 2004; Exploring the Western Mountains, 2004; Exploring the Southwestern United States, 2004; Exploring the Arctic, 2004; Exploring South America, 2004; Exploring Central America, Mexico, and the Caribbean, 2004. SUPREME COURT MILESTONES SERIES WITH R. BLUE: Marbury v. Madison: The Court's Foundation, 2005; Dred Scott: Person or Property?, 2005. **Address:** 140 Clinton Ave., Dobbs Ferry, NY 10522-3006, U.S.A.

NADER, Ralph. American (born United States), b. 1934. **Genres:** Social Commentary, Politics/Government. **Career:** Consumer protection activist; University of Hartford, lecturer in history and government, 1961-63; Princeton University, lecturer, 1967-68; American University Washington College of Law, adjunct faculty. Writer. **Publications:** Unsafe at Any Speed: The Designed-in Dangers of the American Automobile, 1965; (with M. Green and J. Seligman) Constitutionalizing the Corporation: The Case for the Federal Chartering of Giant Corporations, 1976; (with M. Green J. Seligman) and Taming the Giant Corporation, 1976; (with J. Abbotts) Menace of Atomic Energy, 1977; (with W. Taylor) The Big Boys: Styles of Corporate Power, 1986; Nader on Australia, 1986; (with C. Ditlow, L. Polacheck and T. Rhode) Lemon Book: Auto Rights, 1990; (with W.J. Smith) Winning the Insurance Game: The Complete Consumer's Guide to Saving Money, 1990; (with N. Milleron and D. Conacher) Canada Firsts, 1992; (with W.J. Smith) Collision Course: The Truth about Airline Safety, 1994; (with W.J. Smith) No Contest: Corporate Lawyers and the Perversion of Justice in America, 1996; (foreword) More Canada Firsts, 1999; (foreword) Against all Odds, 1999; The Ralph Nader Reader, 2000; Cutting Corporate Welfare, 2000; Crashing the Party: Taking on the Corporate Government in an Age of Surrender, 2002; The Good Fight: Declare Your Independence & Close the Democracy Gap, 2004; In Pursuit of Justice: Collected Writings 2000-2003, 2004; (foreword) Taking Back the Corporation: A Mad as Hell Guide, 2005; The Seventeen Traditions, 2007; Only the Super-rich can Save Us!, 2009; Getting Steamed: To Overcome Corporatism, Build it Together to Win, 2011. EDITOR: (with J. Carper) The Consumer and Corporate Accountability, 1973; (with M.J. Green) Corporate Power in America, 1973; (with M. Green) Verdicts on Lawyers, 1976; (with R. Brownstein and J. Richard) Who's Poisoning America, 1981; Eating Clean: Food Safety and the Chemical Harvest, 1982. Contributor to journals. **Address:** American University Washington College of Law, 4801 Massachusetts Ave. NW, Washington, DC 20016-8180, U.S.A. **Online address:** info@nader.org

NADIS, Fred. American (born United States), b. 1957?. **Genres:** History. **Career:** University of California, lecturer in U.S. History; Doshisha University, visiting associate professor of American studies. Writer and consultant. **Publications:** Wonder Shows: Performing Science, Magic and Religion in America, 2005. **Address:** Rutgers University Press, 100 Joyce Kilmer Ave., Piscataway, NJ 08854-8099, U.S.A. **Online address:** frednadis@yahoo.com

NADKARNI, Nalini. American (born United States), b. 1954. **Genres:** Environmental Sciences/Ecology, Natural History. **Career:** Papua New Guinea

University of Technology, instructor, 1977; Wa Ecology Institute, research assistant, 1977-78; University of California, assistant professor, 1984-89; The Marie Selby Botanical Gardens, director of research, 1989-91, associate research staff; Evergreen State College, faculty, 1991-; University of Washington, staff; College of Forest Resources, associate professor; University of South Florida, Department of Biology, adjunct assistant professor; Missouri Botanical Garden, research associate. Writer, biologist and ecologist. **Publications:** (With J.L. Gressitt) Guide to Mt Kaindi: Background to Montane New Guinea Ecology, 1978; (ed. with M.D. Lowman) Forest Canopies, 1995; (ed. with N.T. Wheelwright) Monteverde: Ecology and Conservation of a Tropical Cloud Forest, 2000; Between Earth and Sky: Our Intimate Connections to Trees, 2008. Contributor to books, periodicals and journals. **Address:** Evergreen State College, Lab II 2259, Olympia, WA 98505, U.S.A. **Online address:** nadkarnn@evergreen.edu

NADLER, John. Hungarian/Canadian (born Canada), b. 1961. **Genres:** Adult Non-fiction, Novels. **Career:** Creston Fire Department, firefighter, 1979-84; British Columbia Ministry of Education, editorial consultant, 1986-90; Budapest Week, writer, 1992-96; Variety Magazine, Budapest correspondent, 1994-; CanWest Newspapers, Balkan correspondent, 1997-, contributing correspondent; Time Magazine, correspondent. **Publications:** Searching for Sofia: A Tale of Obsession, Murder, and War (literary nonfiction), 2003; A Perfect Hell: The True Story of the Black Devils, the Forefathers of the Special Forces, 2006; Prodigal Sons, forthcoming. Contributor to periodicals. **Address:** Variety Magazine, 360 Park Ave. S, New York, NY 10010, U.S.A. **Online address:** john_nadler@yahoo.com

NAGAI, Kaori. British (born England) **Genres:** History, Young Adult Fiction. **Career:** University of Kent, Rutherford College, School of English, honorary research associate and lecturer in English, School of European Culture and Languages assistant lecturer of comparative literature. Writer. **Publications:** On the Strength of a Likeness: Kipling and the Analogical Connections between India and Ireland, 2001; Empire of Analogies: Kipling, India and Ireland, 2006; (ed. with C. Rooney) Kipling and Beyond: Patriotism, Globalisation, 2010. Contributor to periodicals and journals. **Address:** School of English, Rutherford College, University of Kent, Canterbury, KT CT2 7NX, England. **Online address:** k.nagai@kent.ac.uk

NAGATA, Linda. American (born United States), b. 1960. **Genres:** Science Fiction/Fantasy, Novels. **Career:** Novelist. **Publications:** NOVELS: The Bohr Maker, 1995; Tech-Heaven, 1996; Deception Well, 1997; Vast, 1998; Limit of Vision, 2001; Memory, 2003. OTHERS: Skye Object 3270a, 2011; Contributor to books and periodicals. **Address:** c/o Author Mail, Tor Books, 175 5th Ave., New York, NY 10010, U.S.A. **Online address:** nagata@maui.net

NAGEL, Paul C(hester). *See* Obituaries.

NAGEL, Susan. (Susan Ellen Nagel). American (born United States), b. 1954. **Genres:** Humanities, History, Reference. **Career:** Fawcett Books, publicist, 1977-79; Gannett Newspapers, staff, 1976-77; Marymount Manhattan College, professor in humanities. Writer. **Publications:** The Influence of the Novels of Jean Giraudoux on the Hispanic Vanguard Novels of the 1920s-1930s, 1991; Mistress of the Elgin Marbles: A Biography of Mary Nisbet Countess of Elgin, 2004; Marie-Thérèse, Child of Terror: The Fate of Marie Antoinette's Daughter, 2008. **Address:** c/o Author Mail, HarperCollins, 10 E 53rd St., 11th Fl., New York, NY 10020, U.S.A. **Online address:** snagel@mmm.edu

NAGEL, Susan Ellen. *See* **NAGEL, Susan.**

NAGEM, Monique F. American/French (born France), b. 1941. **Genres:** Novels, Novellas/Short Stories, Translations, Romance/Historical. **Career:** McNeese State University, associate professor of languages, 1981-, professor of modern languages, through 2010, retired, 2010. Writer. **Publications:** TRANSLATOR: C. Chawaf, Redemption, 1992; C. Chawaf, Mother Love, Mother Earth, 1992; D. Rolin, The Garden of Delights, 1998; (and intro.) C. Mogador, Memoirs of a Courtesan in Nineteenth-Century Paris, 2001; T. Monenembo, L'aîné des orphelins, (title means: 'The Oldest Orphan'), 2004. **Address:** 507 Contour Dr., Lake Charles, LA 70605-5605, U.S.A. **Online address:** mnagem@mail.mcneese.edu

NAGORSKI, Tom. American (born United States), b. 1962?. **Genres:** History. **Career:** American Broadcasting Co., foreign editor, producer, senior producer, senior broadcast producer, 1984-, foreign managing editor. **Publications:** Miracles on the Water: The Heroic Survivors of a World War II U-Boat Attack, 2006. **Address:** c/o Author Mail, Hyperion Editorial Department, Hyperion Books, 114 5th Ave., New York, NY 10023, U.S.A.

NAGUIB, Nefissa. Norwegian (born Norway), b. 1960?. **Genres:** Social Sciences. **Career:** Oslo University College, Department of Developmental Studies, assistant professor, 1993-97, head of department, 1997-2000, 2003-05, research fellow and associate professor, 2000-03, 2008-09; University of Bergen, Department of Social Anthropology, researcher, 2005-08; Uni Global, senior researcher, 2008-10; Chr. Michelsen Institute (CMI), senior researcher, 2010-; Høgskolen, lecturer; City University of New York, Graduate Center, visiting fellow, Middle East and Middle East American Center, visiting fellow; University of British Columbia, visiting fellow; International Red Cross, consultant; Aga Khan Foundation, consultant; United Nations Children's Fund, consultant; United Nations Educational, Scientific and Cultural Organization, consultant; Journal of Middle East Women's Studies, associate editor. Social anthropologist. **Publications:** (Ed. and contrib. with I.M. Okkenhaug) Interpreting Welfare and Relief in the Middle East, 2008; Women, Water and Memory: Recasting Lives in Palestine, 2009; Food and Foodways in the Middle East, 2009; (ed. and contrib. with B. de Vries) Movements of People in Time and Space, 2010. Contributor to books and periodicals. **Address:** Chr. Michelsen Institute, PO Box 6033, Bergen, N-5892, Norway. **Online address:** nefissa.naguib@cmi.no

NAGURNEY, Anna. American/Canadian (born Canada) **Genres:** Information Science/Computers, Business/Trade/Industry, Economics. **Career:** Systems Consultants Inc., programmer and analyst, 1977-79; Aquidneck Data Corp., senior systems analyst, 1979-80; University of Massachusetts, Isenberg School of Management, Department of Finance and Operations Management, assistant professor, 1983-87, associate professor, 1987-91, professor, 1991-98, John F. Smith Memorial professor, 1998-, Department of Mechanical and Industrial Engineering, associate faculty, 1998-, Department of Civil and Environmental Engineering, Transportation Program, associate faculty, 1998-, doctoral program coordinator in management science, 2000-11, Virtual Center for Supernetworks, director, 2001-, Supernetworks Laboratory for Computation and Visualization, director, 2001-; Royal Institute of Technology, Division of Transportation and Location Analysis, visiting professor, 1999-2001; World Bank, consultant, 2008; Harvard University, Office of Continuing Executive Education, instructor, 2009; University of Gothenburg, School of Business, Economics and Law, visiting professor of operations management, 2012. **Publications:** Network Economics: A Variational Inequality Approach, 1993, rev. ed., 1999; (with D. Zhang) Projected Dynamical Systems and Variational Inequalities with Applications, 1995; (with S. Siokos) Financial Networks: Statics and Dynamics, 1997; (with K.K. Dhanda and P. Ramanujam) Environmental Networks: A Framework for Economic Decision-Making and Policy Analysis, 1999; Sustainable Transportation Networks, 2000; (with J. Dong) Supernetworks: Decision-Making for the Information Age, 2002; (ed.) Innovations in Financial and Economic Networks, 2003; Supply Chain Network Economics: Dynamics of Prices, Flows and Profits, 2006; (with Q. Qiang) Fragile Networks: Identifying Vulnerabilities and Synergies in an Uncertain World, 2009. Contributor to books and journals. **Address:** Department of Finance and Operations Management, Isenberg School of Management, University of Massachusetts, 316 SOM, 121 Presidents Dr., Amherst, MA 01003, U.S.A. **Online address:** nagurney@isenberg.umass.edu

NAGY, Gloria. American (born United States), b. 1946?. **Genres:** Romance/Historical, Novels, Children's Fiction, Mystery/Crime/Suspense. **Career:** Novelist. **Publications:** Virgin Kisses: A Novel, 1978; Unapparent Wounds: A Novel, 1981; Natural Selections, 1985; Radio Blues, 1988; A House in the Hamptons (One Summer Near the End of the Lie): A Novel, 1990; Looking for Leo: A Novel, 1992; Marriage: A Novel, 1995; Wizard Who Wanted to Be Santa, 2000; Beauty: A Novel, 2001; SeaSick, 2009. **Address:** c/o Michael Frankfurt, 488 Madison Ave., New York, NY 10022, U.S.A.

NAHA, Ed. Also writes as Michael McGann, D. B. Drumm. American (born United States), b. 1950. **Genres:** Mystery/Crime/Suspense, Science Fiction/Fantasy, Film, Music, Novellas/Short Stories, Plays/Screenplays, Young Adult Fiction, Horror, Horror. **Career:** CBS Records, manager of east coast publicity, 1972-75, associate producer of east coast artists and repertory, 1975-77; Future Life, co-editor, 1977-80. **Publications:** Horrors-From Screen to Scream: An Encyclopedic Guide to the Greatest Horror and Fantasy Films of All Time, 1975; Science Fiction Aliens, 1977; (comp.) Lillian Roxon's Rock Encyclopedia, 1978; (ed.) 1941: The Official Movie Magazine, 1979; (ed.) The Beatles Forever, 1980; John Lennon and the Beatles Forver, 1980; The Science Fictionary: An A-Z Guide to the World of SF Authors, Films and TV Shows, 1980; (with E. Seidman) Wanted, by the Intergalactic Security Bureau: 20 Full-Color Posters of the Most Wanted Alien Criminals, 1980; The Paradise Plot, 1980; The Films of Roger Corman: Brilliance on a Budget, 1982; The Suicide Plague, 1982; The Making of Dune, 1984; The Con Game, 1986; Robocop, 1987; Breakdown, 1988; Dead-Bang: A Novel, 1989; Ghostbusters II: A Novel, 1989; On the Edge, 1989; Orphans, 1989; Razzle-Dazzle, 1990; Robocop II, 1990; Cracking Up, 1991. NOVELS AS D.B. DRUMM: First, You Fight, 1984; The Road Ghost, 1985; The Stalking Time, 1986; Hell on Earth, 1986; The Children's Crusade, 1987; The Prey, 1987; Ghost Dancers, 1987. NOVELS AS MICHAEL McGANN: The Marauders, 1989; Blood Kin, 1989; Liar's Dice, 1990; Convoy Strike, 1990; The Ghost Warriors, 1990; Blood and Fire, 1991; Fortress of Death, 1991. Contributor to periodicals. **Address:** Harvey Klinger Agency, 301 W 53rd St., New York, NY 10019, U.S.A.

NAHAS, Gabriel G(eorges). American/Egyptian (born Egypt), b. 1920. **Genres:** Education, Ethics, History, Human Relations/Parenting, Humanities, International Relations/Current Affairs, Law, Medicine/Health, Politics/Government, Psychiatry, Psychology, Sciences, Autobiography/Memoirs, Translations. **Career:** Hospital Marie Lannelongue, chief of laboratory of experimental surgery, 1954-55; University of Minnesota, assistant professor of physiology, 1955-57; Walter Reed Army Institute of Research, Department of Cardio Respiratory Disease, chief of respiratory section, 1957-59; George Washington University, Medical School, lecturer in physiology, 1957-59; Columbia University, College of Physicians and Surgeons, associate professor and director of research, 1959-62, professor of anesthesiology, 1962-92, professor emeritus, 1992-; Presbyterian Hospital, attending anesthesiologist, 1967-; University de Paris Faculte de Medicine, Institut d'Anesthesiologie, adjunct professor, 1968-71; New York University Medical School, research professor of anesthesiology, 1992-. Writer. **Publications:** EDITOR: In Vitro and in Vivo Effects of Amine Buffers, 1961; Regulation of Respiration, 1963; (with D.V. Bates) Respiratory Failure, 1965; Current Concepts of Acid-Base Measurement, 1966; (with C.F. Fox) Body Fluid Replacement, 1970; (and trans. with H. Peters and J. Moreau) Hashish and Mental Illness, 1973; (with K. Schaefer) Carbon Dioxide and Metabolic Regulations, 1974; Marihuana: Chemistry, Biochemistry and Cellular Effects, 1976; (with W.D.M. Paton) Cannabis: Biological Effects, 1979; (co-ed.) Marihuana, Biological Effects: Analysis, Metabolism, Cellular Responses, Reproduction and Brain, 1979 (with H.C. Frick) Drug Abuse in the Modern World, 1980; Drogue et Civilisation, 1982; (with D.J. Harvey and W. Paton) Marihuana '84: Proceedings of the Oxford Symposium on Cannabis, 1985; Drogue et Societe, 1990; (with C. Latour) Physiopathology of Illicit Drugs, 1991; (with C. Latour); Cannabis: Physiopathology, Epidemiology and Detection, 1993; (with T. Burks) Drugs of Abuse in the Decade of the Brain, 1996; Operation Overlord, 1996; (T.F. Burks) Drug Abuse in the Decade of the Brain, 1997; (with N. Pace and R. Cancro) Marihuana and Medicine, 1999; (with D. Harvey and C. Latour) Pharmacokinetics and Cannabis Induced Apoptosis, 2001. OTHERS: Body Fluid Replacement in the Surgical Patient, 1970; (ed. with G.A. Robison and L. Triner) Cyclic AMP and Cell Function, 1971; Marihuana-Deceptive Weed, 1972; (with J.C. Salamagne, P. Viars and G. Vourc'h) Le Système cholinergique; en anesthésiologie et en réanimation, 1972; Marihuana, 1973; Keep off the Grass, 1976, 5th ed., 1990; Hashish, Cannabis, Marijuana, 1976; Histoire d'H, 1977; Histoire du Hash, 1983; La Filière du Rail, 1983; Marihuana in Science and Medicine, 1984; Une Epidemie d'amour, 1985; Les Guerres de la Cocaine, 1987; (H.M. Voth) How to Save Your Child from Drugs, 1987; Abrege de Toxicomanie, 1988; Cocaine: The Great White Plague, 1989; A Manual on Drug Dependence, 1992; La Peste Blanche du XX Siecle, 1992; Il n'y a pas deDrogue Douce, 1992; La Drogue Bilan Scientifique et medical, 1994; Network to Freedom, 1999; Drogue, Cerveau, Conscience Exliberte, 2000. **Address:** Department of Anesthesiology, College of Physicians and Surgeons, Columbia University, 630 W 168th St., New York, NY 10032, U.S.A.

NAHAYLO, Bohdan. American (born United States) **Genres:** Politics/Government, History, Social Sciences. **Career:** Radio Free Europe/Radio Liberty, assistant director of research; United Nations High Commissioner for Refugees, senior policy research officer. Writer. **Publications:** (With A. Sheehy) Crimean Tatars, Volga Germans and Meskhetians: Soviet Treatment of Some National Minorities, 1980; (with C.J. Peters) Ukrainians and Georgians, 1981; (with M. Muggeridge) Malcolm Muggeridge/International Commission of Inquiry into the 1932-33 Famine in Ukraine, 1988; (with V. Swoboda) Soviet Disunion: A History of the Nationalities Problem in the U.S.S.R., 1990; New Ukraine, 1992; The Ukrainian Resurgence, 1999. Contributor to periodicals. **Address:** University of Toronto Press, 10 Saint Mary St., Ste. 700, Toronto, ON M4Y 2W8, Canada.

NAHSHON, Edna. American/Israeli (born Israel) **Genres:** Theatre, Art/Art History. **Career:** Jewish Theological Seminary, Hebrew Department, assistant professor of Hebrew, associate professor, professor, chair, 1990-98, Stroock fellow, 1999; Oxford University, Centre for Hebrew and Jewish Studies, Skirball visiting fellow, 1999, senior associate and senior fellow; Educational Film Center, historical adviser. Writer. **Publications:** Yiddish Proletarian Theatre: The Art and Politics of the Artef, 1925-1940, 1998; (ed. and intro.) From the Ghetto to the Melting Pot: Israel Zangwill's Jewish Plays: Three Playscripts, 2006; (ed.) Jews and Shoes, 2008; (ed.) Jewish Theatre: A Global View, 2009; Jews and Theatre in an Intercultural Context, 2012. Contributor to books. **Address:** Jewish Theological Seminary, 603 Kripke Twr., 3080 Broadway, New York, NY 10027, U.S.A. **Online address:** ednahshon@jtsa.edu

NAIDEN, James. American (born United States), b. 1943. **Genres:** Novels, Plays/Screenplays, Poetry, Literary Criticism And History, Politics/Government, Theatre. **Career:** Minneapolis Star Tribune, poetry critic, 1970-85, 1993-96; North Stone Review, editor, 1971-; KFAI-FM, news reporter, 1987-89; Commercial Appeal, book critic, 2001-. **Publications:** The Orange Notebook, 1973; Summer Poems, 2002. **Address:** The North Stone Review, PO Box 14098, Minneapolis, MN 55414-0098, U.S.A. **Online address:** jack123904@aol.com

NAIDOO, Beverley. British/South African (born South Africa), b. 1943. **Genres:** Children's Fiction, Young Adult Fiction, Race Relations, Theatre, Plays/Screenplays, Novellas/Short Stories. **Career:** Researcher, 1988-91; Bournemouth Education Directorate, development officer for arts, 1997-98; University of London, Goldsmith College, part-time tutor for creative writing, 1997-99. Writer. **Publications:** YOUNG ADULTS FICTION: Journey to Jo'burg: A South African Story, 1985; Chain of Fire, 1989; No Turning Back, 1995; The Other Side of Truth, 2000; Out of Bounds, 2001; Web of Lies, 2004. CHILDREN'S FICTION: Letang and Julie Save the Day, 1994; Trouble for Letang and Julie, 1994; Letang's New Friend, 1994; Where Is Zami?, 1998; The Great Tug of War, 2001; (with M. Naidoo) Baba's Gift, 2003. FOR ADULTS: Censoring Reality: An Examination of Books on South Africa, 1984; Through Whose Eyes? Exploring Racism: Reader, Text and Context, 1992; The Playground (play), 2004. EDITOR: Free as I Know, 1987; (with C. Donovan and A. Hicks) Global Tales: Stories from Many Cultures, 1997. OTHER: (intro.) Making it Home: Real-life Stories from Children Forced to Flee, 2004; Burn My Heart, 2007; Call of the Deep, 2008. **Address:** Puffin Marketing Department, Penguin Children's Books, 80 Strand, London, GL WC2R 0RL, England. **Online address:** puffin@penguin.co.uk

NAIDU, Prabhakar S. Indian (born India), b. 1937. **Genres:** Engineering, Sciences. **Career:** Indian Institute of Science, Department of Electrical Communication Engineering, assistant professor, 1971-76, associate professor, 1977-82, professor, 1983-2000, professor emeritus, 2000-; Australian Telecommunication Research Center, visiting scientist. Writer. **Publications:** Modern Spectrum Analysis of Time Series, 1996; Analysis of Geophysical Potential Fields: A Digital Signal Processing Approach, 1998; Sensor Array Signal Processing, 2000, 2nd ed. 2009. **Address:** Indian Institute of Science, Malleswaram, Bangalore, KA 560 012, India. **Online address:** psn@ece.llsc.ernet.in

NAILS, Jennifer. American (born United States) **Genres:** Young Adult Fiction. **Career:** Eastern International College, instructor in English. Writer. **Publications:** Next to Mexico, 2008. **Address:** Brooklyn, NY , U.S.A. **Online address:** jen@jennails.com

NAÍM, Moisés. American/Venezuelan (born Venezuela), b. 1952?. **Genres:** Social Sciences, Economics, Politics/Government. **Career:** Instituto de Estudios Superiores de Administración, professor and dean; Venezuela's Central Bank, director; World Bank, executive director and senior advisor to the president; Venezuela minister of trade and industry, 1990; Foreign Policy (magazine), editor-in-chief, 1996-2010; Carnegie Endowment for International Peace, director of the projects on economic reforms, International Economics Program, senior associate; Group of Fifty (Latin American business organization), chair. **Publications:** Multinacionales: La economía Política De Las Inversiones Extranjeras, 1982; (with R. Piñango) El Caso Venezuela: Una Ilusión De Armonía, 1984; Posibilidades Y Limitaciones Del Funcionamiento De Los Mercados En Los Países Menos Desarrollados: Una Aplicación Delenfoque De Mercados Y Jerarquías Al Caso De Venezuela, 1985; Las Empresas Venezolanas: Su Gerencia, 1989; Paper Tigers and Minotaurs: The Politics of Venezuela's Economic Reforms, 1993; Lessons of the Venezuelan Experience, 1995; Latin America's Journey to the Market: From Macroeconomic Shocks to Institutional Therapy, 1995; (ed. with S. Edwards) Mexico 1994: Anatomy of an Emerging-Market Crash, 1997; (ed. with J.S. Tulchin) Competition Policy, Deregulation, and Modernization in Latin America, 1999; (with G. Smith) Altered States: Globalization, Sovereignty, and Governance, 2000; Illicit: How Smugglers, Traffickers and Copycats are Hijacking the Global Economy, 2005. Contributor to periodicals. **Address:** Carnegie Endowment for International Peace, 1779 Massachusetts Ave. NW, Washington, DC 20036-2103, U.S.A.

NAIRN, Tom (Cunningham). British/Irish/Scottish (born Scotland), b. 1932. **Genres:** Politics/Government. **Career:** University of Birmingham, lecturer in philosophy, 1962-64; Hornsey College of Art, lecturer in liberal studies, 1964-69; Scottish International Institute, director, 1976-80; freelance writer and consultant, 1989-; University of Edinburgh, creator of nationalism studies course, 1995-2000; Royal Melbourne Institute of Technology University, Globalism Research Center, innovation professor of nationalism and cultural diversity, 2002-10; Durham University, research professor, Institute for Advanced Study, fellow, 2009, School of Government and International Affairs, honorary research fellow; University of Strathclyde, visiting professor; University of Aberdeen, Research Institute for Irish and Scottish Studies, fellow. Writer. **Publications:** (With A. Quattrocchi) The Beginning of the End: France, May 1968: What Happened, Why It Happened, 1968; The Left against Europe?, 1973; (contrib.) Against Ulster Nationalism, 1975; The Break-up of Britain: Crisis and Neo-nationalism, 1977, 2nd ed., 1981; (co-author) Nationalismus und Marxismus: Anstoss zu einer notwendigen Debatte, 1978; The Enchanted Glass: Britain and Its Monarchy, 1988; Faces of Nationalism: Janus Revisited, 1998; After Britain: New Labour and the Return of Scotland, 2001; Pariah: Misfortunes of the British Kingdom, 2002; (with P. James) Global Matrix: Nationalism, Globalism and State-terrorism, 2005; (ed. with P. James) Globalization and Violence, 2006. Contributor to periodicals. **Address:** School of Government and International Affairs, Durham University, Al-Qasimi Bldg., Elvet Hill Rd., Durham, DU DH1 3TU, England. **Online address:** nairn@ireland.com

NAJMABADI, Afsaneh. Iranian (born Iran), b. 1946. **Genres:** Novellas/Short Stories, Social Sciences. **Career:** Barnard College, department of women's studies, faculty; Harvard University, professor, 2001-, chair of the Committee on Degrees in Studies of Women, Gender and Sexuality. Writer. **Publications:** Land Reform and Social Change in Iran, 1987; Ma'ayib al-rijal: dar pasukh bih Ta'dib al-nisvan, 1992; Hikayat-i dukhtaran-i Quchan: az yadraftah'ha-yi Inqilab-i Mashrutah, 1995; Bibi Khanum Astarabadi va Khanum-i Afz al Vaziri: Madar va dukhtari az pishgaman-i ma'arif va huquqi zanan, 1996; The Story of the Daughters of Quchan: Gender and National Memory in Iranian History, 1998; (associate ed.) Encyclopedia of Women & Islamic Cultures, 2003; Women with Mustaches and Men without Beards: Gender and Sexual Anxieties of Iranian Modernity, 2005; Nahzat-i nisvan-i sharq, 2005; (ed. with K. Babayan) Islamicate Sexualities: Translations across Temporal Geographies of Desire, 2008. **Address:** Department of History, Harvard University, Robinson Hall, 35 Quincy St., Cambridge, MA 02138, U.S.A. **Online address:** najmabad@fas.harvard.edu

NAKASH, Yitzhak. American (born United States), b. 1958. **Genres:** Theology/Religion, Politics/Government, History. **Career:** Brandeis University, associate professor of modern Middle East studies and director of Islamic and Middle East studies. Writer. **Publications:** The Shi'is of Iraq, 1994, 2nd ed. as The Shi'is of Iraq: With a New Introduction by the Author, 2003; Reaching for Power: The Shi'a in the Modern Arab World, 2006. **Address:** Islamic and Middle Eastern Studies Program, Brandeis University, 415 South St., PO Box 054, Waltham, MA 02454, U.S.A. **Online address:** nakash@brandeis.edu

NAKAYAMA, Shigeru. Japanese (born Japan), b. 1928. **Genres:** Astronomy, History, Sciences, Technology, Translations. **Career:** Heibonsha, editor, 1951-55; University of Tokyo, lecturer in astronomy, 1960-88, associate professor, 1988-89; Charles Scribners' Sons, Dictionary of Scientific Biography, editorial consultant, 1967-; Kanagawa University, professor, 1989-2000, professor emeritus, 2000-; Harvard University, visiting professor, 1972-73; Council of Scientific & Industrial Research, visiting professor, 1977-78; University of California, visiting professor, 1981-82; LaTrobeand Monash University, visiting professor, 1989; Japanese Research Center, visiting professor, 1990, 1998. **Publications:** Astrology, 1964; (with W. Sugimoto) History of Science, 1967; History of Japanese Astronomy, 1969; Japanese Astronomy, 1972; Academic Traditions, 1974; Japanese Views of Science, 1977; Characteristics of Scientific Development in Japan, 1977; Hideyo Noguchi, 1978; The Birth of the Imperial University, 1978; Environmentalist's Cosmology, 1980; The View of Science at the Crossroad, 1980; Contemporary History of Science and Society, 1981; History of the Science of the Heavens, 1984; Science Studies for Citizens, 1984; Academic and Scientific Traditions in China, Japan and the West, 1984; Thoughts on the 21st Century, 1986; Research Guide to the History of Science, 1987; A Trip to American Universities, 1988; Naozo Ichinohe, 1989; Science, Technology and Society in Postwar Japan, 1991; The Social History of Science and Technology in Contemporary Japan, 7 vols., 1995; (with M. Low and H. Yoshioka) Science, Technology and Society in Contemporary Japan, 1999; Nihon no tenmongaku: uranai, koyomi, uchukan, 2000; (with Y.H. Hencho) Kagaku kakumei no genzaishi, 2002; Kagaku gijutsu no kokusai kyosoryoku: Amerika to Nihon sōkoku no hanseiki, 2006; Granting the Seasons: The Chinese Astronomical Reform of 1280, with a Study of Its Many Dimensions and a Translation of its Records, 2009. TRANSLATOR: Modern Scientific Readers, 1955; M. Kline, Mathematics in Western Culture, 1956; Smart, Origin of the Earth, 1962; Dupre and Lakoff, Science and Nation, 1965; Kuhn, Structure of Scientific Revolution, 1971; Charon, Cosmology, 1971; Kearney, Science and Change, 1972; N. Sivin, Copernicus in China, 1984; Stableford and Langford, The Third Mellenium, 1987. EDITOR: (with W. Yuasa) Chronology of Modern Science and Technology, 1961; (co-ed.) Earth and Space Sciences, 1965; International Relations, 1968; (with W. Hirose) Modern Scientific Thought, 1971; (with W. Hirose) Western Learning, 1972; (with W. Sivin) Chinese Science, 1973; (with W. Swain and Yagi) Science and Society in Modern Japan, 1974; The History of Astronomy, 1982; Biographical Dictionary of Astronomers, 1983; Tenmongaku jinmei jiten: tenmongaku nenpyo, 1983; Bakumatsu no yogaku, 1984; Paradaimu saiko, 1984; Western Learning in Mid-nineteenth Century Japan, 1984; Rethinking of Paradigms, 1984; Technological Capacity of Japan, 1986; Nihon no gijutsuryoku: sengoshi to tenbo, 1986; Jozefu Nidamu no sekai: meiyo taoisuto no sei to shiso, 1988; Kagaku gijutsu to ekoroji, 1995; (with K. Masanao and T. Shunsuke) Minkangaku jiten. Jikō hen, 1997. **Address:** 3-7-11 Chuo, Nakano, Tokyo, 1, Japan. **Online address:** kfh00250@nifty.com

NAKHIMOVSKY, Alice Stone. American (born United States), b. 1950. **Genres:** Language/Linguistics, Cultural/Ethnic Topics, Literary Criticism And History, Humanities. **Career:** Colgate University, Department of Russian, assistant professor, 1976-82, associate professor, 1982-91, chair, 1989-, professor of Russian and Jewish studies, 1991-, director of Jewish studies. Writer. **Publications:** (With R.L. Leed and A.D. Nakhimovsky) Beginning Russian, 1981; Laughter in the Void: An Introduction to the Writings of Daniil Kharms and Alexander Vvedenskii, 1982; (ed. with A.D. Nakhimovsky) The Semiotics of Russian Cultural History: Essays, 1985; (with L.S. Paperno and A. Nakhimovsky) Intermediate Russian: The Twelve Chairs, 1985; Russian-Jewish Literature and Identity: Jabotinsky, Babel, Grossman, Galich, Roziner, Markish, 1992; (contrib.) Witness to History: The Photographs of Yevgeny Khaldei, 1997; (trans. and intro.) G. Bruskin, Past Imperfect, 2008. Contributor to journals. **Address:** Department of Russian, Colgate University, 219B Lawrence Hall, 13 Oak Dr., Hamilton, NY 13346-1338, U.S.A. **Online address:** asnakhimovsky@colgate.edu

NAKHNIKIAN, George. American (born United States), b. 1920. **Genres:** Philosophy, Politics/Government. **Career:** Wayne State University, Department of Philosophy, instructor and professor, 1949-68, chairman, 1956-68; Brown University, visiting professor, 1955-56; St. Andrews University, Fulbright lecturer, 1965-66; Indiana University, Department of Philosophy, chairman, 1968-72, professor, 1968-88, professor emeritus, 1988-; Law Forum, consulting editor. **Publications:** (Trans. with W.P. Alston and intro.) Edmund Husserl, The Idea of Phenomenology, 1964; An Introduction to Philosophy, 1967. EDITOR: (and intro.) Nature and Utility of Religion, 1958; (with H.N. Castaneda) Morality and the Language of Conduct, 1963; (with W.P. Alston) Readings in Twentieth-Century Philosophy, 1963; Bertrand Russell's Philosophy, 1974. **Address:** Department of Philosophy, Indiana University, 026 Sycamore Hall, 1033 E 3rd St., Bloomington, IN 47405, U.S.A.

NALLY, Susan W. American (born United States), b. 1947. **Genres:** Theology/Religion. **Career:** Crievewood Baptist Church, Children's S.S. division director. Writer. **Publications:** SPENDING PRIME TIME WITH GOD SERIES: How to Say Yes! to All the Best Choices (and Really Mean It), 1994; (with L. Lee) How to Feel Most Excellent!: About Who You Are (and Really Enjoy It), 1994; How to Stay Way Cool When Things Are Tough (and Really Like It), 1994. **Address:** 713 Shenandoah Dr., Brentwood, TN 37027, U.S.A.

NAMIOKA, Lensey. American/Chinese (born China), b. 1929. **Genres:** Children's Fiction, Young Adult Fiction, Travel/Exploration, Picture/Board Books, Novels. **Career:** Wells College, instructor in mathematics, 1957-58; Cornell University, instructor in mathematics, 1958-61; American Mathematical Society, translator, 1958-66; Japan Broadcasting Corp., broadcasting monitor, 1969. Writer. **Publications:** (Trans.) B.Y. Chao, How to Order and Eat in Chinese, 1974; The Samurai and the Long-Nosed Devils, 1976; White Serpent Castle, 1976; Japan, a Traveler's Companion, 1979; Valley of the Broken Cherry Trees, 1980; Who's Hu?, 1980; Village of the Vampire Cat, 1981; China, a Traveler's Companion, 1985; Phantom of Tiger Mountain, 1986; Island of Ogres, 1989; Coming of the Bear, 1992; Yang the Youngest and His Terrible Ear, 1992; April and the Dragon Lady, 1994; (reteller) The Loyal Cat, 1995; Yang the Third and Her Impossible Family, 1995; Den of the White Fox, 1997; Yang the Second, 1998; Yang the Second and Her Secret Admirers, 1998; The Laziest Boy in the World, 1998; Ties That Bind, Ties That Break, 1999, rev. ed., 2003; Yang the Eldest and His Odd Jobs, 2000; The Hungriest Boy in the World, 2001; Ocean Apart, a World Away: A Novel, 2002; Half and Half, 2003; Mismatch, 2006. Contributor to books, magazines and newspapers. **Address:** 2047 23rd Ave. E, Seattle, WA 98112-2935, U.S.A. **Online address:** lensey@lensey.com

NANCARROW, Mindy. (Mindy Nancarrow Taggard). American (born United States), b. 1951. **Genres:** Literary Criticism And History, Art/Art History, Photography, Young Adult Fiction. **Career:** Oklahoma State University, assistant professor of art history, 1985-88; University of Alabama, assistant professor of art history, associate professor, 1988-2003, professor of art history, 2003-, Graduate Studies, director. Writer. **Publications:** AS MINDY NANCARROW TAGGARD: Murillo's Allegories of Salvation and Triumph: The Parable of the Prodigal Son and The Life of Jacob, 1992; (with B.N. Prieto) Antonio del Castillo y Saavedra: Su vida y su obra, 2004. **Address:** Department of Art and Art History, University of Alabama, 103 Garland Hall, PO Box 870270, Tuscaloosa, AL 35487-0270, U.S.A. **Online address:** mnanc@bama.ua.edu

NAPIER, Bill. (William M. Napier). Irish/Welsh/Scottish (born Scotland), b. 1940. **Genres:** Novels, Astronomy, Young Adult Non-fiction, Sciences. **Career:** Royal Holloway College, lecturer in applied mathematics, 1966-67; Royal Observatory, astronomer, 1967-92; Oxford University, research fellow, 1994-96; Armagh Observatory, Leverhulme fellow, 1996-98, research astronomer, 1996-2001, emeritus researcher, 2001-; University of Cardiff, Institute for Astrobiology, honorary professor, 2001-. Writer. **Publications:** NONFICTION WITH V. CLUBE: The Cosmic Serpent: A Catastrophic View of Earth History, 1982; The Cosmic Winter, 1990; (and M.E. Bailey) The Origin of Comets, 1990. NOVELS: Nemesis, 1998; Revelation, 2000; The Lure, 2002; Shattered Icon, 2004; Splintered Icon, 2005; The Furies, 2009; (with J. Wickramasinghe and C. Wickramasinghe) Comets and the Origin of Life, 2009. Contributor to journals. **Address:** Armagh Observatory, College Hill, Armagh, BT61 9DG, Ireland. **Online address:** wmn@star.arm.ac.uk

NAPIER, Mary. *See* **WRIGHT, (Mary) Patricia.**

NAPIER, Nancy J. American (born United States), b. 1945. **Genres:** Psychology, Self Help, Human Relations/Parenting, Theology/Religion. **Career:** Foundation for Human Enrichment, faculty; Somatic Experiencing Training Institute, faculty. Psychotherapist, hypnotherapist and writer. **Publications:** Recreating Your Self: Help for Adult Children of Dysfunctional Families, 1990; Getting through the Day: Strategies for Adults Hurt as Children, 1993; Sacred Practices for Conscious Living, 1997; (with C.M. Tricomi) Meditations & Rituals For Conscious Living, 2000. Contributor to periodicals. **Address:** 295 Central Park W, PO Box 153, New York, NY 10024, U.S.A. **Online address:** info@nancyjnapier.com

NAPIER, William M. *See* **NAPIER, Bill.**

NAPOLI, Donna Jo. American/Italian (born Italy), b. 1948. **Genres:** Young Adult Fiction, Language/Linguistics, Picture/Board Books. **Career:** Concord Public Schools, instructor of Italian, 1970; Smith College, lecturer in philosophy and Italian, 1973-74; University of North Carolina, lecturer in mathematics and Italian, 1974-75; Georgetown University, assistant professor of linguistics, 1975-80; University of Michigan, linguistics professor, 1980-87, professor, 1981-84, professor, 1984; Swarthmore College, professor, 1987-, chair, 1987-2002; San Francisco State University, Department of English, visiting professor, 1994; University of the Witwatersrand, visiting lecturer in linguistics, 1995; Newcastle University, Leverhulme visiting professor, 2010; Trinity College Dublin, Long Room Hub fellow, 2012. Writer. **Publications:** NONFICTION: (ed.) Elements of Tone, Stress, and Intonation, 1978; (ed. with E.N. Rando) Syntactic Argumentation, 1979; (ed. with E. Rando) Linguistic Muse, 1979; (ed. with W. Cressey) Linguistic Symposium on Romance Languages: 9, 1981; (ed. with E.N. Rando) Meliglossa, 1983; Predication Theory: A Case Study for Indexing Theory, 1989; (ed. with J.A. Kegl) Bridges between Psychology and Linguistics: A Swarthmore Festschrift for Lila Gleitman, 1991; Syntax: Theory and Problems, 1993; (with S. Davis) Prosodic Template in Historical Change: The Passage of the Latin Second Conjugation into Romance, 1994; (with S. Davis) Phonological Factors in Historical Change, 1994; Linguistics: An Introduction, 1996; Language Matters, 2003, (with V. Lee-Schoenfeld), 2nd ed., 2010; (with M. Nespor) L'animale parlante, 2004; (with R. Sutton-Spence) Humour in Sign Languages: The Linguistic Underpinnings, 2009; (ed. with G. Mathur) Deaf Around the World, 2010; (with M. Mai and N. Gaw) Primary Movement in Sign Languages: A Study of Six Languages, 2011. JUVENILE FICTION: The Hero of Barletta, 1988; Soccer Shock, 1991, rev. ed., 1993; The Prince of the Pond: Otherwise Known as De Fawg Pin, 1992, rev. ed., 1994; The Magic Circle, 1993; When the Water Closes over My Head, 1994; Shark Shock, 1994; Jimmy, the Pickpocket of the Palace, 1995; The Bravest Thing, 1995; Zel, 1996; Song of the Magdalene, 1996; On Guard, 1997; Stones in Water, 1997; Trouble on the Tracks, 1997; Sirena, 1998; Changing Tunes, 1998; For the Love of Venice, 1998; (with R. Tchen) Spinners, 1999; Angelwings, 1999-2000; Crazy Jack, 2000; Shelley Shock, 2000; Beast, 2000; Shelley Shock, 2000; Albert, 2001; Three Days, 2001; (with R. Tchen) How Hungry Are You, 2001; Daughter of Venice, 2002; Flamingo Dream, 2002; Rocky the Cat Who Barks, 2002; The Great God Pan, 2003; Breath, 2003; Gracie the Pixie of the Puddle, 2004; North, 2004; (with S. Johnston) Hotel Jungle, 2004; Bound, 2004; Pink Magic, 2005; (with R. Furrow) Sly the Sleuth and the Pet Mysteries, 2005; The King of Mulberry Street, 2005; (with R. Furrow) Sly the Sleuth and the Sports Mysteries, 2006; Ugly, 2006; (with E. Furrow) Bobby the Bold, 2006; Fire in the Hills, 2006; (with R. Furrow) Sly the Sleuth and the Food Mysteries, 2007; Hush, 2007; The Wishing Club, 2007; (with R. Tchen) Corkscrew Counts, 2008; The Smile, 2008; Mogo, The Third Warthog, 2008; (with E. Furrow) Ready to Dream, 2009; The Earth Shook, 2009; (with R. Furrow) Sly the Sleuth and the Code Mysteries, 2009; Alligator Bayou, 2009; (with D. DeLuca) Handy Stories to Read and Sign, 2009; Mama Miti: Wangari Maathai and the Trees of Kenya, 2010; The Wager, 2010; The Crossing, 2011; Lights on the Nile, 2011; A Treasury of Greek Mythology, 2011. ANGELWINGS SERIES: Friends Everywhere, 1999; Little Creatures, 1999; On Her Own, 1999; One Leap Forward, 1999; No Fair, 2000; April Flowers, 2000; Give and Take, 2000; Know-it-all, 2000; Playing Games, 2000; Lies and Lemons, 2000; Running Away, 2000; New Voices, 2000; Left Out, 2000; Happy Holidays, 2000; Partners, 2000; Hang in There, 2001. **Address:** Department of Linguistics, Swarthmore College, Pearson Hall, 500 College Ave., Swarthmore, PA 19081, U.S.A. **Online address:** dnapoli1@swarthmore.edu

NAPORA, Joe. *See* **NAPORA, Joseph S.**

NAPORA, Joseph S. (Joe Napora). American (born United States), b. 1944. **Genres:** Poetry, Translations. **Career:** Ashland Community & Technical College, professor of English, 1991-; Bull Head, publisher, 1994-98. Writer. **Publications:** POETRY: (as Joe Napora) The Name Book, 1984; Bloom Blood, 1985; (as Joe Napora with T. Ely and R. Lingen) Scighte, 1987; To Recognize This Dying, 1987; (ed. as Joe Napora) The Journal of Elizabeth Jennings Wilson, 1987; (as Joe Napora) Snaketrain Freightrain, 1991; (as Joe Napora) Snaketrain, 1992; The Immigrants, 1992; Sentences and Bills, 2011. OTHERS: (trans.) The Walam Olum (title means: 'Delaware Indian Epic Poem') 1992; FINK: A Long Poem, 2010; The Daniel Boone Poems, 2011.

Contributor to periodicals. **Address:** Ashland Community & Technical College, 1400 College Dr., Ashland, KY 41101-3617, U.S.A. **Online address:** barbara2joe@hotmail.com

NAPPA, Mike. American (born United States), b. 1963?. **Genres:** Inspirational/Motivational Literature. **Career:** CBA Frontline Magazine, contributing editor; Nappaland Communications Inc., founder and president, 1995-; Nappaland Public Relations, senior publicist; Nappaland.com, publisher, columnist; Crosswalk.com, columnist; CBNnow.org, columnist; VirutlaHolyLand.com, columnist; Home Life magazine, columnist/cultural commentator; FaithWorks Magazine, columnist/music critic; Nappaland Literary Agency, founder and chief agent; Focus on the Family Magazine, columnist/parenting expert; CCM Magazine, music critic; KPXQ Radio Station, movie critic/radio personality; ParentLife Magazine, columnist; Group Publishing, acquisitions editor, senior creative specialist of marketing; FamilyFans.com, publisher. **Publications:** (With A. Nappa) 52 Fun Family Devotions, 1994; (ed.) Clip-Art Cartoons for Churches, 1995; Bore No More!: For Every Pastor, Speaker, Teacher: 70 Creative Ways to Involve Your Audience in Unforgettable Bible Teaching, 1995; (with S.L. Lingo) Jesus, What's for Lunch?, 1996; (with S.L. Lingo) Little Lamb, Where Did You Go?, 1996; (with S.L. Lingo) Do You See the Star?, 1996; (with A. Nappa and M.D. Warden) Get Real: Making Core Christian Beliefs Relevant to Teenagers, 1996; (with A. Nappa) 52 Fun Family Prayer Adventures: Creative Ways to Pray Together, 1996; (with S.L. Lingo) Noah, Noah, What'll We Do?, 1996; Faith Happens! A Creative Study of the Book of James, 1997; (contrib.) An Introduction to Family Nights, 1997; It's a Sheep's Life: Grazing in the 23rd Psalm, 1997; (with A. Nappa) Imagine That! 365 Wacky Ways to Build a Creative Christian Family, 1998; (with N. Wakefield) Legacy of Joy: A Devotional for Fathers, 1998; (with A. Nappa) Bore No More! 2, 1999; True Stories of Answered Prayer, 1999; A Heart Like His, 1999; (with N. Wakefield) True Stories of Transformed Lives, 1999; What I Wish My Youth Leader Knew about Youth Ministry: A National Survey, 1999; (with A. Nappa) Zachary's Zoo, 2000; (ed. with A. Nappa) A Mind like His, 2000; (with T. Nappa) Lunch Box Laughs, 2000; Lunch Box Trivia, 2000; Lunch Box Promises, 2000; The Courage to Be Christian: Creating a Life of Spiritual Passion, 2001; (with N. Wakefield) The Heart of a Father, 2001; Who Moved My Church, 2001; The Prayer of Jesus: Developing Intimacy with God through Christ's Example, 2001; Growing up Fatherless: Healing from the Absence of Dad, 2003; Tuesdays with Matthew: An Apostle, a Photographer, and Life's Greatest Questions, 2003; (with A. Nappa) Creative Family Prayer Times: 52 Fun Ways to Pray Together, 2007; (with A. Nappa) Creative Family Prayer Times: 52 Fun Ways to Pray Together, 2007; (ed.) Make it Stick, 2007; Interactive Illustrations: The Gospels: For Every Preacher, Teacher, and Small Group Leader, 2010; Instant Small Group, 2011; 77 Reasons Why Your Book was Rejected (and how to be sure it won't happen again!), 2011. Works appear in anthologies. **Address:** Group Publishing Inc., 1515 Cascade Ave., PO Box 481, Loveland, CO 80538, U.S.A.

NAQVI, H. M. Pakistani/British (born England), b. 1974?. **Genres:** Novels. **Career:** World Bank, staff, 1997-2003; Boston University, faculty. Writer. **Publications:** Home Boy, 2009. Contributor to periodicals. **Address:** Karachi, Pakistan. **Online address:** greatglobaldialectic@yahoo.com

NARAGHI, Ehsan. (Ihsān Narāqī). French/Iranian (born Iran), b. 1926. **Genres:** Autobiography/Memoirs, Sociology, Social Sciences. **Career:** National Organization for Statistics, director of sociological problems, 1953-55; University of Teheran, Institute of Social Studies and Research, director, 1958-69, professor of social sciences, 1964-69; UNESCO, Youth Activities Division, director general, 1969-99. Iranian sociologist and writer. **Publications:** L'étude des Populations Dans les Pays à Statistique Incompléte, 1960; Jāmi'ah, Javānān, Dānishgāh, Dīrūz, Imrūz, Fardā, 1972; Ghurbat-i Gharb, 1974; Tama-i khām, 1977; Kayfīyat-i zindagī, 1978; Des Palais du Chah aux Prisons de la Révolution, 1991; Min balāṭ al-shāh ilá sujūn al-thawrah, 1993; From Palace to Prison: Inside the Iranian Revolution, 1994; Naẓarī bih taḥqīqāt-i ijtimāī dar īrān, 2000; Anchih khud dasht, 2003; Iqbāl-i Nāmumkin, 2003; āzād: Majmūah-i maqālātva Muṣ āhabah'hā, 2004. **Address:** Ivan R. Dee Inc., 1332 N Halsted St., Chicago, IL 60622-2637, U.S.A.

NĀRANG, Gopī Chand. Indian (born India), b. 1931. **Genres:** Novellas/Short Stories, Language/Linguistics, Literary Criticism And History, Cultural/Ethnic Topics. **Career:** University of Delhi, St. Stephen's College, lecturer, 1957-58, lecturer, 1959-61, Department of Urdu, reader, 1961-74, professor of Urdu, 1986-95, professor emeritus, 2005-; University of Wisconsin, Department of Indian Studies, visiting professor, 1963-65, 1968-70; Jamia Millia Islamia University, professor and head, 1974-85, acting vice chancellor, 1981-82; National Capital Territory of Delhi, Urdu Academy, vice chairman, 1996-99; University of Oslo, visiting professor, 1997; Sahitya Akademi, president, 2003-07. Writer. **Publications:** Karkhandāri dialect of Delhi Urdu, 1961; Hindustānī qisson semakhūz Urdū masnaviyān, 1962; Urdū kī talīm kelisāniyātī pahlū, 1962; Readings in Literary Urdu Prose, 1967; Manshūrāt, 1968; Urdu: Readings in Literary Urdu Prose, 1968; āsār-i Mahrūm: Pagdandī, Amritsar kā Mahrūmnambar, 1969; Karbal kathā kā lassanī mutālaa, 1970; Armaghān-i Mālik, 1971; Imlā namah, 1974; Iqbāl Jāmiahke musannifīn kī nazar men, 1979; Vazāhatīkitābiyāt, 1980; Anīs shanāsī, 1981; Urdūafsānah: Rivāyat aur masāil: Majmūah-yi maqālātHind o Pāk Urdū Afsānah Semīnār ma Muntakhabmaqālāt, 1981; Safar āshnā, 1982; Iqbāl kā fann, 1983; Uslūbiyāt-i Mīr, 1985; Sānihah-yi Karbalā Bataurshirī istiārah: Urdū shāirī kā ek tahklīqīruhjān, 1986; Intizār Husain aur unke afsāne, 1986; AmīrKhusrau kā Hindvī kalām: Ma nushkah-yi Barlin, zakhīrah-yiIshpringar, 1987; Nayā Urdū Afsānah: Intikhāb, Tajziye, Aur Mubāhis, 1988; Adabī tanqīd aur uslūbiyāt, 1989; Imlā nāmah: Sifārishāt-iImlā Kamītī, Taraqqī-yi Urdū Bord, 1990; AmīraKhusaro kā Hindavī kāvya: śpringara Sangraha kīBarlina Prati Sahita, 1990; Urdu Language and Literature: Critical Perspectives, 1991; Qārīasās tanqīd: Mazhariyat aur qārī kī vāpsī, 1992; Sākhtiyāt, pas sākhtiyāt, aur mashriqīshiriyāt, 1993; Balvant Singh ke bihtarīn afsāne, 1995; Armughān-i Nārang, 1996; Hindūstān ke Urdū musannifīn aur shuarā, 1996; Adabkā badaltā manzar Nāmah: Urdū mabad-i jadīdiyat parmukālalmah, 1998; Dāktar Zākir Husain, shakhsīyat aurkārnāme, 1998; Saṃracanāvāda, uttara-samracanāvāda, evam prācya kāvyaśāstra, 2000; Hindūstānī qiṣ ṣ on se mākhūz Urdūmasnavīyān, 2001; Bīsvīn sadī men Urdū adab, 2002; Urdū ghazal aur Hindustānī zihn va tahzīb, 2002; āzādī ke bāda Urdū afsānā: Eka intikhāba, 2003; Hindūstān kī tahrīk-i āzādī aur Urdūshāirī, 2003; Itlāqī tanqīd: Nae tanāzur, 2003; Taraqqī pasandī jadīdiyat mābad jadīdiyat: GopīC and Nārang ke muntakhab mazāmīn, 2004; Jadīdiyat ke bad, 2005; Valī Daknī: tasavvuf, insāniyat aur muhabbat kāshāir, 2005; Urdū zabān aur lisāniyāt, 2006; Urdūkī naī bastiyān, 2006; Kāghaz-i ātish zadah, 2011. EDITOR: Anthology of Modern Urdu Poetry for Indian Council for Cultural Relations, 1981; Contribution of Writers to Indian Freedom Movement, 1985; (and intro.) Selected Short Stories, 1989; (and intro.) Krishan Chander: Selected Short Stories, 1990; (and intro.) Balwant Singh: Selected Short Stories, 1996; Encyclopaedia of Indian Literature, 6 vols., 1987-94; Masterpieces of Indian Literature, 3 vols., 1997; Let's Learn Urdu, 2000. BOOKS IN HINDI: Amir Khusrau Ka Hindavi Kavya, 1990; Balwant Singh ki Shreshth Kahaniyan, 1997; Paathak Aadhaar Aalochana, 1997; Urdu Kaise Likhen, 2001; Urdu Par Khulta Dareecha, 2005; Beeswein Sadi mein Urdu Sahitya, 2006; Sajjād ẓahīr: adabī khidmāt aur taraqqī pasand taḥrīk, 2007; (with T. va Tahzīb) Firāq Gorakhpūrī: Shāir, naqqād, dānishvar, 2008; Fikshan shiriyāt: Tashkīl o Tanqīd, 2009. **Address:** D-252, Sarvodaya Enclave, New Delhi, DH 110017, India. **Online address:** narang_5@yahoo.co.in

NARĀQĪ, Ihsān. *See* **NARAGHI, Ehsan.**

NARAYAN, Kirin. American (born United States), b. 1959?. **Genres:** Autobiography/Memoirs, Novels. **Career:** University of Wisconsin, Department of Anthropology, professor of anthropology, 1989-. Writer and anthropologist. **Publications:** Storytellers, Saints, and Scoundrels: Folk Narrative in Hindu Religious Teaching, 1989; (ed. with S. Lavie and R. Rosaldo) Creativity/Anthropology, 1993; Love, Stars, and All That (novel), 1994; (with D. Sood) Mondays on the Dark Night of the Moon: Himalayan Foothill Folktales, 1997; (ed. and intro.) Old Deccan Days, or, Hindoo Fairy Legends, 2002; My Family and Other Saints (memoir), 2007; Alive in the Writing: Crafting Ethnography in the Company of Chekhov, 2012. **Address:** Department of Anthropology, University of Wisconsin, 5240 W. H. Sewell Social Science Bldg., 1180 Observatory Dr., Madison, WI 53706, U.S.A. **Online address:** knarayan@wisc.edu

NARDI, Peter M. American (born United States), b. 1947. **Genres:** Sociology, Gay And Lesbian Issues, Sex. **Career:** Pitzer College, assistant professor, 1975-81, associate professor, 1981-86, professor of sociology, 1986-, now professor emeritus, associate dean of faculty, 1995-97, 2000-04, Institutional Research, director, 2001-; Gay and Lesbian Alliance Against Defamation, co-president, 1990-91; Rockefeller Foundation, fellow, 1997; Pacific Sociological Association, president, 2005-06. Writer. **Publications:** Gay Men's Friendships: Invincible Communities, 1999; Doing Survey Research: A Guide to Quantitative Methods, 2003, 2nd ed., 2006; Interpreting Data: A Guide to Understanding Research, 2006. EDITOR AND CONTRIBUTOR: Men's Friendships, 1992; (with D. Sanders and J. Marmor) Growing up before Stonewall:

Life Stories of Some Gay Men, 1994; (with J. Gagnon and M. Levine) In Changing Times: Gay Men and Lesbians Encounter HIV/AIDS, 1997; (with B. Schneider) Social Perspectives in Lesbian and Gay Studies: A Reader, 1998; Gay Masculinities, 2000. **Address:** Pitzer College, 1050 N Mills Ave., Claremont, CA 91711, U.S.A. **Online address:** peter_nardi@pitzer.edu

NARDULLI, Peter F. American (born United States), b. 1947. **Genres:** Law, Politics/Government. **Career:** University of Illinois, Institute of Government and Public Affairs, instructor, 1974-75, assistant professor, associate professor, 1975-80, professor, 1985-, professor of political science, 1997-, acting director, 1985-86, director of graduate studies, 1987-91, head, 1992-2006, Center for the Study of Democratic Governance, founding director, 2004-, Cline Center for Democracy, director, 2004-, College of Law, visiting professor, 1985-86, professor of law, 2005-, Press Book Series, editor, 2006-. **Publications:** The Courtroom Elite: An Organizational Perspective on Criminal Justice, 1978; (ed.) The Study of Criminal Courts: Political Perspectives, 1979; (with J.M. Stonecash) Politics, Professionalism, and Urban Services, 1981; Prisons, Dollars, and Crime, Institute of Government and Public Affairs, 1983; (with J. Eisenstein and R.B. Flemming) The Contours of Justice: Communities and Their Courts, 1988; (with J. Eisenstein and R.B. Flemming) The Tenor of Justice: Criminal Courts and the Guilty Plea Process, 1988; (ed.) Diversity, Conflict, and State Politics: Regionalism in Illinois, 1989; (with J. Eisenstein and R.B. Flemming) The Craft of Justice: Politics and Work in Criminal Court Communities, 1992; (ed.) The Constitution and American Political Development: An Institutional Perspective, 1992; Popular Efficacy in the Democratic Era: A Reexamination of Electoral Accountability in the United States, 1828-2000, 2005; (ed.) International Perspectives on Contemporary Democracy, 2008; (ed.) Domestic Perspectives on Contemporary Democracy, 2008; (contrib.) The Political Dynamics of Thinking and Feeling. Contributor to periodicals. **Address:** Department of Political Science, University of Illinois, 361 Lincoln Hall, 605 E Springfield Ave., Urbana, IL 61801, U.S.A. **Online address:** nardulli@uiuc.edu

NASAR, Jack L. American (born United States), b. 1947. **Genres:** Regional/Urban Planning. **Career:** Shelter Programs Inc., planning consultant, 1970-72; Yonkers, Department of Development, assistant planner, 1972-73; Pennsylvania State University, graduate assistant, 1973-76, instructor in architecture, 1976-77; Westinghouse National Issues Center, research associate, 1976; Institute for Architecture and Urban Studies, consultant programmer, 1977; University of Tennessee, assistant professor of architecture, 1977-80; Ohio State University, assistant professor, associate professor, 1980-84, professor of city and regional planning, 1990-2009; The University of Sydney, fellow, 1988-89. Writer. **Publications:** The Evaluative Image of the City, 1997; Environmental Aesthetics: Theory, Research, and Practice, 1988; Design by Competition, 1999; (ed. with W.F.E. Preiser) Directions in Person-Environment Research and Practice, 1999; (ed. with E. Cowley) Universal Design and Visitability: From Accessibility to Zoning, 2007; (co-ed.) Designing for Designers: Lessons Learned from Schools of Architecture, 2007; Visual Quality by Design, 2008. **Address:** Department of City & Regional Planning, The Ohio State University, 275 W Woodruff Ave., Knowlton Hall, Columbus, OH 43210-1135, U.S.A. **Online address:** nasar.1@osu.edu

NASAR, Sylvia. American/German (born Germany), b. 1947. **Genres:** Biography, Economics. **Career:** New York University, Institute for Economic Analysis, assistant to Wassily Leontief, 1977-80; Institute for Public Information, economist, 1981; Control Data Corp., senior economist, 1981-82; Scientists Institute for Public Information, economist; Fortune, Economic Forecasting Group, associate editor, staff writer, 1983-89; U.S.News & World Report, economics columnist, 1990; New York Times, economics correspondent, 1991-99; Columbia University, Graduate School of Journalism, John S. and James L. Knight professor of business journalism, 2001; Russell Sage Foundation, research fellow, 2007. **Publications:** A Beautiful Mind: A Biography of John Forbes Nash, Jr., Winner of the Nobel Prize in Economics, 1994, 1998; (ed. with H.W. Kuhn) The Essential John Nash, 2002. **Address:** Simon & Schuster Children's Publishing, 1230 Ave. of the Americas, New York, NY 10020-1513, U.S.A. **Online address:** szn1@columbia.edu

NASDIJJ. Also writes as Tim Barrus. American (born United States), b. 1950?. **Genres:** Autobiography/Memoirs, Novels. **Career:** Journalist and educator. **Publications:** The Blood Runs Like a River Through My Dreams: A Memoir, 2000; The Boy and the Dog Are Sleeping (memoir), 2003; Geronimo's Bones: A Memoir of My Brother and Me, 2004. AS TIM BARRUS: My Brother My Lover, 1985; Anywhere, Anywhere, 1987; Genocide The Anthology, 1988; (with R. McCartney-Moore) Selective Service, 1991; To Indigo Dust, 1992. **Address:** c/o Author Mail, Random House, 1745 Broadway, New York, NY 10019, U.S.A.

NASH, (Cyril) Knowlton. Canadian (born Canada), b. 1927. **Genres:** History, Documentaries/Reportage, Social Sciences. **Career:** Globe and Mail, sports reporter, 1945-47; British United Press News Service, manager of news bureaus, 1947-51; United Nations International Federation of Agricultural Producers, director of information and representative, 1951-61; freelance journalist, 1961-64; Canadian Broadcasting Corp., Washington correspondent, 1964-68, CBC Radio and Television, director of information programming, director of television news and current affairs, 1968-78, CBC-TV National News, The National, chief correspondent and anchor person, 1978-88, News in Review and Saturday Report, senior correspondent and anchor, 1990-2004, retired, 1992. **Publications:** History on the Run, 1984; Times to Remember, 1986; Prime Time at Ten, 1987; Kennedy and Diefenbaker: Fear and Loathing across the Undefended Border, 1990; Visions of Canada, 1991; The Microphone Wars, 1994; Cue the Elephant, 1996; Trivia Pursuit: How Showbiz Values Are Corrupting the News, 1998; The Swashbucklers: The Story of Canada's Battling Broadcasters, 2001. **Address:** 29 Whitehall Rd., Toronto, ON M4W 2C5, Canada. **Online address:** cassels@mcmaster.ca

NASH, Elizabeth (Hamilton). American (born United States), b. 1934. **Genres:** Theatre, Biography, Autobiography/Memoirs. **Career:** Coloratura soprano: Pfalztheater, Kaiserslautern 1961-62; Theater am Domh of, Osnabruck, coloratura soprano, 1962-63; Landestheater, Detmold, coloratura soprano, 1963-64; Hessisches Staatstheater, Kassel, coloratura soprano, 1964-67; Indiana University-Bloomington, associate instructor/supervisor in singing, instructor in opera workshop, assistant opera stage director, 1971-74; University of Minnesota-Twin Cities, assistant professor/associate professor of speech and singing for actors, 1975-, professor of speech and singing for actors, head of acting program, 1986-89; Christian Science Monitor Radio Broadcasting, voice production coach and presentation stylist, 1975-90; German Herold Radio Broadcasting, voice production coach and presentation stylist, 1975-; Children's Theater Co., singer and actress, 1979-80. Writer. **Publications:** Always First Class: The Career of Geraldine Farrar, 1981; The Luminous Ones: A History of the Great Actresses, 1991; Pieces of Rainbow, 1994; (with S.O. Lee) Memoirs of Sylvia Olden Lee, 2001; Autobiographical Reminiscences of African-American Classical Singers, 1853-Present: Introducing Their Spiritual Heritage into the Concert Repertoire, 2007. Contributor to magazines. **Address:** Department Theatre Arts & Dance, University of Minnesota, 580 Rarig Ctr., 330 21st Ave. S, Minneapolis, MN 55455, U.S.A. **Online address:** nashx001@tc.umn.edu

NASH, Gary B. American (born United States), b. 1933. **Genres:** History, Politics/Government, Essays. **Career:** Princeton University, instructor, assistant, 1959-62, assistant professor of history, 1964-66; University of California, Department of History, assistant professor, 1966-68, associate professor, 1968-72, professor, 1972-2005, professor emeritus, 2005-, Council on Education Development, dean, 1980-84, dean of undergraduate and intercollege curricular development, 1984-91, National Center for History in the Schools, associate director, 1988-94, director, 1994-; National History Standards Project, co-chair, 1992-96. Writer. **Publications:** And Distinguished Guests, 1962; Quakers and Politics: Pennsylvania 1681-1726, 1968, new ed., 1993; Class and Society in Early America, 1970; Red, White and Black: The Peoples of Early North America, 1974, 6th ed., 2009; The Urban Crucible: Social Change, Political Consciousness and the Origins of the American Revolution, 1979 as The Urban Crucible: The Northern Seaports and the Origins of the American Revolution, 1986; Race, Class, and Politics: Essays on American Colonial and Revolutionary Society, 1986; Forging Freedom: The Formation of Philadelphia's Black Community 1720-1840, 1988; Race and Revolution: The Inaugural Merrill Jensen Lectures, 1990; (with J.R. Soderland) Freedom by Degrees: Emancipation and Its Aftermath in Pennsylvania, 1991; American Odyssey: The United States in the Twentieth Century, 1991, rev. ed. as American Odyssey: The 20th Century and Beyond, 2004; National Standards for United States History: Exploring the American Experience, 1994; National Standards for World History: Exploring Paths to the Present: Grades 5-12, 1994; History Wars of the 1990s, 1996; National Standards for History, 1996; (with C. Crabtree and R.E. Dunn) History on Trial: Culture Wars and the Teaching of the Past, 1997; Forbidden Love: The Secret History of Mixed Race America, 1999, 2nd ed. as Forbidden Love: The Hidden History of Mixed-race America, 2010; (with R.S. Dunn) Sugar and Slaves: The Rise of the Planter Class in the English West Indies, 1624-1713, 2000; First City:

Philadelphia and the Forging of Historical Memory, 2002; Landmarks of the American Revolution, 2003; Unknown American Revolution: The Unruly Birth of Democracy and the Struggle to Create America, 2005; (with C. Carson and E.J. Lapsansky-Werner) African American Lives: The Struggle for Freedom, 2005, 2nd ed., 2011; Forgotten Fifth: African Americans in the Age of Revolution, 2006; (with C. Smith) Atlas of American History, 2007; (with G.R.G. Hodges) Friends of Liberty: A Tale of Three Patriots, Two Revolutions and the Betrayal That Divided a Nation, 2008; The Liberty Bell: An American Icon, 2010. EDITOR/CO-EDITOR: (with R. Weiss) The Great Fear: Race in the Mind of America, 1970; The Private Side of American History: Readings in Everyday Life, 2 vols., 1975, (with C.J. Shelton) 4th ed., 1987; (with D. Sweet) Struggle and Survival in Colonial America, 1981; (with J.R. Jeffrey) The American People, 2 vols., 1985, 7th ed., 2010; Retracing the Past, 2 vols., 1985, 6th ed., 2006; Encyclopedia of American History, 2003, rev. ed., 2010; (with A.F. Young and R. Raphael) Revolutionary Founders: Rebels, Radicals and Reformers in the Making of the Nation, 2011; Encyclopedia of the American Revolution and the Early National Era, 3 vols., forthcoming. **Address:** Deparment of History, University of California at Los Angeles, 6339 Bunche Hall, PO Box 951473, Los Angeles, CA 90095-1473, U.S.A. **Online address:** gnash@ucla.edu

NASH, Joy. American (born United States) **Genres:** Romance/Historical, Novels. **Career:** Writer and architect. **Publications:** ROMANCE NOVELS: My Mobster, 2003; Celtic Fire, 2005; Immortals: The Awakening, 2007; Immortals: The Crossing, 2008; A Little Light Magic, 2009. DRUIDS OF AVALON TRILOGY: The Grail King, 2006; Deep Magic, 2008; Silver Silence, 2009. ANTHOLOGIES: (contrib. With R.T. Popp and J. Ashley) Immortals: The Reckoning, 2009; (contrib. with K. Angell and S. Hill) Santa, Honey, 2009. **Address:** PA , U.S.A. **Online address:** joy@joynash.com

NASH, Joyce D. (Joyce Donovan Nash). American (born United States), b. 1940. **Genres:** Medicine/Health. **Career:** Aluminum Co. of America, secretary, 1960-68; Stanford University, Stanford Heart Disease Prevention Program, research assistant, 1973-76, Diet and Weight Control Clinic, director, 1976-78; Weight Watchers, director of program and training, 1978-81; Lifespring Inc., consultant, 1981-82; Foothill College, student therapist, 1988-89; Pacific Graduate School of Psychology, student therapist, 1989-90; Mount Zion Crisis Clinic, psychological intern, 1991-92; Haight-Ashbury Psychological Services, psychological intern, 1991-92; Kaiser Permanente, psychological assistant, 1992-93; Westside Community Crisis Clinic, psychological intern, 1992-94, on-duty supervisor, 1994-95; Haight-Ashbury Psychological Services, psychological intern, 1991-92. Writer. **Publications:** (With L. Ormiston) Taking Charge of Your Weight and Well Being, 1978; Taking Charge of Your Smoking, 1981; Maximize Your Body Potential: 16 Weeks to a Lifetime of Effective Weight Management, 1986, 3rd ed., 2003; Now That You've Lost It: How to Maintain your Best Weight, 1992; What Your Doctor Can't Tell You about Cosmetic Surgery, 1995; The New Maximize Your Body Potential: Lifetime Skills for Successful Weight Management, 1997; Binge No More: Your Guide to Overcoming Disordered Eating, 1999; Lose Weight, Live Healthy: a Complete Guide to Designing Your Own Weight Loss Program, 2011. Contributor to books and periodicals. **Address:** 1220 University Dr., Ste. 202, Menlo Park, CA 94025, U.S.A. **Online address:** jnash@joycenashphd.com

NASH, Joyce Donovan. *See* **NASH, Joyce D.**

NASH, Mary. Spanish/Irish (born Ireland), b. 1947. **Genres:** Women's Studies And Issues, Social Commentary. **Career:** University of Barcelona, assistant professor, 1976-84, associate professor, 1984-90, professor of contemporary history and department head, 1991-, lecturer, Center for Research in Women's History, founding director, 1982-91, Research Group Multiculturalism and Gender, director; New York University, visiting professor, 1986; University of California, visiting professor, 1992; University of Amsterdam, visiting professor, 1995, 1997; Duke University, visiting professor, 1996; Universidade Aberta, visiting professor, 1997; Spanish Association of Research, founder. Writer. **Publications:** IN SPANISH: Mujeres Libres: Espana, 1936-1939, 1975, 3rd ed., 1977; Mujer y movimiento obrero en Espana, 1931-1939, 1981; Mujer, familia y trabajo en Espana, 1875-1936, 1983; (ed. and contrib.) Presencia y protagonismo: Aspectos de la historia de la mujer, 1984; (ed.) Més enlià del silenci: Les dònes a la historia de Catalunya, 1988; Lasmujeres en la Guerra Civil, 1989; (ed. with J.S. Amelang) Historia y genero: Las mujeres en la Europa Moderna y Contemporanea, 1990; Les dones fanhistoria, 1990; (with S. Tavera) Experiencias desiguales: Conflictossociales y respuestas colectivas (Siglo XIX), 1994; (ed.) Textos para lahistoria de las mujeres en Espana, 1994; (ed. with R. Ballester) Mulheres, trabalho e reproducao: Atitudes sociais e politicas de proteccao a vida, 1996; (ed. with J.D.L. Pascua and G. Espigado) Pautas Historicas de Sociabilidad Femenina Rituales y Modelos de Representacion: Actas del VColoquio Internacional de la Asociacion Espanola de Investigacion Historica de las Mujeres, Cadiz, 5, 6 y 7 de Junio d 1997, 1999; Rojas: las mujeres republicanas en la guerra civil, 1999; (ed. with D. Marre) Multiculturalismos y genero: perspectivas interdisciplinarias, 2001; (ed.with S. Tavera) Las Mujeres y las guerras: el papel de las mujeres en lasguerras de la Edad Antigua a la contemporánea, 2003; (ed. with D. Marre) El Desafío de la diferencia: representaciones culturales eidentidades de género, raza y clase, 2003; Inmigrantes en nuestroespejo: inmigración y discurso periodístico en la prensa Española, 2005. IN ENGLISH: (co-author) Women's Studies and European Integration: With Reference to Current and Future Action Programmes for Equal Opportunities between Women and Men, 1995; Defying Male Civilization: Women in the Spanish Civil War, 1995. CONTRIBUTOR: Marginated Groups in Spanish and Portuguese History, 1989; Visions of Gender and the Rise of the European Welfare States, 1890-1950, 1991; Writing Women's History: International Perspectives, 1991; Contemporary Catalonia in Spain and Europe, 1991; Wayward Girls and Wicked Women: In Memoriam of Angela Carter, 1995; Contested Identities: Women in Contemporary Spanish Society, 1998. OTHERS: (with A. Thompson) Identidades, género y ciudadanía: procesos históricos y cambio social en contextos multiculturales en América Latina, 2005; (ed. with R. Tello and N. Benach) Intersticios: contactos interculturales, género y dinámicas identitarias en Barcelona, 2008; (ed. with G. Torres) Los límites de la diferencia: alteridad cultural, género y prácticas sociales, 2008. **Address:** Department of Contemporary History, University of Barcelona, Montalegre 6, Barcelona, 08001, Spain. **Online address:** nash@ub.edu

NASH, Michael R. American (born United States), b. 1951. **Genres:** Medicine/Health, Psychology. **Career:** Veterans Administration Hospital, clinical psychology trainee, 1977, 1980; Yale University, clinical intern in psychiatry, 1982-83; North Texas State University, assistant professor of psychology, 1983-86; University of Tennessee, assistant professor, 1986-90, associate professor of psychology, 1990-, professor of psychology; American Psychological Association, fellow; Society for Clinical and Experimental Hypnosis, fellow; International Journal of Clinical and Experimental Hypnosis, editor, editor emeritus. **Publications:** (Ed. with E. Fromm and contrib.) Contemporary Hypnosis Research, 1992; (with E. Fromm) Psychoanalysis and Hypnosis, 1995; (with A.J. Barnier) The Oxford Handbook of Hypnosis: Theory, Research and Practice, 2008. Works appear in anthologies. Contributor of articles to journals. **Address:** Department of Psychology, University of Tennessee, 307 Austin Peay Bldg., Knoxville, TN 37996, U.S.A. **Online address:** mnash@utk.edu

NASH, Newlyn. *See* **HOWE, Muriel.**

NASH, Patrick Gerard. Australian (born Australia), b. 1933?. **Genres:** Law, Novels. **Career:** Australian Attorney-General's Department, legal officer, 1956-57; University of Tasmania, lecturer in law, 1957-59; barrister, 1959-62; The Australian Accountant, legal editor, 1962-92; University of Melbourne, lecturer, 1962-64; Monash University, lecturer, professor and dean of law, 1964-66, 1970-80; University of Papua New Guinea, foundation professor and dean of law, 1966-70. **Publications:** Paul's Justices of the Peace, 2nd ed., 1965; Some Problems of Administering Law in the Territory of Papua New Guinea, 1967; Nash on Magistrates Courts, 1975; Civil Procedure Cases and Text, 1976; (Victorian) Justices Manual, 1978; Bourke's Criminal Law, 3rd ed., 1981; Ward and Kelly, Summary Justice, Victorian Commentary, 1984; (with C.K.J. Rao) Homicide: The Law and the Proofs, 1986; Victorian Courts, 1994. **Address:** Owen Dixon Chambers, Rm. 1310, 205 William St., Melbourne, VI 3000, Australia. **Online address:** gerardnash@vicbar.com.au

NASH, Roderick Frazier. American (born United States), b. 1939. **Genres:** Environmental Sciences/Ecology, History, Biography, Economics. **Career:** Dartmouth College, instructor, 1964-66; Hanover Conservation Council, secretary, 1965-; University of California, assistant professor, 1966-69, associate professor, 1969-74, professor of history, 1974-, Department of Environmental Studies, chair, 1970-75, 1992-93, now professor emeritus. Writer. **Publications:** (Contrib.) American History and the Social Sciences, 1964; (with M. Curti) Philanthropy in the Shaping of American Higher Education, 1965; Wilderness and the American Mind, 1967, 3rd ed., 1982; American Environment: Readings in the History of Conservation, 1968, 3rd ed., 1990; (contrib.)

Grand Canyon of The Living Colorado, 1970; Nervous Generation: American Thought, 1917-1930, 1970, rev. ed., 1990; (ed. and intro.) The Call of the Wild: 1900-1916, 1970; (ed.) Environment and Americans: The Problem of Priorities, 1972; (with G. Graves) From These Beginnings: A Biographical Approach to American History, 1973, 7th ed., 2008; (with L.M. Talbot and N.H. Cheek, Jr.) Nature and Human Nature, 1976; Nature in World Development: Patterns in the Preservation of Scenic and Outdoor Recreation Resources, 1978; (with R.O. Collins) The Big Drops: Ten Legendary Rapids of the American West, 1978, rev. ed., 1989; Tourism, Parks and The Wilderness Idea in the History of Alaska, 1981; Rights of Nature: A History of Environmental Ethics, 1989; (ed.) American Environmentalism: Readings in Conservation History, 1990. Contributor to journals. **Address:** Department of History, University of California, Santa Barbara, CA 93106-4160, U.S.A.

NASH, Roger. Canadian/British (born England), b. 1942. **Genres:** Poetry, Philosophy, Sciences, Technology, Environmental Sciences/Ecology. **Career:** League of Canadian Poets, president, 1998-2000; Laurentian University, Department of Philosophy, professor, now professor emeritus, chair, Interdisciplinary Humanities M.A. programme, director, Graduate Diploma in Science Communication, founding member. Writer. **Publications:** POETRY: Settlement in a School of Whales, 1983; Psalms from the Suburbs, 1986; Night Flying, 1990; The Poetry of Prayer, 1994; In the Kosher Chow Mein Restaurant, 1996; Once I was a Wheelbarrow, 2000; Something Blue and Flying Upwards: New and Selected Poems, 2006. OTHERS: Ethics, Science, Technology and the Environment: A Reader, 1993; Ethics, Science, Technology and the Environment: A Study Guide, 1993; Camera and the Cobra and Other Stories, 2011. EDITOR: Spring-fever: Writes of Spring, 1997: An Anthology of Poems from the Ontario Division of the League of Canadian Poets, 1997; Licking Honey Off a Thorn: An Anthology of Poems from the Ontario Division of the League of Canadian Poets: (W)rites of Spring 1998, 1998; Northern Prospects: An Anthology of Northeastern Ontario Poetry, 1998. Contributor to periodicals. **Address:** Department of Philosophy, Laurentian University, L-724, Parker Bldg., 935 Ramsey Lake Rd., Sudbury, ON P3E 2C6, Canada. **Online address:** rnash@laurentian.ca

NASKRECKI, Piotr. American (born United States) **Genres:** Zoology. **Career:** Harvard University, Museum of Comparative Zoology, research associate, Conservation Intl., Center for Applied Biodiversity Science, Invertebrate Diversity Initiative, director, 2002-09. Writer. **Publications:** The Smaller Majority: The Hidden World of the Animals That Dominate the Tropics, 2005; Relics: Travels in Nature's Time Machine, 2011; (co-ed.) Still Counting. . .: Biodiversity Exploration for Conservation: The First 20 Years of the Rapid Assessment Program, 2011. **Address:** Invertebrate Diversity Initiative, Conservation International, Museum of Comparative Zoology, Harvard University, 26 Oxford St., Cambridge, MA 02138, U.S.A. **Online address:** p.naskrecki@conservation.org

NASON, T. *See* **NASON, Tema.**

NASON, Tema. Also writes as T. Nason. American (born United States), b. 1937?. **Genres:** Novels, Novellas/Short Stories, Adult Non-fiction. **Career:** Williams College, junior; Johns Hopkins University, instructor in creative writing, 1969-78; Radcliffe College, Bunting Institute, visiting writer, 1979-80; Brandeis University, senior research associate in sociology, 1980-. Writer. **Publications:** (As T. Nason) A Stranger Here Myself (fiction), 1977; Ethel: The Fictional Autobiography of Ethel Rosenberg (novel), 1990; Full Moon (fiction), 1993. ANTHOLOGIES: Eating Our Hearts Out, 1993; The Times of Our Lives, 1993; The Crimson Edge, 1996. EDITOR: The Rosenbergs: Collected Visions of Artists and Writers, 1988; Vital Lives, 1990. Contributor to periodicals. **Address:** Women's Studies Research Center, Brandeis University, 515 South St., PO Box 079, Waltham, MA 02454-9110, U.S.A. **Online address:** tsnason@aol.com

NASR, Kameel B. American/Lebanese (born Lebanon), b. 1949. **Genres:** Adult Non-fiction, Geography, History. **Career:** Journalist in Jerusalem, 1986-87; De Paul University, teacher of composition. **Publications:** Children of Palestinian Refugees, 1987; The World Up Close: A Cyclist's Adventures on Five Continents, 1990; Bicycle Touring International: The Complete Book on Adventure Cycling, 1992; Cycling the Mediterranean: Bicycle Tours in Spain, France, Italy, Greece and Beyond, 1996; Arab and Israeli Terrorism: The Causes and Effects of Middle East Violence 1936-1993, 1997. **Address:** 578 Silverado Dr., Lafayette, CA 94549, U.S.A.

NASR, Seyyed Hossein. American/Iranian (born Iran), b. 1933. **Genres:** Poetry, Art/Art History, Intellectual History, Philosophy, Theology/Religion, Cultural/Ethnic Topics. **Career:** Teacher, 1955-; Harvard University, teaching assistant, 1955-58, visiting professor, 1962, 1965; Tehran University, associate professor of the history of science and philosophy, 1958-63, professor, 1963-79, dean of the faculty of arts and letters, 1968-72, vice-chancellor, 1970-71; American University of Beirut, first Aga Khan professor of Islamic studies, 1964-65; Aryamehr University, president, 1972, chancellor, 1972-75; Imperial Iranian Academy of Philosophy, founder and president, 1974-79, head; Princeton University, visiting professor, 1975; University of Utah, visiting distinguished professor, 1979; Temple University, professor of Islamic studies, 1979-84; George Washington University, university professor of Islamic studies, 1984-; Al-Furqan Foundation, chief advisor, 1991; University of Edinburgh, faculty. Writer. **Publications:** āshnaī bā Mullā ṣ adrā dar maghrib zamīn, 1961; Three Muslim Sages, 1964; An Introduction to Islamic Cosmological Doctrines: Conceptions of Nature and Methods Used for Its Study by the Ikhwān al-ṣ afā', al-Bīrūni and Ibn Sīnā, 1964, rev. ed., 1978; Naẓar-i mutafakkirān-i Islāmīdarbārah-i ṭabīat, 1964; (with H. Corbin and O. Yahya) Histoirede la Philosophie Islamique, 1964; Ideals and Realities of Islam, 1966, rev. ed., 2000; Islamic Studies: Essays on Law and Society, the Sciences and Philosophy and Sufism, 1967; Science and Civilization in Islam, 1968; The Encounter of Man and Nature, 1968; Sufi Essays, 1972, 3rd ed., 1999; états Spirituels dans le Soufisme, 1973; al-Islām, ahdāfuhuwa-ḥaqāiquh, 1974; Jalāl al-Dīn Rūmī: Supreme Persian Poet and Sage, 1974; Rumi and the Sufi Tradition, 1974; (with W.C. Chittick) An Annotated Bibliography of Islamic Science, 1975; Dirāsāt Islāmīyah: abḥāth mutafarriqah fīal-shar wa-al-mujtamawa-al-ulūm al-sharqīyah, wa-al-falsafah, wa-al-taṣ awwuf fī al-iṭār al-Islāmī, 1975; Dirāsāt Islāmīyah, 1975; Islam and the Plight of Modern Man, 1975; Islam: Perspectives et réalités, 1975; Islamic Science: An Illustrated Study, 1976; Sacred Art in Persian Culture, 1976; Western Science and Asian Cultures, 1976; (ed.) Mélanges offerts á Henry Corbin, 1977; Majmūah-i āsār-i Fārsī-i ShaykhIshrāq, 1977; Ulūm fī al-Islām: dirāsahmuṣ awwarah, 1978; Essais sur le soufisme, 1980; Islamic Life and Thought, 1981; Naẓar-i mutafakkirān-i Islāmī darbārah-i ṭabīat, 1981; Knowledge and the Sacred, 1982; Philosophy, Literature and Fine Arts, 1982; Muḥammad: Man of Allah, 1982; Ideals and Realities of Islam, 1985, rev. ed., 2000; (with J. Pelikan and J. Kitagawa) Comparative Work Ethics: Judeo-Christian, Islamic and Eastern, 1985; Islamic Art and Spirituality, 1986; Traditional Islam in the Modern World, 1987; Islamic Spirituality, 2 vols., 1987-91; (co-author) Expectations of the Millennium: Shi'ism in History, 1988; Shi'ism: Doctrines, Thought and Spirituality, 1988; (with W. Stoddart) Religion of the Heart, 1991; (ed.) The Essential Writings of Frithj of Schuon, 1991; The Need for a Sacred Science, 1993; Spiritualitas dan seni Islam, 1993; Islâm ve bilim, 1993; (with K. O'Brien) In Quest of the Sacred, 1993; Young Muslim's Guide to the Modern World, 1993; Muhammad, Man of God, 1995; (ed. with O. Leaman) The History of Islamic Philosophy, 1996; Religion & the Order of Nature, 1996; The Islamic Intellectual Tradition in Persia, 1996; Sadr al-Din Shirazi and His Transcendent Theosophy: Back Ground, Life and Works, 1997; Man and Nature, 1997; (contrib.) Mecca the Blessed, Medina the Radiant, 1997; Islamic-Christian Dialogue: Problems and Obstacles to be Pondered and Overcome, 1998; Poems of the Way, 1999; Spiritual and Religious Dimensions of the Environmental Crisis, 1999; (ed. with M. Aminrazavi) An Anthology of Philosophy in Persia, vol. I, 1999, vol. II, 2000, vol. III, 2008; Journey Through Persian History and Culture, 2000; Marifat va manavīyat, 2001; The Heart of Islam, 2002; Yād ār zi sham-i murdah, yād ār: majmūah-i maqālāt, 2002; Islam: Religion, History and Civilization, 2003; Farhang-i iṣ ṭilāhāt-i irfān-iIslāmī: (Fārsī-Inglīsī, Inglīsī-Fārsī), 2003; āmūzahhā-yiṣ ūfiyān az dīrūz tāimrūz, 2003; Khamsūna āman alá wafāt al- ārif bi-Allāh al-Shaykh 'Abd al-Wāḥid Yaḥya, 2003; JāvidaMCNnkhirad, 2003; (with F. Jarrār and S. 'ūdah) Dalīl al-shābb al-Muslim fi al-ālamal-hadīth, 2004; Maārif-i Islāmī dar jahān-imūāṣ ir, 2004; Religion et l'ordre de la nature, 2004; Sufism and the Integration of the Inner and Outer Life of Man, 2004; (ed.) Essential Frithjof Schuon, 2005; Al-Tasāmuḥ laysa minnah aw hibah, 2006; (ed. with K. O'Brien) Essential Sophia, 2006; Dar just va jū-yi amr-i qudsī, 2006; Islamic Philosophy from its Origin to the Present: Philosophy in the Land of Prophecy, 2006; The Garden of Truth: The Vision and Promise of Sufism, Islam's Mystical Tradition, 2007; Islam, Science, Muslims, and Technology, 2007; The Essential Seyyed Hossein Nasr, 2007; (foreword) Art of Islam: Language and Meaning, 2009; (with R. Jahanbegloo) In Search of the Sacred, 2010; Islam in the Modern World: Challenged by the West, Threatened by Fundamentalism, Keeping Faith with Tradition, 2011; Islam in the Modern World, 2011;

Muslims and Christians in the New Millennium, 2011. Contributor of articles to journals. **Address:** George Washington University, Gelman Library, Rm. 709R, 2130 H St. NW, Washington, DC 20052-0081, U.S.A. **Online address:** msirat@gwu.edu

NASRIN, Taslima. German/Bangladeshi (born Bangladesh), b. 1962. **Genres:** Adult Non-fiction, Poetry. **Career:** Writer, 1975-; Literary Magazines Senjuti, editor, 1978-83; Health Complex, medical officer, 1986-89, S.S.M.C. and Mitford Hospital, medical officer, 1990-92, Dhaka Medical College Hospital, medical officer, 1993. **Publications:** Sikorey Bipul Khuda (title means: 'Hunger in Roots'), 1986; Nirbasito Bahirey Antorey (title means: 'Banished Without and Within'), 1989; Amar Kichujae Ase Na (title means: 'I Couldn't Care Less'), 1990; Atoley Antorin (title means: 'Captive in the Abyss'), 1991; Nirbachito Column (title means: 'Selected Columns'), 1991; Aparapaksha, 1992; Balikar Gollachut, 1992; Nosto Meyer Nosto Godyo (title means: 'Rotten Proses of a Rotten Girl'), 1992; Fera (title means: 'Return'), 1993; Phyana dao, 1993; Amara kichu yaya asena, 1993; Behula Eka Bhashiyechilo Bhela, 1993; Prasanga nar ibada, sampradayikata, 1994; Dieu fin de siecle: Religions et politique, 1994; Ay Kosto Jhepe, Jibon Debo Mepe (title means: 'Pain Come Roaring Down, I'll Measure Out My Life for You'), 1994; Choto Choto Dukkho Katha (title means: 'Little Little Sad Story'), 1994, rev. ed., Chotòe-chotòeduhòkha, 2005; Dukhoboti Meve (title means: 'Sad Girls'), 1994; The Gamein Reverse (poetry), 1996; Amara Meyebela: Mere Bacapana Ke Dina (memoir), 2 vols., 2000, trans. as My Girlhood: An Autobiography, 2001, rev. ed. as Meyebela: My Bengali Girlhood: A Memoir of Growing Up Female in a Muslim World, 2002; Atmakatha, 2000; Jolopodyo (title means: 'Waterlilies'), 2001; Pharasi Premika, 2001; Sodha, 2001; Utala Haoya, 2002; Khali Khali Lage, 2002; Ka, 2003; Khali Khali Lage (title means: 'Feeling Empty'), 2004; Dvikhanòdòita, 2004; Homecoming /Phera, 2005; All about Women, 2005; Kicchukhan Thako (title means: 'Stay For A While'), 2005; Bhalobaso? Cchai baso (title means: 'It's Your Love! Or a Heap of Trash!), 2007; Bondini (title means: 'Prisoner'), 2008. NOVELS: Oporpokkho (title means: 'The Opponent'), 1992; Shodh (title means: 'Revenge'), 1992; Nimontron (title means: 'Invitation'), 1993; Phera (title means: 'Return'), 1993; Lajja (title means: 'Shame'), 1993; Bhromor Koio Gia (title means: 'Tell Him The Secret'), 1994; Forashi Premik (title means: 'French Lover'), 2002; Shorom (title means: 'Shame Again'), 2009. BIOGRAPHIES: Amar Meyebel (title means: 'My Girlhood'), 1999; Utal Hawa (title means: 'Gusty Wind'), 2002; Ka (title means: 'Speak Up'), 2003; Dwikhondito (title means: 'The Life Divided'), 2003; Sei Sob Andhokar (title means: 'Those Dark Days'), 2004; Ami Bhalo Nei, Tumi Bhalo Theko Priyo Desh (title means: 'My Exile'), 2006. OTHERS: The Game in Reverse: Poems, 1995; Nirbāsita nārīra kabitā, 1995; Tasalimā Nāsarinera nirācita kalāma, 2004; Seisaba andhakāra, 2004; Tui nishiddha, tui katha kaisa nā, 2007; Nārīra konao deśa nei, 2007; Mujhe ghara le calo, 2007; Poems, 2008; (with C. Fourest) Libres de le dire: conversations mécréantes, 2010. **Address:** George Braziller Publishers, 171 Madison Ave., New York, NY 10016, U.S.A. **Online address:** email@taslimanasrin.com

NASSAR, Eugene Paul. American (born United States), b. 1935. **Genres:** Literary Criticism And History, Essays, Biology, Biography. **Career:** Hamilton College, instructor in English, 1962-64; Syracuse University, Utica College, assistant professor, 1964-66, associate professor, 1966-71, professor of English, 1971-, The Eugene Paul Nassar Ethnic Heritage Studies Center, founder, 1981, now professor emeritus of English. Writer. **Publications:** Wallace Stevens: An Anatomy of Figuration, 1965, 1968; The Rape of Cinderella: Essays in Literary Continuity, 1970; The Cantos of Ezra Pound: The Lyric Mode, 1975; Wind of the Land, 1979; Essays Critical and Metacritical, 1983; Illustrations to Dante's Inferno, 1994; (with J.G. Moses) Annotated Index to the Syrian World, 1926-1932, 1994; A Walk around the Block, 1999; Local Sketches, 2003. Contributor to periodicals. **Address:** Department of English, Utica College, Syracuse University, 1600 Burrstone Rd., Utica, NY 13502, U.S.A. **Online address:** pnassar@dreamscape.com

NASSON, Bill. South African (born South Africa), b. 1952. **Genres:** History. **Career:** University of Cape Town, senior lecturer in economic history, 1986-90, associate professor of history, 1992-, Western Cape Oral History Project, director, 1992-, professor; Yale University, Southern African Research Program and Department of History, visiting fellow, 1984; University of Illinois at Urbana, visiting fellow and associate professor of African history, 1990-91; Stanford University, visiting lecturer, 1991; Australian National University, visiting fellow, 1994; Stellenbosch University, professor of history. Writer. **Publications:** (Ed.) Student Research Papers Produced in the Department of Economic History of the University of Cape Town, 1988; (with J. Samuel) Education: From Poverty to Liberty, 1990; Abraham Esau's War, 1991; (with T. Lodge) All, Here and Now, 1991; Uyadela wen'osulapho: Black Participation in Anglo-Boer War, 1999; Turning Points in History, 2004; Britannia's Empire: Making a British World, 2004; Springboks on the Somme: South Africa in the Great War, 1914-1918, 2007; War for South Africa, 2010. **Address:** Department of History, University of Stellenbosch, Rm. 319, Wilcocks Bldg., PO Box X1, Stellenbosch, 7602, South Africa. **Online address:** bill.nasson@uct.ac.za

NATARAJAN, Nalini. American/Indian (born India), b. 1956. **Genres:** Literary Criticism And History, Women's Studies And Issues. **Career:** Jawaharlal Nehru University, assistant professor, 1978-80; University of Delhi, Miranda House, lecturer, 1984-86; Yale University, Department of English, postdoctoral fellow, 1986-87; University of Puerto Rico, assistant professor, 1987-92, associate professor, 1992-98, professor of English, 1998-. Writer. **Publications:** Missionary among the Khasis, 1977; (intro.) Writers of the Indian Diaspora: A Bio-Bibliographical Critical Sourcebook, 1993; (ed.) Handbook of Twentieth-Century Literatures of India, 1996; Woman and Indian Modernity: Readings of Colonial and Postcolonial Novels, 2002; The Resonating Island, 2011. Contributor of articles to books and journals. **Address:** Department of English, University of Puerto Rico, Rm. PED-6, Basement of Pedreira Bldg., PO Box 23356, Rio Piedras, PR 00931-3356, U.S.A. **Online address:** nnatarajan@msn.com

NATHAN, Amy. American (born United States) **Genres:** Human Relations/Parenting, Children's Non-fiction, Music, History, Dance/Ballet. **Career:** Teacher in adult education programs, 1968-71; Off-Broadway Productions, Regional Theater, actress, 1971-80; teacher of creative drama in arts programs, 1972-80; Scholastic Magazines, associate editor, 1980-81; Zillions Magazine, associate editor, 1981-94; freelance writer, 1994-. **Publications:** Everything You Need to Know about Conflict Resolution, 1996; Surviving Homework: Tips from Teens, 1996; The Kids' Allowance Book, 1998; The Young Musician's Survival Guide: Tips from Teens & Pros, 2000; Yankee Doodle Gals: Women Pilots of World War II, 2001; Count on Us: American Women in the Military, 2004; Meet the Musicians: From Prodigy (or not) to Pro, 2006; Take a Seat-Make a Stand, 2006; Meet the Dancers, 2008; Young Musician's Survival Guide: Tips from Teens and Pros, 2008. **Address:** 5 Edgewood Ave., Larchmont, NY 10538, U.S.A. **Online address:** amynbooks@gmail.com

NATHAN, John. American (born United States), b. 1940?. **Genres:** Biography. **Career:** University of California, Takashima professor of Japanese cultural studies; Princeton University, faculty. Writer, translator and director. **Publications:** Mishima: A Biography, Little, 1974; Sony: The Private Life, 1999; (with H. Hibbett, E. McClellan and E. Seidensticker) Words, Ideas and Ambiguities: Four Perspectives on Translating from the Japanese, 2000; Japan Unbound: A Volatile Nation's Quest for Pride and Purpose, 2004; Living Carelessly in Tokyo and Elsewhere: A Memoir, 2008. TRANSLATOR: Yukio Mishima, The Sailor Who Fell from Grace with the Sea, 1965; Kenzaburo Oe, A Personal Matter, 1969; Kenzaburo Oe, Teach Us to Outgrow Our Madness: Four Short Novels, 1977; Kenzaburo Oe, Rouse Up O Young Men of the New Age!, 2002. Contributor to periodicals. **Address:** East Asian Lang. & Cultural Studies Dept., University of California, Santa Barbara, CA 93106-7075, U.S.A. **Online address:** mezameyo@earthlink.net

NATHAN, Linda F. American (born United States), b. 1955. **Genres:** Reference. **Career:** Boston Arts Academy, founding headmaster; Center for Collaborative Education, co-founder; Harvard Graduate School of Education, lecturer. Writer. **Publications:** The Hardest Questions Aren't on the Test: Lessons from an Innovative Urban School, 2009. Contributor to periodicals. **Online address:** linda@lindanathan.com

NATHANSON, Paul. Canadian (born Canada), b. 1947. **Genres:** Ethics, Film, Theology/Religion. **Career:** Jewish Public Library, cataloguer, 1972-76; National Gallery of Canada, cataloguer, 1973-74; Vancouver School of Theology, librarian and instructor, 1979-82; Bishop's University, instructor, 1984; McGill University, instructor, 1988, Centre for Medicine, Ethics and Law, co-investigator, 1988-90, Centre for Medicine, Ethics and Law, senior research associate, 1990-93, faculty of religious studies, research associate, 2002-. Writer. **Publications:** Over the Rainbow: The Wizard of Oz as a Secular Myth of America, 1991; (with K.K. Young) Spreading Misandry: The Teaching of Contempt for Men in Popular Culture, 2001; (with K.K. Young) Legalizing Misandry: From Public Shame to Systemic Discrimination against Men, 2006; (with K.K. Young) Sanctifying Misandry: Goddess Ideology and the Fall of Man, 2010; Transcending Misandry, forthcoming; (with K.K. Toung) The Future of Nature: Reproductive Technologies and the Symbolic Frontier, forthcoming. **Address:** McGill-Queen's University Press, 3430 McTavish St., Montreal, QC H3A 1X9, Canada. **Online address:** wordwatcher@vif.com

NATHANSON, Stephen (Lewis). American (born United States), b. 1943. **Genres:** Philosophy, International Relations/Current Affairs, Economics, Humanities, Politics/Government, Law. **Career:** State University of New York, assistant professor of philosophy, 1969-72; Northeastern University, Department of Philosophy and Religion, assistant professor, 1972-75, associate professor of philosophy and religion, 1975-85, chair, 1975-91, professor of philosophy and religion, 1985-, Center for Effective University Teaching, director, 1996-. Writer. **Publications:** The Ideal of Rationality, 1985, rev. ed. as The Ideal of Rationality: A Defense, within Reason, 1994; An Eye for an Eye?: The Morality of Punishing by Death, 1987, 2nd ed., 2001; Should We Consent to Be Governed?: A Short Introduction to Political Philosophy, 1992, 2nd ed., 2001; Patriotism, Morality, and Peace, 1993; Economic Justice, 1998; Should We Consent to be Governed?: A Short Introduction to Political Philosophy, 2001; (ed. and intro.) Principles of Political Economy: With Some of Their Applications to Social Philosophy, 2004; Terrorism and the Ethics of War, 2010. Contributor to periodicals. **Address:** Department of Philosophy and Religion, Northeastern University, 373 Holmes Hall, 360 Huntington Ave., Boston, MA 02115, U.S.A. **Online address:** s.nathanson@neu.edu

NATION, Kaleb. American (born United States), b. 1988?. **Genres:** Novels. **Career:** The Top 5 (radio program), host, 2006-08. Writer and public speaker. **Publications:** BRAN HAMBRIC NOVEL SERIES: The Farfield Curse, 2009; The Specter Key, 2010. **Address:** c/o Richard Curtis, Richard Curtis Associates, 171 E 74th St., 2nd Fl., New York, NY 10021, U.S.A. **Online address:** kaleb@kalebnation.com

NATION, Mark. (Mark Thiessen Nation). American (born United States) **Genres:** Theology/Religion, Ethics, Sex. **Career:** Evangelist, youth minister, 1972-75; Child Protective Services, Department for Human Services, staff, 1977-79; Champaign-Urbana Peace Initiative, founding director, 1981-86; Grace Community Church, pastor, 1987; pastor, 1987-96; Orestes Christian Church, pastor, 1989-91; Ladera Church of the Brethren, pastor, 1991-95; Glendale Church of the Brethren, interim pastor, 1995-96; London Mennonite Centre, director, 1996-2002; Eastern Mennonite University, Eastern Mennonite Seminary, associate professor of theology, 2002-, professor. Writer. **Publications:** (Ed. with S. Hauerwas and N. Murphy) Theology without Foundations: Religious Practice and the Future of Theological Truth, 1994; (ed. with N. Murphy and B.J. Kallenberg) Virtues and Practices in the Christian Tradition: Christian Ethics after MacIntyre, 1997; (ed. with S. Hauerwas, C.K. Huebner and H.J. Huebner) The Wisdom of the Cross: Essays in Honor of John Howard Yoder, 1999; (ed. with S. Wells) Faithfulness and Fortitude: In Conversation with the Theological Ethics of Stanley Hauerwas, 2000; (ed.) Karl Barth and the Problem of War and Other Essays on Barth by John Howard Yoder, 2003; John Howard Yoder: Mennonite Patience, Evangelical Witness, Catholic Convictions, 2006; (with T. Grimsrud) Reasoning Together: A Conversation on Homosexuality, 2008; (with G.H. Stassen and J.H. Yoder) War of the Lamb: the Ethics of Nonviolence and Peacemaking, 2009; (with A. Siegrist and D. Umbel) Dietrich Bonhoeffer the Assassin?: Challenging a Myth, Recovering Costly Grace, 2012; (co-ed.) Revolutionary Christianity: The 1966 South American Lectures, forthcoming. Contributor of articles to periodicals. **Address:** Seminary Department, Eastern Mennonite University, SB 226, 1200 Park Rd., PO Box 10936, Harrisonburg, VA 22802-2462, U.S.A. **Online address:** mark.nation@emu.edu

NATION, Mark Thiessen. *See* **NATION, Mark.**

NATION, Richard F. American (born United States), b. 1963. **Genres:** Theology/Religion, Agriculture/Forestry, Politics/Government, History. **Career:** Eastern Michigan University, associate professor of history, professor. Writer. **Publications:** At Home in the Hoosier Hills: Agriculture, Politics and Religion in Southern Indiana, 1810-1870, 2005; (ed. with S.E. Towne) Indiana's War: The Civil War in Documents, 2009. **Address:** Department of History and Philosophy, Eastern Michigan University, 701 Pray-Harrold, Ypsilanti, MI 48197, U.S.A. **Online address:** richard.nation@emich.edu

NATOLI, Joseph. American (born United States), b. 1943. **Genres:** Writing/Journalism, Film, International Relations/Current Affairs, Social Commentary, Popular Culture. **Career:** New England College, instructor, 1971-73, assistant professor of English, 1973-75; Bluefield State College, acting director of library and adjunct lecturer in English, 1975-77; Wake Forest University, university library, head of reference and bibliography, 1977-81; University of California, bibliographer and adjunct lecturer in humanities, 1981-83; Michigan State University, Center for Integrative Studies in Arts, adjunct lecturer, 1983-2000, Department of Writing, Rhetoric and American Culture, adjunct professor, 2002-, professor emeritus of writing, rhetoric and American culture. Writer. **Publications:** Twentieth-Century Blake Criticism: Northrop Frye to the Present, 1982; (with F.L. Rusch) Psychocriticism: An Annotated Bibliography, 1984; Mot d'Ordre: Disorder in Literary Worlds, 1992; Hauntings: Popular Film and American Culture, 1990-1992, 1994; A Primer to Postmodernity, 1997; Speeding to the Millennium: Film & Culture, 1993-1995, 1997; Postmodern Journeys: Film and Culture, 1996-1998, 2000; Memory's Orbit, 2003; This is a Picture and Not the World: Movies and A Post-9/11 America, 2007. EDITOR:(and contrib.) Psychological Perspectives on Literature: Freudian Dissidents and Non-Freudians, 1984; (and contrib.) Tracing Literary Theory, 1987; (and contrib.) Literary Theory's Future(s), 1989; (with L. Hutcheon) A Postmodern Reader, 1993; (with Bertens) Postmodernism: Key Figures, 2002. **Address:** 620 Baldwin Ct., East Lansing, MI 48823, U.S.A. **Online address:** josephpnatoli@gmail.com

NATTIEZ, Jean Jacques. Canadian/French (born France), b. 1945. **Genres:** Music. **Career:** Universite de Montréal, professor of musicology, 1972- . Writer. **Publications:** Fidel Castro. Présentation, choix de textes, 1968; Densité 21.5 deVarèse: essai d'analyse sémiologique, 1975; Fondements d'unesémiologie de la musique, 1976; Points de repère, 1981, rev. ed., 1995; (with J. Thomas and P. Mion) Envers d'une Œuvre: De naturasonorum de Bernard Parmegiani, 1982; Tétralogies, Wagner, Boulez, Chéreau: essai sur l'infidélité, 1983; Proust musicien, 1984; (ed.) Orientations: Collected Writings, 1986; Musicologie généraleet sémiologie, 1987; De la sémiologie à la musique, 1988; Proust as Musician, 1989; Music and Discourse: Toward a Semiology of Music, 1990; Wagner Androgyne: essai sur l'interprétation, 1990; Correspondance, 1991; Wagner Androgyne: A Study in Interpretation, 1993; The Boulez-Cage Correspondence, 1993; Combat de Chronos et d'Orphée: essais, 1993; Opera Leméac, 1997; Le Musique, la Recherche et la Vie: un Dialogue et Quelques Dérives, 1999; Enciclopedia della musica, 2001; (ed.) Correspondance et documents, 2002; Battle of Chronos and Orpheus: Essays in Applied Musical Semiology, 2004; Lévi-Strauss musicien: essai sur la tentation homologique, 2008; Quêtes d'absolus, 2009. **Address:** Faculté de musique, Universityersité de Montréal, Rm. B-504, PO Box 6128, Succursale Centre-ville, Montreal, QC H3C 3J7, Canada. **Online address:** jean-jacques.nattiez@umontreal.ca

NATUSCH, Sheila. New Zealander (born New Zealand), b. 1926. **Genres:** History, Natural History, Biography, Autobiography/Memoirs, Young Adult Fiction. **Career:** National Library of New Zealand, staff, 1949; Dominion Museum (now National Museum), staff. Writer. **Publications:** (With N.S. Seaward) Stewart Island, 1951; Native Plants, 1956; Native Rock, 1959; Animals of New Zealand, 1967, rev. ed., 1999; A Bunch of Wild Orchids, 1968, rev. ed., 1999; New Zealand Mosses, 1969; Brother Wohlers: A Biography, 1969; On the Edge of the Bush: Women in Early Southland, 1976, rev. ed., 1999; Hell and High Water: A German Occupation of the Chatham Islands 1843-1910, 1977, rev. ed., 1992; The Cruise of the Acheron: Her Majesty's Steam Vessel on Survey in New Zealand Waters 1848-51, 1978; The Roaring Forties: Glimpses of Foveaux Strait, 1840-1850, 46-48 S: From Old Letters, Diaries, Reports, Notebooks, Memoirs, Sketches, 1978, rev. ed., 1999; Fortnight in Iceland, 1979; Wild Fare for Wilderness Foragers, 1979; Wellington with S.N., 1982, rev. ed. as Wellington Awash, 2000; A Pocketful of Pebbles, 1983; Stewart Island: A Souvenir, 1983; Southward Ho! The Search for a New Edinburgh, 1844, 1985; (with L. Chambers) Granny Gurton's Garden, 1987; (with G. Swainson) William Swainson of Fern Grove, F.R.S., F.L.S., & C: The Anatomy of a Nineteenth-Century Naturalist, 1987; Roy Traill of Stewart Island, 1991; An Island Called Home, 1991; The Natural World of the Traills, 1996; Ruapuke Visited, 1998; Cruise of the Acheron: Her Majesty's Steam Vessel on Survey in New Zealand Waters, 1848-51, 1998; (ed.) My Dear Friend Tuckett: Letters from a Foveaux Strait Outpost in the 1850s, 1998; A Naturalist and a Gentleman (from Letters of Charles Traill), 1999; Out of Our Tree: Sightings of a Scattered Family, 2001. **Address:** 46 Owhiro Bay Parade, Wellington, 6002, New Zealand.

NATWAR-SINGH, K. Indian (born India), b. 1931. **Genres:** Novellas/

Short Stories, Autobiography/Memoirs, Biography, Essays. **Career:** Government of India, Indian Embassy, staff, 1956-58, Permanent Indian Mission to the U.N., staff, 1961-66, Ministry of External Affairs, deputy high commissioner, 1973-77, ambassador to Pakistan, 1980-82, Ministry of External Affairs, secretary, 1982-84, minister of state for steel, 1984-85, minister of state for fertilizer, 1985-86, union minister of state for foreign affairs, 1986-89, 12th Lok Sabha, member, 1998, Rajya Sabha, member, 2002-, minister for external affairs, 2002-05; U.N. General Assembly, alternate Indian delegate, 1963; Prime Minister's Secretariat, deputy secretary, joint secretary, 1966-71; Indian ambassador to Poland, 1971-73; U.N. General Assembly, Indian Delegation, member, 1971. Writer. **Publications:** E.M. Forster: A Tribute, 1964; (ed.) The Legacy of Nehru, 1965; (ed. and intro.) Tales from Modern India, 1966; (ed. and intro.) Stories from India, 1971; Maharaja Suraj Mal, 1707-63, His Life and Times, 1981; Curtain Raisers: Essays, Reviews, Letters, 1984; (ed. with H.Y.S. Prasad) Rajiv Gandhi, Tributes and Memories, 1992; Count Your Blessings, 1993; (ed.) The Legacy of Nehru, 1996; Profiles and Letters, 1998; The Magnificent Maharaja Bhupinder Singh of Patiala (1891-1938), 1998; Heart to Heart, 2003; My China Diary, 1956-88, 2009; Yours Sincerely, 2010. **Address:** 19 Teenmurti Ln., New Delhi, DH 110019, India.

NAU, Henry R(ichard). American (born United States), b. 1941. **Genres:** Economics, International Relations/Current Affairs, Politics/Government, Technology. **Career:** Agency for International Development, Vietnam Bureau, intern, 1966; National Cash Register Co., marketing researcher, 1967; Forschungsinstitut der Deutschen Gesellschaft fuer Auswaertige Politik, visiting research fellow, 1969-70; Williams College, assistant professor of political science, 1971-73; George Washington University, assistant professor, 1973-76, associate professor, 1976-84, professor, 1984-, Elliott School of International Affairs, associate dean, 1988-92, professor of political science and international affairs, U.S.-Japan and U.S-Japan-South Korea Legislative Exchange Programs, director; Department of State, special assistant, 1975-77; Johns Hopkins School of Advanced International Studies, visiting professor, 1975-77; Stanford University, visiting associate professor, 1977; Columbia University, visiting associate professor, 1977-78; Washington Center of Foreign Policy Research, research associate, 1979-80, visiting professor, 1984-85; National Security Council, senior staff and director, 1981-83; Foreign Policy Institute, fellow, 1987; Smithsonian Institution, Woodrow Wilson International Center for Scholars, fellow, 1987; Carnegie Council on Ethics and International Affairs, U.S.-Japan Economic Agenda, co-director, 1989-; Foreign Service Institute, lecturer; Air War College, lecturer; Inter-American Defense College, lecturer; Air Command and Staff College, lecturer; National Defense University, lecturer; SRI Intl., consultant; Bureau of Oceans and International Environmental and Scientific Affairs, consultant; National Academy of Sciences, consultant. Writer. **Publications:** National Politics and International Technology: Nuclear Reactor Development in Western Europe, 1974; (ed.) Technology Transfer and U.S. Foreign Policy, 1976; (contrib.) Oil and the Atom: Issues in US-Japan Energy Relations, 1980; International Reaganomics: A Domestic Approach to World Economy, 1984; (ed. and contrib.) Domestic Trade Politics and the Uruguay Round, 1989; The Myth of America's Decline: Leading the World Economy into the 1990s, 1990; Trade and Security: U.S. Policies at Cross-Purposes, 1995; At Home Abroad: Identity and Power in American Foreign Policy, 2002; Perspectives On International Relations: Power, Institutions and Ideas, 2007, 2nd ed., 2009; (ed.) International Relations in Perspective: A Reader, 2009. **Address:** Elliott School of International Affairs, George Washington University, 1957 E St. NW, Ste. 501, Washington, DC 20052, U.S.A. **Online address:** nau@gwu.edu

NAUGHTON, Jim. American (born United States), b. 1957. **Genres:** Human Relations/Parenting, Documentaries/Reportage, Young Adult Fiction. **Career:** New York Times, sportswriter, 1979-80; Syracuse Post Standard, reporter and editor, 1982-85; New York Daily News, sportswriter, 1985-87; Washington Post, reporter for style section, 1987-92; The Chronicle of Higher Education, senior editor, 1996-; Episcopal Diocese of Washington, director of communications; Episcopal Café, founder and editor-in-chief. **Publications:** My Brother Stealing Second (young adult), 1989; Taking to the Air: The Rise of Michael Jordan, 1992; Catholics in Crisis: An American Parish Fights for Its Soul, 1996. **Address:** Episcopal Diocese of Washington, 3101 Wisconsin Ave. NW, Washington, DC 20016-5015, U.S.A. **Online address:** jnaughton@edow.org

NAUMAN, Eileen. *See* **MCKENNA, Lindsay Gvhdi.**

NAUMAN, Eileen Gvhdi. *See* **MCKENNA, Lindsay Gvhdi.**

NAURECKAS, Jim. American (born United States), b. 1964. **Genres:** Humor/Satire, Documentaries/Reportage, Social Sciences. **Career:** In These Times, staff writer, 1987-88; Washington Report on the Hemisphere, managing editor, 1989; Extra!, editor, 1990-; Fair, program director and co-manager. **Publications:** (Co-author) Real War Stories No.2 Citizen Soldier (Comic), 1991; (with S. Rendall and J. Cohen) The Way Things Aren't: Rush Limbaugh's Reign of Error, 1995; (ed. with J. Jackson) The Fair Reader: An Extra! Review of Press and Politics in the Nineties, 1996. **Address:** FAIR, 104 W 27th St., Ste. 10B, New York, NY 10001, U.S.A. **Online address:** jnaureckas@fair.org

NAVARRA, Tova. American (born United States), b. 1948. **Genres:** Plays/Screenplays, How-to Books, inspirational/Motivational Literature, Medicine/Health, Local History/Rural Topics, Photography, Writing/Journalism, Documentaries/Reportage, Documentaries/Reportage. **Career:** Village Times, correspondent, 1974-75; Seton Hall Prep, teacher, 1975-78; Asbury Park Press, entertainment and feature writer and press correspondent, 1978-85, feature writer, art critic and family writer, 1985-92; New Jersey Music and Arts, staff writer, illustrator and photographer, 1978-81; Shore Affinity, founder and publisher, 1979-81; Associated University Presses, book editor, 1981-82; Jersey Shore Medical Center, copywriter and photographer, 1985; Witmer House, psychiatric charge nurse, 1985; Copley News Service, feature writer and columnist, 1988-93; American Journal of Nursing, contributing editor, 1990-94; Two River Times, feature writer and art columnist, 1993-94, lifestyle editor, 1999-2000; Visiting Nurse Association of Central Jersey, supervisor of grant research, 1993-94; Courier, associate editor, 1998-99, lifestyle editor, 1999-2000. **Publications:** The New Jersey Shore, 1985; Jim Gary: His Life and Art, 1987; Through the Kunai Grass with Dad (staged reading), 1988; Playing It Smart: What to Do When You're on Your Own, 1989 as On My Own: Helping Kids Help Themselves, 1994; Your Body: Highlights of Human Anatomy, 1990; (with M.A. Lipkowitz and J.G. Navarra) Therapeutic Communication, 1990; (with M.A. Lipkowitz) Allergies A-Z, 1994; An Insider's Guide to Home Health Care, 1995; Wisdom for Caregivers, 1995; (with M.A. Lipkowitz and J.G. Navarra) Encyclopedia of Vitamins, Minerals, and Supplements, 1996; Toward Painless Writing: A Guide for Health Professionals, 1998; The American Century Series: Staten Island, 1998; Seton Hall University: A Photographic History, 1999; Encyclopedia of Asthma and Respiratory Disorders, 2001; Young People/Tough Problems, 2002; The Encyclopedia of Complementary and Alternative Medicine, 2004. IMAGES OF AMERICA SERIES: Howell and Farmingdale, 1996; Levittown, 1997, vol. II, 1999; Staten Island, vol. I, 1997, vol. II: A Closer Look, 1999. Contributor of articles to periodicals. **Address:** c/o Faith H. Hamlin, Sanford J. Greenburger Associates, 55 5th Ave., New York, NY 10003, U.S.A.

NAVARRO, Yvonne. American (born United States), b. 1957?. **Genres:** Horror, Science Fiction/Fantasy, Young Adult Fiction. **Career:** Writer. **Publications:** REFERENCE BOOKS: First Name Reverse Dictionary, 1993, 2nd ed., 2007. FICTION: After Age, 1993; Species (novelization of screenplay), 1995; Deadrush, 1995; Aliens: Music of the Spears (novelization of graphic novel), 1996; Final Impact, 1997; Species II (novelization of screenplay), 1998; Red Shadows, 1998; That's Not My Name, 2000; Buffy: Paleo, 2000; The Willow Files, 2001; Tempted Champions, 2002; Mirror Me, 2004; Darkening, 2004; Shattered Twilight, 2004; Broken Sunrise, 2004; Hellboy: A Novelization, 2004; Elektra: A Novelization, 2005; Ultraviolet: A Novelization, 2006; Highborn, 2010; Concrete Savior, 2011; Grimwood Tales, forthcoming; Die With Me, forthcoming; Plague Angel, forthcoming. Contributor to periodicals. **Address:** PO Box 1364, Sierra Vista, AZ 85636-1364, U.S.A. **Online address:** von@yvonnenavarro.com

NAVASKY, Victor. (Victor S(aul) Navasky). American (born United States), b. 1932. **Genres:** Politics/Government. **Career:** State of Michigan, Lansing, special assistant to the Governor, 1959-60; Monocle Political Satire Magazine, founding editor and publisher, 1961-70; U.S. Civil Rights Commission, consultant, 1961, 1970-72; New York Times Magazine, manuscript editor, 1970-72, Book Review, columnist, 1973-77; New York University, adjunct associate professor, 1972-73; Wesleyan University, visiting professor, 1975; Princeton University, Ferris visiting professor of journalism, 1976-77; The Nation, editor-in-chief, 1978-95, editorial director and publisher, 1995-2005, publisher emeritus, 2005-; Columbia University, George T. Delacorte professor in magazine, 1999-, Freedom Forum Media Studies Center, senior fellow, Delacorte Center for Magazine, director; Columbia Journalism Review, chairman, 2004-; Harvard Kennedy School of Government, Institute of Politics, fellow. **Publications:** (Ed. with R.R. Lingeman) The Monocle Peep Show,

1965; Kennedy Justice, 1971; (with D. Paster) Law Enforcement, 1976; Naming Names, 1980; (comp. with C. Cerf) The Experts Speak, 1984, rev. ed., 1998; (ed. with K.V. Heuvel) The Best of the Nation, 2000; A Matter of Opinion, 2005; (with C. Cerf) Mission Accomplished! Or How We Won the War in Iraq: The Experts Speak, 2008. **Address:** Graduate School of Journalism, Columbia University, 2950 Broadway, 116th St., New York, NY 10027, U.S.A. **Online address:** vsn2@columbia.edu

NAVASKY, Victor S(aul). *See* **NAVASKY, Victor.**

NAVES, Elaine Kalman. Canadian (born Canada), b. 1947. **Genres:** Social Sciences, History, Biography. **Career:** Writer. **Publications:** The Writers of Montreal, 1993; Journey to Vaja: Reconstructing the World of a Hungarian-Jewish Family, 1996; Putting Down Roots: Montreal's Immigrant Writers, 1998; (with B. Demchinsky) Storied Streets: Montreal in the Literary Imagination, 2000; Shoshanna's Story: A Mother, a Daughter, and the Shadows of History, 2003; Robert Weaver: Godfather of Canadian Literature, 2007. **Address:** c/o Daphne Hart, Helen Heller Agency, 509 Logan Ave., Toronto, ON M4K 3B2, Canada. **Online address:** elainekalmanaves@sympatico.ca

NAVIA, Luis E. American/Colombian (born Colombia), b. 1940. **Genres:** Philosophy, Bibliography. **Career:** Hofstra University, instructor in foreign languages, 1965-67, adjunct professor of philosophy, 1987-92; City University of New York, Queens College, lecturer in philosophy, 1965-70; New York Institute of Technology, College of Arts and Sciences, professor of philosophy, 1968-, Division of Continuing Education, philosophy coordinator, 1976-77, Department of Social Sciences, chair, associate professor, 1985-93, 2001-, Honors Program, director, 2002-03, School of Arts, Sciences and Communication, dean, 1993-98; New York University, lecturer in philosophy, 1970; School of Visual Arts, adjunct professor of philosophy, 1978-92. Writer. **Publications:** (Ed. with N. Capaldi) Journeys through Philosophy: A Classical Introduction, 1977, rev. ed., 1982; A Bridge to the Stars: Our Ancient Cosmic Legacy, 1977; (ed. with E. Kelly) Ethics and the Search for Values, 1980; (with N. Capaldi and E. Kelly) An Invitation to Philosophy, 1981; (ed. with E. Kelly) The Fundamental Questions: A Selection of Readings in Philosophy, 1985, 2nd ed., 1995; Socrates, the Man and His Philosophy, 1985; Socratic Testimonies, 1987; (with E.L. Katz) Socrates: An Annotated Bibliography, 1988; Pythagoras: An Annotated Bibliography, 1990; The Presocratic Philosophers: An Annotated Bibliography, 1993; The Socratic Presence: A Study of the Sources, 1993; The Philosophy of Cynicism: An Annotated Bibliography, 1995; Classical Cynicism: A Critical Study, 1996; Diogenes of Sinope: The Man in the Tub, 1998; The Adventure of Philosophy, 1999; Antisthenes of Athens: Setting the World Aright, 2001; Diogenes the Cynic: The War against the World, 2005; Socrates: A Life Examined, 2007. **Address:** Department of Social Sciences, College of Arts & Sciences, New York Institute of Technology, Rm. 7, Whitney Lane House, Old Westbury, NY 11568-8000, U.S.A. **Online address:** lnavia@nyit.edu

NAVROZOV, Andrei. Italian/Russian (born Russia), b. 1956. **Genres:** Translations, Politics/Government, Intellectual History, Travel/Exploration. **Career:** Yale Literary Magazine, owner and editor, 1978-85; Wall Street Journal, book reviewer, 1985; freelance literary journalist, 1985-98; novelist, 1998-. **Publications:** (Trans.) B. Pasternak, Second Nature: Forty-Six Poems, 1990; The Gingerbread Race: A Life in the Closing World Once Called Free, 1993; Italian Carousel: Scenes of Internal Exile, 2003. Contributor to periodicals. **Address:** Gillon Aitken Associates Ltd., 29 Fernshaw Rd., London, GL SW10 0TG, England.

NAYFEH, Ali Hasan. American (born United States), b. 1933. **Genres:** Engineering. **Career:** Heliodyne Corp., principal researcher, 1964-68; Aerotherm Corp., principal researcher, 1968-71; Virginia Polytechnic Institute and State University, professor of engineering science and mechanics, 1971-76, distinguished professor, 1976-; Yarmouk University, College of Engineering, founder and dean of engineering, 1980-84. Writer. **Publications:** Perturbation Methods, 1973; (with D.T. Mook) Nonlinear Oscillations, 1979; Introduction to Perturbation Techniques, 1981; Problems in Perturbation, 1985; Method of Normal Forms, 1993; (with B. Balachandran) Applied Nonlinear Dynamics, 1995; (with C.M. Chin) Perturbation Methods with Mathematica, 1999; (with C.M. Chin) Perturbation Methods with Maple, 1999; Nonlinear Interactions, 2000; (with P.F. Pai) Linear and Nonlinear Structural Mechanics, 2004. Contributor to books and journals. **Address:** Department of Engineering Science & Mechanics, Virginia Polytechnic Institute and State Universit, Blacksburg, VA 24061, U.S.A. **Online address:** anayfeh@vt.edu

NAYLOR, Gloria. American (born United States), b. 1950. **Genres:** Novels, Plays/Screenplays, Social Sciences, Literary Criticism And History. **Career:** Cummington Community of the Arts, writer-in-residence, 1983; George Washington University, visiting lecturer, 1983-84; New York University, visiting professor, 1986; New York Times, contributor, 1986; Princeton University, visiting lecturer, 1986-87; Boston University, visiting professor, 1987; Brandeis University, Fannie Hurst Visiting Professor, 1988; Cornell University, Society for the Humanities, senior fellow, 1988; One Way Productions, founder, president and producer, 1990-; University of Kent, visiting professor, 1992; Hartford Stage Co., playwright, 1994. **Publications:** The Women of Brewster Place, 1982; Linden Hills, 1985; Mama Day, 1988; Bailey's Café, 1992; (ed.) Children of the Night: The Best Short Stories by Black Writers, 1967 to the Present, 1995; The Men of Brewster Place, 1998; 1996, 2005. Contributor to periodicals. **Address:** Sterling Lord Literistic Inc., 65 Bleecker St., New York, NY 10012-2420, U.S.A.

NAYLOR, Phyllis Reynolds. American (born United States), b. 1933. **Genres:** Novels, Children's Fiction, Adult Non-fiction, Children's Non-fiction, Science Fiction/Fantasy, Sociology, Young Adult Non-fiction. **Career:** Billings Hospital, clinical secretary, 1953-56; elementary school teacher, 1956; National Education Association, editorial assistant, 1959-60. Writer. **Publications:** The Galloping Goat, 1965; Grasshoppers in the Soup, 1965; What the Gulls Were Singing, 1967; To Shake a Shadow, 1967; The New Schoolmaster, 1967; A New Year's Surprise, 1967; Knee Deep in Ice Cream, 1967; Jennifer Jean, the Cross-Eyed Queen, 1967; When Rivers Meet, 1968; Dark Side of the Moon, 1969; Meet Murdock, 1969; The Private I, and Other Stories, 1969; To Make a Wee Moon, 1969; Making It Happen, 1970; Ships in the Night, 1970; Wrestle the Mountain, 1971; How to Find Your Wonderful Someone, 1971; No Easy Circle, 1972; To Walk the Sky Path, 1973; An Amish Family, 1974; Witch's Sister, 1975; Getting Along in Your Family, 1976; Walking through the Dark, 1976; Witch Water, 1977; Crazy Love: An Autobiographical Account of Marriage and Madness, 1977; The Witch Herself, 1978; How I Came to Be a Writer, 1978; In Small Doses, 1979; Revelations, 1979; Getting Along with Your Friends, 1979; How Lazy Can You Get?, 1979; Change in the Wind, 1979; Eddie, Incorporated, 1980; Shadows on the Wall, 1980; Getting Along with Your Teachers, 1981; All Because I'm Older, 1981; Faces in the Water, 1981; Footprints at the Window, 1981; The Boy with the Helium Head, 1982; Never Born a Hero, 1982; String of Chances, 1982; The Solomon System, 1983; The Mad Gasser of Bessledorf Street, 1983; A Triangle Has Four Sides, 1983; Night Cry, 1984; Old Sadie and the Christmas Bear, 1984; The Dark of the Tunnel, 1985; The Agony of Alice, 1985; The Keeper, 1986; The Bodies in the Bessledorf Hotel, 1986; Unexpected Pleasures, 1986; The Year of the Gopher, 1987; Phyllis Naylor Interview with Kay Bonetti, 1987; Beetles, Lightly Toasted, 1987; The Baby, the Bed, and the Rose, 1987; (with L.S. Reynolds) Maudie in the Middle, 1988; One of the Third Grade Thonkers, 1988; Alice in Rapture, Sort Of, 1989; Keeping a Christmas Secret, 1989; The Craft of Writing the Novel, 1989; Bernie and the Bessledorf Ghost, 1990; Send No Blessings, 1990; The Witch's Eye, 1990; King of the Playground, 1991; Shiloh, 1991; Witch Weed, 1991; Reluctantly Alice, 1991; The Witch Returns, 1992; Josie's Troubles, 1992; All but Alice, 1992; The Boys Start the War, 1993; Alice in April, 1993; The Grand Escape, 1993; The Girls Get Even, 1993; The Face in the Bessledorf Funeral Parlor, 1993; Alice In-Between, 1994; Boys against Girls, 1994; The Fear Place, 1994; Alice the Brave, 1995; Being Danny's Dog, 1995; Ice, 1995; Alice in Lace, 1996; Shiloh Season, 1996; The Bomb in the Bessledorf Bus Depot, 1996; Ducks Disappearing, 1997; Outrageously Alice, 1997; The Healing of Texas Jake, 1997; I Can't Take You Anywhere!, 1997; Treasure of Bessledorf Hill, 1997; Saving Shiloh, 1997; Danny's Desert Rats, 1998; Sang Spell, 1998; Girl's Revenge, 1998; Achingly Alice, 1998; Sweet Strawberries, 1999; Alice on the Outside, 1999; Walkers Crossing, 1999; Traitor among the Boys, 1999; Bernie Magruder and the Drive-Thru Funeral Parlor, 1999; Bernie Magruder and the Pirate's Treasure, 1999; Bernie Magruder and the Bus Station Blow-Up, 1999; The Grooming of Alice, 2000; Jade Green, 2000; Peril in the Bessledorf Parachute Factory, 2000; Carlotta's Kittens, 2000; A Spy among the Girls, 2000; Alice Alone, 2001; The Great Chicken Debacle, 2001; Bernie Magruder and the Case of the Big Stink, 2001; Bernie Magruder and the Disappearing Bodies, 2001; Bernie Magruder and the Haunted Hotel, 2001; Bernie Magruder and the Parachute Peril, 2001; The Boys Return, 2001; Simply Alice, 2002; Please Do Feed the Bears, 2002; Starting with Alice, 2002; The Girls Take Over, 2002; Percy's Picnic, 2002; Blizzard's Wake, 2002; Patiently Alice, 2003; Alice in Blunderland, 2003; Boys in Control, 2003; Alice, Woman of the House, 2003; Bernie Magruder and the Bats in the Belfry, 2003; After, 2003; Girls Rule!, 2004; Shiloh Collection, 2004; Including Alice, 2004; Lovingly Alice, 2004; Boys Rock!, 2005; Polo's Mother, 2005; Anyone Can Eat Squid!, 2005; Alice on Her Way, 2005; Do not Panic, 2006; Alice in the Know, 2006; Roxie and the Hooligans, 2006; Who Won the War?, 2006; Cuckoo Feathers, 2006; Dangerously Alice, 2007; Patches and Scratches, 2007; Eating Enchiladas, 2008; Cricket Man, 2008; Almost Alice, 2008; Faith, Hope and Ivy June, 2009; Intensely Alice, 2009; Emily's Fortune, 2010; Alice in Charge, 2010; Incredibly Alice, 2011; Alice on Board, 2012; Emily and Jackson Hiding Out, 2012. Contributor to magazines and newspapers. **Address:** John Hawkins and Associates Inc., 71 W 23rd St., Ste. 1600, New York, NY 10010-4185, U.S.A.

NAYLOR, Sean. American/Canadian (born Canada) **Genres:** Novels, Young Adult Non-fiction. **Career:** Army Times, senior writer, 1990-. **Publications:** (With T. Donnelly) Clash of Chariots: The Great Tank Battles, 1996; Not a Good Day to Die: The Untold Story of Operation Anaconda, 2005. **Address:** Army Times Publishing Co., 6883 Commercial Dr., Springfield, VA 22159-0500, U.S.A. **Online address:** info@seannaylor.com

NAYMAN, Michele. British/Australian (born Australia), b. 1956. **Genres:** Poetry, Novels, Novellas/Short Stories, Young Adult Non-fiction, Young Adult Fiction. **Career:** The Age, journalist; The National Times, journalist; The Guardian, journalist; Columbia University, teacher of journalism and creative writing. Freelance writer. **Publications:** What You Love You Are (poems), 1977; Faces You Can't Find Again (stories), 1980; Somewhere Else (stories), 1989; Jetlag (novel), 1994. **Address:** The Australian Literature Resource, The University of Queensland, Duhig Bldg., Level 7, Brisbane, QL 4072, Australia. **Online address:** mnayman@mnayman.demon.co.uk

NAZIR-ALI, Michael. Scottish/British/Pakistani (born Pakistan), b. 1949. **Genres:** Institutions/Organizations, Theology/Religion. **Career:** Lahore Cathedral, provost, 1981-84; University of Greenwich, visiting professor of theology and religious studies; Trinity College, chairman of council; Mission Theology Advisory Group of the Board of Mission, chairman, 1992-2001; Church of England, bishop of rochester, 1994-2009; Crown Appointments Review Group, theological consultant, 1998-2001; Oxford Centre for Mission Studies, director; Christian Aid, director. Writer. **Publications:** Islam: A Christian Perspective, 1983; Frontiers in Muslim-Christian Encounter, 1987; Martyrs and Magistrates: Toleration and Trial in Islam, 1989; From Everywhere to Everywhere: A World View of Christian Witness, 1990; The Roots of Islamic Tolerance: Origin and Development, 1990; Mission and Dialogue: Proclaiming the Gospel Afresh in Every Age, 1995; Citizens and Exiles: Christian Faith in a Plural World, 1998; Shapes of the Church to Come, 2001; Understanding My Muslim Neighbor: Some Questions and Answers, 2002; Conviction and Conflict: Islam, Christianity and World Order, 2006; The Unique and Universal Christ, 2008. **Address:** Continuum International Publishing Group, The Tower Bldg., 11 York Rd., London, GL SE1 7NX, England. **Online address:** oxtrad@gmail.com

NDIAYE, Marie. French (born France), b. 1967. **Genres:** Novels. **Career:** Writer. **Publications:** Quant au riche avenir, 1985; Comédie classique, 1987; La Femme changée en bûche, 1989; En famille, 1990; Un temps de saison, 1994; La Sorcière, 1996; Among Family, 1997; Naufrageée: J.M.W. Turner, 1999; Hilda, 1999; Rosie Carpe (novel), 2001; Papa doit manger, 2002; Tous mes amis, 2004; Autoportrait en vert, 2005; Mon coeur à l'étroit, 2007; (with J.Y. Cendrey) Puzzle: trois pièces: théâtre, 2007; Trois Femmes Puissantes: Roman, 2009; Les grandes personnes, 2011. Contributor to periodicals. **Address:** c/o Author Mail, Les Editions de Minuit, 7 rue Bernard-Palissy, Paris, 75006, France.

NEAL, Bill. American (born United States), b. 1936. **Genres:** Law, Young Adult Non-fiction. **Career:** Writer, attorney and journalist. **Publications:** NONFICTION: Our Stories: The Medicine Mound Settlers' Community Scrapbook, 1997; Getting Away with Murder on the Texas Frontier: Notorious Killings & Celebrated Trials, 2006; From Guns to Gavels: How Justice Grew Up in the Outlaw West, 2008; Sex, Murder & the Unwritten Law: Gender and Judicial Mayhem, Texas Style, 2009. OTHER: The Last Frontier: The Story of Hardeman County, 1966. **Address:** Abilene, TX , U.S.A. **Online address:** bill.neal36@gmail.com

NEAL, Frank. British (born England), b. 1932?. **Genres:** Economics, History, Local History/Rural Topics, Social Commentary, Business/Trade/Industry. **Career:** Southport Technical College, assistant lecturer in economics, 1959-61; University of Liverpool, Department of Economics, research assistant, 1962-63, Institute of Irish Studies, honorary professor; Chelmer Institute of Higher Education, principal lecturer in economics, 1963-69; Sheffield Polytechnic, principal lecturer in economics, 1969-74; University of Salford, senior lecturer in economics and social statistics, 1974-96, professor of economics and social history, 1996, European Studies Research Institute, research fellow, research professor, professor of British economic and social history, through 2000; University of Manchester, Simon senior research fellow, 1990-91. Writer. **Publications:** (With R.W. Quincy) Using Mathematics in Economics, 1973; (with R. Shone) Economic Model Building, 1976; (with E. Rick) The Environment of Business, 1983; Sectarian Violence: The Liverpool Experience, 1819-1914, 1988; Black '47: Britain and the Famine Irish, 1998; (ed. with M. Busteed and J. Tonge) Irish Protestant Identities, 2008; Investment in Liverpool Shipping During the Industrial Revolution, forthcoming. **Address:** College Arts and Social Sciences, University of Salford, Crescent House, Salford, GM M5 4WT, England. **Online address:** fneal33544@aol.com

NEALE, Jonathan. British/American (born United States) **Genres:** Novels, Sciences, Young Adult Non-fiction, Sports/Fitness, Plays/Screenplays, Autobiography/Memoirs. **Career:** Novelist, activist and educator. **Publications:** NONFICTION: Memoirs of a Callous Picket, 1983; The Cutlass and the Lash: Mutiny and Discipline in Nelson's Navy, 1985; The American War: Vietnam 1960-1975, 2001; Tigers of the Snow: How One Fateful Climb Made the Sherpas Mountaineering Legends, 2002; You Are G8, We Are Six Billion: The Truth behind the Genoa Protests, 2002; Whats' Wrong with America?: How the Rich and Powerful Have Changed America and Now Want to Change the World, 2004; Stop Global Warming: Change the World, 2008. NOVELS: The Laughter of Heroes, 1993; Lost at Sea, 2002; Himalaya, 2004. **Address:** c/o Author Mail, Houghton Mifflin Co., 222 Berkeley St., Boston, MA 02116-3764, U.S.A.

NEALON, Kevin. (Dirk Storm). American (born United States), b. 1953. **Genres:** Human Relations/Parenting. **Career:** Writer. **Publications:** Yes, You're Pregnant, but What about Me?, 2008. **Address:** United Talent Agency, 9560 Wilshire Blvd., Ste. 500, Beverly Hills, CA 90212-2401, U.S.A.

NEAR, Holly. American (born United States), b. 1949. **Genres:** Autobiography/Memoirs, Songs/Lyrics And Libretti, Plays/Screenplays. **Career:** Redwood Records, founder and operator, 1972-. Writer. **Publications:** (With D. Richardson) Fire in the Rain...Singer in the Storm (autobiography), 1990; The Great Peace March, 1993; (with T. Near) Fire in the Rain...Singer in the Storm-A One-woman Stage Show. Contributor to books. **Address:** PO Box 236, Ukiah, CA 95482, U.S.A. **Online address:** holly@hollynear.com

NEAVERSON, Bob. American (born United States), b. 1967?. **Genres:** Autobiography/Memoirs, Young Adult Non-fiction, Music, Biography, Art/Art History, Literary Criticism And History. **Career:** Writer and educator. **Publications:** The Beatles Movies, 1997; (with D. O'Dell) At the Apple's Core: The Beatles from the Inside, 2002. **Address:** c/o Author Mail, Peter Owen Publishers Inc., 73 Kenway Rd., London, GL SW5 0RE, England.

NECIPOGLU, Gulru. American/Turkish (born Turkey), b. 1956?. **Genres:** Architecture, Autobiography/Memoirs. **Career:** Harvard University, teaching fellow, 1981-84, Aga Khan Program, research assistant, 1984-85, research associate, 1985-86, director, Department of Fine Arts, assistant professor, 1987-89, associate professor, 1989-93, director and professor of Islamic art, 1993-, Aga Khan Professor of Islamic Art; Columbia University, Mellon-David Heyman fellow in urban studies, 1986-87, lecturer, 1986-87; Villa i Tati, visiting post-doctoral fellow, 2005. Writer. **Publications:** Architecture, Ceremonial, and Power: The Topkapi Palace in the Fifteenth and Sixteenth Centuries, 1991; The Topkapi Scroll: Geometry and Ornament in Islamic Architecture; Topkapi Palace Museum Library MS H. 1956, 1995; (with A.N. Arapi) The Age of Sinan: Architectural Culture in the Ottoman Empire, 2005; (ed. and intro.) Sinan's Autobiographies: Five Sixteenth-Century Texts, 2006. Contributor to books. **Address:** Harvard University, 29 Oxford St., Cambridge, MA 02138, U.S.A. **Online address:** agakhan@fas.harvard.edu

NECK, Christopher P. American (born United States) **Genres:** Administration/Management, inspirational/Motivational Literature, Adult Non-fiction. **Career:** Virginia Polytechnic Institute and State University, Pamplin College of Business, associate professor of management, 1994-2009; Arizona State University, associate professor of management, 2009-. Writer. **Publications:** Medicine for the Mind: Healing Words to Help You Soar, 1997; (co-author)

For Team Members Only: Making Your Workplace Team Productive and Hassle-Free, 1997; (with C.C. Manz) Mastering Self-Leadership: Empowering Yourself for Personal Excellence, 1998, 5th ed., 2010; (co-author) The Wisdom of Solomon at Work: Ancient Virtues for Living and Leading Today, 2001; (co-author) Fit to Lead: The Proven 8-week Solution for Shaping up Your Body, Your Mind and Your Career, 2004. Contributor of articles to periodicals. **Address:** Departmentt of Management, W P Carey School of Business, Arizona University, PO Box 874006, Tempe, VA 85287-4006, U.S.A. **Online address:** christopher.neck@asu.edu

NEDER, Dennis W. American (born United States), b. 1959. **Genres:** Adult Non-fiction. **Career:** Full Spectrum Technologies L.L.C, president, 1979-2000; Remington Publications, president, 2000-; BAM! Productions, president and chief executive officer, 2005-11. Writer and musician. **Publications:** Being a Man in a Womans World, 2002; Being a Man in a Womans World II, 2004; Being a Man in a Womans World III, forthcoming; Ten Things Men Wish Women Knew, forthcoming. **Address:** c/o Author Mail, Remington Publications, 3115 Foothill Blvd., Ste. M120, La Crescenta, CA 91214-2691, U.S.A. **Online address:** dwneder@remingtonpublications.com

NEEDHAM, Kate. French/British (born England), b. 1962. **Genres:** Crafts, Language/Linguistics, Children's Non-fiction, Education, Reference. **Career:** Specialist Publications, editor of trade newspapers and magazines, 1986-87; Bright Williamson Public Relations, account executive, 1987-88; Adventurers Ltd. (travel magazine), editor, 1988-90; Usborne Publishing Ltd., editor and writer, 1990-91, 1993-96; freelance writer, 1991-93, 1996-. **Publications:** (With E. O'Brien) The Usborne Book of Origami, 1991; (with P. Holland) The Usborne Book of Paper Superplanes, 1992; Why Do People Eat?, 1992; (with S. Meredith and M. Unwin) You and Your Body, 1993; Essential French Dictionary, 1994; Essential German Dictionary, 1994; Collecting Things, 1995; The Great Undersea Search, 1995; Dinosaurs, 1995; Middle Ages, 1996; First Pony, 1996; Jumping, 1996; (ed.) Showing, 1996; (ed.) Grooming and Stable Management, 1996; (with L. Smith) The Usborne Riding School, 1997; (with C. Young) The Usborne Great Wildlife Search, 1998; Cross Country, 1998; (ed. with R. Treays and L. Miles) Usborne Book of Everyday Words, 1999; (ed. with R. Treays and L. Miles) The Usborne Book of Everyday Words in Irish, 1999; (ed. with R. Treays and L. Miles) The Usborne Book of Everyday Words in French, 1999; (ed. with R. Treays and L. Miles) The Usborne Book of Everyday Words in Spanish, 1999; (ed. with R. Treays and L. Miles) The Usborne Book of Everyday Words in German, 1999; (with N. Irving and L. Colvin) Essential French Phrasebook and Dictionary, 2000; Pony Guide, 2006. **Address:** 17 Ave. Emile Deschanel, Paris, 75007, France.

NEEDLE, Jan. (Frank Kippax). British (born England), b. 1943. **Genres:** Children's Fiction, Literary Criticism And History, Mystery/Crime/Suspense, Novels, Criminology/True Crime, Animals/Pets. **Career:** Portsmouth Evening News, reporter, 1960-64; Daily Herald and Sun, reporter and sub-editor, 1964-68. **Publications:** JUVENILE: Albeson and the Germans, 1977; My Mate Shofiq, 1978; The Size Spies, 1978; A Fine Boy for Killing, 1979, rev. ed., 1996; Rottenteeth, 1980; The Bee Rustlers, 1980; A Sense of Shame and Other Stories, 1980; Wild Wood, 1981; Losers Weepers, 1981; (with P. Thomson) Brecht, 1981; Another Fine Mess, 1982; Piggy in the Middle, 1982; Going Out, 1983; A Pitiful Place, 1984; Tucker's Luck, 1984; Great Days at Grange Hill, 1985; A Game of Soldiers, 1985; Behind the Bike Sheds, 1985; Tucker in Control, 1985; (co-author) Rebels of Gas Street, 1986; Wagstaffe the Wind-Up Boy, 1987; Uncle in the Attic, 1987; Skeleton at School, 1987; In the Doghouse, 1988; The Sleeping Party, 1988; The Thief, 1989; Mad Scramble, 1990; As Seen on TV, 1990; The War of the Worms, 1992; Wagstaffe and the Life of Crime, 1992; Bogeymen, 1992; The Bully, 1993; The Wicked Trade, 1998, 2nd ed., 2001; The Spithead Nymph, 2004; (ed.) Bram Stoker's Dracula, 2004; The Hunchback of Notre Dame, 2005; Moby Dick, 2005; Moby-Dick, or, the Whale, 2006; Undertaker's Wind, 2006. FOR ADULTS AS FRANK KIPPAX: The Scar, 1990; The Butcher's Bill, 1991; Other People's Blood, 1992; Fear of Night and Darkness, 1993. Contributor to periodicals. **Address:** David Higham Associates, 5-8 Lower John St., Golden Sq., London, GL W1F 9HA, England. **Online address:** jan@janneedle.com

NEEDLEMAN, Jacob. American (born United States), b. 1934. **Genres:** Novels, Ethics, History, Philosophy, Money/Finance, Theology/Religion. **Career:** West Haven Veterans Administration Hospital, clinical psychology trainee, 1960-61; Rockefeller Institute, research associate, 1961-62; San Francisco State University, assistant professor, 1962-66, associate professor, 1966, chairman of the department, 1968-69, professor of philosophy, professor emeritus of philosophy; Rockefeller Foundation, fellow, 1977-78; The Graduate Theological Union, Center for Studies on New Religions, director, 1977-83; University of California, lecturer in psychiatry and consultant in medical ethics, 1981-84. Writer. **Publications:** Being-in-the-World, 1963; (trans.) E. Straus, The Primary World of the Senses, 1963; The New Religions, 1970, rev. ed., 1987; A Sense of the Cosmos, 1975; Lost Christianity: A Journey of Rediscovery to the Center of Christian Experience, 1980; Consciousness and Tradition, 1982; The Heart of Philosophy, 1982; The Way of the Physician, 1985; Sin and Scientism, 1986; Sorcerers (novel), 1986; Sense of the Cosmos: The Encounter of Modern Science and Ancient Truth, 1988; Money and the Meaning of Life, 1991; Indestructible Question: Essays on Nature, Spirit, and the Human Paradox, 1994; A Little Book on Love, 1996; Money, Money, Money: The Search for Wealth and the Pursuit of Happiness, 1998; Time and the Soul, 1998; The American Soul: Rediscovering the Wisdom of the Founders, 2002; Why Can't We Be Good?, 2007; (trans. and intro. with J.P. Piazza) Essential Marcus Aurelius, 2008; Spiritual Emerson: Essential Works, 2008; Introduction to the Gurdjieff Work, 2009; What is God?, 2009. EDITOR: Care of Patients with Fatal Illnesses, 1969; (with A.K. Bierman and J.A. Gould) Religion for a New Generation, 1973, 2nd ed., 1977; The Sword of Gnosis, 1974; Sacred Tradition and Present Need, 1975; (with D. Lewis) On the Way to Self Knowledge, 1976; (with G. Baker) Understanding the New Religions, 1978; Speaking of My Life: The Art of Living in the Cultural Revolution, 1979; Real Philosophy, 1990; (with A. Faivre) Modern Esoteric Spirituality, 1992; Gurdjieff, 1996; Inner Journey: Views from the Gurdjieff Work, 2008. **Address:** Department of Philosophy, San Francisco State University, 1600 Holloway Ave., Humanities 444, San Francisco, CA 94132, U.S.A. **Online address:** jneedle@sfsu.edu

NEEL, Jasper. (Jasper Phillip Neel). American (born United States), b. 1946. **Genres:** Education, Writing/Journalism. **Career:** Baylor University, Waco, assistant professor of English, 1975-79; Modern Language Association of America, director of English programs, 1979-84; Northern Illinois University, associate professor of English, 1984-89; Vanderbilt University, professor of English, 1990-; Dedman College, dean; Southern Methodist University, vice provost, Department of English, faculty, 2007-, professor. Writer. **Publications:** (Ed.) Options for the Teaching of English: Freshman Composition, 1978; Plato, Derrida and Writing, 1988; Aristotle's Voice: Rhetoric, Theory and Writing in America, 1994. **Address:** Department of English, Southern Methodist University, Rm. 222 Dallas Hall, 3225 University Blvd., PO Box 750435, Dallas, TX 75275-0435, U.S.A. **Online address:** neel@smu.edu

NEEL, Jasper Phillip. *See* **NEEL, Jasper.**

NEELD, Elizabeth Cowan. *See* **NEELD, Elizabeth Harper.**

NEELD, Elizabeth Harper. Also writes as Elizabeth Cowan, Elizabeth Cowan Neeld. American (born United States), b. 1940. **Genres:** Writing/Journalism, Literary Criticism And History, Theology/Religion, Biography, Self Help, Essays. **Career:** Cleveland State Community College, professor and college administrator, 1967-73, Humanities Division, head, 1967-73; Modern Language Association, director of English programs, 1973-76; Texas A&M University, professor of English, 1976-83, assistant, 1980-81; University of Houston, College of Business Administration, executive professor, 1990-2000; corporate consultant, 1990-2000. Writer. **Publications:** OTHERS: (Ed.) Harper & Row Studies in Language and Literature, 1973; Options for the Teaching of English: The Undergraduate Curriculum, 1975; (ed.) Either Way Will Hurt and Other Essays on English, 1976; (ed.) From the Plow to the Pulpit: A Spiritual Autobiography, 1986; Seven Choices: Taking the Steps to New Life after Losing Someone You Love, 1990, 3rd ed., 1997; (with M.B. Muller) Sister Bernadette: Cowboy Nun from Texas, 1991; A Sacred Primer: The Essential Guide to Quiet Time and Prayer, 1999; Seven Choices: Finding Daylight after Loss Shatters Your World, 2003; Tough Transitions: Navigating Your Way through Difficult Times, 2005. AS ELIZABETH COWAN NEELD: (contrib.) Plain English Rhetoric and Reader, 1982; Writing Brief, 1983, 2nd ed., 1986; The Way a Writer Reads: A College Reader, 1987; Writing: A Short Course, 1988. AS ELIZABETH COWAN: (with G. Cowan) Writing, 1980, 3rd ed., 1990; (ed. with K. Davis) Fairy Tales of the Sea, 1981; Readings for Writing, 1983. Contributor to periodicals. **Address:** 6706 Beauford Dr., Austin, TX 78750-8124, U.S.A. **Online address:** cppaustin@earthlink.net

NEELY, Barbara. American (born United States), b. 1941?. **Genres:** Mystery/Crime/Suspense, Novels, Young Adult Fiction, Literary Criticism And History. **Career:** Writer. **Publications:** NOVELS: Blanche on the Lam, 1992; Blanche among the Talented Tenth, 1994; Blanche Cleans Up, 1998; Blanche Passes Go, 2000. Works appear in anthologies. Contributor to periodicals. **Address:** St. Martin's Press, 175 5th Ave., New York, NY 10010, U.S.A.

NEENAN, Colin. American (born United States), b. 1958. **Genres:** Young Adult Fiction, Novels, Novellas/Short Stories. **Career:** Public Schools-Fairfax, media specialist, 1991-95; Trumbull Public Schools, media specialist, 1995-, Media Center, team leader. Writer and librarian. **Publications:** YOUNG ADULT NOVELS: In Your Dreams, 1995; Live a Little, 1996; Idiot!: A Love Story with Drama, Betrayal and E-Mail, 2004; Thick, 2006. **Address:** Farber Literary Agency Inc., 14 E 75th St., Ste. 2E, New York, NY 10021-2625, U.S.A.

NEES, Lawrence. American (born United States), b. 1949. **Genres:** Art/Art History, Bibliography, History. **Career:** University of Victoria (Canada), Department of History in Art, visiting sessional lecturer, 1976-77; University of Massachusetts, Boston, Department of Art, lecturer, 1977-78; University of Delaware, Department of Art History, assistant professor, 1978-82, associate professor, 1982-88, associate chairman, 1986-87, 2001-02, professor of art history, 1988-, director of graduate studies, 2002-04, Department of Art Conservation, adjunct professor, 1996-99; Harvard University, department of fine arts, visiting assistant professor, 1980; Bryn Mawr College, visiting professor, 1989, 2000; Temple University, visiting Professor, 1998, 2004, 2005. Writer. **Publications:** From Justinian to Charlemagne: European Art, 565-787: An Annotated Bibliography, 1985; The Gundohinus Gospels, 1987; A Tainted Mantle: Hercules and the Classical Tradition at the Carolingian Court, 1991; (ed.) Approaches to Early-Medieval Art, 1998; Early Medieval Art, 2002. **Address:** Department of Art History, University of Delaware, 304A Old College, 150 South College Ave., Newark, DE 19716-7200, U.S.A. **Online address:** nees@udel.edu

NEFEDOVA, Tatyana. Russian (born Russia), b. 1949. **Genres:** Geography, Natural History. **Career:** Institute for Landerkunde, head, 1996-; Moscow State University, associate, 1970-79, researcher, 1974-78; Russian Academy of Science, Institute of Geography, researcher, 1978-86, senior researcher, 1986-; Institute of Regional Geography, head of Moscow branch; Research Center of Russian Land, Department of Agriculture and Environment, head. Writer. **Publications:** Continuity and Change in Rural Russia: A Geographical Perspective, 1997; The Environs of Russian Cities, 2000; (with G. Ioffe and I. Zaslavsky) The End of Peasantry? The Disintegration of Rural Russia, 2006; (with J. Pallot) Russia's Unknown Agriculture, 2007. Contributor to journals. **Address:** Department of Economic & Social Geography, Institute of Geography, Russian Academy of Science, 29 Stromonetnyy Per., Moscow, 109107, Russia. **Online address:** trene12@yandex.ru

NEFF, Lyle. Canadian (born Canada), b. 1969?. **Genres:** Poetry, Young Adult Fiction. **Career:** Writer. **Publications:** Ivanhoe Station, 1997; Hundred Block at Nine, 1998; Full Magpie Dodge, 2000; Bizarre Winery Tragedy, 2005. Works appear in anthology. **Address:** Anvil Press Publishers, 278 E 1st Ave., PO Box 3008, Vancouver, BC V5T 1A6, Canada. **Online address:** lyle.neff@blvdmedia.com

NEGEV, Eilat. Israeli/American (born United States) **Genres:** Adult Nonfiction. **Career:** Yedioth Aharonot, chief literary correspondent, 1990-, journalist; Israeli Radio, documentary radio producer. Writer. **Publications:** Siḥot Intimiyot, 1995; ḥayim Peratiyim, 2001; Close Encounters with Twenty Israeli Writers, 2003; (with Y. Koren) In Our Hearts We Were Giants: The Remarkable Story of the Lilliput Troupe: A Dwarf Family's Survival of the Holocaust, 2004; (with Y. Koren) A Lover of Unreason: The Life and Tragic Death of Assia Wevill, 2006; (with Y. Koren) Lover of Unreason: Assia Wevill, Sylvia Plath's Rival and Ted Hughes's Doomed Love, 2007; (with Y. Koren) The First Lady of Fleet Street: The Life of Rachel Beer: Crusading Heiress and Newspaper Pioneer, 2011. Contributor to books. **Address:** c/o Author Mail, Carroll & Graf Publishers, 245 W 17th St., 11th Fl., New York, NY 10011-5300, U.S.A. **Online address:** negevkoren@yahoo.com

NEGNEVITSKY, Michael. Australian (born Australia), b. 1956. **Genres:** Information Science/Computers, Engineering. **Career:** Belorussian University of Technology, senior research fellow and senior lecturer in electrical and electronic engineering, 1984-91; Scientific and Research Business Corp., Power System Control Research Laboratory, head, 1989-91; Monash University, senior research associate in electrical and computer system engineering, 1992; University of Tasmania, lecturer, 1993-95, senior lecturer, 1996-2001, associate professor of engineering, 2002-; University of Vermont, adjunct full professor in the school of engineering, 2006-. Writer. **Publications:** Artificial Intelligence: A Guide to Intelligent Systems, 2002, 2nd ed., 2005. **Address:** School of Engineering, University of Tasmania, PO Box 252-65, Hobart, TA 7001, Australia. **Online address:** michael.negnevitsky@utas.edu.au

NEHRT, Lee C(harles). American (born United States), b. 1926. **Genres:** Business/Trade/Industry, Economics, International Relations/Current Affairs, Education, Reference. **Career:** North American Aviation, foreign operations supervisor, 1956-60; Indiana University, assistant professor, 1962-65, associate professor, 1967-69, professor of international business, 1969-74; Government of Tunisia, Ford Foundation Adviser, 1965-67; Michigan State University, Academy of International Business, vice president, 1967-69, president, 1972-74, fellow, Fellows of the Academy, dean, 1978-81; Dhaka University, advisor, 1969-71; Wichita State University, R.P. Clinton professor of international management, 1974-78, now chair emeritus; World Trade Institute, director, 1978-81; Ohio State University, Owens Illinois professor of international management, 1981-86, now professor emeritus; Government of Indonesia, adviser, 1986-89; International Museum of Blacksmithing, curator, 1991-93. Writer and consultant. **Publications:** (With S.H. Robock) Education for International Business, 1963; (ed. with S.H. Robock) Education in International Business, 1964; Pre-Investment Study of the Sheet Glass Industry, 1964; International Marketing of Nuclear Power Plants, 1965; Foreign Marketing of Nuclear Power Plants, 1965; Financing Capital Equipment Exports, 1966; (ed.) International Finance for Multinational Business, 1967, 2nd ed., 1972; (with F. Truitt and R. Wright) International Business Research: Past, Present and Future, 1969; The Political Climate for Private Foreign Investment, 1970; (with A.E. Salmi) Managerial Policy and Strategy for the Arab World, 1973; (with Lamp Li and G. Evans) Managerial Policy, Strategy and Planning for South East Asia, 1974; (with E. Soriano) Managerial Strategy in an Asian Context, 1974; (with E. Soriano) Business Policy in an Asian Context, 1976, 2nd ed., 1983; (ed.) Business and International Education, 1977; (ed.) The Internationalization of the Business School Curriculum, 1979; (ed.) Case Studies of Internationalization of the Business School Curriculum, 1981. **Address:** Academy of International Business, Eli Broad College of Business, Michigan State University, 7 Eppley Ctr., East Lansing, MI 48824-1121, U.S.A.

NEIGHBOUR, Mary E. American (born United States), b. 1957?. **Genres:** History, Race Relations, Cultural/Ethnic Topics, Civil Liberties/Human Rights, Novels, Law, Writing/Journalism, Young Adult Fiction, Young Adult Fiction. **Career:** Writer and psychotherapist. **Publications:** Speak Right On: Dred Scott, a Novel, 2006; Gray, forthcoming. **Address:** c/o Author Mail, Toby Press, PO Box 8531, New Milford, CT 06776-8531, U.S.A. **Online address:** author@speakrighton.com

NEILAN, Sarah. British (born England), b. 1936?. **Genres:** Novels, Romance/Historical, Essays. **Career:** Writer, 1974-. **Publications:** The Braganza Pursuit, 1976; An Air of Glory, 1977, 2nd ed., 1978: Charlotte Bronte's Shirley: A Critical Essay, 1977; Paradise: A Novel, 1982; The Old Enchantment, 1991. Contributor of articles to magazines. **Address:** Peters Fraser and Dunlop Group Ltd., Drury House, 34-43 Russell St., London, GL WC2B 5HA, England.

NEILL, Fiona. British (born England), b. 1966?. **Genres:** Novels. **Career:** Times magazine, features writer, columnist; Marie Claire magazine, features editor. **Publications:** The Secret Life of a Slummy Mummy, 2007; Friends, Lovers and Other Indiscretions, 2009; What the Nanny Saw, 2011. **Address:** c/o Simon Trewin, PFD Drury House, 34-43 Russell St., London, GL WC2B 5HA, England.

NEILSON, James Warren. American (born United States), b. 1933. **Genres:** History, Biography, Politics/Government. **Career:** Mayville State College, associate professor, 1958-59, professor of history, Department of Social Science, chairman, 1958-98, professor emeritus, 1998-; Trail County Young Republican Club, charter vice-president, 1960-61. Writer. **Publications:** Shelby M. Cullom: Prairie State Republican, 1962; From Protest to Preservation: What Republicans Have Believed, 1968; The School of Personal Service: A History of Mayville State College, 1980, 2nd ed., 2001. **Address:** Department of Social Science, Mayville State University, 330 3rd St. NE, Mayville, ND 58257, U.S.A.

NEIMAN, Susan. American (born United States), b. 1955. **Genres:** Autobiography/Memoirs, History, Philosophy. **Career:** Yale University, assistant professor, associate professor, 1989-96; Tel Aviv University, associate professor, 1996-2000; Einstein Forum, director, 2000-; University of Michigan, Tanner lecturer, 2010. Author. **Publications:** Slow Fire: Jewish Notes from Berlin, 1992; The Unity of Reason: Rereading Kant, 1994; Evil in Modern Thought: An Alternative History of Philosophy, 2002; (co-ed.) Zum Glück, 2004; Fremde sehen anders: Zur Lage der Bundesrepublik, 2005; In Het Zicht Van De Galg: Helden En Het Kwaad, 2006; Moral Clarity: A Guide for Grown-up Idealists, 2008, rev. ed., 2009; (ed. with I. Nachum) Margherita von Brentano: Das Persönliche und das Politische, Wallstein Verlag, Göttingen, 2010. Contributor to periodicals. **Address:** Einstein Forum, Am Neuem Market 7, Potsdam, 14467, Germany. **Online address:** susan.neiman@einsteinforum.de

NEIMANIS, George J(uris). American (born Latvia), b. 1932. **Genres:** Social Sciences, Documentaries/Reportage, History. **Career:** U.S. Department of the Army, civilian logistics officer, 1958-66; Gannon College, instructor in economics, 1966-68; Niagara University, Everett W. Ockerman lecturer, 1987, Department of Economics and Commerce, professor of economics, 1970-, chairperson, 1975-84, professor emeritus; Riga Business School, visiting professor, 1991, 1993-94, 1996, acting associate dean, 1993; U.S. Agency for International Development, Business, Government and Industry Consultants Inc., consultant; Hudson Institute, consultant; Supreme Council of the Republic of Latvia, consultant. Writer. **Publications:** (Co-author) Niagara County, New York: Resources Exploitation and Environmental Consequences, 1880-1979, 1980; The Collapse of the Soviet Empire: A View from Riga, 1997. Contributor of articles. **Address:** 425 Tryon Dr., Lewiston, NY 14092, U.S.A. **Online address:** gneima5853@aol.com

NEIWERT, David A. American (born United States), b. 1956?. **Genres:** Politics/Government, Adult Non-fiction, Social Commentary, Young Adult Non-fiction. **Career:** MSNBC.com, internet writer and producer, 1996-2000; Crooks & Liars, managing editor; freelance journalist. **Publications:** In God's Country: The Patriot Movement and the Pacific Northwest, 1999; Death on the Fourth of July: The Story of a Killing, A Trial, and Hate Crime in America, 2004; Strawberry Days: How Internment Destroyed a Japanese American Community, 2005; The Eliminationists: How Hate Talk Radicalized The American Right, 2009; (with J. Amato) Over The Cliff: How Obama's Election Drove The American Right Insane, 2010. **Address:** c/o Author Mail, Palgrave Macmillan, 175 5th Ave., New York, NY 10010, U.S.A. **Online address:** dneiwert@hotmail.com

NELL, Victor. South African/Zimbabwean (born Zimbabwe), b. 1935. **Genres:** Psychology. **Career:** University of South Africa, Department of Psychology, instructor, 1977-, senior lecturer in psychology, associate professor of psychology, 1989-94, professor, 1994-, head, Health Psychology Unit, director, 1986-2000; South African Clinical Neuropsychology Association, founding president, 1984-88. Writer. **Publications:** Lost in a Book: The Psychology of Reading for Pleasure, 1988; Cross-cultural Neuropsychological Assessment: Theory and Practice, 2000. **Address:** West Hill House, 6 Swains Ln., Highgate, London, GL N6 6QS, England. **Online address:** psychology@victornell.co.uk

NELSON, Antonya. American (born United States), b. 1961. **Genres:** Novellas/Short Stories, Novels. **Career:** New Mexico State University, Department of English, assistant professor, 1989-95, associate professor, 1995-, Graduate School, professor; University of Houston, Cullen co-chair in creative writing, Department of English, professor; Warren Wilson College, M.F.A. Program, instructor. Writer. **Publications:** FICTION: Family Terrorists: A Novella and Seven Stories, 1984; The Expendables: Stories, 1989; In the Land of Men: Stories, 1992; Talking in Bed, 1996; Nobody's Girl: A Novel, 1998; Living to Tell: A Novel, 2000; Female Trouble: A Collection of Short Stories, 2002; Some Fun: Stories and a Novella, 2006; Nothing Right, 2009, Bound, 2010. OTHERS: (ed. with R. Boswell) American Fiction, vol. X: The Best Unpublished Stories by Emerging Writers, 1999. Contributor to periodicals. **Address:** Department of English, University of Houston, 234B Roy Cullen Bldg., 4800 Calhoun Rd., Houston, TX 77004-5008, U.S.A. **Online address:** antonyanelson@sbcglobal.net

NELSON, Arvid. American (born United States) **Genres:** Humor/Satire, Graphic Novels. **Career:** Writer. **Publications:** (Co-author) Rex Mundi, vol. I: The Guardian of the Temple, 2006, vol. II: The Lost Kings, 2006, vol. III: The River Underground, 2007, vol. IV: Crown and Sword, 2007, vol. V: The Valley at the End of the World, 2008, vol. VI: Gate of God, 2010; Killer 7, 2007; (with L. Tae-Hang) Hellgate: London, vol. I, 2008; (with M. Camp and D. Stewart) Zero Killer, 2010; The Seven Branches, forthcoming. **Address:** c/o Author Mail, Dark Horse Comics, 10956 SE Main St., Milwaukie, OR 97222-7644, U.S.A. **Online address:** arvid@shrunkenheadstudios.com

NELSON, Betty Palmer. American (born United States), b. 1938. **Genres:** Novels, Language/Linguistics, Education, Literary Criticism And History. **Career:** Muskingum College, faculty, 1961-69; Volunteer State Community College, professor of English, 1975-. Writer. **Publications:** (With L.P. Clara) Solving Writing Problems: A Self-Paced Workbook, 1979; Private Knowledge (novel), 1990; The Weight of Light: 1849-1890, 1992; Pursuit of Bliss: 1913 to 1919, 1992; Uncertain April, 1909-1950, 1994; Changing Seasons, 1996; (with D.L. Voltz and M. Jean) Sims Connecting Teachers, Students, and Standards: Strategies for Success in Diverse and Inclusive Classrooms, 2010. Contributor to periodicals. **Address:** 236 Harbor Dr., Hendersonville, TN 37075, U.S.A. **Online address:** betty.nelson@volstate.edu

NELSON, Bob. *See* **NELSON, Bobby Jack.**

NELSON, Bobby Jack. (Bob Nelson). American (born United States), b. 1938. **Genres:** Novels, Business/Trade/Industry. **Career:** Writer. **Publications:** Coast-to-Coast, 1965; The Last Station: A Novel, 1972; Brothers: A Novel, 1975; The Devil to Pay, 1980; The Pull, 1986; Keepers: A Memoir, 1998; One Day in the World of My Brilliant Mind: A Personal View of Real Matters, 2000; (co-author) A Time for White Roses, 2000; (as Bob Nelson) 1001 Ways to Reward Employees, 2005. **Address:** c/o Author Mail, W.W. Norton & Company Inc., 500 5th Ave., New York, NY 10110, U.S.A.

NELSON, Brent. Canadian (born Canada), b. 1966?. **Genres:** Theology/Religion, History. **Career:** University of Saskatchewan, assistant professor, associate professor of English and research chair. Writer. **Publications:** (Ed.) Waterloo Directory of English Newspapers and Periodicals, 1800-1900, 2003; Holy Ambition: Rhetoric, Courtship, and Devotion in the Sermons of John Donne, 2005. Contributor to books and periodicals. **Address:** Department of English, University of Saskatchewan, 317 Arts Bldg., 9 Campus Dr., Saskatoon, SK S7N 5A5, Canada. **Online address:** nelson@arts.usask.ca

NELSON, Bryan. *See* **NELSON, J. Bryan.**

NELSON, Carolyn W(illiamson). American (born United States), b. 1942. **Genres:** Writing/Journalism, Bibliography, Reference. **Career:** Yale University, Wing STC Project, editor, 1980-. **Publications:** (Ed.) Short-Title Catalogue of Books Printed in England, Scotland, Ireland, Wales, and British America, and of English Books Printed in Other Countries, 1641-1700, vol. III: P1- Z28, 2nd ed. 1972, vol. I: A1- England, 2nd ed., 1994; (with M. Seccombe) Periodical Publications, 1641-1700: A Survey With Illustrations, 1986; (comp. with M. Seccombe) British Newspapers and Periodicals, 1641-1700: A Short-Title Catalogue of Serials Printed in England, Scotland, Ireland, and British America: With a Checklist of Serials Printed 1701-March 1702 and Chronological, Geographical, Foreign Language, Subject, Publishers, and Editor Indexes, 1641-1702, 1987; First-Line Index of English Poetry, 1500-1800, 2005. Contributor to periodicals. **Address:** Wing STC Project, Yale University, PO Box 1603A, Yale Station, New Haven, CT 06520, U.S.A. **Online address:** vpfpa@att.net

NELSON, Claudia. American (born United States), b. 1960. **Genres:** Literary Criticism And History, Women's Studies And Issues. **Career:** Book-of-the-Month Club, copy editor, 1980-84; West Chester University, College Literature, managing editor, 1990-91; Texas State University, assistant professor of English, 1993-97, associate professor, 1997-2003; Texas A&M University, associate professor, 2003-06, professor of English, 2006-, affiliated professor of women's and gender studies, 2006-. **Publications:** Boys Will Be Girls: The Feminine Ethic and British Children's Fiction, 1857-1917, 1991; Invisible Men: Fatherhood in Victorian Periodicals, 1850-1910, 1995; Little Strangers: Portrayals of Adoption and Foster Care in America, 1850-1929, 2003; Family Ties in Victorian England, 2007. EDITOR: (with L. Vallone) The Girl's Own: Cultural Histories of the Anglo-American Girl, 1830-1915, 1994; (with A. Holmes) Maternal Instincts: Visions of Motherhood and Sexuality in Britain, 1875-1925, 1997; (with M. Martin) Sexual Pedagogies: Sex Education in Britain, Australia, and America, 1879-2000, 2004. **Address:** Department of English, Texas A&M University, 243B Blocker Bldg., College Station, TX 77843-4227, U.S.A. **Online address:** claudia_nelson@tamu.edu

NELSON, D. A. Ann. British/Scottish (born Scotland), b. 1970. **Genres:** Children's Fiction, Animals/Pets. **Career:** National Health Service, staff; Glasgow University, part-time lecturer in creative writing. Writer. **Publications:** DarkIsle, 2008. Contributor to periodicals. **Address:** Cardross, Scotland. **Online address:** d-a-nelson@tiscali.co.uk

NELSON, Daniel. American (born United States), b. 1941. **Genres:** Environmental Sciences/Ecology, History, Industrial Relations. **Career:** University of Delaware, assistant professor of history, 1967-70; Eleutherian Mills-Hagley Foundation, Eleutherian Mills Historical Library, specialist, 1967-69; Hagley Library, staff, 1967-70; University of Akron, Department of History, associate professor, 1970-77, professor, 1977-2000, chair, 1995-98, professor emeritus, 2000-, director of graduate studies, 1974-79, University of Akron Press, director, 1988-92; Medina-Summit Land Conservancy, president, 2003-05. Writer. **Publications:** A checklist of writings on the economic history of the greater Philadelphia-Wilmington region, 1968; Unemployment Insurance: The American Experience 1915-35, 1969; Managers and Workers: Origins of the New Factory System in the U.S. 1880-1920, 1975, 2nd ed., 1995; Frederick W. Taylor and the Rise of Scientific Management, 1980; American Rubber Workers and Organized Labor 1900-1941, 1988; (ed.) Mental Revolution: Scientific Management Since Taylor, 1992; Farm and Factory: Midwestern Workers, 1880-1990, 1995; Shifting Fortunes, 1997; (ed.) Life, Liberty, and Property: A Story of Conflict and a Measurement of Conflicting Rights, 1998; Northern Landscapes: The Struggle for Wilderness Alaska, 2004; Passion for the Land: John F. Seiberling and the Environmental Movement, 2009. **Address:** Department of History, The University of Akron, 302 Buchtel Common, Akron, OH 44325, U.S.A. **Online address:** nelson@uakron.edu

NELSON, D-L. Lane. Swiss/American (born United States), b. 1942?. **Genres:** Novels. **Career:** Canadian CU Newswire, founder; Webster University, faculty. Novelist. **Publications:** NOVELS: Chickpea Lover 2003; The Card, 2005; Running from the Puppet Master, 2008; Family Value: 392 Chestnut Street, 2010; Murder in Caleb's Landing: A Third-Culture Kid Mystery, 2010; Murder in Argelès: A Third-Culture Kid Mystery, 2011. **Address:** Canadian Credit Union News Wire, 16 Case Postale, Corsier, Geneva, CH 1246, Switzerland. **Online address:** donna-lane.nelson@wanadoo.fr

NELSON, Dorothy. Irish (born Ireland) **Genres:** Novels, Young Adult Fiction. **Career:** Writer. **Publications:** In Nights City, 1982; Tar and Feathers, 1987; (comp. with M.H. Green and D.M. Clevenger) Graceland, 1994. **Address:** Dalkey Archive Press, PO Box 8905, Normal, IL 61790-8905, U.S.A.

NELSON, Eric. American (born United States), b. 1970. **Genres:** Young Adult Non-fiction, Law, Politics/Government. **Career:** University of Oxford, adjunct instructor, 1994-98; University of Newcastle, lecturer in history, 1999-2000; University of Southern Mississippi, associate professor of history, 2000-06; Oxford Brookes University, Institute for Historical and Cultural Research, visiting fellow, 2006; Missouri State University, College of Humanities and Public Affairs, assistant professor of history, associate professor of history, 2006-, Center for Teaching and Learning, provosts fellow for teaching and learning, 2009-10, deans fellow for course transformation, 2010-; University of Saint Andrews, Centre for Reformation Research, James K Cameron faculty fellow, 2006-07. Writer. **Publications:** NONFICTION: (ed. with A. Eickelmann and T. Lansford) Justice and Violence: Political Violence, Pacifism and Cultural Transformation, 2005; The Jesuits and the Monarchy: Catholic Reform and Political Authority in France (1590-1615), 2005. **Address:** Department of History, Missouri State University, 416 Strong Hall, 901 S National Ave., Springfield, MO 65897-0027, U.S.A. **Online address:** ericnelson@missouristate.edu

NELSON, Geoffrey Kenneth. British (born England), b. 1923. **Genres:** Novellas/Short Stories, Science Fiction/Fantasy, Poetry, Local History/Rural Topics, Sociology, Theology/Religion, Autobiography/Memoirs, Young Adult Fiction, Young Adult Fiction. **Career:** Westwood School, teacher, 1956-62; Bournville College, assistant lecturer in sociology, 1962-64; Birmingham Polytechnic (now University of Central England), lecturer, 1964-69, senior lecturer, 1969-75, principal lecturer in sociology, 1975-88, honorable research fellow, 1988-; University of Birmingham, Institute for the Study of Worship and Religious Architecture, honorary fellow, 1969-80, Department of Theology, visiting lecturer; British Association, Sociology Section, honorable secretary, 1972-77; Worcestershire-The County Magazine, wildlife correspondent, 1988-92. **Publications:** Spiritualism and Society, 1969; (with R.A. Clews) Mobility and Religious Commitment, 1971; (contrib.) Religion in the Birmingham Area, 1975; History of Modern Spiritualism, 1976; A Poet's Reading, 1980; Butterfly's Eye, 1980; (co-author) Video-Violence and Children, 1983; Cults, New Religions, and Religious Creativity, 1987; Der Drang zum Spirituellen, 1991; To Be a Farmer's Boy, 1992; Countrywomen on the Land: Memories of Rural Life in the 1920s and '30s, 1992; Caught in the Net, 1992; Seen and Not Heard, 1993; Over the Farmyard Gate: Country Life in the 1930s, 1995. Contributor to magazines and newspapers. **Address:** 32 Clun Rd., Northfield, Birmingham, BK B31 1NU, England.

NELSON, Howard. American (born United States), b. 1947. **Genres:** Poetry, Literary Criticism And History, Natural History. **Career:** Cayuga Community College, professor of English, 1970-. Writer. **Publications:** POETRY: Creatures, 1983; Singing into the Belly, 1990; Gorilla Blessing, 1993; Bone Music, 1997; The Nap by the Waterfall, 2009. OTHERS: Robert Bly: An Introduction to the Poetry, 1984; (ed.) On the Poetry of Galway Kinnell: The Wages of Dying, 1987; (ed.) Earth, My Likeness: Nature Poetry of Walt Whitman, 2010. **Address:** Department of English, Cayuga Community College, 197 Franklin St., Auburn, NY 13021-3011, U.S.A. **Online address:** nelsonh33@hotmail.com

NELSON, Jack Lee. American (born United States), b. 1932. **Genres:** Education, Sex, Social Sciences, Sociology, History. **Career:** Teacher, 1956-58; Citrus College, part-time instructor in sociology and psychology, 1958-63; California State University, instructor, assistant professor of education, 1958-63; State University of New York, associate professor of education, 1963-68, chair, 1966-68; Rutgers University, Graduate School of Education, Department of Science and Humanities Education, professor, 1968-75, chair, 1972-75, distinguished professor of education, 1975-98, professor emeritus, 1998-; University of Colorado, visiting professor, 1968; City University of New York, visiting professor, 1973; Cambridge University, visiting professor, 1974, 1975, 1979 and 1983; Hayden Book Co., Hayden American Values Series, series editor. **Publications:** (With T.E. Linton) Patterns of Power: Social Foundations of Education, 1967, 2nd ed., 1974; (Comp.) Teen-agers and Sex, 1970; (with F. Besag) Sociological Perspectives in Education, 1970; Teaching Elementary Social Studies thru Inquiry, 1970; Population and Survival: Can We Win the Race, 1972; Introduction to Value Inquiry, 1974; Values and Society, 1975; Population and Progress, 1977; Values, Rights and the New Morality, 1977; (with J.U. Michaelis) Secondary Social Studies, 1980; (with F. Besag) Foundations of Education: Stasis and Change, 1984; (with S.B. Palonsky and K. Carlson) Critical Issues in Education, 1990, 7th ed. as Critical Issues in Education: Dialogues and Dialectics, 2010. EDITOR: (with K. Carlson and T.E. Linton) Radical Ideas and the Schools, 1972; (with W.K. Hoy and C.G. Miskel) Educational Administration, 1978; (with V.M. Green) International Human Rights: Contemporary Issues, 1980. **Address:** Policy and Administration, Graduate School of Education, Rutgers University, 10 Seminary Pl., New Brunswick, NJ 08901-1108, U.S.A. **Online address:** jln@gateway.net

NELSON, Jacquelyn S. American (born United States), b. 1950. **Genres:** History. **Career:** High school social studies teacher, 1973-78; Ball State University, instructor in history, 1981-84, office assistant, 1985-88, assistant to dean of Graduate School, 1988-89, acting assistant dean, 1989-93, assistant dean of Graduate School and adjunct professor of history, 1993-; Vincennes University, assistant professor of history, 1984-85. Writer. **Publications:** Indiana Quakers Confront the Civil War, 1991. Contributor of articles to periodicals and newspapers. **Address:** Graduate School, Ball State University, Rm. 100, W Quad, 2000 W University Ave., Muncie, IN 47306, U.S.A. **Online address:** jnelson@bsu.edu

NELSON, James L. American (born United States), b. 1962. **Genres:** Romance/Historical, History, Adult Non-fiction. **Career:** The Landsburg Co. (television production), assistant editor, 1986-88; Golden Hinde (ship), boatswain, 1988-89; Lady Washington (ship), rigger/sailor, 1990-91; H.M.S. Rose (sail training ship), thirdmate, director of education, 1991-92; writer, 1992-. **Publications:** HISTORICAL FICTION: By Force of Arms, 1996; The Maddest Idea, 1997; The Continental Risque, 1998; Lords of the Ocean, 1999; The Guardship, 2000; All the Brave Fellows, 2000; Blackbirder, 2001; (as E. Garrett) The Sweet Trade, 2001, rev. ed. as The Only Life that Mattered: The Short and Merry Lives of Anne Bonny, Mary Read and Calico Jack

Rackam, 2004; The Pirate Round, 2002; Glory in the Name: A Novel of the Confederate Navy, 2003; Only Life that Mattered: The Short and Merry Lives of Anne Bonny, Mary Read and Calico Jack Rackam, 2004; Reign of Iron: The Story of the First Battling Ironclads, the Monitor and the Merrimack, 2004; Thieves of Mercy: A Novel of the Civil War at Sea, 2005; Benedict Arnold's Navy: The Ragtag Fleet that Lost the Battle of Lake Champlain but Won the American Revolution, 2006; George Washington's Secret Navy: How the American Revolution Went to Sea, 2008; General Washington's Great Gamble: And the Sea Battle That Won the American Revolution, 2010; With Fire and Sword: The Battle of Bunker Hill and the Beginning of the American Revolution, 2011. **Address:** c/o Nat Sobel, Sobel Weber Associates Inc., 146 E 19th St., New York, NY 10003-2404, U.S.A. **Online address:** jlnelson@suscom-maine.net

NELSON, J. Bryan. (Bryan Nelson). Scottish/British (born England), b. 1932. **Genres:** Biology, Environmental Sciences/Ecology, Natural History, Sciences, Animals/Pets. **Career:** University of Aberdeen, visiting research fellow, 1966-67, lecturer, 1969-73, senior lecturer, 1973-79, reader in zoology, 1979-, now reader emeritus; Azraq UNESCO Field Station, director, 1968-69; Galapagos Conservation Trust, honorary vice president; Scottish Seabird Centre, director. Writer. **Publications:** Galapagos: Islands of Birds, 1968; Azraq Desert Oasis, 1974; The Sulidae: Gannets and Boobies, 1978; The Gannet, 1978; Seabirds: Their Biology and Ecology, 1979; Living with Seabirds, 1986; The Bass and Its Seabirds, 2000; The Atlantic Gannet, 2002; The Pelecaniiformes, 2005; Pelicans, Cormorants and Their Relatives: Pelecanidae, Sulidae, Phalacrocoracidae, Anhingidae, Fregatidae, Phaethontidae, 2005. Contributor to journals. **Address:** Balkirk, Glenlochar, Castle Douglas, DG7 2LU, Scotland.

NELSON, Jill. American (born United States), b. 1952. **Genres:** Plays/Screenplays, Autobiography/Memoirs, Essays, Novels. **Career:** Freelance writer, 1978-86, 1990-; City University of New York, City College, adjunct lecturer, 1982, professor of journalism, 1998-2003, Hunter College, adjunct lecturer, 1983; Washington Post, staff writer, 1986-90. **Publications:** NON-FICTION: Volunteer Slavery: My Authentic Negro Experience, 1993; Straight, No Chaser: How I Became a Grown-up Black Woman (essays), 1997; (ed.) Police Brutality: An Anthology, 2000; Sexual Healing (novel), 2003; Finding Martha's Vineyard: African Americans at Home on an Island, 2005; Let's Get It On, 2009. Contributor to magazines and newspapers. **Address:** W. W. Norton & Company Inc., 500 5th Ave., New York, NY 10110, U.S.A. **Online address:** talktojill@jillnelson.com

NELSON, Jim A. *See* **STOTTER, Mike.**

NELSON, Keith L(eBahn). American (born United States), b. 1932. **Genres:** History, Politics/Government, Civil Liberties/Human Rights, International Relations/Current Affairs, Theology/Religion. **Career:** University of Texas-Austin, instructor in history, 1963-65; University of California-Irvine, Department of History, assistant professor, 1965-72, associate professor, 1973-91, professor, 1992-2004, emeritus professor of history, School of Humanities, associate dean, 1975, Humanities Core Course, director, 1984-88, Center for Global Peace and Conflict Studies, director, 1988-93, Study Center-Sweden and Denmark, director, 1999-2002, Center for International Education, director, 2002-05, research professor, Religious Studies Program, director, 2010-11; Lund University, Fulbright professor, 1990-91, UC-Study Center on Critical World Issues, co-founder. Writer. **Publications:** Victors Divided: America and the Allies in Germany, 1918-1923, 1975; (with S.C. Olin, Jr.) Why War? Ideology, Theory and History, 1979; The Making of Détente: Soviet-American Relations in the Shadow of Vietnam, 1995. EDITOR: Why We Fought, 1969; The Impact of War on American Life: The Twentieth-Century Experience, 1971; (with P.M. Morgan) Re-Viewing the Cold War: Domestic Factors and Foreign Policy in the East-West Confrontation, 2000. Contributor to periodicals. **Address:** Department of History, University of California, 274 Murray Krieger Hall, Irvine, CA 92697, U.S.A. **Online address:** klnelson@uci.edu

NELSON, Lynn A. American (born United States), b. 1967?. **Genres:** Environmental Sciences/Ecology, Natural History. **Career:** Middle Tennessee State University, associate professor of history. Writer and historian. **Publications:** Pharsalia: An Environmental Biography of a Southern Plantation, 1780-1880, 2007. Contributor to books, periodicals and journals. **Address:** Department of History, Middle Tennessee State University, Rm. 285 Peck Hall, 1301 E Main St., PO Box 23, Murfreesboro, TN 37132, U.S.A. **Online address:** lnelson@mtsu.edu

NELSON, Mariah Burton. American (born United States), b. 1956. **Genres:** Adult Non-fiction, Sports/Fitness, Women's Studies And Issues. **Career:** Women's Sports and Fitness Magazine, editor, 1984-87, columnist; Speaking of Sports, president, 1987-2006; Frances Willard Society, founder, 1998; National Speakers Association, president, 2001-02; American Association for Physical Activity and Recreation, executive director, 2006-; Oxygen Media News, columnist; The Washington Post Magazine, columnist; Knight Ridder/Tribune News, columnist; American Association of Retired Persons, chief speechwriter and acting director; Speaking Success for Athletes, co-founder and co-owner. **Publications:** Are We Winning Yet?: How Women Are Changing Sports and Sports Are Changing Women, Random House 1991; The Stronger Women Get, the More Men Love Football: Sexism and the American Culture of Sports, Harcourt Brace 1994; Embracing Victory: Life Lessons in Competition and Compassion, Morrow 1998; The Unburdened Heart: Five Keys To Forgiveness And Freedom, 2000; We Are All Athletes, Dare Press 2004; Making Money on the Sidelines, AAPAR 2008. Contributor to Contributor to periodicals, newspapers and magazines. **Address:** 2909 N 24th St., Arlington, VA 22207-4914, U.S.A. **Online address:** mariah@mariahburtonnelson.com

NELSON, Mark. *See* **JOHNSTON, Ronald.**

NELSON, Megan Kate. American (born United States), b. 1972?. **Genres:** History, Cultural/Ethnic Topics. **Career:** Harvard University, lecturer, 2002-03; Texas Tech University, assistant professor, 2003-06, director of honors arts and letters program, 2005-06; California State University, assistant professor of history, 2006-. Writer. **Publications:** Trembling Earth: A Cultural History of the Okefenokee Swamp, 2005; Ruin Nation: Destruction and the American Civil War, 2012; Flesh and Stone: Ruins and the Civil War, forthcoming. Contributor to books and journals. **Address:** Department of History, California State University, Rm. H810L, Humanities Bldg., 800 N State College Blvd., 8th Fl., PO Box 6846, Fullerton, CA 92834, U.S.A. **Online address:** megannelson@fullerton.edu

NELSON, Michael. British (born England), b. 1929. **Genres:** Communications/Media, History. **Career:** Reuters News Agency, general manager, 1952-89. Writer. **Publications:** War of the Black Heavens: The Battles of Western Broadcasting in the Cold War, 1997; Queen Victoria and the Discovery of the Riviera, 2001; Americans and the Making of the Riviera, 2008. **Address:** 21 Lansdowne Rd., London, GL W11 3AG, England. **Online address:** michael@menelson.co.uk

NELSON, N. A. British (born England), b. 1971?. **Genres:** Novels. **Career:** Writer and novelist. **Publications:** Bringing the Boy Home (juvenile novel), 2008. **Online address:** nina@ninanelsonbooks.com

NELSON, Peter N. American (born United States), b. 1953. **Genres:** Young Adult Fiction, Plays/Screenplays, Writing/Journalism, Young Adult Non-fiction, Novels, Children's Fiction. **Career:** Rhode Island School of Design, teacher of writing; St. Lawrence University, teacher of creative writing; Emerson College, teacher of creative writing. Freelance journalist, 1981-. **Publications:** OUNG ADULT NOVELS: Sylvia Smith-Smith, 1987; Fast Lane West, 1991; Night of Fire, 1991; Scarface, 1991; Deadly Games, 1992; Dangerous Waters, 1992; Double Dose, 1992; First to Die, 1992; The Third Degree, 1993; Death Threat, 1993; Six Deadly Lies, 1993. OTHER: Real Man Tells All (collected columns), 1988; Marry Like a Man: The Essential Guide for Grooms, 1992; (with J. Brehm) That Others May Live: The True Story of a PJ, a Member of America's Most Daring Rescue Force, 2000; (with J. Brehm) That Others May Live: Real-Life Heroes of the Perfect Storm, 2000; Left for Dead: A Young Man's Search for Justice for the USS Indianapolis, 2002; The Christmas List, 2004; A More Unbending Battle, 2009; The Harlem Hellfightres Struggle for Democracy in WWI and Equality at Home, 2009; I Thought You Were Dead, 2010; (with L. Wiehl) Waking Hours, 2011; Rise and Fall of El Solo Libre, 2012. Contributor to periodicals. **Address:** c/o Zachary-Shuster-Hormsworth, 1776 Broadway, Ste. 1405, New York, NY 10019, U.S.A. **Online address:** petenlson@aol.com

NELSON, R(adell) Faraday. *See* **NELSON, Ray.**

NELSON, Ray. Also writes as Jeffrey Lord, Ray Faraday Nelson, R(adell)

Faraday Nelson, R. N. Elson, Jeffrey Elson. American (born United States), b. 1931. **Genres:** Novels, Science Fiction/Fantasy, Plays/Screenplays, Songs/ Lyrics And Libretti, Cartoons, Illustrations. **Career:** Northside Poster Co., printer, 1954; Artcraft Poster Co., printer and art director, 1955; Jean Linard, translator, 1959; University of California Press, computer programmer and accounting assistant, 1961-62; freelance writer and artist, 1962-; Berkeley Free University, co-director, 1967-68; Adams Junior High School, teaching assistant, 1968-87; Universal Pictures, screenwriter, 1988-. **Publications:** (As Ray Nelson) Perdita: Songs of Love, Sex, and Self Pity, 1960; (with P.K. Dick) The Ganymede Takeover (science fiction), 1967; The Agony of Love, 1969; Girl with the Hungry Eyes, 1969; (as R.N. Elson) How to Do It, 1970; (as R.N. Elson) Black Pussy, 1970; (as R.N. Elson) Sex Happy Hippy, 1970; (as R.N. Elson) The DA's Wife, 1970; Blake's Progress (science fiction), 1975; Then Beggars Could Ride (science fiction), 1976; The Ecolog (science fiction), 1977; The Revolt of the Unemployables (science fiction), 1978; (as Jeffrey Lord) Dimension of Horror (science fiction), 1979; The Prometheus Man (science fiction), 1982; The Branching Forks, 1984; Time Quest (fantasy), 1985; (as Ray Faraday Nelson) Dog-Headed Death (historical), 1989; Virtual Zen (science fiction), 1995. **Address:** 333 Ramona Ave., El Cerrito, CA 94530, U.S.A. **Online address:** rayfaradaynelson@aol.com

NELSON, Ray Faraday. *See* **NELSON, Ray.**

NELSON, Robert M(cDowell). American (born United States), b. 1945. **Genres:** Literary Criticism And History. **Career:** University of Richmond, instructor, 1968-71, assistant professor, 1975-85, professor of English, 1985-2006, professor emeritus, 2006-. Writer. **Publications:** Place and Vision: The Function of Landscape in Native American Fiction, 1993; Leslie Marmon Silko's Ceremony: The Recovery of Tradition, 2008. Works appear in anthologies. Contributor to journals and magazines. **Address:** 2421 Birchwood Rd., Henrico, VA 23294-3513, U.S.A. **Online address:** rnelson@richmond.edu

NELSON, Samuel H. American (born United States), b. 1946. **Genres:** Music, Songs/Lyrics And Libretti. **Career:** Argonne National Laboratory, assistant economist, 1976-77, 1980-83, part-time employee, 1983-2001; Energy System Research Group, economist, 1977-79; Feldenkrais, practitioner, 1987-; Sanford Cohen and Associates, consultant, 2001-. Writer. **Publications:** (With E. Blades-Zeller) Singing with Your Whole Self: The Feldenkrais Method and Voice, 2000. Contributor to periodicals. **Address:** c/o Author Mail, Scarecrow Press, 4501 Forbes Blvd., Ste. 200, Lanham, MD 20706, U.S.A. **Online address:** samnel@aol.com

NELSON, Sharlene (P.). American (born United States), b. 1933. **Genres:** Agriculture/Forestry, Children's Non-fiction, Travel/Exploration, Natural History, History, Sciences. **Career:** Freelance writer, 1956-; Pacific Search, staff writer, 1966-72; Oregonian, correspondent, 1973-82. **Publications:** (With J. LeMieux) Cruising the Columbia and Snake Rivers: Eleven Cruises in the Inland Waterway, 1981, (with J. LeMieux and T.W. Nelson) rev. ed., 1986. WITH T.W. NELSON: The Umbrella Guide to Washington Lighthouses, 1990, rev. ed., 1998; The Umbrella Guide to California Lighthouses, 1993, rev. ed., 1999; The Umbrella Guide to Oregon Lighthouses, 1994; Bull Whackers to Whistle Punks: Logging in the Old West, 1996; The Umbrella Guide to Exploring the Columbia-Snake River Inland Waterway, 1997; Mount St. Helens National Volcanic Monument: True Book, 1997; Olympic National Park, 1997; Hawaii Volcanoes National Park, 1998; Mount Rainier National Park, 1998; William Boeing: Builder of Planes, 1999; Brett Favre, 2001; The Golden Gate Bridge, 2001; The Makah, 2003; The Nez Perce, 2003; Jedediah Smith, 2004. Contributor to periodicals. **Address:** 824 S Marine Hills Way, Federal Way, WA 98003-3183, U.S.A.

NELSON, Steven D. American (born United States), b. 1962. **Genres:** Architecture, Art/Art History. **Career:** Wellesley College, instructor; Tufts University, lecturer and assistant professor, 1996-2000; University of California, associate professor of African and African American art history and department vice chair, 2000-. Writer, academic and art historian. **Publications:** (ed. with L. Gangitano) New Histories: The Institute of Contemporary Art, Boston, 1996; From Cameroon to Paris: Mousgoum Architecture in & Out of Africa, 2007. Contributor of articles to periodicals and journals. **Address:** Department of Art History, University of California, 100 Dodd Hall, 405 Hilgard Ave., Los Angeles, CA 90095-1417, U.S.A. **Online address:** nelsons@humnet.ucla.edu

NELSON, T. G. A. Australian/British (born England), b. 1940. **Genres:** Literary Criticism And History, Film, Theatre, Humor/Satire, History. **Career:** University of New England, associate professor of English, now retired. Writer. **Publications:** Comedy: An Introduction to Comedy in Literature, Drama and Cinema, 1990; Children, Parents and the Rise of the Novel, 1995. **Address:** Department of English, University of New England, Armidale, NW 2351, Australia. **Online address:** tnelson@metz.une.edu.au

NELSON, Theresa. American (born United States), b. 1948. **Genres:** Children's Fiction, Young Adult Fiction. **Career:** Theatre Under the Stars, teacher of creative dramatics, 1971-80; St. Mary's School, director, 1983-90. Freelance writer. **Publications:** The 25 Cent Miracle, 1986; Devil Storm, 1987; And One for All, 1989; The Beggars' Ride, 1992; Earthshine, 1994; The Empress of Elsewhere, 1998; Ruby Electric, 2003. **Address:** 3508 Woodcliff Rd., Sherman Oaks, CA 91403, U.S.A. **Online address:** tnelsonbooks@yahoo.com

NELSON, Tim Blake. American (born United States), b. 1964. **Genres:** Novels, Art/Art History. **Career:** Writer and director. **Publications:** The Grey Zone, 1996; Eye of God, 1997; Kansas, 1998; Anadarko, 1998; The Grey Zone: The Director's Notes and Screenplay, 2003. **Address:** United Talent Agency, 9560 Wilshire Blvd., 5th Fl., Beverly Hills, CA 90212, U.S.A.

NEMEC, James. *See* Obituaries.

NEPAULSINGH, Colbert I(vor). Trinidadian (born Trinidad and Tobago), b. 1943. **Genres:** Literary Criticism And History. **Career:** University of British Columbia, lecturer, 1968; Acadia University, lecturer, 1968-70; University at Albany, State University of New York, assistant professor, 1972-81, associate professor, 1981-87, professor of Latin American and Caribbean studies, 1987-, department head, 1986-88, Center for the Arts and Humanities, acting director, 1987-88, associate vice president for academic affairs, 1988-91, Department of Latin American and Caribbean Studies, chair; Westfield College, speaker, 1972; Southeastern Institute of Medieval and Renaissance Studies, 1978; Guggenheim fellow, 1981; University of California, speaker, 1982; University of Toronto, speaker, 1983; University of Massachusetts, speaker, 1983; Carleton University, speaker, 1984; University Commission for Affirmative Action, faculty, 1985-86; Western Michigan University, speaker, 1986; Universidad del Sagrado Corazon, speaker, 1994. Writer. **Publications:** (Ed. and intro.) Dezir a las Syete Virtudes y Otros Poemas, 1977; Towards a History of Literary Composition in Medieval Spain, 1986; Apples of Gold in Filigrees of Silver: Jewish Writing in the Eye of the Spanish Inquisition, 1995; (contrib.) Another Life: Fully Annotated, 2004. Contributor of articles to books and periodicals. **Address:** Department of Latin American and Caribbean Studies, University at Albany, State University of New York, 250b Social Science, 1400 Washington Ave., Albany, NY 12222, U.S.A. **Online address:** nepaulsi@albany.edu

NEPSTAD, Sharon Erickson. American (born United States), b. 1964. **Genres:** Theology/Religion, History. **Career:** Victim Offender Reconciliation Program, co-founder and president, 1992-96; Regis University, assistant professor of sociology, 1996-99, director of peace and justice studies, 1997-99; Duquesne University, assistant professor, associate professor of sociology, 1999-2005; University of Southern Maine, associate professor, professor of sociology and director of religious studies; University of New Mexico, director of religious studies, 2009-. Sociologist and writer. **Publications:** Convictions of the Soul: Religion, Culture, and Agency in the Central America Solidarity Movement, 2004; Religion and War Resistance in the Plowshares Movement, 2008. Contributor of articles to books and journals. **Address:** Department of Sociology, University of Southern Maine, 96 Falmouth St., PO Box 9300, Portland, ME 04104-9300, U.S.A. **Online address:** snepstad@usm.maine.edu

NERBURN, Kent Michael. American (born United States), b. 1946. **Genres:** Cultural/Ethnic Topics. **Career:** Minneapolis Institute of the Arts, instructor, 1985-86; Saint Paul Pioneer Press & Dispatch, visual arts critic, 1986-87; Robbinsdale school district, lecturer in art criticism, 1987-88; Arts magazine, sculpture writer, 1986-88; Northern Arts Reviewers, founder and visual arts critic, 1988; Minnesota Discipline-Based Art Education Consortium, art criticism specialist, 1988-; Bemidji State University, visiting professor, 1988. **Publications:** (Comp. with L.Mengelkoch) Native American Wisdom, 1991; (ed. and arranger) The Soul of an Indian and Other Writings from Ohiyesa, 1993; Letters to My Son: Reflections on Becoming a Man, 1993, as Letters to

My Son: A Father's Wisdom on Manhood, Women, Life and Love, 1994, 2nd ed., 1999; Neither Wolf nor Dog: On Forgotten Roads with an Indian Elder, 1994, rev. ed., 2002; (comp. and intro.) The Wisdom of the Great Chiefs: The Classic Speeches of Chief Red Jacket, Chief Joseph and Chief Seattle, 1994; Simple Truths: Clear & Gentle Guidance on the Big Issues of Life, 1996, new ed., 2005; A Haunting Reverence: Meditations on a Northern Land, 1996; Small Graces: The Quiet Gifts of Everyday Life, 1998; (comp. and ed.) Wisdom of the Native Americans, 1999; Make Me an Instrument of Your Peace: Living in the Spirit of the Prayer of Saint Francis, 1999; Calm Surrender: Walking the Hard Road of Forgiveness, 2000; Road Angels: Searching for Home on America's Coast of Dreams, 2001; Chief Joseph & the Flight of the Nez Perce: The Untold Story of an American Tragedy, 2005; Hidden Beauty of Everyday Life, 2006; Wolf at Twilight: An Indian Elder's Journey through a Land of Ghosts and Shadows, 2009; (contrib.) Views from the Reservation, 2010; Ordinary Sacred: The Simple Beauty of Everyday Life, 2012. Author of art criticism and reviews for arts magazines and papers. **Address:** c/o Author Mail, 7th Fl. HarperCollins Publishers, 10 E 53rd St., New York, MN 10022, U.S.A.

NERI, G. (Greg Neri). American (born United States) **Genres:** Novels, Young Adult Non-fiction, Young Adult Fiction. **Career:** AnimAction Inc., teacher of animation and storytelling and producer of films. Author, filmmaker, artist and digital media producer. **Publications:** FOR YOUNG ADULTS: Chess Rumble, 2007; Yummy: The Last Days of a Southside Shorty, 2009; Surf Mules, 2009; Caught, 2010. **Address:** c/o Edward Necarsulmer, McIntosh & Otis Inc., 353 Lexington Ave., New York, NY 10016-0941, U.S.A. **Online address:** greg@gregneri.com

NERI, Greg. *See* **NERI, G.**

NERICCIO, William Anthony. American (born United States), b. 1961. **Genres:** Novels, Humanities, Intellectual History, Language/Linguistics, Literary Criticism And History, Philosophy, Photography, Women's Studies And Issues, Graphic Novels, Illustrations, Technology, Theatre, Film, Advertising/Public Relations, Autobiography/Memoirs, Fash Ion/Costume, Humor/Satire, Cultural/Ethnic Topics. **Career:** San Diego State University, Department of English and Comparative Literature, Foundation for International Education, visiting senior lecturer in literature, 2001, 2003, 2005, 2007, professor, chair, 2007-09, The Master of Arts in Liberal Arts and Sciences (MALAS), director; Chicano/Chicana Studies (CCS), professor; Center for Latin American Studies (CLAS), professor; University of Connecticut, faculty; Cornell University, faculty. Writer. **Publications:** Tex[t]-Mex: Seductive Hallucinations of the Mexican in America, 2007; The Hurt Business: Oliver Mayer's Early Works Plus, 2008; (ed.) Homer from Salinas: John Steinbeck's Enduring Voice for California, 2009. Contributor to books. **Address:** Department of English & Comparative Literature, San Diego State University, 5500 Campanile Dr., San Diego, CA 92182-6020, U.S.A. **Online address:** bnericci@mail.sdsu.edu

NERIN, Bill. *See* **NERIN, William F.**

NERIN, William F. (Bill Nerin). American (born United States), b. 1926. **Genres:** Psychology, Human Relations/Parenting, Self Help. **Career:** Catholic priest, 1951-75; University of Oklahoma, Department of Human Relations, adjunct assistant professor, adjunct professor, 1977-; Family Reconstruction Training Institute, co-director. Writer and consultant. **Publications:** Family Reconstruction: A Long Day's Journey Into Light, 1986; You Can't Grow Up Till You Go Back Home: A Safe Journey to See Your Parents as Human, 1993; A Couple Faces Death: My Life After Anne, 2010. Contributor to journals. **Address:** Magic Mountain Publishing Co., PO Box 962, Gig Harbor, WA 98335, U.S.A. **Online address:** nerins@earthlink.net

NERLICH, Graham C. Australian (born Australia), b. 1929. **Genres:** Philosophy, Sciences, Humanities. **Career:** University of Adelaide, Hughes professor of philosophy, 1974, now professor emeritus, research fellow. Writer. **Publications:** The Shape of Space, 1976, 2nd ed., 1994; Values and Valuing: Speculations on the Ethical Life of Persons, 1989; What Spacetime Explains: Metaphysical Essays on Space and Time, 1994. **Address:** School of Humanities, University of Adelaide, Rm. 7 19, Napier Bldg., North Terr. Campus, Adelaide, SA 5005, Australia. **Online address:** graham.nerlich@adelaide.edu.au

NERSESIAN, R. L. *See* **NERSESIAN, Roy L.**

NERSESIAN, Roy L. (R. L. Nersesian). American (born United States) **Genres:** Technology, How-to Books, Education. **Career:** Zapata Naess Shipping, engineer officer, 1971-73; Manufacturers Hanover Trust, project analyst, 1973-76; Poten and Partners, internal advisor to chief lending officer, 1976-85, 1992-; Monmouth University, School of Business, associate professor of management, 1985-, operations management, 1985-; Columbia University, School of International and Public Affairs, adjunct, 1991-, Center for Energy, Marine Transportation and Public Policy, adjunct associate professor of international and public affairs, 2000-. Writer. **Publications:** Ships and Shipping: A Comprehensive Guide, 1981; Computer Simulation in Business Decision Making: A Guide for Managers, Planners and MIS Professionals, 1989; Corporate Planning, Human Behavior and Computer Simulation: Forecasting Business Cycles, 1990; Should Oil Companies Own Tankers?, 1991; Computer Simulation in Financial Risk Management: A Guide for Business Planners and Strategists, 1991; (with J.A. Helly) Global Management Accounting: A Guide for Executives of International Corporations, 1993; (with G.B. Swartz) Computer Simulation in Logistics: With Visual Basic Application, 1996; Trends and Tools for Operations Management: An Updated Guide for Executives and Managers, 2000; Corporate Financial Risk Management: A Computer-based Guide for Nonspecialists, 2004; Energy for the 21st Century: A Comprehensive Guide to Conventional and Alternative Sources, 2007, 2nd ed., 2010; Biofuels: Fuels of the Future?, 2008. **Address:** School of International & Public Affairs, Columbia University, 514 W 113th St., New York, NY 10025, U.S.A. **Online address:** rln39@columbia.edu

NERSESSIAN, V(rej) N. British/Iranian (born Iran), b. 1948. **Genres:** Area Studies, History, Social Commentary, Translations, Bibliography, Theology/Religion, Essays. **Career:** British Library, Christian Middle East Collections, curator in charge, 1976-; Armenian Orthodox Church, priest; Armenian Apostolic Church, senior priest. Writer. **Publications:** An Index of Articles on Armenian Studies in Western Journals, 1976; Catalogue of Early Armenian Books, 1512-1850, 1980; Armenian Illuminated Gospel-Books, 1987; Tondrakian Movement: Religious Movements in the Armenian Church From the Fourth to the Tenth Centuries, 1984; (comp.) Armenia, 1993; (comp.) A Bibliography of Articles on Armenian Studies in Western Journals, 1869-1995, 1997; (intro.) Armenian Sacred and Folk Music, 1998; (trans. and intro.) R. Atayan, The Armenian Neume System of Notation, 1999; The Bible in the Armenian Tradition, 2001; Treasures from the Ark: 1700 Years of Armenian Christian Art, 2001; (comp. and intro.) F.C. Conybeare, The Armenian Church, 2001; (T. Greenwood) Art of the Armenians, 2004. EDITOR: Essays on Armenian Music, 1978; Armenian Church Historical Studies, 1993. Contributor to books. **Address:** British Library, 96 Euston Rd., London, GL NW1 2DB, England. **Online address:** vred.nersessian@mail.bl.uk

NESBITT, John D. American (born United States), b. 1948. **Genres:** Novels, Novellas/Short Stories, Westerns/Adventure, Young Adult Fiction, Mystery/Crime/Suspense, Poetry, Adult Non-fiction, Writing/Journalism. **Career:** Eastern Wyoming College, instructor in English and Spanish, 1981-. Writer. **Publications:** SHORT STORIES: Adventures of the Ramrod Rider, 1991, rev. ed., 1999; One Foot in the Stirrup: Western Stories, 1995; I'll Tell You What: Fiction with Voice, 1996; Antelope Sky: Stories of the Modern West, 1997; Seasons in the Fields: Stories of a Golden West, 1998. OTHERS: (ed.) Wyoming Journeys, 1995; Blue Book of Basic Writing, 1996; Writing for Real, 2000; (ed.) Solid Sam, the Boy Road-Agent, 2001; (co-author) Deer Camp Tales & Recipes, 2008; Done By Friday, 2010; Understanding Fiction, 2011. NOVELS: One-Eyed Cowboy Wild, 1994; One Foot in the Stirrup, 1995, rev. ed., 1997; Twin Rivers, 1995, 2nd ed., 1996; Wild Rose of Ruby Canyon, 1997, 2nd ed., 1999; Black Diamond Rendezvous, 1998; Keep the Wind in Your Face, 1998; A Good Man to Have in Camp, 1999; Coyote Trail, 2000; North of Cheyenne, 2000; Man from Wolf River, 2001; For the Norden Boys, 2002; Black Hat Butte, 2003, 2nd ed., 2004; Red Wind Crossing, 2003; Robert Roripaugh, 2004; West of Rock River, 2004; Rancho Alegre, 2005; Shadows on the Plain, 2005; Lonesome Range, 2006; Raven Springs, 2007; Death at Dark Water, 2008; Poacher's Moon, 2008; Trouble at the Redstone, 2008; Stranger in Thunder Basin, 2009; Not a Rustler, 2010; Gather My Horses, 2011. Works appear in anthologies. Contributor of articles to periodicals. **Address:** Department of English, Eastern Wyoming College, 3200 W C St., Torrington, WY 82240, U.S.A. **Online address:** john.nesbitt@ewc.wy.edu

NESBITT, Marc. American (born United States) **Genres:** Novellas/Short Stories, Young Adult Fiction, Literary Criticism And History. **Career:** Video game producer and fiction writer. **Publications:** Gigantic: Stories, 2002.

Contributor to periodicals. **Address:** c/o Author Mail, Grove Press, Grove-Atlantic, 841 Broadway, 4th Fl., New York, NY 10003, U.S.A.

NESBO, Jo. Norwegian/Swedish (born Sweden), b. 1960. **Genres:** Criminology/True Crime, Mystery/Crime/Suspense. **Career:** Writer. **Publications:** (with E. Sobye) Stemmer fra Balkan (title means: "Figures in the Balkans"), 1999; (trans.) Jo Nesbo, Karusellmusikk: Noveller (title means: "Merry-Go-Round Music"), 2001; (with M. Kildahl, Per Petterson and Helge Fisknes) Rom for alle: det gjelder a fa lov til a vaere menneske, den man er, 2005; (trans.) Jo Nesbo, Det hvite hotellet (title means: "The White Hotel"), 2007; Doktor Proktors Prompepulvet (children's book),2007; trans. as Doctor Proctor's Fart Powder, 2010; HARRY HOLE CRIME NOVELS: (trans.) Jo Nesbo, Flaggermusmannen (title means: "The Bat Man"), 1997; (trans.) Jo Nesbo, Kakerlakkene (title means:"The Cockroaches"), 1998; Rodstrupe, 2000, trans. as The Redbreast, 2007; Marekors, 2003, trans. as The Devil's Star, 2010; Sorgenfri, translated by Don Bartlett as Nemesis, 2009; Frelseren, translated as The Redeemer, 2009; (trans.) Jo Nesbo, Snomannen (title means: "The Snowman"), 2010. **Address:** Salomonsson Agency, Stora Nygatan 20, Stockholm, 11127, Sweden.

NESS, Immanuel. American (born United States), b. 1958. **Genres:** Demography, History, Organized Labor, Politics/Government, Social Sciences, Urban Studies, Reference. **Career:** City University of New York, Brooklyn College, professor of political science, 1995-; Lower East Side Community Labor Association, founder; Working USA: The Journal of Labor and Society, editor. **Publications:** (With J.T. Marlin) Book of World City Rankings, 1986; Trade Unions and the Betrayal of the Unemployed, 1998; Encyclopedia of World Cities, 1999; (with J. Cement) Encyclopedia of Global Population and Demographics, 1999; Encyclopedia of Third Parties in America, 2000; Encyclopedia of Interest Groups and Lobbyists in the United States, 2000; Central Labor Councils and the Revival of American Unionism: Organizing for Justice in Our Communities, 2001; Encyclopedia of American Social Movements, 2004; Immigrants, Unions and the U.S. Labor Market, 2005; (with S. Jayaraman) New Urban Immigrant Workforce: Innovative Models for Labor Organizing, 2005; (ed. with M. Marable and J. Wilson) Race and Labor Matters in the New U.S. Economy, 2006; (ed. with A. Brenner and B. Day) Encylopedia of Strikes in American History, 2008; (ed.) International Encyclopedia of Revolution and Protest: 1500 to the Present, 2009; (ed. with A. Brenner and B. Day) Encyclopedia of Strikes in American History, 2009; (ed. with J.B. McDonald) Beyond the Capitalist Economy: Another World is Possible, 2010; (ed. with D. Azzellini) Ours to Manage and to Own: Worker Control from the Commune to the Present, 2011; Guest Workers and Resistance to U.S. Corporate Despotism, 2011; Encyclopedia of Global Human Migration, 4 vols., 2012. **Address:** Graduate Center for Worker Education, City University of New York, 3417 James Hall, New York, NY 10004, U.S.A. **Online address:** Iness@brooklyn.cuny.edu

NESSE, Randolph M. American (born United States), b. 1948. **Genres:** Botany, Medicine/Health, Psychology. **Career:** University of Michigan, Medical Center, resident in psychiatry, 1974-77, Department of Psychiatry, chief resident, 1976-77, instructor in psychiatry, 1977-79, assistant professor of psychiatry, 1979-85, director of resident and fellow education, 1981-86, associate professor of psychiatry, 1985-93, Anxiety Disorders Program, associate director, 1986-93, Division of Adult Ambulatory Psychiatry, director, 1990-92, professor of psychiatry, 1993-, associate chairman for education and academic affairs, 1993-96, professor of psychology, 2001-, Institute for Social Research, Survey Research Center, Evolution and Human Adaptation Program, director, 1996-, Research Center for Group Dynamics, faculty research associate, 1996-2001, senior research scientist, 2002-03, research professor, 2003-; Stanford University, Department of Psychiatry, visiting associate professor, 1993; University College London, Department of Anthropology, visiting professor, 2002-03; Wissenschaftskolleg zu Berlin, fellow, 2007-08. Writer. **Publications:** (With G.C. Williams) Why We Get Sick: The New Science of Darwinian Medicine, 1994 in UK as Evolution and Healing: The New Science of Darwinian Medicine, 1996; (ed.) Evolution and the Capacity for Commitment, 2001; (ed. with C.B. Wortman and D. Carr) Late Life Widowhood in the United States, 2005; (ed. with D. Carr and C.B. Wortman) Spousal Bereavement in Late Life, 2006; (ed. with L. Wolpert, D. Nutt and C.M. Pariante) Understanding Depression: A Translational Approach, 2009; Why Mental Disorders Exist: Evolutionary Foundations for Psychiatry, forthcoming. Contributor to journals and periodicals. **Address:** Department of Psychology, University of Michigan, 3018 East Hall, 530 Church St., Ann Arbor, MI 48109-1043, U.S.A. **Online address:** nesse@umich.edu

NESSET, Kirk. American (born United States), b. 1957. **Genres:** Novellas/Short Stories, Poetry, Translations, Essays, Adult Non-fiction. **Career:** University of California-Santa Barbara, teaching assistant of English, 1985-91; Whittier College, assistant professor of English, 1991-95; Allegheny College, assistant professor of English, 1995-99, associate professor of English and creative writing, 1999-2009, professor of English and creative writing, 2009-; Chautauqua Literary Institute, writer-in-residence. **Publications:** The Stories of Raymond Carver: A Critical Study, 1995; Paradise Road, 2007; Mr. Agreeable, 2009; (trans.) Alphabet of the World: Selected Works by Eugenio Montejo, 2010; Saint X, 2011. Contributor of stories, poems, articles to journals. **Address:** Department of English, Allegheny College, Oddfellows 206, 520 N Main St., PO Box 174, Meadville, PA 16335, U.S.A. **Online address:** knesset@allegheny.edu

NESTEL, Sheryl. Canadian (born Canada), b. 1950?. **Genres:** Social Sciences, History, Race Relations, Sociology, Women's Studies And Issues. **Career:** Humber College, School of Health Sciences, Women's College Hospital, Multidiscipline Childbirth Educators Certificate Program, program coordinator and instructor, 1993-98; University of Manitoba, Department of Community Health Sciences, postdoctoral fellow, 2000-01; University of Toronto, Ontario Institute for Studies in Education, instructor, 2000, 2003-05, assistant professor, 2001-03, postdoctoral fellow, 2003-04, Institute for Women's Studies and Gender Studies, research chair, 2001-; Mt. Sinai Hospital, Evaluation of Diversity Training for Physicians, principal investigator, 2005. Writer. **Publications:** Obstructed Labour: Race and Gender in the Re-emergence of Midwifery, 2006. Contributor to journals. **Address:** Department of Sociology and Equity Studies, Ontario Institute for Studies in Education, University of Toronto, Rm. 12-266, 252 Bloor St. W, Toronto, ON M5S 1V6, Canada. **Online address:** snestel@oise.utoronto.ca

NESTER, Daniel. American (born United States), b. 1968. **Genres:** Young Adult Non-fiction. **Career:** Painted Bride Quarterly, contributing editor and online archive project coordinator, 1992-2004; Pequod, assistant editor, 1995-96; Film & TV Today, editor and writer, 1995-99; New York University, administrative assistant of film and television, 1996-2000, adjunct writing professor, 2001-; Slack Inc., medical writer and correspondent, 1999-; La Petite Zine, editor-in-chief, 1999-2003; DUCKY, contributing editor, 2000; Slope Editions, board director, 2003-; McSweeney's, assistant web editor, 2003-; Unpleasant Event Schedule, editor, 2003-; TBWA/Chiat/Day, proofreader, 2004; The College of Saint Rose, assistant professor of English, 2005-, director, 2007-. **Publications:** God Save My Queen: A Tribute, 2003; God Save My Queen II: The Show Must Go On, 2004; The History of My World Tonight, 2006; How to be Inappropriate, 2009. Contributor of journals. Works appear in anthologies. **Address:** Department of English, The College of Saint Rose, 432 Western Ave., Albany, NY 12203, U.S.A. **Online address:** danielnester@gmail.com

NESTER, William R. American (born United States), b. 1956. **Genres:** Politics/Government. **Career:** Amvic Language School, teacher of English and French, 1980-81; Berkeley Language School, teacher of English and French, 1983; ABC Language School, teacher of English and French, 1983-84; University of London, School of Oriental and African Studies, lecturer in Far East politics, 1987-89; St. John's University, assistant professor, 1989-95, associate professor, 1995-96, professor of government and politics, 1996-; Teikyo University, lecturer; Villanova University, lecturer; West Chester University, lecturer; State University of New York College, lecturer; St. Francis College, lecturer; University of Nebraska, lecturer. Writer. **Publications:** Japan's Growing Predominance over East Asia and the World Economy, 1990; The Foundation of Japanese Power: Continuities, Changes, Challenges, 1990; Japanese Industrial Targeting: The Neomercantilist Path to Economic Superpower, 1991; Japan and the Third World: Patterns, Power, Prospects, 1992; European Power and the Japanese Challenge, 1993; American Power, the New World Order, and the Japanese Challenge, 1993; International Relations: Geopolitical and Geoeconomic Conflict and Cooperation, 1995; Ends of the Earth, 1995; Power across the Pacific: A Diplomatic History of American Relations with Japan, 1996; The War for America's Natural Resources, 1997; American Industrial Policy: Free or Managed Markets, 1997; A Short History of American Industrial Policies, 1998; From Mountain Man to Millionaire: The Bold and Dashing Life of Robert Campbell, 1999; The First Global War: Britain, France, and the Fate of North America, 1756-1775, 2000; Haughty Conquerors: Amherst and the Great Indian Uprising of 1763, 2000; International Relations: Politics and Economics in the 21st Century, 2000; Great Frontier War: Britain, France, and the Imperial Struggle for North

America, 1607-1755, 2000; The Arikara War: The First Plains Indian War, 1823, 2001; Frontier War for American Independence, 2004; Epic Battles for Ticonderoga, 1758, 2008; Globalization: A Short History of the Modern World, 2010; Globalization, Wealth, and Power in the Twenty-First Century, 2010; Globalization, War, and Peace in the Twenty-First Century, 2010; Revolutionary Years, 1775-1789: The Art of American Power During the Early Republic, 2011; Haunted Victory: The American Crusade to Destroy Saddam and Impose Democracy on Iraq, 2012. Contributor to books. **Address:** Department of Government and Politics, St. John's University, St.John Hall, Rm. 234, 8000 Utopia Pkwy., Jamaica, NY 11439, U.S.A. **Online address:** nesterw@stjohns.edu

NESTLER, Eric J. American (born United States), b. 1954. **Genres:** Medicine/Health, Psychiatry, Animals/Pets. **Career:** Yale University School of Medicine, Elizabeth Mears and House Jameson professor of psychiatry and pharmacology; University of Texas Southwestern Medical Center, Lou and Ellen McGinley distinguished chair in psychiatric research and professor; Parkland Memorial Hospital, chief of the psychiatry service; Mount School Sinai of Medicine, professor of pharmacology and systems therapeutics, 2008-, professor of psychiatry, 2008-, professor and chair of neuroscience, 2008-, Mount Sinai Friedman Brain Institute, director; Nestler Lab, principal investigator. Writer. **Publications:** (With P. Greengard) Protein Phosphorylation in the Nervous System, 1984; (with S.E. Hyman) The Molecular Foundations of Psychiatry, 1993; (ed. with D.S. Charney and B.S. Bunney) Neurobiology of Mental Illness, 1999; (with S.E. Hyman and R.C. Malenka) Molecular Neuropharmacology: A Foundation for Clinical Neuroscience, 2001, 2nd ed., 2008; Neurobiology of Mental Illness, 2004, (ed. with D.S. Charney) 3rd ed., 2009. **Address:** Mount Sinai School of Medicine, Icahn Medical Institute, Rm. 10-23, Fl. 10, 1425 Madison Ave., New York, NY 10029, U.S.A. **Online address:** eric.nestler@mssm.edu

NETANYAHU, Benjamin. (Binyamin Netanyahu). Israeli (born Israel), b. 1949. **Genres:** Area Studies, International Relations/Current Affairs, Politics/Government. **Career:** Boston Consulting Group, consultant, 1976-78; Jonathan Institute, executive director, 1978-80; Rim Industries Ltd., senior manager, 1980-82; Israeli Embassy, deputy chief of mission, 1982-84; United Nations, Israel's ambassador, 1984-88; Israeli Government, deputy minister of foreign affairs, 1988-91, prime minister, 1996-99, 2009-, foreign minister, 2002-03, minister of finance, 2003-05, health minister of Israel, pensioner affairs minister of Israel and economic strategy minister of Israel; Likud (political party), chairman, 1993-. Writer. **Publications:** (Ed.) International Terrorism, Challenge and Response: Proceedings of the Jerusalem Conference on International Terrorism, 1981; (ed.) Terrorism: How the West can Win, 1986; Place Among the Nations: Israel and the World, 1993; Fighting Terrorism: How Democracies can Defeat Domestic and International Terrorists, 1995; Durable Peace: Israel and Its Place Among the Nations, 2000; (foreword and afterword) Letters of Jonathan Netanyahu: The Commander of the Entebbe Rescue Force, 2001. AS BINYAMIN NETANYAHU: (contrib.) Self-Portrait of a Hero: The Letters of Jonathan Netanyahu, 1963-1976, 1980; (contrib.) Pis'ma Ĭoni: portret geroia, 1983; Maḳom Taḥat Ha-Shemesh: Maavaḳo Shel am Yiśrael Le-Atsmaut, Viṭtaḥon Ule-Shalom, 1995; Milḥamah Be-ṭeror: Ketsad Yavisu Ha-Mishṭarim Ha Demoḳraṭiyim et Ha-ṭerorHa-Meḳomi Ṿe-Et Ha-ṭeror Ha-Benle Tumi, 1996. Contributor to newspapers. **Address:** Prime Minister's Office, 3 Kaplan St., PO Box 187, Kiryat Ben-Gurion, Jerusalem, 91919, Israel. **Online address:** email@netanyahu.org

NETANYAHU, Binyamin. *See* **NETANYAHU, Benjamin.**

NETHERY, Mary. American (born United States) **Genres:** Children's Fiction. **Career:** Humboldt County Office of Education, staff development coordinator and editor, 1977-. **Publications:** Hannah and Jack, 1996; Orange Cat Goes to Market, 1997; Mary Veronica's Egg, 1999; (with K. Larson) Two Bobbies: A True Story of Hurricane Katrina, Friendship, and Survival, 2008; (with B. Dennis and K. Larson) Nubs: The True Story of A Mutt, a Marine and a Miracle, 2009; Famous Nini: A Mostly True Story of How a Plain White Cat Became a Star, 2010. Contributor to magazines. **Address:** Humboldt County Office of Education, 901 Myrtle Ave., Eureka, CA 95501, U.S.A. **Online address:** nethery@tidepool.com

NETIFNET, Dadisi Mwende. American (born United States), b. 1959. **Genres:** Poetry, Literary Criticism And History. **Career:** Writer. **Publications:** Poetry for Today's Young Black Revolutionary Minds, 1993; Had I Only Known (poetry collection), 1994. **Address:** 700 Seward, Ste. 306, Detroit, MI 48202, U.S.A.

NETZ, Reviel. American/Israeli (born Israel), b. 1968?. **Genres:** Classics. **Career:** Tel Aviv University, teaching assistant, 1991-92, visiting lecturer, 1996-97; Cambridge University, British council scholar, 1992-93, invited lecturer, 1995-97, affiliated lecturer, 1997-99; Massachusetts Institute of Technology, Dibner Institute for the History of Science and Technology, postdoctoral fellow, 1998-99; Stanford University, assistant professor in classics and philosophy, 1999-. Writer. **Publications:** Adayin ba-huc: shirim, 1998; The Shaping of Deduction in Greek Mathematics: A Study in Cognitive History, 1999; (ed. and trans.) Archimedes, The Works of Archimedes: Translated into English, Together with Eutocius' Commentaries, with Commentary, and Critical Edition of the Diagrams, 2004; The Transformation of Mathematics in the Early Mediterranean World: From Problems to Equations, 2004; Barbed Wire: An Ecology of Modernity, 2004; (with W. Noel) The Archimedes Codex: How a Medieval Prayer Book Is Revealing the True Genius of Antiquity's Greatest Scientist, 2007. **Address:** Department of Classics, Stanford University, Stanford, CA 94305, U.S.A. **Online address:** reviel.netz@stanford.edu

NEU, Jerome. American (born United States), b. 1947. **Genres:** Philosophy, Psychology, History. **Career:** University of California, professor of humanities, 1972-, Writer. **Publications:** Emotion, Thought and Therapy, 1977; (ed.) The Cambridge Companion to Freud, 1991; (comp.) Guia de Freud, 1996; A Tear Is an Intellectual Thing: The Meanings of Emotion, 2000; Sticks and Stones: The Philosophy of Insults, 2008; (ed.) In Memoriam Norman O. Brown, 2007; (ed.) The Challenge of Islam: The Prophetic Tradition, 2009. **Address:** Cowell College, University of California, A110 Cowell Annex, 1156 High St., Santa Cruz, CA 95064, U.S.A. **Online address:** neu@ucsc.edu

NEUBECK, Kenneth J. American (born United States) **Genres:** Sociology, Young Adult Non-fiction, Humanities, Business/Trade/Industry, Economics. **Career:** U.S. Office of Education, Office of Special Assistant to the Commissioner, research aide, 1964, Equal Educational Opportunities Program, research aide, 1964-66, Bureau of Research, research assistant, 1966-68; Washington University, instructor in sociology, 1968, lecturer, 1968-70; University of New Brunswick, lecturer, 1970-71; University of Connecticut, Department of Sociology, instructor, assistant professor, 1971-78, associate professor of sociology, 1978-2003, department associate head, 1986-87, human rights minor director, 2001-03, professor emeritus, 2003-. Writer. **Publications:** Corporate Response to Urban Crisis, 1974; Social Problems: A Critical Approach, 1979, (with M.A. Neubeck and D.S. Glasberg) 5th ed., 2007; (with D.S. Glasberg) Sociology: A Critical Approach, 1996; (with N.A. Cazenave) Welfare Racism: Playing the Race Card Against America's Poor, 2001; (with D.S. Glasberg) Sociology: Diversity, Conflict, and Change, 2005; When Welfare Disappears: The Case for Economic Human Rights, 2006. Contributor to books and periodicals. **Address:** Department of Sociology, University of Connecticut, 344 Mansfield Rd., Ste. 2068, Storrs, CT 06269-2068, U.S.A. **Online address:** kenneth.neubeck@uconn.edu

NEUBERGER, Julia. (Julia Babette Sarah Neuberger). British (born England), b. 1950. **Genres:** Young Adult Fiction, Human Relations/Parenting, Theology/Religion, Literary Criticism And History. **Career:** Rabbi of congregation, 1977-89; Leo Baeck College, lecturer and associate fellow, 1979-97; Newnham College, associate fellow, 1983-96; King's Fund Institute, visiting fellow, 1989-91, chief executive, 1997-2004; Harvard Medical School, visiting fellow, 1991-92; National Health Service Trust, chair, 1993-97; King's Fund College, associate fellow, 1993-97; University of Ulster, chancellor, 1994-2000; Royal College of Nursing, vice-president. Writer. **Publications:** Caring for Dying People of Different Faiths, 1986, 3rd ed., 2004; The Story of the Jews, 1986; Whatever's Happening to Women?, 1991; Ethics and Healthcare: Research Ethics Committees in the U.K., 1992; On Being Jewish, 1995; Good Death, 1996; Dying Well: A Guide to Enabling a Good Death, 1996, 2nd ed., 2004; Moral State We're In, 2005. EDITOR: Days of Decision, 4 vols., 1987; (with J. White) A Necessary End, 1991; (and intro.) Things that Matter: An Anthology of Women's Spiritual Poetry, 1992; (with B. New) Hidden Assets: Values and Decision-Making in the NHS, 2002; The Moral State We're In, 2005; Report on Volunteering, 2008. **Address:** The King's Fund, 11-13 Cavendish Sq., London, GL W1G 0AN, England. **Online address:** paolachurchill@hotmail.com

NEUBERGER, Julia Babette Sarah. *See* **NEUBERGER, Julia.**

NEUFELD, James (E.). Canadian (born Canada), b. 1944. **Genres:** Dance/Ballet, E-books, Art/Art History. **Career:** Trent University, professor of English literature, 1972-2009, Catharine Parr Traill College, principal, 1982-87, vice-president for university services, 1990-95, Department of English Literature, head, 2000-05, professor emeritus, 2009-. Writer. **Publications:** Power to Rise: The Story of the National Ballet of Canada, 1996. Contributor to periodicals. **Address:** Department of English Literature, Trent University, Catharine Parr Traill College, 119 Wallis Hall, 1600 W Bank Dr, Peterborough, ON K9J 7B8, Canada. **Online address:** jneufeld@trentu.ca

NEUFELD, Josh. American (born United States), b. 1967. **Genres:** Illustrations. **Career:** Writer and illustrator. **Publications:** SELF-ILLUSTRATED: A.D.: New Orleans after the Deluge (graphic book), 2009. **Address:** Brooklyn, NY , U.S.A. **Online address:** josh@joshcomix.com

NEUFELD, Michael J. American/Canadian (born Canada), b. 1951. **Genres:** Air/Space Topics, History, Business/Trade/Industry, Sciences. **Career:** Clarkson University, part-time instructor, 1983-84, part-time assistant professor, 1984-85; State University of New York, visiting assistant professor, 1985-86; Colgate University, visiting assistant professor, 1986-88; Smithsonian Institution, National Air and Space Museum, fellow, 1988-90, Aeronautics Division, curator, 1990-99, Space History Division, curator, 1999-, chair, 2007-11; Johns Hopkins University, senior lecturer, 2001. Writer. **Publications:** The Skilled Metalworkers of Nuremberg: Craft and Class in the Industrial Revolution, 1989; The Rocket and the Reich: Peenemüende and the Coming of the Ballistic Missile Era, 1995; (ed. and intro.) Planet Dora: A Memoir of the Holocaust and the Birth of the Space Age, 1997; (ed. with M. Berenbaum) The Bombing of Auschwitz: Should the Allies Have Attempted It?, 2000; Von Braun: Dreamer of Space, Engineer of War, 2007; (ed. with A.M. Spencer) Smithsonian National Air and Space Museum: An Autobiography, 2010. **Address:** Space History Division, National Air and Space Museum, Smithsonian Institution, MRC 311, PO Box 37012, Washington, DC 20013-7012, U.S.A. **Online address:** neufeldm@si.edu

NEUFELD, Thomas R. (Thomas R. Yoder Neufeld). Canadian (born Canada) **Genres:** Theology/Religion. **Career:** University of Waterloo, Conrad Grebel University College, faculty, 1983-, associate professor of religious studies, and peace and conflict studies, professor of religious studies, director of graduate theological studies. Writer. **Publications:** Guilt and Humanness: The Significance of Guilt for the Humanization of the Judicial-Correctional System, 1982; (as Thomas R. Yoder Neufeld) Put on the Armour of God: The Divine Warrior from Isaiah to Ephesians, 1997; (as Thomas R. Yoder Neufeld) Ephesians, 2001; (as Thomas R. Yoder Neufeld) Recovering Jesus: The Witness of the New Testament, 2007; (as Thomas R. Yoder Neufeld) Christus ist unser Friede: Die Kirche und ihr Ruf zu Wehrlosigkeit und Widerstand, 2007; (as Thomas R. Yoder Neufeld) Killing Enmity: Violence and the New Testament, 2011. Contributor to periodicals. **Address:** Conrad Grebel University College, University of Waterloo, 140 Westmount Rd. N, Waterloo, ON N2L 3G6, Canada. **Online address:** tyoderne@uwaterloo.ca

NEUFELD, Thomas R. Yoder. *See* **NEUFELD, Thomas R.**

NEUGEBOREN, Jay. American (born United States), b. 1938. **Genres:** Novels, Autobiography/Memoirs, Plays/Screenplays, Novellas/Short Stories, Psychology. **Career:** General Motors Corp., junior executive, 1960; teacher, 1961-66; Columbia University, preceptor, 1964-66; Stanford University, lecturer, 1966-67; freelance writer, 1967-69; Freiburg, faculty; State University of New York, assistant professor, 1969-70; University of Massachusetts, professor and resident writer, 1971-, professor emeritus, director of the graduate creative writing program, 1980-85. Writer. **Publications:** Big Man, 1966; Listen Ruben Fontanez, 1968; Corky's Brother, 1969; Parentheses: An Autobiographical Journey, 1970; Sam's Legacy, 1974; An Orphan's Tale, 1976; (ed.) The Story of Story Magazine, 1980; The Stolen Jew, 1981; Before My Life Began, 1985; Poli: A Mexican Boy in Early Texas, 1989; Imagining Robert: My Brother, Madness & Survival, 1997; Don't Worry About the Kids (short stories), 1997; Transforming Madness: New Lives for People Living With Mental Illness, 1999; Open Heart: A Patient's Story of Life-saving Medicine and Life-giving Friendship, 2003; (ed. and intro.) The Hillside Diary and Other Writings, 2004; News from the New American Diaspora and Other Tales of Exile, 2005; 1940, Two Dollar Radio, 2008; You are My Heart and Other Stories, 2011. Contributor to periodicals. **Address:** Department of English, University of Massachusetts, 170 Bartlett Hall, Amherst, MA 01003, U.S.A.

NEUHAUS, Denise. British (born England) **Genres:** Novels, Novellas/Short Stories, Young Adult Fiction. **Career:** Sacred Heart University, faculty of English. Writer. **Publications:** Best Short Stories, 1991; The Minerva Book of Short Stories, 1992; First Fictions Introduction, 1992; The Love of Women, 1993; The Christening, 1995. **Address:** c/o Vivien Green, Richard Scott Simon Ltd., 43 Doughty St., London, GL WC1N 2LF, England.

NEUHOUSER, Frederick. American (born United States), b. 1957. **Genres:** Philosophy, Social Commentary, inspirational/Motivational Literature. **Career:** Harvard University, assistant professor of philosophy, 1988-95; University of California, associate professor of philosophy, 1996-98; Cornell University, professor of philosophy, 1998-2003; Columbia University, Barnard College professor of philosophy and Viola Manderfeld professor of German, 2003-, department chair; J.W. Goethe-Universität, visiting professor of philosophy, 2006. Writer. **Publications:** Fichte's Theory of Subjectivity, 1990; Foundations of Hegel's Social Theory: Actualizing Freedom, 2000; (ed.) Foundations of Natural Right: According to the Principles of the Wissenschaftslehre, 2000; Rousseau's Theodicy Of Self-love: Evil, Rationality and the Drive For Recognition, 2008; Rousseau's Julie: Passion, Love and the Price of Virtue, forthcoming; Desire, Recognition and the Relation between Bondsman and Lord, forthcoming. **Address:** Department of Philosophy, Columbia University, 326D Milbank, 708 Philosophy Hall, 1150 Amsterdam Ave., PO Box 4971, New York, NY 10027, U.S.A. **Online address:** fneuhouser@barnard.edu

NEVAI, Lucia. American (born United States), b. 1945. **Genres:** Novels, Novellas/Short Stories, Young Adult Fiction. **Career:** Writer. **Publications:** Star Game, 1987; Normal, 1997; Seriously (novel), 2004; Salvation, 2008. Contributor to periodicals and magazines. Works appear in anthologies. **Address:** Shannon Literary Agency Inc., 20 W 22nd St., Ste. 1603, New York, NY 10010, U.S.A. **Online address:** lnevai@nycap.rr.com

NEVELS, Cynthia Skove. American (born United States), b. 1955. **Genres:** Young Adult Non-fiction. **Career:** Blinn College, history instructor. Writer. **Publications:** Lynching to Belong: Claiming Whiteness through Racial Violence (nonfiction), 2007. **Address:** Blinn College, 2423 Blinn Blvd., PO Box 6030, Bryan, TX 77805, U.S.A. **Online address:** cynthia.nevels@blinn.edu

NEVILLE, Helen F(rances Fowler). Armenian/Canadian (born Canada), b. 1943. **Genres:** Human Relations/Parenting. **Career:** Kaiser Permanente Hospital, Department of Pediatrics, pediatric advice nurse, 1976-96, Temperament Project, coordinator, 1990-. Teacher and writer. **Publications:** (With M. Halaby) No-Fault Parenting, 1984; (with J. Kristal and R. Renner) Teacher's Manual for Temperament-Based Parenting Classes, 1994; (with D. Clarke-Johnson) Temperament Tools: Working with Your Child's Inborn Traits, 1998; Is this a Phase?: Child Development & Parent Strategies, birth to 6 Years, 2007. **Address:** 5409 Thomas Ave., Oakland, CA 94618, U.S.A. **Online address:** helenwork@jong.com

NEVILLE, Katherine. American (born United States), b. 1945. **Genres:** Novels. **Career:** Algerian Government, international consultant, 1970; U.S. Department of Energy, staff; Bank of America, vice president, 1980. Novelist. **Publications:** NOVELS: The Eight, 1988; A Calculated Risk, 1992; The Magic Circle, 1998; The Fire, 2008. **Address:** c/o Author Mail, Ballantine Books, 1540 Broadway, 11th Fl., New York, NY 10036, U.S.A. **Online address:** katherineneville@katherineneville.com

NEVILLE, Leonora. American (born United States), b. 1970. **Genres:** History. **Career:** Catholic University of America, Department of History, assistant professor, 1998-2004, associate professor of history, 2004-10, Center for the Study of Early Christianity, associate director, 2004-; University of Wisconsin-Madison, John W. and Jeanne M. Rowe professor of Byzantine history, 2010, visiting associate. Writer. **Publications:** Authority in Byzantine Provincial Society, 950-1100, 2004; Heroes and Romans in Twelfth-Century Byzantium, forthcoming. Contributor to journals. **Address:** Department of History, University of Wisconsin-Madison, 3211 Mosse Humanities Bldg., 455 N Park St., Madison, WI 53706-1483, U.S.A. **Online address:** nevillel@cua.edu

NEVILLE, Robert. *See* **HUTSON, Shaun P.**

NEVILLE, Robert C(ummings). American (born United States), b. 1939. **Genres:** Philosophy, Theology/Religion. **Career:** Yale University, instructor,

1963-65; Wesleyan University, visiting instructor, 1964-65, assistant professor of philosophy, 1966-67; Fordham University, assistant professor, 1965-68, associate professor, 1968-71; Institute of Society, Ethics and the Life Sciences, associate for behavioral sciences, 1971-73; State University of New York, associate professor, 1971-74, professor, 1974-77; State University of New York at Stony Brook, professor of philosophy and religious studies, 1977-87, Humanities and Arts, dean, 1982-85; Stony Brook Center for Religious Studies, director, 1978-82; Boston University, professor of religion, philosophy and theology, 1987-, School of Theology, dean, 1988-2003, dean of Marsh chapel, 2003-06, Danielson Institute, executive director, 2005-09, chaplain, 2005-09; Association of United Methodist Theological Schools, president, 1998-99; American Academy of Religion, president; International Society for Chinese Philosophy, president; Metaphysical Society of America, president. Writer. **Publications:** God the Creator, 1968; The Cosmology of Freedom, 1974; Soldier, Sage, Saint, 1978; Creativity and God: A Challenge to Process Theology, 1980; Reconstruction of Thinking, 1981; The Tao and the Daimon, 1982; The Puritan Smile: A Look Toward Moral Reflection, 1987; Recovery of the Measure: Interpretation and Nature, 1989; Behind the Masks of God: An Essay Toward Comparative Theology, 1991; A Theology Primer, 1991; The Highroad around Modernism, 1992; Eternity and Time's Flow, 1993; Normative Cultures, 1995; The Truth of Broken Symbols, 1996; The God Who Beckons: Theology in the Form of Sermons, 1999; Boston Confucianism: Portable Tradition in the Late-Modern World, 2001; Symbols of Jesus: A Christology of Symbolic Engagement, 2001; Religion in Late Modernity, 2002; Preaching the Gospel without Easy Answers, 2005; On the Scope and Truth of Theology: Theology as Symbolic Engagement, 2006; Ritual and Deference: Extending Chinese Philosophy in a Comparative Context, 2008; Realism in Religion, 2009. EDITOR: (with W.G.G. Meister) Operating on the Mind, 1975; New Essays in Metaphysics, 1987; (with T.P. Kasulis) Recovery of Philosophy in America: Essays in Honor of John Edwin Smith, 1997; The Human Condition, 2001; Ultimate Realities, 2001; Religious Truth, 2001. **Address:** School of Theology, Boston University, STH 334, 145 Bay State Rd., Boston, MA 02215, U.S.A. **Online address:** rneville@bu.edu

NEVINS, Francis M(ichael). American (born United States), b. 1943. **Genres:** Novellas/Short Stories, Mystery/Crime/Suspense, Film, Literary Criticism And History, Law. **Career:** Clark Boardman Ltd., law publishers, assistant to the editor-in-chief, 1967; St. Peter's College, adjunct instructor in government, 1967; Middlesex County Legal Services Corp., staff attorney, 1970-71; St. Louis University, School of Law, assistant professor, 1971-75, associate professor, 1975-78, professor, 1978-2005, professor emeritus, 2005-; St. Louis Volunteer Lawyers for the Arts, board director, 1980-89. **Publications:** MYSTERY NOVELS: Publish and Perish, 1975; Corrupt and Ensnare, 1978; The 120-Hour Clock, 1986; The Ninety Million Dollar Mouse, 1987; Into the Stone River Twice, 1996; Beneficiaries' Requiem, 2000. EDITOR: The Mystery Writer's Art, 1970; Nightwebs: Stories by Cornell Woolrich, 1972; Multiplying Villainies: Selected Mystery Criticism of Anthony Boucher, 1973; Better Mousetraps: The Best Short Stories of John Lutz, 1988; Little Boxes of Bewilderment: Suspense Comedies by Jack Ritchie, 1989; The Night My Friend: Stories of Crime and Suspense by Edward D. Hoch, 1991; The Anthony Boucher Chronicles, 3 vols., 2001-02; (and intro.) Night and Fear: A Centenary Collection of Stories by Cornell Woolrich, 2004; Tonight, Somewhere in New York: The Last Stories and an Unfinished Novel by Cornell Woolrich, 2005; The Keeler Keyhole Collection, 2005; Love and Night: Unknown Stories by Cornell Woolrich, 2007. COLLECTIONS OF SHORT STORIES: Night of Silken Snowand Other Stories, 2001; Leap Day and Other Stories, 2003. EDITOR WITH M.H. GREENBERG: (J. Shine and W. Shine) The Good Old Stuff: Stories by John D. MacDonald, 1982; Exeunt Murderers: The Best Mystery Stories of Anthony Boucher, 1983; Buffet for Unwelcome Guests: The Best Short Mystery Stories of Christianna Brand, 1983; (J. Shine and W. Shine) More Good Old Stuff: Stories by John D. MacDonald, 1984; Carnival of Crime: The Best Mystery Stories of Fredric Brown, 1985; The Best of Ellery Queen, 1985; Leopold's Way: Detective Stories by Edward D. Hoch, 1985; Darkness at Dawn: Early Suspense Classics by Cornell Woolrich, 1985; Hitchcock in Prime Time, 1985; The Adventures of Henry Turnbuckle: Detective Comedies by Jack Ritchie, 1987; Mr. President-Private Eye, 1988; Death on Television: The Best of Henry Slesar's Alfred Hitchcock Stories, 1989. NONFICTION BOOKS: (co-author) Detectionary, 1971; Royal Bloodline: Ellery Queen, Author and Detective, 1974; (with R. Stanich) The Sound of Detection: Ellery Queen's Adventures in Radio, 1983, 2nd ed., 2002; Missouri Probate: Intestacy, Wills and Basic Administration, 1983; Cornell Woolrich: First You Dream, Then You Die, 1988; The Films of Hopalong Cassidy, 1988; Bar-20: The Life of Clarence E. Mulford, 1993; The Films of the Cisco Kid, 1997; Joseph H. Lewis: Overview, Interview and Filmography, 1998; Paul Landres: A Director's Stories, 2000; (with M. Grams, Jr.) The Sound of Detection: Ellery Queen's Adventures in Radio, 2nd ed. 2002; (with G.D. Keller) The Cisco Kid: American Hero, Hispanic Roots, 2008; Hopalong Cassidy: On the Page, On the Screen, 2008; Cornucopia of Crime, 2010; Night Forms, 2010. OTHERS: Cornell Woolrich: Mörkrets Poet, 1977; (comp.) Edward D. Hoch Bibliography, 1955-1991, 1991; Into the Same River Twice, 1996; Canine Crimes II, 1997. **Address:** School of Law, St. Louis University, 3700 Lindell Blvd., St. Louis, MO 63108, U.S.A. **Online address:** nevinsfm@slu.edu

NEVINS, Joseph. American (born United States), b. 1964. **Genres:** Adult Non-fiction. **Career:** Vassar College, Department Of Earth Science and Geography, associate professor of geography. Writer. **Publications:** Operation Gatekeeper: The Rise of the Illegal Alien and the Making of the U.S.-Mexico Boundary, 2002, 2nd ed. as Operation Gatekeeper and Beyond: The War on Illegals and the Remaking of the U.S.-Mexico Boundary, 2010; A Not-So-Distant Horror: Mass Violence in East Timor, 2005; (ed. with N.L. Peluso) Taking Southeast Asia to Market: Commodities, Nature, and People in the Neoliberal Age, 2008; Dying to Live: A Story of U.S. Immigration in an Age of Global Apartheid, 2008. **Address:** Department of Earth Science and Geography, Vassar College, 109 Ely Hall, 124 Raymond Ave., PO Box 66, Poughkeepsie, NY 12604-0735, U.S.A. **Online address:** jonevins@vassar.edu

NEVO, Joseph. Israeli (born Israel), b. 1942. **Genres:** Politics/Government, History, Adult Non-fiction. **Career:** Carleton University, visiting professor, 1981-82; York University, visiting professor, 1986-87; Princeton University, visiting professor, 1991; Meiji Gakuwin University, visiting professor; University of Haifa, professor of Middle East history, Center for Gulf Studies, senior fellow. Writer. **Publications:** NONFICTION: Ha-'Arvim: el mul ha-tenu'ah ha-tsiyonit yeah-yishuv ha-yehudi, 1946-1950: devarim be-yom 'iyun shenati rishon (745) shel hug ha-mizrah ha-tikhon be-vet ha-sefer le-hinukh shel ha-tenu'ah ha-kibutsit oranim, universittat hefah, 1987; (ed. with I. Pappe) Jordan in the Middle East: The Making of a Pivotal State, 1948-1988, 1994; King Abdallah and Palestine: A Territorial Ambition, 1996; Ha-Mizrah ha-tikhon be- yamenu, 2003; Neighbors Caught in a Maze: Israel-Jordan Relations before and after the Peace Treaty (in Hebrew), 2004; Jordan: In Search of an Identity (in Hebrew), 2005; King Hussein and the Evolution of Jordan's Perception of a Political Settlement with Israel, 1967-1988, 2006. Contributor of articles to books, journals and periodicals. **Address:** Department of Middle Eastern History, University of Haifa, Mount Carmel, Haifa, 31905, Israel. **Online address:** jnevo@research.haifa.ac.il

NEW, Melvyn. American (born United States), b. 1938. **Genres:** Literary Criticism And History. **Career:** University of Tennessee, assistant professor of English, 1962-63; Vanderbilt University, instructor in English, 1965-66; University of Florida, assistant professor, 1966-70, associate professor, 1970-76, professor of English, 1976-2007, chairperson of department, 1979-88, professor emeritus, 2007-. Writer. **Publications:** Laurence Sterne as Satirist: A Reading of Tristram Shandy, 1969; (with J. New): The Text of Tristram Shandy, 1978, vol. III (with R.A. Davies and W.G. Day): The Notes to Tristram Shandy, 1984, vol. IV-V The Sermons, 1996; Laurence Sterne and Tristram Shandy, 1985; Telling New Lies: Essays in Fiction, Past and Present, 1992; Tristram Shandy: A Book for Free Spirits, 1994. EDITOR: (with J. New) The Life and Opinions of Tristram Shandy, Gentleman: The Text, 1978; (with J. New) The Florida Edition of the Works of Laurence Sterne, 1978; The Works of Laurence Sterne, vol. I-II: Approaches to Teaching Sterne's Tristram Shandy, 1989; A New Casebook on Tristram Shandy, 1992; The Complete Novels and Selected Writings of Amy Levy, 1993; Critical Essays on Laurence Sterne, 1998; In Proximity: Emmanuel Levinas and the Eighteenth Century, 2001; (with W.G. Day) A Sentimental Journey Through France And Italy: And, Continuation Of The Bramine's Journal: The Text And Notes, 2002; (with E.D. Taylor) Mary Astell and John Norris: Letters Concerning the Love of God, 2004; (with P. Voogd) The Letters, vol. I: 1739-1764, 2009. Works represented in anthologies. Contributor of articles and reviews to literature journals. **Address:** Department of English, University of Florida, 4344 Turlington Hall, PO Box 117310, Gainesville, FL 32611, U.S.A. **Online address:** mnew@english.ufl.edu

NEW, William Herbert. Canadian (born Canada), b. 1938. **Genres:** Poetry, Literary Criticism And History. **Career:** University of British Columbia, faculty, 1965-, professor of English, 1975-2003, Brenda and David McLean chair of Canadian studies, 1995-97, University Killam professor, professor emeritus, 2003-; Canadian Literature, editor, 1977-95, editor emeritus, 2004-. **Publications:** Introduction to The Stone Angel, 1967; Malcolm Lowry, 1971; Articulating West (essays), 1972; Among Worlds, 1975; Malcolm Lowry: A Reference Guide, 1978; Dreams of Speech and Violence, 1987; A History of Canadian Literature, 1991, rev. ed., 2003; Land Sliding, 1997; Borderlands, 1998; Reading Mansfield and Metaphors of Form, 1999; Grandchild of Empire, 2003; (with M. Dvorak) Tropes and Territories, 2007; (co-author) From a Speaking Place, 2009. POETRY: Science Lessons, 1996; Raucous, 1999; Stone Rain, 2001; Riverbook and Ocean, 2002; Underwood Log, 2004; Touching Ecuador, 2006; Along a Snake Fence Riding, 2007; The Rope-maker's Tale, 2009. CHILDREN'S BOOKS: Vanilla Gorilla, 1998; Llamas in the Laundry, 2002; Dream Helmet, 2005; The Year I Was Grounded, 2008. **Address:** Department of English, University of British Columbia, 1873 E Mall, Vancouver, BC V6T 1Z1, Canada. **Online address:** wnew@interchange.ubc.ca

NEWCOMB, Robert. American (born United States), b. 1951?. **Genres:** Novels, Young Adult Fiction, Literary Criticism And History. **Career:** Writer and consultant. **Publications:** THE CHRONICLES OF BLOOD AND STONE SERIES: The Fifth Sorceress, 2002; The Gates of Dawn, 2003; The Scrolls of the Ancients, 2004. THE DESTINIES OF BLOOD AND STONE SERIES: Savage Messiah, 2006; A March Into Darkness, 2007; The Rise of the Blood Royal, 2008; The League of Whispers, forthcoming. Contributor to periodicals. **Address:** c/o Author Mail, Del Rey Publicity, Random House Publishing Group, 1745 Broadway, 18th Fl., New York, NY 10019, U.S.A.

NEWCOME, Robert. British (born England), b. 1955. **Genres:** Children's Fiction, Animals/Pets. **Career:** John Lewis Partnership, department manager, management trainer, 1983-96; ITMS, consultant, 1996-. Writer. **Publications:** (With Z. Newcome) Herbert the Harmonious Hippo, 1989; Little Lion, 1993. **Address:** 31 Ray Park Ave., Maidenhead, Maidenhead, BR SL6 8DZ, England.

NEWCOMER, James W. American (born United States), b. 1912. **Genres:** Poetry, Literary Criticism And History, Essays. **Career:** Teacher, 1934-37; Elgin Academy, Department of English, chair, 1937-42, assistant headmaster, 1938-42; Junior College, Department of English, chair, 1937-42, assistant headmaster, 1938-42; Hockaday Junior College, Department of English, chair, 1946-51, dean, 1947-51; Olivet College, dean and professor of English, 1952-60; Texas Woman's University, dean of faculty and dean of graduate studies, 1960-65; Texas Christian University, vice-chancellor for academic affairs, 1965-72, vice-chancellor emeritus, 1972-, Trustees' professor of English, 1972-82, University Press, director, 1966-82. Writer. **Publications:** (Contrib.) Why Teach?, 1957; (with E.J. McGrath and K.P. Bunnell) Liberal Education and Pharmacy, 1960; Maria Edgeworth, the Novelist, 1767-1849, a Bicentennial Study, 1967; (contrib.) A Part of Space: Ten Texas Writers, 1969; Maria Edgeworth, 1973; Celebration, For Orchestra, Chorus, and Solo Voices (poetry), 1973; (with R. Newcomer) The Merton Barn Poems, 1981; The Grand Duchy of Luxembourg: The Evolution of Nationhood, 963 A.D. to 1983, 1984; The Resonance of Grace (poetry), 1984; Lady Morgan the Novelist, 1990; The Nationhood of Luxembourg: Eight Essays on the Grand Duchy, 1998. Contributor to journals. **Address:** Texas Christian University, 2800 S University Dr., Fort Worth, TX 76129, U.S.A.

NEWCOMER, Robert (J.). American (born United States), b. 1943. **Genres:** Architecture, Gerontology/Senior Issues, Regional/Urban Planning, Medicine/Health, Social Work. **Career:** Gerontological Planning Associates, director of planning, 1972-73; County of San Diego, Human Resources Agency, Research and Evaluation Section, head, 1974-76; University of California, assistant research scientist, 1976-78, adjunct associate professor, 1979-84, associate professor, 1984-87, professor of social and behavioral sciences, 1987-, department head, 1996-99, 2001-04, chair, Disability Statistics Training Center, co-principal investigator and director, 1998-2003, Institute for Health & Aging, deputy director; Center for Personal Assistance Services, co-principal investigator, 2003-, associate director, director. Writer and consultant. **Publications:** (With L.E. Gelwicks) Planning Housing Environments for the Elderly, 1974; (co-author) Fiscal Austerity and Aging: Shifting Governmental Responsibility for the Elderly, 1983. EDITOR: (with T.O. Byerts and M.P. Lawton) Community Planning for an Aging Society, 1976; (co-ed.) Long Term Care of the Elderly: Public Policy Issues, 1985; (with M.P. Lawton and T.O. Byerts) Housing an Aging Society, 1986; (with A. Wilkinson) Managing Care and Quality Assurance: Integrating Acute and Chronic Care, 1996; (with A.E. Benjamin) Indicators of Chronic Health Conditions: Monitoring Community-Level Delivery Systems, 1997. Contributor to books and journals. **Address:** Department of Social and Behavioral Sciences, University of California, 3333 California St., Ste. LHts-455, San Francisco, CA 94143-0612, U.S.A. **Online address:** robert.newcomer@ucsf.edu

NEWELL, Clayton R. American (born United States), b. 1942. **Genres:** Military/Defense/Arms Control, History. **Career:** Independent military consultant, 1992-. Writer. **Publications:** The Framework of Operational Warfare, 1991; On Operational Art, 1994; Lee vs. McClellan: The First Campaign, 1996; Historical Dictionary of the Persian Gulf War, 1990-1991, 1998; The United States Army: A Historical Dictionary, 2002; General Thoughts: Seventy Years with the Army: Writings of General Frederick J. Kroesen, 2003; (ed. with R.K. Bluhm and J.A. White) U.S. Army Infantry, 2007; The A to Z of the Persian Gulf War: 1990-1991, 2007; (with C.R. Shrader) Of Duty Well and Faithfully Done: A History of the Regular Army in the Civil War, 2011. **Address:** PO Box 303, Galena, MD 21635, U.S.A. **Online address:** migreg@ix.netcom.com

NEWELL, Coke. American (born United States), b. 1958. **Genres:** Novels, Law, Travel/Exploration. **Career:** Melaleuca Inc., vice president; Church of Jesus Christ of Latter-day Saints, national media relations officer; Salt Lake Community College, professor; Edaphica L.L.C., founder. Writer. **Publications:** Dying Words: Colombian Journalists and the Cocaine Warlords, 1991; Cow Chips Aren't for Dippin': A Guide to Life in the New Wild West, 1996, rev. ed., 2009; Latter Days: A Guided Tour through Six Billion Years of Mormonism, 2000; Journey to Edaphica, 2006; On the Road to Heaven (novel), 2007. Contributor to periodicals. **Address:** Edaphica L.L.C., 138 Pebble Beach Dr., Tooele, UT 84074-9649, U.S.A. **Online address:** coke@edaphica.com

NEWELL, Dianne. Canadian (born Canada), b. 1943. **Genres:** History, Business/Trade/Industry, Economics. **Career:** University of British Columbia, professor of history, 1980-, Killam research fellow, 1990-91, associated faculty, associate dean of graduate studies, 1996-98, Peter Wall Institute for Advanced Studies, interim director, 2003-06, director, 2006-; Society for Industrial Archeology, journal editor. **Publications:** The Failure to Preserve the Queen City Hotel, Cumberland, Maryland (booklet), 1975; Technology on the Frontier: Mining in Old Ontario, 1986; (with R. Greenhill) Survivals: Aspects of Industrial Archeology in Ontario, 1989; Tangled Webs of History: Indians and the Law in Canada's Pacific Coast Fisheries, 1993. EDITOR: Development of the Pacific Salmon-Canning Industry: A Grown Man's Game, 1989; (with R.E Ommer) Fishing Places, Fishing People: Traditions and Issues in Canadian Small-Scale Fisheries, 1999. **Address:** Peter Wall Institute for Advanced Studies, University of British Columbia, Rm. 1107 Buchanan Twr., 1873 E Mall, 6331 Crescent Rd., Vancouver, BC V6T 1Z2, Canada. **Online address:** dianne.newell@ubc.ca

NEWELL, Waller R. Canadian (born Canada), b. 1952. **Genres:** Politics/Government, Military/Defense/Arms Control, Philosophy. **Career:** Yale University, instructor, 1979-80; University of Toronto, Victoria College, lecturer, 1981-82; University of Nebraska, assistant professor, 1982-87, associate professor, 1987-88; Carlton University, Department of Political Science, associate professor, 1988-95, professor, 1995-, Centre for Liberal Education and Public Affairs, co-director, 1994-; Books in Canada, contributing editor, 1995-98. **Publications:** (With P.C. Emberley) Bankrupt Education: The Decline of Liberal Education in Canada, 1994; Ruling Passion: The Erotics of Statecraft in Platonic Political Philosophy, 2000; The Search for the Manly Heart: Recovering the Positive Tradition of Manliness, 2000; What Is a Man? 3,000 Years of Wisdom on the Art of Manly Virtue, 2000, rev. ed., 2001; The Code of Man: Love, Courage, Pride, Family, Country, 2003; Understanding the Roots of Modern Terrorism: The French Revolution to Al Qaeda, 2008; The Soul of a Leader: Character, Conviction, and Ten Lessons in Political Greatness, 2009. **Address:** Ottawa, ON , Canada. **Online address:** wnewell@ccs.carleton.ca

NEWELL, William H. Australian (born Australia), b. 1922. **Genres:** Anthropology/Ethnology, Sociology, Autobiography/Memoirs. **Career:** Victoria University of Manchester, lecturer in social anthropology, 1950-53; University of Malaya, fellow in social research unit, 1953-57; Victoria University of Manchester, lecturer in social anthropology, 1957-60; Economic and Political Weekly, foreign correspondent, 1959-68; International Christian University, professor of sociology and head of department, 1960-69; Delhi School of Economics, professor, 1968; University of Sydney, associate professor of anthropology, 1969-89, now retired; University of Hong Kong, professor of sociology, 1971-72; Yu Shan College, Taiwan, professor of social anthropology, 1990-92. Writer. **Publications:** Scheduled Castes and Tribes of Himachel Pradesh, 1961; Treacherous River, 1962. EDITOR: (with K. Morioka) Sociology of Japanese Religion, 1968; Ancestors, 1974; Japan in Asia 1939-1942, 1980. **Address:** 14 Olive St., Ryde, NW 2112, Australia. **Online address:** william.newell@anthropology.usyd.edu.au

NEWEY, Katherine. (Mary Katherine Newey). British/Australian (born Australia), b. 1958. **Genres:** Theatre, Young Adult Non-fiction. **Career:** University of Wollongong, lecturer in English; Lancaster University, senior lecturer in theater studies; University of Birmingham, professor of drama and theater arts. Writer. **Publications:** NONFICTION: Mary Shelley's Frankenstein, 1993; Women's Theatre Writing in Victorian Britain, 2005. Contributor to books and journals. **Address:** Department of Drama and Theatre Arts, University of Birmingham, Edgbaston, Birmingham, WM B15 2TT, England. **Online address:** k.newey@bham.ac.uk

NEWEY, Mary Katherine. *See* **NEWEY, Katherine.**

NEWITZ, Annalee. American (born United States), b. 1969. **Genres:** Cultural/Ethnic Topics, Sciences, Social Sciences. **Career:** Freelance writer, 1992-; Bad Subjects, co-founder, 1992-2000; University of California, English and American Studies, instructor, 1994-98, lecturer, 1998-99; New York Press, west coast correspondent, 1997-99; San Francisco Bay Guardian, culture editor, 2000-04; Electronic Frontier Foundation, policy analyst, 2004-05; Computer Professionals for Social Responsibility, vice president, 2006-07, president, 2007-; io9, lead editor, 2007-. **Publications:** (Ed. with M. Wray) White Trash: Race and Class in America, 1997; (ed.) Bad Subjects Anthology, 1998; (ed. with C. Anders) She's Such a Geek! Women Write about Science, Technology, and Other Nerdy Stuff, 2006; Pretend We're Dead: Capitalist Monsters in American Pop Culture, 2006. Contributor to periodicals. **Address:** Computer Professionals for Social Responsibility, PO Box 20046, Stanford, CA 94309-0046, U.S.A. **Online address:** annalee@techsploitation.com

NEWKIRK, Ingrid E. American/British (born England), b. 1949. **Genres:** Children's Fiction, Animals/Pets. **Career:** Montgomery County, state law enforcement officer, 1970; Commission on Public Health, chief of animal disease control, 1976; People for the Ethical Treatment of Animals (PETA), co-founder and president, 1980; Foundation to Support Animal Protection, director. Writer. **Publications:** Save the Animals! 101 Easy Things You Can Do, foreword by Linda McCartney, 1990; Kids Can Save the Animals! 101 Easy Things to Do, 1991; Free the Animals! The Untold Story of the Animal Liberation Front and Its Founder, Valerie, 1992; The Compassionate Cook, or, "Please Don't Eat the Animals!" A Vegetarian Cookbook, 1993; 250 Things You Can Do to Make Your Cat Adore You, 1998; You Can Save the Animals: 251 Ways to Stop Thoughtless Cruelty, 1999; Free the Animals: The Amazing True Story of the Animal Liberation Front, 2000; (ed.) The PETA Celebrity Cookbook: Delicious Recipes from Your Favorite Stars, 2002; Making Kind Choices: Everyday Ways to Enhance Your Life through Earth-and Animal-Friendly Living, 2005; 50 Awesome Ways Kids Can Help Animals: Fun and Easy Ways to Be a Kind Kid, 2006; (as Ingrid E. Newkirk) Let's Have a Dog Party! 20 Tail-Wagging Celebrations to Share with Your Best Friend, 2007; The PETA Practical Guide to Animal Rights: Simple Acts of Kindness to Help Animals in Trouble, 2009; (with J. Ratcliffe) One Can Make a Difference: How Simple Actions Can Change the World, 2009. Contributor to periodicals. **Address:** People for the Ethical Treatment of Animals, 501 Front St., Norfolk, VA 23510, U.S.A. **Online address:** info@peta.org

NEWLAND, John. *See* **GRESHAM, Stephen.**

NEWLYN, Lucy. British/Ugandan (born Uganda), b. 1956. **Genres:** Poetry, Literary Criticism And History, Romance/Historical, Young Adult Fiction. **Career:** International Wordsworth Summer Conference, tutor and lecturer, 1982-86; Oxford University, Christ Church, lecturer, 1983-86, St. Edmund Hall, tutor in English, 1986-, professor of English, fellow. Writer. **Publications:** (Ed. with R. Gravil and N. Roe) Coleridge's Imagination: Essays in Memory of Pete Laver, 1985; Coleridge, Wordsworth and the Language of Allusion, 1986; Paradise Lost and the Romantic Reader, 1993; Reading, Writing and Romanticism: The Anxiety of Reception, 2000; Chatter of Choughs, 2001; (ed.) The Cambridge Companion to Coleridge, 2002; (ed. with G. Cuthbertson) Branch-lines: Edward Thomas and Contemporary Poetry, 2008. **Address:** St. Edmund Hall, Oxford University, Oxford, OX OX1 4AR, England. **Online address:** lucy.newlyn@seh.ox.ac.uk

NEWMAN, Andrea. British (born England), b. 1938. **Genres:** Novels, Novellas/Short Stories, Plays/Screenplays, Young Adult Non-fiction, Young Adult Fiction. **Career:** London Civil Service, clerical officer, 1960-62; teacher, 1962-64; writer, 1964-. **Publications:** A Share of the World, 1964; Mirage, 1965; The Cage, 1966; Three into Two Won't Go, 1967; Alexa, 1968 in US as The City Lover, 1969; A Bouquet of Barbed Wire, 1969; An Evil Streak, 1977; Another Bouquet, 1978; Mackenzie, 1980; A Sense of Guilt, 1988; A Gift of Poison, 1991; Risking It All, 1995. Works appear in anthologies. **Address:** c/o A.D. Peters, 10 Buckingham St., London, GL WC2, England.

NEWMAN, Andrew. British (born England), b. 1948. **Genres:** Philosophy. **Career:** University of Tulsa, assistant professor of philosophy, 1985-90; University of Nebraska assistant professor, 1990-91, associate professor of philosophy, 1991-, professor of philosophy and chair of the philosophy program. Writer. **Publications:** The Physical Basis of Predication, 1992; The Correspondence Theory of Truth: An Essay on the Metaphysics of Predication, 2002. Contributor of articles to journals. **Address:** Department of Philosophy and Religion, University of Nebraska, 205G Arts and Sciences Hall, Omaha, NE 68182-0265, U.S.A. **Online address:** andrewnewman@unomaha.edu

NEWMAN, Arnold. American (born United States), b. 1941. **Genres:** Environmental Sciences/Ecology, Sciences, Biology, Natural History. **Career:** International Society for the Preservation of the Tropical Rainforest, co-founder; Africa Tomorrow, co-founder; Cathedral Rainforest Science Preserve, and Fossil Ridge Paleontological Park, founder; Arlene Ween L.L.C., manager. Writer. **Publications:** The Tropical Rain Forest: The Lungs of the Planet, 1987; Tropical Rainforest: A World Survey of Our Most Valuable and Endangered Habitat with a Blueprint for Its Survival, 1990, rev. ed. as Tropical Rainforest: Our Most Valuable and Endangered Habitat with a Blueprint for its Survival into the Third Millennium, 2002. **Address:** 3931 Camino de la Cumbre, Sherman Oaks, CA 91423, U.S.A. **Online address:** forest@nwc.net

NEWMAN, Coleman J. *See* **NEWMAN, Jerry.**

NEWMAN, Dan. (Daniel G. Newman). American (born United States), b. 1969. **Genres:** Information Science/Computers, Technology. **Career:** Say I Can Inc., founder and president, 1995-; Waveside Publishing, president. Writer. **Publications:** Talk to Your Computer: Speech Recognition Made Easy, 1999; The Dragon NaturallySpeaking Guide: Speech Recognition Made Fast and Simple, 2000; (as Daniel Newman) Viavoice Guide: Speech Recognition Made Fast and Simple, 2000; The L&H VoiceXpress Guide. **Address:** Say I Can Inc., 1474 University Ave., Ste. 105, Berkeley, CA 94702, U.S.A. **Online address:** newman@sayican.com

NEWMAN, Daniel G. *See* **NEWMAN, Dan.**

NEWMAN, Felice. American (born United States) **Genres:** Sex, Social Sciences. **Career:** Cleis Press, founding co-publisher, 1980-. Writer and translator. **Publications:** (Ed.) Cameos: 12 Small Press Women Poets, 1978; (ed. with F. Delacoste) Fight Back!: Feminist Resistance to Male Violence, 1981; Another Love, 1991; The Whole Lesbian Sex Book: A Passionate Guide for All of Us, 1999, 2nd ed., 2004; (ed. with F. Delacoste) Best Sex Writing 2006, 2006. Contributor to periodicals. **Address:** Cleis Press, 2246 6th St., Berkeley, CA 94710, U.S.A. **Online address:** felice@felicenewman.com

NEWMAN, G(ordon) F. British (born England), b. 1946. **Genres:** Novels, Plays/Screenplays, Law, Young Adult Fiction. **Career:** One-Eyed Dog Ltd., founder, 1994. Film producer and screenwriter. **Publications:** NOVELS: Sir, You Bastard, 1970; Billy: A Family Tragedy, 1972; The Player and the Guest, 1972; You Nice Bastard, 1972; The Split, 1972; Three Professional Ladies, 1973; You Flash Bastard, 1974; The Streetfighter, 1975; A Detective's Tale, 1977; The Guvnor, 1977 in US as Trade-Off, 1979; The List, 1979; The Obsession, 1980; Charlie and Joanna, 1981; The Men with the Guns, 1982; Law and Order, 1983; The Nation's Health, 1984; An Honourable Trade, 1984; Set a Thief, 1986; The Testing Ground, 1987; Trading the Future, 1991; Circle if Poison, 1993; Circle of Poison, 1995; Crime and Punishment, 2009; The Exorcist, 2010. Contributor to periodicals. **Address:** Kempley House, Kempley, GC GL18 2BS, England. **Online address:** mail@gfnewman.com

NEWMAN, Isadore. American (born United States), b. 1942. **Genres:** Mathematics/Statistics, Writing/Journalism, Social Sciences. **Career:** SUMMA Health System, Cardiovascular Health and Rehabilitation Institute, scientific director; University of Akron, distinguished professor of research methodology, 1971-, now distinguished professor emeritus of education, distinguished Harrington professor, 1995-97, Institute for Life-Span Development and Gerontology, associate director, 1980-, fellow; Northeastern Ohio University College of Medicine, Office of Geriatric Medicine, research professor, 1982-84, Department of Psychiatry, adjunct professor, 1990-; Evaluation and Research Associates Inc., president; Journal of Educational Research, research methodology section editor; Ohio Journal of Science, editor; Florida International University, College of Education, director of research and graduate studies. Psychologist. **Publications:** (Co-author) An Introduction to the Basic Concepts of Measurement and Evaluation, 1973; (with J. Fraas) Statistics for Beginners, 1979; (co-author) Rx for Writing a Behavioral Dissertation and Thesis, 1979; (with C. Benz) Multiple Linear Regression, 1983; (with C. Newman) Conceptual Statistics for Beginners, 2nd ed., 1994, (co-author) 3rd ed., 2006; (with K. McNeil and F.J. Kelly) Testing Research Hypotheses with the General Linear Model, 1996; (co-author) Theses and Dissertations: A Guide to Writing in the Social and Physical Sciences, 1997; (with C.R. Benz) Qualitative-Quantitative Research Methodology: Exploring the Interactive Continuum, 1998; (with K. McNeil) Conducting Survey Research in the Social Sciences, 1998; (with K. McNeil and J. Steinhauser) How to be Involved in Program Evaluation: What Every Administrator Needs to Know, 2005; (with C.S. Ridenour) Mixed Methods Research: Exploring the Interactive Continuum, 2008. Contributor to books and journals. **Address:** Institute for Life-Span Development and, Gerontology, University of Akron, College of Arts and Sciences Bldg., Ste. 340, Akron, OH 44325-4307, U.S.A. **Online address:** inewman@uakron.edu

NEWMAN, James L. American (born United States), b. 1939. **Genres:** Geography, Area Studies, Food And Wine, Travel/Exploration. **Career:** Syracuse University, assistant professor, 1967-73, associate professor, 1973-82, professor of geography, 1982-2005, professor emeritus of geography, 2005-. Writer. **Publications:** Ecological Basis for Subsistence Change Among the Sandawe of Tanzania, 1970; (with G. Matzke) Population: Patterns, Dynamics and Prospects, 1984; The Peopling of Africa: A Geographical Interpretation, 1995; Imperial Footprints: Henry Morton Stanley's African Journeys, 2004; (with M.J. Bennett and J.C. Howe) Current Critical Issues in Environmental Law, 2008; Paths Without Glory: Richard Francis Burton in Africa, 2010. EDITOR: Environmental Evaluation and Risk Adjustment in Eastern Africa, 1969; (with C.G. Knight) Contemporary Africa: Geography and Change, 1974; Drought, Famine, and Population Movements in Africa, 1975; (with D. Griffith) Eliminating Hunger in Africa: Technical and Human Perspectives, 1994. Contributor to books and periodicals. **Address:** Department of Geography, Syracuse University, 144 Eggers Hall, Syracuse, NY 13244-1020, U.S.A. **Online address:** jlnewman@maxwell.syr.edu

NEWMAN, Jerry. (Coleman J. Newman). Canadian (born Canada), b. 1935. **Genres:** Novels, Poetry, Children's Fiction. **Career:** Sir George Williams University, lecturer in English, 1960-66, assistant professor of English, 1971-72; McGill University, assistant professor of English, 1966-71; University of British Columbia, assistant professor, associate professor of theatre, film and creative writing, 1971-2000, associate professor emeritus of theatre, film and creative writing, 2000-. Writer. **Publications:** We Always Take Care of Our Own, 1965; A Russian Novel, 1973; Sudden Proclamations: Poems, 1992; Green Earrings and a Felt Hat, 1993. Contributor of articles to journals and periodicals. **Address:** Creative Writing Program, University of British Columbia, Rm. E462, Buchanan, 1866 Main Mall, Vancouver, BC V6T 1Z1, Canada.

NEWMAN, Katherine S. American (born United States), b. 1953?. **Genres:** Economics, Law, Social Sciences, Politics/Government. **Career:** University of California-Berkeley, School of Law, Jurisprudence and Social Policy Program, lecturer, 1979-81; Columbia University, assistant professor, associate professor of anthropology, 1981-92, professor of anthropology, 1992-96, Faculty of the Arts and Sciences, chair, 1993-94; Harvard University, Kennedy School of Government, professor of public policy and Ford Foundation professor of urban studies, 1996-99, Malcolm Wiener professor of urban studies, 1999-2004, Doctoral Programs in Government, Sociology and Social Policy, chair, 1998-2004, Radcliffe Institute for Advanced Study, dean of social science, 2001-04; University of California-Irvine, chancellor's distinguished fellow, 2002; Princeton University, professor of sociology and public affairs, 2004-05, Malcolm Stevenson Forbes '41 professor of sociology and public affairs, 2005-, Institute for International and Regional Studies, director, 2007-, Joint Doctoral Program in Social Policy, Sociology, Politics and Psychology, chair, 2007-; Johns Hopkins University, Zanvyl Krieger School of Arts and Sciences, James B. Knapp dean, 2010-. Writer. **Publications:** Law and Economic Organization: A Comparative Study of Preindustrial Societies, 1983; Falling from Grace: The Experience of Downward Mobility in the American Middle Class, 1988, 2nd ed. as Falling From Grace: Downward Mobility in the Age of Affluence, 1999; Declining Fortunes: The Withering of the American Dream, 1993; No Shame in My Game: The Working Poor in the Inner City, 1999; (with M.M. Chin) High Stakes: Time Poverty, Testing, and the Children of the Working Poor, 2002; A Different Shade of Gray: Mid-Life and Beyond in the Inner City, 2003; (co-author) Rampage: The Social Roots of School Shootings, 2004; Chutes and Ladders: Navigating the Low-wage Labor Market, 2006; (with V.T. Chen) The Missing Class: Portraits of the Near Poor in America, 2007; (ed. with S. Thorat) Labor Market Discrimination and Urban Sector, 2007; (ed.) Laid Off, Laid Low: Political and Economic Consequences of Employment Insecurity, 2008; (ed. with M.A. Centeno) Discrimination in an Unequal World, 2009; (with S.S. Jodhka) In the Name of Gobalization, 2009; (with E.S. Jacobs) Who Cares?: Public Ambivalence and Government Activism from the New Deal to the Second Gilded Age, 2010; (ed. with P. Attewell) Growing Gaps: Educational Inequality Around the World, 2010; (ed. with S. Thorat) Blocked by Caste, 2010; (with R.L. O'Brien) Taxing the Poor: Doing Damage to the Truly Disadvantaged, 2011; The Accordion Family: How Globalization Reshapes the Private World, forthcoming. Contributor to periodicals. **Address:** Zanvyl Krieger School of Arts and Sciences, Johns Hopkins University, 237 Mergenthaler, 3400 N Charles St., Baltimore, MD 21218-2608, U.S.A. **Online address:** knewman@jhu.edu

NEWMAN, Rick. American (born United States), b. 1965?. **Genres:** History, Military/Defense/Arms Control, Politics/Government. **Career:** U.S. News & World Report, chief Pentagon correspondent, 1995-2001, chief business correspondent. Writer. **Publications:** (With D. Shepperd) Bury Us Upside Down: The Misty Pilots and the Secret Battle for the Ho Chi Minh Trail, 2006; (with P. Creed) Firefight: Inside the Battle to Save the Pentagon on 9/11, 2008. Contributor to periodicals. **Address:** U.S. News & World Report, 1050 Thomas Jefferson St. NW, Washington, DC 20007-3837, U.S.A.

NEWMAN, Sharan (Hill). American (born United States), b. 1949. **Genres:** Mystery/Crime/Suspense, Romance/Historical, Science Fiction/Fantasy, History. **Career:** Temple University, instructor in English, 1976; Oxford College, instructor in English, 1977-79. Writer. **Publications:** The Daga's Harp, 1977; Guinevere, 1981; The Chessboard Queen, 1983; Guinevere Evermore, 1985; Death Comes as Epiphany, 1993; The Devil's Door, 1994; The Wandering Arm, 1995; Strong as Death, 1996; Cursed in the Blood, 1998; The Difficult Saint, 1999; To Wear the White Cloak, 2000; Heresy, 2002; The Outcast Dove, 2003; The Witch in the Well, 2004; The Real History behind the Da Vinci Code, 2005; The Real History Behind the Templars, 2007; The Shanghai Tunnel, 2008; The Real History of the End of the World, 2010. **Address:** 18645 SW Farmington Rd., Ste. 255, Aloha, OR 97007, U.S.A. **Online address:** sharannewman@sharannewman.com

NEWMAN, Stephen L. American (born United States), b. 1952. **Genres:** Politics/Government. **Career:** Institute for Humane Studies, visiting fellow, 1978-79; Ripon College, Law and Society Program, director, 1982-85, Department of Politics and Government, director, 1980-85, instructor, 1980-82, acting chair, 1982-83, assistant professor, 1982-85, chairman of department, 1982-83; York University, Department of Political Science, assistant professor, 1985-87, associate professor political science, 1987-, director of undergraduate studies, 1988-92, chair, 1997-2001, professor of political science. Writer. **Publications:** Liberalism at Wit's End: The Libertarian Revolt against the Modern State, 1984; (ed.) Constitutional Politics in Canada and the United States, 2004. Contributor to periodicals. **Address:** Department of Political Science, York University, 4700 Keele St., Toronto, ON M3J 1P3, Canada. **Online address:** snewman@yorku.ca

NEWMAN, Susan. American (born United States) **Genres:** Psychology, Human Relations/Parenting, Social Sciences, How-to Books. **Career:** Rutgers University, part-time lecturer. Social psychologist, host and writer. **Publications:** Memorable Birthdays, 1980; Never Say Yes to a Stranger: What Your Child Must Know to Stay Safe, 1985; You Can Say No To a Drink or a Drug, 1986; It Won't Happen to Me, 1987; Parenting An Only Child: The Joys and Challenges of Raising Your One and Only, 1990, rev. ed., 2001;

Don't be S.A.D.: A Teenage Guide to Handling Stress, Anxiety & Depression, 1991; Little Things Long Remembered: Making Your Children Feel Special Every Day, 1993; Let's Always-: Promises to Make Love Last, 1995; (with J.S. King) Getting Your Child Into College: What Parents Must Know, 1996; Little Things Mean a Lot: Creating Happy Memories with Your Grandchildren, 1996; Little Things Shared: Lasting Connections between Family and Friends, 1998; Nobody's Baby Now: Reinventing Your Adult Relationship with Your Mother and Father, 2003; The Book of NO: 250 Ways to Say It-and Mean It-and Stop People-Pleasing Forever, 2006; Under One Roof Again: All Grown Up and (Re)Learning to Live Together Happily, 2010; The Case for the Only Child: Your Essential Guide, 2011. Contributor to periodicals. **Address:** Carol Mann Agency, 55 5th Ave., New York, NY 10003, U.S.A. **Online address:** snewman9@optonline.net

NEWMAN, William R. American (born United States), b. 1955?. **Genres:** Sciences, Biography. **Career:** Indiana University, Department of History and Philosophy of Science, Ruth Halls professor of history and philosophy of science, faculty, 1996-. Writer. **Publications:** The Summa Perfectionis of Pseudo-Geber: A Critical Edition, Translation and Study, 1991; Gehennical Fire: The Lives of George Starkey, an American Alchemist in the Scientific Revolution, 1994; (ed. with A. Grafton) Secrets of Nature: Astrology and Alchemy in Early Modern Europe, 2001; (ed. with C. Luthy and J.E. Murdoch) Late Medieval and Early Modern Corpuscular Matter Theories, 2001; (with L.M. Principe) Alchemy Tried in the Fire: Starkey, Boyle and the Fate of Helmontian Chymistry, 2002; Promethean Ambitions: Alchemy and the Quest to Perfect Nature, 2004; (ed. with L.M. Principe) Alchemical Laboratory Notebooks and Correspondence, 2004; Atoms and Alchemy: Chymistry and the Experimental Origins of the Scientific Revolution, 2006; (ed. with E.D. Sylla) Evidence and Interpretation in Studies on Early Science and Medicine: Essays in Honor of John E. Murdoch, 2009. **Address:** Department of History and Philosophy of Science, Indiana University, 1011 E 3rd St., Goodbody Hall 130, Bloomington, IN 47405, U.S.A. **Online address:** wnewman@indiana.edu

NEWMARK, Leonard. American (born United States), b. 1929. **Genres:** Language/Linguistics, Reference. **Career:** Ohio State University, instructor in English, 1954-57, assistant professor of English, 1957-61, associate professor of linguistics, 1961-62; Indiana University, associate professor of linguistics, 1962-63; University of California, professor of linguistics, 1963-92, chair of department, 1963-72, professor emeritus, 1992-. Writer. **Publications:** Structural Grammar of Albanian, 1957; (with M. Bloomfield) A Linguistic Introduction to the History of English, 1963; (with J. Hinely and J. Mintz) Using American English, 1964; (co-author) Spoken Albanian, 1980, rev. ed., 1997; Standard Albanian: A Reference Grammar for Students, 1982; Oxford Albanian Dictionary, 1998; (ed.) Albanian-English Dictionary, 1998; (with V. Dervishi) Albanian Handbook: With English and Albanian Glossaries, 1999; (ed.) lbanian-English Dictionary: Fjalor shqip-anglisht, 2000. **Address:** University of California, 9500 Gilman Dr., La Jolla, CA 92093, U.S.A. **Online address:** ldnewmark@ucsd.edu

NEWPORT, Cris. *See* **DIMARCO, Cris K. A.**

NEWSHOLME, Christopher (Mansford). British (born England), b. 1920. **Genres:** Botany, Sciences, Homes/Gardens. **Career:** Veterinary surgeon, 1947-72. Writer. **Publications:** Willows: The Genus Salix, 1992; (contrib.) National Plant Collections Directory, 1993. **Address:** St. Mawgan, Beach Ln., Bromsberrow Heath, Ledbury, HF HR8 1PQ, England.

NEWTH, Mette. Norwegian (born Norway), b. 1942. **Genres:** Children's Fiction, Translations, Novels. **Career:** National College of Art and Design, principal, 1989-93; Norwegian Forum for Freedom of Expression, administrator, 1995-98; Oslo National College of Art, principal, 1999-2002. Illustrator and translator. **Publications:** JUVENILE FICTION: Little Viking, 1975; Lille Skrekk, 1975; Nora og ordene, 1975; Tiny Terror, 1975; Rat Trickery, 1979; (with P. Newth) Benjamins Borg, 1976; (with W. Kreye) Leseratte und die Wasserratte, 1978; (with P. Newth) Ball-sprett, 1980; (with P. Newth) Mammaen min er så høy som stjernene, 1980; (with P. Newth) Ibakgården til Rosa og Fred, 1983; Oppdagelsen: en fabel fra virkeligheten, 1984; (with P. Newth) Soldrengen, 1985; Bortførelesen: ungdomsroman, 1987, trans. as The Abduction, 1989; Vårfuglen, 1989; Gjennom steinen, 1990; Eldsalamanderen, 1994; Det mørke lyset, 1995, trans. as The Dark Light, 1998; Forandringen, 1998, trans. as The Transformation, 2000; Under huden, 1999; Arktis: Jordas Navle, 2007. Contributor to newspapers and magazines. **Address:** PO Box 22, Rykkinn, 1334, Norway. **Online address:** mette@newth.net

NEWTON, Diana. British (born England), b. 1953. **Genres:** Social Sciences, History. **Career:** University of Durham, research fellow; University of Teesside, research fellow, reader in early modern British history, Centre for Regional and Local Historical Research, chair, North East England History Institute, director, 2006-. Writer. **Publications:** Papists, Protestants and Puritans, 1559-1714, 1998; (with J. Lumby) The Grosvenors of Eaton: The Dukes of Westminster and Their Forebears, 2002; The Making of the Jacobean Regime: James VI and I and the Government of England, 1603-1605, 2005; North-East England, 1569-1625: Governance, Culture and Identity, 2006; (ed. with B. Lancaster and N. Vall) An Agenda for Regional History, 2007; (ed. with A.J. Pollard) A History of Newcastle before 1700, 2008; (ed. with D. Newton and A.J. Pollard) Newcastle and Gateshead Before 1700, 2009. Contributor to books and periodicals. **Address:** Department of History, University of Teesside, Rm. M4.16, Middlesbrough, TS1 3BA, England. **Online address:** d.newton@tees.ac.uk

NEWTON, Esther (Mary). American (born United States), b. 1940. **Genres:** Gay And Lesbian Issues. **Career:** City University of New York, Queens College, assistant professor of anthropology, 1968-71; Yale University, visiting professor, 1970; State University of New York, Purchase College, assistant professor, 1971-74, associate professor, 1974-92, professor of anthropology, 1992-2006, professor emerita of anthropology, 2006-, coordinator of women's studies program, 1984-85, 1986, Kempner distinguished research professor, 1992-, now Kempner distinguished research professor emeritus, Lesbian and Gay Studies Program, founder and co-chair; University of Amsterdam, visiting professor, 1993; University of Michigan, professor of American culture and women's studies and lecturer IV. Writer. **Publications:** Mother Camp: Female Impersonators in America, 1972; (with S. Walton) Womanfriends, 1976; Cherry Grove, Fire Island: Sixty Years in America's First Gay and Lesbian Town, 1993; Margaret Mead Made Me Gay: Personal Essays, Public Ideas, 2000; My Butch Career, forthcoming. Works appear in anthologies. Contributor to books and periodicals. **Address:** School of Natural and Social Sciences, Purchase College, State University of New York, 735 Anderson Hill Rd., Purchase, NY 10577-1402, U.S.A. **Online address:** enewt@umich.edu

NEWTON, Francis. *See* **HOBSBAWM, Eric (John Ernest).**

NEWTON, Kenneth. British/Scottish (born Scotland), b. 1940. **Genres:** Politics/Government, Regional/Urban Planning, Sociology, History, Economics. **Career:** University of Birmingham, lecturer in political sociology, 1965-74; Nuffield College, research fellow, 1974-78; University of Dundee, professor of political science, 1978-87; Essex University, Government Department, professor, 1987-2000; European Consortium for Political Research, executive director, 1989-2000; University of Southampton, professor of comparative politics, 2000-, now professor emeritus; Wissenschaftszentrum Berlin, visiting professor; Hertie School of Governance, visiting professor. Writer. **Publications:** (Ed. and contrib. with S. Abrams) Opportunities After O Level: A Guide for Students, Teachers and Parents to Education and Career Opportunities Beyond G.C.E.O-Level, 1965; Method of Dual Analysis in the Study of Social Movements, 1966; Anomie, Alienation, Competence and Marginality, 1966; City Politics in Britain and America, 1968; (with D.S. Morris) Occupational Composition of Party Groups on Birmingham Council, 1920-1966, 1969; (with D.S. Morris) Chairmen and Non-Chairmen of Birmingham Council, 1969; (with D.S. Morris) Ward Volatility and Social Class, 1969; The Sociology of British Communism, 1969; (with D.S. Morris) Profile of a Local Political Elite: Businessmen on Birmingham Council, 1920-1966, 1969; (with D.S. Morris) Onymous Empire: Voluntary Organisations in Birmingham Politics, 1970; (with D.S. Morris) Turnout in Local Elections: Birmingham, 1945-1969, 1970; Community Decision-Makers and Community Decision-Making in England and the United States, 1970; Roles of Elected Representatives in Local Politics, 1971; (with P. Davis) Aggregate Data Analysis of Party Voting in Local Elections, 1971; Aggregate Data Analysis of Turnout in Local Elections, 1971; (with P. Davis) Social and Political Patterns of Immigrant Areas, 1971; Links Between Elite and Non-Elite in a Local Political System, 1972; (with D.S. Morris) Voluntary Organisations in Community Politics, 1973; Second City Politics: Democratic Processes and Decision-Making in Birmingham, 1976; Is Small Really so Beautiful? Is Big Really so Ugly?, 1978; Balancing the Books: Financial Problems of Local Government in West Europe, 1980; (ed.) Urban Political Economy, 1981; (with L.J. Sharpe) Does Politics Matter?: The Determinants of Public Policy, 1984; (with T. Karran) Politics of Local Expenditure, 1985; (with J-E Lane and D. McKay) Political Data Handbook: OECD Countries, 1991, 2nd ed., 1997; (with M. Kaase) Beliefs in Government, 1995, 3rd ed., 2004; The Politics of the New Europe, 1997, 2nd ed., 2001; (co-author) The New British Politics, 3rd ed., 2003; (with J.W.V. Deth) Foundations of Comparative Politics: Democracies of the Modern World, 2005, 2nd ed., 2010; (with S. Zmerli and J.R. Montero) Trust in People, Confidence in Political Institutions and Satisfaction with Democracy Citizenship and Involvement in European Democracies, 2007; (contrib.) The Wit and Humour of Political Science, 2010; (ed. with B. Geissel) Evaluating Democratic Innovations: Curing the Democratic Malaise?, 2011. FORTHCOMING: The Origins of Social and Political Trust in Contemporary Society; Patterns of Social and Political Participation in Western Societies; The Impact of the Mass Media on Government and Politics in Western Democracies. **Address:** School of Social Sciences, University of Southampton, University Rd., Highfield, Southampton, HM SO17 1BJ, England. **Online address:** k.newton@soton.ac.uk

NEWTON, Lionel. American (born United States), b. 1960?. **Genres:** Novels, Young Adult Fiction, Human Relations/Parenting. **Career:** Writer. **Publications:** Getting Right with God: A Novel, 1994; Things to Be Lost, 1995. **Address:** Dutton/Signet, 375 Hudson St., New York, NY 10014-3658, U.S.A.

NEWTON, Mark Charan. British (born England), b. 1981. **Genres:** Science Fiction/Fantasy, Novels. **Career:** Solaris Imprint, co-founder. Writer. **Publications:** The Reef, 2008. LEGENDS OF THE RED SUN FANTASY NOVELS: Nights of Villjamur, 2009; City of Ruin, 2010; The Book of Transformations, 2011. **Address:** Nottingham, NT , England. **Online address:** mark@marknewton.com

NEWTON, Merlin Owen. American (born United States), b. 1935. **Genres:** Law, History, Humanities. **Career:** Auburn University, instructor, 1965-70; Huntingdon College, instructor, associate professor, 1970-95, professor emeritus, 1995-; League of Women Voters, director. Writer. **Publications:** Armed with the Constitution: Jehovah's Witnesses in Alabama and the U.S. Supreme Court, 1939-1946, 1995. Contributor of articles to periodicals. **Address:** Huntingdon College, 1500 E Fairview Ave., Montgomery, AL 36106-2148, U.S.A.

NEWTON, Nerida. Australian (born Australia), b. 1972?. **Genres:** Novels, Young Adult Fiction. **Career:** University of Queensland, Australia, faculty in creative writing. Writer. **Publications:** The Lambing Flat, 2003; Death of a Whaler, 2006. **Address:** University Of Queensland Press, Staff House Rd., PO Box 6042, St Lucia, QL 4067, Australia. **Online address:** letterstonerida@neridanewton.com

NEWTON, Robert. Australian (born Australia), b. 1965?. **Genres:** Novels, Food And Wine, Young Adult Fiction. **Career:** Metropolitan Fire Brigade, firefighter, 1990-; Newton Brother's Rubbish Removal Co., co-founder. Author. **Publications:** NOVELS: My Name Is Will Thompson, 2001; The Khaki Kid, 2002; The Punjabi Pappadum, 2003; Saturday Morning Mozart and Burnt Toast, 2004; Runner, 2005; The Black Dog Gang, 2007. **Address:** Booked Out Speakers Agency, PO Box 580, South Yarra, VI 3141, Australia.

NEWTON, Roger G(erhard). American/German (born Germany), b. 1924. **Genres:** Physics, Mathematics/Statistics, Education. **Career:** Indiana University, Department of Physics, assistant professor, 1955-58, associate professor, 1958-60, professor, 1960-, chairman, 1973-80, distinguished professor, 1978-, Institute for Advanced Study, director, 1982-86, distinguished professor emeritus, 1995-; Journal of Mathematical Physics, editor-in-chief, 1992-2005; American Journal of Physics, associate editor; Inverse Problems, associate editor. **Publications:** (Trans. with J. Bernstein) R. von Mises, Positivism, 1951; The Complex J-Plane, 1964; Scattering Theory of Waves and Particles, 1966, 2nd ed., 2002; Inverse Schroedinger Scattering, 1989; What Makes Nature Tick?, 1993; The Truth of Science, 1997; Thinking about Physics, 2000; Quantum Physics, 2002; Galileo's Pendulum, 2004; From Clockwork to Crapshoot, 2007; How Physics Confronts Reality, 2009. **Address:** Department of Physics, Indiana University, Bloomington, IN 47405, U.S.A. **Online address:** newton@indiana.edu

NEWTON, Steven H. American (born United States) **Genres:** History, Military/Defense/Arms Control, Young Adult Non-fiction. **Career:** Delaware State University, professor of history; North and South Magazine, associate chair. Writer. **Publications:** NONFICTION: (ed.) German Battle Tactics on the Russian Front, 1941-1945, 1994; Retreat from Leningrad, Army Group North, 1944-1945, 1995; Joseph E. Johnston and the Defense of Richmond, 1998; Lost for the Cause: The Confederate Army in 1864, 2000; McPherson's Ridge: The First Battle for the High Ground, July 1, 1863, 2002; (trans. and ed.) Kursk: The German View: Eyewitness Reports of Operation Citadel by the German Commanders, 2002; (trans.) Panzer Operations: The Eastern Front Memoir of General Raus, 1941-1945, 2005; Hitler's Commander: Field Marshal Walther Model: Hitler's Favorite General, 2006. **Address:** Dept. of History Political Science & Philosophy, Delaware State University, Rm. 207, 1200 N DuPont Hwy., Dover, DE 19901, U.S.A. **Online address:** snewton@desu.edu

NEWTON, Suzanne. American (born United States), b. 1936. **Genres:** Children's Fiction, Young Adult Fiction, History. **Career:** Peace Jr. College for Women, writer-in-residence, 1974-75; Meredith College, writer-in-residence, 1982-; Aversboro Elementary School, writer-in-residence, 2004-. **Publications:** Purro and the Prattleberries, 1970; c/o Arnold's Corners, 1974; What Are You Up To, William Thomas, 1977; Reubella and the Old Focus Home, 1978; M. V. Sexton Speaking, 1981; I Will Call It Georgie's Blues, 1983; An End to Perfect, 1984; A Place Between, 1986; An End To Perfect, 1986; Where are You When I Need You?, 1991. **Address:** Aversboro Elementary School, 1605 Aversboro Rd., Garner, NC 27529, U.S.A.

NEWTON, Verne W. American (born United States), b. 1944. **Genres:** International Relations/Current Affairs, Biography, History. **Career:** Franklin D. Roosevelt Library, director, 1991-98; Marist College, James A. Cannavino Library, director. Writer. **Publications:** The Cambridge Spies: The Untold Story of Maclean, Philby and Burgess in America, 1991; (ed.) FDR and the Holocaust, 1996. **Address:** James A. Cannavino Library, Marist College, LB 244, 3399 North Rd., Poughkeepsie, NY 12601, U.S.A. **Online address:** verne.newton@marist.edu

NEY, Ronald E. (Ronald Ellroy Ney). American (born United States), b. 1936. **Genres:** Chemistry, Environmental Sciences/Ecology, Sciences, Education. **Career:** U.S. Department of Welfare, Food and Drug Administration, laboratory group leader and chemist, 1962-65; U.S. Department of Agriculture, Pesticide Registration Division, supervisory chemist, 1965-70; U.S. Environmental Protection Agency, Pesticide Registration Division, Efficacy and Ecological Effects Branch, section chief, 1970-78, Hazard Evaluation Division, Environmental Fate Branch, section chief, 1978-80, Hazard Evaluation Division, staff chemist, 1980-81, Office of Solid Waste, Land Disposal Branch, chemist adviser, 1981-86; realtor and chemical consultant, 1986-2001; Northern Virginia Community College, adjunct instructor, 1991-95. Writer. **Publications:** Where Did That Chemical Go?: A Practical Guide to Chemical Fate and Transport in the Environment, 1990; Your Guide to Safety, 1992; Fate and Transport of Organic Chemicals in the Environment: A Practical Guide, 1995, 3rd ed., 1998; Chemicals: What You Need to Know, 1996. Contributor to journals. **Address:** 5446 Sir Churchill Dr., Leesburg, FL 34748-7915, U.S.A.

NEY, Ronald Ellroy. *See* **NEY, Ronald E.**

NG, Fae Myenne. American (born United States), b. 1956. **Genres:** Novels. **Career:** University of California-Santa Cruz, writing lecturer; University of California-Berkeley, writing lecturer. Writer. **Publications:** Bone, 1993; Steer Toward Rock, 2008. Contributor to periodicals. **Address:** c/o Eric Ashworth, Candida Donadio and Associates, 231 W 22nd St., New York, NY 10011-2765, U.S.A. **Online address:** fmn@berkeley.edu

NG, Franklin. American (born United States), b. 1947?. **Genres:** Anthropology/Ethnology, Young Adult Non-fiction, History, Social Sciences. **Career:** California State University, Ethnic Studies Program, coordinator, 1975-78, Asian American Studies Program, coordinator, 1975-, Chinese Students' Club, advisor, 1975-81, Scion (Japanese American Students club), advisor, 1975-77, Department of Anthropology, assistant professor, professor of anthropology, 1978-; Amerasia Week, advisor, 1975-. Writer. **Publications:** Chinese American Struggle for Equality, 1992; (co-ed.) New Visions in Asian American Studies: Diversity, Community, Power, 1994; (ed. with J.D. Wilson) Asian American Encyclopedia, 1995; (ed. and intro.) Asian American Family Life and Community, 1998; (ed. and intro.) Asian American Interethnic Relations and Politics, 1998; (ed. and intro.) Asian American Issues Relating to Labor, Economics, and Socioeconomic Status, 1998; (ed. and intro.) Asian American Women and Gender, 1998; (ed. and intro.) History and Immigration of Asian Americans, 1998; (ed. and intro.) Adaptation, Acculturation, and

Transnational Ties Among Asian Americans, 1998; Taiwanese Americans, 1998; (ed.) Distinguished Asian Americans: A Biographical Dictionary, 1999; (ed. with L. Bankston) Racial and Ethnic Relations in America, 3 vols., 2000; (with M.Y. Danico) Asian American Issues, 2004. HOUGHTON-MIFFLIN SOCIAL STUDIES SERIES: (with B.J. Armento and G.B. Nash) From Sea to Shining Sea, 1999; (with B.J. Armento and G.B. Nash) Oh, California, 1999; (with B.J. Armento and G.B. Nash) American Will Be, 1999; (with B.J. Armento and G.B. Nash) A Message of Ancient Days, 1999; (with B.J. Armento and G.B. Nash) Across the Centuries, 1999; (with B.J. Armento and G.B. Nash) A More Perfect Union, 1999. Contributor of articles to periodicals. **Address:** Department of Anthropology, California State University, Rm. 389, Peters Business Bldg., 5245 N Backer Ave., PO Box 16, Fresno, CA 93740-8001, U.S.A. **Online address:** franklin_ng@csufresno.edu

NG, Man lun. Chinese (born China), b. 1946. **Genres:** Sex, Psychiatry. **Career:** Queen Mary Hospital, University Psychiatric Unit, medical officer, 1972-73, honorary consultant in psychiatry, 1981-; University of Hong Kong, lecturer, 1973-81, senior lecturer, 1981-93, reader, 1993-96, professor of psychiatry, 1996-; Government of Hong Kong, Supreme Court, medical inspector, 1985-; Hong Kong Sex Education Association, founder and president, 1985; Asian Federation for Sexology, founder and president, 1990-94, director, 1992-; Harmony House, director, 1994-; International Chinese Psychosomatic Medicine Journal, vice-chief editor, 1997-; Medical Council of Hong Kong, assessor, 1997-99; Teen AIDS, advisor, 1997-; HKU Family Institute, honorary professor and associate director. Writer. **Publications:** (Contrib.) The Mentally Ill and Society, 1987; (contrib.) China Review, 1992; (ed. with L.S. Lam) Sexuality in Asia, 1993; (ed. with E.J. Haberle) Sexual Behavior in Modern China: A Report on the Nationwide Survey of 20000 Men and Women, 1997. Contributor to journals. **Address:** University of Hong Kong, HKU Family instituite, 5/F Tsan Yuk Hospital, 30 Hospital Rd., Sai Ying Pun, 1, Hong Kong. **Online address:** hrmcnml@hkucc.hku.hk

NG, Mei. American (born United States), b. 1966?. **Genres:** Novels. **Career:** New York City Gay and Lesbian Anti-Violence Project, counselor. Writer. **Publications:** Eating Chinese Food Naked (novel), 1998. **Address:** Scribner Books, Simon & Schuster Inc., 1230 Ave. of the Americas, 13th Fl., New York, NY 10020-1513, U.S.A.

NGCOBO, Lauretta. British/South African (born South Africa), b. 1931?. **Genres:** Novels, Essays, History. **Career:** Novelist and educator. **Publications:** NOVELS: Cross of Gold, 1981; (ed.) Let It Be Told: Essays by Black Women in Britain, 1987; And They Didn't Die, 1991; Fikile Learns to Like Other People, 1993. **Address:** Macmillan Publishers Ltd., Brunel Rd., Houndmills, Basingstoke, HM RG21 6XS, England.

NGUGI, J(ames) T. *See* **NGUGI WA THIONG.**

NGUGI WA THIONG. Also writes as Ngũgĩ Wa Thiong'o, J(ames) T. Ngugi. American/Kenyan (born Kenya), b. 1938. **Genres:** Novels, Plays/Screenplays, Literary Criticism And History, Politics/Government, Cultural/Ethnic Topics. **Career:** Penpoint Journal, editor, 1963-64; teacher, 1964-70; Zuka Journal, editor, 1965-70; University of Nairobi, Department of Literature, lecturer in English literature, senior lecturer and chair, 1967-77; Makerere University, creative writing fellow, 1969-70; Northwestern University, visiting associate professor of English and African studies, 1970-71; Byreuth University, visiting professor, 1984; Yale University, visiting professor of English and comparative literature, 1989-92; New York University, professor of comparative literature and performance studies, 1999-2002; University of California, distinguished professor of English and comparative literature, International Center for Writing and Translation, director; Mutiiri, founder and editor, 1992-. **Publications:** The Black Hermit, 1963; River Between, 1965; This Time Tomorrow, 1970; Homecoming: Essays on African and Caribbean Literature, Culture and Politics, 1972; Secret Lives and Other Stories, 1972; (with M.G. Mugo) The Trial of Dedan Kimathi, 1976 as Mzalendo Kimathi, 1978; Petals of Blood, 1977; Mtawa Mweusi, 1978; Caitaani mũtharaba-inĩ, 1980, trans. as Devil on the Cross, 1983; Detained: A Writer's Prison Diary, 1981; Education for a National Culture, 1981; Writers in Politics: Essays, 1981, rev. ed., 1997; Njamba Nene na mbaathi i mathagu, 1982; (co-author and trans. with Ngugi wa Mirii) I Will Marry When I Want (play), 1982; Barrel of a Pen: Resistance to Repression in Neo-Colonial Kenya, 1983; Bathitoora ya Njamba Nene, 1984; Decolonizing the Mind: The Politics of Language in African Literature, 1986; Decolonising the Mind, 1986; Writing Against Neocolonialism, 1986; Matigari ma Njiruungi, 1986, trans. as Matigari, 1990; Njambas Nene no Chiubu King'angi'I, 1986; The First Walter Rodney Memorial Lecture, 1987; (contrib.) Mother, Sing for me, 1989; Njamba Nene and the Flying Bus, 1989; Njamba Nene's Pistol, 1989; Moving the Centre: The Struggle for Cultural Freedoms, 1992; Bhāshā, saṃskrti, aura rāshṭrīya asmitā, 1994; Ngugi wa Thiong'o: Texts and Contexts, 1995; Penpoints, Gunpoints and Dreams: Toward A Critical Theory of The Arts and The State In Africa, 1998; Mũrogi wa Kagogo, 2004; Ngugi wa Thiong'o Speaks, 2005; Wizard of the Crow, 2006; (with B. Head) To Stir the Heart, 2007; Something Torn and New: An African Renaissance, 2009; Remembering Africa, 2009; (intro.) A Fine Madness, 2010; Dreams in a Time of War: A Childhood Memoir, 2010; Globalectics, 2012. AS JAMES T. NGUGI: Grain of Wheat, 1967, rev. ed., 2012; Weep Not, Child, 1967. Works appear in anthologies. **Address:** Comparative Literature and English, University of California, 279 Humanities Instructional Bldg., PO Box 2651, Irvine, CA 92697-2651, U.S.A.

NGUYÊN, Kiên. American/Vietnamese (born Vietnam), b. 1967?. **Genres:** Adult Non-fiction, Ethics, Literary Criticism And History, Autobiography/Memoirs, Biography. **Career:** New York University College of Dentistry, clinical instructor in general dentistry and management science. Author and dentist. **Publications:** Sud-Vietnam depuis Dien-Bien-Phu, 1963; Escalade de la Guerre au Vietnam: Vers un Conflit Nucléaire Mondial?, 1965; Vietnam, 15 Years After the Liberation of Saigon, 1990; The Unwanted: A Memoir of Childhood, 2001; Chim Kháchkeìu: taìyp truyeiyn ngaĩn, 2002; TruyênNğn, 2002; The Tapestries: A Novel, 2002; Le Colonial: A Novel, 2004. Contributor to books and periodicals. **Address:** c/o Linda Biagi, Little, Brown & Co., 1271 Ave. of the Americas, New York, NY 10020-1300, U.S.A. **Online address:** spiritnyc@aol.com

NICASTRO, Nicholas. American (born United States), b. 1963. **Genres:** Novels. **Career:** Cornell University, faculty; Hobart and William Smith Colleges, faculty. Writer. **Publications:** Circumference: Eratosthenes and the Ancient Quest to Measure the Globe (nonfiction), 2008. HISTORICAL FICTION: The Eighteenth Captain, 1999; Between Two Fires 2002; Empire of Ashes: A Novel of Alexander the Great, 2004; The Isle of Stone: A Novel of Ancient Sparta, 2005; Antigone's Wake: A Novel of Imperial Athens, 2007. Contributor to periodicals. **Online address:** inquiries@nicastrobooks.com

NICE, David C. American (born United States), b. 1952. **Genres:** Politics/Government, Public/Social Administration, Transportation, International Relations/Current Affairs. **Career:** Indiana University, visiting assistant professor of political science, 1979-80; University of Georgia, assistant professor, 1980-85, associate professor of political science, 1985-88, assistant department head, 1985-88, undergraduate coordinator, 1984-85; Washington State University, Department of Political Science, associate professor, 1988-91, professor of political science, 1991-, chair, 1991-93, undergraduate coordinator, 1994-96. Writer. **Publications:** Federalism: The Politics of Intergovernmental Relations, 1987; (ed. with J.C. Pierce and C.H. Sheldon) Government and Politics in the Evergreen State, 1992; Policy Innovation in State Government, 1994; (with P. Fredericksen) The Politics of Intergovernmental Relations, 1995; Amtrak: The History and Politics of a National Railroad, 1998; (with J.J. Harrigan) Politics and Policy in States & Communities, 2001, 10th ed., 2008; Public Budgeting, 2002; (with J. Cohen) The Presidency, forthcoming; (with J. Cohen) Readings on the American Presidency, forthcoming. Contributor to journals. **Address:** Department of Political Science, Washington State University, 808 Johnson Twr., PO Box 644880, Pullman, WA 99164-4880, U.S.A. **Online address:** dnice@wsu.edu

NICE, Jill. British (born England), b. 1940. **Genres:** Food And Wine, Medicine/Health, Homes/Gardens. **Career:** Sugar and Spice Country Foods, owner, 1970-; Looking Good Naturally, co-owner, 1970-. Writer. **Publications:** Home Made Preserves, 1982, rev. ed. as The Complete Book of Home-Made Preserves, 1995; Looking Good Naturally, 1986; Herbal Remedies: The Complete Guide to Natural Healing, 1990, rev. ed., 2000; Aloe Vera, 2000; Milk Thistle, 2000; (with J.R. Davies) Cranberry: Vaccinium Macrocarpon, 2000; (with C. Foley and M.A. Webb) The New Herb Bible, 2002; Herbal Remedies and Home Comforts, 2005. Contributor to magazines and periodicals. **Address:** Watson, Little Ltd., 12 Egbert St., London, GL NW1 8LJ, England.

NICHOLAS, David M(ansfield). American (born United States), b. 1939. **Genres:** History, Politics/Government, Economics, Business/Trade/Industry, Humanities. **Career:** University of Nebraska, assistant professor, 1967-71, associate professor, 1971-76, professor, 1976-89; Clemson University, professor of history, 1989-2001, Kathryn and Calhoun Lemon professor of history, 2001-06, Kathryn and Calhoun Lemon professor emeritus of history, 2006-. Writer. **Publications:** Town and Countryside: Social, Economic and Political Tensions in Fourteenth-Century Flanders, 1971; Stad en Platteland in de Middeleeuwen, 1971; Medieval West, 400-1450; A Preindustrial Civilization, 1973; Middle East, Its Oil, Economies, and Investment Policies: A Guide to Sources of Financial Information, 1981; The Domestic Life of a Medieval City: Women, Children, and the Family in Fourteenth-Century Ghent, 1985; The Metamorphosis of a Medieval City: Ghent in the Age of the Arteveldes, 1302-1390, 1987; The Van Arteveldes of Ghent: The Varieties of Vendetta and the Hero in History, 1988; (ed. with B.S. Bachrach) Law, Custom, and the Social Fabric in Medieval Europe: Essays in Honor of Bryce Lyon, 1990; The Evolution of the Medieval World: Society, Government, and Thought in Europe, 312-1500, 1992; Medieval Flanders, 1992; Trade, Urbanisation, and the Family: Studies in the History of Medieval Flanders, 1996; The Growth of the Medieval City: From Late Antiquity to the Fourteenth Century, 1997; The Later Medieval City, 1300-1500, 1997; The Transformation of Europe 1300-1600, 1999; Urban Europe, 1100-1700, 2003; Northern Lands: Germanic Europe, c.1270-c.1500, 2009. Contributor to journals. **Address:** Department of History and Geography, Clemson University, 126 Hardin Hall, PO Box 340527, Clemson, SC 29634-0527, U.S.A. **Online address:** nichold@clemson.edu

NICHOLAS, Deborah. *See* **JEFFRIES, Sabrina.**

NICHOLAS, Sian (Helen). American (born United States), b. 1964. **Genres:** History. **Career:** University of London, Institute of Historical Research, research fellow, 1991-92; University of Wales, lecturer in history, 1992-; Aberystwyth University, Department of History and Welsh History, lecturer; Royal Historical Society, fellow. **Publications:** The Echo of War: Home Front Propaganda and the Wartime BBC, 1939-45, 1996. **Address:** Department of History and Welsh History, Aberystwyth University, Rm. C51, Hugh Owen Bldg., Ceredigion, SY23 3DY, Wales. **Online address:** shn@aber.ac.uk

NICHOLLS, C(hristine) S(tephanie). British (born England), b. 1943. **Genres:** History, Biography, Autobiography/Memoirs, Reference, Politics/Government. **Career:** University of London, Institute of Commonwealth Studies, Henry Charles Chapman research fellow, 1968-69; British Broadcasting Corporation (BBC), research assistant, 1969-74; freelance media commentator, 1970-74, research assistant, 1975-76; Oxford University Press, editor, 1977-95; Dictionary of National Biography, Oxford University Press, joint editor, 1977-89, editor, 1989-95, Sutton Pocket Biographies, editor, 1996-; St. Antony's College, Oxford University, associate fellow, 1990-. **Publications:** Swahili Coast: Politics, Diplomacy and Trade on the East African Littoral, 1798-1856, 1971; History Makers: Leaders and Statesmen of the 20th Century, 1973; (with P. Awdry) Cataract, 1985; Health region Statistical Profiles for British Columbia, 1993, 3rd ed., 1996; David Livingstone, 1998; A History of St Antony's College, Oxford, 1950-2000, 2000; Elspeth Huxley: A Biography, 2003; Red Strangers: The White Tribe of Kenya, 2005; A Kenya Childhood, 2011. EDITOR: (with E.T. Williams) Dictionary of National Biography, 1961-1970, 1981; (with L. Blake) The Dictionary of National Biography, 1971-1980: With an Index Covering the Years 1901-1980 in One Alphabetical Series, 1971-1980, 1986; (with L. Blake) Dictionary of National Biography, 1981-1985: With an Index Covering the Years 1901-1985 in One Alphabetical Series, 1990; Power: A Political History of the Twentieth Century, 1990; (co-ed.) Dictionary of National Biography, Missing Persons, 1994; Hutchinson Encyclopedia of Biography, 1996; Dictionary of National Biography, 1986-1990: With an Index Covering the Years 1901-1990 in One Alphabetical Series, 1996; Encyclopedia of Biography, 1997. Contributor to periodicals. **Address:** Dictionary of National Biography, Oxford University, Broad St., Oxford, OX OX1 3BG, England. **Online address:** christine.nicholls@lineone.net

NICHOLLS, Henry. British (born England), b. 1973?. **Genres:** Sciences, Adult Non-fiction, Animals/Pets, Chemistry, Environmental Sciences/Ecology, History, Medicine/Health, Natural History, Zoology. **Career:** Endeavor (history of science magazine), editor-in-chief, 2002-09; Galapagos Matters, editor, 2008-. Freelance science journalist. **Publications:** Lonesome George: The Life and Loves of a Conservation Icon, 2006; The Way of the Panda: The Curious History of China's Political Animal, 2010. **Address:** Profile Books, 3A Exmouth House, Pine St., Exmouth Market, GL EC1R OJH, United Kingdom. **Online address:** henry@henrynicholls.com

NICHOLLS, Sally. British (born England), b. 1983. **Genres:** Children's Fiction. **Career:** Author. **Publications:** Ways to Live Forever, 2008; Season of Secrets, 2009. Contributor to periodicals. **Address:** c/o Rosemary Canter, United Agents, 130 Shaftesbury Ave., London, GL W1D 5EU, England.

NICHOLS, Charlotte. *See* **HICKS, Barbara.**

NICHOLS, Deborah L. American (born United States), b. 1952. **Genres:** Archaeology/Antiquities, Social Sciences, Anthropology/Ethnology, Politics/Government. **Career:** Mimbres Archaeological Center, archaeologist, 1975; Pennsylvania State University, instructor in general education, 1978-80; Pennsylvania State Historical and Museum Commission, field director of excavations, 1979; Southern Illinois University, Black Mesa Archaeological Project in Arizona, assistant director, adjunct assistant professor of anthropology, 1981-85; Dartmouth College, assistant professor, 1985-90, associate professor, 1990-96, department head, 1991-94, professor of anthropology, 1996-, William J. Bryant 1925 Professor of Anthropology, 2002-, department chair. Writer. **Publications:** (Contrib.) Mesoamerican Elites: An Archaeological Assessment, 1992; (contrib.) Economics and Politics in the Aztec Realm, 1994; (contrib.) The Archaeology of Ancient Mexico and Central America: An Encyclopedia, 1999; (contrib.) Prehistoric Culture Change on the Colorado Plateau: Ten Thousand Years on Black Mesa, 1999. EDITOR: (with F.E. Smiley and P.P. Andrews) Excavations on Black Mesa, 1981: A Descriptive Report, 1983; (with F.E. Smiley) Excavations on Black Mesa, 1982: A Descriptive Report, 1984; (with T.H. Charlton and contrib.) The Archaeology of City-States: Cross-Cultural Approaches, 1998; Archaeology Is Anthropology, 2003; (and intro. with P.L. Crown) Social Violence in the Prehispanic American Southwest, 2008; (ed. with C.A. Pool) Oxford Handbook of Mesoamerican Archaeology, 2012. Contributor to books and periodicals. **Address:** Department of Anthropology, Dartmouth College, 6047 Silsby Hall, Hanover, NH 03755, U.S.A. **Online address:** deborah.l.nichols@dartmouth.edu

NICHOLS, Grace. British/Guyanese (born Guyana), b. 1950. **Genres:** Novels, Children's Fiction, Poetry, Young Adult Fiction, Children's Non-fiction. **Career:** Freelance journalist in Guyana, 1967-77; teacher, 1969-70; Georgetown Chronicle, reporter, 1972-73; Government Information Services, information assistant, 1973-76. **Publications:** Trust You, Wriggly (for children), 1980; Baby Fish and Other Stories from Village to Rainforest (for children), 1983; I Is a Long-Memoried Woman (poetry), 1983; Lesly in London (for children), 1984; The Fat Black Woman's Poems, 1984; A Dangerous Knowing: Four Black Women Poets, 1985; The Discovery (for children), 1986; Whole of a Morning Sky (novel), 1986; Come on into My Tropical Garden (poetry for children), 1988; (comp.) Black Poetry, 1988; (comp.) Poetry Jump Up, 1989; Lazy Thoughts of a Lazy Woman and Other Poems, 1989; I is a long Memoried Woman, 1990; (ed.) Can I Buy a Slice of Sky?: Poems from Black, Asian and American Indian Cultures, 1991; (with J. Agrad) No Hickory No Dickory No Dock: A Collection of Caribbean Nursery Rhymes, 1991; (contrib.) Quartet of Poems, 1993; Give Yourself a Hug (poetry for children), 1994; (ed. with J. Agrad) A Caribbean Dozen: Poems from Caribbean Poets, 1994; Sunrise (poetry), 1996; Asana and The Animals: A Book of Pet Poems, 1997; (contrib.) We Couldn't Provide Fish Thumbs, 1997; The Poet Cat, 2000; (ed. with J. Agard) Under the Moon & Over the Sea: A Collection of Caribbean Poems, 2002; (ed. with J. Agard) From Mouth to Mouth: Oral Poems from Around the World, 2004; Paint Me a Poem: New Poems Inspired by Art in Tate, 2004; Everybody's Got a Gift: New and Selected Poems, 2005; Startling the Flying Fish, 2005; Picasso, I Want My Face Back, 2009; I Have Crossed an Ocean: Selected Poems, 2010; Whoa, Baby, Whoa, 2012. **Address:** c/o Anthea Morton-Saner, Curtis Brown Ltd., Haymarket House, 28-29 Haymarket, London, GL SW1Y 4SP, England.

NICHOLS, John. American (born United States), b. 1940. **Genres:** Novels, Plays/Screenplays, Autobiography/Memoirs, Environmental Sciences/Ecology, Photography, Social Commentary, Business/Trade/Industry, Economics, Economics. **Career:** University of New Mexico, visiting professor, 1992, 1993. Photographer and writer. **Publications:** The Sterile Cuckoo, 1965; The Wizard of Loneliness, 1966; The Milagro Beanfield War, 1974; The Magic Journey, 1978; A Ghost in the Music, 1979; If Mountains Die, 1979; The Nirvana Blues (New Mexico trilogy), 1981; The Last Beautiful Days of Autumn, 1982; In Praise of Mountain Lions, 1984; On the Mesa, 1986; American Blood, 1987; A Fragile Beauty, 1987; The Sky's the Limit, 1990; An Elegy for September, 1992; Keep It Simple, 1992; Conjugal Bliss: A Comedy of Marital Arts, 1994; Dancing on the Stones, 2000; The Voice of the Butterfly, 2001; An American Child Supreme: The Education of a Liberation Ecologist, 2001;

(foreword) Enriqueta Vasquez and the Chicano Movement, 2006. **Address:** PO Box 1165, Taos, NM 87571, U.S.A.

NICHOLS, John Gordon. British (born England), b. 1930. **Genres:** Poetry, Literary Criticism And History, Translations, Theology/Religion. **Career:** Teacher, 1954-62; King David School, English Department, head, 1957-62; Edge Hill College of Education, lecturer, 1962-64; Notre Dame College, senior lecturer, 1964-66, principal lecturer in English, 1966, head, 1970-80. Writer. **Publications:** The Flighty Horse, 1968; (with T. Pey) The Poet's Purpose, 1969; The Poetry of Ben Jonson, 1969; The Poetry of Sir Philip Sidney: An Interpretation in the Context of his Life and Times, 1974. TRANSLATOR: G. Gozzano, Colloquies and Selected Letters, 1987; G. d'Annunzio, Halcyon, 1988; G. Leopardi, The Canti: With a Selection of His Prose, 1994; Petrarch, Canzoniere, 2000; U. Foscolo, Last Letters of Jacopo Ortis, 2002; J. von Eichendorff, Life of a Good-for-nothing, 2002; G. Boccaccio, Life of Dante, 2002; G. Leopardi, Thoughts, 2002; L. da Vinci, Prophecies, 2002; Petrarch, My Secret Book, 2002; L. Pirandello, Loveless Love, 2002; G. Casanova, The Duel, 2003; G. Verga, Life in the Country, 2003; Dante, New Life, 2003; G. d'Annunzio, The Book of the Virgins, 2003; I. Svevo, A Perfect Hoax, 2003; G. Boccaccio, Decameron, 2008; N. Machiavelli, The Prince, 2010; U. Foscolo, Sepulchres, 2010; D. Alighieri, Inferno, 2010; Secretum Petrarch, 2010; Letters from London and Europe, 1925-30, 2010; Divine Comedy, 2011. **Address:** 43 Warren Dr., Wallasey, MS CH45 0JP, England.

NICHOLS, Leigh. *See* **KOONTZ, Dean R(ay).**

NICHOLS, Linda. American (born United States), b. 1954?. **Genres:** Novels, Literary Criticism And History. **Career:** Writer. **Publications:** Handyman, 2000; Not a Sparrow Falls, 2002; If I Gained the World, 2003, At the Scent of Water, 2004; In Search of Eden, 2007. Contributor of articles to journals and periodicals. **Address:** c/o Author Mail, Bethany House Publishers, 11400 Hampshire Ave. S, Minneapolis, MN 55438, U.S.A.

NICHOLS, Peter (Richard). British (born England), b. 1927. **Genres:** Plays/Screenplays, Autobiography/Memoirs, Humor/Satire, Poetry, History, Literary Criticism And History. **Career:** National Service, R.I.A., 1945-48, professional actor, 1950-55; teacher, 1956-59; playwright, 1959-. Writer. **Publications:** Day in the Death of Joe Egg, 1967; Joe Egg, 1967; The National Health, or, Nurse Norton's Affair: A Play in Two Acts, 1970; Chez nous: A Domestic Comedy in Two Acts, 1974; Freeway: A Play in Two Acts, 1975; Privates on Parade: A Play with Songs in Two Acts, 1977; Born in the Gardens: A Play in Two Acts, 1980; Passion Play, 1981; Poppy, 1981; Feeling You're Behind: An Autobiography, 1984; Piece of My Mind, 1987; Plays, 1987; Blue Murder: A Play or Two, 1996; Diaries, 1969-77, 2000; So Long Life, 2000; Lingua Franca, 2010. Contributor to periodicals. **Address:** Alan Brodie Representation Ltd., The Courtyard, 55 Charterhouse St., Paddock Ste., London, GL EC1M 6HA, England.

NICHOLS, Stephen J. American (born United States), b. 1970. **Genres:** Theology/Religion. **Career:** Lancaster Bible College and Graduate School, professor; London Theological Seminary, visiting lecturer. Writer, historian and theologian. **Publications:** Jonathan Edwards: A Guided Tour of His Life and Thought, 2001; Martin Luther: A Guided Tour of His Life and Thought, 2002; Martin Luther's Ninety-five Theses, 2002; An Absolute Sort of Certainty: The Holy Spirit and the Apologetics of Jonathan Edwards, 2003; J. Gresham Machen: A Guided Tour of His Life and Thought, 2004; Pages from Church History: Guided Tour of Christian Classics, 2006; Heaven on Earth: Capturing Jonathan Edwards' Vision of Living in Between, 2006; The Reformation: How a Monk and a Mallet Changed the World, 2007; For Us and for Our Salvation: The Doctrine of Christ in the Early Church, 2007; Getting the Blues: What Blues Music Teaches Us about Suffering and Salvation, 2008; Jesus Made in America: A Cultural History from the Puritans to the Passion of the Christ, 2008; (with E.T. Brandt) Ancient Word, Changing Worlds: The Doctrine of Scripture in a Modern Age, 2009; What Is Vocation? ("Basics of the Faith" series), 2010; (with N. Bustard) The Church History ABCs: Augustine and 25 Other Heroes of the Faith, 2010; Welcome to the Story: Reading, Loving, Living God's Word, 2011. EDITOR: (intro.) Jonathan Edwards' Resolutions; And, Advice to Young Converts, 2001; (with D.G. Hart and S.M. Lucas) The Legacy of Jonathan Edwards: American Religion and the Evangelical Tradition, 2003; (intro.) J. Gresham Machen's "The Gospel and the Modern World" and Other Short Writings, 2005. Contributor to periodicals. **Address:** Lancaster, PA , U.S.A. **Online address:** snichols@lbc.edu

NICHOLS, Victoria. *See* **NICHOLS, Victoria (Sorensen).**

NICHOLS, Victoria (Sorensen). (Victoria Nichols). American (born United States), b. 1944. **Genres:** Mystery/Crime/Suspense, Women's Studies And Issues. **Career:** Palo Alto/Stanford Hospital, histology technician, 1960-63; KARA, consultant; California Institute of Transpersonal Psychology, consultant; Microtech Conversion Systems, consultant. Writer. **Publications:** WITH S. THOMPSON: Silk Stalkings: When Women Write of Murder: A Survey of Series Characters Created by Women Authors in Crime and Mystery Fiction, 1988; Silk Stalkings: More Women Write of Murder, 1998. **Address:** c/o Ruth Cohen, PO Box 7626, Menlo Park, CA 94026, U.S.A.

NICHOLSON, Colin. British (born England), b. 1944. **Genres:** Literary Criticism And History, Writing/Journalism. **Career:** University of Edinburgh, reader and professor in English literature, 1969-, professor, 2000-. Writer. **Publications:** EDITOR: (with R. Chatterjee) Tropic Crucible: Self and Theory in Language and Literature, 1984; (with P. Easingwood) Canadian Story and History, 1885-1985; Papers Presented at the Tenth Annual Conference of the British Association for Canadian Studies, 1985; Alexander Pope: Essay for the Tercentenary, 1988; (with G. Carnall) Impeachment of Warren Hastings: Papers From a Bicentenary Commemoration, 1989; Margaret Laurence: Critical Approaches to the Fiction of Margaret Laurence, 1990; (with J. Orr) Cinema and Fiction: New Modes of Adapting, 1992; Iain Crichton Smith: Critical Essays, 1992; Margaret Atwood: Writing and Subjectivity, 1994; (with M. McGuire) Edinburgh Companion to Contemporary Scottish Poetry, 2009. OTHER: Poem, Purpose and Place: Shaping Identity in Contemporary Scottish Verse, 1992; Writing and the Rise of Finance: Capital Satires of The Early Eighteenth Century, 1994; Edwin Morgan: Inventions of Modernity, 2002. **Address:** Department of English Literature, University of Edinburgh, David Hume Tower, Fl. 6, George Sq., Edinburgh, EH8 9JX, Scotland. **Online address:** c.nicholson@ed.ac.uk

NICHOLSON, Deborah L. Canadian (born Canada), b. 1961. **Genres:** Novels, Mystery/Crime/Suspense. **Career:** Centre for the Performing Arts, staff; Theatre Calgary, house manager. Writer. **Publications:** KATE CARPENTER SERIES: MYSTERY NOVELS: House Report, 2004; Evening the Score, 2004; Flirting with Disaster, 2005; Sins of the Mother, 2005; Liar, Liar, 2006. **Address:** c/o Anne Dewe, Andrew Mann Ltd., 39-41 North Rd., London, GL N7 9DP, England. **Online address:** debs.book61@gmail.com

NICHOLSON, E(rnest) W(ilson). British (born England), b. 1938. **Genres:** Theology/Religion. **Career:** University College (now Wolfson College), fellow, 1967-79; Cambridge University, Pembroke College, lecturer in divinity, 1967-79; Trinity College, lecturer in Hebrew and Semitic languages, 1962-67; Oxford University, Oriel College, provost, pro-vice chancellor and fellow, 1979-90, professor of the interpretation of Holy Scripture, 1979-, honorary fellow. Writer. **Publications:** Deuteronomy and Tradition, 1967; Preaching to the Exiles: A Study of the Prose Tradition in the Book of Jeremiah, 1970; Exodus and Sinai in History and Tradition, 1973; (ed. and trans. with J. Baker) The Commentary of Rabbi David Kimhi on Psalms 120-150, 1973; (contrib.) The Book of the Prophet Jeremiah, Chapters 1-25, 1975; (contrib.) The Book of the Prophet Jeremiah, Chapters 26-52, 1975; Interpreting the Old Testament: A Century of the Oriel Professorship, 1981; God and His People: Covenant and Theology in the Old Testament, 1986; The Pentateuch in the Twentieth Century, 1998; (contrib.) Covenant as context, 2003; (ed.) Century of Theological and Religious Studies in Britain, 2003. **Address:** Oriel College, University of Oxford, Oriel Sq., Oxford, OX OX1 4EW, England.

NICHOLSON, Lois P. American (born United States), b. 1949. **Genres:** Young Adult Non-fiction, Biography, Sports/Fitness, Adult Non-fiction. **Career:** Rock Hall Elementary and Middle School, media specialist, 1989-93; Cape St. Claire Elementary School, media specialist, 1994-. Writer. **Publications:** Cal Ripken Jr.: Quiet Hero, 1993, 2nd ed., 1995; George Washington Carver, 1994; Michael Jackson, 1994; Oprah Winfrey, 1994; Babe Ruth: Sultan of Swat, 1995; Casey Stengel, 1995; Georgia O'Keeffe, 1995; Helen Keller: Humanitarian, 1996; Lucille Ball, 1996; Nolan Ryan, 1996; Ken Griffey, Jr., 1997; Oprah Winfrey: Talking With America, 1997; Booker T. Washington, 1997; From Maryland to Cooperstown: Seven Maryland Natives in Baseball's Hall of Fame, 1998; Composite Guide to Lacrosse, 1999; Dian Fossey: Primatologist, 2003. **Address:** 226 S Washington St., Easton, MD 21601-2014, U.S.A. **Online address:** loispn@dmv.com

NICHOLSON, Mavis. Welsh (born Wales), b. 1930. **Genres:** Self Help, Autobiography/Memoirs, Biography, Military/Defense/Arms Control, History. **Career:** Freelance television interviewer and radio host, 1950-; Montgomery Wildlife Trust, president. Writer. **Publications:** Help Yourself: Solutions to the Practical Problems of Everyday Life, 1974; Martha Jane and Me: A Girlhood in Wales (autobiography), 1992; What Did You Do in the War, Mummy?: Women in World War II, 1995. **Address:** J M Thurley Literary Agents, 213 Linen Hall, 162-168 Regent St., West End, London, GL W1R 5TA, England.

NICHTER, Mark (Andrew). American (born United States), b. 1949. **Genres:** Anthropology/Ethnology, Medicine/Health, Social Sciences, Psychology. **Career:** University of Hawaii at Manoa, lecturer in anthropology, 1981-83; University of Colombo, Fulbright professor, 1983-84; University of Arizona, assistant professor, 1985-89, associate professor of anthropology, 1989, Regents professor and professor of anthropology, public health, family medicine, Graduate Medical Anthropology Training Program, coordinator; University of the Philippines, visiting professor, 1991; Mahidol University, visiting professor, 1996-97; Achuta Menon Centre, visiting professor, 1997-98. Writer. **Publications:** Anthropology and International Health: Asian Case Studies, 1989, 2nd ed., (with M. Nichter), 1996; (ed.) Anthropological Approaches to the Study of Ethnomedicine, 1992; (ed. with M. Lock) New Horizons in Medical Anthropology: Essays in Honour of Charles Leslie, 2002; Global Health: Why Cultural Perceptions, Social Representations, and Biopolitics Matter, 2008. Contributor to many journals. **Address:** Department of Anthropology, University of Arizona, Emil W Haury Bldg. 321, PO Box 210030, Tucson, AZ 85721-0030, U.S.A. **Online address:** mnichter@u.arizona.edu

NÍ CHUILLEANÁIN, Eiléan. Irish (born Ireland), b. 1942. **Genres:** Poetry. **Career:** Trinity College, Department of English, lecturer, 1966-85, senior lecturer, 1985-99, fellow, 1993, associate professor of English, 1999-; Cyphers Literary Magazine, co-founder, 1975. Writer. **Publications:** Acts and Monuments, 1972; Site of Ambush, 1975; The Second Voyage, 1977; Cork, 1977; The Rose-Geranium, 1981; (ed.) Irish Women: Image and Achievement, 1985; The Magdalene Sermon, 1989; Magdalene Sermon and Earlier Poems, 1991; (ed. with J.D. Pheifer) Noble and Joyous Histories: English Romances, 1375-1650, 1993; (trans. with M. McGuckian) The Water Horse: Poems, 1999; The Brazen Serpent, 1994; The Girl Who Married the Reindeer, 2001; (ed.) As I was among the Captives: Joseph Campbell's Prison Diary, 1922-1923, 2001; (ed.) Wilde Legacy, 2003; (trans.) I. Mălăncioiu, After the Raising of Lazarus, 2005; (trans.) Verbale, 2005; Selected poems, 2008; Sunfish, 2009; (ed. with C.Ó. Culleanien and D. Parris) Translation and Censorship: Patterns of Communication and Interference, 2009; Heresy and Orthodoxy in Early English Literature, 2010. Contributor to periodicals. **Address:** Department of English, Trinity College Dublin, College Green, DU 2, Ireland. **Online address:** enchullnn@tcd.ie

NICIEZA, Fabian. American/Argentine (born Argentina), b. 1961. **Genres:** Graphic Novels, Novels, Children's Fiction. **Career:** Berkley Publishing, managing editor, through 1985; Marvel Comics, manufacturing assistant, advertising manager and writer, 1985-96, editor, 1992, writer, 1998-; Acclaim Comics, editor-in-chief and writer, 1996-98, president; FunGoPlay, chief creative officer. **Publications:** NFL Superpro: Fourth and Goal to Go, 1991; (co-ed.) Hook: The Official Movie Adaptation, 1991; Bill and Ted's Bogus Journey, 1991; (with R. Liefeld and T. McFarlane) Stan Lee Presents X-Force and Spider-Man in Sabotage, 1992; (with T. DeFalco) The New Warriors: Beginnings, 1992; Gambit and the X-Ternals, 1995; The Amazing X-Men, 1995; X-Men: Fatal Attractions, 1995; (with M. Waid) Justice League: Midsummer's Nightmare, 1996; Deadpool: The Circle Chase, 1997; The Blackburne Covenant, 2003; Stake to the Heart, 2004; Cable/Deadpool: If Looks Could Kill, 2004; Justice League Adventures, 2004; Robin: Search for a Hero, 2009; Batman: Battle for the Cowl Companion, 2009; Batman: The Cat and the Bat, 2009; (with K. Busiek) Trinity, 2009; Tron: The Betrayal, 2010; Azrael: Death's Dark Knight, 2010; Azrael: Angel in the Dark, 2010; Red Robin, forthcoming. **Address:** c/o Author Mail, Dark Horse Comics, 10956 SE Main St., Milwaukie, OR 97222, U.S.A.

NICKEL, Barbara. Canadian (born Canada), b. 1966. **Genres:** Children's Fiction, Novels, Poetry. **Career:** University of British Columbia, Creative Writing Program, instructor; Prism Intl., poetry editor, instructor. **Publications:** FOR CHILDREN: The Secret Wish of Nannerl Mozart, 1996; From the Top of a Grain Elevator, 1999; Hannah Waters and the Daughter of Johann Sebastian Bach, 2005. FOR ADULTS: The Gladys Elegies (poetry), 1997; Domain (poetry), 2007. **Address:** 42550 Yale Rd., Chilliwack, BC V2R 4J4, Canada. **Online address:** barbaranickel@shaw.ca

NICKEL, Douglas R. American (born United States), b. 1961. **Genres:** Adult Non-fiction, Art/Art History, History, Photography. **Career:** Cornell University, Herbert F. Johnson Museum of Art, Photo and Prints Department, intern, 1983-85; Princeton University, The Art Museum, Department of Photography, curatorial assistant, 1986-90; San Francisco Museum of Modern Art, assistant curator of photography, 1993-96, associate curator of photography, 1997-99, curator of photography, 1999-2003; University of Arizona, Center for Creative Photography, director, 2003-07, Department of Art History, associate professor of art history, 2003-07; Brown University, Department of the History of Art and Architecture, Andrea V. Rosenthal professor of modern art, 2007-. Writer. **Publications:** Snapshots: The Photography of Everyday Life, 1888 to the Present, 1998; (intro.) Picturing Modernity: Highlights from the Photography Collection of the San Francisco Museum of Modern Art, 1998; Carleton Watkins: The Art of Perception, 1999; (contrib.) Stranger Passing, 2001; Dreaming in Pictures: The Photography of Lewis Carroll, 2002; Francis Frith in Egypt and Palestine: A Victorian Photographer Abroad, 2004; (contrib.) Self-portraits 1967-2005, 2005; Chuck Close: Self-Portraits 1967-2005, 2005; (contrib.) Trees: National Champions, 2005; (foreword) Milton Rogovin: The Making of a Documentary Photographer, 2006; (intro.) This Side of Paradise: Body and Landscape in Los Angeles Photographs, 2008; (foreword) John Gutmann: The Photographer at Work, 2009. Works appear in anthologies. Contributor to journals. **Address:** Department of the History of Art and Architecture, Brown University, 64 College St., PO Box 1855, Providence, RI 02912, U.S.A. **Online address:** douglas_nickel@brown.edu

NICOL, Jodi. *See* **SAUNDERS, Jean (Innes).**

NICOL, Mary. *See* **RAZZELL, Mary (Catherine).**

NICOLA, Andrée. *See* **MCLAUGHLIN, Andrée Nicola.**

NICOLAISEN, (Agnes) Ida (Benedicte). Danish (born Denmark), b. 1940. **Genres:** Anthropology/Ethnology, Cultural/Ethnic Topics, Third World, History. **Career:** Copenhagen University, associate professor of cultural sociology, 1971-91, associate professor of anthropology, 1991-97; Aarhus University, external lecturer, 1971-73; FOLK journal, editor, 1985-92; Carlsberg Foundation, Nomad Research Project, editor-in-chief; Danish Board of Development Collaboration, vice-chair, 1996-2003; DANIDA's Committee on Information, chair, 1997-2008; Nordic Institute of Asian Studies, senior researcher, 1997-; UN Permanent Forum on Indigenous Issues, vice-chair, 2002-08; Barnard College, visiting research fellow; Hunter College, visiting research fellow. **Publications:** (With T. Damgaard-Soerensen) Building a Longboat, 1988; (with J. Nicolaisen) The Pastoral Tuareg, 2 vols., 1997; Elusive Hunters: The Haddad of Kanem and the Bahr el Ghazal, 2010. EDITOR-IN-CHIEF: Nomads of Luristan: History, Material Culture and Pastoralism in Western Iran, 1993; Mongol Costumes, 1993; Bedouins of Qatar, 1993; Afghan Nomads in Transition: A Century of Change Among the Zala Khān Khel, 1994; Afghan Craftsmen: The Cultures of Three Itinerant Communities, 1994; Mongol Jewelry: Jewelry Collected by the First and Second Danish Central Asian Expeditions, 1995; Caravans and Trade in Afghanistan: The Changing Life of the Nomadic Hazarbuz, 1995; Tibetan Nomads, 1996; Exploring Central Asia I-II, 2002; Afghan Nomads. Caravans, Conflicts and Trade in Afghanistan and British India 1800-1980, 2006; Exploring Central Asia: From the Steppes to the High Pamirs, 1896-1899. Contributor to journals. **Address:** Nordic Institute of Asian Studies, Leifsgade 33, Copenhagen, 2300, Denmark. **Online address:** nicolaisen@nias.ku.dk

NICOLSON, Adam. British (born England), b. 1957. **Genres:** Young Adult Non-fiction, Novellas/Short Stories. **Career:** Sunday Telegraph Magazine, author, naturalist and columnist, 1981-; Sunday Times, journalist and columnist; Daily Telegraph, journalist and columnist. **Publications:** NONFICTION: The National Trust Book of Long Walks in England, Scotland, and Wales, 1981; Long Walks in France, 1983; (contrib.) Landscape in Britain, 1984; (contrib.) Wetland: Life in the Somerset Levels, 1986; (with N. Nicolson) Two Roads to Dodge City, 1986 in US as Two Roads to Dodge City: Two Colorful English Writers, Father and Son, Chronicle Their Wonderful Journeys across America, 1987; (with P. Morter) Prospects of England: Two Thousand Years Seen through Twelve English Towns, 1989; On Foot, 1990; Adam Nicolson's Book of Walks, 1990; Restoration: The Rebuilding of Windsor Castle, 1997; (contrib.) Panoramas of England, 1997; Perch Hill: A New Life, 1999; Regeneration: The Story of the Dome, 1999; The Hated Wife: Carrie Kipling 1862-1939, 2001; Sea Room: An Island Life in the Hebrides, 2002; God's Secretaries: The Making of the King James Bible in UK as Power and Glory: Jacobean England and the Making of the King James Bible, 2003; Seamanship: A Voyage along the Wild Coasts of the British Isles, 2005; Seize the Fire: Heroism, Duty, and the Battle of Trafalgar in UK as Men of Honour: Trafalgar and the Making of the English Hero, 2005; Sissinghurst: An Unfinished History, 2008; Quarrel with the King: The Story of an English Family on the High Road to Civil War in UK as Earls of Paradise, 2008, rev. ed. as Arcadia: The Dream of Perfection in Renaissance England, 2009; (with E. Anderson) About Eton, 2010; Gentry: Stories of the English, 2011. **Address:** HarperCollins Publishers, 10 E 53rd St., New York, NY 10022, U.S.A.

NICOSIA, Gerald (Martin). American (born United States), b. 1949. **Genres:** Poetry, Literary Criticism And History, Biography, Adult Non-fiction, Plays/Screenplays. **Career:** Teacher, 1973-77; The Washington Post, reviewer; The Chicago Tribune, reviewer; The Los Angeles Times, reviewer; The San Francisco Chronicle, reviewer; USA Today, reviewer; The American Book Review, reviewer; The Review of Contemporary Fiction, reviewer; Contemporary Literary Criticism, reviewer; The New York Quarterly, reviewer; University of Illinois, teaching assistant, 1973, faculty of creative writing and journalism, 1986-87; University of California, faculty of creative writing and journalism. **Publications:** (With R. Raff) Bughouse Blues (nonfiction), 1977; Memory Babe: A Critical Biography of Jack Kerouac (biography), 1983; Jack in Ghost-Town (play), 1987; The Two Lowells of Jack Kerouac (chapbook), 1988; Lunatics, Lovers, Poets, Vets, and Bargirls: Poems (poetry), 1991; An Afternoon of Poetry (chapbook), 1993; (ed.) Cranial Guitar: Selected Poems, 1996; (ed.) Baby Driver, 1998; (ed.) Trainsong, 1998; (ed.) Teducation, 1999; Home to War: A History of the Vietnam Veterans Movement (nonfiction), 2001; Love, California Style (poetry), 2002; Embrace of the Lepers (poetry), 2004; (ed.) Jan Kerouac: A Life in Memory, 2009. Contributor to periodicals. Works appear in anthologies. **Address:** PO Box 130, Corte Madera, CA 94976-0130, U.S.A. **Online address:** gerald@geraldnicosia.com

NIDITCH, Susan. American (born United States), b. 1950. **Genres:** Theology/Religion, Adult Non-fiction, Social Sciences, Children's Fiction, History. **Career:** University of Cincinnati, assistant professor of religion, 1977-78; Amherst College, assistant professor, 1978-84, associate professor, 1984-90, chair of department, 1986-87, 1991-93, professor of religion, 1990-, Samuel Green professor of religion, 1992-, Elizabeth Bruss readership, 1987-90. Writer. **Publications:** The Symbolic Vision in Biblical Tradition, 1983; Chaos to Cosmos: Studies in Biblical Patterns of Creation, 1985; Underdogs and Tricksters: A Prelude to Biblical Folklore, 1987; (ed. and intro.) Text and Tradition: The Hebrew Bible and Folklore, 1990; War in the Hebrew Bible: A Study in the Ethics of Violence, 1993; Folklore and the Hebrew Bible, 1993; Oral World and Written Word: Ancient Israelite Literature, 1996; Ancient Israelite Religion, 1997; Judges: A Commentary, 2008; My Brother Esau is a Hairy Man: Hair and Identity in Ancient Israel, 2008. **Address:** Department of Religion, Amherst College, 114 Chapin Hall, PO Box AC 2252, Amherst, MA 01002, U.S.A. **Online address:** sniditch@amherst.edu

NIEBUHR, Gary Warren. American (born United States), b. 1954. **Genres:** Biography, Literary Criticism And History, Young Adult Fiction, Mystery/Crime/Suspense. **Career:** Village of Greendale, library director; Private Investigator Entertainment Service, operator; Bouchercon, coordinator, 1981, 1999; Eyecon, coordinator, 1995; University of Wisconsin, School of Library and Information Science, lecturer; Mystery Writers of America-Midwest, board director, 1997-99. Writer. **Publications:** A Reader's Guide to the Private Eye Novel, 1993; The Long Good Cry, 1998; Make Mine a Mystery: A Reader's Guide to Mystery and Detective Fiction, 2003; Read 'em Their Writes: A Handbook for Mystery and Crime Fiction Book Discussions, 2006; Caught up in Crime: A Reader's Guide to Crime Fiction and Nonfiction, 2009; Make Mine a Mystery II, 2011. EDITOR and CONTRIBUTOR: (with O.A. Hardy-Sayles) The Big Jacuzzi: A Collection of Shallow Short Stories, 1992; (with Hardy-Sayles) Farewell, My Lobby: A Collection of Shameless Short Stories, 1993; The Lady in the 10, 000 Lakes, 1996; The Little Sister in Crime, 1997. Contributor of articles. **Address:** PO Box 341218, Milwaukee, WI 53234, U.S.A. **Online address:** pieshook@execpc.com

NIEBUHR, Gustav. American (born United States), b. 1955. **Genres:** Theology/Religion. **Career:** Berkshire Eagle, reporter, 1980-84; Times Picayune, reporter, 1984-86; Atlanta Journal-Constitution, reporter, 1986-89; Wall Street Journal, staff writer, 1989-92; Washington Post, staff writer, 1992-94; New York Times, national correspondent, 1994-2001; Syracuse University, associate professor of religion and the media, 2004-. Journalist and academic. **Publications:** Beyond Tolerance: Searching for Interfaith Understanding in America, 2008. Contributor to books and periodicals. **Address:** Syracuse University, 313 Tolley, 501 Hall of Languages, Syracuse, NY 13244-1170, U.S.A. **Online address:** rgniebuh@syr.edu

NIEDERHOFFER, Galt. American (born United States), b. 1975?. **Genres:** Novels, Sciences, Young Adult Fiction. **Career:** Giv'en Films, co-founder, 1996-; Plum Pictures, co-founder, 2003, partner. Writer. **Publications:** A Taxonomy of Barnacles, 2006; The Romantics, 2008. **Address:** Plum Pictures, 636 Broadway, Ste. 814, New York, NY 10012, U.S.A. **Online address:** galtn@aol.com

NIEDERMAN, Derrick. American (born United States), b. 1954. **Genres:** Novels, Money/Finance, Economics, Young Adult Fiction, Novellas/Short Stories. **Career:** Worth, investment editor. **Publications:** This Is Not Your Father's Stockpicking Book: Profiting from the Hidden Investment Clues Found in Everyday Life, 1995; Inspector Forsooth's Whodunnits (short stories), 1998; The Inner Game of Investing: Access the Power of Your Investment Personality, 1999; A Killing on Wall Street: An Investment Mystery (novel), 2000; The Little Giant Book of Math Puzzles, 2000; Math Puzzles for the Clever Mind, 2001; (with D. Boyum) What The Numbers Say: A Field Guide to Mastering Our Numerical World, 2003; (with A. Hart-Davis and R. Blum) Mensa Math, 2004; Mind-Stretching Math Puzzles, 2005; (co-author) Classic Brain Twisters, 2005; Number Freak: From 1 to 200- The Hidden Language of Numbers Revealed, 2009; The Puzzler's Dilemma, 2012. Contributor to periodicals. **Address:** c/o Author Mail, John Wiley & Sons Inc., 111 River St., Hoboken, NJ 07030, U.S.A.

NIELDS, Nerissa. American (born United States), b. 1967?. **Genres:** Novels. **Career:** The Nields, founding member, 1991-. Writer and singer. **Publications:** Plastic Angel, 2005; How to Be an Adult, 2008; The Big Idea, 2010; (with K. Nields) All Together Singing in the Kitchen: Creative Ways to Make & Listen to Music as a Family, 2011. **Address:** c/o Ginger Knowlton, Curtis Brown Ltd., 10 Astor Pl., New York, NY 10003-6935, U.S.A. **Online address:** nerissand@gmail.com

NIELSEN, John. American (born United States) **Genres:** Novels, Natural History, Sciences, Environmental Sciences/Ecology. **Career:** Los Angeles Times, journalist; Orange County Register, journalist; Salisbury Evening Post, journalist; Massachusetts Institute of Technology, science journalism fellow; National Public Radio, science correspondent and substitute news program host, 1990-. **Publications:** Condor: To the Brink and Back-The Life and Times of One Giant Bird, 2006. **Address:** Science Desk, National Public Radio, 635 Massachusetts Ave. NW, Washington, DC 20001, U.S.A.

NIELSEN, Kim E. American (born United States), b. 1965. **Genres:** Biography, History. **Career:** University of Wisconsin, professor of history and women's studies, 1999-. Writer, biographer and historian. **Publications:** Un-American Womanhood: Antiradicalism, Antifeminism, and the First Red Scare, 2001; The Radical Lives of Helen Keller, 2004; (ed.) Helen Keller: Selected Writings, 2005; Beyond the Miracle Worker: The Remarkable Life of Anne Sullivan Macy and Her Extraordinary Friendship with Helen Keller, 2009. **Address:** University of Wisconsin, A320 Mary Ann Cofrin Hall, Green Bay, WI 54311, U.S.A. **Online address:** nielsenk@uwgb.edu

NIELSEN, Nancy J. American (born United States), b. 1951. **Genres:** Children's Non-fiction, Education, Civil Liberties/Human Rights, Animals/Pets. **Career:** Teacher, 1979-87; NJN Communications, communications consultant, 1986-. Writer. **Publications:** From Freud to Masters and Johnson: The Feminine Psychology of Helene Deutsch, 1979; Timothy Leary and the Psychedelic Drugs, 1980; Bicycle Racing, 1987; Eric Dickerson, 1987; Helicopter Pilots, 1988; Boundary Waters Canoe Area, 1989; (ed.) Survival Guide for Kids with LD: Learning Differences, 1990; Black Widow Spider, 1990; Teen Alcoholism, 1990; Animal Migration, 1991; Carnivorous Plants, 1992; Killer Whales: The Orcas of the Pacific Ocean, 1995; Reformers and Activists, 1997; Harriet Tubman, 2002. Contributor to books and periodicals. **Address:** 2904 35th Ave. S, Minneapolis, MN 55406, U.S.A. **Online address:** njnc@earthlink.net

NIELSEN, Niels Christian. American (born United States), b. 1921.

Genres: Theology/Religion, Social Commentary, Philosophy. **Career:** Yale College, instructor in religion, 1948-51; Rice University, faculty, 1951, professor of philosophy and religious thought, 1959-91, Newton Rayzor professor of philosophy and religious thought, Department of Religious Studies, chairman, 1968-91, professor emeritus, 1991-; Methodist Church, ordained elder. Writer. **Publications:** Philosophy and Religion in Post-War Japan, 1957; (co-trans.) Geistige Landerkunde, USA, 1960; A Layman Looks at World Religions, 1962; God in Education: A New Opportunity for American schools, 1966; Solzhenitsyn's Religion, 1975; The Religion of President Carter, 1977; The Crisis of Human Rights, 1978; (co-author) Religions of the World, 1983, 3rd ed., 1993; Revolutions in Eastern Europe: The Religious Roots, 1991; Fundamentalism, Mythos and World Religions, 1993; (ed.) Christianity after Communism: Social, Political and Cultural Struggle in Russia, 1994; God in the Obama Era, 2009. **Address:** Rice University, MS-15 Religious Studies, 6100 Main St., Houston, TX 77005-1892, U.S.A. **Online address:** niels@tuf.rice.edu

NIELSON, James. Canadian/American (born United States), b. 1958. **Genres:** Literary Criticism And History, Translations, Young Adult Fiction. **Career:** McGill University, lecturer in English, 1989-92; University of British Columbia, lecturer in English, 1992-95; University of Michigan Press, translator, 1994-95; MediaLinx Interactive, web consultant and researcher, HTML author and internet programmer, 1995-2001, senior web developer, 1995-98; Morris and Helen Belkin Art Gallery, proofreader, 1995; Bell Sympatico, online producer, senior web developer, project manager and home page editor, 1995-2001; One Step Solutions, owner, 2001-. **Publications:** Unread Herrings: Thomas Nashe and the Prosaics of the Real, 1993; (trans. with G. James) M. Serres, Genesis, 1995. Contributor to books and periodicals. **Address:** Onestep Solutions, 194 Lippincott St., Toronto, ON M5S 2P1, Canada. **Online address:** jnielson@sympatico.ca

NIEMANN, Greg. American (born United States), b. 1939. **Genres:** History, Adult Non-fiction. **Career:** United Parcel Service, staff, 1957-58, delivery driver, editor, 1961-95, communications manager, editor, retired, 1995; San Clemente Journal, staff; International Association of Business Communicators, president; Writers Association of California, director. writer. **Publications:** Baja Legends: The Historic Characters, Events, and Locations That Put Baja California on the Map, 2002; Palm Springs Legends: Creation of a Desert Oasis, 2006; Big Brown: The Untold Story of UPS, 2007. **Address:** Sunbelt Publications Inc., 1256 Fayette St., El Cajon, CA 92020, U.S.A. **Online address:** info@gregniemann.com

NIEMANN, Linda (Grant). American (born United States), b. 1946. **Genres:** Autobiography/Memoirs. **Career:** University of California, acting assistant professor of English, 1972-74, lecturer in English, 1986-87, 1975; Cabrillo College, researcher and consultant, 1975-78; Mercury Communications, researcher and consultant, 1976-78; University of San Francisco, instructor, 1986-87; Kennesaw State University, professor, 1999-. Writer. **Publications:** Boomer: Railroad Memoirs, 1990, 7th ed., 2011; On the Rails: A Woman's Journey, 1996; Railroad Voices, 1998; Railroad Noir, 2010. **Address:** American Studies Program, Kennesaw State University, Rm. 5010, Social Sciences Bldg., 1000 Chastain Rd., Ste. 22, Kennesaw, GA 30144, U.S.A. **Online address:** lniemann@kennesaw.edu

NIEMELA, Pirkko. Finnish (born Finland), b. 1939. **Genres:** Psychology, Women's Studies And Issues, Sciences, Mathematics/Statistics. **Career:** University of Turku, assistant teacher of psychology, 1976, professor of psychology, 1983, now professor emeritus; Finnish Academy of Science, researcher, 1976-83; family therapist, 1984-; psychoanalyst, 1989-. Writer. **Publications:** (Co-author) Perceived Peace-Mindedness of the Superpowers: Images of the U.S.A. and the U.S.S.R., 1989; (ed. with K. Bjórkqvist) Of Mice and Women: Aspects of Female Aggression, 1992. Contributor to books and journals. **Address:** Department of Psychology, University of Turku, Assistentinkatu 7, Turku, 20014, Finland. **Online address:** pirkko.niemela@utu.fi

NIERENBERG, Gerard I. American (born United States), b. 1923. **Genres:** Business/Trade/Industry, Communications/Media, Ethics, Human Relations/Parenting, Language/Linguistics, Self Help. **Career:** Nierenberg Zeif and Weinstein, partner, 1947-; The Negotiation Institute, founder, 1966. Writer. **Publications:** Art of Negotiating, 1968; Creative Business Negotiating, 1971; (with H. Calero) How to Read a Person Like a Book, 1971; Fundamentals of Negotiating, 1973; (with H. Calero) Meta-Talk: Guide to Hidden Meanings in Conversations, 1974; How to Give and Receive Advice, 1975; The Art of Creative Thinking, 1982; The Complete Negotiator, 1986; How to Read a Person like a Book, 1986; How to Give Yourself Good Advice, 1986; Workable Ethics, 1987; Negotiating the Big Sale, 1991; (with G.G. Schwendotner) The Non-verbal Selling Power, 1989; You're the Expert, 1991; Do It Right the First Time, 1996; Earn from Your Mistakes-Nierenberg's Error Awareness Systems, 1999; Secrets of a Master Negotiator, 2000; Successful Selling Made E-Z, 2001; (with H.H. Calera) New Art of Negotiating: How to Closeany Deal, 2009, (with H.H. Calero) New How to Read a Person Like a Book, 2010. Contributor to magazines. **Address:** Negotiation Institution Inc., 330 E 38th St., Ste. 7L, New York, NY 10016, U.S.A. **Online address:** george@negotiation.com

NIGAM, Sanjay (Kumar). American/Indian (born India), b. 1959?. **Genres:** Novellas/Short Stories, Medicine/Health, Literary Criticism And History, Young Adult Fiction. **Career:** Harvard Medical School, associate professor of medicine. Writer. **Publications:** The Non-Resident Indian and Other Stories, 1996; The Snake Charmer, 1998; Transplanted Man, 2002. Contributor of short stories to periodicals. **Address:** William Morrow & Co., 1350 Ave. of the Americas, New York, NY 10019, U.S.A.

NIGHBERT, David F(ranklin). American (born United States), b. 1948. **Genres:** Mystery/Crime/Suspense, Science Fiction/Fantasy, Sciences. **Career:** Tower Records, assistant manager, 1989-. Writer and actor. **Publications:** SCIENCE-FICTION: TIMELAPSE SERIES: Timelapse, 1988; The Clouds of Magellan, 1991. BULL COCHRAN MYSTERY SERIES: Strikezone, 1989; Squeezeplay, 1992; Shutout, 1995. Contributor to periodicals. **Address:** Tower Records, 1961 Broadway, New York, NY 10023-5904, U.S.A.

NIGHTINGALE, Pamela. British (born England), b. 1938. **Genres:** History, Business/Trade/Industry, Economics, Social Sciences. **Career:** Archivist, 1963-66; research assistant to the Reverend Honorable Lord Glendevon, 1967-69; Open University, tutor, 1972-79; Worker's Educational Association, lecturer, 1972-79; Buckinghamshire Archaeological Society, honorary librarian, 1974-80; Historical Association, chair, 1974-80; Grocers' Co. of London, historian, 1979-95; Leverhulme research fellow, 1993-98, now emeritus; economic and social research fellow, 1999-2004. Writer. **Publications:** Trade and Empire in Western India, 1784-1806, 1970; (with C. Skrine) Macartney at Kashgar: New Light on British, Chinese and Russian Activities in Singkiang, 1890-1918, 1973; Fortune and Integrity: A Study of Moral Attitudes in the Indian Diary of George Paterson, 1769-74, 1985; A Medieval Mercantile Community: The Grocers Company and the Politics & Trade of London, 1000-1485, 1995; Trade, Money and Power in Medieval England, 2007. Contributor of academic articles on medieval economic and monetary history to scholarly journals. **Address:** Ashmolean Museum, Beaumont St., Oxford, OX OX1 2PH, England.

NIGHTMARE, M. Macha. American (born United States), b. 1943. **Genres:** Cultural/Ethnic Topics, Theology/Religion, Popular Culture. **Career:** Author, interfaith activist and ritualist. **Publications:** Woman Blood: Portraits of Women in Poetry and Prose, 1981; The Pagan Book of Living and Dying: Practical Rituals, Prayers, Blessings, and Meditations on Crossing Over, 1997; Witchcraft and the Web: Weaving Pagan Traditions Online, 2001; Pagan Pride: Honoring the Craft and Culture of Earth and Goddess, 2004. Works appear in anthologies. **Address:** c/o Jennie Dunham, Dunham Literary Inc., 156 5th Ave., Ste. 823, New York, NY 10010-7002, U.S.A. **Online address:** herself@machanightmare.com

NIGRO, August John. American (born United States), b. 1934. **Genres:** Literary Criticism And History, Young Adult Fiction. **Career:** University of Miami, English assistant, 1958-60; University of Maryland, English assistant, 1960-63; University of Maryland (Europe), lecturer, 1963-65; Niagara University, assistant professor of English, 1965-67; Kutztown University, English professor, 1967-, now professor emeritus. Writer. **Publications:** The Diagonal Line: Separation and Reparation in American Literature, 1984; The Net of Nemesis: Studies in Tragic Bond/age, 2000; Wolfsangel: A German City on Trial, 1945-48, 2000. Contributor to periodicals. **Address:** Susquehanna University Press, Susquehanna University, 514 University Ave., Selinsgrove, PA 17870, U.S.A. **Online address:** nigro@kutztown.edu

NIHAN, Christophe. Swiss (born Switzerland), b. 1972?. **Genres:** Reference. **Career:** University of Lausanne, associate professor of Hebrew Bible. Theologian and writer. **Publications:** From Priestly Torah to Pentateuch: A

Study in the Composition of the Book of Leviticus, 2007; (with P. Abadie) Étienne Nodet, Samaritains, Juifs, Temples, 2010. Contributor to journals. **Online address:** christophe.nihan@unil.ch

NI HUA-CHING. Chinese (born China), b. 1925. **Genres:** Philosophy, Self Help, Theology/Religion, Translations. **Career:** Integral Way Society, co-founder; Yo San University, School of Chinese Medicine, co-founder. Taoist master, author and translator. **Publications:** Tao: The Subtle Universal Law and the Integral Way of Life, 1979, 2nd ed., 1993; The Taoist Inner View of the Universe and the Immortal Realm, 1979; 8, 000 Years of Wisdom, 1983; The Book of Changes and the Unchanging Truth, 1983, rev. ed., 1995; Workbook for Spiritual Development of All People, 1984, rev. ed., 1995; The Great Awakening of All People, 1985 as The Uncharted Voyage toward the Subtle Light, 1985 as The Spiritual Expedition: vol. II: Awaken to the Great Path, vol. III: Ascend the Spiritual Mountain, 1992; The Gentle Path of Spiritual Progress, 1987; Stepping Stones for Spiritual Success, 1989; The Wisdom of Three Masters, vol. I: Attaining Unlimited Life: The Teachings of Chuang Tzu; vol. II: Enlightenment: Mother of Spiritual Independence: The Teachings of Hui Neng; vol. III: The Way of Integral Life: The Teachings of a Taoist Master, 1989; Story of Two Kingdoms, 1989; The Esoteric Teachings of the Tradition of Tao, vol. I: The Story of Two Kingdoms, vol. II: Quest of Soul, vol. III: Eternal Light, 1989; Essence of Universal Spirituality, 1990; Guide to the Inner Light, 1990; Nurture Your Spirits, 1990; Internal Growth through Tao, 1990; The Power of Natural Healing, 1990; The Key to All Good Fortune, 1991; Harmony: The Art of Life, 1991, rev. ed., 2000; Moonlight in the Dark Night, 1991; Ageless Counsel for Modern Life, 1991; The Mystical Universal Mother, 1991; Esoteric Tao Teh Ching, 1992; Internal Alchemy, 1992; Mysticism: Empowering the Spirit Within, 1992; The Time Is Now for a Better Life and a Better World, 1992; Workbook for Spiritual Development of all People, 1992; Life and Teaching of Two Immortals, vol. I: Kou Hong, vol. II: Chen Tuan, 1992-93; The Way, the Truth and the Light, 1993; The Majestic Domain of the Heart, 1993; Immortal Wisdom, 1993; (with D. Ni and M. Ni) Strength from Movement, 1993; Attune Your Body with Dao-In, rev. ed., 1994; By the Light of the North Star, 1995; Hua hu ching: The Later Teachings of Lao Tzu, 1995; Concourse of All Spiritual Paths, 1995; The Gate to Infinity, 1995; The Natural Course of Spiritual Life, 1995; The Power of Positive Living, 1995; Seeing the Unseen, 1995; Self-Reliance and Constructive Change, 1995; The Universal Path of Natural Life, 1995; The Reunion of Mind and Spirit, 1996; Spring Thunder, 1996; From Diversity to Unity, 1996; Entering the Tao: Master Ni's Guidance for Self-Cultivation, 1997; The Foundation of a Happy Life, 1999; Enrich Your Life with Virtue, 1999; Harmony: The Art of Life, 2000; The Centermost Way, 2001; (with M. Ni) The New Universal Morality, 2003; (with M. Ni) The Power of the Feminine, 2004; (with M. Ni) Path of Constructive Life: Embracing Heaven's Heart, 2006; Unchartered Voyage Toward the Subtle Light, 2007; Key to Good Fortune: Refining Your Spirit, 2007; (with M. Ni) Love of Mother Universe, 2008; (with M.S. Ni and J. Miller) Tai Chi for a Healthy Body, Mind and Spirit: The Ni Family Tradition, 2010; (with M.S. Ni) Evolve Heaven on Earth, 2012. TRANSLATOR: Complete Works of Lao Tzu, 1979. **Address:** SevenStar Communications Group, 13315 Washington Blvd., Ste. 200, Los Angeles, CA 90066, U.S.A.

NIKITAS, Derek. American (born United States), b. 1974. **Genres:** Novels. **Career:** State University of New York-Brockport, Delta College, educator; Eastern Kentucky University, assistant professor, 2008-. Novelist, short-story writer and educator. **Publications:** Pyres (novel), 2007. Contributor to magazines and periodicals. **Online address:** derek@dereknikitas.com

NIKKEL, David H. American (born United States), b. 1952. **Genres:** Theology/Religion. **Career:** Church of the Good Shepherd, associate pastor, 1981-83; Atwater United Methodist Church, pastor, 1983-87; East Ohio Conference of the United Methodist Church, Commission on the Status and Role of Women, vice chairperson, 1984-92; Smith Corners United Methodist Church, pastor, 1987-92; Ecumenical Christian Counseling Service of Northern Ohio, counselor, 1990-92; Greater Austintown Ecumenical Association, founder, president, 1990-92; Hastings College, assistant professor of religion and philosophy and college chaplain, 1992-98; Hastings and Adams County Ministerial Association, president, 1995-; United Methodist Church, pastor, 1998-2002, University of North Carolina at Pembroke, assistant professor of religion, 2002-08, Tomorrow's Religious Leaders, faculty advisor, 2002-, Department of Philosophy and Religion, chair, 2007-, associate professor of religion, 2008-, Youngstown State University, adjunct professor; Hiram College, adjunct professor; Mt. Union College, adjunct professor; Methodist Theological School, adjunct professor; North American Paul Tillich Society, president. Writer. **Publications:** Panentheism in Hartshorne and Tillich: A Creative Synthesis, 1995; Radical Embodiment, 2010. Contributor to periodicals. **Address:** Department of Philosophy & Religion, University of North Carolina, Rm. 315, Education Ctr., PO Box 1510, Pembroke, NC 28372-1510, U.S.A. **Online address:** david.nikkel@uncp.edu

NIKLAS, Karl J(oseph). American (born United States), b. 1948. **Genres:** Botany, Biology. **Career:** New York Botanical Gardens, curator of paleobotany, 1974-78; Cornell University, faculty, 1978-; Department of Plant Biology, professor of botany, 1985-, Liberty Hyde Bailey professor, chair, 2000-; American Journal of Botany, editor-in-chief, 1995-2004; Botanical Society of America, president, 2008-09. **Publications:** (Ed.) Paleobotany, Paleoecology, and Evolution, 1981; Plant Biomechanics: An Engineering Approach to Plant Form and Function, 1992; Plant Allometry: The Scaling and Form to Process, 1994; Evolutionary Biology of Plants, 1997; (with H. Spatz) Plant Physics, 2012. Contributor to journals. **Address:** Department of Plant Biology, Cornell University, Rm. 208, Plant Science Bldg., Ithaca, NY 14853-5908, U.S.A. **Online address:** kjn2@cornell.edu

NILES, Steve. American (born United States), b. 1965. **Genres:** Novels, Horror. **Career:** Arcane Comics, founder; Creep Entertainment (production company), co-founder, 2003. Novelist, film producer and musician. **Publications:** COMIC BOOK COMPILATIONS/GRAPHIC NOVELS: Dark Days, 2003. Wake the Dead, 2003; (with N. Stakal) Hyde, 2004; Secret Skull, 2004; Aleister Arcane, 2004; Freaks of the Heartland, 2005; (with B.M. Bendis) Hellspawn: The Ashley Wood Collection, 2006; (co-author) Gotham County Line: Batman, 2006; Simon Dark, 2007; 28 Days Later: The Aftermath, 2007; (with J. Mariotte) Eternal Damnation, 2008; Spawn: Book of the Dead, 2008; American Freakshow, 2008; Simon Dark: What Simon Does, 2008; The Lost Ones, 2008; City of Others, 2008; Dead, She Said, 2009; City of Dust, 2009; Epilogue, 2009; Batman, 2009; Simon Dark: Ashes, 2009; Simon Dark: The Game of Life, 2009; The Creeper, 2010; A World of Hurt, 2010. 30 DAYS OF NIGHT SERIES: 30 Days of Night, 2002; The Complete 30 Days of Night, 2003; 30 Days of Night: Bloodsucker Tales, 2003; 30 Days of Night: Return to Barrow, 2004; (with J. Mariotte) 30 Days of Night: Rumors of the Undead, 2006; (with J. Mariotte) 30 Days of Night: Immortal Remains, 2007; Beyond Barrow: 30 Days of Night 9, 2008. CAL McDONALD SERIES: Savage Membrane, 2002; Dial M for Monster, 2003; Guns, Drugs, and Monsters, 2005; Last Train to Deadsville, 2005; Two Red Eyes: Criminal Macabre, 2007; Criminal Macabre: The Complete Cal McDonald Stories, 2007; Criminal Macabre: Cell Block 66, 2009. OTHER: (ed.) Clive Barker, Illustrator, 1990. **Address:** Toluca Lake, CA , U.S.A. **Online address:** steve@steveniles.com

NILSEN, Anders Brekhus. American (born United States), b. 1973. **Genres:** Art/Art History. **Career:** Artist and writer. **Publications:** Big Questions vol. I, 1999, vol. III: Astrophysics, 2000, vol. IV: Asomatognosia, 2001, vol. V: Nothingness, 2002, vol. VI: Anoesia and the Matrideicidic Theophany, 2004, vol. VII: Dinner and a Nap, 2005, vol. VIII: Theory and Practice, 2005, vol. IX: The Lost and Found, 2006, vol. X: Monologues for the coming Plague, 2006; The Hand That Feeds, 2007; Dogs and Water, 2007; Don't Go Where I Can't Follow, 2007; The End, 2007; Monologues for Calculating the Density of Black Holes, 2008; Big Questions, 2011. **Address:** 3844 W Wrightwood Ave., Chicago, IL 60647, U.S.A. **Online address:** ndrs@hotmail.com

NILSEN, Anna. *See* **BASSIL, Andrea.**

NILSSON, Eleanor. Australian/Scottish (born Scotland), b. 1939. **Genres:** Children's Fiction, Novels, Humor/Satire. **Career:** High school teacher, 1960-61; Adelaide Teachers' College, lecturer in English, 1962-68; South Australia College of Advanced Education, lecturer in English, 1971-90; University of South Australia, lecturer in English, 1991-92; full-time writer, 1992-. **Publications:** Parrot Fashion, 1983; The Rainbow Stealer, 1984; Tatty, 1985; A Bush Birthday, 1985; Heffalump?, 1986; The 89th Kitten, 1987; Pomily's Wish, 1987; Mystery Meals, 1987; There's a Crocodile There Now Too, 1987; Heffalump? and the Toy Hospital, 1989; A Lamb Like Alice, 1990; The Black Duck, 1991; The House Guest, 1991; Writing for Children, 1992; Graffiti Dog, 1995; Outside Permission, 1996; The Experiment, 1996; Pearl's Pantry, 1990; Tiptoe round a [illegible]; [illegible], 1999; The Doll of Germelshausen, 1999; The Way Home, 2001; Helping Out, 2003. **Address:** 410 Main Rd., Coromandel Valley, Adelaide, SA 5051, Australia.

NILSSON, **Jenny Lind.** American (born United States), b. 1957. **Genres:** Young Adult Fiction, Music, Children's Fiction. **Career:** Musician and author of children's books. **Publications:** (With G. Keillor) The Sandy Bottom Orchestra, 1996; (with G. Keillor) Sommerstücke (Ab 12 J.), 2003. **Address:** Hyperion Books, 114 5th Ave., 13th Fl., New York, NY 10011-5645, U.S.A.

NILSSON, **Per.** Swedish (born Sweden), b. 1954. **Genres:** Novels, Young Adult Fiction. **Career:** Swedish Secondary School, teacher in maths and music; freelance writer, 1999-. **Publications:** YOUNG-ADULT NOVELS: Hjärtans fröjd, 1992; Anarkai, 1998; Du & Du & Du, 1998; Ett annat sätt attvara ung, 2000; Lilla Livet, Lilla Döden, 2001; You & You & You, 2005; Seventeen, 2007. Contributor to periodicals. **Address:** c/o Author Mail, Rabén Sjögren, PO Box 2052, Stockholm, 10312, Sweden.

NIMAN, **Michael I.** American (born United States), b. 1957. **Genres:** Anthropology/Ethnology, Area Studies, Civil Liberties/Human Rights, International Relations/Current Affairs, Race Relations, Writing/Journalism. **Career:** Buffalo State College, assistant professor, 1994-, associate professor of journalism, 2002-; State University of New York-Buffalo, visiting assistant professor, 1997-98; Buffalo Coalition for Progressive Media, co-founder, 1997-2004; Buffalo Beat Newspaper, columnist, media critic, 2001; ArtVoice, columnist, 2001-; Coldtype, columnist, 2005-; New York Sociologist, editor, 2007-. Consultant. **Publications:** People of the Rainbow: A Nomadic Utopia (ethnography), 1997, 2nd ed., 2011. Contributor to magazines and newspapers. **Address:** Department of Communication, Buffalo State College, 210 Bishop Hall, 1300 Elmwood Ave., Buffalo, NY 14222, U.S.A. **Online address:** nimanmi@buffalostate.edu

NIMMO, **Jenny.** Welsh/British (born England), b. 1944. **Genres:** Children's Fiction, Novels, Young Adult Fiction. **Career:** Theatre Southeast, actress and assistant stage manager, 1960-63; Governess in Amalfi, staff, 1963; British Broadcasting Corp., photographic researcher, 1964-66, assistant floor manager, 1966-68, 1971-74. Writer and director. **Publications:** CHILDREN OF THE RED KING: Midnight for Charlie Bone, 2002; Charlie Bone and the Time Twister, 2002; Charlie Bone and the Blue Boa, 2004; Charlie Bone and the Invisible Boy, 2004; Charlie Bone and the Castle of Mirrors, 2005; Charlie Bone and the Hidden King, 2006; Charlie Bone and the Wilderness Wolf, 2007; Charlie Bone and the Beast, 2007; Charlie Bone and the Shadow, 2008; Charlie Bone and the Red Knight, 2009. BOX BOYS: The Box Boys and the Bonfire Cat, 1999; The Box Boys and the Dog in the Mist, 1999; The Box Boys and the Fairground Ride, 1999; The Box Boys and the Magic Shell, 1999. DELILAH: Delilah and the Dogspell, 1991; Delilah and the Dishwasher Dogs, 1993; Delilah Alone, 1995. SNOW SPIDER: The Snow Spider, 1986; Emlyn's Moon, 1987; The Chestnut Soldier, 1989; The Snow Spider Trilogy, 1993. NOVELS: The Bronze Trumpete, 1974; Ultramarine, 1990; Rainbow and Mr. Zed, 1992; Griffins Castle, 1994; The Rinaldi Ring, 1999; Milo's Wolves, 2001; Secret Creatures, 2007. PICTURE BOOKS: The Bears Will Get You, 1990; The Starlight Cloak, 1990; The Witches and the Singing Mice, 1993; Gwion and the Witch, 1996; Esmeralda and the Children Next Door, 1999; The Strongest Girl in the World, 2001; Branwen, 2001; Something Wonderful, 2001; Pig on a Swing, 2003; The Beasties, 2010. SELF-ILLUSTRATED: Tatty Apple, 1984; The Red Secret, 1989; Jupiter Boots, 1990; The Stone Mouse, 1993; The Breadwitch, 1993; Wilfred's Wolf, 1994; Ronnie and the Giant Millipede, 1995; Granny Grimm's Gruesome Glasses, 1995; The Witch's Tears, 1996; The Alien on the 99th Floor, 1996; Hot Dog Cool Cat, 1997; Seth and the Strangers, 1997; The Owl Tree, 1997; The Dragon's Child, 1997; The Dog Star, 1999; Toby in the Dark, 1999; Ill Will Well Nell, 2000; The Bodygulpa, 2001; Tom and the Pterosaur, 2001; Beak and Whisker, 2002; Matty Mouse, 2003; The Night of the Unicorn, 2003; Invisible Vinnie, 2003. CHRONICLES OF THE RED KING: Secret Kingdom, 2011; The Stones of Ravenglass, 2012. **Address:** David Highham Associates, 5-8 Lower John St., Golden Sq., London, GL W1F 9HA, England. **Online address:** jennynimmo@aol.com

NIMOY, **Adam.** American (born United States), b. 1956. **Genres:** Autobiography/Memoirs, Biography. **Career:** New York Film Academy, faculty. Writer and television director. **Publications:** My Incredibly Wonderful, Miserable Life: An Anti-Memoir, 2008. **Address:** The Gersh Agency, 9465 Wilshire Blvd., 6th Fl., Beverly Hills, CA 90212, U.S.A.

NINEHAM, **Dennis Eric.** British (born England), b. 1921. **Genres:** Theology/Religion, History, Social Sciences. **Career:** Oxford University, Queen's College, fellow, 1946-54, honorable fellow, 1991-, Keble College, warden, 1969-79, honorable fellow, 1980-; University of London, King's College, professor of Biblical and historical theology, 1954-58, professor of divinity, 1958-64, fellow, 1963-; Cambridge University, Regius professor of divinity and fellow of Emmanuel College, 1964-69; University of Bristol, Department of Theology, professor of theology and head, 1980-86. Writer. **Publications:** A New Way of Looking at the Gospels, 1961; The Gospel of St. Mark, 1963, rev. ed., 1968; (co-author) Historicity and Chronology in the New Testament, 1965; History and the Gospel: The Charles Gore Memorial Lecture Delivered in Westminister Abbey on 8th November 1966, 1967; (contrib.) Christ for Us Today, 1968; Use and Abuse of the Bible: A Study of the Bible in an Age of Rapid Cultural Change, 1976; New Testament Interpretation in an Historical Age, 1976; (contrib.) The Myth of God Incarnate, 1977; Explorations in Theology, 1977; Christianity, Mediaeval and Modern: A Study in Religious Change, 1993. EDITOR: Studies in the Gospels: Essays in Memory of R.H. Lightfoot, 1955, 2nd ed., 1957; On the Authority of the Bible, 1960; Church's Use of the Bible, Past and Present, 1963; The Church's Use of the Bible, 1965; New English Bible Reviewed, 1965. Contributor to periodicals. **Address:** 9 Fitzherbert Close, Oxford, OX OX4 4EN, England.

NIR, **Yossi.** Israeli (born Israel), b. 1955?. **Genres:** Mystery/Crime/Suspense. **Career:** Weizmann Institute of Science, professor. Writer. **Publications:** (With H.R. Quinn) The Mystery of the Missing Antimatter, 2008. **Address:** Department of Particle Physics, Weizmann Institute of Science, Rehovot, 76100, Israel. **Online address:** yosef.nir@weizmann.ac.il

NISBET, **Jack.** American (born United States), b. 1949. **Genres:** Earth Sciences, Geography, History, Biography, Autobiography/Memoirs, Sciences, Technology, Travel/Exploration, Travel/Exploration, Ethics. **Career:** Farallon Islands National Wildlife Refuge, winter field assistant, 1975-82; teacher, 1986-2004; writer, 2004-; Whitworth College, teacher; Northwest Museum of Arts and Culture, consultant; Canadian Broadcasting Corp., consultant. **Publications:** Sky People, 1984; Sources of the River: Tracking David Thompson through Western North America, 1994; Purple Flat Top: In Pursuit of a Place, 1996; Singing Grass, Burning Sage: Discovering Washington's Shrub-Steppe, 1999; Visible Bones: Journeys across Time in the Columbia Country, 2003; The Mapmaker's Eye: David Thompson and the Moment of Contact on the Columbia Plateau, 2005; The Collector: David Douglas and the Natural History of the Pacific Northwest, 2009; Purple Flat Top: In Pursuit of a Place, 2011. Contributor to periodicals. **Address:** Ann Rittenberg Literary Agency, 1201 Broadway, Ste. 708, New York, NY 10001, U.S.A. **Online address:** jack@jacknisbet.com

NISH, **Ian Hill.** British (born England), b. 1926. **Genres:** History, International Relations/Current Affairs, Essays. **Career:** University of Sydney, lecturer in history, 1958-62; University of London, London School of Economics and Political Science, senior lecturer, 1963-72, reader, 1972-80, professor of international history, 1980-91, professor emeritus, 1991-; European Association for Japanese Studies, president, 1985-88; British Association for Japanese Studies, secretary; Suntory Toyota International Centre for Economics and Related Disciplines, honorary senior research associate. Writer. **Publications:** The Anglo-Japanese Alliance: The Diplomacy of Two Island Empires, 1894-1907, 1966; The Story of Japan in US as Short History of Japan, 1968; Alliance in Decline: A Study in Anglo-Japanese Relations, 1908-23, 1972; Britain and Japan, 1600-1975, 1975; Japanese Foreign Policy, 1869-1942: Kasumigaseki to Miyakezaka, 1977; (with D. Steeds) China, Japan and 19th-Century Britain, 1977; (ed. with C. Dunn) European Studies on Japan, 1979; (ed.) Indonesian Experience: The Role of Japan and Britain, 1943-1948, 1979; (ed.) Anglo-Japanese Alienation, 1919-1952: Papers of the Anglo-Japanese Conference on the History of the Second World War, 1982; The Origins of the Russo-Japanese War, 1985; (ed.) Contemporary European Writing on Japan: Scholarly Views from Eastern and Western Europe, 1988; British Documents on Foreign Affairs-Reports and Papers from the Foreign Office Confidential Print. Part I, From the Mid-Nineteenth Century to the First World War. Series E, Asia, 1860-1914, 1989; (contrib.) Conflict and Amity in East Asia: Essays in Honour of Ian Nish, 1992; Japan's Struggle with Internationalism: Japan, China and the League of Nations, 1993; (ed.) Britain and Japan: Biographical Portraits, 1994; (ed. with G. Redding and N. Sek-hong) Work and Society: Labour and Human Resources in East Asia, 1996; The Iwakura Mission in America and Europe, 1998; (ed. with C. Hosoya) The History of Anglo-Japanese Relations, 2000; (co-author) Nichi-Ei Kōryūshi, 1600-2000, 2000; Collected Writings, 2 vols., 2001-02; Japanese Foreign Policy in the Interwar Period, 2002; (contrib.) Problems of the Far East, 2002; (ed. with M. Light) Cabinet Decisions On Foreign Policy: The British Experience, October 1938-June 1941, 2002; Turkish Foreign Policy During The Second World War: An Active Neutrality, 2004; The Japanese in War and Peace, 1942-48, 2011; (with K. Fumitaka) Rekishi to Wakai, 2011. **Address:** London School of Economics and Political Science, University of London, Houghton St., London, GL WC2A 2AE, England. **Online address:** a.swain@lse.ac.uk

NISHIMURA, Kae. American (born United States) **Genres:** Animals/Pets, Illustrations, Children's Fiction. **Career:** Author and illustrator. **Publications:** SELF-ILLUSTRATED: Dinah!: A Cat Adventure, 2004. OTHERS: I am Dodo: Not a True Story, 2005; Bunny Lune, 2007. **Address:** c/o Author Mail, Houghton Mifflin Co., 215 Park Ave. S, New York, NY 10003-1603, U.S.A. **Online address:** kae@thesoupgroup.net

NISKALA, Brenda. Canadian (born Canada), b. 1955?. **Genres:** Poetry, Young Adult Fiction. **Career:** Saskatchewan Writers Guild, electronic writer-in-residence, 1994-95; Saskatchewan Publishers Group, co-executive director; University of Regina, Department of Extension, creative writing teacher, staff; ACTRA, branch representative. **Publications:** POETRY: Ambergris Moon, 1983; (co-author) Open 24 Hours, 1997; Of All the Ways to Die, 2009; For The Love of Strangers, 2010. Works appear in anthologies. Contributor of articles to magazines and periodicals. **Address:** Saskatchewan Publishers Group, 2405 11th Ave., Regina, SK S4P 0K4, Canada. **Online address:** bniskala@saskpublishers.sk.ca

NISSANOFF, Daniel. American (born United States), b. 1965?. **Genres:** Marketing, Business/Trade/Industry. **Career:** Weil, Gotshal and Manges L.L.P., associate attorney; PartMiner Inc., founder, chief executive officer and chairman, 1994-2002; Portero, founder, 2004-07; Make Meaning, founder and chief executive officer, 2007-. Writer and public speaker. **Publications:** FutureShop: How the New Auction Culture Will Revolutionize the Way We Buy, Sell, and Get the Things We Really Want, 2006. **Address:** c/o Jennifer Joel, International Creative Management, 40 W 57th St., New York, NY 10019, U.S.A. **Online address:** dnissanoff@auctionculture.com

NISSEN, Bruce. American (born United States), b. 1948. **Genres:** Organized Labor, Business/Trade/Industry. **Career:** Wagner College, assistant professor of philosophy, 1980-81; Indiana University-Purdue University, assistant professor of labor studies, 1981-84, Labor Studies program, director, 1981-84; Indiana University Northwest, assistant professor of labor studies, 1985-88, associate professor, 1988-97, professor, External Degree Program, director, 1990-97, Labor Studies program, director, 1985-90; Policy Studies Journal, special issue editor, 1990; Florida International University, Center for Labor Research and Studies, director, 1997-, Research Institute on Social and Economic Policy, director, 2004-09, Department of Global and Sociocultural Studies, lecturer in sociology, 2010-; United Faculty of Florida, South Florida Unit Service, director, 2009-10. Writer and consultant. **Publications:** Fighting for Jobs: Case Studies of Labor-Community Coalitions Confronting Plant Closings, 1995; Ethics in the Hospitality and Tourism Industry, 2nd ed., 2008. EDITOR and CONTRIBUTOR: (with S. Larson) Theories of the Labor Movement, 1987; U.S. Labor Relations, 1945-1989: Accommodation and Conflict, 1990; (with C. Craypo) Grand Designs: The Impact of Corporate Strategies on Workers, Unions and Communities, 1993; Unions and Workplace Reorganization, 1997; Which Direction for Organized Labor? Essays on Organizing, Outreach and Internal Transformation, 1999; Unions in a Globalized Environment: Changing Borders, Organizational Boundaries and Social Roles, 2002. Contributor to books and periodicals. **Address:** Department of Global & Sociocultural Studies, Florida International University, LC312, Modesto A. Maidique Campus, 11200 SW 8th St., Miami, FL 33199, U.S.A. **Online address:** nissenb@fiu.edu

NISSENSON, Hugh. American (born United States), b. 1933. **Genres:** Novels. **Career:** Writer. **Publications:** A Pile of Stones, 1965; Notes from the Frontier, 1968; In the Reign of Peace, 1972; My Own Ground, 1976; (with Esther Menascé) Eight Stories, 1976; The Tree of Life, 1985; The Elephant and My Jewish Problem, 1988; Chaim Potok and Jewish-American Clture: A Memorial Symposium, 2002; The Days of Awe, 2005; The Pilgrim: A Novel, 2011. SELF-ILLUSTRATED: The Song of the Earth, 2001. **Address:** c/o Author Mail, 1935 Brookdale Rd., Ste. 139, Sourcebooks Inc., Naperville, IL 60563, U.S.A.

NISSENSON, Marilyn. American (born United States), b. 1939. **Genres:** Popular Culture, Photography, Social Sciences. **Career:** Television writer, 1964-90; CBS News, researcher and associate producer, 1962-68; NBC News, researcher and associate producer, 1969-70; non-fiction writer, 1990-. **Publications:** WITH SUSAN JONAS: Cuff Links, 1991; The Ubiquitous Pig, 1992; Going, Going, Gone: Vanishing Americana, 1994; Snake Charm, 1995; Friends for Life: Enriching the Bond between Mothers and their Adult Daughters, 1997; Jeweled Bugs and Butterflies, 2000. OTHERS: Lady Upstairs: Dorothy Schiff and the New York Post, 2007. Contributor to periodicals. **Address:** 411 W End Ave., New York, NY 10024, U.S.A.

NISSMAN, Blossom S. American (born United States), b. 1928. **Genres:** Children's Fiction, Children's Non-fiction, Education, Speech/Rhetoric, Adult Non-fiction. **Career:** Teacher, 1951-53, 1953-57, 1964-66; Willingboro School District, elementary teacher, 1966-69, learning disabilities consultant, 1970-72; Rider College, adjunct assistant professor, 1969-; Trenton State College, adjunct assistant professor, 1969-; Central Burlington County Region, specialist in curriculum and instruction, 1972-76, coordinator, 1976-84, executive director, 1984-; educational consultant, 1972-2000; Long Beach Island School, assistant superintendent, superintendent, 1986-90; Georgian Court College, professor of education, 1990-2000, now retired; Beach Haven Times, weekly columnist. **Publications:** Counselor's Handbook, 1955; Alphabet Land, 1970; Ask Counselor, 1970; (with M.L. Stamm) New Dimensions in Elementary Guidance, 1971; (with M.L. Stamm) Your Child and Drugs: A Preventive Approach, 1973; What You Always Wanted to Know about Tests But Were Afraid to Ask!, 1973; The Implications and Applications of Assessment Procedures for Counselors and Teachers, 1976; Practical Guidance for Space Age Children, 1979; (with M.L. Stamm) Improving Middle School Guidance, 1979; Mainstreaming: Who? Why? When? How?, 1979; Career Assessment Guidelines for Middle and High School Students with Special Needs, 1980; Job Preparation, Selection, Performance, Retention, 1981; Tips for Teachers, 1981; Teacher Tested Alternatives for Use in Classroom Management, 1981; Answers to Questions Most Frequently Asked about Classfied Students, 1981; Searching for Teaching Excellence, 1982; Burlington County Job File, 1983; Community Job File, 1984; Teaching Alternatives, 1999; Teacher-Tested Classroom Management Strategies, 2000, 3rd ed., 2009. Contributor to professional journals. **Address:** Central Burlington County Region, for Special Education, Westampton School, 700 Rancocas Mount Holly Rd., Westampton, NJ 08060-5610, U.S.A. **Online address:** drblossom@attbi.com

NITCHIE, George Wilson. *See* Obituaries.

NITTO, Tomio. Japanese (born Japan), b. 1945. **Genres:** Cartoons, Environmental Sciences/Ecology. **Career:** K2 Design, illustrator, through 1971; Reactor Art and Design, illustrator, 1986. Writer. **Publications:** The Red Rock: A Graphic Fable, 2006. **Address:** Reactor Art and Design, Ltd., 51 Camden St., Toronto, ON M5V 1V2, Canada.

NIVEN, Alastair (Neil Robertson). British/Scottish (born Scotland), b. 1944. **Genres:** Literary Criticism And History. **Career:** University of Ghana, commonwealth fellow, 1966-68, lecturer in English, 1968-69; University of Leeds, lecturer in English, 1969-70; University of Stirling, lecturer in English studies, 1970-78; University of London, School of Oriental and African Studies, honorary lecturer, 1979-85; Journal of Commonwealth Literature, co-editor, 1979-92; University of London, Institute of Commonwealth Studies, Henry Charles Chapman visiting fellow, 1984-85; Cumberland Lodge, principal, 2001-. Writer. **Publications:** (Ed.) The Commonwealth Writer Overseas: Themes of Exile and Expatriation, 1976; D.H. Lawrence: The Novels, 1978; The Yoke of Pity: The Fictional Writings of Mulk Raj Anand, 1978, rev. ed. as Yoke of Pity: Study of the Fictional Writings of Mulk-Raj Anand, 1981; Truth Within Fiction: A Study of Raja Rao's The Serpent & the Rope, 1978; D.H. Lawrence: The Writer and His Work, 1980; (ed.) Notes on Golding's Lord of the Flies, 1980; Elechi Amadi's Concubine, 1981; (ed. and intro.) Under Another Sky: An Anthology of Commonwealth Poetry Prize Winners, 1987; (with H. Springer) The Commonwealth of Universities: The Story of the Association of Commonwealth Universities, 1963-1988, 1988; (ed. with M. Schmidt) Enigmas & Arrivals: An Anthology of Commonwealth Writing, 1997. Contributor to books and periodicals. **Address:** Eden House, 28 Weathercock Ln., Woburn Sands, BK MK17 8NT, England. **Online address:** aniven@cumberlandlodge.ac.uk

NIVEN, Larry. American (born United States), b. 1938. **Genres:** Novels, Novellas/Short Stories, Mystery/Crime/Suspense, Science Fiction/Fantasy, Graphic Novels, Literary Criticism And History. **Career:** Writer, 1964-. **Publications:** World of Ptavvs, 1966; A Gift from Earth, 1968; Neutron Star, 1969;

The Shape of Space, 1969; Ringworld, 1970; (with D. Gerrold) The Flying Sorcerers, 1971; All the Myriad Ways, 1971; (with J. Brunner and J. Vance) Three Trips in Time and Space; Original Novellas of Science Fiction, 1973; Protector, 1973; The Flight of the Horse, 1973; Inconstant Moon, 1973; (with J. Pournelle) The Mote in God's Eye, 1974; A Hole in Space, 1974; Tales of Known Space, 1975; A World Out of Time, 1976; The Long Arm of Gil Hamilton, 1976; (with J. Pournelle) Infemo, 1976; (with J. Pournelle) Lucifer's Hammer, 1977; The Magic Goes Away, 1978; (with J. Pournelle) Inferno, 1978; Convergent Series, 1979; The Patchwork Girl, 1980; The Ringworld Engineers, 1980; (with S. Barnes) Dream Park, 1981; (with J. Pournelle) Oath of Fealty, 1981; (ed.) The Magic May Return, 1981; (with S. Barnes) The Descent of Anansi, 1982; The Integral Trees, 1984; Niven's Laws, 1984; The Time of the Warlock, 1984; (ed.) More Magic, 1984; (with J. Pournelle) Footfall, 1985; Limits, 1985; The Smoke Ring, 1987; (with S. Barnes and J. Pournelle) The Legacy of Heorot, 1987; (with P. Anderson and D. Ing) The Man-Kzin Wars II, 1988; (with D. Ing and S.M. Stirling) Man-Kzin Wars II, 1989; (with S. Barnes) Dream Park II: The Barsoom Project, 1989; (co-author) Man-Kzin Wars III, 1990; N-Space, 1990; (co-author) Man-Kzin Wars IV, 1991; (with S. Barnes) Achilles' Choice, 1991; (with J. Pournelle and M. Flynn) Fallen Angels, 1991; Playgrounds of the Mind, 1991; (with D. Kingsbury, M.O. Martin and G. Benford) Man-Kzin Wars V, 1992; (with S. Barnes) The California Voodoo Game, 1992; (with J. Byrne) Green Lantern: Ganthet's Tale, 1992; (ed.) Alien Sex: Nineteen Tales by the Masters of Science Fiction and Dark Fantasy, 1992; (with J. Pournelle) The Gripping Hand, 1993; (with D. Kingsbury, M.O. Martin and G. Benford) Man-Kzin Wars VI, 1994; Crashlander, 1994; (co-author) Man-Kzin Wars VII, 1995; Flatlander, 1995; (with J. Pournelle and S. Barnes) Beowulf's Children, 1995; Three Books of Known Space, 1996; The Ringworld Throne, 1996; Destiny's Road, 1997; The Best of All Possible Wars: The Best of the Man-Kzin Wars, 1998; Rainbow Mars, 1999; (with J. Pournelle) The Burning City, 2000; (with S. Barnes) Saturn's Race, 2000; Man-Kzin Wars IX, 2002; The Wunder War: Man-Kzin Wars X, 2003; Scatterbrain, 2003; (with D. Gerrold) The Flying Sorcerers, 2004; Ringworld's Children, 2004; (with H. Colebatch and M. Harrington) Man-Kzin Wars XI, 2005; (with B. Cooper) Building Harlequin's Moon, 2005; (with J. Pournelle) Burning Tower, 2005; The Draco Tavern, 2006; (with E.M. Lerner) Fleet of Worlds, 2007; Destiny's Forge, 2007; (with E.M. Lerner) Juggler of Worlds, 2008; (with J. Pournelle) Escape from Hell, 2009; Man-Kzin Wars XII, 2009; (with E.M. Lerner) Destroyer of Worlds, 2009; Passing Perry Crater Base, Time Uncertain, 2009; Scatterbrain II, 2010; (with J. Pournelle) Dream Park IV: Burning Mountain, 2010; (with G. Benford) Bowl of Heaven, 2010; (with J. Pournelle, M. Flynn) The Moon Bowl, 2010; Stars and Gods, 2010; (with E.M. Lerner) Betrayer of Worlds, 2010; The Best of Larry Niven, 2010; (with S. Barnes) The Moon Maze Game, 2011; (contrib.) Man-Kzin wars XIII, 2012. Works appear in anthologies. Contributor to magazines and periodicals. **Address:** Spectrum Literary Agency, 320 Central Pk. W, Ste. 1-D, New York, NY 10025-7659, U.S.A. **Online address:** fithb@aol.com

NIX, Garth. Australian (born Australia), b. 1963. **Genres:** Young Adult Fiction. **Career:** Gotley Nix Evans Private Ltd., marketing communications consultant, 1996-98; Curtis Brown, part-time agent, 1999-2002. Writer. **Publications:** YOUNG ADULT FICTION: The Ragwitch, 1990; Sabriel, 1995; The Calusari (novelization of an episode of the television show The X Files), 1997; Shade's Children, 1997; Lirael: Daughter of the Clayr, 2001; The Creature in the Case, 2005. HUMOR/SATIRE: Very Clever Baby's First Reader: A Simple Reader for Your Child Featuring Freddy the Fish and Easy Words, 1988; Very Clever Baby's Ben Hur: Starring Freddy the Fish as Charlton Heston, 1989; Very Clever Baby's Guide to the Greenhouse Effect, 1992; Very Clever Baby's First Christmas, 1999. FOR CHILDREN: Bill the Inventor, 1998; Blackbread the Pirate, 1999; Serena and the Sea Serpent, 2000. SEVENTH TOWER SERIES: The Fall, 2000; Castle, 2000; Aenir, 2001; Into battle, 2001; Above the Veil, 2001; The Violet Keystone, 2001. OTHER: Abhorsen, 2003; Mister Monday, 2003; Grim Tuesday, 2004; Ragwitch, 2004; Drowned Wednesday, 2005; (co-author) The Year's Best Science Fiction and Fantasy for Teens, 2005; Across the Wall: Tales of the Abhorsen and Other Stories, 2005; Sir Thursday, 2006; One Beastly Beast, 2007; Lady Friday, 2007; Superior Saturday, 2008; Abhorsen Chronicles, 2009; Lord Sunday, 2010; Troubletwisters, 2011; A Confusion of Princes, 2012. Contributor to periodicals. **Address:** Nix Entertainment Private Ltd., PO Box 2308, Clovelly, NW 2031, Australia. **Online address:** garthnix@ozemail.com.au

NIXON, Cornelia. American (born United States) **Genres:** Novels, Novellas/Short Stories, Literary Criticism And History. **Career:** Occident, poetry editor, 1974-76; Indiana University, assistant professor of English, 1981-85, associate professor of English, 1985-92, professor of English, 1992-2000; Mills College, associate professor of English, 2000-02, W.M. Keck Foundation professor of creative writing, 2002-04, professor of English and creative writing, 2004-, chair of English, 2006-07, director of creative writing, 2006-08, Sarlo professor of English, 2007-08. **Publications:** Lawrence's Leadership Politics and the Turn Against Women (criticism), 1986; Now You See It (novel), 1991; Angels Go Naked (novel), 2000; Jarrettsville: A Novel, 2009; Beach Bunny, forthcoming; Wherever We Are, forthcoming; My Life as a Goat, forthcoming. Contributor to periodicals. **Address:** Department of English, Mills College, 312 Mills Hall, 5000 MacArthur Blvd., Oakland, CA 94613, U.S.A. **Online address:** cnixon@mills.edu

NIXON, Mignon. British (born England) **Genres:** Art/Art History, Photography. **Career:** University of London, Courtauld Institute of Art, lecturer in the art history of American art and senior lecturer in art history, professor of art history, associate dean for academic affairs. Writer. **Publications:** (Ed. with M. Buskirk) The Duchamp Effect, 1996; (ed.) Eva Hesse, 2002; Fantastic Reality: Louise Bourgeois and a Story of Modern Art, 2005. **Address:** Courtald Institute of Art, University of London, Somerset House, Strand, London, GL WC2R 0RN, England. **Online address:** mignon.nixon@courtauld.ac.uk

NIXON, Rob. South African/American/Irish (born Ireland), b. 1954?. **Genres:** Literary Criticism And History. **Career:** Columbia University, professor of English and comparative literature, through 2000; University of Wisconsin, Rachel Carson professor of English, 2000-, Nelson Institute for Environmental Studies, affiliated. Writer. **Publications:** Nadine Gordimer, 1991; London Calling: V.S. Naipaul, Postcolonial Mandarin, 1992; Homelands, Harlem and Hollywood: South African Culture and the World Beyond, 1994; Dreambirds: The Natural History of a Fantasy, 2000; Slow Violence and Environmental Time of the Poor, 2011. Contributor to periodicals. **Address:** Department of English, University of Wisconsin, 7125 Helen C. White Hall, 600 N Park St., Madison, WI 53706, U.S.A. **Online address:** rdnixon@wisc.edu

NIXSON, Frederick Ian. British (born England), b. 1943. **Genres:** Business/Trade/Industry, Economics, Third World, History. **Career:** Makerere University, lecturer in economics, 1968-71; University of Manchester, lecturer, 1971-79, senior lecturer, 1979-90, reader in economics, 1990-, professor of development economics, 1996-. Writer. **Publications:** Economic Integration and Industrial Location: An East African Case Study, 1973; (with D. Colman) Economics of Change in Less Developed Countries, 1978, 3rd ed., 1994; (with C.H. Kirkpatrick and N. Lee) Industrial Structure and Policy in Less Developed Countries, 1984; (with R.R. Jordan) Language for Economics: Integrated Study Skills and Advanced Language Practice, 1986; Development Economics, 1996; Vietnamese Enterprises towards Global Competitiveness, 2010. EDITOR: (with C.H. Kirkpatrick) The Industrialisation of Less Developed Countries, 1983; (with P. Collins) Management Development and Economic Restructuring in the Mongolian Peoples Republic: Issues and Options, 1991; (with M. Artis) Economics of the European Union: Policy and Analysis, 1994, 4th ed., 2007; (with P. Cook) The Move to the Market?: Trade and Industry Policy Reform in Transitional Economies, 1995; (with P. Cook and C.H. Kirkpatrick) Privatization, Enterprise Development, and Economic Reform: Experiences of Developing and Transitional Economies, 1998; (co-ed.) Mongolian Economy: A Manual of Applied Economics For a Country in Transition, 2000. Contributor to journals. **Address:** School of Social Sciences, University of Manchester, Oxford Rd., Manchester, GM M13 9PL, England. **Online address:** fred.nixson@man.ac.uk

NKALA, Nathan. Nigerian (born Nigeria), b. 1941. **Genres:** Plays/Screenplays, Novels, Novellas/Short Stories, Mystery/Crime/Suspense, Adult Nonfiction, Young Adult Fiction. **Career:** Civil Service of Eastern Nigeria, administrative staff, 1965, director general and administrative secretary, 1992-; freelance writer, 1988-. **Publications:** (Co-author) The Insider, Stories of War & Peace from Nigeria, 1971; Mezie, the Ogbanje Boy (novel), 1981; Bridal Kidnap, 1988; Drums and the Voice of Death (novel), 1996; (with P. Davison) Lobedu (nonfiction), 1997; (with P.U. Emejulu) Twenty-One Years of Petrogas LTD: The Spirit of Partnership in Development, 1999. Contributor to books. **Address:** Fouth Dimension Publishing Company Ltd., House 16, 5th Ave., City Layout, PO Box 01164, Enugu, 23442, Nigeria.

NOAH, Harold J. (Harold Julius Noah). American (born United States), b. 1925?. **Genres:** Economics, Education. **Career:** Columbia University, Teachers College, instructor in comparative education, 1962-64, assistant professor of economics and education, 1964-66, associate professor, 1966-69, associate chairman, 1967-71, professor, 1969-, Department of Philosophy and the Social Sciences, acting chairman, 1971-72, dean, 1976-81, Gardner Cowles professor of economics and education, now professor emeritus; Comparative Educational Review, editor, 1966-71. **Publications:** Financing Soviet Schools, 1967; (trans. and ed.) The Economics of Education in the U.S.S.R., 1969; (with M.A. Eckstein) Toward a Science of Comparative Education, 1969; (ed. with M.A. Eckstein) Scientific Investigations in Comparative Education, 1969; Reviews of National Policies for Education: Germany, 1972; (co-author) The National Case Study: An Empirical Comparative Study of Twenty-One Educational Systems, 1976; Educational Financing and Policy Goals for Primary Schools: General Report, 1979; Secondary School Examinations: International Perspectives on Policies and Practice, 1993; Doing Comparative Education: Three Decades of Collaboration, 1998; Fraud in Education: The Worm in the Apple, 2001. **Address:** Department of International Studies, Teachers College, Columbia University, 525 W 120th St., New York, NY 10027, U.S.A. **Online address:** hjn9@columbia.edu

NOAH, Harold Julius. *See* **NOAH, Harold J.**

NOAH, Robert. American (born United States), b. 1926?. **Genres:** Young Adult Fiction, Romance/Historical, Art/Art History, Mystery/Crime/Suspense. **Career:** Writer and television producer. **Publications:** All the Right Answers, 1988; The Man Who Stole the Mona Lisa, 1998. **Address:** St. Martin's Press, 175 5th Ave., New York, NY 10010, U.S.A.

NOAM, Eli Michael. American/Israeli (born Israel), b. 1946. **Genres:** Technology, Communications/Media, Economics, Politics/Government. **Career:** Princeton University, Woodrow Wilson School, Department of Economics, visiting assistant professor, 1975-76; Columbia University, Business School, assistant professor, professor of finance and economics, 1976-, Institute for Tele-Information, director, 1983-87, 1991-; New York State Public Service Commission, commissioner, 1987-90; University of St. Gallen, virtual visiting professor, 1998-2002. Writer. **Publications:** The Impact of Information Technologies on the Service Sector, 1986; (with S.R. Barnett and M. Botein) Law of International Telecommunications in the United States, 1988; Telecommunications in Europe, 1992; Television in Europe, 1992; The Telecommunications Revolution, 1992; Impending Doom of Common Carriage, 1993; Interconnecting the Network of Networks, 2001; Media Ownership and Concentration in America, 2007; The Last Bottleneck of the Information Revolution: Competing for Attention Span, forthcoming. EDITOR: Telecommunications Regulation Today and Tomorrow, 1983; Video Media Competition: Regulation, Economics and Technology, 1985; (with G. Faulhaber and R. Tasley) Services in Transition: The Impact of Information Technology on the Service Sector, 1986; (with E.E. Dennis) The Cost of Libel: Economic and Policy Implications, 1989; Technologies without Boundaries: On Telecommunications in a Global Age, 1990; (with J.C. Millonzi) The International Market in Film and Television Programs, 1993; (with S. Komatsuzaki and D.A. Conn) Telecommunications in the Pacific Basin: An Evolutionary Approach, 1994; (with G. Pogorel) Asymmetric Deregulation: The Dynamics of Telecommunications Policy in Europe and the United States, 1994; (with A. NíShúilleabháin) Private Networks Public Objectives, 1996; Telecommunications in Western Asia and the Middle East, 1997; (with A.J. Wolfson) Globalism and Localism in Telecommunications, 1997; Telecommunications in Latin America, 1998; Telecommunications in Africa, 1999; (with J. Alleman) New Investment Theory of Real Options and Its Implication for Telecommunications Economics, 1999; (with D. Steinbock) Competition for the Mobile Internet, 2003; (with J. Groebel and D. Gerbarg) Internet Television, 2004; (with J. Groebel and V. Feldmann) Mobile Media: Content and Services for Wireless Communications, 2006; (with L.M. Pupillo) Peer-to-Peer Video: The Economics, Policy and Culture of Today's New Mass Medium, 2008. Contributor to journals. **Address:** Columbia Institute for Tele-Information, Columbia University, 3022 Broadway Uris Hall, Ste. 1-A, New York, NY 10027, U.S.A. **Online address:** noam@columbia.edu

NOBBS, David. British (born England), b. 1935. **Genres:** Novels, Plays/Screenplays, Young Adult Fiction, Autobiography/Memoirs, Young Adult Non-fiction. **Career:** Sheffield Star, reporter, 1958-60; Saint Pancras Chronicle, reporter, 1961-62. Writer. **Publications:** REGINALD PERRIN NOVELS: The Death of Reginald Perrin, 1975 as The Fall and Rise of Reginald Perrin, 1976; The Return of Reginald Perrin, 1977; The Better World of Reginald Perrin, 1978; The Complete Reginald Perrin, 1990; The Legacy of Reginald Perrin, 1995. OTHER NOVELS: The Itinerant Lodger, 1965; Ostrich Country, 1968; A Piece of the Sky Is Missing, 1969; Second from Last in the Sack Race: A Play, 1983; A Bit of a Do, 1986; Pratt of the Argus, 1988; Fair Do's, 1990; The Cucumber Man, 1994; The Complete Pratt: Containing: Second from Last in the Sack Race, Pratt of the Argus, The Cucumber Man, 1998; Going Gently, 2000; I Didn't Get Where I Am Today (autobiography), 2003; Sex and Other Changes?, 2004; Pratt à Manger, 2006; Obstacles to Young Love, 2010; Life After Deborah, 2011; It Had To Be You, 2011; Wide Skies, forthcoming. OTHERS: And it's Goodnight From Him: The Autobiography of the Two Ronnies, 2006; Cupid's Dart, 2007; The Maltby Collection, 2008. Contributor to periodicals. **Address:** Jonathan Clowes Ltd., 10 Iron Bridge House, Bridge Approach, London, GL NW1 8BD, England.

NOBILE, Philip. American (born United States), b. 1941. **Genres:** Literary Criticism And History, Documentaries/Reportage, Social Sciences, Human Relations/Parenting, Sex, Sciences, Medicine/Health. **Career:** Cobble Hill School of American Studies, teacher in history; Commonweal, assistant editor, 1968-70, acting drama editor, 1969-70; National Catholic Reporter, press critic, 1969-70; Universal Press Syndicate, syndicated columnist, 1971-; History News Network, contributor. Media analyst and writer. **Publications:** EDITOR: Catholic Nonsense, 1970; The New Eroticism: Theories, Vogues and Canons, 1970; (with W.V.E. Casey) The Berrigans, 1971; Favorite Movies: Critics Choice, 1973; (and intro.) Judgment at the Smithsonian: The Uncensored Script of the Smithsonian's 50th Anniversary Exhibit of the Enola Gay, 1995. OTHERS: (with C.A. Reich) The Con III Controversy: The Critics Look at the Greening of America, 1971; (with J. Deedy) Complete Ecology Fact Book, 1972; Intellectual Skywriting: Literary Politics and the New York Review of Books, 1974; King Cancer: The Good, The Bad and the Cure of Cancer, 1975; (with E. Nadler) United States of America vs. Sex: How the Meese Commission Lied about Pornography, 1986; (with E. Eichel) The Perfect Fit: How to Achieve Mutual Fulfillment and Monogamous Passion through the New Intercourse, 1992. Contributor to periodicals. **Address:** 390 South St., Morristown, NJ 07960, U.S.A.

NOBISSO, Josephine. Also writes as Nuria Wood, Nadja Bride. American/Italian (born Italy), b. 1953. **Genres:** Novels, Children's Fiction, Children's Non-fiction, Writing/Journalism, Picture/Board Books, Education. **Career:** Writer, 1972-; speaker, 1975-; writing consultant, 1980-; Winslow Press, senior editor, 1996-97; Gingerbread Publishing House L.L.C., publisher, 1999-. **Publications:** FOR YOUNG READERS: Grandpa Loved, 1989, rev. ed., 2000; Grandma's Scrapbook, 1991, rev. ed., 2000; Shh! The Whale is Smiling, 1992; (with A.C. Krajnc) For the Sake of a Cake, 1993; Hot Cha-Cha!, 1998, rev. ed., 2010; Forest Fires: Run for Your Life!, 2000; John Blair and the Great Hinckley Fire, 2000; The Moon's Lullaby, 2001. NOVELS: (as Nuria Wood) With No Regrets, 1983; (as Nuria Wood) The Family Plan, 1984; (as Nadja Bride) Hide and Seek, 1985; In English, of Course, 2002; The Weight of a Mass: A Tale of Faith, 2002; Saint Juan Diego and Our Lady of Guadalupe, 2002; Josephine Nobisso's Show, Don't Tell!: Secrets of Writing, 2004; The Numbers Dance: A Counting Comedy, 2005; Take it to the Queen: A Tale of Hope, 2008; Francis Woke Up Early, 2011. Contributor of articles to periodicals. **Address:** Gingerbread House, 602 Montauk Hwy., Westhampton Beach, NY 11978, U.S.A. **Online address:** joi@josephinenobisso.com

NOBLE, Dennis L. American (born United States), b. 1939. **Genres:** History, Military/Defense/Arms Control, Marine Sciences/Oceanography, Biography. **Career:** U.S. Coast Guard, marine science technician, 1957-78; Delphi Public Library, library director, 1978-80; U.S. Army, historian, 1985; Port Angeles Public Library, reference librarian, 1985-88, 1996-98; Peninsula College, adjunct history professor, 1988-91; Clallam Bay Correctional Center, prison librarian, 1990-92; full-time writer, 1992-94, 1994-96, 1998-; Eastern Montana College, history instructor, 1994. Writer. **Publications:** (Comp.) United States Life Saving Service Annotated Bibliography, 1975, rev. ed., 1976; Recollections of Vice Admiral J. E. Stika, U.S. Coast Guard, Retired, On the Revenue Cutter Service and Bering Sea Patrol, 1975; (ed. with B.C. Nalty and T.R. Strobridge) Wrecks, Rescues and Investigations: Selected Documents of the U.S. Coast Guard and Its Predecessors, 1978; (with T.M. O' Brien) Sentinels of the Rocks: From Graveyard Coast to National Lakeshore, 1979; The Eagle and the Dragon: The United States Military in China, 1901-1937, 1990; (comp.) Historical Register, U.S. Revenue Cutter Service officers, 1790-1914, 1990; Forgotten Warriors: Combat Art from Vietnam, 1992; That Others Might Live: The U.S. Life Saving Service, 1878-1915, 1994; Lighthouses and Keepers: The U.S. Lighthouse Service and Its Legacy, 1997; (with T.R. Strobridge) Alaska and the U.S. Revenue Cutter Service 1867-1915, 1999; Lifeboat Sailors: The U.S. Coast Guard's Small Boat Stations, 2000; Lifeboat Sailors: Disasters, Rescues, and the Perilous Future of the Coast Guard's Small Boat Stations, 2000; (ed.) Gunboat on the Yangtze: The Diary of Captain Glenn F. Howell of the U.S.S. Palos, 1920-1921, 2002; The Rescue of the Gale Runner: Death, Heroism, and the U.S. Coast Guard, 2002; U.S. Coast Guard, 2005; Rescued by the U.S. Coast Guard: Great Acts of Heroism Since 1878, 2005; (with T.R. Strobridge) Captain "Hell Roaring" Mike Healy: From American Slave to Arctic Hero, 2009; U.S. Coast Guard's War on Human Smuggling, 2011. Contributor to periodicals. **Address:** University Press of Florida, 15 NW 15th St., Gainesville, FL 32611, U.S.A. **Online address:** dln@olypen.com

NOBLE, Kathleen. American (born United States), b. 1950. **Genres:** Mythology/Folklore, Psychology, Theology/Religion, Women's Studies And Issues, inspirational/Motivational Literature, Paranormal, Social Sciences. **Career:** University of Washington-Seattle, Child Development and Mental Retardation Center, research assistant, 1976-77, Center for the Study of Capable Youth, assistant director and psychologist, 1989-2000, research assistant professor of educational psychology, 1990-93, research assistant professor of women's studies, 1993-96, research associate professor of women's studies, 1996-2000, associate professor of women's studies, 2000-03, professor of women's studies, 2003-09, Robinson Center for Young Scholars, director, 2000-08, Halbert and Nancy Robinson professor, 2000-08; Highline-West Seattle Mental Health Center, emergency services therapist and intern, 1978; Kitsap Mental Health Center, Primary Prevention/Natural Helpers Project, coordinator, 1979-81; Central Washington University, adjunct lecturer of psychology, 1980-83; Kent Valley Youth Services, specialist in drug/alcohol education and prevention, 1982; University of Washington-Bothell, professor of science and technology, 2010-. Writer. **Publications:** The Sound of a Silver Horn: Reclaiming the Heroism in Contemporary Women's Lives, 1994; (ed. with K.D. Arnold and R.F. Subotnik) Remarkable Women: Perspectives on Female Talent Development, 1996; Riding the Windhorse: Spiritual Intelligence and the Growth of the Self, 2001. Contributor to books. **Address:** University of Washington, PO Box 358530, Bothell, WA 98011-8246, U.S.A. **Online address:** kdnoble@u.washington.edu

NOBLE, W. C. *See* **NOBLE, William Charles.**

NOBLE, William Charles. (W. C. Noble). British (born England), b. 1935. **Genres:** Biology, Environmental Sciences/Ecology, Medicine/Health, Biography, Sciences. **Career:** Medical Research Council, Air Hygiene Unit, staff, 1957-61; St. Mary's Hospital Medical School, Boots research fellow, 1961-64; St. John's Hospital for Diseases of the Skin, Department of Bacteriology, head, 1964-; Hospital Epidemiology, consultant, 1970-80; Middx Hospital Medical School, honarary lecturer in microbiology, 1971-82; British Journal of Dermatology, assistant editor, 1972-; University of London, professor of microbiology, 1980-; Journal of Epidemiology and Infection, editor, 1980-95. **Publications:** Coli, Great Healer of Men: The Biography of Dr. Leonard Colebrook, 1974; (with D.A. Somerville) Microbiology of Human Skin, 1974; (with J. Naidoo) Microorganisms and Man, 1979; Prevent Infection, 1983; Microbial Skin Disease, Its Epidemiology, 1983; (ed.) The Skin Micro-Flora and Microbial Skin Disease, 1992. **Address:** Department of Microbial Diseases, Institute of Dermatology, Saint Thomas, London, GL SE1 7EH, England.

NODELMAN, Perry. Canadian (born Canada), b. 1942. **Genres:** Picture/Board Books, Young Adult Fiction, Literary Criticism And History, Adult Non-fiction. **Career:** University of Winnipeg, Department of English, assistant professor, professor, 1968-2005. now professor emeritus; Children's Literature Association Quarterly, editor, 1983-87; writer, 1993-; CCL/LCJ, editor, 2004-08; Children's Literature Association, president. **Publications:** ADULT NONFICTION: (Ed. with J.P. May) Festschrift, A Ten Year Retrospective, 1983; Words about Pictures: The Narrative Art of Children's Picture Books, 1988; The Pleasures of Children's Literature, 1991, 3rd ed., 2003; Not a Nickle to Spare: The Great Depression Diary of Sally Cohen, 2007; The Hidden Adult: Defining Children's Literature, 2008. YOUNG ADULT FICTION: The Same Place but Different, 1995; (with C. Matas) Of Two Minds, 1995; (with C. Matas) More Minds, 1996; A Completely Different Place, 1996; (with C. Matas) Out of Their Minds, 1998; Behaving Bradley, 1998; (with C. Matas) A Meeting of Minds, 1999. PICTURE BOOKS: Alice Falls Apart, 1996. OTHERS: (With C. Matas) The Proof that Ghosts Exist, 2008; (with C. Matas) The Curse of the Evening Eye, 2009; (with C. Matas) The Hunt for the Haunted Elephant, 2010; The Hidden Adult: Characteristics of Children's Literature, forthcoming. Contributor to journals, books and periodicals. **Address:** Department of English, University of Winnipeg, 515 Portage Ave., Winnipeg, MB R3B 2E9, Canada. **Online address:** perry_nodelman@shaw.ca

NOE, Kenneth W. American (born United States), b. 1957. **Genres:** History. **Career:** Virginia Tech, teaching assistant, 1979-81; Kentucky Department for Library and Archives, intern, 1982-83; Blue Ridge Regional Library, librarian, 1983-85; University of Illinois, teaching assistant, 1985-87, archivist, 1988-90; Berea College, instructor in library science, 1987-88; University of West Georgia, West Georgia College, assistant professor, 1990-95, associate professor of history, 1995-2000; University of Michigan, outside tenure reviewer, 1995-96; Auburn University, associate professor, 2000-02, Alumni Professor, Draughon professor of Southern history, 2002-; Alabama Historical Commission, consultant, 2005; National Civil War Memorial, consultant, 2007; Alabama Historical Association, vice president, 2007-08, president, 2008-09. Writer. **Publications:** Southwest Virginia's Railroad: Modernization and the Sectional Crisis, 1994; Perryville: This Grand Havoc of Battle, 2001; Reluctant Rebels: The Confederates Who Joined the Army after 1861, 2010. EDITOR: A Southern Boy in Blue: The Memoir of Marcus Woodcock, 9th Kentucky Infantry (U.S.A.), 1996; (with S.H. Wilson) Acoustic Shadows: Essays on Appalachia's Civil War, 1997; (with D. McDonough) Politics and Culture of the Civil War Era: Essays in Honor of Robert W. Johannsen, 2006. Contributor of articles and reviews to history journals. **Address:** Department of History, Auburn University, 310 Thach Hall, Auburn, AL 36849-5207, U.S.A. **Online address:** noekenn@auburn.edu

NOEGEL, Scott B. American (born United States), b. 1962. **Genres:** Language/Linguistics, Literary Criticism And History, Bibliography. **Career:** New Community, founder and affiliate, 1986-89; Galivant Media, co-founder and affiliate, 1987-2000; Cornell University, Department of Near Eastern Studies, graduate research assistant, 1989-90, graduate teaching assistant, 1990-93, lecturer, 1993-94; Ithaca College, Department of Philosophy and Religion, lecturer, 1994; Human Code Inc., consultant, 1994-95; University of Washington, Henry M. Jackson School of International Studies, Department of Jewish Studies, Hazel Cole fellow and visiting lecturer, 1995-96, visiting summer lecturer, 1996, Department of Near Eastern Languages and Civilization, visiting assistant professor, 1997-98, adjunct assistant professor of history and assistant professor, 1998-2002, adjunct associate professor of history and associate professor, 2002-06, chair and professor, 2006-, Central Asian Studies Program, co-director, 2006-; Rice University, visiting assistant professor of religious studies, 1996-97; Jewish Federation of Greater Seattle, teacher at Community High School of Jewish Studies, 1997-98; Temple Beth Am, university instructor, 1997, 2002; Smiles Productions, consultant, 2000-02; American Research Center in Egypt, founder and president, 2004-06. Writer. **Publications:** Janus Parallelism in the Book of Job, 1996; (with B.M. Wheeler) Historical Dictionary of Prophets in Islam and Judaism, 2002; Nocturnal Ciphers: The Allusive Language of Dreams in the Ancient Near East, 2007; (with G.A. Rendsburg) Solomon's Vineyard: Literary and Linguistic Studies in the Song of Songs, 2009. EDITOR: Puns and Pundits: Word Play in the Hebrew Bible and Ancient Near Eastern Literature, 2000; (with J. Walker and B.M. Wheeler) Prayer, Magic, and the Stars in the Ancient and Late Antique World, 2003; (with A.S. Kaye) Afroasiatic Linguistics, Semitics, and Egyptology: Selected Writings of Carleton T. Hodge, 2004. Contributor to books, articles and journals. **Address:** Department of Near Eastern, Language and Civilization, University of Washington, PO Box 353120, Seattle, WA 98195-3120, U.S.A. **Online address:** snoegel@uw.edu

NOEL, Katharine. American (born United States) **Genres:** Novels. **Career:** Gould Farm, staff, 1992-94; Stanford University, Stegner Fellow, 2000-02, Creative Writing Program, Jones lecturer in creative writing. Writer. **Publications:** Halfway House, 2006. **Address:** c/o Deb Seager, Grove/Atlantic Inc., 841 Broadway, 4th Fl., New York, NY 10003-4704, U.S.A. **Online address:** katharine.noel@gmail.com

NÖEL, Roger. *See* **NÖEL, Roger Arthur.**

NÖEL, Roger Arthur. (Roger Nöel). American (born United States), b. 1942. **Genres:** Language/Linguistics, Translations, Social Commentary. **Career:** University of Missouri-St. Louis, instructor in French and Italian, 1970-86; Washington University, Evening College, adjunct faculty, 1985-86; St. Louis University, instructor, 1985-86; Monmouth College, assistant professor, 1986-90, associate professor of modern foreign languages and chair of department, 1990-91; Georgia College and State University, professor of modern foreign languages and chair of department, 1992-. Writer. **Publications:** Joufroi de Poitiers: Traduction critique, 1987; (trans. and ed.) Official Guide to the XXIVth Olympiad, 1988; (with H.G. Danner) An Introduction to an Academic Vocabulary, 1990; (with H.G. Danner) A Thesaurus of Word Roots of the English Language, 1992; (with H.G. Danner) A Thesaurus of Medical Word Roots, 1996; (with H.G. Danner) Discover It!, 1996, 2nd ed., 2004; (ed. with E. Demm and W. Urban) The Independence of the Baltic States, 1996; (with H.G. Danner) The English Tree of Roots and Words from Around the World, 2004; (with H.G.Danner) Discover It!: A Better Vocabulary, A Better Way, 2004. Contributor to periodicals. **Address:** Department of Modern Foreign Languages, Georgia College & State University, 112 Terrell Hall, PO Box 46, Milledgeville, GA 31061, U.S.A. **Online address:** roger.noel@gcsu.edu

NOER, David M. American (born United States), b. 1939. **Genres:** Administration/Management. **Career:** Commercial Credit Co., senior vice president of personnel and administration, 1975-82; Control Data Business Advisors, president and chief executive officer, 1982-86; Control Data Academy of Management, dean and vice president of human resource development, 1986-88; Noer Consulting, president, 1987-90, 1996-2001, consultant, speaker, coach, 2009-; consultant, 1988-90; Center for Creative Leadership, vice president of training and education, 1990-96, honorary senior fellow; Elon University, Frank S. Holt Jr. professor of leadership, 2002-09, now professor emeritus of business leadership. Writer. **Publications:** Multinational People Management: A Guide for Organizations and Employees, 1975; How to Beat The Employment Game, 1975; Jobkeeping: A Hireling's Survival Manual, 1976; Healing the Wounds: Overcoming the Trauma of Layoffs and Revitalizing Downsized Organizations, 1993, rev. ed., 2009; Breaking Free: A Prescription for Personal and Organizational Change, 1997. **Address:** 1911 Falmouth Dr., Greensboro, NC 27410-2166, U.S.A. **Online address:** david@davidnoer.com

NOF, Shimon Y. American (born United States), b. 1946. **Genres:** Engineering, Information Science/Computers, Sciences, Technology. **Career:** Shenkar College, instructor in production and operations management, 1971-72; Manufacturing Data Systems Inc., senior systems analyst, 1976-77; Purdue University, faculty, 1977-, visiting assistant professor, 1977-79, assistant professor, 1979-82, associate professor, 1982-88, professor of industrial engineering, 1988-; Tel-Aviv University, visiting senior lecturer, 1980-81; Israel Institute of Technology, adjunct senior lecturer, 1980-81, visiting professor, 1984-86; Scitex Inc., corporate consultant, 1984-86; Tadiran Ltd., corporate consultant, 1984-86; United Nations, North Atlantic Treaty Organization (NATO), consultant; Ben-Gurion University, lecturer; Laval University, lecturer; University of Puerto Rico, lecturer; Tokyo Institute of Technology, lecturer; Waseda University, lecturer; University of Rochester, lecturer; Georgia Institute of Technology, lecturer; Boston University, lecturer; Universidad Panamericana, lecturer; Universidad Iberoamericana, lecturer; Clemson University, lecturer; National Technological University, lecturer; Columbia University, lecturer; Production, Robotics and Integration Software for Manufacturing and Management (PRISM), director. Writer. **Publications:** (With W.E. Wilhelm and H.J. Warnecke) Industrial Assembly, 1997. EDITOR: Handbook of Industrial Robotics, 1985, 2nd ed., 1999; Robotics and Material Flow, 1986; (with R.C. Dorf) The International Encyclopedia of Robotics: Applications and Automation, 3 vols., 1988; (with C.L. Moodie) Advanced Information Technology for Industrial Material Flow Systems, 1989; (with R.C. Dorf) The Concise International Encyclopedia of Robotics, Applications, and Automation, 1990; Information and Collaboration Models of Integration, 1994; Springer Handbook of Automation, 2009. Contributor of articles to journals. **Address:** School of Industrial Engineering, Purdue University, Grissom Hall, 315 N Grant St., West Lafayette, IN 47907-2023, U.S.A. **Online address:** nof@purdue.edu

NOGEE, Joseph L(ippman). American (born United States), b. 1929. **Genres:** Politics/Government. **Career:** Yale University, instructor, 1956-57; University of Houston, assistant professor, 1958-61, associate professor, 1961-66, Department of Political Science, chair, 1966-68, professor, 1966-99, Russian Studies Program, director, 1974-, professor emeritus, 1999-. Writer. **Publications:** The Diplomacy of Disarmament, 1960; Soviet Policy toward International Control of Atomic Energy, 1961; (with J.W. Spanier) The Politics of Disarmament, 1962; (with R. Donaldson) Soviet Foreign Policy since World War II; (with J.W. Spanier) Peace Impossible-War Unlikely, 1988; (with R.J. Mitchell) Russian Politics, the Struggle for a New Order, 1997; (with R.H. Donaldson) The Foreign Policy of Russia, Changing Systems, Enduring Interest, 1998, 4th ed., 2009. EDITOR: Man, State and Society in the Soviet Union, 1972; (with J.W. Spanier) Congress, The Presidency, and American Foreign Policy, 1981; Soviet Politics: Russia After Brezhnev, 1985. **Address:** Department of Political Science, University of Houston, 447 Philip Guthrie Hoffman Hall, 4800 Calhoun Rd., Houston, TX 77004, U.S.A. **Online address:** josephnogee@aol.com

NOJUMI, Neamatollah. American/Afghani (born Afghanistan) **Genres:** Politics/Government, Military/Defense/Arms Control. **Career:** George Mason University, Institute for Conflict Analysis and Resolution, Center for World Religions, Diplomacy and Conflict Resolution, senior research associate, senior research fellow; United States Agency for International Development, consultant; Harvard Law School, fellow. Writer and speaker. **Publications:** The Rise of the Taliban in Afghanistan: Mass Mobilization, Civil War, and the Future of the Region, 2001; Mass Mobilization in Afghanistan, 2001; (with D. Mazurana and E. Stites) After the Taliban: Life and Security in Rural Afghanistan, 2009. **Address:** Institute for Conflict Analysis and Resolution, George Mason University, Truland Bldg., 3330 Washington Blvd., 5th Fl., Arlington, VA 22201, U.S.A. **Online address:** nojumi@aol.com

NOLAN, Chuck. *See* **EDSON, J(ohn) T(homas).**

NOLAN, David (Joseph). American (born United States), b. 1946. **Genres:** Architecture, History, Literary Criticism And History, Race Relations, Travel/Exploration, Art/Art History. **Career:** Penn Center, administrative aide, 1969-71; St. Regis Paper Co., staff, 1971-72; Nabisco, staff, 1972-77; Historic St. Augustine Preservation Board, historic sites specialist, 1978-80; educator and writer, 1980-; Anniversary to Commemorate the Civil Rights Demonstrations Inc. (ACCORD), founder. **Publications:** Fifty Feet in Paradise: The Booming of Florida, 1984; The Book Lover's Guide to Florida, 1992; The Houses of St. Augustine, 1995; Story of Castlemoate House, 1996; I Swear I Was There: Sex Pistols and the Shape of Rock, 2001; The Illusionist, 2006; Bernard Sumner, 2007. Contributor to magazines and newspapers. **Address:** Anniversary to Commemorate the Civil Rights, Demonstrations Inc., PO Box 697, St. Augustine, FL 32085-0697, U.S.A.

NOLAN, Han. American (born United States), b. 1956. **Genres:** Young Adult Fiction, Children's Fiction. **Career:** Teacher, 1981-84; Hollins University, writer-in-residence, 2002, visiting associate professor, 2004-05. Writer. **Publications:** YOUNG ADULT FICTION: If I Should Die before I Wake, 1994; Send Me Down a Miracle, 1996; Dancing on the Edge, 1997; A Face in Every Window, 1999; Born Blue, 2001; When We Were Saints, 2003; A Summer of Kings, 2006; Crazy, 2010; Pregnant Pause, 2011. Contributor to periodicals. **Address:** Houghton Mifflin Harcourt, 222 Berkeley St., Boston, MA 02116, U.S.A. **Online address:** han@hannolan.com

NOLAN, James L. American (born United States), b. 1962. **Genres:** Sociology, History. **Career:** Oxford University, Williams College, assistant professor of sociology, 1996-, associate professor of sociology, professor of sociology, chair, Williams-Exeter Programme, director. Writer. **Publications:** (Ed.) The American Culture Wars: Current Contests and Future Prospects, 1996; The Therapeutic State: Justifying Government at Century's End, 1998; Reinventing Justice: The American Drug Court Movement, 2001; (ed.) Drug Courts in Theory and in Practice, 2002; Legal Accents, Legal Borrowing: The International Problem-solving Court Movement, 2009. **Address:** Department of Anthropology and Sociology, Williams College, Hollander Hall, 85 Mission Park Dr., Williamstown, MA 01267, U.S.A. **Online address:** james.l.nolan@williams.edu

NOLAN, Janne E. American/French (born France), b. 1944?. **Genres:** Military/Defense/Arms Control. **Career:** U.S. Arms Control and Disarmament Agency, specialist in technology transfer policy and delegate to U.S.-Soviet negotiations on arms transfer limitations, 1977-80; Science Applications International Corp., senior consultant, 1982-83; Brookings Institution, senior fellow, 1987-; Georgetown University, faculty, 1987-, adjunct professor, 1989-; U.S. Secretary of Defense, advisor, 1993-2000; Stanford University Center on International Security and Arms Control, Georgetown Center for Strategic and International Studies, faculty; Harvard University Center for Science and International Affairs, faculty; University of Pittsburgh, Graduate School of Public and International Affairs, professor; American Security Project, director for nuclear security; Eisenhower Institute, director. Writer. **Publications:** Military Industry in Taiwan and South Korea, 1986; Guardians of the Arsenal: The Politics of Nuclear Strategy, 1989; Trappings of Power: Ballistic

Missiles in the Third World, 1991; (ed.) Global Engagement: Security and Cooperation in the 21st Century, 1994; (co-author) Report of the Presidential Advisory Board on Arms Proliferation Policy, 1996; An Elusive Consensus: Nuclear Weapons and American Security after the Cold War, 1999; (ed. with B.I. Finel and B.D. Finlay) Ultimate Security: Combating Weapons of Mass Destruction, 2003; Diplomacy and Security in the Twenty-first Century, 2009. **Address:** Matthew B. Ridgway Center, Graduate School of Public/International Affairs, University of Pittsburgh, 230 S Bouquet St., 3930 Wesley W Posvar Hall, Pittsburgh, PA 15260, U.S.A. **Online address:** jnolan@pitt.edu

NOLAN, Simon. *See* **MAGINN, Simon.**

NOLAN, William F(rancis). Also writes as Terence Duncan. American (born United States), b. 1928. **Genres:** Novels, Novellas/Short Stories, Mystery/Crime/Suspense, Horror, Science Fiction/Fantasy, Plays/Screenplays, Bibliography, Biography, Humor/Satire, Illustrations, Ghost Writer, Poetry. **Career:** Hallmark Cards Inc., staff; freelance book and magazine editor, 1952-91; freelance writer, 1956-. **Publications:** (With J. Fitch) Adventure on Wheels, 1959; Barney Oldfield: The Life and The Times of America's Legendary Speed King, 1961, rev. Ed., 2002; Phil Hill: Yankee Champion; First American to Win the Driving Championship of the World, 1962; Men of Thunder, Fabled Daredevils of Motor Sport, 1964; John Huston: King Rebel, 1965; Sinners and Supermen, 1965; (with G.C. Johnson) Logan's Run, A Novel, 1967; Death Is for Losers, 1968; The White Cad Cross-Up, 1969; Dashiell Hammett: A Casebook, 1969; Space for Hire, 1971; Steve McQueen: Star on Wheels, 1972; Carnival of Speed, 1973; Hemingway: Last Days of the Lion, 1974; The Ray Bradbury Companion, 1975; Logan's World, 1977; Logan's Search, 1980; Hammett: A Life at the Edge, 1983; McQueen, 1984; Look Out for Space, 1985; The Black Mask Boys, 1985; The Work of Charles Beaumont (bibliography), 1986; Dark Encounters (poetry), 1986; Logan: A Trilogy, 1986; (with B. Clarke) The Work of William F. Nolan (bibliography), 1988; (as Terence Duncan) Rio Renegades, 1989; How to Write Horror Fiction, 1990; Blood Sky, 1991; Helltracks, 1991; Helle on Wheels, 1992; The Black Mask Murders, 1994; The Marble Orchard, 1995; Sharks Never Sleep, 1998; The Winchester Horror, 1998; The Logan Chronicles, 2003; With Marlowe in L.A., 2003; Far Out: The Incredible Adventures of Sam Space, 2004; Jack and Sam: A Dynamic Duo, 2004; Logan's Run: Last Day, 2010. STORIES: Impact 20, 1963; Alien Horizons, 1974; Wonderworlds 1977; Things beyond Midnight, 1984; 3 for Space, 1992; Night Shapes, 1995; The Brothers Challis, 1996; Down the Long Night, 2000; Dark Universe, 2003; Have You Seen the Wind?, 2003; Ships in the Night, 2004; Far Out, 2004; Nightworlds, 2004; (and intro.) Wild Galaxy, 2005; Let's Get Creative!: Writing Fiction that Sells!, 2007; Nightshadows, 2007; Dark Dimensions, 2010; Kincaid: A Paranormal Casebook, 2011. EDITOR: Ray Bradbury Review, 1952; (with C. Beaumont) Omnibus of Speed: An Introduction to The World of Motor Sport, 1958; (with C. Beaumont) The Fiend in You, 1962; (with C. Beaumont) When Engines Roar, 1964; Man against Tomorrow, 1965; The Pseudo-People: Androids in Science Fiction, 1965; Il Meglio della Fantascienza, 1967; 3 to the Highest Power, 1968; A Wilderness of Stars: Stories of Man in Conflict with Space, 1969; A Sea of Space, 1970; The Future Is Now, 1970; The Human Equation, 1971; The Edge of Forever, 1971; (with M. Greenberg) Science Fiction Origins, 1980; (and intro.) Max Brand's Best Western Stories, 3 vols., 1981-87; Max Brand: Western Giant, 1986; (with M. Greenberg) Urban Horrors, 1990; (with M. Greenberg) The Bradbury Chronicles, 1991; Tales of the Wild West, 1997; More Tales of the Wild West, 1999; California Sorcery, 1999; Off-Beat, 2002. WESTERNS AS TERENCE DUNCAN: Mustang Warriors, 1987; Apache Raiders, 1987; Unchained Lightning, 1987; Red River Desperadoes, 1988; Rocky Mountain Showdown, 1988; Robbers Roost, 1988; Rio Renegades, 1989; Missouri Woodhawks, 1989. Contributor of articles to books and periodicals. **Address:** c/o John Silbersack, Trident Media Group, 41 Madison Ave., 36th Fl., New York, NY 10010, U.S.A. **Online address:** phantom@phantoms.com

NOLAND, Marcus. American (born United States), b. 1959. **Genres:** Politics/Government, International Relations/Current Affairs, Military/Defense/Arms Control. **Career:** Peterson Institute for International Economics, senior fellow and deputy director, 1985-; National Graduate Institute for Policy Studies (GRIPS), visiting professor, 1988-89; University of Southern California, assistant professor, 1990-91; Johns Hopkins University, visiting associate professor, 1991-98; Council of Economic Advisers, Executive Office of the President of the United States, senior economist, 1993-94; Tokyo University, visiting professor, 1996; University of Ghana, visiting professor, 1997; International Food Policy Research Institute, consultant, 1999; East-West Center, POSCO visiting fellow, 2000, non-resident senior fellow; Yale University, faculty, 2007-; East-West Center, senior fellow. Writer. **Publications:** (With B.A. Balassa) Japan in the World Economy, 1988; Pacific Basin Developing Countries: Prospects for the Future, 1990; (with C.F. Bergsten) Reconcilable Differences? United States-Japan Economic Conflict, 1993; (ed. with C.F. Bergsten) Pacific Dynamism and the International Economic System, 1993; (co-author) Global Economic Effects of the Asian Currency Devaluations, 1998; (ed.) Economic Integration of the Korean Peninsula, 1998; The New Protectionists, 1999; Avoiding the Apocalypse: The Future of the Two Koreas, 2000; (with C.F. Bergsten and T. Ito) No More Bashing: Building a New Japan-United States Economic Relationship, 2001; (with H. Pack) Industrial Policy in an Era of Globalization: Lessons from Asia, 2003; Korea after Kim Jong- Il, 2004; (with S. Haggard) Hunger and Human Rights: The Politics of Famine in North Korea, 2005; (ed. with S. Haggard) The North Korean Refugee Crisis: Human Rights and International Responses, 2006; (with B. Spector) Diamonds and Development in Southern Africa, 2006; (with H. Pack) The Arab Economies in a Changing World, 2007; (with S. Haggard) Famine in North Korea: Markets, Aid, and Reform, 2007; (with S. Haggard) Witness to Transformation: Refugee Insights into North Korea, 2011. Contributor to periodicals. **Address:** Peterson Institute for International Economics, 1750 Massachusetts Ave. NW, Washington, DC 20036-1207, U.S.A. **Online address:** mnoland@petersoninstitute.org

NOLD, Robert. American (born United States), b. 1951?. **Genres:** Homes/Gardens. **Career:** Writer. **Publications:** Penstemons, 1999; Columbines: Aquilegia, Paraquilegia, and Semiaquilegia, 2003; High and Dry: Gardening with Cold-hardy Dryland Plants, 2008. Contributor to magazines. **Address:** Lakewood, CO , U.S.A. **Online address:** penstemon@q.com

NOLEN-HOEKSEMA, Susan. American (born United States), b. 1959. **Genres:** Psychology. **Career:** Stanford University, Department of Psychology, assistant professor, 1986-93, associate professor, 1993-95; University of Michigan, Department of Psychology, associate professor, 1995-99, professor, 1999-2004, Department of Psychiatry, professor, 2002-04, Institute for Research on Women and Gender, director, 2003-04; Yale University, Department of Psychology, professor, 2004-, chair, 2011-, director of graduate studies, 2006-11, Depression and Cognition Program, faculty. Writer. **Publications:** Sex Differences in Depression, 1990; Clashing Views on Abnormal Psychology: A Taking Sides Custom Reader, 1998; Abnormal Psychology, 1998, 5th ed., 2011; (with J. Larson) Coping with Loss, 1999; (with E.E. Smith and D.J. Bem) Fundamentals of Psychology, 2001; Women Who Think Too Much: How to Break Free of Overthinking and Reclaim Your Life, 2003; Eating, Drinking, Overthinking: The Toxic Triangle of Food, Alcohol, and Depression-and How Women Can Break Free, 2006; (ed. with L.M. Hilt) Handbook of Depression in Adolescents, 2008; Power of Women: Harness Your Unique Strengths at Home, at Work, and in Your Community, 2010. Contributor to periodicals. **Address:** Department of Psychology, Yale University, Rm. K 205, PO Box 208205, New Haven, CT 06520-8205, U.S.A. **Online address:** susan.nolen-hoeksema@yale.edu

NOLES, James L. *See* **NOLES, Jim.**

NOLES, Jim. (James L. Noles). American (born United States), b. 1968. **Genres:** History, Military/Defense/Arms Control. **Career:** U.S. Army, officer and aviator; University of Alabama, faculty, School of Law, adjunct professor; Balch & Bingham L.L.P., partner. Writer and attorney. **Publications:** NONFICTION AS JAMES L. NOLES, JR.: Camp Rucker during World War II, 2002; Thomas W. Martin: Alabama Dynamo, 2003; Hearts of Dixie: Fifty Alabamians and the State They Called Home, 2004; John Pelham: The Gallant Pelham, 2004; Twenty-three Minutes to Eternity: The Final Voyage of the Escort Carrier U.S.S. Liscome Bay, 2004; (with J.L. Noles) Mighty by Sacrifice: The Destruction of an American Bomber Squadron, August 29, 1944, 2009. OTHER: A Pocketful of History: Four Hundred Years of America-One State Quarter at a Time, 2008. Contributor to periodicals. **Address:** Balch & Bingham L.L.P., 1901 6th Ave. N, Ste. 1500, Birmingham, AL 35203-4642, U.S.A. **Online address:** jnoles@balch.com

NOLL, Ingrid. German/Chinese (born China), b. 1935. **Genres:** Mystery/Crime/Suspense, Novels, Novellas/Short Stories, Biography. **Career:** Writer. **Publications:** IN ENGLISH TRANSLATION: Die Apothekerin, 1994, trans. as The Pharmacist, 1998; Head Count, 1997; Hell Hath No Fury, 1998; Lady-like: Roman, 2006. UNTRANSLATED WORKS: Der Hahn ist Tot, 1991; Die Häupter meiner Lieben: Roman, 1993; Kalt ist der Abendhauch: Roman,

1996; Röslein rot: Roman, 1998; Selige Witwen: Roman, 2001; Falsche Zungen: gesammelte Geschichten, 2004; Kuckuckskind, 2008; Ehrenwort, 2010. **Address:** c/o Author Mail, HarperCollins Inc., 10 E 53rd St., 7th Fl., New York, NY 10022, U.S.A.

NOLL, Richard. American (born United States), b. 1959. **Genres:** History, Psychiatry, Psychology. **Career:** Ancora Psychiatric Hospital, staff clinical psychologist, 1985-88; West Chester University, Department of Psychology, instructor, 1992-94; Harvard University, postdoctoral fellow, Department of the History of Science, lecturer, 1994-98; Dibner Institute for the History of Science and Technology, resident fellow, 1995-96; DeSales University, assistant professor of psychology, 2000, associate professor of psychology and clinical psychologist. Writer. **Publications:** Bizarre Diseases of the Mind, 1990; (ed. and intro.) Vampirism, Lycanthropy and Demonical Possession: Twentieth Century Case Reports in the Psychiatric Literature, 1991; The Encyclopedia of Schizophrenia and the Psychotic Disorders, 1992, 3rd ed., 2007; (ed.) Vampires, Werewolves and Demons: Twentieth Century Reports in the Psychiatric Literature, 1992; The Jung Cult: Origins of a Charismatic Movement, 1994; The Aryan Christ: The Secret Life of Carl Jung, 1997; American Madness: The Rise and Fall of Dementia Praecox, 2011. Contributor to journals. **Address:** Department of Social Sciences, DeSales University, 104 Tucker House, Center Valley, PA 18034, U.S.A. **Online address:** richard.noll@desales.edu

NOLLEN, Scott Allen. American (born United States), b. 1963. **Genres:** Film, Adult Non-fiction, Biography. **Career:** Writer. **Publications:** The Boys: The Cinematic World of Laurel and Hardy, 1989; Boris Karloff: A Critical Account of His Screen, Stage, Radio, Television and Recording Work, 1991; Robert Louis Stevenson: Life, Literature and the Silver Screen, 1994; Sir Arthur Conan Doyle at the Cinema, 1996; Vincent Price, 1998; Robin Hood: A Cinematic History of the English Outlaw and His Scottish Counterparts, 1999; Boris Karloff: A Gentleman's Life: The Authorized Biography, 1999; Peter Lorre, 1999; Jethro Tull: A History of the Band, 1968-2001, 2002; Cinema of Sinatra: The Actor, on Screen and in Song, 2003; Peter Cushing, 2004; Louis Armstrong: The Life, Music and Screen Career, 2004; Warners Wiseguys: All 112 Films that Robinson, Cagney and Bogart made for the Studio, 2008; Jilly!: Sinatra's Right Hand Man, 2009; Abbott and Costello on the Home Front: A Critical Study of the Wartime Films, 2009; Paul Robeson: Film Pioneer, 2010. **Address:** c/o Author Mail, McFarland & Co., PO Box 611, Jefferson, NC 28640, U.S.A. **Online address:** snollen@hoover.nara.gov

NOLLETTI, Arthur (E.). American (born United States), b. 1941. **Genres:** Film, Art/Art History. **Career:** Danforth Museum, staff, 1976-89; Framingham State College, assistant professor, professor of film and literature, 1971-96, professor in English, 1996-2009, Department of English and Film Studies, retired, now professor emeritus. Writer. **Publications:** (Ed. with D. Desser) Reframing Japanese Cinema: Authorship, Genre, History, 1992; (ed.) The Films of Fred Zinnemann: Critical Perspectives, 1999; The Cinema of Gosho Heinosuke: Laughter through Tears, 2005. Contributor to periodicals. **Address:** Department of English and Film Studies, Framingham State College, 100 State St., PO Box 9101, Framingham, MA 01701-9101, U.S.A. **Online address:** anollet@frc.mass.edu

NOLTINGK, Bernard Edward. British (born England), b. 1918. **Genres:** Administration/Management, Technology, Theology/Religion, Reference, Biography, Autobiography/Memoirs. **Career:** Motor Industry Research Association, Electronics Department, head, 1941-47; Mullard Research Laboratories, Ultrasonics Department, head, 1947-52; Mining Research Establishment, National Coal Board, Strata Control Group, head, 1952-55; Tube Investments Research Laboratories, Electronics and Ultrasonics, head, 1955-60; Central Electricity Research Laboratories, Instrumentation Section, research engineer and head, 1960-81. Writer. **Publications:** The Human Element in Research Management, 1959; The Art of Research: A Guide for the Graduate, 1965. EDITOR: Jone's Instrument Technology, 4th ed., 1985; Instrumentation Reference Book, 1988, 1995; Dissenting Conformist, 1997. Contributor of articles to journals. **Address:** Windwhistle, Nutcombe Ln., Dorking, SR RH4 3DZ, England.

NOMANI, Asra Q. American/Indian (born India), b. 1965?. **Genres:** Women's Studies And Issues, Theology/Religion, Travel/Exploration, Biography. **Career:** Reuters News Agency, stringer, 1980; Wall Street Journal, reporter, 1988-; Salon Magazine, foreign correspondent, 2001; Muslims for Peace, cofounder, 2006; Georgetown University, Pearl Project, leader, 2007-. **Publications:** Tantrika: Traveling the Road of Divine Love, 2003; Standing Alone in Mecca: An American Woman's Struggle for the Soul of Islam, 2005. Contributor to periodicals. **Address:** Kris Dahl, International Creative Management, 40 W 57th St., 17th Fl., New York, NY 10019-4001, U.S.A. **Online address:** asra@asranomani.com

NOMANI, Farhad. French/Iranian (born Iran), b. 1944. **Genres:** Theology/Religion, Politics/Government, Economics. **Career:** University of Tehran, faculty, 1972-83; American University of Paris, lecturer, professor of economics and international business administration and co-chair of the department of economics, 1984-. Writer. **Publications:** (with A. Rahnema) The Secular Miracle: Religion, Politics, and Economic Policy in Iran, 1990; (with A. Rahnema) Islamic Economic Systems, 1994; (ed. with S. Behdad) Islam and the Everyday World: Public Policy Dilemmas, 2006; (with S. Behdad) Class and Labor in Iran: Did the Revolution Matter?, 2006. Contributor to journals. **Address:** American University of Paris, 31 Ave. Bosquet, Paris, 75007, France. **Online address:** nomani@aup.fr

NOON, Jeff. British (born England), b. 1957. **Genres:** Science Fiction/Fantasy, Plays/Screenplays, Novels, Young Adult Fiction. **Career:** Musician and writer. **Publications:** Vurt (novel), 1993; Pollen (sequel to Vurt), 1996; Automated Alice, 1996; Pixel Juice, 2000; Nymphomation, 2000; Needle in the Groove, 2001; Cobralingus, 2001; Falling Out of Cars, 2002. Contributor to books and periodicals. **Address:** Barbara J. Zitwer Agency, 525 W End Ave., Ste. 11H, New York, NY 10024, U.S.A.

NOONAN, Peggy. American (born United States), b. 1950. **Genres:** Politics/Government. **Career:** Aetna Insurance Co., clerk, 1968-70; WEEI (radio station), news and editorial writer, 1974-77; CBS News, broadcast writer and producer, 1977-84; New York University, adjunct professor of journalism, 1978, 1979; U.S. White House, special assistant to President Ronald Reagan, 1984-86; freelance writer, 1986-; speech writer, 1988-89; The Wall Street Journal, author and columnist. **Publications:** What I Saw at the Revolution: A Political Life in the Reagan Era, 1990; Life, Liberty and the Pursuit of Happiness, 1994; Simply Speaking: How to Communicate Your Ideas With Style, Substance and Clarity, 1998; On Speaking Well, 1999; The Case against Hillary Clinton, 2000; When Character Was King: A Story of Ronald Reagan, 2002; A Heart, A Cross and A Flag, 2003; John Paul The Great: Remembering a Spiritual Father, 2005; (intro.) Silver Chalice, 2006; Patriotic Grace: What It Is and Why We Need It Now, 2008. Contributor to periodicals. **Address:** The Wall Street Journal, 1211 Ave. of the Americas, New York, NY 10036, U.S.A.

NORAC, Carl. French/Belgian (born Belgium), b. 1960. **Genres:** Poetry, Novels. **Career:** Royal Conservatorium of Mons, professor of literature, 1996; Hans Christian Andersen ambassador, 2005; Children's book author; poet; French teacher, television scriptwriter and journalist. **Publications:** Le lion fanfaron, 1991; La semaine de Monsieur Gris, 1994; Dimanche aux Hespérides, 1994; Romulus et Rémi une fable lopra, 1994; Coeur de singe, 1995; Un loup dans la nuit bleue, 1996; Les mots doux, 1996; La candeur, 1996; Nemo et le volcan, 1996; Beau comme au cinéma, 1997; I Love You so Much, 1997; Lespoir Pélican, 1998; Lîle aux câlins, 1998; Le sourire de Kiawak, 1998; La carnival des animaux, 1999; I Love to Cuddle, 1999; Eloge de la patience: poèmes, 1999; Bonjour mon petit coeur, 1999; La grande ourse, 1999; Le message de la baleine, 2000; Hello, Sweetie Pie, 2000; Le rêve de lours, 2000; La petite souris d'Halloween, 2000; Marine et Louisa, 2000; Donne-moi un ours!, 2001; Le pre Noël ma écrit, 2001; Un Bisou cest trop court, 2001; Le dernier voyage de Saint-Exupéry, 2001; Luli et le sorcier, 2001; Je suis un amour, 2001; Je veux un bisou!, 2001; Une visite chez la sorcire, 2002; Zeppo, 2002; Tu m'aimes ou tu m'aimes pas?, 2002; Pierrot d'amour, 2002; Lettres du géant á l'enfante qui passé et autres pomes, 2002; Un secret pour grandir, 2003; Tu es si gentil mon ours, 2003; Métrpolitaines: tentative de photographier avec le language métro de Paris hiver 1999-2000, 2003; Akli prince du désert, 2004; My Daddy is a Giant, 2004; Tout pres de maman, 2004; Angakkeg: la légende de loiseau, 2004; Le petit sorcier de la pluie, 2004; Mon papa est un géant, 2004; Coeur de papier, 2004; Quiero un beso!=I want a Kiss!, 2005; Mon meilleur ami du monde, 2005; Le géant de la grande tour, 2005; My Mommy is Magic, 2007. Contributor to periodicals. **Address:** 269, rue de la Source, Olivet, 45160, France. **Online address:** carlnorac@wanadoo.fr

NORBROOK, David. British (born England), b. 1950. **Genres:** Language/

Linguistics, Literary Criticism And History, Poetry. **Career:** University of Oxford, Magdalen College, fellow and tutor in English language and literature, 1978-98, Merton College, Merton professor of Renaissance English literature, 2002-, fellow, Centre for Early Modern Studies, director; University of Maryland, professor of English, 1999-2002. Writer. **Publications:** Poetry and Politics in the English Renaissance, 1984, rev. ed., 2002; (ed. and intro.) The Penguin Book of Renaissance Verse, 1993; Writing the English Republic: Poetry, Rhetoric, and Politics, 1627-1660, 1999; (ed.) Order and Disorder, 2001. **Address:** Merton College, Oxford University, Merton St., Oxford, OX OX1 4JD, England. **Online address:** david.norbrook@merton.ox.ac.uk

NORCROSS, Lisabet. *See* **GLADSTONE, Arthur M.**

NORD, Deborah Epstein. American (born United States), b. 1949. **Genres:** Literary Criticism And History, Women's Studies And Issues. **Career:** Princeton University, Program in the Study of Women and Gender, director, 1996-2003, professor of English. Writer. **Publications:** The Apprenticeship of Beatrice Webb, 1985; Walking the Victorian Streets: Women, Representation, and the City, 1995; (ed. and intro.) Sesame and Lilies, 2002; Gypsies and the British Imagination, 1807-1930, 2006. **Address:** U.S.A. **Online address:** dnord@princeton.edu

NORDAN, Lewis. (Lewis Alonzo Nordan). American (born United States), b. 1939. **Genres:** Novels, Novellas/Short Stories, Autobiography/Memoirs. **Career:** Auburn University, instructor in English, 1966-71; University of Georgia, instructor in English, 1971-74; University of Arkansas, assistant professor of English, 1981-83; University of Pittsburgh, assistant professor of English, 1983-, professor emeritus of creative writing, 2005-. Writer. **Publications:** SHORT STORY COLLECTIONS: Welcome to the Arrow-Catcher Fair, 1983; The All-Girl Football Team, 1986; Music of the Swamp, 1991; Sugar Among the Freaks: Selected Stories, 1996. NOVELS: Wolf Whistle, 1993; The Sharpshooter Blues, 1995; Lightning Song, 1997. OTHER: Boy with Loaded Gun: A Memoir, 2000. Contributor to periodicals. **Address:** Department of English, University of Pittsburgh, 526 Cathedral of Learning, 4200 5th Ave., Pittsburgh, PA 15260, U.S.A. **Online address:** nordan@pitt.edu

NORDAN, Lewis Alonzo. *See* **NORDAN, Lewis.**

NORDHAUS, Jean. American (born United States), b. 1939. **Genres:** Poetry, History, Philosophy. **Career:** University of Maryland, assistant professor of German, 1964-65; University of the District of Columbia, assistant professor of English, 1971-73; Folger Shakespeare Library, programs coordinator for poetry, 1980-83, 1991-92, coordinator. Freelance writer and poet. **Publications:** POETRY: A Language of Hands (chapbook), 1982; A Bracelet of Lies, 1987; My Life in Hiding, 1991; A Purchase of Porcelain (chapbook), 1998; The Porcelain Apes of Moses Mendelssohn, 2002; Innocence, 2006. Works appear in anthologies. Contributor to periodicals. **Address:** 623 E Capitol St. SW, Washington, DC 20003-1234, U.S.A. **Online address:** jnordhaus@att.net

NORDLUND, Willis J. American (born United States), b. 1942. **Genres:** Business/Trade/Industry. **Career:** West Virginia University, assistant professor, 1973-74; Oregon State University, assistant professor, 1974-75; U.S. Department of Labor, regional director, 1976-95; College of West Virginia, associate professor, professor and dean of business, 1995-; New River Community and Technical College, chair, associate professor, 2003-10, professor, 2010-, director; Bluefield State College, Business Division, dean and adjunct professor; Little League, baseball manager; Amateur Athletic Union, baseball manager; Concord University, adjunct professor. Writer. **Publications:** (With R.T. Robson) Energy and Employment, 1980; A History of the Federal Employees' Compensation Act, 1992; The Quest for a Living Wage, 1997; Silent Skies: The Air Traffic Controllers' Strike, 1998. **Address:** Department of Business and Economics, New River Community and Technical College, 167 Dye Dr., Beckley, WV 25801-2637, U.S.A.

NORELL, Mark. *See* **NORELL, Mark A.**

NORELL, Mark A. (Mark Norell). American (born United States), b. 1957. **Genres:** Zoology, Animals/Pets, Young Adult Non-fiction. **Career:** American Museum of Natural History, Paleontology Division, Fossil Reptiles, Amphibians, and Birds, curator-in-charge and chairman. Writer. **Publications:** NONFICTION: (as Mark Norell) All You Need to Know about Dinosaurs, 1991; (with L. Dingus and E.S. Gaffney) Discovering Dinosaurs in the American Museum of Natural History, 1995, rev. ed. as Discovering Dinosaurs: Evolution, Extinction, and the Lessons of Prehistory, 1995; (with L. Dingus) Searching for Velociraptor, 1996; (with L. Dingus) A Nest of Dinosaurs: The Story of Oviraptor (young adult), 1999; (as Mark Norell) Unearthing the Dragon: The Great Feathered Dinosaur Discovery, 2005; Oviraptor Adventure: Mark Norell and the Egg Thief, 2007; (with L. Dingus) Barnum Brown, 2010; (with D.P. Leidy and L. Ross) Traveling the Silk Road: Ancient Pathway to the Modern World, 2011. Contributor to books and journals. **Address:** Division of Paleontology, American Museum of Natural History, 79th St., Central Pk. W, New York, NY 10024-5192, U.S.A. **Online address:** norell@amnh.org

NORÉN, Lars. Swedish (born Sweden), b. 1944. **Genres:** Poetry, Plays/Screenplays. **Career:** Poet and dramatist, 1963-; Royal Dramatic Theater, director, 1999-2007; National Theater, artistic director, 1999-2009; Peoples Theater, artistic director, 2009-, children's theater director, 2011-, artist in residence, 2012-; Folk Theatre, artistic director, 2009-, artist in residence. **Publications:** Syrener, snö, 1963; De verbala resterna avden bildprakt som förgår, 1964; Inledning n: r 2 till Schizz, 1965; Encyklopedi, 1966; Salome-Sfinxerna, 1968; Stupor, 1968; Revolver, 1969; En hungersaga, 1970; Biskötarna, 1970; Solitära dikter, 1972; Viltspeglar, Författarfölaget, 1972; I den underjordiska himlen: Biskötarna II, 1972; Dagliga och nattliga dikter, 1972; Kung Mej ochandra dikter, 1973; Fursteslickaren, 1973; Dagbokaugusti-oktober 1975, 1976; Nattarbete, 1976; Order: dikter, 1978; (contrib.) Bilder från åren 1934-1950, 1978; Den ofullbordade stjärnan: dikter, 1979; Murlod, 1979; Orestes, 1979; Tre skådespel, 1980; Hjärta i hjärta: dikter, 1980; Akt utan nåd, 1980; En fruktensvärd lycka, 1981; Natten är dagens mor, 1982; Underjordens leende, 1982; Kaos är granne med Gud, 1983; Två skådespel, 1983; Demoner, 1984; The Courage to Kill, 1984; Nattvarden, 1985; Stillheten, 1986, 1987; Hebriana, 1989; Höst och vinter, 1989; Endagsvarelser, 1989; Och ge oss skuggorna, 1991; Bobby Fischer bor in Pasadena, 1991; Löven i Vallambrosa, 1991; Tiden är vårt hem, 1992; Tre borderliga kvartetter, 1992; De döda pjäserna, 4 vols., 1995; Radiopjäser 1971-1995, 1996; En sorts Hades, 1996; Personkrets 3: 1 Morire di classe, 1998; Skuggpojkarna: Morire di classe, 1999; Stilla vatten, 2002; Detaljer, 2002; Kyla, 2002; Vinterfövaring, 2003; Le 20 novembre, 2006. **Address:** c/o Bonniers, PO Box 3159, Stockholm, 103 63, Sweden.

NORFLEET, Celeste O. American (born United States), b. 1959. **Genres:** Romance/Historical, Novels. **Career:** CON Graphics, owner, 1991-. Art director and novelist. **Publications:** ROMANCE NOVELS: A Christmas Wish, 2002; Priceless Gift, 2002; Since Forever, 2003; One Sure Thing, 2003; Reflections of You, 2004; Irresistible You, 2004; The Fine Art of Love, 2005; Only You, 2005; (with S. Kitt and D. Savoy) Back in Your Arms, 2006; Love is For Keeps, 2006; Following Love, 2007; Love After All, 2007; Pushing Pause, 2007; When Love Calls, 2008; (with J. Norfleet) She Said, She Said, 2008; Fast Forward, 2009; Then There Was Love. 2009; When it Feels so Right, 2009; Love Me Now, 2009; Sultry Storm, 2009; Cross My Heart, 2010; Heart's Choice, 2010; Flirting With Destiny, 2010; Getting Played, 2011. **Address:** PO Box 7346, Woodbridge, VA 22195-7346, U.S.A. **Online address:** conorfleet@aol.com

NORFOLK, Lawrence. British (born England), b. 1963. **Genres:** Novels, Children's Fiction. **Career:** Writer and teacher. **Publications:** NOVELS: Lemprière's Dictionary, 1991; The Pope's Rhinoceros, 1996; In the Shape of a Boar, 2000. Contributor to periodicals. **Address:** c/o Carole Blake, Blake Friedmann Literary, Film & TV Agency Ltd., 122 Arlington Rd., London, GL NW1 7HP, England.

NORGREN, Jill. American (born United States), b. 1943?. **Genres:** Young Adult Non-fiction, Children's Non-fiction, History, Law, Civil Liberties/Human Rights. **Career:** City University of New York, John Jay College of Criminal Justice, Department of Political Science, professor, now professor emeritus. Writer. **Publications:** (With S. Nanda) American Cultural Pluralism and Law, 1988, 3rd ed., 2006; (with P.T. Shattuck) Partial Justice: Federal Indian Law in a Liberal Constitutional System, 1991; The Cherokee Cases: The Confrontation of Law and Politics, 1996; The Cherokee Cases: Two Landmark Federal Decisions in the Fight for Sovereignty, 2004; Belva Lockwood: The Woman Who Would Be President, 2007; Belva Lockwood: Equal Rights Pioneer, 2009. **Address:** Department of Political Science, John Jay College of Criminal Justice, City University of New York, Rm. 3247N, North Hall, 445 W 59th St., New York, NY 10019, U.S.A. **Online address:** jnorgren@gc.cuny.edu

NORIEGA, Chon A. American (born United States), b. 1961. **Genres:** Film, Art/Art History. **Career:** Maryland Film Commission, National Film Laboratory for Minority Professionals Think Tank, founding member, 1990; University of New Mexico, assistant professor of American studies, 1991-92, Southwest Hispanic Research Institute, research faculty associate, 1991-92; University of California, assistant professor of film and television, 1992-, Department of Film, Television and Digital Media, professor, Chicano Studies Research Center, director; Guadalupe Cultural Arts Center, humanities adviser for Cine Festival, 1993; National Latino Communications Center, consultant; National Association of Latino Independent Producers, co-founder, 1999; Independent Television Service, director. Writer. **Publications:** (Ed. and contrib.) Chicanos and Film: Representation and Resistance, 1992; Cine Chicano, 1993; (ed. with S. Ricci) The Mexican Cinema Project, 1994; (ed.) From the West: Chicano Narrative Photography, 1995; (A.A. López) The Ethnic Eyes: Latino Media Arts, 1996; (ed.) Urban Exile: Collected Writings of Harry Gamboa, Jr., 1998; Shot in America: Television, the State and the Rise of Chicano Cinema, 2000; Shot in America, 2000; (ed.) The Future of Latino Independent Media, 2000; (ed.) Visible Nations: Latin American Cinema and Video, 2000; (ed.) The Future of Latino Independent Media: A NALIP Sourcebook, 2000; (ed.) East of the River: Chicano Art Collectors Anonymous, 2000; (ed.) I, Carmelita Tropicana, 2000; (ed.) Just Another Poster?: Chicano Graphic Arts in California, 2001; (co-ed.) The Chicano Studies Reader: An Anthology of Aztlán, 1970-2000, 2001, 2nd ed., 2010; (ed. with W. Belcher) I am Aztlán: The Personal Essay in Chicano Studies, 2004; (foreword) Gronk, 2007; (with R. Gonzalez and H.N. Fox) Phantom Sightings: Art After the Chicano Movement, 2008; (ed. with T. Romo and P. Tompkins) L.A. Xicano, 2011. Works appear in anthologies. Contributor to journals. **Address:** School of Theatre, Film and Television, University of California, 3329 Macgowan Hall, Los Angeles, CA 90095-1622, U.S.A. **Online address:** cnoriega@ucla.edu

NORMAN, Barry. British (born England), b. 1933. **Genres:** Novels, Film, Adult Non-fiction. **Career:** Daily Mail, business editor, through 1971; British Broadcasting Corp., writer and presenter of the weekly film review film, 1972-98, writer and presenter of Omnibus, 1982; Sky Premiere, presenter. **Publications:** NOVELS: The Matter of Mandrake, 1967; The Hounds of Sparta, 1968; End Product, 1976; A Series of Defeats, 1977; To Nick a Good Body, 1978; Have a Nice Day, 1981; Sticky Wicket, 1984; The Story of Hollywood, 1987; The Birddog Tape, 1992; The Mickey Mouse Affair, 1995 in US as The Butterfly Tattoo, 1996; Death on Sunset, 1998. NONFICTION: Tales of the Redundance Kid, 1975; The Hollywood Greats, 1979; The Movie Greats, 1981; The Film Greats, 1985; Talking Pictures, 1987; One Hundred Best Films of the Century, 1992, rev. ed., 1998; (with E. Norman) Barry Norman's Video Guide, 1993, 3rd ed., 1995; (with E. Norman) The Radio Times Family Video Guide, 1995; And Why Not?, 2002. **Address:** Curtis Brown Ltd., 28/29 Haymarket, London, GL SW1Y 4SP, England.

NORMAN, Edward R(obert). British (born England), b. 1938. **Genres:** History, Theology/Religion. **Career:** Beaconsfield Secondary Modern School, assistant master, 1957-58; Selwyn College, fellow, 1962-64; Jesus College, fellow, 1964-71; University of Cambridge, lecturer in history, 1965-68, dean, 1971-88; NATO, research fellow, 1966-68; Addenbrooke's Hospital, associate chaplain, 1971-78; Peterhouse, fellow, 1971-88, emeritus fellow, 1989-, dean; British Broadcasting Corp., Reith Lecturer, 1978; University of Torlnto, Wilkinson professor of church history, 1981-82; Canterbury Cathedral, six preacher, 1984-; Christ Church College, dean and chaplain, 1988-95; University of York, professor of history. Writer. **Publications:** The Catholic Church and Irish Politics in the 1860s, 1965; The Catholic Church and Ireland 1859-1863, 1965; The Conscience of the State in North America, 1968; Anti-Catholicism in Victorian England, 1968; The Early Development of Irish Society, 1969; A History of Modern Ireland, 1971; Church and Society in Modern England, 1976; Christianity and World Order, 1979; Christianity in the Southern Hemisphere, 1981; The English Catholic Church in the Nineteenth Century, 1983; Ethics and Nuclear Arms: European and American Perspectives, 1985; Roman Catholicism in England from the Elizabethan Settlement to the Second Vatican Council, 1985; The Victorian Christian Socialists, 1987; A History of Churches, 1989; The House of God: Church Architecture, Style, and History, 1990; Entering the Darkness: Christianity and Its Modern Substitutes, 1991; Anglican Catechism, 2001; Out of the Depths, 2001; Secularisation: Sacred Values in a Secular World, 2003; Mercy of God's Humility: The Daily Telegraph Meditations, 2004; Anglican Difficulties, 2004; Roman Catholic Church: An Illustrated History, 2007. **Address:** Peterhouse, Trumpington St., Cambridge, CB2 1RD, England.

NORMAN, Howard A. American (born United States), b. 1949. **Genres:** Novels, Literary Criticism And History, Mythology/Folklore, Translations, Novellas/Short Stories, Young Adult Fiction. **Career:** University of Maryland, Master of Fine Arts Program, instructor in native American literature, 1989-, Department of English, professor of creative writing; Middlebury College, faculty, 1999; Goucher College, writer-in-residence, 2003; University of Vermont, James Marsh professor-at-large, 2006; World Society for the Protection of Animals, translator. **Publications:** (Comp. and trans.) The Wishing Bone Cycle: Narrative Poems from the Swampy Cree Indians, 1976, rev. ed., 1982; (trans.) The Woe Shirt: Caribbean Folk Tales, 1980; (comp. and trans.) Cree Songs to the Newborn, 1981; (comp. and trans.) Where the Chill Came From: Cree Windigo Tales and Journeys, 1982; The Owl Scatterer (juvenile), 1986; The Northern Lights (novel), 1987; Who-Paddled-Backward-With-Trout, 1987; Kiss in the Hotel Joseph Conrad and Other Stories, 1989; (reteller) How Glooskap Outwits the Ice Giants and Other Tales of the Maritime Indians, 1989; (comp. and ed.) Northern Tales, 1990; The Bird Artist, 1994; (foreword) Indian Tales, 1997; (reteller) Girl Who Dreamed Only Geese and Other Tales of the Far North, 1997; The Museum Guard (novel), 1998; (reteller) Trickster and the Fainting Birds, 1999; (intro.) Lafayette Life: Words and Images Since 1928, 1999; The Haunting of L, 2002; The Chauffeur: Stories, 2002; Disobedient Pelican Daughter, 2004; My Famous Evening: Nova Scotia Sojourns, Diaries and Preoccupations, 2004; Between Heaven and Earth: Bird Tales from Around the World, 2004; In Fond Remembrance of Me, 2005; The Devotion, 2007; What is Left the Daughter, 2010. Contributor to periodicals and magazines. **Address:** Department of English, University of Maryland, 3205 Tawes Hall, College Park, MD 20742-8815, U.S.A. **Online address:** hnorman@umd.edu

NORMAN, Lilith. Australian (born Australia), b. 1927. **Genres:** Children's Fiction, Plays/Screenplays, History, Children's Non-fiction, Geography. **Career:** Newtown Library, library assistant, 1947-49; Angus and Robertson Books, sales assistant, 1951-53; Balmain District Hospital, nursing trainee, 1953-56, nurse, 1975-78; Sydney Public Library, library assistant, 1956-58, research officer, 1958-66, children's librarian, 1966-70; Children's Book Council of New South Wales, treasurer, 1968-70; Library Association of Australia, branch councillor, 1969-70, New South Wales Division, president, 1969-71; New South Wales Department of Education School Magazine, assistant editor, 1970-75, editor, 1975-78; full-time writer, 1978-. **Publications:** The City of Sydney: Official Guide, 1959; Facts about Sydney, 1959; Asia: A Select Reading List, 1959; Some Notes on the Early Land Grants at Potts Point, 1959; A History of the City of Sydney Public Library, 1960; Notes on the Glebe, 1960; Historical Notes on Paddington, 1961; Historical Notes on Newtown, 1962; Climb a Lonely Hill, 1971; The Shape of Three, 1971; The Flame Takers, 1973; Mockingbird-Man (reader), 1977; A Dream of Seas, 1978; My Simple Little Brother, 1979; The Brown and Yellow: Sydney Girls' High School 1883-1983, 1983; The Laurel and Hardy Kids, 1989; The Hex, 1989; The Paddock, 1992; Aphanasy, 1994; The Beetle, 1995; Grandpa, 1998. Contributor to periodicals. **Address:** Margaret Connolly & Associates, 37 Ormond St., Paddington, NW 2021, Australia.

NORMAN, Marsha. American (born United States), b. 1947. **Genres:** Novels, Plays/Screenplays, Humanities. **Career:** Kentucky Department of Health, teacher, 1969-70; Jefferson County Public Schools, teacher, 1970-72; Kentucky Arts Commission, teacher, 1972-76; Louisville Times, book reviewer and editor, 1974-79; Actors Theatre of Louisville, director, 1980-81, writer-in-residence; Juilliard School, Lila Acheson Wallace American Playwrights Program, co-director, 1984-; Dramatists Guild of America, vice president. **Publications:** PLAYS: Third and Oak-The Laundromat, 1980; Night, Mother, 1983; Collected Plays of Marsha Norman, 1998; Getting Out, 1998. OTHERS: The Fortune Teller, 1987; Traveler in the Dark, 1988; Secret Garden, 1991; Loving Daniel Boone, 1992; The Secret Garden: Book and Lyrics, 1993; Red Shoes, 1993; Marsha Norman: A Casebook, 1996; Trudy Blue, 2002; Last Dance, 2004; Samantha: An American Girl Holiday, 2004; The Color Purple, 2005; The Master Butchers Singing Club, 2010. Works appear in anthologies. Contributor to journals and newspapers. **Address:** Playwrights Program, Drama Division, Juilliard School, 60 Lincoln Center Plz., New York, NY 10023-6588, U.S.A.

NORMAN, Michael Lewis. American (born United States), b. 1947. **Genres:** Autobiography/Memoirs. **Career:** New York University, Arthur L. Carter Journalism Institute, faculty; New York Times, reporter and columnist;

Home News, staff; Trenton Times, staff. **Publications:** These Good Men: Friendships Forged from War (memoir), 1989; (with E.M. Norman) Tears in the Darkness: The Story of the Bataan Death March and Its Aftermath, 2009. Contributor to periodicals. **Address:** Montclair, NJ , U.S.A. **Online address:** michael@tearsinthedarkness.com

NORMAN, Rick (J.). American (born United States), b. 1954. **Genres:** Young Adult Fiction, Business/Trade/Industry, Ethics, Novels. **Career:** U.S. Department of Justice, assistant attorney, 1983-85, associate attorney, city attorney; McNeese State University, instructor, 1986-93; Woodly, Williams, Boudreau, Norman, Brown & Doyle L.L.C., partner; Association of Professional Arbitrators and Mediators, staff; Tara High School, staff. Writer. **Publications:** (With J.S. Holliday, Jr.) Louisiana Corporations, 1983; Employment Law, 2005. NOVELS: Fielder's Choice, 1991; Cross Body Black, 1996. **Address:** 500 Kirby St., Lake Charles, LA 70601-5221, U.S.A. **Online address:** rnorman@normanble.com

NORMENT, Lisa. American (born United States), b. 1966. **Genres:** Young Adult Fiction, Human Relations/Parenting, Children's Fiction. **Career:** Writer and education administrator. **Publications:** Once upon a Time in Junior High (juvenile fiction), 1994; The Black House; Down the Street. **Address:** c/o Whitny Reid, 2207 Washington Ave., Silver Spring, MD 20910-2616, U.S.A.

NORNES, Abé Mark. American (born United States) **Genres:** Art/Art History, History. **Career:** Colby College, lecturer, 1995; Vanderbilt University, lecturer, 1996; University of Michigan, Department of Asian Languages and Cultures, instructor, 1996-2007, associate chair, 2002-04, professor, 2007-, Department of Screen Arts & Cultures, professor and chair, 1996-, Center for Japanese Studies Press, director of publications, 2002-04; Kinema Club.com, founder. Writer. **Publications:** (With F. Yukio) Media Wars, Then and Now: Pearl Harbor 50th Anniversary: Yamagata International Documentary Film Festival '91, October 7-10, 1991; (ed. with F. Yukio) The Japan/America Film Wars: World War II Propaganda and Its Cultural Contexts, 1994; Japanese Documentary Film: The Meiji Era through Hiroshima, 2003; Forest of Pressure: Ogawa Shinsuke and Postwar Japanese Documentary, 2007; Cinema Babel: Translating Global Cinema, 2007; (with A. Gerow) Research Guide to Japanese Film Studies, 2009. **Address:** Department of Screen Arts & Cultures, University of Michigan, 6348 N Quad, 105 S State St., Ann Arbor, MI 48109-1285, U.S.A. **Online address:** amnornes@umich.edu

NORRANDER, Barbara. American (born United States), b. 1954. **Genres:** Politics/Government, Social Sciences. **Career:** College of William and Mary, acting assistant professor, 1982-83; University of Wisconsin-Milwaukee, visiting assistant professor, 1983-84; University of Kentucky, visiting assistant professor, 1984-85; San Jose State University, Department of Political Science, assistant professor of political science, 1985-89, associate professor, 1989-90; University of Arizona, Department of Political Science, associate professor, 1990-99, professor, 1999-. Writer. **Publications:** Super Tuesday: Regional Politics and Presidential Primaries, 1992; (ed. with C. Wilcox) Understanding Public Opinion, 1997, 3rd ed., 2010; (with M. Corbett) American Government: Using Micro Case ExplorIt, 9th ed., 2006; Can Presidential Primaries Be Reformed?, 2010; The Imperfect Primary: Oddities, Biases and Strengths of U.S. Presidential Nomination Politics, 2010. Contributor to journals. **Address:** Departement of Political Science, University of Arizona, 315 Social Sciences Bldg., PO Box 210027, Tucson, AZ 85721, U.S.A. **Online address:** norrande@u.arizona.edu

NORRELL, Gregory T. American (born United States), b. 1960. **Genres:** Novels, Novellas/Short Stories, Poetry, Information Science/Computers. **Career:** Idaho National Engineering Laboratory, scientist/writer, 1992-95; Dandelion Press, author and publisher, 1995-; Dandelion Media, author and publisher, 1995-; Dandelion Studios, owner; Web Poets Society, founder. **Publications:** Til Death Do Us Part (short stories), 1997; (ed. with J. Bishop) 95 Windows: An Unofficial Poetry Collection from the Microsoft Network (poetry anthology), 1997; Amongst the Shadows (poetry), 1997; The River of No Return (novel), 1998; Impact, 1999; The Poet's Web: A Guide to Poetry on the World Wide Web, forthcoming. **Address:** 1935 E 113 South St., Idaho Falls, ID 83404, U.S.A. **Online address:** dandelion@dandelion-multimedia.com

NORRELL, Robert J(efferson). American (born United States), b. 1952. **Genres:** Young Adult Non-fiction, History, Biography. **Career:** University of Alabama, associate professor, 1988-94, professor, 1994; University of Tennessee, Bernadotte Schmitt chair of excellence, Department of History, professor of history, 1998-; University of Tuebingen, Fulbright distinguished chair in American studies, 2010-11. Writer. **Publications:** Reaping the Whirlwind: The Civil Rights Movement in Tuskegee, 1985; A Promising Field: Engineering at Alabama, 1837-1987, 1990; (ed. with H.J. Knopke and R.W. Rogers) Opening Doors: Perspectives on Race Relations in Contemporary America, 1991; James Bowron: The Autobiography of a New South Industrialist, 1991; The Alabama Story, 1992; The Making of Modern Alabama, 1992; We Want Jobs!: A Story of The Great Depression, 1993; The Alabama Journey: State History and Geography, 1998; House I Live In: Race in the American Century, 2005; Up from History: The Life of Booker T. Washington, 2009. Contributor to books and journals. **Address:** Department of History, University of Tennessee, Dunford Hall, 915 Volunteer Blvd., 6th Fl., PO Box 870212, Knoxville, TN 37996-4065, U.S.A. **Online address:** rnorrell@utk.edu

NORRETRANDERS, Tor. Danish (born Denmark), b. 1955. **Genres:** Sciences, Psychology. **Career:** Writer and scientist. **Publications:** Om kapitalistisk naturvidenskab: forholdet mellem teori og empiri i marxistiske studier af naturvidenskaberne belyst udfra en analyse af forskningen om liv udenfor jorden, 1976; Kraftens frie spil: dansk miljøpolitik efter PVC-sagen fra Skalskør, 1980; Udelelige: Niels Bohrs aktualitet i fysik, mystik og politik, 1985; Videnskabsvurdering: forskning, fremtid og folkestyre, 1987; (with T. Haaland) Dansk dynamit: dansk forsknings internationale status vurderet ud fra bibliometriske indikatorer, 1990; Verden vokser: tilfaeldighedens historie, 1994; The User Illusion: Cutting Consciousness Down to Size, 1998; The Generous Man: How Helping Others Is The Sexiest Thing You Can Do, 2005; Børnespørgehjørne, 2008. **Address:** Penguin Group Inc., 375 Hudson St., New York, NY 10014-3657, U.S.A.

NORRIS, Frances. American (born United States) **Genres:** Novels. **Career:** Harvard-Westlake School, teacher of English and creative writing. Writer. **Publications:** Blue Plate Special: A Novel of Love, Loss, and Food, 2005. Contributor to periodicals. **Address:** c/o Author Mail, St. Martins Press, 175 5th Ave., New York, NY 10010-7703, U.S.A. **Online address:** fnorris@hw.com

NORRIS, Geoffrey. British (born England), b. 1947?. **Genres:** Music, Biography. **Career:** Royal Northern College of Music, lecturer in music history, 1975-77; The New Oxford Companion to Music, supervising and commissioning editor, 1977-83; Daily Telegraph, music critic, 1983-95, chief music critic, 1995-. **Publications:** The Wright Brothers, 1961; Jet Adventure: Airmen Today and Tomorrow, 1962; The Royal Flying Corps: A History, 1965; Rakhmaninov, 1976, 2nd ed., 1993; (with R. Threlfall) A Catalogue of the Compositions of S. Rachmaninoff, 1982; (with C. Norris) Shostakovich: The Man and His Music, 1982; Rachmaninoff, 1994. **Address:** D44 Du Cane Ct., London, GL SW17 7JH, England.

NORRIS, Kathleen. American (born United States), b. 1947. **Genres:** Poetry, inspirational/Motivational Literature, Autobiography/Memoirs, Biography, Psychology. **Career:** Academy of American Poets (AAP), program assistant, 1969-74; Leaves of Grass Inc., president and manager, 1974-97; Lemmon Public Library, assistant librarian, 1976-91; North Dakota Arts Council, poet-in-residence, 1979-92; Family Ranch Corp., manager; poet and writer, 1997-. **Publications:** POETRY: Falling Off, 1971; From South Dakota: Four Poems, 1978; The Middle of the World, 1981; The Year of Common Things (chapbook), 1988; How I Came to Drink My Grandmother's Piano: Some Benedictine Poems, 1989; The Astronomy of Love, 1994; Little Girls in Church, 1995; Journey: New and Selected Poems, 2001. NONFICTION: Dakota: A Spiritual Geography, 1993; The Cloister Walk, 1996; Amazing Grace: A Vocabulary of Faith, 1998; The Quotidian Mysteries: Laundry, Liturgy, and Women's Work, 1998; (contrib.) Meditations on Mary, 1999; The Virgin of Bennington, 2001. EDITOR: Leaving New York: Writers Look Back, 1995. OTHER: (with T. de Paola) The Holy Twins: Benedict and Scholastica, 2001; Acedia & Me: A Marriage, Monks, and a Writer's Life, 2008. Contributor to periodicals. Works appear in anthologies. **Address:** Steven Barclay Agency, 12 Western Ave., Petaluma, CA 94952, U.S.A.

NORRIS, Ken. (Murphre Roos). Canadian/American (born United States), b. 1951. **Genres:** Poetry, Literary Criticism And History. **Career:** Cross Country Press, co-editor, 1975-80; Vehicule Press, editor, 1975-80; McGill University, writer-in-residence, 1983-84; University of Maine, assistant professor, 1985-90, associate professor, 1990-96, professor of Canadian literature, 1996-; Concordia University, faculty; Dawson College, faculty; McGill University, faculty. **Publications:** POETRY: Vegetables, 1975; Under the Skin, 1976; (with T. Konyves) Proverbsi, 1977; Report on the Second Half of the Twentieth Century, 1977; The Perfect Accident, 1978; The Book of Fall, 1979; Autokinesis, 1980; (with J. Mele as Murphre Roos) Sonnets and Other Dead Forms, 1980; To Sleep, To Love, 1982; Eight Odes, 1982; Whirlwinds, 1983; The Better Part of Heaven: Pacific Writings, 1984; One Night, 1985; In the Spirit of the Times, 1986; Islands, 1986; In the House of No, 1991; Alphabet of Desire, 1991; A New World: Essays on Poetry and Poetics, 1994; The Music, 1995; Odes, 1997; Limbo Road, 1998; Hotel Montreal: New and Selected Poems, 2001; Going Home, 2007. EDITOR: (with A. Farkas) Montreal: English Poetry of the Seventies, 1977; Violent Duality: A Study of Margaret Atwood, 1980; (with P. Van Toorn) The Insecurity of Art: Essays on Poetics, 1982; (with P. Van Toorn) Cross/Cut: Contemporary English Quebec Poetry, 1982; Canadian Poetry Now: Twenty Poets of the Eighties, 1984; (with B. Hilderley) Poets 88, 1988; Vehicule Days: An Unorthodox History of Montreal's Vehicule Poets, 1993; (and intro.) Full Sun: Selected Poems, 1993; (with M. Fournier) Take This Waltz: A Celebration of Leonard Cohen, 1994; (with J. Battson) Word Up: Spoken Word Poetry in Print, 1995; Sleepwalking Among the Camels: New and Selected Poems, 1995; (and comp. with E. Farkas) Collected Books of Artie Gold, 2010. OTHERS: The Little Magazine in Canada, 1925-1980: Its Role in the Development of Modernism and Post-Modernism in Canadian Poetry, 1984; (trans.) Symphony, by E. Letelier-Ruz, 1988; (with E. Farkas) Howl Too, Eh? & Other Poems, 1991; Report on the Second Half of the Twentieth Century: Books 1-4, 1988; (trans.) Silence, by E. Letelier-Ruz, 1992; Report on the Second Half of the 20th Century, 2000; The Way Life should Be, 2002; Fifty, 2003; Hôtel Montréal, 2005; Report on the Second Half of the Twentieth Century, Books 16-22, 2005; Dominican Moon, 2005; (trans. with M. Stenbaek) A. Lynge, Taqqat uummammut aqqutaannut takorluukkat apuuffiannutt (title means: 'The Veins of the Heart to the Pinnacle of Mind'), 2008; Asian Skies, 2010; Floating Up to Zero, 2011. Contributor to periodicals. **Address:** Department of English, University of Maine, Rm. 317, 5752 Neville Hall, 168 College Ave., Orono, ME 04469-5752, U.S.A. **Online address:** ken_norris@umit.maine.edu

NORRIS, Pamela. British (born England), b. 1946?. **Genres:** Theology/Religion, Biology, Novels, Humor/Satire, Poetry, Literary Criticism And History. **Career:** Writer and educator. **Publications:** Story of Eve, 1998 in US as Eve: A Biography, 1999; Words of Love: Passionate Women from Heloise to Sylvia Plath, 2006. EDITOR: Sound the Deep Waters: Women's Romantic Poetry in the Victorian Age, 1992; Come Live with Me and Be My Love, 1993; Pride and Prejudice, 1993; Between the Apple-Blossom & the Water: Women Writing about Gardens, 1994; Through the Glass Window Shines the Sun: An Anthology of Medieval Poetry and Prose, 1995; (with C. Michon) Jane Austen's Little Advice Book, 1996. **Address:** New York University Press, 838 Broadway, 3rd Fl., New York, NY 10003-4812, U.S.A.

NORRIS, Shana. American (born United States), b. 1980. **Genres:** Novels. **Career:** Writer. **Publications:** Something to Blog About (novel), 2008. **Address:** Stephen Barbara,, Donald Maass Literary Agency, 121 W 27th St., Ste. 801, New York, NY 10001, U.S.A. **Online address:** shana@shananorris.com

NORRIS, William R. American (born United States), b. 1973?. **Genres:** Novels, Young Adult Fiction. **Career:** Hofstra University, adjunct assistant professor of writing and literature; KGB Literary Bar, Emerging Voices Reading Series, curator; New School and Gotham Writer's Workshop, teacher. Writer. **Publications:** Snapshots, 2001. **Address:** 697 Sackett St., Ste. 3, Brooklyn, NY 11217-3119, U.S.A. **Online address:** william.r.norris@hofstra.edu

NORTH, Charles. American (born United States), b. 1941. **Genres:** Poetry. **Career:** Freelance copy editor, 1965-66; Pace University, instructor, 1967-71, adjunct faculty, 1971-82, poet-in-residence, 1982-. **Publications:** POETRY: Lineups, 1972; Elizabethan & Nova Scotian Music, 1974; Six Buildings, 1977; Leap Year, 1978; (with T. Towle) Gemini, 1981; The Year of the Olive Oil, 1989; (with E. Robinson and S. Ngai) Re: Chapbook 2, 1996; New & Selected Poems, 1999; The Nearness of the Way You Look Tonight, 2000, rev. ed., 2001; (with T. Winkfield) Tulips, 2004; Cadenza, 2007; Complete Lineups, 2009; What It Is Like: New and Selected Poems, 2011. PROSE: No Other Way: Selected Prose, 1998; Ode to Asparagus, Peonies and Manet, 2010. EDITOR: (with J. Schuyler) Broadway: A Poets and Painters Anthology, 1979; (with J. Schuyler) Broadway 2: A Poets and Painters Anthology, 1989; (co-ed.) The Green Lake is Awake: Selected Poems by Joseph Ceravolo, 1994. Works appear in anthologies. **Address:** Department of English, Pace University, Rm. 1517, 1 Pace Plz., New York, NY 10038, U.S.A. **Online address:** cnorth@pace.edu

NORTH, Darian. American (born United States) **Genres:** Novels, Mystery/Crime/Suspense, Young Adult Fiction. **Career:** Novelist. **Publications:** NOVELS: Criminal Seduction, 1993; Bone Deep, 1995; Thief of Souls, 1997; Violation, 1998. **Address:** Dutton, 375 Hudson St., New York, NY 10014, U.S.A.

NORTH, Kate. *See* **CONLON, Kathleen (Annie).**

NORTH, Rick. *See* **BRENNER, Mayer Alan.**

NORTHCUTT, Wayne. American (born United States), b. 1944. **Genres:** History, International Relations/Current Affairs. **Career:** Monterey Institute of International Studies, Western European Area Studies Program, head, 1975-78; Schiller College, lecturer in history and international relations, 1978; University of California, teaching associate, 1979-80; Niagara University, assistant professor, 1980-83, associate professor, 1983-88, professor of history, 1988-, International Studies Program, coordinator, 1985-2003; Chinese People's University, foreign expert, 1983. Writer. **Publications:** The French Socialist and Communist Party under the Fifth Republic, 1958-1981: From Opposition to Power, 1985; (ed.) Historical Dictionary of the French Fourth and Fifth Republics, 1946-1991, 1992; Mitterrand: A Political Biography, 1992; The Regions of France: A Reference Guide to History and Culture, 1996. Contributor to periodicals. **Address:** Department of History, Niagara University, Timon Hall, PO Box 1941, Niagara University, NY 14109-1941, U.S.A. **Online address:** northcutt@niagara.edu

NORTHEAST, Brenda V(ictoria). Australian/British (born England), b. 1948. **Genres:** Children's Fiction, Art/Art History. **Career:** Writer and educator. **Publications:** SELF-ILLUSTRATED: For the Love of Vincent, 1995; For the Love of Auguste, 1997. **Address:** PO Box 888, Gawler, SA 5118, Australia. **Online address:** bearne@sa.chariot.net.au

NORTHROP, Douglas. American (born United States), b. 1967?. **Genres:** Theology/Religion, History. **Career:** Pitzer College, assistant professor of history, 1998-99; University of Georgia, assistant professor of history, 1999-2004; University of Michigan, associate professor of history, 2004-. Writer. **Publications:** (with G. Chiesa) Transition to Democracy: Political Change in the Soviet Union, 1987-1991, 1993; Veiled Empire: Gender & Power in Stalinist Central Asia, 2004; An Imperial World: Empires and Colonies since 1750, 2010. **Address:** Department of History, University of Michigan, 1029 Tisch Hall, Ann Arbor, MI 48109, U.S.A. **Online address:** northrop@umich.edu

NORTHRUP, Jim. American (born United States), b. 1943. **Genres:** Poetry, Novellas/Short Stories, Travel/Exploration, Crafts. **Career:** COMPAS, Writer in the Schools Program, roster artist, 1990-92, Loft Inroads Program, mentor. Writer. **Publications:** Walking the Rez Road (short stories and poems), 1993; The Rez Road Follies: Canoes, Casinos, Computers, and Birch Bark Baskets (essays), 1997; Anishinaabe Syndicated: A View from the Rez, 2011. Contributor to books. **Address:** Voyageur Press, PO Box 59, McGregor, MN 55760, U.S.A. **Online address:** northrup@cp.duluth.mn.us

NORTHRUP, Mary (Wirtz). American (born United States), b. 1952. **Genres:** Librarianship, Education, Information Science/Computers. **Career:** Roman Catholic School, teacher, 1975-76; Johnson Controls Inc., librarian, 1979-82; Mid-Continent Public Library, librarian, 1992-2000; Metropolitan Community College, Maple Woods Library, reference librarian, 1996-. Writer. **Publications:** American Computer Pioneers, 1998; (contrib.) Chocolate for a Lover's Heart, 1999; Short on Time, Long on Learning: Activities for Those Teachable Moments, 2000; Teaching Time-Savers, 2002. Contributor to books and periodicals. **Address:** Maple Woods Library, Metropolitan Community College, 2601 NE Barry Rd., Kansas City, MO 64156, U.S.A.

NORTON, Augustus Richard. American (born United States), b. 1946. **Genres:** Cultural/Ethnic Topics, Politics/Government, Third World, Bibliography, Self Help, Military/Defense/Arms Control. **Career:** University of Illinois, assistant professor of military science, 1974-78, adjunct assistant professor of political science, 1975-77; Old Dominion University, adjunct assistant professor of political science, 1979-80; U.S. Military Academy, assistant professor, 1981-84, associate professor of international studies, 1984, associate professor of comparative politics, 1984-90, professor of political science, 1990-93; Norwegian Institute of International Affairs, Fulbright senior research professor, 1989, 1999-2000; International Peace Academy, senior research fellow, 1990-92; New York University, visiting research professor, 1992-95, Civil Society in the Middle East Program, director of civil society, 1992-94; Boston University, Department of International Relations, professor of international relations, 1993-, Department of Anthropology, professor of anthropology, 1996-, Institute for Iraqi Studies, director; University of Oxford, visiting professor in the politics of the Middle East, Center for Islamic Studies, distinguished visiting fellow, 2000; Iraq Study Group, adviser, 2006-. Writer. **Publications:** NONFICTION: (with M.H. Greenberg) International Terrorism: An Annotated Bibliography and Research Guide, 1980; (co-author) NATO: A Bibliography and Resource Guide, 1984; (co-author) The Emergence of a New Lebanon, 1984; Amal and the Shi'a: Struggle for the Soul of Lebanon, 1987; (with T.G. Weiss) UN Peacekeepers: Soldiers with a Difference, 1990; (with M. Muslih) Political Tides in the Arab World, 1991. OTHERS: Moscow and the Palestinians: A New Tool of Soviet Policy in the Middle East, 1974; Hizballah, 2000; Amnīyat dar Khāvar' miyānah: jihat' gīrīhā-yi nuvīn, 2001; Hezbollah: A Short History, 2007. EDITOR: (with M.M. Greenberg) Studies in Nuclear Terrorism: An Annotated Bibliography and Research Guide, 1979; (with Greenberg) International Terrorism: An Annotated Bibliography and Research Guide, 1980; (with M.H. Greenberg) Touring Nam: The Vietnam War Reader, 1985; (with M.H. Greenberg) The International Relations of the Palestine Liberation Organization, 1989; Civil Society in the Middle East, 1995. Contributor to magazines and periodicals. **Address:** Department of International Relations, Boston University, Rm. 440, 152 Bay State Rd., Boston, MA 02215-1501, U.S.A. **Online address:** arn@bu.edu

NORTON, Bryan G(eorge). American (born United States), b. 1944. **Genres:** Environmental Sciences/Ecology, Philosophy, Politics/Government, Social Sciences, Sciences. **Career:** University of Michigan, teaching fellow, lecturer, Danforth Teaching Training Supervisor, 1967-70; New College of the University of South Florida, assistant professor of philosophy, 1970-77, assistant professor, 1977-85, professor, 1985-88; University of Maryland, Institute for Philosophy and Public Policy, research associate, 1981-83, School of Public Affairs, Executive Degree Program, visiting lecturer, 1992; Resources for the Future, Gilbert White fellow, 1985-86; Georgia Institute of Technology, School of Public Policy, professor of philosophy, 1988-, Philosophy, Science and Technology Program, acting director, 1996-98, 2001-02, distinguished professor; Zoo Atlanta, associated scientist, 1989-2004; Hastings Institute, fellow. Writer. **Publications:** Linguistic Frameworks and Ontology: A Re-Examination of Carnap's Metaphilosophy, 1977; (ed.) The Preservation of Species: The Value of Biological Diversity, 1986; Why Preserve Natural Diversity?, 1987; Toward Unity among Environmentalists, 1991; (ed. with R. Costanza and B.D. Haskell) Ecosystem Health: New Goals for Environmental Management, 1992; (co-ed.) Ethics on the Ark: Zoos, Animal Welfare, and Wildlife Conservation, 1995; (ed. with S. Donnelley and V.A. Sharpe) Wolves and Human Communities: Biology, Politics, and Ethics, 2001; Searching for Sustainability: Interdisciplinary Essays in the Philosophy of Conservation Biology, 2003; Sustainability: A Philosophy of Adaptive Ecosystem Management, 2005. **Address:** School of Public Policy, Georgia Institute of Technology, DM Smith 300, 685 Cherry St., Atlanta, GA 30332, U.S.A.

NORTON, Melissa. American (born United States) **Genres:** Novels, Sports/Fitness, Travel/Exploration. **Career:** Writer and educator. **Publications:** Just the Two of Us: A Cycling Journey Across America, 2001. **Address:** c/o Author Mail, Chandler House Press, 335 Chandler St., PO Box 20100, Worcester, MA 01602, U.S.A.

NORTON, M. Grant. American (born United States), b. 1989?. **Genres:** Sciences. **Career:** Washington State University, School of Mechanical and Materials Engineering, faculty, 1991-, professor, College of Engineering and Architecture, associate dean of research and graduate programs. Writer. **Publications:** (With C. Suryanarayana) X- Ray Diffraction: A Practical Approach, 1998; (with C.B. Cater) Ceramic Materials: Science and Engineering, 2007; (contrib.) Handbook of Nanoceramics and Their Based Nanodevices, 2007. Contributor to journals. **Address:** School of Mechanical & Materials Engineering, Washington State University, Dana 145, PO Box 642920, Pullman, WA 99164-2920, U.S.A. **Online address:** norton@mme.wsu.edu

NORTON, Philip. British (born England), b. 1951. **Genres:** History, Politics/Government. **Career:** University of Sheffield, lecturer, 1975-76; Wroxton College, Fairleigh Dickinson University, lecturer, 1977; University of Hull, Department of Politics, lecturer, 1977-82, senior lecturer, 1982-84, reader, 1984-86, professor of government, 1986-, head, 2002-07, Center for Legislative Studies, director, 1992-; Conservative Academic Group, chairman; King Edward VI Grammar School, governor; Hull Open Public Access Ltd., director. Writer. **Publications:** Discipline, Dissent and The Prevalence of Unity: The Conservative Party in Opposition, 1945-1951, 1975; Conservative Dissidents: Dissent Within the Parliamentary Conservative Party, 1970-74, 1978; The House of Commons in the 1970s: Three Views on Reform, 1978; Dissension in the House of Commons 1974-79, 1980; The Commons in Perspective, 1981; (with A. Aughey) Conservatives and Conservatism, 1981; The Commons in Perspective, 1981; The Constitution in Flux, 1982; The British Polity, 1984, 5th ed., 2011; Parliament in the 1980s, 1985; Parliament in Perspective, 1987; (co-author) Politics U.K., 1991, rev. ed., 1997; Parliament and Politics in Britain, 1993; Does Parliament Matter? 1993; (co-author) Back from Westminster: British Members of Parliament and Their Constituents, 1993; (with P. Cowley) Are Conservative MPs Revolting?: Dissension by Government MPs in the British House of Commons, 1979-96, 1996; Parliaments and Citizens in Western Europe, 2002; Politics U.K., with Bill Jones and Others, 5th ed., 2004; Parliament in British Politics, 2005. EDITOR: (comp.) Dissension in the House of Commons: Intra-Party Dissent in the House of Commons' Division Lobbies, 1945-74, 1975; Law and Order and British Politics, 1984; (with J. Hayward) The Political Science of British Politics, 1986; Legislatures, 1990; (contrib.) Parliaments in Western Europe, 1990; New Directions in British Politics?: Essays on the Evolving Constitution, 1991; (with M. Franklin) Parliamentary Questions, 1993; National Parliaments and the European Union, 1996; The Conservative Party, 1996; (with D. Olson) The New Parliaments of Central and Eastern Europe, 1996; Legislatures and Legislators, 1998; Parliaments and Governments in Western Europe, 1998; Parliaments in Contemporary Western Europe, 1998; Parliaments and Pressure Groups in Western Europe, 1999; (with N. Ahmed) Parliaments in Asia, 1999; Century of Constitutional Reform, 2011. Contributor to periodicals. **Address:** Department of Politics and International Studies, University of Hull, Office 218, Wilberforce Bldg., Cottingham Rd., Hull, SU HU6 7RX, England. **Online address:** p.norton@hull.ac.uk

NORTON, Rictor. American (born United States), b. 1945. **Genres:** Literary Criticism And History, Gay And Lesbian Issues, Sex. **Career:** Florida State University, instructor, 1970-72; Gay News, research editor, 1974-78; Western Publishing Co., foreign rights manager, 1979-90; freelance publishing consultant, 1991-94; freelance writer and editor, 1995-. **Publications:** The Homosexual Literary Tradition: An Interpretation, 1974; Mother Clap's Molly House: The Gay Subculture in England, 1700-1830, 1992, 2nd ed., 2006; The Myth of the Modern Homosexual: Queer History and the Search for Cultural Unity, 1997; Mistress of Udolpho: The Life of Ann Radcliffe, 1999. EDITOR: My Dear Boy: Gay Love Letters through the Centuries, 1998; Gothic Readings: The First Wave, 1764-1840, 2000; Eighteenth-Century British Erotica, vol. V, 2002. Contributor to books and periodicals. **Address:** 29 Huddleston Rd., Tufnell Pk., London, GL N7 0AD, England. **Online address:** rictor_norton@yahoo.co.uk

NORTON, Robert L. American (born United States), b. 1939. **Genres:** Education, Engineering, Technology, Reference. **Career:** Polaroid Corp., product design engineer, 1959-66, senior engineer, 1979-81; Jet Spray Cooler Inc., project engineer, 1966-69; Northeast Medical Center Hospitals, Northeastern University, lecturer, 1967-82, Tufts Surgical Research Department, biomedical engineer, 1969-71; Tufts University, Surgery Department, instructor, 1970-82, assistant professor, 1974-79; Boston City Hospital, Tufts Surgical Service, research associate, 1971-74; Norton Associates Engineering, president, 1971-; Franklin Institute, lecturer in biomedical engineering, 1973-76; Worcester Polytechnic Institute, Milton P. Higgins II distinguished professor of mechanical engineering, 1981-. Writer. **Publications:** (With C.F. Leck) An annotated checklist of the birds of the U.S. Virgin Islands, 1991; Design of Machinery: An Introduction to the Synthesis and Analysis of Mechanisms and Machines, 1992, 5th ed., 2011; Machine Design: An Integrated Approach, 1996, 4th ed., 2011; Cam Design and Manufacturing Handbook, 2002, 2nd ed., 2009; Kinematics and Dynamics of Machinery, 2008. Works appear in anthologies. Contributor to journals. **Address:** Department of Mechanical Engineering, Worcester Polytechnic Institute, Higgins Labs 204, 100 Institute Rd., Worcester, MA 01609, U.S.A. **Online address:** norton@wpi.edu

NORTON, Sheila. (Olivia Ryan). British (born England) **Genres:** Novels, Travel/Exploration. **Career:** Broomfield Hospital, St. Andrews Center for Plastic Surgery and Burns, medical secretary. Writer. **Publications:** NOV-

ELS: The Trouble with Ally, 2003; Other People's Lives in US as Would I Lie to You?, 2003; Body & Soul in US as Will She Or Won't She?, 2004; The Travel Bug, 2005; Sweet Nothings, 2006. AS OLIVIA RYAN: Tales from a Hen Weekend, 2007; Tales from a Wedding Day, 2008; Tales from a Honeymoon Hotel, 2009. Contributor to journals. **Address:** c/o Author Mail, Piatkus Books Ltd., 5 Windmill St., London, GL W1T 2JA, England.

NORWICH, John Julius (Cooper). (Viscount Norwich). British (born England), b. 1929. **Genres:** Architecture, Art/Art History, History, Travel/Exploration. **Career:** Majesty's Foreign Service, British Embassy, third secretary, 1952-64, second secretary, 1957-60, Foreign Office, first secretary, 1961-64; Writer. **Publications:** (With R. Sitwell) Mount Athos, 1966; The Normans in the South in US as The Other Conquest, 1967; Sahara, 1968; The Kingdom in the Sun, 1130-1194, 1970; (ed.) Great Architecture of the World, 1975; Venice: The Rise to Empire, 1977; Christmas Crackers, 1980; Venice: The Splendour and the Fall, 1981; A History of Venice, vol. I: The Rise to Empire, vol. II: The Greatness and the Fall, 1982; The Architecture of Southern England, 1985; Glyndebourne, 1985; Byzantium: The Early Centuries, 1988; More Christmas Crackers, 1990; Byzantium: The Apogee, 1991; Byzantium: The Decline and Fall, 1995; Shakespeare's Kings: The Great Plays and the History of England in the Middle Ages, 1337-1485, 2000; The Normans in Sicily, 2000; (ed.) A Traveller's Companion to Venice, 2002; (ed.) Treasures of Britain: The Architectural, Cultural, Historical and Natural History of Britain, 2002; The Illustrated Christmas Cracker, 2003; Paradise of Cities: Venicein the 19th Century, 2003; (ed.) The Duff Cooper Diaries, 1915-1951, 2005; The Middle Sea: A History of the Mediterranean, 2006; Trying to Please (memoirs), 2008. The Popes: A History, 2011. **Address:** c/o Felicity Bryan, 2A N Parade Ave., Oxford, OX OX2 6LS, England. **Online address:** jjnorwich@dial.pipex.com

NORWICH, Viscount. *See* **NORWICH, John Julius (Cooper).**

NORWICH, William. American (born United States), b. 1954. **Genres:** Novels, Architecture. **Career:** New York Daily News, columnist, 1985-; New York Observer, columnist; Vogue, editor-at-large; Town & Country Magazine, editor-in-chief. **Publications:** Learning to Drive (novel), 1996; Yabu Pushelberg, 2009. Contributor to periodicals. **Address:** Atlantic Inc., 841 Broadway, 4th Fl., New York, NY 10003, U.S.A.

NORWOOD, Mandi. American/British (born England), b. 1963. **Genres:** Sex, Fash Ion/Costume. **Career:** Look Now (magazine), sub-editor and deputy chief sub-editor, 1986-87; Clothes Show (magazine), features editor, 1987; More! (magazine), deputy editor, 1987-89; Looks (magazine), editor, 1989-90; Co. (magazine), editor, 1990-95; British Cosmopolitan, editor, 1995-2000; Mademoiselle, editor-in-chief, 2000-01; SHOP Etc., editor-in-chief, 2004-. **Publications:** Sex and the Married Girl: From Clicking to Climaxing: The Complete Truth about Modern Marriage, 2003; Hitched Chick's Guide to Modern Marriage: Essential Advice for Staying Single-Minded and Happily Married, 2004; (with S. Hoppus and A. Denoon) Rock Star Momma: The Hip Guide to Looking Gorgeous Through All Nine Months and Beyond, 2007; Michelle Style: Celebrating the First Lady of Fashion, 2009. Contributor to periodicals. **Address:** 312 E 69th St., New York, NY 10021, U.S.A.

NOSSITER, Adam. American (born United States), b. 1961?. **Genres:** Documentaries/Reportage, Politics/Government, Biography, History, Young Adult Non-fiction, Military/Defense/Arms Control. **Career:** Atlanta Journal-Constitution, journalist; New York Times, journalist, 1995-97. **Publications:** Of Long Memory: Mississippi and the Murder of Medgar Evers, 1994; The Algeria Hotel: France, Memory, and the Second World War, 2001; France and the Nazis: Memory, Lies, and the Second World War, 2003. **Address:** 2828 Coliseum St., New Orleans, LA 70115, U.S.A.

NOSTRAND, Richard L(ee). American (born United States), b. 1939. **Genres:** Geography. **Career:** University of Massachusetts, instructor, assistant professor of geography, 1967-73; University of Texas, postdoctoral fellow, 1971-72; University of Oklahoma, associate professor, professor of geography, 1973-96, David Ross Boyd professor, 1996-2004, David Ross Boyd professor emeritus, 2004-; Mid-American State Universities Association, honor lecturer, 1980-81; Association of American Geographers, visiting geographical scientist, 1983-84; Universidad de las Américas, Fulbright lecturer, 1990-91. Writer. **Publications:** (Ed. with E.R. Stoddard and J.P. West) Borderlands Sourcebook: A Guide to the Literature on Northern Mexico and the American Southwest, 1983; (ed. with S.B. Hilliard) The American South, 1988; The Hispano Homeland, 1992; (ed. with L.E. Estaville) Homelands: A Geography of Culture and Place across America, 2001; El Cerrito, New Mexico: Eight Generations in a Spanish Village, 2003. Contributor to books and periodicals. **Address:** Department of Geography, University of Oklahoma, SEC 664, 100 E Boyd St., Ste. 510, Norman, OK 73019-1006, U.S.A. **Online address:** rnostrand@ou.edu

NOTAR, Beth E. American (born United States), b. 1963. **Genres:** Cultural/Ethnic Topics. **Career:** National Palace Museum, translator, 1986-87; University of Michigan, Institute for Social Research interviewer, 1989, teaching assistant, 1990-92, instructor in anthropology, 1997; Fulbright-Hays doctoral dissertation research fellow, 1994; Cornell University, teaching assistant in Asian studies, 1997; University of Washington, lecturer in anthropology, 1998; Smith College, lecturer in Asian studies, 1999; Trinity College, assistant professor, 2000-07, associate professor of anthropology, 2007-; Mount Holyoke College, Department of Anthropology, visiting assistant professor, 1998-2000. Academic, anthropologist and writer. **Publications:** Displacing Desire: Travel and Popular Culture in China, 2006. Contributor to periodicals and journals. **Address:** Department of Anthropology, Trinity College, 300 Summit St., Hartford, CT 06106, U.S.A. **Online address:** beth.notar@trincoll.edu

NOVACEK, Michael. (Michael John Novacek). American (born United States), b. 1948. **Genres:** Natural History. **Career:** San Diego State University, lecturer, 1976-77, assistant professor, 1977-79, associate professor of zoology, 1979-82; American Museum of Natural History, staff, 1982, assistant curator, 1983-85, associate curator, 1985-89, curator of vertebrate paleontology, 1989-, vice president and dean of science, 1989-95, senior vice president and provost of science curator, 1994-. Writer. **Publications:** Insectivora and Proteutheria of the later Eocene (Uintan) of San Diego County, California, 1976; Early Tertiary Vertebrate Faunas, Vieja Group, Trans-Pecos Texas, Insectivora, 1976; Review of Paleocene and Eocene Leptictidae (Eutheria, Mammalia) from North America, 1977; Dinosaurs of the Flaming Cliffs, 1996; Time Traveler: In Search of Dinosaurs and Ancient Mammals from Montana to Mongolia, 2002; Terra: Our 100-Million-Year-Old Ecosystem and the Threats that Now Put It at Risk, 2007. EDITOR: (with Q.D. Wheeler) Extinction and Phylogeny, 1992; (with F. Szalay and M. McKenna) Mammal Phylogeny, 1993; The Biodiversity Crisis: Losing What Counts, 2001. **Address:** American Museum of Natural History, 79th St., Central Park W, New York, NY 10024-5192, U.S.A. **Online address:** novacek@amnh.org

NOVACEK, Michael John. *See* **NOVACEK, Michael.**

NOVACK, Sandra. American (born United States), b. 1972. **Genres:** Novels, Young Adult Fiction. **Career:** Duke University, instructor; North Carolina State University, instructor; University of Cincinnati, instructor; Writers.com, online writing instructor. Writer. **Publications:** Precious: A Novel, 2009; Everyone But You: Stories, 2011. Works appear in anthologies. Contributor to magazines. **Address:** Random House Inc., 1745 Broadway, New York, NY 10019, U.S.A. **Online address:** sandra@sandranovack.com

NOVAK, David. American (born United States), b. 1953?. **Genres:** Biography, Business/Trade/Industry. **Career:** Tracey-Locke BBDO, executive vice president, through 1986; PepsiCo, Pizza Hut, senior vice president of marketing, 1986-90, Pepsi-Cola, executive vice president of marketing and national sales, 1990-92, Pepsi-Cola-North America, chief operating officer, 1992-94, KFC-North America, president and chief executive officer, 1994-96, KFC, group president and chief executive officer, 1996-97, Pizza Hut, group president and chief executive officer, 1996-97; Yum! Brands, acting vice chairman, director and president, 1997-, chief executive officer, 2000-, chair, 2001-, executive chairman; Tricon Global Restaurants, vice chair and president, 1997-99, chief executive officer and president, 1999-2001, chair, chief executive officer and president, 2001-02; JPMorgan Chase & Co., independent director, 2001-; Bank One Corp., director, 2001-04. Writer. **Publications:** (With J. Boswell) The Education of an Accidental CEO: My Journey from the Trailer Park to the Corner Office (nonfiction), 2007; Taking People with You, 2011. **Address:** Yum! Brands, 1441 Gardiner Ln., Louisville, KY 40213, U.S.A.

NOVAK, Jana. American (born United States) **Genres:** Theology/Religion, Biography, Autobiography/Memoirs. **Career:** Crisis, editorial assistant, 1994-95; Rising Tide Magazine, assistant editor, 1995-96; freelance editor, 1997, 2004-; Office of the Speaker, writer, 1997-99, senior writer, 1999; U.S. Representative Tillie Fowler, communication director, 1999; Senator Kay Bailey Hutchison, senior communications advisor, 2001-02; Sam Brownback, senior policy advisor, 2002-03; National Endowment for the Arts, congressional relations, 2003-04; freelance writer, 2004-. **Publications:** Knipling Spiztze Lace, 1988; (with M. Novak) Tell Me Why: A Father Answers His Daughter's Questions about God, 1998; (ed.) Don't Play Away Your Cards, Uncle Sam: The American Difference, 2002; (with M. Novak) Washington's God: Religion, Liberty, and the Father of Our Country, 2006. **Address:** 241 10th St. NE, Washington, DC 20002-6213, U.S.A.

NOVAK, Karen. American (born United States), b. 1958. **Genres:** Novels, Horror. **Career:** Writer and translator. **Publications:** NOVELS: Five Mile House, 2000; Ordinary Monsters, 2002; Innocence, 2003; The Wilderness: A Leslie Stone Novel, 2005. Contributor to periodicals. **Address:** c/o Author Mail, Bloomsbury Publishing, 175 5th Ave., New York, NY 10010, U.S.A.

NOVAK, Maximillian Erwin. American (born United States), b. 1930. **Genres:** Intellectual History, Literary Criticism And History. **Career:** University of Michigan, instructor, 1958-61, assistant professor, 1961-62; University of California, assistant professor, 1962-67, associate professor, 1965-68, professor of English, 1969-2000, Clark Library professor, 1973-74, distinguished professor emeritus, 2000-, now professor emeritus; Augustan Reprint Society, associate editor. **Publications:** Economics and the Fiction of Daniel Defoe, 1962; Defoe and the Nature of Man, 1963; (with H. Davis) The Uses of Irony, 1966; Congreve, 1971; (with A. Williams) Congreve Considered, 1971; (with E. Dudley) The Wildman Within, 1972; Realism, Myth and History in Defoe's Fiction, 1983; English Literature in the Eighteenth Century, 1983; Daniel Defoe Master of Fictions, 2001. EDITOR: (with E. Dudley) The Wild Man Within, 1972; Oroonoko, 1976; English Literature in the Age of Disguise, 1977; California Edition of the Works of John Dryden, vol. X, 1970, vol. XIII, 1984; (co-ed.) An Essay Upon Projects, 1999; (with A. Mellor) Passionate Encounters in a Time of Sensibility, 2000; (co-ed.) The Consolidator, 2000; (with J. Lewis) Enchanted Ground: Reimagining John Dryden, 2004; (with C. Fisher) Approaches to Teaching Defoe's Robinson Crusoe, 2005; The Age of Projects, 2008. **Address:** Department of English, University of California, 149 Humanities Bldg., PO Box 951530, Los Angeles, CA 90095, U.S.A. **Online address:** novak@humnet.ucla.edu

NOVAK, Michael. American (born United States), b. 1933. **Genres:** Novels, Cultural/Ethnic Topics, Ethics, Philosophy, Social Commentary, Theology/Religion. **Career:** Stanford University, assistant professor, 1965-68; Commonweal, associate editor, 1966-69; State University of New York-Old Westbury, associate professor philosophy and religious studies, 1968-73; Rockefeller Foundation, Humanities Program, associate director, 1973-74; Syracuse University, Ledden-Watson distinguished professor of religion, 1977-79; American Enterprise Institute, George Frederick Jewett chair in religion and public policy, director of social and political studies, 1978-; United Nations Human Rights Commission, U.S. representative and chief of U.S. Delegation, 1981-82; United Nations Human Rights Commission, U.S. Ambassador, 1981; Institute on Religion and Democracy, director, 1981; National Center for Urban and Ethnic Affairs, director, 1982-86; University of Notre Dame, faculty, 1986-87; visiting professor, 1987-88. **Publications:** The Tiber Was Silver (novel), 1961; A New Generation: American and Catholic, 1964; The Open Church: Vatican II: Act II, 1964; The Men Who Make the Council, 1964; The Experience of Marriage, 1964; Belief and Unbelief, 1965; (with R.M. Brown and A.J. Heschel) Vietnam: Crisis Of Conscience, 1967; A Time to Build, 1967; American Philosophy and the Fugure (essays), 1968; A Theology for Radical Politics, 1969; Naked I Leave (novel), 1970; Story in Politics, 1970; The Experience of Nothingness, 1970; All the Catholic People, 1971; (and intro.) Ascent of the Mountain, Flight of the Dove: An Invitation to Religious Studies, 1971, 3rd ed., 2009; Politics: Realism and Imagination, 1971; (with K.L. Novak) A Book of Elements: Reflections On Middle-Class Days, 1972; The Rise of the Unmeltable Ethnics, 1972; Choosing Our King: Powerful Symbols In Presidential Politics, 1974; The Joy of Sports: End Zones, Bases, Baskets, Balls, and the Consecration Of The American Spirit, 1976, rev. ed., 1993; Further Reflections on Ethnicity, 1977; (ed. with M. Novak and R.J. Vecoli) The Other Catholics, 1978; The Guns of Lattimer, 1978; The American Vision, 1979; The Spirit of Democratic Capitalism, 1982, rev. ed., 1991; Confession of a Catholic, 1983; Freedom with Justice, 1984; Human Rights and the New Realism, 1986; Character and Crime, 1986; Will It Liberate?, 1986; Taking Glasnost Seriously, 1988; Free Persons and the Common Good, 1989; This Hemisphere of Liberty, 1990; Choosing Presidents: Symbols of Political Leadership, 1992; The Catholic Ethic and the Spirit of Capitalism, 1993; Awakening from Nihilism: Why True Matters, 1995; Business as a Calling: Work and the Examined Life, 1996; (ed.) To Empower People, 1996; The Future of the Corporation, 1996; On Corporate Governance: The Corporation as it Ought to be, 1997; Fire of Invention: Civil Society and The Future of The Corporation, 1997; (with J. Novak) Tell Me Why: A Young Woman Questions Her Father About God, 1998; Is There a Third Way?, 1998; On Cultivating Liberty: Reflections on Moral Ecology, 1999; In Praise of the Free Economy, 1999; God's Country: Taking The Declaration Seriously, 2000; (ed. with W. Brailsford and C. Heesters) A Free Society Reader: Principles For The New Millennium, 2000; Three in One: Essays on Democratic Capitalism, 1976-2000, 2001; On Two Wings: Humble Faith And Common Sense at the American Founding, 2001; The Open Church, 2002; Cattolicesimo, Liberalismo, Globalizzazione, 2002; The Universal Hunger for Liberty: A Surprising Look Ahead at the Culture, Economics and Politics of the 21st Century, 2004; Frederick Hart: Changing Tides, 2005; (with J. Novak) Washington's God: Religion, Liberty and The Father of Our Country, 2006; The Universal Hunger for Liberty: Why the Clash of Civilizations Is Not Inevitable, 2006; No One Sees God: The Dark Night of Atheists and Believers, 2008; (with W.E. Simon, Jr.) Living the Call: An Introduction to the Lay Vocation, 2011; All Nature is a Sacramental Fire: Moments of Beauty, Sorrow and Joy, 2011. **Address:** American Enterprise Institute, 1150 17th St. NW, Washington, DC 20036-4603, U.S.A. **Online address:** michaelnovak33@gmail.com

NOVAKOVICH, Josip. Canadian/Croatian (born Croatia), b. 1956. **Genres:** Novellas/Short Stories, Essays. **Career:** Nebraska Indian Community College, instructor, 1989-91; Summer Literary Seminars, core faculty, 1998-; Bard College, faculty, 1999; University of Cincinnati, assistant professor of English, associate professor; Pennsylvania State university, professor of English, 2001-09; Moorhead State University, lecturer; Antioch University, lecturer; Breadloaf Writers' Conference, fiction instructor, 2006-; Concordia University, Department of English, professor, 2009-. Writer. **Publications:** Apricots From Chernobyl (a collection of essays), 1994; Yolk: Short Stories, 1995; Fiction Writer's Workshop (a textbook), 1995, 2nd ed. as Fiction Writer's Workshop: The Key Elements of a Writing Workshop, 2008; Salvation and Other Disasters: Short Stories, 1998; Writing Fiction Step by Step, 1998; (ed. with R. Shapard) Stories in the Stepmother Tongue, 2000; Trazeći grob u Clevelandu, 2003; Plum Brandy: Croatian Journeys, 2003; April Fool's Day: A Novel, 2004; Infidelities: Stories of War and Lust, 2005; Three Deaths, 2010. Contributor to periodicals. **Address:** Department of English, Concordia University, LB 644.3 1455 de Maisonneuve Blvd. W, Montreal, QC H3G 1M8, Canada. **Online address:** jnovakov@alcor.concordia.ca

NOVARO, María. Mexican (born Mexico), b. 1951. **Genres:** Novels, Plays/Screenplays, Art/Art History. **Career:** Film director, cinematographer, producer and author. **Publications:** (With B. Novaro) Danzón, 1994. Contributor to periodicals. **Address:** AltaVista Films, 6121 Santa Monica Blvd., Ste. 102, Hollywood, CA 90038-1711, U.S.A.

NOVAS, Himilce. American/Cuban (born Cuba), b. 1944. **Genres:** Plays/Screenplays, Novels, History. **Career:** Vanidades, journalist, magazine editor and publicist; The New York Times, journalist, magazine editor and publicist; The Connoisseur, journalist, magazine editor and publicist; The Christian Science Monitor, journalist, magazine editor and publicist; Novas Report, broadcaster; KQSB-Radio, broadcaster; KTMS, broadcaster. **Publications:** Free This Day (play), 1994; (with L. Cao) Everything You Need to Know about Latino History, 1994; The Hispanic 100: A Ranking of Latino Men and Women Who Have Most Influenced American Thought and Culture, 1995; Remembering Selena: A Tribute in Pictures and Words, 1995; Mangos, Bananas and Coconuts: A Cuban Love Story (novel), 1996; (with L. Cao) Everything You Need to Know about Asian American History, 1996; (with R.E. Silva) Passport Spain: Your Pocket Guide to Spanish Business, Customs & Etiquette, 1997; (with R. Silva) Latin American Cooking Across the U.S.A., 1997; Secada!, 1997; La Buena Mesa: La Auténtica Cocina Latinoamericana en los Estados Unidos, 1997; Princess Papaya: A Novel, 2003. **Address:** Arte Publico Press, University of Houston, 452 E Cullen Performance Hall, Houston, TX 77204-2004, U.S.A.

NOVGORODOFF, Danica. American (born United States), b. 1980?. **Genres:** Graphic Novels, Illustrations. **Career:** Teacher, 2002; freelance writer, 2004-; First Second Books, book designer, 2005-. **Publications:** SELF-ILLUSTRATED GRAPHIC NOVELS: Circus Song, 2005; A Late Freeze, 2006; Slow Storm, 2008; (with J. Ponsoldt and B. Percy) Refresh, Refresh, 2009. **Address:** Brooklyn, NY , U.S.A. **Online address:** danica.novgorodoff@aya.yale.edu

NOVICK, Sheldon M. American (born United States), b. 1941. **Genres:**

Environmental Sciences/Ecology, Biography, Law. **Career:** Environment Magazine, staff, associate editor, editor and publisher, 1964-77; Washington University, Center for Biology of Natural Systems, administrator, 1966-69; Milgrim Thomajan and Jacobs, associate, 1977-78; U.S. Environmental Protection Agency, regional counsel, 1978-86; Municipal Government, town agent and grand juror, 1987-97; Vermont Law School, adjunct professor of law and history, 2004-. **Publications:** The Careless Atom, 1969; The Electric War: The Fight over Nuclear Power, 1976; Honorable Justice: The Life of Oliver Wendell Holmes, 1989; Henry James: The Young Master, 1996; Henry James: The Mature Master, 2007. EDITOR: (with D. Cottrell) Our World in Peril: An Environment Review, 1967; (with D.W. Stever and M.G. Mellon) Law of Environmental Protection, 1987; Collected Works of Justice Holmes: Complete Public Writings and Selected Judicial Opinions of Oliver Wendell Holmes, 1995. Contributor to periodicals. **Address:** Vermont Law School, 168 Chelsea St., PO Box 96, South Royalton, VT 05068, U.S.A. **Online address:** serge.novick@yahoo.com

NOYES, Deborah. American (born United States), b. 1965. **Genres:** Novels, Novellas/Short Stories, Young Adult Fiction, Picture/Board Books, Young Adult Non-fiction. **Career:** Boston Review, managing editor, 1991-92; freelance writer, 1992-; Western New England College, adjunct lecturer, 1994-2002; Candlewick Press, copywriter, 1997-2000, assistant editor and associate editor, 2000-02, editor, 2002-05, senior editor, 2005-07, executive editor, 2007-10, editor-at-large, 2010-; freelance photographer, 2000-; Emerson College, adjunct lecturer, 2003; Lesley University, visiting writer, 2005. **Publications:** (Ed.) Gothic! Ten Original Dark Tales, 2004; Hana in the Time of the Tulips, 2004; Angel and Apostle, 2005; When I Met the Wolf Girls, 2007; Red Butterfly: How a Princess Smuggled the Secret of Silk out of China, 2007; (ed.) The Restless Dead: Ten Original Stories of the Supernatural, 2007; The Ghosts of Kerfol, 2008; Prudence and Moxie, 2008; (ed.) Sideshow: Ten Original Tales of Freaks, Illusionists, and Other Matters Odd and Magical, 2009. OTHERS: One Kingdom: Our Lives with Animals, 2006; Encyclopedia of the End: Mysterious Death in Fact, Fancy, Folklore and More, 2008; Captivity, 2010. Contributor of articles to periodicals. **Address:** c/o Jill Grinberg, Jill Grinberg Literary Management, 16 Court St., Ste. 3306, Brooklyn, NY 11241, U.S.A. **Online address:** deborahnoyes@gmail.com

NOZAKI, Yoshiko. American (born United States), b. 1956. **Genres:** Reference. **Career:** SUNY-University at Buffalo, associate professor of educational leadership and policy; Asia-Pacific Journal, associate. Writer and historian. **Publications:** (Ed. and contrib. with R. Openshaw and A. Luke) Struggles over Difference: Curriculum, Texts, and Pedagogy in the Asia-Pacific, 2005; War Memory, Nationalism and Education in Postwar Japan, 1945-2007: The Japanese History Textbook Controversy and Ienaga Saburo's Court Challenges, 2008. Contributor to books and journals. **Address:** University at Buffalo, 428 Baldy Hall, Buffalo, NY 14260, U.S.A. **Online address:** ynozaki@buffalo.edu

NRIAGU, Jerome O. American/Nigerian (born Nigeria), b. 1942. **Genres:** Environmental Sciences/Ecology. **Career:** Environment Canada, environmental research scientist, 1972-93; Science of the Total Environment, editor, 1983-; University of Waterloo, adjunct professor, 1985-2000; University of Michigan, School of Public Health, professor of environmental health sciences, 1993-, Environmental Health Program, director, 1996-2001, Center for Human Growth and Development, research professor, 1997-; Science of the Total Environment (journal), editor-in-chief, 2001-. Writer. **Publications:** Lead and Lead Poisoning in Antiquity, 1983; (co-author) Predicting Fate and Transformation of Oxy-Anions in Wastewater Treatment, 2001. EDITOR: Environmental Biogeochemistry, 2 vols., 1976; Biogeochemistry of Lead in the Environment, 2 vols., 1978; Sulfur in the Environment, 2 vols., 1978; Advances in Environmental Science and Technology, 1978; Copper in the Environment, 2 vols., 1979; The Biogeochemistry of Mercury in the Environment, 1979; Zinc in the Environment, 2 vols., 1980; Nickel in the Environment, 1980; Cadmium in the Environment, 2 vols., 1980; Aquatic Toxicology, 1983; (with P.B. Moore) Phosphate Minerals, 1984; (with M.S. Simmons) Toxic Contaminants in the Great Lakes, 1984; The Environmental Impacts of Smelters, 1984; Changing Metal Cycles and Human Health, 1984; (with V. Cairns and P.V. Hodson) Contaminant Effects on Fish, 1984; (with C.I. Davidson) Toxic Metals in the Atmosphere, 1986; (with J. Sprague) Cadmium in the Aquatic Environment, 1987; (with E. Nieboer) Chromium in the Natural and Human Environment, 1988; (with J.A.S. Lakshminarayana) Aquatic Toxicology and Water Quality Management, 1989; (with M.S. Simmons) Food Contamination from Environmental Sources, 1990; Gaseous Pollutants: Characterization and Cycling, 1992; (with E. Nieboer) Nickel and Human Health, 1992; Arsenic in the Environment, 2 vols., 1994; (with M.S. Simmons) Environmental Oxidants, 1994; Thallium in the Environment, 1998; Vanadium in the Environment, 1998; (with P. Sefer) Mineral Components in Foods, 2007; Encyclopedia of Environmental Health, 5 vols., 2011. **Address:** Department of Environmental Health Sciences, School of Public Health, University of Michigan, 6623 SPH I Twr., 1415 Washington Heights, Ann Arbor, MI 48109-2029, U.S.A. **Online address:** jnriagu@umich.edu

NUECHTERLEIN, Jonathan E. American (born United States), b. 1964?. **Genres:** Adult Non-fiction, Bibliography, Communications/Media. **Career:** U.S. Court of Appeals for the District of Columbia Circuit, legal clerk, 1990-91; U.S. Supreme Court, legal clerk, 1991-92; Office of the Solicitor General, assistant, 1996-2000; Federal Communications Commission, deputy general counsel, 2000-01; Wilmer Cutler Pickering Hale and Dorr L.L.P., partner, 2001-, Communications, Privacy and Internet Law Practice Group, chair. Writer. **Publications:** (With P.J. Weiser) Digital Crossroads: American Telecommunications Policy in the Internet Age, 2005. Contributor to periodicals. **Address:** Wilmer Cutler Pickering Hale and Dorr L.L.P., 1875 Pennsylvania Ave. NW, Washington, DC 20006-3642, U.S.A. **Online address:** jon.nuechterlein@wilmerhale.com

NUGENT, Benjamin. American (born United States), b. 1977. **Genres:** Biography, Autobiography/Memoirs, Social Sciences. **Career:** Time Magazine, pop culture reporter, 1999-. Journalist and fiction writer. **Publications:** Elliott Smith and the Big Nothing, 2004; American Nerd: The Story of My People, 2008. Works appear in anthologies. Contributor to periodicals. **Address:** New York, NY , U.S.A. **Online address:** bnugent@americannerdbook.com

NUGENT, (Donald) Christopher. American (born United States), b. 1930. **Genres:** History, Theology/Religion, Humanities. **Career:** University of Alberta, instructor in history, 1961-62; University of Nebraska, assistant professor of history, 1964-66; University of Kentucky, associate professor of history, 1966-95, now professor emeritus; National University of Ireland, University College, visiting lecturer, 1972-73; Ecumenical Institute of Theology, resident fellow, 1979. Writer. **Publications:** Ecumenism in the Age of the Reformation: The Colloquy of Poissy, 1974; Masks of Satan: The Demonic in History, 1983; Mysticism, Death and Dying, 1994. Contributor to periodicals. **Address:** Department of History, University of Kentucky, 1715 Patterson Office Twr., Lexington, KY 40506-0027, U.S.A.

NUGENT, Neill. British (born England), b. 1947. **Genres:** History, Politics/Government, Business/Trade/Industry. **Career:** Manchester Polytechnic, lecturer, senior lecturer and reader in politics, 1972; Duke University, visiting professor; State University of New York, academic director; The College of Europe, visiting professor; University of Bonn, Center for European Integration Studies, visiting professor; Manchester Metropolitan University, professor of politics and Jean Monnet professor of European integration. Writer. **Publications:** EDITOR: (with R. King) The British Right: Conservative and Right Wing Politics in Britain, 1977; (with R. King) Respectable Rebels: Middle Class Campaigns in Britain in the 1970s, 1979; (with R. O'Donnell) The European Business Environment, 1994; The European Union: Annual Review of Activities, 1997; At the Heart of the Union: Studies of the European Commission, 1997, 2nd ed., 2000; (with L. Cram and D. Dinan) Developments in the European Union, 1999; European Union Enlargement, 2004; (with M. Egan and W.E. Paterson) Research Agendas in EU Studies: Stalking the Elephant, 2010. OTHER: (with D. Lowe) The Left in France, 1983; The Government and Politics of the European Community, 1989, 7th ed., 2010; The European Commission, 2001. **Address:** Department of Politics and Philosophy, Manchester Metropolitan University, Geoffrey Manton Bldg., Rm. 313, Rosamond St. W, off Oxford Rd., Manchester, LC M15 6LL, England. **Online address:** n.nugent@mmu.ac.uk

NUGENT, Ted. (Theodore Anthony Nugent). American (born United States), b. 1948. **Genres:** Young Adult Non-fiction, Food And Wine. **Career:** Amboy Dukes, guitarist, 1967-75; solo artist, 1975-; Michigan County Sheriff Department, deputy, 1978-; Damn Yankees, guitarist, 1989-96; Ted Nugent United Sportsmen of America, president. Guitarist, songwriter and singer. **Publications:** NONFICTION: God, Guns & Rock'n'roll, 2000; Kill It & Grill It: A Guide to Preparing and Cooking Wild Game and Fish, 2002; Blood Trails II: The Truth about Bowhunting, 2004; Ted, White, and Blue: The Nugent Manifesto, 2008. **Address:** Nugent USA, 4008 W Michigan Ave., Jackson, MI 49202-1829, U.S.A.

NUGENT, Theodore Anthony. *See* **NUGENT, Ted.**

NUGENT, Walter. American (born United States), b. 1935. **Genres:** History. **Career:** Indiana University, assistant professor, 1963-64, associate professor, 1964-68, professor, 1968-84, associate dean and director of overseas study, 1967-76, Department of History, chairman, 1974-77; Notre Dame University, Tackes professor of history, 1984-2000, professor emeritus, 2000-. Writer. **Publications:** The Tolerant Populists, 1963; Creative History: An Introduction to Historical Method, 1967, 2nd ed., 1973; The Money Question during Reconstruction, 1967; Money and American Society 1865-1880, 1968; Modern America, 1973; From Centennial to World War: American Society 1876-1917, 1977; Structures of American Social History, 1981; Crossings: The Great Transatlantic Migrations, 1870-1914, 1992; (with M. Ridge) The American West: The Reader, 1999; Into the West: The Story of Its People, 1999; Making Our Way: A Family History, 2003; Habits of Empire: A History of American Expansion, 2008; Progressivism: A Very Short Introduction, 2010. **Address:** Department of History, University of Notre Dame, 219 O'Shaughnessy, Notre Dame, IN 46556, U.S.A. **Online address:** wnugent@nd.edu

NULAND, Sherwin. (Sherwin B. Nuland). American (born United States), b. 1930. **Genres:** Medicine/Health, Social Sciences, Theology/Religion. **Career:** Yale-New Haven Hospital, surgeon, 1962-91; Yale University, School of Medicine, clinical professor of surgery, 1962-2009, Institution for Social and Policy Studies, fellow. Writer. **Publications:** Doctors: The Biography of Medicine, 1988; Medicine: The Art of Healing, Hugh, 1992; (co-author) The Face of Mercy: A Photographic History of Medicine at War, 1994; How We Die: Reflections on Life's Final Chapter, 1994; (author of intro.) The Collected Short Stories of William Carlos Williams, 1996; The Wisdom of the Body, 1997, as How We Live, 1998; Leonardo da Vinci, 2000; The Mysteries Within: A Surgeon Reflects on Medical Myths, 2001; (with D. Libeskind and L. Wieseltier) Monument and Memory: September 27, 2002; (ed. and foreword) Jewish Insights on Death and Mourning, 2002; Lost in America: A Journey with My Father, 2003; The Doctors' Plague: Germs, Childbed Fever, and the Strange Story of Ignác Semmelweis, 2003; The Columbia Seminar on Art in Society, 2003; Maimonides, 2005; The Art of Aging: A Doctor's Prescription for Well-Being, 2007; The Best of the Bellevue Literary Review, 2008; The Uncertain Art: Thoughts on a Life in Medicine, 2008; The Soul of Medicine: Tales from the Bedside, 2009. Contributor to books and magazines. **Address:** Glen Hartley, Writers' Representatives L.L.C., 116 W 14th St., 11th Fl., New York, NY 10011-7305, U.S.A. **Online address:** snuland@comcast.net

NULAND, Sherwin B. *See* **NULAND, Sherwin.**

NUMEROFF, Laura Joffe. American (born United States), b. 1953. **Genres:** Children's Fiction, Young Adult Fiction, Picture/Board Books. **Career:** Educator and writer. **Publications:** SELF-ILLUSTRATED FOR CHILDREN: (with A. Richter) Emily's Bunch, 1978; (with A. Richter) You Can't Put Braces on Spaces, 1979. OTHER FOR CHILDREN: Amy for Short, 1976; Phoebe Dexter Has Harriet Peterson's Sniffles, 1977; Walter, 1978; The Ugliest Sweater, 1980; Does Grandma Have an Elmo Elephant Jungle Kit?, 1980; Beatrice Doesn't Want To, 1981; Digger, 1983; If You Give a Mouse a Cookie, 1985; If You Give a Moose a Muffin, 1991; Dogs Don't Wear Sneakers, 1993; Why a Disguise?, 1994; Chimps Don't Wear Glasses, 1995; Mouse Cookies: Ten Easy-to-Make Cookie Recipes, 1995; (with B. Saltzberg) Two for Stew, 1996; The Chicken Sisters, 1997; Mothers/Fathers, 1998; Sometimes I Wonder If Poodles Like Noodles, 1998; If You Give a Pig a Pancake, 1998; Monster Munchies, 1998; The Best Mouse Cookies, 1999; (with W.S. Harpham) The Hope Tree: Kids Talk about Breast Cancer, 1999; If You Take a Mouse to the Movies, 2000; If You Take a Mouse to School, 2002; Laura Numeroff's 10-Step Guide to Living with Your Monster, 2002; If You Give an Author a Pencil, 2002; (with N. Evans) Sherman Crunchley, 2003; Beatrice Doesn't Want To, 2004; If You Give a Pig a Party, 2005; When Sheep Sleep, 2006; Mouse Cookies & More: a Treasury, 2006; Chimps Don't Wear Glasses, 2006; Merry Christmas, Mouse!, 2007; Mouse Cookie First Library, 2007; Time for School, Mouse!, 2008; (with N. Evans) Jellybeans and the Big Dance, 2008; If You Give a Cat a Cupcake, 2008; I Wouldn't Trade My Parents, 2009; Happy Valentine's Day, Mouse!, 2009; Would I Trade My Parents?, 2009; Happy Easter, Mouse!, 2010; Otis & Sydney and the Best Birthday Ever, 2010; (with N. Evans) Jellybeans and the Big Book Bonanza, 2010; (with N. Evans) Ponyella, 2011; (with N. Evans) Jellybeans and the Big Camp Kickoff, 2011; If You Give a Dog a Donut, 2011; (with N. Evans) The Jellybeans and the Big Art Adventure, 2012. DO BEST SERIES: What Mommies Do Best, 1998; What Daddies Do Best, 1998; What Grandmas Do Best, 2000; What Sisters Do Best, 2003; What Aunts Do Best; What Uncles Do Best, 2004; What Puppies Do Best, 2011. **Address:** c/o Author Maily, HarperCollins Publishers, 10 E 53rd St., New York, NY 10022, U.S.A. **Online address:** email@lauranumeroff.com

NUNBERG, Geoffrey. American (born United States), b. 1945. **Genres:** Cultural/Ethnic Topics. **Career:** University of California, professor, 2001- ; Xerox Palo Alto Research Center, principal researcher; Universities of Rome, faculty. Writer. **Publications:** The Linguistics of Punctuation, 1990; (ed.) The Future of the Book, 1996; The Way We Talk Now Commentaries on Language and Culture from NPR's Fresh Air, 2001; Going Nucular: Language, Politics, and Culture in Confrontational Times, 2004; Talking Right: How Conservatives Turned Liberalism into a Tax-Raising, Latte-Drinking, Sushi- Eating, Volvo-Driving, New York Times-Reading, Body-Piercing, Hollywood- Loving, Left-Wing Freak Show, 2006; The Years of Talking Dangerously, 2009. Contributor of articles to periodicals. **Address:** School of Information, University of California, Berkeley, CA 94720, U.S.A. **Online address:** nunberg@berkeley.edu

NUNEZ, Sigrid. American (born United States), b. 1951. **Genres:** Novels, Autobiography/Memoirs, Adult Non-fiction. **Career:** Columbia University, New School University, faculty; Amherst College, Smith College, Washington University, Baruch College (CUNY), University of California at Irvine, Vassar College, Boston University, visiting writer or writer-in-residence. **Publications:** NOVELS: A Feather on the Breath of God, 1995; Naked Sleeper, 1996; Mitz: The Marmoset of Bloomsbury, 1998; For Rouenna, 2001; The Last of Her Kind, 2006; Salvation City, 2010. MEMOIR: Sempre Susan: A Memoir of Susan Sontag, 2011. **Address:** c/o Joy Harris, The Joy Harris Literary Agency, 381 Park Ave. S, Ste. 428, New York, NY 10016, U.S.A. **Online address:** sigrid@sigridnunez.com

NUNN, Frederick McKinley. American (born United States), b. 1937. **Genres:** History, Military/Defense/Arms Control, Politics/Government, Literary Criticism And History. **Career:** Portland State University, assistant professor, 1965-67, associate professor 1967-72, professor of history, 1972, Pacific Rim Studies Center, assistant director, 1972-73, head of the department, 1980-82, assistant dean, 1982-83, associate dean, 1983-92, acting dean, 1992, director of international affairs, 1992-97, vice-provost, 1997-, now professor emeritus; University of Arizona, visiting professor of history and Latin American studies. Writer. **Publications:** Chilean Politics, 1920-31: The Honorable Mission of the Armed Forces, 1970; The Military in Chilean History: Essays on Civil-Military Relations, 1810-1973, 1976; El profesionalismo militar chileno en el siglo XX: pensamiento y autopercepción de la clase de oficiales hasta 1973, 1976; Militares chilenos: desarrollo institucional, relaciones cívico-militares, consideraciones de política, 1977; Chile antiguo y el nuevo: la política de transición, 1973-79, 1979; Yesterday's Soldiers: European Military Professionalism in South America 1890-1940, 1983; The Time of the Generals: Latin American Professional Militarism in World Perspective, 1992; Collisions with History: Latin American Fiction and Social Science from El Boom to the New World Order, 2001. **Address:** Office of International Affairs, Portland State University, Rm. 301 EH, PO Box 751, Portland, OR 97207, U.S.A. **Online address:** nunnf@pdx.edu

NUNN, John. British (born England), b. 1955. **Genres:** Recreation, Technology. **Career:** Chess grandmaster, 1978. Writer. **Publications:** The Pirc for the Tournament Player, 1980; Tactical Chess Endings, 1981; (ed. and foreword) Draw, 1982; (with M. Stean) Sicilian Defence: Najdorf Variation, 1982; The Benoni for the Tournament Player, 1982; Beating the Sicilian, 1984; Solving in Style, 1985; (with P. Griffiths) Secrets of Grandmaster Play, 1987; Najdorf for the Tournament Player, 1988; The Complete Pirc, 1989; Beating the Sicilian II: A Complete New Repertoire for White, 1990; (with T. Harding) The Marshall Attack, 1990; The Classical King's Indian, 1990; Secrets of Rook Endings, 1993; New Ideas in the Four Knights, 1993; New Ideas in the Pirc Defence, 1993; Secrets of Pawnless Endings, 1994; John Nunn's Best Games 1985-93, 1995; Secrets of Minor-Piece Endings, 1995; Complete Najdorf, 1996; (with G. Burgess) Main Line King's Indian, 1996; (with W. Cozens) King Hunt, 1996; Secrets of Grandmaster Chess, 1997; (with G. Burgess and J. Emms) Mammoth Book of the World's Greatest Chess Games, 1998, rev. ed., 2010; Secrets of Practical Chess, 1998; Nunn's Chess Openings, 1999; John Nunn's Chess Puzzle Book, 1999; 101 Brilliant Chess Miniatures, 2000; Understanding Chess Move by Move, 2001; Endgame Challenge, 2002; Learn Chess Tactics, 2004; Grandmaster Chess Move by Move, 2005; Understanding Chess Endgames, 2009; Nunn's Chess Endings, vol. I, 2010. **Address:** 228 Dover House Rd., London, GL SW15 5AH, England.

NUNN, Pamela Gerrish. New Zealander (born New Zealand), b. 1953. **Genres:** Art/Art History, Photography, Architecture. **Career:** University of Canterbury, Department of Fine Arts, professor, 1980. Writer. **Publications:** (Ed. and intro.) Canvassing: Recollections by Six Victorian Women Artists, 1986; Victorian Women Artists, 1987; (with J. Marsh) Women Artists and the Pre-Raphaelite Movement, 1989; Problem Pictures: Women and Men in Victorian Painting, 1995; (with J. Marsh) Pre-Raphaelite Women Artists, 1999; From Victorian to Modern: Innovation and Tradition in the Work of Vanessa Bell, Gwen John and Laura Knight, 2006; Present and Incorrect: Women, Art, Tradition and Modernity, forthcoming. **Address:** School of Fine Arts, University of Canterbury, 223, Block 2, PO Box 4800, Christchurch, 8140, New Zealand. **Online address:** gerrish.nunn@canterbury.ac.nz

NUNNALLY, Tiina. American (born United States), b. 1952. **Genres:** Novels, Translations, Young Adult Fiction. **Career:** University of Washington, Department of Scandinavian Studies, affiliate faculty; Fjord Press & Oso Books, co-editor. Freelance translator. **Publications:** FICTION: Maija: A Novel, 1995; Runemaker: A Margit Andersson Mystery, 1996; Fate of Ravens: A Margit Andersson Mystery, 1998. TRANSLATIONS: Kvindelige Danske Forfattere: Bibliografi Over Prosa i Bogform 1820-1910, 1979; (intro.) T. Ditlevsen, Early Spring (memoirs), 1985; W. Heinesen, Laterna Magica (short stories), 1987; (with S. Murray) M. Newth, The Abduction (young adult fiction), 1989; (ed. with S. Murray) M.A. Nexo, Pelle the Conqueror, 1989, vol. II: Apprenticeship (novel), 1991; (with S. Murray) V. Sorensen, Another Metamorphosis and Other Fictions (short stories), 1990; J.P. Jacobsen, Niels Lyhne (novel), 1990; H. Bang, Katinka (novel), 1990; T. Ditlevsen, The Faces (novel), 1991; K. Hamsun, Night Roamers and Other Stories (short stories), 1992; (with S. Murray) J. Guillou, Enemy's Enemy (suspense novel), 1993; P. Hoeg, Smilla's Sense of Snow (suspense novel), 1993; J.P. Jacobsen, Mogens and Other Stories, 1994; (with S. Murray) K. Rifbjerg, War (poems), 1995; The Wreath, 1997; L. Ullmann, Before You Sleep (novel), 1999; The Wife, 1999; G. Kopperud, The Time of Light (novel), 2000; The Cross, 2000; P.O. Enquist, The Royal Physician's Visit (novel), 2001; The Unknown Sigrid Undset: Jenny and Other Works (novel and letters), 2001; B. Jonsson, Unwinding the Clock (nonfiction), 2001; Jenny: A Novel, 2002; B. Reuter, The Ring of the Slave Prince (YA novel), 2003; H.C. Andersen, Fairy Tales, 2004; S. Undset, Kristin Lavransdatter (novel), 2005; P.O. Enquist, Lewi's Journey (novel), 2005; J. Andersen, Hans Christian Andersen: A New Life (biography), 2005; H. Varmer, Hans Christian Andersen: His Fairy Tale Life (biography for children), 2005; H. Mankell, Chronicler of the Winds (novel), 2006; P.O. Enquist, The Book About Blanche and Marie (novel), 2006; M. Jungstedt, Unseen (mystery), 2006; P.O. Enquist, Book about Blanche and Marie, 2006; J.P. Jacobsen, Niels Lyhne, 2006; M. Jungstedt, Unspoken, 2007; A. Lindgren, Pippi Longstocking, 2007; P.O. Enquist, Three Cave Mountain, 2007; K. östergren, Gentlemen: A Novel, 2007; P.H. Fogtdal, Tsar's Dwarf, 2008; M. Jungstedt, Inner Circle, 2008; M. Ramsland, Doghead, 2009; M. Birkegaard, The Library of Shadows, 2009; K. östergren, Hurricane Party, 2009; M. Jungstedt, Döda av sommaren, (title means: 'The Dead of Summer'), 2011; K. östergren, Gangsters, forthcoming. Contributor to periodicals. **Address:** Department of Scandinavian Studies, University of Washington, 318 Raitt Hall, PO Box 353420, Seattle, WA 98195-3420, U.S.A. **Online address:** tiinanunnally@gmail.com

NURKSE, D(ennis). American (born United States), b. 1949. **Genres:** Poetry, Natural History. **Career:** Defense for Children Intl., program officer and translator, 1988-93; New School University, adjunct poetry faculty, 1998-2001; Sarah Lawrence College, faculty; University of Southern Maine, Stonecoast MFA Program in Creative Writing, professor; Rutgers University, Department of English, faculty, 2007. Writer. **Publications:** Isolation in Action, 1988; Shadow Wars, 1988; Staggered Lights, 1990; Voices Over Water: Poetry, 1993; Leaving Xaia, 1999; The Rules of Paradise, 2001; The Fall, 2002; Burnt Island: Three Suites, 2005; Border Kingdom: Poems, 2008; A Night in Brooklyn: Poems, 2012. **Address:** Knopf Doubleday Publishing Group, 1745 Broadway, New York, NY 10019, U.S.A. **Online address:** dnurkse@hotmail.com

NURSTEN, Jean Patricia (Frobisher). British (born England), b. 1927?. **Genres:** Education, Social Work, Sociology, Social Sciences, Reference. **Career:** University of Reading, psychiatric social worker, 1950-64, visiting senior lecturer, 1989-94, visiting professor, 1994-; University of Bradford, senior lecturer in applied social studies, 1964-76; London School of Economics, senior lecturer in social work, 1979-84; The Queen's University of Belfast, visiting professor in social work, 1992-95. Writer. **Publications:** (With J.H. Kahn) Unwillingly to School: The Place of the Child Guidance Clinic in the Treatment of School Phobia, 1964, (ed. with I. Berg) 4th ed., 1996; (ed.) Social Work Series (Pergamon), 24 vols., 1965; Process of Casework, 1974. **Address:** 3 Cintra Ave., Reading, BR RG2 7AU, England.

NUSSBAUM, Jeff. American (born United States), b. 1975. **Genres:** History, Adult Non-fiction. **Career:** Speechwriter for vice president Al Gore; Gore-Lieberman, senior speechwriter, 2000; Senator Daschle, staff, 2001; Obama-Biden campaign, speechwriter for Vice President Biden; West Wing Writers Group (speechwriters), partner, Humor Cabinet, founder. Writer. **Publications:** (With J. Carville) Had Enough? A Handbook for Fighting Back, 2003; (with B. Graham) Intelligence Matters: The CIA, the FBI, Saudi Arabia and the Failure of America's War on Terror, 2004. **Address:** West Wing Writers Group, 1150 Connecticut Ave. NW, Ste. 505, Washington, DC 20036-4104, U.S.A.

NUSSBAUM, Martha Craven. American (born United States), b. 1947. **Genres:** Philosophy. **Career:** Harvard University, junior fellow, 1972-75; Harvard University, assistant professor, 1975-80, associate professor, 1980-83, professor; Princeton University, humanities fellow, 1977-78; Wellesley College, visiting professor, 1983-84; Brown University, associate professor, 1984-95, professor of philosophy, classics and comparative literature, 1985-87, David Benedict Professor, 1987-88, professor, 1988-95; National Institutes of Health, fellow, 1986-87; United Nations University, World Institute for Development Economics Research, research advisor, 1986-93; All Souls College, visiting fellow, 1986-87; Northwestern University, Alexander Rosenthal Lecturer, 1991; University of Edinburgh, Gifford lecturer, 1993; University of Chicago, professor, 1995-, Ernst Freund distinguished service professor of law and ethics, Department of Classics, associate, Department of Political Science Department, associate; British Academy, corresponding fellow, 2008; Center for Comparative Constitutionalism, founder and coordinator. Writer. **Publications:** The Fragility of Goodness: Luck and Ethics in Greek Tragedy and Philosophy, 1986, rev. ed., 2001; (with A. Sen) Internal Criticism and Indian Rationalist Traditions, 1987; Non-relative Virtues: An Aristotelian Approach, 1987; Nature, Function, and Capability: Aristotle on Political Distribution, 1987; Love's Knowledge: Essays in Philosophy and Literature, 1990; The Therapy of Desire: Theory and Practice in Hellenishe Ethics, 1994; Poetic Justice: The Literary Imagination and Public Life, 1995; For Love of Country: Debating the Limits of Patriotism, 1996; Feminist Critique of Liberalism, 1997; Cultivating Humanity: A Classical Defense of Reform in Liberal Education, 1997; Plato's Republic: The Good Society and the Deformation of Desire, 1998; Sex & Social Justice, 1999; Women and Human Development: The Capabilities Approach, 2000; Vom Nutzen der Moraltheorie für das Leben, 2000; Upheavals of Thought: The Intelligence of Emotion, 2001; Für eine aristotelische Sozialdemokratie, 2002; For Love of Country?, 2002; Hiding from Humanity: Disgust, Shame, and The Law, 2004; Essays on Gender and Governance, 2005; Nascondere l'umanità: il disgusto, la vergogna e la legge, 2005; Frontiers of Justice: Disability, Nationality, Species Membership, 2006; The Clash Within: Democracy, Religious Violence, and India's Future, 2007; Liberty of Conscience: In Defense of America's Tradition of Religious Equality, 2008; Not for Profit: Why Democracy Needs the Humanities, 2010; From Disgust to Humanity: Sexual Orientation and Constitutional Law, 2010. EDITOR: (and trans.) Aristotle's De Motu Animalium, 1978; (with M. Schofield) Language and Logos: Studies in Ancient Greek Philosophy Presented to G.E.L. Owen, 1982; Logic, Science and Dialectic: Collected Papers in Greek Philosophy, 1985; (with A. Rorty) Essays on Aristotle and De Anima, 1992; (with A. Sen) The Quality of Life, 1993; (with J. Brunschwig) Passions and Perceptions: Studies in Hellenistic Philosophy of Mind: Proceedings of the Fifth Symposium Hellenisticum, 1993; (with J. Glover) Women, Culture, and Development: A Study of Human Capabilities, 1995; (with D. Estlund) Shaping Sex, Preference, and Family: Essays on Law and Nature, 1997; (with S.M. Olyan) Sexual Orientation & Human Rights in American Religious Discourse, 1998; (with C.R. Sustein) Clones and Clones: Facts and Fantasies about Human Cloning, 1998; (ed. with J. Cohen and M. Howard) Is Multiculturalism Bad for Women?, 1999; (with J. Sihvola) Sleep of Reason: Erotic Experience and Sexual Ethics in Ancient Greece and Rome, 2002; (with C.R. Sunstein) Animal Rights: Current Debates and New Directions, 2004; (with A. Gleason and J. Goldsmith) On Nineteen Eighty-Four: Orwell and Our Future, 2005; (with S. Levmore) Offensive Internet: Speech, Privacy, and Reputation, 2010. OTHERS: (trans. with R.A. Kaster) Anger,

Mercy, Revenge/Seneca, 2010; (contrib.) The Air we Breathe: Artists and Poets Reflect on Marriage Equality, 2011; Creating Capabilities: The Human Development Approach, 2011; Philosophical Interventions: Book Reviews, 1986-2011, 2012. Contributor to periodicals. **Address:** The Law School, Univeristy of Chicago, Rm. 520, 1111 E 60th St., Chicago, IL 60637-2776, U.S.A. **Online address:** martha_nussbaum@law.uchicago.edu

NUSSBAUM, Paul David. American (born United States), b. 1963. **Genres:** Medicine/Health, Psychology. **Career:** University of Arizona, Clinical Neuropsychological Practicum, assistant, professor, 1989; Veterans Neuropsychiatric Hospital, intern in clinical neuropsychology, 1990-91; University of Pittsburgh, Western Psychiatric Institute and Clinic, postdoctoral fellow, 1991-92, assistant professor of neurology, 1994-2000, adjunct associate professor of Neurosurgery, 2004-, adjunct professor of neurosurgery; Lutheran Affiliated Services, Outpatient Memory Disorders Clinic, co-director, 1994-2001, chairperson of internal review board and Main Street Quality of Life Program, 1994-2000, senior manager, 1994-96, executive manager, 1996-97, 1998-, Aging Research and Education Center, director, 1994-97, 1998-, director of senior healthcare partners, 1997-98; Medical College of Pennsylvania, assistant professor; Geriatric Care Services Inc., developer, Outpatient Memory Disorders Clinic, co-director, 1994-2000; Slippery Rock University, Ann T. Bicknell Memorial lecturer, 1996, adjunct faculty; Shadyside Hospital, allied health associate; Vincentian Regency Nursing Home, behavioral program consultant, 2003-; Metlife, consultant on brain health, 2004-; Pittsburgh Neuropsychology Associates, president, 2005-; Brain Health Lifestyle, international leader; Brain Health for Emeritus Assisted Living, National director, 2005-; Brain Fit, chief scientific officer; Vivity Labs, chief scientific officer, 2007-; Library's of the Future, brain health consultant, 2007-; Fitbrains Inc., chief scientific officer; International Center for Leadership in Education, senior advisor on brain health and education, 2007-, senior vice president; My Way Village, chief brain health officer, 2010-; Vibrant Brains Inc., chief scientific officer and chief brain health officer, 2010-; Moxxor, senior brain health advisor; presenter of clinical workshops and symposia. Consultant and writer. **Publications:** (Contrib.) Progress in Behavior Modification, 1996; (ed. with G. Goldstein and S.R. Beers and contrib.) Handbook of Human Brain Function: Assessment and Rehabilitation, vol. I: Neuropsychology, 1997; (ed.) Handbook of Neuropsychology and Aging, 1997; Brain Health and Wellness, 2003; (ed. with P.J. Snyder) Clinical Neuropsychology: A Pocket Handbook for Assessment, 2005, 2nd ed., (with P.J. Snyder and D.L. Robins) 2006; Your Brain Health Lifestyle: A Proactive Program to Preserve your Life Story, 2007, 2nd ed. as Your Brain Health Lifestyle: Application to the School, Library, Corporate Setting and Home, 2009; What Brain Health Teaches Us about Rigor, Relevance, and Relationships, 2008; Save Your Brain: 5 Things You Must do to Keep Your Mind Young and Sharp, 2010; Brain Health and Optimal Engagement for Older Adults, 2010; Brain Health, forthcoming. Contributor to books and journals. **Address:** 2120 W Grove Dr., Gibsonia, PA 15044, U.S.A. **Online address:** ageon@zoominternet.net

NÜSSLEIN-VOLHARD, Christiane. German (born Germany), b. 1942. **Genres:** Sciences, Medicine/Health. **Career:** Max-Planck-Institut für Virusforschung, supervisor, 1969-74; University of Freiburg, Laboratory of Dr. K. Sander, faculty, 1977; European Molecular Biology Laboratory, faculty of head group, 1978-81; Friedrich-Miescher Laboratorium, Max-Planck Gesellschaft, faculty, 1981-84, scientific faculty, 1985-90, secretary general, through 2009; Max-Planck Institut für Entwicklungsbiologie, director, 1985-; Christine Nüsslein-Volhard Foundation, founder, 2004-. Writer. **Publications:** (Ed. with J. Krätzschmar) Of Fish, Fly, Worm, and Man: Lessons from Developmental Biology for Human Gene Function and Disease, 2000; (ed. with R. Dahm) Zebrafish: A Practical Approach, 2002; Coming to Life: How Genes Drive Development, 2006; (ed.) Wachstum: Eskalation, Steuerung und Grenzen, 2009. **Address:** Max Planck Institute for Developmental Biology, Abteilung 3, Spemannstr 35, Tubingen, 72076, Germany. **Online address:** christiane.nuesslein-volhard@tuebingen.mpg.de

NUTE, Kevin. American/British (born England), b. 1958. **Genres:** Architecture, Humanities, Psychology, Photography. **Career:** Millard-Davies, architectural assistant, 1981-82; YRM Intl., architectural assistant, 1982-83; Archiplan Team, architectural assistant, 1983; Richard Seifert and Partners, assistant architect, 1985-86; Percy Thomas Partnership, assistant architect, 1986; Cambridge University, supervisor and part-time lecturer in architectural history and theory, 1993-94; University of Tokyo, Japan Foundation fellow, 1995-96; Muroran Institute of Technology, associate professor of architecture, 1996-2000; University of Tasmania, visiting teaching fellow, 1997; University of Oregon, associate professor of architecture, 2000-07, professor of architecture, 2007-; University of Queensland, visiting fellow, 2009. Writer. **Publications:** Frank Lloyd Wright and Japan: The Role of Traditional Japanese Art and Architecture in the Work of Frank Lloyd Wright, 1993; Place, Time, and Being in Japanese Architecture, 2004; The Mirror and the Frame: John Yeon and the Landscape Art of China and Japan, 2010; Time in Architectural Space, forthcoming. **Address:** Department of Architecture, University of Oregon, Rm. 1206, Lawrence Hall, Eugene, OR 97403-1206, U.S.A. **Online address:** knute@uoregon.edu

NUTINI, Hugo G(ino). American/Chilean (born Chile), b. 1928. **Genres:** Anthropology/Ethnology, History. **Career:** Los Angeles State College, instructor in anthropology, 1962; Pan American Union, senior researcher, 1962-63; University of Puerto Rico, assistant professor, 1962-63; George Washington University, assistant professor of anthropology, 1963-70; University of Pittsburgh, associate professor, 1970-, distinguished university professor. Writer. **Publications:** San Bernardino Contla: Marriage and Family Structure in a Tlaxcalan Municipio, 1968; (with B.L. Isaac) Los Pueblos de Habla Náhuatl de la Región de Tlaxcala y Puebla, 1974; (with B. Bell) Ritual Kinship: The Structure and Historical Development of the Compadrazgo System in Rural Tlaxcala, 2 vols., 1984; Todos Santos in Rural Tlaxcala: A Syncretic, Expressive, and Symbolic Analysis of the Cult of the Dead, 1988; (with J.M. Roberts) Bloodsucking Witchcraft: An Epistemological Study of Anthropomorphic Supernaturalism in Rural Tlaxcala, 1993; Wages of Conquest: The Mexican Aristocracy in the Context of Western Aristocracies, 1995; Mexican Aristocracy: An Expressive Ethnography, 1910-2000, 2004; Social Stratification and Mobility in Central Veracruz, 2005; (with B.L. Isaac) Social Stratification in Central Mexico, 1500-2000, 2009. EDITOR: (with I.R. Buchler) Game Theory in the Behavioral Sciences, 1969; (with P. Carrasco and J.M. Taggart) Essays on Mexican Kinship, 1976. **Address:** Department of Anthropology, University of Pittsburgh, 3302 WWPH, 4200 5th Ave., Pittsburgh, PA 15260, U.S.A. **Online address:** hnutini@pitt.edu

NUTT, Paul C. American (born United States), b. 1939. **Genres:** Novels, Children's Fiction, Plays/Screenplays, Administration/Management, Business/Trade/Industry, Autobiography/Memoirs. **Career:** University of Michigan, Industrial Engineering Department, research assistant, teaching assistant, 1962-63; University of Wisconsin, Industrial Engineering Department, instructor, 1974; Ohio State University, Fisher College of Business, graduate program in hospital and health services administration, associate professor, 1978-83, Department of Management Sciences, professor, 1990-2006, emeritus professor of management sciences, 2006-, Decisions Sciences Institute, fellow. Writer. **Publications:** Evaluation Concepts and Methods: Shaping Policy for the Health Administrator, 1981; Planning Methods: For Health and Related Organizations, 1984; Making Tough Decisions: Tactics for Improving Managerial Decision Making, 1989; Managing Planned Change, 1992; (with R.W. Backoff) Strategic Management of Public and Third Sector Organizations: A Handbook for Leaders, 1992; Why Decisions Fail: Avoiding the Blunders and Traps That Lead to Decision Debacles, 2002; (ed. with D.C. Wilson) Handbook of Decision Making, 2010. Contributor to journals. **Address:** Fisher College of Business, Ohio State University, 2100 Neil Ave., Columbus, OH 43210, U.S.A. **Online address:** nutt.1@osu.edu

NUTZLE, Futzie. (Bruce John Kleinsmith). American (born United States), b. 1942. **Genres:** Cartoons, Autobiography/Memoirs. **Career:** Artist and cartoonist; Balloon Newspaper, staff, 1968-72; Rolling Stone Magazine Letters, staff, 1975-80; Japan Times, staff, 1985-2002. Writer. **Publications:** Futzie Nutzle, 1983; Futzie Nutzle's Modern Loafer (cartoons), 1981; Run the World: 50 Cents, 1991. **Address:** PO Box 325, San Juan Bautista, CA 95045-0325, U.S.A. **Online address:** fnutzle@aol.com

NUWER, Hank. American (born United States), b. 1946. **Genres:** Social Commentary, Writing/Journalism, Biography. **Career:** Freelance writer, 1969-; Chic Magazine, editorial staff, 1976-77; Clemson University, assistant professor, 1982-83; Ball State University, assistant professor, 1985-89; Rodale Press, senior writer, 1990-91; Arts Indiana Magazine, editor-in-chief, 1993-95; University of Richmond, associate professor of journalism, 1995-97; Indiana University, adjunct professor of journalism, 1995-2007; Anderson University, adjunct professor of journalism, 1998-2007; Franklin College, professor of journalism, 2002-. **Publications:** (With W. Boyles) The Deadliest Profession, 1980; (with W. Boyles) A Killing Trade, 1981; (with W. Boyles) The Wild Ride, 1981; (with W. Boyles) Blood Mountain, 1982; (with C. Shaw) Come Out, Come Out, Wherever You Are, 1982; (ed. with R.G. Waite) Rendezvous at the Ezra Pound Centennial Conference, 1986; Strategies of the Great Football Coaches, 1987; Rendezvousing with Contemporary Authors, 1988; Recruiting in Sports, 1989; Steroids, 1990; Broken Pledges: The Deadly Rite of Hazing, 1990; Sports Scandals, 1994; How to Write Like an Expert about Anything, 1995; The Legend of Jesse Owens, 1998; Wrongs of Passage: Fraternities, Sororities, Hazing, and Binge Drinking, 1999; High School Hazing: When Rites Become Wrongs, 2000; To the Young Writer: Nine Writers Talk about Their Craft, 2002; (ed.) The Hazing Reader, 2004; The Freelance Writer's Desktop Companion: Your Quick-reference Guide to a Career as an Author, 2009; One Long, Wild Conversation, 2010. Contributors to periodicals. **Address:** c/o Kevin Moore, Contemporary Issues Agency, 809 Turnberry Dr., Waunakee, WI 53597-2256, U.S.A. **Online address:** hnuwer@franklincollege.edu

NYAMNJOH, Francis B. South African (born South Africa), b. 1961?. **Genres:** Novels, Adult Non-fiction. **Career:** Council for the Development of Social Science Research, Africa, associate professor and head of publications and dissemination, 2003-09; African Council for Communication Education, vice-president, 1996-2003; University of Cape Town, Department of Social Anthropology, professor, 2009-. Writer. **Publications:** NONFICTION: Mind Searching (novel), 1991, 2nd ed., 2007; (ed.) The Cameroon G.C.E. Crisis: A Test of Anglophone Solidarity, 1996; Mass Media and Democratisation in Cameroon, 1996; (ed. with P.N. Nkwi) Regional Balance and National Integration in Cameroon: Lessons Learned and the Uncertain Future, 1997; (with N. Forcheh and M. Maphanyane) Survey on the Level and Perception of Freedom of Expression in Botswana: Report, 2002; (with P. Konings) Negotiating an Anglophone Identity: A Study of the Politics of Recognition and Representation in Cameroon, 2003; (ed. with H. Englund) Rights and Politics of Recognition in Africa, 2004; Africa's Media: Democracy and the Politics of Belonging, 2005; Insiders and Outsiders: Citizenship and Xenophobia in Contemporary Southern Africa, 2006; (ed. with A. Rwomire) Challenges and Responsibilities of Social Research in Africa: Ethical Issues, 2007; Mobile Phones: The New Talking Drums of Everyday Africa, 2009. NOVELS: A Nose for Money, 2006; The Disillusioned African, 1995, 2nd ed., 2007; Stories from Abakwa, 2007; Souls Forgotten, 2008; The Travail of Dieudonné, 2008; Married but Available, 2009; Intimate Strangers, 2010. OTHERS: The Convert: A Two-Act Play, 2003; Homeless Waters, 2011. CONTRIBUTOR: Le Role des Medias dans le Processus Democratique au Cameroun, 1993; The Past Tense of Shit (Book One), 1993; Media and Sustainable Development, 1995; (ed. with P.N. Nkwi) Regional Balance and National Integration in Cameroon: Lessons Learned and the Uncertain Future, 1997; Tam Tam to Internet, 1998; Walking on the Other Side of the Information Highway: Communication, Culture and Development in the 21st Century, 2000; Magical Interpretations, Material Realities: Modernity, Witchcraft an the Occult in Postcolonial Africa, 2001; Africa at the Crossroads: Between Regionalism and Globalization, 2004; The Cultures and Globalization, 2007; Indigenous Experience Today, 2007; Strength beyond Structure: Social and Historical Trajectories of Agency in Africa, 2007. Contributor to periodicals. **Address:** Department of Social Anthropology, University of Cape Town, 5.23 Arts Bldg., PO Box X3, Cape Town, 7701, South Africa. **Online address:** nyamnjoh@yahoo.com

NYE, David E. American (born United States), b. 1946. **Genres:** Adult Nonfiction, History, Technology. **Career:** Union College, assistant professor of American studies, 1974-78, director of American studies, 1978-81; Odense University, American Studies, associate professor, 1982-87; Copenhagen University, associate professor of American studies, 1987-91; University of Southern Denmark, professor of history and American studies, 1992-; Syddansk University, Center for American Studies, founder and chair, 1992-96, 1998, 2003-04, 2006-; Notre Dame University, Welch visiting professor in American studies, 2003; Warwick University, professor of history and American studies, 2005-06. Writer. **Publications:** Henry Ford, Ignorant Idealist, 1979; The Invented Self: An Anti-biography, from Documents of Thomas A. Edison, 1983; Image Worlds: Corporate Identities at General Electric, 1890-1930, 1985; (ed. with C.K. Thomsen) American Studies in Transition: Essays, 1985; Electrifying America: Social Meanings of a New Technology, 1880-1940, 1990; (ed. with C. Pedersen) Consumption and American Culture, 1991; American Technological Sublime, 1994; (ed. with M. Gidley) American Photographs in Europe, 1994; Narratives and Spaces: Technology and the Construction of American Culture, 1997; Consuming Power: A Social History of American Energies, 1998; (ed.) Technologies of Landscape: From Reaping to Recycling, 1999; America as Second Creation: Technology and Narratives of New Beginnings, 2003; Technology Matters: Questions to Live With, 2006; Introducing Denmark and the Danes: A Two Hour Briefing, 2006; When the Lights Went Out: A History of Blackouts in America, 2010. **Address:** Department of American Studies, University of Southern Denmark, Campusvej 55, Odense, 5230, Denmark. **Online address:** nye@hist.sdu.dk

NYE, Joseph S(amuel). American (born United States), b. 1937. **Genres:** Institutions/Organizations, International Relations/Current Affairs, Politics/Government. **Career:** Harvard University, instructor, 1964-66, assistant professor, 1966-69, associate professor 1969-71, professor of international security, 1971-, Center for International Affairs, director, 1971-, Clarence Dillon professor of international affairs, 1984-87, John F. Kennedy School of Government, dean, 1995-, now dean emeritus, Sultan of Oman professor of international relations, university distinguished service professor; Universitaire des Hautes Etudes Internationales, visiting professor, 1968; Carleton University, School of International Affairs, visiting professor, 1973; Royal Institute of International Affairs, visiting fellow, 1974; Marquette University, Allis Chalmers distinguished professor, 1985; Aspen Institute, senior fellow, Aspen Strategy Group, director. Writer. **Publications:** Pan-Africanism and East African Integration, 1965; Central American Regional Integration, 1967; International Regionalism, 1968; Peace in Parts: Integration and Conflict in Regional Organization, 1971; (with E.B. Haas and R.L. Butterworth) Conflict Management by International Organizations, 1972; (with R.O. Keohane) Transnational Relations and World Politics, 1972; (with R.O. Keohane) Power and Interdependence, 1977, 4th ed., 2012; Living with Nuclear Weapons, 1983; Nuclear Ethics, 1986; Fateful Visions, 1988; American Strategy after the Cold War, 1990; Bound to Lead: The Changing Nature of American Power, 1990; Understanding International Conflicts, 1993, 7th ed., 2009; Estimating the Future?, 1994; The Paradox of American Power: Why the World's Only Superpower Can't Go It Alone, 2002; (with Y. Satoh and P. Wilkinson) Addressing the New International Terrorism, 2003; Soft Power: The Means to Success in World Politics, 2004; Power Game: A Washington Novel, 2004; (with B. Scowcroft) The Challenge of Proliferation, 2005; Power in the Global Information Age, 2005; (with R.L. Armitage) CSIS Commission on Smart Power, 2007; Powers to Lead, 2008; (with D. Welch) Understanding Global Conflict and Cooperation: An Introduction to Theory and History, 2011; The Future of Power, 2011. EDITOR: (with D. Deese) Energy and Security, 1980; The Making of America's Soviet Policy, 1984; (with S.P. Huntington) Global Dilemmas, 1985; (co-ed.) Hawks, Doves, and Owls, 1985; (with R.K. Smith) After the Storm: Lessons from the Gulf War, 1992; (ed. with R.K. Smith) After the Storm: Lessons from the Gulf War, 1992; (with R.O. Keohane and S. Hoffmann) After the Cold War, 1993; (with P.D. Zelikow and D.C. King) Why People don't Trust Government, 1997; (with J.D. Donahue) Governance in a Globalizing World, 2000; (with J.D. Donahue) Market-Based Governance, 2002; (with E.C. Kamarck) Governance.com, 2003; (with J.D. Donahue) For the People, 2003. Contributor to periodicals. **Address:** Harvard University, John F. Kennedy School of Government, 162 Taubman, 79 John F. Kennedy St., PO Box 124, Cambridge, MA 02138-5801, U.S.A. **Online address:** joseph_nye@harvard.edu

NYE, Mary Jo. American (born United States), b. 1944?. **Genres:** Physics, Sciences. **Career:** University of Oklahoma, assistant professor, 1970-, professor, through 1994; Oregon State University, Horning professor of humanities and professor of history, 1994-, now professor emeritus of history; University of Pittsburgh, postdoctoral fellow; Institute for Advanced Study, fellow; Harvard University, visiting professor; University of Cambridge, Churchill College, fellow. Writer. **Publications:** Molecular Reality: A Perspective on the Scientific Work of Jean Perrin, 1972; (ed. and intro.) The Question of the Atom: From the Karlsruhe Congress to the First Solvay Conference, 1860-1911: A Compilation of Primary Sources, 1984; Science in the Provinces: Scientific Communities and Provincial Leadership in France, 1860-1930, 1986; (ed. with J.L. Richards and R.H. Stuewer) The Invention of Physical Science: Intersections of Mathematics, Theology, and Natural Philosophy since the Seventeenth Century: Essays in Honor of Erwin N. Hiebert, 1992; From Chemical Philosophy to Theoretical Chemistry: Dynamics of Matter and Dynamics of Disciplines, 1800-1950, 1993; Before Big Science: The Pursuit of Modern Chemistry and Physics, 1800-1940, 1996; (ed. with D.C. Lindberg and R.L. Numbers) The Cambridge History of Science, vol. V: Modern Physical and Mathematical Sciences, 2002; Blackett: Physics, War, and Politics in the Twentieth Century, 2004. **Address:** Department of History, Oregon State University, 306 Milam Hall, Corvallis, OR 97331-5104, U.S.A. **Online address:** nyem@onid.orst.edu

NYE, Naomi Shihab. American (born United States), b. 1952. **Genres:** Children's Fiction, Poetry, Young Adult Fiction. **Career:** Freelance visiting writer, 1974-; Texas Commission on the Arts' Writers in the Schools Project, affiliate, 1974-86; University of California, Holloway lecturer; University of Hawaii, visiting writer, 1991; University of Alaska, staff, 1994; Michener Center for Writers at Austin, visiting writer, 1995, 2001; University of Texas, Austin, staff, 1995, 2001; U.S. Information Agency Arts America Program, traveling writer and workshop leader; Texas Observer, poetry editor. **Publications:** POETRY: Tattooed Feet, 1977; Eye-to-Eye, 1978; Different Ways to Pray, 1980; On the Edge of the Sky, 1981; Hugging the Jukebox, 1982;

Yellow Glove, 1986; Invisible, 1987; (trans. with M. Jayyusi) Muhammad Al-Maghut, Fan of Swords: Poems, 1991; Mint, 1991; Travel Alarm, 1993; Red Suitcase, 1994; Words under the Words: Selected Poems, 1995; Fuel: Poems, 1998; Mint Snowball, 2001; 19 Varieties of Gazelle: Poems of the Middle East, 2002; The Flag of Childhood: Poems from the Middle East, 2002; You & Yours: Poems, 2005; Honeybee: Poems, 2008. EDITOR: This Same Sky: A Collection of Poems from around the World, 1992; That Tree Is Older Than You Are: Poems & Paintings from Mexico, 1995; (with P.B. Janeczko) I Feel a Little Jumpy around You, 1996; The Space between Our Footsteps: Poems and Paintings from the Middle East, 1998; What Have You Lost?, 1999; Salting the Ocean: 100 Poems by Young Poets, 2000; Is this Forever, or What?: Poems & Paintings from Texas, 2004; Between Heaven and Texas, 2006; Time You Let Me In: 25 Poets Under 25, 2010; Transfer: Poems, 2011. FICTION FOR CHILDREN: Sitti's Secrets, 1994; Benito's Dream Bottle, 1995; Habibi, 1997; Lullaby Raft, 1996; Come with Me, 2000; Baby Radar, 2003. OTHERS: (with R.S. Gwynn, J.E. Seale and W.V. Davis) Texas Poets in Concert, 1990; (trans.) Tuqan, Fadwa, Mountainous Journey: An Autobiography, 1990; Never in a Hurry: Essays on People and Places, 1996; Maze Me: Poems for Girls, 2005; Going Going, 2005; I'll Ask You Three Times, Are You Ok?: Tales of Driving and Being Driven, 2007; There is no Long Distance Now: Very Short Stories, 2011. Contributor to books and periodicals. Works appear in anthologies. **Address:** Steven Barclay Agency, 12 Western Ave., Petaluma, CA 94952, U.S.A. **Online address:** sjbarclay@aol.com

NYE, Robert. Irish/British (born England), b. 1939. **Genres:** Novels, Novellas/Short Stories, Children's Fiction, Young Adult Fiction, Plays/Screenplays, Poetry, Translations, Autobiography/Memoirs, Autobiography/Memoirs, Literary Criticism And History, History. **Career:** Freelance writer, 1961-; Scotsman, poetry editor, 1967-; The Times, poetry critic, 1971-96; University of Edinburgh, writer-in-residence, 1976-77. **Publications:** Juvenilia 1, 1961; Juvenilia 2, 1963; Taliesin, 1966; March Has Horse's Ears, 1966; Doubtfire: A Novel, 1967; Bee Hunter: Adventures of Beowulf, 1968; Tales I Told My Mother, 1969; (with W. Watson) Sawney Bean, 1969; Sisters, 1969; Darker Ends, 1969; Wishing Gold, 1970; Lines Review 38, 1971; Poor Pumpkin, 1971; Reynolds, Reynolds, 1971; The Mathematical Princess and Other Stories, 1972; Agnus Dei, 1973; (trans.) Aucassin and Nicolette, 1973; Two Prayers, 1974; Five Dreams, 1974; The Seven Deadly Sins: A Mask, 1974; Mr. Poe: A Public Lecture with Private Illustrations, 1974; Penthesilia, 1975; Cricket: Three Stories, 1975; Divisions on a Ground, 1976; Falstaff, 1976; Out of this World and Back Again (juvenile), 1977; Once upon Three Times (juvenile), 1978; Merlin, 1978; The Bird of the Golden Land (juvenile), 1980; The Devil's Jig, 1980; Faust, 1980; Harry Pay the Pirate (juvenile), 1981; The Facts of Life and Other Fictions, 1983; Three Tales (for children), 1983; A Collection of Poems 1955-1988, 1989; Fourteen Poems, 1993; Mrs. Shakespeare: The Complete Works, 1993; Henry James and Other Poems, 1995; Collected Poems 1995, 1995; Lord Fox and Other Spine-Chilling Tales, 1997; Rain and The Glass: 99 Poems, New and Selected, 2004. NOVELS: Beowulf: A New Telling, 1968; The Voyage of the Destiny, 1982; The Memoirs of Lord Byron, 1989; The Life and Death of My Lord Gilles de Rais, 1990; The Good Thief, 1997; The Late Mr. Shakespeare, 1998. EDITOR: A Choice of Sir Walter Ralegh's Verse, 1972; A Choice of Swinburne's Verse, 1973; William Barnes: A Selection of His Poems, 1973; The Faber Book of Sonnets, 1976; The English Sermon 1750-1850, 1976; P.E.N. New Poetry 1, 1986; (and intro. with E. Friedmann and A.J. Clark) First Awakenings: The Early Poems of Laura Riding, 1992; (and intro.) A Selection of the Poems of Laura Riding, 1996. **Address:** Penguin Group Inc., 375 Hudson St., New York, NY 10014-3658, U.S.A.

NYE, Simon (Beresford). British (born England), b. 1958. **Genres:** Novels, Plays/Screenplays, Literary Criticism And History. **Career:** Worked in the theater, 1980-85; freelance translator, 1985-88; Credit Suisse, staff translator, 1988-91; full-time writer, 1991-; NBC sitcom Men Behaving Badly, executive consultant, 1996-97. **Publications:** NOVELS: Men Behaving Badly, 1989; Wide Boy, 1990; Best of Men Behaving Badly, 2000. TRANSLATOR: The Vienna Opera, 1987; Matisse's Graphic Work, 1988; Braque, 1988; Don Juan, 2001; Accidental Death of an Anarchist, 2003. **Address:** c/o Rod Hall Agency, Fairgate House, 78 New Oxford St., 6th Fl., London, GL WC1A 1HB, England. **Online address:** simonnye@compuserve.com

NYHART, Nina. American (born United States), b. 1934. **Genres:** Poetry, Young Adult Fiction. **Career:** Massachusetts Arts and Humanities Foundation, poet-teacher for elementary and middle school workshops, 1971-74; Brookline School System, visiting poet, 1973-76; Pine Manor Open College, instructor in poetry, 1976-77; Newton Arts Center, instructor in poetry, 1977-78; Cambridge Center for Adult Education, instructor in poetry, 1983-87; Belmont High School, visiting poet, 1983; Radcliffe College, instructor in poetry, 1988. Writer. **Publications:** (With K. Gensler) The Poetry Connection: An Anthology of Contemporary Poems with Ideas to Stimulate Children's Writing, 1978; (with M. Lockwood) Openers and Temper (poems), 1979; French for Soldiers (poems), 1987. Contributor to magazines. **Address:** 185 Warren St., Brookline, MA 02445, U.S.A.

NYIRI, Pal. Australian (born Australia) **Genres:** Anthropology/Ethnology. **Career:** Macquarie University, senior lecturer, director of the program in applied anthropology, 2004-09; Free University, faculty, 2009-; University of Amsterdam, faculty. Writer. **Publications:** New Chinese Migrants in Europe: The Case of the Chinese Community in Hungary, 1999; (ed. with J. Toth and M. Fullerton) Diasporas and Politics, 2001; (ed. with I. Saveliev) Globalizing Chinese Migration: Trends in Europe and Asia, 2002; (with F.N. Pieke, M. Thuno and A. Ceccagno) Transnational Chinese: Fujianese Migrants in Europe, 2004; (ed. with J. Breidenbach) China Inside Out: Contemporary Chinese Nationalism and Transnationalism, 2005; (co-author) Nem kivAnt gyerekek? KulfOldi gyerekek magyar iskolkban, 2006; Scenic Spots: Chinese Tourism, the State and Cultural Authority, 2006; Chinese in Eastern Europe and Russia: A Middleman Minority in a Transnational Era, 2007; (with J. Breidenbach) Seeing Culture Everywhere: From Genocide to Consumer Habits, 2009; Mobility and Cultural Authority in Contemporary China, 2010. Contributor to books and periodicals. **Address:** Department of Anthropology, Macquarie University, Sydney, NW 2109, Australia. **Online address:** pnyiri@scmp.mq.edu.au

NYLANDER, Jane C. American (born United States), b. 1938. **Genres:** Local History/Rural Topics, Antiques/Furnishings, Humanities. **Career:** Historical Society of York County, curator, 1961-62; New Hampshire Historical Society, curator, 1962-69; New England College, instructor, 1963-64; Monadnock Community College, instructor, 1964-68; Old Sturbridge Village, curator of ceramics and textiles, 1969-84, senior curator, 1985-86; Boston University, adjunct associate professor, 1978-85, adjunct professor, 1993-; Worcester Historical Museum, trustee, 1978-84; Historic Deerfield Inc., trustee, 1981-; Jones Museum, trustee, 1986-88; Strawbery Banke Inc., director, 1986-92; University of New Hampshire, adjunct assistant professor, 1987-92; Portsmouth Athenaeum, trustee, 1987-90; Society for the Preservation of New England Antiquities, director, 1992-93, president, 1993-2002; consultant to museums. Writer. **Publications:** Fabrics for Historic Buildings: A Guide to Selecting Reproduction Fabrics, 1977, 5th ed., 1995; Our Own Snug Fireside: Images of the New England Home, 1760-1860, 1993; (with D. Viera) Windows on the Past: Four Centuries of New England Homes, 2000; (with R.C. Nylander) Fabrics and Wallpapers for Historic Buildings, 2005. Contributor to journals and periodicals. **Address:** 17 Franklin St., Portsmouth, NH 03801, U.S.A.

NYLUND, Eric. *See* **NYLUND, Eric S.**

NYLUND, Eric S. (Eric Nylund). American (born United States), b. 1964. **Genres:** Novels, Novellas/Short Stories, Technology, Mystery/Crime/Suspense, Science Fiction/Fantasy. **Career:** Microsoft Corp., Encarta Encyclopedia, Game Studios, editor and writer. **Publications:** Pawn's Dream, 1995; A Game of Universe, 1997; Dry Water, 1997; Signal to Noise, 1998; A Signal Shattered, 1999; Halo: The Fall of Reach, 2001; Crimson Skies, 2002; Halo: First Strike, 2003; Halo: Ghosts of Onyx, 2006; Halo: Evolutions, 2009; Mortal Coils, 2009; Battlestar Galactica: The Cylon Wars, 2009; Halo Wars: Genesis, 2009; All That Lives Must Die, 2010; The Resisters, 2011. **Address:** c/o Lynn Seligman, 400 Highland Ave., Upper Montclair, NJ 07043, U.S.A. **Online address:** nylund@accessone.com

O

O, **Hugo.** *See* **HAMILTON, Hugo.**

OAKDALE, Suzanne. American (born United States) **Genres:** Autobiography/Memoirs. **Career:** Indiana University, Department of Anthropology, visiting lecturer, 1995-96; Williams College, Department of Anthropology and Sociology, visiting assistant professor, 1997-98; University of New Mexico, Department of Anthropology, associate professor of anthropology, 1998- . Writer. **Publications:** I Foresee My Life: The Ritual Performance of Autobiography in an Amazonian Community, 2005. Contributor to books and journals. **Address:** Department of Anthropology, University of New Mexico, MSC01-1040, Anthropology 1, Albuquerque, NM 87131, U.S.A. **Online address:** soakdale@unm.edu

OAKES, Andy. British (born England), b. 1952?. **Genres:** Novels, Mystery/Crime/Suspense, Young Adult Fiction. **Career:** Writer and photographer. **Publications:** Dragon's Eye: A Novel, 2004; Citizen One, 2006. **Address:** c/o Author Mail, Overlook Press, 141 Wooster St., New York, NY 10012, U.S.A.

OAKES, James. American (born United States), b. 1953. **Genres:** History. **Career:** University of California, instructor in history, 1980-81; Purdue University, assistant professor of history, 1981-82; Princeton University, assistant professor of history, 1982-86, professor of history, 1986-97; Northwestern University, professor of history, 1986-97; City University of New York, Graduate Center, professor of history, 1997-, distinguished professor of history, 2008-. Writer. **Publications:** The Ruling Race: A History of American Slaveholders, 1982; Slavery and Freedom: An Interpretation of the Old South, 1990; The Radical and the Republican: Frederick Douglass, Abraham Lincoln, and the Triumph of Antislavery Politics, 2007; Of the People: A History of the United States, 2010. **Address:** Graduate Center, City University of New York, Rm. 5114.07, 365 5th Ave., New York, NY 10016, U.S.A. **Online address:** joakes@gc.cuny.edu

OAKES, Kaya. American (born United States), b. 1971. **Genres:** Cultural/Ethnic Topics. **Career:** University of California, writing teacher, 1999-; Kitchen Sink magazine, co-founder, editor and writer, 2002-07. **Publications:** Slanted and Enchanted: The Evolution of Indie Culture, 2009. Contributor to periodicals. **Address:** Northern, CA , U.S.A. **Online address:** kaya@oakestown.org

OAKES, Meredith. British/Australian (born Australia), b. 1946. **Genres:** Translations, Plays/Screenplays. **Career:** Sydney Daily Telegraph, music critic, 1968-70; Gate Theatre, writer-in-residence, 1994; Royal Court Theatre, writer-in-residence, 1995; Casarotto Ramsay & Associates Ltd., playwright. **Publications:** PLAYS: The Neighbor, 1993; The Editing Process, 1994; Mind the Gap, 1995; Faith, 1997; (trans.) M. Rinke, Man Who Never Saw Yet Saw Woman's Nakedness, 2001; Man for Hire, 2002; Shadowmouth, 2006; Scenes from the Back of Beyond, 2006; (trans. with A. Tierney) T. Bernhard, Heldenplatz, 2010; Collected Plays, 2010. Contributor to periodicals. **Address:** Casarotto Ramsay & Associates Ltd., Waverley House, 7-12 Noel St., London, GL W1F 8GQ, England.

OAKLEY, Ann. (Rosamund Clay). British (born England), b. 1944. **Genres:** Anthropology/Ethnology, Sociology, Women's Studies And Issues, Novels, Autobiography/Memoirs, Medicine/Health. **Career:** University of Leeds, Institute of Education, Schools Council Project on Teaching English to Immigrant Children, research assistant, 1965-66; Usher Institute, Department of Social Medicine, Survey of Careers of Medical Graduates, research assistant, 1966-67; Institute of Community Studies, Parents' Attitudes to School Survey, research assistant, 1967-68; University of London, Bedford College, Department of Sociology, research officer, 1974-79, Institute of Education, Thomas Coram Research Unit, deputy director, 1985-90, Social Science Research Unit, director, 1990-2005, founding director, 2005-, professor of sociology and social policy, 1991-; University of Oxford, National Perinatal Epidemiology Unit, consultant, 1979-80, Wellcome Research Fellow, 1980-83, senior research officer, 1983-84, Somerville College, honorary fellow, 2001-; University of Warwick, Department of Sociology, visiting fellow, 1983-87; University of Lund, visiting professor, 1986; University of Auckland, visiting professor, 1989; University of Tulane, visiting professor, 1990; University College, Institute of Child Health, Division of Public Health Medicine, honorary professor in social sciences, 1996-; University of Uppsala, Swedish Collegium for Advanced Study in the Social Sciences, Torgny Segerstedt distinguished visiting professor of higher education and learning, 1997. Writer. **Publications:** NOVELS: The Men's Room, 1988; (as Rosamund Clay) Only Angels Forget, 1990; Matilda's Mistake, 1990; The Secret Lives of Eleanor Jenkinson, 1993; Scenes Originating in the Garden of Eden, 1993; A Proper Holiday, 1996. OTHERS: Sex, Gender and Society, 1972; Housewife, 1974; The Sociology of Housework, 1974; Woman's Work: The Housewife, Past and Present, 1975; Becoming a Mother, 1979; Women Confined: Towards a Sociology of Childbirth, 1980; Subject Women, 1981; (with A. McPherson and H. Roberts) Miscarriage, 1984, rev. ed., 1990; Taking It Like a Woman, 1984; The Captured Womb: A History of the Medical Care of Pregnant Women, 1984; Telling the Truth about Jerusalem: Selected Essays, 1986; (with S. Houd) Helpers in Childbirth: Midwifery Today, 1990; Social Support and Motherhood: The Natural History of a Research Project, 1992; Essays on Women, Medicine and Health, 1993; (with J. Brannen, K. Dodd and P. Storey) Young People, Health and Family Life, 1994; Man and Wife: Richard and Kay Titmuss: My Parents' Early Years, 1996; Experiments in Knowing: Gender and Method in the Social Sciences, 2000; (and ed.) Ann Oakley Reader: Gender, Women, and Social Science, 2005; Fracture: Adventures of a Broken Body, 2007; A Critical Woman: Barbara Wootton, Social Science and Public Policy in the Twentieth Century, 2011. EDITOR: (and intro. with J. Mitchell) The Rights and Wrongs of Women, 1976; (with J. Mitchell) What Is Feminism?, 1986; (with S. Williams) The Politics of the Welfare State: Seeing through the Backlash, 1994; (with M. Mitchell) Who's Afraid of Feminism?, 1997; (with J. Ashton) The Gift Relationship, 1997; (with J. Popay and F. Williams) Welfare Research: A Critique Review, 1999; (with P. Alcock, H. Glennerster and A. Sinfield) Welfare and Wellbeing: Richard Titmuss's Contribution to Social Policy, 2001; Gender on Planet Earth, 2002; (with J. Barker) Private Complaints and Public Health: Richard Titmuss on the National Health Service, 2004. **Address:** Social Science Research Unit, Institute of Education, University of London, Rm. 102, 18 Woburn Sq., London, GL WC1H ONR, England. **Online address:** a.oakley@ioe.ac.uk

OAKLEY, Barbara A. American (born United States), b. 1955. **Genres:** Sciences, Psychology. **Career:** South Pole Station, radio operator; Oakland University, School of Engineering and Computer Science, associate professor of engineering; Ford Motor Co., staff; Institute of Electrical and Electronics Engineers, Engineering in Medicine and Biology Society, vice president. Writer. **Publications:** Hair of the Dog: Tales from aboard a Russian Trawler, 1996; Evil Genes: Why Rome Fell, Hitler Rose, Enron Failed and My Sister Stole My Mother's Boyfriend, 2007; (with G. Madhavan and L. Kun) Career Development in Bioengineering and Biotechnology, 2008; (co-author) Pathological Altruism, 2011; Cold-blooded Kindness: Neuroquirks of a Codependent Killer, or Just Give Me a Shot at Loving You, Dear, and Other Reflections on Helping that Hurts, 2011. **Address:** Department of Industrial and Systems Engineering, Oakland University, 648 Science and Engineering Bldg., Rochester, MI 48309-4478, U.S.A. **Online address:** oakley@oakland.edu

OAKLEY, Graham. British (born England), b. 1929. **Genres:** Children's Fiction, Young Adult Fiction, Children's Non-fiction, Young Adult Non-fiction, Animals/Pets. **Career:** Scenic artist in theatres, 1950-55; Royal Opera House, design assistant, 1955-57; Crawford's Advertising Agency, staff, 1960-62; BBC TV, designer, 1962-67, staff, 1967-77. Freelance writer, 1977- . **Publications:** SELF-ILLUSTRATED CHILDREN'S BOOKS: Graham Oakley's Magical Changes, 1979; Hetty and Harriet, 1981; Henry's Quest, 1986; Once upon a Time: A Prince's Fantastic Journey, 1990; The Foxbury Force, 1994; The Foxbury Force and the Pirates, 1995; Foxbury Force and the Ghost, 1997. THE CHURCH MICE SERIES: The Church Mouse, 1972; The Church Cat Abroad, 1973; The Church Mice and the Moon, 1974; The Church Mice Spread Their Wings, 1975; The Church Mice Adrift, 1976; The Church Mice at Bay, 1978; The Church Mice at Christmas, 1980; The Church Mice in Action, 1982; The Diary of a Church Mouse, 1986; More Church Mice Chronicles, 1990; The Church Mice and the Ring, 1992; Humphrey Hits the Jackpot, 1998; The Church Mice Take a Break, 2000. Illustrator of books by others. Contributor to periodicals. **Address:** Macmillan Publishers Ltd., 25 Eccleston Pl., London, GL SW1W 9NF, England. **Online address:** graham@grahamoakley.co.uk

OAKLEY, John H. American (born United States), b. 1949. **Genres:** Classics, History, Art/Art History. **Career:** College of William and Mary, assistant professor, 1980-86, associate professor, 1986-93, chair, 1989-92, 2001-05, professor of classical studies and chancellor professor, 1993-2000, Forrest D. Murden Jr. professor, 2000-; American School of Classical Studies at Athens, Gertrude Smith professor, 1986, senior research fellow, 1986-87, 1993-94, Elizabeth G. Whitehead visiting professor, 1997-98, Andrew W. Mellon professor, 2005-08; University of Canterbury, Department of Classics, visiting professor, 1997; Princeton University, Department of Classics, visiting fellow, 2000-01; Albert-Ludwigs-Freiburg University, visiting professor, 2003. Writer. **Publications:** The Phiale Painter, 1990; (with S.I. Rotroff) Debris from a Public Dining Place in the Athenian Agora, 1992; Corpus Vasorum Antiquorum, 1992; (with R.H. Sinos) The Wedding in Ancient Athens, 1993; (ed. with W.D.E. Coulson and O. Palagia and contrib.) Athenian Potters and Painters: The Conference Proceedings, 1996, (ed. with O. Palagia and contrib.) vol. II, 2009; The Achilles Painter, 1997; (with J. Niels) Coming of Age in Ancient Greece: Images of Childhood from the Classical Past, 2003; Picturing Death in Classical Athens: The Evidence of the White Lekythoi, 2004. Contributor to journals. **Address:** Department of Classical Studies, College of William and Mary, 333 Morton Hall, Williamsburg, VA 23187-8795, U.S.A. **Online address:** jxoakl@wm.edu

OAKS, Dallin H. American (born United States), b. 1932. **Genres:** Law. **Career:** University of Chicago Law Review, editor-in-chief, 1956-57; Church of Jesus Christ of Latter-Day Saints, church official; U.S. Supreme Court Chief Justice Earl Warren, law clerk, 1957-58; Kirkland, Ellis, Hodson, Chaffetz & Masters, attorney, 1958-61; University of Chicago Law School, associate professor, 1961-64, professor of law, 1964-71; Brigham Young University, president, 1971-80. **Publications:** Effects of Griffin Illinois on the States Administration of the Criminal Law, 1957; (ed.) The Wall Between Church and State, 1963; (with W. Lehman) A Criminal Justice System and the Indigent: A Study of Chicago and Cook County, 1968; The Criminal Justice Act in the Federal District Courts, 1969; (with M. Hill) Carthage Conspiracy: The Trial of the Accused Assassins of Joseph Smith, 1975; (with G. Bogert) Cases on the Law of Trusts, 5th ed., 1978; Religious freedom and the Supreme Court, 1981; Trust Doctrines in Church Controversies, 1984; Pure in Heart, 1988; The Lord's Way, 1991; His Holy Name, 1998; With Full Purpose of Heart, 2002. **Address:** The Church of Jesus Christ of Latter-day Saints, 50 NE Temple St., Salt Lake City, UT 84150, U.S.A. **Online address:** dhos@law.uchicago.edu

OAKSEY. Also writes as John Oaksey. British (born England), b. 1929. **Genres:** Sports/Fitness, History, Autobiography/Memoirs, Animals/Pets. **Career:** Daily Telegraph, racing correspondent, 1956-. Writer. **Publications:** AS JOHN OAKSEY: (with G. Cranham and R. Pitman) The Guinness Guide to Steeple Chasing, 1979; (with J. Kidd) The Race of the Championship: American Amateur Wins British Title, 1979; Oaksey on Racing: Thirty Years of Writing and Riding: Selections from Horse and Hound, 1991; Pride of the Shires: The Story of the Whitbread Horses, 1979. OTHERS: (co-author) History of Steeplechasing, 1966; The Story of Mill Reef, 1974; Mince Pie for Starters, 2003. **Address:** Hill Farm, Oaksey, Malmesbury, WT SN16 9HS, England. **Online address:** coaksey@freenetname.co.uk

OAKSEY, John. *See* **OAKSEY.**

OATES, Joyce Carol. Also writes as Lauren Kelly, Rosamond Smith. American (born United States), b. 1938. **Genres:** Novels, Plays/Screenplays, Poetry, Literary Criticism And History, Sports/Fitness, Essays, Novellas/Short Stories, Romance/Historical, Young Adult Non-fiction. **Career:** University of Detroit, instructor, 1961-65, assistant professor, 1965-67; University of Windsor, Department of English, faculty, 1967-78; Princeton University, writer-in-residence, 1978-81, Lewis Center for the Arts, professor of creative writing, 1987-, Roger S. Berlind distinguished professor in the humanities, Roger S. Berlind '52 professor of the humanities. **Publications:** By the North Gate (stories), 1963; With Shuddering Fall, 1964; Upon the Sweeping Flood and Other Stories, 1966; A Garden of Earthly Delights, 1967; Women in Love and Other Poems, 1968; Expensive People, 1968; Anonymous Sins and Other Poems, 1969; Them, 1969; The Wheel of Love (stories), 1970; Love and Its Derangements (poetry), 1970; Cupid and Psyche, 1970; Wonderland, 1971; The Edge of Impossibility: Tragic Forms in Literature, 1972; Marriage and Infidelities (stories), 1972; Do with Me What You Will, 1973; The Hostile Sun: The Poetry of D.H. Lawrence, 1973; Angel Fire: Poems, 1973; Dreaming America, 1973; New Heaven, New Earth: Visionary Experience in Literature, 1974; Miracle Play, 1974; The Hungry Ghosts: Seven Allusive Comedies, 1974; The Goddess and Other Women (stories), 1974; Where Are You Going, Where Have You Been: Stories of Young America, 1974, 1994; The Poisoned Kiss and Other Stories from the Portuguese, 1975; The Seduction and Other Stories, 1975; The Assassins: A Book of Hours, 1975; The Fabulous Beasts (poetry), 1975; Childworld, 1976; Crossing the Border (stories), 1976; The Triumph of the Spider Monkey, 1976; Night-Side (stories), 1977; Season of Peril, 1977; Son of the Morning, 1978; Women Whose Lives Are Food, Men Whose Lives Are Money (poetry), 1978; Unholy Loves, 1979; Cybele, 1979; (ed. with S. Ravenel) The Best American Short Stories 1979, 1979; The Step-Father, 1979; Bellefleur, 1980; Three Plays, 1980; Angel of Light, 1981; Sentimental Education, 1981; Celestial Timepiece, 1981; Contraries: Essays, 1981; A Bloodsmoor Romance, 1982; Invisible Woman: New and Selected Poems, 1970-1972, 1982; The Profane Ant: Essays and Reviews, 1983; The Luxury of Sin, 1983; Mysteries of Winterthurn, 1984; Last Days, 1984; Solstice, 1985; Marya: A Life, 1986; Raven's Wing (stories), 1986; On Boxing (non-fiction), 1987; (with E.T. Bender) Artist in Residence, 1987; You Must Remember This, 1987; Writer: Occasions and Opportunities, 1988; The Assignation (stories), 1988; Conversations with Joyce Carol Oates, 1989; American Appetites, 1989; The Time Traveler: Poems 1983-1989, 1989; Because It Is Bitter, and Because It Is My Heart, 1990; I Lock My Door upon Myself, 1990; I Stand before You Naked, 1991; In Darkest America (plays), 1991; The Rise of Life on Earth, 1991; Heat and Other Stories, 1992; Black Water, 1992; Where Is Here? (stories), 1992; Foxfire: Confessions of a Girl Gang, 1993; Haunted: Tales of the Grotesque, 1994; What I Lived For, 1994; The Perfectionist and Other Plays, 1995; Will You Always Love Me? and Other Stories, 1995; Zombie, 1995; George Bellows: American Artist, 1995; We Were the Mulvaneys, 1996; First Love, 1996; Tenderness, 1996; Man Crazy, 1997; My Heart Laid Bare, 1998; Come Meet Muffin!, 1998; Collector of Hearts, 1998; New Plays, 1998; Broke Heart Blues, 1999; Where I've Been and Where I'm Going: Essays, 1999; Blonde, 2000; Middle Age: A Romance, 2001; I'll Take You There, 2002; Beasts, 2002; The Tattooed Girl, 2003; Where is Little Reynard?, 2003; I Am No One You Know (stories), 2004; The Falls, 2004; Female of the Species: Stories of Mystery and Suspense, 2005; Missing Mom, 2005; Sexy, 2005; Uncensored: Views and (Re) Views, 2005; Flew Away, 2006; Black Girl, White Girl, 2006; High Lonesome: Stories 1966-2006, 2006; The Museum of Dr. Moses: Tales of Mystery And Suspense, 2007; The Gravedigger's Daughter, 2007; Naughty Cherie!, 2008; Wild Nights!, 2008; A Fair Maiden, 2009; Dear Husband, 2009; Little Bird of Heaven, 2009; In Rough Country, 2010; Sourland, 2010; (co-author) Between the Dark and the Daylight, 2010; Give Me Your Heart: Tales of Mystery and Suspense, 2011; (co-author) What You Wish For: A Book for

Darfur, 2011; The Corn Maiden, 2011; A Widow's Story, 2011; Mudwoman, 2012; Black Dahlia & White Rose, 2012; Carthage, 2012. AS ROSAMOND SMITH: Lives of the Twins, 1987; Soul/Mate, 1989; Nemesis, 1990; Snake Eyes, 1992; You Can't Catch Me, 1995; Double Delight, 1997; Starr Bright Will be With You Soon, 1999; The Barrens, 2001. OTHERS: Faithless: Tales of Transgression, 2001; The Faith of a Writer: Life, Craft, Art, 2003; Joyce Carol Oates: Conversations, 1970-2006, 2006. EDITOR/COMPLIER: Scenes from American Life: Contemporary Short Fiction, 1973; Best American Short Stories of 1979; Night Walks, 1982; First-Person Singular: Writers on Their Craft, 1983; Story: Fictions Past and Present, 1985; (with D. Halpern) Reading the Fights: The Best Writing about the Most Controversial of Sports, 1988; The Best American Essays, 1991; Twelve Plays, 1991; The Oxford Book of American Short Stories, 1992; (with D. Halpern) The Sophisticated Cat: An Anthology, 1992; George Bellows: American Artist, 1995; The Essential Dickinson, 1996; American Gothic Tales, 1996; Story: The Art and the Craft of Narrative Fiction, 1997; The Best of H.P. Lovecraft, 1997; (with R.V. Cassill) The Norton Anthology of Contemporary Fiction, 1997; (with J. Berliner) Snapshots: Twentieth-Century Mother-Daughter Fiction, 2000; The Best American Essays of the Century, 2000; The Best New American Voices 2003, 2002; (with O. Penzler) Best American Mystery Stories, 2005. AS LAUREN KELLY: Take Me, Take Me with You, 2004; The Stolen Heart, 2005; Blood Mask, 2006. FOR YOUNG ADULTS: Big Mouth & Ugly Girl, 2002; Small Avalanches and Other Stories, 2003; Freaky Green Eyes, 2003; Rape: A Love Story, 2003; After the Wreck, 2006; The Journal of Joyce Carol Oates: 1973-1982, 2007; My Sister, My Love: The Intimate Story of Skyler Rampike, 2008; (with A. Haley and N. Mailer) Muhammad Ali: Ringside, 2009. Contributor of articles to periodicals. **Address:** John Hawkins and Associates Inc., 71 W 23rd St., Ste. 1600, New York, NY 10010-4185, U.S.A. **Online address:** jcsmith@princeton.edu

OATES, Stephen B(aery). American (born United States), b. 1936. **Genres:** History, Biography, Adult Non-fiction, Autobiography/Memoirs. **Career:** University of Texas, instructor, 1964-67, assistant professor of history, 1967-68; University of Massachusetts, assistant professor, 1968-70, associate professor, 1970-71, professor of history, 1971-80, adjunct professor of English, 1980-85, Paul Murray Kendall professor of biography, 1985-98, Department of History, professor emeritus, 1998-. Writer. **Publications:** Confederate Cavalry West of The River, 1961; (ed. and intro.) Rip Ford's Texas, 1963; (ed.) Republic of Texas, 1968; Visions of Glory, Texans on the Southwestern Frontier, 1970; To Purge This Land with Blood: A Biography of John Brown, 1970, 2nd ed., 1984; (ed.) Portrait of America, 1973, 10th ed. as Portrait of America: From the European Discovery of America to the End of Reconstruction, 2010; The Fires of Jubilee: Nat Turner's Fierce Rebellion, 1975; With Malice Toward None: The Life of Abraham Lincoln, 1977; Our Fiery Trial: Abraham Lincoln, John Brown and The Civil War Era, 1979; Builders of The Dream: Abraham Lincoln and Martin Luther King, Jr., 1982; Let the Trumpet Sound: The Life of Martin Luther King, Jr., 1982, 3rd ed., 1985; Abraham Lincoln, The Man Behind the Myths, 1984; (ed.) Biography as High Adventure: Life-Writers Speak on Their Art, 1986; William Faulkner, The Man and The Artist: A Biography, 1987; Biography as History, 1991; Woman of Valor: Clara Barton and The Civil War, 1994; Approaching Fury: Voices of the Storm, 1820-1861, 1997; Whirlwind of War: Voices of the Storm, 1861-1865, 1998. Contributor to periodicals. **Address:** Department of History, University of Massachusetts, 161 Presidents Dr., Herter Hall, 300 Massachusetts Ave., Amherst, MA 01002, U.S.A. **Online address:** sboates@history.umass.edu

OATES, Wallace Eugene. American (born United States), b. 1937. **Genres:** Environmental Sciences/Ecology. **Career:** San Diego State College, part-time instructor in economics, 1961-62; San Jose State College, part-time instructor in economics, 1962-65; Princeton University, assistant professor of economics, 1965-71, associate professor of economics, 1971-74, professor of economics, 1974-79; University of Maryland, professor of economics, 1979-, distinguished university professor; Eastern Economic Association, president, 1989-90; Southern Economic Association, president, 1993-94. Writer. **Publications:** Fiscal Federalism, 1972; (with H. Kelejian) Introduction to Econometrics: Principles and Applications, 1974, 3rd ed. 1989; (with E.S. Mills) Fiscal Zoning and Land Use Controls: The Economic Issues, 1975; (with W.J. Baumol) Theory of Environmental Policy, 1975, 2nd ed., 1988; (ed.) Political Economy of Fiscal Federalism, 1977; (ed. with O.C. Ashenfelter) Essays in Labor Market Analysis, 1977; (with W.J. Baumol) Economics, Environmental Policy, and the Quality of Life, 1979; Studies in Fiscal Federalism, 1991; (ed.) The Economics of the Environment, 1992; The Economics of Environmental Regulation, 1996; (ed.) The Economics of Fiscal Federalism and Local Finance, 1998; (contrib.) Local Government Tax and Land Use Policies in the United States, 1998; (ed.) RFF Reader in Environmental and Resource Management, 1999, 2nd ed., 2006; (ed.) Property Taxation and Local Government Finance, 2001; Environmental Policy and Fiscal Federalism, 2004. **Address:** Department of Economics, University of Maryland, Tydings Hall 3147E, 3105 Tydings Hall, College Park, MD 20742, U.S.A. **Online address:** oates@econ.umd.edu

OATIS, Steven J. American (born United States), b. 1970. **Genres:** History, Young Adult Non-fiction. **Career:** Georgia State University, faculty; Emory University, faculty; University of the Ozarks, Department of History, assistant professor, 1999, associate professor. Writer. **Publications:** A Colonial Complex: South Carolina's Frontiers in the Era of the Yamasee War, 1680-1730, 2004. **Address:** Department of History, University of the Ozarks, 154 Walton Fine Arts Ctr., 415 N College Ave., Clarksville, AR 72830, U.S.A. **Online address:** soatis@ozarks.edu

OBADELE-STARKS, Ernest. American (born United States), b. 1959?. **Genres:** History. **Career:** Sterling High School, instructor in history; Sam Houston State University, instructor in history; Texas A&M University-College Station, Department of History, assistant professor, associate professor, professor; Texas A&M University-Qatar, associate professor, 2005-09. Writer. **Publications:** Black Unionism in the Industrial South, 2000; Freebooters and Smugglers: The Foreign Slave Trade in the United States after 1808, 2007. Contributor to books and journals. **Address:** Texas A&M University, PO Box 4236, College Station, TX 77843-4236, U.S.A. **Online address:** obad@tamu.edu

OBAID, Nawaf E. American/Saudi (born Saudi Arabia), b. 1974?. **Genres:** History, Adult Non-fiction, Social Sciences. **Career:** Saudi National Security Assessment Project, managing director; Center for Strategic and International Studies, adjunct fellow, Arleigh A. Burke chair in strategy, Saudi strategic affairs adviser; Office of the U.S. Secretary of Defense, special project director; Washington Institute for Near East Policy, fellow. Security consultant and writer. **Publications:** The Oil Kingdom at 100: Petroleum Policymaking in Saudi Arabia, 2000; (with A.H. Cordesman) National Security in Saudi Arabia: Threats, Responses and Challenges, 2000. Contributor to periodicals. **Address:** Center for Strategic & International Studies, 1800 K St. NW, Washington, DC 20006, U.S.A.

O'BARR, Jean (Fox). American (born United States), b. 1942. **Genres:** Women's Studies And Issues. **Career:** Purdue University, lecturer, 1964; University of Dar es Salaam, research associate and field researcher, 1967-68, 1972, 1981; Duke University, lecturer, 1969, 1972-78, adjunct associate professor, 1978-91, professor of the practice of women's studies and adjunct professor of political science, 1991-, director of continuing education, 1970-83, founding director of women's studies, 1983-, Margaret Taylor Smith director of women's studies, 1998-2001, university distinguished service professor, 2000-, university distinguished service professor emeritus of the practice of education, chair, 2003-05; University of North Carolina, visiting assistant professor, 1970-72; Displaced Homemakers, chairperson, 1979-81; Oxford University, Queen Elizabeth House, visiting fellow, 1983; University of Barcelona, Fulbright lecturer; Friends of Duke University Libraries, chair, 2003-05. Writer, speaker and consultant. **Publications:** (With J. Mlela) Shindano: Swahili Essays and Other Stories, 1971; Third World Women (monograph), 1976; (intro.) Passbook Number F.47927: Women and Mau Mau in Kenya, 1985; Feminism in Action, 1994. EDITOR: (with W.M. O'Barr) Language and Politics, 1976; Perspectives on Power, 1982; (with S. Harding) Sex and Scientific Inquiry, 1987; (with E. Minnich and R. Rosenfeld) Reconstructing the Academy, 1988; Women and a New Academy: Gender and Cultural Contexts, 1989; (with M.R. Malson, S. Westphal-Wihl and M. Wyer) Feminist Theory in Practice and Process, 1989; (co-ed.) Sisters and Workers in the Middle Ages, 1989; (with M.R. Malson, E. Mudimbe-Boyi and M. Wyer) Black Women in America, 1989; (with M. Wyer and D. Pope) Ties That Bind, 1990; (with M. Wyer) Engaging Feminism, 1992; (with R.H. Bates and V.Y. Mudimbe) Africa and the Disciplines, 1993; (with N. Hewitt and N. Rosebaugh) Talking Gender, 1996; (with E.C. DeLamotte and N. Meeker) Women Imagine Change, 1997. Contributor of articles to books and periodicals. **Address:** Duke University, 2138 Campus Dr., PO Box 90586, Durham, NC 27708, U.S.A. **Online address:** jeanobar@duke.edu

O'BEIRNE, Kate. American (born United States), b. 1949?. **Genres:** Women's Studies And Issues. **Career:** U.S. Department of Health and Human Services, deputy assistant secretary for legislation, 1986-88; Heritage Foundation, deputy director of domestic policy studies, vice president of government relations; National Review, Washington editor, 1995-. **Publications:** Women Who Make the World Worse: And How Their Radical Feminist Assault Is Ruining Our Families, Military, Schools and Sports, 2006. Contributor of articles to journals and periodicals. **Address:** National Review, 215 Lexington Ave., New York, NY 10016, U.S.A.

OBEJAS, Achy. American/Cuban (born Cuba), b. 1956. **Genres:** Novels, Novellas/Short Stories, Writing/Journalism, Essays, Translations. **Career:** Chicago Tribune, journalist; University of Chicago, Springer writer-in-residence; University of Hawaii, distinguished writer-in-residence; DePaul University, Sor Juana visiting writer. Translator. **Publications:** We Came All the Way from Cuba So You Could Dress Like This?, 1994; Memory Mambo, 1996; Days of Awe, 2001; (ed.) Havana Noir, 2007; Aguas y otros cuentos, 2009; Ruins, 2009; (trans.) E.L. Portela, One Hundred Bottles, 2010. Contributor of articles to newspapers. **Address:** Department of English, DePaul University, SAF 5A-H 513, 802 W Belden Ave., Ste. 255, Chicago, IL 60614-3280, U.S.A. **Online address:** aobejas@depaul.edu

OBERLE, Joseph. American (born United States), b. 1958. **Genres:** Sports/Fitness, Biography, Humor/Satire. **Career:** TV Guide (magazine), editor, 1984-88; Training (magazine), editor, 1989; freelance writer, 1990-91; Skyway News Publications, Minnesota Sports magazine, editor, Skyway News, editor, 1991-92; Timberwolves Publications Department, editorial manager, 1994-2000; TPG Sports, publications manager, 2000-02; Whittier Globe newspaper, staff writer; Minnesota Golfer magazine, managing editor. **Publications:** (Ed. and contrib.) Papal Bull (humorous dictionary), 1989; Anchorage, 1990; Diary of a Mad Househusband, 1996; (with G.L. Mikan) Unstoppable: The Story of George Mikan The First NBA Superstar, 1997. **Address:** Greenhouse Group Communications, 5770 Washington St. NE, Fridley, MN 55432, U.S.A. **Online address:** joe@josephgoberle.com

OBERLIN, Loriann Hoff. American (born United States), b. 1961. **Genres:** Money/Finance, Psychology, Young Adult Non-fiction. **Career:** Loriann Oberlin Counseling & Mediation L.L.C., clinical professional counselor. Educator and writer. **Publications:** Writing for Money, 1994; Working at Home While the Kids Are There, Too, 1997; Surviving Separation and Divorce: A Woman's Guide to Making It Through the First Years, 2000, 2nd ed., 2005; (with T.F. Murphy) The Angry Child: Regaining Control When Your Child Is Out of Control, 2001; The Everything American History Book: People, Places, and Events That Shaped Our Nation, 2001, 2nd ed., 2007; Writing for Quick Cash: Turn Your Way with Words into Real Money, 2004; (with T. Murphy) Overcoming Passive-Aggression: How to Stop Hidden Anger from Spoiling Your Relationships, Career, and Happiness, 2005. Contributor to periodicals and magazines. **Address:** c/o Author Mail, Marlowe & Co., 245 W 17th St., 11th Fl., New York, NY 10011-5300, U.S.A. **Online address:** loriann@loriannoberlin.com

OBERLY, James W. American (born United States), b. 1954. **Genres:** History. **Career:** Ulster County Community College, professor, 1979-81; College of William and Mary, professor, 1981-83; University of Wisconsin-Eau Claire, professor of history, 1983-. Writer. **Publications:** Sixty Million Acres: American Veterans and the Public Lands before the Civil War, 1990; (comp. with L.A. Merriam) United States History: A Bibliography of the New Writings on American History, 1995; A Nation of Statesmen: The Political Culture of the Stockbridge-Munsee Mohicans, 1815-1972, 2005. **Address:** Department of History, University of Wisconsin-Eau Claire, 713 Hibbard Hall, 105 Garfield Ave., PO Box 4004, Eau Claire, WI 54701, U.S.A. **Online address:** joberly@uwec.edu

OBERNDORF, Charles G. American (born United States), b. 1959. **Genres:** Science Fiction/Fantasy, Literary Criticism And History. **Career:** Dartmouth College, assistant teacher, 1982-83; University School, English and social studies, teacher, 1984-. Writer. **Publications:** NOVELS: Sheltered Lives, 1992; Testing, 1993; Foragers, 1996; Abe Osheroff, forthcoming. Contributor to periodicals. **Address:** Shaker Campus, University School, Grades K-8, 20701 Brantley Rd., Shaker Heights, OH 44120, U.S.A. **Online address:** coberndorf@us.edu

OBIKA, Akili Addae. (Akili Addae). American (born United States), b. 1969. **Genres:** Poetry, Literary Criticism And History, Philosophy, Young Adult Fiction, Essays. **Career:** Richmond Times-Dispatch, black literature columnist, 1992-94. **Publications:** Makantagara (poems), 1990; (with Y. Oforiwaa) The Wisdom of the Ages: Themes and Essences of Truth, Love, Struggle and High-Culture in the Works of Ayi Kwei Armah and Kiarri T-H. Cheatwood (literary essays), 1995. **Address:** 830 E State St., Trenton, NJ 08609-1412, U.S.A. **Online address:** aaobika@myexcel.com

OBMASCIK, Mark. American (born United States), b. 1962?. **Genres:** Environmental Sciences/Ecology, Natural History. **Career:** Miami Herald, reporter; Denver Post, journalist, 1985-2002. **Publications:** A Consumer's Guide to Water Conservation: Dozens of Ways to Save Water, the Environment, and a Lot of Money, 1993; A Consumer's Guide to Drinking Water, 2000; The Big Year: A Tale of Man, Nature, and Fowl Obsession, 2004; Halfway to Heaven: My White-knuckled-and Knuckleheaded-Quest for the Rocky Mountain High (memoir), 2009. Contributor to magazines. **Address:** The Miami Herald, 1 Herald Plz., Miami, FL 33132, U.S.A. **Online address:** mark.obmascik@yahoo.com

OBRADOVIĆ, Nadežda. American (born United States), b. 1936. **Genres:** Translations, Novellas/Short Stories, Literary Criticism And History, Young Adult Fiction. **Career:** Medjunarodna Politika, proofreader of French materials, 1959-61; Brodoimpex, translator, 1965-70; University of Belgrade, Faculty of Electrical Engineering, translator, 1970-; Radio Belgrade, broadcaster; Radio Sarajevo, broadcaster. Writer. **Publications:** Determinante Prostorno Funkcionalnih Veza Izmedu Komuna i Regiona u SRSrbiji van Pokrajina, 1982; (ed.) Looking for a Rain God (African stories), 1990; (ed.) African Rhapsody (African stories): Short Stories of the Contemporary African Experience, 1994; Majka je bila Sjajan Covek: AfriCke zenske PriCe, 1995; Bezglasni Krik: Savremenazenska PriCa, 1997; (ed.) The Prince of Fire (Serbian stories): An Anthology of Contemporary Serbian Short Stories, 1998; Anchor Book of Modern African Stories, 2002; Videla Sam Urmine Palme: Egipatskazenska priCa, 2003. Contributor to periodicals. **Address:** c/o Marlene Connor, Connor Literary Agency, 2911 W 71st St., Minneapolis, MN 55423, U.S.A. **Online address:** nadezda@biblioteka.etf.bg.ac.yu

O'BRIANT, Walter H(erbert). American (born United States), b. 1937. **Genres:** Philosophy, Intellectual History, Translations, Young Adult Fiction. **Career:** Wofford College, assistant professor of philosophy and acting chair of department, 1962-65; University of Georgia, assistant professor, 1965-69, associate professor of philosophy, 1969-95; North Carolina State University, visiting professor, 1967; trainer in computer technology and programs and service technician, 1996-2009. Writer. **Publications:** Introduction to Philosophy, 1968, 2nd ed., 1973; (trans.) Gottfried Wilhelm Leibniz's General Investigations Concerning the Analysis of Concepts and Truths, 1968. Contributor to journals. **Address:** 1840 S Creek Dr., Austell, GA 30106, U.S.A. **Online address:** walter.obriant@gmail.com

O'BRIEN, Ally. *See* **GUNN, Ali.**

O'BRIEN, Charles. American (born United States), b. 1927?. **Genres:** Mystery/Crime/Suspense, Criminology/True Crime. **Career:** Western Illinois University, Department of History, professor, 1964-94, professor emeritus, 1994-. Writer. **Publications:** HISTORICAL MYSTERY NOVELS: Mute Witness, 2001; Black Gold, 2002; Noble Blood, 2004; Lethal Beauty, 2005; Fatal Carnival, 2006; Cruel Choices, 2007; Assassins' Rage, 2008; Deadly Quarrel, 2009; False Patriots, 2010. **Address:** Department of History, Western Illinois University, 438 Morgan Hall, 1 University Cir., Macomb, IL 61455, U.S.A. **Online address:** obrien@bcn.net

O'BRIEN, David M(ichael). American (born United States), b. 1951. **Genres:** Law, Politics/Government, Public/Social Administration, Theology/Religion, Civil Liberties/Human Rights. **Career:** University of California, Department of Political Science, lecturer, 1976-77; University of Puget Sound, Department of Politics, assistant professor, 1977-79, chair, 1978-79; University of Virginia, assistant professor, 1979-83, associate professor, 1983-88, graduate advisor, 1983-85, 1989-92, professor, 1989-96, Department of Politics, Leone Reaves and George W. Spicer professor, 1996-; Russell Sage Foundation, visiting postdoctoral fellow, 1981-82; Supreme Court of the United States, Office of Administrative Assistant to the Chief Justice, judicial fellow, 1982-83, research associate, 1983-84; Oxford University, Nuffield College, Fulbright lecturer and visiting professorial fellow in constitutional studies, 1987-88. Writer. **Publications:** Privacy, Law and Public Policy, 1979, (comp.) The Right of Privacy-Its Constitutional & Social Dimensions: A Comprehensive Bibliography, 1980; The Public's Right to Know: The Supreme Court and the

First Amendment, 1981; (ed. with D.A. Marchand) The Politics of Technology Assessment: Institutions, Processes and Policy Disputes, 1982; (and ed. with M.W. Cannon) Views from the Bench: The Judiciary and Constitutional Politics, 1985; Storm Center: The Supreme Court in American Politics, 1986, 8th ed., 2008; What Process is Due? Courts and Science Policy Disputes, 1987; Supreme Court Watch, 1990; Constitutional Law and Politics, 1991, 7th ed., 2008; (with B.H. Craig) Abortion and American Politics, 1993; (with S. Wayne) The Politics of American Government, 1994, 3rd ed., 1999; (with Y. Ohkoshi) To Dream of Dreams: Religious Freedom in Postwar Japan, 1996; (and ed.) Judges on Judging: Views from the Bench, 1997, 3nd ed., 2009; (ed. with P.H. Russell) Judicial Independence in the Age of Democracy: Critical Perspectives from Around the World, 2001; (ed.) Lanahan Feadings in Civil Rights and Civil Liberties, 2003; Animal Sacrifice and Religious Freedom: Church of the Lukumi Babalu Aye v. City of Hialeah, 2004; (co-author) Government by the People, 21st ed., 2005; Constitutional Law and Politics, 2005; (with C.P. Banks) Courts and Judicial Policymaking, 2008; Congress Shall Make No Law: The First Amendment, Unprotected Expression and the U.S. Supreme Court, 2010. Contributor of articles to periodicals. **Address:** Department of Politics, University of Virginia, PO Box 400787, Charlottesville, VA 22904-4787, U.S.A. **Online address:** dmo2y@virginia.edu

O'BRIEN, D(enis) P(atrick). British (born England), b. 1939. **Genres:** Economics, Industrial Relations, Adult Non-fiction, Essays. **Career:** Queens University, assistant lecturer, lecturer, reader in economics, 1963-72; University of Durham, professor of economics, 1972-97, professor emeritus, 1998-. Writer. **Publications:** (With D. Swann) Information Agreements, Competition, and Efficiency, 1968; J.R. McCulloch: A Study in Classical Economics, 1970; Correspondence of Lord Overstone, 3 vols., 1971; (co-author) Competition in British Industry, 1974; Whither Economics?: An Inaugural Lecture, 1974; (ed.) J.R. McCulloch: Treatise on Taxation, 1975; The Classical Economists, 1975; (co-author) Competition Policy, Profitability and Growth, 1979; (ed. and contrib. with J.R. Presley) Pioneers of Modern Economics in Britain, 1981; (with A.C. Darnell) Authorship Puzzles in the History of Economics, 1982; (ed. and contrib. with J. Creedy) Economic Analysis in Historical Perspective, 1984; Lionel Robbins, 1988; Thomas Joplin and Classical Macroeconomics, 1993; (ed.) Foundations of Monetary Economics, 6 vols., 1994; Methodology, Money and the Firm: The Collected Essays of D.P. O'Brien, 2 vols., 1994; (intro.) Classical Writings on Economics, 1995; (ed.) Foundations of Business Cycle Theory, 1997; (ed.) History of Taxation, 1999; Classical Economists Revisited, 2004; The Development of Monetary Economics: A Modern Perspective on Monetary Controversies, 2007; History of Economic Thought as an Intellectual Discipline, 2007; (ed. with J. Creedy) Taxation and the Promotion of Human Happiness: An Essay, 2009; (with J. Creedy) Darwin's Clever Neighbour: George Warde Norman and His Circle, 2010. Contributor to periodicals. **Address:** Edward Elgar Publishing Ltd., The William Pratt House, 9 Dewey Ct., Northampton, MA 01060-3815, U.S.A. **Online address:** d.p.obrien@durham.ac.uk

O'BRIEN, Edna. British/Irish (born Ireland), b. 1930. **Genres:** Novels, Novellas/Short Stories, Children's Fiction, Plays/Screenplays, Young Adult Non-fiction, Picture/Board Books, Romance/Historical, Biography, Biography. **Career:** City College, creative writing teacher. Writer. **Publications:** COUNTRY GIRLS TRILOGY: The Country Girls, 1960; The Lonely Girl, 1962 as The Girl with Green Eyes, 1975; Girls in Their Married Bliss, 1964. NOVELS: August Is a Wicked Month, 1965; Casualties of Peace, 1966; A Pagan Place, 1970; Zee and Co., 1971; Night, 1972; Johnny I Hardly Knew You, 1977; Arabian Days, 1977; I Hardly Knew You, 1978; The Dazzle, 1981; A Christmas Treat, 1982; The Rescue, 1983; High Road, 1988; Far from the Land, 1989; On the Bone, 1989; Time and Tide, 1992; House of Splendid Isolation, 1994; Down by the River, 1997; Wild Decembers, 2000; In the Forest, 2002; Iphigenia, 2003; Triptych and Iphigenia, 2003; The Light of Evening, 2006. COLLECTIONS: The Love Object, 1968; A Scandalous Woman: And Other Stories, 1974; Mrs. Reinhardt and Other Stories; Collector's Choice, 1978 as A Rose in the Heart: Love Stories, 1979; Returning, 1982; A Fanatic Heart: Selected Stories, 1984; Lantern Slides, 1990; An Edna O'Brien Reader, 1994; Irish Revel, 1998; (co-author) Poolside, 2007; Saints and Sinners, 2011. NON FICTION: Mother Ireland, 1976; James and Nora: A Portrait of Joyce's Marriage, 1981; James Joyce: A Biography, 1999. OTHERS: (intro.) Dubliners, 2007; Fanatic Heart: Selected Stories of Edna O'Brien, 2008; Byron in Love: A Short Daring Life, 2009; Haunted, 2010. Contributor to magazines. **Address:** The Wylie Agency Ltd., 17 Bedford Sq., London, GL WC1B 3JA, England.

O'BRIEN, George. Irish (born Ireland), b. 1945. **Genres:** Autobiography/Memoirs, Literary Criticism And History, History, Ethics, Young Adult Fiction. **Career:** University of Warwick, lecturer in English, 1976-80; Vassar College, visiting assistant professor of English, 1980-84; Georgetown University, assistant professor, 1984-90, associate professor of English, 1990-97, professor of English, 1997-. Writer. **Publications:** The Village of Longing (autobiography), 1987; Dancehall Days (autobiography), 1988; Brian Friel (literary criticism), 1990; Out of Our Minds (autobiography), 1994; Brian Friel: A Reference Guide (literary criticism), 1995; (intro.) The Ireland Anthology, 1997; (ed.) Playing the Field: Irish Writers on Sport, 2000. **Address:** Department of English, Georgetown University, 342 New North, 37th and O St. NW, Washington, DC 20057, U.S.A. **Online address:** obriengl@georgetown.edu

O'BRIEN, Kevin. American (born United States), b. 1955. **Genres:** Mystery/Crime/Suspense. **Career:** Association of American Railroads, clerk, through 1980. Writer. **Publications:** NOVELS: Actors, 1986; Only Son, 1997; The Next to Die (thriller), 2001; Make Them Cry (thriller), 2002; Watch Them Die (thriller), 2003; Left for Dead (thriller), 2004; The Last Victim (thriller), 2005; Killing Spree (thriller), 2007; One Last Scream (thriller), 2008; Final Breath (thriller), 2009; Vicious (thriller), 2010. contributor to periodicals. **Address:** Seattle, WA , U.S.A. **Online address:** authorkev@aol.com

O'BRIEN, Lucy. British (born England), b. 1961. **Genres:** Music, Biography. **Career:** University of Leeds, Leeds Student, music editor; New Musical Express, staff writer and sub-editor, 1985-87; City Limits Magazine, music editor, 1987-89; Select Magazine, commissioning editor, 1990-91; Everywoman Magazine, books editor, 1994-96; Middlesex University, tutor; Brighton University, faculty; University of West London, London College of Music, faculty; Westminster University, lecturer in commercial music; University of London, Goldsmiths College, faculty; Southampton Solent University, Faculty of Media, Arts and Society, associate lecturer. Journalist. **Publications:** Dusty (biography), 1989; Annie Lennox: Sweet Dreams are Made of This, 1991; She Bop: The Definitive History of Women in Rock, Pop, and Soul (music reference), 1995, 2nd ed. as She Bop II, 2002; Madonna: Like an Icon, 2007. Contributor to books and periodicals. **Address:** c/o Jane Turnbull, 58 Elgin Cres., London, GL W11 2JJ, England. **Online address:** info@lucyobrien.com

O'BRIEN, Martin. (Jack Drummond). British (born England), b. 1951?. **Genres:** Novels, Travel/Exploration, Young Adult Fiction, Mystery/Crime/Suspense. **Career:** Conde Nast, travel editor; Vogue (magazine), travel editor, 1973. **Publications:** All the Girls (travel), 1982; The Dying Minutes, 2012. JACQUOT SERIES: Jacquot and the Waterman (mystery novel), 2005; Jacquot and the Angel, 2005; Jacquot and the Master, 2007; Jacquot and the Fifteen, 2007; Confession, 2009; Blood Counts, 2010. AS JACK DRUMMOND: Avalanche, 2007; Dive, 2008; Storm, 2009. **Address:** c/o Author Mail, Publicity Department, St. Martin's Press, 175 5th Ave., New York, NY 10010-7703, U.S.A.

O'BRIEN, Matthew. American (born United States) **Genres:** Novels. **Career:** Las Vegas CityLife, staff writer, news editor and managing editor, 2000-08. Journalist. **Publications:** Beneath the Neon: Life and Death in the Tunnels of Las Vegas, 2007; My Week at the Blue Angel: And Other Stories from the Storm Drains, Strip Clubs, and Trailer Parks of Las Vegas, 2010. Contributor to periodicals. **Address:** Huntington Press, 3665 Procyon St., Las Vegas, NV 89103, U.S.A. **Online address:** thesewersofparis@yahoo.com

O'BRIEN, Maureen. British (born England), b. 1943. **Genres:** Mystery/Crime/Suspense, Plays/Screenplays, Novels. **Career:** Actress and writer. **Publications:** MYSTERY NOVELS: Close-up on Death, 1989; Deadly Reflection, 1993; Mask of Betrayal, 1998; Dead Innocent, 1999; Revenge, 2001; Unauthorized Departure, 2003; Every Step You Take, 2004. PLAYS: The Cutting, 2003. OTHER: À l'inattendu les dieux livrent passage, 2006. Contributor to periodicals. **Address:** Kate Feast Management, 10 Primrose Hill Studios, Fitzroy Rd., London, GL NW1 8TR, England.

O'BRIEN, Pat. American (born United States), b. 1948. **Genres:** Sports/Fitness, Young Adult Non-fiction. **Career:** Fox Sports Radio Network, contributor to programming, 2001-; KCBS-TV, journalist. Board of the Special Olympics, director. Writer. **Publications:** Talkin' Sports: A BS-er's Guide, 1998. **Address:** Access Hollywood, NBC-TV, 3000 W Alameda Ave., Trailer E, Burbank, CA 91523, U.S.A.

O'BRIEN, Patrick K. (Patrick Thomas O'Brien). British (born England), b. 1932. **Genres:** Economics, History. **Career:** London University, School of Oriental and African Studies, research fellow, 1960-63, lecturer, 1963-70, reader in economics and economic history, 1967-70, professor of economic history and institute of historical research, director, 1990-98, emeritus professor, 1998-, Institute of Historical Research, senior research fellow and convenor, 1998-2002, London School of Economics, Department of Economic History, centennial professor of economic history, 1999-2009, professor of global economic history, European Research Council Research Project, principal investigator, 2009-12; Institute of National Planning, visiting fellow, 1963; Harvard University, Center For Middle Eastern Studies, Department of Economics, visiting lecturer and fellow, 1968; University of California, Department of Economics, visiting associate professor, 1969; Oxford University, Saint Antony's College, university lecturer, 1970-84, university reader, 1984-90, emeritus fellow, 1990-; Columbia University, Department of History, visiting professor, 1990; Carlos III University, Banca Bilbao Viscaya visiting professor, 1993; University of Minnesota, Union Pacific visiting professor, 1999; University of Manchester, visiting Simon professor, 1999; British Economic History Society, president, 1999-2001; University of Munich, Centre for Economic Studies, visiting fellow, 2003; Netherlands Institute of Advanced Study, visiting fellow, 2004; University of Ghent, Wallerstein visiting professor, 2006; Free University, Liebman visiting professor, 2006; Tsinghua University, visiting professor, 2008, Erasmus Mundus visiting professor, 2010. Writer. **Publications:** Revolution in Egypt's Economic System: From Private Enterprise to Socialism, 1952-1965, 1966; (with G. Briscoe and D.J. Smyth) Measurement of Capacity Utilisation in the United Kingdom, 1970; Two Paths to the Twentieth Century Economic Growth in Britain and France 1780-1914, 1974; The New Economic History of Railways, 1977; (ed.) Railways and the Economic Development of Western Europe 1830-1914, 1983; (ed.) Productivity in the Economies of Europe, 1983; Economic Effects on the American Civil War, 1988; (with R. Quinault) Industrial Revolution and British Society, 1993; (ed. and intro.) Industrial Revolution in Europe, 1994; (ed. with K. Bruland) From Family Firms to Corporate Capitalism: Essays in Business and Industrial History in Honour of Peter Mathias, 1998; (ed.) Philip's Atlas of World History, 1999; (ed.) Urban Achievement in Early Modern Europe: Golden Ages in Antwerp, Amsterdam and London, 2001; (ed. with A. Clesse) Two Hegemonies: Britain 1846-1914 and the United States 1941-2001, 2002; (ed.) Atlas of World History, 2002; (ed.) Industrialisation, 1998; (ed. with D. Winch) Political Economy of British Historical Experience, 1688-1914, 2002; (ed.) Philip's Atlas of World history, 2002; (contrib.) Exceptionalism and Industrialisation: Britain and Its European Rivals, 1688-1815, 2004; Atlas of World History, 2010. Contributor to journals. **Address:** Department of Economic History, London School of Economics & Political Science, Houghton St., Rm. V204, London, GL WC2A 2AE, England. **Online address:** p.obrien@lse.ac.uk

O'BRIEN, Patrick Thomas. *See* **O'BRIEN, Patrick K.**

O'BRIEN, Robyn. American (born United States), b. 1972?. **Genres:** Food And Wine, Medicine/Health. **Career:** Author of nonfiction, financial analyst. **Publications:** (With R. Kranz) The Unhealthy Truth: How Our Food Is Making Us Sick and What We Can Do about It, 2009. **Address:** AllergyKids, PO Box 20236, Boulder, CO 80308, U.S.A.

O'BRIEN, Sean. British (born England), b. 1952. **Genres:** Poetry, Essays. **Career:** Beacon School, teacher, 1981-89; University of Dundee, fellow in creative writing, 1989-90; The Printer's Devil literary magazine, founding editor, 1990-; Sheffield Hallam University, professor of poetry, 1998-2006; Newcastle University, professor of creative writing, 2006-. Writer. **Publications:** POETRY: The Indoor Park, 1983; The Frighteners, 1987; Boundary Beach, 1989; HMS Glasshouse, 1991; A Rarity, 1993; Ghost Train, 1995; Deregulated Muse, 1995; (ed.) Firebox, 1998; Downriver, 2001; (P. Porter and J. Kinsella) Rivers, 2002; (contrib.) The Birds, 2002; Cousin Coat: Selected Poems, 1976-2001, 2002. OTHERS: Bloody Ambassadors: The Gruesome Stories of Irish People Tried for Murder Abroad, 1993; The Deregulated Muse: Essays in Contemporary British and Irish Poetry, 1998; Keepers of the Flame, 2003; (trans.) D. Alighieri, Inferno, 2006; The Drowned Book, 2007; Silence Room, 2008; Afterlife, 2009; (with B. Aris) Night Train, 2009; Andrew Marvell, 2010; November, 2011; Journeys to the Interior, 2012. Contributor to books and periodicals. **Address:** School of English Literature, Language and Linguistics, University of Newcastle, Percy Bldg., Upon, TW NE1 7RU, England. **Online address:** s.p.obrien@ncl.ac.uk

O'BRIEN, Tim. (William Timothy O'Brien). American (born United States), b. 1946. **Genres:** Novels, Young Adult Fiction, History. **Career:** Washington Post, national affairs reporter, 1973-74; Texas State University-San Marcos, MFA Program, endowed chair, 2003-04, 2005-06, 2008-09. **Publications:** NOVELS: Northern Lights, 1975; Going after Cacciato, 1978; The Nuclear Age, 1985; In the Lake of the Woods, 1994; Tomcat in Love, 1998; July, July, 2002. OTHERS: If I Die in a Combat Zone, Box Me Up and Ship Me Home, 1973; From How to Tell a True War Story, 1987; Tennessee: Off the Beaten Path, 1990; The Things They Carried: A Work of Fiction, 1990. Contributor to books and periodicals. **Address:** ICM, 40 W 57th St., New York, NY 10019, U.S.A.

O'BRIEN, Timothy L. American (born United States), b. 1961?. **Genres:** Novels, Young Adult Non-fiction, Business/Trade/Industry. **Career:** Wall Street Journal, reporter, 1992-97, staff writer; New York Times, reporter, 1997-2000, staff writer, 2003-06, Sunday Business Section, editor, 2006-10; Talk Magazine, senior feature writer, 2000-02, staff writer; Huffington Post, national editor, 2010-, executive editor. **Publications:** NONFICTION: Bad Bet: The Inside Story of the Glamour, Glitz, and Danger of America's Gambling Industry, 1998; TrumpNation: The Art of Being the Donald, 2005. **Address:** c/o Andrew Blauner, Blauner Books, 12 E 86th St., Ste. 633, New York, NY 10028-0512, U.S.A. **Online address:** blauner@aol.com

O'BRIEN, (Warren) Greg(ory). American (born United States), b. 1966. **Genres:** Novels, History. **Career:** University of Wyoming, instructor in history, 1995; University of Kentucky, instructor in history, 1998; University of Southern Mississippi, visiting assistant professor, 1998-2000, assistant professor, 2000-02, associate professor of history, 2002-08, director of graduate studies in history, 2002-04; Dartmouth College, visiting professor of native American studies, 2004; University of North Carolina, Department of History, associate professor and director of graduate studies, 2008-; University of Nebraska Press, Native South, associate editor, 2008-. **Publications:** Choctaws in a Revolutionary Age, 1750-1830, 2002; (ed. with T. Harvey) George Washington's South, 2004; (ed.) Pre-removal Choctaw History: Exploring New Paths, 2008; The Timeline of Native Americans: The Ultimate Guide to North America's Indigenous Peoples, 2008. **Address:** Department of History, University of North Carolina, 2110 Moore Humanities and Research, Administration Bldg., PO Box 26170, Greensboro, NC 27402-6170, U.S.A. **Online address:** wgobrien@uncg.edu

O'BRIEN, William Timothy. *See* **O'BRIEN, Tim.**

OBST, Lynda (Rosen). American (born United States), b. 1950. **Genres:** Autobiography/Memoirs, Humor/Satire, Film. **Career:** Producer and writer. **Publications:** Rolling Stone History of the Sixties, 1974; (ed.) The Sixties: The Decade Remembered Now, by the People Who Lived it Then, 1977; Dirty Dreams, 1990; Hello, He Lied: And Other Truths from the Hollywood Trenches, 1996. **Address:** Lynda Obst Productions, 10202 W Washington Blvd., Astaire Bldg., Ste. 1000, Culver City, CA 90232, U.S.A.

O'CALLAGHAN, Sean. American/Irish (born Ireland), b. 1954?. **Genres:** Autobiography/Memoirs, History, Social Sciences. **Career:** Writer. **Publications:** Down by the Glenside: Memoirs of an Irish Boyhood, 1992; The Informer, 1998; To Hell or Barbados, 2000. Contributor to periodicals. **Address:** TransWorld Publications, 2400 41st St. NW, Apt. 100, Washington, DC 20007, U.S.A.

O'CALLAHAN, Jay. American (born United States), b. 1938. **Genres:** Children's Fiction, Songs/Lyrics And Libretti, Novels. **Career:** Wyndham School, teacher and dean. Writer and storyteller. **Publications:** FOR CHILDREN: Tulips, 1992; Orange Cheeks, 1993; Herman and Marguerite: An Earth Story, 1996; Raspberries, 2009. FOR ADULTS: Harry's Our Man, 2011. Works appear in anthologies. **Address:** PO Box 1054, Marshfield, MA 02050, U.S.A. **Online address:** jay@ocallahan.com

OCAMPO, José Antonio. American/Colombian (born Colombia), b. 1952. **Genres:** Economics, Social Sciences, Marketing, Business/Trade/Industry. **Career:** Universidad de los Andes, researcher, 1976-79, professor of economics, 1976-84, 1988, 1993, Centro de Estudios sobre Desarrollo Econímico, director, 1980-82; Journal Desarrollo y Sociedad, director, 1980-82; Fedesarrollo (foundation for higher education and development), alternative executive director and research officer, 1983-84, executive director, 1984-88, senior research officer, 1988-89, 1991-93; Journal Coyuntura Economica, co-editor,

1984; Chenery (employment mission), national director, 1985-86; Colombian Government, advisor on coffee affairs, 1989-90, minister of agriculture and social development, 1993-94, Ministry of Planning, director of national planning department, 1994-96, minister of finance and public credit, 1996-97; WIDER-SIDA, head of mission to Nicaragua, 1989-91; Universidad Nacional, professor of history, 1990; Colombian Foreign Trade Board, advisor, 1990-91; Economic Commission for Latin America and the Caribbean, executive secretary, 1998-2003; United Nations, under-secretary general for economic and social affairs, 2003-07; Columbia University, School of International and Public Affairs, professor of professional practice in international and public affairs, fellow and director of economic and political development concentration, 2007-; Yale University, visiting professor; Oxford University, visiting professor; Cambridge University, visiting professor. **Publications:** Metodología para calcular el efecto de la retroactividad de lacesantia, 1982; En defensa de la continuidad del régimen cambiario, 1983; La reforma fiscal, 1982-1983, 1983; Crisis mundial, protección eindustrialización: ensayos de historia económica colombiana, 1984; Colombia y la economía mundial, 1830-1910, 1984; La política económica en la encrucijada, 1984; Hacia un nuevo modelo de Desarrollo? Un debate, 1987; El problema laboral Colombiano: informes especiales de la nisión de empleo, 1987; Stabilization and Adjustment Policies and Programmes: Colombia, 1987; Historica económica de Colombia, 1987; Planes antinflacionares: reciente en la America Latina, 1987; Lecturas de economia cafetera, 1987; Lecturas de macroeconomia colombiana, 1988; El sector comercio en Colombia, 1988; Colombia y ladeuda externa, 1988; Economía post Keynesiana, 1988; Los dilemas de la política comercial en América Latina, 1988; Introducción a lamacroeconoma Colombiana, 1989; Ciclo cafetero y comportameinto macroeconómico en Colombia, 1940-1987, 1989; Efectos de laliberación y del control de importanciones sobre la industria manufacturera Colombiana, 1976-1988, 1989; Inflación y estabilización e América Latina: nuevos modelos e structuralistas, 1990; La coyuntura cafetera internacional en perspectiva, 1990; Granenciclopedia de Colombia: temática, 1991; Recurrent Hyperinflation and Stabilization in Nicaragua, 1991; La internacionalizacion de la economia colombiana, 1993; Fuentes de competitividad de las exportaciones industriales de Colombia, 1993; Situación actual y perspectivas delsector agropecuario colombiano, 1994; Foreign Capital in Latin America, 1994; El giro de la politica agropecuaria, 1995; Participación privadaen la provisión de servicios sociales: el caso Colombiano, 1996; Seminario Internacional sobre Descentralización Fiscal en AméricaLatina: mejores prácticas y lecciones de política: Cartagena delndias, 1996; Reforming the International Financial Architecture: Consensus and Divergence, 1999; Políticas e instituciones para eldesarrollo sostenible en América Latina y el Caribe, 1999; The Poorest Countries and the Emerging International Financial Architecture, 1999; International Financial Reform: An Ongoing Debate, 1999; Hacia una reforma finaciera internacional: cinco temas esentiales, 2000; Financial Globalization and the Emerging Economies, 2000; An Economic History of Twentieth-Century Latin America, 2000; Equidad, desarrollo ycuidadanía, 2000; Equity, Development, and Citizenship, 2001; Rethinking the Development Agenda, 2001; Una decada de luces y sombres. America Latina y el Caribe en los años noventa, 2001; Un futuro económico para Colombia, 2001; Small Economies in the Face of Globalization, 2003; (ed. with J. Martin) Globalization and Development: A Latin American and Caribbean Perspective, 2003; Asymmetries and Cooperation in the Free Trade Area of the Americas, 2003; Returning to an Eternal Debate: The Terms of Trade for Commodities in the Twentieth Century, 2003; La era de las exportaciones latinoaméricanas: de finesdel siglo XIX a principios del XX, 2003; Industrialización y Estado enla América Latina: la leyenda negra de la posguerra, 2003; A Decade of Light and Shadow: Latin America and The Caribbean in the 1990s, 2003; Counter-Cyclical Prudential and Capital Account Regulations in Developing Countries, 2003; What Progress on International Financial Reform? Why So Limited?, 2003; Rethinking Development Strategies, 2003; El desarrollo económico en los albores del siglo XXI, 2003; Entre las reformas y elconflicto: economía y política en Colombia, 2004; América Latina y el Caribe en la era global, 2004; Gobernabilidad e integración financiera: ámbito global y regional, 2004; Reconstruir el futuro: globalización, desarrollo y democracia en América Latina, 2004; (ed.) Beyond Reforms: Structural Dynamics and Macroeconomic Vulnerability, 2005; (ed.) Regional Financial Cooperation, 2006; (ed.) Cooperación Financiera Regional, 2006; (ed. with J. Kregel and S. Griffith-Jones) International Finance and Development, 2007; (ed. with Jomo K.S.) Towards Full and Decent Employment, 2007; (ed. with R. Vos and Jomo K.S.) Growth Divergences: Explaining Differences in Economic Performance, 2007; (comp.) Historia económica de Colombia, 2007; (ed. with R. Vos) Uneven Economic Development, 2008; (ed. with J.E. Stiglitz) Capital Market Liberalization and Development, 2008; (with C. Rada and L. Taylor) Growth and Policy in Developing Countries: A Structuralist Approach, 2009; (ed. with B. Herman and S. Spiegel) Overcoming Developing Country Debt Crises, 2010; (ed. with S. Griffith-Jones and J.E. Stiglitz) Time for a Visible Hand, 2010; (with J. Ros) Oxford Handbook of Latin American Economics, 2011; (ed. with J.A. Alonso) Development Cooperation in Times of Crisis, 2012. Contributor to books and periodicals. **Address:** School of International and Public Affairs, Columbia University, Rm. 1315, International Affairs Bldg., 420 W 118th St., New York, NY 10027-7235, U.S.A. **Online address:** jao2128@columbia.edu

O'CARROLL, Brendan. Irish (born Ireland), b. 1955?. **Genres:** Novels, Human Relations/Parenting. **Career:** Writer. **Publications:** The Mammy, 1994; The Chisellers, 1995; The Granny, 1996; The Course, 1996; Sparrows Trap, 1997; Mrs. Browns Last Wedding, 1999; Agnes Brown, 1999; The Young Wan: An Agnes Browne Novel, 2003. Contributor to periodicals. **Address:** c/o Author Mail, Penguin Group, 345 Hudson St., New York, NY 10014-4502, U.S.A.

OCHART (TORRES), (Luz) Yvonne. American (born United States), b. 1949. **Genres:** Novellas/Short Stories, Poetry, Plays/Screenplays, Administration/Management, Advertising/Public Relations, Architecture, Art/Art History, Cultural/Ethnic Topics, Film, History, Institutions/Organizations, Politics/Government, Young Adult Fiction, Literary Criticism And History. **Career:** Long Island University, professor in linguistics, Spanish and Spanish literature, 1982-83; Universidad de Puerto Rico, School of Public Communications, adjunct professor of psycholinguistics, 1984-86; Universidad del Sagrado Corazon, adjunct professor of literature, 1984-90; West Indies Advertising, copywriter, 1986-87; Premier Maldonado and Associates, senior copywriter, 1987-89; Instituto de Cultura Puertorriquena, executive assistant director, 1993-96, administrator, 1996-98. Writer. **Publications:** Rantamplan (poems), 1975; Este es nuestro paraiso (poems), 1981; El salto domado, 1989; Poemas de Nueva York, 1989; Obra poética, 1989; El fuego de todas las cosas (stories), 1990; El libro del agua, 1996; La Historiadel Instituto de Cultura Puertorriquena 1955-2003: Camino al Cincuentenario, 2003. Contributor to periodicals. **Address:** Calle Antolin Nin 385, Hato Rey, San Juan, PR 00918, U.S.A.

OCHOA, Enrique C(orrado). American (born United States), b. 1964. **Genres:** Politics/Government, History, Race Relations, Organized Labor. **Career:** California State University-Dominguez Hills, lecturer, 1990-95; University of California, Latin American Center Publications, assistant editor, 1990-92, lecturer, 1993-95; Los Angeles Valley Community College, instructor, 1993; Santa Monica Community College, instructor, 1994; California State University-Los Angeles, assistant professor, 1995-99, associate professor, 1999-2004, professor of history and latin american studies, 2004-, associate coordinator of Latin American studies, 1998-2002, director of Latin American studies, 2008-; California State Polytechnic University-Pomona, Michi and Walter Weglyn endowed chair of multicultural studies, 2006-08. Writer. **Publications:** (Co-ed.) Statistical Abstract of Latin America, 1988; (ed. with D. Lorey and contrib.) Estado y agricultura en México: antecedentes e implicaciones de las reformas salinistas, 1994; Feeding Mexico: The Political Uses of Food since 1910, 2000; (ed. and contrib.) Encyclopedia of Social Welfare History in North America, 2005; (co-ed.) Latina/o Los Angeles: Migrations, Communities and Political Activism, 2005; (ed. with G. Ochoa) Latino Los Angeles: Transformations, Communities and Activism, 2005. Contributor of articles to books and periodicals. **Address:** Department of History, California State University, C4034 King Hall, 5151 State University Dr., Los Angeles, CA 90032, U.S.A. **Online address:** eochoa3@calstatela.edu

OCHS, Vanessa (L.). American (born United States), b. 1953. **Genres:** Theology/Religion, Women's Studies And Issues, Writing/Journalism. **Career:** University of Maryland, Department of English and Drama, lecturer, 1978-79; Colgate University, Department of English and Writing, senior lecturer, 1980-86; Yale University, Department of English, visiting lecturer, 1986-87; Drew University, Graduate School of Drew University, adjunct assistant professor, 1990-93; Department of Religion, adjunct assistant professor, 1993-97; University of Virginia, Department of Religious Religious and Jewish Studies, director, associate professor of religious studies; CLAL-The National Jewish Center for Learning and Leadership, Dorot fellow, 1994-95, senior fellow, 1995-2001; Women of the Wall, director. Writer. **Publications:** Words on Fire: One Woman's Journey into the Sacred, 1990, rev. ed., 1999; Safe and Sound: Protecting Children in an Unpredictable World, 1995; The Book of Sacred Jewish Practices, 2001; The Book of Jewish Dream Interpretation,

2003; Sarah Laughed, 2005; Inventing Jewish Ritual, 2007. Contributor of articles to periodicals. Works appear in anthologies. **Address:** Department of Religious Studies, University of Virginia, PO Box 400126, Charlottesville, VA 22904-4126, U.S.A. **Online address:** vanessa@virginia.edu

OCKER, Christopher (Michael). American (born United States), b. 1958. **Genres:** Sex, Theology/Religion, Politics/Government, History, Biography. **Career:** Federal Republic of Germany, research fellow, 1988-91; San Francisco Theological Seminary, assistant professor, 1991-95, associate professor, 1995-2001, professor, 1997, professor of church history, 2001-, Center for Hermeneutical Studies, associate director, 1991-94, Muilenberg-Koenig history of religions seminar, coordinator, convener, 2009-; Graduate Theological Union, convener, 1996-98, 2007-08; University of California, Department of History, affiliated faculty, 2001-, Center for the Study of Religion and Culture, co-director, 1999-2009, professor. Writer. **Publications:** (Ed.) From Intercourse to Discourse: Control of Sexuality in Rabbinic Literature, 1992; (ed.) Break: Habermas, Heidegger and the Nazis, 1992; Johannes Klenkok: A Friar's Life, 1310-1374, 1993; Biblical Poetics Before Humanism and Reformation, 2002; Church Robbers and Reformers in Germany, 1525-1547: Confiscation and Religious Purpose in the Holy Roman Empire, 2006; (co-ed.) Politics and Reformations: Histories and Reformations: Essays in Honor of Thomas A. Brady, Jr., 2007; Politics and Reformations: Communities, Polities, Nations, and Empires: Essays in Honor of Thomas A. Brady, Jr., 2007. Contributor to books and journals. **Address:** San Francisco Theological Seminary, 105 Seminary Rd., San Anselmo, CA 94960, U.S.A. **Online address:** ocker@sfts.edu

O'COLLINS, Gerald Glynn. Australian/Irish (born Ireland), b. 1931. **Genres:** Theology/Religion, Biography. **Career:** Ordained Roman Catholic priest, 1963; Heythrop College, external lecturer, 1966-67; University of Leicester, external lecturer, 1967; University of Cambridge, Pembroke College, research fellow, 1967-69; Weston School of Theology, visiting professor, 1968-72; Corpus Christi College, lecturer in theology, 1969-73; Jesuit Theological College, lecturer in theology, 1969-73; Gregorian University, visiting professor, 1973, professor of theology, 1974-2006, dean of faculty, 1985-91; Marquette University, visiting professor, 1994, 1998, 2006; St Mary's University College, research professor, 2006-09; Melbourne College of Divinity, fellow, 2009-; Australian Catholic University, adjunct professor, 2010-. Writer. **Publications:** Patrick McMahon Glynn, a Founder of Australian Federation, 1965; Theology and Revelation, 1968; Man and His New Hopes, 1969; Foundations of Theology, 1971; The Easter Jesus, 1973; The Resurrection of Jesus Christ, 1973; The Theology of Secularity, 1974; Faith Under Fire, 1974; Case Against Dogma, 1975; Has Dogma a Future?, 1975; Cross Today: An Evaluation of Current Theological Reflections on the Cross of Christ, 1977; The Calvary Christ, 1977; What Are They Saying about Jesus?, 1977, 2nd ed., 1983; What Are They Saying about the Resurrection?, 1978; A Month with Jesus, 1978; The Second Journey, 1978, rev. ed., 1995; Fundamental Theology, 1981; Finding Jesus: Living Through Lent with John's Gospel, 1983; Interpreting Jesus, 1983; The People's Christmas, 1984; Jesus Today, 1986; Jesus Risen: An Historical, Fundamental And Systematic Examination Of Christ's Resurrection, 1987; Interpreting The Resurrection: Examining The Major Problems In The Stories Of Jesus' Resurrection, 1988; Friends In Faith: Living the Creed Day by Day, 1989; (with M. Venturini) Believing: Understanding The Creed, 1991; Luca-Atti: Studi In Onore di P. Emilio Rasco Nel Suo 70o Compleanno, 1991; A Concise Dictionary of Theology, 1991, rev. ed., 2000; Retrieving Fundamental Theology: The Three Styles of Contemporary Theology, 1993; Resurrection of Jesus Christ: Some Contemporary Issues, 1993; Faith And The Future: Studies In Christian Eschatology, 1994; Experiencing Jesus, 1994; Christology: A Biblical, Historical And Systematic Study Of Jesus Christ, 1995; Focus On Jesus, 1996, rev. ed., 2009; (with D. Kendall) The Bible For Theology: Ten Principles For The Theological Use of Scripture, 1997; All Things New: The Promise Of Advent, Christmas and The New Year, 1998; Tripersonal God: Understanding and Interpreting The Trinity, 1999; Following The Way: Jesus, Our Spiritual Director, 2001; Convergence of Theology: A Festschrift Honoring Gerald O'Collins, 2001; The Incarnation, 2002; Easter Faith, 2003; Catholicism: The Story Of Catholic Christianity, 2003; Living Vatican II: The 21st Council For The 21st Century, 2006; Jesus Our Redeemer: A Christian Approach to Salvation, 2007; Salvation for all: God's Other Peoples, 2008; Jesus: A Portrait, 2008; Catholicism. A Very Short Introduction, 2008; Reflections for Busy People, 2009; Christology, 2nd ed., 2009; (with M.K. Jones) Jesus Our Priest: A Christian Approach to the Priesthood of Christ, 2010; Philip Pullman's Jesus, 2010; Pause for Thought, 2011; Rethinking Fundamental Theology, 2011; A Short Guide to Writing a Thesis, 2011. EDITOR: Patrick McMahon Glynn: Letters To His Family (1874-1927), 1974; Problems And Perspectives Of Fundamental Theology, 1982; Luke and Acts, 1993; Resurrection: An Interdisciplinary Symposium on the Resurrection of Jesus, 1997; The Trinity: An Interdisciplinary Symposium on the Trinity, 1999; The Incarnation. An Interdisciplinary Symosium on the Incarnation of the Son of God, 2002; In Many And Diverse Ways: In Honor Of Jacques Dupuis, 2003; The Redemption: An Interdisciplinary Symposium On Christ As Redeemer, 2004; Pope John Paul II: A Reader, 2007; The Legacy of John Paul II, 2008; Seek God Everywhere, 2010. Contributor to periodicals. **Address:** Jesuit Theological College, 175 Royal Parade, Parkville, VI 3052, Australia. **Online address:** ocollins@unigre.it

O'CONNELL, Caitlin. American (born United States), b. 1965?. **Genres:** Animals/Pets, History. **Career:** HNU Photonics, scientific consultant, 2000-; Namibian Ministry of Environment and Tourism, Etosha National Park, contract researcher; Stanford University, School of Medicine, Center for Conservation Biology, collaborating scientist, 2002-, Clark Center Bio-X Program, fellow, Department of Otolaryngology, research associate, 2005-07, Department of Otolaryngology-Head and Neck Surgery, assistant professor, 2007-09, instructor, 2009-, Continuing Studies Program, lecturer, 2008-; Utopia Scientific (formerly Keystone Species Intl.), co-founder, chief executive officer and co-director, 2002-. Writer. **Publications:** SELF-ILLUSTRATED: (with D.M. Jackson) Elephant Scientist, 2011. OTHERS: The Elephant's Secret Sense: The Hidden Life of the Wild Herds of Africa, 2007; Elephant's Life: An Intimate Portrait from Africa, 2011; The Boy's Club: An Elephantine Take on Male Society, forthcoming. **Address:** Department of Otolaryngology-Head & Neck Surgery, School of Medicine, Stanford University, 801 Welch Rd., Stanford, CA 94305-5739, U.S.A. **Online address:** ceoconnell@utopiascientific.org

O'CONNELL, Carol. American (born United States), b. 1947. **Genres:** Novels, Novellas/Short Stories, Mystery/Crime/Suspense. **Career:** Writer. **Publications:** Mallory's Oracle, 1994; The Man Who Cast Two Shadows, 1995; Killing Critics, 1996; Stone Angel, 1997; Judas Child, 1998; Shell Game, 1999; Crime School, 2002; Dead Famous, 2003; Winter House, 2004; Find Me, 2006; Bone by Bone, 2008; The Chalk Girl, 2011. **Address:** Hutchison of Random House UK, 20 Vauxhall Bridge Rd., London, GL SW1V 25A, England.

O'CONNELL, David F. American (born United States), b. 1953. **Genres:** Psychiatry, Medicine/Health, Psychology. **Career:** Alvernia College, instructor in addictions studies, 1981-2000; private practice of psychology, 1989-; Caron Foundation, Impaired Professionals Program, attending psychologist, 1989-, psychological consultant; St. Joseph Hospital, attending psychologist, 1990-; Berks Counseling Center, clinical director; Terraces, staff psychologist; Recovery Centers of America, consulting psychologist; Reading Police Academy, consultant. Writer. **Publications:** (Ed.) Managing the Dually Diagnosed Patient: Current Issues and Clinical Approaches, 1990, 2nd ed., 2002; (ed. with C.N. Alexander) Self-Recovery: Treating Addictions Using Transcendental Meditation and Maharishi Ayur-Veda, 1994; Dual Disorders: Essentials for Assessment and Treatment, 1998; Awakening the Spirit: A Guide to Developing a Spiritual Program in Addictions Recovery, 2003; (with D. Bevvino) Managing your Recovery from Addiction: A Guide for Executives, Senior Managers and Other Professionals, 2007. Contributor to books and journals. **Address:** West Lawn Professional Plz., 25 Stevens Ave., Galen Hall Rd., PO Box 150, West Lawn, PA 19609, U.S.A. **Online address:** doconnell@caronfoundation.org

O'CONNELL, Jack. American (born United States), b. 1959. **Genres:** Novels, Mystery/Crime/Suspense, Literary Criticism And History. **Career:** Writer. **Publications:** QUINSIGAMOND SERIES: Box Nine, 1992; Wireless, 1993; The Skin Palace, 1996; Word Made Flesh, 1998. NOVEL: The Resurrectionist, 2008. Contributor to books and periodicals. **Address:** Sobel Weber Associates Inc., 146 E 19th St., New York, NY 10003-2404, U.S.A.

O'CONNELL, Jennifer. (Jenny O'Connell). American (born United States) **Genres:** Novels, Young Adult Fiction, Romance/Historical. **Career:** Writer. **Publications:** Bachelorette No. 1, 2003; Dress Rehearsal, 2005; Off the Record, 2005; (as Jenny O'Connell) Plan B (young adult novel), 2006; (ed.) Everything I Needed to Know about Being a Girl I Learned from Judy Blume, 2007; (with V. King) The Divorced Girls' Society: Your Initiation into the Club You Never Thought You'd Join, 2007; The Book of Luke, 2007; Insider Dating, 2007; (as Jenny O'Connell) Local Girls: An Island Summer Novel, 2008; (as Jenny O'Connell) Rich Boys: An Island Summer Novel, 2008. **Address:** c/o Author Mail, Publicity Department, Penguin Group, 375 Hudson St., New York, NY 10014, U.S.A. **Online address:** jennifer@jenniferoconnell.com

O'CONNELL, Jenny. *See* **O'CONNELL, Jennifer.**

O'CONNELL, Laurence J. American (born United States), b. 1945. **Genres:** Ethics, Theology/Religion, Sciences. **Career:** Catholic Health Association, vice president for theology, mission and ethics, 1985-89; The Park Ridge Center for Health Faith and Ethics, president and chief executive officer, 1989-; Advocate Health Care, chief ethics officer; Commission of the European Community, international advisor. Writer. **Publications:** (Trans. with A.M. Schneider) W.A. de Pater, Reden van Gott: Reflexionen sur analytischen Philosophie der religioesen Sprache, 1974; (with R. Craig and C.L. Middleton) Ethics Committees: A Practical Approach, 1986. EDITOR: (with E.R. Dubose and R.P. Hamel) A Matter of Principles' Ferment in US Bioethics, 1994; (with R.C. Fox and S.J. Youngner) Organ Transplantation: Meanings and Realities, 1996. Contributor of articles to journals and periodicals. **Address:** 507 W Barry Ave., Chicago, IL 60657-5416, U.S.A. **Online address:** ljo@prchfe.org

O'CONNELL, Marvin R(ichard). American (born United States), b. 1930. **Genres:** Theology/Religion, History, Novels. **Career:** College of St. Thomas, Department of History, instructor, 1958-59, assistant professor, 1959-63, associate professor, 1963-72; University of Notre Dame, Department of History, associate professor, 1972-77, professor, 1977-, chair, 1974-80, now professor emeritus, Undergraduate Program, director, 1993-95. Writer. **Publications:** Dowling Decade in Saint Paul, 1955; Thomas Stapleton and the Counter Reformation, 1964; The Oxford Conspirators: A History of the Oxford Movement 1833-45, 1969; The Counter Reformation, 1559-1610, 1974; McElroy (novel), 1980; John Ireland and the American Catholic Church, 1988; Critics on Trial: An Introduction to the Catholic Modernist Crisis, 1994; Blaise Pascal: Reasons of the Heart, 1997; Edward Sorin, 2001; Pilgrims to the Northland: The Archdiocese of St. Paul, 1840-1962, 2009. Contributor to journals. **Address:** Department of History, University of Notre Dame, 219 O'Shaughnessy Hall, Notre Dame, IN 46556, U.S.A. **Online address:** marvin.r.oconnell.1@nd.edu

O'CONNELL, Rebecca. (Rebecca Tova Ben-Zvi). American (born United States), b. 1968. **Genres:** Young Adult Fiction, Self Help. **Career:** Carnegie Library of Pittsburgh, children's librarian, 1992-, senior librarian. Writer. **Publications:** Myrtle of Willendorf (young adult novel), 2000; The Baby Goes Beep, 2003; (as Rebecca Tova Ben-Zvi) Four Sides, Eight Nights, 2005; Penina Levine is a Hard-Boiled Egg, 2007; Penina Levine is a Potato Pancake, 2008; Danny is Done With Diapers: A Potty ABC, 2010; Done with Diapers!, 2011. Contributor to periodicals. **Address:** BookStop Literary Agency, 67 Meadow View Rd., Orinda, CA 94563, U.S.A. **Online address:** rebecca@rebeccaoconnell.com

O'CONNOR, Alan. Canadian/Irish (born Ireland), b. 1955. **Genres:** Cultural/Ethnic Topics, Literary Criticism And History, Young Adult Fiction. **Career:** Ohio State University, assistant professor of communication, 1987-90; Trent University, Cultural Studies, assistant professor of cultural studies, 1990-, associate professor, professor, director of cultural studies. Writer. **Publications:** Raymond Williams: Writing, Culture, Politics, 1989; Raymond Williams, 2005; Voice of the Mountains: Radio and Anthropology, 2006. EDITOR: Raymond Williams on Television: Selected Writings, 1989; Community Radio in Bolivia: The Miner's Radio Stations, 2004; Punk Record Labels and the Struggle for Autonomy: The Emergence of DIY, 2008. Contributor to periodicals. **Address:** Department of Cultural Studies, Trent University, Scott House, Rm. 202, 300 London St., Peterborough, ON K9H 7P4, Canada. **Online address:** aoconnor@trentu.ca

O'CONNOR, Carol A. American (born United States), b. 1946. **Genres:** Biography, History. **Career:** Phillips Exeter Academy, instructor, 1972-73; Knox College, assistant professor, 1974-77; Utah State University, Department of History, assistant professor, 1977-80, associate professor, 1980-86, professor, 1986-2002, director of graduate studies, 1988-99; Arkansas State University, professor of history, 2002-, College of Humanities and Social Sciences, dean, 2003-09, interim dean, 2009-. Writer and historian. **Publications:** A Sort of Utopia, Scarsdale, 1891-1981, 1983; (ed. C.A. Milner II and M.A. Sandweiss) The Oxford History of the American West, 1994; (with C.A. Milner II) As Big as the West: The Pioneer Life of Granville Stuart, 2009. Contributor to journals and periodicals. **Address:** College of Humanities and Social Sciences, Arkansas State University, State University, AR 72467-1150, U.S.A. **Online address:** coconnor@astate.edu

O'CONNOR, Colin. Australian (born Australia), b. 1928. **Genres:** Engineering. **Career:** Queensland State Public Service, engineer, 1949-53; University of Queensland, lecturer, 1954-70, professor of civil engineering, 1970, dean of civil engineering, 1972-74, now professor emeritus; Royal Military College, external examiner, 1965-67. Writer. **Publications:** Design of Bridge Superstructures, 1971; Design of Bridges: An Historical Study, 1975; Numbers of Engineering Graduates in Queensland, 1977; Spanning Two Centuries: Historic Bridges of Australia, 1985; Roman Bridges, 1993; (with P.A. Shaw) Bridge Loads: An International Perspective, 2000. Contributor to periodicals. **Address:** University of Queensland, Brisbane, St. Lucia, QL 4072, Australia.

O'CONNOR, Erin. American (born United States), b. 1965. **Genres:** History. **Career:** Bridgewater State University, assistant professor of history, CART research fellow. Writer and historian. **Publications:** Gender, Indian, Nation: The Contradictions of Making Ecuador, 1830-1925, 2007; (ed. with L.J. Garofalo) Documenting Latin America, 2011. **Address:** Bridgewater State University, 131 Summer St., Bridgewater, MA 02325, U.S.A. **Online address:** eoconnor@bridgew.edu

O'CONNOR, Francis V(alentine). American (born United States), b. 1937. **Genres:** Poetry, Art/Art History, History, Psychology. **Career:** University of Maryland, assistant professor, 1964-70; Johns Hopkins University, Evening College, assistant professor of art history, 1966-67; National Collection of Fine Arts, Smithsonian Institution, senior visiting research associate, 1970-72; Corcoran School of Art, faculty, 1970-72; American University, faculty, 1970-72; Whitney Museum of American Art Independent Study Program, adjunct professor and tutor, 1973-77; Raphael Research, director, 1973-; Federal Art Patronage Notes, editor, 1974-86; Williams College, Robert Sterling Clark visiting professor of art history, 1990; Institute for the Medical Humanities, Rockefeller fellow, 1991; National Humanities Center, 1994-95. Writer. **Publications:** Federal Art Patronage 1933-1943, 1966; Jackson Pollock, 4 vols., 1978; Federal Support for the Visual Arts: The New Deal and Now, 1969, 2nd ed., 1971; (contrib.) Creative Lives, 1997; Charles Seliger: Redefining Abstract Expressionism, 2002; (contrib.) Edwin Dickinson, 2002; The Mural in America: Wall Painting in the United States from Prehistory to the Present, 2010. EDITOR: The New Deal Art Projects: An Anthology of Memoirs, 1972; (and intro.) Art for the Millions: Essays from the 1930s by Artists and Administrators of the WPA Federal Art Project, 1973; Supplement Number One to the Pollock Catalogue, 1995. **Address:** 250 E 73rd St., Apt. 11C, New York, NY 10021-4310, U.S.A. **Online address:** fvoc@aol.com

O'CONNOR, Laura. American (born United States), b. 1959?. **Genres:** History. **Career:** University of California, associate professor of humanities. Writer. **Publications:** Haunted English: The Celtic Fringe, the British Empire, and De-Anglicization, 2006. Contributor to books and periodicals. **Address:** University of California, 352 Humanities Instructional Bldg., PO Box 2650, Irvine, CA 92697, U.S.A. **Online address:** loconnor@uci.edu

O'CONNOR, Leo F. American (born United States), b. 1936. **Genres:** Literary Criticism And History, Language/Linguistics, Young Adult Fiction. **Career:** Columbia Broadcasting System (CBS) News, administrator, 1959-60; Fairfield University, assistant professor, 1965-74, associate professor, 1975-86, professor, 1987-director of American studies; Town of Fairfield, representative, 1973-74; University of San Diego, visiting professor, 1985-86; Fairfield University, professor of American studies. Writer. **Publications:** Religion in the American Novel, 1984; The Protestant Sensibility in the American Novel, 1992. **Address:** Department of American Studies, Fairfield University, 1073 N Benson Rd., Fairfield, CT 06824, U.S.A. **Online address:** lfoconnor@fairfield.edu

O'CONNOR, Mallory McCane. American (born United States), b. 1943. **Genres:** Archaeology/Antiquities. **Career:** Ohio University, graduate assistant, 1966-69, instructor in art history, 1969; University of Florida, instructor in humanities, 1972-73, instructor in art history, 1973-78, Office of Development, staff writer, 1982-83, visiting assistant professor, 1986-87, University Gallery, assistant director, 1987-88; freelance writer, 1978-; Business to Business Magazine, feature writer, 1983-84; Thomas Center Gallery, Department of Cultural and Nature Operations, visual arts coordinator and director, 1985-

94; Nova University, instructor, 1985; Santa Fe Community College, Santa Fe Gallery, chief curator, 1994-99, associate professor of art history, 1994-2005, professor emeritus, 2005-; O'Connor L.L.C, president and founder, 2010-. **Publications:** Lost Cities of the Ancient Southeast, 1995; (with G. Monroe) Florida's American Heritage River: Images from the St. Johns Region, 2009. Contributor to books and periodicals. **Address:** Santa Fe Community College, Bldg. M-147, A-228, 3000 NW 83rd St., Gainesville, FL 32606-6210, U.S.A. **Online address:** mallory.oconnor@sfcc.edu

O'CONNOR, Pat. Irish (born Ireland), b. 1950. **Genres:** Sociology, Women's Studies And Issues, Medicine/Health. **Career:** Economic and Social Research Institute, research assistant, 1970-73; University of London, Bedford College, research officer, 1973-79, Royal Holloway College, research officer, 1973-79; National Institute for Social Work, Social Research Unit, project director, 1979-82; Waterford Institute of Technology, lecturer and course director, 1982-92; University of Limerick, lecturer in sociology, 1992-2000, professor of sociology and social policy, 1997-, course director, 1992-97, College of Humanities, dean, 2000-07, Faculty of Arts, Humanities and Social Sciences, dean, 2008-. Writer. **Publications:** (With I. Sinclair, A.Vicery and D. Crosbie) Bridging Two Worlds: Social Work with the Elderly, 1989; Friendships between Women: A Critical Review, 1992; The Barriers to Women's Promotion in the Health Boards, 1995; Emerging Voices: Women in Contemporary Irish Society, 1998; Irish Children and Teenagers in a Changing World, 2008. Contributor to journals. **Address:** Department of Sociology, University of Limerick, National Technological Pk., Limerick, LI 1, Ireland. **Online address:** patrick.oconnor@ul.ie

O'CONNOR, Patricia W. American (born United States), b. 1931. **Genres:** Literary Criticism And History, Theatre, Plays/Screenplays, Translations, inspirational/Motivational Literature, Romance/Historical. **Career:** University of Cincinnati, instructor, 1962-63, assistant professor, professor, 1963-83, director of University of Cincinnati programs in Spain, 1966-69, Department of Romance Languages, acting head, 1976-77, Charles Phelps Taft professor of romance languages and literatures, through 1983, now professor emeritus; Estreno magazine, editor. **Publications:** Women in the Theatre of Gregorio Martinez Sierra, 1966; Gregorio andMaría Martinez Sierra: Cronica de una colaboracion, 1977; Plays of Protest from the Franco Era, 1981; Contemporary Spanish Theatre: The Social Comedies of the Sixties, 1983; Gregorio y Maria Martinez Sierra: cronica de una colaboracion, 1987; Dramaturgas españolas de hoy: Unaintroducción, 1988; (trans.) A. Diosdado, Yours for the Asking, 1995; Antonio Buero Vallejo en sus espejos, 1996; Mujeres sobre mujeres: teatrobreve español: One-Act Spanish Plays by Women about Women, 1998; (trans.) Story of a Stairway, The Basement Window, Dawn, 2003; Mito yrealidad de una dramaturga española: María Martínez Sierra, 2003; Mujeres sobre mujeres en los albores del siglo XXI: teatro breve español=One-act Plays by Women about Women in the Early Years of the 21st Century, 2006. EDITOR: (with A.M. Pasquariello) El traguluz, 1977; (with A.M. Pasquariello) Contemporary Spanish Theater: Seven One-Act Plays, 1980; Plays of the New Democratic Spain (1975-1990), 1992; (trans.) A. Buero-Vallejo, Antonio Buero-Vallejo: Four Tragedies of Conscience (1949-1999), 2008; Elena Cánovas y Las Yeses: teatro carcelario, teatro liberador: colección de ensayos con dos obras teatrales "Libertas, libertatis" y "El más preciado bien que nos dieron los cielos", 2009; (trans.) Patenting Destiny: A Tale of Two Shoes (Ventanilla de Patentes), 2010. **Address:** Department of Romance Languages and Literatures, University of Cincinnati, 714 Old Chem, PO Box 210377, Cincinnati, OH 45221-0377, U.S.A. **Online address:** pat.oconnor@uc.edu

O'CONNOR, Rebecca K. American (born United States), b. 1971. **Genres:** Romance/Historical, Young Adult Non-fiction, Young Adult Fiction, Novels, Natural History, Autobiography/Memoirs. **Career:** Grace's Attorney Services, owner, 1993-98; Natural Encounters, bird trainer and supervisor, 1998-2001; Living Desert, animal trainer and development associate, 2001-04; Girl Scouts, development associate and director of development, 2004-08; Ducks Unlimited, director of development, 2008-. Writer. **Publications:** Falcon's Return (romance fiction), 2002; Endangered Animals and Habitats (young adult nonfiction), 2002; Frogs and Toads, 2003; Owls, 2003; Acid Rain, 2004; (with D. Myers) Uniquely Nevada, 2004; Is there Life After Death?, 2005; (ed.) How Should the World Respond to Natural Disasters?, 2006; A Parrot for Life, 2007; Finches, 2008; Lift (memoir), 2009; Lories & Lorikeets, 2011. **Address:** c/o Dawn G. Stuart, Terra Communications Inc., 1300 NE 8th St., Bend, OR 97701, U.S.A. **Online address:** rebecca@rebeccakoconnor.com

O'CONNOR, Richard. American (born United States) **Genres:** Medicine/Health, Self Help, Psychology. **Career:** Northwest Center for Family Service and Mental Health, executive director. Writer. **Publications:** Undoing Depression: What Therapy Doesn't Teach You and Medication Can't Give You, 1997, 2nd ed., 2010; Active Treatment of Depression, 2001; Undoing Perpetual Stress, 2005; Happy at Last: The Thinking Person's Guide to Finding Joy, 2008; Happiness: The Thinking Person's Guide, 2009. **Address:** 117 Main St., Canaan, CT 06018, U.S.A. **Online address:** hapatlast@gmail.com

O'CONNOR, Robert. American (born United States), b. 1959. **Genres:** Novels, Plays/Screenplays. **Career:** Syracuse University, university fellow, 1982-84, instructor, 1985-91; State University of New York College, lecturer in fiction, drama and literature, 1985-, associate professor; Auburn Correctional Facility, instructor, 1990-92. Writer. **Publications:** Buffalo Soldiers, 1993; Army Go Home, 2002. **Address:** Department of English, State University of New York, P324 Poucher Hall, 327 Campus Ctr., 7060 Rte. 104, Oswego, NY 13126-3599, U.S.A. **Online address:** robert.oconnor@oswego.edu

O'CONNOR, Stephen. American (born United States), b. 1952. **Genres:** Adult Non-fiction, Novellas/Short Stories. **Career:** Columbia University, adjunct professor of creative writing, professor in fine arts program, 2002-, MFA Program, teacher; Sarah Lawrence College, adjunct professor of creative writing, professor in fine arts program, 2002-; City University of New York, Lehman College, adjunct professor of creative writing; New School University, adjunct professor of creative writing; Vista College, creative writing teacher; Money and Esquire, fact checker and reporter; Rutgers University, adjunct professor; American University, professor; ABC News, desk assistant; Easter Seals Center, teacher; T&W, director. **Publications:** ISBN 0-943568-01-3, 1983; Rescue (short stories), 1989; Will My Name Be Shouted Out?: Reaching Inner City Students through the Power of Writing, 1996; Orphan Trains: The Story of Charles Loring Brace and the Children He Saved and Failed, 2001; Here Comes Another Lesson: Stories, 2010. Contributor of articles to newspapers and periodicals. **Address:** Witherspoon Associates Inc., 235 E 31st St., New York, NY 10016-6302, U.S.A. **Online address:** smoconn@aol.com

O'CONNOR, Timothy Edward. American (born United States), b. 1951. **Genres:** History. **Career:** College of St. Thomas, administrative assistant, 1981-82; University of Northern Iowa, assistant professor, 1982-87, associate professor, 1987-92, professor of history, 1992-, leader of study tour of the U.S.S.R., 1989. Writer. **Publications:** The Politics of Soviet Culture: Anatolii Lunacharskii, 1983; Diplomacy and Revolution: G.V. Chicherin and Soviet Foreign Affairs, 1918-1930, 1988; The Engineer of Revolution: L.B. Krasin and the Bolsheviks, 1870-1926, 1992. Contributor of articles to journals. **Address:** Department of History, University of Northern Iowa, 330 Seerley Hall, 1227 W 27th St., Cedar Falls, IA 50614, U.S.A. **Online address:** timothy.oconnor@uni.edu

O CUILLEANAIN, Cormac. (Cormac Millar). Irish (born Ireland), b. 1950. **Genres:** Literary Criticism And History, Translations, Novels. **Career:** Institute of Public Administration, editor, 1977-78; Trinity College, lecturer in Italian, 1978-79; Ward River Press, editor, 1979-83; National University of Ireland, University College, lecturer in Italian, 1983-86; Trinity College, lecturer in Italian, 1986-97, senior lecturer, 1997-, associate professor and head of Italian, 2006-; Foundation for Italian Studies, board of director, 1986-; Irish Translators' Association, chairperson, 1986-91; Irish Writers' Centre, chairperson, 1991-93. **Publications:** Religion and the Clergy in Boccaccio's Decameron, 1984. AS CORMAC MILLAR: An Irish Solution, 2004; The Grounds, 2006. TRANSLATOR: R. Gervaso, Cagliostro, 1974; P. Valpreda, The Valpreda Papers, 1975; E. Cantarella, Bisexuality in the Ancient World, 1992; Boccaccio, Decameron, 2004. EDITOR: (with E.G. Haywood and contrib.) Italian Storytellers: Essays on Italian Narrative Literature, 1989; (with J.C. Barnes) Dante and the Middle Ages: Literary and Historical Essays, 1995; (with M. Cronin) The Languages of Ireland, 2003; (with C. Salvadori and J. Scattergood) Italian Culture: Interactions, Transpositions, Translations, 2006; (with E. Ni Chuilleanain and D. Parris) Translation and Censorship, 2008. Work represented in anthologies. Contributor of articles, translations, and reviews to language and Italian studies journals. **Address:** Department of Italian, Trinity College, Rm. 4087, Arts Bldg., Dublin, 2, Ireland. **Online address:** cocullnn@tcd.ie

ODAGA, Asenath (Bole). Kenyan (born Kenya), b. 1937. **Genres:** Novels, Novellas/Short Stories, Children's Fiction, Plays/Screenplays, Language/Linguistics, Literary Criticism And History, Mythology/Folklore, Reference,

Reference. **Career:** Church Missionary Society Teacher Training College, teacher, 1957-58; Kambare School, teacher, 1957-58; Butere Girls School, teacher, 1959-60; Nyakach Girls School, founder and headmistress, 1961-63; Kenya Railways, assistant secretary, 1964; Kenya Dairy Board, assistant secretary, 1965-67; Kenya Library Services, secretary, 1968; East African Standard Newspaper, advertising assistant, 1969-70; Kerr Downey and Selby Safaris, advertising assistant and office manager, 1969-70; Christian Churches Educational Association, Curriculum Development Program, assistant director, 1974-75; University of Nairobi, Institute of African Studies, research fellow, 1976-81; freelance writer, 1982-; Lake Publishers & Enterprises Ltd., founder and managing director, 1982-; Future in Africa, country coordinator, 1990-. **Publications:** CHILDREN'S FICTION: Jande's Ambition, 1966; The Secret of the Monkey Rock, 1966; The Diamond Ring, 1967; The Angry Flames, 1968; Sweets and Sugar Cane, 1969; The Villager's Son, 1971; Kip on the Farm, 1972; Kip on the Coast, 1977; Kip Goes to the City, 1977; The Rag Ball, 1987; Munde Goes to the Market, 1987; Munde and His Friends, 1987; The Silver Cup, 1988; A Night on a Tree, 1992; (ed.) Why the Hyena Has a Crooked Neck, 1992; The Cloud Boy, 1994. ADULT FICTION: The Shade Changes, 1984; The Storm, 1986; Between the Years, 1987; A Bridge in Time, 1987; A Taste of Life, 1988; Love Potion, A Reed on the Roof, Block Ten, with Other Stories, 1988; Riana, 1989; Endless Road, 1995; Rosa, Love Ash and Other Stories, 1995. FOLKTALES: The Hare's Blanket and Other Tales, 1967; Poko Nyar Mugumba, 1978; Thu Tinda: Stories from Kenya, 1980; The Two Friends, 1981; Kenyan Folktales, 1981; Ogilo nungo piny kirom, 1983; Nyamgondho the Son of Ombare and Other Luo Stories, 1986; Weche, Sigendigi Timbe Luo Moko, 1987; Story Time, 1987; The Honey River, 1994; Secrets, 1999; Jood Ogango, 1999; Wat Ng'ue, forthcoming. NON-FICTION: Nyathini Koa e Nyuolne Nyaka Higni Adek, 1976; Oral Literature: A School Certificate Course, 1982. PLAYS: Simbi Nyaima, 1982. OTHERS: (ed. with D. Kirui and D. Crippen) God, Myself and Others (Christian stories), 1976; Sigendini gi Timbe Luo Moko, 1982; Block Ten, with Other Stories, 1982; Look and Learn, 1982; My Home (reader), 1983; Yesterday's Today: A Study of Oral Literature, 1984; Literature for Children and Young People in Kenya, 1985, Luo Sayings, 1991; Luo-English Dictionary, 1991; Luo-English Phrases, 1993; English-Dholuo Dictionary, 1997; Holding the Center, 1998; The Night Runners, 1998; (ed. with H.A. Shiloli) The Survivors, 2000; (ed. with H.A. Shiloli) Moving to the Centre, 2000; Something for Nothing, 2001; Simbi Nyaima gi sigendini Luo moko, 2002; Kisera, 2002; Nyangi gi Otis, 2004; The Luo Oral Literature: Educational Values of their Narratives, 2010. Contributor to periodicals. **Address:** Lake Publishers & Enterprises Ltd., Wananchi Enterprise Ctr., Jomo Kenyatta Hwy., PO Box 1743-4100, Kisumu, 40100, Kenya.

O'DALY, William. American (born United States), b. 1951. **Genres:** Poetry, Translations, Young Adult Fiction, Literary Criticism And History. **Career:** Spectrum, assistant editor, 1972; Willow Springs, editor, 1979-86; Eastern Washington University, assistant professor, 1981-86; Microsoft Corp., senior instructional designer, 1987-96; Antioch University, adjunct faculty, 1988-95. **Publications:** POEMS: The Whale in the Web, 1979. TRANSLATOR OF POEMS BY PABLO NERUDA: Still Another Day, 1984, 2nd ed., 2005; The Separate Rose, 1985, 2nd ed., 2005; Winter Garden, 1986, 2nd ed., 2002; The Sea and the Bells, 1988, 2nd ed., 2001; The Yellow Heart, 1990, 2nd ed., 2002; The Book of Questions, 1991, 2nd ed., 2001; Hands of Day, 2008; World's End, 2009. **Address:** 2129 Stonebrook Ct., Auburn, CA 95603, U.S.A. **Online address:** wodaly@mindsync.com

O'DAY, Alan (Earl). British/American (born United States) **Genres:** Area Studies, History, Bibliography. **Career:** University of Maryland, lecturer in history, 1969-70; University of Newcastle, junior research officer, 1970-71; University of Salford, research assistant, 1971-72; University of East Anglia, lecturer in economic and social history, 1972-74; University of Giessen, lecturer in American studies, 1974-76; University of North London, lecturer, 1976-77, senior lecturer in history, 1977-2001; Concordia University, adjunct professor, 1992-94; University of Oxford, Greyfriars Hall, senior fellow in history and politics, senior associate, St Bede's Hall, fellow in modern history, 2001-; Rothermere American Institute, visiting fellow, 2002-03; St. John's, visiting fellow; Wolfson College, visiting fellow; St. Antony's, visiting fellow; Mansfield College, visiting fellow; University of Durham, visiting fellow; University of Edinburgh, Institute for Advanced Study in the Humanities, visiting fellow; University of London, School of Advanced Study, visiting fellow; Queen's University, Institute of Irish Studies, senior visiting fellow; Trinity College, visiting professor. Writer. **Publications:** The English Face of Irish Nationalism: Parnellite Involvement in British Politics, 1880-86, 1977, 2nd ed., 1993; Parnell and the First Home Rule Episode, 1986; (and intro.) Reactions to Irish Nationalism, 1865-1914, 1987; Charles Stewart Parnell, 1998; Irish Home Rule, 1867-1921, 1998; (with N.C. Fleming) Longman Handbook of Modern Irish History Since 1800, 2005; (with N.C. Fleming) Charles Stewart Parnell and His Times, 2011. EDITOR: The Edwardian Age, 1979; (with Y. Alexander) Terrorism in Ireland, 1984; (with Y. Alexander) Ireland's Terrorist Dilemma, 1986; (with T.R. Gourvish and contrib.) Later Victorian Britain, 1988; (with Y. Alexander) Ireland's Terrorist Trauma, 1989; (and intro.) A Survey of the Irish in England, 1872, 1990; (with T.R. Gourvish) Britain since 1945, 1991; (with D.G. Boyce and contrib.) Parnell in Perspective, 1991; (with Y. Alexander) The Irish Terrorism Experience, 1991; (with A. Kappeler and F. Adanir) Comparative Studies on Governments and Non-Dominant Ethnic Groups in Europe, 1850-1940, vol. VI: The Formation of National Elites, 1992; (with J. Stevenson) Irish Historical Documents since 1800, 1992; Dimensions of Irish Terrorism, 1994; Government and Institutions in the Post-1832 United Kingdom, 1994; (and contrib.) Terrorism's Laboratory: The Case of Northern Ireland, 1995; Government and Institutions in the Post-1832 United Kingdom, 1995; (with D.G. Noyce) Making of Modern Irish History, 1996; Political Violence in Northern Ireland, 1997; (with D.G. Bryce) Defenders of the Union, 2001; Cyberterrorism, 2004; War on Terrorism, 2004; Weapons of Mass Destruction and Terrorism, 2004; Dimensions of Terrorism, 2004; (with D.G. Boyce) Ireland in Transition, 1867-1921, 2004; (with D.G. Bryce) Ulster Crisis: 1885-1921, 2006; (with N.C. Fleming) Ireland and Anglo-Irish relations since 1800: Critical Essays, 2008; (with D.G. Boyce) Gladstone And Ireland: Politics, Religion and Nationality in the Victorian Age, 2010. Work represented in anthologies. Contributor of articles and reviews to periodicals. **Address:** 6 York Pl., Oxford, OX OX4 1YL, England.

ODBER (DE BAUBETA), Patricia (Anne). British/Scottish (born Scotland), b. 1953. **Genres:** Language/Linguistics, Literary Criticism And History, Women's Studies And Issues, Translations, Autobiography/Memoirs, Business/Trade/Industry. **Career:** University of Glasgow, lecturer in Portuguese, 1978-80; University of Birmingham, lecturer in Portuguese and linguistics, 1981-, senior lecturer in Hispanic studies, 1996-, tutor and director of Portuguese studies, convenor, academic adviser to international students, head of department, director of the cátedra gil vicente. Educator and writer. **Publications:** Ingles: Curso Basico para Portugueses, 1990; Anticlerical Satire in Medieval Portuguese Literature, 1992; Igreja, Pecado, e Sátira Socialna Idade Média Portuguesa, 1997; Anthology in Portugal: A New Approach to the History of Portuguese Literature in the Twentieth Century, 2007. EDITOR: (with T.J. Dadson and R.J. Oakley) New Frontiers in Hispanic and Luso-Brazilian Scholarship: Como se Fue el Maestro for Derek W. Lomax, in Memoriam, 1994; (with M. Coulthard) Theoretical Issues and Practical Cases in Portuguese-English Translation, 1996; (with M. Coulthard) The Knowledges of the Translator: From Literary Interpretation to Machine Classification, 1996; Actas del XII Congreso de la Asociacion Internacional de Hispanistas, 1998; (with D. Flitter) Ondas do Mar de Vigo, 1998; (with J. Cannon and R. Warner) Advertising and Identity in Europe: The I of the Beholder, 2000; (trans. with I.R. Carlsen) The Creation of the World, 2001; The Anthology in Portugal. Selected Essays, 2009. Contributor to books and journals. **Address:** The Department of Hispanic Studies, University of Birmingham, Edgbaston Campus, Birmingham, WM B15 2TT, England. **Online address:** p.a.odber-de-baubeta@bham.ac.uk

O'DEA, Brian. Canadian (born Canada), b. 1948. **Genres:** Novels. **Career:** CTV, executive producer, 2006. Writer. **Publications:** High: Confessions of a Pot Smuggler, 2006; High: Confessions of an International Drug Smuggler, 2009. **Address:** Flamingo Neck Pictures, 1400 Kingston Rd., Toronto, ON M1N 1R3, Canada. **Online address:** brianodea@brianodea.com

O'DELL, Carol D. American (born United States) **Genres:** Autobiography/Memoirs. **Career:** Hot Psychology Magazine, health editor. Educator. **Publications:** Mothering Mother: A Daughter's Humorous and Heartbreaking Memoir, 2007, 2nd ed., Mothering Mother: A Daughter's Humorous and Heartbreaking Memoir: An Unflinchingly Honest Look at Family Caregiving, 2009. Contributor to magazines, periodicals, and journals. **Address:** 96280 Light Wind Dr., Fernandina Beach, FL 32034, U.S.A. **Online address:** writecarolodell@gmail.com

ODELL, George H. *See* Obituaries.

O'DELL, Holly. American (born United States) **Genres:** Romance/Historical. **Career:** Writer. **Publications:** Spin Control, 2006. Contributor to periodicals. **Address:** Avalon Books, 160 Madison Ave., Ste. 5, New York, NY 10016-5412, U.S.A. **Online address:** hollyodell1@gmail.com

ODELL, Jonathan. American (born United States), b. 1951?. **Genres:** Novels. **Career:** Sanderson Farms, sales manager, 1975-77; Development Consultants, trainer and consultant, 1977-79; Conklin Co., trainer, 1980-81, vice president of human resources, 1982-86; Jonathan Consulting Group, founder and president, 1986-89; Institute for Authentic Dialogue, co-founder, 2003-04. Novelist, essayist and lecturer. **Publications:** The View from Delphi: A Novel, 2004; The Healing, 2012; The Last Safe Place, forthcoming; (with J. Kuether) Just Call Me A Dinosaur, forthcoming. **Address:** c/o Author Mail, MacAdam/Cage Publishing, 155 Sansome St., Ste. 520, San Francisco, CA 94104-3615, U.S.A. **Online address:** jon.odell@earthlink.net

ODELL, Peter R(andon). Dutch/British (born England), b. 1930. **Genres:** Earth Sciences, Economics, Geography, International Relations/Current Affairs. **Career:** Shell Intl., economist, 1958-61; University of London, London School of Economics and Political Science, lecturer in economic geography, 1961-68, Lord Stamp lecturer, 1976-; Erasmus University, professor of economic geography and director of economic geography institute, 1968-, now professor emeritus of international energy studies. Energy consultant and writer. **Publications:** An Economic Geography of Oil, 1963; Oil: The New Commanding Height, 1965; Natural Gas in Western Europe: A Case Study in the Economic Geography of Energy Resources, 1969; Oil and World Power: Background to the Oil Crisis, 1970, 8th ed., 1986; (with D.A. Preston) Economics and Societies in Latin America: A Geographical Interpretation, 1973, 2nd ed., 1978; Energy Needs and Resources, 1974, 2nd ed., 1977; (with K.E. Rosing) The North Sea Oil Province: An Attempt to Simulate Its Exploration and Exploitation, 1975; The West European Energy Economy: The Case for Self-Sufficiency, 1976; (with K.E. Rosing) Optimal Developments of North Sea Oilfields, 1976; (with L. Vallenilla) The Pressures of Oil: A Strategy for Economic Revival, 1978; British Oil Policy, 1980; The Development of Britain's Offshore Oil Resources: A Radical Alternative, 1980; (with K.E. Rosing) The Future of Oil, 1980, 2nd ed., 1983; (with J.A. van Reyn) Energie: Geen Probleem?, 1981; (ed. with J. Rees) The International Oil Industry: An Interdisciplinary Perspective, 1987; Global and Regional Energy Supplies: Recent Fictions and Fallacies Revisited, 1991; Energy in Europe: Resources and Choices, 1998; Fossil Fuel Resources in the 21st Century, 1999; Oil and Gas, Crises and Controversies, 1961-2000, vol. I: Global Issues, 2001, vol. II: Europe's Entanglement, 2002; Why Carbon Fuels will Dominate the 21st Century's Global Energy Economy, 2004. **Address:** Erasmus University, Burgemeester Oudlaan 50, PO Box 1738, Rotterdam, 3062 PA, Netherlands. **Online address:** peter@odell.u-net.com

ODELL, Robin Ian. British (born England), b. 1935. **Genres:** Criminology/True Crime, Environmental Sciences/Ecology, Mystery/Crime/Suspense, Young Adult Fiction, Horror. **Career:** University of Southampton, School of Education, Department of Zoology, laboratory technician, 1951-54, assistant museum curator, 1956-62; University Institute of Education-Southampton, technical demonstrator, 1962-68; Water Research Centre, publications manager, 1968-; Water and Environmental Manager Magazine, editor, 1996-2001. **Publications:** Jack the Ripper in Fact and Fiction, 1965; (comp. with T. Barfield) Humanist Glossary, 1967; Crime and Punishment, 1975; Exhumation of a Murder, 1975; (with J.H.H. Gaute) Murderers' Who's Who, 1979, (with W. Gregg) new ed. as Murderers' Row: An International Murderers' Who's Who, 2006; (with J.H.H. Gaute) Lady Killers, 1980; (with J.H.H. Gaute) Murder Whatdunit, 1982; (with J.H.H. Gaute) Murder Whereabouts, 1986; (with C. Wilson) Jack the Ripper: Summing Up and Verdict, 1987; (with C. Berry-Dee) Dad Help Me Please, 1990; (with J.H.H. Gaute) The New Murderers' Who's Who, 1991; (with C. Berry-Dee) The Long Drop, 1993; Landmarks in Twentieth Century Murder, 1995; International Murderers Who's Who, 1996; Ripperology: A Study of the World's First Serial Killer and A Literary Phenomenon, 2006; (with C. Berry-Dee) Prime Suspect: The True Story of John Cannan, the Only Man Police Want to Investigate for the Murder of Suzy Lamplugh, 2007; (and ed.) The Mammoth Book of Bizarre Crimes, 2010. **Address:** 11 Red House Dr., Sonning Common, Reading, BR RG4 9NT, England. **Online address:** bobodel@compuserve.com

O'DELL, Tawni. American (born United States), b. 1964?. **Genres:** Documentaries/Reportage, Novels, Young Adult Fiction, Women's Studies And Issues. **Career:** Writer. **Publications:** NOVELS: Back Roads, 1999; Coal Run, 2000; Sister Mine, 2007; Fragile Beasts, 2010. Contributor to periodicals. Works appear in anthologies. **Address:** c/o Author Mail, Penguin Putnam, 375 Hudson St., New York, NY 10014, U.S.A. **Online address:** todell@literati.net

ODELL-SCOTT, David W. American (born United States), b. 1953. **Genres:** Demography. **Career:** Vanderbilt University, Department of Philosophy, graduate teaching assistant, 1980-82, adjunct instructor, 1984-90; Belmont University, Department of Philosophy, adjunct instructor, 1985-87, assistant professor, 1985-87; Fisk University, Department of Philosophical and Religious Studies, assistant professor, 1987-90, chair, 1989-90; Kent State University, Department of Philosophy, assistant professor, 1990-95, associate professor, 1995-2005, chair 2003-, professor, 2005-, Religion Studies Program, coordinator, 1996-; Ohio Pluralism Project, co-founder and co-director. Writer. **Publications:** A Post-Patriarchal Christology, 1991; Paul's Critique of Theocracy: A/Theocracy in Corinthians and Galatians, 2003; (ed.) Democracy and Religion: Free Exercise and Diverse Visions, 2004; (ed.) Reading Romans with Contemporary Philosophers and Theologians, 2007. Contributor to books. **Address:** Department of Philosophy, Kent State University, 320 Bowman Hall, Kent, OH 44242-0001, U.S.A. **Online address:**

ODENWALD, Neil G. American (born United States), b. 1935. **Genres:** Horticulture, Homes/Gardens. **Career:** Louisiana State University, Louisiana Cooperative Extension Service, specialist, 1959-72, professor of landscape architecture, 1972-, School of Landscape Architecture, director, chairman, professor emeritus of landscape architecture. Writer. **Publications:** Plants for Designers, 1980; (with J.R. Turner) Plants for the South: A Guide for Landscape Design, 1980; Southern Plants, 1985; (with J.R. Turner) Identification, Selection and Use of Southern Plants for Landscape Design, 1987, 4th ed., 2006; (with J. Feltwell) Live Oak Splendor: Gardens of the Mississippi from Natchez to New Orleans, 1992; (with C.F. Fryling, Jr. and T.E. Pope) Attracting Birds to Southern Gardens, 1993; (with C.F. Fryling, Jr. and T.E. Pope) Plants for American Landscapes, 1996; (with W.C. Welch) The Bountiful Flower Garden, 2000. **Address:** School of Landscape Architecture, Louisiana State University, 302 Design Bldg., Baton Rouge, LA 70803, U.S.A. **Online address:** ngoden@aol.com

ODENWALD, Sten F. American (born United States), b. 1956?. **Genres:** Astronomy, Sciences, Physics. **Career:** NASA IMAGE Satellite Program, education and public outreach manager. Writer. **Publications:** Astronomy Café: 365 Questions and Answers from Ask the Astronomer, 1998; The 23rd Cycle: Learning to Live with a Stormy Star, 2001; Patterns in the Void: Why Nothing is Important, 2002; Concepts in Space Science, 2002; Back to the Astronomy Café: More Questions and Answers About the Cosmos from Ask the Astronomer, 2003; Stepping Through the Stargate, 2004. Contributor to periodicals. **Address:** NASA Goddard Space Flight Center, PO Box 672, Greenbelt, MD 20771-0024, U.S.A. **Online address:** odenwald@bolero.gsfc.nasa.gov

ODERMAN, Stuart (Douglas). American (born United States), b. 1940. **Genres:** Film, Music, Humor/Satire, Biography, Autobiography/Memoirs. **Career:** Newark School System, writer and teacher, through 2005, retired. **Publications:** Roscoe Fatty Arbuckle: A Biography of the Silent Film Comedian, 1887-1933, 1994; Lillian Gish: A Life on Stage and Screen, 2000; Talking to the Piano Player: Silent Film Stars, Writers and Directors Remember, 2005; The Keystone Krowd: Mack, Mabel, the Kops and the Girls (1908/1915), 2007. Contributor of articles to periodicals. **Address:** 243 S Harrison St., Apt. 9H, East Orange, NJ 07018, U.S.A.

ODETS, Walt (Whitman). American (born United States), b. 1947. **Genres:** Medicine/Health, Psychology, Social Sciences. **Career:** Gay Men's Health Crisis (GMHC), consultant; Shanti Project, consultant. Writer. **Publications:** Love in the Shadow: Being HIV-Negative in the Age of AIDS, 1995; (ed. with M. Shernoff) The Second Decade of AIDS: A Mental Health Practice Handbook, 1995; In the Shadow of the Epidemic: Being HIV-Negative in the Age of AIDS, 1995. Contributor to books and periodicals. **Address:** 2904 Florence St., Berkeley, CA 94705-2004, U.S.A. **Online address:** odets@comcast.net

ODHIAMBO, David Nandi. Canadian/Kenyan (born Kenya), b. 1965. **Genres:** Poetry, Novels, Children's Fiction, Literary Criticism And History. **Career:** Banff Centre for the Arts, resident at writing studio, 1994, 1996; Ontario Human Rights Commission, mitigation officer, 1989; Carleton University, researcher and writer for CKDU-Radio, 1990; United Nations Association, Africa 2000 Program, educator, 1991-93, Africa Focus: Model U.N.

for Youth, coordinator and publicist, 1992; Co-Development Canada, coordinator and facilitator of youth dialogue on race relations, 1992; Alternate Shelter Society, youth care worker, 1995-96; Vingee and Associates, youth care worker, 1998. Writer. **Publications:** Diss/ed Banded Nation, 1998; Kipligat's Chance, 2003; The Reverend's Apprentice, 2008. Contributor of articles to periodicals. **Address:** c/o Author Mail, Penguin Books Canada Ltd., 90 Eglinton Ave. E, Ste. 700, Toronto, ON M4P 2Y3, Canada. **Online address:** dvdnandi@gmail.com

O'DOHERTY, Malachi. Irish (born Ireland), b. 1951. **Genres:** Documentaries/Reportage, Theology/Religion, Autobiography/Memoirs, Social Sciences. **Career:** British Broadcasting Corp., writer; Belfast Telegraph, columnist; Fortnight magazine, managing editor; Audio blog Arts Talk, producer and presenter. **Publications:** The Trouble with Guns: Republican Strategy and the Provisional IRA, 1998; I Was Teenage Catholic, 2003; The Telling Year: Belfast 1972, 2007; Empty Pulpits: Ireland's Retreat From Religion, 2008; Under His Roof, 2009. Contributor of political articles to periodicals. **Address:** 62 N Parade, Belfast, BF BT7 2GJ, Northern Ireland. **Online address:** malachi@malachiodoherty.com

O'DONNELL, Brennan (Patrick). American (born United States), b. 1958. **Genres:** Literary Criticism And History, Education. **Career:** Pennsylvania State University, John W. White fellow, 1981-82; University of North Carolina, Pogue fellow, 1981-83; Loyola College, assistant professor of English, 1987-93, associate professor, 1994-2001, professor of English, 2001-04; Fordham College, dean and professor of English, 2004-09; Manhattan College, president and professor of English, 2009-. Writer. **Publications:** Numerous Verse: A Guide to the Stanzas and Metrical Structures of Wordsworth's Poetry, 1989; The Passion of Meter: A Study of Wordsworth's Metrical Art, 1995; (co-editor) The Work of Andre Dubus, 2002. Contributor of articles to books and periodicals. **Address:** Office of the President, Manhattan College, 4513 Manhattan College Pkwy., Bronx, NY 10471, U.S.A. **Online address:** brennan.odonnell@manhattan.edu

O'DONNELL, Edward T. American (born United States), b. 1963?. **Genres:** Business/Trade/Industry. **Career:** City University of New York, Hunter College, associate professor of history, 1995-2001; College of the Holy Cross, associate professor of history, 2001-; Fordham University, visiting associate professor, 2001. Writer and historian. **Publications:** 1001 Things Everyone Should Know about Irish American History, 2002; Ship Ablaze: The Tragedy of the Steamboat General Slocum, 2003; (with J. Keene and S. Cornell) Visions of America: A History of the United States, 2009. FORTHCOMING: The Ethnic Crucible: New York City's Lower East Side, 1820-2000; Talisman of a Lost Hope; The Road Well Traveled: 101 Stories of Wisdom, Achievement, and Inspiration from the American Past; Henry George for Mayor! Irish Nationalism, Labor Radicalism, and Independent Politics in Gilded Age New York City; Land of Promise. Contributor to books and periodicals. **Address:** Department of History, College of the Holy Cross, O'Kane 361, 1 College St., Worcester, MA 01610-2322, U.S.A. **Online address:** eodonnell@holycross.edu

O'DONNELL, Guillermo A. Argentine (born Argentina) **Genres:** International Relations/Current Affairs, Politics/Government. **Career:** Universidad d'El Salvador, professor of political science, 1971-75; Princeton University, Institute for Advance Study, fellow, 1974-77; University of Michigan, visiting professor, 1974; IUPERJ, senior researcher, 1978-80; CEBRAP, senior researcher, 1980-83; University of Notre Dame, Helen Kellogg professor of government, 1983-, Helen Kellogg Institute for International Studies, academic director, 1983-88, senior fellow, now professor emeritus; University of California, visiting professor, 1983. Writer. **Publications:** Modernization and Bureaucratic-Authoritarianism: Studies in South American Politics, 1972, 3rd ed., 1998; Reflexiones sobre las tendencias generales de cambio en el estado burocrático-autoritario, 1975; Estado y alianzas en la Argentina, 1956-1976, 1976; Y a mi, que me importa?: notas sobre sociabilidad y política en Argentina y Brasil, 1984; Bureaucratic Authoritarianism: Argentina 1966-1973, in Comparative Perspective, 1988; Contrapuntos, 1997; Counterpoints, 1999; Disonancias, 2007; Dissonances, 2007; Catacumbas, 2008; Democracy, Agency and the State: Theory with Comparative Intent, 2010; (co-author) Democracia Delegativa, 2011. EDITOR: (with P. Schmitter and L. Whitehead) Transitions from Authoritarian Rule: Prospects for Democracy, 4 vols., 1986; (with A. Foxley and M.S. McPherson) Development, Democracy, and the Art of Trespassing: Essays in Honor of Albert O. Hirschman, 1986; (with F.W. Reis) A Democracia no Brasil: Dilemas e Perspectivas, 1988; (with S. Mainwaring and J.S. Valenzuela) Issues in Democratic Consolidation: The New South American Democracies in Comparative Perspective, 1992; (with V. Tokman) Poverty and Inequality in Latin America: Issues and New Challenges, 1998; (with J. Méndez and P.S. Pinheiro) The (Un)Rule of Law and the Underprivileged in Latin America, 1999; (with J.V. Cullell and O.M. Lazzetta) Quality of Democracy, 2004. Contributor to books and journals. **Address:** Kellogg Institute for International Studies, University of Notre Dame, 219 Hesburgh Ctr., 130 Hesburgh Ctr., Notre Dame, IN 46556, U.S.A. **Online address:** godonnel@nd.edu

O'DONNELL, Jan. *See* **KLAVENESS, Jan O'Donnell.**

O'DONNELL, M. R. *See* **ROSS-MACDONALD, Malcolm (John).**

O'DONNELL, Patrick K. American (born United States), b. 1969?. **Genres:** History, Military/Defense/Arms Control, Biography, Autobiography/Memoirs. **Career:** Drop Zone, founder. Author and historian. **Publications:** Beyond Valor: World War II's Ranger and Airborne Veterans Reveal the Heart of Combat, 2001; Into the Rising Sun: In Their Own Words, World War II's Pacific Veterans Reveal the Heart of Combat, 2002; Operatives, Spies, and Saboteurs: The Unknown History of the Men and Women of World War II's OSS, 2004; We Were One: Shoulder to Shoulder with the Marines Who Took Fallujah, 2006; The Brenner Assignment, 2008; They Dared Return, 2009; Give Me Tomorrow: The Epic Story of a Legendary Marine Unit in Korea, 2010. Contributor to periodicals. **Address:** Zack Company Inc., 243 W 70th St., Ste. 8D, New York, NY 10023, U.S.A. **Online address:** wrestlerncaa@yahoo.com

O'DONNELL, Pierce. American (born United States), b. 1947. **Genres:** History, Law, Social Commentary. **Career:** Williams, Connolly and Califano, partner, 1975-78; Beardsley, Hufstedler and Kemble, partner, 1978-81; Commission on Judicial Performance, special counsel staff, 1979; Hufstedler, Miller, Carlson and Beardsley, partner, 1981-82; O'Donnell and Gordon, partner, 1982-87; Kaye, Scholer, Fierman, Hays and Handler, partner, 1987-96; Harvard Law School, visiting lecturer, 1993-; University of California, Independent Film and Television Producers Program, adjunct professor, 1994-97; O'Donnell Shaeffer Mortimer LLP, partner, 1996-. Writer. **Publications:** (With M.J. Churgin and D.E. Curtis) Toward a Just and Effective Sentencing System: Agenda for Legislative Reform, 1977; (with D. McDougal) Fatal Subtraction: The Inside Story of Buchwald v. Paramount, 1992, 2nd ed., 1996; Dawn's Early Light, 2001; In Time of War: Hitler's Terrorist Attack on America, 2005; Funny You Asked about That, 2006. Contributor to periodicals and journals. **Address:** O'Donnell Shaeffer Mortimer L.L.P., 550 S Hope St., Ste. 2000, Los Angeles, CA 90071, U.S.A.

O'DONNELL, Sunshine. American (born United States), b. 1971?. **Genres:** Novels, Literary Criticism And History. **Career:** Creative writing, visual arts and quantum physics, instructor; Coffeehouse Project, founder and publisher, 1994-. Poet, essayist and educator. **Publications:** Open Me (novel), 2007. Contributor to periodicals. **Address:** MacAdam Cage Publishing, 155 Sansome St., Ste. 550, San Francisco, CA 94104, U.S.A. **Online address:** sunshine.odonnell@gmail.com

O'DONOGHUE, Bernard. British/Irish (born Ireland), b. 1945. **Genres:** Poetry, Translations. **Career:** Intl. Business Machine, systems analyst, 1968-69; Magdalen College, lecturer in medieval English language and literature, 1971-95; Wadham College, tutor and fellow in English, 1995-, CUF Lecturer. Poet and writer. **Publications:** POETRY: Razorblades and Pencils, 1984; Poaching Rights, 1987; The Absent Signifier, 1990; The Weakness, 1991; Gunpowder, 1995; Here nor There, 1999; Outliving, 2003. OTHERS: (ed. and intro.) Selected Poetry of Thomas Hoccleve, 1982; The Courtly Love Tradition, 1982; Seamus Heaney and The Language of Poetry, 1994; Oxford Irish Quotations, 1999; (ed. with D. Constantine, H. Lee) Oxford Poets 2000: An Anthology, 2000; (ed. with D. Constantine, H. Lee) Oxford Poets 2002: An Anthology, 2002; Medieval Secular Lyrics, 2002; Outliving, 2003; (ed. with D. Constantine) Oxford Poets 2004: An Anthology, 2004; (trans.) Z. Hejda, Stay in a Sanatorium & Other Poems, 2005; (trans.) Sir Gawain and the Green Knight, 2006; (ed.) Cambridge Companion to Seamus Heaney, 2009. **Address:** Wadham College, Parks Rd., Oxford, OX OX1 3PN, England. **Online address:** bernard.odonoghue@wadham.ox.ac.uk

O'DONOHOE, Nicholas Benjamin. *See* **O'DONOHOE, Nick.**

O'DONOHOE, Nick. (Nicholas Benjamin O'Donohoe). American (born United States), b. 1952. **Genres:** Mystery/Crime/Suspense, Science Fiction/Fantasy, Novels, History. **Career:** Virginia Polytechnic Institute and State University, instructor, 1981-83, assistant professor, 1983-; C.I. Hayes, staff and writer; Parker Group Inc., writer and account executive. **Publications:** NOVELS: April Snow, 1982; Too, Too Solid Flesh, 1989; The Gnomewrench in the Dwarfworks, 1999; The Gnomewrench in the Peopleworks, 2000. MYSTERY NOVELS. NATHAN PHILLIPS SERIES: Wind Chill, 1985; Open Season, 1986. FANTASY/SCIENCE FICTION NOVELS. CROSSROADS SERIES: The Magic and the Healing, Book 1, 1994; Under the Healing Sign, 1995; The Healing of Crossroads, 1996. **Address:** Parker Group Inc., 394 Angell St., Providence, RI 02906, U.S.A. **Online address:** nicko@parkergroup.com

O'DONOVAN, Oliver. (Oliver Michael Timothy O'Donovan). British (born England), b. 1945. **Genres:** Theology/Religion, Politics/Government. **Career:** St. Helen's Church, assistant curate, 1972-76; University of Oxford, Wycliffe Hall, tutor, 1972-77, Chevasse lecturer, 1985, Regius professor of moral and pastoral theology and canon of Christ Church, 1982-2006, director of graduate studies, Faculty of Theology, chair, 1990-92, faculty, 1995-99, Christ Church, librarian, 2002-06, preacher, Bampton lecturer, 2003; Toronto School of Theology, Wycliffe College, assistant professor of systematic theology, 1977-81, associate professor, 1981-82; Bishop of Toronto, examining chaplain, 1978-82; Queen's University, Church of Ireland Theological lecturer, 1986, 2006; University of Durham, pastoral theology lecturer, 1987; Birmingham Cathedral, assize preacher, 1988; University of Cambridge, Hulsean preacher, 1989, Hulsean lecturer, 1994; Saint Patrick's College, visiting lecturer, 1989; Fuller Theological Seminary, Payton lecturer, 1989; General Theological Seminary, Paddock lecturer, 1990-; McMaster University, Hooker lecturer, 1996; Society for Study of Christian Ethics, president, 1997-2001; Gregorian University, McCarthy visiting professor, 2001; Saint John's College, Cheung Siu Kwai lecturer, 2002; University of Edinburgh, New College, professor of Christian ethics and practical theology, 2006-; McGill University, Birks Lecturer, 2009; Society for the Study of Christian Ethics, president. Writer. **Publications:** In Pursuit of a Christian View of War, 1977; Measure for Measure: Justice in Punishment and the Sentence of Death, 1977; The Problem of Self-Love in St. Augustine, 1980; Begotten or Made?, 1984; Principles in the Public Realm: The Dilemma of Christian Moral Witness, 1984; On the Thirty-Nine Articles: A Conversation with Tudor Christianity, 1986; Resurrection and Moral Order: An Outline for Evangelical Ethics, 1986; Peace and Certainty: A Theological Essay on Deterrence, 1989; (ed. with J. Atkinson, D.H. Field and A.F. Holmes) New Dictionary of Christian Ethics & Pastoral Theology, 1995; The Desire of the Nations: Rediscovering the Roots of Political Theology, 1996; (ed. with J.L. O'Donovan) From Irenaeus to Grotius: A Sourcebook in Christian Political Thought, 100-1625, 1999; Common Objects of Love: Moral Reflection and the Shaping of Community, 2002; The Just War Revisited, 2003; (with J.L. O'Donovan) Bonds of Imperfection: Christian Politics, Past and Present, 2004; The Ways of Judgment, 2005; A Conversation Waiting to Begin/ US: Church in Crisis: the Gay Controversy and the Anglican Communion, 2008; The Word in Small Boats: Sermons from Oxford, 2010. **Address:** School of Divinity, New College, Mound Pl., Edinburgh, EH1 2LX, Scotland. **Online address:** oliver.odonovan@ed.ac.uk

O'DONOVAN, Oliver Michael Timothy. *See* **O'DONOVAN, Oliver.**

O'DONOVAN, Susan Eva. American (born United States), b. 1953. **Genres:** History. **Career:** University of California, teaching assistant, 1988-90; University of Maryland, Freedmen and Southern Society Project, assistant editor, 1993-96, associate editor, 1996-2001; University of Maryland, lecturer, 1997-2000; Harvard University, assistant professor, 2001-05, associate professor of history and African and African American studies, 2005-09; University of Memphis, assistant professor, 2009-. Writer, historian, reviewer and consultant. **Publications:** Becoming Free in the Cotton South, 2007; (co-author) Freedom: A Documentary History of Emancipation, 1861-1867, vol. I: Land and Labor, 1865, 2008. Contributor to books, periodicals and journals. **Address:** Department of History, University of Memphis, 219 Mitchell Hall, Memphis, TN 38152, U.S.A. **Online address:** odonovan@fas.harvard.edu

O'DOR, Ronald Keith. Canadian/American (born United States), b. 1944. **Genres:** Biology, Zoology, Illustrations, Sciences. **Career:** Cambridge University, postdoctoral fellow in zoology, 1971-73; Dalhousie University, assistant professor, associate professor, 1973-83, professor of biology, 1983-, director of aquatron laboratory, 1986-93; Laboratoire Arago, summer scientist, 1979-85; Pacific Biological Station, visiting scientist, 1980; Bamfield Marine Station, sessional professor, 1987; University of British Columbia, visiting professor, 1987; Cephalopod International Advisory Council, president, 1988-91; University of the Azores, visiting scientist, 1989-90; University of Papua New Guinea, visiting scientist, 1989-91; Hokkaido University, visiting professor, 1991; Port Elizabeth Museum, visiting scientist, 1994; Lizard Island Research Station, visiting scientist, 1996, 2000; Kennedy Space Center, principal investigator, ARF-1, STS-77, NASA, USA, 1996; Biology Department, chair, 1997-2000; Lincoln Marine Science Centre, visiting scientist, 1999; Census of Marine Life, senior scientist, 2000-; Dalhousie University, associate dean of science for research and development, 2004-08, professor; Fisheries and Ocean Science, Uinversity of Alaska, Fairbanks, visiting scientist, 2005; City University of Hong Kong, visiting professor of electronic engineering, 2008. Writer. **Publications:** (With T. Okutani and T. Kubodera) Recent Advances in Cephalopod Fishery Biology, 1993; (with H.O. Poertner and D.L. Macmillan) The Physiology of Cephalopod Molluscs: Lifestyle and Performance Adaptations, 1994; (with P. Rodhouse and E.G. Dawe) Squid Recruitment Dynamics, 1998; The Unknown Ocean: Baseline Report of the Census of Marine Life Program, 2003. Contributor to journals. **Address:** Department of Biology, Dalhousie University, 1355 Oxford St., Halifax, NS B3H 4R2, Canada. **Online address:** ron.odor@dal.ca

O'DRISCOLL, Dennis. Irish (born Ireland), b. 1954. **Genres:** Poetry, Essays, Autobiography/Memoirs, Literary Criticism And History, Art/Art History. **Career:** Revenue Commissioners, executive officer, 1970-76, higher executive officer, 1976-83, assistant principal officer, 1983-; Dublin Arts Festival, literary organizer, 1977-79; Poetry Ireland Review, editor, 1986-87; University College, writer-in-residence, 1987-88; Harvard University, reader; Agenda magazine, advisor; Harvard Review, contributing editor. **Publications:** (Ed. with P. Fallon) The First Ten Years: Dublin Arts Festival Poetry, 1979; Kist, 1982; Hidden Extras, 1987; Five Irish Poets, 1990; Long Story Short, 1993; The Bottom Line, 1994; Quality Time, 1997; Weather Permitting, 1999; Troubled Thoughts, Majestic Dreams: Selected Prose Writings, 2001; Exemplary Damages, 2002; New and Selected Poems, 2004; 50 O'Clock, 2005; (ed.) The Bloodaxe Book of Poetry Quotations, 2006; Reality Check, 2007; Stepping Stones: Interviews with Seamus Heaney, 2008; (ed.) Quote Poet Unquote: Contemporary Quotations on Poets and Poetry, 2008; All the Living, 2008; Sing for the Taxman: Revenue and Exemptions in the Life of a Poet, 2009. **Address:** Anvil Press Poetry, Neptune House, 70 Royal Hill, London, GL SE10 8RF, England.

ŌE, Kenzaburō. Japanese (born Japan), b. 1935. **Genres:** Novels, Novellas/Short Stories, Essays, Young Adult Fiction. **Career:** Novelist and short story writer, 1952-. **Publications:** Shisha no ogori, Shiiku (novella); Memushiri kouchi, 1958; Ishihara Shintarō bunko, 1964; Kojinteki na taiken, 1964; Nihon reinen, 1965; Man'engannen no futtobōru, 1971; Opozdavshaia molodezh: Roman, 1973; Kaikō Takeshi, ōe Kenzaburō shū, 1976; Pinchi ranna chosho, 1976; Teach Us to Outgrow Our Madness: Four Short Novels, 1977; Hiroshimano hikari, 1980; Hiroshima Notes, 1981, rev. ed., 1995; Shuppatsuten, 1980; Okinawa keiken, 1981; Seinen e, 1981; Sengo bungakusha, 1981; Sōzōryoku to jōkyō, 1981; The Catch and other War Stories, 1981; (with N. Yūjirō and Y. Masao) Chūshin to shūen, 1981; (with N. Yūjirō and Y. Masao) Shomotsu: Sekai no in yu, 1981; Yomu kōi, 1981; Kaku kōi, 1981; Kotoba to jōkyō, 1981; Mirai no bungakusha, 1981; (with N. Yūjirō and Y. Masao) Bunka no kasseika, 1982; Hiroshima kara Oiroshima e: 82 Yōroppa nohankaku heiwa undō o miru, 1982; Kaku no taika to ningen no koe, 1982; Rein tsurio kiku onnatachi, 1982; Atarashii hito yo mezameyo, 1983; Zapiski Pinchrannera: Roman, 1983; Ikani ki o korosu ka, 1984; Nihon gendai no yumanisutoWatanabe Kazuo o yomu, 1984; (with Y. Ryōsuke) Sekai no 40-nen: sengoo minaosu, soshite, ima, 1984; (ed. and intro.) The Crazy Iris and Other Stories of the Atomic Aftermath, 1985; (ed.) Nan to mo shirenai mirai ni, 1985; Ikikata no teigi: futatabi jōkyō e, 1985; Kaba ni kamareru, 1985; Fire from the Ashes, 1985; Shōsetsu no takurami chi no tanoshimi, 1985; Natsukashii toshi e notegami, 1987; Atarashii bungaku no tame ni, 1988; Kirupu no gundan, 1988; Saigo no shōsetsu, 1988; Jinsei no Shinseki, 1989; ōoka Shōhei no sekai, 1989; Jiritsu to kyōseio kataru: shōgaisha, kōreisha to kazoku, shakai, 1990; Chiryōtō: kinmirai SF, 1990; Shizuka na seikatsu, 1990; (with T. Tōru) Opera o tsukuru, 1990; Chiryōtō wakusei: kinmirai SF, 1991; Hiroshima no seimei no ki, 1991; Boku ga hontoni wakakatta koro, 1992; Jinsei no habitto, 1992; Moeagaru midori no ki, 1993; Shinnen no aisatsu, 1993; Shōsetsu nohōhō, 1993; Shōsetsu no keikō, 1994; Japan, the Ambiguous, and Myself; The Nobel Prize Speech and Other Lectures, 1995; (with G. Grass) Gestern, vor 50 jahren: Ein deutch-japanischer briefwechsel, 1995; Kaifuku-surukazoku, 1995; Nihongo to Nihonjin nokokoro, 1996; (with ō. Yukari ga) Yuruyaka na kizuna, 1996; A Healing Family (essays), 1996; Two Novels: Seventeen, J., 1996; (with I. Hisashi and T. Yasutaka) Yūtopiasagashi, monogatari sagashi: bungaku no mirai ni muke te, 1998; Watakushito iu shōsetsuka no tsukurikata, 1998; Chugaeri, 1999; ōe Kenzaburō saihakken, 2001; (with A. Siganos and P. Forest) Nostalgies et autres labyrinthes: entretiens avecAndré Siganos et Philippe Forest, 2005. FICTION: Warera no jidai, 1959; Okurete kita seinen, 1961; Sakebigoe, 1962; The Perverts, 1963; Adventures in Daily Life, 1964; Nichijo seikatsu no boken, 1971; Kozui wawaga tamashii ni oyobi, 1973; Seinen no omei, 1974; M/T to mori no fushgino monogatari, 1986; Aimai na Nohon no watakushi, 1995; Doitsu to Nihon no sengo bungaku o kakeru, 1997; Watakushi to iu shosetsuka no tsukurikata, 1998; (with I. Hishashi and T. Yasutaka) Yutopia sagashi, monogatari sagashi: bungaku no mirai ni muke te, 1998; (with G. Grass) Just Yesterday, Fifty Years Ago: A Critical Dialogue on the Anniversary of the End of the Second World War, 1999; Oe Kenzaburosaihakken, 2001; Rouse Up O Young Men of the New Age!, 2002; (with A. Siganos) Nostalgies et autres labyrinthes: entretiens avec André Siganos et Philippe Forest, 2005; ōe Kenzaburō sakka jishin o kataru, 2007. THE FLAMING GREEN TREE SERIES: Sukuinushi ga nagurareru made, 1993; Yureugoku: vashireshon, 1994; Oinaru hi ni, 1995. SHORT STORIES: Kodokuna seinen no kyuka, 1960; Seiteki ningen, 1968; ōe Kenzaburō shu, 1969; Warera no hyoki o ikinobiru michi o oshieyo, 1975; Oe Kenzaburo, 1971; Mizukara waga namida o nugui-tamau hi, 1972; Sora no kaibutsu Agui, 1972. ESSAYS: Sekai no wakamonotachi, 1962; Oe Kenzaburo zensakuhin, 1966-67; Jizokusuru kokorozashi, 1968; Oe Kenzaburo shu, 1969; Kakujidaino sozoryoku, 1970; Kowaremono to shite no ningen, 1970; Okinawa noto, 1970; Itami Mansaku essei shu, 1971; Kujira no shimetsusuru hi, 1972; Dojidai to shite no sengo, 1973; Jokyo e, 1974; Bungaku noto, 1974; Genshuku na tsunawatari, 1974; Kotoba no yotte, 1976. **Address:** 585 Seijo-machi, Setagaya-Ku, Tokyo, 154-0017, Japan.

OELSCHLAEGER, Max. American (born United States), b. 1943. **Genres:** Environmental Sciences/Ecology, Economics, Social Sciences. **Career:** University of North Texas, professor of the philosophy of ecology, postmodern thought, and environmental ethics and chair of department of philosophy and religion studies; Northern Arizona University, Frances B. McAllister chair in community, culture, and environment, through 2006, Department of Humanities, Arts, and Religion, professor. Writer. **Publications:** The Environmental Imperative: A Socio-Economic Perspective, 1977; The Idea of Wilderness: From Prehistory to the Age of Ecology, 1991; (ed.) The Wilderness Condition: Essays on Environment and Civilization, 1992; (ed.) After Earth Day: Continuing the Conservation Effort, 1992; Caring for Creation: An Ecumenical Approach to the Environmental Crisis, 1994; (ed.) Postmodern Environmental Ethics, 1995; (with P.A.Y. Gunter) Texas Land Ethics, 1997; The End of Faith?, forthcoming; Survival, forthcoming. Contributor to periodicals. **Address:** Department of Humanities, Arts, and Religion, Northern Arizona University, 111 Riles Bldg., S San Francisco St., PO Box 6031, Flagstaff, AZ 86011, U.S.A. **Online address:** max.oelschlaeger@nau.edu

O'FAOLAIN, Julia. Also writes as Julia Martines. British (born England), b. 1932. **Genres:** Novels, Women's Studies And Issues, Translations, inspirational/Motivational Literature, Young Adult Fiction, Autobiography/Memoirs. **Career:** Council of Europe, translator, 1955-57; Reed College, instructor in French, 1957-61; Scuola Interpreti, teacher, 1962-65. Writer. **Publications:** We Might See Sights! and Other Stories, 1968; Godded and Codded, 1970; Three Lovers: A Novel, 1971; (ed. with L. Martines) Not in God's Image, 1973; Man in the Cellar: Stories, 1974; Women in the Wall, 1975; Melancholy Baby and Other Stories, 1978; No Country for Young Men, 1980; Daughters of Passion: Stories, 1982; The Obedient Wife, 1985; Irish Signorina: Divertimento, 1986; Judas Cloth, 1993; Ercoli e il Guardiano Notturno, 1999; Adam Gould, 2009. TRANSLATOR AS JULIA MARTINES: Two Memoirs of Renaissance Florence: The Diaries of Buonaccorso Pitti and Gregorio Dati, 1967; A Man of Parts, 1968. Works appear in anthologies. Contributor to periodicals. **Address:** Rogers, Coleridge & White Ltd., 20 Powis Mews, London, GL W11 1JN, England.

OFFER, Avner. British/Israeli (born Israel) **Genres:** History, Politics/Government, Public/Social Administration, Economics. **Career:** Oxford University, Merton College, junior research fellow, 1976-78; University of York, lecturer in economic and social history, 1979-90, reader in economic and social history, 1990-91; University of Southampton, Hartley research fellow, 1981-82; Australian National University, Institute of Advanced Studies, research fellow, 1985-88; Rutgers University, Center for Historical Analysis, senior fellow, 1991-; Oxford University, Nuffield College, professorial fellow and reader in recent social and economic history, 1992-2000, professor of economic history, 2000-11, All Souls College, fellow, 2000-; New York University, Remarque Institute, senior visiting fellow, 1999, Inet research fellow, 2011-12. Writer. **Publications:** Property and Politics, 1981; The Sod House vs. the Manor House: British and Overseas Farming, 1870-1914, 1986; The First World War: An Agrarian Interpretation, 1989; Between the Gift and the Market: The Economy of Regard, 1996; The American Automobile Frenzy of the 1950s, 1996; (ed.) In Pursuit of the Quality of Life, 1996; Epidemics of Abundance: Overeating and Slimming in the USA and Britain since the 1950s, 1998; Economic Welfare Measurements and Human Well-being, 2000; Why Has the Public Sector Grown So Large in Market Societies?: The Political Economy of Prudence in the U.K., 1870-2000, 2003; The Challenge of Affluence: Self-Control and Well-Being in the United States and Britain since 1950, 2006; The Markup for Lemons: Quality and Uncertainty in American and British Used Car Markets, 2007. **Address:** All Souls College, Oxford University, High St., Oxford, OX OX1 4AL, England. **Online address:** avner.offer@all-souls.ox.ac.uk

OFFIT, Paul A. American (born United States), b. 1951. **Genres:** Medicine/Health, History, Human Relations/Parenting, Sciences. **Career:** University of Pennsylvania School of Medicine, Henle professor of immunologic and infectious diseases, Department of Pediatrics, instructor in pediatrics, 1982-84, clinical assistant professor in pediatrics, 1984-85, assistant professor, 1987-92, associate professor, 1992-2000, professor, 2000-; The Wistar Institute of Anatomy and Biology, research investigator, 1982-85, assistant professor, 1987-92, adjunct associate professor, 1991-; Stanford University School of Medicine, Department of Medical Microbiology, research associate, 1985-87, Division of Pediatric Infectious Diseases, clinical assistant professor, 1986-87; Childrens Hospital of Philadelphia, chief of infectious diseases, 1992-, Vaccine Education Center, director. Writer. **Publications:** (With L.M. Bell) What Every Parent Should Know about Vaccines, 1998, rev. ed. as Vaccines: What Every Parent Should Know, 1999, 3rd ed., 2003; (with B. Fass-Offit and L.M. Bell) Breaking the Antibiotic Habit: A Parent's Guide to Coughs, Colds, Ear Infections and Sore Throats, 1999; The Cutter Incident: How America's First Polio Vaccine Led to the Growing Vaccine Crisis, 2005; Vaccinated: One Man's Quest to Defeat the World's Deadliest Diseases, 2007; Autism's False Prophets: Bad Science, Risky Medicine and the Search for a Cure, 2008; Deadly Choices: How the Anti-Vaccine Movement Threatens Us All, 2011; (with C.A. Moser) Vaccines and Your Child: Separating Fact from Fiction, 2011. **Address:** Division of Infectious Diseases, Childrens Hospital of Philadelphia, Rm. 1202D Abramson Research Bldg., 3615 Civic Center Blvd., Philadelphia, PA 19104, U.S.A. **Online address:** offit@email.chop.edu

OFFLEY, Ed. (Edward Peyton Offley). American (born United States), b. 1948. **Genres:** Writing/Journalism, Military/Defense/Arms Control, Trivia/Facts. **Career:** Virginia Gazette, reporter, 1972-; Ledger-Star, associate editorial page editor for military and defense issues, 1981-85; Seattle Post-Intelligencer, associate editorial page editor for military and defense issues, 1985-87, military reporter, 1987-2000; Stars and Stripes, editor-in-chief, 2000; Military Reporters and Editors, founder and director, 2002-; Defense Watch, editor, 2001-05; News Herald, staff, 2005-. **Publications:** (With B. Owens as Edward Offley) Lifting the Fog of War, 2000; Pen & Sword: A Journalist's Guide to Covering the Military, 2001; Scorpion Down: Sunk by the Soviets, Buried by the Pentagon: The Untold Story of the USS Scorpion, 2007; Turning The Tide: How A Small Band of Allied Sailors Defeated The U-Boats and Won The Battle of the Atlantic, 2011. **Address:** Basic Books, 387 Park Ave. S, New York, NY 10016, U.S.A. **Online address:** ed_offley@yahoo.com

OFFLEY, Edward Peyton. *See* **OFFLEY, Ed.**

O'FLYNN, Catherine. British (born England), b. 1970?. **Genres:** Novels, Young Adult Fiction. **Career:** Writer. **Publications:** What Was Lost: A Novel, 2007; (ed.) Roads Ahead, 2009; The News Where You Are, 2010. **Address:** Lucy Luck, Lucy Luck Associates, 18-21 Cavaye Pl., London, GL SW10 9PT, England.

OFRAT, Gideon. Israeli (born Israel), b. 1945. **Genres:** Art/Art History, Philosophy, Language/Linguistics. **Career:** Hebrew University, lecturer in drama, 1970-81; Bezalel Academy of Arts and Design, senior lecturer on aesthetics, 1971-95; Time for Art (art center), artistic director and curator, 2002-04. Writer. **Publications:** The Definition of Art, 1975; Ha-Teạtòron Ha-radiḳali: Ha-teạtòron He-ḥadash Shel Sof Shenot Ha-shishim, 1976;

The Artistic Judgment, 1978; The Israeli Drama, 1978; Adamah, Adam, Dam: Mitoshe-ḥaluts U-fulḥan Ha-adamah Be-maḥazot Ha-hityashvut, 1980; Earth, Man, Blood, 1980; (co-author) The Story of Israeli Art, 1980; Ha-Masa El Matityahu, 1982; Kan: Al meḳomiyut ạeret Be-omanut Yiśrael, 1984; Here, 1984; Altòernạtòivah, 1986; Home: The Art of Abraham Offek, 1986; Bayit: Avraham Ofeḳ: Avodot, 1956-1986, 1987; Betsalel He-hadash, 1935-1955, 1987; Liṭvinovsḳi, 1987; Litòvinovskòi Touch: Israeli Postmodernism, 1988; Ludvig Blum/Ludwig Blum: 1891-1974, 1988; 1948-dor 708 Be-omanut Yiśrael, 1988; Back to the Sea, 1992; Hanging Gardens, 1993; Al Ha-arets: Ha-omanutha-Eretsyiśreelit: Pirḳe-avot, 1993; On the Ground, 2 vols., 1994; The Art of Shalom Sebba, 1994; Noishṭain, Tsaig ṿe-Grosmanbemartefe Ha-Sifriyah Ha-leumit: Ha-Bienaleh Be-ṿenetsyah 1995, Ha-Bitan Ha-Yiśreeli, 1995; (with G.D. Bolas and M. Sgan-Cohen) Ketav: Flesh and Word in Israeli Art, 1996; Nimrod with Tefilin, 1996; Triple Darkness: Plato, Kant, Kierkegaard, 1997; Shamah: Teologyah Shelalaṭah, 1998; Deridah Ha-Yehudi: Al Yahadut Ke-fetsa ṿe-al Hagutoshel Zaḳ Deridah, 1998; One Hundred Years of Art in Israel, 1998; Defuse Ha-yofi: śiḥot Im Gamad, 1998; Yonder: Theology of the Obscure, 1998; Patterns of Beauty, 1998; Yoḥanan Simon: Monografyah, 1999; Exile, 1999; Shivḥe Galut, 2000; Be-sifriyato Shel Aryeh Arokh, 2001; Be-heḳsher Meḳomi, 2004; Naftali Bezem, 2005; Biḳureomanut: Peraḳim Al Omanim Yiśreelim, 2005; Luiz Shats: 1916-1997, 2006; Kive-tokh Shelo: Tanakh Bi-reshut Ha-yahid, 2006; Li-reotba-ḥashekhah: Miron Simah, 2006; Mosheh Tamir: Ha-epos Veha-mitos, 2007; Zivah Kronzon: Remets, 2007; Voshington Hotseh Et Ha-Yarden: Mivhar Maamarim, 1984-2008, 2008; He-Aśor Ha-rishon: Hegemonya Ve-ribui, 2008; Ha-Holkhim El Ha-har: Avraham Ofek: Rishume Akedah, 2008; Berit Veha-milah Shel Zak Deridah, 2008; Ani ha-homer: Hanah Yitshaki, keramika it, 2008; ha-Shivah el ha-shṭeṭl: ha-Yahadut ke-dimui be-omanut Yiśra'el, 2011. Contributor of articles to journals and newspapers. **Address:** 6 Mevo-Hamatmid, Jerusalem, 94593, Israel.

OGAWA, Dennis M. (Dennis Masaaki Ogawa). American (born United States), b. 1943. **Genres:** Cultural/Ethnic Topics, History. **Career:** University of Hawaii, American Studies Department, professor, 1969-, chair, Press, general editor; Japanese Cultural Center, consultant, vice chairperson; Olelo, director. **Publications:** From Japs to Japanese: Evolution of Japanese-American Stereotypes, 1971; Jan Ken Po: The World of Hawaii's Japanese Americans, 1973, 2nd ed., 1978; (with G. Grant) Kodomo No Tame Ni: For the Sake of Our Children, 1977; Ellison Onizuka: A Remembrance, 1987; Unlikely Revolutionary: Matsuo Takabuki and the Making of Modern Hawaii, 1998; First Among Nisei: The Life and Writings of Masaji Marumoto, 2007; (with J.M. Blink and M. Gordon) California Hotel and Casino: Hawai'I's Home Away from Home, 2008. Contributor of articles to journals. **Address:** American Studies Department, University of Hawaii, Moore Hall 324, 1890 East-West Rd., Honolulu, HI 96822-4733, U.S.A.

OGAWA, Dennis Masaaki. *See* **OGAWA, Dennis M.**

OGBAA, Kalu. American/Nigerian (born Nigeria), b. 1945. **Genres:** Cultural/Ethnic Topics, Literary Criticism And History. **Career:** Alvan Ikoku College of Education, assistant lecturer, 1974-76; Ohio State University, teaching associate, 1977; University of Texas, assistant instructor of English, 1978-81, lecturer of English, 1981; Imo State University, assistant professor, 1982-85, associate professor of English, 1985-89, Division of General Studies, acting director, 1986-89; Oral Roberts University, visiting associate professor of English, 1989-90; Clark Atlanta University, visiting associate professor of English, 1990-92; Southern Connecticut State University, associate professor of English, 1992-95, professor of English, 1995-. Writer. **Publications:** Gods, Oracles and Divination: Folkways in Chinua Achebe's Novels, 1992; (ed.) The Gong and the Flute: African Literary Development and Celebration, 1994; Igbo, 1995; Understanding Things Fall Apart: A Student Casebook To Issues, Sources, And Historical Documents, 1999; A Century of Nigerian Literature: A Select Bibliography, 2003; The Nigerian Americans, 2003; General Ojukwu: The Legend of Biafra, 2007; Blood and Bravery: Voices of Biafran Veterans of the Nigeria-Biafra War, 2010. Contributor to books. **Address:** Department of English, Southern Connecticut State University, EN 225D, 501 Crescent St., New Haven, CT 06515, U.S.A. **Online address:** ogbaak1@southernct.edu

OGDEN, Christopher. American (born United States), b. 1945. **Genres:** Writing/Journalism, Biography, Autobiography/Memoirs. **Career:** Time Magazine, correspondent, 1973-76, Washington chief state department correspondent, 1976-79, chief White House correspondent, 1979-81, Midwest bureau chief, 1981-85, London bureau chief, 1985-89, chief diplomatic correspondent, 1989-91, foreign affairs columnist, 1992-; United Press Intl., correspondent; Portsmouth Abbey School, board director. **Publications:** Maggie: An Intimate Portrait of a Woman in Power, 1990; Life of the Party: The Biography of Pamela Digby Churchill Hayward Harriman, 1994; Legacy: A Biography of Moses and Walter Annenberg, 1999. Contributor to periodicals. **Address:** Time Magazine, 555 12th St. NW, Ste. 600, Washington, DC 20004, U.S.A.

OGEDE, Ode. American/Nigerian (born Nigeria), b. 1956. **Genres:** Literary Criticism And History. **Career:** Ahmadu Bello University, assistant lecturer, lecturer, senior lecturer in English, 1981-94; University of Pennsylvania, Andrew Mellon faculty fellow, 1994, 1995; Lincoln University, visiting lecturer, 1995-96; North Carolina Central University, Department of English and Mass Communication, associate professor, 1996-2000, professor, 2001-. Writer. **Publications:** Art, Society and Performance: Igede Praise Poetry, 1997; Ayi Kwei Armah, Radical Iconoclast, 2000; Achebe and the Politics of Representation, 2001; (ed.) Teacher Commentary on Student Papers, 2002; Achebe's Things Fall Apart: Reader's Guide, 2007; Intertextuality in Contemporary African Literature: Looking Inward, 2011. Contributor of to periodicals. **Address:** Department of English & Mass Communication, North Carolina Central University, 318 Farrison-Newton, Durham, NC 27707, U.S.A. **Online address:** oogede@nccu.edu

OGILVIE, Brian W. American (born United States) **Genres:** Natural History. **Career:** University of Massachusetts, graduate program director & associate professor of history. Writer and historian. **Publications:** The Science of Describing: Natural History in Renaissance Europe, 2006. **Address:** Department of History, University of Massachusetts, Rm. 614, Herter Hall, 161 Presidents Dr., Amherst, MA 01003-9312, U.S.A. **Online address:** ogilvie@history.umass.edu

OGILVIE, Marilyn. *See* **OGILVIE, Marilyn Bailey.**

OGILVIE, Marilyn Bailey. (Marilyn Ogilvie). American (born United States), b. 1936. **Genres:** Biography, Bibliography, Women's Studies And Issues. **Career:** Phoenix Union High School, teacher, 1959-61; St. Andrew's College, teacher, 1961-62; Portland State University, assistant professor of the history of science, 1971-75; Oscar Rose Jr. College, adjunct instructor in American history, 1975-76; University of Oklahoma, visiting assistant professor of the history of science, 1977-83, associate professor of bibliography, 1991-94, adjunct associate professor of history of science, 1991-94, curator of the history of science collections, 1991-2008, professor of the history of science and bibliography, 1994-2008, professor emeritus, 2008-; Oklahoma Baptist University, adjunct assistant professor of the history of science, 1979-80, assistant professor of natural science, 1980-85, associate professor of natural science, 1985-91, Division of Natural Sciences and Mathematics, chair. Writer. **Publications:** Women in Science: Antiquity through the Nineteenth Century, A Biographical Dictionary with Annotated Bibliography, 1986; (with K.L. Meek) Women and Science: An Annotated Bibliography, 1996; (with C.J. Choquette) A Dame Full of Vim and Vigor: A Biography of Alice Middleton Boring, Biologist in China, 1999; (ed. with J. Harvey) The Biographical Dictionary of Women in Science: Pioneering Lives from Ancient Times to the Mid-20th Century, 2000; (ed.) Biographical Dictionary of Scientists, 3rd ed., 2000; Marie Curie: A Biography, 2004. Contributor to anthologies and periodicals. **Address:** Department of the History of Science, University of Oklahoma- Libraries, 601 Elm, Rm. 521, 401 W Brooks St., Norman, OK 73019, U.S.A. **Online address:** mogilvie@ou.edu

OGLETREE, Thomas Warren. American (born United States), b. 1933. **Genres:** Theology/Religion, Social Sciences. **Career:** Birmingham-Southern College, assistant professor of philosophy and religion, 1963-65; Chicago Theological Seminary, assistant professor of constructive theology, 1965-68, associate professor of constructive theology, 1968-70; Vanderbilt University, Divinity School, associate professor of theological ethics, 1970-75, professor of theological ethics, 1975-81, Institute for Public Policy Studies, senior research associate, 1975-81, Graduate Department of Religion, chair, 1980-81; Drew University, Theological School, professor of theological ethics, 1981-90, dean, 1981-90; Society of Christian Ethics, vice president, 1982-83, president, 1983-84; Yale University, Divinity School, professor of theological ethics, 1990-, dean, 1990-96. Writer. **Publications:** Christian Faith and History: A Critical Comparison of Ernst Troeltsch and Karl Barth, 1965; The Death of God Controversy, 1966; Openings for Marxist-Christian Dialogue,

1968; (with H. Aptheker and S. Bliss) From Hope to Liberation, 1974; (ed. with G.R. Lucas, Jr.) Lifeboat Ethics: The Moral Dilemmas of World Hunger, 1976; The Use of the Bible in Christian Ethics: A Constructive Essay, 1983; Hospitality to the Stranger: Dimensions of Moral Understanding, 1985; The World Calling: The Church's Witness in Politics and Society, 2004; Critical Inquiry in Christian Social Ethics, 2004; Biblical Foundations for Christian Social Teaching, 2006. **Address:** Yale Divinity School, 409 Prospect St., New Haven, CT 06511, U.S.A. **Online address:** thomas.ogletree@yale.edu

O'GRADY, Desmond (James Bernard). Irish (born Ireland), b. 1935. **Genres:** Poetry, Translations, Biography, History. **Career:** American University in Cairo, Harvard distinguished visiting professor, 1971, visiting poet-in-residence, 1975-76; Tabriz University, visiting professor of English literature, 1976-77; University of Alexandria, visiting professor of English literature, 1978-80. Poet and translator. **Publications:** POEMS: Chords and Orchestrations, 1956; (co-author) New Work by Five Poets, 1957; (co-author) A Reading of New Poems, 1958; (co-author) Poems, 1959; Reilly, 1961; Professor Kelleher and the Charles River, 1964; Eat From God's Hand; Paul Gauthier and the Chruch of the Poor, 1965; The Dark Edge of Europe, 1967; Separazioni, 1968; The Dying Gaul, 1968; Hellas, 1971; Separations, 1973; Stations, 1976; Sing Me Creation, 1977; The Headgear of the Tribe: New and Selected Poems, 1979; His Skaldcrane's Nest, 1979; These Fields in Springtime, 1984; The Wandering Celt, 1984; Alexandrian Notebook, 1989; Tipperary, 1991; My Fields This Springtime, 1993; The Road Taken: Poems 1956-96, 1997; The Wandering Celt, 2001; The Battle of Kinsale, 1601, 2002; The Song of Songs: A Version, 2003; On My Way, 2006; My Alexandria: Poems and Prose, 2006. TRANSLATOR: Off Licence, 1968; The Gododdin, 1977; A Limerick Rake, 1978; Grecian Glances: Versions from the Classical Anthology, 1981; The Seven Arab Odes, 1990; Ten Modern Arab Poets, 1992, rev. ed., 2007; Alternative Manners, 1993; Trawling Tradition: Translations 1954-1994, 1994; Il Galata Morente, 1996; Zlatko Tomici'c, Croatia My Love: Poems, 2003. OTHERS: Correggio Jones and the Runaways: The Italo-Australian Connection, 1995; (with A.M. Greeley) The Turned Card: Christianity Before and After the Wall, 1997. **Address:** Rincurran Hermitage, Kinsale, CK 4, Ireland.

O'GRADY, John P. American (born United States), b. 1958. **Genres:** Novels, Environmental Sciences/Ecology, Essays, Natural History, Young Adult Fiction. **Career:** University of California, lecturer, 1991-94; Boise State University, assistant professor of English, 1994-; Allegheny College, assistant professor of English. Writer. **Publications:** Pilgrims to the Wild: Everett Ruess, Henry David Thoreau, John Muir, Clarence King, Mary Austin, 1993; (comp. with L. Anderson and S. Slovic) Literature and the Environment: A Reader on Nature and Culture, 1999; Grave Goods: Essays of a Peculiar Nature, 2001; The Infrared Flaneur, forthcoming; The Mountain Austerities, forthcoming. **Address:** The University of Utah Press, J. Willard Marriott Library, 295 South 1500 East, Ste. 5400, Salt Lake City, UT 84112, U.S.A. **Online address:** johnpogrady@comcast.net

O'GRADY, Paul. Irish (born Ireland), b. 1964. **Genres:** Philosophy, Ethics. **Career:** Saint Catherine's College, lecturer in philosophy, 1996-97; Trinity College, lecturer in philosophy, 1997-, fellow, 2003-. Writer. **Publications:** Relativism, 2002; (ed.) The Consolations of Philosophy: Reflections in an Economic Downturn, 2010; Aquinas' Philosophy of Religion, 2011. **Address:** Department of Philosophy, Trinity College, Rm. 5017, Arts Bldg., 5th Fl., College Green, DU 2, Ireland. **Online address:** pogrady@tcd.ie

O'GRADY, Rohan. Also writes as A. Carleon, June O. Skinner. Canadian (born Canada), b. 1922. **Genres:** Romance/Historical, Novels, Literary Criticism And History, Young Adult Fiction. **Career:** Librarian and author. **Publications:** O'Houlihan's Jest: A Lament for the Irish, 1961; Pippin's Journal, or, Rosemary is for Remembrance, 1962 in US as Master of Montrolfe Hall, 1965; Let's Kill Uncle, 1963; Bleak November, 1970; (as A. Carleon) The May Spoon, 1981; The Curse of the Montrolfes, 1983. **Address:** McIntosh, McKee, and Dodds, 30 E 60th St., New York, NY 10022, U.S.A.

OGRIN, Dušan. Slovenian (born Slovenia), b. 1929. **Genres:** Architecture, Art/Art History, Environmental Sciences/Ecology, Homes/Gardens, Horticulture. **Career:** University of Ljubljana, Department of Landscape Architecture, assistant professor, 1957-60, lecturer, 1960-65, associate professor, 1965-86, professor, 1986-, biotechnical faculty; Harvard University, visiting professor. Writer. **Publications:** Zelenje v urbanem okolju: Zbornik mednarodnega simpozija, 1972; (co-author) The Oxford Companion to Gardens, 1986; The World Heritage of Gardens, 1993; Varstvo narave zunaj zavarovanih obmocij, 1996. UNTRANSLATED WORKS: Zelenje v nasem okolju, 1964; Cvetne grmovnice, 1967; Zelenje v urbanem okolju. Zbornik mednarodnega simpozija, 1972; Natura e progetto del parco contemporaneo, 1988; Vrtna Umetnost Sveta, 1993; (co-author) Sven Ingvar Andersson, Arkitektens Forlag, 1994; (co-author) Hommage a Ravnikar Edvard, 1995; Varstvo narave zunajzavarovanih obmocij: Zbornik mednarodne konference ob evropskem letuvarstva narave, 1995, 1996; Giardini del mondo, 1995; Slovenske krajine: 304 strani, 310 barvnih slik, 1997. **Address:** Department of Landscape Architecture, University of Ljubljana, Jamnikarjeva 101, Ljubljana, 1000, Slovenia. **Online address:** dusan.ogrin@bf.uni-lj.si

OGUIBE, Olu. American/Nigerian (born Nigeria), b. 1964. **Genres:** Poetry, Literary Criticism And History, Art/Art History. **Career:** West Africa Magazine, literary and theatre critic writer; University of London, Goldsmiths College, senior lecturer, 1994-95, School of Oriental and African Studies, faculty; University of Illinois, assistant professor, 1995-96; University of South Florida, Stuart Golden endowed chair, 1996-99; Smithsonian Institution, senior fellow; The New School, Vera List Center for Art and Politics, senior fellow, 2000-; University of Connecticut, professor of art and African-American studies, Institute for African American Studies, associate director, interim director. Art historian and art curator. **Publications:** A Song from Exile, 1990; A Gathering Fear (poetry), 1992; (ed.) Democracy in Nigeria, 1993; Songs for Catalina, 1994; (ed. and intro.) Sojourners: New Writing by Africans in Britain, 1994; (with P. Ntuli) The Battle for South Africa's Mind: Towards a Post-Apartheid Culture, 1995; Uzo Egonu: An African Artists in the West, 1995; Crossing: Time. Space. Movement, 1998; (ed. with O. Enwezor) Reading the Contemporary: African Art from Theory to the Marketplace, 1999; (ed. with S. Hassan) Authentic/ Ex-Centric: Conceptualism in Contemporary African Art, 2001; The Culture Game, 2004. **Address:** Department of Art & Art History, University of Connecticut, 830 Bolton Rd., Ste. 1099, Storrs, CT 06269-1099, U.S.A. **Online address:** ooguibe@camwood.org

OGUNYEMI, Chikwenye Okonjo. Nigerian (born Nigeria), b. 1939?. **Genres:** Literary Criticism And History, Women's Studies And Issues, Humanities. **Career:** City University of New York, Queen's College, instructor, 1971-72; University of Ibadan, professor of literature, 1972-89, instructor in literature, 1972-; Sarah Lawrence College, professor of literature, 1989-2008, now professor emeritus; Barnard College, African women's writing, 1997-2007; Writer. **Publications:** Richard Wright's Black Boy, 1987; Africa Wo/Man Palava: The Nigerian Novel by Women, 1996; Juju Fission: Women's Alternative Fictions from the Sahara, the Kalahari and the Oases In-between, 2007; (co-ed.) The Twelve Best Books by African Women: Critical Readings, 2008. Works appear in anthologies. Contributor to journals and books. **Address:** Sarah Lawrence College, 1 Mead Way, Bronxville, NY 10708, U.S.A. **Online address:** ogunyemi@slc.edu

OGUNYEMI, Yemi D(iploman). American/Nigerian (born Nigeria), b. 1950?. **Genres:** Novels, Novellas/Short Stories, Children's Fiction, Young Adult Fiction, Poetry, Philosophy. **Career:** Writer, 1983-; Vienna News, reporter; Diplomats, reporter; Austro-Nigerian Society, founder, 1983; Development News, publisher and director, 1983-; Institute of Creative Writing, director, 1983-93; Liberty University, associate professor of philosophy and letters, 1993-94; Harvard University, associate fellow, 1994-95, research fellow, W.E.B. Du Bois Institute, associate professor of Afro-American studies, 1994-95; Bircham International University, professor, faculty of arts and humanities, 2007, academic supervisor for journalism, academis dean; Diaspora Press of America, founder, 1995; Institute of Yoruba, founder and director, 2000; International University of Diaspora, founder, 2005; Foundation University, Faculty of Arts and Humanities, professor. **Publications:** Trans-Continental Poems, 1974; The Myths of the Coffee Boys, 1985; Women in Europe, 1986; Dreams of Joy, 1986; Press-Media in Africa, 1986; The Source of the River Koku, 1987; How Dogs Became Friends of Men, 1987; The New Intellectuals for Peace and Development, 1987; The African Soul, 1989; (ed.) My Contact with Africans and Africa, 1989; Studying Creative Writing in Nigeria, 1991; The Writers and Politics, 1991; The Literary Philosophy for the Year 2000, 1991; The Covenant of the Earth, 1993, 2nd ed., 1998; Facts, Fictions and Feelings of Moremi, 1997; Introduction to Yoruba Philosophy, Religion and Literature, 1998; Literatures of the Diaspora, 2000; The Charmed Comforter, 2000; The Peddlers Strike, 2000; Farmers' Burden, 2000; The Political Philosophy of Wole Soyinka and Other Narratives, 2001; Path to Life Therapy and Its Healing Poems, 2002; The Melodrama of the Last Word, 2003; Literatures of the African Diaspora, 2003; My Gazar with

My Geisha, 2008; The Literary/Political Philosophy of Wole Soyinka, 2009; The Oral Traditions in Ile-Ife, 2010. FORTHCOMING: A Hundred Week-Days in Paradise; The Last Cowrie Queen; Modicums of O; Twice Anagram; Thieves among the Citizens; Make Me Your Own; The Republic of Happiness. **Address:** Diaspora Press of America, PO Box 200981, Boston, MA 02120-0018, U.S.A. **Online address:** princeyemi36@hotmail.com

OHAEGBULAM, Festus Ugboaja. American (born United States) **Genres:** Politics/Government, Cultural/Ethnic Topics, Local History/Rural Topics, History. **Career:** Assemblies of God School, headmaster, 1957-60; Regis College, teaching fellow, 1966-67; Southern University, associate professor of political science, 1967-72; University of South Florida, associate professor, 1972-76, professor of government and international affairs, 1977-99, professor emeritus, 1999-, director of Africana studies, 1977-91; Louisiana State University, visiting professor, 1970-72; University of Florida, Center for African Studies, visiting research associate, 2001. Writer. **Publications:** Nationalism in Colonial and Post-Colonial Africa, 1977; Nigeria and the UN Mission to the Democratic Republic of the Congo: A Case Study of the Formative Stages of Nigeria's Foreign Policy, 1982; The Post-Colonial Erain Africa: Traumas and Opportunities; A Foreign Affairs Special Anthology, 1990; Towards an Understanding of the African Experience from Historical and Contemporary Perspectives, 1990; A Concise Introduction to American Foreign Policy, 1999; Africa in World Affairs: A Concise Companion Compendium; A Foreign Affairs Custom Anthology, 2001; West African Responses to European Imperialism in the Nineteenth and Twentieth Centuries, 2002; U.S. Policy in Postcolonial Africa: Four Case Studies in Conflict Resolution, 2005; A Culture of Deference: Congress, the President and the Course of the U.S. led Invasion and Occupation of Iraq, 2007. **Address:** Department of Government and International Affairs, University of South Florida, 270 FAO, 4202 E Fowler Ave., Tampa, FL 33620-5550, U.S.A. **Online address:** ohaegbul@chuma1.cas.usf.edu

O'HAGAN, Andrew. British/Scottish (born Scotland), b. 1968?. **Genres:** Novels, Documentaries/Reportage, Adult Non-fiction, Westerns/Adventure. **Career:** London Review of Books, contributing editor, 1991-95; Trinity College, visiting fellow in creative writing, 2008; Granta Magazine, contributing editor; Esquire, editor-at-large; King's College, creative writing, fellow. **Publications:** The Missing, 1995; Our Fathers, 1999; The End of British Farming, 2001; Personality, 2003; (co-ed.) Weekenders: Adventures in Calcutta, 2004; Be Near Me, 2006; The Atlantic Ocean, 2008; (ed.) A Night Out With Robert Burns: The Greatest Poems, 2008; The Life and Opinions of Maf the Dog, and of His Friend Marilyn Monroe, 2010. Contributor to newspapers and periodicals. **Address:** c/o Author Mail, A. P. Watt Ltd., 20 John St., London, GL WC1N 2DR, England.

O'HAGAN, Christine. (Christine Kehl O'Hagan). American (born United States) **Genres:** Novels. **Career:** Writer. **Publications:** Benediction at the Savoia, 1992; (as Christine Kehl O'Hagan) The Book of Kehls, 2005. Contributor to periodicals. **Address:** Ann Rittenberg Literary Agency Inc., 15 Maiden Ln., Ste. 206, New York, NY 10038, U.S.A. **Online address:** christine@christinekehlohagan.com

O'HAGAN, Christine Kehl. *See* **O'HAGAN, Christine.**

OHANIAN, Hans C. American/German (born Germany), b. 1941. **Genres:** Physics, Sciences. **Career:** Rensselaer Polytechnic Institute, assistant professor, 1968-76, adjunct professor, 1979-94; Union College, associate professor, 1977-83; Dudley Observatory, senior scientist, 1990-94; University of Vermont, Department of Physics, adjunct professor of physics, 2004-; University of Rome, faculty. Writer and physicist. **Publications:** NONFICTION: Gravitation and Spacetime, 1976, (with R. Ruffini) 2nd ed., 1994; Physics, 1985, 2nd ed., 1989; Modern Physics, 1987, 2nd ed., 1995; Classical Electrodynamics, 1988, 2nd ed., 2007; Principles of Quantum Mechanics, 1990; Principles of Physics, 1994; Relativity: A Modern Introduction, 2001; (with J.T. Markert) Physics for Engineers and Scientists, 3rd ed., 2007; Einstein's Mistakes: The Human Failings of Genius, 2008. **Address:** Department of Physics, University of Vermont, Rm. A413, Cook Physical Sciences Bldg., 82 University Pl., Burlington, VT 05405-0125, U.S.A. **Online address:** hans.ohanian@uvm.edu

O'HANLON, Ardal. Irish (born Ireland), b. 1965. **Genres:** Novels, Young Adult Fiction. **Career:** Writer and actor. **Publications:** The Talk of the Town, 1998; Knick Knack Paddy Whack: A Novel, 2000. **Address:** Dawn Sedgwick Management, 3 Goodwins Ct., Covent Garden, London, GL WC2N 4LL, England.

O'HANLON, Michael E(dward). American (born United States) **Genres:** Military/Defense/Arms Control, Theology/Religion, Anthropology/Ethnology. **Career:** Congressional Budget Office, National Security Division, defense and foreign policy budget analyst, 1989-94; Institute for Defense Analyses, research assistant; Columbia University, adjunct professor; Georgetown University, adjunct professor, 1996-; Brookings Institution, senior fellow in foreign policy, 1994-, Sydney Stein, Jr. chair, Brookings-ABC Opportunity 08 Project, director; Princeton University, visiting lecturer. Writer. **Publications:** U.S. Costs of Verification and Compliance under Pending Arms Treaties, 1990; The Art of War in the Age of Peace: U.S. Military Posture for the Post-Cold War World, 1992; Limiting Conventional Arms Exports to the Middle East, 1992; Defense Planning for the Late 1990s: Beyond the Desert Storm Framework, 1995; (with C. Graham) A Half Penny on the Federal Dollar: The Future of Development Aid, 1997; Saving Lives with Force: Military Criteria for Humanitarian Intervention, 1997; How to Be a Cheap Hawk: The 1999 and 2000 Defense Budgets, 1998; Technological Change and the Future of Warfare, 2000; (with I.H. Daalder) Winning Ugly: NATO's War to Save Kosovo, 2000; (with J.M. Lindsay) Defending America: The Case for Limited National Missile Defense, 2001; Defense Policy Choices for the Bush Administration, 2001-2005, 2001; (co-author) Protecting the American Homeland: A Preliminary Analysis, 2002; Expanding Global Military Capacity for Humanitarian Intervention, 2003; (with M. Mochizuki) Crisis on the Korean Peninsula: How to Deal with a Nuclear North Korea, 2003; Neither Star Wars nor Sanctuary: Constraining the Military Uses of Space, 2004; Defense Strategy for the Post-Saddam Era, 2005; (with M.A. Levi) The Future of Arms Control, 2005; U.S. Defense Strategy after Saddam, 2005; (with K.M. Campbell) Hard Power: The New Politics of National Security, 2006; (with R.C. Bush) War like No Other: The Truth about China's Challenge to America, 2007; Science of War, 2009; Budgeting for Hard Power, 2009; Skeptic's Case for Nuclear Disarmament, 2010; (with H. Sherjan) Toughing it out in Afghanistan, 2010. EDITOR: (co-ed.) The Anthropology of Landscape: Perspectives on Space and Place, 1997; (with R.L. Welsch) Hunting the Gatherers: Ethnographic Collectors, Agents and Agency in Melanesia, 1870s-1930s, 2000; Opportunity 08: Independent Ideas for America's Next President, 2007. Contributor to periodicals. Works appear in anthologies. **Address:** Brookings Institution, 1775 Massachusetts Ave. NW, Washington, DC 20036, U.S.A. **Online address:** meo14@columbia.edu

O'HARA, David. American (born United States), b. 1969?. **Genres:** Science Fiction/Fantasy, Theology/Religion, Literary Criticism And History. **Career:** Augustana College, Department of Religion, Philosophy, and the Classics, assistant professor, 2005-, Philosophy Program, director. Writer. **Publications:** (With M.T. Dickerson) From Homer to Harry Potter: A Handbook on Myth and Fantasy, 2006; (with M.T. Dickerson) Narnia and the Fields of Arbol: The Environmental Vision of C.S. Lewis, 2008. Contributor of articles to journals. **Address:** Augustana College, 2001 S Summit Ave., Sioux Falls, SD 57197-0001, U.S.A. **Online address:** david.ohara@augie.edu

O'HARA, Kevin. American (born United States), b. 1949. **Genres:** Autobiography/Memoirs. **Career:** Berkshire Medical Center, psychiatric nurse, 1973-; Berkshire Eagle, columnist. **Publications:** Last of the Donkey Pilgrims (memoir), 2004; A Lucky Irish Lad (memoir), 2010. **Address:** Pittsfield, MA , U.S.A. **Online address:** kohara@kevin-ohara.com

O'HARA, Marjorie (Doreen). British (born England), b. 1928. **Genres:** Novels, Children's Fiction, Young Adult Fiction, Science Fiction/Fantasy. **Career:** Suffolk County Council, deputy county officer, retired, 1979. Writer. **Publications:** NOVELS: The Cunning Man's Glass (juvenile), 1989; Piper's Gate, 1991. **Address:** 84 Station Rd., Framlingham, SU IP13 9EE, England. **Online address:** mmarjd@hotmail.com

O'HARE, Jeff(rey A.). American (born United States), b. 1958. **Genres:** Children's Fiction, Plays/Screenplays, Young Adult Non-fiction, Children's Non-fiction, Humor/Satire. **Career:** Suffolk County News, sports reporter. **Publications:** (With R.S. Pitt and P.C. Fenlon, Jr.) Creatures of Middle Earth, 1988; Knee Slappers, Side Splitters, and Tummy Ticklers: A Book of Riddles and Jokes, 1992; Searchin Safari: Natures Hidden Wonders, 1992 as Searchin Safari: Looking for Camouflaged Creatures, 1992; What Might I Be?, 1992; Cat & Dog Mysteries: 14 Exciting Mini-Mysteries with Hidden Pictures,

1993; (ed.) Globe Probe Featuring Cincinnati Holmes: Exciting Geographical Adventures All around the World from the Journals of Dr. Croftsford Holmes, 1993; Hanukkah, Happy Hanukkah: Crafts, Recipes, Games, Puzzles, Songs, and More for the Joyous Celebration of the Festival of Lights, 1994; Secret Codes and Hidden Messages, 1997; Giant Book of Mazes, 1997; Puzzlemania Super Challenge, 1998; Bogus Beasts: In Search of Imaginary Animals, 1999; Hanukkah, Festival of Lights: Celebrate with Songs, Decorations, Food, Games, Prayers, and Traditions, 2000; (ed.) Halloween Book of Fun: Puzzles, Games, Jokes, Ideas and More, 2001; (ed.) Winter Book of Fun: Puzzles, Games, Jokes, Ideas, and More, 2002; Beastly Behaviors: Find the Baffling Bonds Between Amazing Animals, 2002; Travel Puzzles and Games from Highlights, 2002; Frogs and Toads, 2003; Puzzlemania Series, 2003; Mathmania, 2004; Dragonball Z: Book of Heroes (& Villains), 2005. **Address:** Boyds Mills Press, 815 Church St., Honesdale, PA 18431, U.S.A. **Online address:** jeffhfc@aol.com

O'HARE, Mick Richard. British (born England), b. 1964?. **Genres:** History, Sports/Fitness. **Career:** Autosport Magazine, production editor; New Scientist Magazine, production editor. **Publications:** (With D. Farrar and P. Lush) Touch and Go: The History of Professional Rugby League in London, 1995; Tries in the Valleys: A History of Rugby League in Wales, 1998; How to Fossilize Your Hamster: And Other Amazing Experiments for the Armchair Scientist, 2008. EDITOR: (with A. Anderson) Bizarre Tales from New Scientist, 1998; The Last Word: New Scientist, 1998; The Last Word 2: New Scientist, 2000; Does Anything Eat Wasps? And 101 Other Questions, 2005; Why Don't Penguins Feet Freeze? And 114 Other Questions, 2006. Contributor to books. **Address:** New Scientist, Lacon House, 84 Theobald's Rd., London, GL WC1X 8NS, England.

O'HEARN, Denis. American (born United States), b. 1953?. **Genres:** Economics, History, Local History/Rural Topics, Adult Non-fiction. **Career:** University of New Mexico, Department of Political Science, research assistant, 1973-75, Department of Economics, research assistant, 1974-75; University of Michigan, research assistant, 1975-78, research associate, 1978-83; University College Dublin, visiting professor, 1992; University of Wisconsin-Madison, assistant professor, 1988-93, associate professor, 1994; Queen's University, professor of sociology, 1994-95, professor, 2003-08; Binghamton University, professor of sociology, 2006-. Writer. **Publications:** (Ed. with B. Barham and S.G. Bunker) States, Firms, and Raw Materials: The World Economy and Ecology of Aluminum, 1994; Inside the Celtic Tiger: The Irish Economy and the Asian Model, 1998; (ed. with R. Munck) Critical Development Theory: Contributions toward a New Paradigm, 1999; The Atlantic Economy: Britain, the U.S. and Ireland, 2001; Nothing but an Unfinished Song: Bobby Sands, the Irish Hunger Striker Who Ignited a Generation, 2006; (with L. McKeon) D'éirigh mé ar maidin: Beathaisńis Roibeaird Uí Sheachnasaigh do Léitheoirí Níos Óige, 2006; (intro.) Wobblies and Zapatistas: Converstions on Anarchism, Marxism, and Radical History, 2008. Contributor to professional journals. **Address:** Department of Sociology, Binghamton University, PO Box 6000, Binghamton, NY 13902-6000, U.S.A. **Online address:** dohearn@binghamton.edu

OHL, Vicki. American (born United States), b. 1950?. **Genres:** Biography, Music. **Career:** Heidelberg University, associate vice president for academic affairs, Arts and Science, dean of undergraduate faculty, professor of piano and music theory, faculty coordinator of honors program, division director for arts, humanities and communication. **Publications:** Fine and Dandy: The Life and Work of Kay Swift (biography), 2004. **Address:** Department of Music, Heidelberg University, Honors House, 310 E Market St., Tiffin, OH 44883-2462, U.S.A. **Online address:** vohl@heidelberg.edu

OHLMEYER, Jane H. Irish/American/Zambian (born Zambia), b. 1962. **Genres:** History. **Career:** University of California, lecturer in history, 1991, visiting lecturer, 1992; Yale University, lecturer in history, 1994-95; University of Aberdeen, lecturer, 1995-2000, professor of history, 2000-03; University of Aberdeen, senior lecturer in history, 1999-2000, professor in Irish history, 2000-03, Head of the School of History and History of Art, 2001-03; Leverhulme Trust, research fellow, 1999-2001; Caledonian Research Foundation, board governor, 2001-; Trinity College, Irish Research Council for the Humanities and Social Sciences, external assessor, 2002, Erasmus Smith's professor of history, 2003-, Erasmus Smith's chair of modern history, principal investigator; Folger Shakespeare Library, seminar director; National Library of Scotland, trustee, 2000-; Maunsel Publishing House, editor, 2001-; Ecole des hautes Etudes en Sciences Sociales, visiting professor, 2005. **Publications:** Civil War and Restoration in the Three Stuart Kingdoms: The Career Of Randal Macdonnell, Marquis Of Antrim, 1609-1683, 1993, 2nd ed., 2001; Making Ireland English, 2012. EDITOR: Ireland From Independence to Occupation, 1641-1660, 1995; (with E.ÓCiardha) The Irish Statute Staple Books, 1596-1687, 1998; (with J. Kenyon and J. Morrill) The Civil Wars: A Military History of England, Scotland and Ireland 1638-1660, 1998; Political Thought in Seventeenth-Century Ireland: Kingdom or Colony?, 2000; (with A.I. Macinnes) The Stuart Kingdoms In The Seventeenth Century: Awkward Neighbours, 2002; (with C. Brady) British Interventions in Early Modern Ireland, 2004; (with E. O'Halpin and R. Armstrong) Intelligence, Statecraft and International Power, 2006; (with D. Dickson and J. Parmentier) Irish And Scottish Mercantile Networks In Europe And Overseas In The Seventeenth And Eighteenth Centuries, 2007. **Address:** Department of History, Trinity College, College Green, Dublin, DU 2, Ireland. **Online address:** jane.ohlmeyer@tcd.ie

OHYE, Bonnie. American (born United States) **Genres:** Human Relations/Parenting, Psychology. **Career:** Massachusetts Psychological Association, Early Career Psychology Initiative, co-founder, 1995; Harvard Medical School/Massachusetts General Hospital, clinical psychologist, OPD supervisor, assistant clinical professor of psychology; Red Sox Foundation and Massachusetts General Hospital, Home Base Family Support Program, clinical director. Writer. **Publications:** Love in Two Languages: Lessons on Mothering in a Culture of Individuality, 2001. **Address:** Department of Psychiatry, Massachusetts General Hospital, YAW 6A, 55 Fruit St., Boston, MA 02114-2696, U.S.A.

OIWA, Keibo. (Shinichi Tsuji). Japanese (born Japan) **Genres:** Anthropology/Ethnology, Environmental Sciences/Ecology, Essays, Translations, History, Social Sciences. **Career:** Meiji Gakuin University, associate professor of international studies, 1991-, professor. Writer. **Publications:** (Ed. with J.V. Koschmann and Y. Shinji) International Perspectives on Yanagita Kunio and Japanese Folklore Studies, 1985; (ed.) Stone Voices: Wartime Writings of Japanese Canadian Issei, 1991; (with D.T. Suzuki) Japan We Never Knew: A Journey of Discovery, 1997; (with D.T. Suzuki) The Other Japan: Voices Beyond the Mainstream, 1999; Rowing the Eternal Sea: The Story of a Minamata Fisherman, 2001. AS SHINICHI TSUJI: Harlem Speaks, 1985; Black Music sae Areba, 1986; Tokoyo no Fune o Kogite: Minamata-byo Shishi, 1986; Here and There: Essays on Japanese and North American Cultures, 1988; Hia ando Zea, 1988; Nikkei Kanadajin, 1990; Redressing the Past: Self-Portraits of Japanese Canadians, 1990; (trans.) Robert F. Murphy, Body Silent, 1992; Slow Is Beautiful: Culture as Slowness, 2001. **Address:** Meiji Gakuin University, 1518 Kamikurata-Cho, Totsuka-Ku, Yokohama, 244-8539, Japan. **Online address:** oiwa@k.meijigakuin.ac.jp

OJA, Carol J. American (born United States), b. 1953. **Genres:** Music. **Career:** City University of New York, Brooklyn College, Conservatory of Music, associate professor, 1985-, Graduate School, associate professor, 1985-; Institute for Studies in American Music, director; Harvard University, Department of Music, professor, William Powell Mason professor of music, graduate advisor in historical musciology; Society for American Music, presdient. Writer. **Publications:** Stravinsky in Modern Music, 1982; Colin McPhee: Composer in Two Worlds, 1990; Making Music Modern: New York in the 1920s, 2000; Bernstein's Broadway: A Musical and Cultural History of the Early Shows, forthcoming. EDITOR: American Music Recordings: A Discography of 20th Century U.S. Composers, 1982; (with R. Crawford and R.L. Lott) A Celebration of American Music: Words and Music in Honor of H. Wiley Hitchcock, 1990; (with R. Allen) Henry Cowell's Musical Worlds: A Program Book for the Henry Cowell Centennial Festival, 1997; (with J. Tick) Aaron Copland and His World, 2005. Contributor to periodicals. **Address:** Department of Music, Harvard University, 304S, Music Bldg., Cambridge, MA 02138, U.S.A. **Online address:** coja@fas.harvard.edu

OJAIDE, Tanure. American/Nigerian (born Nigeria), b. 1948. **Genres:** Poetry, Literary Criticism And History, Autobiography/Memoirs. **Career:** St. Kevin's College, teacher, 1971-73; Federal Government College, English teacher, 1973-75; Petroleum Training Institute, lecturer in English and communication, 1975-77; University of Maiduguri, lecturer in English/communications, 1977-85, senior lecturer, 1985-87, reader, 1987-89; Whitman College, visiting Johnston professor of third world literatures, 1989-90; University of North Carolina, assistant professor, 1990-93, associate professor, 1993-98, professor of African-American and African studies, 1998-, Frank Porter Graham professor of Africana studies, 2006-, African Studies Academy, chairman; Albright College, National Endowment for the Humanities professor, 1996-97. Writer. **Publications:** POETRY: Children of Iroko and Other Poems, 1973; (with S.S. Ugheteni) Yono Urhobo: Obe Rerha, 1981; Labyrinths of the Delta, 1986; The Eagle's Vision, 1987; Poems, 1988; The Endless Song, 1989; The Fate of Vultures and Other Poems, 1990; The Blood of Peace, 1991; The Daydream of Ants and Other Poems, 1997; Cannons for the Brave, 1998; Delta Blues and Home Songs: Poems, 1998; When It No Longer Matters Where You Live, 1998; Invoking the Warrior Spirit: New and Selected Poems, 1999. OTHERS: The Poetry of Wole Soyinka (criticism), 1994; Poetic Imagination in Black Africa: Essays on African Poetry (criticism), 1996; Great Boys: An African Childhood (autobiography), 1998; (ed. with T.M. Sallah) The New African Poetry: An Anthology, 1999; In the Kingdom of Songs: A Trilogy of Poems, 1952-2000, 2002; (with J. Obi) Culture, Society and Politics in Modern African Literature, 2002; Poetry, Performance and Art: Udje Dance Songs of the Urhobo People, 2003; I Want to Dance and Other Poems, 2003; God's Medicine-Men and Other Stories, 2004; The Activist, 2006; In the House of Words, 2006; Waiting for the Hatching of a Cockerel, 2008; Debt-Collector and Other Stories, 2009; Theorizing African Oral Poetic Performance and Aesthetics: Udje Dance Songs of the Urhobo People, 2009; Matters of the Moment, 2009; Beauty I Have Seen, 2010; (ed.) Contemporary African Writers, 2011; Contemporary African Literature, 2011. Contributor of articles to books and periodicals. Works appear in anthologies. **Address:** Department of Africana Studies, University of North Carolina, 138 Garinger, 9201 University City Blvd., Charlotte, NC 28223-0001, U.S.A. **Online address:** tojaide@email.uncc.edu

OJEDA, José Promis. *See* **PROMIS, José.**

O'KANE, Bernard. Egyptian/Irish (born Ireland) **Genres:** Regional/Urban Planning, Photography. **Career:** British Institute of Persian Studies, assistant director, 1976-79; University of London, School of Examinations Department, assistant examiner, 1979-; American University in Cairo, Department of Arabic Studies, instructor, 1980-82, assistant professor, 1982-86, Center for Arabic Studies, assistant director, 1985-86, director, 1989-91, associate professor, 1986-93, professor of Islamic art and architecture, 1993-; Harvard University, Department of Fine Arts, visiting associate professor, 1991-92; University of California, Departments of Near Eastern Studies and History of Art, visiting professor, 1995-96. Writer. **Publications:** Timurid Architecture in Khurasan, 1987; Studies in Persian Art and Architecture, 1995; Early Persian Painting: Kalila and Dimna Manuscripts of the Late Fourteenth Century, 2003; (ed.) The Iconography of Islamic Art: Studies in Honour of Robert Hillenbrand, 2005; (ed.) The Treasures of Islamic Art in the Museums of Cairo, 2006; Treasures of Islam: Artistic Glories of the Muslim World, 2007; The Appearance of Persian on Islamic Art, 2009. Contributor to books and periodicals. **Address:** American University in Cairo, PO Box 2511, Cairo, 11511, Egypt. **Online address:** bokane@aucegypt.edu

O'KANE, James M. American (born United States), b. 1941. **Genres:** Sociology, Criminology/True Crime, Young Adult Non-fiction. **Career:** St. Francis College, instructor in sociology, 1964-67; Drew University, instructor, 1967-68, assistant professor, 1968-72, associate professor, 1972-78, professor of sociology, 1978-, chair of department, 1970-78, 1980-86, 1989-90, Center for Public and Corporate Affairs, member of advisory council, 1982-83, professor of sociology emeritus; New York University, member of summer faculty, 1969-70, Resident Center, teacher, 1969; Focus House, Department of Water Resources, director, 1970, 1971; University of Navarra, visiting research professor, 1973; Social Science Research Associates, founder, 1974, research director, 1974-; Discovery Club (boys' club), founder, 1979, director, 1979-85; Media Methods Inc., consultant to U.S. Department of Housing and Urban Development; Madison Community Pool Corp., vice-president of board, 1981, president, 1982. Writer. **Publications:** Pamplona: A Sociological Analysis of Migration and Urban Adaptation Patterns, 1981; The Crooked Ladder: Gangsters, Ethnicity, and the American Dream, 1992; Wicked Deeds: Murder in America, 2005. Work represented in anthologies. Contributor of articles and reviews to journals in the social sciences and to newspapers. **Address:** Department of Sociology, Drew University, Rm. 24, Gilbert House, Madison, NJ 07940, U.S.A.

O'KANE, Rosemary H.T. British (born England), b. 1947. **Genres:** Politics/Government, History, Social Sciences. **Career:** University of Keele, professor of comparative political theory, 1973-, now professor emeritus of comparative political theory. Writer. **Publications:** The Likelihood of Coups, 1987; The Revolutionary Reign of Terror: The Role of Violence in Political Change, 1991; Terror, Force and States: The Path from Modernity, 1996; (ed. and intro.) Revolution: Critical Concept in Political Science, 4 vols., 2000; Paths to Democracy: Revolution and Totalitarianism, 2004; (ed.) Terrorism, 2 vols., 2005. Contributor to journals. **Address:** Department of Politics, University of Keele, Rm. CBA 1.017, Chancellor's Bldg., Keele, ST ST5 5BG, England. **Online address:** r.h.t.okane@pol.keele.ac.uk

OKANIMA, Dorothy. *See* **SEGUN, Mabel D.**

O'KEEFE, Deborah (Janney). American (born United States), b. 1939. **Genres:** Science Fiction/Fantasy, History, Young Adult Fiction. **Career:** Hobart-William Smith College, assistant professor of English, 1960-61; Reader's Digest Educational Division, assistant editor, 1961-62; Vassar College, visiting assistant professor of English, 1977-79; Manhattanville College, director of writing program and assistant professor of English, 1980-86; Johns Hopkins University, Center for Gifted and Talented Youth, expository writing program teacher, 1987-90. **Publications:** Good Girl Messages: How Young Women Were Misled by Their Favorite Books, 2000; Readers in Wonderland: The Liberating Worlds of Fantasy Fiction: From Dorothy to Harry Potter, 2003. Contributor to periodicals, newspapers and magazines. **Address:** c/o Publicity Director, The Continuum International Publishing Group Ltd., 80 Maiden Ln., Ste. 704, New York, NY 10038, U.S.A.

O'KEEFE, Kevin. American (born United States) **Genres:** Adult Non-fiction, Novels. **Career:** Lawyer, 1982-99; Prairielaw.com, founder, 1998-2001; Quintus, managing director and head, 1999-2001; Martindale-Hubbell, vice president of business development, 2001-02; LexBlog Inc., chief executive officer and publisher, 2003-, ProPolo, chief executive, 2007-10; EverBank, consultant, 2010-. Journalist and consultant. **Publications:** The Average American: The Extraordinary Search for the Nation's Most Ordinary Citizen, 2005. Contributor to periodicals. **Address:** LexBlog Inc., 95 S Jackson St., Ste. 200, Seattle, WA 98104-4418, U.S.A. **Online address:** kevin@lexblog.com

O'KEEFE, Susan Heyboer. American (born United States), b. 1953. **Genres:** Picture/Board Books. **Career:** Writer. **Publications:** One Hungry Monster: A Counting Book in Rhyme, 1989; A Season for Giving, 1990; A Bug from Aunt Tillie, 1991; Who Will Miss Me If I Don't Go to Church?, 1992; Countdown to Christmas: Advent Thoughts Prayers and Activities, 1995; Administrative Assistants and Secretarys Handbook, 1995; Sleepy Angels First Bedtime Story, 1999; Master the ACT, 1999; Good Night God Bless, 1999; Angel Prayers: Prayers for All Children, 1999; Its Great to Be Catholic!, 2001; Love Me Love You, 2001; My Life and Death by Alexandra Canarsie, 2001; What Does a Priest Do?: What Does a Nun Do?, 2002; Death by Eggplant, 2004; Christmas Gifts, 2004; Be the Star that You Are!: A Book for Kids Who Feel Different, 2005; Baby Day, 2006; Hungry Monster ABC, 2007; Frankenstein's Monster: A Novel, 2010. **Address:** c/o Steven Chudney, The Chudney Agency, 72 N State Rd., Ste. 501, Briarcliff Manor, NY 10510, U.S.A. **Online address:** susan@susanheyboerokeefe.com

O'KEEFFE, Frank. Canadian/Irish (born Ireland), b. 1938. **Genres:** Children's Fiction, Young Adult Fiction, Novels, Natural History. **Career:** Yellowhead School Division, teacher-librarian and teacher, 1973-88, substitute teacher, 1988-96; Lakehead College, creative writing educator; Lakehead College, teacher; Edmonton Public School, teacher; writer, 1985-. **Publications:** Guppy Love, or, The Day the Fish Tank Exploded, 1986; School Stinks!, 1991; (with M. Godfrey) There's a Cow in My Swimming Pool, 1991; It's Only a Game, 1992; Weekend at the Ritz, 1993; Nancy Nylen-Ordinary Farm Girl/Explorer Extraordinaire, 1994; If It Rains Again Tomorrow, Can We Go Home?, 1996; Mad about Marvin and Harry Flammable, forthcoming. **Address:** The Writer's Union of Canada, 90 Richmond St. E, Ste. 200, Toronto, ON M5C 1P1, Canada.

OKIMOTO, Jean Davies. American (born United States), b. 1942. **Genres:** Young Adult Fiction, Picture/Board Books, Novels, E-books, Psychology, Plays/Screenplays, Novellas/Short Stories, Children's Fiction, Adult Non-fiction, Human Relations/Parenting. **Career:** Mount Baker Community Club, vice president, 1968; teacher, 1972-73; University of Washington, editorial consultant in child psychiatry, 1973-74; Mount Baker Youth Service Bureau, assistant, 1974-75. Writer. **Publications:** My Mother Is Not Married to My Father, 1979; It's Just Too Much, 1980; Norman Schnurman, Average Person, 1982; Who Did It, Jenny Lake?, 1983; Jason's Women, 1986; (with P.J. Stegall) Boomerang Kids: How to Live with Adult Children who Return Home, 1987; Blumpoe the Grumpoe Meets Arnold the Cat, 1990; Molly by

Any Other Name, 1990; Take a Chance, Gramps!, 1990; A Place for Grace, 1993; Hum It Again, Jeremy (one-act play), 1990; No Dear, Not Here: The Marbled Murrelets' Quest for a Nest in the Pacific Northwest, 1995; Talent Night, 1995; Uncle Hideki, 1995; The Eclipse of Moonbeam Dawson, 1997; To Jaykae: Life Stinx, 1999; Dear Ichiro, 2002; (with E.M Aoki) The White Swan Express: A Story about Adoption, 2002; Uncle Hideki and the Empty Nest, 2006; Winston of Churchill: One Bear's Battle Against Global Warming, 2007; The Love Ceiling, 2009; Maya and the Cotton Candy Boy, 2011; Walter's Muse, 2012. Works appear in anthologies. **Address:** PO Box 13305, Burton, WA 98013, U.S.A. **Online address:** jokim12345@aol.com

OKKER, Patricia. American (born United States), b. 1960. **Genres:** Literary Criticism And History, Women's Studies And Issues, Young Adult Fiction. **Career:** University of Missouri, Department of English, assistant professor, 1990-96, associate professor, 1996-2004, William T. Kemper fellow, 2003, professor of English, 2004-, associate chair, chair, Provost Office, faculty fellow. Writer. **Publications:** Our Sister Editors: Sarah J. Hale and the Tradition of Nineteenth-Century American Women Editors, 1995; Social Stories: The Magazine Novel in Nineteenth-Century America, 2003; (ed.) Transnationalism and American Serial Fiction, 2011. Contributor of articles to books and periodicals. **Address:** Department of English, University of Missouri, TBA, 107 Tate Hall, Columbia, MI 65211-1500, U.S.A. **Online address:** okkerp@missouri.edu

OKORAFOR-MBACHU, Nnedi. American (born United States), b. 1974. **Genres:** Children's Fiction, Novels, Science Fiction/Fantasy, Young Adult Fiction. **Career:** The Star Newspapers Tinley Park, columnist, 1998-; Afrique Newsmagazine, editor, 1999-2000; freelance writer, 2000-03; University of Illinois, Chancellor's Office, graduate assistant, 2000-01, Department of English, teaching assistant, 2003-07; Black Issues Book Review, writer, 2003-; Governors State University, Department of English, adjunct professor, 2002-; Chicago State University, visiting professor of creative writing, 2008-09, assistant professor of creative writing, 2009-, professor of creative writing. **Publications:** NOVELS: Zahrah the Windseeker, 2005; The Shadow Speaker, 2007; Long Juju Man, 2008; Who Fears Death?, 2010; Akata Witch, 2011. Works appear in anthologies. Contributor to periodicals. **Address:** c/o Donald Maass, Donald Maass Literary Agency, 121 W 27th St., Ste. 801, New York, NY 10001-6262, U.S.A. **Online address:** nnedi@netscape.com

OKORO, Anezi. Nigerian (born Nigeria), b. 1929. **Genres:** Children's Fiction, Medicine/Health, Environmental Sciences/Ecology, Picture/Board Books, Education. **Career:** University College Hospital, house surgeon, 1956-57; Ministry of Health-Lagos, medical officer, 1957-64, consultant dermatologist, 1965-66; University of Lagos, College of Medicine, associate lecturer, 1964-66; Ministry of Health-Enugu, consultant dermatologist, 1966-74; University of Nigeria, senior lecturer, 1967-74, reader, 1974-75, professor of medicine, 1975-; Nigerian National Petroleum Corp., director, 1977-81; African Association for Dermatology, president, 1986-91; Medical College of Georgia, visiting professor, 1987; University of Minnesota, visiting professor, 1988; King Faisal University, professor of dermatology, 1989-95. Writer. **Publications:** The Village School, 1966; The Village Headmaster, 1967; New Broom at Amanzu, 1967; Febechi down the Niger, 1971; Febechi and Group in Cave Adventure, 1972; One Week in Trouble, 1973; Dr. Amadi's Postings, 1974; Pictorial Handbook of Common Skin Diseases, 1981; Education Is Great, 1986; Double Trouble, 1990; Pariah Earth and Other Stories, 1994; The Second Great Flood, 2000; Hands Off!, Young Doctor, 2003; Flying Tortoise, 2004; Ringing Verses for African Schools, 2004; Eclipse Fever, 2007. **Address:** Skin Clinic, University of Nigeria Teaching Hospital, PO Box 01129, Enugu, 00176, Nigeria. **Online address:** anokese@infoweb.com.ng

OKPARA, Mzee Lasana. *See* **HORD, Frederick (Lee).**

OKRANT, Robyn. American (born United States), b. 1973?. **Genres:** Biography. **Career:** Writer, actor, educator and director. **Publications:** Living Oprah: My One-Year Experiment to Walk the Walk of the Queen of Talk, 2010. **Address:** Chicago, IL , U.S.A. **Online address:** robyn@robynokrant.com

OKRI, Ben. Nigerian (born Nigeria), b. 1959. **Genres:** Novels, Novellas/Short Stories, Poetry. **Career:** West Africa Magazine, journalist and poetry editor, 1981-87; West Africa magazine, poetry editor, 1983-86; BBC World Service, host, 1984-85; Royal Society of Literature, fellow, 1987; Trinity College, visiting fellow, fellow commoner, 1991-93; International PEN, English Centre, vice-president; Royal Society of Literature, fellow; University of California, Department of English, Robert Bennett lecturer. **Publications:** Flowers and Shadows (novel), 1980; The Landscapes Within (novel), 1981; Incidents at the Shrine: Short Stories, 1986; Stars of the New Curfew (short stories), 1988; The Famished Road (novel), 1991; An African Elegy, 1992; Songs of Enchantment, 1993; Astonishing the Gods, 1995; Birds of Heaven, 1995; Dangerous Love, 1996; A Way of Being Free, 1997; Infinite Riches, 1999; Mental Flight, 1999; Awakening Age, 2001; In Arcadia, 2002; Starbook: A Magical Tale of Love and Regeneration, 2007; Tales of Freedom, 2009; A Time for New Dreams, 2011. Contributor of articles to periodicals. **Address:** c/o Author Mail, The Orion Publishing Group Ltd., Orion House, 5 Upper St. Matrin's Ln., London, GL WC2H 9EA, England.

OKTENBERG, Adrian. American (born United States), b. 1947. **Genres:** Poetry, Essays, Literary Criticism And History, Young Adult Fiction. **Career:** Writer, 1979-. **Publications:** POETRY: The Bosnia Elegies, 1997; Drawing in the Dirt (chapbook), 1997; Swimming with Dolphins, 2002. Contributor to periodicals. **Address:** c/o Paris Press, PO Box 487, Ashfield, MA 01330, U.S.A.

OKWU, Julian C. R. American/British (born England), b. 1966. **Genres:** Photography, History, Biography. **Career:** MacWorld, staff, 1989. Photographer and writer. **Publications:** Face Forward: Young African American Men in a Critical Age (photographs and commentaries), 1997; As I Am: Young African American Women in a Critical Age, 1999. **Address:** Chronicle Books, 85 2nd St., San Francisco, CA 94105, U.S.A. **Online address:** julian@jujustudios.com

OLALEYE, Isaac O. American/Nigerian (born Nigeria), b. 1941. **Genres:** Novellas/Short Stories, Children's Fiction, Poetry, Adult Non-fiction, Children's Non-fiction, Race Relations, Young Adult Fiction, History, Social Sciences. **Career:** Nigeria's Department of Public Prosecutions, messenger; Pan American Airways, sales agent. Writer. **Publications:** Did God Make Them Black?, 1990; Bitter Bananas (juvenile), 1994; Distant Talking Drums (juvenile), 1995; Lake of the Big Snake (juvenile), 1998; In the Rainfield: Who is the Greatest?, 2000; Bikes for Rent! (Juvenile), 2001. Contributor to magazines. **Address:** PO Box 38, Chula Vista, TX 91912, U.S.A.

OLASKY, Marvin. American (born United States), b. 1950. **Genres:** History, Politics/Government, Social Commentary, Writing/Journalism, Business/Trade/Industry, Theology/Religion, Social Sciences. **Career:** Boston Globe, reporter and correspondent, 1970-71, 1973; Bulletin, Bend, reporter, 1971-72; San Diego State University, lecturer, 1976-77; Du Pont Co., academic affairs coordinator and speech writer, 1978-83; University of Texas at Austin, assistant professor, 1983-88, associate professor of journalism, 1988-93, professor of journalism, 1993-; World Magazine, editor, 1994-; Progress and Freedom Foundation, senior fellow, 1995-96; Austin American-Statesman, biweekly columnist, 1996-2003; Acton Institute for the Study of Religion and Liberty, senior fellow, 1999-; Princeton University, visiting professor, 2004-06. Writer. **Publications:** Corporate Public Relations: A New Historical Perspective, 1987; Patterns of Corporate Philanthropy: Public Affairs and the Forbes 100, 1987; (with H. Schlossberg) Turning Point: A Christian Worldview Declaration, 1987; Prodigal Press: The Anti-Christian Bias of the News Media, 1988; The Press and Abortion, 1838-1988, 1988; (ed.) Freedom, Justice and Hope: Toward a Strategy for the Poor and the Oppressed, 1988; (with S. Olasky) More than Kindness: A Compassionate Approach to Childbearing, 1990; Central Ideas in the Development of American Journalism, 1991; Patterns of Corporate Philanthropy, 1991; The Tragedy of American Compassion, 1992; Abortion Rites: A Social History of Abortion in America, 1992; Philanthropically Correct: The Story of the Council on Foundations, 1993; (ed.) Loving Your Neighbor: A Principled Guide to Charity, 1995; Fighting for Liberty and Virtue: Political and Cultural Wars in Eighteenth-Century America, 1995; Renewing American Compassion, 1996; Telling the Truth: How to Revitalize Christian Journalism, 1996; (with J. Belz) Whirled Views: Tracking Today's Culture Storms, 1997; The American Leadership Tradition: Moral Vision from Washington to Clinton, 1999, rev. ed. as The American Leadership Tradition: The Inevitable Impact of a Leader's Faith on a Nation's Destiny, 2000; Compassionate Conservatism: What It Is, What It Does and How It Can Transform America, 2000; Standing for Christ in a Modern Babylon, 2003; Religions Next Door: What We Need to Know About Judaism, Hinduism, Buddhism and Islam and What Reporters are Missing, 2004; Monkey Business: The True Story of the Scopes Trial, 2005; Scimitar's Edge, 2006; The Politics of Disaster, 2006; Unreliable Witnesses, 2007. Contributor to periodicals. **Address:** School of Journalism, University of Texas, PO Box A1000, Austin, TX 78712, U.S.A. **Online address:** molasky@aol.com

OLBERMANN, Keith. American (born United States), b. 1959. **Genres:** Humor/Satire, Social Sciences. **Career:** UPI Radio Network, sports reporter, 1979-80; RKO Radio, sports reporter, 1980-82; WNEW-AM, sports reporter, 1980-83; Cable News Network (CNN), national sports reporter and anchor, 1981-84; WCVB-TV, national sports reporter and anchor, 1984; KTLA-TV, weeknight sports reporter and anchor, 1985-88; KCBS-TV, sports anchor and host of the Keith Olbermann Show, 1988-91; Entertainment and Sports Programming Network (ESPN), ESPN Sports Radio, weekend co-host, 1992-93, co-host, 2005-07, ESPN2, co-anchor of Sports Night, 1993-94, ESPN, SportsCenter, co-anchor and co-host, 1992-97; National Broadcasting Co. (NBC)/ MSNBC, columnist and television host, 1997-98, Countdown, host, 2003-; Fox Sports News, 1999-2001; Salon.com, columnist, 2002-03; NBC Sports, Football Night in America, co-host, 2007-. Writer and sports commentator. **Publications:** NONFICTION: The Big Show: Inside ESPN's SportsCenter, 1997; The Worst Person in the World: And 202 Strong Contenders, 2006; Truth and Consequences: Special Comments on the Bush Administration's War on American Values, 2007. **Address:** MSNBC Cable L.L.C., 30 Rockefeller Plz., 38th Fl., New York, NY 10112-3899, U.S.A.

OLCOTT, Jocelyn. (Jocelyn Harrison Olcott). American (born United States), b. 1970. **Genres:** Women's Studies And Issues, History. **Career:** California State University, assistant professor, 2000-02; Duke University, Department of History, Andrew W. Mellon associate professor and associate chair, 2002-. Writer. **Publications:** Revolutionary Women in Postrevolutionary Mexico, 2005; (ed. with M.K. Vaughan and G. Cano) Sex in Revolution: Gender, Politics, and Power in Modern Mexico, 2006. Contributor to journals. **Address:** Department of History, Duke University, 315 Carr Bldg., PO Box 90719, Durham, NC 27708-0719, U.S.A. **Online address:** olcott@duke.edu

OLCOTT, Jocelyn Harrison. *See* **OLCOTT, Jocelyn.**

OLDENBURG, Carl. *See* **OLDENBURG, Ray.**

OLDENBURG, Ramon A. *See* **OLDENBURG, Ray.**

OLDENBURG, Ray. Also writes as Carl Oldenburg, Ramon A. Oldenburg. American (born United States), b. 1932. **Genres:** Social Commentary, Urban Studies, Theology/Religion, Humor/Satire, Social Sciences. **Career:** High school teacher, 1957-58; University of Minnesota, instructor in sociology, 1963-65; Stout State University, assistant professor of sociology, 1965-66; University of Nevada, assistant professor of sociology, 1966-67; University of West Florida, assistant professor, 1967-68, Department of Sociology, Anthropology, Earth and Atmospheric Sciences, chair, 1968-71, 1975-77, 1979-81, associate professor of sociology, 1968-, professor of sociology, through 2001, professor emeritus of sociology and anthropology, 2001-, Kairos Halfway House for Boys, president, 1970-72. Writer. **Publications:** (As Carl Oldenburg) Frog Croaks: Haiku Tongue-in-Cheek, 1975; The Great Good Place: Cafes, Coffee Shops, Community Centers, Beauty Parlors, General Stores, Bars, Hangouts, at the Heart of Community, 1989, 3rd ed., 1999; (ed. with intro.) Celebrating the Third Place: Inspiring Stories About The Great Good Places At The Heart Of Our Communities, 2001. Contributor of articles to journals and newspapers. **Address:** 4635 Tree Line Dr., Pensacola, FL 32504, U.S.A. **Online address:** rayoldenburg@msn.com

OLDERR, Steven. American (born United States), b. 1943. **Genres:** Sports/Fitness, Bibliography, Reference. **Career:** Teacher, 1970-71; Eisenhower Public Library, assistant director, 1972-74; Riverside Public Library, director, 1974-88; Naperville Public Libraries, assistant director, 1992-96; Prevention First Inc., library manager, 1998-99; Institute for Clinical Social Work, library manager/webmaster, 1999-; Saint Paul's Parish, librarian and webmaster. Writer. **Publications:** (Comp.) Symbolism: A Comprehensive Dictionary, 1986; Olderr's Fiction Index, 1987; Mystery Index: Subjects, Settings and Sleuths of 10000 Titles, 1987; Olderr's Young Adult Fiction Index, 1989; Olderr's Fiction Subject Headings: A Supplement and Guide to the LC Thesaurus, 1991; (comp.) Reverse Symbolism Dictionary: Symbols Listed by Subject, 1992; Pan American Games: A Statistical History, 1951-1999, 2003. **Address:** St. Paul's Parish, 60 Akenside Rd., Riverside, IL 60546, U.S.A. **Online address:** olderr@ameritech.net

OLDFIELD, Jenny. Also writes as Jodie Mellor, Donna King, Jasmine Oliver, Kate Pennington. British (born England), b. 1949. **Genres:** Children's Fiction, Children's Non-fiction, Literary Criticism And History, Novels, Picture/Board Books, Animals/Pets. **Career:** Edgbaston High School, English teacher, 1972-74; Fairleigh Dickinson University, Wroxton College, lecturer in English, 1976; King Edward's High School for Girls, English teacher, 1977. Writer, 1977-. **Publications:** Tomorrow Shall Be My Dancing Day, 1975; Mr. Hardisty's Kind Offer, 1975; Secret of the Seasons, 1976; Jane Eyre and Wuthering Heights: A Study Guide, 1976; Fancy That! 1979; Going Soft, 1979; Yours Truly..., 1979; The Terrible Pet, 1979; The True Loves of Tannockburn, 1980; Rough Remedies, 1981; Fitzwilliam Frog: His Problem at the Pool, 1986; Said the Blind Man (adult novel), 1986; Vincent Viper, 1987; Ricardo Rat, 1987; Leonardo Lizard, 1988; Smile Please, 1989; Bad Company, 1989; January's Child, 1989; Misfits and Rebels: Short Stories, 1990; Rings on Her Fingers, 1992; Camping Paradiso, 1994; The Hidden Tomb, 1995; Pardise Court, 1995; After Hours, 1996; Deadline, 1996; All Fall Down, 1997; Extra Time, 1999; Off-Side, 2001; Silver Cloud, 2002; Iron Eyes, 2002; Bad Heart, 2003. ANIMAL ALERT SERIES: Abandoned, 1997; Killer on the Loose, 1997; Quarantine, 1997; Intensive Care, 1997; Skin and Bone, 1998; Living Proof, 1998; Blind Alley, 1998; Grievous Bodily Harm, 1998; Crash, 1998; Running Wild, 1998; Lost and Found, 1999; Heatwave, 1999. ONE FOR SORROW SERIES: One for Sorrow, 1999; Two for Joy, 1999; Three for a Girl, 1999; Four for a Boy, 1999; Five for Silver, 2000; Six for Gold, 2000; Seven for a Secret, 2000; Eight for a Wish, 2000; Nine for a Kiss, 2000. HOME FARM TWINS SERIES: Speckle: The Stray, 1996; Solo: The Homeless, 1996; Susie: The Orphan, 1996; Snip and Snap: The Truants, 1996; Spike: The Tramp, 1996; Sinbad: The Runaway, 1996; Home Farm Twins, 1997; Sunny: The Hero, 1997; Stevie: The Rebel, 1997; Sampson: The Giant, 1997; Scruffy: The Scamp, 1997; Socks: The Survivor, 1997; Smoky the Mystery, 1998; Skye: The Champion, 1998; Stanley: The Troublemaker, 1998; Sorrel: The Substitute, 1998; Sultan: The Patient, 1998; Sugar and Spice: The Pickpockets, 1998; Sophie: The Show-Off, 1998; Smoky: The Mystery, 1998; Silky: The Foundling, 1999; Stalky: The Mascot, 1999; Shelley: The Shadow, 1999; Spot: The Prisoner, 1999; Scott: The Braveheart, 1999; Samantha: The Snob, 1999; Star: The Surprise, 1999; Maisie Wants Her Mum, 2000; Short Story Collections Snapshots, 2000; Mitch Goes Missing, 2000; Smarty: The Outcast, 2000; Mac Climbs a Mountain, 2000; Home Farm Friends: Short Story Collection, 2000; Titch Plays Tricks, 2001; Tess Gets Trapped, 2001; Toby Takes the Plunge, 2001. HORSES OF HALF MOON RANCH SERIES: Wild Horses, 1999; Midnight Lady, 1999; Crazy Horse, 1999; Johnny Mohawk, 1999; Rodeo Rocky, 1999; Third-Time Lucky, 1999; Navaho Joe, 2000; Jethro Junior, 2000; Danny Boy, 2000; Hollywood Princess, 2000; Little Vixen, 2000; Gunsmoke, 2000; Golden Dawn, 2000; Starlight, 2000; Moondance, 2001; Skylark, 2001; Steamboat Charlie, 2001; Lady Roseanne, 2001; Silver Spur, 2001; Eagle Wing, 2001; El Dorado, 2001; Santa Ana, 2001; Chiquitita, 2001; Diamond Charm, 2002. DEFINITELY DAISY SERIES: You're a Disgrace, Daisy!, 2001; Just You Wait, Winona!, 2001; You Must Be Joking, Jimmy!, 2001; I'd Like a Little Word, Leonie!, 2001; Not Now, Nathan!, 2001; What's the Matter, Maya?, 2001; Dream on, Daisy!, 2001; Daisy Dares, 2005; Not Again, Daisy!: Books 4-6, 2005; Watch Out, Daisy!: Books 1-3, 2005. TOTALLY TOM SERIES: Tell Me the Truth, Tom!, 2002; Watch out, Wayne, 2002; Get Lost, Lola!, 2002; Keep the Noise Down, Kingsley, 2002; Drop Dead, Danielle, 2002; Don't Make Me Laugh, Liam, 2002; Tough It Out, Tom, 2003. MY LITTLE LIFE SERIES: When Ellie Cheated, 2002; When Scott Got Lost, 2002; When Geri and I Fell Out, 2002; When Dad Went on a Date, 2002; When I Won a Prize, 2002; When Shah Went Weird, 2002. AS KATE PENNINGTON: Tread Softly, 2004; Brief Candle, 2004; Charley Feather, 2005; Nightingale's Song, 2006. AS JODIE MELLOR: MYSTERY PUPS SERIES: Dognapped!, 2008; Framed!, 2008; Diamond Dogs!, 2009; Missing!, 2009. AS JASMINE OLIVER: MATERIAL GIRLS SERIES: Gucci Girls, 2005; Armani Angels, 2005; Prada Princesses, 2006. AS DONNA KING: GOING FOR THE GOLD SERIES: Double Twist, 2007; Game, Set, and Match, 2007; Kick Off, 2007; Slam Dunk, 2007. AS DONNA KING: UNBEATABLE SERIES: Balancing Act, 2008; Riding High, 2008. SHAKESPEARE TODAY SERIES: As You Like It, 2009; Much Ado About Nothing, 2011. DRESSING-UP DREAMS SERIES: Ruby's Satin Dress, 2008; Ruby's Diamond Tiara, 2008; Ruby's Velvet Cloak, 2008; Ruby's Glass Slippers, 2008; The Silver Mirror, 2008; The Flowered Apron, 2008; The Pearly Comb, 2008; The Lace Gown, 2008; The Red Cloak, 2009; The Party Frock, 2009; The Picnic Basket, 2009; The Frilly Nightdress, 2009. MY MAGICAL PONY: Shining Star, 2005; Silver Mist, 2005; Bright Eyes, 2006; Dawn Light, 2006; Falling Leaves, 2006; Midnight Snow, 2006; North Star, 2006; Pale Moon, 2006; Red Skies, 2006; Sea Haze, 2006; Summer Shadows, 2006; Summertime Blues, 2006; New

Beginnings, 2007; Secret Whispers, 2007; Starlight Dreams, 2007. WILDE FAMILY: Running Wilde, 2003; Wilde Child, 2003; Wilde Day Out, 2003; Wild Style, 2003; Wilde Party, 2004; Wilde Ride, 2004. BLACK PEARL PONIES SERIES: Red Star, 2011; Wildflower, 2011; Miss Molly, 2011; Stormcloud, 2011; Snickers, 2011; Ghost Horse, 2011. OTHERS: Paradise Court/After Hours, 2002; Callum Mccoodle: Streetwise, 2004; Harmony Harris Cuts Loose, 2004; Live the Dream!, 2004; Marsha Martinez Meets the Stars, 2005; Pet School, 2005; The Runaway, 2005; The Dreamseeker Trilogy, 2005; (comp.) The Kingfisher Book of Horse and Pony Stories, 2005; Wings of Icarus: White Wolves, 2007; Mystery Pups, 2008. **Address:** Caroline Sheldon Literary Agency Ltd., 71 Hillgate Pl., London, GL W8 7SS, England. **Online address:** mail@jennyoldfield.com

OLDFIELD, J(ohn) R(ichard). British/Welsh (born Wales), b. 1953. **Genres:** History, Social Sciences, Politics/Government. **Career:** University of Leicester, lecturer in history, 1980-83; University of Southampton, lecturer, 1983-95, senior lecturer in history, 1995-, professor; University of South Carolina, visiting research professor, 1988, 1993-94. Writer. **Publications:** Alexander Crummell (1819-1898) and the Creation of an African-American Church in Liberia, 1990; Printers, Booksellers and Libraries in Hampshire, 1750-1800, 1993; (ed.) Civilization and Black Progress: Selected Writings of Alexander Crummell on the South, 1995; Popular Politics and British Anti-Slavery: The Mobilisation of Public Opinion Against the Slave Trade, 1787-1807, 1995; On the Beat: Black Policemen in Charleston, South Carolina, 1868-1921, 2001; Transatlanticism, Slavery and Race, 2002; (ed.) The British Transatlantic Slave Trade, vol. III: The Abolitionist Struggle: Opponents of the Slave Trade, 2003; Chords of Freedom: Commemoration, Ritual and British Transatlantic Slavery, 2007; (ed. with C. Kaplan) Imagining Transatlantic Slavery, 2010. Contributor of articles to books and journals. **Address:** Department of History, University of Southampton, 65 Bldg., Avenue Campus, Highfield, Southampton, HM SO17 1BF, England. **Online address:** jro1@soton.ac.uk

OLDFIELD, Michael. British (born England), b. 1953. **Genres:** Writing/Journalism, Music. **Career:** Middlesex Advertiser, journalist, 1967-70; Melody Maker, journalist, 1970-78, editor, 1980-84; Daily Mail, journalist, 1978-80; freelance journalist, 1984-. **Publications:** Dire Straits, 1984; Born in the U.K., 1988. Contributor to periodicals. **Address:** 7 Highlever Rd., London, GL W10 6PP, England.

OLDFIELD, Pamela. British (born England), b. 1931. **Genres:** Novellas/Short Stories, Romance/Historical, Children's Fiction, Picture/Board Books, Novels. **Career:** Writer and educator. **Publications:** FOR CHILDREN: Melanie Brown Goes to School, 1970; Melanie Brown Climbs a Tree, 1972; The Adventures of Sarah and Theodore Bodgitt, 1974; Melanie Brown and the Jar of Sweets, 1974; The Hallowe'en Pumpkin, 1974; Simon's Extra Gran, 1974; A Witch in the House, 1976; The Terribly Plain Princess and Other Stories, 1977; The Adventures of the Gumby Gang, 1978; The Gumby Gang Again, 1978; Katy and Dom, 1978; More about the Gumby Gang, 1979; Katy and Dom and the Lost Cat, 1979; Children of the Plague, 1979; The Gumby Gang Strikes Again, 1980; The Gumby Gang on Holiday, 1980; The Rising of the Wain, 1980; The Riverside Cat, 1980; Cloppity, 1981; Parkin's Storm, 1982; Tommie Dobbie and the Witch Next Door, 1983; The Princess Well-I-May, 1983; Ghost Stories, 1984; Hurdy-Gurdy, 1984 in US as Merry-Go-Round, 1985; Barnaby and Bell and the Lost Button, 1985; Barnaby and Bell and the Birthday Cake, 1985; The Christmas Ghost, 1985; Ginger's Nine Lives, 1986; Roller Coaster, 1986; The Return of the Gumby Gang, 1986; Toby and the Donkey, 1986; The Ghosts of Bellering Oast, 1987; The Magic Toys, 1987; Spine Chillers, 1987; (reteller) Tales from Ancient Greece, 1988; Stories from Ancient Greece (retellings), 1988; Sam, Sue and Cinderella, 1989; Bomb Alert, 1989; Secret Persuader, 1989; A Shaggy Dog Story, 1990; The Mill Pond Ghost and Other Stories, 1991; A Ginger Cat and a Shaggy Dog, 1992; All About Melanie Brown, 1992; The Haunting of Wayne Briggs and Other Spinechilling Stories, 1993; (with C. Sloan and S. Sheringham) The Marvellous Magical Storybook, 1993; The Melanie Brown Stories, 1994; Cat with No Name, 1994; Ben's Fantastic Plant, 2005. NOVELS: The Rich Earth, 1980; This Ravished Land, 1980; After the Storm, 1981; White Water, 1982; Green Harvest, 1983; Summer Song, 1984; Golden Tally, 1985; The Gooding Girl, 1985; The Stationmaster's Daughter, 1986; Lily Golightly, 1987; Betrothed, 1987; Turn of the Tide, 1988; A Dutiful Wife, 1989; Sweet Sally Lunn, 1990; The Halliday Girls, 1991; Long Dark Summer, 1992; Passionate Exile, 1993; String of Blue Beads, 1994; Falling from Grace, 1995; The Butterfly Box, 1996; The Gilded Land, 1997; Lowering Skies, 1998; Lady of the Night, 1998; (with J. Henley) Somebody's Lover, 1998; Pieces of Silver, 1998; A Woman Alone, 1999; Yesterday's Shadow, 1999; The Bright Dawning, 1999; Riding the Storm, 2000; All Our Tomorrows, 2001; Early One Morning, 2001; Great Plague, 2001; Changing Fortunes, 2002; New Beginnings, 2003; Matters of Trust, 2003; Victorian Workhouse, 2004; Dangerous Secrets, 2004; Intricate Liaisons, 2004; Henry's Women, 2005; Summer Lightning, 2005; Turning Leaves, 2005; Jack's Shadow, 2006; Loving and Losing, 2007; Fateful Voyage, 2007; Full Circle, 2007; The Longest Road, 2008; The Queen's Token: White Wolves, 2008; The Fairfax Legacy, 2008; The Birthday Present, 2009; Truth Will Out, 2009; The Boat House, 2010; The Penningtons, 2010; The Great Betrayal, 2011. WILLERBYS SERIES: Willerbys and the Burglar, 1981; Willerbys and the Haunted Mill, 1981; Willerbys and the Old Castle, 1982; Willerbys and the Sad Clown, 1982; Willerbys and the Bank Robbers, 1983; Willerbys and the Mystery Man, 1984. EDITOR: Helter-Skelter: Stories for Six-Year-Olds, 1983. **Address:** Faber and Faber Ltd., 3 Queen Sq., London, GL WC1N 3AU, England.

OLDHAM, John (M.). American (born United States), b. 1940. **Genres:** Psychiatry, Medicine/Health. **Career:** Saint Luke's Hospital, intern in pediatrics, 1967-68; New York State Psychiatric Institute, resident, 1968-71, deputy director, 1984-89, acting director, 1989-90, director, 1989-2002; Columbia University, resident in psychiatry, 1968-71, Columbia Presbyterian Medical Center, chief resident in psychiatry, 1970-71, College of Physicians and Surgeons, instructor, 1974-76, associate, 1976-77, lecturer, 1977-84, Department of Psychiatry, associate professor, 1984-88, associate chairman, 1986-96, professor of clinical psychiatry, 1988-86, vice chairman, 1996-2000, Elizabeth K. Dollard professor of clinical psychiatry, medicine, and the law, 1996-2002, acting chairman, 2000-02, Center for Psychoanalytic Training and Research, training and supervising psychoanalyst, 1983-; Washington Psychoanalytic Institute, auditor, 1971-72; American Board of Psychiatry and Neurology, diplomate and examiner, 1973; Roosevelt Hospital, director of psychiatric emergency services, 1973-74, director of residency training, 1974-77; Cornell University, Medical College, assistant professor, 1977-83, associate professor, 1983-84, Department of Psychiatry, consultant, 1997; New York Hospital, Short Term Diagnostic and Treatment Unit, director, 1977-80, Division of Acute Treatment Services, director, 1980-84, Acute Division Research Group, chairman, 1981-84, co-project director for Borderline Research Group, 1982-84, Department of Psychiatry, consultant, 1997; Presbyterian Hospital, associate attending psychiatrist, 1984-88, attending psychiatrist, 1988-; New York State Office of Mental Health, chief medical officer, 1988-2002; Research Foundation for Mental Hygiene Inc., board director, 1989-; Association for Psychoanalytic Medicine, president, 1989-91; Project for Psychiatric Outreach to the Homeless Inc., board director, 1993-2000; Journal of Psychiatric Practice, editor, 1997-, board director, 1998-2000; Association for Research on Personality Disorders, president, 1997-99, board director, 2003-06; Medical University of South Carolina, Institute of Psychiatry, executive director, 2002-06, Department of Psychiatry and Behavioral Sciences, professor and chairman, 2002-06; American Psychiatric Association, distinguished psychiatrist lecturer, 2002, American Psychiatric Institute for Research and Education, board director, 2003-06, distinguished life fellow, 2005-, American Psychiatric Foundation, board director, 2010-, president, 2011; South Carolina Psychiatric Association, vice president, 2004-05, president, 2006; North Shore University Hospital, Department of Psychiatry, Judge Bernard Thompson memorial lecturer, 2004; American College of Psychiatrists, treasurer, 2004-07, vice president, 2007-09, president, 2010-11, fellow; Jefferson Medical College, Albert M. Biele, M.D. visiting professor in psychiatry, 2005; American Psychiatric Publishing Inc., board director, 2005-; Emory University, School of Medicine, clinical professor of psychiatry and behavioral sciences, 2005-06; Baylor College of Medicine, Menninger Department of Psychiatry and Behavioral Sciences, executive vice chair for clinical affairs and development and professor of psychiatry and behavioral sciences, 2007-, The Menninger Clinic, senior vice president and chief of staff, 2007-; American College of Psychoanalysts, fellow; American Psychopathological Association, fellow; 7th International Congress on Personality Disorders, fellow; Journal of Personality Disorders, contributing editor. Consultant. **Publications:** (With L.M. Russakoff) Dynamic Therapy in Brief Hospitalization, 1987; (with L.B. Morris) The Personality Self-Portrait: Why You Think, Work, Love, and Act the Way You Do, 1990; Psychiatric Research: New Findings and Future Directions, 1992. EDITOR: Columbia University College of Physicians and Surgeons Complete Home Guide to Mental Health, 1992; (with M.B. Riba and A. Tasman) American Psychiatric Press Review of Psychiatry, vol. XII, 1992; (with S. Bone) Paranoia, 1994; (with E. Hollander and A.E. Skodol) Impulsivity and Compulsivity, 1996; (co-ed.)

American Psychiatric Publishing Textbook of Personality Disorders, 2005; (with F.B. Dickerson and S.S. Sharfstein) Textbook of Hospital Psychiatry, 2009; (with A.E. Skodol and D.S. Bender) Essentials of Personality Disorders, 2009. EDITOR AND CONTRIBUTOR: (with R.S. Liebert) The Middle Years: New Psychoanalytic Perspectives, 1989; Personality Disorders: New Perspectives on Diagnostic Validity, 1991; (with F.I. Kass and H. Pardes) The Columbia Guide to Emotional and Mental Health, 1992. Works appear in anthologies. Contributor to journals. **Address:** The Menninger Clinic, Baylor College of Medicine, 2801 Gessner Dr., Houston, TX 77080, U.S.A. **Online address:** joldham@menninger.edu

OLDHAM, **June.** British (born England) **Genres:** Novels, Novellas/Short Stories, Children's Fiction, Young Adult Fiction, Horror, Young Adult Nonfiction. **Career:** Writer, 1973-; Ilkley Literature Festival, director, 1982; Corby, writer-in-residence, 1983; Arts Council of Great Britain, fellow in creative writing, 1984, 1985. **Publications:** FOR CHILDREN: (with A. Strugnell) A Narrow Escape, 1973. NOVELS FOR YOUNG ADULTS: Wraggle Taggle War (novel), 1977; The Raven Waits, 1979; Enter Tom, 1985; Grow Up, Cupid!, 1986; Moving In, 1987; Double Take, 1988; Foundling, 1995 in US as Found, 1996; Escape, 1996; Undercurrents, 1998; Smoke Trail, 2002; In the Blood, 2003. NOVELS FOR ADULTS: Flames, 1986; A Little Rattle in the Air, 1990. Contributor to periodicals. **Address:** Virago Press, 100 Victoria Embankment, London, GL EC4Y 0DY, England. **Online address:** juneroseoldham@blueyonder.co.uk

OLDMAN, **Mark.** American (born United States), b. 1969. **Genres:** Food And Wine. **Career:** Vault.com, co-founder, 1997, president, through 2007; wine course teacher. Writer. **Publications:** Princeton Review Student Access Guide to America's Top One Hundred Internships, 1994; The Internship Bible, 1996; (with S. Hamadeh and H.S. Hamadeh) The Job Vault, 1997; (H.S. Hamadeh, S. Hamadeh and M. Oldman) Vault Reports Guide to Starting Your Own Business, 1998; Law Firms: The Vault.com Guide to America's Top Fifty Law Firms, 1998; The Vault Guide to Schmoozing, 2001; Vault Guide to Top Internships, 2004; Oldman's Guide to Outsmarting Wine: 108 Ingenious Shortcuts to Navigate the World of Wine with Confidence and Style, 2004; Oldman's Brave New World of Wine: Pleasure, Value and Adventure Beyond Wine's Usual Suspects, 2010. **Address:** W. W. Norton & Company Inc., 500 5th Ave., New York, NY 10110, U.S.A.

OLDMIXON, **Elizabeth Anne.** American (born United States), b. 1974?. **Genres:** Politics/Government, Theology/Religion. **Career:** University of Florida, Department of Political Science, associate director, 1997-99; D-MA, legislative fellow, 2002; University of North Texas, Department of Political Science, assistant professor, 2002-08, assistant chair, 2008-10, associate professor of political science, 2008-; Brandeis University, Schusterman Center for Israel Studies Summer Institute, faculty, 2008-. Writer. **Publications:** Uncompromising Positions: God, Sex, and the U.S. House of Representatives, 2005; (contrib.) Representing God at the Statehouse: Religion and Politics in the American States, 2005; (contrib.) Religion in World Politics, 2006; (contrib.) Oxford Handbook on Religion and American Politics, 2009. Contributor to journals. **Address:** Department of Political Science, University of North Texas, Rm. 125 Wooten Hall, 1155 Union Cir., PO Box 305340, Denton, TX 76203-5340, U.S.A. **Online address:** oldmixon@unt.edu

OLDRIDGE, **Darren.** British (born England), b. 1966. **Genres:** History. **Career:** University of Worcester, senior lecturer in history. Writer. **Publications:** Religion and Society in Early Stuart England, 1998; (ed.) The Witchcraft Reader, 2002, 2nd ed., 2008; Strange Histories: The Trial of the Pig, the Walking Dead and Other Matters of Fact from the Medieval and Renaissance Worlds, 2005; Devil in Tudor and Stuart England, 2010; Devil: A Very Short Introduction, 2012. **Address:** University of Worcester, St. Johns Campus, Henwick Grove, Worcester, HW WR2 6AJ, England. **Online address:** d.oldridge@worc.ac.uk

OLDS, **Bruce.** American (born United States), b. 1951. **Genres:** Novels, Young Adult Fiction. **Career:** Writer. **Publications:** NOVELS: Raising Holy Hell, 1995; Bucking the Tiger, 2001; The Moments Lost: A Midwest Pilgrim's Progress, 2007; The Camp, forthcoming. **Address:** The Wylie Agency, 250 W 57th St., Ste. 2114, New York, NY 10107-2199, U.S.A.

OLDS, **Sharon.** American (born United States), b. 1942. **Genres:** Poetry. **Career:** Theodor Herzl Institute, lecturer in residence on poetry, 1976-80; Manhattan Theater Club, visiting teacher of poetry, 1982; Nathan Mayhew Seminars of Martha's Vineyard, visiting teacher of poetry, 1982; Young Men's Christian Association of New York City, Poetry Center, visiting teacher of poetry, 1982; Poetry Society of America, visiting teacher of poetry, 1983; New York University, visiting teacher of poetry, 1983, 1985; Sarah Lawrence College, visiting teacher of poetry, 1984; Goldwater Hospital, visiting teacher of poetry, 1985-90; Columbia University, visiting teacher of poetry, 1985-86; State University of New York College, visiting teacher of poetry, 1986; Brandeis University, Fanny Hurst chair, 1986-87; New York University, Department of English, associate professor, 1992-, professor, Graduate Program in Creative Writing, director; New York University workshop program, Goldwater Hospital, founding director; New York State Poet, 1998-2000. Writer. **Publications:** POETRY: Satan Says, 1980; The Dead and the Living: Poems, 1984; The Gold Cell: Poems, 1987; The Matter of this World: New and Selected Poems, 1987; The Sign of Saturn, 1991; The Father, 1992; The Wellspring: Poems, 1996; Blood, Tin, Straw, 1999; Unswept Room, 2002; Strike Sparks: Selected Poems, 1980-2002, 2004; Selected Poems, 2005; One Secret Thing, 2008. OTHERS: (foreword) What Silence Equals, 1993; (intro.) The Orgy: An Irish Journey of Passion and Transformation, 1997; Stag's Leap, 2012. Works appear in anthologies. Contributor of articles to journal. **Address:** Department of English, New York University, Rm. 200, 19 University Pl., 5th Fl., New York, NY 10003, U.S.A. **Online address:** so1@nyu.edu

O'LEARY, **Don.** Irish (born Ireland), b. 1955?. **Genres:** History. **Career:** University College Cork, Biosciences Institute, senior technical officer. Writer. **Publications:** Vocationalism and Social Catholicism in Twentieth-Century Ireland: The Search for a Christian Social Order, 2000; Roman Catholicism and Modern Science: A History, 2006. **Address:** Department Of Anatomy, Biosciences Institute, University College Cork, Rm. G9, Cork, 0000, Ireland. **Online address:** d.oleary@ucc.ie

O'LEARY, **Kevin.** American (born United States) **Genres:** Politics/Government. **Career:** University of California, Center for the Study of Democracy, political scientist, senior research fellow, 2004-07; Campaigns and Elections, national correspondent; OC Metro Magazine, editor; Pasadena Star-News, editorial page editor; Los Angeles Times, reporter. **Publications:** Saving Democracy: A Plan for Real Representation in America, 2006. **Address:** Stanford University Press, 1450 Page Mill Rd., Palo Alto, CA 94304-1124, U.S.A.

O'LEARY, **Patrick.** American (born United States), b. 1952. **Genres:** Novels, Poetry, Marketing, Literary Criticism And History, Novellas/Short Stories, Songs/Lyrics And Libretti, Film, Photography, Photography. **Career:** Campbell-Ewald, copywriter, 1975-2002, Chevrolet Website, associate creative director, 1995-2008, creative director, 1995-96, National Fatherhood Account, creative director, 1995-2008, associate creative director, 1997-2008; fiction writer, 1975-2009; freelance writer, 2009-10; Apple Inc., specialist, 2010-. **Publications:** Door Number Three, 1995; The Gift, 1997; Other Voices, Other Doors (collection), 2001; The Impossible Bird, 2002; The Black Heart, 2009. Contributor to periodicals. **Address:** Tor Books, 175 5th Ave., New York, NY 10010-7703, U.S.A. **Online address:** patri10629@wowway.com

O'LEARY, **Patsy Baker.** American (born United States), b. 1937. **Genres:** Adult Non-fiction, Novels, Children's Fiction. **Career:** Film production and secretary, 1959-79; Get Smart (television series), assistant to the producer, 1966-70; freelance writer, 1979-; Pitt Community College, instructor in creative writing, 1980-; East Carolina University, lecturer in English, 1980-81, lecturer in communications, 1990-95. **Publications:** With Wings as Eagles (novel), 1997. **Address:** Barrie Van Dyck Agency Inc., 217 Spruce St., Philadelphia, PA 19106-3906, U.S.A.

O'LEARY, **Rosemary.** American (born United States), b. 1955. **Genres:** Public/Social Administration, Environmental Sciences/Ecology, Business/Trade/Industry, Economics. **Career:** State of Kansas, legislative analyst in the office of the governor, 1981-82, attorney, 1982-83, director of policy planning, 1983-85; Indiana University, assistant professor, 1988-90, associate professor of public and environmental affairs, 1994-, professor of public and environmental affairs, Indiana Conflict Resolution Institute, co-founder and co-director; Syracuse University, assistant professor, 1990-93, associate professor, 1993-94, professor, 1998-2004, Ph.D. Program, interim director, 2000-01, coordinator, 2001-04, Maxwell Graduate School of Syracuse University, Department of Public Administration and Policy, distinguished professor of public administration and international affairs, 2004-, Program for the Advancement of Research on Conflict and Collaboration, co-director, 2005-09; Howard G. and S. Louise Phanstiel endowed chair in strategic management and leadership,

2008-; Campbell Public Affairs Institute, senior research associate, Center for Environmental Policy and Administration, senior research associate, 1998-. Writer. **Publications:** Environmental Change: Federal Courts and the EPA, 1993; Emergency Planning: Local Government and the Community Right-to-Know Act, 1993; (with D.H. Rosenblum and J. Chanin) Public Administration and Law, 1997, 3rd ed., 2010; (co-author) Managing for the Environment: Understanding the Legal, Organizational, and Policy Challenges, 1999; (ed. with L.B. Bingham) The Promise and Performance of Environmental Conflict Resolution, 2003; (ed. with R.F. Durant and D.J. Fiorino) Environmental Governance Reconsidered: Challenges, Choices, and Opportunities, 2004; Ethics of Dissent: Managing Guerrilla Government, 2006; (ed. with L.B. Bingham) Big Ideas in Collaborative Public Management, 2008; (ed. with L.B. Bingham) Collaborative Public Manager: New Ideas for the Twenty-first Century, 2009; (ed. with D.V. Slyke and S. Kim) The Future of Public Administration Around the World: The Minnowbrook Perspective, 2010. **Address:** Campbell Public Affairs Institute, The Maxwell School of Syracuse University, 400 Eggers Hall, Syracuse, NY 13244, U.S.A. **Online address:** roleary@maxwell.syr.edu

OLEKSIW, Susan (Prince). American (born United States), b. 1945. **Genres:** Novels, Mystery/Crime/Suspense, Novellas/Short Stories, Literary Criticism And History. **Career:** Larcom Press, editor and co-founder, 1998-2003; Level Best Books, editor and co-founder, 2003-10. **Publications:** A Reader's Guide to the Classic British Mystery, 1988; (ed.) Oxford Companion to Crime and Mystery Writing, 1999; (ed. with R. Herbert) Undertow: Crime Stories by New England Writers, 2003; (ed. with S. Alexander and K. Flora) Riptide: Crime Stories by New England Writers, 2004; (ed. with K. Flora and R. McCarty) Seasmoke: Crime Stories by New England Writers, 2006. NOVELS: Murder in Mellingham, 1993; Double Take: A Mellingham Mystery, 1994; Family Album: A Mellingham Mystery, 1995; Friends and Enemies: A Mellingham Mystery, 2001; Murderous Innocence: A Mellingham Mystery, 2006; Under the Eye of Kali: An Anita Ray Mystery, 2010. Contributor of articles to periodicals. **Address:** PO Box 161, Prides Crossing, MA 01965, U.S.A. **Online address:** spo2@earthlink.net

OLESON, James A. American (born United States) **Genres:** Biography, Autobiography/Memoirs. **Career:** Writer. **Publications:** In Their Own Words: True Stories and Adventures of the American Fighter Ace, 2007. Contributor to periodicals. **Address:** IA , U.S.A. **Online address:** jkoleson@yahoo.com

OLICK, Jeffrey K. American (born United States), b. 1964. **Genres:** Politics/Government. **Career:** Columbia University, instructor, 1993-94, assistant professor of sociology, 1994-2000, associate professor of sociology, 2000-04, Society of Fellows, associate, 1994-2004, Center for Social Sciences, organizer, 1995-97; University of Virginia, associate professor, 2004-07, professor of sociology and history, 2007-, director of graduate admissions in sociology and director of graduate studies in sociology, 2006-09. Writer. **Publications:** (Ed.) States of Memory: Continuities, Conflicts, and Transformations in National Retrospection, 2003; In the House of the Hangman: The Agonies of German Defeat, 1943-1949, 2005; The Politics of Regret: On Collective Memory and Historical Responsibility, 2007; (ed., trans. and intro. with A.J. Perrin) Guilt and Defense: On the Legacies of National Socialism in Postwar Germany, 2010; (ed. with V. Vinitzky-Seroussi and D. Levy) The Collective Memory Reader, 2011; (ed., trans. and intro. with A.J. Perrin) Group Experiment and Other Writings: The Frankfurt School on Public Opinion in Postwar Germany, 2011. Contributor to periodicals and journals. **Address:** Department of Sociology, University of Virginia, 502 Cabell Hall, Dynamics Bldg., 3rd Fl., 2015 Ivy Rd., PO Box 400766, Charlottesville, VA 22904, U.S.A. **Online address:** jko3k@virginia.edu

OLIPHANT, B. J. *See* **TEPPER, Sheri S.**

OLIPHANT, Dave (Edward Davis). American (born United States), b. 1939. **Genres:** Poetry, Education, Literary Criticism And History, Music. **Career:** University of the Americas, director of creative writing and translation workshops, 1975-76; University of Texas, assistant professor, 1976-78, instructor, 1990-2002, senior lecturer, 2003-06; Harry Ransom Humanities Research Center, Library Chronicle, editor of quarterly journal, 1979-97; Austin Community College, part-time instructor of English, 1978-2004, now retired. Poet, editor and translator. **Publications:** POETRY: Maria's Poems, 1987; Memories of Texas Towns & Cities, 2000; Backtracking, 2004. NONFICTION: Texan Jazz, 1996; The Early Swing Era, 1930-1941, 2002; Jazz Mavericks of the Lone Star State, 2007; Harbingers of Books to Come: A Texan's Literary Life, 2009. OTHER: (trans.) Figures of Speech, 1999; After-Dinner Declarations, 2009. **Address:** 1402 Mimosa Pass, Cedar Park, TX 78613, U.S.A. **Online address:** doliphant@mail.utexas.edu

OLITZKY, Kerry M. American (born United States), b. 1954. **Genres:** Theology/Religion, Education, Self Help, Cultural/Ethnic Topics, Gerontology/Senior Issues. **Career:** Mature Adult Day Care Center, program manager, 1976; American Jewish Archives, assistant archivist, 1978-81; B'nai B'rith Youth Organization, assistant regional director, 1978-81; Beth Israel, assistant rabbi and director of religious education for congregation, 1981-84; Hebrew Union College, School of Education, Jewish Institute of Religion, director of graduate studies program, 1984-98, Research and Educational Development, national director, 1991-96, Adult Jewish Learning and Living, national dean, 1996-98; Wexner Heritage Foundation, vice president, 1998-99; Jewish Outreach Institute, executive director, 2000-. Writer. **Publications:** EDUCATION AND REFERENCE BOOKS: Aging and Judaism (textbook), 1980; Critical Issues Facing American Jewish Youth: A Resource Book for Educators, Experimental Ed, 1982; Come Dance with Me: Life in the Jewish Shtetl, 1983; I Am a Reform Jew (student workbook), 1986; Explaining Reform Judaism (teacher's guide), 1986; My Jewish Community (student workbook), 1986; A Jewish Mourner's Handbook, 1991; (with R.H. Isaacs) A Glossary of Jewish Life, 1992; When Your Jewish Child Asks Why: Answers for Tough Questions, 1993; Reform Judaism in America: A Biographical Dictionary and Source Book, 1824-1980, 1993; The How to Book of Jewish Living, 1993; Sacred Celebrations: A Jewish Holiday Handbook, 1994; Eight Nights, Eight Lights: Family Values for Each Night of Hanukkah, 1994; Doing Mitzvot, Mitzvah Projects for Bar/Bat Mitzvah, 1994; The Journey of the Soul: Traditional Sources on Teshuvah, 1995; Critical Documents of Jewish History, 1995; The American Synagogue: A Historical Dictionary and Sourcebook, 1996. SELF-HELP BOOKS: (with S.A. Copans) Twelve Jewish Steps to Recovery: A Personal Guide to Turning from Alcoholism and Other Addictions, 1991, 2nd ed., 2009; Renewed Each Day: Daily Twelve Step Recovery Meditations Based on the Bible, 2 vols., 1992; Recovery from Codependence: A Jewish Twelve Steps Guide to Healing Your Soul, 1993; One Hundred Blessings Every Day: Daily Twelve Step Recovery Affirmations, Exercises for Personal Growth & Renewal Reflecting Seasons of the Jewish Year, 1993; The Second How-To Handbook for Jewish Living, 1995; Healing Essays, 1996. OTHERS: (ed. with J. Stevens) An Index to the Sound Recordings Collection of the American Jewish Archives, 1980; To Grow Old in Israel: A Survey of Recent Trends and Developments, 1988; In Celebration: An American Jewish Perspective on the Bicentennial of the U.S. Constitution, 1988; An Interfaith Ministry to the Aged: A Survey of Models, 1988; The Synagogue Confronts the Jewish Family of the Twenty-first Century, 1988; (ed.) The Safe Deposit Box: And Other Stories about Grandparents, Old Lovers and Crazy Old Men, 1989; Leaving Mother Russia: Chapters in the Russian Jewish Experience, 1990; The Discovery Haggadah, 1992; Hebrew, Heroes, and Holidays: The Great Jewish Fun Book, 1992; Pirke Avot: A New Translation and Commentary, 1993; Documents of Jewish Life, 1993; (ed. and trans. with L. Kravitz) Pirke Avot: A Modern Commentary on Jewish Ethics, 1993; (with R.H. Isaacs) The How-to Handbook for Jewish Living, 1993; (with L.S. Kushner) Sparks Beneath the Surface: A Spiritual Commentary on the Torah, 1993; Will the Real Hero of Purim Please Stand Up?, 1995; Sacred Moments: Tales of the Jewish Life Cycle, 1995; Striving Toward Virtue: A Contemporary Guide for Jewish Ethical Behavior, 1996; Jewish Wedding Ceremony, 1996; Preparing Your Heart for the High Holy Days: A Guided Journal, 1996; (ed. with C. Ochs) Paths of Faithfulness: Personal Essays on Jewish Spirituality, 1997; (with C. Ochs) Jewish Spiritual Guidance: Finding Our Way to God, 1997; Rediscovering Judaism: Bar and Bat Mitzvah for Adults, 1997; Grief in Our Seasons: A Mourner's Kaddish Companion, 1998; Sacred Intentions: Daily Inspiration to Strengthen the Spirit, Based on Jewish Wisdom, 1999; (with L.S. Kravitz) Shemonah Perakim: A Treatise on the Soul, 1999; From Your Father's House: Reflections for Modern Jewish Men, 1999; (with R.H. Isaacs) I Believe: The Thirteen Principles of Faith: A Confirmation Textbook, 1999; An Encyclopedia of American Synagogue Ritual, 2000; Jewish Paths Toward Healing and Wholeness: A Personal Guide to Dealing with Suffering, 2000; (ed. with L. Forman) Restful Reflections: Nighttime Inspiration to Calm the Soul: Based on Jewish Wisdom, 2001; The Rituals & Practices of a Jewish Life: A Handbook for Personal Spiritual Renewal, 2002; (with R.H. Isaacs) The Third How to Handbook for Jewish Living, 2002; (with L.S. Kravitz) Mishlei: A Modern Commentary on Proverbs, 2002; Preparing Your Heart for Passover: A Guide for Spiritual Readiness, 2002; (with L.S. Kravitz) Kohelet: A Modern Commentary, 2003; (with J.P. Littman) Making a Successful Jewish Interfaith Marriage: The Jewish Outreach Institute Guide to Opportunities, Challenges, and Resources, 2003; (trans. with L.S. Kravitz) Shir Hashirim: A Modern Commentary on the Song of Songs, 2004; (with R.H. Isaacs) The Complete How to Handbook for Jewish Living, 2004; Introducing My Faith and My Community: The Jewish Outreach Institute Guide for the Christian in a Jewish Interfaith Relationship, 2004; Ruth: A Modern Commentary, 2005; (with D. Judson) Jewish Ritual: A Brief Introduction for Christians, 2005; (with L.S. Kravitz) Jonah: A Modern Commentary, 2006; (with D. Judson) Jewish Holidays: A Brief Introduction for Christians, 2007; (trans. with L.S. Kravitz) Eichah: A Modern Commentary on the Book of Lamentations, 2008; Life's Daily Blessings: Inspiring Reflections on Gratitude and Joy for Every Day, Based on Jewish Wisdom, 2009; (trans. with L.S. Kravitz) Esther: A Modern Commentary, 2010. Works appear in anthologies. Contributor to journals and magazines. **Address:** Jewish Outreach Institute, 1270 Broadway, Ste. 609, New York, NY 10001-3224, U.S.A. **Online address:** kolitzky@joi.org

OLIVEIRA, Robin Frazier. American (born United States), b. 1954?. **Genres:** Novels, History. **Career:** Upstreet Magazine, fiction editor; Narrative Magazine, assistant editor. Nurse. **Publications:** My Name Is Mary Sutter (historical novel), 2010. Contributor to periodicals. **Address:** Marly Rusoff and Associates Inc., PO Box 524, Bronxville, NY 10708, U.S.A.

OLIVELLE, Patrick. American/Sri Lankan (born Sri Lanka), b. 1942. **Genres:** Theology/Religion, Translations. **Career:** Indiana University, Department of Religious Studies, assistant professor, 1974-78, associate professor, 1978-83, professor of religious studies, 1983-91, chair, 1984-90; University of Texas, Austin, Department of Asian Studies, professor of Sanskrit and Indian religions, 1991-, Jacob and Frances Sanger Mossiker chair in the humanities, chair, 1994-2007, Center for Asian Studies, director, 1994-2000, Alma Cowden Madden centennial professor, 2000-06, South Asia Institute, interim director, 2003-04, Marlene and Morton Meyerson centennial fellow; University of Western Michigan, Mircea Eliade lecturer in comparative religion, 1997; Oxford University Press, U.S. delegate, 1998-; University of Vienna, Numata professor, 2001. Writer. **Publications:** (Ed.) The Origin and the Early Development of Buddhist Monachism, 1974; (ed., intro. and trans.) Vāsudevāśrama Yatidharmaprakāśa: A Treatise on World Renunciation, vol. I: Sanskrit Text, 1976, vol. II: Annotated English Translation, 1977; (ed. and intro.) Saṃnyāsapaddhati of Rudra Deva, 1986; Renunciation in Hinduism: A Medieval Debate, vol. I: The Debate and the Advaita Argument, 1986, vol. II: The Visistadvaita Argument, 1987; (trans. and intro.) The Saṃnyāsa Upaniṣ hads: Hindu Scriptures on Asceticism and Renunciation, 1992; The āśrama System: The History and Hermeneutics of a Religious Institution, 1992; (ed. and trans.) Rules and Regulations of Brahmanical Asceticism: Yatidharmasamuccaya of Yadava Prakasa, 1995; (trans.) Upaniṣ ads, 1996; (trans.) Pañcatantra: The Book of India's Folk Wisdom, 1997; Early Upaniṣ ads: Annotated Text and Translation, 1998; (trans. and ed.) Dharmasūtras: The Law Codes of āpastamba, Gautama, Baudhāyana, and Vasiṣ ṭha, 1999; (trans.) Law Code of Manu, 2004; Manu's Code of Law: A Critical Edition and Translation of the Manava-Dharmasastra, 2005; Language, Texts and Society: Explorations in Ancient Indian Culture and Religion, 2005; (ed. and trans.) Dharmasūtra Parallels: Containing the Dharmasūtras of āpastamba, Gautama, Baudhāyana, and Vasisòtòha, 2005; (ed.) Between the Empires: Society in India 300 BCE to 400 CE, 2006; (trans.) Viṣ ṇuśarman, The Five Discourses on Worldly Wisdom, 2006; (trans.) Aśvaghoṣ a, Life of the Buddha, 2007; (trans.) Upaniṣ hads, 2008; Aśoka: In History and Historical Memory, 2009; (ed.) Dharma, rev. ed., 2009; (trans. and ed.) Dharmasutras: The Law Codes of Ancient India, 2009. Contributor to periodicals. **Address:** Department of Asian Studies, University of Texas, WCH 4.112, 1 University Sta., PO Box Z, Austin, TX 78712-0587, U.S.A. **Online address:** jpo@uts.cc.utexas.edu

OLIVER, Bill. American (born United States), b. 1949. **Genres:** Adult Non-fiction, Novellas/Short Stories, Young Adult Fiction. **Career:** Virginia Military Institute, assistant professor of English, 1983-87, institute writing program, director of the writing center, 1996-; University of Texas, assistant professor of English, 1987-91; Washington and Lee University, visiting professor, 1991-96, VMI's Writing Center, director. Writer. **Publications:** Women and Children First (short stories), 1998; (ed. with B. Lyons) Passion and Craft: Conversations with Notable Writers, 1998; Asunder (short story collection); Necessary Evils, forthcoming. Contributor to periodicals. **Address:** 205 Carroll Hall, Lexington, VA 24450, U.S.A. **Online address:** oliverb@vmi.edu

OLIVER, James (Anthony). British (born England), b. 1956. **Genres:** Civil Liberties/Human Rights, History, Politics/Government. **Career:** British Gas, intern, 1980-81; Energy Conscious Design Partnership, consultant, 1985-86; A Company of Writers Ltd., director, 1988-90; James A. Oliver Consulting, principal, 1991-; World Editorial Network, founder, 1997. Writer. **Publications:** (With P. Lashmar) Britain's Secret Propaganda War 1948-1977, 1998. Contributor to periodicals. **Address:** c/o Author Mail, Sutton Publishing, Phoenix Mill, Thrupp, Stroud, GC GL5 2BU, England.

OLIVER, Jasmine. *See* **OLDFIELD, Jenny.**

OLIVER, Kelly. American (born United States), b. 1958. **Genres:** Literary Criticism And History. **Career:** University of Texas, Departments of Philosophy, associate professor; State University of New York, faculty; Vanderbilt University, faculty, 2005-, W. Alton Jones chair of philosophy, professor of African American and diaspora studies, film studies, and women's and gender studies. Feminist and writer. **Publications:** (Ed.) Ethics, Politics and Difference in Julia Kristeva's Writing, 1993; Reading Kristeva: Unraveling the Double-bind, 1993; Womanizing Nietzsche: Philosophy's Relation to the Feminine, 1995; (ed.) The Portable Kristeva, 1997, rev. ed., 2002; Family Values: Subjects Between Nature and Culture, 1997; (ed. with M. Pearsall) Feminist Interpretations of Friedrich Nietzsche, 1998; Subjectivity Without Subjects: From Abject Fathers to Desiring Mothers, 1998; (ed. with C. Hendricks) Language and Liberation: Feminism, Philosophy and Language, 1999; Enigmas: Essays on Sarah Kofman, 1999; (ed.) French Feminism Reader, 2000; Witnessing: Beyond Recognition, 2001; (ed. with S. Edwin) Between the Psyche and the Social: Psychoanalytic Social Theory, 2002; (with B. Trigo) Noir Anxiety, 2003; The Colonization of Psychic Space: A Psychoanalytic Social Theory of Oppression, 2004; (ed. with L. Walsh) Contemporary French Feminism, 2004; Women as Wweapons of War: Iraq, Sex and the Media, 2007; (co-ed.) Living Attention: On Teresa Brennan, 2007; Women as Weapons of War: Iraq, Sex and the Media, 2007; Animal Lessons: How They Teach Us To Be Human, 2009; (ed. with S.K. Keltner) Psychoanalysis, Aesthetics and Politics in the Work of Kristeva, 2009. Contributor to periodicals. **Address:** Departments of Philosophy, Vanderbilt University, 103 Furman Hall, Nashville, TN 37240, U.S.A. **Online address:** kelly.oliver@vanderbilt.edu

OLIVER, Kitty. American (born United States), b. 1947. **Genres:** Cultural/Ethnic Topics, Race Relations, Autobiography/Memoirs, Social Sciences, History, Anthropology/Ethnology. **Career:** Miami Herald, staff writer and columnist, 1971-90; Nova Southeastern University, presidential research fellow, 1986, Dolores Auzenne fellow, 1992-93, assistant, 1992-94; Kitty O Enterprises Inc., president, 1992-; Florida International University, visiting instructor, 1994-96; Florida Atlantic University, visiting associate professor and writer-in-residence, 1995; Sun-Sentinel, staff writer and freelance columnist, 1998-; Wavelengths Web Cast Radio Show, consulting producer, 2006-; WBEC-TV Public Broadcasting Station, consulting producer, writer and host; Sunshine magazine, columnist. **Publications:** Reflections of Broward: Ethnic Diversity, 1991; New Reflections: Ethnic Diversity, 1991; Multicolored Memories of a Black Southern Girl, 2001; Voices of America: Race & Change in Hollywood, 2001; (comp. and ed.) Multicultural Reflections On Race and Change: Featuring Archival Interviews from the Race and Change Oral History Collection, African American Research Library and Cultural Center, 2006. **Address:** Kitty O Enterprises Inc., 1323 SE 17th St., Ste. 108, Fort Lauderdale, FL 33316-1707, U.S.A. **Online address:** kittyo@kittyoliveronline.com

OLIVER, Lawrence J. American (born United States), b. 1949. **Genres:** Literary Criticism And History, Politics/Government. **Career:** Texas AandM University, College of Liberal Arts, assistant professor, 1984-90, associate professor of English, 1990-98, professor of English, 1998-, College of Liberal Arts, associate dean, 1998-. Writer. **Publications:** Brander Matthews, Theodore Roosevelt and the Politics of American Literature, 1880-1920, 1992; (ed.) The Letters of Theodore Roosevelt and Brander Matthews, 1995; (ed. with K.M. Price) Critical Essays on James Weldon Johnson, 1997. **Address:** Dean's Office, College of Liberal Arts, Texas A&M University, 301 Coke Bldg., College Station, TX 77843-4223, U.S.A. **Online address:** l-oliver@tamu.edu

OLIVER, Maria Antònia. Spanish (born Spain), b. 1946. **Genres:** Novels, Novellas/Short Stories, Plays/Screenplays, Children's Fiction. **Career:** Writer. **Publications:** NOVELS: Cròniques d'un Mig Estiu (title means: 'Chronicles of a Half Summer'), 1970; Cròniques de la Molt Anomendada Ciutat de Montcarrà (title means: 'Chronicles of the Very Renowned City of Montcarrà'), 1972, rev. ed., 1991; El Vaixell d'iràs I no Tornaràs (title means:

'The Ship that Never Returned'), 1976; Punt d'arròs (title means: 'Knit-Purl'), 1979; Crineres de Foc (title means: 'Manes of Fire'), 1985; Estudi en Lila, 1985; Antípodes, 1988; Joana E., 1992; El Sol Que fa L'ànec (title means: 'The Sun That Makes the Duck'), 1994; Amor de Cans (title means: 'Dogs' Love'), 1995. STORIES/NOVELLAS: Coordenades Espai-temps Perguardar-hi Les Ensaïmades (title means: 'E-Time Coordinates for Keeping Ènsaïmades'), 1975; Figues d'un Altre Paner (title means: 'A Horse of a Different Color'), 1979; Tríptics, 1989; Tallats de Lluna (title means: 'Moon Sliced'), 2000. FOR CHILDREN: Margalida Perla Fina, 1985; Elpacaticú, 1988. OTHERS: Illes: Mallorca, Menorca, Eivissa, Formentera, Cabrera, 1978; Study in Lilac: A Worldkrime Mystery, 1987; Antipodes, 1989; Croniques de la Molt Anomenada Ciutat de Montcarrà, 1991; (co-author) Espejo de Agua: Reflejos Del Puerto, 1992; (co-author) Through the Waterglass: Reflections of the Port, 1992; Negroni de Ginebra (title means: 'Gin Negroni'), 1993; Dida, 1996; Blue Roses for a Dead Lady?, 1998; (contrib.) Univers Tísner: 1912-2000: Gairebé un Segle, 2001; Illai la Dona: Trenta-cinc Anys de Contes, 2003. **Address:** c/o Trigo, Marisa, Peu de la Creu, Barcelona, 4 08001, Spain.

OLIVER, Marilyn Tower. American (born United States), b. 1935. **Genres:** Crafts, Biography, Documentaries/Reportage, Gay And Lesbian Issues, History. **Career:** Metropolitan Opera Western Regional Auditions, publicity director. Journalist and educator. **Publications:** Natural Crafts: 72 Easy Projects, 1994; Gangs: Trouble in the Streets, 1995; Drugs: Should They Be Legalized?, 1996; Prisons: Today's Debate, 1997; Alcatraz Prison in American History, 1998; Gay and Lesbian Rights: A Struggle, 1998; The Importance of Muhammad, 2003; Henry VIII, 2004; Attila the Hun, 2006. Contributor to books. **Address:** 2646 Lake View Terr. E, Los Angeles, CA 90039-2605, U.S.A. **Online address:** mtowriter@yahoo.com

OLIVER, Mary. American (born United States), b. 1935. **Genres:** Poetry, Education. **Career:** Fine Arts Work Center, Department of Writing, chair, 1972-73; Case Western Reserve University, Mather visiting professor, 1980, 1982; Bucknell University, poet-in-residence, 1986; University of Cincinnati, Elliston visiting professor, 1986; Sweet Briar College, Margaret Banister writer-in-residence, 1991-95; Bennington College, Catharine Osgood Foster chair for distinguished teaching, 1996-2001. **Publications:** No Voyage, and Other Poems, 1963; The River Styx, Ohio, and Other Poems, 1972; The Night Traveler, 1978; Twelve Moons, 1979; American Primitive, 1983; Dream Work, 1986; House of Light, 1990; New and Selected Poems, 1992, vol. II, 2004; A Poetry Handbook, 1994; White Pine, 1994; Blue Pastures, 1995; West Wind, 1997; Rules for the Dance, 1998; Winter Hours, 1999; The Leaf and the Cloud, 2000; What Do We Know, 2002; Owls and Other Fantasies, 2003; Long Life, 2004; Blue Iris, 2004; Why I Wake Early: New Poems, 2004; Thirst, 2006; (contrib.) Our World, 2007; Red Bird, 2008; Truro Bear and Other Adventures, 2008; Evidence, 2009; Swan: Poems and Prose Poems, 2010; Fury of Light, 2010. Contributor to periodicals. **Address:** Beacon Press, 25 Beacon St., Boston, MA 02108, U.S.A.

OLIVER, Richard W. American/Canadian (born Canada), b. 1946. **Genres:** How-to Books, Business/Trade/Industry, Technology. **Career:** DuPont Co., United States division, marketing manager, 1969-71, Canadian Division, assistant to chairman for public policy and investor relations, 1973-76, consultant; U.S. Department of Transportation, staff, 1972; Northern Telecom Inc., manager of global product support through vice president marketing, 1976-92, vice president of business and residential services; Vanderbilt University, Owen Graduate School of Management, adjunct professor of management, 1985-92, 2000-, professor of management, 1991-2000; Duke University, Fuqua School of Business, faculty, 1991-97; Applied Innovation Inc., board director, 1992-; Quality Industries, board director, 1992-; Comptronix Corp., board director, 1993-96; Communications Central Inc., board director, 1993-97; Prime Office Products, investor and founding board member, 1995-2002; SymmetriCom Inc., chairman of the board, 1997-; First Union National Bank of Tennessee, board director, 1990-99; Cornell University, Johnson School of Management, adjunct professor of management; American Learning Solutions (ALS), co-founder, 2001, chief executive officer; American Graduate School of Management (AGSM), co-founder, 2001, chief executive officer; Berwind Industries, consultant; Central Parking, Law & Economics, consultant; Dominion Securities, consultant; J.C. Bradford, consultant; Tetrapak Inc., consultant; BellSouth, consultant; NYNEX, consultant; Honeywell, consultant; Canadian Broadcasting Corp., consultant; Hudson Bay Co., consultant; Allied Clinical Labs, consultant; Tennessee Pride; consultant; Nashville Institute for the Arts, faculty; Global Market Associates, principal. Writer. **Publications:** (With W.A. Jenkins) The Eagle and the Monk: Seven Principles of Successful Change, 1998; The Shape of Things to Come: Seven Imperatives for Winning in the New World of Business, 1999; (with C. Leipold) Hockey-Tonk: The Amazing Story of the Nashville Predators, 2000; The Coming Biotech Age: The Business of Bio-Materials, 2000; (with C.Leipold) Hockey Tonk, 2000; The Biotech Age: The Business of Biotech and How to Profit from It, 2003; What Is Transparency?, 2004; (with T. Leffel) Hip-Hop, Inc.: Success Strategies of the Rap Moguls, 2006. **Address:** Owen Graduate School of Management, Vanderbilt University, 401 21st Ave. S, Nashville, TN 37203, U.S.A. **Online address:** rick.oliver@owen.vanderbilt.edu

OLIVER, Roland Anthony. British/Indian (born India), b. 1923. **Genres:** Area Studies, History, Autobiography/Memoirs, Social Sciences. **Career:** British Foreign Office, staff, 1942-45; School of Oriental and African Studies, lecturer, 1948-58; University of London, reader, 1958-63, professor, 1963-86, professor emeritus of African history, 1986-; University of Brussels, Franqui professor, 1961, visiting professor; Northwestern University, visiting professor, 1962; Royal Africa Society, honorary vice president, 1965-; Harvard University, visiting professor, 1967; British Institute in Eastern Africa, president; Journal of African History, co-editor. **Publications:** The Missionary Factor in East Africa, 1952, 2nd ed., 1965; How Christian Is Africa?, 1956; Sir Harry Johnston and the Scramble for Africa, 1957; (with J.D. Fage) A Short History of Africa, 1962, 6th ed., 1988; African History for the Outside World, 1964; (with A.E. Atmore) Africa Since 1800, 1967, 5th ed., 2005; (with B.M. Fagan) Africa in the Iron Age: c 500 B.C. to A.D. 1400, 1975; (with R. Oliver and A. Atmore) L'Africa, 1980; (with A. Atmore) The African Middle Ages 1400-1800, 1980, 2nd ed., 2008; The African Experience, 1991, 2nd ed. as The African Experience: From Olduvai Gorge to the 21st Century, 2000; In the Realms of Gold: Pioneering in African History, 1997; The African Experience: From Olduvai Gorge to the21st Century, 2000; (with A. Atmore) Medieval Africa, 1250-1800, 2001. EDITOR: The Dawn of African History, 1961, 2nd ed., 1968; (with G. Mathew) A History of East Africa, 1963; (with C. Oliver) Africa in the Days of Exploration, 1965; The Middle Age of African History, 1967; (with J.D. Fage) Papers in African Prehistory, 1970; (with J.D. Fage) Cambridge History of Africa, 8 vols., 1975-86; (with M. Crowder) The Cambridge Encyclopedia of Africa, 1981. Contributor to periodicals. **Address:** School of Oriental and African Studies, University of London, Thornhaugh St., Russell Sq., London, GL WC1H 0XG, England. **Online address:** smiersoliver@aol.com

OLKIN, Rhoda. American (born United States), b. 1953. **Genres:** Psychology, Social Sciences. **Career:** University of California, counselor, 1975-78, director of handicapped services, 1976-77; University of California-San Diego, intern, 1979-80; Behavioral Psychology Center, counselor, 1975-76; Planned Parenthood, counselor, 1976; Social Advocates for Youth, family counselor, 1978-79; licensed marriage, family and child counselor, 1982-; Veterans Administration Medical Center, Outpatient Alcohol Clinic and Family Therapy Unit, fellow, 1982, research psychologist with psychiatry service, 1982-85; California State University-Sacramento, assistant professor, associate professor, 1985-90; Journal of Family Psychology, adhoc reviewer, 1988-; California School of Professional Psychology, professor, 1990-; Journal of Counseling and Development, adhoc reviewer, 1991-; Disability Studies Quarterly, adhoc reviewer, 1995-; Professional Psychology: Research & Practice, adhoc reviewer, 1995-; Institute on Disability Rehabilitation and Research, Department of Education, principal investigator, 1999-2003; Through the Looking Glass, staff, research psychologist, 1999-; Alliant International University, distinguished professor, Institute on Disability and Health Psychology, executive director. Writer. **Publications:** What Psychotherapists Should Know about Disability, 1999. Contributor to books and journals. **Address:** Alliant International University, 1 Beach St., San Francisco, CA 94133, U.S.A. **Online address:** rolkin@alliant.edu

OLLESTAD, Norman. American (born United States), b. 1967. **Genres:** Autobiography/Memoirs. **Career:** Writer. **Publications:** Crazy for the Storm: A Memoir of Survival, 2009. **Address:** Venice, CA , U.S.A. **Online address:** norman@crazyforthestorm.com

OLLIER, C. D. *See* **OLLIER, Cliff(ord) David.**

OLLIER, Cliff(ord) David. (C. D. Ollier). Australian (born Australia), b. 1931. **Genres:** Earth Sciences, Geography, History. **Career:** Department of Agriculture, soil scientist, 1956-58; University of Melbourne, senior lecturer in geology, 1959-66; University of Papua New Guinea, Geology Department, head, 1967-69; Canberra College of Advanced Education, faculty, 1969-75; Australian National University, Research School of Pacific Studies, research fellow, 1975-; University of Western Australia, School of Earth and Geographical Sciences, professor of geography, 1979-89, emeritus professor, 1989-, adjunct and honorary staff. Writer. **Publications:** Weathering, 1969, 2nd ed., 1984; Volcanoes, 1969, 2nd ed., 1988; (as C.D. Ollier) Earth History in Maps and Diagrams, 1973; Weathering and Landforms, 1974; Ayers Rock and the Olgas in Colour, 1976; Tectonics and Landforms, 1981; (ed.) Morphotectonics of Passive Continental Margins, 1985; (comp.) Glossary of Morphotectonics, 1988; Ancient Landforms, 1991; An Ancient Land, 1993; (with C. Pain) Regolith, Soils and Landforms, 1996; (with C. Pain) The Origin of Mountains, 2000. **Address:** School of Earth & Environment, University of Western Australia, 35 Stirling Hwy., Crawley, WA 6009, Australia. **Online address:** cliff.ollier@uwa.edu.au

OLMERT, Michael. American (born United States), b. 1940. **Genres:** History, Architecture, Natural History. **Career:** Institute for Defense Analyses, editor, 1964-66; Arinc Research, editor, 1966-68; Resource Management Corp., director of publications, 1968-72; freelance writer, 1972-; Catholic University, lecturer, 1981; University of Maryland at College Park, instructor in English, 1986-95, professor of English, 1995-. **Publications:** The Tradition of Sport in Medieval Literature, 1980; The Official Guidebook to Williamsburg, 1985, rev. ed., 1998; The Smithsonian Book of Books, 1992; Milton's Teeth and Ovid's Umbrella: Curiouser and Curiouser Adventures in History, 1996; Shakespeare and Doctor Lopez, 2004; Great Creating Nature, 2005; Kitchens, Smokehouses and Privies: Outbuildings and The Architecture Of Daily Life In The Eighteenth-century Mid-Atlantic, 2009. Contributor to magazines and newspapers. **Address:** c/o Leona Schecter, 3748 Huntington St., Washington, DC 20015, U.S.A. **Online address:** olmert@umd.edu

OLMSTEAD, Earl P. American (born United States), b. 1920. **Genres:** Biography, History, Social Sciences. **Career:** Tuscarawas County Historical Society, president; Hardware and Supply Co., vice president for sales and marketing, 1948-76; Pissicra Realty Co., manager, 1976-90; Ohio State University, president, now emeritus. Writer. **Publications:** Blackcoats among the Delaware: David Zeisberger on the Ohio Frontier, 1991; A Day of Shame, 1991; A Documentary History of the Ohio and Erie Canal in Tuscarawas County, 1996; David Zeisberger: A Life among the Indians, 1997. Contributor to magazines. **Address:** 862 E Iron Ave., Apt. 217, Dover, OH 44622-2080, U.S.A. **Online address:** epolmstead@earthlink.net

OLMSTEAD, Robert. American (born United States), b. 1954. **Genres:** Novels, Novellas/Short Stories, Autobiography/Memoirs. **Career:** Jordan High School, English teacher, 1977-85, Dickinson College, senior writer-in-residence, 1985-; Ohio Wesleyan University, associate professor of English, professor of English, 2002-, Creative Writing Program, director; Boise State University, Creative Writing Program, director. Writer. **Publications:** NOVELS: Soft Water, 1988; America by Land, 1993; A Trail of Heart's Blood Wherever We Go: A Novel, 1998; Coal Black Horse, 2007; Far Bright Star: A Novel, 2009; Cold Dark Night, 2012. SHORT STORIES: River Dogs, 1987. OTHER: Stay Here With Me: A Memoir, 1996; Elements of the Writing Craft, 1997. Contributor to periodicals. **Address:** Department of English, Ohio Wesleyan University, 211 Sturges, 61 S Sandusky St., Delaware, OH 43015, U.S.A. **Online address:** rmolmste@owu.edu

OLMSTED, Robert W(alsh). American (born United States), b. 1936. **Genres:** Children's Fiction, Poetry, History, Biography. **Career:** Sunbury Daily Item, reporter and photographer, 1965-67; teacher of high school English, 1970-76; Patick County High School, teacher, 1978-; Conservatory of American Letters, publisher and president, 1987-; A Magazine for Writers, Northwoods Journal, editor; Northwoods Press Inc., president. **Publications:** Northern Lights, 1969; The First Christmas Ever, 1973, rev. ed., 1976; (with D. Spohn) Shadows on Cassiopeia, 1976; Wild Strawberries at 3000 Feet, 1986. EDITOR: New England Voices, 1972; Summertime, 1972; Man: When Born of Fire, 1973; Spring Songs, 1973; Rendevous with the Sea, 1976; Poems for Coffee Breaking, 1976; Two Hundred Years to Here, 1976; The Poetry Book, 1976; Showcase 1976, 1977. Works appear in anthologies. Contributor to magazines and newspapers. **Address:** Conservatory of American Letters, PO Box 298, Thomaston, ME 04861, U.S.A.

OLNEY, E. Price. *See* **OLNEY, Ross R(obert).**

OLNEY, Ross R(obert). (E. Price Olney). American (born United States), b. 1929. **Genres:** Children's Non-fiction, Recreation, Sports/Fitness, Biography, Young Adult Non-fiction, Military/Defense/Arms Control, Children's Non-fiction. **Career:** Writer, 1958-. Journalist and photographer. **Publications:** The Young Sportsman's Guide to Surfing, 1965; Americans in Space: A History of Manned Space Travel, 1966, rev. ed., 1970; The Young Sportsman's Guide to Water Safety, 1966; Daredevils of the Speedway, 1966; Light Motorcycle Riding, 1967; The Inquiring Mind: Astronomy, 1967; Sound All Around: How Hi-Fi and Stereo Work, 1967; The Story of Traffic Control, 1968; King of the Drag Strip, 1968; Let's Go Sailing: A Handbook for Young Sailors, 1969; Internal Combustion Engines, 1969; The Inquiring Mind: Oceanography, 1969; Men Against the Sea, 1969; (ed.) Tales of Time and Space, 1969; (with R.W. Graham) Kings of the Surf, 1969; Great Moments in Speed, 1970; Kings of Motor Speed, 1970; Great Dragging Wagons, 1970; The Incredible A. J. Foyt, 1970; The Indianapolis 500, 1970; Simple Gasoline Engine Repair, 1972; Air Traffic Control, 1972; Shudders, 1972; Drag Strip Danger, 1972; How To Keep Your Car Running, Your Money in Your Pocket, and Your Mind Intact!, 1973; Great Auto Racing Champions, 1973; Simple Bicycle Repair and Maintenance, 1973; (with R. Grable) The Racing Bugs: Formula Vee and Super Vee, 1974; Driving: How to Get a License (and Keep It!), 1974; Motorcycles, 1974; (with P. Olney) Quick and Easy Magic Fun, 1974; Superstars of Auto Racing, 1975; Light Motorcycle Repair and Maintenance, 1975; Motorcycling, 1975; Photographing Action Sports, 1976; Simple Appliance Repair, 1976; Superstars of Auto-Racing, 1976; How to Buy a Used Car, 1976; Gymnastics, 1976; Hang Gliding, 1976; How to Understand Soccer, 1976; Auto Racing's Young Lions, 1977; (with C. Bush) Better Skateboarding for Boys and Girls, 1977; (with M.A. Duganne) How to Make Your Car Run Better, 1977; Pocket Calculator Fun & Games, 1977; This Game Called Hockey: Great Moments in the World's Fastest Team Sport, 1978; The Young Runner, 1978; A.J. Foyt: The Only Four Time Winner, 1978; Illustrated Auto Racing Dictionary for Young People, 1978; Keeping Insects as Pets, 1978; How to Understand Soccer, 1978; Drama on the Speedway, 1978; Janet Guthrie, 1978; Modern Auto-Racing Superstars, 1978; Modern Racing Cars, 1978; (with C. Bush) Roller Skating, 1979; Tricky Discs: Frisbee Saucer Flying 1979; How to Understand Auto Racing, 1979; (with P. Olney) Easy to Make Magic, 1979; They Said It Couldn't Be Done, 1979; Out to Launch: Model Rockets, 1979; Keeping our Cities Clean, 1979; Modern Motorcycle Superstars, 1980; Auto Racing: R/C Micro Style, 1980; (with C. Bush) Better Kite Flying for Boys and Girls, 1980; The Amazing Yo-Yo, 1980; Model Airplanes, R/C Style, 1980; The Young Bicyclist, 1980; Auto Racing-R/C Micro Style, 1980; Riding High: Bicycling for Young People, 1981; Offshore!: Oil and Gas Platforms in the Ocean, 1981; Modern Drag Racing Superstars, 1981; Listen to Your Car: An Easy Guide to Identifying Car Troubles, 1981; Farm Giants, 1982; Modern Speed Record Superstars, 1982; Super Champions of Ice Hockey, 1982; Windsurfing: A Complete Guide, 1982; Winners, 1982; Construction Giants, 1983; (with P. Olney) Time: How to Have More of It, 1983; (with P. Olney) How Long?: To Go, To Grow, To Know, 1984; The Farm Combine, 1984; Super-Champions of Auto Racing, 1984; Lacrosse is For Me, 1984; Ocean-Going Giants, 1985; (with P.J. Olney) Imaging: Think Your Way to Success in Sports and Classroom, 1985; (with P.J. Olney) Up Against the Law: Your Legal Rights as a Minor, 1985; Car of the Future, 1986; The Shell Auto Care Guide: Tips on Everything You Need to Know as a Car Owner and Driver, 1986; (with R.D. Olney) The Amazing Transistor: Key to the Computer Age, 1986; (with P. Olney) Imagining, 1987; (with P. Olney) Up Against the Law, 1987; The Disposable Camera Guide, 1993; Combat, He Wrote, 1994; Landmark Decisions: Furman v. Georgia, 1996; (with B. Henson) Furman v. Georgia: The Death Penalty and The Constitution, 1996; Lyn St. James: Driven to Be First, 1997; History of Auto Racing, 1997. Contributor of articles to journals. **Address:** 2335 Sunset Dr., Ventura, CA 93001-2450, U.S.A. **Online address:** rohimself@aol.com

O'LOUGHLIN, Ed. Irish/Canadian (born Canada), b. 1966?. **Genres:** Novels. **Career:** Irish Times, reporter, Africa correspondent, 1994-; Sydney Morning Herald, Middle East correspondent, 2002-08; Melbourne Age, Middle East correspondent, 2002-08. **Publications:** Not Untrue and Not Unkind (novel), 2009; Toploader (novel), 2011. Contributor to periodicals. **Address:** c/o Peter Straus, Rogers, Coleridge & White Literary Agency, 20 Powis Mews, London, GL W11 1JN, England.

OLOWU, (Claudius) Dele. Nigerian (born Nigeria), b. 1952. **Genres:** Third World, Politics/Government, Public/Social Administration, Institutions/Organizations, Area Studies. **Career:** Obafemi Awolowo University, lecturer, 1977-83, senior lecturer, 1983-91, head of department, 1984-85, 1988, Department of Public Administration, professor, 1991-96, professor emeritus,

1996-; Redeemed Christian Church of God, area pastor, 1981-, ordained full pastor, 1986; Indiana University, research associate at workshop in political theory and policy analysis, 1985-87; Commonwealth Secretariat, consultant, 1986-87; World Bank, consultant, 1987-90; African Association for Public Administration and Management, consultant, 1989-91; United Nations Economic Commission for Africa, staff, 1991; Institute of Social Studies, professor, 1998-2004; IASIA Public Sector Reform Working Group, co-director, 2000-08; Addis Ababa University, faculty; University of Namibia, faculty. Writer. **Publications:** (Ed.) Administration of Social Services in Nigeria: The Challenge to Local Governments, 1981; (with D. Ayo) Managing the Nigerian Federal System: Issues and Policy Options: Abstracts of a High-Level Policy Workshop, 1985; Administration of the Nigerian Federal System, 1985; (ed. with B. Oshionebo) Report on the National Workshop on Manpower Utilisation and Development in Nigeria: A Post-Udoji Evaluation, 4th-5th September 1985, 1986; African Local Governments as Instrument of Economic and Social Development, International Union of Local Authorities, 1988; (ed. with L. Adamolekun and M. Laleye) Local Government in West Africa since Independence, 1988; Achievements and Problems of Federal and State Transfers to Local Governments in Nigeria Since Independence, 1989; African Local Governments as Instruments of Economic and Social Development, 1989; (ed. with A.O. Sanda and S. Ojo) Managing Performance in Nigeria's Public Sector, 1989; (ed. with J.S. Wunsch) The Failure of the Centralized State: Institutions and Self-Governance in Africa, 1990; Lagos State Governance, Economy and Society & Economy: Constitutionalism and Development in Nigeria, 1990; Local Government in Nigeria, 1991; (ed. with M. Laleye and V. Ayeni) Monograph Series on Administrative Responses to the African Economic Crisis: The Case of Nigeria, 1991; (with S.B. Ayo and J. Erero) Nigerian Public Administration: Past, Present, and Future: Essays in Honour of Professor Ladipo Adamolekun, 1991; (ed. with S.B. Ayo and B. Akande) Local Institutions and National Development in Nigeria, 1991; (ed. with S. Rasheed) Ethics and Accountability in African Public Services, 1993; (ed. with K. Soremekun and A. Williams) Governance and Democratisation in Nigeria, 1995; Faillite de l'Etat Centralisé en Afrique, 1995; (ed.with J. Erero) Indigenous Governance Systems in Nigeria, 1997; (with A. Williams and K. Soremekun) Governance and Democratisation in West Africa, 1999; (ed. with W.O.O. Ogendo and G. Hyden) African Perspectives on Governance, 2000; Decentralization Policies and Practices Under Structural Adjustment and Democratization in Africa, 2001; (ed. with S. Sako) Better Governance and Public Policy: Capacity Building for Democratic Renewal in Africa, 2002; (with J.S. Wunsch) Local Governance in Africa: The Challenges of Democratic Decentralization, 2004; Local Governance and Poverty Reduction, 2006; Local Governance Reform in Comparative Perspective, 2009. Contributor to books and journals. **Address:** Suze Groeneweg Erf 357, 3315 XK, Dordrecht, 1, Netherlands. **Online address:** dolowu2@yahoo.com

OLSEN, Brad. American/Norwegian/German (born Germany), b. 1965. **Genres:** Travel/Exploration, Reference, Theology/Religion, Cultural/Ethnic Topics, E-books, Illustrations. **Career:** Consortium of Collective Consciousness Publishing, founder, 1995-. Travel writer, photographer and graphic artist. **Publications:** SELF-ILLUSTRATED: World Stompers: A Young Persons Ultra-Budget Guide to Travel, 1996, 5th ed. as World Stompers: A Global Travel Manifesto, 2001; Extreme Adventures: Hawaii, 1998; Extreme Adventures: Northern California, 1998; Sacred Places: 101 Spiritual Sites Around the World, 2001; Sacred Places North America: 108 Destinations, 2003, 2nd ed., 2008; Sacred Places Around the World: 108 Destinations, 2nd ed., 2004; Sacred Places Europe: 108 Destinations, 2006. **Address:** CCC Publishing, 530 8th Ave., Ste. 6, San Francisco, CA 94118-3755, U.S.A. **Online address:** brad@cccpublishing.com

OLSEN, Edward A. American (born United States), b. 1941. **Genres:** Economics. **Career:** George Williams College, lecturer in international relations; U.S. State Department, Bureau of Intelligence and Research, Office of East Asian and Pacific Affairs, political intelligence analyst, 1975-80; Naval Postgraduate School, professor of national security affairs, 1980-, Asian Studies, director. Academic and writer. **Publications:** Japan: Economic Growth, Resource Scarcity and Environmental Constraints, 1978; (ed. with T.H. Kwak and W. Patterson) The Two Koreas in World Politics, 1983; U.S.-Japan Strategic Reciprocity: A Neo-internationalist View, 1985; (ed. with S. Jurika) The Armed Forces in Contemporary Asian Societies, 1986; (ed. with J.H. Shin and T.H. Kwak) Northeast Asian Security and Peace: Toward the 1990s, 1988; U.S. Policy and the Two Koreas, 1988; (ed. with T.H. Kwak) The Major Powers of Northeast Asia: Seeking Peace and Security, 1996; Toward Normalizing U.S. Korea Relations: In Due Course?, 2002; U.S. National Defense for the Twenty-first Century: The Grand Exit Strategy, 2002; Korea, the Divided Nation, 2005. Contributor to periodicals and journals. **Address:** National Security Affairs Department, Naval Postgraduate School, 1411 Cunningham Rd., Monterey, CA 93943, U.S.A. **Online address:** eolsen@nps.edu

OLSEN, Gary. American (born United States), b. 1948. **Genres:** Information Science/Computers, Sciences, Technology. **Career:** KDTH Radio, broadcaster, news reporter, advertising writer and producer, 1968-74; Deere and Co., graphic artist, photographer, video grapher, 1974-77, editor of employee communication, 1977-93; Hardie Interactive, media designer, 1993-97; Frank Hardie Advertising, manager, 1994, creative director, 1994-95, creative technology director, 1995-96, lead media designer and webmaster, 1996-97; University of Dubuque, adjunct faculty; National Computer Systems, graphic designer and new media specialist, 1997-. Writer. **Publications:** Getting Started in Computer Graphics, 1989, rev. ed., 1993; Getting Started in Multimedia Design, 1997; Windows 2000 Active Directory Design and Migration, 2000; (with B. Howard) Windows Server 2003 on HP ProLiant Servers, 2005. **Address:** National Computer Systems, 2510 N Dodge St., Iowa City, IA 52245, U.S.A. **Online address:** olsega@mchsi.com

OLSEN, Klaus Malling. Danish (born Denmark), b. 1955. **Genres:** Zoology, Sciences, Natural History. **Career:** Carsten Murmann Night School, staff, 1969-75. Ornithologist and writer. **Publications:** BIRDING GUIDES: (with H. Larsson) Terns of Europe and North America, 1995; (with H. Larsson) Skuas and Jaegers: A Guide to the Skuas and Jaegers of the World, 1997; (with H. Larsson) Gulls of North America, Europe and Asia, 2003. Contributor to books. **Address:** c/o Author Mail, Princeton University Press, 41 William St., Princeton, NJ 08540-5237, U.S.A. **Online address:** calidris@worldonline.dk

OLSEN, Lance (M.). American (born United States), b. 1956. **Genres:** Novels, Novellas/Short Stories, Poetry, Literary Criticism And History. **Career:** University of Iowa, instructor, 1979-80; University of Virginia, instructor, 1981-85; University of Kentucky, assistant professor of English, 1985-90; University of Idaho, associate professor, 1990-96, professor of English, 1996-2001, writer-in-residence, 1996-98; University of Utah, professor of English, 2007-. Writer. **Publications:** LITERATURE: Ellipse of Uncertainty: An Introduction to Postmodern Fantasy, 1987; Circus of the Mind in Motion: Postmodernism and the Comic Vision, 1990; William Gibson, 1992; Lolita: A Janus Text, 1995; Rebel Yell: A Short Guide to Fiction Writing, 1998. NOVELS: Live from Earth, 1990; Tonguing the Zeitgeist, 1994; Burnt, 1996; Time Famine, 1996; Freaknest, 2000; Girl Imagined by Chance, 2002; Nietzsche's Kisses, 2006; Anxious Pleasures, 2007; Head in Flames, 2009; Calendar of Regrets, 2010. STORIES: My Dates with Franz, 1993; Scherzi, I Believe, 1994; Sewing Shut My Eyes, 2000; Hideous Beauties, 2003. OTHER: (with J. Worley) Natural Selections (poetry), 1993. **Address:** Department of English, University of Utah, 255 S Central Campus Dr., Rm. 3500, Salt Lake City, UT 84112, U.S.A. **Online address:** lance.olsen@utah.edu

OLSEN, Mark Andrew. American (born United States) **Genres:** Novels, Mystery/Crime/Suspense, Theology/Religion. **Career:** Novelist and screenwriter. **Publications:** NOVELS: The Assignment, 2004; (with T. Tenney) Hadassah: One Night with the King, 2004; (with T. Tenney) Hadassah: The Girl Who Became Queen Esther, 2004; (with T. Tenney) The Hadassah Covenant, 2005; (with J. Bevere) Rescued: A Novel, 2006; The Watchers, 2007; (with T. Tenney) The Road Home, 2007; Warriors, 2008; Ulterior Motives, 2009. **Address:** c/o Author Mail, Bethany House, 11400 Hampshire Ave. S, Minneapolis, MN 55438, U.S.A.

OLSHAN, Matthew. American (born United States) **Genres:** Novels, Young Adult Fiction. **Career:** Writer. **Publications:** Finn: A Novel, 2001; The Flown Sky, 2007; The Boxer Lalouche, forthcoming; Marshlands, forthcoming. **Address:** Bancroft Press, PO Box 65360, Baltimore, MD 21209, U.S.A. **Online address:** writing@matthewolshan.com

OLSON, Arielle North. American (born United States), b. 1932. **Genres:** Literary Criticism And History, Children's Fiction. **Career:** Morristown Daily Record, feature writer, 1953-54; St. Louis Post-Dispatch, children's book reviewer, 1969-95. **Publications:** Hurry Home, Grandma!, 1984; Ven Deprisa, Abuela!/Hurry Home, Grandma!, 1985; The Lighthouse Keeper's Daughter, 1987; Noah's Cats and The Devil's Fire, 1992; (with H. Schwartz) Ask the Bones: Scary Stories from Around the World, 1999; (with H. Schwartz) More Bones: Scary Stories from Around the World, 2008. **Address:** 236 N Elm

Ave., Webster Groves, MO 63119, U.S.A.

OLSON, David Richard. Canadian (born Canada), b. 1935. **Genres:** Education, Language/Linguistics, Psychology, Essays, Biography, Reference. **Career:** Dalhousie University, assistant professor of educational psychology, 1963-65; Harvard University, Center for Cognitive Studies, post-doctoral fellow, research fellow, 1965-66; University of Toronto, Ontario Institute for Studies in Education, professor of applied psychology, 1966-71, professor of applied psychology, 1971-, now professor emeritus; Stanford Center for Research and Development in Teaching, fellow, 1969-70; Oxford University, Wolfson College, visiting fellow, 1974-75. Writer. **Publications:** Cognitive Development: The Child's Acquisition of Diagonality, 1970; (with E. Bialystok) Spatial Cognition: Spatial Cognition: The Structure and Development of Mental Representations of Spatial Relations, 1983; Few Die Well, 1991; The World on Paper: The Conceptual and Cognitive Implications of Writing and Reading, 1994. EDITOR: Media and Symbols: The Forms of Expression Communication and Education, 1974; Social Foundations of Language and Thought: Essays in Honor of J.S. Bruner, 1980; (with N. Torrance and A. Hildyard) Literacy, Language and Learning: The Nature and Consequences of Reading and Writing, 1985; (with F. Holthoon) Common Sense: A Foundation for the Social Sciences, 1987; (with J. Astington and P. Harris) Developing Theories of Mind, 1988; (with N. Torrance) Literacy and Orality, 1991; (with I. Taylor) Scripts and Literacy: Reading and Learning to Read Alphabets, Syllabaries and Characters, Kluwer, 1995; (with N. Torrance) Modes of Thought: Explorations in Culture and Cognition, 1996; (with N. Torrance) The Handook of Education and Human Development: New Models of Learning, Teaching and Schooling, 1996; (with F. Zalozo and J. Astington) Children's Discovery of Intention, 1999; (with P.D. Zelazo and J.W. Astington) Developing Theories of Intention: Social Understanding and Self-Control, 1999; (with N. Torrance) The Making of Literate Societies, 2001; Psychological Theory and Educational Reform: How School Remakes Mind and Society, 2003; Technology, Literacy and the Evolution of Society: Implications of the Work of Jack Goody, 2005; Jerome Bruner: The Cognitive Revolution in Educational Theory, 2008; (with N. Torrance) The Cambridge Handbook of Literacy, 2009. **Address:** Ontario Institute for Studies in Education, University of Toronto, 252 Bloor St. W, 9th Fl., Toronto, ON M5S 1V6, Canada. **Online address:** dolson@oise.utoronto.ca

OLSON, Gary A. American (born United States), b. 1954. **Genres:** Education, Writing/Journalism. **Career:** Indiana University, Writing Center, director, 1978-80; Shelton State Community College, adjunct instructor, 1980; University of Alabama, instructor in English and director of writing center, 1980-82; University of North Carolina, assistant professor of English, 1982-85, director of developmental writing, 1982-83, Center for Writing, director, 1982-84; Alabama Council of Teachers of English, board director, 1982; Technical Communication, associate editor, 1983-87; Journal of Advanced Composition, associate editor, 1984-85; University of South Florida, assistant professor, 1985-87, associate professor, 1987-92, professor of rhetoric and composition, 1992-2004, Institute for Interpretive Human Studies, associate, 1991-2004; St. Thomas University, coordinator of writing across the curriculum, 1988; Rhetoric Society of America, board director, 1990-95; Association of Teachers of Advanced Composition, presdient, 1994-; Illinois State University College of Arts and Sciences, dean, 2004-, professor of English, 2004-09; Idaho State University, provost and vice president for academic affairs. Writer. **Publications:** (With R. Ray and J. DeGeorge) Style and Readability in Technical Writing: A Sentence-Combining Aapproach, 1984; (with Ray and DeGeorge) Style and Readability in Business Writing, 1985; Justifying Belief: Stanley Fish and the Work of Rhetoric, 2002; (with L. Worsham) Postmodern Sophistry: Stanley Fish and the Critical Enterprise, 2004; (with L. Worsham) Politics of Possibility: Encountering the Radical Imagination, 2007. EDITOR: Writing Centers: Theory and Administration, 1984; (with R.E. Ray and J. DeGeorge) The Process Reader, 1986; (with E. Metzger and E. Ashton-Jones) Advanced Placement English: Theory, Politics, and Pedagogy, 1989; (with E. Ashton-Jones) The Gender Reader, 1991, 2nd ed., 2000; (with I. Gale) Cross-Disciplinary Perspectives on Rhetoric and Literacy, 1991; Philosophy, Rhetoric, Literary Criticism, 1994; (with S.I. Dobrin) Composition Theory for the Postmodern Classroom, 1994; (with E. Hirsh) Women Writing Culture, 1995; (with J. Drew) Landmark Essays on Advanced Composition, 1996; (with T.W. Taylor) Publishing in Rhetoric and Composition, 1997; (with L. Worsham) Race, Rhetoric, and the Postcolonial, 1999; (with L. Worsham and S.I. Dobrin) The Kinneavy Papers: Theory and the Study of Discourse, 2000; Rhetoric and Composition as Intellectual Work, 2002; (with L. Worsham) Critical Intellectuals on Writing, 2003; (with L. Worsham) Plugged In: Technology, Rhetoric, and Culture in a Posthuman Age, 2008; (with J.W. Presley) Future of Higher Education: Perspectives from America's Academic Leaders, 2009. Contributor to books and academic journals. **Address:** Office of the Provost & VP for Academic Affairs, Idaho State University, 921 S 8th Ave., PO Box 8063, Pocatello, ID 83209-8063, U.S.A.

OLSON, Gretchen. American (born United States) **Genres:** Novels, Psychology. **Career:** Hands and Words Are Not for Hurting Project, president. Author. **Publications:** Joyride, 1998; Call Me Hope, 2007. **Address:** Little, Brown Book Group, 100 Victoria Embankment, London, GL EC4Y 0DY, England. **Online address:** gretchen@gretchenolson.com

OLSON, James S. (James Stuart Olson). American (born United States), b. 1946. **Genres:** Young Adult Non-fiction, History, Bibliography, Social Sciences. **Career:** Dowling College, lecturer in history, instructor, 1970-71; State University of New York, lecturer in history, 1971-72, instructor of history, 1971; Sam Houston State University, assistant professor, 1972-78, associate professor, 1978-84, professor of history, 1984-96, Regents professor of history, distinguished professor of history, 1996-, chair of department, 1988-; Church of Jesus Christ of Latter-day Saints, bishop and stake president, North American Southwest Area, area authority, 1996-, New Testament Institute of Religion, instructor. Writer. **Publications:** (Contrib.) Black Labor in America, 1970; Historical Dictionary of the 1920s: From World War I to the New Deal, 1919-1933, 1988; (comp.) The History of Cancer: An Annotated Bibliography, 1989; The Indians of Central and South America: An Ethnohistorical Dictionary, 1991; The Peoples of Africa: An Ethnohistorical Dictionary, 1996; An Ethnohistorical Dictionary of China, 1998; Historical Dictionary of the 1950s, 2000. NONFICTION: (as James Stuart Olson) Herbert Hoover and the Reconstruction Finance Corporation, 1931-1933, 1977; (as James Stuart Olson with H.O. Beal) The Ethnic Dimension in American History, 1979, 4th ed., 2010; Slave Life in America: A Historiography and Selected Bibliography, 1983; (contrib.) War and Crisis in Modern America, 1983; (with R. Wilson) Native Americans in the Twentieth Century, 1984; Catholic Immigrants in America, 1987; Saving Capitalism: The Reconstruction Finance Corporation and the New Deal, 1933-1940, 1988; (with R. Roberts) Winning Is the Only Thing: Sports in America since 1945, 1989; (with R.H. Fritze and R. Roberts) Reflections on Western Civilization: A Reader, 2 vols., 1991; (with R. Roberts) Where the Domino Fell: America and Vietnam, 1945-1990, 1991, 5th ed., 2008; (with R.H. Fritze and R. Roberts) Reflections on World Civilization: A Reader, 2 vols., 1992; Honest Graft: The World of George Washington Plunkitt, 1993; (with J.E. Olson) Cuban Americans: From Trauma to Triumph, 1995; (with R. Roberts) John Wayne: American, 1995; (with R. Roberts) My Lai: A Brief History with Documents, 1998; (with R. Roberts) A Line in the Sand: The Alamo in Blood and Memory, 2001; Bathsheba's Breast: Women, Cancer and History, 2002; Equality Deferred: Race, Ethnicity and Immigration in America since 1945, 2003; Making Cancer History: Disease and Discovery at the University of Texas M.D. Anderson Cancer Center, 2008. EDITOR: NONFICTION: Historical Dictionary of the New Deal: From Inauguration to Preparation for War, 1985; (with R. Roberts) American Experiences: Readings in American History, 2 vols., 1986, 8th ed., 2008; Dictionary of the Vietnam War, 1988; Historical Dictionary of European Imperialism, 1991; (with S.W. Morgan) Dictionary of United States Economic History, 1992; (editor-in-chief) Historical Dictionary of the Spanish Empire, 1402-1975, 1992; The Vietnam War: Handbook of the Literature and Research, 1993; An Ethnohistorical Dictionary of the Russian and Soviet Empires, 1994; (with R.D. Marcus and D. Burner) The United States in the Twentieth Century, 2 vols., 1995; (with R. Shadle) Historical Dictionary of the British Empire, 2 vols., 1996; Encyclopedia of American Indian Civil Rights, 1997; Historical Dictionary of War Journalism, 1997; Historical Dictionary of the 1960s, 1999; Historical Dictionary of the 1970s, 1999; Historical Dictionary of the Great Depression, 1929-1940, 2001; Encyclopedia of the Industrial Revolution in America, 2002. Contributor to periodicals. **Address:** Department of History, Sam Houston State University, PO Box 2239, Huntsville, TX 77341-2239, U.S.A. **Online address:** his_jso@shsu.edu

OLSON, James Stuart. *See* **OLSON, James S.**

OLSON, Jeannine. *See* **OLSON, Jeannine E.**

OLSON, Jeannine E. (Jeannine Olson). American (born United States), b. 1939. **Genres:** History, Social Sciences, Theology/Religion. **Career:** Rhode Island College, Department of History, professor. Historian and writer. **Publications:** (as Jeannine Olson) Histoire de l'église: vingt siècles et six continents, 1972; Calvin and Social Welfare: Deacons and the Bourse francaise, 1989; One Ministry Many Roles: Deacons and Deaconesses through the Centuries, 1992, rev. ed. as Deacons and Deaconesses through the Centuries, 2005. Contributor to books. **Address:** Department of History, Rhode Island College, 600 Mount Pleasant Ave., Providence, RI 02908-1991, U.S.A. **Online address:** jolson@ric.edu

OLSON, Karen. American (born United States), b. 1943. **Genres:** Adult Nonfiction, Women's Studies And Issues, History, Social Sciences. **Career:** Community College of Baltimore County, professor of history and anthropology. Writer, historian and anthropologist. **Publications:** Wives of Steel: Voices of Women from the Sparrows Point Steelmaking Communities, 2005. **Address:** Community College of Baltimore County, Dundalk, 7200 Sollers Point Rd., Baltimore, MD 21222-4649, U.S.A. **Online address:** kolson@ccbcmd.edu

OLSON, Kirby. American (born United States), b. 1956. **Genres:** Theatre, Translations, Humor/Satire, Literary Criticism And History. **Career:** University of Washington, acting instructor, 1994-95; University of Tampere, assistant professor, 1995-2000; State University of New York-Delhi, assistant professor, 2001-, associate professor in English and humanities, professor of liberal arts and science. Writer. **Publications:** (Trans. with X. Callahan and M. Borch-Jacobsen) Remembering Anna O: A Century of Mystification, 1996; Comedy after Postmodernism: Rereading Comedy from Edward Lear to Charles Willeford, 2001; Gregory Corso: Doubting Thomist, 2002; Andrei Codrescu and the Myth of America, 2005; Temping, 2006. **Address:** Liberal Arts and Sciences Division, State University of New York-Delhi, 2 Main St., Delhi, NY 13753, U.S.A. **Online address:** kirbyolson2@hotmail.com

OLSON, Laura R. American (born United States), b. 1967. **Genres:** Politics/Government, Theology/Religion, Young Adult Non-fiction, Bibliography. **Career:** Clemson University, assistant professor, 1996-2001, associate professor, 2001-06, director of undergraduate studies, 2002-08, professor of political science, 2006-. Writer. **Publications:** NONFICTION: (with T.G. Jelen) The Religious Dimension of Political Behavior: A Critical Analysis and Annotated Bibliography, 1998; (with R.B. Fowler and A.D. Hertzke) Religion and Politics in America: Faith, Culture and Strategic Choices, 1999; Filled with Spirit and Power: Protestant Clergy in Politics, 2000; (ed. with S.E.S. Crawford) Christian Clergy in American Politics, 2001; (ed. with P.A. Djupe) Encyclopedia of American Religion and Politics, 2003; (with S.E.S. Crawford and M.M. Deckman) Women with a Mission: Religion, Gender and the Politics of Women Clergy, 2005; (ed. with P.A. Djupe) Religious Interests in Community Conflict: Beyond the Culture Wars, 2007; (ed. with J.C. Green) Beyond Red State, Blue State: Electoral Gaps in the Twenty-first Century American Electorate, 2009. Contributor of articles to periodicals. **Address:** Department of Political Science, Clemson University, 232 Brackett Hall, Clemson, SC 29634-1354, U.S.A. **Online address:** laurao@clemson.edu

OLSON, Lester C. American (born United States), b. 1955. **Genres:** Art/Art History, Communications/Media, History, Speech/Rhetoric, Literary Criticism And History, Humanities. **Career:** Pennsylvania State University, Department of Speech Communication, teaching assistant, 1977-80; University of Wisconsin, Department of Communication Arts, teaching assistant, 1980-84; University of Pittsburgh, Department of Communication, assistant professor, 1984-90, associate professor, 1990-2005, professor, 2005-, director of graduate studies, 1991-92, 1994-96, chancellor's distinguished teacher; University of California, Department of Rhetoric and Communication, visiting assistant professor, 1988-. Writer. **Publications:** Emblems of American Community in the Revolutionary Era: A Study in Rhetorical Iconology, 1991; Benjamin Franklin's Vision of American Community: A Study in Rhetorical Iconology, 2004; Visual Rhetoric: A Reader in Communication and American Culture, 2008; Human Rights Rhetoric: Traditions of Witnessing and Testifying, 2012; Audre Lorde's Public Advocacy: Poet Orator, Wounded Warrior, forthcoming. Contributor of articles to journals. **Address:** Department of Communication, School of Arts & Sciences, University of Pittsburgh, 1109 M Cathedral of Learning, Pittsburgh, PA 15260, U.S.A. **Online address:** olson@pitt.edu

OLSON, Linda. American (born United States), b. 1949. **Genres:** Education, Sociology. **Career:** Johns Hopkins University, senior research assistant, 1991, associate research scientist. Writer. **Publications:** (With D.R. Entwisle and K.A. Alexander) Children, Schools, and Inequality, 1997. **Address:** Center for Social Organizaton of Schools, School of Education, Johns Hopkins Univeristy, 2701 N Charles St., Ste. 300, Baltimore, MD 21218-2685, U.S.A. **Online address:** lsolson@jhu.edu

OLSON, Lynne. American (born United States), b. 1952?. **Genres:** History, Biography, Autobiography/Memoirs. **Career:** Associated Press, reporter, 1971-72, 1974-76; Baltimore Sun, correspondent, 1977-81; freelance writer, 1981-; American University, assistant professor of journalism. **Publications:** (With S. Cloud) The Murrow Boys: Pioneers on the Front Lines of Broadcast Journalism, 1996; Freedom's Daughters: The Unsung Heroines of the Civil Rights Movement from 1830 to 1970, 2001; (with S. Cloud) A Question of Honor: The Kościuszko Squadron: Forgotten Heroes of World War II as For Your Freedom and Ours: The Kosciuszko Squadron: Forgotten Heroes of World War II, 2003; (with S. Cloud) Sprawa Honoru, 2007; Troublesome Young Men: The Rebels Who Brought Churchill to Power and Helped Save England, 2007; Citizens of London, 2010. **Address:** c/o Author Mail, Knopf Publishing, 1745 Broadway, New York, NY 10019, U.S.A.

OLSON, Michael Keith. American (born United States) **Genres:** History, Business/Trade/Industry, Economics, Military/Defense/Arms Control, Novels. **Career:** San Francisco Chronicle, writer and photographer; Australian Broadcast Commission, producer; KQED Public Television, producer; NBC, examiner; ABC, examiner; Food Chain Syndicated Radio Program, producer and host; MO MultiMedia Group, president. Journalist. **Publications:** Metro-Farm: The Guide to Growing for Big Profit on a Small Parcel of Land, 1994; Tales from a Tin Can: The USS Dale from Pearl Harbor to Tokyo Bay, 2007. **Address:** Zenith Press, 400 1st Ave. N, Ste. 300, Minneapolis, MN 55401-1721, U.S.A. **Online address:** michael@tincan.us

OLSON, Robert W(illiam). American (born United States), b. 1940. **Genres:** History, Area Studies, Social Sciences, Humanities. **Career:** High school teacher, 1962-65; Indiana University-Bloomington, associate instructor in history, 1969-72; Clemson University, lecturer in history, 1972-73; University of Kentucky, assistant professor, 1973-77, associate professor, 1977-86, professor of Middle East and Ottoman history, 1986-, Hallam memorial professor, 1994-2000, university research professor, 1995-96, Albert D. and Elizabeth H. Kirwan memorial university professor, 1999-2000, College of Arts and Science's, distinguished professor, 2000-01. Writer. **Publications:** The Siege of Mosul and Ottoman-Persian Relations, 1718-1743, 1975; (contrib.) The Discoverers: An Encyclopedia of Explorers and Exploration, 1980; The Ba'th and Syria, 1947-1982: An Interpretative Historical Essay, 1980, rev. ed. as The Ba'th and Syria, 1947-1982: The Evolution of Ideology, Party and State from French Withdrawal to the Era of Hafizal-Asad, 1982; (ed. with A. Jabbari) Iran: Essays on a Revolution in the Making, 1981; (ed.) The Fundamental Principles and Precepts of Islam and Precepts of Islamic Government, 1981; (ed.) J.A. Ahmad, Iranian Society, 1982; (ed. with A. Hussain and J. Qureshi) Orientalism, Islam and Islamists, 1984; (ed.) Islamic and Middle Eastern Societies, 1987; The Emergence of Kurdish Nationalism and the Sheikh Said Rebellion, 1880-1925, 1989; (ed.) Kurdish Nationalist Movement in the 1990s, 1996; Imperial Meanderings and Republican By-Ways, 1996; The Kurdish Question and Turkish-Iranian Relations: From World War I to 1998, 1998; (comp.) Ellen White Comments on the Crisis Ahead, 2000; Turkey's Relations with Iran, Syria, Israel and Russia, 1991-2000, 2001; Turkey-Iran Relations, 1979-2004, 2004; The Goat and the Butcher: Nationalism and State Formation in Kurdistan-Iraq Since the Iraqi War, 2005; Blood, Beliefs and Ballots: The Management of Kurdish Nationalism in Turkey, 2007-2009, 2009. **Address:** Department of History, University of Kentucky, 1751 Patterson Office Twr. 0027, Lexington, KY 40506-0027, U.S.A. **Online address:** hisposta@uky.edu

OLSON, Steve E. American (born United States), b. 1956. **Genres:** Sciences, Theology/Religion, Sciences. **Career:** Freelance writer, 1978-88, 1991-; The Futurist magazine, writer and editor, 1978-79; Science 84-86 magazine, contributing editor; Executive Office of the President, Office of Science and Technology Policy, Special Assistant for Communications, 1989-92; White House Science Office, writer, 1988-91; National Academy Op-Ed Service, director, 1992-98. **Publications:** Biotechnology: An Industry Comes of Age, 1986; Shaping the Future: Biology and Human Values, 1989; Mapping Human History: Discovering the Past through Our Genes, 2002; Evolution in Hawaii: A Supplement to Teaching about Evolution and the Nature of Science, 2004; Count Down: Six Kids Vie for Glory at the World's Toughest Math Competition, 2004; (ed.) The National Academies Summit on America's Energy Future: Summary of a Meeting, 2008; (with G. Graffin) Anarchy Evolution: Faith, Science, and Bad Religion in a World Without God, 2010; (contrib.)

Emerging Threat of Drug-Resistant Tuberculosis in Southern Africa, 2011; Toward an Integrated Science of Research on Families, 2011; (with L.M. Troy and E.A. Miller) Hunger and Obesity: Understanding a Food Insecurity Paradigm, 2011; (with A.C. Berger) Etablishing Precompetitive Collaborations to Stimulate Genomics-Driven Drug Development, 2011. Contributor to magazines. **Address:** Rafe Sagalyn, 7201 Wisconsin Ave., Ste. 675, Bethesda, MD 20814, U.S.A. **Online address:** steve@steveolson.com

OLSON, Steven. American (born United States), b. 1950. **Genres:** Literary Criticism And History, Poetry. **Career:** University of Texas, instructor and teaching assistant, 1977-79; University of Illinois, teaching assistant, 1980-86; Northern Montana College, assistant professor of English, 1986-89; Central Washington University, Department of English, professor, 1989-. Writer. **Publications:** The Prairie in Nineteenth-Century American Poetry, 1994. Contributor of articles to periodicals. **Address:** Depatment of English, Central Washington University, Rm. 416A, Language and Literature Bldg., 400 E University Way, Ellensburg, WA 98926-7553, U.S.A. **Online address:** olsons@cwu.edu

OLSON, Susan M. American (born United States), b. 1949. **Genres:** Law, Politics/Government, History. **Career:** University of Utah, professor of political science, 1986-. Writer. **Publications:** Clients and Lawyers: Securing the Rights of Disabled Persons, 1984; Calendaring Practices of the Eastern District of North Carolina, 1987; (with D. McCool and J.L. Robinson) Native Vote: American Indians, the Voting Rights Act, and the Right to Vote, 2007. Contributor of articles to periodicals. **Address:** Department of Political Science, University of Utah, Rm. 252, 260 S Central Campus Dr., Salt Lake City, UT 84112-9199, U.S.A. **Online address:** susan.olson@utah.edu

OLSON, Ted. American (born United States), b. 1960?. **Genres:** Poetry, Music, Mythology/Folklore, Natural History, Local History/Rural Topics, Writing/Journalism, Area Studies, Autobiography/Memoirs, Autobiography/Memoirs, Humanities, Environmental Sciences/Ecology, Cultural/Ethnic Topics, Race Relations, Literary Criticism And History, Regional/Urban Planning, Film, Photography, Popular Culture. **Career:** University of Kentucky, teaching assistant, 1988-91; University of Mississippi, teaching assistant, 1991-95; Maryville College, adjunct professor of Appalachian studies and English, 1995-97; Union College, assistant professor of English, 1997-99; East Tennessee State University, professor of Appalachian studies and English, 1999-, Appalachian, Scottish, and Irish Studies Program, director, 1999-2004, Center for Appalachian Studies and Services, interim director, 2002-03. Writer. **Publications:** So Far: Poems, 1994; Blue Ridge Folklife (nonfiction), 1998; (ed.) From the Mountain, From the Valley: New and Collected Poems, 2001; (ed.) CrossRoads: A Southern Culture Annual, 2004; (ed.) The Country of the Pointed Firs and Selected Short Fiction, 2005; (ed. with C.K. Wolfe) The Bristol Sessions: Writings about the Big Bang of Country Music (nonfiction), 2005; (ed.) Cross Roads: A Southern Culture Annual, 2005; Breathing in Darkness: Poems, 2006; (ed.) CrossRoads: A Southern Culture Annual, 2006; (ed. with K.H. Olson) James Still: Critical Essays on the Dean of Appalachian Literature (nonfiction), 2007; James Still in Interviews, Oral Histories and Memoirs (nonfiction), 2009; (ed.) CrossRoads: A Southern Culture Annual, 2009; (ed. with A. Cavender) A Tennessee Folklore Sampler: Selected Readings from the Tennessee Folklore Society Bulletin, 1934-2009 (nonfiction), 2009; (ed.) Winesburg, Ohio, 2010; (with T. Russell) The Bristol Sessions, 1927-1928: The Big Bang of Country Music (nonfiction), 2011; (ed.) The Encyclopedia of Appalachia On-line Music Section (nonfiction), 2011; Impossible Wind: The Formative Poetry of Robinson Jeffers (nonfiction), 2012; (ed.) The Hills Remember: The Complete Short Stories of James Still, 2012. **Address:** East Tennessee State University, PO Box 70556, Johnson City, TN 37614-1700, U.S.A. **Online address:** olson@etsu.edu

OLSON, Toby. American (born United States), b. 1937. **Genres:** Novels, Poetry, Young Adult Fiction, Literary Criticism And History. **Career:** Long Island University, Aspen Writers Workshop, co-founder and associate director, 1964-67; The New School For Social Research, faculty, 1967-75; Long Island University, assistant professor, 1966-74; State University of New York College at Cortland, poet-in-residence, 1972; State University of New York at Cortland, poet-in-residence, 1972; Friends Seminary, writer-in-residence, 1974-75; Temple University, associate professor, 1975, professor, 1975-99; Friends Seminary, poet-in-residence, 1974-75. Writer. **Publications:** POETRY: The Hawk-Foot Poems, 1968; Maps, 1969; Worms into Nails, 1969; The Brand, 1969; Pig's Book, 1969; Cold House, 1970; (contrib.) Inside Outer Space, 1970; Poems, 1970; Tools, 1971; Shooting Pigeons, 1971; Home, 1972; Vectors, 1972; (contrib.) Loves, Etc., 1973; Fishing, 1974; A Kind of Psychology, 1974; The Wrestlers and Other Poems, 1974; City, 1974; (contrib.) Active Anthology, 1974; Changing Appearance: Poems 1965-70, 1975; A Moral Proposition, 1975; Priorities, 1975; Seeds, 1975; Standard-4, 1975; Home, 1976; Three and One, 1976; Doctor Miriam: Five Poems by Her Admiring Husband, 1977; Aesthetics, 1978; The Florence Poems, 1978; Aesthetics, 1978; Bird songs, 1980; Two Standards, 1982; Still/Quiet, 1982; Sitting in Gusevik, 1983; We Are the Fire: A Selection of Poems, 1984; Unfinished Building (poetry), 1993; Human Nature (poetry), 2000. NOVELS: (intro.) Goodrich, 1972; (intro.) Arctic Summer, 1974; (intro.) One Armed Flyer, 1976; The Life of Jesus: An Apocryphal Novel, 1976; Seaview, 1982; (ed. with M.E. Siegel) Writing Talks: Views on Teaching Writing from Across the Professions, 1983; We Are in the Fire, 1984; The Woman Who Escaped from Shame, 1986; Utah, 1987, 5th ed., 2003; Dorit in Lesbos, 1990; Pool: From the Novel Dorit in Lesbos, 1991; At Sea, 1993; Unfinished Buildings: Poems, 1993; At Sea, 1993; Write Letter to Billy, 2000; The Blond Box, 2003; The Bitter Half, 2006; Sea View, 2006; Tampico, 2008. Works appear in anthologies. Contributor of articles. **Address:** 275 S 19th St., Ste. 7, Philadelphia, PA 19103-5710, U.S.A. **Online address:** toby.olson@verizon.net

OLSON, Walter K. American (born United States), b. 1954. **Genres:** Law, Politics/Government. **Career:** U.S. House of Representatives, policy analyst, 1980; American Enterprise Institute for Public Policy Research, associate editor, 1980-85; Manhattan Institute for Policy Research, senior fellow, 1985-2010; Cato Institute, Center for Constitutional Studies, senior fellow, 2010-. **Publications:** (Ed.) New Directions in Liability Law, 1988; The Litigation Explosion: What Happened When America Unleashed the Lawsuit, 1991; The Excuse Factory: How Employment Law is Paralyzing the American Workplace, 1997; The Rule of Lawyers: How the New Litigation Elite Threatens America's Rule of Law, 2003; Schools for Misrule: Legal Academia and an Overlawyered America, 2011. Contributor to periodicals. **Address:** Cato Institute, 1000 Massachusetts Ave. NW, Washington, DC 20001, U.S.A. **Online address:** wo@walterolson.com

OLTION, Jerry. (Ryan Hughes). American (born United States), b. 1957. **Genres:** Science Fiction/Fantasy, Young Adult Fiction, Novels, Literary Criticism And History, Young Adult Non-fiction. **Career:** Writer. **Publications:** Frame of Reference, 1987; Humanity, 1990; Alliance, 1990; Love Songs of a Mad Scientist, 1993; Tales from the Yuletide, 1994; Twilights End, 1996; Buried Treasures, 1996; Mudd in Your Eye, 1997; Singing in the Rain, 1998; Prophets Power, 1998; Where Sea Meets Sky, 1998; (with K. Oltion) The Flaming Arrow, 2000; Abandon in Place, 2000; The Getaway Special, 2001; With Stars in Their Eyes, 2003; Twenty Questions, 2003; Paradise Passed, 2004; Anywhere But Here, 2005; Analog Science Fiction and Fact, 2011. AS RYAN HUGHES: The Darkness before the Dawn, 1995; You Only Die Twice, 1997; Hard Crash, 1997; Prophet's Power, 1998. Contributor to periodicals. **Address:** c/o Author Mail, Tor Books, 175 5th Ave., 14th Fl., New York, NY 10010, U.S.A. **Online address:** j.oltion@sff.net

OLUPONA, Jacob K. (Jacob Obafemi Kehinde Olupona). American/Nigerian (born Nigeria), b. 1951. **Genres:** Theology/Religion, Cultural/Ethnic Topics. **Career:** University of California, professor and director of African American and African studies, 1991-2006; Harvard University, visiting professor, Harvard Divinity School, professor and chair of Committee on African Studies, 2006-; Florida International University, visiting professor; Muhlenberg College, visiting professor; Smith College, visiting professor; Beyreuth University, visiting professor; Selly Oak Colleges, visiting professor. Writer. **Publications:** (ed.) African Traditional Religions in Contemporary Society, 1991; Kingship, Religion, and Rituals in a Nigerian Community: A Phenomenological Study of Ondo Yoruba Festivals, 1991; (ed.) Religion and Peace in Multi-faith Nigeria, 1992; (ed. with S.S. Nyang) Religious Plurality in Africa: Essays in Honour of John S. Mbiti, 1993; (ed.) African Spirituality: Forms, Meanings, and Expressions, 2000; (ed.) Beyond Primitivism: Indigenous Religious Traditions and Modernity, 2004; (ed. with R. Gemignani) African Immigrant Religions in America, 2007; (ed. with T. Rey) Òrìṣà Devotion as World Religion: The Globalization of Yorùbá Religious Culture, 2008. **Address:** Harvard Divinity School, 45 Francis Ave., Cambridge, MA 02138-1911, U.S.A. **Online address:** olupona@fas.harvard.edu

OLUPONA, Jacob Obafemi Kehinde, *See* **OLUPONA, Jacob K.**

OLWELL, Russell B. American (born United States), b. 1969?. **Genres:** History, Business/Trade/Industry. **Career:** Eastern Michigan University, assistant professor, associate professor of history of technology, professor of history, EMU Gear Up Project, director; Kyoritsu Women's University, Fulbright lecturer, 2007. Writer and historian. **Publications:** At Work in the Atomic City: A Labor and Social History of Oak Ridge, Tennessee, 2004; International Atomic Energy Agency, 2009. Contributor to journals. **Address:** Department of History & Philosophy, Eastern Michigan University, 110 Hoyt, 701 Pray-Harrold, Ypsilanti, MI 48197, U.S.A. **Online address:** rolwell@emich.edu

O'MALLEY, Padraig. Irish (born Ireland), b. 1942?. **Genres:** Sociology, International Relations/Current Affairs, Politics/Government. **Career:** University of Massachusetts, John W. McCormack Institute of Public Affairs, Center for Democracy and Development, senior fellow, 1982-2006, policy analyst, McCormack Graduate School of Policy Studies, John Joseph Moakley distinguished professor of Peace and Reconciliation, 2007-, Irish Studies Program, lecturer; New England Journal of Public Policy, editor. **Publications:** The Uncivil Wars: Ireland Today, 1983, 3rd ed., 1997; Biting at the Grave: The Irish Hunger Strikes and the Politics of Despair, 1990; Northern Ireland: Questions of Nuance, 1990; Northern Ireland-The Changing Paradigm: Politics and the Constitution, 1993; The Prospects for Democracy in Southern Africa, 1993; Uneven Paths: Advancing Democracy in Southern Africa, 1993; Religion and Conflict: The Case of Northern Ireland, 1995; Northern Ireland, 1983-1996: For Every Step Forward, 1996; Ramaphosa and Meyer in Belfast: The South African Experience; How the New South Africa Was Negotiated, 1996; Shades of Difference: Transition in South Africa 1989-1999, 2007. EDITOR: AIDS: A Special Issue of the New England Journal of Public Policy, 1988, as The AIDS Epidemic: Private Rights and the Public Interest (essays), 1989; Homelessness: New England and Beyond, 1992; Uneven Paths: Advancing Democracy in Southern Africa, 1993; Southern Africa: The People's Voices, 1999; Sticks & Stones: Living with Uncertain Wars, 2006. **Address:** John W. McCormack Graduate School, University of Massachusetts, 100 Morrissey Blvd., Boston, MA 02125, U.S.A. **Online address:** padraig.omalley@umb.edu

O'MALLEY, Patrick R. American (born United States) **Genres:** Reference, Writing/Journalism. **Career:** Georgetown University, associate professor of English. Writer. **Publications:** Catholicism, Sexual Deviance and Victorian Gothic Culture, 2006. Contributor of articles to journals. Works appear in anthologies. **Address:** Department of English, Georgetown University, Box 571131, New North 306, Washington, DC 20057-1131, U.S.A. **Online address:** pro@georgetown.edu

O'MALLEY, Penelope Grenoble. American (born United States) **Genres:** Urban Studies, Transportation, Geography, Environmental Sciences/Ecology, Autobiography/Memoirs, Travel/Exploration, History. **Career:** Santa Catalina Island Conservancy, director of communications; Santa Barbara Museum of Natural History, research assistant, research associate. Writer. **Publications:** Takeoffs Are Optional, Landings Are Mandatory: Airline Pilots Talk about Deregulation, Safety and the Future of Commercial Aviation, 1993; Malibu Diary: Notes from an Urban Refugee, 2004. Contributor to magazines and periodicals. **Address:** c/o Author Mail, University of Nebraska Press, PO Box 166, Reno, NV 89557, U.S.A.

O'MALLEY, Thomas. British (born England), b. 1967?. **Genres:** Novels. **Career:** University of Iowa, returning writer fellow, Department of English, assistant professor; Omega Institute, faculty. Writer. **Publications:** In the Province of Saints: A Novel, 2005. **Address:** Omega Institute, 150 Lake Dr., Rhinebeck, NY 12572-3252, U.S.A. **Online address:** thomas.omalley@dartmouth.edu

O'MALLEY, Vincent (J.). American (born United States), b. 1945. **Genres:** inspirational/Motivational Literature, Biography, Theology/Religion. **Career:** Ordained Roman Catholic priest, 1973-; Saint John the Baptist, pastor; Saint Josephs Roman Catholic Church, pastor, religious leader; Niagara University, assistant, 1990-91, executive vice-president, 1991-95, senior assistant, 1995-, Department of Religious Education, instructor. Writer. **Publications:** Saintly Companions: A Cross-Reference of Sainted Relationships, 1995; Ordinary Suffering of Extraordinary Saints, 2000; Saints of Africa, 2001; Saints of North America, 2004; Saints of Asia: 1500 to the Present, 2007. Contributor to periodicals. **Address:** Saint Josephs Roman Catholic Church, 47 DePaul St., PO Box 376, Emmitsburg, MD 21727, U.S.A. **Online address:** vomcm@attglobal.net

OMANG, Joanne (Brenda). American (born United States), b. 1943. **Genres:** Novels, Communications/Media, Military/Defense/Arms Control, Young Adult Fiction, History. **Career:** United Press Intl., reporter, 1967-68, bureau chief, 1968-69, editor, 1969-71; Washington Post, staff and bureau chief, 1973-74, chief correspondent for Latin America, 1975-77, staff writer, 1978-79, diplomatic and foreign policy correspondent, 1982-87, assistant national editor, 1989-91; freelance writer, 1991-. **Publications:** (With A. Neier) Psychological Operations in Guerrilla Warfare, 1985; Incident at Akabal (novel), 1992. **Address:** c/o Timothy Seldes, Russell & Volkening Inc., 50 W 29th St., Ste. 7E, New York, NY 10001, U.S.A. **Online address:** omangj@aol.com

O'MARA, Peggy (Noreen). American (born United States), b. 1947. **Genres:** Human Relations/Parenting, Essays, Medicine/Health. **Career:** Zia School, special education teacher, 1972-73; University of Utah, Holloman Air Force Base, MBA coordinator, 1973; freelance writer, 1974-; Mothering Magazine, editor, publisher and owner, 1980-, editor-in-chief. **Publications:** (Co-ed.) Mother Poet, 1983; The Way Back Home: Essays on Life and Family, 1993; (with J. McConnell) Natural Family Living: The Mothering Magazine Guide to Parenting, 2000; (with W. Ponte) Mothering Magazine's Having a Baby, Naturally: The Mothering Magazine Guide to Pregnancy and Childbirth, 2003; A Quiet Place: Essays on Life and Family, 2006; (foreword) Feeding the Whole Family: Cooking with Whole Foods: Recipes for Babies, Young Children, and Their Parents, 2008. EDITED WITH A. PEDERSEN: Being a Father: Family, Work, and Self, 1990; Schooling at Home: Parents, Kids, and Learning, 1990; Teens: A Fresh Look, 1991. Contributor to periodicals. **Address:** Mothering Magazine, PO Box 1690, Santa Fe, NM 87504, U.S.A. **Online address:** peggyo@mothering.com

OMMUNDSEN, Wenche. Australian/Norwegian (born Norway), b. 1952. **Genres:** Writing/Journalism, Social Sciences, Cultural/Ethnic Topics. **Career:** Monash University, tutor in English, 1986; Deakin University, senior lecturer in literature and journalism, 1986-, Faculty of Arts, research manager, 2000-; University of Wollongong, professor of English literatures, 2006, Faculty of Arts, associate dean, 2007-09, dean, 2009-. Writer. **Publications:** Metafictions?: Reflexivity in Contemporary Texts, 1993; (ed. with M. Boreland) Refractions: Asian/Australian Writing, 1995; (ed. with H. Rowley) From a Distance: Australian Writers and Cultural Displacement, 1996; (ed. with B. Edwards) Appreciating Difference: Writing Postcolonial Literary History, 1998; (ed.) Bastard Moon: Essays on Chinese-Australian Writing, 2001; (ed. with M. Leach and A. Vandenberg) Cultural Citizenship and the Challenges of Globalization, 2010. **Address:** Faculty of Arts, School of English Literature and Philosophy, University of Wollongong, Wollongong, NW 2522, Australia. **Online address:** wenche@uow.edu.au

OMOTO, Kathryn Bishop. *See* **ECKERT, Kathryn Bishop.**

O'MURCHU, Diarmuid. British/Irish (born Ireland), b. 1950?. **Genres:** Theology/Religion. **Career:** Priest, writer and social psychologist. **Publications:** The Seed Must Die: Religious Life-Survival or Extinction?, 1980; The God Who Becomes Redundant, 1986; Religious Life: A Prophetic Vision: Hope and Promise for Tomorrow, 1991; Quantum Theology, 1997, rev. ed. as Quantum Theology: Spiritual Implications of the New Physics, 2004; Reclaiming Spirituality: A New Spiritual Framework for Today's World, 1998; Poverty, Celibacy, and Obedience: A Radical Option for Life, 1999; Our World in Transition: Making Sense of a Changing World, 2000; Religion in Exile: A Spiritual Homecoming, 2000; Evolutionary Faith: Rediscovering God in Our Great Story, 2002; Catching Up with Jesus: A Gospel Story for Our Times, 2005; Consecrated Religious Life: The Changing Paradigms, 2005; The Transformation of Desire: How Desire Became Corrupted and How We Can Reclaim It, 2007; Ancestral Grace: Meeting God in Our Human Story, 2008; Jesus in the Power of Poetry: A New Voice for Gospel Truth, 2009; Adult Faith: Growing in Wisdom and Understanding, 2010. **Address:** London, GL , England. **Online address:** diarmuid.13@gmail.com

ONDAATJE, Michael. (Philip Michael Ondaatje). Canadian/Sri Lankan (born Sri Lanka), b. 1943. **Genres:** Novels, Plays/Screenplays, Poetry, Literary Criticism And History. **Career:** University of Western Ontario, instructor, 1967-71, 1967-71; York University, Glendon College, Department of English, faculty of English literature, 1971-90; Mongrel Broadsides, editor; University of Hawaii, Honolulu, visiting professor, 1979-; Brown University, visiting professor, 1990-. Writer. **Publications:** The Dainty Monsters, 1967; The Man with Seven Toes, 1971; The Collected Works of Billy the Kid, Left Handed Poems, 1970; Leonard Cohen, 1970; (ed.) The Broken Ark, 1971; Rat Jelly,

1973; Personal Fictions: Stories by Munro, Wiebe, Thomas & Blaise, 1977; Elimination Dance, 1978; Rat Jelly and Other Poems, 1979; (ed.) The Long Poem Anthology, 1979; There's a Trick with a Knife I'm Learning to do: Poems, 1963-1978, 1979; Tin Roof, 1982; Running in the Family, 1982; Secular Love (poems), 1984; Two Poems, 1986; In the Skin of a Lion (novel), 1987; (ed. with R. Banks and D. Young) Brushes with Greatness: An Anthology of Chance Encounters with Greatness, 1989; (ed. with L. Spalding) The Brick Anthology, 1989; (ed.) From Ink Lake, 1990; The Cinnamon Peeler: Selected Poems, 1991; (ed. with G. Bowering) H in the Heart, 1994; Coming through Slaughter (novel), 1984; The English Patient: A Screenplay, 1996; Handwriting (poems), 1999; Anil's Ghost, 2000; (ed. with M. Redhill, E. Spalding and L. Spalding) Lost Classics, 2000; Conversations: Walter Murch and the Art of Editing Film, 2002; (ed. and intro.) Paris Stories, 2002; Vintage Ondaatje, 2004; Story, 2005; Divisadero, 2007; (contrib.) 100 Journeys for the Spirit, 2010; Cat's Table, 2011. Contributor to books and periodicals. **Address:** Bloomsbury Publishing plc, 38 Soho Sq., London, GL W1D 3HB, England.

ONDAATJE, Philip Michael. *See* **ONDAATJE, Michael.**

ONDEGO, Ogova. Kenyan (born Kenya), b. 1968. **Genres:** Novellas/Short Stories, Children's Fiction, Young Adult Fiction, Poetry, Communications/Media, Cultural/Ethnic Topics, Fash Ion/Costume, Gay And Lesbian Issues, Literary Criticism And History, Writing/Journalism, Autobiography/Memoirs. **Career:** Artmatters.com, publisher and editor; Kenya Broadcasting Corp., researcher, 2001-; Stepafrica (bimonthly magazine), editorial/research staff; Africa Film and Television, East Africa correspondent; Rootz Africa magazine, East Africa correspondent. **Publications:** Heroes Stand Alone, 1994; A Virgin in God's Hands, 1995; Matatu Terror (autobiography), 1995; African Cine Week: Kenya, 2003; Same Gender Unions, 2004; From Terror to Hope, 2009. FORTHCOMING: African Film Kenya; Braggart's Day. Contributor to books. **Address:** Artmatters.Info, Philadelphia House, 4th Fl., Tom Mboya St., Hakati Rd., PO Box 20775, Nairobi, 00100, Kenya.

ONDRA, Nancy J. American (born United States) **Genres:** Agriculture/Forestry, Horticulture. **Career:** Rodale Press (magazine publisher), editor, through 1995; freelance garden writer and editor, 1995-; Pendragon Perennials (rare-plant nursery), owner. **Publications:** Rodales Successful Organic Gardening: Annuals and Bulbs, 1995; Soil and Composting: The Complete Guide to Building Healthy Fertile Soil, 1998; Easy Plant Propagation: Filling Your Garden with Plants from Seeds Cuttings Divisions and Layers, 1998; Landscaping with Herbs: Beautify Your Yard and Garden with Easy-care Herbs, 2000; Taylor's Guide to Roses: How to Select Grow and Enjoy More than 380 Roses, 2001; Grasses: Versatile Partners for Uncommon Garden Design, 2002; (with S. Cohen) The Perennial Gardeners Design Primer, 2005; (with S. Cohen) Fallscaping: Extending Your Garden Season into Autumn, 2007; Foliage: Astonishing Color and Texture beyond Flowers, 2007; (ed.) Mulch Magic!: Secrets for Making and Using Compost and Mulch in Your Garden, 2007; The Perennial Care Manual: A Plant-by-Plant Guide: What to Do and When to Do It, 2009. **Address:** Storey Publishing, 210 MASS MoCA Way, North Adams, MA 01247, U.S.A. **Online address:** hayefield@comcast.net

ONEAL, Elizabeth. (Zibby Oneal). American (born United States), b. 1934. **Genres:** Children's Fiction, Children's Non-fiction, Young Adult Fiction, Novels, Picture/Board Books, Technology, Literary Criticism And History, Art/Art History, Reference. **Career:** University of Michigan, lecturer in English, 1976-85. Writer. **Publications:** AS ZIBBY ONEAL: War Work, 1971; The Improbable Adventures of Marvelous O'Hara Soapstone, 1972; Turtle and Snail, 1979; The Language of Goldfish: A Novel, 1980; A Formal Feeling: A Novel, 1982; In Summer Light, 1985; Maude and Walter, 1985; Grandma Moses: Painter of Rural America, 1986; A Long Way to Go: A Story of Women's Right to Vote, 1990. Contributor to periodicals. **Address:** c/o Marilyn Marlow, Curtis Brown Ltd., 10 Astor Pl., New York, NY 10003-6935, U.S.A.

O'NEAL, Hank. American (born United States), b. 1940. **Genres:** Biography, Autobiography/Memoirs, Art/Art History, Music, Photography, History, Young Adult Non-fiction. **Career:** Central Intelligence Agency, staff, 1963-77; Chiaroscuro Records Inc., owner and chief producer, 1970-78, 1987-; Downtown Sound, owner, 1973-80; Hammond Music Enterprises, executive vice-president, 1981-84; HOSS Inc., owner and executive vice-president, 1984-; SOS Productions, president, 1987-. Writer. **Publications:** (With E. Condon) The Eddie Condon Scrapbook of Jazz, 1973; Vision Shared: A Classic Portrait of America and Its People, 1935-1943, 1976; Berenice Abbott: American Photographer, 1982; Life is Painful, Nasty, and Short: In My Case it has Only Been Painful and Nasty: Djuna Barnes, 1978-1981: An Informal Memoir, 1990; Sincerely, Ty Cobb: The Funky Blues Date, 1995; (contrib.) The Graphic Art of Paul Bacon, 1999; Hank O'Neal: Portraits, 1971-2000, 2000; (intro.) Gay Day: The Golden Age of the Christopher Street Parade 1974-1983, 2006; The Ghosts of Harlem, 2009; Bernice Abbott, 2010. **Address:** Chiaroscuro Records Inc., 830 Broadway, 3rd Fl., New York, NY 10003-4827, U.S.A. **Online address:** chiarohank@aol.com

ONEAL, Zibby. *See* **ONEAL, Elizabeth.**

O'NEIL, Robert M. American (born United States), b. 1934. **Genres:** Law, Politics/Government. **Career:** Tufts University, instructor in speech, 1956-61; San Francisco State College, visiting instructor in speech, 1962; U.S. Supreme Court Justice, law clerk, 1962-63; University of California, Berkeley, professor of law, 1963-67, 1969-72; State University of New York, professor of law and executive assistant, 1967-69; University of Cincinnati, professor of law, 1972-75, vice-president and provost for academic affairs, 1972-73, executive vice-president for academic affairs, 1973-75; Council on Legal Education Opportunity, chairman, 1972-74; Indiana University, professor of law and vice-president of the university, 1975-80; University of Wisconsin, professor of law and president of university system, 1980-85; University of Virginia, president of the university, 1985-90, professor of law emeritus, 1985-, university professor emeritus, Thomas Jefferson Center for the Protection of Free Expression, director. Writer. **Publications:** (Co-author) A Guide to Debate, 1964; (with J.A. Lynch) Crime and Law Enforcement, 1965; (with D. Parker and N. Econopouly) Civil Liberties: Case Studies and the Law, 1965; Free Speech: Responsible Communication under Law, 1966, 2nd ed., 1972; (with J.A. Lynch) Combating Crime, 1967; The Price of Dependency: Civil Liberties in the Welfare State, 1970; (with J.P. Morris and R. Mack) No Heroes, No Villains, 1972; The Courts, Government and Higher Education, 1972; (with A. DAmato) The Judiciary and Vietnam, 1972; (co-author) Civil Liberties Today, 1974; Discriminating Against Discrimination: Preferential Admissions and the DeFunis Case, 1975; Minorities in Medicine: Report of a Conference, 1977; The Rights of Government Employees: The Basic ACLU Guide to a Government Employees, 1978; Handbook of the Law of Public Employment, 1978, 2nd ed., 1993; Classrooms in the Crossfire: The Rights and Interests of Students, Parents, Teachers, Administrators, Librarians and the Community, 1981; The Rights of Public Employees: The Basic ACLU Guide to the Rights of Public Employees, 1993; Free Speech in the College Community, 1997; Alcohol Advertising on the Air: Beyond the Reach of Government, 1997; The First Amendment and Civil Liability, 2001; Academic Freedom in the Wired World: Political Extremism, Corporate Power and the University, 2008. Contributor to journals and magazines. **Address:** Virginia School of Law, University of Virginia, WB104E, 580 Massie Dr., Charlottesville, VA 22903, U.S.A. **Online address:** rmo@virginia.edu

O'NEILL, Jamie. Irish (born Ireland), b. 1962?. **Genres:** Novels, Young Adult Fiction. **Career:** Writer. **Publications:** Disturbance, 1989; Kilbrack, or, Who is Nancy Valentine?, 1990; At Swim, Two Boys, 2001. **Address:** c/o Author Mail, Simon & Schuster Inc., 1230 Ave. of the Americas, New York, NY 10020-1513, U.S.A. **Online address:** atswim@iol.ie

O'NEILL, Joseph. Irish (born Ireland), b. 1964. **Genres:** Novels, History, Literary Criticism And History. **Career:** Novelist and writer. **Publications:** This is the Life, 1991; The Breezes, 1995; Blood-Dark Track: A Family History, 2000; Netherland, 2008; (intro.) Actual, 2009. Contributor to periodicals. **Address:** Chambers of James Guthrie Q.C., 3 Hare Ct., Temple, London, GL EC4Y 7BJ, England. **Online address:** josephoneill@earthlink.com

O'NEILL, Kevin M. American (born United States), b. 1953. **Genres:** Biology, Environmental Sciences/Ecology. **Career:** ColoradoStateUniversity, graduate research assistant, 1976-81; Montana State University, Entomology Research Laboratory, research associate, 1985-90, Department Of Land Resources and Environmental Sciences, assistant professor, 1990-96, associate professor, 1996-2003, professor, 2003-05; biologist; entomologist. Writer. **Publications:** (With H.E. Evans) The Natural History and Behavior of North American Beewolves, 1988; Solitary Wasps: Behavior and Natural History, 2001; (with H.E. Evans) The Sand Wasps: Natural History and Behavior, 2007; (with A. Moore) League of Extraordinary Gentlemen: Black Dossier, 2008; (with P. Mills) Marshal Law: Origins, 2008. Contributor to periodicals. **Address:** Department of Land Resources and, Environmental Sciences, Montana State University, PO Box 172220, Bozeman, MT 59717-2220, U.S.A. **Online address:** koneill@montana.edu

O'NEILL, Robert John. British/Australian (born Australia), b. 1936. **Genres:** Military/Defense/Arms Control, History, Biography, Bibliography, Politics/Government. **Career:** German Universities and Archives, historical researcher, 1964-65; Royal Military College, senior lecturer in history, 1967-69, senior fellow, 1969-77, professorial fellow, 1977-82; Australian National University, Institute of Advanced Studies, senior fellow in international relations, 1970-82, Strategic and Defence Studies Centre, head, 1971-82; University of Oxford, All Souls College, Chichele Professor of the History of War and fellow, 1987-2001, now Chichele Professor of the History of War and fellow, 2001-, Foreign Policy Studies Programme, director, 1987-2001, director of graduate studies in the modern history, International Institute for Strategic Studies, director, 1982-87; Australian Strategic Policy Institute, chairman of the council, 2000-05; University of Sydney, Graduate School of Government, deputy chairman, 2003-05, United States Studies Centre, planning director, 2006-07; Lowy Institute for International Policy, director, 2003-; University of London, Kings College, chairman of the committee of management of the Sir Robert Menzies Centre for Australian Studies. Writer. **Publications:** (Contrib.) The Theory and Practice of War, 1965; The German Army and the Nazi Party 1933-39, 1966; Vietnam Task, 1968; Indo-China Tragedy, 1945-54, 1968; General Giap: Politician and Strategist, 1969; Strategy of General Giap since 1964, 1969; The Army in Papua-New Guinea; Current Role and Implications for Independence, 1971; Peking-Hanoi Relations in 1970, 1971; (with J. Fielding) A Select Bibliography of Australian Military History 1891-1939, 1978; (with J. Tie and J.O. Langtry) Australia's Defence Resources: A Compendium of Data, 1978; Australia in the Korean War 1950-53, 1981; Australia, Britain and International Security: Retrospect and Prospect, 1985; (intro. with D. Schwartz) Hedley Bull on Arms Control, 1987; Alliances and International Order: An Inaugural Lecture Delivered Before the University of Oxford on 20 November 1987, 1988; Security Challenges for Southeast Asia after the Cold War, 1992; (with R. Hart and S. Hart) World War II: Northwest Europe, 1944-1945, 2010; World War II: The Mediterranean, 1940-1945, 2010; (with J.T. Glatthaar) Civil War: Sherman's Capture of Atlanta and Other Western Battles, 1863-1865, 2011; (with R.K. Kricks) Civil War: Gettysburg and Other Eastern Battles, 1863-1865, 2011; (with S.D. Engle) Civil War: The Siege of Vicksburg and Other Western Battles, 1861-July 1863, 2011. EDITOR: The Strategic Nuclear Balance: An Australian Perspective: Papers from a Conference Held by the Strategic and Defence Studies Centre, Research School of Pacific Studies, the Australian National University, Canberra, 1974, 1975; The Defence of Australia: Fundamental New Aspects: The Proceedings of a Conference Organized by the Strategic and Defence Studies Centre, The Australian National University, October 1976, 1977; Insecurity! The Spread of Weapons in Indian and Pacific Oceans, 1978; (with D.M. Horner) New Directions in Strategic Thinking, 1981; (with D.M. Horner) Australian Defence Policy for the 1980s, 1982; Security in East Asia, 1984; The Conduct of East-West Relations in the 1980's, 1985; New Technology and Western Security Policy, 1985; Doctrine, the Alliance and Arms Control, 1987; East Asia, the West and International Security, 1987; Prospects for Security in the Mediterranean, 1988; (with R.J. Vincent) The West and the Third World: Essays in Honor of J.D.B. Miller, 1990; (with B. Heuser) Securing Peace in Europe 1945-62: Thoughts for the Post-Cold War Era, 1992; (with L. Freedman and P. Hayes) War, Strategy and International Politics: Essays in Honour of Sir Michael Howard, 1992; (with J. Baylis) Alternative Nuclear Futures: The Role of Nuclear Weapons in the Post-Cold War World, 2000; World War II: The Pacific, 2010; World War II: The Eastern Front 1941-1945, 2010; World War II. Europe, 1939-1943, 2010; World War II: The War at Sea, 2010; (with G.W. Gallagher) Civil War: Bull Run and Other Eastern Battles, 1861-May 1863, 2011; Road to Victory: From Pearl Harbor to Okinawa, 2011. **Address:** All Souls College, 27 High St., City Ctr., Oxford, OX OX1 4AL, England.

O'NEILL, Tom. American (born United States), b. 1961?. **Genres:** Novels, Young Adult Fiction. **Career:** Attorney and writer. **Publications:** Shark Tank, 2004. **Address:** Kate's Mystery Books, 2211 Massachusetts Ave., Cambridge, MA 02140-1211, U.S.A.

O'NEILL, Tony. American/British (born England), b. 1978. **Genres:** Novels, Autobiography/Memoirs, Poetry. **Career:** Writer and musician. **Publications:** COLLECTED WORKS: Seizure Wet Dreams, 2006; Songs from the Shooting Gallery: Poems, 1999-2006, 2007; Notre Dame Du Vide, 2009. FICTION: Digging the Vein (novel), 2006; Down and Out on Murder Mile, 2008; Sick City, 2010. NON-FICITON: (with J. Peter) Hero of the Underground: A Memoir, 2008; (with C. Currie) Neon Angel: Diary of a Runaway, 2010. **Address:** New York, NY , U.S.A. **Online address:** mailinglist@tonyoneill.net

O'NEILL, William L. American (born United States), b. 1935. **Genres:** History. **Career:** University of Pittsburgh, assistant professor, 1963-64; University of Colorado, assistant professor, 1964-66; University of Wisconsin, assistant professor, associate professor, 1966-71; Rutgers University, professor of history, 1971-2006, professor emeritus of history, 2006-. Writer. **Publications:** Divorce in the Progressive Era, 1967; Everyone was Brave, 1969; Coming Apart: An Informal History of America in the 1960s, 1971; (L.C. Gardner) Looking Backward: A Reintroduction to American History, 1974; The Progressive Years, 1975; (with W.E. Pulliam and C.M. Bowman) America Rediscovered, Its Political Life, 1977; The Last Romantic: A Life of Max Eastman, 1978; A Better World: The Great Schism-Stalinism and the American Intellectuals, 1982; American High: The Years of Confidence, 1945-1960, 1986; Feminism in America, 2nd ed., 1989; A Democracy at War: America's Fight at Home and Abroad in World War II, 1993; The Oxford Essential Guide to World War II, 2002. EDITOR: Echoes of Revolt, 1966; The Woman Movement, 1969; (and intro.) American Society since 1945, 1969; Women at Work, 1972; The American Sexual Dilemma, 1972; (ed.) Insights and Parallels, 1973; (with S. Hook and R. O'Toole) Philosophy, History, and Social Action, 1988; World War II, 1999; The New Left, 2001; (contrib.) Ours to Fight For, 2003; (ed.) The Scribner Encyclopedia of American Lives, 2003; A Bubble in Time: America During the Interwar Years, 1989-2001, 2009. **Address:** Department of History, Rutgers University, 16 Seminary Pl., New Brunswick, NJ 08903, U.S.A. **Online address:** wlohp@aol.com

ONESS, Elizabeth. American (born United States), b. 1960. **Genres:** Novellas/Short Stories, Poetry, Novels, Young Adult Fiction. **Career:** Taoist Health Institute, assistant to the director, 1986-92; Sutton Hoo Press, director of marketing and development, 1999-; Winona State University, assistant professor of English, associate professor of English, 2001-; River Valley Welsh, vice president. Writer. **Publications:** In the Blue before Night (poetry chapbook), 1991; Sure Knowledge (poetry chapbook), 1999; Articles of Faith (short stories), 2000; Departures (novel), 2004; Twelve Rivers of the Body (novel), 2008; Fallibility (poems), 2009. **Address:** Department of English, Winona State University, 302 Minne Hall, PO Box 5838, Winona, MN 55987, U.S.A. **Online address:** eoness@winona.edu

ONG, Han. American/Filipino (born Philippines), b. 1968. **Genres:** Plays/Screenplays, Novels. **Career:** Novelist. **Publications:** Fixer Chao, 2001; Disinherited, 2004. **Address:** Farrar, Strauss & Giroux, 19 Union Sq. W, New York, NY 10003, U.S.A.

ONSTAD, Chris. American (born United States), b. 1975. **Genres:** Graphic Novels. **Career:** Novelist. **Publications:** GRAPHIC NOVELS: Achewood, vol. I: The Great Outdoor Fight, 2008, vol. II: Worst Song, Played on Ugliest Guitar, 2008, vol. III: A Home for Scared People, 2010; Achewood Comics: 2001-2004, 2010. **Address:** Portland, OR , U.S.A. **Online address:** chris@achewood.com

ONUF, Nicholas. (Nicholas Greenwood Onuf). American (born United States), b. 1941. **Genres:** Law, Politics/Government, History, Military/Defense/Arms Control, Essays. **Career:** American University, faculty; Ritsumeikan University, faculty; University of Colombo, faculty; Howard University, faculty; Columbia University, faculty; Georgetown University, faculty; Florida International University, School of International and Public Affairs, Department of Politics and International Relations, professor, professor emeritus, 2005-. Writer. **Publications:** Reprisals: Rituals, Rules, Rationales, 1974; (ed. as Nicholas Greenwood Onuf) Law-Making in the Global Community, 1982; (as Nicholas Greenwood Onuf) World of Our Making: Rules and Rule in Social Theory and International Relations, 1989; (with P. Onuf) Federal Union, Modern World: The Law of Nations in an Age of Revolutions, 1776-1814, 1993; (as Nicholas G. Onuf with C.P. Arvanitopoulos) The Cold War and the Paradox of Nonalignment, 1994; (ed. with V. Kubálková and P. Kowert) International Relations in a Constructed World, 1998; (as Nicholas Greenwood Onuf) The Republican Legacy in International Thought, 1998; (with P. Onuf) Nations, Markets, and War: Modern History and the American Civil War, 2006; International Legal Theory: Essays and Engagements, 1966-2006, 2008. **Address:** Department of Politics & International Relations, School of International and Public Affairs, Florida International University, Rm. 440, SIPA Bldg., 11200 SW 8th St., Miami, FL 33199-2516, U.S.A. **Online address:** onufn@fiu.edu

ONUF, Nicholas Greenwood. *See* **ONUF, Nicholas.**

ONUF, Peter S. American (born United States), b. 1946. **Genres:** History. **Career:** University of Virginia, Thomas Jefferson Memorial Foundation professor, 1989-; Worcester Polytechnic Institute, assistant professor. Writer and historian. **Publications:** The Origins of the Federal Republic: Jurisdictional Controversies in the United States, 1775- 1787, 1983; Statehood and Union: A History of the Northwest Ordinance, 1987; (with A.R.L. Cayton) The Midwest and the Nation: Rethinking the History of an American Region, 1990; (with C.D. Matson) A Union of Interests: Political and Economic Thought in Revolutionary America, 1990; (ed. and intro.) Establishing the New Regime: The Washington Administration, 1991; (ed. and intro.) The Federal Constitution, 1991; (ed. and intro.) New American Nation, 1775-1820, 1991; (ed. and intro.) Patriots, Redcoats and Loyalists, 1991; (ed. and intro.) Ratifying, Amending, and Interpreting the Constitution, 1991; (ed. and intro.) Federalists and Republicans, 1991; (ed. and intro.) The Revolution in the States, 1991; (ed. and intro.) America and the World: Diplomacy, Politics, and War, 1991; (ed. and intro.) American Culture, 1776-1815, 1991; (ed. and intro.) Congress and the Confederation, 1991; (ed. and intro.) The Revolution in American Thought, 1991; (ed. and intro.) State and Local Politics in the New Nation, 1991; (with N. Onuf) Federal Union, Modern World: The Law of Nations in an Age of Revolutions, 1776- 1814, 1993; (ed.) Jeffersonian Legacies, 1993; (intro.) The Life of Washington, 1996; (with E.L. Ayers, P.N. Limerick and S. Nissenbaum) All Over the Map: Rethinking Region and Nation in the United States, 1996; (ed. with J.E. Lewis) Sally Hemings & Thomas Jefferson: History, Memory, and Civic Culture, 1999; Jefferson's Empire: The Language of American Nationhood, 2000; (with L.J. Sadosky) Jeffersonian America, 2002; (ed. with J. Horn and J.E. Lewis) The Revolution of 1800: Democracy, Race, and the New Republic, 2002; (ed. with E.H. Gould) Empire and Nation: The American Revolution in the Atlantic World, 2005; (ed. with D.Seefeldt and J.L. Hantman) Across the Continent: Jefferson, Lewis and Clark, and the Making of America, 2005; (with N. Onuf) Nations, Markets, and War: Modern History and the American Civil War, 2006; The Mind of Thomas Jefferson, 2007; (ed. with C.Y. Dupont) Declaring Independence: The Origin and Influence of America's Founding Document: Featuring the Albert H. Small Declaration of Independence Collection, 2008. Contributor of articles to journals. **Address:** Corcoran Department of History, University of Virginia, Randall Hall, PO Box 400180, Charlottesville, VA 22904, U.S.A. **Online address:** pso2k@virginia.edu

ONWUEME, Tess Osonye. (Tess Akaeke). Nigerian (born Nigeria), b. 1955. **Genres:** Novels, Plays/Screenplays, Cultural/Ethnic Topics, Theatre, Women's Studies And Issues, Autobiography/Memoirs. **Career:** University of Ife, assistant lecturer in English, 1980-82; Federal University of Technology, assistant professor of English and head of performing arts program, 1982-85; Association of Nigeria Authors (ANA), vice president, 1987-88, acting president, 1988-89; Imo State University (now Abia State University), associate professor of English, 1986-88, head of performing arts unit, 1988-89; Wayne State University, associate professor of Africana studies and Martin Luther King Jr., professor of multicultural literary studies, Rosa Parks distinguished writer, 1989-90; Montclair State University, associate professor of English and multicultural literary studies, 1990-92, professor of Africana studies; Vassar College, associate professor of Africana studies and English, 1992-93; University of Wisconsin, distinguished professor of cultural diversity and professor of English, 1994-. **Publications:** A Hen Too Soon, 1983; The Broken Calabash, 1984; The Desert Encroaches, 1985; A Scent of Onion, 1986; Ban Empty Barn, 1986; The Artist's Homecoming, 1986; Cattle Egret versus Nama, 1986; Mirror for Campus, 1987; The Reign of Wazobia, 1988; Go Tell it to the Women: An Epic Drama for Women, 1992; Three Plays, 1993; Riot in Heaven: Musical Drama for the Voices of Color, 1996; Tell It to Women: An Epic Drama for Women, 1997; The Missing Face: Musical Drama for the Voices of Color, 1997; Shakara-Dance-Hall Queen, 2000; Why The Elephant Has No Butt (a novel), 2000; Then She Said It, 2002; Acada Boys and Riot in Heaven, 2003; Acada Boys and Mirror For Campus, 2003; What Mama Said: An Epic Drama, 2003; No Vacancy!, 2004. Works appear in anthologies. Contributor to periodicals. **Address:** Department of English, University of Wisconsin, 7195 Helen C. White, 600 N Park St., Madison, WI 53706, U.S.A. **Online address:** onwuemto@uwec.edu

ONYEAMA, Dillibe. Nigerian (born Nigeria), b. 1951. **Genres:** Novels, Race Relations, Autobiography/Memoirs, Biography. **Career:** Drum Publications, sub-editor, 1974-75; West Africa magazine, journalist, 1978; Delta Publications Ltd., chief executive officer, 1981-, managing director, 1988-; Satellite Books, editor. Writer. **Publications:** Nigger at Eton, 1972, rev. ed., 1982; John Bull's Nigger, 1974; (comp.) Book of Black Man's Humour, 1975; Sex is a Nigger's Game, 1976; Juju: A Novel, 1977; Secret Society, 1978; Return, 1978; Female Target, 1979; Revenge of the Medicine Man, 1980; Rules of the Game, 1981; Night Demon, 1982; Chief Onyeama, 1982; Modern Messiah, 1983; African Legend: The Incredible Story of Francis Arthur Nzeribe, 1984; Godfathers of Voodoo, 1985; Correct English, 1986; Notes of a So-Called Afro-Saxon, 1988; A Message to My Compatriots, 1996; The Boomerang, 1998; (ed. and comp.) The Joys of African Humour, 2000; The New Man: A Perspective in Evil, 2002; And the Last Shall be First: The Sam Egwu Phenomenon, 2006; Anti-Christ, 2008; The Story of an African God: Life and Times of Paramount Chief Onyeama, 2nd ed., 2010. **Address:** PO Box 1172, Enugu, 23401, Nigeria.

OOSTERHUIS, Harry. Dutch (born Netherlands), b. 1958. **Genres:** Gay And Lesbian Issues, Psychiatry, Social Sciences, History, Politics/Government. **Career:** Groniek, editor, 1980-82; Homologie, editor, 1983-86; Ministry of Welfare, Public Health and Culture, Fascism and Homosexuality Research Project, coordinator and editor, 1984-85; Catholic University, Faculty of Philosophy, lecturer in lesbian and gay studies, 1991-92; Maastricht University, Faculty of Arts and Social Sciences, lecturer in history, 1992-; Huizinga Institute, Research School for Cultural History, lecturer in history, 1992-. **Publications:** (Ed. and intro.) Homosexuality and Male Bonding in Pre-Nazi Germany: The Youth Movement, the Gay Movement, and Male Bonding before Hitler's Rise: Original Transcripts from Der Eigene, the First Gay Journal in the World, 1991; Homoseksualiteit in Katholiek Nederland: Een Social Geschiedenis 1900-1970, 1992; (ed. with G. Hekma and J. Steakley) Gay Men and the Sexual History of the Political Left, 1995; Stepchildren of Nature: Krafft-Ebing, Psychiatry, and the Making of Sexual Identity, 2000. **Address:** Faculty of Arts and Social Sciences, Maastricht University, Rm. D. 2.06, Grote Gracht 90-92, PO Box 616, Maastricht, 6211 SZ, Netherlands. **Online address:** harry.oosterhuis@maastrichtuniversity.nl

OOSTINDIE, Gert. Dutch (born Netherlands), b. 1955. **Genres:** History. **Career:** Utrecht University, Department of Anthropology, chair in Caribbean studies, 1993-2006; Royal Netherlands Academy of Arts and Sciences, Institute of Southeast Asian and Caribbean Studies, head, 1993-2000, director, 2000-; Leiden University, Department of History, professor of Caribbean history, 2006-. Writer and anthropologist. **Publications:** (With E. Maduro) Antillianen en Surinamers in Nederland, 1634/1667-1954, 1986; (with I. Koulen, P. Verton and R. Hoefte) The Netherlands Antilles and Aruba: A Research Guide, 1987; Roosenburg en mon Bijou: Twee Surinaamse Plantages, 1720-1870, 1989; (comp. with R. Hoefte) Echo Van Eldorado, 1996; (with P. Verton, H. Napel and Römer) Ki Sorto Di Reino?=What Kind of Kingdom?: Visies en Verwachtingen van Antillianen en Arubanen Omtrent het Koninkrijk, 1998; Het Paradijs Overzee: De Nederlandse Caraïben en Nederland, 1998, trans. as Paradise Overseas: The Dutch Caribbean: Colonialism and Its Transatlantic Legacies, 2005; (with I. Klinkers) Knellende Koninkrijksbanden: Het Nederlandse Dekolonisatiebeleid in de Caraïben, 1940-2000, 2001; (with I. Klinkers) Decolonising the Caribbean: Dutch Policies in a Comparative Perspective, 2003; De Parels en de Kroon: Het Koningshuis en de Koloniën, 2006; Postkoloniaal Nederland, 2010; Postkoloniale monumenten van Nederland, 2011. EDITOR: (with I. Koulen and P. Verton) Sociaal-wetenschappelijk Onderzoek Nederlandse Antillen: Inventarisatie (1967-1984) en Prioriteiten, 1984; (and contrib.) Fifty Years Later: Antislavery, Capitalism and Modernity in the Dutch Orbit, 1995; Ethnicity in the Caribbean: Essays in Honor of Harry Hoetink, 1996; (co-ed.) Etnicidad como estratega en América Latina y el Caribe, 1996; Dromen en Littekens: Dertig Jaar Na de Curaçaose Revolte, 30 Mei 1969, 1999; Het Verleden Onder Ogen: Herdenking van de Slavernij, 1999; Curaçao, 30 Mei 1969: Verhalen over de Revolte, 1999; Facing Up to the Past: Perspectives on the Commemoration of Slavery from Africa, the Americas and Europe, 2001; Dutch Colonialism, Migration and Cultural Heritage, 2008; Gouverneurs van de Nederlandse Antillen sinds 1815, 2011; (with U. Bosma and J. Lucassen) Postcolonial Migrants and Identity Politics, 2012. Contributor to journals. **Address:** Institute of Southeast Asian and Caribbean Studies, Royal Netherlands Academy of Arts and Sciences, Reuvensplaats 2, PO Box 9515, Leiden, 2311 BE, Netherlands. **Online address:** g.j.oostindie@hum.leidenuniv.nl

OPHULS, Patrick. *See* **OPHULS, William.**

OPHULS, William. (Patrick Ophuls). American (born United States), b. 1934. **Genres:** Environmental Sciences/Ecology, Politics/Government, Sciences. **Career:** U.S. Foreign Service, 1959-67, Department of State, researcher on middle eastern affairs, 1959-61, consular and political officer at embassy, 1961-63, language officer and ambassador's assistant at embassy, 1963-67; Northwestern University, visiting associate professor of political science and urban affairs, 1979-81. Writer and consultant. **Publications:** Ecology and the Politics of Scarcity: Prologue to a Political Theory of the Steady State, 1977; (with A.S. Boyan, Jr.) Ecology and the Politics of Scarcity Revisited: The Unraveling of the American Dream, 1992; Requiem for Modern Politics: The Tragedy of the Enlightenment and the Challenge of the New Millennium, 1997; (as P. Ophuls) Buddha Takes No Prisoners: A Meditator's Survival Manual, 2007; Plato's Revenge: Politics in the Age of Ecology, 2011; Immoderate Greatness: Why Civilizations Fail, forthcoming. **Address:** 313 Meigs Rd., Ste. A-511, Santa Barbara, CA 93109, U.S.A. **Online address:** pophuls@west.net

OPIE, Anne. New Zealander (born New Zealand), b. 1946. **Genres:** Gerontology/Senior Issues, Human Relations/Parenting, Law, Social Sciences, Social Work, Women's Studies And Issues, Criminology/True Crime. **Career:** Victoria University of Wellington, research fellow and senior research fellow, 1989-98; Legal Services Board, research manager, 1998-2000, research consultant, 2000-08. Writer. **Publications:** Caring Alone, 1991; There's Nobody There, 1992; Beyond Good Intentions: Support Work with Older People, 1995; Thinking Teams/Thinking Clients: Knowledge-Based Team Work, 2000. Contributor to books and journals. **Address:** 72 Woodside Rd., RD1, Greytown, Wellington, 5794, New Zealand. **Online address:** anne.opie@clear.net.nz

OPIE, Iona. British (born England), b. 1923. **Genres:** Children's Fiction, Language/Linguistics, Literary Criticism And History, Mythology/Folklore, inspirational/Motivational Literature. **Career:** May Hill Arbuthnot, lecturer, 1991. Writer and folklorist. **Publications:** (With B. Alderson and R. Opie) The Treasures of Childhood: Books, Toys and Games from the Opie Collection, 1989. WITH P. OPIE: Christmas Party Games, 1957; The Lore and Language of Schoolchildren, 1959; Puffin Book of Nursery Rhymes, 1963 in US as A Family Book of Nursery Rhymes, 1964; Fee Fi Fo Fum, 1965; Children's Games in Street and Playground: Chasing, Catching, Seeking, Hunting, Racing, Dueling, Exerting, Daring, Guessing, Acting, Pretending, 1969; Three Centuries of Nursery Rhymes and Poetry for Children, 1973, rev. ed., 1977; A Nursery Companion, 1980; The Singing Game, 1985; Tail Feathers from Mother Goose: The Opie Rhyme Book, 1988; The Opie Collection of Children's Literature: A Guide to the Microfiche Collection, 1990; (foreword) Children and Their Books: A Celebration of the Work of Iona and Peter Opie, 1990; The People in the Playground, 1993; Children's Games with Things: Marbles, Five stones, Throwing and Catching, Gambling, Hopscotch, Chucking and Pitching, Ball-bouncing, Skipping, Tops, and Tipcat, 1997; The Puffin Book of Nursery Rhymes: Gathered, 1997. EDITOR (most with P. Opie): I Saw Esau, 1947, as I Saw Esau: The Schoolchild's Pocket Book, 1992; (with P. Opie) The Oxford Dictionary of Nursery Rhymes, 1951; Ditties for the Nursery, 1954; The Oxford Nursery Rhyme Book, 1955; (with P. Opie) The Oxford Book of Children's Verse, 1973; (comp. with P. Opie) The Classic Fairy Tales, 1974; (with P. Opie) The Oxford Book of Narrative Verse, 1983; (With M. Tatem) A Dictionary of Superstitions, 1989; (with P. Opie) Babies: An Unsentimental Anthology, 1990; My Very First Mother Goose, 1996; Humpty Dumpty and Other Rhymes, 1997; Little Boy Blue and Other Rhymes, 1997; Pussycat Pussycat and Other Rhymes, 1997; Wee Willie Winkie and Other Rhymes, 1997; Here Comes Mother Goose, 1999; Mother Goose's Little Treasures, 2007. **Address:** Mells House, West Liss, HM GU33 6JQ, England.

OPPEGAARD, David. American (born United States), b. 1979?. **Genres:** Novels. **Career:** Writer. **Publications:** The Suicide Collectors (novel), 2008; Wormwood, Nevada (novel), 2009. **Address:** c/o Jonathan Lyons, Lyons Literary L.L.C., 540 President St., 3rd Fl., Brooklyn, NY 11215, U.S.A. **Online address:** oppegaard@gmail.com

OPPEL, Kenneth. Canadian (born Canada), b. 1967. **Genres:** Children's Fiction, Young Adult Fiction, Picture/Board Books, Picture/Board Books. **Career:** Novelist and screenwriter, 1988-; Scholastic Canada, associate editor, 1989; Quill and Quire, Books for Young People, editor, 1995-96. **Publications:** JUNIOR FICTION: Colin's Fantastic Video Adventure, 1985; (with R. Ricci) Cosimo Cat, 1990; Follow That Star, 1992; A Bad Case of Ghosts, 1993; A Bad Case of Magic, 1993; Cosmic Snapshots, 1993; Galactic Snapshots, 1993; A Bad Case of Dinosaurs, 1994; A Bad Case of Robots, 1994; Emma's Emu, 1995; A Bad Case of Super-Goo, 1996; Peg and the Whale, 2000; A Creepy Case of Vampires, 2002; Peg and the Yeti, 2004; The King's Taster, 2009. YOUNG ADULT FICTION: The Live-Forever Machine, 1990; Dead Water Zone, 1992; Silverwing, 1997; Sunwing, 1999; Firewing, 2002; Airborn, 2004; Skybreaker, 2005; Darkwing, 2007; Starclimber, 2008; Half Brother, 2010; This Dark Endeavor, 2011. **Address:** HarperCollins Canada, 2 Bloor St. E, 20th Fl., 20th Fl., Toronto, ON M4W 1A8, Canada. **Online address:** kenneth.oppel@sympatico.ca

OPPELT, Norman T. American (born United States), b. 1930. **Genres:** Archaeology/Antiquities, Cultural/Ethnic Topics, Bibliography, Sciences, Education, Social Sciences, Politics/Government, History, History. **Career:** University of Northern Colorado, dean of men, 1960-64, dean of students, 1964-70, professor of psychology and higher education, 1967-87, chair of department, 1972-83, adviser to American Indian students, 1977-87; University of Hawaii at Manoa, faculty, 1968, 1976; Mesa Verde National Park, park ranger and archaeological interpreter, 1987-2001; Disabled American Veterans Service Center, volunteer psychologist, 1989-90. **Publications:** Southwestern Pottery: An Annotated Bibliography and List of Types And Wares, 1976, 2nd ed., 1988; Guide to Prehistoric Ruins of the Southwest, 1981, 2nd ed., 1989; The Tribally Controlled Indian Colleges: The Beginnings of Self Determination in American Indian Education, 1990; Earth, Water and Fire: The Prehistoric Pottery of Mesa Verde, 1991; List of Southwestern Pottery: Types and Wares: With Dates And References To Descriptions And Illustrations, 2002; Soda and Mineral Water Bottles and Bottlers of Colorado, 1860 to 1915, 2005. **Address:** 2218 25th St., Greeley, CO 80631-8144, U.S.A. **Online address:** tpoppelt54@aol.com

OPPENHEIM, Felix E. American/German (born Germany), b. 1913. **Genres:** Philosophy, Politics/Government, Ethics, Law, Social Sciences. **Career:** University of Delaware, assistant professor, associate professor, 1946-57; Yale University, visiting associate professor, 1951-52; Stanford University, research associate, visiting associate professor, 1955-56; Princeton University, visiting lecturer, 1960; New School for Social Research, faculty, 1960-61; University of Massachusetts, professor of government, 1961-83, professor emeritus of political science, 1983-. Writer. **Publications:** Outline of a Logical Analysis of Law, 1944; Dimensions of Freedom, 1961; Moral Principles in Political Philosophy, 1968, 2nd ed., 1975; Political Concepts: A Reconstruction, 1981; The Place of Morality in Foreign Policy, 1991. Contributor to journals. **Address:** Department of Political Science, University of Massachusetts, Thompson Hall, 200 Hicks Way, 181 Presidents Dr., Amherst, MA 01003-9305, U.S.A. **Online address:** soppenheim@iopener.net

OPPENHEIM, Lois Hecht. American (born United States), b. 1948. **Genres:** Administration/Management, Area Studies, Politics/Government. **Career:** Washington University, instructor in political science, 1972; Facultad Latinoamericana de las Ciencias Sociales, visiting researcher, 1972-73; University of Iowa, research assistant, 1975-76; University of Copenhagen, Whittier College, instructor, 1976-80, assistant professor, 1980-84, associate professor, 1984-88, professor of political science, 1988-93, department head, 1987-88, Latin American Studies Committee, head, 1985-91, Danish International Studies Program, director in residence, 1988; Program in Labor Economics, visiting researcher, 1987; University of Judaism, College of Arts & Sciences, chair, visiting professor, 1991-93, professor of political science, 1991-, department head, 1991-, head, 1994-95, 1998-99; Economic Commission for Latin America and the Caribbean, Women's Division, affiliated researcher, 1997; University of Chile, Department of Sociology, visiting professor, 1997, acting provost, 2000, vice president for academic affairs, 2001-04. Writer. **Publications:** Politics in Chile: Democracy, Authoritarianism and the Search for Development, 1993, 3rd ed. as Politics in Chile: Socialism, Authoritarianism, and Market Democracy, 2007; (ed. with S. Borzutzky) After Pinochet: The Chilean Road to Democracy and the Market, 2006. Contributor to Latin American studies journals. **Address:** Sunny & Isadore Familian Campus, University of Judaism, 15600 Mulholland Dr., Los Angeles, CA 90077, U.S.A. **Online address:** loppenheim@uj.edu

OPPENHEIM, Michael. American (born United States), b. 1940. **Genres:** Plays/Screenplays, Medicine/Health, Sports/Fitness, Sciences. **Career:** Physician and writer, 1973-. **Publications:** Commonsense Health, 1981; The Complete Book of Better Digestion: A Gut-level Guide to Gastric Relief, 1990; The Doctor's Guide to the Best Medical Care: A Practical, No-nonsense Evaluation of Your Treatment Options for Over 100 Conditions and Diseases, 1992; The Man's Health Book, 1994; 100 Drugs that Work: A Guide to the Best Prescription and Non-Prescription Drugs, 1994. Contributor of articles to magazines. **Address:** 2366 Veteran Ave., Los Angeles, CA 90064, U.S.A. **Online address:** michaeloppen@yahoo.com

OPPENHEIM, Micha Falk. American/German (born Germany), b. 1937. **Genres:** Theology/Religion, Bibliography, History. **Career:** Brooklyn College of the City University of New York, catalog librarian, 1961-63; National Conference of Christians and Jews, librarian, 1963-65; NYC Community College, branch librarian, 1965-66; Jewish Theological Seminary of America, senior cataloger, 1966-88, head of bibliographic control, 1988-; Fashion Institute of Technology, adjunct assistant librarian, 1967-76; Temple Sholom of West Essex, librarian, 1976-89. Writer. **Publications:** Jewish Life Index, 1946-1960: Supplement, 1960-1965, 1968; Guide to the Study and Practice of Judaism; A Selected List, 1972; The Study and Practice of Judaism: A Selected, Annotated List, 1979; (with C. Cutter) Jewish Reference Sources: A Selective, Annotated Bibliographic Guide, 1982, 2nd ed. as Judaica Reference Sources: A Selective, Annotated Bibliographic Guide, 1993. Works appear in anthologies. Contributor to periodicals. **Address:** Library of the Jewish Theological Seminary, 3080 Broadway, New York, NY 10027, U.S.A.

OPPENHEIMER, Andres. American/Argentine (born Argentina), b. 1951. **Genres:** Documentaries/Reportage. **Career:** Siete Dias (magazine), reporter and editor, 1970-75; Associated Press, reporter and editor, 1977-83; Miami Herald (newspaper), Latin American correspondent and writer, 1983-; National Public Radio, reporter; British Broadcasting Corp., reporter. **Publications:** Castro's Final Hour: The Secret Story behind the Coming Downfall of Communist Cuba, 1992; Bordering on Chaos: Guerrillas, Stockbrokers, Politicians and Mexico's Road to Prosperity, 1996; Crónicas de héroes y Bandidos, 1998; Bordering on Chaos: Mexico's Roller-Coaster Journey to Prosperity, 1998; Ojos vendados: Estados Unidos y el negocio de la corrupción en América Latina, 2001; Cuentos chinos: el engaño de Washington, la mentira populista y la esperanza de América Latina, 2005; Saving the Americas, 2007; iBasta de historias!: la obsesión Latinoamericana con el pasado y las doce claves del futuro, 2010. Contributor of articles to periodicals. **Address:** Latin American Correspondent, Miami Herald, 1 Herald Plz., Miami, FL 33132, U.S.A. **Online address:** aoppenheimer@herald.com

OPPENHEIMER, Gregg. American (born United States), b. 1951. **Genres:** Adult Non-fiction, Art/Art History, Law, Biography, Humor/Satire. **Career:** O'Melveny and Myers, attorney, 1977-96, partner, 1986-96; DVD Producer, 2000-. Writer. **Publications:** Originality in Art Reproductions: Variations in Search of a Theme, 27 Copyright Law Symposium 207, 1983; (with J. Oppenheimer) Laughs, Luck...and Lucy: How I Came to Create the Most Popular Sitcom of all Time, 1996. **Address:** 524 9th St., Santa Monica, CA 90402, U.S.A. **Online address:** gopp@aol.com

OPPENHEIMER, Todd. American (born United States) **Genres:** Education, Technology, Young Adult Non-fiction. **Career:** The Writers Grotto, journalist. Investigative reporter and calligrapher. **Publications:** The Flickering Mind: The False Promise of Technology in the Classroom, and How Learning Can Be Saved, 2003. Contributor to periodicals. **Address:** c/o Author Mail, Random House Inc., 1745 Broadway, New York, NY 10019-4368, U.S.A.

OPPENNEER, Betsy. *See* Obituaries.

OPPERSDORFF, Tony. American/British (born England), b. 1945. **Genres:** Travel/Exploration, Essays. **Career:** Riley School, photography teacher, 1978-88. Writer. **Publications:** Coastal Labrador: A Northern Odyssey, 1991. **Address:** c/o Connie Leavitt, 5 Free St., Camden, ME 04843, U.S.A.

ORBACH, Benjamin. American (born United States) **Genres:** Adult Non-fiction, Writing/Journalism. **Career:** Creative Associates International (an international development Co.), project manager, 2007-, Creative Learning, director, resident country director, through 2009; AmeriCorps, special education social studies teacher; U.S. Department of State, Middle East Partnership Initiative (MEPI), deputy regional coordinator, 2004-07; Washington Institute, research fellow. Writer. **Publications:** Live from Jordan: Letters Home from My Journey through the Middle East, 2007. Contributor to books and periodicals. **Address:** Pittsburgh, PA , U.S.A. **Online address:** benjaminorbach@yahoo.com

ORBAN, Christine. Also writes as Olivier Orban, Christine Rheims. Moroccan (born Morocco), b. 1954. **Genres:** Novels, Autobiography/Memoirs, Biography. **Career:** Writer. **Publications:** AS CHRISTINE ORBAN: Une Année Amoureuse De Virginia Woolf: Roman, 1990; La Femme Adultère, 1992; Le Collectionneur: Roman, 1993; (with O.Orban) Une Folie Amoureuse: Roman, 1997; L'Âme Saeur, 1998; L'attente: Roman, 1999; J'étais L'origine De Monde: Roman, 2000; Fringues: Roman, 2002; Le Silence Des Hommes: Roman, 2003; One Day My Sister Disappeared, 2004; Deux Fois Par Semaine: Roman, 2005; N'Oublie pas d' être heureuse, 2009; Vie m'a dit--, 2009; Collectionneur, 2010; Pays de l'absence: Roman, 2011. AS CHRISTINE RHEIMS: Les Petites Filles ne Meurent Jamais, 1986; Le Fil De Soi, 1988. **Address:** c/o Author Mail, Random House Inc., 1745 Broadway, New York, NY 10019, U.S.A.

ORBAN, Olivier. *See* **ORBAN, Christine.**

ORBINSKI, James Jude. Canadian/Irish (born Ireland), b. 1960?. **Genres:** International Relations/Current Affairs. **Career:** University of Toronto, professor of medicine and political science; Dalla Lana School of Public Health, Global Health, chair; Massey College, Founding Saul Rae, fellow and senior fellow; Munk School of Global Affairs, senior fellow; Dignitas Intl., co-founder; St. Michael's Hospital, physician. Writer. **Publications:** An Imperfect Offering: Humanitarian Action in the Twenty-first Century (current affairs), 2008. **Address:** Dalla Lana School of Public Health, University of Toronto, 155 College St., Ste. 400, Toronto, ON M5T-3M7, Canada. **Online address:** james.orbinski@utoronto.ca

ORDE, A. J. *See* **TEPPER, Sheri S.**

ORDINANS, Nicholas J. Australian/British (born England), b. 1950. **Genres:** Mystery/Crime/Suspense, Novels. **Career:** Novelist. **Publications:** Home Run, 2001; The Celluloid Kid, 2010; Whingeblade: The Soonar Stories, vol. I, 2010, vol. II, forthcoming; Where There Be Tygers, 2010. FORTHCOMING: Whose Zoo?; Jaffa-Lost and Found; Lily and the Drifters; Dream Soldier; Just Four Men; Yesterday; Things That Came. **Address:** CreateSpace, 345 Boren Ave. N, SEA27-4th Fl., Seattle, WA 98109, U.S.A. **Online address:** nickjo@bigfoot.com.au

O'REGAN, Valerie R. American (born United States), b. 1956?. **Genres:** Politics/Government, Industrial Relations. **Career:** University of California, instructor, 1995-98, lecturer and internship director, 1997-98; San Bernardino Valley College, instructor, 1997-98; North Dakota State University, Coordinate Model United Nations Program, faculty, 1998-2000, Department of Political Science, assistant professor, 1998-2003; California State University, lecturer, 2004-05, assistant professor, 2005-. Writer. **Publications:** Gender Matters: Female Policymakers Influence in Industrialized Nations, 2000. Contributor to periodicals. **Address:** Division of Politics, Administration and Justice, California State University, UH542, PO Box 6848, Fullerton, CA 92834-6848, U.S.A. **Online address:** voregan@fullerton.edu

O'REILLY, Kenneth. American (born United States), b. 1951. **Genres:** History, Race Relations, Adult Non-fiction. **Career:** Marquette University, faculty; University of Alaska-Anchorage, professor of history, 1983-, professor emeritus. Writer. **Publications:** Hoover and the Un-Americans: The FBI, HUAC and the Red Menace, 1983; Racial Matters: The FBI's Secret File on Black America, 1960-1972, 1989; Black Americans: The FBI Files, 1994; Nixon's Piano: Presidents and Racial Politics from Washington to Clinton, 1995; Walking on the Sun: The Infamous Presidency of George W. Bush, 2009. **Address:** Department of History, University of Alaska, 147 Admin, 3211 Providence Dr., Anchorage, AK 99508, U.S.A. **Online address:** afko@uaa.alaska.edu

O'REILLY, Victor. American/Irish (born Ireland), b. 1944?. **Genres:** Mystery/Crime/Suspense. **Career:** Photojournalist. Writer. **Publications:** Games of the Hangman, 1991 in UK as Games of Vengeance, 1994; Rules of the Hunt, 1995; The Devil's Footprint, 1996; Satan's Smile, 2010; The Dragon's Response, forthcoming. Contributor to periodicals. **Address:** Sterling Lord Literistic Agency, 65 Blecker St., 12th Fl., New York, NY 10012, U.S.A. **Online address:** victororeilly@comcast.net

O'REILLY HERRERA, (C.) Andrea. American (born United States), b. 1959. **Genres:** Novels, Cultural/Ethnic Topics, Literary Criticism And History, Race Relations, Women's Studies And Issues, Art/Art History, Autobiography/Memoirs. **Career:** State University of New York, Department of English, faculty, 1993-99; University of Colorado, professor of literature, 1999-, Ethnic Studies Program, director, 1999-, Academic Diversity and Development Program, assistant vice chancellor, 2002-, Women's and Ethnic Studies Program, assistant director, director, 2008-. Writer. **Publications:** (Ed. with E.M. Nollen and S.R. Foor.) Family Matters in the British and American Novel, 1997; (ed.) A Secret Weavers Anthology, 1998; (ed.) Remembering Cuba: Legacy of a Diaspora, 2001; The Pearl of the Antilles (novel), 2001; Cuba: Idea of a Nation Displaced, 2007; (co-ed.) The Matrix Reader: Examining the Dynamics of Oppression and Privilege, 2008; Cuban Artists Across the Diaspora: Setting the Tent Against the House, 2011. Contributor of articles to books and periodicals. **Address:** Women's & Ethnic Studies Program, University of Colorado, Rm. 1025D, Columbine Hall, 1420 Austin Bluffs Pkwy., Colorado Springs, CO 80918, U.S.A. **Online address:** aherrera@uccs.edu

OREL, Harold. American (born United States), b. 1926. **Genres:** Literary Criticism And History, Novellas/Short Stories, History, Essays. **Career:** University of Maryland, instructor in English, 1952-56, instructor in overseas program, 1954-55; General Electric, publications specialist, 1957; University of Kansas, College of Liberal Arts and Sciences, Department of English, associate professor, 1957-62, professor of English, 1962-74, university distinguished professor of English, 1974-, now university distinguished professor emeritus; Midwest Research Institute, consultant. Writer. **Publications:** The World of Victorian Humor, 1961; Thomas Hardy's Epic-Drama, 1963; The Development of William Butler Yeats 1885-1900, 1968; English Romantic Poets and the Enlightenment, 1973; The Final Years of Thomas Hardy 1912-1928, 1976; Victorian Literary Critics, 1984; The Victorian Short Story, 1986; The Literary Achievement of Rebecca West, 1986; The Unknown Thomas Hardy, 1987; (comp.) Critical Essays on Rudyard Kipling, 1989; A Kipling Chronology, 1990; Popular Fiction in England, 1914-1918, 1992; The Historical Novel from Scott to Sabatini, 1995. EDITOR: (with G.J. Worth) Six Studies in Nineteeth-Century English Literature and Thought, 1962; Thomas Hardy's Personal Writings: Prefaces, Literary Opinions, Reminiscences, 1966; Thomas Hardy's Personal Writings, 1967; (with P. Wiley) British Poetry 1880-1920, 1969; (with G.J. Worth) The Nineteenth-Century Writer and His Audience, 1969; Irish History and Culture, 1976; The Dynasts, 1978; (co-ed.) The Scottish World, 1981; Kipling: Interviews and Recollections, 2 vols., 1983; Victorian Short Stories: An Anthology, 1987; Victorian Short Stories 2: The Trials of Love, 1990; Sir Arthur Conan Doyle: Interviews and Recollections, 1991; Critical Essays on Sir Arthur Conan Doyle, 1992; Gilbert and Sullivan: Interviews and Recollections, 1994; Critical Essays on Thomas Hardy's Poetry, 1995; The Brontës: Interviews and Recollections, 1997; Charles Darwin: Interviews and Recollections, 2000; William Wordsworth: Interviews and Recollections, 2005. **Address:** Department of English, College of Liberal Arts & Sciences, University of Kansas, 1445 Jayhawk Blvd., Lawrence, KS 66045-2115, U.S.A. **Online address:** horel@ku.edu

OREN, Dan A. American (born United States), b. 1958. **Genres:** History, Race Relations, Adult Non-fiction, Sciences. **Career:** Camp Interlaken, program director, 1978-80; BB Camp, program and waterfront director, 1981; Yale University, School of Medicine, Department of Psychiatry, postdoctoral fellow, 1984-86, associate clinical professor of psychiatry, adjunct faculty; Bristol-Myers Squibb Co., Pharmaceutical Research Institute, director. Writer. **Publications:** Joining the Club: A History of Jews and Yale, 1985, 2nd ed., 2001; (co-author) How to Beat Jet Lag: A Practical Guide for Air Travelers, 1993. Contributor of articles to periodicals. **Address:** Department of Psychiatry, School of Medicine, Yale University, 300 George St., Ste. 901, New Haven, CT 06511-6662, U.S.A. **Online address:** dan.oren@yale.edu

OREN, Michael B(ornstein). Israeli/American (born United States), b. 1955. **Genres:** International Relations/Current Affairs, Novels. **Career:** Harvard University, visiting professor, 2006; Yale University, visiting professor, 2006; Shalem Center, senior fellow, distinguished fellow, Middle East history project, head; The New Republic, contributing editor; Israel's Department of Inter-Religious Affairs under Prime Minister Yitzhak Rabin, director; Hebrew University, Lady Davis Fellow; Georgetown University, visiting professor; Tel-Aviv University, Moshe Dayan Fellow; School of foreign service, faculty; Israeli ambassador to the United States. Writer. **Publications:** Origins of the Second Arab-Israel War: Egypt, Israel and the Great Powers, 1952-56, 1992; Sand Devil (three novellas), 2001; Six Days of War: June 1967 and the Making of the Modern Middle East, 2002; Reunion (novel), 2003; (co-ed.) New Essays on Zionism, 2006; Power, Faith and Fantasy: America in the Middle East, 1776 to the Present, 2007. Contributor to periodicals and journals. **Address:** The Shalem Center, 13 Yehoshua Bin-Nun St., Jerusalem, 93102, Israel.

ORENSTEIN, Catherine. American (born United States) **Genres:** Novels, Social Sciences. **Career:** The OpEd Project, founder and director; Woodhull Institute for Ethical Leadership, fellow; Echoing Green Foundation, fellow. Writer. **Publications:** Little Red Riding Hood Uncloaked: Sex, Morality, and the Evolution of a Fairy Tale, 2002. **Address:** c/o Author Mail, Basic Books, 387 Park Ave. S, 17th Fl., New York, NY 10016-8810, U.S.A.

ORENSTEIN, Peggy. American (born United States), b. 1961. **Genres:** Psychology, Women's Studies And Issues. **Career:** Esquire, associate editor, 1983-86; Manhattan Inc., senior editor, 1986-87; 7 Days, senior editor, 1987-88; Mother Jones, writer, managing editor, 1988-91; Farallon Films, producer and writer; New York Times Magazine, contributing writer; The Los Angeles Times, contributing writer; USA Today, contributing writer; Vogue Magazine, contributing writer; Elle Magazine, contributing writer; Discover Magazine, contributing writer; More Magazine, contributing writer; Salon Magazine, contributing writer; O: The Oprah Magazine, contributing writer; The New Yorker, contributing writer. **Publications:** Schoolgirls: Young Women, Self-Esteem, and the Confidence Gap, 1994; Flux: Women on Sex, Work, Love, Kids and Life in a Half-Changed World, 2000; Waiting for Daisy: A Tale of Two Continents, Three Religions, Five Infertility Doctors, an Oscar, an Atomic Bomb, a Romantic Night and One Woman's Quest to Become a Mother, 2007; Cinderella Ate My Daughter: Dispatches From the Frontlines of the New Girlie-Girl Culture, 2011. Contributor to periodicals. **Address:** Sandra Dijkstra Literary Agency, 1155 Camino Del Mar, Ste. 515, Del Mar, CA 92014-2605, U.S.A. **Online address:** peggy@peggyorenstein.com

ORENSTEIN, Ronald I. American (born United States), b. 1946?. **Genres:** Animals/Pets, Environmental Sciences/Ecology, Sciences, Children's Fiction, Bibliography. **Career:** International Wildlife Coalition, project director. Writer. **Publications:** (With J.C. Barlow) Variation in the Jaw Musculature of the Avian Family Vireonidae, 1981; Elephants: The Deciding Decade, 1991; How on Earth?: A Question-and-Answer Book about How Animals and Plants Live, 1994; How on Earth?: A Question-and-Answer Book about How Our Planet Works, 1995; Songbirds: Celebrating Natures Voices, 1997; New Animal Discoveries, 2001; Turtles Tortoises and Terrapins: Survivors in Armor, 2001. **Address:** International Wildlife Coalition, 1825 Shady Creek Ct., Mississauga, ON L5L 3W2, Canada. **Online address:** ornstn@inforamp.net

ORENT, Wendy. American (born United States), b. 1951?. **Genres:** Anthropology/Ethnology, Medicine/Health, Sciences, History. **Career:** Writer and anthropologist. **Publications:** (With I.V. Domaradskij) Biowarrior: Inside the Soviet/Russian Biological War Machine, 2003; Plague: The Mysterious Past and Terrifying Future of the Worlds Most Dangerous Disease, 2004. Contributor to periodicals. **Address:** c/o Author Mail, Simon Schuster Inc., 1230 Ave. of the Americas, New York, NY 10020, U.S.A. **Online address:** orentw@mindspring.com

OREY, Michael. American (born United States) **Genres:** Documentaries/Reportage, Law, Adult Non-fiction. **Career:** Simpson Thacher & Bartlett, attorney; The American Lawyer, writer and editor; Wall Street Journal, reporter, senior writer and editor; Ziff Brothers Investments, legal analyst; Business Week, senior writer, 2005-. **Publications:** Assuming the Risk: The Mavericks, the Lawyers and the Whistle-Blowers Who Beat Big Tobacco, 1999. **Address:** BusinessWeek, 1221 Ave. of the Americas, New York, NY 10020, U.S.A.

ORGEL, Doris. Also writes as Suzanne Altman, Doris Adelberg. American/Austrian (born Austria), b. 1929. **Genres:** Children's Fiction, Children's Non-fiction, Translations, Animals/Pets, Novellas/Short Stories, Young Adult Fiction, Picture/Board Books. **Career:** Writer and translator of children's books, 1955-; Bank Street College of Education, Writer's Lab, conductor, 1985-94; Bank Street Publications and Media Group, senior staff writer and editor, 1991-94. **Publications:** FOR CHILDREN: (as Doris Adelberg) Grandma's Holidays, 1963; Sarah's Room, 1963; (as Doris Adelberg) Lizzie's Twins, 1964; Cindy's Snowdrops, 1966; The Good-byes of Magnus Marmalade, 1966; Cindy's Sad and Happy Tree, 1967; In a Forgotten Place, 1967; Whose Turtle?, 1968; On the Sand Dune, 1968; Phoebe and the Prince, 1969; Merry, Rose, and Christmas-Tree June, 1969; Next Door to Xanadu, 1969; The Uproar, 1970; The Mulberry Music, 1971; Bartholomew, We Love You!, 1973; A Certain Magic, 1975; Merry, Merry Fibruary (poetry), 1977; The Devil in Vienna, 1978, 2nd ed., 2004; Next-Door Neighbors, 1979; Risking Love, 1985; My War with Mrs. Galloway, 1985; Whiskers Once and Always, 1986; Midnight Soup and a Witch's Hat, 1987; Starring Becky Suslow, 1989; Crack in the Heart, 1989; Nobodies and Somebodies, 1991; The Mouse Who Wanted to Marry, 1993; Button Soup, 1994; (with E. Schecter) The Flower of Sheba, 1994; Ariadne Awake!, 1994; The Spaghetti Party, 1995; Two Crows Counting, 1996; The Princess and the God, 1996; Don't Call Me Slob-o, 1996; Friends to the Rescue, 1996; We Goddesses: Athena, Aphrodite, Hera, 1999; My Mother's Daughter: Four Greek Goddesses Speak, 2003. RE-TELLER: STORIES AND FAIRY TALES: The Tale of Gockel, Hinkel, and Gackeliah, 1961; Schoolmaster Whackwell's Wonderful Sons, A Fairy Tale, 1962; The Heart of Stone, 1964; The Story of Lohengrin, The Knight of the Swan, 1966; A Monkey's Uncle, 1969; The Child from Far Away, 1971; Baron Munchausen: 15 Truly Tall Tales, 1971; Little John, 1972; Godfather Cat and Mousie, 1986; Next Time I Will: An Old English Tale, 1993; (with E. Coplon and E. Schecter) She'll Be Coming Round the Mountain, 1994; (as Suzanne Altman with E. Schecter) Worst Days Diary, 1995; The Princess and the God, 1996; The Lion and the Mouse and Other Aesop Fables, 2000; The Bremen Town Musicians and Other Animal Tales from Grimm, 2004; Doctor All-Knowing: A Folk Tale from the Brothers Grimm, 2008. TRANSLATOR: W. Hauff, Dwarf Long-Nose, 1960; W. Grieder, The Enchanted Drum, 1969; M. Lobe, The Grandma in the Apple Tree, 1970; Nero Corleone: A Cat's Story, 1997; Daniel Half Human: And the Good Nazi, 2004; Crazy Diamond; 2008; The Cat's Tale: Why the Years are Named for Animals, 2008. Contributor to periodicals. **Address:** Writers House, 21 W 26th St., New York, NY 10010-1083, U.S.A. **Online address:** dorisorgel@aol.com

ORION, **Doreen.** American (born United States), b. 1959. **Genres:** Autobiography/Memoirs, Psychiatry. **Career:** University of Colorado, Health Sciences Center, faculty. Writer and psychiatrist. **Publications:** MEMOIRS: I Know You Really Love Me: A Psychiatrist's Journal of Erotomania, Stalking, and Obsessive Love, 1997; Queen of the Road: The True Tale of 47 States, 22, 000 Miles, 200 Shoes, 2 Cats, 1 Poodle, a Husband, and a Bus with a Will of Its Own, 2008. **Address:** CO , U.S.A. **Online address:** doreen@doreenorion.com

O'RIORDAN, **Michelle.** Irish (born Ireland) **Genres:** History, Poetry, Literary Criticism And History. **Career:** Dublin Institute for Advanced Studies, School of Celtic Studies, assistant professor and publications officer. Writer. **Publications:** The Gaelic Mind and the Collapse of the Gaelic World, 1990; Irish Bardic Poetry and Rhetorical Reality, 2007. Contributor to periodicals. **Address:** School of Celtic Studies, Dublin Institute for Advanced Studies, 10 Burlington Rd., Dublin, DU 4, Ireland.

ORIZIO, **Riccardo.** Kenyan/Italian (born Italy), b. 1961?. **Genres:** History, Social Sciences, Sociology, Autobiography/Memoirs, Politics/Government. **Career:** Corriere Della Sera, foreign correspondent; La Repubblica, foreign correspondent; CNN, foreign correspondent. **Publications:** Lost White Tribes: Journeys among the Forgotten, 2000 in US as Lost White Tribes: The End of Privilege and the Last Colonials in Sri Lanka, Jamaica, Brazil, Haiti, Namibia and Guadeloupe, 2001; Talk of the Devil: Encounters with Seven Dictators, 2003. **Address:** Shirley Stewart Literary Agency, 21 Denmark St., London, GL WC2H 8NA, England. **Online address:** info@riccardoorizio.com

ORKENY, **Antal.** Hungarian (born Hungary), b. 1954. **Genres:** Politics/Government. **Career:** Eotvos Lorand University, Faculty of Social Sciences, assistant professor, 1978-86, associate professor of sociology, 1987-97, professor of sociology, 1997-; University of California, Educational Abroad Program, lecturer, 1988-89, 1990-91, 1992-, academic director, 1992-; University of Wisconsin, Educational Abroad Program, lecturer, 1988-89, 1990-91, 1992-, academic director, 1992-, Ethnic and Minority Studies Program, director, 1993-97, PhD Program director, 1997-, ELTE-UNESCO Minority Studies Department, head, 2006-, Institute for Social Relations, director, 2010-; American University, Budapest Program, lecturer, 1991-93; Minority Research Institute, director, 1995-; Hungarian Film Academy, lecturer, 1995-99. Writer. **Publications:** (With G. Csepeli and M. Székelyi) Grappling with National Identity. How Nations See each Other in Central Europe, 2000; (ed. with K. Phalet) Ethnic Minorities and Inter-Ethnic Relations in Context: A Dutch-Hungarian Comparison, 2001; (with G. Csepeli) Gyülölet és politika, 2002; (with G. Csepeli and S. Mária) Nemzetek egymás tükrében: interetnikus viszonyok a Kárpát-medencében, 2002; Menni vagy maradni?: kedvezménytörvény és migrációs várakozások, 2003. **Address:** Faculty of Social Sciences, Eotvos Lorand University, 1117, Pazmany Peter Setany 1A, Budapest, H-1117, Hungary. **Online address:** orkeny@tatk.elte.hu

ORLEAN, **Susan.** American (born United States), b. 1955. **Genres:** Urban Studies, Cultural/Ethnic Topics, Geography. **Career:** Wilamette Week, reporter; Boston Phoenix, staff writer, 1983-86; Boston Globe, columnist, 1986-87; Rolling Stone, contributing editor, 1987-; freelance writer, 1987-; The New Yorker, staff writer, 1992-. **Publications:** Red Sox and Bluefish: And Other Things That Make New England New England 1987; Saturday Night, 1990; The Orchid Thief, 1998; The Bullfighter Checks Her Makeup, 2000; My Kind of Place, 2004; (ed. and intro.) Best American Travel Writing 2007, 2007; Lazy Little Loafers, 2008; Rin Tin Tin: the Life and the Legend, 2011. Contributor of articles to periodicals. **Address:** The New Yorker, 4 Times Sq., New York, NY 10036, U.S.A. **Online address:** webmail@susanorlean.com

ORLECK, **Annelise.** American (born United States), b. 1959. **Genres:** Women's Studies And Issues. **Career:** City of New York, Mayor's Task Force on the Holocaust, coordinator, 1981; Princeton University, lecturer in history, 1989-90; Dartmouth College, assistant professor of history, 1990-96, associate professor, 1996-2005, professor of history, 2005-. Writer. **Publications:** Common Sense and a Little Fire: Women and Working-Class Politics in the United States, 1900-1965, 1995; (ed. with A. Jetter and D. Taylor) The Politics of Motherhood: Activist Voices From Left to Right, 1997; The Soviet Jewish Americans, 1999; Storming Caesars Palace: How Black Mothers Fought their Own War on Poverty, 2005; (ed. with L.G. Hazirjian) The War on Poverty: A New Grassroots History, 1964-1980, 2011. **Address:** Department of History, Dartmouth College, 402 Carson Hall, Hanover, NH 03755, U.S.A. **Online address:** annelise.orleck@dartmouth.edu

ORLEDGE, **Robert.** British (born England), b. 1948. **Genres:** Music, Theatre. **Career:** University of Liverpool, lecturer, 1971-80, senior lecturer in music, 1980-85, reader, 1986-91, head of department, 1991-93, professor of music, 1991-2004, senior research fellow, professor emeritus, 2004-. Writer. **Publications:** Gabriel Fauré, 1979, rev. ed., 1983; (ed.) Ballade for Piano and Orchestra, Op. 19, 1981; (ed.) Elégie for violoncello and orchestra, Op. 24, 1981; (ed.) Masques et Bergamasques: Suite for Orchestra, Op. 112, 1981; (ed.) Pavane for orchestra with chorus ad Libitum, Op. 50, 1981; Pelléas et Mélisande: Suite for Orchestra, Op. 80, 1981; Debussy and the Theatre, 1982; Charles Koechlin (1867-1950): His Life and Works, 1989; Satie the Composer, 1990; (contrib.) Trois Pièces Op. 34 Pour Basson et Piano, 1990; (contrib.) Pastorale Pour Flute, Clarinette et Piano, Opus 75 Bis, 1990; 6ème Nocturne Pour Piano (œuvre posthume), 1994; (ed. and comp.) Satie Remembered, 1995; (ed.) Deux œuvres Pour Violon et Piano, 1995; (ed.) Statue Retrouvée: Pour Trompette en ut et Orgue (ou piano), 1995; (ed.) Chœur des marins: Pourténor, chœur D'hommes et Piano, 1997; (contrib.) The Dreamy Fish: The Angora Ox: Pour Piano, 1997; (ed.) Trois pièces Pour Piano, 1998; (contrib.) Piéces ultimes/Last Pieces, 2005; (contrib.) Portrait de Daisy Hamilton: opus 140: 1934-38, 2007. Contributor of articles to periodicals. **Address:** Department of Music, University of Liverpool, Liverpool, MS L69 3BX, England. **Online address:** rorledge@liv.ac.uk

ORLEV, **Uri.** Israeli/Polish (born Poland), b. 1931. **Genres:** Novels, Young Adult Fiction, Translations, Poetry, Children's Fiction. **Career:** Writer, 1962-. **Publications:** ḥayale-Oferet, 1956; ḥayat ha-ḥoshekh, 1976; Meshaga'at Pilim, 1977; Maḥshevot Tsohorayim, 1978; ḳasheh li-heyot Aryeh, 1979; Motsets ha-mazal, 1980; Ha-I bi-Rehov Ha-tsiporim, 1981; Savta Soreget, 1981; Rosh ha-'ir ten La-shir, 1981; Keter Ha-draḳon, 1984; ḥafifat rosh, 1986; Ish min Ha-tsad ha-aher, 1988; Lidyah, Malkat Erets Yisra'el, 1991; Hagueret Im Hamigbaat, 1990; ḳeṭanah-Gedolah, 1996; Shirat Ha-liṿyatanim, 1997; Hairy Tuesday, 1999; Lion for Michael, 2001; Ruts, Yeled, Ruts, 2001; Ha-Baitah Me-'aravot Ha-Shemesh, 2010. **Address:** Yemin Moshe, 4 Ha-berakhah, Jerusalem, 4, Israel.

ORLOVA, **Alexandra (Anatol'evna).** American/Ukranian (born Ukraine), b. 1911. **Genres:** Young Adult Fiction, Music, Biography, Autobiography/Memoirs. **Career:** Leningrad Conservatoire, bibliographer, 1933-35; Leningrad Philharmonic, library bibliographer, 1935-37, library director, 1941-44; Tchaikovsky Museum, scientific worker, 1938-39; Leningrad Scientific Research, Music and Theater Institute, scientific worker, 1945-50; writer, 1950-. **Publications:** (Co-author) Dni i gody P.Tchaikovsky, 1940, M.I. Glinka: Letopis' zhizni b itvorchestva, 1952; M.I. Glinka: Literaturnoe nasledie, 2 vols., 1952-53; M.I. Glinka: Zapiski, Commentaryee, 1953; Mikhail Ivanovich Glinka, 1954; Petr Il'ich Chaikovskii, 1840-1893 (juvenile), 1955; Glinka v vospominaniakhsovremennikov, 1955; Trudy i dni M.P. Musorgskogo, 1963 as Musorgsky's Days and Works: A Biography in Documents, 1983; (with V.N. Rimskii-Korsakov) Stranitsy zhizni N.A. Rimskogo-Korsakova, 4 vols., 1969-73; Glinka v Peterburge, Lenizdat, 1970; (ed. with M.S. Pekelis) Literaturnoe nasledie M.P. Musorgskogo, 2 vols., 1971; Musorgskii v Peterburge, 1974; P.I. Chaikovskii: O muzyke, o zhizni, o sebe, 1976; Mikhail Glukh, Ocerk zhisni i tvorchestva, 1977; Glinka's Life in Music: A Chronicle, 1988; (comp.) Tchaikovsky: A Self-Portrait, 1990; (comp. and ed.) Musorgsky Remembered, 1991; Tchaikovsky Bez Retushi, 2001; Chaikovski: Un Autorretrato, 2007. **Address:** 97 Van Wagenen Ave., Apt. 1D, Jersey City, NJ 07306-5378, U.S.A.

ORME, David John. British (born England) **Genres:** Novels, Children's Fiction, Education. **Career:** Writer. **Publications:** Joshua's Junk, 1994; Red Bird, 1994; Rainy Days, 1994; Ten Tired Tigers, 1994; I Hear Thunder, 1994; Wibble Wobble, 1994; Monster's Baking Day, 1994; Planets, Stars, and Galaxies, 1996; Losing My Roof (autobiography), 1996; The Haunted Asteroids, 1996; The City of the Roborgs, 1996; (with M. Andrew) Curriculum Bank: Speaking and Listening, 1997; Clever Cat's Hide and Seek, 1998; Planet of the Robots, 1998; Read Me Another, Dad!, 1999; Writers in Britain: The BrontEs, 1999; (with S. Wright) It's Official: Language of World War 2, 2000; Beyond This World, 2000; Sci-fi Danger! (short stories), 2000; Pre-1914 Classics: Charles Dickens, 2000; NET: An English Resource, 2001; Word Play Smiles, 2001; Danger at Sea, 2002; Soldiers in Training, 2002; How Fit Are You?, 2002; Survival Guide, 2002; Starship Football, 2002; Macbeth: Warlord of Space (graphic novel), 2002; Is There Life Beyond Earth?, 2003; Danger Mountain, 2003; (with J. Langford) Mysterious?, 2003; Ghostly Places, 2003; Ghostly Animals, 2003; (with S. Ransford) Spooky Jokes, Puzzles and Poems, 2003; Ghost Hunting, 2004; The Donkey That Was Too Fast, 2005; Tsunamis: Why Are These Waves So High?, 2005; Tornadoes: What Do We Call Tornadoes over the Sea?, 2005; Dinosaur Planet, 2005; The Thirsty Moose: Based on a Native American Folktale, 2005; Animals under Threat: Orangutan, 2005; Space Pirates, 2006; Something Evil, 2006; Space Wreck, 2006; Scary!, 2006; Space Games, 2007; Trapped in Space, 2007; Doorway to Darkness, 2007; Spook Manor, 2007; The Valley of Wisdom, 2007; Space Plague, 2007; Hurricane Season, 2008; Monster Planet, 2008; Mutants from the Deep, 2009; Mind Thief, 2009; The Red Wolf, 2009; Secrets of the Ninja, 2009; The Lost City, 2009; Water Pirates from Outer Space, 2009; The Ice Caves of Pluto, 2009; The Frozen Men of Mars, 2009; The Evil Swarm, 2009; The Time Warriors, 2009; The Cryptic Code, 2009; Attack of the Rock Men, 2009. WITH H. ORME: Walking with Dinosaurs: Dinosaur World, 2000; Changing Schools, 2001; Blue Planet: Ocean World, 2001; Jenny's Story, 2003; What on Earth? Tsunamis, 2005; What on Earth? Tornadoes, 2005; Let's Explore Comets and Asteroids, 2007; Let's Explore Earth, 2007; Let's Explore Jupiter, 2007; Let's Explore Mars, 2007; Let's Explore Mercury, 2007; Let's Explore Neptune, 2007; Let's Explore Pluto and Beyond, 2007; Let's Explore Saturn, 2007; Let's Explore the Moon, 2007; Let's Explore the Sun, 2007; Let's Explore Uranus, 2007; Let's Explore Venus, 2007. POETRY: A Fear of Bells, 1983; (with J. Sale) The Poetry Show, 3 vols., 1987; The Gravedigger's Sandwich, 1992; The Essential Guide to Poetry, 1992; Ere We Go!, 1993; Dracula's Auntie Ruthless, 1994; (ed.) Cheating at Conkers, 1994; (ed.) Penny Whistle, 1995; You'll Never Walk Alone, 1995; Snoggers, 1995; Heroes and Villains, 1995; Poetry Workshop, 1997; Dear Future: A Time Capsule of Poems, 1997; We Woz Robbed!, 1997; While Shepherds Washed Their Socks, 1997; They Think It's All Over!, 1998; Revenge of the Man-Eating Gerbils, 1998; (ed. with B. Moses) Classic Poems, 1999; (ed. with B. Moses) Poems from Around the World, 1999; (ed. with B. Moses) What Kind of Poem?, 1999; (ed.) Prayers and Poems from Around the World, 1999; (ed.) Weaving Words, 2000; (ed.) Stories and Extracts from Shakespeare, 2000; Nothing Tastes Quite Like a Gerbil, 2000; The Ghoul School Bus, 2000; The Final Whistle, 2000; Freaky Families, 2001; A Magic Nation, 2002; (ed.) Ghostly Verse, 2002; Unlocking the Poet in Every Child, 2011. **Address:** United Kingdom. **Online address:** mail@davidorme.co.uk

ORME, Nicholas. British (born England) **Genres:** History, Race Relations, Education, Theology/Religion, Translations. **Career:** University of Exeter, Department of History, tutor, 1964, lecturer, 1965-81, senior lecturer, 1977, reader in history, 1980-88, professor of history, 1988-2007, professor emeritus, 2007-; Merton College, visiting research fellow, 1982; University of Minnesota, Union-Pacific visiting professor, 1998. Writer. **Publications:** English Schools in the Middle Ages, 1973; Education in the West of England, 1066-1548: Cornwall, Devon, Dorset, Gloucestershire, Somerset, Wiltshire, 1976; The Minor Clergy of Exeter Cathedral, 1300-1548: A List of the Minor Officers, Vicars Choral, Annuellars, Secondaries and Choristers, 1980; Early British Swimming, 55 BC-AD 1719: With the First Swimming Treatise in English, 1595, 1983; From Childhood to Chivalry: The Education of the English Kings and Aristocracy 1066-1530, 1984; Education and Society in Medieval and Renaissance England, 1989; A Guide to St. Peter's Church, Brampford Speke, 1989; Unity and Variety: A History of the Church in Devon and Cornwall, 1991; (ed.) Nicholas Roscarrock's Lives of the Saints: Cornwall and Devon, 1992; (with M. Webster) The English Hospital, 1070-1570, 1995; White Bird Flying (juvenile), 1995; English Church Dedications: With a Survey of Cornwall and Devon, 1996; The Cap and the Sword: Exeter and the Rebellions of 1497, 1997; Education in Early Tudor England: Magdalen College Oxford and Its School, 1998; The Saints of Cornwall, 2000; Medieval Children, 2001; (ed. with D. Lepine) Death and Memory in Medieval Exeter, 2003; (ed. with J. Chynoweth and A. Walsham) The Survey of Cornwall, 2004; Medieval Schools: From Roman Britain to Renaissance England, 2006; (ed.) Cornish Wills, 1342-1540, 2007; Cornwall and the Cross: Christianity 500-1560, 2007; (ed.) The Victoria History of the County of Cornwall: vol. II: Religious History to 1561, 2007; Exeter Cathedral: The First Thousand Years, 400-1550, 2009; (ed. and trans) Fleas, Flies and Friars, 2012. **Address:** Department of History, University of Exeter, Amory Bldg., Rennes Dr., Streatham Campus, Exeter, DN EX4 4RJ, England. **Online address:** n.i.orme@exeter.ac.uk

ORMEROD, Neil. (Neil James Ormerod). Australian (born Australia), b. 1954. **Genres:** Theology/Religion, History, Philosophy. **Career:** Australian Catholic University, professor of theology, 2005-, Institute of Theology, Philosophy, and Religious Education, director, 2005-. Writer and theologian. **Publications:** Grace and Disgrace: A Theology of Self-Esteem, Society, and History, 1992; Why Marry?, 1992; A New Handbook for Today's Catholic: Beliefs, Practices, Prayers, 1992; (ed. with G. Moses) Human Beings and Nature: Historical and Philosophical Studies, 1992; (with T. Ormerod) When Ministers Sin: Sexual Abuse in the Churches, 1995; Introducing Contemporary Theologies: The What and the Who of Theology Today, 1997; Method, Meaning, and Revelation: The Meaning and Function of Revelation in Bernard Lonergan's Method in Theology, 2000; The Trinity: Retrieving the Western Tradition, 2005; Creation, Grace, and Redemption, 2007; (ed.) Identity and Mission in Catholic Agencies, 2008; (as Neil J. Ormerod with J.W. O'Malley, J.A. Komonchak and S. Schloesser) Vatican II: Did Anything Happen?, 2008; (as Neil J. Ormerod with S. Clifton) Globalization and the Mission of the Church, 2009; (ed. as Neil James Ormerod with R. Konig and D.M. Braithwaite) Fifty Years of Insight, 2011; Trinitarian Primer, 2011. Contributor to journals. **Address:** Australian Catholic University, Edmund Rice Bldg., Level 2-E2.72, 25A Barker Rd., PO Box 2002, Strathfield, NW 2135, Australia. **Online address:** neil.ormerod@acu.edu.au

ORMEROD, Neil James. *See* **ORMEROD, Neil.**

ORMEROD, Roger. British (born England), b. 1920. **Genres:** Mystery/Crime/Suspense, Novels, Criminology/True Crime. **Career:** County court clerk, 1937-48; social security clerk; Department of Social Security, county court officer, executive officer and inspector, 1948-72. Writer. **Publications:** Time to Kill, 1974; The Silence of the Night, 1974; Full Fury, 1975; A Spoonful of Luger, 1975; Sealed with a Loving Kill, 1976; The Colour of Fear, 1976; A Glimpse of Death, 1976; Too Late for the Funeral, 1977; This Murder Come to Mind, 1977; A Dip into Murder, 1978; The Weight of Evidence, 1978; The Bright Face of Danger, 1979; The Amnesia Trap, 1979; Cart Before the Hearse, 1979; More Dead than Alive, 1980; Double Take, 1980; One Deathless Hour, 1981; Face Value, 1983 in US as The Hanging Doll Murder, 1984; Seeing Red, 1985; Dead Ringer, 1986; Still Life with Pistol, 1986; A Death to Remember, 1987; An Alibi Too Soon, 1987; The Second Jeopardy, 1987; An Open Window, 1988; By Death Possessed, 1988; Guilt on the Lily, 1989; Death of an Innocent, 1989; No Sign of Life, 1990; Hung in the Balance, 1990; Farewell Gesture, 1991; Bury Him Darkly, 1991; When the Old Man Died, 1991; Third Time Fatal, 1992; The Key to the Case, 1992; A Shot at Nothing, 1993; Shame the Devil, 1993; Mask of Innocence, 1994; And Hope to Die, 1995; Stone Cold Dead, 1995; Farewell Gesture, 1995; Landscape with Corpse, 1996; Curtain of Beads, 1996; The Vital Minute, 1996; The Night She Died, 1997; Parting Shot, 1998; The Seven Razors of Occam, 1998; Final Toll, 1999. Contributor to periodicals. **Address:** Laurence Pollinger Ltd., 18 Maddox St., Mayfair, London, GL W1R 0EU, England.

ORMONDROYD, Edward. American (born United States), b. 1925. **Genres:** Children's Fiction, Recreation, Poetry, Novels. **Career:** Writer, librarian and merchant seaman. **Publications:** David and the Phoenix, 1957; The Tale of Alain, 1960; Time at the Top, 1963; Jonathan Frederick Aloysius Brown (poetry), 1964; Theodore, 1966; Michael, the Upstairs Dog, 1967; Broderick, 1969; Theodores Rival, 1971; Castaways on Long Ago, 1973; Imagination Greene, 1973; All in Good Time, 1975; Johnny Castleseed, 1985; (with R. Bradfield and C. Geer) Time at the Top and All in Good Time, 2011. **Address:** 5258 Curry Rd., Trumansburg, NY 14886-9552, U.S.A. **Online address:** jlo5@cornell.edu

ORMSBY, Frank. Irish (born Ireland), b. 1947. **Genres:** Poetry, Literary Criticism And History. **Career:** Honest Ulsterman Magazine, editor, 1969-89; Royal Belfast Academical Institution, English teacher, 1971-, head of English; Contributor to periodicals. **Publications:** Ripe for Company, 1971; Business as Usual, 1973; A Store of Candles, 1977; Being Walked by a Dog, 1978; A Northern Spring, 1986; The Ghost Train, 1995. EDITOR: Poets from the North of Ireland, 1979; Northern Windows, 1987; The Long Embrace: Twentieth-Century Irish Love Poems, 1987; Thine in Storm and Calm: An Amanda McKittrick Ros Reader, 1988; The Collected Poems of John Hewitt, 1991; A Rage for Order: Poetry of the Northern Ireland Troubles, 1992; The Hip Flask: Short Poems from Ireland, 2002; The Blackbird's Nest, 2006; (with M. Longley) Selected Poems, 2007; Fireflies, 2009. Contributor to periodicals. **Address:** Royal Belfast Academical Institution, College Sq. E, Belfast, AT BT1 6DL, Northern Ireland.

ORNISH, Dean. American (born United States), b. 1953. **Genres:** Food And Wine, Medicine/Health, Self Help. **Career:** University of California, School of Medicine, Division of General Internal Medicine, assistant clinical professor of medicine and attending physician, 1984-, Preventive Medicine Research Institute, founder and president, 1984-; Presbyterian Hospital, California Pacific Medical Center, medical staff and attending physician, 1984; Google Health Advisory Council, chair, 2007-09; Massachusetts General Hospital, medical internship and residency. Writer. **Publications:** Stress, Diet and Your Heart, 1983; Dr. Dean Ornish's Program for Reversing Heart Disease: The Only System Scientifically Proven to Reverse Heart Disease without Drugs or Surgery, 1990; Eat More, Weigh Less: Dr. Dean Ornish's Life Choice Program for Losing Weight Safely While Eating Abundantly, 1993, rev. ed., 2001; (co-author) Everyday Cooking with Dr. Dean Ornish: 150 Easy, Low-fat, High-flavor Recipes, 1996; Love and Survival: The Scientific Basis for the Healing Power of Intimacy, 1998; The Spectrum: A Scientifically Proven Program to Feel Better, Live Longer, Lose Weight, and Gain Health, 2007. Contributor of articles to periodicals. **Address:** Preventive Medicine Research Institute, 900 Bridgeway, Sausalito, CA 94965, U.S.A.

OROS, Andrew L. American (born United States), b. 1969?. **Genres:** Politics/Government. **Career:** Washington College, associate professor of political science and international studies; National Institute for Defense Studies, research fellow, 2009; Millennium: Journal of International Studies, editor. Political scientist. **Publications:** (Ed. with D. Jacquin-Berda and M. Verweij) Culture in World Politics, 1998; Normalizing Japan: Politics, Identity, and the Evolution of Security Practice, 2008; (with Y. Tatsumi) Global Security Watch-Japan, 2010. Contributor to journals. **Address:** U.S.A. **Online address:** aoros2@washcoll.edu

OROSZ, Joel J. American (born United States), b. 1957. **Genres:** Money/Finance, Homes/Gardens. **Career:** Kalamazoo Public Museum, curator of interpretation, 1983-86; W.K. Kellogg Foundation, program director, 1986-2001; Grand Valley State University, distinguished professor of philanthropic studies, 2001-, Dorothy A. Johnson Center for Philanthropy and Nonprofit Leadership, founding director; The Grantmaking School, director and lead faculty. Writer. **Publications:** The Eagle That Is Forgotten, 1988; Curators and Culture: The Museum Movement in America, 1740-1870, 1990; (ed.) For the Benefit of All: A History of Philanthropy in Michigan: An Engaging Look at the Philanthropic Traditions of the Great Lakes State and Its People, 1997; The Insider's Guide to Grantmaking: How Foundations Find, Fund and Manage Effective Programs, 2000; Effective Foundation Management: 14 Challenges of Philanthropic Leadership-and How to Outfox Them, 2007. Contributor to periodicals. **Address:** School of Public & Nonprofit Administration, Grand Valley State University, 200 Bicycle Factory, 2nd Fl., DeVos Ctr., 401 W Fulton St., Grand Rapids, MI 49504, U.S.A. **Online address:** oroszj@gvsu.edu

O'ROURKE, Erin. (Lance Hawvermale). American (born United States), b. 1972?. **Genres:** Novels, Mystery/Crime/Suspense. **Career:** University of Arkansas, Marketing and Communications Department, editor and instructor of English, 2006-10; Ranger College, webmaster, 2010-, Department of English, instructor, 2010-. Writer and counselor. **Publications:** NOVELS: Seeing Pink, 2003; Fugitive Shoes, 2006; (as Lance Hawvermale) The Tongue Merchant, 2008. **Address:** Department of English, Ranger College, 1100 College Cir., Ranger, TX 76470, U.S.A. **Online address:** mail@lancehawvermale.com

O'ROURKE, James S. (James Scofield O'Rourke). American (born United States), b. 1946. **Genres:** Communications/Media, Business/Trade/Industry. **Career:** Temple University, graduate teaching assistant, 1969-70; Communications Institute of Ireland, visiting professor, 1970; Syracuse University, assistant professor of aerospace studies, 1975-78; United States Air Force Academy, instructor of English, 1978-80, assistant professor of English, 1980-81, associate professor of English, 1981-83; University of Colorado, adjunct associate professor of communication, 1981-83; Defense Information School, professor of public affairs, 1983-86, Public Affairs Department, Policy and Information Division, chief, 1984-86; Indiana University, adjunct professor of communication, 1984-86; Auburn University, adjunct professor of communication, 1986-90; Air University, associate professor of public affairs, 1986-89, professor of public affairs, 1989-90; University of Notre Dame, associate professor of business, 1990-, professor of management, Fanning Center for Business Communication, founder, Arthur F. and Mary J. O'Neil, director and professional specialist, 1990-, Eugene D. Fanning Center for Business Communication, founder, 1990-; Business Communication Quarterly, reviewer, 1993-98; CHOICE: Current Review for Academic Libraries, reviewer, 1993-99; The Conference on Corporate Communication, founding director, 1997-; ABC Ethics Interest Group, founding director, 2000-05; Management Communication Association, conference host, 2002; The Education Review of Business Communication, associate editor, 2003-05. Writer. **Publications:** (With T.W. Portre and J.J. Zigerell) Television in Community and Junior Colleges: An Overview and Guidelines, 1980; Reflections in the Dome: Sixty Years of Life at Notre Dame, 1986; Beginning Your Career Search: A Hands-on Approach to Building Your Career Portfolio, 1998, 4th ed. 2007; (with M.J. O'Hair and H.D. O'Hair) Business Communication: A Framework for Success, 2000; Management Communication: A Case-Analysis Approach, 2001, 4th ed., 2010; Casebook for Business Communication, 2002, 2nd ed., 2007; Effective Communication, 2009. EDITOR: Public Affairs Handbook, 1985; Meeting the Media, 1986; Reflections in the Dome: Sixty Years of Life at Notre Dame, 1988; (with B. Yarbrough) Leading Groups and Teams, 2002; (with C. Boulger) e-Technology and the Fourth Economy, 2003; (with S. Collins) Interpersonal Communication: Listening and Responding, Truth About Confident Presenting, 2005; (with E. Tuleja) Intercultural Communication for Business, 2005; (co-ed.) Graphics and Visual Communication for Managers, 2007; (with S. Collins) Communication in a Virtual Organization; (with S. Collins) Persuasion, 2008; (with C. Karlson) Writing and Presenting a Business Plan, 2008; (with S. Collins) Managing Conflict and Workplace Relationships, 2009. **Address:** Fanning Center for Business Communication, University of Notre Dame, 234B Mendoza College of Business, Notre Dame, IN 46556-5646, U.S.A. **Online address:** jorourke@nd.edu

O'ROURKE, James Scofield. *See* **O'ROURKE, James S.**

O'ROURKE, P. J. American (born United States), b. 1947. **Genres:** Poetry, Social Commentary, Humor/Satire, Politics/Government. **Career:** New York Herald, feature editor, 1971-72; freelance writer, 1972-73; National Lampoon, executive editor and managing editor, 1972-77, editor-in-chief, 1978-81; freelance journalist, 1981-; Rolling Stone Magazine, head of international affairs desk, 1981-2001, contributor; Atlantic Monthly, correspondent, 2001-. **Publications:** Nancy Adler Poems, 1970; Our Friend the Vowel (poems), 1976; Modern Manners: An Etiquette Book for Rude People, 1983; Republican Party Reptile, 1986; The Bachelor Home Companion, 1987; Holidays in Hell, 1988; (comp.) The Official American Spectator Enemies List, 1990; Parliament of Whores, 1991; Give War a Chance, 1992; All the Trouble in the World, 1994; Age and Guile Beat Youth, Innocence and a Bad Haircut, 1995; (comp.) Enemies List, 1996; Eat the Rich, 1998; The CEO of the Sofa, 2001; National Lampoon 1964 High School Yearbook, 2003; Peace Kills, 2004; On the Wealth of Nations, 2007; Driving Like Crazy: Thirty Years of Vehicular Hell-bending, Celebrating America the Way It's Supposed To Be-With an Oil Well in Every Backyard, 2009; Don't Vote It Just Encourages the Bastards, 2010. EDITOR: (with D.C. Kenney) The 1964 High School Yearbook, 1974; National Lampoon: A Dirty Book, 1976; Sunday Newspaper Parody, 1978;

(with J. Hughes) National Lampoon Sunday Newspaper Parody, 2005. **Address:** Grove/Atlantic Inc., 841 Broadway, 4th Fl., New York, NY 10003, U.S.A.

O'ROURKE, William. American (born United States), b. 1945. **Genres:** Novels, Civil Liberties/Human Rights, Social Commentary, Adult Non-fiction, Social Sciences. **Career:** Kean College of New Jersey, instructor in journalism, 1973-75; Rutgers University, assistant professor, 1975-78; Mt. Holyoke College, assistant professor, 1978-81; University of Notre Dame, professor of English, 1981-. Writer. **Publications:** The Harrisburg 7 and the New Catholic Left, 1972; (ed. and intro.) On the Job: Fiction about Work by Contemporary American Writers, 1977; Signs of the Literary Times: Essays, Reviews, Profiles, 1970-1992, 1993; Campaign America 96: The View from the Couch, 1997, 2nd ed., 2000; Campaign America 2000: The View from the Couch, 2001; On Having A Heart Attack: A Medical Memoir, 2006; (ed. and intro. with J. Matthias) Notre Dame Review: The First Ten Years, 2009. NOVELS: The Meekness of Isaac, 1974; Idle Hands, 1981; Criminal Tendencies, 1987; Notts, 1996. Contributor to periodicals. **Address:** Department of English, University of Notre Dame, 465 Decio Faculty Hall, 356 O'Shaughnessy Hall, Notre Dame, IN 46556, U.S.A. **Online address:** worourke@nd.edu

ORR, D. Alan. American (born United States) **Genres:** Law, Politics/Government. **Career:** Queen's University, faculty; Carleton University, faculty; Maryland Institute College of Art, faculty, 2004-. Writer. **Publications:** Treason and the State: Law, Politics and Ideology in the English Civil War, 2002. Contributor to journals. **Address:** Maryland Institute College of Art, 1300 Mount Royal Ave., Baltimore, MD 21217, U.S.A. **Online address:** aorr0405@yahoo.com

ORR, David W. American (born United States), b. 1944?. **Genres:** Economics, Earth Sciences, Adult Non-fiction, Cultural/Ethnic Topics, Environmental Sciences/Ecology, Social Sciences, Reference, Architecture, Architecture. **Career:** Oberlin College, Department of Environmental Studies, professor, chair, Paul Sears distinguished professor of environmental studies and politics, Environmental Studies Center, director; University of Vermont, James Marsh professor-at-large; Conservation Biology, contributing editor. **Publications:** (Ed. with M.S. Soroos) The Global Predicament: Ecological Perspectives on World Order, 1979; Ecological Literacy: Education and the Transition to a Postmodern World, 1992; Earth in Mind: On Education, Environment, and the Human Prospect, 1994; The Nature of Design: Ecology, Culture, and Human Intention, 2002; The Last Refuge: The Corruption of Patriotism and Environment in the Age of Terror, 2004; Design on the Edge: The Making of a High-Performance Building, 2006; Down to the Wire: Confronting Climate Collapse, 2009; Hope is an Imperative: The Essential David Orr, 2011. Contributor of articles to periodicals. **Address:** Environmental Studies Program, Adam Joseph Lewis Ctr., Oberlin College, 122 Elm St., Oberlin, OH 44074-1526, U.S.A. **Online address:** david.orr@oberlin.edu

ORR, Gregory. *See* **ORR, Gregory (Simpson).**

ORR, Gregory (Simpson). (Gregory Orr). American (born United States), b. 1947. **Genres:** Poetry, Literary Criticism And History, Autobiography/Memoirs, inspirational/Motivational Literature, Essays. **Career:** University of Virginia, assistant professor, 1975-80, associate professor, 1980-88, professor of English, 1988-; Virginia Quarterly Review, poetry consultant, 1976-2003; University of Hawaii, visiting writer, 1982-. **Publications:** AS GREGORY ORR: POETRY: Burning the Empty Nests, 1973, 2nd ed., 1997; Gathering the Bones Together, 1975; Salt Wings, 1980; The Red House, 1980; We Must Make a Kingdom of It, 1986; New and Selected Poems, 1987; City of Salt, 1995; Orpheus and Eurydice: A Lyric Sequence, 2001; The Caged Owl: New and Selected Poems, 2002; How Beautiful the Beloved, 2009. OTHER: Large White Rock Called the Sleeping Angel, 1974; Stanley Kunitz: An Introduction to the Poetry, 1985; Richer Entanglements: Essays and Notes on Poetry and Poems, 1993; (ed. with E.B. Voigt) Poets Teaching Poets: Self and the World, 1996; Poetry as Survival, 2002; The Blessing: A Memoir, 2002; Concerning the Book that is the Body of the Beloved, 2005; City of Poetry, 2012. Contributor to books, journals and magazines. **Address:** Department of English, University of Virginia, 431 Bryan Hall, PO Box 400121, Charlottesville, VA 22904-4121, U.S.A. **Online address:** gso@virginia.edu

ORR, Wendy. (Sally George). Australian/Canadian (born Canada), b. 1953. **Genres:** Novels, Children's Fiction, Young Adult Fiction, Picture/Board Books. **Career:** Albury Community Health, occupational therapist, 1975-80; Language and Development Clinic, occupational therapist, 1982-91; author, 1988-. **Publications:** Amanda's Dinosaur, 1988; The Tin Can Puppy, 1990; Bad Martha, 1991; Aa-Choo!, 1992; Leaving It to You, 1993; The Great Yackandandah Billy Cart Race, 1993; Mindblowing!, 1994, as A Light in Space, 1994; The Laziest Boy in the World, 1994; Yasou Nikki, 1995; Dirtbikes, 1995; The Bully Biscuit Gang, 1995; Jessica Joan, 1995; Grandfather Martin, 1996; Alroy's Very Nearly Clean Bedroom, 1996; Peeling the Onion (young adult), 1997; Paradise Palace, 1997; Arabella, 1998; Paradise Gold, 1999; Ark in the Park, 1999; Poppy's Path (young reader), 2000; Nim's Island, 2001; Mokie & Bik, 2007; Nim At Sea, 2007. MICKI AND DANIEL (picture book series): Micki Moon and Daniel Day, 1993; Pegasus and Ooloo Mooloo, 1993; The Train to the City, 1993; The Wedding, 1993; Spook's Shack, 2002; The Princess and Her Panther, 2010, Lost! A Dog Called Bear, 2011; Missing! A Cat Called Buster, 2011; Wanted! A Guinea Pig Named Henry, 2012. OTHER: The House at Evelyn's Pond (novel), 2001. AS SALLY GEORGE: Bad Dog, George, 1994; Breakfast in Bed, 1994; George at the Zoo, 1994; Abandoned! A Lion Called Kiki, 2012. **Address:** c/o Debbie Golvan, Golvan Arts Management, PO Box 766, Kew, VI 3101, Australia. **Online address:** wendyorr@bigpond.com

ORSENNA, érik. French (born France), b. 1947. **Genres:** Young Adult Fiction. **Career:** Writer. **Publications:** Loyola's Blues, 1974; La Vie Comme à Lausanne, 1977; (ed.) L. De Rouvroy Saint-Simon, Mémoires. 15, 1718-1720, 1979; Une Comédie Française, 1980; (with J. Terrasse) Villes D'eaux (history), 1981; L'Exposition Coloniale, 1988; (with C. Guillemin and E. Fottorino) Besoin d'Afrique, 1992; Grand Amour, éditions Du Seuil (Paris, France), 1993; (with E. Kuligowski) Rochefort Et La Corderie Royale (history), 1995; Docks: Photographies, 1995; Histoire Du Monde En Neufguitares, 1996; (with B. Matussière) Mésaventures Du Paradis: Mélodie Cubaine (travel), 1996; Deux étés, 1997; (with H. Amiard) L'atelier De Alain Senderens: Les maîtres De La Gastronomie, 1997; Longtemps, 1998; (with B. Poirot-Delpech) Discours de Réception De Erik Orsennaà l'Académie Française Et Résponse de Bertrand Poirot-Delpech, 1999; (with D. Mordzinski) Lumieres Du Sud: Portraits Etrécits d'écrivains d'Amérique Latine, 1999; Portrait D'unhomme Heureux: André Le Nôtre, 1613-1700 (biography), 2000; Lagrammaire Est Une Chanson Douce, 2001; (foreword) City and Landscapes as Henri Cartier-Bresson: City and Landscapes, 2001; (preface) Europe En Première Ligne, 2002; Madame Bâ, 2003; Chevaliers Du Subjonctif, 2004; Portrait Du Gulf Stream: éloge Des Courants: Promenade, 2005; Dernières Nouvelles Des Oiseaux, 2005; Voyage Aux Pays Du Coton: Petit Précis De Mondialisation, 2006; (with I. Autissier) Salut Au Grand Sud, 2006; Révolte Des Accents, 2007; (with Isabella and T. Vaughan) Kerdalo: Le Jardin Continu, 2007; Monde De Ressources Rares, 2007; A380, 2007; Avenir De L'eau: Petit Précis De Mondialisation II, 2008; Quels espaces pour demain?, 2008; Chanson De Charles Quint, 2008; (P. Bernasconi) Et si on dansait?: éloge de la ponctuation, 2009; L' entreprise des Indes: roman, 2010; The Indies Enterprise, 2011. **Address:** c/o Author Mail, George Braziller Inc., 171 Madison Ave., New York, NY 10016, U.S.A.

ORTEGA, Julio. American (born United States), b. 1942. **Genres:** Translations. **Career:** Universidad San Agustí, visiting professor, 1968; University of Texas, visiting professor, 1977; Universidad de Puerto Rico, visiting professor, 1983; Brandeis University, professor and chairperson, 1987-88; University of London, King's College, visiting professor, 1987; Brown University, professor of hispanic studies, 1989-, chair hispanic studies, 1995-98, Center for Latin American Studies, director, 2004-05, director of graduate studies, 2004-; Universidad Central de Venezuela, visiting professor, 1995; University of Cambridge, visiting professor, 1995-96; Archives Collection, Editorial Council, coordinator. Writer. **Publications:** Las Vinas de Moro: Poemas, 1968; Figuracion de la Persona, 1971; Relato De La Utopia: Notas Sobre Narrativa Cubana de la Revolucion, 1973; La Imaginacion Critica: Ensayos Sobre la Modernidad en el Peru, 1974; Tierra en el Dia: Noticia Provechosa Acerca de las Costumbres y Creencias en la Ciudad Deseada, y Otros Varios Ejemplos Amenos, 1975, (trans. with E. Campbell) as The Land in the Day, 1978; Rituales: Poemas, 1976; La Contemplacion y la Fiesta: Notas Sobre la Novela Latinoamericana Actual, 1979; Texto, Comunicacion y Cultura: Los Rios Profundos de Jose Maria Arguedas, 1982; Acto Subversivo, 1984; Poetics of Change: The New Spanish-American Narrative, 1984; (co-author) Los Cuatro Continentes, 1986; Cultura y Modernizacion en la Lima del 900, 1986; La Teoria Poetica de Cesar Vallejo, 1986; Critica de la Identidad: La Pregunta por el Peru en Su Literatura, 1988; Diario Imaginario, 1988; Rayuela, 1991; El Oro de Moscu, 1991; Una Poetica del Cambio, 1991; Reapropiaciones:

Cultura y Nueva Escritura en Puerto Rico, 1991; (contrib.) Tradiciones Peruanas, 1993; Arte de Innovar, 1994; Ayacucho, Goodbye: Moscow's Gold, 1994; El Hilo del Habla: La Narrativa de Alfredo Bryce Echenique, 1994; Las Islas Blancas: Relatos de Pesca, rev. ed., 1994; La Mesa del Padre, 1995; El Principio Radical de lo Nuevo: Postmodernidad, Identidad y Novela en America Latina, 1997; (co-author) El Combate de Los Angeles: Literatura, Genero, Diferencia, 1999; Habanera, 1999; Taller de la Escritura: Conversaciones, Encuentros, 2000; Caja de Herramientas: Practicas Culturales para el Nuevo Siglo Chileno, 2000; Transatlantic Translations: Dialogues in Latin American Literature, 2006; The Art of Reading: Stories and Poems, 2007; Imagen de Carlos Fuentes, 2008; COMPILER: (and intro.) El Reino de la Imagen, 1981; Poemas para Combatir la Calvicie: Muestra De Antipoesia, 1993; Antologia del Cuento Latinoamericano del Siglo XXI: Las Horas y las Hordas, 1997; Gaborio: Artes de Releer a Gabriel Garcia Marquez, 2003; (with M.F. Lander and intro.) Alfredo Bryce Echenique Ante la Critica, 2004; (and intro. with J.F. Ferre) Mutantes: Narrativa Espanola de Ultima Generacion, 2007. EDITOR: (and intro.) La Utopia Incaica: Primera Parte de los Comentarios Reales, 1972; (and intro.) La Casilla de los Morelli, 1973; Versiones del Surrealismo, 1974; Palabra de Escandalo, 1974; Cesar Vallejo, 1975; Latin America in Its Literature, 1980; (with M.H. Forster) De la Cronica a la Nueva Narrativa Mexicana: Coloquio Sobre Literatura Mexicana, 1986; (and intro.) Antologia de la Poesia Hispanoamericana Actual, 1987; Gabriel Garcia Marquez and the Powers of Fiction, 1988; Trilce, 1991; La Cervantiada, 1993; (with J.A.Y. Vazquez) Conquista y Contraconquista: La Escritura del Nuevo Mundo: Actas Del XXVIII Congreso Del Instituto Internacional de Literatura Iberoamericana, 1994; Guia del Nuevo Siglo, 1998; (with C. Fuentes) The Picador Book of Latin American Stories, 1999; Viaje Hacia la Noche, 1999; (with C. Fuentes) The Vintage Book of Latin American Stories, 2000; The Fox from Up Above and the Fox from Down Below, 2000; (with M.F. Lander) La Vida Exagerada de Martin Romana, 2000; (with E.R. Parra) El Aleph, 2001; (with E.R. Parra) El Hombre Que Hablaba de Octavia de Cadiz: Cuaderno de Navegacion en un Sillon Voltaire, 2003; Lagartija sin Cola, 2007; Capital Mexicana, 2007; (with C. Palacio) Mexico Trasatlantico, 2008; Nuevos hispanismos interdisciplinarios y trasatlánticos, 2010; Lizard's Tale: A Novel, 2011. Contributor to periodicals. **Address:** Brown University, 45 Prospect St., PO Box 1876, Providence, RI 02912, U.S.A. **Online address:** julio_ortega@brown.edu

ORTEGO, Sheila. American (born United States), b. 1952. **Genres:** Novels, Literary Criticism And History. **Career:** Santa Fe Community College, faculty and administrator, 1983-, adjunct professor, executive vice president and vice president of instruction and student services, president, 2006, GROW Santa Fe Community College Foundation, president. Writer. **Publications:** The Road from La Cueva (novel), 2008. Contributor to journals and periodicals. **Address:** Santa Fe Community College, 6401 Richards Ave., Santa Fe, NM 87508-4887, U.S.A.

ORTENBERG, Veronica. British/Romanian (born Romania), b. 1961. **Genres:** Anthropology/Ethnology, Art/Art History, Cultural/Ethnic Topics, Film, History, Intellectual History, Popular Culture, Theology/Religion, Women's Studies And Issues, Music. **Career:** Oxford University, St. Hugh's College, junior research fellow, 1987-89, British Academy postdoctoral fellow, 1989-92; European College for Adult Education, director, 1991-92; University of Durham, lecturer in medieval history, 1992-93; University of Wales, lecturer in medieval history, 1994-99; Victoria County History of England, editor, 1999-2005, county editor, 2005-; University College Northampton, Department of History, senior lecturer, 2005-; University of London, Victoria County History, staff. **Publications:** The English Church and the Continent in the Tenth and Eleventh Centuries: Cultural, Spiritual and Artistic Exchanges, 1992; In Search of the Holy Grail: The Quest for the Middle Ages, 2006. **Address:** Department of History, University College of Northampton, Park Campus, Broughton Green Rd., Northampton, NH NN2 7AL, England. **Online address:** veronica.ortenberg@mohist.ox.ac.uk

ORTH, John V. American (born United States), b. 1947. **Genres:** Young Adult Non-fiction, History. **Career:** U.S. Third Circuit Court of Appeals, law clerk, 1977-78; University of North Carolina, assistant professor, 1978-81, associate professor of law, 1981-84, associate dean, 1985-86, William Rand Kenan, Jr. professor of law, 1993 . Writer. **Publications:** NONFICTION: The Judicial Power of the United States: The Eleventh Amendment in American History, 1987; Combination and Conspiracy: A Legal History of Trade Unionism, 1721-1906, 1991; The North Carolina State Constitution: A Reference Guide, 1993; The North Carolina State Constitution: With History and Commentary, 1995; Due Process of Law: A Brief History, 2003; How Many Judges Does It Take to Make a Supreme Court? And Other Essays on Law and the Constitution, 2006; Reappraisals in the Law of Property, 2010; North Carolina State Constitution, 2011. **Address:** University of North Carolina School of Law, Van Hecke-Wettach Hall, 160 Ridge Rd.,CB 3380, Chapel Hill, NC 27599-3380, U.S.A. **Online address:** jvorth@email.unc.edu

ORTH, Lucia. Italian (born Italy), b. 1953. **Genres:** Novels. **Career:** Haskell Indian Nations University, faculty. Writer. **Publications:** Baby Jesus Pawnshop (novel), 2008. **Address:** Trento, Italy. **Online address:** lucia.orth@gmail.com

ORTIZ, Paul. American (born United States), b. 1964. **Genres:** History. **Career:** Duke University, research coordinator of "Behind the Veil" documentary project, 1996-2001, visiting assistant professor of history and documentary studies, 2000-01; University of California, associate professor of community studies, 2001-08; University of Florida, Samuel Proctor Oral History Program, director, 2008-, Department of History, associate professor; KAOS radio program "Pathways to Justice", producer; United Farm Workers Union, labor activist. Writer. **Publications:** (Contrib.) The Human Cost of Food: Farmworkers' Lives, Labor and Advocacy, 2002; Emancipation Betrayed: The Hidden History of Black Organizing and White Violence in Florida from Reconstruction to the Bloody Election of 1920, 2005. Contributor to journals. **Address:** Department of History, University of Florida, 210 Keene-Flint Hall & 241 Pugh Hall, PO Box 117320, Gainesville, FL 32611-7320, U.S.A. **Online address:** rpeacock@history.ufl.edu

ORTIZ-TAYLOR, Sheila. American (born United States), b. 1939. **Genres:** Novels, Poetry, Gay And Lesbian Issues. **Career:** Florida State University, professor of English, 1973-2006, professor emerita, 2006-. Writer. **Publications:** NOVELS: Faultline, 1982; Spring Forward/Fall Back, 1985; Southbound, 1990; Coachella (novel), 1998; Out Rageous, 2006; Assisted Living, 2007; Homestead, 2011. OTHERS: Slow Dancing at Miss Polly's (poetry), 1989; Imaginary Parents (memoir), 1996. **Address:** Department of English, Florida State University, Tallahassee, FL 32306, U.S.A. **Online address:** sortiztaylor@me.com

ORTNER, Robert. American (born United States), b. 1927. **Genres:** Economics, Mathematics/Statistics, Money/Finance, Business/Trade/Industry, Politics/Government. **Career:** University of Pennsylvania, lecturer in economic statistics, 1955-62; Carl M. Loeb, economist, 1962-64; Rhodes and Co., economist, 1962-64; Bank of New York, senior vice-president and chief economist, 1965-81; North American Reinsurance Corp., director, 1973-81, 1989-; U.S. Department of Commerce, chief economist, 1981-86, under secretary for economic affairs, 1986-89, Bureau of the Census, director, Bureau of Economic Analysis and Office of Productivity, Technology and Innovation, director, 1986-89; U.S. Air Force, operations research consultant. Writer. **Publications:** Voodoo Deficits, 1990. Contributor to periodicals. **Address:** 374 White Oak Ridge Rd., Short Hills, NJ 07078, U.S.A.

ORTNER, Sherry B(eth). American (born United States), b. 1941. **Genres:** Anthropology/Ethnology, Cultural/Ethnic Topics, History, Social Sciences, Women's Studies And Issues, Philosophy, Archaeology/Antiquities, Psychology, Psychology. **Career:** Princeton University, lecturer in anthropology, 1969-70; Sarah Lawrence College, assistant professor of anthropology, 1971-77; Institute for Advanced Study, fellow, 1973-74; University of Michigan, associate professor, 1977-84, professor of anthropology, 1984-94; Center for Advanced Study in the Behavioral Sciences, fellow, 1982-83; University of California, professor of anthropology, 1994-96, distinguished professor of anthropology, 2004-; Columbia University, professor of anthropology, 1996-, chair, 2003-. Writer. **Publications:** (Contrib.) Women, Culture, and Society, 1974; Sherpas (documentary film), 1977; Sherpas Through Their Rituals, 1978; High Religion: A Cultural and Political History of Sherpa Buddhism, 1989; La Teoría Antropológica Desde losAños Sesenta, 1993; Making Gender: The Politics and Erotics of Culture, 1996; Life and Death on Mt. Everest: Sherpas and Himalayan Mountaineering, 1999; New Jersey Dreaming: Capital, Culture, and the Class of '58, 2003; Anthropology and Social Theory: Culture, Power, and the Acting Subject, 2006. EDITOR: (with H. Whitehead) Sexual Meanings: The Cultural Construction of Gender and Sexuality, 1981; (with N.B. Dirks and G. Eley) Culture/Power/History: A Reader in Contemporary Social Theory, 1994; Fate of Culture: Geertz and Beyond, 1999. **Address:** Department of Anthropology, University of California, Los Angeles,

341 Haines Hall, PO Box 951553, Los Angeles, CA 90095-1553, U.S.A. **Online address:** sortner@anthro.ucla.edu

ORTON, Anthony. British (born England), b. 1937. **Genres:** Education, Mathematics/Statistics, Young Adult Non-fiction, Education. **Career:** Colne Valley High School, teacher, 1960-70; Edge Hill College of Higher Education, senior lecturer, 1971-74; University of Leeds, faculty, 1974-2001. Writer. **Publications:** (Co-author) Mathematics in Biology, 1981; Learning Mathematics, 1987, 3rd ed., 2004; (with L. Frobisher) Insights into Teaching Mathematics, 1996; (co-author) Learning to Teach Number, 1999; (with L. Frobisher, A. Frobisher and J. Orton) Learning to Teach Shape and Space, 2007. EDITOR: Studies in Mechanics Learning, 1985; (with J. Jagger) The Composition of Forces and the Problem of Vectors, 1990; (with G. Wain) Issues in Teaching Mathematics, 1994; Pattern in the Teaching and Learning of Mathematics, 1999. **Address:** Centre for Studies in Science, Mathematics Education, University of Leeds, Leeds, WY LS2 9JT, England. **Online address:** a.orton@education.leeds.ac.uk

ORTTUNG, Robert W. American (born United States), b. 1964. **Genres:** International Relations/Current Affairs, History, Politics/Government. **Career:** Open Media Research Institute, senior research analyst, 1995-97; East West Institute, head of regional studies, 1997-; Jefferson Institute, staff; American University, Transnational Crime and Corruption Center, staff; Swiss Federal Institute of Technology, professor, Center for Security Studies, director; Resource Security Institute, president; George Washington University, Institute for European, Russian, and Eurasian Studies, assistant director. Writer. **Publications:** From Leningrad to St. Petersburg: Democratization in a Russian City, 1995; (with L. Belin) The Russian Parliamentary Elections of 1995: The Battle for the Duma, 1997; (ed.) The Republics and Regions of the Russian Federation: A Guide to Politics, Policies and Leaders, 2000; (ed. with P. Reddaway) Dynamics of Russian Politics: Putin's Reform of Federal-Regional Relations, 2004; (ed. with A. Wenger and J. Perovic) Russian Business Power: The Role of Russian Business in Foreign and Security Relations, 2006; (ed. with A. Makarychev) National Counter-Terrorism Strategies: Legal, Institutional, and Public Policy Dimensions in the U.S., U.K., France, Turkey, and Russia, 2006; (ed. with A. Latta) Russia's Battle with Crime, Corruption and Terrorism, 2008; (ed. with A. Wenger and J. Perovic) Russian Energy Power and Foreign Relations: Implications for Conflcit and Cooperation, 2009; (ed. with A. Wenger and J. Perovic) Energy and the Transformation of International Relations: Toward a New Producer-Consumer Framework, 2009. **Address:** Resource Security Institute, 1514 N Longfellow St., Arlington, VA 22205, U.S.A. **Online address:** rorttung@gmail.com

OSBORN, David (D.). (David E. Osborn). American (born United States), b. 1923. **Genres:** Novels, Plays/Screenplays, Mystery/Crime/Suspense, Young Adult Fiction, Theology/Religion. **Career:** Test pilot, television director, screenwriter and novelist. **Publications:** The Glass Tower, 1971; Open Season, 1974; The French Decision, 1980; Love and Treason, 1982; Jessica and the Crocodile Knight, 1984; Heads, 1985; Murder on Martha's Vineyard, 1988; Murder on the Chesapeake, 1992; Murder in the Napa Valley, 1993; The Last Pope, 2004. **Address:** c/o Robert G. Diforio, D4EO Literary Agency, 7 Indian Valley Rd., Weston, CT 06883, U.S.A.

OSBORN, David E. *See* **OSBORN, David (D.).**

OSBORN, Ian. American (born United States), b. 1946?. **Genres:** Psychology, Medicine/Health, Autobiography/Memoirs. **Career:** University of Iowa, medical resident; Centre Community Hospital, State College, physician, 1980-90; Pennsylvania State University, professor of psychiatry and department head, director of mental health, 1980-90; Clearfield-Jefferson Mental Health Center, psychiatrist, 1990-2000; University of New Mexico, psychiatrist, 2000-, assistant professor. Writer. **Publications:** Tormenting Thoughts and Secret Rituals: The Hidden Epidemic of Obsessive-Compulsive Disorder, 1998; Can Christianity Cure Obsessive-Compulsive Disorder?: A Psychiatrist Explores the Role of Faith in Treatment, 2008. **Address:** c/o Regina Ryan, Regina Ryan Publishing Enterprises Inc., 251 Central Pk. W, New York, NY 10024, U.S.A. **Online address:** iosborn@salud.unm.edu

OSBORN, Karen. American (born United States), b. 1954. **Genres:** Poetry, Novels, Young Adult Fiction. **Career:** Arkansas Poetry in the Schools, poet, 1979-83, director, 1982-83; Clemson University, instructor of English, 1983-87; University of Kentucky, part-time instructor of English, 1988-93. Clark Equipment Inc., technical writer, 1990; Mount Holyoke College, visiting assistant professor in English. Novelist and poet. **Publications:** NOVELS: Patchwork, 1991; Between Earth and Sky, 1996; River Road: A Novel, 2002. Works appear in anthologies. Contributor to periodicals. **Address:** Mount Holyoke College, 34 8 Park St., South Hadley, MA 01075, U.S.A. **Online address:** karenosborn@comcast.net

OSBORN, Susan (E.). American (born United States), b. 1954. **Genres:** Antiques/Furnishings, Novels, Fash Ion/Costume, Homes/Gardens, Writing/Journalism, Business/Trade/Industry. **Career:** Empire State Labor College, instructor in writing, 1983-84; State University of New York College, instructor in writing, 1984-85; Rutgers University, visiting lecturer, 1985-90; The New School for Social Research, instructor in writing, 1996-97; Purdue University, editor. **Publications:** Kitchen Antiques, 1980; Pine, 1980; A Collector's Guide to Glass, 1981; A Collector's Guide to Wicker, 1981; The Book of Country Living, 1981; The Free Things Series: Teachers, Gardeners, Campers, 1982; (ed.) The Great American Guide to Diet and Health, 1982; The Information Age Sourcebook, 1982; The Black Woman's Daybook, 1983; American Rustic Furniture, 1984; Real Clothes, 1984; (co-author) The Official Redhead Handbook, 1984; Dial An Expert: The Consumer's Sourcebook of Free and Low-Cost Expertise Available by Phone, 1986; Surviving the Wreck, 1993; What's in a Name?, 1999; (ed. and contrib.) Elizabeth Bowen: New Critical Perspectives, 2009. **Address:** c/o Philip Lief, Philip Lief Group, 6 W 20th St., New York, NJ 10011, U.S.A. **Online address:** susosborn@patmedia.net

OSBORNE, Charles. British/Australian (born Australia), b. 1927. **Genres:** Novellas/Short Stories, Poetry, Literary Criticism And History, Music, Biography, Translations, Language/Linguistics, Autobiography/Memoirs, Autobiography/Memoirs. **Career:** Ballad Bookshop, co-owner, 1947-51; writer and editor, 1953-; British Broadcasting Corp., broadcaster of musical and literary programs, 1957-; London Magazine, assistant editor, 1958-66; Alan Ross Ltd., chief editor, 1965-; Arts Council of Great Britain, assistant, 1966-71, literature director, 1971-86; Poetry Intl., director, 1967-; Daily Telegraph, chief theatre critic, 1986-91. **Publications:** EDITOR: Australian Stories of Today, 1961; Opera 1966, 1966; Twelve Poets, 1967; Australia, New Zealand and the South Pacific: A Handbook, 1970; Letters of Giuseppe Verdi, 1972; (and intro.) Richard Wagner' Stories and Essays, 1973; The Bram Stoker Bedside Companion, 1973; New Poems, 1973; (with P. Porter) New Poetry: An Anthology, 1975; The Dictionary of Composers, 1978; (and comp. with K. Thomson) Klemperer Stories: Anecdotes, Sayings and Impressions of Otto Klemperer, 1980; An Anthology of Poetry for Shakespeare, 1988. OTHERS: (with B. Brophy and M. Levey) Fifty Works of English and American Literature We Could Do Without, 1967; Kafka, 1967; Swansong, 1968; The Complete Operas of Verdi, 1969; Ned Kelly, 1970; The Concert Song Companion: A Guide to the Classical Repertoire, 1974; Richard Wagner and His World in UK as Wagner and His World, 1977; Verdi, 1978; The Complete Operas of Mozart: A Critical Guide, 1978; (trans.) Frida Leider, Playing My Part, 1978; Rigoletto: A Guide to the Opera, 1979; W.H. Auden: The Life of a Poet, 1979; The Opera House Album: A Collection of Turn-of-the Century Postcards, 1979; The Complete Operas of Puccini: A Critical Guide, 1981; (trans.) Schnitzler, The Round Dance and Other Plays, 1982; The Life and Crimes of Agatha Christie, 1982; The World Theatre of Wagner: A Celebration of One Hundred Fifty Years of Wagner Productions, 1982; The Dictionary of Opera, 1983; How to Enjoy Opera, 1983; Collected Poems, 1941-81, 1984; Letter to W.H. Auden and Other Poems, 1984; Schubert and His Vienna, 1985; Giving It Away: The Memoirs of an Uncivil Servant, 1986; Verdi: A Life in the Theatre, 1987; The Complete Operas of Richard Strauss, 1988; Max Oldaker, 1988; Favourite Love Poems, 1988; The Complete Operas of Richard Wagner, 1991; The Bel Canto Operas of Rossini, Donizetti and Bellini, 1994; Black Coffee, 1998; The Pink Danube: A Novel, 1999; (adapter) Spider's Web: Agatha Christie, 2000; Importance of Being Earnest, 2000; Opera Lover's Companion, 2004. Contributor to periodicals. **Address:** John Johnson Ltd., 45-47 Clerkenwell Green, London, GL EC1R 0HT, England.

OSBORNE, David. *See* **SILVERBERG, Robert.**

OSBORNE, Frances. British (born England), b. 1969. **Genres:** Biography, Novels, History. **Career:** Journalist, barrister and biographer. **Publications:** Lilla's Feast: A True Story of Food, Love, and War in the Orient, 2004; The Bolter: Idina Sackville, the Woman Who Scandalised 1920's Society and Became White Mischief's Infamous Seductress, 2008 in US as The Bolter, 2009. Contributor to newspapers and periodicals. **Address:** c/o Melanie Jackson,

Melanie Jackson Agency, 41 W 72nd St., Ste. 3F, New York, NY 10023, U.S.A.

OSBORNE, Milton (Edgeworth). Australian (born Australia), b. 1936. **Genres:** Area Studies, History, Politics/Government. **Career:** University of Sydney, temporary lecturer, 1962-63; Monash University, senior lecturer and associate professor of history, 1967-71; American University, associate professor of history, 1972-74; British Institute in South-East Asia, director, 1975-79; Asia Branch, Office of National Assessments, head, 1982-93; Australian National University, visiting fellow, adjunct professor, 1993-; Lowy Institute for International Policy, visiting fellow, 2004-. Writer and consultant. **Publications:** Singapore and Malaysia, 1964; Strategic Hamlets in South Viet-Nam, 1965; Southeast Asian Reactions to Possible Alternative American Policies in Asia, 1968; (with D.K. Wyatt) The Abridged Cambodian Chronicle: A Thai version of Cambodian History, 1968; The French Presence in Cochinchina and Cambodia: Rule and Response (1859-1905), 1969; Region of Revolt: Focus on Southeast Asia, 1970; Politics and Power in Cambodia, 1974; River Road to China: The Mekong River Expedition, 1866-1873, 1975; From Conviction to Anxiety: The French Self-Image in Vietnam, 1976; Southeast Asia: An Introductory History, 1979, rev. ed., 2000; Before Kampuchea: Preludes to Tragedy, 1979; Refugees: Four Political Case-studies, 1981; (ed.) Ho Chi Minh, 1982; Southeast Asia: An Illustrated Introductory History, 1985; Fear and Fascination in the Tropics: A Reader's Guide to French Fiction in Indochina, 1986; Sihanouk: Prince of Light, Prince of Darkness, 1994; River Road to China: The Search for the Sources of the Mekong, 1866-73, 1996; Strategic Hamlets in South Viet-Nam: A Survey and Comparison, 1997; The Mekong: Turbulent Past, Uncertain Future, 2000; (with C. Summer) Arts of Southeast Asia: From the Powerhouse Museum Collection, 2001; Exploring Southeast Asia: A Traveller's History of the Region, 2002; (trans.) T. Zephir, Angkor: A Tour of the Monuments, 2004; River at Risk: The Mekong and the Water Politics of China and Southeast Asia, 2004; Phnom Penh: A Cultural History, 2008; (foreword) Writing from Asia, 2010. **Address:** The Lowy Institute for International Policy, 31 Bligh St., Sydney, NW 2000, Australia. **Online address:** mosborne@zip.com.au

OSBORNE, Roy Martin. British (born England), b. 1948. **Genres:** Art/Art History. **Career:** New Constructivists, artist. Writer and educator. **Publications:** Lights and Pigments, 1980; From Prism to Paintbox, 1989; The Cycad Collection of the Durban Botanic Gardens, 1993; Teaching Colour in Art, 1995; (intro.) On Colours: 1528, 2002; Color Influencing Form, 2004. EDITOR: The Color Compendium, 1989; Colour and Humanism, 2003; (with T. Walters) Cycad Classification, 2004; (and comp.) Books on Colour 1500-2000, 2004; (with A.P. Vovides and D.W. Stevenson) Proceedings of Cycad 2005, 2007; His Life and Work, 2009; Colour Symbolism, 2009; Colour Engrained in the Mind, 2010. **Address:** 17 Hepplestone Close, Dover Park Dr., London, GL SW15 5DE, England. **Online address:** art.school@virgin.net

OSBORNE, Thomas M. American (born United States), b. 1972?. **Genres:** Philosophy, Cultural/Ethnic Topics. **Career:** Duke University, instructor in philosophy, 1999-2001; Pontifical Institute of Mediaeval Studies, Gilson fellow, 2001-02; University of Nevada, visiting assistant professor, 2002-03; University of St. Thomas, Center for Thomistic Studies, assistant professor, 2003-09, associate professor, 2009-. Writer. **Publications:** Love of Self and Love of God in Thirteenth-Century Ethics, 2005. Contributor to journals. **Address:** Center for Thomistic Studies, University of St. Thomas, 3800 Montrose, Houston, TX 77006-4626, U.S.A.

OSBORNE, Will. American (born United States), b. 1949. **Genres:** Children's Fiction, Young Adult Fiction, Plays/Screenplays, Songs/Lyrics And Libretti, Children's Non-fiction, Young Adult Non-fiction, Children's Nonfiction, Natural History, Natural History. **Career:** Actor, 1972-. Writer. **Publications:** 13 Ghosts: Strange but True Stories, 1988; (with A. Herrea) Smoke & Mirrors (play), 1993. WITH M.P. OSBORNE: The Deadly Power of Medusa, 1988; Jason and the Argonauts, 1988; Dinosaurs, 2000; Knights and Castles, 2000; Mummies and Pyramids: A Nonfiction Companion to Mummies in the Morning, 2001; Pirates, 2001; Rain Forests: A Nonfiction Companion to Afternoon on the Amazon, 2001; Space, 2002; Titanic: A Nonfiction Companion to Tonight on the Titanic, 2002; Twisters and Other Terrible Storms: A Nonfiction Companion to Twister on Tuesday, 2003; Time to Dance, 2003; Sleeping Bobby, 2005. **Address:** Sheldon Fogelman Agency Inc., 10 E 40th St., New York, NY 10016-0200, U.S.A.

OSBORNE-MCKNIGHT, Juilene. American (born United States) **Genres:** Novels. **Career:** DeSales University, assistant professor. Writer and educator. **Publications:** NOVELS: I Am of Irelaunde: A Novel of Patrick and Osian, 2000; Daughter of Ireland, 2002; Bright Sword of Ireland, 2004; Song of Ireland, 2006. **Address:** DeSales University, 2755 Station Ave., Center Valley, PA 18034, U.S.A. **Online address:** juilene@jmcknight.com

OSEN, James L. American (born United States), b. 1934. **Genres:** History, Autobiography/Memoirs, Biography, Theology/Religion. **Career:** High school English teacher, 1958-59; Beloit College, instructor, professor of history, 1962-, now Corlis professor emeritus; Newberry Library, faculty fellow in humanities, 1967-68, fellow, 1983. Writer. **Publications:** Prophet and Peacemaker: The Life of Adolphe Monod, 1984; Royalist Political Thought during the French Revolution, 1995. Contributor to journals. **Address:** Department of History, Beloit College, Rm. 103, 718 Church St., Beloit, WI 53511, U.S.A.

OSER, Marie. American (born United States), b. 1946. **Genres:** Food And Wine, Medicine/Health, Sports/Fitness. **Career:** Childbirth Education Association, counselor for pregnant and newly delivered mothers, 1980-83; Time, Education Program, marketing and educator support representative, 1984-87; VegTV Inc. (television network), producer, president, chief executive officer; freelance writer, 1990-; Ecomii L.L.C., managing editor. **Publications:** Luscious Low-Fat Desserts, 1994; Soy of Cooking: Easy-to-Make Vegetarian, Low-Fat, Fat-Free, and Antioxidant-Rich Gourmet Recipes, 1996; More Soy Cooking: Healthful Renditions of Classic Traditional Meals, 2000; The Enlightened Kitchen: Eat Your Way to Better Health, 2002. Contributor to magazines and newspapers. **Address:** c/o Author Mail, John Wiley & Sons Inc., 111 River St., Hoboken, NJ 07030-5774, U.S.A. **Online address:** marie@veggiechef.com

OSERS, Ewald. British/Czech (born Czech Republic), b. 1917. **Genres:** Poetry, Translations. **Career:** Translators Association, chair, 1971, 1980-81, 1983-84; Translators' Guild, chair, 1975-79; Institute of Linguists, vice-chair, 1975-80; World Congresses of Translators, leader of British delegation, 1977, 1981, 1984, 1987; International Federation of Translators, vice-president, 1977-81, 1984-87; Babel, editorial director, 1979-87; Harvard University, lecturer and translation workshop leader; Brown University, lecturer and translation workshop leader; Cornell University, lecturer and translation workshop leader; Georgetown University, lecturer and translation workshop leader; Brandeis University, lecturer and translation workshop leader; Rutgers University, lecturer and translation workshop leader; International PEN, fellow; Institute of Translation and Interpreting, fellow. **Publications:** (Ed. and trans. with J.K. Montgomery) Modern Czech Poetry: An Anthology, 1945; (with F. Giffin) The Boys' Book of Modern Chemical Wonders, 1966 in UK as The Burke Book of Modern Chemical Wonders; (ed. and trans.) O. Lysohorsky, Selected Poems, 1971; Voices from across the Water: Translations from Twelve Languages by Ewald Osers, 1985; Arrive Where We Started (poems), 1995; Snows of Yesteryear: A Translator's Story, 2007. TRANSLATOR: (with G. Theiner) Three Czech Poets: Vitezslav Nezval, Antonin Bartusek, Josef Hanzlik, 1971; R. Kunze, With the Volume Turned Down, and Other Poems, 1973; Contemporary German Poetry, 1976; R. Auslaender, Selected Poems, 1977; R. Langer, Wounded No Doubt: Selected Poems, 1979; N. Kuchak, A Hundred and One Hayrens, 1979; J. Seifert, The Plague Column, 1979; W.H. Fritz, Without Remission: Selected Poems, 1981; (with H. Hammelmann) The Correspondence between Richard Strauss and Hugo Von Hofmannsthal, 1981; S. Haffner, The Meaning of Hitler, 1983; Seifert, An Umbrella from Piccadilly, 1983; M. Holub, On the Contrary, and Other Poems, 1984; N. Vaptsarov, Nineteen Poems, 1984; K. Capek, War with the Newts, 1985, new trans., 1990; L. Levchev, Stolen Fire: Selected Poems, 1986; (with G. Gibian) Seifert, The Selected Poetry of Jaroslav Seifert, 1986; (with J. Milner and G. Theiner) Holub, The Fly, 1987; (with J. Cejka and M. Cernik) New Czech Poetry, 1988; V. Janovic, The House of the Tragic Poet, 1988; M. Matevski, Footprints of the Wind: Selected Poems, 1988; (with I. Milner, J. Milner and G. Theiner) Holub, Poems before and After: Collected English Translations, 1990; R. Safranski, Schopenhauer and the Wild Years of Philosophy, 1990; (with P.S. Falla and D.S. McMurry) W. Deist, Germany and the Second World War, vol. I: The Build-up of German Aggression, 1991; (with D.S. McMurry) K.A. Maier, vol. II: Germany's Initial Conquests in Europe, 1991; (trans.) Ivan Klima, Love and Garbage (novel), 1991; (with I. Milner and J. Milner) J. Hanzlik, Selected Poems, 1992; M. Kruger, The End of the Novel, 1992; The Man in the Ice, 1994; H. Piontek, Selected Poems, 1994; (with D.S. McMurry and L. Willmot) G. Schreiber, B. Stegemann,

D. Vogel, vol. III: The Mediterranean, South-East Europe, and North Africa, 1995; A. Folsing, Albert Einstein: A Biography, 1997; R. Safranski, Martin Heidegger: A Master from Germany, 1997; H. Harrer, Return to Tibet: Tibet after the Chinese Occupation, 1998; A. Lustig, Levely Green Eyes: A Novel, 2002; M. Rufus, And That's the Truth, 2006; Snows of Yesteryear: A Translator's Story: An Autobiography, 2007; V. Nezval, Prague with Fingers of Rain, 2009. Works appear in anthologies. **Address:** 33 Reades Ln., Sonning Common, Reading, BR RG4 9LL, England. **Online address:** osers@aol.com

OSGOOD, Kenneth. (Kenneth Alan Osgood). American (born United States), b. 1971. **Genres:** History, Military/Defense/Arms Control, Autobiography/Memoirs, Politics/Government. **Career:** University of California-Santa Barbara, Department of History, lead teaching assistant, 1995-98, Center for Cold War Studies, associate coordinator, 1997-99, graduate instructor in writing program, 1998-99; University of California-San Diego, Department of History, lecturer, 2001; Florida Atlantic University, assistant professor of history, 2001-, Larkin Symposium, director; Ohio State University, Mershon Center, postdoctoral fellow, 2003-04; University College Dublin, Mary Ball Washington chair in American history, 2006-07. Writer. **Publications:** (Ed., intro. and contrib. with K. Larres) The Cold War after Stalin's Death: A Missed Opportunity for Peace?, 2006; Total Cold War: Eisenhower's Secret Propaganda Battle at Home and Abroad, 2006; (ed. with B.C. Etheridge) The United States and Public Diplomacy: New Directions in Cultural and International History, 2010; (ed. with A.K. Frank) Selling War in a Media Age: The Presidency and Public Opinion in the American Century, 2010. Contributor of articles to books and journals. **Address:** Department of History, Florida Atlantic University, 777 Glades Rd., PO Box 3091, Boca Raton, FL 33431-6424, U.S.A. **Online address:** kosgood@fau.edu

OSGOOD, Kenneth Alan. *See* **OSGOOD, Kenneth.**

O'SHAUGHNESSY, Andrew J. (Andrew Jackson O'Shaughnessy). American/British (born England), b. 1959. **Genres:** History. **Career:** Oxford University, Lincoln College, lecturer, 1986-87; Davidson College, tutor, 1987-90; The Forest School, teacher, 1988; Eton College, master, 1988-89; Southern Methodist University, visiting assistant professor of American history, 1989-90; University of Wisconsin, assistant professor, 1990-97, associate professor, 1997-2002, professor of American history, 2002, Department of History, chair, 1998-2003; University of Virginia, Corcoran Department of History, professor, 2002-; Thomas Jefferson Foundation, Robert H. Smith International Center for Jefferson Studies, Saunders director, 2003-, staff. Writer. **Publications:** (As Andrew Jackson O'Shaughnessy) An Empire Divided: The American Revolution and the British Caribbean, 2000; (ed. with L.J. Sadosky, P. Nicolaisen and P.S. Onuf) The Old World, New World: America and Europe in the Age of Jefferson, 2010. **Address:** Thomas Jefferson Foundation, Ivy Business Pk., 556 Dettor Rd., Ste. 107, PO Box 316, Charlottesville, VA 22903, U.S.A. **Online address:** ao2k@virginia.edu

O'SHAUGHNESSY, Andrew Jackson. *See* **O'SHAUGHNESSY, Andrew J.**

O'SHAUGHNESSY, Ellen Cassels. American (born United States), b. 1937. **Genres:** Education, How-to Books, Human Relations/Parenting, Communications/Media, Literary Criticism And History. **Career:** Monterey Peninsula Unified School District, teacher's aide and art instructor, 1968-74; Pacific Grove Unified School District, school teacher and teacher's aide, 1974-82, special education consultant, 1984-85; Psychological Services, intern, 1976; Synthesis (publishing company), owner, writer and publisher, 1984-; Gift Horse Gallery, owner and artist, 1990; Easter Seals, staff, 1993-95; Monterey Peninsula Unified School, special education assistant, 1993-95. **Publications:** Teaching Art to Children, 1974; Synthesis (symbolic-language series for developmentally disabled and non-reading adults), 1981; You Love to Cook Book (symbolic-language cookbook), 1983; I Could Ride on the Carousel Longer, 1989; (with D. Garner) Somebody Called Me a Retard Today... and My Heart Felt Sad, 1992; The Easiest Piano Lesson-in the Whole Universe!, 1994. Contributor to periodicals. **Address:** PO Box 51063, Pacific Grove, CA 93950, U.S.A.

O'SHEA, Donal B. American/Canadian (born Canada) **Genres:** Novels, Mathematics/Statistics. **Career:** Mt. Holyoke College, assistant professor, 1980-86, associate professor, 1986-91, professor of mathematics, 1991-, Elizabeth T. Kennan professor of mathematics and statistics, dean of mathematics faculty, 1998-, vice president of academic affairs; University of Kaiserslautern, visiting professor, 1988-89; University of Hawai, visiting professor, 1991-92, 1997-98; University of Edinburgh, visiting professor, 2004-05; University of Miami, visiting professor, 2004-05. Writer. **Publications:** An Exposition of Catastrophe Theory and Its Applications to Phase Transitions, 1977; (with D. Cox and J. Little) Ideals, Varieties, and Algorithms: An Introduction to Computational Algebraic Geometry and Commutative Algebra, 1992, 3rd ed., 2007; (with D. Cox and J. Little) Using Algebraic Geometry, 1998, 2nd ed., as Using Algebraic Geometry, 2005; The Poincare Conjecture: In Search of the Shape of the Universe, 2007. **Address:** Dean of Faculty Office, Mt. Holyoke College, 102 Mary Lyon Hall, 50 College St., South Hadley, MA 01075, U.S.A. **Online address:** doshea@mtholyoke.edu

O'SHEA, Kathleen A. American (born United States), b. 1944. **Genres:** Bibliography, Women's Studies And Issues. **Career:** Parochial School, teacher, 1964-65; teacher, 1965-75, 1977-79, 1984-91; Beacon Lodge Camp for the Blind, counselor and director of adult unit, 1975-76; Migrant Education Program, counselor and teacher, 1979-81; Innisfree Village, counselor, 1979-85; Parochial High School, teacher of English and Spanish, 1980-83; Beardall Senior Center, creator and director of Elder theatre, 1984-89; Florida Peace and Justice Coalition, interpreter, 1984-89. Writer. **Publications:** (Contrib.) Women Prisoners: A Forgotten Population, 1993; (comp. with B.R. Fletcher) Female Offenders: An Annotated Bibliography, 1997; Women and the Death Penalty in the United States, 1900-1998, 1999; Women on the Row: Revelations from Both Sides of the Bars, 2000. Contributor to books and periodicals. **Address:** 5505 Walnut Level Rd., Crozet, VA 22932-1633, U.S.A. **Online address:** sisterko@aol.com

O'SHEA, Mick. Australian (born Australia), b. 1975?. **Genres:** History, Reference, Travel/Exploration. **Career:** Wildside Asia, co-founder, chief executive officer; Mekong Descent Foundation, founder. Writer and eco-tourism consultant. **Publications:** Zootopia Tree (children's book), 2002; The Early Days of the Sex Pistols: Only Anarchists Are Pretty, 2004; (with A. Parker) And Now for Something Completely Digital: The Complete Illustrated Guide to Monty Python CDs and DVDs, 2006; In the Naga's Wake: The First Man to Navigate the Mekong, from Tibet to the South China Sea, 2007. **Address:** Mekong Descent Foundation, 200 Varden St., Kalgoorlie, WA 6430, Australia.

OSHEROW, Jacqueline. American (born United States), b. 1956. **Genres:** Poetry. **Career:** University of Utah, assistant professor of English, 1989-, professor of English, distinguished professor. Writer. **Publications:** Looking for Angels in New York (poems), 1988; Conversations with Survivors (poems), 1994; With a Moon in Transit, 1996; Dead Men's Praise, 1999; Hoopoe's Crown: Poems, 2005; Whitethorn: Poems, 2010. Works appear in anthologies. **Address:** Department of English, University of Utah, 3401 Languages & Communication Bldg., Rm. 3500, 255 S Central Campus Dr., Salt Lake City, UT 84112-0499, U.S.A. **Online address:** j.osherow@english.utah.edu

OSHINSKY, David M. American (born United States), b. 1944?. **Genres:** History, Law. **Career:** Rutgers University, professor; University of Texas, College of Liberal Arts, Department of History, distinguished visiting professor, professor, Jack S. Blanton chair. Writer. **Publications:** Senator Joseph McCarthy and the American Labor Movement, 1976; A Conspiracy So Immense: The World of Joe McCarthy, 1983; (with R.P. McCormick and D. Horn) The Case of the Nazi Professor, 1989; Worse Than Slavery: Parchman Farm and the Ordeal of Jim Crow Justice, 1996; A Conspiracy so Immense: The World of Joe McCarthy, 2005; Polio: An American Story, 2005; Capital Punishment on Trial: Furman V. Georgia and the Death Penalty in Modern America, 2010. **Address:** Department of History, University of Texas, 3.504 GAR, PO Box B7000, Austin, TX 78712-0220, U.S.A. **Online address:** oshinsky@mail.utexas.edu

O'SIADHAIL, Micheal. Irish (born Ireland), b. 1947. **Genres:** Poetry, Language/Linguistics. **Career:** Trinity College, lecturer, 1969-73; Dublin Institute for Advanced Studies, professor, 1974-87; University of Iceland, visiting professor, 1982; full-time writer, 1987-; Ireland Literature Exchange, chairman. **Publications:** POETRY: Springnight, 1983; The Image Wheel, 1985; The Chosen Garden, 1990; Hail! Madam Jazz: New and Selected Poems, 1992; A Fragile City, 1995; Our Double Time, 1998; Poems 1975-1995, 1999; The Gossamer Wall: Poems in Witness to the Holocaust, 2002; Love Life, 2005; Globe, 2007; Tongues, 2010. OTHERS: Córas Fuaimeanna na Gaeilge: Na canúintí Agus anCaighdeán, 1975; Téarmaí Tógálá Agus tís as Inis Meáin, 1978; Learning Irish, 1980, rev. ed. as Lehrbuch der Irischen Sprache, 1985;

Learning Irish: An Introductory Self-tutor, 1988; Modern Irish, 1989. **Address:** 5 Trimleston Ave., Booterstown, DU 4, Ireland. **Online address:** info@osiadhail.com

OSING, Gordon T. American (born United States), b. 1937. **Genres:** Poetry, Translations. **Career:** University of Memphis, English faculty, 1973, now professor emeritus; University of Hong Kong, senior Fulbright lecturer, 1989-90, 1990-91. Writer. **Publications:** (Co-author) Hello, Hello, 1975; Blooming Alone in Winter: Fifty Poems of Su Dong-Po, 1990; Forever Tonight at My Window: Thirty Ci of Li Qing-Zhao, 1991; Things That Never Happened: Fictions of Family Eros, 2004; Slaughtering the Buddha, 2010. POETRY: From the Boundary Waters, 1981; Town Down River, 1985; The Water Radical, 1999; The Jagger and the Loitering Lady, 1999; Crossing Against the Sun, 1999; Apo/Calypso: Lakeside in Delta Bluffs Woods, a Four Years Dao in the Blues: Poems and Journals, 2002; Meanwhile: Poems Within the Moment, 2011. EDITOR: The Good People of Gomorrah: A Memphis Miscellany, 1979; (and co-trans.) City at the End of Time, 1992; (and co-trans.) The Mists of My Heart: Poems and Prose by Shu Ting, 1994. **Address:** Department of English, University of Memphis, 467 Patterson Hall, Memphis, TN 38152-3530, U.S.A.

OSMER, Richard Robert. American (born United States), b. 1950. **Genres:** Theology/Religion, Essays. **Career:** Ordained Presbyterian minister; Princeton Theological Seminary, Department of Practical Theology, Thomas W. Synnott professor of Christian education. Writer. **Publications:** A Teachable Spirit: Recovering the Teaching Office in the Church, 1990; Teaching for Faith: A Guide for Teachers of Adult Classes, 1992; Confirmation: Presbyterian Practices in Ecumenical Perspective, 1996; (with F.L. Schweitzer) Religious Education between Modernization and Globalization: New Perspectives on the United States and Germany, 2003; The Teaching Ministry of Congregations, 2005; Practical Theology: An Introduction, 2008. EDITOR: (with L.B. Lewis and A.S. Vaughn) Devotion and Discipline: Training for Presbyterian Leaders, 1999; (with L.B. Lewis and A.S. Vaughn) Foundations of Faith: Education for New Church Members, 1999; (with L.B. Lewis and A.S. Vaughn) Can We Talk?: Conversations for Faith: Teacher's Guide, 1999; (with F.L. Schweitzer) Developing a Public Faith: New Directions in Practical Theology: Essays in Honor of James W. Fowler, 2003; (with K.C. Dean) Youth, Religion and Globalization, 2006. **Address:** Department of Practical Theology, Princeton Theological Seminary, 23 Tennent Hall, 64 Mercer St., PO Box 821, Princeton, NJ 08542-0803, U.S.A. **Online address:** richard.osmer@ptsem.edu

OSMOND, John. Welsh (born Wales), b. 1946. **Genres:** Adult Non-fiction, History, Social Sciences, Geography. **Career:** Yorkshire Post, reporter; Western Mail, reporter, political correspondent, 1972-80; Arcade: Wales Fortnightly, editor, 1980-82; HTV Television, producer, 1982-88; Wales on Sunday, assistant editor, 1988-90; Well Area of Writers, chairperson, 1988-94; freelance writer and television producer, 1990-96; Institute of Welsh Affairs, director, 1996-; School of Public Policy, honorary senior research fellow; University of Wales Institute, fellow. **Publications:** The Centralist Enemy, 1974; Creative Conflict: The Politics of Welsh Devolution, 1977; Alternatives, 1984; Police Conspiracy?, 1984; Work in the Future: Alternatives to Unemployment, 1986; The Divided Kingdom, 1988; The Democratic Challenge, 1992; The Reality of Dyslexia, 1993; Welsh Europeans, 1995; Reforming the Lords and Changing Britain, 1998; Craft as Art: Projecting the Makers of Wales within the Global Economy, 2001; The Future of Welsh Devolution, 2002; Crossing the Rubicon: Coalition Politics Welsh Style, 2007. EDITOR: The Future of the Word, 1985; The National Question Again: Welsh Political Identity in the 1980s, 1985; A Parliament for Wales, 1994; The National Assembly Agenda, 1998; Period of De-Stabilisation: Monitoring the National Assembly: May to August 2001, 2001; (with J.B. Jones) Inclusive Government and Party Management: The National Assembly for Wales and the Work of its Committees, 2001; Building a Civic Culture, 2002; (with S. Cymru) Engaging with Europe, 2002; Birth of Welsh Democracy, 2003; Second Term Challenge, 2003; Welsh Politics Come of Age, 2005; Myths, Memories and Futures: The National Library and National Museum in the Story of Wales, 2007. **Address:** Institute of Welsh Affairs, 4 Cathedral Rd., Cardiff, CF11 9LJ, Wales. **Online address:** johnosmond@iwa.org.uk

OSMOND, Jonathan. British/Welsh (born Wales), b. 1953. **Genres:** Art/Art History, History. **Career:** Institute of Bavarian History, Theodor Heuss Research Fellow, 1977-78; University of Leicester, lecturer in history, 1979-93; Humboldt University, research fellow, 1993; Central European University, visiting professor, 1993; Cardiff University, professor of modern European history, 1994-96, head of department, 1996-2006, Cardiff Centre for Modern German History, director and pro vice-chancellor, 2007-; Potsdam University, Alexander von Humboldt Foundation, research fellow, 2007. Writer. **Publications:** German Reunification: A Reference Guide and Commentary, 1992; Rural Protest in the Weimar Republic: The Free Peasantry in the Rhineland and Bavaria, 1993; (ed. with P. Major) The Worker's and Peasant's State: Communism and Society in East Germany under Ulbricht 1945-71, 2002; (ed. with A. Cimdina) Power and Culture: Hegemony, Interaction, and Dissent, 2006. **Address:** Cardiff School of History and Archaeology, Cardiff University, Humanities Bldg., Colum Dr., Cardiff, CF10 3EU, United Kingdom. **Online address:** osmond@cardiff.ac.uk

OSOKINA, Elena A(leksandrovna). Russian (born Russia), b. 1959. **Genres:** History. **Career:** Russian Academy of Sciences, senior research associate, 1991-2002; University of North Carolina, faculty, 1995-96; Donaueschingen Academy, visiting lecturer, 1997; Harvard University, Davis Center for Russian Studies, postdoctoral fellow, 2000-01; Oberlin College, visiting assistant professor of history, 2001-03; Missouri State University, assistant professor, 2003-05; University of South Carolina, professor, 2005-. Writer. **Publications:** Hierarchy of Consumption: Life under the Stalinist Rationing System, 1928-1935, 1993; Behind the Facade of Stalin's Plenty, 1927-1940, 1998; Our Daily Bread: Socialist Distribution and the Art of Survival in Stalin's Russia, 1927-1941, 2001; Gold for Industrialization: Torgsin, 2009. Contributor to books and periodicals. **Address:** Department of Hitory, University of South Carolina, 218 Gambrell Hall, Columbia, SC 29208, U.S.A. **Online address:** osokina@mailbox.sc.edu

OSSERMAN, Robert. American (born United States), b. 1926. **Genres:** Mathematics/Statistics, Young Adult Fiction, Sciences. **Career:** University of Colorado, instructor, 1952-53; Stanford University, acting assistant professor, 1955-57, assistant professor, 1957-60, associate professor, 1960-66, professor of mathematics, 1966-94, chairman of maths department, 1973-79, Mellon professor of interdisciplinary studies, 1987-90, professor emeritus, 1994-; New York University Institute of Mathematical Sciences, member, 1957-58; Office of Naval Research, head of math branch, 1960-61; Harvard University, visiting lecturer and research associate, 1961-62; University of Paris, Fulbright lecturer, 1965-66; University of Warwick, fellow; Math Sciences Research Institute, member, 1983-84, deputy director, 1990-95, special projects director, 1995-. Writer. **Publications:** Two-Dimensional Calculus, 1968; A Survey of Minimal Surfaces, 1969, 2nd ed., 1986; (with D.A. Hoffman) The Geometry of the Generalized Gauss Map, 1980; Poetry of the Universe: A Mathematical Exploration of the Cosmos, 1995. EDITOR: (with S.S. Chern) Differential Geometry, Proceedings of the Symposium in Pure Mathematics, 1975; (with A. Weinstein) Geometry of the Laplace Operator, Proceedings of the Symposium in Pure Mathematics, 1980; Encyclopaedia of Mathematical Sciences, vol. IX0: Minimal Surfaces, 1997. Contributor to periodicals. **Address:** Mathematical Sciences Research Institute, 17 Gauss Way, Berkeley, CA 94720-5070, U.S.A.

OSTER, Clinton Victor. American (born United States), b. 1947. **Genres:** Air/Space Topics, Business/Trade/Industry, Transportation. **Career:** U.S. Public Health Service, National Institute for Occupational Safety and Health, engineer, 1969-71; U.S. Department of Labor, Office of the Assistant Secretary for Policy, Evaluation, and Research, budget analyst, 1972; Harvard University, research fellow in business administration, 1977-79, lecturer in economics, 1978-79, John F. Kennedy School of Government, research fellow, 1981-82; Indiana University, School of Public and Environmental Affairs, assistant professor, 1979-84, associate professor, 1984-88, professor of business and public and environmental affairs, 1988-2011, associate dean, 1989-92, 2005-08, professor emeritus of business and public and environmental affairs, 2011-, Center for Urban and Regional Analysis, associate director, 1982-85, Transportation Research Center, director, 1985-89, Highway and Transportation Management Institute, associate director, 1988-92, Faculty of Public Finance and Policy Analysis, chair, 1998-2004, Kelley School of Business, adjunct professor of business. Writer and consultant. **Publications:** The Financing of Hawaii's Highways, 1964; (ed. with J.R. Meyer) Airline Deregulation: The Early Experience, 1981; (co-author) Deregulation and the New Airline Entrepreneurs, 1984; (co-author) Deregulation and the Future of Intercity Passenger Travel, 1987; (with P. Forsyth) Free to Fly: Practical Airline Deregulation, 1987; (with J.S. Strong and C.K. Zorn) Why Airplanes Crash: Aviation Safety in a Changing World, 1992; (with C.F. Bonser and E.B. McGregor) Policy Choices and Public Action, 1996; (ed. with J.S. Hansen) Taking Flight: Education and Training for Aviation Careers, 1997; (with C.F. Bonser and E.B. McGregor) American Public Policy Problems: An Introductory Guide, 2000; (with J.S. Strong) Managing the Skies: Public Policy, Organization and Financing of Air Traffic Management, 2007. Contributor to journals. **Address:** School of Public and Environmental Affairs, Indiana University, Rm. 451, 1315 E 10th St., Bloomington, IN 47405, U.S.A. **Online address:** oster@indiana.edu

OSTERMAN, Paul. American (born United States) **Genres:** Business/Trade/Industry, Administration/Management. **Career:** Brooklyn College, assistant, 1971; Boston University, assistant professor of economics, associate professor of economics; Instituto de Empressa (Madrid), visiting professor, 1995-; Massachusetts Institute of Technology, Sloan School of Management, Department of human resources and management, associate professor, professor, Department of Behavioral and Policy Sciences, area head, 2001-03, deputy dean, 2003-07; Nanyang Technological University, professor of human resources and management; International Labor Review, co-editor, 2006-; Inter-American Development Bank, Consultant, 2008-; Jobs For the Future, director, 2008-; SEEDCO, Board advisors. Writer. **Publications:** (With R. Gross) Individualism: Man in Modern Society, 1971; (ed. with R. Gross) High School, 1971; (ed. with R. Gross) New Professionals, 1972; Getting Started: The Youth Labor Market, 1980; (ed.) Internal Labor Markets, 1984; Employment Futures: Reorganization, Dislocation, and Public Policy, 1988; Workforce Policies for the 1990s, 1989; (with R. Batt) Workplace Training Policy: Case Studies of State and Local Experiments, 1993; (with R. Batt) National Policy for Workplace Training: Lessons from State and Local Experiments, 1993; (with T.A. Kochan) The Mutual Gains Enterprise: Forging a Winning Partnership among Labor, Management, and Government, 1994; (ed.) Broken Ladders: Managerial Careers in the New Economy, 1996; Securing Prosperity: The American Labor Market: How It Has Changed and What to Do about It, 1999; (co-ed.) Working in America: A Blueprint for the New Labor Market, 2001; Gathering Power: The Future of Progressive Politics in America, 2003; Truth about Middle Managers: Who They are, how They Work, Why they Matter, 2008; Nuevas Fronteras del Management, 2009; Good Jobs America, 2011. **Address:** Sloan School of Management, Massachusetts Institute of Technology, Rm. E62-336, 100 Main St., Cambridge, MA 02142, U.S.A. **Online address:** osterman@mit.edu

OSTERWEIL, Adam. American (born United States), b. 1972?. **Genres:** Children's Fiction. **Career:** Springs Public School, teacher of English. Writer. **Publications:** The Comic Book Kid, 2001; The Amulet of Komondor, 2003; The Lost Treasure of Talus Scree, 2005; The Baseball Card Kid, 2009. **Address:** Springs School, 48 School St., East Hampton, NY 10036, U.S.A. **Online address:** adam@adamosterweil.com

OSTLER, Rosemarie. American (born United States), b. 1954. **Genres:** Bibliography. **Career:** Writer, etymologist and librarian. **Publications:** Theoretical Syntax, 1980- 1990: An Annotated and Classified Bibliography, 1992; Dewdroppers, Waldos, and Slackers: A Decade-by-Decade Guide to the Vanishing Vocabulary of the Twentieth Century, 2003; Let's Talk Turkey: The Stories behind America's Favorite Expressions, 2008. **Online address:** rostler@efn.org

OSTLUND, Lori. American (born United States), b. 1965?. **Genres:** Novellas/Short Stories. **Career:** California Art Institute, writing instructor. Writer. **Publications:** The Bigness of the World: Stories, 2009. Contributor to periodicals. **Address:** c/o Terra Chalberg, Susan Golomb Literary Agency, 540 President St., 3rd Fl., Brooklyn, NY 11215, U.S.A. **Online address:** lori@loriostlund.com

OSTOW, Micol. American (born United States), b. 1976. **Genres:** Romance/Historical, Novels, Young Adult Fiction, Children's Fiction, Literary Criticism And History. **Career:** Media Bistro, writing workshop, instructor; Simon and Schuster, editor. **Publications:** (Comp. with S. Brezenoff) The Quotable Slayer, 2003; Westminster Abby, 2005; Changeling Places, 2005; 30 Guys in 30 Days, 2005; Changeling Places: An Original Novel, 2005; (with N. Harlan) Mind your Manners, Dick and Jane, 2006; House of Shards, 2006; Emily Goldberg Learns to Salsa, 2006; Ultimate Travel Games, 2006; Crush du jour, 2007; (contrib.) First Kiss (Then Tell), 2007; Gettin' Lucky, 2007; Popular Vote, 2008; Golden Girl, 2009, Fashionista, 2009; So Punk Rock (and Other Ways to Disappoint Your Mother): A Novel, 2009; (with N. Harlan) Up Over Down Under, 2010; Family, 2011; What Would My Cellphone Do?, 2011. **Address:** c/o Author Mail, Simon Pulse/Simon and Schuster, 1230 Ave. of the Americas, New York, NY 10020, U.S.A. **Online address:** micol@micolostow.com

OSTRANDER, Rick. American (born United States), b. 1965?. **Genres:** Theology/Religion. **Career:** University of Notre Dame, adjunct instructor, 1993-95; Grand Canyon University, assistant professor of history, 1996-97; John Brown University, Department of History, assistant professor, 1997-2002, chair, 1999-, associate professor, 2002-, Division of Social and Behavioral Studies, chair, 2001-, dean of undergraduate studies, 2002-. Writer. **Publications:** The Life of Prayer in a World of Science: Protestants, Prayer and American Culture, 1870-1930, 2000; Head, Heart and Hand: John Brown University and Modern Evangelical Higher Education, 2003; Why College Matters to God: Academic Faithfulness and Christian Higher Education, 2009. Contributor to periodicals. **Address:** Office of Academic Affairs, John Brown University, 2000 W University St., Siloam Springs, AR 72761, U.S.A. **Online address:** jbuinfo@jbu.edu

OSTROM, Hans. American (born United States), b. 1954. **Genres:** Novels, Poetry, Education, Literary Criticism And History. **Career:** University of California, teaching assistant, 1977-80, assistant director of composition, 1981-82, lecturer, 1981-83; Johannes Gutenberg University, visiting lecturer, 1980-81; University of Puget Sound, distinguished professor of English, 1983-, Center for Writing across the Curriculum, director, 1984-88, Department of English, chair, African American Studies and English, professor of African American studies and English, 2008-, James Dolliver NEH distinguished teaching professor; Uppsala University, senior Fulbright lecturer, 1994. Writer. **Publications:** (With L.A. Morris and L.P. Young) The Living Language: A Reader, 1984; (with T. Lulofs) Leigh Hunt: A Reference Guide, 1985; (comp.) Lives and Moments: An Introduction to Short Fiction (anthology), 1991; Three to Get Ready (novel), 1991; (with W. Bishop) Water's Night: Poems (chapbook), 1992; Langston Hughes: A Study of the Short Fiction, 1993; Subjects Apprehended: Poems, 2000; (with W. Bishop and K. Haake) Metro: Journeys in Creative Writing, 2001; A Langston Hughes Encyclopedia, 2002; Coast Starlight: Collected Poems, 1976-2006, 2006; Honoring Juanita, 2010. EDITOR: (with M.T. Turnbull and R.F. Garratt) Spectrum: A Reader, 1987; (with W. Bishop) Colors of a Different Horse: Rethinking How We Teach Creative Writing, 1994; (ed. with W. Bishop) Genre and Writing, 1997; (with W. Bishop) The Subject is Story, 2003; (with D. Macey, Jr.) Greenwood Encyclopedia of African American Literature, 2005. Work appears in anthologies. Contributor of articles. **Address:** Department of English, University of Puget Sound, Howarth 328, 1500 N Warner St., Tacoma, WA 98416, U.S.A. **Online address:** ostrom@ups.edu

OSTROVSKY, Eugene. American/Russian (born Russia), b. 1938. **Genres:** Documentaries/Reportage, Translations, Adult Non-fiction, History. **Career:** U.S. Information Agency, Voice of America, international broadcaster, 1983-. Writer. **Publications:** The Modern Chess Sacrifice, 1978; Russian Doctor, 1984; (trans.) V. Golyakhovsky, The Price of Freedom: A Russian Doctor Immigrates to America, 1986; (trans.) Y.B. Shvets, Washington Station: My Life as a KGB Spy in America, 1994. **Address:** Voice of America, International Broadcasting Bureau, U.S. Information Agency, 330 Independence Ave. SW, Washington, DC 20237, U.S.A.

OSTROW, Joel M. American (born United States) **Genres:** Politics/Government, History. **Career:** Benedictine University, Department of Political Science, associate professor, professor and chair; Crain's Communications, Moscow correspondent. **Publications:** Comparing Post-Soviet Legislatures: A Theory of Institutional Design and Political Conflict, 2000; (with G.A. Satarov and I.M. Khakamada) The Consolidation of Dictatorship in Russia: An Inside View of the Demise of Democracy, 2007. **Address:** Department of Political Science, Benedictine University, 5700 College Rd., Lisle, IL 60532, U.S.A. **Online address:** jostrow@ben.edu

OSTROW, Ronald J. American (born United States), b. 1931. **Genres:** Criminology/True Crime, Law, Politics/Government, Adult Non-fiction. **Career:** Wall Street Journal, reporter, 1956-60; Business Week, assistant editor, 1961-62; Los Angeles Times, financial writer, 1962-65, Nieman fellow, 1965, Washington bureau, reporter, 1966-98. **Publications:** (With J. Nelson) The FBI and the Berrigans: The Making of a Conspiracy, 1972; (with G.B. Bell) Taking Care of the Law, 1982. **Address:** c/o Michael Hamilburg, Mitchell J. Hamilburg Agency, 8671 Wilshire Blvd., Ste. 500, Beverly Hills, CA 90211, U.S.A. **Online address:** ronjostrow@aol.com

OSTROWER, Gary B. American (born United States), b. 1939. **Genres:** History, Politics/Government, International Relations/Current Affairs. **Career:** Vassar College, instructor, 1967-68; Alfred University, professor of history, 1969-, Margaret and Barbara Hagar professor of humanities, 1996-99, Kruson distinguished professor, 2009-; University of Pennsylvania, visiting assistant professor, 1979-80; Alfred City, mayor, 1999-2005. Writer. **Publications:** Collective Insecurity: The United States and the League of Nations During the Early Thirties, 1979; The League of Nations: From 1919-1929, 1996; The United States and the United Nations: 1940 to 1998, 1998. **Address:** Department of Human Studies, Alfred University, Kanakadea Hall, 1 Saxon Dr., Alfred, NY 14802-1205, U.S.A. **Online address:** ostrower@alfred.edu

OSTROWSKI, Jan K. Polish (born Poland), b. 1947. **Genres:** History, Translations, Art/Art History. **Career:** Jagiellonian University, assistant professor, 1973-83, associate professor, 1983-91, professor of art history, 1991-; Wawel Royal Castle, director, 1989-. Writer. **Publications:** Arte popolare polacca, 1981; Anton Van Dyck et la peinture génoise du XVIIe siècle: Aux Sources du baroque dans un milieu artistique italien, 1981; Piotr Michalowski, 1985; Pięć Studiów o Piotrze Michałowskim, 1988; Kraków, 1989; Die Polnische Malerei: vom Ende des 18. Jahrhunderts bis zum Beginn der Moderne, 1989; (ed.) Materialy do dziejów sztuki sakralnej na ziemiach wschodnich dawnej Rzeczypospolitej, 1993; (ed.) Sztuka kresów wschodnich, 1994; (with A. Małkiewicz) Wstęp do historii sztuki: materiały bibliograficzne, 1995; Mistrzowie Malarstwa Polskiego, 1996; Lwów: Dzieje i Sztuka, 1997; Kresy Bliskie i Dalekie, 1998; (co-ed.) Kraj skrzydlatych jezdzców: sztuka w Polsce, 1572-1764, 2000; Podhorce: dzieje wnętrz pałacowych i galerii obrazów, 2001; (foreword) Encyklopedia sztuki polskiej, 2001; (foreword) Wielka encyklopedia malarstwa polskiego, 2011; (foreword) Sztuka Krakowa, 2011. Contributor to periodicals. **Address:** Wawel Royal Castle, Wawel 5, Krakow, 31-001, Poland.

OSUNDARE, Niyi. American/Nigerian (born Nigeria), b. 1947. **Genres:** Novellas/Short Stories, Poetry. **Career:** University of Ibadan, faculty, 1974-, lecturer, 1982-, professor, 1989-, Department of English, chair, 1993-97; University of Wisconsin, lecturer, 1990-92; University of New Orleans, lecturer, 1990-, associate professor of English, 1991-92, professor, 1997-, research professor, 2001-. Freelance journalist. **Publications:** Songs of the Marketplace, 1983; Village Voices: Poems, 1984; A Nib in the Pond, 1986; The Eye of the Earth: Poems, 1986; The Writer as Righter: The African Literary Artist and His Social Obligations, 1986; Moonsongs, 1988; Songs of the Season, 1990; Waiting Laughters: A Long Song in Many Voices, 1990; Selected Poems, 1992; African Literature and the Crisis of Post-Structuralist Theorising, 1993; Midlife, 1993; Horses of Memory, 1998; The Word Is an Egg: Poems, 2000; Thread in the Loom: Essays on African Literature and Culture, 2002; Pages from the Book of the Sun: New and Selected Poems, 2002; State Visit: Drama, 2002; (ed. with A. Na'Allah) People's Poet: Emerging Perspectives on Niyi Osundare, 2003; Early Birds. Book One: Poems for Junior Secondary, 2004; Tender Moments: Love Poems, 2006; The Universe in the University: A Scholar-Poet's Look from Inside Out: Valedictory Lecture, University of Ibadan, July 26, 2007; Dialogue with My Country: Selections from the Newswatch Column (1986-2003), 2007; Style and Literary Communication in African Prose Fiction in English, 2008. Contributor of articles to periodicals. Works appear in anthologies. **Address:** Department of English, University of New Orleans, 313 Liberal Arts Bldg., 2000 Lakeshore Dr., New Orleans, LA 70148, U.S.A. **Online address:** oosunda1@uno.edu

O'TATE, Ann. *See* **COX, Ana Marie.**

OTIS, Johnny. American (born United States), b. 1921. **Genres:** Music, Art/Art History. **Career:** Johnny Otis Music School, owner; Johnny Otis Cabaret, owner; Landmark Church (non-demoninational Christian church), pastor; Johnny Otis Center for the Arts (JOCA), executive director; Nocturne Organic Farm (manufacturers of Johnny Otis Organic Apple Juice), co-owner; University of California, African American music, teacher of history. Writer. **Publications:** Listen to the Lambs, 1968; Upside Your Head! Rhythm and Blues on Central Avenue, 1994; Colors and Chords: The Art of Johnny Otis, 1995; Red Beans & Rice and Other Rock 'n' Roll Recipes, 1997; Midnight at the Barrelhouse, forthcoming. **Address:** Johnny Otis World, PO Box 2435, Sebastopol, CA 95473, U.S.A. **Online address:** tgould@johnnyotisworld.com

OTOMO, Katsuhiro. Japanese (born Japan), b. 1954. **Genres:** Cartoons, Graphic Novels, Science Fiction/Fantasy, Humor/Satire. **Career:** Graphic artist, comic book creator, film animator and writer. **Publications:** Domu: A Child's Dream, 1996, 2nd ed., 2001; Akira, 1988, vol. I, 2009, vol. II-III, 2010; Legend of Mother Sarah: Tunnel Town (collection), 1996; The Memory of Memories, 1996; Hipira, 2002; Steamboy, 2004. **Address:** c/o Author Mail, Dark Horse Comics, 10956 SE Main St., Milwaukie, OR 97222, U.S.A.

O'TOOLE, Fintan. Irish (born Ireland), b. 1958. **Genres:** Politics/Government, Cultural/Ethnic Topics, Biography, History, Politics/Government, Theatre. **Career:** The Irish Times, journalist, 1988-, assistant editor, columnist, drama critic; New York Daily News, drama critic, 1997-2001; In Dublin Magazine, drama critic; The Sunday Tribune, drama critic; Abbey Theatre, literary adviser. **Publications:** The Politics of Magic: The Work and Times of Tom Murphy, 1987, rev. ed. as Tom Murphy: The Politics of Magic, 1994; The Southern Question, 1987; No More Heroes: A Radical Guide to Shakespeare, 1990; A Mass for Jesse James: A Journey through 1980's Ireland, 1990; Black Hole, Green Card: The Disappearance of Ireland, 1994; (co-author) Diverse Communities: The Evolution of Gay and Lesbian Politics in Ireland, 1994; (co-author) Ireland: The Emigrant Nursery and the World Economy, 1994; Meanwhile Back at the Ranch: The Politics of Irish Beef, 1995; (co-author) Women and the New Reproductive Technologies in Ireland, 1995; A Radical Guide to Macbeth and Hamlet, 1995; (ed.) Rethinking the War on Drugs in Ireland, 1996; (co-author) Imeall nah Eorpa: The Edge of Europe, 1996; (intro.) Three Plays, 1996; The Ex-Isle of Erin: Images of a Global Ireland, 1997; (intro.) Plays, 1997; A Traitor's Kiss: The Life of Richard Brinsley Sheridan, 1997 in US as A Traitor's Kiss: The Life of Richard Brinsley Sheridan, 1751-1816, 1998; The Lie of the Land: Irish Identities, 1998 in Ireland as The Irish Times Book of the Century: 1900-1999, 1999; (co-author) Irish Art Now: From the Pacific to the Political, 1999; (intro.) Shrines, 2001; Shakespeare Is Hard, but So Is Life: A Radical Guide to Shakespearean Tragedy, 2002; After the Ball, 2003; (afterword) Critical Moments: Fintan O'Toole on Modern Irish Theater, 2003; (contrib.) Dancing on the Edge of Europe: Irish Choreographers in Conversation, 2003; (with T. Kinsella) Post Washington: Why America Can't Rule the World, 2005; White Savage: William Johnson and the Invention of America, 2005; (with S. Hegarty) The Irish Times Book of the 1916 Rising, 2006; Ship of Fools: How Stupidity and Corruption Sank the Celtic Tiger, 2009; Enough is Enough: How to Build a New Republic, 2010; (intro.) Radiant Life, 2011. Contributor to periodicals. **Address:** Irish Times, Tara St., Dublin, DU 02, Ireland. **Online address:** otoole.fintan@gmail.com

O'TOOLE, Judith Hansen. American (born United States), b. 1953. **Genres:** Art/Art History, Literary Criticism And History, Photography. **Career:** Wilkes University, Sordoni Art Gallery, director, 1982-93, associate professor, 1985-93; Westmoreland Museum of American Art, director and chief executive officer, 1993-, board trustee, 2005-; Pittsburgh Social Innovation Accelerator, board director and secretary, 2005-; Greensburg Community Development Corp., board director and president, 2005-; Citizens for the Arts in Pennsylvania, board director. Writer. **Publications:** Severin Roesen, 1992; Different Views in Hudson River School Painting, 2005. **Address:** Westmoreland Museum of American Art, 221 N Main St., Greensburg, PA 15601, U.S.A. **Online address:** jotoole@wmuseumaa.org

O'TOOLE, Lawrence. Canadian (born Canada), b. 1951?. **Genres:** Autobiography/Memoirs, Travel/Exploration. **Career:** Corcoran, associate; Coldwell Banker Village Green, producer. Journalist. **Publications:** Heart's Longing: Newfoundland, New York and the Distance Home, 1994. Contributor to books and periodicals. **Address:** Douglas & McIntyre Publishing Group, 2323 Quebec St., Ste. 201, Vancouver, BC V5T 4S7, Canada. **Online address:** lawrence.otoole@coldwellbanker.com

O'TOOLE, Patricia E. American (born United States), b. 1946. **Genres:** Adult Non-fiction, History, Biography. **Career:** Columbia University, School of the Arts, adjunct assistant professor, 1995-2002, lecturer, 2002-03, assistant professor, 2004-05, associate professor, 2005-, vice-chair. Journalist and biographer. **Publications:** Corporate Messiah: The Hiring and Firing of Million-Dollar Managers, 1984, rev. ed., 1985; The Five of Hearts: An Intimate Portrait of Henry Adams and His Friends, 1880-1918, 1990; White House Fellows: A Sense of Involvement, a Vision of Greatness, 1995; Money and Morals in America: A History, 1998; When Trumpets Call: Theodore Roosevelt after the White House, 2005. Contributor to periodicals. **Address:** School of the Arts, Columbia University, 415 Dodge Hall, 2960 Broadway, PO Box 1808, New York, NY 10027-6950, U.S.A. **Online address:** peo4@columbia.edu

OTT, Thomas. Swiss (born Switzerland), b. 1966. **Genres:** Novels, Graphic Novels, Humor/Satire. **Career:** Writer. **Publications:** Phantom Der Superheld, 1995; Grettings from Hellville, 1995; Dead End, 2002. Contributor of periodicals. **Address:** Fantagraphics Books Inc., 7563 Lake City Way NE, Seattle, WA 98115, U.S.A.

OTT, Victoria E. American (born United States), b. 1971. **Genres:** History. **Career:** University of Tennessee, teaching assistant, 1999-2002, graduate lecturer, 2002-03, adjunct faculty, 2003-04; Birmingham-Southern College, assistant professor of American history, 2004-. Writer and historian. **Publications:** Confederate Daughters: Coming of Age during the Civil War, 2008. Contributor to periodicals. **Address:** Birmingham-Southern College, 900 Arkadelphia Rd., PO Box 549031, Birmingham, AL 35254, U.S.A. **Online address:** vott@bsc.edu

OTTAVIANI, Jim. American (born United States), b. 1963. **Genres:** Sciences, Biography, Children's Fiction. **Career:** United Engineers and Constructors Inc., nuclear-mechanical engineer, 1988-90; University of Michigan, library associate, 1990-92, Mechanical Engineering Department, special librarian, 1992-95, Engineering Library, head of reference, 1994-96, Art, Architecture and Engineering Library, head of reference, 1996-2006, Media Union Library, head of reference, 1996; Deep Blue, coordinator, 2006-; G.T. Labs, founder, director and chief research scientist. Writer. **Publications:** Two-fisted Science, 1997; Dignifying Science: Stories about Women Scientists, 1999; Fallout: J. Robert Oppenheimer, Leo Szilard and the Political Science of the Atomic Bomb, 2001; Suspended in Language: Niels Bohr's Life, Discoveries and the Century He Shaped, 2004; Bone Sharps, Cowboys and Thunder Lizards: A Tale of Edward Drinker Cope, Othniel Charles Marsh and the Gilded Age of Paleontology, 2005; (ed.) Charles R. Knight: Autobiography of an Artist, 2005; (with D. Meconis) Wire Mothers: Harry Harlow and the Science of Love, 2007; (with J. Johnston) Levitation: Physics and Psychology in the Service of Deception, 2007; (with Z. Cannon and K. Cannon) T-Minus: The Race to the Moon, 2009. **Address:** G.T. Labs, PO Box 8145, Ann Arbor, MI 48107, U.S.A. **Online address:** jimo@gt-labs.com

OTTAWAY, David B. American (born United States), b. 1939. **Genres:** Politics/Government, History. **Career:** Washington Post, foreign correspondent, Journalist, 1971-2006; Woodrow Wilson International Center for Scholars, fellow senior scholar, 2006-. Writer. **Publications:** (With M. Ottaway) Algeria: The Politics of a Socialist Revolution, 1970; (with M. Ottaway) Ethiopia: Empire in Revolution, 1978; (with M. Ottaway) Afrocommunism, 1981, 2nd ed., 1986; Chained Together: Mandela, De Klerk, and the Struggle to Remake South Africa, 1993; The King's Messenger: Prince Bandar Bin Sultan and America's Tangled Relationship with Saudi Arabia, 2008. **Address:** Woodrow Wilson International Center for Scholars, 1 Woodrow Wilaon Plaza, 1300 Pennsylvania Ave. NW, Washington, DC 20004, U.S.A. **Online address:** david.ottaway@wilsoncenter.org

OTTAWAY, Marina (Seassaro). American/Italian (born Italy), b. 1943. **Genres:** International Relations/Current Affairs, Politics/Government. **Career:** Georgetown University, instructor in sociology, 1972-73; American University-Cairo, instructor in sociology, 1973-74, assistant professor of sociology, associate professor of political science, 1981-85; University of Addis Ababa, assistant professor of sociology, 1974-77; University of Zambia, assistant professor of social development, 1977-79; Johns Hopkins University, School of Advanced International Studies, adjunct professor, 1980-81, 1985-89, 1992, 1997-; George Mason University, adjunct professor of political science, 1985-86; American University-Washington, associate professor of international service, 1986-89; Brookings Institution, non-resident research associate, 1990-92; University of the Witwatersrand, visiting professor, 1990, 1991; American University, distinguished adjunct professor of international service, 1992-93; Georgetown University, School of Foreign Service, visiting professor, 1993-97; Carnegie Endowment for International Peace, senior associate, 1998-. Writer. **Publications:** Sociology of Development: Ethiopian Case Studies, 1977; Soviet and American Influence in the Horn of Africa, 1992; South Africa: The Struggle for a New Order, 1993; Democratization and Ethnic Nationalism, 1994; Africa's New Leaders: Democracy or State Reconstruction?, 1999; Democracy Challenged: The Rise of Semi-Authoritarianism, 2003; (co-author) Bāzsāzī-i Afghānistān, 2004. WITH D. OTTAWAY: Algeria: The Politics of a Socialist Revolution, 1970; Ethiopia: Empire in Revolution, 1978; Afrocommunism, 1981, 2nd ed., 1986. EDITOR: The Political Economy of Ethiopia, 1990; Democracy in Africa, 1997; (with T. Carothers) Funding Virtue, 2000; (with T. Carothers) Uncharted Journey: Promoting Democracy in the Middle East, 2005; (with J. Choucair-Vizoso) Beyond the Façade: Political Reform in the Arab World, 2008; (with A. Hamzawy) Getting to Pluralism, 2009; (with C. Boucek) Yemen on the Brink, 2010. Work represented in anthologies. Contributor of articles to journals. **Address:** Carnegie Endowment for International Peace, 1779 Massachusetts Ave. NW, Washington, DC 20036-2103, U.S.A. **Online address:** mottaway@ceip.org

OTTEN, Charlotte F(ennema). American (born United States), b. 1926. **Genres:** Poetry, Humanities, Biography, History, Young Adult Fiction. **Career:** University of Michigan, Extension Center, lecturer, 1972; Grand Valley State University, assistant professor, 1972-74, associate professor of English, 1974-77; Calvin College, Department of English, professor, 1977-91, professor emeritus, 1991-; University College of Wales, director of interim course, 1983, 1984; Greater Grand Rapids Women's History Council, director, 1995-. Writer. **Publications:** Environ'd with Eternity (nonfiction), 1985; January Rides the Wind: A Book of Poems for Children, 1997; Home in a Wilderness Fort: Copper Harbor, 1844, 2006. EDITOR: A Lycanthropy Reader: Werewolves in Western Culture, 1986; (with G.D. Schmidt) The Voice of the Narrator in Children's Literature: Insights from Writers and Critics, 1989; English Women's Voices: An Anthology of Women Writers, 1540-1700, 1992; Book of Birth Poetry, 1995; The Literary Werewolf: An Anthology, 2002. **Address:** Department of English, Calvin College, 1795 Knollcrest Cir., 3201 Burton SE, Grand Rapids, MI 49546, U.S.A.

OTTENBERG, Simon. American (born United States), b. 1923. **Genres:** Anthropology/Ethnology, Art/Art History, Sociology, Technology, Theology/Religion. **Career:** University of Chicago, instructor in anthropology, 1954; Washington State University, acting instructor in anthropology, 1954-55; University of Washington, instructor, 1955-57, assistant professor, 1957-63, associate professor, 1963-68, professor, 1968-90, professor emeritus of anthropology, 1990-; University of Ghana, honorary visiting professor, 1970-71. Writer. **Publications:** Double Descent in an African Society: The Afikpo Village Group, 1968; Leadership and Authority in an African Society: The Afikpo Village Group, 1971; Anthropology and African Aesthetics, 1971; Masked Rituals of Afikpo, 1975; Boyhood Rituals in an African Society: An Interpretation, 1989; Seeing with Music: The Lives of Three Blind African Musicians, 1996; New Traditions from Nigeria: Seven Artists of the Nsukka Group, 1997; Farmers and Townspeople in a Changing Nigeria: Abakaliki During Colonial Times (1905-1960), 2005; Igbo Religion, Social Life, And Other Essays, 2006. EDITOR: (with P.V. Ottenberg) Cultures and Societies of Africa, 1960; African Religious Groups and Beliefs, 1982; The Nsukka Artists and Nigerian Contemporary Art, 2002; (with D.A. Binkley) Playful Performers: African Children's Masquerades, 2006; Olayinka, 2011. Contributor to journals. **Address:** Department of Anthropology, University of Washington, PO Box 353100, Seattle, WA 98195, U.S.A. **Online address:** otten@u.washington.edu

OTTO, Beatrice K. Swiss (born Switzerland), b. 1963. **Genres:** Business/Trade/Industry. **Career:** Editor and translator, 1986-89; freelance consultant, 1994-. **Publications:** Fools are Everywhere: The Court Jester Around the World, 2001. Contributor to periodicals. **Address:** c/o Author Mail, University of Chicago Press, 1427 E 60th St., Chicago, IL 60637, U.S.A. **Online address:** ottobeatrice@hotmail.com

OTTO, Lon. American (born United States), b. 1948. **Genres:** Novels, Novellas/Short Stories, Young Adult Fiction. **Career:** University of St. Thomas, assistant professor, 1974-78, associate professor, 1978-82, professor of English, 1982-; University of Iowa, teacher, 1997-2006; University of Michigan, writer-in-residence; Northwest Missouri State University, writer-in-residence; Creighton University, writer-in-residence. **Publications:** Nest of Hooks, 1978; Water Bodies, 1986; Cover Me: Short Stories, 1988. **Address:** Department of English, University of St. Thomas, JRC 354, 2115 Summit Ave., St. Paul, MN 55105-1096, U.S.A. **Online address:** l9otto@stthomas.edu

OTTO, Whitney. American (born United States), b. 1955. **Genres:** Novels, Novellas/Short Stories, Young Adult Fiction. **Career:** University of California, staff, 1975-78, instructor in creative writing and composition, 1987-89; bookkeeper, 1980-86; Irvine Valley College, instructor in composition, 1990. Novelist and educator. **Publications:** How to Make an American Quilt, 1991; Now You See Her, 1994; The Passion Dream Book: A Novel, 1997; A Collection of Beauties at the Height of Their Popularity: A Novel, 2002. Contributor to books. **Address:** c/o Joy Harris, Robert Lantz-Joy Harris Literary Agency, 156 5th Ave., New York, NY 10010, U.S.A.

OTWAY-WARD, Patricia. *See* **WEENOLSEN, Patricia.**

OUELLETTE, Jennifer. American (born United States) **Genres:** Physics. **Career:** Writer, 1992-; American Institute of Physics, freelance writer, 1995-2008; APS News, columnist, associate editor. **Publications:** Black Bodies and Quantum Cats: Tales from The Annals of Physics, 2005; The Physics of the Buffyverse, 2007; Calculus Diaries: How Math Can Help You Lose Weight, Win in Vegas, and Survive a Zombie Apocalypse, 2010. Contributor to periodicals. **Address:** c/o Mildred Marmur, Mildred Marmur Associates Ltd., 2005 Palmer Ave., PO Box 127, Larchmont, NY 10538-2437, U.S.A. **Online address:** jenluc@gmail.com

OUELLETTE, Pierre. (Pierre Davis). American (born United States), b. 1945?. **Genres:** Novels, Science Fiction/Fantasy. **Career:** KVO Inc., founding partner. Writer and advertising executive. **Publications:** The Deus Machine: A Novel, 1994; The Third Pandemic: A Novel, 1996; (as Pierre Davis) A Breed Apart, 2009; (as Pierre Davis) Origin Unknown, 2011. **Address:** Bantam-Dell Publishing Group, 1745 Broadway, New York, NY 10019-4368, U.S.A. **Online address:** pierre-ouellette@tumblr.com

OUGH, Richard N. British/Canadian (born Canada), b. 1946. **Genres:** Law. **Career:** Writer. **Publications:** The Mareva Injunction and Anton Piller Order, 1987, (with W. Flenley) 2nd. ed. as The Mareva Injunction and Anton Piller Order: Practice and Precedents, 1993. **Address:** Lamb Chambers, Temple, London, GL EC4Y 7AS, England. **Online address:** richardough@lambchambers.co.uk

OUGHTON, Jerrie. American (born United States), b. 1937. **Genres:** Children's Fiction, Young Adult Fiction, Mythology/Folklore. **Career:** Teacher, 1963-64, 1974-85; Fayette County Public Schools, secretary, 1989-2000. Writer. **Publications:** How the Stars Fell into the Sky: A Navajo Legend, 1992; The Magic Weaver of Rugs: A Tale of the Navajo, 1994; Music from a Place Called Half Moon, 1995; The War in Georgia, 1997; Perfect Family, 2000. Contributor to periodicals. **Address:** c/o Kathleen Rouark, Houghton Mifflin Co., 222 Berkely St., Boston, MA 02116, U.S.A. **Online address:** jerrieoughton@cs.com

OUGHTON, John P. Canadian (born Canada), b. 1948?. **Genres:** Poetry, Illustrations. **Career:** Sheridan College, part-time professor of communications, 2000-; Ontario College of Art and Design, part-time professor of communications and literature, 2000-; Acadia University, teacher; Centennial College, professor learning and teaching. Poet, journalist and photographer. **Publications:** SELF-ILLUSTRATED: Gearing of Love, 1984. OTHERS: Zoogeographical Study of the Land Snails of Ontario, 1948. POETRY: Taking Tree Trains, 1973; Mata Haris Lost Words, 1988; Counting out the Millennium, 1996; Take With You What You've Left, 2003; Time Slip, 2010. Works appear in anthologies. Contributor to periodicals. **Address:** Pecan Grove Press, 1 Camino Santa Maria, San Antonio, TX 78228-8608, U.S.A. **Online address:** john.oughton@sheridanc.on.ca

OUST, Gail. (Elizabeth Turner). American (born United States), b. 1943?. **Genres:** Novels. **Career:** Writer. **Publications:** BUNCO BABES MYSTERY SERIES: Whack 'N' Roll (novel), 2009; 'Til Dice Do Us Part, 2010; Shake, Murder, and Roll, 2011. NOVELS AS ELIZABETH TURNER: Sweet Possession, 1986; Forbidden Fires, 1988; Fortune's Captive, 1991; Midnight Rain, 1994; Inside Paradise, 1996; Bayou Magic, 1999; Wild and Sweet, 2000; Just before Daybreak, 2002; Rebel's Treasure, 2002. **Address:** Penguin Group Inc., 375 Hudson St., New York, NY 10014-3657, U.S.A. **Online address:** gboust@wctel.net

OUTHWAITE, (Richard) William. British (born England), b. 1949. **Genres:** Area Studies, Philosophy, Social Sciences, Sociology. **Career:** University of Sussex, lecturer, 1973-87, reader, 1987-93, professor of sociology, 1993-2007, visiting professor, Centre for Critical Social Theory; Sociology, deputy editor, 1985-88; Current Sociology, editor, 1987-93; European Journal of Social Theory, associate editor, 1997-; Newcastle university, professor of sociology, 2007-. **Publications:** Understanding Social Life: The Method Called Verstehen, 1975, 2nd ed., 1986; Concept Formation in Social Science, 1983; New Philosophies of Social Science: Realism, Hermeneutics and Critical Theory, 1987; Habermas: A Critical Introduction, 1994, 2nd ed., 2009; (with L. Ray) Social Theory and Postcommunism, 2005; Future of Society, 2006; European Society, 2008. EDITOR: Max Weber and Karl Marx, 1982; (with M. Mulkay) Social Theory and Social Criticism: Essays for Tom Bottomore, 1987; The Habermas Reader, 1996; (with T. Bottomore) The Blackwell Dictionary of Twentieth-Century Social Thought, 1993, 2nd ed., 2003; (with L. Martell) The Sociology of Politics, 1998; (with M.S. Archer) Defending Objectivity: Essays in Honour of Andrew Collier, 2004; (with S.P. Turner) SAGE Handbook of Social Science Methodology, 2007. **Address:** School of Geography, Politics and Sociology, Newcastle university, Newcastle upon Tyne, TW NE1 7RU, England. **Online address:** william.outhwaite@ncl.ac.uk

OUTLAND, Robert B. American (born United States) **Genres:** History, Business/Trade/Industry, Economics. **Career:** Louisiana State University, instructor in history, 2002-. Writer. **Publications:** Tapping the Pines: The Naval Stores Industry in the American South, 2004. Contributor to periodicals and journals. **Address:** Department of History, Louisiana State University, 217F Himes Hall, Baton Rouge, LA 70803, U.S.A. **Online address:** old160@aol.com

OVASON, David. British (born England) **Genres:** Intellectual History, Art/Art History, Architecture. **Career:** Teacher of astrology and writer. **Publications:** The Secrets of Nostradamus: The Medieval Code of the Master Revealed in the Age of Computer Science, 1997; The Nostradamus Code, 1998; (intro.) The Zelator: A Modern Initiate Explores the Ancient Mysteries, 1998; The Book of the Eclipse: The Hidden Influences of Eclipses, 1999; The Secret Zodiacs of Washington DC: Was the City of Stars Planned by Masons?, 1999 in US as The Secret Architecture of Our Nation's Capital: The Masons and the Building of Washington, 2000; The Secrets of Nostradamus: A Radical New Interpretation of the Master's Prophecies, 2001; Nostradamus: Prophecies for America, 2001; The Two Children: A Study of the Two Jesus Children in Literature and Art, 2001; The Secret Symbols of the Dollar Bill, 2004; History of the Horoscope, 2005; Shakespeare's Secret Booke: Deciphering Magical and Rosicrucian Codes, 2010; Michel Nostradamus and Rudolf Steiner, 2011. **Address:** c/o Author Mail, HarperCollins Publishers, 10 E 53rd St., 7th Fl., New York, NY 10022-5244, U.S.A.

OVE, Robert S. American (born United States), b. 1927. **Genres:** Theology/Religion, Documentaries/Reportage, Education, Biography. **Career:** Lutheran Churches, pastor, 1958-91, Evangelical minister, now retired; Wyoming Tribune Eagle, Preacher Feature Weekly Column, editor, 1994-97; Mescalero Apache Reservation, teacher. Writer. **Publications:** Christian Voices from Nepal, 1997; (with H.H. Stockel) Geronimo's Kids: A Teacher's Lessons on the Apache Reservation, 1997. **Address:** 6171 Roadrunner Loop NE, Rio Rancho, NM 87144-5116, U.S.A.

OVED, Yaacov. Israeli (born Israel), b. 1929?. **Genres:** History, Theology/Religion, Cultural/Ethnic Topics. **Career:** Tel Aviv University, Department of History, professor; International Communal Studies Association, board director, co-founder, president. Writer. **Publications:** Anarquismo y el movimiento obrero en Argentina, 1978; Matayim shenot ḳomunah be-Artsot-ha-Berit, 1986; (with Y. Gorni and I. Paz) Communal Life: An International Perspective, 1987; Two Hundred Years of American Communes, 1988; Aḥim reḥoḳim: toldot ha-yeḥasim ben ha-tenu'ah ha-ḳibutsit la-Bruderhof, 1993; The Witness of the Brothers: A History of the Bruderhof, 1996; 'Edut ha-aḥim: toldot ha-ḳomunot shel ha-Bruderhof, 1996; ḳomunot u-ḳehilot shituf ba-maḥatsit ha-sheniyah shel ha-me'ah ha-20 (1950-2000), 2009. **Address:** International Communal Studies Association, Yad Tabenkin, Ramat Efal, 52960, Israel. **Online address:** ovedyac@post.tau.ac.il

OVERALL, Christine. Canadian (born Canada), b. 1949. **Genres:** Philosophy, Women's Studies And Issues, Social Commentary, Writing/Journalism. **Career:** Marianopolis College, professor of philosophy and humanities, 1975-84; Queen's University, assistant professor, 1986-87, associate professor, 1987-92, professor of philosophy, 1992-, Faculty of Arts and Science, associate dean, 1997-2005, John and Ella G. Charlton professor in philosophy, 2004-05, research chair, 2005-10; University of Waterloo, Department of Philosophy, Alex P. Humphrey professor in feminist philosophy, 2003; Mount Saint Vincent University, Nancy's chair in women's studies, 2006-07. Writer. **Publications:** Ethics and Human Reproduction: A Feminist Analysis, 1987; Human Reproduction: Principles, Practices, Policies, 1993; A Feminist I: Reflections from Academia, 1998; Thinking Like a Woman: Personal Life and Political Ideas, 2001; Aging, Death and Human Longevity: A Philosophical Inquiry, 2003; Why Have Children?: The Ethical Debate, 2012. EDITOR:

(with L. Code and S. Mullett) Feminist Perspectives: Philosophical Essays on Method and Morals, 1988; The Future of Human Reproduction, 1989; (with W.P. Zion) Perspectives on AIDS: Ethical and Social Issues, 1991. CONTRIBUTOR: This Fine Place So Far from Home: Voices of Academics from the Working Class, 1995; Philosophical Perspectives on Bioethics, 1996. **Address:** Department of Philosophy, Queen's University, 313 John Watson Hall, Kingston, ON K7L 3N6, Canada. **Online address:** cdo@queensu.ca

OVERALL, Sonia. British (born England), b. 1973. **Genres:** Novels. **Career:** Writer and educator. **Publications:** A Likeness, 2004; The Realm of Shells, 2006. **Address:** c/o Simon Trewin, United Agents Ltd., 12-26 Lexington St., London, GL W1F OLE, England. **Online address:** soniaoverall@hotmail.com

OVEREND, William George. British (born England), b. 1921. **Genres:** Chemistry, Education, Biography, Sciences. **Career:** University College, assistant lecturer of chemistry, 1946-47; Dunlop Rubber Company Ltd., research chemist, 1947-49; British Rubber Producers Research Association, research chemist, 1947-49; University of Birmingham, honorable research fellow, 1947-49, lecturer of chemistry, 1949-55; Pennsylvania State College, associate professor, 1951-52; University of London, reader in organic chemistry, 1955-57, professor of chemistry, 1957-87, senator, 1978-87, professor emeritus, 1987, Leverhulme emeritus fellow, 1987-89; Birkbeck College of London, Department of Chemistry, head, 1957-79, vice-master, 1974-78, master, 1979-87, professor; English University Press, Chemical Science Texts Series, editor, 1960-. **Publications:** The Use of Tracer Elements in Biology, 1951; (ed.) Programmes in Organic Chemistry, 8 vols., 1973. **Address:** The Retreat, Nightingales Ln., Chalfont St. Giles, BK HP8 4SG, England.

OVERMAN, Dean L. American (born United States), b. 1943. **Genres:** Theology/Religion, Language/Linguistics. **Career:** Winston & Strawn, senior partner, 1977-; University of Virginia Law School, faculty, 1978; Van Raalte Institute, visiting senior research fellow; White House, fellow, special assistant and associate director. Writer. **Publications:** Effective Writing Techniques, 1980; A Case against Accident and Self-Organization, 1997; A Case for the Existence of God, 2008; A Case for the Divinity of Jesus: Examining the Earliest Evidence, 2009. **Address:** Rowman & Littlefield Publishers, 4501 Forbes Blvd., Suite 200, Lanham, MD 20706, U.S.A. **Online address:** deanoverman@gmail.com

OVERMYER, Eric. American (born United States), b. 1951. **Genres:** Plays/Screenplays, Novels, Young Adult Fiction. **Career:** Yale University School of Drama, professor, 1991-92. Writer. **Publications:** PLAYS: Native Speech, 1984; In a Pig's Valise, 1984; On the Verge or The Geography of Yearning, 1985; In Perpetuity Throughout the Universe, 1988; Don Quixote de La Jolla, 1990; Mi Vida Loca, 1991; Dark Rapture, 1992; Eric Overmyer: Collected Plays, 1993; The Heliotrope Bouquet by Scott Joplin & Louis Chauvin, 1993; Amphitryon, 1996; Marriage of Figaro/Figaro Gets a Divorce, 1996. **Address:** American Conservatory Theater, 415 Geary St., San Francisco, CA 94102, U.S.A.

OVERMYER, James E. American (born United States), b. 1946. **Genres:** History, Biography, Autobiography/Memoirs, Politics/Government. **Career:** Berkshire Eagle, reporter, 1972-79; Berkshire County District Attorney, administrator, 1979-83; Massachusetts State Senate, legislative staff, 1983-86; New York State Assembly, budget analyst, 1986-92; New York State Division of the Budget, budget examiner, 1992-95. **Publications:** Effa Manley and the Newark Eagles, 1993; Queen of the Negro Leagues: Effa Manley and the Newark Eagles, 1998. Contributor to books and periodicals. **Address:** 7 Fairview Ave., Lenox, MA 01240-2301, U.S.A.

OVERMYER-VELAZQUEZ, Mark. American (born United States), b. 1970. **Genres:** History. **Career:** Pomona College, faculty member, 2002; Wesleyan University, Center for the Humanities, Andrew Mellon Postdoctoral Fellow, 2003-04; University of Connecticut, associate professor of history and director of the Center for Latin American and Caribbean Studies, 2008-. Writer. **Publications:** Visions of the Emerald City: Modernity, Tradition, and the Formation of Porfirian Oaxaca, Mexico, 2006; (ed.) Latino America: A State-by-State Encyclopedia, 2008. Contributor to journals. **Address:** Department of History, University of Connecticut, 241 Glenbrook Rd., Storrs, CT 06269-2103, U.S.A. **Online address:** mark.velazquez@uconn.edu

OVERTON, Jenny (Margaret Mary). British (born England), b. 1942. **Genres:** Children's Fiction, Local History/Rural Topics, Education. **Career:** Cambridge University, Newnham College, appeals secretary, 1965-66, principal's secretary, 1966-67, Aluminium Federation, assistant editor, 1967-69; Macmillan & Co., book editor, 1969-71; Lutterworth Press, editor, 1971-84; freelance editor, 1984-. **Publications:** Creed Country, 1969; The Thirteen Days of Christmas, 1972; Nightwatch Winter, 1973; Ship from Simnel Street, 1986; A Suffragette Nest: Peaslake, 1910 and After, 1998; (ed.) Sausages, Pickles, Cure for a Cough: Recipes of a Country Butcher's Wife, 1999. Contributor to periodicals. **Address:** Raines & Raines, 244 Madison Ave., New York, NY 10016, U.S.A.

OVERTON, Ron. American (born United States), b. 1943. **Genres:** Poetry, Literary Criticism And History. **Career:** Barrington College, instructor, 1967-69; Phillips Academy, poet-in-residence, 1979; Empire State College of the State University, mentor, 1982-84; Stony Brook University, lecturer in English, 1983-. Writer. **Publications:** POETRY: Dead Reckoning, 1979; Love on the Alexander Hamilton, 1985; Hotel Me: Poems for Gil Evans and Others, 1994; Psychic Killed by Train, 2002. Contributor of articles to periodicals. Works appear in anthologies. **Address:** The Writing Center, Program in Writing & Rhetoric, Stony Brook University, 2111 Humanities Bldg., 100 Nicolls Rd., Stony Brook, NY 11794-5350, U.S.A. **Online address:** roverton@notes.cc.sunysb.edu

ØVSTEDAL, Barbara. Also writes as Barbara Paul, Rosalind Laker. British (born England), b. 1925?. **Genres:** Novels, Romance/Historical. **Career:** Writer. **Publications:** Norway, 1973, Red Cherry Summer, 1973; Valley of the Reindeer, 1973; Souvenir from Sweden, 1974. AS ROSALIND LAKER: Sovereign's Key, 1969; Far Seeks the Heart, 1970, rev. ed., 1988; Sail a Jewelled Ship, 1971; The Shripney Lady, 1972, rev. ed., 1989; Fair Wind of Love, 1974, rev. ed., 1988; The Smuggler's Bride, 1975; Ride the Blue Riband, 1977; Warwyck's Woman, 1978 in UK as Warwyck's Wife, 1979; Claudine's Daughter, 1979, 2nd ed., 1983; Warwyck's Choice in UK as The Warwycks of Easthampton, 1980; Banners of Silk, 1981; Gilded Splendour, 1982; Jewelled Path, 1983; What the Heart Keeps, 1984; This Shining Land, 1985; Tree of Gold, 1986; The Silver Touch, 1987, 2nd ed., 1989; To Dance with Kings, 1988; Circle of Pearls, 1990; The Golden Tulip, 1991; The Venetian Mask, 1993; The Sugar Pavilion, 1994; The Fortuny Gown, 1994; Orchids and Diamonds, 1995; The Fragile Hour, 1997; New World, New Love, 2002; To Dream of Snow, 2004; Garlands of Gold, 2007; Brilliance, 2007; House by the Fjord, 2011. AS BARBARA PAUL: The Seventeenth Stair, 1975; The Curse of Halewood, 1977 in US as Devil's Fire, Love's Revenge, 1976; The Frenchwoman, 1977; To Love a Stranger, 1978; A Cadenza for Caruso, 1984; The Renewable Virgin, 1984; Kill Fee, 1985; Prima Donna at Large, 1985; But He Was Already Dead When I Got There, 1986; Good King Sauerkraut, 1989; He Huffed and He Puffed, 1989; In-laws and Outlaws, 1990; You Have the Right to Remain Silent: A Mystery with Marian Larch, 1992; A History of East Brandywine Township: Chester County, Pennsylvania, 1992; The Apostrophe Thief: A Mystery with Marian Larch, 1993; Fare Play: A Mystery with Marian Larch, 1995; Full Frontal Murder: A Mystery with Marian Larch, 1997. **Address:** Juliet Burton Literary Agency, 2 Clifton Ave., London, GL W12 9DR, England. **Online address:** info@rosalindlaker.com

OWEN, David. American (born United States), b. 1955. **Genres:** Economics. **Career:** Harper's, senior writer; Atlantic Monthly, contributing editor; New Yorker, staff writer, 1991-; Golf Digest, contributing editor, 1995-. **Publications:** High School, 1981; None of the Above: Behind the Myth of Scholastic Aptitude, 1985, rev. ed. as None of the Above Revised: The Truth behind the SATs, 1999; The Man Who Invented Saturday Morning: And Other Adventures in American Enterprise, 1988; The Walls around Us: The Thinking Person's Guide to How a House Works, 1991; My Usual Game, 1996; Around the House: Reflections on Life under a Roof, 1998; (ed. with J. Bingham) Lure of the Links: Great Golf Stories, 1999; The Complete Office Golf, 1999; Life under a Leaky Roof, 2000; The Chosen One: Tiger Woods and the Dilemma of Greatness, 2001; The Making of the Masters: Clifford Roberts, Augusta National, and Golf's Most Prestigious Tournament, 2003; Copies in Seconds: How a Lone Inventor and an Unknown Company Created the Biggest Communication Breakthrough since Gutenberg'Chester Carlson and the Birth of Xerox, 2005; Hit & Hope: How the Rest of Us Play Golf, 2005; Sheetrock & Shellac: A Thinking Person's Guide to the Art and Science of Home Improvement, 2007; The First National Bank of Dad: A Foolproof Method for Teaching Your Kids the Value of Money, 2007; Green Metropolis: Why Living Smaller, Living Closer, and Driving Less Are Keys to Sustainability, 2009. **Address:** Washington, CT , U.S.A. **Online address:** green.metropolis.owen@gmail.com

OWEN, David (Anthony Llewellyn). British (born England), b. 1938. **Genres:** Medicine/Health, Politics/Government. **Career:** St. Thomas's Hospital, Medical Unit, research fellow, 1966-67; parliamentary under-secretary of state for Defense for the Royal Navy, 1968-70; Parliament (U.K.) for the Devonport Division of Plymouth, member, 1974-92; parliamentary under-secretary of state for Health, 1974; Department of Health and Social Security, minister of state, 1974-76; Foreign and Commonwealth Office, minister of state, 1976-77; secretary of state for Foreign and Commonwealth Affairs, 1977-79; Social Democratic Party, co-founder, 1981, leader, 1983-87, 1988-92; International Conference on the Former Yugoslavia, EU co-chairman, 1992-95; Global Natural Energy, chairman, 1995-2006; Abbott Laboratories, director, 1996-2011; Liverpool University, chancellor, 1996-2009; Europe Steel, chair, 2000-; Yukos Intl., chair, 2002-05; Intelligent Energy, director, 2003-06; Gallagher Holdings, consultant, 2006-; Hyperdynamics Corp., director, 2009-. Writer. **Publications:** A Unified Health Service, 1968; The Politics of Defence, 1972; In Sickness and in Health, 1976; Human Rights, 1978; Face the Future, 1981; A Future that Will Work, 1984; A United Kingdom, 1986; Our NHS, 1988; Time to Declare (autobiography), 1991; Seven Ages (poetry anthology), 1992; Balkan Odyssey, 1995; Hubris Syndrome, 2007; In Sickness and In Power: Illness in Heads of Government During the Last 100 years, 2008; Time to Declare: Second Innings (autobiography) 2009; Nuclear Papers, 2009. **Address:** House of Lords, London, GL SW1A 0PW, England. **Online address:** lordowen@gotadsl.co.uk

OWEN, Howard (Wayne). American (born United States), b. 1949. **Genres:** Novels, Communications/Media. **Career:** Martinsville Bulletin, sports writer, 1971-73; Gastonia Gazette, sports editor, 1973-74; Tallahassee Democrat, executive sports editor, 1977-78; Richmond Times-Dispatch, assistant sports editor, 1978-83, sports news editor, 1983-92, sports editor, 1992-95, deputy managing editor, 1995-2006; Free Lance-Star, business editor. **Publications:** NOVELS: Littlejohn, 1992; Fat Lightning, 1994; Answers to Lucky, 1996; The Measured Man, 1997; Harry and Ruth, 2000; The Rail, 2002; Turn Signal, 2004; Rock of Ages, 2006; Reckoning, 2010. SHORT STORIES: (contrib.) Richmond Noir, 2009. Contributor to periodicals. **Address:** Free Lance-Star, 616 Amelia St., Fredericksburg, VA 22401-3887, U.S.A. **Online address:** howen@freelancestar.com

OWEN, Maureen. American (born United States), b. 1943. **Genres:** Poetry, Romance/Historical. **Career:** Saint Marks-in-the-Bowery, Poetry Project, administrative assistant, 1973-76, coordinator and director, 1976-80, program coordinator, 2001-03; freelance creative writing and book production workshop leader, 1980; Inland Book Co., catalog manager, 1982-96; Morton Publishing Co., senior editor of series publications, 1996-2000; Naropa University, Summer Writing Program, faculty, 1998, 2001, 2003-06, adjunct professor, 2003; Swarthmore College, honors examiner in English literature, 1999, 2002; Edinboro University, creative writing and composition faculty, 1999; LPC Group, In-House Press, managing editor, 2000-01. **Publications:** POETRY: Country Rush, 1973; No Travels Journal, 1975; Hearts in Space, 1980; AE (Amelia Earhart), 1984; Zombie Notes, 1985; Imaginary Income, 1992; Untapped Maps, 1993; American Rush: Selected Poems, 1998; Erosion's Pull, 2006. Works appear in anthologies. **Address:** Naropa University, 2130 Arapahoe Ave., Boulder, CO 80302, U.S.A. **Online address:** pomowen@ix.netcom.com

OWENS, David M. American (born United States), b. 1954?. **Genres:** Military/Defense/Arms Control. **Career:** United States Military Academy, faculty; Purdue University, faculty; Valparaiso University, faculty, 2000-, associate professor of English, 2001-, assistant provost. Writer. **Publications:** The Devil's Topographer: Ambrose Bierce and the American War Story, 2006. Contributor to journals. **Address:** Department of English, Valparaiso University, 220 Huegli Hall, 1409 Chapel Dr., Valparaiso, IN 46383, U.S.A. **Online address:** david.owens@valpo.edu

OWENS, E(dwin) J(ohn). Welsh/British (born England), b. 1950. **Genres:** Archaeology/Antiquities, Urban Studies, Architecture. **Career:** University of Wales, University College of Swansea (now Swansea University), lecturer in classics and ancient history, 1978-. Writer. **Publications:** (Co-author) Roman Public Buildings, 1990; The City in the Greek and Roman World, 1991; (co-author) Roman Domestic Buildings, 1996; (co-author) Cremna in Pisidia, 1996. **Address:** College of Arts and Humanities, Swansea University, Singleton Pk., Swansea, WG SA2 8PP, Wales. **Online address:** e.j.owens@swansea.ac.uk

OWENS, Janis E(llen). American (born United States), b. 1960. **Genres:** Novels, Adult Non-fiction, Food And Wine. **Career:** Novelist. **Publications:** My Brother Michael, 1997; Myra Sims, 1999; The Schooling of Claybird Catts, 2003; Cracker Kitchen: A Cookbook in Celebration of Cornbread-fed, Down-home Family Stories and Cuisine, 2009; American Ghost, 2013. **Address:** c/o Joy Harris, Joy Harris Literary Agency Inc., 381 Park Ave. S, Ste. 428, New York, NY 10016, U.S.A. **Online address:** janiseowens@juno.com

OWENS, John E. British (born England), b. 1948. **Genres:** Politics/Government, Institutions/Organizations, Social Sciences. **Career:** Polytechnic of Central London, lecturer, 1978-85; University of Essex, ESRC Data Archive, visiting fellow, 1984-87, 1993-95; lecturer in government, 1985-86; University of Westminster, senior lecturer in political science, 1986-98, reader in U.S. government and politics, 1998-2002, Centre for the Study of Democracy, professor of United States government and politics, 2002-; Texas A&M University, Center for Presidential Studies, visiting fellow, 1999-; American University, School of Public Affairs, visiting research fellow, 2002-; University of London, School of Advanced Study, Institute for the Study of the Americas, associate fellow, 2002-; Library of Congress, consultant; British Broadcasting Corp., consultant. Writer. **Publications:** (With J. Keane) After Full Employment, 1986; (with M. Foley) Congress and the Presidency: Institutional Politics in a Separated System, 1996. EDITOR: (with D. McSweeney and contrib.) The Republican Takeover of Congress, 1998; (with E.C. Hargrove, Jr.) Political Leadership in Context, 2003; (with J. Dumbrell) America's War on Terrorism: New Dimensions in U.S. Government and National Security, 2008; (with R. Pelizzo) The Impact of the Post 9/11 War on Terror on Executive-Legislative Relations: A Global Perspective, 2009; (ed. with R. Pelizzo) The War on Terror and the Growth of Executive Power?: A Comparative Analysis, 2010. Contributor to journals. **Address:** The Centre for the Study of Democracy, The University of Westminster, 32-38 Wells St., London, GL W1T 3UW, England. **Online address:** owensj@wesminster.ac.uk

OWENS, Kenneth N. American (born United States), b. 1933. **Genres:** History, Biography, Natural History. **Career:** Northern Illinois University, assistant professor, associate professor, 1959-68; California State University, associate professor, professor of history and ethnic studies, 1968-2000, professor emeritus of history and ethnic studies, 2000-, Native American Ethnic Studies Program, director, 1969-71, Capital Campus Public History Program, director, 1983-2000. Writer. **Publications:** Galena, Grant, and the Fortunes of War, 1963; (ed. and intro.) The Wreck of the Sv. Nikolai: Two Narratives of the First Russian Expedition to the Oregon Country, 1808-1810, 1985; (ed.) John Sutter and a Wider West, 1994; (ed.) Perilous Passage: A Narrative of the Montana Gold Rush by Edward Ruthven Purple, 1995; Riches for All: The California Gold Rush and the World, 2002; Fishing the Hatch: New West Romanticism and Fly-Fishing in the High Country, Montana The Magazine of Western History, 2002; (ed. and intro.) A Tenderfoot in Montana by Franklin Thompson, 2004; (ed.) John Sutter and His Grant by John Laufkotter, 2004; Gold Rush Saints: California Mormons and the Great Rush for Riches, 2004; (with I.W. Engstrand) John Sutter: Sutter's Fort and the California Gold Rush, 2004; Frontiersman for the Tsar: Timofei Tarakanov and the Expansion of Russian America, Montana The Magazine of Western History, 2006; Blue Ribbon Tailwaters: The Unplanned Role of the U.S. Bureau of Reclamation in Western Fly Fishing, 2007. **Address:** Department of History, Sacramento State University, Sacramento, CA 95819-6059, U.S.A. **Online address:** kenowens44@yahoo.com

OWENS, Rochelle. American (born United States), b. 1936. **Genres:** Novellas/Short Stories, Plays/Screenplays, Poetry, Literary Criticism And History, Translations, Young Adult Fiction. **Career:** University of California, visiting lecturer, 1982; University of Oklahoma, adjunct professor of creative writing; Brown University, writer-in-residence; University of Southwestern Louisiana, staff. **Publications:** POETRY: Not Be Essence That Cannot Be, 1961; (co-author) Four Young Lady Poems, 1962; Salt and Core, 1968; I Am the Babe of Joseph Stalin's Daughter: Poems 1961-1971, 1972; Poems from Joe's Garage, 1973; The Joe Eighty-Two Creation Poems, 1974; The Joe Chronicles, 1979; Shemuel, 1979; French Light, 1984; Constructs, 1985; W.C. Fields in French Light, 1986; How Much Paint Does the Painting Need, 1988; Paysanne: And Selected Earlier Poems, 1992; New and Selected Poems, 1961-1996, 1997; Luca: Discourse on Life and Death, 2001; Triptych: Poems, 2006. PLAYS: Futz, 1965; Beclch, 1967; Futz and What Came After, 1968; He Wants Shih!, 1969; (ed. and contrib.) Spontaneous Combustion: Eight New American Plays, 1972; The Karl Marx Play, 1973; The Karl Marx Play and Others, 1974; Emma Instigated Me, 1976; The Widow and the

Colonel, 1977; Mountain Rites, 1978; Chucky's Hunch, 1981; Who Do You Want, Peire Vidal?, 1981; Futz and Who Do You Want, Peire Vidal?, 1986; (trans.) Three Front, 1991. OTHER: Black Chalk: Discourse on Life and Death, 1992; (trans.) The Passersby, 1993; Journey to Purity, 2009; Solitary Workwoman, 2011. Contributor to magazines and journals. **Address:** 226 W Rittenhouse Sq., Apt. 1001, Philadelphia, PA 19103, U.S.A. **Online address:** geno@mycidco.com

OWENS, Thomas S(heldon). (Tom Owens). American (born United States), b. 1960. **Genres:** Sports/Fitness, How-to Books, History, Transportation, Autobiography/Memoirs, Novellas/Short Stories. **Career:** Sports Collectors Digest, columnist, avid sports collector, 1969-, co-editor, 1987-88; Freelance writer and author-in-the-schools, 1988-; Marshalltown Times Republican, reporter, 1979-80; Iowa State Daily, staff writer, 1980-84; Des Moines Register, sports correspondent, 1984-86. **Publications:** AS TOM OWENS: Collecting Sports Autographs, 1989; Official Baseball Card Price Guide, 1990; (with D. Craft) Redbirds Revisited: Great Stories and Memories from St. Louis Cardinals (oral histories for adults), 1990; Book of 1993 Baseball Cards, 1993. OTHERS: Complete Book of Baseball Cards, 1988; Greatest Baseball Players of All Time, 1990; Collecting Baseball Cards, 1993; Collecting Comic Books: A Young Person's Guide, 1995; (with D.S. Helmer) Inside Collectible Card Games: Play It Your Way, 1996; Collecting Baseball Memorabilia, 1996; Beyond Baseball Cards, 1996; Remember When: A Nostalgic Look at America's National Pastime, 1996; Ken Griffey, Jr: Super Center Fielder, 1997; Michael Jordan: Legendary Guard, 1997; Mike Piazza: Phenomenal Catcher, 1997; Mount Rushmore, 1997; The Chicago Bulls Basketball Team, 1997; Dan Marino: Record-setting Qarterback, 1997; David Robinson: All-Star Center, 1997; Ellis Island, 1997; The Golden Gate Bridge, 1997; Great Catchers, 1997; Jerry Rice: Speedy Wide Receiver, 1997; The Atlanta Braves Baseball Team, 1998; Collecting Basketball Cards, 1998; (with D.S. Helmer) Football, 1998; (with D.S. Helmer) Teamwork, the Los Angeles Sparks in Action, 1999; (with D.S. Helmer) Teamwork, the New York Liberty inAction, 1999; (with D.S. Helmer) Teamwork, the Phoenix Mercury in Action, 1999; (with D.S. Helmer) Teamwork, the Sacramento Monarchs in Action, 1999; (with D.S. Helmer) Teamwork, the Utah Starzz in Action, 1999; The Story of Basketball, 1999; (with D.S. Helmer) Baseball, 1999; (with D.S. Helmer) Basketball, 1999; (with D.S. Helmer) Hockey, 1999; (with D.S. Helmer) Teamwork, the Charlotte Sting in Action, 1999; (with D.S. Helmer) Teamwork, the Cleveland Rockers in Action, 1999; (with D.S. Helmer) Teamwork, the Houston Comets in Action, 1999; Free to Learn, 2000; Mother of Invention, 2000; (with D.S. Helmer) NASCAR, 2000; A New Mother, 2000; (with D.S. Helmer) Soccer, 2000; Flames of Freedom, 2000; (with D.S. Helmer) The History of Baseball, 2000; (with D.S. Helmer) The History of Basketball, 2000; (with D.S. Helmer) The History of Figure Skating, 2000; (with D.S. Helmer) The History of Football, 2000; (with D.S. Helmer) The History of Hockey, 2000; (with D.S. Helmer) The History of Soccer, 2000; The Bravest Blacksmith, 2000; Baseball Parks, 2001; Collecting Baseball Cards: 21st Century Edition, 2001; Collecting Stock Car Racing Memorabilia, 2001; Football Stadiums, 2001; (with D.S. Helmer) Stock Car Racing, 2001; Basketball Arenas, 2002; Immigrants and Neighbors, 2003; On Both Sides of the Civil War, 2003; The Star-Spangled Banner: The Flag and Its Anthem, 2003; (with D.S. Helmer) The Statue of Liberty, 2003; Traveling on the Freedom Machines of the Transportation Age, 2003; Washington, D.C., 2003; Muhammad Ali: Boxing Champ & Role Model, 2011. **Address:** c/o Barbara Kouts, PO Box 558, Bellport, NY 11713, U.S.A.

OWENS, Tom. *See* **OWENS, Thomas S(heldon).**

OWENSBY, Brian P(hilip). American (born United States), b. 1959?. **Genres:** Area Studies, Law, History. **Career:** University of Virginia, assistant professor of Latin American studies, 1994-, Corcoran Department of History, assistant professor of history, associate professor, professor and department chair, 1994-. Writer. **Publications:** Intimate Ironies: Modernity and the Making of Middle-Class Lives in Brazil, 1999; Empire's Law and Indian Justice in Colonial Mexico, 2008. Contributor to periodicals. **Address:** Corcoran Department of History, University of Virginia, 382 Nau Hall, 1540 Jefferson Park Ave., PO Box 400180, Charlottesville, VA 22904, U.S.A. **Online address:** bpo3a@virginia.edu

OWINGS, Alison. American (born United States), b. 1944. **Genres:** Documentaries/Reportage, Cultural/Ethnic Topics, Women's Studies And Issues, History, Social Commentary, Social Sciences, Writing/Journalism. **Career:** Congressional Quarterly, writer and researcher, 1966; ABC, news assistant, 1967-69; WRC-TV, associate producer of documentary series, 1969-71; WNBC-TV, associate producer, 1971-73; CBS, television news writer, 1973-77; freelance television news writer, 1982-99; freelance editor, 1999-. **Publications:** The Wander Woman's Phrasebook: How to Meet or Avoid People in Three Romance Languages, 1987; Frauen: German Women Recall the Third Reich, 1993; Hey, Waitress! The USA from the Other Side of the Tray, 2002; Indian Voices: Listening to Native Americans. 2011. **Address:** c/o Ellen Levine, Trident Media Group, 41 Madison Ave., New York, NY 10010, U.S.A. **Online address:** ajowings@sbcglobal.net

OWNBY, David. Canadian (born Canada), b. 1958. **Genres:** History. **Career:** University of Montreal, professor of history, Center for East Asian Studies, director. Writer and historian. **Publications:** (Ed. with M.S. Heidhues) Secret Societies Reconsidered: Perspectives on the Social History of Modern South China and Southeast Asia, 1993; Brotherhoods and Secret Societies in Early and Mid-Qing China: The Formation of a Tradition, 1996; Falun Gong and the Future of China, 2008. **Address:** Canada. **Online address:** ownbyd@cetase.umontreal.ca

OXENBURY, Helen. British (born England), b. 1938. **Genres:** Children's Fiction, Illustrations, Animals/Pets. **Career:** Tel-Aviv, stage designer, 1961; television designer, 1963. Writer and illustrator of children's books. **Publications:** SELF-ILLUSTRATED FOR CHILDREN: Numbers of Things, 1968 as Helen Oxenbury's Numbers of Things, 1983; Helen Oxenbury's ABC of Things, 1971; ABC of Things, 1972; Pig Tale, 1973; (with I. Cutler) Animal House, 1977; (with F. Maschler) Child's Book of Manners, 1978; The Queen and Rosie Randall, 1979; 729 Curious Creatures, 1980 as Curious Creatures, 1985; 729 Merry Mix-ups, 1980 as Merry Mix-ups, 1985 in UK as 729 Animal Allsorts, 1980; 729 Puzzle People, 1980 as Puzzle People, 1985, 2nd ed., 1995; Bill and Stanley, 1981; Dressing, 1981; Family, 1981; Friends, 1981; Playing, 1981; Working, 1981; Tiny Tim: Verses for Children, 1982; Bedtime, 1982; Mother's Helper, 1982; Shopping Trip, 1982, 2nd ed., 1991; Good Night, Good Morning, 1982; Beach Day, 1982; The Birthday Party, 1983; The Car Trip in UK as The Drive, 1983; The Checkup in UK as The First Check-Up, 1983; The Dancing Class, 1983; Eating Out, 1983; First Day of School in UK as Playschool, 1983; Grandma and Grandpa in UK as Gran and Granpa, 1984; The Important Visitor in UK as The Visitor, 1984; Our Dog, 1984; The Helen Oxenbury Nursery Story Book, 1985; I Can, 1985; I Hear, 1985; I See, 1986; I Touch, 1986; Baby's First Book and Doll, 1986; All Fall Down, 1987; Say Goodnight, 1987; Tickle, Tickle, 1987; Clap Hands, 1987; Monkey See, Monkey Do, 1991; (reteller) The Helen Oxenbury Nursery Treasury, 1992; It's My Birthday, 1994; Animal Scramble, 1995; Helen Oxenbury's Big Baby Book, 2003. TOM AND PIPPO SERIES: Tom and Pippo Go for a Walk, 1988; Tom and Pippo Make a Mess, 1988; Tom and Pippo in the Garden, 1988; Tom and Pippo Read a Story, 1988; Tom and Pippo and the Washing Machine, 1988; Tom and Pippo Go Shopping, 1989; Tom and Pippo See the Moon, 1989; Tom and Pippo's Day, 1989; Tom and Pippo in the Snow, 1989; Tom and Pippo Make a Friend, 1989; Pippo Gets Lost, 1989; Tom and Pippo and the Dog, 1989; Tom and Pippo and the Bicycle, 1993; Tom and Pippo on the Beach, 1993. Illustrator of books by others. **Address:** Greene and Heaton Ltd., 37 Goldhawk Rd., London, GL W12 8QQ, England.

OXENDINE, Bess Holland. American (born United States), b. 1933. **Genres:** Biography, Children's Non-fiction, Literary Criticism And History, Young Adult Fiction. **Career:** Kannapolis City Schools, teacher and literary adviser, 1961-90; North Carolina Governor's School for Gifted, philosophy teacher, 1979-80; Rowan-Cabarrus Community College, English teacher, 1989-. Speaker, reader and writer. **Publications:** Miriam, 1994; Samuel, 2000; Grace Beyond Measure, 2000. **Address:** 1193 Daybrook Dr., Kannapolis, NC 28081, U.S.A.

OXENHANDLER, Noelle. (Noelle Fintushel). American (born United States), b. 1952. **Genres:** Human Relations/Parenting, Autobiography/Memoirs. **Career:** Sarah Lawrence College, faculty; Sonoma State University, assistant professor of English, associate professor of English. Writer. **Publications:** (With N. Hillard as Noelle Fintushel) A Grief Out of Season: When Your Parents Divorce in Your Adult Years, 1991; The Eros of Parenthood: Explorations in Light and Dark, 2001; The Wishing Year: A House, a Man, My Soul: A Memoir of Fulfilled Desire, 2008; (ed. with J. Kornfield) Buddha is Still Teaching: Contemporary Buddhist Wisdom, 2010. Contributor to journals and periodicals. **Address:** Department of English, Sonoma State University, Rm. 362, Nichols Hall, 1801 E Cotati Ave., Rohnert Park, CA 94928-3609, U.S.A. **Online address:** noelle.oxenhandler@sonoma.edu

OXHORN, **Philip D.** American (born United States) **Genres:** Politics/Government, Social Sciences. **Career:** Facultad Latinoamericana de Ciencias Sociales, visiting researcher, 1985-87; Kellogg Institute for International Studies, residential fellow, 1988; McGill University, associate professor of political science, professor, McGill-Cuba Project, co-director, 1994, Institute for the Study of International Development, founding director; Project Muse, Latin American Research Review, editor-in-chief. **Publications:** Democracia y Participacioń Popular: Organizaciones Poblacionales en la Futura Democracia Chilena, 1986; (trans.) M.A. Garreton, The Chilean Political Process, 1989; Organizing Civil Society: The Popular Sectors and the Struggle for Democracy in Chile, 1995; (ed. with G. Ducatenzeiler) What Kind of Democracy? What Kind of Market?: Latin America in the Age of Neoliberalism, 1998; (ed. with P.K. Starr) Markets & Democracy in Latin America: Conflict or Convergence?, 1999; (ed. with A.D. Selee and J.S. Tulchin) Decentralization, Democratic Governance, and Civil Society in Comparative perspective: Africa, Asia, and Latin America, 2004; (ed. with K.M. Roberts and J. Burdick) Beyond Neoliberalism in Latin America?: Societies and Politics at the Crossroads, 2009; Sustaining Civil Society: Economic Change, Democracy and the Social Construction of Citizenship in Latin America, 2011. Contributor to books and journals. **Address:** Department of Political Science, McGill University, Rm. 414, Leacock Bldg., 855 Sherbrooke St. W, Montreal, QC H3A 2T7, Canada. **Online address:** philip.oxhorn@mcgill.ca

OXLEY, **William.** British (born England), b. 1939. **Genres:** Plays/Screenplays, Poetry, Literary Criticism And History, Philosophy, Travel/Exploration, Autobiography/Memoirs, Translations. **Career:** Articled clerk, 1957-64; Deloitte and Co., chartered accountant, 1964-68; Lazard Brothers and Company Ltd., chartered accountant, 1968-76; writer, 1976-; Torbay, millennium poet-in-residence, 2000-01; Institute of Chartered Accountants, fellow. Writer. **Publications:** The Dark Structures, and Other Poems, 1967; New Workings, 1969; Passages from Time (poems), 1971; The Icon Poems, 1972; Sixteen Days in Autumn(travel), 1972; Opera Vetera, 1973; Mirrors of the Sea, 1973; Eve Free, 1974; Fightings, 1974; Mundane Shell, 1975; Superficies, 1976; The Exile, 1979; The Notebook of Hephaestus and Other Poems, 1981; (trans.) Poems of a Black Orpheus, 1981; The Synopthegms of a Prophet (aphorisms), 1981; The Idea and Its Imminence, 1982; Of Human Consciousness, 1982; The Cauldron of Inspiration, 1983; A Map of Time, 1984; The Triviad and Other Satires, 1984; The Inner Tapestry, 1985; Vitalism and Celebration (essays), 1987; The Mansands Trilogy, 1988; Mad Tom on Tower Hill, 1988; Distinguishing Poetry: Writings on Poetry, 1989; Forest Sequence, 1991; The Patient Reconstruction of Paradise, 1991; The Playboy, 1992; In the Drift of Words, 1992; Cardboard Troy, 1993; The Hallsands Tragedy, 1993; Collected Longer Poems, 1994; (ed.) Completing the Picture: Exiles, Outsiders & Independents, 1995; Three Plays, 1996; The Green Crayon Man, 1997; No Accounting for Paradise (autobiography), 1999; Firework Planet (for children), 2000; Reclaiming the Lyre: Selected Poems, 2001; Namaste: Nepal Poems, 2004; London Visions, 2004; Poems Antibes, 2006; Working Backwards (a poet's notebook), 2008; Sunlight in a Champagne Glass, 2009; Everyman His Own God, 2010. **Address:** 6 The Mount, Furzeham, Brixham, South Devon, TQ5 8QY, England. **Online address:** pwoxley@aol.com

OZERSKY, **Josh.** American (born United States), b. 1967. **Genres:** History, Communications/Media. **Career:** Citysearch Local Guide Website, restaurant editor, 2008-; Feedbag Website, editor; New York Magazine Website, food editor. **Publications:** (Comp. with W. Vesterman) Readings for the 21st Century: Tomorrow's Issues for Today's Students, 2nd ed., 1994, 4th ed., 2000; Archie Bunker's America: TV in an Era of Change, 1968-1978, 2003; The Hamburger: A History, 2008. Contributor to periodicals. **Address:** New York, NY , U.S.A. **Online address:** editor@the-feedbag.com

OZICK, **Cynthia.** American (born United States), b. 1928. **Genres:** Novels, Novellas/Short Stories, Plays/Screenplays, Theatre, Essays, Young Adult Non-fiction, Humanities, Literary Criticism And History, Literary Criticism And History. **Career:** Filene's Department Store, advertising copywriter, 1952-53; New York University, instructor in English, 1964-65; City University of New York, City College, distinguished artist-in-residence, 1981-82; Harvard University, faculty, 1985. Writer and translator. **Publications:** Trust (novel), 1966; The Pagan Rabbi and Other Stories, 1971; Bloodshed and Three Novellas, 1976; Levitation: Five Fictions, 1982; The Cannibal Galaxy, 1983; Art & Ardor (essays), 1983; Seymour Adelman, 1906-1985: A Keepsake, 1985; The Messiah of Stockholm: A Novel, 1987; The Shawl, 1989; Metaphor and Memory (essays), 1989; What Henry James Knew and Other Essays on Writers, 1993; Portrait of the Artist as a Bad Character: And Other Essays on Writing, 1996; Fame & Folly, 1996; Cynthia Ozick Reader, 1996; (intro.) Seize the Day, 1996; The Puttermesser Papers, 1997; (ed. and intro. with R. Atwan) Best American Essays 1998, 1998; Quarrel & Quandary: Essays, 2000; From New York to Jerusalem, 2001; (intro.) Complete Works of Isaac Babel, 2002; Heir to the Glimmering World, 2004; Bear Boy, 2005; Din in the Head: Essays, 2006; Collected Stories, 2006; Dictation: A Quartet, 2008; Foreign Bodies, 2010. Contributor to books and periodicals. Works appear in anthologies. **Address:** Alfred A. Knopf Inc., 201 E 50th St., New York, NY 10022-7799, U.S.A.

OZSVATH, **Zsuzsanna.** American (born United States), b. 1934. **Genres:** Literary Criticism And History, Area Studies, Translations. **Career:** Hockaday School of Dallas, teacher, 1968-69; Bishop College, assistant professor, 1969-79; University of Texas-Dallas, School of Arts and Humanities, lecturer, 1976-80, senior lecturer, 1980-82, visiting professor, 1982-83, assistant professor, 1983-88, associate professor, 1988-98, professor of literature and the history of ideas, 1998-, Holocaust Studies Program, director, 1980-, Leah and Paul Lewis chair in holocaust studies; Common Knowledge, assistant editor. **Publications:** In the Footsteps of Orpheus: The Life and Times of Miklos Radnoti, 2000; Orpheus Nyomában: Radnóti Miklós élete és kora, 2004. TRANSLATIONS: (with F. Turner) M. Radnoti, Foamy Sky: The Major Poems of Miklos Radnoti, 1992; (with F. Turner) A. Jozsef, The Iron-Blue Vault: Selected Poems of Attila Jozsef, 1999; When the Danube ran red, 2010. Contributor of essays. **Address:** School of Arts & Humanities, University of Texas, JO 5.116B, Jonsson Bldg., 800 W Campbell Rd., Richardson, TX 75080-3021, U.S.A. **Online address:** zozsvath@utdallas.edu

OZYUREK, **Esra.** American (born United States) **Genres:** Politics/Government. **Career:** University of California, assistant professor. Writer. **Publications:** (ed.) Turkiye'nin toplumsal hafizasi: hatirladiklariyla ve unuttuklariyla (title means: 'Remembering and Forgetting: Social Memory in Turkey'), 2001; Nostalgia for the Modern: State Secularism and Everyday Politics in Turkey, 2006; (ed.) The Politics of Public Memory in Turkey, 2007. Contributor to books and periodicals. **Address:** University of San Diego, 5998 Alcala Pk., San Diego, CA 92110, U.S.A. **Online address:** eozyurek@ucsd.edu

P

PACE, Alison. American (born United States) **Genres:** Novels, Children's Fiction, Animals/Pets. **Career:** Sothebys Institute, fine art researcher. Writer. **Publications:** If Andy Warhol Had a Girlfriend (novel), 2005; Pug Hill (novel), 2006; Through Thick and Thin (novel), 2007; City Dog, 2008; A Pug's Tale, 2011. **Address:** c/o Megan Swartz, Penguin Group, 375 Hudson St., New York, NY 10014, U.S.A. **Online address:** alison@alisonpace.com

PACE, Robert F. American (born United States), b. 1966. **Genres:** Travel/Exploration, History, Young Adult Non-fiction. **Career:** Texas Christian University, graduate assistant, 1988-90, instructor in history, 1990-92; Longwood College, assistant professor, 1992-98, associate professor, 1998-99; McMurry University, associate professor, 1999-2004, department of history, chair, 2001-06, professor of history, 2004-, Grady McWhiney Research Foundation, fellow, 1996-, senior director, 1999-2004, vice president and chief operating officer, 2004-. Writer and historian. **Publications:** (Ed. with G. McWhiney and W.O. Moore) Fear God and Walk Humbly: The Agricultural Journal of James Mallory, 1843-1877, 1997; (ed.) Two Hundred Years in the Heart of Virginia: Perspectives on Farmville's History, 1798-1998, 1998; Halls of Honor: College Men in the Old South, 2004; (with D.S. Frazier) Frontier Texas: History of a Borderland to 1880, 2004; (ed.) Buffalo Days: Stories from J. Wright Mooar, 2005; (with D.S. Frazier and R.P. Wettemann, Jr.) The Texas You Expect: The Story of Buffalo Gap Historic Village, 2006; (with D.S. Frazier) Abilene Historic Landmarks: An Illustrated Tour, 2008. Contributor to journals. **Address:** Department of History, McMurry University, PO Box 638, McMurry Sta., Abilene, TX 79697, U.S.A. **Online address:** rpace@mcm.edu

PACELLE, Mitchell. American (born United States) **Genres:** Documentaries/Reportage, Business/Trade/Industry. **Career:** Wall Street Journal, columnist, reporter. **Publications:** Empire: A Tale of Obsession, Betrayal, and the Battle for an American Icon, 2001. Contributor of articles to newspapers. **Address:** c/o Author Mail, John Wiley & Sons Inc., 111 River St., Hoboken, NJ 07030-5773, U.S.A.

PACK, Robert. American (born United States), b. 1929. **Genres:** Poetry, Literary Criticism And History, Essays, Novellas/Short Stories, Music. **Career:** Barnard College, associate in poetry, 1957-63; Bread Loaf Writers Conference, staff, 1963-72, director, 1973-94; Middlebury College, professor of English, 1964-98, Abernathy professor, 1970-78; University of Montana, adjunct assistant professor, 1998-. Writer. **Publications:** The Irony of Joy, 1955; Wallace Stevens: An Approach to His Poetry and Thought, 1958; A Strangers Privilege, 1959; The Forgotten Secret, 1959; Then What Did You Do?, 1961; (trans. with M. Lelach) W.A. Mozart, Three Mozart Libretti: Complete in Italian and English, 1961, rev. ed., 1993; Guarded by Women, 1963; Selected Poems, 1964; How to Catch a Crocodile, 1964; Wallace Stevens: An Approach to His Poetry and Thought, 1968; Home from the Cemetery, 1969; Nothing but Light, 1972; Keeping Watch, 1976; Waking to My Name: New and Selected Poems, 1980; Faces in a Single Tree: A Cycle of Monologues, 1984; Affirming Limits: Essays on Mortality, Choice and Poetic Form, 1985; Clayfield Rejoices, Clayfield Laments: A Sequence of Poems, 1987; Before It Vanishes: A Packet for Professor Pagels, 1989; The Octopus Who Wanted to Juggle, 1990; The Long View: Essays on the Discipline of Hope and Poetic Craft, 1991; Inheritance (poetry), 1992; Fathering the Map: New and Selected Later Poems, 1993; Minding the Sun, 1996; Rounding It Out: A Cycle of Sonnetelles, 1999; Belief and Uncertainty in the Poetry of Robert Frost, 2003; Elk in Winter, 2004; Composing Voices: A Cycle of Dramatic Monologues, 2005; (with F. Vagnini) The Side Effects Bible: The Dietary Solution to Unwanted Side Effects of Common Medications, 2005; (with R. Hoffman) Alternative Cures That Really Work: For the Savvy Health Consumer a Must-have Guide to more than 100 Food Remedies, Herbs, Supplements, and Healing Techniques, 2006; Willing to Choose: Volition & Storytelling in Shakespeares Major Plays, 2007; (with N. Taylor and J. Yazdany) Arthritis for Dummies, 2007; (with G.T. Grossberg) The Essential Herb-drug-vitamin Interaction Guide: The Safe Way to Use Medications and Supplements Together, 2008; Laughter Before Sleep, 2011. EDITOR: (with D. Hall and L. Simpson) New Poets of England and America, 1957; (with D. Hall) New Poets of England and America: Second Selection, 1962; (with T.F. Driver) Poems of Doubt and Belief: An Anthology of Modern Religious Poetry, 1964; (with M. Klein) Literature for Composition on the Theme of Innocence and Experience, 1966; (with M. Klein) Short Stories: Classic, Modern, Contemporary, 1967; (and intro.) The Selected Letters of John Keats, 1974; (with S. Lea and J. Parini) The Bread Loaf Anthology of Contemporary American Poetry, 1985; (with J. Parini) The Bread Loaf Anthology of Contemporary American Short Stories, 1987; (with J. Parini) The Bread Loaf Anthology of Contemporary American Essays, 1989; (with J. Parini) Writers on Writing, 1991; (with J. Parini) Poems for a Small Planet: Contemporary American Nature Poetry, 1993; (with J. Parini) American Identities: Contemporary Multicultural Voices, 1994; (with J. Parini)Touchstones: Merican Poets on a Favorite Poem, 1996; (with J. Parini) Introspections: American Poets on One of Their Own Poems, 1997; (with J. Parini) Contemporary Poetry of New England, 2002. Contributor to periodicals. **Address:** David R. Godine Publishers Inc., 9 Hamilton Pl., Boston, MA 02108-4715, U.S.A. **Online address:** cnd3199@blackfoot.net

PACK, Spencer J. American (born United States), b. 1953. **Genres:** Economics, Business/Trade/Industry. **Career:** Connecticut College, instructor, 1981-83, assistant professor, 1983-88, associate professor of economics, 1988-93, professor of economics, 1993-, chair of department, 1988-91; Yale University, visiting associate professor, 1990-91, Dana fellow, 1990. Writer. **Publications:** Reconstructing Marxian Economics: Marx Based upon a Sraffian Commodity Theory of Value, 1985; Capitalism as a Moral System: Adam Smith's Critique of the Free Market Economy, 1991; Aristotle, Adam Smith and Karl Marx: On Some Fundamental Issues in 21st Century Political Economy, 2010. Works appear in anthologies. Contributor of articles to periodicals. **Address:** Department of Economics, Connecticut College, 270 Mohegan Ave., PO Box 5381, New London, CT 06320, U.S.A. **Online address:** sjpac@conncoll.edu

PACKARD, Robert. American/Canadian (born Canada), b. 1916. **Genres:** Travel/Exploration, Writing/Journalism. **Career:** Stevens Institute of Technology, College of Arts and Letters, instructor, 1960-, professor of humanities, now professor emeritus. Writer. **Publications:** Refractions: Writers and Places, 1990. Contributor to periodicals. **Address:** Department of Literature & Communications, College of Arts & Letters, Stevens Institute of Technology, Castle Point on Hudson, Hoboken, NJ 07030-5991, U.S.A. **Online address:** rpackard@stevens.edu

PACKER, James Innell. Canadian/British (born England), b. 1926. **Genres:** Theology/Religion. **Career:** Latimer House, warden, 1961-69; Tyndale Hall Theological College, principal, 1969-71; Trinity College, associate principal, 1971-79; Regent College, professor of theology, 1979-, Regent College's Anglican Studies Program, director; Anglican theological college, principal. Writer. **Publications:** (With O.R. Johnston) Martin Luther on the Bondage of the Will: A New Translation of De Servo Arbitrio (1525) Martin Luther's Reply to Erasmus of Rotterdam, 1957; Fundamentalism and the Word of God, Some Evangelical Principles, 1958; (with O.R. Johnston) Luther's Bondage of the Will, 1958; Evangelism and the Sovereignty of God, 1961; (ed.) Church of England and the Methodist Church: A Consideration of the Report, Conversations between the Church of England and the Methodist Church: Ten Essays, 1963; Our Lord's Understanding of the Law of God, 1962; (co-ed.) New Bible Dictionary, 1962, 3rd ed., 1996; Keep Yourselves from Idols, 1964; (ed.) All in Each Place, 1965; God Speaks to Man; Revelation and the Bible, 1965; Tomorrow's Worship, 1966; (ed.) Guidelines: Anglican Evangelicals Face the Future, 1967; (with A.M. Stibbs) The Spirit within You, 1967; (ed.) Guidelines, 1967; (with G.O. Buchanan and G.E. Duffield) Fellowship in the Gospel: Evangelical Comment on Anglican-Methodist Unity and Intercommunion Today, 1968; (ed.) Fellowship in the Gospel, 1968; Relations between English Churchmen and Roman Catholics: Some Guiding Principles; A Memorandum Issued by the Church Society, 1968; (co-author) Growing into Union, 1970; Knowing God, 1973; I Want to Be a Christian, 1977; Ten Commandments, 1977; For Man's Sake, 1978; (with R.T. Beckwith and G.E. Duffield) Across the Divide, 1978; The Evangelical Anglican Identity Problem, 1978; God Has Spoken, 1979; (ed. with M.C. Tenney and W. White) Bible Almanac, 1980; Beyond the Battle for the Bible, 1980; A Kind of Noah's Ark?, 1981; God's Words: Studies of key Bible Themes, 1981; All the People and Places of the Bible, 1982; (ed. with M.C. Tenney and W. White) Daily Life in Bible Times, 1982; (ed. with M.C. Tenney and W. White) World of the New Testament, 1982; Freedom, Authority and Scripture, 1982; (with R.T. Beckwith) The 39 Articles, 1984; Keep in Step with the Spirit, 1984; (ed. with M.C. Tenney and W. White) Land of the Bible, 1985; (ed. with M.C. Tenney and W. White) Public Life in Bible Times, 1985; (with T. Howard) Christianity, the True Humanism, 1985; (ed.) The Best in Theology, vol. I-IV, 1986-89; Through the Year with J.I. Packer, 1986; Your Father Loves You: Daily Insights for Knowing God, 1986; God in Our Midst, 1987; Hot Tub Religion, 1987; (ed.) Here We Stand, 1988; (ed. with M.C. Tenney and W. White) Everyday Life in the Bible: The Old and New Testaments, 1989; A Quest for Godliness: The Puritan Vision of the Christian Life, 1990; (ed. with L. Wilkinson) Alive to God: Studies in Spirituality Presented to James Houston, 1992; Rediscovering Holiness, 1992; Hot Tub Religion: Christian Living in a Materialistic World, 1993; Concise Theology: A Guide to Historic Christian Beliefs, 1993; Growing in Christ, 1994; A Passion for Faithfulness: Wisdom from the Book of Nehemiah, 1995; Knowing Christianity, 1995; (ed. with L. Wilkinson) Nelson's Ilustrated Ecyclopedia of Bible Facts, 1995; Knowing and Doing the Will of God, 1995; Life in the Spirit: A 30-Day Devotional, 1996; Truth & Power: The Place of Scripture in the Christian Life, 1996; Great Grace: A 31-Day Devotional, 1997; Grief Sanctified: Passing Through Grief to Peace and Joy, 1997; Great Power: A 31-Day Devotional, 1997; Great Joy: A 30 Day Devotional, 1998; Collected Shorter Writings of J.I. Packer, vol. I-IV, 1999-2000; (ed. with S.K. Soderlund) Way of Wisdom: Essays in Honor of Bruce K. Waltke, 2000; (ed.) Puritan Papers, 2000; J.I. Packer Answers Questions for Today, 2001; (with C. Nystrom) Never beyond Hope: How God Touches & Uses Imperfect People, 2000; God's Plans for You, 2001; Faithfulness and Holiness, 2002; The Redemption and Restoration of Man in the Thought of Richard Baxter, 2003; (with T.C. Oden) One Faith: The Evangelical Consensus, 2004; Knowing God Through the Year, 2004; Keep in Step with the Spirit: Finding Fullness in our Walk with God, 2005; (with C. Nystrom) Praying: Finding Our Way Through Duty to Delight, 2006; Keeping the 10 Commandments, 2007; Praying the Lord's Prayer, 2007; Affirming the Apostles' Creed, 2008; (with C. Nystrom) Guard Us, Guide Us: Divine Leading in Life's Decisions, 2008; (with M. Dever) In My Place Condemned He Stood: Celebrating the Glory of the Atonement, 2008; Evangelism & the Sovereignty of God, 2009; Knowing God Devotional Journal: A One-year Guide, 2009; (with C. Nystrom) Abiding in Christ: 8 Studies for Individuals and Groups, 2009; (with G.A. Parrett) Grounded in the Gospel: Building Believers the Old-fashioned Way, 2010. **Address:** Regent College, [illegible] University Blvd., Vancouver, BC V6T 2E4, Canada.

PACKER, Joan Garrett. American (born United States), b. 1948. **Genres:** Bibliography, Biography, Literary Criticism And History. **Career:** Houston Lighting and Power, corporate librarian, 1969-70; Central Connecticut State University, assistant curriculum librarian, 1971-81, head reference librarian, 1981-2003, adjunct librarian, 2003-. Writer. **Publications:** Margaret Drabble: An Annotated Bibliography, 1988; Rebecca West: An Annotated Bibliography, 1991. Contributor to books. **Address:** Elihu Burritt Library Reference Department, Central Connecticut State University, 1615 Stanley St., New Britain, CT 06050, U.S.A. **Online address:** packerj@ccsu.edu

PACKER, Mez. British (born England), b. 1966?. **Genres:** Novels. **Career:** British Broadcasting Corp., broadcast journalist; Step Forward Publishing, magazine editor; Coventry University, visiting lecturer, 2005-; Interactive Media, associate senior lecturer. **Publications:** Among Thieves (novel), 2009. Contributor to periodicals. **Address:** Leamington Spa, England. **Online address:** m.packer@coventry.ac.uk

PACKER, Vin. *See* **MEAKER, Marijane (Agnes).**

PACKETT, Charles Neville. British (born England), b. 1922?. **Genres:** Travel/Exploration, Business/Trade/Industry, History, Cultural/Ethnic Topics, Social Sciences. **Career:** Sydney Packett and Sons Ltd., director, 1941-91, consultant, 1991-; Ashville College, governor, 1970-2002; City & Guilds of London Institute, honorary fellow, 2000. Writer. **Publications:** History of the Greek Order of St. Dennis of Zante, 1962; City of Bradford Local Savings Committee Year Book, 1962; Guide to the Republic of San Marino, 1964; The Orders of Knighthood of the Most Serene Republic of San Marino, 1970; Guide to the Republic of Nauru, 1971; A History and A to Z of Her Majesty's Lieutenancy of Counties (1547-1972) with Particular Reference to the West Riding of Yorkshire, 1973; The County Lieutenancy in the U.K. 1547-1975, 1975; Kingdom of Tonga: Travel and Holiday Guide to Tongatapu Island, 1976; Association of Lieutenants of Counties & Custodes Rotulorum: A Brief History (1907/1977), 1977; (ed.) A Short History of the Republic of San Marino, 1979; Diamond Jubilee History (1920-1980) of Sydney Packett and Sons Ltd., 1980; The Texas Navy: A Brief History, 1983; A History of the Bradford Club, 1986; A History of the Lieutenancy of the City of London, 1987; (comp.) Bradfords Around the World, 1997; Surprise Packett, 1998. **Address:** 20 Wells Ct., Wells Promenade, Ilkley, WY LS29 9LG, England.

PACULT, F. Paul. American (born United States), b. 1949. **Genres:** Adult Non-fiction. **Career:** New York Times, special projects editor; Spirit Journal Inc., president, publisher and editor, 1984-; Delta Sky, columnist; Wine Enthusiast Magazine, columnist and spirits-tasting director; Beverage Dynamics, contributing editor; Wine and Spirits, contributing editor. Educator and consultant. **Publications:** The Beer Essentials: The Spirit Journal Guide to over 650 of the World's Beers, 1997; Kindred Spirits: The Spirit Journal Guide to the World's Distilled Spirits and Fortified Wines, 1997; American Still Life: The Jim Beam Story and the Making of the World's #1 Bourbon, 2003; A Double Scotch: How Chivas Regal and The Glenlivet Became Global Icons, 2005; Kindred Spirits 2: 2,400 Reviews of Whiskey, Brandy, Vodka, Tequila, Rum, Gin, and Liqueurs from F. Paul Pacult's Spirit Journal 2000-2007, 2008. **Address:** Spirit Journal Inc., 241 Old Reservoir Rd., PO Box 126, Wallkill, NY 12589-4033, U.S.A. **Online address:** pacult@interport.net

PACZKOWSKI, Andrzej. Polish (born Poland), b. 1938. **Genres:** Novels, History, Social Sciences. **Career:** Institute of Literary Researches of PAS, assistant, 1966-74; National Library, assistant, 1975-80; Institute of Political Studies, Polish Academy of Sciences, assistant professor, 1975-91, professor of history, 1991-, director of political history laboratory; Institute of History of PAS, assistant professor, 1980-90; University of Bialystok, assistant professor, 1991-94; Collegium Civitas, professor, 1999-; Woodrow Wilson Center, fellow. Writer. **Publications:** Zakopane i okolice, 1968, 4th ed., 1984; Prasa Polityczna Ruchu Ludowego (1918-1939), 1970; Czwarta wladza; prasa dawniej i dziś, 1973; Prasapolonijna w latach 1870-1939: zarys problematyki, 1977; Prasa ispoleczność polska we Francji w latach, 1920-1940, 1979; Prasapolska w latach 1918-1939, 1980; Prasa codzienna Warszawy w latach 1918-1939, 1983; Polska prasa konspiracyjna (1939-1945) i powstaniawarszawskiego w zbiorach Biblioteki Narodowej: katalog, 1984; Opozycja iopór spoleczny w Polsce, 1945-1980: materialy konwersatorium z 20lutego 1991; Stanislaw Mikolajczyk, czyli, Kleska Realisty: zarysbiografii politycznej, 1991; Referendum z 30 czerwca 1946 r.: przebieg iwyniki, 1993; Zdobycie wladzy: 1945-1947, 1993; Aparat bezpieczeństwaw latach 1944-1956: taktyka, strategia, metody, 1994; Powrótzolnierzy AK z sowieckich lagrów, 1995; Zaciskanie petli. [illegible] Czechoslowacji 1968 r., 1995; Krajowa Komisja Porozumiewawcza NSZZ Solidarnosc, posiedzenie 9 10 kwietnia 1981r., 1996; Pól wieku dziejów Polski: 1939-1989, 1996; NKWD o

Polscei Polakach: rekonesans archiwalny; 1996; Polska 1986-1989: od kooptacji donegocjacji: kilka uwag o wchodzeniu w proces zmiany systemowej; 1997; Rozmowy z rzadem PRL: negocjacje pomiędzy NSZZ Solidarność a rządem w dniach 15-18 pazdziernika 1981, 1998; Tajne dokumentyBiura Politycznego: PRL-ZSRR 1956-1970, 1998; Od sfalszowanego zwyciestwado prawdziwej kleski: szkice do portretu PRL, 1999; The Black Book of Communism: Crimes, Terror, Repression, 1999; Aparat bezpieczeństwa w Polsce w latach 1950-1952: taktyka, strategia, metody, 2000; Droga domniejszego zla: strategia i taktyka obozu wadzy, lipiec 1980-styczeń1982, 2000; System nomenklatury kadr w Polsce (1950-1970), 2000; Strajki, bunty, manifestacje jako polska droga przez socjalizm, 2003; The Spring Will Be Ours: Poland and the Poles from Occupation to Freedom, 2003; Diariusz premiera Stanislawa Mikolajczyka prowadzony przez Stefanie Liebermanowa: 13 XII 1944-14 VI 1945, 2003; Centrum wladzy w Polsce: 1948-1970, 2003; Aparat bezpieczeństwa w Polsce w latach 1953-1954: taktyka, strategia, metody, 2004; Wojna polsko-jaruzelska: stan wojenny w Polsce 13 XII 1981 22 VII 1983, 2006; (ed. with M. Byrne) From Solidarity to Martial Law: The Polish Crisis of 1980-1981: A Documentary History, 2007; (co-ed.) Od Pilsudskiego do Wałęsy: studia z dziejów Polski w XX wieku, 2008; Wywiad polski w roku 1949: sprawozdanie z dzialaności, 2009; Trzy twarze Józefa światly: przyczynek do historii komunizmu w Polsce, 2009. **Address:** c/o Author Mail, Penn State University Press, 820 N University Dr., University Support Bldg. 1, Ste. C, University Park, PA 16802-1003, U.S.A. **Online address:** apaczkow@isppan.waw.pl

PADANILAM, George J. American/Indian (born India), b. 1939. **Genres:** Novels, Philosophy, Psychology. **Career:** Medical College of Ohio, resident in surgery, 1972. Writer. **Publications:** The Fig Leaf Conspiracy: Improve Your Life, Eliminate False Perceptions, 2004. **Address:** c/o Cynthia Sterling, Lee Shore Literary Agency, 7436 Washington Ave., Ste. 100, Pittsburgh, PA 15218-2521, U.S.A. **Online address:** gjpad01@yahoo.com

PADDISON, Sara. (Sara Hatch Paddison). American (born United States), b. 1953. **Genres:** Self Help, Psychology. **Career:** Institute of HeartMath, vice-president, 1970-93, chief financial officer, 1992-, president and chief executive officer, 1998-. Writer. **Publications:** Just Love the People, 1991; The Hidden Power of the Heart: Achieving Balance and Fulfillment in a Stressful World, 1992; (ed.) Parenting Manual, 1995; (ed.) Teaching Children to Love, 1996; (with. D. Childre) HeartMath Discovery Program: Daily Readings and Self-Discovery Exercises for Creating a More Rewarding Life, 1998; Hidden Power of the Heart: Discovering an Unlimited Source of Intelligence, 1998. **Address:** Institute of HeartMath, 14700 W Park Ave., Boulder Creek, CA 95006, U.S.A.

PADDISON, Sara Hatch. *See* **PADDISON, Sara.**

PADDOCK, Jennifer. American (born United States) **Genres:** Novels, Young Adult Fiction. **Career:** Writer. **Publications:** A Secret Word: A Novel, 2004; Point Clear, 2006. Contributor to Journals. Works appears in anthologies. **Address:** c/o Author Mail, Simon Schuster Inc., 1230 Ave. of the Americas, New York, NY 10020, U.S.A.

PADDOCK, Lisa. (Lisa Olson Paddock). American (born United States), b. 1951. **Genres:** Law, Literary Criticism And History, Biography, Autobiography/Memoirs. **Career:** University of Toronto, lecturer, 1981-82; Merrill Lynch, financial adviser, 1982-86; Carter, Ledyard and Milburn, legal associate, 1989-92; Davis and Gilbert, legal associate, 1992; Great American Trials, editor, 1994. **Publications:** (Co-ed.) Great American Trials, 1994, 2nd ed., 2002; Facts about the Supreme Court of the United States, 1996; (with C.S. Rollyson) Student's Guide to Scandinavian American Genealogy, 1996; (with C.S. Rollyson) Student's Guide to Polish American Genealogy, 1996; (co-ed.) Courtroom Drama: 120 of the World's Most Notable Trials, 1998; Susan Sontag: The Making of an Icon, 2000; Contrapuntal in Integration, 2000; Herman Melville A to Z, 2001; Encyclopedia of American Literature, vol. II, 2002; The Supreme Court for Dummies, 2002; (with C. Rollyson) Brontës A to Z: The Essential Reference to Their Lives and Work, 2003; (co-author) Critical Companion to Herman Melville: A Literary Reference to His Life and Work, 2007. Contributor to periodicals. **Address:** 52 Alexandra Way, Cape May Court House, NJ 08210, U.S.A. **Online address:** lisa_paddock@yahoo.com

PADDOCK, Lisa Olson. *See* **PADDOCK, Lisa.**

PADEL, Ruth. British (born England), b. 1946. **Genres:** Poetry, Theology/Religion, Psychology, Theatre, Literary Criticism And History, Natural History. **Career:** Oxford University, research fellow and lecturer, 1976-80; University of London, Birkbeck College, lecturer in classics, 1980-84. Freelance writer, 1984-. **Publications:** Alibi (poems), 1985; Summer Snow (poems), 1990; In and Out of the Mind: Greek Images of the Tragic Self, 1992; Angel (poems), 1993; Whom Gods Destroy: Elements of Greek and Tragic Madness, 1995; Fusewire (poems), 1996; Rembrandt Would Have Loved You (poems), 1998; I'm a Man: Sex, Gods and Rock 'n' Roll, 2000; 52 Ways of Looking at a Poem or How Reading Modern Poetry Can Change Your Life, 2002; Voodoo Shop, 2002; The Soho Leopard, 2004; Tigers in Red Weather, 2006; Poem and the Journey: And Sixty Poems to Read Along the Way, 2007; Darwin: A Life In Poems, 2009; Silent Letters of the Alphabet, 2010; Where the Serpent Lives, 2010. **Address:** United Agents, 12 Lexington St., London, GL W1F 7QL, England. **Online address:** mail@ruthpadel.com

PADEN, William E. American (born United States), b. 1939. **Genres:** Theology/Religion. **Career:** University of Vermont, Department of Religion, instructor, 1965-67, assistant professor, 1967-74, chairman, 1972-78, 1990-2005, associate professor, 1974-90, professor, 1990-2009, professor emeritus, 2009-. Writer. **Publications:** Religious Worlds: The Comparative Study of Religion, 1988, 2nd ed., 1994; Interpreting the Sacred: Ways of Viewing Religion, 1992, rev. ed., 2003. Contributor to journals. Works appear in anthologies. **Address:** Department of Religion, University of Vermont, 481 Main St., Burlington, VT 05405, U.S.A. **Online address:** william.paden@uvm.edu

PADFIELD, Peter. British/Indian (born India), b. 1932. **Genres:** Novels, History, Military/Defense/Arms Control, Autobiography/Memoirs, Biography, Young Adult Fiction. **Career:** Shaw Savill & Albion Shipping Line, cadet, 1950-53; Peninsular and Oriental Steam Navigation Co., officer, 1953-58; Shipbuilding and Shipping Record, editorial assistant, 1960; Angula Engineering Company Ltd., director, 1960-63; writer, 1963-. **Publications:** OTHERS: The Sea is a Magic Carpet (autobiography), 1959; The Merchant Navy as a Career, 1962; Maritime Dominion and the Triumph of the Free World: Naval Campaigns that Shaped the Modern World 1852-2001, 2009; The Sunday Times, forthcoming. HISTORY: The Titanic and The Californian, 1965; An Agony of Collisions, 1966; The Battleship Era, 1972, rev. ed. as Battleship, 2000; Guns at Sea, 1973; The Great Naval Race, 1974; Nelson's War, 1975; Tide of Empires, 2 vols., 1979-82; Rule Britannia: The Victorian and Edwardian Navy, 1981; Beneath the Houseflag of the P&O, 1982; Armada, 1988; War beneath the Sea: Submarine Conflict 1939-1945, 1995; Maritime Supremacy and the Opening of the Western Mind, 1999; Maritime Power and the Struggle for Freedom, 2005. BIOGRAPHY: Aim Straight, 1967; Broke and the Shannon, 1969; Donitz: The Last Führer, 1983, rev. ed., 1993; Himmler: Reichsführer-SS, 1990, rev. ed., 2001; Hess: Flight for the Führer, 1991, rev. ed. as Hess: The Führer's Disciple, 2001. NOVELS: The Lion's Claw, 1978; The Unquiet Gods, 1980; Gold Chains of Empire, 1982; Salt and Steel, 1986. **Address:** Andrew Lownie Literary Agency Ltd., 36 Great Smith St., London, GL SW1P 3BU, England.

PADGETT, (Mary) Abigail. American (born United States), b. 1942. **Genres:** Mystery/Crime/Suspense, Social Sciences, Young Adult Fiction, Gay And Lesbian Issues. **Career:** Teacher, 1964-69; Malcolm Bliss Mental Health Center, vocational rehabilitation specialist, 1971-76; Washington University, adjunct teacher of sociology, 1976-79; Houston/Galveston American Civil Liberties Union, director, 1980-82; Sociological Abstracts, writer, 1983-85; San Diego County Department of Social Services, Child Protective Services, court investigator, 1986-88. Writer. **Publications:** Child of Silence, 1993; Strawgirl, 1994; Turtle Baby, 1995; Moonbird Boy, 1996; The Dollmaker's Daughters, 1997; Blue, 1998; The Last Blue Plate Special, 2001. **Address:** c/o Sandra Dijkstra, Sandra Dijkstra Literary Agency, 1155 Camino del Mar., Ste. 515, Del Mar, CA 92014-3115, U.S.A.

PADGETT, Ron. American (born United States), b. 1942. **Genres:** Novels, Novellas/Short Stories, Plays/Screenplays, Poetry, Translations, Biography, Literary Criticism And History. **Career:** St. Mark's-in-the-Bowery, poetry workshop instructor, 1968-69; Full Court Press, co-founder, 1973-, editor, 1973-88; South Carolina Arts Commission, writer in the community, 1976-78; St. Mark's Poetry Project, director, 1978-81; Teachers and Writers Collaborative, director of publications, 1982-99; Atlantic Center for the Arts, lecturer; Columbia University, lecturer; Brooklyn College, faculty. **Publications:** (With T. Berrigan) Seventeen: Plays, 1964; 2/2 Stories for Andy Warhol, 1965; In Advance of the Broken Arm: Poems, 1965; Sky: An Opener, 1966; (with T. Berrigan) Bean Spasms: Poems and Prose, 1967; Tone Arm,

1967; (with J. Brainard) 100, 000 Fleeing Hilda, 1967; (with T. Clark) Bun, 1968; (with T. Berrigan and J. Brainard) Some Thing, 1968; Great Balls of Fire, 1969, rev. ed., 1990; (with J. Dine) The Adventures of Mr. and Mrs. Jim and Ron, 1970; Sweet Pea, 1971; Poetry Collection, 1971; Sufferin' Succotash, with Joe Brainard, with Kiss My Ass, 1971; (with J. Stanton) Chrononhotonothologos, 1971; (with T. Berrigan and T. Clark) Back in Boston Again, 1972; (with J. Dine) Oo La La, 1973; (with T. Veitch) Antlers in the Treetops, 1973; Crazy Compositions, 1974; Toujours L'amour, 1976; (with G. Schneeman) Pullman, Arrive, 1978; Tulsa Kid, 1979; Triangles in the Afternoon, 1979; (with T. Winkfield) How to Be a Woodpecker, 1983; (contrib. with G. Peck) Cubist Prints, Cubist Books, 1983; (with T. Winkfield) How to Be Modern Art, 1984; Among the Blacks: Two Works, 1988; Pantoum, 1988; (with Dorny) Wish, 1988; Light as Air, 1989; The Big Something, 1990; (with C. Coolidge) Supernatural Overtures, 1990; Blood Work: Selected Prose, 1993; Ted: A Personal Memoir of Ted Berrigan, 1993; New & Selected Poems, 1995; Creative Reading, 1997; Albanian Diary, 1999; The Straight Line, 2000; Poems I Guess I Wrote, 2001; You Never Know, 2002; Yodeling into a Kotex, 2002; Oklahoma Tough, 2003; Joe: A Memoir of Joe Brainard, 2004; Selected Poems, 2007; How to be Perfect, 2007; How Long, 2011. EDITOR: (with T. Berrigan) Literary Days, 1964; (with D. Shapiro) An Anthology of New York Poets, 1970; (with B. Zavatsky) The Whole Word Catalogue 2, 1977; (with N.L. Shapiro) The Point: Where Teaching and Writing Intersect, 1983; (and intro.) Complete Poems, 1986; Teachers & Writers Handbook of Poetic Forms, 1987, 2nd ed., 2000; The Teachers and Writers Guide to Walt Whitman, 1991; (with C. Edgar) Educating the Imagination: Essays and Ideas for Teachers and Writers, 1994; (with C. Edgar) Old Faithful: 18 Writers Present Their Favourite Writing Assignments, 1995; World Poets: An Encyclopedia for Students, 2000; Painter Among Poets: The Collaborative Art of George Schneeman, 2004; (with S. Berrigan) Dear Sandy, Hello, 2010. TRANSLATOR: The Poet Assassinated, 1968; Dialogues with Marcel Duchamp, 1970; (with D. Ball) Rldasedlrad les Dlcmhypbdf, 1971; (with B. Zavatsky) V. Larbaud, The Poems of A.O. Barnabooth, 1974; Kodak, 1976; The Poet Assassinated and Other Stories, 1984; B. Cendrars, Complete Poems, 1992. Contributor to books and periodicals. **Address:** Coffee House Press, 79 Thirteenth Ave. NE, Ste. 110, Minneapolis, MN 55413, U.S.A.

PADGETT, Stephen. Scottish/British (born England), b. 1951. **Genres:** History, International Relations/Current Affairs, Politics/Government, Economics. **Career:** Loughborough University of Technology, faculty, 1979-90; University of Essex, lecturer in European politics, 1991-95; University of Liverpool, professor of politics, 1995-2000; University of Strathclyde, professor of politics, 2000-; German Politics, founding co-editor, managing editor. **Publications:** (With T. Burkett) Political Parties and Elections in West Germany: The Search for a New Stability, 1986; (with W.E. Paterson) A History of Social Democracy in Postwar Europe, 1991; Organizing Democracy in Eastern Germany: Interest Groups in Post-Communist Society, 2000; (with S. Bulmer, D. Dolowitz and P. Humphreys) Policy Transfer in European Union Governance, 2007. EDITOR: (with W.E. Paterson and G. Smith) Developments in German Politics, 1992, rev. ed., 1996; Parties and Party Systems in the New Germany, 1993; Adenauer to Kohl: The Development of the German Chancellorship, 1994; (with T. Saalfeld) Bundestagswahl '98: End of an Era?, 2000; (with T. Poguntke) Continuity and Change in German Politics: Beyond the Politics of Centrality?: A Festschrift for Gordon Smith, 2002; (with K. Dayson) The Politics of Economic Reform in Germany: From Rhineland Capitalism to Hybrid Capitalism?, 2006; (with S. Bulmer and C. Jeffery) Rethinking Germany and Europe, 2010. **Address:** University of Strathclyde, 16 Richmond St., Glasgow, G1 1XQ, Scotland. **Online address:** stephen.padgett@strath.ac.uk

PADILLA, Ignacio. American/Mexican (born Mexico), b. 1968?. **Genres:** Literary Criticism And History, Mystery/Crime/Suspense. **Career:** National library of Mexico, director, 2007-; Mexican Embassy, cultural attache. Diplomat and author. **Publications:** Subterraneos: cuentos del asfalto y la vereda, 1990; (with J. Volpi and E. Urroz) Tres bosquejos del mal, 1994; La catedral de los ahogados, 1995; Si volviesen sus majestades, 1996; Ultimos trenes, 1996; Amphitryon, 2000; Las antpodas y el siglo, 2001; Crónicas Africanas: Espejismo y utopía en el reino de Swazilandia; 2001; Shadow Without a Name, 2003; Espiral de artillería, 2003; Antípodas, 2006; Cinito Del Tuscano, 2006; El peso de las cosas: Ensayos, 2004-2006, 2006; (with R. Gallo) Heterodoxos Mexicanos: Una Antología Dialogada, 2006; Teología de los Fractales, 2008; Vida íntima de los Encendedores: Animismo en la sociedad ultramoderna, 2009; Anacrónicos y otros cuentos, 2010; Isla de las Tribus Perdidas, 2010. **Address:** c/o Author Mail, Farrar, Straus & Giroux, 19 Union Sq. W, New York, NY 10001, U.S.A.

PADILLA, Mark Benjamin. American (born United States), b. 1969. **Genres:** Adult Non-fiction. **Career:** University of Michigan, assistant professor of health behavior and health education, Population Studies Center, research affiliate. Writer. **Publications:** Caribbean Pleasure Industry: Tourism, Sexuality, and AIDS in the Dominican Republic, 2007; Love and Globalization: Transformations of Intimacy in the Contemporary World, 2007. Contributor to books. **Address:** School of Public Health, University of Michigan, 3830 SPH 1, 1415 Washington Heights, Ann Arbor, MI 48109-2029, U.S.A. **Online address:** padillam@umich.edu

PADILLA, Raymond V. American/Mexican (born Mexico), b. 1944. **Genres:** Education, Information Science/Computers, Language/Linguistics. **Career:** University of Michigan, admissions counselor, 1970-71; University of California, Survey Research Center, research assistant and acting project director, 1972, Chicano Studies Program, researcher assistant, 1973; Michigan Department of Education, higher education consultant and coordinator of Latino education, 1975-77; Eastern Michigan University, Department of Social Foundations, assistant professor, 1977-80, Department of Foreign Languages and Bilingual Studies, director, 1977-82, associate professor, 1981; Arizona State University, Center for Bilingual, associate, 1982-85, Department of Higher and Adult Education, associate professor, professor of educational leadership and policy studies, 1982-97, Hispanic Research Center, director and associate research professor, 1986-91, College of Liberal Arts and Sciences, Department of Chicana and Chicano Studies, professor, 1997-2000; University of Texas, College of Education and Human Development, professor, 2001-, Department of Educational Leadership and Policy Studies, interim department chair, 2004-05. Writer. **Publications:** Chicano Studies Revisited: Still in Search of the Campus and the Community, 1987; HyperQual: MacIntosh Program for Qualitative Data Analysis, 1991; (with M. Montiel) Debatable Diversity: Critical Dialogues on Change in American Universities, 1998. EDITOR: Bilingualism and Public Policy, Puerto Rican Perspectives, 1979; Ethnoperspectives in Bilingual Education Research, Bilingual Programs, vol. I: Bilingual Education and Public Policy in the United States, 1979, vol. II: Theory in Bilingual Education, 1980, Bilingual Education Technology, 1981; Theory, Technology, and Public Policy in Bilingual Education, 1983; (with M. Montiel) Chicanos and the Higher Learning, 1985; (with E.E. Garcia) Advances in Bilingual Education Research, 1985; (with A.H. Benavides) Critical Perspectives on Bilingual Education Research, 1992; (with R.C. Chávez) The Leaning Ivory Tower: Latino Professors in American Universities, 1995; (with K.P. Gonzalez) Doing the Public Good: Latina/o Scholars Engage Civic Participation, 2008; Student Success Modeling: Elementary School to College, 2009. Contributor to books. **Address:** College of Education & Human Development, University of Texas, 6900 N Loop 1604 W, San Antonio, TX 78249-0654, U.S.A. **Online address:** raymond.padilla@utsa.edu

PADILLA, Tanalís. American (born United States), b. 1973. **Genres:** History. **Career:** Dartmouth College, associate professor of history. Writer and historian. **Publications:** Rural Resistance in the Land of Zapata: The Jaramillista Movement and the Myth of the Pax Priísta, 1940-1962, 2008. **Address:** Department of History, Dartmouth College, 409 Carson Hall, Hanover, NH 03755, U.S.A. **Online address:** tanalis.padilla@dartmouth.edu

PADMORE, Sandra. American/Barbadian (born Barbados), b. 1957. **Genres:** Essays, Poetry, Songs/Lyrics And Libretti, Novellas/Short Stories. **Career:** Bank of New York, administrator, 1988-94; Port Authority of New York and New Jersey, staff accountant, 1994-. Writer. **Publications:** Some Things I Have Noticed, 1996. **Address:** Port Authority of New York and New Jersey, PO Box 2018, Jersey City, NJ 07030, U.S.A. **Online address:** splewis@panynj.gov

PADOVANO, Anthony T. American (born United States), b. 1934. **Genres:** Theology/Religion. **Career:** Ordained Catholic priest, 1959; Roman Echoes, editor-in-chief, 1959; Darlington Seminary, professor of systematic theology, 1962-74; Saint Catharine's, parish assistant, 1963-74; Ramapo College, founding faculty, 1971-, distinguished professor of literature and philosophy, 1971-; National Catholic Reporter, feature writer, 1971-; National Association for Married Priesthood, president, 1980-90; Fordham University, adjunct theology professor; Saint Elizabeth College, adjunct theology professor. **Publications:** The Cross of Christ, Measure of the World, 1962; The Estranged

God, 1966; Who is Christ?, 1967; Belief in Human Life, 1969; American Culture and the Quest for Christ, 1970; Dawn without Darkness, 1971; Free to Be Faithful, 1972; Eden and Easter, 1974; Presence and Structure, 1976; A Case for Worship, 1976; America: Its People, Its Promise, 1976; The Human Journey: Thomas Merton, Symbol of a Century, 1981; Trilogy, 1982; Contemplation and Compassion, 1984; Winter Rain, 1984; His Name Is John, 1985; Christmas to Calvary, 1987; Love and Destiny, 1987; Summer Lightning, 1988; Conscience and Conflict, 1988; Reform and Renewal, 1990; A Celebration of Life, 1990; The Church Today, 1990; Scripture in the Streets, 1992; A Retreat with Thomas Merton, 1995; Hope is a Dialogue, 1998; Resistance and Renewal, 2002; Clergy Sexual Abuse: Out of the Shadows, 2002; Life Choices, 2004; A Path to Freedom, 2011. **Address:** School of American & International Studies, Ramapo College of New Jersey, 505 Ramapo Valley Rd., Mahwah, NJ 07430-1680, U.S.A. **Online address:** apadovan@ramapo.edu

PAE, Sung Moon. American/Korean (born Korea (South)), b. 1939. **Genres:** Politics/Government, Social Sciences, Economics, Business/Trade/Industry. **Career:** Bellevue University, College of Arts and Sciences, professor of global and political studies, 1975-, Con Agra distinguished professor of political science, Division of Behavioral and Social Sciences, chair, 1981-2000. Writer. **Publications:** Testing Democratic Theories in Korea, 1986, trans. as Minjujuŭi haksŏl Han guk esŏ ŭi sirhŏm, 1988; Korea Leading Developing Nations: Economy, Democracy and Welfare, 1992. **Address:** Department of Global and Political Studies, College of Arts & Sciences, Bellevue University, 513 Learning Ctr., 1000 Galvin Rd. S, Bellevue, NE 68005, U.S.A. **Online address:** sung.pae@bellevue.edu

PAESLER, Michael. American (born United States), b. 1946. **Genres:** Physics. **Career:** North Carolina State University, Physics Department, assistant professor, 1980-85, associate professor, 1985-90, professor of physics, 1990-, director of graduate programs, 1997-2005, department head, 2005-, principal investigator; American Physical Society, fellow. Writer. **Publications:** (Ed. with P.J. Moyer) Near-Field Optics: 9-10 July, 1995, San Diego, California, 1995; (with P.J. Moyer) Near-Field Optics: Theory, Instrumentation and Applications, 1996. **Address:** Department of Physics, North Carolina State University, Riddick Hall, Ste. 421, PO Box 8202, Raleigh, NC 27695, U.S.A. **Online address:** paesler@ncsu.edu

PAETRO, Maxine. American (born United States), b. 1946. **Genres:** Novels, Business/Trade/Industry, Autobiography/Memoirs. **Career:** Saatchi and Saatchi Advertising, executive vice president and director of creative operations; Ogilvy and Mather, executive vice president and manager of creative department; Young and Rubicam, vice president and associate manager of creative services; Foote, Cone and Belding Communications Inc., vice president and manager of creative department; DFS/Dorland Worldwide, vice president and director of creative operations, 1981-87. Writer. **Publications:** How to Put Your Book Together and Get a Job in Advertising, 1979; Manshare: A Novel, 1986; Babydreams, 1989; Windfall, 1991; (with D. Darin) Dream Lovers: The Magnificent Shattered Lives of Bobby Darin and Sandra Dee, 1994. WITH J. PATTERSON: 4th of July: A Novel, 2005; 5th Horseman, 2006; The 6th Target: A Novel, 2007; 7th Heaven, 2008; 8th Confession, 2009; Swimsuit: A Novel, 2009; Private, 2010; 9th Judgment, 2010; 10th Anniversary, 2011; 11th Hour, 2012; Private: #1 Suspect, 2012. Contributor to periodicals. **Address:** c/o Joni Evans, William Morris Agency, 1325 Ave. of the Americas, New York, NY 10019, U.S.A.

PAFFENROTH, Kim. American (born United States), b. 1966. **Genres:** Novels, Young Adult Non-fiction. **Career:** Southwestern Michigan College, instructor, 1993; University of Notre Dame, tutor, 1993-95, teaching fellow, 1994-95, adjunct assistant professor, 1995-96, visiting assistant professor, 1996-97; Iona College, assistant professor, 2001-, associate professor of religious studies, department chair; University of Notre Dame, presidential fellow, 1990-94; Salvatori fellow, Heritage Foundation, 1997; Villanova University, Arthur Ennis fellow, 1997-99; Acton Institute, research fellow, 1998; Westar Institute, fellow, 2003. Academic and writer. **Publications:** NONFICTION: The Story of Jesus according to L, 1997; (ed. with K.L. Hughes) Augustine and Liberal Education, 2000; Judas: Images of the Lost Disciple, 2001; (ed. with R.P. Kennedy) A Reader's Companion to Augustine's Confessions, 2003; In Praise of Wisdom: Literary and Theological Reflections on Faith and Reason, 2004; The Heart Set Free: Sin and Redemption in the Gospels, Augustine, Dante and Flannery O'Connor, 2005; (ed. with J.D. Kevin and L. Hughes) Augustine and Politics, 2005; (ed. with R.P. Kennedy and J. Doody) Augustine and Literature, 2006; (with T. Bertonneau) The Truth Is out There: Christian Faith and the Classics of TV Science Fiction, 2006; Gospel of the Living Dead: George Romero's Visions of Hell on Earth, 2006; (ed. with B. Brown and J. Doody) Augustine and World Religions, 2008; (ed. with K.L. Hughes) Augustine and Liberal Education, 2008; (ed. with C.T. Daly and J. Doody) Augustine and History, 2008. NOVELS: Dying to Live, 2007; Dying to Live 2, 2008; Orpheus and the Pearl, 2008. Contributor to periodicals and journals. **Address:** Department of Religious Studies, Iona College, 715 North Ave., New Rochelle, NY 10801, U.S.A. **Online address:** kpaffenroth@iona.edu

PAGÁN, Victoria Emma. American (born United States), b. 1965. **Genres:** History, Homes/Gardens, Politics/Government, Sciences. **Career:** University of Florida, Department of Classics, assistant professor, 1997-98, associate professor, 2005-10, professor and chair, 2010-, College of Liberal Arts and Sciences, Waldo W. Neikirk term professor, 2008; University of Wisconsin-Madison, Department of Classics, assistant professor, 1998-2005, associate professor, 2005. Writer. **Publications:** Conspiracy Narratives in Roman History, 2004; Rome and the Literature of Gardens, 2006; A Sallust Reader: Selections from Bellum Catilinae, Bellum Iugurthinum, and Historiae, 2009; (ed.) A Companion to Tacitus, 2012. Contributor to periodicals and journals. **Address:** Department of Classics, University of Florida, 115C Dauer Hall, PO Box 117435, Gainesville, FL 32611-7435, U.S.A. **Online address:** vepagan@ufl.edu

PAGE, Carl. New Zealander (born New Zealand), b. 1957. **Genres:** Philosophy, History. **Career:** University of Auckland, assistant lecturer, 1982; Pennsylvania State University, part-time instructor, 1984-85; Emory University, assistant professor of philosophy, 1987-94, Sears Writing Program, fellow, 1989-90; Georgia State University, lecturer, 1988; Ohio Northern University, lecturer, 1989; Rochester Institute of Technology, lecturer, 1990; University of Georgia, lecturer, 1993; St. John's College, tutor, 1994-; Boston University, lecturer, 1995; Brock University, lecturer, 1996. Writer. **Publications:** Philosophical Historicism and the Betrayal of First Philosophy, 1995. Contributor of articles to books and journals. **Address:** St. John's College, 60 College Ave., Annapolis, MD 21401-1687, U.S.A. **Online address:** carl.page@sjca.edu

PAGE, Christopher H. British (born England), b. 1952. **Genres:** Music. **Career:** Oxford University, Jesus College, research fellow in English, 1977-80, New College, lecturer in Old and Middle English, 1980-85; Cambridge University, Sidney Sussex College, senior research fellow, 1985-89, lecturer in English, 1989-, fellow and vice master. Writer. **Publications:** (Ed.) Sequences and Hymns, 1983; Voices and Instruments of the Middle Ages, 1986; The Owl and the Nightingale, 1990; (ed., trans. and intro.) Summa Musice, 1991; Discarding Images: Reflections on Music and Culture in Medieval France, 1993; Songs of the Trouveres, 1995; Latin Poetry and Conductus Rhythm in Medieval France, 1997; (ed.) Music and Instruments of the Middle Ages: Studies on Texts and Performance, 1997; (ed.) Jerusalem: Vision of Peace, 1998; The Christian West and Its Singers: The First Thousand Years, 2010. **Address:** Department of English, Sidney Sussex College, Cambridge University, Sidney St., Cambridge, CB CB2 3HU, England. **Online address:** chp1000@cam.ac.uk

PAGE, Clarence. American (born United States), b. 1947. **Genres:** Essays, Social Sciences, Race Relations, Sociology, Literary Criticism And History. **Career:** Dayton Herald, intern, 1960; Middletown Journal, writer and photographer, 1964; Cincinnati Enquirer, writer and photographer, 1964; reporter and freelance writer, 1969-; Chicago Tribune, reporter and assistant city editor, 1969-80, columnist, 1984-, bureau, 1991-; WBBM-TV, director of community affairs, 1980-82, news department reporter and planning editor, 1982-84. **Publications:** (Ed. and intro.) A Foot in Each World: Essays and Articles, 1986; Showing My Color: Impolite Essays on Race and Identity, 1996. Contributor to periodicals. **Address:** Chicago Tribune, 435 N Michigan Ave., Chicago, IL 60611-4066, U.S.A. **Online address:** cptime@aol.com

PAGE, Geoff(rey Donald). Australian (born Australia), b. 1940. **Genres:** Novels, Novellas/Short Stories, Poetry, Literary Criticism And History, Biography, Documentaries/Reportage, Photography. **Career:** Teacher of history and English, 1964-74; Narrabundah College, senior English teacher, 1974-2001. Writer. **Publications:** POETRY: Smalltown Memorials, 1975; Collecting the Weather, 1978; Cassandra Paddocks, 1980; Clairvoyant in Autumn, 1983; Collected Lives, 1986; Smiling in English, Smoking in French, 1987; Footwork, 1988; Selected Poems, 1991; Gravel Corners, 1992; Human Interest, 1994; Mrs. Schnell Arrives in Heaven and Other Light Verse, 1995; (with B.H. Pooaraar) The Great Forgetting, 1996; The Secret, 1997; Collateral Damage, 1999; The Scarring (verse novel), 1999; Darker and Lighter, 2001; Carte Postales, 2004. NOVELS: Benton's Conviction, 1985; Winter Vision, 1989; Drumming on Water, 2003; Freehold: Verse Novel, 2005. OTHER: (with P. Roberts) Two Poets, 1971; (trans. with W. Coutts) Century of Clouds: Poems of Guillaume Apollinaire, 1985; Invisible Histories (stories), 1990; A Reader's Guide to Contemporary Australian Poetry, 1995; Bernie McGann: A Life in Jazz (biography), 1997; (trans. with R.F. Brissenden and L. NardiFord) Day after Day: Selected Poems of Salvatore Quasimodo, 2002; Lawrie and Shirley: The Final Cadenza: A Movie in Verse, 2006; 80 Great Poems from Chaucer to Now, 2006. EDITOR: Shadows from the Wire: Poems and Photographs of Australians in the Great War, 1983; On the Move: Australian Poets in Europe, 1992; The Indigo Book of Modern Australian Sonnets, 2003. **Address:** 8/40 Leahy Close, Narrabundah, AC 2604, Australia. **Online address:** geoffdpage@ozemail.com.au

PAGE, Karen. American (born United States), b. 1962. **Genres:** Food And Wine, Business/Trade/Industry. **Career:** Lehman Brothers, investment banker, 1983-85; New York City Magazine, publisher and manager, 1985-87; Braxton Associates, strategy consultant, 1989-92; Country Music, executive vice-president, 1992-94; Harvard Business School Network of Women Alumnae, chair, 1992-; Karen Page and Associates, president, 1994-. Writer. **Publications:** WITH A. DORNENBURG: Becoming a Chef: With Recipes and Reflections from America's Leading Chefs, 1995, rev. ed., 2003; Culinary Artistry, 1996; Dining Out: Secrets from America's Leading Critics, Chefs and Restaurateurs, 1998; Chef's Night Out, Four-Star Restaurants to Neighborhood Favorites: 100 Top Chefs Tell You Where (and How!) to Enjoy America's Best, 2001; The New American Chef: Cooking with the Best Flavors and Techniques from around the World, 2003; What to Drink with What You Eat: The Definitive Guide to Pairing Food with Wine, Beer, Spirits, Coffee, Tea-Even Water-Based on Expert Advice from America's Best Sommeliers, 2006; The Flavor Bible: The Essential Guide to Culinary Creativity, Based on the Wisdom of America's Most Imaginative Chefs, 2008; Food Lover's Guide to Wine, 2011; On Mastering Wine, forthcoming. **Address:** 527 3rd Ave., Ste. 130, New York, NY 10016, U.S.A. **Online address:** karenapage@aol.com

PAGE, Katherine Hall. American (born United States), b. 1947. **Genres:** Mystery/Crime/Suspense, Young Adult Fiction, Novels, Young Adult Nonfiction, Horror. **Career:** Teacher of English and history and director of programs for adolescents with special emotional needs, 1969-80; writer, 1980-; educational consultant, 1985-. **Publications:** FAITH FAIRCHILD MYSTERY SERIES: The Body in the Belfry, 1989; The Body in the Kelp, 1990; The Body in the Bouillon, 1991; The Body in the Vestibule, 1992; The Body in the Cast, 1993; The Body in the Basement, 1994; The Body in the Bog, 1996; The Body in the Fjord, 1997; The Body in the Bookcase, 1998; The Body in the Big Apple, 1999; The Body in the Moonlight, 2001; The Body in the Bonfire, 2002; The Body in the Lighthouse, 2003; The Body in the Attic, 2004; The Body in the Snowdrift, 2005; The Body in the Ivy, 2006; The Body in the Gallery, 2008; The Body in the Sleigh, 2009; The Body in the Gazebo, 2011; The Body in the Boudoir, 2012. CHRISTIE AND COMPANY MYSTERIES: Christie & Company, 1996; Down East, 1997; In the Year of the Dragon, 1997; Bon Voyage, 1998. NOVEL: Club Meds, 2006. NONFICTION: Have Faith in Your Kitchen, 2010. OTHERS: (with C. Ridgway, J. McCoy and J. Pence) Mistletoe and Mayhem, 2004. **Address:** c/o Faith Hamlin, Sanford J. Greenburger Associates Inc., 55 5th Ave., New York, NY 10003, U.S.A.

PAGE, Norman. British (born England), b. 1930. **Genres:** Literary Criticism And History, Biography. **Career:** High school teacher of English, 1951-60; Ripon College of Education, principal lecturer in English and head of department, 1960-69; University of Alberta, assistant professor, 1969-70, associate professor, 1970-75, professor of English, 1975-85; University of Nottingham, professor of modern English, 1985-93, chair of English literature, 1985, head of department, 1987-90, emeritus professor, 1993-. Writer. **Publications:** EDITOR: Bleak House, 1971; Wilkie Collins: The Critical Heritage, 1974; Hardy's Jude the Obscure: An Authoritative Text: Backgrounds and Contexts Criticism, 1970, 2nd ed., 1999; Dickens, Hard Times, Great Expectations and Our Mutual Friend: A Casebook, 1979; Thomas Hardy: The Writer and His Background, 1980; D.H. Lawrence: Interviews and Recollections, 1981; Nabokov: The Critical Heritage, 1982; A Thomas Hardy Annual, 5 vols., 1982-87; Tennyson: Interviews and Recollections, 1983; Henry James: Interviews and Recollections, 1984; The Language of Literature, 1984; William Golding: Novels 1954-67: Lord of the Flies, The Inheritors, Pincher Martin, Free Fall, The Spire, The Pyramid: A Casebook, 1985; Byron: Interviews and Recollections, 1985; Dr. Johnson: Interviews and Recollections, 1987; Bleak House: A Novel of Connections, 1990; (with P. Preston) The Literature of Place, 1993; (and intro.) Mad Monkton and Other Stories, 1994; (and intro.) Man and Wife, 1995; Alfred Lord Tennyson: Selected Poetry, 1995; The Picture of Dorian Gray, 1998; (with T. Sasaki) Wilkie Collins: Selection, 1999; (and intro. with T. Sasaki) John Marchmont's Legacy, 1999; (and intro. with R. Sasaki) Miss or Mrs?: The Haunted Hotel, 1999; The Guilty River, 1999; Oxford Reader's Companion to Hardy, 2000; (and intro.) The Old Curiosity Shop, 2000. OTHERS: The Language of Jane Austen, 1972; Speech in the English Novel, 1973, 2nd ed., 1988; (and intro.) Thomas Hardy, 1977; E.M. Forster's Posthumous Fiction, 1977; A.E. Housman: A Critical Biography, 1983; A Dickens Companion, 1984, 2nd ed., 1988; A Kipling Companion, 1984; A Conrad Companion, 1986; E.M. Forster, 1987; A Dickens Chronology, 1989; A Byron Chronology, 1988; Bleak House: A Novel of Connections, 1990; Muriel Spark, 1990; The Thirties in Britain, 1990; A Dr. Johnson Chronology, 1990; An Oscar Wilde Chronology, 1991; Tennyson: An Illustrated Biography, 1992; An Evelyn Waugh Chronolgy, 1997; Auden and Isherwood: The Berlin Years, 1998; (with V. Purton) Palgrave Literary Dictionary of Tennyson, 2010. Contributor of articles to books and journals. **Address:** School of English Studies, University of Nottingham, Trent Bldg., University Pk., Nottingham, NT NG7 2RD, England.

PAGE, Penny B(ooth). American (born United States), b. 1949. **Genres:** Adult Non-fiction, Food And Wine, Education. **Career:** Rutgers Center of Alcohol Studies, bibliographic assistant, 1977-78, research assistant, 1978-81, librarian, 1981-, director of information services; Substance Abuse Librarians and Information Specialists, chair, 1984-85, vice chair, 1985-87, archivist, 1987-. Writer and speaker. **Publications:** Alcohol Use and Alcoholism: A Guide to the Literature, 1986; Children of Alcoholics: A Sourcebook, 1991. Contributor to books and periodicals. **Address:** Center of Alcohol Studies, Rutgers University, 607 Allison Rd., Piscataway, NJ 08854-8001, U.S.A.

PAGE, Reba Neukom. American (born United States), b. 1942. **Genres:** Education. **Career:** Teacher, 1972-80; University of Wisconsin, lecturer, 1984-85; Bowdoin College, assistant professor, 1985-87; Spencer Foundation, Spencer fellow, 1986-87; University of California, faculty, 1987-95, associate professor, professor; Howard University, associate professor of education, 1987-95, associate professor 1995-97, professor of education, 1997-. Writer. **Publications:** (Ed. with L. Valli) Curriculum Differentiation: Interpretive Studies of U.S. Secondary Schools, 1990; Lower-Track Classrooms: A Curricular and Cultural Perspective, 1991. **Address:** Graduate School of Education, University of California, Sproul Hall 2128, Riverside, CA 92521-0128, U.S.A. **Online address:** reba.page@ucr.edu

PAGE, Tim. Australian/British (born England), b. 1944. **Genres:** Local History/Rural Topics. **Career:** U.S. AID, staff, 1963-65; United Press Intl., freelance photographer; Agence France-Presse, freelance photographer, TIME-LIFE, freelance photographer; Associated Press, freelance photographer; Bloomberg Magazine, photographer; Griffith University, adjunct professor of photojournalism, Australian Rivers Institute, postdoctoral fellow; ÂSOUTH, founding member. Writer. **Publications:** Tim Page's Nam, 1983; Sri Lanka, 1984; Ten Years After: Vietnam Today, 1987; Page after Page: Memoirs of a War-Torn Photographer (autobiography), 1989; Derailed in Uncle Ho's Victory Garden: Return to Vietnam and Cambodia, 1995; Mid-Term Report, 1995; (ed. with H. Faas) Indochina Requiem: Images from Vietnam, Cambodia and Laos Remembered, 1997; (intro.) Delta: The Perils, Profits and Politics of Water in South and Southeast Asia, 1997; (ed. with H. Faas) Requiem: By the Photographers who Died in Vietnam and Indochina, 1997; Mindful Moment, 2001; Another Vietnam: Pictures of the War from the Other Side, 2002. **Address:** Australian Rivers Institute, Griffith University, Nathan Campus, Rm. N13 1.33, 170 Kessels Rd., Nathan, QL 4111, Australia. **Online address:** t.page@griffith.edu.au

PAGE, Tim. American (born United States), b. 1954. **Genres:** Music, History, Humor/Satire. **Career:** Soho News, music critic, 1979-82; New York Times, music writer, 1982-87; The Manhattan School of Music, lecturer in the humanities, 1985-88; The Juilliard School, Graduate Level Seminar in Criticism, teacher, 1986-94; Newsday, chief music critic, 1987-95; New York Newsday, chief music critic, 1987-95; Washington Post, chief classical music critic, 1995-99, music critic, 2000-, staff writer; St. Louis Symphony

Orchestra, artistic advisor and creative chair, 1999-2000; University of Missouri, professor of music, 1999-2000; Peabody Conservatory, Graduate Level Seminar in Criticism, teacher, 2005-06; University of Southern California, professor of journalism and music, 2008-; Catalyst, co-founder. Music critic and biographer. **Publications:** (Co-ed.) Hip Pocket Guide to New York City, 1982; (ed. and intro.) Glenn Gould Reader, 1984; (ed. with V.W. Page) Selected Letters of Virgil Thomson, 1988; Music From the Road: Views and Reviews, 1978-1992, 1992; (comp.) William Kapell: A Documentary Life History of the American Pianist, 1992; (ed. and intro.) Dawn Powell at Her Best, 1994; (contrib.) Glenn Gould: Photographische Suiten, 1995; (ed. and intro.) Diaries of Dawn Powell, 1931-1965, 1995; Dawn Powell: A Biography, 1998; (ed. and intro. with M. Sexton) Four Plays, 1999; (ed. and intro.) Unknown Sigrid Undset: Jenny and Other Works, 2001; Tim Page on Music: Views and Reviews, 2002; (ed. and intro.) What's God Got To Do With It?: Robert G. Ingersoll on Free Thought, Honest Talk, and The Separation of Church and State, 2005; (intro.) Glenn Gould: A Life in Pictures, 2007; Parallel Play: Growing Up with Undiagnosed Asperger's, 2009; (contrib.) 50 Years of Music: The Saint Paul Chamber Orchestra, 2009; Parallel Play, 2010; (with C. Hall) Carnegie Hall Treasures, 2011. **Address:** Washington Post, 1150 15th St. NW, Washington, DC 20071-0001, U.S.A. **Online address:** ellispag@usc.edu

PAGE, Tyler. American (born United States), b. 1976. **Genres:** Graphic Novels. **Career:** Minneapolis College of Art and Design, director of print technology. Writer and artist. **Publications:** STYLISH VITTLES SERIES: GRAPHIC NOVELS: Stylish Vittles: I Met a Girl, 2002; Stylish Vittles: All the Way, 2003; Stylish Vittles: Fare Thee Well, 2005. **Address:** Dementian Comics, 4849 Emerson Ave. S, Minneapolis, MN 55419-5331, U.S.A. **Online address:** mail@stylishvittles.com

PAGEL, Tempa. American (born United States) **Genres:** Mystery/Crime/Suspense. **Career:** Writer and educator. **Publications:** Here's the Church, Here's the Steeple: An Andy Gammon Mystery, 2006. **Address:** Five Star Press, 295 Kennedy Memorial Dr., Waterville, ME 04901-4535, U.S.A. **Online address:** tempapagel@yahoo.com

PAGELS, Elaine. American (born United States), b. 1943. **Genres:** Theology/Religion. **Career:** Columbia University, Barnard College, assistant professor, 1970-74, associate professor, professor of history of religion and head of department, 1974-82; Princeton University, Harrington Spear Paine Foundation, professor of religion, 1982-. Writer. **Publications:** The Johannine Gospel in Gnostic Exegesis, 1973; The Gnostic Paul: Gnostic Exegesis of the Pauline Letters, 1975; The Gnostic Gospels, 1979; (contrib.) Nag Hammadi Codex III, 5, The Dialogue of the Savior, 1984; Adam, Eve, and the Serpent, 1988; The Origin of Satan, 1995; Beyond Belief, 2003; Reading Judas: The Gospel of Judas and the Shaping of Christianity, 2007. Contributor to periodicals. **Address:** Department of Religion, Princeton University, Rm. 240, 1879 Hall, Washington Rd., Princeton, NJ 08544-1006, U.S.A. **Online address:** epagels@princeton.edu

PAGET, Julian (Tolver). British (born England), b. 1921. **Genres:** History, Military/Defense/Arms Control. **Career:** Full-time writer, 1968-. **Publications:** Counter-Insurgency Campaigning in US as Counter-Insurgency Operations: Techniques of Guerilla Warfare, 1967; Last Post: Aden, 1964-67, 1969; Story of the Guards, 1976; The Pageantry of Britain, 1979; The Yeomen of the Guard: Five Hundred Years of Service, 1485-1985, 1984; Discovering London's Ceremonial and Traditions, 1989; Wellington's Peninsular War: The Battles and Battlefields, 1990; (with D. Saunders) Hougoumont: The Key to Victory at Waterloo, 1992; No Problem Too Difficult: A History of the Forces Help Society and Lord Roberts Workshops, 1999; (ed.) Second to None: The Coldstream Guards, 1650-2000, 2000. Contributor to books. **Address:** 4 Trevor St., London, GL SW7 1DU, England.

PAGLEN, Trevor. American (born United States), b. 1974?. **Genres:** Military/Defense/Arms Control, Politics/Government. **Career:** University of California, researcher. Writer, artist and geographer. **Publications:** (With A.C. Thompson) Torture Taxi: On the Trail of the CIA's Rendition Flights, 2006; I Could Tell You but Then You Would Have to Be Destroyed by Me: Emblems from the Pentagon's Black World, 2007; The Other Night Sky, 2008; (contrib.) Experimental Geography: Radical Approaches to Landscape, Cartography, and Urbanism, 2008; Blank Spots on the Map: The Dark Geography of the Pentagon's Secret World, 2009. Contributor to magazines. **Address:** Department of Geography, University of California, 507 McCone Hall, Berkeley, CA 94720-4740, U.S.A. **Online address:** trevor@paglen.com

PAGLIA, Camille. (Camille Anna Paglia). American (born United States), b. 1947. **Genres:** Art/Art History, Communications/Media, Film, Humanities, Sex, Gay And Lesbian Issues, Essays. **Career:** Bennington College, Literature and Languages Division, faculty, 1972-80; Wesleyan University, visiting lecturer in English, 1980; Yale University, Ezra Stiles College, fellow, 1981, visiting lecturer in comparative literature, 1981, 1984, visiting lecturer in English, 1981-83, Silliman College, fellow, 1984; Philadelphia College of Performing Arts (now University of the Arts), assistant professor, 1984-86, associate professor, 1987-91, professor of humanities, 1991-2000, university Wesleyan professor of humanities and media studies, 2000-; Salon.com, cofounding contributor, 1995-, columnist, 1995-2001; Interview magazine, contributing editor, 2001-. **Publications:** Sexual Personae: Art and Decadence from Nefertiti to Emily Dickinson, 1990; Sex, Art and American Culture: Essays, 1991; Vamps and Tramps: New Essays, 1994; The Birds, 1998; Break, Blow, Burn: Camille Paglia Reads 43 of the World's Best Poems, 2005; The Race to the White House, 2008; (contrib.) Camp Nest, 2008. Contrbutor to periodicals. **Address:** Department of Humanities, University of the Arts, 320 S Broad St., Philadelphia, PA 19102, U.S.A.

PAGLIA, Camille Anna. *See* **PAGLIA, Camille.**

PAGONIS, William G. German/American (born United States), b. 1941. **Genres:** Military/Defense/Arms Control. **Career:** U.S. Army Military Personnel Center, staff, 1973-75; Office of the Chief of Legislative Liaison, staff officer, 1975-76; U.S. Army Transportation School and Center, deputy chief, 1978-79; Sears Roebuck Co., executive vice president for supply chain, 1993-2004, senior vice president for supply chain; Sears Logistics Services Inc., director, president, 1993-2004; Rail America Inc., chairman, director; GENCO Supply Chain Solutions, vice chairman, chairman, chief executive officer. Writer. **Publications:** (With J.L. Cruikshank) Moving Mountains: Lessons in Leadership and Logistics from the Gulf War, 1992; Leadership in a Combat Zone, 2001. Contributor to journals. **Address:** GENCO Supply Chain Solutions, 100 Papercraft Pk., Pittsburgh, PA 15238-3200, U.S.A.

PAHOR, Boris. Italian (born Italy), b. 1913. **Genres:** Novels, Novellas/Short Stories, Essays, Autobiography/Memoirs. **Career:** Freelance writer, 1947-53; teacher in Slovenian schools, 1953-75. **Publications:** Moj trzaški Naslov (short stories), 1948; Mesto v Zalivu (title means: 'The City on the Bay'), 1955; Vila Ob Jezeru (title means: 'The Villa along the Lake'), 1955; Onkraj Pekla So Ljudje (title means: 'There Are People Beyond the Hell'), 1958 as Spopad s Pomladjo, 1978; Kres V pristanu (short stories), 1959; Na Sipini (title means: 'Sinking'), 1960; Parnik Trobi Nji (title means: 'The Steamer's Horn Blows for Her'), 1964; Nomadi Brez Oaze (title means: 'Nomads without an Oasis'), 1965; Nekropola (memoir), 1967; Odisej Objamboru (title means: 'Odysseus at the Mast'), 1969; Skarabej v Srcu (journal), 1970; Odisej ob jamboru, 1971; Grmada v Pristanu (short stories), 1972; Varno naročje: 12 Brane Novele in Crtice (short stories), 1974; Zatemnitev (title means: 'Blackout'), 1975; Trzaški Mozaik: Izborobčasnih Zapiskov, (title means: 'Triestian Mosaic'), 1983; Vlabirintu (title means: 'In the Labyrinth'), 1984; Ta Ocean Strasno Odprt (title means: 'The Fearful Ocean'), 1990; Zlahtne Transverzale (memoir), 1991; Napoved Nove Plovbe: Dnevniski Zapiski 1986-1989 (title means: 'A New Start'), 1992; Slovenska Svatba (title means: 'Slovenian Night'), 1995; V Vodoravni Legi (novel), 1997; Pogled Iz Jamborovega Kosa, 1998; Zibelka Sveta: Roman (novel), 1999; Dihanje Morja (short stories), 2001; Notranji Odmevi, 2003; Zibelka Sveta; Zgodba Oreki, Kripti in Dvorljivem Golobu, 2003; Letteratura Slovena Del Litorale: Vademecum, 2004; Villa Sul Lago: Romanzo Breve, 2004; Meni Pojejo Fantje, Meni Pojejo!, 2004; Trst in Slovenski Cas, 2006; Trg Oberdan, 2006; Srecko Kosovel: Pricevalec Zaznamovanega Stoletja, 2008; Difficult Spring, 2009; Necropolis, 2010. **Address:** Salita a Contovello-Kontovel 71, Trieste, 34136, Italy.

PAIETTA, Ann C. (Ann Catherine Paietta). American (born United States), b. 1956. **Genres:** Literary Criticism And History, Bibliography, Reference. **Career:** University of Illinois, Library of the Health Sciences, information services librarian, 1985-86, facilities manager, 1986-87; Yale University, Cushing/John Jay Whitney Medical Library, access services librarian, 1987-92; New York Academy of Medicine, head of library access services and information services, 1992-94, Middle Atlantic Region, network programs coordinator for health science libraries, 1994-97; Dependent Care Connection, research specialist and director of research and development, 1997-99;

Deep River Public Library, library director, 1999-; Fairfield University, part-time reference librarian, 1997-2000; Manhattanville College, instructor in information literacy, 1999; Southern Connecticut State University, reference librarian and adjunct faculty member, 2000-01. Writer. **Publications:** Access Services: A Handbook, 1991; (with J.L. Kauppila) Animals on Screen and Radio: An Annotated Sourcebook, 1994; (with J.L. Kauppila) Health Professionals on Screen, 1999; Saints, Clergy, and Other Religious Figures on Film and Television, 1895-2003, 2005; Teachers in the Movies: A Filmography of Depictions of Grade School, Preschool, and Day Care Educators, 1890s to the Present, 2007. **Address:** Deep River Public Library, 150 Main St., Deep River, CT 06417, U.S.A. **Online address:** apaietta@att.net

PAIETTA, Ann Catherine. *See* **PAIETTA, Ann C.**

PAIGE, Robin. *See* **ALBERT, Susan Wittig.**

PAINE, Tom. American (born United States) **Genres:** Novellas/Short Stories, Young Adult Fiction. **Career:** Middlebury College, teacher of creative writing. Writer. **Publications:** Scar Vegas: And Other Stories, 2000; The Pearl of Kuwait, 2003. Contributor to books. **Address:** c/o Author Mail, Harcourt Inc., 6277 Sea Harbor Dr., Orlando, FL 32887, U.S.A.

PAINTER, John. Australian (born Australia), b. 1935. **Genres:** History, Theology/Religion, Humanities, Philosophy. **Career:** University of Durham, tutor, 1965-68; University of Cape Town, senior lecturer, 1971-73, associate professor, 1973-76; La Trobe University, reader, associate professor, 1977-96; Australian Academy of the Humanities, fellow, 1991-; Charles Sturt University, reverend professor, professor of theology, 1997-. Writer. **Publications:** John: Witness and Theologian, 1975, 3rd ed., 1986; Reading John's Gospel Today, 1979; Theology as Hermeneutics, 1987; The Quest for the Messiah, 1991, 2nd ed., 1993; Mark: Worlds in Conflict, 1997; Just James: The Brother of Jesus in History and Tradition, 1997, 2nd ed., 2004; 1, 2, 3 John, 2002; Word, Theology and Community, 2002. **Address:** St Mark's National Theological Centre, School of Theology, Charles Sturt University, 15 Blackall St., Barton, AC 2600, Australia. **Online address:** jpainter@csu.edu.au

PAIRO, Preston (A.). American (born United States), b. 1958. **Genres:** Novels, Mystery/Crime/Suspense, Young Adult Fiction, Travel/Exploration. **Career:** Pairo & Pairo L.L.C., attorney, 1984-. Writer. **Publications:** NOVELS: The Captain Drowns, 1986; Winner's Cut, 1986; Razor Moon, 1988; Haitian Red, 1989; Midnight Razz, 1991; Beach Money, 1991; One Dead Judge, 1993; Breach of Trust, 1995; Bright Eyes, 1996; The Angel's Crime, 1998. Contributor to magazines. **Address:** Pairo & Pairo L.L.C., 9050-A Frederick Rd., Ellicott City, MD 21042, U.S.A. **Online address:** pairo@pairo.com

PAISNER, Daniel. American (born United States), b. 1960?. **Genres:** Novels, Adult Non-fiction, Autobiography/Memoirs, Biography. **Career:** Long Island University, adjunct professor of journalism. Writer. **Publications:** Tele-Shopping: A Guide to Televisions Home Shopping Networks, 1987; (with W. Scott) America Is My Neighborhood, 1987; (with M.J. Warner) Theo and Me: Growing up Okay, 1988; Heartlands: An American Odyssey, 1989; The Imperfect Mirror: Inside Stories of Television Newswomen, 1989; Obit, 1990; (with G. Rivera) Exposing Myself, 1991; (with E.I. Koch) Citizen Koch: An Autobiography, 1992; Horizontal Hold: The Making and Breaking of a Network Television Pilot, 1992; (with A. Quinn) One Man Tango, 1995; (with M. Williams) Mountain, Get out of My Way: Life Lessons and Learned Truths, 1996; (with Emme) True Beauty: Positive Attitudes and Practical Tips from the Worlds Leading Plus-Size Model, 1996; (with G.E. Pataki) Pataki: An Autobiography, 1998; (with S. Jones) You Have to Stand for Something, or Youll Fall for Anything, 1998; The Ball: Mark McGwires 70th Home Run Ball and the Marketing of the American Dream, 1999; (contrib.) Im Not Done Yet!: Keeping at It, Remaining Relevant, and Having the Time of My Life, 2000; The Full Catastrophe, 2000; (with E. Hommer) Hill: A True Story of Tragedy, Recovery, and Redemption on North Americas Highest Peak, 2001; (with M. Williams) Dozen Ways to Sunday: Stories of Hope and Courage, 2001; (with R. Picciotto) Last Man Down: A Firefighters Story of Survival and Escape from the World Trade Center, 2002; (with L.H. Lavin) Winners Make It Happen: Reflections of a Self-Made Man, 2003; (contrib.) Say What You Mean and Mean What You Say!: 7 Simple Strategies to Help Our Children Along the Path to Purpose and Possibility, 2003; (with J. Brown) Price of Their Blood: Profiles in Spirit, 2003; Mourning Wood: A Novel, 2004; (with B. Rancic) You're Hired: How to Succeed in Business and Life, 2004; (with H.R. Foote) Get Your Own Damn Beer, Im Watching the Game!: A Womans Guide to Loving Pro Football, 2005; (with C. Moneymaker) Moneymaker: How an Amateur Poker Player Turned 40 Dollars into 2.5 Million Dollars at the World Series of Poker, 2005; (with C.R.V. Zandt) Facing Down Evil: Reflections of an FBI Hostage Negotiator, 2006; (comp. with D. Washington) Hand to Guide Me, 2006; (with D. John) Display of Power: How FUBU Changed a World of Fashion, Branding and Lifestyle, 2007; (with J. McElwain) Game of My Life: A True Story of Challenge, Triumph, and Growing up Autistic, 2008; (with M. McEwen) Change in the Weather: Life After Stroke, 2008; (with D. DeGette) Sex, Science, and Stem Cells: Inside the Right Wing Assault on Reason, 2008; (with K. Chiger) The Girl in the Green Sweater: A Life in Holocausts Shadow, 2008; (with S. Williams) On the Line, 2009; (with M. Brzezinski) All Things at Once, 2009; (with R. Darling) The Complete Game: Reflections on Baseball, Pitching, and Life on the Mound, 2009; (with J. Kasich) Every Other Monday: Twenty Years of Life, Lunch, Faith, and Friendship, 2010. Nobodys Perfect: Two Men, One Call, and a Game for Baseball History, 2011. Contributor to periodicals. **Address:** Long Island University, 720 Northern Blvd., Brookville, NY 11548, U.S.A. **Online address:** danpaisner@aol.com

PAK, Chŏng-dong. *See* **PARK, Jung-Dong.**

PAKULA, Hannah (Cohn). American (born United States), b. 1933. **Genres:** Biography, Autobiography/Memoirs. **Career:** Writer. **Publications:** The Last Romantic: A Biography of Queen Marie of Roumania, 1984; Uncommon Woman: The Empress Frederick, Daughter of Queen Victoria, Wife of the Crown Prince of Prussia, Mother of Kaiser Wilhelm, 1995; The Last Empress, 2009. Contributor of articles and book reviews to periodicals. **Address:** c/o Kelly Welsh, Simon & Schuster, 1230 6th Ave., New York, NY 10020, U.S.A.

PAL, Pratapaditya. American/Bangladeshi (born Bangladesh), b. 1935. **Genres:** Archaeology/Antiquities, Art/Art History, Humanities, Theology/Religion. **Career:** Cambridge University, lecturer in Indian studies, 1963-64; American Academy of Benares, research associate, 1966-67; Museum of Fine Arts, keeper of the Indian Collection, 1967-69; University of California-Los Angeles, visiting professor, 1970; Los Angeles County Museum of Art, senior curator of Indian and Southeast Asian art, 1970-95, acting director, 1979, retired, 1995; University of Southern California, professor of fine arts, 1971-89; National Endowment for the Arts, fellow, 1974; University of California-Santa Barbara, visiting professor, 1980; Oxford University, William Cohn Lecturer, 1983; Pierpont Morgan Library, Catherine Mead memorial lecturer, 1986; Prince of Wales Museum, Ananda K. Coomaraswamy memorial lecturer, 1987; University of Texas, D. J. Sibley lecturer in prehistoric art, 1989; Victoria and Albert Museum, Anthony Gardner memorial lecturer, 1993; MARG Publications, general editor, 1993-; University of California-Irvine, visiting professor, 1994-95; Art Institute of Chicago, visiting curator of Indian, Himalayan and Southeast Asian Art, 1996-2003; Norton Simon Museum, research fellow and consulting curator, 1996-. Writer. **Publications:** Ragamala Paintings in the Museum of Fine Arts, Boston, 1967; (with D. Bhattacaryya) The Astral Divinities of Nepal, 1968; The Art of Tibet, 1969; (with H.C. Tseng) Lamaist Art, 1969; (with J. Fontein) Oriental Art, 1969; Vaishnava Iconology in Nepal, 1970; Indo-Asian Art: The John G. Ford Collection, 1971; Krishna: The Cowherd King, 1972; The Art of Nepal, vol. I: Sculpture, 1974, vol. II: Painting, 1978; Buddhist Art in Licchavi Nepal, 1974; Nepal: Where the Gods are Young, 1975; Bronzes of Kashmir, 1975; The Sensuous Immortals, 1977; The Divine Presence, 1978; The Ideal Image, 1978; The Classical Tradition in Rajput Painting, 1978; Elephants and Ivories, 1981; Hindu Religion and Iconology, 1981; Indian Paintings in Los Angeles Museums, 1982; A Buddhist Paradise, 1982; Art of Tibet, 1983; Court Paintings of India, 1983; Light of Asia, 1984; Tibetan Paintings: A Study of Tibetan thankas, Eleventh to Nineteenth Centuries, 1984; Art of Nepal, 1985; From Merchants to Emperors, 1986; Indian Sculpture, vol. I, 1986, vol. II, 1988; Icons of Piety, Images of Whimsy, 1987; (with J. Meech) Buddhist Book Illuminations, 1988; (co-author) Romance of the Taj Mahal, 1989; Art of the Himalayas, 1992; Indian Painting, vol. I, 1993; The Peaceful Liberators: Jain Art from India, 1994; (co-author) Dancing to the Flute, 1997; A Collecting Odyssey, 1997; Divine Images, Human Visions, 1997; Tibet: Tradition and Change, 1997; Desire and Devotion, 2001; (with B. Seid) The Holy Cow and Other Animals, 2002; Himalayas: An Aesthetic Adventure, 2003; Asian Art at the Norton Simon Museum, vol. I: Art from the Indian Subcontinent, 2003, vol. II: Art from the Himalayas and China, 2004, vol. III: Art from Sri Lanka and SE Asia, 2004; (with K. Desai) A Centennial Bouquet, the Karl Khandalavala Collection of Indian Art, 2004; Painted Poems: Rajput Paintings from the Ramesh and Ur-mil Kapoor Collection, 2004; Arts of Kashmir, 2007; (contrib.) E.O. Hoppe's Santiniketan, 2010. EDITOR: Aspects of Indian Art, 1972; Islamic Art: The Nasli M. Heeramaneck Collection, 1974; American Collectors of Asian Art, 1986; Pot-pourri of Indian Art, 1988; Art and Architecture of Ancient Kashmir, 1989; Calcutta Through 300 Years: Changing Visions, Lasting Images, 1990; Master Artists of the Imperial Mughal Court, 1991; Ganesh, the Benevolent, 1995; Path to Void, 1996; 2000, Reflections on the Arts in India, 2000; Orissa Revisited, 2001; (with J. Pereira) India & Portugal: Cultural Interactions, 2001; Indian Terracotta Sculpture: Early Phase, 2002; Bengal, Sites and Sights, 2003; Nepal, Old Images, New Insights, 2004; Buddhist Art: Form & Meaning, 2007; Sindh, Past Glory, Present Nostalgia, 2008; Goddess Durga: The Power and the Glory, 2009; (with S. Mukherjee and R. Poddar) East Meets West: A Selection of Asian and European Art from the Tata Collection in the Chhatrapati Shivaji Maharaj Vastu Sangrahalaya, Formerly Prince of Wales Museum of Western India, 2010. **Address:** Norton Simon Museum, 411 W Colorado Blvd., Pasadena, CA 91105-1825, U.S.A.

PALANDRI, Enrico. Italian (born Italy), b. 1956?. **Genres:** Novels, Plays/Screenplays, Translations, Songs/Lyrics And Libretti, Communications/Media. **Career:** University College London, writer-in-residence, 2002, Centre for Italian Studies, director; Universita di Venezia Ca Foscari, associate professor of theory of literature. **Publications:** Bologna marzo 1977, 1977; Boccalone, 1979; (with M. Bellocchio) Diavolo incorpo, 1986; Le pietre e il sale, 1986, trans. as Ages Apart, 1989; La viadel ritorno, 1990, trans. as The Way Back, 1993; Allegro fantastico, 1993; Le colpevoli ambiguità di Herbert Markus, 1997; Angela prende il volo, 2000; La deriva Romantica, 2002; L'altra Sera, 2003; Pier, 2005; I fratelli minori, 2010. Contributor to newspapers. **Address:** University College London, Gower St., via Andegari 6, London, GL WC1E 6BT, England. **Online address:** e.palandri@ucl.ac.uk

PALAZCHENKO, Pavel. Russian (born Russia), b. 1949. **Genres:** Autobiography/Memoirs, Biography, History. **Career:** Moscow Linguistic University (formerly Moscow Institute of Foreign Languages), teacher; freelance interpreter; Gorbachev Foundation, consultant; Foreign Ministry, staff, 1980-91; U.S.S.R. President's executive Office, staff. **Publications:** My Years with Gorbachev and Shevardnadze: The Memoir of a Soviet Interpreter, 1997; Vse poznaetsia v sravnenii, ili, Nesistematicheskiislovar trudnostei, tonkostei I premudrostei angliiskogo iazyka vsopostavlenii s russkim: Learn by Comparing: An Unsystematic Dictionary of Difficult, Fine and Tricky Points of the English Language Compared to Russian, 1999; Moĭ nesistematicheskiĭ slovar: Iz zapisnoĭknizhki perevodchika, 2002; Nesistematicheskiĭ Slovar, 2005; Russko-angliiskiĭ, Anglo-russkiĭ, 2005. Contributor to periodicals. **Address:** Penn State University Press, 820 N University Dr., Ste. C, USB 1, University Park, PA 16802-1003, U.S.A. **Online address:** pavelpal@mtu-net.ru

PALAZZOLO, Daniel J. American (born United States), b. 1961. **Genres:** Politics/Government, Social Sciences. **Career:** University of Richmond, Department of Political Science, associate professor, 1989-, professor of political science, assistant, School of Arts and Sciences, Center for Government and Policy, director. Writer. **Publications:** The Speaker and the Budget: Leadership in the Post-Reform House of Representatives, 1992; Done Deal?: The Politics of the 1997 Budget Agreement, 1999; (ed. with J.W. Ceaser) Election Reform: Politics and Policy, 2005. Works appear in anthologies. Contributor to journals. **Address:** Department of Political Science, University of Richmond, 215 Weinstein Hall, 28 Westhampton Way, Richmond, VA 23173-0001, U.S.A. **Online address:** dpalazzo@richmond.edu

PALDA, Filip. Canadian (born Canada), b. 1962. **Genres:** Economics, Politics/Government, Social Sciences, Money/Finance. **Career:** University of Ottawa, professor of economics, 1987-91; Fraser Institute, senior economist, 1991-94, senior fellow; Universite du Quebec, école nationale d'administration publique, professor of economics, 1994-. Writer. **Publications:** Election Finance Regulation in Canada: A Critical Review, 1991; (with I. Horry and M.A. Walker) Tax Facts 8, 1992; How Much is Your Vote Worth?: The Unfairness of Campaign Spending Limits, 1994; (with I. Horry and M.A. Walker) Tax Facts 9, 1994; (ed.) Provincial Trade Wars: Why the Blockade Must End, 1994; L'Etat Interventionniste, 1994; (ed.) Essays in Canadian Surface Transportation, 1995; It's No Gamble: The Economic and Social Benefits of Stock Markets, 1995; Here the People Rule: A Toolbook for Reforming Democracy, 1997; (with I. Horry, J. Emes and M.A. Walker) Tax Facts 10, 1997; Home on the Urban Range: An Idea Map for Reforming the City, 1998; (with M. Boucher) Ici, le Peuple Gouverne: Pour une Réforme de la Deémocratie, 2000; Tax Evasion and Firm Survival in Competitive Markets, 2001. **Address:** école nationale d'administration publique, Universite du Quebec, 555, boul. Charest Est, Quebec, QC G1K 9E5, Canada. **Online address:** filip.palda@enap.ca

PALDIEL, Mordecai. American/Israeli/Belgian (born Belgium), b. 1937. **Genres:** Theology/Religion, History, Philosophy, Autobiography/Memoirs, Military/Defense/Arms Control, Humanities. **Career:** Yad Vashem: Holocaust Martyrs' and Heroes' Remembrance Authority, Department for the Righteous, director, 1982-; Yeshiva College, lecturer; Queens College, lecturer; International Raoul Wallenberg Foundation, director of special projects, 2008-. Writer. **Publications:** Kol ha-meḳayem Nefesh Aḥat: ḥaside Umot ha-olam Ṿe-Yiḥudam, 1992; The Path of the Righteous: Gentile Rescuers of Jews during the Holocaust, 1993; Whosoever Saves (in Hebrew), 1993; Sheltering the Jews: Stories of Holocaust Rescuers, 1996; Es Gab auch Gerechte, 1999; Saving the Jews: Amazing Stories of Men and Women Who Defied the Final Solution, 2000; Churches and the Holocaust: Unholy Teaching, Good Samaritans and Reconciliation, 2006; Righteous among the Nations, 2007; Diplomat Heroes of the Holocaust, 2007. Contributor to periodicals. **Address:** The Jewish Foundation for the Righteous, 305 7th Ave., 19th Fl., New York, NY 10001, U.S.A. **Online address:** paldiel@bezeqint.net

PALEČEK, Libuše. Czech (born Czech Republic), b. 1937. **Genres:** Children's Fiction, Plays/Screenplays, Animals/Pets. **Career:** ULD Theater, director and set designer, 1962-67; freelance writer and director, 1967-. **Publications:** FOR CHILDREN: Mir gefaellt es nicht ueberall, 1972; Wer ist der Moechtigste auf der Welt, 1973; Der lustige Mann, 1974; The Little Black White Cat, 1974; Maly Tiger, 1974 in UK as The Timid Little Tiger, 1980; Tylinek, 1975; The Little Hippo Pummel, 1975; Tralala, 1977; The Mightiest Mouse in the World, 1980; The Bird of Happiness, 1980; Piccoli concerti della sera, 1980; The Surprise Kitten, 1981; Der Zauberhain, 1983; The Magic Ribbon, 1988; Stupsi, 1990; Nein, ichfuerchte mich nicht, 1995. OTHERS: (reteller) The Magic Grove, 1984; Silocary (poems), 1998. **Address:** Wad Zamecnici 15, Praha Five-Smichov, 15000, Czech Republic.

PALENCIA, Elaine Fowler. (Laurel Blake). American (born United States), b. 1946. **Genres:** Novels, Novellas/Short Stories, Poetry, Essays, Young Adult Fiction, Literary Criticism And History. **Career:** Illinois Wesleyan University, creative writing teacher, 2000; Red Herring Fiction Workshop, moderator; Green River Writers Workshop, instructor; Local Young Men's Christian Association, aerobics instructor; Pegasus, editor. **Publications:** Heart on Holiday, 1980; Small Caucasian Woman: Stories, 1993; Fiction in Murderous Intent, 1998; Essay in Bloodroot, 1998; Brier Country: Stories from Blue Valley, 2000. POETRY: Taking the Train, 1997; Poetry in Pegasus, 1998; The Sow's Ear Poetry Review, 1998; River King Poetry Supplement, 1998; The Dailiness of It, 2002. AS LAUREL BLAKE: Stormy Passage, 1982; Stranger in Paradise, 1983; Into the Whirlwind, 1984. Contributor to periodicals. Works appear in anthologies. **Address:** 3006 Valley Brook Dr., Champaign, IL 61822-6114, U.S.A. **Online address:** epalenci@uiuc.edu

PALESTINI, Robert. (Robert H. Palestini). American (born United States), b. 1941. **Genres:** Education, Administration/Management. **Career:** Roman Catholic High School, teacher, 1963-70, assistant principal, 1970-75; Pennsylvania State University, director of evening division, 1969-76; Roman Catholic Archdiocese of Philadelphia, Office of Catholic Education, director of planning, 1976-78, director of secondary-school personnel, 1977-82, assistant superintendent of secondary-school services, 1982-87, superintendent of schools, 1987-90; Saint Joseph's University, College of Arts and Sciences, Program Development in Education, director, associate professor of education, 1990-, Graduate and Continuing Studies, dean, 1992-, now dean emeritus. Writer. **Publications:** The Ten-Minute Guide to Educational Leadership: A Handbook of Insights, 1998; Educational Administration: Leading with Heart and Mind, 1998, 2nd ed., 2005; Ten Steps to Educational Reform: Making Change Happen, 2000; (with K.F. Palestini) Law and American Education, 2001, 2nd ed., 2006; The Human Touch in Educational Leadership: A Postpositivist Approach to Understanding Educational Leadership, 2003; Path to Leadership: The Heroic Follower, 2006; Game Plan for Effective Leadership: Lessons from 10 Successful Coaches in Moving from Theory to Practice, 2008; From Leadership Theory to Practice, 2009; Practical Leadership Strategies, 2010. Contributor of articles to periodicals. **Address:** Department of Education, College of Arts & Sciences, St. Joseph's University, 5600 City Ave., Philadelphia, PA 19131-1395, U.S.A. **Online address:** rpalesti@sju.edu

PALESTINI, Robert H. *See* **PALESTINI, Robert.**

PALEY, Vivian Gussin. American (born United States), b. 1929. **Genres:** Novellas/Short Stories, Education. **Career:** Teacher, 1952-56, 1963-70; University of Chicago, Laboratory School, teacher, 1971-95, now retired. Writer. **Publications:** White Teacher, 1979; Wally's Stories: Conversations in the Kindergarten, 1981; Boys and Girls: Superheroes in the Doll Corner, 1984; Mollie is Three: Growing Up in School, 1986; Bad Guys Don't Have Birthdays: Fantasy Play at Four, 1988; The Boy Who Would Be a Helicopter, 1990; You Can't Say You Can't Play, 1992; Kwanzaa and Me: A Teacher's Story, 1995; The Girl with the Brown Crayon, 1997; The Kindness of Children, 1999; In Mrs. Tully's Room: A Childcare Portrait, 2001; (intro.) Under Deadman's Skin: Discovering the Meaning of Children's Violent Play, 2001; A Child's Work: The Importance of Fantasy Play, 2004; Boy on the Beach: Building Community Through Play, 2010. **Address:** 5422 S Blackstone Ave., Chicago, IL 60615, U.S.A.

PALFREY, Evelyn. American (born United States), b. 1950. **Genres:** Novels, Romance/Historical. **Career:** Author and attorney. **Publications:** Three Perfect Men, 1996; The Price of Passion, 1997; Dangerous Dilemmas, 2001; Everything in Its Place, 2002; (with S. Kitt and L. Castoro) Cougar Tales, 2009. **Address:** Moon Child Books, PO Box 142495, Austin, TX 78714-2495, U.S.A. **Online address:** evelyn@evelynpalfrey.com

PALIN, Michael (Edward). British (born England), b. 1943. **Genres:** Novels, Novellas/Short Stories, Children's Fiction, Plays/Screenplays, Organized Labor, Travel/Exploration, Humor/Satire, E-books, E-books, History. **Career:** Python Feature Films, co-writing and co-starring, 1971-83. **Publications:** HUMOR: (co-author) Monty Python's Big Red Book, 1972; (co-author) The Brand New Monty Python Book, 1973 as Brand New Monty Python Paperbook, 1974; Monty Python's Flying Circus, 1974; (with T. Jones) Bert Fegg's Nasty Book for Boys and Girls, 1974, rev. ed. as Dr. Fegg's Encyclopaedia of All World Knowledge, 1985; (with T. Jones) More Ripping Yarns, 1978; (co-author) Ripping Yarns, 1979; (with T. Jones) Monty Python's Life of Brian, 1979; The Missionary, 1983; Limericks, 1985, 2nd ed., 1987; The Complete Ripping Yarns, 1990; (co-author) Pocketful of Python, 2000. TRAVEL: (co-author) Great Railway Journeys of the World, 1981, vol. II, 1994; Around the World in Eighty Days, 1990, rev. ed. as Around the World in 80 Days: Companion to the PBS Series, 1995; Pole to Pole, 1992; Pole to Pole-The Photographs, 1994; Full Circle: A Pacific Journey, 1997; Michael Palin's Hemingway Adventure, 1999; Sahara, 2003; Himalaya, 2004; (intro.) Explorer's Eye: First-hand Accounts of Adventure and Exploration, 2005; (foreword) Traveller: Observations from an American in Exile, 2009. CHILDREN'S FICTION: Small Harry and the Toothache Pills, 1981; The Mirrorstone: A Ghost Story with Holograms, 1986; The Cyril Stories, 1986. OTHERS: Their Finest Hours: Two Short Plays, Under hill's Finest Hour and Buchanan's Finest Hour, 1976; The Complete Works of Shakespeare and Monty Python: Volume One-Monty Python, 1981; (contrib.) Brazil/Brazil Productions, 1985; (contrib.) A Private Function, 1985; East of Ipswich, 1987; Happy Holidays: The Golden Age of Railway Posters, 1987; Number 27, 1988; The Complete Monty Python's Flying Circus: All the Words, 1989; The Weekend (play), 1994; Hemingway's Chair (novel), 1995, 2nd ed., 1998; Pole to Pole with Michael Palin: North to South by Camel, River Raft, and Balloon, 1995; Diaries 1969-1979: The Python Years, 2007. Contributor of articles to journels. **Address:** Python Pictures Ltd., 68A Delancey St., London, GL NW1 7RY, England. **Online address:** thecommittee@michaelpalinforpresident.com

PALING, Chris. British (born England), b. 1956. **Genres:** Novels, Mystery/Crime/Suspense, Young Adult Fiction. **Career:** British Broadcasting Corp., radio producer, 1980-. Writer. **Publications:** NOVELS: After the Raid, 1995; Deserters, 1996; Morning All Day, 1997; The Silent Sentry, 1999; Newton's Swing, 2000; The Repentant Morning, 2003; A Town by the Sea, 2005; Minding, 2007; Nimrod's Shadow, 2011. **Address:** c/o Deborah Rogers, Rogers Coleridge & White Ltd., 20 Powis Mews, London, GL W11 1JN, England. **Online address:** chris.paling@bbc.co.uk

PALKOVIC, Mark. American (born United States), b. 1954. **Genres:** Music, Bibliography, Translations. **Career:** Georgia Southern College, catalog librarian, 1978-79; Auburn University, catalog librarian, 1979-81; University of Cincinnati, College-Conservatory of Music Library, audio visual media librarian, 1981-2001, head librarian, 2001-; American Harp Journal, associate editor, 1993-; Music Library Association Index and Bibliography Series, editor, 2001-; Miniature Book Society, treasurer. **Publications:** Musical Boxes, 1983; (ed. and trans.) Harp Music in the Nineteenth Century, 1992; Harp Music Bibliography, 1995; Index to CD and Record Reviews, 1987-1997, 1999; Harp Music Bibliography: Chamber Music and Concertos, 2001; Harp Music Bibliography Supplement: Compositions for Solo Harp and Harp Ensemble, 2002; Chekhov's Chameleon. **Address:** College-Conservatory of Music Library, University of Cincinnati, 600 Blegen Library, PO Box 210152, Cincinnati, OH 45221-0152, U.S.A. **Online address:** mark.palkovic@uc.edu

PALLIS, Athanasios A. Greek (born Greece), b. 1966. **Genres:** International Relations/Current Affairs, Institutions/Organizations, Geography, Industrial Relations. **Career:** University of Piraeus, research fellow, 1999-2001, teaching fellow, 2000-01; University of Ioannina, teaching fellow, 2001-02; University of the Aegean, adjunct lecturer, 2001-03, lecturer, 2003-06, assistant professor, 2007-, Department of Shipping, Trade and Transport, Jean Monnet chair; University of Antwerp, Institute of Transport and Maritime Management, visiting professor, 2006-; Hellenic Association of Maritime Economists, secretary general, 2006-; University of Dalhouse University, visiting professor, 2007, International Trade and Transportation, adjunct professor, 2007-; PortEconomics.gr, co-director and founding member; PortEconomics.eu, co-director and founding member. Writer. **Publications:** The Common EU Maritime Transport Policy: Policy Europeanisation in the 1990s, 2002; (with C.I. Chlomoudis) European Union Port Policy: The Movement Towards a Long-Term Strategy 2002; (co-author) European Policies for Shipping, 2006; Maritime Transport: The Greek Paradigm, 2007; (co-author) Greek Shipping, Employment, Competitiveness, 2008; (with P. Verhoeven) European Port Policy in the 21 Century, forthcoming. **Address:** Department of Shipping Trade & Transport, University of the Aegean, 2 Korai St., Chios, 82100, Greece. **Online address:** apallis@stt.aegean.gr

PALLISER, Charles. American (born United States), b. 1947. **Genres:** Novels, Plays/Screenplays. **Career:** Huddersfield Polytechnic, lecturer, 1972-74; University of Strathclyde, lecturer in English, 1974-90, professor of English, 1974-90; The Literary Review, editor, 1979; Rutgers University, visiting teacher in creative writing, instructor in creative writing, 1986; University of Poitiers, writer-in-residence, 1997. **Publications:** NOVELS: The Quincunx, 1990; The Sensationist, 1991; Betrayals, 1995; The Unburied, 1999. **Address:** 120 Highbury Hill, London, GL N5 1AT, England. **Online address:** 106063.1716@compuserve.com

PALLITO, Robert M. American (born United States), b. 1964?. **Genres:** Law. **Career:** University of Texas, assistant professor, 2002-07; Seton Hall University, faculty, 2007-, Department of Political Science and Public Affairs, assistant professor, associate professor. Writer. **Publications:** (With W.G. Weaver) Presidential Secrecy and the Law, 2007; (ed.) Torture and State Violence in the United States, 2011. **Address:** Department of Political Science, Seton Hall University, Rm. 565, Jubilee Hall, 400 S Orange Ave., South Orange, NJ 07079, U.S.A. **Online address:** robert.pallitto@shu.edu

PALLONE, Dave. American (born United States), b. 1951. **Genres:** Sports/Fitness, Autobiography/Memoirs, Biography. **Career:** National League baseball, umpire, 1979-88. Writer. **Publications:** (With A. Steinberg) Behind the Mask: My Double Life in Baseball (memoir), 1990; (with J. Markbreit) Born to Referee: My Life on the Gridiron 1999. **Address:** PO Box 1013, Denver, CO 80201-1013, U.S.A. **Online address:** dave@davepallone.com

PALM, Carl. American (born United States), b. 1949. **Genres:** Adult Nonfiction, History, Travel/Exploration, Cultural/Ethnic Topics. **Career:** Franklin Federal Bancorp., vice president, 1985-91; The Palm Agency, agent and owner, 1991-2005; Austin Insurance Group, director of marketing, 2005-; Austin Community College, lecturer, 2009-, Department of English, adjunct professor, associate professor. Writer. **Publications:** The Great California Story: Real-Life Roots of an American Legend, 2004; This Day in California History, 2008. **Address:** Department of English, Austin Community College, 5930 Middle Fiskville Rd., Austin, TX 78752-4390, U.S.A. **Online address:** cpalm@austincc.edu

PALMER, Alan Warwick. British (born England), b. 1926. **Genres:** History, Biography, International Relations/Current Affairs, Autobiography/Memoirs, Military/Defense/Arms Control. **Career:** Highgate School, assistant master, 1951-53, senior history master, 1953-69, Department of History, head, now retired. Writer. **Publications:** (With C.A. Macartney) Independent Eastern Europe: A History, 1962; Dictionary of Modern History 1789-1945, 1962; Yugoslavia, 1964; Gardeners of Salonika, 1965; Napoleon in Russia, 1967, rev.

ed., 2003; (ed.) Age of Optimism, 1970, rev. ed., 1974; The Lands Between: A History of East-Central Europe since the Congress of Vienna, 1970; Metternich, 1972; Life and Times of George IV, 1972; Russia in War and Peace, 1972; Alexander I: Tsar of War and Peace, 1974; (ed.) Nations and Empires, 1974; Frederick the Great, 1974; (contrib.) A Military Atlas of the First World War, 1975; Bismarck, 1976; (comp. with V. Palmer) Quotations in History: A Dictionary of Historical Quotations, 1976; Kings and Queens of England, 1976, rev. ed., 1985; The Kaiser: Warlord of the Second Reich, 1978; Dictionary of Twentieth Century History, 1979; Princes of Wales, 1979; The Facts on File Dictionary of 20th Century History, 1979; The Penguin Dictionary of Twentieth-Century History, 1979, 2nd ed. as Penguin Dictionary of Modern History, 1789-1945, 1983; Who's Who in Modern History, 1980; (with V. Palmer) Who's Who in Shakespeare's England, 1981; The Chancelleries of Europe, 1983; (with V. Palmer) Royal England: A Historical Gazetteer, 1983; An Encyclopaedia Napoleon's Europe, 1984; Crowned Cousins: The Anglo-German Royal Connection, 1985; The Banner of Battle: The Story of the Crimean War, 1987; (with V. Palmer) Who's Who in Bloomsbury, 1987; The East End: Four Centuries of London Life, 1989; (with Michael) The Royal House of Greece, 1990; Bernadotte, 1990; The Decline and Fall of The Ottoman Empire, 1992; (with V. Palmer) The Chronology of British History, 1992; (contrib.) The New Penguin Dictionary of Modern History, 1789-1945, 1994; Twilight of the Habsburgs: The Life and Times of Emperor Francis Joseph, 1995; Dictionary of British Empire and Commonwealth, 1996; (with V. Palmer) The Pimlico Chronology of British History: From 250, 000 BC to the Present, 1996; Who's Who in World Politics: From 1860 to the Present Day, 1996; Victory 1918, 1998; Napoleon & Marie Louise: The Emperor's Second Wife, 2001; Northern Shores: A History of the Baltic Sea and its Peoples, 2005; The Baltic: A New History of the Region and its Peoples, 2006; The Salient: Ypres, 1914-18, 2007. **Address:** Campbell Thomson & McLaughlin Ltd., 50 Albemarle St., London, GL W1S 4BD, England.

PALMER, Beverly Wilson. American (born United States), b. 1936. **Genres:** History, Biography, Autobiography/Memoirs. **Career:** Pitzer College, lecturer in writing, 1976-83, editor of the correspondence of Charles Sumner, 1983-86; Pomona College, lecturer in writing, 1985-, editor of the correspondence of Charles Sumner, research associate, 1986-90, Thaddeus Stevens papers, editor, 1991-97, correspondence of Lucretia Mott, 1997-. **Publications:** EDITOR: Charles Sumner Papers, 1988; Selected Letters of Charles Sumner, 1990; The Selected Papers of Thaddeus Stevens, 1997; The Thaddeus Stevens Papers: Selected Correspondence and Speeches, 1997; Woman's Wit & Whimsy: The 1833 Diary of Anna Cabot Lowell Quincy, 2003; (with K.K. Sklar) The Selected Letters of Florence Kelley, 1869-1931, 2009. OTHER: Selected Letters of Lucretia Coffin Mott, 2002. Contributor to periodicals. **Address:** Department of History, Pomona College, 300 E Bonita Ave., Claremont, CA 91711, U.S.A. **Online address:** bpalmer@pomona.edu

PALMER, Bryan D. *See* **PALMER, Bryan D(ouglas).**

PALMER, Bryan D(ouglas). (Bryan D. Palmer). Canadian (born Canada), b. 1951. **Genres:** Local History/Rural Topics, History, Theology/Religion. **Career:** State University of New York, lecturer in general studies, 1974; Queen's University, assistant professor of history, 1977-79, associate professor, 1984-86, professor of history, 1986-; McGill University, assistant professor of history, 1979-81; Simon Fraser University, associate professor of history, 1981-84; University of Victoria, visiting professor, 1984; Duke University, Center for International Studies, visiting professor, 1986; Beijing Normal University, visiting professor, 1992; Trent University, professor, Canada research chair in Canadian studies, 2007-. Writer. **Publications:** A Culture in Conflict: Skilled Workers and Industrial Capitalism in Hamilton, Ontario, 1860-1914, 1979; The Making of E.P. Thompson: Marxism, Humanism and History, 1981; (with G.S. Kealey) Dreaming of What Might Be: The Knights of Labor in Ontario, 1880-1900, 1982; Working-Class Experience: The Rise and Reconstitution of Canadian Labour, 1800-1980, 1983, rev. ed. as Working-Class Experience: Rethinking the History of Canadian Labour, 1800-1991, 1992; (ed. and contrib.) The Character of Class Struggle: Essays in Canadian Working-Class History, 1850-1985, 1986; Solidarity: The Rise and Fall of an Opposition in British Columbia, 1987; (ed. and intro.) A Communist Life: Jack Scott and the Canadian Workers Movement, 1927-1985, 1988; Work and Unions in Canada, 1988; Descent Into Discourse: The Reification of Language and the Writing of Social History, 1990; E.P. Thompson: Objections and Oppositions, 1994; Goodyear Invades the Backcountry: The Corporate Takeover of a Rural Town, 1994 as Capitalism Comes to the Backcountry: The Goodyear Invasion of Napanee, 1994; Cultures of Darkness: Night Travels in the Histories of Transgression, 2000; (ed.) Labouring the Canadian Millennium: Writings on Work and Workers, History and Historiography, 2000; James P. Cannon and the Origins of the American Revolutionary Left, 1890-1928, 2007; Canada's 1960s: The Ironies of Identity in a Rebellious Era, 2009. Contributor of articles to books and journals. **Address:** Department of History, Trent University, 1600 W Bank Dr., Peterborough, ON K9J 7B8, Canada. **Online address:** bpalmer@trentu.ca

PALMER, Catherine. American (born United States), b. 1956?. **Genres:** Romance/Historical, Theology/Religion. **Career:** Novelist. **Publications:** Down to Earth Beauty, 1982; The Burning Plains, 1988; The Wild Winds, 1990; Land of Enchantment, 1990; Forbidden, 1991; Weeping Grass, 1992; Outlaw Heart, 1992; Red Hot, 1992; Gunman's Lady, 1993; Renegade Flame, 1993; For the Love of a Child, 1994; Falcon Moon, 1994; His Best Friend's Wife, 1995; Sometimes Forever, 1996; (with J. Odell, D.W. Smith and P. Stoks) A Victorian Christmas Cottage, 1997; (with G. Aiken, D.W. Smith and P. Stoks) A Victorian Christmas Quilt, 1998; (with G. Aiken, L. Copeland and D. Crawford) With This Ring, 1998; (with K. Chute, D. Crawford and P. Stoks) A Victorian Christmas Tree, 1998; Lone Star, 1998; (with P. Stoks and E. White) Prairie Christmas, 2000; (with G. Aiken and K. Billerbeck) A Victorian Christmas Keepsake, 2001; A Dangerous Silence, 2001; English Ivy, 2002; The Happy Room, 2002; Wild Heather, 2003; Love's Proof, 2003; (with P. Stoks) Loved One, 2003; Fatal Harvest, 2003; (with G.G. Martin) That Christmas Feeling, 2004; (with L. Goodnight and L. Harris) Cowboy Christmas, 2004; Thread of Deceit, 2004; Love's Haven, 2005; Sweet Violet, 2005; (with J. Hart) A Merry Little Christmas, 2006; Bachelor's Bargain, 2006; Affectionate Adversary, 2006; (with G. Chapman) It Happens Every Spring, 2006; Leaves of Hope, 2006; (with G. Chapman) Falling for You Again, 2007; (with G. Chapman) Summer Breeze, 2007; The Briton, 2008; (with G. Chapman) Winter Turns to Spring, 2008; Stranger in the Night, 2009; A Victorian Christmas, 2009; The Maverick's Bride, 2009; The Courteous Cad, 2010; The Outlaw's Bride, 2010; The Gunman's Bride, 2011. FINDERS KEEPERS SERIES: Finders Keepers, 1999; Hide and Seek, 2001. TREASURES OF THE HEART SERIES: The Treasure of Zanzibar, 1997 as A Whisper of Danger, 2000; The Treasure of Timbuktu, 1997 as A Kiss of Adventure, 2000; A Touch of Betrayal, 2000; Sunrise Song, 2003. A TOWN CALLED HOPE SERIES: Prairie Rose, 1997; Prairie Fire, 1998; Prairie Storm, 1999. Works appear in anthologies. Contributor to books and periodicals. **Address:** c/o Author Mail, Tyndale House Publishers, 351 Executive Dr., Carol Stream, IL 60188-2420, U.S.A.

PALMER, Dexter. American (born United States), b. 1974. **Genres:** Novels. **Career:** Writer. **Publications:** The Dream of Perpetual Motion, 2010. **Address:** c/o Susan Golomb, Susan Golomb Literary Agency, 540 President St., 3rd Fl., Brooklyn, NY 11215, U.S.A.

PALMER, Diana. *See* **KYLE, Susan S(paeth).**

PALMER, Elizabeth. British (born England), b. 1942. **Genres:** Novels, Young Adult Fiction. **Career:** Mirror Group, Publicity Department, graphic designer; Financial Times, Publicity Department, graphic designer; freelance book designer; writer, 1990-. **Publications:** Scarlet Angel (novel) in UK as The Stainless Angel, 1993; Plucking the Apple, 1994; Old Money, 1995; Flowering Judas, 1996; The Golden Rule, 1997; The Dark Side of the Sun, 1999; The Distaff Side, 2004. **Address:** c/o. Felicity Bryan, 2A North Parade Banbury Rd., Oxford, GL OX2 6PE, England. **Online address:** elizabeth7.palmer@dial.pipex.com

PALMER, Frank Robert. British (born England), b. 1922. **Genres:** Language/Linguistics, Education. **Career:** University of London, School of Oriental and African Studies, lecturer in linguistics, 1950-60; University of Wales, University College of North Wales, professor of linguistics and head, 1960-65; University of Reading, professor of linguistics and head, 1965-87, professor emeritus of linguistic science, 1987-. Writer. **Publications:** The Morphology of the Tigre Noun, 1962; A Linguistic Study of the English Verb, 1965; (ed.) Selected Papers of J. R. Firth, 1952-59, 1968; (ed.) Prosodic Analysis, 1970; Grammar, 1971, 2nd ed., 1984; The English Verb, 1974, 2nd ed., 1988; Semantics: A New Outline, 1976, 2nd ed., 1981; Modality and the English Modals, 1979, 2nd ed., 1990; Linguistic Controversies: Essays in Linguistic Theory and Practice in Honour of F.R. Palmer, 1982; Mood and Modality, 1986, 2nd ed., 2001; (ed. with T. Bynon) Studies in the History of Western Linguistics: In Honour of R.H. Robins, 1986; Grammatical Roles and Relations, 1994; (ed.) Grammar and Meaning: Essays in Honour of Sir John Lyons, 1995; (ed. with R. Facchinetti and M. Krug) Modality in Contemporary English, 2003; (ed. with R. Facchinetti) English Modality in Perspective: Genre Analysis and Contrastive Studies, 2004; Studies on English Modality, 2009. **Address:** School of Languages and European Studies, University of Reading, Whiteknights, Reading, BR RG6 6AA, England.

PALMER, Hap. American (born United States), b. 1942. **Genres:** Songs/Lyrics And Libretti, Education. **Career:** Los Angeles City Schools, special education teacher, 1967-81; University of California, Department of Cultural And Recreational Affairs, instructor, 1983-88, education extension, staff, 1984-89; Educational Activities, educational recording artist, 1968-87; Hap-Pal Music Inc., educational recording artist, producer and music publisher, 1976-. Writer. **Publications:** Homemade Band: Songs to Sing, Instruments to Make, 1990. **Address:** c/o FS Management, Hap-Pal Music Inc., PO Box 5955, Sherman Oaks, CA 91413-5955, U.S.A. **Online address:** hap.palmer@gmail.com

PALMER, John D. American (born United States), b. 1932. **Genres:** Biology, Sciences, Science Fiction/Fantasy, Animals/Pets. **Career:** University of Illinois, instructor, assistant professor, 1961-63; University of Bristol, national science postdoctoral fellow, 1963-64; New York University, professor of biology and department head, 1964-74; University of Massachusetts, professor of biology and department head, 1974-, professor emeritus, 1998-. Writer. **Publications:** Textbook of Modern Biology, 1968; (with F.A. Brown, Jr. and J.W. Hastings) The Biological Clock: Two Views, 1970; Biological Clocks in Marine Organisms: The Control of Physiological and Behavioral Tidal Rhythms, 1974; An Introduction to Biological Rhythms, 1976; Biological Rhythms and Living Clocks, 1977; Human Biological Rhythms, 1983; The Biological Rhythms and Clocks of Intertidal Animals, 1995; The Living Clock: The Orchestrator of Biological Rhythms, 2002. Contributor of articles to journals. **Address:** Department of Biology, University of Massachusetts, 221 Morrill Science Ctr., 611 N Pleasant St., Amherst, MA 01003-5810, U.S.A. **Online address:** ftodd@bio.umass.edu

PALMER, John Philip. *See* **PALMER, Philip.**

PALMER, Larry I. American (born United States), b. 1944. **Genres:** Medicine/Health, Law. **Career:** Law clerk to Judge A. Leon Higginbotham, Jr., 1969-70; Rutgers University, School of Law, assistant professor, 1970-73, associate professor of law, 1973-75, director of Summer Institute for the Study of Problems of Children and the Law, 1974-75; Cornell University, associate professor, 1975-79, professor of law, 1979-, vice provost, 1979-84, vice president for academic programs and campus affairs, 1987-94, now professor emeritus; University of Louisville, endowed chair in urban health policy, 2002-, professor; Georgetown University, visiting professor; University of Virginia, visiting professor; Virginia Commonwealth University and the College of William and Mary, director of health policy and law initiative. Writer. **Publications:** Law, Medicine and Social Justice, 1989; Endings and Beginnings: Law, Medicine and Society in Assisted Life and Death, 2000. Contributor of articles to books and journals. **Address:** School of Public Health and Information Sciences, University of Louisville, Rm. 4051, K-WING,, 555 S Floyd St., Louisville, KY 40292, U.S.A. **Online address:** lipalm01@louisville.edu

PALMER, Maria. *See* **STRACHAN, Ian.**

PALMER, Maria. *See* **BRENNAN, Herbie.**

PALMER, Maria. *See* **BRENNAN, J(ames) H(erbert).**

PALMER, Martin (Giles). British (born England), b. 1953. **Genres:** Theology/Religion, Philosophy. **Career:** Christian Education Movement, regional organizer, 1977-79; Centre for the Study of Religion and Education in the Inner City, founder and director, 1977-83; Christian Statesman Magazine, founder, 1978-; International Labour Reports Magazine, founder, 1983-; International Consultancy on Religion, Education and Culture, director, 1983-; HRH Prince Philip of England, religious advisor, 1986-; Sacred Earth Drama, co-founder, 1991; Alliance of Religions and Conservation (ARC), secretary general, 1995-, director; Sikh World Council India, external advisor, 1996-; Sacred Land Project, founder and director, 1997-, World Wildlife Fund, advisor; international lecturer. Writer. **Publications:** Faiths and Festivals, 1984; Sacred Trinity, Salford, 1635-1985, 1985; (with E. Bisset) Worlds of Difference, 1985; (with M. Kwok and J. OBrien) The Fortune Tellers I Ching, 1986; (with S. Tang) Chinese Herbal Prescriptions: A Practical and Authoritative Self-Help Guide, 1986; (with P.K. Man Ho and J. OBrien) Lines of Destiny: How to Read Faces and Hands the Chinese Way, 1986; (with K. Man Ho and J. OBrien) The Fortune Tellers I Ching, 1986; (with M. Kwok and K. Brown) Three Lives, 1987; Genesis or Nemesis, 1988; (with M. Kwok and J. OBrien) The Eight Immortals of Taoism, 1990; Faith in the Future, 1991; What Should We Teach?: Christians and Education in a Pluralist World, 1991; (with J. OBrien and E. Breuilly) Religion for a Change, 3 vols., 1991; (with E. Jennings) Living the Changes, 1992; Creation Harvest Handbook, 1993; Lord of Creation, 1993; (with A. Patterson) A Way to Whithorn, 1993; Coming of Age, 1993; Living Christianity, 1993; (with J. OBrien) The State of Religion Atlas, 1993 trans. as Weltatlas der Religionen, 1994; The Elements of Taoism, 1995; (with J. Ramsay) I Ching: The Shamanic Oracle of Change, 1995; (with E. Breuilly) After the Ark, 1996; (with Z. Xiaomin) Essential Chinese Mythology, 1997; (with O.B. Duane) Mysticism, 1997; (with E. Breuilly and J. OBrien) Religions of the World: The Illustrated Guide to Origins, Beliefs, Traditions & Festival, 1997; (with N. Palmer and D. Bellamy) Sacred Britain, 1997; (with J. Westwood) Sacred Journeys, 1997; Travels through Sacred China: Guide to the Soul and Spiritual Heritage of China, 1997; (with J. OBrien and Z. Xiaomin) The Feng Shui Workbook: A Room-by-Room Guide to Effective Feng Shui in Your Home and Workplace, 1998; (with J. Ramsay and M. Kwok) Kuan Yin: Myths and Revelations of the Chinese Goddess of Compassion, 1998; Yin & Yang: Understanding the Chinese Philosophy of Opposites and How to Apply It to Your Everyday Life, 1998; (with D. Manning) Sacred Gardens: A Guide to the Traditions, Meaning and Design of Beautiful and Tranquil Places, 2000; (with N. Palmer) The Spiritual Traveler: England, Scotland, Wales: The Guide to Sacred Sites and Pilgrim Routes in Britain, 2000; (with Z. Xiaomin and R. Craze) Chinese Fortune Sticks, 2000; (co-author) The Jesus Sutras: Rediscovering the Lost Scrolls of Taoist Christianity, 2001; (with N. Palmer) The Sacred History of Britain: Landscape, Myth and Power: The Forces That Have Shaped Britain's Spirituality, 2002; (ed.) The Times World Religions: A Comprehensive Guide To The Religions Of The World, 2002; (with Z. Xiaomin) Tao Stones: Chinese Meditations for Every Day, 2002; (with J. O'Brien and E. Breuilly) Festivals of the World: The Illustrated Guide to Celebrations, Customs, Events and Holidays, 2002; (with V. Finlay) Faith in Conservation: New Approaches to Religions and the Environment, 2003; (with J. OBrien) The Atlas of Religion, 2007; (with J. Ramsay and M.H. Kwok) The Kuan yin Chronicles: The Myths and Prophecies of the Chinese Goddess of Compassion, 2009. EDITOR: Essential Teachings of Islam, 1987; (with A. Nash and I. Hattingh) Faith and Nature, 1987; (with E. Breuilly) Christianity and Ecology, 1992; (with J. OBrien) The Book of Reincarnation and the Afterlife, 1997. TRANSLATOR: (with M. Kwok and J. Ramsay and intro.) Lao Tzu, The Tao Te Ching, 1996; (co-author) The Book of Chuang-Tzu, 1996. EDITOR AND TRANSLATOR: (co-author) Tung Shu, the Ancient Chinese Almanac, 1986; Tao te Ching: A New Translation, 1993; (with M. Kwok and J. Ramsay) The Illustrated Tao Te Ching, 2002. Contributor to periodicals. **Address:** International Consultancy of Religion, Education and Culture, 3 Wynnstay Grove, Manchester, GM M14 6XG, England.

PALMER, Michael Denison. British/Australian (born Australia), b. 1933. **Genres:** History, Social Sciences, Politics/Government. **Career:** Aldenham School, history master, 1958-63; City of Leicester School, senior history master, 1963-68; Rickmansworth School, senior history master, 1968-72; Oxford University, Christ Church, schoolmaster fellow, 1970; The Littlehampton School, deputy headmaster, 1972-77; DeBurgh School, headmaster, 1977-89; Surrey County Council, archive development officer, 1989-. Writer. **Publications:** (Co-author) Handbook of European Organizations, 1968; European Unity: A Survey of the European Organisations, 1968; Government, 1970; Cities, 1971; Ships and Shipping, 1971; The Prospects for a European Security Conference, 1971; Henry VIII, 1971, 2nd ed., 1983; Warfare, 1972; World Population, 1973; World Resources and Energy, 1975; European Parliament: What it is, What it Does, How it Works, 1981; Elizabeth I, 1988; From Ensor to Magritte: Belgian Art, 1880-1940, 1994, 2nd ed., 1998; (comp. and ed.) Elements of a Christian Worldview, 1998. **Address:** 13 Denham Rd., Epsom, SR KT17 3AA, England. **Online address:** michael@thepalmers0.freeserve.co.uk

PALMER, Peter John. Australian (born Australia), b. 1932. **Genres:** Geography, History, Reference, Young Adult Fiction. **Career:** Ouyen High School, faculty, 1954-57; Alexandra High School, faculty, 1958-63; Burwood High School, faculty, 1964-68; University of Melbourne, part-time tutor, 1965-67; Monash University, part-time lecturer, 1969; Ashwood High School, faculty, 1969; Waverley High School, faculty, 1970-76; Koonung High School, deputy principal, 1977-80; Preston East High School, principal, 1981-88. Writer.

Publications: The Past and Us, 1957; The Twentieth Century, 1964; Geography 10, 1992; (ed.) Macmillan Australian Atlas, 1983, 4th ed., 1993. EDITOR and CO-AUTHOR: Confrontation, 1971; Interaction, 1973; Expansion, 1974; Survival, 1975; Three Worlds, 1977; Earth and Man, 1980; Man on the Land, 1981; Man and Machines, 1983; Challenge, 1985. **Address:** 34 Ardgower Ct., Lower Templestowe, VI 3107, Australia.

PALMER, Philip. (John Philip Palmer). British (born England), b. 1960?. **Genres:** Novels. **Career:** Writer and script editor. **Publications:** Debatable Space (novel), 2008. **Address:** London, GL , England. **Online address:** webguy@philippalmer.net

PALMER, Scott W. American (born United States), b. 1967. **Genres:** Young Adult Non-fiction. **Career:** Western Illinois University, adjunct assistant professor, 1997-98, assistant professor, 1998, associate professor. Writer. **Publications:** Dictatorship of the Air: Aviation Culture and the Fate of Modern Russia (nonfiction), 2006. **Address:** Department of History, 438 Morgan Hall, 1 University Cir., Macomb, IL 61455-1390, U.S.A. **Online address:** sw-palmer@wiu.edu

PALMER, Stanley H. American (born United States), b. 1944. **Genres:** History, Economics, Essays. **Career:** Harvard University, teaching fellow and tutor, 1970-72; University of Texas, College of Liberal Arts, Department of History, assistant professor, 1973-78, associate professor, 1978-88, professor of history, 1988-, graduate advisor, 1981-82, 1990-94, acting chair, 1982-83, chair, 1983-87, assistant chair, 1995, 1996-2001, acting chair, 1995-96, graduate advisor, 1997-2002. Writer. **Publications:** Economic Arithmetic: A Guide to the Statistical Sources of English Commerce, Industry, and Finance, 1700-1850, 1977; (co-author) Essays on Modern European Revolutionary History, 1977; (ed. with G. Wolfskill) Essays on Frontiers in World History, 1981; Police and Protest in England and Ireland, 1780-1850, 1988; (ed. with D. Reinhartz) Essays on the History of North American Discovery and Exploration, 1988. **Address:** Department of History, University of Texas, 345 University Hall, PO Box 19529, Arlington, TX 76019, U.S.A. **Online address:** spalmer@uta.edu

PALMER, Stephen. British/Welsh (born Wales), b. 1962?. **Genres:** Novels. **Career:** Writer, musician and artist. **Publications:** NOVELS: Memory Seed, 1996; Glass, 1997; Muezzinland, 2002; Flowercrash, 2002; Hallucinating, 2004; Urbis Morpheos, 2010. **Address:** England. **Online address:** dekray@yahoo.com

PALMER, William J. American (born United States), b. 1943. **Genres:** Novels, Film, Literary Criticism And History, Theatre, Humor/Satire. **Career:** Purdue University, professor of English, 1969-, assistant teacher, 2004-, director of the department's film studies program, 2005-, director of graduate studies. Writer. **Publications:** The Fiction of John Fowles: Tradition, Art and the Loneliness of Selfhood, 1974; The Films of the Seventies: A Social History, 1987; The Films of the Eighties: A Social History, 1993; Dickens and New Historicism, 1997. NOVELS: The Detective and Mr. Dickens: Being an Account of the Macbeth Murders and the Strange Events Surrounding Them, 1990; The Highwayman and Mr. Dickens: An Account of the Strange Events of the Medusa Murders, 1992; The Hoydens and Mr. Dickens: The Strange Affair of the Feminist Phantom, 1997; (ed.) The Dons and Mr. Dickens: The Strange Case of the Oxford Christmas Plot: A Secret Victorian Journal, Attributed to Wilkie Collins, 2000; Films of the Nineties: The Decade of Spin, 2009; The Wabash Trilogy: The Wabash Baseball Blues, The Redneck Mafia, Civic Theater, 2010. Contributor to books, journals and newspapers. **Address:** Department of English, Purdue University, Heavilon 313, West Lafayette, IN 47907, U.S.A. **Online address:** wjpalmer@purdue.edu

PALMIÉ, Stephan. American/German (born Germany), b. 1959. **Genres:** Anthropology/Ethnology, Social Sciences. **Career:** University of Munich, Department of American Cultural History, instructor, 1984-85, 1986-87, acting assistant professor, 1987-89, assistant professor, 1991-94, 1996; University of Miami, School of Medicine, Department of Psychiatry, Office of Transcultural Education and Research, research intern, 1985; University of Virginia, Carter G. Woodson Institute for African and Afro-American Studies, visiting lecturer, 1990; German National Research Foundation, postdoctoral fellow, 1991; University of Maryland, Department History, assistant professor, 1997-2002, associate professor, 2002; University of Chicago, Department of Anthropology, associate professor of anthropology, 2003-, professor of anthropology. Writer. **Publications:** Das Exil der Götter: Geschichte und Vorstellungswelt einer afrokubanischen Religion, 1991; (ed.) Slave Cultures and the Cultures of Slavery, 1995; Kommentierte Ausgabe der vollständigen Geschichte der Mission der evangelischen Brüder auf den caraibischen Inseln S. Thomas S. Croix und S. Jan von C.G.A. Oldendorp, 2000; Wizards and Scientists: Explorations in Afro-Cuban Modernity and Tradition, 2002; (ed.) Africas of the Americas: Beyond the Search for Origins in the Study of Afro-Atlantic Religions, 2008; (ed. with G. Baca and A. Khan) Empirical Futures, 2009; (ed. with F.A. Scarano) The Caribbean: A History of the Region and Its Peoples, 2011. Contributor of articles to books and periodicals. **Address:** Department of Anthropology, University of Chicago, 1126 E 59th St., Chicago, IL 60637-1580, U.S.A. **Online address:** palmie@uchicago.edu

PALOMINO, Rafael. American/Colombian (born Colombia), b. 1963. **Genres:** Food And Wine, Regional/Urban Planning. **Career:** Metropolis Cafe, executive chef, 1986-94; Inca Grill, co-owner and chef, 1994-95; Bistro Latino, co-owner and chef, 1995-98; Sonora Restaurant, proprietor and chef, 1998-; Greenwich Tavern, proprietor, 2009-; Pacifico in New Haven, proprietor, 2009; Pacifico in Center Valley, proprietor, 2009-; Blackrock Tavern, proprietor, 2009-. Writer. **Publications:** (With J. Moskin) Bistro Latino: Home Cooking Fired Up with the Flavors of Latin, 1998; (with R. Navarro-Valls and S.C. Arribas) Estado y Religión: Textos Para Una Reflexión Crítica, 2000. WITH A. GARGALIANO: Viva la Vida: Festive Recipes for Entertaining Latin-Style, 2002; Nueva Salsa: Recipes to Spice It Up, 2003; Fiesta Latina: Fabulous Food for Sizzling Parties, 2006; Palomino's Latin Grill: Sultry and Simple Food for Red-Hot Dinners and Parties, 2010; Sabor Latino, forthcoming. **Address:** Sonora Restaurant, 179 Rectory St., Port Chester, NY 10573, U.S.A. **Online address:** info@pasioncatering.com

PALUDI, Michele A. American (born United States), b. 1954. **Genres:** Administration/Management, Psychology, Women's Studies And Issues. **Career:** Michele Paludi and Associates (consultants in sexual harassment), principal; Franklin & Marshall College, visiting assistant professor, 1980-81; Kent State University, visiting assistant professor, 1981-82, assistant professor, associate professor of psychology, 1981-86; Hunter College, Department of Psychology, professor, 1986-93, director of women's studies, Minorities Access to Research Careers Program, director, Masters Program in Psychology, director, Sexual Harassment Panel, director, Psychological Advising Office, director; City University of New York, visiting associate professor, 1986-92, professor of psychology, 1992-, Women's Studies Program, director, 1991-92; Union College, visiting professor of psychology and graduate management, 1992-, president of human resources management solutions, School of Management, faculty, adjunct full professor, 1992-; Union Graduate College, full professor, 1992-, School of Management Certificate Programs in Human Resource Management, Financial Management, Health Management and Management and Leadership, director; Human Resources Management Solutions, president. Writer. **Publications:** Exploring/Teaching the Psychology of Women: A Manual of Resources, 1990, 2nd ed., 1996; (with R.B. Barickman) Academic and Workplace Sexual Harassment: A Resource Manual, 1991; (with J.A. Doyle) Sex & Gender: The Human Experience, 1991; The Psychology of Women, 1992, 2nd ed., 2002; (with J.N. Tedisco) Missing Children: A Psychological Approach to Understanding the Causes and Consequences of Stranger and Non-Stranger Abduction of Children, 1996; (with A. Levy) Workplace Sexual Harassment, 1997, 2nd ed., 2002; (with R.B. Barickman) Sexual Harassment, Work and Education: A Resource Manual For Prevention, 1998; Human Development in Multicultural Contexts: A Book of Readings, 2001; (co-author) Understanding Workplace Violence: A Guide for Managers and Employees, 2006. EDITOR: Ivory Power: Sexual Harassment on Campus, 1990; (with G.A. Steuernagel) Foundations for a Feminist Restructuring of the Academic Disciplines, 1990; (with F.L. Denmark) Handbook on the Psychology of Women, 1993; (with F.L. Denmark) Psychology of Women: A Handbook of Issues and Theories, 1993; Sexual Harassment on College Campuses: Abusing the Ivory Power, 1996; The Psychology of Sexual Victimization: A Handbook, 1999; Human Development in Multicultural Contexts: A Book of Readings, 2002; (with C. Paludi) Academic and Workplace Sexual Harassment: A Handbook of Social Science, Legal, Cultural and Management Perspectives, 2003; Praeger Guide to the Psychology of Gender, 2004; (with P. Neidermeyer) Work, Life and Family Imbalance: How to Level the Playing Field, 2007; (with F.L. Denmark) Psychology of Women: A Handbook of Issues and Theories, 2008; Psychology of Women at Work: Challenges and Solutions for Our Female Workforce, 2008; Understanding and Preventing Campus Violence, 2008; (with F.L. Denmark) Victims of Sexual Assault and Abuse: Resources and Responses for Individuals and Families, 2010; Feminism and Women's Rights Worldwide, 2010; (with B.E. Coates) Women as

Transformational Leaders, 2011; (with M.A. Paludi and E.R. DeSouza) Praeger Handbook on Understanding and Preventing Workplace Discrimination, 2011; (with P.K. Lundberg-Love and K.L. Nadal) Women and Mental Disorders, 2012. Contributor to journals. **Address:** Union College, UGC - School of Management, 303 Graduate Ctr., 807 Union St., Schenectady, NY 12308, U.S.A. **Online address:** mpaludi@aol.com

PALUMBI, **Stephen R.** American (born United States), b. 1956. **Genres:** Biology, Zoology, Sciences, History. **Career:** University of Hawaii, Department of Zoology, assistant professor, 1985-90, associate professor, 1990-94, professor, 1994-96, Kewalo Marine Lab, director, 1995-96; Harvard University, Department of Organismic and Evolutionary Biology, professor, 1996-2002; Stanford University, Department of Biological Sciences, Harold A Miller professor in marine sciences, 2002-, Hopkins Marine Station, director, 2008-, Woods Institute for the Environment, senior fellow. Writer. **Publications:** (Ed. with J.D. Ferraris) Molecular Zoology: Advances, Strategies, and Protocols, 1996; The Evolution Explosion: How Humans Cause Rapid Evolutionary Change, 2001; (with C. Sotka) Death and Life of Monterey Bay: A Story of Revival, 2011. Contributor to periodicals. **Address:** Department of Biological Sciences, Stanford University, 120 Ocean View Blvd., Pacific Grove, CA 93950-3024, U.S.A. **Online address:** spalumbi@stanford.edu

PALUMBO, **Donald E.** American (born United States), b. 1949. **Genres:** Science Fiction/Fantasy, Philosophy, Sex. **Career:** Lamar University, adjunct instructor in English, 1976-78; Northern Michigan University, associate professor of English, 1978-83; Lorain County Community College, chair of language and humanities division, 1983-87; Shippensburg University of Pennsylvania, professor of English, 1987-92; High Point University, International Association for the Fantastic in the Arts, president; East Carolina University, professor of English, 1992-, School of Anything Goes Anime, faculty advisor. Writer. **Publications:** (Ed.) Eros in the Mind's Eye: Sexuality and the Fantastic in Art and Film, 1986; (ed.) Erotic Universe: Sexuality and Fantastic Literature, 1986; (ed.) Spectrum of the Fantastic: Selected Essays from the Sixth International Conference on the Fantastic in the Arts, 1988; Chaos Theory, Asimov's Foundations and Robots, and Herbert's Dune: The Fractal Aesthetic of Epic Science Fiction, 2002; The Monomyth in American Science Fiction, forthcoming. **Address:** Department of English, East Carolina University, Bate 2121, E 5th St., Greenville, NC 27858-4353, U.S.A. **Online address:** palumbod@ecu.edu

PALUMBO-LIU, **David.** American (born United States) **Genres:** Literary Criticism And History, History. **Career:** Kyoto University, Faculty of Letters, research fellow, 1985-86; Georgetown University, English and the School of Foreign Service, assistant professor, 1988-90; Stanford University, assistant professor in comparative literature, 1990-94, Stanford Humanities Center, teaching fellow, 1994-95, associate professor of comparative literature, 1995-2001, Asian American Studies Program, director, 1999-2000, Program in Modern Thought and Literature, director, 1999, professor of comparative literature, 2001-, director of comparative literature. Writer. **Publications:** The Poetics of Appropriation: The Literary Theory and Practice of Huang Tingjian, 1993; Asian/American: Historical Crossings of a Racial Frontier, 1999. EDITOR: The Ethnic Canon: Histories, Institutions, and Interventions, 1995; (co-ed.) On Becoming Filipino: Selected Writings of Carlos Bulosan, 1995; (with H.U. Gumbrecht) Streams of Cultural Capital: Transnational Cultural Studies, 1997; (with B. Robbins and N. Tanoukhi) Immanuel Wallerstein and the Problem of the World: System, Scale, Culture, 2011. TRANSLATOR: Chi Chun, Ah-yu, 1983; J-F Lyotard, Marie á Narita, 1993. Contributor to periodicals. **Address:** Department of Comparative Literature, Stanford University, Rm. 229, Bldg. 260, 450 Serra Mall, Stanford, CA 94305-2031, U.S.A. **Online address:** palumbo-liu@stanford.edu

PALWICK, **Susan.** American (born United States), b. 1961?. **Genres:** Young Adult Fiction, Science Fiction/Fantasy, Novels. **Career:** University of Nevada, associate professor of English, School of Medicine, adjunct faculty. Writer. **Publications:** FANTASY AND SCIENCE FICTION: Flying in Place, 1992; The Necessary Beggar, 2005; Shelter, 2007; Fate of Mice, 2007; Driving to November, forthcoming. Contributor to journals. **Address:** Department of English, University of Nevada, 1664 N Virginia St., PO Box 0098, Reno, NV 89557 0098, U.S.A. **Online address:** palwick@unr.edu

PAMPEL, **Fred C.** American (born United States), b. 1950. **Genres:** Gerontology/Senior Issues, Sociology, Medicine/Health, Social Commentary, Adult Non-fiction, Reference. **Career:** University of Iowa, assistant professor, 1977-81, associate professor, 1981-87, faculty of scholars fellowship, 1985-88, professor of sociology, 1987-89, 1993-94; University of North Carolina, Department of Sociology, visiting associate professor, 1984-85; Florida State University, Institute on Aging, professor of sociology and research director, 1989-90; University of Colorado, population program, professor of sociology and faculty research associate, 1990-, Bureau of Sociological Research, director, 1995-96, associate vice chancellor for research, 2004-06; University of Essex, Essex Summer School in Social Science Data Analysis and Collection, instructor, 2003-04; London School of Economics and Political Science, Graduate School, faculty associate, 2007-. Writer. **Publications:** Social Change and the Aged: Recent Trends in the United States, 1981; (with J.B. Williamson) Age, Class, Politics and the Welfare State, 1989; (ed. with M.B. Tracy) International Handbook of Old-Age Insurance, 1991; (with J.B. Williamson) Old-Age Security in Comparative Perspective, 1993; Aging, Social Inequality and Public Policy, 1998; Logistic Regression: A Primer, 2000; Sociological Lives and Ideas: An Introduction to the Classical Theorists, 2000; The Institutional Context of Population Change: Patterns of Fertility and Mortality Across High-Income Nations, 2001; (with S. Pauley) Progress Against Heart Disease, 2004; Racial Profiling, 2004; Tobacco Industry and Smoking, 2004, rev. ed., 2009; Threats To Food Safety, 2006; Drugs and Sports, 2007; Sociological Lives and Ideas: An Introduction to the Classical Theorists, 2007; Rights of the Elderly, 2008; Disaster Response, 2008; Prescription Drugs, 2010; Public Policy and the Genetics of Smoking, forthcoming. **Address:** Population Program, University of Colorado, Rm. 102A, IBS Bldg. 3, 484 UCB, 219 Ketcham Hall UCB 327, Boulder, CO 80309, U.S.A. **Online address:** fred.pampel@colorado.edu

PANAGARIYA, **Arvind.** American/Indian (born India), b. 1952. **Genres:** Economics, International Relations/Current Affairs. **Career:** Rajasthan University, lecturer in economics, 1973-74; University of Maryland, assistant professor of economics, 1978-83, associate professor of economics, 1983-89, professor of economics, 1989-2004, Center for International Economics, co-director, 1993-2004; World Bank, principal economist and senior economist, 1989-93; Asian Development Bank, chief economist, 2001, consultant; Institute for Social and Economic Change, V.K.R.V. Rao endowment professor, 2002-03; World Trade Organization, consultant; Columbia University, School of International and Public Affairs, Jagdish Bhagwati Professor of Indian Political Economy and professor of economics, 2004-; Brookings Institution, non-resident senior fellow, 2007-; India Policy Forum, editor. **Publications:** How Should Tariffs be Structured?, 1990; (with M. Schiff) Commodity Exports and Real Income in Africa, 1990; Input Tariffs and Duty Drawbacks in the Design of Tariff Reform, 1990; (with M. Schiff) Taxes Versus Quotas: The Case of Cocoa Exports, 1991; Unraveling the Mysteries of Chinas Foreign Trade Regime: A View from Jiangsu Province, 1991; (with D. Rodrik) Political-Economy Arguments for Uniform Tariff, 1991; (with J. de Melo and C. Montenegro) Regional Integration Old and New, 1992; (with J. de Melo) The New Regionalism in Trade Policy, 1992; (with J. de Melo and D. Rodrik) The New Regionalism: A Country Perspective, 1993; (ed. with J. de Melo) New Dimensions in Regional Integration, 1993; Should East Asia go Regional?: No, No, and Maybe, 1993; (with R. Findlay) A Political-Economy Analysis of Free Trade Areas and Customs Unions, 1994; (with S. Dhar) Is East Asia Less Open than North America and the European Economic Community? No, 1994; (with M.G. Quibria and N. Rao) The Emerging Global Trading Environment and Developing Asia, 1996; (ed. with J. Bhagwati) The Economics of Preferential Trade Agreements, 1996; (with S. Shah and D. Mishra) Demand Elasticities in International Trade: Are They Really Low?, 1996; (ed. with M.G. Quibria and N. Rao) The Global Trading System and Developing Asia, 1997; (with I. Dīwān) Khiyārāt al-siyāsātal-tijārīyah lil-Diffah al-Gharbīyah wa-Qitā Ghazzah, 1997; Lectures on International Trade, 1998; (ed. with J. Bhagwati and P. Krishna) Trading Blocs: Alternative Approaches to Analyzing Preferential Trade Agreements, 1999; Regionalism in Trade Policy, 1999; (ed. with P.R. Portney and R.M. Schwab) Environmental and Public Economics: Essays in Honor of Wallace E. Oates, 1999; E-Commerce, WTO and Developing Countries, 2000; (ed. with D. Mitra) The Political Economy of Trade, Aid and Foreign Investment Policies, 2004; (ed. with E. Dinopoulos, P. Krishna and K. Wong) Trade, Globalization, and Poverty, 2008; India: The Emerging Giant, 2008; India's Reforms: How they Produced Inclusive Growth, 2012. **Address:** School of International & Public Affairs, Columbia University, Rm. 829, International Affairs Bldg., 420 W 118th St., New York, NY 10027, U.S.A. **Online address:** ap2231@columbia.edu

PANAYI, **Panikos.** British (born England), b. 1962. **Genres:** History, Race Relations, Food And Wine. **Career:** University of Keele, lecturer in history,

1989-90; De Montfort University, lecturer in history, 1990-93, senior lecturer, 1993-97, principal lecturer and reader, 1997-99, professor of European history, 1999-. Writer. **Publications:** The Enemy in Our Midst: Germans in Britain during the First World War, 1991; Immigration, Ethnicity, and Racism in Britain, 1815-1945, 1994; German Immigrants in Britain during the Nineteenth Century, 1815-1914, 1995; Outsiders: History of European Minorities, 1999; Ethnic Minorities in Nineteenth and Twentieth Century Germany, 2000; Life and Death in a German Town: Osnabrnck from the Weimar Republic to World War Two and Beyond, 2007; Spicing Up Britain: The Multicultural History of British Food, 2008; An Immigration History of Britain: Multicultural Racism Since c1800, 2010. EDITOR: Racial Violence in Britain, 1840-1950, 1993, 1996; Minorities in Wartime, 1993; Germans in Britain since 1500, 1996; (with K. Larres) The Federal Republic of Germany since 1949, 1996; Weimar and Nazi Germany, 2001; (with K. Burrell) Histories and Memories: Migrants and Their History in Britain, 2006. **Address:** Faculty of Humanities, De Montfort University, Leicester, LE1 9BH, England. **Online address:** ppanayi@dmu.ac.uk

PANCAKE, Ann. American (born United States), b. 1963. **Genres:** Novellas/Short Stories, Novels. **Career:** California Language Institute, teacher of English, 1986-87; American Samoa Community College, instructor in English, 1988-90; Vongchavalitkul College, instructor in English, 1992-93; Pennsylvania State University, Behrend College, assistant professor of creative writing and literature, 1998-, Smith Reading Series, director, 1999-2000; Pacific Lutheran University, Low-residency MFA Program, faculty. Writer. **Publications:** Given Ground (short stories), 2001; Strange as this Weather has Been: A Novel, 2007. Works appear in anthologies. Contributor of articles to periodicals. **Address:** School of Humanities and Social Sciences, Behrend College, Pennsylvania State University, 170 Irvin Kochel Ctr., 4951 College Dr., Erie, PA 16563-4119, U.S.A. **Online address:** asp6@psu.edu

PANCHYK, Richard. American (born United States), b. 1970. **Genres:** Engineering, Children's Non-fiction, History, Biography, Reference, Art/Art History, Archaeology/Antiquities, Adult Non-fiction, Adult Non-fiction. **Career:** Pocumtuck Valley Memorial Association, teacher, 1994-95; Gannett Fleming Engineers and Architects, marketing coordinator, 1996-; Hazen and Sawyer, marketing manager. Writer. **Publications:** NONFICTION FOR ADULTS: A History of Westbury, Long Island, 2007; Forgotten Tales of Long ISland, 2008; 101 Glimpses of Long Island's North Shore, 2008; German New York City, 2008; Keys to American History: Understanding Our Most Important Historic Documents, 2008; Catholic New York City, 2009; New York City Skyscrapers, 2010. NONFICTION FOR CHILDREN: (with M. Levy) Engineering the City: How Infrastructure Works, Projects and Principles for Beginners, 2000; Archaeology for Kids: Uncovering the Mysteries of Our Past: 25 Activities, 2001; World War II for Kids, 2002; American Folk Art for Kids, 2004; Galileo for Kids, 2005; Our Supreme Court, 2006; Franklin Delano Roosevelt for Kids, 2007. OTHERS: (with K. Panchyk) The CADD Department, 1991; (with K. Panchyk) CAD Management, 1998; Quakers, Tycoons, Aviators, 2007; 101 Glimpses of the South Fork, 2009; Charting the World, 2011. **Address:** 210 Lewis Ave., 1 Penn Plz., Ste. 2222, Westbury, NY 11590, U.S.A. **Online address:** panchyk@yahoo.com

PANCOL, Katherine. French/Moroccan (born Morocco), b. 1954?. **Genres:** Novels. **Career:** Journalist and novelist. **Publications:** Moi d'abord, 1979; La barbare, 1981; Scarlett, si possible, 1985; Les hommes cruels ne courent pas les rues, 1990; Vu de l'extérieur, 1993; Une si belle image, 1994; Encore une danse, 1998; J'étais là avant, 1999; Et monter lentement dans un immense amour, 2001; Un homme à distance, 2002; Embrassez-moi, 2003; Les Yeux jaunes des crocodiles: Roman, 2006; Valse lente des tortues: Roman, 2008; Les écureuils de Central Park Sont Tristes le Lundi, 2010. **Address:** Les éditions Albin Michel, 22 Rue Huyghens, Paris, 75014, France. **Online address:** kpancol@noos.fr

PANEK, Richard. American (born United States) **Genres:** Sciences, Astronomy. **Career:** Goddard College, MFA in Creative Writing Program, faculty advisor; Barnard College, creative writing instructor and adjunct associate professor. Journalist. **Publications:** Waterloo Diamonds, 1995; Seeing and Believing: How the Telescope Opened Our Eyes and Minds to the Heavens, 1998; The Invisible Century: Einstein, Freud, and the Search for Hidden Universes, 2004; The 4 Percent Universe: Dark Matter, Dark Energy, and the Race to Discover the Rest of Reality, 2010; Let There Be Dark: At the Dawn of the Next Universe, forthcoming. Works appear in anthologies. Contributor of articles to periodicals. **Address:** Viking Publicity, Penguin Group Inc., 375 Hudson St., New York, NY 10014-3658, U.S.A. **Online address:** richardpanek@yahoo.com

PANFORD, Kwamina. American/Ghanaian (born Ghana), b. 1955. **Genres:** Area Studies, Law, Social Sciences, Business/Trade/Industry, Economics. **Career:** Northeastern University, Department of African American Studies, associate professor, 1991-, associate vice provost, 2003-; Ghana Association, adviser and editor-in-chief. Consultant. **Publications:** African Labor Relations and Workers' Rights: Assessing the Role of the International Labor Organization, 1994; Assessing Africa's Global Competitiveness, 2001; IMF-World Bank and Labor's Burdens in Africa: Ghana's Experience, 2001; (co-ed.) 21st Century Africa Challenges and Opportunities, 2005; (ed. with K. Konadu-Agyemang) Africa's Development in the Twenty-First Century: Pertinent Socio-Economic and Development Issues, 2006; Ghana's Industrial Relations and Labor Laws, 2008. **Address:** Department of African American Studies, Northeastern University, 132 Nightingale Hall, 360 Huntington Ave., Boston, MA 02115-5005, U.S.A. **Online address:** k.panford@neu.edu

PANIK, Sharon. American (born United States), b. 1952. **Genres:** Children's Fiction, Mythology/Folklore, Language/Linguistics, Sports/Fitness. **Career:** Poudre School District R-1, teacher, 1974-2005. Writer. **Publications:** QUETZALCOATL SERIES WITH M. PARKE: A Quetzalcóatl Tale of Corn, 1992; A Quetzalcóatl Tale of the Ball Game, 1992; A Quetzalcóatl Tale of Chocolate, 1994; A Quetzalcóatl Tale of Colored Cotton. **Address:** 1100 Pheasant Dr., Fort Collins, CO 80525-9129, U.S.A. **Online address:** mphaberstroh@frii.com

PANITCH, Leo (Victor). Canadian (born Canada), b. 1945. **Genres:** Economics, Politics/Government, Sociology, Organized Labor, History, International Relations/Current Affairs, Industrial Relations, Social Sciences, Social Sciences. **Career:** Carleton University, lecturer, 1972-74, assistant professor, 1974-77, associate professor, 1977-82, professor of political science, 1982-84; York University, professor of political science, 1984-, distinguished research professor, senior Canada research chair in comparative political economy; The Socialist Register, co-editor, 1985-. **Publications:** Social Democracy and Industrial Militancy: The Labour Party, the Trade Unions and Incomes Policy 1945-1974, 1976; Workers, Wages and Controls: The Anti-Inflation Programme and its Implications for Canadian Workers, 1976; (ed. and co-author) The Canadian State: Political Economy and Political Power, 1977; (with D. Swartz) From Consent to Coercion: The Assault on Trade Union Freedoms, 1985, 3rd ed., 2003; Working-class Politics in Crisis: Essays on Labour and the State, 1986; Assault on Trade Union Freedoms: From Consent to Coercion Revisited, 1988, rev. ed., 2003; (ed. with G. Albo and D. Langille) A Different Kind of State? Popular Power and Democratic Administration, 1993; (ed. with R. Miliband) Real Problems, False Solutions: Socialist Register, 1993; Globalization and the State, 1994; (with C. Leys) The End of Parliamentary Socialism: From New Left to New Labour, 1997, rev. ed., 2001; (ed. with C. Leys) Necessary and Unnecessary Utopias: Socialist Register 2000, 1999; (co-author) Strategie der Neuen Mitte: Verabschiedet sich die Moderne Sozialdemokratie als Reformpartei?, 1999; Renewing Socialism: Democracy, Strategy, and Imagination, 2001, 2nd ed., 2008; (with S. Gindin) Global Capitalism and American Empire 2004; American Empire and the Political Economy of Global Finance, 2008, (ed. with M. Konings) 2nd ed., 2009; In and Out of Crisis (with G. Albo and S. Gindin) 2010. **Address:** Department of Political Science, York University, 4700 Keele St., Ross S660, Toronto, ON M3J 1P3, Canada. **Online address:** lpanitch@yorku.ca

PANKHURST, Richard (Keir Pethick). British (born England), b. 1927. **Genres:** History, Travel/Exploration. **Career:** Addis Ababa University, Institute of Ethiopian Studies, professor of Ethiopian studies, 1957-76, founder, 1962, director, 1963-73; Royal Asiatic Society, librarian, 1980-86. Writer. **Publications:** (With E.S. Pankhurst) Ethiopia and Eritrea, 1953; William Thompson (1775-1833): Britain's Pioneer Socialist, Feminist and Co-operator, 1954; Kenya: The History of Two Nations, 1954; The Saint Simonians, Mill and Carlyle, 1957; An Introduction to the Economic History of Ethiopia, from Early Times to 1800, 1961; Great Ethiopian Famine of 1888-1892, 1964; Some Factors Depressing the Standard of Living of Peasants in Traditional Ethiopia, 1965; (ed.) Travellers in Ethiopia, 1965; State and Land in Ethiopian History, 1966; (ed.) The Ethiopian Royal Chronicles, 1967; Brief Note on the Economic History of Ethiopia from 1800 to 1935, 1967; An Introduction to the History of the Ethiopian Army, 1967; Primitive Money, Money and Banking in Ethiopia, 1967; Economic History of Ethiopia, 1800-1935, 1968; (with G. Last) A History of Ethiopia in Pictures, 1969; History and Traditional

Treatment of Rabies in Ethiopia, 1969; Language and Education in Ethiopia; Historical Background to the Post-War Period, 1969; Traditional Ethiopian Army and Its Weapons, 1969; History of Ethiopia, 1970; Some Notes on the Historical and Economic Geography of the Massawa Area, 1520-1885, 1973; Saint Simonians, Mill and Carlyle: A Preface to Modern Thought, 1974; (ed. with B. Michael and S. Chojnacki) Dictionary of Ethiopian Biography, 1975; Some Notes for the History of Typhus in Ethiopia, 1975; Sylvia Pankhurst, Artist and Crusader: An Intimate Portrait, 1979; (ed.) Tax Records and Inventories of Emperor Tweodros of Ethiopia, 1979; History of Ethiopian Tents from Mediaeval Times to the Reign of Emperor Tewodros II, 1982; History of Ethiopian Towns from the Middle Ages to the Early Nineteenth Century, 1982; (with G. Hancock and D. Willetts) Under Ethiopian Skies, 1983, 4th ed., 2009; Let's Visit Ethiopia, 1984; (with D. Appleyard) Letters from Ethiopian Rulers, 1985; The History of Famine and Epidemics in Ethiopia Prior to the 20th Century, 1985; (with L. Ingrams) Ethiopia Engraved: An Illustrated Catalogue of Engravings by Foreign Travellers from 1681 to 1900, 1988; (ed.) Historical Geography of Ethiopia: From the First Century AD to 1704, 1989; History of Ethiopian Towns: From the Middle Ages to 1935, 2 vols., 1989; (ed. with T. Beyene and S. Bekele) Kasa and Kasa, Papers on the Lives, Times and Images of Téwodros II and Yohannes IV, (1885-1889), 1990; Introduction to the Medical History of Ethiopia, 1990; A Social History of Ethiopia: The Northern and Central Highlands from Early Medieval Times to the Rise of Emperor Téwodros II, 1990; (ed. with I. Bullock) Sylvia Pankhurst: From Artist to Anti-Fascist, 1992; Prelude to Magdala: Emperor Theodore of Ethiopia and British Diplomacy, 1992; (with D. Gerard) Ethiopia Photographed, 1996; The Ethiopian Borderlands: Essays in Regional History form Ancient Times to the End of the 18th Century, 1997; The Ethiopians, 1999; (with S.S. Jayasuriya) African Diaspora in the Indian Ocean, 2001; The Ethiopians: A History, 2001; Sylvia Pankhurst: Counsel for Ethiopia: A Biographical Essay on Ethiopian, Anti-Fascist and Anti-Colonialist History, 1934-1960, 2003; (with F.A. Sharf and D. Northrup) Abyssinia, 1867-1868: Artists on Campaign: Watercolors and Drawings from the British Expedition under Sir Robert Napier, 2003; Historic Images of Ethiopia, 2005. **Address:** 22 Lawn Rd., London, GL NW3 2XR, England. **Online address:** pankhurst@ethionet.et

PANNICK, David. British (born England), b. 1956. **Genres:** Law, Biography. **Career:** Barrister at law, 1978-; All Souls College, fellow, 1978-; Times, columnist, 1991-; Deputy High Court, judge, 1998-2005; Hertford College, honorary fellow, 2004-. **Publications:** Judicial Review of the Death Penalty, 1982; Sex Discrimination in Sport, 1983; Sex Discrimination Law, 1985; Judges, 1987; Advocates, 1992; (ed. with A. Lester) Human Rights Law and Practice, 1999, (ed. with L. Lester and J. Herberg) 3rd ed., 2009; I Have to Move My Car: Tales of Unpersuasive Advocates and Injudicious Judges, 2008. **Address:** Blackstone Chambers, Blackstone House, Temple, London, GL EC4Y 9BW, England.

PANOFSKY, Ruth. Canadian (born Canada), b. 1958. **Genres:** Poetry, Literary Criticism And History. **Career:** Ryerson University, professor of English. Writer. **Publications:** Adele Wiseman: An Annotated Bibliography, 1992; (ed. with J. Lennox) Selected Letters of Margaret Laurence and Adele Wiseman, 1997; (ed.) Adele Wiseman: Essays on Her Works, 2001; Lifeline (poetry), 2001; The Force of Vocation: The Literary Career of Adele Wiseman, 2006; Laike and Nahum: A Poem in Two Voices (poetry), 2007; At Odds in the World: Essays on Jewish Canadian Women Writers, 2008. Contributor of articles to books and periodicals. **Address:** Department of English, Ryerson University, 350 Victoria St., Toronto, ON M5B 2K3, Canada. **Online address:** panofsky@ryerson.ca

PANOURGIA, Neni K(onstantinou). (Nenny Panourgia). American/Greek (born Greece), b. 1958. **Genres:** Classics, History, Anthropology/Ethnology. **Career:** Intercultural Action Learning Program, teacher of Greek and anthropology, 1981, 1982; Indiana University, lecturer in Greek, William Hammond Mathers Museum, practicum, 1983-85, associate instructor in anthropology, 1989; De Paul University, lecturer, 1987; University of Colorado, exhibit coordinator, 1987; Ohio State University, lecturer, 1991; Columbia University, lecturer in Greek, 1991, assistant professor of anthropology, associate professor; Museum of Children's Health, coordinator of operations, 1994-95; University of Lund, lecturer, 1992; Harvard University, lecturer, 1994; Selwyn College, lecturer, 1994; New York University, lecturer, 1994; Pantion University of Social and Political Sciences, visiting research fellow, 1994-95; Princeton University, visiting fellow in Hellenic studies, 1995-96, teacher of Greek language and literature, 1996-97; Rutgers University, lecturer of anthropology. Writer. **Publications:** Fragments of Death, Fables of Identity: An Athenian Anthropography, 1995; (ed. with G.E. Marcus) Ethnographica Moralia: Experiments in Interpretive Anthropology, 2008; Dangerous Citizens: The Greek Left and the Terror of the State, 2009; Oedipal Sightings: Anthropology, Ethnography, and the Deconstruction of the Site, forthcoming; Deforming Bodies Forming Subjects, forthcoming; Greek-Americans: Workings of an Ethnic Presence, forthcoming. Contributor to books and periodicals. **Address:** Department of Anthropology, Columbia University, Rm. 458, Schermerhorn Ext., 1200 Amsterdam Ave. W, 119th St., New York, NY 10027-5523, U.S.A. **Online address:** np255@columbia.edu

PANOURGIA, Nenny. *See* **PANOURGIA, Neni K(onstantinou).**

PANTAEVA, Irina. American/Russian (born Russia), b. 1972. **Genres:** Autobiography/Memoirs, Women's Studies And Issues. **Career:** Fashion model, actress, jewelry designer and writer. **Publications:** Siberian Dream: A Memoir, 1998. Contributor to periodicals. **Address:** c/o Avon Books, 1350 Ave. of the Americas, New York, NY 10019, U.S.A.

PANZER, Mary (Caroline). American (born United States), b. 1955. **Genres:** Art/Art History. **Career:** University of Kansas, assistant professor, 1989-91; Spencer Museum of Art, curator of photographs, 1989-91; SMART Museum of Art, assistant director, 1991; National Portrait Gallery, Smithsonian Institution, curator of photographs, 1992-2000; New York University, Department of History, adjunct professor, 2001-06; Wall Street Journal, freelance writer, 2007-; Brooklyn Navy Yard Development Corp., exhibition consultant, 2008-; historian. Writer. **Publications:** Philadelphia Naturalistic Photography, 1865-1906, 1982; In My Studio: Rudolf Eickmeyer, Jr. and the Art of the Camera, 1885-1930, 1986; (contrib.) Splendors of the American West: Thomas Moran's Art of the Grand Canyon and Yellowstone: Paintings, Watercolors, Drawings, and Photographs from the Thomas Gilcrease Institute of American History and Art, 1990; Mathew Brady and the Image of History, 1997; Mathew Brady, 2001; Lewis Hine, 2002; (contrib.) Separate, But Equal: The Mississippi Photographs of Henry Clay Anderson, 2002; Things as They Are, 2005. Contributor to periodicals. **Address:** National Portrait Gallery, 8th & F St. NW, Washington, DC 20560, U.S.A.

PAOLA, Suzanne. *See* **ANTONETTA, Susanne.**

PAPADIMITRIOU, Dimitri B. American/Greek (born Greece), b. 1946. **Genres:** Money/Finance, Economics, Business/Trade/Industry. **Career:** William Penn Life Insurance Co., executive vice president, secretary and treasurer, 1969-77, director, 1972-; New School University, adjunct professor of graduate faculty, 1975-76; Bard College, executive vice president and provost, 1977-, Jerome Levy professor of economics, 1977-, Jerome Levy Economics Institute, president, 1986-; Aspen Institute, Wye Fellow, 1985; Trade Deficit Review Commission, United States Congress, vice chairman, 1999-2001. Writer. **Publications:** EDITOR: (with S.M. Fazzari) Financial Conditions and Macroeconomic Performance: Essays in Honor of Hyman P. Minsky, 1992; Profits, Deficits and Instability, 1992; (with E.N. Wolff) Poverty and Prosperity in the U.S.A. in the Late Twentieth Century, 1993; Aspects of Distribution of Wealth and Income, 1994; The Stability of the Financial System, 1996; Modernizing Financial Systems, 2000; (and intro.) Induced Investment and Business Cycles, 2005; The Distributional Effects of Government Spending and Taxation, 2006; Government Spending on the Elderly, 2007; (with L.R. Wray) Stabilizing an Unstable Economy, 2008; (with L.R. Wray) John Maynard Keynes, 2008; (with L.R. Wray) The Elgar Companion to Hyman Minsky, 2010; (with G. Zezza) Contributions in Stock-flow Modelling: Essays in Honour of Wynne Godley, 2012. Contributor of articles to periodicals. **Address:** Office of the Provost, Bard College, 30 Campus Rd., PO Box 5000, Annandale-On-Hudson, NY 12504-5000, U.S.A. **Online address:** dbp@levy.org

PAPANIKOLAS, Zeese. American (born United States), b. 1942. **Genres:** History, Novels. **Career:** Stanford University, faculty, Stegner fellow, 1965-66; Sonoma State College, faculty; Aristotle University, Fulbright senior specialist; San Francisco Art Institute, professor of humanities, 1968-. Writer. **Publications:** (Ed. with F. Bergon) Looking Far West: The Search for the American West in History, Myth, and Literature, 1978; Buried Unsung: Louis Tikas and the Ludlow Massacre, 1982; Trickster in the Land of Dreams, 1995; American Silence, 2007; Rivers: A Novel, forthcoming; Syncopated Civilization: A Study in American Style, forthcoming. Contributor to periodicals. **Address:** University of Nebraska Press, 1111 Lincoln Mall, Lincoln, NE 68588-0630, U.S.A.

PAPE, Robert A. (Robert Anthony Pape). American (born United States), b. 1960. **Genres:** International Relations/Current Affairs, Military/Defense/Arms Control, Air/Space Topics, Social Commentary, Adult Non-fiction, Social Sciences, Politics/Government. **Career:** Dartmouth College, teacher of international relations, 1991-96; United States Air Force School of Advanced Airpower Studies, Maxwell Air Force Base, teacher of air power strategy, 1996-99; University of Chicago, Department of Political Science, professor of political science, 1999-, Program for International Security Politics, director, Chicago Project on Security and Terrorism, founder and director, 2003-. Writer. **Publications:** NONFICTION: Bombing to Win: Air Power and Coercion in War, 1996; Dying to Win: The Strategic Logic of Suicide Terrorism, 2005; (with J.K. Feldman) Cutting the Fuse: The Explosion of Global Suicide Terrorism and How to Stop It, 2010. Contributor to periodicals. **Address:** Department of Political Science, University of Chicago, Pick Hall 418 A, 5828 S University Ave., Chicago, IL 60637-1553, U.S.A. **Online address:** r-pape@uchicago.edu

PAPE, Robert Anthony. *See* **PAPE, Robert A.**

PAPER, Lewis Jay. American (born United States), b. 1946. **Genres:** Politics/Government, Biography, Sports/Fitness. **Career:** Harvard University, teaching fellow in government, 1969-71; Citizens Communications Center, attorney, 1972-73; legislative counsel to Senator Gaylord Nelson, 1973-75; Lowenstein, Sandler, Brochin, Kohl and Fisher, associate attorney, 1975-78; Federal Communications Commission, assistant general counsel, 1978-79, associate general counsel, 1979-81; Grove, Engelberg and Gross, partner, 1981-86; Georgetown University Law Center, adjunct professor of law, 1983-86; Keck, Mahin and Cate, staff, 1986-95; Dickstein Shapiro L.L.P., partner, 1995-. Writer. **Publications:** The Promise and the Performance: The Leadership of John F. Kennedy, 1975; John F. Kennedy: The Promise and the Performance, 1980; Brandeis, 1983; Empire: William S. Paley and the Making of CBS, 1987; Perfect: Don Larsen's Miraculous World Series Game and the Men who Made it Happen, 2009. Contributor to periodicals and journals. **Address:** Dickstein Shapiro L.L.P., 1825 Eye St. NW, Washington, DC 20006-5403, U.S.A. **Online address:** paperl@dicksteinshapiro.com

PAPES, Robert. American (born United States), b. 1943. **Genres:** Business/Trade/Industry, Economics, Marketing. **Career:** General Electric Co., staff, 1966-85; James River Co., general manager, 1986-90; International Paper, general manager, 1990-92; General Services Industry, general manager, 1992-95; American P&Ds Paper, general manager, 1995-98; ITW, general manager, 1998-2002; Papes Consulting, owner and consultant. Writer. **Publications:** Turnaround, 2002; Management During an Economic Crisis, 2010. **Address:** 3241 Pimlico Blvd., Stow, OH 44224, U.S.A. **Online address:** consulting@robertpapes.com

PAPINEAU, David. British (born England), b. 1947. **Genres:** Philosophy. **Career:** University of Reading, lecturer in sociology, 1974-77; Macquarie University, lecturer in philosophy, 1977-79; University of London, Birkbeck College, lecturer in philosophy, 1979-80; Cambridge University, lecturer in philosophy of science, 1981-90; King's College, professor of philosophy, 1990-. Writer. **Publications:** For Science in the Social Sciences, 1978; Theory and Meaning, 1979; Reality and Representation, 1987; Philosophical Naturalism, 1993; (ed.) The Philosophy of Science, 1996; Thinking about Consciousness, 2002; The Roots of Reason: Philosophical Essays on Rationality, Evolution and Probability, 2003; (ed.) Western Philosophy: An Illustrated Guide, 2004; (ed. with G. MacDonald) Teleosemantics: New Philosophical Essays, 2006; (ed.) Philosophy, 2008. **Address:** Department of Philosophy, King's College, The Strand, London, GL WC2R 2LS, England. **Online address:** david.papineau@kcl.ac.uk

PAPKE, David (Ray). American (born United States), b. 1947. **Genres:** Criminology/True Crime. **Career:** Yale University, Davenport College, dean and lecturer in American studies, 1975-78; Indiana University School of Law, visiting assistant professor of law, 1983-86, assistant professor of law, 1983-86, associate professor of law and adjunct associate professor of American studies, 1986-91, professor of law, 1991-96, professor of liberal arts, 1991-2001, R. Bruce Townsend professor of law, 1996-2001; Tamkang University, Fullbright professor of American studies, 1986-87; University of Illinois College of Law, visiting professor of law, 1991; Marquette University Law School, Robert F. Boden visiting professor of law, 1998, professor of law, 2002-; Association of American Law Schools, Section on Law and Humanities, program coordinator, 2001-02. Writer. **Publications:** Framing the Criminal: Crime, Cultural Work, and the Loss of Critical Perspective, 1830-1900 (monograph), 1987; Narrative & The Legal Discourse, 1991; Heretics in the Temple: Americans Who Reject the Nation's Legal Faith (monograph), 1998; The Pullman Case: The Clash of Labor and Capital in Industrial America (monograph), 1999, 2nd ed. 2000; Law and Popular Culture: Text, Notes, and Questions, 2007, 2nd ed., 2012. **Address:** Marquette University Law School, Sensenbrenner Hall, 1103 W Wisconsin Ave., PO Box 1881, Milwaukee, WI 53233, U.S.A. **Online address:** david.papke@marquette.edu

PAPPANO, Marilyn. (Rachel Butler). American (born United States) **Genres:** Romance/Historical, Adult Non-fiction, Novels. **Career:** Author. **Publications:** The Lights of Home, 1987; Guilt by Association, 1988; Room at the Inn, 1988; Cody Daniels' Return, 1988; Somebody's Baby, 1989; Something of Heaven, 1989; Not Without Honor, 1990; Safe Haven, 1990; Probable Cause, 1991; A Dangerous Man, 1991; Operation Homefront, 1992; Somebody's Lady, 1992; No Retreat, 1992; Memories of Laura, 1993; Sweet Annie's Pass, 1993; Finally a Father, 1993; In Sinful Harmony, 1995; Within Reach, 1995; Survive the Night, 1996; Passion, 1996; Suspicion, 1997; Murphy's Law, 1998; Older, Wiser...Pregnant, 1998; (with M. Shayne) Who Do You Love?: Two Hearts and A Little Bit Dangerous, 2000; Honourable Intentions, 2001; The Truth About Tate, 2001; My Secret Valentine, 2001; The Princess and the Mercenary, 2002; (co-author) Snowy Nights, 2003; The Trouble with Josh, 2003; (as Rachel Butler) The Assassin, 2005; (as Rachel Butler) Deep Cover, 2005; Somebody's Hero, 2006; More Than A Hero, 2007; One Stormy Night, 2007; (as Rachel Butler) Scorched, 2007; Forbidden Stranger, 2008; Intimate Enemy, 2008; Scandal in Copper Lake, 2009; Passion To Die For, 2009; Criminal Deception, 2010; Protector's Temptation, 2010; Copper Lake Secrets, 2011. SOUTHERN KNIGHTS SERIES: Michael's Gift, 1994; Regarding Remy, 1994; A Man like Smith, 1995; Convincing Jamey, 1997; The Taming of Reid Donovan, 1997; Knight Errant, 1997. BETHLEHEM SERIES: A Season for Miracles, 1997; Some Enchanted Season, 1998; Father to Be, 1999; First Kiss, 2000; Getting Lucky, 2001; Heaven on Earth, 2002; Cabin Fever, 2003; Small Wonders, 2003. HEARTBREAK CANYON SERIES: Cattleman's Promise, 1999; The Horseman's Bride, 1999; Rogue's Reform, 2000; The Sheriff's Surrender, 2001; Lawman's Redemption, 2002; One True Thing, 2004; The Bluest Eyes in Texas, 2005. **Address:** PO Box 643, Sapulpa, OK 74067-0643, U.S.A. **Online address:** marilyn@marilynpappano.com

PAPPAS, Milt. American (born United States), b. 1939. **Genres:** Autobiography/Memoirs. **Career:** Writer. **Publications:** (With W. Mausser) Bringing the Heat: The Autobiography of Milt Pappas, 1998; (with W. Mausser and L. Names) Out at Home: Triumph and Tragedy in the Life of a Major Leaguer, 2000. **Address:** 502 Highlington Ct., Beecher, IL 60401-3576, U.S.A.

PAPPÉ, Ilan. British/Israeli (born Israel), b. 1954. **Genres:** History, International Relations/Current Affairs. **Career:** Dayan Center, research fellow, 1985-87; Haifa University, senior lecturer in political science, 1984-2006; Research Institute for Peace, academic director, 1992-; Academic Institute for Peace, founder and academic director, 1992-2000; Emil Tuma Institute for Palestine Studies, chair, 2000-06; University of Exeter, Department of History, chair, 2007-09, professor of history, Exeter Centre for Ethno-Political Studies, co-director, European Centre for Palestine Studies, director. Writer. **Publications:** Britain and the Arab-Israeli Conflict, 1948-51, 1988; The Making of the Arab-Israeli Conflict, 1947-51, 1992; Profil shel sakinai: metsuḳah ṿe-alimut Palesṭinit, 1993; 'Arvim ṿi-Yehudim bi-teḳufat ha-Mandaṭ, 1995; (ed. with J. Nevo) Jordan in the Middle East: The Making of a Pivotal State, 1948-1988, 1996; Politics and Ideas in the Middle East, 1996; (ed. with M. Ma'oz) Middle Eastern Politics and Ideas: A History from Within, 1997; (ed.) The Israel/Palestine Question, 1999, 2nd ed. as Israel/Palestine Question: A Reader, 2007; Atsulat ha-arets, 2002; A History of Modern Palestine: One Land, Two Peoples, 2004, 2nd ed., 2006; The Modern Middle East, 2005, 2nd ed., 2010; The Ethnic Cleansing of Palestine, 2006; (ed. with J. Hilal) Across the Wall, 2010; (with N. Chomsky) Gaza in Crisis, 2010; Forgotten Palestinians: A History of the Palestinians in Israel, 2011. **Address:** Department of History, University of Exeter, Cornwall Campus, Penryn, CW TR10 9EZ, England. **Online address:** i.pappe@exeter.ac.uk

PAQUET, Laura Byrne. Canadian (born Canada), b. 1965. **Genres:** Adult

Non-fiction, Romance/Historical, inspirational/Motivational Literature, Novels. **Career:** Ottawa Business News, reporter, 1986-88; Capital Publishers, editor, 1988-92; Cornerstone Word Co., co-founder; Editors Association of Canada, directory chair, 2002-03. **Publications:** Secret Ottawa: The Unique Guidebook to Ottawa's Hidden Sites, Sounds and Tastes, 2000; The Urge to Splurge: A Social History of Shopping, 2003; (with A. Holden and K. Huntington) On Bended Knee, 2003; (with L. Collum and H.A. Solomon) Wife for Papa, 2004; Honorable Match, 2004; Incomparable Cassandra, 2004; Rakish Spy, 2004; Wanderlust: A Social History of Travel, 2007. ROMANCE NOVELS: Lord Langdon's Tutor, 2000; Miss Scott Meets Her Match, 2002; Mr. McAllister Sets His Cap, 2003. EDITOR: Ottawa: A Guide to Heritage Structures, 2000; Secret Guides, 2001. Contributor to periodicals. Works appear in anthologies. **Address:** c/o Robert Lecker, Robert Lecker Agency, 4055 Melrose Ave., Montreal, QC H4A 2S5, Canada. **Online address:** laura@cornerstoneword.com

PARADIS, Adrian Alexis. *See* Obituaries.

PARADISE, Paul R. American (born United States), b. 1950. **Genres:** Animals/Pets, Law, Criminology/True Crime, Economics. **Career:** T.F.H. Publications, staff writer, 1975-79; Matthew Bender and Company Inc., New York City, legal indexer, 1980-86; writer, 1986-. **Publications:** (Co-author) All about Canaries, 1976; African Grey Parrots, 1979; Amazon Parrots, 1979; Gerbils, 1980; Rabbits, 1983; Cockatiels, 1988; Racoons; (contrib.) Police; Trademark Counterfeiting, Product Privacy, and the Billion Dollar Threat to the U.S. Economy, 1999; Fancy Goldfish, 2000. Contributor to magazines. **Address:** Quorum Books, 88 Post Rd. W, Westport, CT 06880-4208, U.S.A.

PARANJAPE, Makarand (Ramachandra). Indian (born India), b. 1960. **Genres:** Novels, Novellas/Short Stories, Poetry, Literary Criticism And History. **Career:** University of Illinois, teaching assistant, 1980-86; University of Hyderabad, lecturer, reader, 1986-94; Indian Institute of Technology, Department of Humanities and Social Sciences, associate professor of humanities and social sciences, 1994-99; Indian Institute of Advanced Study, visiting professor, 1996; Jawaharlal Nehru University, School of Language, Literature, and Culture Studies, Centre for English Studies, professor of English, 1999-; UGC Special Assistance Programme, coordinator, 2003-; China-India Intercultural Dialogue, joint coordinator, 2004-05; National University of Singapore, Indian Council for Cultural Relations, chair of Indian Studies and professor, 2010-. Writer. **Publications:** Mysticism in Indian English Poetry, 1988; Decolonization and Development: Hind Svaraj Revisioned, 1993; (trans.) H.G. Joglekar, Boats, 1994; This Time I Promise It'll Be Different: Short Stories, 1994; The Narrator (novel), 1995; Towards a Poetics of the Indian English Novel, 2000; Another Canon: Indian Texts and Traditions in English, 2009; Altered Destinations: Self, Society, and Nation in India, 2009. POETRY: The Serene Flame, 1991; Playing the Dark God, 1992; Used Book, 2001; Partial Disclosure, 2004. EDITOR: (and intro.) Sarojini Naidu: Selected Poetry and Prose, 1993; An Anthology of New Indian English Poetry, 1993; Indian Poetry in English, 1993; (and intro.) Sarojini Naidu: Selected Letters, 1996; Nativism: Essays in Literary Criticism, 1997; The Best of Raja Rao, 1998; The Penguin Sri Aurobindo Reader, 1999; In Diaspora: Theories, Histories, Texts, 2001; The Little Book of Sri Aurobindo, 2001; (with H.V. Dehejia) Saundarya, 2003; (S.K. Sareen) Sabda, 2004; Dharma and Development, 2005; (with S. Sengupta) The Cyclonic Swami: Vivekananda in the West, 2005; Sacred Australia, 2009. **Address:** Centre for English Studies, School of Language, Literature, & Culture Studies, Jawaharlal Nehru University, New Mehrauli Rd., New Delhi, DH 110067, India. **Online address:** makarand@mail.jnu.ac.in

PARASCANDOLA, Louis J. American (born United States), b. 1952. **Genres:** Literary Criticism And History, Novels, History. **Career:** Long Island University, associate professor of English, 1992-, professor of English. Writer. **Publications:** Puzzled Which to Choose: Conflicting Socio-Political Views in the Works of Captain Frederick Marryat, 1997; Winds Can Wake Up the Dead: An Eric Walrond Reader, 1998; (ed.) Look for Me all Around You: Anglophone Caribbean Immigrants in the Harlem Renaissance, 2005. **Address:** Department of English, Long Island University, Brooklyn Campus, Humanities 464, Brooklyn, NY 11201, U.S.A. **Online address:** louis.parascandola@liu.edu

PARATORE, Coleen Murtagh. American (born United States), b. 1958. **Genres:** Novels, Picture/Board Books. **Career:** Russell Sage College, director of communications, adjunct professor; freelance public relations consultant; Books Worth Writing, founder. Writer. **Publications:** JUVENILE: 26 Big Things Small Hands Do, 2004; How Prudence Proovit Proved the Truth about Fairy Tales, 2004; Compatibly Cupid, 2006; Mack McGinn's Big Win, 2007; Catching the Sun, 2008; The Funeral Director's Son, 2008; Sunny Holiday, 2009; A Pearl Among Princes, 2009; Forget Me Not: From the Life of Willa Havisham, 2009; Kip Campbell's Gift, 2009; Mermaid Wedding Cakes, 2010; Sweet and Sunny, 2010; Wish I Might: From the Life of Willa Havisham, 2010; From Willa, With Love: From the Life of Willa Havisham, 2011; Dreamsleeves, 2012. THE WEDDING PLANNER'S DAUGHTER SERIES: The Wedding Planner's Daughter, 2005; The Cupid Chronicles, 2006; Willa by Heart, 2008. **Address:** Scholastic Inc., 557 Broadway, New York, NY 10012, U.S.A. **Online address:** cmparatore@aol.com

PARAVISINI-GEBERT, Lizabeth. American/Puerto Rican (born Puerto Rico), b. 1953. **Genres:** Cultural/Ethnic Topics, Literary Criticism And History, Local History/Rural Topics, Biography, Novellas/Short Stories, Bibliography. **Career:** Herbert H. Lehman College, City University of New York, Puerto Rican studies, associate professor, 1981-91; Vassar College, Hispanic studies, associate professor, 1991-96, professor, Randolph distinguished professor chair, 1997-, Africana Studies Program, director. Writer. **Publications:** (Ed. with C.C. Esteves) Green Cane and Juicy Flotsam: Short Stories by Caribbean Women, 1991; (contrib.) Luz y sombra, 1991; (with M.F. Olmos) El Placer de la Palabra: Literatura erótica Femininade América Latina: Antología crítica, 1991; (comp. with O.T. Seda) Caribbean Women Novelists: An Annotated Bibliography, 1992, 2nd ed., 1993; (with M.F. Olmos) Pleasure in the Word: Erotic Writings by Latin American Women, 1993, 2nd ed., 1994; Phyllis Shand Allfrey: A Caribbean Life, 1993, 2nd ed., 1996; (ed. with M.F. Olmos) Remaking a Lost Harmony: Stories from the Hispanic Caribbean, 1995; (ed. with M.F. Olmos) Sacred Possessions: Vadou, Santeria, Obeah and the Caribbean, 1997; Jamaica Kincaid: A Critical Companion, 1999; (ed. with M.F. Olmos) Healing Cultures: Art and Religion as Curative Practices in the Caribbean and Its Diaspora, 2001; (ed. with I.R. Cesareo) Women at Sea: Travel Writing and The Margins of Caribbean Discourse, 2001; (with M.F. Olmos) Creole Religions of the Caribbean: An Introduction from Vodou and Santeria to Obeah and Espiritismo, 2003, 2nd ed., 2011; Literatures of the Carribean, 2004; (ed.with I.R. Cesareo) Displacements and Transformations in Caribbean Cultures, 2008; Glimpses of Hell, forthcoming; Jose Marti: A Biography of the Cuban Patriot, forthcoming. **Address:** Department of Hispanic Studies, Vassar College, CH-144, 124 Raymond Ave., PO Box 266, Poughkeepsie, NY 12604, U.S.A. **Online address:** liparavisini@vassar.edu

PARBERRY, Ian. American/British (born England), b. 1959?. **Genres:** Information Science/Computers, Technology, Sciences. **Career:** Pennsylvania State University, assistant professor of computer science, 1984-90; University of North Texas, Department of Computer Science and Engineering, associate professor, 1990-95, professor of computer sciences, 1995-, interim chair, 2009-11, Center for Research in Parallel and Distributed Computing, director, 1990-95; Third Hemisphere Interactive, owner, 1997-; InfoMover Inc., consultant, 1998-2007; Lasso Technologies, consultant, 2001-01. Writer. **Publications:** Parallel Complexity Theory, 1987; Circuit Complexity and Neural Networks, 1994; Problems on Algorithms, 1995, 2nd ed., 2007; Learn Computer Game Programming with DirectX 7.0, 2000; Introduction to Computer Game Programming with DirectX 8.0, 2001; (with F. Dunn) 3D Math Primer for Graphics and Game Development, 2002, 2nd ed., 2011. Contributor of articles to books and journals. **Address:** Department of Computer Science and Engineering, University of North Texas, Rm. F209, Discovery Pk., 3940 N Elm, 1155 Union Cir., Ste. 311366, Denton, TX 76207-7102, U.S.A. **Online address:** ian@unt.edu

PARDES, Ilana. Israeli (born Israel), b. 1956. **Genres:** Biography. **Career:** Princeton University, assistant professor, 1990-92; Hebrew University, professor, 1992-, Department of Comparative Literature, chair, 2003-08; University of California, visiting professor, 1996, 2006. Contributor to periodicals. **Publications:** Countertraditions in the Bible: A Feminist Approach, 1992; The Biography of Ancient Israel: National Narratives in the Bible, 2000; (ed. with R. Ginsburg) New Perspectives on Freud's "Moses and Monotheism", 2006; Melville's Bibles, 2008. Contributor to books and periodicals. **Address:** Jerusalem, Israel. **Online address:** mspardes@huji.ac.il

PARDOE, Blaine. American (born United States), b. 1962. **Genres:** Novels, Military/Defense/Arms Control, Information Science/Computers, Science Fiction/Fantasy. **Career:** Ford, staff; GM, staff; Chrysler, staff; Ernst & Young LLP, staff; GM Life, editorial columnist. **Publications:** BATTLETECH SE-

RIES: Highlander Gambit, 1995; Impetus of War, 1996; Exodus Road, 1997; Roar of Honor, 1999; (with M. Odom) By Blood Betrayed, 1999; Measure of a Hero, 2000; Call of Duty, 2001; Operation Audacity, 2002. BATTLETECH: MECHWARRIOR DARK AGE SERIES: Target of Opportunity, 2005; Surrender Your Dreams, 2006; Fire at Will, 2007. OTHERS: Cubicle Warfare: Self-defense Tactics for Today's Hypercompetitive Workplace, 1997; The Cruise of the Sea Eagle: The Amazing True Story of Imperial Germany's Gentleman Pirate, 2005; Terror of the Autumn Skies: The True Story of Frank Luke, America's Rogue Ace of World War I, 2008; Lost Eagles: One Man's Mission to Find Missing Airmen in Two World Wars, 2010; Secret Witness, 2012; Virginia Creeper, 2012; Business Rules, 2012; The Bad Boy, 2012. Contributor of articles to magazines. **Address:** 1551 Freeman Dr., Amissville, VA 20106, U.S.A. **Online address:** bpardoe870@aol.com

PARDUE, Diana. (Diana F. Pardue). American (born United States), b. 1951. **Genres:** Cultural/Ethnic Topics, Fash Ion/Costume, Archaeology/Antiquities, History, Art/Art History, Literary Criticism And History. **Career:** National Park Services, staff, 1974, Division of Museum Services, staff curator, 1978-86, chief of museum services, 1986-90; Statue of Liberty National Monument and Ellis Island, chief curator, 1990-; Heard Museum, chief curator, 2007. Writer. **Publications:** AS DIANA F. PARDUE: (with K.L. Howard) Inventing the Southwest: The Fred Harvey Company and Native American Art, 1996; (contrib.) The Collecting Passions of Dennis and Janis Lyon, 2004; Shared Images: The Innovative Jewelry of Yazzie Johnson and Gail Bird, 2007; Contemporary Southwestern Jewelry, 2007; (contrib.) Generations, 2010; (with N.L. Sandfield) Native American Bolo Ties, 2011. Contributor to periodicals. **Address:** Statue of Liberty Natl Monument, Ellis Island Immigration Museum, New York, NY 10004, U.S.A. **Online address:** diana_pardue@nps.gov

PARDUE, Diana F. *See* **PARDUE, Diana.**

PARENTE, Stephen L. American (born United States), b. 1961. **Genres:** Adult Non-fiction, E-books, Economics. **Career:** University of Minnesota, Department of Economics, instructor, 1985-89; U.S. Department of Justice, economist, 1989-91; Georgetown University, Department of Economics, adjunct assistant professor, 1990; Northeastern University, Department of Economics, assistant professor, 1991-96; University of Pennsylvania, Department of Economics, visiting lecturer, 1996-99; Federal Reserve Bank of Philadelphia, consultant, 1998; University of Illinois-Urbana-Champaign, Department of Economics, assistant professor, 1999-2001, associate professor, 2001-; University of Lausanne, Walras-Pareto lecturer. Writer. **Publications:** The Problem of Economic Development, 1997; (with E.C. Prescott) Monopoly Rights: Barriers to Riches, 2000; The American Economic Review, forthcoming. Contributor to periodicals. **Address:** Department of Economics, University of Illinois, 410 David Kinley Hall, 1407 W Gregory Dr., Urbana, IL 61801, U.S.A. **Online address:** parente@illinois.edu

PARETSKY, Sara. American (born United States), b. 1947. **Genres:** Mystery/Crime/Suspense, Education, Novels. **Career:** Urban Research Corp., publications and conference manager, 1974-76; CNA Insurance, manager of direct mail marketing programs, 1977-86; writer, 1986-; Sisters in Crime, co-founder and president; Northwestern University, writer-in-residence, 1998. **Publications:** Case Studies in Alternative Education, 1975; Indemnity Only, 1982; Deadlock, 1984; Killing Orders, 1985; Bitter Medicine, 1987; Blood Shot in UK as Toxic Shock, 1988; Beastly Tales, 1989; Burn Marks, 1990; Guardian Angel, 1992; Tunnel Vision, 1994; Windy City Blues, 1995; Ghost Country, 1998; Hard Time, 1999; Total Recall, 2001; VI x 2: Photo Finish and Publicity Stunts, 2001; Blacklist, 2003; Black List, 2004; Fire Sale, 2005; Writing In an Age of Silence, 2007; Bleeding Kansas, 2008; Hardball, 2009; Body Work, 2010; Breakdown, 2012. EDITOR: A Woman's Eye, 1991; Eye of a Woman (story anthology), 1990; Women on the Case, 1996; Sisters on the Case: Celebrating Twenty Years of Sisters in Crime, 2007. Works appear in anthologies. Contributor to periodicals. **Address:** Dominick Abel Literary Agency Inc., 146 W 82nd St. 1A, New York, IL 10024, U.S.A. **Online address:** viwarshawski@mindspring.com

PARFITT, Tudor (Vernon). British (born England), b. 1944. **Genres:** History, Theology/Religion, Travel/Exploration. **Career:** University of Toronto, lecturer, 1972-74; University of London, School of Oriental and African Studies, professor of Hebrew and Jewish studies, 1974-, Centre of Near and Middle East Studies, chairman, 1996; University of Southampton, Parkes Fellow, 1977. Writer. **Publications:** (Trans. with G. Abramson) Y. Amichai, Great Tranquillity: Questions and Answers, 1983; (ed. with G. Abramson) The Great Transition: The Recovery of the Lost Centers of Modern Hebrew Literature, 1985; (with D. Kessler) The Falashas: The Jews of Ethiopia, 1985; Operation Moses: The Untold Story of the Secret Exodus of the Falasha Jews from Ethiopia, 1985; The Jews in Palestine, 1800-1882, 1987; The Thirteenth Gate: Travels among the Lost Tribes of Israel, 1987; The Jews of African and Asia, 1987; The Jews of Arab Countries and Iran: A Survey, 1988; Las Tribus Perdidas de Israel, 1989; Journey to the Vanished City: The Search for a Lost Tribe of Israel, 1993; (ed. with E.T. Semi and R.D. Ceccato) L'altro Visto Dall'altro: Letteratura Araba ed Ebraica a Confronto, 1993; (ed. with G. Abramson) Jewish Education and Learning: Published in Honour of Dr. David Patterson on the Occasion of His Seventieth Birthday, 1995; (ed. with S. Kaplan and E.T. Semi) Between Africa and Zion: Proceedings of the First International Congress of the Society for the Study of Ethiopian Jewry, 1995; The Road to Redemption: The Jews of the Yemen, 1900-1950, 1996; (ed. with E.T. Semi) The Beta Israel in Ethiopia and Israel: Studies on Ethiopian Jews, 1999; (ed.) Israel and Ishmael: Studies in Muslim-Jewish Relations, 2000; (with E.T. Semi) Judaising Movements: Studies in the Margins of Judaism, 2002; The Lost Tribes of Israel: the History of a Myth, 2002; (ed. with Y. Egorova) Jews, Muslims, and Mass Media: Mediating the Other, 2003; (with Y. Egorova) Genetics, Mass Media, and Identity: A Case Study of the Genetic Research on the Lemba and Bene Israel, 2005; (ed. with E.T. Semi) The Jews of Ethiopia: The Birth of an Elite, 2005; The Lost Ark of the Covenant: The Remarkable Quest for the Legendary Ark, 2008; Lost Ark of the Covenant: Solving The 2, 500 Year Old Mystery of the Fabled Biblical Ark, 2008. **Address:** Department of the Languages, School of Oriental & African Studies, University of London, Thornhaugh St., Russell Sq., London, GL WC1H 0XG, England. **Online address:** tp@soas.ac.uk

PARFITT, Will. British (born England), b. 1950. **Genres:** Psychology, Self Help, inspirational/Motivational Literature, Philosophy, Theology/Religion, Poetry, Young Adult Non-fiction. **Career:** P.S. Avalon, co-founder and director. Psychotherapist and writer. **Publications:** (Ed.) Test Tube: An Anthology of Experimental Poetry, 1969; Midnight on the Diamond Air: Poems, 1970; (with A. Drylie) A Crowley Cross-index, 1976; Walking through Walls, 1990; The Elements of Psychosynthesis, 1990; Walking Through Walls, 1990; The Elements of the Qabalah, 1995; The New Living Qabalah, 1996; Qabalah, 1997; The Complete Guide to the Kabbalah, 2001; Psychosynthesis: The Elements and Beyond, 2003, rev. ed., 2006; Through the Gates of Matter, 2003; Kabbalah for Life, 2007; The Something and Nothing of Death, 2008; Kabbalah: The Tree of Life Meditations on the Pathways to Paradise, 2010. **Address:** P.S. Avalon, PO Box 1865, Somerset, GC BA6 8YR, England. **Online address:** will@willparfitt.com

PARGIN, Jason Keith. American (born United States), b. 1975. **Genres:** Novels. **Career:** Cracked.com, assistant editor, 2007-, editor. **Publications:** John Dies at the End (novel), 2007. Contributor to periodicals. **Address:** c/o Jeff Moores, Dunow, Carlson and Lerner, 27 W 20th St., Ste. 1107, New York, NY 10011, U.S.A. **Online address:** dwong187@gmail.com

PARI, Susanne. American (born United States), b. 1957?. **Genres:** Novels, Young Adult Fiction, Literary Criticism And History. **Career:** Christian Science Monitor, intern to stringer; Book Group Expo, program director; Afghan Womens' Writing Project, teacher. Writer and journalist. **Publications:** The Fortune Catcher, 1997; Glücksfänger, 1999; De waarzegger, 2001; Bis wir uns wiedersehen, 2001. Contributor to periodicals. **Address:** Warner Books, Time Life Bldg., 1271 Ave. of the Americas, New York, NY 10020, U.S.A. **Online address:** sspari@aol.com

PARILLO, Mark P. American (born United States), b. 1955. **Genres:** Military/Defense/Arms Control, History, Biography, Autobiography/Memoirs. **Career:** University of Alabama, faculty; Pennsylvania State University, faculty; Kansas State University, associate professor of history, 1992-, Institute of Military History and 20th Century Studies, faculty; World War II Studies Association, chairman and newsletter editor; National World War II Museum, presidential counselor. **Publications:** The Japanese Merchant Marine in World War II, 1993; (ed.) We Were in the Big One: Experiences of the World War II Generation, 2002. Contributor to books. **Address:** Department of History, Kansas State University, 221 Eisenhower Hall, Manhattan, KS 66506-1002, U.S.A. **Online address:** parillo@ksu.edu

PARINI, Jay. American (born United States), b. 1948. **Genres:** Literary Criticism And History, Novels, Poetry, Cultural/Ethnic Topics, Young Adult Fiction, Biography. **Career:** University of St. Andrews, teaching fellow, 1972-

75; Dartmouth College, assistant professor of English, 1975-82; Middlebury College, professor of English, 1982-, D.E. Axinn professor of English and creative writing; American Council of Learned Societies, fellow, 1985-86; Christ Church College, visiting fellow, 1993-94; University of London, visiting fellow, 2005-06; Oxford University, faculty. Writer. **Publications:** POETRY: Singing in Time (poetry), 1972; Theodore Roethke: An American Romantic (literary criticism), 1979; The Love Run (novel), 1980; Anthracite Country: Poems, 1982; (co-ed.) The Breadloaf Anthology of Contemporary American Poetry, 1985; The Patch Boys (novel), 1986; An Invitation to Poetry (textbook), 1987; Town Life: Poems, 1988; The Art of Subtraction: New and Selected Poems, 1988, new ed., 2005; A Vermont Christmas, 1988; The Last Station: A Novel of Tolstoys Last Year, 1990; Bay of Arrows, 1992; The Columbia History of American Poetry, 1993; House of Days: Poems, 1998; Why Poetry Matters, 2008. BIOGRAPHIES: Theodore Roethke: An American Romantic, 1979; John Steinbeck: A Biography, 1995; (ed.) The Columbia Anthology of American Poetry, 1995; Benjamins Crossing: A Novel, 1997; House of Days (poetry), 1998; Robert Frost: A Life, 1999; One Matchless Time: A Life of William Faulkner, 2004. NOVELS: The Love Run, 1980; The Patch Boys, 1986; The Last Station: A Novel of Tolstoys Last Year, 1990; Bay of Arrows, 1992; Benjamins Crossing, 1996; The Apprentice Lover, 2002; Promised Land: Thirteen Books that Changed America, 2008. EDITOR: (with M.R. Barone and S. Lea) Richard Eberhart: A Celebration, 1980; Gore Vidal: Writer against the Grain, 1992; Bay of Arrows, 1992; The Columbia Anthology of American Poetry, 1995; The Norton Book of American Autobiography, 1999; World Writers in English, 2004; The Oxford Encyclopedia of American Literature, 2004; (with D. Kuspit and T. Roberts) Anthony Quinns Eye: A Lifetime of Creating and Collecting Art, 2004; Selected Essays of Gore Vidal, 2008; (with R. Bauer) The Wadsworth Themes in American Literature Series, 1492-1820, 2009; (with S. Samuels) The Wadsworth Themes in American Literature Series, 1800-1865, 2009; (with A. Bendixen) The Wadsworth Themes in American Literature Series, 1865-1915, 2009; (with M.J. Cutter) The Wadsworth Themes in American Literature Series, 1910-1945, 2009; (with H. Hart) The Wadsworth Themes in American Literature Series, 1945-present, 2009; British Writers. Retrospective Supplement III, 2010. EDITOR WITH ROBERT PACK: The Bread Loaf Anthology of Contemporary American Poetry, 1985; The Bread Loaf Anthology of Contemporary American Short Stories, 1987; The Bread Loaf Anthology of Contemporary American Essays, 1989; Poems for a Small Planet: Contemporary American Nature Poetry, 1993; American Identities: Contemporary Multicultural Voices, 1994; Touchstones: American Poets on a Favorite Poem, 1996; Introspections: American Poets on One of Their Own Poems, 1997; Contemporary Poetry of New England, 2002. BRITISH WRITER: Supplement VI, 2001; Supplement VII, 2002; Retrospective Supplement I, 2002; Retrospective Supplement II, 2002; Supplement VIII, 2003; Supplement IX, 2004; Supplement X, 2005; Supplement XI, 2006; Supplement XII, 2006; Supplement XIII, 2008; Supplement XV, 2009; Supplement XIV, 2009; Retrospective Supplement III, 2009; Supplement XVI, 2010; Supplement XVII, 2010. WITH A. KENNETH CIONGOLI: Beyond the Godfather: Italian American Writers on the Real Italian American Experience, 1997; Passage to Liberty: The Story of Italian Immigration and the Rebirth of America, 2002. OTHER: Theodore Roethke, an American Romantic, 1979; An Invitation to Poetry, 1987; A Vermont Christmas, 1988; Writers on Writing, 1991; Some Necessary Angels: Essays on Writing and Politics, 1997; The Art of Teaching, 2005; An American Revolution, 2004; (comp.) Wadsworth Anthology of Poetry, 2005; (intro.) The Complete Poetry of Edgar Allan Poe, 2008; The Passages of H.M.: A Novel of Herman Melville, 2010. Contributor to journals. **Address:** Department of English & American Literatures, Axinn Ctr. at Starr Library, Middlebury College, 15 Old Chapel Rd., Middlebury, VT 05753, U.S.A. **Online address:** parini@middlebury.edu

PARIS, Barry. American (born United States), b. 1948. **Genres:** Biography, Autobiography/Memoirs, Art/Art History, Literary Criticism And History. **Career:** American Political Items Collectors, presidential biography researcher, 1965-; Columbia University Tutorial Service, instructor, 1965-69; Manhattan Commercial Corp., translator, 1967; Catholic Diocesan Schools, instructor, 1969-70; Wichita Eagle, film and theater critic and reporter, 1969-72; Wichita State University, instructor, 1970-76; University of Southern Illinois, editor, 1971; Prairie Journal, editor and publisher, 1972-74; KAKE-TV, performing arts critic, 1972-76; Wichita Sun, feature editor and film critic, 1974-76; Pittsburgh Post-Gazette, editorial writer and editor, 1976-79, film and music critic and reporter, 1980-86, senior film critic; Miami Herald, feature editor, 1979-80; Sunday Arts Magazine, WQED-FM, co-founder, co-creator, host and critic-at-large, 1981-. **Publications:** Louise Brooks, 1989; (with T. Curtis) Tony Curtis: The Autobiography, 1993; Garbo: A Biography, 1995; Audrey Hepburn, 1996; (ed. and intro.) Stella Adler, vol. I: On Ibsen, Strindberg & Chekhov, 1999, vol. II: On O'Neill, Odets & Tennessee Williams, 2012; Song of Haiti: The Lives of Dr. Larimer and Gwen Mellon at Albert Schweitzer Hospital of Deschapelles, 2000; Pierce in Oblivion: The Life of Franklin Pierce, 2013. Contributor to periodicals. **Address:** c/o Daniel A. Strone, Trident Media Group, 41 Madison Ave., 36th Fl., New York, NY 10010, U.S.A.

PARIS, Bernard Jay. American (born United States), b. 1931. **Genres:** Literary Criticism And History, Psychology, Biography. **Career:** Lehigh University, instructor, 1956-60; Michigan State University, assistant professor, professor, 1960-81; University of Florida, professor of English, 1981-96, emeritus professor, 1996-, Institute for Psychological Study of the Arts, director, 1985-92. Writer. **Publications:** Experiments in Life: George Eliot's Quest for Values, 1965; A Psychological Approach to Fiction: Studies in Thackeray, Stendhal, George Eliot, Dostoevsky and Conrad, 1974; Character and Conflict in Jane Austen's Novels: A Psychological Approach, 1978; Bargains with Fate: Psychological Crises and Conflicts in Shakespeare and His Plays, 1991; Character as a Subversive Force in Shakespeare: The History and the Roman Plays, 1991; Karen Horney: A Psychoanalyst's Search for Self-Understanding, 1994; Imagined Human Beings: A Psychological Approach to Character and Conflict in Literature, 1997; Rereading George Eliot, 2003; Conrad's Charlie Marlow, 2005; Dostoevsky's Greatest Characters: A New Approach to Notes from Underground, Crime and Punishment, and The Brothers Karamazov, 2008; Heaven and its Discontents: Milton's Characters in Paradise Lost, 2010. EDITOR: Third Force Psychology and the Study of Literature, 1986; (with N. Holland and S. Homan) Shakespeare's Personality, 1989; The Therapeutic Process: Essays and Lectures, 1999; The Unknown Karen Horney, 2000. **Address:** 1430 NW 94th St., Gainesville, FL 32606, U.S.A. **Online address:** bjparis@ufl.edu

PARIS, David C. American (born United States), b. 1949. **Genres:** Education, History. **Career:** Virginia Polytechnic Institute and State University, faculty, 1975-79; Hamilton College, faculty, 1979-, chair, 1984-94, associate dean of the faculty, 1996-99, vice president of academic affairs and dean faculty, 1999-2005, Leonard C. Ferguson professor of government, 2006-; New Leadership Alliance for Student Learning and Accountability, executive director, 2012-. Writer. **Publications:** (With J.F. Reynolds) Logic of Policy Inquiry, 1983; Ideology and Educational Reform: Themes and Theories in Public Education, 1995. **Address:** Hamilton College, 198 College Hill Rd., Clinton, NY 13323, U.S.A. **Online address:** dparis@hamilton.edu

PARIS, Jenell Williams. American (born United States), b. 1972. **Genres:** Adult Non-fiction, Anthropology/Ethnology. **Career:** American University, adjunct faculty, 1995-96; Council of Christian Colleges and Universities, American Studies Program, adjunct faculty, 1996-97; Mission Year, curriculum developer, 1997-98; Bethel University, professor of anthropology, 1999-2007; Messiah College, professor of anthropology and sociology, 2007-. Writer. **Publications:** (With M.O. Eyring) Urban Disciples: A Beginner's Guide to Serving God in the City, 2000; Birth Control for Christians: Making Wise Choices, 2003; (with B.M. Howell) Introducing Cultural Anthropology, 2010; Sex is Not a Big Deal, 2010; End of Sexual Identity: Why Sex is too Important to Define Who We are, 2011; We Are Family: A Book of Questions, forthcoming; Prayers of Consolation, forthcoming. **Address:** Messiah College, Boyer 364, PO Box 3057, Grantham, PA 17027, U.S.A. **Online address:** jparis@messiah.edu

PARIS, Michael. British (born England), b. 1949. **Genres:** History, Bibliography, Film. **Career:** Open University, teacher; Middlesex Polytechnic, lecturer in history; University of Central Lancashire, Lancashire Polytechnic, senior lecturer in modern history, now emeritus professor of modern history. Writer. **Publications:** (With C. Comber) Jimmie the Kid: The Life of Jimmie Rodgers, 1977; Silvertown, 1917, 1986; (ed.) The Novels of World War Two: Annotated Bibliography of World War Two Fiction, 1990; Winged Warfare, 1859-1917, 1992; From the Wright Brothers to Top Gun: Aviation, Nationalism and Popular Cinema, 1995; (ed.) The First World War and Popular Cinema: 1914 to the Present, 2000; Warrior Nation: Images of War in British Popular Culture, 1850-2000, 2000; Over the Top: The Great War and Juvenile Literature in Britain, 2004. Contributor to periodicals. **Address:** School of Education and Social Science, University of Central Lancashire, Preston, LC PR1 2HE, England. **Online address:** mparis@uclan.ac.uk

PARIS, Roland. Canadian (born Canada), b. 1967. **Genres:** Politics/Government, Social Sciences. **Career:** Government of Canada, Privy Council Office, policy analyst, 1991-92, staff, 2004-05, foreign policy advisor, 2003-05, Department of Foreign Affairs, staff, 2003-04; Johns Hopkins University, Paul H. Nitze School of Advanced International Studies, visiting researcher, 1997-98; University of Colorado, assistant professor of political science, 1999-2003, 2006; Conference Board of Canada, director of research, 2005-06; University of Ottawa, Graduate School of Public and International Affairs, associate professor, 2006-, University Research chair in international security and governance, 2007-, Centre for International Policy Studies, founding director, 2007-; Research Partnership on Postwar Statebuilding, co-director. Writer. **Publications:** (Contrib.) The Iraq War and Its Consequences: Thoughts of Nobel Peace Laureates and Eminent Scholars, 2003; At War's End: Building Peace after Civil Conflict, 2004; (contrib.) Oxford Handbook of the United Nations, 2007; (ed. with T.D. Sisk) The Dilemmas of Statebuilding: Confronting the Contradictions of Postwar Peace Operations, 2008; (ed. with E. Newman and O.P. Richmond) New Perspectives on Liberal Peacebuilding, 2009. Contributor to journals. **Address:** Grad School of Public and International Affairs, University of Ottawa, Rm. 11121, 55 Laurier Ave. E, Ottawa, ON K1N 6N5, Canada. **Online address:** rparis@uottawa.ca

PARISH, James Robert. (Frances Maugham). American (born United States), b. 1944. **Genres:** Communications/Media, Film, Theatre, Trivia/Facts, Biography, Reference. **Career:** Cape Playhouse, publicist and properties manager, 1961-64; Entertainment Copyright Research Company Inc., founder and president, 1965-68, director, 1967-68; Variety, reviewer and interviewer, 1968-69; Motion Picture Daily, reporter, 1969; Harold Rand & Company Inc. (publicity firm), entertainment publicist, 1969-70; freelance writer and consultant, 1970-; MCRB, executive, 1978-79, 1981-87; Homeowners Marketing Services, executive, 1987-88; Renaissance Books, acquisition editor, 1996-99; JRP Media Inc., founder. **Publications:** (With A.G. Barbour and A.H. Marill) Karloff, 1969; (ed. with P. Michael) American Movies Reference Book, 1969; (ed. with L. Maltin) Television Movies, 1969; (with P. Michael) The Emmy Awards, 1970; The Great Movie Series, 1971; The Fox Girls, 1971; (with A.H. Marill) The Cinema of Edward G. Robinson, 1972; The Paramount Pretties, 1972; (with R.L. Bowers) The MGM Stock Company, 1973; The Slapstick Queens, 1973; Actors Television Credits, 1973; (with M.R. Pitts) The Great Pictures, 1974, vol. II, 1986; (with S. Whitney) The George Raft File, 1974; (with S. Whitney) Vincent Price Unmasked, 1974; (with M.R. Pitts) Film Directors Guide: United States, 1974; The RKO Gals, 1974; Hollywood's Great Love Teams, 1974; The Great Movie Heroes, 1974; Good Dames, 1974; (with D.E. Stanke) The Glamour Girls, 1975; (with D.E. Stanke) The Debonairs, 1975; (with L. DeCarl) Hollywood Players: The 40's, 1975; (with J. Ano) Liza!: An Unauthorized Biography, 1975; (with J. Ano) Liza!: Her Cinderella Nightmare, 1975; (with M.R. Pitts) The Great Gangster Pictures, 1975, vol. II, 1987; (co-author) Film Directors Guide: Western Europe, 1975; The Elvis Presley Scrapbook, 1975; Great Western Stars, 1976, rev. ed., 1996; (with L. DeCarl, W.T. Leonard and G.W. Mank) Hollywood Players: The Forties, 1976; (with W.T. Leonard) Hollywood Players: The Thirties, 1976; Jeanette MacDonald Story, 1976; The Tough Guys, 1976; (with M.R. Pitts) The Great Science Fiction Pictures, 1976, vol. II, 1990; (with M.R. Pitts) The Great Western Pictures, 1976, vol. II, 1988; (with D.E. Stanke) The Swashbucklers, 1976; Film Actors Guide: Western Europe, 1977; (with D.E. Stanke) The All-Americans, 1977; (with D.E. Stanke) The Leading Ladies, 1977; Hollywood Character Actors, 1978; (with G.W. Mank and D.E. Stanke) The Hollywood Beauties, 1978; (with M.R. Pitts) Hollywood on Hollywood, 1978; (with W.T. Leonard) The Funsters, 1979; (with D.E. Stanke) The Forties Gals, 1979; (as Frances Maugham) Hollywood Happiness, 1979; (with G. Mank) The Hollywood Regulars, 1980; (with G. Mank) The Best of MGM, 1980; (with G. Mank) Hollywood reliables, 1980; (with M.A. Trost) Actors TV Credits, vol. I, 1980, (with V.A. Terrace) vol. II, 1982, vol. III, 1986; Black Action Pictures, 1989; (with M.R. Pitts) Great Detective Pictures, 1990; Great Combat Pictures, 1990; Great Cop Pictures 1990; (with V.A. Terrace) Complete Actors Television Credits, 2 vols., 1990; (with M.R. Pitts) Hollywood Songsters, 1991; Prison Pictures from Hollywood, 1991; (with M.R. Pitts) Great Hollywood Musicals, 1991; (with D.E. Stanke) Hollywood Baby Boomers, 1992; Prostitution in Hollywood Films, 1992; The Hollywood Celebrity Death Book, 1992; Let's Talk, 1992; Gays & Lesbians in Mainstream Cinema, 1993; Ghosts & Angels on the Screen, 1994; Pirates & Seafaring Swashbucklers, 1995; Today's Black Hollywood, 1995; The Unofficial Murder, She Wrote Casebook, 1997; Rosie: Rosie O'Donnell's Biography, 1997, rev. ed., 1998; Whoopi Goldberg: Her Journey from Poverty to Megastardom, 1997, rev. ed. 1999; Jason Biggs, 2000; The Hollywood Book of Death, 2001; Gus Van Sant, 2001; Hollywood Bad Boys, 2002; Hollywood Book of Death, 2002; Jet Li: A Biography, 2002; (and ed. with A.Taylor) Encyclopedia of Ethnic Groups in Hollywood, 2003; Hollywood Book of Love: An Irreverent Guide to the Films that Raised our Romantic Expectations, 2003; Hollywood Divas: The Good, the Bad and the Fabulous, 2003; Whitney Houston, 2003, rev. ed. as Whitney Houston: The Return of the Diva, 2009; Hollywood Book of Scandals, 2004; Steven Spielberg, Filmmaker, 2004; Tom Hanks: Actor, 2004; Denzel Washington, Actor, 2005; Halle Berry: Actor, 2005; Katharine Hepburn: The Untold Story, 2005; Katie Couric: TV News Broadcaster, 2005; Stephen King: Author, 2005; Twyla Tharp: Dancer and Choreographer, 2005; Fiasco: A History of Hollywood's Iconic Flops, 2006; Hollywood Book of Breakups, 2006; Jennifer Lopez: Actor and Singer, 2006; Jim Henson: Puppeteer and Filmmaker, 2006; Stan Lee: Comic-Book Writer and Publisher, 2006; Gloria Estefan Singer, 2006; (with A.Taylor) Career Opportunities in Writing, 2006; Hollywood Book of Extravagance, 2007; It's Good to be the King: The Seriously Funny Life of Mel Brooks, 2007; (with A. Taylor) Career Opportunities in Television and Cable, 2007; (with A. Taylor) Career Opportunities in the Internet, Video Games, and Multimedia, 2007; (with A. Taylor) Opportunities in the Internet, Video Games, and Multimedia, 2007; (with A. Taylor) Career Opportunities in the Energy Industry, 2008; (with A. Taylor) Career Opportunities in Library and Information Science, 2009. Contributor to newspapers. **Address:** c/o Stuart Bernstein, Representation for Artists, 63 Carmine St., 3D, New York, NY 10014-4368, U.S.A. **Online address:** jrparish@sbcglobal.net

PARISH, Steven M. American (born United States), b. 1953. **Genres:** Anthropology/Ethnology, Social Sciences, Philosophy, Psychiatry, Humanities. **Career:** Boston University, assistant professor of anthropology, 1988-93; consultant, 1994-96; University of California, assistant professor, 1996-98, associate professor of anthropology, 1998-, professor of anthropology. Writer. **Publications:** Moral Knowing in a Hindu Sacred City: An Exploration of Mind, Emotion, and Self, 1994; Hierarchy and Its Discontents: Culture and the Politics of Consciousness in Caste Society, 1996; Subjectivity and Suffering in American Culture: Possible Selves, 2008. **Address:** Department of Anthropology, University of California San Diego, Social Science Bldg., 9500 Gilman Dr., La Jolla, CA 92093-0532, U.S.A. **Online address:** sparish@ucsd.edu

PARK, Bob. *See* **PARK, Robert L.**

PARK, David. Irish/British (born England), b. 1953?. **Genres:** Novels. **Career:** Writer and educator. **Publications:** NOVELS: UNLESS OTHERWISE NOTED: Oranges from Spain (stories), 1991; The Healing, 1992; The Rye Man, 1994; Stone Kingdoms, 1996; The Big Snow, 2002; Swallowing the Sun, 2004; The Truth Commissioner, 2008. **Address:** The Sayle Literary Agency, 8b King's Parade, Cambridge, CB CB2 1SJ, England.

PARK, Ed. American (born United States), b. 1970?. **Genres:** Novels. **Career:** Village Voice, copy editor, senior editor, reviewer and supplement editor, through 2006; Believer Magazine, founding editor; Poetry Foundation, editor. **Publications:** Personal Days (novel), 2008. Contributor to periodicals. **Address:** New York, NY , U.S.A. **Online address:** info@ed-park.com

PARK, Jung-Dong. (Chŏng-dong Pak). Korean (born Korea (South)), b. 1960. **Genres:** International Relations/Current Affairs, Economics. **Career:** University of Tokyo, postdoctoral research fellow, 1992-93; Korea Development Institute, research fellow, 1995-; Kingdom of Cambodia, economic consultant, 2001-02. Writer. **Publications:** AS CHŎNG-DONG PAK: Hyŏndae Chungguk kyŏngjeron: kyŏngje tŭkku ŭi kyŏngjejŏk hyokwa, 1993; Pukhan ŭi kyŏngje t'ŭkku: Chungguk kwaŭi pigyo, 1996; Pukhan ŭi kyŏngje kaebal chŏllyak e taehan il koch'al, 2000; (with A. Chong-sok) 21-segi Tongbuga kyŏngje hyŏmnyŏk e kwanhan yŏn'gu: Chungguk e chinch'urhan Han'guk pŏbindŭl ŭi hyŏnjihwa rŭl t'onghan kyŏngyŏng sŏngkwa chego rŭl chungsim ŭro, 2002; Kaebal kyŏngjeron: Chungguk kwa Pukhan ŭi pigyo, 2003; Han-Chung kyoryu ŭi ŏje, onŭl, naeil, 2004. OTHERS: Modern Chinese Economics (in Korean), 1993; Total Review of Special Economic Zones (in Japanese), 1996; The Economic Impact of the Rajin-Sunbong Free Economic and Trade Zone of the Democratic People's Republic of Korea (in Korean), 1996; The Special Economic Zones of China and Their Impact on Its Economic Development, 1997. Contributor to periodicals. **Address:** Korea Development Institute, Hoegiro 49 Dongdaemun-gu, Seoul, 130-868, Korea (South). **Online address:** jdpark00@hanmail.net

PARK, Katharine. American (born United States), b. 1950. **Genres:** Medicine/Health, History, Women's Studies And Issues, Young Adult Fiction. **Career:** Harvard University, professor of history. Writer. **Publications:** NONFICTION: Doctors and Medicine in Early Renaissance Florence, 1985; (with L. Daston) Wonders and the Order of Nature, 1150-1750, 1998; Secrets of Women: Gender, Generation, and the Origins of Human Dissection, 2006; (ed. with L. Daston) The Cambridge History of Science, vol. III: Early Modern Science, 2006. Contributor of articles to periodicals. **Address:** Department of the History of Science, Harvard University, 371 Science Ctr., Cambridge, MA 02138, U.S.A. **Online address:** park28@fas.harvard.edu

PARK, Roberta J. American (born United States), b. 1931. **Genres:** Philosophy, Sports/Fitness, Medicine/Health, History. **Career:** University of California, assistant supervisor of physical education, 1959-63, associate supervisor of physical education, 1963-69, supervisor of physical education, 1969-76, associate professor, 1976-80, professor of physical education (now human biodynamics), through 1980, chairman of department, 1982-92, Center for Studies in Higher Education, associate, through 1984, now professor emeritus; Springfield College, Peter V. Karpovich lecturer, 1991; Catholic University, lecturer, 1992. Writer. **Publications:** (Co-author) The Philosophic Process in Physical Education, 3rd ed., 1977; The Body as Icon and Object: Sport, Exercise and Gender, 1660-1980. EDITOR: (with J.C. Harris) Play, Games and Sports in Cultural Contexts: Readings in the Anthropology of Sport, 1983; (with J.A. Mangan) From Fair Sex to Feminism: Sport and the Socialization of Women in the Industrial and Post-Industrial Eras, 1987; (with H.M. Eckert) New Possibilities?/New Paradigms!, 1991; (with J.W. Berryman) Sport and Exercise Science: Essays in the History of Sports Medicine, 1992. Contributor to periodicals. Works appear in anthologies. **Address:** Department of Integrative Biology, University of California, 207 Hearst Gym, 3060 Valley Life Sciences Bldg., Ste. 3140, Berkeley, CA 94720-3140, U.S.A. **Online address:** rjpark@berkeley.edu

PARK, Robert L. Also writes as Bob Park. American (born United States), b. 1931. **Genres:** Sciences. **Career:** University of Maryland, professor of physics, 1974-, professor emeritus; American Physical Society Office of Public Information, director, 1983-2006; Sandia National Laboratories, director. Writer. **Publications:** NONFICTION: (ed. with M.G. Lagally) Solid State Physics: Surfaces, 1985; Voodoo Science: The Road from Foolishness to Fraud, 2000; Superstition: Belief in the Age of Science, 2008. Contributor of articles to periodicals. **Address:** Adelphi, MD , U.S.A. **Online address:** bobpark@umd.edu

PARK, Timothy K. American/Korean (born Korea (South)), b. 1948. **Genres:** Theology/Religion, Administration/Management, Education, History. **Career:** Woo-E Central Presbyterian Church, youth pastor, 1971-72; Chongshin University, dormitory supervisor, 1974-75, School of World Mission, visiting associate professor, 1996-97; Daebang Presbyterian Church, associate pastor and missionary candidate, 1980-81; Presbyterian Theological Seminary-Philippines, co-founder, 1983, assistant professor, 1983-91, associate professor, 1992-96, president, 1984-96, 1992-96; Evangelical Presbyterian Mission, field director, 1991-93; Fuller Theological Seminary, associate professor of Asian mission and director of Korean studies, 1996-; Institute for Asian Mission, president, director, 1997-; Bethesda Christian University, visiting associate professor, 1998-2000; All Nations Church, cooperative pastor, 1999-; Ttokamsa Home Mission Church, mission pasator, 2004-; David J. Cho Missiological Institute, associate director, 2004-; David J. Cho Mission Museum and Library, director, 2009-. Writer and pastor. **Publications:** Missionary Movement of the Korean Church, 1999; Mission Pathfinder: Korean Mission in the 21st Century, 2001; Cross-Cultural Church Planting, 2005; (ed.) Mission History of the Asian Churches, 2010; Korean Church in Global Mission, forthcoming. **Address:** Fuller Theological Seminary, 135 N Oakland Ave., Pasadena, CA 91182, U.S.A. **Online address:** timpark@fuller.edu

PARKE, Marilyn. American (born United States), b. 1928. **Genres:** Children's Fiction, How-to Books, Politics/Government. **Career:** Teacher-Poudre R-1, chapter I teacher, 1973-. Writer. **Publications:** QUETZALCOATL SERIES WITH SHARON PANIK: A Quetzalcoatl Tale of Corn, 1992; A Quetzalcoatl Tale of the Ball Game, 1992; A Quetzalcoatl Tale of Chocolate, 1994. Contributor to periodicals. **Address:** 1209 Parkwood Dr., Fort Collins, CO 80525, U.S.A.

PARKER, Alan Michael. American (born United States), b. 1961. **Genres:** Novels. **Career:** Davidson College, faculty, 1998-, professor of English, director of creative writing; Queens University, Low-Residency MFA Program, core faculty; Rutgers University, faculty; Penn State Erie University, faculty. Poet. **Publications:** (Ed. with M. Willhardt) The Routledge Anthology of Cross-Gendered Verse, 1996; Days Like Prose (poems), 1997; The Vandals: Poems, 1999; (ed. with M. Willhardt) Who's Who in Twentieth-Century World Poetry, 2000, 2nd ed., 2002; Love Song with Motor Vehicles: Poems, 2003; (ed.) The Imaginary Poets, 2005; Cry Uncle (novel), 2005; Elephants & Butterflies: Poems, 2008. Contributor to journals and periodicals. **Address:** PO Box 7010, Davidson, NC 28035-7010, U.S.A. **Online address:** amparker@davidson.edu

PARKER, Barbara Keevil. American (born United States), b. 1938. **Genres:** Novels, Young Adult Non-fiction, Children's Non-fiction, Animals/Pets. **Career:** Rhode Island College, Department of Economics and Management, Center for Economic Education, coordinator, 1976-78; consultant, 1978-79; Rhode Island Hospital, manager of employee education and training staff, 1979-84; Salve Regina College, graduate instructor in health services administration, 1981-82; Wesley Homes, director of education, 1985-91, coordinator of employee assistance program, 1987-91; Covenant Counseling Institute, therapist and director of education, 1991-94; Interfaith Counseling Center, therapist, 1995-98; Institute of Children's Literature, writing instructor, 2000-. Writer. **Publications:** FOR CHILDREN: Christian Celebrations, 1998; The Lord Is My Shepherd, 1998; The Good Samaritan, 1998; North American Wolves, 1998; Susan B. Anthony: Daring to Vote, 1998; (with D.F. Parker) Miguel de Cervantes, 2003; Giraffes, 2004; Cheetahs, 2005; (with D.F. Parker) Lynxes, 2005; Ticks, 2007. OTHER: Healthcare Education: A Guide to Staff Development, 1986. **Address:** c/o Author Mail, Lerner Publications Company Inc., 241 1st Ave. N, Minneapolis, MN 55401-1699, U.S.A. **Online address:** bkparker@comcast.net

PARKER, David. Hong Kong (born Hong Kong), b. 1943?. **Genres:** Philosophy, Literary Criticism And History. **Career:** Chinese University of Hong Kong, research professor, 2001-, Research Centre for Human Values, director. Writer. **Publications:** Building on Sand (novel), 1989; The Mighty World of Eye: Stories/Anti-Stories (short stories), 1990; Ethics, Theory, and the Novel, 1994; (ed. with R. Dalziell and I. Wright) Shame and the Modern Self, 1996; (ed. with J. Adamson and R. Freadman) Renegotiating Ethics in Literature, Philosophy, and Theory, 1998; The Self in Moral Space: Life Narrative and the Good, 2007. Contributor to journals. **Address:** Department of English, Chinese University of Hong Kong, 3/F Fung King Hey Bldg., Shatin, 1, Hong Kong. **Online address:** dparker@cuhk.edu.hk

PARKER, David. British (born England), b. 1941. **Genres:** History, Humanities. **Career:** University of Leeds, history teacher, 1985-, chair of department, now professor emeritus. Writer. **Publications:** La Rochelle and the French Monarchy: Conflict and Order in Seventeenth-century France, 1980; The Making of French Absolutism, 1983; Class and State in Ancient Régine France: The Road to Modernity?, 1996; (ed.) Revolutions: The Revolutionary Tradition in The West, 1560-1991, 2000. Contributor to periodicals. **Address:** School of History, University of Leeds, Leeds, WY LS2 9JT, England.

PARKER, D(avid) C. British (born England), b. 1953. **Genres:** Theology/Religion, History. **Career:** Queen's Theological College, tutor, 1985-93; University of Birmingham, Edward Cadbury Professor of Theology, International Greek New Testament Project, co-editor. **Publications:** Codex Bezae: An Early Christian Manuscript and Its Text, 1992; The Living Text of the Gospels, 1997; Manuscripts, Texts, Theology: Collected Papers 1977, 2007; An Introduction to the New Testament Manuscripts and Their Texts, 2008; Codex Sinaiticus: The Story of the World's Oldest Bible, 2010. **Address:** Department of Theology & Religion, Institute of Textual Scholarship & Electronic Edit, University of Birmingham, Elinfeld House, Birmingham, WM B29 6LQ, England. **Online address:** d.c.parker@bham.ac.uk

PARKER, Gary E. American (born United States), b. 1953. **Genres:** Novels, Theology/Religion, Literary Criticism And History. **Career:** First Baptist Church, associate pastor, 1976-79; Hilltop Lakes Chapel, pastor, 1979-82; Warrenton Baptist Church, pastor, 1982-85; Grace Baptist Church, pastor, 1985-90; First Baptist Church, pastor, 1990-96. Writer. **Publications:** The Gift of Doubt: From Crisis to Authentic Faith, 1990; Creative Tensions: Personal Growth through Stress, 1991; Principles Worth Protecting, 1993; Desert Water, 1995; Dark Road to Daylight, 1996; A Capital Offense, 1998; The Ephesus Fragment, 1999; The Last Gift, 1999; Rumors of Peace: A World at Peace in What Everyone Longs for-Or is It?, 2000; The Wedding Dress, 2001;

Shepherd's Cross: A Christmas Carol of Hope, 2001; Secret Tides, 2004; Midnight Miracle, 2005; Fateful Journeys, 2005; Her Daddy's Eyes, 2006; Distant Shores, 2006; Church on a Mission, 2009. NOVELS: Beyond a Reasonable Doubt, 1994; Death Stalks a Holiday, 1996; Highland Hopes, 2001; Highland Mercies, 2002; Highland Grace, 2003; Constantine Conspiracy, 2010. Contributor to periodicals. **Address:** c/o Author Mail, Bethany House Publishers, 11400 Hampshire Ave. S, Minneapolis, MN 55438, U.S.A.

PARKER, Glenn M. American (born United States), b. 1938. **Genres:** Administration/Management. **Career:** Glenn M. Parker Associates Inc., team-building consultant, 1971-; Rider University, adjunct faculty. Writer. **Publications:** Team Players and Teamwork: The New Competitive Business Strategy, 1990, 2nd ed. as Team Players and Team Work: New Strategies for Developing Successful Collaboration, 2008; Parker Team Player Survey, 1991; Team Development Survey, 1992; Cross-Functional Teams: Working With Allies, Enemies, and Other Strangers, 1994, 2nd ed., 2003; Handbook of Best Practices for Teams, vol. I, 1996, vol. II, 1998; Cross-Functional Teams: The Simulation Game, 1998; Team Players!, 1998; (with S. Thiagarajan) Teamwork and Teamplay: Games and Activities for Building and Training Teams, 1999; (with J. McAdams and D. Zielinski) Rewarding Teams: Lessons from the Trenches, 2000; Being a Team Player, 2000; (with R. Kropp) Team Workout: A Trainer's Sourcebook of 50 Team-Building Games and Activities, 2001; Team Depot: A Warehouse of over 600 Tools to Reassess, Rejuvenate and Rehabilitate Your Team, 2002; (with R. Hoffman) Meeting Excellence: 33 Tools to Lead Meetings that Get Results, 2006. FACILITATOR HANDBOOKS: (with R.P. Kropp) Fifty Activities for Team Building, vol. I, 1992; (with R.P. Kropp) Fifty Activities for Self-Directed Teams, 1994; The Team Kit, 1995; Cross-Functional Team Toolkit, 1997; Team Building Workshop Facilitator's Guide, 1997; (with P. Glenn) Twenty-Five Instruments for Team Building, 1998; Teamwork: Twenty Steps for Building Powerful Teams, 1998; Team Workout: Fifty Interactive Activities, 2000. **Address:** 36 Otter Creek Rd., Skillman, NJ 08558-2365, U.S.A. **Online address:** glenn@glennparker.com

PARKER, Gordon. British (born England), b. 1940. **Genres:** Novels, Plays/Screenplays, Novellas/Short Stories, Mystery/Crime/Suspense, Young Adult Fiction. **Career:** Clark Chapman Ltd., area sales representative, 1962-67, area sales manager, 1967-78, sales manager in Engineering Division, 1978-80; Essen Steels Ltd., sales manager, 1980-; BBC-Radio, book reviewer. Writer. **Publications:** The Darkness of the Morning, 1975; Lightning in May, 1976; The Pool, 1978; Action of the Tiger, 1981. **Address:** David Higham Associates Ltd., 5/8 Lower John St., Golden Sq., London, GL W1R 4HA, England.

PARKER, Jade. *See* **HEATH, Lorraine.**

PARKER, Jeff. Canadian/American (born United States), b. 1974. **Genres:** Novels. **Career:** Eastern Michigan University, teacher of creative writing; University of Toronto, assistant professor, Creative Writing MA Program, acting director; Summer Literary Seminars, Russia Program, director. Writer. **Publications:** (Ed. with M. Iossel) Amerika: Russian Writers View the United States (anthology), 2004; Ovenman: A Novel, 2007; (ed. with M. Iossel) Rasskazy: New Fiction from a New Russia, 2009; The Taste of Penny, 2009. Contributor to periodicals and journals. Works appear in anthologies. **Address:** Department of English, University of Toronto, 170 Saint George St., Toronto, ON M5R 2M8, Canada. **Online address:** js.parker@utoronto.ca

PARKER, John W. American (born United States), b. 1945. **Genres:** History. **Career:** U.S. Department of State, Bureau of Intelligence and Research, deputy office director, Office for Russian and Eurasian Analysis, Division for Caucasus and Central Asia, chief, Office for Soviet and East European Analysis, analyst of Soviet foreign policy; American Embassy-Moscow, chief of political/internal section, 1989-91; National Defense University, visiting research fellow, 2010. Writer, political scientist and analyst. **Publications:** Kremlin in Transition, 1991; Persian Dreams: Moscow and Tehran since the Fall of the Shah, 2009. **Address:** Arlington, VA , U.S.A. **Online address:** john.parker@ndu.edu

PARKER, Julie Faith. American (born United States), b. 1961. **Genres:** Adult Non-fiction, Women's Studies And Issues. **Career:** United Methodist Church, ordained minister, 1987-; Hofstra Protestant Chaplaincy, chaplain, 1991-99; Yale University, Department of Religious Studies, faculty in Old Testament studies, 1999-; Colby College, visiting assistant professor in religious studies, 2010-. Writer. **Publications:** Careers for Women as Clergy, 1993; Everything You Need to Know about Living in a Shelter, 1995; Everything You Need to Know about Decision Making, 1996, rev. ed., 1998; High Performance through Leadership, 1996. **Address:** Department of Religious Studies, Colby College, Lovejoy 354, 4640 Mayflower Hill, Waterville, ME 04901-8846, U.S.A. **Online address:** jfparker@colby.edu

PARKER, L. P. E. British (born England), b. 1933. **Genres:** Classics, Humanities. **Career:** University of London, assistant lecturer, 1957-60; University of Newcastle, lecturer, 1960-67; Oxford University, St. Hugh's College, fellow and lecturer, 1971-, now emeritus fellow. Writer. **Publications:** The Songs of Aristophanes, 1995; (ed. and intro.) Alcestis, 2007. **Address:** St. Hugh College, Oxford University, St. Margaret, Oxford, OX OX2 9EY, England.

PARKER, Matthew. British/American (born United States), b. 1970?. **Genres:** Novels, Business/Trade/Industry. **Career:** Author and editorial consultant. **Publications:** The Battle of Britain July-October 1940: An Oral History of Britains Finest Hour, 2000; Monte Cassino: The Hardest-Fought Battle of World War II, 2004; Panama Fever: Epic History of One of the Greatest Engineering Triumphs of All Time: The Building of the Panama Canal, 2008 in UK as Hell's Gorge: The Battle to Build the Panama Canal, 2009; The Sugar Barons, 2011. Contributor to periodicals. **Address:** c/o Hutchinson, Random House, 20 Vauxhall Bridge Rd., London, GL SW1V 2SA, England.

PARKER, Nancy W(inslow). American (born United States), b. 1930. **Genres:** Children's Fiction, Children's Non-fiction, Young Adult Non-fiction, Young Adult Fiction, Illustrations, Literary Criticism And History, Adult Non-fiction, Westerns/Adventure, Westerns/Adventure. **Career:** National Broadcasting Company Inc., sales promoter, 1956-60; New York Soccer Club, sports promoter, 1961-63; Radio Corporation of America (RCA), sales promoter, 1964-67; Appleton-Century-Crofts Inc., art director, 1968-70; Holt, Rinehart and Winston Inc., graphic designer, 1970-72; freelance writer, illustrator of children's books, 1972-. **Publications:** SELF-ILLUSTRATED: The Man with the Take-Apart Head, 1974; The Party at the Old Farm: A Halloween Story, 1975; Mrs. Wilson Wanders Off, 1976; Love from Uncle Clyde, 1977; The Crocodile Under Louis Finneberg's Bed, 1978; The President's Cabinet And How It Grew, 1978, rev. ed., 1991; The Ordeal of Byron B. Blackbear, 1979; Puddums, the Cathcarts' Orange Cat, 1980; Poofy Loves Company, 1980; The Spotted Dog: The Strange Tale Of A Witch's Revenge, 1980; The President's Car (non-fiction), 1981; Love from Aunt Betty, 1983; Christmas Camel, 1983; The United Nations from A to Z, 1985; (with J.R. Wright) Bugs (non-fiction), 1987; (with J.R. Wright) Frogs, Toads, Lizards and Salamanders (non-fiction), 1990; Working Frog, 1992; Money, Money, Money: The Meaning of the Art and Symbols on United States Paper Currency, 1995; Locks, Crocs, and Skeeters: The Story of the Panama Canal, 1996; Land Ho! Fifty Glorious Years in the Age of Exploration with Twelve Important Explorers, 2001; Organs!: How They Work, Fall Apart, and Can Be Replaced, 2009. OTHER: Cooper, The McNallys' Big Black Dog, 1981. Illustrator of books by others. **Address:** 51 E 74th St., Apt. 3R, New York, NY 10021-2717, U.S.A. **Online address:** nwparker52@aol.com

PARKER, Peter (Robert Nevill). British (born England), b. 1954. **Genres:** Biography, Adult Non-fiction, Literary Criticism And History, Military/Defense/Arms Control, History, Young Adult Fiction, Novels. **Career:** Freelance writer, 1985-; The Oxford Dictionary of National Biography, associate editor. **Publications:** The Old Lie: The Great War and the Public-School Ethos, 1987; Ackerley: The Life of J.R. Ackerley, 1989; (ed. with F. Kermode) A Reader's Guide to the Twentieth-Century Novel, 1995; (ed. with F. Kermode) A Reader's Guide to Twentieth-Century Writers, 1996; Isherwood: A Life Revealed, 2004; Last Veteran: Harry Patch and the Legacy of War, 2009. Works appear in anthologies. Contributor to magazines and newspapers. **Address:** David Higham Associates Ltd., 5-8 Lower John St., Golden Sq., London, GL W1F 9HA, England.

PARKER, Steve. American (born United States), b. 1954. **Genres:** Medicine/Health. **Career:** Austin Medical Education Foundation, internal medicine resident, 1981-84; Advanced Cardiac Specialists, hospitalist, 2001-03; Prodigee Inpatient Physicians Group, hospitalist, 2003-09; Midwestern University, Arizona College of Osteopathic Medicine, Division of Clinical Medicine, adjunct assistant professor, 2003-10; pxHealth, chief executive officer, 2007; Desert Vista Medical Associates, hospitalist, 2010-. Writer. **Publications:** The Advanced Mediterranean Diet: Lose Weight, Feel Better, Live

Longer, 2007, 2nd ed., 2012; Conquer Diabetes and Prediabetes: The Low-Carb Mediterranean Diet, 2011; KMD: Ketogenic Mediterranean Diet, 2012. **Address:** pxHealth, PO Box 27276, Scottsdale, AZ 85255-0137, U.S.A. **Online address:** steveparkermd@gmail.com

PARKER, T. H. L. *See* **PARKER, Thomas (Henry Louis).**

PARKER, Thomas (Henry Louis). (T. H. L. Parker). British (born England), b. 1916. **Genres:** Theology/Religion. **Career:** Church of England, ordained deacon, 1939, priest, 1940; curate, 1939-48; air raid warden, 1940-45; University of Durham, lecturer, 1971-75, reader in theology, 1975-81, dean of faculty of divinity, 1979-81, now reader emeritus. Writer. **Publications:** Oracles of God: An Introduction to the Preaching of John Calvin, 1947; The Doctrine of Knowledge of God, 1952, rev. ed. as Calvin's Doctrine of Knowledge of God, 1970; Portrait of Calvin, 1954; Supplementa Calviniana, 1962; Doctrine of the Knowledge of God, 2nd ed., 1969; Karl Barth, 1970; Calvin's New Testament Commentaries, 1971, 2nd ed., 1993; John Calvin: A Biography, 1975, rev. ed., 2006; Calvin's Old Testament Commentaries, 1986; Romans 1532-1542, 1986; Calvin's Preaching, 1992; Calvin, An Introduction to His Thought, 1995; Calvini Commentarius in Epistolam ad Hebraeos, 1996; Commentaries on Romans, 1999. EDITOR: (and trans.) Calvin's Sermons on Isaiah 53, 1956; Essays in Christology for Karl Barth, 1956; English Reformers, 1966; (with J.I. McCord) Service in Christ, 1966; Calvini Commentarius in Epistolam ad Romanos, 1981; Iohannis Calvini Commentarius in Epistolam Pauli and Romanos, 1981; (with F.M. Higman and L. Thorpe) Sermons sur Le Livre d 'Esaie, Chapitres 30-41, 1993; (with D.C. Parker) Calvini Commentarius in Epistolam ad Romanos, 1999. TRANSLATOR: Barth's Church Dogmatics, 1957; Calvin's Commentary on John, vol. I, 1959, vol. II, 1961; (with D. Cairns and E. Brunner) Dogmatics, vol. III, 1962; Calvin's Commentary on Galatians, 1965; Calvin's Commentary on Psalms, vol. II, 1965; The Epistles of Paul the Apostle to the Galatians, Ephesians, Phillippians, and the Colossians, 1966; Calvin's Commentary on the Harmony of the Gospels, 1972; Calvin's Commentary on Gospels, vol. II, 1973; Calvin's Lectures on Dan 1-6, 1993; Daniel I, 1993. **Address:** Department of Theology and Religion, Durham University, Abbey House, Palace Green, DU DH1 3RS, England.

PARKER, Tom. American (born United States), b. 1943. **Genres:** Business/Trade/Industry, Sports/Fitness, Autobiography/Memoirs, Novels. **Career:** Writer. **Publications:** Small Business: A Novel, 1986; (with D. Winfield) Winfield: A Player's Life, 1988; Anna, Ann, Annie, 1993; (with S.L. Kurtzig) CEO: Building a $400 Million Company from the Ground Up, 1991; (with G. Heil and R. Tate) Leadership and the Customer Revolution, 1994; (with G. Heil and D. Stephens) One Size Fits One, 1996. Works appear in anthologies. **Address:** 535 Ramona St., Ste. 6, Palo Alto, CA 94301, U.S.A. **Online address:** tom@tomparkerwrites.com

PARKER, Una-Mary. British (born England), b. 1930. **Genres:** Novels, Young Adult Fiction. **Career:** Novelist. **Publications:** Riches, 1987; Scandals, 1988; Temptations, 1989; Veil of Secrets, 1990; Enticements, 1990; The Palace Affair, 1992; Forbidden Feelings, 1993; Only the Best, 1993; A Guilty Pleasure, 1994; False Promises, 1995; Taking Control, 1996; A Dangerous Desire, 1997; Dark Passions, 1998; Secrets of the Night, 1999; Broken Trust, 1999; Sweet Vengeance, 2000; Moment of Madness, 2001; The Granville Affaire, 2005; The Granville Sisters, 2005; The Granville Legacy, 2006; Alexia's Secrets, 2008; Echoes of Betrayal, 2009. **Address:** 9 Cheval Pl., London, GL SW7 1DY, England.

PARKES, M(alcolm) B(eckwith). British (born England), b. 1930. **Genres:** Bibliography, Language/Linguistics, Classics, History, Intellectual History. **Career:** Lambeth Palace Library, archivist, 1957-58; Oxford University, lecturer in English, 1961-71, Keble College, fellow, 1965-, tutor, 1965-97, lecturer, 1971-93, reader in paleography, 1993-96, professor, 1997-98, emeritus professor of paleography, 1998-; University of Durham, lecturer, 1972; University of Konstanz, visiting professor, 1974, 1980; University of London, lecturer, 1976; Victoria University of Manchester, Mont Follick lecturer, 1986; University of Rochester, Robert F. Metzdorf lecturer, 1987; University of Minnesota-Twin Cities, James J. Hill professor, 1991; University of Pennsylvania, James L. Rosier lecturer, 1995; Institute for Advanced Study, School of Historical Studies, member, 1997; Harvard University, visiting professor, 1998; Medieval Academy of America, corresponding fellow; British Academy, senior fellow; University of Oxford, James P.R. Lyell reader in bibliography, 1999. Writer. **Publications:** English Cursive Book Hands, 1250-1500, 1969, rev. ed., 1979; (intro. with E. Salter) Troilus and Criseyde, 1978; (with R. Beadle) Poetical Works, 1979; (ed. with A.G. Watson) Medieval Scribes, Manuscripts and Libraries: Essays Presented to N.R. Ker, 1978; (comp.) Medieval Manuscripts of Keble College, Oxford: A Descriptive Catalogue, 1979; Scribes, Scripts and Readers, 1991; Pause and Effect: An Introduction to the History of Punctuation in the West, 1993; (intro. with J. Tschann) Facsimile of Oxford, Bodleian Library, MS Digby 86, 1996; Their Hands before Our Eyes: A Closer Look at Scribes: The Lyell Lectures Delivered in the University of Oxford, 1999, 2008. Contributor to periodicals. **Address:** Keble College, Oxford University, Parks Rd., Oxford, OX OX1 3PG, England.

PARKES, Walter. *See* **PARKES, Walter F.**

PARKES, Walter F. (Walter Parkes). American (born United States), b. 1951. **Genres:** Plays/Screenplays, Film, Young Adult Non-fiction. **Career:** Amblin Entertainment, president, 1994-; DreamWorks SKG, Motion Picture Division, co-head, 1994-2005. Writer and studio musician. **Publications:** (With R. Scott and D. Landau) Gladiator: The Making of the Ridley Scott Epic, 2000. Contributor to journals. **Address:** Creative Artists Agency, 9830 Wilshire Blvd., Beverly Hills, CA 90212-1804, U.S.A.

PARKHURST, Brooke. American (born United States), b. 1980?. **Genres:** Novels, Food And Wine. **Career:** American Broadcasting Co. (ABC), host; Fox News, production assistant. Writer. **Publications:** Belle in the Big Apple: A Novel with Recipes, 2008. **Address:** c/o Bill Contardi, Brandt & Hochman Literary Agents, 1501 Broadway, New York, NY 10036, U.S.A. **Online address:** brooke@brookeparkhurst.com

PARKIN, Frank. British (born England), b. 1940. **Genres:** Sociology, Novels, Mythology/Folklore, Social Sciences. **Career:** Oxford University, fellow and tutor in politics. Writer. **Publications:** NONFICTION: Middle Class Radicalism: The Social Bases of the British Campaign for Nuclear Disarmament, 1968; Class Inequality and Political Order: Social Stratification in Capitalist and Communist Societies, 1971; (ed.) The Social Analysis of Class Structure, 1975; Marxism and Class Theory: A Bourgeois Critique, 1979; Max Weber, 1982; Durkheim, 1992. FICTION: Krippendorf's Tribe, 1985; The Mind and Body Shop, 1986; Makesi Weibo, 1987. Contributor to periodicals. **Address:** 29 Western Rd., Oxford, OX OX1 4LF, England.

PARKIN, Gaile. Zambian (born Zambia), b. 1957. **Genres:** Novels. **Career:** Writer, counselor and consultant. **Publications:** Baking Cakes in Kigali (novel), 2009. **Address:** Christine Green Authors' Agent, 6 Whitehorse Mews, Westminster Bridge Rd., London, GL SE1 7QD, England.

PARKIN, Sara Lamb. Scottish (born Scotland), b. 1946. **Genres:** Environmental Sciences/Ecology, Business/Trade/Industry, Economics. **Career:** University of Edinburgh, research assistant, 1973-74; Leeds Area Health Authority, family planning nurse, 1976-80; Green Party, international liaison secretary, 1983-90, speaker, 1989-92, executive chairperson, 1992; European Green Coordination, co-secretary and spokesperson, 1985-90; Forum for the Future, founding director and trustee, 1992-, programme director. Writer. **Publications:** Green Parties: An International Guide, 1989; Green Futures: Agenda for the Twenty-First Century, 1991; (ed.) Green Light on Europe, 1991; The Life and Death of Petra Kelly, 1994; The Positive Deviant: Sustainability Leadership in a Perverse World, 2010. Contributor of books and periodicals to magazines. **Address:** Forum for the Future, Overseas House, 19-23 Ironmonger Row, London, GL EC1V 3QN, England. **Online address:** saraparkinoffice@forumforthefuture.org

PARKINSON, Alan F. British (born England) **Genres:** Social Sciences, Politics/Government, History. **Career:** London South Bank University, Education Department, senior lecturer in history and education. Writer. **Publications:** Ulster Loyalism and the British Media, 1998; Belfast's Unholy War: The Troubles of the 1920s, 2004; 1972 and the Ulster troubles: "A Very Bad Year", 2010; (ed. with E. Phoenix) Conflicts in the North of Ireland, 1900-2000: Flashpoints and Fracture Zones, 2010. **Address:** Education Department, London South Bank University, 103 Borough Rd., London, GL SE1 0AA, England. **Online address:** parkinaf@lsbu.ac.uk

PARKINSON, Siobhan. Irish (born Ireland), b. 1954. **Genres:** Children's Fiction, Young Adult Fiction, Novels, Young Adult Non-fiction, Children's Non-fiction. **Career:** Royal Irish Academy, assistant editor, 1980-83; freelance editor, 1983-87; C.J. Fallon Ltd., editor, 1987-89; CBT Systems, head of technical writing, 1989-95; Focus Ireland, editor and writer, 1995-97; Town House Publishers, managing editor, 1998-; Marino Institute of Education, writer-in-residence; Children's Books Ireland, The Magazine of Children's Books, co-editor. **Publications:** OFF WE GO SERIES: The Dublin Adventure, 1992; The Country Adventure, 1992; The Leprechaun Who Wished He Wasn't, 1993. FOR CHILDREN: All Shining in the Spring, 1995; Cows are Vegetarians, 2001; Animals Don't Have Ghosts, 2002. FOR YOUNG ADULTS: Amelia, 1993; No Peace for Amelia, 1994; Sisters...No Way!, 1996; Four Kids, Three Cats, Two Cows, One Witch (Maybe), 1998; The Moon King, 1998; Breaking the Wishbone, 1999; Call of the Whales, 2000; The Love Bear, 2002; Kathleen: The Celtic Knot, 2003. FOR ADULTS: The Thirteenth Room, 2003; Something Invisible, 2006; Second Fiddle, or, How to Tell a Blackbird from a Sausage, 2007; Blue like Friday, 2008; The Henny Penny Tree, 2008; Dialann: sár-rúnda, Amy Ní Chonchúir, 2008; Painted Ladies, 2010; Bruised, as Long Story Short, 2011. EDITOR: Home: An Anthology of Modern Irish Writing, 1996; A Part of Ourselves: Laments for Lives that Ended Too Soon, 1997. **Address:** 7 Kenilworth Pk., Dublin, 6W, Ireland. **Online address:** parkbenn@indigo.ie

PARKINSON, Stanley. American (born United States), b. 1941. **Genres:** Psychology, Medicine/Health. **Career:** Arizona State University, Somerville Lab, professor of psychology, 1971-, chair, 1983-88, now emeritus professor. Writer. **Publications:** (With G. Levine) Experimental Methods in Psychology, 1993. **Address:** Department of Psychology, Arizona State University, 950 S McAllister, Rm. 237, PO Box 871104, Tempe, AZ 85287-1104, U.S.A. **Online address:** stanley.parkinson@asu.edu

PARKS, Adele. British (born England), b. 1969?. **Genres:** Young Adult Fiction, Novels, Romance/Historical, Novellas/Short Stories. **Career:** Writer and educator. **Publications:** NOVELS: Playing Away, 2000; Game Over, 2001; Larger Than Life, 2002; The Other Woman's Shoes as in US as Lust for Life, 2003; Still Thinking of You, 2004; Husbands, 2005; Young Wives' Tales, 2007; Tell Me Something, 2008; Love Lies, 2009; Men I've Loved Before, 2010; About Last Night, 2011; Whatever It Takes, 2012. OTHER: Happy Families, 2008. **Address:** c/o Jonny Geller, Curtis Brown Group Ltd., Haymarket House, 28-29 Haymarket, London, GL SW1Y 4SP, England. **Online address:** adele@adeleparks.com

PARKS, Brad. American (born United States), b. 1974. **Genres:** Mystery/Crime/Suspense. **Career:** Washington Post, reporter; Star-Ledger, reporter. **Publications:** CARTER ROSS MYSTERY SERIES: Faces of the Gone, 2009; Eyes of the Innocent, 2011. **Address:** c/o Jeanne Forte Dube, Forte Associates, 250 W 57th St., Ste. 2302, New York, NY 10107, U.S.A.

PARKS, Deborah A. (Deborah Amel Parks). American (born United States), b. 1948. **Genres:** Travel/Exploration, Biography, Engineering. **Career:** Freelance researcher and writer, 1971-72; BBDO Advertising Agency, market researcher and writer, 1972-73; Somers High School, Westchester Board of Co-Operative Education, secondary school teacher, 1973-76; freelance editor, writer, educational consultant, 1976-77; Prentice Hall Inc., associate editor, 1977-79; Scholastic Inc., staff writer and editor, 1979-81; Harcourt Brace Jovanovich Inc., senior supervisory editor, 1981-85; Editorial Directions, president and owner, 1985-91; editorial consultant and author, 1991-. **Publications:** Climb Away!: A Mountaineer's Dream (adventure), 1996; (with M.L. Ware) Eleanor Roosevelt: Freedom's Champion, 1999; Jane Addams: Freedom's Innovator, 1999; John Paul II: The Pope from Poland, 2002; Nature's Machines: The Story of Biomechanist Mimi Koehl, 2005. Contributor of articles to books and periodicals. **Address:** 1167 Rte. 52, Ste. 220, Fishkill, NY 12524, U.S.A.

PARKS, Deborah Amel. *See* **PARKS, Deborah A.**

PARKS, Gregory S. American (born United States) **Genres:** Sociology. **Career:** The African-American Institute, intern, 1993-94; Saint Elizabeth's Psychiatric Hospital, psychology extern, 1995; Federal Bureau of Prisons Office of Research, intern, 1995-96; Manhattan Psychiatric Center, psychology extern, 1999; University of Kentucky, Department of Psychology, teaching assistant, 1999, 2000, Lyman T. Johnson post-doctoral fellow, 2004-06, psychology faculty, Department of Psychiatry, neuropsychology extern, 2000-01; Harris Psychological Services Center, psychology extern, 2000-03; University of Kentucky Office of Greek Affairs, Greek affairs advisor, 2002-03; Eastern State Psychiatric Hospital, psychology extern, 2003; DC Superior Court, Child Guidance and Family Counseling Clinic, pre-doctoral clinical psychology internship, 2003-04; U.S. District Court for the District of Columbia, judicial intern, 2006; Cornell University Office of Minority Student Affairs, prelaw advisor, 2007-; District of Columbia Court of Appeals, judicial clerkship, 2008-09. Writer. **Publications:** Freedom, Justice and Equality: The Teachings of the Nation of Islam, 1992; (co-ed.) African American Fraternities and Sororities: The Legacy and the Vision, 2005; (co-ed.) Critical Race Realism: Intersections of Psychology, Race and Law, 2008; (ed.) Black Greek-Letter Organizations in the Twenty-First Century: Our Fight has Just Begun, 2008; (ed. with C.L. Torbenson) Brothers and Sisters: Diversity in College Fraternities and Sororities, 2009; (ed. with M.W. Hughey) The Obamas and a (post) Racial America?, 2010; (ed. with M.W. Hughey) 12 Angry Men, 2010; (ed. with M.W. Hughey) Black Greek-letter Organizations 2.0, 2011. **Address:** Department of Psychology, University of Kentucky, 106-B Kastle Hall, Lexington, KY 40506, U.S.A. **Online address:** gsp28@cornell.edu

PARKS, Peggy J. American (born United States), b. 1951. **Genres:** Children's Non-fiction, History, Documentaries/Reportage. **Career:** Freelance writer, 1995-. **Publications:** (Contrib.) Greater Grand Rapids: The City that Works, 1998; Benjamin Franklin, 2002; News Media, 2002; Music, 2002; Great Depression, 2003; The Internet, 2003; Global Warming, 2003; Aswan High Dam, 2003; Music, 2003; Police Officer, 2003; Doctor, 2003; Computer Programmer, 2003; Teacher, 2003; Lawyer, 2003; Musician, 2003; Writer, 2003; Jonas Salk, 2003; Robert Fulton, 2003; Afghanistan, 2003; Iraq, 2003; North Korea, 2003; Global Warming, 2004; The Sydney Opera House, 2004; Firefighter, 2004; Veterinarian, 2004; Exploring Mars, 2004; Global Resources, 2004; The Great Barrier Reef, 2004; Sand Dunes, 2004; Clothing, 2004; The Loch Ness Monster, 2005; Oil Spills, 2005; Entertainment, 2005; Exploration, 2005; Weapons, 2005; Joseph Lister, 2005; Killer Asteroids, 2006; Toxic Waste, 2006; Tsunamis, 2006; Acid Rain, 2006; Astronaut, 2006; Computer Animator, 2006; Constellations, 2006; Ecotourism, 2006; Fighter Pilot, 2006; Foods of France, 2006; Hurricanes, 2006; Aliens, 2007; Driving Under the Influence, 2007; Impressionism, 2007; Monsoons, 2007; Predicting Earthquakes, 2007; Street Crime, 2007; Street Racing, 2007; Water Pollution, 2007; Health Care, 2008; HPV, 2008; School Violence, 2008; Sun, 2008; Video Games, 2008; Garbage and Recycling, 2008; Witches, 2008; Animal Experimentation, 2008; Autism, 2008; Computer Hacking, 2008; Down Syndrome, 2008; Drunk Driving, 2008; Earth, 2008; ESP, 2008; Gay Rights, 2008; Alzheimer's Disease, 2009; Anorexia, 2009; Epilepsy, 2009; Drug Legalization, 2009; SIDS, 2009; Stem Cells, 2009; DNA Evidence and Investigation, 2009; Coal Power, 2009; Sudden Infant Death Syndrome, 2009; Leukemia, 2009; Genetic Disorders, 2009; Wind Power, 2010; Solar Power, 2010; Obsessive-Compulsive Disorder, 2010; Learning Disabilities, 2010; Ghosts, 2010; Gangs, 2010; Does the Death Penalty Deter Crime?, 2010; Drugs and Sports, 2010; Space Research, 2011; Self-injury Disorder, 2011; Schizophrenia, 2011; Online Social Networking, 2011; Brain Tumors: Part of the Compact Research Series, 2011; Influenza, 2011; Anxiety Disorders, 2011; The Death Penalty, 2012; The Green Movement, 2012; Teenage Eating Disorders, 2012; Teenage Sex and Pregnancy, 2012; Teenage Suicide, 2012. Contributor to periodicals. **Address:** 1623 E Harbour Towne Cir., Muskegon, MI 49441, U.S.A. **Online address:** pj@pjparks.com

PARKS, Suzan Lori. American (born United States), b. 1964. **Genres:** Plays/Screenplays, Novels. **Career:** University of Michigan, faculty, 1990; Eugene Lang College, professor of playwriting, 1990; Yale University, faculty, 1990-91; New York University, faculty, 1990-91; New School for Social Research (now New School University), writer-in-residence, 1991-92; Yale School of Drama, associate artist; Wilma Theater, playwriting residency; California Institute of the Arts, Audrey Skirball Kernis Theater Projects writing for performance program, director, 2000-. Playwright. **Publications:** In the Blood, 2000; Topdog/Underdog, 2001; Getting Mother's Body, 2003. Contributor to periodicals. **Address:** c/o Author Mail, Theatre Communications Group, 520 8th Ave., 24th Fl., New York, NY 10018-4156, U.S.A.

PARLAKIAN, Nishan. American (born United States), b. 1925. **Genres:** Plays/Screenplays. **Career:** City University of New York, Bronx Community College, instructor in English and speech, 1961-63; Pace University, associate professor of speech and drama, 1963-70; City University of New York, John Jay College of Criminal Justice, professor of drama, speech and English literature, 1972-, now professor emeritus; Armenian Church of America, artistic director, 1972-. Theatrical producer and writer. **Publications:** Grandma, Pray for Me, 1990; (ed. with S.P. Crowe) Modern Armenian Drama: An Anthology, 2001; (ed.) Contemporary Armenian American Drama: An Anthology of Ancestral Voices, 2004; (ed.) Notable Women in Modern Armenian

Drama: An Anthology, 2009. **Address:** Department of Speech, Theater, & Media, John Jay College of Criminal Justice, City University of New York, Rm. 336, 899 10th Ave., New York, NY 10019, U.S.A. **Online address:** nparlakian@jjay.cuny.edu

PARLOFF, Roger (Harris). American (born United States), b. 1955. **Genres:** Law, Young Adult Non-fiction. **Career:** Law clerk, 1982-83; Office of the District Attorney, assistant district attorney, 1983-84; Goldman and Hafetz, criminal defense attorney, 1984-87; journalist, 1988-; American Lawyer Media, senior writer, 1988-2000; Inside.com/Brill's Content, staff, 2000-01; FORTUNE, senior writer, senior editor, contributor, 2002-. **Publications:** (With K. Andersen and M. O'Donnell) Tools of Power: The Elitist's Guide to the Ruthless Exploitation of Everybody and Everything, 1980; Triple Jeopardy: A Story of Law at Its Best-and Worst, 1996. **Address:** FORTUNE, Time & Life Bldg., Rockefeller Ctr., New York, NY 10020, U.S.A. **Online address:** rparloff@fortunemail.com

PARMELEE, John H. American (born United States), b. 1970. **Genres:** Politics/Government, Money/Finance, Young Adult Non-fiction. **Career:** Kiplinger's Personal Finance, reporter, 1994-97; Congressional Quarterly, reporter, 1997-98; University of North Florida, associate professor of communication, 2001. Writer. **Publications:** (With S. Godin) If You're Clueless about Financial Planning and Want to Know More, 1998; Meet the Candidate Videos: Analyzing Presidential Primary Campaign Videocassettes, 2003; Politics and the Twitter Revolution: How Tweets Influence the Relationship Between Political Leaders and the Public, 2011. **Address:** Department of Communication, University of North Florida, 1 UNF Dr., Jacksonville, FL 32224, U.S.A. **Online address:** jparmele@unf.edu

PARMET, Herbert S. American (born United States), b. 1929. **Genres:** History, Biography. **Career:** Mineola High School, teacher, 1954-68, Department of Social Studies, chairman, 1961-68; City University of New York, Queensborough Community College, assistant professor, 1968-73, associate professor, 1973-75, professor, 1975-83, distinguished professor of history, 1983-95, distinguished professor emeritus of history, 1995-. Writer. **Publications:** (With M.B. Hecht) Aaron Burr: Portrait of an Ambitious Man, 1967; (with M.B. Hecht) Never Again: A President Runs for a Third Term, 1968; Eisenhower and the American Crusades, 1972, rev. ed., 1999; The Democratic Umbrella: The Years After FDR, 1976; Jack: The Struggles of John F. Kennedy, 1980; JFK: The Presidency of John F. Kennedy, 1983, rev. ed., 1986; 200 Years of Looking Ahead: Commemorating the Bicentennial of the Founding of the Bank of New York, 1784-1984, 1984; Richard Nixon and His America, 1990; George Bush: The Life of a Lone Star Yankee, 1997; Presidential Power from the New Deal to the New Right, 2002; Richard M. Nixon: An American Enigma, 2008. CONTRIBUTOR: Our Presidents, 1969; Makers of American Diplomacy, 1974; The Presidency, 1976. **Address:** Department of History, Queensborough Community College, Rm. M-408, Medical Arts Bldg., 4th Fl., Bayside, NY 11364, U.S.A. **Online address:** hparmet@gmail.com

PARNELL, Mary Davies. Welsh (born Wales), b. 1936. **Genres:** Autobiography/Memoirs, Biography, History. **Career:** New Welsh Review, editorial assistant, deputy editor. Educator. **Publications:** Block Salt and Candles: A Rhondda Childhood, 1991; Snobs and Sardines: Rhondda Schooldays, 1993; Plateaux, Gateaux, Chateaux, 1997. **Address:** New Welsh Review Ltd., PO Box 170, Aberystwyth, DY SY23 1WZ, Wales.

PAROTTI, Phillip (Elliott). American (born United States), b. 1941. **Genres:** Novels, Novellas/Short Stories, Young Adult Fiction. **Career:** U.S. Naval Reserve, staff, 1967-83; Sam Houston State University, professor of English, 1972-2004, professor emeritus of English, 2004-; Texas Review, fiction editor, 1976-84. **Publications:** The Greek Generals Talk: Memoirs of the Trojan War, 1986; The Trojan Generals Talk: Memoirs of the Greek War, 1988; Fires in the Sky, 1990. **Address:** Department of English, Sam Houston State University, 1901 University Ave., PO Box 2146, Huntsville, TX 77341-2146, U.S.A. **Online address:** eng_pxp@shsu.edu

PARR, Ann. (Danny Parr). American (born United States), b. 1943. **Genres:** Young Adult Non-fiction. **Career:** Elementary music teacher, 1965-68. Writer. **Publications:** (With J. Parr) We Care: An Education Effectiveness Process, 1990; Gordon Parks: (contrib.) No Excuses, 2006, (contrib.) Jeremy Mayfield, 2006; Coach Tex Winter: Triangle Basketball, 2006; Allisons, 2007; (ed.) Stories of World War II, 2011. AS DANNY PARR: Lowriders, 2001, 2nd ed., 2005; Extreme In-line Skating Moves, 2001; Extreme Bicycle Stunt Riding Moves, 2001; Dirt Bikes, 2002. **Address:** 926 Pheasant Run, PO Box 24, Lindsborg, KS 67456-1712, U.S.A. **Online address:** annmparr@gmail.com

PARR, Danny. *See* **PARR, Ann.**

PARRIS, Matthew (Francis). British/South African (born South Africa), b. 1949. **Career:** London Foreign Office, affiliated, 1974-76, Conservative Research Department, staff, 1976-77; Office of the Margaret Thatcher, staff, 1977-79; House of Commons, Parliament for Derbyshire West, member, 1979-86; London Weekend Television, presenter, 1986-88; Times, parliamentary sketchwriter, 1988-2002, columnist; The Spectator, columnist. Radio and television broadcaster. **Publications:** (With P. Blaker and J. Critchley) Coping with the Soviet Union: A New Tory View, 1977; Inca-Kola: A Traveller's Tale of Peru, 1990; So Far So Good, 1992; Look Behind You: Sketches and Follies from the Commons, 1993; Scorn, 1994; Great Parliamentary Scandals: Four Centuries of Calumny, Smear and Innuendo, 1995; Read My Lips; A Treasury of Things Politicians Wish They Hadn't Said, 1997; I Couldn't Possibly Comment, 1996; I Couldn't Possibly Comment: Sketches and Follies from the Commons Again, 1998; Off Message, 2001; Chance Witness: An Outsider's Life in Politics, 2002; The Great Unfrocked: 2000 Years of Church Scandal, 2002. **Address:** c/o Xandra Hardie, 9 Elsworthy Terr., London, GL NW3 3DR, England.

PARRISH, Patt. *See* **BUCHEISTER, Patt.**

PARRISH, Richard. American (born United States) **Genres:** Novels, Law. **Career:** Edge Hill College, lecturer in law. Criminal defense lawyer and author. **Publications:** NOVELS: Our Choice of Gods, 1989; Abandoned Heart, 1996; Sports Law and Policy in the European Union, 2003. JOSHUA RABB SERIES: The Dividing Line, 1993; Versions of the Truth, 1994; Nothing but the Truth, 1995; Wind and Lies, 1997; Defending the Truth, 1998. OTHERS: (ed. with S. Gardiner and R.C.R. Siekmann) EU, Sport, Law and Policy: Regulation, Re-Regulation and Representation, 2009. **Address:** Onyx Books, 375 Hudson St., New York, NY 10014, U.S.A. **Online address:** rparrishlaw@aol.com

PARRISH, T(homas) Michael. American (born United States), b. 1953. **Genres:** Military/Defense/Arms Control, History, Bibliography, Biography, Autobiography/Memoirs, Local History/Rural Topics. **Career:** Jenkins Rare Book and Publishing Co., manager, 1976-91; T. Michael Parrish, Rare Americana, proprietor, 1992-93; Lyndon Baines Johnson Library and Museum, archivist and historian, 1994-; Louisiana State University, U.S. Civil War Center, national board of directors; Society of Civil War Historians, president, 1997-99; Louisiana State University Press, Conflicting Worlds: New Dimensions of the Civil War, series editor, 1997-; University of North Carolina Press, Littlefield History of the Civil War Era, co-editor, 1997-2003; University of Baylor, Department of History, Linden G. Bowers professor of American history, 2003-. **Publications:** (With R.M. Willingham Jr.) Confederate Imprints: A Bibliography of Southern Publications from Secession to Surrender, 1984; (ed. and intro.) Reminiscences of the War in Virginia, 1989; (ed. and intro.) As It Was: Reminiscences of a Soldier of the Third Texas Cavalry and the Nineteenth Louisiana Infantry, C.S.A., 1990; Richard Taylor, Soldier Prince of Dixie, 1992; (ed. with N.D. Brown and intro.) The Campaigns of Walker's Texas Division, 1993; (ed. and intro.) The Military Operations of General Beauregard in the War between the States, 1994; (ed. with T.W. Cutrer) Brothers in Gray: The Civil War Letters of the Pierson Family, 1997; P.G.T. Beauregard: The Civil War and Southern Power, forthcoming. Works appear in anthologies. **Address:** Department of History, Baylor University, Tidwell Bible Bldg., 1 Bear Pl., Ste. 97306, 600 Speight Ave., Waco, TX 76798-7306, U.S.A. **Online address:** michael_parrish@baylor.edu

PARRISH, Tim. American (born United States), b. 1958. **Genres:** Novellas/Short Stories, Young Adult Fiction, History, Literary Criticism And History. **Career:** Southern Connecticut State University, professor of English, 1994-, Creative Writing/Fiction, instructor. Fiction writer. **Publications:** Red Stick Men: Stories, 2000; Walking Blues: Making Americans from Emerson to Elvis, 2001. Contributor to books and periodicals. **Address:** Department of English, Southern Connecticut State University, Rm. EN 235D, 501 Crescent St., New Haven, CT 06515-1355, U.S.A. **Online address:** parrisht1@southernct.edu

PARRISH, William E. American (born United States), b. 1931. **Genres:** History, Biography, Essays. **Career:** University of Missouri, instructor, 1952-

55, visiting associate professor of history, 1956, 1962, Westminster College, associate professor, 1955-63, professor of history, 1966-71, chairman of department, 1966-78, Harry S. Truman professor of American history, 1971-78, dean of the college, 1973-75; Missouri American Revolution Bicentennial Commission, chairman, 1974-76; Mississippi State University, professor, 1978-96, emeritus professor of history, 1996-; Sesquicentennial History of Missouri, general editor. **Publications:** David Rice Atchison of Missouri, Border Politician, 1961; The Morphology of the Tigre Noun, 1962; Turbulent Partnership: Missouri and the Union, 1861-1865, 1963; Missouri under Radical rule, 1865-1870, 1965; A Linguistic Study of the English Verb, 1965; (ed.) Selected Papers of J.R.Firth 1952-1959, 1968; (ed.) The Civil War: A Second American Revolution?, 1970; (ed.) Prosodic Analysis, 1970; Westminster College; An Informal History, 1851-1969, 1971; Grammar, 1971, 2nd ed., 1984; The English Verb, 1974, 2nd ed., 1988; Semantics, 1975, 2nd ed., 1981; Semantics: A New Outline, 1976; Modality and the English Modals, 1979, 2nd ed., 1990; (with C.T. Jones and L.O. Christensen) Missouri, The Heart of the Nation, 1980, 3rd ed. 2004; Linguistic Controversies: Essays in Linguistic Theory and Practice in Honour of F.R. Palmer, 1982; Mood and Modality, 1986, 2nd ed., 2001; (ed. with T. Bynon) Studies in the History of Western Linguistics: In Honour of R.H. Robins, 1986; Grammatical Roles and Relations, 1994; (ed.) Grammar and Meaning: Essays in Honour of Sir John Lyons, 1995; Frank Blair: Lincoln's Conservative, 1998; The History of Phi Gamma Delta, 1925-1996: Tomos Gamma, 1998; (ed.) A History of Missouri, 1971, rev. ed., 2003; Modality, 2001; (ed. with R. Facchinetti and M. Krug) Modality in Contemporary English, 2003; (ed. with R. Facchinetti) English Modality in Perspective: Genre Analysis and Contrastive Studies, 2004; (ed. and intro.) The Civil War in Missouri: Essays from the Missouri Historical Review, 1906-2006, 2006. **Address:** Department of History, Mississippi State University, 214 Allen Hall, Mississippi State, MS 39762, U.S.A.

PARROTT, Horace Ian. *See* **PARROTT, Ian.**

PARROTT, Ian. (Horace Ian Parrott). Welsh/British (born England), b. 1916. **Genres:** Music. **Career:** Malvern College, assistant director of music, 1937-39; University of Birmingham, lecturer in music, 1946-50; University College of Wales, Gregynog professor of music, 1950-83, Gregynog chair of music, through 1983, now professor emeritus; Trinity College of Music, external examiner, 1949-, faculty, 1954-. Writer. **Publications:** Pathways to Modern Music, 1947; A Guide to Musical Thought, 1955; Method in Orchestration, 1957; The Music of An Adventure, 1966; The Spiritual Pilgrims, 1969; Elgar, 1971; Second Impression, 1977; The Music of Rosemary Brown, 1978; Suite No. 2 for Organ, 1986; Fantasy for Piano, 1986; Cyril Scott and His Piano Music, 1992; The Crying Curlew: Peter Warlock: Family and Influences, Centenary 1994, 1994. **Address:** University of Wales, King Edward VII Ave., Cathays Park, Cardiff, CF10 3NS, England.

PARROTT, Les. American (born United States) **Genres:** Human Relations/ Parenting, Psychology. **Career:** Seattle Pacific University, assistant professor, 1989-92, associate professor of psychology, 1993-98, professor of psychology, 1999-, School of Social and Behavioral Sciences, Center for Relationship Development, co-director; Fuller Theological Seminary, Graduate School of Psychology, senior teaching assistant, 1986-89, assistant professor, 1989-92, adjunct professor, 1990-, associate professor, 1993-98; University Washington School of Medicine, fellow; Foundation for Healthy Relationships, co-founder, 2000-, president. Writer. **Publications:** Helping the Struggling Adolescent: A Guide to Thirty Common Problems for Parents, Counselors and Youth Workers, 1993, as Helping the Struggling Adolescent: A Guide to Thirty-Six Common Problems for Counselors, Pastors and Youth Workers (includes counseling guide), 2000; Helping the Struggling Adolescent: A Counseling Guide: With Forty Rapid Assessment Tests, 1993; How to Write Psychology Papers, 1994; Love's Unseen Enemy: How to Overcome Guilt to Build Healthy Relationships, 1994; Seven Secrets of a Healthy Dating Relationship, 1995; High-Maintenance Relationships: How to Handle Impossible People, 1996; Once upon a Family: Building a Healthy Home When Your Family Isn't a Fairy Tale, 1996; Counseling and Psychotherapy (includes study guide), 1997, 2nd ed., 2003; The Control Freak, 2000; Helping Your Struggling Teenager: A Parenting Handbook on Thirty-Six Common Problems, 2000; (with L. Parrott) The Life You Want Your Kids to Live, 2001; (with N.C. Warren) Love the Life you Live: 3 Secrets to Feeling Good, Deep Down in Your Soul, 2003; Shoulda, Coulda, Woulda: Live in the Present, Find your Future, 2003; 25 Ways to Win with People: How to Make Others Feel Like a Million Bucks, 2005. WITH L.L. PARROTT: The Marriage Mentor Manual: How You Can Help the Newlywed Couple Stay Married, 1995; Becoming Soul Mates: Cultivating Spiritual Intimacy in the Early Years of Marriage, 1995; Saving Your Marriage before It Starts: Seven Questions to Ask Before (and after) You Marry, 1995, rev. ed., 2006; The Career Counselor: Guidance for Planning Careers and Managing Career Crises, 1995; Questions Couples Ask: Answers to the Top 100 Marital Questions, 1996; Like a Kiss on the Lips: Meditations on Proverbs for Couples, 1997; Mentoring Engaged and Newlywed Couples: Leader's Guide: Building Marriages That Love for a Lifetime, 1997; Relationships: An Open and Honest Guide to Making Bad Relationships Better and Good Relationships Great (includes workbook), 1998; A Good Friend: Ten Traits of Enduring Ties, 1998; Love Is-: Meditations for Couples on 1 Corinthians 13, 1999; Saving Your Second Marriage before It Starts: Nine Questions to Ask before (and after) You Remarry, 2001, rev. ed., 2006; When Bad Things Happen to Good Marriages: How to Stay Together When Life Pulls You Apart (separate workbooks are available for husband and wife), 2001; Building Better Marriages in Oklahoma, 2001; The Love List: Eight Healthy Habits for Married Couples, 2002; Pillow Talk for Couples: Drawing Closer Before the Lights Go Out, 2002; Lemonade in the Desert: a Good Friend Refreshes the Soul, 2004; Love Talk: Speak Each Other's Language Like You Never have Before, 2004; Lovetalk Starters: 275 Questions to Get Your Conversations Going, 2004; The Complete Guide to Marriage Mentoring: Connecting Couples to Build Better Marriages, 2005; I Love You More: How Everyday Problems Can Strengthen Your Marriage, 2005; Marriage Mentor Training Manual for Wives: a Ten Session Program for Equipping Marriage Mentors, 2006; The Marriage Mentor Training Manual for Husbands, 2006; 51 Creative Ideas for Marriage Mentors: Connecting Couples to Build Better Marriages, 2006; Time Together: Meditations for Your Time Starved Marriage, 2006; Your Time-starved Marriage Work Book for Women: How to Stay Connected at the Speed of Life, 2006; The Parent you Want to Be: Who You Are Matters More Than What You Do, 2007; 3 Seconds: the Power of Thinking Twice, 2007; Trading Places: the Best Move You'll Ever Make in Your Marriage, 2008; L.O.V.E.: Putting Your Love Styles to Work for You, 2009; Crazy Good Sex: Putting to Bed the Myths Men Have About Sex, 2009; (with B. Dallas) You're Stronger than You Think: the Power to Do What You Feel You Can't, 2010; Dot.com Dating, 2010; Real Relationships: From Bad to Better and Good to Great, 2011; (with S. Allen and T. Kuna) Hour that Matters Most: The Surprising Power of the Family Meal, 2011. EDITOR: Getting Ready for the Wedding: All You Need to Know before You Say I Do, 1998; The Marriage Devotional Bible, 2000. Contributor to books and periodicals. **Address:** School of Psychology, Family & Community, Seattle Pacific University, 115 Marston Hall, 3307 3rd Ave. W, Seattle, WA 98119, U.S.A. **Online address:** lpiii@spu.edu

PARROTT, Leslie L. American (born United States), b. 1964?. **Genres:** Human Relations/Parenting, Psychology. **Career:** Olivet Nazarene University, president, 1975-91; University of Washington School of Medicine, fellow; Seattle Pacific University, professor of clinical psychology, Center for Relationship Development, founder and co-director. Writer. **Publications:** If You Ever Needed Friends, It's Now, 2000. WITH L. PARROTT, III: The Marriage Mentor Manual: How You Can Help the Newlywed Couple Stay Married, 1995; Becoming Soul Mates: Cultivating Spiritual Intimacy in the Early Years of Marriage, 1995; Saving Your Marriage before It Starts: Seven Questions to Ask Before (and after) You Marry, 1995; (with L. Parrott III) The Career Counselor: Guidance for Planning Careers and Managing Career Crises, 1995; Questions Couples Ask: Answers to the Top 100 Marital Questions, 1996; Like a Kiss on the Lips: Meditations on Proverbs for Couples, 1997; Mentoring Engaged and Newlywed Couples: Leader's Guide: Building Marriages That Love for a Lifetime, 1997; Relationships: An Open and Honest Guide to Making Bad Relationships Better and Good Relationships Great (includes workbook), 1998; Relationships 101, 1998; A Good Friend: Ten Traits of Enduring Ties, 1998; (ed.) Getting Ready for the Wedding: All You Need to Know before You Say I Do, 1998; Love Is: Meditations for Couples on 1 Corinthians 13, 1999; (ed.) The Marriage Devotional Bible, 2000; Saving Your Second Marriage before It Starts: Nine Questions to Ask before (and after) You Remarry, 2001; Building Better Marriages in Oklahoma, 2001; When Bad Things Happen to Good Marriages: How to Stay Together When Life Pulls You Apart, 2001; The Love List: Eight Healthy Habits for Married Couples, 2002; God Made You Nose to Toes, 2002; Marshmallow Clouds, 2003; Love Talk: Speak Each Other's Language Like You Never Have Before, 2004; Just the Two of Us: Love Talk Meditations for Couples, 2004; Lemonade in the Desert: A Good Friend Refreshes the Soul, 2004; Lovetalk Starters: 275 Questions to get Your Conversations Going, 2004; I Love You More: How Everyday Problems can Strengthen Your Marriage, 2005; Complete Guide to Marriage Mentoring: Connecting Couples to Build Better Marriages, 2005; Saving Your Second Marriage before It Starts: Nine Questions to Ask before-and after-You Remarry: Workbook for Men, 2006; Time Together: Meditations for Your Time Starved Marriage, 2006; Marriage Mentor Training Manual for Wives: A Ten Session Program for Equipping Marriage Mentors, 2006; Your Time-Starved Marriage: How to Stay Connected at the Speed of Life, 2006; Your Time-starved Marriage Workbook for Women: How to Stay Connected at the Speed of Life, 2006; 51 Creative Ideas for Marriage Mentors: Connecting Couples to Build Better Marriages, 2006; Marriage Mentor Training Manual for Husbands, 2006; You Matter More than You Think: What a Woman Needs to Know about the Difference She Makes, 2006; Parent You Want to Be: Who You are Matters More Than What You Do, 2007; Trading Places: The Best Move You'll Ever Make in Your Marriage, 2008; Trading Places: Workbook for Men, 2008; (with Les) L.O.V.E.: Putting Your Love Styles to Work for You, 2009; First Drop of Rain, 2009; Dot. com Dating: Finding Your Right Someone Online: Avoiding the Liars, Losers and Freaks, 2010; (with S. Allen and T. Kuna) The Hour that Matters Most: The Surprising Power of the Family Meal, 2011; One Year Love Talk Devotional For Couples, 2011; Real Relationships: From Bad to Better and Good to Great, 2011. Contributor to periodicals and books. **Address:** Psychology Department, Seattle Pacific University, 408 Alexander Hall, 3307 3rd Ave. W, Seattle, WA 98119, U.S.A.

PARRY, Graham. British (born England), b. 1940. **Genres:** Art/Art History, Poetry, History. **Career:** Columbia University, preceptor, 1962-65; University of British Columbia, assistant professor, 1965-67, visiting professor, 1993-94; University of Leeds, lecturer in English, 1967-76; Universite de Toulouse, visiting professor, 1972-73; City College of New York, visiting professor, 1975-76; University of York, lecturer in English, 1977, professor of Renaissance literature, now professor emeritus of English; Doshisha University, visiting professor, 1981-82, 1997-98. Writer. **Publications:** Lady Mary Wroth's Urania, 1975; Wenceslaus Hollar in England: A Tercentenary Exhibition [held at the] Ashmolean Museum 1 October-27 November, 1977, 1977; The Pre-Raphaelite Image: Style and Subject 1848-56, 1978; Hollar's England: A Mid-Seventeenth Century View, 1980; The Golden Age Restor'd: The Culture of the Stuart Court 1603-1642, 1981; Seventeenth-Century Poetry: The Social Context, 1985; The Seventeenth Century: The Intellectual and Cultural Context of English Literature, 1603-1700, 1989; The Trophies of Time: English Antiquarians of the Seventeenth Century, 1995; The Life and Letters of John Talman, 1997; (ed. with J. Raymond) Milton and the Terms of Liberty, 2002; The Arts of the Anglican Counter-Reformation: Glory, Laud and Honour, 2006. Contributor to periodicals. **Address:** English and Related Literature, University of York, Heslington, WY YO10 5DD, England. **Online address:** gp8@york.ac.uk

PARSHALL, Jonathan B. American (born United States), b. 1962. **Genres:** History. **Career:** U.S. Naval War College, adjunct professor; www.combinedfleet.com, founder, 1995. Host and writer. **Publications:** (with A.P. Tully) Shattered Sword: The Untold Story of the Battle of Midway, 2005. **Address:** Minneapolis, MN , U.S.A. **Online address:** jonp@combinedfleet.com

PARSHALL, Karen Hunger. American (born United States), b. 1955. **Genres:** Mathematics/Statistics, Education. **Career:** Sweet Briar College, assistant professor of mathematics, 1982-87; University of Illinois, assistant professor of mathematics, 1987-88; University of Virginia, assistant professor, 1988-93, associate professor, 1993-99; professor of mathematics and history, 1999-, associate dean for social science; Historia Mathematica, book review editor, 1990-94, managing editor, 1994-96, editor, 1996-99. **Publications:** (With D.E. Rowe) The Emergence of the American Mathematical Research Community, 1876-1900, 1994; (ed. with P.H. Theerman) Experiencing Nature: Proceedings of a Conference in Honor of Allen G. Debus, 1997; James Joseph Sylvester: Life and Work in Letters, 1998; (ed. with A.C. Rice) Mathematics Unbound: The Evolution of an International Mathematical Research Community, 1800-1945, 2002; James Joseph Sylvester: Jewish Mathematician in a Victorian World, 2006; (ed. with J.J. Gray) Episodes in the History of Modern Algebra (1800- 1950), 2007. Contributor to professional journals. **Address:** Departments of Mathematics, University of Virginia, 226 Kerchof Hall, 141 Cabell Dr., PO Box 400137, Charlottesville, VA 22904, U.S.A. **Online address:** khp3k@virginia.edu

PARSON-NESBITT, Julie. American (born United States), b. 1957. **Genres:** Poetry, Novellas/Short Stories. **Career:** University of Illinois, College of Architecture and the Arts, grants and communications specialist. Writer. **Publications:** Clark St. Lullabye, Poems, 1985; (co-ed.) Naming the Daytime Moon: Stories and Poems by Chicago Women, 1988; (ed. with M. Warr and L. Rodriguez) Power Lines: A Decade of Poetry from Chicago's Guild Complex, 1993; Finders: Poems by Julie Parson-Nesbitt, 1996. **Address:** College of Architecture and the Arts, University of Illinois, 303 Jefferson Hall, 929 W Harrison St., Chicago, IL 60607-7038, U.S.A. **Online address:** parsonnesbitt@earthlink.net

PARSONS, Alexandra. British (born England), b. 1947. **Genres:** Animals/Pets, Young Adult Fiction, Children's Non-fiction, Young Adult Non-fiction, Children's Fiction, Sciences, History, Architecture, Architecture. **Career:** Mitchell Beazley, senior executive editor, 1978-83; The Watermark Press, co-founder, 1983-88; writer, 1988-. **Publications:** EYEWITNESS JUNIORS SERIES IN UK AS AMAZING WORLDS SERIES: Amazing Birds, 1990; Amazing Mammals, 1990; Amazing Snakes, 1990; Amazing Spiders, 1990; Amazing Cats, 1990; Amazing Poisonous Animals, 1990. MICKEY WONDERS WHY? SERIES: Can You Really Fry an Egg on a Stone?, 1992; How Far Is It to the Moon?, 1992; How Do Birds Fly?, 1992; Were Dinosaurs Smart?, 1992; What Is Toothpaste Made Of?, 1992; Where Do Rainbows End?, 1992; Why Do Boomerangs Come Back?, 1992; Why Do Camels Have Humps?, 1992; Why Do Puppies Chew Slippers?, 1992; Why Do Some Kids Have Freckles?, 1992; Why Do Tigers Have Stripes?, 1992; Why Do Whales Sing?, 1992; Why Is Grass Green?, 1992; Are Jellyfish Made of Jelly?, 1993. WHAT'S INSIDE? SERIES: Toys, 1991; Shells, 1991; Small Animals, 1991; Baby, 1992; Boats, 1992; Everyday Things, 1992; Trucks, 1992; Plants, 1992; Insects, 1992; Spacecraft, 1992; Great Inventions, 1993; Sea Creatures, 1993; Cars, 1993; Animal Homes, 1993. MAKE-IT-WORK SCIENCE SERIES: Earth: A Creative, Hands-on Approach to Science, 1993; Electricity: A Creative, Hands-on Approach to Science, 1993; Sound: A Creative, Hands-on Approach to Science, 1993; (with C. Watts) Plants: A Creative Hand-on Approach to Science, 1993. MAKE-IT-WORK HISTORY SERIES (with A. Haslam): Ancient Egypt, 1995; Arctic Peoples, 1995; North American Indians, 1995; (with C. Watts) Plants, 1998. LIFE EDUCATION SERIES: An Amazing Machine, 1996; Being Me, 1996; Fit for Life, 1996; Me and My World, 1996; I'm Happy, I'm Healthy, 1997; I Am Special, 1997; My Wonderful Body, 1997; You're Special, Too, 1997. OTHERS: (ed.) Music in Time, 1983; Facts and Phalluses: A Collection of Bizarre and Intriguing Truths, Legends and Measurements, 1990; A Proper Breakfast (cookbook), 1991; Araminta Goes Shopping, 1991; (with I. Parsons) Making It from 12 to 20: How to Survive Your Teens, 1991; Dead Fishy!, 1999; Road Rage!, 1999; Spell Bound!, 1999; Slap Head!, 1999; High Speed!, 2000; Dream Baby!, 2000; Make it Work! Sound, 2001; (with S. Hoppen) Stephanie Hoppen's Decorating with Style: Elegant Details and Creative Solutions for Transforming Your Home, 2002; The Perfect Kitchen, 2004; Victoria Romantic Window Style, 2004; (with H. Spencer-Churchill) Blenheim and the Churchills: The Ancestral Estate of One of England's Most Venerable Families, 2005; (with H. Spencer-Churchill) Blenheim and the Churchill Family: A Personal Portrait, 2005. **Address:** c/o Author Mail, Hearst Books, 300 W 57th St., New York, NY 10019-3741, U.S.A. **Online address:** parsons@globalnet.co.uk

PARSONS, George W. American (born United States), b. 1927. **Genres:** Local History/Rural Topics, History. **Career:** General Foods Corp., maintenance worker, 1950-84. Writer. **Publications:** Put the Vermonters Ahead: The First Vermont Brigade in the Civil War, 1996; Marking of Medal of Honor Gravesites of Men of the First Vermont Brigade; The Third Vermont. Contributor to periodicals. **Address:** White Mane Publishing Company Inc., 63 W Burd St., PO Box 152, Shippensburg, PA 17257-1250, U.S.A.

PARSONS, Mikeal C. American (born United States), b. 1957?. **Genres:** Adult Non-fiction, Theology/Religion. **Career:** Baylor University, College of Arts and Sciences, Department of Religion, professor and Macon chair in religion. Writer. **Publications:** NONFICTION: The Departure of Jesus in Luke-Acts, 1987; (ed. with J.B. Tyson) Cadbury, Knox, and Talbert: American Contributions to the Study of Acts, 1992; (with R.I. Pervo) Rethinking the Unity of Luke and Acts, 1993; (ed. with R.B. Sloan) Perspectives on John: Methods and Interpretation in the Fourth Gospel, 1993; (ed. with H.J. Hornik) Interpreting Christian Art: Reflections on Christian Art, 2003; (with M.M. Culy) Acts: A Handbook on the Greek Text, 2003; (with H.J. Hornik) Illuminating Luke, vol. I: The Infancy Narrative in Italian Renaissance Painting, 2003, vol. II: The Public Ministry of Christ in Italian Renaissance and Baroque Painting, 2005; Body and Character in Luke and Acts: The Subversion of Physiognomy in Early Christianity, 2006; Luke: Storyteller, Interpreter, Evangelist, 2007; (with M.M. Culy and J.J. Stigall) Luke: A Handbook on the Greek Text, 2010. **Address:** Department of Religion, College of Arts and Sciences, Baylor University, 1 Bear Pl., PO Box 97284, Waco, TX 76798-7284, U.S.A. **Online address:** mike_parsons@baylor.edu

PARSONS, Paul. British (born England), b. 1971?. **Genres:** Astronomy, Sciences, History, Technology, Philosophy. **Career:** Writer, 1988-; BBC Focus Magazine, editor. **Publications:** (With G. Privett) The Deep-Sky Observer's Year: A Guide to Observing Deep-Sky Objects throughout the Year, 2001; The Big Bang: The Birth of Our Universe, 2001; (ed.) 30-Second Theories: The 50 Most Thought-Provoking Theories in Science, 2009; The Science of Doctor Who, 2010; Science 1001, 2010. Contributor of articles to periodicals. **Address:** c/o Author Mail, DK Publishing, 95 Madison Ave., New York, NY 10023, U.S.A.

PARSONS, Peter John. *See* **PARSONS, P. J.**

PARSONS, P. J. (Peter John Parsons). British (born England), b. 1936. **Genres:** History, Translations. **Career:** University of Oxford, lecturer in documentary papyrology, 1960-65, lecturer in papyrology, 1965-80, Regius professor of Greek, 1989-2003, professor emeritus, 2003-; University of Cambridge, J.H. Gray lecturer, 1982; University of California, Heller lecturer, 1988. Writer. **Publications:** EDITOR AND TRANSLATOR: GRAECO-ROMAN MEMOIRS SERIES: (with J.R. Rea and E.G. Turner) Oxyrhynchus Papyri 33, 1968; (with L. Ingrams and J.R. Rea) Oxyrhynchus Papyri 34, 1968; Oxyrhynchus Papyri 42, 1974; (with A.K. Bowman, H.M. Cockle and T.C. Skeat) Oxyrhynchus Papyri 50, 1983; (with R.A. Coles and H. Maehler) Oxyrhynchus Papyri 54, 1987; (with E.W. Handley, H.G. Ioannidou and J.E.G. Whitehorne) Oxyrhynchus Papyri 59, 1992; (with N. Gonis and D. Obbink) Oxyrhynchus Papyri 68, 2003; (with R. Hatzilambrou) Oxyrhynchus Papyri 71, 2007. OTHERS: (with E. Málašek and J. Pradel) The Volume Reduction of Low-Activity Solid Wastes, 1970; (ed. as Peter Parsons with H. Lloyd-Jones) Supplementum Hellenisticum, 1983; (ed.) Greek Manuscripts of the Ancient World, 2nd ed., 1987; (contrib.) Greek Minor Prophets scroll from Naḥal ḥever, 1990; (as Peter Parsons) City of the Sharp-Nosed Fish: Greek Lives in Roman Egypt, 2007; (co-ed.) Oxyrhynchus: A City and Its Texts, 2007. Contributor to books and periodicals. **Address:** Faculty of Classics, University of Oxford, Ioannou Ctr. for Classical and Byzantine Studies, 66 St. Giles, Oxford, OX OX1 3LU, England. **Online address:** peter.parsons@classics.ox.ac.uk

PARSONS, (Quentin) Neil. British (born England), b. 1944. **Genres:** Area Studies, History, Biography. **Career:** University of Zambia, lecturer in history, 1971-75; University of Swaziland, lecturer in history, 1975-79; Oxford University, research associate, 1979-80; University of Botswana, senior research fellow, 1980-82, associate professor, 1996-99, professor of history, 1999-; National Museum and Art Gallery, research associate, 1983-88; Institute of Commonwealth Studies, research associate, 1988-92; University of Cape Town, visiting research fellow, 1993; Botswana Society, research associate, 1995-96. Writer. **Publications:** Word of Khama, 1972; High Commission Territories, 1909-1964: A Bibliography, 1976; (comp. with D.L. Kgathi) The Brigade Movement in Botswana, 1981; A New History of Southern Africa, 1982, 2nd ed., 1993; Consolidated Checklist of Theses and Dissertations on Botswana, 1982; Report on the Botswana Brigades, 1965-83, 1983; Research Sector in Botswana: A Survey Conducted on Behalf of the Royal Norwegian Ministry for Development Cooperation, 1987; (contrib.) Succession to High Office in Botswana, 1990; (with R.K. Hitchcock) Index to Publications, 1969-1989, 1991; (with W. Henderson and T. Tlou) Seretse Khama, 1921-1980, 1995; King Khama, Emperor Joe, and the Great White Queen: Victorian Britain through African Eyes, 1998; Clicko: The Wild Dancing Bushman, 2009. EDITOR: (with R. Palmer) The Roots of Rural Poverty in Central and Southern Africa (monograph), 1977; Working Harder for Botswana, 1985; (with R. Hitchcock and J. Taylor) Research for Development in Botswana, 1987; (with M. Crowder) Monarch of All I Survey: Bechuanaland Diaries, 1929-37, 1988; Botswana Society Social Studies Atlas, 1988. **Address:** Department of History, University of Botswana, PO Box UB 00704, Gaborone, 1, Botswana. **Online address:** nparsons@mopipi.ub.bw

PARTHASARATHY, R(ajagopal). American/Indian (born India), b. 1934. **Genres:** Poetry, Area Studies, Translations, History. **Career:** Ismail Yusuf College, lecturer in English, 1959-62; Mithibai College, lecturer in English, 1962-63, 1964-65; British Council, lecturer in English language teaching, 1965-66; Presidency College, assistant professor of English, 1966-67; South Indian Education Society College, lecturer in English, 1967-71; Oxford University Press, regional editor, 1971-78, editor-Delhi, 1978-82; University of Texas, assistant instructor in English, 1982-86; Skidmore College, assistant professor of English and Asian studies, 1986-92, associate professor, 1992-, professor of English, director of Asian studies, 1994-98. **Publications:** EDITOR: (with J.J. Healy) Poetry from Leeds: Ken Smith, 1968; Ten Twentieth-Century Indian Poets, 1976. POETRY: Rough Passage, 1977; (trans. and intro.) Cilappatikāram of Ilanko Atikal: An Epic of South India, 1993, rev. ed., 2004. **Address:** Department of English, Skidmore College, 313 Palamountain Hall, 815 N Broadway, Saratoga Springs, NY 12866-1632, U.S.A. **Online address:** rparthas@skidmore.edu

PARTOW, Donna. American (born United States), b. 1961. **Genres:** Race Relations. **Career:** Writer. **Publications:** Homemade Business, 1992; (with C. Partow) How to Work with the One You Love--and Live to Tell about It, 1995; No More Lone Ranger Moms: Women Helping Women in the Practical Everyday-ness of Life, 1995; Families That Play Together Stay Together!, 1996; Becoming a Vessel God Can Use, 1996; A Woman's Guide to the Temperaments: How Understanding Your Personality Type Can Enrich Your Relationship with Your Husband and Your Kids, 1998; Walking in Total God-Confidence, 1999; Living in Absolute Freedom, 2000; A Ten-Week Journey to Standing Firm, 2001; Becoming a Vessel God Can Use Prayer Journal: A Guided Devotional Journey, 2002; A Woman's Guide to Personality Types: Enriching Your Family Relationships by Understanding the Four Temperaments, 2002; (with L. Johnson) Extracting the Precious from 2 Corinthians: A Bible Study for Women, 2003; (with L. Johnson) Extracting the Precious from Isaiah: A Bible Study for Women, 2003; This Isn't the Life I Signed Up For, 2003; (with L. Johnson) Extracting the Precious from Galatians: A Bible Study for Women, 2004; (with L. Johnson) Extracting the Precious from Nehemiah, 2004; Becoming the Woman I Want to Be: 90 Days to Renew Your Spirit, Soul, and Body, 2004; Soon to Be a Major Motion Picture: New Direction for Life's Dramas, 2005; Let Your Life Count: Make a Difference Right Where You Are, 2006; Becoming a Vessel of God's Power: Give God Thirty Days and See What He Will Do, 2007; Becoming the Woman God Wants Me to Be: A 90-day Guide to Living the Proverbs 31 Life, 2008; Making Money from Home: How to Run a Successful Home-based Business, 2010; Personalities in Love: Understanding Yourself and the Man in Your Life, 2011. Contributor to periodicals. **Address:** Donna Partow Ministries, PO Box 975, Scottsdale, AZ 85252, U.S.A. **Online address:** info@donnapartow.com

PARTRIDGE, Jenny (Lilian). British (born England), b. 1947. **Genres:** Novellas/Short Stories, Children's Fiction, Novels, Literary Criticism And History. **Career:** Presentation Colour Ltd., retoucher, 1967-72; Romany Studio Workshop, co-founder and artist, 1972-; Romany Studio, co-founder, 2003-. Writer. **Publications:** Mr. Squint, 1980; Peterkin Pollensnuff, 1980; Hopfellow, 1980; Colonel Grunt, 1981; Grandma Snuffles, 1981; Dominic Sly, 1981; Harriet Plume, 1981; Lop-Ear, 1981; Oakapple Wood Stories, 1982; A Tale of Oakapple Wood, 1983; Four Friends in Oakapple Wood, 1984; Jack Flax, 1986; Rafferty's Return, 1986; Rifkins, 1986; Clara Quince, 1986; Green as Grass, Blue as Sky, 1991; Tales of Oakapple Wood (compliation), 1993; Rhymes for All Seasons, 1994. **Address:** Romany Studio, Woodbridge Rd., Tunstall, Woodbridge, SU IP12 2JE, England.

PARTRIDGE, Norman. American (born United States), b. 1958. **Genres:** Horror, Novels, Young Adult Fiction, Novellas/Short Stories. **Career:** Writer. **Publications:** Mr. Fox and Other Feral Tales, 1992; Slippin' into Darkness, 1994; The Bars on Satan's Jailhouse, 1995; Spyder, 1995; Bad Intentions, 1996; (ed. with M.H. Greenberg) It Came from the Drive-In, 1996; Saquaro Riptide, 1997; Red Right Hand, 1998; Ten Ounce Siesta, 1998; Wildest Dreams, 1998; Wild Times: Deathblow No. 1, 1999; The Crow: Wicked Prayer, 2000; The Man with the Barbed-Wire Fists, 2001; Dark Harvest, 2007; Lesser Demons, 2010. Contributor to magazines and books. **Address:** Subterranean Press, PO Box 190106, Burton, MI 48519, U.S.A. **Online address:** normanpartridge@aol.com

PASCAL, Francine. American (born United States), b. 1938. **Genres:** Novels, Young Adult Fiction, Young Adult Non-fiction. **Career:** Writer and educator. **Publications:** YOUNG ADULT FICTION: Hangin' Out with Cici, 1977; My First Love and Other Disasters, 1979; The Hand-Me-Down Kid, 1980; Love and Betrayal and Hold the Mayo!, 1985; Road Trip, 2001; Me, Me, Me, 2001; Love, 2001; Flee, 2001; Control Freak, 2001; Close to You, 2001; Max's Choice, 2001; I Need You, 2001; Too Many Good-byes, 2001; He's the One, 2001; Where We Belong, 2001; Twins, 2002; Touch and Go, 2002; Tia in the Middle, 2002; Sex, 2002; Senior Cut Day, 2002; Prom Night, 2002; Never Give Up, 2002; It Takes Two, 2002; Get a Clue, 2002; Fear,

2002; Cruise Control, 2002; Blind, 2002; Betrayed, 2002; Best of Enemies, 2002; Before Gaia, 2002; Be Mine, 2002; Alone, 2002; Sweet 18, 2003; Shock, 2003; My Mother was Never a Kid, 2003; Lust, 2003; Lost, 2003; Gaia Abducted, 2003; Freak, 2003; Escape, 2003; Chase, 2003; Wired, 2004; Terror, 2004; The Ruling Class, 2004; Normal, 2004; Gone, 2004; Fake, 2004; Exposed, 2004; Live Bait, 2005; Kill Game, 2005. SWEET VALLEY HIGH SERIES: Double Love, 1984; Secrets, 1984; Playing with Fire, 1984; Power Play, 1984; All Night Long, 1984; Dangerous Love, 1984; Dear Sister, 1984; Heartbreaker, 1984; Racing Hearts, 1984; Wrong Kind of Girl, 1984; Too Good to Be True, 1984; When Love Dies, 1984; Kidnapped!, 1984; Deceptions, 1984; Promises, 1985; Rags to Riches, 1985; Love Letters, 1985; Head over Heels, 1985; Showdown, 1985; Crash Landing!New York, 1985; Runaway, 1985; Too Much in Love, 1986; Say Goodbye, 1986; Memories, 1986; Nowhere to Run, 1986; Hostage! New York, 1986; Lovestruck, 1986; Alone in the Crowd, 1986; Bitter Rivals, 1986; Jealous Lies, 1986; Taking Sides, 1986; The New Jessica, 1986; Starting Over, 1987; Forbidden Love, 1987; Out of Control, 1987; Last Chance, 1987; Rumors, 1987; Leaving Home, 1987; Secret Admirer, 1987; On the Edge, 1987; Outcast, 1987; Caught in the Middle, 1988; Pretenses, 1988; Hard Choices, 1988; Family Secrets, 1988; Decisions, 1988; Slam Book Fever, 1988; Playing for Keeps, 1988; Troublemaker, 1988; Out of Reach, 1988; In Love Again, 1989; Against the Odds, 1989; Brokenhearted, 1989; Teacher Crush, 1989; Perfect Shot, 1989; White Lies, 1989; Two-Boy Weekend, 1989; That Fatal Night, 1989; Lost at Sea, 1989; Second Chance, 1989; Ms. Quarterback, 1990; The New Elizabeth, 1990; The Ghost of Tricia Martin, 1990; Friend Against Friend, 1990; Trouble at Home, 1990; Who's to Blame, 1990; The Parent Plot, 1990; Boy Trouble, 1990; Who's Who?, 1990; The Love Bet, 1990; Amy's True Love, 1991; Miss Teen Sweet Valley, 1991; The Perfect Girl, 1991; Regina's Legacy, 1991; Rock Star's Girl, 1991; Starring Jessica! New York, 1991; Cheating to Win, 1991; The Dating Game, 1991; The Long-Lost Brother, 1991; The Girl They Both Loved, 1991; Rosa's Lie, 1992; Kidnapped by the Cult, 1992; Steven's Bride, 1992; The Stolen Diary, 1992; Soap Star, 1992; Jessica Against Bruce, 1992; My Best Friend's Boyfriend, 1992; Love Letters for Sale, 1992; Elizabeth Betrayed, 1992; Don't Go Home with John, 1993; In Love with a Prince, 1993; She's Not What She Seems, 1993; Stepsisters, 1993; Are We in Love? New York, 1993; The Morning After, 1993; The Arrest, 1993; The Verdict, 1993; The Wedding, 1993; Beware the Babysitter, 1993; Almost Married, 1994; The Boyfriend War, 1994; A Date with a Werewolf, 1994; Death Threat, 1994; Double-Crossed, 1994; Jessica's Secret Love, 1994; Left at the Altar, 1994; Love and Death in London, 1994; Operation Love Match, 1994; College Weekend, 1995; Crash Landing, 1995; The Cousin War, 1995; Jessica's Older Guy, 1995; Jessica Quits the Squad, 1995; Jessica the Genius, 1995; Meet the Stars of Sweet Valley High, 1995; The Morning After, 1995; Nightmare in Death Valley, 1995; The Pom-Pom Wars, 1995; She's Not What She Seems, 1995; V for Victory, 1995; The Treasure of Death Valley, 1995; When Loves Dies, 1995; The Arrest, 1996; Beware of the Babysitter, 1996; Camp Killer, 1996; Dance of Death, 1996; Elizabeth's Rival, 1996; The High School War, 1996; In Love With the Enemy, 1996; Kiss Before Dying, 1996; Kiss of a Killer, 1996; Left at the Alter, 1996; Meet Me at Midnight, 1996; Out of Control, 1996; Tall, Dark, and Deadly, 1996; Fashion Victim, 1997; Happily Ever After, 1997; Lila's New Flame, 1997; Model Flirt, 1997; Once Upon A Time, 1997; To Catch a Thief, 1997; Too Hot to Handle, 1997; The Big Night, 1998; Elizabeth Is Mine, 1998; Fight Fire With Fire, 1998; Picture Perfect Prom?, 1998; Please Forgive Me, 1998; What Jessica Wants, 1998; Earthquake, 1998; Sweet Valley Confidential: Ten Years Later, 2011. SWEET VALLEY HIGH SUPER EDITIONS: Perfect Summer, 1985; Malibu Summer, 1986; Special Christmas, 1986; Spring Break, 1986; Spring Fever, 1987; Winter Carnival, 1987; Murder in Paradise, 1995; Return of the Evil Twin, 1995; Falling for Lucas, 1996; Cover Girls, 1997; Jessica Takes Manhattan, 1997; Mystery Date, 1997; Last Wish, 1998. SWEET VALLEY HIGH SUPER THRILLER SERIES: Double Jeopardy, 1987; On the Run, 1988; No Place to Hide, 1988; Deadly Summer, 1989; Murder on the Line, 1992; Beware the Wolfman, 1994; A Deadly Christmas, 1994; Double Jeopardy, 1995; A Killer on Board, 1995; Murder in Paradise, 1995; A Stranger in the House, 1995; (with K. William) R for Revenge, 1997. SWEET VALLEY HIGH SUPER STAR SERIES: Lila's Story, 1989; Bruce's Story, 1990; Enid's Story, 1990; Olivia's Story, 1991; Todd's Story, 1992. SWEET VALLEY MAGNA EDITIONS: The Wakefields of Sweet Valley, 1991; The Wakefield Legacy: The Untold Story, 1992; A Night to Remember, 1993; The Evil Twin, 1993; Elizabeth's Secret Diary, vol. I, 1994, vol. II, 1996, vol. III, 1997; Jessica's Secret Diary, vol. I, 1994, vol. II, 1996, vol. III, 1997. SWEET VALLEY TWINS SERIES: Best Friends, 1986; Teacher's Pet, 1986; The Haunted House, 1986; Choosing Sides, 1986; Sneaking Out, 1987; The New Girl, 1987; Three's a Crowd, 1987; First Place, 1987; Against the Rules, 1987; One of the Gang, 1987; Buried Treasure, 1987; Keeping Secrets, 1987; Stretching the Truth, 1987; Tug of War, 1987; The Bully, 1988; Playing Hooky, 1988; Left Behind, 1988; Claim to Fame, 1988; Center of Attention, 1988; Jumping to Conclusions, 1988; Second Best, 1988; The Older Boy, 1988; Out of Place, 1988; Elizabeth's New Hero, 1989; Standing Out, 1989; Jessica on Stage, 1989; Jessica the Rock Star, 1989; Jessica's Bad Idea, 1989; Taking Charge, 1989; Big Camp Secret, 1989; Jessica and the Brat Attack, 1989; April Fool!, 1989; Princess Elizabeth, 1989; Elizabeth's First Kiss, 1990; War Between the Twins, 1990; Summer Fun Book, 1990; The Twins Get Caught, 1990; Lois Strikes Back, 1990; Mary Is Missing, 1990; Jessica's Secret, 1990; Jessica and the Money Mix-Up, 1990; Danny Means Trouble, 1990; Amy's Pen Pal, 1990; Amy Moves In, 1991; Jessica's New Look, 1991; Lucky Takes the Reins, 1991; Mademoiselle Jessica, 1991; Mansy Miller Fights Back, 1991; The Twins' Little Sister, 1991; Booster Boycott, 1991; Elizabeth the Impossible, 1991; Jessica and the Secret Star, 1991; The Slime That Ate Sweet Valley, 1991; The Big Party Weekend, 1991; Brooke and Her Rock-Star Mom, 1992; The Wakefields Strike It Rich, 1992; Big Brother's in Love!, 1992; Elizabeth and the Orphans, 1992; Barnyard Battle, 1992; Ciao, Sweet Valley, 1992; Jessica the Nerd, 1992; Sarah's Dad and Sophia's Mom, 1992; Poor Lila!, 1992; The Charm School Mystery, 1992; Patty's Last Dance, 1993; The Great Boyfriend Switch, 1993; Jessica the Thief, 1993; The Middle School Gets Married, 1993; Won't Someone Help Anna?, 1993; Psychic Sisters, 1993; Jessica Saves the Trees, 1993; The Love Potion, 1993; Lila's Music Video, 1993; Elizabeth the Hero, 1993; Jessica and the Earthquake, 1994; Yours for a Day, 1994; Todd Runs Away, 1994; Steven the Zombie, 1994; Jessica's Blind Date, 1994; The Gossip War, 1994; Robbery atthe Mall, 1994; Steven's Enemy, 1994; Amy's Secret Sister, 1994; Deadly Voyage, 1995; Don't Go in the Basement, 1995; Elizabeth the Seventh-Grader, 1995; Escape from Terror Island, 1995; It Can't Happen Here, 1995; Jessica's Cookie Disaster, 1995; The Middle School Gets Married, 1995; The Mother-Daughter Switch, 1995; Romeo and Two Juliets, 1995; Steven Gets Even, 1995; The Battle of the Cheerleaders, 1996; The Beast is Watching You, 1996; The Beast Must Die, 1996; Don't Talk to Brian, 1996; Elizabeth the Spy, 1996; Elizabeth's First Kiss, 1996; The Incredible Madame Jessica, 1996; The Mysterious Dr. Q, 1996; Too Scared to Sleep, 1996; Twins in Love, 1996; Twins Little Sister, 1996; Holiday Mischief, 1996; If I Die Before I Wake, 1997; Big Brother's inLove Again, 1997; Breakfast of Enemies, 1997; Cammi's Crush, 1997; Elizabeth Solves It All, 1997; Jessica's First Kiss, 1997; Jessica's Lucky Millions, 1997; Pumpkin Fever, 1997; Sister's at War, 1997; The Twins Hit Hollywood, 1997; The Boyfriend Game, 1998; The Boyfriend Mess, 1998; Down With Queen Janet, 1998; Happy Mother's Day, Lila, 1998; If Looks Could Kill, 1998; Jessica Takes Charge, 1998. SWEET VALLEY TWINS SUPER SERIES: Class Trip, 1988; Holiday Mischief, 1988; The Big Camp Secret, 1989; The Unicorns Go Hawaiian, 1991; Lila's Secret Valentine, 1994; Jessica's Animal Instincts, 1996; The Twins Go To College, 1997; The Year Without Christmas, 1997; Good-Bye Middle School, Countdown to Junior High, 1997; Jessica's No Angel, 1998. SWEET VALLEY TWINS SUPER CHILLER SERIES: The Christmas Ghost, 1989; The Carnival Ghost, 1990; The Ghost in the Graveyard, 1990; The Ghost in the Bell Tower, 1992; The Curse of the Ruby Necklace, 1993; The Curse of the Golden Heart, 1994; The Haunted Burial Ground, 1994; The Secret of the Magic Pen, 1995; Evil Elizabeth, 1995; The Curse of the Ruby Necklace, 1995. SWEET VALLEY TWINS MAGNA EDITIONS: The Magic Christmas, 1992; A Christmas Without Elizabeth, 1993; BIG for Christmas, 1994. SWEET VALLEY KIDS SERIES: Surprise! Surprise!, 1989; Runaway Hamster, 1989; Teamwork, 1989; Lila's Secret, 1990; Elizabeth's Valentine, 1990; Elizabeth's Super-Selling Lemonade, 1990; Jessica's Big Mistake, 1990; Jessica's Cat Trick, 1990; Jessica's Zoo Adventure, 1990; The Twins and the Wild West, 1990; Starring Winston, 1990; The Substitute Teacher, 1990; Sweet Valley Trick or Treat, 1990; Crybaby Lois, 1990; Bossy Steven, 1991; Carolyn's Mystery Dolls, 1991; Fearless Elizabeth, 1991; Jessica and Jumbo, 1991; The Twins Go to the Hospital, 1991; Jessica the Babysitter, 1991; Jessica and the Spelling Bee Surprise, 1991; Lila's Haunted House Party, 1991; Sweet Valley Slumber Party, 1991; Cousin Kelly's Family Secret, 1991; Left-Out Elizabeth, 1992; Jessica's Snobby Club, 1992; The Sweet Valley Cleanup Team, 1992; Elizabeth Meets Her Hero, 1992; Andy and the Alien, 1992; Jessica's Unburied Treasure, 1992; Elizabeth and Jessica Run Away, 1992; Left Back!, 1992; Caroline's Halloween Spell, 1992; The Best Thanksgiving Ever, 1992; Elizabeth's Broken Arm, 1993; Elizabeth's Video Fever, 1993; The Big Race, 1993; Good-bye, Eva, 1993; Ellen Is Home Alone, 1993; Robin in the Middle, 1993; The Missing Tea Set, 1993; Jessica's Monster Nightmare, 1993; Jessica Gets Spooked, 1993; The Twins Big Pow-Wow, 1993; Elizabeth's Piano Lessons, 1994; Get the Teacher!, 1994; Elizabeth the Tattletale, 1994; Lila's April Fool, 1994; Jessica's Mermaid, 1994; Steven's Twin, 1994; Lois and the Sleepover, 1994; Julie the Karate Kid, 1994; The Magic Puppets, 1994; Star of the Parade, 1994; The Halloween War, 1995; Jessica's Big Mistake, 1995; The Jessica and Elizabeth Show, 1995; Jessica + Jessica = Trouble, 1995; Jessica Plays Cupid, 1995; Lila's Birthday Bash, 1995; Lila's Christmas Angel, 1995; Lila's Secret, 1995; Lila's Secret Valentine, 1995; The Magic Puppets, 1995; No Girls Allowed, 1995; Scaredy-Cat Elizabeth, 1995; The Amazing Jessica, 1996; And the Winner Is Horseback Adventure, 1996; A Roller Coaster for the Twins!, 1996; The Secret of Fantasy Forest, 1996; Steven's Big Crush, 1996; Class Picture Day!, 1997; Good-Bye, Mrs. Otis, 1997; Jessica's Secret Friend, 1997; The MacAroni Mess, 1997; The Witch in the Pumpkin Patch, 1997; Danger: Twins at Work!, 1998; Little Drummer Girls, 1998; Sweet Valley Blizzard!, 1998. SWEET VALLEY KIDS SUPER SNOOPER SERIES: The Case of the Secret Santa, 1990; The Case of the Magic Christmas Bell, 1991; The Case of the Haunted Camp, 1992; The Case of the Christmas Thief, 1992; The Case of the Hidden Treasure, 1993; The Case of the Million-Dollar Diamonds, 1993; The Case of the Alien Princess, 1994. SWEET VALLEY KIDS SUPER SPECIAL SERIES: The Easter Bunny Battle, 1996; Elizabeth Hatches an Egg, 1996; Jessica's Animal Instincts, 1996. SWEET VALLEY KIDS HAIR RAISER SUPER SPECIAL SERIES: A Curse on Elizabeth, 1995; Elizabeth Hatches an Egg, 1996. SWEET VALLEY UNIVERSITY SERIES: College Girls, 1993; Love, Lies, and Jessica Wakefield, 1993; What Your Parents Don't Know ..., 1994; Anything for Love, 1994; A Married Woman, 1994; The Love of Her Life, 1994; Home for Christmas, 1994; Behind Closed Doors, 1995; College Cruise, 1995; Deadly Attraction, 1995; No Means No, 1995; The Other Woman, 1995; Shipboard Wedding, 1995; Sorority Scandal, 1995; S.S. Heartbreak, 1995; Take Back the Night, 1995; Billie's Secret, 1996; Broken Promises, Shattered Dreams, 1996; Busted, 1996; Elizabeth's Summer Love, 1996; For the Love of Ryan, 1996; Here Comes the Bride, 1996; His Secret Past, 1996; Sweet Kiss of Summer, 1996; The Trial of Jessica Wakefield, 1996; Beauty and the Beach, 1997; The Boys of Summer, 1997; Elizabeth and Todd Forever, 1997; Elizabeth's Heartbreak, 1997; One Last Kiss, 1997; Out of the Picture, 1997; Spy Girl, 1997; The Truth About Ryan, 1997; Undercover Angels, 1997; Breaking Away, 1998; Channel X: Thriller Edition, 1998; Elizabeth: New York, 1998; Escape to New York, 1998; Good-Bye, Elizabeth, 1998; Have You Heard About Elizabeth?, 1998; Private Jessica, 1998; Sneaking In, 1998; The First Time, 2000; Who Knew?, 2000; Secret Love Diaries: Sam, 2000; Secret Love Diaries: Jessica, 2000; Secret Love Diaries, Elizabeth, 2000; Secret Love Diaries, Chloe, 2000; Rush Week, 2000; Elizabeth in Love, 2000; Dropping Out, 2000; The Dreaded Ex, 2000. SWEET VALLEY UNIVERSITY THRILLER EDITIONS: Kiss of the Vampire, 1995; Wanted for Murder, 1995; He's Watching You, vol. I, 1995, vol. II, 1995; The House of Death, 1996; The Roommate, 1996; Running for Her Life, 1996; Dead Before Dawn, 1997; Killer at Sea, 1997; What Winston Saw, 1997; Don't Answer the Phone, 1998; Love and Murder, 1998; Very Bad Things, 2000; Face It, 2000. UNICORN CLUB SERIES: Save the Unicorns, 1994; Maria's Movie Comeback, 1994; The Best Friend Game, 1994; Lila's Little Sister, 1994; Unicorns in Love, 1994; Too Close for Comfort, 1995; The Unicorns at War, 1995; Unicorns in Love, 1995; Ellen's Family, 1996; Lila on the Loose, 1996; Mandy in the Middle, 1996; Five Girls and a Baby, 1996; Who Will Be Miss Unicorn?, 1996; Bon Voyage, Unicorns, 1997; Boyfriends for Everyone, 1997; The Most Beautiful Girls in the World, 1997; Rachel's In, Lila's Out, 1997; Snow Bunnies, 1997; In Love With Mandy, 1997; Jessica's Dream Date, 1998; Trapped in the Mall, 1998. SWEET VALLEY SENIOR YEAR SERIES: Boy Meets Girl, 1999; Broken Angel, 1999; Can't Stay Away, 1999; I've Got a Secret, 1999; If You Only Knew, 1999; Maria Who?, 1999; Say It to My Face, 1999; So Cool, 1999; Take Me On, 1999; The One That Got Away, 1999; Your Basic Nightmare, 1999; Bad Girl, 2000; Three Girls and a Guy, 2000; The It Guy, 2000; Split Decision, 2000; So Not Me, 2000; On My Own, 2000; All about Love, 2000; As If I Care, 2000; Backstabber, 2000; Falling Apart, 2000; Nothing Is Forever, 2000; It's My Life, 2000; Never Let Go, 2000; Straight Up, 2001; Too Late, 2001; Playing Dirty, 2001; Meant to Be, 2001; Tearing Me Apart, 2001; Stay or Go, 2001. UNICORN CLUB SUPER EDITION: Angels Keep Out, 1996. CAITLIN SERIES: The Love Trilogy: vol. I: Loving, vol. II: Love Lost, vol. III: True Love, 1986; The Promise Trilogy: vol. I: Tender Promises, 1986, vol. II: Promises Broken, 1986, vol. III: A New Promise, 1987; The Forever Trilogy: vol. I: Dreams of Forever, vol. II: Forever and Always, vol. III: Together Forever, 1987. FOR ADULTS: (with J. Pascal) The Strange Case of Patty Hearst, 1974; Save Johanna! (novel), 1981; If Wishes Were Horses (novel), 1994. SWEET VALLEY JUNIOR HIGH SERIES: Boy. Friend. 1999; Cheating on Anna, 1999; Get Real, 1999; Got a Problem?, 1999; How to Ruina Friendship, 1999; Lacey's Crush, 1999; One 2 Many, 1999; Soulmates, 1999; The Cool Crowd, 1999; Too Popular, 1999; Twin Switch, 1999; Third Wheel, 1999; What You Don't Know, 2000; Wild Child, 2000; Whatever, 2000; True Blue, 2000; Three Days, Two Nights, 2000; She Loves Me Real, 2000; Invisible Me, 2000; I'm So Outta Here, 2000; Clueless, 2000; Dance Fever, 2001; Drama Queen, 2001; No More Mr. Nice Guy, 2001; She's Back He's Back, 2002. ELIZABETH SERIES: University, Interrupted, 2001; London Calling, 2001; Royal Pain, 2001; Downstairs, Upstairs, 2001. FEARLESS SERIES: Fearless, 1999; Sam, 1999; Run, 2000; Twisted, 2000; Kiss, 2000; Payback, 2000; Rebel, 2000; Heat, 2000; Blood, 2000; Liar, 2000; Trust, 2000; Killer, 2000; Bad, 2001; Missing, 2001; Tears, 2001; Naked, 2001; Agent Out, 2006; Naked Eye, 2006. OTHERS: Sweet Valley High, 2011; Fearless, 2012. **Address:** c/o Amy Berkower, Writers House, 21 W 26th St., New York, NY 10010-1003, U.S.A.

PASCALE, Richard Tanner. British/American (born United States), b. 1938. **Genres:** Administration/Management, Politics/Government, Business/Trade/Industry, Economics, Reference, History, Psychology. **Career:** Stanford University, Graduate School of Business, assistant professor, 1971-73, associate professor, professor of business, 1974-94; National Commission on Productivity, consultant, 1972-73; Oxford University, Templeton College, associate fellow; White House Task Force, senior staff; McKinsey & Co., consultant. Writer. **Publications:** (With G.P. Barbour) Shared Power: A Study of Four Federal Funding Systems in Appalachia, 1977; (with A.G. Athos) The Art of Japanese Management: Applications for American Executives, 1981; Managing on the Edge: How the Smartest Companies Use Conflict to Stay Ahead, 1990; Surfing the Edge of Chaos: The Laws of Nature and the New Laws of Business, 2000; (with J. Sternin and M. Sternin) The Power of Positive Deviance: How Unlikely Innovators Solve the World's Toughest Problems, 2010. **Address:** Templeton College, University of Oxford, Egrove Pk., Oxford, OX OX1 5NY, England.

PASCARELLA, Perry. American (born United States), b. 1934. **Genres:** Business/Trade/Industry, Theology/Religion, Technology. **Career:** Dun & Bradstreet, credit reporter, 1960-61; IndustryWeek Magazine, executive editor, 1961-70, managing editor, 1970-71, executive editor, 1971-86, editor-in-chief, 1986-89; Steel Magazine, assistant editor, business editor, 1961-69, managing editor, 1969-70; Penton Publishing Inc., vice president for editorial and graphics operations, 1989-96, retired, 1996; BrownHerron Publishing, founding member, author and associate editor, 2001-. **Publications:** Technology Fire in a Dark World, 1979; Industry Week's Guide to Tomorrow's Executive: Humanagement in the Future Corporation, 1981; The New Achievers: Creating a Modern Work Ethic, 1984; (with M.A. Frohman) The Purpose-Driven Organization: Unleashing the Power of Direction and Commitment, 1989; The Ten Commandments of the Workplace and How to Break Them Every Day, 1996; (with B.A. Nagle) Leveraging People and Profit: The Hard Work of Soft Management, 1998; Christ-centered Leadership: Thriving in Business by Putting God in Charge, 1999; Earning Trust, 2000; (with S. Lombardo and M. Frohman) Asserting Yourself-Appropriately, 2000; (with J.L. Mariotti) Collaborating for Success, 2000; (with M. Frohman) Involving Others in Problem Solving, 2000; (with G.M. Bellman) Unleashing the Power of Shared Dreams, 2005. Contributor of articles to journals. **Address:** Brown-Herron Publishing, PO Box 23680, Louisville, KY 40223-0680, U.S.A. **Online address:** perry@brownherron.com

PASCHEN, Elise (Maria). American (born United States), b. 1959. **Genres:** Poetry, Social Sciences. **Career:** Oxford Poetry Magazine, co-founder, 1983; Poetry Society of America, executive director, 1988-2001; Poetry in Motion, co-founder; Newberry Library, Frances Allen Fellow; Three Oaks, poet laureate; School of the Art Institute of Chicago, MFA Writing Program, instructor, 1999-; The New York Times Magazine, editor. **Publications:** POETRY: Houses: Coasts, 1985; Infidelities, 1996; Bestiary, 2009. EDITOR: (with M. Peacock and N. Neches) Poetry in Motion: 100 Poems from the Subways and Buses, 1996; (with R.P. Mosby) Poetry Speaks: Hear Great Poets Read Their Work from Tennyson to Plath Read Their Own Work, 2001, 2nd ed., 2007; (with B.F. Lauer) Poetry in Motion Coast to Coast: 120 Poems from the Subways and Buses, 2002; Poetry Speaks to Children, 2005; (with D. Raccah) Poetry Speaks Who I Am, 2010. Works appear in anthologies. Contributor of poems to periodicals. **Address:** c/o Ileanna Portillo, Red Hen Press, PO Box 40820, Pasadena, CA 91114, U.S.A. **Online address:** elise@poetry.chicago.il.us

PASCOE, Bruce. (Leopold Glass). Australian (born Australia), b. 1947.

Genres: Novels, Novellas/Short Stories, History, Literary Criticism And History, Animals/Pets, Young Adult Fiction, Adult Non-fiction. **Career:** Writer, educator and publisher. **Publications:** Night Animals, 1986; Fox, 1988; (with D. McRae) The Great Australian Novel, 1988; Dearly Beloved (drama), 1995; Ruby-Eyed Coucal, 1996; Cape Otway, Coast of Secrets, 1998; Shark, 1999; (as Leopold Glass) Ribcage, 2000; Nightjar, 2000; Earth, 2001; Ocean, 2002; Wathaurong The People Who Said No, 2003; Foxies in a Firehose, 2006; Convincing Ground: Learning to Fall in Love with Your Country, 2007; (with S.H. Krishna-Pillay) Dictionary of Wathawoorroong, 2008; The Little Red Yellow Black Book, 2008; Bloke, 2009; The Chainsaw File, 2011. EDITOR: (with L. Harwood and P. White) The Babe Is Wise: Contemporary Stories by Australian Women, 1987; (with L. Harwood) Fabulous at Fifty: Fifty of the Best From Australian Short Stories, 1995; Wathaurong Too Bloody Strong, 1997; (with S. Pillay) Dictionary of Wathaurong Language, 2002. Contributor to periodicals. **Address:** Pascoe Publishing, PO Box 42, Apollo Bay, VI 3233, Australia. **Online address:** brucepascoe@westnet.com.au

PASCOE, C. J. American (born United States), b. 1974. **Genres:** Social Sciences, Human Relations/Parenting, Education, Gay And Lesbian Issues. **Career:** Colorado College, assistant professor of sociology. Writer. **Publications:** Dude, You're a Fag: Masculinity and Sexuality in High School, 2007; (co-author) Hanging Out, Messing Around, and Geeking Out: Kids Living and Learning with New Media, 2009. **Address:** Department of Sociology, Colorado College, 14 E Cache la Poudre St., Colorado Springs, CO 80903, U.S.A. **Online address:** c.j.pascoe@coloradocollege.edu

PASCOE, David. *See* **LAWRENCE, David.**

PASEWARK, William Robert. American (born United States), b. 1924. **Genres:** Administration/Management, Business/Trade/Industry, Technology, Information Science/Computers, Education. **Career:** University of Houston, director of MBA programs; ExxonMobil, staff; Frost Bank, staff; New York University, instructor in business education, 1949-51; Meredith College, associate professor of business education, 1951-52; Michigan State University, assistant professor of business education, 1952-56; University of Georgia, professor; University of Houston, professor; Texas Tech University, professor of business education and chair, 1956-83, Webster professor of business, now professor emeritus; West Texas Business Education Association, president, 1958; California State University, visiting professor, 1959; Lions Intl., director, 1968; North Arizona State University, visiting professor, 1969; Central Connecticut State College, visiting professor, 1974; American Vocational Association, president and director, 1976-77; Office Management Consultants, owner, 1977. Writer. **Publications:** (With P.L. Agnew) Key-Driven Calculator Course, 1962; (with P.L. Agnew) Rotary Calculator Course, 1962; (with P.L. Agnew) Full-Keyboard Adding Listing Machine Course, 1963; (with P.L. Agnew) Ten-key Adding-listing Machine and Printing Calculator Course, 3rd ed., 1963; (with P.L. Agnew and J.R. Meehan) Clerical Office Practice, 4th ed., 1967; (with N.J. Cornelia and P.L. Agnew) Office Machines Course: Adding and Calculating Machines, 1971, (with N.J. Cornelia) 5th ed., 1979; Duplicating Machine Processes, 1971; (with J.R. Meehan and M.E. Oliverio) Secretarial Office Procedures, 8th ed., 1972, (with M.E. Oliverio) 10th ed., 1982; (with J.R. Meehan and M.E. Oliverio) Clerical Office Procedures, 5th ed., 1973, 7th ed., 1983; (ed. with D. Kilchenstein) Individualized Instruction in Business and Office Education, 1973; (with N.J. Cornelia) Ten-Key Adding-Listing Machine Course, 1974; Electronic and Mechanical Printing Calculator Course, 1974, 4th ed., 1991; Electronic Display Calculator, 1975; Machine Transcription Word Processing, 1979; Electronic Calculating Machines Simulation, 1982; Procedures for the Modern Office, 1983; Electronic Display/Printing Calculator, 1983; Reprographics, 1984; (with J. Willis) SuperCalc 3, 1986; (with J. Willis) Working with SuperCalc 4, 1987; Electronic Office Machines, 6th ed., 1987; (co-author) The Office: Procedures and Technology, 1988, 2nd ed., 1993; Electronic Printing Calculator, 1990; Calculating Machines Simulation, 1991; Electronic Calculators, 2nd ed., 1992; Calculator Math for Job and Personal Use, 1992; Microsoft Works: Tutorial and Applications, IBM Version, 1991, Macintosh Version, 1992; Ten-Key Skill Builder, 1992; PFS: First Publisher: Tutorial and Applications, 1993; Publish It!, Apple Versions 3.0 and 4.0, 1993, IBM Version 2.0, 1993; Microsoft Works for Windows, 1994; Microsoft Works for Windows 3.0 Tutorial and Applications, 1994 Express Publisher Tutorial and Applications, 1994; Microsoft Works DOS 3.0 Quick Course, 1994; Microsoft Works DOS versions 2.0 and 3.0 Applications for Reinforcement, 1995; Microsoft Works WIN 3.0 Quick Course, 1995; Microsoft Works Macintosh 4.0 Quick Course, 1995; Machine Transcription Document Production, 1995; Microsoft Office 4.3 for Windows 3.1 Tutorial and Applications, 1996; Microsoft Office for Windows 95, 1996; Microsoft Works 4.0 for Windows 95 Quick Course, 1996; Microsoft Works for Windows 95 Quick Course, 1996; Microsoft Works for Windows 95 Tutorial and Applications, 1996; Microsoft Works versions 2.0 and 3.0 for Windows Applications for Reinforcement, 1995; Microsoft Works Versions 3.0 and 4.0 for Macintosh Applications for Reinforcement, 1996; Microsoft Works for Windows 95 Applications for Reinforcement, 1996; Pagemaker 5.0 for Windows and Macintosh QuickTorial, 1996; Pagemaker 6.0 for Windows 95 and Macintosh QuickTorial, 1996; Machine Transcription for Document Processing, 1997; Microcomputer Office Applications, 1997; Microsoft Office for Windows 97, 1997; Microsoft Works for Windows 95 version 4.5, 1998; ClarisWorks, Macintosh Tutorial and Applications, 4.0, 1996, 5.0, 1998; Calculators: Printing and Display, 1998; Calculating Machines Simulation, 1999; Microsoft Office 2000 Introductory, 1999; Microsoft Works for Windows 2000, 2000; Machine Transcription and Dictation, 2000; Microsoft Office for Windows XP, 2000; Microsoft Office Applications Introductory, 2003, Supplements for Office 2000, 2003; Microsoft Office Applications Advanced, Supplements for Office 2000, XP, 2003; Microsoft Office 2003, Introductory, 2004; Understanding Corporate Annual Reports, 5th ed., 2004, 6th ed. as Understanding Corporate Annual Reports: A Financial Analysis Project, 2007; Microsoft Office 2003, Basics, 2004. Contributor of articles to journals. **Address:** Area of Accounting, Rawls College of Business, Texas Tech University, Rm. 411, 15th St., Flint Ave., PO Box 42101, Lubbock, TX 79409-2101, U.S.A. **Online address:** w.pasewark@ttu.edu

PASHKOW, Fredric J. American (born United States), b. 1945. **Genres:** Medicine/Health, How-to Books, Education. **Career:** University of Colorado, clinical fellow in cardiology, clinical associate professor of cardiology, Fellows Teaching Clinic, staff; University of Chicago, intern, resident in internal medicine and in cardiology; consultant in internal medicine, 1976-88; Cleveland Clinic Foundation, adjunct staff, Division of Education, vice chair, Exercise Testing Laboratories, Cardiac Consultation Service, Preventive Cardiology Program, director, 1988-99; University of Hawaii, John A. Burns School of Medicine, professor, Queens Medical Center, Heart Institute, medical director, 1999-2003; vice president of U.S. medical affairs, through 2006; Cardax Pharmaceuticals, executive vice president and chief medical officer, 2006-. Writer. **Publications:** (With P. Pashkow, M. Schafer and C. Ferguson) Successful Cardiac Rehabilitation: The Complete Guide for Building Cardiac Rehab Programs, 1988; (ed. with W.A. Dafoe) Clinical Cardiac Rehabilitation: A Cardiologist's Guide, 1993, 2nd ed., 1999; (with C. Libov) The Woman's Heart Book: The Complete Guide to Keeping Your Heart Healthy and What to Do If Things Go Wrong, 1993; (with C. Libov) 50 Essential Things to Do When the Doctor Says It's Heart Disease, 1995; (ed. with W.A. Dafoe) Clinical Cardiac Rehabilitation: A Cardiologist's Guide, 1999. Contributor to medical journals. **Address:** Cardax Pharmaceuticals, 2800 Woodlawn Dr., Honolulu, HI 96822, U.S.A. **Online address:** fpashkow@cardaxpharma.com

PASHMAN, Susan. American (born United States), b. 1942. **Genres:** Novels, Essays, Young Adult Fiction. **Career:** Adelphi University, instructor in philosophy, 1966-78; New York State Council for the Humanities, director of humanities project, 1977-79; attorney, 1985-91; Public Access Continuing Education, director, 1992-; Vermont Studio Center, writer-in-residence, 1995; Djerassi Resident Artists Program, writer-in-residence, 1997; Virginia Center for the Creative Arts, writer-in-residence, 1999-. Writer. **Publications:** NOVEL: The Speed of Light, 1997. Contributor to periodicals. Works appear in anthologies. **Address:** c/o Carolyn Krupp, Julian Bach Literary Agency, 22 East 71st St., New York, NY 10021, U.S.A.

PASICK, Robert. American (born United States), b. 1946. **Genres:** Self Help. **Career:** Hawthorn Center, director of early intervention service, 1975-80; Ann Arbor Center for the Family, psychologist, director of research and training, 1980-2000; executive coach, 1995-; Ford Motor Co., executive; Michigan Bank, chief executive officer; Small Pharmaceutical Co., chief executive officer; Japanese Medical Device Co., chief executive officer; University of Michigan, Ross School of Business, William Davidson Institute, executive education faculty, 1998-, faculty affiliate, 2003-; Leaders Connect, founder and president; CEO Connect, founder and president. Writer. **Publications:** (With R.L. Meth) Men in Therapy, 1990; Awakening from the Deep Sleep, 1992; What Every Man Needs to Know, 1994; Conversations with My Old Dog, 2000; Pet Loss, 2002. Contributor of articles to periodicals. **Address:** Stephen M. Ross School of Business, University of Michigan, 701 Tappan

St., Ann Arbor, MI 48109-1234, U.S.A. **Online address:** rpasick@umich.edu

PASLES, Paul C. American (born United States), b. 1968. **Genres:** Mathematics/Statistics. **Career:** Villanova University, associate professor of mathematics. Writer and mathematician. **Publications:** Benjamin Franklin's Numbers: An Unsung Mathematical Odyssey, 2008. Contributor to periodicals. **Address:** Department of Mathematics and Statistics, Villanova University, 800 Lancaster Ave., Villanova, PA 19085, U.S.A. **Online address:** paul.pasles@villanova.edu

PASQUARELLO, Michael. American (born United States), b. 1951?. **Genres:** Theology/Religion. **Career:** United Methodist Church, pastor, 1983-2001; Asbury Theological Seminary, School of Biblical Interpretation and Proclamation, associate professor of preaching, 2001-, professor, Granger E. and Anna A. Fisher professor of preaching. Writer. **Publications:** (Ed. with J.B. Green) Narrative Reading, Narrative Preaching: Reuniting New Testament Interpretation and Proclamation, 2003; Sacred Rhetoric: Preaching as a Theological and Pastoral Practice of the Church, 2005; Christian Preaching: A Trinitarian Theology of Proclamation, 2006; We Speak Because We Have First Been Spoken, 2009; John Wesley, 2010. **Address:** Asbury Theological Seminary, 204 N Lexington Ave., Wilmore, KY 40390, U.S.A.

PASSARELLA, J. G. *See* **GANGEMI, Joseph G.**

PASSARO, Maria (C. Pastore). American/Italian (born Italy), b. 1943. **Genres:** Literary Criticism And History, Translations. **Career:** Mamaroneck Schools, curriculum specialist, 1978-81; City University of New York, Herbert H. Lehman College, adjunct professor, 1981-88; Fordham University, adjunct professor, 1981-88; Yonkers Public School, instructor, 1988-89; Central Connecticut State University, Department of Modern Languages, assistant professor, 1989-94, associate professor, 1994-99, professor, 1999-. Writer and translator. **Publications:** Representation of Women in Medieval and Renaissance Texts, 2005. TRANSLATOR: (and intro.) T. Tasso, King Torrismondo, 1997; Selected Writings of Girolamo Savonarola: Religion and Politics, 1490-1498, 2006; T. Tasso, Rhymes of Love 2011. TRANSLATOR INTO ITALIAN: J. Tusiani, Gente Mia e Altre Poesie, 1982; J.W. Longfellow, Michelangelo, 1986; J. Tusiani, Mallo e Gheriglio e La Quinta Stagione, 1986. Contributor of articles to books and periodicals. **Address:** Department of Modern Languages, Central Connecticut State University, Rm. LD 208, 1516 Stanley St., New Britain, CT 06050, U.S.A. **Online address:** passaro@ccsu.edu

PASSERON, Jean Claude. French (born France), b. 1930. **Genres:** Philosophy, Social Sciences, Sociology, Education, Reference. **Career:** Sorbonne, assistant professor of sociology, 1961-65; University of Nantes, maitre de conferences, 1965-68; Paris-VIII Vincennes, Department of Sociology, head, 1969-75; Center National Recherche Scientifique, director of research, 1975-80, scientific consultant, 1982-85; Ecole des Hautes Etudesen Sciences Sociales, professor, 1984-, director of studies; Conseil Scientifique de l'Observatoire de la Vie Etudiante, center for sociological research, head, 1985-96, president; Mediterranean Institute of Research and Creation, founder, 1986, director, 1986-92; Enquete: histoire, sociolgie, anthropoligie, director, 1994-. Writer and translator. **Publications:** IN ENGLISH TRANSLATION: (with P. Bourdieu) Les HâcRitiers: LesâcTudiants Et La Culture, Editions de Minuit, 1966, trans. as (with P. Bourdieu) The Inheritors, 1979; (with C. Grignon) Etudes de cas sur l'innovation dans l'enseignement superieur, trans. as (with C. Grignon) French Experience Before 1968, 1970; (with Bourdieu and J.C. Chamboredon) Le Metier de sociologue: Prealables Epistemologiques, 1968, 5th ed., 2005, trans. as The Craft of Sociology, 1991; (with Bourdieu) La Reproduction; éléments pour unethéorie du système d'enseignement, 1970, trans. as Reproduction in Education, Society and Culture, 1977; (with Bourdieu and M. de Saint Martin) Academic Discourse, 1994; (co-author) Academic Discourse: Linguistic Misunderstanding and Professorial Power, 1996. IN FRENCH: (with G. Antoine) La réforme de l'Universite, 1966; (ed. with R. Castel) éducation, développement et démocratie, Algérie, Espagne, France, Gréce, Hongrie, Italie, Pays arabes, Yougoslavie, 1967; Métier de sociologue, 1968; Les mots de lasociologie, 1980; (co-author) L'ceil à la page: enqueête sur lesimages et les bibliothèques, 1984; (with C. Grignon) Le savant et lepopulaire, 1989; Le Raisonnement sociologique, 1991; (contrib. with P.M. Menger) L'art de la recherche, melanges en l'honneur de R. Moulin, 1994; (ed. with L.A. Gerard-Varet) Modèle et l'enqueête: les usages duprincipe de rationalité dans les sciences sociales, 1995; (with J.P. Grossein) Sociologie des religions de Max Weber, 1996; (comp.) Richard Hoggart en France, 1999; Goût de l'enquête, 2001; (with P. Bourdieu) Los Herederos, 2003; (with J. Revel) Qu'est-ce qu'une discipline, 2006. OTHERS: (ed.) Les étudiants et leurs études, 1964; (with P. Bourdieu and M.S. Martin) Rapport pédagogique et communication, 1965; Penser par cas, 2005; (with J. Revel) Les arts moyens aujourd'hui: actes du colloque international d'Albi, 30-31 mars, 1er avril 2006. Contributor to books and periodicals. **Address:** Ecole des Hautes Etudes, en Sciences Sociales-Marseille, 2 rue de la Charite, Marseille, 13002, France. **Online address:** jean-claude.passeron@univmed.fr

PASSET, Joanne E. American (born United States), b. 1954. **Genres:** Women's Studies And Issues, Sex. **Career:** University of California, Graduate School of Library and Information Science, assistant professor, 1988-90; Indiana University, School of Library and Information Science, assistant professor, 1990-94; Bluffton College, director of libraries, 1998-2000; Dominican University, associate professor of library and information science, 2000-01; Indiana University East, School of Humanities and Social Sciences, assistant professor of history, 2001-, professor of history, Indiana Association of Historians, president, 2004-05. Writer. **Publications:** Cultural Crusaders: Women Librarians in the American West, 1900-1917, 1994; (with M.N. Maack) Aspirations and Mentoring in an Academic Environment, 1994; Sex Radicals and the Quest for Women's Equality, 2003; Sex Variant Woman: The Life of Jeannette Howard Foster, 2008. Contributor to periodicals. **Address:** School of Humanities & Social Sciences, Indiana University, Tom Raper Hall 270, 2325 Chester Blvd., Richmond, IN 47374-1289, U.S.A. **Online address:** jpasset@indiana.edu

PASTAN, Linda. American (born United States), b. 1932. **Genres:** Poetry, inspirational/Motivational Literature, Essays, Literary Criticism And History. **Career:** American University, instructor; Breadloaf Writers Conference, lecturer. Writer. **Publications:** POETRY: A Perfect Circle of Sun, 1971; On the Way to the Zoo: Poems, 1975; Aspects of Eve: Poems, 1975; The Five Stages of Grief, 1978; Selected Poems of Linda Pastan, 1979; Setting the Table: Poems, 1980; Even as We Sleep, 1980; Waiting for My Life: Poems, 1981; PM/AM: New and Selected Poems, 1983; A Fraction of Darkness: Poems, 1985; The Imperfect Paradise: Poems, 1988; Heroes in Disguise: Poems, 1991; An Early Afterlife: Poems, 1995; Carnival Evening: New and Selected Poems 1968-1998, 1998; The Last Uncle: Poems, 2002; Queen of a Rainy Country, 2006; Traveling Light: Poems, 2011. Contributor to periodicals. **Address:** 11710 Beall Mountain Rd., Potomac, MD 20854, U.S.A. **Online address:** lpastan@att.net

PASTAN, Rachel. American (born United States) **Genres:** Novels. **Career:** Swarthmore College, writing instructor; Bennington Writing Seminars, writing instructor; Edgewood College, writing instructor; Writers' Place, writing instructor. Novelist and educator. **Publications:** This Side of Married (novel), 2004; Lady of the Snakes (novel), 2008. Contributor to periodicals. **Address:** Philadelphia, PA , U.S.A. **Online address:** rachelpastan@yahoo.com

PASTI, Umberto. Italian (born Italy) **Genres:** Writing/Journalism, Translations. **Career:** Writer. **Publications:** (Trans.) Marcel Proust's Letters to His Mother, 1986; L'Età Fiorita, 2000; Accademia del dottor Pastiche, 2008; Più felice del mondo, 2011. Contributor to periodicals. **Address:** c/o Author Mail, Pushkin Press, 12 Chester Terr., London, GL NW1 4ND, England.

PASTOR, Ben. American/Italian (born Italy), b. 1950. **Genres:** Novels. **Career:** Norwich University, associate professor of graduate studies. Writer. **Publications:** Lumen, 1999; Liar Moon, 2001; The Water Thief, 2007; The Fire Waker, 2008; (co-author) Camicie rosse, storie nere: tredici giallisti per mille garibaldini, 2011. Contributor of articles to periodicals. **Address:** School of Graduate and Continuing Studies, Norwich University, 158 Harmon Dr., Northfield, VT 05663-1000, U.S.A. **Online address:** info@benpastor.com

PASTORE, Christopher. American (born United States), b. 1975. **Genres:** Sports/Fitness, Archaeology/Antiquities. **Career:** New School for Social Research, creative writing faculty. Writer. **Publications:** Temple to the Wind: The Story of America's Greatest Naval Architect and His Masterpiece, Reliance, 2005. Contributor to periodicals. **Address:** Lyons Press, PO Box 480, Guilford, CT 06437-0480, U.S.A.

PASTORELLO, Karen. American (born United States), b. 1956. **Genres:** History, Biography. **Career:** State University of New York, Tompkins Cortland Community College, professor of history, 1990-, women and gender studies chair. Writer and historian. **Publications:** A Power among Them:

Bessie Abramowitz Hillman and the Making of the Amalgamated Clothing Workers of America, 2008. **Address:** Tompkins Cortland Community College, State University of New York, 170 North St., PO Box 139, Dryden, NY 13053, U.S.A.

PATE, J'Nell L(aVerne). American (born United States), b. 1938. **Genres:** History, Local History/Rural Topics, Military/Defense/Arms Control, Biography. **Career:** Teacher, 1960-67; Tarrant County Junior College, part-time instructor, 1968-72, assistant professor, associate professor, professor of history, 1972-2000, professor emeritus, 2000-. Writer and historian. **Publications:** Livestock Legacy: The Fort Worth Stockyards, 1887-1987, 1988; (ed.) Document Sets for Texas and the Southwest in U.S. History, 1991; Ranald Slidell Mackenzie: Brave Cavalry Colonel, 1994; North of the River: A Brief History of North Fort Worth, 1994; Hazel Vaughn Leigh and the Fort Worth Boys' Club, 2000; America's Historic Stockyards: Livestock Hotels, 2005; From Syria to Seminole: Memoir of a High Plains Merchant, 2006; Fort Worth Stockyards, 2009; Texas Sesqicentennial Wagon Train, 2011; Arsenal of Defense: Fort Worth's Military Legacy, 2011. Works appear in anthologies. Contributor to periodicals. **Address:** 1104 Carpenter St., Azle, TX 76020-3312, U.S.A. **Online address:** jnellpate@charter.net

PATEL, Eboo. American (born United States), b. 1975?. **Genres:** Biography, Social Sciences. **Career:** Interfaith Youth Core (IFYC), founder and president, 1998-, executive director; Ashoka, Ashoka fellow. Writer and educator. **Publications:** (Ed. with P. Brodeur) Building the Interfaith Youth Movement: Beyond Dialogue to Action, 2006; Acts of Faith: The Story of an American Muslim, the Struggle for the Soul of a Generation, 2007. **Address:** Interfaith Youth Core, 910 W Van Buren St., 4th Fl., Chicago, IL 60607, U.S.A. **Online address:** eboo@ifyc.org

PATEL, Raj. American/British (born England), b. 1972?. **Genres:** Agriculture/Forestry, Business/Trade/Industry, Marketing. **Career:** World Bank, staff; World Trade Organization, staff; United Nations, staff; University of KwaZulu-Natal, School of Development Studies, research associate. Writer. **Publications:** Promised Land: Competing Visions of Agrarian Reform, 2006; Stuffed and Starved: Markets, Power and the Hidden Battle for the World Food System, 2007 in US as Stuffed and Starved: The Hidden Battle for the World Food System, 2008; (with E. Holt-Gimenez and A. Shattuck) Food Rebellions! Crisis and the Hunger for Justice, 2009; The Value of Nothing: How to Reshape Market Society and Redefine Democracy, 2009. **Address:** Berkeley, CA , U.S.A. **Online address:** stuffedandstarved@gmail.com

PATENAUDE, Bertrand M. American (born United States), b. 1956. **Genres:** History. **Career:** Naval Postgraduate School, Department of National Security Affairs, lecturer, 1992-2000; Stanford University, Hoover Institution, research fellow. Writer. **Publications:** (Ed. with A. Dallin) Soviet Scholarship under Gorbachev, 1988; (ed. and intro.) The Russian Revolution, 1992; (ed. and intro. with A. Dallin) Stalin and Stalinism, 1992; (ed., intro. and comp. with T. Emmons) War, Revolution, and Peace in Russia: The Passages of Frank Golder, 1914-1927, 1992; The Big Show in Bololand: The American Relief Expedition to Soviet Russia in the Famine of 1921, 2002; A Wealth of Ideas: Revelations from the Hoover Institution Archives, 2006; Stalin's Nemesis: The Exile and Murder of Leon Trotsky, 2009 in US as Trotsky: Downfall of a Revolutionary, 2010. Contributor to journals and periodicals. **Address:** Hoover Institution, Stanford University, 434 Galvez Mall, Stanford, CA 94305-6010, U.S.A.

PATEREK, Josephine. American (born United States), b. 1916. **Genres:** Plays/Screenplays, Fash Ion/Costume, Theatre, Social Sciences, History. **Career:** Substitute art teacher, 1941-43; University of Minnesota, instructor in communications, 1955-60; KUOM-Radio, program host, 1956; University of Wisconsin, assistant professor, professor of English, speech and theater, 1961-78, professor emeritus, 1978-; KTCA-TV, communications teacher, 1963-67; WRFW-Radio, program host, 1970-75; State Service for Blind, reader, 1982-92; Clark College, teacher, 2000. Writer. **Publications:** Costuming for the Theatre, 1959; Benjy and the Gillygoo: Three Plays for Children, 1983; The Encyclopedia of American Indian Costume, 1994. **Address:** 5801 NE 119th St., Vancouver, WA 98686-3447, U.S.A.

PATERSON, Alistair (Ian Hughes). New Zealander (born New Zealand), b. 1929. **Genres:** Novels, Poetry, Novellas/Short Stories. **Career:** Royal New Zealand Navy, career officer, 1954-74, senior instructor officer aboard H.M.N.Z.S. Philomel, 1970-74; New Zealand Police Department, dean of general studies, 1974-78; New Zealand Education Department, continuing education officer, 1979-89; Poetry New Zealand, editor, 1994-; New Zealand Order of Merit for Services to Literature, officer, 2007-. Writer. **Publications:** Caves in the Hills: Selected Poems, 1965; Birds Flying: Poems, 1973; Cities & Strangers, 1976; The Toledo Room: A Poem for Voices, 1978; Qu'appelle, 1982; The New Poetry, 1982; Odysseus Rex, 1986; Incantations for Warriors, 1987; How to Be a Millionaire by Next Wednesday (novel), 1994; Summer on the Coted' Azur, 2003. EDITOR: 15 Contemporary New Zealand Poets, 1980; Short Stories from New Zealand, 1988. **Address:** 34B Methuen Rd., Avondale, Auckland, 0600, New Zealand. **Online address:** alstair@iconz.co.nz

PATERSON, Janet M. Canadian/Swiss (born Switzerland), b. 1944. **Genres:** Literary Criticism And History, Biography, History, Young Adult Fiction, Translations. **Career:** University of Toronto, Department of French, professor of French, 1981-, chairperson for graduate studies, 1991-95, associate dean for humanities, 1996-98, Department of French, chairperson, 1998-, Innis College, principal. Writer. **Publications:** Anne Hébert: Architexture Romanesque, 1985; Moments Postmodernes dans le Roman Québécois, 1990; (with M. Randall) Hubert Aquin: Trou de Memoire (critical edition), 1993; Anne Hébert en Revue, 2006. EDITOR: (with J. Lennox) Challenges, Projects, Texts: Canadian Editing, 1993; (with J. Cotnam) La Didactique À l'oeuvre: Perspectives Théoriques et Pratiques, 1995; Sexuation, Espace, écriture: La Littérature Québécoise en Transformation, 2002. **Address:** Department of French, University of Toronto, 2 Sussex Ave., Toronto, ON M5S 1J5, Canada.

PATERSON, Katherine (Womeldorf). American/Chinese (born China), b. 1932. **Genres:** Children's Fiction, Children's Non-fiction, Literary Criticism And History, Translations, History, Picture/Board Books, Young Adult Nonfiction, Novels, Plays/Screenplays. **Career:** Lovettsville Elementary School, teacher, 1954-55; Pennington School for Boys, master of sacred studies and English, 1963-65; Messiah College, Boyer Center, distinguished professional-in-residence, 2002. Writer. **Publications:** HISTORICAL FICTION FOR CHILDREN AND YOUNG ADULTS: The Sign of the Chrysanthemum, 1973; Of Nightingales That Weep, 1974; The Master Puppeteer, 1975; Rebels of the Heavenly Kingdom, 1983; Lyddie, 1991; (ed. with A. Durell and J.C. George) The Big Book for Our Planet, 1993; Jip: His Story, 1996; Parzival: The Quest of the Grail Knight, 1998; Preacher's Boy, 1999. CONTEMPORARY REALISTIC FICTION FOR CHILDREN AND YOUNG ADULTS: Bridge to Terabithia, 1977; The Great Gilly Hopkins, 1978; Jacob Have I Loved, 1980; Come Sing, Jimmy Jo, 1985; Park's Quest, 1988; Flip-flop Girl, 1994; The Same Stuff as Stars, 2002. MARVIN SERIES FOR BEGINNING READERS: The Smallest Cow in the World, 1988, new ed., 1991; Marvin's Best Christmas Present Ever, 1997; Marvin One Too Many, 2001. FOR CHILDREN AND YOUNG ADULTS: Angels and Other Strangers: Family Christmas Stories, 1979; Star of Night: Stories for Christmas, 1980; (with J. Paterson) Consider the Lilies: Plants of the Bible, 1986; (trans.) The Tongue-cut Sparrow, 1987; (co-author) The World in 1492, 1992; A Midnight Clear: Stories for the Christmas Season, 1995; The Angel and the Donkey, 1996; Celia and the Sweet, Sweet Water, 1998; (with J. Paterson) Images of God: Views of the Invisible, 1998; Più bel regalo di Marco, 1998; The Wide-awake Princess, 2000; Katherine Paterson Treasury, 2001; The Field of the Dogs, 2001; (co-author) Acting Out, 2008; Read for Your Life, vol. I-II, IV-VIII, 2010, vol. XI-XIII, XV-XVI, 2011. RELIGIOUS EDUCATION MATERIALS FOR CHILDREN: To Make Men Free, 1973; Justice for All People, 1973; Who Am I? 1992. NON FICTION FOR ADULTS: Gates of Excellence: On Reading and Writing Books for Children, 1981; The Spying Heart: More Thoughts on Reading and Writing Books for Children, 1989; Stick to Reality and a Dream: Celebrating America's Young Readers: A Lecture for the Year of the Young Reader, 1990; The Tale of the Mandarin Ducks, 1990; A Sense of Wonder: On Reading and Writing Books for Children, 1995; The Invisible Child: On Reading and Writing Books for Children, 2000; The Tale of Jemima Puddle-Duck, 2002. OTHERS: The King's Equal, 1992; (with J. Paterson) Blueberries for the Queen, 2004; Bread and Roses, Too, 2006; (afterword) Best Shorts: Favorite Short Stories for Sharing, 2006; Light of the World: The Life of Jesus for Children, 2008; The Day of the Pelican, 2009; (with J. Paterson) Flint Heart, 2011; Brother Sun, Sister Moon, 2011; Under the Spell of the Moon, 2012. Contributor of articles to periodicals. **Address:** Clarion Books, 215 Park Ave. S, New York, NY 10003-1603, U.S.A.

PATERSON, Ronald (William Keith). British/Scottish (born Scotland), b. 1933. **Genres:** Education, Philosophy, Biography, Paranormal, Theology/Religion, Ethics, Literary Criticism And History, Young Adult Fiction, Young

Adult Fiction. **Career:** Bromsgrove College of Further Education, assistant lecturer, 1958-59; University of Manchester, Holly Royde College, Department of Extra-Mural Studies, staff tutor, 1959-61; University of Hull, lecturer, senior lecturer in philosophy, 1962-94. Writer. **Publications:** The Nihilistic Egoist: Max Stirner, 1971; Values, Education, and the Adult, 1979; Philosophy and the Belief in a Life after Death, 1995; The New Patricians: An Essay on Values and Consciousness, 1998. Contributor of articles and reviews. **Address:** 292 Cottingham Rd., Hull, HU6 8QA, England.

PATEY, Douglas Lane. American (born United States), b. 1952. **Genres:** Literary Criticism And History, Essays, Biography, History, Education. **Career:** Smith College, assistant professor, 1979-85, associate professor, 1985-91, professor, 1991-2003, Sophia Smith professor of English language and literature, 2003-. Writer. **Publications:** Probability and Literary Form: Philosophic Theory and Literary Practice in the Augustan Age, 1984; (ed. with T. Keegan) Augustan Studies: Essays in Honor of Irvin Ehrenpreis, 1985; The Life of Evelyn Waugh: A Critical Biography, 1998; (ed.) Of Human Bondage: Historical Perspectives on Addiction, 2003; Imitation and the Transmission of Culture: The Emergence of the Modern Division Between the Arts and the Sciences, forthcoming. **Address:** Department of English Language & Literature, Smith College, 3/09 Neilson Library, 7 Elm St., Northampton, MA 01063-6304, U.S.A. **Online address:** dpatey@smith.edu

PATIN, Thomas A. American (born United States), b. 1958. **Genres:** Art/Art History, Adult Non-fiction, Natural History, Social Sciences. **Career:** Cornish College for the Arts, instructor in art history, 1989-91; University of Washington, instructor in writing, 1991-92; Western Washington University, visiting lecturer in art history, 1992-93; University of Washington, Writing Center, director, 1993-94; Ohio University, assistant professor of art history, theory and criticism, 1995-2007, Graduate Certificate Program in Critical Cultural Studies, director, 1997-2007, co-director of art in France program, 1997; Northern Arizona University, College of Arts and Letters, professor of art history, 2007-, School of Art, director, 2007-. Writer. **Publications:** (With J.McLerran) Artwords: A Glossary of Contemporary Art Theory, 1997; Discipline and Varnish: Rhetoric, Subjectivity and Counter-Memory in the Museum, 1999; (ed.) Observation Points: The Visual Poetics of National Parks, 2012; Techniques of the Subject: Art History, the Order of Things and Subjectivity, forthcoming; Savage Graces in the Museum: Indians, Museums and the Re/Presentation of Ethnicity, forthcoming; How to Do Things with Signs, forthcoming; Naturalizing Rhetoric: Environmental Politics and the Visual Poetics of National Parks, Monuments and Wilderness Areas, forthcoming; Nature's Masterpiece; Naturalizing Culture in the National Parks, forthcoming. Contributor to books and periodicals. **Address:** College of Arts and Letters, Northern Arizona University, 212 Fine and Performing Arts Bldg., PO Box 5064, Flagstaff, AZ 86011, U.S.A. **Online address:** tom.patin@nau.edu

PATNEAUDE, David. American (born United States), b. 1944. **Genres:** Children's Fiction, Young Adult Fiction, Mystery/Crime/Suspense, Science Fiction/Fantasy, Social Commentary. **Career:** Writer. **Publications:** Someone Was Watching, 1993; Dark, Starry Morning: Stories of this World and Beyond, 1995; The Last Man's Reward, 1996; Framed in Fire, 1999; Haunting at Home Plate, 2000; Colder Than Ice, 2003; Thin Wood Walls, 2004; Deadly Drive, 2005, Piece of the Sky, 2007; Epitaph Road, 2010; Caught in the Wake, forthcoming. **Address:** 12606 NE 166th Ct., Woodinville, WA 98072, U.S.A. **Online address:** david@patneaude.com

PATON, Priscilla. American (born United States), b. 1952. **Genres:** Children's Fiction. **Career:** University of Texas, lecturer in English, 1982-83; Texas A&M University, assistant professor of English, 1986-93; Florida Atlantic University, assistant professor of English, 1994-97; Luther College, assistant professor of English, 1997-; Denison University, associate professor of English. Writer. **Publications:** Howard and the Sitter Surprise, 1996; Abandoned New England: Landscape in the Works of Homer, Frost, Hopper, Wyeth, and Bishop, 2003. Contributor to periodicals. **Address:** Denison University, 100 W College St., Granville, OH 43023, U.S.A. **Online address:** paton@denison.edu

PATRICK, James. *See* **PRELLER, James.**

PATRICK, Jennifer. American (born United States), b. 1965?. **Genres:** Novels. **Career:** Small Craft Warnings, staff; University of Georgia, financial aid counselor and program specialist, 1992-, academic adviser, 2003-, Center for Counseling and Testing, therapist; Franklin College of Arts and Science, academic advisor. Writer. **Publications:** The Night She Died (novel), 2004. Contributor to periodicals. **Address:** c/o Author Mail, Soho Press Inc., 853 Broadway, New York, NY 10003, U.S.A. **Online address:** jlpatrick@franklin.uga.edu

PATRICK, Jim. American (born United States) **Genres:** Documentaries/Reportage, Local History/Rural Topics, Marine Sciences/Oceanography, Romance/Historical. **Career:** Nantucket Short Play Festival and Competition, founder. Writer. **Publications:** (With R. Benchley) Scallop Season: A Nantucket Chronicle, 2002. **Address:** c/o Autopscot Press, PO Box 600, Siasconset, MA 02564, U.S.A.

PATRICK, Maxine. *See* **MAXWELL, Patricia Anne.**

PATRICK, Robert. American (born United States), b. 1937. **Genres:** Plays/Screenplays, Novels, Gay And Lesbian Issues, Novellas/Short Stories, Film. **Career:** Old Reliable Theatre, playwright-in-residence, 1967-71; Astrology Magazine, feature editor, 1971-72. **Publications:** Golden Circle: A Fantastic Farce: A Two Act Play, 1970; Robert Patrick's Cheap Theatricks!, 1972; Play-by-Play: A Spectacle of Ourselves, 1975; Kennedy's Children, 1975; One Man, One Woman: Six One Act Plays, 1978; My Cup Ranneth Over, 1979; Mutual Benefit Life, 1979; T-Shirts, 1979; Mercy Drop and Other Plays, 1980; Michelangelo's Models, 1983; Judas, 1984; Untold Decades: Seven Comedies of Gay Romance, 1988; Temple Slave (novel), 1994. **Address:** 1837 N Alexandria Ave., Ste. 211, Los Angeles, CA 90027, U.S.A. **Online address:** rbrtptrck@aol.com

PATRICK, Susan. *See* **LORRIMER, Claire.**

PATRON, Susan. American (born United States), b. 1948. **Genres:** Children's Fiction, Children's Non-fiction, Picture/Board Books, Young Adult Fiction. **Career:** Los Angeles Public Library, children's librarian, 1972-79, senior children's librarian, 1979-2007, now retired. Writer. **Publications:** Burgoo Stew, 1991; Five Bad Boys, Billy Que and the Dustdobbin, 1992; Bobbin Dustdobbin, 1993; Maybe Yes, Maybe No, Maybe Maybe, 1993; Dark Cloud Strong Breeze, 1994; The Higher Power of Lucky, 2006; Lucky Breaks, 2009; Lucky for Good, 2011. Works appear in anthologies. **Address:** Writers House, 21 W 26th St., New York, NY 10010, U.S.A. **Online address:** susanpatron@susanpatron.com

PATT, Richard B. American (born United States), b. 1954. **Genres:** Medicine/Health, Sciences. **Career:** Strong Memorial Hospital, medical director of pain treatment center and founder of cancer pain initiative, 1986-88; University of Texas, Anesthesia Pain Service, director, 1993-, Anderson's Pain and Symptom Management, deputy chief; Patt Center for Cancer Pain and Wellness, president and chief medical officer; Texas Medical Center, Inpatient Services at the Hospice, director. Writer. **Publications:** (With W. Pfisterer) Keywords and Concepts for Anesthesia Boards, 1986; (ed.) Cancer Pain, 1993; (with S. Lang) You Don't Have to Suffer: A Family's Guide to Cancer Pain Management, 1994; (co-ed.) Assessment and Treatment of Cancer Pain, 1998; (with S.S. Lang) The Complete Guide to Relieving Cancer Pain and Suffering, 2004. Works appear in anthologies. **Address:** Patt Center for Cancer Pain & Wellness, 1920 Woodbury Bldg., Houston, TX 77030, U.S.A.

PATTEN, Alan. American/Canadian (born Canada) **Genres:** Politics/Government, Philosophy. **Career:** McGill University, associate professor of political science; University of Exeter, lecturer in politics; Princeton University, Laurance S. Rockefeller visiting fellow, 2001-02, Department of Politics, associate professor of politics, professor of politics, Fund for Canadian Studies, chair, Program in Law and Public Affairs, LAPA Faculty Associate. Writer, political scientist and philosopher. **Publications:** Hegel's Idea of Freedom, 1999; (ed. with W. Kymlicka) Language Rights and Political Theory, 2003; Equal Recognition: The Moral Foundations of Minority Cultural Rights, 2009. Contributor to books and periodicals. **Address:** Department of Politics, Princeton University, 246 Corwin Hall, Princeton, NJ 08544-1012, U.S.A. **Online address:** apatten@princeton.edu

PATTEN, Brian. British (born England), b. 1946. **Genres:** Novels, Children's Fiction, Plays/Screenplays, Poetry, Young Adult Fiction, Novellas/Short Stories, Literary Criticism And History. **Career:** University of California, regents lecturer, 1985; Liverpool University, Royal Society of Litrature, fellow; John Moores University, Royal Society of Litrature, fellow; poet; journalist; gardener; newspaper vendor. **Publications:** Little Johnny's Confession, 1967; (with A. Henri and R. McGough) The Mersey Sound, 1967, rev. ed., 1983; Atomic Adam, 1968; Note to the Hurrying Man: Poems, Winter '66-Summer '68, 1969; Home Coming, 1969; The Elephant and the Flower: Almost Fables, 1970; The Irrelevant Song, 1971, 2nd ed., 1975; Unreliable Nightingale, 1973; Jumping Mouse, 1973; Mr. Moon's Last Case, 1975; The Pig and the Junkle (play), 1975; Vanishing Trick, 1976; Emma's Doll (juvenile), 1976; The Sly Cormorant and the Fishes (juvenile): New Adaptations into Poetry of the Aesop Fables, 1977; Grave Gossip, 1979; Clare's Countryside, 1981; Love Poems, 1981; Blind Love (play), 1982; (with A. Henri and R. McGough) New Volume, 1983; Gargling with Jelly: A Collection of Poems, 1985; Jimmy Tag-along, 1988; Storm Damage, 1988; Gargling with Jelly-The Play, 1988; Thawing Frozen Frogs (comic verse), 1990; Grizzelda Frizzle and Other Stories, 1992; The Magic Bicycle, 1993; Impossible Parents, 1994; The Utter Nutters (comic verse), 1994; Grinning Jack: Selected Poems, 1995; Armada, 1996; Beowulf, a Re-telling, 1999; The Blue and Green Ark: An Alphabet for Planet Earth, 2000; Impossible Parents Go Green, 2000; Juggling with Gerbils (children's poetry), 2000; The Story Giant (novel), 2001; Collected Love Poems, 2007. EDITOR: (with P. Krett) The House that Jack Built: Poems for Shelter, 1973; Gangsters, Ghosts, and Dragonflies, 1981; Clare's Countryside, 1981; The Puffin Book of Twentieth Century Children's Verse, 1991. Contributor to periodicals. **Address:** c/o Rogers Coleridge & White, 20 Powis Mews, London, GL W11 1JN, England.

PATTEN, Chris. British (born England), b. 1944. **Genres:** Politics/Government, History. **Career:** Conservative Research Department, director, 1974-79; British Cabinet Office, junior official, official in the Home Office, 1970-72; personal assistant and political secretary, 1972-74; British Government, member, 1983-92; governor, 1992-97; European commissioner for external relations, 1999-2004; Newcastle University, chancellor, 1999-; Oxford University, chancellor, 2003-. Politician, civil servant, campaign staffer. **Publications:** The Tory Case, 1983; Great Britain and the World: Three Talks at Berkeley, 1990; Letters to Hong Kong, 1997; East and West: China, Power and the Future of Asia, 1998; Conflict Prevention and Peace-Building, 2003; Not Quite the Diplomat: Home Truths About World Affairs, 2005; Cousins and Strangers: America, Britain, and Europe in a New Century, 2006; What Next?: Surviving the Twenty-first Century, 2008. **Address:** Coutts & Co., 440 Strand, London, GL WC2R 0QS, England.

PATTEN, Thomas H. American (born United States), b. 1929. **Genres:** Administration/Management, Industrial Relations, Sociology. **Career:** Ford Motor Co., staff, 1957-65; University of Detroit, College of Commerce and Finance and College of Arts and Sciences, professor of management and sociology, 1965-67; Michigan State University, School of Labor and Industrial Relations, professor of industrial relations and associate director, 1967-; California State Polytechnic University, professor of management and human resources, 1984-, now professor emeritus. Writer. **Publications:** (With M. Lieberman) When School Districts Bargain, 1968; The Foreman: Forgotten Man of Management, 1968; Manpower Planning and the Development of Human Resources, 1971; (ed.) OD: Emerging Dimensions and Concepts: A Collection of Papers, 1973; Bibliography on Compensation Planning and Administration, 1960-74, 1975, 3rd ed. as Bibliography of Compensation Planning and Administration Publications, 1975-1985, 1987; Pay: Employee Compensation and Incentive Plans, 1977; (ed.) Classics of Personnel Management, 1979; Organizational Development through Teambuilding, 1981; (with R.M. Madigan) Compensation Planning and Administration: A Bibliography, 1960-1980, 1981; A Manager's Guide to Performance Appraisal: Pride, Prejudice and the Law of Equal Opportunity, 1982; Fair Pay: The Managerial Challenge of Comparable Job Worth and Job Evaluation, 1988; Exercises for Developing Human Resources Management Skills, 1996. **Address:** Department of Management and Human Resources, California State Polytechnic University, Rm. 279, Bldg. 94, 3801 W Temple Ave., Pomona, CA 91768-2557, U.S.A. **Online address:** thpatten@csupomona.edu

PATTERSON, Amy S. (Amy Stephenson Patterson). American (born United States) **Genres:** Politics/Government, Medicine/Health. **Career:** Indiana University, Department of Political Science, associate instructor; Anderson University, adjunct professor of political science, 1996-97; Elmhurst College, Department of Political Science, assistant professor of political science, 1997-2001, acting chairperson, 1998; Calvin College, associate professor of political science, 2001-. Political scientist, consultant and writer. **Publications:** (ed. and contrib.) The African State and the AIDS Crisis, 2005; The Politics of AIDS in Africa, 2006. Contributor of articles to books and journals. **Address:** Calvin College, 1810 E Beltline Ave. SE, Grand Rapids, MI 49546-5951, U.S.A. **Online address:** apatters@calvin.edu

PATTERSON, Amy Stephenson. *See* **PATTERSON, Amy S.**

PATTERSON, Bradley H. (Bradley Hawkes Patterson). American (born United States), b. 1921. **Genres:** Politics/Government. **Career:** Cranbrook School for Boys, teacher, 1943-45; U.S. Department of State, affiliate, 1945-54; White House staff, deputy cabinet secretary, assistant secretary to the cabinet, 1954-61; Bureau of Budget, management analyst, 1961; U.S. Peace Corps, executive secretary, 1961-62; Office of the Secretary of the Treasury, national security adviser, 1962-64; National War College, affiliate, 1965-66; National Advisory Commission on Selective Service, executive director, 1966-67; National Advisory Council on Economic Opportunity, executive director, 1967-69; White House, special consultant to the President, executive assistant, 1969-74, Presidential Personnel Office, assistant director for operations, 1974-76, President for Native American Programs, special assistant, 1976-77; Brookings Institution, Center for Public Policy Education, fellow, 1977-, senior staff, 1977-88; consultant, 1988-. Writer. **Publications:** (As Bradley Hawkes Patterson) Adam Hawkes, 1608-1672: His Life and Times, 1957; The Ring of Power: The White House Staff and Its Expanding Role in Government, 1988; The White House Staff: Inside the West Wing and Beyond, 2000; To Serve the President: Continuity and Innovation in the White House Staff, 2008. Contributor to periodicals. **Address:** 6705 Pemberton St., Bethesda, MD 20817, U.S.A.

PATTERSON, Bradley Hawkes. *See* **PATTERSON, Bradley H.**

PATTERSON, Dan. American (born United States), b. 1953. **Genres:** History, Military/Defense/Arms Control, Communications/Media, Local History/Rural Topics, History, Design, Photography, Air/Space Topics, Transportation, Documentaries/Reportage. **Career:** Photographer and graphic designer. Writer. **Publications:** Shoo Shoo Baby, 1988; The Lady, 1991; The Soldier, 1992; Mustang, 1995; Lancaster, 1996; Messerschmitt Bf 109, 1996; Spitfire, 1996; (with R. Dick) War and Peace in the Air, 2006; (with R. Dick) 50 Aircraft that Changed the World, 2007; Mock the Week: 1001 Scenes We'd Like, 2008. AVIATION CENTURY SERIES WITH R. DICK: The Early Years, 2003; World War II, 2004; The Golden Age, 2004; (with R. Dick) Aviation Century World War II, 2004; Wings of Change, 2005; (with R. Dick) Aviation Century Wings of Change, 2005. **Address:** c/o Author Mail, Boston Mills Press, 132 Main St., Erin, ON N0B 1T0, Canada. **Online address:** dan@flyinghistory.com

PATTERSON, E. Britt. American (born United States), b. 1954. **Genres:** Criminology/True Crime, Civil Liberties/Human Rights, Social Sciences, Politics/Government. **Career:** Washington County Juvenile Detention Center, house parent, 1976-77; Youth Development Center of Pennsylvania, counselor, 1979-81; Children and Youth Services of Greene County, caseworker, 1981-82; University of Maryland at College Park, Institute of Criminal Justice and Criminology, instructor, 1984-86; National Institute of Justice, research assistant, 1985-87; Florida State University, assistant professor of criminology and criminal justice, 1987-92; Shippensburg State University, assistant professor of criminal justice, 1992, associate professor. Writer. **Publications:** (Ed. with M.J. Lynch and contrib.) Race and Criminal Justice, 1991; (ed. with M.J. Lynch) Justice with Prejudice: Race and Criminal Justice in America, 1996; (ed. with K.K. Childs and M.J. Lynch) Racial Divide, Racial and Ethnic Bias in the Criminal Justice System, 2008. Contributor to journals. Works appear in anthologies. **Address:** Department of Criminal Justice, College of Education and Human Services, Shippensburg University, SPH 313, 1871 Old Main, Shippensburg, PA 17257, U.S.A. **Online address:** ebpatt@ship.edu

PATTERSON, Francine (G.). (Penny Patterson). American (born United States), b. 1947. **Genres:** Animals/Pets, Children's Non-fiction. **Career:** Stanford University, teaching assistant, 1971-74, research assistant, 1974-75, undergraduate research supervisor, 1975-80; Gorilla Foundation, co-founder, president and research director, 1976-; San Jose State University, Department of Anthropology, adjunct research associate and lecturer and Center for Anthropological Research, lecturer, 1982-; University of Santa Clara, adjunct professor of psychology, 1984-; Gorilla Journal, editor-in chief; Center for Cross Cultural Communication, board consultant. **Publications:** (With E. Linden) The Education of Koko, 1981; Koko's Kitten, 1985; Koko's Story,

1987; Koko-Love!: Conversations with a Signing Gorilla, 1999. Contributor to books and periodicals. **Address:** The Gorilla Foundation, PO Box 620530, Woodside, CA 94062, U.S.A. **Online address:** info@koko.org

PATTERSON, George N(eilson). Scottish (born Scotland), b. 1920. **Genres:** International Relations/Current Affairs, Medicine/Health, Theology/Religion, Autobiography/Memoirs. **Career:** Engineer, 1947-50; Journalist, 1950-61; British Broadcasting Corp., host, 1961-63; International Committee for the Study of Group Rights (now Minority Rights Group), co-founder and director; freelance writer, broadcaster and lecturer, 1963-. **Publications:** Tibetan Journey, 1952; Journey with Loshay, 1954; God's Fool, 1954; Up and Down Asia, 1956; Tragic Destiny, 1958; Tibet in Revolt, 1960; Peking versus Delhi, 1964; The Unquiet Frontier, 1964; Christianity in Communist China, 1968; A Fool at Forty: Raid into Tibet, 1970; (with M. Patterson) Addictions Can Be Cured, 1975; (with M. Patterson) Getting off the Hook, 1983; Christianity and Marxism, 1983; (with M. Patterson) The Power Factor, 1987; Requiem for Tibet, 1990; The China Paradox: Christ versus Marx, 1990; (with M. Patterson) The Paradise Factor, 1992; (with M. Patterson) Healing Power: The Lost Dimension, 1992; Patterson of Tibet: Death Throes of a Nation, 1998; Mary Magdalene: The Greatest Love Story Never Told, 2006; Countdown To Armageddon, 2010. Works appear in anthologies. Contributor to magazines and newspapers. **Address:** c/o Author Mail, Curtis Brown Ltd., 10 Astor Pl., New York, NY 10003-6935, U.S.A. **Online address:** patlamegla@sprintmail.com

PATTERSON, Glenn. Irish/British (born England), b. 1961. **Genres:** Novels, Young Adult Non-fiction. **Career:** Arts Council of Northern Ireland, writer in the community, 1989-91; University of East Anglia, writer-in-residence, 1992; University of Cork, writer-in-residence; National University of Ireland, University College, writer-in-residence, 1993-94; Queen's University Belfast, writer-in-residence, 1994-97, lecturer in creative writing; RTE (Irish television network), presenter of the arts review program Black Box, 1995-96; Tinderbox Theatre Co., director. **Publications:** NOVELS: Burning Your Own, 1988; Fat Lad, 1992; Black Night at Big Thunder Mountain, 1995; The International, 1999; Number 5, 2003; That Which Was, 2004; Third Party, 2007; Once Upon a Hill: Love in Troubled Times, 2008. OTHER: Lapsed Protestant, 2006. **Address:** Seamus Heaney Centre For Poetry, Queen's University Belfast, Rm. 01.010, 48 University Rd., Belfast, BT7 1NN, Ireland. **Online address:** glenn.patterson@qub.ac.uk

PATTERSON, Horace L. American (born United States), b. 1947. **Genres:** inspirational/Motivational Literature, Biography, Autobiography/Memoirs, Theology/Religion. **Career:** Pastor of Baptist churches, 1966-67, 1969-74; Mount Canaan Baptist Church, pastor, 1974-; Alabama Institute for the Deaf and Blind, behavior specialist; Rushing Springs School of Theology, president; Talladega College, systematic theology, professor, criminal justice, research specialist, Retired Senior Volunteer Program, director. Writer. **Publications:** Clean but Empty, 1990; Climbing the Sacred Ladder, 1992; When People Do You Wrong, 1996; Unbroken and Unbound: A Life Dedicated to God, Justice and the South, 2002. **Address:** 101 Harrison Dr., Talladega, AL 35160, U.S.A. **Online address:** patterson.horace@aidb.state.al.us

PATTERSON, (Horace) Orlando. Also writes as H. Orlando L. Patterson, H. Orlando Patterson, Horace Orlando Lloyd Patterson. American/Jamaican (born Jamaica), b. 1940. **Genres:** Novels, Sociology, History, Social Commentary. **Career:** University of London, London School of Economics, assistant lecturer in sociology, 1965-67; New Left Review, member of editorial board, 1965-66; University of the West Indies, Department of Sociology, lecturer, 1967-70; Harvard University, visiting lecturer, 1970-71, Allston Burr senior tutor, 1971-73, professor of sociology, 1971-93, acting chairman, 1989-90, John Cowles professor of sociology, 1993-; Cambridge University, Wolfson College, visiting fellow, 1978-79; University of Chicago, visiting professor, 1994-95; American Sociological Review, associate editor, 1989-92; American Sociological Association, chair, 1990-91; American Academy of Political and Social Sciences, Ernest W. Burgess fellow; American Academy of Arts and Sciences, fellow; American Sociological Review, associate editor, 1989-92; American Sociological Association, chair, 1990-91. **Publications:** The Children of Sisyphus, 1964; Children of Sisyphus, 1965; An Absence of Ruins, 1967; The Sociology of Slavery: An Analysis of the Origins, Development, and Structure of Negro Slave Society in Jamaica, 1969; Die the Long Day, 1972; Ethnic Chauvinism: The Reactionary Impulse, 1977; Slavery and Social Death: A Comparative Study, 1982; Freedom, 1991; Freedom in the Making of Western Culture, 1991; (with P. Levine and N. Rush) Earth, Stars, and Writers, 1992; The Ordeal of Integration: Progress and Resentment in America's Racial Crisis, 1998; Rituals of Blood: Consequences of Slavery in Two American Centuries, 1998; Chronology of World Slavery, 1999. **Address:** Department of Sociology, Harvard University, 520 William James Hall, 33 Kirkland St., Cambridge, MA 02138, U.S.A. **Online address:** opatters@fas.harvard.edu

PATTERSON, Horace Orlando Lloyd. *See* **PATTERSON, (Horace) Orlando.**

PATTERSON, H. Orlando. *See* **PATTERSON, (Horace) Orlando.**

PATTERSON, H. Orlando L. *See* **PATTERSON, (Horace) Orlando.**

PATTERSON, Ian. British (born England), b. 1948?. **Genres:** Economics. **Career:** Cambridge University, Queens' College, instructor in English. Writer and translator. **Publications:** (Ed. and trans.) The Theory of the Four Movements, 1996; Guernica and Total War, 2007. **Address:** Cambridge, CB , England. **Online address:** ikp1000@cam.ac.uk

PATTERSON, Jerry L. (Jerry Mumford Patterson). American (born United States), b. 1934. **Genres:** Novels, Plays/Screenplays, Poetry, Young Adult Fiction. **Career:** Rotary Intl., fellow, 1961; State of Arkansas, assistant attorney general, 1962-64; Cumberland Presbyterian Church, minister. Actor and writer. **Publications:** The Delta and Other Poems, 1985; Teacher, Oh Teacher (novel), 1988; One Hundred Prayers for Everyday People, 1993. **Address:** 7007 Whitaker Ave., Van Nuys, CA 91406, U.S.A.

PATTERSON, Jerry Mumford. *See* **PATTERSON, Jerry L.**

PATTERSON, Kevin. Canadian (born Canada), b. 1964. **Genres:** Autobiography/Memoirs, Novels, Young Adult Non-fiction. **Career:** Dalhousie University, resident in internal medicine. Writer and doctor. **Publications:** The Water in Between: A Journey at Sea, 1999; Country of Cold: Stories of Sex and Death, 2003; Consumption: A Novel, 2006; (ed. with J. Warren) Outside the Wire: The War in Afghanistan in the Words of Its Participants, 2007. **Address:** c/o Author Mail, Random House of Canada Ltd., 1 Toronto St., Ste. 300, Toronto, ON M5C 2V6, Canada. **Online address:** contact@outsidethewire.ca

PATTERSON, Martha H. American (born United States), b. 1966. **Genres:** Women's Studies And Issues. **Career:** Carleton College, rhetoric assistant, 1987-88; University of Iowa, General Education Program, writing tutor for athletic student services, 1988-92, teaching assistant, 1990-95, Department of English, visiting assistant professor, 1996-97; Grinnell College, visiting assistant professor, 1997-98; University of Michigan, instructor, 1998-2000; Spring Hill College, assistant professor, 2000-04; McKendree University, associate professor of English, 2004-. Writer. **Publications:** Beyond the Gibson Girl: Reimagining the American New Woman, 1894-1915, 2005; (ed.) American New Woman Revisited: A Reader, 1894-1930, 2008. Contributor of articles to periodicals. **Address:** Department of English, McKendree University, Rm. 206, Carnegie Hall, 701 College Rd., Lebanon, IL 62254, U.S.A. **Online address:** mhpatterson@mckendree.edu

PATTERSON, Michael. British (born England), b. 1939. **Genres:** Theatre, Translations, History, Literary Criticism And History. **Career:** Queen's University, lecturer in German, 1965-70; University College, lecturer in drama, 1970-74; University of Leeds, senior lecturer in drama and theatre arts, 1974-87; University of Ulster, reader in theatre studies, 1987-94; De Montfort University, professor of theatre, 1994-2004, emeritus professor of theatre, 2004-. Writer. **Publications:** German Theatre Today: Post-War Theatre in West and East Germany, Austria and Northern Switzerland, 1976; (ed.) Woyzeck, 1979; The Revolution in German Theatre, 1900-1933, 1981; Peter Stein: Germany's Leading Theatre Director, 1981; The Theatre of Goethe, Schiller, Kleist and Buechner, 1984; (ed. and intro.) The Complete Plays, 1987; The First German Theatre: Schiller, Goethe, Kleist and Buchner in Performance, 1990; German Theatre: A Bibliography, 1996; Strategies of Political Theatre: Post-War British Playwrights, 2003; Oxford Dictionary of Plays, 2005. Contributor to periodicals. **Address:** Department of Performing Arts, De Montfort University, 2.03 CL, 52 1/2 Gateway St., Leicester, LE LE1 9BH, England. **Online address:** mwp@dmu.ac.uk

PATTERSON, Penny. *See* **PATTERSON, Francine (G.).**

PATTERSON, Richard North. American (born United States), b. 1947.

Genres: Novels, Mystery/Crime/Suspense. **Career:** Office of the Attorney General, assistant attorney general, 1971-73; U.S. Securities and Exchange Commission, trial attorney, 1973-75, attorney, 1978-; Berkowitz, Lefkovits & Patrick (law firm), partner in firm, 1975-78; McCotchers, Doyle, Brown & Emersen, partner, 1985-93. Writer. **Publications:** NOVELS: The Lasko Tangent, 1979; The Outside Man: A Novel, 1981; Escape the Night, 1983; Private Screening, 1985; Degree of Guilt, 1993; Eyes of a Child, 1995; Final Judgement, 1995; Caroline Masters, 1995; Silent Witness, 1997; No Safe Place, 1998; Dark Lady, 1999; Protect and Defend: A Novel, 2000; Two Complete Novels, 2002; Balance of Power, 2003; Conviction: A Novel, 2005; Race: A Novel, 2007; Exile: A Novel, 2007; The Spire: A Novel, 2009; Eclipse: A Novel, 2009; In the Name of Honor: A Novel, 2010; Devil's Light: A Novel, 2011; Fall From Grace, 2012. Contributor of articles to periodicals. **Address:** c/o Melanie DeNardo, Henry Holt and Co., 175 5th Ave., New York, NY 10010, U.S.A.

PATTERSON, Sparrow L. American (born United States), b. 1974?. **Genres:** Novels, Sex, Adult Non-fiction. **Career:** Poet, 2000-. **Publications:** Synthetic Bi Products, 2001; Diary of a Suicide Queen, forthcoming. **Address:** c/o Author Mail, Akashic Books, PO Box 1456, New York, NY 10009, U.S.A. **Online address:** sparrow@sparrowcantread.com

PATTERSON, Tiffany Ruby. American (born United States), b. 1946. **Genres:** History. **Career:** State University of New York, Binghamton University, associate professor of history; Hamilton College, associate professor of Africana Studies. Writer. **Publications:** Zora Neale Hurston and a History of Southern Life (nonfiction) , 2005. Contributor to journals. **Address:** Hamilton College, 198 College Hill Rd., Clinton, NY 13323, U.S.A. **Online address:** tpatters@hamilton.edu

PATTILLO, Mary E. (Mary Pattillo-McCoy). American (born United States), b. 1970. **Genres:** Politics/Government, Race Relations, History. **Career:** University of Chicago, research assistant, 1993-96, lecturer, 1996; Illinois Institute of Technology, lecturer, 1995; University of Michigan, postdoctoral fellow and research associate, 1997-98; Northwestern University, assistant professor, 1998-2001, associate professor, 2001-06, Arthur Andersen Research and Teaching Professor, 2004-07, professor of sociology and African American studies, 2006-, Department of African American Studies, chair, 2001-02, faculty fellow, 1998-2004, faculty associate, 2004-, Department of Sociology, chair, 2006-. Writer and researcher. **Publications:** Black Picket Fences: Privilege and Peril among the Black Middle Class, 1999; (ed. with D. Weiman and B. Western) Imprisoning America: The Social Effects of Mass Incarceration, 2004; Black on the Block: The Politics of Race and Class in the City, 2007. Contributor to books, journals and periodicals. **Address:** Northwestern University, 1810 Chicago Ave., Evanston, IL 60208-0812, U.S.A. **Online address:** m-pattillo@northwestern.edu

PATTILLO-MCCOY, Mary. *See* **PATTILLO, Mary E.**

PATTON, Phil. American (born United States), b. 1952. **Genres:** History, Novellas/Short Stories, Technology, Design, Art/Art History, Architecture, Transportation. **Career:** Esquire, contributing editor, 1975-76; ID magazine, contributing editor; Wired, contributing editor; Departures, contributing editor; The New York Times, automotive design writer; School of Visual Arts, DCrit program, teacher. **Publications:** Razzle Dazzle: The Curious Marriage of Television and Professional Football, 1984; Open Road: A Celebration of the American Highway, 1986; (with J. Yeager and D. Rutan) Voyager, 1987; Made in U.S.A.: The Secret Histories of the Things That Made America, 1992; Highway, 1996; (with B. Polster) Highway: America's Endless Dream, 1997; Technofollies: An Anthology of B, 1997; Bill Traylor: High Singing Blue, 1997; Dreamland: Inside the Secret World of Roswell and Area 51, 1998; Bug: The Strange Mutations of the World's Most Famous Automobile, 2002; Michael Graves Designs: The Art of the Everyday Object, 2004; (with T.V. Boyce and M. Lamm) Art and Colour of General Motors, 2008; (with J. Heimann) Classic Cars of the 20th Century, 2009. **Address:** Department of Design Criticism, School of Visual Arts, 209 E 23 St., New York, NY 10010-3994, U.S.A. **Online address:** philpatton@msn.com

PATTON, Robert H. (Robert Holbrook Patton). American (born United States), b. 1957. **Genres:** Novels, History. **Career:** Writer. **Publications:** The Pattons: A Personal History of an American Family, 1994; Life between Wars (novel), 1997; Up, Down & Sideways (novel), 1997; Patriot Pirates: The Privateer War for Freedom and Fortune in the American Revolution, 2008. **Address:** Darien, CT , U.S.A. **Online address:** rhpatton@optonline.net

PATTON, Robert Holbrook. *See* **PATTON, Robert H.**

PATTON, Stacey. American (born United States), b. 1978. **Genres:** History, Race Relations. **Career:** N.A.A.C.P. Legal and Educational Defense Fund, writer & editor; Baltimore Sun, journalist; Washington Post, journalist; Montclair State University, adjunct professor of history. **Publications:** That Mean Old Yesterday (memoir), 2007. **Address:** Montclair State University, Montclair, NJ 07043, U.S.A. **Online address:** info.meanoldyesterday@yahoo.com

PATTOU, Edith. American (born United States) **Genres:** Novels, Picture/Board Books, Children's Fiction. **Career:** Writer. **Publications:** SONGS OF EIRREN: Hero's Song, 1991; Fire Arrow: The Second Song of Eirren, 1998. PICTURE BOOKS: Mrs. Spitzers Garden, 2001. NOVELS: East, 2003; North Child, 2006. Contributor to periodicals. **Address:** c/o Author Mail, Harcourt International, 6277 Sea Harbor Dr., Orlando, FL 32887, U.S.A.

PATTULLO, Polly. British (born England), b. 1946. **Genres:** Documentaries/Reportage, Travel/Exploration. **Career:** Observer Magazine, features editor, 1986; Caribbean Insight, deputy editor, 1990-; Guardian Newspaper, desk editor, 1991-; Traveller's Tree (travel and tour operators), co-founder; Papillote Press (publisher), co-founder. **Publications:** (Co-author) Women and Work, 1977; (co-author) Power and Prejudice, 1990; Last Resorts: The Cost of Tourism in the Caribbean, 1996, 2nd ed., 2005; (with A.J. Baptiste) The Gardens of Dominica, 1998; Fire from the Mountain: The Tragedy of Montserrat and the Betrayal of its People, 2000; (with O. Minelli) Ethical Travel Guide: Your Passport to Exciting Alternative Holidays, 2006; (with C. Sorhaindo) Home Again: Stories of Migration and Return, 2009. **Address:** Papillote Press, 23 Rozel Rd., London, GL SW4 0EY, England. **Online address:** pattul@guardian.co.uk

PATURI, Felix R. German/Polish (born Poland), b. 1940. **Genres:** Adult Non-fiction, Business/Trade/Industry. **Career:** ZDF, editor; publicist. **Publications:** IN ENGLISH: The Escalator Effect: How to Get to the Top without Effort, 1973; Geniale Ingenieure der Natur: wodurch uns, Pflanzen technisch überlegen sind, 1974; Nature, Mother of Invention: The Engineering of Plant Life, 1976; Prehistoric Heritage, 1979. IN GERMAN: Baumeister unserer Zukunft: kühne Projekte der Forscher, Erfinder und Ingenieure in aller Welt, 1975; Zeugen der Vorzeit: auf d. Spuren europ. Vergangenheit, 1976; Natur erleben in Europa: faszinierende Schönheit am Rande europ. Reisewege, 1978; (with M.J.B. Rauck and G. Volke) Mit dem Rad durch zwei Jahrhunderte: das Fahrrad und seine Geschichte, 1979; Chaos oder Paradies: Alternativen zur Menschheitskrise, 1981; Unbekannter Nachbar Orient: erlebter Islam, 1982; Von der Erde zu den Sternen: 200 Jahre Luftfahrt, 1983; Die Geschichte vom Glas, 1986; (with R.R. Box) Jahrhundert Automobil, 1986; Die Geschichte des Fahrrads, 1988; Reisen zu Gott: christliche Pilgerfahrten in Europa, 1989; Harenberg Schlüsseldaten Astronomie: von den Sonnenuhred der Babylonier bis zu den Raumsonden im 21. Jahrhundert, 1996. Contributor to periodicals. **Address:** Sanford J. Greenburger Associates Inc., 55 5th Ave., 15th Fl., New York, NY 10003, U.S.A.

PATZER, Gordon. American (born United States), b. 1952. **Genres:** Business/Trade/Industry, Medicine/Health, Advertising/Public Relations, Administration/Management, Adult Non-fiction, Civil Liberties/Human Rights, Fash Ion/Costume, Art/Art History, Education, Gay And Lesbian Issues, International Relations/Current Affairs, Money/Finance, Popular Culture, Psychiatry, Psychology, E-books, Novels, Romance/Historical. **Career:** Appearance Research Institute (API) for Research, founder, director, chief executive officer. Writer, educator and speaker. **Publications:** NON-FICTION: Looks: The Physical Attractiveness Phenomena, 1985; Using Secondary Data in Marketing Research: United States and Worldwide, 1995; Experiment-Research Methodology in Marketing: Types and Applications, 1996; Why Physically Attractive People Are More Successful: The Scientific Explanation, Social The Power and Paradox of Physical Attractiveness, 2006; Consequences and Ethical Problems, 2007; Looks: Why They Matter More Than You Ever Imagined, 2008. FICTION: Fall In Fargo, forthcoming. **Address:** Roosevelt University, 430 S Michigan Ave., Chicago, IL 60605, U.S.A. **Online address:** gordon@gordonpatzer.com

PAUKER, Ted. *See* **CONQUEST, (George) Robert (Acworth).**

PAUKETAT, Timothy R. American (born United States), b. 1961?. **Genres:** Archaeology/Antiquities, History. **Career:** University of Oklahoma, associate professor, 1992-96; State University of New York, associate professor, 1996-98; University of Illinois, associate professor, 1998-2005, professor, 2005-; U.S. Army Corps of Engineers, intern; Center for American Archaeology, staff archaeologist; Southern Illinois University, research assistant. Writer. **Publications:** (Co-author) The Lohmann Site: An Early Mississippian Center in the American Bottom (11-S-49), 1992; (ed. with A.W. Barker) Lords of the Southeast: Social Inequality and the Native Elites of Southeastern North America, 1992; (with J.R. Bozell and S.L. Dunavan) Temples for Cahokia Lords: Preston Holder's 1955-1956 Excavations of Kunnemann Mound, 1993; The Ascent of Chiefs: Cahokia and Mississippian Politics in Native North America, 1994; (ed. with T.E. Emerson) Cahokia: Domination and Ideology in the Mississippian World, 1997; (with P. Miracle and S.L. Dunavan) The Archaeology of Downtown Cahokia: The Tract 15A and Dunham Tract Excavations, 1998; (co-author) An Archaeological Survey of the Horseshoe Lake State Park, Madison County, Illinois, 1998; (ed.) The Archaeology of Traditions: Agency and History before and after Columbus, 2001; Ancient Cahokia and the Mississippians, 2004; (with N.S. Bernard) Cahokia Mounds (juvenile nonfiction), 2004; (co-ed.) The Archaeology of the East St. Louis Mound Center, vol. 1: The Southside Excavations, 2005; (ed. with D.D. Loren) North American Archaeology, 2005; Chiefdoms and Other Archaeological Delusions, 2007; Cahokia: Ancient America's Great City on the Mississippi, 2009. **Address:** University of Illinois, 123 Davenport Hall, M/C 148, 607 S Mathews, Urbana, IL 61801, U.S.A. **Online address:** pauketat@illinois.edu

PAUL, Ann Whitford. American (born United States), b. 1941. **Genres:** Children's Fiction, Poetry, Children's Non-fiction, Picture/Board Books. **Career:** Social worker, 1965-70. Writer. **Publications:** Owl at Night, 1985; Eight Hands Round: A Patchwork Alphabet, 1991; Shadows Are About, 1992; The Seasons Sewn, 1996; Hello Toes! Hello Feet!, 1998; Silly Sadie, Silly Samuel, 1998; Everything to Spend the Night, 1999; All by Herself, 1999; Little Monkey Says Goodnight, 2002; Mañana Iguana, 2004; Hop! Hop! Hop!, 2005; Fiesta Fiasco, 2007; Snail's Good Night, 2007; Count on Culebra, 2008; If Animals Kissed Good Night, 2008; Writing Picture Books: A Hands-on Guide from Story Creation to Publication, 2009; Word Builder, 2009; Tortuga in Trouble, 2009. Contributor to books. **Address:** 2531 N Catalina St., Los Angeles, CA 90027, U.S.A. **Online address:** ann@annwhitfordpaul.net

PAUL, Anthea. American (born United States) **Genres:** Novels, Young Adult Fiction. **Career:** Photographer, editor, art director, trend forecaster, creative director. **Publications:** Girlosophy: A Soul Survival Kit, 2000; Girlosophy 2: The Love Survival Kit, 2002; (with J. Glisic and J. Adams) 21st Century Goddess, 2002; Girlosophy: The Oracle, 2003; Girlosophy: The Breakup Survival Kit, 2003; Real Girls Stories: Girlosophy, 2004; Girlosophy: Real Girls Eat, 2005. Contributor to periodicals. **Address:** c/o Author Mail, Allen & Unwin Private Ltd., PO Box 8500, St. Leonards, NW 1590, Australia.

PAUL, Barbara. American (born United States), b. 1931. **Genres:** Mystery/Crime/Suspense, Science Fiction/Fantasy. **Career:** Berry College, instructor, 1957-61; Erskine College, assistant professor and drama director, 1961-65; University of Pittsburgh, instructor, 1969-73, professor; American Crime Writers League, treasurer; Sisters in Crime, founder and president. Writer. **Publications:** SCIENCE FICTION: An Exercise for Madmen, 1978; Pillars of Salt, 1979; Bibblings, 1979; Under the Canopy, 1980; The Three-Minute Universe, 1988. MYSTERIES: The Fourth Wall, 1979; Liars and Tyrants and People Who Turn Blue, 1980; First Gravedigger, 1980; Your Eyelids Are Growing Heavy, 1981; The Renewable Virgin, 1984; A Cadenza for Caruso, 1984; Kill Fee, 1985; Prima Donna at Large, 1985; But He Was Already Dead When I Got There, 1986; A Chorus of Detectives, 1987; He Huffed and He Puffed, 1989; Good King Sauerkraut, 1989; In-Laws and Outlaws, 1990; You Have the Right to Remain Silent, 1992; The Apostrophe Thief, 1993; Fare Play, 1995; Full Frontal Murder, 1997; Jack Be Quick and Other Crime Stories (collection), 1999; (with D. Candeloro) Chicago Heights Revisited, 2000. Contributor of short stories to periodicals. **Address:** c/o Dominick Abel, Dominick Abel Literary Agency Inc., 146 W 82nd St., Ste. 1B, New York, NY 10024, U.S.A. **Online address:** bp@barbarapaul.com

PAUL, Barbara. *See* **ØVSTEDAL, Barbara.**

PAUL, Caroline. American (born United States), b. 1963. **Genres:** Novels, Autobiography/Memoirs. **Career:** San Francisco Fire Department, firefighter. Journalist. **Publications:** Fighting Fire (memoir), 1998; East Wind, Rain (historical novel), 2006. **Address:** c/o Author Mail, William Morrow & Co., 10 E 53rd St., 7th Fl., New York, NY 10022-5244, U.S.A. **Online address:** webmaster@carolinepaul.com

PAUL, George F(ranklin). American (born United States), b. 1954. **Genres:** Advertising/Public Relations, Antiques/Furnishings, Communications/Media, History, Technology, Sciences, Homes/Gardens. **Career:** State of New York, J.N. Adam DDSO, speech and language pathologist, 1977-90; State of New York, Craig DDSO, Department of Speech and Language, coordinator, 1990-94, Finger Lakes DDSO, Department of Speech and Language, coordinator, 1994-2009, retired 2009. Writer. **Publications:** Column Phonograph Forum in The New Amberola Graphic, 1983; (with T.C. Fabrizio) The Talking Machine Compendium, 1877-1929, 1997, 2nd ed., 2005; Antique Phonograph Gadgets, Gizmos and Gimmicks, 1999; (with T.C. Fabrizio) Discovering Antique Phonographs, 2000; (with T.C. Fabrizio) Phonographs with Flair, 2001; (with T.C. Fabrizio) Antique Phonograph Advertising, 2002; (with T.C. Fabrizio) Antique Phonograph Accessories and Contraptions, 2003; (with T.C. Fabrizio) Phonographica, 2004; (with T.C. Fabrizio) World of Antique Phonographs, 2007. **Address:** 126 S Main St., Mount Morris, NY 14510, U.S.A. **Online address:** gpaul2000@aol.com

PAUL, Tessa. British/Zimbabwean (born Zimbabwe), b. 1944. **Genres:** Homes/Gardens, Natural History, Animals/Pets, Theology/Religion, History. **Career:** Writer and illustrator. **Publications:** NONFICTION: Art of Louis Comfort Tiffany, 1987; Tiles for a Beautiful Home, 1990; (with M. Lloyd and J. Blackmore) Glass for a Beautiful Home, 1990; New Flowers: Growing the New Garden Varieties, 1990; Christmas Long Ago: Christmas Past with Changing Pictures, 1992; Tiffany, 1992; (contrib.) The Gardener's Handbook: The Essential Guide for Success with Plants, 1993. FIESTA! SERIES: Israel, 1997; Russia, 1997; Turkey, 1998. ANIMAL TRACKERS SERIES: In Fields and Meadows, 1997; By Lakes and Rivers, 1997; In Woods and Forests, 1997; By the Seashore, 1997; At the Poles, 1998; Down Under, 1998; In the Jungle, 1998; On Safari, 1998. OTHERS: (with R. Creighton-Jobe) The Illustrated World Encyclopedia of Saints, 2009; An Illustrated History of Saints and Sainthood, 2012. Contributor to periodicals. **Address:** 164 Shirland Rd., London, GL W9 2BT, England.

PAULEY, Garth E. American (born United States), b. 1971. **Genres:** Civil Liberties/Human Rights, Race Relations, Education, History. **Career:** Calvin College, Department of Communication Arts and Sciences, assistant professor of rhetoric, 2005-. Writer. **Publications:** The Modern Presidency and Civil Rights: Rhetoric on Race from Roosevelt to Nixon, 2001; LBJ's American Promise: The 1965 Voting Rights Address, 2007. **Address:** Department of Communication Arts and Sciences, Calvin College, DeVos Communication Ctr., 1810 E Beltline SE, Grand Rapids, MI 49546-5951, U.S.A. **Online address:** gpauley@calvin.edu

PAULEY, Kimberly. American (born United States), b. 1973. **Genres:** Horror, Young Adult Fiction, Adult Non-fiction. **Career:** Young Adult (and Kids!) Book Central Web site, founder. Writer and book reviewer. **Publications:** Sucks to Be Me: The All- True Confessions of Mina Hamilton, 2008; Still Sucks to Be Me: The All-True Confessions of Mina Hamilton, 2010; Cat Girl's Day Off, 2012. **Address:** PO Box 303, Grayslake, IL 60030, U.S.A. **Online address:** kim@kimberlypauley.com

PAULOS, John A(llen). American (born United States), b. 1945. **Genres:** Mathematics/Statistics, Philosophy. **Career:** Temple University, Department of Mathematics, assistant professor, associate professor, 1974-, professor of mathematics, 1980-; Guardian, columnist; ABCNews.com, columnist; Columbia University School of Journalism, visiting professor, 2000. **Publications:** Mathematics and Humor, 1980; I Think, Therefore I Laugh: An Alternative Approach to Philosophy, 1985, 2nd ed., 2000; Innumeracy: Mathematical Illiteracy and Its Consequences, 1989; Beyond Numeracy: The Ruminations of a Numbers Man, 1991; A Mathematician Reads the Newspaper, 1995; Once Upon a Number, 1999; A Mathematician Plays the Stock Market, 2003; Irreligion: A Mathematician Explains Why the Arguments for God Just Don't Add Up, 2008. **Address:** Department of Mathematics, Temple University, Rm. 638 Wachman Hall, 1805 N Broad St., Philadelphia, PA 19122, U.S.A. **Online address:** paulos@temple.edu

PAULSEN, Gary. American (born United States), b. 1939. **Genres:** Novels, Novellas/Short Stories, Children's Fiction, Children's Non-fiction, Homes/

Gardens, Social Commentary, Young Adult Non-fiction, Mystery/Crime/Suspense, Mystery/Crime/Suspense. **Career:** Writer, 1960-. Teacher and director. **Publications:** CHILDREN'S FICTION: Mr. Tucket, 1969; The C.B. Radio Caper, 1977; The Curse of the Cobra, 1977; The Foxman, 1977; The Golden Stick, 1977; Tiltawhirl John, 1977; Winterkill, 1977; (with R. Peekner) The Green Recruit, 1978; Hope and a Hatchet, 1978; The Night the White Deer Died, 1978; The Spitball Gang, 1980; Dancing Carl, 1983; Popcorn Days and Buttermilk Nights, 1983; Tracker, 1984; Dogsong, 1985; Sentries, 1986; The Crossing, 1987; Hatchet, 1987; The Island, 1988; The Voyage of the Frog, 1989; The Winter Stories, 1989; The Tent: A Tale in One Sitting, 1995; Call Me Francis Tucket, 1995; Amos Gets Married, 1995; Amos's Killer Concert Caper, 1995; Brian's Winter, 1996; Dunc and Amos Go to the Dogs, 1996; The Schernoff Discoveries, 1997; Tucket's Ride, 1997; Soldier's Heart: A Novel of the Civil War, 1998; The Transall Saga, 1998; Tucket's Gold, 1999; My Life in Dog Years, 1998; Canoe Days, 1998; White Fox Chronicles, 1999; Brian's Return, 1999; Alida's Song, 1999; (foreword) Adventures of Huckleberry Finn, 1999; Tucket's Home, 2000; Brian's Hunt, 2003; The Quilt, 2004; The Time Hackers, 2005; The Legend of Bass Reeves: Being the True and Fictional Account of the Most Valiant Marshal in the West, 2006; The Amazing Life of Birds: The Twenty-day Puberty Journal of Duane Homer Leech, 2006; Lawn Boy, 2007; Mudshark, 2009; Notes from the Dog, 2009; Woods Runner, 2010; Masters of Disaster, 2010; Lawn Boy Returns, 2010; Liar, Liar: The Theory, Practice, and Destructive Properties of Deception, 2011. CHILDREN'S NON-FICTION: Dribbling, Shooting and Scoring Sometimes, 1976; The Grass Eaters: Real Animals, 1976; (with D. Theis) Martin Luther King: The Man Who Climbed the Mountain, 1976; The Small Ones, 1976; Careers in an Airport, 1977; Hitting, Pitching, and Running Maybe, 1977; Tackling, Running, and Kicking-Now and Again, 1977; Riding, Roping, and Bulldogging-Almost, 1977; Forehanding and Backhanding-If You're Lucky, 1978, rev. ed. (with R. Barrett) as Tennis: Focus on Sport, 1980; (with J. Morris) Hiking and Backpacking, 1978; Running, Jumping, and Throwing-If You Can, 1978, rev. ed. (with R. Barrett) as Athletics: Focus on Sport, 1980; (with J. Morris) Canoeing, Kayaking, and Rafting, 1979; Downhill, Hotdogging, and Cross-Country-If the Snow Isn't Sticky, 1979, rev. ed. (with R. Barrett) as Skiing: Focus on Sport, 1980; Facing Off, Checking, and Goaltending-Perhaps, 1979, rev. ed. (with R. Barrett) as Ice Hockey: Focus on Sport, 1980; Going Very Fast in a Circle-If You Don't Run Out of Gas, 1979, rev. ed. (with R. Barrett) as Motor Racing: Focus on Sport, 1980; Launching, Floating High, and Landing-If Your Pilot Light Doesn't Go Out, 1979, rev. ed. as Full of Hot Air: Launching, Floating High, and Landing, 1993; Pummeling, Falling, and Getting Up-Sometimes, 1979; Track, Enduro, and Motocross-Unless You Fall Over, 1979, rev. ed. (with R. Barrett) as Motor Cycling: Focus on Sport, 1980; (with A. Browne, Jr.) TV and Movie Animals, 1980; Sailing: From Jibs to Jibing, 1981; Puppies, Dogs, and Blue Northers: Reflections on Being Raised by a Pack of Sled Dogs, 1996; Molly McGinty Has a Really Good Day, 2004. NOVELS FOR ADULTS: The Death Specialists, 1976; The Implosion Effect, 1976; C.B. Jockey, 1977; The Sweeper, 1980; Meteorite-Track 291, 1981; Survival Guide, 1981; Compkill, 1981; Clutterkill, 1981; The Meatgrinder, 1984; Murphy, 1987; Murphy's Gold, 1988; Night Rituals, 1989; The Madonna Stories, 1989; Murphy's Herd, 1989; Murphy's War, 1990; The Boy Who Owned the School: A Comedy of Love, 1990; Canyons, 1990; The Cookcamp, 1991; The River, 1991; The Winter Room, 1991; A Christmas Sonata, 1992; Dunc Gets Tweaked, 1992; Clabbered Dirt, Sweet Grass, 1992; The Haymeadow, 1992; The Case of the Dirty Bird, 1992; Culpepper's Cannon, 1992; Dunc's Doll, 1992; Dunc and the Flaming Ghost, 1992; Dunc's Halloween, 1992; Dunc Breaks the Record, 1992; Nightjohn, 1993; Sisters/Hermanas, 1993; Amos Gets Famous, 1993; Dunc and Amos Hit the Big Top, 1993; Murphy's Stand, 1993; Dunc's Dump, 1993; Dunc's Undercover, 1993; Dunc and Amos and the Red Tattoos, 1993; Dunc and the Haunted House, 1993; Amos's Last Stand, 1993; The Wild Culpepper Cruise, 1993; Legend of Red Horse Cavern, 1994; Rodomonte's Revenge, 1994; Dunc and the Greased Sticks of Doom, 1994; Cowpokes and Desperadoes, 1994; Prince Amos, 1994; Coach Amos, 1994; Amos and the Alien, 1994; Dunc and Amos Meet the Slasher, 1994; Danger on Midnight River, 1995; Hook 'Em, Snotty!, 1995; Amos Goes Bananas, 1995; The Tortilla Factory, 1995; Murphy's Ambush, 1995; Amos and the Vampire, 1996; Amos and the Chameleon Caper, 1996; Murphy's Trail, 1996; Amos Binder, Secret Agent, 1997; Worksong, 1997; Sarny: A Life Remembered, 1997; Super Amos, 1997; Dunc and Amos on Thin Ice, 1997; Escape, Return, Breakout, 2000; Woodsong, 2002. OTHER FOR ADULTS: (with R.F. Locke) The Special War, 1966; Some Birds Don't Fly, 1968; The Building a New, Buying an Old, Remodeling a Used, Comprehensive Home and Shelter How to Do It Book, 1976; Farm; A History and Celebration of the American Farmer, 1977; Successful Home Repair: When Not to Call the Contractor, 1978; Money-Saving Home Repair Guide, 1981; Beat the System: A Survival Guide, 1983; Kill Fee, 1990; Night Rituals, 1991; Dogteam, 1992; The Monument, 1993; Harris and Me: A Summer Remembered, 1993; Eastern Sun, Winter Moon: An Autobiographical Odyssey, 1993; The Car, 1994; Winterdance: The Fine Madness of Running the Iditarod, 1994; Father Water, Mother Woods: Essays on Fishing and Hunting in the North Woods, 1994; The Rifle, 1995; Pilgrimage on a Steelride: A Memoir about Men and Motorcycles, 1997; The Beet Fields: Memories of a Sixteenth Summer, 2000; Guts: The True Stories behind Hatchet and the Brian Books, 2001; Caught by the Sea: My Life on Boats, 2001; How Angel Peterson Got His Name: And Other Outrageous Tales About Extreme Sports, 2003; Glass Cafe, or, The Stripper and the State: How My Mother Started a War with the System That Made Us Kind of Rich and a Little Bit Famous, 2003; (ed.) Shelf Life: Stories by the Book, 2003; Gary Paulsen Collection, 2004; World of Adventure Trio, 2006; Paintings from the Cave, 2011; Flat Broke, 2011; Crush, 2012. WORLD OF ADVENTURE SERIES: FOR CHILDREN: Escape from Fire Mountain, 1995; Rock Jockeys, 1995; Captive!, 1996; Skydive!, 1996; The Treasure of El Patron, 1996; The Seventh Crystal, 1996; The Creature of Black Water Lake, 1997; The Grizzly, 1997; Thunder Valley, 1998; Curse of the Ruins, 1998; Time Benders, 1998; Flight of the Hawk, 1998. Contributor to periodicals. **Address:** Children's Publicity, Random House Inc., 1540 Broadway, New York, NY 10036-4039, U.S.A.

PAULSON, Michael G. (Michael George Paulson). American (born United States), b. 1945. **Genres:** Literary Criticism And History. **Career:** Muhlenberg College, assistant professor, 1986-87; Kutztown University, associate professor of foreign language, 1987-93, professor of foreign language, 1993-. Writer. **Publications:** NONFICTION: (with T. Alvarez-Detrell) Cervantes, Hardy, and La fuerza de la sangre, 1985; Lepanto: Fact, Fiction and Fantasy, 1986; The Queens' Encounter: The Mary Stuart Anachronism in Dramas by Diamante, Boursault, Schiller and Donizetti, 1988; The Possible Influence of Montaigne's Essais on Descartes' Treatise on the Passions, 1988; A Critical Analysis of De La Fayette's La Princesse de Cleves as a Royal Novel: Kings, Queens, and Splendor, 1991. OTHER (with T. Alvarez-Detrell) (trans.) La corona tragica de Lope de Vega, trans. as: Lope de Vega's The Tragic Crown, 1982; Youth and the Beach, 1993; Facets of a Princess, 1998; Catherine de Medici: Five Portraits, 2002; (with T. Alvarez-Detrell) Figure of Louis XIII in Modern French Literature, 2008; (with T. Alvarez-Detrell) The Portrayal of Anne of Austria in Modern French Literature, 2010. **Address:** Department of Foreign Languages, Kutztown University, 300 NE 2nd Ave., Miami, FL 33132, U.S.A. **Online address:** mpaulson@mdcc.edu

PAULSON, Michael George. *See* **PAULSON, Michael G.**

PAULSON, Ronald (Howard). American (born United States), b. 1930. **Genres:** Art/Art History, Literary Criticism And History. **Career:** University of Illinois, instructor, 1958-59, assistant professor, 1959-62, associate professor, 1962-63; Rice University, professor of English, 1963-67; Johns Hopkins University, Department of English, professor, 1967-75, chairman, 1968-75, 1985-91, Andrew W. Mellon professor of humanities, 1973-75, Mayer professor of humanities, 1985-, School of Arts and Sciences, William D. and Robin Mayer professor emeritus; Yale University, Department of English, professor, 1975-84, director of graduate studies, 1976-83, Thomas E. Donnelley professor, 1980-84. Writer. **Publications:** Theme and Structure in Swift's Tale of a Tub, 1960; Hogarth's Graphic Works, 1965, 1970, 1989; Novelette Before 1900, 1965; The Fictions of Satire, 1967; Satire and the Novel, 1967; Hogarth: His Life, Art and Times, 1971; Rowlandson: A New Interpretation, 1972; Emblem and Expression in English Art of the 18th Century, 1975; The Age of Hogarth, 1975; Popular and Polite Art in the Age of Hogarth and Fielding, 1979; Literary Landscape: Turner and Constable, 1982; Representations of Revolution, 1983; Book and Painting: Shakespeare, Milton, and the Bible, 1983; Breaking and Remaking, 1989; Figure and Abstraction in Contemporary Painting, 1990; Hogarth, I: The Modern Moral Subject, 1991; Hogarth, II: High Art and Low, 1992; Hogarth, III: Art and Politics, 1993; The Beautiful, Novel, and Strange: Aesthetics and Heterodoxy, 1996; Don Quixote in England: The Aestetics of Laughter, 1997; The Life of Henry Fielding: A Critical Biography, 2000; Hogarth's Harlot: Sacred Parody in Enlightenment England, 2003; Sin and Evil: Moral Values in Literature, 2007; The Art of Riot in England and America, 2010. EDITOR: Fielding: A Collection of Critical Essays, 1962; The Novelette, 1965; Henry Fielding: The Critical Heritage, 1969; Satire: Modern Essays in Criticism, 1971, The Field of Quality, 5 vols., 1979; Fleetwood, 1979; The History of Miss Betsy Thoughtless, 4 vols., 1979, Memoirs of Bryan Perdue, 3 vols., 1979; Julia de Roubiggne,

2 vols., 1979; Barham Downs, 2 vols., 1979; James Wallace, 3 vols., 1979; Virtuous Orphan; or, The Life of Marianne, Countess Of-, 4 vols., 1979; The Adventures of Telemachus, 2 vols., 1979; Chrysal; or, The Adventures of a Guinea, 4 vols., 1979; Mount Henneth, 2 vols., 1980; The Analysis of Beauty: William Hogarth, 1997. **Address:** Department of English, The Johns Hopkins University, 14 Gilman Hall, 3400 N Charles St., Baltimore, MD 21218, U.S.A. **Online address:** pauls_r@jhu.edu

PAULSSON, Gunnar S. (Gunnar Steve Paulsson). Canadian (born Canada) **Genres:** Novels. **Career:** Oxford Centre for Hebrew and Jewish Studies, lecturer. Writer. **Publications:** The Holocaust Exhibition at the Imperial War Museum, 2000; (ed.) Barbara Engelking, Holocaust and Memory: The Experience of the Holocaust and Its Consequences: An Investigation Based on Personal Narratives, 2001; Secret City: The Hidden Jews of Warsaw, 1940-1945, 2002. Contributed articles to Journal. **Online address:** gspaulsson@sympatico.ca

PAULSSON, Gunnar Steve. *See* **PAULSSON, Gunnar S.**

PAULSSON, Martin W. American (born United States), b. 1942. **Genres:** History. **Career:** Trenton State College, adjunct professor, 1976-92, assistant professor, 1992-; The College of New Jersey, Department of History, historian, faculty. Writer. **Publications:** The Social Anxieties of Progressive Reform: Atlantic City, 1854-1920, 1994. Contributor to periodicals. **Address:** Department of History, The College of New Jersey, 2000 Pennington Rd., PO Box 7718, Ewing, NJ 08628-0718, U.S.A. **Online address:** paulsson@tcnj.edu

PAULY, Louis W. American/Canadian (born Canada), b. 1952?. **Genres:** Economics, Money/Finance. **Career:** Irving Trust Co., Foreign Credit Analyst, 1975-76; Royal Bank of Canada, manager, 1978-82; Institute for Fiscal and Monetary Policy, Ministry of Finance, research fellow, 1985; International Monetary Fund, Policy Development and Review Department, staff, 1988-89; University of Toronto, assistant professor of political science, 1987-91, associate professor, 1991-96, professor of political science, 1996-, Center of International Studies, director, 1997-, Canada research chair in globalization and governance, 2002-; Munk Centre, acting director, 2002-03, International Organization, 2007-10, Munk School of Global Affairs, deputy director and research, 2011-. Writer. **Publications:** Foreign Banks in Australia: The Politics of Deregulation, 1987; Regulatory Politics in Japan: The Case of Foreign Banking, 1987; Opening Financial Markets: Banking Politics on the Pacific Rim, 1988; (ed. with J.G. Stein) Choosing to Cooperate: How States Avoid Loss, 1993; The League of Nations and the Foreshadowing of the International Monetary Fund, 1996; Who Elected the Bankers?: Surveillance and Control in the World Economy, 1997; The Myth of the Global Corporation, 1998; (ed. with M. Greven) Democracy Beyond the State: The European Dilemma and the Emerging Global Order, 2000; (ed. with D.M. Andrews and C.R. Henning) Governing the World's Money, 2002; (ed. with E. Grande) Complex Sovereignty: Reconstituting Political Authority in the Twenty-first Century, 2005; (ed. with S. Bernstein) Global Liberalism and Political Order: Toward a New Grand Compromise?, 2007; Global Ordering: Institutions and Autonomy in a Changing World, 2008. **Address:** University of Toronto, Centre for International Studies, Munk School of Global Affairs, 1 Devonshire Pl., Toronto, ON M5S 3K7, Canada. **Online address:** lpauly@chass.utoronto.ca

PAULY, Rebecca M. American (born United States), b. 1942. **Genres:** Film, Language/Linguistics, Literary Criticism And History, Art/Art History. **Career:** Newark Center for Creative Learning, teacher and curriculum developer, 1971-74, 1975-78; Gruppo LePetit, teacher of English as a foreign language, 1974-75; Tower Hill School, French teacher, 1982; University of Delaware, lecturer, 1982-84, assistant professor of French and Italian, 1984-87; West Chester University, assistant professor, 1987-92, associate professor of French and Italian, 1992-96, professor of French and Italian, 1996-, French Section, coordinator, 1989-. Writer. **Publications:** Le Berceau et la Bibliothèque: Le Paradoxe de l'écriture Autobiographique, 1989; The Transparent Illusion: Image and Ideology in French Text and Film, 1993, rev. ed., 2003. **Address:** Department of Languages and Cultures, West Chester University, 105 Main Hall, 700 S High St., West Chester, PA 19383, U.S.A. **Online address:** rpauly@wcupa.edu

PAUSEWANG, Gudrun. German (born Germany), b. 1928. **Genres:** Young Adult Fiction, Novels, Translations, Travel/Exploration, History. **Career:** Writer and teacher. **Publications:** YOUNG ADULT FICTION: IN ENGLISH TRANSLATION: Die letzten Kinder von Schewenborn, 1985, trans. as The Last Children of Schevenborn, 1988, as The Last Children, 1989; Die Wolke, 1987, trans. as Fall-Out, 1992; Eine Reise im August, 1992, trans. as The Final Journey, 1996. IN GERMAN: Unddann kommt Emilio, 1974; Kunibert und Killewamba, 1976; Der Streik der Dienstmaedchen, 1979; Rosenkawiesen, 1980; Die Not der Familie Caldera, 1981; Die Prinzessin springt ins Heu, 1982; Auf einem langen Weg, 1982; Wer hat Angst vor Raeuber Grapsch, 1983; Ich habe Hunger, Ich habe Durst, 1984; Etwas laesst sich doch bewirken, 1984; Friedens: Geschichten (stories), 1985; Ein wilder Winter fuer Raeuber Grapsch, 1986; Ein Eigenheim fuer Raeuber Grapsch, 1987; Die Kinder in der Erde, 1988; Kreuzund quer ubers Meer, 1988; Fern von der Rosinkawiese, 1989; Geliebte Rosinkawiese, 1990; Das Tor zum Garten der Zambranos, 1991; Es ist dochalles gruen, 1991; Das grosse Buch vom Raeuber Grapsch, 1992; Der Schlund, 1993; Der Weihnachtsmann im Kittchen, 1995; Die Verraeterin, 1995; Wie es den Leuten von der Rosinkawiese nach dem Krieg erging, 1996; Einfach abhauen, 1996; Adi: Jugend eines Diktators, 1997; Ich geb' dir noch eine Chance, Gott!, 1997; Wiedersehen mit Anna, 1997; Warum eigentlich nicht, 1998; Hinterm Haus der Wassermann, 1998; 1996-1997 Germanistikstudium, 1998; Horst du den Fluss, Elin?, 1998; Was wisst ihrdenn von mir?, 1998; Barfuss durch die grosse stadt, 1999; Dudarfst nichtschreien, 2000; Roller und Rosenkranz, 2000; Macht euch euern Kriegallein, 2000; Onkel Hugo und der Zauberer, 2002; Dort, wo zwei Mondescheinen, 2002; Und was mach ich?, 2003; Der Spinatrampir, 2003; Ich wardabei. Geschichten gene das Vergessen, 2004; Roller und Rosenkranz, 2004; überleben!, 2005; Ärmer werden, na und!: Denkanstösse nichtnur für junge Leute, 2006; Die Meute, 2006; Erlaubter Humor im Nationalsozialismus (1933-1945), 2007; Ein wunderbarer Vater, 2009; Die Oma im Drachenbauch und andere Omageschichten, 2010. **Address:** Brueder-Grimm-Weg 11, Schlitz, 36110, Germany.

PAVELICH, Matt. American (born United States) **Genres:** Novels, Young Adult Fiction, Romance/Historical, Humanities. **Career:** Writer and attorney. **Publications:** SHORT STORIES: Beasts of the Forest, Beasts of the Field, 1991; Our Savage: A Novel, 2004. **Address:** PO Box 403, Hot Springs, MT 59845, U.S.A.

PAVEY, Don. (Jack Adair). British (born England), b. 1922. **Genres:** Art/Art History, Communications/Media, Design, Education, Psychology, Self Help, History. **Career:** Kingston University, Kingston College of Art, lecturer in design and history of art, 1950-69, senior lecturer in charge of the experimental art and design workshop, 1969-82; Micro Academy, founder, director, 1986; Color Academy on Internet, director; Royal College of Art, Colour Reference Library, co-founder; Leeds University, National Art Education Archive, co-founder. Writer. **Publications:** (Ed.) Methuen Handbook of Colour and Colour Dictionary, 1963; Art-Based Games, 1979; Genius, 1980; Colour, 1981; The Artist's Colourmen's Story, 1985; First Facts about Colour, 1986; Colour and Effect, 1987; Design and Colour, 1988; Advertising and the Dream-makers, 1989; Design and Communication, 1990; Style in Painting, 1991; Supergames, 1993; Virtual Genius, 1996; Psychology of Colour, 1999; ProMICAD, 2000; On Colour (trans. Of Telesio's De Coloribus, 1528); Colour and Humanism, 2003; Psychobox, 2004; Buddhist Colour, 2005. Contributor to journals. **Address:** Micro Academy, Studio House, 30 Wayside, London, GL SW14 7LN, England. **Online address:** studio@coloracademy.co.uk

PAVLIK, John V. American (born United States) **Genres:** Business/Trade/Industry, Communications/Media, Marketing, Social Sciences. **Career:** American Family Insurance Group, public relations officer, 1977-78; University of Minnesota-Twin Cities, instructor in journalism, mass communication and marketing, 1981-82; Pennsylvania State University, assistant professor of communications, 1982-88, School of Journalism, graduate studies director, 1984-86; Columbia University, Freedom Forum Media Studies Center, associate director for research and technology studies, staff and developer of computer software, 1988-94, director of library, 1988-93, co-director of research group, 1990-94; San Diego State University, professor of communication, 1994-95, School of Communication, director, 1994-95; Columbia University, Center for New Media, executive director, professor, 1996-2002, Institute for Learning Technologies, Teacher's College, senior research associate, 1997-; Rutgers University, School of Communication, Information and Library Studies, department of journalism and media studies, professor, 2002-, chair, 2002-, director, 2002-. Writer. **Publications:** Public Relations: What Research Tells Us, 1987; (ed. with E.E. Dennis) Demystifying Media Technology: Readings from the Freedom Forum Center, 1993; (ed. with F. Williams) The People's Right to Know: Media, Democracy, and the Information Highway, 1994; New Media Technology and the Information Superhighway, 1996, rev. ed. as New Media Technology: Cultural and Commercial Perspectives, 1998; (ed. with S. Chang, D. Anastassiou and A. Eleftheriadis) Video on Demand Systems: Technology, Interoperability, and Trials, 1997; Journalism and New Media, 2001; (with S. McIntosh) Converging Media: An Introduction to Mass Communication, 2004, 2nd ed., 2011; Media in the Digital Age, 2008. Contributor of articles to books and journals. **Address:** Department of Journalism and Media Studies, Rutgers University, 185 College Ave., Rm. 207B, Journalism Hall, New Brunswick, NJ 08901, U.S.A. **Online address:** jpavlik@rutgers.edu

PAVLOU, Stel. British (born England), b. 1970. **Genres:** Novels, Science Fiction/Fantasy, Young Adult Fiction. **Career:** Writer. **Publications:** NOVELS: Decipher, 2002; Gene, 2005. **Address:** Ed Victor Ltd., 6 Bayley Sq., London, GL WC1B 3HB, England.

PAVLOWITCH, Stevan K. British/Yugoslav (born England), b. 1933. **Genres:** History, International Relations/Current Affairs, Humanities. **Career:** Journalist, 1958-65; University of Southampton, staff, 1965-97, emeritus professor of history, 1997-. **Publications:** Anglo-Russian Rivalry in Serbia 1837-1839, 1961; Yugoslavia, 1971; Bijou d'Art: Histoires de la vie, de l'oeuvre et du milieu de Bojidar Karageorgevitch, artiste parisien et prince balkanique (1862-1908), 1978; (with E. Biberaj) The Albanian Problem in Yugoslavia: Two Views, 1982; Unconventional Perceptions of Yugoslavia 1940-1945, 1985; The Improbable Survivor: Yugoslavia and its Problems 1918-1988, 1988; Yugoslavia's Great Dictator: Tito, a Reassessment, 1992; A History of the Balkans 1804-1945, 1999; Serbia: The History behind the Name, 2001; Serbia: The History of an Idea, 2002; Hitler's New Disorder: The Second World War in Yugoslavia. 2008. **Address:** Centre for the Study of the Balkans, Goldsmiths College, University of London, New Cross, London, GL SE14 6NW, England. **Online address:** pavlowitch@btinternet.com

PAWEL, Miriam. American (born United States), b. 1958?. **Genres:** Economics. **Career:** Newsday, reporter and assistant managing editor; Los Angeles Times, assistant managing editor, through 2004, reporter, 2004-06. **Publications:** The Union of Their Dreams: Power, Hope, and Struggle in Cesar Chavez's Farm Worker Movement, 2009. **Address:** c/o Gloria Loomis, Watkins-Loomis Literary Agency, 133 E 35th St., New York, NY 10016, U.S.A. **Online address:** mpawel@unionoftheirdreams.com

PAWLAK, Mark. American (born United States), b. 1948. **Genres:** Poetry, Literary Criticism And History, Writing/Journalism. **Career:** University of Massachusetts Boston, instructor in mathematics, 1978-, Academic Support Programs, director; Hanging Loose Press, co-editor, 1980-. **Publications:** POETRY: The Buffalo Sequence, 1978; All the News, 1985; Special Handling: Newspaper Poems New and Selected, 1993; Official Versions, 2006; Jefferson's New Image Salon, 2010. EDITOR (with D. Lourie) Smart Like Me: High School-Age Writing from the Sixties to Now, 1988; Bullseye: Stories and Poems by Outstanding High School Writers, 1994; Shooting the Rat: More Outstanding Poems and Stories by High School Writers, 2003; Present/Tense: Poets in the World, 2004; (with R. Hershon) When We Were Countries: Outstanding Poems and Stories By High School Writers, 2010. **Address:** Academic Support Programs, University of Massachusetts Boston, CC 1-1300, 100 Morrissey Blvd., Boston, MA 02125-3393, U.S.A. **Online address:** mark.pawlak@umb.edu

PAWLIKOWSKI, John Thaddeus. American (born United States), b. 1940. **Genres:** Theology/Religion, Law. **Career:** University of Chicago, Calvert House, chaplain's assistant, 1967-; Catholic Theological Union, assistant professor, 1968-, professor of social ethics, dean of students, 1969-72, acting president, 1975-76, Catholic-Jewish Studies Program, director; National Council of Churches' Faith and Order Study Commission on Israel, chairman, 1972-73; Chicago Institute for Inter-religious Research, chairman, 1973; International Institute of Community Service, fellow, 1975; American Foundation for the Institute of Polish-Jewish Studies, vice president, 1986-; Chicago Clergy and Laity Concerned, vice president, 1987-; International Council of Christian and Jews, president, 2002. Writer. **Publications:** Epistle Homilies, 1966; Proposals for Church Sponsored New Housing, 1971; Catechetics and Prejudice, 1973; Sinai and Calvary, 1976; The Challenge of the Holocaust for Christian Theology, 1978; What Are They Saying about Christian-Jewish Relations?, 1980; Christ in the Light of the Christian-Jewish Dialogue, 1982; (intro.) Justice in the Marketplace, 1985; (with J.A. Wilde) When Catholics Speak about Jews, 1987; Jesus and The Theology of Israel, 1989; (co-author) Jewish-Christian Dialogue: Drawing Honey from the Rock, 2008. EDITOR: (with D. Senior) Biblical and Theological Reflections on the Challenge of Peace, 1984; (with D. Senior) Economic Justice: CTU's Pastoral Commentary on the Bishop's Letter on the Economy, 1988; (with R. Fragomeni) The Ecological Challenge: Ethical, Liturgical, and Spiritual Responses, 1994; (with D. Bergant) Harvest of a Dialogue: Reflections of a Rabbi/Scholar on a Catholic Faculty, 1997; (ed. with J. Bemporad and J. Sievers) Good and Evil after Auschwitz: Ethical Implications for Today, 2000; (with H.G. Perlmuter) Reinterpreting Revelation and Tradition: Jews and Christians in Conversation, 2000; (and intro. with J. Banki) Ethics in the shadow of the Holocaust: Christian and Jewish Perspectives, 2001; (with E.B. Korn) Two Faiths, One Covenant? Jewish and Christian Identity in the Presence of the Other, 2005. **Address:** Catholic Theological Union, 5401 S Cornell Ave., Chicago, IL 60615-5698, U.S.A. **Online address:** jtmp@ctu.edu

PAXSON, Diana L(ucile). American (born United States), b. 1943. **Genres:** Science Fiction/Fantasy, Novels, Young Adult Non-fiction. **Career:** Educator, 1971-81; Center for Non-Traditional Religions, chairman, instructor of clergy in training, 1981-86, president, 1986-89; Fellowship of the Spiral Path, ordained minister, 1982; Fiction Writers of America, Board of Science, western regional director, 1990-96. Writer. **Publications:** FANTASY NOVELS: White Mare, Red Stallion, 1976; Brisingamen, 1984; The Paradise Tree, 1987; The White Raven, 1988; The Serpent's Tooth, 1991; (with M.Z. Bradley) The Forest House, 1993; (with M.Z. Bradley) Lady of Avalon, 1997; (with M.Z. Bradley) Priestess of Avalon, 2000; (with M.Z. Bradley) Ancestors of Avalon, 2004; (with M.Z. Bradley) Ravens of Avalon, 2007; (with M.Z. Bradley) Sword of Avalon, 2009. WESTRIA SERIES: Lady of Light, 1982; Lady of Darkness, 1983; Silverhair the Wanderer, 1986; The Earthstone, 1987; The Sea Star, 1988; The Wind Crystal, 1990; The Mistress of the Jewels, 1991; The Jewel of Fire, 1992; The Golden Hills of Westria, 2006. FIONN MAC CUMHAIL SERIES WITH A. MARTINE-BARNES: Master of Earth and Water, 1992; The Shield between the Worlds, 1994; Sword of Fire and Shadow, 1995. WODAN'S CHILDREN TRILOGY: The Wolf and the Raven, 1993; The Dragons of the Rhine, 1995; The Lord of Horses, 1996. HALLOWED ISLE SERIES: The Book of the Sword, 1999; The Book of the Spear, 1999; The Book of the Cauldron, 1999; The Book of the Stone, 2000. OTHERS: (with Z.E. Budapest) Celestial Wisdom: For Every Year of Your Life: Discover the Hidden Meaning of Your Age, 2003; Taking Up the Runes: A Complete Guide to Using Runes in Spells, Rituals, Divination, and Magic, 2005; Essential Asatru: Walking the Path of Norse Paganism, 2006; Trance-portation: Learning to Navigate the Inner World, 2008. Illustrator of books by others. **Address:** PO Box 472, Berkeley, CA 94701-0472, U.S.A. **Online address:** d.studebake1@genie.com

PAXTON, John. British (born England), b. 1923. **Genres:** Business/Trade/Industry, History, International Relations/Current Affairs, Politics/Government, Social Sciences. **Career:** Millfield School, economics teacher and department head, 1952-63; Statesmans Year-Book, assistant editor, 1963-68, deputy editor, 1968-69, editor, 1969-90; writer, 1990-. **Publications:** (With A.E. Walsh) Trade in the Common Market Countries, 1965; The Structure and Development of the Common Market, 1968; (with A.E. Walsh) Trade And Industrial Resources of the Common Market and EFTA Countries: A Comparative Statistical Analysis, 1970; Smuggling, 1971; (with A.E. Walsh) Into Europe: The Structure and Development of the Common Market, 2nd ed., 1972; World Legislatures, 1974; (with A.E. Walsh) Competition Policy: European and International Trends and Practices, 1974; Dictionary of Abbreviations, 1974; (with A.E. Walsh) Competition Policy: European and International Trends and Practices, 1975; The Statesmans Year-Book World Gazetteer, 1975, 4th ed., 1991; The Developing Common Market, 1976; A Dictionary of the European Communities, 1977, 2nd ed., 1982; (with C. Cook) Commonwealth Political Facts, 1978; (with S. Fairfield) A Calendar of Creative Man, 1980; Companion to Russian History, 1984, rev. ed. as Encyclopedia of Russian History, 1993; Companion to the Revolution, 1986; Penguin Dictionary of Abbreviations, 1989; (with G. Payton) Penguin Dictionary of Proper Names, 1990; European Communities, 1992; Penguin Encyclopedia of Places, 1999; Imperial Russia: A Reference Handbook, 2000; Dictionary of Financial Abbreviations, 2002; Leaders of Russia and the Soviet Union: From the Romanov Dynasty to Vladimir Putin, 2004. EDITOR: (and comp.) Everymans Dictionary of Abbreviations, 1974, 2nd ed., 1986; New Illustrated Everymans Encyclopaedia, 1983; Statesmans Year-book Historical Companion, 1988; (with E.W. Knappman) The Wilson Calendar of World History, 1999. EUROPEAN POLITICAL FACTS WITH C. COOK: European Political Facts 1918-73, 1975; European Political Facts, 1848-1918, 1978; European Political Facts, 1918-84, 1986; European Political Facts, 1918-90, 1992;

European Political Facts, 1900-1996, 1998; European Political Facts of the Twentieth Century, 2001. Contributor to periodicals. **Address:** Moss Cottage, Hardway, Bruton, SM BA10 0LN, England.

PAYNE, Alan. *See* **JAKES, John.**

PAYNE, Daniel G. American (born United States), b. 1958. **Genres:** Plays/Screenplays, Literary Criticism And History, Writing/Journalism, Sciences. **Career:** Monroe Community College, instructor in English, 1993-94; Union College, visiting assistant professor of English, 1996-97; State University of New York, assistant professor of English, 2001, associate professor. Writer. **Publications:** Voices in the Wilderness: American Nature Writing and Environmental Politics, 1996; (ed. with R.S. Newman) The Palgrave Environmental Reader, 2005; (ed.) Writing the Land: John Burroughs and His Legacy: Essays from the John Burroughs Nature Writing Conference, 2008. Contributor to journals. **Address:** Department of English, State University of New York at Oneonta, Netzer 319, Oneonta, NY 13820, U.S.A. **Online address:** paynedg@oneonta.edu

PAYNE, Darwin. American (born United States), b. 1937. **Genres:** History, Biography. **Career:** Fort Worth Press, reporter, 1960-72; Dallas Times Herald, reporter, 1960-72; KERA-TV, reporter, 1960-72; Southern Methodist University, professor, 1967-68, 1972-80, professor emeritus, 1980-, Division of Journalism, acting chair, 1973-74, chair, 1980-; The Suburban Tribune, editor and publisher, 1985-89. **Publications:** Press Corps and the Kennedy Assassination, 1970; The Man of Only Yesterday: Frederick Lewis Allen, 1975; (ed.) Dissenting Opinion: Carl Brannin's Letters to the Editor, 1933-1976, 1977; Initiative in Energy: Dresser Industries, 1880-1978, 1979; Dallas: An Illustrated History, 1982; Owen Wister: Chronicler of the West, Gentleman of the East, 1985; (ed.) Sketches of a Growing Town: Episodes and People of Dallas from Early Days to Recent Times, 1991; Texas Chronicles: The Heritage and Enterprise of the Lone Star State, 1994; Big D: Triumphs and Tribulations of an American Supercity in the 20th Century, 1994, rev. ed., 2000; (ed.) Reporting the Kennedy Assassination: Journalists Who Were There Recall Their Experiences, 1996; As Old as Dallas Itself: A History of the Lawyers of Dallas, the Dallas Bar Association and the City They Helped Build, 1999; (with K. Fitzpatrick) From Prairie to Planes: How Dallas and Fort Worth Overcame Politics and Personalities to Build One of the World's Biggest and Busiest Airports, 1999; Dynamic Dallas: An Illustrated History, 2002; Indomitable Sarah: The Life of Judge Sarah T. Hughes, 2004; Quest for Justice: Louis A. Bedford Jr. and the Struggle for Equal Rights in Texas, 2009; In Honor of the Mustangs: The Centennial History of SMU Athletics, 2010. Contributor to periodicals. **Address:** 9021 Gunnison Dr., Dallas, TX 75231, U.S.A. **Online address:** dpayne@smu.edu

PAYNE, Deborah C. *See* **PAYNE FISK, Deborah C.**

PAYNE, Donald Gordon. Also writes as Donald Gordon, James Vance Marshall, Ian Cameron. British (born England), b. 1924. **Genres:** Novels, Travel/Exploration, Biography, Mystery/Crime/Suspense, Politics/Government, Literary Criticism And History. **Career:** Christopher Johnson Publishers Ltd., trainee, 1949-52; Robert Hale Ltd., editor, 1952-56. Writer. **Publications:** AS IAN CAMERON: The Midnight Sea, 1958; Red Duster, White Ensign: The Story of the Malta Convoys, 1959; The Lost Ones, 1961 in US as The Island at the Top of the World, 1970; Wings of the Morning, 1962; Lodestone and Evening Star, 1965; The Impossible Dream: Building of the Panama Canal, 1972; The Mountains at the Bottom of the World, 1972; Magellan and the First Circumnavigation of the World, 1973; Antarctica: The Last Continent, 1974; The White Ship, 1975; The Young Eagles, 1979; To the Farthest Ends of the Earth: 150 Years of World Exploration by the Royal Geographical Society, 1980; Mountains of the Gods: The Himalayas and the Mountains of Central Asia, 1984; Exploring Antarctica, 1984; Exploring Africa, 1984; Exploring Australia, 1985; Exploring the Himalayas, 1985; Lost Paradise: The Exploration of the Pacific, 1987; (contrib.) Into the Unknown, 1987; Kingdom of the Sun God: A History of the Andes and Their People, 1990; Explorers and Exploration, 1991; Riders of the Storm: The Story of the Royal National Lifeboat Institution, 2002. AS JAMES VANCE MARSHALL: The Children, 1959 in US as Walkabout, 1961; A River Ran Out of Eden, 1963 as The Golden Seal, 1986; My Boy John That Went to Sea, 1966; A Walk to the Hills of the Dreamtime, 1970; The Wind at Morning, 1973; Still Waters, 1982; White-Out, 2000. AS DONALD GORDON: Star-Raker, 1962; Flight of the Bat, 1963; The Golden Oyster, 1967; Leap in the Dark, 1970. **Address:** c/o John Johnson, 211 W 80th St., Lower Level, London, GL EC1R 0HT, England.

PAYNE, Holly. American (born United States) **Genres:** Novels. **Career:** California College of the Arts, MFA Program in Writing, adjunct professor; Academy of Art University, faculty; Skywriter Series Fiction Workshops, founder; Skywriter Ranch, founder. Novelist, screenwriter and educator. **Publications:** NOVELS: The Virgin's Knot, 2002; The Sound of Blue, 2005; Kingdom of Simplicity, 2009. **Address:** California College of the Arts, 1111 8th St., San Francisco, CA 94107-2247, U.S.A. **Online address:** holly@holly-payne.com

PAYNE, Jason Julian. *See* **PAYNE, J. Julian.**

PAYNE, J. Gregory. American (born United States), b. 1949. **Genres:** History, Biography, Communications/Media, Theatre, Ethics, Area Studies, Humanities, Politics/Government, Politics/Government. **Career:** California Lutheran College, associate professor of communications, 1976-77; Occidental College, assistant professor of rhetoric and director of debate, 1976-83, British Debate Tour, president and director, 1980, 1981; Emerson College, Department of Communication Studies, associate professor and co-director of news study group, 1983-, chair, Center for Ethics in Political and Health Communication, director, 1983-, Los Angeles Program, director, 1986, 1987; Young Physicians of America, president, 1987-; Bechtel Corp., consultant; U.S. Treasury Department, consultant; California Credit Union, consultant; Saudi American Exchange, founding director; International Academy of Business Disciplines, president; NCA Political Communication Division, chair. Writer. **Publications:** Mayday: Kent State, 1981; (with S.C. Ratzan) Tom Bradley: The Impossible Dream, 1986. Contributor to articles. **Address:** Department of Communication Studies, Emerson College, 8th Fl., 120 Boylston St., Boston, MA 02116-4624, U.S.A.

PAYNE, J. Julian. (Jason Julian Payne). Canadian (born Canada), b. 1970. **Genres:** Adult Non-fiction, Humor/Satire, Reference. **Career:** Anecdotage Press, founder and editor, 2000-. **Publications:** Celebrity Anecdotes: Funny Stories About the Stars, 2005. **Address:** Anecdotage Press, 220 Glenrose Ave., Toronto, ON M4T 1K9, Canada. **Online address:** imastandup@comic.com

PAYNE, Ladell. American (born United States), b. 1933. **Genres:** Biography, Literary Criticism And History, Cultural/Ethnic Topics, Social Sciences. **Career:** Claremont Men's College (now Claremont McKenna College), instructor, 1960-, assistant professor, associate professor, professor of English, 1975-79, chair of department of literature, 1974-77, assistant, 1976-79; University of Vienna, Fulbright lecturer in American studies, 1971-72; Randolph-Macon College, president, 1979-97, president emeritus, 1997-; Center for the Study of Southern Culture, consultant, 1980-. Writer. **Publications:** Thomas Wolfe, 1969; Black Novelists and the Southern Literary Tradition, 1981; (co-ed.) Achievement of William Faulkner: A Centennial Tribute, 1997. Contributor to books and journals. **Address:** Office of the President, Randolph-Macon College, Peele Hall, 204 Henry St., PO Box 5005, Ashland, VA 23005-5505, U.S.A.

PAYNE, Leigh A. British/Korean/American (born United States), b. 1956. **Genres:** Politics/Government, Area Studies. **Career:** Yale University, lecturer, 1990-91; University of Wisconsin, assistant professor, 1991-98, associate professor, 1998-2001, professor of political science, 2001-09; University of Minnesota Law School, visiting professor in the political science, 2008-11; University of Oxford, St Antony's College, fellow, Latin American Center, professor, 2009-. Writer. **Publications:** Brazilian Industrialists and Democratic Change, 1994; (with E. Bartell) Business and Democracy in Latin America, 1995; Uncivil Movements: The Armed Right Wing and Democracy in Latin America, 2000; Unsettling Accounts: Neither Truth Nor Reconciliation in Confessions of State Violence, 2008; (with T.D. Olsen and A.G. Reiter) Transitional Justice in Balance: Comparing Processes, Weighing Efficacy, 2010; (ed. with K. Bilbija) Accounting for Violence: Marketing Memory in Latin America, 2011. **Address:** The Latin American Center, St. Antony's College, University of Oxford, Woodstock Rd., Oxford, OX OX2 6JF, England. **Online address:** lpayne@polisci.wisc.edu

PAYNE, Neil F. American (born United States), b. 1939. **Genres:** Environmental Sciences/Ecology, Natural History. **Career:** Newfoundland Wildlife Division, furbearer biologist, 1967-71; University of Washington, research assistant professor, 1973-75; University of Wisconsin-Stevens Point, professor, 1975-98, professor emeritus of wildlife, 1998-. Writer. **Publications:** (Co-author) Environmental Impacts of Harvesting Wood for Energy, 1987; (with F. Copes) Wildlife and Fisheries Habitat Improvement Handbook, 1990; Techniques for Wildlife Habitat Management of Wetlands, 1992; (with F.C. Bryant) Techniques for Wildlife Habitat Management of Uplands, 1994; Wildlife Habitat Management of Wetlands, 1998; (with F.C. Bryant) Wildlife Habitat Management of Forestlands, Rangelands, and Farmlands, 1998; More Wildlife on Your Land: A Guide for Private Landowners, 2002; (with R.D. Taber) Wildlife, Conservation, and Human Welfare: A United States and Canadian Perspective, 2003; Wildlife Delights and Dilemmas: Newfoundland and Labrador, 2011. Contributor to periodicals. **Address:** College of Natural Resources, University of Wisconsin-Stevens Point, Stevens Point, WI 54481, U.S.A. **Online address:** npayne@uwsp.edu

PAYNE, (William) David. American (born United States), b. 1955. **Genres:** Novels, History, Romance/Historical. **Career:** Hollins University, writer-in-residence. **Publications:** Confessions of a Taoist on Wall Street: A Chinese American Romance, 1984; Early from the Dance, 1989; Ruin Creek, 1993; Gravesend Light: A Novel, 2000; Back to Wando Passo, 2006. **Address:** c/o Tina Bennett, Janklow & Nesbit Associates, 445 Park Ave., New York, NY 10022-2606, U.S.A. **Online address:** david@davidpaynebooks.com

PAYNE FISK, Deborah C. (Deborah C. Payne). American (born United States), b. 1952. **Genres:** Theatre, Literary Criticism And History. **Career:** Trinity University, assistant professor of literature, 1984-85; American University, assistant professor, 1985-92, associate professor of literature, 1992-, affiliate professor of theatre, 2002-. Writer. **Publications:** (Ed. with J.D. Canfield) Cultural Readings of Restoration and Eighteenth-Century English Theater, 1995; (ed.) Cambridge Companion to English Restoration Theatre, 2000; (ed. and intro.) Four Restoration Libertine Plays, 2005. **Address:** Department of Literature, American University, Battelle Tompkins 218, 4400 Masschusetts Ave. NW, Washington, DC 20016-8047, U.S.A. **Online address:** dfisk@american.edu

PAYTON, Rodney J. (Rodney Johns Payton). American (born United States), b. 1940. **Genres:** Literary Criticism And History, Translations, Social Sciences, Young Adult Fiction, Humanities. **Career:** Western Washington University, lecturer, 1970-71, assistant professor, 1971-75, associate professor, 1976-92, professor of liberal studies, 1992-2005, professor emeritus, 2005-. Writer. **Publications:** A Modern Reader's Guide to Dante's Inferno, 1992; (trans. with U. Mammitzsch) J. Huizinga, The Autumn of the Middle Ages, 1996. Contributor to professional journals. Works appear in anthologies. **Address:** Department of Liberal Studies, Western Washington University, Bond Hall 152, PO Box 9064, Bellingham, WA 98225, U.S.A.

PAYTON, Rodney Johns. *See* **PAYTON, Rodney J.**

PAZZI, Roberto. Italian (born Italy), b. 1946. **Genres:** Poetry, Novels. **Career:** V. Monti Institute, teacher; University of Urbino, Sociology of Art and Literature Department, chair; Contrappunto (poetry journal), editor, 1984-85; Sinopia (poetry journal), founder. **Publications:** L'esperienza anteriore (poems), 1973; Versi occidentali (poems), 1976; Il re, le parole, 1980; Cercando l'imperatore: Storia di un reggimento russo disperso nella Siberia durante la Rivoluzione in cerca dello Zar prigioniero, 1985; La principessa e il drago (novel), 1986; Calma di vento (poems), 1987; La malattia del tempo, 1987; (co-author) Giardini e cortili di Ferrara, 1988; Vangelo di Giuda (title means: 'The Gospel of Judas'), 1989; (with P. Zappaterra) Ferrara interni, 1990; Il bambino, 1991; La stanza sull'acqua (title means: The Room on the Water), 1991; Le città del dottor Malaguti, 1993; Il filo delle bugie: poesie edite ed inedite, 1966-1994 (poems), 1994; Incerti di viaggio: Romanzo, 1996; Domani sarò re: Romanzo, 1997; La gravità dei corpi, 1998; La città volante (novel), 1999; Vangelo di Guida (novel), 1999; L'immaginario contemporaneo: Atti del convegno letterario internazionale, Ferrara, 21-23 maggio 1999, 2000; Conclave (novel), 2001; Maldicenza e altri racconti, 2001; Erede, 2002; Signore degli occhi: Romanzo, 2004; Ombra del padre, 2005; Qualcuno mi insegue, 2007; Forbici di Solingen: romanzo, 2007; Dopo Primavera, 2008; Mi spiacerà morire per non vederti più: romanzo, 2010. Contributor to periodicals. **Address:** c/o Author Mail, Random House Publicity, 1745 Broadway, New York, NY 10019, U.S.A.

PEABODY, Richard (Myers). American (born United States), b. 1951. **Genres:** Novellas/Short Stories, Poetry, Administration/Management, Biography, Autobiography/Memoirs, Literary Criticism And History, Science Fiction/Fantasy. **Career:** Gargoyle Magazine, co-founder and editor, 1976-90; WPFW-FM, co-host of weekly radio show, 1978-79; Paycock Press, founder, 1979; Saint John's College, fiction workshops instructor, 1985-87; Writer's Center, fiction workshops instructor, 1987-99, 2006-; Georgetown University, creative writing instructor, 1993; University of Maryland, creative writing instructor, 1993-97; University of Virginia, fiction workshops instructor, 1993-97; Atticus Books, co-owner, 1995-99. Poet and Writer. **Publications:** I'm in Love with Morton Salt Girl, 1979; Monaural (fiction), 1980; Paraffin Days (stories), 1995; Open Joints on Bridge (stories), 1999; Sugar Mountain (novella), 2000. POEMS: I'm in Love with the Morton Salt Girl, 1979; Echt and Ersatz/I'm in Love with the Morton Salt Girl, 1985; Sad Fashions, 1990; Buoyancy and Other Myths, 1995; Mood Vertigo, 1999; Rain Flowers, 2002; Last of the Red Hot Magnetos, 2004. EDITOR: DC Magazines: A Literary Retrospective, 1982; Mavericks: Nine Independent Publishers, 1983; (with L. Ebersole) Mondo Barbie, 1993; (with L. Ebersole) Mondo Elvis, 1994; (with L. Ebersole) Coming to Terms: A Literary Response to Abortion, 1995; (with L. Ebersole) Mondo Marilyn, 1995; (with L. Ebersole) Mondo James Dean, 1996; A Different Beat: Writings by Women of the Beat Generation, 1997; Grace and Gravity: Fiction by Washington Area Women, 2004; (with L. Ebersole) Conversations with Gore Vidal, 2005. Alice Redux: New Stories of Alice, Lewis and Wonderland, 2005; (with L. Ebersole) Sex and Chocolate: Tasty Morsels for Mind and Body, 2006; Enhanced Gravity: More Fiction by Washington Area Women, 2006; Kiss the Sky: Fiction and Poetry Starring Jimi Hendrix, 2007. Contributor of stories and reviews to magazines. **Address:** Anne Edelstein Literary Agency, 310 Riverside Dr., Ste. 1811, New York, NY 10025, U.S.A. **Online address:** hedgehog2@erols.com

PEACE, David. Japanese/British (born England), b. 1967. **Genres:** Criminology/True Crime, Novels. **Career:** Writer and educator. **Publications:** Nineteen Seventy Four, 1999, 2nd ed., 2000; Nineteen Seventy Seven, 2000; Nineteen Eighty, 2001; Nineteen Eighty Three, 2002; GB84, 2004; The Damned Utd, 2006; Tokyo Year Zero, 2007; Occupied City, 2009; Tokyo Regained, 2010. **Address:** Serpent's Tail, 3A Exmouth House, Pine St., London, GL EC1R 0JH, England.

PEACE, Richard (Arthur). British (born England), b. 1933. **Genres:** Literary Criticism And History, Novels. **Career:** University of Bristol, lecturer, senior lecturer in Russian, 1963-75, professor of Russian, 1984-94, professor emeritus, 1994-; University of Hull, professor of Russian, 1975-84. Writer. **Publications:** Dostoyevsky: An Examination of the Major Novels, 1971; Russian Literature and the Fictionalisation of Life, 1976; The Enigma of Gogol: An Examination of the Writings of N.V. Gogol and Their Place in the Russian Literary Tradition, 1981; Chekhov: A Study of the Four Major Plays, 1983; Oblomov: A Critical Examination of Goncharov's Novel, 1991; Dostoevsky: Notes from Underground, 1993. EDITOR: (and intro.) Woe from Wit, 1995; Fyodor Dostoevsky's Crime and Punishment: A Casebook, 2006; Plays and Petersburg Tales, 2008. INTRODUCTION: Gogol: Village Evenings near Dihanka and Mirgorod, 1994; Petersburg Tales: Marriage: The Government Inspector, 1995; Crime and Punishment, 1995. Contributor to books. **Address:** Department of Russian Studies, University of Bristol, 17 Woodland Rd., Bristol, BS8 1TE, England. **Online address:** richard@richardpeace.myzen.co.uk

PEACHMENT, Christopher. American (born United States) **Genres:** Novels, Biography, Young Adult Fiction, Literary Criticism And History. **Career:** Royal Court Theatre, stage manager; Time Out (magazine), film editor; Times, deputy literary editor and arts editor. **Publications:** Caravaggio, 2003; The Green and the Gold, 2003; The Green and the Gold: A Novel of Andrew Marvell: Spy, Politician, Poet, 2004. Contributor to periodicals. **Address:** St. Martins Press, 175 5th Ave., New York, NY 10010, U.S.A.

PEACOCK, Alan (Turner). British (born England), b. 1922. **Genres:** Economics, Education, Music. **Career:** University of St. Andrews, lecturer, 1947-48; London School of Economics, lecturer in economics, 1948-51, reader in public finance, 1951-56; University of Edinburgh, professor of economic science, 1956-62; University of York, professor of economics, 1962-78, Department of Economics, founder; Departments of Trade, Industry and Consumer Protection, chief economic adviser, 1973-76; University of Buckingham, professor of economics, 1978-84; principal and vice-chancellor, 1980-84; David Hume Institute, co-founder and executive director, 1985-91; Heriot Watt University, research professor in public finance. Writer. **Publications:** Economics of National Insurance, 1952; (trans.) H. von Stackelberg, Theory of the Market Economy, 1953; (ed.) Income Redistribution and Social Policy, 1954; (with H. Edey) National Income and Social Accounting,

1954, 3rd rev. ed., 1968; (with D. Dosser) National Income of Tanganyika, 1958; (with R.A. Musgrave) Classics in Public Finance, 1958; (with J. Wiseman) Growth of Public Expenditure in the United Kingdom, 1961, 2nd ed., 1967; (ed. with D. Robertson) Public Expenditure, 1963; (with J. Wiseman) Education for Democrats, 1964; Welfare Society, 1966; (with H. Glennerster and R. Lavers) Educational Finance, 1968; (ed.) Quantitative Analysis in Public Finance, 1969; (with A.J. Culyer) Economic Aspects of Student Unrest, 1969; (with G. Shaw) Economic Theory of Fiscal Policy, 1971, 2nd ed., 1976; (with G.K. Shaw) Fiscal Policy and the Employment Problem in Less Developed Countries, 1971; (with R. Weir) The Composer in the Market Place, 1975; The Oil Crisis and the Professional Economist, 1975; (with C. Rowley) Welfare Economics, 1975; Credibility of Liberal Economics, 1977; The Economic Analysis of Government, 1979; Structural Economic Policies in West Germany and the United Kingdom, 1980; (ed. with F. Forte) Political Economy of Taxation, 1981; The Regulation Game, 1984; (ed. with F. Forte) Public Expenditure and Government Growth, 1985; Waltz Contrasts, 1988; (with G. Bannock) Governments and Small Business, 1989; (ed.) Germanys Social Market Economy: Origins and the Funding Problem, 1989; (ed. with H. Willsgerodt) German Neo-liberals and the Social Market Economy, 1989; Public Choice Analysis in Historical Perspective, 1991; (with G. Bannock) Corporate Takeovers and the Public Interest: Report of an Inquiry Conducted for the Joseph Rowntree Foundation, 1991; Paying the Piper: Culture, Music and Money, 1993; (ed. with R.A. Classics in the Theory of Public Finance, 1994; (ed. with I. Rizzo) Cultural Economics and Cultural Policies, 1994; The Political Economy of Economic Freedom, 1997; (with B. Main) What Price Civil Justice?, 2000; Calling the Tune: A Critique of Arts Funding in Scotland, 2001; The Enigmatic Sailor: Memoirs of a Seagoing Intelligence Officer, 2003; (with I. Rizzo) The Heritage Game: Economics, Policy and Practice, 2008. Contributor to journals and magazines. **Address:** David Hume Institute, 21 George Sq., Edinburgh, EH8 9LD, Scotland. **Online address:** peacock@ebs.hw.ac.uk

PEACOCK, Molly. American/Canadian (born Canada), b. 1947. **Genres:** Poetry, Essays, Homes/Gardens, Literary Criticism And History, Women's Studies And Issues, Autobiography/Memoirs, Biography, Art/Art History, Biography, Plays/Screenplays. **Career:** State University of New York, director of academic advising, 1970-73, coordinator of innovational projects in office of the dean, 1973-76; Johns Hopkins University, Danforth fellow, 1975-77, honorary fellow, 1977-78; Delaware Arts Council, poet-in-residence, 1978-81; Friends Seminary, learning specialist, 1981-92; Hofstra University, visiting lecturer, 1986, 1988; Columbia University, visiting lecturer, 1987; New York University, visiting lecturer, 1989; Sarah Lawrence College, visiting lecturer; Barnard College, visiting lecturer, 1989-90; Poetry Society of America, president, 1989-95, 1999-2001; One-to-One Poetry Consulting, staff, 1990-; Bucknell University, poet-in-residence, 1993-94; University of Western Ontario, writer-in-resident, 1995-96; American Poets' Corner, Cathedral of Saint John the Divine, poet-in-residence, 2000-05; Spalding University, graduate faculty, 2003-; The City University of New York, Leon Levy Center, fellow, 2009. Writer. **Publications:** And Live Apart: Poems, 1980; Raw Heaven, 1984; Take Heart, 1989; Original Love, 1995; (ed. with E. Paschen and N. Neches) Poetry in Motion: 100 Poems from the Subways and Buses, 1996; (intro.) Understory, 1996; Paradise, Piece by Piece, 1998; How to Read a Poem and Start a Poetry Circle, 1999; (ed.) The Private I: Privacy in a Public World, 2001; Cornucopia: New and Selected Poems, 1975-2002, 2002; The Shimmering Verge: A One-Woman Show in Poems, 2003; The Second Blush: Poems, 2008; The Paper Garden, 2010. **Address:** c/o Kathleen Anderson, Anderson Literary Management, 12 W 19 St., 2nd Fl., New York, NY 10011, U.S.A. **Online address:** molly@mollypeacock.org

PEACOCK, Sandra J. American (born United States), b. 1955?. **Genres:** Biography. **Career:** Georgia Southern University, Department of history, chair, 2002-08, associate professor, professor of history, Women's and Gender Studies Program, director. Writer. **Publications:** Jane Ellen Harrison: The Mask and the Self, 1988; The Theological and Ethical Writings of Frances Power Cobbe, 1822-1904, 2002; (with R.S. Davis) Judge Faye Sanders Martin: Head Full of Sense, Heart Full of Gold, 2004. Contributor to periodicals. **Address:** Department of History, Georgia Southern University, 1207 Forest Drive Bldg., PO Box 8054, Statesboro, GA 30460-8054, U.S.A. **Online address:** speacock@georgiasouthern.edu

PEACOCK, Shane. Canadian (born Canada), b. 1957?. **Genres:** Biography, Young Adult Fiction, Mystery/Crime/Suspense. **Career:** Writer. **Publications:** BIOGRAPHIES: The Great Farini: The High-Wire Life of William Hunt, 1995; Unusual Heroes: Canada's Prime Ministers and Fathers of Confederation, 2002; DYLAN MAPLES ADVENTURE SERIES: The Mystery of Ireland's Eye, 1999; The Secret of the Silver Mines, 2000; Bone Beds of the Badlands, 2001; Monster in the Mountains, 2003; THE BOY SHERLOCK HOLMES SERIES: Eye of the Crow: The Boy Sherlock Holmes, His First Case, 2007; Death in the Air: The Boy Sherlock Holmes, His Second Case, 2008; The Dragon Turn: The Boy Sherlock Holmes, 2011; Master Sherlock: The Boy Sherlock Holmes, 2012. PLAYS: The Great Farini: The Play, 1994; The Devil and Joseph Scriven, 1999; The Art of Silent Killing, 2006. TELEVISION DOCUMENTARIES: Dangerous Dreams: The Life of The Great Farini, 2000; The Passion of Joseph Scriven, 2001; (co-producer) Team Spirit: The Jordin and Terence Tootoo Story, 2004; (ed.) Exhibit Eh! Exposing Canada, 2006. Contributor to magazines and newspapers. **Address:** Pamela Paul Agency, 12 Westrose Ave., Toronto, ON M8X 1Z2, Canada.

PEAK, John A. American (born United States) **Genres:** Novels, Literary Criticism And History. **Career:** Colorado Court of Appeals, clerk for justice William F. Dwyer; Office of the City Attorney for the City and County of San Francisco, defense attorney, 1980-93. Writer. **Publications:** NOVELS: Spare Change, 1994; Blood Relations, 1997; Mortal Judgments, 1999; M and M, 2002. **Address:** St. Martin's Press Inc., Rm. 1715, 175 5th Ave., New York, NY 10010-7703, U.S.A. **Online address:** japeak@earthlink.net

PEAR, David (Adrian). Australian/British (born England), b. 1957. **Genres:** Biography, Music, Autobiography/Memoirs, Art/Art History. **Career:** Australian National University, Humanities Research Centre, visiting fellow, 2002-04; Monash University, part-time senior lecturer, research fellow. Writer. **Publications:** (Ed. with M. Gillies) The All-Round Man: Selected Letters of Percy Grainger, 1914-1961, 1994; (with M. Gillies) Portrait of Percy Grainger, 2002; (ed. with M. Gillies and M. Carroll) Self-portrait of Percy Grainger, 2006; (comp. and ed.) Facing Percy Grainger, 2006. CONTRIBUTOR: (with R. Gordon) Australian Dictionary of Biography vol. XI, 1891-1939, 1988. Contributor to periodicals. **Address:** Humanities Research Centre, The Australian National University, Sir Roland Wilson Bldg., Ste. 120, McCoy Circuit, Canberra, AC 0200, Australia. **Online address:** david.pear@anu.edu.au

PEARCE, Edward. British (born England), b. 1939?. **Genres:** Novels. **Career:** Daily Express, lead writer, 1977-79; Daily Telegraph, commons sketch writer & lead writer 1979- 87; Sunday Times, columnist, 1987-90; New Statesman, sketch writer, 1990-95. **Publications:** The Senate of Lilliput, 1983; Hummingbirds and Hyenas, 1985; Looking Down on Mrs. Thatcher, 1987; The Quiet Rise of John Major, 1991; Election Rides, 1992; Machiavelli's Children, 1993; The Lost Leaders: The Best Prime Ministers We Never Had, 1998; Lines of Most Resistance: The Lords, the Tories and Ireland, 1886-1914, 1999; Denis Healey: A Life in Our Times, 2002; Reform! The Fight for the 1832 Reform Act, 2003; (ed. with D. Pearce) The Diaries of Charles Greville, 2005; The Great Man: Scoundrel, Genius and Britain's First Prime Minister, 2007. **Address:** Yorkshire Post Newspapers Ltd., Wellington St., PO Box 168, Leeds, LS1 1RF, England.

PEARCE, Margaret. (Jacqueline Webb). Australian (born Australia) **Genres:** Romance/Historical, Children's Fiction, Young Adult Fiction, Westerns/Adventure, Novels. **Career:** Writer. **Publications:** FOR CHILDREN: The Circus Runaways, 1978; Altar of Shulaani: An Exciting Science Fiction Adventure, 1981; Wanted! A Horse, 1983; The Misfit, 1984; One Day in the Life of a Maidservant (series), 1987; The Castle Hill Uprising (series), 1987; Marmaduke, 1988; Weekend of Herman John (series), 1989; When Doggo Went Purple, 1989; The Secret in the Compost Bin, 1990; The Convertible Couch, 1991; Caught in Willaburra, 1992; The Old Man in the Park, 1992; Bolton Road Spy Catchers, 1992; Rilla and the School Play, 1997; Birthday Surprise, 1998; Party Poopers, 1999; Carrington, 2006; Jewellers to the Palace, 2006; Edge of Forever, 2006. FOR YOUNG ADULTS: The Look of Love, 1988; Bobby and Frank, 1989; Three's a Crowd, 1991; The Togetherness Routine, 1991; Weekend Territory, 1993; The Secret of the Third Seal, 1995. ROMANCE NOVELS AS JACQUELINE WEBB: The Lonely Heart, 1990; Roses are for Romance, 1991; Shadows over Taralon, 1992. Works appear in anthologies. **Address:** PO Box 253, Belgrane, VI 3160, Australia. **Online address:** mpearceau@gmail.com

PEARCE, Mary E. British (born England), b. 1932. **Genres:** Novels, Natural History, Children's Fiction. **Career:** Writer, 1960-. **Publications:** APPLE TREE SAGA SERIES: Apple Tree Lean Down, 1973; Jack Mercybright,

1974; The Sorrowing Wind, 1975. OTHERS: Cast a Long Shadow, 1977; The Land Endures, 1978; Seedtime and Harvest, 1980; Polsinney Harbour, 1983; The Two Farms, 1985; The Old House At Railes, 1993. Contributor to books. **Address:** Owls End, Shuthonger, Tewkesbury, GC GL20 6EQ, England.

PEARCEY, Nancy. American (born United States), b. 1952?. **Genres:** Theology/Religion, inspirational/Motivational Literature, Social Commentary, Adult Non-fiction, Philosophy. **Career:** Break Point (radio), founding editor, 1991-, executive editor; Wilberforce Forum, policy director, senior fellow; Origins and Designs (journal), managing editor; Philadelphia Biblical University, professor; Discovery Institute, senior fellow; The Pearcey Report, editor-at-large. **Publications:** (Ed.) Our Amazing World, 1985; (ed.) Our Orderly World, 1986; (with C.B. Thaxton) The Soul of Science: Christian Faith and Natural Philosophy, 1994; Total Truth: Liberating Christianity from its Cultural Captivity, 2004, 2nd ed., 2005. WITH C.W. COLSON: A Dance with Deception: Revealing the Truth Behind the Headlines, 1993; How Now Shall We Live?, 1999, 2nd ed., 2000; Developing a Christian Worldview of Science and Evolution, 2001; Developing a Christian Worldview of the Christian in Today's Culture, 2001; Developing a Christian Worldview of the Problem of Evil, 2001. Contributor to periodicals. **Address:** c/o Author Mail, Tyndale House Publishers, 351 Executive Dr., Carol Stream, IL 60188, U.S.A. **Online address:** npearcey@worldji.com

PEARL, David. British (born England), b. 1944. **Genres:** Law, Medicine/Health. **Career:** Cambridge University, university lecturer, 1967-89; University of East Anglia, professor of law, 1989-94, School of Law, dean, 1989-94; Immigration Appeals Authority, chief adjudicator, 1994-98; Immigration Appeals Tribunal, chief adjudicator, 1994, president, 1998-99; Judicial Studies Board, director of studies, 1999-2002; Care Standards Tribunal, president, 2002-; Fitzwilliam College, fellow. Writer. **Publications:** A Textbook on Muslim Law, 1979, (with W. Menski) 3rd ed. as Muslim Family Law, 1998; Interpersonal Conflict of Laws in India, Pakistan, and Bangladesh, 1981; (with J. Khayat) Mourir utile, 1981; (with K. Gray) Social Welfare Law, 1981; Family Law and Society, 1983, 5th ed., 2002; Family Law and the Immigrant Communities, 1986; (with A. Grubb) Blood Testing, AIDS, and DNA Profiling: Law and Policy, 1990; Islamic Family Law and Its Reception by the Courts in England, 2000; (with D. Hershman) Care Standards Legislation Handbook, 2002, (ed.) 7th ed., 2009; Piano Exercises for Dummies, 2008. EDITOR: (with J.M. Eekelaar) An Aging World: Dilemmas and Challenges for Law and Social Policy, 1989; (with A. Bainham) Frontiers of Family Law, 1993. **Address:** Jordan Publishing Ltd., 21 St. Thomas St., Bristol, BS1 6JS, England. **Online address:** david.pearl@cst.gsi.gov.uk

PEARL, Matthew. American (born United States), b. 1975. **Genres:** Mystery/Crime/Suspense, Novels, Young Adult Non-fiction, Literary Criticism And History, Horror. **Career:** Harvard University, instructor of literature and creative writing, 2000-, Harvard Law School, visiting lecturer; Emerson College, instructor of literature and creative writing. Writer. **Publications:** (Ed. and intro.) Inferno, 2003; The Dante Club (novel), 2003; The Poe Shadow (novel), 2006; (ed. and intro.) Murders in the Rue Morgue: The Dupin Tales, 2006; (ed. and intro.) Mystery of Edwin Drood, 2009; Last Dickens: A Novel, 2009; (co-author) No Rest for the Dead, 2011; The Technologists, 2012. Contributor to periodicals and journals. **Address:** c/o Author Mail, Random House Inc., 1745 Broadway, New York, NY 10019, U.S.A. **Online address:** mpearl@matthewpearl.com

PEARLMAN, Daniel D. (Daniel David Pearlman). American (born United States), b. 1935. **Genres:** Novels, Novellas/Short Stories, Science Fiction/Fantasy, Literary Criticism And History, Young Adult Fiction. **Career:** Brooklyn College, faculty; Long Island University, faculty; University of Arizona, faculty; Monmouth College, faculty; University of Seville, faculty; Lehman College, faculty; University of Rhode Island, Department of English, professor, 1980-2005, chair, 1980-83, professor emeritus, 2005-, Council for the Literature of the Fantastic, coordinator, Puck/Clf Newsletter, co-editor; Paideuma, editorial associate. **Publications:** The Barb of Time: on the Unity of Ezra Pound's Cantos (literary criticism), 1969; (with P.R. Pearlman) Guide to Rapid Revision (textbook), 1974, 8th ed., 2003; (with A. DuBose) Letter Perfect: An ABC for Business Writers (textbook), 1985. NOVELS: Black Flames, 1997; Memini, 2003; Weeds in Franco's Garden, forthcoming. SHORT STORIES: The Final Dream and Other Fictions, 1995; The Best-Known Man in the World and Other Misfits, 2001. Contributor of short stories to magazines and journals. **Address:** Department of English, University of Rhode Island, 114 Swan Hall, 60 Upper College Rd., Kingston, RI 02881, U.S.A. **Online address:** dpearl@uriacc.uri.edu

PEARLMAN, Daniel David. *See* **PEARLMAN, Daniel D.**

PEARLMAN, Jeff. American (born United States) **Genres:** Biography, Sports/Fitness. **Career:** Tennessean, features writer, 1994-96, food and fashion writer; Sports Illustrated, reporter, 1996-, senior writer, SI.com, columnist and contributor; Newsday, features writer; ESPN.com, columnist. **Publications:** The Bad Guys Won: A Season of Brawling, Boozing, Bimbo-chasing, and Championship Baseball with Straw, Doc, Mookie, Nails, the Kid, and the Rest of the 1986 Mets, the Rowdiest Team to Put on a New York Uniform, and Maybe the Best, 2004; Love Me, Hate Me: Barry Bonds and The Making of an Antihero, 2006; Boys will be Boys: The Glory Days and Party Nights of the Dallas Cowboys Dynasty, 2008; Rocket that Fell to Earth: Roger Clemens and the Rage for Baseball Immortality, 2009; Sweetness: The Enigmatic Life of Walter Payton, 2011. Contributor to periodicals. **Address:** c/o Author Mail, HarperCollins Publishers, 10 E 53rd St., New York, NY 10022, U.S.A.

PEARLMAN, Mickey. American (born United States), b. 1938. **Genres:** Literary Criticism And History, Women's Studies And Issues. **Career:** College of New Rochelle, teacher, 1977-80; Iona College, teacher, 1980-88; educator and writer, 1988-; Hartwick College, visiting Babcock lecturer, 1991; Boston Globe, book reviewer; Minneapolis Star Tribune, book reviewer; The Forward, book reviewer. **Publications:** (With K.U. Henderson) Inter/View: Talks with America's Writing Women, 1990, as A Voice of One's Own, 1990; (with A.H.P. Werlock) Tillie Olsen, 1991; Listen to Their Voices, 1993; What to Read, 1994, rev. ed., 2003; Re-Inventing Reality: Patterns and Characters in the Novels of Muriel Spark, 1996. EDITOR: (and contrib.) American Women Writing Fiction: Memory, Identity, Family, Space, 1989; (and intro.) Mother Puzzles: Daughters and Mothers in Contemporary American Literature, 1989; The Anna Book: Searching for Anna in Literary History, 1991; Canadian Women Writing Fiction, 1992; Between Friends, 1994; Place Called Home: Twenty Writing Women Remember, 1996; A Few Thousand Words about Love, 1998. Contributor to periodicals. **Address:** Vicky Bijur Literary Agency, 333 W End Ave., Ste. 5B, New York, NY 10023-8129, U.S.A. **Online address:** mickey@mickeypearlman.com

PEARLSTINE, Norman. American (born United States), b. 1942. **Genres:** Politics/Government, Writing/Journalism, Social Sciences. **Career:** Wall Street Journal, reporter, 1968-73, Tokyo bureau chief, 1973-76, managing editor of Asian edition, 1976-78, national news editor, 1980-82, European Edition, editor and publisher, 1982-83, managing editor, 1983-91, executive editor, 1991-92; Forbes, executive editor, 1978-80; Friday Holdings (media investment group), founder, 1992, general partner, 1993-94; Time Warner Inc., senior advisor, Time Inc., staff, 1994, editor-in-chief, 1995-2005; Carlyle Group, Telecom and Media Team, senior advisor, 2006-; Bloomberg L.P., chief content officer, 2008-; American Academy in Berlin, president and chief executive officer; Atsuko Chiba Foundation, president; Business Week, chairman. **Publications:** Off the Record: The Press, the Government, and the War over Anonymous Sources, 2007. **Address:** c/o Lynn Nesbit, Janklow & Nesbit Associates, 445 Park Ave., New York, NY 10022, U.S.A. **Online address:** norm@normanpearlstine.com

PEARS, Tim. British (born England), b. 1956. **Genres:** Novels, Children's Fiction, Young Adult Fiction. **Career:** Oxford Brookes University, royal literary fund fellow, 2006-. Librarian and writer. **Publications:** NOVELS: In the Place of Fallen Leaves, 1993; In a Land of Plenty, 1997; A Revolution of the Sun, 2000; Wake Up, 2002; Blenheim Orchard, 2007; Landed, 2010; Disputed Land, 2011. Contributor to periodicals. **Address:** c/o Victoria Hobbs, A. M. Heath & Company Ltd., 6 Warwick Ct., London, GL WC1R 5DJ, England.

PEARSALL, Derek (Albert). British (born England), b. 1931. **Genres:** Literary Criticism And History, Bibliography, Art/Art History, Poetry, Biography, Documentaries/Reportage. **Career:** University of London, King's College, assistant lecturer, 1959-61, lecturer in English, 1961-65; University of Toronto, visiting professor, 1963-64; University of York, Kings Manor, lecturer, 1965-68, senior lecturer, 1968-71, reader, 1971-76, professor of English, 1976-86, honorary professor, now professor emeritus, Center for Medieval Studies, founder, co-director, 1978-86; University of Minnesota, visiting professor, 1974; University of Connecticut, visiting professor, 1981-84; Harvard University, visiting professor, 1985-87, Gurney professor of English, 1987-2000, Gurney professor emeritus of English, 2000-; Union College, Lamont distinguished visiting professor, 1990; University of California, visiting professor, 1991, Center for Medieval and Renaissance Studies, distinguished visiting professor, 1991. Writer. **Publications:** Gover and Lydgate: Writers and Their Work, 1969; John Lydgate, 1970; (with E. Salter) Landscapes and Seasons of the Medieval World, 1973; Old English and Middle English Poetry, 1977; (intro.) The Auchinleck Manuscript, 1977; Piers Plowman: An Edition of the C-Text, 1978; The Canterbury Tales, 1985; An Annotated Critical Bibliography of Langland, 1990; The Life of Geoffrey Chaucer: A Critical Biography, 1992; John Lydgate: A Bio-bibliography, 1997; Gothic Europe 1200-1450, 2000; Arthurian Romance: A Short Introduction, 2003; William Langland, William Blake and the Poetry of Hope, 2003. EDITOR: The Floure and the Leafe and The Assembly of Ladies, 1962, rev. ed., 1980; (with E. Salter) Piers Plowman: Selections from the C-Text, 1967; (with R.A. Waldron) Medieval Literature and Civilization: Studies in Memory of G.N. Garmonsway, 1969; Gower and Lydgate, 1969; (with A.S.G. Edwards) Middle English Prose, 1981; Manuscripts and Readers in 15th Century England: The Literary Implications of Manuscript Study: Essays from the 1981 Conference at the University of York, 1983; (with N. Zeeman) Fourteenth-Century English Poetry: Contexts and Readings, 1984; The Nun's Priest's Tale, 1984; Manuscripts and Texts: Editorial Problems in Later Middle English Literature, 1987; (with N. Zeeman) English and International: Studies in the Literature, Art and Patronage of Medieval England, 1988; (with J. Griffiths) Book Production and Publishing in Britain, 1375-1475, 1989; Studies in the Vernon Manuscript, 1990; The Floure and the Leafe, The Assembly of Ladies, The Isle of Ladies, 1990; (with K. Scott and intro.) Piers Plowman: A Facsimile of Bodleian Library, Oxford, MS Douce 104, 1992; Chaucer to Spenser: An Anthology, 1998; Chaucer to Spenser: A Critical Reader, 1999; Chaucer to Spenser: An Anthology of Writings in English 1375-1575, 1999; New Directions in Later Medieval Manuscript Study: Essays from the 1998 Harvard Conference, 2000; Book Production and Publishing in Britain 1375-1475, 2007. FORTHCOMING: John Lydgate: A Documentary Biography; The Chaucer Portraits. Contributor to books. **Address:** Department of English and Related Literature, University of York, Heslington, York, NY Y010 5DD, England. **Online address:** derek@apearsall.fsnet.co.uk

PEARSALL, Shelley. American (born United States), b. 1966?. **Genres:** Novels. **Career:** Public school teacher; museum historian; James Thurber House, children's writer-in-residence, 2005. **Publications:** Remarkable Ohioans: Stories, 1997; Trouble Don't Last, 2002; Crooked River, 2005; All of the Above, 2006; All Shook Up, 2008; Jump into the Sky, 2012. **Address:** Alfred A Knopf Inc., 1745 Broadway, New York, NY 10019, U.S.A. **Online address:** shellquill@yahoo.com

PEARSE, Meic. American/British (born England), b. 1955. **Genres:** History. **Career:** Evangelical Theological Seminary, visiting professor of church History, 1995-; London School of Theology, faculty, head of theology program; Houghton College, professor; Oxford University, faculty; University of Newcastle, faculty; SS. Cyril and Methodius University, faculty; Osijek University, faculty; Timisoara University, faculty; St. Bonaventure University, faculty. Writer. **Publications:** Why the Rest Hates the West: Understanding the Roots of Global Rage, 2004; The Gods of War: Is Religion the Primary Cause of Violent Conflict?, 2007. **Address:** U.S.A. **Online address:** meic.pearse@houghton.edu

PEARSON, Carol Lynn. American (born United States), b. 1939. **Genres:** Novels, Novellas/Short Stories, Poetry, Autobiography/Memoirs. **Career:** Schoolteacher, 1962-63; freelance writer, 1963-. **Publications:** Daughters of Light, 1973; The Flight and the Nest, 1975; My Turn On Earth, 1977; Will I Ever Forget This Day?, 1980; Overheard at the Dance, 1981; A Lasting Peace (novel), 1983; Today, Tomorrow, and Four Weeks from Tuesday (novel), 1983; A Stranger for Christmas (novel), 1984; Goodbye, I Love You, 1986; One on the Seesaw: The Ups and Downs of a Single-Parent Family, 1988; The Modern Magi (novella), 1994; The Christmas Thief (novella), 1995; Morning Glory Mother (novella), 1997; The Lesson (fable), 1998; The Stocking Stuffer's Story, 1998; What Love Is (fable), 1999; Will You Still Be My Daughter? (fable), 2000; Girlfriend, You Are the Best! (fable), 2000; Fuzzy Red Bathrobe: Questions from the Heart for Mothers and Daughters, 2000; Day-old Child and Other Celebrations of Motherhood, 2001; The Gift: A Fable for Our Times, 2001; Strong Man: A Fable for Our Times, 2001; Consider the Butterfly: Transforming Your Life through Meaningful Coincidence (biography), 2002; Embracing Coincidence, 2002; A Sister (fable), 2002; Modern Magi, 2003; Christmas Thief, 2003; Stranger for Christmas, 2003; The Christmas Play, 2004; The Christmas Moment, 2005; The Runaway Mother, 2006; No More Goodbyes: Circling the Wagons around Our Gay Loved Ones, 2007; Summer of Truth, 2007; Dance, 2007; Priceless Moments: Snapshots of Motherhood, 2008; I'll Always be Your Daughter, 2009; Lord is My Shepherd, 2009; Girlfriend!, 2010; In Dog Years I'm Dead: Growing Old, 2010; Lesson: A Fable of Hope, 2010; Do These Depends Make My Butt Look Bigger?, 2010; What Love is: A Fable for Couples, 2010; I'm Still a Hot Babe, but Now it Comes in Flashes, 2011. POETRY: Beginnings, 1967; The Search, 1970; The Growing Season, 1976; Call It Mother, 1979; A Widening View, 1983; I Can't Stop Smiling, 1984; Women I Have Known and Been, 1992; Picture Window, 1996 as Beginnings and Beyond, 2005; In Love Again and Always, 2007; The Sweet, Still Waters of Home, 2011. **Address:** PivotPoint Books, 1384 Cornwall Ct., Walnut Creek, CA 94597, U.S.A. **Online address:** clp@clpearson.com

PEARSON, Diane (Margaret). (Diane Margaret McClelland). British (born England), b. 1931. **Genres:** Novels. **Career:** Jonathan Cape Ltd., Production Department, book production assistant, 1948-52; County Hall, local government, staff, 1952-60; Purnells Publishing, Department of Advertising, staff, 1962-63; Transworld Publishers Ltd., senior editor, 1963-; Corgi Books Ltd., editor, 1964-; Romantic Novelists Association, president. **Publications:** Bride of Tancred, 1967; The Marigold Field, 1969; Sarah Whitman, 1971; Sarah, 1971; Csardas, 1975; The Summer of the Barshinskeys, 1984; Voices of Summer: A Novel, 1992. Contributor to periodicals. **Address:** Curtis Brown Ltd., 1 Craven Hill, 28/29 Haymarket, London, GL W2 3EP, England.

PEARSON, Jo. *See* **PEARSON, Joanne (E.).**

PEARSON, Joanne (E.). (Jo Pearson). Welsh/British (born England) **Genres:** Theology/Religion, Psychology, Humanities. **Career:** Open University, lecturer in religious studies, through 2002; University of Cardiff, faculty, 2002-05; Liverpool Hope University, senior lecturer in comparative religions, 2005-; Belief beyond Boundaries, founder; University of Winchester, Department of Theology and Religious Studies, senior lecturer and programme leader of theology and religious studies, head of academic development. Writer. **Publications:** (Ed. with R.H. Roberts and G. Samuel) Nature Religion Today: Paganism in the Modern World, 1998; (ed. and contrib.) Belief beyond Boundaries: Wicca, Celtic Spirituality, and the New Age, 2002; A Popular Dictionary of Paganism, 2002; Wicca: Magic, Spirituality, and the Mystic Other, 2003; (ed.) The Development of European Paganism: Histories, Influences, and Contexts, c. 1880-2002, 2005; The Cultural Criticism of Witchcraft: Magic, Spirituality and the Mystic Other, 2006; Wicca and the Christian Heritage: Ritual, Sex, and Magic, 2007. Contributor to books. **Address:** Department of Theology and Religious Studies, University of Winchester, Winchester, SO22 4NR, England. **Online address:** jo.overend@winchester.ac.uk

PEARSON, John. British (born England), b. 1930. **Genres:** Novels, Biography, Documentaries/Reportage, History. **Career:** The Times, staff reporter; The Sunday Times, staff reporter, columnist; BBC Television, scriptwriter; freelance writer, 1965-. **Publications:** Gone to Timbuctoo (novel), 1961; (with G. Turner) The Persuasion Industry, 1965; Bluebird and the Dead Lake, 1965; The Life of Ian Fleming, 1966; The Last Hero; The Gallant Story of Donald Campbell and the Land Speed Record, 1966; The Colosseum, 1968; The Life of James Bond, 1970; The Profession of Violence: The Rise and Fall of the Kray Twins, 1972, 3rd ed., 1984; Arena: The Story of the Colosseum, 1973; Edward the Rake, 1974; Bellamy Saga, 1976; Facades, 1978; The Life of Biggles, 1978; Sitwells, 1979; The Kindness of Dr. Avicenna, 1982; Stags and Serpents: The Story of the House of Cavendish and the Dukes of Devonshire, 1983; Serpent and the Stag, 1984; The Ultimate Family: The Making of the Royal House of Windsor, 1986; The Selling of the Royal Family: The Mystique of the British Monarchy, 1986; The Private Lives of Winston Churchill, 1991; Painfully Rich: J. Paul Getty and His Heirs, 1995; Blood Royal: The Spencers and the Royals, 1999; The Cult of Violence, 2001. **Address:** c/o Peters Fraser Dunlop, 34 Russell St., London, GL WC2B 5MA, England.

PEARSON, Kit. Canadian (born Canada), b. 1947. **Genres:** Children's Fiction, Mythology/Folklore, Literary Criticism And History, Novels, Picture/Board Books. **Career:** North York Public Library, children's librarian, 1990. Writer. **Publications:** CHILDREN'S NOVELS: The Daring Game, 1986; A Handful of Time, 1987; The Sky Is Falling, 1989; Looking at the Moon, 1991; The Lights Go on Again, 1993; Awake and Dreaming, 1996; Whispers of War: The War of 1812 Diary of Susanna Merritt, 2002; A Perfect Gentle Knight, 2007; The Whole Truth, 2011. OTHERS: The Singing Basket, 1989; (ed.) This Land: A Cross-Country Anthology of Canadian Fiction for Young Readers, 1998. **Address:** Transatlantic Literary Agency Inc., 2 Bloor St. E, Ste. 3500, Toronto, ON M4W 1A8, Canada. **Online address:** comments@kitpearson.com

PEARSON, Ridley. (Wendell McCall). American (born United States), b. 1953. **Genres:** Novels, Mystery/Crime/Suspense, Young Adult Fiction. **Career:** Oxford University, Raymond Chandler Fulbright fellow, 1990; Fudan University, College of International Language and Literature, visiting professor, 2008-09. Writer. **Publications:** AS WENDELL MCCALL: Dead Aim: a Chris Klick Mystery, 1988; Aim for the Heart: a Chris Klick Mystery, 1990; Concerto in Dead Flat: a Chris Klick Novel, 1999. OTHERS: Never Look Back: A Novel of Espionage and Revenge, 1985; Blood of the Albatross: A Thriller, 1986; The Seizing of the Yankee Green Mall: A Novel, 1987; Undercurrents: A Novel, 1988; Probable Cause, 1990; Hard Fall, 1992; The Angel Maker: A Novel, 1993; No Witnesses: A Novel, 1994; Chain of Evidence, 1995; Beyond Recognition, 1997; The Pied Pipper, 1998; The First Victim, 1999; Middle of Nowhere: A Novel, 2000; The Diary of Ellen Rimbauer, 2001; Parallel Lies, 2001; The Art of Deception, 2002; The Body of David Hayes, 2004; (with D. Barry) Peter and the Starcatchers, 2004; Kingdom Keepers, 2005; (with D. Barry) Missing Mermaid: A Neverland Island Book, 2005; Cut and Run, 2005; (with D. Barry) Peter and the Shadow Thieves, 2006; (with D. Barry) Peter and the Secret of Rundoon, 2007; (with D. Barry) Cave of the Dark Wind: A Never Land Book, 2007; Killer Weekend, 2007; (with D. Barry) Blood Tide: A Never Land Book, 2008; Killer View, 2008; Disney at Dawn, 2008; (with D. Barry) Science Fair: A Story of Mystery, Danger, International Suspense and a Very Nervous Frog, 2008; Steel Trapp: the Challenge, 2008; Rise of Chernabog, 2008; Killer Summer, 2009; (with D. Barry) Peter and the Sword of Mercy, 2009; In Harm's Way, 2010; Kingdom Keepers IV, 2011. **Address:** c/o Albert Zuckerman, Writer's House Inc., 21 W 26th St., New York, NY 10010, U.S.A. **Online address:** email@ridleypearson.com

PEARSON, Roger A. G. British (born England) **Genres:** Translations, Music, History. **Career:** University of Oxford, Queen's College, college lecturer, 1973-77, fellow and praelector in French, 1977-, assistant dean, 1977-80, university lecturer, 1977-97, acting dean, 1981, tutor for admissions, 1985-90, senior tutor, 1994, 1995-96, professor of French, 1997-; Government of France, Ordre des Palmes Académiques, officer, 2005-. Writer and translator. **Publications:** Early Civilisations of the Nordic Peoples, 1966; Stendhal's Violin: A Novelist and His Reader, 1988; (trans. and intro.) E. Zola, The Masterpiece, 1993; The Fables of Reason: A Study of Voltaire's Contes Philosophiques, 1993; (ed. and intro.) Stendhal: The Red and the Black and The Charterhouse of Parma, 1994; Unfolding Mallarmé: The Development of a Poetic Art, 1996; (trans. and intro.) E. Zola, La bête humaine, 1996; (trans. and intro.) Voltaire, Candide and Other Stories, 1998, new. ed., 2006; (trans. and intro.) G. de Maupassant, A Life, 1999; (trans. and intro.) E. Zola, Germinal, 2004; Mallarmé and Circumstance: The Translation of Silence, 2004; Voltaire Almighty: A Life in Pursuit of Freedom, 2005. Contributor to periodicals. **Address:** Queen's College, University of Oxford, High St., Oxford, OX OX1 4AW, England. **Online address:** roger.pearson@queens.ox.ac.uk

PEARSON, Scott Roberts. American (born United States), b. 1938. **Genres:** Economics, Agriculture/Forestry. **Career:** U.S. Peace Corps, Sokoto Training College, teacher of African history and geography, 1961-63; U.S. Agency for International Development, consultant, 1965-; Stanford University, Food Research Institute, assistant professor, 1968-74, associate professor, 1974-80, professor of economics, 1980-, associate director, 1977-92, director, 1992-96; Commission on International Trade and Investment Policy, staff economist, 1970-71; International Bank for Reconstruction and Development, consultant, 1971-. Writer. **Publications:** (Contrib.) Public Policy, 1966; (contrib.) Growth and Development of the Nigerian Economy, 1970; Petroleum and The Nigerian Economy, 1970; (contrib.) The Energy Question, 1974; (co-author) Commodity Exports and African Economic Development, 1974; (co-author) Rice in West Africa: Policy and Economics, 1981; (with T.E. Josling and M. Langworthy) Options for Farm Policy in the European Community, 1981; (with T.E. Josling) Developments in the Common Agricultural Policy of the European Community, 1982; (with C.P. Timmer and W.P. Falcon) Food Policy Analysis, 1983; (contrib.) The Cassava Economy of Java, 1984; (co-author) Portuguese Agriculture in Transition, 1987; (with Eric Monke) The Policy Analysis Matrix for Agricultural Development, 1989; (co-author) Rice Policy in Indonesia, 1991; Structural Change and Small Farm Agriculture in Northwest Portugal, 1993; Agricultural Policy in Kenya: Application of the Policy Analysis Matrix, 1995; (ed. with E. Monke and F. Avillez) Small Farm Agriculture in Southern Europe: CAP Reform and Structural Change, 1998; (with C. Gotsch and S. Bahri) Applications of the Policy Analysis Matrix in Indonesian Agriculture, 2004. Contributor to journals. **Address:** 691 Mirada Ave., Stanford, CA 94305, U.S.A.

PEARSON, Sybille. American/Czech (born Czech Republic), b. 1937. **Genres:** Plays/Screenplays, Novellas/Short Stories, Young Adult Fiction. **Career:** City College of New York, teacher and writer; New York University, Tisch School of the Arts, Graduate Musical Theatre Writing Program, adjunct professor; Vineyard Theater, artistic resident. **Publications:** A Little Going Away Party, 1984; Baby, 1984; Sally and Marsha (two-act play), 1985; Phantasie, 1989; Unfinished Stories, 1993. **Address:** c/o Audrey Wood, International Creative Management, 730 5th Ave., New York, NY 10019, U.S.A.

PEARSON, T(homas) R(eid). (T. Reid Pearson). American (born United States), b. 1956. **Genres:** Novels. **Career:** Peace College, teacher of English, 1980-81; painter and carpenter, 1981-84; writer, 1984-; University of Mississippi, writer-in-residence, 1993. **Publications:** A Short History of a Small Place, 1985; Off for the Sweet Hereafter, 1986; The Last of How It Was, 1987; Call and Response, 1989; Gospel Hour, 1991; Cry Me A River, 1993; Last of How it Was, 1996; Blue Ridge, 2000; Polar, 2002; True Cross, 2003; Glad News of the Natural World, 2005; Seaworthy: Adrift with William Willis in the Golden Age of Rafting, 2006; (with A. Nieto) Augie's Quest: One Man's Journey from Success to Significance, 2007; Red Scare, 2008; Jerusalem Gap, 2010. Contributor to books. **Address:** Bloomsbury Publishing, 175 5th Ave., New York, NY 10010, U.S.A.

PEARSON, Thomas S(pencer). American (born United States), b. 1949. **Genres:** History, Young Adult Non-fiction, Local History/Rural Topics, Politics/Government. **Career:** Monmouth University, Department of History and Anthropology, assistant professor, 1978-85, chairman, 1981-88, 1989-92, associate professor of history, 1985-94, professor of history, 1994-, vice-president for academic affairs and provost, 1992-, coordinator of graduate studies, 1989-90. Writer. **Publications:** Russian Officialdom in Crisis: Autocracy and Local Self-Government, 1861-1900, 1989. Contributor to journals and periodicals. **Address:** Department of History and Anthropology, Monmouth University, 211 Wilson Hall, 400 Cedar Ave., West Long Branch, NJ 07764-1898, U.S.A. **Online address:** pearson@monmouth.edu

PEARSON, T. Reid. *See* **PEARSON, T(homas) R(eid).**

PEASE, Allan. Australian (born Australia), b. 1951?. **Genres:** Sex, Psychology. **Career:** Pease international Pty Ltd., co-founder. Writer and educator. **Publications:** Body Language: How to Read Others Thoughts by Their Gestures, 1981; Signals: How to Use Body Language for Power, Success and Love, 1984; (with B. Pease) Why Men Don't Listen & Women Can't Read Maps: How We're Different and What to Do about It, 2000; (with B. Pease) Why Men Don't Have a Clue and Women Always Need More Shoes: The Ultimate Guide to the Opposite Sex, 2004; (with B. Pease) The Definitive Book of Body Language, 2006; (with B. Pease) Are You Made for Each Other?, 2006; Easy Peasey: People Skills for Life, 2006; (with B. Pease) Why Men want Sex and Women Need Love: Unraveling the Simple Truth, 2009. **Address:** Pease International Pty Ltd., PO Box 1260, Buderim, QL 4556, Australia. **Online address:** info@peaseinternational.com

PEAVLER, Terry J. American (born United States), b. 1942. **Genres:** Literary Criticism And History, Language/Linguistics, Novels, Essays. **Career:** Pennsylvania State University, University Park Campus, assistant professor, 1971-79, associate professor, 1979-88, professor of Spanish, 1988-2001, professor emeritus of Spanish, 2001-, associate dean for undergraduate studies, Department of Spanish, Italian and Portuguese, interim head; Colorado Off Highway Vehicle Coalition, director and vice chairman. Writer. **Publications:** Individuations: The Novel as Dissent, 1987; El texto en llamas: El artenarrativo de Juan Rulfo, 1988; Julio Cortázar, 1990; (ed. with P. Standish) Structures of Power: Essays on Twentieth-Century Spanish-American Fiction, 1996. **Address:** Colorado Off Highway Vehicle Coalition, PO Box 1091, Buena Vista, CO 81211, U.S.A. **Online address:** tpeavler@cohvco.org

PECHT, Michael G. American (born United States), b. 1952. **Genres:** Sciences, Engineering. **Career:** University of Maryland, professor of mechanical engineering, 1983-, Westinghouse professor, 1987-88, chair professor, professor in applied mathematics, Computer Advanced Life Cycle Engineering

(CALCE) Electronic Packaging Research Center, founder and director, 1985-; Institute for Defense Analyses, consultant; IEEE, chief editor on reliability, Microelectronics Reliability, chief editor, Transactions on Components and Packaging Technology, associate editor. **Publications:** EDITOR: Handbook of Electronic Package Design, 1991; Soldering Processes and Equipment, 1993; (with L.T. Nguyen) Electronic Packaging Reliability, 1993; Placement and Routing of Electronic Modules, 1993; (with R. Hannemann and A. Kraus) Quality Conformance and Qualification of Electronic Packages, 1994; Reliability Engineering, 1994; Integrated Circuit, Hybrid, and Multichip Module Package Design Guidelines, 1994; (with R.J. Hannemann and A.D. Kraus) Physical Architecture of VLSI Systems, 1994; (with L. Nguyen and Hakim) Plastic Encapsulated Microelectronics: Materials, Processes, Quality, Reliability, and Applications, 1994; Product Reliability, Maintainability, and Supportability Handbook, 1995; (with Y.T. Yong) Advanced Routing of Electronic Modules, 1996; (with R. Radojcic and G. Rao) Guidebook for Managing Silicon Chip Reliability, 1999; (with S. Ganesan) Lead-Free Electronics, 2003; Parts Selection and Management, 2004. OTHERS: (with P. Lall and E. Hakim) The Influence of Temperature on Microelectronic Device Reliability, 1994; (with J. Pecht) Long-Term Non-Operating Reliability of Electronic Products, 1995; (with Chung-Shing Lee) The Taiwan Electronics Industry, 1997; (with D. Bean and Shukla) The Singapore and Malaysia's Electronics Industries, 1997; (S.B. Lee and M. Lee) The Korean Electronic Industry, 1997; (with W. Nakayama and W. Boulton) The Japanese Electronics Industry, 1999; (co-author) The Chinese Electronics Industry, 1999; (co-author) Electronic Packaging Materials and Their Properties, 1999; (R. Radojcic and G. Rao) Guidebook for Managing Silicon Chip Reliability, 1999; Life-Cycle Forecasting, Mitigation Assessment and Obsolescence Strategies, 2002; Contamination of Electronic Assemblies, 2003; (with W. Liu) IC Component Sockets, 2004; (with D. Das and N. Pendsé) Rating and Uprating of Electronic Parts, 2005; (with Y.C. Chan) China's Electronic Industry, 2006; Prognostics and Health Management of Electronics, 2007. Contributor to scientific journals. Works appear in anthologies. **Address:** CALCE Electronic Products & Systems Consortium, University of Maryland, Rm. S1103, Bldg. 89, College Park, MD 20742, U.S.A. **Online address:** pecht@calce.umd.edu

PECK, Dale. American (born United States), b. 1967. **Genres:** Novels, Young Adult Non-fiction, Young Adult Fiction, Children's Fiction, Autobiography/Memoirs, Literary Criticism And History. **Career:** New School University, Graduate Writing Program, adjunct professor of writing, 1999-; Out Magazine, contributing editor, 2006-; novelist. **Publications:** Martin and John: A Novel in UK as Fucking Martin, 1993; The Law of Enclosures, 1996; Now It's Time to Say Goodbye, 1998; What we Lost, 2003; Hatchet Jobs: Writings on Contemporary Fiction, 2004; Drift House: The First Voyage, 2005; The Lost Cities: A Drift House Voyage, 2007; (foreword) Vital Signs: Essential AIDS Fiction. 2007; The Garden of Lost and Found, 2007; Body Surfing, 2009; Sprout, 2009; (with T. Kring) Shift, 2010; Caretaker, forthcoming. Contributor to periodicals. **Address:** Irene Skolnick Agency, 22 W 23rd St., Fl. 5, New York, NY 10010, U.S.A. **Online address:** mail@dalepeck.com

PECK, David R. American (born United States), b. 1938. **Genres:** Literary Criticism And History, Education, How-to Books, Language/Linguistics. **Career:** California State University, professor of English, 1967-99, professor emeritus, 1999-; University of Ljubljana, Fulbright lecturer, 1984-85; University of Leeds, visiting professor, 1990-91. Writer. **Publications:** American Marxist Literary Criticism, 1926-1941, 1975; (comp. with C. Bullock) Guide to Marxist Literary Criticism, 1980; (with B. Brinkman, E. Hoffman and J. Blum) A Guide to the Whole Writing Process, 1984; Novels of Initiation: A Guidebook for Teaching Literature to Adolescents, 1989; American Ethnic Literatures, 1992; (ed. with J.R. Maitino) Teaching American Ethnic Literatures, 1996; (ed.) Identities and Issues in Literature, 1997; (ed.) American Ethnic Writers, 2000. **Address:** Department of English, California State University, MHB 419, 1250 Bellflower Blvd., Long Beach, CA 90840, U.S.A.

PECK, Jeffrey M. American (born United States), b. 1950. **Genres:** Young Adult Non-fiction, Literary Criticism And History, Theology/Religion. **Career:** University of Washington, assistant professor of German, 1979-86, associate professor of germanics and comparative literature, 1986-92; Free University, Institute for General and Comparative Literature, visiting professor, 1990-91; Georgetown University, associate professor, 1992-96, professor, 1996-2000, senior fellow-in-residence, visiting professor, 2003-04; American Institute for Contemporary German Studies, faculty, 1992-99, 2002-08; York University, professor, 1999-2002, Canadian Centre for German and European Studies, director, 1999-2002, Institute of European Studies, co-director, 2000-02; University of Montreal, professor, 1999-2002, Canadian Centre for German and European Studies, director, 1999-2002; University of Toronto, adjunct faculty and associate graduate faculty, 2000-02; Humboldt University, Leo Baeck Summer University in Jewish Studies, director, 2007-09, Department of Cultural Studies, Walter Benjamin chair in Jewish culture and history, 2007-09; City University of New York, Baruch College, Weissman School of Arts and Sciences, dean, 2008-, Department of Modern Languages and Comparative Literature, professor. Writer. **Publications:** NONFICTION: Hermes Disguised: Literary Hermeneutics and the Interpretation of Literature: Kleist, Grillparzer, Fontane, 1983; (ed. with R. Cohen, C. Camuto and C. Bowen) New Literary History International Bibliography of Literary Theory and Criticism, 1988; (with J. Borneman) Sojourners: The Return of German Jews and the Question of Identity, 1995; (ed. with E.V. Daniel) Culture/Contexture: Explorations in Anthropology and Literary Studies, 1996; (ed. with K.J. Milich) Multiculturalism in Transit: A German-American Exchange, 1998; Being Jewish in the New Germany, 2006. Contributor to books. **Address:** Office of the Dean, Baruch College, City University of New York, 1 Bernard Baruch Way, New York, NY 10010, U.S.A. **Online address:** jeffrey.peck@baruch.cuny.edu

PECK, Merton Joseph. American (born United States), b. 1925. **Genres:** Economics, Public/Social Administration, Administration/Management, Transportation. **Career:** Harvard University, teaching fellow and instructor in economics, 1951-55, assistant professor, 1956-60, associate professor of business administration, 1960-61; University of Michigan, assistant professor of economics, 1955-56; Office of the Secretary of Defense, director of systems analysis, 1961-63; Yale University, Department of Economics, Thomas DeWitt Cuyler professor of economics, 1963-2002, chair, 1967-68, Thomas DeWitt Cuyler professor emeritus of economics, 2002-; Brookings Institution, senior staff, 1963-. Writer and consultant. **Publications:** (Co-author) The Maintenance of Way Employment on U.S. Railroads, 1957; (co-author) Economics of Competition in the Transportation Industries, 1959; Competition in the Aluminum Industry, 1945-1958, 1961; (with F.M. Scherer) Weapons Acquisition Process: An Economic Analysis, 1962; Competitive Policy for Transportation?, 1965; (with R.R. Nelson and E.D. Kalachek) Technology, Economic Growth, and Public Policy: A Rand Corporation and Brookings Institution Study, 1967; (co-author) Federal Regulation of Television, 1973; (with R.G. Noll and J.J. McGowan) Economic Aspects of Television Regulation, 1973. EDITOR: The World Aluminum Industry in a Changing Energy Era, 1988; (with T.J. Richardson) What is to Be Done: Proposals for the Soviet Transition to the Market, 1991; (with H.H. Landsberg and J.E. Tilton) Competitiveness in Metals: The Impact of Public Policy, 1992; (with L. Gokhberg and J. Gács) Russian Applied Research and Development: Its Problems and Its Promise, 1997. **Address:** Department of Economics, Yale University, 28 Hillhouse Ave., PO Box 208268, New Haven, CT 06511, U.S.A.

PECK, Richard (Wayne). American (born United States), b. 1934. **Genres:** Novels, Children's Fiction, Young Adult Fiction, Picture/Board Books, Young Adult Non-fiction, Literary Criticism And History, Humor/Satire, Novellas/Short Stories, Novellas/Short Stories. **Career:** Southern Illinois University, instructor in English, 1958-60; Glenbrook North High School, teacher, 1961-63; Scott, Foresman Co., textbook editor, 1963-65; City University of New York, Hunter College, instructor in English and education, 1965-71; Council for Basic Education, assistant director, 1969-70; writer, 1971-; Jesus College, English-speaking union fellow, 1973; Louisiana State University, School of Library and Information Science, adjunct professor. **Publications:** (With N. Strasma) Old Town, A Complete Guide: Strolling, Shopping, Supping, Sipping, 1965; (ed. with N.E. Hoopes) Edge of Awareness: 25 Contemporary Essays, 1966; Sounds and Silences: Poetry for Now, 1970; (ed.) Mindscapes: Poems for the Real World, 1971; Don't Look and It Won't Hurt, 1972; (ed.) Leap into Reality: Essays for Now, 1972; (with M. Smith and G. Weber) A Consumer's Guide to Educational Innovations, 1972; Dreamland Lake, 1973; Through a Brief Darkness, 1973; Urban Studies: A Research Paper Casebook, 1974; Representing Super Doll, 1974; Transitions: A Literary Paper Casebook, 1974; (with S.N. Judy) The Creative Word, 1974; The Ghost Belonged to Me: A Novel, 1975, 2nd ed., 1989; Are You in the House Alone?, 1976; (ed.) Pictures That Storm inside My Head, 1976; Ghosts I Have Been, 1977; Monster Night at Grandma's House, 1977; Father Figure, 1978; Secrets of the Shopping Mall, 1979; Amanda/Miranda, 1980; (contrib.) Literature for Today's Young Adults, 1980; New York Time, 1981; Close Enough to Touch, 1981; The Dreadful Future of Blossom Culp, 1983; This Family of Women, 1983; (contrib.) Sixteen: Short Stories by Outstanding Young Adults Writers, 1984; Remembering the Good Times, 1985; Blossom Culp and the Sleep of

Death, 1986; Princess Ashley, 1987; (contrib.) Visions: Nineteen Short Stories by Outstanding Writers for Young Adults, 1987; Write a Tale of Terror, 1987; Those Summer Girls I Never Met, 1988; (contrib.) Connections: Short Stories by Outstanding Writers for Young Adults, 1989; Voices After Midnight: A Novel, 1990; Unfinished Portrait of Jessica, 1991; Anonymously Yours, 1991; Bel-Air Bambi and the Mall Rats, 1993; Love and Death at the Mall: Teaching and Writing for the Literate Young, 1994; The Last Safe Place on Earth, 1995; Lost in Cyberspace, 1995; The Great Interactive Dream Machine: Another Adventure in Cyberspace, 1996; A Long Way from Chicago: A Novel in Stories, 1998; Strays like Us, 1998; London Holiday, 1998; A Year Down Yonder, 2000; Fair Weather: A Novel, 2001; Invitations to the World: Teaching and Writing for the Young, 2002; (with D. Freeman) Gregory's Shadow, 2002; The River Between Us, 2003; The Teacher's Funeral: A Comedy in Three Parts, 2004, 2nd ed., 2005; Past Perfect, Present Tense: New and Collected Stories, 2004; Here Lies The Librarian, 2006; On The Wings of Heroes, 2007; Particular Heroes, 2007; (co-author) Acting Out, 2008; A Season of Gifts, 2009; Three Quarters Dead, 2010; Secrets at Sea, 2011. Contributor to books and periodicals. Works appear in anthologies. **Address:** Dial Books for Young Readers, 375 Hudson St., New York, NY 10014-3657, U.S.A.

PECK, Robert S(tephen). American (born United States), b. 1953. **Genres:** Civil Liberties/Human Rights, Social Sciences, Law. **Career:** U.S. House of Representatives, legislative aide, 1972-73; Matthew Bender and Co., editor, 1977-78; Public Education Association, staff attorney and director of educational rights, 1978-82; American Bar Association, staff director, 1982-89; Citizens Information Service of Illinois, director, 1985-87; Freedom to Read Foundation, president, 1988-90; U.S. Supreme Court, judicial fellow, 1990-91; American Civil Liberties Union, legislative counsel, 1991-95; American University, adjunct lecturer, 1991-; Association of Trial Lawyers of America, senior director of legal affairs and policy research, 1995-2001; Center for Constitutional Litigation P.C., president, 2001-. Writer. **Publications:** We the People: The Constitution in American Life, 1987; The Bill of Rights and the Politics of Interpretation, 1992; Libraries, Cyberspace and the First Amendment: A Practical Guide to the Legal Issues, 2000. EDITOR: (with C.J. White) Understanding the Law: A Handbook on Educating the Public, 1983; (with M. Manemann) Speaking & Writing Truth: Community Forums on the First Amendment, 1985; (with R.S. Pollock) The Blessings of Liberty: Bicentennial Lectures at the National Archives, 1986; To Govern a Changing Society: Constitutionalism and the Challenge of New Technology, 1990. Contributor to journals. **Address:** Center for Constitutional Litigation P.C., 777 6th St. NW, Ste. 520, Washington, DC 20001, U.S.A.

PECK, Sylvia. American (born United States), b. 1953. **Genres:** Children's Fiction, Young Adult Fiction. **Career:** Solar Utilities Co., administrative assistant, 1978; English Language Services, teacher, 1979; Neighborhood Legal Services Inc., law clerk, 1980; Michael McGlinn, law clerk, 1981; Kopelman and Paige, law clerk, 1981; Federal Defenders, intern, 1981; Legal Aid Society, associate appellate counsel for Federal Defender Services Unit, 1983-85; Sullivan and Worcester, legal writing consultant, 1985-86; Suffolk University, instructor in legal writing and research, 1985-88, adjunct professor, 1988-91; Department of Environmental Protection, Office of General Counsel, assistant general counsel, 1989-95; Emerson College, adjunct professor, 1992. Writer. **Publications:** FOR CHILDREN: Seal Child, 1989; Kelsey's Raven, 1992; The Kingdom of the Tigers: A Novel, forthcoming. Contributor to periodicals. **Address:** c/o Roberta Pryor, 24 W 55th St., New York, NY 10019, U.S.A.

PECORA, Vincent P. (Vincent Pitt Pecora). American (born United States), b. 1953. **Genres:** Cultural/Ethnic Topics, Theology/Religion. **Career:** University of Arkansas, assistant professor, 1984-85; University of California, assistant professor, 1985-90, associate professor, 1990-95, professor, and director of Center for Modern and Contemporary Studies, 1995, director of humanities consortium, 1998-2005; University of Utah, Gordon B. Hinckley Professor of British Literature and Culture, English Department chair, British Studies Program, English Program director, 2005-. Writer. **Publications:** Self & Form in Modern Narrative, 1989; Households of the Soul, 1997; (ed.) Nations and Identities: Classic Readings, 2001; Secularization and Cultural Criticism: Religion, Nation, & Modernity, 2006. **Address:** University of Utah, Rm. 3500, English Languages and Communication Bldg., 255 S Central Campus Dr., Salt Lake City, UT 84112-0499, U.S.A. **Online address:** v.pecora@utah.edu

PECORA, Vincent Pitt. *See* **PECORA, Vincent P.**

PEDAHZUR, Ami. American/Israeli (born Israel), b. 1970. **Genres:** Civil Liberties/Human Rights, Politics/Government, Adult Non-fiction. **Career:** University of Haifa, assistant instructor, 1998-2000, lecturer, 2000-02, senior lecturer, 2002-05; National Security Studies Center, senior fellow, 1999-2004; The Hebrew University, visiting lecturer, 2002; University of Texas, Donald D. Harrington Fellow, 2004-05, Department of Government, associate professor, 2005-09, professor, 2010-, Department of Middle Eastern Studies, faculty affiliate, 2005-10, Center for Middle Eastern Studies, faculty affiliate, 2005-10, Robert S. Strauss Center for International Security and Law, senior fellow, 2007-, Center for European Studies, faculty affiliate, 2008-, Schusterman Center for Jewish Studies, faculty affiliate, 2009-, distinguished fellow, 2009-, Tiger Lab, head; Studies in Conflict and Terrorism, associate editor. **Publications:** The Israeli Response to Jewish Extremism and Violence: Defending Democracy, 2002; (with L. Weinberg) Political Parties and Terrorist Groups, 2003, 2nd ed. (with A. Perliger and L. Weinberg), 2009; (ed. with L. Weinberg) Religious Fundamentalism and Political Extremism, 2004; Ha-Demokratiyah Ha-Mitgonenet be-Yiśrael, 2004; (with A. Perliger and G. Parhan) Hitmodedut mul Teror Bi-Yerushalayim 1967-2002, 2005; (ed.) Root Causes of Suicide Terrorism: The Globalization of Martyrdom, 2006; (with A. Perliger) Jewish Terrorism in Israel, 2009; The Israeli Secret Services and the Struggle Against Terrorism, 2009. Contributor to periodicals. **Address:** Department of Government, University of Texas, MEZ 3.140, 1 University Sta., PO Box A1800, Austin, TX 78712-0119, U.S.A. **Online address:** pedahzur@austin.utexas.edu

PEDDICORD, Jo (Anne). American (born United States), b. 1925. **Genres:** Fash Ion/Costume, Gerontology/Senior Issues, Self Help, Medicine/Health. **Career:** Teacher, 1984-. Writer. **Publications:** Look Like a Winner after 50 with Care, Color and Style, 1992, 3rd ed., 1997; Feel Nifty after 50: Top Tips to Help Women Grow Young, 1999, 2nd. ed., 2000; How to Fell and Look Nifty After 50!, 2000. Contributor to periodicals. **Address:** Golden Aspen Publishing, PO Box 370333, Denver, CO 80237-0333, U.S.A.

PEDELTY, Mark. American (born United States), b. 1964. **Genres:** Popular Culture. **Career:** Anthropologist; Miami University, assistant professor, 1995-99; University of Minnesota-Morris, Anthropology and Sociology, assistant professor, 1994-95; University of Minnesota-Twin Cities, assistant professor, 1999-2002, associate professor, 2003-. Writer. **Publications:** War Stories: The Culture of Foreign Correspondents, 1995; (contrib.) Reinventing Ourselves: Interdisciplinary Education, Collaborative Learning, and Experimentation in Higher Education, 2001; Musical Ritual in Mexico City: From the Aztec to NAFTA, 2004. Contributor to periodicals. **Address:** School of Journalism and Mass Communication, University of Minnesota, 111 Murphy Hall, 206 Church St. SE, Minneapolis, MN 55455, U.S.A. **Online address:** pedeltmh@umn.edu

PEDEN, W. Creighton. American (born United States), b. 1935. **Genres:** Philosophy, Theology/Religion, Biography, Politics/Government, Military/Defense/Arms Control. **Career:** Radford University, Department of Philosophy, head, 1965-68; Millikan University, Department of Philosophy, head, 1968-69; Augusta State University, Fuller E. Callaway professor of philosophy, 1969-93, Fuller E. Callaway professor emeritus of philosophy, 1993-; Georgia Consortium for International Education, founding executive director, 1970-73; Augusta Forum, founding president, 1977-78; University of Glasgow, visiting professor, 1982-83; Highlands Institute for American Religious Thought Inc., founding executive director, 1987-92, founding president, 1992-; Twentieth World Congress of Philosophy, executive director, 1988-93; Free University of Amsterdam, visiting professor, 1991. Writer. **Publications:** Wieman's Empirical Process Philosophy, 1977; (with C. Hartshorne) Whitehead's View of Reality, 1981; The Chicago School: Voices in Liberal Religious Thought, 1987; The Philosopher of Free Religion: Francis Ellingwood Abbot, 1836-1903, 1992; Civil War Pulpit to World's Parliament of Religion: The Thought of William James Potter, 1829-1893, 1996; A Good Life in a World Made Good: Albert Eustace Haydon, 1880-1975, 2006; Intellectual Biography of David Atwood Wasson (1828-1887): An American Transcendentalist Thinker, 2008; Evolutionary Theist: An Intellectual Biography of Minot Judson Savage, 1841-1918, 2009; (comp. and contrib.) Life and Thought of Henry Nelson Wieman (1884-1975): An American Philosopher, 2010; Empirical Tradition in American Liberal Religious Thought, 1860-1960, 2010. EDITOR: (with L.E. Axel) Creative Freedom, Vocation of Liberal Religion, 1982; (with C. Willig) Science Serving Faith, 1987; (with Y. Hudson) Philosophical Essays on the Ideas of a Good Society, 1988; (with L.E. Axel) God, Values, and Empiricism: Issues in Philosophical Theology, 1989; (with J.P.

Sterba) Freedom, Equality, and Social Change, 1989; (with Y. Hudson) Revolution, Violence, and Equality, 1990; (with Y. Hudson) Terrorism, Justice, and Social Values, 1990; (with D.M. Speak) American Constitutional Experiment, 1991; (with Y. Hudson) Communitarianism, Liberalism, and Social Responsibility, 1991; (with J.K. Roth) Rights, Justice, and Community, 1992; (with Y. Hudson) Bill of Rights: Bicentennial Reflections, 1993; (with Y. Hudson) Freedom, Dharma, and Rights, 1993; (with L.E. Axel) New Essays in Religious Naturalism, 1993; (with Y. Hudson) The Social Power of Ideas, 1995; (with Y. Hudson) Liberalism, Oppression, and Empowerment, 1995; (with J.A. Stone) The Chicago School of Theology: Pioneers in Religious Inquiry, 1996; (with E.J. Tarbox) The Collected Essays of Francis Ellingwood Abbot (1836-1903), American Philosopher and Free Religionist, 1996; (with E.J. Tarbox) Essays and Sermons of William James Potter (1829-1893), Unitarian Minister and Freethinker, 2003; (with J.N. Gaston) Pragmatism and the Rise of Religious Humanism: The Writings of Albert Eustace Haydon (1880-1975), 2006. Contributor of articles to journals and periodicals. **Address:** Department of Philosophy, Augusta State University, 2500 Walton Way, Augusta, GA 30904-2200, U.S.A.

PEDERSEN, Laura. American (born United States), b. 1965. **Genres:** Business/Trade/Industry, Novels. **Career:** New York Times, finance columnist, 1990; Booker T. Washington Learning Center, teacher. Writer. **Publications:** (With F.P. Model) Play Money: My Brief but Brilliant Career on Wall Street, 1991; Street-Smart Career Guide: A Step-by-Step Program for Your Career Development, 1993. NOVELS: Going Away Party, 2001; Beginner's Luck, 2003; Last Call, 2004; Heart's Desire, 2005; Full House, 2005; The Sweetest Hours, 2005; The Big Shuffle, 2006; Buffalo Gal: A Memoir, 2008; Best Bet, 2009; Buffalo Unbound, 2010; Fool's Mate, 2011; Planes, Trains, and Auto-Rickshaws, 2012. Contributor to periodicals. **Address:** c/o Author Mail, Ballantine Books, Random House Inc., 1745 Broadway, New York, NY 10019, U.S.A.

PEDERSEN, Vernon L. American (born United States), b. 1955. **Genres:** History, Politics/Government, Organized Labor. **Career:** Shepherd College, adjunct professor of history, 1991-94; American University in Bulgaria, associate professor of history, 1994-2001, associate vice president for academic affairs and dean of faculty, 2001-03; Montana State University, College of Technology, associate dean of academic affairs and student services, 2003-06; University of Great Falls, Science and Humanites Division, chair, Department of History and Political Science, head, 2006-, professor of history. Writer. **Publications:** The Communist Party of Maryland, 1919-1957, 2001. Contributor to journals. **Address:** University of Great Falls, FOS 110, Library Bldg., 1301 20th St. S, Great Falls, MT 59405, U.S.A. **Online address:** vpedersen01@ugf.edu

PEDERSON, Rena. American (born United States) **Genres:** Women's Studies And Issues. **Career:** United Press Intl., reporter, 1970-72; Associated Press, reporter, 1972; Dallas Morning News, reporter, 1973-, features writer, television critic, editor, 1986-2002, vice president and editorial page editor, 2002-; American College of Education, director of communications; U.S. Department of State, Undersecretary of State for Public Diplomacy and Public Affairs, senior advisor for strategic communications; National Math and Science Initiative, communication director. **Publications:** (With R. Lee Smith) What's Next? Women Redefining Their Dreams in the Prime of Life, 2001; What's Missing? Inspiration for Women Seeking Faith and Joy in Their Lives, 2003; The Lost Apostle: Searching for the Truth about Junia, 2006. **Address:** National Math & Science Initiative, 325 N St. Paul St., Ste. 2900, Dallas, TX 75201, U.S.A. **Online address:** rena@renapederson.com

PEDERSON, William D(avid). American/Irish (born Ireland), b. 1946. **Genres:** History, International Relations/Current Affairs, Law, Politics/Government, Social Sciences, Reference, Young Adult Non-fiction, Children's Non-fiction, Autobiography/Memoirs. **Career:** Lamar University, teacher, 1977-79; Westminster College, teacher, 1979-80; Yankton College, teacher, 1980-81; Louisiana State University, professor of political science, 1981-, American Studies Program, founding director, 1982-91, 1995-, Intl. Lincoln Center for American Studies, founding director, 1982-, founder of presidential conference series, 1992, American studies chair in liberal arts, 1999; Georgetown University, professor, 1997-; Centenary College of Louisiana, teacher, 1999, 2005. Writer. **Publications:** CONTRIBUTOR: Dimensions of the Modern Presidency, 1981; Glimpses of Shreveport, 1985; Morality and Conviction in American Politics, 1990; Theodore Roosevelt: Many-Sided American, 1992; The Presidency and Domestic Policies of Jimmy Carter, 1994. EDITOR: (with A.M. McLaurin and contrib.) The Rating Game in American Politics, 1987; (with N.W. Provizer and contrib.) Grassroots Constitutionalism: Shreveport, the South, and the Supreme Law of the Land, 1988; The Barberian Presidency, 1989; Governmental Gridlock: Congressional-Presidential Relations in the U.S., 1991; Lincoln and Leadership, 1993; (with N.W. Provizer) Great Justices of the U.S. Supreme Court, 1993; (with F.J. Williams and V.J. Marsala) Abraham Lincoln: Sources and Style of Leadership, 1994; (with F.J. Williams) Abraham Lincoln: Contemporary, 1995; (with M.J. Rozell) FDR and the Modern Presidency, 1997; (with B.W. Daynes and M.P. Riccards) The New Deal and Public Policy, 1998; (with J.Y. Simon and H. Holzer) Lincoln Forum: Abraham Lincoln, Gettysburg, and the Civil War, 1999; (with M.J. Rozell and F.J. Williams) George Washington and the Origins of the American Presidency, 2000; (with E. Fishman and M.J. Rozell) George Washington, Foundation of Presidential Leadership and Character, 2001; (with N.B. Young and B.W. Daynes) Franklin D. Roosevelt and the Shaping of American Political Culture, 2001; Franklin D. Roosevelt and Congress, 2001; (with F.J. Williams) Franklin Roosevelt and Abraham Lincoln, 2003; (with N.W. Provizer) Leaders of the Pack: Polls & Case Studies of Great Supreme Court Justices, 2003; (with T.C. Howard) Franklin D. Roosevelt and the Formation of the Modern World, 2003; (with S.K. Shaw and F.J. Williams) Franklin Roosevelt and the Transformation of the Supreme Court, 2004; (with F.J. Williams) Creative Breakthroughs in Leadership: James Madison, Abraham Lincoln, and Mahatma Gandhi, 2007; (with J.R. Vile and F.J. Williams) James Madison: Philosopher, Founder, and Statesman, 2008; (with F.J. Williams) Lincoln Lessons: Reflections on America's Greatest Leader, 2009: (with Robert P. Watson) Lincoln's Enduring Legacy: Great Thinkers, Great Leaders, 2010; (with J. Tripathy) Abraham Lincoln Without Borders: Lincoln's Legacy Outside America, 2010; A Companion to Franklin D. Roosevelt, 2011. OTHER: FDR Years, 2006. Contributor to journals. **Address:** International Lincoln Center for American Studies, Louisiana State University, 321 BH, 1 University Pl., Shreveport, LA 71115-2301, U.S.A. **Online address:** william.pederson@lsus.edu

PEDRAZAS, Allan. American (born United States) **Genres:** Mystery/Crime/Suspense, Novels, Young Adult Fiction. **Career:** Novelist. **Publications:** The Harry Chronicles, 1995; Angel's Cove, 1997. **Address:** St. Martin's Press, Rm. 1715, 175 5th Ave., New York, NY 10010, U.S.A.

PEEBLES, Curtis. American (born United States), b. 1955. **Genres:** History, Military/Defense/Arms Control, Air/Space Topics, Sciences, History. **Career:** Smithsonian Institution, aerospace historian; National Aeronautics and Space Administration, Dryden Flight Research Center, aerospace historian. Writer. **Publications:** COLD WAR: Battle for Space, 1983; Guardians: Strategic Reconnaissance Satellites, 1987; The Moby Dick Project: Reconnaissance Balloons over Russia, 1991; The Corona Project: America's First Spy Satellites, 1997; Shadow Flights: America's Secret Air War against the Soviet Union, 2000; Twilight Warriors: Covert Air Operations against the USSR, 2005. FLIGHT TECHNOLOGY DEVELOPMENT: Dark Eagles: A History of Top Secret U.S. Aircraft Programs, 1995; The Spoken Word: Recollections of Dryden History, the Early Years, 2003; From Runway to Orbit: Reflections of a NASA Engineer, 2004; Road to Mach 10: Lessons Learned from the X-43A Flight Research Program, 2008. SPACE EXPLORATION: Watch the Skies! A Chronicle of the Flying Saucer Myth, 1994; High Frontier: The U.S. Air Force and the Military Space Program, 1997; Flying without Wings: NASA Lifting Bodies and the Birth of the Space Shuttle, 1999; Asteroids: A History, 2000. OTHER: Eleven Seconds into the Unknown, 2010. Contributor of numerous articles to books and periodicals. **Address:** Dryden Flight Research Center, National Aeronautics and Space Administration, PO Box 273, Edwards, CA 93523-0273, U.S.A.

PEEL, Ellen S. American (born United States), b. 1951?. **Genres:** Politics/Government, History, Literary Criticism And History. **Career:** Cambridge Computer Associates, technical writer and editor, 1973-75; Second Wave, staff writer and editor, 1974-75; Massachusetts Feminist Federal Credit Union, co-founder and publications editor, 1974-75; University of Cincinnati, Department of English and Comparative Literature, assistant professor, 1983-89, associate professor, 1989; San Francisco State University, Department of English and Comparative Literature, assistant professor, 1990-92, associate professor, 1992-99, professor, 1999-. **Publications:** Politics, Persuasion and Pragmatism: A Rhetoric of Feminist Utopian Fiction, 2002. Contributor to books and periodicals. **Address:** San Francisco State University, 1600 Holloway Ave., San Francisco, CA 94132, U.S.A. **Online address:** epeel@sfsu.edu

PEEL, H(azel) M(ary). British (born England), b. 1930. **Genres:** Novels, Children's Fiction, History. **Career:** Bristol Siddeley Engines Ltd., typist, 1953-57; freelance journalist; writer, 1957-. **Publications:** Fury, Son of the Wilds, 1959; Pilot, the Hunter, 1962; Pilot, The Chaser, 1964; Easter, The Show Jumper, 1965; Jago, 1966; Nightstorm, the Flat Racer, 1966; Dido and Rogue, 1967; Gay Darius, 1968; Untamed, 1969; Land and Power, 1974; Law of the Wilds, 1974; Pocket Dictionary of the Horse, 1978, rev. ed., 2000; Miner, forthcoming. Contributor to periodicals. **Address:** Society of Authors, 84 Drayton Gardens, London, GL SW10, England.

PEEL, Kendal J. *See* **STACEY, Tom.**

PEELER, Tim. American (born United States), b. 1957. **Genres:** Poetry. **Career:** Catawba Valley Community College, instructor in English, 1992-, Learning Assistance Center, English coordinator and director. Writer. **Publications:** Touching All the Bases: Poems from Baseball, 2000; Waiting for Godot's First Pitch: More Poems from Baseball (poetry), 2001; Writers on the Storm (short stories and essays), 2001; (with B. McLawhorn) Baseball in Catawba County, 2004; Blood River (poetry), 2005; (with R.G. Utley and A. Peeler) Outlaw Ballplayers: Interviews and Profiles from the Independent Carolina Baseball League, 2006; Fresh Horses (poetry), 2007; (with F. Mofford) Voices from Baseball in Catawba County, 2008; Checking Out (poetry), 2010; (with T. Pope) Waiting for Charlie Brown (poetry), 2011. **Address:** Learning Assistance Center, Catawba Valley Community College, 2550 US Hwy. 70 SE, Hickory, NC 28602-8302, U.S.A. **Online address:** tpeeler@cvcc.edu

PEERADINA, Saleem. American/Indian (born India), b. 1944. **Genres:** Poetry, Autobiography/Memoirs. **Career:** Kirti College, lecturer, 1969-71; Forsyth Country Day School, instructor, 1973-74; Indian Institute of Technology, lecturer, 1974-75; St. Xavier's College, lecturer, 1976-77; Sophia College, lecturer, 1977-84; Hindustan Thompson Associates, copywriter, 1984-87; Adrian College/Alma College, professor, 1988-89; Siena Heights University, associate professor of English, 1989-. Writer. **Publications:** POETRY: First Offence, 1980; Group Portrait, 1992; Meditations on Desire, 2003; The Ocean in My Yard, 2005. EDITOR: Contemporary Indian Poetry in English, 1972; Cultural Forces Shaping India, 1980. **Address:** Department of English, Siena Heights University, 308C Sacred Heart Hall, 1247 E Siena Heights Dr., Adrian, MI 49221-1755, U.S.A. **Online address:** speerad2@sienaheights.edu

PEERENBOOM, Randall. British/American (born United States), b. 1958. **Genres:** Law, History. **Career:** Freshfields Solicitors, staff, 1994-98; PRC Legal Issues, consultant, 1998-; University of California, Law School, acting professor, 1998-2002, professor of law, 2003-07; Yiwen Law Firm, counsel, 1999-; Ford Foundation, consultant, 2002; Asian Development Bank, consultant, 2004-05; Wolfson College, Foundation for Law, Justice and Society, Rule of Law in China Program, director, 2008-; University of Oxford, Centre for Socio-Legal Studies, associate research fellow; La Trobe University, law professor. Writer and lawyer. **Publications:** Law and Morality in Ancient China: The Silk Manuscripts of Huang-Lao, 1993; Lawyers in China: Obstacles to Independence and the Defense of Rights, 1998; China's Long March toward Rule of Law, 2002; China Modernizes: Threat to the West or Model for the Rest?, 2007. EDITOR: (with T. Jones and C. Salbaing) Doing Business in China, 2000; Asian Discourses of Rule of Law: Theories and Implementation of Rule of Law in Twelve Asian Countries, France, and the U.S., 2004; (with C. Petersen and A. Chen) Human Rights in Asia: A Comparative Legal Study of Twelve Asian Jurisdictions, France, and the U.S., 2006; (with J. Gillespie) Regulation in Asia, 2009; (ed.) Judicial Independence in China: Lessons for Global Rule of Law Promotion, 2010; (with M. Zurn and A. Nollkaemper) Rule of Law Dynamics: In an Era of International and Transnational Governance, 2012. Contributor to books and journals. **Address:** Foundation for Law, Justice and Society, Wolfson College, Linton Rd., Oxford, OX OX2 6UD, England. **Online address:** peerenbo@mail.law.ucla.edu

PEERY, Janet. American (born United States), b. 1948. **Genres:** Novels, Novellas/Short Stories. **Career:** Sweet Briar College, teacher; Warren Wilson [illegible] teacher; Old Dominion University, Department of English, professor of creative writing; Kansas [illegible]; GLEN Workshop, faculty; Antioch University, Rappahannock Fiction Writers Workshop, faculty. Writer. **Publications:** COLLECTION: Alligator Dance (short stories), 1993, 2nd ed., 1998. NOVELS: The River beyond the World, 1996; What the Thunder Said, 2007. Contributor to periodicals. **Address:** Department of English, Old Dominion University, 5012 Batten Arts & Letters Bldg., 5115 Hampton Blvd., Norfolk, VA 23529, U.S.A. **Online address:** jpeery@odu.edu

PEET, Mal. British (born England) **Genres:** Novels, Young Adult Non-fiction, Young Adult Fiction, Animals/Pets, Education. **Career:** Educator, illustrator and cartoonist; freelance writer, 1986-. **Publications:** EDUCATIONAL READERS; FOR YOUNG READERS: (with E. Graham) Spending a Penny, 1995; (with E. Graham) Never Sell a Hen on a Wet Day, 1996; Wicked, 1996; (with E. Graham) What's Cooking, 1996; (with E. Graham and M. Morgan) Read Aloud and Talk about Duck Green School Stories (readers), 1999; Keep Your Hamster Happy, 1999; (with E. Graham) Creatures, Kings and Scary Things, 2000; The Giants, 2000; A Bird in the Bush, 2000; (with E. Graham) Wolves, Eyes, and Stormy Skies, 2000; (with E. Graham) Spiders, Chips, and Rocket Ships, 2000; The Wolf Whistle, 2000; (with E. Graham) Moonlight, Seas, and Chocolate Trees, 2000; The Troll's Hat, 2001; The Spooky Eyes, 2001; Life: An Exploded Diagram, 2011; Painting Out the Stars, 2011; Catching the Moon, 2011; Haunted, 2011; I Spy Fly, 2011. YOUNG-ADULT NOVELS: Keeper, 2003; Tamar, 2005; Penalty, 2006; Exposure, 2008. FOR YOUNG READERS: SELF-ILLUSTRATED: A Floating World, 1998; (with E. Graham) Cloud Tea Monkeys, 1999. **Address:** c/o Author Mail, Walker Books Ltd., 87 Vauxhall Walk, London, GL SE11 5HJ, England.

PEETERS, Frederik. Swiss (born Switzerland), b. 1974?. **Genres:** Novels. **Career:** Writer. **Publications:** Blue Pills: A Positive Love Story, 2008. Contributor to comic magazines. **Address:** Geneva, Switzerland. **Online address:** frederik@peeters.ch

PEETERS, Schuiten. *See* **SCHUITEN, François Louis Marie.**

PEETZ, David. Australian (born Australia), b. 1957?. **Genres:** Adult Non-fiction, Politics/Government, Economics, Women's Studies And Issues. **Career:** Griffith University, professor of economics, Department of Employment Relations and Human Resources, academic staff, professor of employment relations. Writer and economist. **Publications:** (Ed. with J. Langmore) Wealth, Poverty, and Survival: Australia in the World, 1983; Unions in a Contrary World: The Future of the Australian Trade Union Movement, 1998; (contrib.) Australia in Accord: An Evaluation of the Prices and Incomes Accord in the Hawke-Keating Years, 2001; (contrib.) Trade Unions and the Crisis of Democracy: Strategies and Perspectives, 2004; Brave New Workplace: How Individual Contracts Are Changing Our Jobs, 2006; (with G. Murray) Women of the Coal Rushes, 2010. Contributor to periodicals and journals. **Address:** Department of Employment Relations & Human, Resources, Griffith University, N50 1.07, 170 Kessels Rd., Nathan, QL 4111, Australia. **Online address:** d.peetz@griffith.edu.au

PEGG, Mark Gregory. Australian/American (born United States), b. 1963. **Genres:** Young Adult Non-fiction. **Career:** University College, University of London, research assistant, 1988-89; University of Sydney, tutor & lecturer in medieval history, 1990, visiting fellow, 1997-98; Princeton University, preceptor & lecturer, 1993, 1996, research assistant, 1996-97, chair & co-ordinator of Medieval Seminar, 1997; Washington University, visiting assistant professor, 1998, assistant professor, 1999-2004, associate professor of history, 2004-; The Inquisition (documentary), consultant, 1991-96. Writer. **Publications:** NONFICTION: The Corruption of Angels: The Great Inquisition of 1245-1246, 2001; A Most Holy War: The Albigensian Crusade and the Battle for Christendom, 2008. Contributor to books and periodicals. **Address:** Washington University, 1 Brookings Dr., St. Louis, MO 63130, U.S.A. **Online address:** mpegg@wustl.edu

PEGRAM, Thomas R. American (born United States), b. 1955. **Genres:** History, Local History/Rural Topics, Politics/Government, Social Sciences. **Career:** Suffolk University, lecturer in history, 1986-88; Simmons College, special instructor, 1987-88; Ohio State University, instructor in history, 1988-90; Loyola College, Department of History, assistant professor of history, 1990-94, associate professor of history, 1995-2001, chair, 1998-2001, professor of history, 2001. Writer. **Publications:** Partisans and Progressives: Private Interest and Public Policy, 1870-1922, 1992; [illegible], The Struggle for a Dry America, 1800-1933, 1998; One Hundred Percent American: The Rebirth and Decline of the Ku Klux Klan in the 1920s, 2011. Contributor of articles to periodicals. **Address:** Department of History, Loyola College, 4501 N Charles St., Baltimore, MD 21210-2699, U.S.A. **Online address:** tpegram@loyola.edu

PEHNT, Wolfgang. German (born Germany), b. 1931. **Genres:** Architecture, Art/Art History. **Career:** Verlag Gerd Hatje, lecturer, 1957-63; Deutschlandfunk (broadcasting Co.), editor of arts and architecture, 1963-95, Department of Literature and Art in Germany radio, head, 1974-95; Ruhr University, Department of History of Architecture, professor, 1995-2009. Writer. **Publications:** Knaurs Lexikon der modernen Architektur, 1963; (ed.) Encyclopedia of Modern Architecture, 1964; Die Stadt in der Bundesrepublik Deutschland: Lebensbedingungen, Aufgaben, Planung: Mit 31 Tab., 1974; Das Ende der Zuversicht: Architektur in diesem Jahrhundert: Ideen, Bauten, Dokumente, 1983; Der Anfang der Bescheidenheit, 1983; (contrib.) Encyclopedia of 20th-century Architecture, 1983; Architekturzeichnungen des Expressionismus, 1985; Engelbert Kremser: Baukunst, 1967-1987, 1986; Hans Hollein Museum in Mönchengladbach: Architektur als Collage, 1986; Karljosef Schattner, ein Architekt ausEichstätt, 1988; Die Erfindung der Geschichte: Aufsätze undGespräche zur Architektur unseres Jahrhunderts, 1989; Hauptstädteder Deutschen: Residenzen, Regierungssitze, Metropolen: eine Sendereihedes Deutschlandfunks, 1991; (contrib.) Rudolf Steiner, Goetheanum, Dornach, 1991; (intro.) Axel Schultes in Bangert, Jansen, Scholz, Schultes: Projects, 1985-1991, 1992; Egon Eiermann: die Kaiser-Wilhelm-Gedächtnis-Kirche, 1994; Klaus Kinold: Architektur-Photographie, 1995; Kister Scheithauer & Partner, 1996; Bewohnte Bilder: Rudolf Schwarz 1897-1961: Architekt einer anderen Moderne: Werkverzeichnis, 1997; Die Architektur des Expressionismus, 1998; Gottfried Böhm, 1999; Deutsche Architektur seit 1900, 2005; (contrib.) Peter Kulka: Bosch Haus Heidehof, Stuttgart, 2005; (with M. Schirren) Hans Poelzig, Architekt Lehrer Kuenstler, 2007; Die Plangestalt des Ganzen, 2011. **Address:** Danziger Str. 2A, Northrhine-Westfalia, Cologne, D 50858, Germany. **Online address:** pehnt@netcologne.de

PEIRCE, Neal R. American (born United States), b. 1932. **Genres:** Politics/Government, Social Commentary, International Relations/Current Affairs. **Career:** Citistates Group, chairman; Washington Post Writers Group, syndicated columnist; Congressional Quarterly, political editor, 1960-69; National Broadcasting Corp., consultant and commentator, 1964-66; CBS Broadcasting Inc., consultant and commentator, 1967-76; The National Journal, co-founder and contributing editor, 1969-96; Smithsonian Institution, Woodrow Wilson International Center for Scholars, fellow, 1971-74; Princeton University, Woodrow Wilson School of Public Affairs, John L. Weinberg distinguished visiting professor, 1992. **Publications:** The People's President, 1968, (with L.D. Longley) rev. ed., 1981; The Megastates of America, 1972; The Pacific States of America, 1972; The Mountain States of America, 1972; The Great Plains States of America, 1973; The Deep South States of America, 1974; (ed. with J.L. Mayer) Prospects for New England, 1975; The Border South States, 1975; The New England States, 1976; (with M. Barone) The Mid-Atlantic States of America, 1977; (with J. Hagstrom and C. Steinbach) Economic Development: The Challenge of the 1980s, 1979; (with J. Hagstrom and C. Steinbach) Democratizing the Development Process, 1979; (with J. Keefe) The Great Lakes States of America, 1980; (with J. Hagstrom) The Book of America, 1983; (with C.F. Steinbach) Corrective Capitalism, 1987; (with C.F. Stainbach) Enterprising Communities: Community-Based Development in America, 1990, 1990; Over New England, 1990; (with C.W. Johnson and J.S. Hall) Citistates: How Urban America Can Prosper in a Competitive World, 1993; (with R. Guskind) Breakthroughs: Re-Creating the American City, 1993; (with L.D. Longley) The Electoral College Primer, 1996; (with C. Johnson) Boundary Crossers: Community Leadership for a Global Age, 1997; (with L.D. Longley) The Electoral College Primer 2000, 1999; Century of the City: No Time To Lose, 2008. **Address:** 610 G St. SW, Washington, DC 20024, U.S.A. **Online address:** npeirce@citistates.com

PEKÁRKOVÁ, Iva. American/Czech (born Czech Republic), b. 1963. **Genres:** Novels. **Career:** Writer. **Publications:** Péra a Perutě, 1989, trans. as Truck Stop Rainbows, 1992; Kulatý Svět, 1993, trans. as The World Is Round, 1994; Dej mi ty prachy, 1996, 2nd ed., 2001; Můj I.Q., 1999; Gimme the Money, 2000; Třicet dva chwanů, 2000; Jaxi taksikařím, 2009. Contributor to periodicals. **Address:** Farrar Straus & Giroux, 19 Union Sq. W, New York, NY 10003, U.S.A. **Online address:** ivapekarkova@gmail.com

PEKKANEN, Sarah. American (born United States), b. 1968?. **Genres:** Novels. **Career:** E! Entertainment Network, on-air reporter; USA Today, reporter; Baltimore Sun, reporter. **Publications:** The Opposite of Me: A Novel, 2010; Skipping a Beat: A Novel, 2011. **Address:** Washington, DC , U.S.A. **Online address:** sarah@sarahpekkanen.com

PELAN, John. American (born United States), b. 1957. **Genres:** Science Fiction/Fantasy, Horror, Young Adult Fiction. **Career:** Axolotl Press, founder, 1986; Darkside Press, founder; Silver Salamander, founder; Midnight House, co-founder; Darkside Press, founder, owner. Author, teacher and publisher. **Publications:** Axolotl special 1, 1989; (with E. Lee) Goon, 1996; (with E. Lee) Cotter's Field; or, The Scene That Started It All, 1996; (with E. Lee) The Case of the Police Officer's Cock Ring and the Piano Player Who Had No Fingers, 1997; Girl's Night Out, 1998; (with E. Lee) Refrigerator Full of Sperm, 1998; (with E. Lee) Sideshow, 1998; (with E. Lee) Prologue, 1998; (with E. Lee) Shifters, 1998; (with E. Lee) Splatterspunk: The Micah Hayes Stories, 1998; An Antique Vintage, 1999; Darkness, My Old Friend (stories), 2002; Colour Out of Darkness, 2004; (with E. Lee) Family Tradition, 2002. EDITOR: Darkside: Horror for the New Millenium, 1995; (and contrib.) The Last Continent: New Tales of Zothique, 1999; Fearful Rock and Other Precarious Locales, 2001; (with B. Adams) The Children of Cthulhu: Chilling New Tales Inspired by H.P. Lovecraft, 2002; The Devil Is Not Mocked and Other Warnings: The Selected Stories of Manly Wade Wellman, Vol2, 2002; K. Fleming, Can Such Things Be? or The Weird of the Beresfords, 2002; The Darker Side, 2002; L. Baldwin, The Shadow on the Blind, 2002; Sin's Doorway and Other Ominous Entrances, 2003; Owls Hoot in the Daytime and Other Omens, 2003; (with M. Reaves) Shadows over Baker Street, 2003; (with R. Kirk) What Shadows We Pursue: Ghost Stories, vol. II, 2003; A Walk on the Darkside: Visions of Horror, 2004; Crazy Little Thing Called Love, 2004; Lost on the Darkside: Voices from the Edge of Horror, 2005; Alone on the Darkside: Echoes from Shadows of Horror, 2006; Century's Best Horror Fiction, 2006, vol. I, 2010, vol. II, 2011; Dark Arts, 2006; City of Night, 2007; Sailing on Strange Seas: An Anthology Tribute to William Hope Hodgson, forthcoming. Contributor to magazines. **Address:** Darkside Press, 4128 Woodland Park Ave. N, Seattle, WA 98103, U.S.A. **Online address:** jpelan@cnw.com

PELEG, Ilan. American/Israeli (born Israel), b. 1944?. **Genres:** International Relations/Current Affairs, Politics/Government. **Career:** Lafayette College, Department of Government and Law, assistant professor, 1974-80, associate professor, 1980-88, head, 1985-95, professor of government and law, 1988-90, Charles A. Dana professor of government and law, 1990-, International Affairs Program, head, 1978-85; Princeton University, research fellow, 1983-84; University of Pennsylvania, fellow-in-residence, 1984-85, Middle East Research Institute, research fellow, 1985-87; Atlantic Council of the United States, academic associate, 1985-; Pennsylvania Humanities Council, lecturer, 1987, 1990, 1992-93; Columbia University, Center for the Study of Human Rights, fellow, 1990; Bethlehem Chamber Music Society, board director, 1993-; Association for Israel Studies, president, 1995-97; Israel Studies Forum, editor-in-chief, 2000-; Reconstructionist Rabbinical College, Israeli Society, adjunct professor. **Publications:** Begin's Foreign Policy, 1977-1983: Israel's Move to the Right, 1987; Human Rights in the West Bank and Gaza, 1995; Democratizing the Hegemonic State: Political Transformation in the Age of Identity, 2007; Legacy of George W. Bush's Foreign Policy: Moving beyond Neoconservatism, 2009; The Foreign Policy of George W. Bush, forthcoming. EDITOR AND CONTRIBUTOR: (with O. Seliktar) The Emergence of Binational Israel: The Second Republic in the Making, 1989; Patterns of Censorship around the World, 1993; The Peace Process in the Middle East: Interdisciplinary Perspectives, 1997; Middle East Peace Process: Interdisciplinary Perspectives, 1998; (with L.S. Bell and A.J. Nathan) Negotiating Culture and Human Rights, 2001. Contributor of articles to books and journals. **Address:** Department of Government & Law, Lafayette College, 207 Kirby Hall of Civil Rights, Easton, PA 18042-1780, U.S.A. **Online address:** pelegi@lafayette.edu

PELKA, Fred. American (born United States), b. 1954. **Genres:** Civil Liberties/Human Rights, Adult Non-fiction, Social Sciences. **Career:** Hospital News, reporter, 1986-87; freelance writer; Boston Center for Independent Living, co-founder, 1984-86; University of California, Bancroft Library Regional Oral History Office, researcher and interviewer, 2000-. Writer. **Publications:** The ABC-Clio Companion to the Disability Rights Movement, 1997; (ed. and intro.) The Civil War Letters of Colonel Charles F. Johnson, Invalid Corps, 2004; John Simon Guggenheim Memorial, fellow, 2004. Works appear in anthologies. Contributor to magazines. **Address:** 54 Burncolt Rd., Florence, MA 01062-1054, U.S.A.

PELL, Ed(ward). (Edward Sergei Pell). American (born United States), b. 1950. **Genres:** Adult Non-fiction, Young Adult Non-fiction, History, Biography. **Career:** ESP Ventures (marketing consultant firm), president. Journalist and marketing consultant. **Publications:** Maryland, 2003; Connecticut, 2003; Indiana, 2003; John Winthrop: Governor of the Massachusetts Bay Colony, 2004. **Address:** c/o Author Mail, Capstone Press, 151 Good Counsel Dr., PO Box 669, Mankato, MN 56001-3143, U.S.A. **Online address:** espvent@bellatlantic.net

PELL, Edward Sergei. *See* **PELL, Ed(ward).**

PELLETIER, Cathie. (K. C. McKinnon). American (born United States), b. 1953. **Genres:** Novels, Novellas/Short Stories, Children's Fiction, Young Adult Fiction. **Career:** Writer. **Publications:** The Funeral Makers, 1986; Once Upon a Time on the Banks, 1989; The Weight of Winter: A Novel, 1991; The Bubble Reputation: A Novel, 1993; A Marriage Made at Woodstock, 1994; (ed. with P.B. Cox and J. Glaser) A Country Music Christmas, 1996; Beaming Sonny Home, 1996; (with S. Davis) The Christmas Note, 1997; A Country Music Christmas, 1997; (as K.C. McKinnon) Dancing at the Harvest Moon, 1997; (as K.C. McKinnon) Candles on Bay Street, 1999; Running the Bulls: A Novel, 2005. Contributor to periodicals. **Address:** Crown Publishing, 201 E 50th St., New York, NY 10022, U.S.A. **Online address:** cathpell@aol.com

PELLETIER, Nancy. American (born United States), b. 1923. **Genres:** Novels, Plays/Screenplays, Young Adult Fiction, Literary Criticism And History. **Career:** Parkersburg Community College, lecturer, 1969-70, assistant professor, 1970-75, associate professor of English, 1975-81, chairman of humanities division, 1978-81; Eve Inc., vice president, 1985-86; Marietta College, teacher of creative writing to the elderly, 1987-88. Writer. **Publications:** The Rearrangement: Novel, 1985 in UK as Happy Families, 1986. **Address:** 1308 Cisler Dr., 624 5th St., Marietta, OH 45750, U.S.A.

PELLEY, Kathleen T. British/Scottish (born Scotland), b. 1955. **Genres:** Children's Fiction. **Career:** Children's writer. **Publications:** The Giant King (juvenile), 2003; Inventor McGregor (juvenile), 2006; Magnus Maximus, a Marvelous Measurer, 2010; Raj the Bookstore Tiger, 2011. **Address:** c/o Author Mail, Child Welfare League of America Inc., 1726 M St. NW, Ste. 500, Washington, DC 20036, U.S.A. **Online address:** ktpelley@aol.com

PELLI, Moshe. American/Israeli (born Israel), b. 1936. **Genres:** Novels, Children's Fiction, Intellectual History, Literary Criticism And History. **Career:** University of Texas at Austin, assistant professor of Hebrew, 1967-71, Hebrew Language Program, coordinator, 1969; Ben Gurion University of the Negev, senior lecturer in Hebrew literature, 1971-74; Cornell University, associate professor of modern Hebrew language and literature, 1974-78, Hebrew Language Program, coordinator, 1975-77; Yeshiva University, Erna Michael College, associate professor of modern Hebrew language and literature, 1978-84; University of Central Florida, associate professor, 1985-88, Judaic Studies Program, director, 1985-, professor of Judaic studies, 1989-, Abe and Tess Wise endowed professor of Judaic studies, 2004-; Hebrew Day School of Central Florida, board director, 1986-; National Association of Professors of Hebrew, vice president, 2005-07, president, 2007-09. Writer. **Publications:** Al deateft, 1961; Elohim bamahapechet, 1965; The Impact of Deism on the Hebrew Literature of the Enlightenment in Germany, 1971; Naphtali Herz Wessely's Attitude toward the Jewish Religion as a Mirror of a Generation in Transition, 1971; The Hebrew Story in the Eighteenth and Nineteenth Centuries, 1971; The Hebrew Satire in the Eighteenth and Nineteenth Centuries, 1971; Moshe Mendelssohn: Bechavlei masoret (Moses Mendelssohn: Bonds of Tradition); Introduction to Modern Hebrew Literature in the 18th and 19th Centuries, 1972; Mordechai Gumpel Schnaber: The First Religious Reformer of the Hebrew Haskalah in Germany, 1972; The Attitude of the First Maskilim toward the Hebrew Language, 1972; Isaac Satanow's 'Mishlei Asaf' as Reflecting the Ideology of the German Hebrew Haskalah, 1972; The Age of Haskalah: Studies in Hebrew Literature of the Enlightenment in Germany, 1979, new ed., 2006; Getting By in Hebrew, 1984; Bema'avqei temurah (Struggle for Change), 1988; Hatarbut Ha'ivrit Ba'America, 80 Shnot Hatenu'ah Ha'ivrit Be'artzot Habrit, 1998; Sugot vesugyot besifrut ha Haskalah ha Ivrit: ha genre ha maskili, 1999; Shaar le haskalah: mafteah muar leha Measef, ketav ha et ha Ivri ha rishon, 2000; Dor ha-Measfim be-shahar ha-Haskalah: terumatam ha-sifrutit shel halutse ha-Measef, ketav ha et ha-Ivri ha-rishon le Haskalah ha-Ivrit be-reshitah, 2001; Bikurei Ha'itim the First Fruits of Haskalah, 2005; In Search of Genres: Hebrew Enlightenment and Modernity, 2005; Haśkalah u modernizm: hatḥalot ṿe-hemshekhim: hitḳablut ha-Haśkalah ha-muḳdemet ba-meah ha-19 u-beshilhe ha-teḳufah, 2007; Haśkalah u-modernizm: hatḥalot ṿe-hemshekhim: hitḳablut ha-Haśkalah ha-muḳdemet ba-me ah ha-19 u-beshilhe ha-teḳufah, 2007; Shadow of Death: Letters in Flames, 2008; Kerem ḥemed: ḥokhmat Yiśra el hi Yavneh ha-ḥadashah: mafteaḥ muar le-Kerem ḥemed: ketav-ha-et ha-Ivri shel ha-Haśkalah be-Galitsiyah uve-Iṭalyah, 593-616, 2009; Haskalah and Beyond: the Reception of the Hebrew Enlightenment and the Emergence of Haskalah Judaism, 2010. CHILDREN'S BOOKS IN HEBREW: Giborei Hag Getto, 1963; Ha Ayarah, 1964; Ivrit baolam hehadash, 1965; Shalom Aleichem, 1966; Itzhak Ben Tzvi (biography), 1971; Shalom (Peace), 1980. **Address:** Judaic Studies Program, College of Arts & Sciences, University of Central Florida, Rm. CNH415, Colbourn Hall, 4000 Central Florida Blvd., PO Box 161992, Orlando, FL 32816-1992, U.S.A. **Online address:** judaicst@ucf.edu

PELOSI, Nancy. American (born United States), b. 1940. **Genres:** Autobiography/Memoirs, Self Help. **Career:** Congressional representative (U.S. federal government), politician; United States House of Representatives, minority leader, House minority whip, 2002-03, House minority leader, 2003-07. Writer. **Publications:** (With A.H. Hearth) Know Your Power: A Message to America's Daughters, 2008. **Address:** U.S House of Representatives, 235 Cannon HOB, Washington, DC 20515, U.S.A.

PÉLOT, Pierre. (Pierre Suragne). French (born France), b. 1945. **Genres:** Science Fiction/Fantasy, Literary Criticism And History. **Career:** Writer. **Publications:** Les croix en feu, 1966; La piste du Dakota, 1966; Dylan Stark, la couleurde Dieu, 1967; L'unique rebelle, 1971; Sierra Brulante, 1971; (as Pierre Suragne) Laseptième saison, 1972; Les légendes de Terre, 1973; Le coeur sousla cendre, 1974; Les neiges du coucou, 1976; Transit, 1977; Foetus-party, 1977; Delirium Circus, 1977; Les barreaux de l'éden, 1977; Canyon Street, 1978; Le sommeil du chien, 1978; Le canard à trois pattes, 1978; La guerre olympique, 1980; Quatre hommes pour lenfer, 1980; Le ciel bleu d'Irockee, 1980; KidJésus, 1981; L'été en pente douce: engrenage, 1981; Lesîles du vacarme, 1981; Les pieds dans la tête, 1982; Le hibou sur la porte, 1982; La marche des bannis, 1982; Nos armessont de miel, 1982; La forêt muette, 1982; Mourir au hasard, 1982; Pour un cheval qui savait rire, 1982; Saison de rouille, 1982; Soleilshurlants: les hommes sans futur, 1983; La nuit sur terre, 1983; Deuxhommes sont venus, 1983; Le train ne sifflera pas trois fois, 1983; Bluespour Julie, 1984; Le père de feu, 1984; Le chien courant surl'autoroute en criant son nom, 1984; Natural Killer, 1985; Noires racines, 1985; Le bruit des autres, 1985; Ce chasseur-là, 1985; L'heured'hiver, 1985; Paradis zéro, 1985; Fou dans la tête de Nazi Jones, Belladone et compagnie, 1986; Les passagers du mirage, 1986; Lesconquerrants immobiles, 1986; Mémoires d'un épouvantailblessé au combat, 1986; Observation du virus en temps de paix, 1986; Purgatoire, 1986; Elle qui ne sait pas dire je, 1987; Alabama un neuf neufsix, 1987; Offensive du virus sous le champs de bataille, 1987; Sécession bis, 1987; Une jeune fille au sourire fragile, 1988; Si loinde Caïn, 1988; Le 16e round, 1990; Le ciel sous la pierre, 1990; Lerêve de Lucy, 1990; Le présent du fou, 1990; Les forains du borddu gouffre, 1990; Le fils du grand Konnar, 1990; La nuit du sagittaire, 1990; Les faucheurs de temps, 1990; Le pain perdu, 1991; La drave, 1991; Ultimes aventures en territoires fourbes, 1991; Sur la piste des rollmops, 1991; Rollmops Dream, 1991; Gilbert le barbant, le retour, 1991; Lebonheur des sardines, 1993; Le Père Noël s'appelle Basile, 1993; Les épaules du diable, 1993; Ce soir, les souris sont bleues, 1994; L'expédition perdue, 1994; Pauvres zhéros, 1995; Une autre saisoncomme le printemps, 1995; Après le bout du monde, 1995; Lescaïmans sont des gens comme les autres, 1996; Messager destempêtes lointaines, 1996; Qui regarde la montagne au loin, 1996; Lesourire des crabes, 1996; Sous le vent du monde qui regarde la montagne auloin, 1996; La peau de l'orage; Duz; Je suis la brume; Brouillards, 1997; Le nom perdu du soleil: sous le vent du monde, 1997; L'assassin de Dieu, 1998; Les pirates du Graal, 1998; Hanuman: entrez dans la légende dudieu singe, 1998; Debout dans le ventre blanc du silence, 1999; Le jour del'enfant tueur: Le livre de Ahorn, 1999; Cimetière aux étoiles, 1999; Avant la fin du ciel: sous le vent du monde, 2000; L'ombre de lalouve: Le livre de Ahorn, 2000; Ceux qui parlent au bord de la pierre, 2001; C'est ainsi que les hommes vivent, 2003; Méchamment dimanche, 2005; L'ombre des voyageuses, 2006; Normales saisonnières: roman, 2007; La croque buissonnière, 2008; L'ange étrange et Marie-McDo: roman, 2010; Maria: Roman, 2011. **Address:** c/o Author Mail, Heloise d'Ormesson Editions, 87 Blvd. Saint-Michel, Paris, 75005, France.

PELZER, Richard B. American (born United States), b. 1965. **Genres:** Biography, Young Adult Fiction, Human Relations/Parenting, Self Help. **Career:** Writer. **Publications:** A Brothers Journey: Surviving a Childhood of Abuse, 2005; A Teenager's Journey: Overcoming a Childhood of Abuse, 2006; Closer: A Man's Journey, forthcoming. Contributor to periodicals. **Address:** c/o Author Mail, Warner Books, 1271 Ave. of the Americas, New York, NY 10020-1300, U.S.A.

PEMBERTON, Margaret. Also writes as Christina Harland, Maggie Hudson, Rebecca Dean, Carris Carlise. British (born England), b. 1943. **Genres:** Novels, Young Adult Fiction. **Career:** Freelance writer, 1974-. **Publications:** Rendezvous with Danger, 1974; The Mystery of Saligo Bay, 1976; Shadows over Silver Sands, 1976; Tapestry of Fear, 1979; The Guilty Secret, 1979; Vengeance in the Sun, 1979; Harlot, 1981 as The Far Morning, 1998; Lion of Languedoc, 1980; Pioneer Girl, 1981; Some Distant Shore, 1981; Flower Garden, 1982; African Enchantment, 1982; Flight to Verechenko, 1983 in UK as A Rebellious Heart, Severn House, 2002; Forever, 1983; Devil's Palace, 1984; Silver Shadows, 1985; Goddess, 1985; Never Leave Me, 1986; A Multitude of Sins, 1988; (as Carris Carlisle) Party in Peking, 1987, rev. ed., 1993; (as Christina Harland) White Christmas in Saigon, 1990; (as Christina Harland) Waiting Wives, 1991; An Embarrassment of Riches, 1992; Moonflower Madness, 1993; Zadruga, 1994; Forget-Me-Not Bride, 1995; Londoners, 1995; Magnolia Square, 1996; The Girl Who Knew Too Much, 1997; Yorkshire Rose, 1996; Coronation Summer, 1997; The Far Morning, 1998; Last Letter, 1998; (as Maggie Hudson) Tell Me No Secrets, Tell Me No Lies, 1999; Undying Love, 1999; A Year to Eternity, 2000; From China with Love, 2000; (as Maggie Hudson) Fast Women, 2000; A Dark Enchantment, 2001; (as Maggie Hudson) Looking for Mr. Big, 2001; (as Maggie Hudson) Nowhere to Run, 2002; The Reckless Miss Grainger, 2002; A Many Splendoured Thing, 2003; The Four of Us, 2004; The Turbulent Years, 2005; Unforgettable Days, 2005; Violins of Autumn, 2006; A Time to Remember, 2007; The Last Goodbye, 2007. AS REBECCA DEAN: Enemies of the Heart, 2008; A Dangerous Desire, 2008 in US as The Palace Circle, 2009; Golden Prince, 2010; Shadow Queen, 2012. **Address:** 13 Manor Ln., London, GL SE13 5QW, England.

PEÑA, Charles V. American (born United States) **Genres:** Politics/Government, Military/Defense/Arms Control, History, Social Sciences. **Career:** Cato Institute, director of defense policy studies, defense policy and program expert, senior manager; MSNBC-TV, television analyst; Global TV (Canada), television analyst; Channel One News, television analyst; Independent Institute, senior fellow; Coalition for a Realistic Foreign Policy, senior fellow; Straus Military Reform Project, adviser; George Washington University, Homeland Security Policy Institute, senior fellow. Writer. **Publications:** (Co-author) Exiting Iraq: Why the U.S. Must End the Military Occupation and Renew the War against Al Qaeda, 2004; Winning the Un-War: A New Strategy for the War on Terrorism, 2006; (co-author) The Search for WMD: Non-Proliferation, Intelligence and Pre-emption in the New Security Environment, 2006. Contributor to periodicals. **Address:** Independent Institute, 100 Swan Way, Oakland, CA 94621-1428, U.S.A.

PENA, Milagros. American (born United States), b. 1955. **Genres:** Anthropology/Ethnology, Sociology. **Career:** Spanish teacher, 1978-80; State University of New York, instructor in sociology, 1986-87; Occidental College, adjunct professor of sociology, 1989; Bowling Green State University, Departments of Ethnic Studies and Sociology, assistant professor, 1990-94, associate professor of sociology and ethnic studies, 1995-96, graduate coordinator of ethnic studies, 1993-96; City University of New York, Graduate School and University Center, Program for the Analysis of Religion among Latinos, vice president, 1995; New Mexico State University, Department of Sociology and Anthropology, assistant professor of sociology, 1996-97, associate professor, 1995-99; University of Florida, Department of Sociology, associate professor, 1999-2007, professor of sociology and women's studies, 2007-, Center for Women's Studies and Gender Research, director, 2005-, College of Arts and Sciences, associate dean for social and behavioral sciences, Writer. **Publications:** Theologies and Liberation in Peru: The Role of Ideas in Social Movements, 1995; (with C. Malott) Punk Rockers' Revolution: A Pedagogy of Race, Class, and Gender, 2004; (with E.I. Hernandez and K.G. Davis) Emerging Voices, Urgent Choices: Essays on Latinoa Religious Leadership, 2006; Latina Activists Across Borders: Women's Grassroots Organizing in Mexico and Texas, 2007. Contributor of articles to journals. **Address:** Dept. of Sociology & Ctr. for Women's Studies, University of Florida, 2014 Turlington Hall, Gainesville, FL 32611-7330, U.S.A. **Online address:** mpena@soc.ufl.edu

PENCAK, William. (William A. Pencak). American (born United States), b. 1951. **Genres:** Politics/Government, History, Military/Defense/Arms Control, Economics. **Career:** Pennsylvania State University, Department of History, assistant professor, professor, 1983-. Writer. **Publications:** War, Politics & Revolution in Provincial Massachusetts, 1981; America's Burke: The Mind of Thomas Hutchinson, 1982; (ed. with C.E. Wright) Authority and Resistance in Early New York, 1988; For God & Country: The American Legion, 1919-1941, 1989; (ed. with W.W. Holt, Jr.) The Law in America, 1607-1861, 1989; (ed. with C.E. Wright) New York and the Rise of American Capitalism: Economic Development and the Social and Political History of an American State, 1780-1870, 1989; (ed. with S. Berrol and R.M. Miller) Immigration to New York, 1991; (ed. with P.A. Gilje) New York in the Age of the Constitution, 1775-1800, 1992; History, Signing In: Essays in History and Semiotics, 1993; (ed. with F. Freidel) The White House: The First Two Hundred Years, 1994; The Conflict of Law and Justice in the Icelandic Sagas, 1995; (ed.) Worldmaking, 1996; (ed. with J.B. Frantz) Beyond Philadelphia: The American Revolution in the Pennsylvania Hinterland, 1998; (ed. with J.R. Lindgren) New Approaches to Semiotics and the Human Sciences: Essays in Honor of Roberta Kevelson, 1998; (co-ed.) The Law vs. the People: Twelfth Round Table on Law and Semiotics, 2000; (ed. with W. Blair) Making and Remaking Pennsylvania's Civil War, 2001; (ed. with R.M. Miller) Pennsylvania: A History of the Commonwealth, 2002; (ed. with J. Dorinson) Paul Robeson: Essays on His Life and Legacy, 2002; The Films of Derek Jarman, 2002; (ed. with M. Dennis and S.P. Newman) Riot and Revelry in Early America, 2002; (ed. with C. Palecek) From Absurdity to Zen: The Wit and Wisdom of Roberta Kevelson, 2002; (ed. with D.K. Richter) Friends and Enemies in Penn's Woods: Indians, Colonists, and the Racial Construction of Pennsylvania, 2004; Jews and Gentiles in Early America, 1654-1800, 2005; (ed. with A. Wagner) Images in Law, 2006; (ed. with P.A. Gilje) Pirates, Jack Tar, and Memory: New Directions in American Maritime Histor, 2007; Historic Pennsylvania: An Illustrated History, 2008. Contributor to journals. **Address:** Dept of History & Religious Studies Prog, Pennsylvania State University, 108 Weaver Bldg., University Park, PA 16802, U.S.A. **Online address:** wap1@psu.edu

PENCAK, William A. *See* **PENCAK, William.**

PENCAVEL, John (H.). American/British (born England), b. 1943. **Genres:** Business/Trade/Industry, Economics, Organized Labor. **Career:** Princeton University, Jane Eliza Proctor visiting fellow, 1966-67, Industrial Relations Section, affiliated, 1968-69; Stanford University, department of economics, professor, 1969-, Levin professor of economics, Stanford Center for International Development, director, Stanford Institute for Economic Policy Research, senior fellow; Institute for the Study of Labor, research fellow; Hoover Institution on War, Revolution, and Peace, National fellow, 1972-73; Journal of Economic Literature, associate editor, 1982-85, editor, 1986-. Writer. **Publications:** An Analysis of the Quit Rate in American Manufacturing Industry, 1970; Labor Markets under Trade Unionism: Employment, Wages, and Hours, 1991; Role of Labor Unions in Fostering Economic Development, 1995; Worker Participation: Lessons From the Worker Co-ops of the Pacific Northwest, 2001; Earnings Inequality and Market Work in Husband-Wife Families, 2006; (with L. Pistaferri and F. Schivardi) Wages, Employment, and Capital in Capitalist and Worker-Owned Firms, 2006. Contributor of articles to periodicals. Works appear in anthologies. **Address:** Department of Economics, Stanford University, Rm. 262, Landau Economics Bldg., 579 Serra Mall, PO Box 6072, Stanford, CA 94305-6072, U.S.A. **Online address:** pencavel@stanford.edu

PENCE, Caprial A. American (born United States), b. 1963. **Genres:** Food And Wine. **Career:** Fullers Restaurant, chef, 1987-92; Caprials Bistro, chef and co-owner, 1992-; Caprial and John's Kitchen, co-owner, 2002-; The Learning Channel, Caprials Café, host; Public Broadcasting Service, Cooking with Caprial and John, host. Cookbook author and television chef. **Publications:** Caprial's Seasonal Kitchen: An Innovative Chef's Menus and Recipes for Easy Home Cooking, 1988; Caprial's Café Favorites, 1994; Cooking with Caprial: American Bistro Fare, 1996; Caprial's Bistro Style Cuisine, 1998; (with M. Dowers) Caprial's Soup and Sandwiches, 1998; Caprial's Bistro, 1999; Caprial Cooks for Friends, 2000; (with M. Carey) Caprial's Desserts, 2001; Caprial and John's Kitchen: Recipes for Cooking Together, 2003. **Address:** Caprial & John's Kitchen, 609 SE Ankeny, Portland, OR 97214, U.S.A. **Online address:** caprial@caprial.com

PENCE, Gregory E. American (born United States), b. 1948. **Genres:** Design, Medicine/Health, Philosophy, Theology/Religion, Cultural/Ethnic Topics. **Career:** University of Alabama, professor of philosophy, 1976-, professor of medical ethics, 1977-, Early Health Professions Acceptance Program, director. Writer. **Publications:** Ethical Options in Medicine, 1980; Classic Cases in Medical Ethics: Accounts of Cases That Have Shaped Medical Ethics, with Philosophical, Legal and Historical Backgrounds, 1990, 5th ed., 2008; (with L. Stephens) Seven Dilemmas in World Religion, 1994; (ed.) Classic Works in Medical Ethics: Core Philosophical Readings, 1998; (ed.) Flesh of My Flesh: The Ethics of Cloning Humans: A Reader, 1998, 2nd ed. as The Ethics of Cloning Humans: A Companion to Bioethics, 2009; Who's Afraid of Human Cloning?, 1998; A Dictionary of Common Philosophical Terms, 2000; Re-creating Medicine: Ethical Issues at the Frontiers of Medicine, 2000; (ed.) The Ethics of Food: A Reader for the Twenty-First Century, 2002; Brave New Bioethics, 2002; Designer Food: Mutant Harvest or Breadbasket of the World?, 2002; Cloning after Dolly: Who's Still Afraid of Human Cloning?, 2004; Elements of Bioethics, 2007; Medical Ethics: Accounts of Ground-Breaking Cases, 2010; How to Build a Better Human: An Ethical Blueprint, forthcoming. Contributor to periodicals. **Address:** Department of Philosophy, University of Alabama, HB 414A, 900 13th St. S, Birmingham, AL 35294-1260, U.S.A. **Online address:** pence@uab.edu

PENCE, Joanne. American (born United States) **Genres:** Administration/Management, Mystery/Crime/Suspense, Novels. **Career:** Social Security Administration, operations analysis manager, 1970-98. Mystery writer and educator. **Publications:** NOVEL: Armed and Dangerous, 1987. ANGIE AMALFI SERIES: Something's Cooking, 1993; Too Many Cooks, 1994; Cooking up Trouble, 1995; Cooking Most Deadly, 1996; Cook's Night Out, 1998; Cooks Overboard, 1998; A Cook in Time, 1999; To Catch a Cook, 2000; Bell, Cook and Candle, 2002; If Cooks Could Kill, 2003; Two Cooks A-Killing, 2003; Courting Disaster, 2004; Red Hot Murder, 2006; The Da Vinci Cook, 2007. **Address:** HarperCollins Publishers, 10 E 53rd St., New York, NY 10022, U.S.A. **Online address:** joanne@joannepence.com

PENDERGAST, John S. American (born United States), b. 1963. **Genres:** Theology/Religion, Plays/Screenplays, Literary Criticism And History. **Career:** Southern Illinois University, assistant professor of English. Writer. **Publications:** Love's Labour's Lost: A Guide to the Play, 2002; Religion, Allegory and Literacy in Early Modern England, 1560-1640: The Control of the Word, 2006. **Address:** Department of English, Southern Illinois University, 3206 Peck Hall, PO Box 1431, Edwardsville, IL 62026, U.S.A. **Online address:** jpender@siue.edu

PENDLE, Karin. American (born United States), b. 1939. **Genres:** Music, Reference. **Career:** Oberlin College, instructor in music, 1964-69; University of Western Ontario, assistant professor, associate professor of music, 1970-76; University of Cincinnati, assistant professor, professor of music, 1970-, now professor emeritus. Writer. **Publications:** Eugéne Scribe and French Opera of the Nineteenth Century, 1979; (ed.) Women and Music: A History, 1991, 2nd ed., 2001; (co-author) L'opera-comique en France des origines a 1789, 1992; Women in Music: A Research and Information Guide, 2005, 2nd ed., 2010. **Address:** College-Conservatory of Music, University of Cincinnati, Mary Emery Hall, PO Box 210003, Cincinnati, OH 45221-0003, U.S.A. **Online address:** pendleka@email.uc.edu

PENDLETON, Thomas. Also writes as Lee Thomas, Dallas Reed. American (born United States), b. 1965?. **Genres:** Novels, Mystery/Crime/Suspense. **Career:** Writer. **Publications:** Mason, 2008. WICKED DEAD SERIES WITH S. PETRUCHA: Lurker, 2007; Torn, 2007; Snared, 2007; Skin, 2008; Crush, 2008; Prey, 2008. AS DALLAS REED: Shimmer, 2008; The Calling, 2009. AS LEE THOMAS: Stained, 2004; Parish Damned, 2005; The Dust of Wonderland, 2007; In the Closet, under the Bed (stories), 2009; Damage, 2009; The German, 2011; Focus, 2011. Works appear in anthologies. Contributor to periodicals. **Address:** Lethe Press, 118 Heritage Ave., Maple Shade, NJ 08052, U.S.A. **Online address:** leethomaswriter@gmail.com

PENDREIGH, Brian. American (born United States), b. 1957?. **Genres:** Film, Travel/Exploration, Biography, Photography. **Career:** The Scotsman, senior feature writer, film correspondent and cinema editor, 1987-97; Hotdog magazine, associate editor; freelance film journalist, 1997-. **Publications:** On Location: The Film Fan's Guide to Britain and Ireland, 1995; Mel Gibson and His Movies, 1997; Ewan McGregor, 1998; The Scot Pack: The Further Adventures of the Trainspotters and Their Fellow Travellers, 2000; The Legend of The Planet of the Apes: Or How Hollywood Turned Darwin Upside Down, 2001; The Pocket Scottish Movie Book, 2002. Contributor to periodicals. **Address:** c/o Author Mail, Mainstream Publishing, 7 Albany St., Edinburgh, LT EH1 3UG, Scotland.

PENELOPE *See* **Shaw, Carolyn V.**

PENELOPE, Julia. American (born United States), b. 1941. **Genres:** Writing/Journalism, Gay And Lesbian Issues, Poetry, Language/Linguistics, Women's Studies And Issues, Essays. **Career:** University of Georgia, instructor, 1968-71, assistant professor, 1971-74; University of South Dakota, visiting assistant professor, 1976; University of Nebraska, assistant professor, 1976-77, associate professor, 1977-87; Washington University, visiting associate professor, 1986-87; writer, 1987-; University of Massachusetts, visiting associate professor, 1988; Green Party of Texas-Lubbock County, founder and co-chair. **Publications:** (With M. Gray) Found Goddesses: From Asphalta to Viscera, 1988; Speaking Freely: Unlearning the Lies of the Fathers' Tongues, 1990; Call Me Lesbian: Lesbian Lives, Lesbian Theory, 1992; Flinging Wide the Eyed Universe, 1999. EDITOR: Effective Writing, 1973; (with A.P. Nilsen and others) Sexism and Language, 1977; (with S.J. Wolfe) The Coming Out Stories, 1980, 2nd as The Original Coming Out Stories, 1989; (with S.L. Hoagland) For Lesbians Only: Separatist Writing, 1988; (with S. Valentine) Finding the Lesbians: Personal Accounts from Around the World, 1990; (with S. Valentine) International Feminist Fiction, 1992; (with S.J. Wolfe) Sexual Practice/Textual Theory: Lesbian Cultural Criticism, 1993; (with S.J. Wolfe) Lesbian Culture: An Anthology: The Lives, Work, Ideas, Art and Visions of Lesbians Past and Present, 1993; Out of the Class Closet: Lesbians Speak, 1994. Contributor to periodicals. **Address:** 1916 37th St., Lubbock, TX 79412, U.S.A. **Online address:** JPenel6280@aol.com

PENMAN, Sharon Kay. American (born United States), b. 1945. **Genres:** Mystery/Crime/Suspense. **Career:** Writer, tax lawyer and educator. **Publications:** HISTORICAL THRILLERS: The Sunne in Splendour, 1982; Here Be Dragons, 1985; Falls the Shadow, 1988; The Reckoning, 1991; When Christ and His Saints Slept, 1995; The Queen's Man: A Medieval Mystery, 1996; Cruel as the Grave: A Medieval Mystery, 1998; Time and Chance, 2002; Dragon's Lair: A Medieval Mystery, 2003; Prince of Darkness: A Medieval Mystery, 2005; Devil's Brood, 2008; Lionheart, 2011. Contributor to periodicals. **Address:** c/o Author Mail, Henry Holt & Co., 115 W 18th St., New York, NY 10011, U.S.A.

PENN, Mark J. American (born United States), b. 1954. **Genres:** Novels. **Career:** McDonald's, polling analyst & advisor; AT & T, polling analyst & advisor, Coca-Cola, polling analyst & advisor; American Express, polling analyst & advisor; Ford Motor Co., polling analyst & advisor; Microsoft, polling analyst & advisor; Penn, Schoen and Berland (PSB, polling firm), president & cofounder, 1975-; Burson-Marsteller (B-M, public relations firm), worldwide chief executive officer, 1995-. Writer. **Publications:** (with E.K. Zalesne) Microtrends: The Small Forces behind Tomorrow's Big Changes (nonfiction), 2007. Contributor to periodicals. **Address:** The Leigh Bureau, 92 E Main St., Ste. 400, Somerville, NJ 08876, U.S.A. **Online address:** markjpenn@bm.com

PENN, Michael Philip. American (born United States) **Genres:** Theology/Religion, History, Biography. **Career:** National Aeronautics and Space Administration, Ames Research Center, electron microscopy researcher, 1987-89; Weizmann Institute, recombinant DNA researcher, 1989; Palo Alto Veterans Hospital, immuno-cytochemistry researcher, 1989; Apple Computers, software engineer, 1989-93; Pinewood High School, teacher, debate and speech coach, 1990-91; Princeton High School, teacher and debate coach, 1991-93; Durham Academy High School, teacher and director of forensics program, 1994-99; Duke University, teaching assistant, 1996-98, instructor, 1998-99; Bryn Mawr College, visiting lecturer, 2000; Haverford College, visiting assistant professor, 2000-01; Brandeis University, postdoctoral fellow, 2001-02; Mt. Holyoke College, assistant professor, 2002-08, associate professor, 2008-. Writer. **Publications:** Kissing Christians: Ritual and Community in the Late Ancient Church, 2005. Contributor of articles to books. **Address:** Department of Religion, Mount Holyoke College, 205 Skinner Hall, South Hadley, MA 01075, U.S.A. **Online address:** mpenn@mtholyoke.edu

PENN, W(illiam) S. American (born United States), b. 1949. **Genres:** Novels, Essays, Adult Non-fiction, History. **Career:** State University of New York, assistant professor, 1981-84; City University of New York, Hostos

Community College, assistant professor, 1986-87; Michigan State University, Department of English, associate professor of English, 1987-, professor of creative writing. Writer. **Publications:** The Absence of Angels (novel), 1994; All My Sins Are Relatives (essays), 1995; The Telling of the World: Native American Stories & Art, 1996; (ed.) As We Are Now: Mixblood Essays on Race and Identity, 1997; This is the World, 2000; Killing Time with Strangers (novel), 2000; Feathering Custer (essays), 2001; Hazing: A Novel in Ten Satires, forthcoming; The Revenge of King George, forthcoming. Contributor to journals. **Address:** Department of English, Michigan State University, 206A Morrill Hall, East Lansing, MI 48824, U.S.A. **Online address:** penn@msu.edu

PENNA, Dennis Roy. American (born United States), b. 1947. **Genres:** Biography, Plays/Screenplays, Adult Non-fiction. **Career:** Writer. **Publications:** (With J. Lanza) Russ Columbo and the Crooner Mystique, 2003. **Address:** c/o Author Mail, Feral House, PO Box 39910, Los Angeles, CA 90039, U.S.A.

PENNAC, Daniel. French/Moroccan (born Morocco), b. 1944?. **Genres:** Novels, Essays, Young Adult Fiction, Children's Fiction, Mystery/Crime/Suspense, Autobiography/Memoirs. **Career:** High school teacher. Mystery writer, novelist and author of nonfiction. **Publications:** FOR CHILDREN: Le grand rex, 1980; Cabot-Caboche, 1982; L'oeil du loup, 1982; Kamo et moi, 1992; Kamo, l'agence Babel, 1992; Kamo, l'idée du siècle, 1993; Comme au théâtre, 1996; L'evasion Kamo, 1997. ADULT FICTION: (with T. Eliad) Les enfants de Yalta, 1978; Messieurs les enfants, 1997; Le dictateur et le hamac: Roman, 2003. MALAUSSENESAGA FICTION: Le Fée carabine, 1987; Le petite marchande de prose, 1993; Au bonheur des ogres, 1993; Monsieur Malaussène: Roman, 1995; Monsieur Malaussène au théâtre, 1996; Des crétiens et des maures, 1997; Aux fruits de la Passion: Roman, 1999. OTHERS: Le service militaire au service de qui?, 1973; La sens de la Houppelande, 1991; Comme un roman, 1992; (with J. Marigny) Sang pour sang, le-réveil des vampires, 1993; Vercors d'en haute: La réserve naturelle des Hauts Planteaux, 1996; Merci, 2004; Nemo, 2006; écrire, 2007; Chagrin d'école, 2007; Rights Of The Reader, 2008; School Blues, 2010. **Address:** Editions Gallimard, 5 rue Sébastian-Bottin, Paris, 75328, France.

PENNER, Fred (Ralph Cornelius). Canadian (born Canada), b. 1946. **Genres:** Songs/Lyrics And Libretti, Children's Fiction. **Career:** CBC, Fred Penner's Place, host, 1985-97; Oak Street Music, executive vice president, 1987-98; MTV/Nickelodeon (U.S.), host, 1989-; Children's entertainer and television performer. Writer. **Publications:** OTHERS: The Bump, 1984; Ebeneezer Sneezer, 1985; Rollerskating, 1987; (with S. Oberman) Julie Gerond and the Polka Dot Pony, 1988; Sing Along Play Along (contains songs from Penner's first four albums), 1990; Proud, 1997; The Cat Came Back, 2005; (with S. Fatus) Here We Go Round the Mulberry Bush, 2007; Whole World, 2007. **Address:** Oak Street Music, 93 Lombard Ave., Ste. 108, Winnipeg, MB R3B 3B1, Canada.

PENNER, Jonathan. American (born United States), b. 1940. **Genres:** Novels, Novellas/Short Stories. **Career:** New School for Social Research, instructor in English, 1968; Housatonic Community College, lecturer in English, 1968-70; Southern Illinois University, lecturer in English, 1976-77; University of Arizona, assistant professor, 1978-84, associate professor, 1984-90, professor of English, 1990-; University of Edinburgh, postdoctoral fellow, 1978-; Vanderbilt University, faculty; University of Hawaii, faculty. Writer. **Publications:** Going Blind (novel), 1977; The Intelligent Traveler's Guide to Chiribosco (novella), 1983; Private Parties (short stories), 1983; Natural Order (novel), 1990; This is My Voice, 2003. Contributor to periodicals. **Address:** Department of English, The University of Arizona, Rm. 445, Modern Languages Bldg., PO Box 210067, Tucson, AZ 85721-0001, U.S.A. **Online address:** exlibris@u.arizona.edu

PENNEY, Sue. Welsh/British (born England), b. 1957. **Genres:** Theology/Religion, Humanities, Environmental Sciences/Ecology, Children's Fiction. **Career:** Teacher, 1980-91; writer, 1991-. **Publications:** DISCOVERING RELIGIONS SERIES: Christianity, 1987, rev. ed., 2008; Islam, 1987, rev. ed., 2008; Judaism, 1987, rev. ed., 2008; Sikhism, 1988, rev. ed., 2008; Buddhism, 1988, rev. ed., 2008; Hinduism, 1988, rev. ed., 2008. EXAMINING SOCIAL ISSUES SERIES: (with I. Happs) Examining Health, 1993; Examining Environmental Issues, 1993; Examining Relationships, 1993. OTHERS: Understanding Christianity, 1999. **Address:** c/o Author Mail, Heinemann Library, 100 N La Salle, Ste. 1200, Chicago, IL 60602, U.S.A.

PENNIE, Hester. *See* **TAYLOR, Elisabeth (D.).**

PENNINGTON, Kate. *See* **OLDFIELD, Jenny.**

PENROD, Diane. (Diane Marie Penrod). American (born United States), b. 1958. **Genres:** Adult Non-fiction, Education. **Career:** JCHD Advertising, copywriter and media buyer, 1980; marketing consultant, 1980-86; Jones Colad, industrial sales representative, 1982-85; Bryan and Stratton Business Institute, instructor, 1987-91; State University of New York, instructor, 1989, 1994; Syracuse University, instructor, 1989-94; Rowan University, associate professor, 1994-2004, professor, 2004-, director; Communications Institute, Center for Research, director, 1997-99; National Writing Project, site director; editor. **Publications:** (Ed.) Miss Grundy Doesn't Teach Here Anymore: Popular Culture and the Composition Classroom, 1997; Composition and Convergence: The Impact of New Media on Writing Assessment, 2005; Using Blogs to Enhance Literacy: The Next Powerful Step in 21st-Century Learning, 2007. **Address:** Department of Writing Arts, College of Communication, Rowan University, 201 Mullica Hill Rd., Glassboro, NJ 08028, U.S.A. **Online address:** penrod@rowan.edu

PENROD, Diane Marie. *See* **PENROD, Diane.**

PENROSE, Antony. British (born England), b. 1947. **Genres:** Agriculture/Forestry, Art/Art History, Photography, Autobiography/Memoirs, Biography, Photography, Children's Fiction. **Career:** Filmmaker, 1977-88; The Farley's Yard Trust, founder. Writer. **Publications:** Lee Miller in Sussex: A Gardner Centre Gallery Touring Exhibition, 1984; The Lives of Lee Miller, 1985; (ed.) Lee Miller's War: Photographer and Correspondent With the Allies in Europe, 1944-45, 1992; Legendary Lee Miller, 1998; Roland Penrose: The Friendly Surrealist: A Memoir, 2001; Home of the Surrealists: Lee Miller, Roland Penrose and Their Circle at Farley Farm, 2001; Ecrits d'une femmesurréaliste, 2001; Roland Penrose: The Friendly Surrealist, 2001; Boy Who Bit Picasso, 2010. **Address:** Farley's Yard Trust, Farley Farm, Chiddingly, ES BN8 6HW, England. **Online address:** ami@farleysyard.org.uk

PENROSE, Roger. British/American (born United States), b. 1931. **Genres:** Mathematics/Statistics, Physics, Science Fiction/Fantasy, Sciences, Reference. **Career:** National Research Development Corp., mathematician, 1956-, consultant, 1956-57; Bedford College, assistant lecturer in pure mathematics, 1956-57; St. John's College, research fellow, 1957-60; Princeton University, (NATO) research fellow, 1959-61; Syracuse University, (NATO) research fellow, 1959-61; Cornell University, (NATO) research fellow, 1959-61; King's College, research associate, 1961-63; University of Texas, visiting associate professor, 1963-64; Birkbeck College, reader, 1964-66, professor of applied mathematics, 1966-73; Battelle Institute, lecturer, 1966-67, 1969; University of Oxford, Rouse Ball professor of mathematics, 1973, now Rouse Ball professor emeritus of mathematics; Rice University, Edgar Odell Lovett professor of mathematics, 1982-87; Syracuse University, visiting distinguished professor of physics and mathematics, 1987; London Mathematical Society and New Zealand Mathematical Society, Forder Lecturer, 1992-93; Yeshiva University, visiting professor; Cornell University, visiting professor. Writer. **Publications:** This is Oxford and Cambridge, 1962; An Analysis of the Structure of Space-Time, 1970; Techniques of Differential Topology in Relativity, 1972; (ed. with C.J. Isham and D.W. Sciama) Quantum Gravity: An Oxford Symposium, 1975; (with W. Rindler) Spinors and Space-Time, vol. I: Two-Spinor Calculus and Relativistic Fields, 1975, vol. II: Spinor and Twistor Methods in Space-Time Geometry, 1981; (ed. with C.J. Isham and D.W. Sciama) Quantum Gravity 2: An Oxford Symposium, 1981; (ed. with C.J. Isham) Quantum Concepts in Space and Time, 1986; (co-ed.) M.C. Escher, Art and Science, 1986; Hermann Weyl, 1885-1985: Centenary Lectures, 1986; The Emperor's New Mind: Concerning Computers, Minds and the Laws of Physics, 1989; Shadows of the Mind: A Search for the Missing Science of Consciousness, 1994; (with S.W. Hawking) Nature of Space and Time, 1996; (coauthor) The Large, the Small and the Human Mind, 1997, rev. ed., 1999; (with B.W. Aldiss) White Mars: Or, The Mind Set Free, a 21st-Century Utopia, 2000; The Road to Reality: A Complete Guide to the Laws of the Universe, 2004; Science, Sporutuality and the Nature of Reality: A Discussion between Roger Penrose and T.D. Singh, 2005; Cycles of Time: An Extraordinary New View of the Universe, 2010; Roger Penrose: Collected Works, 2010. Contributor to journals, books and periodicals. **Address:** Mathematical Institute, Oxford University, 24-29 St. Giles, Oxford, OX OX1 3LB, England. **Online address:** rouse@maths.ox.ac.uk

PENSKY, Max. American (born United States), b. 1961. **Genres:** Philosophy, Social Sciences, Sociology. **Career:** Boston College, Department of Philosophy, teaching fellow, 1984-88; State University of New York, Binghamton University, assistant professor of philosophy, 1990-96, associate professor, 1996-2005, professor of philosophy, 2005-, department chair; Oxford University, Balliol College, Oliver Smithies lecturer and fellow, 2006-07, Centre for the Study of Social Justice, senior research fellow, 2006-07. Writer. **Publications:** Melancholy Dialectics: Walter Benjamin and the Play of Mourning, 1993; (trans. and ed.) The Past as Future, 1994; (ed. and intro.) Actuality of Adorno: Critical Essays on Adorno and the Postmodern, 1997; (ed. and intro.) Postnational Constellation: Political Essays, 2001; (ed.) Globalizing Critical Theory, 2005; (with D. Levy and J. Torpey) Old Europe, New Europe, Core Europe: Transatlantic Relations After the Iraq War, 2005; (ed. and trans. with C. Cronin) J. Habermas, Time of Transitions, 2006; Ends of Solidarity: Discourse Theory in Ethics and Politics, 2008. **Address:** Department of Philosophy, Binghamton University, LT 1208, 4400 Vestal Pkwy. E, PO Box 6000, Binghamton, NY 13902-6000, U.S.A. **Online address:** mpensky@binghamton.edu

PENSLAR, Derek J(onathan). Canadian/American (born United States), b. 1958. **Genres:** History, Politics/Government, Theology/Religion. **Career:** Indiana University, assistant professor, associate professor of history and Jewish studies, 1987-98, associate director of Jewish studies, 1991-98; University of Toronto, Samuel Zacks professor of Jewish history, 1998-, Centre for Jewish Studies, director, 2002-08; Harvard University, visiting professor of Israel studies, 2006; Columbia University, visiting professor of Israel studies, 2009; Oxford University, Stanley Lewis professor of Israel studies, 2012-. Writer. **Publications:** Indiana Jewish history, 1988; Anti-Semitism: The Jewish Response, 1989; Zionism and Technocracy: The Engineering of Jewish Settlement in Palestine, 1870-1918, 1991; Mumhim be-sherut ha-hityashvut ha-Tsiyonit, 1994; (ed. with M. Brenner) In Search of Jewish Community: Jewish Identities in Germany and Austria, 1918-1933, 1998; Shylocks Children: Economics and Jewish Identity in Modern Europe, 2001; Tikhnun ha-ọtopyah ha-Tsiyonit: Itsuv ha-hityashvut ha-Yehuditbe-Erets-Yiśrael, 1870-1918, 2001; (with A. Shapira) Israeli Historical Revisionism: From Left to Right, 2003; (with I.D. Kalmar) Orientalism and the Jews, 2005; (with M. Marrus and J.G. Stein) Contemporary Antisemitism: Canada and the World, 2005; Israel in History: The Jewish State in Comparative Perspective, 2007; (with E. Kaplan) The Origins of Israel 1882-1948: A Documentary History, 2011. **Address:** Department of History, University of Toronto, SS 2064, Rm. 2074, 100 St. George St., Toronto, ON M5S 3G3, Canada. **Online address:** derek.penslar@utoronto.ca

PENTCHEVA, Bissera V. American (born United States) **Genres:** Theology/Religion, History, Art/Art History. **Career:** Columbia University, postdoctoral fellow; Stanford University, assistant professor of art history, 2003-, associate professor of art history. Writer and art historian. **Publications:** Icons and Power: The Mother of God in Byzantium, 2006; Sensual Icon: Space, Ritual, and the Senses in Byzantium, 2010. **Address:** Department of Art & Art History, Nathan Cummings Art Bldg, Stanford University, Stanford, CA 94305, U.S.A. **Online address:** bissera@stanford.edu

PENYCATE, John (Vincent George). British (born England), b. 1943. **Genres:** Documentaries/Reportage, Psychology, History. **Career:** British Broadcasting Corp., correspondent, producer; ITV, researcher. **Publications:** (With T. Clark) Psychopath: The Case of Patrick Mackay, 1976; (with T. Mangold) The Tunnels of Cu Chi, 1985; (with T. Mangold) Tunnel Warfare, 1987; (with T. Mangold) Ham Cu Chi: câu chuyên khó tin vecuôc chien tranh o Viêt Nam, 1988. **Address:** British Broadcasting Corp., 201 Wood Ln., London, GL W12 7TQ, England.

PEPPÉ, Rodney (Darrell). British (born England), b. 1934. **Genres:** Children's Fiction, Crafts, Picture/Board Books, Graphic Novels, Children's Nonfiction, Illustrations, Young Adult Fiction. **Career:** S.H. Benson and J. Walter Thompson, art director, 1960-65; Ross Foods Ltd., consultant designer, 1965-73; freelance graphic designer and illustrator, 1965-. Writer. **Publications:** The Alphabet Book, 1968; Circus Numbers, 1969; The House That Jack Built, 1970; Hey Riddle Diddle!, 1971; Little Painter, 1971; Simple Simon, 1972; [illegible], 1973; Odd One Out, 1974; Humpty Dumpty, 1975; Henry's Exercises, 1975; Henry's Garden, 1975; [illegible]; Henry's Sunbathe, 1975; Picture Stories, 1976; Puzzle Book, 1977; Ten Little Bad Boys, 1978; Henry Gets Out, 1978; Henry's Toy Cupboard, 1978; Henry's Aeroplane, 1978; Humphrey the Number Horse: Fun with Counting and Multiplication, 1979; Three Little Pigs, 1979; Indoors, 1980; Outdoors, 1980; Rodney Peppe's Moving Toys, 1980; The Mice Who Lived in a Shoe, 1981; Run Rabbit, Run!, 1982; The Kettleship Pirates, 1983; Little Dolls, 1983; Little Toy Board Books (series, 5 vols.), 1983; Make Your Own Paper Toys, 1984; Hello Henry, 1984; Hurrah for Henry, 1984; Block Books series, vol. IV, 1985; The Mice and the Flying Basket, 1985; Press Out Circus, 1986; Press Out Train, 1986; Tell the Time with Mortimer, 1986; The Mice and the Clockwork Bus, 1986; Open House, 1987; Thumbprint Circus, 1988; First Nursery Rhymes, 1988; Rodney Peppe's Noah's Ark Frieze, 1989; Here Comes Huxley Pig, 1989; Huxley Pig the Clown, 1989; Huxley Pig at the Circus, 1989; Here Comes Huxley Pig in the Haunted House, 1989; Huxley Pig's Aeroplane, 1989; Rodney Peppe's ABC Frieze, 1990; Huxley Pig's Model Car, 1990; Huxley Pig at the Beach, 1990; Huxley Pig at the Restaurant, 1990; Animal Directory: A First Counting Book, 1990; Summer Days, 1991; The ABC Index, 1991; Winter Days, 1991; Huxley Pig's Dressing-Up Book, 1990; The Shapes Finder, 1991; The Mice on the Moon, 1993; The Colour Catalogue, 1992; The Mice and the Travel Machine, 1993; Farm Animals Rockers, 1995; Wild Animal Rockers, 1995; Gus and Nipper, 1996; The Magic Toy Box, 1996; Hippo Plays Hide-and-Seek, 1998; Angelmouse series, vol. VI, 1999; Automata and Mechanical Toys, 2002; Toys and Models, 2003. **Address:** Stoneleigh House, 6 Stoneleigh Dr., Livermead, Torquay, DN TQ2 6TR, England.

PEPPER, Andrew. Irish (born Ireland) **Genres:** Novels, Mystery/Crime/Suspense. **Career:** Queen's University, professor. Writer. **Publications:** The Contemporary American Crime Novel: Race, Ethnicity, Gender, Class, 2000; American History and Contemporary Hollywood Film, 2005. PYKE MYSTERY SERIES: The Last Days of Newgate, 2007; The Revenge of Captain Paine, 2008; Kill-Devil and Water, 2008; The Detective Branch, 2008. **Address:** Belfast, AT , Northern Ireland. **Online address:** a.pepper@qub.ac.uk

PERABO, Susan. American (born United States), b. 1969?. **Genres:** Young Adult Fiction, Novels, Mystery/Crime/Suspense. **Career:** Dickinson College, writer-in-residence and associate professor of English, 1996-, chair. Writer. **Publications:** Writers in the Schools: A Guide to Teaching Creative Writing in the Classroom, 1998; Who I Was Supposed to Be, 1999; The Broken Places (novel), 2001. Works appear in anthologies. Contributor to periodicals. **Address:** Department of English, Dickinson College, Rm. 307, East College, 28 N College St., PO Box 1773, Carlisle, PA 17013, U.S.A. **Online address:** perabo@dickinson.edu

PERANI, Judith. American (born United States) **Genres:** Area Studies, History, Art/Art History. **Career:** Ohio University, School of Art, professor of art history and interim director, African Studies Program, faculty. Writer. **Publications:** (With C. Kinzelman) Sacred and Secular Art of West Africa, 1976; (with L. Aronson) Nigerian Textiles, Evolution of Surface Design, 1979; (with E.B. Chokr) Art of the Congo River Basin, 1983; (with M. Hunt-Nishi) Ritual Art of the Sepik River, 1984; (with M. Hunt-Nishi) Art of the Sepik River and the Papuan Gulf, 1987; (with F.T. Smith) The Visual Arts of Africa: Gender, Power, and Life Cycle Rituals, 1998; (with N.H. Wolff) Cloth, Dress, and Art Patronage in Africa, 1999. **Address:** Department of History, Ohio University, Bentley Annex, 4th Fl., Athens, OH 45701-2979, U.S.A. **Online address:** perani@ouvaxa.cats.ohiou.edu

PERCHARD, Tom. British (born England), b. 1976?. **Genres:** Biography. **Career:** University of Westminster, visiting lecturer, 2004-06, senior lecturer in music sociology, 2006-, programme director; University of London, Goldsmiths College, visiting lecturer, 2004-06, Department of Music, lecturer, 2008-, departmental senior tutor, senior lecturer; Equinox Publishing Ltd., editor. **Publications:** Lee Morgan: His Life, Music and Culture, 2006. Contributor to periodicals. **Address:** Department of Music, Goldsmiths College, University of London, Lewisham Way, New Cross, London, GL SE14 6NW, England. **Online address:** postmaster@tomperchard.com

PERCY, Benjamin. American (born United States), b. 1979. **Genres:** Young Adult Fiction. **Career:** Marquette University, visiting assistant professor; University of Wisconsin, assistant professor; Iowa State University, assistant professor of English and creative writing, 2008-. Writer. **Publications:** The Language of Elk (short fiction), 2006; Refresh, Refresh: Stories (short fiction), 2007; The Wilding (novel), 2010; Red Moon (novel), 2013. Contributor of articles to books and periodicals. **Address:** c/o Katherine Fausset, Curtis Brown Ltd., 10 Astor Pl., New York, NY 10003, U.S.A. **Online address:** benjaminpercy@aol.com

PERCY, John R(ees). Canadian (born Canada), b. 1941?. **Genres:** Astronomy, Education. **Career:** University of Toronto, Erindale College, assistant professor, 1968-73, associate professor, 1973-78, professor of astronomy, 1978-2008, associate dean for sciences and vice principal for research and graduate studies, 1989-94, professor of education, 2000-08; professor emeritus, astronomy and science education, 2008-; Ontario Science Centre, chair and board trustee; International Astronomical Union (IAU), Commission on the Teaching of Astronomy, vice president, 1991-94, president; Science Teachers' Association, honorary president, vice-chair, 1992-98; Royal Astronomical Society, president; American Association of Variable Star Observers, president; Astronomical Society of the Pacific, president. Writer. **Publications:** (Co-author) Science 10: An Introductory Study, 1988; Understanding Variable Stars, 2007. EDITOR: The Study of Variable Stars Using Small Telescopes, 1986; (with J.M. Pasachoff) The Teaching of Astronomy, 1990; (with J. Mattei and C. Sterken) Variable Star Research: An International Perspective, 1992; Astronomy Education: Current Developments, Future Coordination, 1996; (with L. Gouguenheim and D. McNally) New Trends in Astronomy Teaching, 1998; (with J.B. Wilson) Amateur-Professional Partnerships in Astronomy, 2000; (with J.M. Pasachoff) Teaching and Learning Astronomy, 2005; (with S. Abbas) Celebrating 40 Years of History at the University of Toronto Mississauga, 2007; Understanding Variable Stars, 2007. **Address:** Department of Astronomy & Astrophysics, University of Toronto, 50 St. George St., Toronto, ON M5S 3H4, Canada. **Online address:** john.percy@utoronto.ca

PERDRIZET, Marie-Pierre. French (born France), b. 1952. **Genres:** Young Adult Non-fiction, Novels, Translations, Children's Non-fiction. **Career:** Lycee Francais de San Salvador, elementary school teacher, 1974-75. Writer. **Publications:** JUVENILE: Les Hommes de la prehistoire, 1982, trans. as Ask about Prehistoric Life, 1987; Les Batisseurs de cathedrales, 1990, trans. as The Cathedral Builders, 1992. OTHER: (with C. Cohen and L. Pelpel) La formation architecturale au dix-huitième siecle en France: Rapport de recherche, 1977; (co-author) A la Decouverte de l'histoire, 1982; (co-author) A la Decouverte de la terre, 1983; Marie Curie, 1983; Le Moyen Age au temps des chevaliers et des chateaux forts, 1985; Les hommes d'autrefois, 1987; Les chateaux forts, 1987; (co-author) 1000 Reponses, 1988; Le temps des Celtes, des Romains, des Germains, 1989; (co-author) Memo Junior, 1990; (co-author) Memo Benjamin, 1991; Le petit citoyen, 1994. **Address:** 106 rue de la Fraternite, Bagnolet, 93170, France.

PERDUE, Peter C. American (born United States), b. 1949. **Genres:** Intellectual History, Business/Trade/Industry. **Career:** Massachusetts Institute of Technology, Department of History, instructor, 1980-81, assistant professor, 1982-87, associate professor, 1987-94, faculty head, 1990-99, professor of history, 1994-2008, professor emeritus, 2008-, T.T. and Wei Fong Chao professor of Asian civilizations, 2000-08, acting head of history faculty, 2002-03, advisor on Asian studies, 1985-, Yale University, Department of History, professor of history, 2008-. Writer and historian. **Publications:** Exhausting the Earth: State and Peasant in Hunan, 1500-1850, 1987; China Marches West: The Qing Conquest of Central Eurasia, 2005; (ed. with A.L. Stoler and C. McGranahan) Imperial Formations, 2007; (ed. with H. Islamoğlu) Shared Histories of Modernity, 2009. CONTRIBUTOR: Chinese History in Economic Perspective, 1992; Does Technology Drive History? The Dilemma of Technological Determinism, 1994; Warfare in Chinese History, 2000; Land, Property, and the Environment, 2002; Warfare in Inner Asian History, 2002; The Oxford Encyclopedia of Economic History, 2003; Constituting Modernity: Private Property in the East and West, 2004; Untaming the Frontier in Anthropology, Archaeology, and History, 2005. Contributor to periodicals. **Address:** Department of History, Yale University, 2682 Hall of Graduate Studies, 320 York St., PO Box 208324, New Haven, CT 06511, U.S.A. **Online address:** peter.c.perdue@yale.edu

PERDUE, Tito. American/Chilean (born Chile), b. 1938?. **Genres:** Novels. **Career:** Iowa State University, social sciences bibliographer, 1970-80, University Library, faculty, 1968-70; State University of New York, assistant director, 1980-82; Emory University Library, associate director, 1982-83. Novelist, 1983-. **Publications:** Lee: A Novel, 1991; The New Austerities, 1994; Opportunities in Alabama Agriculture: A Novel, 1994; The Sweet-Scented Manuscript, 2004; Fields of Asphodel, 2007. **Address:** Brent, AL , U.S.A. **Online address:** leepefley@aol.com

PERELMAN, Bob. American (born United States), b. 1947. **Genres:** Poetry, Literary Criticism And History, Language/Linguistics. **Career:** University of Pennsylvania, assistant professor 1990-95, associate professor, 1995-99, professor, 1999-, associate chair. Writer. **Publications:** Braille, 1975; Seven Works, 1978; a.k.a., 1979; Primer, 1981; To the Reader, 1984; (ed.) Writing/Talks, 1985; The First World, 1986; Face Value, 1988; Captive Audience, 1988; Virtual Reality, 1993; The Trouble with Genius: Reading Pound, Joyce, Stein, and Zukofsky, 1994; The Marginalization of Poetry: Language Writing and Literary History, 1996; The Future of Memory, 1998; Ten to One: Selected Poems, 1999; (with F. Shaw) Playing Bodies, 2004; Iflife, 2006. **Address:** Department of English, University of Pennsylvania, Rm. 317, Fisher-Bennett Hall, 3340 Walnut St., Philadelphia, PA 19104-6273, U.S.A. **Online address:** perelman@english.upenn.edu

PERETTI, Burton W(illiam). American (born United States), b. 1961. **Genres:** History, Music. **Career:** University of Kansas, visiting assistant professor of history, 1989-92; Colorado College, visiting assistant professor of history, 1993-94; University of California, visiting lecturer, 1992-93, 1994; Middle Tennessee State University, assistant professor, 1994-95; Pellissippi State Technical Community College, professor, 1995-; Western Connecticut State University, History Department, professor. Writer. **Publications:** The Creation of Jazz: Music, Race, and Culture in Urban America, 1992; Jazz in American Culture, 1997; Nightclub City: Politics and Amusement in Manhattan, 2007; Lift Every Voice: The History of African-American Music, 2008; The Leading Man: The Presidential Image and Hollywood, forthcoming. Contributor to periodicals. **Address:** Department of History, Western Connecticut State University, Warner Hall 221, 181 White St., Danbury, CT 06810, U.S.A. **Online address:** perettib@wcsu.edu

PERETTI, Frank E. American/Canadian (born Canada), b. 1951. **Genres:** Novels, Children's Fiction, Picture/Board Books, Young Adult Non-fiction. **Career:** Community Church, associate pastor, 1978-84; K-2 Ski Factory, production worker, 1985-88; Ordained minister; writer and public speaker, 1986- . **Publications:** COOPER KIDS ADVENTURES SERIES: The Door in the Dragon's Throat, 1985; Escape from the Island of Aquarius, 1986; The Tombs of Anak, 1987; Trapped at the Bottom of the Sea, 1988; The Secret of the Desert Stone, 1996; The Deadly Curse of Toco-Rey, 1996; The Legend of Annie Murphy, 1996; Flying Blind, 1998; Mayday at Two Thousand Five Hundred Feet, 1998. THE VERITAS PROJECT: Hangman's Curse, 2001; Nightmare Academy, 2002. OTHERS: This Present Darkness, 1986; Tilly, 1988; Piercing the Darkness, 1989; All is Well, 1991; Prophet, 1992; The Oath, 1995; The Visitation, 1999; The Wounded Spirit, 2000; No More Victims, 2001; No More Bullies: For Those Who Wound or Are Wounded, 2003; Monster, 2005; (with T. Dekker) House, 2006; Out of the Darkness, forthcoming. **Address:** c/o Author Mail, Blanton Harrell Cooke & Corzine, 5250 Virginia Way, Ste. 110, Brentwood, TN 37027, U.S.A.

PEREZ, George. American (born United States), b. 1954. **Genres:** Cartoons, Graphic Novels. **Career:** CrossGen Entertainment Inc., senior artist. Writer and graphic artist. **Publications:** COLLECTIONS: (co-author) The Project Pegasus Saga Starring the Thing, 1988; (with Peter David) The Incredible Hulk: Future Imperfect, 1994; Superman: Whatever Happened to the Man of Tomorrow?, 1997; (with M. Wolfman) New Teen Titans Archives, 1999; (co-author) History of the DC Universe, 2002; (with L. Wein and G. Potter) Wonder Woman, 2004; The New Teen Titans: Who is Donna Troy?, 2005; (with P. David) Sachs & Violens, 2006; George Perez on His Work and Career, 2008; (co-author) The Brave and the Bold, 2008; (with G. Conway) Justice League of America, vol. I, 2009. **Address:** CrossGen Entertainment Inc., 4023 Tampa Rd., Ste. 2400, Oldsmar, FL 34677-0105, U.S.A.

PEREZ, Gilberto (Guillermo). American/Cuban (born Cuba), b. 1943. **Genres:** Film. **Career:** Princeton University, lecturer in film history and theory, 1972-80; Cornell University, visiting lecturer in cinema studies, 1980-81; William Paterson College, professor, 1981-82; Harvard University, professor, 1982-83; Sarah Lawrence College, professor of film history, 1983-, Department of Film History, head, Noble Foundation chair in art and cultural history. Writer. **Publications:** The Material Ghost: Films and Their Medium, 1998. Contributor to periodicals. **Address:** Department of Film History, Sarah Lawrence College, 1 Mead Way, Bronxville, NY 10708, U.S.A.

PEREZ, Lana. *See* **PEREZ, Marlene.**

PEREZ, Marlene. (Lana Perez). American (born United States) **Genres:** Novels. **Career:** Writer. **Publications:** Unexpected Development, 2004; Love in the Corner Pocket, 2008; Dead is the New Black, 2008; Dead is So

Last Year, 2009; Dead is a State of Mind, 2009; Comeback, 2009; Dead is Just a Rumor, 2010; Dead is Not an Option, 2011. AS LANA PEREZ: Bright Lights for Bella, 2005; Figure in the Frost, 2005; Bella Goes Hollywood, 2006. **Address:** c/o Author Mail, Roaring Brook Press, 2 Old New Milford Rd., Brookfield, CT 06804, U.S.A. **Online address:** marlene@marleneperez.com

PEREZ, Rolando. American/Cuban (born Cuba), b. 1957. **Genres:** Novels, Plays/Screenplays, Poetry, Art/Art History, Literary Criticism And History, Philosophy. **Career:** Chelsea Vocational High School, librarian, 1990-94; Hunter College of the City University of New York, Wexler Library, reference librarian, 1994-, Department of Africana and Puerto Rican/Latino Studies, professor, 2009-, Department of Romance Languages, associate professor. Writer. **Publications:** Understanding the Psychology and Morality of the Overman, 1983; Severo Sarduy and the Religion of the Text, 1988; On An(archy) & Schizoanalysis, 1990; Janus Dies?: A One Act Play, 1990; The Odyssey, 1990; Plays & Playthings: Nine One Acts, 1991; The House That Ate Their Brains (play), 1992; H Is for Box: A Play, 1993; The Lining of Our Souls, 1995, rev. ed. as The Lining of Our Souls: Excursions into Selected Paintings of Edward Hopper, 2002; (comp. with T. Cordero and I. Dobles) Dominación social y subjetividad: contribuciones de la psicología social, 1996; The Divine Duty of Servants: A Book of Worship Based on the Artwork of Bruno Schulz, 1999; The Electric Comedy (poetry), 2000; Plays & Playthings: 8 One-acts of Eros and Death, 2003; Severo Sarduy and the Neo-Baroque Image of Thought in the Visual Arts, 2011. Contributor to books. **Address:** Hunter College of the City University of New York, Wexler Library, Rm. 412, 695 Park Ave., New York, NY 10065, U.S.A. **Online address:** rperez@hunter.cuny.edu

PEREZ, Sofia A(na). Iranian (born Iran), b. 1963?. **Genres:** Economics, Politics/Government. **Career:** Woodrow Wilson Institute for International Scholars, research intern, 1984-85; George Washington University, Department Political Science, teaching fellow, 1985-90; Centro de Estudios Avanzados en Ciencias Sociales, visiting researcher, 1991-92; Wissenschaftszentrum-Berlin fuer Sozialforschung, Labor Market and Employment Division, researcher, 1993; Boston University, assistant professor of political science, 1994-2000, associate professor of political science, 2000-; Harvard University, Minda de Gunzburg Center for European Studies, affiliate. Writer. **Publications:** (Coauthor) Capital Ungoverned: Liberalizing Finance in Interventionist States, 1997; Banking on Privilege: The Politics of Spanish Financial Reform, 1997; The Left and Immigration in Europe, forthcoming. Contributor to books and periodicals. **Address:** Department of Political Science, Boston University, Rm. PLS 301, 232 Bay State Rd., Boston, MA 02215, U.S.A. **Online address:** sperez@bu.edu

PÉREZ-ORAMAS, Luis. (Luis Enrique Pérez-Oramas). American/Venezuelan (born Venezuela), b. 1960?. **Genres:** Poetry, Adult Non-fiction, Art/Art History. **Career:** Patricia Phelps de Cisneros Collection, curator, 1995-2003; Museum of Modern Art, Department of Drawings, adjunct curator, 2003-06, Estrellita Brodsky curator of Latin American art, 2006-. Poet. **Publications:** Poemas, 1978; Salmos y Boleros de la casa, 1986; Armando Reveron, de los Prodigios de la luz a los Trabajos del arte, 1990; La Decada Impensable y otros Escritos Fechados, 1996; (with A. Jimenez) La Invención de la Continuidad: Galeria Arte Nacional, Mayo-Agosto de 1997, 1997; Mirar Furtivo, 1997; La Cocina de Jurassic Park y otros Ensayos Visuales, 1998; Gacelas y otros poemas, 1999; Carlos Raúl Villanueva: Un Moderno en Sudamérica, 2000; Arte Contemporaneo Venezolano en la Coleccion Cisneros, 1990-2004, 2004; La Construccion de un Personage, Imagenes de Armando Reveron, 2004; Gego: Anudamientos, 2004; La Resistencia de las Sombras: Alejandro Otero y Gego: The shadows Resistance: Alejandro Otero and Gego, 2005; An Atlas of Drawings: Transforming Chronologies, 2006; (with J. Elderfield) Armando Reveron, 2007; León Ferrari and Mira Schendel: Tangled Alphabets, 2009. **Address:** Department of Drawings, Museum of Modern Art, 11 W 53rd St., New York, NY 10019-5497, U.S.A.

PÉREZ-ORAMAS, Luis Enrique. *See* **PÉREZ-ORAMAS, Luis.**

PEREZ-ROMERO, Antonio. American/Spanish (born Spain), b. 1949. **Genres:** Young Adult Non-fiction. **Career:** John Carroll University, associate professor of Spanish. Writer. **Publications:** NONFICTION: Subversion and Liberation in the Writings of St. Teresa of Avila, 1996; The Subversive Tradition in Spanish Renaissance Writing, 2005. Contributor of articles to journals. **Address:** John Carroll University, 126 O'Malley Center, University Heights, OH 44118, U.S.A. **Online address:** aperezromero@jcu.edu

PEREZ-STABLE, Marifeli. Cuban (born Cuba), b. 1949?. **Genres:** History, Anthropology/Ethnology, Sociology. **Career:** State University of New York, Politics, Economy and Society Program, instructor, 1976-85, convener, 1985-86, assistant professor, 1985-88, associate professor, 1988-, professor, 1996-2001, PES program, chair, 1985-86, 1996-97; Policy Alternatives for the Caribbean and Central America (PACCA), associate, 1987; New School for Social Research, Center for Studies of Social Change, adjunct professor, 1990, National Science Foundation, visiting professor, 1991-92; New York University, visiting professor, 1993; Florida International University, Department of Sociology and Anthropology, visiting professor, 2000-01, professor of sociology, 2001-, Caribbean Center and Cuban Research Institute, project director, 2002-04; Inter-American Dialogue, vice president for democratic governance, 2004-09, senior non-resident fellow, 2009. Writer. **Publications:** The Cuban Revolution: Origins, Course and Legacy, 1993, 2nd ed., 1999; (ed.) Rough Riders, 2003; (ed.) Looking Forward: Comparative Perspectives on Cuba's Transition, 2007; United States and Cuba: Intimate Enemies, 2011. **Address:** Department of Global & Sociocultural Studies, Florida International University, Modesto A. Maidique Campus, DM 334, Miami, FL 33199, U.S.A.

PERFETTI, Charles A. American (born United States), b. 1940. **Genres:** Education, Psychology, Language/Linguistics. **Career:** University of Michigan, Department of Psychology, lecturer, 1967; University of Pittsburgh, assistant professor to professor of psychology, 1967-83, Learning Research and Development Center, research scientist, senior scientist, 1967-, associate director, 2000-08, director, 2008-, Program in Learning, Development & Cognition, chair, 1983-92, Graduate Program in Cognitive Psychology, chair, 1983-92, professor of psychology and linguistics, 1984-, Department of Psychology, chair, 1992-98, Department of Linguistics, interim chair, 1999, distinguished university professor of psychology, 2001-; Netherlands Institute for Advanced Studies, fellow, 1988; University of Auckland, honorary visiting professor, 1996; University of Sussex, Leverhulme visiting research fellow, 2003; Pittsburgh Science of Learning Center, chief scientist, 2007-08; co-director, 2008-; University of Texas at Austin, lecturer; City University of New York, lecturer; University of Bielefeld, lecturer. Writer. **Publications:** (Ed. with A.M. Lesgold and contrib.) Interactive Processes in Reading, 1981; Reading Ability, 1985; (ed. with L. Rieben and contrib.) L'Apprentilecteur: Recherches empiriques et implications pedagogiques, 1989, trans. as Learning to Read: Basic Research and Its Implications, 1991; (with M.A. Britt and M.C. Georgi) Text-based Learning and Reasoning: Studies in History, 1995; (ed. with L. Rieben and M. Fayol) Learning to Spell: Research, Theory, and Practice across Languages, 1997; (ed. with F. Schmalhofer) Higher Level Language Processes in the Brain: Inference and Comprehension Processes, 2007. Works appear in anthologies. **Address:** Learning Research and Development Center, University of Pittsburgh, 3939 O'Hara St., Pittsburgh, PA 15260, U.S.A. **Online address:** perfetti@pitt.edu

PERIN, Roberto. Canadian (born Canada), b. 1948. **Genres:** International Relations/Current Affairs, History, Politics/Government. **Career:** Simon Fraser University, Department of History, visiting lecturer, 1973; University of Edinburgh, lecturer, 1975-77; York University, Atkinson College, Department of History, assistant professor, 1977-81, associate professor, 1981-2004, professor of history, 2004-, Glendon College, Department of History, professor of history, 2004-; University of Toronto, Canadian Studies Programme, visiting professor, 1981; Canadian Academic Centre in Italy, director, 1983-85; School of Public and International Affairs, graduate programme director, 2008. Writer. **Publications:** Rome in Canada: The Vatican and Canadian Affairs in the Late Victorian Age, 1990 in France as Rome et le Canada: la bureaucratie vaticane et laquestion nationale 1870-1903, 1993; Ignace de Montréal, artisan d'une identité nationale, 2008. EDITOR: (with F. Sturino) Arrangiarsi: The Italian Immigration Experience in Canada, 1989; (with D. Drache) Negotiating with a Sovereign Québec, 1992; (with T. Murphy) A Concise History of Christianity in Canada, 1996; (with F. Iacovetta and A. Principe) Enemies Within: Italian and Other Internees in Canada and Abroad, 2000. **Address:** Department of History, Glendon College, York University, 236 York Hall, 2275 Bayview Ave., Toronto, ON M4N 3M6, Canada. **Online address:** rperin@yorku.ca

PERKEL, Colin N. Afghani/Canadian (born Canada), b. 1956. **Genres:** Documentaries/Reportage. **Career:** Freelance writer, 1983-; London Free

Press, reporter, 1984-86; Canadian Broadcasting Corp., reporter and editor for national radio and television news programs, 1986-88; Canadian Press, reporter and editor, 1988-, senior correspondent; Ontario Legislature, political correspondent; Canadian Media Guild, CP/BN National Branch, president. **Publications:** Well of Lies: The Walkerton Water Tragedy, 2002. Contributor to magazines and newspapers. **Address:** c/o Author Mail, McClelland & Stewart Ltd., 75 Sherbourne St., 5th Fl., Toronto, ON M5A 2P9, Canada. **Online address:** perkx@sympatico.ca

PERKINS, Diane. *See* **GASTON, Diane.**

PERKINS, D. M. *See* **PERKINS, Michael.**

PERKINS, Dwight Heald. American (born United States), b. 1934. **Genres:** Economics, History, International Relations/Current Affairs. **Career:** Harvard University, instructor, associate professor, 1963-69, professor of economics, 1969-81, East Asian Research Center, associate director, 1973-77, Department of Economics, chairman, 1977-80, Harvard Institute for International Development, director, 1980-95, H.H. Burbank professor of political economy, 1981-2006, H.H. Burbank research professor of political economy, 2006-, Asia Center, director, 2002-05; Hitotsubashi University, Institute of Economic Research, research associate, 1968-69; China Development Research Foundation, distinguished fellow, 2008-09. Writer. **Publications:** (With M.H. Halperin) Communist China and Arms Control, 1965; Market Control and Planning in Communist China, 1966; Agricultural Development in China 1368-1968, 1969; China's Modern Economy in Historical Perspective, 1975; (co-author) Rural Small-Scale Industry in the People's Republic of China, 1977; (co-author) Rural Development in Korea, 1980; (co-author) Economic and Social Modernization in Korea, 1980; (co-author) Economics of Development, 1983, 5th ed., 2001; (with S. Yusuf) Rural Development in China, 1984; China: Asia's Next Economic Giant?, 1986; (with M. Roemer) Reforming Economic Systems in Developing Countries, 1990; (co-author) Industrialization and the State: The Korean Heavy and Chemical Industry Drive, 1995; (co-author) Assisting Development in a Changing World, 1997; (co-author) Industrialization and the State, 2001; (co-author) Under New Ownership: Privatizing China's State Owned Enterprises, 2006. **Address:** Department of Economics, Harvard University, Littauer M-14, Cambridge, MA 02138, U.S.A. **Online address:** dwight_perkins@harvard.edu

PERKINS, Emily. New Zealander (born New Zealand), b. 1970?. **Genres:** Novellas/Short Stories, Novels. **Career:** University of Auckland, creative writing tutor, faculty in the School of Languages, 2007; AUT University, lecturer. Writer. **Publications:** Not Her Real Name and Other Stories, 1996; Leave Before You Go, 1998; (ed.) The Picnic Virgin: New Writers, 1999; The New Girl, 2001; Novel About My Wife: A Novel, 2008. **Address:** c/o Anchor Books, Doubleday, 1540 Broadway, New York, NY 10036, U.S.A.

PERKINS, George (Burton). American (born United States), b. 1930. **Genres:** Novels, Literary Criticism And History, Travel/Exploration, Humor/Satire, Young Adult Fiction. **Career:** Cornell University, teaching assistant, 1955-57; Washington University, instructor, 1957-60; Baldwin-Wallace College, assistant professor, 1960-63; Fairleigh Dickinson University, assistant professor, 1963-66; University of Edinburgh, lecturer in American literature, 1966-67, Institute for Advanced Studies in the Humanities, fellow, 1981; Eastern Michigan University, associate professor, 1967-70, director of graduate studies in English, 1969-73, professor of English, 1970-2001, professor emeritus of American literature, 2001-; University of Newcastle, senior Fulbright fellow, 1989; Collegium for Advanced Studies, director, 1995-97; Duke University, fellow; Cornell University, fellow; The Journal of Narrative Technique, founding editor, associate editor, 1993. **Publications:** Writing Clear Prose, 1964; Varieties of Prose, 1966; (contrib.) Contemporary Novelists, 1972; Realistic American Short Fiction, 1972; (comp.) American Poetic Theory, 1972; (with N. Frye and Baker) The Practical Imagination: An Introduction to Poetry, 1983; (with B. Perkins and F. McHugh) Diagnostic and Achievement Tests, 1984; (with N. Frye and Baker) The Harper Handbook to Literature, 1985, (with N. Frye, Baker and Perkins) 2nd ed., 1997; A Season in New South Wales, 1989; (with B. Perkins and R. Warhol) Women's Work: An Anthology of American Literature, 1994. EDITOR: (and intro.) The Theory of the American Novel, 1970; (with B. Perkins) The American Tradition in Literature, 4th ed., 1974, 12th ed., 2009; (with N. Frye and S. Baker) The Practical Imagination, 1980, rev. ed., 1987; (with B. Perkins) Contemporary American Literature, 1987; (with B. Perkins and P. Leininger) The Harper Collins Reader's Encyclopedia of American Literature, 1991, 2nd ed., 2002; (with B. Perkins and P. Leininger) Benét's Reader's Encyclopedia of American Literature, 1991; (with B. Perkins) Kaleidoscope: Stories of the American Experience, 1993; Stones Stand, Waters Flow: A New England Story, 2007; Rare Days in Lost Valley: The Bellwether University Book of Universal Truths, 2007. **Address:** Department of English Language and Literature, Eastern Michigan University, 603-B Pray-Harrold Hall, Ypsilanti, MI 48197, U.S.A. **Online address:** george.perkins@emich.edu

PERKINS, John. American (born United States), b. 1945. **Genres:** Adult Non-fiction, Business/Trade/Industry, Economics. **Career:** Chas. T. Main, economic consultant and chief economist, 1971-80; Independent Power Systems, founder and chief executive officer, 1982-90; Dream Change Coalition, founder and chair, 1991-. Writer. **Publications:** The Stress-free Habit: Powerful Techniques for Health and Longevity from the Andes Yucatan and Far East, 1989; Psycho Navigation: Techniques for Travel beyond Time, 1990; The World is as You Dream It: Shamanic Teachings from the Amazon and Andes, 1994; Shape shifting: Shamanic Techniques for Global and Personal Transformation, 1997; Spirit of the Shuar: Wisdom from the Last Unconquered People of the Amazon, 2001; Confessions of an Economic Hit Man, 2004; The Secret History of the American Empire: Economic Hit Men, Jackals, and the Truth about Global Corruption, 2007; Hoodwinked: An Economic Hit Man Reveals Why the World Financial Markets Imploded-and What We Need to Do to Remake Them, 2009. **Address:** Dream Change, PO Box 503, Langley, WA 98260, U.S.A. **Online address:** john@johnperkins.org

PERKINS, John H. American (born United States), b. 1942. **Genres:** Agriculture/Forestry, Environmental Sciences/Ecology, History, Sciences. **Career:** National Research Council, principal staff officer, 1971-74; Miami University, assistant professor, associate professor, 1974-80; Evergreen State College, faculty, 1980-2007, senior academic dean, 1980-86, faculty emeritus, 2007-, Graduate Program on the Environment, director, 1999-2005; Environmental Practice Magazine, founding editor-in-chief, 1999-2008; National Council for Science and the Environment, senior fellow, 2010-. **Publications:** (Ed. with D. Pimentel) Pest Control: Cultural and Environmental Aspects, 1980; Insects, Experts, and the Insecticide Crisis: The Quest for New Pest Management Strategies, 1982; Geopolitics and the Green Revolution: Wheat, Genes, and the Cold War, 1997; (with R. Conlon) Wheels and Deals: The Automotive Industry in Twentieth-Century Australia, 2001. **Address:** The Evergreen State College, 2700 Evergreen Pkwy. NW, Olympia, WA 98505, U.S.A. **Online address:** perkinsj@evergreen.edu

PERKINS, Kelly. American (born United States), b. 1961?. **Genres:** Autobiography/Memoirs. **Career:** HydraCoach Inc. (a manufacturer of hydration monitoring products for athletes and consumers), co-founder. Writer. **Publications:** The Climb of My Life: Scaling Mountains with a Borrowed Heart (memoir), 2007. **Online address:** info@theclimbofmylife.com

PERKINS, Lynne Rae. American (born United States), b. 1956. **Genres:** Children's Fiction, Illustrations, Westerns/Adventure, Young Adult Fiction, Humor/Satire. **Career:** Graphic designer, author and illustrator. **Publications:** Home Lovely, 1995; Clouds for Dinner, 1997; All Alone in the Universe, 1999; The Broken Cat, 2002; Snow Music, 2003; Criss Cross, 2005; Pictures from Our Vacation, 2007; The Cardboard Piano, 2008; As Easy as Falling off the Face of the Earth, 2010. Illustrator of books by others. **Address:** c/o Author Mail, Greenwillow Books, 1350 Ave. of the Americas, New York, NY 10019, U.S.A.

PERKINS, Michael. (D. M. Perkins). American (born United States), b. 1942. **Genres:** Novels, Poetry, Sex, Literary Criticism And History, Sciences, History, Science Fiction/Fantasy. **Career:** Tompkins Square Press, editor, 1966-68; Milky Way Productions, managing editor, 1969-, contributing editor; Croton Press Ltd., editorial director, 1969-72; Artists' Cooperative, co-founder and director, 1973-75; Ulster Arts, editor, 1978-79; Woodstock Guild, program director, 1985-95, chairman of advisory board, 1985-95; State Council on the Arts, writer-in-residence, 1985-; Masquerade Books, senior editor, 1992-98; New York State University, writing panelist Thayer fellow in arts, 1996-98. **Publications:** Third Street Poems, 1965, The Blue Woman, and Other Poems, 1966; Blue Movie, 1968; Queen of Heat, 1968; Shorter Poems, 1968; Evil Companions, 1968; The Tour: Hell's Heated Vacancies, 1969; Renie Perkins: The Life and Work of a Young Artist Who Died by Her Own Hand at the Age of Twenty-five, 1969; Whacking Off, 1969; Terminus, 1969; (contrib.) Renie Perkins, 1969; Estelle, 1969; Down Here, 1969; The Secret Record: Modern Erotic Literature, 1976; The Persistence of Desire,

1977; (contrib.) Twentieth Century Science Fiction Writers, 1982; Praise in the Ears of Clouds, 1982; Gift of Choice, 1992; (ed.) An Anthology of Classic Anonymous Erotic Writing, 1993; The Good Parts: An Uncensored Guide to Literary Sexuality, 1994; (co-ed.) Case Studies in Clinical Linguistics, 1995; (ed.) Coming Up: The World's Best Erotic Writing, 1996; Dark Matter, 1996; (co-ed.) Deep Frying: Chemistry, Nutrition and Practical Applications, 1996; (co-ed.) New Directions in Language Development and Disorders, 2000; Dark Games, 2000; Night Moves, 2000; Cermonies of the Flesh, 2000; Dark Star, 2002; Burn, 2002; The Friends of the Library Guide to Woodstock, 2002; I Could Walk All Day, 2002. AS D.M. PERKINS: Jennifer, 1996; Jennifer and Nikki, 1982; Jennifer on Tour, 2003. **Address:** 750 Ohayo Mountain Rd., Glenford, NY 12433, U.S.A. **Online address:** m.perkins@netstep.net

PERKINS, Mitali. American/Indian (born India), b. 1963. **Genres:** Young Adult Fiction, Children's Fiction, Novels. **Career:** Writer. **Publications:** The Sunita Experiment, 1993; (contrib.) Stories from Where We Live: The California Coast, 2001; Islam and Christianity, 2003; Monsoon Summer, 2004; Not-So-Star-Spangled Life of Sunita Sen: A Novel, 2005; Ambassador Families: Equipping Your Kids to Engage Popular Culture, 2005; First Daughter: Extreme American Makeover, 2007; White House Rules, 2008; Rickshaw Girl, 2007; Secret Keeper, 2009; Bamboo People, 2011. Contributor to periodicals. **Address:** c/o Laura Rennert, Andrea Brown Literary Agency Inc., 2225 E Bayshore Rd., Ste. 200, Palo Alto, CA 94303, U.S.A. **Online address:** mitaliperk@yahoo.com

PERKINS, Suzetta M. American (born United States), b. 1962?. **Genres:** Novels. **Career:** Fayetteville State University, secretary. Writer and administrator. **Publications:** NOVELS: Behind the Veil, 2006; A Love So Deep, 2007; Ex-Terminator: Life after Marriage, 2008; Déjà Vu, 2009; Nothing Stays the Same, 2010. Works appear in anthologies. **Address:** PO Box 64424, Fayetteville, NC 28306, U.S.A. **Online address:** nubianqe2@aol.com

PERKINS, Thomas J. *See* **PERKINS, Tom James.**

PERKINS, Tom James. (Thomas J. Perkins). American (born United States), b. 1932. **Genres:** Novels, Romance/Historical. **Career:** University Laboratories (now Spectra-Physics), founder, 1960-; Hewlett-Packard, administrative head of the research, general manager, 1963-, director, 2002, 2004-06; Kleiner Perkins Caufield & Byers (venture capital co.), co-founder, 1972-2001; Tandem Computers Inc., chairman, 1974-97, director; Genentech, chair, 1976-90, director; The News Corp., non-executive director, director, 1996-; Compaq Computer, director, 1997-2002; Applied Materials Inc, director; Acuson, director; Hybritech Inc., director; Philips Electronics NV, director; Symantec, director; LSI Logic, director; Corning Glass Works, director. Writer. **Publications:** Sex and the Single Zillionaire (romance novel), 2006; The Art of Letter Carving in Stone, 2007; Valley Boy: The Education of Tom Perkins, 2007. AS THOMAS J. PERKINS: Classic Supercharged Sports Cars, 1984. **Address:** c/o Author Mail, HarperCollins Publishers Inc., 10 E 53rd St., 6th Fl., New York, NY 10022-5244, U.S.A.

PERKINSON, Robert. American (born United States), b. 1969?. **Genres:** History. **Career:** University of Hawaii, Department of American Studies, professor. Writer. **Publications:** Texas Tough: The Rise of America's Prison Empire, 2010. **Address:** Department of American Studies, University of Hawaii, 1890 East-West Rd., Moore Hall 324, Honolulu, HI 96822, U.S.A. **Online address:** perk@texastough.com

PERKOWITZ, Sidney. American (born United States), b. 1939. **Genres:** Physics, Humanities, Intellectual History, Popular Culture, Science Fiction/Fantasy, Art/Art History, Astronomy, Engineering, Engineering. **Career:** General Telephone and Electronics, research physicist, 1966-69; Emory University, assistant professor, 1969-74, associate professor, 1974-79, professor, 1979-87, chairman of physics department, 1980-83, Charles Howard Candler professor of physics, 1987-; University of California, visiting professor, 1983-84; Santa Barbara Research Center, consultant, 1983-87; National Research Council of Canada, consultant, 1988-91; Atlanta College of Arts, adjunct professor of humanities, 1989; National Institute of Science and Technology, consultant, 1990-94. Writer. **Publications:** Optical Characterization of Semiconductors; Infrared, Raman, and Photoluminescence Spectroscopy, 1993; Survey of Optical Characterization Methods for Materials, Processing, and Manufacturing in the Semiconductor Industry, 1995; Empire of Light: A History of Discovery in Science and Art, 1996; Universal Foam: From Cappuccino to the Cosmos, 2000; Digital People: From Bionic Humans to Androids, 2004; Hollywood Science: Movies, Science, and the End of the World, 2007; Slow Light: Invisibility, Teleportation, and Other Mysteries of Light, 2011. **Address:** Department of Physics, Emory University, N244 Mathematics & Science Center Bldg., 400 Dowman Dr., Atlanta, GA 30322, U.S.A. **Online address:** physp@emory.edu

PERL, Jed. American (born United States), b. 1951?. **Genres:** Art/Art History. **Career:** Vogue, contributing editor, 1980-94, art critic; New Republic, art critic, 1994-; Art in America and Arts Magazine, art critic; Salmagundi, columnist; New Criterion, contributor; University of Chicago, lecturer; Princeton University, lecturer; Harvard's Kennedy School, teacher; New York Studio School, teacher; Kansas City Art Institute, teacher; Stanford University, faculty; Parson's School of Design, teacher; Philadelphia College, faculty; Pratt Institute, faculty; New School for Social Research, teacher. **Publications:** Paris without End: On French Art since World War I, 1988; (contrib.) Man Ray, 1988; Gallery Going: Four Seasons in the Art World, 1991; Trevor Winkfield's Pageant, 1997; (ed.) Louisa Matthiasdottir, 1999; Eyewitness: Reports from An Art World in Crisis, 2000; New Art City: Manhattan at Mid-Century, 2005; Antoine's Alphabet: Watteau and His World, 2008. Contributor to books and periodicals. **Address:** New Republic, 1331 H St. NW, Ste. 700, Washington, DC 20005, U.S.A.

PERL, Ruth June. American (born United States), b. 1929. **Genres:** Autobiography/Memoirs. **Career:** Pacific Telephone and Telegraph Co., long distance operator, 1945-47; California state offices, clerk and accounting clerk, 1947-49; Hebrew Christian Witness, founder, 1955-, secretary, treasurer, 1956-. Writer. **Publications:** Thy People Shall Be My People, 1968 in UK as Let My People Know, 1969. **Address:** Hebrew Christian Witness, PO Box 2, San Bernardino, CA 92402, U.S.A. **Online address:** ruth@hcwperl.org

PERLE, Liz. (Elizabeth Perle McKenna). American (born United States) **Genres:** Young Adult Fiction, Biography, Autobiography/Memoirs, Adult Non-fiction. **Career:** Harper & Row, Department of Marketing, staff and manager; Bantam Books, Department of Marketing, staff and associate publisher; Prentice Hall Press, publisher, vice president; Addison Wesley, vice president and publisher of general books; Hearst Book Group (William Morrow/Avon), vice president and editorial director, 1991-93, General Book Division, publisher, 1993-94, vice president and publisher, 1994-95; Common Sense Media Inc. (nonpartisan media watchdog organization), co-founder, 2002-, editor-in-chief. **Publications:** NON FICTION: (as Elizabeth Perle McKenna) When Work Doesn't Work Anymore: Women, Work and Identity, 1997; Money, A Memoir: Women, Emotions, and Cash, 2006. **Address:** Common Sense Media Inc., 650 Townsend, Ste. 435, San Francisco, CA 94103, U.S.A.

PERLIN, John. American (born United States), b. 1944. **Genres:** Agriculture/Forestry, Environmental Sciences/Ecology, Technology, Engineering, Natural History, Sciences, Biology, Mathematics/Statistics, Mathematics/Statistics. **Career:** Writer, lecturer and consultant. **Publications:** (With K. Butti) A Golden Thread: 2500 Years of Solar Architecture and Technology, 1980; A Forest Journey: The Role of Wood in the Development of Civilization, 1989; From Space to Earth: The Story of Solar Electricity, 1999. Contributor to periodicals. **Address:** The Rahus Institute, 8026 Washington Ave., Sebastopol, CA 95472, U.S.A. **Online address:** johnperlin@cox.net

PERLMAN, Rhea. American (born United States), b. 1948. **Genres:** Humor/Satire, Children's Non-fiction. **Career:** Author and television producer. **Publications:** OTTO UNDERCOVER SERIES: Born to Drive, 2006; Canyon Catastrophe, 2006; Water Balloon Doom, 2006; Toxic Taffy Takeover, 2006; The Brink of Ex-Stink-Tion, 2007; Brain Freeze, 2007. Contributor to periodicals. **Address:** International Creative Management, 8942 Wilshire Blvd., Beverly Hills, CA 90211-1908, U.S.A.

PERLOFF, Marjorie (Gabrielle). American/Austrian (born Austria), b. 1931. **Genres:** Literary Criticism And History, Humanities, Translations, Art/Art History, Poetry. **Career:** Catholic University of America, assistant professor, 1966-68, associate professor of English, 1968-71; University of Maryland, associate professor, 1971-73, professor of English, 1973-76; University of Southern California, Florence R. Scott professor of English and comparative literature, 1976-86, Florence R. Scott professor emeritus of English, 2009-; Stanford University, professor of English and comparative literature, [illegible], Sadie Dernham Patek professor of humanities, 1990-2000, Sadie Dernham Patek emeritus professor of humanities, 2001-. Writer. **Publications:** Rhyme and Meaning in the Poetry of Yeats, 1970; The Poetic Art of

Robert Lowell, 1973; Frank O'Hara: Poet among Painters, 1977; The Poetics of Indeterminacy: Rimbaud to Cage, 1981; The Dance of the Intellect: Studies in the Poetry of the Pound Tradition, 1985; The Futurist Moment: Avant-Garde, Avant Guerre, and the Language of Rupture, 1986; (co-ed.) Columbia Literary History of the U.S., 1988; (ed.) Postmodern Genres, 1989; Poetic License: Essays on Modernist and Postmodernist Lyric, 1990; Radical Artifice: Writing Poetry in the Age of Media, 1991; (ed. with C. Junkerman) John Cage: Composed in America, 1994; Wittgenstein's Ladder: Poetic Language and the Strangeness of the Ordinary, 1996; Poetry On & Off the Page: Essays for Emergent Occasions, 1998; American Poetry: The Twentieth Century, vol. II, 2000; 21st-Century Modernism: The New Poetics, 2002; Differentials: Poetry, Poetics, Pedagogy, 2004; Vienna Paradox: A Memoir, 2004; (ed. with C. Dworkin) The Sound of Poetry, the Poetry of Sound, 2009; Unoriginal Genius, 2010. Contributor of articles to books and journals. **Address:** Department of English, Stanford University, 460 Bldg., Margaret Jacks Hall, Stanford, CA 94305-2087, U.S.A. **Online address:** mperloff@earthlink.net

PERLOFF, Richard M. American (born United States), b. 1951. **Genres:** Communications/Media, Medicine/Health, Politics/Government. **Career:** Ohio State University, postdoctoral fellow in psychology, journalism and communication, 1978-79; Cleveland State University, faculty, 1979-, School of Communication, assistant professor, 1980-85, associate professor, 1985-94, professor of communication, 1994-, director, founding director, 2004-11. Writer. **Publications:** (Ed. with S. Kraus) Mass Media and Political Thought: An Information Processing Approach, 1985; (with L.M. Jeffres) Mass Media: Processes and Effects, 1986; The Dynamics of Persuasion, 1993, 4th ed. as The Dynamics of Persuasion: Communication and attitudes in the 21st Century, 2010; (with L.W. Jeffres) Mass Media Effects, 1997; Political Communication, 1998; Persuading People to Have Safer Sex: Applications of Social Science to the AIDS Crisis, 2001. Contributor to journals. **Address:** School of Communication, Cleveland State University, Rm. 231, Music and Communication Bldg., 2121 Euclid Ave., Cleveland, OH 44115, U.S.A. **Online address:** r.perloff@csuohio.edu

PERNICE, Joe T. Canadian (born Canada), b. 1967?. **Genres:** Novels. **Career:** Writer, musician and producer. **Publications:** Meat Is Murder, 2003; It Feels So Good When I Stop (novel), 2009. Contributor to journals and magazines. **Address:** c/o Ali Hedrick, Billions Corp., 3522 W Armitage Ave., Chicago, IL 60647, U.S.A.

PERNU, Dennis. Also writes as James Koons, James Koons. American (born United States), b. 1970. **Genres:** Children's Non-fiction. **Career:** Borders Inc., bookseller, 1992-95; Graywolf Press, editorial intern, 1992; New Rivers Press, editorial intern, 1994; Callan Publishing, editor, 1995-. **Publications:** (As James Koons) U.S. Army Rangers, 1995; Hot Rods, 1995; (as James Koons) Monster Trucks, 1996; (as James Koons) Pickup Trucks, 1996; (ed.) Route 66, Lost & Found: Ruins and Relics Revisited, 2004; (ed. with L. Hitch) BMX Trix & Techniques for the Track, 2004; (ed.) GE Evolution Locomotives, 2007. **Address:** Capstone Press, 151 Good Counsel Dr., Mankato, MN 56001, U.S.A.

PERONE, James E. American (born United States), b. 1958. **Genres:** Music, Bibliography, Biography. **Career:** Capital University, music teacher, 1977-79; Nelson's Music and Williams's Music, music teacher, 1978-80; Western New York Institute for the Arts in Education, teaching artist in music, 1983-87; University of New York, teaching assistant, 1983-87; U-Crest Music Center, music teacher, 1984-88; State University of New York, lecturer, 1986-88, visiting lecturer, 1993-94; Canisius College, assistant to dean, 1988-91, adjunct professor of music and department head, 1988-94; Community Music School of Buffalo, music teacher, 1992-94; Villa Maria College, woodwind instructor, 1992-94; Mount Union College (now University of Mount Union), assistant professor of music, 1994-2000, department head, 1996-2001, associate professor of music, 2000-06, professor of music, 2006-, Margaret Morgan Ramsey professor in music, 2009-; Tuscarawas Philharmonic Orchestra, principal clarinetist, 1996-; Canton Community Band, first clarinetist, 1996-, assistant conductor, 1998; Ohio District of Kiwanis Intl., Division 17, distinguished lieutenant fovernor, 2003-04; Kiwanis Club of Alliance, president. Writer. **Publications:** Howard Hanson: A Bio-Bibliography, 1993; Musical Anthologies for Analytical Study: A Bibliography, 1995; (comp.) Orchestration Theory: A Bibliography, 1996; (comp.) Harmony Theory: A Bibliography, 1997; (comp.) Form and Analysis Theory: A Bibliography, 1998; Elvis Costello: A Bio-Bibliography, 1998; Carole King: A Bio-Bibliography, 1999; Paul Simon: A Bio-Bibliography, 2000; Songs of the Vietnam Conflict, 2001; Louis Moreau Gottschalk: A Bio-Bibliography, 2002; Music of the Counterculture Era, 2004; Woodstock: An Encyclopedia of The Music and Art Fair, 2005; Words and Music of Carole King, 2006; Sound of Stevie Wonder: His Words and Music, 2006; Words and Music of David Bowie, 2007; Words and Music of Prince, 2008; Mods, Rockers, and the Music of the British Invasion, 2009. Contributor to journals and periodicals. **Address:** Department of Music, Mount Union College, 1972 Clark Ave., Alliance, OH 44601, U.S.A. **Online address:** peroneje@mountunion.edu

PERRETT, Bryan. Also writes as R. Eldworth, R. Eldworth. British (born England), b. 1934. **Genres:** Children's Fiction, History, Military/Defense/Arms Control. **Career:** Liverpool Echo, defense correspondent. Writer. **Publications:** Fighting Vehicles of the Red Army, 1969; NATO Armour, 1971; The Valentine in North Africa 1942-43, 1972; The Matilda, 1973; The Churchill, 1974; Through Mud and Blood, 1975; Tank Tracks to Rangoon, 1978; The Lee/Grant Tank in British Service, 1978; Allied Tank Destroyers, 1979; Armour in Battle: Wavell's Offensive, 1979; Sturmartillerie and Panzerjager, 1979; The Churchill Tank, 1980; The Stuart Light Tank Series, 1980; The Panzerkampfwagen III IV and V, 3 vols., 1980-81; British Tanks in North Africa 1940-42, 1981; (with A. Lord) Czar's British Squadron, 1981; The Tiger Tanks, 1981; German Armoured Cars, 1982; German Light Panzers, 1982; Weapons of the Falklands Conflict, 1982; History of Biltzkrieg, 1983; Mechanized Infantry, 1984; The Hawks, 1984; (ed. and contrib.) Elite Fighting Units, 1984; Lightning War, 1985; Allied Tanks Italy, 1985; Allied Tanks North Africa, 1986; Knights of the Black Cross, 1986; A Hawkat War, 1986; Soviet Armour since 1945, 1987; Hitler's Panzers: The Years of Aggression, 1987; Desert Warfare, 1988; (with I. Hogg) Encyclopedia of the Second World War, 1989; Canopy of War, 1990; Tank Warfare, 1990; Liverpool: A City at War, 1990; Last Stand!, 1991; The Battle Book, 1992; At All Costs, 1993; Seize and Hold, 1994; Iron Fist, 1995; Against All Odds!, 1995; Impossible Victories, 1996; Hampshire Tigers: The Story of the Royal Hampshire Regiment, 1945-1992, 1997; The Real Hornblower: The Life & Times of Admiral Sir James Gordon, 1997; Megiddo, 1999; Gunboat, 2000; The Taste of Battle, 2000; The Changing Face of Battle, 2000; (as R. Eldworth) Last Convoy, 2000; (as R. Eldworth) Beach Assault, 2000; Heroes of the Hour, 2001; Gunboat!: Small Ships at War, 2001; Trafalgar, 2002; The Crimea, 2002; Waterloo, 2003; For Valour-Victoria Cross & Medal of Honor Battles, 2003; Megiddo 1918: Lawrence, Allenby, and the March on Damascus, 2004; North Sea Battleground, 2011. **Address:** 7 Maple Ave., Burscough, LC L40 5SL, England. **Online address:** bbperrett@aol.com

PERRIAM, Wendy. British (born England), b. 1940. **Genres:** Novels, Novellas/Short Stories. **Career:** Author and creative writing tutor. **Publications:** NOVELS: Absinthe for Elevenses, 1980 in US as Bourbon for Breakfast, 1982; Cuckoo, 1981; After Purple, 1982; Born of Woman, 1984; The Stillness the Dancing, 1985; Sin City, 1987; Devils, for a Change, 1989; Fifty-Minute Hour, 1990; Bird Inside, 1993; Michael, Michael, 1994; Breaking and Entering, 1994; Coupling, 1996; Second Skin, 1999; Lying, 2000; Tread Softly, 2002; Broken Places, 2010; Fire on Dark Water, 2011. SHORT STORIES: Dreams, Demons and Desire (short stories), 2001; Virgin in the Gym and Other Stories, 2004; Laughter Class and Other Stories, 2006; The Biggest Female in the World and Other Stories, 2006; Little Marvel, 2008; The Queen's Margarine, 2009. OTHERS: A Wounded Deer, 2006; Willa Cather and the Dance, 2009. Works appear in anthologies. **Address:** Curtis Brown Ltd., 5th Fl, Haymarket House, 28-29 Haymarket, London, GL SW1Y 4SP, England. **Online address:** wendy@wendyperriman.com

PERRIN, Dennis. American (born United States) **Genres:** Novels, Biography, Military/Defense/Arms Control, History. **Career:** Writer. **Publications:** Mr. Mike: The Life and Work of Michael O'Donoghue, 1998; American Fan: Sports Mania and the Culture That Feeds It, 2000; Savage Mules: The Democrats and Endless War, 2008. Contributor to periodicals. **Address:** c/o Author Mail, Avon Books, 1350 Ave. of the Americas, New York, NY 10019-4702, U.S.A. **Online address:** dperrin@comcast.net

PERRIN, Don. American/German (born Germany), b. 1964. **Genres:** Science Fiction/Fantasy. **Career:** Software Kinetics, director of electronic warfare research, 1992-93; writer, 1993-; Gamer Magazine, owner, 2005-; Archangel Entertainment, associate; MWAN Magazine, publisher; True North Miniature, owner. **Publications:** MAG FORCE 7 SERIES: WITH M. WEIS: Knights of the Black Garth (science fiction), 1995; Robot Blues (science fiction), 1996; Hung Out, 1998. DRAGONLANCE SERIES: (with M. Weis) Theros Ironfeld (fantasy), 1996; (with M. Weis) The Doom Brigade (fantasy), 1996; (with M. Weis) Brothers in Arms, 1999; Draconian Measures, 2000; (with M.H. Herbert and Stan) Bertrem's Guide to the War of Souls, vol. II, 2002. OTHER: (with M. Weis) Raistlin Chronicles, 2010. Contributor to books. **Address:** Archangel Entertainment, PO Box 481, Lake Geneva, WI 53147, U.S.A.

PERRIN, Kayla. American (born United States), b. 1970?. **Genres:** Novels. **Career:** Writer. **Publications:** ROMANCE NOVELS, EXCEPT WHERE NOTED: Again, My Love, 1997; Everlasting Love, 1998; Sweet Honesty, 1999; Holiday of Love, 2000; (with J. Sims and C. Wright) A Very Special Love, 2000; The Disappearance of Allison Jones, 2000; If You Want Me, 2001; Flirting with Danger, 2001; The Sisters of Theta Phi Kappa (thriller), 2001; In an Instant, 2002; Say You Need Me, 2002; Fool for Love, 2003; In a Heartbeat, 2003; Tell Me You Love Me, 2003; The Delta Sisters (thriller), 2004; Gimme an O!, 2005; Midnight Dreams, 2006; Getting Even, 2006; The Sweet Spot, 2006; Getting Some, 2007; (with B. Mott) How to Kill a Guy in 10 Days, 2007; Irresistible Desire, 2007; Love, Lies & Videotape, 2007; We'll Never Tell (crime novel), 2007; Obsession, 2008; Single Mama Drama, 2008; Single Mama's Got More Drama (sequel to Single Mama Drama), 2009; Spring Break, 2010; Island Fantasy, 2010. Contributor to books. **Online address:** kayla@kaylaperrin.com

PERRONE, Charles A. American (born United States), b. 1951. **Genres:** Cultural/Ethnic Topics, Music, Translations. **Career:** University of Florida, assistant professor, 1985-90, associate professor of Portuguese and Luso-Brazilian literature and culture, 1990-98, professor, 1998-. Writer. **Publications:** Letras e letras (da MPB), 1988, 2008; Masters of Contemporary Brazilian Song: MPB, 1965-1985, 1989; (trans.) Adriano Espinola, Taxi or, Poem of Love in Transit, 1992; Seven Faces: Brazilian Poetry since Modernism, 1996; Brazil, Lyric and the Americas, 2010. EDITOR: (co-ed.) Crônicas Brasileiras Nova Fase, 1994; (with C. Dunn) Brazilian Popular Music and Globalization, 2001; First World Third Class and Other Tales of the Global Mix (by Regina Rheda), 2005. **Address:** University of Florida, Dauer Hall 170, PO Box 117405, Gainesville, FL 32611-7405, U.S.A. **Online address:** perrone@ufl.edu

PERROTTA, Tom. American (born United States), b. 1961. **Genres:** Novels. **Career:** Yale University, writing tutor and part-time instructor, 1988-93; Harvard University, preceptor, 1994-98. Writer. **Publications:** FICTION: Bad Haircut: Stories of the Seventies, 1994; The Wishbones, 1997; Election, 1998; Joe College, 2000; Little Children, 2004; (with W. Leitch) My Life as a Loser, 2005; (intro.) Little Children: The Shooting Script, 2006; Abstinence Teacher, 2007; The Leftovers, 2011. **Address:** c/o Dori Weintraub, St. Martin's Press, 175 5th Ave., New York, NY 10010, U.S.A. **Online address:** tom@tomperrotta.net

PERRY, Anne. Scottish/British (born England), b. 1938. **Genres:** Mystery/Crime/Suspense. **Career:** Muldoon & Adams (insurance company), property underwriter, 1967-72; writer, 1972-. **Publications:** THOMAS PITT MYSTERY SERIES: The Cater Street Hangman, 1979; Callander Square, 1980; Paragon Walk, 1981; Resurrection Row, 1981; Rutland Place, 1983; Bluegate Fields, 1984; Death in the Devil's Acre, 1985; Cardington Crescent, 1987; Silence in Hanover Close, 1988; Bethlehem Road, 1990; Highgate Rise, 1991; Belgrave Square, 1992; Farriers' Lane, 1993; The Hyde Park Headsman, 1994; Traitor's Gate, 1995; Pentecost Alley, 1996; Ashworth Hall, 1997; Brunswick Gardens, 1998; Bedford Square, 1998; Half Moon Street, 1998; The Whitechapel Conspiracy, 2001; Southampton Row, 2002; Seven Dials, 2003; Long Spoon Lane, 2005; Buckingham Palace Gardens, 2008; Anne Perry's Silent Nights: Two Victorian Christmas Mysteries, 2009; Treason at Lisson Grove, 2011. WILLIAM MONK MYSTERY SERIES: The Face of a Stranger, 1990; A Dangerous Mourning, 1991; Defend and Betray, 1992; A Sudden, Fearful Death, 1993; The Sins of the Wolf, 1994; Cain His Brother, 1995; Weighed in the Balance, 1996; The Silent Cry, 1997; The Whited Sepulchres, 1997; The Twisted Root, 1999; Slaves of Obsession, 2000; A Funeral in Blue, 2001; Death of a Stranger, 2002; The Shifting Tide, 2004; Dark Assassin, 2006; Anne Perry Christmas: Two Holiday Novels, 2006; Execution Dock, 2009. WORLD WAR ONE SERIES: No Graves as Yet, 2003; Shoulder the Sky, 2004; Angels in the Gloom, 2005; At Some Disputed Barricade, 2006; We Shall Not Sleep, 2007. CHRISTMAS NOVELLAS: A Christmas Journey, 2003; A Christmas Visitor, 2004; A Christmas Guest, 2005; A Christmas Secret, 2006; A Christmas Beginning, 2007; A Christmas Grace, 2008; (with G. Haigh) Making Your Way in Headship, 2008. NOVELS: Fashionable Funeral, 1992; Tathea, 1999; A Dish Taken Cold, 1999; The One Thing More, 2000; Come Armageddon, 2001; (co-author) Naked Came the Phoenix, 2001; (co-author) I'd Kill for That, 2004; Letter From The Highlands, 2004; Heroes, 2007; Christmas Promise, 2009; Sheen on the Silk, 2010; Christmas Odyssey, 2010. NONFICTION: Letters From The Highlands, 2004. OTHERS: (ed.) Much Ado about Murder, 2002; (ed.) Death by Dickens, 2004; (ed.) Thou Shalt not Kill, 2005; Acceptable Loss, 2011. **Address:** c/o Meg Davis, MBA Literary Agency, 62 Grafton Way, London, GL W1P 5DW, England. **Online address:** contact-anne@anneperry.net

PERRY, Bruce D. American (born United States), b. 1955. **Genres:** Psychiatry, Children's Non-fiction. **Career:** University of Chicago, School of Medicine, faculty, 1988-91, Child and Adolescent Psychiatry, fellow; Texas Childrens Hospital, chief of psychiatry, 1990; Baylor College of Medicine, Thomas S. Trammell research professor of child psychiatry, 1992-2001, Department of Psychiatry, vice-chairman for research, 1993-2001; Alberta Mental Health Board, medical director for provincial programs in children's mental health, 2001-03; Child Trauma Center, senior fellow; Alberta Ministry of Children's Services, senior consultant; Northwestern University, Feinberg School of Medicine, adjunct professor of psychiatry and behavioral sciences. Clinician, researcher and writer. **Publications:** (With M. Szalavitz) The Boy Who Was Raised as a Dog: And Other Stories from a Child Psychiatrist's Notebook: What Traumatized Children Can Teach Us about Loss, Love and Healing, 2006; (with M. Szalavitz) Born for Love: Why Empathy Is Essential and Endangered, 2010. **Address:** Child Trauma Academy, 5161 San Felipe, Ste. 320, Houston, TX 77056, U.S.A.

PERRY, Curtis. American (born United States) **Genres:** Literary Criticism And History. **Career:** Arizona State University, associate professor of English; University of Illinois, professor of English, 2006-, department head. Writer. **Publications:** The Making of Jacobean Culture: James I and the Renegotiation of Elizabethan Literary Practice, 1997; (ed.) Material Culture and Cultural Materialisms in the Middle Ages and Renaissance, 2001; Literature and Favoritism in Early Modern England, 2006; (ed.) Eros and Power in English Renaissance Drama, 2008; (ed. with J. Watkins) Shakespeare and the Middle Ages, 2009. **Address:** Department of English, University of Illinois at Urbana-Champaign, 208 English, 608 S Wright St., Urbana, IL 61801, U.S.A. **Online address:** cperry@illinois.edu

PERRY, Dayn. American (born United States), b. 1972. **Genres:** Young Adult Non-fiction, Biography. **Career:** Writer. **Publications:** Winners: How Good Baseball Teams Become Great Ones (and It's Not the Way You Think) (nonfiction), 2006; Reggie Jackson: The Life and Thunderous Career of Baseball's Mr. October (biography), 2010. Contributor to periodicals. **Address:** Chicago, IL , U.S.A. **Online address:** daynperry@yahoo.com

PERRY, Douglas. American (born United States), b. 1968. **Genres:** Young Adult Non-fiction. **Career:** Oregonian, online features editor. **Publications:** (With J. Guinn) The Sixteenth Minute: Life in the Aftermath of Fame (nonfiction), 2005; The Girls of Murder City: Fame, Lust, and the Beautiful Killers Who Inspired Chicago (nonfiction), 2010. Contributor to newspapers and magazines. **Address:** Jim Donovan Literary, 4515 Prentice, Ste. 109, Dallas, TX 75206, U.S.A. **Online address:** doug.perry@hotmail.com

PERRY, Jeffrey B. (Jeffrey Babcock Perry). American (born United States), b. 1946. **Genres:** Biography, History, Social Commentary. **Career:** United States Postal Service, mail sorting facility worker, now retired. Writer. **Publications:** (Ed.) A Hubert Harrison Reader, 2001; Hubert Harrison: The Voice of Harlem Radicalism, 1883-1918, 2009. **Address:** Columbia University Press, 1 Oldlands Way, Bognor Regis, WS 22 9SA, England. **Online address:** jeffreybperry@gmail.com

PERRY, Jeffrey Babcock. *See* **PERRY, Jeffrey B.**

PERRY, Margaret. American (born United States), b. 1933. **Genres:** Literary Criticism And History, Novellas/Short Stories, Bibliography. **Career:** New York Public Library, reference and young adult librarian, 1954-55, 1957-58; U.S. Army, civilian librarian, 1959-63, 1964-67; U.S. Military Academy, reference librarian, 1967-68, chief of circulation, 1968-70; University of Rochester, head of education library, 1970-75, assistant professor, 1973-75, assistant professor of education, 1974-82, associate professor of English, 1975-82, Reader Services Division, head, 1975-78, acting director of libraries, 1976-77, assistant director of libraries for reader services, 1978-82; Urban League of Rochester, assistant treasurer, 1977-78, vice-president, 1978-80, board director; Valparaiso University, director of libraries, 1982-93, associate professor, now professor emeritus; Afro-Americans in New York Life and History, contributing editor. **Publications:** A Bio-Bibliography of Countée P. Cullen, 1903-1946, 1971; Silence to the Drums: A Survey of the Literature of the Harlem Renaissance, 1976; The Harlem Renaissance: An Annotated Bibliography and Commentary, 1982; (ed. and intro.) The Short Fiction of Rudolph Fisher, 1987. Contributor of articles to journals. **Address:** Valparaiso University, 1700 Chapel Dr., Valparaiso, IN 46383-4520, U.S.A. **Online address:** mperry@aliens.com

PERRY, Michael Charles. British (born England), b. 1933. **Genres:** Paranormal, Theology/Religion, Essays, Reference. **Career:** Church of England, assistant curate, 1958-60, ordained priest, 1959, archdeacon of Durham, 1970-93; Ripon Hall, chaplain at Theological College, 1961-63; Society for Promoting Christian Knowledge, chief assistant for home publishing, 1963-70; Archbishops Commission on Christian Doctrine, secretary, 1967-71; The Church Quarterly, editor, 1968-71; St. John's College, Selwyn Lecturer, 1976; Trinity College, Marshall Memorial Lecturer, 1976; College of Psychic Studies, Beard Memorial Lecturer, 1977; The Christian Parapsychologist, editor, 1978-; Durham Cathedral, sub-dean, 1985-98; Bishop of Durham, senior chaplain, 1993-98, emeritus, 1998-. **Publications:** Easter Enigma: An Essay on the Resurrection with Speical Reference to the Data of Psychical Research, 1959; The Pattern of Matins and Evensong, 1961; Meet the Prayer Book, 1963; (co-author) The Churchman's Companion, 1964; Anglican-Methodist Unity: A Short Guide, 1968; (with D. Morgan) Declaring the Faith: The Printed Word, 1969; Sharing in One Bread, 1973, rev. ed., 1980; The Resurrection of Man, 1975; Handbook of Parish Worship, 1977, rev. ed., 1989; The Paradox of Worship, 1977; (with P. Carter) Handbook of Parish Finance, 1981, rev. ed., 1992; Psychic Studies: A Christian's View, 1987; Gods Within, 1992; Psychical and Spiritual, 2003. EDITOR: Crisis for Confirmation in US as Confirmation Crisis, 1967; (with I. Ramsay) Faith Alert, 1968; Deliverance, 1987, rev. ed., 1996. **Address:** 57 Ferens Pk., Durham, DU DH1 1NU, England. **Online address:** mandmperry@totalserve.co.uk

PERRY, Pamela. American (born United States), b. 1955?. **Genres:** Race Relations, Sociology, Social Sciences, Anthropology/Ethnology. **Career:** University of California-Berkeley, teaching assistant, 1989-97; Harvard University, Harvard Children's Initiative, postdoctoral fellow, 1998-2000; University of California-Santa Cruz, assistant professor of community studies, 2000- . Writer. **Publications:** Shades of White: White Kids and Racial Identities in High School, 2002. Contributor to journals. **Address:** Department of Community Studies, University of California, 231 Oakes College, 1156 High St., Santa Cruz, CA 95064-1077, U.S.A. **Online address:** pperry@cats.ucsc.edu

PERRY, Paul. American (born United States), b. 1950. **Genres:** Theology/Religion, Medicine/Health, Children's Fiction, Literary Criticism And History. **Career:** Runner's World, managing editor, 1978-80; Running, editor-in-chief, 1980-83; American Health Magazine, executive editor, 1984-88, full-time writer, 1988-; Columbia University, prestigious Gannett Center for Media Studies, fellow; University of Oregon, teacher of magazine writing. **Publications:** Fasting Safely: The Chronicle of a Seven-Day Fast, 1982; Paul Perry's Complete Book of the Triathlon, 1983; (with R. Phaigh) Athletic Massage, 1984; (with R. Moody) The Light Beyond, 1988; (with M. Morse) Closer to the Light, 1990; (with H. Hellerstein) Healing Your Heart, 1990; (with K. Babbs) On the Bus, 1990; (with R.A. Moody, Jr.) Coming Back, 1991; (with R. Moody) Life before Life: Regression into Past Lives, 1991; (with R. Callahan) Why Do I Eat When I'm Not Hungry?: How to Use your Body's Own Energy System to Treat Food Addictions with the Revolutionary Callahan Techniques, 1991; (with M. Morse) Transformed by the Light, 1992; Fear and Loathing: The Strange and Terrible Saga of Hunter S. Thompson, 1992, 2nd ed., 2004; (with R.A. Moody, Jr.) Reunions: Visionary Encounters with Departed Loved Ones, 1993; (with D. Brinkley) Saved by the Light: The True Story of a Man Who Died Twice and the Profound Revelations He Received, 1994; (with M. Morse) Parting Visions: Uses and Meanings of Pre-Death, Psychic and Spiritual Experiences, 1994; (with D. Brinkley) At Peace in the Light: The Further Adventures of a Reluctant Psychic Who Reveals the Secret of Your Spiritual Powers, 1995; (with H. Liu) Mastering Miracles: The Healing Art of Qi Gong as Taught by a Master, 1997; (with C. Steiner) Achieving Emotional Literacy: A Personal Program to Increase Your Emotional Intelligence, 1997; (with B. Clifford) The Black Ship: The Quest to Recover an English Pirate Ship and Its Lost Treasure, as Expedition Whydah: The Story of the World's First Excavation of a Pirate Treasure Ship and the Man Who Found Her, 1999; (with V.S. Cherewatenko) The Diabetes Cure: A Medical Approach That Can Slow, Stop, Even Cure Type 2 Diabetes, 1999; (with B. Clifford) Expedition Whydah, 1999; (with M. Morse) Where God Lives: The Science of the Paranormal and How Our Brains Are Linked to the Universe, 2000; (with V.S. Cherewatenko) Stress Cure: A Simple 7-Step Plan to Balance Mood, Improve Memory and Restore Energy, 2003; (with B. Clifford) Return to Treasure Island and the Search for Captain Kidd, 2003; Jesus in Egypt: Discovering the Secrets of Christ's Childhood Years, 2003; Evidence of the Afterlife: The Science of Near-death Experience, 2010; (with R.A. Moody, Jr.) Glimpses of Eternity: Sharing a Loved One's Passage from this Life to the Next, 2010; (with R. Moody) Paranormal: My Life in Pursuit of the Afterlife, 2012. Contributor to periodicals. **Address:** c/o Nat Sobel, Sobel Weber Associates Inc., 146 E Nineteenth St., New York, NY 10003, U.S.A. **Online address:** pperry87@home.com

PERRY, Phyllis Alesia. American (born United States), b. 1961?. **Genres:** Novels, Novellas/Short Stories, Young Adult Fiction, Literary Criticism And History. **Career:** Alabama Journal, assistant city editor, editor, copy editor; Atlanta Journal-Constitution, editor, copy editor, reporter. **Publications:** Stigmata: A Novel, 1998; A Sunday in June: A Novel, 2004. Contributor to periodicals. **Address:** c/o Author Mail, Hyperion Editorial Department, 77 W 66th St., 11th Fl., New York, NY 10023, U.S.A. **Online address:** phyllis@phyllisalesiaperry.com

PERRY, Phyllis J. American (born United States), b. 1933. **Genres:** Children's Fiction, Children's Non-fiction, Education, Sports/Fitness. **Career:** Boulder Valley Public Schools, teacher, curriculum specialist, educational programs specialist, instructional design specialist, director of talented and gifted education, principal, 1968-91. Writer. **Publications:** FOR CHILDREN NONFICTION: Spiders, 1964; Lets Look at the Birds, 1965; A Trip through the Zoo, 1968; One Dozen Swimmers, 1968; Lets Look at Moths and Butterflies, 1969; Lets Look at Frogs, 1969; Lets Look at Snails, 1969; Lets Look at Seashells, 1971; The Fiddle Hoppers, 1995; Ballooning, 1996; Sea Stars & Dragons, 1996; Armor to Venom: Animal Defenses, 1997; The Crocodilians, 1997; Hide and Seek: Creatures in Camouflage, 1997; The Snow Cats, 1997; Soaring, 1997; Bats, 1998; Crafty Canines, 1999; Freshwater Giants, 1999; Board Sailing, 2000; Keeping the Traditions: A Multicultural Resource, 2000; Trains, 2001; Animals Under the Ground, 2001; Animals That Hibernate, 2001; Animals That Live under Ground, 2001; The Musical ABC, 2001; Science Companion for Library, Home & School, 2002; Under the Old Oak Tree, 2003; Secrets of the Rock, 2004; Kids Look at Colorado, 2005; Animals, Animals: Buffalo, 2005; Sounds Around Us: Poems to Tickle Kids' Ears, 2005; The Case of the Three-Legged Buffalo, 2006; Case of the Hidden Masterpiece, 2006; Alien, the Giant and Rocketman, 2007; Sherlock Hounds: Our Heroic Search and Rescue Dogs, 2007; The Secrets of the Sea Chest, 2007. FICTION: Mr. Crumb's Secret, 2003; The Secret of the Silver Key, 2003. BOOKS FOR TEACHERS: Full Flowering: A Parent and Teacher Guide to Programs for the Gifted, 1985; A Guide to Independent Research, 1986; Colorado History: Creative Activities for Curious Kids, 1994; A Teachers Science Companion: Resources and Activities in Science and Math, 1994; Getting Started in Science Fairs: From Planning to Judging, 1995; (with P. Rillero) 365 Science Projects and Activities, 1996; Guide to Math Materials, 1997; Reading Activities & Resources That Work, 1997; Myths, Legends and Tales, 1999; Science Fair Success with Plants, 1999; Ten Tall Tales: Origins, Activities, and More, 2001; Teaching Fantasy Novels: From The Hobbit to Harry Potter and the Goblet of Fire, 2003. LITERATURE BRIDGES TO SCIENCE SERIES: Bridges to theWorld of Water, 1995; Rainy, Windy, Snowy, Sunny Days, 1996; The Worlds Regions & Weather, 1996; Exploring the World of Animals, 1997. LITERATURE BRIDGES TO SOCIAL STUDIES SERIES: Exploring the World of Sports, 1998; Exploring Our Countrys History, 1998. OTHERS: Lets Learn about Mushrooms, 1974; Mexican American Sketches, 1976; A Look at Colorado, 1976; Jazz upYour Journal Writing, Grades 1-2, 2003, Grades 3-4, 2003, Grades 5-6, 2003; Colorado Fun: Activities for On the Road and At Home, Big Earth, 2007; The Field Guide to Ocean Animals, 2007; It Happened in Rocky Mountain National Park, 2008; Images of America: Rocky Mountain National Park, 2008; Clue School: The Ghost in the Music Room, 2008; Ace Your Ecology and Environmental Science Project, 2009; Pandas' Earthquake Escape, 2010; Speaking Ill of the Dead; Jerks in Colorado History, 2011. Contributor to books and periodicals. **Address:** 3190 Endicott Dr., Boulder, CO 80305, U.S.A. **Online address:** phyllisperry@q.com

PERRY, Roland. Australian (born Australia), b. 1946. **Genres:** Sports/Fitness, Recreation, Biography, Autobiography/Memoirs, Young Adult Non-fiction. **Career:** Age newspaper, journalist, 1969-73. Freelance writer. **Publica-**

tions: BIOGRAPHY: The Exile: Burchett, Reporter of Conflict, 1988; Shane Warne, Master Spinner, 1993; Lethal Hero: The Mel Gibson Biography, 1993; The Fifth Man, 1994; The Don, 1995; Mel Gibson: Actor, Director, Producer, 1996; Bold Warnie: Shane Warne and Australia's Rise to Cricket Dominance, 1999; Waugh's Way: The Steve Waugh Story-Learner, Legend, Leader, 2000, rev. ed., 2002; Monash: The Outsider Who Won a War, 2004; Last of the Cold War Spies: The Life of Michael Straight, the Only American in Britain's Cambridge Spy Ring, 2005; Miller's Luck: The Life and Loves of Keith Miller, Australia's Greatest All-Rounder, 2005; Sailing to the Moon, 2008; Bradman's Invincibles, 2008; Changi Brownlow, 2010. NOVELS: Programme for a Puppet, 1979 as Program for a Puppet, 1980; Blood Is a Stranger, 1988; Faces in the Rain, 1990. NONFICTION: Hidden Power: The Programming of the President as The Programming of the President: The Hidden Power of the Computer in World Politics Today, 1984; Captain Australia: A History of the Celebrated Captains of Australian Test Cricket, 2000, rev. ed., 2001; Bradman's Best: Sir Donald Bradman's Selection of the Best Team in Cricket History, 2001; Bradman's Best Ashes Teams: Sir Donald Bradman's Selection of the Best Ashes Teams in Cricket History, 2003; The Ashes: A Celebration, 2006; Australian Light Horse, 2009. **Address:** Andrew Lownie Literary Agency Ltd., 36 Great Smith St., London, GL SW1P 3BU, England. **Online address:** rolandjp@bigpond.net.au

PERRY, Steve. American (born United States), b. 1947. **Genres:** Novellas/Short Stories, Mystery/Crime/Suspense, Science Fiction/Fantasy, Plays/Screenplays, Novels, Horror. **Career:** University of Washington, teacher; Ruby-Spears Productions, staff writer. **Publications:** The Tularemia Gambit, 1981; Civil War Secret Agent, 1984; (with M. Reaves) Sword of the Samurai, 1984; The Hero Curse, 1991; The Harriers: Of War and Honor, 1991; The Mask, 1994; The Trinity Vector, 1996; The Digital Effect, 1997; Men in Black, 1997; (with G.A. Braunbeck) Time Was: Isaac Asimov's I-Bots, 1998; (with D. Perry) Titan A.E., 2000; Windowpane, 2003; Bristlecone, 2010; Champion of the Dead, 2010; Curse the Darkness: Tyrone Candle Mystery, 2010. VENTURE SILK SERIES: Spindoc, 1994; The Forever Drug, 1995. CONAN SERIES: Conan the Fearless, 1986; Conan the Defiant, 1987; Conan the Indomitable, 1989; Conan the Free Lance, 1990; Conan the Formidable, 1990. MATADOR SERIES: The Man Who Never Missed, 1985; Matadora, 1986; The Machiavelli Interface, 1986; (with M. Reaves) The Omega Cage, 1988; The 97th Step, 1989; The Albino Knife, 1991; Black Steel, 1992; Brother Death, 1992; Musashi Flex, 2005. SCIENCE FICTION WITH M. REAVES: Hellstar, 1984; Dome, 1987. STAR WARS SERIES: Shadows of the Empire, 1996; (with R. Randall and T. Simmon) Shadows of the Empire: Evolution, 2000; (with M. Reaves) Death Star, 2007. STAR WARS: CLONE WARS SERIES WITH M. REAVES: Medstar I: Battle Surgeons, 2004; Medstar II: Jedi Healer, 2004. ALIENS SERIES: Earth Hive, 1992; Nightmare Asylum, 1993; (with S. Perry) The Female War, 1993. ALIENS VS. PREDATOR SERIES: (with S. Perry) Prey, 1994; (with D. Bischoff) Hunters Planet, 1994. STELLAR RANGERS SERIES: Peacemaker, 1993; Guns and Honor, 1993; Stellar Ranger, 1994; Lone Star, 1994. NET FORCE SERIES WITH TOM CLANCY: (with S. Pieczenik) Net Force, 1999; (with S. Pieczenik) Breaking Point, 2000; (with S. Pieczenik) Point of Impact, 2001; (with S. Pieczenik) Cybernation, 2001; State of War, 2003; (with L. Segriff) Changing of the Guard, 2003; (with L. Segriff) Springboard, 2005; (with L. Segriff) Archimedes Effect, 2006. OTHERS: (contrib.) Another Dimension 2: The Little Book, 1994; Batman and the Ninja, 1995; Leonard Nimoy's Primortals: Target Earth, 1997; Immune Response, 2006; (with D. Perry) Chris Bunch's the Gangster Conspiracy: A Star Risk, Ltd. Novel, 2007; Turnabout: A Novel, 2008; Indiana Jones and the Army of the Dead, 2009. Works appear in anthologies. Contributor to magazines. **Address:** Jean V. Naggar Literary Agency Inc., 216 E 75th St., Ste. 1E, New York, NY 10021-2921, U.S.A. **Online address:** perry1966@comcast.net

PERRY, Thomas Kennedy. American (born United States), b. 1952. **Genres:** Sports/Fitness, Young Adult Fiction. **Career:** Velux-Greenwood Corp., purchasing and personnel manager, 1979-80; Kendall Co., training manager, 1981-83; Corporate Office, assistant to labor relations director, 1983-85; American Fiber and Finishing Co., assistant personnel manager, 1985-91, personnel manager, 1991-; Aveleigh Presbyterian Church, member, 1991-96; Piedmont Technical College, adjunct faculty, 1993-94. Writer. **Publications:** Textile League Baseball: South Carolinas Mill Teams 1880-1955, 1993; Shoeless Joe, 1995; (with M.C. Kirkpatrick) The Southern Textile Basketball Tournament: A History 1921-1997, 1997; Just Joe: Baseball's Natural, as Told by His Wife, 2007. **Address:** McFarland & Company Inc., 960 NC Hwy. 88 W, PO Box 611, Jefferson, NC 28640, U.S.A.

PERSICO, Joseph E. American (born United States), b. 1930. **Genres:** History, Biography, Young Adult Non-fiction, Novels. **Career:** New York Governor Averell Harriman, consumer advocate, 1956-59; U.S. Information Agency, foreign service officer, 1959-62; New York State Department of Health, speech writer, 1964-66; chief speech writer for Governor, 1966-74, chief speech writer for Vice President Nelson A. Rockefeller, 1974-77; writer, 1977-. **Publications:** My Enemy, My Brother: Men and Days of Gettysburg, 1977; Piercing the Reich: The Penetration of Nazi Germany by American Secret Agents During World War II, 1979; The Spiderweb, 1979; The Imperial Rockefeller: A Biography of Nelson A. Rockefeller, 1982; (with G. Sunderland) Keeping Out of Crime's Way: The Practical Guide for People Over 50, 1985; Edward R. Murrow: An American Original, 1988; Casey: From the OSS to the CIA, 1990; The Lives and Secrets of William J. Casey, 1990; Nuremberg: Infamy on Trial, 1994; Collaborator: Autobiography of General Colin L. Powell, 1995; (with C.L. Powell) My American Journey, 1995 in UK as A Soldier's Way: An Autobiography, 1995; Roosevelt's Secret War: FDR and World War II Espionage, 2001; Eleventh Month, Eleventh Day, Eleventh Hour: Armistice Day, 1918, World War I and Its Violent Climax, 2004; Franklin and Lucy: President Roosevelt, Mrs. Rutherfurd, and the Other Remarkable Women in His Life, 2008; Franklin and Lucy: Mrs. Rutherfurd and the Other Remarkable Women in Roosevelt's Life, 2009; Roosevelt's Centurions: FDR and the Commanders He Led to Victory in World War II, 2012. **Address:** c/o Karen Fink, Random House Inc., 1745 Broadway, New York, NY 10019-4368, U.S.A. **Online address:** jp@josephpersico.com

PERSON, James E(llis). American (born United States), b. 1955. **Genres:** Biography, Social Sciences, Biography, Philosophy. **Career:** Ford Motor Co., Michigan Truck Plant, part-time automotive worker, 1974-77; Bonded Security, security guard, 1978; Gale Group, editorial assistant, 1979, assistant editor, 1979-81, senior assistant editor, 1981-82, associate editor, 1982-84, co-editor, 1984-85, editor, 1985-95, senior editor, 1995-2001, content database manager, 2001-. **Publications:** The Unbought Grace of Life: Essays in Honor of Russell Kirk, 1994; Russell Kirk: A Critical Biography of a Conservative Mind, 1999; Earl Hamner: From Walton's Mountain to Tomorrow, 2005. Contributor to periodicals. **Address:** Gale, Cengage Learning, 27500 Drake Rd., Farmington Hills, MI 48331, U.S.A.

PESANTUBBEE, Michelene. (Michelene E. Pesantubbee). American (born United States), b. 1953?. **Genres:** Social Sciences, Women's Studies And Issues. **Career:** San Diego State University, lecturer, 1984-85; Bacone College, lecturer, 1988-89; University of Colorado, 1994, instructor, 1994, assistant professor, 1995-2003; Harvard Divinity School, lecturer, 2002; University of Iowa, Department of Religious Studies and American and Indian and Native studies, assistant professor, 2003-06, associate professor, 2006-. Writer. **Publications:** (As Michelene E. Pesantubbee) Choctaw Women in a Chaotic World: The Clash of Cultures in the Colonial Southeast, 2005; (contrib.) Millennialism, Persecution and Violence, 2000; (contrib.) Native Voices: American Indian Identity and Resistance, 2003; Religion and Peacebuilding, 2004. Contributor to journals. **Address:** Department of Religious Studies, University of Iowa, 312 Gilmore Hall, Iowa City, IA 52242, U.S.A. **Online address:** michelene-pesantubbe@uiowa.edu

PESANTUBBEE, Michelene E. *See* **PESANTUBBEE, Michelene.**

PESIC, Peter. American (born United States), b. 1948. **Genres:** Music, Writing/Journalism, Philosophy, Mathematics/Statistics, Physics. **Career:** Stanford Linear Accelerator Center, research assistant and associate, 1970-75; Stanford University, lecturer, 1976-80, Ronald James Alexander memorial lecturer on musicology, 2008; St. John's College, tutor, 1980-; University of North Carolina, Dorr lecturer, 2003; University of Nevada, Paul Leonard lecturer in philosophy, 2009. Writer. **Publications:** (Ed. and intro.) Lectures in Theoretical Physics, 1998; Labyrinth: A Search for the Hidden Meaning of Science, 2000; (ed. and intro.) Theory of Heat, 2001; Seeing Double: Shared Identities in Physics, Philosophy and Literature, 2002; Abel's Proof: An Essay on the Sources and Meaning of Mathematical Unsolvability, 2003; Sky in a Bottle, 2005; (ed. and intro.) General Investigations of Curved Surfaces, 2005; (intro.) Elementary Treatise on Electricity, 2005; (ed. and intro.) Beyond Geometry: Classic Papers from Riemann to Einstein, 2007; (ed. and intro.) Mind and Nature: Selected Writings on Philosophy, Mathematics and Physics, 2009. Contributor to periodicals. **Address:** St. John's College,

1160 Camino Cruz Blanca, Santa Fe, NM 87505, U.S.A. **Online address:** peter.pesic@sjcsf.edu

PESSAR, Patricia R. American (born United States) **Genres:** History, Travel/Exploration, Social Sciences, Theology/Religion. **Career:** Yale University, adjunct professor of American studies and anthropology. Writer. **Publications:** Kinship Relations of Production in the Migration Process: The Case of Dominican Emigration to the United States, 1982; (ed.) When Borders Don't Divide: Labor Migration and Refugee Movements in the Americas, 1988; Fronteras permeables: MigraciOn laboral y movimientos de refugiados en America, 1991; (with S. Grasmuck) Between Two Islands: Dominican International Migration, 1991; A Visa for a Dream: Dominicans in the United States, 1995; (ed.) Caribbean Circuits: New Directions in the Study of Caribbean Migration, 1997; From Fanatics to Folk: Brazilian Millenarianism and Popular Culture, 2004; Gendered Migrations and Geographies of Power: A Critical Feminist Engagement with Migration Studies, forthcoming. **Address:** Yale University, PO Box 208236, New Haven, CT 06520-8236, U.S.A. **Online address:** patricia.pessar@yale.edu

PESTANA, Carla Gardina. American (born United States), b. 1958. **Genres:** Cultural/Ethnic Topics, History, Theology/Religion. **Career:** John Carter Brown Library, research associate, 1985-86; Ohio State University, assistant professor, 1987-93, associate professor of history, 1993-, Lilly teaching fellow, 1990-92; Miami University, W.E. Smith professor of history, 2003-; Canterbury University, lecturer. Writer. **Publications:** Liberty of Conscience and the Growth of Religious Diversity in Early America, 1636-1786, 1986; Quakers and Baptists in Colonial Massachusetts, 1991; (ed. with S.V. Salinger) Inequality in Early America, 1999; The English Atlantic in an Age of Revolution, 1640-1661, 2004; Protestant Empire: Religion and the Making of the British Atlantic World, 2009. Works appear in anthologies. Contributor of articles to journals. **Address:** Department of History, Miami University, Rm. 271, Upham Hall, 501 E High St., Oxford, OH 45056, U.S.A. **Online address:** pestancg@muohio.edu

PETE, Eric E. American (born United States), b. 1968. **Genres:** Novels, Young Adult Fiction, Novellas/Short Stories. **Career:** E-fect Publishing, owner and publisher, 2000-. Writer. **Publications:** Real for Me, 2000; Someone's in the Kitchen, 2002; After Hours, 2002; Twilight Moods, 2002; Gets No Love, 2004; Don't Get It Twisted, 2005; Lady Sings the Cruels, 2006; Blow Your Mind, 2007; Sticks and Stones, 2009; Reality Check, 2009; Crushed Ice, 2010; Piano in the Dark, 2010. Works appear in anthologies. **Address:** E-fect Publishing, PO Box 2262, Spring, TX 77383-2262, U.S.A. **Online address:** heyeric@att.net

PETERS, Brian. *See* **STOKOE, E(dward) G(eorge).**

PETERS, Curtis H. American (born United States), b. 1942. **Genres:** Philosophy. **Career:** Concordia Senior College, lecturer and assistant professor of philosophy, 1970-76; Indiana University Southeast, Division of Humanities, dean; Department of Philosophy, assistant professor, 1976-80, associate professor, 1980-86, overseas study director, 1982-83, 1991-92, professor, 1986-, now professor emeritus; Grace Lutheran Church, assistant pastor; Concordia Lutheran Church, pastor, retired; Camp Cedarbrook, board director; Lutheran Family Services, board director; Writer. **Publications:** (Trans. with P.J. Bossert) Introduction to the Logical Investigations, 1975; Kant's Philosophy of Hope, 1993; Reasoning Well, forthcoming. **Address:** Indiana University Southeast, 4201 Grant Line Rd., New Albany, IN 47150, U.S.A. **Online address:** cpeters@ius.edu

PETERS, Elizabeth. *See* **MERTZ, Barbara (Louise) G(ross).**

PETERS, John Durham. American (born United States), b. 1958?. **Genres:** Philosophy, History, Law. **Career:** University of Iowa, assistant professor, 1986-92, associate professor, 1992-2000, professor of communication studies, 2000-01, F. Wendell Miller distinguished professor, 2002-10, director of graduate studies, 2003-04, 2006-08, chair, 2008-11, A. Craig Baird professor in communication studies, 2010-; Catholic University of Nijmegen, exchange professor, 1990; University of Athens, Department of Mass Media and Communication, Fulbright professor, 1998-99; University of London, Goldsmiths College, Leverhulme fellow, 1999-2000. Writer. **Publications:** Speaking into the Air: A History of the Idea of Peters Communication, 1999; (co-ed.) Are There Any? Should There Be? How about These?, 2003; (ed. with P. Simonson) Mass Communication and American Social Thought: Key Texts, 1919-1968, 2004; Courting the Abyss: Free Speech and the Liberal Tradition, 2005; Promiscuous Knowledge: The Information Age in Historical Perspective, forthcoming. Contributor to books and periodicals. **Address:** Department of Communication Studies, University of Iowa, 149 Becker Communication Studies Bldg., Iowa City, IA 52242-1498, U.S.A. **Online address:** john-peters@uiowa.edu

PETERS, Julie Anne. American (born United States), b. 1952. **Genres:** Children's Fiction, Young Adult Fiction. **Career:** Teacher, 1974-75; Tracom Corp., research assistant and computer programmer, 1975-84; Electronic Data Systems, computer systems designer, 1985-88; writer, 1989-; Jefferson County School District, educational assistant, 1990-94. **Publications:** The Stinky Sneakers Contest, 1992; Risky Friends, 1993; B.J.'s Billion-Dollar Bet, 1994; How Do You Spell Geek?, 1996; Revenge of the Snob Squad, 1998; Romance of the Snob Squad, 1999; Love Me, Love My Broccoli, 1999; Define Normal, 2000; A Snitch in the Snob Squad, 2001; Keeping You a Secret, 2003; Luna, 2004; Far from Xanadu, 2005; Between Mom and Jo, 2006; Grl2grl: Short Fictions, 2007; Rage: A Love Story, 2009; By the Time You Read This, I'll be Dead, 2010; She Loves You, She Loves You Not..., 2011. Contributor to periodicals. **Address:** 14 Twilight Dr., Lakewood, CO 80215, U.S.A. **Online address:** julie@julieannepeters.com

PETERS, Kate. British (born England) **Genres:** History. **Career:** University of Birmingham, lecturer in history; University College London, lecturer and course director, 1998-2005, honorary research associate; Cambridge University, Churchill College, teaching bi-fellow in history, 2007-. Writer. **Publications:** (Contrib.) The Emergence of Quaker Writing: Dissenting Literature in Seventeenth-Century England, 1994; (contrib.) Gender and Christian Religion, 1998; (with I. Green) The Cambridge History of the Book in Britain, vol. IV: 1557-1695, 2002; Print Culture and the Early Quakers, 2005; Can You Hear Me Now?: Harnessing The Power of Your Vocal Impact in 31 Days, 2006. Contributor to periodicals. **Address:** Churchill College, Cambridge University, Cambridge, CB CB3 0DS, England. **Online address:** mkp30@cam.ac.uk

PETERS, Lisa Westberg. American (born United States), b. 1951. **Genres:** Children's Fiction, Poetry, Children's Non-fiction. **Career:** Freelance writer and educator. **Publications:** The Sun, the Wind and the Rain, 1988; Serengeti, 1989; Tania's Trolls, 1989; The Condor, 1990; Good Morning, River!, 1990; Water's Way, 1991; Purple Delicious Blackberry Jam, 1992; This Way Home, 1994; When the Fly Flew In, 1994; Meg and Dad Discover Treasure in the Air, 1995; The Hayloft, 1995; October Smiled Back, 1996; Cold Little Duck, Duck, Duck, 2000; Our Family Tree: An Evolution Story, 2003; Earthshake: Poems from the Ground Up, 2003; We're Rabbits!, 2004; Sleepyhead Bear, 2006; Volcano Wakes Up!, 2010; Frankie Works the Night Shift, 2010. **Address:** 521 2nd St. SE, Ste. 402, Minneapolis, MN 55414, U.S.A. **Online address:** lisawpeters@gmail.com

PETERS, Margot (McCullough). (Margret Pierce). American (born United States), b. 1933. **Genres:** Novels, Literary Criticism And History, Theatre, Women's Studies And Issues, Biography, Young Adult Fiction. **Career:** Northland College, assistant professor of English, 1963-66; University of Wisconsin-Whitewater, professor of English, 1969-91, professor emeritus, 1991-; Dartmouth College, Kathe Tappe Vernon chair of biography, 1978; Harvard University, lecturer. Writer. **Publications:** Charlotte Bronte: Style in the Novel, 1973; Unquiet Soul: A Biography of Charlotte Bronte, 1975; (contrib.) The Genius of Bernard Shaw, 1979; Bernard Shaw and the Actresses, 1980; Mrs. Pat: The Life of Mrs. Patrick Campbell, 1984; The House of Barrymore, 1990; (as Margret Pierce) Wild Justice, 1995; (ed. with D.H. Laurence) Unpublished Shaw, 1996; May Sarton: A Biography, 1997; Design for Living: Lunt and Fontanne, 2003; Biography of Lorine Niedecker, 2011. **Address:** College of Letters & Sciences, University of Wisconsin, 800 W Main St., Whitewater, WI 53190-1790, U.S.A. **Online address:** margot@gdinet.com

PETERS, Michael (Adrian). American/New Zealander (born New Zealand), b. 1948. **Genres:** Education, Philosophy, Intellectual History, Public/Social Administration, Politics/Government, Social Sciences, Economics, Humanities, Humanities. **Career:** University of Auckland, Department of Education, university tutor, 1982-85, senior research fellow, 1985-88, lecturer in education, 1985-90, Research Unit for Research in Maori Education, member, 1993-, School of Education, senior lecturer, 1993-96, associate professor and head of cultural and policy studies, 1995-98, professor of education, 2000-03, adjunct professor, 2003-05, chair, 2000-03; Auckland Institute of Technology, research officer, 1989; Northern Region Tutor Training Centre, visiting research fellow, 1989; research analyst and consultant, 1985-90; University of Canterbury, lecturer in education, 1991-92; University of Glasgow, Faculty of education, research professor of education, 2000-03, professor of education, 2003-05, adjunct professor of education, 2005-08; Auckland University of Technology, adjunct professor of communication studies, 2000-05; University of Illinois, College of Education, professor of educational policy studies, 2005-; University of Hong Kong, visiting professor, 2005; Universidad Santiago de Cali, visiting professor, 2006; California State University, visiting professor, 2006-08; Royal Melbourne Institute of Technology, School of Fine Arts, adjunct professor, 2008-; Guangzhou University, School of Foriegn Studies, adjunct professor, 2010-. Writer. **Publications:** (Co-author) Counternarratives: Cultural Studies and Critical Pedagogies in Postmodern Spaces, 1996; (with J. Marshall) Individualism and Community: Education and Social Policy in the Postmodern Condition, 1996; Poststructuralism, Politics, and Education, 1996; (with P. Roberts) University Futures and the Politics of Reform, 1998; (with J. Marshall) Wittgenstein: Philosophy, Postmodernism, and Pedagogy, 1999; (with P. Roberts) University Futures and the Politics of Reform, 1999; Pós-estruturalismo e filosofia da diferença Uma introdução, 2000; Poststructuralism, Marxism and Neoliberalism: Between Theory and Politics, 2001; (with N. Burbules) Poststructuralism and Educational Research, 2004; (with T. Besley) Building Knowledge Cultures: Education and Development in the Age of Knowledge Capitalism, 2006; Knowledge Economy, Development and the Future of Higher Education, 2007; (with F. Kessl) New Europe, Old America, 2007; (with T. Besley) Por Que Foucault? Novas Diretrizes Para a Pesquisa Educacional, 2008; (with N. Burbules and P. Smeyers) Showing and Doing: Wittgenstein as a Pedagogical Philosopher, 2008; (with H. Biesta) Derrida, Politics and Pedagogy: Deconstructing the Humanities, 2008; (with T. Besley) Subjectivity and Truth: Foucault, Education and the Culture of the Self, 2008; (with P. Murphy and S. Marginson) Creativity and the Global Knowledge Economy, 2009; (with P. Murphy and S. Marginson) Imagination: Three Models of Imagination in the Age of the Knowledge Economy, 2010; (with P. Roberts) The Virtues of Openness, 2011; The Last Book of Postmodernism, 2011; Neoliberalism and After?, 2011; Educational Philosophy and Politics, 2012; (with P. Robert) Neoliberalism, Scholarship and Intellectual Life. EDITOR: Education and the Postmodern Condition, 1995; (with S. Webstee, W. Hope and J.D. Marshall) Critical Theory, Poststructuralism, and the Social Context, 1996; Cultural Politics and the University in Aotearoa/New Zealand, 1997; Naming the Multiple: Poststructuralism and Education, 1998; (with P. Roberts) Virtual Technologies and Tertiary Education: A National Vision?, 1998; (with J. Marshall) Education Policy, 1999; After the Disciplines: The Emergence of Cultural Studies, 1999; (with C. Lankshear, E. Gonzalez and A. de Alba) The Curriculum in the Postmodern Condition, 2000; (with J. Marshall and P. Smeyers) Nietzsche's Legacy for Education: Past and Present Values, 2001; (with P. Ghiraldelli, Jr.) Richard Rorty: Education, Philosophy and Politics, 2001; Heidegger, Education and Modernity, 2002; (with C. Lankshear and M. Olssen) Futures of Critical Theory: Dreams of Difference, 2003; (with C. Lankshear and M. Olssen) Critical Theory: Founders and Praxis, 2003; (with C. Lankshear and M. Olssen) Critical Theory and the Human Condition, 2003; (with P.P. Trifonas) Derrida, Deconstruction and Education, 2004; Education, Globalization and the State in the Age of Terrorism, 2004; (with P.P. Trifonas) Deconstructing Derrida: Tasks for the New Humanities, 2005; (with P. Smeyers) Postfoundationalist Themes in the Philosophy of Education: Festschrift for James D. Marshall, 2006; (with J. Freeman-Moir) Edutopias: New Utopian Thinking in Education, 2006; (with C. Kapitzke) Global Knowledge Cultures, 2007; (with T. Besley) Why Foucault? New Directions in Educational Research, 2007; (with H. Blee and A. Britton) Global Citizenship Education: Philosophy, Theory and Pedagogy, 2008; (with E.J. Gonzalez-Gaudiano) Environmental Education Today: Identity, Politics and Citizenship, 2008; (with T. Kvernbekk and H. Simpson) Military Pedagogies and Why They Matter, 2008; (with R. Britez) Open Education and Education for Openness, 2008; (with J. York) Leo Strauss, Political Philosophy and Education, 2008; (with M. Olssen) Varieties of Liberalism: Handbook on Educational Politics, 2008; (with C. Russell, P. Hart and A. Reid) Companion to Educational Research, 2008; (with M. Simons and M. Olssen) Re-Reading Education Policies: Studying the Policy Agenda of the 21 st Century, 2009; (with M. Olssen and T. Besley) Governmentality Studies in Education, 2009; Academic Writing, Philosophy and Genre, 2009, (with P. Murphy and S. Marginson) Global Creation: Space, Connection and Universities in the Age of the Knowledge Economy, 2010, (with D. Araya) Education in the Creative Economy, 2010; (with J. York) Leo Strauss, Education, and Political Thought, 2010; (with E.J. White) Bakhtinian Pedagogy, 2011; (with E. Bulut) Cognitive Capitalism, Education, and Digital Labor, 2011; (with M. Olssen, T. Besley and S. Weber) Governmentality, Education and the Rise of Neoliberalism. Contributor of articles to books and journals. **Address:** College of Education, University of Illinois, Education Bldg., 1310 S 6th St., Champaign, IL 61820-6925, U.S.A. **Online address:** mpet001@illinois.edu

PETERS, Rick. American (born United States) **Genres:** Industrial Relations, Homes/Gardens, Architecture, Crafts. **Career:** ShopNotes Magazine, editor; Woodsmith Magazine, editor. **Publications:** (With R. Hazelton) Ron Hazelton's House Calls: America's Most Requested Home Improvement Projects, 1999; Plumbing Basics, 2000; Flooring Basics, 2000; Air Tools: How to Choose, Use, and Maintain Them, 2000; Woodworker's Guide to Wood: Softwoods, Hardwoods, Plywoods, Composites, Veneers, 2000; Electrical Basics, 2000; Drills and Drill Presses: How to Choose, Use, and Maintain Them, 2000; Controlling Dust in the Workshop, 2000; Framing Basics, 2000; Woodworker's Hand Tools: An Essential Guide, 2001; Great Windows & Doors: A Step-by-Step Guide, 2001; Great Decks & Porches: A Step-by-Step Guide, 2001; Jointers and Planers: How to Choose, Use and Maintain Them, 2001; Woodworkers Power Tools: An Essential Guide, 2002; Building Garden & Patio Furniture, 2002; Popular Mechanics Router Fundamentals: The Complete Guide, 2004; Popular Mechanics Moneysmart Makeovers: Bathrooms, 2004; Sheds and Garages, 2004; Table Saw Fundamentals, 2004; Kitchens: Moneysmart Makeovers, 2004; Popular Mechanics Moneysmart Makeovers: Bathrooms, 2004; Popular Mechanics Workshop. Scroll Saw Fundamentals: The Complete Guide, 2005; Kitchen Makeovers, 2005; Popular Mechanics Moneysmart Makeovers: Living Spaces, 2005; Popular Mechanics: Lathe Fundamentals, 2005; Popular Mechanics MoneySmart Makeovers: Porches, Decks & Patios, 2005; Popular Mechanics Scroll Saw Fundamentals, 2005; Home How-to Handbook: Plumbing, 2006; Popular Mechanics Workshop. Miter Saw Fundamentals: The Complete Guide, 2006; Popular Mechanics Workshop: Band Saw Fundamentals: The Complete Guide, 2006; Home How-to-Handbook: Electrical, 2006; Remodeling for Easy-Access Living, 2006; Popular Mechanics Garage Makeovers: Adding Space Without Adding On, 2006; Home How-to Handbook: Tile, 2007; Popular Mechanics Jointer & Planer Fundamentals, 2007; Popular Mechanics Trim Carpentry, 2008; Home How-to Handbook: Trim, 2008. Contributor of articles to magazines. **Address:** c/o Author Mail, Hearst Books, 300 W 57th St., New York, NY 10019-3741, U.S.A.

PETERS, Robert. American (born United States), b. 1924. **Genres:** Novellas/Short Stories, Plays/Screenplays, Poetry, Gay And Lesbian Issues, Literary Criticism And History, Autobiography/Memoirs, Biography, Essays, Humor/Satire. **Career:** University of Idaho, instructor in English, 1951-52; Boston University, assistant professor of humanities, 1952-54; Ohio Wesleyan University, assistant professor of English, 1954-57; Wayne State University, associate professor of English, 1957-63; University of California-Riverside, associate professor, 1963-66, professor, 1966-68; University of California-Irvine, professor of English and comparative literature, 1968-92, professor emeritus, 1993-. Writer. **Publications:** Victorians on Literature and Art, 1961; The Crowns of Apollo: Swinburne's Principles of Literature and Art; A Study in Victorian Criticism and Aesthetics, 1965; Fuck Mother (play), 1970; Red Midnight Moon, 1974; Shaker Light, 1975; The Great American Poetry Bake-Off (criticism), 4 vols., 1979-91; Celebrities: In Memory of Margaret Dumont, Dowager of the Marx Brothers Movies (1890-1965), 1981; The Peters Black and Blue Guides to Literary Journals (criticism), 1984; Ludwig of Bavaria: A Verse Biography and a Play for Single Performer, 1986; Crunching Gravel (memoir): Growing Up in the Thirties, 1988; Hunting the Snark: A Compendium of New Poetic Terminology, 1989; Snapshots for a Serial Killer, 1992; Crunching Gravel: A Wisconsin Boyhood in the Thirties, 1993; Zapped (novellas), 1993; Where the Bee Sucks (criticism): Workers, Drones and Queens of Contemporary American Poetry, 1994; (with R. Peters) Nell's Story (memoir): A Woman from Eagle River, 1995; For You, Lili Marlene: A Memoir of World War II, 1995; Feather: A Child's Death and Life, 1997; Mad Ludwig of Bavaria and Other Short Plays, 2001. POETRY: Songs for a Son, 1967; The Sow's Head and Other Poems, 1968; Connections in the English Lake District: A Verse Suite, 1972; Byron Exhumed, 1973; Holy Cow: Parable Poems, 1974; Cool Zebras of Light, 1974; Gabriel: A Poem, 1974; Bronchial Tangle, Heart System, 1974; The Gift to Be Simple: A Garland for Ann Lee, 1975; The Poet as Ice-Skater, 1976; Gauguin's Chair, 1977; Hawthorne, 1977; The Drowned Man to the Fish, 1978; The Picnic in the Snow: Ludwig II of Bavaria, 1982, Great American Poetry Bake Off, 1982; Eighteen Poems, 1983; What Dillinger Meant to Me, 1983; Hawker, 1984; Kane, 1985; Shaker Light: Mother Ann Lee in America, 1987; Breughel's Pig,

1989; Haydon: An Artist's Life, 1989; Good Night, Paul, 1992; Love Poems for Robert Mitchum, 1992; Poems: Selected and New, 1992; Familial Love and Other Misfortunes, 2001; Makars' Dozens, 2006. EDITOR: America: The Diary of a Visit by E. Gosse, 1966; Pioneers of Modern Poetry, 1967; (with H.M. Schueller) The Letters of John Addington Symonds, 3 vols., 1967-69; Letters to a Tutor, 1988. **Address:** Department of English, University of California, 369 Humanities Instructional Bldg., 160 Aldrich Hall, Irvine, CA 92697, U.S.A. **Online address:** ptrachrp@aol.com

PETERS, Rudolph. Dutch (born Netherlands), b. 1943. **Genres:** Theology/Religion, Law, Bibliography, History. **Career:** University of Amsterdam, Department of Arabic and Islamic Studies, lecturer, 1968, associate professor, 1987-92, professor, 1992-, director of the Institute for Mediterranean Studies, 1992-99; Netherlands Institute for Archeology and Arabic Studies, director, 1982-87; American University, history teacher, 1983-87. Writer. **Publications:** Jihad in Mediaeval and Modern Islam: The Chapter on Jihad from Averroes' Legal Handbook Bidayat Al-mudjtahid and the Treatise Koran and Fighting by the Late Shaykh-al-Azhar, Mahmud Shaltut, 1977; Islam and Colonialism: The Doctrine of Jihad in Modern History, 1979; Proceedings of the Ninth Congress of the Union of Europeans, Arabs, and Islamics: Amsterdam, 1st to 7th September 1978, 1981; Van Vreemde Herkomst: Achtergronden Van Turkse En Marokkaanse Landgenoten, 1982; The Challenge of the Middle East: Middle Eastern Studies at the University of Amsterdam, 1982; Inspiratie En Kritiek: Moslimse Intellectuelen over De Islam, 1992; Hidden Futures: Death and Immortality in Ancient Egypt, Anatolia, the Classical, Biblical and Arabic-Islamic World, 1994; A Bibliography of Islamic Law, 1980-1993, 1994; Jihad in Classical and Modern Islam: A Reader, 1996, 2nd ed., 2008; Islamic Criminal Law in Nigeria, 2003; The Islamic School of Law: Evolution, Devolution, and Progress, 2005; Crime and Punishment in Islamic Law: Theory and Practice from the Sixteenth to the Twenty-first Century, 2005; Dispensing Justice in Islam: Qadis and Their Judgements, 2006. Contributor to journals. **Address:** Oudemanhuispoort 4-6, Amsterdam, 1012 CN, Netherlands. **Online address:** r.peters@uva.nl

PETERS, Shawn Francis. American (born United States), b. 1966. **Genres:** Adult Non-fiction, Social Sciences. **Career:** W.H. Freeman (publisher), Scientific American Books, assistant project editor, 1988-89; New Hampshire Premier, political reporter, 1989-92; University of New Hampshire, instructor, 1991-92; University of Massachusetts, Amherst College, writing instructor for summer programs, 1991-95; freelance journalist and editor, 1995-96; Des Moines Art Center, manager, 1996-97; University of Wisconsin, School of Journalism and Mass Communication, student services coordinator, 1997-2001, writing and study skills specialist; freelance journalist, 2001-. **Publications:** Judging Jehovah's Witnesses: Religious Persecution and the Dawn of the Rights Revolution, 2000; Defending the Faith: The Yoder Case and the First Amendment, 2003; Yoder Case: Religious Freedom, Education, and Parental Rights, 2003; When Prayer Fails: Faith Healing, Children, and the Law, 2007. Contributor to periodicals. **Address:** Center for Educational Opportunity, University of Wisconsin, 16 Ingraham Hall, 1155 Observatory Dr., Madison, WI 53706, U.S.A. **Online address:** shawn_peters@msn.com

PETERSEN, David. American (born United States), b. 1977. **Genres:** Children's Fiction, Graphic Novels, Picture/Board Books. **Career:** Artist and graphic novelist, 2006-. **Publications:** SELF-ILLUSTRATED MOUSE GUARD SERIES: Fall 1152, 2008; Winter 1152, 2009. CHILDREN'S BOOKS: Papa Bear, Rest in Peace Bailey Bear, 2004; The Mouse and the Cardinal, Maddie Plus the Monster, What Emma Will Be, 2005; Kate's Escape, 2005; (contrib.) Voices, 2004; (contrib.) Ye Olde Lore of Yore, vol. I, 2005. SELF-ILLUSTRATED: Snowy Valentine, 2011. **Address:** HarperCollins Publishers, 10 E 53rd St., New York, NY 10022, U.S.A. **Online address:** ericebon@hotmail.com

PETERSEN, P(eter) J(ames). American (born United States), b. 1941. **Genres:** Young Adult Fiction, Children's Fiction, Novels, Novellas/Short Stories, Picture/Board Books. **Career:** Shasta College, English instructor, 1964-2000, now retired. Writer. **Publications:** YOUNG ADULT FICTION: Would You Settle for Improbable?, 1981; Nobody Else Can Walk It for You, 1982; The Boll Weevil Express, 1983; Here's to the Sophomores, 1984; Corky and the Brothers Cool, 1985; Going for the Big One, 1986; The Freshman Detective Blues, 1987; Good-bye to Good Ol' Charlie, 1987; How Can You Hijack a Cave?, 1988; The Fireplug Is First Base, 1990; I Hate Camping, 1991; Liars, 1992; The Sub, 1993; I Want Answers and a Parachute, 1993; The Amazing Magic Show, 1994; I Hate Company, 1994; Some Days, Other Days, 1994; White Water, 1997; Can You Keep a Secret?, 1997; My Worst Friend, 1999; I Hate Weddings, 2000; Rising Water, 2002; Rob&Sara.com, 2004; Wild River, 2009. **Address:** 1243 Pueblo Ct., Redding, CA 96001, U.S.A. **Online address:** pjpetersen@charter.net

PETERSEN, Tore T. Norwegian (born Norway), b. 1954. **Genres:** History, Politics/Government. **Career:** Norwegian University of Science and Technology, professor of history. Writer. **Publications:** NONFICTION: The Middle East between the Great Powers: Anglo-American Conflict and Cooperation, 1952-7, 2000; (ed.) Controlling the Uncontrollable? The Great Powers in the Middle East, 2006; The Decline of the Anglo-American Middle East, 1961-1969: A Willing Retreat, 2006; Richard Nixon, Great Britain and the Anglo-American Alignment in the Persian Gulf and Arabian Peninsula: Making Allies out of Clients, 2009; (ed.) Challenging Retrenchment: The United States, Great Britain and the Middle East 1950-1980, 2010. **Address:** Norwegian University of Science and Technology, Edvard Bulls veg 1, Bldg 6, Level 4, Dragvoll, 7491, Norway. **Online address:** tore.petersen@hf.ntnu.no

PETERSILIA, Joan. American (born United States), b. 1951. **Genres:** Adult Non-fiction. **Career:** RAND Corp., senior researcher of criminal justice program, 1974-89, director of criminal justice program, 1989- 94, corporate fellow, 1992-94; Research in Corrections, founder and editor, 1985-91; University of California, School of Social Ecology, professor of criminology, law, and society, 1992-2009, Center for Evidence-Based Corrections, director, 2005-09; Stanford Law School, visiting professor, 2005-06, Adelbert H. Sweet professor of law and faculty co-director of Stanford criminal justice center, 2009-; California Policy Research Center, director; National Institute of Justice, special adviser; National Institute of Corrections, special adviser; Urban Institute, special adviser; RAND Corp., special adviser; Office of Juvenile Justice and Delinquency Prevention, special adviser. **Publications:** NONFICTION: (with J.M. Chaiken and P.W. Greenwood) The Criminal Investigation Process: A Summary Report, 1976; (with J.M. Chaiken and P.W. Greenwood) The Criminal Investigation Process, 1977; (with P.W. Greenwood and M.Lavin) Criminal Careers of Habitual Felons, 1977; (with P.W. Greenwood) Mandatory Prison Sentences: Their Projected Effects on Crime and Prison Populations, 1977; Which Inmates Participate in Prison Treatment Programs?, 1978; (with P.W. Greenwood and F.E. Zimring) Age, Crime, and Sanctions: The Transition from Juvenile to Adult Court, 1980; (with P. Honig and C. Hubay, Jr.) The Prison Experience of Career Criminals, 1980; Racial Disparities in the Criminal Justice System, 1983; (co-author) Granting Felons Probation: Public Risks and Alternatives, 1985; (with S. Turner) Guideline-Based Justice: The Implications for Racial Minorities, 1985; (with S. Turner and J. Peterson) Prison Versus Probation in California: Implications for Crime and Offender Recidivism, 1986; Expanding Options for Criminal Sentencing, 1987; The Influence of Criminal Justice Research, 1987; (with A. Abrahamse and J.Q. Wilson) Police Performance and Case Attrition, 1987; (with S.P. Klein and S. Turner) Racial Equity in Sentencing, 1988; (with S. Turner) Diverting Prisoners to Intensive Probation: Results of an Experiment in Oregon, 1990; (with S. Turner) Intensive Supervision for High-Risk Probationers: Findings from Three California Experiments, 1990; Reforming Probation and Parole in the 21st Century, 2002; When Prisoners Come Home: Parole and Prisoner Reentry, 2003. EDITOR: (with J.M. Byrne and A.J. Lurigio) Smart Sentencing: The Emergence of Intermediate Sanctions, 1992; (with J.Q. Wilson) Crime, 1995; Community Corrections: Probation, Parole, and Intermediate Sanctions, 1998; (with J. Lane) Criminal Justice Policy, 1998; (with J. Foote and N.A. Crowell) Crime Victims with Developmental Disabilities: Report of a Workshop, 2001; (with J.Q. Wilson) Crime: Public Policies for Crime Control, 2002; (with J.Q. Wilson) Crime and Public Policy, 2nd ed., 2010. Contributor of articles to books and journals. **Address:** Stanford Law School, Crown Quadrangle, 559 Nathan Abbott Way, Stanford, CA 94305-8610, U.S.A. **Online address:** petersilia@law.stanford.edu

PETERSON, Carol R. American (born United States), b. 1942. **Genres:** Botany, Medicine/Health, Homes/Gardens. **Career:** Norcliffe Foundation, manager, 1982-91; Fresh from the Garden, owner, 1993-; Mountain Garden Publishing Inc., president. Writer. **Publications:** Herbs You Can Master: A Primer for Herbal Enthusiasts, 1994; More Herbs You Can Master: Twelve Wondrous Plants for Extra Nutrition, Improved Health, Natural Beauty, 1999. **Address:** Fresh From the Garden, PO Box 98, Snoqualmie, WA 98065, U.S.A. **Online address:** herbmaster@comcast.net

PETERSON, Christian A. American (born United States), b. 1953. **Genres:** Photography, Bibliography, Art/Art History. **Career:** Minneapolis Institute of Arts, Department of Photography and New Media, staff, 1980-, associate curator of photographs. Writer. **Publications:** Pictorialism in America: The Minneapolis Salon of Photography, 1932-1946: The Minneapolis Institute of Arts, January 15-April 3, 1983, 1983; The Creative Camera Art of Max Thorek, 1984; Edward Steichen: The Portraits, 1984; Camera Work: Process & Image, 1985; Photographs Beget Photographs, 1987; The Lyrical Documents of Robert Gene Wilcox, 1988; (with D. Mrázková) The Modern Pictorialism of D.J. Ruzicka, 1990; (ed.) Alfred Stieglitz's Camera Notes, 1993; Index to the Annuals of the Pictorial Photographers of America, 1993; (contrib.) The Pictorial Artistry of Adolf Fassbender, 1994; (ed.) Index to the American Annual of Photography, 1996; After the Photo-Secession: American Pictorial Photography, 1910-1955, 1997; The Poetics of Vision: Photographs from the Collection of Harry M. Drake, 1997; Chaining the Sun: Portraits by Jeremiah Gurney, 1999; Walker Evans: The Collection of the Minneapolis Institute of Arts, 2003; Annotated Bibliography on Pictorial Photography: Selected Books From the Library of Christian A. Peterson, 2004; Quiet Landscapes of William B. Post, 2005; San Francisco Psychedelic, 2007; Masterpiece Photographs from the Minneapolis Institute of Arts: The Curatorial Legacy of Carroll T. Hartwell, 2008; Peter Henry Emerson and American Naturalistic Photography, 2008. Contributor to periodicals. **Address:** Department of Photography and New Media, Minneapolis Institute of Arts, 2400 3rd Ave. S, Minneapolis, MN 55404, U.S.A. **Online address:** cpeterson@artsmia.org

PETERSON, Chris(tine Louise). American (born United States), b. 1957. **Genres:** Technology, Engineering. **Career:** Alpha Industries, product engineer, 1979-82, product manager, 1983-85; American Information Exchange Co., director of marketplace operations, 1991-92; Foresight Institute, co-founder and vice president of public policy, 1997-, president, editor; Blue Ribbon Task Force on Nanotechnology, staff. **Publications:** (With G. Pergamit and K.E. Drexler) Unbounding the Future: The Nanotechnology Revolution, 1991; (with G. Pergamit) Leaping the Abyss: Putting Group Genius to Work, 1997; I Love the Internet, But I Want My Privacy, Too!: Simple Steps Anyone Can Take to Enjoy the Net Without Worry, 1998. **Address:** Foresight Institute, PO Box 61058, Palo Alto, CA 94306, U.S.A. **Online address:** peterson@foresight.org

PETERSON, Christmas. *See* **CHRISTMAS, Joyce.**

PETERSON, Cris. American (born United States), b. 1952. **Genres:** Children's Fiction, Children's Non-fiction, Young Adult Non-fiction, Young Adult Fiction, Animals/Pets, History. **Career:** Four Cubs Farm, chief financial officer, 1973-; Dairy farmer, writer and public speaker, 1973-; Local Historical Society, president, 1974-86; Universal Press Syndicate, nationally syndicated columnist, 1992-2000. **Publications:** Extra Cheese, Please!: Mozzarella's Journey from Cow to Pizza, 1994; Family Literacy Book, 1995; Harvest Year, 1996; Horsepower: The Wonder of Draft Horses, 1997; Century Farm: One Hundred Years on a Family Farm, 1999; Amazing Grazing, 2002; Wild Horses: Black Hills Sanctuary, 2003; Fantastic Farm Machines, 2006; Clarabelle: Making Milk and So Much More, 2007; Birchbark Brigade: A Fur Trade History, 2009; Seeds, Soil, Sun: Earth's Recipe for Food, 2010. Contributor to periodicals. **Address:** Four Cubs Farm, 23250 S Williams Rd., Grantsburg, WI 54840-9059, U.S.A. **Online address:** cris@crispeterson.com

PETERSON, Elmer. American (born United States), b. 1930. **Genres:** Literary Criticism And History, Writing/Journalism. **Career:** Colorado College, assistant professor, 1961-65, associate professor, 1965-70, professor of French, 1970-77, director of development and special projects, 1977-, dean of summer session, 1982-87, professor emeritus of French, 2000-. Writer. **Publications:** Tristan Tzara: Dada and Surrational Theorist, 1971; Z1 with Notes, 1972; (contrib.) Duchamp du signe, 1975; Dentelle Indented (poetry anthology), 1982. EDITOR: (with M. Sanouillet) Salt Seller, 1973; (with M. Sanouillet) Writings of Marcel Duchamp, 1989; Paris Dada, 2001. **Address:** Department of Romance Languages, Colorado College, 336 Armstrong Hall, 14 E Cache La Poudre St., Colorado Springs, CO 80903, U.S.A. **Online address:** epeterson@coloradocollege.edu

PETERSON, Eugene H. American (born United States), b. 1932. **Genres:** Theology/Religion, inspirational/Motivational Literature. **Career:** Christ Our King Presbyterian Church, founding pastor, 1962-91, retired, 1991; Regent College, James M. Houston professor of spiritual theology, professor of spiritual theology, through 2006, professor emeritus of spiritual theology, 2006-. Writer. **Publications:** Growing Up in Christ: A Guide for Families with Adolescents, 1976; A Year with the Psalms: 365 Meditations and Prayers, 1979; Five Smooth Stones for Pastoral Work, 1980; A Long Obedience in the Same Direction: Discipleship in an Instant Society, 1980; Traveling Light: Reflections on the Free Life, 1982; Run with the Horses: The Quest for Life at Its Best, 1983, 2nd ed., 2009; Earth and Altar: The Community of Prayer in a Self-Bound Society, 1985; Forces Concealed in Quiet: Meditations from the Writings of John the Apostle, 1985; Weddings, Funerals, and Special Events, 1987; Growing Up with Your Teenager, 1987; Working the Angles: The Shape of Pastoral Integrity, 1987; Reversed Thunder: The Revelation of John and the Praying Imagination, 1988; Traveling Light: Modern Meditations on St. Paul's Letter of Freedom, 1988; Answering God: The Psalms as Tools for Prayer, 1989; The Contemplative Pastor: Returning to the Art of Spiritual Direction, 1989; (ed.) Stories for the Christian Year, 1992; Under the Unpredictable Plant: An Exploration in Vocational Holiness, 1992; The Contemplative Pastor: Returning to the Art of Spiritual Direction, 1993; Praying with Jesus: A Year of Daily Prayers and Reflections on the Words and Actions of Jesus, 1993; Praying with the Psalms: A Year of Daily Prayers and Reflections on the Words of David, 1993; Where Your Treasure Is: Psalms That Summon You from Self to Community, 1993; Like Dew Your Youth: Growing Up with Your Teenager, 1994; Praying with Moses: A Year of Daily Prayers and Reflections on the Words and Actions of Moses, 1994; Praying with the Early Christians: A Year of Daily Prayers and Reflections on the Words of the Early Christians, 1994; Praying with Paul: A Year of Daily Prayers and Reflections on the Words and Actions of Paul, 1995; Praying with the Prophets: A Year of Daily Prayers and Reflections on the Words and Actions of the Prophets, 1995; Perseverance, 1996; Excellence, 1996; Take and Read: Spiritual Reading: An Annotated List, 1996; Leap over a Wall: Earthy Spirituality for Everyday Christians, 1997; Subversive Spirituality, 1997; Not a Day Goes by without His Unfolding Grace, 1998; The Wisdom of Each Other: A Conversation between Spiritual Friends, 1998; The Psalms: An Artist's Impression, 1999; First and Second Samuel, 1999; The Unnecessary Pastor: Rediscovering the Call, 2000; A Long Obedience in the Same Direction: Discipleship in an Instant Society, 2000; Allegories of Heaven: An Artist Explores the Greatest Story Ever Told, 2002; (ed. with E. Griffin) Epiphanies: Stories for the Christian Year, 2003; (with A. Kaai) In a Word, 2003; Psalm 67: For SATB Chorus, Congregation, Optional Descant and Organ, 2004; The Christmas Troll, 2004; The Power of a Mother: Words to Speak and Pray from the Message, 2005; Christ Plays in Ten Thousand Places: A Conversation in Spiritual Theology, 2005; Eat This Book: A Conversation in the Art of Spiritual Reading, 2006; Living the Resurrection: The Risen Christ in Everyday Life, 2006; NIV, The Message: Parallel Bible, 2006; A Year with Jesus: Daily Readings and Meditations, 2006; The Jesus Way: A Conversation on the Ways That Jesus Is the Way, 2007; Conversations: The Message With Its Translator, 2007; The Message Remix, 2007; The Message-NKJV Parallel Bible, 2007; (with P. Santucci) The Jesus Way Study Guide, 2007; The Invitation: A Simple Guide to the Bible, 2008; Tell It Slant: A Conversation on the Language of Jesus in His Stories and Prayers, 2008; (with P. Santucci) Tell It Slant: Study Guide, 2008; Practice Resurrection: A Conversation on Growing Up in Christ, 2010; The Pastor: A Memoir, 2011. THE MESSAGE SERIES: The New Testament in Contemporary English, 1993; The Message: The New Testament with Psalms, 1994; The Message: New Testament with Psalms and Proverbs, 1995; The Message: Proverbs, 1995; The Message: Job: Led by Suffering to the Heart of God, 1996; The Message: The Wisdom Books, 1996; Living the Message: Daily Reflections with Eugene H. Peterson, 1996, rev. ed. as Living the Message: Daily Help for Living the God-Centered Life, 2003; The Message Promise Book, 1997; The Message: Sayings of Jesus, 1998; The Message: The Prophets, 2000; The Message: The Old Testament Books of Moses, 2001; The Message: The History Books, 2002; The Message: The Gospel of John in Contemporary Language, 2003; The Message: The New Testament in Contemporary Language, 2003; The Message: The Bible in Contemporary Language, 2003; Are You Talking to Me, God?: Guidelines for Life from the Message, 2004; God's Message for Each Day: Wisdom from the Word of God, 2004; God's Message of Christmas Love, 2004; The Power of a Blessing: Words to Speak and Pray from the Message, 2004; The Power of a Friend: Words to Speak and Pray from the Message, 2005; The Power of a Prayer: Words to Speak and Pray from the Message, 2005; The Message Three-Way Concordance: Word, Phrase, Synonym, 2006; (contrib.) The Great Pursuit: The Message for Those in Search of God, 2007; My First Message: A Devotional Bible for Kids, 2007; The Message of Leadership: 31 Essential Insights from Proverbs, 2007. **Address:** Regent College, 5800 University Blvd., Vancouver, BC V6T 2E4, Canada.

PETERSON, Fred W. American (born United States), b. 19[illegible]. **Genres:** Homes/Gardens, Architecture, History. **Career:** University of Minnesota, professor of art history, 1961-92, professor emeritus, 1993-. Writer. **Publications:** Homes in the Heartland: Balloon Frame Farmhouses of the Upper Midwest, 1850-1920, 1992; Building Community, Keeping the Faith: German Catholic Vernacular Architecture in a Rural Minnesota Parish, 1998. **Address:** Department of Art History, University of Minnesota, 600 E 4th St., Morris, MN 56267, U.S.A.

PETERSON, Jean Sunde. American (born United States), b. 1941. **Genres:** Human Relations/Parenting, Education, Psychology, Education, Cultural/Ethnic Topics. **Career:** Teacher, 1962-66, 1972-91; Truman State University, counselor of education, 1995-99; Purdue University, counselor of education, 1999-, professor of educational studies. Writer. **Publications:** Talk with Teens about Self and Stress: 50 Guided Discussions for School and Counseling Groups, 1993; Talk with Teens about Feelings, Family, Relationships, and the Future: 50 Guided Discussions for School and Counseling Groups, 1995; (with J.M. Littrell) Portrait and Model of a School Counselor, 2005; (ed. with S. Mendaglio) Models of Counseling Gifted Children, Adolescents, and Young Adults, 2007; The Essential Guide to Talking with Teens: Ready-to-Use Discussions for School and Youth Groups, 2007; The Essential Guide to Talking with Gifted Teens: Ready-to-Use Discussions About Identity, Stress, Relationships, and More, 2008; Gifted at Risk: Poetic Portraits, 2009; Talk with Teens about What Matters to Them, 2011. Contributor to books, journals and magazines. **Address:** Department of Educational Studies, Purdue University, Beering Hall of Liberal Arts and Education, 100 N University St., West Lafayette, IN 47907-2098, U.S.A. **Online address:** jeanp@purdue.edu

PETERSON, Keith R. *See* **KLAVAN, Andrew.**

PETERSON, Michael L. American (born United States), b. 1950. **Genres:** Philosophy, Theology/Religion. **Career:** Roberts Wesleyan College, professor of philosophy, 1974-78; Asbury College, professor of philosophy and chair of the department, 1978-96, 1997-, Lilly Transformations Project, director, 2003-; Faith and Philosophy: Journal of the Society of Christian Philosophers, managing editor, 1984-; Trinity Western University, doctor of human letters honoris causa, 2010; Asbury Theological Seminary, professor of philosophy of religion, 2011-. **Publications:** Evil and the Christian God, 1982; Philosophy of Education: Issues and Options, 1986; (co-author) Reason and Religious Belief: An Introduction to the Philosophy of Religion, 1990, 4th ed., 2008; God and Evil: An Introduction to the Issues, 1998; With All Your Mind: A Christian Philosophy of Education, 2001. EDITOR/CO-EDITOR: A Spectrum of Thought, 1982; The Problem of Evil: Selected Readings, 1992; Philosophy of Religion: Selected Readings, 1996, 4th ed., 2010; Exploring the Philosophy of Religion Series, 2001; Contemporary Debates in Philosophy of Religion, 2003. Contributor to philosophy journals. Works appear in anthologies. **Address:** Department of Philosophy of Religion, Asbury Theological Seminary, 1 Macklem Dr., Wilmore, KY 40390, U.S.A. **Online address:** mike.peterson@asburyseminary.edu

PETERSON, Peter G. American (born United States), b. 1926. **Genres:** Economics, Social Sciences. **Career:** Market Facts Inc., market analyst, 1947-49, associate director, 1949, executive vice president, 1951; McCann-Erickson (advertising firm), director of marketing services, 1953, vice president, 1954, general manager of Chicago office, 1955, director and assistant, 1957; Bell and Howell, executive vice president and director, 1958, president, 1961, chief executive officer and chairman, 1963-71; Council on International Economic Policy, executive director, 1971; U.S. Government, secretary of commerce, 1972-73; Lehman Brothers Kuhn Loeb Inc., chief executive officer and chair of the board, 1973-84; The Blackstone Group, chairman, senior chairman and co-founder, 1985-2008; Federal Reserve Bank of New York, chair, 2000-04; Council on Foreign Relation, chairman, through 2007, now chairman emeritus; Peter G. Peterson Foundation, founder and chairman, 2008-; Sony Corp., director; 3M Co., director; Federated Department Stores, director; Black & Decker, director; The Continental Group, director; General Foods, director; RCA, director; Minnesota Mining and Manufacturing Co, director; Rockefeller Center Properties Inc., director; Peterson Institute for International Economics, founding chairman. Writer. **Publications:** The United States in a Changing World Economy, 1971; U.S.-Soviet Commercial Relationships in a New Era, 1972; Deficits, Debts and Demographics: Three Fundamentals Affecting Our Long-Term Economic Future, 1985; (with N. Howe) On Borrowed Time: How the Growth in Entitlement Spending Threatens America's Future, 1988; The 1990s: Decade of Reckoning or a Decade of a New Partnership?, 1991; Facing Up: How To Rescue the Economy from Crushing Debt and Restore the American Dream, 1993; Facing Up: Paying Our Nation's Debt and Saving Our Children's Future, 1994; Will America Grow up Before it Grows Old?: How the Coming Social Security Crisis Threatens You, Your Family and Your Country, 1996; Gray Dawn: How the Coming Age Wave Will Transform America: And the World, 1999; (with C.A. Hills) Safeguarding Prosperity in a Global Financial System: The Future International Financial Architecture: Report of an Independent Task Force Sponsored by the Council on Foreign Relations, 1999; (co-author) Finding America's Voice, 2003; Running on Empty: How the Democratic and Republican Parties are Bankrupting Our Future and What Americans Can Do About It, 2004; Education of an American Dreamer: How a Son of Greek Immigrants Learned His Way from a Nebraska Diner to Washington, Wall Street and Beyond, 2009. Contributor to periodicals. **Address:** Peter G. Peterson Foundation, 1383 Ave. of the Americas, PO Box 278, New York, NY 10019, U.S.A.

PETERSON, Richard Austin. *See* Obituaries.

PETERSON, Richard S(cot). American/Scottish (born Scotland), b. 1938. **Genres:** Literary Criticism And History, Language/Linguistics, Poetry. **Career:** Princeton University, instructor in English, 1966-69, assistant professor of English, 1969-72; University of Virginia, lecturer in English, 1972-75; Yale University, assistant professor of English, 1976-80, British Studies Program, director of undergraduate studies, 1978-80; University of Connecticut, assistant professor, associate professor, 1980-87, professor of English, 1987-, Academic Placement for English Graduate Students, head, 1982-85, 1987-88, 1990-92, Faculty Research Foundation, Humanities and Fine Arts Panel, head, 1985-86, English Department, graduate coordinator, 1988-89, professor of English and comparative literature, 1990-. Writer. **Publications:** Imitation and Praise in the Poems of Ben Jonson, 1981, 2nd ed., 2011; (ed.) Essays in Art and Literature, 1986; (ed.) Envies Scourge and Vertues Honour, 2010; (ed.) Jonsonian Soundings: Essays on the Poems and Masques, 2011. Contributor to periodicals and journals. **Address:** Department of English, University of Connecticut, 215 Glenbrook Rd., PO Box U-4025, Storrs, CT 06269-4025, U.S.A. **Online address:** richard.peterson@uconn.edu

PETERSON, Tracie. (Janelle Jamison). American (born United States), b. 1959?. **Genres:** Westerns/Adventure, Young Adult Non-fiction, Novels. **Career:** Bethany House Publishers, writer; Kansas Christian (newspaper), columnist. **Publications:** HEARTSONG PRESENTS SERIES: A Place to Belong, 1992; Perfect Love, 1993; Tender Journeys, 1993; (as Janelle Jamison) A Light in the Window, 1993; (as Janelle Jamison) The Willing Heart, 1993; Destiny's Road, 1993; (as Janelle Jamison) Beyond Today, 1994; Iditarod Dream, 1994; If Given a Chance, 1994; Kingdom Divided, 1995; The Heart's Calling, 1994; Forever Yours, 1994; Angel's Cause, 1995; Alas, My Love, 1995; Come Away, My Love, 1996; If Only, 1996; My Valentine, 1996; Wings like Eagles, 1996; A Wing and a Prayer, 1996; (with J. Peterson) Crossroads, 1997; Logan's Lady, 1997; Wings of the Dawn, 1997; The House on Windridge, 1998; Five Geese Flying, 1998; Stormy Weather, 1999. RIBBONS OF STEEL SERIES (with J. Pella): Distant Dreams, 1996; A Hope Beyond, 1997; A Promise for Tomorrow, 1998. ANTHOLOGIES: (co-author) Christmas Treasures, 1996; (co-author) An Old-Fashioned Christmas, 1997; (co-author) Summer Dreams, 1997; Alaska, 1998; (co-author) Season of Love, 1998; (co-author) Spring's Promise, 1999; Colorado Wings, 2000; Tidings of Peace, 2000; New Mexico Sunrise, 2001; New Mexico Sunset, 2001; (with J.M. Miller) Kansas, 2001; Julotta, 2002. NOVELS: Entangled, 1997; Controlling Interests, 1998; Framed, 1998; Seasons of Love, 1998; A Slender Thread, 2000; The Long-Awaited Child, 2001; Eyes of the Heart, 2002; Silent Star, 2003; Castles, 2004; What She Left for Me, 2005; One More Sunrise, 2007; Where My Heart Belongs, 2007. WESTWARD CHRONICLES SERIES: A Shelter of Hope, 1998; Hidden in a Whisper, 1999; A Veiled Reflection, 2000. NON-FICTION: A Celebration of Life, 1999; (with A. Bottke and D. O'Brian) I Can't Do It All, 2006. RIBBONS WEST SERIES (with J. Pella): Westward the Dream, 1999; Separate Roads, 1999; Ties That Bind, 2000. SHANNON SAGA SERIES (with J.S. Bell): City of Angels, 2001; Angels Flight, 2001; Angel of Mercy, 2002. YUKON QUEST SERIES: Treasures of the North, 2001; Ashes and Ice, 2001; Rivers of Gold, 2002. DESERT ROSES SERIES: Shadows of the Canyon, 2002; Across the Years, 2003; Beneath a Harvest Sky, 2003. BELLS OF LOWELL SERIES (with J. Miller): Daughter of the Loom, 2003; A Fragile Design, 2003; These Tangled Threads, 2003. HEIRS OF MONTANA SERIES: Land of My Heart, 2004; The Coming Storm, 2004; To Dream Anew, 2004; The Hope Within, 2005. LIGHTS OF LOWELL SERIES (with J. Miller): A Tapestry of Hope, 2004; A Love Woven True, 2005; The Pattern of Her Heart, 2005. ALASKAN QUEST

SERIES: Summer of the Midnight Sun, 2006; Under the Northern Lights, 2006; Whispers of Winter, 2006. LADIES OF LIBERTY SERIES: A Lady of High Regard, 2007; A Lady of Hidden Intent, 2008; A Lady of Secret Devotion, 2008. BROADMOOR LEGACY SERIES (with J. Miller): A Daughter's Inheritance, 2008; An Unexpected Love, 2008; A Surrendered Heart, 2009. BRIDES OF GALLATIN COUNTY SERIES: A Promise to Believe in, 2008; A Love to Last Forever, 2009; A Dream to Call My Own, 2009. SONG OF ALASKA: Dawn's Prelude, 2009; Morning's Refrain, 2010; Twilight's Serenade, 2010. STRIKING A MATCH: Embers of Love, 2010; Hearts Aglow, 2011; Hope Rekindled, 2011; To Have and to Hold, 2011; House of Secrets, 2011; Chasing the Sun, 2012. Contributor to periodicals. **Address:** Baker Publishing Group, 6030 E Fulton Rd., 11400 Hampshire Ave. S, Ada, MI 49301, U.S.A. **Online address:** tracie@traciepeterson.com

PETERSON, V. Spike. American (born United States), b. 1946. **Genres:** International Relations/Current Affairs, Politics/Government, Women's Studies And Issues, Economics. **Career:** American University, teaching assistant, 1982-83, adjunct assistant professor of western tradition, women and development, and world politics, 1989-90; University of Southern California, adjunct assistant professor of gender and international relations theory, 1989; University of Arizona, Department of Political Science, assistant professor, 1990-96, associate professor, 1996-2004, professor, 2004-, Center for Latin American Studies, faculty, School of Government and Public Policy, professor; London School of Economics, Gender Institute, associate fellow, 2008-11. Writer. **Publications:** Clarification and Contestation: Exploring the Integration of Feminist and International Relations Theory, 1989; (ed.) Gendered States: Feminist (Re)Visions of International Relations Theory, 1992; (with A.S. Runyan) Global Gender Issues, 1993, 3rd ed. as Global Gender Issues in the New Millennium, 2010; A Critical Rewriting of Global Political Economy: Integrating Reproductive, Productive, and Virtual Economies, 2003. Contributor of articles to journals. **Address:** Department of Political Science, University of Arizona, Rm. 314C, Social Sciences Bldg., PO Box 210027, Tucson, AZ 85721-0027, U.S.A. **Online address:** spikep@email.arizona.edu

PETERSON, Wallace C(arroll). American (born United States), b. 1921. **Genres:** Air/Space Topics, Economics, Military/Defense/Arms Control, Politics/Government. **Career:** Lincoln Journal, reporter, 1946; University of Nebraska, Department of Economics, instructor, 1951-54, assistant professor, 1954-57, associate professor, 1957-62, professor, 1962-66, chair, 1965-75, George Holmes professor of economics, 1966-91, George Holmes professor emeritus of economics, 1991-; Fulbright lecturer in Greece, 1964-65. Writer. **Publications:** The Welfare State in France, 1960; Income, Employment, and Economic Growth, 1962, (with P.S. Estenson) 8th ed., 1996; Personal Income in Nebraska and Nebraska Counties: 1950-1962, 1965; Elements of Economics, 1973; Our Overloaded Economy: Inflation, Unemployment, and the Crisis in American Capitalism, 1982; (ed.) Market Power and the Economy: Industrial, Corporate, Governmental, and Political Aspects, 1988; Transfer Spending, Taxes, and the American Welfare State, 1991; Silent Depression: The Fate of the American Dream, 1994; (with F.R. Strobel) The Coming Class War and How to Avoid It: Rebuilding the American Middle Class, 1999; Social Security Primer: What Every Citizen Should Know, 1999; Pylon: The Omaha Air Races, 1931-1934, 2002. **Address:** Department of Economics, University of Nebraska, College of Business 340, PO Box 880489, Lincoln, NE 68588-0489, U.S.A.

PETIEVICH, Gerald. American (born United States), b. 1944. **Genres:** Mystery/Crime/Suspense, Plays/Screenplays, Novels, Criminology/True Crime. **Career:** Writer. **Publications:** Money Men, 1981; One Shot Deal, 1983; To Die in Beverly Hills, 1983; To Live and Die in L.A., 1984; The Quality of the Informant, 1985; Shakedown, 1988; Earth Angels, 1989; Paramour, 1991; The Sentinel, 2003. **Address:** 551 Twin Palms Dr., San Gabriel, CA 91775, U.S.A. **Online address:** gpetievich@aol.com

PETIT, Susan. American (born United States), b. 1945. **Genres:** Literary Criticism And History, History. **Career:** College of San Mateo, professor of English and French, 1968-2008, president of academic senate, 1978-79, Writing Center, staff; San Mateo County Community College District, president of academic senate, 1981-82; Academic Senate for California Community Colleges, publications editor, 1984-86. **Publications:** Michel Tournier's Metaphysical Fictions, 1991; Françoise Mallet-Joris, 2001, trans. as Femme de papier: Françoise Mallet-Joris et son oeuvre. Works appear in anthologies. Contributor of articles and reviews to journals. **Address:** College of San Mateo, 1700 W Hillsdale Blvd., San Mateo, CA 94402, U.S.A. **Online address:** petit@smccd.edu

PETKOVŠEK, Marko. Slovenian (born Slovenia), b. 1955. **Genres:** Mathematics/Statistics. **Career:** Institute Jozef Stefan, mathematician, 1976-78, 1987-88; University of Ljubljana, associate professor of mathematics, Institute of Mathematics, Physics and Mechanics, researcher, 1980-, professor; Wolfram Research Inc., mathematician, 1989; Carnegie-Mellon University, visiting scientist, 1995-96, adjunct assistant professor, 1996-. Writer. **Publications:** (With H.S. Wilf and D. Zeilberger) A=B, 1996. Contributor to journals. **Address:** Department of Mathematics, University of Ljubljana, Rm. 4.09, Jadranska 21/IV, Jadranska Ul. 19, Ljubljana, 1000, Slovenia. **Online address:** marko.petkovsek@fmf.uni-lj.si

PETLEY, Dexter. French/British (born England), b. 1955. **Genres:** Novels, Young Adult Fiction. **Career:** English teacher, 1979-81; British Broadcasting Corp., World Service, journalist and broadcaster, 1981-85; full-time writer, 1995-. **Publications:** NOVELS: Little Nineveh, 1995; Joyride, 1999; White Lies, 2003; One True Void, 2008. **Address:** c/o Mark Stanton, Jenny Brown Associates, 33 Argyle Pl., Edinburgh, EH9 1JT, Scotland. **Online address:** dexter@dexterpetley.com

PETRAKIS, Harry Mark. American (born United States), b. 1923. **Genres:** Novels, Plays/Screenplays, Young Adult Fiction, Biography, Novellas/Short Stories, Science Fiction/Fantasy. **Career:** Freelance writer and lecturer, 1960-; Indiana University Writer's Conference, teacher at writing workshops, 1964-65, 1970, 1974; Ohio University, McGuffey visiting lecturer, 1971; Chicago Public Library, writer-in-residence, 1976-77; Chicago Board of Education, writer-in-residence, 1976-77; Illinois Wesleyan University, teacher at writing workshops, 1978-79; Ball State University, teacher at writing workshops, 1978, 1980; University of Wisconsin, teacher at writing workshops, 1978-80; University of Rochester, teacher at writing workshops, 1979-80; San Francisco State University, Nikos Kazantzakis professor, 1992, writer-in-residence. **Publications:** FICTION: Lion at My Heart, 1959; The Odyssey of Kostas Volakis, 1963; Pericles on 31st Street, 1965; A Dream of Kings, 1966; The Waves of Night and Other Stories, 1969; Stelmark: A Family Recollection, 1970; In the Land of Morning, 1973; Hour of the Bell: A Novel of the 1821 Greek War of Independence Against the Turks, 1976; A Petrakis Reader, 1978; Nick the Greek, 1979; Days of Vengeance, 1983; Reflections: A Writer's Life-A Writer's Work, 1983; Collected Stories, 1987; Ghost of the Sun: A Novel, 1990; Tales of the Heart: Dreams and Memories of a Lifetime, 1999; Twilight of the Ice, 2003; The Orchards of Ithaca, 2004. OTHERS: The Founder's Touch: The Life of Paul Galvin of Motorola (biography), 1965, 3rd ed., 1991; (contrib.) The Writer's World, 1969; Stelmark: A Family Recollection, 1970; Reflections: A Writer's Life, a Writer's Work, 1984; Legends of Glory and Other Stories, 2005; The Hour of the Bell, 2008; Shepherds of Shadows, 2008; Cavafy's Stone and Other Village Tales, 2010. Contributor of articles to periodicals. **Address:** Duneland Books, PO Box 2028, Chesterton, IN 46304, U.S.A. **Online address:** info@harrymarkpetrakis.com

PETRE, William. *See* **ADAMS, Will.**

PETRIE, Anne. Canadian (born Canada), b. 1946. **Genres:** History, Local History/Rural Topics, Young Adult Non-fiction, Literary Criticism And History. **Career:** CBC-TV, Midday, regular contributor, 1980, 24 Hours Late Night, host, 1985-89. Writer. **Publications:** Ethnic Vancouver, 1982; Vancouver Secrets, 1984; More Vancouver Secrets, 1985; Gone to an Aunt's: Remembering Canada's Homes for Unwed Mothers, 1998. Contributor to periodicals. **Address:** The Writers Union of Canada, 40 Wellington St. E, 3rd Fl., Toronto, ON M5E 1C7, Canada.

PETRIE, Duncan. British/New Zealander/Scottish (born Scotland), b. 1963. **Genres:** Film, Documentaries/Reportage. **Career:** British Film Institute, research officer, 1990-95; University of Strathclyde, lecturer, 1992, 1993, 1994; London Consortium, faculty, 1993-; University of Glasgow, visiting lecturer, 1994; University of Exeter, senior lecturer in English and American studies, 1996-, Bill Douglas Centre for the History of Cinema and Popular Culture, director, 1996-2002, School of English, reader in film, 2001-; South West Media Development Agency, vice chairperson of board of directors, 1996-, chair; University of Warwick, seminar presenter, 1998; University of Auckland, Department of Film, Television and Media Studies, professor and department head, 2004-09; University of York, Department of Theatre, Film and Television, professor, 2009-; University Exeter, School of English, faculty; Mixed

Cinema Network, co-supervisor. Writer. **Publications:** Creativity and Constraint in the British Film Industry, 1991; The British Cinematographer, 1996; Screening Scotland, 2000; Contemporary Scottish Fictions: Film, Television and the Novel, 2004; (with D. Stuart) A Coming of Age: Thirty Years of New Zealand Film, 2008. EDITOR: (intro.) Screening Europe: Image and Identity in Contemporary European Cinema, 1992; (intro.) New Questions of British Cinema, 1992; (with E. Dick and A. Noble) Bill Douglas: A Lanternist's Account, 1993; Cinema and the Realms of Enchantment, 1993; (with J. Willis) Television and the Household: Reports from the BFI's Audience Tracking Study, 1995; (with C. MacCabe) New Scholarship from BFI Research, 1996; Inside Stories: Diaries of British Film-Makers at Work, 1996; (with R. Kruger) A Paul Rotha Reader, 1999; (with M. Hjort) Cinema of Small Nations, 2007. Contributor to periodicals. **Address:** Department of Theatre, Film & Television, University of York, Baird Ln., Heslington, NY YO10 5DD, England. **Online address:** dp547@york.ac.uk

PETRIE, Paul (James). American (born United States), b. 1928. **Genres:** Poetry. **Career:** University of Rhode Island, instructor, 1959-62, assistant professor, 1962-66, associate professor, 1966-69, professor of English, 1969-90, professor emeritus of English, 1990-. Writer. **Publications:** Confessions of a Non-Conformist, 1963; The Race with Time and the Devil, 1965; The Leader: For Martin Luther King, Jr., 1968; From under the Hill of Night: Poems, 1969; The Idol, 1973; The Academy of Goodbye, 1974; Light from the Furnace Rising, 1978; Time Songs, 1979; Not Seeing Is Believing, 1983; Strange Gravity: Songs, Physical and Metaphysical, 1984; The Runners, 1988; Rooms of Grace: New and Selected Poems by Paul Petrie, 2005. **Address:** Department of English, University of Rhode Island, 114 Swan Hall, 60 Upper College Rd., Kingston, RI 02881, U.S.A.

PETRINO, Elizabeth. American (born United States), b. 1962. **Genres:** Biography. **Career:** Louisiana Tech University, assistant professor of English; Wake Forest University, assistant professor of English; Fairfield University, assistant professor of English, 2000-05, associate professor English-American literature, 2005-. Writer. **Publications:** Emily Dickinson and Her Contemporaries: Women's Verses in America, 1820-1885, 1998; (ed. with J.M. Boryczka) Jesuit and Feminist Education: Intersections in Teaching and Learning in the Twenty-first Century, 2011. **Address:** Department of English, Fairfield University, Rm. 109, Donnarumma Hall, 1073 N Benson Rd., Fairfield, CT 06824, U.S.A. **Online address:** epetrino@fairfield.edu

PETRO, Nicolai N. American/German (born Germany), b. 1958. **Genres:** Politics/Government. **Career:** University of Virginia, instructor, 1979, White Burkett Miller Center of Public Affairs, research fellow, 1984-85; Sweet Briar College, visiting instructor, 1982; Monterey Institute of International Studies, assistant professor of international policy studies, 1985-88, Center for Contemporary Russian Studies, founder and director, 1987; U.S. Department of State, Office of Soviet Union Affairs, special assistant for policy, 1989-90, U.S. Embassy, attache in political section, 1990; University of Pennsylvania, lecturer in political science, 1990-91; University of Rhode Island, assistant professor of political science, 1991-, professor of political science; Brown University, Center for Foreign Policy Development, visiting research associate, 1991-; Dialog Municipal Research and Training Center, staff consultant, 2001-02. Writer. **Publications:** The Predicament of Human Rights: The Carter and Reagan Policies, 1983; (ed. and contrib.) Christianity and Russian Culture in Soviet Society: Sources of Stability and Change, 1989; (ed.) Reflections on Russia, 1991; The Rebirth of Russian Democracy: An Interpretation of Political Culture, 1995; (with A.Z. Rubinstein) Russian Foreign Policy: From Empire to Nation-State, 1997; Crafting Democracy: How Novgorod has Coped with Rapid Social Change, 2004; Vzlet Demokratii: Novgorodskaia Model Uskorennykh Sotsialnykh Izmeneniĭ, 2004. Contributor of articles to journals. **Address:** Department of Political Science, University of Rhode Island, 0002A Washburn Hall, 80 Upper College Rd., Ste. 4, Kingston, RI 02881-0817, U.S.A. **Online address:** nnpetro@gmail.com

PETRO, Pamela J. American (born United States), b. 1960. **Genres:** Travel/Exploration, Romance/Historical, Art/Art History, Biography, Autobiography/Memoirs. **Career:** Limited Editions Club, editor, 1985-86; Brown University, Learning Community, instructor, 1993, 1994, 1997; New York Public Library, book consultant; Lesley University, Master of Fine Arts in Creative Writing Program, faculty and interdisciplinary advisor; Smith College, faculty. **Publications:** The Newport and Narragansett Bay Book: A Complete Guide, 1994, 2nd ed., 1998; Travels in an Old Tongue: Touring the World Speaking Welsh, 1997; Sitting up with the Dead: A Storied Journey through the American South, 2002; Slow Breath of Stone: A Romanesque Love Story, 2005. Contributor to periodicals, magazines and newspapers. **Address:** Lesley University, 29 Everett St., Cambridge, MA 02138, U.S.A. **Online address:** pamelapetro@att.net

PETRO, Peter. Canadian/Slovak (born Slovakia), b. 1946. **Genres:** Literary Criticism And History, Translations. **Career:** University of British Columbia, professor, 1977-, Department of Germanic Studies, Russian Program, coordinator, Program in Modern European Studies, chair. Writer. **Publications:** Modern Satire: Four Studies, 1982; (trans.) M.M. Simecka, The Year of the Frog: A Novel, 1993; A History of Slovak Literature, 1995; (ed.) Critical Essays on Milan Kundera, 1999; (trans.) Rivers of Babylon, 2007. Contributor of articles to journals. **Address:** Department of CENES, The University of British Columbia, 212 Buchanan Twr., Vancouver, BC V6T 1Z1, Canada. **Online address:** petro@interchange.ubc.ca

PETROPOULOS, Jonathan G. American (born United States), b. 1961. **Genres:** Art/Art History. **Career:** Harvard University, History and in the Core Program, teaching fellow, 1985-90, lecturer on history and literature, 1990-93; Loyola College, assistant professor of history, 1993-97, associate professor of history, 1997-99; Claremont McKenna College, associate professor of history, 1999-2000, professor of history, 2000-01, John V. Croul professor of European history, 2001-, Committee for Rhodes and Marshall Scholarships, chair, 1999-, director, 2001-, associate director, 2003-; Presidential Commission on Holocaust Assets in the United States, research director for art and cultural property, 1999-2000; Family of Benjamin Z. Gould Center for Humanistic Studies, director, 2001-; Cambridge University, visiting fellow, 2004-05. Writer. **Publications:** Art as Politics in the Third Reich, 1996; (co-ed.) User's Guide to German Cultural Studies, 1997; The Faustian Bargain: The Art World in Nazi Germany, 2000; (ed.) Gray Zones: Ambiguity and Compromise in the Holocaust and its Aftermath, 2005; Royals and the Reich: The Princes Von Hessen in Nazi Germany, 2006. Contributor of articles and reviews to periodicals. **Address:** Department of History, Claremont McKenna College, 850 Columbia Ave., Claremont, CA 91711-6420, U.S.A. **Online address:** jonathan_petropoulos@mckenna.edu

PETROSKI, Henry. American (born United States), b. 1942. **Genres:** Design, Engineering, History, Technology, Sciences. **Career:** University of Illinois, instructor in theoretical and applied mechanics, 1966-68; University of Texas, assistant professor of engineering mechanics, 1968-74; Argonne National Laboratory, Analysis and Safety Division, mechanical engineer, 1975-80; Duke University, Department of Civil and Environmental Engineering, associate professor, 1980, professor, 1987-93, chair, 1991-2000, Aleksandar S. Vesic professor, 1993-, director of graduate studies, 1981-86, professor of history, 1995-; American Scientist, engineering columnist, 1991-; ASEE Prism, columnist, 2000-. **Publications:** To Engineer is Human: The Role of Failure in Successful Design, 1985; To Engineer is Human: The Role of Failure in Successful Design, 1985; Beyond Engineering: Essays and Other Attempts to Figure without Equations, 1986; The Pencil: A History of Design and Circumstance, 1990; The Evolution of Useful Things, 1992; Design Paradigms, 1994; Engineers of Dreams: Great Bridge Builders and the Spanning of America, 1995; Invention by Design: How Engineers Get from Thought to Thing, 1996; Remaking the World, 1997; The Book on the Bookshelf, 1999; Paperboy: Confessions of a Future Engineer, 2002; Small Things Considered, 2003; Pushing the Limits, 2004; Success Through Failure: The Paradox of Design, 2006; The Toothpick: Technology and Culture, 2007; The Essential Engineer: Why Science Alone will not Solve our Global Problems, 2010; Engineer's Alphabet, 2011. **Address:** Department of Civil and Environmental Engineering, Pratt School of Engineering, Duke University, 133 Hudson Engineering Bldg., Durham, NC 27708-0287, U.S.A. **Online address:** petroski@duke.edu

PETRUCCI, Armando. Italian (born Italy), b. 1932. **Genres:** Librarianship, History, Cultural/Ethnic Topics. **Career:** Accademia dei Lincei, librarian, 1958-72; University of Salerno, professor, 1972-74; University of Rome, professor, 1974-91; Scuola Normale Superiore, professor of Latin paleography, 1991-, director of the center for medieval culture, now professor emeritus. Writer. **Publications:** Notarii: documenti per la storia del notariato italiano, 1958; Codicediplomatico del Monastero benedettino di S. Maria di Tremiti (1005-1237), 1961; Il protocollo notarile di Coluccio Salutati (1372-1373), 1963; Le Tavolette Cerate Fiorentine di Casa Majorfi, 1965; La Scrittura di F. Petrarca (title means: 'The Writings of Petrarch'), 1967; Epistoleautografe, 1968; Coluccio Salutati, 1972; Viazo da Venesia al Sancto Iherusalem, 1972;

(with G. Barone) Primo, Non Leggere: Biblioteche e Pubblica Lettura in Italia dal 1861 ai Nostri Giorni (title means: 'First, Not to Read: Libraries and Public Reading in Italy from 1861 to the Present), 1976; Libri, Scrittura, e Pubblico nel Rinascimento: Guida Storica e Critica (title means: 'Books, Writing and the Public in the Rennaissance: A Historical and Critical Guide'), 1977; Scrittura e Popolonella Roma Barocca (title means: 'Writing and the People in Baroque Rome'), 1982; La Descrizione del Manoscritto: Storia, Problemi, Modelli (title means: The Description of the Manuscript: History, Problems, Models), 1984; La Scrittura: Ideologia e Rappresentazione (title means: The Writings: Ideology and Representation), 1986; La Scrittura (title means: 'Writing'), 1986; (intro.) Alfabeto delle Maiuscole antiche romane, 1986; Scrivere e No, 1987; (co-author) Disegnare il libro: grafica editoriale in Italia dal 1945 ad oggi, 1988; (comp.) Libros, editores y público enla Europa moderna, 1990; (with C. Romeo) Scriptores in Urbibus: Alfabetismo e Cultura Scritta nell'Italia Altomedievale, 1992; Medioevo da Leggere: Guida allo Studio delle Testimonianze Scritte del Medioevo Italiano, 1992; Jeux de lettres: formes et usages de l'inscription en Italie, 11e-20e siècles, 1993; Public Lettering: Script, Power and Culture, 1993; I più Antichi Documenti Originali del Commune di Lucera(1232-1496), 1994; Le Scritture Ultime: Ideologia della Morte e Strategiedello Scrivere nella Tradizione Occidentale, 1995; Escribir y leer enoccidente, 1995; Writers and Readers in Medieval Italy: Studies in the History of Written Culture, 1995; Writing the Dead: Death and Writing Strategies in the Western Tradition, 1998; La descrizione del manoscritto: Storia, problemi, modelli, 2001; Segni: Per Armando Petrucci, 2002; Primalezione di paleografia, 2002; (co-author) Lettere originali del Medioevo latino: VII-XI sec., 2004. EDITOR: Catologo Sommatio dei Manoscritti del Fondo Rossi, Sezione corsiniana, 1977; (with A. Pratesi) Un Secolo di Paleografia e Diplomatica (1887-1986): Per il Centenario dell Instituto di Paleografia dell 'Universita di Roma (title means: A Century of Paleography and Diplomatics (1887-1986): For the Centenary of the Institute of Paleography of the University of Rome), 1988. OTHERS: Studi epigrafici ed epigrafia nuova nel Rinascimento umanistico / Augusto Campana, 2005; Writing Relations: American Scholars in Italian Archives, 2008; Scrivere lettere: una storia plurimillenaria, 2008; Libros, Escrituras y Bibliotecas, 2011; A History of Epistolography: In the Middle Ages, forthcoming. Contributor to books. **Address:** Scuola Normale Superiore, Piazza dei Cavalieri, 7, Pisa, 56126, Italy. **Online address:** a.petrucci@sns.it

PETRUSICH, Amanda. American (born United States), b. 1980?. **Genres:** Music. **Career:** Pitchfork TV, on-air contributor; Paste Magazine, senior contributing editor; Pitchforkmedia.com., staff writer; Charlottesville Writing Center, creative nonfiction writing instructor; New York University, Gallatin School of Individualized Study, part-time faculty. **Publications:** Pink Moon, 2007; It Still Moves: Lost Songs, Lost Highways, and the Search for the Next American Music, 2008. Contributor to periodicals. **Address:** Gallatin School of Individualized Study, New York University, Rm. 503, 1 Washington Pl., New York, NY 10003, U.S.A. **Online address:** petrusich@gmail.com

PETRY, Alice Hall. American (born United States), b. 1951. **Genres:** Women's Studies And Issues, Novellas/Short Stories, Essays, Literary Criticism And History, Young Adult Fiction. **Career:** Rhode Island School of Design, instructor, 1979-80, assistant professor, 1980-86, associate professor of English, 1986-95, chair, 1993-95; Southern Illinois University, professor of English, 1995-, chair of department of English, 1995-2001, now professor emeritus; University of Colorado, visiting professor, 1987. Writer. **Publications:** A Genius in His Way: The Art of Cable's Old Creole Days, 1988; Fitzgerald's Craft of Short Fiction: The Collected Stories, 1920-1935, 1989; Understanding Anne Tyler, 1990; (ed.) Critical Essays on Anne Tyler, 1992; (ed.) Critical Essays on Kate Chopin, 1996; (ed.) On Harper Lee: Essays and Reflections, 2007. Contributor to journals. **Address:** Department of English Language and Literature, Southern Illinois University at Edwardsville, 3206 Peck Hall, PO Box 1431, Edwardsville, IL 62026-1431, U.S.A. **Online address:** apetry@siue.edu

PETRY, Yvonne. Canadian (born Canada), b. 1962?. **Genres:** History, Women's Studies And Issues. **Career:** University of Regina, Luther College, history instructor, associate professor. Writer. **Publications:** (With W. Stahl, R.A. Campbell and G. Diver) Webs of Reality: Social Perspectives on Science and Religion, 2002; Gender, Kabbalah, and the Reformation: The Mystical Theology of Guillaume Postel, 1510-1581, 2004. **Address:** Luther College, University of Regina, Rm. LC 114, 3737 Wascana Pkwy., Regina, SK S4S 0A2, Canada. **Online address:** yvonne.petry@uregina.ca

PETSALIS-DIOMIDIS, Nicholas. Greek (born Greece), b. 1943. **Genres:** Art/Art History, Politics/Government, Biography, Autobiography/Memoirs, History, Literary Criticism And History. **Career:** Historian, 1969-. Writer. **Publications:** Greece at the Paris Peace Conference, 1919, 1978; Chatzekyriakos-Ghikas: pleres katalogos tou zographikou ergou, 1921-1940, 1979; Spyrou Vassiliou, Oi xylografies, 1981; He Helladatōn dyo kyverneseōn, 1916-17: kathestōtika, diplōmatika kai oikonomika provlemata tou ethnikou dichasmou, 1988; He agnōste Kallas, 1998, trans. as The Unknown Callas: The Greek Years, 2001. **Address:** Amadeus Press, 133 SW 2nd Ave., Ste. 450, Portland, OR 97204, U.S.A.

PETTIFER, James. British (born England), b. 1949. **Genres:** History, Travel/Exploration, Politics/Government. **Career:** Oxford University, Queen Elizabeth House, Leverhulme research fellow, 1991-92; University of Sofia, Institute of Balkan Studies, research associate, 1992-93; Institute of Balkan Studies, research associate, 1992-, visiting professor, 1996-; University of Bath, research fellow, 1999; Defence Academy of the United Kingdom, professor, 2000-; University of Birmingham, honorary fellow, 2004; State University of Tetovo, visiting professor, 2006-; Princeton University, Stanley J. Seeger research fellow, 2007. Writer. **Publications:** (Ed.) Cockburn in Spain: Despatches from the Spanish Civil War, 1986; The Greeks: The Land and the People since the War, 1993; Blue Guide to Albania, 1994; (with M. Vickers) Albania: From Anarchy to a Balkan Identity, 1997, 2nd ed., 2000; (ed.) The Turkish Labyrinth: Atatürk and the New Islam, 1997; Blue Guide to Bulgaria, 1997; Bulgaria, 1998; The New Macedonian Question, 1999; Koncept për realitetin e ri: dialog me Hashim Thacin, 2001; Albania & Kosovo, 2001; Shqipëria dhe Kosova, 2003; Ekspresi i Kosoves, 2005; Kosova Express, 2005; Bulgarian Elections, 2005: A Difficult Result for EU Accession, 2005; (with J. Pettifer) Butrint: Environs and the Southern Albanian Coast: A Visitors Guide, 2006; (ed. with M. Nazarko) Strengthening Religious Tolerance for a Secure Civil Society in Albania and the Southern Balkans, 2007; Macedonia: Names, Nomenclaturas and NATO, 2008; Woodhouse, Zerva dhe Çamët: eksplorim në trashëgimineë e Luftës së Dytë Botërore, 2010. Contributor to periodicals. **Address:** Curtis Brown Ltd., 28/9 Haymarket, London, GL SW1Y 4SP, England. **Online address:** james@balkan.demon.co.uk

PETTIFER, Julian. British (born England), b. 1935. **Genres:** Natural History, Theology/Religion, Transportation. **Career:** Southern Television, reporter, writer and presenter, 1958-62; BBC, reporter, writer and presenter, 1962-75; freelance television reporter, writer and presenter, 1975-; Nature Watch, presenter, 1980-92; Central Television, writer and presenter of series, 1986-88; BBC Correspondent Series and Crossing Continents, BBC Radio 4, 1995-99; Royal Society for the Protection of Birds, president; Wildlife Trust, vice president; Order of the British Empire, officer, 2010. **Publications:** (With K. Hudson) Diamonds in the Sky: A Social History of Air Travel, 1979; (with R. Brown) Nature Watch, 1981; (with N. Turner) Automania: Man and the Motor Car, 1984; (with R. Brown) The Nature Watchers, 1985; (with R. Bradley) Missionaries, 1991. Contributor to periodicals. **Address:** Ste. 9, Roland Gardens, London, GL SW7 3PE, England.

PETTIGREW, Judy. American (born United States), b. 1943. **Genres:** Essays. **Career:** Procter & Gamble, field researcher in market research, 1965-66; JP's Distinctive Marketing, freelance marketing writer, 1968-76; United Air Specialist, manager of product marketing, 1976-80; Union Central Life, manager of marketing communications, 1980-82; Creative Consortium Inc. (brokerage firm for marketing professionals), founder and president, 1982-2001; Consortium for Nonprofit Marketing, executive director, 1994-98; Wow! Unlimited Inc. (creator of programs and products for women), founder and chief executive officer, 1995-2001; Long Term Care: A Family Affair, consultant, 2001-. **Publications:** Cincinnati Women: Jewels in the Crown, 1988; Sure I Can Rollerskate on Jell-O!, 1989; Been There, Done That, Bought the T-Shirt!, 1995; (with D. Simpson) From Hot Flashes to Power Surges, 1996; If I Should Die before I Wake..., 1998; (as Judy Hoyt Pettigrew with E. Miller) The Secret Gardens of Laguna Beach, 2003. **Address:** Wow! Unlimited Inc., 4850 Marieview Ct., Ste. 402, Cincinnati, OH 45236-2012, U.S.A. **Online address:** judypettigrew@fuse.net

PETTIT, Rhonda S(ue). American (born United States), b. 1955. **Genres:** Literary Criticism And History, Essays. **Career:** Georgetown News & Times, journalist, 1977-79; Daily Enterprise, journalist, 1977-79; Hi-Pro Review, journalist, 1977-79; Kentucky Energy Cabinet Laboratory, publications manager and editor, 1979-88; Northern Kentucky University, lecturer in English, 1996-98; Awakenings Café co-coordinator of faculty-student reading series,

1997-98; Xavier University, adjunct professor, 1997; University of Cincinnati, Raymond Walters College, adjunct professor, assistant professor of English, 1998-, associate professor, Women's, Gender and Sexuality Studies, affiliate faculty; Art Academy of Cincinnati, adjunct professor, 1997. Writer. **Publications:** Joy Harjo, 1998; A Gendered Collision: Sentimentalism and Modernism in Dorothy Parker's Poetry and Fiction, 2000; (ed.) The Critical Waltz: Essays on the Work of Dorothy Parker, 2005. Works appear in anthologies. Contributor of articles to periodicals. **Address:** Department of English and Communication, Raymond Walters College, University of Cincinnati, 9555 Plainfield Rd., Office S 132, Blue Ash, OH 45236-1096, U.S.A. **Online address:** rhonda.pettit@uc.edu

PETTY, W(illiam) H(enry). *See* Obituaries.

PETUCH, Edward J. American (born United States), b. 1949?. **Genres:** Environmental Sciences/Ecology, Botany, Sciences. **Career:** Florida Atlantic University, Department of Geosciences, professor, faculty; Pangea Institute, faculty. Writer, oceanographer and paleontologist. **Publications:** Twelve New Indo-Pacific Gastropods, 1979; (with D.M. Sargent) Atlas of the Living Olive Shells of the World, 1986; New Caribbean Molluscan Faunas, 1987; Field Guide to the Ecphoras, 1988; Neogene History of Tropical American Mollusks: Biogeography & Evolutionary Patterns of Tropical Western Atlantic Mollusca, 1988; The Edge of the Fossil Sea: Life along the Shores of Prehistoric Florida, 1992; Coastal Paleoceanography of Eastern North America: (Miocene-Pleistocene), 1997; Cenozoic Seas: The View from Eastern North America, 2004; (with C.E. Roberts) The Geology of the Everglades and Adjacent Areas, 2007; The Geology of the Florida Keys and Everglades: An Illustrated Field Guide to Florida's Hidden Beauty, 2008; (with M. Drolshagen) Molluscan Paleontology of the Chesapeake Miocene, 2010. **Address:** Department of Geosciences, Florida Atlantic University, PS 338, 777 Glades Rd., Boca Raton, FL 33431, U.S.A. **Online address:** epetuch@fau.edu

PEVSNER, Stella. American (born United States) **Genres:** Young Adult Fiction, Children's Fiction, Plays/Screenplays, Animals/Pets, Children's Nonfiction. **Career:** Writer for children, 1969-; teacher. **Publications:** FICTION FOR CHILDREN: Break a Leg!, 1969; Footsteps on the Stairs, 1970; Call Me Heller, That's My Name, 1973; A Smart Kid Like You, 1975; Keep Stompin' till the Music Stops, 1977; Me, My Goat & My Sister's Wedding, 1985; The Night the Whole Class Slept Over, 1991; Jon, Flora and the Odd-Eyed Cat, 1994; Would My Fortune Cookie Lie?, 1996. FOR YOUNG ADULTS: And You Give Me a Pain, Elaine, 1978; Cute Is a Four-Letter Word, 1980; I'll Always Remember You--Maybe, 1981; Lindsay, Lindsay, Fly Away Home, 1983; Sister of the Quints, 1987; How Could You Do It, Diane?, 1989; I'm Emma, I'm a Quint, 1993; (with F. Tang) Sing for Your Father, Su Phan, 1997; Is Everyone Moonburned but Me?, 2000. **Address:** Clarion Books, 222 Berkeley St., Boston, IL 02116, U.S.A. **Online address:** stelauthor@aol.com

PEYER, Bernd C. German/Austrian (born Austria), b. 1946. **Genres:** Cultural/Ethnic Topics, Anthropology/Ethnology, Communications/Media, Travel/Exploration, Young Adult Fiction, Adult Non-fiction. **Career:** American College of Switzerland, instructor in sports, 1966-67; University of Frankfurt, Institut fuer England-und Amerikastudien, academic tutor, 1977-79, research assistant, 1980-83, lecturer, 1982-2008, APL Professor, 2008-, research associate; Deganawidah Quetzalcoatl University, instructor, 1979-80; Dartmouth College, Native American Studies Center, Gordon Russell Visiting Professor, 1995. Writer. **Publications:** Hyemeyohsts Storm's Seven Arrows: Fiction and Anthropology in the Native American Novel, 1979; (with P. Bolz) Indianische Kunst Nordamerikas, 1987; Hildebrand's Urlaubsfuehrer: Dominikanische Republik, 1991, 4th ed., 1993; The Tutor'd Mind: Indian Missionary-Authors in Antebellum America, 1997; The Thinking Indian: Native American Writers, 1850s-1920s, 2007. EDITOR: The Elders Wrote: An Anthology of Early Prose by North American Indians, 1768-1931, 1982; The Singing Spirit: Early Short Stories by North American Indians, 1989; American Indian Nonfiction: An Anthology of Writings, 1760s-1930s, 2007. Contributor to books and periodicals. **Address:** Center for North American Studies, University of Frankfurt, Senckenberganlage 31, Frankfurt, D-60325, Germany. **Online address:** berndpeyer@aol.com

PEYTON, A(nthony) J(oseph). British (born England), b. 1962. **Genres:** Technology, Sciences. **Career:** Kratos Analytical Ltd., engineer, 1986-89; The University of Manchester (formerly Victoria University of Manchester), lecturer, 1990-96, professor of electromagnetic tomography engineering, 2004-, chair of electromagnetic tomography engineering; Lancaster University, senior lecturer, 1996-2001, reader, 2001-04, professor, 2004. Writer. **Publications:** (With V. Walsh) Analog Electronics with Op Amps: A Source Book of Practical Circuits, 1993. **Address:** School of Electrical and Electronic Engineering, The University of Manchester, Bldg. E48A, Sackville St., Manchester, GM M13 9PL, England. **Online address:** a.peyton@manchester.ac.uk

PEYTON, K. M. (Kathleen Herald). British (born England), b. 1929. **Genres:** Children's Fiction, Young Adult Non-fiction, Novels, Picture/Board Books, Illustrations, Animals/Pets. **Career:** Art teacher, 1952-56; writer, 1956-. **Publications:** SELF-ILLUSTRATED: Fly-by-Night, 1969. AS KATHLEEN HERALD: Sabre the Horse from the Sea, 1947; The Mandrake: A Pony, 1949; Crab the Roan, 1953. OTHERS: North to Adventure, 1959; Stormcock Meets Trouble, 1961; The Hard Way Home, 1962 in US as Sing a Song of Ambush, 1964; Windfall, 1962 in US as Sea Fever, 1963; Brownsea Silver, 1964; The Maplin Bird, 1965; The Plan for Birdsmarsh, 1966; Thunder in the Sky, 1966; Flambards, 1967; The Edge of the Cloud, 1969; Pennington's Seventeenth Summer, 1970 in US as Pennington's Last Term, 1971; Flambards in Summer, 1970; The Beethoven Medal, 1971; A Pattern of Roses, 1972; Pennington's Heir, 1973; The Team, 1975; So Once Was I, 1976; The Right-Hand Man, 1977; Prove Yourself a Hero, 1977; A Midsummer Night's Death, 1979; Marion's Angels, 1979; The Flambards Trilogy, 1980; Dear Fred, 1981; Flambards Divided, 1982; Going Home, 1982; Who, Sir? Me, Sir?, 1983, 2nd ed., 2000; Free Rein, 1983; The Last Ditch, 1983; Froggett's Revenge, 1985; The Sound of Distant Cheering, 1986; Downhill All the Way, 1988; Plain Jack, 1988; Skylark, 1989; Darkling, 1989; Poor Badger, 1990; No Roses Round the Door, 1990; The Boy Who Wasn't There, 1992; Late to Smile, 1992; Apple Won't Jump, 1992; The Wild Boy and Queen Moon, 1993; The Swallow Tale, 1995; Mr. Brown, 1995; Swallow Summer, 1996; Windy Webley, 1997; Unquiet Spirits, 1997; Swallow the Star, 1997; The Pony That Went to Sea, 1997; Danger Offshore, 1998; Firehead, 1998; Snowfall, 1998; The Pied Piper, 1999; The Paradise Pony, 1999; The Scruffy Pony, 1999; Horses, 2000; Pony in the Dark, 2001; Blind Beauty, 2001; Stealaway, 2001; Small Gains, 2003; Greater Gains, 2005; My Alice, 2006; Minnas Quest: Roman Pony Adventures, 2007; Blue Skies and Gunfire, 2007; No Turning Back, 2008; Horses: Wild Reads, 2009; Far From Home, 2009; Paradise House, 2011. **Address:** c/o Author Mail, Oxford University Press, Great Clarendon St., Oxford, EX OX1 6DP, England.

PEZESHKI, Charles. American (born United States), b. 1962. **Genres:** Environmental Sciences/Ecology, Engineering, Biography. **Career:** Jones and Laughlin Steel Corp., process control engineer, 1982-83; Duke University, Department of Electrical Engineering, teaching assistant, 1983-84, research assistant, 1985-87, system administrator, 1985-87, instructor, 1986-87, research assistant professor, 1987-88; Washington State University, School of Mechanical and Materials Engineering, assistant professor, 1988-94, associate professor, 1994-2005, professor, Faculty Senate, chair, 2004-05, 2006-07, associate director, 2005-08, Industrial Design Clinic, director, 1994-. Writer. **Publications:** Wild to the Last: Environmental Conflict in the Clearwater Country, 1998. Contributor of articles to periodicals. **Address:** School of Mechanical and Materials Engineering, Washington State University, EE/ME 143, PO Box 642920, Pullman, WA 99164-2920, U.S.A. **Online address:** pezeshki@mme.wsu.edu

PEZZULLO, Ralph. American (born United States), b. 1954. **Genres:** Novels, Mystery/Crime/Suspense, Plays/Screenplays, International Relations/Current Affairs, Writing/Journalism, Young Adult Fiction, Military/Defense/Arms Control. **Career:** Author. **Publications:** At the Fall of Somoza, 1994; The Leap into Haiti, 2002; Eve Missing, 2003; Jawbreaker: The Attack on Bin Laden and Al Qaeda: A Personal Account by the CIA's Key Field Commander, 2005; Plunging into Haiti: Clinton, Aristide and the Defeat of Diplomacy, 2006; The Walk-In, 2008; Most Evil, 2009; Inside SEAL Team Six, 2011; Hunt the Wolf, 2012; Blood of My Blood, 2012; Saigon, forthcoming; Committed to the Invincible Sun, forthcoming. **Address:** 2345 Westwood Blvd., Ste. 7, Los Angeles, CA 90064-2197, U.S.A. **Online address:** ralph@ralphpezzullo.com

PFAELZER, Jean. American (born United States), b. 1944?. **Genres:** Literary Criticism And History, History, Young Adult Fiction. **Career:** University of London, External Degree Division, part-time supervisor and part-time tutor, 1968-70; California State University, visiting assistant professor, 1974-75; University of California, assistant professor of literature and director of humanities, 1975-82; National Labor Law Center, executive director, 1982-83; University of Delaware, visiting professor of American studies, 1985-87, associate professor of American studies and English, 1987-95, professor of English, 1996-, Department of Women's Studies, professor, faculty of East Asian studies. Writer. **Publications:** The Utopian Novel in America, 1886-1896: The Politics of Form, 1984; (ed. and intro.) A Rebecca Harding Davis Reader, 1995; Parlor Radical: Rebecca Harding Davis and the Origins of American Social Realism, 1996; (ed. and intro.) Mizora: A Prophecy, 2000; Driven Out: The Forgotten War Against Chinese Americans, 2007; Driven Out: Roundups and Resistance of Chinese People in Rural California in the 19th Century, forthcoming. **Address:** Department of English, University of Delaware, 316 Memorial Hall, Newark, DE 19716, U.S.A. **Online address:** pfaelzer@udel.edu

PFAFF, Daniel W. American (born United States), b. 1940. **Genres:** Biography. **Career:** Pennsylvania State University, assistant professor, associate professor of journalism, 1971-85, professor of journalism, 1985-92, associate professor of communications, 1985-90, School of Communications, associate dean, 1990-94, acting dean, 1992, College of Communications, now professor emeritus. Writer. **Publications:** Joseph Pulitzer II and Advertising Censorship, 1929-1939, 1982; Joseph Pulitzer II and the Post-Dispatch: A Newspaperman's Life, 1991; No Ordinary Joe: A Life of Joseph Pulitzer III, 2005. Contributor of articles to books. **Address:** 260 Homan Ave., State College, PA 16801, U.S.A. **Online address:** dwp1@psu.edu

PFAFF, Steven. American (born United States), b. 1970. **Genres:** History, Sociology. **Career:** Sociological Theory, assistant editor, 1994-99; University of Washington, professor, 2001-, Jackson School of International Studies, Center for West European Studies, director; American Journal of Sociology, consulting editor, 2005-06. **Publications:** (Co-ed.) Classical Sociological Theory, 2002, 2nd ed., 2007; Exit-Voice Dynamics and the Collapse of East Germany: The Crisis of Leninism and the Revolution of 1989, 2006. Contributor of articles to books and journals. **Address:** Department of Sociology, University of Washington, 202 Savery Hall, PO Box 353340, Seattle, WA 98195-3340, U.S.A. **Online address:** pfaff@u.washington.edu

PFAFF, William (Wendel). French/American (born United States), b. 1928. **Genres:** International Relations/Current Affairs, Politics/Government, History, Military/Defense/Arms Control. **Career:** Commonweal, associate editor, 1949-55, editor; American Broadcasting Co., News and Public Affairs, writer, 1955-57; Free Europe Committee Inc., executive, 1957-61; Hudson Research Europe Ltd., deputy director, 1972-78; New Yorker, political commentator, 1972-92; International Herald Tribune, columnist, 1978-; Los Angeles Times Syndicate, columnist, 1978-. **Publications:** (With E. Stillman) The New Politics: America and the End of the Postwar World, 1961; (with E. Stillman) The Politics of Hysteria: The Sources of Twentieth-Century Conflict, 1964; (with E. Stillman) Power and Impotence: The Failure of America's Foreign Policy, 1966; (co-author) Can We Win in Vietnam?, 1968; Condemned to Freedom, 1971; Barbarian Sentiments: How the American Century Ends, 1989, rev. ed. as Barbarian Sentiments: America in the New Century, 2000; The Wrath of Nations: Civilization and the Furies of Nationalism, 1993; Fear, Anger and Failure: A Chronicle the Bush Administration's War Against Terror from the Attacks in September 2001 to Defeat in Baghdad, 2004; Bullet's Song: Romantic Violence and Utopia, 2004; The Irony of Manifest Destiny: The Tragedy of America's Foreign Policy, 2010. Contirbutor to books and periodicals. **Address:** 72 Ave. Victor Hugo, Paris, 75116, France. **Online address:** cnil@williampfaff.com

PFANNER, (Anne) Louise. Australian (born Australia), b. 1955. **Genres:** Children's Fiction, Picture/Board Books, Young Adult Fiction, Homes/Gardens, Literary Criticism And History. **Career:** Freelance writer and illustrator. **Publications:** SELF ILLUSTRATED: Louise Builds a House, 1987; Louise Builds a Boat, 1988; The Town Mouse and The Country Mouse, 1997; Little Red Hen, 1997; Little Lucie's Diary, 2004. OTHER: (contrib.) Favourite Stories of Playschool, 1991. Illustrator of books by others. **Address:** c/o Barbara Mobbs, PO Box 126, Edgecliff, NW 2027, Australia. **Online address:** delecta@bigpond.com

PFEFFER, Wendy. American (born United States), b. 1929. **Genres:** Children's Fiction, Children's Non-fiction, How-to Books, Animals/Pets. **Career:** First grade teacher, 1950-53, Pennington Presbyterian Nursery School, co-founder, director, early childhood specialist, 1961-91; freelance writer, 1981-; Jointure for Community Adult Education, Writer's Workshop, teacher. **Publications:** Writing Children's Books, 1985; Starting a Family Day Care, 1989; The Gooney War, 1990; All about Me, 1990; The World of Nature, 1990; Popcorn Park Zoo: A Haven with a Heart, 1992; From Tadpole to Frog, 1994; Marta's Magnets, 1995; What's It Like to Be a Fish?, 1996; Polar Bears, 1996; Swans, 1996; Snowy Owls, 1997; Arctic Wolves, 1997; A Log's Life, 1997; Sounds All Around, 1999; The Big Flood, 2001; Mallard Duck at Meadow View Pond, 2001; Living on the Edge Series, 2002; Hot Deserts, 2002; Thunder and Lightning, 2002; Dolphin Talk: Whistles, Clicks, and Clapping Jaws, 2003; Arctic Frozen Reaches, 2003; Deep Oceans, 2003; High Mountains, 2003; Icy Antarctic Waters, 2003; The Shortest Day: Celebrating the Winter Solstice, 2003; Firefly at StonyBrook Farm, 2004; From Seed to Pumpkin, 2004; Wiggling Worms at Work, 2004; We Gather Together: Celebrating the Harvest Season, 2006; New Beginning: Celebrating the Spring Equinox, 2008; Many Ways to be a Soldier, 2008; Life in a Coral Reef, 2009; The Longest Day: Celebrating the Summer Solstice, 2010; World of Sharks, 2011; Wolf Pup, 2011. **Address:** 3 Timberlane Dr., Pennington, NJ 08534, U.S.A. **Online address:** tomwendypf@aol.com

PFEIFER, Michael J. (Michael James Pfeifer). American (born United States) **Genres:** Social Sciences. **Career:** Evergreen State College, faculty, 1999-2006; University of Western Ontario, Department of History, faculty, 2006-07; City University of New York, John Jay College of Criminal Justice, associate professor of American history, 2007-. Writer. **Publications:** Rough Justice: Lynching and American Society, 1874-1947, 2004; The Roots of Rough Justice: Origins of American Lynching, 2011. Contributor to periodicals. **Address:** Department of History, John Jay College of Criminal Justice, City University of New York, 445 W 59th St., New York, NY 10019, U.S.A. **Online address:** mpfeifer@jjay.cuny.edu

PFEIFER, Michael James. *See* **PFEIFER, Michael J.**

PFEIFFER, Janet (B.). American (born United States), b. 1949. **Genres:** Children's Fiction, Education, inspirational/Motivational Literature, Self Help. **Career:** Home Maintenance Service, past owner; Battered Women's Shelter, instructor and director; Educational Institutions, teacher; Reunion of Hearts: Reconciling and Reconnecting Estranged Families, founder; Pfeiffer Power Seminars, president, chief executive officer; Writer, speaker and consultant. **Publications:** The Seedling's Journey, 1994; The Angel and the Gift: A Second Chance, 1996; The Orchids of Gateway Lane: Galen's Message of Peace, 1997; Jordan's Promise, 1998; Dying to Be Safe: Ultimate Solutions to Violence, 2000; (co-author) 101 Great Ways to Improve Your Life, vol. III, 2007; The Secret Side of Anger, 2009. **Address:** Pfeiffer Power Seminars L.L.C., 5716 Berkshire Valley Rd., PO Box 2773, Oak Ridge, NJ 07438, U.S.A. **Online address:** janet@pfeifferpowerseminars.com

PFISTER, Patrick. Spanish/American (born United States), b. 1949. **Genres:** Travel/Exploration, Reference. **Career:** Writer. **Publications:** Pilgrimage: Tales from the Open Road (travel book), 1995; Over Sand & Sea: A Traveler's Tales, 2007. **Address:** Lauria 81, 3, 1a, Barcelona, 08009, Spain.

PFLIEGER, Pat. American (born United States), b. 1955. **Genres:** Literary Criticism And History, Children's Fiction. **Career:** University of Minnesota, teaching associate in composition, 1980-86, Hess Collection, cataloguer, 1982-86; Illinois State University, Department of English, assistant professor of children's literature, 1987-88; West Chester University, Department of English, assistant professor of children's literature, 1988-. Writer. **Publications:** (Ed. with H.M. Hill) A Reference Guide to Modern Fantasy for Children, 1984; Beverly Cleary (biography), 1991; The Fog's Net (picturebook), 1994; (ed.) Letters from Nineteenth-Century Children to Robert Merry's Museum Magazine, 2001. Contributor to books. **Address:** Department of English, West Chester University, 516 Main Hall, West Chester, PA 19383, U.S.A. **Online address:** ppflieger@wcupa.edu

PHARES, Walid. American/Lebanese (born Lebanon), b. 1957?. **Genres:** Politics/Government, History. **Career:** Publisher, 1982-87; Florida Atlantic University, professor of Middle East studies, 1993-2006; Fox News Channel, Middle East correspondent, contributor, 2007-; European Foundation for Democracies, visiting fellow, 2006-09; National Defense University, School for National Security Executive Education (SNSEE), visiting professor, 2006-, faculty; Florida International University, lecturer; University of Miami, lecturer; Foundation for the Defense of Democracies, senior fellow and director of future terrorism project, 2001-10; U.S. House of Representatives Caucus on Counter Terrorism, advisor, 2007-; Trans-Atlantic Parliamentary Group, co-ordinator, co-secretary general, 2008-; Saint Joseph University, faculty. **Publications:** Lebanese Christian Nationalism: The Rise and Fall of an Ethnic

Resistance, 1995; Future Jihad: Terrorist Strategies against America, 2005; The War of Ideas: Jihadism Against Democracy, 2007; Confrontation: Winning the War Against Future Jihad, 2008; Coming Revolution: Struggle for Freedom in the Middle East, 2010. **Address:** National Defense University, Marshall Hall, 300 5th Ave. SW, Washington, DC 20319-5066, U.S.A. **Online address:** phares@walidphares.com

PHARIES, David (Arnold). American (born United States), b. 1951. **Genres:** Bibliography, History, Language/Linguistics. **Career:** Arizona State University, visiting assistant professor, 1979-80; University of Florida, assistant professor, 1980-85, associate professor of Spanish, 1985-89, professor of Spanish, 1989-, Department of Romance Languages and Literatures, chair, 2003-08, Department of Spanish and Portuguese, chair, 2008-, College of Liberal Arts and Sciences, associate dean for humanities; Universitat Heidelberg, visiting professor, 1987-88, 1991-92. Writer. **Publications:** AS DAVID A. PHARIES: Charles S. Pierce and the Linguistic Sign, 1985; Structure and Analogy in the Playful Lexicon of Spanish, 1986; The Origin and Development of the Ibero-Romance-nc/-ng Suffixes, 1990; Bibliography of Latin and Ibero-Romance Suffixation, 1994; University of Chicago Spanish Dictionary: Spanish-English, English-Spanish, 5th ed., 2002; Diccionario Etimológico de los Españoles y de Otros Elementos Finales, 2002; A Brief History of the Spanish Language, 2007; Breve historia de lalengua española, 2007. Contributor of articles to periodicals. **Address:** Department of Spanish and Portuguese, University of Florida, 170A Dauer Hall, Gainesville, FL 32611, U.S.A. **Online address:** pharies@ufl.edu

PHATHANOTHAI, Sirin. French/Thai (born Thailand), b. 1947. **Genres:** Novels. **Career:** Thailand's Minister of Commerce, adviser; Thailand's Ministry of Interior, adviser, 1997-. Writer. **Publications:** The Dragon's Pearl, 1994; La petite otage de la Chine rouge, 1995. **Address:** Georges Borchardt Inc., 136 E 57th St., New York, NY 10022-2707, U.S.A. **Online address:** dutasia@worldnet.fr

PHAYER, Michael. American (born United States), b. 1935. **Genres:** History, Social Sciences, Theology/Religion, Autobiography/Memoirs. **Career:** Marquette University, Department of History, faculty, 1970-90, professor of history, 1990-2002, professor emeritus, 2002-. Writer. **Publications:** Protestant and Catholic Women in Nazi Germany, 1990; (with E. Fleischner) Cries in the Night: Women who Challenged the Holocaust, 1997; The Catholic Church and the Holocaust, 1930-1965, 2000; Pius XII, the Holocaust, and the Cold War, 2008. **Address:** Department of History, Marquette University, 303A Coughlin Hall, 607 N 13th St., PO Box 1881, Milwaukee, WI 53201-1881, U.S.A. **Online address:** michael.phayer@marquette.edu

PHELAN, Anna Hamilton. American (born United States) **Genres:** Plays/Screenplays, Film, Picture/Board Books. **Career:** Screenwriter, 1985-; Actress and part-time hospital worker. **Publications:** Mask, 1985; Into the Homeland, 1987; Gorillas in the Mist, 1988; (with A. Scott and C. Sigal) In Love and War, 1996; Girl, Interrupted, 1999. Contributor to periodicals. **Address:** New Line Cinema Corp., 116 N Robertson Blvd., Ste. 200, Los Angeles, CA 90048-3105, U.S.A.

PHELAN, Jay. American (born United States) **Genres:** Biology, Sciences. **Career:** University of California, biology professor. Writer. **Publications:** (With T. Burnham) Mean Genes: From Sex to Money to Food: Taming Our Primal Instincts, 2000; What is Life?: A Guide to Biology With Physiology, 2010. Contributor to periodicals. **Address:** Department of Biology, University of California, 405 Hilgard Ave., PO Box 951361, Los Angeles, CA 90095-1606, U.S.A. **Online address:** jay@ucla.edu

PHELAN, Joseph. (J. P. Phelan). British (born England), b. 1963?. **Genres:** Poetry. **Career:** De Montfort University, Department of English and Creative Writing, senior lecturer in English, reader in nineteenth-century literature. Writer. **Publications:** (Ed. as J.P. Phelan) Clough: Selected Poems, 1995; The Nineteenth-Century Sonnet, 2005; (ed. with J. Woolford and D. Karlin) The Poems of Robert Browning, vol. III, 2007, vol. IV, 2012; (with J. Woolford and D. Karlin) Robert Browning: Selected Poems, 2010; The Music of Verse: Metrical Experiment in Nineteenth-Century Poetry, 2011. Contributor to books and journals. **Address:** Faculty of Humanities, De Montfort University, Clephan Bldg., The Gateway, Leicester, LC LE1 9BH, England. **Online address:** jphelan@dmu.ac.uk

PHELAN, J. P. *See* **PHELAN, Joseph.**

PHELAN, Shane. American (born United States), b. 1956. **Genres:** Gay And Lesbian Issues, Politics/Government, Sex, Regional/Urban Planning, Social Sciences. **Career:** Haverford College, visiting assistant professor, 1987-88; University of New Mexico, assistant professor, 1988-94, associate professor, 1994-98, professor, 1998-. Writer. **Publications:** Identity Politics: Lesbian Feminism and the Limits of Community, 1989; Getting Specific: Postmodern Lesbian Politics, 1994; (ed. with M. Blasius) We Are Everywhere: A Historical Sourcebook of Gay and Lesbian Politics, 1997; (ed.) Playing with Fire: Queer Politics, Queer Theories, 1997; Sexual Strangers: Gays, Lesbians, and Dilemmas of Citizenship, 2001. Contributor to periodicals. **Address:** Department of Political Science, University of New Mexico, 1 University of New Mexico, PO Box 05-3070, Albuquerque, NM 87131-0001, U.S.A. **Online address:** sphelan@unm.edu

PHELAN, Tom (Thomas Joseph). Irish/American (born United States), b. 1940. **Genres:** Novels, Essays, History. **Career:** Harriman College, assistant professor of English. Writer and priest. **Publications:** NOVELS: In the Season of the Daisies, 1993; Iscariot, 1995; Derrycloney, 1999; The Canal Bridge, 2005; Nailer, 2011. **Address:** Glanvil Enterprises, 53 East Merrick Rd., Ste. 132, Freeport, NY 11520, U.S.A. **Online address:** glanvil3@aol.com

PHELPS, Barry. British (born England), b. 1941. **Genres:** Biography, History, Adult Non-fiction, Writing/Journalism. **Career:** Laing and Cruickshank, stockbrokers' authorized clerk; Union Acceptances, portfolio manager; Guinness Mahon, portfolio manager and investment analyst; M and G Unit Trust Group, investment research manager, 1968-69; Keyser Ullmann, investment manager, 1969-71; Euromoney, deputy editor, editor, 1971-73; Daily Mail, assistant city editor of City Page, 1973-83; Broad Street Associates Ltd., executive director, 1983-86; APT Data Services Ltd., chair, 1985-; Abbatt Phelps Tanous Ltd., founder, 1986, managing director, 1986-88; Politics International Ltd., director and consultant, 1986-89; MMI Strategic Communications, executive director, 1988-90; Capital Markets Partners Ltd., director, 1990-96; Ribstone Ltd., consultant; The Royal Borough of Kensington and Chelsea, Earl's Court Ward, councilor, 1994-2010. Writer. **Publications:** (Ed. with P. Sergeant) Daily Mail Inflation Fighter's Handbook, 1975; Power and the Party: A History of the Carlton Club, 1932-1982, (non-fiction), 1982; P.G. Wodehouse: Man and Myth, 1992; Wooster of Yaxley and Wodehouse of Kimberley: Parallel Peerages, 1992; Two Little Known East Anglian Authors Compared: Sir Pelhan Wodehouse & Mr. Bertram Wooster, 1993; You Don't Say: The Dictionary of Misquotations, 1995. **Address:** Maisonette, 26 Nevern Pl., London, GL SW5 9PP, England. **Online address:** cllr.phelps@rbkc.gov.uk

PHELPS, Christopher. American (born United States), b. 1965. **Genres:** Biography. **Career:** Against the Current, co-editor, 1994-; Simon Fraser University, visiting assistant professor, 1995-96; University of Oregon, department of history, tutor, 1996-97; Monthly Review Press, editorial director, 1998-99; Ohio State University, assistant professor of history, 1999-2003, associate professor of history, 2003-09; University of Pecs, senior lecturer in history of philosophy, 2000; University of Lodz, distinguished chair in American studies and literature, 2004-05; University of Nottingham, associate professor of intellectual and cultural history. Writer. **Publications:** (Contrib.) From Hegel to Marx: Studies in the Intellectual Development of Karl Marx, 1994; Young Sidney Hook: Marxist and Pragmatist, 1997; (ed. and intro.) Jungle, 2004. Contributor of articles to periodicals and magazines. **Address:** Department of American and Canadian Studies, University of Nottingham, Rm. B83 Trent, University Park, Nottingham, NG7 2RD, United Kingdom. **Online address:** christopher.phelps@nottingham.ac.uk

PHELPS, Edmund S. American (born United States), b. 1933. **Genres:** Economics. **Career:** Yale University, assistant instructor in economics, 1958-59, assistant professor of economics, 1960-62, associate professor of economics, 1963-66; RAND Corp., economist, 1959-60; Massachusetts Institute of Technology, visiting associate professor of economics, 1962-63; Cowles Foundation, staff and associate professor of economics, 1963-66; University of Pennsylvania, professor of economics, 1966-71; U.S. Treasury Department, consultant, 1969; Columbia University, professor of economics, 1971-77, 1978-82, McVickar professor of political economy, 1983-, senior advisor, 1997-2000, Center on Capitalism and Society, Arts and Sciences, director, 2001-, research fellow, 2001-; New York University, professor of economics, 1978-79; University of Siena, International School of Economic Research, co-director, 1987-90; European Bank for Reconstruction and Development, resident consultant, 1992-93. Writer. **Publications:** The Goal of

Economic Growth: Sources, Costs, Benefits, 1962, rev. ed., 1969; Fiscal Neutrality Toward Economic Growth, 1965; Golden Rules of Economic Growth; Studies of Efficient and Optimal Investment, 1967; (with A.A. Alchian and D.T. Mortensen) Microeconomic Foundations of Employment and Inflation Theory, 1970; Inflation Policy and Unemployment Theory: The Cost-Benefit Approach to Monetary Planning, 1972; Economic Justice; Selected Readings, 1973; Studies in Macroeconomic Theory, vol. I: Employment and Inflation, 1979, vol. II: Redistribution and Growth, 1980; Political Economy: An Introductory Text, 1985; (with J-P Fitoussi) The Slump in Europe: Open Economy Theory Reconstructed, 1988; Seven Schools of Macroeconomic Thought: The Arne Ryde Memorial Lectures, 1990; (co-author) Needed Mechanisms of Corporate Governance and Finance in Eastern Europe, 1993; (with H. Kierzkowski and G. Zoega) Mechanisms of Economic Collapse and Growth in Eastern Europe, 1994; (with H.T. Hoon, G. Kanaginis and G. Zoega) Structural Slumps: The Modern Equilibrium Theory of Unemployment, Interest and Assets, 1994; Rewarding Work: How to Restore Participation and Self-Support to Free Enterprise, 1997; Enterprise and Inclusion in Italy, 2002. EDITOR: The Goal of Economic Growth: Sources, Costs, Benefits, 1962; Private Wants and Public Needs: Issues Surrounding the Size and Scope of Government Expenditure, 1962; (co-ed.) Problems of the Modern Economy, 1966; Altruism, Morality and Economic Theory, 1975; (with R. Frydman) Individual Forecasting and Aggregate Outcomes: Rational Expectations Examined, 1983; (with Aldershot and Hants) Recent Developments in Macroeconomics, 3 vols., 1991; (with M. Baldassarri and L. Paganetto) Risparmio, Accumulazione, Sviluppo, 1991; (with M. Baldassarri and L. Paganetto) International Economic Interdependence, Patterns of Trade Balances and Economic Policy Coordination, 1992; (with M. Baldassarri and L. Paganetto) Le Diversità Nell'economia Mondiale: Tassi de Crescita, aree economiche e globalizzazione del mercato, 1993; (with M. Baldassarri and L. Paganetto) Privatization Processes in Eastern Europe: Theoretical Foundations and Empirical Results, 1993; (with M. Baldassarri and L. Paganetto) World Saving, Prosperity and Growth, 1993; (with M. Baldassarri, L. Paganetto and A. Alesina) Crisi e Disoccupazione Degli Anni '90: Cause e Rimedi, 1994; (with M. Baldassarri and L. Paganetto) International Differences in Growth Rates: Market Globalization and Economic Areas, 1994; (with M. Baldassarri and L. Paganetto) Equita, Eefficienza eCcrescita: il Futuro del Welfare State, 1995; (with M. Baldassarri and L. Paganetto) Equity, Efficiency and Growth: The Future of the Welfare State, 1996; (with M. Baldassarri and L. Paganetto) The 1990s Slump: Causes and Cures, 1996; (with M. Baldassarri and L. Paganetto) Institutions and Economic Organization in the Advanced Economies: The Governance Perspective, 1998; (with L. Paganetto) Finance Research, Education and Growth, 2003; Designing Inclusion: Tools to Raise Low-End Pay and Employment in Private Enterprise, 2003; (with L. Paganetto) Finance, Research, Education, and Growth, 2003; (with H. Sinn) Perspectives on the Performance of the Continental Economies, 2011. Contributor to books. **Address:** Department of Economics, Columbia University, Rm. 1004, International Affairs Bldg., 420 W 118th St., PO Box 3308, New York, NY 10027, U.S.A. **Online address:** esp2@columbia.edu

PHILANDER, **S. George H.** American/South African (born South Africa), b. 1942. **Genres:** Meteorology/Atmospheric Sciences. **Career:** Massachusetts Institute of Technology, research associate, 1970-71; Princeton University, research associate, 1971-78, Department of Geological and Geophysical Sciences, full professor, 1990-, Atmospheric and Oceanic Sciences Program, director, 1990-2006, Department of Geological and Geophysical Sciences, chair, 1994-2001, Knox Taylor professor of geosciences, 2005-; Princeton University, research associate, 1971-77; World Meteorological Organization, consultant, 1973-74; Geophysical Fluid Dynamics Lab, senior research oceanographer, 1978-89; National Oceanographic and Atmospheric Administration, Department of Commerce, senior research oceanographer, 1978; Museum National d'Histoire Naturelle, visiting professor, 1982; America Meteorological Society, fellow, 1986; American Geophysical Union, fellow, 1991; American Academy of Arts and Sciences, fellow, 2003; University of Cape Town, research professor, 2007-; African Centre for Climate and Earth System Science, research director, 2007. Writer. **Publications:** (With H. Charnock) Dynamics of the Coupled Atmosphere and Ocean: Proceedings of a Royal Society Discussion Meeting Held on 13 and 14 December 1988, 1989; El Niño, La Niña, and the Southern Oscillation, 1990; Is the Temperature Rising?: The Uncertain Science of Global Warming, 1998; Our Affair with El Niño: How We Transformed an Enchanting Peruvian Current into a Global Climate Hazard, 2004; Encyclopedia of Global Warming and Climate Change, 2008. **Address:** Atmospheric & Oceanic Science Program, Princeton University, 209 Forrestal Campus Sayre Hall, Princeton, NJ 08544, U.S.A. **Online address:** gphlder@princeton.edu

PHILBRICK, **Nathaniel.** American (born United States), b. 1956. **Genres:** Local History/Rural Topics, Marine Sciences/Oceanography. **Career:** Egan Maritime Institute, founding director, 1996-98-; Nantucket Historical Association, research fellow in history; Sailing World Magazine, writer. **Publications:** (Ed.) Yaahting: A Parody, 1984; The Passionate Sailor, 1986; Away Off Shore, 1994; (intro.) Miriam Coffin, or, The Whale-Fishermen, 1995; Abram's Eyes, 1998; Second Wind: A Nantucket Sailor's Odyssey, 1998; Abram's Eyes: The Native American Legacy of Nantucket Island, 1998; (ed. and intro. with T. Philbrick) Loss of the Ship Essex, Sunk by a Whale, 2000; In the Heart of the Sea, 2000; Revenge of the Whale, 2002; Sea of Glory: America's Voyage of Discovery: The U.S. Exploring Expedition, 1838-1842, 2003; Sea of Glory: The Epic South Seas Expedition 1838-42, 2004; (ed. and intro. with T. Philbrick) The Private Journal of William Reynolds: United States Exploring Expedition, 1838-1842, 2004; Mayflower: A Story of Courage, Community and War, 2006; (ed. and intro. with T. Philbrick) Mayflower Papers: Selected Writings of Colonial New England, 2007; Mayflower and the Pilgrims' New World, 2008; Last Stand: Custer, Sitting Bull and the Battle of the Little Bighorn, 2010; Why read Moby-Dick?, 2011. Contributor to periodicals. **Address:** Tandem Literary, 2387 North Ave., Scotch Plains, NJ 07076, U.S.A.

PHILBRICK, **(W.) Rodman.** Also writes as Chris Jordan. American (born United States), b. 1951. **Genres:** Mystery/Crime/Suspense, Children's Fiction, Novels, Sports/Fitness, Social Commentary. **Career:** Writer, 1987-. **Publications:** Shooting Star (mystery), 1982; Slow Dancer: A Connie Kale Investigation, 1984; Shadow Kills: A Novel of Mystery, 1985; Ice for the Eskimo: A J.D. Hawkins Mystery, 1986; Neon Flamingo: A T.D. Stash Crime Adventure, 1987; The Crystal Blue Persuasion (crime), 1988; Tough Enough (crime), 1989; Paint It Black: A J.D. Hawkins Mystery, 1989; The Big Chip, 1990; Walk on the Water (mystery), 1991; Freak the Mighty (young adult), 1993; (with L. Harnett) The Final Nightmare, Book III, 1995; The Fire Pony (juvenile), 1996; (with Harnett) The Werewolf Chronicles, Number 01: Night Creature, 1996; (with Harnett and J. Feiwel) Children of the Wolf, 1996; The Mighty, 1997; (with Harnett) Strange Invaders, vol. I, 1997; (with Harnett) Things, vol. II, 1997; (with Harnett) Brain Stealers, vol. III, 1997; (with Harnett) Abduction, 1998; Max the Mighty, 1998; REM World, 2000; Last Book in the Universe, 2000; Journal of Douglas Allen Deeds: The Donner Party Expedition, 2001; Coffins, 2002; Young Man and the Sea, 2004; Taken, 2006; Mostly True Adventures of Homer P. Figg, 2009. AS WILLIAM R. DANTZ: Seventh Sleeper, 1991; Hunger, 1992; Nine Levels Down, 1995. AS CHRIS JORDAN: Taken, 2006; Trapped, 2007; Torn, 2009. **Address:** St. Martin's Press, 175 5th Ave., New York, NY 10010, U.S.A. **Online address:** philbrick@earthlink.net

PHILIP, **George.** British (born England), b. 1951. **Genres:** Economics, Politics/Government. **Career:** University of London, Institute of Latin American Studies, research fellow, 1975-76, lecturer in Latin American politics, 1976-86, reader in Latin American politics, 1986-91, London School of Economics and Political Science, lecturer in Latin American politics, 1976-86, reader in Latin American politics, 1986-91, reader in comparative and Latin American politics, 1991-2001, professor of comparative and Latin American politics, 2001-, Department of Government, head, 2004-07, team leader for Latin America. Writer. **Publications:** The Rise and Fall of the Peruvian Military Radicals, 1968-1976, 1978; Oil and Politics in Ecuador, 1972-1976, 1979; Oil and Politics in Latin America, 1982; The Military in South American Politics, 1985; (ed.) Politics in Mexico, 1985; (ed. with C. Clapham) The Political Dilemmas of Military Regimes, 1985; (ed. with R. Enriquez) The Mexican Economy, 1988; (ed.) British Documents on Foreign Affairs-Reports and Papers from the Foreign Office Confidential Print, 20 vols., 1989-1992; The Presidency in Mexican Politics, 1992; The Political Economy of International Oil, 1994; Democracy in Latin America: Surviving Conflict and Crises?, 2003; Democracy and Development in Latin America, 2005; (with F. Panizza) The Return of the Left, 2011. **Address:** London School of Economics and Political Science, University of London, H505, Connaught House, Houghton St., London, GL WC2A 2AE, England. **Online address:** g.philip@lse.ac.uk

PHILIP, **M(arlene) Nourbese.** Canadian/Trinidadian (born Trinidad and Tobago), b. 1947. **Genres:** Young Adult Fiction, Novels, Essays, Plays/Screenplays, Poetry. **Career:** Carswell Publishing, staff, 1981-88; Ontario Legal

Aid, interviewing lawyer, 1983-86; Workers Compensation Appeals Tribunal, vice chair, 1986-88; York University, creative fiction lecturer, 1989-91; Banff Centre of the Arts, resident, 1990, 1993-94; University of Toronto, lecturer, 1992-; Ontario College of Art, lecturer and course director; McMaster University, writer-in-residence; University of Windsor, writer-in-residence. **Publications:** YOUNG ADULT FICTION: Harriet's Daughter (Caribbean Writers), 1988. ADULT FICTION: Looking for Livingstone: An Odyssey of Silence, 1991. POETRY: Thorns, 1980; Salmon Courage, 1983; She Tries Her Tongue, Her Silence Softly Breaks, 1989; Zong!, 2008. NOVEL: Harriet's Daughter, 1988. OTHERS: Frontiers: Selected Essays And Writings on Racism and Culture, 1984-1992, 1992; A Genealogy of Resistance: And Other Essays, 1997; Coups and Calypsos: A Play, 2001. Contributor to journals. Works appear in anthologies. **Address:** The Mercury Press, PO Box 672, Sta. P, Toronto, ON M5S 2Y4, Canada. **Online address:** nourbese@nourbese.com

PHILIPPE, Daniel. *See* **MASON, Daniel.**

PHILIPSEN, Dirk. American/German (born Germany), b. 1959. **Genres:** History, Economics. **Career:** Virginia State University, professor of history, Institute for the Study of Race Relations, founder and director; Duke University, John Hope Franklin Humanities Institute, Andrew W. Mellon Foundation fellow, 2009-10. Writer. **Publications:** We Were the People: Voices from East Germany's Revolutionary Autumn of 1989, 1993; Who Counts? What We Measure Matters: A History of the GDP, 2013. **Address:** Department of History, Virginia State University, Colson 101 D, 1 Hayden Dr., Petersburg, VA 23806-1000, U.S.A. **Online address:** dphilipsen@vsu.edu

PHILLIPPY, Patricia Berrahou. American (born United States), b. 1960. **Genres:** Poetry, Literary Criticism And History, Biography. **Career:** Texas A&M University, assistant professor, associate professor, professor, 1989-2010; Kingston University, Faculty of Arts and Social Sciences, professor of English literature and creative writing. Writer. **Publications:** Love's Remedies: Recantation and Renaissance Lyric Poetry, 1995; Women, Death and Literature in Post-Reformation England, 2002; Painting Women: Cosmetics, Canvases and Early Modern Culture, 2006. **Address:** Faculty of Arts and Social Sciences, Kingston University, Penrhyn Rd., HH32, Kingston upon Thames, SR KT1 2EE, England. **Online address:** p.phillippy@kingston.ac.uk

PHILLIPS, Carl. American (born United States), b. 1959. **Genres:** Poetry, Translations, Essays, Young Adult Fiction. **Career:** Falmouth High School, high school teacher, 1985-91; Washington University, assistant professor, 1993-96, associate professor, 1996-, professor of English and African and African-American studies writing program, faculty and writer. **Publications:** POEMS: In the Blood, 1992; Cortège, 1995; From the Devotions, 1998; Pastoral, 2000; (ed. and intro.) The Drowned City, 2000; The Tether, 2001; (trans.) Philoctetes, 2001; Rock Harbor, 2002; The Rest of Love, 2004; Coin of the Realm: Essays on the Life and Art of Poetry, 2004; Rest of Love, 2004; Riding Westward, 2006; Quiver of Arrows: Selected Poems, 1986-2006, 2007; Speak Low, 2009; Double Shadow, 2011. Works appear in anthologies. **Address:** Department of English, Washington University, 1 Brookings Dr., PO Box 1122, St. Louis, MO 63130-4899, U.S.A. **Online address:** cphillips@wustl.edu

PHILLIPS, Caryl. American/West Indian (born British West Indies), b. 1958. **Genres:** Novels, Plays/Screenplays, Travel/Exploration. **Career:** Observer Festival of Theatre, founding chair, 1978, artistic director, 1979; Factory Arts Center, Arts Council of Great Britain, writer-in-residence, 1980-82; Arvon Foundation, writing instructor, 1983-95; The Bush Theatre, director, 1985-89; University of Mysore, Literary Criterion Centre, writer-in-residence, 1987; Literary Criterion Centre, staff, 1987; University of Kent, honorary senior staff, 1988-; The Caribbean Writer, board director, 1989-; University of Stockholm, writer-in-residence, 1989; Stockholm University, faculty, 1989; University of Ghana, visiting lecturer, 1990; Amherst College, visiting writer, 1990-92, writer-in-residence, 1992-98, professor of English, 1994-98, Creative Writing Center, co-director, 1992-97; University of Poznan, visiting lecturer, 1991; Faber Inc., consulting editor, 1992-94, Caribbean series editor, 1996-; Humber College, visiting writer, 1992, 1993; Bomb Magazine, contributing editor, 1993-; National Institute of Education, writer-in-residence, 1994; Graywolf Press, consultant editor, 1994-; Heartland Productions Ltd., director, 1994-2000; Wasifiri Magazine, advisory editor, 1995-; Columbia University, Barnard College, professor of English, Henry R. Luce Professor of Migration and Social Order, 1998-2005, Initiatives in the Humanities, director, 2002-05, visiting professor of English and Weiss international fellow in literature and the arts, 2005-06, Barnard Forum on Migration, director; University of the West Indies, visiting professor in the humanities, 1999, 2000; British Council, senior advisor for literature, 2002-; New York Public Library, Dorothy and Lewis B. Cullman Center for Scholars and Writers, Mel and Lois Tukman fellow, 2002-03; Yale University, professor of English, 2005-; North American Network of Cities of Asylum, vice president, 2005-09; Het Beschrijf, writer-in-residence, 2007; Dartmouth College, Montgomery fellow-in-residence and visiting professor of English, 2008; University of Oxford, Department of English, visiting professor, 2009; Oxford University, Queen's College, honorary fellow. **Publications:** PLAYS: Where There is Darkness, 1982; The Shelter, 1984; The Final Passage, 1985. NONFICTION: A State of Independence, 1986; The European Tribe, 1987; Higher Ground: A Novel in Three Parts, 1989; Crossing the River, 1993; The Atlantic Sound, 2000; In the Falling Snow, 2009; Conversations with Caryl Phillips, 2009. EDITOR: Extravagant Strangers, 1997; The Right Set: A Tennis Anthology, 1999; The Right Set: The Faber Book of Tennis, 1999. OTHERS: Cambridge: A Novel, 1992; The Nature of Blood, 1997; A New World Order, 2001; A Distant Shore, 2003; Dancing in the Dark, 2005; Foreigners, 2007; Color me English, 2011. **Address:** Judy Daish Associates, 2 St. Charles Pl., London, GL W10 6EQ, England.

PHILLIPS, Christopher. American (born United States), b. 1959. **Genres:** Philosophy, Social Sciences, Politics/Government. **Career:** Society of Philosophical Inquiry, co-founder and executive director. Freelance journalist and educator. **Publications:** The Philosophers' Club, 2001; Socrates Café: A Fresh Taste of Philosophy, 2001; Six Questions of Socrates: A Modern-Day Journey of Discovery through World Philosophy, 2004; (as Chris Phillips) Ceci Ann's Day of Why, 2006; Socrates in Love: Philosophy for a Passionate Heart, 2007; Constitution Café: Jefferson's Brew for a True Revolution, 2011. Contributor of articles to newspapers and magazines. **Address:** Society for Philosophical Inquiry, PO Box 3718, Williamsburg, VA 23187-3718, U.S.A. **Online address:** christopher_phillips@mac.com

PHILLIPS, Clyde. American (born United States) **Genres:** Novels, Mystery/Crime/Suspense, Adult Non-fiction, Criminology/True Crime, Literary Criticism And History, Young Adult Fiction. **Career:** Television producer; film and television writer. **Publications:** Fall from Grace, 1998; Blindsided: A Mystery, 2000; Sacrifice, 2003. Contributor to periodicals. **Address:** c/o Author Mail, William Morrow, HarperCollins Publishers, 10 E 53rd St., New York, NY 10022, U.S.A.

PHILLIPS, Delores. American (born United States), b. 1950?. **Genres:** Novels, Young Adult Fiction, Literary Criticism And History. **Career:** Writer and psychiatric nurse. **Publications:** The Darkest Child, 2004. Contributor to periodicals. **Address:** c/o Author Mail, Soho Press Inc., 853 Broadway, New York, NY 10003, U.S.A.

PHILLIPS, Derek L. Dutch/American (born United States), b. 1934. **Genres:** Art/Art History, History, Philosophy, Sociology, Politics/Government. **Career:** Wellesley College, instructor in sociology, 1962-63; Dartmouth College, assistant professor of sociology, 1963-66; New York University, associate professor, professor of sociology, 1966-71; Universiteit van Amsterdam, Sociologisch Instituut, professor of sociology, 1971-99, emeritus professor of sociology, 1999-. Writer. **Publications:** (Ed.) Studies in American Society, 1965, vol. II, 1967; Knowledge from What? Theories and Methods in Social Research, 1971; Abandoning Method, 1973; Wittgenstein and Scientific Knowledge: A Sociological Perspective, 1977; Equality, Justice, and Rectification: An Exploration in Normative Sociology, 1979; De Naakte Nederlander, 1985; Toward a Just Social Order, 1986; Looking Backward: A Critical Appraisal of Communitarian Thought, 1993; (with K. Muizelaar) Picturing Men and Women in the Dutch Golden Age: Paintings and People in Historical Perspective, 2003; Well-being in Amsterdam's Golden Age, 2008. Contributor to journals. **Address:** Sociologisch Instituut, Universiteit van Amsterdam, Oude Hoogstraat 24, Amsterdam, 1012 CE, Netherlands.

PHILLIPS, Holly. Canadian (born Canada), b. 1969. **Genres:** Novels, Novellas/Short Stories. **Career:** Writer. **Publications:** In the Palace of Repose (short stories), 2005; The Burning Girl (novel), 2006; The Engine's Child (novel), 2008; (ed. with C. Doctorow) Tesseracts Eleven (short story collection), 2008. CONTRIBUTOR OF SHORT STORIES: Horror: The Best of the Year, 2006; Best of the Rest 4, 2006; Eidolon I, 2006; Fantasy Anthology, 2007; Interfictions, 2007; A Book of Wizards, 2008. Contributor to magazines. **Address:** Victoria, BC , Canada. **Online address:** milligan@netidea.com

PHILLIPS, Hugh D. American (born United States), b. 1952. **Genres:** Biography. **Career:** Vanderbilt University, Department of History, teaching fellow, 1981-85, visiting professor of history, 2000-; Troy State University, Department of History and Social Sciences, visiting assistant professor of history, 1985-86; University of Alabama, Department of History, assistant professor of history, 1986-88; Western Kentucky University, Department of History, assistant professor, 1988-90, associate professor of history, 1990-99, professor, 1999-, Russian and East European Studies, director, 1989-. Writer. **Publications:** Between the Revolution and the West: A Political Biography of Maxim M. Litvinov, 1992. **Address:** Department of History, Western Kentucky University, 230A Cherry Hall, 1906 College Heights Blvd., Bowling Green, KY 42101-1000, U.S.A. **Online address:** hugh.phillips@wku.edu

PHILLIPS, Jason. American (born United States), b. 1973. **Genres:** History. **Career:** Mississippi State University, assistant professor of history. Writer. **Publications:** Diehard Rebels: The Confederate Culture of Invincibility, 2007. Contributor of articles and essays to books, periodicals and journals. **Address:** MS , U.S.A. **Online address:** jphillips@history.msstate.edu

PHILLIPS, Jayne Anne. American (born United States), b. 1952. **Genres:** Novels, Novellas/Short Stories, Literary Criticism And History. **Career:** Humboldt State University, lecturer, 1978-79; New York University, faculty; Williams College, faculty; Radcliffe College, assistant professor, 1980-81; Boston University, assistant professor of English, 1982-83; Brandeis University, chair of letters, 1986-87, fiction writer-in-residence, 1987-; Harvard University, visiting senior lecturer, 1990, 1993-94; Rutgers-The State University of New Jersey, professor of English, MFA Program, director. Writer. **Publications:** Sweethearts, 1976; Counting, 1978; Black Tickets, 1979; How Mickey Made It, 1981; The Secret Country, 1983; Machine Dreams, 1984; Fast Lanes, 1987; The Last Day of Summer, 1993; Shelter: A Novel, 1994; Motherkind: A Novel, 2000; Lark and Termite: A Novel, 2009. Works appear in anthologies. Contributor to magazines. **Address:** Department of English, Rutgers-Newark-State University of New Jersey, 43 Bleeker St., Newark, NJ 07102-1801, U.S.A. **Online address:** japhillips@andromeda.rutgers.edu

PHILLIPS, John Lawrence. American (born United States), b. 1923. **Genres:** Education, Mathematics/Statistics, Psychology, Medicine/Health. **Career:** Carbon College, director of guidance and instructor in psychology, 1953-54; University of Utah, instructor in educational psychology, 1954; Boise Junior College, Department of psychology, chair, director of student personnel services, 1954-57, dean, 1957-59, Division of Social Sciences, chair, 1959-68; Boise State University, chairman, Division of Social Sciences, 1959-68, Department of Psychology, professor and chairman, 1968-88, professor emeritus, 1988-; American College Testing Program, state coordinator, 1959-66. Writer. **Publications:** (Ed.) Counselor's Guide to Idaho Colleges, 1965, 4th ed., 1971; (co-author) Counseling and Confidentiality, 1968; (co-author) Freedom and Determinism in Counseling Psychology, 1968; The Origins of Intellect: Piaget's Theory, 1969, 2nd ed., 1975; Statistical Thinking: A Structural Approach, 1973, 2nd ed., 1988; Piaget's Theory: A Primer, 1981; How to Think about Statistics, 1988, 6th ed., 2000. Contributor to journals. **Address:** Department of Psychology, Boise State University, 1910 University Dr., Boise, ID 83707, U.S.A.

PHILLIPS, Jonathan P. British (born England) **Genres:** History, Race Relations, Theology/Religion. **Career:** University of London, Royal Holloway College, Department of History, senior lecturer in medieval history, reader, professor of crusading history. Writer. **Publications:** Defenders of the Holy Land: Relations Between the Latin East and the West, 1119-1187, 1996; (ed.) The First Crusade: Origins and Impact, 1997; (foreword) De Expugnatione Lyxbonensi = The Conquest of Lisbon, 2000; (ed. with M. Hoch) The Second Crusade: Scope and Consequences, 2002; The Crusades, 1095-1197, 2002; (contrib.) The Experience of Crusading, 2003; The Fourth Crusade and the Sack of Constantinople, 2004; Second Crusade: Extending the Frontiers of Christendom, 2007; Holy Warriors: A Modern History of the Crusades, 2009. **Address:** Department of History, Royal Holloway College, University of London, 321 McCrea Bldg., Egham Hill, Egham, SR TW20 0EX, England. **Online address:** j.p.phillips@rhul.ac.uk

PHILLIPS, Kate. American (born United States), b. 1966. **Genres:** Novels, Literary Criticism And History, Biography, Young Adult Fiction. **Career:** Beijing Normal University, teacher, 1988-89; Irish Immigration Center, grant writer and newsletter editor, 1992-95. **Publications:** White Rabbit, 1996; Helen Hunt Jackson: A Literary Life, 2003; Santa Clara, forthcoming. Contributor to periodicals. **Address:** c/o Anne Borchardt, Georges Borchardt Literary Agency, 136 E 57th St., New York, NY 10022, U.S.A.

PHILLIPS, Kenneth J. H. British (born England), b. 1946. **Genres:** Sciences. **Career:** National Aeronautics and Space Administration, Goddard Space Flight Center, National Research Council, postdoctoral fellow, 1972-75; University of Hawaii, National Science Foundation postdoctoral fellow, 1975-76; Rutherford Appleton Laboratory, research scientist, 1977-2002; Queen's University, honorary lecturer, 1997-2002, senior research associate, 2002-05; University College London, research fellow, 2006-08, visiting professor, 2008-. Writer. **Publications:** Guide to the Sun, 1992; (ed. with D.N. Mishev) First Results of 1999 Total Eclipse Observations: Proceedings of the International Conference Held in Varna, Bulgaria, 11-15 September, 2000, 2002; (with U. Feldman and E. Landi) Ultraviolet and X-ray Spectroscopy of the Solar Atmosphere, 2008. Contributor of articles to journals and magazines. Works appear in anthologies. **Address:** Cambridge University Press, 32 Ave. of the Americas, New York, NY 10013-2473, U.S.A. **Online address:** phillips@stars.gsfc.nasa.gov

PHILLIPS, Leroy. *See* Obituaries.

PHILLIPS, Lisa. American (born United States), b. 1956. **Genres:** Art/Art History, Young Adult Fiction, Photography. **Career:** Whitney Museum of American Art, curator, 1980-98; Yale University, visiting professor; Chase Manhattan Bank, consulting curator; New Museum of Contemporary Art, director, 1999-. Writer. **Publications:** Third Dimension: Sculpture of the New York School, 1984; (intro.) High Styles: Twentieth-century American Design, 1985; (with P. Shjeldahl) Cindy Sherman, 1986; Frederick Kiesler 1989; Image World: Art and Media Culture, 1989; (with K. Kertess) Terry Winters, 1991; Richard Prince, 1992; (with M.E. Gonzalez) Photoplay: Works from the Chase Manhattan Collection, 1993; Beat Culture and the New America, 1950-1965, 1995; Biennial Exhibition, 1997; (with P. Schimmel) Charles Ray, 1998; Vital Signs: Organic Abstraction from the Permanent Collection, 1998; The American Century: Art & Culture, 1950-2000, 1999; Paul McCarthy, 2000; (intro.) 13 Alumni Artists, 2000; Carrol Dunham: Paintings, 2002; (with M. Heiferman) John Waters: Change of Life, 2004; Obsession Everlasting, 2009; Knight Everlasting, 2010; Rogue Everlasting, 2011. **Address:** New Museum of Contemporary Art, 235 Bowery, New York, NY 10002, U.S.A. **Online address:** lphillips@newmuseum.org

PHILLIPS, Marie. British (born England), b. 1976. **Genres:** Novels. **Career:** Writer. **Publications:** Gods Behaving Badly (novel), 2007; (co-author) Because I Am a Girl, 2010. **Address:** c/o David Godwin, David Godwin Associates Ltd., 55 Monmouth St., London, GL WC2H 9DG, England.

PHILLIPS, Mike. Guyanese (born Guyana), b. 1941?. **Genres:** Novels, Novellas/Short Stories, Plays/Screenplays, Social Commentary, Race Relations, Biography. **Career:** British Broadcasting Corp., journalist and broadcaster, 1972-83; University of Westminster, London, senior lecturer in media studies, 1983-92; writer, 1992-; Gresham College, professor of music. **Publications:** Community Work and Racism, 1982; Smell of the Coast and Other Stories, 1987; Blood Rights, 1989; The Late Candidate, 1990; Notting Hill in the Sixties, 1991; Boyz N the Hood: A Novel, 1991; (contrib.) Whose Cities?, 1991; (contrib.) Shelter Anniversary Book, 1991; Point of Darkness, 1995; Fast Road To Nowhere, 1996; An Image to Die For, 1997; The Dancing Face, 1997; (with T. Philips) Windrush: The Irresistible Rise of Multi-Racial Britain, 1998; A Shadow of Myself, 2000; London Crossings: A Biography of Black Britain, 2001; Kind of Union, 2005. Works appear in anthologies. Contributor of articles to periodicals. **Address:** c/o Anthony Harwood, Curtis Brown Ltd., Haymarket House, 28-29 Haymarket, London, GL SW1Y 4SP, England.

PHILLIPS, Patrick. American (born United States), b. 1970. **Genres:** Poetry. **Career:** Poet. **Publications:** Chattahoochee (poems), 2004; Boy (poems), 2008. **Address:** Brooklyn, NY , U.S.A. **Online address:** patrick@patrickthemighty.com

PHILLIPS, Roderick (Goler). Canadian/New Zealander (born New Zealand), b. 1947?. **Genres:** Food And Wine, History, Demography, Human Relations/Parenting, Women's Studies And Issues. **Career:** University of Auckland, lecturer, 1976-78, senior lecturer in history, 1978-83; Queen's University, assistant professor of history, 1983-86; Brock University, professor of history, 1987-89; Carleton University, professor of history, 1989-; University of Texas, Walter Prescott Webb memorial lecturer, 1990; Journal of Family History, editor, 1996-; Sage Publications, general editor, 1996-; Ottawa Citizen, wine columnist; Research Institute for the Culture and History of Food and Drink, director. **Publications:** (Ed.) Alternatives to ANZUS, 1977; Family Breakdown in Late Eighteenth-Century France: Divorces in Rouen, 1792-1803, 1980; Divorce in New Zealand: A Social History, 1981; Putting Asunder: A History of Divorce in Western Society, 1988; Untying the Knot: A Short History of Divorce in the Western World, 1991; Society, State and Nation in Twentieth-Century Europe, 1996; A Short History of Wine, 2000; Ontario Wine Country, 2006; The 500 Best Value Wines in the LCBO, 2007. **Address:** Department of History, Carleton University, 1125 Colonel By Dr., Ottawa, ON K1S 5B6, Canada. **Online address:** roderick_phillips@carleton.ca

PHILLIPS, Sarah T. American (born United States), b. 1974. **Genres:** History. **Career:** Columbia University, assistant professor of history. Writer. **Publications:** This Land, This Nation: Conservation, Rural America and the New Deal, 2007. Contributor to books and periodicals. **Address:** Department of History, Columbia University, 611 Fayerweather Hall, 1180 Amsterdam Ave., New York, NY 10027-7039, U.S.A. **Online address:** sp2313@columbia.edu

PHILLIPS, Scott. American (born United States), b. 1961?. **Genres:** Novels, Mystery/Crime/Suspense, Young Adult Fiction. **Career:** Writer and photographer. **Publications:** NOVELS: The Ice Harvest, 2000; The Walkaway, 2003; Cottonwood, 2004; (with L.C. Templeton) Investing the Templeton Way: The Market-beating Strategies of Value Investing's Legendary Bargain Hunter, 2008; Adjustment: A Novel, 2011. **Address:** c/o Nicole Aragi, Aragi Inc., 143 W 27th St., Ste. 4F, New York, NY 10001, U.S.A. **Online address:** scott@scottphillipsauthor.com

PHILLIPS, Sky. American (born United States), b. 1921. **Genres:** Romance/Historical, History. **Career:** Air Force Officers Wives Club, president. Writer. **Publications:** Secret Mission to Melbourne, November 1941, 1992. **Address:** c/o Sara Sheppard Landis, 271 Ave. C, New York, NY 10009, U.S.A.

PHILLIPS, Stephen H. American (born United States), b. 1950. **Genres:** Philosophy, Humanities, Social Sciences. **Career:** University of Texas, professor of philosophy and Asian studies, 1982-; University of Hawaii, visiting professor, 1995. Writer. **Publications:** Aurobindo's Philosophy of Brahman, 1986; (ed. with R. Kane) Hartshorne, Process Philosophy, and Theology, 1989; (ed. with D. Bonevac and W. Boon) Beyond the Western Tradition: Readings in Moral and Political Philosophy, 1992; (ed. with D. Bonevac) Understanding Non-Western Philosophy: Introductory Readings, 1993; Classical Indian Metaphysics: Refutations of Realism and the Emergence of New Logic, 1995; Philosophy of Religion: A Global Approach, 1996; (with R. Tatacharya) Gangeśa on the Upādhi, the Inferential Undercutting Condition: Introduction, Translation, and Explanation, 2002; Epistemology of Perception, 2004; Yoga, Karma and Rebirth: A Brief History and Philosophy, 2009; (with D. Bonevac) Introduction to World Philosophy: A Multicultural Reader, 2009; Proof of Momentariness By Positive Correlation: The Ksanabhangasiddhi Anvayatmika by Ratnakirti, forthcoming. **Address:** Department of Philosophy & Asian Studies, University of Texas, Waggener Hall 301, C3500, Austin, TX 78712, U.S.A. **Online address:** phillips@mail.utexas.edu

PHILLIPS, Susan E. American (born United States), b. 1970?. **Genres:** Adult Non-fiction, History, Social Sciences, Literary Criticism And History. **Career:** Northwestern University, Weinberg College of Arts and Sciences, Department of English, associate professor and associate chair; Medievalists' Writing Workshop, co-director. Writer. **Publications:** Transforming Talk: The Problem with Gossip in Late Medieval England, 2007. **Address:** Department of English, Weinberg College of Arts and Sciences, Northwestern University, Rm. 315, University Hall, 1897 Sheridan Rd., Evanston, IL 60208-2240, U.S.A. **Online address:** susie-phillips@northwestern.edu

PHILLIPS, Susan S. American (born United States), b. 1954. **Genres:** Human Relations/Parenting, Sociology, Theology/Religion. **Career:** New College Berkeley, adjunct professor of sociology, 1985-, academic dean, 1992-94, executive director, 1994-, professor of sociology and Christianity; University of California, adjunct professor; Fuller Theological Seminary, adjunct professor; Regent College, adjunct professor; Ontario Theological Seminary, adjunct professor. Writer. **Publications:** (With P. Benner) The Crisis of Care: Affirming and Restoring Caring Practices in the Helping Professions, 1994; Candlelight: Illuminating the Art of Spiritual Direction, 2008. **Address:** New College Berkeley, 2029 Durant Ave., Berkeley, CA 94704-1564, U.S.A. **Online address:** suphillips@aol.com

PHILLIPS, Suzanne. American (born United States) **Genres:** Novels. **Career:** Writer. **Publications:** Chloe Doe in UK as Miss America, 2007; Burn, 2008. **Address:** Jodie Rhodes Literary Agency, 8840 Villa La Jolla Dr., Ste. 315, La Jolla, CA 92037, U.S.A.

PHILLIPS, Timothy. British/Irish (born Ireland) **Genres:** Theology/Religion, History, Young Adult Fiction. **Career:** British Broadcasting Corp., translator, principal translator. Writer. **Publications:** Beslan: The Tragedy of School No. 1, 2007. **Address:** David Higham Associates, 5-8 Lower John St., Golden Sq., London, GL W1F 9HA, England.

PHILLIPS, T. J. *See* **SAVAGE, Tom.**

PHILLIPSON, David W. British (born England), b. 1942. **Genres:** Anthropology/Ethnology, Archaeology/Antiquities. **Career:** Zambia National Monuments Commission, secretary and inspector, 1964-72; British Institute in Eastern Africa, assistant director, 1973-79; Glasgow Museums and Art Galleries, keeper of archaeology, ethnography, and history, 1979-81; Cambridge University, Museum of Archaeology and Anthropology, director and curator, 1981-2006, reader in African prehistory, 1991-2001, professor of African archaeology, 2001-, faculty chair, now professor emeritus, Gonville and Caius College, professorial fellow, now emeritus fellow. Writer. **Publications:** (With B.M. Fagan and S.G.H. Daniels) Iron Age Cultures in Zambia, 1967, vol. II, 1969; (comp.) An Annotated Bibliography of the Archaeology of Zambia, 1968; Prehistoric Rock Paintings and Engravings of Zambia: Exhibition Catalogue, 1972; Historical Notes on Political Development in Zambia, 1972; National Monuments of Zambia: An Illustrated Guide, 1972; (ed.) Mosi-oa-Tunya: A Handbook to the Victoria Falls Region, 1975, 2nd ed., 1990; Iron Age in Zambia, 1975; (contrib.) Supplementary Bibliography of the Archaeology of Zambia, 1967-1973, 1975; The Prehistory of Eastern Zambia, 1976; The Later Prehistory of Eastern and Southern Africa, 1977; (with L. Phillipson) East Africa's Prehistoric Past, 1978; African Archaeology, 1985, 3rd ed., 2005; (ed.) Excavations at Aksum: An Account of Research at the Ancient Ethiopian Capital Directed in 1972-4 by the Late Dr. Neville Chittick, 1989; (ed.) The Monuments of Aksum: An Illustrated Account, 1997; Ancient Ethiopia: Aksum, Its Antecedents and Successors, 1998; Archaeology at Aksum, Ethiopia, 1993-7, 2000; Archaeology in Africa and in Museums: Inaugural Lecture Delivered at the University of Cambridge, 22 October 2002, 2003; Ancient Churches of Ethiopia: Fourth-Fourteenth Centuries, 2009. **Address:** Gonville & Caius College, Cambridge University, Trinity St., Cambridge, CB CB2 1TA, England. **Online address:** dw.l.phillipson@btinternet.com

PHILLIPSON, Michael. British (born England), b. 1940. **Genres:** Art/Art History, Communications/Media, Cultural/Ethnic Topics, Philosophy, Sociology, History. **Career:** Medical Research Council, research officer, 1964-66; University of London, Bedford College, research officer, 1966; Political and Economic Planning, research officer, 1967; University of London, Goldsmiths College, senior lecturer in sociology, communications and art, 1967-91; Middlesex University, Department of Fine Art, part-time teacher; freelance writer. **Publications:** Making Fuller Use of Survey Data, 1968; Sociological Aspects of Crime and Delinquency, 1971; (with P. Filmer, D. Silverman and D. Walsh) New Directions in Sociological Theory, 1972; Understanding Crime and Delinquency: A Sociological Introduction, 1974; (co-author) Problems of Reflexivity and Dialectics in Sociological Inquiry, 1975; Painting, Language, and Modernity, 1985; In Modernity's Wake: The Ameurunculus Letters, 1989. Contributor to books. **Address:** Derlwyn, Glandwr, Hebron, Whitland, SA34 0YD, Wales. **Online address:** mikphillipson@aol.com

PHILMUS, Robert M(ichael). Canadian/American (born United States), b. 1943. **Genres:** Literary Criticism And History, Science Fiction/Fantasy, Humanities. **Career:** Carleton College, instructor in English, 1967-68; Concordia University, Loyola Campus, assistant professor, 1968-72, associate professor, 1973-77, professor of English, 1977-98, emeritus professor, 1998-. Writer. **Publications:** Into the Unknown: The Evolution of Science Fiction from Francis Godwin to H.G. Wells, 1970; (ed. with D.Y. Hughes) H.G. Wells: Early Writings in Science and Science Fiction, 1975; (ed.) H.G. Wells and Modern Science Fiction, 1977; (ed. with P. Parrinder) H.G. Wells's Literary Criticism, 1980; (ed.) Island of Doctor Moreau: A Variorum Text, 1993; Visions and Revisions: (Re)constructing Science Fiction, 2006. Contributor to journals. **Address:** Department of English, Concordia University, Loyola Campus, 1455 De Maisonneuve Blvd., Montreal, QC H3G 1M8, Canada.

PHILP, Richard B(lain). Canadian (born Canada), b. 1934. **Genres:** Environmental Sciences/Ecology, Medicine/Health. **Career:** University of Western Ontario, professor, 1965-, adjunct professor of physiology and pharmacology, now professor emeritus of pharmacology and toxicology; Pharmaceutical Industry, consultant. Writer. **Publications:** Methods of Testing Proposed Antithrombotic Drugs, 1981; Environmental Hazards and Human Health, 1995; Ecosystems and Human Health: Environmental Hazards and Toxicology, 2001; Herbal-Drug Interactions and Adverse Effects: An Evidence-based Quick Reference Guide, 2004. Contributor to books and journals. **Address:** University of Western Ontario, 1151 Richmond St., London, ON N6A 3K7, Canada. **Online address:** rphilp@uwo.ca

PHILPOTT, Don. American/British (born England), b. 1946. **Genres:** Travel/Exploration, Food And Wine. **Career:** Reuters-Press Association, senior correspondent, 1968-88, editor; Mediawise Communications-London, founder and president, 1988-94; Mediawise Communications-Orlando, founder and president, 1994-; Institute of Public Relations, media trainer. Writer. **Publications:** The Vineyards of France, 1987; Visitor's Guide to Iceland, 1989; Wine and Food of Bulgaria, 1990; Florida: A Home Buyer's Guide, 1992; Champagne Almanac, 1993; The Wine Drinker's Almanac, 1993; Food, Fact, and Fantasy, 1994; (co-author) Off the Beaten Track: Austria, 2nd ed., 1994; Visitor's Guide to Norway, 1995; Visitor's Guide to USA: Vermont, New Hampshire, and Maine, 1995; Visitor's Guide to Burgundy and Beaujolais, 1995; Visitor's Guide to the Windward Islands, 1996; Antigua & Barbuda, 1999; (with P. Philpott) The Trailside Cookbook: A Handbook for Hungry Campers and Hikers, 2005; (with M.W. Kuenstle) Education Facility Security Handbook, 2007; (with D. Grimme) Workplace Violence Prevention Handbook, 2009; (with J. Hill) Wounded Warrior Handbook: A Resource Guide for Returning Veterans, 2009; (ed. with P. Serluco) Public School Emergency Preparedness and Crisis Management Plan, 2010; (with J. Hill and C. Lawhorne) Military Marriage Manual: Tactics for Successful Relationships, 2010; (with R.T. Jordan) Is America Safe?: Terrorism, Homeland Security, and Emergency Preparedness, 2010; (with C. Lawhorne) Combat-related Traumatic Brain Injury and PTSD, 2010; (with J. Hill and C. Lawhorne) Life After the Military: A Handbook for Transitioning Veterans, 2011; (with J. Hill) Special Needs Families in the Military: A Resource Guide, 2011; (ed.) Guide to Federal Terms and Acronyms, 2011. CARIBBEAN SUNSEEKERS SERIES: Grenada, 1994; St. Lucia, 1994; St. Vincent & Grenadines, 1994; U.S. Virgin Islands, 1996; Dominica, 1996. **Address:** Florida Features, 375 Douglas Ave., Ste. 1002, Altamonte Springs, FL 32714, U.S.A. **Online address:** dp@donphilpott.com

PHONGPAICHIT, Pasuk. Thai (born Thailand), b. 1946. **Genres:** Social Commentary, Adult Non-fiction, Psychology. **Career:** Monash University, teaching fellow, faculty of economics, 1970-71; Chulalongkorn University, lecturer, faculty of economics, 1971-73, Economic Research Unit, senior lecturer and director, 1979-80, associate professor, 1985-99, professor of economics, 1999-, Political Economy Center, director, 1990-93; University of Cambridge, part-time teaching fellow, 1978-79; International Labour Office, Asian Regional Team for Employment, expert and developmental economist, 1980-84; Institute of Southeast Asian Studies, research fellow, 1988-89; Johns Hopkins University, School of Advanced International Studies, visiting professor, 2001; Griffith University, Jackson Memorial fellow, 2003; Center of Southeast Asian Studies, research fellow, 2004-05; University of Washington, Ames Visiting Professor, 2005; University of Tokyo, Institute of Social Science, visiting professor, 2006-07. Writer. **Publications:** (Ed. with N. Vitchapan) Khāchāng læ ræcngngān samphan nai utsāhakam Thai, 1972; (co-author) Employment, Income and the Mobilisation of Local Resources in Three Thai Villages, 1982; From Peasant Girls to Bangkok Masseuses, 1982; (contrib.) Women, Work and Society, 1985; (ed. with B. Kunasirin and B. Rutchatorn) The Lion and the Mouse? Japan, Asia and Thailand, 1986; (contrib.) Structures of Patriarchy: State, Community and Household in Modernizing Asia, 1988; The New Wave of Japanese Investment in ASEAN: Determinants and Prospects, 1990; (with S.P. bannāthikān) Phonlawat Thai, 1991; (with P. Phongphaichit, bannānhikān and S. Phiriyarangsan) Rat, thun, chaophō thōngthin, kap sangkhom Thai, 1992; (contrib.) The May 1992 Crisis in Thailand: Background and Aftermath, 1993; (ed. with S. Piriyarangsan) Chon chan klāng bon kras prachæhipatai Thai, 1993; (I.S. Hen) Tai no keizai hatten to infōmaru sekutā, 1993; (with S. Phiriyarangsan and bannāthikān) Krachāi amnāt yāngrai sāng prachāthipatai, 1994; (with S. Phiriyarangsan) Khōrapchan kap prachāthipatai Thai, 1994; (with S. Piriyarangsan and N. Treerat) Corruption and Democracy in Thailand, 1994; (with C. Baker) Thailand: Economy and Politics, 1995, 2nd ed., 2002; Challenging Social Exclusion: Rights and Livelihood in Thailand, 1996; (with S. Phiriyarangsan and bannāthikān) Chit samnuk l 'udomkān khōng khabūankān prachāthipatai rūam samai, 1996; (with C. Baker) Thailand's Boom!, 1996, rev. ed. as Thailand's Boom and Bust, 1998; (with S. Piriyarangsan and N. Treerat) Guns, Girls, Gambling, Ganja: Thailand's Illegal Economy and Public Policy, 1998; Phatthanākān utsāhakam l phatthanākān setthakit, prasopkān khōng Kaoli Tai, Brāsin, Thai, 1998; (trans. and intro. with C. Baker) C. Nartsupha, The Thai Village Economy in the Past, 1999; Wikrit setthakit l watthanatham niyom: pāthakathā Prīdī Phanomyong, 1999; (with C. Baker) Thailand's Crisis, 2000; (trans. and intro. with C. Baker) P. Banomyong, Pridi by Pridi, 2000; (co-author) 'Utsāhakam kānphanan Thai, 'Angkrit, Saharat 'Amerikā, 'Otsatrelīa, l Mālesīa, 2000; (contrib.) Thailand beyond Crisis, 2001; (co-author) Withī chīwit withī sū: khabūankan prachāchon rūamsamai, 2002; (with C. Baker) Thaksin: The Business of Politics in Thailand, 2004; (contrib.) After the Storm: Crises, Recovery and Sustaining Development in East Asia, Singapore, 2004; (with C. Baker) A History of Thailand, 2005, 2nd ed., 2009; (contrib.) Populism and Reformism in Asia, 2005; (contrib.) Thailand: Beyond the Crisis, 2005; Kāntōsū khōng thun Thai, 2006; (with C. Baker) Thai Capital After the 1997 Crisis, 2008; (with S. Takashi) The Rise of Middle Classes in Southeast Asia, 2008; Thun Chīang Mai: khrōngsāng khōng thun l kānplīanplng khōng nakthurakit nai Mūang Chīang Mai, 2009; (ed. and trans. with C. Baker) The Tale of Khun Chang, Khun Phaen, 2010; Phāsuk Phongphaichit: panyāchon Sayām wiphāk, 2010. Contributor to periodicals and journals. **Address:** Faculty of Economics, Chulalongkorn University, Phayathai Rd., Bangkok, 10330, Thailand. **Online address:** ppasuk@chula.ac.th

PIANKA, Eric R(odger). *See* Obituaries.

PIASCIK, Andy. American (born United States), b. 1957. **Genres:** History. **Career:** Writer. **Publications:** The Best Show in Football: The 1946-1955 Cleveland Browns, Pro Football's Greatest Dynasty, 2007; Gridiron Gauntlet: The Story of the Men Who Integrated Pro Football, in Their Own Words, 2009. Contributor to magazines. **Address:** CT , U.S.A. **Online address:** andypiascik@yahoo.com

PIATT, Bill. (Robert William Piatt). American (born United States), b. 1950. **Genres:** Law, Novels, Language/Linguistics. **Career:** New Mexico State University, visiting assistant professor of law, 1976-78; University of Oklahoma, assistant professor of law, 1978-79; Washburn University of Topeka, associate professor of law, 1983-87; Southern Illinois University, visiting professor of law, 1987-88; Texas Tech University, associate professor, 1988-90, J. Hadley Edgar professorship of law, 1988, professor of law, 1990-98; St. Mary University School of Law, Ryan professor of law and dean, 1998-. Writer. **Publications:** A Layperson's Guide to New Mexico Law, 1977; Only English? Law and Language Policy in the United States, 1990; (contrib.) Language Loyalties: A Source Book on the Official English Controversy, 1992; Language on the Job: Balancing Business Needs and Employee Rights, 1993; Immigration Law: Cases and Materials, 1994; Black and Brown in America: The Case for Cooperation, 1997; (as Robert William Piatt, Jr.) Catholic Legal Perspectives, 2012. Contributor to periodicals and books. **Address:** School of Law, St. Mary's University, 1 Camino Santa Maria, San Antonio, TX 78228-8503, U.S.A. **Online address:** bpiatt@stmarytx.edu

PIATT, Robert William. *See* **PIATT, Bill.**

PIAZZA, Tom. American (born United States), b. 1955. **Genres:** Novels, Novellas/Short Stories, Music. **Career:** Jazz Magazine, associate editor, 1976-79; freelance music journalist and jazz pianist, 1977-91; Iowa Writer's Workshop, Maytag Fellow and teaching-writing fellow, 1991-93; University of Iowa, teacher of fiction writing, 1992-93; Loyola University, visiting writer-in-residence, 2001-03, Department of English, faculty, 2009; Virginia Center for Creative Arts, writer-in-residence. **Publications:** The Guide to Classic Recorded Jazz, 1995; Blues and Trouble: Twelve Stories (fiction), 1996; (ed.) Setting the Tempo, 1996; Blues Up and Down: Jazz in Our Time, 1997; True Adventures with the King of Bluegrass, 1999; My Cold War (novel), 2003; Understanding Jazz: Ways to Listen, 2005; Why New Orleans Matters, 2008; City of Refuge: A Novel, 2008; Devil Sent The Rain, 2011. Contributor to periodicals. **Address:** c/o Amy Williams, McCormick and Williams,

37 W 20th St., Ste. 606, New York, NY 10011, U.S.A. **Online address:** bluealias@aol.com

PICANO, Felice. American (born United States), b. 1944. **Genres:** Novels, Medicine/Health, Young Adult Fiction. **Career:** New York City Department of Welfare, social worker, 1964-66; Art Direction, assistant editor, 1966-68; Doubleday Bookstore, assistant manager, 1969-70; Rizzoli's Bookstore, assistant manager and buyer, 1972-74; writer, 1974-; Sea Horse Press Ltd., founder and publisher, 1977-94; Gay Presses of New York, co-founder and co-publisher 1980-94; Antioch University, adjunct professor, 2011. **Publications:** Smart as the Devil (novel), 1975; Eyes (novel), 1975; The Mesmerist (novel), 1977; The Deformity Lover and Other Poems, 1978; The Lure (novel), 1979 (ed.) A True Likeness: An Anthology of Lesbian and Gay Writing Today, 1980; An Asian Minor: The True Story of Ganymede, 1981; Late in the Season (novel), 1981; Slashed to Ribbons in Defense of Love and Other Stories, 1983; House of Cards (novel), 1984; Ambidextrous: The Secret Lives of Children (memoir), 1985; Window Elegies (poetry), 1986; Immortal (play with music, based on Picano's novella An Asian Minor: The True Story of Ganymede), 1986; One o'Clock (one-act play), 1986; Men Who Loved Me: A Memoir in the Form of a Novel, 1989; To the Seventh Power, 1990; (with C. Silverstein) The New Joy of Gay Sex, 1992, 3rd ed. as The Joy of Gay Sex, 2003; Like People in History (novel), 1995; Dryland's End, Masquerade Books, 1995; A House on the Ocean, a House on the Bay: A Memoir, 1997; Looking Glass Lives: A Novel, 1998; The Book of Lies (novel), 2000; The New York Years: Stories, 2000; Onyx (novel), 2001; The Bombay Trunk (play), 2002; Fred in Love (memoir), 2005; Tales: From a Distant Planet, 2006; Art and Sex in Greenwich Village: Gay Literary Life after Stonewall, 2007; Ambientes, 2011. Contributor of articles to periodicals. Works appear in anthologies. **Address:** c/o Malaga Baldi, Malaga Baldi Agency, 204 W 84th St., Ste. 3C, New York, NY 10024, U.S.A. **Online address:** felicepic@aol.com

PICCIRILLI, Tom. American (born United States), b. 1965. **Genres:** Novellas/Short Stories, Mystery/Crime/Suspense, Horror, Young Adult Fiction, Adult Non-fiction, Novels, Poetry. **Career:** Pirate Writings Magazine, co-editor; Epitaph Magazine, fiction editor; Space and Time Magazine, fiction editor. **Publications:** NOVELS: Dark Father, 1990; Shards, 1996; (with G.D. Houarner and E. Lee); Inside the Works, 1997; Hexes, 1999; The Deceased, 2000; The Night Class, 2000; A Lower Deep, 2001; Grave Men, 2002; Fuckin' Lie Down Already, 2003; A Choir of Ill Children, 2003; Thrust, 2005; November Mourns, 2005; Headstone City, 2006; The Dead Letters, 2006; The Midnight Road, 2007; The Fever Kill, 2007; Hellboy: Emerald Hell, 2008; The Cold Spot, 2008; The Coldest Mile, 2009; Shadow Season, 2009. COLLECTIONS: Pentacle, 1995; The Hanging Man and Other Strange Suspensions, 1996; The Dog Syndrome and Other Sick Puppies, 1997; Deep into that Darkness Peering, 1999; A Student of Hell, (poems), 2000; (co-author) Four Dark Nights, 2002; This Cape Is Red Because I've Been Bleeding (poetry), 2002; Mean Sheep, 2003; Coffin Blues, 2004; (ed.) The Devil's Wine, 2004. FELICITY GROVE MYSTERY NOVEL SERIES: The Dead Past, 1997; Sorrow's Crown, 1998. NON-FICTION: Welcome to Hell: A Working Guide for the Beginning Writer, 2000; (with E.J. McFadden and J. Yolen) Deconstructing Tolkien: A Fundamental Analysis of the Lord of the Rings, 2004. CHAPBOOKS: (with E. Gorman) Cast in Dark Waters, 2002. OTHER: The Nobody, 2009. Works appear in anthologies. Contributor to periodicals. **Address:** 53 Whitman Ave., Islip, NY 11751-2113, U.S.A. **Online address:** picself1@aol.com

PICK, Alison. Canadian (born Canada), b. 1975?. **Genres:** Poetry, Novels. **Career:** The Banff Centre, program faculty. Poet. **Publications:** Question & Answer (poems), 2003; The Sweet Edge (novel), 2005; The Dream World (poems), 2008; Far to Go, 2010. Works appear in anthologies. Contributor to periodicals. **Address:** c/o Laura Repas, House of Anansi Press, 110 Spadina Ave., Ste. 801, Toronto, ON M5V 2K4, Canada. **Online address:** aliepick@gmail.com

PICK, Hella. British/Austrian (born Austria), b. 1929?. **Genres:** Biography, Law, History. **Career:** Guardian, United Nations correspondent, 1960-, diplomatic editor, Washington correspondent, associate foreign affairs editor, 1961-; Club of Three, coordinator, 1998-; Institute for Strategic Dialogue (ISD), arts and culture programme director. **Publications:** Simon Wiesenthal: A Life in Search of Justice, 1996; Guilty Victim: Austria from the Holocaust to Haider, 2000. Contributor to periodicals. **Address:** Institute for Strategic Dialogue, 48 Charles St., London, GL W1J 5EN, England.

PICK, John Barclay. Scottish/British (born England), b. 1921. **Genres:** Novels, Recreation, Biography, Humor/Satire, Sports/Fitness, Literary Criticism And History. **Career:** J. Pick and Sons Ltd., sales manager to director, 1959-81. Writer. **Publications:** (Ed.) Gangrel: Literature, Philosophy, Poetry, Music, 1940; Under the Crust, 1946; Out of the Pit, 1951; The Lonely Aren't Alone, 1952; Phoenix Dictionary of Games: Outdoor, Covered Court and Gymnasium, Indoor; How to Play 458 Games, 1952; 180 Games for One Player: How to Play 180 Games of all Kinds; Outdoor and Indoor; On Board, Table or Floor; With Pencil and Paper or in the Head; From Bounce Ball and One Man Fives to Cat's Cradle, Cryptographs and Carlton, 1954; Spectators' Handbook: An Aid to the Appreciation of Athletics, Boxing, Cricket, Association and Rugby Football and Lawn Tennis, 1956; (with J. Atkins) A Land Fit for Eros, 1957; The Fat Valley, 1959 in US as The Last Valley, 1960; (with C. Wilson and E.H. Visiak) The Strange Genius of David Lindsay: An Appreciation, 1970; 100 Games for One Player, 1974; 100 More Games for One Player, 1975; (ed.) Violet Apple & The Witch, 1976; Freedom Itself, 1979; (with F.R. Hart) Neil M. Gunn: A Highland Life, 1981; (ed.) Selected Letters of Neil Gunn, 1987; (co-author) Neil Gunn's Country, 1991; A Voyage to Arcturus, 1992; The Great Shadow House: Essays on the Metaphysical Tradition in Scottish Fiction, 1993. **Address:** Hollins, Balmaclellan, Castle Douglas, Kirkcudbrightshire, DG DG7 3QH, Scotland.

PICK, Lucy K. American/Canadian (born Canada), b. 1966. **Genres:** History, Theology/Religion. **Career:** University of Chicago, Divinity School, faculty, 1996-, John Nuveen instructor, director of undergraduate studies and senior lecturer in the history of Christianity, 2001-, Department of History, associate faculty. Writer. **Publications:** Conflict and Coexistence: Archbishop Rodrigo and the Muslims and Jews of Medieval Spain, 2004. Contributor to periodicals and journals. **Address:** Divinity School, University of Chicago, 400 C Swift Hall, 1025 E 58th St., Chicago, IL 60637, U.S.A. **Online address:** lucypick@uchicago.edu

PICKARD, Nancy. American (born United States), b. 1945. **Genres:** Mystery/Crime/Suspense, Writing/Journalism, Young Adult Fiction. **Career:** Writer, 1967-; The Squire, reporter and editor, 1967-69; Western Auto, writer and supervisor, 1969-72; Mystery Writers of America, board director; Sisters In Crime, founding member and president. **Publications:** MYSTERIES: Generous Death, 1984; Say No to Murder, 1985; No Body, 1986; Marriage Is Murder, 1987; Dead Crazy, 1988; Bum Steer, 1990; IOU, 1991; The 27-Ingredient Chili Con Carne Murders, 1993; But I Wouldn't Want to Die There, 1993; Confession, 1994; Twilight, 1995; The Blue Corn Murders, 1998; Storm Warnings, 1999; (ed.) The First Lady Murders, 1999; (ed.) Mom, Apple Pie, and Murder, 2000; The Whole Truth, 2000; The Secret Ingredient Murders, 2001; Ring of Truth, 2001; The Truth Hurts, 2002; Virgin of Small Plains: A Novel, 2006; Scent of Rain and Lightning, 2010. OTHERS: (co-author) Mary Higgins Clark Presents The Plot Thicken, 1997. NONFICTION: (with L. Lott) Seven Steps on the Writer's Path, 2003. **Address:** Meredith Bernstein Literary Agency, 2112 Broadway, Ste. 503A, New York, NY 10023, U.S.A. **Online address:** npickard@kc.rr.com

PICKARD, Tom. British (born England), b. 1946. **Genres:** Novellas/Short Stories, Plays/Screenplays, Poetry, Songs/Lyrics And Libretti, Documentaries/Reportage, inspirational/Motivational Literature, Humanities. **Career:** Morden Tower poetry Center, co-founder, 1963, manager, 1963-72; King Ida's Watch Chain (arts magazine), editor, 1965; Ultima Thule Book Shop, founder, 1969-73; Eruption Magazine, co-founder. Writer. **Publications:** High on the Walls, 1967; New Human Unisphere, 1969; An Armpit of Lice, 1970; (ed.) The Lesser Known Shagg, 1971; The Order of Chance, 1971; Guttersnipe, 1971; Dancing under Fire, 1973; Hero Dust: New and Selected Poems, 1979; OK Tree, 1980; Serving My Time to a Trade, 1980; Domestic Art, 1981; In Search of Ingenuous, 1981; The Jarrow March, 1982; Custom & Exile, 1985; Shedding Her Skirts, 1985; Dragon Story, 1985; We Make Ships, 1989; Tiepin Eros: New & Selected Poems, 1994; Fuckwind, 1999; Hole in the Wall: New & Selected Poems, 2002; Thrice and a Half, 2003; The Dark Months of May, 2004; Ballad of Jamie Allan, 2007. **Address:** Morden Twr., Back Stowell St., West Walls, Newcastle upon Tyne, NM NE1 4XG, England. **Online address:** tompickard@onetel.net.uk

PICKELL, David. American (born United States) **Genres:** Cultural/Ethnic Topics, Travel/Exploration. **Career:** Writer. **Publications:** (With K. Muller) Underwater Indonesia: A Guide to the World's Greatest Diving, 1995; (with K. Muller) New Guinea: Journey into the Stone Age, 1996; (with W. Siagian) The Underwater Jewel of Southeast Asia, 2000; (comp.) Freeport Project

Area, South Coast of Irian Jaya (Papua), Indonesia, 2001; Kamoro: Between the Tides in Irian Jaya, 2001; Between the Tides: A Fascinating Journey among the Kamoro of New Guinea, 2003. EDITOR: Borneo: Journey into the Tropical Rainforest, 1990, 2nd ed., 1996; East of Bali: From Lombok to Timor: Periplus Adventure Guide, 1991; Kalimantan: Indonesian Borneo, 1996; Maluku: Indonesian Spice Islands, 1997; Diving Indonesia: A Guide to World's Greatest Diving, 1999. Contributor to periodicals. **Address:** c/o Author Mail, Tuttle Publishing, Airport Business Pk., 364 Innovation Dr., North Clarendon, VT 05759-9436, U.S.A.

PICKERING, David (Hugh). British (born England), b. 1958. **Genres:** Cultural/Ethnic Topics, Language/Linguistics, Mythology/Folklore, Theatre, Theology/Religion, Biography, History, Poetry, Humor/Satire, Music, Art/Art History, Popular Culture, Trivia/Facts, Novels, Novellas/Short Stories, Plays/Screenplays, Illustrations, Autobiography/Memoirs. **Career:** Market House Books Ltd., assistant editor, 1984-92; freelance writer and illustrator, 1992-. **Publications:** (Ed. with W. Packard and C. Savidge) Sphere/Facts on File Dictionary of the Theatre, 1988; (ed. with A. Isaacs and E. Martin) Brewers Dictionary of 20th-Century Phrase and Fable, 1991; Gale Research Encyclopedia of Pantomime, 1991; Cassell Dictionary of Soccer, 1994; Brewers Twentieth-Century Music Phrase and Fable, 1994; Cassell Dictionary of Superstitions, 1995; (ed.) St James Press International Dictionary of Theatre: Actors, Directors and Designers, 1996; Cassell Dictionary of Witchcraft, 1996; Cassell Dictionary of Abbreviations, 1996; Cassell Dictionary of Proverbs, 1997; Cassell Companion to Twentieth-Century Music, 1997; Cassell Dictionary and Thesaurus, 1999; Cassell Dictionary of Folklore, 1999; The Penguin Dictionary of First Names, 1999; (ed. with R. Fergusson and M. Manser) New Penguin Thesaurus, 2000; Cassell's Sports Quotations, 2000; Penguin Pears Factfinder, 2001; (ed. with M.H. Manser) Facts on File Dictionary of Foreign Words and Phrases, 2002; (ed. with M.H. Manser) Facts on File Dictionary of Classical and Biblical Allusions, 2003; (ed.) HarperCollins Best-Loved Hymns and Readings, 2004; (ed. with M.H. Manser) Collins Dictionary of Saints, 2004; Collins Best-Loved Christmas Carols, Readings and Poetry, 2005; Penguin Pocket Babies' Names, 2005; (ed. with M.H. Manser) Facts on File Dictionary of Proverbs, 2006; Collins Pirates, 2006; Penguin Pocket Jokes, 2006; (with M.H. Manser) Weidenfeld and Nicolson Buttering Parsnips, Twocking Chavs, 2007; Collins Ancient Egypt, 2007; Collins Ancient Greece, 2007; Collins Ancient Rome, 2007; (ed. with M.H. Manser) Facts on File Dictionary of Allusions, 2007; Random House Perfect Pub Quiz, 2007; Random House Perfect Family Quiz, 2009; Penguin Book of Baby Names, 2009; (with A. Pickering) Witch-Hunting in England, 2010. Contributor to books. **Address:** 25 Mitre St., Buckingham, BK MK18 1DW, England. **Online address:** david@pickering96.freeserve.co.uk

PICKERING, Eileen Marion. *See* **FALCON, Mark.**

PICKERING, Robert B. American (born United States), b. 1950. **Genres:** Anthropology/Ethnology, Children's Non-fiction, Adult Non-fiction. **Career:** U.S. Army Central Identification Laboratory, physical anthropologist, 1975-76; Field Museum of Natural History, Adult Education Program, instructor, 1977-80, program developer and adult educator, 1982-86, research associate, 1987-92; Northwestern University, instructor, 1979-80; Oakton Community College, instructor, 1980; Pacific Studies Institute, Yap Island Mortuary Site Project, director, 1980; Center for American Archaeology, Northern Illinois Programs, director, 1981-82; Children's Museum of Indianapolis, educator and curator of anthropology, 1988-91; Indiana University-Purdue University, adjunct associate professor, 1989-91; Denver Museum of Nature and Science, Department of Anthropology, curator and chairman, 1991-99; University of Colorado, adjunct associate professor, 1993-; Buffalo Bill Historical Center, Collier-Read Deputy Director for Collections and Education, 1999-2009; University of Tulsa, applied associate professor of museum science and management and anthropology, Museum Science and Management Program, founding director, 2009-, Gilcrease Museum, senior curator, 2009-. Writer and consultant. **Publications:** I Can Be an Archaeologist (juvenile nonfiction), 1987; Prehistoric North America: The People (juvenile nonfiction), 1996; (with D.C. Bachman) The Use of Forensic Anthropology, 1997, 2nd ed., 2009; Seeing the White Buffalo, 1997; (with K. Tankersely) Sitting Bull's Pipe, 2006. Contributor to books and periodicals. **Address:** Gilcrease Museum, University of Tulsa, 800 S Tucker Dr., Tulsa, OK 74104-9700, U.S.A. **Online address:** bob-pickering@utulsa.edu

PICKERING, Samuel F(rancis). American (born United States), b. 1941. **Genres:** Essays, Literary Criticism And History, Young Adult Non-fiction, Autobiography/Memoirs. **Career:** Montgomery Bell Academy, instructor, 1965-66; University of Tulsa, Institute of Modern Letters, fellow, 1970; Dartmouth College, assistant professor, 1970-78; University of Connecticut, assistant professor, associate professor, 1978-84, professor, 1984-2010; University of Western Australia, research associate, 1993-94; University of Edinburgh, Institute for Advanced Studies in the Humanities, fellow, 2005. Writer. **Publications:** ESSAY COLLECTIONS: A Continuing Education, 1985; The Right Distance, 1987; May Days, 1988; Still Life, 1990; Let It Ride, 1991; Trespassing, 1994; Walkabout Year: Twelve Months in Australia, 1995; Living to Prowl, 1997; The Blue Caterpillar and Other Essays, 1997; Deprived of Unhappiness, 1998; A Little Fling and Other Essays, 1999; The Last Book, 2001; Waltzing the Magpies: A Year in Australia, 2004. The Best of Pickering, 2004; Indian Summer: Musings on the Gift of Life, 2005; Letters to a Teacher, 2005. Edinburgh Days, or Doing What I Want to Do, 2007; Autumn Spring, 2007; Comfortable Boy: A Memoir, 2010; Journeys, 2010; Dreamtime: A Happy Book, 2011; A Tramps Wallet, 2011. OTHERS: The Moral Tradition in English Fiction, 1785-1850, 1976; John Locke and Children's Books in Eighteenth Century England, 1981; Moral Instruction and Fiction for Children, 1993. Contributor to magazines and journals. **Address:** Department of English, University of Connecticut, Rm. 230, 215 Glenbrook Rd., PO Box U-4025, Storrs Mansfield, CT 06269, U.S.A. **Online address:** samuel.pickering@uconn.edu

PICKETT, Rex. American (born United States), b. 1952. **Genres:** Novels, Film, Literary Criticism And History, Young Adult Fiction. **Career:** Author, film director and editor. **Publications:** Sideways, 2004; Shambolic, forthcoming. Contributor to periodicals. **Address:** St. Martins Press, 175 5th Ave., New York, NY 10010, U.S.A.

PICKOVER, Clifford A. American (born United States), b. 1957. **Genres:** Information Science/Computers, Sciences, Art/Art History, Technology, Philosophy, Mathematics/Statistics. **Career:** IBM T.J. Watson Research Center, research staff, 1982-, IBM Journal of Research and Development, associate editor; writer, 1990-; Discover Magazine, Brain-Boggler Columnist, 1995-; Computers in Physics, associate editor; Odyssey Magazine, Brain-Strain Columnist; Computers & Graphics Journal, associate editor. **Publications:** Computers, Pattern, Chaos, and Beauty: Graphics from an Unseen World, 1990; Computers and the Imagination: Visual Adventures beyond the Edge, 1991; Mazes for the Mind: Computers and the Unexpected, 1992; Chaos in Wonderland: Visual Adventures In A Fractal World, 1994; Keys to Infinity, 1995; Black Holes: A Traveler's Guide, 1996; Loom of God: Mathematical Tapestries at the Edge of Time, 1997; Alien IQ Test, 1997; Science of Aliens, 1998; Strange Brains and Genius: The Secret Lives of Eccentric Scientists and Madmen, 1998; Time, 1998; Surfing Through Hyperspace: Understanding Higher Universes in Six Easy Lessons, 1999; (with P. Anthony) Spider Legs, 1999; Cryptorunes: Codes and Secret Writing, 2000; Girl who Gave Birth to Rabbits: A True Medical Mystery, 2000; Wonders of Numbers: Adventures in Mathematics, Mind, and Meaning, 2001; The Stars of Heaven, 2001; Paradox of God and the Science of Omniscience, 2001; Dreaming the Future: The Fantastic Story of Prediction, 2001; Liquid Earth, 2002; The Lobotomy Club, 2002; Sushi Never Sleeps, 2002; Mathematics of Oz: Mental Gymnastics from Beyond the Edge, 2002; Egg Drop Soup, 2002; The Zen of Magic Squares, Circles, and Stars, 2002; Calculus and Pizza: A Cookbook for the Hungry Mind, 2003; Passion for Mathematics: Numbers, Puzzles, Madness, Religion, and the Quest for Reality, 2005; Sex, Drugs, Einstein and Elves, 2005; Möbius Strip: Dr August Möbius's Marvelous Band in Mathematics, Games, Literature, Art, Technology, and Cosmology, 2006; Beginner's Guide to Immortality: Extraordinary People, Alien Brains, and Quantum Resurrection, 2007; The Heaven Virus, 2007; Archimedes to Hawking: Laws of Science and the Great Minds Behind Them, 2008; The Math Book, 2009; Jews in Hyperspace, 2009; The Loom of God: Tapestries of Mathematical and Mysticism, 2009; The Physics Book, 2011. EDITOR: (with I. Hargittai) Spiral Symmetry, 1992; Visions of the Future: Art, Technology, and Computing in the Next Century, 1993; (with S. Tweksbury) Frontiers of Scientific Visualization, 1994; The Pattern Book: Fractal, Nature, and Art, 1995; Future Health, 1995; Visualizing Biological Information, 1995; Fractal Horizons, 1996; Chaos and fractals, 1998. Contributor of articles to periodicals. **Address:** IBM T. J. Watson Research Center, 1101 Kitchawan Rd., Rte. 134, Yorktown Heights, NY 10598, U.S.A. **Online address:** cliffp@us.ibm.com

PICKUS, Keith H. American (born United States), b. 1959?. **Genres:** History, Social Commentary, Biography. **Career:** Wichita State University, assistant professor, 1995-2001, associate professor, 2001-09, professor, 2009-, coordinator of the graduate program in history, 2000-01, interim associate dean, 2001-02, associate dean for budget, 2002-07, associate provost for strategic planning and operations, 2007-11, interim provost, 2011, Community Center for Support and Research, acting director, 2008-09. Writer. **Publications:** Constructing Modern Identities: Jewish University Students in Germany, 1815-1914, 1999; Our Only Hope: Eddie's Holocaust story and the Weisz Family Correspondence, 2008. Contributor to books. **Address:** Department of History, Wichita State University, 1845 Fairmount St., PO Box 45, Wichita, KS 67260, U.S.A. **Online address:** keith.pickus@wichita.edu

PICKUS, Noah. (Noah M. Jedidiah Pickus). American (born United States), b. 1964. **Genres:** Adult Non-fiction, Civil Liberties/Human Rights, Philosophy. **Career:** Duke University, assistant professor of public policy, 1996-2002, Terry Sanford Institute of Public Policy, director, 2004-, Kenan Institute for Ethics, associate director, 2004-07, Fuqua School of Business, adjunct instructor, 2006-, Nannerl O. Keohane director, 2007-; North Carolina State University, Institute for Emerging Issues, founding director, 2002-04; Middlebury College, faculty; Department of Homeland Security, adviser; Arbor Group, senior policy advisor. Writer. **Publications:** (Ed.) Immigration and Citizenship in the Twenty-first Century, 1998; True Faith and Allegiance: Immigration and American Civic Nationalism, 2005. Contributor to journals. **Address:** Kenan Institute for Ethics, Duke University, 102 W Duke Bldg., PO Box 90432, Durham, NC 27708, U.S.A. **Online address:** pickus@duke.edu

PICKUS, Noah M. Jedidiah. *See* **PICKUS, Noah.**

PICTON, Bernard. *See* **KNIGHT, Bernard.**

PIDERIT, John J. American (born United States), b. 1944. **Genres:** Adult Non-fiction, Economics, Education, Theology/Religion. **Career:** Regis High School, mathematics teacher, 1967-68; Roman Catholic Church, ordained Jesuit priest, 1971; Fordham University, assistant campus minister, 1971-72, assistant professor, 1978-89, associate professor of economics, 1989-90, Department of Economics, assistant chairperson, 1979-82, 1988-89, Program for International Political Economics and Development, director, 1981-83, 1987-88, Graduate Studies, assistant chairperson, 1984-88; Princeton University, assistant campus minister, 1975-78, preceptor, 1976-77; Queen's Court Residential College, master, 1987-90; Marquette University, corporate vice president, 1990-93; Loyola University of Chicago, president, 1993-2001; Catholic Education Institute, president, 2001-. Writer. **Publications:** The Ethical Foundations of Economics, 1993; (with M.M. Morey) Catholic Higher Education: A Culture in Crisis, 2006; (with M.M. Morey) Renewing Parish Culture: Building for a Catholic Future, 2008; Sexual Morality, 2011; (ed. with M.M. Morey) Teaching the Tradition, 2012; (with W.J. Donnelly) The Just Society, forthcoming. **Address:** The Catholic Education Institute, St. Helena Hall, Ste. 202, 925 Hutchinson River Pkwy., Bronx, NY 10465, U.S.A.

PIELKE, Roger A. American (born United States), b. 1968. **Genres:** Earth Sciences. **Career:** National Center for Atmospheric Research, scientist, 1993-2001; University of Colorado, professor of environmental studies, 2001-, Cooperative Institute for Research in Environmental Sciences (CIRES), fellow, director of the Center for Science and Technology Policy Research, 2001-07; James Martin Institute for Science and Civilization, Oxford University, associate fellow, 2007; Breakthrough Institute, senior fellow. Writer. **Publications:** (with R.A. Pielke, Sr.) Hurricanes: Their Nature and Impacts on Society, 1997; (ed. with D. Sarewitz and R. Byerly, Jr.) Prediction: Science, Decision Making and the Future of Nature, 2000; (ed. with R.A. Pielke, Sr.) Storms, 2000; The Honest Broker: Making Sense of Science in Policy and Politics, 2007. **Address:** Center for Science and Technology Policy Research, 1333 Grandview Ave., PO Box 488, Boulder, CO 80309-0488, U.S.A. **Online address:** pielke@colorado.edu

PIERARD, Richard V(ictor). American (born United States), b. 1934. **Genres:** Politics/Government, Theology/Religion, Bibliography, History, Cultural/Ethnic Topics, Reference. **Career:** University of Lowa, instructor in history, 1964; Indiana State University, assistant professor, 1964-67, associate professor, 1967-72, professor of history, 1972-2000, emeritus professor of history, 2000-; Bibelschule Bergstrasse, visiting professor, 1971; Greenville College, visiting professor, 1972-73; Regent College, visiting professor, 1975-; University of Aberdeen, research fellow, 1978; Trinity Evangelical Divinity School, visiting professor, 1982-; University of Frankfurt, Fulbright professor, 1984-85; Northern Baptist Theological Seminary, visiting professor, 1987-; Fuller Theological Seminary, visiting professor, 1988, 1991-; De Pauw University, visiting professor, 1989; University of Halle, Fulbright professor, 1989-90; Gordon College, Stephen Phillips professor of history; Liverpool Hope University, adjunct professor. Writer. **Publications:** (Ed. with R.G. Clouse and R.D. Linder) Protest and Politics: Christianity and Contemporary Affairs, 1968; The Unequal Yoke: Evangelical Christianity and Political Conservatism, 1970; (ed. with R.G. Clouse and R.D. Linder) The Cross and the Flag, 1972; (with R.D. Linder) Politics: A Case for Christian Action, 1973; (with R.D. Linder) The Twilight of the Saints: Christianity and Civil Religion in Modern America, 1978; (with R.G. Clouse) Streams of Civilization, vol. II, 1980; Bibliography on the New Christian Right, 1981; Bibliography on the Religious Right in America, 1986; (with R.D. Linder) Civil Religion and the Presidency, 1988; (ed.) New Twentieth-Century Encyclopedia of Religious Knowledge, 2nd ed., 1991; (with R.G. Clouse and E.M. Yamauchi) Two Kingdoms: The Church and Culture through the Ages, 1993; (ed.) The Revolution of the Candles: Christians in the Revolution of the German Democratic Republic, 1996; (with R.G. Clouse and R.N. Hosack) The New Millennium Manual: A Once and Future Guide, 1999; The Story of the Church, 2002; The American Church Experience: A Concise History, 2004. Contributor to books and reference books. **Address:** Department of History, Indiana State University, 621 Chestnut St., Stalker Hall 104, Terre Haute, IN 47809, U.S.A. **Online address:** hipper@ruby.indstate.edu

PIERCE, Chonda. American (born United States) **Genres:** Humor/Satire, Children's Non-fiction, Theology/Religion, Autobiography/Memoirs, Animals/Pets. **Career:** Writer, music publisher and actress. **Publications:** Second Row, Piano Side: With Humor, Heartache, and Hope, Chonda Pierce Tells Her Story (memoir), 1996; It's Always Darkest before the Fun Comes Up, 1998; Chonda Pierce on Her Soapbox, 1999; (with D. Pierce) Tales from the Ark, 2000; I Can See Myself in His Eyeballs: God Is Closer than You Think, 2001; (with D. Pierce) Tales from the Manger, 2004; Roadkill on the Highway to Heaven: No Animals were Injured in the Writing of This Book!, 2006; Laughing in the Dark: A Comedian's Journey through Depression, 2007. **Address:** William Morris Agency, 1600 Division St., Ste. 300, Nashville, TN 37203-2755, U.S.A. **Online address:** laugh@chonda.org

PIERCE, David. British (born England), b. 1947. **Genres:** Literary Criticism And History, Translations, History, inspirational/Motivational Literature, Cultural/Ethnic Topics. **Career:** British Council, teacher, 1970-71; high school teacher, 1974-78; York St. John University, professor of English and Irish literature, 1978-, reader in English and Irish, principal lecturer in literature; University College of Ripon, instructor, 1978-; University of York, instructor, 1978-, honorary research fellow, 1992. Writer. **Publications:** (With M. Eagleton) Attitudes to Class in the English Novel from Walter Scott to David Storey, 1979; W. B. Yeats: A Guide through the Critical Maze, 1989; James Joyce's Ireland, 1992; Yeats's Worlds: Ireland, England, and the Poetic Imagination, 1995; (ed. with P. de Voogd) Laurence Sterne in Modernism and Postmodernism, 1996; (ed.) W.B. Yeats Critical Assessments, 4 vols., 2000; (ed.) Irish Writing in the Twentieth Century: A Reader, 2000; Light, Freedom and Song: A Cultural History of Modern Irish Writing, 2005; Joyce and Company, 2006; Reading Joyce, 2008. **Address:** York St. John University, Lord Mayor's Walk, York, NY YO31 7EX, England. **Online address:** d.pierce@yorksj.ac.uk

PIERCE, F(ranklin) David. American (born United States), b. 1947. **Genres:** Medicine/Health, Business/Trade/Industry. **Career:** Westinghouse Electric Corp., manager of safety, environment and security, 1984-; Strategic Solutions Inc., director, 1994-; Leadership Solution Consultants Inc., co-founder, vice president and principal consultant. Writer. **Publications:** Total Quality for Safety and Health Professionals, 1995; Shifting Safety and Health Paradigms, 1996; Managing Change for Safety & Health Professionals: A 6 Step Process, 1997; Mastering Change: A Safety and Health Professional's Guide to Future Success, 1997; Project Management for Environmental, Safety & Health Professionals: 18 Steps to Success, 1998. Contributor to magazines. **Address:** Leadership Solution Consultants Inc., 1505 Waters Ln., Sandy, UT 84093, U.S.A. **Online address:** dave.pierce@att.net

PIERCE, Margret. *See* **PETERS, Margot (McCullough).**

PIERCE, Nora Elena. American (born United States) **Genres:** History. **Career:** Stanford University, Wallace Stegner Fellow, lecturer in creative writing; Cité Internationale des arts Paris, artist-in-residence. Writer. **Publi-**

cations: The Insufficiency of Maps: A Novel, 2007. **Address:** c/o J. Adams, Levine Greenberg Literary Agency Inc., 307 7th Ave., Ste. 2407, New York, NY 10001, U.S.A. **Online address:** nepierce@stanford.edu

PIERCE, Patricia Jobe. American (born United States), b. 1943. **Genres:** Plays/Screenplays, Poetry, Art/Art History, Biography, Business/Trade/ Industry. **Career:** Pierce Galleries Inc., owner and president, 1968-. Freelance writer. **Publications:** (With R.H. Kristiansen) John Joseph Enneking: American Impressionist Painter, 1972; The Ten: Frank W. Benson, Joseph R. DeCamp, Thomas W. Dewing, Childe Hassam, Willard L. Metcalf, Robert Reid, Edward Simmons, Edmund C. Tarbell, John H. Twachtman, J. Alden Weir and William Merritt Chase (Who Replaced Twachtman, 1902), 1976; Edmund C. Tarbell and the Boston School of Painting, 1889-1980, 1980; The Watercolored World of J.W.S. Cox, 1981; Richard Earl Thompson, American Impressionist: A Prophetic Odyssey in Paint, 1982; Edward Henry Potthast: More than One Man (international art collection), 1991; The Ultimate Elvis: Elvis Presley Day by Day, 1994; Love, 2000; Painters of the American Beach, 2000; How to Invest and Collect Art in the Twenty-first Century, 2001; Art Collecting and Investing, 2003; Edward Henry Potthast, 2006. Contributor of articles to periodicals. **Address:** Pierce Galleries Inc., 5 S Water St., Nantucket, MA 02554-6108, U.S.A. **Online address:** info@piercegalleries.com

PIERCE, Sharon. *See* **MCCULLOUGH, Sharon Pierce.**

PIERCESON, Jason. American (born United States), b. 1972. **Genres:** Gay And Lesbian Issues. **Career:** St. Norbert College, instructor, 2003-05; University of Illinois, Department of Political Science, assistant professor of political and legal studies, 2005-, associate professor of political science and legal studies, chair. Writer. **Publications:** Courts, Liberalism, and Rights: Gay Law and Politics in the United States and Canada, 2005; (ed. with G.A. Babst and E.R. Gill) Moral Argument, Religion, and Same-Sex Marriage: Advancing the Public Good, 2009; (ed. with A. Piatti-Crocker and S. Schulenberg) Same-Sex Marriage in the Americas: Policy Innovation for Same-Sex Relationships, 2010. **Address:** Department of Political Science, University of Illinois, Public Affairs Ctr. 360, 1 University Plz., Springfield, IL 62703, U.S.A. **Online address:** jpier2@uis.edu

PIERCY, Marge. American (born United States), b. 1936. **Genres:** Novels, Plays/Screenplays, Poetry, Essays, Young Adult Non-fiction, Science Fiction/ Fantasy, Young Adult Fiction. **Career:** Indiana University, instructor, 1960-62; University of Kansas, poet-in-residence, 1971; New York State Council on the Arts, consultant, 1971; Lower Cape Women's Center, consultant, 1973-76; Thomas Jefferson College, distinguished visiting lecturer, 1975, 1978, 1980; Grand Valley State College, distinguished visiting lecturer, 1975, 1978, 1980; Holy Cross University, fiction writer-in-residence, 1976; Fine Arts Work Center, staff, 1976-77; State University of New York, Butler chair of letters, 1977; Ohio State University, fiction writer-in-residence, 1985; St. James Press, contemporary novelist, 1985-; University of Cincinnati, poet-in-residence, 1986; Tikkun, poetry editor, 1988-96; University of Michigan, DeRoy distinguished visiting professor, 1992; Leapfrog Press, editor, 1997-; Lilith, poetry editor, 2000-; Center for the Book, resident poet, 2000; Seattle Review, fiction editor, 2003-; World Fellowship Center, writer-in-residence, 2005. **Publications:** Breaking Camp: Poems, 1968; Hard Loving: Poems, 1969; Going down Fast, A Novel, 1969; Dance the Eagle to Sleep, A Novel, 1970; (with B. Hershon, E. Jarrett and D. Lourie) 4-Telling, Poetry, 1971; To Be of Use: Poems, 1973; Small Changes, A Novel, 1973; Woman on the Edge of Time, A Novel, 1976; Living in the Open: Poems, 1976; The Twelve-spoked Wheel Flashing, Poetry, 1978; The High Cost of Living, A Novel, 1978; The Moon Is Always Female, Poetry, 1980; Vida: A Novel, 1980; Circles on the Water: Selected Poems of Marge Piercy, 1982; Braided Lives: A Novel, 1982; Parti-colored Blocks For A Quilt, 1982; Stone, Paper, Knife, 1983; Fly Away Home: A Novel, 1984; My Mother's Body, 1985; Gone to Soldiers: A Novel, 1987; Available Light, 1988; Paths of Resistance: The Art and Craft of the Political Novel, 1989; Summer People: A Novel, 1989; (with N. Blaine) The Earth Shines Secretly: A Book of Days, 1990; Mars and Her Children: Poems, 1992; He, She, and It: A Novel, 1991 in UK as Body of Glass, 1992; The Longings of Women, 1994; City of Darkness, City of Light: A Novel, 1996; What Are Big Girls Made Of?: Poems, 1997; (with I. Wood) Storm Tide, 1998; Early Grrrl: The Early Poems of Marge Piercy, 1999; The Art of Blessing the Day: Poems with a Jewish Theme, 1999; Three Women, 1999; (with I. Wood) So You Want To Write: How To Master The Craft Of Fiction And The Personal Narrative, 2001; Sleeping With Cats: A Memoir, 2002; Third Child, 2003; Colors Passing Through Us: Poems, 2003; Sex Wars, 2005; The Crooked Inheritance: Poems, 2006; Pesach For The Rest of Us: Making The Passover Seder Your Own, 2007; (intro.) Painting Cats, 2009; Hunger Moon: Selected Poems, 1980-2010, 2011. Works appear in anthologies. Contributor to periodicals. **Address:** c/o Lois Wallace, Wallace Literary Agency Inc., 301 E 79th St., Ste. 14 J, New York, NY 10075, U.S.A. **Online address:** hagolem@c4.net

PIERIBONE, Vincent A. American (born United States), b. 1964?. **Genres:** Sciences. **Career:** Karolinska Institute, Nobel Institute of Neurophysiology, National Science Foundation and Fogarty international fellow, 1990-92; Rockefeller University, assistant professor, 1995-97, adjunct professor; Yale University School of Medicine, Department of Cellular And Molecular Physiology and Neurobiology, associate professor; John B. Pierce Laboratory, associate fellow, 1997-. Writer. **Publications:** (With D.F. Gruber) Aglow in the Dark: The Revolutionary Science of Biofluorescence, 2005. Contributor to journals. **Address:** Department of Cellular & Molecular Physiology, Yale University School of Medicine, JPL 215, 333 Cedar St., Rm.B-147, PO Box 208026, New Haven, CT 06520-8026, U.S.A. **Online address:** vincent.pieribone@cmp.yale.edu

PIERPOINT, Katherine. British (born England), b. 1961?. **Genres:** Poetry. **Career:** Freelance writer, editor, researcher and translator, 1990-; King's School, poet-in-residence, 2006; University of Kent, Royal Literary Fund fellow. **Publications:** Truffle Beds (poetry), 1995; (trans. with T. Boll) Coral Bracho's Poems, 2008. Contributor of poems to periodicals and anthologies. **Address:** Faber & Faber Ltd., 3 Queen Sq., London, GL WC1N 3AU, England. **Online address:** katherine@kpierpoint.freeserve.co.uk

PIERRE, D. B. C. *See* **FINLAY, Peter (Warren).**

PIERSANTI, Claudio. Italian (born Italy), b. 1954?. **Genres:** Novels. **Career:** Novelist. **Publications:** Casa di Nessuno: Romanzo, 1981; Charles, 1986; L'amore Degli Adulti, 1989; Gli Sguardi Cattivi Della Gente, 1992; Cinghiali, 1994; Vesna va Veloce, 1996; Luisa e il Silenzio, 1997; Stigmate, 1999; L'appeso, 2000; Luisa and the Silence, 2002; Comanó il Padre, 2003; Ritorno a Casa di Enrico Metz, 2006; Giorni Nudi, 2010; (with L. Mattotti) Stigmata, 2011; (with E.O. Foster and W. Ewing) C Photo, 2011. **Address:** c/o Author Mail, Marlboro/Northwestern University Press, 629 Noyes St., Evanston, IL 60208-4210, U.S.A.

PIERSON, Christopher. British (born England), b. 1956. **Genres:** Politics/Government, History, Philosophy, Social Sciences. **Career:** University of Stirling, reader in politics, 1985-; University of Nottingham, professor of politics, director of teaching; Australian National University, visiting professor; Johns Hopkins University, visiting professor; University of California, visiting professor; British Journal of Politics and International Relations, editor. **Publications:** Marxist Theory and Democratic Politics, 1986; Beyond the Welfare State?: The New Political Economy of Welfare, 1991, 2nd ed., 1998; Socialism After Communism: The New Market Socialism, 1995; The Modern State, 1996, 3rd ed., 2011; (with A. Giddens) Conversations with Anthony Giddens: Making Sense of Modernity, 1998; (ed. with S. Tormey) Politics at the Edge: The PSA Yearbook 1999, 2000; (ed. with F.G. Castles) The Welfare State: A Reader, 2000, 2nd ed., 2006; Hard Choices: Social Democracy in the Twenty-First Century, 2001; (ed. with N. Ellison) Developments in British Social Policy 2, 2003; Late Industrializers and the Development of the Welfare State, 2004. **Address:** School of Politics and International Relations, University of Nottingham, Rm. C2 Law and Social Sciences, University Pk., Nottingham, NG7 2RD, England. **Online address:** chris.pierson@nottingham.ac.uk

PIERSON, Melissa Holbrook. American (born United States), b. 1957. **Genres:** Adult Non-fiction, Environmental Sciences/Ecology, Art/Art History, Autobiography/Memoirs. **Career:** Writer. **Publications:** The Perfect Vehicle: What It Is about Motorcycles, 1997; (ed. with L. Sante) O.K. You Mugs: Writers on Movie Actors, 1999; Dark Horses and Black Beauties: Animals, Woman, a Passion, 2000; The Place You Love Is Gone: Progress Hits Home, 2006; The Man Who Would Stop at Nothing: Long-Distance Motorcycling's Endless Road, 2011. Contributor to periodicals. **Address:** c/o Betsy Lerner, Dunow, Carlson & Lerner Agency, 27 W 20th St., Ste. 1107, New York, NY 10011, U.S.A. **Online address:** mmpierson@earthlink.net

PIERSON, Paul. American (born United States), b. 1950. **Genres:** Politics/ Government. **Career:** Harvard University, assistant professor, 1989-93, associate professor, 1993-96, professor of government, 1996-2003, Harold Hitchings Burbank professor of political economy, 2003-04; European University Institute, Jean Monnet visiting professor, 1997; University of California, professor of political science, 2004-, John Gross professor of political science, Avice Saint chair of public policy, Department of Political Science, chair, 2007-10, John Gross endowed chair. Writer and political philosopher. **Publications:** CONTRIBUTOR: Do Institutions Matter? Government Capabilities in the United States and Abroad, 1993; Economic Security and Intergenerational Justice, 1994; Policy-Making in the European Community, 1996; Policy-Making in the European Union, 2000; Capitalism and Democracy in Central and Eastern Europe: Assessing the Legacy of Communist Rule, 2003; Rethinking Political Institutions: The Art of the State, 2006. OTHERS: Dismantling the Welfare State? Reagan, Thatcher and the Politics of Retrenchment, 1994; (ed. with L. Leibfried) European Social Policy: Between Fragmentation and Integration, 1995; (ed.) The New Politics of the Welfare State, 2001; Politics in Time: History, Institutions and Social Analysis, 2004; (with J.S. Hacker) Off Center: The Republican Revolution and the Erosion of American Democracy, 2005; (ed. with T. Skocpol) The Transformation of American Politics: Activist Government and the Rise of Conservatism, 2007; (with J.S. Hacker) Winner-Take-all Politics: How Washington made the Rich Richer-and Turned its Back on the Middle Class, 2010. Contributor of articles to periodicals. **Address:** University of California, 850B Barrows Hall, Berkeley, CA 94720-1950, U.S.A. **Online address:** pierson@berkeley.edu

PIETRUSZA, David. American (born United States), b. 1949. **Genres:** Sports/Fitness, Young Adult Non-fiction, Documentaries/Reportage, Biography, History. **Career:** National Perspectives Inc., president; Total Sports, editor-in-chief, 1997-98; New York State Governor's Office of Regulatory Reform, public information officer, 1998-. Television producer. **Publications:** Baseball's Canadian-American League: A History of it's Inception, Franchises, Participants, Locales, Statisics, Demise and Legacy, 1936-1951, 1990; Major Leagues: The Formation, Sometimes Absorption and Mostly Inevitable Demise of 18 Professional Baseball Organizations, 1871 to Present, 1991; (co-ed.) Total Baseball, 6th ed., 1999; End of the Cold War, 1995; The Battle of Normandy, 1995; Minor Miracles: The Legend and Lure of Minor League Baseball, 1995; The Battle of Waterloo, 1996; (co-ed.) Total Indians, 1996; (co-ed.) Total Braves, 1996; The Invasion of Normandy, 1996; The Chinese Cultural Revolution, 1996; John F. Kennedy, 1997; Smoking, 1997; Lights On!: The Wild Century-Long Saga of Night Baseball, 1997; The Phoenix Suns Basketball Team, 1997; The Boston Celtics Basketball Team, 1998; The New York Yankees Baseball Team, 1998; Judge and Jury: The Life and Times of Judge Kenesaw Mountain Landis, 1998; (with B. Carrol, P. Palmer and J. Thorn) The Hidden Game of Football: The Next Edition, 1998; (co-ed.) Total Baseball Catalog: Great Baseball Stuff and How to Buy It, 1998; The Roaring Twenties, 1998; The Los Angeles Dodgers Baseball Team, 1999; Michael Jordon, 1999; Top 10 Baseball Managers, 1999; Michael Jordan, 1999; The Baltimore Orioles Baseball Team, 2000; The San Francisco Giants Baseball Team, 2000; Baseball: The Biographical Encyclopedia, 2000; The Cleveland Indians Baseball Team, 2001; The St. Louis Cardinals Baseball Team, 2001; (with T. Williams) Ted Williams: My Life in Pictures, 2001; (with T. Williams) Teddy Ballgame: My Life in Pictures, 2002; Rothstein: The Life, Times and Murder of the Criminal Genius Who Fixed the 1919 World Series, 2003; Major Leagues: The Formation, Sometimes Absorption and Mostly Inevitable Demise of 18 Professional Baseball Organizations, 1871 to present, 2006; 1920: The Year Of The Six Presidents, 2007; 1960: LBJ vs. JFK vs. Nixon: The Epic Campaign that Forged Three Presidencies, 2008; 1948: Harry Truman's Improbable Victory and the Year that Transformed America's Role in the World, 2011. Works appear in anthologies. Contributor to journals. **Address:** 49 Heritage Pkwy., Scotia, NY 12302, U.S.A. **Online address:** webmaster2@davidpietrusza.com

PIGGOTT, Alan (Derek). British (born England), b. 1922. **Genres:** Recreation, Autobiography/Memoirs, Sports/Fitness, Reference. **Career:** Lasham Gliding Center, chief flying instructor, 1953-89. Writer. **Publications:** Gliding: A Handbook on Soaring Flight, 1958, 7th ed., 1997; Beginning Gliding: The Fundamentals of Soaring Flight, 1975; Understanding Gliding: The Principles of Soaring Flight, 1977; Delta Papa: A Life of Flying (autobiography), 1977; Going Solo, 1978; Understanding Flying Weather, 1988; Derek Piggott on Gliding, 1989; Gliding Safety, 1991, 2nd ed. 1997. Author of scripts for a cassette series on gliding and soaring. **Address:** A.P. Watt Ltd., 26/28 Bedford Row, London, GL WC1R 4HL, England. **Online address:** derek@boyd-piggott.demon.co.uk

PIIRTO, Jane. American (born United States), b. 1941. **Genres:** Novels, Novellas/Short Stories, Poetry, Education, Psychology. **Career:** Northern Michigan University, editor of university newspaper, 1962-63; Kent State University, Department of English, graduate assistant, 1964-65; Northern Michigan University, English Department, faculty, 1966-71; Bowling Green State University, fellow, 1975-76; City University of New York, Hunter College, Laboratory School, principal, 1983-88; Ashland University, professor and director of talent development, 1988-, Trustees' distinguished professor, 1998; University of Georgia, visiting professor in educational psychology, 1996; American Educational Research Association, board director, 2001-09; National Association for Gifted Children, board director, 2002; University of Helsinki, external reviewer; University of Calgary, external reviewer; University of British Columbia, external reviewer; Monash University, external reviewer; Department of State, Overseas Schools, consultant. Writer. **Publications:** Postcards from the Upper Peninsula, 1983; The Three-Week Trance Diet (novel), 1985; Understanding Those Who Create, 1992, 3rd ed., 2007; Talented Children and Adults: Their Development and Education, 1993, 3rd ed., 2007; A Location in the Upper Peninsula (essays, stories, and poems), 1994; Luovuus (nonfiction), 1999; My Teeming Brain: Understanding Creative Writers (nonfiction), 2002. Understanding Creativity, 2004; Saunas, 2008. Contributor to periodicals. **Address:** Ashland University, 401 College Ave., Ashland, OH 44805, U.S.A. **Online address:** jpiirto@ashland.edu

PIKE, David L. American (born United States), b. 1963?. **Genres:** Literary Criticism And History, Film, Urban Studies. **Career:** Columbia University, Mellon postdoctoral fellow, 1993-95; American University, professor of literature and film studies. Writer. **Publications:** Passage through Hell: Modernist Descents, Medieval Underworlds, 1997; Subterranean Cities: The World beneath Paris and London, 1800-1945, 2005; Metropolis on the Styx: The Underworlds of Modern Urban Culture, 1800-2001, 2007; (ed. with D. Damrosch) Longman Anthology of World Literature, 2004, 2nd ed., 2008; Canadian Cinema since the 1980s: At the Heart of the World, 2012. **Address:** Department of Literature, American University, 237 Battelle-Tompkins, 4400 Massachusetts Ave. NW, Washington, DC 20016-8047, U.S.A. **Online address:** dpike@american.edu

PIKE, Robert W(ilson). American (born United States), b. 1931. **Genres:** Recreation, Adult Non-fiction, Children's Non-fiction. **Career:** Sales and marketing representative, 1958-82; Abbott Laboratories Inc., senior manager in sales, marketing and new product development, vice president, International Division, general manager, 1982-88; Jefferson Rubber Works Inc., vice president for sales and marketing, 1988-95; Curriculum Media Inc., chief executive officer, 1995-. Writer. **Publications:** Winning Checkers for Kids of All Ages, 1993; An Endless Adventure, 1994; Checker Problem Solving, 1996; Checker Power: A Game of Problem Solving, 1997; Play Winning Checkers: Official American Mensa Game Book, 1999; 101 Checker Puzzles, 2000; Little Giant Encyclopedia of Checker Puzzles, 2001. **Address:** Curriculum Media Inc., 1076 Torrey Pines Rd., Chula Vista, CA 91915, U.S.A. **Online address:** rpike63@aol.com

PIKE, R. William. American (born United States), b. 1956. **Genres:** Education, Plays/Screenplays, Sciences, Sports/Fitness. **Career:** Ticonderoga Central School District, secondary English teacher, 1978-80; Sachem Central School District, secondary English teacher, 1980-81; Holt, Rinehart and Winston, School Division, freelance writer, 1981-82; William Floyd Central School District, secondary English teacher, 1981-; Family Life Journal, book reviewer, 1992-. Writer. **Publications:** Act for Health: Using Theater to Teach Tough Teen Topics, 1991; Stop, Look, Listen Up! And Other Dramas for Confronting Social Issues in Elementary School, 1993; Facing Violence: Discussion-Starting Skits for Teenagers, 1995; Facing Substance Abuse: Discussion-Starting Skits for Teenagers, 1996. Contributor to periodicals. **Address:** 38 Adelia Path, Riverhead, NY 11901, U.S.A. **Online address:** capike@aol.com

PIKER, Joshua. American (born United States), b. 1967?. **Genres:** Adult Non-fiction, History. **Career:** University of Oklahoma, assistant professor of history, adjunct associate professor of native American studies, associate professor of history. Writer. **Publications:** Okfuskee: A Creek Indian Town in Colonial America, 2004; The Deaths of Acorn Whistler, forthcoming. Contributor to journals. **Address:** Department of History, University of Oklahoma, Rm. 403A, 455 W Lindsey St., Norman, OK 73019-2004, U.S.A. **Online address:** jpiker@ou.edu

PILARDI, Jo-Ann. American (born United States), b. 1941?. **Genres:** Philosophy, Women's Studies And Issues, Humanities, History. **Career:** Towson University, chair of women's studies, 1995-2003, professor of philosophy and women's studies, director of graduate program and women's studies, professor emeritus, 2007-. Writer and feminist activist. **Publications:** Simone de Beauvoir Writing the Self: Philosophy Becomes Autobiography, 1999. **Address:** Department of Philosophy and Religious Studies, Towson University, 8000 York Rd., Towson, MD 21252-0001, U.S.A. **Online address:** jpilardi@towson.edu

PILARZ, Scott R. American (born United States), b. 1959. **Genres:** Young Adult Non-fiction. **Career:** University of Ibadan, lecturer in philosophy department; St. Joseph's University, faculty member, 1994-; Georgetown University, assistant professor, 1996-, interim University Chaplain, 2002; University of Scranton, member of board of trustees, 2000-, president, 2003-. Writer. **Publications:** Robert Southwell and the Mission of Literature, 1561-1595: Writing Reconciliation (nonfiction), 2003. Contributor to journals. **Address:** President's Office, University of Scranton, Scranton Hall, Scranton, PA 18510, U.S.A. **Online address:** pilarzs2@scranton.edu

PILBEAM, Pamela M. British (born England) **Genres:** Biography. **Career:** University of London, Royal Holloway College, professor of French history, 1995-, now professor emeritus. Writer. **Publications:** The Middle Classes in Europe, 1789-1914: France, Germany, Italy and Russia, 1990; The French Revolution of 1830, 1991; Republicanism in Nineteenth-Century France, 1814-1871, 1995; (ed.) Themes in Modern European History, 1780-1830, 1995; The Constitutional Monarchy in France, 1814-1848, 1999; French Socialists before Marx: Workers, Women and the Social Question in France, 2000; Madame Tussaud and the History of Waxworks, 2003. **Address:** 28 Lisburne Rd., London, GL NW3 2NR, England. **Online address:** p.pilbeam@rhul.ac.uk

PILCHER, Jeffrey M. American (born United States), b. 1965. **Genres:** History. **Career:** The Citadel, assistant professor, 1994-99; University of Minnesota, professor of history. Writer and historian. **Publications:** Que Vivan los Tamales! Food and the Making of Mexican Identity, 1998; Cantinflas and the Chaos of Mexican Modernity, 2001; (ed.) The Human Tradition in Mexico, 2003; The Sausage Rebellion: Public Health, Private Enterprise, and Meat in Mexico City, 1890- 1917, 2006; Food in World History, 2006. Contributor to periodicals and magazines. **Address:** Department of History, University of Minnesota, 1118 Heller H271, 19th Ave. S,, Minneapolis, MN 55455, U.S.A. **Online address:** pilcherj@umn.edu

PILCHER, Robin. Scottish/British (born England), b. 1950. **Genres:** Novels, Humor/Satire. **Career:** Red Barn Recording Studios, founder. Novelist and marketing consultant. **Publications:** An Ocean Apart, 1999; Starting Over, 2002; A Risk Worth Taking, 2004; Starburst, 2007; A Matter of Trust in US as The Long Way Home, 2010. **Address:** Monorgan Farm, Longforgan, Dundee, DD2 5HT, Scotland. **Online address:** contact@robinpilcher.co.uk

PILCHER, Rosamunde. (Jane Fraser). Scottish/British (born England), b. 1924. **Genres:** Novels, Novellas/Short Stories, Young Adult Fiction. **Career:** Writer. **Publications:** AS JANE FRASER: The Brown Fields, 1951; Dangerous Intruder, 1951; Young Bar, 1952; A Day Like Spring, 1953; Dear Tom, 1954; Bridge of Corvie, 1956; A Family Affair, 1958; The Keeper's House, 1963; A Long Way from Home, 1963. OTHERS: A Secret to Tell, 1955; April, 1957; On My Own, 1965; Sleeping Tiger, 1967; Another View, 1969; The End of the Summer, 1971; Snow in April, 1972; The Empty House, 1973; The Day of the Storm, 1975; Under Gemini, 1976; Wild Mountain Thyme, 1978; The Carousel, 1981; Voices in Summer, 1984; The Blue Bedroom and Other Stories, 1985; The Shell Seekers, 1987; September, 1990; Flowers in The Rain & Other Stories, 1991; The Blackberry Day: And Other Stories, 1992; (intro.) Love Stories, 1995; Coming Home, 1995; The World of Rosamunde Pilcher, 1995; Three Complete Novels, 1995; The Key, 1996; New Collection of Three Complete Books, 1997; Christmas With Rosamunde Pilcher, 1998; Shadows, 1999; Flowers, 1999; Winter Solstice, 2000; Dziki tymianek, 2005. Contributor to magazines. **Address:** Penrowan, Main St., Longforgan, DD2 5ET, Scotland.

PILGER, John Richard. British/Australian (born Australia), b. 1939. **Genres:** Politics/Government, Social Commentary, Documentaries/Reportage. **Career:** Australian Consolidated Press, cadet journalist; London Daily Mirror, chief foreign correspondent, 1963-85; Granada Television, filmmaker, 1969-72; World in Action, reporter, 1969-71; Associated Television Ltd., filmmaker, 1974-81; Central Television, filmmaker, 1981-; News on Sunday, editor-in-chief and founder, 1986-88. **Publications:** NONFICTION: The Last Day, 1975; (with A. Barnett) Aftermath: The Struggle of Cambodia and Vietnam, 1982; The Outsiders, 1984; Heroes, 1986; A Secret Country, 1989; Distant Voices, 1992, rev. ed., 1994; Hidden Agendas, 1998; Reporting The World, 2001; In The Name of Justice, 2001; The New Rulers of the World, 2002; (ed.) Tell Me no Lies: Investigative Journalism that Changed the World, 2005; Freedom Next Time: Resisting the Empire, 2007. Contributor to periodicals. **Address:** 57 Hambalt Rd., London, GL SW4 9EQ, England. **Online address:** jpmarheene@hotmail.com

PILIPP, Frank. German (born Germany), b. 1961. **Genres:** Literary Criticism And History, Novels. **Career:** University of Georgia, graduate teaching assistant, 1982-84; University of North Carolina, graduate teaching assistant, 1985-89; North Carolina State University, visiting lecturer, 1989-90; Lynchburg College, assistant professor of German, 1990-95; Georgia Institute of Technology, assistant professor to professor of German, 1995-97, associate professor of German, 1997-2003, professor of German, 2003-. Writer. **Publications:** The Novels of Martin Walser: A Critical Introduction, 1991; Ingeborg Bachmanns Erzahlband Das dreissigste Jahr: Kritischer Kommentar und Deutung, 2001. EDITOR: New Critical Perspectives on Martin Walser, 1994; Legacy of Kafka in Contemporary Austrian Literature, 1997; (with D. Coury) Works of Peter Handke: International Perspectives, 2005; (ed. with C. Anton) Beyond Political Correctness: Remapping German Sensibilities In The 21st Century, 2010. Contributor to periodicals. **Address:** Ivan Allen College, Georgia Institute of Technology, 217 Swann Bldg., 781 Marietta St., Atlanta, GA 30332-0525, U.S.A. **Online address:** frank.pilipp@modlangs.gatech.edu

PILLEMER, David B. American (born United States), b. 1950?. **Genres:** Medicine/Health, Psychiatry. **Career:** Wellesley College, instructor in Education, 1977-78, instructor in psychology, 1978-79, assistant professor, 1979-84, associate professor, 1985-91, professor of psychology, 1991-2003, Child Study Center, psychological director, 1980-89, 1992-2002, Department of Psychology, chairperson, 1987-89, Learning and Teaching Center, faculty director, 1994-2003, William R. Kenan Jr. professor, 1999-2001; University of New Hampshire, College of Liberal Arts, Dr. Samuel E. Paul professor of developmental psychology, 2003-, Samuel E. Paul chair in developmental psychology, 2003-, professor of psychology, 2003-; Carsey Institute for Families and Communities, senior fellow, 2005-. Psychologist and writer. **Publications:** (With R.J. Light) Summing Up: The Science of Reviewing Research, 1984; Momentous Events, Vivid Memories: How Unforgettable Moments Help Us Understand the Meaning of Our Lives, 1998; (with S.H. White) Developmental Psychology and Social Change: Research, History and Policy, 2005. **Address:** Psychology Department, University of New Hampshire, Conant 01 314D, Library Way, Durham, NH 03824, U.S.A. **Online address:** david.pillemer@unh.edu

PILLING, Ann. British (born England), b. 1944. **Genres:** Novels, Children's Fiction, Novellas/Short Stories, Ghost Writer, Young Adult Fiction, Young Adult Non-fiction. **Career:** Secondary schools, English teacher; Federation of Children's Book Groups, publications officer, 1978-81. Writer. **Publications:** GHOST NOVELS AS ANN CHEETHAM: Black Harvest, 1983; The Beggar's Curse, 1984; The Witch of Lagg, 1986; The Pit, 1987; The Empty Frame, 1997. FOR CHILDREN: The Year of the Worm, 1984; Henry's Leg, 1985; The Friday Parcel, 1986; No Guns, No Oranges, 1986; (ed. with A. Wood) Our Best Stories, 1986; The Big Pink, 1987; The Beast in the Basement, 1988; Dustbin Charlie, 1988; On the Lion's Side, 1988; Stan, 1988; The Big Biscuit, 1989; The Jungle Sale, 1989; Our Kid, 1989; Getting Rid of Aunt Mildred, 1990; The Donkey's Day Out, 1990; Before I Go to Sleep, 1990; The Boy with His Leg in the Air, 1991; Vote for Baz, 1992; Considering Helen, 1993; The Kingfisher Children's Bible: Stories from the Old and New Testaments, 1993; Realms of Gold: Myths & Legends from Around the World, 1993; The Baked Bean Kids, 1993; Dustbin Charlie Cleans Up, 1994; Mother's Daily Scream, 1995; Amber's Secret, 2000; The Catnappers, 2002; Kingfisher Treasury of Myths and Legends, 2003. FOR ADULTS: A Broken Path, 1991; Considering Helen, 1993. Noah's Ark, 1996; The Life of Jesus, 1996; The Hutchinson Illustrated Encyclopedia of British History, 1998; Why Bear Has a Stumpy Tail and Other Creation Stories, 2000; Watching for the

Otter, forthcoming; The Dancing Sailors, forthcoming. **Address:** 22 Norham Gardens, Oxford, OX OX2 6QD, England.

PILLING, Christopher (Robert). British (born England), b. 1936. **Genres:** Poetry, Theatre, Essays, Translations, inspirational/Motivational Literature, Young Adult Fiction, History. **Career:** Ecole Normale, assistant in English, 1957-58; Wirral Grammar School, athletics and physical education teacher, 1959-61; King Edward's Grammar School, athletics and physical education teacher, 1961-62; Ackworth School, athletics and physical education teacher, 1962-73; Knottingley High School, Department of Modern Languages, head, 1973-78; University of Newcastle upon Tyne, tutor in English, 1978-80; Keswick School, Department of French, 1980-88; full-time writer, 1988-. **Publications:** Snakes & Girls, 1970; Fifteen Poems, 1970; In All the Spaces on All the Lines, 1971; Wren and Owl, 1971; Andrée's Bloom and the Anemones, 1973; Light Leaves, 1975; Question of Angels, 1976; War Photographer from the Age of 14, 1983; Foreign Bodies, 1992; Cross Your Legs and Wish, 1994; The Lobster Can Wait, 1998; In the Pink, 1999; (with C. Fleming) The Ghosts of Greta Hall, 2001; Tree Time (poetry), 2003; Life Classes, 2004; (ed.) Inside Story: Selected Poems, 2008. TRANSLATOR: These Jaundiced Loves, 1995; Les Amours Jaunes, 1995; (with D. Kennedy) The Press, 2000; (with D. Kennedy) The Dice Cup, 2000; Love at the Full, 2004; Springing From Catullus, 2009. **Address:** 25 High Hill, Keswick, CM CA12 5NY, England. **Online address:** chrispilling@onetel.net.uk

PILLING, John. British (born England), b. 1946. **Genres:** Literary Criticism And History, Biography, Adult Non-fiction, Autobiography/Memoirs. **Career:** University of Reading, Department of English Language and Literature, lecturer in English, 1971-85, reader in English, 1985-93, professor of English and European literature, 1993-, now professor emeritus; Journal of Beckett Studies, editor, 1978-85; University of California, visiting professor of English, 1984-85; The Beckett International Foundation, director, 1993-2004. **Publications:** Samuel Beckett, 1976; (with J. Knowlson) Frescoes of the Skull: The Later Prose and Drama of Samuel Beckett, 1979; Autobiography and Imagination: Studies in Self-Scrutiny, 1981; An Introduction to Fifty Modern European Poets in UK as A Reader's Guide to Fifty Modern European Poets, 1982; Beckett before Godot, 1997; A Companion to Dream of Fair to Middling Women, 2004; Samuel Beckett Chronology, 2006; Samuel Beckett's More Pricks Than Kicks, 2011. EDITOR: (with M. Bryden) The Ideal Core of the Onion: Reading Beckett Archives, 1992; The Cambridge Companion to Beckett, 1994; Beckett's Dream Notebook, 1999. **Address:** Department of English Language and Literature, University of Reading, Whiteknights, PO Box 218, Reading, BR RG6 6AA, England. **Online address:** j.pilling@reading.ac.uk

PIMENTEL, David. American (born United States), b. 1925?. **Genres:** Environmental Sciences/Ecology, Agriculture/Forestry, Biology. **Career:** U.S. Public Health Service (USPHS) Tropical Research Laboratory, chief, 1951-55, USPHS Technical Development Laboratory, project leader, 1954-55; Cornell University, assistant professor of insect ecology, 1955-63, Department of Entomology and Limnology, professor and chair, 1963-, now professor emeritus. Writer. **Publications:** Pesticides, Pollution, and Food Supply, 1972; Genetics and Ecology of Population Control, 1973; (with M. Pimentel) Food, Energy, and Society, 1979, 3rd ed., 2008; Food, Energy, and the Future of Society, 1980; Food, Energy, and Society, 2008. EDITOR: World Food, Pest Losses, and the Environment, 1978; (with E.H. Smith) Pest Control Strategies, 1978; (with T.J. Sheets) Pesticides: Contemporary Roles in Agriculture, Health, and Environment, 1979; Handbook of Energy Utilization in Agriculture, 1980; (with J.H. Perkins) Pest Control: Cultural and Environmental Aspects, 1980; CRC Handbook of Pest Management in Agriculture, 1981; Handbook of Pest Management in Agriculture, 3 vols., 1981, 2nd ed., 1991; (with C.W. Hall) Food and Energy Resources, 1984; Some Aspects of Integrated Pest Management, 1986; (with C.W. Hall) Food and Natural Resources, 1989; (ed. with C.V. Kidd) Integrated Resource Management: Agroforestry for Development, 1992; (with H. Lehman) The Pesticide Question: Environment, Economics, and Ethics, 1993; World Soil Erosion and Conservation, 1993; Techniques for Reducing Pesticide Use: Economic and Environmental Benefits, 1997; (with L. Westra and R.F. Noss) Ecological Integrity: Integrating Environment, Conservation, and Health, 2000; Encyclopedia of Pest Management, 2001; Biological Invasions: Economic and Environmental Costs of Alien Plant, Animal, And Microbe Species, 2002; U.S. Energy Conservation and Efficiency, 2004; Environmental, Energetic, and Economic Comparisons of Organic and Conventional Farming Systems, 2005; Soil Erosion, 2006; Encyclopedia of Pest Management, vol. II, 2007; Ecology of Increasing Diseases: Population growth and Environmental Degradation, 2007; Energy Efficiency and Conservation for Individual Americans, 2007; Area-Wide Pest Management: Environmental, Economic and Food Issues, 2007; (with M. Pimentel) Soil Erosion: A Food and Environmental Threat, 2007; After Silent Spring: Ecological Effects of Pesticides on Public Health and on Birds an Other Organisms. 2008; (co-ed.) Reducing Energy Inputs in the U.S. Food System, 2008; Ethanol Wastes More Energy Than it Produces, 2008; Renewable and Solar Energy Technologies: Energy and Environmental Issues, 2008; (with T. Patzek) Ethanol Production: Energy and Economic Issues Related to U.S. and Brazilian Sugarcane, 2008; (co-ed.) Food Versus Biofuels: Environmental and Economic Costs, 2009; Corn and Cellulosic Ethanol Problems and Soil Erosion, 2010. Contributor to journals and periodicals. **Address:** Department of Entomology, College of Agriculture & Life Sciences, Cornell University, 5126 Comstock Hall, Ithaca, NY 14853, U.S.A. **Online address:** dp18@cornell.edu

PIMM, Stuart L(eonard). American/British (born England), b. 1949. **Genres:** Environmental Sciences/Ecology, Natural History, Zoology, Sciences. **Career:** Clemson University, assistant professor, 1974-75; Texas Tech University, assistant professor, 1975-79, associate professor, 1979-82; University of Tennessee, associate professor, 1982-86, Science alliance, 1984-99, professor of zoology and ecology, 1986-99; Sigma Xi, national lecturer, 1993-95; Columbia University, professor of ecology, 1999-2002; University of Pretoria, extraordinary professor, 2001-; Duke University, Doris Duke professor of conservation ecology, 2002-. Writer. **Publications:** Food Webs, 1982, 2nd ed., 2002; The Balance of Nature?: Ecological Issues in the Conservation of Species and Communities, 1991; The Birdwatcher's Handbook: A Guide to the Natural History of the Birds of Britain and Europe, 1994; World According to Pimm: A Scientist Audits the Earth, 2001. Contributor to periodicals. **Address:** Nicholas School of the Environment, Duke University, Rm. A 301 LSRC Bldg., PO Box 90328, Durham, NC 27708, U.S.A. **Online address:** stuartpimm@me.com

PINA-CABRAL, João de. Portuguese (born Portugal), b. 1954. **Genres:** Anthropology/Ethnology, Social Sciences. **Career:** I.S.C.T.E., lecturer in social anthropology, 1982-84; University of Southampton, Calouste Gulbenkian fellow in Portuguese studies, 1984-86, researcher; University of Lisbon, Institute of Social Sciences, senior research fellow in social anthropology, 1984-88, research coordinator; Portuguese Association of Anthropology, founding president, 1988-91; London School of Economics and Political Science, Malinowski Memorial Lecturer, 1992; European Association of Social Anthropology, founding member, 1995-97, president, 2003-04; Universidade Atlantica, founder and rector, 1996-97; University of Kent, Stirling Memorial Lecturer, 2003; Royal Anthropological Institute of Great Britain and Ireland, honorary fellow; Instituto Superior de Ciencias do Trabalho e da Empresa, Department of Anthropology, co-founder; University of Coimbra, Faculty of Sciences and Technology, staff; Universidade Estadual de Campinas, Program of Postgraduation in Social Anthropology, inaugural lecturer. Writer. **Publications:** Sons of Adam, Daughters of Eve: The Peasant Worldview of the Alto Minho, 1986; Os Contextos da Antropologia, 1991; Aromas de Urze e de Lama, 1993; (with N. Lourenço) Em Terra de tufões: Dinâmicas da Ethicidate Macaense, 1993; (with J. Yuan and L.L. Zhu) Tai Feng zhi Xiang: Aomen tu Sheng zu qun Dong Tai, 1995; Elite: Choice, Leadership and Succession, 2000; Between China and Europe: Person, Culture, and Emotion in Macao, 2002; A Persistência daHistória: Passado e Contemporaneidade Em Africa, 2004; (with S.M. Viegas) Nomes, 2007; Aromas de urze e de lama, 2008; (with L. Schmidt) Ciência e cidadania, 2008. EDITOR: (with H. Martins and R. Feijó) Death in Portugal, 1983; (with J. Campbell) Europe Observed, 1992; (with F. Pine) On the Margins of Religion, 2008; (with C. Toren) The Challenge of Epistemology, 2011. Contributor to journals. **Address:** Institute of Social Sciences, University of Lisbon, Ave. Anibal de Bettencourtt 9, Lisbon, 1600-189, Portugal. **Online address:** pina.cabral@ics.ul.pt

PINCH, Richard G. E. (Richard Gilmour Eric Pinch). British (born England), b. 1954. **Genres:** Mathematics/Statistics, Sciences. **Career:** Cambridge University, Queen's College, lecturer in pure mathematics, 1993-98. Writer. **Publications:** (With C.M. Goldie) Communication Theory, 1991. **Address:** 2 Eldon Rd., Cheltenham, GC GL52 6TU, England. **Online address:** rgep@chalcedon.demon.co.uk

PINCH, Richard Gilmour Eric. *See* **PINCH, Richard G. E.**

PINCH, Trevor (John). Irish/American (born United States), b. 1952.

Genres: Sociology, Technology, Sciences, Humanities, Music. **Career:** University of Bath, School of Humanities and Social Sciences, research officer, 1975-77, research fellow, 1980-82; University of York, Department of Sociology, temporary lecturer, 1983-85, lecturer, 1983-90, senior lecturer, 1990-91, Institute for Research in the Social Sciences, assistant director, 1987-90; Cornell University, Department of Science and Technology Studies, associate professor, 1990-94, professor, 1994-, chair, 1999-2007, Department of Sociology, professor, 1999-; University of Twente, visiting research fellow, 1982-83; Virginia Polytechnic Institute and State University, Mullins distinguished lecturer, 1991. Writer. **Publications:** (With H.M. Collins) Frames of Meaning, 1982; Confronting Nature, 1986; (with M. Ashmore and M. Mulkay) Health and Efficiency, 1989; (with H.M. Collins) The Golem: What Everyone Should Know about Science, 1993, 2nd ed., 1998; (with C. Clark) The Hard Sell: The Language and Lessons of Street-Wise Marketing, 1995; (with H.M. Collins) The Golem at Large: What You Should Know about Technology, 1998; (with F. Trocco) Analog Days: The Invention and Impact of the Moog Synthesizer, 2002; Dr. Golem: How to Think about Medicine, 2005. EDITOR: (with T.P. Hughes and W.E. Bijker) The Social Construction of Technological Systems, 1987; (with D. Gooding and S. Schaffer) The Uses of Experiment, 1989; (co-ed. and contrib.) Dependency to Enterprise, 1991; (co-ed.) Handbook of Science and Technology Studies, 1994; (with N. Oudshoorn) How Users Matter: The Co-construction of Users and Technologies, 2003; (with R. Swedberg) Living in a Material World: Economic Sociology Meets Science and Technology Studies, 2008; (with K. Bijsterveld)The Oxford Handbook of Sound Studies, 2011. **Address:** Department of Science and Technology Studies, Cornell University, Rm. 309, Rockefeller Hall, Ithaca, NY 14853, U.S.A. **Online address:** tjp2@cornell.edu

PINCH, Winifred. *See* **PINCH, Winifred J. Ellenchild.**

PINCH, Winifred J. Ellenchild. (Winifred Pinch). American (born United States), b. 1938. **Genres:** Novels, Medicine/Health, Philosophy, Ethics. **Career:** Taylor Hospital, staff nurse, 1959-60; Bryn Mawr Hospital, staff nurse, 1961-62; Merritt Hospital School of Nursing, instructor, 1966-67; Christian Hospital, staff nurse, assistant director, 1967-70; Providence Hospital, staff nurse, 1971; St. Anselm College, assistant professor, 1974-82; Midland Lutheran College, assistant professor, 1982-85; Creighton University, associate professor, 1985-93, Center for Health Policy and Ethics, professor, 1989-, School of Nursing, professor, 1993-. Writer. **Publications:** When the Bough Breaks: Parental Perceptions of Ethical Decision-making in NICU, 2002; (ed. with A.M. Haddad) Nursing and Health Care Ethics: A Legacy and a Vision, 2008. **Address:** Creighton University Medical Center, Center for Health Policy and Ethics, Rm. 210, 2500 California Plz., Omaha, NE 68178, U.S.A. **Online address:** wpinch@creighton.edu

PINCHER, (Henry) Chapman. British/Indian (born India), b. 1914. **Genres:** Writing/Journalism, Novels, Biology, Young Adult Non-fiction. **Career:** Liverpool Institute, staff, 1936-40; Daily Express, Beaverbrook Newspapers, editor, columnist, special writer, 1946-79, chief defense correspondent, 1972-79; King's College, fellow, 1979; freelance journalist and consultant, 1979-. **Publications:** The Breeding of Farm Animals, 1946; Into the Atomic Age, 1948; A Study of Fishes, 1948; Study of Fish, with Drawings by the Author, 1948; Spotlight on Animals, 1950; Evolution, 1950; Sleep, and How to Get More of It, 1954; Not with a Bang, 1965; The Giantkiller, 1967; The Penthouse Conspirators, 1970; Sex in Our Time, 1973; The Skeleton at the Villa Wolkonsky, 1975; The Eye of the Tornado, 1976; The Four Horses, 1978; Inside Story: A Documentary of the Pursuit of Power, 1978; Dirty Tricks: A Novel, 1980; Their Trade Is Treachery, 1981; The Private World of St. John Terrapin: A Novel of the Café Royal, 1982; Too Secret Too Long, 1984; The Secret Offensive, 1985; Traitors, 1987; Traitors: The Anatomy of Treason, 1987; A Web of Deception, 1987; Spycatcher Affair, 1988; Contamination, 1989; The Truth about Dirty Tricks: From Harold Wilson to Margaret Thatcher, 1991; One Dog and Her Man, 1991; A Box of Chocolates, 1993; Pastoral Symphony, 1993; (contrib.) My Life as a Real Dog, 1995; Life's a Bitch!, 1996; Tight Lines!, 1997; Treachery: Betrayals, Blunders, and Cover-Ups, 2009. **Address:** Church House, 16 Church St., Kintbury, Hungerford, BR RG17 9TR, England. **Online address:** harry.chapman-pincher@dial.pipex.com

PINCUS, Fred L. (Fred Leonard Pincus). American (born United States), b. 1942. **Genres:** Sociology, Race Relations, Social Sciences. **Career:** University of Maryland, associate professor, professor of sociology, 1968-. Writer. **Publications:** Bridges to Opportunity: Are Community Colleges Meeting the Transfer Needs of Minority Students?, 1989; (ed. with H.J. Ehrlich) Race and Ethnic Conflict: Contending Views on Prejudice, Discrimination, and Ethnoviolence, 1994, 2nd ed., 1999; Reverse Discrimination: Dismantling the Myth, 2003; Understanding Diversity: An Introduction to Class, Race, Gender, and Sexual Orientation, 2006, 2nd ed., 2011. Contributor of articles to books and periodicals. **Address:** Department of Sociology and Anthropology, University of Maryland Baltimore County, Rm. 223, Public Policy Bldg., 1000 Hilltop Cir., Baltimore, MD 21250-0001, U.S.A. **Online address:** pincus@umbc.edu

PINCUS, Fred Leonard. *See* **PINCUS, Fred L.**

PINCZES, Elinor J(ane). American (born United States), b. 1940. **Genres:** Novels, Novellas/Short Stories, Children's Fiction. **Career:** Montana State University, Animal and Range Science, research technician, 1959-63; Soil Conservation Service State Office, secretary, 1964-67. Writer. **Publications:** Pirate Walks the Plank, 1992; One Hundred Hungry Ants, 1993; A Remainder of One, 1995; Arctic Fives Arrive, 1996; Inchworm and a Half, 2001; My Full Moon is Square, 2002. **Address:** 315 N Teton, Bozeman, MT 59718, U.S.A. **Online address:** ladybug@imt.net

PINDELL, Terry. American (born United States), b. 1947. **Genres:** Travel/Exploration, Autobiography/Memoirs, Regional/Urban Planning. **Career:** Keene School District, high school English teacher, 1971-88, department head, 1982-88. Writer. **Publications:** Making Tracks: An American Rail Odyssey, 1990; Last Train to Toronto: A Canadian Rail Odyssey, 1992; A Good Place to Live: America's Last Migration, 1995; (with L.R. Mallis) Yesterday's Train: A Rail Odyssey through Mexican History, 1997. Contributor to periodicals. **Address:** c/o Joe Spieler, 95 Circle Dr., Hastings on Hudson, NY 10706-1905, U.S.A.

PINE, Charles R. *See* **GILMAN, George G.**

PINE, Nicholas. Also writes as Andrew Colman, Nicholas Adams. American (born United States), b. 1951. **Genres:** Horror, Mystery/Crime/Suspense, Novels, Education. **Career:** Writer. **Publications:** AS NICHOLAS ADAMS (YOUNG ADULT HORROR): Horror High, 1991; Mr. Popularity, 1991; Resolved: You're Dead, 1991; Heartbreaker, 1991; Hard Rock, 1991; The New Kid on the Block, 1991. TERROR ACADEMY SERIES (YOUNG ADULT HORROR): Lights Out, 1993; Stalker, 1993; Sixteen Candles, 1993; Spring Break, 1993; The New Kid, 1993; Student Body, 1993; The In-Crowd, 1993; Night School, 1993; Breaking Up, 1994; Summer School, 1994; Science Project, 1994; In crowd, 1994; The Prom, 1994; The Substitute, 1994; School Spirit, 1995; Boy Crazy, 1995. AS ANDREW COLEMAN (YOUNG ADULT SUSPENSE): Mirror Image, 1996; Attitude Problem, 1996. OTHER: Concise Encyclopedia and 2000 Price Guide to Goss China, 1999. **Address:** The Vines Agency Inc., 648 Broadway, Ste. 901, New York, NY 10012, U.S.A.

PINEIRO, R. J. (Rogelio J. Pineiro). American/Cuban (born Cuba), b. 1961. **Genres:** Novels, Information Science/Computers, Mystery/Crime/Suspense, Young Adult Fiction. **Career:** Advanced Micro Devices, engineering manager, 1983-, computer engineer. Writer. **Publications:** NOVELS: Siege of Lightning, 1993; Ultimatum, 1994; Retribution, 1995; Exposure, 1996; Breakthrough, 1997; 01-01-00: A Novel of the Millennium, 1999; Y2K, 1999; Shutdown, 2000; Conspiracy.com, 2001; Firewall, 2002; Cyberterror, 2003; Havoc, 2005; Spyware, 2007; The Eagle and the Cross, 2008; Meltdown: The Global Climate Thriller, 2010; Beyond The Crooked Mile, 2011. **Address:** William Morris Agency, 1325 Ave. of the Americas, New York, NY 10019-6026, U.S.A. **Online address:** author@rjpineiro.com

PINEIRO, Rogelio J. *See* **PINEIRO, R. J.**

PINES, Ayala Malach. Israeli/Russian (born Russia), b. 1945. **Genres:** Psychology, Translations, Romance/Historical. **Career:** Ben-Gurion University, Department of Business Administration, head, researcher, dean, professor of clinical, social and organizational psychologist, 1995, School of Management, faculty. Psychologist, lecturer and writer. **Publications:** (With E. Aronson and D. Kafry) Burnout: From Tedium to Personal Growth, 1981; (with C. Maslach) Experiencing Social Psychology: Readings and Projects, 1984, 4th ed., 2002; Sheḥiḳah be-ahavah uve-haye ha-nísu'in, 1987, Career Burnout: Causes and Cures, 1988, (trans.) Keeping the Spark Alive: Preventing Burnout in Love and Marriage, 1988; ha-Lahaṭutanit: ha-ishah ha-ʾovedet, be'ayot u-fitronit (title means: 'The Juggler Working Woman'), 1989; Tsilah shel ahava: kin'ah romantit, 1992, trans. as Romantic Jealously: Understanding and Conquering the Shadow of Love; Couple Burnout: Causes and Cures, 1996; Falling in Love: Why We Choose the Lovers We Choose, 1999, 2nd ed., 2005; Hitahavut: ekh anu boḥarim be-mi le-hit'ahev' 2002; (with C. Maslach) Experiencing Social Psychology: Readings and Projects, 2002; (with G. Kenan) Laḥats u-sheḥiḳah ba-avodat shoṭre Magav, 2003; Laḥats u-sheḥiḳah ba-Shabas: gormim, totsaot ṿe-darkhe hitmodedut, 2003; (ed. with M.F. Ozbilgin) Career Choice in Management and Entrepreneurship: A Research Companion, 2007. **Address:** Department of Business Administration, Ben-Gurion University, PO Box 653, Beer-Sheva, 84105, Israel. **Online address:** pinesa@inter.net.il

PINKARD, Susan K. American (born United States), b. 1953. **Genres:** Food And Wine, Young Adult Non-fiction. **Career:** Georgetown University, visiting assistant professor. Writer and historian. **Publications:** A Revolution in Taste: The Rise of French Cuisine, 1650-1800 (nonfiction), 2009. **Address:** U.S.A. **Online address:** pinkards@georgetown.edu

PINKER, Susan. Canadian (born Canada), b. 1957. **Genres:** Psychology, Novels. **Career:** Private psychology practice, 1982-; Globe and Mail, columnist. McGill University, faculty of psychology. **Publications:** The Sexual Paradox: Men, Women and the Real Gender Gap, 2008. Contributor to periodicals. **Address:** Bukowski Agency, 14 Prince Arthur Ave., Ste. 202, Toronto, ON M5R 1A9, Canada. **Online address:** spinker@globeandmail.com

PINKWATER, Daniel Manus. American (born United States), b. 1941. **Genres:** Children's Fiction, Animals/Pets, Novels, Picture/Board Books, Young Adult Non-fiction, Biography, Social Sciences, Humor/Satire, Humor/Satire. **Career:** Children's Aid Society, art instructor, 1967-69; Lower West Side Visual Arts Center, art instructor, 1969; Henry Street Settlement, art instructor, 1969; Bonnie Brae Farm for Boys, art instructor, 1969; Inner City Summer Arts Program, assistant project director, 1970; National Public Radio, occasional commentator, 1987-. Writer. **Publications:** MAGIC MOSCOW SERIES: The Magic Moscow, 1980; Attila the Pun, 1981; Slaves of Spiegel, 1982. SNARKOUT BOYS SERIES: The Avocado of Death, 1982; The Baconburg Horror, 1984. BIG BOB SERIES: Big Bob and the Thanksgiving Potatoes, 1998; Big Bob and the Magic Valentine's Day Potato, 1999; Big Bob and the Winter Holiday Potato, 1999; Big Bob and the Halloween Potatoes, 2002. IRVING AND MUKTUK SERIES: Two Bad Bears, 2001; Bad Bears in the Big City, 2003; Bad Bears and a Bunny, 2005; Bad Bear Detectives, 2006; Bad Bears Go Visiting, 2007. NOVELS: Wizard Crystal, 1973; Magic Camera, 1974; Wingman, 1975; Lizard Music, 1976; Around Fred's Bed, 1976; Fat Men from Space, 1977; The Hoboken Chicken Emergency, 1977; The Last Guru, 1978; Alan Mendelsohn: The Boy from Mars, 1979; Return of the Moose, 1979; Yobgorgle, 1979; (with L. Keele) Java Jack, 1980; The Worms of Kukumlima, 1981; The Snarkout Boys & the Baconburg Horror, 1984; Borgel, 1990; The Phantom of the Lunch Wagon, 1992; Spaceburger: A Kevin Spoon and Mason Mintz Story, 1993; Blue Moose and Return of the Moose, 1993; The Time Tourists, 1993; The Afterlife Diet, 1995; Mush, a Dog from Space, 1995; Goose Night, 1996; The Magic Goose, 1997; The Education of Robert Nifkin, 1998; The Magic Pretzel, 2000; The Lunchroom of Doom, 2000; Meets Dorkula, 2001; Fat Camp Commandos, 2001; The Hound of the Basketballs, 2001; Meets Oliver Twit, 2002; Fat Camp Commandos Go West, 2002; Mush's Jazz Adventure, 2002; Looking for Bobowicz, 2004; The Artsy Smartsy Club, 2005; The Neddiad: How Neddie Took the Train, Went to Hollywood, and Saved Civilization, 2007; Sleepover Larry, 2007; The Yggyssey: How Iggy Wondered What Happened to all the Ghosts, Found out Where They Went, and Went There, 2009; Adventures of a Cat-Whiskered Girl, 2010; Bushman Lives!, 2012. OMNIBUS: 5 Novels, 1997; 4 Fantastic Novels, 2000; Once Upon a Blue Moose, 2006. COLLECTIONS: (co-author) It's Fine to Be Nine, 2000; Uncle Boris in the Yukon: And Other Shaggy Dog Stories, 2001. PICTURE BOOKS: The Terrible Roar, 1970; Bear's Picture, 1972; Fat Elliot and the Gorilla, 1974; Three Big Hogs, 1975; Blue Moose, 1975; The Blue Thing, 1977; The Big Orange Splot, 1977; Pickle Creature, 1979; The Wuggie Norple Story, 1980; Tooth-Gnasher Superflash, 1981; Roger's Umbrella, 1982; I Was a Second Grade Werewolf, 1983; Devil in the Drain, 1984; Ducks!, 1984; Jolly Roger: A Dog of Hoboken, 1985; The Muffin Fiend, 1986; The Moosepire, 1986; The Frankenbagel Monster, 1986; Aunt Lulu, 1988; Guys from Space, 1989; Uncle Melvin, 1989; Wempires, 1991; Doodle Flute, 1991; I Was a Class Two Werewolf, 1992; Author's Day, 1993; Ned Feldman, Space Pirate, 1994; Wallpaper from Space, 1996; Young Larry, 1997; Second-Grade Ape, 1998; Bongo Larry, 1998; At the Hotel Larry, 1998; Wolf Christmas, 1998; Ice-Cream Larry, 1999; Rainy Morning, 1999; Cone Kong: The Scary Ice Cream Giant, 2001; The Picture of Morty & Ray, 2003; Dancing Larry, 2007; Yo-Yo Man, 2007; I am the Dog, 2010; Beautiful Yetta: The Yiddish Chicken, 2010; Bear in Love, 2012. NON FICTION: (with J. Pinkwater) Superpuppy, 1982, rev. ed. as Superpuppy: How to Choose, Raise, and Train the Best Possible Dog for You, 2002; Fish Whistle: Commentaries, Uncommentaries, and Vulgar Excesses, 1989; Chicago Days Hoboken Nights, 1992; Hoboken Fish & Chicago Whistle, 2000; Music and Dance, 2002. OTHER: Mrs. Noodlekugel, 2012. Contributor of articles to books and periodicals. **Address:** c/o Jennifer Laughran, Andrea Brown Literary Agency Inc., 1076 Eagle Dr., Salinas, CA 93905-4466, U.S.A.

PINN, Anthony B(ernard). American (born United States), b. 1964. **Genres:** Theology/Religion. **Career:** Gordon-Conwell Theological Seminary, Center for Urban Ministerial Education, instructor, 1993-94; Suffolk University, senior lecturer, 1993-94; Macalester College, assistant professor, 1994-99, associate professor, 1999-2002, professor of religious studies, 2002-, African-American Studies Program, director; University of New Mexico, visiting professor, 1995; Rice University, Agnes Cullen Arnold professor of humanities, professor of religious studies, director of graduate studies, Wiess College, associate; American Academy of Religion's Black Theology Group, co-chair. Writer. **Publications:** Why, Lord? Suffering and Evil in Black Theology, 1995; Varieties of Black Religious Experience, 1998; (ed.) Making the Gospel, 1999; (ed. with S.W. Angell) Social Protest Thought in the AME Church, 2000; (ed.) By These Hands: A Documentary History of African-American Humanism, 2001; (ed. with B. Valentin) The Ties That Bind: African American and Hispanic American/Latino: A Theology in Dialogue, 2001; Redemptive Suffering and Moral Evil, 2002; Fortress Introduction to Black Church History, 2002; The Black Church in the Post-Civil Rights Era, 2002; (ed.) Moral Evil and Redemptive Suffering: A History of Theodicy in African-American Religious Thought, 2002; Noise and Spirit: The Religious and Spiritual Sensibilities of Rap Music, 2003; Terror and Triumph: The Nature of Black Religion, 2003; African American Humanist Principles: Living and Thinking Like the Children of Nimrod, 2004; (R. Moore and M.R. Sawyer) Peoples Temple and Black Religion in America, 2004; (ed. with D.N. Hopkins) Loving the Body: Black Religious Studies and the Erotic, 2004; African American Religious Experience in America, 2006; (ed. And intro.) Pauli Murray: Selected Sermons and Writings, 2006; (ed. with A.D. Callahan) People of African Descent and the Story of Nimrod, 2007; (ed. with A.D. Callahan) African American Religious Life and the Story of Nimrod, 2008; (co-ed.) African American Religious Cultures, 2009; (ed. with B. Valentn) Creating Ourselves: African Americans and Hispanic Americans on Popular Culture and Religious Expression, 2009; (ed.) Black Religion and Aesthetics, 2009; Understanding & Transforming the Black Church, 2010; Embodiment and the New Shape of Black Theological Thought, 2010; (ed. with S.M. Floyd-Thomas) Liberation Theologies in the United States, 2010; (C.F. Levander and M.O. Emerson) Teaching and Studying the Americas: Cultural Influences from Colonialism to the Present, 2010; What is African American Religion?, 2011; The End of God-Talk, 2012. Contributor of articles to periodicals. **Address:** Department of Religious Studies, Rice University, 213 Humanities Bldg., 6100 Main MS-15, Houston, TX 77005, U.S.A. **Online address:** pinn@rice.edu

PINNER, Patty. American (born United States), b. 1957. **Genres:** Food And Wine, Regional/Urban Planning. **Career:** U.S. Postal Service, trainer, 1981-2004. Writer. **Publications:** Sweets: A Collection of Soul Food Desserts and Memories, 2003; Sweets: Soul Food Desserts & Memories, 2006; Sweety Pies: An Uncommon Collection Of Womanish Observations, With Pie, 2007. Contributor to periodicals. **Address:** c/o Lisa Ekus, 57 North St., Hatfield, MA 01038, U.S.A.

PINNEY, Lucy (Catherine). British (born England), b. 1952. **Genres:** Novels, Autobiography/Memoirs, History. **Career:** Penguin Books, copy editor, 1973-75; freelance writer, 1975-. **Publications:** NOVELS: The Pink Stallion, 1988; Tender Moth, 1994; A Country Wife, 2004. Works appear in anthologies. Contributor to periodicals. **Address:** c/o PFD, Drury House, 34-43 Russell St., London, GL WC2B 5HA, England. **Online address:** lucy@egremont.eurobell.co.uk

PINNOCK, Winsome. British (born England), b. 1961?. **Genres:** Plays/Screenplays, Novels, Young Adult Fiction. **Career:** Tricycle Theatre, playwright-in-residence, 1989-90; Royal Court Theatre, playwright-in-residence, 1991-; Clean Break Theatre Co., playwright-in-residence; Royal Holloway College, visiting lecturer in script writing, 1996-97; Cambridge University, senior visiting fellow in creative writing workshops, 1997-98; BBC Television, script editor, 1998-2000; Bath Spa University College, lecturer in creative writing, 2000-01; London Metropolitan University, senior lecturer in creative writing, 2002-. **Publications:** PLAYS: Talking in Tongues, 1995; Mules, 1996; The Rebirth of Robert Samuels, 1996; One Under, 2005. **Address:** Faculty of Arts and Social Sciences, Kingston University, HH25, Penrhyn Rd., Kingston upon Thames, SR KT1 2EE, England. **Online address:** w.pinnock@kingston.ac.uk

PIÑOL, Albert Sánchez. Spanish (born Spain), b. 1965?. **Genres:** Novels, Literary Criticism And History. **Career:** Writer and anthropologist. **Publications:** Pallassos i monstres: la història tragicòmica de 8 dictadors africans, 2000; Les edats d'or, 2001; Pell freda, 2002; Tretze tristos tràngols, 2008. Contributor to journals and periodicals. **Address:** c/o Author Mail, Farrar, Straus and Giroux, 19 Union Sq. W, New York, NY 10003-3304, U.S.A.

PINON, Nelida. Brazilian (born Brazil), b. 1937. **Genres:** Novels, Novellas/Short Stories, Theology/Religion. **Career:** Author and educator; Pontifica Universideade Catolica, faculty of philosophy; Federal University of Rio de Janeiro, creator of chair in literary creation, 1970; University of Miami, Dr. Henry King Stanford professor of humanities, 1990-2003; Columbia University, lecturer; Johns Hopkins University, lecturer; Harvard University, lecturer; Georgetown University, lecturer. **Publications:** Guia mapa de Gabriel Arcanjo, 1961; Madeira Feita Cruz, 1963; Tempo dasfrutas, 1966; Fundador, 1969, rev. ed., 1976; Casa da paixão, 1972; Sala de armas; contos, 1973; Tebas do meu coração, 1974; Forçado destino, 1977; Calor das Coisas: Contos, 1980; A república dos Sonhos: Romance, 1984, 3rd ed., 1987; Doce Canção de Caetana, 1987; Fernando Casás: Ocos: Marzo, 1992, Casa da Parra, Santiagode Compostela, 1992; Pão de Cada dia, 1994; Até Amanhã, Outravez: crônicas, 1999; Presumível Coração da América, 2002; Vozes do deserto, 2004; Seduccín de la Memoria, 2006; (ed.) Século XX: A Mulher Conquista o Brasil, 2006; Aprendiz de Homero: Ensaio, 2008; Coração Andarilho, 2009; Voices of the Desert, 2009; (contrib.) Mulheres Que Escrevem, Mulheres Que Lêem, 2009. **Address:** Agencia Carmen Balcells, Diagonal 580, Barcelona, 08021, Spain.

PINSKER, Sanford S. American (born United States), b. 1941. **Genres:** Poetry, Literary Criticism And History. **Career:** Franklin and Marshall College, assistant professor, 1967-73, associate professor, 1974-84, professor of English, 1984-88, Shadek Humanities professor, 1988-2004, emeritus professor of English, 2004-; University of California, visiting professor, 1973, 1975. Writer. **Publications:** The Schlemiel as Metaphor, 1971, rev. ed., 1992; Still Life (poetry), 1975; The Comedy That Hoits: An Essay on the Fiction of Philip Roth, 1975; The Languages of Joseph Conrad, 1978; Between Two Worlds: The American Novel in the 1960's, 1980; Memory Breaks Off (poetry), 1983; Conversations with Contemporary American Writers, 1985; Whales at Play (poetry), 1987; Three Pacific Northwest Poets: William Stafford, Richard Hugo, and David Wagoner, 1987; The Uncompromising Fictions of Cynthia Ozick, 1987; Bearing the Bad News: Contemporary American Literature and Culture, 1990; Understanding Joseph Heller, 1991; (ed. with J. Fishel) Jewish-American Literature and Culture: An Encyclopedia, 1992; Jewish-American Fiction, 1917-1987, 1992; Sketches of Spain (chapbook), 1992; The Catcher in the Rye, 1993; Worrying about Race, 1985-1995, 1996; Oedipus Meets the Press and Other Tragi-Comedies of Our Time, 1997; (with A. Pinsker) Understanding The Catcher in the Rye: A Student Casebook to Issues, Sources, and Historical Documents, 1999. EDITOR: Critical Essays on Philip Roth, 1982; (with J.L. Fischel) America and the Holocaust, 7 vols., 1984-91; (with J. Fischel) Jewish-American Fiction, 1992. **Address:** 4280 Galt Ocean Dr., Plaza S, Apt. 11-5, Fort Lauderdale, FL 33308, U.S.A. **Online address:** spinsker@aol.com

PINSKY, Mark I. American (born United States), b. 1947?. **Genres:** Theology/Religion, Art/Art History. **Career:** Duke University, faculty; Columbia University, Graduate School of Journalism, head; New China News Agency, editorial adviser, 1982-83; Los Angeles Times, staff writer, 1985-95; Orlando Sentinel, religion writer and senior reporter, 1995-. **Publications:** The Gospel According to The Simpsons: The Spiritual Life of the World's Most Animated Family, 2001; (with S.F. Parvin) The Gospel According to The Simpsons: Leader's Guide for Group Study, 2002, 2nd ed. as Gospel According to the Simpsons. Bigger and Possibly Even Better! Edition: Leader's Guide for Group Study, 2009; The Gospel According to Disney: Faith, Trust and Pixie Dust, 2004; A Jew Among the Evangelicals: A Guide for the Perplexed, 2006; The Gospel According to the Simpsons: Bigger and Possibly Even Better! Edition With a New Afterword Exploring South Park, Family Guy, and Other Animated TV Shows, 2007; Amazing Gifts: Stories of Faith, Disability and Inclusion, 2011. **Address:** DeChant-Hughes and Associates Inc., 1440 N Kingsbury St., Ste. 123, Chicago, IL 60622, U.S.A. **Online address:** mark@markpinsky.com

PINSKY, Robert. American (born United States), b. 1940. **Genres:** Poetry, Literary Criticism And History, Translations. **Career:** University of Chicago, assistant professor of humanities, 1967-68; Wellesley College, professor of English, 1968-80; Harvard University, visiting lecturer, 1979-80; University of California, professor of English, 1980-88; Washington University, Hurst professor, 1981; Boston University, College of Arts and Sciences, professor of English and creative writing, 1988-; Library of Congress, poet laureate consultant, 1997-2000. Poet. **Publications:** Landor's Poetry, 1968; Sadness and Happiness: Poems, 1975; The Situation of Poetry: Contemporary Poetry and Its Traditions, 1976; An Explanation of America, 1979; (co-author) Five American Poets, 1979; History of My Heart, 1984; (trans.) The Separate Notebooks, 1984; Poetry and the World, 1988; The Want Bone, 1990; (trans.) The Inferno of Dante: A New Verse Translation, 1994; The Figured Wheel: New and Collected Poems, 1966-1996, 1996; Rhyme of Reb Nachman, 1998; The Sounds of Poetry: A Brief Guide, 1998; (comp.) The Handbook of Heartbreak: 101 Poems of Lost Love and Sorrow, 1998; Jersey Rain, 2000; (intro.) Carved Memories: Heritage in Stone from the Russian Jewish Pale, 2000; (ed. with M. Dietz) Americans' Favorite Poems: The Favorite Poem Project Anthology, 2000; (ed.) World's Tallest Disaster: Poems, 2001; Democracy, Culture, and the Voice of Poetry, 2002; (ed. with M. Dietz) Poems to Read: A New Favorite Poem Project Anthology, 2002; (ed. with M. Dietz and R. Ellis) Invitation to Poetry: A New Favorite Poem Project anthology, 2004; (ed.) Selected Poems, 2004, 1st ed., 2011; Life of David, 2005; First Things to Hand: Poems, 2006; (contrib.) Writing a Modern Jewish History: Essays in Honor of Salo W. Baron, 2006; Gulf Music, 2007; Thousands of Broadways: Dreams and Nightmares of the American Small Town, 2009; (ed.) Essential Pleasures, 2009; (trans.) I'll Tell What I Saw, 2009. **Address:** Department of English, College of Arts and Sciences, Boston University, Rm. 215, 236 Bay State Rd., Boston, MA 02215, U.S.A. **Online address:** rpinsky@bu.edu

PINSON, William M(eredith). American (born United States), b. 1934. **Genres:** Human Relations/Parenting, Social Commentary, Theology/Religion. **Career:** Southwestern Baptist Theological Seminary, professor of Christian ethics, 1963-75; First Baptist Church, pastor, 1975-77; Golden Gate Theological Seminary, president, 1977-82; Baptist General Convention of Texas, executive director, 1982-2000, executive director emeritus, 2000-, Baylor University, George W. Truett Theological Seminary, distinguished visiting professor in Christian ethics. Writer. **Publications:** Ambassadors and Christian Citizenship, 1963; How to Deal with Controversial Issues, 1966; Resource Guide to Current Social Issues, 1968; No Greater Challenge, 1969; (with T.B. Maston) Right or Wrong, 1971; (with C.E. Fant) Twenty Centuries of Great Preaching, 13 vols., 1971; A Program of Application for the Local Church, 1972; (with B. Glass) Don't Blame the Game, 1972; (with C.E. Fant) Contemporary Christian Trends, 1972; The Local Church in Ministry, 1973; The Five Worlds of Youth, 1974; Applying the Gospel: Suggestions for Christian Social Action in a Local Church, 1975; (with N.P. Howington and A.H. McEachern) Growing Disciples Through Preaching, 1976; Families with Purpose, 1978; Introduction to Christian Ethics, 1979; (ed.) An Approach to Christian Ethics: The Life, Contribution and Thought of T. B. Maston, 1979; The Biblical View of the Family, 1981; The Word Topical Bible of Issues and Answers, 1981; Ready to Minister, 1984; (contrib.) Unto the Least of These, 1992; (with C.E. Fant) A Treasury of Great Preaching: An Encyclopedia of Preaching, 1995; Issues Testing Baptist Policy, 2003; (co-author) The Book of Revelation, 2005; Baptists and Religious Liberty: The Freedom Road, 2007. **Address:** Baptist General Convention of Texas, 333 N Washington, Dallas, TX 75246, U.S.A. **Online address:** william.pinson@bgct.org

PINTER, Jason. American (born United States), b. 1979. **Genres:** Novels. **Career:** Three Rivers Press, editor, 2003-06; Crown Publishers, editor, 2006-07; St. Martin's Press, editor, 2007-; Waxman Literary Agency, agent, 2010-; Warner Books, book editor; Random House, book editor; St. Martin's Press, book editor; Huffington Post, columnist. **Publications:** HENRY PARKER SERIES: The Mark, 2007; The Guilty (sequel to The Mark), 2008; The Stolen, 2008; The Fury, 2009; The Darkness, 2009. OTHERS: (co-author) Killer Year, 2007; Zeke Bartholomew: Superspy, 2011; The Great Divide, 2012. Works appear in anthologies. **Address:** The Veltre Co., 78 5th Ave., 3rd Fl., New York, NY 10011, U.S.A. **Online address:** jason@jasonpinter.com

PINTO, António Costa. Portuguese (born Portugal), b. 1953. **Genres:** History, Travel/Exploration, Social Sciences, Politics/Government. **Career:** Instituto Superior de Ciencias do Trabalho e da Empresa, Portugal, professor of modern European history and politics; Contemporary Portuguese History Resource Center, assistant director; University of Lisbon, Institute of Social Sciences, senior fellow, research professor, professor of politics and contemporary European history; Stanford University, visiting professor, 1993; St Antony's College, senior associate, 1995; Princeton University, senior visiting fellow, 1996; Contemporary Portuguese History Resource Centre, deputy director, 1998-; Institut détudes Politiques, visiting professor, 1999-2003; University of California, senior visiting fellow, 2000; Georgetown University, visiting professor, 2004; Portuguese Political Science Association, president, 2006-10; Daily News, columnist. **Publications:** (With N.A. Ribeiro) A Acção Escolar Vanguarda, 1933-1936: a juventude nacionalista nos primórdios do estado novo, 1980; O Salazarismo e o fascismo europeu: problemas de interpretação nas ciências sociais, 1992; Os Camisas Azuis: ideologia, elites e movimentos fascistas em Portugal, 1914-1945, 1994; (ed. and contrib.) Modern Portugal, 1998; (ed. with N.S. Teixeira) A Primeira Republica Portuguesaentre o Liberalismo e o Autoritarismo, 1999; The Blue Shirts: Portuguese Fascists and the New State, 2000; (ed. and contrib.) Portugal Contemporâneo, 2000; O fim do império portugues: a cena internacional, a guerra colonial, e a descolonização, 1961-1975, 2001; (ed. with M.I. Rezola) Os presidentes de República Portuguesa, 2001; (ed. with N.S. Teixeira) Southern Europe and the Making of the European Union, 1945-1980s, 2002; (ed. with P.T. de Almeida and N. Bermeo) Who Governs Southern Europe: Regime Change and Ministerial Recruitment, 1850-2000, 2003; (ed.) Contemporary Portugal: Politics, Society and Culture, 2003; (ed. with S. Lloyd-Jones and contrib.) The Last Empire: Thirty Years of Portuguese Decolonization, 2003; (ed. with A. Freire) Elites, sociedades e mudança politica, 2003; (ed.) 25 de Abril: os desafios para Portugal nos próximos 30 anos, 2004; (with J.M.L Viegas) Democracia, novos desafios e novos horizontes, 2004; (contrib.) Dicionário Parliamentary biography, 1935-1974, 2004-05; (with N.S. Teixeira) A Europa do Sul e a construcão da União Europeia 1945-2000, 2005; (with P.T. Almeida and N. Bermeo) Quem governa a Europa do Sul?: o recrutamento ministerial, 1850-2000, 2006; O corporativismo em português: estado, política e sociedade no salazarismo e no varguismo, 2008; (ed.) Ruling Elites and Decision-making in Fascist-era Dictatorships, 2009; (ed.) Rethinking the Nature of Fascism: Comparative Perspectives, 2010; (with A. Freire) O poder presidencial em Portugal, 2010; (intro. with M.B.D. Cruz) A transição mpossível, 2010. Contributor to books. **Address:** Institute of Social Science, University of Lisbon, Av. Professor Aníbal Bettencourt 9, Lisbon, 1600-189, Portugal. **Online address:** acpinto@ul.pt

PINTO, Jacqueline. Also writes as Jacqueline Blairman, Jacqueline Blairman. British (born England), b. 1927?. **Genres:** Children's Fiction, Children's Non-fiction, Young Adult Fiction. **Career:** Homes and Gardens Magazine, sub-editor. **Publications:** (As Jacqueline Blairman) Triplets at Royders, 1948; (as Jacqueline Blairman) The Headmistress in Disgrace, 1949; Rebel at St. Agatha's, 1949; Moses Mendelssohn, 1960; School Dinner Disaster, 1983; School Gala Disaster, 1985; School Library Disaster, 1986; School Outing Disaster, 1987; School Donkey Disaster, 1988; School Hobby Disaster, 1990. **Address:** 19 Hartsbourne Pk., 180 High Rd., Bushey Heath, HF WD23 1SD, England.

PIOTROWSKI, Thaddeus (Tadeusz). American/Polish (born Poland), b. 1940. **Genres:** Sociology, History, Biography, Social Sciences, Anthropology/Ethnology. **Career:** Archbishop Ryan High School, teacher of Spanish and English literature and chair of foreign language department, 1968-71; University of New Hampshire, professor of sociology, 1972-, associate dean of faculty, 2001-04. Writer. **Publications:** HISTORY: Vengeance of the Swallows: Memoir of a Polish Family's Ordeal under Soviet Aggression, Ukrainian Ethnic Cleansing and Nazi Enslavement, and Their Emigration to America (autobiography), 1995; Poland's Holocaust: Ethnic Strife, Collaboration with Occupying Forces and Genocide in the Second Republic, 1918-1947, 1998; (ed.) Genocide and Rescue in Wolyn: Recollections of the Ukrainian Nationalist Ethnic Cleansing Campaign against the Poles during World War II, 2000; (ed.) The Indian Heritage of New Hampshire and Northern New England, 2002; (ed.) The Polish Deportees of World War II: Recollections of Removal to the Soviet Union and Dispersal throughout the World, 2004. **Address:** Department of Sociology, University of New Hampshire, 400 Commercial St., Manchester, NH 03101, U.S.A. **Online address:** thaddeus@cisunix.unh.edu

PIOTT, Steven L. American (born United States), b. 1948. **Genres:** History, Politics/Government, Social Commentary. **Career:** Clarion University, professor of history, 1985-; Massey University, Fulbright teaching fellow, 1992. Writer. **Publications:** (With R. Jensen and C.C. Gibbs) Grass Roots Politics: Parties, Issues and Voters, 1983; The Anti-Monopoly Persuasion: Popular Resistance to the Rise of Big Business in the Midwest, 1985; Holy Joe: Joseph W. Folk and the Missouri Idea, 1997; Giving Voters a Voice: The Origins of the Initiative and Referendum in America, 2003; American Reformers, 1870-1920: Progressives in Word and Deed, 2006; Daily Life in the Progressive Era, 2011. **Address:** Department of History, Clarion University of Pennsylvania, Rm. 208, Founders Hall, 840 Wood St., Clarion, PA 16214, U.S.A. **Online address:** spiott@clarion.edu

PIPER, Adrian (Margaret Smith). German/American (born United States), b. 1948. **Genres:** Art/Art History, Philosophy. **Career:** Harvard University, graduate teaching assistant, 1976-77; University of Michigan, assistant professor, 1979-82, 1984-86; Stanford University, Mellon research fellow, 1982-84; Georgetown University, associate professor, 1986-88; University of California, associate professor, 1988-90; Wellesley College, professor of philosophy, 1990-2005; APRA Foundation, founder, 2005-; New York University, New York Institute for the Humanities, fellow. Writer. **Publications:** Here and Now, 1968; Parlando a me stessa: l 'autobiografia progressiva diun oggetto d'arte, 1975; Adrian Piper, Reflections, 1967-1987: Alternative Museum, New York City, April 18-May 30, 1987, Travelling to Nexus Contemporary Art Center, Atlanta, Georgia, Nov. 21-December 19, 1987, 1987; Colored People, 1991; Decide Who You Are, 1992; Out of Order, Out of Sight, vol. I: Selected Writings in Meta-Art, 1968-1992, vol. II: Selected Writings in Art Criticism, 1967-1992, 1996; On Wearing Three Hats, 1996; On Becoming a Warrior, 2001; Adrian Piper Seit 1965: Metakunst und Kunstkritik, 2002; Adrian Piper: textes d'oeuvres et essais, 2003; Rationality and the Structure of the Self, vol. I: The Humean Conception, 2008, vol. II: A Kantian Conception, 2008; Kant's Metaethics: First Critique Foundations, forthcoming. Contributor to books and periodicals. **Address:** APRA Foundation Berlin gGmbH, Reinickendorfer StraBe 117, Berlin, D-13347, Germany. **Online address:** contact@adrianpiper.com

PIPER, Jon Kingsbury. American (born United States), b. 1957. **Genres:** Agriculture/Forestry, Environmental Sciences/Ecology. **Career:** Washington State University, visiting assistant professor of biology, 1985; Land Institute, research associate, 1985-97, research coordinator, 1989-, Program in Natural Systems Agriculture, director; Benedictine College, adjunct faculty, 1989; Bethel College, associate professor of biology, 1997-2003, professor of biology, 2003-, Katherine Esau distinguished chair in plant sciences; Kansas State University, adjunct assistant professor. Writer. **Publications:** (With J.D. Soule) Farming in Nature's Image: An Ecological Approach to Agriculture, 1992. Contributor to journals. **Address:** Department of Biology, Bethel College, 300 E 27th St., North Newton, KS 67117, U.S.A. **Online address:** smilax@bethelks.edu

PIPES, Daniel. American (born United States), b. 1949. **Genres:** History, International Relations/Current Affairs, Area Studies. **Career:** Princeton University, visiting fellow, 1977-78; University of Chicago, Harper fellow and research associate, 1978-82; U.S. Department of State, policy planning staff, 1982-83, special adviser, 1983; Harvard University, lecturer in history, 1983-84; Naval War College, professor of strategy, 1984-86; National Institute for Research Advancement, visiting fellow, 1985-; Foreign Policy Research Institute, director, 1986-93; Washington Institute for Near East Policy, visiting fellow, 1986-; Kuwait University, visiting professor, 1989-; Middle East Forum, director, 1994-2011, president, 2011-. Writer. **Publications:** Slave Soldiers and Islam: The Genesis of a Military System, 1981; An Arabist's Guide to Egyptian Colloquial, 1983; In the Path of God: Islamand Political Power, 1983, rev. ed., 2002; The Long Shadow: Culture and Politics in the Middle East, 1989; The Rushdie Affair: The Ayatollah, the Novelist, and the West, 1990, rev. ed., 2003; Greater Syria: The History of Ambition, 1990; Damascus Courts the West: Syrian Politics, 1989-91, 1991; Syria beyond the Peace Process, 1995; The Hidden Hand: Middle East Fears of Conspiracy, 1996; Conspiracy: How the Paranoid Style Flourishes and Where it Comes from, 1997; Militant Islam Reaches America (essays), 2002; Miniatures (essays), 2004. EDITOR: (with A. Garfinkle) Friendly Tyrants: An American Dilemma, 1991; Sandstorm: Middle East Conflicts and America, 1993. Contributor to periodicals. Works appear in anthologies. **Address:** Middle East Forum, 1500 Walnut St., Ste. 1050, Philadelphia, PA 19102, U.S.A. **Online address:** daniel.pipes@gmail.com

PIPES, Richard. American/Polish (born Poland), b. 1923. **Genres:** History, Intellectual History, International Relations/Current Affairs, Politics/Government, Social Sciences. **Career:** Harvard University, faculty, 1950, professor of history, 1958-75, Frank B. Baird Jr. professor of history, 1975-96, Frank B. Baird Jr. professor emeritus of history, 1996-, Russian Research Center, associate director, 1962-64, director, 1968-73; Stanford Research Institute, senior consultant, 1973-78; Central Intelligence Agency-Team B, chairman, 1976. Writer. **Publications:** Formation of the Soviet Union, 1954, rev. ed. as The Formation of the Soviet Union: Communism and Nationalism, 1917-1923, 1964; Moslems of Soviet Central Asia: Trends and Prospects, 1954; Karamzin's Memoir on Ancient and Modern Russia, 1959, new ed. as Karamzin's Memoir on Ancient and Modern Russia: A Translation and Analysis, 2005; Social Democracy and the St. Petersburg Labor Movement, 1885-1897, 1963, 2nd ed., 1985; Of the Russe Commonwealth, 1966; Europe since 1815, 1970; Struve, Liberal on the Left, 1870-1905, 1970; (with J.H. Hexter and A. Molho) Europe since 1500, 1971; International Negotiation: Some Operational Principles of Soviet Foreign Policy, 1972; Russia Under the Old Regime, 1974, 2nd ed., 1995; Struve, Liberal on the Right, 1905-1944, 1980; U.S.-Soviet Relations in the Era of Détente, 1981; Modern Europe, 1981; Survival Is Not Enough: Soviet Realities and America's Future, 1984; Russia Observed: Collected Essays on Russian and Soviet History, 1989; The Russian Revolution, 1990; Russia under the Bolshevik Regime, 1990; Communism, the Vanished Specter, 1993; A Concise History of the Russian Revolution, 1995; Three Whys of the Russian Revolution, 1997; Property and Freedom, 1999; Communism: A History, 2001; Land Tenure in Pre-Roman Antiquity and Its Political Consequences, 2001; The Degaev Affair: Terror and Treason in Tsarist Russia, 2003; Vixi: The Memoir of a Non-Belonger, 2003; Russian Conservatism and Its Critics: A Study in Political Culture, 2005; The Trial of Vera Z, 2010. EDITOR: The Russian Intelligensia, 1961; Revolutionary Russia, 1968; Peter Berngardovich Struve: Collected Works in Fifteen Volumes, 1970; Soviet Strategy in Europe, 1976; Bibliography of the Published Writings of Peter Berngardovich Struve, 1980; (with D. Brandenberger) The Unknown Lenin: From the Secret Archive, 1996. Contributor to periodicals. **Address:** Department of History, Harvard University, 201 Robinson Hall, 35 Quincy St., Cambridge, MA 02138-3880, U.S.A. **Online address:** rpipes23@aol.com

PIPHER, Mary (Bray). American (born United States), b. 1947. **Genres:** Novels, Psychology, Autobiography/Memoirs. **Career:** University of Nebraska, faculty; Nebraska Wesleyan University, faculty. Writer. **Publications:** Hunger Pains, 1987, rev. ed., 1995; The Shelter of each Other: Rebuilding our Families, 1996; Another Country: Navigating the Emotional Terrain of Our Elders, 1999; Middle of Everywhere: The World's Refugees Come to Our Town, 2002; Letters to a Young Therapist: Stories of Hope and Healing, 2003; Writing to Change the World, 2006; Seeking Peace: Chronicles of the Worst Buddhist in the World, 2009; Memoir, forthcoming. **Address:** 3150 S 58th St., Lincoln, NE 68506, U.S.A. **Online address:** jimpipher@gmail.com

PIPKIN, John. American (born United States), b. 1967. **Genres:** Novels. **Career:** Writers' League of Texas, executive director; Saint Louis University, faculty; Boston University, faculty; Southwestern University, faculty. Writer. **Publications:** Woodsburner: A Novel, 2009. Contributor to periodicals. **Address:** Austin, TX , U.S.A. **Online address:** pipkinjohn@hotmail.com

PIPKIN, Turk. American (born United States), b. 1953. **Genres:** Young Adult Non-fiction, Young Adult Fiction, Humor/Satire, Biography. **Career:** Rodney Dangerfield, stand-up comedian; Nobelity, director. Writer. **Publications:** NONFICTION: Be a Clown!, 1989; (with H. Anderson) Harry Anderson's Games You Can't Lose: A Guide for Suckers, 1989; The Winners Guide to the Texas Lottery, 1992; (with M. Frech) Barton Springs Eternal: The Soul of a City, 1993; Born of the River: The Colorado River and the LCRA, 1995; The Old Man and the Tee: How I Took Ten Strokes off My Game and Learned to Love Golf All Over Again (memoir), 2004; (with W. Nelson) The Tao of Willie: A Guide to the Happiness in Your Heart, 2006. FICTION: Fast Greens, 1994; When Angels Sing: A Christmas Story, 1999. Contributor to periodicals. **Address:** Algonquin Books, PO Box 2225, Chapel Hill, NC 27515-2225, U.S.A. **Online address:** tpipkin1@aol.com

PIRARO, Dan. American (born United States), b. 1958?. **Genres:** Cartoons, Essays, Social Commentary, Humor/Satire, Animals/Pets. **Career:** Writer. **Publications:** Bizarro, 1986; Too Bizarro, 1988; Mondo Bizarro, 1989; More Bizarro, 1990; Sumo Bizarro, 1990; Glasnost Bizarro, 1990; Post-Modern Bizarro, 1991; The Book of Lame Excuses, 1991; The Best of Bizarro, 1992; The Best of Bizarro, vol. II, 1994; Bizarro Number 9: A Collection of Bizarro Cartoons, 1995; Bizarro Number 10, 1996; Bizarro among the Savages: A Relatively Famous Guy's Experiences on the Road and in the Homes of Strangers, 1997; Life Is Strange and So Are You, 2001; The Three Little Pigs Buy the White House, 2004; Bizarro and Other Strange Manifestations of the Art of Dan Piraro, 2006; Bizarro Buccanneers, Nuttin' But Pirate Cartoons, 2008. **Address:** King Features, 300 W 57th St., 15th Fl., New York, NY 10019, U.S.A. **Online address:** piraro@earthlink.net

PIRIE, Bruce A. Canadian (born Canada), b. 1953. **Genres:** Education, Reference. **Career:** Peel District School Board, secondary school teacher, 1977-2009, now retired. Writer. **Publications:** Reshaping High School English, 1997; Teenage Boys and High School English, 2002. Contributor to books and periodicals. **Address:** 1337 Clarkson Rd. N, Mississauga, ON L5J 2W6, Canada. **Online address:** brucepirie@mac.com

PISANI, Elizabeth. British (born England) **Genres:** Medicine/Health, Sciences. **Career:** Reuters Ltd., staff correspondent, 1987-93; Economist, Indonesia correspondent, 1990-91; Centre for Population Studies, independent consultant, 1994-95; Asia Times, Indochina bureau chief, 1995-96, European Union correspondent, 1996; independent consultant on HIV/AIDS epidemiology, 1997-2001; Family Health Intl.-Asia, senior technical officer of surveillance and evaluation, 2001-05; Chinese Centre for Disease Control and Prevention, consultant of estimates and data use, 2005. Journalist and medical researcher. **Publications:** The Wisdom of Whores: Bureaucrats, Brothels, and the Business of AIDS, 2008. Contributor to books and journals. **Address:** Felicity Bryan Literary Agency, 2a North Parade Ave., Oxford, OX OX2 6LX, England. **Online address:** pisani@ternyata.org

PISSARRO, Joachim. American/French (born France) **Genres:** Art/Art History. **Career:** Art Institute of Chicago, freelance researcher, 1981; Wildenstein Institute, faculty, 1983-; Yeshiva University, Department of Art History, visiting professor, 1984; Phillips Auction House, director of impressionist and modern paintings and sculpture, 1984-88; Dallas Museum of Art, independent curator, 1988-93; Philadelphia Museum of Art, independent curator, 1988-93; Royal Academy of London, independent curator, 1988-93; Muśe de la Foundation de l'Hermitage, director, 1993-94; Kimbell Art Museum, chief curator, 1994-97; University of Texas, visiting lecturer, 1994-97; Yale University, Department of the History of Art, adjunct professor, 1997-2002, Art Gallery, Seymour H. Knox, Jr., curator of European and contemporary art, 1997-2001; Melbourne University, visiting lecturer, 1999; Brisbane Art Gallery, visiting lecturer, 1999; Sydney University, visiting lecturer, 1999; Museum of Modern Art, co-curator, curator, 2003-07, Department of Painting and Sculpture, adjunct curator, 2007-; City University of New York, Hunter College, visiting professor, 2002-04, Bershad professor of art history, 2007-, Hunter College Galleries, director, 2007-. Writer. **Publications:** Monet's Cathedral: Rouen, 1892-1894, 1990; (with R.R. Brettell) The Impressionist and the City: Pissarro's Series Paintings, 1992; Camille Pissarro, 1992; (ed. with D. Kosinski and M. Stevens) From Manet to Gauguin: Masterpieces from Swiss Private Collections, 1995; Monet and the Mediterranean, 1997; (G. Garrels and R.S. Field) Jasper Johns: New Paintings and Works on Paper, 1999; Individualism and Inter-Subjectivity in Modernism, 2001; Pioneering Modern Painting: Cézanne & Pissarro 1865-1885, 2005; (with C.D.R. Snollaerts) Pissarro: Critical Catalogue of Paintings, 2005; (with J. Wilmerding) Robert Indiana: The Artist and His Work, 1955-2005, 2006; Cézanne/Pissarro, Johns/Rauschenberg: Comparative Studies on Intersubjectivity in Modern Art, 2006; (with R.R. Brettell) Manet to Matisse: Impressionist Masters from the Marion and Henry Bloch Collection, 2007; (with S. Heugten and C. Stolwijk) Van Gogh and the Colors of the Night, 2008; (with D. Carrier) Wild Art: Art Outside the Art World, forthcoming. **Address:** Department of Hunter Art, Hunter College, City University of New York, 695 Park Ave., 11th Fl., North Bldg., New York, NY 10021, U.S.A. **Online address:** joachim.pissarro@hunter.cuny.edu

PISTOR, Katharina. American/German (born Germany), b. 1963. **Genres:** Law. **Career:** Max Planck Institute for Foreign and International Private Law, 1998-99; Harvard University, Kennedy School of Government, assistant professor, 2000-01; Columbia University School of Law, associate professor, 2001-04, professor of law, 2005-, Michael I. Sovern professor of law, 2008-. Writer. **Publications:** (Ed. with J.D. Sachs) The Rule of Law and Economic Reform in Russia, 1997; (co-author) The Role of Law and Legal Institutions in Asian Economic Development: 1960-1995, 1999; (ed. with G. Bermann) Law and Governance in an Enlarged European Union, 2004; (with C.J. Milhaupt) Law and Capitalism: What Corporate Crises Reveal about Legal

Systems and Economic Development around the World, 2008. Contributor to books and journals. **Address:** New York, NY , U.S.A. **Online address:** kpisto@law.columbia.edu

PITBLADO, Bonnie L. American (born United States), b. 1968. **Genres:** Archaeology/Antiquities. **Career:** University of Arizona, Department of Anthropology, teaching assistant and associate, 1992-96; Western State College, visiting professor, 2000-01, assistant professor of anthropology, 2001-02; Utah State University, assistant professor of anthropology, 2002-08, associate professor of anthropology, 2008-, Museum of Anthropology, director. Writer. **Publications:** Late Paleoindian Occupation of the Southern Rocky Mountains, 2003; (ed. with R.H. Brunswig) Frontiers in Colorado Paleoindian Archaeology: From the Dent Site to the Rocky Mountains, 2007. Contributor to books. **Address:** Department of Sociology, Social Work and Anthropology, Utah State University, 0730 Old Main Hill, Logan, UT 84322-0730, U.S.A. **Online address:** bpitblado@hass.usu.edu

PITCHER, Caroline (Nell). British (born England), b. 1948. **Genres:** Children's Fiction, Young Adult Fiction, Picture/Board Books, Novels. **Career:** Teacher, 1971-84; writer, 1985-. **Publications:** CHILDREN'S BOOKS: Diamond, 1987; Gruff Treatment, 1988; The Red-Spotted Reindeer, 1988; Mr. Duckbody Superstar, 1988; Gold in the Garden Shed, 1988; The Runaway Reptiles, 1988; The Chocolate Bar Burglar, 1988; The Sue Tribe, 1991; Gerald and the Pelican, 1993; Kevin the Blue, 1993; Jo's Storm, 1994; The Snow Whale, 1996; Kylie and the Can-Can Beans, 1997; The Time of the Lion, 1998; Run with the Wind, 1998; Don't Be Afraid, Little Foal, 1998; On the Pond, 1998; Mariana and the Merchild, 2000; (with C. Wright) Are You Spring?, 2000; Please Don't Eat My Sister, 2001; Nico's Octopus, 2003; Castaway, 2006; Shaman Boy, 2007; Monster Piano, 2007; The Littlest Owl, 2008; Time for Bed, Little One, 2009; Home, Sweet Home, 2009; Fox Fire, forthcoming. YOUNG ADULT FICTION: On the Wire, 1989; Mine, 1997; Silkscreen, 2000; Cast Away, 2000; 11 O'clock Chocolate Cake, 2002; (with S. Williams) The Winter Dragon, 2002; The Gods Are Watching, 2004; (with J. Morris) Lord of the Forest, 2004; Cloud Cat, 2005; Sky Shifter, 2005. Contributor to periodicals. **Address:** 532 Kedleston Rd., Allestree, Derby, DB DE22 2NG, England. **Online address:** liney@carolinepitcher.co.uk

PITCHER, George. American (born United States), b. 1925. **Genres:** Philosophy, Autobiography/Memoirs, Young Adult Non-fiction. **Career:** Princeton University, instructor, 1956-60, assistant professor, 1960-63, associate professor, 1963-70, professor, 1970-81, emeritus professor of philosophy, 1981-. Writer. **Publications:** The Philosophy of Wittgenstein, 1964; A Theory of Perception, 1971; Berkeley, 1977; A Life of Grace, 1987; Berkeley on Vision: A Nineteenth-Century Debate, 1988; The Dogs Who Came to Stay, 1995. EDITOR: Truth, 1964; Wittgenstein: A Collection of Critical Essays, 1966; (with O.P. Wood) Ryle: A Collection of Critical Essays, 1970. **Address:** Department of Philosophy, Princeton University, 1879 Hall, Princeton, NJ 08544-1006, U.S.A. **Online address:** pitcher@princeton.edu

PITCHER, Harvey John. British (born England), b. 1936. **Genres:** Novellas/Short Stories, Area Studies, Literary Criticism And History, Translations, Plays/Screenplays, Young Adult Fiction. **Career:** University of Glasgow, assistant lecturer in Russian, 1961-63; University of St. Andrews, lecturer in Russian, 1963-71; writer, 1971-. **Publications:** Understanding the Russians, 1964; (ed. and intro.) The Tale of How Ivan Ivanovich Quarrelled with Ivan Nikiforovich, 1970; The Chekhov Play: A New Interpretation, 1973; When Miss Emmie Was in Russia: English Governesses Before, During, and After the October Revolution, 1977; Chekhov's Leading Lady: A Portrait of the Actress Olga Knipper, 1979; The Smiths of Moscow: A Story of Britons Abroad, 1984; Lily: An Anglo-Russian Romance, 1987; Muir and Mirrielees: The Scottish Partnership that Became a Household Name in Russia, 1994; Witnesses of the Russian Revolution, 1994; (ed.) Everyday Russian: A Reader, 1996. TRANSLATOR: (with J. Forsyth) Chuckle with Chekhov, 1975; (with P. Miles) A.P. Chekhov, Chekhov, The Early Stories, 1883-88, 1982; (and intro. with P. Miles) A.P. Chekhov, Early Stories, 1994; (and intro.) A.P. Chekhov, The Comic Stories, 1999; (and ed.) V. Kataev, If Only We Could Know!: An Interpretation of Chekhov, 2002. **Address:** 37 Bernard Rd., Cromer, NF NR27 9AW, England.

PITE, Ralph. British/Welsh (born Wales), b. 1961. **Genres:** Novels, Young Adult Fiction, History, Poetry, Romance/Historical. **Career:** University of Cambridge, faculty; University of Liverpool, School of English, faculty, 1994-; University of Cardiff, professor of English literature; University of Bristol, Department of English, professor of English literature. Writer. **Publications:** The Circle of Our Vision: Dante's Presence in English Romantic Poetry, 1994; (ed.) Lives of the Great Romantics II by their Contemporaries, 1997; Hardy's Geography: Wessex and the Regional Novel, 2002; (co-ed.) Lives of Victorian Literary Figures. I, Eliot, Dickens, and Tennyson, 2003; Paths and Ladders, 2003; (ed.) Lives of Victorian Literary Figures. II, The Brownings, the Brontes, and the Rossettis, 2004; (ed. with H. Jones) W.S. Graham: Speaking towards You, 2004; (ed.) Lives of Victorian Literary Figures. III, Elizabeth Gaskell, the Carlyles and John Ruskin, 2005; Thomas Hardy: The Guarded Life, 2007; (ed.) Lives of Victorian Literary Figures. V, Mary Elizabeth Braddon, Wilkie Collins and William Thackeray, 2007. **Address:** Department of English, University of Bristol, Rm. 2.16, 11 Woodland Rd., Clifton, Bristol, BS8 1TB, England. **Online address:** egrrgp@bristol.ac.uk

PITINO, Rick. American (born United States), b. 1952. **Genres:** Sports/Fitness, Self Help, Business/Trade/Industry. **Career:** University of Hawaii, assistant coach, 1974-76; Syracuse University, assistant coach, 1976-78; Boston University, head coach, 1978-83; New York Knicks (NBA), assistant coach, 1983-85, head coach, 1987-89; Providence College, head coach, 1985-87; University of Kentucky, head coach, 1989-97; Boston Celtics (NBA), president and head coach, 1997-2001; Rick Pitino Classic Italian food Co., founder, 1998; Daniel Pitino Foundation, founder; University of Louisville, head basketball coach, 2001-; Puerto Rico National Team, head coach, 2010-. Writer. **Publications:** (With B. Reynolds) Born to Coach: A Season with the New York Knicks, 1988; (with D. Weiss) Full-Court Pressure: A Year in Kentucky Basketball, 1992; (with B. Reynolds) Success Is a Choice: Ten Steps to Overachieving in Business and Life, 1997; Lead to Succeed: The Ten Traits of Great Leadership in Business and Life, 2000; (with P. Forde) Rebound Rules: The Art of Success 2.0, 2008. Contributor to periodicals. **Address:** c/o Hyperion, 114 5th Ave., New York, NY 10011, U.S.A.

PITLUK, Adam. American (born United States) **Genres:** Theology/Religion. **Career:** American Airlines Publishing, editorial director; University of Texas, faculty. Journalist and educator. **Publications:** Standing Eight: The Inspiring Story of Jesus "El Matador" Chavez, Who Became Lightweight Champion of the World, 2006; Damned to Eternity: The Story of the Man Who They Said Caused the Flood, 2007. Contributor to periodicals. **Address:** American Airlines Publishing, 4333 Amon Carter Blvd., Fort Worth, TX 76155, U.S.A. **Online address:** aspitluk@yahoo.com

PITSULA, James (Michael). Canadian (born Canada), b. 1950. **Genres:** Local History/Rural Topics, History. **Career:** University of Winnipeg, lecturer in history, 1977-78; University of Regina, lecturer, 1978-79, assistant professor, 1979-84, associate professor of history, 1984-94, professor of history, 1994-. Writer. **Publications:** Let the Family Flourish: History of the Regina Family Service Bureau 1913-1982, 1982; An Act of Faith: The Early Years of Regina College, 1988; (with K. Rasmussen) Privatizing a Province: The New Right in Saskatchewan, 1990; (ed.) New Perspectives on the Canadian Constitutional Debate, 1997; Helping Families through Life: A History of Family Service Regina, 2001; As One Who Serves: The Making of the University of Regina, 2006; For All We Have and Are: Regina and the Experience of the Great War, 2008. Works appears in anthologies. Contributor to journals. **Address:** Department of History, University of Regina, AH 334, 3737 Wascana Pkwy., Regina, SK S4S 0A2, Canada. **Online address:** james.pitsula@uregina.ca

PITT, David Charles. New Zealander (born New Zealand), b. 1938. **Genres:** Anthropology/Ethnology, Environmental Sciences/Ecology, Geography, International Relations/Current Affairs, Sociology, Politics/Government. **Career:** University of Victoria, assistant professor of anthropology and sociology, 1965-67; University of Waikato, professor of sociology and head of the department, 1968-71; International Labour Organization, consultant, 1968-71; University of Auckland, professor of sociology, head of the department, European Studies committee, chairman, 1971-79; World Health Organization, consultant, 1979-83; Chargé de Recherches, Institut International de recherches pour la paix, 1984-; University of Bern, visiting professor, 1985-86. Writer. **Publications:** Tradition and Economic Progress, 1970; Historical Documents in Anthropology and Sociology, 1972; (with C. MacPherson) Emerging Pluralism: The Samoan Community in New Zealand, 1974; Socioeconomic Development in the Pacific, 1974; Development from Below, 1976; Social Dynamics of Development, 1976; (ed.) Social Class in New Zealand, 1976; Population and Development, 1977; Social Processes in New Zealand's Future: The Relevance of European Models: A Discussion Paper, 1978; (ed.) Society and Environment, the Crisis in the Mountains, 1978; (ed. with G.

Sterky) Child Labour: A Threat to Health and Development, 1981; (co-ed.) Children and War: Proceedings of Symposium at Siuntio Baths, Finland, 24.3.-27.3.1983, 1983; (with J. McNeely) Culture and Conservation: The Human Dimension in Environmental Planning, 1984; (with T. Weiss) The Nature of United Nations Bureaucracy, 1986; Rethinking Population, Environment and Development, 1986; (ed. with G. Thompson) Nuclear Free Zones, 1987; (ed. with S. Briceno) New Ideas in Environmental Education, 1988; (ed. with J. Ives) Deforestation: Social Dynamics in Watersheds and Mountain Ecosytems, 1988; The Future of the Environment, 1988; (ed. with P.R. Turner) The Anthropology of War and Peace: Perspectives on the Nuclear Age, 1989; Mountain World in Danger, 1991, 2nd ed. (with S. Nilsson), 2009; (with S. Nilsson) Protecting the Atmosphere: The Climate Change Convention and Its Context, 1994; Water in a Warmer World, 1995; AIDS and the Grass Roots, 1996; The Biosphere and Noosphere Reader, 1999; Historical Dictionary of Pacifism and Peace Movements, 2005; AIDS-A Cross Cultural Companion, 2005. **Address:** Institut de Recherches pour la Paix, 34 Blvd. du Pont D, Geneva, 1205, Switzerland. **Online address:** dpitt@freesurf.ch

PITT-KETHLEY, (Helen) Fiona. British/Spanish (born Spain), b. 1954. **Genres:** Novels, Poetry, Travel/Exploration, Writing/Journalism. **Career:** Teacher. Writer, 1978-. **Publications:** London, 1984; Rome, 1985; The Tower of Glass, 1985; Sky Ray Lolly, 1986; Gesta, 1986; Private Parts, 1987; Journeys to the Underworld, 1988; The Perfect Man, 1989; Abacus, 1989; The Misfortunes of Nigel, 1991; The Literary Companion to Sex: An Anthology of Prose and Poetry, 1992; The Maiden's Progress, 1992; Too Hot to Handle, 1992; Dogs, 1993; The Pan Principle, 1994; The Literary Companion to Low Life, 1995; Double Act, 1996; Mom for a Muse, 1999; Red Light Districts of the World, 2000; My Schooling, 2000; Baker's Dozen, 2000; Selected Poems, 2008. Contributor to periodicals. **Address:** Calle Era Baja 30, Santa Lucia, Cartagena, 30202, Spain. **Online address:** livinginspain@hotmail.com

PITTOCK, Joan (Hornby). (Joan Wesson). Scottish/British (born England), b. 1930. **Genres:** Cultural/Ethnic Topics, Literary Criticism And History, History, Young Adult Fiction, Biography. **Career:** Teacher, 1955-57; University of Keele, lecturer in English, 1957; University of Aberdeen, assistant lecturer, 1964-66, lecturer, 1966-78, senior lecturer in English, 1978-, Cultural History Group, convener, 1985-, Thomas Reid Institute for Research into Interdisciplinary Studies, director, 1991-95, honorary research fellow in English, 1995-; British Society for 18th Century Studies, editor, 1976-78, president, 1980-82; British Journal for 18th Century Studies, founding editor, 1978-80; International Society for Eighteenth-Century Studies, fellow, 1980-; Modern Humanities Research Association, fellow; Association of Scottish Literary Studies, fellow; Scottish Georgian Society, fellow; Magdalen College, visiting research fellow, 1986; Edinburgh University, Institute for Advanced Studies in the Humanities, fellow, 1986. **Publications:** The Ascendancy of Taste: The Achievement of Joseph and Thomas Warton, 1973; Henry Birkhead, Founder of the Oxford Chair of Poetry: Poetry and the Redemption of History, 1999. EDITOR: Joseph Warton: Odes on Various Subjects 1746, 1977; George Hardinge: Rowley and Chatterton in the Shades 1782, 1979; (with J.J. Carter) Aberdeen and the Enlightenment: Proceedings of a Conference held at the University of Aberdeen, 1987; (with A. Wear) Interpretation and Cultural History, 1991. Contributor to periodicals. **Address:** Department of English, King's College, University of Aberdeen, Taylor Bldg., Old Aberdeen, AB9 2UB, Scotland.

PITTS, Jennifer G. American (born United States), b. 1970?. **Genres:** History. **Career:** The New Republic Magazine, staff; Yale University, assistant professor, 2000-04; Princeton University, Center for Human Values, visiting research associate, 2003-04, assistant professor of politics, 2004-; Institute for Advanced Study, School of Social Science, faculty, 2006-07; University of Chicago, faculty, 2007, Department of Political Science, associate professor. Writer. **Publications:** (Ed. and trans.) Alexis de Tocqueville (title means: 'Writings on Empire and Slavery'), 2001; A Turn to Empire: The Rise of Imperial Liberalism in Britain and France, 2005. Contributor to books and journals. **Address:** Department of Political Science, University of Chicago, 243 Corwin Hall, 5801 S Ellis Ave., Chicago, IL 60637, U.S.A. **Online address:** jpitts@uchicago.edu

PITTS, Michael R. American (born United States), b. 1947. **Genres:** Film, Photography. **Career:** Teacher, 1970-72; Anderson Daily Bulletin, city government reporter and entertainment editor, 1972-74; Madison County Council of Governments, public relations director, 1974-77; General Electric Cablevision, film reviewer, 1974-78; Anderson Herald, copy editor, reporter and entertainment editor, 1977-78; Franklin Life Insurance Co., insurance agent, 1978-79; Metropolitan Life Insurance Co., insurance agent, 1979-80; H&R Block, tax preparer, 1981; freelance writer, 1981-; Anderson Public Library, genealogy librarian, 1991-. **Publications:** Radio Soundtracks: A Reference Guide, 1976, 2nd ed., 1986; (with L.H. Harrison) Hollywood on Record: The Film Stars' Discography, 1978; Famous Movie Detectives, 1979, vol. III, 2004; Horror Film Stars, 1981, 3rd ed., 2002; (with R.H. Campbell) The Bible on Film: A Checklist 1897-1980, 1981; Hollywood and American History: A Filmography of Over 250 Motion Pictures Depicting U.S. History, 1984; Western Movies: A TV and Video Guide to 4200 Genre Films, 1986, 2nd ed., 1997; Kate Smith: A Bio-Bibliography, 1988; (with R.H. Hayes) Kate Smith on the Radio: A Log, 1929-47, 1992; Poverty Row Studios, 1929-1940, 1997; Charles Bronson: The 95 Films and The 156 Television Appearances, 1999; The Crooners, 2002; Western Film Series of the Sound Era, 2009; Columbia Pictures Horror, Science Fiction and Fantasy Films, 1928-1982, 2010. WITH J.R. PARISH: The Great Spy Pictures, 1974, vol. II, 1986; Film Directors: A Guide to their American Films, 1974; Great Gangster Pictures, 1976, vol. II, 1987; The Great Western Pictures, 1976, vol. II, 1988; (and D.E. Stanke) The All-Americans, 1977; The Great Science Fiction Pictures, 1977, vol. II, 1990; Hollywood on Hollywood, 1978; The Great Detective Pictures, 1990; Hollywood Songsters, 1990, 2nd ed., 2002; The Great Hollywood Musical Pictures, 1992. Contributor to film journals and history magazines. **Address:** 512 North St., Chesterfield, IN 46017, U.S.A. **Online address:** mirpitts@yahoo.com

PITTS, Vincent J. American (born United States), b. 1947. **Genres:** Politics/Government, Economics. **Career:** Quinnipiac University, part-time faculty. Historian and writer. **Publications:** France and the German Problem: Politics and Economics in the Locarno Period, 1924-1929, 1987; The Man Who Sacked Rome: Charles De Bourbon, Constable of France (1490-1527), 1993; Du Palais Du Roi Au Palais De Justice: L'histoire Du Palais De La Cité (360-1439), 1999; La Grande Mademoiselle at the Court of France: 1627-1693, 2000; Henri IV of France: His Reign and Age, 2009. **Address:** U.S.A. **Online address:** vincent.pitts@quinnipiac.edu

PITZEL, Steve. (Steve Zell). American (born United States) **Genres:** Horror, Novels, Young Adult Fiction. **Career:** Mattel Inc., senior artist; Intel Corp., animator and senior technical marketing engineer; Tombstone Epitaph, editorial cartoonist, courtroom sketch artist. Writer. **Publications:** (As Steve Zell) Wizrd, 1994. **Address:** c/o Publicity Department, St. Martin's Press, 175 5th Ave., New York, NY 10010, U.S.A. **Online address:** steve.pitzel@intel.com

PIVEN, Hanoch. Spanish/Uraguayian (born Uruguay), b. 1963. **Genres:** Children's Non-fiction. **Career:** Artist, editorial caricaturist, illustrator and educator. **Publications:** FOR CHILDREN: What Presidents Are Made Of, 2004. OTHER: The Perfect Purple Feather, 2002; Faces: 78 Portraits from Madonna to the Pope, 2002; Piven in America, 2002; Scary Show of Mo and Jo, 2005; What Athletes are Made of, 2006; My Dog is as Smelly as Dirty Socks: And Other Funny Family Portraits, 2007; What Cats are Made of, 2009; My Best Friend is as Sharp as a Pencil: And Other Funny Classroom Portraits, 2010. **Address:** Heflinreps, 10 Linden Terr., Leonia, NJ 07605, U.S.A. **Online address:** hanoch@pivenworld.com

PIXLEY, Marcella. American (born United States) **Genres:** Novels. **Career:** Writer and educator. **Publications:** Freak, 2007; Without Tess, 2011. Contributor to periodicals. **Address:** Westford, MA , U.S.A.

PIZER, John. (John David Pizer). American (born United States), b. 1953. **Genres:** Literary Criticism And History, History, Young Adult Fiction. **Career:** Microsoft Corp., proofreader and editor of software user manuals, 1985; Louisiana State University, Department of Foreign Languages and Literatures, professor, 1987-. **Publications:** (As John David Pizer) The Historical Perspective in German Genre Theory: Its Development from Gottsched to Hegel, 1985; Toward a Theory of Radical Origin: Essays on Modern German Thought, 1995; Ego-Alter Ego: Double and/as Other in the Age of German Poetic Realism, 1998; Idea of World Literature: History and Pedagogical Practice, 2006; Imagining the Age of Goethe in German Literature, 1970-2010, 2011. Contributor to books and journals. **Address:** Department of Foreign Languages & Literatures, Louisiana State University, 314 Hodges Hall, Baton Rouge, LA 70803, U.S.A. **Online address:** pizerj@lsu.edu

PIZER, John David. *See* **PIZER, John.**

PIZZICHINI, Lilian. British (born England), b. 1965?. **Genres:** Biography, History, Poetry. **Career:** Writer. **Publications:** Dead Men's Wages: Secrets of a London Conman and His Family, 2002; The Blue Hour: A Life of Jean Rhys, 2009. **Address:** Annette Green Authors Agency, 1 E Cliff Rd., Tunbridge Wells, KT TN4 9AD, England. **Online address:** lilian_pizzichini@yahoo.co.uk

PLACE, Milner. British (born England), b. 1930. **Genres:** Poetry, Natural History, Young Adult Fiction. **Career:** Poetry Circle, editor. **Publications:** POETRY: En Busca de mi Alma, 1977; The Confusion of Anglers, 1988; Where Smoke Is, 1990; Piltdown Man and Bat Woman, 1994; In a Rare Time of Rain, 1995; The City of Flowers, 1998; Caminante, 2003; Certain Matters, 2007; Naked Invitation, 2009; Odersfelt, 2008; Wild Music, forthcoming. Works appear in anthologies. Contributor to magazines. **Address:** 11A Sunny Bank Rd., Edgerton, Huddersfield, WY HD3 3DE, England.

PLACH, Eva. Canadian (born Canada), b. 1969. **Genres:** History, Politics/Government, Cultural/Ethnic Topics. **Career:** Wilfrid Laurier University, associate professor and undergraduate officer. Writer and historian. **Publications:** The Clash of Moral Nations: Cultural Politics in Pilsudski's Poland, 1926-1935, 2006. Contributor of articles, book to journals. **Address:** Wilfrid Laurier University, 75 University Ave. W, Waterloo, ON N2L 3C5, Canada. **Online address:** eplach@wlu.ca

PLANK, Geoffrey. British (born England), b. 1960. **Genres:** Social Sciences. **Career:** University of Cincinnati, Department of History, assistant professor, 1994-2000, associate professor, 2000-06, professor, 2006-; University of Pennsylvania, McNeil Center for Early American Studies, fellow, 2007-08; University of East Anglia, professor of American studies, 2010-. Writer. **Publications:** An Unsettled Conquest: The British Campaign Against the Peoples of Acadia, 2001; (co-author) The Conquest of Acadia, 1710: Imperial, Colonial and Aboriginal Constructions, 2004; Rebellion and Savagery: The Jacobite Rising of 1745 and the British Empire, 2006; John Woolman's Path to the Peaceable Kingdom: A Quaker in the British Empire, 2012. Contributor of articles to periodicals. **Address:** School of American Studies, University of East Anglia, 1.22 Arts Bldg., Norwich Research Pk., Norwich, NF NR4 7TJ, United Kingdom. **Online address:** g.plank@uea.ac.uk

PLANT, Deborah G. American (born United States), b. 1956. **Genres:** Philosophy, Politics/Government, Biography. **Career:** Memphis State University, assistant professor of African American literature, 1988-93; University of South Florida, associate professor of Africana studies, 1993-, director of graduate program, 2002-08, interim chair, 2006-07, chair, 2008-. Writer. **Publications:** Every Tub Must Sit on Its Own Bottom: The Philosophy and Politics of Zora Neale Hurston, 1995; Zora Neale Hurston: A Biography of the Spirit, 2007; (ed.) The Inside Light, 2010; Alice Walker: Truth Teller, Freedom Writer, forthcoming. Contributor to journals. **Address:** Department of Africana Studies, University of South Florida, FAO 259, 4202 East Fowler Ave., Tampa, FL 33620-5550, U.S.A.

PLANT, Sadie. British (born England), b. 1964?. **Genres:** Cultural/Ethnic Topics, Adult Non-fiction, Social Sciences, Philosophy, Photography. **Career:** University of Birmingham, lecturer in cultural studies; University of Warwick, Cybernetic Culture Research Unit, director, research fellow. Writer. **Publications:** The Most Radical Gesture: The Situationist International in a Postmodern Age, 1992; Zeros and Ones: Digital Women Plus the New Technoculture, 1997; Writing on Drugs, 1999, 2nd ed., 2000; On the Mobile the Effects of Mobile Telephones on Social and Individual Life, 2001. Contributor to periodicals. **Address:** A.P. Watt Ltd., 20 John St., London, GL WC1N 2DR, England. **Online address:** s.j.plant@warwick.ac.uk

PLANTE, David (Robert). British/American (born United States), b. 1940. **Genres:** Novels, Translations, Gay And Lesbian Issues, Autobiography/Memoirs, Biography, Medicine/Health, Literary Criticism And History, Gay And Lesbian Issues, Gay And Lesbian Issues. **Career:** Teacher, 1961-62; Hart's Guide to New York, researcher, 1962-64; Boston School of Modern Languages, teacher, 1964-65; St. John's Preparatory School, teacher, 1965-66; University of East Anglia, writer-in-residence, 1976-77; University of Tulsa, writer-in-residence, 1980-83; Cambridge University, visiting fellow, 1984-85; King's College, writer-in-residence, 1985-86; Adelphi University, writer-in-residence, 1989; Columbia University, School of the Arts, professor; Gorki Institute of Literature, writer-in-residence. **Publications:** (Trans. with N. Stangos) A. Embiricos, Argo or, The Voyage of a Balloon, 1967; The Ghost of Henry James, 1970; Slides: A Novel, 1971; Relatives, 1972; The Darkness of the Body, 1974; Figures in Bright Air, 1976; The Family, 1978; The Country: A Novel, 1981; The Woods: A Novel, 1982; The Francoeur Novels, 1983; Difficult Women: A Memoir of Three, 1983; The Foreigner, 1984; The Catholic, 1986; My Mother's Pearl Necklace, 1987; The Native, 1988; (contrib.) Jean Rhys, 1989; The Accident, 1991; Annunciation, 1994; The Age of Terror, 1999; Keith Milow: New Work, 2000; American Ghosts, 2005; ABC: A Novel, 2007; (intro.) Pure Reason: Poems, 2007; Pure Lover: A Memoir of Grief, 2009. Works appear in anthologies. Contributor to journals. **Address:** c/o Lynn Nesbit, Janklow & Nesbit Associates, 445 Park Ave., New York, NY 10022-2606, U.S.A.

PLASCHKE, Bill. American (born United States), b. 1958. **Genres:** Biography. **Career:** Los Angeles Times, journalist, 1987-96; sports columnist, 1996-. **Publications:** (With C. Knox) Hard Knox: The Life of an NFL Coach, 1988; (with D. Williams) No More Mr. Nice Guy: A Life of Hardball, 1990; Plaschke: Good Sports, Spoil Sports, Foul Balls, and Odd Balls, 2002; (with T. Lasorda) I Live for This! Baseball's Last True Believer, 2007; (with H. Cejudo) American Victory: Wrestling, Dreams, and A Journey Toward Home. **Address:** Houghton Mifflin Harcourt, 222 Berkeley St., Boston, MA 02116, U.S.A. **Online address:** bill.plaschke@latimes.com

PLATT, Brian. American (born United States), b. 1970. **Genres:** History. **Career:** George Mason University, associate professor and chair of the department of history and art history. Writer. **Publications:** Burning and Building: Schooling and State Formation in Japan, 1750-1890, 2004. **Address:** Department of History & Art History, George Mason University, Robinson Hall B 351, 4400 University Dr., MSN 3G1, Fairfax, VA 22030-4444, U.S.A. **Online address:** bplatt1@gmu.edu

PLATT, Colin. British/Chinese (born China), b. 1934. **Genres:** Archaeology/Antiquities, History, Social Sciences, Art/Art History. **Career:** University of Leeds, lecturer in medieval archaeology, 1962-64; University of Southampton, lecturer, 1964-74, senior lecturer, 1974-79, reader, 1979-83, professor of history, 1983-. Writer. **Publications:** The Monastic Grange in Medieval England, 1969; Medieval Archaeology in England: A Guide to the Historical Sources, 1969; Medieval Southampton: The Port and Trading Community, A.D. 1000-1600, 1973; (with R. Coleman-Smith and ed.) Excavations in Medieval Southampton, 1953-1969, 2 vols., 1975; The English Medieval Town, 1976; Medieval England, 1978; The Atlas of Medieval Man, 1980; The Parish Churches of Medieval England, 1981; The Castle in Medieval England and Wales, 1982; The Abbeys and Priories of Medieval England, 1984; Medieval Britain from the Air, 1984; Traveller's Guide to Medieval England, 1985; National Trust Guide to Late Medieval and Renaissance Britain, 1986; The Architecture of Medieval Britain: A Social History, 1990; The Great Rebuildings of Tudor and Stuart England, 1994; King Death: The Black Death and Its Aftermath in Late-Medieval England, 1996; Marks of Opulence: The Why, When, and Where of Western Art, 1000-1900 AD, 2004; Concise History of Jersey: A New Perspective, 2009. **Address:** Department of History, University of Southampton, University Rd., Southampton, DN SO17 1BJ, England.

PLATT, Donald. American (born United States), b. 1957. **Genres:** Poetry, Gerontology/Senior Issues, Gay And Lesbian Issues, Human Relations/Parenting, Race Relations, Art/Art History. **Career:** Purdue University, Department of English, associate professor, 2000-07, professor, 2007-; University of Virginia, Henry Hoyns fellow. Writer. **Publications:** POETRY: Fresh Peaches, Fireworks & Guns, 1994; Cloud Atlas, 2002; My Father Says Grace, 2007; Dirt Angels, 2009. Contributor of books to periodicals. **Address:** Department of English, Purdue University, Rm. HEAV 311B, 500 Oval Dr., West Lafayette, IN 47907-2038, U.S.A. **Online address:** plattd@purdue.edu

PLATT, Harold L. (Harold Lawrence Platt). American (born United States), b. 1945?. **Genres:** Social Sciences, Environmental Sciences/Ecology. **Career:** Rice University, teaching assistant, 1972-73; Houston Community College, instructor, 1973-74; Loyola University, Department of History, assistant professor, 1974-81, associate professor, 1981-90, professor of history, 1990-, Loyola Video History Project, historical director and executive editor, 1984-88, Facilities for the Regional Final of the Chicago Metro History Fair, coordinator, 1990-95, director of graduate programs, 1991-94, internship coordinator, 2003-06; Houston Metropolitan Archives, consultant, 1974-75; Commonwealth Edison Co., director of corporate archives project, 1983-84, Centennial Museum Project, historical director, 1984-85; History Teaching Alliance, project director for bicentennial graduate seminar, 1986, coordinator, 1990-92. Consultant and writer. **Publications:** City Building in the New

South: The Growth of Public Services in Houston, Texas, 1830-1910, 1983; The Electric City: Energy and the Growth of the Chicago Area, 1880-1930, 1991; (ed. with G. Massard-Guilbaud and D. Schott) Cities and Catastrophes: Coping with Emergency in European History, 2002; Shock Cities: The Environmental Transformation and Reform of Manchester and Chicago, 2005. CONTRIBUTOR: The Age of Urban Reform, 1977; Technology and the Rise of the Networked City in Europe and America, 1988; The Constitution, Law and American Life: Critical Aspects of the Nineteenth-Century Experience, 1992; Oxford Companion to American History, 2001; Encyclopedia of Chicago, 2004. Contributor to books, periodicals and journals. **Address:** Department of History, Loyola University Chicago, Crown Ctr. 509, 6525 N Sheridan Rd., Chicago, IL 60626-5385, U.S.A. **Online address:** hplatt@luc.edu

PLATT, Harold Lawrence. *See* **PLATT, Harold L.**

PLATT, James R. (Jim Platt). American (born United States), b. 1972. **Genres:** Sports/Fitness, Biography, Autobiography/Memoirs. **Career:** Sports Immortals Inc., vice president, 1998-, Sports Immortals Experience, president. Writer. **Publications:** (As Jim Platt with J. Buckley, Jr.) Sports Immortals: Stories of Inspiration and Achievement, 2002. **Address:** Sports Immortals Inc., 6830 N Federal Hwy., Boca Raton, FL 33487-1626, U.S.A. **Online address:** legends@sportsimmortals.com

PLATT, Jim. *See* **PLATT, James R.**

PLATT, Peter G(odfrey). American (born United States), b. 1961. **Genres:** Literary Criticism And History. **Career:** Teacher, 1983-87, 1992-94; Villiers Park Program, tutor, 1990; Barnard College, assistant professor, 1994-2002, associate professor of English, 2002-, professor of English and chair; University of Edinburgh, Institute for Advanced Studies in the Humanities, fellow, 1998. Writer. **Publications:** Reason Diminished: Shakespeare and the Marvelous, 1997; (ed.) Wonders, Marvels, and Monsters in Early Modern Culture, 1999; Shakespeare and the Culture of Paradox, 2009. Contributor of articles to books and periodicals. **Address:** Department of English, Barnard College, 421 Barnard Hall, 3009 Broadway, New York, NY 10027, U.S.A. **Online address:** pplatt@barnard.edu

PLATT, Randall. (Randall Beth Platt). American (born United States), b. 1948. **Genres:** Novels, Young Adult Fiction, Westerns/Adventure, Humor/Satire, Plays/Screenplays, Language/Linguistics, Reference. **Career:** Eddie Bauer Inc., data processing supervisor, 1969-73, private secretary, 1976-79; freelance writer, 1983-. **Publications:** The Four Arrows Fe-As-Ko, (filmed as Promise The Moon) 1991; Out of a Forest Clearing: An Environmental Fable, 1991; Seahorse Stables (German trans.), 1992; Honor Bright (young adult fiction), 1997; The Royalscope Fe-As-Ko (silent film spoof), 1997; The Cornerstone, 1998; The Likes of Me (young adult fiction), 2000; The 1898 Base-ball Fe-As-Ko (humorous western), 2000; Hellie Jondoe (young adult novel), 2009. **Address:** 1126 Point Fosdick Dr. NW, Gig Harbor, WA 98335-8810, U.S.A. **Online address:** randall@plattbooks.com

PLATT, Randall Beth. *See* **PLATT, Randall.**

PLATT, Rutherford H. American (born United States), b. 1940. **Genres:** Law, Environmental Sciences/Ecology, Sciences, Young Adult Fiction. **Career:** University of Chicago, research assistant, 1966-67; Open Lands Project, staff attorney, 1968-72; University of Massachusetts-Amherst, assistant professor, 1972-78, associate professor, 1978-83, professor of geography, 1983-2007, professor emeritus of geography, 2007-; City University of New York, Insitute for Sustainable Cities, senior fellow, Ecological Cities Project, director. Writer. **Publications:** (With B.J.L. Berry, S.J. Parsons and R.H. Platt) The Impact of Urban Renewal on Small Business, 1968; Open Land in Urban Illinois: Roles of the Citizen Advocate, 1972; The Open Space Decision Process, 1972; Intergovernmental Management of Floodplains, 1980; This Green World, 2nd ed., 1988; Land Use Control: Geography, Law and Public Policy, 1991, rev. ed., 1995; (co-author) Coastal Erosion: Has Retreat Sounded?, 1992; Land Use and Society: Geography, Law and Public Policy, 1996, rev. ed., 2004; Disasters and Democracy: The Politics of Extreme Natural Events, 1999; (co-author) The Practice of Sustainable Development, 2000. EDITOR: (with G. Macinko) Beyond the Urban Fringe: Land Use Issues of Nonmetropolitan America, 1983; Regional Management of Metropolitan Floodplains, 1987; (with B.K.R. Burbank and S.G. Pelczarski) Cities on the Beach: Management of Developed Coastal Barriers, 1987; (with R.A. Rowntree and P.C. Muick) The Ecological City: Preserving and Restoring Urban Biodiversity, 1994; The Humane Metropolis: People and Nature in the 21st Century City, 2006. Contributor to books. **Address:** The Humane Metropolis, 1 Short St., Northampton, MA 01062, U.S.A. **Online address:** platt@geo.umass.edu

PLATTNER, Andy. American (born United States) **Genres:** Novellas/Short Stories. **Career:** Wire-to-Wire Daily Florida Racing Journal, writer. **Publications:** Winter Money, 1997; Kentucky Derby Vault: A History of the Run for the Roses, 2009; A Marriage of Convenience, 2011. Contributor to periodicals. **Address:** c/o Author Mail, University of Georgia Press, 330 Research Dr., Athens, GA 30602-4901, U.S.A.

PLATTNER, Marc F. American (born United States), b. 1945. **Genres:** Essays, Novels. **Career:** The Public Interest, managing editor, 1971-75; Century Foundation (formerly the Twentieth Century Fund), program officer, 1975-81; United States Mission to the United Nations, advisor on economic and social affairs, 1981-83; National Humanities Center in Research Triangle Park, staff, 1983-84; National Endowment for Democracy (NED), vice-president for research and studies, director, 1984-89; International Forum for Democratic Studies, co-director; European University Institute, Robert Schuman Centre for Advanced Studies, visiting professor, 2002-03; Journal of Democracy, founding co-editor. **Publications:** Rousseau's State of Nature: An Interpretation of the Discourse on Inequality, 1979; (co-author) Democracy: Theory and Practice, 1995; Democracy without Borders?: Global Challenges to Liberal Democracy, 2008. EDITOR: Human Rights in Our Time: Essays in Memory of Victor Baras, 1984; (with L. Diamond) Capitalism, Socialism and Democracy Revisited, 1993; (with L. Diamond) The Global Resurgence of Democracy, 1993, 2nd ed., 1996; (with L. Diamond) Nationalism, Ethnic Conflict and Democracy, 1994; (with L. Diamond) Economic Reform and Democracy, 1995; (with L. Diamond) Civil-Military Relations and Democracy, 1996; (with L. Diamond) Democracy in East Asia, 1998; (with L. Diamond and A. Schedler) The Self-Restraining State: Power and Accountability in New Democracies, 1999; (with L. Diamond) Democratization in Africa, 1999, 2nd ed. as Democratization in Africa: Progress and Retreat, 2010; (with J.C. Espada) The Democratic Invention, 2000; (with A. Smolar) Globalization, Power and Democracy, 2000; (with J.C. Espada and A. Wolfson) The Liberal Tradition in Focus: Problems and New Perspectives, 2000; (with L. Diamond) The Global Divergence of Democracies, 2001; (with L. Diamond) Democracy after Communism, 2002; (with L. Diamond and D. Brumberg) Islam and Democracy in the Middle East, 2003; (with L. Diamond and P.J. Costopoulos) World Religions and Democracy, 2005; (with L. Diamond) Electoral Systems and Democracy, 2006; (with S. Ganguly and L. Diamond) The State of India's Democracy, 2007; (with L. Diamond) How People View Democracy, 2008; (with L. Diamond and D.A. Brun) Latin America's Struggle for Democracy, 2008; (with L. Diamond) Democracy: A Reader, 2009; (with L. Diamond and P.J. Costopoulos) Debates on democratization, 2010; (with F. Fukuyama and L. Diamond) Poverty, Inequality and Democracy, 2012. Contributor to journals. **Address:** Journal of Democracy, 1025 F St. NW, Ste. 800, Washington, DC 20004, U.S.A.

PLATZKER, David. American (born United States), b. 1965. **Genres:** Art/Art History, Photography, Crafts. **Career:** Printed Matter Inc., executive director, 1998-. Writer. **Publications:** Multiples in Retrospect, 1990; Multiples Store, 1996; (with R.H. Axsom) Printed Stuff: Prints, Posters and Ephemera by Claes Oldenburg: A Catalog Raisonnee, 1958-1996, 1997; (with E. Wyckoff) Hard Pressed: 600 Years of Prints and Process, 2000; History of Artists Publications, 1917-2001, forthcoming. **Address:** Printed Matter Inc., 535 W 22nd St., New York, NY 10011, U.S.A. **Online address:** dplatzker@printedmatter.org

PLAUT, Eric A. American (born United States), b. 1927. **Genres:** Psychology, Music. **Career:** Montefiore Hospital, intern, 1952-54; Worcester State Hospital, resident in psychiatry, 1954-55; Massachusetts Memorial Hospital, resident in psychiatry, 1956-57; Mills College, lecturer in occupational therapy, 1958-60; Kaiser Hospital, staff psychiatrist, 1958-62; Cowell Memorial Hospital, staff psychiatrist, 1958-62; University of California-San Francisco, assistant clinical professor of psychiatry, 1958-74; American Civil Liberties Union, board director, 1960-65; Herrick-Berkeley Psychiatric Clinic, director, 1962-68; U.S. Department of the Interior, Bureau of Indian Affairs, consulting psychiatrist, 1967-68; Berkeley Mental Health Services, program chief, 1968-71; University of California-Berkeley, lecturer, 1969-74; Vanguard Investments, general partner, 1971-77; Indiana Department of Mental Health and Developmental Disabilities, deputy commissioner, 1974-76; University of Indiana, associate clinical professor, 1975-76; Connecticut Department of

Mental Health, commissioner, 1976-81; University of Connecticut, clinical professor, 1978-81; Yale University, clinical professor, 1979-81; Northwestern Memorial Hospital, Institute of Psychiatry, associate director, 1981-91; Northwestern University, professor, 1981-94, professor emeritus, 1994-; Magnum Medical Software Corp., vice-president, 1987-89. Writer. **Publications:** Grand Opera: Mirror of the Western Mind, 1993; (intro. and ed. with K. Anderson and trans. with G. Edgcomb and K. Anderson) Marx on Suicide, 1999. Contributor of articles to journals. **Address:** Northwestern University, 633 Clark St., Evanston, IL 60208, U.S.A.

PLAUT, Joshua Eli. American (born United States), b. 1957. **Genres:** Theology/Religion, Anthropology/Ethnology, History, Social Sciences, Cultural/Ethnic Topics. **Career:** Jerusalem Center for Public Policy, archivist, 1977; U.S. Department of State, analyst of investment aid, 1978; Congregation Kol Haverim, rabbi, 1986-93; Trinity College, B'nai B'rith Hillel Director, 1986-93; Martha's Vineyard Hebrew Center, rabbi, 1993-; Massachusetts Institute of Technology, Hillel Jewish chaplain, 1993-, university rabbi; American Friends of Rabin Medical Center, executive director. Writer. **Publications:** Scattered Lights: The Remnant of Israel in Rural Greece, 1985; Greek Jewry in the Twentieth Century, 1913-1983: Patterns of Jewish Survival in the Greek Provinces Before and After the Holocaust, 1996; A Kosher Christmas, 2012; Silent Night? Being Jewish at Christmas-time in America: Proclaiming Identity in the Face of Seasonal Marginality, forthcoming. **Address:** PO Box 692, Vineyard Haven, MA 02568, U.S.A. **Online address:** rjplaut@mit.edu

PLAUT, Melissa. American (born United States), b. 1975?. **Genres:** Novels. **Career:** Writer. **Publications:** Hack: How I Stopped Worrying about What to Do with My Life and Started Driving a Yellow Cab, 2007. **Address:** Villard Books, 1745 Broadway, New York, NY 10019-4368, U.S.A. **Online address:** newyorkhack@gmail.com

PLAUT, W. Gunther. Canadian/German (born Germany), b. 1912. **Genres:** Novels, History, Theology/Religion, Autobiography/Memoirs, Novellas/Short Stories. **Career:** Rabbi, 1939-48, 1948-61; Macalester College, visiting lecturer in philosophy, 1952-54; Saint Paul Gallery and School of Art, president, 1953-59; Minnesota Governor's Committee on Ethics in Government, chair, 1958-61; Holy Blossom Temple, senior rabbi, 1961-77, now rabbi emeritus; World Federalists of Canada, national president, 1966-69; Ontario Human Rights Commission, vice-chair, 1977-85; Canadian Jewish Congress, national president, 1977-80; St. Paul Council of Arts and Sciences, vice-president; Haifa University, visiting lecturer in Jewish thought, 1978. Writer. **Publications:** Die materielle Eheungultigkeit im deutschen und schweizerischen internationalen Privatrecht, 1935; Mount Zion, 1856-1956: The First Hundred Years, 1956; The Jews in Minnesota, 1959; The Book of Proverbs: A Commentary, 1961; Judaism and the Scientific Spirit, 1962; The Rise of Reform Judaism, 1963; The Case for the Chosen People: The Role of the Jewish People Yesterday and Today, 1965; The Growth of Reform Judaism, 1965; Your Neighbor Is a Jew, 1967; Your Neighbour is a Jew, 1967; Israel Since the Six-Day War, 1968; The Sabbath as Protest: Thoughts on Work and Leisure in the Automated Society, 1970; Page Two: Ten Years of News and Views, 1971; Genesis: A Modern Commentary, 1974; Children's Services for the High Holy Days, 1975; Time to Think, 1977; Hanging Threads, 1978 in US as The Man in the Blue Vest and Other Stories, 1980; Numbers: A Commentary, 1979; Midrash as an Aid to Preaching, 1979; (ed.) The Torah, A Modern Commentary, 1979, rev. ed., 2005; Exodus: A Commentary, 1980; Unfinished Business (autobiography), 1981; Through the Sound of many Voices, 1982; Refugee Determination in Canada: A Report to the Honourable Flora MacDonald, Minister of Employment and Immigration, 1985; The Letter, 1986; The Man Who Would Be Messiah, 1988; Rabbi's Manual, 1988; The Magen David: How the Star of David Became the Jewish Symbol, 1991; German-Jewish Bible Translations: Linguistic Theology as a Political Phenomenon, 1992; Asylum-A Moral Dilemma, 1995; The Haftarah Commentary, 1996; The Haftarah Commentary, 1996; (with M. Washofsky) Teshuvot for the Nineties, 1997; More Unfinished Business (autobiography), 1997; Price and Privilege of Growing Old, 2000; (comp. with M.A. Meyer) The Reform Judaism Reader, 2001; Eight Decades, 2008. **Address:** Holy Blossom Temple, 1950 Bathurst St., Toronto, ON M5P 3K9, Canada. **Online address:** gplaut@yorku.ca

PLEASANT, Barbara. American (born United States) **Genres:** Homes/Gardens, Horticulture. **Career:** Organic Gardening Magazine, contributing editor, 1984-90; Mother Earth News, contributing editor; The Herb Companion, contributing editor. Master Gardener organizations, lecturer. Writer, mental health counselor and child welfare. **Publications:** The Handbook of Southern Vegetable Gardening, 1984; Warm-Climate Gardening: Tips, Techniques, Plans, Projects for Humid or Dry Conditions, 1993; The Gardener's Bug Book: Earth-safe Insect Control, 1994; The Gardener's Guide to Plant Diseases: Earth-safe Remedies, 1995; The Gardener's Weed Book: Earth-safe Controls, 1996; Controlling Garden Weeds, 1997; Cutting Gardens, 1997; Easy Garden Projects for All Seasons, 1997; Container Gardens, 1997; Lawns & Ground Covers, 1997; Beds and Borders, 1998; (with K.L. Smith) Ortho's All about Vegetables, 1999; Gardening Essentials, 1999; Annual Flowers, 2000; Better Gardens, Less Work, 2001; Garden Stone: Creative Ideas, Practical Projects and Inspiration for Purely Decorative Uses, 2002; The Southern Garden Advisor, 2003; The Whole Herb: For Cooking, Crafts, Gardening, Health and Other Joys of Life, 2004; The Complete Houseplant Survival Manual: Essential Know-How For Keeping (not Killing) More Than 160 Indoor Plants, 2005; Easy Garden Projects To Make, Build and Grow: 200 Do-It-Yourself Ideas to Help You Grow Your Best Garden Ever, 2006; (with D.L. Martin) The Complete Compost Gardening: A New Time-saving System for more Flavorful Vegetables, Bountiful Blooms and the Richest Soil You've Ever Seen, 2008; (with D.L. Martin) The Complete Compost Gardening Guide: Banner Batches, Grow Heaps, Comforter Compost and Other Amazing Techniques for Saving Time and Money and Producing the Most Flavorful, Nutritious Vegetables Ever, 2008; (with H. Cotten and P. Crawford) Easy Gardens for the South, 2009; Starter Vegetable Gardens: 24 No-Fail Plans for Small Organic Gardens, 2010. **Address:** c/o Author Mail, Storey Publishing, 210 MASS MoCA Way, North Adams, MA 01247, U.S.A. **Online address:** barbara@swva.net

PLEIJ, Herman. Dutch (born Netherlands), b. 1943. **Genres:** Cultural/Ethnic Topics. **Career:** University of Amsterdam, lecturer on Dutch historical literature, professor of historical Dutch literature, 1981-2008, Faculty of Arts, dean, 1990-92, professor emeritus of old Dutch literature, 2008-. Writer. **Publications:** He gilde van de Blauwe Schuit: literatuur, volksfeest en burgermoraal in de late middeleeuwen, 1979; De blauwe schuit, 1979; (co-ed.) Een Nyeuwe clucht boeck: een zestiende-eeuwse anekdotenverzameling, 1983; Het literaire leven in de middeleeuwen, 1984; Van schelmen en schavuiten: laatmiddeleeuwse vagebondteksten, 1985; 't Is al vrouwenwerk: refreinen van Anna Bijns, 1987; De sneeuwpoppen van 1511: literatuur en tussen middeleeuwen en modern tijd, 1988; Nederlandse literatuur van de late middeleeuwen, 1990; Sprekend over de middeleeuwen, 1991; Het Nederlandse onbehagen, 1992; Kleuren van de middeleeuwen, 1994; Zandgrond, 1994; Mooi meegenomen?: Over de genietbaarheid van oudere teksten uit de Nederlandse letterkunde, 1997; Dromen van Cocagne: middeleeuwse fantasieandeumln over volmaakte leve, 1997, translated by D. Webb as Dreaming of Cockaigne: Medieval Fantasies of the Perfect Life, 2001; Hollands welbehagen, 1998; Tegen de barbarij: tien stukken over vaderlandse beschaving, 1999; Van karmijn, purper en blauw: over kleuren van de Middeleeuwen en daarna, 2002; (ed. with J. Reynaert) Geschreven en gedrukt: boekproductie van handschrift naar druk in de overgang van Middeleeuwen naar moderne tijd, 2004; (ed. with W. Blockmans) Nederland van prehistorie tot Beeldenstorm, 2007; Gevleugelde woord: geschiedenis van de Nederlandse literatuur 1400-1560, 2007; Komt een vrouwtje bij de drukker-: over gezichtsveranderingen van de literatuur uit de late Middeleeuwen, 2008. **Address:** University of Amsterdam, Rm. 433, Spuistraat 134, Binnengasthuisstraat 9, Amsterdam, 1012 VB, Netherlands. **Online address:** h.pleij@uva.nl

PLESCH, Veronique Brigitte. Swiss (born Switzerland), b. 1957?. **Genres:** Art/Art History. **Career:** Mills College, lecturer, 1990; San Francisco State University, lecturer, 1990-91; Colby College, professor, 1994-; International Association of Word & Image Studies, president, 2008-. Writer. **Publications:** (With K. Ashley) The Cultural Processes of Appropriation, 2002; Le Christ peint, Le cycle de la Passion dans les chapelles peintes du XVe siecle dans les Etats de Savoie, 2004; (with C. Cluever and L. Hoek) Orientations: Space/Time/Image/Word, 2005; Painter and Priest: Giovanni Canavesio's Visual Rhetoric and the Passion Cycle at La Brigue, 2006. Contributor of articles to books and journals. **Address:** Colby College, 5634 Mayflower Hill, Waterville, ME 04901-8856, U.S.A. **Online address:** vbplesch@colby.edu

PLESKO, Les. (Leslie Plesko). American/Hungarian (born Hungary), b. 1954. **Genres:** Novels, Young Adult Fiction. **Career:** University of California, instructor of creative writing. Writer. **Publications:** The Last Bongo Sunset: A Novel, 1995; Slow Lie Detector, 2009. **Address:** Goldstein and Associates, 1150 Yale St., Ste. 12, Santa Monica, CA 90403, U.S.A.

PLESKO, Leslie. *See* **PLESKO, Les.**

PLESS, Vera. American (born United States), b. 1931. **Genres:** Mathematics/Statistics, Information Science/Computers. **Career:** United States Air Force, mathematician, 1962-72; Massachusetts Institute of Technology, research associate, 1972-75; University of Illinois, Department of Mathematics, Statistics, and Computer Science, professor, 1975-, now professor emeritus; California Technical College, visiting professor, 1985-86; The Technion, visiting professor, researcher and scientist. Writer. **Publications:** An Introduction to The Theory of Error-Correcting Codes, 1982, 3rd ed., 1998; (ed. with W.C. Huffman and R.A. Brualdi) Handbook of Coding Theory, 1998; (with W.C. Huffman) Fundamentals of Error-Correcting Codes, 2003; (with J. Beissinger) Cryptoclub: Using Mathematics to Make and Break Secret Codes, 2006. Contributor of articles to journals. **Address:** Department of Mathematics, University of Illinois, 507 Science and Engineering Offices, 851 S Morgan St., Chicago, IL 60607-7045, U.S.A. **Online address:** vpless@uic.edu

PLETSCH, Carl (Erich). American (born United States), b. 1943. **Genres:** History, Biography, Philosophy. **Career:** University of North Carolina, assistant professor of history, 1979-85; Miami University, associate professor of history, 1988-; University of Colorado, Department of History, associate professor. Writer. **Publications:** Psychoanalytic Study of Friedrich Nietzsche, 1977; Young Nietzsche: Becoming a Genius, 1991. EDITOR: (with S.H. Baron) Introspection in Biography: The Biographer's Quest for Self-Awareness, 1985; (with A.D. Baldwin and I.D. Luce) Beyond Preservation: Restoring and Inventing Landscapes, 1994. **Address:** Department of History, University of Colorado, King Ctr. 550, PO Box 182, Denver, CO 80217-3364, U.S.A. **Online address:** carl.pletsch@ucdenver.edu

PLITT, Jane R(uth). American (born United States), b. 1948. **Genres:** Autobiography/Memoirs. **Career:** Rochester Telephone Co., labor relations manager, 1969-; National Organization for Women, executive director, 1973-; Cresap, McCormick and Paget, consultant, 1975-; New York State Department of Commerce, business ombudsperson, 1977-; JP Associates, president, 1979-; State of New York, arbitrator, 1979-; WXXI Public Radio and Television, board chair, 1983-99; Unite and Write, board chair, 1996-99; Rochester Women's Network, founder; Rochester Chamber of Commerce, Small Business Council, president. Writer. **Publications:** Martha Matilda Harper and the American Dream: How One Woman Changed the Face of Modern Business, 2000. Contributor to books and periodicals. **Address:** Rochester Women's Network, 249 Highland Ave., Ste. 200, Rochester, NY 14620, U.S.A. **Online address:** bruen2@att.net

PLOEGER, Katherine (M.). American (born United States), b. 1955. **Genres:** Education, Writing/Journalism, Language/Linguistics, Young Adult Non-fiction, Young Adult Fiction. **Career:** Timesavers, administrative support staff, 1979-81; Castlee Publications, travel writer, 1980-88; TAB Products Co., training coordinator, 1981-84; Stanford University, administrative assistant, 1984-91; Old World Gift Shoppe, owner and operator, 1988-91; San Joaquin Delta College, adjunct instructor in English, 1994; Modesto Junior College, adjunct and associate instructor, 1994-99; Chapman University, Modesto Center, adjunct, associate, lecturer in English, 1994-2002; California State University, lecturer, 1995-2002, Stanislaus Extended Education, teacher, 2000-02; Valley Commercial College, adjunct instructor, 1995; Ploeger's Services, owner and operator, 1999-; Saddleback College, adjunct and associate professor of English, 2004-05; California State University, adjunct and associate professor of English, 2007-08. Writer. **Publications:** Character Workshop, 1994, 2nd ed., 1999; Plot Workshop, 1994, 2nd ed., 1999; Brainstorming Workshop, 1995, 2nd ed., 1999; Basic Writer's Toolkit, 1995; Writer's Toolkit, 1995; Simplified Paragraph Skills, 2000; Simplified Essay Skills, 2001. Contributor to periodicals. **Address:** 2850 SW Cedar Hills Blvd., Ste. 244, Beaverton, OR 97005, U.S.A. **Online address:** katieploeger@gmail.com

PLOKHY, Serhii. Canadian (born Canada), b. 1957?. **Genres:** Politics/Government, History, Theology/Religion. **Career:** Dnipropetrovsk University, Department of World History, chair; National Academy Sciences of Ukraine, Institute of Archeography and Source Studies, researcher and head of the department of the history of culture; University of Alberta, adjunct professor of history and classics, 1999-, professor of history, Peter Jacyk Centre for Ukrainian Historical Research, associate director, 2008-; Harvard University, Department of History, Mykhailo Hrushevsky professor of Ukrainian history, chair, 2007-; Canadian Institute of Ukrainian Studies, Church Studies Program, director. Historian and author. **Publications:** Pershyi Vseukralns'kyi pravoslavnyi t's'erkovnyi sobor UAPT'S', 14-30 z'h'ovtni'a' 1921 roku: dokumenty i materialy, 1999; The Cossacks and Religion in Early Modern Ukraine, 2001; Tsars and Cossacks: A Study in Iconography, 2002; (with F.E. Sysyn) Religion and Nation in Modern Ukraine, 2003; Unmaking Imperial Russia: Mykhailo Hrushevsky and the Writing of Ukrainian History, 2005; (ed. with F.E. Sysyn) Synopsis: A Collection of Essays in Honour of Zenon E. Kohut, 2005; The Origins of the Slavic Nations: Premodern Identities in Russia, Ukraine and Belarus, 2006; Ukraine's Quest for Europe: Borders, Cultures, Identities, 2007; Ukraine and Russia: Representations of the Past, 2008; Yalta: The Price of Peace, 2010. **Address:** Jacyk Center for Ukrainian Historical Research, University of Alberta, 450 Athabasca Hall, Edmonton, AB T6G 2E8, Canada.

PLOTKIN, Bill. American (born United States), b. 1950. **Genres:** Sciences, Natural History, Theology/Religion, Self Help. **Career:** State University of New York, professor of psychology, 1979; Animas Valley Institute (nonprofit organization), founder and guide, 1981-. Writer and depth psychologist. **Publications:** Soulcraft: Crossing into the Mysteries of Nature and Psyche, 2003; Nature and the Human Soul: Cultivating Wholeness and Community in a Fragmented World, 2008. **Address:** Animas Valley Institute, PO Box 1020, Durango, CO 81302, U.S.A. **Online address:** soulcraft@animas.org

PLOTKIN, Diane M. American (born United States), b. 1942. **Genres:** Biography, Social Sciences, History. **Career:** Greene Family Camp, camp nurse, 1977-92; Brookhaven College, instructor, 1984-, professor of world literature and Holocaust studies. Writer. **Publications:** (With R.A. Ritvo) Sisters in Sorrow: Voices of Care in the Holocaust, 1998; (contrib.) Problems Unique to the Holocaust, 1999; (ed.) Yesterday: My Story, 2002; Medical Care of Concentration Camp Survivors, forthcoming. **Address:** Texas A&M University Press, 4354 TAMU, John H. Lindsey Bldg., Lewis St., College Station, TX 77843-4354, U.S.A. **Online address:** dmartin@dcccd.edu

PLOURDE-BARKER, Michele. *See* **BARKER, M. P.**

PLOWDEN, David. American (born United States), b. 1932. **Genres:** History, Photography, Adult Non-fiction. **Career:** Writer and photographer, 1962-; Illinois Institute of Technology, Institute of Design, visiting associate professor, 1978-80, associate professor, 1980-86; University of Iowa, School of Journalism and Mass Communications, lecturer, 1985-88; Grand Valley State University, visiting professor, 1988-90, 1991-2007; University of Baltimore, Yale Gordon College of Liberal Arts, Institute for Publication Design, artist-in-residence and senior fellow, 1990-91. **Publications:** Farewell to Steam, 1966; (contrib.) Gems, 1967; (contrib.) America the Vanishing, 1969; (ed.) Lincoln and His America 1809-1865, 1970; The Hand of Man on America, 1971; (contrib.) Nantucket, 1971; The Floor of the Sky: The Great Plains, 1972; (contrib.) Cape May to Montauk, 1973; Commonplace, 1974; Bridges: The Spans of North America, 1974, rev. ed., 2002; (with R. Berton) Desert and Plain, the Mountains and the River: A Celebration of Rural America, 1975; Tugboat: Text and Photographs, 1976; (contrib.) Iron Road: A Portrait of American Railroading, 1978; Steel, 1981; An American Chronology: Photographs of David Plowden, 1982; Industrial Landscape, 1985; A Time of Trains, 1987; A Sense of Place, 1988; End of an Era: The Last of the Great Lakes Steamboats, 1992; Small Town America, 1994; Imprints: David Plowden, A Retrospective, 1997; David Plowden: The American Barn, 2003; Handful of Dust: Photographs of Disappearing America, 2006; David Plowden: Vanishing Point: Fifty Years of Photography, 2007; Requiem for Steam, 2010. Contributor to periodicals. **Address:** c/o Scott Gould, RLR Associates, 7 W 51st St., New York, IL 10019, U.S.A. **Online address:** david@davidplowden.com

PLOWDEN, Martha Ward. American (born United States), b. 1948. **Genres:** Sports/Fitness, Women's Studies And Issues. **Career:** Southern Bell Telephone Co., operator; Taliaferro County Elementary and High School, librarian; Grady Memorial Hospital, food service supervisor; Clark College, librarian; Atlanta Public School System, media specialist, now retired; Metro Atlanta Skills Center, mathematics instructor; Clark Atlanta University, adjunct professor. Writer. **Publications:** Famous Firsts of Black Women, 1993, 2nd ed., 2002; Olympic Black Women, 1996, NAACP One Hundredth Year Anniversary, 1909-2009: A Historical Perspective of the Georgia State Conference, 2009. **Address:** Pelican Publishing Company, 1000 Burmaster St., Gretna, LA 70053-2246, U.S.A. **Online address:** nplowden@bellsouth.net

PLUM, Jennifer. *See* **KURLAND, Michael (Joseph).**

PLUMLEY, Lisa. American (born United States) **Genres:** Novels, Romance/Historical, Novellas/Short Stories. **Career:** Author. **Publications:** Surrender, 1997; The Honeymoon Hoax, 1998; My Best Friend's Baby, 1999; Outlaw, 1999; Lawman, 1999; Man of the Year, 2000; Her Best Man, 2000; Making Over Mike, 2001; Falling for April, 2002; Reconsidering Riley, 2002; The Drifter, 2002; The Matchmaker, 2003; Perfect Together, 2003; Perfect Switch, 2004; Josie Day Is Coming Home, 2005; Once upon a Christmas, 2005; Mad about Max, 2006; The Rascal, 2006; The Scoundrel, 2006; Let's Misbehave, 2008; Home for the Holidays, 2008; My Favorite Witch, 2009; Holiday Affair, 2010; The Mail-Order Groom, 2010; The Bride Raffle, 2011; Melt Into You, 2012; The Honor-Bound Gambler, 2012; Together for Christmas, 2012. Works appear in anthologies. **Address:** AZ , U.S.A. **Online address:** lisa@lisaplumley.com

PLUMLY, Stanley (Ross). American (born United States), b. 1939. **Genres:** Poetry, Literary Criticism And History, Biography. **Career:** Louisiana State University, visiting poet, 1968-70; Ohio Review, poetry editor, 1970-75; Ohio University, visiting poet, 1970-73, professor of English, 1970-74; University of Iowa, visiting lecturer, 1975-76; Iowa Review, poetry editor, 1976-78; Princeton University, visiting lecturer, 1976-78; Columbia University, visiting lecturer, 1977-79; University of Michigan, faculty, 1979; University of Houston, professor of English, 1979, visiting poet, 1979-85; University of Maryland, distinguished university professor, 1985-, professor of English, director of creative writing. **Publications:** In the Outer Dark, 1970; Giraffe, 1973; How the Plains Indians Got Horses, 1975; Out-of-the-Body Travel, 1977; Summer Celestial, 1983; Boy on the Step: Poems, 1989; The Marriage in the Trees, 1997; (ed. with M. Collier) New Bread Loaf Anthology of Contemporary American Poetry, 1999; Now That My Father Lies Down Beside Me: New and Selected Poems, 1970-2000, 2000; (ed. with S. Matthews) Poetry Blues: Essays and Interviews, 2001; Argument and Song: Sources and Silences in Poetry, 2003; (ed. with S. Matthews) Search Party: Collected Poems of William Matthews, 2004; Old Heart: Poems, 2007; Posthumous Keats: A Personal Biography, 2008; New Hope for the Dead: Uncollected William Matthews, 2010. **Address:** Department of English, University of Maryland, 2119 Tawes Hall, College Park, MD 20742-0001, U.S.A. **Online address:** splumly@umd.edu

PLUMMER, Brenda Gayle. American (born United States), b. 1946. **Genres:** History, Social Commentary, Local History/Rural Topics. **Career:** Fisk University, Department of History, instructor, 1973-75; University of California, Department of Black Studies, lecturer and research fellow, 1979-81; University of Minnesota, assistant professor, 1981-87, associate professor, 1987-90, adjunct professor, 1987-90; University of Wisconsin-Madison, associate professor of history and Afro-American studies, 1991-94, professor of history and Afro-American studies, 1994-. **Publications:** Haiti and the Great Powers: 1902-1915, 1988; Haiti and the United States: The Psychological Moment, 1992; Rising Wind: Black Americans and U.S. Foreign Affairs, 1935-1960, 1996; (ed.) Window on Freedom: Race, Civil Rights and Foreign Affairs, 1945-1988, 2003; America's Dilemma: Race, Civil Rights and Foreign Affairs, forthcoming. **Address:** Department of History, University of Wisconsin, 5111 Mosse Humanities, 455 N Park St., Madison, WI 53706, U.S.A. **Online address:** bplummer@macc.wisc.edu

PLUMMER, Louise. American (born United States), b. 1942?. **Genres:** Novels, Essays. **Career:** Brigham Young University, associate professor of English. Writer. **Publications:** YOUNG ADULT NOVELS: (with L. Taylor and T. Cooke) A Walk to Grow On, 1985; The Romantic Obsessions and Humiliations of Annie Sehlmeier, 1987; My Name Is Sus5an Smith, the 5 Is Silent, 1991; The Unlikely Romance of Kate Bjorkman, 1995; A Dance for Three, 2000; Finding Daddy, 2007. FOR ADULTS: Thoughts of a Grasshopper: Essays and Oddities, 1992; (with T. Plummer) Eating Chocolates and Dancing in the Kitchen: Sketches of Marriage and Family, 1998. Contributor to periodicals. **Address:** 5757 W South Temple, Salt Lake City, UT 84111, U.S.A. **Online address:** louiseplummer@byu.edu

PLUTZER, Eric. American (born United States), b. 1958. **Genres:** Politics/Government. **Career:** Indiana University, postdoctoral fellow, 1987-89; Iowa State University, assistant professor, 1989-94; Pennsylvania State University, associate professor, 1994-2005, professor of political science and sociology, 2005-, academic director, 2006-. Writer. **Publications:** (with M.B. Berkman) Ten Thousand Democracies: Politics and Public Opinion in America's School Districts, 2005. Contributor to books and journals. **Address:** Department of Political Science, Pennsylvania State University, 219 Pond Lab, University Park, PA 16802, U.S.A. **Online address:** plutzer@psu.edu

POAGUE, Leland. (Leland Allen Poague). American (born United States), b. 1948. **Genres:** Film, Novels, Bibliography. **Career:** State University of New York College, instructor, 1973-74, assistant professor of English, 1974-78; Iowa State University, assistant professor, 1978-81, associate professor, 1981-86, professor, 1986-. Writer. **Publications:** The Cinema of Frank Capra: An Approach to Film Comedy, 1975; The Cinema of Ernst Lubitsch: The Hollywood Films, 1978; The Hollywood Professionals: Billy Wilder and Leo McCarey, vol. VII, 1980; Howard Hawks, 1982; (with W. Cadbury) Film Criticism: A Counter Theory, 1982; Another Frank Capra, 1994; (comp. with K.A. Parsons) Susan Sontag: An Annotated Bibliography 1948-1992, 2000. EDITOR: (with M. Deutelbaum) A Hitchcock Reader, 1986, 2nd ed., 2009; Conversations with Susan Sontag, 1995; Frank Capra: Interviews, 2004; (with T. Leitch) A Companion to Alfred Hitchcock, 2011. Contributor to journals. **Address:** Department of English, Iowa State University, 321 Ross Hall, Ames, IA 50011-1201, U.S.A. **Online address:** lpoague@iastate.edu

POAGUE, Leland Allen. *See* **POAGUE, Leland.**

POBLOCKI, Dan. American (born United States), b. 1981. **Genres:** Children's Fiction, Mystery/Crime/Suspense. **Career:** Author. **Publications:** The Stone Child, 2009; The Nightmarys, 2010. **Address:** Brooklyn, NY , U.S.A. **Online address:** danpoblocki@yahoo.com

POCESKI, Mario. (Cheng Chien Bhikshu). American (born United States), b. 1964?. **Genres:** Adult Non-fiction. **Career:** University of Iowa, visiting assistant professor of Chinese religions, 2000-01; University of Florida, assistant professor of Buddhist studies and Chinese religions and affiliate faculty of Asian studies program, 2001-08, associate professor of Buddhist studies and Chinese religions, 2008-. Writer. **Publications:** NONFICTION: (as Cheng Chien Bhikshu) Manifestation of the Tathagata: Buddhahood according to the Avatamsaka Sutra, 1993; (as Cheng Chien Bhikshu) Sun-Face Buddha: The Teachings of Ma-tsu and the Hung-chou School of Ch'an, 1993; Ordinary Mind as the Way: The Hongzhou School and the Growth of Chan Buddhism, 2007; Introducing Chinese Religions, 2009. Contributor to books and journals. **Address:** Department of Religion, University of Florida, 107 Anderson Hall, Gainesville, FL 32611-7410, U.S.A. **Online address:** mpoceski@religion.ufl.edu

POCH, John. American (born United States), b. 1966. **Genres:** Poetry. **Career:** Texas Tech University, associate professor of creative writing and director of the creative writing program; Colgate University, creative writing fellow, 2000-01; Lynchburg College, Thornton Writer-in-Residence, 2007; 32 Poems, editor; MacDowell Colony, writer-in-residence; Headlands Center for the Arts, writer-in-residence; Blue Mountain Center, writer-in-residence. Academic. **Publications:** In Defense of the Fall (chapbook), 2000; Poems, 2004; (with C. Davidson) Hockey Haiku: The Essential Collection, 2006; Ghost Towns of the Enchanted Circle (letterpress/art book), 2007; Two Men Fighting with a Knife (poetry), 2008; Dolls (poetry), 2009. Contributor to periodicals and journals. **Address:** Department of English, Texas Tech University, PO Box 43091, Lubbock, TX 79409-3091, U.S.A. **Online address:** john.poch@ttu.edu

POCHODA, Ivy. American (born United States), b. 1977. **Genres:** Novels. **Career:** Harvard University, Crimson Newspaper, staff writer, 1995-97; James Merrill House, writer-in-residence, 2009; Baby, editor. **Publications:** The Art of Disappearing (novel), 2009. Contributor to periodicals. **Address:** New York, NY , U.S.A. **Online address:** ivy@ivypochoda.com

PODELL, Diane K(opperman). American (born United States), b. 1931. **Genres:** Librarianship, Bibliography. **Career:** Maywood Public Library, reference librarian and assistant director, 1975-78; Long Island University, C.W. Post Campus, professor of library and periodicals librarian, 1979-, Palmer School of Library and Information Science, adjunct lecturer, 1985-89, now professor emeritus, adjunct librarian; Queens College of the City University of New York, adjunct lecturer, 1980-89; Queensborough Community College of the City University of New York, adjunct reference librarian, 1990-94. Writer. **Publications:** Thematic Atlases for Public, Academic, and High School Libraries, 1994. **Address:** Department of Periodicals, C.W. Post

Campus, Long Island University, B. Davis Schwartz Library, Brookville, NY 11548, U.S.A. **Online address:** dpodell@liu.edu

PODHORETZ, John. American (born United States), b. 1961. **Genres:** Politics/Government. **Career:** Weekly Standard, co-founder and deputy director, 1995-97, contributing editor, 1997-; New York Post, associate editor, 1997-2000, columnist, 2000-; Fox News Channel, contributor, 1997-; White House Writers Group (corporate speechwriting and public relations firm), co-founder; Time magazine, researcher and reporter; Regan Books, consulting editor; Commentary magazine, staff, 2007, editor, 2009-, editorial director. **Publications:** Hell of a Ride: Backstage at the White House Follies 1989-1993, 1993; (ed.) A Passion for Truth: The Selected Writings of Eric Breindel, 1999; Bush Country: How Dubya Became a Great President while Driving Liberals Insane, 2004; Can She be Stopped?: Hillary Clinton will be the Next President of the United States Unless, 2006. **Address:** New York Post, 1211 Ave. of the Americas, New York, NY 10036-8790, U.S.A. **Online address:** podhoretz@nypost.com

PODHORETZ, Norman. American (born United States), b. 1930. **Genres:** International Relations/Current Affairs, Literary Criticism And History, Social Commentary, Autobiography/Memoirs, Intellectual History. **Career:** Commentary Magazine, assistant editor, 1955, associate editor, 1956-58, editor, 1960-95, editor-at-large, 1995-; Looking Glass Library, editor-in-chief, 1958-60; Hudson Institute, senior fellow, 1995-2008. **Publications:** Doings and Undoings: The Fifties and After in American Writing, 1964; (ed.) The Commentary Reader: Two Decades of Articles and Stories, 1966; Making It (autobiography), 1967; Breaking Ranks: A Political Memoir, 1979; The Present Danger, 1980; Why We Were in Vietnam, 1982; State of World Jewry Address, 1983, 1984; The Bloody Crossroads: Where Literature and Politics Meet, 1986; Ex-Friends (memoir), 1999; My Love Affair with America: The Cautionary Tale of a Cheerful Conservative, 2000; The Prophets: Who They Were, What They Are, 2002; Norman Podhoretz reader, 2004; World War IV: The Long Struggle Against Islamofascism, 2007; Why Are Jews Liberals?, 2009. **Address:** Commentary, 165 E 56th St., New York, NY 10022, U.S.A. **Online address:** npodhoretz@gmail.com

PODWAL, Mark. American (born United States), b. 1945. **Genres:** Theology/Religion, Illustrations. **Career:** New York University, Langone Medical Center and School of Medicine, clinical associate professor of dermatology, 1974-; Tisch University Hospital, associate attending physician, 1974-; Bellevue Hospital, associate attending physician, 1974-. Writer and artist. **Publications:** The Decline and Fall of the American Empire, 1971; Freud's da Vinci, 1977; A Book of Hebrew Letters, 1978; Leonardo di Freud, 1982; A Jewish Bestiary, 1984; The Book of Tens, 1994; Golem: A Giant Made of Mud, 1995; Zidovsk'sny=Jewish Dreams, 1997; The Menorah Story, 1998; A Sweet Year: A Taste of the Jewish Holidays, 2003; Jerusalem Sky: Stars, Crosses, and Crescents, 2005; Doctored Drawings, 2007; Built by Angels: The Story of the Old-New Synagogue, 2009. Contributor to periodicals. **Address:** 55 East 73 St., New York, NY 10021, U.S.A. **Online address:** infomarkpodwal@gmail.com

POËPPEL, Ernst. German (born Germany), b. 1940. **Genres:** Biology, Sciences, Medicine/Health. **Career:** Max-Planck-Institute of Behavioral Physiology, fellow, 1965-70, research associate, 1973-76; Massachusetts Institute of Technology, Department of Psychology and Brain Science, research associate, 1971-73; Volkswagen Foundation, postdoctoral fellow, 1969-70; Department of Neurophysiology, postdoctoral fellow, 1969-70; Neuroscience Research Program, staff scientist, 1972-73; Max-Planck-Institute of Psychiatry, researcher, 1973-76, postdoctoral fellow, 1969-70; University of Munich, professor of medical psychology, 1976; Leopold-Franzens-University, faculty of natural sciences; Ludwig-Maximilians-University, faculty of medicine, Institute of Medical Psychology, founder and chairman, 1977-2008, Human Studies Center, chairman, 1997-; Juelich (a research center), board director, 1992-97; Generation Research Program, director, 2000; Parmenides Center for the Study of Thinking, co-director, 2001-; Peter-Schilffarth-Institute of Sociotechnology, scientific director, 2009-. Writer. **Publications:** Lust und Schmerz: Grundlagen menschlichen Erlebens und Verhaltens, 1982; Grenzen des Bewusstseins: Uber Wirklichkeit und Welterfahrung, 1985; Geheimmisvolles Kosmos Gehim, 1994; (with M. Kerner) Zeit und Mensch, 1996; (with C. Kolo and T. Christaller) Bioinformation. Problemlosung fur die Wissengesellschaft, 1999. EDITOR: (with I. Rentschler and D. Epstein) Beauty and the Brain: Biological Aspects of Aesthetics, 1988; (with N. von Steinbüechel and D.V. van Cramon) Neuropsychological Rehabilitation, 1992; (with C. Maar and T. Christaller) Die Technik auf dem Weg zur Seele, 1996; (with E. Kraft and B. Gulyás) Neural Correlates of Thinking, 2009. Contributor to books and journals. **Address:** Institute of Medical Psychology, Ludwig-Maximilians-University, Goethestrasse 31/ 1, Munich, 80336, Germany. **Online address:** ernst.poeppel@med.uni-muenchen.de

POGGE, Thomas. American (born United States), b. 1953. **Genres:** Social Sciences, Politics/Government, Philosophy, Essays. **Career:** Columbia University, assistant professor, associate professor, 1983-2006, professor, 2006-08; Australian National University, Centre for Applied Philosophy and Public Ethics, professorial fellow, 2004-11; Yale University, professor of philosophy and international affairs, Leitner professor of philosophy and international affairs, 2008-, Global Justice Program, director; University of Oslo, Centre for the Study of Mind in Nature, research director, 2007-; University of Central Lancashire, Centre for Professional Ethics, adjunct professor of political philosophy, 2005-, professor of political philosophy; Stanford Encyclopedia of Philosophy, editor. Philosopher. **Publications:** (As Thomas W. Pogge) Realizing Rawls, 1989; (as Thomas W. Pogge) World Poverty and Human Rights: Cosmopolitan Responsibilities and Reforms, 2002; Gerechtigkeit in der Einen Welt, 2009; Politics as Usual, 2010. EDITOR: (as Thomas W. Pogge with L. Meyer and S.L. Paulson) Rights, Culture, and the Law: Themes from the Legal and Political Philosophy of Joseph Raz, 2003; (with C. Barry) Global Institutions and Responsibilities, 2005; (with A. Follesdal) Real World Justice: Grounds, Principles, Human Rights, and Social Institutions, 2005; Freedom from Poverty as a Human Right: Who Owes What to the Very Poor?, 2007; (with R.E. Goodin and P. Pettit) A Companion to Contemporary Political Philosophy, 2007; (with D. Moellendorf) Global Justice: Seminal Essays, 2008; (with D. Moellendorf) Global Responsibilities, 2008; (with K. Horton) Global Ethics: Seminal Essays, 2008; (with M. Rimmer and K. Rubenstein) Incentives for Global Public Health, 2010; (with M.J. Selgelid) Health Rights, 2010; (with P. Illingworth and L. Wenar) Giving Well, 2011; (with N. Dobos and C. Barry) Global Financial Crisis, 2011. Contributor of articles to journals. **Address:** Department of Philosophy and International Affairs, Yale University, PO Box 208306, New Haven, CT 06520-8306, U.S.A. **Online address:** thomas.pogge@yale.edu

POGREBIN, Letty Cottin. American (born United States), b. 1939. **Genres:** Novels, Politics/Government, Sociology, Theology/Religion, Women's Studies And Issues, Writing/Journalism, Biography. **Career:** Simon & Schuster Inc., part-time secretary and assistant, 1957-59; Coward-McCann Inc., editorial assistant, 1959-60; Sussman & Sugar, copywriter, 1960; Bernard Geis Associates, director of publicity, advertising and subsidiary rights, 1960-70, vice-president, 1970; Ladies Home Journal, columnist, 1971-81; Ms. Magazine, co-founder, 1971, editor and writer, 1971-90, editor at large, 1987-89, columnist, 1988, contributing editor and writer, 1990-91; New York Times, columnist, 1983; Newsday, columnist, 1986; Tukkun, editor and writer, 1988-; Moment Magazine, editor and writer, 1989-; Family Circle, editor and writer, 1989-. **Publications:** How to Make It in a Man's World, 1970; Getting Yours: How to Make the System Work for the Working Woman, 1975; Growing Up Free: Raising Your Child in the '80s, 1980; (ed.) Stories for Free Children, 1982; Family Politics: Love and Power on an Intimate Frontier, 1983; Among Friends: Who We Like, Why We Like Them and What We Do with Them, 1987; Deborah, Golda, and Me: Being Female and Jewish in America, 1991; Getting over Getting Older: An Intimate Journey, 1996; Three Daughters (novel), 2002. Contributor to newspapers. **Address:** Rosenstone/ Wender, 38 E 29th St., 10th Fl., New York, NY 10016, U.S.A. **Online address:** lettycp@aol.com

POGUE, Bill. (William Reid Pogue). American (born United States), b. 1930. **Genres:** Air/Space Topics, Science Fiction/Fantasy, Technology, Literary Criticism And History. **Career:** National Aeronautics and Space Administration, Johnson Space Center, astronaut, 1966-77; technical services contractor to aerospace firms, 1978-; Public Service Co., staff consultant, 1979-83. Writer. **Publications:** Astronaut Primer, 1985; How Do You Go to the Bathroom in Space?, 1985, rev. ed., 1999; (with B. Bova) The Trikon Deception, 1992. **Address:** Vutara Services, 4 Cromer Dr., Bella Vista, AR 72715-5318, U.S.A.

POGUE, Carolyn. Canadian (born Canada), b. 1948?. **Genres:** Human Relations/Parenting, Cultural/Ethnic Topics. **Career:** Art of Peace (children's art camp), co-founder. Writer. **Publications:** The Weekend Parent: Learning to Live without Full-time Kids, 1990; Mother's Children and Other Plays, 1992; (ed.) Treasury of Celebrations: Create Celebrations That Reflect Your Values and Don't Cost the Earth, 1996; Language of the Heart: Rituals, Stories, and Information about Death, 1997; A Creation Story, 1998; Part-time Parent: Learning to Live without Full-time Custody, 1998; A New Day: Peacemaking Stories and Activities, 2005; Remember Peace, 2005; After the Beginning, 2006; Seasons of Peace: A Teaching Resource, 2007; A World of Faith: Introducing Spiritual Traditions to Teens, 2007; Gwen, 2009. Contributor to magazines. **Address:** Calgary, AB , Canada. **Online address:** info@carolynpogue.ca

POGUE, Charles (Edward). American (born United States), b. 1950. **Genres:** Plays/Screenplays, Young Adult Fiction, Literary Criticism And History. **Career:** Mercury II Theatre, co-founder and artistic director, 1969-71; Globe of the Great Southwest, artist-in-residence, 1972-73; stage actor, 1973-81; screenwriter, 1982-; Writers Guild of America, director, 1997-2001. **Publications:** Dragonheart, 1996. Contributor to periodicals. **Address:** GSO, 15260 Ventura Blvd., Ste. 2100, Sherman Oaks, CA 91403-5360, U.S.A. **Online address:** cepogue@email.msn.com

POGUE, William Reid. *See* **POGUE, Bill.**

POHL, Frederik. American (born United States), b. 1919. **Genres:** Novels, Novellas/Short Stories, Science Fiction/Fantasy, History, Sciences, Business/Trade/Industry, Economics, Young Adult Non-fiction, Young Adult Non-fiction. **Career:** Popular Publications, editor, 1939-43; Popular Science Publishing Co., editor in book department and assistant circulation manager, 1946-49; literary agent, 1946-53; freelance writer, 1953-60; Galaxy magazine, editor, 1959-69; American Management Association, staff lecturer, 1966-69; Ace Books, executive editor, 1971-72; Bantam Books, science fiction editor, 1973-79; The Harbour School, trustee, 1972-75; First Unitarian Church of Monmouth City, trustee, 1973-75; U.S. Department of State in Yugoslavia, Romania and the Soviet Union, cultural exchange lecturer in science fiction, 1974. **Publications:** (With C.M. Kornbluth) The Space Merchants, 1953; (with C.M. Kornbluth) Search the Sky, 1954; (with J. Williamson) Undersea Quest, 1954; (with C.M. Kornbluth) A Town Is Drowning, 1955; (with C.M. Kornbluth) Gladiator-at-Law, 1955; Alternating Currents (short stories), 1956; (with C.M. Kornbluth) Presidential Year, 1956; (with J. Williamson) Undersea Fleet, 1956; Slave Ship, 1957; Edge of the City, 1957; The Case against Tomorrow, 1957; (with J. Williamson) Undersea City, 1958; Tomorrow Times Seven, 1959; (with C.M. Kornbluth) Wolfbane, 1959; The Man Who Ate the World, 1960; Turn Left at Thursday (short stories), 1961; (with C.M. Kornbluth) The Wonder Effect, 1962; A Plague of Pythons, 1963, rev. ed. as Demon in the Skull, 1984; The Abominable Earthman, 1963; (with J. Williamson) The Reefs of Space, 1964; (with J. Williamson) Starchild, 1965; Drunkard's Walk, 1966; The Frederik Pohl Omnibus, 1966; Digits and Dastards, 1968; The Age of Pussyfoot, 1969; (with J. Williamson) Rogue Star, 1969; Day Million (short stories), 1970; Practical Politics 1972, 1971; Farthest Star: The Saga of Cuckoo, 1975; The Early Pohl, 1976; Man Plus, 1976; Gateway, 1977; (with J. Williamson) The Starchild Trilogy, 1977; The Way the Future Was: A Memoir, 1978; Jem, 1979; Survival Kit, 1979; Beyond the Blue Event Horizon, 1980; The Cool War, 1981; (foreword and afterword) Not this August, 1981; Planets Three, 1981; Science Fiction, Studies in Film, 1981; Syzygy, 1982; (intro.) The New Visions: A Collection of Modern Science Fiction Art, 1982; Starburst, 1982; Yesterday's Tomorrows: Favorite Stories from Forty Years as a Science Fiction Editor, 1982; Bipohl: Two Complete Novels, 1982; (with J. Williamson) Wall Around a Star, 1983; Midas World, 1983; Heechee Rendezvous, 1984; The Merchants' War, 1984; Pohlstars, 1984; The Years of the City, 1984; Black Star Rising, 1985; The Coming of the Quantum Cats, 1986; Chernobyl, 1987; The Annals of the Heechee, 1987; Narabedla Ltd., 1988; (with J. Williamson) Land's End, 1988; Csernobil, 1988; The Day the Martians Came, 1988; Homegoing, 1989; The World at the End of Time, 1990; The Gateway Trip: Tales and Vignettes of the Heechee, 1990; Outnumbering the Dead, 1991; (with J. Williamson) The Singers of Time, 1991; (with I. Asimov) Our Angry Earth, 1991; Stopping at Slowyear, 1991; Mining the Oort, 1992; The Voices of Heaven, 1994; (with T. Thomas) Mars Plus, 1994; Prince Henry Sinclair: His Expedition to the New World in 1398, 1995; The Other End of Time, 1996; Siege of Eternity, 1997; O Pioneer!, 1998; Far Shore of Time, 1999; Chasing Science: Science as Spectator Sport, 2000; The Boy Who Would Live Forever, 2004; Platinum Pohl: The Collected Best Stories, 2005; (with A.C. Clarke) The Last Theorem, 2008; The Hated and Other Stories, 2010; All the Lives He Led, 2011. EDITOR: Beyond the End of Time, 1952; Star Science Fiction Stories, 3 vols., 1953-54; (and intro.) Assignment in Tomorrow: An Anthology, 1954; Star Short Novels, 1954; Star of Stars, 1960; The Expert Dreamers, 1962; Time Waits for Winthrop, and Four Other Short Novels from Galaxy, 1962; The Seventh Galaxy Reader, 1964; Star Fourteen, 1966; The If Reader of Science Fiction, 1966; Nightmare Age, 1970; (with C. Pohl) Science Fiction: The Great Years, 1974; The Science Fiction Roll of Honor: An Anthology of Fiction and Nonfiction by Guests of Honor at World Science Fiction Conventions, 1975; (and intro.) The Best of C.M. Kornbluth, 1976; (with M.H. Greenberg and J. Olander) Science Fiction of the Forties, 1978; (with M.H. Greenberg and J.D. Olander) Galaxy, Thirty Years of Innovative Science Fiction, 1980; (with M.H. Greenberg and J. Olander) The Great Science Fiction Series: Stories from the Best of the Series from 1944 to 1980 by Twenty All-time Favorite Writers, 1980; (with E.A. Hull) Tales from the Planet Earth, 1986; SFWA Grand Masters, 1999. Contributor to periodicals. **Address:** 855 S Harvard Dr., Palatine, IL 60067-7026, U.S.A.

POHLMANN, Marcus D. American (born United States), b. 1950. **Genres:** Politics/Government, Law, Race Relations, Education, Reference. **Career:** Metropolitan Applied Research Center, research associate, 1975-76; The Spence School, instructor in political science and economics, 1975-76; Bates College, visiting assistant professor, 1976-77; College of Wooster, assistant professor, 1977-83, Urban Studies Program, chair, 1978-82; Arkansas State University, associate professor of political science, 1983-86, Master of Arts Program, coordinator, 1985-86; Rhodes College, Department of Political Science, professor, 1986-, chair, 1986-93, 1997-2002. Writer. **Publications:** Political Power in the Postindustrial City: An Introduction to Urban Politics, 1986; Black Politics in Conservative America, 1990, 3rd ed., 2008; Governing the Postindustrial City, 1993; (with M.P. Kirby) Racial Politics at the Crossroads: Memphis Elects Dr. W.W. Herenton, 1996; (with L.V. Whisenhunt) Student's Guide to Landmark Congressional Laws on Civil Rights, 2002; (ed. and intro.) African American Political Thought, 2003; Opportunity Lost: Race and Poverty in the Memphis City Schools, 2008. Contributor of articles to periodicals. **Address:** Department of Political Science, Rhodes College, 301 Buckman Hall, 2000 N Pkwy., Memphis, TN 38112-1624, U.S.A. **Online address:** pohlmann@rhodes.edu

POHL-WEARY, Emily. Canadian (born Canada) **Genres:** Biography, Autobiography/Memoirs, Young Adult Fiction, Children's Fiction. **Career:** Broken Pencil Magazine, co-editor; Kiss Machine, founder, writer and editor. Filmmaker. **Publications:** (With J. Merril) Better to Have Loved: The Life of Judith Merril, 2002; (ed.) Girls Who Bite Back: Witches, Mutants, Slayers and Freaks, 2004; A Girl Like Sugar, 2004; Iron-on Constellations, 2005; Strange Times at Western High, 2006. Contributor to periodicals. **Address:** Kiss Machine, PO Box 108, Sta. P, Toronto, ON M5S 2S8, Canada. **Online address:** emily@kissmachine.com

POINAR, Roberta. American (born United States) **Genres:** Natural History, Animals/Pets, Sciences. **Career:** Berkeley University, fellow researcher; University of California, faculty; Oregon State university, The Amber Institute, co-founder. Writer. **Publications:** (With G. Poinar, Jr.) The Quest for Life in Amber, 1994; (with G. Poinar, Jr.) The Amber Forest: A Reconstruction of a Vanished World, 1999; (with G. Poinar, Jr.) What Bugged the Dinosaurs?: Insects, Disease, and Death in the Cretaceous, 2008. **Address:** c/o Author Mail, Princeton University Press, 41 William St., Princeton, NJ 08540-5237, U.S.A.

POINTER, Richard W(ayne). American (born United States), b. 1955. **Genres:** History, Social Sciences. **Career:** Christian liberal arts colleges, faculty, 1980; Wheaton College, visiting assistant professor, 1982-83; Trinity College, assistant professor, 1983-87, associate professor of history, 1987-94; Philadelphia Center for Early American Studies, fellow, 1985-86; Westmont College, visiting associate professor, 1988-89, associate professor, 1994-96, professor, 1996-, provost, 2009-11. Writer. **Publications:** Protestant Pluralism and the New York Experience: A Study of Eighteenth-Century Religious Diversity, 1988; Encounters of the Spirit: Native Americans and European Colonial Religion, 2007. **Address:** Department of History, Westmont College, Deane Hall, 955 La Paz Rd., Ste. 205, Santa Barbara, CA 93108-1099, U.S.A. **Online address:** pointer@westmont.edu

POINTS, Larry (Gene). American (born United States), b. 1945. **Genres:** Children's Non-fiction. **Career:** Mt. Rainier National Park, park ranger, 1969-70; Hopewell Furnace National Historic Site, supervisory park ranger, 1970-74; Assateague Island National Seashore, chief of park interpretation, 1974-2000, retired, 2000. Writer. **Publications:** (With A. Jauck) Assateague: Island of the Wild Ponies, 1993, rev. ed., 1997; (with A. Jauck) Ribbons of Sand: Exploring Atlantic Beaches, 1997; (with A. Jauck) Barrier Islands Are for the Birds, 2000. Contributor to periodicals. **Address:** 103 W Chestnut St., Delmar, MD 21875, U.S.A. **Online address:** larry@seacritters.com

POIRIER, Juliane. *See* **LOCKE, Juliane Poirier.**

POIRIER, Mark Jude. American (born United States) **Genres:** Novellas/Short Stories. **Career:** Bennington College, faculty. Writer. **Publications:** Naked Pueblo (short stories), 1999; Unsung Heroes of American Industry: Stories, 2001; Goats, 2001; Modern Ranch Living, 2004; (ed.) Worst Years of Your Life: Stories for the Geeked-Out, Angst-Ridden, Lust-Addled and Deeply Misunderstood Adolescent in All of Us, 2007. Contributor of short stories to publications. **Address:** c/o Author Mail, Talk Miramax/Hyperion Books, 77 W 66th St., 11th Fl., New York, NY 10023, U.S.A.

POIRIER-BURES, Simone. (See-mun Pwar-yea-Bursh). American/Canadian (born Canada), b. 1944. **Genres:** Novels, Novellas/Short Stories, Autobiography/Memoirs, Biography, Young Adult Fiction. **Career:** Virginia Polytechnic Institute, English instructor, 1982-; State University, English instructor, 1982-; University of Dubuque, director of continuing education; Bures and Associate Inc., consultant; school teacher; property manager. Writer. **Publications:** Candyman (novel), 1994; That Shining Place (memoir), 1995; Nicole (short stories), 2000. Works appear in anthologies. Contributor of to periodicals. **Address:** Department of English, Virginia Tech University, 323 Shanks Hall, Blacksburg, VA 24061, U.S.A. **Online address:** poirier@vt.edu

POLACCO, Patricia. American (born United States), b. 1944. **Genres:** Children's Fiction, Illustrations, Young Adult Fiction. **Career:** Babushka Inc., founder. Author and illustrator, 1986-. **Publications:** SELF-ILLUSTRATED FOR CHILDREN: Meteor!, 1987; Rechenka's Eggs, 1988; (with L. Two Blossom) Boatride, 1988; The Keeping Quilt, 1988; Uncle Vova's Tree, 1989; Babushka's Doll, 1990; Just Plain Fancy, 1990; Thunder Cake, 1990; Some Birthday!, 1991; Appelemando's Dreams, 1991; Chicken Sunday, 1992; Mrs. Katz and Tush, 1992; Picnic at Mudsock Meadow, 1992; Babushka Baba Yaga, 1993; The Bee Tree, 1993; My Rotten, Redheaded, Older Brother, 1994; Pink and Say, 1994; Tikvah Means Hope, 1994; Babushka's Mother Goose, 1995; My Ol' Man, 1995; Aunt Chip and the Great Triple Creek Dam Affair, 1996; I Can Hear the Sun: A Modern Myth, 1996; The Trees of the Dancing Goats, 1996; In Enzo's Splendid Gardens, 1997; Pink y Say, 1997; El pollo de los domingos, 1997; Uncle Isaaco, 1997; Mrs. Mack, 1998; Thank you, Mr. Falker, 1998; Welcome Comfort, 1999; Luba and the Wren, 1999; The Butterfly, 2000; Betty Doll, 2001; Mr. Lincoln's Way, 2001; When Lightning Comes in a Jar, 2002; A Christmas Tapestry, 2002; G is for Goat, 2003; The Graves Family, 2003; John Philip Duck, 2004; Oh, Look!, 2004; An Orange for Frankie, 2004; Emma Kate, 2005; The Graves Family Goes Camping, 2005; Mommies Say Shhh!, 2005; Rotten Richie and the Ultimate Dare, 2006; Something About Hensley's, 2006; Ginger and Petunia, 2007; The Lemonade Club, 2007; For the Love of Autumn, 2008; Someone for Mr. Sussman, 2008; In Our Mothers' House, 2009; January's Sparrow, 2009; The Junk Yard Wonders, 2010; Junkyard Wonders, 2010; Bun Bun Button, 2011; Just in Time, Abraham Lincoln, 2011; The Art of Miss Chew, 2012. OTHERS: Firetalking, 1994. **Address:** Babuska Inc., 118 Barry St., Union City, MI 49094, U.S.A.

POLAKOFF, Keith (Ian). American (born United States), b. 1941. **Genres:** History, Politics/Government, Social Sciences. **Career:** City University of New York, Herbert H. Lehman College, lecturer in history, 1967-69; California State University, assistant professor, 1969-73, associate professor, 1973-78, professor of history, 1978-, School of Fine Arts, acting dean, 1984-85, School of Social and Behavioral Sciences, acting dean, 1985-86, assistant vice-president for academic affairs, 1986-92, dean of graduate studies, 1986-98, associate vice-president for academic affairs, 1992-, dean of undergraduate studies, 1998-2001, professor emeritus, 2004-; The History Teacher Magazine, editor, 1972-77, production manager, 1977-80. **Publications:** The Politics of Inertia: The Election of 1876 and the End of Reconstruction, 1973; (co-author) Generations of Americans: A History of the United States, 1976; Political Parties in American History, 1981. **Address:** Division of Academic Affairs, California State University, 1250 Bellflower Bivd., Long Beach, CA 90840, U.S.A. **Online address:** kip@csulb.edu

POLAKOW-SURANSKY, Sasha. American (born United States), b. 1979. **Genres:** History, Politics/Government. **Career:** Foreign Affairs, senior editor, Historian. **Publications:** The Unspoken Alliance: Israel's Secret Relationship with Apartheid South Africa, 2010. Contributor to periodicals. **Address:** Brooklyn, NY , U.S.A. **Online address:** spolakow@cfr.org

POLANSKY, Ronald M. American (born United States), b. 1948. **Genres:** Philosophy, Medicine/Health. **Career:** Purdue University, assistant professor of philosophy, 1974-75; Duquesne University, professor of philosophy, 1975-; Mathesis Publications, editor. **Publications:** Philosophy and Knowledge: A Commentary on Plato's Theaetetus, 1992; (ed. with M.G. Kuczewski) Bioethics: Ancient Themes in Contemporary Issues, 2000; Aristotle: De Anima, 2007. **Address:** Department of Philosophy, Duquesne University, 600 Forbes Ave., Pittsburgh, PA 15282, U.S.A. **Online address:** polansky@duq.edu

POLANSKY, Steven. American (born United States), b. 1949?. **Genres:** Novels, Novellas/Short Stories. **Career:** St. Olaf College, professor of English; Macalester College, visiting professor; University of Minnesota, MFA Program, visiting professor. Writer. **Publications:** Dating Miss Universe: Nine Stories, 1999; Bradbury Report: A Novel, 2009. **Address:** c/o Judith Hottensen, Weinstein Books, 345 Hudson St., 13th Fl., New York, NY 10014-4502, U.S.A. **Online address:** smpolansky@hotmail.com

POLASKI, Sandra Hack. American (born United States), b. 1964. **Genres:** Novels. **Career:** St. Mary's College (now St. Mary's School), instructor, 1994; Elon College, instructor, 1994; Furman University, assistant professor of religion, 1995-96; Baptist Theological Seminary at Richmond, assistant professor, 1996-2000, associate professor of new testament studies, 2000-. Writer. **Publications:** Paul and the Discourse of Power, 1999; A Feminist Introduction to Paul, 2005; Inside the Red Tent, 2006; Great Sayings of Paul, 2008. Contributor of numerous articles to journals. **Address:** Baptist Theological Seminary at Richmond, 3400 Brook Rd., Richmond, VA 23227, U.S.A. **Online address:** sandra.hack.polaski@btsr.edu

POLASTRON, Lucien X. French (born France), b. 1944?. **Genres:** Translations. **Career:** Maisons d'Hier et d'Aujourd'hui (monthly magazine), deputy chief editor, 1966-; Far East cultural reporter, 1976-; Le Rivage des Livres for France 3, producer, 1980; France Culture radio service, staff, 1980-90. **Publications:** Calligraphie chinoise: Initiation, 1995; Le Papier: 2000 ans d'histoire et de savoir-faire, 1999; Decouverte des calligraphies de l'arabe, 2003; Decouverte de l'enluminure medievale, 2003; Calligraphie chinoise en trois styles, 2004; Calligraphie japonaise, 2004; Livres en feu: Histoire de la destruction sans fin des bibliotheques, 2004; La grande numerisation: Y a-t-il une pensee apres le papier?, 2006; Books on Fire: The Destruction of Libraries Throughout History, 2007; Great Digitization: And the Quest to Know Everything, 2009. **Address:** PO Box 388, Rochester, VT 05767-0388, U.S.A. **Online address:** message@polastron.com

POLHEMUS, Robert M(ackinlay). American (born United States), b. 1935. **Genres:** Literary Criticism And History, Theology/Religion, Social Sciences. **Career:** Stanford University, assistant professor, 1963-68, associate professor, 1968-79, professor of English, 1979-, Department of English, chair, 1980-84, 2000-05, now professor emeritus, Howard H. And Jessie T. Watkins university professor, 1992-97, Joseph S. Atha professor in humanities, 2000-, Stanford Humanities Center, fellow; Guggenheim fellow, 1980-81. Writer. **Publications:** The Changing World of Anthony Trollope, 1968; Comic Faith: The Great Tradition From Austen to Joyce, 1980; Erotic Faith: Being in Love from Jane Austen to D.H. Lawrence, 1990; (ed. with R.B. Henkle) Critical Reconstructions: The Relationship of Fiction and Life, 1994; Lot's Daughters: Sex, Redemption, and Women's Quest for Authority, 2005; A Device to Root Out Evil, forthcoming. **Address:** Department of English, Stanford University, 201C Margaret Jacks Hall, 460 Bldg., 450 Serra Mall, Stanford, CA 94305-2087, U.S.A. **Online address:** polhemus@stanford.edu

POLICOFF, Stephen Phillip. American (born United States), b. 1948. **Genres:** Novels, Children's Fiction, Songs/Lyrics And Libretti, Writing/Journalism, Animals/Pets. **Career:** Center for Creative Youth, director of creative writing, 1978-95; Medicine Show Theater Ensemble, literary manager, 1979-86; New York University, adjunct assistant professor of creative writing, 1986-94, master teacher of writing, 1994-. Writer. **Publications:** (With J. Skinner) Real Toads in Imaginary Gardens: Suggestions and Starting Points for Young Creative Writers, 1991; The Dreamer's Companion: A Young Person's Guide to Understanding Dreams and Using them Creatively, 1997; Cesar's Amazing Journey, 1999; Beautiful Somewhere Else (novel), 2004. Contributor to periodicals. **Address:** c/o Author Mail, Carroll & Graf Publishers, 245 W 17th St., 11th Fl., New York, NY 10011-5300, U.S.A.

POLIKOFF, Barbara G(arland). American (born United States), b. 1929. **Genres:** Novels, Children's Fiction, Biography, Autobiography/Memoirs, Animals/Pets. **Career:** Von Steuben Public High School, teacher, 1951-52;

Chicago Natural History Museum, associate editor of the bulletin, 1952-55; Sullivan House, director, 1970-90; Chicago Public Schools, teacher, 1973-93. **Publications:** (And photographer) My Parrot Eats Baked Beans, 1988; James Madison, 4th President of the United States, 1989; Herbert C. Hoover: 31st President of the United States (biography), 1990; Life's a Funny Proposition, Horatio (novel), 1992; Riding the Wind, 1995; With One Bold Act: The Story of Jane Addams, 1999; Why Does the Coquí Sing?, 2004. **Address:** c/o Jane Jordan Browne, Browne & Miller Literary Associates, 410 S Michigan Ave., Ste. 460, Chicago, IL 60605, U.S.A. **Online address:** barbarapol@aol.com

POLIKOFF, Nancy D. American (born United States), b. 1952. **Genres:** Law. **Career:** Catholic University of America, Columbus School of Law, instructor, 1975-76; Hunter, Polikoff, Bodley & Bottum P.C., attorney and founding partner, 1976-81; Women's Legal Defense Fund, staff attorney, 1982-87; American University, Washington College of Law, assistant professor of law, 1987-90, associate professor, 1990-93, professor, 1993-; University of Arizona, James E. Rogers College of Law, visiting professor, 2004-05. Writer and activist. **Publications:** Beyond Straight and Gay Marriage: Valuing All Families under the Law, 2008. Contributor to books, periodicals and journals. **Address:** Washington College of Law, American University, Rm. 450, 4801 Massachusetts Ave. NW, Washington, DC 20016, U.S.A. **Online address:** npoliko@wcl.american.edu

POLING(-KEMPES), Lesley. American (born United States), b. 1954. **Genres:** Novels, History. **Career:** Ghost Ranch, historian and leader of women's studies seminars, 1976-; writer, producer, co-director and researcher, 1979-84. **Publications:** The Harvey Girls: Women Who Opened the West, 1989; Far from Home: West by Rail with the Harvey Girls, 1995; Canyon of Remembering, 1996; Valley of Shining Stone: The Story of Abiquiu, 1997; (with F.W. Turner and B. Lynes) Georgia O'Keeffe and New Mexico: A Sense of Place, 2004; Ghost Ranch, 2005. Contributor to periodicals. **Address:** Ghost Ranch, HC77, PO Box 11, Abiquiu, NM 87510, U.S.A.

POLISAR, Barry Louis. American (born United States), b. 1954. **Genres:** Children's Fiction, Music, Animals/Pets. **Career:** Rainbow Morning Music, owner. Writer, musician and singer. **Publications:** JUVENILE: Dinosaurs I Have Known, 1986; Don't Do That!: A Child's Guide to Bad Manners, Ridiculous Rules, and Inadequate Etiquette, 1986; The Haunted House Party, 1987; Snakes! and the Boy Who was Afraid of Them, 1988; The Snake Who was Afraid of People, 1988; The Trouble with Ben, 1992; Peculiar Zoo, 1993; Insect Soup, 1999; A Little Less Noise, 2001; Stolen Man: The Story of the Amistad Rebellion, 2006; Telling the Story: A Passover Haggadah Explained, 2007; Curious Creatures, 2010; Something Fishy, forthcoming. Contributor to periodicals. **Address:** Rainbow Morning Music, 2121 Fairland Rd., Silver Spring, MD 20904-5427, U.S.A. **Online address:** barrylou@barrylou.com

POLISI, Joseph W. American (born United States), b. 1947. **Genres:** Art/Art History, History. **Career:** Yale University, School of Music, executive officer, 1976-80; Manhattan School of Music, dean of faculty, 1980-83; University of Cincinnati, College-Conservatory of Music, dean, 1983-84; Juilliard School, president, 1984-. Writer. **Publications:** The Artist as Citizen, 2005; American Muse: The Life and Times of William Schuman, 2008. **Address:** Office of the President, The Juilliard School, 60 Lincoln Center Plz., New York, NY 10023-6588, U.S.A. **Online address:** jwpolisi@juilliard.edu

POLITO, Robert. American (born United States), b. 1951. **Genres:** Literary Criticism And History, Poetry, Biography. **Career:** Harvard University, instructor in English, 1976-81; Wellesley College, assistant professor of English, 1981-89; New York University, Writing Program, assistant director, 1990-92; New School for Social Research, Writing Program, director, 1992-. Writer. **Publications:** At the Titan's Breakfast: Three Essays on Byron's Poetry, 1987; (ed. and intro. with M. McCauley) Fireworks: The Lost Writings of Jim Thompson, 1988; (comp.) A Reader's Guide to James Morrill's The Changing Light at Sandover, 1994; Doubles (poems), 1995; Savage Art: A Biography of Jim Thompson, 1995; (ed.) Crime Novels: American Noir of the 1930s and 1940s, 1997; (ed.) Crime Novels: American Noir of the 1950s, 1997; (ed.) Selected Poems, 2004; Hollywood & God, 2009; (ed.) Farber on Film, 2009; Detours: 7 Noir Lives, forthcoming. Contributor to magazines and newspapers to periodicals. **Address:** New School for Social Research, 66 W 12th St., New York, NY 10011, U.S.A. **Online address:** politor@newschool.edu

POLIZZOTTI, Mark. American (born United States), b. 1957. **Genres:** Biography, Translations, Art/Art History, Film, Essays, Literary Criticism And History, Music. **Career:** Random House, assistant editor, 1983-85; Grove Weidenfeld, senior editor, 1985-90; David R. Godine Publishers, editorial director, 1993-99; Museum of Fine Arts, director of publications, 1999-2001, Department of Intellectual Property and Publisher, director, 2001-; The Metropolitan Museum of Art, publisher and editor-in-chief. Biographer, translator and historian. **Publications:** TRANSLATOR: Pure War, 1983; Speed and Politics, 1986; J. Echenoz, Cherokee, 1987; Compact, 1988; Popular Defense and Ecological Struggles, 1990; (ed. and intro.) R. Daumal, The Powers of the Word: Selected Essays and Notes, 1927-1943, 1991; J. Echenoz, Double Jeopardy, 1993; Conversations: The Autobiography of Surrealism, 1993; J. Hoestlandt, Star of Fear, Star of Hope, 1995; Plan of Occupancy, 1995; The Lost Steps, 1996; J. Echenoz, Big Blondes, 1997; (and intro.) A. Breton, Anthology of Black Humor, 1997; My Heart through Which Her Heart Has Passed, 1998; M. Duras, fWriting, 1998; Royal Sculptor, 1998; P. Chamoiseau, Seven Dreams of Elmira, 1999; (with M.A. Caws) A. Breton, Break of Day, 1999; J. Echenoz, I'm Gone, 2001; C. Oster, A Cleaning Woman, 2002; D.V. Cauwelaert, One-Way, 2003; Gauguin Tahiti, 2004; J. Echenoz, Chopin's Move, 2004; J. Echenoz, Piano, 2004; A Key to the Louvre, 2004; D.V. Cauwelaert, Out of My Head, 2004; G. Flaubert, Bouvard and Pécuchet, 2005; M. Duras, Yann Andréa Steiner, 2006; L. Lê, Three Fates, 2010; (and intro.) R. Roussel, Impressions of Africa, 2011. OTHERS: Lautreamont Nomad, 1994; M. Polizzotti, Revolution of the Mind: The Life of Andre Breton, 1995, rev. ed., 2009; (co-author) S.: A Novel, 1997; The New Life: Poems, 1998; (ed. and intro.) André Breton: Selections, 2003; Luis Bunuel's Los Olvidados, 2006; Bob Dylan: Highway 61 Revisited, 2006. **Address:** MFA Publications, 465 Huntington Ave., Boston, MA 02115, U.S.A. **Online address:** mp@mfa.org

POLKING, Kirk. American (born United States), b. 1925. **Genres:** Adult Non-fiction, Children's Non-fiction, Writing/Journalism. **Career:** U.S. War Department, administrative assistant, 1943-45; Writer's Digest, editorial assistant, 1948-52, editor, 1963-73, Writer's Digest School, director, 1976-91; F&W Publishing Corp., editorial assistant, 1948-52; Farm Quarterly, circulation manager, 1952-57; freelance writer and editor, 1957-62, 1991-. **Publications:** Let's Go with Lewis and Clark, 1963; Let's Go on the Half Moon with Henry Hudson, 1964; Let's Go to See Congress at Work, 1966; Let's Go to an Atomic Energy Town, 1968; The Private Pilot's Dictionary and Handbook, 1974, 2nd ed., 1986; Oceans of the World: Our Essential Resource, 1983; Freelance Jobs for Writers, 1984; Writing Family Histories and Memoirs, 1995; Oceanographers and Explorers of the Sea, 1999. EDITOR: (with J. Chimsky) Beginning Writer's Handbook, 1968; (with J. Polking) The Beginning Writer's Answer Book 1971, 5th ed., 1993; How to Make Money in Your Spare Time by Writing, 1971; Artist's Market, 1974; (with L.S. Meranus) Law and the Writer, 1978, 3rd ed., 1984; Jobs for Writers, 1980; Internships, 1981; (with J. Bloss and C. Cannon) Writer's Encyclopedia, 1986; The Beginner's Guide to Getting Published, 1987; Writer's Friendly Legal Guide, 1989; Writing A to Z, 1990. **Address:** 529 Constitution Sq., Cincinnati, OH 45255-3304, U.S.A.

POLKINGHORNE, John Charlton. British (born England), b. 1930. **Genres:** Physics, Theology/Religion, Sciences, Technology, Autobiography/Memoirs. **Career:** Trinity College, fellow, 1954-86, Trinity Hall, dean and chaplain, 1986-89; California Institute of Technology, Commonwealth Fund fellow, 1955-56; University of Edinburgh, lecturer in mathematical physics, 1956-58; Cambridge University, lecturer in applied mathematics, 1958-65, reader in theoretical physics, 1965-68, professor of mathematical physics, 1968-79; St. Andrew's, curate, 1981-82; St. Michael's, curate, 1982-84; vicar in Kent, England, 1984-86; Queen's College, president, 1989-96, fellow, 1996-. Writer, theoretical physicist and Anglican priest. **Publications:** (Co-author) The Analytic S-Matrix, 1966; The Particle Play, 1979; Models of High Energy Processes, 1980; The Way the World Is: The Christian Perspective of a Scientist, 1983, rev. ed., 1992; The Quantum World, 1984; Science and Christian Belief, 1984; One World: The Interaction of Science and Theology, 1986, rev. ed., 2007; Science and Creation, 1988; Science and Providence, 1989, rev. ed., 2007; Science and Creation: The Search for Understanding, 1989; Rochester Round About: The Story of High Energy Physics, 1989; Reason and Reality: The Relationship between Science and Theology, 1992; The Faith of a Physicist: Reflections of A Bottom-up Thinker, 1994; Quarks, Chaos and Christianity: Questions to Science and Relition, 1994; Serious Talk: Science and Religion in Dialogue, 1995; Beyond Science: The Wider Human Context, 1996; Scientists as Theologians, 1996; Searching for Truth: Lenten Meditations on Science and Faith, 1996; Beyond Science,

1996; Belief in God in an Age of Science, 1998; Science and Theology: An Introduction, 1998; Faith, Science and Understanding, 2000; (ed. with M. Welker) End of the World and the Ends of God: Science and Theology on Eschatology, 2000; (with M. Welker) Faith in the Living God, 2001; (ed.) The Work of Love: Creation as Kenosis, 2001; The God of Hope and the End of the World, 2002; Traffic in Truth: Exchanges Between Science and Theology, 2002; Quantum Theory: A Very Short Introduction, 2002; Living with Hope: A Scientist Looks at Advent, Christmas and Epiphany, 2003; Exploring Reality: The Intertwining of Science and Religion, 2005; Quantum Physics and Theology: An Unexpected Kinship, 2007; From Physicist to Priest: An Autobiography, 2007; Theology in the Context of Science, 2009; (with N. Beale) Questions of Truth: Fifty-one Responses to Questions About God, Science and Belief, 2009; (ed.) The Trinity and An Entangled World: Relationality in Physical Science and Theology, 2010; Encountering Scripture: A Scientist Explores the Bible, 2010; The Polkinghorne Reader: Science, Faith and the Search for Meaning, 2010; (ed.) Meaning in Mathematics, 2011. **Address:** Oxford University Press, 198 Madison Ave., New York, NY 10016, U.S.A.

POLKINHORN, Harry. American (born United States), b. 1945. **Genres:** Poetry. **Career:** Teacher; San Diego State University, Department of English and Comparative Literature, professor, 1979-, University Press, director, 1989-. Writer and critic. **Publications:** POETRY: Excisions, 1976; Radix Zero, 1981; Volvox, 1981; Anaesthesia, 1985; Bridges of Skin Money (visual), 1986; Summary Dissolution (visual), 1988; Begging for Remission, 1989; Teraphim (visual), 1995; Mount Soledad, 1996; Throat Shadow, 1997; Blueshift, 1998; Tayet's Bandages, 1999; Demos oneiron, 2011; (with A. Velasco) Calo: a Dictionary of Spanish Barrio & Border Slang, 2011. EXPERIMENTAL FICTION: Travelling with Women, 1983; Lorenia La Rosa: A Travelogue, 1989. OTHER: (with A. Velasco and M. Lambert) El Libro de Calo: Pachuco Slang Dictionary, 1983; (with Velasco and Lambert) El Libro de Calo: Chicano Slang Dictionary, 1986; Jerome Rothenberg: A Descriptive Bibliography, 1988; The Illusion of Reality: An Interview with Dick Higgins, 1990. EDITOR: Border Literature/Literatura Fronteriza: A Binational Conference, 1987; (co-ed.) Literatura Frontera Mexico-Estados Unidos/ Mexican-American Border Writing, 1987; (co-ed.) Mexican/American Border Literature: Short Stories, 1987; (with R. Reyes and G.T. Muñoz) The Line: Essays on Mexican/American Border Literature: Short Stories, 1988; (and intro.) Post-Art: International Exhibition of Visual/Experimental Poetry, 1988; (co-ed.) Border Literature: Proceedings of the Border Literature Conference (Tijuana, June-July, 1988), 1989; (co-ed.) Border Literature: Towards an Integrated Perspective XIII, 1990; (co-ed.) Visual Arts on the U.S./Mexican Border, 1991; (with R. Reyes and G.T. Muñoz) The Flight of the Eagle: Poetry on the U.S.-Mexico Border, 1993; (with G.T. Muñoz and R. Reyes and trans.) Bodies beyond Borders: Dance on the U.S.-Mexico Border, 1993; (with R. Reyes and G.T. Muñoz) Open Signs: Language and Society on the U.S.-Mexico Border, 1993; (co-ed. and trans.) Visual Poetry: An International Anthology, 1994; (co-ed.) Border Lives, 1995; R. Starr, San Diego State University: A History in Word and Image, 1995; (with M. Weiss and trans.) Across the Line/Al otro lado: The Poetry of Baja California, 2002. TRANSLATOR: Corrosive Signs (essays on experimental poetry), 1990; J.M. Di Bella, Nailed to the Wound (short fiction), 1993; (contrib.) The Border: The Future of Postmodernity (critical essays), 1994; P. Menezes, Poetics and Visuality: A Trajectory of Contemporary Brazilian Poetry (theoretical text), 1995; C. Padin, Art for Life, 1997. Contributor of articles to periodicals. **Address:** 3232 Governor Dr., Ste. J, San Diego, CA 92122, U.S.A. **Online address:** h.polkinhorn.1@alumni.nyu.edu

POLLACK, Henry N. American (born United States), b. 1936. **Genres:** Environmental Sciences/Ecology, Natural History. **Career:** University of Michigan, professor of geophysics; Climate Project, science adviser. Writer, scientist and geophysicist. **Publications:** (Ed. with V.R. Murthy) Structure and Evolution of the Continental Lithosphere, 1984; Uncertain Science ... Uncertain World, 2003; A World without Ice, 2009. **Address:** Ann Arbor, MI , U.S.A. **Online address:** worldwithoutice@gmail.com

POLLACK, Howard. (Howard J. Pollack). American (born United States), b. 1952. **Genres:** Music. **Career:** University of Houston, assistant professor, 1987-93, associate professor of music, 1993-, John and Rebecca Moores professor of music, 2005; Cornell University, Rochester Institute of Technology, faculty; Empire State College, faculty. Writer. **Publications:** Walter Piston, 1982; Harvard Composers: Walter Piston and His Students, From Frederic Krewski to Elliott Carter, 1992; (ed. with C. Reschke) German Literature and Music: An Aesthetic Fusion, 1890-1989, 1992; Skyscraper Lullaby: The Life and Music of John Alden Carpenter, 1995; John Alden Carpenter: A Chicago Composer, 1995; Aaron Copland: The Life andWork of an Uncommon Man, 1999; George Gershwin: His Life and Work, 2006. **Address:** School of Music, University of Houston, MSM 223, 120 School of Music Bldg., Houston, TX 77204-4017, U.S.A. **Online address:** hpollack@uh.edu

POLLACK, Howard J. *See* **POLLACK, Howard.**

POLLACK, Jill S. American (born United States), b. 1963. **Genres:** Gay And Lesbian Issues, Biography, Social Sciences, History. **Career:** Writer, 1993-; Story Studio Chicago, founder and director, 2003-; Women in Communications Inc., president. **Publications:** Shirley Chisholm (juvenile biography), 1994; Lesbian and Gay Families: Redefining Parenting in America, 1995; Women on the Hill: A History of Women in Congress, 1996. **Address:** StoryStudio Chicago, 4043 N Ravenswood, Ste. 222, Chicago, IL 60613-5682, U.S.A. **Online address:** jill@storystudiochicago.com

POLLACK, Kenneth M(ichael). American (born United States), b. 1966. **Genres:** Administration/Management, History, Military/Defense/Arms Control. **Career:** Middle East policy analyst. Central Intelligence Agency, Iran-Iraq military analyst, 1988-95; National Security Council, Near East and South Asian affairs, director, 1995-96, Persian Gulf Affairs, director, 1999-2001; National Defense University, senior research professor, 1998-99, 2001; Council of Foreign Relations, director, National Security Studies, senior fellow and deputy director, director, 2001-02; Brookings Institution, Saban Center for Middle East Policy, Foreign Policy Studies, director of research and senior fellow; National Defense University, senior research professor, 1998-99, 2001. National security advisor, educator and writer. **Publications:** Saudi Military Effectiveness in the 1990s, 1999; Arabs at War: Military Effectiveness, 1948-1991, 2002; The Threatening Storm: The Case for Invading Iraq, 2002; The Persian Puzzle: The Conflict between Iran and America, 2004; A Switch in Time: A New Strategy for America in Iraq, 2006; (with D.L. Byman) Things Fall Apart: Containing the Spillover From an Iraqi Civil War, 2007; A Path Out of the Dessert: A Grand Strategy for America in the Middle East, 2008; (co-author) Which Path to Persia?: Options for a New American Strategy toward Iran, 2009; (co-author) Unfinished Business: An American Strategy for Iraq Moving Forward, 2011. Contributor to journals. **Address:** Saban Center for Middle East Policy, The Brookings Institution, 1775 Massachusetts Ave. NW, Washington, DC 20036, U.S.A. **Online address:** sabancenter@brookings.edu

POLLACK, Rachel. American (born United States), b. 1933. **Genres:** Gay And Lesbian Issues, Sex, Young Adult Non-fiction, Literary Criticism And History, Self Help. **Career:** Journalist and consultant, 1980-. **Publications:** (With C. Schwartz) The Journey Out: A Guide for and about Lesbian, Gay, and Bisexual Teens, 1995. Contributor to periodicals. **Address:** c/o Author Mail, Viking Penguin, 375 Hudson St., New York, NY 10014, U.S.A.

POLLACK, Rachel (Grace). American (born United States), b. 1945. **Genres:** Novels, Paranormal, Young Adult Fiction, Adult Non-fiction. **Career:** Goddard College, faculty, 2002-, MFA in Creative Writing Program, faculty advisor; State University of New York, faculty; New York State University, faculty. Writer. **Publications:** NOVELS: Golden Vanity, 1980; Alqua Dreams, 1987; Unquenchable Fire, 1988; Temporary Agency, 1994; Godmother Night, 1996. NONFICTION: 78 Degrees of Wisdom: A Book of Tarot, 2 vols., 1980-83; Salvador Dali's Tarot, 1985; A Practical Guide to Fortune Telling: Palmistry, The Crystal Ball, Runes, Tea Leaves, The Tarot, 1986; Teach Yourself Fortune Telling, 1986; Tarot: The Open Labyrinth, 1986; The New Tarot, 1990; Tarot Readings and Meditations, 1990; (with C. Schwartz) The Journey Out: A Guide for and about Lesbian, Gay, and Bisexual Teens, 1995. EDITOR: (with C. Matthews) Tarot Tales, 1989; (with M.K. Greer) New Thoughts on Tarot: Transcripts from the First International Newcastle Tarot Symposium, 1989. OTHERS: Burning Sky, 1995; The Vertigo Tarot, 1995; Body of the Goddess: Sacred Wisdom in Myth, Landscape and Culture, 1997; Haindl Tarot: A Reader's Handbook, 1999; Complete Illustrated Guide to Tarot, 1999; Power of Ritual, 2000; Shining Tribe Tarot: Awakening the Universal Spirit, 2001; Forest of Souls: A Walk through the Tarot, 2002; Haindl Tarot, the Major Arcana, 2002; A Secret Woman, 2002; The Kabbalah Tree: A Journey of Balance and Growth, 2004; Seeker: The Tarot Unveiled, 2005; Rachel Pollack's Tarot Wisdom: Spiritual Teachings and Deeper Meanings, 2008; (foreword) Best Tarot Practices: Everything You Need to Know to Learn the Tarot, 2009; Fairy Tales, forthcoming; Simon Wisdom!, forthcoming. **Address:** c/o Author Mail, St. Martin's Press, 175 5th Ave., New York, NY 10010, U.S.A. **Online address:** rachel@rachelpollack.com

POLLACK, Robert (Elliot). American (born United States), b. 1940. **Genres:** Medicine/Health, Psychiatry, Sciences, Theology/Religion, Biology, Natural History. **Career:** New York University, Medical Center, Department of Pathology, instructor, 1968-69, assistant professor, 1969-70; Cold Spring Harbor Laboratory, senior scientist, 1970-74, director of summer program, 1972-74; State University of New York, School of Medicine, adjunct assistant professor, 1971-75, associate professor, 1975-77, professor, 1977-78; Columbia University, Department of Biological Sciences, professor, 1978-, Columbia College, dean, 1982-89, Center for Environmental Research and Conservation, adjunct professor, 1994-, College of Physicians and Surgeons, Center for Psychoanalytic Training and Research, Department of Psychiatry, lecturer, 1999-, Earth Institute, Center for the Study of Science and Religion, founder and director, 1999-, professor of biological sciences, 2009-, Departments of Religion, adjunct professor, 2000-, Heyman Center for the Humanities, fellow, 2005-06; Albert Einstein College of Medicine, visiting associate professor, 1977-93; Union Theological Seminary, adjunct professor of science and religion, 2002-. Writer. **Publications:** (With S. Pfeiffer) Animal Cell Culture Cell Manual, 1970; (ed. with A. Hellman and M.N. Oxman) Biohazards in Biological Research, 1973; (ed.) Readings in Mammalian Cell Culture, 1973, rev. ed., 1981; Signs of Life: The Language and Meanings of DNA, 1994; The Missing Moment: How the Unconscious Shapes Modern Science, 1999; (contrib.) Genetics & Your Health: A Guide for the 21st Century Family, 1999; The Faith of Biology and the Biology of Faith: Order, Meaning, and Free Will in Modern Medical Science, 2000. Contributor to periodicals. **Address:** Department of Biological Sciences, Columbia University, 749 Mudd Bldg., 1212 Amsterdam Ave., PO Box 2419, New York, NY 10027-7003, U.S.A. **Online address:** pollack@columbia.edu

POLLAK, Mark. American/French (born France), b. 1947. **Genres:** Recreation, Sports/Fitness. **Career:** Piper and Marbury (law firm), partner, 1972-99; Wilmer, Cutler and Pickering (law firm), partner, 1999-. Writer. **Publications:** Sports Leagues and Teams: An Encyclopedia, 1871-1996, 1998. **Address:** Wilmer, Cutler & Pickering, 100 Light St., Baltimore, MD 21202, U.S.A. **Online address:** pollak@wilmerhale.com

POLLAK, Vivian R. American (born United States), b. 1938. **Genres:** Biography, Literary Criticism And History. **Career:** Cheyney University, assistant professor, 1970-74, associate professor, 1974-76, professor of English, 1976-86; University of Pennsylvania, lecturer in English and women's studies, 1975-77; University of Washington, visiting associate professor, 1985-86, associate professor, 1986-91, professor of English, 1991-95; Washington University, professor of English, 1995-, professor of women, gender and sexuality studies, 2007-. Writer. **Publications:** Dickinson: The Anxiety of Gender, 1984; (ed.) A Poet's Parents: The Courtship Letters of Emily Norcross and Edward Dickinson, 1988; (ed.) New Essays on Daisy Miller and The Turn of the Screw, 1993; Erotic Whitman, 2000; (ed.) Historical Guide to Emily Dickinson, 2004. Contributor to journals. **Address:** Department of English, Washington University, 1 Brookings Dr., PO Box 1122, St. Louis, MO 63130, U.S.A. **Online address:** vrpollak@wustl.edu

POLLAND, Madeleine A(ngela). Spanish/Irish (born Ireland), b. 1918. **Genres:** Novels, Children's Fiction, Young Adult Fiction, History, Romance/Historical. **Career:** Letchworth Public Library, assistant librarian, 1938-42; writer, 1958-. **Publications:** Children of the Red King, 1959; The Town across the Water, 1961; Beorn the Proud, 1961; Fingal's Quest, 1961; The White Twilight, 1962; Chuiraquimba and the Black Robes, 1962; The City of the Golden House, 1963; The Queen's Blessing, 1963; Flame Over Tara, 1964; Mission to Cathay, 1964; Queen without Crown, 1965; Thicker than Water, 1965; Deirdre, 1967; Minutes of a Murder in UK as The Little Spot of Bother, 1967; To Tell My People, 1968; Stranger in the Hills, 1968; Random Army, 1969 in UK as Shattered Summer, 1970; Alhambra, 1970; To Kill a King, 1971; A Family Affair, 1971; Package to Spain, 1971; Daughter of the Sea in UK as Daughter to Poseidon, 1972; Prince of the Double Axe, 1976; (as Frances Adrian) Double Shadow, 1977; Sabrina: A Novel, 1979; All Their Kingdoms, 1980; The Heart Speaks Many Ways: A Novel, 1982; No Price Too High: A Novel, 1984; As It Was in the Beginning, 1987; Rich Man's Flowers, 1990; The Pomegranate House, 1992. Contributor to periodicals. **Address:** Edificio Hercules 634, Avenida Gamonal, Arroyo de la Miel, Malaga, 29631, Spain.

POLLARD, A(nthony) J(ames). British (born England), b. 1941. **Genres:** History, Biography, Autobiography/Memoirs. **Career:** University of Teesside, fellow, lecturer, 1969-73, senior lecturer, 1973-80, principal lecturer, 1980-89, reader in local history, 1989-92, professor of history, 1992-, now professor emeritus, Centre for Regional and Local Historical Research, research staff. Writer. **Publications:** John Talbot and the War in France, 1427-1453, 1983; The Wars of the Roses, 1988, rev. ed., 2001; North-Eastern England during the Wars of the Roses, 1990; Richard III and the Princes in the Tower, 1991; Late-Medieval England, 1399-1509, 2000; The Worlds of Richard III, 2002; Imagining Robin Hood: The Late-Medieval Stories in Historical Context, 2004; Warwick the Kingmaker: Politics, Power and Fame, 2007. EDITOR: Property and Politics: Essays in Late Medieval History, 1986; The Wars of the Roses: Problems in Focus, 1995; (with R.H. Britnell) The McFarlane Legacy, 1995; The North of England in the Age of Richard III, 1996; Middlesbrough: Town and Community, 1830-1950, 1996; (with P.W.M. Freeman) Fields of Conflict: Progress and Prospect in Battlefield Archaeology, 2001; (with A. Green) Regional Identities in North-East England, 1300-2000, 2007; (with D. Newton) Newcastle and Gateshead Before 1700, 2009. **Address:** School of Law, Arts & Humanities, University of Teesside, Tees Valley, Middlesbrough, CL TS1 3BA, England. **Online address:** a.pollard@tees.ac.uk

POLLARD, Helen Perlstein. American (born United States), b. 1946. **Genres:** Anthropology/Ethnology, Social Sciences, History. **Career:** University of California, Archaeological Field School, crew chief, 1965; State of California, staff archaeologist for a highway salvage program, 1965; Columbia University, Department of Anthropology, laboratory assistant, 1966-67, Woodrow Wilson fellow, 1967-68, 1970-71, teaching assistant, 1970, Barnard College, teaching assistant, 1969-70; Lerma River Basin Survey, field director and ceramic consultant, 1972; State University of New York, instructor, 1972-73, assistant professor of environmental science, 1973-77, adjunct assistant professor of anthropology, 1975-85, associate director of research project, 1976-81, visiting assistant professor of anthropology, 1985-86; Michigan State University, assistant professor of anthropology, 1986-91, associate professor of anthropology, 1991-96, professor of anthropology, 1996-, Michigan State University Museum, adjunct curator; Hickory Hill Condominium Association, director, 1992-95. Writer. **Publications:** (With S. Gorenstein) Tarascan Civilization: A Late Prehispanic Cultural System, 1983; Taríacuri's Legacy: The Prehispanic Tarascan State, 1993. Contributor of articles and journals. **Address:** Department of Anthropology, Michigan State University, 354 Baker Hall, East Lansing, MI 48824, U.S.A. **Online address:** pollardh@msu.edu

POLLARD, Irina. Australian (born Australia), b. 1939. **Genres:** Biology, Education, Ethics, Medicine/Health, Sciences, Social Commentary. **Career:** Macquarie University, associate professor in biology, 1973-. Researcher and writer. **Publications:** A Guide to Reproduction: Social Issues and Human Concerns, 1994; Bioscience Ethics, 2009. Contributor to books and journals. **Address:** Department of Biological Sciences, Macquarie University, E8C 171, Sydney, NW 2109, Australia. **Online address:** irina.pollard@mq.edu.au

POLLARD, John (Richard Thornhill). Welsh/British (born England), b. 1914. **Genres:** History, Humanities, Travel/Exploration, Biography, Autobiography/Memoirs, Theology/Religion. **Career:** Herne Bay College, classics master, 1938-39; St. Andrews University, assistant in classics, 1948-49; University College of North Wales (now Bangor University), lecturer and senior lecturer in classics, 1949-82, 1987-89. Writer. **Publications:** Journey to the Styx, 1955; Adventure Begins in Kenya, 1957; Africa for Adventure, 1961; African Zoo Man, 1963; Wolves and Werewolves, 1964; Helen of Troy, 1965; Seers, Shrines and Sirens, 1965; The Long Safari, 1967; (with C. Day Lewis) Virgil: The Aeneid Appreciation, 1969; Birds in Greek Life and Myth, 1977; Divination and Oracles: Greece, Civilization of the Ancient Mediterranean, 1988; No County to Compare, 1994. Contributor to books and journals. **Address:** The Yard, Red Wharf Bay, Anglesey, LL75 8RX, Wales.

POLLARD, Lisa. American (born United States), b. 1963?. **Genres:** Politics/Government, History. **Career:** Leland Stanford Junior University, lecturer, 1996; University of North Carolina, assistant professor, 1997-2003, associate professor of history, 2003-; North Carolina Humanities Council Speakers' Forum, speaker, 1999-; American Research Center in Egypt, scholar-in-residence, 2005-06. Writer. **Publications:** (ed. with L. Haney) Families of a New World: Gender, Politics, and State Development in a Global Context, 2003; Nurturing the Nation: The Family Politics of Modernizing, Colonizing and Liberating Egypt (1805- 1923), 2005; Contributor to anthologies. **Ad-**

dress: 601 S College Rd., Wilmington, NC 28403, U.S.A. **Online address:** pollardl@uncwil.edu

POLLEN, Daniel A. American (born United States), b. 1935. **Genres:** Medicine/Health, History, Sciences. **Career:** Massachusetts General Hospital, associate professor, 1966-79; Barrow Neurological Institute, research director, 1979-83; University of Massachusetts, School of Medicine, Department of Neurology, professor of neurology and physiology, 1983-. Writer. **Publications:** Hannah's Heirs: The Quest for the Genetic Origins of Alzheimer's Disease, 1993. **Address:** Ruth Wreschner Literary Agency, 10 W 74th St., New York, NY 10023-2403, U.S.A. **Online address:** pollend@ummhc.org

POLLETTA, Francesca. American (born United States) **Genres:** Social Sciences. **Career:** Columbia University, assistant professor, associate professor; University of California, professor of sociology. Writer and sociologist. **Publications:** (ed. with J. Goodwin and J.M. Jasper) Passionate Politics: Emotions and Social Movements, 2001; Freedom Is an Endless Meeting: Democracy in American Social Movements, 2002; It Was Like a Fever: Storytelling in Protest and Politics, 2006. Contributor to books and periodicals. **Address:** University of California, 4183 Social Science Plz., PO Box 5100, Irvine, CA 92697, U.S.A. **Online address:** polletta@uci.edu

POLLEY, Judith Anne. (Valentina Luellen). Portuguese/British (born England), b. 1938. **Genres:** Novels, Romance/Historical, Literary Criticism And History. **Career:** Writer. **Publications:** ROMANCE NOVELS: The Flowering Desert, 1970; The Secret of Val Verde, 1974; Val Verde, 1974; The King's Shadow, 1975; The Laird's French Bride, 1978; Love and Pride, 1988; Dark Star, 1989; The Web of Love, 1989; Winter Embers-Summer Fire, 1991; To Please a Lady, 1992; One Love, 1993; Hostage of Love, 1994. ROMANCE NOVELS UNDER PSEUDONYM JUDITH HAGAR: Journey into Love, 1968; Master of Karatangi, 1968; A Man for Melanie, 1970; Dangerous Deception, 1972; Keeper of the Flame, 1977; The Captive Heart, 1978; The Place of Happiness, 1978; To Touch the Stars, 1979; Beloved Enemy, 1980; Don't Run from Love, 1981; Shadow of the Eagle, 1982; Beloved Adversary, 1982; The Wind of Change, 1982; The Measure of Love, 1983; The Peaceful Homecoming, 1983. ROMANCE NOVELS UNDER PSEUDONYM VALENTINA LUELLEN: The Countess, 1967; Maria and Elena, 1968; A Pride of MacDonalds, 1968; Slightly Scarlet, 1969; Children of the Devil, 1970; Madelon, 1970; The King's Cavalier, 1971; Castle of the Mist, 1972; Francesca, 1977; Moonshadow, 1981; Prince of Deception, 1981; Silver Salamander, 1982; Wild Wind in the Heather, 1983; The Valley of Tears, 1984; The Moonflower, 1984; Elusive Flame of Love, 1984; Mistress of Tanglewood, 1984; Black Ravenswood, 1985; The Lord of Darkness, 1985; The Devil of Talland, 1985; The Passionate Pirate, 1986; Where the Heart Leads, 1986; Love the Avenger, 1986; The Devil's Touch, 1987; My Lady Melisande, 1987; The Way of Love. **Address:** Quinta Sombra da Lua, Calcada, 8150 S Bráz de Alportel, Algarve, 31700-008, Portugal.

POLLITT, Michael G(erald). British (born England), b. 1967. **Genres:** Economics. **Career:** Oxford University, Trinity College, lecturer, 1991-94, Brasenose College, lecturer, 1991-94, Worcester College, lecturer, 1991-94, Balliol College, lecturer, 1991-94; Cambridge University, lecturer in applied industrial organization, 1994-99, Sidney Sussex College, fellow and director of studies in economics, 1994-, dean of discipline, 1997-2000, lecturer in business economics, 1999-2001, university senior lecturer in business economics, 2001-, director of programmes, Electricity Policy Research Group, assistant director, acting executive director and team leader, Studies in Management and Economics, director; European School of Management, visiting lecturer, 1994-95; London Business School, visiting lecturer, 1996; Association of Christian Economists, convenor, 2000-; Massachusetts Institute of Technology, Electricity Project, co-leader, 2001-05, Department of Economics, visiting associate professor; ESRC Electricity Policy Research Group, acting executive director, 2005-06; Ofgem, external economic advisor, 2007-11; Centre for Business Research, research associate. Writer and speaker. **Publications:** Ownership and Performance in Electric Utilities: International Evidence on Privatization and Efficiency, 1995; (co-author) A European Market for Electricity, 1999. EDITOR AND CONTRIBUTOR: (with I.W. Jones) The Role of Business Ethics in Economic Performance, 1998; (with I.W. Jones) Understanding How Issues in Business Ethics Develop, 2002; (with S. Berg and M. Tsuji) Private Initiatives in Infrastructures: Priorities, Incentives and Performance, 2002; (with T. Jamasb and W.J. Nuttall) Future Electricity Technologies and Systems, 2006; (with I.W. Jones and D. Bek) Multinationals in Their Communities: A Social Capital Approach to Corporate Citizenship Projects, 2007; (with T. Jamasb and M.G. Pollitt) Delivering a Low-carbon Electricity System: Technologies, Economics and Policy, 2008; (with T. Jamasb) Future of Electricity Demand: Customers, Citizens, and Loads, 2011. Contributor of articles to periodicals. **Address:** Judge Business School, University of Cambridge, Trumpington St., Cambridge, CM CB2 1AG, England. **Online address:** m.pollitt@jbs.cam.ac.uk

POLLOCK, Dale. (Dale M. Pollock). American (born United States), b. 1950. **Genres:** Film, Biography. **Career:** Orson Welles Theatre, co-founder and manager, 1968-72; freelance writer, 1973-75; Santa Cruz Sentinel, general assignment reporter and entertainment editor, 1975-77; Daily Variety, film and television reporter and critic, 1977-80; Los Angeles Times, staff writer, 1980-85; Gelten Films, development executive, 1985-86; A and M Films, president, 1986-93; University of Southern California, lecturer; University of California, lecturer; University of North Carolina, School of the Arts, School of Filmmaking, dean, 1999-2006, professor of cinema studies, 2007-, professor of producing, 2008-. **Publications:** Skywalking: The Life and Films of George Lucas, 1983, rev. ed., 1999. Contributor to magazines. **Address:** School of the Arts, University of North Carolina, 1533 S Main St., Winston-Salem, NC 27127-2738, U.S.A. **Online address:** dmpollock@dalempollock.com

POLLOCK, Dale M. *See* **POLLOCK, Dale.**

POLLOCK, Donald Ray. American (born United States), b. 1954. **Genres:** Novellas/Short Stories. **Career:** Writer, 2005-. **Publications:** Knockemstiff (short stories), 2008. Contributor of articles to periodicals. **Address:** Inkwell Management, 521 5th Ave., 26th Fl., New York, NY 10175, U.S.A. **Online address:** don@donaldraypollock.com

POLLOCK, John Charles. British (born England), b. 1923. **Genres:** History, Theology/Religion, Travel/Exploration, Biography, Autobiography/Memoirs. **Career:** Wellington College, assistant master of history and divinity, 1947-49; Saint Paul's Church, curate, 1951-53. Writer. **Publications:** Candidate for Truth, 1950; A Cambridge Movement, 1953; The Cambridge Seven, 1955; Way to Glory: Life of Havelock of Lucknow, 1957, rev. ed., 1996; Shadows Fall Apart, 1958; The Good Seed, 1959; Earth's Remotest End, 1960; Hudson Taylor and Maria, 1962; The Christians from Siberia in US as The Faith of the Russian Evangelicals, 1964; The Keswick Story, 1964, rev. ed., 2008; Crusade '66: Britain Hears Billy Graham, 1966; Moody without Sankey, 1966; Billy Graham, 1966; The Apostle: A Life of Saint Paul, 1969; Victims of the Long March and Other Stories, 1970; A Foreign Devil in China: The Life of Nelson Bell, 1971, 1988; George Whitefield and the Great Awakening, 1973; Wilberforce, 1977; Billy Graham: Evangelist to the World, 1979; The Siberian Seven, 1979; Amazing Grace: John Newton's Story, 1981; Moody, 1983; The Master: A Life of Jesus, 1984; Billy Graham: Highlights of the Story in US as To All the Nations, 1984, rev. ed., 2003; Shaftesbury, the Poor Man's Earl, 1985; A Fistful of Heroes, 1988; John Wesley, 1989; On Fire for God, 1990; Fear No Foe: A Brother's Story, 1992; Language and Learning: An Introduction for Teaching, 1992; Gordon: The Man behind the Legend, 1993; The Master and the Apostle, 1995; Kitchener: The Road to Omdurman, 1998; Billy Graham Story: The Authorized Biography, 2003. **Address:** Rose Ash House, South Molton, DN EX36 4RB, England.

POLLOCK, Leland W(ells). American (born United States), b. 1943. **Genres:** Biology, Natural History. **Career:** Wellcome Marine Laboratory, Federal Water Quality Administration, fellow, 1969-71; Marine Biological Laboratory, Federal Water Quality Administration, fellow, 1969-71; Drew University, assistant professor, 1972-79, associate professor, 1979-85, professor of biology, 1985-2005, department head, 1981-86, 1990-93, 1999-2002, chairperson of science division, 1994-95, 1998-99, 1999-2000, professor emeritus, 2005-; Shoals Marine Laboratory, core faculty, 1974-83; AquaVets Program, adjunct faculty, 1978-2001; New Jersey Governor's School in the Sciences, teacher for biology laboratories and research projects, 1984-2000. Writer. **Publications:** A Practical Guide to the Marine Animals of Northeastern North America, 1998. Contributor to books and journals. **Address:** Department of Biology, Drew University, Hall of Sciences, 36 Madison Ave., Madison, NJ 07940, U.S.A. **Online address:** lpollock@drew.edu

POLLOCK, (Mary) Sharon. Canadian (born Canada), b. 1936. **Genres:** Plays/Screenplays, Theatre, Film, Children's Fiction, Literary Criticism And History. **Career:** University of Alberta, affiliated with the drama department, [illegible], visiting lecturer, [illegible]; Banff Center School of Fine Arts, head of playwright's colony, 1977-80; Alberta Theater Projects, playwright-in-residence, 1977-79; National Arts Center, artist-in-residence, 1981-83; Theater Calgary, dramaturge and assistant artistic director, 1983-84, artistic director, 1984; Regina Public Library, playwright-in-residence, 1986-87; Manitoba Theater Center, associate artistic director, 1988; Theater New, artistic director, 1988-90; Garry Theater, co-founder of independent theater group, 1992; Alberta Playwrights Network, president, 1998; Theater Junction, playwright-in-residence, 1999-. Director and actress. **Publications:** STAGE PLAYS: And Out Goes You, 1975; Tracings: The Fraser Story, 1977; Mail vs. Female, 1979; One Tiger to a Hill, 1980; Generations, 1980; Whiskey Six Cadenza, 1983; Egg, 1988; A Death in the Family, 1993; Moving Pictures, 1999; End Dream, 2000; Angel's Trumpet, 2001; Death in the Family, 2008; Kabloona Talk, 2008; Man Out of Joint, 2008. PLAYS FOR CHILDREN: New Canadians, 1973; Superstition Throu' the Ages, 1973; The Great Drag Race, 1974, rev. ed. as Choked and Croaked, 1974; Wudjesay?, 1974; The Happy Prince, 1974; The Rose and the Nightingale, 1974; Star-child, 1974; Lessons in Swizzlery, 1978; The Wreck of the National Line Car, 1978; Chautaqua Spelt E-N-E-R-G-Y, 1979. OTHERS: A Compulsory Option, 1970, rev. ed. as No! No!No!, 1977; Walsh, 1973, 3rd ed., 1983; My Name Is Lisabeth, 1976, rev. ed. as Blood Relations: And Other Plays, 1981, rev. ed., 2002; The Komagata Maru Incident, 1978; Doc, 1986, rev. ed., 2003; Getting It Straight: Heroines: Three Plays, 1989; Playhouse: Six Fantasy Plays For Children, 1989; Saucy Jack, 1994; It's All Make-Believe, Isn't It?: Marilyn Monroe, 1994; Fair Liberty's Call, 1995, rev. ed., 2002; Three Plays, 2003; Sharon Pollock: Collected Works, 2005. **Address:** 319 Manora Dr. NE, Calgary, AB T2A 4R2, Canada. **Online address:** spdrama@telus.net

POLLOCK, Nancy J. New Zealander/British (born England), b. 1934. **Genres:** Anthropology/Ethnology, Food And Wine, Medicine/Health, Natural History, Humanities, Social Sciences. **Career:** ICI Ltd., indexer, 1952-54; school secretary, 1954-61; Victoria University of Wellington, lecturer, 1970-, senior lecturer in anthropology, coordinator of Pacific studies. Writer. **Publications:** These Roots Remain: Food Habits in Islands of the Central and Eastern Pacific since Western Contact, 1992; (comp.) Nauru Bibliography, 1994. EDITOR: (with R. Crocombe) French Polynesia: A Book of Selected Readings, 1988; (with M. Young) The Power of Kava, 1995; (with I. de Garine) Social Aspects of Obesity, 1995. Contributor to academic journals. **Address:** Department of Anthropology and Developement Studi, Victoria University, PO Box 600, Wellington, 6140, New Zealand. **Online address:** nancy_pollock@paradise.net.nz

POLONSKY, Michael Jay. Australian/American (born United States), b. 1959. **Genres:** Marketing, Advertising/Public Relations, Business/Trade/Industry, Ethics. **Career:** Temple University, instructor in economics, 1985-86; University of the Witwatersrand, lecturer in business economics, 1986-88; State of New Jersey, Department of Treasury, Office of Budget and Management, project specialist, 1985-86; Massey University, visiting lecturer in finance, 1988; Charles Sturt University, lecturer in marketing and economics, 1989-90; University of Newcastle, lecturer in management, 1990-97, senior lecturer, 1997-2001, coordinator of marketing group, 1992-95, associate professor of marketing, 2001; Australian Catholic University, lecturer, 1991; Victoria University, School of Tourism, Hospitality and Marketing, Melbourne Airport chair, professor of marketing, 2001-, Marketing Group, chair, 2001-; Deakin University, professor of marketing. Writer. **Publications:** (With H.T. Suchard) Country Education Profiles-South Africa: A Comparative Study, 1993; (with D.S. Waller) Designing and Managing a Research Project: A Business Student's Guide, 2005. EDITOR: (with H. Lozada and A. Mintu) Environmental Issues in the Curricula of International Business: The Green Imperative, 1993; (with A.T. Mintu-Wimsatt) Environmental Marketing: Strategies, Practice, Theory and Research, 1995. Contributor to books. **Address:** School of Management and Marketing, Deakin University, Lb 5.105, 221 Burwood Highway, Burwood, VI 3125, Australia. **Online address:** michael.polonsky@deakin.edu.au

POLOWETZKY, Michael. American/British (born England), b. 1956?. **Genres:** Adult Non-fiction, History. **Career:** Researcher and writer. **Publications:** A Bond Never Broken: The Relations between Napoleon and the Authors of France, 1993; Jerusalem Recovered: Victorian Intellectuals and the Birth of Modern Zionism, 1995; Prominent Sisters: Mary Lamb, Dorothy Wordsworth and Sarah Disraeli, 1996. **Address:** 34 Gramercy Pk., New York, NY 10003, U.S.A.

POLSGROVE, Carol. American (born United States), b. 1945. **Genres:** History, Documentaries/Reportage, Politics/Government, Civil Liberties/Human Rights. **Career:** Associated Press, writer, 1967-68; Maysville Community College, instructor, 1973-74; Eastern Kentucky University, associate professor, 1974-77; San Jose State University, lecturer, 1978-80, 1982-83; Progressive, associate editor, 1980-81; Mother Jones, editor, 1983-85; San Francisco State University, lecturer, 1986-87; California State University, lecturer, 1987-89; Indiana University, School of Journalism, professor of journalism, 1989-. **Publications:** It Wasn't Pretty, Folks, But Didn't We Have Fun?: Esquire in the Sixties, 1995, rev. ed. as It Wasn't Pretty, Folks, But Didn't We Have Fun?: Surviving the '60s with Esquire's Harold Hayes, 2001; Divided Minds: Intellectuals and the Civil Rights Movement, 2001; Ending British Rule in Africa: Writers in a Common Cause, 2009. Contributor of articles to journals and magazines. **Address:** School of Journalism, Indiana University, Ernie Pyle Hall, 940 E 7th St., Bloomington, IN 47405-7108, U.S.A. **Online address:** cpolsgro@indiana.edu

POLSKY, Andrew J. American (born United States), b. 1955. **Genres:** Politics/Government, History. **Career:** Princeton University, Department of Politics, lecturer in politics, 1981-82; Barnard College, adjunct instructor in political science, 1982; City University of New York, John Jay College of Criminal Justice, adjunct instructor in government, 1983-84, adjunct instructor in public administration, 1984, Baruch College, adjunct instructor, 1984, Hunter College, Department of Political Science, assistant professor, 1984-90, associate professor of political science, 1991-2004, chair, 1993-96, professor, 2005-, acting chair, 2008-09, Social Science Institute, director, 1993-94; Polity, editor, 2005-. **Publications:** The Rise of the Therapeutic State, 1991; Elusive Victories: The American Presidency at War, 2012. Contributor of articles to journals. **Address:** Department of Political Science, Hunter College, City University of New York, Rm. 1723 Hunter W, 695 Park Ave., New York, NY 10065, U.S.A. **Online address:** apolsky@hunter.cuny.edu

POLUKHINA, Valentina. British/Russian (born Russia), b. 1936. **Genres:** Literary Criticism And History, Biography, Poetry, Cultural/Ethnic Topics. **Career:** Moscow Lumumba University, lecturer in Russian language, 1962-68, 1972-73; Keele University, assistant in Russian studies, 1973-76, lecturer, 1976-91, senior lecturer in Russian literature, 1991-, reader in Russian literature, 1991-95, professor of Russian literature, 1995-2001, professor emeritus, 2001-. Writer. **Publications:** Joseph Brodsky: A Poet for Our Time, 1989; Brodsky Through the Eyes of His Contemporaries, 1992, 2nd ed., 2008; (with I. Piarli) Slovar' Tropov Brodskogo: Na Materiale Sbornika Chast' Rechi, 1995; (with U. Parli) The Dictionary of Brodsky's Tropes, 1995; Brodskiĭ Glazami Sovremennikov, 1997; Bol'she Samogo Sebia: O Brodskom, 2009. EDITOR: (with L. Loseff) Brodsky's Poetics and Aesthetics, 1990; (with F. Andrew and R. Reid) Literary Tradition and Practice in Russian Culture, 1993; (and intro.) The Silk of Time: Bilingual Selected Poems, 1994; (with R. Reid and J. Andrew) Structure and Tradition in Russian Society, 1994; Brodsky's Genres, 1995; (with L. Loseff) Joseph Brodsky: The Art of a Poem, 1999; Brodsky as a Critic, 2000; Selected Poems, 2001; (with D. Weissbort) Russian Women Poets, 2002; (with L. Loseff) Kak Rabotaet Stikhotvorenie Brodskogo, 2002; (with D. Weissbort) Anthology of Contemporary Russian Women Poets, 2005. Contributor to periodicals. **Address:** School of Humanities, Keele University, Walter Moberly Bldg., Keele, ST ST5 5BG, England. **Online address:** valentina@polukhina.fsnet.co.uk

POMERANTZ, Charlotte. American (born United States), b. 1930. **Genres:** Children's Fiction, Poetry, Animals/Pets. **Career:** Writer. **Publications:** (Ed.) A Quarter-Century of Un-Americana, 1938-1963, 1963; JUVENILE FICTION: The Bear Who Couldn't Sleep, 1965; Harb al-sāmitah, 1966; The Moon Pony, 1967; Ask the Windy Sea, 1968; Why You Look Like You Whereas I Tend to Look Like Me, 1969; The Day They Parachuted Cats on Borneo: A Drama of Ecology (play), 1971; The Piggy in the Puddle, 1974; The Princess and the Admiral, 1974; The Ballad of the Long-Tailed Rat (rhyme), 1975; Detective Poufy's First Case: Or, The Missing Battery-Operated Pepper Grinder, 1976; The Mango Tooth, 1977; The Downtown Fairy Godmother, 1978; The Tamarindo Puppy and Other Poems, 1979; Noah's and Namah's Ark, 1980; If I Had a Paka: Poems in Eleven Languages, 1982; Buffy and Albert, 1982; Posy, 1983; Whiff, Sniff, Nibble and Chew: The Gingerbread Boy Retold, 1984; Where's the Bear?, 1984, 1st ed., 2003; The Half-Birthday Party, 1984; All Asleep, 1984; One Duck, Another Duck, 1984; How Many Trucks Can A Two Truck Tow?, 1987; Timothy Tall Feather, 1987; The Chalk Doll, 1989; Flap Your Wings and Try (rhyme) 1989; The Outside Dog, 1992; You're Not My Friend, 1992; Serena Katz, 1992; Halfway to Your House, 1993; Here

Comes Henny, 1994; Mangaboom, 1997; You're Not My Best Friend Anymore, 1998; The Mousery, 2000; The Birthday Letter, 2000; Thunderboom!: Poems for Everybody, 2005. Works appear in anthologies. **Address:** 261 W 21st St., New York, NY 10011, U.S.A.

PON, Cindy. American/Taiwanese (born Taiwan), b. 1973?. **Genres:** Novels, Science Fiction/Fantasy. **Career:** Author and artist. **Publications:** Silver Phoenix: Beyond the Kingdom of Xia (fantasy novel), 2009. **Address:** c/o Bill Contardi, Brandt & Hochman Literary Agents, 1501 Broadway, Ste. 2310, New York, NY 10036, U.S.A. **Online address:** pon.cindy@gmail.com

PONCE, Mary Helen. AmericanMexican (born Mexico), b. 1938. **Genres:** Novellas/Short Stories, Local History/Rural Topics, Autobiography/Memoirs, Biography, Translations, Biography, Translations, Young Adult Fiction, Young Adult Fiction. **Career:** California State University, Northridge, instructor of Chicano studies, 1982-87, adjunct professor, 1987-88; University of New Mexico, Women's Studies program, adjunct faculty, 1988-92; University of California Los Angeles, adjunct faculty, 1992-93. Writer. **Publications:** Taking Control, 1987; The Wedding, 1989, rev. ed., 2008; The Lives and Works of Five New Mexican Women Writers, 1936-1990 (monograph), 1992; Hoyt Street: An Autobiography, 1993; Calle Hoyt: Recuerdos de una Juventud Chicana, 1995; The Life and Works of Fabiola Cabeza de Baca, New Mexican Hispanic Woman Writer, 1995. Contributor of articles to journals. Works appear in anthologies. **Address:** 7837 Denivelle Rd., Sunland, CA 91040-2209, U.S.A. **Online address:** mhpon@aol.com

PONDER, Patricia. *See* **MAXWELL, Patricia Anne.**

PONG, David (B. P. T.). American (born United States), b. 1939. **Genres:** Area Studies, History, Education, Reference. **Career:** Institute of Historical Research, University of London, research fellow, 1965-66; Harvard University, East Asian Research Center, research associate, 1968; University of Delaware, assistant professor, 1969-73, associate professor, 1973-89, professor of history, 1989-, East Asian studies program, director, 1989-2009, head of department, 1992-98; American Council of Learned Societies, research fellow, 1973-74; Australian National University, research fellow in far eastern history, 1978-82; Princeton University, visiting associate professor, 1988; The Hong Kong Baptist University, Modern History Research Centre, honorary research fellow, 2002-. Writer. **Publications:** (Ed. and intro.) Lo Tach'un, T'ai-wan hai-fang ping k'ai-shan jih-chi, 1972; A Critical Guide to the Kwangtung Provincial Archives Deposited at the Public Record Office of London, 1975; (ed. with E.S.K. Fung) Ideal and Reality: Social and Political Change in Modern China, 1860-1949, 1985; Shen Pao-chen and China's Modernization in the Nineteenth Century, 1994; Shen Baozhen pingzhuan: Zhongguo jindaihua de changshi (title means: 'A Critical Biography of Shen Baozhen: China's Venture in Modernization'), 2000; (ed.) Resisting Japan: Mobilizing for War in China, 1935-1945, 2008; (ed.) Encyclopedia of Modern China, 2009. Contributor of articles to journals. **Address:** Department of History, University of Delaware, 46 W Delaware Ave., 224 John Munroe Hall, Newark, DE 19716, U.S.A. **Online address:** dpong@udel.edu

PONSONBY, Laura. British (born England), b. 1935. **Genres:** Art/Art History, Botany, Horticulture, Women's Studies And Issues, Travel/Exploration. **Career:** Royal Botanic Gardens, guide lecturer and education officer, 1965-94; Haslemere Educational Museum, honorary botanist; Grove Park School, governor, 1992-; educator, 1994-. Writer, naturalist and musician. **Publications:** (With J. Stubbs) List of the Flowering Plants and Ferns of Haslemere District, 1978; Marianne North at Kew Gardens, 1990; (with R.L.A. Stiff) Margaret Mee-Marianne North: Exploratrices Intrepides, 2007; (with J. Stubbs) Kew Souvenir Guide and Junior Guide HMSO. **Address:** 17 South End, Kensington, London, GL W8 5BU, England. **Online address:** laura_ponsonby@hotmail.com

PONTING, Clive. Welsh/British (born England), b. 1947?. **Genres:** Novels, Technology, Engineering, Social Sciences, Adult Non-fiction. **Career:** University of Wales, reader in politics and international relations, through 2004, now retired. British Ministry of Defense, assistant secretary. Writer. **Publications:** The Right to Know: The Inside Story of the Belgrano Affair, 1985; Whitehall: Tragedy and Farce, 1986; Breach of Promise: Labour in Power, 1964-1970, 1989; 1940: Myth and Reality, 1990; Secrecy in Britain, 1990; Decision Making in the Gulf: Lessons to Be Learned, 1991; A Green History of the World, 1991; Churchill, 1994; Armageddon: The Reality Behind the Distortions, Myths, Lies, and Illusions of World War II, 1995; Progress and Barbarism: The World in the Twentieth Century, 1998; The Twentieth Century: A World History, 1999; World History: A New Perspective, 2000; Thirteen Days: The Road to the First World War, 2002; The Crimean War, 2004; Gunpowder, 2005; A New Green History of the World: The Environment And The Collapse Of Great Civilizations, 2007. Contributer to periodicals. **Address:** University of Wales, Singleton Pk., Swansea, WG SA2 8PP, Wales. **Online address:** c.ponting@swansea.ac.uk

POOL, Gail. American (born United States), b. 1946. **Genres:** Literary Criticism And History, Adult Non-fiction, Local History/Rural Topics. **Career:** Boston Review, editor; Radcliffe Quarterly, book review editor; Wilson Library Bulletin, book review editor; Harvard University, Radcliffe Seminars, instructor in writing for publication. Freelance journalist. **Publications:** (Ed. and intro.) Other People's Mail: An Anthology of Letter Stories, 2000; Faint Praise: The Plight of Book Reviewing in America, 2007. Contributor to periodicals. **Address:** 60 Shepard St., Cambridge, MA 02138, U.S.A. **Online address:** gailpool@comcast.net

POOLE, Elizabeth. British (born England), b. 1969. **Genres:** Politics/Government, Theology/Religion. **Career:** Staffordshire University, Faculty of Arts, Media and Design, senior lecturer in media studies, 2000-. Writer. **Publications:** Reporting Islam: Media Representations of British Muslims, 2002; (ed. with J.E. Richardson) Muslims and the News Media, 2006. **Address:** Faculty of Arts, Media and Design, Staffordshire University, L402 Flaxman Bldg., College Rd., Stoke-on-Trent, ST ST4 2DE, England. **Online address:** e.poole@staffs.ac.uk

POOLE, Eric. American (born United States), b. 1960. **Genres:** Autobiography/Memoirs. **Career:** Fox Radio, vice president of radio marketing. Writer and memoirist. **Publications:** Where's My Wand? One Boy's Magical Triumph over Alienation and Shag Carpeting (memoir), 2010. **Address:** c/o Rebecca Oliver, William Morris Endeavor Entertainment, 1325 Ave. of the Americas, New York, NY 20019, U.S.A. **Online address:** eric@ericpoole.net

POOLE, Josephine. British (born England), b. 1933. **Genres:** Novels, Novellas/Short Stories, Mystery/Crime/Suspense, Children's Fiction, Young Adult Fiction, Plays/Screenplays, Songs/Lyrics And Libretti, Picture/Board Books, Picture/Board Books. **Career:** British Broadcasting Corp., Features Department, secretary, 1954-56. Writer. **Publications:** A Dream in the House, 1961; Moon Eyes, 1965; The Lilywhite Boys, 1968; Catch as Catch Can, 1969; Yokeham, 1970; Billy Buck in US as The Visitor, 1972; Touch and Go, 1976; When Fishes Flew, 1978; The Open Grave, 1979; The Forbidden Room, 1979; Hannah Chance, 1980; Kings, Ghosts and Highwaymen, 1981; Diamond Jack, 1983; Country Diary Companion, 1983; Three for Luck, 1985; Wildlife Tales, 1986; Puss in Boots, 1987; The Sleeping Beauty, 1988; The Loving Ghosts, 1988; Angel, 1989; This is Me Speaking, 1990; Snow White, 1991; Paul Loves Amy Loves Christo, 1992; Scared to Death, 1994; Pinocchio (retelling), 1994; Deadly Inheritance, 1995; The Water Babies (retelling), 1996; Jack and the Beanstalk, 1997; Hero, 1997; Joan of Arc, 1998; Run Rabbit, 2000; Fair Game, 2000; Scorched, 2003; Anne Frank, 2005. Contributor to periodicals. **Address:** A.P. Watt Ltd., 20 John St., London, GL WC1N 2DR, England. **Online address:** charlottehelyar@ntlworld.com

POOLE, Richard. British (born England), b. 1945. **Genres:** Novellas/Short Stories, Poetry, Songs/Lyrics And Libretti, Young Adult Fiction. **Career:** Coleg Harlech, tutor in literature, 1970-2000; Poetry Wales, editor, 1992-96. Writer. **Publications:** Venus and Adonis, 1984; Richard Hughes: A Novelist, 1986. EDITOR: In the Lap of Atlas, 1979; Fiction as Truth: Selected Literary Writings, 1983. POETRY: "Goings" and Other Poems, 1978; Words before Midnight, 1981; Natural Histories, 1989; Autobiographies and Explorations, Sixty-two Sonnets, 1994; That Fool July, 2003; The Posthumous Club, 2006; The Sleeping Lady, 2007; Two Tots of Irish, 2007. BOOK OF LOWMOOR: Jewel and Thorn, 2005; Brass Key, 2007; Iron Angel: The Third Book of Lowmoor, 2007; The Day I Found My Childhood Erased, forthcoming. Works appear in anthologies. **Address:** Glan-y-Werydd, Llandanwg, Harlech, GY LL46 2SD, Wales.

POOLE, Scott. American (born United States), b. 1951. **Genres:** Architecture, Biography. **Career:** University of Texas, faculty; Virginia Tech, School of Architecture and Design, associate professor of architecture, professor of architecture, 1986-, founding director, 2004-; Commonwealth of Virginia, architect; University of Calgary, Gillmor visiting lecturer, 2000; Virginia Society of the American Institute of Architects, president and board director,

2008-10. Writer. **Publications:** The New Finnish Architecture, 1992; Material Matters: Architecture and Material Practice, 2006. **Address:** School of Architecture and Design, Virginia Tech University, 201 Cowgill Hall, PO Box 0205, Blacksburg, VA 24061-0001, U.S.A. **Online address:** spoole@vt.edu

POOR, Sara S. American (born United States), b. 1963. **Genres:** Women's Studies And Issues. **Career:** Duke University, instructor in German and literature, 1987-95; University of Erlangen, faculty, 1995-96; Stanford University, assistant professor of German studies and gender studies, 1996-2002; Princeton University, Department of German, assistant professor, 2002-06, Charles Osgood bicentennial preceptor, 2005-08, associate professor, 2006-, director of graduate studies, 2006-08; Medieval Feminist Forum, associate editor, 2002-04, editor, 2004-05; The Medieval Review, book review editor, 2003-06. **Publications:** Mechthild of Magdeburg and Her Book: Gender and the Making of Textual Authority, 2004; (ed. with J.K. Schulman) Women and Medieval Epic: Gender, Genre and the Limits of Epic Masculinity, 2007. Contributor of articles to journals. **Address:** Department of Germanic Languages & Literature, Princeton University, 211 E Pyne Ave., Princeton, NJ 08544, U.S.A. **Online address:** spoor@princeton.edu

POORE, Carol. American (born United States), b. 1949. **Genres:** Cultural/Ethnic Topics, Travel/Exploration. **Career:** Ripon College, visiting assistant professor, 1981; Brown University, assistant professor, 1982-88, associate professor, 1988-2000, professor, 2000-. Writer. **Publications:** (Ed. with J. Elliott and J. Pelzer) Stereotyp und Vorurteil in der Literatur: Unters. zu Autoren d. 20. Jh., 1978; (ed.) Die Anfänge der Deutschen Arbeiterbewegung in Amerika, 1984; (ed.) Reminiscenzen: Seine Rede Vor Richter Gary, Sozialpolitische Abhandlungen, Briefe, Notizen, Etc., 1984; (ed.) Deutsch-Amerikanische Sozialistische Literatur, 1865-1900: Anthologie, 1987; The Bonds of Labor: German Journeys to the Working World, 1890-1990, 2000; Disability in Twentieth-Century German Culture, 2007. Contributor of articles to books, periodicals and journals. **Address:** U.S.A. **Online address:** carol_poore@brown.edu

POORTINGA, Y(pe) H. Dutch (born Netherlands), b. 1939?. **Genres:** Education, Psychology, Social Sciences, Young Adult Non-fiction. **Career:** Catholic University, faculty; Tilburg University, professor of cross-cultural psychology, now professor emeritus; University of Leuven, now professor emeritus. Writer. **Publications:** Cross-Cultural Comparison of Maximum Performance Tests, 1971; (with B.I.M. Foden) A Comparative Study of Curiosity in Black and White South African Students, 1975; Basic Problems in Cross-Cultural Psychology, 1977; (with L.H. Echensberger and W.J. Lonner) Cross-Cultural Contributions to Psychology, 1979; (with M.H. Segall, P.R. Dasen and J.W. Berry) Human Behavior in Global Perspective: An Introduction to Cross-Cultural Psychology, 1990; (with M.H. Segall, P.R. Dasen and J.W. Berry) Cross-Cultural Psychology: Research and Applications, 1991, 2nd ed. as Handbook of Cross-Cultural Psychology, 1997. EDITOR: (with I.R. Laguines) From a Different Perspective: Studies of Behavior across Cultures, 1985; (with H. Keller and A. Scholmerich) Between Culture and Biology: Perspectives on Ontogenetic Development, 2002; (with F.J.R. van de Vijver and D.A. van Hemert) Multilevel Analysis of Individuals and Cultures, 2008. **Address:** Tilburg University, Rm. P 208, PO Box 90153, Tilburg, 5000 LE, Netherlands. **Online address:** y.h.poortinga@uvt.nl

POORVU, William J. American (born United States), b. 1935. **Genres:** Economics, Money/Finance, Business/Trade/Industry. **Career:** WCVB-TV, Channel 5, owner and founder, 1963-82; Boston Broadcasters Inc., officer and director, 1963-83; Bank of Boston Pooled Real Estate Investment Fund, staff, 1971-91; Harvard University, Harvard Business School, lecturer, 1973-81, adjunct professor, 1981-89, professor emeritus, 1989-, Class of 1961 Adjunct Professor in Emeritus Entrepreneurship, Harvard Graduate School of Design, Department of City Planning, faculty; Connecticut General Mortgage and Realty Investments Inc., trustee, 1980-81; Baupost Group Inc., co-founder and chair, 1982-; Massachusetts Financial Services Group, trustee and director; Sonesta International Corp., director, 1985-92; Trammell Crow Real Estate Investors, trustee, 1986-92; CBL & Associates Properties, director, 1993; National Public Radio Foundation, vice chairman; Boston Symphony Orchestra, treasurer, vice chair and trustee; Gardner Museum, trustee and treasurer; New England Medical Center, trustee emeritus. Writer and entrepreneur. **Publications:** Real Estate: A Case Study Approach, 1993; The Real Estate Challenge: Capitalizing on Change, 1996; (with J.L. Cruikshank) The Real Estate Game: The Intelligent Guide to Decision-making and Investment, 1999; (with J.L. Cruikshank) Creating and Growing Real Estate Wealth: The 4 Stages to a Lifetime of Success, 2008. **Address:** Graduate School of Business, Harvard University, T-15 Morgan Hall, Soldiers Field, Boston, MA 02163, U.S.A. **Online address:** wpoorvu@hbs.edu

POOS, Lawrence Raymond. *See* **POOS, L. R.**

POOS, L. R. (Lawrence Raymond Poos). American (born United States), b. 1954. **Genres:** History, Law. **Career:** Cambridge University, Fitzwilliam College, fellow, 1980-83; University of East Anglia, visiting lecturer, 1983; The Catholic University of America, Department of History, assistant professor of history, 1983-89, associate professor of history, 1989-94, professor of history, 1994-, chair, 1995-2001, School of Arts and Sciences, dean, 2002-. Writer and historian. **Publications:** (With R.S. Wieck, V. Reinburg and J. Plummer) Time Sanctified: The Book of Hours in Medieval Art and Life, 1988; A Rural Society after the Black Death: Essex, 1350-1525, 1991; (ed. with L. Bonfield) Select Cases in Manorial Courts, 1250-1550: Property and Family Law, 1998; (ed.) Lower Ecclesiastical Jurisdiction in Late-Medieval England: The Courts of the Dean and Chapter of Lincoln, 1336-1349, and the Deanery of Wisbech, 1485-1484, 2001; Love, Hate, and The Law in Tudor England: The Three Wives of Ralph Rishton, forthcoming. Contributor to journals. **Address:** Department of History, Catholic University of America, 101 Cardinal Hall W, 620 Michigan Ave. NE, Washington, DC 20064-0001, U.S.A. **Online address:** poos@cua.edu

POPE, Deborah. American (born United States) **Genres:** Poetry, Education, Essays. **Career:** Duke University, professor of English, 1979-; Duke Writers Conference, co-founder. Writer. **Publications:** A Separate Vision: Isolation in Contemporary Women's Poetry, 1984; Ties that Bind: Essays on Mothering and Patriarchy, 1990; blood Spell, 1992; Fanatic Heart, 1992; Mortal World, 1995; Falling Out of Sky, 1999; Symphony and Chorale Composition, 2003. EDITOR: (with N. Quinn) The Ideology of Mothering: Disruption and Reproduction of Patriarchy, 1990. FORTHCOMING: (ed. with W. Lottrell) Matters of Course: Conversations on Gender, Teaching and Learning; Book of Hours; How it Happens. **Address:** Department of English, Duke University, 304B Allen Bldg., PO Box 90014, Durham, NC 27708, U.S.A. **Online address:** dpope@duke.edu

POPE, Hugh. British/South African (born South Africa) **Genres:** Local History/Rural Topics, Adult Non-fiction, Travel/Exploration, Reference. **Career:** United Press Intl., correspondent, 1982-84; Reuters, correspondent, 1984-89; The Independent, correspondent, 1990-97; The Wall Street Journal, correspondent, 1997-2005, Istanbul bureau, chief; International Crisis Group, Turkey/Cyprus project director. **Publications:** (With N. Pope) Turkey Unveiled: Ataturk and After, 1997; (with N. Pope) Turkey Unveiled: A History of Modern Turkey, 1998; Sons of the Conquerors: The Rise of the Turkic World, 2005; Dining with al-Qaeda: Three Decades Exploring the Many Worlds of the Middle East, 2010. **Address:** c/o Author Mail, Overlook Press, 1 Overlook Dr., Woodstock, NY 12498, U.S.A.

POPE, Rebecca A. American (born United States), b. 1955. **Genres:** Literary Criticism And History, Adult Non-fiction, History, Philosophy. **Career:** Columbia College, instructor in English, 1982-87; Catholic University of America, instructor in English, 1987-89; Montgomery College, instructor, 1987; Georgetown University, instructor in English, 1989-; University of the District of Columbia, lecturer, 1992; Smithsonian Institution, Campus on the Mall, instructor, 1995; University of Maryland, lecturer, 1996-97; University of Illinois, office manager; University of Memphis, Methodist Le Bonheur Center for Healthcare Economics, graduate research assistant, 2005-06; Amerigroup Corp., healthcare economist, 2006-08; First Horizon National Corp., senior statistical analyst, 2008-09; University of Tennessee, Health Science Center, Division of Internal Medicine, healthcare economist, 2009-10; University of Arkansas for Medical Sciences, Center for Clinical and Translational Research, program manager, 2010-11, Arkansas Foundation for Medical Care, statistician, 2011-. Writer. **Publications:** Vamping the Text (Microform): Frame- and Multiple-Tale Narrative Structures in Nineteenth-Century British Gothic Fiction, 1992; (contrib.) Embodied Voices: Female Vocality in Western Culture, 1994; (contrib.) Feminism in Women's Detective Fiction, 1995; (with S.J. Leonardi) The Divas Mouth: Body, Voice, Prima Donna Politics, 1996; (contrib.) The Erotics of Instruction, 1997; (contrib.) The Work of Opera, forthcoming; Ida and Louise Cook, forthcoming. Contributor to books and journals. **Address:** Little Rock Offices, Arkansas Foundation for Medical Care, 1020 W 4th St., Ste. 300, Little Rock, AZ 72201, U.S.A. **Online address:** poper@georgetown.edu

POPESCU, Petru. American/Romanian (born Romania), b. 1944. **Genres:** Novels. **Career:** Writer and filmmaker. **Publications:** The Last Wave (novelization of the film The Last Wave by Peter Weir), 1977; Amazon Beaming, 1991; Almost Adam (novel), 1996; The Return: A Family Revisits Their Eastern European Roots, 1997; Prins, 1998; The Oasis: A Memoir of Love and Survival in a Concentration Camp, 2001; Birth of the Pack, 2007; Footprints in Time, 2008; Girl Mary, 2009. **Address:** Beverly Hills, CA , U.S.A. **Online address:** petru@petrupopescu.com

POPKIN, Samuel L(ewis). American (born United States), b. 1942. **Genres:** Politics/Government. **Career:** Simulatics Corp., project director for urban analysis and Vietnam studies, 1965-67, consultant, 1968-72; Yale University, lecturer, 1967-68; Rand Corp., consultant, 1968-72; Harvard University, assistant professor, 1968-73; University of Texas, faculty, 1973-75; University of California, associate professor of political science, 1975-90, professor of political science, 1991-; CBS, consultant, 1983-90. Writer. **Publications:** (With I.S. Pool and R.P. Abelson) Candidates, Issues, and Strategies: A Computer Simulation of the 1960 Presidential Election, 1964, rev. ed. as Candidates, Issues and Strategies: A Computer Simulation of the 1960 and 1964 Presidential Elections, 1965; The Rational Peasant: The Political Economy of Rural Society in Vietnam, 1979; (ed. with S. Kernell) Chief of Staff: Twenty-Five Years of Managing the Presidency, 1986; The Reasoning Voter: Communication and Persuasion in Presidential Campaigns, 1991, 2nd ed., 1994; (ed. with A. Lupia and M.D. McCubbins) Elements of Reason: Cognition, Choice, and the Bounds of Rationality, 2000. **Address:** Department of Political Science, University of California, Rm. 396, Social Sciences Bldg., 9500 Gilman Dr., Ste. 0521, La Jolla, CA 92093-0521, U.S.A. **Online address:** spopkin@ucsd.edu

POPLOFF, Michelle. American (born United States), b. 1956. **Genres:** Children's Fiction, Illustrations, Children's Non-fiction. **Career:** Bantam Doubleday Dell Publishing Co., staff, 1979-; Random House, Delacorte Press Books, vice president and executive editor; Dell Books for Young Readers, executive editor. **Publications:** Busy O'Brien and the Great Bubble Gum Blowout, 1990; Busy O'Brien and the Caterpillar Punch Bunch, 1992; Splash-a-Roo and Snowflakes, 1996; Tea Party for Two, 1997; Bat Bones and Spider Stew, 1998; The First Fangs-Giving, 2001; Ghoul School Rules!, 2001; Roses Are Dread, Violets Are Boo: A Vampire Valentine Story, 2001; Field Trip to Flying Feathers Farm, 2002; The 100th Greatest Day of School, 2002; Pajama Party!, 2002; First Fangs-Giving, 2002; Triple Checkup, 2004. **Address:** c/o Publicity Director, Walker Books, 720 5th Ave., New York, NY 10019, U.S.A.

POPPER, Frank James. American (born United States), b. 1944. **Genres:** Environmental Sciences/Ecology, Geography, Regional/Urban Planning, Urban Studies. **Career:** Twentieth Century Fund (now Century Fund), research associate, 1968-69, State Land-Use Planning Project, director, 1975-81; Public Administration Service, staff associate, 1971-73; American Society of Planning Officials (now American Planning Association), senior research associate, 1973-74; Environmental Law Institute, senior associate, 1979-80; consultant, 1980-; Resources for the Future, Gilbert White fellow, 1982-83; Rutgers University, Department of Urban Studies, associate professor, professor, 1983-, chair, 1986-91, 1994, Center for Russian, Central and East European Studies, staff, 1987-91, Department of American Studies, staff, 1993-, Department of Political Science, staff, 2008-; Princeton University, Department of Civil and Environmental Engineering, visiting professor, 2001-02, 2003-. Writer. **Publications:** The President's Commissions, 1970; (with E. Finkler and W.J. Toner) Urban Nongrowth, 1976; The Politics of Land-Use Reform, 1981; (ed. with C.G. Geisler) Land Reform, American Style, 1984; (with D.E. Popper) The Great Plains: From Dust to Dust, 1987. Contributor to journals. **Address:** Bloustein School of Planning & Public Policy, Rutgers University, Rm. 535, Civic Square Bldg., 33 Livingston Ave., New Brunswick, NJ 08901-1958, U.S.A. **Online address:** fpopper@rci.rutgers.edu

PORCELLINO, John. American (born United States), b. 1968. **Genres:** Graphic Novels, Animals/Pets. **Career:** Writer and cartoonist. **Publications:** King-Cat Collection, 1998; King-Cat Nummer Eins, 1998; Perfect Example, 2000; Diary of a Mosquito Abatement Man, 2005; Moon Lake Trails, 2006; King-Cat Classix: The Best of King-Cat Comics and Stories, 2007; Thoreau at Walden, 2008; Map of My Heart: Celebrating the 20th Century of the King Cat Zine, 2009. **Address:** PO Box 142, South Beloit, IL 61080, U.S.A. **Online address:** johnp_kingcat@hotmail.com

PORTAL, Ellis. *See* **POWE, Bruce Allen.**

PORTALE, Alfred. American (born United States), b. 1945. **Genres:** Food And Wine, Regional/Urban Planning. **Career:** Gotham Bar and Grill, executive chef and co-owner, 1984-; Striped Bass, consulting chef. Writer. **Publications:** Alfred Portales Gotham Bar and Grill Cookbook, 1997; (with A. Friedman) Alfred Portales Twelve Seasons Cookbook, 2000; (with A. Friedman) Alfred Portales Simple Pleasures: Home Cooking from the Gotham Bar and Grills Acclaimed Chef, 2004. Contributor to periodicals. **Address:** c/o Author Mail, William Morrow & Co., 10 E 53rd St., 7th Fl., New York, NY 10022, U.S.A.

PORTALES, Marco. American (born United States), b. 1948. **Genres:** Cultural/Ethnic Topics. **Career:** University of California, assistant professor of English, 1974-79; University of Houston, associate professor of English, 1979-91; Texas Southmost College, dean of arts and sciences, 1986-88; Texas A&M University, professor of English, 1991-, executive assistant to the president, 1996-97. Public speaker and writer. **Publications:** Youth and Age in American Literature, 1989; Crowding Out Latinos: Mexican Americans in the Public Consciousness, 2000; (with R. Portales) Quality Education for Latinos and Latinas: Print and Oral Skills for all Students, K-College, 2005; Latino Sun, Rising: Our Spanish-Speaking U.S. World, 2005; Why Pancho Villa & Emiliano Zapata Wore Cananas: A Photo History on the 100th Year of the Mexican Revolution, 1910-1928, 2010. **Address:** Department of English, Texas A&M University, 218A Blocker, College Station, TX 77843-4229, U.S.A. **Online address:** mportales@tamu.edu

PORTE, Barbara Ann. American (born United States), b. 1943. **Genres:** Novellas/Short Stories, Children's Fiction, Young Adult Fiction, Social Commentary, Picture/Board Books, Novels. **Career:** Freeport Memorial Library, department head; Prince George's County Memorial Library System, head of programs; Nassau Library System, Children's Services Division, chief, 1974-86. Writer. **Publications:** Harry's Visit, 1983; Jesse's Ghost and Other Stories, 1983; Harry's Dog, 1984; Harry's Mom, 1985; The Kidnapping of Aunt Elizabeth, 1985; I Only Made Up the Roses, 1987; Harry in Trouble, 1989; The Take-Along Dog, 1989; Ruthann and Her Pig, 1989; Fat Fanny, Beanpole Bertha, and the Boys, 1991; Harry Gets an Uncle, 1991; Taxicab Tales, 1992; A Turkey Drive and Other Tales, 1993; Something Terrible Happened (for young adults): A Novel, 1994; Harry's Birthday, 1994; Black Elephant with a Brown Ear (in Alabama), 1996; Harry's Pony, 1997; Hearsay: Strange Tales from the Middle Kingdom, 1998; He's Sorry, She's Sorry, They're Sorry, Too (short stories for adults): Stories, 1998; If You Ever Get Lost, the Adventures of Julia and Evan, 2000; Beauty and the Serpent, Thirteen Tales of Unnatural Animals, 2001. PICTURE BOOKS: Leave That Cricket Be, Alan Lee, 1993; When Grandma Almost Fell off the Mountain and Other Stories, 1993; When Aunt Lucy Rode a Mule and Other Stories, 1994; Chickens! Chickens!, 1995; Surprise! Surprise! It's Grandfather's Birthday, 1997; Tale of a Tadpole, 1997; Ma Jiang and the Orange Ants, 2000. Contributor of stories to magazines. Works appear in anthologies. **Address:** PO Box 16627, Arlington, VA 22215, U.S.A.

PORTE, Joan. American (born United States), b. 1955. **Genres:** Literary Criticism And History, Essays, Women's Studies And Issues. **Career:** Democratic Representative Robert Roe, legislative assistant, 1976-79; Consumer Action Now, assistant, 1979-81; National Society of Professional Engineers, political director, 1981-84; Associated Builders and Contractors, political director, 1984-86; Blue Horizons Travel Inc. (formerly Travel Partners Inc.), president, 1986-; Card Pal Inc., founder. Writer. **Publications:** Forty-Ish: Lessons for the Ages From a Baby Boomer, 1996; Guide for the Irritated Citizen: Make Your Imprint on Society, 1996. Contributor to books. **Address:** Blue Horizons Travel Inc., 5800 N 23rd St., Arlington, VA 22205-3329, U.S.A. **Online address:** joanstravel@verizon.net

PORTEN, Bezalel. Israeli/American (born United States), b. 1931. **Genres:** Archaeology/Antiquities, Theology/Religion, Translations. **Career:** Jewish Theological Seminary of America, Teachers Institute, instructor, 1958; College of Jewish Studies, lecturer, 1958-60, assistant professor of Bible, 1962-64; Roosevelt University, lecturer in history, 1963-64; University of California-Berkeley, visiting assistant professor, 1964-65; University of California-Davis, assistant professor, 1965-68, associate professor of Hebrew and Bible, 1968-69, Haifa University, teaching fellow, 1968-72, York University, visiting associate professor, 1975-76; University of Pennsylvania, senior fellow, 1979-81; Cambridge University, visiting fellow, 1994; Yale University, visiting professor, 1997-98; Hebrew University, teaching fellow, 1969-72, senior lecturer in Jewish history, 1972-83, associate professor, professor,

1983-99, now professor emeritus. Writer. **Publications:** Archives from Elephantine: The Life of an Ancient Jewish Military Colony, 1968; Yehudim mi-Yev va-Aramim mi-Suvan, 1973; (with J.C. Greenfield) Jews of Elephantine and Arameans of Syene: Fifty Aramaic Texts with Hebrew and English Translations, 1974; (with J.C. Greenfield) The Bisitun Inscription of Darius the Great: Aramaic Version, 1982; (ed. and trans. with A Yardeni) Textbook of Aramaic Documents from Ancient Egypt, 4 vols., 1986-99; (co-author) Dictionary of the North-West Semitic Inscriptions, 1995; (co-author) The Elephantine Papyri in English: Three Millennia of Cross-Cultural Continuity and Change, 1996, 2nd ed., 2011; (with T. Muraoka) A Grammar of Egyptian Aramaic, 1998, 2nd ed., 2003; (with J. Lund) Aramaic Documents from Egypt: A Key-Word-in-Context Concordance, 2002. Contributor of articles to journals. **Address:** Department of Jewish History, Hebrew University, Jerusalem, 91905, Israel. **Online address:** msporten@mscc.huji.ac.il

PORTER, Andrew. American (born United States), b. 1972?. **Genres:** Novellas/Short Stories. **Career:** Trinity University, assistant professor of English and creative writing. Writer. **Publications:** The Theory of Light and Matter, 2008. Contributor to periodicals. **Address:** San Antonio, TX , U.S.A. **Online address:** andrewporter3@mac.com

PORTER, Anna. Canadian/Hungarian (born Hungary) **Genres:** Novels, Mystery/Crime/Suspense, Adult Non-fiction. **Career:** Cassell and Co., junior editor, proofreader; Collier Macmillan, sales representative, editor; McClelland & Stewart, from editorial coordinator to president and publisher of Seal Books imprint, 1969-82; Key Porter Books, co-founder, publisher, chief executive officer, 1982-2005, president; Bantam-Seal Books, president; Maritime Life Insurance Co., director; Argus Corp., director; Doubleday Canada Ltd., chairman; The Order of Canada, officer. **Publications:** (Ed. with M. Harris) Farewell to the 70s: A Canadian Salute to a Confusing Decade, 1979; Hidden Agenda, 1985; Mortal Sins, 1988; The Bookfair Murders, 1996. NONFICTION: The Storyteller: Memory, Secrets, Magic and Lies, 2000; Kasztner's Train, 2007; Ghosts of Europe: Central Europe's Past and Uncertain Future, 2011. **Address:** Key Porter Books, 70 The Esplanade, Bolton, ON M5E 1R2, Canada.

PORTER, Barbara Nevling. American (born United States), b. 1946. **Genres:** Archaeology/Antiquities, Art/Art History, Politics/Government, Theology/Religion. **Career:** Chebeague Marine Enterprises Inc., secretary, treasurer, sales representative and sales officer, 1981-; Bowdoin College, Assyrian Art and Archaeology, consultant to Museum of Art, 1986-90, lecturer in history, 1990; Bates College, Department of Philosophy and Religion, lecturer, 1990-91; Brandeis University, Department of Near Eastern and Judaic Studies, lecturer in Akkadian, 1994-95, visiting lecturer in Akkadian literature, 2003-04; Harvard University, Harvard Semitic Museum, research associate, 1996-; Chebeague Island Parents Association, founder and president; The Casco Bay Assyriological Institute, director, 1996-. Writer. **Publications:** Assyrian Bas-Reliefs at the Bowdoin College Museum of Art, 1989; Images, Power, and Politics: Figurative Aspects of Esarhaddon's Babylonian Policy, 1993; (ed.) One God or Many? Concepts of Divinity in the Ancient World, 2000; Trees, Kings, and Politics: Studies in Assyrian Iconography, 2003; (ed.) Ritual and Politics in Ancient Mesopotamia, 2005; (ed.) What is a God, 2009; (ed. with J. Stackert and D.P. Wright) Gazing on the Deep, 2010. Contributor of articles to books and journals. **Address:** The Casco Bay Assyriological Institute, 27 Soule Rd., Chebeague Island, ME 04017, U.S.A. **Online address:** bnporter@fas.harvard.edu

PORTER, Bernard (John). British (born England), b. 1941. **Genres:** History, Politics/Government. **Career:** Cambridge University, Corpus Christi College, research fellow, 1966-68; University of Hull, lecturer, 1968-78, senior lecturer, 1978-87, reader in history, 1987-92; University of Newcastle, School of Historical Studies, chair, Faculty of Humanities, Arts and Social Sciences, professor of modern history, 1992-2002, emeritus professor, 2002-; Yale University, visiting professor, 1999-2000. Writer. **Publications:** Critics of Empire: British Radical Attitudes to Colonialism in Africa 1896-1914, 1968; The Lion's Share: A Short History of British Imperialism 1850-1970, 1975, 4th ed. as The Lion's Share: A Short History of British Imperialism, 1850-2004, 2004; The Refugee Question in Mid-Victorian Politics, 1979; Britain, Europe and the World 1850-1982: Delusions of Grandeur, 1983; The Origins of the Vigilante State: The London Metropolitan Police Special Branch before the First World War, 1987; Plots and Paranoia: A History of Political Policing in Britain, 1790 to the Present Day, 1989; Britannia's Burden: The Political Evolution of Modern Britain 1851-1990, 1994; The Absent-Minded Imperialists: Empire, Society, and Culture in Britain, 2004; Empire and Superempire: Britain, America and the World, 2006; Battle of the Styles, 2011. **Address:** School of Historical Studies, Faculty of Humanities, Arts & Social Sciences, Newcastle University, Claremont Rd., Newcastle upon Tyne, TW NE1 7RU, England. **Online address:** kajsa@kajsa.karoo.co.uk

PORTER, Burton F. American (born United States), b. 1936. **Genres:** Philosophy, Humanities. **Career:** University of Maryland, assistant professor of philosophy, 1966-69, lecturer in philosophy, European Division, 1968-71; King's College, associate professor of philosophy, 1969-71; Russell Sage College, associate professor, 1971-87, professor of philosophy and chairman of department, 1971-; Drexel University, professor, Department of Humanities and Communications, head, 1987-91; Western New England College, School of Arts and Sciences, dean, 1991-99, professor of philosophy, 1991-. Writer. **Publications:** Deity and Morality, with Regard to the Naturalistic Fallacy, 1968; Philosophy: A Literary and Conceptual Approach, 1974, 3rd ed., 1995; Personal Philosophy: Perspectives on Living, 1976; The Good Life: Alternatives in Ethics, 1980, 3rd ed., 2001; Reasons for Living: A Basic Ethics, 1988; (ed.) Religion & Reason, 1993; Instructor's Manual to Accompany The Voice of Reason: Fundamentals of Critical Thinking, 2002; The Voice of Reason, 2002; Philosophy through Fiction and Film, 2004, 2nd ed., 2009; Head & the Heart: Philosophy in Literature, 2006; What the Tortoise Taught Us: The Story of Philosophy, 2010; Good Life: Options in Ethics, 2010. **Address:** Department of Communications & Humanities, Western New England College, Herman 206D, 1215 Wilbraham Rd., PO Box 5214, Springfield, MA 01119, U.S.A. **Online address:** bporter@wnec.edu

PORTER, Edgar A(dwell). American (born United States), b. 1949. **Genres:** Area Studies, Education. **Career:** Berea College, Students for Appalachia Program, director, 1974-76; Kentucky Prisoners Support Council, executive director, 1976-78; Henan Teachers University, instructor in English, 1979-81; East-West Center, professional associate, vice-president and assistant to the president, 1981-83; Bethel College, director of special programs, 1983-86; Center for Implementing Alternatives to Incarceration, director, 1986-87; University of Hawai'i, director of student academic services and associate professor in Asian studies, 1988-93, director of student academic services, 1988-2002, associate dean, 1993-2002, interim dean, 2002-06; The Freedom Forum Asian Studies Fellowship Program, curator, 1989-93; Japan American Institute of Management Science, adjunct professor, 1996-2003; Ritsumeikan Asia Pacific University, deputy executive director of the institutes, 2006-07, Institute of Language Culture Studies, director, 2006-07, Institute of International Strategic Studies, director, 2006-07, Division of Academic Affairs, dean, 2007-, professor, now professor emeritus. Writer. **Publications:** (Ed.) Journalism from Tiananmen, 1990; Foreign Teachers in China: Old Problems for a New Generation, 1979-1989, 1990; The People's Doctor: George Hatem and China's Revolution, 1997; (ed. with T. Wesley-Smith) China in Oceania: Reshaping the Pacific?, 2010. Contributor to periodicals. **Address:** School of Hawaiian Asian and Pacific Studies, University of Hawaii at Manoa, 315 Moore Hall, 1890 East-West Rd., Honolulu, HI 96822, U.S.A. **Online address:** porter@apu.ac.jp

PORTER, Joe Ashby. American (born United States), b. 1942. **Genres:** Novels, Novellas/Short Stories, Literary Criticism And History. **Career:** University of California, teaching assistant, 1966-67; University of Virginia, assistant professor, 1970-73; University of Baltimore, assistant professor of English, 1976-77; University of Maryland, Shoreline Community College, instructor, assistant professor, 1977-78; Towson State University, assistant professor, 1976-77; Murray State University, assistant professor, 1978-80; Duke University, assistant professor, 1980-88, associate professor, 1988-95, professor, 1995-; South Atlantic Modern Language Association, president, 1992-93; Brown University, writer-in residence; Universite Francois Rabelais, visiting professor. Writer. **Publications:** Eelgrass (novel), 1977; The Drama of Speech Acts: Shakespeare's Lancastrian Tetralogy, 1979; The Kentucky Stories, 1983; (co-ed.) Renaissance Papers 1983-90, vol. VIII, 1984-91; Shakespeare's Mercutio: His History and Drama, 1989; Lithuania: Short Stories, 1990; Critical Essays on Shakespeare's Romeo and Juliet, 1997; Resident Aliens (novel), 2000; Touch Wood: Short Stories, 2002; The Near Future (novel), 2006; All Aboard: Stories, 2008; (ed.) New Variorum Othello, forthcoming. Contributor of articles to magazines and journals. Works appear in anthologies. **Address:** Department of English, Duke University, 304J/K Allen Bldg., PO Box 90015, Durham, NC 27708, U.S.A. **Online address:** japorter@duke.edu

PORTER, Julia C. *See* **PORTER, Michael C.**

PORTER, Laurin. American (born United States), b. 1945. **Genres:** Literary Criticism And History. **Career:** St. Mary's University, assistant professor of English, 1976-78; University of Texas-Dallas, lecturer, 1979-82, visiting assistant professor of English, 1984-86; University of Texas-Arlington, visiting associate professor, 1986-88, adjunct assistant professor, 1988-90, assistant professor, 1990-94, associate professor, 1994-2002, professor of English, 2002-. Writer and literary critic. **Publications:** The Banished Prince: Time, Memory and Ritual in the Late Plays of Eugene O'Neill, 1988; Orphans' Home: The Voice and Vision of Horton Foote, 2003. Contributor of articles to books and periodicals. **Address:** Department of English, University of Texas, 203 Carlisle Hall, PO Box 19035, Arlington, TX 76019-0035, U.S.A. **Online address:** lporter@uta.edu

PORTER, Linda. British (born England), b. 1947?. **Genres:** Biography, History. **Career:** British Telecommunications, international public relations senior advisor. Writer, educator and historian. **Publications:** Mary Tudor: The First Queen, 2007 in US as The First Queen of England: The Myth of Bloody Mary, 2008; Katherine the Queen: The Remarkable Life of Katherine Parr, 2010. Contributor to magazines. **Address:** Andrew Lownie Literary Agency Ltd., 36 Great Smith St., London, GL SW1P 3BU, England. **Online address:** mailmaster@lindaporter.net

PORTER, Michael C. (Julia C. Porter). American (born United States), b. 1970?. **Genres:** Novels. **Career:** NetIQ (software company), technical Writer. **Publications:** Gunning for the Buddha (short stories), 2005; (as J.C. Porter) Heart's Revenge, 2006; The Wannoshay Cycle, 2008; A Gathering of Doorways, 2008. **Address:** Wake Forest, NC , U.S.A. **Online address:** mjasper@gmail.com

PORTER, Michael E(ugene). American (born United States), b. 1947. **Genres:** Business/Trade/Industry. **Career:** Harvard University, School of Business, assistant professor, 1973-77, associate professor, 1977-82, professor, 1982-90, C. Roland Christensen professor of business administration, 1990-, Bishop William Lawrence university professor; Alpine Inc., board director, 1983-85; Anatar Investments, board director, 1983-85; Council on Competitiveness, board director, 1983-85; Hyatt Legal Plans, board director, 1983-85; Lotus Development Corp., board director, 1983-85; Alpha-Beta Technologies, board director, 1983-85; Initiative for a Competitive Inner City, founder, 1994; Review of Economics and Statistics, associate editor. **Publications:** Interbrand Choice, Strategy and Bilateral Market Power, 1976; (co-author) Studies in Canadian Industrial Organization, 1978; Competitive Strategy: Techniques for Analyzing Industries and Competitors, 1980; (with R.E. Caves, A.M. Spence and J.T. Scott) Competition in the Open Economy, 1980; Cases in Competitive Strategy, 1983; Competitive Advantage: Creating and Sustaining Superior Performance, 1985; (ed.) Competition in Global Industries, 1986; The Competitive Advantage of Nations, 1990; Canada at the Crossroads, 1991; (ed. with C.A. Montgomery) Strategy: Seeking and Securing Competitive Advantage, 1991; (with ö. Sölvell and I. Zander) Advantage Sweden, 1991, 2nd ed., 1993; Capitol Choices, 1992; Lifting All Boats, 1995; On Competition, 1998; (H. Takeuchi and M. Sakakibara) Can Japan Compete?, 2000; (with D.V. Opstal) U.S. Competitiveness 2001: Strengths, Vulnerabilities and Long-Term Policies, 2001; (with C.H.M. Ketels) U.K. Competitiveness: Moving to the Next Stage, 2003; (with E.O. Teisberg) Redefining Health Care: Creating Value-Based Competition On Results, 2006. **Address:** Graduate School of Business, Harvard University, Soldiers Field, Boston, MA 02163, U.S.A. **Online address:** mporter@hbs.edu

PORTER, Roger B. (Roger Blaine Porter). American (born United States), b. 1946. **Genres:** Politics/Government, Economics. **Career:** White House, fellow, 1974-75, Economic Policy Board, executive secretary, 1974-77, special assistant to the president, 1981-82, deputy assistant to the president and director of policy development, 1981-85, Secretary of the Treasury, counselor, 1981-85; assistant to the President for Economic and Domestic Policy, 1989-93; Harvard University, John F. Kennedy School of Government, assistant professor, 1977-, faculty, 1978, associate professor of public policy, through 1981, professor of business and government, 1985-89, IBM professor of business and government, 1993-. Writer. **Publications:** Presidential Decision Making: The Economic Policy Board, 1980; The U.S.-U.S.S.R. Grain Agreement, 1984; (co-ed.) Efficiency, Equity and Legitimacy: The Multilateral Trading System at the Millennium, 2001; (ed. with R.R. Glauber and T.J. Healey) New Directions in Financial Services Regulation, 2011. **Address:** John F. Kennedy School of Government, Harvard University, Belfer-414, 79 John F. Kennedy St., PO Box 82, Cambridge, MA 02138-5801, U.S.A. **Online address:** roger_porter@harvard.edu

PORTER, Roger Blaine. *See* **PORTER, Roger B.**

PORTER, Sheena. British (born England), b. 1935. **Genres:** Children's Fiction, History, Psychiatry, Novels. **Career:** Leicester City Library, library assistant, 1954-57; Nottinghamshire County Library, regional children's librarian, 1957-60; Oxford University Press, editorial assistant, 1960-61; Shropshire County Library, regional children's librarian, 1961-62. **Publications:** The Bronze Chrysanthemum, 1961; Hills and Hollows, 1962; Jacob's Ladder, 1963; Nordy Bank, 1964; The Knockers, 1965; Deerfold, 1966; The Scapegoat, 1968; The Valley of Carreg-wen, 1971; The Hospital, 1973. **Address:** 7 St. Mary Mews, Lower Corve St., Ludlow, SA SY8 1DZ, England.

PORTER, Sue. British (born England), b. 1951. **Genres:** Children's Fiction, Children's Non-fiction, Theatre, Illustrations, Music, Literary Criticism And History. **Career:** Writer and illustrator. **Publications:** Baa, Baa, Black Sheep, 1982; One Potato, 1989; Action Packed: 30 Ideas for Drama, 1990; Play It Again: Suggestions for Drama, 1990; Little Wolf and the Giant, 1990; Chloe's Eggs, 1994; Moose Music, 1994; My Little Rabbit Tale, 1994; Sweet Dreams: A Lift-the-Flap Bedtime Story, 1996; In Bed before Dark, 1997; Parsnip: A Lift-the-Flap Book, 1997; Parsnip and the Runaway Tractor: A Lift-the-Flap Book, 1999; Parsnip and the Pink Blanket, 2000; It's Me, Parsnip, 2008; Parsnip, 2008. Illustrator of books by others. **Address:** Eunice McMullen Children's Literary Agent Ltd., 38 Clewer Hill Rd., Windsor, BR SL4 4BW, England.

PORTER, Tracey. American (born United States) **Genres:** Children's Fiction, Young Adult Fiction, Novels. **Career:** Crossroads School for Arts and Sciences, middle-school teacher. Writer. **Publications:** YOUNG ADULT NOVELS: Treasures in the Dust, 1997; A Dance of Sisters, 2002; Billy Creekmore, 2007; Lark, 2011. **Address:** HarperCollins Publishers Ltd., 77-85 Fulham Palace Rd., Hammersmith, GL W6 8JB, England.

PORTIS, Charles (McColl). American (born United States), b. 1933. **Genres:** Westerns/Adventure, Novels, Literary Criticism And History. **Career:** Commercial Appeal, reporter, 1958; Arkansas Gazette, reporter, 1959-60; New York Herald-Tribune, reporter and London correspondent, 1960-64; freelance writer, 1964-. **Publications:** Norwood, 1966, 3rd ed., 1999; True Grit: A Novel, 1968, 4th ed., 2003; The Dog of the South, 1979, 3rd ed., 1999; Masters of Atlantis: A Novel, 1985, 3rd ed., 2000; Gringos: A Novel, 1991, 2nd ed., 2000. Contributor to periodicals. **Address:** c/o Lynn Nesbit, Janklow and Nesbit Associates, 598 Madison Ave., New York, NY 10022, U.S.A.

PÖRTNER, Hans O. German (born Germany), b. 1955. **Genres:** Marine Sciences/Oceanography, Zoology, Sciences, Animals/Pets. **Career:** Alfred Wegener Institute fur Polar und Meeresforschung, professor, 1994-. Writer. **Publications:** (With R.K. O'Dor and D. Macmillan) Physiology of Cephalopod Molluscs, 1994; (ed. with R. Playle) Cold Ocean Physiology, 1998. **Address:** Alfred-Wegener-Inst fur Polar-und Meeresforschung, Bldg. E-2515, Am Handelshafen 12, Bremerhaven, D-27570, Germany. **Online address:** hans.poertner@awi.de

POSAMENTIER, Alfred S. American (born United States), b. 1942. **Genres:** Mathematics/Statistics, Education. **Career:** City College of the City University of New York, professor emeritus of mathematics education, 1970-2010, Science Lectures Program, coordinator, 1981-90, director of international exchange programs, 1983-2009, director for extension center, 1984-2009, School of Education, associate dean, 1986-95, dean, 1999-2009; Select Program in Science and Engineering, director, 1978-2003; City College, Northeast Resource Center for Science and Engineering, coordinator, 1981-89, Center for Science and Mathematics Education, director, 1986-90, Staff Development Program in Mathematics, director, 1983-90; Mathematics Teacher Retraining Program, director, 1984-96; Technical University of Vienna, University of Vienna, visiting professor; Humboldt University, visiting professor; University of Warsaw, visiting professor; Technical University of Berlin, visiting professor; Mercy College, School of Education, dean, 2010-. Educator and writer. **Publications:** A Study Guide for the Scholastic Aptitude Test Mathematics Section, 1968, 3rd ed., 2003; (with J.H. Banks and R.L. Bannister) Geometry: Its Elements and Structure, 1972, 2nd ed., 1977; (with J. Stepelman) Teaching Secondary School Mathematics: Techniques and Enrichment Units, 1981, 8th ed., 2010; (with G.H. Elgarten and S.E. Moresh) Using Computers in Mathematics, 1983, 2nd ed., 1986; (with G.H. Elgarten) Using Computers: Programming and Problem Solving, 1984; Excursions in Advanced Euclidean Geometry, 1984; (with W. Wernick) Advanced Geometric Constructions, 1988; (with C.T. Salkind) Challenging Problems in Geometry, 1988; Arbeitsmaterialien: Mathematik, 1994; The Art of Problem Solving: A Resource for the Mathematics Teacher, 1996; (with C.T. Salkind) Challenging Problems in Algebra, 1996; Students! Get Ready for the Mathematics for SAT I: Problem-Solving Strategies and Practice Tests, 1996; (with I. Lewisch) Wörterbuch für den Mathematik-Unterricht, 1996; (with S. Krulik) Teachers! Prepare Your Students for the Mathematics for SAT I: Methods and Problem-Solving Strategies, 1996; Students, Get Ready for the Mathematics SAT I, 1996; (with H. Hartman and C. Kaiser) Tips for the Mathematics Teacher: Research-Based Strategies to Help Students Learn, 1998; (with S. Krulik) Problem Solving Strategies for Efficient and Elegant Solutions, 1998; Making Geometry Come Alive, 2000; Making Pre-Algebra Come Alive, 2000; Making Algebra Come Alive, 2000; (with H.A. Hauptman) 101 Great Ideas for Introducing Key Concepts in Mathematics, 2001, 2nd ed. as 101+ Great Ideas for Introducing Key Concepts in Mathematics, 2006; Advanced Euclidean Geometry: Excursions for Secondary Teachers and Students, 2002; Math Wonders to Inspire Teachers and Students, 2002; Math Charmers: Tantalizing Tidbits for the Mind, 2003; Pi: A Biography of the World's Most Mysterious Number, 2004; (with D. Jaye) What Successful Math Teachers Do, Grades 6-12: 79 Research-based Strategies for the Standards-based Classroom, 2006; (with E.S. Wall) What Successful Math Teachers Do, Grades PreK-5: 47 Research-based Strategies for the Standards-based Classroom, 2007; (with D. Jaye and S. Krulik) Exemplary Practices for Secondary Math Teachers, 2007; (with I. Lehmann) Fabulous Fibonacci Numbers, 2007; (with S. Krulik) Problem-solving Strategies for Efficient and Elegant Solutions, Grades 6-12: A Resource for the Mathematics Teacher, 2008; (with S. Krulik) Problem Solving in Mathematics, Ggrades 3-6: Powerful Strategies to Deepen Understanding, 2009; (with I. Lehmann) Mathematical Amazements and Surprises: Fascinating Figures and Noteworthy Numbers, 2009; Progress in Mathematics, 6 vols., The Pythagorean Theorem, Its Power and Beauty, 2010; (with I. Lehmann) The Glorious Golden Ratio, 2011; The Art of Motivating Students for Mathematics Instruction, 2011. **Address:** School of Education, Mercy College, 555 Broadway, Dobbs Ferry, NY 10522, U.S.A. **Online address:** asp2@juno.com

POSEN, Barry R. American (born United States), b. 1952. **Genres:** Military/Defense/Arms Control, Politics/Government, International Relations/Current Affairs. **Career:** Harvard University, Center for Science and International Affairs, graduate student fellow, 1979-81, post-doctoral fellow, 1981-82; RAND Corp., consultant, 1980-81, 1984; OSD/PAE, analyst for Europe Division, 1982-83; Princeton University, Woodrow Wilson School, assistant professor of political science, 1984-87; Smithsonian Institution, Woodrow Wilson Center, fellow, 1986; Massachusetts Institute of Technology, associate professor, 1987-91, Ford international professor of political science, 1991-, Security Studies Program, director, 2006, Seminar XXI Program, co-director; Christian Science Monitor, military expert consultant, 1991. Writer. **Publications:** (With Y.B. Horin) Israel's Strategic Doctrine, 1981; The Sources of Military Doctrine: France, Britain and Germany between the World Wars, 1984; Inadvertent Escalation: Conventional War and Nuclear Risks, 1991; A Nuclear-Armed Iran: A Difficult but Not Impossible Policy Problem, 2006. Works appear in anthologies. Contributor of articles to periodicals. **Address:** Department of Political Science, Massachusetts Institute of Technology, E40-463, 77 Massachusetts Ave., Cambridge, MA 02139, U.S.A. **Online address:** posen@mit.edu

POSKITT, Kjartan. British (born England), b. 1956?. **Genres:** Mystery/Crime/Suspense, Mathematics/Statistics, Plays/Screenplays. **Career:** British Broadcasting Corp., Swap Shop and Saturday Superstore, co-writer. Author, musician, composer, playwright and consultant to television shows. **Publications:** The Mystery of the Magic Toy, 1989; (with S. Appleby) The 99 Don'ts: A Guide to Unrecommendable Practices, 1992; Decode the Deadliest Joke in the Universe, 1993; (with S. Appleby) The 122 Turn-Offs: A Catalogue of Unnerving Encounters, 1993; Find the Phantom of Ghastly Castle, 1994; (with S. Appleby) The 1113 at K-UPS: A Nightmare of Inadvertent Calamities, 1995; Attack of the Killer Puzzles, 1996; Murderous Maths, 1997; The Gobsmacking Galaxy, 1997; More Murderous Maths, 1998; Titus O'Skinty's Gruesome Game Show, 1998; Practical Jokes, 1998; Secret Codes, 1999; The Essential Arithmetricks: How to Plus, Minus, Multiply and Divide, 1999; Isaac Newton and His Apple, 1999; Desperate Measures, 2000; The Mean and Vulgar Bits: Fractions and Averages, 2000; Do You Feel Lucky? The Secrets of Probability, 2001; Maths: Exam Success without the Stress, 2001; Warp Maze, 2002; Professor Fiendish's Book of Diabolical Brainbenders, 2002; Numbers: The Key to the Universe, 2002; Vicious Circles and Other Savage Shapes, 2002; The Phantom X, 2003; The Fiendish Angletron, 2004; The Magic of Pants: A Conjuror's Compendium of Underpants Tricks to Delight All Ages, 2004; A Brief History of Pants: The Rudiments of Pantology, 2005; The Perfect Sausage, 2005; Kakuro and Other Fun Number Puzzles, 2006; Sudoku: 100 Fun Number Puzzles, 2006; Urgum the Axeman, 2006; Urgum and the Seat of Flames, 2007; Urgum and the Goo Goo Bah!, 2008; Everyday Math Tricks for Grown-ups, 2011. PLAYS: Sammy's Magic Garden: A Ghost Musical, 1990; Henry the Tudor Dude: A Musical Play, 1995; The Rumpelstiltskin Racket: A Musical Play, 1996; Fawkes'the Quiet Guy: A Musical, 1998; Nell's Belles: The Swinging Sixteen-Sixties Show: A Musical, 2002. Contributor to magazines. **Address:** Reader Digest, 750 3rd Ave., 4th Fl., New York, NY 10017, U.S.A. **Online address:** kjweb@kjartan.co.uk

POSNER, Daniel N. American (born United States) **Genres:** Politics/Government, Social Sciences. **Career:** Institute for the Study of World Politics, dissertation fellow, 1992-93; Social Science Research Council, international predissertation fellow, 1993-94; University of California, assistant professor of political science, 1998-2005, Cattell fellow, 2000-01, Working Group in African Political Economy (WGAPE), co-organizer, 2002-, associate professor of political science, 2005-10, Center for Economic History, faculty associate, 2006-, Global Fellows Program, director, 2007-08, professor of political science, 2010-; Stanford University, Hoover Institution, national fellow, 2001-02, Center for Advanced Study in the Behavioral Sciences, fellow, 2010-11; California Institute of Technology, visiting associate in political science, 2005-07. Writer. **Publications:** Institutions and Ethnic Politics in Africa, 2005. Contributor to journals and periodicals. **Address:** Department of Political Science, University of California, 4289 Bunche Hall, PO Box 951472, Los Angeles, CA 90095-1472, U.S.A. **Online address:** dposner@polisci.ucla.edu

POSNER, Eric A. American (born United States), b. 1965. **Genres:** Law, Economics. **Career:** Office of Legal Counsel, Department of Justice, attorney advisor, 1992-93; University of Pennsylvania, assistant professor of law, 1993-98; University of Chicago Law School, professor of law, 1998-2003, Kirkland and Ellis professor of law, 2003-; The Journal of Legal Studies, editor, 1998-. Writer. **Publications:** (Ed.) Chicago Lectures in Law and Economics, 2000; Law and Social Norms, 2000; Law and Economics, 2001; (ed. with M.D. Adler) Cost-Benefit Analysis: Legal, Philosophical and Economic Perspectives, 2001; (with J.L. Goldsmith) The Limits of International Law, 2005; (with M.D. Adler) New Foundations of Cost-benefit Analysis, 2006; (ed.) Social Norms, Nonlegal Sanctions and the Law, 2007; (with A. Vermeule) Terror in the Balance: Security, Liberty and the Courts, 2007; Perils of Global Legalism, 2009; (with D. Weisbach) Climate Change Justice, 2010; Law and Happiness, 2010; (ed.) Economics of Public International Law, 2010 (with A. Vermeule) Executive Unbound: After the Madisonian Republic, 2011. **Address:** University of Chicago Law School, Rm. 420, 1111 E 60th St., Chicago, IL 60637, U.S.A. **Online address:** eposner@uchicago.edu

POSNER, Gerald L. American (born United States), b. 1954. **Genres:** Adult Non-fiction, Biography, Criminology/True Crime, Social Sciences, Documentaries/Reportage. **Career:** Cravath, Swaine and Moore (law firm), litigation attorney, 1978-80; Posner and Ferrara (law firm), partner, 1980-86, counsel, 1986-. Writer. **Publications:** (With J. Ware) Mengele: The Complete Story, 1986; Warlords of Crime: Chinese Secret Societies-The New Mafia, 1988; The Bio-Assassins (novel), 1989; Hitler's Children: Sons and Daughters of Leaders of the Third Reich Talk about Themselves and Their Fathers, 1991; Case Closed: Lee Harvey Oswald and the Assassination of JFK, 1993; Citizen Perot: His Life and Times, 1996; Killing the Dream: James Earl Ray and the Assassination of Martin Luther King, Jr., 1998; Motown: Music, Money, Sex, and Power, 2002; Why America Slept: The Failure to Prevent 9/11, 2003; Secrets of the Kingdom: The Inside Story of the Saudi-U.S. Connection, 2005; Miami Babylon: A Tale of Crime, Wealth and Power, 2009. Contributor to periodicals. **Address:** Area 51 L.L.C., 1521 Alton Rd., Ste. 442, Miami Beach, FL 33139, U.S.A. **Online address:** feedback@posner.com

POSNER, Rebecca. British (born England), b. 1929. **Genres:** Language/Linguistics, Romance/Historical, Humanities. **Career:** Girton College, fellow, 1960-63; University of Ghana, professor of romance languages, 1963-65; York University, reader in language, 1965-78; Columbia University, visiting professor of romance philology, 1971-72; Oxford University, St. Hugh's College, professor of the romance languages and fellow, 1978-96, emeritus professor and honorary fellow, 1996-; Princeton University, visiting senior fellow, 1983; Philological Society, president, 1996-2000. Writer. **Publications:** Consonantal Dissimilation in the Romance Languages, 1961; The Romance Languages: A Linguistic Introduction, 1966; (with J. Orr and I. Iordan) Introduction to Romance Linguistics: Its Schools and Scholars, 1970; (co-ed.) Trends in Romance Linguistics and Philology, 1980, vol. V, 1991; Variation and Change in French: Essays Presented to Rebecca Posner on the Occasion of Her Sixtieth Birthday, 1990; The Romance Languages: Language Survey, 1996; Linguistic Change in French, 1997; Las Lenguas Romances, 1997. **Address:** St Hugh's College, Oxford University, St Margaret's Rd., Oxford, OX OX2 6LE, England. **Online address:** rebecca.posner@st-hughs.oxford.ac.uk

POSNER, Richard. Also writes as Iris Foster, Erica Mitchell, Paul Todd, Alayna Richards, Dayle Courtney. American (born United States), b. 1944. **Genres:** Novels, Mystery/Crime/Suspense, Romance/Historical, Science Fiction/Fantasy, Children's Fiction, Horror. **Career:** Scott Meredith Literary Agency Inc., editor, 1967-72; full-time writer, 1972-; teacher, 1978; Sachem High School, English teacher; Adelphi University, Queensborough Community College, instructor of composition; Suffolk Community College, instructor of composition, assistant adjunct professor. **Publications:** (With J. Craig) The New York Crime Book, 1972; The Mafia Man, 1973; The Seven-Ups, 1973; The Trigger Man, 1974; Welcome, Sinner, 1974; The Image and the Flesh, 1975; Lucas Tanner: A Question of Guilt, 1975; Lucas Tanner: A Matter of Love, 1975; Lucas Tanner: For Her to Decide, 1975; The Lovers, 1978; The Impassioned, 1980; Infidelities, 1982; (with M. Castoire) The Gold Shield, 1982; Sweet Pain, 1987; Sparrow's Flight, 1988; Goodnight, Cinderella, 1989; Someone to Die For, 1993; Sweet Sixteen and Never Been Killed, 1993; Can You Hear Me Scream?, 1994; Terror Runs Deep, 1995. AS DAYLE COURTNEY: Operation Doomsday, 1981; Flight to Terror, 1981; Escape from Eden, 1981; The Ivy Plot, 1981; The Knife with Eyes, 1981; Omen of the Flying Light, 1981; The Foxworth Hunt, 1982; Tower of Flames, 1982; Jaws of Terror, 1982; Three-Ring Inferno, 1982; Mysterious Strangers, 1982; The Foxworth Hunt, 1982; The Hidden Cave, 1982; The House that Ate People, 1983; The Trail of Bigfoot, 1983; Shadow of Fear, 1983; The Sinister Circle, 1983; Secret of Pirates' Cave, 1984; The Great UFO Chase, 1984; The Olympic Plot, 1984; Jaws of Terror, 1991; Public Intellectuals: A Study of Decline, 2002. AS IRIS FOSTER: The Moorwood Legacy, 1972; Deadly Sea, Deadly Sand, 1972; Nightshade, 1973; The Sabath Quest, 1973; The Crimson Moon, 1973. AS ERICA MITCHELL: Jade Moon, 1984; Bright Desire, 1985. AS BEATRICE MURRAY: The Dark Sonata, 1971. AS ALAYNA RICHARDS: Tycoon, 1983. AS PAUL TODD: Blood All Over, 1975. AS DICK WINE: Allegro with Passion, 1973. **Address:** Henry Morrison Inc., PO Box 235, Bedford Hills, NY 10507, U.S.A. **Online address:** rpoz@yahoo.com

POSNER, Richard A. American (born United States), b. 1939. **Genres:** Law, Economics, Philosophy, Sex, Business/Trade/Industry, Reference. **Career:** Supreme Court of the United States, law clerk, 1962-63; Federal Trade Commission, assistant, 1963-65; Solicitor General's Office, assistant, 1965-67; President's Task Force on Communications Policy, general counsel, 1967-68; Stanford University, associate professor of law, 1968-69; University of Chicago, Law School, professor of law, 1969-78, Lee and Brena Freeman professor of law, 1978-81, senior lecturer, 1981-; National Bureau of Economic Research, research associate, 1971-81; Lexecon Inc. (economic and legal consultants), president, 1977-81; United States Court of Appeals for the Seventh Circuit, judge, 1981-, chief judge, 1993-2000. Writer. **Publications:** Cable Television: The Problem of Local Monopoly, 1970; Economic Analysis of Law, 1972, 8th ed., 2011; Regulation of Advertising by the FTC, 1973; Antitrust Cases, Economic Notes, and Other Materials, 1974, (with F.H. Easterbrook) 2nd ed., 1981; (with G. Casper) A Study of the Supreme Court's Caseload, 1974; The Social Costs of Monopoly and Regulation, 1975; Antitrust Law: An Economic Perspective, 1976, 2nd ed., 2002; The Robinson-Patman Act: Federal Regulation of Differences, 1976; (with G. Casper) The Workload of the Supreme Court, 1976; (with J.H. Langbein) Market Funds and Trust-Investment Law, II, 1977; (with A.T. Kronman) The Economics of Contract Law, 1979; (ed. with K.E. Scott) Economics of Corporation Law and Securities Regulation, 1980; Cases and Economic Notes on Antitrust, 2nd ed., 1981; The Economics of Justice, 1981, (with F.H. Easterbrook) 1982-83 Supplement to Antitrust Cases, Economic Notes, and Other Materials, 1982; Tort Law: Cases and Economic Analysis, 1982; The Federal Courts: Crisis and Reform, 1985; (with W.M. Landes) The Economic Structure of Tort Law, 1987; Law and Literature: A Misunderstood Relation, 1988, 3rd ed., 2009; The Problems of Jurisprudence, 1990; Cardozo: A Study in Reputation, 1990; A Theory of Sexuality, 1992; Sex and Reason, 1992; (ed. and intro.) The Essential Holmes: Selections from the Letters, Speeches, Judicial Opinions, and Other Writings of Oliver Wendell Holmes, 1992; (with T.J. Philipson) Private Choices and Public Health: The Aids Epidemic in an Economic Perspective, 1993; Economics, Time, and Age, 25th Geary Lecture, 1994; Aging and Old Age, 1995; Overcoming Law, 1995; The Federal Courts: Challenge and Reform, 1996; Law and Legal Theory in England and America, 1996; (with K. Silbaugh) A Guide to America's Sex Laws, 1996; (ed. with F. Parisi) Law and Economics, 1997; An Affair of State: The Investigation, Impeachment, and Trial of President Clinton, 1999; Natural Monopoly and Its Regulation, 1999; The Problematics of Moral and Legal Theory, 1999; The Economic Structure of the Law, 2000; Frontiers of Legal Theory, 2001; Breaking the Deadlock, 2001; Public Intellectuals: A Study of Decline, 2001; (ed. with F. Parisi) Economic Foundations of Private Law, 2002; Law, Pragmatism, and Democracy, 2003; (with W.M. Landes) Economic Structure of Intellectual Property Law, 2003; Catastrophe: Risk and Response, 2004; (with W.M. Landes) Political Economy of Intellectual Property Law, 2004; Remaking Domestic Intelligence, 2005; Preventing Surprise Attacks: Intelligence Reform in the Wake of 9/11, 2005; Not a Suicide Pact: The Constitution in a Time of National Emergency, 2006; Uncertain Shield: The U.S. Intelligence System in the Throes of Reform, 2006; The Little Book of Plagiarism, 2007; Countering Terrorism: Blurred Focus, Halting Steps, 2007; How Judges Think, 2008; Failure of Capitalism: The Crisis of '08 and the Descent into Depression, 2009; (with G.S. Becker) Uncommon Sense: Economic Insights, from Marriage to Terrorism, 2009; (foreword) Quotable Judge Posner: Selections from Twenty-five Years of Judicial Opinions, 2010; The Crisis of Capitalist Democracy, 2010. Contributor to journals. **Address:** Law School, University of Chicago, Rm. 611, 1111 E 60th St., Chicago, IL 60637-2776, U.S.A. **Online address:** rposner@law.uchicago.edu

POSPÍŠIL, Leopold Jaroslav. American/Czech (born Czech Republic), b. 1923. **Genres:** Anthropology/Ethnology, Economics, Law, Social Sciences, Essays. **Career:** Yale University, Division of Anthropology, Peabody Museum, research assistant, 1953-56, instructor in anthropology, 1956-57, assistant curator, 1956-60, assistant professor, 1957-60, associate professor and associate curator, 1960-65, professor of anthropology, curator and director, University Publishers in Anthropology, editor, 1965-93, professor and curator emeritus of anthropology and law, 1993-. **Publications:** Law Among the Kapauku of Netherlands New Guinea, 1956; Kapauku Papuans and their Law, 1958; Kapauku Papuan Economy, 1963; The Kapauku Papuans of West New Guinea, 1963, 2nd ed., 1978; (contrib.) Explorations in Cultural Anthropology: Essays in Honor of George Peter Murdock, 1964; (contrib.) Introduction to Cultural Anthropology: Essays in the Scope and Methods of the Science of Man, 1968; Anthropology of Law: A Comparative Theory, 1971; The Ethnology of Law, 1972, 2nd ed., 1978; Anthropologie des Rechts, 1982; Obernberg: A Quantitative Analysis of a Tirolean Peasant Economy, 1995; Sociocultural Anthropology, 2004. **Address:** Department of Anthropology, Yale University, Rm. 206, 51 Hillhouse Ave., PO Box 208277, New Haven, CT 06520-8277, U.S.A. **Online address:** leopold.pospisil@yale.edu

POST, Jennifer C. (Jennifer Post Quinn). American (born United States) **Genres:** Music, Anthropology/Ethnology, Area Studies. **Career:** Musical Instrument Museum, associate curator of musical instruments, curator of musical instruments; Middlebury College, Helen Hartness Flanders Ballad Collection, curator, Ethnomusicology Archives, curator, assistant professor of music. Writer. **Publications:** (Comp. as Jennifer Post Quinn) An Index to the Field Recordings in the Flanders Ballad Collection at Middlebury College, Middlebury, Vermont, 1983; Music in Rural New England Family and Community Life, 1870-1940, 2004; Ethnomusicology: A Guide to Research, 2004, 2nd ed. as Ethnomusicology: A Research and Information Guide, 2011; (ed.) Ethnomusicology: A Contemporary Reader, 2006. **Address:** Musical Instrument Museum, 4725 E Mayo Blvd., Phoenix, AZ 85050, U.S.A. **Online address:** post.jennifer@gmail.com

POST, Robert C(harles). American (born United States), b. 1937. **Genres:** History, Technology, Biography. **Career:** Motor Vehicle Division, Los Angeles County, Department of Beaches, supervisor, 1958-68; Manhattan Beach, maitre'd and bartender, 1961-65; Pacific Historical Review, editorial assistant, 1966-71; Los Angeles Metropolitan History Project, principal investigator, 1969-71; National Museum of History and Technology, Division of Electricity, research fellow, 1971-72, Division of Engineering, museum specialist, 1973-74, Office of the director, historian, 1974-77, Exhibits Task Force, supervising historian, 1977-79, Division of Transportation, curator, Department of History of science and technology, vice chair, 1980-82; Smithsonian Exposition Books, editor, 1979-80; National Museum of American History, editor-in-chief of technology and culture, 1981-95, curator-at-large, 1982-95, associate director of the Lemelson Center for Invention and Innovation, 1995-96; University of Maryland, professor of history, 1996-2001. **Publications:** Physics, Patents, and Politics: A Biography of Charles Grafton Page, 1976; American Maritime Enterprise, 1978; The Tancook Whalers: Origins, Rediscovery, and Revival, 1985; Street Railways and the Growth of Los Angeles: Horse, Cable, Electric Lines, 1989; High Performance: The Culture and Technology of Drag Racing, 1950-2000, 1994, rev. ed., 2001; Technology, Transport, and Travel in American History, 2003; The SAE Story: One Hundred Years of Mobility, 2005; Urban Mass Transit: The Life Story of a Technology, 2007. EDITOR: 1876: A Centennial Exhibition, 1976; (with A. Doster and J. Goodwin) The American Land, 1979; (and contrib.) Every Four Years, 1980, rev. ed., 1984; (with O. Mayr) Yankee Enterprise: Rise of the American System of Manufactures, 1981, rev. ed., 1995; (and contrib.) American Enterprise, 1984; (with S.H. Cutcliffe) In Context: History and the History of Technology: Essays in Honor of Melvin Kranzberg, 1989; (and contrib.) The Spirit of American Invention, 1989; (with N.L. Rosenblum) Civil Society and Government, 2003; Urban Mass Transit: The Life Story of a Technology, 2007, 2nd ed., 2009. Contributor to books and periodicals. **Address:** 544 S Aurora St., Easton, MD 21601, U.S.A. **Online address:** rpost@intercom.net

POSTER, Jem. (Jem Paul Poster). Welsh (born Wales), b. 1949. **Genres:** Novels, Poetry. **Career:** English Heritage, archaeologist; Cambridge University, Institute of Continuing Education, administrator; Oxford University, Department for Continuing Education, administrator and professor, through 2003; Aberystwyth University, professor and director of creative writing, 2003-. Poet and novelist. **Publications:** (ed.) Selected Poetry, 1986; The Thirties Poets, 1993; By Some Other Route, 1994; Brought to Light, 2001; Rifling Paradise, 2006; Courting Shadows (novel), 2008. Contributor to periodicals. **Address:** Department of English & Creative Writing, Aberystwyth University, Hugh Owen Bldg., Aberystwyth, SY23 3DY, Wales. **Online address:** ppp@aber.ac.uk

POSTER, Jem Paul. *See* **POSTER, Jem.**

POSTER, Mark. American (born United States), b. 1941. **Genres:** Intellectual History, Philosophy. **Career:** University of California, assistant professor, 1969-74, associate professor of European history of ideas, 1974-78, professor of history, 1978-, now professor emeritus of film and media studies and history, Department of Information and Computer Science, faculty. Writer. **Publications:** The Utopian Thought of Restif de la Bretonne, 1971; (ed. and intro.) Harmonian Man: Selected Writings of Charles Fourier, 1971; Existential Marxism in Postwar France: From Sartre to Althusser, 1975; (trans.) Jean Baudrillard, The Mirror of Production, 1975; Critical Theory of the Family, 1978; Sartre's Marxism, 1979; Foucault, Marxism, and History: Mode of Production Versus Mode of Information, 1984; (ed. and intro.) Selected Writings, 1988, 2nd ed., 2001; Critical Theory and Poststructuralism: In Search of a Context, 1989; The Mode of Information: Poststructuralism and Social Context, 1990; (ed. with R. Kling and S. Olin) Postsuburban California: The Transformation of Orange County Since World War II, 1991; (ed.) Politics, Theory, and Contemporary Culture, 1993; The Second Media Age, 1995; Cultural History and Postmodernity: Disciplinary Readings and Challenges, 1997; What's the Matter With the Internet?, 2001; Information Please: Culture and Politics in the Age of Digital Machines, 2006; (ed. with D. Savat) Deleuze and New Technology, 2009; (intro.) Does Writing Have a Future?, 2011. **Address:** Department of History, University of California, 230 Murray Krieger Hall, Irvine, CA 92697-3275, U.S.A. **Online address:** poster@uci.edu

POSTGATE, John (Raymond). British (born England), b. 1922. **Genres:** Biology, Medicine/Health, Sciences, Biography. **Career:** Chemical Research Laboratory, Department of Scientific and Industrial Research, senior research fellow, 1948-50, senior scientific officer, 1950-52, principal scientific officer, 1952-59; Microbiological Research Establishment, principal scientific officer, 1959-61, senior principal scientific officer, 1961-63; University of Illinois, visiting professor, 1962-63; Agricultural and Food Research Council, Unit of Nitrogen Fixation, assistant director, 1963-80, deputy chief scientific officer, 1973-87, director, 1980-87; University of Sussex, professor of microbiology, 1965-87, professor emeritus, 1987-; Oregon State University, visiting professor, 1977-78. Writer. **Publications:** Microbes and Man, 1969, 4th ed., 2000; (ed.) Chemistry and Biochemistry of Nitrogen Fixation, 1971; Biological Nitrogen Fixation, 1972; A Plain Man's Guide to Jazz, 1973; (ed. with T.R.G. Gray) Survival of Vegetative Microbes, 1976; (ed. with W. Newton and C. Rodriguez-Barrueco) Recent Developments in Nitrogen Fixation, 1977; Nitrogen Fixation, 1978, 3rd ed., 1998; The Sulphate-Reducing Bacteria, 1979, 2nd ed., 1984; The Fundamentals of Nitrogen Fixation, 1982; (ed. with F.J. Bergersen) Century of Nitrogen Fixation Research, 1987; The Outer Reaches of Life, 1994; (with M. Postgate) A Stomach for Dissent: The Life of Raymond Postgate, 1896-1971, 1994; Lethal Lozenges and Tainted Tea: A Biography of John Postgate, 1820-1881, 2001. Contributor of articles to journals and magazines. **Address:** University of Sussex, Sussex House, Brighton, ES BN1 9RH, England. **Online address:** johnp@biols.susx.ac.uk

POSTLEWAIT, Heidi. American (born United States) **Genres:** Young Adult Fiction, History. **Career:** United Nations Department of Peacekeeping Operations, staff development program manager. Writer. **Publications:** (With K. Cain and A. Thomson) Emergency Sex and Other Desperate Measures: A True Story from Hell on Earth, 2004. Contributor to periodicals. **Address:** c/o Author Mail, Hyperion Books, 77 W 66th St., 11th Fl., New York, NY 10023, U.S.A.

POSTMAN, Andrew. American (born United States), b. 1961. **Genres:** Information Science/Computers, Trivia/Facts, Novels, Sports/Fitness. **Career:** Drexel Burnam Lambert, pianist. Writer. **Publications:** Using Hal: A Guide to Achieving Greater Productivity with Lotus 1-2-3's Companion Product, 1987; The Ultimate Book of Sports Lists, 1990; Now I Know Everything (novel), 1995; What's in an Age?: Who Did What When, From Age 1 to 100, 1999; (with E. O'Kelly) Chasing Daylight: How My Forthcoming Death Transformed My Life: A Final Account, 2006; Sports Know it All, 2008. Contributor to magazines. **Address:** Markson Thoma Literary Agency, 44 Greenwich Ave., New York, NY 10011, U.S.A.

POTI, Barbara. *See* **CROOKER, Barbara.**

POTKAY, Adam. American (born United States), b. 1961. **Genres:** History. **Career:** Rutgers University, lecturer, 1986-88; College of William and Mary, professor of English, 1990-, William R. Kenan professor of humanities, 2009-; University of Aberdeen, visiting lecturer, 1997; Columbia University, visiting professor, 2001. Writer. **Publications:** The Fate of Eloquence in the Age of Hume, 1994; (ed. with S. Burr and intro.) Black Atlantic Writers of the Eighteenth Century: Living the New Exodus in England and the Americas, 1995; An Education on the Delaware: St. Mary's Hall and Doane Academy, 1837-1999, 2000; The Passion for Happiness: Samuel Johnson and David Hume, 2000; The Story of Joy: From the Bible to Late Romanticism, 2007; (ed.) The History of the Adventures of Joseph Andrews, 2008. Contributor to books and periodicals. **Address:** College of William and Mary, PO Box 8795, Williamsburg, VA 23187-8795, U.S.A. **Online address:** aspotk@wm.edu

POTTER, Carol. American (born United States), b. 1950. **Genres:** Poetry, Human Relations/Parenting, Young Adult Fiction, Literary Criticism And History. **Career:** Rhetoric University of Massachusetts, instructor, 1979-81; Fort River School, instructor, 1982-84; Adjunct Holyoke Community College, instructor of English, 1984-86; Holyoke Community College, professor of English, 1986-2004; Antioch University, MFA Program, core faculty, 2002-, BA Program, associate professor, 2004-; Ohio State University, visiting faculty, 2003; Indiana University MFA Program, visiting poet, 2003-04; Santa Monica College, instructor, 2004-; Los Angeles City College, instructor, 2004-; University of California-Los Angeles Writer's Extension, instructor, 2005-. Writer. **Publications:** POETRY: Before We Were Born, 1990; Upside Down in the Dark: Poems, 1995; Short History of Pets, 2000; Otherwise Obedient, 2008. Contributor to magazines. Works appear in anthologies. **Address:** MFA Program, Antioch University, 400 Corporate Pointe, Culver City, CA 90230, U.S.A. **Online address:** carol_potter57@yahoo.com

POTTER, Franz J. American (born United States), b. 1969?. **Genres:** History, Race Relations, Humanities. **Career:** Southern New Hampshire University, adjunct professor, 2003-05; Plymouth State University, adjunct professor, 2003-05; National University, assistant professor, 2005-. Writer. **Publications:** (Ed.) The Monster Made by Man: A Compendium of Gothic Adaptations, 2004; The History of Gothic Publishing, 1800-1835: Exhuming the Trade, 2005; Romances and Gothic Tales, 2006. **Address:** Department of Arts and Humanities, National University, 11355 N Torrey Pines Rd., La Jolla, CA 92037, U.S.A. **Online address:** fpotter@nu.edu

POTTER, Harry (D.). British/Scottish (born Scotland), b. 1954. **Genres:** Civil Liberties/Human Rights, History, Institutions/Organizations, Law, Theology/Religion. **Career:** Curate, 1981-84; Cambridge University, Selwyn College, fellow, 1984-87; Her Majesty's Prison Service, chaplain, 1987-92; barrister at law, 1992-. Writer. **Publications:** Hanging in Judgment: Religion and the Death Penalty in England from the Bloody Code to Abolition, 1993; Hanging and Heresy, 1993; (ed.) Father Diamond of Deptford, 1994; Bloodfeud: The Stewarts and Gordons at War in the Age of Mary Queen of Scots, 2002; Edinburgh Under Siege, 1571-1573, 2003. **Address:** 3 Grays Inn Sq., Holborn, GL WC1R 5AH, England.

POTTER, Simon J. British (born England), b. 1975. **Genres:** Communications/Media, Adult Non-fiction. **Career:** National University of Ireland, lecturer in history; IRCHSS Government of Ireland, research fellow, 2004-05; Menzies Centre for Australian Studies, Rydon fellow; National Library of Australia, Harold White fellow. Historian and writer. **Publications:** News and the British World: The Emergence of an Imperial Press System, 1876-1922, 2003; (ed.) Newspapers and Empire in Ireland and Britain: Reporting the British Empire, 1857-1921, 2004; (ed.) Imperial Communication: Australia, Britain and the British Empire, 1830-50, 2005; Elitism, the ABC and the BBC, 1922-70, 2008. Contributor of articles to books and journals. **Address:** Department of History, National University of Ireland, Rm. 413, Galway, 4, Ireland. **Online address:** simon.potter@nuigalway.ie

POTTINGER, Stanley. American (born United States), b. 1940?. **Genres:** Mystery/Crime/Suspense, Novels. **Career:** United States Department of Health, Education and Welfare, Civil Rights Division, director; United States Department of Justice, Civil Rights Division, assistant attorney general; Barnstorm Books, president and publisher. Writer and entrepreneur. **Publications:** The Fourth Procedure, 1995; A Slow Burning, 2000; The Last Nazi, 2003; The Final Procedure, 2004; The Boss, 2006. Contributor to journals and periodicals. **Address:** c/o Author Mail, Penguin Group (USA) Inc., 375 Hudson St., New York, NY 10014, U.S.A.

POTTS, Richard. British (born England), b. 1938. **Genres:** Children's Fiction, Children's Non-fiction. **Career:** Great Ouseburn Primary School, head teacher, 1977-, now retired. Writer. **Publications:** An Owl for His Birthday, 1966; The Haunted Mine, 1968; A Boy and His Bike, 1976, rev. ed., 2005; Tod's Owl, 1980; Battleground, 1987; Mollie with Ginger, 1993; Ghost in the Mine, 1998; Brockson's Ball, 2000; (with F. Manders) Crossing the Tyne, 2001. **Address:** Gorilla Books, 1A Ogleforth Mews, York, NY YO1 7JW, England.

POTTS, Rolf. American (born United States), b. 1970. **Genres:** Travel/Exploration. **Career:** Salon.com, columnist; World Hum, columnist. Writer. **Publications:** Vagabonding: An Uncommon Guide to the Art of Long-term World Travel, 2003; Marco Polo Didn't Go There: Stories and Revelations from One Decade as a Postmodern Travel Writer, 2008. Contributor to books and periodicals. Works appear in anthologies. **Address:** KS , U.S.A. **Online address:** rolf@rolfpotts.com

POTTS, Stephen W(ayne). American (born United States), b. 1949. **Genres:** Literary Criticism And History, Novels, History. **Career:** University of Wuerzburg, Fulbright lecturer, 1980-81; San Diego State University, instructor in writing, 1981-84, National Center for the Study of Children's Literature, Department of English and Comparative Literature, lecturer; University of California, Center for Human Development, Department of Literature, lecturer, adjunct professor of literature, 1984-. Writer. **Publications:** From Here to Absurdity: The Moral Battlefields of Joseph Heller, 1982, rev. ed., 1995; Catch-22: Antiheroic Anti-Novel, 1989; The Second Marxian Invasion: The Fiction of the Strugatsky Brothers, 1991; The Price of Paradise: The Magazine Career of F. Scott Fitzgerald, 1993. Contributor to books and periodicals. **Address:** Literature Department, University of California San Diego, LIT 147, 9500 Gilman Dr., La Jolla, CA 92093-0410, U.S.A. **Online address:** swpotts@ucsd.edu

POTVIN, Elizabeth Ann. *See* **POTVIN, Liza.**

POTVIN, Liza. (Elizabeth Ann Potvin). Canadian/French (born France), b. 1958. **Genres:** Adult Non-fiction, Novellas/Short Stories, Biography, Autobiography/Memoirs. **Career:** New Canadians Society, English literacy tutor, 1979-80, 1982; University of Calgary, English Immersion Program, tutor, 1982-83; Queen's University, Department of English, teaching assistant, 1983-84; McMaster University, Department of English, teaching assistant, 1984-87; Malaspina University College, Writing Centre, instructor, 1993-94; Nanaimo Montessori School, poetry teacher, 1997; Fairview Elementary School, poetry teacher, 1998-99; Tibetan Cultural Association, literary assistant, 2001-02; Malaspina University College, Department of English, professor, 1990-2008; Vancouver Island University, professor in English, 2008-. Writer. **Publications:** White Lies for My Mother, 1992; The Traveller's Hat, 2003; Cougarman: Percy Dewar, 2005; (with C. Matthews) Dog Days: Between The Lines, 2009. **Address:** Department of English, Vancouver Island University, Rm. 236, Bldg. 340, 900 5th St., Nanaimo, BC V9R 5S5, Canada. **Online address:** liza.potvin@viu.ca

POULIN, Jacques. Canadian (born Canada), b. 1937. **Genres:** Novels, Novellas/Short Stories, Young Adult Fiction, Translations. **Career:** Writer and translator. **Publications:** NOVELS: Mon cheval pour un royaume (novella), 1967; Jimmy: Roman, 1969; La coeur de la baleine bleue, 1970; Faites de beaux rêves, 1974; Les Grandes marés, 1978; Grandes marées, 1978; The Jimmy Trilogy (includes My Horse for a Kingdom, Jimmy, and The Heart of the Blue Whale), 1979; Volkswagen Blues, 1984; Le Vieux Chagrin, 1989; Les yeux bleus de Mistassini, 2002; La traduction estune histoire d'amour, 2006; Anglais n'est pas une Langue Magique, 2009. OTHERS: La tournée d'automne, 1993; La traduction est une histoire d'amour, 2006. **Address:** Union des écrivains québecois, 3492 avenue Laval, Montreal, QC H2X 3C8, Canada.

POULIN, Stephane. Canadian (born Canada), b. 1961. **Genres:** Children's Fiction, Illustrations, History. **Career:** Illustrator, 1984-. Writer. **Publications:** FOR CHILDREN: Les Amours de ma mere: contes et mensonges de mon enfance, 1990, English ed. as My Mother's Loves: Stories and Lies from My Childhood, 1990; Un Voyage pour deux: contes et mensonges de mon enfance, 1991, trans. as Travels for Two: Stories and Lies from My Childhood, 1991. SELF-ILLUSTRATED FOR CHILDREN: Ah! Belle Cite!/A Beautiful City ABC, 1985; Album de famille, 1986, trans. as Family Album, 1991; As-tu vu Josephine?, 1986, trans. as Have You Seen Josephine?, 1986; Peux-tu attraper Josephine?, 1987, trans. as Can You Catch Josephine?, 1987; Les Jeux zoolympiques, 1988; Pourrais-tu arreter Josephine?, 1988, trans. as Could You Stop Josephine?, 1988; Benjamin et la saga des oreillers, 1989, trans. as Benjamin and the Pillow Saga, 1989. OTHER: Bestiaire, 2002. Illustrator of books by others. **Address:** 4597 des Erables, Montreal, QC H2H 2E1, Canada.

POULSON, Christine. British (born England) **Genres:** Mystery/Crime/Suspense, Art/Art History. **Career:** Birmingham Museum and Art Gallery, curator of ceramics; William Morris Society, Kelmscott House, curator; Open University, tutor; University of Cambridge, faculty of architecture and history of art, Homerton College, senior lecturer in history of art; Centre for Nineteenth-Century Studies, research fellow. Writer. **Publications:** William Morris, 1989; William Morris on Art and Design, 1996; The Quest for the Grail: Arthurian Legend in British Art, 1840-1920, 1999; Dead Letters, 2002; Stage Fright: A Cambridge Mystery, 2003; Murder is Academic: A Cambridge Mystery, 2004; Footfall, 2006. **Address:** c/o David Grossman, David Grossman Literary Agency, 118b Holland Park Ave., London, GL W11 4UA, England. **Online address:** christine@christinepoulson.co.uk

POULSON, Stephen C. American (born United States), b. 1966?. **Genres:** Social Commentary, History, Sociology, Anthropology/Ethnology. **Career:** James Madison University, Department of Political Science, adjunct faculty, 1990-96, Department of Sociology and Anthropology, assistant professor, 2004-10, associate professor, 2010-; Washington and Lee University, Department of Sociology and Anthropology, visiting assistant professor, 2003-04; Roanoke College, Department of International Relations, adjunct assistant professor, 2004-05. Writer. **Publications:** Social Movements in Twentieth-Century Iran: Culture, Ideology and Mobilizing Frameworks, 2005. Contributor of articles to newspapers and journals. **Address:** James Madison University, Sheldon Hall, MSC 7501, Harrisonburg, VA 22807, U.S.A. **Online address:** poulsosc@jmu.edu

POULTNEY, David. American (born United States), b. 1939. **Genres:** Music, History, Literary Criticism And History. **Career:** Texas Technological College, assistant professor of music and chairperson of music history and literature division, 1967-68; Illinois State University, Department of Music, assistant professor, 1968-72, associate professor, 1973-76, professor of musicology, 1977-. Writer. **Publications:** (Ed.) La Vergine addolorata, 1971; Studying Music History: Learning, Reasoning and Writing about Music History and Literature, 1983, 2nd ed., 1995; Dictionary of Western Church Music, 1991. Contributor to periodicals. **Address:** Department of Music, Illinois State University, Centennial E 230, PO Box 5600, Normal, IL 61790-5660, U.S.A.

POUNDSTONE, William. American (born United States), b. 1955. **Genres:** Trivia/Facts, Business/Trade/Industry, Economics, Marketing. **Career:** New York Times, critic, 1992; Dave Bell Associates, co-producer, 1993-94, producer, 1994-95; Economist, critic, 1996. Writer. **Publications:** Big Secrets: The Uncensored Truth about All Sorts of Stuff You Are Never Supposed to Know, 1983; The Recursive Universe: Cosmic Complexity and the Limits of Scientific Knowledge, 1985; Bigger Secrets: More Than 125 Things They Prayed You'd Never Find Out, 1986; Labyrinths of Reason: Paradox, Puzzles and the Frailty of Knowledge, 1988; The Ultimate, 1990; Prisoner's Dilemma: John von Neumann, Game Theory and the Puzzle of the Bomb, 1992; Biggest Secrets: More Uncensored Truth about All Sorts of Stuff You Are Never Supposed to Know, 1993; Carl Sagan: A Life in the Cosmos, 1999; How Would You Move Mount Fuji?: Microsoft's Cult of the Puzzle, How the World's Smartest Companies Select the Most Creative Thinkers, 2003; Fortune's Formula: The Untold Story of the Scientific Betting System that Beat the Casinos and Wall Street, 2005; Gaming The Vote: Why Elections Aren't Fair (and What We Can Do About It), 2008; Priceless: The Myth of Fair Value (and How to Take Advantage of It), 2010; Priceless: The Hidden Psychology of Value, 2010; Are You Smart Enough to Work At Google?: Trick Questions, Zen-Like Riddles, Insanely Difficult Puzzles, and Other Devious Interviewing Techniques You Need to Know to Get a Job in the New Economy, 2012. Contributor to periodicals. **Address:** c/o Mitch Douglas, International Creative Management, 825 8th Ave., New York, NY 10019, U.S.A. **Online address:** info@williampoundstone.net

POUPEYE, Veerle. (Veerle Henriette Gabriella Maria Poupeye). Jamaican/Belgian (born Belgium), b. 1958. **Genres:** History, Art/Art History, Graphic Novels. **Career:** Edna Manley College of the Visual and Performing Arts, lecturer, 1984-97, senior lecturer in art history, head of department of art history and liberal arts, 1998-, research fellow; Institute of Jamaica, inaugural lecturer, 1987; National Gallery of Jamaica, docent, 1985-87, assistant curator, 1987-94, executive director; MultiCare Foundation, The Visual Arts Programme, coordinator, 1994-98, adviser, 1998-; Emory University, faculty; New York University, faculty. Writer. **Publications:** (Contrib.) 1492-1992: Un Nouveau Regard sur les Caraibes, 1992; Caribbean Art, 1998; (with D. Boxer) Modern Jamaican Art, 1998. Contributor to periodicals. **Address:** Department of Art History and Liberal Arts, Edna Manley College of the, Visual & Performing Arts, Arthur Wint Dr., Kingston, 5, Jamaica. **Online address:** veerle.poupeye@emc.edu.jm

POUPEYE, Veerle Henriette Gabriella Maria. *See* **POUPEYE, Veerle.**

POVERMAN, C(harles) E. American (born United States), b. 1944. **Genres:** Novellas/Short Stories, Novels. **Career:** Yale University, visiting lecturer, 1973-75; Connecticut Center for Continuing Education, teacher, 1974-75; University of Arizona, assistant professor, 1977-80, associate professor, 1980-86, professor of English, 1986-, director creative writing program, 1993-95. Writer. **Publications:** NOVELS: The Black Velvet Girl, 1976; Susan, 1977; Solomon's Daughter, 1981; My Father in Dreams, 1988; On the Edge, 1997; Love by Drowning, forthcoming. OTHER: Skin (stories), 1992. Contributor to periodicals. **Address:** Department of English, University of Arizona, Rm. 445, 1423 E University Blvd., Modern Languages Bldg., PO Box 210067, Tucson, AZ 85721, U.S.A. **Online address:** poverman@email.arizona.edu

POWE, Bruce Allen. (Ellis Portal). Canadian (born Canada), b. 1925. **Genres:** Novels, Science Fiction/Fantasy, Humor/Satire, Young Adult Fiction, Natural History. **Career:** Canadian Army Overseas, staff, 1943-45; Minister of Mines and Technical Surveys, special assistant, 1951-57; Imperial Oil Ltd., editorial assistant, 1957-60; Ontario Liberal Association, executive director, 1960-63; Baker Advertising Ltd., vice president of public relations, 1964-66; Canadian Life and Health Insurance Association, director of public relations, 1966-90; Powe Communications, sole proprietor. Writer. **Publications:** Expresso '67; A Compleat Guide to Canada's Centennial of Conflagration, 1867-19--?, 1966; (as Ellis Portal) Killing Ground: The Canadian Civil War, 1968; The Last Days of the American Empire, 1974; The Aberhart Summer, 1983; The Ice Eaters, 1987; Aldershot, 1945: The Novel, 2004. **Address:** 158 Ridley Blvd., Toronto, ON M5M 3M1, Canada. **Online address:** bapowe@aol.com

POWE-ALLRED, Alexandra. *See* **ALLRED, Alexandra Powe.**

POWELL, Alan. Australian/New Zealander (born New Zealand), b. 1936. **Genres:** History, Sciences, Politics/Government, Adult Non-fiction, Military/Defense/Arms Control. **Career:** Darwin Institute of Technology, senior lecturer in history, 1974-86; University College of the Northern Territory, dean of arts, 1986-88; Charles Darwin University, dean of arts, 1989-92, professor of history, 1993-97, emeritus professor of history and political science, 1997-; Northern Territory History, editor; Historical Society of the Northern Territory, publications editor. **Publications:** Patrician Democrat: The Political Life of Charles Cowper, 1843-1870, 1977; Far Country: A Short History of the Northern Territory, 1982, rev. ed., 2000; (co-author) Extraction Practices and Technology on the Charters Towers Goldfield/Diane Menghetti. Trees to Burn: Settlement in the Atherton-Evelyn Rainforest, 1880-1900, 1982; The Shadow's Edge: Australia's Northern War, 1988, rev. ed., 1992; (ed.) Northern Territory Dictionary of Biography, vol. I, 1990; War by Stealth: Australians and the Allied Intelligence Bureau, 1942-1945, 1996; The Third Force: ANGAU's New Guinea War, 1942-1946, 2003. Contributor to books and periodicals. **Address:** School of Creative Arts and Humanities, Faculty of Law, Business and Arts, Charles Darwin University, Orange 6.3, Darwin, NT 0909, Australia. **Online address:** alan.powell@cdu.edu.au

POWELL, Ardal. American/British (born England), b. 1958. **Genres:** Music, Sociology, Bibliography. **Career:** Folkers and Powell (flute makers), partner, 1984-2009; Traverso, founder and editor, 1989; National Endowment for the Humanities, fellow, 1993-94; Folkers Flute Company Ltd., president, 1999-; Full Circle Flute Company Ltd., staff, 1999-2009; Pendragon Press, staff, 2007-. Performer, soloist and lecturer; brand-new multimedia co., chief executive officer. **Publications:** The Flute, 2002; (ed.) The Baroque Flute Fingering Book, 2nd ed., 2002; (ed.) Traverso: Historical Flute Newsletter: The Second Decade, 1999-2008: With a Bibliography of Publications on Historical Flutes, 1999-2008, 2009; (ed.) Lindsay's Elements of Flute-playing (1828-30): A Study in Performance Practice, 2009. EDITOR AND TRANSLATOR: J.G. Tromlitz, The Virtuoso Flute-Player, 1991; (and intro.) J.G. Tromlitz, The Keyed Flute, 1996; Max Weber's Sociology of Music, 2011. Works appear in anthologies. Contributor to music journals. **Address:** Folkers & Powell, 49 Rte. 25, PO Box 148, Hudson, NY 12534, U.S.A.

POWELL, Barry B. American (born United States), b. 1942. **Genres:** Classics, Mythology/Folklore, History, Language/Linguistics, Novels, Theology/Religion. **Career:** Northern Arizona University, assistant professor of classics, 1969-73; University of Wisconsin, Department of classics, assistant professor, 1973-75, associate professor, 1975-80, professor, 1980-, Halls-Bascom professor, 1992-, now Halls-Bascom professor emeritus; University of California, visiting professor, 1984-85; University of New Mexico, visiting professor, 2007. Writer. **Publications:** Composition by Theme in The Odyssey, 1977; Homer and the Origin of the Greek Alphabet, 1991; Classical Myth, 1995, 7th ed., 2011; (ed. with I. Morris) A New Companion to Homer, 1997; A Short Introduction to Classical Myth, 2001; Writing and the Origins of Greek Literature, 2002; Homer, 2004, 2nd ed., 2007; The War at Troy: A True History, 2006; Rooms Containing Falcons, Poems, 2006; The Greeks: History, Culture, and Society, 2006, 2nd ed., 2009; Ramses in Nighttown, A Novel, 2006; Writing: Theory and History of the Technology of Civilization, 2008; Ilias, Odysseia, 2009; 30-Second Mythology, 2011; World Myth, 2012. Contributor to journals. **Address:** Department of Classics, University of Wisconsin, 910 Van Hise Hall, 1220 Linden Dr., Madison, WI 53706, U.S.A. **Online address:** bbpowell@wisc.edu

POWELL, Corey S. American (born United States), b. 1966?. **Genres:** Sciences. **Career:** Discover magazine, editor, senior editor and executive web editor, editor-in-chief; New York University, adjunct professor of science journalism; Scientific American, editor; Physics Today, editor. **Publications:** God in the Equation: How Einstein Became the Prophet of the New Religious Era, 2002. **Address:** Discover Magazine, 275 7th Ave., 21st Fl., New York, NY 10001, U.S.A. **Online address:** corey@corey-powell.com

POWELL, Craig. Australian (born Australia), b. 1940. **Genres:** Poetry, Music, Young Adult Fiction. **Career:** Royal Prince Alfred Hospital, junior resident medical officer, 1965; Western Suburbs Hospital, senior resident medical officer, 1966; Parramatta Psychiatric Hospital, staff psychiatrist, 1968-72; Brandon Mental Health Centre, team III clinical director, 1972-75; St. Joseph's Hospital, chief resident in psychiatry, 1976; London Psychiatric Hospital, staff psychiatrist, 1976-82; Westmead Hospital, psychiatry, visiting medical officer, 1984-88; Prince of Wales Hospital, visiting medical officer of mental health, 2001-. Writer. **Publications:** A Different Kind of Breathing, 1966; I Learn by Going: Poems, 1968; A Country without Exiles: Poems, 1972; Rehearsal for Dancers, 1978; Minga Street: New and Selected Poems, 1993; Music and Women's Bodies, 2002. Contributor to journals. **Address:** Five Islands Press, University of Melbourne, PO Box 4429, Parkville, VI 3052, Australia.

POWELL, D. A. American (born United States), b. 1963. **Genres:** Poetry, Literary Criticism And History, Autobiography/Memoirs. **Career:** Harvard University, Briggs-Copeland lecturer in poetry; University of San Francisco, associate professor of English; Davidson College, McGee visiting writer. **Publications:** POETRY: Explosions and Small Geometries, 1991; (with C. Ciavonne and P. Hartnett) Con Sequences, 1993; Tea, 1998; Lunch, 2000; Cocktails, 2004; Chronic, 2009. AUTOBIOGRAPHY/MEMOIRS: (with D. Trinidad) By Myself: An Autobiography, 2009. LITERARY CRITICISM AND HISTORY: (with K. Prufer) Dunstan Thompson, 2010. **Address:** Department of English, University of San Francisco, 2130 Fulton St., San Francisco, CA 94117, U.S.A. **Online address:** dapowell@usfca.edu

POWELL, Dannye Romine. American (born United States), b. 1941. **Genres:** Writing/Journalism, Poetry, Communications/Media, Children's Fiction, History, Adult Non-fiction, Homes/Gardens, Social Commentary, Social Commentary. **Career:** Charlotte Observer, book editor and feature writer, 1975-92, restaurant critic, 1980-87, metropolitan columnist, 1992-. **Publications:** Parting the Curtains: Interviews with Southern Writers, 1994; At Every Wedding, Someone Stays Home (poems), 1994; Parting the Curtains: Voices of the Great Southern Writers, 1995; Ecstasy of Regret (poems), 2002; Necklace of Bees, Poems, 2008. Contributor to magazines. **Address:** The Charlotte Observer, 600 S Tryon St., Charlotte, NC 28202, U.S.A. **Online address:** dannye700@aol.com

POWELL, David. British (born England), b. 1925. **Genres:** Literary Criticism And History, Librarianship. **Career:** Northampton Public Library, reference librarian, 1955-72; Northampton College of Education, librarian, 1972-75; Nene College, technical-services librarian, 1975-85, senior librarian, now retired. Writer. **Publications:** (Comp.) Catalogue of the John Clare Collection in the Northampton Public Library, 1964; (comp. with V.A. Hatley) Catalogue of the Leather and Footwear Collections in the Northampton Central Reference Library and the Library of the Northampton Central College of Further Education, 1968; (intro.) The Parish: A Satire, 1985; The Life and Times of John Clare, 1993. EDITOR: The Wood Is Sweet: Poems for Young Readers, 1966; Doves and Pomegranates: Poems for Young Readers, 1969; (with E. Robinson) John Clare, 1984; (with E. Robinson and M. Grainger) The Later Poems of John Clare, 2 vols., 1984; (with E. Robinson and M. Grainger) The Early Poems of John Clare, 1804-1822, 2 vols., 1989; (with G. Summerfield) The Shepherd's Calendar, 1993; (with E. Robinson and P.M.S. Dawson) Cottage Tales, 1993; (with E. Robinson and P.M.S. Dawson) Northborough Sonnets, 1995; (with E. Robinson and P.M.S. Dawson) Poems of the Middle Period, 1822-1837, 1996; (with E. Robinson) John Clare by Himself, 1996; John Clare's Proverbs, 2000; (with P.M.S. Dawson and E. Robinson) John Clare: A Champion for the Poor (verses and prose), 2000; John Clare's Aphorisms, 2002; (and intro. with E. Robinson) Major Works, 2004. **Address:** Curtis Brown Group Ltd., Haymarket House, 28-29 Haymarket, London, GL SW1 4SP, England.

POWELL, David A. American (born United States), b. 1952. **Genres:** Literary Criticism And History, Gay And Lesbian Issues. **Career:** Universite de Strasbourg, lecturer, 1978-79; Universite de Paris X, lecturer, 1981-83; University of Pennsylvania, lecturer in French, 1983-84; Barnard College, instructor in French, 1984-86; Hofstra University, Department of Romance Languages and Literatures, assistant professor, 1986-95, associate professor, 1996-2001, professor of French, 2001-, chair, 2004-10, associate dean for student academic affairs, 1990-94, LGBT Studies Program, director, 2006-. Writer. **Publications:** George Sand, 1990; Le Siècle de George Sand, 1998; While the Music Lasts: The Representation of Music in the Works of George Sand, 2001. EDITOR: (with N. Datlof and J. Fuchs) The World of George Sand, 1991; George Sand Today, 1992; 21st-Century Gay Culture, 2008; (with T. Powell) Queer Exoticism, 2010. Contributor of articles to journals. **Address:** Department of Romance Languages & Literatures, Hofstra University, 327 Calkins Hall, Hempstead, NY 11549-1000, U.S.A. **Online address:** david.a.powell@hofstra.edu

POWELL, Eric. American (born United States), b. 1975. **Genres:** Children's Fiction, Picture/Board Books, Literary Criticism And History, Young Adult Fiction. **Career:** Freelance comic book writer and illustrator, 1995-. **Publications:** The Goon: Rough Stuff, 2004; The Goon: Nothin' but Misery, 2004; The Goon: My Murderous Childhood (and Other Grievous Yarns), 2004. **Address:** Diamond Comic Distributors Inc., 1966 Greenspring Dr., Ste. 300, Timonium, MD 21093, U.S.A.

POWELL, E. S. *See* **POWELL, E. Sandy.**

POWELL, E. Sandy. (E. S. Powell). American (born United States), b. 1947. **Genres:** Young Adult Non-fiction, Young Adult Fiction, Human Relations/Parenting, Sports/Fitness, Children's Fiction. **Career:** Southwestern Oregon Community College, instructor. Writer. **Publications:** FOR YOUNG READERS: Geranium Morning, 1990; Daisy, 1991; A Chance to Grow, 1992; (as E.S. Powell) Washington, 1993; Rats, 1994. OTHER: Heart to Heart Caregiving: A Sourcebook of Family Day Care Activities, Projects and Practical Provider Support, 1990; Reading Women's Lives, 3rd ed., 2002; What's Up?: Activities for Responding to Children's Lives, 2003; (Manuscript ed.) Elmo Williams: A Hollywood Memoir, 2006. Contributor to periodicals. **Address:** c/o Author Mail, Thomson Delmar Learning, Executive Woods, 5 Maxwell Dr., PO Box 8007, Clifton Park, NY 12065-8007, U.S.A.

POWELL, H. Jefferson. American (born United States), b. 1954. **Genres:** Politics/Government, History. **Career:** Yale Law School, research associate, 1983-84; University of Iowa, associate professor, 1984-88, professor of law, 1988-89; Duke University, visiting professor, visiting associate professor, 1987-88, 1988-89, Frederic Cleaveland professor of law and divinity, 1989-2010; United States Department of Justice, Office of Legal Counsel, deputy assistant attorney general, 1993-96, principal deputy solicitor general, 1996; George Washington University, Law School, professor of law, 2010-. Writer. **Publications:** (Comp.) The Languages of Power: A Sourcebook of Early American Constitutional History, 1991; The Moral Tradition of American Constitutionalism: A Theological Interpretation, 1993; The Constitution and the Attorneys General, 1999; (foreword and intro.) Our Chief Magistrate and His Powers, 2002; The President's Authority over Foreign Affairs: An Essay in Constitutional Interpretation, 2002; A Community Built on Words: The Constitution in History and Politics, 2002; Constitutional Conscience: The Moral Dimension of Judicial Decision, 2008; (intro.) A View of the Constitution, 2nd ed., 2009; (with D.L. Lange) No Law: Intellectual Property in the Image of an Absolute First Amendment, 2009; (ed. with J.B. White) Law and Democracy in the Empire of Force, 2009. Contributor to books, journals and periodicals. **Address:** Law School, George Washington University, 2000 H St. NW, Washington, DC 20052, U.S.A. **Online address:** jpowell2@law.gwu.edu

POWELL, Joseph. American (born United States), b. 1952. **Genres:** Poetry, Young Adult Fiction. **Career:** Central Washington University, Department of English, adjunct professor, 1982-83, 1984-89, assistant professor, associate professor, 1989-96, professor of English, 1996-; Sequim High School, English teacher, 1983-84; Ellensburg's Arts Commission, vice-chair, 1986-88, president, 1990-92. Writer. **Publications:** POETRY: Counting The Change, 1986; Winter Insomnia, 1993; Getting Here, 1997; Aegean Dialogues (chapbook), 1998; The Greatest Hits 1980-2001, 2001; A Ring in Air, 2003; (with M. Halperin) Accent on Meter: A Handbook for Readers of Poetry, 2004; Fish Grooming and Other Stories, 2007; Hard Earth, forthcoming. Works appear in anthologies. Contributor to periodicals. **Address:** Department of English, Central Washington University, 416C Language and Literature Bldg., 400 E University Way, Ellensburg, WA 98926-7553, U.S.A. **Online address:** powellj@cwu.edu

POWELL, Kevin. American (born United States), b. 1966. **Genres:** Poetry, Documentaries/Reportage, Politics/Government. **Career:** New York University, instructor of English, 1990-92; Vibe magazine, senior writer, 1992-96. **Publications:** (Ed.) In the Tradition: An Anthology of Young Black Writers, 1993; Recognize: Poems, 1995; Keepin' It Real: Post-MTV Reflections on Race, Sex and Politics, 1997; (ed.) Step into a World: A Global Anthology of the New Black Literature, 2000; (ed.) Who Shot Ya?: Three Decades of Hiphop Photography, 2002; Who's Gonna Take the Weight?: Manhood, Race and Power in America, 2003; Someday We'll All Be Free, 2006; (ed.) Black Male Handbook: A Blueprint for Life, 2008; No Sleep Till Brooklyn, New and Selected Poems, 2008; Open Letters to America, 2009; My Own Private Ghetto, 2012; The Kevin Powell Reader, 2013; Homeboy Alone, forthcoming. Contributor to periodicals. **Address:** c/o Marisa King-Redwood, Buzz Brand Marketing, 419 Lafayette St., 2nd Fl., New York, NY 10003, U.S.A. **Online address:** gene@kevinpowell.net

POWELL, Martyn J. Welsh (born Wales), b. 1972. **Genres:** Politics/Government, History. **Career:** Aberystwyth University, Department of History & Welsh History, lecturer in modern British history. Writer. **Publications:** Britain and Ireland in the Eighteenth-Century Crisis of Empire, 2003; The Politics of Consumption in Eighteenth-Century Ireland, 2005; Piss-Pots, Printers and Public Opinion in Eighteenth-century Dublin: Richard Twiss's Tour in Ireland, 2009. **Address:** Department of History & Welsh History, Aberystwyth University, Hugh Owen Bldg., Aberystwyth, DY SY23 3DY, Wales. **Online address:** mpp@aber.ac.uk

POWELL, Nate. American (born United States), b. 1978?. **Genres:** Graphic Novels, Illustrations. **Career:** Harlan Records, owner and manager. Writer and record producer. **Publications:** SELF-ILLUSTRATED: Sounds of Your Name, 2nd ed., 2007. OTHERS: Tiny Giants, 2003; It Disappears, 2004; Please Release, 2006; Swallow Me Whole (graphic novel), 2008; Any Empire, 2011; The Year Of The Beasts, 2012; The Silence Of Our Friends, 2012. Works appear in anthologies. Illustrator of books by others. **Address:** Roaring Brook Press, 175 5th Ave., New York, NY 10010, U.S.A. **Online address:** seemybrotherdance@yahoo.com

POWELL, Neil. British (born England), b. 1948. **Genres:** Novels, Poetry, Literary Criticism And History, Biography, Novellas/Short Stories, Art/Art History, Autobiography/Memoirs. **Career:** Kimbolton School, teacher, 1971-74; Saint Christopher School, teacher, 1974-86; Baldock Bookshop, owner, 1986-90; freelance writer and editor, 1990-. **Publications:** At Little Gidding, 1974; Afternoon Dawn, 1975: Suffolk Poems, 1975; At the Edge, 1977; Out of Time, 1979; Carpenters of Light: A Critical Study of Contemporary British Poetry, 1979; A Season of Calm Weather, 1982; True Colours: New and Selected Poems, 1991; Unreal City, 1992; The Stones on Thorpeness Beach, 1994; Roy Fuller: Writer and Society, 1995; The Language of Jazz, 1997; Selected Poems, 1998; George Crabbe: An English Life, 2004; A Halfway House, 2004; Amis and Son: Two Literary Generation, 2008. EDITOR: Selected Poems, 1990; Gay Love Poetry, 1997; D. Davie, Collected Poems, 2001. Contributor to magazines. **Address:** Carcanet Press, Alliance House, 30 Cross St., 4th Fl., Manchester, GM M2 7AQ, England.

POWELL, Padgett. American (born United States), b. 1952. **Genres:** Novels, Novellas/Short Stories. **Career:** University of Florida, professor, 1984-. Writer. **Publications:** Edisto: A Novel, 1984; A Woman Named Drown, 1987; (contrib.) A World Unsuspected: Portraits of Southern Childhood, 1987; Edisto Revisted, 1996; Mrs. Hollingsworth's Men, 2000. STORIES: Typical, 1991; Aliens of Affection: Stories, 1998; The Interrogative Mood, 2009; You & I, 2011. **Address:** Department of English, University of Florida, 4211E Turlington Hall, PO Box 117310, Gainesville, FL 32611-7310, U.S.A. **Online address:** powell@english.ufl.edu

POWELL, Randy. American (born United States), b. 1956. **Genres:** Young Adult Fiction, Novels, Sports/Fitness. **Career:** Teacher, 1984-88; writer, 1988-; The Boeing Co., technical writer, 1989-; Vermont College, faculty of MFA in writing. **Publications:** YOUNG ADULT FICTION: My Underrated Year, 1988; Is Kissing a Girl Who Smokes Like Licking an Ashtray?, 1992; Dean Duffy, 1995; The Whistling Toilets, 1996; Tribute to Another Dead Rock Star, 1999; Run if You Dare, 2001; Three Clams and an Oyster, 2002; Swiss Mist, 2008. **Address:** c/o Author Mail, Farrar, Straus and Giroux, 19 Union Sq. W, New York, NY 10003, U.S.A.

POWELL, Robert. Singaporean/British (born England), b. 1942. **Genres:** Architecture, Art/Art History, Photography. **Career:** Richard Turley Associates, assistant architect, 1963-64; Ainsworth Spark Associates, architect to partner, 1966-83; Morowali Nature Reserve, creator of management plan, 1979-80; National University of Singapore, senior lecturer, 1984-90, associate professor of architecture, 1990-97, adjunct associate professor, 1998-99; RPA Consultants, partner, planner, and urban designer, 1984-; Operation Raleigh, selection coordinator, 1984-90; Singapore Ministry of National Development, planning appeals inspector, 1988-97; Akimedia Ltd., managing director, 1997-. Writer. **Publications:** Innovative Architecture of Singapore, 1989; Ken Yeang: Rethinking the Environmental Filter, 1989; The Asian House: Contemporary Houses of Southeast Asia, 1993; Living Legacy: Singapores Architectural Heritage Renewed, 1994; The Tropical Asian House, 1996; Line Edge and Shade: The Search for a Design Language in Tropical Asia, 1997; The Urban Asian House: Living in the Tropical City, 1998; Rethinking the Skyscraper: The Complete Works of Ken Yeang, 1999; History of Houses, 1999; Singapore: Architecture of a Global City, 2000; Architecture of Learning: New Singapore Schools, 2001; New Asian House, 2001; No Limits: Articulating William Lim, 2002; New Thai House, 2003; Singapore Architecture, 2003; (with A. Betsky) SCDA Architects: Selected and Current Works, 2004; (with R. Sheard and P. Bingham-Hall) Stadium: Architecture for the New Global Culture, 2005; The New Malaysian House, 2008; Singapore Houses, 2009. EDITOR: Architecture and Identity, 1986; Regionalism in Architecture, 1987; The Architecture of Housing: Proceedings of an International Seminar Sponsored by the Aga Khan Award for Architecture, the African Union of Architects, and the Association of Architects of Tanzania, held in Zanzibar, the United Republic of Tanzania, 12-15 October 1988, 1990; Regionalism: Forging an Identity, 1991; Renovation Guide for Homes, 1992; Fragments of a Journey, 2001. Contributor to books and journals. **Address:** Block 1, Pandan Valley, Ste. 04-103, Singapore, 597625, Singapore. **Online address:** rpacon@mbox3.singnet.com.sg

POWELL, Yolanda White. American (born United States), b. 1961. **Genres:** Antiques/Furnishings, Theology/Religion, Reference. **Career:** Voice of Calvary Ministries, assistant director of development, 1989-91; freelance writer, 1991-94; Onondaga Council on Alcoholism and Addiction, public information officer, 1994-96; Creative Inspirations, creative director, 1996-; The Spoken Word Intl., president and chief executive officer, 1999-. **Publications:** (With L.B. Cillie) From Darkness to Light: A Modern Guide to Recapturing Historical Riches-Understanding Auctions, Collectibles and Estate Sales, 1997; (with W.J. Powell) Soul Food & Living Water: Spiritual Nourishment and Practical Help for African American Families, 2003. Contributor to periodicals. **Address:** The Spoken Word Intl., PO Box 1214, Huntingtown, MD 20639-1214, U.S.A. **Online address:** thepowells@the-spoken-word.org

POWER, Patrick C. (Patrick Carthage Power). Irish (born Ireland), b. 1928. **Genres:** Area Studies, History, Literary Criticism And History, Travel/Exploration, Law, Young Adult Fiction, Social Sciences. **Career:** Educator, now retired; lecturer on local history. Writer. **Publications:** The Story of Anglo-Irish Poetry, 1800-1922, 1967; A Literary History of Ireland, 1969; The Book of Irish Curses, 1974; (trans.) F. O'Brien, The Poor Mouth (from Gaelic-An Beal Bocht): A Bad Story about the Hard Life, 1974; Carrick-on-Suir and Its People, 1976; Sex and Marriage in Ancient Ireland, 1976; Heritage Trails in South Tipperary, 1987; History of South Tipperary, 1989; History of Waterford: City and County, 1990, rev. ed., 1998; St. Mary's Parochial School Clonmel, 1993; The Courts Martial of 1798-9, 1997; (trans.) B. Merriman, Cúirt an mheán oíche (title means: 'The Midnight Court), 1999; History of Dungarvan Town and District, 2000; (with S. Duffy) Timechart History of Ireland, 2001; Carrick-on-Suir Town and District 1800-2000, 2003. **Address:** c/o Helen Walsh, 93 Willow Pk., Clonmel, TP 1, Ireland. **Online address:** pecpower@eircom.net

POWER, Patrick Carthage. *See* **POWER, Patrick C.**

POWER, Samantha. American/Irish (born Ireland), b. 1970. **Genres:** Documentaries/Reportage, History. **Career:** U.S. News and World Report, reporter, 1993-96; Economist Newspaper, reporter, 1993-96; International Crisis Group, political analyst, 1996; Harvard University, John F. Kennedy School of Government, Carr Center for Human Rights Policy, adjunct lecturer in public policy, founding executive director, 1998-2002, Anna Lindh professor of practice of global leadership and public policy, 2007-; Time Magazine, foreign policy correspondent, 2007-, foreign policy columnist; National Security Council, Office of Multilateral Affairs and Human Rights, senior director of multilateral affairs, 2009-. **Publications:** (Comp.) Breakdown in the Balkans: A Chronicle of Events, January 1989 to May, 1993, 1993; (ed. with G. Allison) Realizing Human Rights: Moving from Inspiration to Impact, 2000; A Problem from Hell: America and the Age of Genocide, 2002; Missions, 2005; Talk of the Town: Boltonism, 2005; (intro.) Axis Rule in Occupied Europe: Laws of Occupation, Analysis of Government, Proposals for Redress, 2005; Punishing Evildoers, 2006; (with M. Abramowitz) Democrats: Get Loud, Get

Angry!, 2006; Chasing the Flame: Sergio Vieira de Mello and the Fight to Save the World, 2008; (ed. with D. Chollet) Unquiet American, 2011. Contributor to books and periodicals. **Address:** Carr Center for Human Rights Policy, John F. Kennedy School of Government, Harvard University, 79 John F. Kennedy Kennedy St., Cambridge, MA 02138, U.S.A. **Online address:** samantha_power@ksg.harvard.edu

POWERS, Alan. British (born England), b. 1955. **Genres:** Architecture, Art/Art History, Education, Reference. **Career:** Judd Street Gallery, director, 1985-91; Prince of Wales's Institute of Architecture, librarian, 1993-99; University of Greenwich, School of Architecture and Construction, associate senior lecturer, 1999-, professor of architecture and cultural history, 2007-; Pollock's Toy Museum, chairman, 1999-, Twentieth Century Architecture, editor. **Publications:** (With C. Aslet) The National Trust Book of the English House, 1986; H.S. Goodhart-Rendel, 1987; Oliver Hill: Architect and Lover of Life, 1887-1968, 1989; Shop Fronts, 1989; Modern Block Printed Textiles, 1992; In the Line of Development, 1992; (co-author) God's Architect: A Life of Raymond McGrath, 1995; (with J. Sharples and M. Shippobottom) Charles Reilly and the Liverpool School of Architecture, 1904-1933, 1996; John Campbell, 1997; (with E. Harwood) Tayler and Green, 1998; Living with Books, 1999; (ed.) Modern Britain: 1929-1939, 1999; Nature in Design, 1999; Francis Pollen, 1999; Living with Pictures, 2000; Apartment: Stylish Solutions for Apartment Living, 2001; Front Cover: Great Book Jackets and Cover Design, 2001; Serge Chermayeff, 2001; (ed.) Twentieth Century Architecture 5: Festival of Britain and Brief City, 2001; Children's Book Covers, 2003; Eric Ravilious: Imagined Realities, 2003; (ed. with E. Harwood) The Heroic Period of Conservation, 2004; Elements of Style: An Encyclopedia of Domestic Architectural Detail, 2005; (ed. with S. Charlton and E. Harwood) British Modern: Architecture and Design in the 1930s, 2007; (ed. with E. Harwood) Housing the Twentieth Century Nation, 2008; Art and Print: The Curwen Story, 2008; Aldington, Craig and Collinge, 2009; Robin Hood Gardens Re-Visions, 2010. Contributor to periodicals. **Address:** Old Royal Naval College, University of Greenwich, Rm. R111, Park Row, London, GL SE10 9LS, England. **Online address:** a.powers@gre.ac.uk

POWERS, Janet M. American (born United States), b. 1939?. **Genres:** Sociology. **Career:** Pak-American Cultural Center, ESL instructor, 1962-63; Gettysburg College, Department of English, instructor, 1963-65, Department of History, instructor, 1966-79, adjunct assistant professor, 1979-87, adjunct associate professor, 1991-98, associate professor, 1998-, professor of interdisciplinary studies and womens studies, now professor emeritus, Area Studies Symposium, program coordinator, 1985-86, 1986-87, 1988-89, 1993-, Global Studies Program, coordinator, 1998-; Phi Beta Kappa, president, 1995-97; Middle Atlantic Region/Association for Asian Studies, vicepresident, 1996-97, president, 1997-98; Western Maryland College, adjunct instructor of cross-cultural studies, 1992-98; South India Term Abroad, director, 1994; Central Pennsylvania Consortium, director. Writer. **Publications:** Blossoms on the Olive Tree: Israeli and Palestinian Women Working for Peace, 2006; Difficult to Subdue as the Wind, 2008; Kites Over the Mango Tree: Restoring Harmony between Hindus and Muslims in Gujarat, 2009. Contributor to periodicals. **Address:** Women, Gender and Sexuality Studies, Gettysburg College, 311 Weidensall, 300 N Washington St., PO Box 2450, Gettysburg, PA 17325, U.S.A. **Online address:** jpowers@gettysburg.edu

POWERS, Jessica. *See* **POWERS, J. L.**

POWERS, J. L. (Jessica Powers). American (born United States) **Genres:** Human Relations/Parenting, Novels, Literary Criticism And History. **Career:** Cinco Puntos Press, senior editor; Skyline Community College, faculty. **Publications:** The Confessional (young-adult novel), 2007; This Thing Called the Future: a Novel, 2011. UNDER NAME JESSICA POWERS: A Bark in the Park: The Forty-five Best Places to Hike with Your Dog in the El Paso/Las Cruces Region, 2003; (ed.) Labor Pains and Birth Stories: Essays on Pregnancy, Childbirth and Becoming a Parent, 2009. **Address:** Alfred A. Knopf Books for Young Readers, 1745 Broadway 10th fl., New York, NY 10019, U.S.A. **Online address:** jlpowers@evaporites.com

POWERS, Lyall H(arris). American (born United States), b. 1924. **Genres:** Literary Criticism And History, Biography, History. **Career:** University of Wisconsin, instructor in English, 1955; University of British Columbia, visiting associate professor, 1963; University of Michigan, professor of English, 1967-93, professor emeritus, 1994-; University of Gottingen, visiting professor, 1974; University of Hawaii, visiting professor, 1982. Writer. **Publications:** Henry James and French Naturalism, 1956; The Portable Henry James, rev. ed., 1968; The Merrill Guide to Henry James, 1969; (comp.) The Merrill Studies in The Portrait of a Lady, 1970; Henry James: An Introduction and Interpretation, 1970; Henry James and the Naturalist Movement, 1971; Faulkner's Yoknapatawpha Comedy, 1980; The Portrait of a Lady: Maiden, Woman and Heroine, 1991. EDITOR: (intro.) Henry James's Major Novels: Essays in Criticism, 1973; (intro. with L. Edel) The Complete Notebooks of Henry James, 1988; (with C.V. Eby) Leon Edel and Literary Art, 1988; Henry James and Edith Wharton: Letters, 1900-1915, 1989; (intro.) Henry James at Work, 2006. **Address:** Department of English, University of Michigan, 4202 Angell Hall, 435 S State St., Ann Arbor, MI 48109-1003, U.S.A. **Online address:** lhpowers@umich.edu

POWERS, Martin J. (Martin Joseph Powers). American (born United States), b. 1949?. **Genres:** Art/Art History, Politics/Government. **Career:** University of Chicago, William Rainey Harper fellow, 1975-76; University of California, assistant professor, 1977-85, associate professor, 1985-87; University of Michigan, associate professor, 1987-98, professor, 1998-, Sally Michelson Davidson professor of Chinese arts and cultures, 1999-; University of Victoria, Lansdowne visiting professor, 2001; Tsinghua University, Weilun visiting professor, 2005, visiting professor, 2006-09; Princeton Institute for Advanced Study, School of Historical Studies, fellow, 2008-09. Writer. **Publications:** Art & Political Expression in Early China, 1991; Pattern and Person: Ornament, Society, and Self in Classical China, 2006. Contributor to books and periodicals. **Address:** Department of the History of Art, University of Michigan, 120A Tappan Hall, 855 S University Ave., Ann Arbor, MI 48109-1357, U.S.A. **Online address:** mpow@umich.edu

POWERS, Martin Joseph. *See* **POWERS, Martin J.**

POWERS, Richard Gid. American (born United States), b. 1944?. **Genres:** History. **Career:** City University of New York, College of Staten Island, professor of history and american studies, CORE Program, director, Graduate Center, American Studies Program, coordinator, 1996-2002, Freshmen General Education Program, co-director. Writer. **Publications:** G-Men: Hoovers FBI in American Popular Culture, 1983; Secrecy and Power: The Life of J. Edgar Hoover, 1987; (ed. with H. Kató, B. Stronach) Handbook of Japanese Popular Culture, 1989; Not without Honor: The History of American Anticommunism, 1995; Broken: The Troubled Past and Uncertain Future of the FBI, 2004. **Address:** Department of History, College of Staten Island, City University of New York, Rm. 209, 2N Bldg., 535 E 80th St., New York, NY 10021, U.S.A. **Online address:** rgpsi@earthlink.net

POWERS, Richard (S.). American (born United States), b. 1957. **Genres:** Novels. **Career:** Computer programmer and freelance data processor; University of Illinois, writer-in-residence, 1992-, Swanlund chair in English, 1996-, Department of English, professor; Beckman Institute for Advanced Science and Technology, full-time faculty. Novelist. **Publications:** NOVELS: Three Farmers on Their Way to a Dance, 1985; Prisoner's Dilemma, 1988; The Gold Bug Variations, 1991; Operation Wandering Soul: A Novel, 1993; Galatea 2.2, 1995; Gain, 1998; Plowing the Dark, 2000; The Time of Our Singing, 2003; The Echo Maker, 2006; Generosity: An Enhancement, 2009. Contributor to periodicals. **Address:** Beckman Institute for Advanced Science and, Technology, University of Illinois, 2215 Beckman Institute, 405 N Mathews Ave., Urbana, IL 61801, U.S.A. **Online address:** rpowers@illinois.edu

POWERS, Steve. American (born United States), b. 1934. **Genres:** Communications/Media, Adult Non-fiction, Writing/Journalism. **Career:** WADS, newscaster, 1961-; WMCA Radio, anchor, through 1972; ABC Radio Network News, correspondent, 1972-; RKO Radio Network News, staff; WNYW-TV Channel 5 News, anchor and reporter, 1980-93; St. John's University, associate professor, 1993-98; New York Times Radio, anchor, WQXR-FM, writer, producer and newscaster, retired, 2007; Columbia School of Journalism, adjunct professor; The New School, adjunct professor; New York University, adjunct professor. **Publications:** (With N. Postman) How to Watch TV News, 1992, rev. ed., 2008; Listen to Your Neighbor's Heart: A Book about the Awesome Power of Listening, 1997. **Address:** c/o Elaine Markson, Elaine Markson Literary Agency Inc., 44 Greenwich Ave., New York, NY 10011-8347, U.S.A. **Online address:** spsp@optonline.net

POWERS, William T. American (born United States), b. 1926. **Genres:** Psychology, Medicine/Health, Social Sciences. **Career:** Veterans Administration Research Hospital, medical physicist, 1954-60; Northwestern University,

Department of Astronomy, electronic systems engineer, 1960-73; freelance consulting engineer and writer, 1973-79; Chicago Sun-Times, Department of Technical Services, electronic systems engineer, 1979-90. Writer. **Publications:** Behavior: The Control of Perception, 1973, 2nd ed., 2005; (contrib.) A Cybernetic Approach to the Assessment of Children, 1979; (contrib.) Communication and Control in Society, 1979; Living Control Systems: Selected Papers of William T. Powers, 1989; (ed. with R.J. Robertson) Introduction To Modern Psychology: The Control-Theory View, 1990; Living Control Systems II: Selected Papers, 1992; (contrib.) Mind Readings: Experimental Studies of Purpose, 1992; Making Sense of Behavior: The Meaning of Control, 1998; Living Control Systems III: The Fact of Control, 2008; Living Control Systems III: Models and Simulations, forthcoming. Contributor to journals and magazines. **Address:** 73 Ridge Pl., Durango, CO 81303-8136, U.S.A. **Online address:** powers_w@frontier.net

POWLEDGE, Fred. American (born United States), b. 1935. **Genres:** Children's Non-fiction, Civil Liberties/Human Rights, Environmental Sciences/Ecology, Race Relations, Sciences. **Career:** Associated Press, editor and reporter, 1958-60; Atlanta Journal, reporter, 1960-63; New York Times, reporter, 1963-66; freelance writer, 1966-. **Publications:** Black Power/White Resistance, 1967; To Change a Child: A Report on the Institute for Developmental Studies, 1967; Model City, 1971; Mud Show: A Circus Season, 1975; Born on the Circus, 1976; The Backpacker's Budget Food Book: How to Select and Prepare Your Provisions from Supermarket Shelves, 1977; Journeys through the South: A Rediscovery, 1977; So You're Adopted, 1982; Water: The Nature, Uses, and Future of Our Most Precious and Abused Resource, 1982; A Forgiving Wind: On Becoming a Sailor, 1983; Fat of the Land, 1984; The New Adoption Maze and How to Get Through It, 1985; You'll Survive: Late Blooming, Early Blooming, Loneliness, Klutziness, and Other Problems of Adolescence, and How to Live Through Them, 1986; Free at Last? The Civil Rights Movement and the People Who Made It, 1991; We Shall Overcome: Heroes of the Civil Rights Movement, 1993; Working River, 1995; Pharmacy in the Forest: How Medicines are Found in the Natural World, 1998. **Address:** 1427 E Waverly St., Tucson, AZ 85719, U.S.A. **Online address:** fredpowledge@nasw.org

POWLES, William E(arnest). Canadian/Japanese (born Japan), b. 1919. **Genres:** Psychiatry, Psychology. **Career:** University of British Columbia, clinical instructor in psychiatry, 1953-59; University of Cincinnati, assistant professor of psychiatry and occupational health, 1959-66; Queen's University, associate professor, professor of psychiatry, 1966-94, professor emeritus, 1994-. Writer. **Publications:** Human Development and Homeostasis: The Science of Psychiatry, 1992. **Address:** Queen's University, 99 University Ave., Kingston, ON K7L 3N6, Canada. **Online address:** wep@queensu.ca

POWLING, Chris. British (born England), b. 1943. **Genres:** Children's Fiction, Children's Non-fiction, Biography. **Career:** Primary school teacher, 1966-75, head teacher, 1975-85; King Alfreds College, senior lecturer in English, 1985-96; Books for Keeps Journal, editor, 1989-96; freelance writer and broadcaster, 1996-; The Guardian, critic; The Observer, critic; Books For Keeps, critic; Carousel, critic; The Times Educational Supplement, critic; British Broadcasting Corp., broadcaster; Classic FM, editor. **Publications:** CHILDREN'S FICTION: Daredevils or Scaredycats, 1979; Mog and the Rectifier, 1980; The Mustang Machine, 1981; Uncle Neptune, 1982; The Conker as Hard as a Diamond, 1984; Stuntkid, 1985; The Phantom Carwash, 1986; Fingers Crossed, 1987; Flyaway Frankie, 1987; Bellas Dragon, 1988; (with S. Anderson) Hiccup Harry, 1988, 2nd ed., 1990; Hoppity-Gap, 1988; Ziggy and the Ice Ogre, 1988; Harrys Party, 1989; The Golden Years of Mother Goose, 1989; A Spook at the Superstore, 1990; ELF 61, 1990; Harry with Spots On, 1990; Butterfingers, 1991; Old Chap Dragon, 1991; Dracula in Sunlight, 1992; Where the Quaggy Bends, 1992; Wesley at the Water Park, 1992; Harry Moves House, 1993; A Razzle-Dazzle Rainbow, 1993; Its That Dragon Again, 1993; (comp.) The Kingfisher Book of Scary Stories, 1994, rev. ed., 2002; (comp.) Faces in the Dark: A Book of Scary Stories, 1994; Famous with Smokey Joe, 1995; Harry the Superhero, 1995; Kits Castle, 1996; Harry on Holiday, 1997; Sophies Nu-Pet, 1998; Talkback, 1998; Gorgeous George, 1998; My Sisters Name Is Roser, 1999; Long John Santa, 1999; All about Us, 1999; Astra in the Attic, 1999; (reteller) The Tempest, 2001; Roger McGough, 2001; The Multi-Million Pound Mascot, 2001; The Ghost Behind the Stars, 2002; Insiders, 2002; Anne Fine, 2003; Mettings with the Minister, 2003; Pirates, 2003; Treasure at the Flea Market, 2006. OTHER: Roald Dahl, 1983; Whats It Like to Be (non-fiction series), 1990; Jan Hoy: A Personnel Manager, 1990; Quentin Blake: An Illustrator, 1990; Michael Rosen: A Poet, 1990; Trish Cooke: A Television Presenter, 1990; (ed.) The Best of Books for Keeps, 1994; A Guide to Poetry 0-13, 1996; Storytelling in Schools, 1997; Dick King-Smith, 1999; Shirley Hughes, 1999; Readers Who Dont, 2000; Shark, 2000; Windows on the World, 2000; The Book about Books, 2000; Blade, 2005; Treasure at the Flea Market, 2005; (comp.) Supershorts: Seriously Spooky Stories, 2007; On the Ghost Trail, 2007; Flint, 2008. Contributor to periodicals. **Address:** 9 Guilford Grove, Greenwich, London, GL SE10 8JY, England.

POWNALL, David. British (born England), b. 1938. **Genres:** Novels, Children's Fiction, Plays/Screenplays, Poetry, Travel/Exploration, Novellas/Short Stories. **Career:** Ford Motor Co., personnel officer, 1960-63, staff, 1960-69; Anglo-American PLC, personnel manager, 1963-69; writer, 1969-; Century Theatre Touring Group, resident writer, 1970-72; Duke's Playhouse, resident playwright, 1972-75; Paines Plough Theatre, founder and resident writer, 1975-80. **Publications:** POETRY: (with J. Hill) An Eagle Each, 1972; Another Country, 1978; The Setting of Nets, Caldy War Memorial, 1979; Madjez-el-Bab, Tunisia, 1980; Thoughts From The Night Ferry, 2007; Poems, 2007. FICTION: The Raining Tree War, 1974; African Horse, 1975; My Organic Uncle and Other Stories 1976; God Perkins, 1977; Light on a Honeycomb, 1978; Beloved Latitudes, 1981; The White Cutter, 1988; The Gardener, 1990; Stagg and His Mother, 1991; The Sphinx and The Sybarites, 1993; The Catalogue of Men, 1999. OTHERS: Motocar and Richard III Part Two, 1979; Between Ribble and Lune: Scenes from the North-West, 1980; (co-ed.) The Fisherman's Bedside Book, 1980; The Bunch from Bananas (for children), 1980; Master Class, 1983; Le Tailleur de Pierre, 1990; El Maestro de Piedra, 1990; Stenmasteren, 1992; The Composer Plays, 1994; Nijinsky: Death of a Faun, 1996; Getting the Picture, 1998; Radio Plays, 1998; Plays One, 2000; Catalogue of Men, 2000; Plays Two, 2002; Plays for One Person: Rousseau's Tale, Crates on Barrels, Later, 2003; The Lancaster Plays, 2006; Innocent Screams, 2007; The Ruling Passion, 2008; Archivist, 2010. **Address:** c/o Johnson & Alcock, 45-47 Clerkenwell Green, Clerkenwell House, London, GL EC1R OHT, England.

POWNING, Beth. Canadian/American (born United States), b. 1949?. **Genres:** Photography, Novels, Children's Fiction, Adult Non-fiction, Poetry. **Career:** Writer and photographer. **Publications:** Seeds of Another Summer: Finding the Spirit of Home in Nature, 1996; Home: Chronicle of a North Country Life, 1996; Shadow Child: An Apprenticeship in Love and Loss, 1999; The Hatbox Letters, 2004; Edge Seasons, 2005; The Sea Captain's Wife, 2010. Works appear in anthologies. Contributor of articles to periodicals. **Address:** c/o Jackie Kaiser, Westwood Creative Artists, 94 Harbord St., Toronto, ON M5S 1G6, Canada. **Online address:** beth@powning.com

POWTER, Susan. American (born United States), b. 1957. **Genres:** Food And Wine, Medicine/Health, How-to Books, Self Help. **Career:** The Susan Powter Show, organizer, 1994. Writer. **Publications:** Stop the Insanity!, 1993; The Pocket Powter: Questions and Answers to Help You Change the Way You Look and Feel Forever, 1994; Food, 1995; C'mon America, Let's Eat!: Susan Powter's Favorite Low-Fat Recipes to Fit Your Lifestyle, 1996; Hey Mom! I'm Hungry!: Great-Tasting, Low-Fat, Easy Recipes to Feed Your Family, 1997; Sober-and Staying That Way: The Missing Link in the Cure for Alcoholism, 1997; Women's Voices Rising, 1998; The Politics of Stupid, 2002. **Address:** Crone Inc., 4509 Interlake N, Ste. 227, Seattle, WA 98103, U.S.A. **Online address:** susanpowterinquiries@yahoo.com

POYER, Joe. American (born United States), b. 1939. **Genres:** Novels, Antiques/Furnishings, Military/Defense/Arms Control. **Career:** Michigan Tuberculosis and Respiratory Disease Association, assistant director of public information, 1961-62; Pratt and Whitney Aircraft, proposal writer and editor, 1963-65; Beckman Instruments Inc., proposal writer and editor, 1965-67; Bioscience Planning Inc., interdisciplinary communications manager, 1968-69; Allergan Pharmaceuticals Inc., senior project manager and research administrator, 1968-77; Golden West College, instructor in novel writing, 1973-75; KCAL-TV, on-camera military analyst, 1990-94; North Cape Publications Inc., owner and publisher, 1991-. **Publications:** EDITOR: Instrumentation Methods for Predictive Medicine, 1966; Biomedical Sciences Instrumentation, 1967. NOVELS: Operation Malacca, 1968; North Cape, 1969; The Balkan Assignment, 1971; The Chinese Agenda, 1972; Hell Shot, 1973; The Shooting of the Green, 1973; The Day of Reckoning, 1976; The Contract, 1978; Tunnel War, 1979; Vengeance 10, 1980; Devoted Friends, 1982; A Time of War, vol. I: The Transgressors, 1984, vol. II: Come Evil Days, 1985. NON-FICTION: (comp.) Milspeak: A Dictionary of International Military

Acronyms & Abbreviations, 1986; (with A. Lightbody) Illustrated History of Tanks, 1989; Illustrated History of Helicopters, 1990; (with A. Lightbody) Helicopter Fighters, 1990; U.S. Combat: America's Land-Based Weaponry, 1990; (with A. Lightbody) Complete Book of U.S. Fighting Power, 1990; Submarines: Hunter/Killers and Boomers, 1990; The Great Book of Fighter Planes, 1990; The Complete Book of Top Gun, 1990; The Complete Book of U.S. Naval Power, 1991; (with C. Riesch) The 45-70 Springfield, 1991, 5th ed., 2011; U.S. Winchester Trench and Riot Guns And Other U.S. Combat Shotguns, 1992; (with C. Riesch) The M1 Garand: 1936-1957, 1995; (co-author) The SKS Carbine (CKC45g), 1996; M14-Type Rifle: A Shooter's and Collector's Guide, 1997; The SAFN-49 Battle Rifle, 1998; (with S. Kehaya) The Swedish Mauser Rifles, 1999; The M16/AR15 Rifle, 2000, 3rd ed., 2007; M1903 Springfield Rifle and Its Variations, 2001; The American Krag Rifle and Carbine, 2001; The Swiss Magazine Loading Rifles 1869-1958, 2003; The AK-47 and AK-74 Kalashnikov Rifles and their Variations: A Shooter's and Collector's Guide, 2nd ed., 2006; The .58- and .50 Caliber Rifles and Carbines of the Springfield Armory, 1865-1872, 2006; U.S. M1 Carbine: Wartime Production, 6th ed., 2007; The Model 1911 and Model 1911A1 Military and Commercial Pistols, 2008. Contributor of articles to periodicals. **Address:** North Cape Publications Inc., PO Box 1027, Tustin, CA 92781, U.S.A. **Online address:** ncape@ix.netcom.com

POYNOR, Robin. American (born United States), b. 1942. **Genres:** Art/Art History, Cultural/Ethnic Topics, History, Photography. **Career:** Purdue University, visiting assistant professor, 1970; University of Minnesota, instructor and curator, 1972-78; University of Florida, visiting assistant professor, 1978-79, adjunct assistant professor, 1979-80, assistant professor, 1980-85, associate professor, 1985-95, professor of art, 1995-, Graduate Study for Art History, director. Writer. **Publications:** African Art at the Harn Museum: Spirit Eyes, Human Hands, 1995; (ed.) Cultural Vibrations: A History of Art n Africa, 2000; (with M.B. Visonà and H.B. Cole) A History of Art in Africa, 2001, 2nd ed., 2008; (ed. with A. Carlson) Africa in Florida, forthcoming. Contributor to books and journals. **Address:** School of Art and Art History, University of Florida, 101 FAC, PO Box 115801, Gainesville, FL 32611-5801, U.S.A. **Online address:** rpoynor@ufl.edu

POYNTER, Jane. American/British (born England), b. 1962?. **Genres:** Social Sciences. **Career:** Paragon Space Development Corp., president; Yogi & Co. (multimedia firm), head; SPACEHAB's experimental ecosystem, chief scientist; Seawater Foundation's carbon-sequestration project, chief scientist. Consultant, writer, speaker, environmental researcher and memoirist. **Publications:** The Human Experiment: Two Years and Twenty Minutes inside Biosphere 2, 2006. **Address:** Yogi & Co., 3481 E Michigan St., Tucson, AZ 85714, U.S.A. **Online address:** info@janepoynter.com

POZNER, Vladimir. American/Russian/French (born France), b. 1934. **Genres:** Writing/Journalism, Autobiography/Memoirs, Military/Defense/Arms Control. **Career:** Translator, 1958-60; Novosty Press Agency, senior editor and managing editor, 1961-67; Soviet Life Magazine, executive editor, 1967-70; Sputnik Magazine, executive editor, 1967-70; North American Service of Radio, commentator, 1970-86; Soviet Central TV, political commentator and talk show host, 1986-91; Academy of Russian Television, president. **Publications:** Parting with Illusions (memoir), 1990; (comp. with H. Keyssar) Remembering War: A U.S.-Soviet Dialogue, 1990; Eyewitness: A Personal Account of the Unraveling of the Soviet Union, 1992; (contrib.) Ėkzamen pered zerkalom: Vladimir Pozner otvechaet na voprosy zhurnalista, 1994; Tur de Frans: puteshestvie po Frantsii s Ivanom Urgantom, 2011. Contributor to periodicals. **Address:** Frederick Hill Associates, 1842 Union St., San Francisco, CA 94123-4308, U.S.A. **Online address:** poznerv@mail.ru

PRADO, Holly. American (born United States), b. 1938. **Genres:** Novels, Poetry. **Career:** English teacher, 1965-73; teacher of writing, 1973-; University of Southern California, Master of Professional Writing Program, teacher of poetry, 1989-2009, instructor, creative writing. **Publications:** Feasts, 1976; Nothing Breaks Off at the Edge, 1976; Losses, 1977; How the Creative Looks Today, 1980; Gardens (novel), 1985; Specific Mysteries, 1990; Esperanza: Poems for Orpheus (poetry), 1998; These Mirrors Prove It: Selected Poems and Prose, 1970-2003, 2004; From One to the Next, 2008; Monkey Journal, 2008. Contributor to periodicals. **Address:** 1256 N Mariposa Ave., Los Angeles, CA 90029, U.S.A. **Online address:** hollyprado@earthlink.net

PRAG, John. British (born England), b. 1941. **Genres:** Archaeology/Antiquities, Social Sciences, Politics/Government. **Career:** Oxford University, Ashmolean Museum, temporary assistant keeper, 1966-67; University of Manchester, Manchester Museum, keeper of archaeology, 1969-, honorary lecturer in history, 1977-83, archaeology, 1984-, reader in classics and ancient history, 2002-, professor of archaeological studies, 2004-, now professor emeritus, Department of Classics and Ancient History, honorary research fellow, professor emeritus of classics; McMaster University, visiting professor of classics, 1978; British School at Athens, visiting fellow, 1994; Manchester Musto University, professor of archaeological studies, 2004-. Writer. **Publications:** The Oresteia: Iconographic and Narrative Tradition, 1985; (with R. Neave) Making Faces: Using Forensic and Archaeological Evidence, 1997, rev. ed., 1999. EDITOR AND CONTRIBUTOR: (with G.R. Tsetskhladze and A.M. Snodgrass) Periplous: Papers on Classical Art and Archaeology Presented to Sir John Boardman, 2000; (with J. Swaddling) Seianti Hanunia Tlesnasa: The Story of an Etruscan Noblewoman, 2000, 2nd ed., 2002; The Story of Alderley Edge, 2002; (ed. with S. Timberlake) The Archaeology of Alderley Edge, 2005. Contributor to journals. **Address:** Manchester Museum, University of Manchester, Oxford Rd., Manchester, GM M13 9PL, England. **Online address:** john.prag@manchester.ac.uk

PRAGER, Emily. American (born United States), b. 1952?. **Genres:** Novellas/Short Stories, Novels, Biography. **Career:** Simon & Schuster, novelist, 1981-82; Random House U.K., novelist, 1983-; New York Times, columnist, 1993-95; New York University, School of Continuing and Professional Studies, teacher, adjunct professor of humanities, 1999-2009, adjunct instructor; Columbia Graduate School of Journalism, adjunct professor, 2000-01; National Lampoon Magazine, contributing editor; Village Voice, columnist; Daily Telegraph, columnist; Penthouse, columnist; The Guardian, columnist; Shanghai American School, teacher. **Publications:** World War II Resistance Stories, 1979; The Official I-Hate-Video Games Handbook, 1982; A Visit from the Footbinder and Other Stories, 1982; (ed.) Titters 101: An Introduction to Women's Literature, 1984; Clea & Zeus Divorce, 1987; Eve's Tattoo, 1991; Roger Fishbite: A Novel, 1999; Wuhu Diary: On Taking My Adopted Daughter Back to Her Hometown in China, 2001; (intro.) After Claude, 2010. **Address:** Random House, 1745 Broadway, New York, NY 10019, U.S.A.

PRALL, Stuart E. American (born United States), b. 1929. **Genres:** History, Humanities. **Career:** Queens College of the City University of New York, lecturer in history, 1955-58, instructor, 1960-63, assistant professor, 1964-66, associate professor, 1967-71, professor of history, 1972-2001, executive, 1988-94, professor emeritus, 2001-; Newark State College, assistant professor of history, 1958-60. Writer. **Publications:** The Agitation for Law Reform during the Puritan Revolution 1640-1660, 1966; (ed.) The Puritan Revolution: A Documentary History, 1968; The Bloodless Revolution: England 1688, 1972; (with D.H. Willson) A History of England, 4th ed., 1991; Church and State in Tudor and Stuart England, 1993; The Puritan Revolution and the English Civil War, 2002. **Address:** 7050 Owl's Nest Terr., Bradenton, FL 34203, U.S.A.

PRANCE, Ghillean Tolmie. British (born England), b. 1937. **Genres:** Botany, Environmental Sciences/Ecology. **Career:** New York Botanical Garden, research assistant, 1963-66, associate curator, 1966-68, curator, 1968-75, director of research, 1975-81, vice president, 1977-81, Institute of Economic Botany, senior vice president and director, 1981-88; Instituto Nacional de Pesquisas da Amazonia, director of graduate studies, 1973-75; Royal Botanical Gardens, Kew, director, 1988-99; University of Reading, visiting professor, 1988-; Malvern College, governor, 1993-; Eden Project, scientific director, 1998-; National Tropical Botanical Garden, McBryde professor, 2000-02. Writer. **Publications:** Leaves: The Formation, Characteristics and Uses of Hundreds of Leaves Found in All Parts of the World, 1986; Manual de Botanica Economica doMaranhao, 1988; Wild Flowers for All Seasons, 1989; Out of the Amazon, 1992; (with A.E. Prance) Bark: The Formation, Characteristics, and Uses of Bark around the World; Rainforests of the World, 1998; (co-author) The Biological Monograph, 1998. EDITOR: Biological Diversification in the Tropics, 1981; Amazonia: Key Environments, 1985; Tropical Forests and World Climate, 1986; (with T.C. Whitmore) Biogeography and Quaternary History in Tropical America (monographs), 1987; White Gold: The Diaries of an Amazon Rubber Tapper, 1989; (with C.B. Dewitt) Missionary Earthkeeping, 1992; (with M. Nesbitt) The Cultural History of Plants, 2004; (with H. Holcroft) Rainforest Light and Spirit, 2008. Contributor to scientific journals and magazines. **Address:** The Old Vicarage, Silver St., Lyme Regis, DS DT7 3HS, England. **Online address:** siriain01@yahoo.co.uk

PRANTERA, Amanda. Italian/British (born England), b. 1942. **Genres:**

Novels, Young Adult Fiction. **Career:** Writer, 1984-. **Publications:** Strange Loop, 1984; The Cabalist, 1986; Conversations with Lord Byron on Perversion, 163 Years After His Lordship's Death, 1987; The Side of the Moon, 1991; Proto Zoë, 1993; Young Italians, 1993; Kingdom of Fànes, 1995; Zoë Trope, 1996; Letter to Lorenzo, 1999; Don Giovanna, 2000; Capri File, 2001; Spoiler, 2003; (as A.P.) Sabine, 2005; The Loft, 2010. Contributor to periodicals. **Address:** Bloomsbury Publishing, 50 Bedford Sq., London, GL WC1B 3DP, England. **Online address:** info@amandaprantera.net

PRAP, Lila. Slovenian (born Slovenia), b. 1955. **Genres:** Children's Fiction, Animals/Pets. **Career:** Architect, 1980-81; teacher, civil engineering, 1981-84; Gorenje Velenje, industrial designer, 1986-89; freelance artist, 1989-. Writer. **Publications:** CHILDRENS BOOKS: Zivalske Uspavanke, 2000; Why?, 2005; Animal Lullabies, 2006; Daddies, 2007, Doggy Whys?, 2011. Illustrator of books by others. **Address:** NorthSouth Books, 350 7th Ave., Ste. 1400, New York, NY 10001, U.S.A. **Online address:** lilijana.praprotnik@guest.arnes.si

PRATCHETT, Terry. British (born England), b. 1948. **Genres:** Science Fiction/Fantasy, Children's Fiction, Young Adult Fiction. **Career:** Journalist, 1965-80; Central Electricity Generating Board, Western Region, press officer, 1980-87; Order of the British Empire, officer, 1998. **Publications:** The Carpet People, 1971, rev. ed., 1992; The Dark Side of the Sun, 1976; Strata, 1981; The Unadulterated Cat, 1989; (with N. Gaiman) Good Omens, 1990; Only You Can Save Mankind, 1992; Johnny and the Dead, 1993; Johnny and the Bomb, 1995; Where's My Cow? 2005; The Illustrated Wee Free Men, 2007; I Shall Wear Midnight, 2010; Snuff, 2011. DISCWORLD NOVEL SERIES: The Colour of Magic, 1983; The Light Fantastic, 1986; Equal Rites, 1987; Mort, 1987; Sourcery, 1988; Wyrd Sisters, 1988; Pyramids, 1989; Eric, 1989; Guards! Guards!, 1989; Moving Pictures, 1990; Reaper Man, 1991; Witches Abroad, 1991; Small Gods, 1992; Lords and Ladies, 1993; Men at Arms, 1993; (with S. Briggs) The Streets of Ankh-Morpork, 1993; (with S. Briggs) The Discworld Companion, 1994, rev. ed., 2003; Soul Music, 1994; Interesting Times, 1994; Maskerade, 1995; (with S. Briggs) The Discworld Mapp, 1995; Feet of Clay, 1996; Hogfather, 1996; Jingo, 1997; The Last Continent, 1998; (with S. Briggs) A Tourist Guide to Lancre, 1998; Carpe Jugulum, 1998; (with P. Kidby) Death's Domain, 1999; (with I. Stewart and J. Cohen) The Science of Discworld, 1999, vol. II: The Globe, 2002, vol. III: Darwin's Watch, 2005; The Fifth Elephant, 1999; The Truth, 2000; Thief of Time, 2001; The Last Hero, 2001; Night Watch, 2002; Monstrous Regiment, 2003; Going Postal, 2004; (with P. Kidby) The Art of Discworld, 2004; Thud!, 2005; Making Money, 2007; Wit & Wisdom of Discworld, 2007; Discworld Graphic Novels, 2008; Unseen Academicals, 2009. BROMELIAD TRILOGY: Truckers, 1989; Diggers, 1990; Wings, 1990; Bromeliad Trilogy, 2003. FOR YOUNG ADULTS: The Amazing Maurice and His Educated Rodents, 2001; The Wee Free Men, 2003; A Hat Full of Sky, 2004; Wintersmith, 2006; Nation, 2008; (with J. Simpson) The Folklore of Discworld, 2008. **Address:** Colin Smythe Ltd., 38 Mill Ln., PO Box 6, Gerrards Cross, BK SL9 8BA, England. **Online address:** tp@colinsmythe.co.uk

PRATHAP, G(angan). Indian/Singaporean (born Singapore), b. 1951. **Genres:** Engineering. **Career:** National Aeronautical Laboratory, research associate, 1978-80; National Aerospace Laboratories, scientist, 1980-2000; DLR Institute of Structural Mechanics, DAAD exchange fellow, 1983-84; Fibre Reinforced Plastics Research Centre, research assistant, 1977-78; Center for Mathematical Modelling and Computer Simulation, scientist-in-charge, 2000-08; Cochin University of Science and Technology (CUSAT), vice chancellor, 2008-09; National Institute of Science Communication and Information Resources (NISCAIR), director; Jawaharlal Nehru Centre for Advanced Scientific Research, honorary senior fellow. Writer. **Publications:** The Finite Element Method in Structural Mechanics: Principles and Practice of Design of Field-Consistent Elements for Structural and Solid Mechanics, 1993. **Address:** Natl Inst of Science Comm & Info Resources, 14, Satsang Vihar Marg, Special Institutional Area, New Delhi, DH 110 067, India. **Online address:** gp@niscair.res.in

PRATT, Anna. (Anna Christine Pratt). Canadian (born Canada), b. 1964?. **Genres:** Military/Defense/Arms Control, History. **Career:** York University, associate professor of criminology. Writer, academic and criminologist. **Publications:** Securing Borders: Detention and Deportation in Canada, 2005. Contributor to periodicals and journals. **Address:** York University, S722 Ross, 4700 Keele St., Toronto, ON M3J 1P3, Canada. **Online address:** apratt@yorku.ca

PRATT, Anna Christine. *See* **PRATT, Anna.**

PRATT, David. British (born England), b. 1973. **Genres:** Politics/Government, History. **Career:** Downing College, archivist, keeper of art and artifacts and fellow in history. Writer, archivist and historian. **Publications:** The Political Thought of King Alfred the Great, 2007. Contributor to books, periodicals and journals. **Address:** England. **Online address:** david.pratt@dow.cam.ac.uk

PRATT, Geraldine. Canadian (born Canada), b. 1955. **Genres:** Young Adult Non-fiction. **Career:** Clark University, faculty member, 1984-86; University of British Columbia, professor of geography, 1986-. Writer. **Publications:** NONFICTION: (ed. with R. Harris) Housing Tenure and Social Class, 1987; Gender, Work and Space, 1995; Working Feminism, 2004; (co-ed.) Dictionary of Human Geography, 5th ed., 2007. Contributor to books and journals. **Address:** Department of Geography, University of British Columbia, 1984 W Mall, Vancouver, BC V6T 1Z2, Canada. **Online address:** gpratt@geog.ubc.ca

PRATT, James Michael. American (born United States) **Genres:** Novels. **Career:** PowerThink Publishing L.L.C., co-founder and owner; Spiritual counselor, businessman and author. **Publications:** The Last Valentine, 1998; The Lighthouse Keeper, 2000; Ticket Home, 2001; Paradise Bay, 2002; Dad, The Man Who Lied to Save The Planet: 12 Timeless Virtues Handed Down to a Son by an Everyday Dad, 2003; Mom, The Woman Who Made Oatmeal Stick to My Ribs, 2004; The Good Heart, 2005; Sneak Peek, forthcoming. **Address:** c/o Author Mail, St. Martin Press, 175 5th Ave., New York, NY 10010, U.S.A. **Online address:** james@jmpratt.com

PRATT, John Clark. American (born United States), b. 1932. **Genres:** Novels, Poetry, History, Literary Criticism And History, Writing/Journalism, Humor/Satire, Essays, Young Adult Fiction, Young Adult Fiction. **Career:** U.S. Air Force Academy, assistant professor, 1960-68, associate professor, 1968-73, professor of English, 1973-74; Colorado State University, professor of English, 1974-2002, chair of department, 1974-80, professor of English, 1980-2001, professor emeritus, 2002-; Pratt Publishing Company Inc., founder and president, 1988-; University of Lisbon, Fulbright lecturer, 1974-75; State University of Leningrad, Fulbright lecturer, 1980; United States Industries Inc., consultant. Writer. **Publications:** The Meaning of Modern Poetry, 1962; John Steinbeck, 1970; The Laotian Fragments, 1974; (with V.A. Neufeldt) George Eliot's Middlemarch Notebooks: An Edition, 1979; Vietnam Voices, 1984, rev. ed., 1999; (with T. Lomperis) Reading the Wind: The Literature of the Vietnam War, 1986; Writing from Scratch: The Essay, 1987; The Royal Lao Air Force: 1959-70, 1995; American Affairs, 2010. EDITOR: One Flew over the Cuckoo's Nest, 1973, rev. ed., 1996; Writing from Scratch: for Business, 1990; Writing from Scratch: Freelancing, 1990; The Quiet American, 1996. **Address:** Department of English, Colorado State University, Ft. Collins, CO 80523, U.S.A. **Online address:** jcpratt@lamar.colostate.edu

PRATT, Pierre. Canadian (born Canada), b. 1962. **Genres:** Children's Fiction, Illustrations, Young Adult Fiction, Children's Non-fiction. **Career:** Writer. **Publications:** SELF-ILLUSTRATED: Follow That Hat!, 1992; Marcel & Andre, 1994; Beaux Dimanches, 1996; Hippo Beach, 1996; Léon sans son chapeau, 1997; Collection pied de nez, vol. I-vol. IV, 1997; La vie exemplaire de Marthaet Paul, 1998; (with H. Roche) Have You Ever seen a Chick Hatch?, 1998; (with H. Roche) Have You Ever Picked a Dandelion?, 1998; Car, 2001; Home, 2001; Park, 2001; Shopping, 2001; I See... My Mom, I See... My Dad, 2001; (with J. Godbout) Mes petites fesses, 2003; Lejour où Zoé zozota, 2005. Illustrator of books others. **Address:** 5976 rue Jeanne Mance, Montreal, QC H2V 4K8, Canada. **Online address:** pierre@pierrepratt.com

PRATT, Steven. *See* **PRATT, Steven G.**

PRATT, Steven G. (Steven Pratt). American (born United States) **Genres:** Food And Wine, Self Help. **Career:** Medical practitioner, 1985-; Scripps Memorial Hospital, senior staff ophthalmologist; La Jolla Laser Vision Eye Center, ophthalmologist; San Diego Eye Bank, vice president. Writer. **Publications:** NONFICTION: WITH KATHY MATTHEWS: Superfoods Rx: Fourteen Foods That Will Change Your Life, 2004; Superfoods Healthstyle: Proven Strategies for Lifelong Health, 2006; The SuperfoodsRx Diet: Lose Weight with the Power of Supernutrients, 2008; Superhealth: 6 Simple Steps, 6 Easy Weeks, 1 Longer, Healthier Life, 2009. Contributor to periodicals.

Address: La Jolla Laser Vision Eye Center, 9850 Genesee Ave., Ste. 310, La Jolla, CA 92037, U.S.A.

PRATT, T. A. *See* **PRATT, Tim.**

PRATT, Tim. (T. A. Pratt). American (born United States), b. 1976. **Genres:** Novellas/Short Stories, Poetry. **Career:** Flytrap (literary magazine), co-editor; Locus magazine, editor and book reviewer, senior editor; poet. **Publications:** (With H. Shaw) Living Together in Mythic Times (chapbook), 2001; (with H. Shaw) Floodwater (chapbook), 2002; (with H. Shaw) Wintering Away (chapbook), 2003; Little Gods (short stories and poetry), 2003; (with E. Donahoe) Love: Sensual, Subversive, and Erotic Poetry and Art, 2003; Pook's Original Miscellany (chapbook), 2004; The Strange Adventures of Rangergirl, 2005; Hart & Boot & Other Stories, 2007; If There Were Wolves, 2006; Blood Engines, 2007; Poison Sleep, 2008; Dead Reign, 2008; Spell Games, 2009; Bone Shop, 2009; Sympathy for the Devil, 2010; Broken Mirrors, 2010; The Nex, 2010; Briarpatch, 2011; Silver Linings, 2011. Contributor to periodicals. **Address:** c/o Author Mail, Night Shade Books, 1470 NW Saltzman Rd., Portland, OR 97229, U.S.A. **Online address:** timpratt@gmail.com

PRAWER, S(iegbert) S(alomon). British/German (born Germany), b. 1925. **Genres:** Film, Language/Linguistics, Literary Criticism And History. **Career:** University of Birmingham, assistant lecturer, 1948-51, lecturer, 1951-58, senior lecturer in German, 1958-63; Westfield College, professor of German, 1964-69; London University Institute of Germanic Studies, honorary director, 1966-68, honorary fellow, 1987-; Harvard University, visiting professor, 1968; Hamburg University, visiting professor, 1969; Queen's College, fellow, 1969-, dean of degrees, 1969-93, honorary fellow, 1993-; University of Oxford, Taylor professor of German language and literature, 1969-86, Taylor emeritus professor of German language and literature, 1986-; Oxford German Studies, co-editor, 1971-75; Anglica Germanica, co-editor, 1973-79; Knox College, visiting fellow, 1976; Australian National University, Humanities Research Centre, visiting fellow, 1980; Brandeis University, Tauber Institute, visiting fellow, 1981-82; Freelance graphic artist, 1986-; Russell Sage Foundation, visiting fellow, 1988. **Publications:** German Lyric Poetry: A Critical Analysis of Selected Poems from Klopstockto Rilke, 1952; Mörike und seine Leser, 1960; Heine's Buch der Lieder: Critical Study, 1960; Heine, The Tragic Satirist, 1961; The Uncanny in Literature (lecture), 1965; Heine's Shakespeare: A Study on Contexts, 1970; Comparative Literary Studies: An Introduction, 1973; Karl Marx and World Literature, 1976; Caligari's Children: The Film as Tale of Terror, 1980; Heine's Jewish Comedy: A Study of His Portraits of Jews and Judaism, 1983; N. Stencl: Poet of Whitechapel, 1984; Coal-Smoke and Englishmen: A Study of Verbal Caricature in the Writings of Heinrich Heine, 1984; Frankenstein's Island: England and the English in the Writings of Heinrich Heine, 1986; Israel at Vanity Fair: Jews and Judaism in the Writings of W.M. Thackeray, 1992; Breeches and Metaphysics: Thackeray's German Discourse, 1997; William Thackeray's European Sketch Books: A Study of Literary and Graphic Portraiture, 2000; The Blue Angel: A Film Classic, 2002; Herzog's Nosferatu: A Modern Classic, 2004; Between Two Worlds: The Jewish Presence in German and Austrian Film, 1910-1933, 2005; Cultural Citizen of the World: Sigmund Freud's Knowledge and Use of British and American Writings, 2009; EDITOR: (trans.) The Penguin Book of Lieder, 1964; (with R.H. Thomas and L. Forster) Essays in German Language, Culture and Society, 1969; The Romantic Period in Germany, 1970; Seventeen Modern German Poets, 1971; Das Cabinet des Dr. Caligari: Drehbuch von Carl Mayer und HansJanowitz zu Robert Wienes Film von 1919/20, 1995. **Address:** University of Oxford, Wellington Sq., Oxford, OX OX1 2JD, England.

PRAZNIAK, Roxann. American (born United States) **Genres:** Area Studies, History, Politics/Government. **Career:** Hampden-Sydney College, associate professor of history, 1990-95, Elliott professor of history, 1996-; University of Oregon, Robert D. Clark Honors College, assistant professor of history, 2002-03, associate professor of history; Soka University of America, visiting professor of history, 2006-07. Writer. **Publications:** Dialogues across Civilization: Sketches in World History From the Chinese and European Experiences, 1996; Of Camel Kings and Other Things: Rural Rebels against Modernity in Late Imperial China, 1999; (ed. with A. Dirlik) Places and Politics in an Age of Globalization, 2001; Sudden Appearances: The Mongol Era in the Making Of Modernities, forthcoming. **Address:** Department of History, Robert D. Clark Honors College, University of Oregon, 221 Chapman Hall, Eugene, OR 97403-1293, U.S.A. **Online address:** prazniak@uoregon.edu

PRECHEL, Harland. American (born United States), b. 1949. **Genres:** Sociology, Social Sciences, Politics/Government. **Career:** State University of New York, instructor, 1985-86, assistant professor, 1986-87; University of Maryland, Department of Sociology and Policy Sciences, 1987-91, affiliate assistant professor, 1990-91; Texas A&M University, Department of Sociology, assistant professor, 1991-93, associate professor, 1993-2001, professor of sociology, 2001-, George Bush School of Government and Public Service, professor, 1997-2002; Comparative and Historical Section of the American Sociological Association, treasury-secretary, 1993-96. Writer. **Publications:** Steel and the State: Industry Politics and Business Policy Formation, 1940-1989, American Sociological Review, 55: 648-668, 1990; Conflict and Historical Variation in Steel Capital-State Relations: The Emergence of State Structures and a More Prominent, Less Autonomous State, American Sociological Review, 56: 693-698, 1991; Economic Crisis and the Centralization of Control Over the Managerial Process: Corporate Restructuring and Neo-Fordist Decision Making, American Sociological Review, 59: 723-745, 1994; (with J. Boies) Capital Dependence, Financial Risk and Change From the Multidivisional to the Multilayered Subsidiary Form, Sociological Forum, 13: 321-362, 1997; Big Business and the State: Historical Transitions and Corporate Transformation, 1880s-1990s, 2000; (with J. Boies) Capital Dependence, Political Behavior and Change to the Multilayered Subsidiary Form, Social Problems, 49: 301-326, 2002; (with T. Morris) Selected Articles: The Effects of Organizational and Political Embeddedness on Financial Malfeasance in the Largest U.S. Corporations: Dependence, Incentives and Opportunities, American Sociological Review, 75: 331-354, 2010. **Address:** Department of Sociology, Texas A&M University, Rm. 429A Academic Bldg., College Station, TX 77843-4351, U.S.A. **Online address:** hprechel@tamu.edu

PRECHTER, Robert R(ougelot). American (born United States), b. 1949. **Genres:** Money/Finance. **Career:** Merrill Lynch, technical market specialist, 1975-79; Elliott Wave Intl., founder, president and chief executive officer, 1979-; Foundation for the Study of Cycles, board director, 1997-2001; Socionomics Institute, founder and principal, 2002-. Writer. **Publications:** (With A.J. Frost) Elliott Wave Principle: Key to Stock Market Profits, 1978, 2nd ed., 1981; (ed. and foreword) The Major Works of R. N. Elliott, 1980, 2nd ed., 1990; A Turn in the Tidal Wave, 1989; (ed. and foreword) R. N. Elliott's Market Letters, 1938-1946, 1993; (ed. and foreword) R.N. Elliott's Masterworks: The Definitive Collection, 1994; At the Crest of the Tidal Wave: A Forecast for the Great Bear Market, 1995; Prechter's Perspective, 1996; (ed.) The Elliott Wave Writings of A.J. Frost and Richard Russell, 1996; Introduction to the Wave Principle of Human Social Behavior, 1998; The Wave Principle of Human Social Behavior and the New Science of Socionomics, 1999; Socionomics: The Science of History and Social Prediction, 1999; View from the Top of the Grand Supercycle, 2001; (ed.) Market Analysis for the New Millennium, 2002; You Can Survive and Prosper in a Deflationary Crash and Depression, 2002; Conquer the Crash: You Can Survive and Prosper in a Deflationary Depression, 2002; Beautiful Pictures from the Gallery of Phinance, 2003, 2nd ed., 2010; View from the Top, 2003; Pioneering Studies in Socionomics, 2003; How to Forecast Gold and Silver Using the Wave Principle, 2006. **Address:** Elliott Wave Intl., PO Box 1618, Gainesville, GA 30503, U.S.A.

PREDA, Alex. Scottish (born Scotland), b. 1960. **Genres:** Social Sciences, Economics. **Career:** University of Edinburgh, lecturer in sociology, professor of sociology. Writer and educator. **Publications:** AIDS, Rhetoric and Medical Knowledge, 2004; (ed. with K.K. Cetina) The Sociology of Financial Markets, 2005; Information, Knowledge and Economic life: An Introduction to the Sociology of Markets, 2009; Framing Finance: The Boundaries of Markets and Modern Capitalism, 2009. Contributor to periodicals and journals. **Address:** School of Social and Political Studies, University of Edinburgh, 5.06 Chrystal Macmillan Bidg., 15a George Sq., Edinburgh, EH8 9LD, Scotland. **Online address:** a.preda@ed.ac.uk

PREGRACKE, Chad. American (born United States), b. 1974. **Genres:** Autobiography/Memoirs, Environmental Sciences/Ecology. **Career:** Living Lands & Waters, founder and president, 1998-. Writer. **Publications:** (With J. Barrow) From the Bottom Up: One Man's Crusade to Clean America's Rivers, 2007. **Address:** Living Lands & Waters, 17624 Rte. 84 N, East Moline, IL 61244-9712, U.S.A. **Online address:** chad@livinglandsandwaters.org

PRELLER, James. Also writes as Mitzi Kafka, James Patrick. American (born United States), b. 1961. **Genres:** Children's Fiction, Children's Nonfiction, Sports/Fitness, Ghost Writer, Picture/Board Books, Young Adult Non-fiction. **Career:** Scholastic Inc., copywriter and promotion manager, 1985-90; freelance writer and editor, 1990-. **Publications:** CHILDREN'S FICTION: Maxx Tax: Avalanche Rescue!, 1986; Maxx Trax II: Monster Truck Adventure, 1988; The Fox and the Hound, 1988; Big Top Pee Wee: Pee-Wee and the Circus, 1988; Wake Me in Spring, 1994; Hiccups for Elephant, 1994; Kratts' Creatures: Off to Elephant School, 1996; Space Jam, 1996; Bugs Bunny's Space Jam Scrapbook, 1996; (with M. Preller) The Boastful Frog, 1996; Kratts' Creatures: What's Buggin You?, 1997; The Lost World, Jurassic Park: The Complete Dinosaur Scrapbook, 1997; Stinkers, 1997; Cardinal and Sunflower, 1998; (adaptor) Godzilla, 1998; The Godzilla Movie Scrapbook, 1998; The Iron Giant: A Novelization, 1999; Along came Spider, 2008; Six Innings: A Game in the Life, 2008; Mighty Casey, 2009; Bystander, 2009; Justin Fisher Declares War!, 2010; A Pirate's Guide To First Grade, 2010. JIGSAW JONES SERIES: The Case of Missing Hamster, 1998; The Case of the Christmas Snowman, 1998; The Case of the Secret Valentine, 1999; Case of the Stolen Baseball Cards, 1999; The Case of the Spooky Sleepover, 1999; Case of the Runaway Dog, 1999; Case of the Great Sled Race, 1999; The Case of the Baseball Card Caper, 1999; The Case of the Mummy Mystery, 1999; The Case of the Ghostwriter, 2000; The Case of the Class Clown, 2000; Rain, Rain, Go Away, 2000; The Case of the Stinky Science Project, 2000; The Case of the Detective in Disguise, 2001; The Case of the Sneaker Sneak, 2001; Case of the Bicycle Bandit, 2001; The Case of the Haunted Scarecrow, 2001; The Case of the Golden Key, 2002; The Case of the Disappearing Dinosaur, 2002; The Case of the Million-Dollar Mystery, 2002; The Case of the Buried Treasure, 2002; The Case of the Bear Scare, 2002; The Case of the Rainy Day Mystery, 2003; The Case of the Race against Time, 2003; The Case of the Perfect Prank, 2004; The Case of the Santa Claus Mystery, 2004; The Case of the Glow-in-the-Dark Ghost, 2004; The Case of the Double Trouble Detectives, 2005; The Case Of The Frog-jumping Contest, 2005; The Case of the Food Fight, 2005; Case of the Groaning Ghost, 2006; Case of the Snowboarding Superstar, 2006; Case of the Spoiled Rotten Spy, 2007; Case of the Kidnapped Candy, 2007. NONFICTION: Meet the Authors and Illustrators, 1993; In Search of the Real Tasmanian Devil, 1996; How I Saved the World, 1996; NBA Action from A to Z, 1996; Lost World Scrapbook, 1997; NBA Book of Big and Little, 1998; The Next Generation with Poster, 1998; McGwire and Sosa, 1998; (adaptor)The Mummy: Movie Scrapbook, 1999; (with J. Layden) Inside the WNBA, 1999; The NBA Book of Opposites, 2000; Rock Solid, 2000; Meet the Stars of Professional Wrestling, 2000; The Big Book of Picture-book Authors & Illustrators, 2001; Baseball Power Players, 2002; Major League Baseball Card Collectors's Kit with Book, 2002; Football Power Playes, 2002; The Major League Baseball Guide to Card Collecting, 2003; Behind The Scenes, 2003; Fantasy Football, 2003; Megastars: NFL, 2003; NFL Team Tracker, 2003; National Football League Megastars, 2004; World Series Scrapbook, 2005; Super Bowl Super Touchdowns: NFL, 2005. SPORTS: How to Play Little League Baseball, 1990; Sports Shots: Michael Jordan, 1994; The Ultimate NBA Postcard Book, 1996; Extreme Sports Photo Scrapbook, 1997; (with J. Layden) NBA Game Day, 1997; 3-in-1 Table Top Sports, 2003. AS MITZI KAFKA: The Norfin Trolls: Too Many Trolls, 1993; The Norfin Trolls: The Best Costume Party Ever, 1993. AS JAMES PATRICK: Buyer be Aware: The Complete Car Buyers' Text, 1993; Men in Black, 1997; Quest for Camelot, 1998; Baby Geniuses Movie Scrapbook, 1998; Football Madness: The Road to Super Bowl XXXVII, 2003. GHOSTWRITER: Shaquille O'Neal, Shaq and the Beanstalk and Other Very, Very Tall Tales, 1999; Ghost Cat and Other Spooky Tales, 2006. **Address:** Scholastic Books, 557 Broadway, New York, NY 10012, U.S.A. **Online address:** jimmyprell@aol.com

PRELUTSKY, Jack. American (born United States), b. 1940. **Genres:** Children's Fiction, Poetry, Translations, Adult Non-fiction. **Career:** Writer. **Publications:** POEMS: A Gopher in the Garden and Other Animal Poems, 1967; Lazy Blackbird and Other Verses, 1969; Three Saxon Nobles and Other Verses, 1969; The Terrible Tiger, 1969; Toucans Two and Other Poems, 1971; Circus, 1974; The Pack Rat's Day and Other Poems, 1974; Nightmares: Poems to Trouble Your Sleep, 1976; It's Halloween Christmas, Thanksgiving, Valentine's Day, 4 vols., 1977-83; The Snopp on the Sidewalk and Other Poems, 1977; The Mean Old Mean Hyena, 1978; The Queen of Eene, 1978; The Headless Horseman Rides Tonight: More Poems to Trouble Your Sleep, 1980; Rainy Day Saturday, 1980; Rolling Harvey down the Hill, 1980; The Sheriff of Rottenshot: Poems, 1982; Kermit's Garden of Verses, 1982; The Baby Uggs are Hatching, 1982; The Random House Book of Poetry for Children, 1983; It's Snowing! It's Snowing!, 1984; What I Did Last Summer, 1984; New Kid on the Block, 1984; My Parents Think I'm Sleeping, 1985; Ride a Purple Pelican, 1986; Tyrannosaurus Was a Beast, 1988; Beneath a Blue Umbrella, 1990; Something Big Has Been Here, 1990; (ed.) For Laughing Out Loud: More Poems to Tickle Your Funnybone, 1991; Twickham Tweer, 1991; There'll be a Slight Delay and Other Poems for Grown Ups, 1991; Jack Prelutsky's Sweet & Silly Muppet Poems, 1992; The Dragons Are Singing Tonight, 1993; A. Nonny Mouse Writes Again!: Poems, 1993; Monday's Troll, 1996; A Pizza the Size of the Sun, 1996; (ed.) Beauty of the Beast, 1997; (ed.) Imagine That!: Poems of Never-Was, 1998; (with Seuss and L. Smith) Hooray for Diffendoofer Day!, 1998; Dog Days, 1999; Gargoyle on the Roof, 1999; (ed.) 20th Century Children's Poetry Treasury, 1999; It's Raining Pigs and Noodles, 2000; Awful Ogre's Awful Day, 2000; The Frogs Wore Red Suspenders, 2002; Halloween Countdown, 2002; Scranimals, 2002; The Wild Witches' Ball, 2004; If Not for the Cat, 2004; Read a Rhyme, Write a Rhyme, 2005; Behold the Bold Umbrellaphant: And Other Poems, 2006; What a Day it was at School!: Poems, 2006; In Aunt Giraffe's Green Garden, 2007; Wizard, 2007; Good Sports: Rhymes About Running, Jumping, Throwing, and More, 2007; In Old Giraffe's Green Garden: Rhymes, 2007; Me I Am!, 2007; It's Thanksgiving!, 2007; My Dog May be a Genius: Poems, 2008; Awful Ogre Running Wild, 2008; Pizza, Pigs, and Poetry: How to Write a Poem, 2008; It's Christmas!, 2008; It's Valentine's Day!, 2009; The Swamps of Sleethe: Poems from Beyond the Solar System, 2009; (ed.) There's No Place like School: Classroom Poems, 2010; Carnival of the Animals by Camille Saint-Saëns: New Verses, 2010; Fabulous Skating Potato, 2012; Stardines Swim High Across the Sky and Other Poems, 2012. TRANSLATOR: R. Neumann, The Bad Bear, 1967; H. Hoffman, The Mountain Bounder, 1967; W. Blecher, No End of Nonsense, 1968; J. Kruess, The Proud Wooden Drummer, 1969. **Address:** c/o Author Mail, Greenwillow Books, 1350 Ave. of the Americas, New York, NY 10019-4702, U.S.A.

PREMO, Bianca. (Bianca C. Premo). American (born United States), b. 1969. **Genres:** Law, History. **Career:** Instituto de Estudios Peruanos, researcher, 1997-99; University of North Carolina, instructor, 2000; Duke University, visiting instructor of history, 2000; Emory University, assistant professor of history, 2001-07; Florida International University, associate professor of history, 2007-; Universidad Nacional Mayor de San Marcos, GÉnero e Historia Program, affiliate. Writer and historian. **Publications:** Children of the Father King: Youth, Authority, & Legal Minority in Colonial Lima, 2005; (ed. with O.E. Gonzalez) Raising an Empire: Children in Early Modern Iberia and Colonial Latin America, 2007. Contributor to books and periodicals. **Address:** Department of History, Florida International University, DM 391-C, University Pk., Miami, FL 33199, U.S.A. **Online address:** premob@fiu.edu

PREMO, Bianca C. *See* **PREMO, Bianca.**

PRENDERGAST, John. American (born United States), b. 1958. **Genres:** Novels, Young Adult Fiction. **Career:** University of Pennsylvania, assistant editor, 1982, staff writer in Development Office, 1982-84, Wharton School, staff writer, 1984; Agency at Centrum, editor, 1984-85; Thomas Jefferson University, development writer, 1985-87; Inform Inc., associate director of development, 1988-89; American Society of Civil Engineers, associate editor, 1989-91, managing editor, 1991-96, civil engineering; The Pennsylvania Gazette, editor. **Publications:** Jump (novel), 1995. Contributor of articles to periodicals. **Address:** The Pennsylvania Gazette, 3910 Chestnut St., 3rd Fl., Philadelphia, PA 19104-3111, U.S.A. **Online address:** jprender@ben.dev.upenn.edu

PRENDERGAST, Mark J(oseph Anthony). British/Irish (born Ireland), b. 1959. **Genres:** Adult Non-fiction, History, Literary Criticism And History. **Career:** Irish Times, journalist, 1981-83; Irish Rock, journalist, 1983-85; Hi-Fi Choice, reviewer, writer, and interviewer, 2002-. **Publications:** Irish Rock: Roots, Personalities, Directions, 1987; The Isle of Noises, 1990; Classical Music, 1994; Tangerine Dream Tangents, 1994; Jimi Hendrix Companion, 1996; The Ambient Century: From Mahler to Trance: The Evolution of Sound in the Electronic Age, 2000, rev. ed., 2003. Contributor to journals. **Address:** 2 Liphook Cres., Forest Hill, London, GL SE2 33BW, England. **Online address:** prenderg@ohio.edu

PRESCOTT, Casey. *See* **MORRIS, Chris(topher Crosby).**

PRESCOTT, J(ohn) R(obert) V(ictor). (Victor Prescott). Australian (born Australia), b. 1931?. **Genres:** Geography, Politics/Government. **Career:** University College, lecturer in geography, 1956-61; University of Melbourne, faculty, 1961-, professor of geography, chair in geography, through, 1996, professor emeritus, 1996-. Writer. **Publications:** The Geography of Frontiers and Boundaries, 1965, rev. ed. as Frontiers and Boundaries, 1978; The Geography of State Policies, 1968; The Evolution of Nigeria's International and Regional Boundaries 1861-1971, 1971; Political Geography, 1972; The Political Geography of the Oceans, 1975; The Map of Mainland Asia by Treaty, 1975; (with W.G. East) Our Fragmented World: An Introduction to Political Geography, 1975; (with H.J. Collier and D.F. Prescott) The Frontiers of Asia and Southeast Asia, 1976; Boundaries and Frontiers, 1978; (with J.F. Lovering) The Last of Lands: Antarctica, 1979; (ed.) Australia's Continental Shelf, 1979; Maritime Jurisdiction in Southeast Asia, 1981; Australia's Maritime Boundaries, 1985; (with C. Schofield) The Maritime Political Boundaries of the World, 1986, (with C. Schofield) 2nd ed., 2005; Political Frontiers and Boundaries, 1987; Maritime Jurisdiction In East Asian Seas, 1987; (with S.L. Davis) Aboriginal Frontiers and Boundaries in Australia, 1992; (as Victor Prescott) South China Sea: Limits of National Claims, 1996; (with D. Hancox) Secret Hydrographic Surveys in the Spratly Islands, 1997; The Gulf of Thailand: Maritime Limits to Conflict and Cooperation, 1998; (with G. Boyes) Undelimited Maritime Boundaries in the Pacific Ocean Excluding the Pacific Rim, 2000; (with C. Schofield) Undelimited Maritime Boundaries of the Asian Rim in the Pacific Ocean, 2001; (with G.D. Triggs) International Frontiers and Boundaries, 2008. **Address:** Department of Geography and Environmental Studies, University of Melbourne, 801 Swanston St., Parkville, VI 3010, Australia. **Online address:** johnrvp@unimelb.edu.au

PRESCOTT, Victor. *See* **PRESCOTT, J(ohn) R(obert) V(ictor).**

PRESNALL, Judith (Ann) Janda. American/Polish/Slovak (born Slovakia), b. 1943. **Genres:** Animals/Pets, Children's Non-fiction, Young Adult Non-fiction, Biography, Picture/Board Books, Children's Fiction. **Career:** John Marshall Junior High School, business teacher, 1967-69; Pierce Community College, typing teacher, 1982-86; Merit College, typing teacher, 1984-88; writer, 1985-. **Publications:** Animals That Glow, 1993; Rachel Carson, 1994; Animal Skeletons, 1995; Artificial Organs, 1995; Circuses: Under the Big Top, 1996; The Giant Panda, 1997; Oprah Winfrey, 1998; Mount Rushmore, 1999; Life on Alcatraz, 2000; Guide Dogs, 2002; Horse Therapists, 2002; Police Dogs, 2002; Animal Actors, 2002; Navy Dolphins, 2002; Circus Animals, 2003; Capuchin Monkey Aides, 2003; Rescue Dogs, 2003; Rodeo Animals, 2003; Canine Companions, 2003; Carrier Pigeons, 2004; Racehorses, 2004; Sled Dogs, 2004; Hearing Dogs, 2005. **Address:** 6311 Crebs Ave., Tarzana, CA 91335, U.S.A. **Online address:** judypresnall@hotmail.com

PRESNELL, Barbara. American (born United States), b. 1954. **Genres:** Poetry, Industrial Relations. **Career:** North Carolina Arts Council, artist-in-residence, 1977-79, fellow, 2002; Kentucky Arts Council, artist-in-residence, 1987-95; University of Kentucky, adjunct instructor in English, 1990-95; Catawba College, assistant professor of English, 1995-2000; University of North Carolina, lecturer, 2000. Writer. **Publications:** POETRY: Snake Dreams, 1994; Unravelings, 1998; Los Hijos, 2002; Sherry's Prayer, 2004; Piece Work, 2007. Works appear in anthologies. Contributor to journals. **Address:** 17 Hege Dr., Lexington, NC 27292-2321, U.S.A. **Online address:** bpresnell@lexcominc.net

PRESS, Frank. (Frank D. Press). American (born United States), b. 1924. **Genres:** Earth Sciences, Young Adult Fiction. **Career:** Columbia University, research associate, 1946-49, instructor, 1949-51, assistant professor, 1951-52, associate professor of geophysics and oceanography, 1952-55; California Institute of Technology, professor of geophysics, 1955-65, Caltech Seismological Laboratory, director, 1957-65; Massachusetts Institute of Technology, professor of geology and geophysics and Department of Earth and Planetary Sciences, chairman, 1965-77, professor, 1981; Executive Office of the President, Office of Science and Technology Policy, director and adviser to the president, 1977-80; U.S. National Academy of Sciences, president, 1981-93. Writer. **Publications:** (With M. Ewing) Two Applications of Normal Mode Sound Propagation in the Ocean, 1948; (co-author) Air-Coupled Flexural Waves in Floating Ice, 1950; (with R. Siever) Earth, 1974, 4th ed., 1986; (ed. with Siever) Planet Earth: Readings from Scientific American, 1974; (with Siever) A Study Guide to the Earth, 1974; (contrib.) High Technology Gap?: Europe, America and Japan, 1987; Understanding Earth, 1997, (with J. Grotzinger, T.H. Jordon and R. Siever) 4th ed., 2004. **Address:** 2500 Virginia Ave., Ste. 616 S, Washington, DC 20037-1001, U.S.A.

PRESS, Frank D. *See* **PRESS, Frank.**

PRESS, O(tto) Charles. American (born United States), b. 1922. **Genres:** Politics/Government, Public/Social Administration, Urban Studies, Biography. **Career:** North Dakota Agricultural College, faculty, 1954-56, instructor in political science, 1956-57; Grand Rapids Metropolitan Area Study, director, 1956-57; University of Wisconsin, assistant professor, 1957-58; Michigan State University, Institute of Community Development, staff, assistant professor, 1958-62, associate professor, 1962-65, Department of Political Science, professor, 1965-91, chairman, 1965-72, now professor emeritus; Midwest Political Science Association, president, 1974-75. Writer. **Publications:** When One Third of a City Moves to the Suburbs; A Report on the Grand Rapids Metropolitan Area, 1959; (with C. Adrian) Convention Report, 1962; Main Street Politics; (with C.R. Adrian) The American Political Process, 1965; (with C.R. Adrian) Choice Theory: AGlossary of Terms, 1966; (with C. Adrian)Politics Reappraisal, American 1974; (with C.R. Adrian) Governing Urban America, 5th ed., 1977; (with K. VerBurg) State and Community Governments in a Feral System, 1979, 2nd ed., 1983; (with K. VerBurg) American Policy Studies, 1981; The Political Cartoon, 1981; (with K. VerBurg) State and Community Governments in the Federal System, 1983; Primer for Board of Review Members, 4th ed., 1987; (with K. VerBurg) American Politicians and Journalists, 1988; (with K. VerBurg) State and Community Governments in a Dynamic Federal System, 3rd ed., 1991; Looking over Sir Arthur's Shoulder: How Conan Doyle Turned the Trick, 2004. EDITOR: (with O.P. Williams) Democracy in Urban America, 1964; (with A. Arian) Empathy and Ideology, 1966; (ed. with O.P. Williams) Democracy in the Fifty States, 1966. **Address:** Department of Political Science, Michigan State University, 303 S Kedzie Hall, East Lansing, MI 48824, U.S.A. **Online address:** pressc@msu.edu

PRESSER, Stephen B. (Stephen Bruce Presser). American (born United States), b. 1946. **Genres:** Law, Business/Trade/Industry, Politics/Government. **Career:** Rutgers University, assistant professor of law, 1974-76, associate professor, 1976-77; University of Virginia, visiting associate professor of law, 1976-77; Northwestern University, associate professor, 1977-79, professor of law, 1979-, Raoul Berger professor of legal history, 1992-, Department of Management and Strategy, adjunct professor, 1992-99, professor of business law, 1999-. Writer. **Publications:** (Ed. with J.S. Zainaldin) Law and Jurisprudence in American History: Cases and Materials, 1980, 7th ed., 2008; Studies in the History of the United States Courts of the Third Circuit, 1982; Piercing the Corporate Veil, 1991; The Original Misunderstanding: The English, The Americans, and The Dialectic of Federalist Jurisprudence, 1991; Recapturing the Constitution: Race, Religion and Abortion Reconsidered, 1994; An Introduction to the Law of Business Organizations: Cases, Notes and Questions, 2005, 3rd ed., 2010. **Address:** Law School, Northwestern University, 357 E Chicago Ave., Chicago, IL 60611, U.S.A. **Online address:** s-presser@law.northwestern.edu

PRESSER, Stephen Bruce. *See* **PRESSER, Stephen B.**

PRESSLER, Mirjam. German (born Germany), b. 1940. **Genres:** Children's Fiction, Novels. **Career:** Author and translator. **Publications:** Novemberkatzen: Kinderroman, 1982; Unter der Steinhaut: Treffen Junger Autoren '93, 1994; Jola und Nickel in der Schule, 1994; The Diary of a Young Girl: The Definitive Edition, 1995; Halinka, 1998; The Story of Anne Frank, 1999; Shylocks Tochter: Venedig im Jahre 1568, 1999; Anne Frank: A Hidden Life, 2000; Shylock's Daughter, 2001; Malka, 2002; Zeit der schlafenden Hunde: Roman, 2003; Wenn das Gluck Kommt, Muss Man ihm einen Stuhl Hinstellen, Neuausg, 2004; Rosengift, 2004; Wundertütentage: Roman für Kinder, 2005; Golem stiller Bruder, 2007; Let Sleeping Dogs Lie, 2007; Grüsse und Küsse an alle: die Geschichte der Familie von Anne Frank, 2009; Nathan und seine Kinder: Roman, 2009; The Diary of a Young Girl, 2010; (with G. Elias) Treasures from the Attic: The Extraordinary Story of Anne Frank's Family, 2011. Contributor to periodicals. **Address:** Verlag Beltz und Gelberg, Werderstrasse 10, Weinheim, 69469, Germany.

PRESSMAN, Jeremy. American (born United States), b. 1969. **Genres:** Politics/Government. **Career:** Carnegie Endowment for International Peace, project associate, 1991-96; University of Connecticut, assistant professor of political science, 2003-09, associate professor, 2009-10, Alan R. Bennet Honorary Professor of Political Science, 2010-. Writer and political scientist. **Publications:** Point of No Return: The Deadly Struggle for Middle East Peace, 1997; Warring Friends: Alliance Restraint in International Politics, 2008. Contributor to books, periodicals and journals. **Address:** U.S.A. **Online address:** jeremy.pressman@uconn.edu

PRESSNER, Amanda. American (born United States), b. 1978?. **Genres:** Travel/Exploration. **Career:** Condé Nast Publications, copywriter, 2002-03; Self, editorial assistant, 2003-04, assistant editor, 2004-05; Shape, senior editor, 2007-09; freelance writer, 2009-. **Publications:** (With J. Baggett and H.C. Corbett) The Lost Girls: Three Friends, Four Continents, One Unconventional Detour around the World, 2010. Contributor to periodicals. **Address:** New York, NY , U.S.A. **Online address:** pressner@gmail.com

PRESTON, Andrew. British (born England), b. 1973. **Genres:** History, Theology/Religion. **Career:** Yale University, Center for International and Area Studies, Fox international fellow, 1999-2000, International Security Studies, post doctoral fellow, 2001-03, International Security Studies, visiting assistant professor, 2005-06, John M Olin fellow, 2005-06; University of Victoria, faculty; London School of Economics, Cold War Studies Centre, fellow, 2006-09; Graduate Institute of International and Development Studies, visiting professor of history, 2007; Cambridge University, Clare College, fellow, senior lecturer in american history. Writer and historian. **Publications:** The War Council: McGeorge Bundy, the NSC and Vietnam, 2006; (ed. with F. Logevall) Nixon in the World: American Foreign Relations, 1969-1977, 2008; Sword Of The Spirit, Shield of Faith: Religion In American War And Diplomacy, 2012. Contributor to periodicals. **Address:** Clare College, Cambridge University, Trinity Ln., West Rd., Cambridge, CB2 1TL, England. **Online address:** amp33@cam.ac.uk

PRESTON, Ben. *See* **SANNA, Ellyn.**

PRESTON, Caroline. American (born United States) **Genres:** Novels, Humor/Satire, Young Adult Fiction. **Career:** Harvard University, Houghton Library, archivist and manuscript librarian; Peabody Essex Museum, manuscript librarian. Writer. **Publications:** Jackie by Josie, 1997; Lucy Crocker 2.0, 2000; Gatsby's Girl, 2006; The Scrapbook of Frankie Pratt: A Novel in Pictures, 2011. **Address:** Scribner, 1230 Ave. of the Americas, New York, NY 10020, U.S.A.

PRESTON, Diana. British (born England), b. 1952?. **Genres:** History, Travel/Exploration. **Career:** Canadian Broadcasting Corp., broadcaster; British Broadcasting Corp., broadcaster. Journalist. **Publications:** The Road to Culloden Moor: Bonnie Prince Charlie and the 45 Rebellion, 1995; A First Rate Tragedy: Captain Scott's Antarctic Expeditions, 1997; The Boxer Rebellion, The Dramatic Story of China's War on Foreigners That Shook the World in the Summer of 1900, 2000; Brief History of the Boxer Rebellion: China's War on Foreigners, 1900, 2000; Lusitania: An Epic Tragedy, 2002; Remember the Lusitania, 2003; (with M. Preston) A Pirate of Exquisite Mind: Explorer, Naturalist, and Buccaneer: The Life of William Dampier, 2004; Before the Fallout: From Marie Curie to Hiroshima, 2005; Before the Fall-Out: The Human Chain Reaction from Marie Curie to Hiroshima, 2005; Cleopatra and Antony: Power, Love, and Politics in the Ancient World, 2009. **Address:** c/o Author Mail, Walker & Co., 104 5th Ave., New York, NY 10011, U.S.A.

PRESTON, Douglas. American (born United States), b. 1956. **Genres:** Novels, Archaeology/Antiquities, Art/Art History, Natural History, Young Adult Non-fiction, Horror. **Career:** American Museum of Natural History, editor, writer, manager of publications, 1978-85; Editions Alecto Ltd., director and executive vice president, 1985-87; Princeton University, lecturer in English, 1989-90; Laboratory of Anthropology, research associate; Smithsonian, contributing writer; The Atlantic Monthly, contributing writer; The New Yorker, contributing writer; Curator, managing editor; Natural History Magazine, columnist. **Publications:** Dinosaurs in the Attic: An Excursion into the American Museum of Natural History, 1986; Cities of Gold: A Journey Across the American Southwest in Pursuit of Coronado, 1992; Jennie, 1994; Talking to the Ground: One Family's Journey on Horseback Across the Sacred Land of the Navajo, 1995; (with J.A. Esquibel) The Royal Road: El Camino Real From Mexico City to Santa Fe, 1998; The Codex, 2003; Tyrannosaur Canyon, 2005; (contrib.) Ribbons of Time: The Dalquest Research Site, 2006; (M. Spezi) Monster of Florence, 2008; Blasphemy, 2008; Impact, 2010. WITH L. CHILD: The Relic, 1994; Mount Dragon: A Novel, 1996; Reliquary, 1997; Riptide, 1998; Thunderhead, 1999; The Ice Limit, 2000; The Cabinet of Curiosities, 2002; Still Life with Crows, 2003; Brimstone, 2004; Dance of Death, 2005; The Book of the Dead, 2006; The Wheel of Darkness, 2007; Cemetery Dance, 2009; Fever Dream, 2010; Cold Vengeance, 2011; Gideon's Sword, 2011; Gideon's Corpse, 2012. Contributor to periodicals. **Address:** c/o Author Mail, Grand Central Publishing, 237 Park Ave., New York, NY 10017-3140, U.S.A.

PRESTON, Ivy (Alice). (Ivy (Alice) Kinross Preston). New Zealander (born New Zealand), b. 1914. **Genres:** Romance/Historical, Autobiography/Memoirs, Novels, Young Adult Fiction, Mystery/Crime/Suspense. **Career:** Romance novelist. **Publications:** The Silver Stream (autobiography), 1959; Where Rats Twine, 1960; None So Blind, 1961; Magic in Maoriland, 1962; Rosemary for Remembrance, 1962; Island of Enchantment, 1963; Tamarisk in Bloom, 1963; Hearts Do Not Break, 1964; The Blue Remembered Hills, 1965; Secret Love of Nurse Wilson, 1965; Enchanted Evening, 1966; Hospital on the Hill, 1967; Nicolette, 1967; Red Roses for a Nurse, 1968; Ticket of Destiny, 1969; April in Westland, 1969; A Fleeting Breath, 1970; Interrupted Journey, 1970; (co-author) Springbrook: Seventy-Five Years of Progress, 1971; A Fleeting Breath, 1971; Portrait of Pierre, 1971; Petals in the Wind, 1972; Release the Past, 1973; Romance in Glenmore Street, 1974; Voyage of Destiny, 1974; Moonlight on the Lake, 1975; House above the Bay, 1976; Sunlit Seas, 1977; Where Stars May Lead, 1978; One Broken Dream, 1979; Mountain Magic, 1979; Summer at Willowbank, 1980; Interlude in Greece, 1982; Nurse in Cofusion, 1983; Enchantment at Hillcrest, 1984; Fair Accuser, 1985; To Dream Again, 1985; Flight from Heartbreak, 1986; Landscapes of the Past (autobiography), 1986; Threads of Destiny, 1986; Stranger from the Sea, 1987; Pacific Magic, 1987; Tumult of the Heart, 1988; Spring at Granite Peaks, 1990; Love in Las Vegas, 1993; Rainbow in My Hand, 1997. **Address:** 95 Church St., Timaru, 7910, New Zealand.

PRESTON, Ivy (Alice) Kinross. *See* **PRESTON, Ivy (Alice).**

PRESTON, Marcia K. (M. K. Preston). American (born United States), b. 1944. **Genres:** Mystery/Crime/Suspense, Young Adult Fiction. **Career:** National Cowboy & Western Heritage Museum, public relations and publications director. Writer and educator. **Publications:** FICTION: (as M.K. Preston) Perhaps She'll Die: A Chantalene Mystery, 2001; (as M.K. Preston) Song of the Bones: A Chantalene Mystery, 2003; The Butterfly House, 2005; The Piano Man, 2005; Trudy's Promise, 2008; The Wind Comes Sweeping, 2009. Contributor to periodicals. **Address:** OK , U.S.A. **Online address:** marcia@marciapreston.com

PRESTON, M. K. *See* **PRESTON, Marcia K.**

PRESTON-MAFHAM, Rod(ney Arthur). British (born England), b. 1942. **Genres:** Zoology, Natural History, Young Adult Non-fiction, Animals/Pets, Sciences, Education, Reference. **Career:** Grammar School, Biology teacher and department head, 1974-88; Premaphotos Wildlife (picture library), partner and photographer, 1976-. Writer. **Publications:** WITH K. PRESTON-MAFHAM: Spiders of the World, 1984; Butterflies of the World, 1988; The Book of Spiders and Scorpions, 1991; Cacti: The Illustrated Dictionary, 1991; Primates of the World, 1992; The Encyclopedia of Land Invertebrate Behaviour, 1993; The Natural History of Spiders, 1996; The Natural History of Insects, 1996; Natural World of Bugs & Insects, 2001; Bears, 2002; Encyclopedia of Insects and Spiders, 2005; (with A. Campbell and A.J. Beer) Insects & Other Invertebrates, 2006; Spiders, 2007. **Address:** Premaphotos Wildlife, Amberstone, 1 Kirland Rd., Bodmin, CW PL30 5JQ, England. **Online address:** library@premaphotos.co.uk

PRESTOWITZ, Clyde V. American (born United States), b. 1941. **Genres:** Economics. **Career:** U.S. Foreign Service, diplomat; Reagan Administration, counselor to the secretary of commerce, 1981; Carnegie Endowment (foreign-policy think tank), senior associate, 1988; Economic Strategy Institute, founder and president. Writer. **Publications:** Lessons from the Fall and Rise of Nations: The Future for America, 1987; Trading Places: How We Allowed Japan to Take the Lead, 1988 as Trading Places: How We Are Giving Our Future to Japan and How to Reclaim It, 1989. (ed. with R.A. Morse and A. Tonelson) Powernomics: Economics and Strategy after the Cold War, 1991; (co-author) The New North American Order: A Win-Win Strategy for U.S.-Mexico Trade, 1991; (with E. Schulz) The Networked Economy: Lessons from the Trenches, 2000; Rogue Nation: American Unilateralism and the Failure of Good Intentions, 2003; Three Billion New Capitalists: The Great Shift of Wealth and Power to the East, 2005; The Betrayal of American Prosperity: Free Market Delusions, America's Decline, and How We Must Compete in the Post-dollar Era, 2010. Contributor to periodicals. **Address:** Economic Strategy Institute, 3050 K St. NW Ste. 200, Washington, DC 20007, U.S.A. **Online address:** presto@econstrat.org

PRESTWICH, Michael (Charles). British (born England), b. 1943. **Genres:** History, Politics/Government. **Career:** Oxford University, lecturer, 1965-69;

University of St. Andrews, lecturer in medieval history, 1969-79; University of Durham, reader in medieval history, 1979-86, professor of history, 1986-2008, pro-vice-chancellor, 1993-99; emeritus professor 2008-. Writer. **Publications:** War, Politics, and Finance Under Edward I, 1972; (trans.) York Civic Ordinances, 1301, 1976; The Three Edwards: War and State in England, 1272-1377, 1980, 2nd ed., 2003; (ed.) Documents Illustrating the Crisis of 1297-98 in England, 1980; Edward I, 1988; English Politics in the Thirteenth Century, 1990; (ed. with D. Rollason and M. Harvey) Anglo-Norman Durham: 1093-1193, 1994; Armies and Warfare in the Middle Ages: The English Experience, 1996; (ed. with R. Britnell and R. Frame) Thirteenth Century England IX: Proceedings of the Durham Conference, 2001, 2003; (ed. with intro.) Place of War in English History, 1066-1214, 2004; Plantagenet England 1225-1360, 2005; Knight, 2010. **Address:** 46 Albert St., Durham, DU DH1 4RJ, England. **Online address:** m.c.prestwich@durham.ac.uk

PREVAS, John. American (born United States), b. 1947?. **Genres:** History, Language/Linguistics, Biography, Autobiography/Memoirs. **Career:** Towson University, senior lecturer in Greek; Eckerd College, assistant professor of classics, professor of Latin and ancient history. Writer. **Publications:** Hannibal Crosses the Alps: The Enigma Re-Examined, 1998; Xenophon's March: Into the Lair of the Persian Lion, 2002; Envy of the Gods: Alexander the Greats Ill-fated Journey across Asia, 2004, 2nd ed., 2005; (with S. Forbes) Power Ambition Glory, 2009. **Address:** c/o Author Mail, Da Capo Press, 11 Cambridge Ctr., Cambridge, MA 02142, U.S.A.

PRÉVAUX, Aude Yung-De. French (born France), b. 1943?. **Genres:** History, Biography. **Career:** Liberation, journalist. Writer. **Publications:** Un amour dans la tempête de l'histoire: Jacques et Lotka dePrévaux, 1999, trans. as Jacques and Lotka: A Resistance Story, 2000, rev. ed. as Love in the Tempest of History: A French Resistance Story, 2001. Contributor to publications and periodicals. **Address:** c/o Author Mail, The Free Press/Simon & Schuster, 1230 Ave. of the Americas, 11th Fl., New York, NY 10020, U.S.A.

PREVIN, André (George). (Andreas Ludwig Prewin). American/German (born Germany), b. 1929. **Genres:** Music, Young Adult Fiction. **Career:** Metro-Goldwyn-Mayer, Department of Music, rehearsal conductor and orchestrator, 1945-50; film score composer and conductor, 1952-59; Houston Symphony, conductor-in-chief, music director, 1967-69; London Symphony Orchestra, music director and principal conductor, 1968-79, conductor emeritus, 1979-; Pittsburgh Symphony Orchestra, music director, 1976-84; Royal Philharmonic Orchestra, principal conductor, 1985-90, director, 1985-; Los Angeles Philharmonic Orchestra, music director, 1986-89; Houston University, faculty; Berkshire Music Center, instructor. Writer. **Publications:** (With A. Hopkins) Music Face to Face, 1971; (ed.) Orchestra, 1979; Andre Previn's Guide to Music, 1983; (ed.) Andre Previn's Guide to the Orchestra: With Chapters on the Voice, Keyboards, Mechanical and Electronic Instruments, 1986; No Minor Chords: My Days in Hollywood, 1991. **Address:** Columbia Artists Management Inc., 165 W 57th St., New York, NY 10019-2201, U.S.A.

PREVOTS, Naima. (Naima Wallenrod Prevots). American (born United States), b. 1935. **Genres:** History, Dance/Ballet, Adult Non-fiction. **Career:** American University, professor of dance, 1967-83, 1988-2002, chair of performing arts, professor emeritus, 2002-; Hollywood Bowl Museum, director and curator, 1983-87; Office of Education, consultant, 1985-; Fulbright Association, director, 1990-93; National Endowment for the Humanities, panelist, 1991. Writer. **Publications:** (Ed.) Dance in the Public Schools, 1973; A Vision for Music, 1985; Sound Waves, 1986; Dancing in the Sun, 1987; American Pageantry: A Movement for Art and Democracy, 1990; Dance for Export: Cultural Diplomacy and the Cold War, 1998. Contributor to periodicals. **Address:** Department of Performing Arts, American University, 4400 Massachusetts Ave., Washington, DC 20016, U.S.A. **Online address:** prevots@american.edu

PREVOTS, Naima Wallenrod. *See* **PREVOTS, Naima.**

PREWIN, Andreas Ludwig. *See* **PREVIN, André (George).**

PREWITT, Kenneth. American (born United States), b. 1936. **Genres:** Politics/Government. **Career:** Washington University, assistant professor of political science, 1963-64; Makerere University College, visiting professor of political science, 1964-65; University of Chicago, faculty, 1965-, assistant professor, professor of political science, 1976-82; Stanford University, research associate in political science, 1968-69; University of Nairobi, Institute of Development Studies, teacher, 1970-72; National Opinion Research Center, director, 1979-; Center for Advanced Study in the Behavioral Sciences, fellow, 1983-84; United States Census Bureau, director, 1998-2001; New School University, Graduate Faculty of Political and Social Science, dean, 2001-02; Columbia University, School of Intl. and Public Affairs, Carnegie professor of public affairs, vice-president for global initiatives; Center for the Advanced Study in the Behavioral Sciences, fellow. Writer. **Publications:** (With Eliot, Chambers and Salisbury) American Government: Readings and Problems for Analysis, 1965; Uganda Extramural Students and Political development, 1966; (with R.E. Dawson) Political Socialization: An Analytic Study, 1968; (ed. with L.L. Knowles) Institutional Racism in America, 1970; Recruitment of Political Leaders: A Study of Citizen-Politicians, 1970; (with D.K. Leonard) Methodological Notes on Quantification, Productivity and Groups in Administrative Research, 1971; (with D. Shepard) Cross-Tabulation of Means: Description of Computer Program SO4B, 1971; Education and Political Values, 1971; Education and Social Equality in Kenya, 1972; (with D. Court) Nation Versus Region: Social Learning in Kenyan Secondary Schools, 1972; (with H. Eulau) Labyrinths of Democracy: Adaptations, Linkages, Representation and Policies in Urban Politics, 1973; (with A. Stone) Elites and American Democracy, 1973; (with A. Stone) Ruling Elites: Elite Theory, Power and American Democracy, 1973; (with S. Verba) Introduction to American Government, 1974, 6th ed., 1991; Introductory Research Methodology: East African Applications, 1975; (with S. Verba) Principles of American Government, 1975, 3rd ed., 1980; (with R.E. Dawson and K.S. Dawson) Political Socialization: An Analytic Study, 1977; (ed.) Research Opportunities in China for American Humanists and Social Scientists, 1982; (with J.D. Miller) National Survey of the Non-Governmental Leadership of American Science and Technology: A Report to the National Science Foundation, 1982; (with S. Verba) Introduction to American Government, 6th ed., 1991; (ed.) Networks in International Capacity Building: Cases from Sub-Saharan Africa, 1998; Politics and Science in Census Taking, 2003; The Hard Count, 2006; (ed.) The Legitimacy of Philanthropic Foundations: United States and European Perspectives, 2006; (ed. with M. Dogan) Fondations philanthropiques en Europe et aux États-Unis, 2007. Contributor to periodicals. **Address:** School of International Affairs, Columbia University, Rm. 1314 IAB, 420 W 118th St., PO Box 3328, New York, NY 10027, U.S.A. **Online address:** kp2058@columbia.edu

PRICE, Alan. American (born United States), b. 1943. **Genres:** Literary Criticism And History. **Career:** Pennsylvania State University, instructor, 1966-76, assistant professor, 1976-88, associate professor, 1988-97, professor of English, 1995-2005, now professor emeritus; Hazelton Community Concert Association, vice president, 1988-94; Edith Wharton Society, president. Writer. **Publications:** (And ed. with K. Joslin) Wretched Exotic: Essays on Edith Wharton in Europe, 1993; The End of the Age of Innocence: Edith Wharton and the First World War, 1996. Contributor to books and journals. **Address:** Department of English, Pennsylvania State University, 76 University Dr., Hazleton, PA 18202, U.S.A.

PRICE, Anthony. British (born England), b. 1928. **Genres:** Mystery/Crime/Suspense, Novels, Young Adult Non-fiction, Military/Defense/Arms Control. **Career:** Westminster Press, journalist, 1952-88; Oxford Times, deputy editor, editor, 1972-88, retired, 1988. **Publications:** MYSTERY NOVELS: The Labyrinth Makers, 1970; The Alamut Ambush, 1971; Colonel Butler's Wolf, 1972; October Men, 1973; Other Paths to Glory, 1974; Our Man in Camelot, 1975; War Game, 1976; The '44 Vintage, 1978; Tomorrow's Ghost, 1979; The Hour of the Donkey, 1980; Soldier No More, 1981; The Old Vengeful, 1982; Gunner Kelly, 1983; Sion Crossing, 1984; Here Be Monsters, 1985; For the Good of the State, 1986; A New Kind of War, 1987; A Prospect of Vengeance, 1988; The Memory Trap, 1989. OTHER: The Eyes of the Fleet: A Popular History of Frigates and Frigate Captains, 1793-1815, 1996. **Address:** AP Watt Ltd., 20 John St., London, GL WC1N 2DR, England.

PRICE, Christopher. American (born United States) **Genres:** Young Adult Non-fiction, Sports/Fitness. **Career:** Metro Boston, football writer, 2001-. **Publications:** NONFICTION: Baseball by the Beach: A History of America's Pastime on Cape Cod, 1997; The Blueprint: How the New England Patriots Beat the System to Create the Last Great NFL Superpower, 2007. Contributor of periodicals. **Address:** Metro Boston, 320 Congress St., 5th Fl., Boston, MA 02210, U.S.A. **Online address:** capeleaguer@hotmail.com

PRICE, Glanville. Welsh (born Wales), b. 1928. **Genres:** Language/Linguistics, Bibliography. **Career:** Wade Deacon Grammar School, French master,

1954-55; University of Saint Andrews, lecturer in French, 1958-64; University of Leeds, lecturer in French, 1965-66; University of Stirling, professor of French, 1967-72; University of Wales, professor of French, 1972-92, professor of romance languages, 1975-87; research professor, 1992-95, professor emeritus, 1995-; University of California, visiting professor, 1982. Writer. **Publications:** The Present Position of Minority Languages in Western Europe, 1969; The French Language: Present and Past, 1971; (with K.F. Bach) Romance Linguistics and the Romance Languages: A Bibliography of Bibliographies, 1977; The Languages of Britain, 1984; An Introduction to French Pronunciation, 1991, rev. ed., 2005; A Comprehensive French Grammar, 6th ed., 2007. EDITOR: William, Count of Orange: Four Old French Epics, 1975; The Celtic Connection, 1992; (with C. Lupu) Hommages Offerts à Maria Manoliu-Manea, 1994; Discourse and Pragmatic Constraints on Grammatical Choices, 1994; Encyclopedia of the Languages of Europe, 1998; Languages of Europe, 1998; Languages in Britain and Ireland, 2000. **Address:** Department of European Languages, University of Wales, Hugh Owen Bldg., Penglais, Aberystwyth, SY23 3DY, Wales. **Online address:** gap@aber.ac.uk

PRICE, Hugh B(ernard). American (born United States), b. 1941. **Genres:** Speech/Rhetoric, Social Sciences, Education. **Career:** New Haven Legal Assistance Association, neighborhood attorney, 1966-68; Black Coalition of New Haven, executive director, 1968-70; Cogen, Holt & Associates, partner, 1970-76; City of New Haven Human Resources Administration, director, 1977-78; New York Times, editorial board, 1978-82; WNET/Thirteen TV, senior vice president, 1982-88; National Association for the Advancement of Colored People Legal Defense and Education Fund, board director, 1986-88; Rockefeller Foundation, vice president, 1988-94; National Urban League, president and chief executive officer, 1994-2003; Brookings Institution, economic studies, non-resident senior fellow, 2006-; Princeton University, Woodrow Wilson School of Public and International Affairs, John L. Weinberg and Goldman Sachs visiting professor, 2008-. Writer. **Publications:** The Role of the Urban League Movement in Overcoming Inner-City Poverty: Challenges for the 21st Century, 1995; Education Accountability: Saving Schools and Students, 1999; To Be Equal, 1999; Destination: The American Dream, 2001; To Be Equal: A Look at Our Nation, 2001; Achievement Matters: Getting Your Child the Best Education Possible, 2002; Mobilizing the Community to Help Students Succeed, 2008. Contributor to periodicals. **Address:** Eonomic Studies, Brookings Institution, 1775 Massachusetts Ave., NW, Washington, DC 20036, U.S.A. **Online address:** huprice@yahoo.com

PRICE, John (T.). American (born United States), b. 1966. **Genres:** Autobiography/Memoirs, Literary Criticism And History, Young Adult Fiction. **Career:** University of Nebraska, Department of English, associate professor of English, professor, Jefferis Endowed chair of English and creative writing, faculty in advanced writing. Writer. **Publications:** Not Just Any Land: A Personal and Literary Journey into the American Grasslands, 2004; Man Killed by Pheasant: And Other Kinships (a memoir), 2008. Contributor to periodicals. **Address:** Department of English, University of Nebraska, 403 ASH, 6001 Dodge St., Omaha, NE 68182-0315, U.S.A. **Online address:** jtprice@mail.unomaha.edu

PRICE, Matthew A(rlen). American (born United States), b. 1960?. **Genres:** Theology/Religion, History. **Career:** Starsong Communications, vice president; Tyndale House Publishers, director of development; Jubilee Publishers, manager; Upland Publishing, president; Publishing Services Corp., founder and president; Smart Data Strategies Inc., director of marketing, 2000-; American University, associate professor of history. Writer. **Publications:** (With M. Collins) The Story of Christianity: A Celebration of 2000 Years of Faith, 1999; Blessings of Hope from the Letters of Paul, 2002; Blessings of Encouragement from Psalm 139, 2002; (with J. Anderson) Questions I'd Like to Ask God, 2004. **Address:** c/o DK Publishing Inc., 375 Hudson St., New York, NY 10014, U.S.A.

PRICE, Nancy. American (born United States), b. 1925?. **Genres:** Novels, Young Adult Fiction, Women's Studies And Issues. **Career:** University of Northern Iowa, faculty, 1964-68, professor of creative writing, 1979-, now professor emeritus; Karolyi Foundation, writer-in-residence, 1975. **Publications:** A Natural Death, 1973; An Accomplished Woman, 1979; Sleeping With the Enemy, 1987; Night Woman, 1992; Bonfire's Daughter, 1998; Snake in the Blackberries, 2001 in US as No One Knows, 2004; Two Liars and a Bride, 2004; Two Hundred Men, One Woman, 2009; Stolen Away, 2010. Contributor to periodicals. **Address:** Malmarie Press Inc., 4387 Rummell Rd., St. Cloud, FL 34769, U.S.A. **Online address:** nancypricebooks@aol.com

PRICE, Richard. American (born United States), b. 1949. **Genres:** Novels, Plays/Screenplays, Westerns/Adventure. **Career:** Hostos Community College, lecturer in English, 1973; New York University, lecturer in urban affairs, 1973, lecturer in creative writing, 1974, 1977; State University of New York-Stony Brook, lecturer in creative writing, 1974-; State University of New York-Binghamton, lecturer in creative writing, 1976; Hofstra University, lecturer in creative writing, 1978-79; Yale University, lecturer in creative writing, 1980. Writer and producer. **Publications:** NOVELS: The Wanderers, 1974; Bloodbrothers, 1976; Ladies' Man, 1978; The Breaks, 1983; Clockers, 1992; Freedomland, 1998; Samaritan, 2003; Jux, 2008; Lush Life, 2008. **Address:** c/o Dorothy Vincent, Janklow & Nesbit Associates, 445 Park Ave., New York, NY 10022, U.S.A.

PRICE, Robert M. American (born United States), b. 1941. **Genres:** International Relations/Current Affairs, Politics/Government, Social Sciences, History. **Career:** University of California, Charles and Louise Travers Department of Political Science, assistant professor, 1970-75, associate professor, 1976-90, professor of political science, 1991-, chair, 1996-2001, associate vice chancellor for research. Writer. **Publications:** Society and Bureaucracy in Contemporary Ghana, 1975; U.S. Foreign Policy in Sub-Saharan Africa: National Interest and Global Strategy, 1978; (ed. with C.G. Rosberg) The Apartheid Regime: Political Power and Racial Domination, 1980; The Apartheid State in Crisis: Political Transformation in South Africa, 1975-1990, 1991. Works appear in anthologies. Contributor to journals and newspapers. **Address:** Travers Department of Political Science, University of California, 210 Barrows Hall, Ste. 1950, Berkeley, CA 94720-1950, U.S.A. **Online address:** rprice@berkeley.edu

PRICE, Roger (David). Welsh (born Wales), b. 1944. **Genres:** History, Humanities. **Career:** University of East Anglia, lecturer, 1968-82, senior lecturer, 1983, reader in social history, 1984, professor of European history, 1991-94; University of Wales, professor of history; Aberystwyth University, Department of History and Welsh History, professor. Writer. **Publications:** The French Second Republic: A Social History, 1972; The Economic Modernisation of France 1975; (ed.) Revolution and Reaction: 1848 and the Second French Republic, 1975; (ed.) 1848 in France, 1975; An Economic History of Modern France, 1730-1914, 1981; The Modernization of Rural France: Communications Networks and Agricultural Market Structures in Nineteenth-century France, 1983; A Social History of Nineteenth-Century France, 1987; The Revolutions of 1848, 1988; A Concise History of France, 1993, 2nd ed., 2005; (ed.) Documents on the French Revolution of 1848, 1996; Napoleon III and the Second Empire, 1997; The French Second Empire: An Anatomy of Political Power, 2001; People and Politics in France, 1868-1870, 2004; Fear of God is the Basis of Social Order: The Roman Catholic Church and Counter-Revolution in Nineteenth Century France, forthcoming. Contributor to journals and periodicals. **Address:** Department of History & Welsh History, Aberystwyth University, Rm. C47, Hugh Owen Bldg., Aberystwyth, DY SY23 3DY, Wales. **Online address:** rdp@aber.ac.uk

PRICE, Susan. British (born England), b. 1955. **Genres:** Children's Fiction, Novellas/Short Stories, Young Adult Fiction, Science Fiction/Fantasy, Horror, Mythology/Folklore, Novels, Education, Education. **Career:** Cooperative Society, supermarket shelf-filler, 1973-75; North Riding College of Education, resident creative writer, 1980. **Publications:** Devil's Piper, 1973; Twopence a Tub, 1975; Sticks and Stones, 1976; Home from Home, 1977; Christopher Uptake, 1981; The Carpenter (stories), 1981; In a Nutshell, 1983; From Where I Stand, 1984; Ghosts at Large, 1984; Odin's Monster, 1986; The Ghost Drum: A Cat's Tale, 1987; Ghostly Tales, 1987; Here Lies Price, 1987; The Bone Dog, 1988; Master Thomas Katt, 1988; (ed.) Horror Stories, 1988; Crack-a-Story, 1989; Feasting of Trolls, 1990; (co-author) Haunting Christmas Tales, 1991; Ghost Song, 1992; Ghost Dance, 1993; (co-author) Thirteen More Tales of Horror, 1994; The Saga of Aslak, 1995; Elfgift, 1995; Elfking, 1996; Pedro, 1997; The Sterkarm Handshake, 1998; The Story Collector, 1998; Ghosts and Lies, 1998; A True Spell and a Dangerous, 1998; The Ghost Wife, 1999; Official Guide, 2000; The Wolf Sisters, 2001; The Bearwood Witch, 2001; The King's Head, 2002; The Wolf's Footprint, 2003; Sterkarm Kiss, 2003; Olly Spellmaker and the Hairy Horror, 2004; Olly Spellmaker and the Sulky Smudge, 2004; Elf Alert!, 2005; Odin's Voice, 2005; Odin's Queen, 2006; (ed.) Dark Side: Truly Terrifying Tales, 2007; Feasting the Wolf, 2007; Odin's Son, 2007. Contributor to periodicals. **Address:** Scholastic Ltd., Commonwealth House, 1-19 New Oxford St., London, GL WC1A 1NU, England. **Online address:** susanprice@susanprice.org.uk

PRICE, Victor (Henry John). Irish (born Ireland), b. 1930. **Genres:** Novels, Plays/Screenplays, Poetry, Translations, Novellas/Short Stories, Mystery/Crime/Suspense. **Career:** Lurgan College, teacher, 1952-54; Oberschule, teacher, 1954-55; Annadale Grammar School, teacher, 1955-56; British Broadcasting Corp.-Northern Ireland, announcer, 1956-59; Radio Hong Kong, feature producer, 1960-63; British Broadcasting Corp.-London, External Services, script writer, 1963-64, North American and Pacific Service, senior producer, 1964-65, Greek programme organizer, 1965-66, assistant program editor, 1966-71, general program editor, 1971-. **Publications:** NOVELS: The Death of Achilles, 1963; The Other Kingdom, 1964; Caliban's Wooing, 1966. OTHERS: (trans. and intro.) The Plays of Georg Büchner, 1971; (ed.) Apollo in Mourne: Poems, Plays & Stories, 1978; (trans. and intro.) G. Büchner, Danton's Death; Leonce and Lena; Woyzeck, 1988; Two Parts Water (verse), 1982; Strange Meeting, 2000; Deborah, 2000; Confessions of a Centaur, 2007. **Address:** Curtis Brown Ltd., 575 Madison Ave., New York, NY 10022-2511, U.S.A. **Online address:** vprice@ntlworld.com

PRICE-SMITH, Andrew T. American/Canadian (born Canada), b. 1968?. **Genres:** Medicine/Health. **Career:** Columbia University, Earth Institute, postdoctoral research scientist and adjunct assistant professor; University of South Florida, Center for Globalization, interdisciplinary professor; Colorado College, assistant professor, 2005-10, associate professor of political science, 2010-; University of Oxford, lecturer; Dartmouth College, lecturer; University of California-Los Angeles, lecturer; Columbia University, lecturer; United States Institute of Peace, advisor; United Nations Development Program, advisor; World Bank, advisor; U.S. Environmental Protection Agency, advisor. Writer and political scientist. **Publications:** (Ed.) Plagues and Politics: Infectious Disease and International Policy, 2001; The Health of Nations: Infectious Disease, Environmental Change, and Their Effects on National Security and Development, 2002; Contagion and Chaos: Disease, Ecology, and National Security in the Era of Globalization, 2009. Contributor to journals and periodicals. **Address:** Department of Political Science, Colorado College, 14 E Cache La Poudre, Colorado Springs, CO 80903, U.S.A. **Online address:** aps@coloradocollege.edu

PRICE-THOMPSON, Tracy. American (born United States), b. 1963?. **Genres:** Novels, Writing/Journalism. **Career:** Writer. **Publications:** NOVELS: Black Coffee, 2002; Chocolate Sangria, 2003; (ed. with T. Stovall) Proverbs for the People, 2003; A Woman's Worth, 2005; Knockin' Boots, 2005; (with V. McGlothin and C. Greene) Indecent Exposure, 2006; (ed. with T. Stovall) Other People's Skin: Four Novellas, 2007; Gather Together in My Name, 2008; 1-900-A-N-Y-T-I-M-E: A Novel, 2009; (with T. Stovall) My Blue Suede Shoes: Four Novellas, 2011. Works appear in anthologies. Contributor to periodicals. **Address:** c/o Author Mail, Random House Inc., 1745 Broadway, New York, NY 10019, U.S.A. **Online address:** tracythomp@aol.com

PRICKETT, (Alexander) (Thomas) Stephen. *See* **PRICKETT, Stephen.**

PRICKETT, Stephen. ((Alexander) (Thomas) Stephen Prickett). Scottish/Sierra Leonean (born Sierra Leone), b. 1939. **Genres:** Mystery/Crime/Suspense, Architecture, Literary Criticism And History. **Career:** Methodist College, English teacher, 1962-64; University of Sussex, School of English and American Studies, assistant lecturer, lecturer, 1967-78, sub-dean, 1972-75, Department of English, reader, 1978-82, chairman, 1980-82; Australian National University, Department of English, professor, 1983-89, head, 1985-88, visiting fellow, 1997-98; Smith College, visiting lecturer, 1970-71; University of Minnesota, Fulbright visiting professor, 1979-80; University of Glasgow, Department of English Language and Literature, Regius professor, 1988-2001, head, 1990-93, Regius professor emeritus, 2001-, Centre for the Study of European Romanticism, director, 1996-; European Society for the Study of Literature and Theology, president, 1991-2000; Duke University, visiting professor of English, 2001-02; Baylor University, Armstrong Browning Library, director, 2003-08; University of Kent, honorary professor; National University of Singapore, Department of English, distinguished visiting professor. Writer. **Publications:** Do It Yourself Doom (crime), 1962; Coleridge and Wordsworth, 1970; Wordsworth and Coleridge: The Lyrical Ballads, 1975; Romanticism and Religion, 1976; Victorian Fantasy, 1979, 2nd ed., 2005; Words and the Word, 1986; England and the French Revolution, 1988; (with R. Barnes) The Bible, 1991; Origins of Narrative: The Romantic Appropriation of the Bible, 1996; Narrative, Religion, and Science: Fundamentalism Versus Irony, 1700-1999, 2002; Modernity and the Reinvention of Tradition: Backing into the Future, 2009. EDITOR: Cambridge New Architecture, 1970; The Romantics, 1981; Reading the Text, 1991; (and intro. with R. Carroll) The Bible: Authorized King James Version, 1997; (with D. Jasper and A. Hass) The Bible and Literature: A Reader, 1999; (with P. Hill) Education! Education! Education!: Managerial Ethics and the Law of Unintended Consequences, 2002; European Romanticism: A Reader, 2010. **Address:** Department of English Literature, University of Glasgow, 5 University Gardens, Glasgow, G12 8QQ, Scotland. **Online address:** atsp@eh.quik.co.uk

PRIEST, Christopher (McKenzie). British (born England), b. 1943. **Genres:** Novels, Science Fiction/Fantasy, Children's Non-fiction, Film, Adult Non-fiction, Novellas/Short Stories. **Career:** Full-time freelance writer, 1968-; The Times, journalist; The Guardian, journalist; The Independent, journalist; The New Statesman, journalist; The Scotsman, journalist; H.G. Wells Society, vice president. **Publications:** Indoctrinaire, 1970; Fugue for a Darkening Island in US as Darkening Island, 1972; Inverted World, 1974; Your Book of Film-Making, 1974; Real-Time World, 1974; The Space Machine: A Scientific Romance, 1976; A Dream of Wessex in US as The Perfect Lover, 1977; An Infinite Summer, 1979; The Affirmation, 1981; The Glamour, 1984; The Book on the Edge of Forever: An Enquiry into the Non-Appearance of Harlan Ellison's the Last Dangerous Visions, 1985; The Last Deadloss Visions, 1987; The Quiet Woman, 1990; The Prestige, 1995, 2nd ed., 2006; The Extremes, 1998; (with G. Morrison and M. Waid) JLA: Strength in Numbers, 1998; (co-author) Impulse: Bart Saves the Universe, 1999; The Dream Archipelago, 1999; The Separation, 2002; The Islanders, 2011. EDITOR: Anticipations, 1978; (co-ed.) Stars of Albion, 1979. **Address:** c/o Robert Kirby, Peters Fraser and Dunlop, 34-43 Russell St., London, GL WC2B 5HA, England. **Online address:** cp@christopher-priest.co.uk

PRIEST, John Michael. American (born United States), b. 1949. **Genres:** History, Adult Non-fiction, Military/Defense/Arms Control, Art/Art History, Social Sciences. **Career:** Washington County Board of Education, Hagerstown, teacher, 1980-; South Hagerstown High School, teacher. Writer. **Publications:** Antietam: The Soldiers' Battle, 1989; (co-ed.) From New Bern to Fredericksburg: Captain James Wren's Diary: B Company, 48th Pennsylvania Volunteers, February 20, 1862-December 17, 1862, 1990; Before Antietam: The Battle of South Mountain, 1992; (ed.) John T. McMahon's Diary of the 136th New York, 1861-1864, 1993; (ed.) Stephen Elliott Welch of the Hampton Legion, 1994; Antietam: The Soldiers' Battlefield, 1994; Turn Them Out to Die Like a Mule, 1995; (co-ed.) One Surgeon's Private War: Doctor William W. Potter of the 57th New York, 1996; Into the Fight: Pickett's Charge at Gettysburg, 1998; (co-ed.) 16th Connecticut Volunteer Infantry, 2002. THE BATTLE OF THE WILDERNESS SERIES: Nowhere to Run: The Wilderness, May 4th & 5th, 1864, 1995; Victory Without Triumph: The Wilderness, May 6th & 7th, 1864, 1996. **Address:** South Hagerstown High School, 1101 S Potomac St., Hagerstown, MD 21740, U.S.A. **Online address:** priesjoh@wcboe.k12.md.us

PRIEST, Stephen. British (born England), b. 1954. **Genres:** Intellectual History, Humanities, Philosophy, Theology/Religion, Ethics. **Career:** Council of Europe, press and information administrator, 1977; British Universities, lecturer, senior lecturer and reader, 1980-2000; Dartmouth College, visiting professor in philosophy, 1992; University of Rhode Island, distinguished visiting professor in humanities, 1994; Université de Bretagne Occidentale, visiting professor, 1999; University of Edinburgh, lecturer in philosophy and director of studies in philosophy; University of Oxford, lecturer, 2001-, Blackfriars Hall, fellow and tutor, senior research fellow, 2004-, Wolfson College, member; University of Nijmegen, visiting professor, 2006; Westfälischen Wilhelms-Universität Münster, visiting professor, 2006; Saint Cyrill and Methodius University, visiting professor, 2007; Macedonian Academy of Sciences and Arts, visiting professor, 2007; Nippon University, visiting professor, 2008. Writer. **Publications:** The British Empiricists: Hobbes to Ayer, 1990, 2nd ed., 2007; Theories of the Mind, 1991; Merleau-Ponty, 1998, 2nd ed., 2003; The Subject in Question: Sartre's Critique of Husserl in The Transcendence of the Ego, 2000. EDITOR: Hegel's Critique of Kant, 1987, new ed., 1992; Jean-Paul Sartre, Basic Writings, 2001; (with A. Flew) A Dictionary of Philosophy, 2002. **Address:** Blackfriars Hall, University of Oxford, 64 Saint Giles, Oxford, OX OX1 3LY, England.

PRIESTLEY, Chris. British (born England), b. 1958?. **Genres:** Novels, Novellas/Short Stories, Young Adult Non-fiction, Military/Defense/Arms Control. **Career:** Author, illustrator, artist and cartoonist. **Publications:** SELF-ILLUSTRATED: Dog Magic!, 2000; Jail-Breaker Jack, 2001. TOM MARLOWE ADVENTURE SERIES: Death and the Arrow, 2003; The White Rider, 2004; Redwulf's Curse, 2005. OTHERS: (with S. Woodcock and

K. Wildgust) Routeing around the Heart of England, 1988; Battle of Britain: Harry Woods, England, 1939-1941, 2002 as Battle of Britain: A Second World War Spitfire Pilot, 1939-1941, 2008; Witch Hunt, 2003; The Battle of Hastings, 2003; Billy Wizard, 2005; Uncle Montague's Tales of Terror, 2007; New World, 2007; Tales of Terror from the Black Ship, 2008. **Address:** c/o Philippa Milnes-Smith, Lucas Alexander Whitley Ltd., 14 Vernon St., London, GL W14 0RJ, England.

PRIESTMAN, Martin. British (born England), b. 1949. **Genres:** Literary Criticism And History, Natural History, Art/Art History, Criminology/True Crime, Poetry. **Career:** Teacher, 1972-77; Roehampton University, lecturer in drama and English, 1977-79, senior lecturer in English, 1979-92, reader in English, 1992-99, professor of English, 1999-. Writer. **Publications:** (Ed. with K. Parkinson) Peasants and Countrymen in Literature: A Symposium Organised by the English Department of the Roehampton Institute in February 1981, 1982; Cowper's Task: Structure and Influence, 1983; Detective Fiction and Literature: The Figure on the Carpet, 1991; Crime Fiction from Poe to the Present, 1998; Romantic Atheism: Poetry and Freethought 1780-1830, 1999; (ed.) Cambridge Companion to Crime Fiction, 2003. Contributor to periodicals. Works appear in anthologies. **Address:** School of Arts, Roehampton University, Digby Stuart College, Fi108, Roehampton Ln., London, GL SW15 5PH, England. **Online address:** m.priestman@roehampton.ac.uk

PRIETO, Jose Manuel. (Jose Manuel Prieto Gonzalez). American/Cuban (born Cuba), b. 1962?. **Genres:** Novels. **Career:** Centro de Investigacion y Docencia Económicas, faculty, 1994-; Seton Hall University, Joseph A. Unanue Latino Institute, head. Writer. **Publications:** (As José Manuel Prieto González) Nunca Antes Habías Visto El Rojo, 1996; Enciclopedia de una vida en Rusia, 1997; Livadia (novel), 1999; Trenta días en Moscú, 2001; El tartamudo y la rusa, 2002; (ed. and intro.) Los Mejores Cuentos Mexicanos: Edición 2005, 2005; Rex, 2009. **Address:** New York, NY , U.S.A. **Online address:** livadia@josemanuelprieto.com

PRIMACK, Alice Lefler. American (born United States), b. 1939. **Genres:** Librarianship, Sciences. **Career:** Ohio State University, library intern, 1962-63, reference librarian, 1963-66; University of Florida, assistant librarian, university librarian, 1972-91, now university librarian emeritus. Writer. **Publications:** How to Find Out in Pharmacy, 1969; Finding Answers in Science and Technology, 1984; Journal Literature of the Physical Sciences: A Manual, 1992. Contributor to periodicals. **Address:** 3657 NW 40th Pl., Gainesville, FL 32605-1467, U.S.A. **Online address:** primack@uflib.ufl.edu

PRIMACK, Richard B. American (born United States), b. 1950. **Genres:** Environmental Sciences/Ecology, Biology, Mathematics/Statistics. **Career:** University of Canterbury, post-doctoral fellow, 1976-78; Boston University, assistant professor, 1978-85, associate professor, 1985-91, associate director of environmental studies, 1996-98, professor of biology, 1991-; Harvard University, post-doctoral fellow, 1980-81, Bullard fellow, 1999-2000, Putnam fellow, 2006-07; Sarawak Forest Department, visiting researcher, 1980-81, 1985-90, 1999-2000; University of Hong Kong, visiting professor, 1990; Tokyo University, visiting professor, 2006-07; John Simon Guggenheim Memorial Foundation, Guggenheim fellow, 2006-07; Charles University, visiting professor, 2007. Writer. **Publications:** (With C.K. Levy) A Field Guide to Poisonous Plants and Mushrooms of North America, 1984; Forester's Guide to the Moraceace of Sarawak, 1985; Essentials of Conservation Biology, 1993, 5th ed., 2010; Naturschutzbiologie, 1995; A Primer of Conservation Biology, 1995, 4th ed., 2008, trans. as Osnovi sokhranenia bioraznoobrazia, 2002; (ed. with T.E. Lovejoy) Ecology, Conservation and Management of Southeast Asian Forests, 1995; (co-ed.) Timber, Tourists and Temples: Conservation and Development in the Maya Forest of Belize, Guatemala and Mexico, 1997; An Invitation to Conservation Biology, 1997; Conservation and Community Development in the Maya Forest of Belize, Guatemala and Mexico, 1998; CoSo Sinh Hoc Bao Ton, 1999; Elementos de Conservation Biologica: Perspectivas Latinamericanas, 2001; Biologické principy Ochrany přírody, 2001; Biologia da Conservacao, 2001; Introduction a la Biologica de la Conservacion, 2002; Conservasione della Natura, 2003; (with R. Corlett) Tropical Rain Forests: An Ecological and Biogeographical Comparison, 2005, 2nd ed., 2011; Principe de base de la conservation de labiodiversité, 2005. **Address:** Department of Biology, Boston University, 5 Cummington St., Boston, MA 02215, U.S.A. **Online address:** primack@bu.edu

PRIME, Derek James. British (born England), b. 1931. **Genres:** Children's Non-fiction, Theology/Religion, Travel/Exploration, Ethics, Cultural/Ethnic Topics. **Career:** Battersea Grammar School, head of religious instruction, 1954-57; Lansdowne Evangelical Free Church, minister of fellowship, 1957-, president, 1965-67, minister, 1957-66; Independent Evangelical Churches, president, 1966-67; Charlotte Baptist Chapel, minister, 1969-87. Writer. **Publications:** TELL ME THE ANSWER SERIES: A Christian's Guide to Prayer, 1963; Tell Me the Answer about the Bible and about God, 1965, rev. ed. as Tell Me about the Bible and About God, Moody, 1967; Tell Me the Answer about the Lord Jesus Christ, 1965, rev. ed. as Tell Me about the Lord Jesus Christ, 1967; Tell Me the Answer about the Holy Spirit and the Church, 1965; Tell Me the Answer about the Lord's Prayer, 1965, rev. ed. as Tell Me about the Lord's Prayer, 1967; Questions on the Christian Faith Answered from the Bible, 1967; A Christian's Guide to Leadership, 1966, rev. ed. as Christian Leadership, 1980; Tell Me the Answer about Becoming a Christian, 1967; Tell Me the Answer about the Ten Commandments, 1967, rev. ed. as Tell Me About the Ten Commandments, 1969; This Way to Life, 1968; Bible Guidelines, 1979; Created to Praise, 1981; From Trials to Triumphs, 1982; Baker's Bible Study Guide, 1982; Practical Prayer, 1985; Directions for Christian Living, 1986; Pastors and Teachers, 1989; Drawing Power: Evangelism in the Acts, 1991; Women in the Church, 1992; Let's Say the Grace Together, 1994; Focus on the Bible: James, 1995; Gofors and Grumps: An A-Z of Bible Characters, 1995; Jesus: His Life and Ministry, 1995; The Lord's Prayer for Today, 1996; The Ascension: The Shout of the King, 1999; Let's Study 2 Corinthians, 2000; Unspoken Lessons About the Unseen God: Esther Simply Explained, 2001; Bible Answers, 2001; Active Evangelism, 2003; On Being a Pastor, 2004; Living for God's Pleasure, 2004; Opening up 1 Corinthians, 2005; Travel with Robert Murray McCheyne, 2007; Under God's Smile, 2008. **Address:** 7/14 Perdrixknowe, Edinburgh, LT EH14 1AF, Scotland. **Online address:** derek@primed.freeserve.co.uk

PRIME, Jim H. Canadian (born Canada), b. 1948. **Genres:** Sports/Fitness, Recreation, Biography, History. **Career:** Gage Publishing Ltd., sales manager, 1972-; writer, 1980-. **Publications:** (With T. Williams) Ted Williams' Hit List, 1995; (ed. and comp. with B. Nowlin) Ted Williams: A Tribute, 1997; (with B. Nowlin and M. Ross) Fenway Saved, 1999; Tales from the Red Sox Dugout, 2000; (with T. Williams) Ted Williams' Hit List: The Best of the Best Ranks the Best of the Rest, 2003; (with B. Lee) Little Red (Sox) Book: A Revisionist Red Sox History, 2003; (ed.) Mr. Red Sox: The Johnny Pesky Story, 2004; (with B. Nowlin) Blood Feud: The Red Sox, the Yankees and the Struggle of Good Versus Evil, 2005; Red Sox Essential: Everything You Need to Know to be a Real Fan, 2006; (with B. Lee) Baseball Eccentrics: The Most Entertaining, Outrageous and Unforgettable Characters in the Game, 2006; (with P. Jim) Boston Red Sox World Series Encyclopedia, 2008; How Hockey Explains Canada, 2011. **Address:** 1061 Evergreen Ave., New Minas, NS B4N 4J5, Canada. **Online address:** jprime@gagelearning.com

PRINCE, Alison. Scottish/British (born England), b. 1931. **Genres:** Children's Fiction, Adult Non-fiction, Animals/Pets, Children's Non-fiction, Novellas/Short Stories, Biography, Poetry, Novels, Novels. **Career:** Elliott Comprehensive School, Art Department, head, 1954-58; Jordanhill College of Education, fellow in creative writing, 1988. Writer. **Publications:** CHILDREN'S FICTION: Joe and the Horse, 1969; The House on the Common, 1969; The Red Alfa, 1971 in US as The Red Jaguar, 1972; (with C. Connor) Ben's Fish, 1972; The Doubting Kind, 1975; The Turkey's Nest, 1979 in US as Willow Farm, 1980; The Night I Sold My Boots, 1979; Haunted Children (stories), 1982; Mill Green on Fire, 1982; Mill Green on Stage, 1982; The Sinister Airfield, 1983; Goodbye Summer, 1983; Night Landings, 1983; A Spy at Mill Green, 1983; The Ghost Within (stories), 1984; Hands Off Mill Green!, 1984; The Others, 1984; Scramble!, 1984; Rock On, Mill Green, 1985; A Job for Merv, 1986; Nick's October, 1986; The Type One Super Robot, 1987; How's Business, 1987; The Blue Moon Day, 1988; A Haunting Refrain (stories), 1988; Merv on the Road, 1993; A Dog Called You, 1993; The Sherwood Hero, 1995; Magic Dad, 1996; Fergus, Fabulous Ferret, 1997; Fatso's Rat, 1997; Hans Christian Andersen: The Fan Dancer (biography), 1998; Screw Loose, 1998; Dear Del, 1999; Cat Number Three, 2000; (and illustrator) Second Chance, 2000; A Nation Again, 2000; Bird Boy, 2000; My Tudor Queen, 2001; The Fortune Teller, 2001; Bumble, 2001; Boojer, 2002; Oranges and Murder, 2002; Spud, 2003; Three Blind Eyes, 2003; Anne Boleyn and Me, 2004; Luck, 2004; The Summer House, 2004; Tower-Block Pony, 2004; Smoke, 2005; Jacoby's Game, 2006; Speed, 2006; Doodlebug Summer, 2006; Outbreak, 2008. CHILDREN'S NON-FICTION: (with J. Hickson) Whosaurus? Dinosaurus!, 1975; Who Wants Pets?, 1988; On the Money, 2009. FOR ADULTS: All who Love us, 1977; Friend in Need, 1977; The Good Pets Guide, 1981; The Necessary Goat (essays on creative thinking), 1992; On Arran (essays), 1994; Kenneth Grahame: An Innocent in the Wild Wood (biography), 1994; Having Been in the City (poetry), 1994; The Witching Tree (novel), 1996; Turnaround, 2002; The Whifflet Train (poetry), 2003; Help!, 2008; The Sherwood Nightmare, 2008; Catherine of Aragon, 2010; Web, 2010; No Ordinary Love Song, 2011; Henry VIII's Wives, 2011. Contributor to periodicals. **Address:** Burnfoot House, Whiting Bay, Isle of Arran, KA27 8QL, Scotland. **Online address:** alison.prince1@virgin.net

PRINCE, Hugh. British (born England), b. 1927. **Genres:** Geography, Local History/Rural Topics, History, Sciences. **Career:** University College London, faculty, 1951-65, reader in geography, 1965-92, emeritus reader and honorary research fellow, 1992-; University of Minnesota-Twin Cities, visiting professor, 1966, 1968, 1990; Clark University, visiting professor, 1971; German Academic Exchange Service, fellow, 1978; University of Wuerzburg, fellow, 1978. Writer. **Publications:** (Ed. with J.T. Coppock) Greater London, 1964; Parks in England, 1967; (with R.J.P. Kain) The Tithe Surveys of England and Wales, 1985; Wetlands of the American Midwest: A Historical Geography of Changing Attitudes, 1997; (with R.J.P. Kain) Tithe Surveys for Historians, 2000; Geographers Engaged in Historical Geography in British Higher Education, 1931-1991, 2000. **Address:** Department of Geography, University College London, Pearson Bldg., Gower St., London, GL WC1E 6BT, England. **Online address:** h.prince@ucl.ac.uk

PRINCE, Maggie. British (born England) **Genres:** Children's Fiction, Young Adult Fiction, Autobiography/Memoirs. **Career:** Writer and educator. **Publications:** Dragon in the Drainpipe, 1981; Witch Hill, 1982; The Glory Hole, 1984; Rachel on the Run, 1985; Dragon in the Family, 1985; Wishing Powder, 1986; Memoirs of a Dangerous Alien, 1994; Pulling the Plug on the Universe, 1995; Here Comes a Candle to Light You to Bed, 1996 in US as The House on Hound Hill, 1998; Raider's Tide, 2002; North Side of the Tree, 2003; Tomorrow the Fox Will Come to Town, forthcoming. Contributor to periodicals. **Address:** c/o Anthony Sheil, Sheil Land Associates, 43 Doughty St., London, GL WC1N 2LF, England.

PRINCE, Russ Alan. American (born United States), b. 1958. **Genres:** Marketing. **Career:** Prince & Associates Inc. (market research firm), president; Private Wealth magazine, founder. Writer and business and financial expert. **Publications:** The Seven Faces of Philanthropy: A New Approach to Cultivating Major Donors, 1994; (with E.K. Phillips and H.I. Apolinsky) Physician Financial Planning in a Changing Environment, 1996; Winning the War for the Wealthy: How Life Insurance Companies Can Dominate the Upscale Markets, 1999; (with A.A. Bavelas) Creating a Pipeline of New Affluent Clients: Building Strategic Partnerships with Lawyers & Accountants, 2003; (with H.S. Grove) Women of Wealth: Understanding Today's Affluent Female Investor, 2004; (with B.V. Bortel) RainMaker: Strategic Partnering with Attorneys and Accountants to Create a Pipeline of New Affluent Clients, 2006; (with L. Schiff) The Middle-Class Millionaire: The Rise of the New Rich and How They Are Changing America, 2008. WITH KAREN MARU FILE: Marketing to Family Business Owners: A Toolkit for Life Insurance Professionals, 1995; Marketing through Advisors: A Toolkit for Life Insurance Professionals, 1996; Building Your Business: Marketing Your Way to a $ 100 Million Investment Advisory Business, 1997; (with G.L. Rathbun) The Perfect Legacy: How to Establish Your Own Private Foundation, 1998. **Address:** Redding, CT , U.S.A. **Online address:** princeasoc@aol.com

PRINCE, Stephen. American (born United States), b. 1955?. **Genres:** Film, Theatre. **Career:** Virginia Polytechnic Institute and State University, Department of Theatre and Cinema, associate professor of communication studies, professor of communication studies; Society for Cinema and Media Studies, president. Historian and writer. **Publications:** The Warrior's Camera: The Cinema of Akira Kurosawa, 1991; Visions of Empire: Political Imagery in Contemporary American Film, 1992; Movies and Meaning: An Introduction to Film, 1997, 5th ed., 2010; (ed.) Sam Peckinpah's The Wild Bunch, 1998; Savage Cinema: Sam Peckinpah and the Rise of Ultraviolent Movies, 1998; A New Pot of Gold: Hollywood Under the Electronic Rainbow, 1980-1989, 1999; (ed. and intro.) Screening Violence, 2000; Classical Film Violence: Designing and Regulating Brutality in Hollywood Cinema, 1930-1968, 2003; (ed. and intro.) Horror Film, 2004; (ed.) American Cinema of the 1980s: Themes and Variations, 2007; Firestorm: American Film in the Age of Terrorism, 2009; Kurosawa at 100, 2010. Contributor to publications. **Address:** Department of Theatre & Cinema, Virginia Polytechnic Institute & State University, 242 E Henderson Hall, Blacksburg, VA 24061-0311, U.S.A. **Online address:** sprince@vt.edu

PRINCE-HUGHES, Dawn. American (born United States), b. 1964. **Genres:** Autobiography/Memoirs, Novels, Sciences, Adult Non-fiction, Gay And Lesbian Issues. **Career:** Woodland Park Zoo, part-time researcher; Western Washington University, adjunct professor of anthropology. Writer. **Publications:** Gorillas Among Us: A Primate Ethnographers Book of Days, 2001; (ed.) Aquamarine Blue 5: Personal Stories of College Students with Autism, 2002; Songs of the Gorilla Nation: My Journey through Autism, 2004; Expecting Teryk: An Exceptional Path to Parenthood, 2005. **Address:** Western Washington University, 516 High St., Bellingham, WA 98225-9009, U.S.A.

PRINCESS ANNE. British (born England), b. 1950. **Genres:** Animals/Pets, Sociology, Autobiography/Memoirs, Social Sciences, Biography. **Career:** University of London, chancellor, 1981-. Writer. **Publications:** (With M. Phillips) Princess Anne and Mark Phillips Talking about Horses with Genevieve Murphy, 1976; (with I. Herbert) Riding through My Life, 1991; What Is Punishment For and How Does It Relate to the Concept of Community?, 1991. Contributor to periodicals. **Address:** Buckingham Palace, London, GL SW1 A1AA, England.

PRINCIPE, Lawrence M. American (born United States), b. 1962. **Genres:** Sciences, Art/Art History, Chemistry, Philosophy, History. **Career:** Johns Hopkins University, professor of humanities, Drew professor of the humanities, Charles Singleton center, director. Writer. **Publications:** The Triumphal Chariot Reexamined: A Study and Chemical Evaluation of Basil Valentine's Triumphal Chariot of Antimony, 1983; The Aspiring Adept: Robert Boyle and His Alchemical Quest: Including Boyle's Lost Dialogue on the Transmutation of Metals, 1998; (contrib.) Instruments and Experimentation in the History of Chemistry, 2000; (contrib.) Secrets of Nature: Astrology and Alchemy in Early Modern Europe, 2001; (ed. with M. Hunter and A. Clericuzio) The Correspondence of Robert Boyle, 1636-1691, 2001; (with W.R. Newman) Alchemy Tried in the Fire: Starkey, Boyle, and the Fate of Helmontian Chymistry, 2002; (with L. DeWitt) Transmutations-Alchemy in Art: Selected Works from the Eddleman and Fisher Collections at the Chemical Heritage Foundation, 2002; (ed. with W.R. Newman) Alchemical Laboratory Notebooks and Correspondence, 2004; (contrib.) Newton and Newtonianism: New Studies, 2004; (ed.) Chymists and Chymistry: Studies in the History of Alchemy and Early Modern Chemistry, 2007; (ed. with M. Beretta and A. Clericuzio) Accademia del Cimento and its European Context, 2009; Scientific Revolution: A Very Short Introduction, 2011. Contributor to journals. **Address:** Department of History of Science and Technology, Johns Hopkins University, 376 Gilman Hall, 3505 N Charles St., Baltimore, MD 21218, U.S.A. **Online address:** lmafp@jhu.edu

PRINDLE, David F. American (born United States), b. 1948. **Genres:** Politics/Government, Area Studies, Economics. **Career:** University of Texas, Austin, College of Liberal Arts, Department of Government, professor. Writer. **Publications:** Petroleum and Politics: The Texas Railroad Commission, 1980; Petroleum Politics and the Texas Railroad Commission, 1981; Shale Oil, Water and the Politics of Ambiguity, 1982; (ed.) Texas Monthly Political Reader, 1985; The Politics of Glamour: Ideology and Democracy in the Screen Actors Guild, 1988; Risky Business: The Political Economy of Hollywood, 1993; (with R.H. Kraemer and C. Newell) Essentials of Texas Politics, 1996, 10th ed., 2008; (with R.H. Kraemer and C. Newell) Texas Politics, 1996, 11th ed., 2009; 1996 Elections and the Public Good: To Accompany American Democracy and the Public Good by Steven Kelman, 1997; The Paradox of Democratic Capitalism: Politics and Economics in American Thought, 2006; Stephen Jay Gould and the Politics of Evolution, 2009. **Address:** Department of Government, University of Texas, 430 Burdine Hall, 1 University Sta. A1800, PO Box Z, Austin, TX 78713-8926, U.S.A. **Online address:** dprindle@austin.utexas.edu

PRINGLE, David (William). British/Scottish (born Scotland), b. 1950. **Genres:** Science Fiction/Fantasy, Adult Non-fiction, Bibliography. **Career:** Leeds City Libraries, librarian, 1973-78; Leeds Polytechnic, information officer, 1979-82; Foundation, editor, 1980-86; Interzone, editor, 1982-, publisher, 1988-2004; GW Books, series editor, 1988-91; Million, publisher, 1990-93. **Publications:** (Ed. and comp. with J. Goddard) J. G. Ballard, The First Twenty Years, 1976; Earth is the Alien Planet: J.G. Ballard's Four-Dimensional Nightmare, 1979; J.G. Ballard: Primary and Secondary Bibliography, 1984, Science Fiction: The Hundred Best Novels: An English Language Selection, 1949-1984, 1985; (ed. with J. Clute and C. Greenland) Interzone: The 1st Anthology: New Science Fiction and Fantasy Writing, 1985; Science Fiction: The 100 Best Novels: An English-Language Selection, 1985, 2nd ed., 1997;

Imaginary People: A Who's Who of Fictional Characters from the 18th Century to the Present Day, 1987, 2nd ed., 1996; Modern Fantasy, 1988; Imaginary People: A Who's Who of Modern Fictional Characters, 1988; Modern Fantasy: The Hundred Best Novels: An English-Language Selection, 1946-1987, 1989; The Ultimate Guide to Science Fiction, 1990, 2nd ed. as Ultimate Guide to Science Fiction: An A-Z of Science-Fiction Books by Title, 1995; (ed.) St. James Guide to Fantasy Writers, 1996; (ed.) The Ultimate Encyclopedia of Science Fiction, 1996; (ed.) The Best of Interzone, 1997; (ed.) St. James Guide to Horror, Ghost & Gothic Writers, 1998; (ed.) Ultimate Encyclopedia of Fantasy: The Definitive Illustrated Guide, 1999. ROMANS: Deathwing, 1993; The Laughter of Dark Gods, 2002. BLOEMLEZINGEN: The Interzone Pulp Anthology, 1999; The Ant Men of Tibet and Other Stories, 1999. Contributor to periodicals. **Address:** Black Library, Games Workshop, Willow Rd., Nottingham, NT NG7 2WS, England.

PRINGLE, Laurence P(atrick). American (born United States), b. 1935. **Genres:** Children's Fiction, Children's Non-fiction. **Career:** Lima Central School, science teacher, 1961-62; American Museum of Natural History, Nature and Science (children's magazine), associate editor, 1963-65, senior editor, 1965-67, executive editor, 1967-70; freelance writer and photographer, 1970-; New School for Social Research, faculty, 1976-78; Kean College of New Jersey, writer-in-residence, 1985-86; Highlights for Children Writers Workshop, faculty, 1987-2004, 2007, 2009. **Publications:** FOR CHILDREN NONFICTION: Dinosaurs and Their World, 1968; The Only Earth We Have, 1969; From Field to Forest, 1970; In a Beaver Valley, 1970; One Earth, Many People, 1971; Ecology, 1971; Cockroaches, 1971; This Is a River, 1972; From Pond to Prairie, 1972; Pests and People, 1972; Estuaries, 1973; Into the Woods, 1973; Follow a Fisher, 1973; Twist, Wiggle, and Squirm: A Book about Earthworms, 1973; Recycling Resources, 1974; Energy: Power for People, 1975; City and Suburb, 1975; Chains, Webs, and Pyramids, 1975; Water Plants, 1975; The Minnow Family, 1976; Listen to the Crows, 1976; Our Hungry Earth, 1976; Death Is Natural, 1977; The Hidden World, 1977; The Controversial Coyote, 1977; The Gentle Desert, 1977; Animals and Their Niches, 1977; The Economic Growth Debate, 1978; Dinosaurs and People, 1978; Wild Foods, 1978; Nuclear Power, 1979; Natural Fire, 1979; Lives at Stake, 1980; What Shall We Do with the Land?, 1981; Frost Hollows and Other Microclimates, 1981; Vampire Bats, 1982; Water, 1982; Radiation, 1983; Wolfman, 1983; Feral, 1983; The Earth Is Flat, and Other Great Mistakes, 1983; Being a Plant, 1983; Animals at Play, 1985; Nuclear War, 1985; Here Come the Killer Bees, 1986, rev. ed. as Killer Bees, 1990; Throwing Things Away, 1986; Home: How Animals Find Comfort and Safety, 1987; Restoring Our Earth, 1987; Rain of Troubles, 1988; The Animal Rights Controversy, 1989; Bearman, 1989; Nuclear Energy, 1989; Living in a Risky World, 1989; The Golden Book of Insects and Spiders, 1990; Global Warming, 1990; Saving Our Wildlife, 1990; Batman, 1991; Living Treasure, 1991; Antarctica, 1992; The Golden Book of Volcanoes, Earthquakes, and Powerful Storms, 1992; Jackal Woman, 1993; Chemical and Biological Warfare, 1993, rev. ed., 2000; Oil Spills, 1993; Scorpion Man, 1994; Coral Reefs, 1995; Dinosaurs Strange and Wonderful, 1995; Dolphin Man, 1995; Fire in the Forest, 1995; Vanishing Ozone, 1995; Smoking, 1996; Taking Care of the Earth, 1996; Animal Monsters, 1997; Drinking, 1997; An Extraordinary Life: The Story of a Monarch Butterfly, 1997; Elephant Woman, 1997; Everybody Has a Belly Button, 1997; Nature! Wild and Wonderful, 1997; One Room School, 1998; Bats! Strange and Wonderful, 2000; The Environmental Movement, 2000; Sharks! Strange and Wonderful, 2001; Global Warming: The Threat of Earth's Changing Climate, 2001; A Dragon in the Sky: The Story of a Green Darner Dragonfly, 2001; Scholastic Encyclopedia of Animals, 2001; Strange Animals, New to Science, 2002; Crows! Strange and Wonderful, 2002; Dog of Discovery: A Newfoundland's Adventures with Lewis and Clark, 2002; Whales! Strange and Wonderful, 2003; Come to the Ocean's Edge, 2003; Snakes! Strange and Wonderful, 2004; American Slave, American Hero: York of the Lewis and Clark Expedition, 2006; Penguins! Strange and Wonderful, 2007; Imagine a Dragon, 2008.; Alligators and Crocodiles! Strange and Wonderful, 2009; Cicadas! Strange and Wonderful, 2010; Billions of Years, Amazing Changes: The Story of Evolution, 2011. NONFICTION FOR ADULTS: Wild River, 1972; Rivers and Lakes, 1985. PICTURE BOOKS: Jesse Builds a Road, 1989 in UK as Simon Builds a Road, 1990; Octopus Hug, 1993; Naming the Cat, 1997; Bear Hug, 2003. EXPLORE YOUR SENSES SERIES: Sight, 1999; Smell, 1999; Hearing, 1999; Touch, 1999; Taste, 1999. **Address:** 11 Castle Hill Ln., PO Box 252, West Nyack, NY 10994, U.S.A. **Online address:** octopushug@aol.com

PRINS, Harald E. L. Dutch (born Netherlands), b. 1951. **Genres:** Anthropology/Ethnology. **Career:** Radboud University, assistant professor of comparative history, 1976-78; Association of Aroostook Indians, director of research and development, 1981-82; Aroostook Band of Micmac Indians, research director, 1982-90; Micmac Indian Artisans in Northern Maine, film project director, 1983-85; Bowdoin College, lecturer in anthropology, 1986-88, 1990; Colby College, visiting professor of anthropology, 1988-89; University of Maine, adjunct professor, 1989; Kansas State University, assistant professor, 1990-94, associate professor, 1994-96, professor of anthropology, 1996-2005, distinguished professor of anthropology, 2005-, American Ethnic Studies Program, acting director, 1995; Amnesty Intl., international observer. Writer. **Publications:** (Co-ed. and contrib.) American Beginnings: Exploration, Culture, and Cartography in the Land of Norumbega, 1994; The Mikmaq: Resistance, Accommodation, and Cultural Survival, 1996; (co-author) Cultural Anthropology, 2004; (co-author) The Essence of Anthropology, 2005; (with B. McBride) Asticou's Island Domain: Wabanaki Peoples at Mount Desert Island, 1500-2000: Acadia National Park Ethnographic Overview and Assessment, 2007; (with B. McBride) Indians in Eden: Wabanakis & Rusticators on Maine's Mount Desert Island, 1840s-1920s, 2009; From Indian Island to Omaha Beach, 2010. Contributor to books. **Address:** Department of Sociology & Anthropology, Kansas State University, 207 Waters Hall, Manhattan, KS 66506, U.S.A. **Online address:** prins@ksu.edu

PRIOR, Charles W.A. British (born England), b. 1969. **Genres:** Theology/Religion. **Career:** Queen's University, teaching fellow, 2000-03, adjunct assistant professor, 2003-04, 2006-07; University of Cambridge, research fellow, 2004-06; University of Hull, lecturer, 2007-; International Study Centre, visiting fellow, 2004. Historian, educator and author. **Publications:** (ed.) Mandeville and Augustan Ideas: New Essays, 2000; Defining the Jacobean Church: The Politics of Religious Controversy, 1603-1625, 2005. Contributor to periodicals. **Address:** University of Hull, Cottingham Rd., Hull, HU6 7RX, England. **Online address:** c.prior@hull.ac.uk

PRIOR, Kenneth Francis William. (K(enneth) F. W. Prior). British (born England), b. 1926. **Genres:** Theology/Religion, Social Sciences. **Career:** Curator, 1949-53; St. Paul's Church, vicar, 1953-65; Hannington Memorial Church, bishop, 1965-70; rector of Sevenoaks, 1970-86; St. John's Downshire Hill, minister, 1987-90. Writer. **Publications:** God and Mammon, 1965; The Way of Holiness: The Christian Doctrine of Sanctification, 1967, rev. ed., 1994; (ed.) Services of Baptism and Confirmation, 1967; The Gospel in a Pagan Society, 1975, rev. ed., 1995; The Gospel in a Pagan Society: The Relevance for Today of Paul's Ministry in Athens, 1975; The Way of Holiness: A Study in Christian Growth, 1982; Perils of Leadership, 1990. Contributor to periodicals. **Address:** 22 Barnfield Rd., Torquay, DN TQ2 6TN, England.

PRIOR, K(enneth) F. W. *See* **PRIOR, Kenneth Francis William.**

PRIOR, Natalie Jane. Australian (born Australia), b. 1963. **Genres:** Children's Fiction, Young Adult Fiction, Children's Non-fiction, Social Sciences. **Career:** Writer and librarian. **Publications:** Bog Bodies: Mummies and Curious Corpses, 1981; The Amazing Adventures of Amabel, 1990; Amabel Abroad-More Amazing Adventures, 1992; (with T. Denton) The Paw, 1993; Mysterious Ruins, Lost Cities and Buried Treasure, 1994; Tasha's Witch, 1995; Dance Crazy: Star Turns from Ballet to Belly Dancing, 1995; Yesterday's Heroes, 1995; The Paw in Destination Brazil, 1995; Caves, Graves and Catacombs: Secrets from Beneath the Earth, 1996; The Demidenko Diary, 1996; West End Shuffle, 1996; London Calling, 1997; The Loft, 1997; The Paw in the Purple Diamond, 1998; Cleopatra: Last Queen of Egypt, 1998; Nero: Evil Emperor of Rome, 1998; The Recorder, 2000; Chocolate, 2000; Chewing Gum, 2000; Fireworks and Darkness, 2002; Squish, 2002; Encyclopedia of Preserved People: Pickled, Frozen and Mummified Corpses from Around the World, 2002; Lily Quench and the Lighthouse of Skellig Mor, 2003; Lily Quench and the Black Mountains, 2003; Lily Quench and the Magicians' Pyramid, 2003; Lily Quench and the Treasure of Mote Ely, 2004; Lily Quench and the Hand of Manuelo in UK as The Secret of Manuelo, 2004; Lily Quench and the Dragon of Ashby, 2004; Lily Quench and the Search for King Dragon, 2005; The Star Locket, 2006; (with C. Orisini) Minnie Pearl and the Undersea Bazaar, 2007; Lily Quench's Companion: And Guide to Dragons and the Art of Quenching, 2007; Star, 2008; Sun, 2008; Minivers On the Run, 2008; Minivers in Danger: Minivers Fight Back, 2010; Minivers and the Secret Room, 2010; Minivers Rule!, 2011. THE DOLLS SERIES: Fashion Follies, 2005; Susannah's Notebook, 2005; Horse Fever, 2005; Kiki's Caravan, 2006. **Address:** Margaret Connolly & Associates, PO Box 945, Wahroonga, NW 2076, Australia. **Online address:** njpenquiries@mac.com

PRIOR, Robin. Australian (born Australia) **Genres:** History, Military/Defense/Arms Control. **Career:** University of Adelaide, visiting research fellow, 1979-82, Australian Research Council, fellow, 1983-85; Australian Defence Force Academy, University of New South Wales, School of History, lecturer in history, 1986-98, associate professor, 1998-2005, professor, 2005-, head, 1998-2003, School of Humanities and Social Sciences, head, 2003-. Writer and historian. **Publications:** WITH T. WILSON: HISTORIES: Command on the Western Front: The Military Career of Sir Henry Rawlinson, 1914-18, 1992; Passchendaele: The Untold Story, 1996, 2nd ed., 2002; The First World War, 1999; The Somme, 2005. OTHERS: Churchill's World Crisis as History, 1983; (co-author) The Oxford Companion to Australian Military History, 1995; (with J. O'Connor) Successful Selling With Nlp: The Way Forward in the New Bazaar, 1995; (with M. Leibling) Coaching Made Easy: Step-By-Step Techniques That Get Results, 2003; (with M. Leibling) The A-z Of Learning: Tips And Techniques For Teachers, 2004; Gallipoli: The End of the Myth, 2009. **Address:** University of New South Wales, Australian Defence Force Academy, Northcott Dr., PO Box 7916, Canberra, AC 2600, Australia. **Online address:** robin.prior@adelaide.edu.au

PRITCHARD, Ray. American (born United States), b. 1952. **Genres:** inspirational/Motivational Literature, Theology/Religion, History, Reference. **Career:** East Los Angeles School of Ministry, professor, 1981-83; Calvary Memorial Church, senior pastor, 1989-; Trinity Evangelical Divinity School, visiting instructor, 1994-98; Keep Believing Ministries, president and founder. Writer. **Publications:** The Road Best Traveled: Knowing God's Will For Your Life, 1995; Names of the Holy Spirit, 1995; Man of Honor: Living the Life of Godly Character, 1996; Keep Believing: God in the Midst of Our Deepest Struggles, 1997; The ABCs of Wisdom: Building Character with Solomon, 1997; (with B. Briner) The Leadership Lessons of Jesus: A Timeless Model for Today's Leaders, 1997; (with B. Briner) More Leadership Lessons of Jesus: A Timeless Model for Today's World, 1998, rev. ed., 2001; Something New Under the Sun: Ancient Wisdom for Contemporary Living, 1998; What a Christian Believes, 1998; Green Pastures, Quiet Waters: Refreshing Moments in the Psalms, 1999; An Anchor for the Soul: Help for the Present, Hope for the Future, 2000; Faith: The Way of Excellence, 2001; FAQ: Frequently Asked Questions about the Christian Life, 2001; In the Shadow of the Cross, 2001; Hope: The Way of Excellence, 2001; In the Shadow of the Cross: The Deeper Meaning of Calvary, 2001; (contrib.) A Reason For Hope, 2001; Love: The Way of Excellence, 2001; Anchor for the Soul: Bible Study, 2002; (contrib.) What the Cross Means to Me, 2002; And When You Pray: The Deeper Meaning of the Lord's Prayer, 2002; God You Can Trust, 2003; He's God and We're Not: The Seven Laws of the Spiritual Life, 2003; Beyond all You Could Ask or Think: How to Pray Like the Apostle Paul, 2004; Discovering God's Will for Your Life, 2004; Healing Power of Forgiveness, 2005; Incredible Journey of Faith, 2005; Credo: Believing in Something to Die For, 2005; Why Did This Happen to Me?, 2006; Stealth Attack: Arming Yourself Against Satan's Plan to Destroy Your Life, 2007; Fire and Rain: The Wild-Hearted Faith of Elijah, 2007. Contributor to periodicals. **Address:** Calvary Memorial Church, 931 Lake St., Oak Park, IL 60301, U.S.A. **Online address:** ray@keepbelieving.com

PRITCHARD, R(obert) John. American (born United States), b. 1945. **Genres:** Adult Non-fiction, Area Studies, Civil Liberties/Human Rights, History, International Relations/Current Affairs, Law, Military/Defense/Arms Control, Politics/Government, Social Sciences, Documentaries/Reportage, Reference. **Career:** University of California, teaching assistant, 1968-70; freelance writer and broadcaster on historical and legal studies, 1970-; Millennium, managing editor, 1974-76; London School of Economics, research assistant, consulting editor in international history, 1974-87; Independent Television, historical consultant, 1984-85; Integrated Dictionary Systems Ltd. (now Integrated Document Systems Ltd.), founding director and secretary, 1986-90, 1999-; University of Kent, part-time lecturer in history, 1989-91; University of London, Kings College, Department of War Studies, consultant visiting fellow in war studies, 1990-93; Victoria University of Manchester, Simon visiting senior research fellow in history, 1993-94; Notre Dame University (London Programme), adjunct assistant professor of history, 1993; Legal and Historical Enterprises, director, 1993-; St Antony's College, Nissan Institute of Japanese Studies, inter-faculty research fellow, 1994-96; Right Search, director, 1996-; Robert M.W. Kempner Collegium, director, 1996-2000. Writer. **Publications:** The Reichstag Fire: Ashes of Democracy, 1972; Far Eastern Influences upon British Strategy towards the Great Powers 1937-1939, 1979; (ed. and comp. with S.M. Zaide) The Tokyo War Crimes Trial, 2 vols., 1981, Index and Guide, 5 vols., 1981-87; (with L. Gleeck) General History of the Philippines, vol. I: The American Half-Century, 1898-1946, 1984; Far Eastern Influences upon British Strategy towards the Great Powers, 1937-1939, 1987; An Overview of the Historical Importance of the Tokyo War Trial, 1987; (with P. Calvocoressi and G. Wint) Total War: The Causes and Courses of the Second World War, 1989, 2nd ed., 1990; (with P. Williams and D. Wallace) Unit 731: The Japanese Army's Secret of Secrets, 1989; (with Lady T. Marks) Japan and the Second World War, 1989; (with P. Calvocoressi and G. Wint) The Causes and Courses of the Second World War, 1989; (co-author) From Pearl Harbor to Hiroshima, 1994; (co-author) La Deportation, 1995; An Introduction and Guide to the British War Crimes Trials in the Far East, 1946-1948, 1997; (co-author) World War Two in Asia and the Pacific and the War's Aftermath, 1998; (ed. and comp.) Tokyo Major War Crimes Trial: The Records of the International Military Tribunal for the Far East: With an Authoritative Commentary and Comprehensive Guide, 1998; (co-author) International Criminal Law, III: Enforcement, 1999; (co-author) 1945: War and Peace in the Pacific, 1999; (ed.) Hostilities without Declaration of War, 2002; (ed. with J. Carey and W.V. Dunlap) International Humanitarian Law, 2003. Contributor to journals. **Address:** 11 Charlotte Sq., Margate, KT CT9 1LR, England.

PRITCHARD, William H. American (born United States), b. 1932. **Genres:** Literary Criticism And History, Biography, Essays. **Career:** Amherst College, instructor, 1958-61, assistant professor, 1961-65, associate professor, 1965-70, professor, 1970-, Henry Clay Folger professor of English; Hudson Review, editor. **Publications:** Wyndham Lewis, 1968; Wyndham Lewis: Profile in Literature, 1972; Seeing through Everything: English Writers 1918-1940, 1977; Lives of the Modern Poets, 1980, 2nd ed., 1996; Frost: A Literary Life Reconsidered, 1984, 2nd ed., 1993; Randall Jarrell: A Literary Life, 1990; Playing It by Ear: Literary Essays and Reviews, 1994; English Papers: A Teaching Life, 1995; Talking Back to Emily Dickinson and Other Essays, 1998; Updike: America's Man of Letters, 2000; Shelf Life: Literary Essays and Reviews, 2003; On Poets & Poetry, 2009. EDITOR: W.B. Yeats, 1972; (co-ed.) The Norton Anthology of American Literature, 1979, 4th ed., 1993; Randall Jarrell: Selected Poems, 1990. Contributor to periodicals. **Address:** Department of English, Amherst College, Rm. 2, Johnson Chapel, PO Box AC 2234, Amherst, MA 01002-5000, U.S.A. **Online address:** whpritchard@amherst.edu

PRITCHETT, Kay. American (born United States), b. 1946. **Genres:** Literary Criticism And History, Translations, Novels. **Career:** University of Seville, Instituto de Idiomas, instructor in English language, 1975-76; Center for Cross-Cultural Studies, instructor in Spanish literature and culture, 1976-78, instructor in English, 1978-80, University of North Carolina's Year-at-Sevilla Program, director, 1980-81, lecturer in the program, 1981-82; University of Arkansas, instructor, 1982-84, assistant professor, 1984-91, associate professor, 1991-98, professor of Spanish, 1998-. Writer. **Publications:** Nature's Colloquy with the Word: Pureza Canelo's First Poetics, 2004; In Pursuit of Poem Shadows: Pureza Canelo's Second Poetics, 2011. TRANSLATOR: (ed. and trans.) Four Postmodern Poets of Spain: A Critical Introduction with Translations of the Poems, 1991; J.W. Montes Vannuci, Jonah and the Pink Whale (novel), 1991; J. Urzagasti, The Land of Silence (novel), 1994; (ed.) P. Canelo, Pureza Canelo's Celda Verde/Green Cell: A Critical Introduction with Translations of the Poems, 2000. **Address:** Department of World Language,, Literature and Cultures, University of Arkansas, Kimpel Hall, Fayetteville, AR 72701, U.S.A. **Online address:** pritche@uark.edu

PRITCHETT, Wendell. American (born United States) **Genres:** Adult Non-fiction, Law. **Career:** Wolf, Block, Schorr and Solis-Cohen, attorney, 1991-92; Regional Housing Legal Services, staff attorney, 1993-95; executive director of district offices, 1996-97; City University of New York, Baruch College, assistant professor of history, 1997-2002; University of Pennsylvania, visiting assistant professor, 2001-02, assistant professor of law, 2002-06, professor of law, 2006-07, associate dean for academic affairs, 2006-07, professor of law, 2008-09; Office of Mayor Michael A. Nutter, deputy chief of staff and director of policy, 2008; State University of New Jersey, Camden Campus of Rutgers, chief executive officer, chancellor, 2009-. Writer. **Publications:** Brownsville, Brooklyn: Blacks Jews and the Changing Face of the Ghetto, 2002; Robert Clifton Weaver and the American City: The Life and Times of an Urban Reformer, 2008; (co-author) Property Law and Policy: A Comparative Institutional Perspective, 2nd ed., 2009. Contributor to books and periodicals. **Address:** State University of New Jersey, 303 Cooper St., Camden, NJ 08102-1519, U.S.A. **Online address:** chancellor@camden.rutgers.edu

PRITTS, Kim Derek. American (born United States), b. 1953. **Genres:** Adult Non-fiction, Plays/Screenplays, Technology, Engineering, Mystery/Crime/Suspense. **Career:** State conservation officer, 1981-; freelance writer, 1985-; Ethnic Minority Screenwriters Contests, prejudge, 1992-95. **Publications:** The Mystery of Sadler Marsh, 1993; Ginseng: How to Find, Grow, and Use America's Forest Gold, 1995, 2nd ed., 2010; The Eagle of Seldomridge, forthcoming; Necessity, forthcoming; Recognizing Occult Crime Scenes, forthcoming; Handcuffing Techniques, forthcoming. Contributor of articles to magazines. **Address:** Lancaster, PA , U.S.A.

PROBST, Mark. American (born United States), b. 1925. **Genres:** Novels, Novellas/Short Stories. **Career:** District Attorney's Office, assistant district attorney, 1951-53; Merrill Lynch, Pierce, Fenner & Smith Inc., financial consultant, 1966-. Writer. **Publications:** Winter Losses, 1989. **Address:** c/o Gloria Loomis, Watkins Loomis Agency Inc., 150 E 35th St., New York, NY 10016-4102, U.S.A.

PROBYN, Clive T. Australian/British (born England), b. 1944. **Genres:** Literary Criticism And History, Young Adult Fiction, Art/Art History, Biography, Autobiography/Memoirs, Romance/Historical. **Career:** University of Lancaster, lecturer, 1968-68, senior lecturer in English literature, 1978-, School of English, chair, 1976-78, Department of English Literature, head, 1980-; County College, dean, 1973-75; University of Baghdad, visiting professor, 1975-; University of Sokoto, foundation professor of modern European languages (English and French) and dean of faculty of arts and Islamic studies, 1978-80; Monash University, visiting professor, 1981-, professor of English, 1982-, chairperson of department, 1983-92, School of Literary, Visual and Performance Studies, head, 1998-; Ehrenpreis Centre for Swift Studies, founding member, 1986-; University of Melbourne, professorial associate, 1988-. Writer. **Publications:** The Art of Jonathan Swift, 1978; Jonathan Swift, The Contemporary Background, 1979; Chinua Achebe: A Man of the People (biography), 1980; Alexander Pope: Collected Poems, 1980; Wole Soyinka: The Road (biography), 1981; Gabriel Okara: The Voice (biography), 1982; English Poetry: A Handbook, 1984; English Fiction of the Eighteenth Century, 1700-1789, 1987; Gulliver's Travels: Critical Study, 1987; Monash Swift Studies, 1988; Jonathan Swift, Gulliver's Travels, 1989; The Sociable Humanist: The Life and Works of James Harris, 1709-80: Provincial and Metropolitan Culture in Eighteenth-Century England, 1991. EDITOR: Gulliver's Travels, 1975; (with K. Williams) A Tale of a Tub and Other Satires, 1975; Jonathan Swift: The Contemporary Background, 1978; (with M.C. Battestin) The Correspondence of Henry and Sarah Fielding, 1993; (with W.B. Steele) Maurice Guest, 1998; (with R. Solomon, B. Steele and P. O'Neill) Henry Handel Richardson: The Letters, 2000; (with B. Steele) The Getting of Wisdom, 2000. OTHER: Jonathan Swift and the Black Art, forthcoming. Contributor of articles to books and periodicals. **Address:** School of English Studies, Monash University, Wellington Rd., PO Box 11A, Victoria, VI 3800, Australia. **Online address:** clive.probyn@arts.monash.edu.au

PROCHASKA, F. K. *See* **PROCHASKA, Frank.**

PROCHASKA, Frank. (F. K. Prochaska). American/British (born England), b. 1941. **Genres:** History, Politics/Government, Adult Non-fiction. **Career:** Northwestern University, instructor, 1969-72; University of Missouri, assistant professor, 1973-74; University of Wisconsin, associate professor, 1976; University College, tutor, 1976-87; Yale University, Institute of Historical Research, honorary fellow, lecturer and senior research scientist; Wellcome Institute for the History of Medicine, London University, research fellow, 1987-90; University College, honorary research fellow, 1987-93; All Souls College, visiting fellow, 1997-98; St. Hugh's College, instructor; Royal Holloway College, London University, instructor. Writer. **Publications:** (As F.K. Prochaska) Women and Philanthropy in Nineteenth-Century England, 1980; (ed. with A. Prochaska) Margaretta Acworth's Georgian Cookery Book, 1987; The Voluntary Impulse: Philanthropy in Modern Britain, 1989; (contrib.) Cambridge Social History of Britain, 1750-1950, 1990; (as F.K. Prochaska) Philanthropy and the Hospitals of London: The King's Fund, 1897-1990, 1992; Royal Bounty: The Making of a Welfare Monarchy, 1995; The Republic of Britain, 1760-2000, 2000; Schools of Citizenship: Charity and Civic Virtue, 2002; (contrib.) Royal Lives, 2002; Christianity and Social Service in Modern Britain: The Disinherited Spirit, 2006; The Eagle and the Crown: Americans and the British Monarchy, 2008; Eminent Victorians on American Democracy, 2012. Contributor to periodicals and journals. **Address:** Department of History, Yale University, 213 HGS, 500 College St., PO Box 208234, New Haven, CT 06511-8962, U.S.A. **Online address:** frank.prochaska@yale.edu

PROFUMO, David. British (born England), b. 1955. **Genres:** Novels, Sports/Fitness, Biography, Autobiography/Memoirs. **Career:** Eton College, assistant master of English, 1978; The Royal School, assistant master of English and drama, 1978-79; King's College, part-time lecturer of English, 1981-83; The Fiction Magazine, deputy editor, 1982-84; Daily Telegraph, columnist, 1987-95. **Publications:** (Ed. and intro. with G. Swift) The Magic Wheel: An Anthology of Fishing in Literature, 1985; Sea Music, 1988; In Praise of Trout, 1989; The Weather in Iceland (novel), 1993; Bringing the House Down, 2006. Contributor to periodicals. **Address:** Aitken Alexander Associates Ltd., 18-21 Cavaye Pl., London, GL SW10 9PT, England.

PROKES, Mary T(imothy). American (born United States), b. 1931?. **Genres:** Theology/Religion, Young Adult Non-fiction. **Career:** College of Notre Dame of Maryland, teacher of religious studies, 1976-81; Ain Karim Centre, co-founder, 1978; Kroger International University, visiting lecturer, 1982-83; University of Saskatchewan, St. Thomas More College, assistant professor of religious studies, 1984-93; Christendom College, Notre Dame Graduate School, professor of theology and spirituality, 1994-; Roman Catholic, Permanent Diaconate Program, member of faculty, 1994-; Newman Theological College, faculty, 1992. Writer. **Publications:** Women's Challenge: Ministry in the Flesh, 1977; Women, Men and the Call to Mutuality, Ecumenism, 73, 1984; The Nuptial Meaning of the Body in Light of Mary's Assumption, Communio: International Catholic Review, vol. XI, 2, Summer, 1984; Trinitarian Relationships and Their Reflections in Woman and Man in Proceedings of the Canadian Theological Society, 1988; The Challenge of HIV/AIDS: Caring in Faith, 1991; Transcendence: An Interdisciplinary Issue, 1992; Mutuality: The Human Image of Trinitarian Love, 1993; Toward a Theology of the Body, 1997; Convergence of Trinitarian Mutuality and Technological Truth in The Family of the Future, the Future of the Family, 1999; At the Interface: Theology and Virtual Reality, 2004. Contributor of articles and poems to magazines. **Address:** Christendom College, 4407 Sano St., Alexandria, VA 22312, U.S.A.

PROMIS, José. (José Promis Ojeda). American/Chilean (born Chile), b. 1940. **Genres:** Cultural/Ethnic Topics, Literary Criticism And History. **Career:** Teacher, 1962-67; University of Chile, assistant professor, 1966-70, professor of Chilean literature, 1968-75; Catholic University of Valparaiso, professor, 1967-75, director, 1969-71, Department of Literature, head, 1971-72; Catholic University of Chile, professor, 1973-76; University of Arizona, visiting professor, 1976-77, professor of Spanish-American literature and literary criticism, 1976-83, acting department head, 1983-84, professor emeritus of Spanish, 1987-, Guadalajara Summer School, academic adviser, 1986-87, Center for Latin American Studies, faculty; Texas Christian University, Green honor professor, 1987; University of Playa Ancha, visiting faculty consultant, 1991-. Writer. **Publications:** AS JOSé PROMIS OJEDA: (co-author) Ernesto Cardenal, poeta de la liberación latinoamericana, 1975; (co-author) José Donoso: la destrucción de un mundo, 1975; (intro.) Poesía romántica chilena, 1975. IN SPANISH: Manual de Castellano, 1968; Lectura y Lenguaje, 1970; Laconciencia de la realidad en la literature espanola (Siglos XII-XVI), 1972; (comp.) Testimonios y documentos de la literatura chilena (1842-1975), 1977; La novela chilena actual: orígenes y desarrollo, 1977; (with J. Roman-Lagunas) La prosa hispanoamericana: Evolucion y Antologia, 1988; La novela chilena del último siglo, 1993. OTHERS: La identidad de Hispanoamérica: Ensayo sobre literatura colonial, 1987; (comp.) La Literatura del Reino de Chile, 2002. Works appear in anthologies. Contributor to journals. **Address:** Department of Spanish and Portuguese, University of Arizona, 545 Modern Languages, Tucson, AZ 85721-0067, U.S.A. **Online address:** jpromis@email.arizona.edu

PROSEK, James. American (born United States), b. 1975. **Genres:** Recreation, Biography, Sports/Fitness. **Career:** The New York Times, contributor; Peabody Museum of Natural History, curatorial affiliate; Yale Institute for Biospheric Studies, director. Author and artist. **Publications:** Trout: An Illustrated History, 1996; Joe and Me: An Education in Fishing and Friendship, 1997; The Complete Angler: A Connecticut Yankee Follows in the Footsteps of Walton, 1999; Early Love and Brook Trout, 2000; Fly-Fishing the 41st: Around the World on the 41st Parallel, 2003; Trout of the World, 2003; (contrib.) Fly Fishing is Spoken Here, 2003; Good Day's Fishing, 2004; Tight Lines, 2007; The Day My Mother Left, 2007; Bird, Butterfly, Eel, 2009; Eels: An Exploration of the World's Most Mysterious Fish, from New Zealand to the Sargasso, 2010. **Address:** c/o Elaine Markson, Markson Thoma Literary Agency, 44 Greenwich Ave., New York, NY 10011, U.S.A.

PROTHERO, Stephen (Richard). American (born United States), b. 1960. **Genres:** Theology/Religion, Politics/Government, Sociology. **Career:** Harvard University, instructor, 1988; Yale University, visiting lecturer in religious studies and American studies, 1990; Georgia State University, assistant professor of religious studies, 1990-95; Boston University, Department of Religion, assistant professor, 1996-2000, associate professor, 2000-04, professor, 2004-, director of undergraduate studies, 1996-99, chair, 2003-08, Division of Religious and Theological Studies, associate director, 2000-02, director, 2003-06. Writer. **Publications:** (With G. Shattuck, Jr. and E. Queen II) The Encyclopedia of American Religious History, 1996, 3rd ed., 2009; The White Buddhist: The Asian Odyssey of Henry Steel Olcott, 1996; (ed. with T.A. Tweed) Asian Religions in America: A Documentary History, 1999; Purified by Fire: A History of Cremation in America, 2001; American Jesus: How The Son Of God Became A National Icon, 2003; Is America's Jesus good for the Jews?, 2005; (ed.) A Nation Of Religions: The Politics Of Pluralism In Multireligious America, 2006; Religious Literacy: What Every American Needs To Know-And Doesn't, 2007; God Is Not One: The Eight Rival Religions That Run the World-and Why Their Differences Matter, 2010. Contributor of articles and journals. **Address:** Department of Religion, Boston University, 145 Bay State Rd., Boston, MA 02215, U.S.A. **Online address:** prothero@bu.edu

PROTOPOPESCU, Orel. (Orel Odinov Protopopescu). American (born United States) **Genres:** Picture/Board Books, Children's Non-fiction, Humor/Satire, Poetry, Children's Fiction. **Career:** Writer, producer and educator. **Publications:** (With S. Liu) A Thousand Peaks: Poems from China, 2001; Metaphors and Similes You Can Eat and Twelve More Great Poetry Writing Lessons, 2003; Two Sticks, 2007; Thelonious Mouse, 2011; What Remains, 2011. AS OREL ODINOV PROTOPOPESCU: Since Lulu Learned the Cancan, 1991; The Perilous Pit, 1993. **Address:** PO Box 709, Miller Place, NY 11764, U.S.A. **Online address:** orelprotopopescu@gmail.com

PROTOPOPESCU, Orel Odinov. *See* **PROTOPOPESCU, Orel.**

PROUDFOOT, Lindsay. (Lindsay J. Proudfoot). Irish/British (born England), b. 1950. **Genres:** History, Geography. **Career:** Queen's University, lecturer, 1977-96, reader in historical geography, 1994-. Writer. **Publications:** (With B.J. Graham) Urban Improvement in Provincial Ireland, 1700-1840, 1994; Urban Patronage and Social Authority: The Management of the Duke of Devonshire's Towns in Ireland, 1760-1890, 1995. EDITOR: (with B.J. Graham and contrib.) An Historical Geography of Ireland, 1993; (contrib.) County Down: History and Society: Interdisciplinary Essays on the History of an Irish County, 1996; (with R. King and B.J. Smith and contrib.) The Mediterranean: Environment and Society, 1996; (ed.) Down: History & Society, 1997; (ed. with P. Borsay) Provincial Towns in Early Modern England and Ireland: Change, Convergence, and Divergence, 2002; (with M.M. Roche) (Dis)placing Empire: Renegotiating British Colonial Geographies, 2005. Contributor of articles to books and journals. **Address:** Department of Geosciences, School of Geography, Archaeology & Palaeoecology, Queen's University, Belfast, BT7 1NN, Northern Ireland. **Online address:** l.proudfoot@qub.ac.uk

PROUDFOOT, Lindsay J. *See* **PROUDFOOT, Lindsay.**

PROULX, Annie. *See* **PROULX, E(dna) Annie.**

PROULX, E(dna) Annie. (Annie Proulx). American (born United States), b. 1935. **Genres:** Novels, Novellas/Short Stories, Young Adult Fiction. **Career:** Harvard University, Kress Fellow, 1974; writer, 1975-; Behind the Times, founder and editor, 1984-86. **Publications:** (With L. Nichols) Sweet & Hard Cider: Making It, Using It, & Enjoying It, 1980; What'll You Take for It?: Back to Barter, 1981; (with L. Nichols) Complete Dairy Foods Cookbook: How to Make Everything from Cheese to Custard in Your Own Kitchen, 1982; Gardener's Journal and Record Book, 1983; Plan and Make Your Own Fences & Gates, Walkways, Walls & Drives, 1983; Fine Art of Salad Gardening, 1985; Gourmet Gardener: Growing Choice Fruits and Vegetables With Spectacular Results, 1987; Heart Songs and Other Stories, 1988; Postcards (novel), 1992; The Shipping News (novel), 1993; Fiction, Flyfishing & the Search for Innocence, 1994; Accordion Crimes (novel), 1996; Treadwell: Photographs, 1996; (with L. Nichols) Cider: Making, Using & Enjoying Sweet & Hard Cider, 1997, 3rd ed., 2003; Brokeback Mountain, 1998; Close Range: Wyoming Stories, 1999; That Old Ace in the Hole: A Novel, 2002; Bad Dirt: Wyoming Stories 2, 2004; (ed.) Roaring in the Blood: Remembering Robert F. Jones, 2006; Brokeback Mountain: Story to Screenplay, 2006; William Matthews: Working the West, 2007; Fine Just the Way It Is: Wyoming Stories 3, 2008; (ed.) Red Desert: History of a Place, 2008; (contrib.) Aidan Higgins: The Fragility of Form, 2010; Bird Cloud, 2011; Cloud Bird, 2011; (intro.) The Photographs of Carl Mydans, 2011. Contributor of articles and short stories to periodicals. **Address:** c/o Liz Darhansoff, Darhansoff, Verrill & Feldman Literary Agents, 236 W 26th St., Ste. 802, New York, NY 10001-6736, U.S.A.

PROULX, Monique. Canadian (born Canada), b. 1952. **Genres:** Novels, Novellas/Short Stories, Plays/Screenplays, Young Adult Fiction. **Career:** Writer. **Publications:** Sans Coeur et Sans Reproche (short stories), 1983; Le Sexe des étoiles (novel), 1987; Homme Invisible à la Fenêtre (novel), 1993; Invisible Man at the Window, 1994; Les Aurores Montreales (short stories), 1996; Aurores montréales, 1997; Le Coeur est un muscle involontaire (novel), 2002; Heart is an Involuntary Muscle, 2003; Champagne: Roman, 2008, trans. as Wildlives, 2009. **Address:** 4563 rue Hutchison, Montreal, QC H2V 4A1, Canada.

PROULX, Suzanne. American (born United States) **Genres:** Novels, Young Adult Non-fiction, Medicine/Health. **Career:** Left Coast Crime, co-chair; Editor and freelance writer. **Publications:** Bad Blood, 1999; Bad Luck, 2000; Bad Medicine, 2001; Declared Dead, 2002. **Address:** c/o Author Mail, Random House Inc., 1745 Broadway, New York, NY 10019, U.S.A. **Online address:** cslproulx@yahoo.com

PROVENCE, Michael. American (born United States), b. 1966. **Genres:** History, Area Studies. **Career:** Southern Methodist University, assistant professor, 2001-04; University of California, assistant professor, 2004-07, associate professor, 2007-, Middle East Studies Programs, director; Zentrum Moderner Orient, Alexander von Humboldt fellow. Writer. **Publications:** The Great Syrian Revolt and the Rise of Arab Nationalism, 2005. Contributor to journals and periodicals. **Address:** Department of History, University of California, 9500 Gilman Dr., Ste. 0104, La Jolla, CA 92093-0104, U.S.A. **Online address:** mprovence@ucsd.edu

PROVINE, Robert R(aymond). American (born United States), b. 1943. **Genres:** Psychology, Humor/Satire. **Career:** Washington University, visiting scientist, 1971, research assistant professor, 1971-74; University of Maryland, assistant professor of psychology, 1974-76, associate professor of psychology, 1976-83, professor of psychology, 1983-, Neuroscience Program, assistant director; National Institutes of Health, principle investigator. Writer and consultant. **Publications:** Laughter: A Scientific Investigation, 2000. Contributor to journals. **Address:** Department of Psychology, University of Maryland, Rm. 331, Math/Psychology Bldg., 1000 Hilltop Cir., Baltimore, MD 21250-0001, U.S.A. **Online address:** provine@umbc.edu

PROWELL, Sandra West. American (born United States) **Genres:** Mystery/Crime/Suspense. **Career:** Montana Authors' Coalition, co-founder, 1989-. Writer and photographer. **Publications:** PHOEBE SIEGEL MYSTERIES: By Evil Means, 1993; The Killing of Monday Brown, 1994; When Wallflowers Die, 1996. Contributor to periodicals. **Address:** Walker & Co., 435 Hudson St., New York, NY 10014-3941, U.S.A.

PROWN, Jonathan. American (born United States) **Genres:** Antiques/Furnishings, Local History/Rural Topics, Homes/Gardens, Photography, Art/Art History. **Career:** Arthur Page Conservation Studio, apprentice paintings conservator, 1985; Colonial Williamsburg Foundation, furniture conservation intern and technician, 1986-90, assistant curator of furniture, 1988-95, associate curator of furniture and sculpture, Department of Collections, 1995-. Writer. **Publications:** (With R.L. Hurst) Southern Furniture, 1680-1830: The Colonial Williamsburg Collection, 1997; (intro.) American Furniture 1999, 2000. Contributor of articles to periodicals. **Address:** 1500 E Lilac Ln., Fox Point, WI 53217-2961, U.S.A.

PROWSE, Brad A. American (born United States), b. 1935. **Genres:** Mystery/Crime/Suspense, Science Fiction/Fantasy, Westerns/Adventure, Plays/Screenplays, Food And Wine, History, Literary Criticism And History, Young Adult Fiction, Young Adult Fiction. **Career:** U.S. Army, civilian electronic technician and manager; The Union, staff. Writer. **Publications:** Home Jerky Making for the Home, Trail, and Campfire, 1997. NOVELS: Thundermaker (western), 2000; Dakota Territory (western), 2000; Incident in a Ghost Town, 2000; Cold Storage, 2000; Hard-Rock, High-Grading and Harlots: Tales of Nevada County in the Days of Gold, 2002. Contributor to history magazines. **Address:** PO Box 403, Rough and Ready, CA 95975, U.S.A.

PROZAN, Charlotte (Krause). American (born United States), b. 1936. **Genres:** Psychology, Women's Studies And Issues, Medicine/Health, Sciences, Human Relations/Parenting, Social Sciences. **Career:** Private practice of psychotherapy, 1967-. Writer. **Publications:** Feminist Psychoanalytic Psychotherapy, 1992; The Technique of Feminist Psychoanalytic Psychotherapy, 1993; (ed.) Construction and Reconstruction of Memory: Dilemmas of Childhood Sexual Abuse, 1997. **Address:** 156 16th Ave., San Francisco, CA 94118, U.S.A. **Online address:** cprozan@pacbell.net

PRUD'HOMME, Alex. American (born United States) **Genres:** Biography, Novels. **Career:** New York Magazine, fact-checker, 1988; BusinessMonth Magazine, writer; Talk Magazine, staff writer, 2011. **Publications:** Rosie O'Donnell: A Biography, 1999; (with M. Cherkasky) Forewarned: Why the Government Is Failing to Protect Us, and What We Must Do to Protect Ourselves, 2003; The Cell Game: Sam Waksal's Fast Money and False Promises-And the Fate of ImClone's Cancer Drug, 2004; (with J. Child) My Life in France, 2006; Troubled Waters, forthcoming. **Address:** c/o Tina Bennett, Janklow & Nesbit Associates, 445 Park Ave., New York, NY 10022-2606, U.S.A.

PRUETT, Candace (J.). American (born United States), b. 1968. **Genres:** Children's Fiction. **Career:** Poudre Valley Health System, human resources consultant, nurse recruiter and project director, 1993-; Project Self-Sufficiency, counselor. Writer. **Publications:** A Visit with My Uncle Ted, 2003. **Address:** Poudre Valley Health System, 2315 E Harmony Rd., Ste. 200, Fort Collins, CO 80528-8620, U.S.A. **Online address:** cjp2@pvhs.org

PRUETT, Kyle D(ean). American (born United States), b. 1943. **Genres:** Human Relations/Parenting, Medicine/Health, Psychology, Self Help, Adult Non-fiction, Social Sciences. **Career:** Mount Auburn Hospital, intern, 1969-70; Boston City Hospital, intern, 1969-70; Tufts New England Medical Center, resident in psychiatry, 1970-72; Yale Child Study Center, child psychiatry fellow, 1972-74, assistant clinical professor, 1975-79, associate clinical professor, 1979-87, Child Development Unit, coordinator of training, 1979-87, clinical professor of psychiatry, 1987-, coordinator of education and training, 1995-98, director of medical studies, 1999-2007, director of undergraduate studies, 1999-2007; St. Rafael's Hospital, Adolescent Crisis Unit for Treatment and Evaluation, staff child psychiatrist, 1974-76; Hampstead Child Therapy Clinic, visiting fellow, 1975; Yale-New Haven Hospital, attending physician, 1976-2008; Yale University School of Nursing, clinical professor, 1993-; Connecticut Infant-Toddler Development Assessment Program, consultant; Performing Arts Medicine Clinic, consultant. Writer. **Publications:** The Nurturing Father: Journey toward the Complete Man, 1987; Me, Myself and I, 1999; Fatherneed: Why Father Care is as Essential as Mother Care for Your Child, 2000; (with M.K. Pruett) Partnership Parenting, 2009. Contributor to journals. **Address:** Yale Child Study Center, Yale School of Medicine, 230 S Frontage Rd., PO Box 207900, New Haven, CT 06512-7900, U.S.A. **Online address:** kyle.pruett@yale.edu

PRUETT, Lynn. American (born United States), b. 1960?. **Genres:** Business/Trade/Industry, Novels. **Career:** University of Kentucky, instructor in writing, 1995-. Writer. **Publications:** Ruby River, 2002. Works appear in anthologies. Contributor to periodicals. **Address:** 543 Boonesboro Ave., Lexington, KY 40508-1953, U.S.A. **Online address:** contact@lynnpruett.com

PRUNIER, Gerard. Ethiopian/French (born France), b. 1942. **Genres:** History, Politics/Government. **Career:** Centre National de la Recherche Scientifique (CNRS), researcher, 1984-, research fellow, 1984-2001, senior researcher; Centre Francais des Etudes Ethiopiennes, director, 2001-06; Rift Valley Institute, fellow; Peace Dividend, board advisor. Writer and historian. **Publications:** (Ed. with J. Chrétien) Les Ethnies ont une Histoire, 1989; L'Ouganda et la Question Indienne: 1896-1972, 1990; (co-ed.) L'Invention Religieuse en Afrique: Histoire et Religion en Afrique Noire, 1993; (with B. Calas) L'Ouganda Contemporain, 1994; Rwanda Crisis, 1959-1994: History of a Genocide, 1995; The Rwanda Crisis: History of a Genocide, 1995, 2nd ed., 1999; (ed. with F. Grignon) Le Kenya Contemporain, 1998; Of What I Saw and Heard, 2004; Darfur: The Ambiguous Genocide in Paris as Le Darfour: Un Génocide Ambigu, 2005, trans. as Darfur: The Ambiguous Genocide, 2005, 3rd ed. as Darfur: A 21st Century Genocide, 2008; (ed.) L'éthiopie Contemporaine, 2007; From Genocide to Continental War, 2009; Africa's World War: Congo, the Rwandan Genocide, and the Making of a Continental Catastrophe, 2009. Contributor to books. **Address:** Centre National de la Recherche Scientifique, 3 rue Michel-Ange, Paris, 75794, France. **Online address:** gerard.prunier@wanadoo.fr

PRUTER, Robert. American (born United States), b. 1944. **Genres:** Music, Sports/Fitness, Reference, History, Literary Criticism And History. **Career:** Standard Educational Corp., assistant editor, 1969-74, associate editor, 1974-79, senior editor social sciences, 1979-96; Goldmine (magazine), columnist and feature writer, 1977-84, rhythm and blues editor, 1984-2006, R&B editor, 1985-2006; Bowling Green State University, advisory editor, 1995; Planning/Communications, senior research editor, 1996-97; Charles D. Spencer and Associates, assistant editor, 1997-98, associate editor, 1999-2001; Lewis University, government documents librarian/reference, 2001-. **Publications:** Chicago Soul, 1991; (ed.) Blackwell's Guide to Soul Recordings, 1993; Doo Wop: The Chicago Scene, 1996; (foreword) Give em Soul, Richard!: Race, Radio and Rhythm and Blues in Chicago, 2010. Contributor of articles to journals. **Address:** Government Documents Library, Lewis University, 1 University Pkwy., Romeoville, IL 60446-2200, U.S.A. **Online address:** pruterro@lewisu.edu

PRYBYLA, Jan S(tanislaw). *See* Obituaries.

PRYCE, Lois. British (born England), b. 1973. **Genres:** Travel/Exploration. **Career:** British Broadcasting Corp. (BBC), product manager. Freelance journalist and speaker. **Publications:** Lois on the Loose: One Woman, One Motorcycle, 20, 000 Miles across the Americas, 2007; Red Tape and White Knuckles, 2009. **Address:** Faye Bender Literary Agency, 19 Cheever Pl., Brooklyn, NY 11231-3004, U.S.A. **Online address:** lois@loisontheloose.com

PRYCE-JONES, David. British/Austrian (born Austria), b. 1936. **Genres:** Novels, History, Travel/Exploration, Documentaries/Reportage, Essays. **Career:** Financial Times, literary editor, 1959-61; Time and Time, literary editor, 1960-61; The Spectator, literary editor, 1961-63; National Review magazine, senior editor, 1999-; University of Iowa, visiting writer-in-residence, 1964-65, teacher writers workshop; California State College, visiting lecturer, 1966, 1968, teacher writers workshop, 1968, 1970; The Daily Telegraph, special correspondent, 1966-82; University of California, visiting lecturer, 1970, teacher writers workshop, 1972. **Publications:** Owls and Satyrs, 1961; Graham Greene, 1962; (trans.) M. Rheims, Art on the Market, 1962; (trans.) G. Prassinos, The Traveller, 1962; The Sands of Summer, 1963; Next Generation: Travels in Israel, 1964; Quondam, 1965; The Stranger's View, 1967; The Hungarian Revolution, 1968; Running Away, 1969; The Face of Defeat, 1972; (ed.) Evelyn Waugh and His World, 1973; The England Commune, 1975; Unity Mitford: A Quest, 1976; (trans.) P. Marsay, Leaving Standing Still, 1977; Vienna, 1978; Shirley's Guild, 1979; Paris in the Third Reich, 1981; Cyril Connolly, Journal and Memoir, 1983; The Afternoon Sun, 1986; The Closed Circle: An Interpretation of Arabs, 1989; (with W. Shaw) The World Almanac of the Soviet Union: From 1905 to the Present, 1990; (with W. Shaw) Encyclopedia of the USSR: From 1905 to the Present: Lenin to Gorbachev, 1990; Inheritance, 1992; You Can't Be too Careful: Cautionary Tales, 1992; The War That Never Was: The Fall of the Soviet Empire, 1985-1991, 1995; The Strange Death of the Soviet Empire, 1995; Closed Circle: An Interpretation of the Arabs, 2002; Betrayal: France, the Arabs and the Jews, 2006; Safe Houses, 2007; Treason of the Heart: From Thomas Paine to Kim Philby, 2011. Contributor to periodicals. **Address:** Christopher Sinclair-Stevenson, 3 South Terr., London, GL SW7 2TB, England.

PRYMAK, Thomas M. Canadian (born Canada), b. 1948. **Genres:** Cultural/Ethnic Topics, History, Biography, Autobiography/Memoirs, Social Sciences. **Career:** Steppe to Prairie Productions, producer and director, 1973-75; University of Saskatchewan, instructor in Ukrainian history, 1984-85; University of Toronto, instructor in Ukrainian studies, 1987-88, Center for Russian and East European Studies, faculty member; McMaster University, instructor in Russian studies, 1989-92. Writer. **Publications:** Mykhailo Hrushevsky: The Politics of National Culture, 1987; Maple Leaf and Trident: The Ukrainian Canadians during the Second World War, 1988; Mykola Kostomarov: A Biography, 1996. Contributor of articles and reviews to scholarly journals and periodicals and books. **Address:** 46 Priscilla Ave., Toronto, ON M6S 3W2, Canada.

PRYNNE, J. H. British (born England), b. 1936. **Genres:** Poetry. **Career:** Harvard University, Frank Knox fellow, 1960-61; University of Cambridge, Gonville and Caius College, fellow, lecturer in English, 1962-2005, director of studies in English, through 2005, librarian, through 2006, emeritus reader in English poetry; University of Sussex, honorary professor of English; Sun Yat-sen University, visiting professor. Writer. **Publications:** Stars, Tigers and the Shape of Words, 1993; They That Haue Powre to Hurt: A Specimen of a Commentary on Shakespeares Sonnets, 94, 2001; Field Notes: The Solitary Reaper and Others, 2007; Streak Willing Entourage Artesian, 2009. POEMS: Force of Circumstance and Other Poems, 1962; Kitchen Poems, 1968; Day Light Songs, 1968; Aristeas, 1968; The White Stones, 1969; Fire Lizard, 1970; Brass, 1971; Into the Day, 1972; A Night Square, 1973; Wound Response, 1974; High Pink on Chrome, 1975; News of Warring Clans, 1977; Down Where Changed, 1979; Poems, 1982, 2nd ed., 2005; The Oval Window, 1983; Marzipan, 1986; Bands Around the Throat, 1987; Word Order, 1989; Jie ban mi Shi Hu, 1992; Not-You, 1993; Her Weasels Wild Returning, 1994; For the Monogram, 1997; Collected Poems, 1998; Red D Gypsum, 1998; Pearls That Were, 1999; Triodes, 1999; Unanswering Rational Shore, 2001; Acrylic Tips, 2002; Biting the Air, 2003; Blue Slides At Rest, 2004; To Pollen, 2006; Sub Songs, 2010. Contributor to magazines. **Address:** Gonville and Caius College, University of Cambridge, Trinity St., Cambridge, CB CB2 1TA, England. **Online address:** jhp13@cam.ac.uk

PRYOR, Bonnie H. American (born United States), b. 1942. **Genres:** Children's Fiction, Young Adult Fiction, Illustrations, History, Romance/Historical. **Career:** Public speaker and writer, 1985-. **Publications:** CHILDREN'S BOOKS: Grandpa Bear, 1985; Grandpa Bear's Christmas, 1986; Amanda and April, 1986; Rats, Spiders and Love, 1986; Mr. Z and the Time Clock, 1986; The House on Maple Street, 1987; Vinegar Pancakes and Vanishing Cream, 1987; Seth of the Lion People, 1988; Porcupine Mouse, 1988, rev. ed., 2002; Jenny's New Baby Sister, 1988; Happy Birthday Mama, 1988; Mr. Munday and the Rustlers, 1987; Plum Tree War, 1989; Perfect Percy, 1989; Mr. Munday and the Space Creature, 1989; The Twenty-Four-Hour Lipstick Mystery, 1989; Greenbrook Farm, 1991; Merry Christmas, Amanda and April Pig, 1990; Beaver Boys, 1992; Horses in the Garage, 1992; Jumping Jenny, 1992; Lottie's Dream, 1992; Poison Ivy and Eyebrow Wigs, 1993; Birthday Blizzard, 1993; Houses in the Garden, 1994; Marvelous Marvin and the Wolfman Mystery, 1994; Marvelous Marvin and the Pioneer Ghost, 1995; Dream Jar, 1996; Toenails, Tonsils and Tornados, 1997; Louie & Dan Are Friends, 1997; Toenails Tonsils and Tornadoes, 1997; Thomas, 1998; American Adventure: Thomas, 1998; American Adventure: Luke, 1999; American Adventure: Joseph, 1999; Thomas in Danger, 1999; Joseph: A Rumble of War, 1861, 1999; Luke: On the Golden Trail, 1849, 1999; Luke on the High Seas, 2000; Joseph's Choice, 1861, 2000; Hannah Pritchard: Pirate of the Revolution, 2008; Pirate Hannah Pritchard: Captured!, 2009; Iron Dragon: The Courageous Story of Lee Chin, 2010; Simon's Escape: A Story of the Holocaust, 2010; Captain Hannah Pritchard: The Hunt for Pirate Gold, 2011. Contributor to magazines and periodicals. **Address:** 19600 Baker Rd., Gambier, OH 43022, U.S.A. **Online address:** bonniepryor@rocketmail.com

PRYOR, Vanessa. *See* **YARBRO, Chelsea Quinn.**

PTACEK, Kathryn. Also writes as Kathleen Maxwell, Kathryn Grant, Les Simons. American (born United States), b. 1952?. **Genres:** Young Adult Fiction, Natural History, Science Fiction/Fantasy, Horror. **Career:** University of New Mexico, Department of Speech and Hearing, secretary and technical writer, Computer Center, editor. **Publications:** (As Les Simons) Gila!, 1981; Satans Angel, 1981; Renegade Lady, 1982; The Wayward Widow, 1982; Shadow-Eyes, 1984; The Lawless Heart, 1984; Blood Autumn, 1984; Kachina, 1986; My Lady Rogue, 1986; The Phoenix Bells, 1987; Aurora, 1987; (ed.) Women of Darkness, 1988; In Silence Sealed, 1988; Ghost Dance, 1990; (ed.) Women of the West: An Anthology of Short Stories by Contemporary Women Writers, 1990; (ed.) Women of Darkness II: More Original Horror and Dark Fantasy by Contemporary Women Writers, 1990; The Hunted, 1992. AS KATHRYN GRANT: The Pheonix Bells, 1987; The Willow Garden, 1989; The Black Jade Road, 1989. AS KATHLEEN MAXWELL: The Devil's Heart, 1983; Winter Masquerade, 1984. **Address:** PO Box 97, Newton, NJ 07860-0097, U.S.A.

PUAR, Jasbir K. American (born United States), b. 1967. **Genres:** History. **Career:** University of California, Department of Women's Studies, teaching assistant, 1994-96; San Francisco State University, instructor of women's studies, 1998-99; Rutgers University, Department of Women's and Gender Studies, assistant professor, 2000-, Department of Geography, graduate faculty. Writer. **Publications:** Terrorist Assemblages: Homonationalism in Queer Times, 2007. Contributor to books and journals. **Address:** Department of Women's & Gender Studies, Rutgers University, 162 Ryders Ln., Douglass Campus, New Brunswick, NJ 08901, U.S.A. **Online address:** jpuar@rci.rutgers.edu

PUCCI, Pietro. American/Italian (born Italy), b. 1927. **Genres:** Classics, Philosophy, Literary Criticism And History. **Career:** University of Florence, assistant professor of classics, 1951-52, visiting professor, 1970; University of Ottawa, assistant professor of classics, 1959-61; University of Kansas, assistant professor of classics, 1961-62; Cornell University, Department of Classics, assistant professor, 1962-67, associate professor, 1967-72, professor, 1972-, head, 1983-87, 1990-91, Goldwin Smith professor; University of California, visiting professor, 1969; Ecole des Hautes Etudes, director of studies, 1984, 1989. Writer. **Publications:** Aristofane e Euripide: Studi Stilistici e Metrici, 1961; (trans.) Platone: Simposio, Fedro, Alcibiade I, Alcibiade II, Teage, Ipparco, Carmide, Lachete, Liside, Bari, 1966; Hesiod and the Language of Poetry, 1977; The Violence of Pity in Euripides' Medea, 1980; Odysseus Polutropos: Intertextual Studies on the Odyssey and the Iliad, 1987; (ed.) Language and the Tragic Hero: Essays on Greek Tragedy in Honor of Gordon M. Kirkwood, 1988; Oedipus and the Fabrication of the Father: Oedipus Tyrannus in Modern Criticism and Philosophy, 1992; Enigma, Segreto, Oracolo, 1996; The Song of the Sirens: Essays on Homer, 1998; (trans. and intro.) Inno alle muse, 2007. Works appear in anthologies. Contributor to journals. **Address:** Department of Classics, Cornell University, Rm. 125, Goldwin Smith Hall, Ithaca, NY 14853-3201, U.S.A. **Online address:** pp26@cornell.edu

PUCHNER, Eric. American (born United States) **Genres:** Novellas/Short Stories, Novels. **Career:** San Francisco State University, instructor; Stanford University, instructor, Wallace Stegner fellow, John L'Heureux fellow; Claremont McKenna College, assistant professor. Writer. **Publications:** Music through the Floor: Stories, 2005; Model Home: A Novel, 2010. Works appear in anthologies. Contributor to periodicals. **Address:** c/o Dorian Karchmar, William Morris Endeavor Entertainment, 1325 Ave. of the Americas, New York, NY 10019-6026, U.S.A. **Online address:** eric.puchner@cmc.edu

PUFF, Helmut. American/German (born Germany), b. 1961?. **Genres:** History, Sex. **Career:** Institute for the Late Middle Ages and the Reformation, research assistant, 1982-83; Museum for the History of Hamburg, research assistant, 1985-87; University of Basel, German Seminar, assistant, 1988-92, 1995, Research Project on Renaissance Marriage Treatises in German Language, research fellow, 1992-95; University of Michigan, Department of Germanic Languages and Literatures, visiting assistant professor, 1995-96, Department of Germanic Languages and Literatures and Department of History, assistant professor, 1996-2002, associate professor, 2002-, History of Art and Program in History and Anthropology, affilate, 2004-, interim chair, 2007-08. Writer. **Publications:** (Ed.) Lust, Angst und Provokation: Homosexualität in der Gesellschaft, 1993; Von dem Schlüssel aller künsten, nemblich der Grammatica: Deutsch im lateinischen grammatikunterricht 1480-1560, 1995; (with C. Wild) Zwischen den Disziplinen? Perspektiven der Frühneuzeitforschung, 2003; Sodomy in Reformation Germany and Switzerland, 1400-1600, 2003; (ed. with S. Spector and D. Herzog) After the History of Sexuality: German Genealogies with and Beyond Foucault, 2012. Contributor of article to books and professional journals. **Address:** Department of History, University of Michigan, 3142 MLB, 812 E. Washington St., Ann Arbor, MI 48109-1003, U.S.A. **Online address:** puffh@umich.edu

PUGH, Dianne G. American (born United States) **Genres:** Mystery/Crime/Suspense, Novels, Literary Criticism And History. **Career:** Writer and investment counselor. **Publications:** IRIS THORNE MYSTERY SERIES: Cold Call, 1993; Slow Squeeze, 1994; Fast Friends, 1997; Foolproof, 1997. NOVELS: Body Blow, 1995; Pushover, 1999. Contributor to periodicals. **Address:** Pocket Books, 1230 Ave. of the Americas, 11th Fl., New York, NY 10020-1513, U.S.A.

PUGSLEY, Alex. (Alexander Hunter Pugsley). Canadian (born Canada), b. 1963?. **Genres:** Plays/Screenplays, Novels, Literary Criticism And History. **Career:** Writer. **Publications:** (With L. MacDonald) Kay Darling (novel), 1994. **Address:** 273 Crawford St., Ste. 2, Toronto, ON M6J 2V7, Canada.

PUGSLEY, Alexander Hunter. *See* **PUGSLEY, Alex.**

PUIGGRÓS, Adriana (Victoria). Argentine (born Argentina), b. 1941. **Genres:** Politics/Government, Social Commentary, Adult Non-fiction. **Career:** University of Buenos Aires, director of department of educational sciences and director of Institute of educational sciences, 1973-74, dean of philosophy and letters faculty, 1974, professor of Latin American educational history; Confederation of Education Workers of the Republic of Argentina, director of research institute; Secretary of State for Technology, Science and Productive Innovation Ministry of Education of Argentina, staff, 2001; Province of Buenos Aires, advisor, 2002-05. Writer. **Publications:** Imperialismo y Educacíon en América Latina, 1980; (comp. with M. Gomez) La Educación Popular en América Latina: Orígenes, Polémicas Y Perspectivas, 1984; Democracia y Autoritarismo en laPedagogía Argentina y Latino Americana, 1986; Discusiones Sobre Educación y Política: Aportes al Congreso Pedagógico Nacional, 1987; (with S. Jose and J. Balduzzi) Hacia una Pedagogía de laImaginación para América Latina, 1988; Imperialism and Education in Latin America, 1988; Discusiones sobre educación y politíca, 1990; Sujetos, Disciplina y Curriculum: En los Orígenes del Sistema Educativo Argentino, 1990; América Latina: Crisis y Prospectiva de la Educacíon, 1991; Crisis y educacion popular, 1992; (with G.T. Bertussi and M.A.C. Franco) Estudos Comparados e Educação na América Latina, 1992; Crisis y educacion popular, 1992; Universidad, Proyecto Generacional y el Imaginario Pedagógico, 1993; Imaginación y crisis en la educación Latino Americana, 1994; (co-author) La Educacion: Hacia que Futuro Mira?, 1994; (co-author) Discursos Pedagógicos e Imaginario Social en el Peronismo, 1945-1955, 1995; Volver a Educar: el Desafío de la Enseñanza Argentina aFinales del Siglo XX, 1995; (comp. with C. Lozano) Historia de laEducación en Iberoamérica, 1945-1992, 1995; Qué Paso en la Educación Argentina: Desde la Conquista Hasta el Menemismo, 1996, 2nd ed., 2003; La Otra Reforma: Desde la Educación Menemista al Fin deSiglo, 1997; (co-author) Dictaduras y Utopías enla Historia Reciente de la Educación Argentina (1955-1983), 1997; Neoliberalism & Education in the Americas, 1999; (co-author) En LosLímites de la Educación: Ninos y Jóvenes del Fin de Siglo, 1999; Educar Entre el Acuerdo y la Libertad: Propuestas Para laEducación del Siglo XXI, 1999; Paulo Freire e a Agenda da Educação Latino-Americana no Século XXI, 2001; El Lugar del Saber: Conflictos y Alternativas Entre Educación, Conocimiento yPolitica, 2003; La Fábrica del Conocimiento: Los Saberes Socialmente Productivos en América Latina, 2004; De Simón Rodriguez a Paulo Freire: Educación para la Integración Ibero Americana, 2004; (with L. Rodríguez) Saberes: Reflexiones, Experiencias y debates, 2009; Tremenda Sugestión De Pensar Que no es Posible: Luchas Por Una Democracia Educativa, 1995-2010, 2010; Rodolfo Puiggrós: retrato familiar de un intelectual militante, 2010. EDITOR: Sociedad Civil y Estado en los Origenes del Sistema Educativo Argentino, 1991; Escuela, Democracia y Orden (1916-1943), 1992; (with J.L. Bernetti) Peronismo: Cultura Política y Educacíon (1945-1955), 1993; (co-ed.) Alternativas Pedagógicas: Sujetos y Prospectiva de la Educación Latino Americana, 1994; (with C.A. Torres) Latin American Education: Comparative Perspectives, 1997. Contributor to books and periodicals. **Address:** University of Buenos Aires, Viamonte 430 st., Buenos Aires, 1430, Argentina. **Online address:** apuiggros@ibm.net

PULECIO, Ingrid Betancourt. *See* **BETANCOURT, Ingrid.**

PULLEIN-THOMPSON, Diana. (Diana Farr). British (born England), b. 1925. **Genres:** Novels, Children's Fiction, Literary Criticism And History, Writing/Journalism, Autobiography/Memoirs, Biography, Young Adult Fiction. **Career:** Grove Riding Schools, director; Rosica Colin Ltd., staff of literary agency, 1950-52; Faith Press, part-time editor, 1957-59. **Publications:** I Wanted a Pony, 1946; (with J. Pullein-Thompson and C. Pullein-Thompson) It Began with Picotee, 1946; Three Ponies and Shannan, 1947; The Penny Fields, 1949; A Pony to School, 1950; A Pony for Sale, 1951; Janet Must Ride, 1953; Horses at Home, and Friends Must Part, 1954; Riding for Children, 1957; The Boy and the Donkey, 1958; The Donkey Race, 1958; The Hidden River, 1960; The Boy Who Came to Stay, 1960; The Battle of Clapham Common, 1962; Bindi Must Go, 1962; The Secret Dog, 1970; The Hermit's Horse, 1973; (with C. Pullein-Thompson and J. Pullein-Thompson) Black Beauty's Family, 1975 as Black Beauty's Clan, 1975; Ponies in the Valley, 1976; Ponies on the Trail, 1978; Ponies in Peril, 1979; Cassidy in Danger, 1979, rev. ed. as This Pony is Dangerous, 1990; Only a Pony, 1980; The Pony Seekers, 1981; Foal for Candy, 1981; Candy Has Her Foal, 1981; Riding with the Lyntons, 1982; Black Beauty's Family 2, 1982; A Pony Found, 1983; Black Princess, 1983; Once a Pony, 1986; Dear Pup (humour): Letters to a Young Dog, 1988; Star Riders, 1990; The Long Ride Home, 1996; (with C. Pullein-Thompson and J. Pullein-Thompson) Fair Girls and Grey Horses: Memories of a Country Childhood, 1996; Classic Horse & Pony Stories: The World's Best Horse and Pony Stories in their Real-Life Settings, 1999; (with C. Pullein-Thompson and J. Pullein-Thompson) More from Black Beauty's Family, 2001. AS DIANA FARR: Gilbert Cannan: A Georgian Prodigy, 1978; Five at 10: Prime Ministers' Consorts since 1957, 1985; Choosing (adult novel), 1988. Contributor to books and periodicals. **Address:** Orchard Hill, Swan Barn Rd., Haslemere, SR GU27 2HY, England.

PULLEIN-THOMPSON, Josephine. British (born England), b. 1924. **Genres:** Mystery/Crime/Suspense, Children's Fiction, Animals/Pets, Autobiography/Memoirs, Literary Criticism And History. **Career:** P.E.N., English Centre, general secretary, 1976-93, president, 1993-97. Writer. **Publications:** Six Ponies, 1946; I Had Two Ponies, 1947; Plenty of Ponies, 1949; Pony Club Team, 1950; The Radney Club, 1951; Prince Among Ponies, 1952; One Day Event, 1954; Show Jumping Secret, 1955; Patrick's Pony, 1956; Pony Club Camp, 1957; The Trick Jumpers, 1958; Gin and Murder, 1959; They Died in the Spring, 1960; All Change, 1961 as The Hidden Horse, 1992; How Horses Are Trained, 1961; Ponies in Color, 1962; Murder Strikes Pink, 1963; Learn to Ride Well, 1966; Horses and Their Owners, 1970; Race Horse Holiday, 1971; (as Josephine Mann) A Place with Two Faces, 1972; Proud Riders, 1973; Ride Better and Better, 1974; (with C. Pullein-Thompson and D. Pullein-Thompson) Black Beauty's Clan, 1975; Star Riders of the Moor, 1976, rev. ed. as Star-Riders of the Moor, 1990; Fear Treks the Moor, 1978; (with C. Pullein-Thompson and D. Pullein-Thompson) Black Beauty's Family, 1978; Night Shade, 1978; Ride to the Rescue, 1979; Black Ebony, 1979; Ghost Horse on the Moor, 1980; The No Good Pony, 1981; Treasure on the Moor, 1982; The Prize Pony, 1982; The Hidden Horse, 1982; Black Raven, 1982; Pony Club Cup, 1983; Save the Ponies, 1983; Mystery on the Moor, 1984; Pony Club Challenge, 1984; Pony Club Trek, 1985; Suspicion Stalks the Moor, 1986; Black Swift, 1991; A Job with Horses, 1994; Treasury of Horse and Pony Stories, 1995; Pony Stories, 1996; (with C. Pullein-Thompson and D. Pullein-Thompson) Fair Girls and Grey Horses: Memories of A Country Childhood, 1996; How to Ride Well, 1996; (with C. Pullein-Thompson and D. Pullein-Thompson) More from Black Beauty's Family, 2001. Contributor to books and periodicals. **Address:** 16 Knivet Rd., London, GL SW6 IJH, England.

PULLMAN, Philip. British (born England), b. 1946. **Genres:** Children's Fiction, Plays/Screenplays, Children's Non-fiction, Novels, Novellas/Short Stories. **Career:** Westminster College, lecturer, 1988-95. Writer. **Publications:** FOR YOUNG ADULTS FICTION: The Ruby in the Smoke, 1985; The Shadow in the Plate, 1987 in US as The Shadow in the North, 1988; The Tiger in the Well, 1990; Spring-heeled Jack, 1991; The Broken Bridge, 1992; The White Mercedes, 1993 as The Butterfly Tattoo, 1998; The Tin Princess, 1994; Detective Stories: Chosen by Philip Pullman, 1998; (intro.) Paradise Lost, 2005; Golden Compass, 2006. HIS DARK MATERIALS TRILOGY: Northern Lights, 1995 in US as The Golden Compass, 1996; The Subtle Knife, 1997; The Amber Spyglass, 2000; Lyra's Oxford, 2003; His Dark Materials, 2007. FOR CHILDREN FICTION: Ancient Civilizations, 1978; Count Karlstein, 1982; How to Be Cool, 1987; The Wonderful Story of Aladdin and the Enchanted Lamp, 1993 as Aladdin and the Enchanted Lamp, 2005; Thunderbolt's Waxwork, 1994; The Gas Fitter's Ball, 1995; Clockwork or All Wound Up, 1998; The Firework Maker's Daughter, 1999; I Was a Rat!, 2000; Puss in Boots: The Adventures of That Most Enterprising Feline, 2000; The Scarecrow and His Servant, 2005; Good Man Jesus and the Scoundrel Christ, 2010. FOR ADULTS NOVELS: Galatea, 1979. NON-FICTION: Ancient Civilisations, 1978; Using the Oxford Junior Dictionary, 1978. THE NEW CUT GANG SERIES: Thunderbolt's Waxworks, 1994; The Gas-Fitter's Ball, 1995. OTHERS: Once Upon a Time in the North, 2008; (co-author) Magic Beans: A Handful of Fairytales from the Storybag, 2011; The Adventures of the New Cut Gang, 2011; Two Crafty Criminals!: And How they were Captured by the Daring Detectives of the New Cut Gang, 2012. Contributor to periodicals. **Address:** c/o Caradoc King, A.P. Watt Ltd., 20 John St., London, GL WC1N 2DR, England.

PULS, Mark. American (born United States), b. 1963. **Genres:** Biography. **Career:** Detroit News, investigative reporter; journalist. Writer. **Publications:** Samuel Adams: Father of the American Revolution, 2006; (with M. Claxton) Uncommon Valor: A Story of Race, Patriotism, and Glory in the Final Battles of the Civil War, 2006; Henry Knox: Visionary General of the American Revolution, 2008. Contributor to periodicals. **Address:** c/o Author Mail, Palgrave Macmillan, 175 5th Ave., New York, NY 10010, U.S.A.

PULSFORD, Petronella. British (born England), b. 1946. **Genres:** Novels,

Mystery/Crime/Suspense. **Career:** Writer. **Publications:** Lee's Ghost, 1990. **Address:** 8 Thomas St. W, Halifax, WY HX1 3HF, England.

PULTZ, John Francisco. American (born United States), b. 1952. **Genres:** Photography, Art/Art History. **Career:** Museum of Modern Art, Department of Photography, Beaumont and Nancy Newhall curatorial fellow, 1981-84; J. Paul Getty Museum, Department of Photographs, consultant, 1985; Bard College, visiting assistant professor, 1986; Temple University, Tyler School of Art, visiting assistant professor, 1986; Kean College, instructor, 1991; New York University, instructor, 1992; University of Kansas, Spencer Museum of Art, curator of photography, 1992-2006, Kress Foundation Department of Art History, assistant professor, 1992-98, associate professor, graduate advisor and director of graduate admissions, 1999-; Denver Art Museum, consulting curator of photography and new media, 2001-02. Writer. **Publications:** (With C.B. Scallen) Cubism and American Photography, 1910-1930, 1981; The Body and the Lens: Photography 1839 to the Present, 1995; (with A. de Mondenard) Le Corps Photographié, 1995; (with A.W. Lee) Diane Arbus: Family Albums, 2003. **Address:** Kress Foundation Department of Art History, University of Kansas, 209 Spencer Museum of Art, 1301 Mississippi St., Lawrence, KS 66045, U.S.A. **Online address:** pultz@ku.edu

PULVER, Robin. American (born United States), b. 1945. **Genres:** Children's Fiction, Picture/Board Books, Young Adult Fiction. **Career:** Writer. **Publications:** Mrs. Toggle's Zipper, 1990; The Holiday Handwriting School, 1991; Mrs. Toggle and the Dinosaur, 1991; Nobody's Mother Is in Second Grade, 1992; Mrs. Toggle's Beautiful Blue Shoe, 1994; Homer and the House Next Door, 1994; Alicia's Tutu, 1997; Axle Annie, 1999; Way to Go, Alex!, 1999; Mrs. Toggle's Class Picture Day, 2000; Punctuation Takes a Vacation, 2003; Christmas for a Kitten, 2003; Axle Annie and the Speed Grump, 2005; Author Day for Room 3T, 2005; Nouns and Verbs have a Field Day, 2006; Silent Letters Loud and Clear, 2008; Never Say Boo!, 2009; Christmas Kitten, Home at Last, 2010; Thank You, Miss Doover!, 2010; Happy Endings: A Story About Suffixes, 2011; Case of the Incapacitated Capitals, 2012. Contributor to periodicals. **Address:** 19 Cricket Hill Dr., Pittsford, NY 14534, U.S.A. **Online address:** robinpulvernews-subscribe@yahoogroups.com

PULVERTAFT, (Isobel) Lalage. (Hilary March). British (born England), b. 1925?. **Genres:** Novels, Young Adult Fiction, Romance/Historical. **Career:** C.A. Doxiadis, editorial assistant, 1971-73. **Publications:** No Great Magic, 1956; The Thing Desired, 1957; Golden October, 1965; (as Hilary March) A Question of Love, 1966. **Address:** 96A Chalmers Rd., Cambridge, CB CB1 3SX, England. **Online address:** lalpulvertaft@aol.com

PULZER, Peter George Julius. British/Austrian (born Austria), b. 1929. **Genres:** History, Politics/Government, Theology/Religion. **Career:** Magdalen College, lecturer in politics, 1957-62; Christ Church, lecturer in politics, 1957-62; University of Oxford, lecturer in Politics, 1957-62, tutor in politics, 1962-84, All Souls College, Gladstone professor of government and public administration and fellow, 1984-96, now emeritus fellow and professor emeritus; University of Birmingham, Institute for German Studies, professorial fellow, 1996-99. Writer. **Publications:** The Rise of Political Anti-Semitism in Germany and Austria, 1964, rev. ed., 1988; Entstehung des politischen Antisemitismus in Deutschland und Osterreich, 1867 bis 1914, 1966; Political Representation and Elections: Parties and Voting in Great Britain, 1967; Political Representation and Elections in Britain, 1967, rev. ed., 1972; Jews and the German State: The Political History of a Minority, 1848-1933, 1992, rev. ed., 2003; German Politics, 1945-1995, 1995; Germany, 1870-1945: Politics, State Formation, and War, 1997; (ed. with K.R. Luther) Austria 1945-95: Fifty Years of the Second Republic, 1998; (ed. with W. Benz and A. Paucker) JüDisches Leben in der Weimarer Republik: Jews in the Weimar Republic, 1998; German Antisemitism Revisited, 1999; What About the Jewish Non-Intellectuals in Germany?: Some Remarks on the Image of Pre-1933 German Jewry, 2001; (ed. with H. Tewes) Liberalism, Anti-semitism and Democracy, 2001; Jews and the German State: The Political History of a Minority, 1848-1933, 2003; German Historians and Germany's Jews, 2007. Contributor to periodicals and journals. **Address:** All Souls College, University of Oxford, 14 High St., Oxford, OX OX1 4AL, England.

PUN, Ngai. Hong Kong/Chinese (born China), b. 1970. **Genres:** Humanities, Industrial Relations, History, Social Sciences. **Career:** City University of Hong Kong, lecturer, 1998-99; University of Hong Kong, research assistant professor, 1999-2001; Hong Kong University of Science and Technology, Division of Social Science, assistant professor, 2001-, associate professor; Chinese Working Women Network, founder and chair; anthropologist. Writer. **Publications:** (Ed. with A.S. Ku) Remaking Citizenship in Hong Kong: Community, Nation and the Global City, 2004; Made in China: Women Factory Workers in a Global Workplace, 2005. Contributor of articles to journals. **Address:** Division of Social Science, Hong Kong University of Science and Technology, Rm. 3372, Academic Bldg., Clear Water Bay, Kowloon, 1, Hong Kong. **Online address:** sonpun@atsust.hk

PUNKE, Michael. American (born United States), b. 1964. **Genres:** Novels, History. **Career:** White House, National Security Council and the National Economic Council, director for international economic affairs, 1993-95; Office of the United States Trade Representative, senior policy advisor, 1995-96, deputy united states trade representative; University of Montana, Department of Political Science, adjunct instructor and professor; World Trade Organization, U.S ambassador and permanent representative. Lawyer and writer. **Publications:** The Revenant, 2002; Fire and Brimstone: The North Butte Mining Disaster of 1917, 2006; Last Stand: George Bird Grinnell, The Battle to Save the Buffalo and the Birth of the New West, 2007; No More Forever, forthcoming. **Address:** Department of Political Science, University of Montana, 350 Liberal Arts Bldg, 32 Campus Dr., Missoula, MT 59812, U.S.A. **Online address:** mpunke@michaelpunke.com

PURCELL, Anne G. American (born United States), b. 1932. **Genres:** Theology/Religion, Autobiography/Memoirs, History, Biography. **Career:** Writer. **Publications:** (With B. Purcell) Love and Duty: The Remarkable Story of a Courageous MIA Family and the Victory They Won with Their Faith, 1992. **Address:** Richard Curtis Associates Inc., 171 E 74th St., New York, NY 10021, U.S.A. **Online address:** dunrovin@alltel.net

PURCELL, Ben. *See* **PURCELL, Benjamin H.**

PURCELL, Benjamin H. (Ben Purcell). American (born United States), b. 1928. **Genres:** Documentaries/Reportage, History, Biography, Autobiography/Memoirs. **Career:** Writer. **Publications:** (With A. Purcell) Love and Duty: The Remarkable Story of a Courageous MIA Family and the Victory They Won with Their Faith, 1992. **Address:** 1581 Hwy., 197 N, Clarkesville, GA 30523, U.S.A. **Online address:** dunrovin@alltel.net

PURCELL, Leah. Australian (born Australia), b. 1970. **Genres:** Children's Fiction, Young Adult Fiction. **Career:** RED Music Channel, show host, 1995. Singer, actress, song writer and director. **Publications:** (With S. Rankin) Box the Pony, 1999; Black Chicks Talking, 2002. **Address:** Bain Stewart Personal Management, PO Box 1008, Leichhardt, NW 2040, Australia. **Online address:** bspm@leahpurcell.com

PURDY, Dwight H(illiard). American (born United States), b. 1941. **Genres:** Literary Criticism And History, Poetry, Theology/Religion. **Career:** University of Texas, teaching assistant and instructor in English, 1967-72; University of Minnesota, assistant professor, 1972-82, associate professor, 1982-88, professor of English, 1988-2005, professor emeritus, 2005-. Writer. **Publications:** Joseph Conrad's Bible, 1984; Biblical Echo and Allusion in the Poetry of W.B. Yeats: Poetics and The Art of God, 1994. Contributor of articles to journals. **Address:** Division of Humanities, University of Minnesota, 600 E 4th St., Morris, MN 56267-2132, U.S.A.

PURDY, Laura M. American (born United States), b. 1946. **Genres:** Ethics, Philosophy, Women's Studies And Issues. **Career:** San Jose State University, extension instructor, 1975; Cornell University, Program on Science, Technology and Society, post-doctoral research associate, 1975-77, lecturer in women's studies, 1979; Science, Technology and Society, research and postdoctoral fellow, 1977-78; Bowling Green State University, Retrospective Indexing Project, assistant editor, 1978; Wells College, lecturer, 1979, assistant professor, 1979-85, associate professor, 1986-92, professor of philosophy, 1992-, Ruth and Albert Koch professor of humanities; Hamilton College, visiting associate professor, 1989-90, Irwin chair, 1988-90, McCullough distinguished visiting chair of political philosophy, 2008-09; University Health Network, bioethicist, 1997-2000; University of Toronto, Joint Centre for Bioethics, bioethicist, 1997-2000, Department of Philosophy, professor, 1997-2000. Writer. **Publications:** In Their Best Interest?: The Case against Equal Rights for Children, 1992; (ed. with H.B. Holmes) Feminist Perspectives in Medical Ethics, 1992; Reproducing Persons: Issues in Feminist Bioethics, 1996; (ed. with S. French and W. Teays) Violence against Women: Philosophical Perspectives, 1998; (ed. with A. Donchin) Embodying Bioethics: Recent Feminist Advances, 1999; (ed. with W. Teays) Bioethics, Justice and Health Care, 2001. **Address:** Division of Social Science, Wells College, 170 Main St., Aurora, NY 13026, U.S.A. **Online address:** lpurdy@wells.edu

PURKISS, Diane. British/Australian (born Australia), b. 1961. **Genres:** Literary Criticism And History, Young Adult Fiction, Humanities. **Career:** University of East Anglia, lecturer in English, 1991-93; University of Reading, lecturer in English, 1993-98; Exeter University, professor of English, 1998-2000; Keble College, fellow and tutor of English, 2000-. Writer. **Publications:** The Witch in History: Early Modern and Twentieth-Century Representations, 1996; At the Bottom of the Garden: A Dark History of Fairies, Hobgoblins, and Other Troublesome Things, 2000 in UK as Troublesome Things: A History of Fairies and Fairy Stories, 2000; Literature, Gender, and Politics during the English Civil War, 2005; English Civil War: A People's History, 2006; English Civil War: Papists, Gentlewomen, Soldiers, and Witchfinders in the Birth of modern Britain, 2006; Fairies and Fairy Stories: A History, 2007. EDITOR: (with C. Brant) Women, Texts, and Histories: 1575-1760, 1992; (ed. and intro.) Renaissance Women: The Plays of Elizabeth Cary: The Poems of Aemilia Lanyer, 1994. Works appear in anthologies. Contributor to periodicals. **Address:** Keble College, Oxford, OX OX1 3PG, England. **Online address:** diane.purkiss@keble.ox.ac.uk

PURPURA, Lia. American (born United States), b. 1964. **Genres:** Poetry, Essays, Translations. **Career:** Loyola University, writer-in-residence, 1990-; Pacific Lutheran University, Rainier Writing Workshop, faculty, 2004-. **Publications:** The Brighter the Veil (poetry), 1996; (trans.) Poems of Grzegorz Musial: Taste of Ash and Berliner Tagebuch, 1998; Increase (essays), 2000; Stone Sky Lifting (poems), 2000; On Looking: Essays, 2006; King Baby, 2008; Rough Likeness, 2012. **Address:** Department of Writing, Loyola University, Humanities 243-B, 4501 N Charles St., Baltimore, MD 21210, U.S.A. **Online address:** lpurpura@loyola.edu

PURSER, Ann. British (born England), b. 1933?. **Genres:** Novels, Mystery/Crime/Suspense, Young Adult Non-fiction, Young Adult Fiction. **Career:** SHE magazine, columnist. **Publications:** Looking Back at Popular Entertainment, 1901-1939, 1978; You and Your Handicapped Child, 1981. NOVELS: Pastures New, 1994; Spinster of this Parish, 1995; Orphan Lamb, 1996; New Every Morning, 1996; Thy Neighbour's Wife, 1997; Mixed Doubles, 1998; Murder on Monday, 2002; Terror on Tuesday, 2003; Weeping on Wednesday, 2003; Theft on Thursday, 2005; Fear on Friday, 2005; Secrets on Saturday, 2006; Sorrow on Sunday, 2007; Warning at One, 2008; Tragedy at Two, 2009; The Hangman' s Row Enquiry, 2009; Threats at Three, 2010; Measby Murder Enquiry, 2011; Foul Play At four, 2011. **Address:** David Higham Associates, 5-8 Lower John St., Golden Square, GL W1F 9HA, England. **Online address:** annphil.purser@btinternet.com

PURSER, John W(hitley). Scottish (born Scotland), b. 1942?. **Genres:** Plays/Screenplays, Poetry, Music, Literary Criticism And History. **Career:** Lanarkshire Country Council, cello teacher, 1964-67; freelance writer and composer, 1965-; Glasgow University, Extramural Department, freelance lecturer, 1965-77; The Scotsman, freelance music critic, 1967-70; Scottish Intl., director, 1968-70; Occasional Words Ltd., director, 1969; Scottish Music Information Centre, manager, 1985-87; Elgol and Torrin Historical Society, secretary, 1996-2002; Gaelic College, Sabhal Mòr Ostaig, research fellow, honorary research fellow, 2004; Strathaird Community Association, vice chairman, 2004-; Stretto Magazine, joint editor. **Publications:** POETRY: The Counting Stick, 1976; A Share of the Wind, 1980; The Wren Boys, 1983; Amoretti, 1985. OTHERS: Is the Red Light On?: The Story of the BBC Scottish Symphony Orchestra, 1987; The Literary Works of Jack B. Yeats, 1991; Scotland's Music, 1992. Contributor to periodicals. **Address:** Sabhal Mòr Ostaig, ACC, Sleat, IV44 8RQ, Scotland.

PURSER, Philip (John). British (born England), b. 1925. **Genres:** Novels, Plays/Screenplays, Autobiography/Memoirs, Mystery/Crime/Suspense. **Career:** British Army, Royal engineers, 1943-47; Bon Accord, editorial assistant, 1950-51; Scottish Daily Mail, reporter, 1951-55; Daily Mail, London, television reporter, 1955-56; News Chronicle, television critic, 1957-60; The Sunday Telegraph, television critic, 1961-87. **Publications:** Peregrination 22, 1962; Four Days to the Fireworks, 1964; The Twentymen, 1967; Night of Glass, 1968; The Holy Father's Navy, 1971; The Last Great Tram Race, 1974; Where Is He Now?, 1978; The One and Only Phyllis Dixey, 1978; (ed. and intro.) A Small Explosion, 1979; (with L. Halliwell) Television Companion, 1982, rev. ed., 1986; Friedrich Harris: Shooting the Hero, 1990; Poeted, 1991; Done Viewing, 1992; Phyllis Purser, 1893-1989, 1994; Lights in the Sky, 2005. **Address:** Flat 10, 184 Gloucester Pl., London, GL NW1 6DS, England. **Online address:** annphil.purser@btinternet.com

PURTILL, Richard L. American (born United States), b. 1931. **Genres:** Ethics, Theology/Religion, Philosophy, Young Adult Fiction. **Career:** Western Washington University, Department of Philosophy, instructor, 1962-65, assistant professor, 1965-68, associate professor, 1968-72, professor, 1972, acting chairman, 1970-71, now professor emeritus of philosophy; San Francisco State College (now San Francisco State University), visiting lecturer, 1968-69. Writer. **Publications:** NONFICTION: Logic for Philosophers, 1971; Logical Thinking, 1972; Lord of the Elves and Eldils: Fantasy and Philosophy in C.S. Lewis and J.R.R. Tolkien, 1974, 2nd ed. 2006; Reason to Believe, 1974; (contrib.) Ethics and Public Policy, 1975; Philosophically Speaking, 1975; Thinking About Ethics, 1976; (contrib.) The Longing for a Form: Essays on the Fiction of C.S. Lewis, 1977; Thinking About Religion: A Philosophical Introduction to Religion, 1978; Logic: Argument Refutation and Proof, 1979; C.S. Lewis Case for the Christian Faith, 1981, new ed., 2004; J.R.R. Tolkien: Myth, Morality and Religion, 1984; (ed.) Moral Dilemmas: Readings in Ethics and Social Philosophy, 1985; (co-author) Philosophical Questions: An Introductory Anthology, 1985; A Logical Introduction to Philosophy, 1989; Reason to Believe: Why Faith Makes Sense, 2009. THE KAPHTU TRILOGY: The Golden Gryphon Feather, 1979; The Stolen Goddess, 1980; The Mirror of Helen, 1983. LOST TALES OF KAPHTU: The Gryphon Seal, 2005; The Eleusinian Gate, 2006; Letter To Nausicaa: Lost Tales of Kaphtu, 2008. OTHER NOVELS: Murdercon, 1982; The Parallel Man, 1984; Enchantment at Delphi, 1986; Parallel Worlds of Richard Purtill, 2011; Beyond the Rock of Sybil, forthcoming. **Address:** Department of Philosophy, College of Humanities and Social Sciences, Western Washington University, 302 Bond Hall, 516 High St., Bellingham, WA 98225-9054, U.S.A. **Online address:** purtill@cc.wwu.edu

PURVES, Libby. British (born England), b. 1950. **Genres:** Novels, Architecture, How-to Books, Sports/Fitness. **Career:** British Broadcasting Corp., studio manager, 1971, reporter and presenter, 1975-; Today programme, presenter, 1976; Radio 4 Midweek, presenter, 1983-; Times, major columnist, 1993-; novelist, 1995-; Order of the British Empire, officer, 1999-; Tatler Magazine, editor; Oxford Union, librarian. **Publications:** (Ed. with S. Purcell) Happy Unicorns: The Poetry Of The Under Twenty-Fives, 1971; (ed. and intro.) Adventures Under Sail: Selected Writings of H.W. Tilman, 1982. NONFICTION: Britain at Play, 1982; The Sailing Weekend Book, 1985; How Not to Be a Perfect Mother, 1986; How to Find the Perfect Boat, 1987; Where Did You Leave the Admiral?, 1987; (with P. Heiney) The English and Their Horses, 1988; One Summer's Grace: A Family Voyage Round Britain, 1989; How Not to Raise the Perfect Child, 1991; Working Times, 1993; How Not to Be a Perfect Family, 1994; Holy Smoke, 1998; (reteller) Favorite Bible Stories, 1998; Radio: A True Love Story, 2002; A Little Learning: Broodings from the Back of the Class, 2006. NOVELS: Casting Off, 1995; A Long Walk in Wintertime, 1996; Home Leave, 1997; More Lives Than One, 1998; Regatta, 1999; Nature's Masterpiece, 2000; Passing Go, 2000; A Free Woman, 2001; Mother Country, 2002; Continental Drift, 2003; Acting Up, 2004; Love Songs and Lies, 2007; Shadow Child, 2009. **Address:** BBC Radio 4, Broadcasting House, Portland Pl., London, GL W1A 1AA, England.

PURVIS, Alston W. American (born United States), b. 1943?. **Genres:** Art/Art History, Adult Non-fiction, Crafts. **Career:** Cooper Union, instructor, 1969-70; Royal Academy of Fine Arts, associate professor, 1971-82; Boston University, College of Fine Arts, Department of Graphic Design, chairman, 1982-, associate professor of art, professor of art, head; School of Visual Arts, director and interim, 1998-2002. Writer, graphic designer and translator. **Publications:** Dutch Graphic Design, 1918-1945, 1992; (contrib.) Wendingen 1918-1932, 2001; (contrib.) Wendingen: A Journal for the Arts, 1918-1932, 2001; (with M.F.L. Coultre) A Century of Posters, 2002; (with M.F.L. Coultre) Graphic Design 20th Century, 2003; (with A. Tresinowski) The Vendetta: FBI Hero Melvin Purvis's War against Crime, and J. Edgar Hoover's War against Him, 2005; (with C.W. de Jong and F. Friedl) Creative Type: A Sourcebook of Classic and Contemporary Letterforms, 2005; (with P.B. Meggs) Meggs' History of Graphic Design, 4th ed., 2006, 5th ed., 2012; (with M.F.L. Coultre) Jan Tschichold: Posters Of The Avant-garde, 2007; (ed. with P. Rand and A. Winestein) Ballets Russes And The Art Of Design, 2009; (contrib.) Type: A Visual History of Typefaces and Graphic Styles, 2009; (ed. with C.W. de Jong and M.F.L. Coultre) Poster: 1, 000 Posters from Toulouse-

Lautrec to Sagmeister, 2010. **Address:** School of Visual Arts, College of Fine Arts, Boston University, 855 Commonwealth Ave., Boston, MA 02215-1303, U.S.A. **Online address:** apurvis@bu.edu

PUSHKAREV, Boris S. American/Czech (born Czech Republic), b. 1929. **Genres:** Cultural/Ethnic Topics, Regional/Urban Planning, Transportation, Architecture. **Career:** Maurice E.H. Rotival & Associates, planner, 1954-57; Yale University, instructor in city planning, 1957-61; Yale University, Instructor, 1958-61; Regional Plan Association, chief planner, 1961-68, planning director, 1968-69, vice-president of research and planning, 1969-90; New York University, adjunct assistant professor, adjunct professor, 1967-78; National Alliance of Russian Solidarists, director, 1979-; Russian Research Foundation for the Study of Alternatives to Soviet Policy, chairman, 1981-. Writer. **Publications:** (With C. Tunnard) Man-Made America: Chaos or Control, 1963; (ed. and intro.) How to Save Urban America: Regional Plan Association, Choices for '76, 1973; Urban Space for Pedestrians: A Quantitative Approach, 1975; (with J. Zupan) Public Transportation and Land Use Policy, 1977; (ed. with P.J. Bearse) Regional Accounts: Structure and Performance of the New York Region's Economy in the Seventies, 1980; Urban Rail in America: An Exploration of Criteria for Fixed-Guideway Transit, 1982; Rossií i opyt zapada: izbrannye stat i 1955-1995, 1995; (co-author) Kommunisticheskíĭ rezhim i narodnoe soprotivlenie v Rossii 1917-1991, 1997; Belaía Rossiía 1917-1922, 2003; (co-author) Dve Rossii XX veka: obzor istorii 1917-1993, 2008. **Address:** 770 Anderson Ave. 20F, Cliffside Park, NJ 07010, U.S.A.

PUSHKER, Gloria (Teles). American (born United States), b. 1927. **Genres:** Children's Fiction, Biography, Autobiography/Memoirs. **Career:** Storyteller, 1983-; Xavier University, instructor of children's literature; Loyola University, faculty; fashion coordinator. Writer. **Publications:** Toby Belfer Never Had a Christmas Tree, 1990; Toby Belfer's Seder: A Passover Story Retold, 1994; A Belfer Bar Mitzvah, 1995; Toby Belfer and the High Holy Days, 2001; Toby Belfer Visits Ellis Island, 2003; (with M. Tarman) Toby Belfer Learns about Heroes and Martyrs, 2009. Contributor to periodicals. **Address:** Loyola University, 6363 St., Charles Ave., New Orleans, LA 70118, U.S.A.

PUTNAM, Constance E(lizabeth). American (born United States), b. 1943. **Genres:** Writing/Journalism, Biography, Writing/Journalism, Autobiography/Memoirs, Translations, Social Sciences, Medicine/Health, Education, History. **Career:** Teacher, 1965-73, 1985-; Houghton Mifflin Co., consulting editor and product manager, 1974-81, executive editor of foreign languages, 1981-83; Northeastern University, director of graphic arts program, 1983-85; freelance writer, 1985-. **Publications:** German Today 1 Tests, 1982; German Today 2 Tests, 1982; (trans.) Criminological Research in the Eighties and Beyond, 1988; (with M.L. Radelet and H.A. Bedau) In Spite of Innocence: Erroneous Convictions in Capital Cases, 1992; (with O.S. Hayward) Improve, Perfect & Perpetuate: Dr. Nathan Smith and Early American Medical Education, 1998; Hospice or Hemlock?: Searching for Heroic Compassion, 2002; The Science We Have Loved and Taught: Dartmouth Medical School's First Two Centuries, 2004. Contributor to periodicals. **Address:** Dartmouth Medical School, 1 Medical Center Dr., PO Box 7070, Lebanon, NH 03756, U.S.A. **Online address:** cputconcord@hotmail.com

PUTNAM, Douglas. (Douglas T. Putnam). American (born United States), b. 1953?. **Genres:** Sports/Fitness, Children's Non-fiction. **Career:** County Commissioners Association of Ohio, attorney; sports fantasy league commissioner. Writer. **Publications:** (As Douglas T. Putnam) Controversies of the Sports World, 1999. **Address:** Greenwood Press, Greenwood Publishing Group Inc., 88 Post Rd. W, Westport, CT 06881, U.S.A.

PUTNAM, Douglas T. *See* **PUTNAM, Douglas.**

PUTNAM, William L(owell). American (born United States), b. 1924. **Genres:** Earth Sciences, Environmental Sciences/Ecology, Meteorology/Atmospheric Sciences, Biography. **Career:** Mount Washington Volunteer Ski Patrol, founder and secretary/treasurer, 1947-52; Tufts College, instructor in geology, 1948-50; Springfield Chamber of Commerce Merchants Bureau and Industrial Bureau, affiliated, 1950-52, Springfield Television Corp., founder, president, chief executive officer, 1952-84; Maximum Service Telecasters, director and vice chair, 1975-84; NBC Affiliates, secretary/treasurer, 1977-82; Carroll Travel Bureau, director, 1984-98; Tip Off Classic, chair, 1984, treasurer, 1986-91; National Conference of Christians and Jews, national director, 1985-88; International Association of Alpine Societies, vice president, 1991-94; American Mountain Guides Association, director, 1991-97; Lowell Observatory, director. Writer. **Publications:** (With J.M. Thorington) A Climber's Guide to the Rocky Mountains of Canada, 6th ed., 1966; Climber's Guide to the Interior Ranges of British Columbia, 1971; (with G.W. Boles) Climber's Guide to the Rocky Mountains of Canada-South, 1973; (with C. Jones and R. Kruszyna) Climber's Guide to the Rocky Mountains of Canada-North, 1973; (with R. Kruszyna) Climber's Guide to the Interior Ranges of British Columbia-South, 1977; (with R. Kruszyna and G.W. Boles) Rocky Mountains of Canada, South, 1979; Great Glacier and Its House: The Story of the First Center of Alpinism in North America, 1885-1925, 1982; (with R. Kruszyna) Rocky Mountains of Canada, North, 7th ed., 1985; (with A.J. Kauffman) Guiding Spirit, 1986; Joe Dodge: One New Hampshire Institution, 1986; (with G.W. Boles and R.W. Laurilla) Place Names of the Canadian Alps, 1990; Worst Weather on Earth, 1991; A Yankee Image: The Life and Times of Roger Lowell Putnam, 1991; Green Cognac: The Education of a Mountain Fighter, 1991; (with A.J. Kauffman) K2: The 1939 Tragedy, 1992; (co-author) The Explorers of Mars Hill: A Centennial History of Lowell Observatory, 1894-1994, 1994; John Peter Zenger and the Fundamental Freedom, 1997; Kaiser's Merchant Ships in World War I, 2001; Percival Lowell's Big Red Car: The Tale of an Astronomer and a 1911 Stevens-Duryea, 2002; (with B.C. Post) Mountaineer's Pontiff: Achille Ratti, 2006; (with G.W. Boles and R.W. Laurilla) Canadian Mountain Place Names: The Rockies and Columbia Mountains, 2006; Great Railroad Tunnels of North America, 2011. **Address:** Lowell Observatory, 1400 W Mars Hill Rd., Flagstaff, AZ 86001, U.S.A.

PUTNEY, Clifford. American (born United States), b. 1963. **Genres:** History. **Career:** Bentley University, senior lecturer of history, assistant professor, 1997-. Writer. **Publications:** Muscular Christianity: Manhood and Sports in Protestant America, 1880-1920, 2001; Missionaries in Hawai'i: The Lives of Peter and Fanny Gulick, 1797-1883, 2010. **Address:** Department of History, Bentley University, AAC 129, 175 Forest St., Waltham, MA 02452, U.S.A. **Online address:** cputney@bentley.edu

PUTNEY, Gail J. *See* **FULLERTON, Gail.**

PUTNEY, Mary Jo. American (born United States) **Genres:** Romance/Historical, Novels, Young Adult Fiction. **Career:** Writer and graphic designer. **Publications:** ROMANCE NOVELS: Lady of Fortune, 1988; The Controversial Countess, 1989; Carousel of Hearts, 1989; The Rogue and the Runaway, 1990; Dearly Beloved, 1990; The Rake and the Reformer, 1991; Silk and Shadows, 1991; Uncommon Vows, 1991; Silk and Secrets, 1992; The Would Be Widow, 1992; Veils of Silk, 1992; Petals in the Storm, 1993; Thunder and Roses, 1993 in UK as Fallen Angel, 2009; The Diabolical Baron, 1994; Dancing on the Wind, 1994; Angel Rogue, 1995; River of Fire, 1996; Shattered Rainbows, 1996; One Perfect Rose, 1997; The Rake, 1998; The Wild Child, 1999; The Burning Point, 2000; The China Bride, 2000; Arco Iris Roto, 2000; Christmas Revels, 2002; Bartered Bride, 2002; Spiral Path, 2002; Twist of Fate, 2003; Kiss of Fate: A Novel, 2004; Stolen Magic, 2005; Marriage Spell: A Novel, 2006; Distant Magic, 2007; Loving a Lost Lord, 2009; (co-author) Chalice of Roses, 2010; Never Less Than A Lady, 2010; Dark Mirror, 2011; Dark Passage, 2011; Nowhere Near Respectable, 2011; No Longer A Gentleman, 2012. Works appear in anthologies. **Address:** Kensington Publishing Corporation, 119 W 40th St., New York, NY 10018, U.S.A. **Online address:** mjp624@aol.com

PUTTER, Ad. British/Welsh/Dutch (born Netherlands), b. 1967. **Genres:** Literary Criticism And History, Poetry, Humanities. **Career:** University of Utrecht, lecturer in English, 1991-92; Cambridge University, Jesus College, research fellow in medieval studies, 1992-94; University of Bristol, reader in English, 1994-, lecturer in English, 1994-, professor of medieval English literature, Centre for Medieval Studies, director, 2011-, School of Humanities, graduate officer. Writer. **Publications:** Sir Gawain and the Green Knight and French Arthurian Romance, 1995; An Introduction to the Gawain-Poet, 1996; (ed. with J. Gilbert) The Spirit of Medieval English Popular Romance, 2000; (ed. with C. Muessig) Envisaging Heaven in the Middle Ages, 2006; (ed. with E. Archibald) A Cambridge Companion to the Arthurian Legend, 2009. Contributor to journals. **Address:** Department of English, University of Bristol, Rm. 2.10, 11 Woodland Rd., Bristol, AV BS8 1TB, England. **Online address:** a.d.putter@bristol.ac.uk

PUTTERMAN, Louis (G.). American (born United States), b. 1952. **Genres:**

Economics, Social Sciences, History. **Career:** Brown University, assistant professor, 1980-82, associate professor, 1982-87, professor of economics, 1987-, Center for the Comparative Study of Development, associate director, 1989-96, acting director, 1990, 1992, Watson Institute for International Studies, research associate. Writer. **Publications:** Peasants, Collectives, and Choice: Economic Theory and Tanzania's Villages, 1986; (with J.P. Bonin) Economics of Cooperation and the Labor-Managed Economy, 1987; Division of Labor and Welfare: An Introduction to Economic Systems, 1990; Continuity and Change in China's Rural Development: Collective and Reform Eras in Perspective, 1993; Dollars and Change: Economics in Context, 2001. EDITOR AND CONTRIBUTOR: The Economic Nature of the Firm: A Reader, 1986, 3rd ed., 2009; (with D. Rueschemeyer) State and Market in Development: Synergy or Rivalry?, 1992; (with A. Ben-Ner) Economics, Values and Organization, 1998. Contributor to books. **Address:** Department of Economics, Brown University, PO Box B, Providence, RI 02912-9000, U.S.A. **Online address:** louis_putterman@brown.edu

PUXLEY, Ray. British (born England), b. 1948. **Genres:** Language/Linguistics, Humor/Satire, History, Reference. **Career:** Newspaper sports columnist, 1996-; The Singing News, columnist. **Publications:** Cockney Rabbit: A Dick n Arry of Rhyming Slang, 1992; Fresh Rabbit, 1998; Fresh Rabbit: A Dick n Arry of Contemporary Rhyming Slang, 2000; Britslang: The Uncensored A-Z of Slang, Rhyming and Otherwise, 2003, rev. ed., 2004; Complete Cockney Rabbit: The Ultimate Dick n Arry of Rhyming Slang, 2008. **Address:** 14 Peartree Gardens, Dagenham, EX RM10 8YU, England.

PWAR-YEA-BURSH, See-mun. *See* **POIRIER-BURES, Simone.**

PYBRUM, Steven (Mark). American (born United States), b. 1951. **Genres:** Money/Finance, Adult Non-fiction, Business/Trade/Industry, Human Relations/Parenting. **Career:** Pybrum and Co. (financial planning firm), founder, chief executive officer, president, 1979-; Tax Tips (radio program), host, 1980-; Business Cents, syndicated columnist, 1980-; Agri-Business Tax Tips, syndicated columnist, 1980-; International Business Machines, consultant; Bank of America, consultant; McDonald's, consultant; U.S. Senate, consultant. **Publications:** NONFICTION: Money and Marriage: Making it Work Together: A Guide to Smart Money Management and Harmonious Communications, 1996; Money and Marriage: For Engaged Couples, 2003. **Address:** Pybrum & Co., 817 Garden St., Ste. 201, PO Box 23209, Santa Barbara, CA 93101, U.S.A.

PYBUS, Cassandra. Australian (born Australia), b. 1927. **Genres:** Adult Non-fiction, History, Social Sciences. **Career:** Full-time writer and historian, 1985-; Island Magazine, editor, 1989-94; Australian Humanities Review, founding editor; The Age, frequent contributor; The Australian, frequent contributor; La Trobe University, visiting fellow in humanities; University of Sydney, professor, Australian Research Council, professorial fellow, 2007- ; University of Texas, distinguished visiting professor, 2008. **Publications:** (Ed. with R. Flanagan) The Rest of the World is Watching: Tasmania and the Greens, 1990; Community of Thieves, 1992; Gross Moral Turpitude: The Orr Case Reconsidered, 1993 as Seduction and Consent: A Case of Gross Moral Turpitude, 1994; (ed.) Columbus' Blindness, and Other Essays, 1994; White Rajah: A Dynastic Intrigue, 1996; The White Rajahs of Sarawak, Dynastic Intrigue and the Forgotten Canadian Heir, 1997; Till Apples Grow on an Orange Tree (autobiography), 1998; Devil and James McAuley, 1999, rev. ed., 2001; Raven Road, 2001; Woman Who Walked to Russia, 2002; (with H. Maxwell-Stewart) American Citizens, British Slaves: Yankee Political Prisoners in an Australian Penal Colony 1839-1850, 2002; Black Founders: The Unknown Story of Australia's First Black Settlers, 2006; Epic Journeys of Freedom: Runaway Slaves of the American Revolution and Their Global Quest for Liberty, 2006; (ed. with M. Rediker and E. Christopher) Many Middle Passages: Forced Migration and the Making of the Modern World, 2007. **Address:** Department of History, University of Sydney, Rm. S505, Bldg. A14, Sydney, NW 2006, Australia. **Online address:** cassandra.pybus@arts.usyd.edu.au

PYBUS, Rodney. British (born England), b. 1938. **Genres:** Poetry, Music. **Career:** The Journal, feature writer and literary editor, 1962-64; Tyne Tees Television, writer and producer, 1964-76; University of Newcastle upon Tyne, poetry workshops, tutor, 1973-76; Macquarie University, School of English and Linguistics, lecturer in mass communication, 1976-79; Northern Arts, literature officer, 1979-81; University of Liverpool, tutor, 1981-82; full-time writer, 1982-. **Publications:** POEMS: In Memoriam Milena, 1973; Bridging Loans, 1976; At the Stone Junction, 1978; (ed. with W. Scammell) Adam's Dream: Poems from Cumbria and Lakeland, 1981; The Loveless Letters, 1981; (co-author) Wall, 1981; (with D. Constantine) Talitha Cumi, 1983; Cicadas in Their Summers: New and Selected Poems, 1965-1985, 1988; Still Mine: For Baritone and Orchestra, 1991-92, 1993; Flying Blues: Poems, 1988-1993, 1994; Veronica Lake, forthcoming. Contributor to magazines. **Address:** Carcanet Press, Alliance House, 4th Fl., 30 Cross St., Manchester, M2 7AQ, England. **Online address:** rodneypybus@gmail.com

PYE, Michael (Kenneth). Portuguese/British (born England), b. 1946. **Genres:** Novels, Film, Translations, Young Adult Fiction. **Career:** The Scotsman, staff writer, 1967-71, columnist; The Sunday Times, financial reporter, editor, 1971-78; STV, presenter, 1976-78; freelance writer, 1978-; Daily Telegraph, columnist; Esquire, columnist; Geo, columnist; Atlantic Monthly, columnist; Coco-Cola, consultant. **Publications:** (With L. Myles) The Movie Brats: How the Film Generation Took over Hollywood, 1979; Moguls: Inside the Business of Show Business, 1980; The King over the Water: The Windsors in the Bahamas, 1981 as The Windsors in Exile, 1982; (contrib.) The Pirelli Calendar Album, 1988; Maximum City: The Biography of New York, 1991. NOVELS: Eldorado, 1983 in US as Kingdom Come, 1985; Reckoning, 1987; Chaos, 1991; The Drowning Room, 1995; Taking Lives, 1999; The Pieces from Berlin, 2003, (trans.) J. Schuhl, Ingrid Caven, 2004. **Address:** Irene Skolnick Agency, 22 W 23rd St., 5th Fl., New York, NY 10010, U.S.A.

PYENSON, Lewis (Robert). (Tom Sriver). American/Canadian (born Canada), b. 1947. **Genres:** History, Intellectual History, Sciences. **Career:** University of Montreal, lecturer to professor, 1973-86, professor of the history of science, 1986-95; Joint Atlantic Seminar in the History of Physics, founder, 1974; Universite Louis Pasteur, visiting lecturer, 1975; Johns Hopkins University, visiting professor, 1978; David M. Stewart Museum, honorary curator of scientific instruments, 1991-95; University of Louisiana, professor of history and dean of the graduate school, 1995-2001, professor history of science, 2001, Center for Louisiana Studies, research professor of history, adjunct professor of cognitive science, philosophy, physics, and modern languages; Western Michigan University, Department of History, professor of history, 2006-, Graduate College, dean, 2006-10. Writer. **Publications:** (Ed. and intro.) Why I Left Canada: Reflections on Science and Politics, 1978; Neohumanism and the Persistence of Pure Mathematics in Wilhelmian Germany, 1983; The Young Einstein: The Advent of Relativity, 1985; Cultural Imperialism and Exact Sciences: German Expansion Overseas, 1900-1930, 1985; Empire of Reason: Exact Sciences in Indonesia, 1840-1940, 1989; Civilizing Mission: Exact Sciences and French Overseas Expansion, 1830-1940, 1993; (ed.) Teaching and Research in the University, 1996; (ed.) Disciplines and Interdisciplinarity in the New Century, 1997; (ed.) Word and Icon: Saying and Seeing, 1998; (with S. Sheets-Pyenson) Fontana History of Science in Society, 1998; (ed.) Fortiter, Feliciter, Fideliter: The Centennial Lectures of the Graduate School of the University of Southwestern Louisiana, 1999; (ed.) Value: Pondering Goodness, 1999; (with S. Sheets-Pyenson) Servants of Nature: A History of Scientific Institutions, Enterprises and Sensibilities, 1999; The Passion of George Sarton: A Modern Marriage and Its Discipline, 2007; (as Tom Sriver) True Jacob, 2009. **Address:** Department of History, Western Michigan University, 1903 W Michigan Ave., Kalamazoo, MI 49008-5334, U.S.A. **Online address:** lewis.pyenson@wmich.edu

PYE-SMITH, Charlie. British (born England), b. 1951. **Genres:** Travel/Exploration. **Career:** Writer and journalist, 1980-. **Publications:** (With C. Rose) Crisis and Conservation, 1984; Conservation, 1984; (with R. North) Working the Land, 1985; The Other Nile, 1986; (ed. with C. Hall) The Countryside We Want: A Manifesto for the Year 2000, 1987; The Sequestered Kingdom: Travels in Nepal, 1988; In Search of Neptune: A Celebration of the National Trust's Coastline, 1990; In Search of Wild India, 1993; Barcelona: A Celebration and a Guide, 1993; (with G.B. Feyerabend and R. Sandbrook) The Wealth of Communities: Stories of Success in Local Environmental Management, 1994; The Philippines: In Search of Justice, 1997; Rebels and Outcasts: A Journey Through Christian India, 1998; The Subsidy Scandal: How Your Government Wastes Your Money to Wreck Your Environment, 2002; Aid that Works, 2006; Farming Trees, Banishing Hunger, 2008; Rural Revival in Tanzania, 2010; Fruits of Success, 2010; Window on a Better World, 2010. Contributor to periodicals. **Address:** c/o Vivien Green, Sheil Land Associates Ltd., 52 Doughty St., London, GL WC1N 2LS, England. **Online address:** cpyesmith@blueyonder.co.uk

PYLE, Gerald F. American (born United States), b. 1937. **Genres:** Demography, Medicine/Health, Reference. **Career:** Rand McNally, research cartographer, 1962-64; Encyclopedia Britannica, research geographer, 1964-65; University of Chicago, Center for Urban Studies, staff cartographer, 1965-70; University of Akron, assistant professor of geography, 1970-73, associate professor of geography and urban studies, 1973-78, professor of urban studies, 1978-80; University of North Carolina, professor of geography and earth sciences, 1980-96, professor of epidemiology, 1995-, professor of health behavior and administration, 2002-, now professor emeritus; Macquarie University, visiting fellow, 1988; Queen's College, adjunct professor, 1990; International Symposium on Medical Geography, organizer and conference director, 1992. Writer. **Publications:** Heart Disease, Cancer and Stroke in Chicago: A Geographical Analysis with Facilities Plans for 1980, 1971; Ohio Geographers, 1973; (co-author) The Spatial Dynamics of Crime, 1974; Applied Medical Geography, 1979; (ed.) New Directions in Medical Geography, 1980; The Diffusion of Influenza: Patterns and Paradigms, 1986; (with G.W. Shannon and R.L. Bashshur) The Geography of AIDS, 1991; (with Shannon) Disease and Medical Care in the United States: A Medical Atlas of the Twentieth Century, 1993. Contributor to books and periodicals. **Address:** Department of Health Behavior and Administration, University of North Carolina, 9201 University City Blvd., Charlotte, NC 28223-0001, U.S.A. **Online address:** gfpyle@email.uncc.edu

PYLE, Kenneth B. American (born United States), b. 1936. **Genres:** History, Politics/Government, Social Sciences. **Career:** Stanford University, visiting lecturer, 1964-65; University of Washington, Henry M. Jackson School of International Studies, assistant professor, 1965-69, associate professor of history, 1969-75, professor, 1975-, Henry M. Jackson professor of history and Asian studies, 1975-, chairman of Japanese and Korean studies, 1972-78, 1991-95, director, 1978-88, Institute for Comparative and Foreign Area Studies, acting director, 1975; Yale University, visiting associate professor of history, 1969-70; Journal of Japanese Studies, editor, 1974-86; University of Pittsburgh, provost, 1986; Association of Asian Studies, distinguished lecturer, 1988; The National Bureau of Asian Research, founding president, 1989-99; Johns Hopkins University, Walter Hines Page fellow in international relations. Consultant. **Publications:** The New Generation in Meiji Japan: Problems of Cultural Identity, 1885-1895, 1969; The Making of Modern Japan, 1978, 2nd ed., 1996; (ed.) The Trade Crisis: How Will Japan Respond?, 1987; The Japanese Question: Power and Purpose in a New Era, 1992, 2nd ed., 1996; (ed. with D.C. Hellmann) From APEC to Xanadu: Creating a Viable Community in the Post-Cold War Pacific, 1997; Japan Rising: The Resurgence of Japanese Power and Purpose, 2007. **Address:** Henry M. Jackson School of International Studies, University of Washington, 229 Thomson Hall, PO Box 353650, Seattle, WA 98195-3650, U.S.A. **Online address:** kbp@u.washington.edu

PYLE, Kevin C. American (born United States), b. 1964. **Genres:** Medicine/Health, Young Adult Fiction, Graphic Novels, Adult Non-fiction, Documentaries/Reportage. **Career:** Illustrator, 1988-; Minor Injury Gallery, director, 1990-91; author, 2001-; artist, 2007-. **Publications:** SELF-ILLUSTRATED: Lab U.S.A.: Illuminated Documents, 2001; Prison Town: Paying the Price (comic book), 2005. OTHERS: Blindspot (graphic novel), 2007; Katman (graphic novel), 2009; Take What You Can Carry (graphic novel), 2012. Contributor to periodicals. **Online address:** kcp@boatfire37.com

PYNCHON, Thomas. American (born United States), b. 1937. **Genres:** Novels, Novellas/Short Stories, Literary Criticism And History, Young Adult Fiction, Mystery/Crime/Suspense. **Career:** Boeing Aircraft Corp., writer. **Publications:** Entropy, 1962; V: A Novel, 1963; The Crying of Lot 49, 1966; Mortality and Mercy in Vienna, 1970; Gravity's Rainbow, 1973; Low-lands, 1978; Secret Integration, 1980; Small Rain, 1982; (intro.) Been Down So Long It Looks Like Up to Me, 1983; Journey into the Mind of Watts, 1983; Slow Learner: Early Stories, 1984; Vineland, 1990; (intro.) The Teaching of Don B, 1992; (co-author) Deadly Sins, 1993; Mason and Dixon, 1997; Against the Day: A Novel, 2006; Inherent Vice, 2009. Contributor to magazines and periodicals. **Address:** c/o Author Mail, Little, Brown & Company Inc., 1271 Ave. of the Americas, New York, NY 10020-1300, U.S.A.

Q

QAZWINI, Hassan. (Hasan Al-Qazwini). American/Iraqi (born Iraq), b. 1964?. **Genres:** Social Sciences, Theology/Religion. **Career:** Azzahra Islamic Center, director, 1992-97; Islamic Center of America, religious leader, 1997-; Young Muslim Association (YMA), founder, 1998; Annibras, editor. Religious leader and memoirist. **Publications:** (As Imam Hassan Qazwini with B. Crawford) American Crescent: A Muslim Cleric on the Power of His Faith, the Struggle against Prejudice, and the Future of Islam and America, 2007; (as Hasan al-Qazwini) Min arīj al-Qur'ān, 2010. **Address:** Islamic Center of America, 19500 Ford Rd., Dearborn, MI 48128-2404, U.S.A. **Online address:** imamqazwini@icofa.com

QUALE, G(ladys) Robina. American (born United States), b. 1931. **Genres:** History, Human Relations/Parenting, Social Sciences. **Career:** Albion College, instructor, 1957-60, assistant professor, 1960-65, associate professor, 1965-70, professor of history, 1970-92, professor emeritus, 1992-. Writer. **Publications:** Eastern Civilizations, 1966, 2nd ed., 1975; History of Marriage Systems, 1988; Families in Context: A World History of Population, 1992. **Address:** Albion College, 611 E Porter St., Albion, MI 49224-1831, U.S.A.

QUALEY, Marsha. American (born United States), b. 1953. **Genres:** Young Adult Fiction, Children's Non-fiction, Literary Criticism And History. **Career:** Writer, 1990-; Bard College, Loft Literary Center, faculty; Hamline University, faculty, 2007-. **Publications:** YOUNG ADULT FICTION: Everybody's Daughter, 1991; Revolutions of the Heart, 1993; Come in from the Cold, 1994; Hometown, 1995; Thin Ice, 1997; Close to a Killer, 1999; Every Friend a Stranger, 2001; One Night, 2002; Yankee Doodle, 2003; Too Big a Storm, 2004; Just Like That, 2005. PICTURE BOOKS (as Ann Owen): Protecting Your Home, 2004; Delivering Your Mail, 2004; Keeping You Safe, 2004; Keeping You Healthy, 2004. **Address:** Hamline University, 1536 Hewitt Ave., Saint Paul, MN 55104-1284, U.S.A. **Online address:** mqualey@charter.net

QUANDT, Richard (Emeric). American/Hungarian (born Hungary), b. 1930. **Genres:** Economics, Business/Trade/Industry, Translations. **Career:** Princeton University, Department of Economics, assistant professor of economics, 1957-59, associate professor of economics, 1959-64, Hughes-Rogers professor of economics, 1964-95, senior research economist, Ford Foundation research professor, 1967-68, chairman, 1968-71, 1985-88, director of graduate studies, 1973-80, Financial Research Center, director, 1982-95, now professor emeritus; Mathematica Inc., consultant, 1961-67; University of London, Birkbeck College, visiting professor, 1981; Oxford University Press, executive editor, 2001-. Consultant and writer. **Publications:** (With J.M. Henderson) Microeconomic Theory: A Mathematical Approach, 1958, 3rd ed., 1980; (with W.L. Thorp) The New Inflation, 1959; (with B.G. Malkiel) Strategies and Rational Decisions in the Securities Options Market, 1969; (with S.M. Goldfeld) Nonlinear Methods in Econometrics, 1972; (with D. Ann Hsu) Statistical Analyses of Aircraft Hijackings and Political Assassinations, 1976; (with P. Asch) Racetrack Betting: The Professors' Guide to Strategies, 1986; (with H.S. Rosen) The Conflict between Equilibrium and Disequilibrium Theories: The Case Of The U.S. Labor Market, 1988; The Econometrics of Disequilibrium, 1988; The Collected Articles of Richard E. Quandt, 1992; The Changing Landscape in Eastern Europe: Personal Reflections on Philanthropy and Technology Transfer, 2002; (trans.) If Dogs Could Talk, 2005. EDITOR: The Demand for Travel: Theory and Measurement, 1970; (with S.M. Goldfeld) Studies in Nonlinear Estimation, 1976; (with M.H. Peston) Prices, Competition and Equilibrium, 1986; (with with D. Triska) Optimal Decisions in Markets and Planned Economies, 1990; (with R. Ekman) Technology and Scholarly Communication, 1999; (with A. Lass) Library Automation in Transitional Societies: Lessons from Eastern Europe, 2000; (with A. Lass) Union Catalogs at the Crossroad, 2004. **Address:** Department of Economics, Princeton University, Fisher Hall, Princeton, NJ 08544-1021, U.S.A. **Online address:** quandt@sprynet.com

QUANDT, William Bauer. American (born United States), b. 1941. **Genres:** Politics/Government. **Career:** University of California, lecturer, 1969-71; Rand Corp., staff, 1968-72, National Security Council, staff, 1972-74, Senior Staff, 1977-79, office director for Middle East affairs, 1977-79; University of Pennsylvania, associate professor of political science, 1974-76; Brookings Institution, senior fellow, 1979-94; Massachusetts Institute of Technology, visiting lecturer, 1979; University of Virginia, Edward R. Stettinius, Jr. professor of politics, 1994-, vice provost for international affairs, 2000-03. Writer. **Publications:** Revolution and Political Leadership: Algeria 1954-58, 1969; The Comparative Study of Political Elites, 1970; Palestinian Nationalism: Its Political and Military Dimensions, 1971; Algerian Military Development: The Professionalization of a Guerrilla Army, 1972; (with F. Jabber and A.M. Lesch) The Politics of Palestinian Nationalism, 1973; Decade of Decisions: American Policy toward the Arab-Israeli Conflict 1967-1976, 1977; Saudi Arabia in the 1980s: Foreign Policy, Security, and Oil, 1981; Saudi Arabia's Oil Policy: A Staff Paper, 1982; (with D.R. Bohi) Energy Security in the 1980s: Economic and Political Perspectives: A Staff Paper, 1984; Camp David: Peacemaking and Politics, 1986; (ed.) Middle East: Ten Years After Camp David, 1988; United States and Egypt: An Essay on Policy for the 1990s, 1990; Peace Process: American Diplomacy and the Arab-Israel Conflict since 1967, 1993, 3rd ed., 2005; (with A.J. Pierre) Algerian Crisis: Policy Options for the West, 1996; Between Ballots and Bullets: Algeria's Transition from Authoritarianism, 1998. **Address:** Department of Politics, The University of Virginia, 255 Cabell Hall, Gibson S-164, PO Box 400787, Charlottesville, VA 22904-4787, U.S.A. **Online address:** wbq8f@virginia.edu

QUANTIC, Diane Dufva. American (born United States), b. 1941. **Genres:** Literary Criticism And History, Local History/Rural Topics, Biography. **Career:** Wichita State University, assistant professor, 1973-95, associate professor of English, 1995-; director of writing program, 1995-2000, coordinator of graduate programs in English, 2001-04; coordinator of Great Plains studies certificate, 2001-; Fulbright senior lecturer in Bulgaria, 1986-87; Western Literature, president, 1992-93. Writer. **Publications:** William Allen White, 1993; The Nature of the Place: A Study of Great Plains Fiction, 1995; (ed. with P.J. Hafen) A Great Plains Reader, 2003. **Address:** Wichita State University, 608B Lindquist Hall, Wichita, KS 67260, U.S.A. **Online address:** diane.quantic@wichita.edu

QUARTZ, Steven R. American (born United States) **Genres:** Biology, Sciences, Biography, Autobiography/Memoirs, Psychology. **Career:** California Institute of Technology, instructor, 1998-99, assistant professor, 1999-2002, associate professor, 2002-10, professor, 2010-, Social Cognitive Neuroscience Laboratory, director; Salk Institute, Sloan Center for Theoretical Neurobiology, fellow. Writer. **Publications:** (With T.J. Sejnowski) Liars, Lovers, and Heroes: What the New Brain Science Reveals About How We Become Who We Are, 2002. **Address:** Division of the Humanities and Social Sciences, California Institute of Technology, 209 Dabney Hall, Pasadena, CA 91125, U.S.A. **Online address:** steve@hss.caltech.edu

QUASTHOFF, Thomas. British/German (born Germany), b. 1959. **Genres:** Autobiography/Memoirs. **Career:** Hanns Eisler School of Music, professor; Musikakademie, professor for life; Barbican Hall, artist-in-residence. Writer. **Publications:** Die Stimme: Autobiographie, 2004. **Address:** London, GL , England. **Online address:** machreich@rbartists.at

QUATTLEBAUM, Mary. American (born United States), b. 1958. **Genres:** Children's Fiction, Young Adult Fiction, Poetry, Picture/Board Books, Novels. **Career:** Children's National Medical Center, medical writer and editor, 1986-88; Arts Project Renaissance, part-time director of creative writing program for older adults, 1986-98; Georgetown University, School for Summer and Continuing Education, writing instructor, 1986-; freelance writer and editor, 1989-. **Publications:** MIDDLE-GRADE NOVELS: Jackson Jones and the Puddle of Thorns, 1994; Jazz, Pizzazz and the Silver Threads, 1996; The Magic Squad and the Dog of Great Potential, 1997; Grover G. Graham and Me, 2001; Jackson Jones and Mission Greentop, 2004; Winter Friends, 2005; Jackson Jones and the Curse of the Outlaw Rose, 2006; Why Sparks Fly High at Dancing Point: A Colonial American Folktale, 2006. PICTURE BOOKS: (reteller) In the Beginning, 1995; (reteller) Jesus and the Children, 1995; Underground Train, 1997; Aunt CeeCee, Aunt Belle, and Mama's Surprise, 1999; The Shine Man: A Christmas Story, 2001. POETRY: A Year on My Street, 1996; Family Reunion, 2004. OTHERS: Jackson Jones and Mission Greentop, 2004; Winter Friends, 2005; (reteller) Sparks Fly High: The Legend of Dancing Point, 2006; Jackson Jones and the Curse of the Outlaw Rose, 2006; Pirate vs Pirate, 2011; Hungry Ghost of Rue Orleans, 2011; Jo MacDonald saw a Pond, 2011; Jo MacDonald had a Garden, 2012. Contributor of articals to magazines and newspapers. **Address:** Eerdmans Books for Young Readers, 255 Jefferson Ave. SE, Grand Rapids, MI 49503, U.S.A. **Online address:** mary@maryquattlebaum.com

QUAYE, Kofi. American/Ghanaian (born Ghana), b. 1947?. **Genres:** Novels, Novellas/Short Stories, Young Adult Fiction, Biography, Autobiography/Memoirs. **Career:** Accra Registrar General's Office, clerk. Writer. **Publications:** FICTION: Sammy Slams the Gang, 1970; The Murder in Kumasi, 1970; The Takoradi Kidjackers, 1971; Foli Fights the Forgers, 1991; Jojo in New York, 1993; No Deal, 1994; Crisis in the Family, 2002; (with G. Davis) Free from Death Road, 2003. Contributor of articles to periodicals. **Address:** Macmillan Publishers Ltd., 4 Crinan St., London, GL N1 9XW, England.

QUAYLE, Dan. *See* **QUAYLE, (James) Dan(forth).**

QUAYLE, (James) Dan(forth). (Dan Quayle). American (born United States), b. 1947. **Genres:** Politics/Government, Autobiography/Memoirs, Economics. **Career:** Huntington Herald Press, court reporter and pressman, 1965-69, associate publisher and general manager, 1974-76; State of Indiana, administrative assistant, 1971-73, Indiana Inheritance Tax Division, director, 1973-74; State Bar of Indiana, staff, 1974; Huntington College, instructor in business law, 1975; U.S. House of Representatives, congressman from 4th Indiana district, 1976-81; U.S. Senate, senator from Indiana, 1981-89; vice president of the United States, 1989-93; Circle Investors, chairman, 1993-94; speaker, author, 1994-2001; Cerberus Global Capital, chairman, 2001-. **Publications:** NATO and the Economic Recession: Report of Dan Quayle to the Committe on Armed Services, 1982; (co-ed.) Strategic Defense and the Western Alliance, 1986; Standing Firm: A Vice-Presidential Memoir, 1994; (with D. Medved) The American Family: Discovering the Values that Make Us Strong, 1996; Worth Fighting For, 1999; (intro.) Freedom's Fortress: Vincennes' History of Service to the United States, 2009. **Address:** Paradise Valley, AZ , U.S.A.

QUEENAN, Joe. American (born United States), b. 1950. **Genres:** Politics/Government, Humor/Satire, Autobiography/Memoirs. **Career:** Barron's, writer, 1987-89; Forbes, senior editor, 1989-90; writer, 1990-. **Publications:** Imperial Caddy: The Rise of Dan Quayle in America and the Decline and Fall of Practically Everything Else, 1992; If You're Talking to Me Your Career Must Be in Trouble: Movies, Mayhem and Malice, 1994; The Unkindest Cut: How a Hatchet-Man Critic Made His Own $7,000 Movie and Put It All on His Credit Card, 1995; Joe Queenan's America, 1997; Red Lobster, White Trash, Blue Lagoon, 1998; Confessions of a Cineplex Heckler: Celluloid Tirades and Escapades, 2000; My Goodness: A Cynic's Short-Lived Search for Sainthood, 2000; Balsamic Dreams: A Short but Self-Important History of the Baby Boomer Generation, 2001; (ed.) The Malcontents: The Best Bitter, Cynical, and Satirical Writing in the World, 2002; True Believers: The Tragic Inner Life of Sports Fans, 2003; Queenan Country: A Reluctant Anglophile's Pilgrimage to the Mother Country, 2004; Closing Time: A Memoir, 2009. Contributor to periodicals. **Address:** c/o Joe Vallecy, 320 Riverside Dr., New York, NY 10012, U.S.A.

QUEENEY, Courtney. American (born United States), b. 1978?. **Genres:** Poetry, Literary Criticism And History. **Career:** Poet, 2005-. **Publications:** (With S.C. Harwell and F. Marklevits) Three New Poets, 2006; Filibuster to Delay a Kiss: And Other Poems, 2007. Contributor of poetry to periodicals. **Address:** Brooklyn, NY , U.S.A. **Online address:** courtneyqueeney@hotmail.com

QUEFFÉLEC, Yann. French (born France), b. 1949. **Genres:** Novels, Young Adult Fiction. **Career:** Le Nouvel Observateur, journalist. **Publications:** Béla Bartók, 1981; Le Charme noir, 1983; Les Noces barbares, 1985; La Femme sous l'horizon, 1988; Le Maître deschimres, 1990; Prends garde au loup (novel), 1992; La Ménace, 1993; Disparue dans la nuit: Roman, 1994; Et la force d'aimer, 1996; Happy Birthday, Sara (novel), 1997; Noir animal, ou, La Menace, 1997; Toi, l'horizon, 1999; Osmose, 2000; Le Soleil se lve louest, 2001; Boris après l'amour, 2002; (with J. Champion) Idoles, 2002; Vert cruel, 2003; Moi et toi: roman, 2004; Les Affamés: nouvelles, 2004; Ma première femme (novel), 2005; La Dégustation: 1973-1974, 2005; Mineure, 2006; Tendre est la mer, 2006; Lamour est fou: roman, 2006; Amante: roman, 2006; Le plus heureux des hommes: roman, 2007; (with K. Legendre and B. Bergman) A.N.A.T.O.L.E, 2007; (with K. Legendre) Inside, 2007; Tabarly, 2008; Adieu Bugaled Breizh, 2009; La puissance des corps: roman, 2009; Sables du Jubaland, 2010; Piano de ma mère, 2010; Oubliés du vent, 2010. **Address:** c/o Author Mail, Librairie Arthme Fayard, 13 rue du Montparnasse, Paris, 75006, France.

QUELLER, Jessica. American (born United States), b. 1969. **Genres:** Novels, Biography. **Career:** Writer. **Publications:** Pretty Is What Changes: Impossible Choices, the Breast Cancer Gene, and How I Defied My Destiny, 2008. **Address:** Cara Stein, William Morris Agency, 1325 Ave. of the Americas, New York, NY 10019, U.S.A.

QUESADA, Roberto. Spanish (born Spain), b. 1962?. **Genres:** Novels, Theology/Religion. **Career:** SobreVuelo, founder and director; Honduras Embassy, delegate. journalist. **Publications:** El Desertor, 1985; Los Barcos (novel), 1988; The Ships, 1992; El Humano y la Diosa, 1996; (comp.) When the Road is Long, Even Slippers Feel Tight: A Collection of Latin American Proverbs, 1998; The Big Banana, 1999; Nunca Entres por Miami, 2002. Contributor to periodicals. **Address:** Arte Público Press, University of Houston, 452 Cullen Performance Hall, Houston, TX 77204-2004, U.S.A.

QUESTER, George (Herman). American (born United States), b. 1936. **Genres:** International Relations/Current Affairs. **Career:** Harvard University, instructor, assistant professor of government, 1965-70; Cornell University, associate professor, 1970-73, professor of government, 1973-82; National War College, teacher, 1981-82; University of California, teacher, 1981-82; U.S. Naval Academy, teacher, 1981-82; University of Maryland, Department of Government and Politics, professor and head of department, 1982-, chair, Center for International Development and Conflict Management, associate, professor emeritus; National Defense University, faculty, 1999; George Washington University, Elliott School of International Affairs, J.B. and Maurice C. Shapiro visiting professor; United States Army War College, Strategic Studies Institute, external researcher. Writer. **Publications:** Deterrence Before Hiroshima, 1966; Nuclear Diplomacy, 1970; (ed.) Power, Action, and Interaction: Readings on International Politics, 1971; The Politics of Nuclear Proliferation, 1973; The Continuing Problem of International Politics, 1974; Offense and Defense in the International System, 1977; Peaceful P.A.L, 1977; Defense Over Offense in Central Europe, 1978; (ed.) Navies and Arms Control, 1978; Nuclear Proliferation: Breaking the Chain, 1981; American Foreign Policy: The Lost Consensus, 1982; The Future of Nuclear Deterrence, 1986; The International Politics of Television, 1990; Nuclear Pakistan and Nuclear India: Stable Deterrent or Proliferation Challenge?, 1992; (ed.) Nuclear Challenge in Russia and the New States of Eurasia, 1995; Nuclear Monopoly, 2000; Before and After the Cold War: Using Past Forecasts to Predict the

Future, 2002; Nuclear First Strike: Consequences of a Broken Taboo, 2006; Preemption, Prevention and Proliferation, 2009; The Last Time We Were at Global-Zero, 2010. **Address:** Department of Government and Politics, University of Maryland, 3140 Tydings Hall, College Park, MD 20742, U.S.A. **Online address:** gquester@gwu.edu

QUETCHENBACH, Bernard W. American (born United States), b. 1955?. **Genres:** Art/Art History, Literary Criticism And History. **Career:** Florida Southern College, assistant professor of English, associate professor of English. Writer. **Publications:** Back from the Far Field: American Nature Poetry in the Late Twentieth Century, 2000; The Hermit's Act, 2004; (ed. with J. Haldeman) Lake Hollingsworth: Reflections and Studies, 2005. Contributor of articals to periodicals. **Address:** Department of English, Florida Southern College, 111 Lake Hollingsworth Dr., Lakeland, FL 33801-5698, U.S.A. **Online address:** bquetchenbach@flsouthern.edu

QUIATT, Duane. American (born United States), b. 1929. **Genres:** Poetry, Anthropology/Ethnology. **Career:** University of Colorado-Boulder, instructor in English, 1959-62; University of Missouri, assistant professor of anthropology, 1966-69; University of Colorado-Denver, assistant professor, professor of anthropology, 1970-, now professor emeritus. Writer. **Publications:** EDITOR: Primates on Primates, 1972; (with J. Itani) Hominid Culture in Primate Perspective, 1994. OTHERS: (with V. Reynolds) Primate Behaviour: Information, Social Knowledge and the Evolution of Culture, 1993. Contributor of articles to journals. **Address:** Department of Anthropology, University of Colorado, 1201 5th St., Ste. 270, PO Box 173364, Denver, CO 80204, U.S.A. **Online address:** duane.quiatt@ucdenver.edu

QUICK, Matthew. (Matthew M. Quick). American (born United States), b. 1973. **Genres:** Novels, Young Adult Fiction. **Career:** Haddonfield Memorial High School, teacher, 1997-2004. Writer. **Publications:** The Silver Linings Playbook (novel), 2008; Sorta Like a Rockstar (young-adult novel), 2010; Boy21, 2012. **Address:** Collingswood, NJ , U.S.A. **Online address:** matthew@matthewmquick.com

QUICK, Matthew M. *See* **QUICK, Matthew.**

QUICK, William K(ellon). American (born United States), b. 1933. **Genres:** Theology/Religion, History, Local History/Rural Topics. **Career:** Broad Street Methodist Church, associate, 1953-54; United Methodist Church-Zebulon, pastor, 1959-63; United Methodist Church-Greenville, pastor, 1963-69; Saint James Methodist, pastor, 1963-69; Methodist Children's Home, trustee, 1963-69; Trinity Methodist Church, senior pastor, 1969-74; United Methodist Church-Durham, senior pastor, 1969-74; Metropolitan United Methodist Church, senior pastor, 1974-98, emeritus, 1998-; Methodist Retirement Homes, trustee, 1976-84; WDIV-TV, host, 1977-95; Michigan Christian Advocate, trustee, 1980-85; New Center Area Council, director, 1980-95; Duke University, Duke Divinity School, trustee, 1982-92, visiting faculty, 1999-2005; Asbury Theological Seminary, trustee, 1983-88; Radio host, 1987-2005; United Theological Seminary, board of advisor, 1989-90, trustee, 1991-2003; Protestant Radio and Television Center, trustee, 1991-; Ecumenical Theological Seminary, trustee, 1993-98; World Methodist Council, associate general secretary, 2000-06. Writer. **Publications:** Signs of Our Times: A Vision for the Church, 1989; Worship and the Arts, 1994; The Past Speaks to the Future, 1995; Take Five, 5 Minutes with Bill Quick, 1996; Will the City Lose the Church, 1998; Good New from Detroit: Sermons for Living the Practical Christian Life, Preached from a City Pulpit, 1998. Contributor to books and periodicals. **Address:** Duke Divinity School, Duke University, 108 Gray, PO Box 90970, Durham, NC 27708-0968, U.S.A. **Online address:** wkquick@aol.com

QUIGLEY, David. American (born United States), b. 1966?. **Genres:** History, Politics/Government. **Career:** John Jay High School, social studies teacher and community outreach coordinator, 1988-91; New York University, Department of History, instructor, 1994-97, John W. Draper Interdisciplinary M.A. Program in the Humanities and Social Thought, visiting assistant professor, 1997-98; Boston College, College of Arts and Sciences, faculty, 1998-, associate professor and director of graduate studies, professor of history, acting associate dean, 2007-08, interim dean, 2008-09, dean, 2009-, Institute for the Liberal Arts, founding director, 2008-09, Graduate School of Arts and Sciences, interim dean, 2008-09, dean, 2009-. Writer. **Publications:** (Ed. with D.N. Gellman) Jim Crow New York: A Documentary History of Race and Citizenship, 1777-1877, 2003; (ed. with J.M. O'Toole) Boston's Histories: Essays in Honor of Thomas H. O'Connor, 2004; Second Founding: New York City, Reconstruction and the Making of American Democracy, 2004; (contrib.) Slavery in New York, 2005; (contrib.) Encyclopedia of African-American History, vol. I: The Colonial World and the New Nation, 2006; (contrib.) Globalizing American History, 2008. Contributor of articles to periodicals. **Address:** Department of History, Boston College, Maloney Hall, 140 Commonwealth Ave., Chestnut Hill, MA 02467-3859, U.S.A. **Online address:** david.quigley@bc.edu

QUIGLEY, Declan. British (born England), b. 1956. **Genres:** Anthropology/Ethnology, Industrial Relations, Medicine/Health, Self Help. **Career:** Cambridge University, postdoctoral research fellow, 1986-89, lecturer in social anthropology, 1990-92; Queen's University of Belfast, lecturer, reader in social anthropology, 1992-99; St. Andrews University, lecturer in social anthropology, 1999-2002; Barcelona Alexander Technique School, teacher, 2005-. Writer. **Publications:** The Interpretation of Caste, 1993; (with V. Srivastava) L'Inde des tribus oubliees, 1993; (ed. with D.N. Gellner) Contested Hierarchies: A Collaborative Ethnography of Caste among the Newars of the Kathmandu Valley, Nepal, 1995; (contrib.) Tribes of India, 2000; (ed.) The Character of Kingship, 2005. **Address:** calle Santa Anna 28, 1-2, Barcelona, 08002, Spain. **Online address:** declanqui@gmail.com

QUIGLEY, Kevin F. F. American (born United States), b. 1952. **Genres:** Politics/Government. **Career:** U.S. Senate, legislative director to senator John Heinz, 1986-88; Office of Management and Budget, budget examiner, presidential management intern; Pew Charitable Trusts, director of public policy, 1989-95; Asia Society, vice president of policy and business, 1997-; Global Alliance for Workers and Communities, executive director; Vietnam Veterans of America Foundation, acting chief executive officer; National Peace Corps Association, president; Johns Hopkins University, The Paul H. Nitze School of Advanced International Studies, adjunct faculty; George Mason University, School of Public and International Affairs, adjunct faculty; Quigley and Associates, principal and consultant to international affairs organizations; Worldwide Responsible Apparel Production, director; Institute for Sustainable Communities, vice chairman; Carnegie Endowment for International Peace, resident associate. Writer. **Publications:** For Democracy's Sake: Foundations and Democracy Assistance in Central Europe, 1997. **Address:** National Peace Corps Association, 1900 L St. NW, Ste. 404, Washington, DC 20036, U.S.A. **Online address:** president@peacecorpsconnect.org

QUIGLEY, Sarah. American (born United States), b. 1976?. **Genres:** Young Adult Fiction, Romance/Historical. **Career:** Author and educator. **Publications:** TMI, 2009. **Address:** San Francisco, CA , U.S.A. **Online address:** sarah@sarahquigley.com

QUILTER, Deborah. American (born United States), b. 1950. **Genres:** Medicine/Health, Sports/Fitness, Gerontology/Senior Issues, inspirational/Motivational Literature, Travel/Exploration. **Career:** San Francisco Bay Guardian, consumer reporter, 1981-83; Andrews Publications, legal correspondent, 1982-85; Better Health and Living, travel and entertainment editor, 1985-87; Pilates Style Magazine, founding editor; Dance Spirit Magazine, contributing editor; Stage Directions Magazine, contributing editor; RSIhelp.com, founder, 1996-; Mt. Sinai Hospital, Martha Stewart Center, director of yoga; H&D Physical Therapy, movement therapist. Educator. **Publications:** (With E. Pascarelli) Repetitive Strain Injury: A Computer User's Guide, 1994; (contrib.) Total Health for Women, 1995; The Repetitive Strain Injury Recovery Book, 1998. Contributor to periodicals. **Address:** 140 Riverside Blvd., Ste. 1106, New York, NY 10069-0610, U.S.A. **Online address:** dquilter@earthlink.net

QUINDLEN, Anna. American (born United States), b. 1953. **Genres:** Documentaries/Reportage, Essays, Novels, Young Adult Fiction, Travel/Exploration, Reference. **Career:** New York Post, reporter, 1974-77; New York Times, general assignment and city hall reporter, 1977-81, columnist, 1981-94, deputy metropolitan editor, 1983-85; Newsweek, staff, 1999-2009. **Publications:** Living Out Loud (columns), 1988; Object Lessons (novel), 1991; The Tree That Came to Stay, 1992; Thinking Out Loud, 1993; One True Thing, 1994; (intro.) Little Women or Meg, Jo, Beth, and Amy, 1994; (with N. Kelsh) Naked Babies, 1996; Happily Ever After, 1997; Black and Blue: A Novel, 1998; How Reading Changed My Life, 1998; (with N. Kelsh) Siblings, 1998; A Short Guide to a Happy Life, 2000; Blessings: A Novel, 2002; Loud and Clear, 2004; Imagined London: A Tour of the World's Greatest Fictional City, 2004; Being Perfect, 2005; Rise and Shine: A Novel, 2006; A Wrinkle in Time, 2007; Good Dog, Stay, 2007; Every Last One: A Novel, 2010; Lots of

Candles, Plenty of Cake, 2012. **Address:** c/o Amanda Urban, International Creative Management, 730 5th Ave., New York, NY 10019, U.S.A.

QUINLAN, David. British (born England), b. 1942. **Genres:** Film, Biography, Autobiography/Memoirs. **Career:** TV Times, film editor, 1971-, film critic, 1972-2006. **Publications:** Roman Catholicism, 1966; Quinlan's Illustrated Registry of Film Stars, 1981, 5th ed. as Quinlan's Film Stars, 2000 in UK as Quinlan's Illustrated Directory of Film Stars, 1981; Quinlan's Illustrated Guide to Film Directors, 1983; Quinlan's Illustrated Directory of Film Character Actors, 1985, 2nd ed., 1993; British Sound Films: The Studio Years 1928-1959, 1985; Illustrated Encyclopedia of Movie Character Actors, 1986; Wicked Women of the Screen, 1988; Quinlan's Illustrated Directory of Film Comedy Actors, 1992; The Film Lover's Companion: Nearly 2000 Stars and the Movies They Made, 1997; Tom Hanks: A Career in Orbit, 1997; Quinlan's Character Stars, 2004. **Address:** Andrew Mann Ltd., 39-41 North Rd., London, GL N7 9DP, England.

QUINLAN, Mary Lou. American (born United States), b. 1953?. **Genres:** Women's Studies And Issues, Business/Trade/Industry. **Career:** Saint Joseph's University, lecturer, advertising executive, director of communications, 1975-78, adjunct professor of marketing; Avon, director of advertising, 1978-89; Ally & Gargan, senior vice president, 1989-91; DDB Needham Worldwide, executive vice president and managing partner, 1991-94; NW Ayer & Partners, president, 1994-99, chief executive officer, 1995-99; MacManus Group, vice chair, 1999; Just Ask a Woman, founder and chief executive officer, 1999-; St. Joseph's University, board director; 1800flowers.com, board director. **Publications:** Just Ask a Woman: Cracking the Code of What Women Want and How They Buy, 2003; Time off for Good Behavior: How Hardworking Women Can Take a Break and Change Their Lives, 2005; (with J. Drexler and T. Chapman) What She's Not Telling You, Why Women Hide the Whole Truth and What Marketers Can Do About It, 2009. **Address:** Just Ask a Woman, 670 Broadway, Ste. 301, New York, NY 10012, U.S.A. **Online address:** marylou@justaskawoman.com

QUINLAN, Patrick. American (born United States) **Genres:** Novels, Young Adult Non-fiction. **Career:** Journalist, political worker and copywriter. **Publications:** NOVELS: Smoked, 2006; The Takedown, 2007; The Drop-Off, 2008; The Hit, 2009. NON-FICTION: (with R. Hauer) All Those Moments: Stories of Heroes, Villains, Replicants, and Blade Runners, 2007; All Those Moments. **Address:** St. Martin's Press, 175 5th Ave., New York, NY 10010-7703, U.S.A. **Online address:** patrick@patrickquinlan.com

QUINLAN, Susan E(lizabeth). American (born United States), b. 1954. **Genres:** Children's Non-fiction, Sciences, Animals/Pets. **Career:** Alaska Cooperative Wildlife Research Unit, research fellow, 1976-77; U.S. Forest Service, biological technician, 1978-79; U.S. Fish and Wildlife Service, biological technician, 1980; Alaska Department of Fish and Game, game biologist, 1981-88; Linnaea Associates, partner and consultant, 1988-. Writer. **Publications:** (With N. Tankersley and P.D. Arneson) A Guide to Wildlife Viewing in Alaska, 1983; The Case of the Mummified Pigs and Other Mysteries in Nature (for children), 1995; Puffins (for children), 1999; (contrib.) A Manual of Selected Neotropical Migrant Birds of Alaska National Forests, rev. ed., 1999; The Case of the Monkeys that Fell from the Trees: And Other Mysteries in Tropical Nature, 2003; Caribou, 2005. Contributor to books and periodicals. **Address:** Linnaea Associates, 3697 Frenchman Rd., PO Box 82115, Fairbanks, AK 99709-5966, U.S.A. **Online address:** nature@ptialaska.net

QUINN, D. Michael. American (born United States), b. 1944. **Genres:** History, Theology/Religion, History, Biography, Autobiography/Memoirs. **Career:** Brigham Young University, professor, 1976-88; Henry E. Huntington Library, research fellow, 1988-89, 1992-93; KUED-TV, historical consultant, 1989-90, 1994-95; Indiana University-Purdue University, research fellow, 1990-91; National Endowment for the Arts, fellow, 1993-94; Yale University, Department of History, Beinecke senior fellow and associate, 2002-03. Writer. **Publications:** J. Reuben Clark: The Church Years, 1983; Early Mormonism and the Magic World View, 1987, rev. ed., 1998; (ed.) The New Mormon History: Revisionist Essays on the Past, 1992; The Mormon Hierarchy: Origins of Power, 1994; Same-Sex Dynamics among Nineteenth-Century Americans: A Mormon Example, 1996; The Mormon Hierarchy: Extensions of Power, 1997; Elder Statesman: A Biography of J. Reuben Clark, 2002. Contributor to periodicals. **Address:** Signature Books, 564 West 400 North, Salt Lake City, UT 84116, U.S.A.

QUINN, Helen R. American/Australian (born Australia), b. 1943?. **Genres:** Physics, Sciences. **Career:** SLAC National Accelerator Laboratory, research associate, 1967-68, visiting scientist, 1977-78, research associate, 1978-79, scientific staff, 1979-2003, education coordinator, 1988-93, Education and Public Outreach, assistant to the director, 1993-, professor, 2003-; Harvard University, honorary research fellow, 1971-72, assistant professor, 1972-76, associate professor, 1976-77. Writer. **Publications:** (With R.M. Barnett and H. Muhry) The Charm of Strange Quarks: Mysteries and Revolutions of Particle Physics, 2000; NASA's Elementary and Secondary Education Program: Review and Critique, 2008; (with Y. Nir) The Mystery of the Missing Antimatter, 2008. Contributor to periodicals. **Address:** SLAC National Accelerator Laboratory, 2575 Sand Hill Rd., Menlo Park, CA 94025, U.S.A. **Online address:** quinn@slac.stanford.edu

QUINN, Jennifer Post. *See* **POST, Jennifer C.**

QUINN, Pat. New Zealander (born New Zealand), b. 1947. **Genres:** Children's Fiction, Novels, Young Adult Fiction, Law. **Career:** Computer system analyst, writer. **Publications:** How to Appeal Your Illinois Property Taxes Without a Lawyer, 1988; Moving the Earth, 1992; The Value of X, 1993; Sailing with New Zealand Endeavour, 1993; Free Fall, 1994; Sounds Crazy, 1995; Kirsty and Lionel (adult), 1996; Too Chicken, 1997; Go, Horatio!, 1998; Dragor (picture book), 2000; Ratz, 2002; Starz, 2004; Leopold the Wondercat (picture book), 2006. Contributor to periodicals. **Address:** c/o Scholastic New Zealand Ltd., 21 Lady Ruby Dr., PO Box 94407, Auckland, 1730, New Zealand. **Online address:** patq@actrix.gen.nz

QUINN, Peter (John). Australian (born Australia), b. 1941?. **Genres:** Biology, Sciences, Botany, Education. **Career:** University of Sydney, research fellow, 1967; A.R.C. Institute of Animal Physiology, Biochemistry Department, research fellow, 1968-69; Washington University Medical School, Department of Psychiatry, research instructor, 1970; University of Oxford, Department of Biochemistry, senior research fellow, 1972-74; Weizmann Institute of Science, Department of Biochemistry, visiting research fellow, 1973; Hadassah Medical School, visiting research fellow, 1973; University of London, King's College, lecturer, 1974-79, senior lecturer, 1980-85, reader-in-biophysical chemistry, 1985-89; professor of biochemistry, 1989-2009; professor emeritus of biochemistry, 2009-; University of Guelph, visiting professor, 1988; Nagoya University, Monbusho professor, 1993; Robert Gordon University, visiting professor, 1993-99; University of Pittsburgh, adjunct professor of environmental and occupational health, 1997-. Writer. **Publications:** The Molecular Biology of Cell Membranes, 1976; (ed. with C.A. Pasternak) The Molecular Basis of Movement through Membranes, 1985; (ed. with J.L. Harwood) Plant Lipid Biochemistry, Structure and Utilization: The Proceedings of the Ninth International Symposium on Plant Lipids, held at Wye College, Kent, July 1990, 1990; (ed. with R.J. Cherry) Structural and Dynamic Properties of Lipids and Membranes, 1992; Fat-Soluble Vitamins, 1998; (co-ed.) Recent Advances in the Biochemistry of Plant Lipids, 2000; (ed. with V.E. Kagan) Coenzyme Q: Molecular Mechanisms in Health and Disease, 2001; (co-ed.) Phospholipid Metabolism in Apoptosis, 2002; (ed.) Membrane Dynamics and Domains, 2004; (co-author) Lipids: Structure, Physical Properties and Functionality, 2006; (co-ed.) Lipids in Health and Disease, 2008; (ed. with X. Wang) Endotoxins: Structure, Function and Recognition, 2010. **Address:** Department of Biochemistry, King's College, Franklin-Wilkins Bldg., 150 Stamford St., London, GL SE1 9NN, England. **Online address:** p.quinn@kcl.ac.uk

QUINN, Rob. American (born United States), b. 1972. **Genres:** Literary Criticism And History, Novels, Young Adult Fiction, Biography, Autobiography/Memoirs. **Career:** Chelsea House Publishers, web site copywriter and editor. **Publications:** Oscar De La Hoya, 2001. Contributor of articles to newspapers. **Address:** Chelsea House Publishers, 132 W 31st St. 17th Fl., New York, NY 10001, U.S.A. **Online address:** rob_quinn@chelseahouse.com

QUINN, Simon. *See* **SMITH, Martin Cruz.**

QUINN, Sunny. American (born United States), b. 1949. **Genres:** Communications/Media, Music, Photography. **Career:** Connecticut School of Broadcasting, director of education and lead instructor; Top Hat Productions, co-owner; Sunny 104.3, host. Writer, voice-over artist and producer. **Publications:** Morning Mosh, 1998; Put Your Mouth Where the Money Is!: How to Build a Successful Radio and TV Voiceover Business, 1998; Tales of the American Band: Grand Funk Railroad, 1999; On Air, forthcoming. **Address:** Airwave Publications, PO Box 753, Jupiter, FL 33468-0753, U.S.A. **Online address:** sunnyq@airwav.com

QUINN, Tara Taylor. American (born United States) **Genres:** Romance/Historical, Novels. **Career:** Romance Writers of America, president; Dayton Daily News, freelance reporter. Educator. **Publications:** ROMANCE NOVELS: Yesterday's Secrets, 1993; McGillus V. Wright, 1994; No Cure for Love, 1994; Dare to Love, 1994; The Birth Mother, 1996; The Heart of Christmas, 1998; My Babies and Me, 1999; Gabe's Special Delivery, 2000; His Brother's Bride, 2002; For the Children, 2003, rev. ed., 2005; Where the Road Ends, 2003; Street Smart, 2004; Hidden, 2005; The Promise of Christmas, 2005; In Plain Sight, 2006; Merry Christmas, Babies, 2006; A Child's Wish, 2006; The Night We Met, 2007; Sara's Son, 2007; Behind Closed Doors, 2007; At Close Range, 2008; Trusting Ryan, 2008; The Holiday Visitor, 2008; The Sheriff's Daughter, 2008; A Daughter's Trust, 2009; It Happened on Maple Street, 2011. SHELTER VALLEY STORIES: Becca's Baby, 2000; My Sister, Myself, 2000; White Picket Fences, 2000; Just Around the Corner, 2001; Sheltered in His Arms, 2001; The Sheriff of Shelter Valley, 2002; Born in the Valley, 2003; Nothing Sacred, 2004; What Daddy Doesn't Know, 2004; Somebody's Baby, 2005; Full Contact, 2011. OTHERS: Jacob's Girls, 1995; Another Man's Child, 1997; Shotgun Baby, 1997; Father: Unknown, 1998; Her Secret, His Child, 1999; Cassidy's Kids, 2000; Mother's Day, 2001; The Secret Son, 2002; The Rancher's Bride, 2002; (with A. Stevens) Yesterday's Memories, 2003; (with M. Early and J. Macdonald) Celebrates 25 years, 2005; (K.R. Smith and I. Cooper) From Here to Maternity, 2006; The Baby Gamble, 2007; (with J. Brashear and L. Cardillo) The Valentine Gift, 2008; Sophie's Secret, 2009; (co-author) More Than Words, 2009. CHAPMAN FILES SERIES: The First Wife, 2010; The Second Lie, 2010; The Third Secret, 2010; The Fourth Victim, 2010. Works appear in anthologies. **Address:** c/o Author Mail, Harlequin Enterprises Ltd., PO Box 5190, Buffalo, NY 14240-5190, U.S.A. **Online address:** staff@tarataylorquinn.com

QUINNEY, Richard. American (born United States), b. 1934. **Genres:** Criminology/True Crime, Sociology, Autobiography/Memoirs. **Career:** St. Lawrence University, instructor in anthropology and sociology, 1960-62; University of Kentucky, assistant professor, 1962-65; New York University, associate professor, 1965-70, professor, 1970-72; Brooklyn College, visiting professor, 1974-75; Graduate Center of the City University of New York, visiting professor, 1974-75; Society for the Study of Social Problems, chairperson, 1975-77; Brown University, visiting professor, 1975-78, adjunct professor of sociology, 1978-83; American Sociological Association, chairperson, 1977-78; Boston College, distinguished visiting professor, 1978-79, adjunct professor of sociology, 1980-83; University of Wisconsin, visiting professor, 1980; Northern Illinois University, professor, 1983-97, emeritus professor, 1998-. Writer. **Publications:** (With M. Clinard) Criminal Behavior Systems: A Typology, 1967, 2nd ed., 1973; The Problem of Crime, 1970, 3rd ed., 1991; The Social Reality of Crime, 1970; Critique of Legal Order: Crime Control in Capitalist Society, 1974; Criminology: Analysis and Critique of Crime in America, 1975, 2nd ed., 1979; Class, State, and Crime, 1977; Capitalist Society: Readings for a Critical Sociology, 1979; Providence: The Reconstruction of Social and Moral Order, 1980; Social Existence: Metaphysics, Marxism and the Social Sciences, 1982; Journey to a Far Place: Autobiographical Reflections, 1991; For the Time Being: Ethnography of Everyday Life, 1998; Erich Fromm and Critical Criminology, 2000; Bearing Witness to Crime and Social Justice, 2000; Borderland, 2001; Where Yet the Sweet Birds Sing, 2006; Once again the Wonder, 2006; Of Time and Place: A Farm in Wisconsin, 2006; Tales from the Middle Border, 2007; Field Notes, 2008; Things Once Seen, 2008. EDITOR: Crime and Justice in Society, 1969; Criminal Justice in America, 1974; (ed. with P. Beirne) Marxism and Law, 1982; (with H.E. Pepinsky) Criminology as Peacemaking, 1991; (with R.J. Berger) Storytelling Sociology: Narrative as Social Inquiry, 2005; A Lifetime Burning, 2010; Once Upon an Island, 2011; A Farm in Wisconsin, 2012. Contributor to periodicals. **Address:** Northern Illinois University, 1425 W Lincoln Hwy., DeKalb, IL 60115-2828, U.S.A. **Online address:** rquinney@earthlink.net

QUIÑONES, Magaly. Also writes as Marta Magaly Quiñones Perez. American (born United States), b. 1945?. **Genres:** Poetry, Literary Criticism And History. **Career:** University of Puerto Rico, Library Planning, librarian. Writer. **Publications:** Entre me voz y el tiempo, 1969; Era que el mundo era, 1974; Zambayllu, 1976; Cantándole a la noche misma, 1978; En la pequeña Antilla, 1982; Nombrar, 1985; Razón de lucha razón de amor, 1989; Sueños de papel, 1996; Mi Mundo/My World, 2003; Patio de fondo, 2003. **Address:** University of Puerto Rico, PO Box 23301, San Juan, PR 00931-3301, U.S.A. **Online address:** mquinone@rrpac.upr.clu.edu

QUINONES, Ricardo J(oseph). American (born United States), b. 1935. **Genres:** Literary Criticism And History, Adult Non-fiction. **Career:** Harvard University, teaching assistant, 1960-62, history and literature, tutor, 1962-63, visiting professor, 1970; Claremont McKenna College, assistant professor of comparative literature, 1963-69, associate professor of comparative literature, 1969-75, professor of English and comparative literature, 1975-, Department of Literature, chair, 1977-80, 1990-92, Claremont Graduate Center, faculty, 1965, Villaci Tatti visiting fellow, 1981, Benjamin Z. Gould Center for Humanistic Studies, director, 1986-, Josephine Olp Weeks professor of comparative literature, 1987-, now professor emeritus of literature; City University of New York, visiting professor, 1970-71; University of California, faculty, 1987-90; University of Kansas, distinguished visiting professor, 1998-2000. Writer. **Publications:** The Renaissance Discovery of Time, 1972; Dante Alighieri, 1979; Mapping Literary Modernism: Time and Development, 1985; (ed. with M. Chefdor and A. Wachtel) Modernism: Challenges and Perspectives, 1986; The Changes of Cain: Violence and the Lost Brother in Cain and Abel Literature, 1991; Foundation Sacrifice in Dante's Commedia, 1994; Dualisms: The Agons Of The Modern World, 2007; Erasmus and Voltaire, 2007; Through the Years, 2010; Sorting of the Ways, 2011. **Address:** Department of Comparative Literature, Claremont McKenna College, ACB-CGU, 888 Columbia Ave., Kravis Ctr., Claremont, CA 91711, U.S.A. **Online address:** ricardo.quinones@claremontmckenna.edu

QUINONES, Sam. American/German (born Germany), b. 1958. **Genres:** Cultural/Ethnic Topics, Classics, Young Adult Non-fiction. **Career:** Orange County Register, journalist, 1987; Stockton Record, crime reporter, 1988-92; Tacoma News-Tribune, 1992-94; Mexico Insight (magazine), reporter, 1994; freelance writer, 1994-2004; Los Angeles Times, reporter on immigration and gangs, 2004-. **Publications:** True Tales from Another Mexico: The Lynch Mob, the Popsicle Kings, Chalino, and the Bronx, 2001; Antonio's Gun and Delfino's Dream: True Tales of Mexican Migration, 2007. **Address:** Los Angeles Times, 202 W 1st St., Los Angeles, CA 90012, U.S.A. **Online address:** samquinones7@yahoo.com

QUIÑONES PEREZ, Marta Magaly. *See* **QUIÑONES, Magaly.**

QUIÑONEZ, Ernesto. American (born United States), b. 1966?. **Genres:** Novels, Young Adult Fiction. **Career:** City of New York, Board of Education, teacher, 1996-2000; Indiana University, Writers Conference, faculty, 2001; Cornell University, Department of English, assistant professor. Writer. **Publications:** Bodega Dreams, 2000; El Fuego de Chango, trans. as Chango's Fire, 2004; Taina's Song, forthcoming; Botanica Tales, forthcoming. **Address:** Department of English, Cornell University, 267 Goldwin Smith, Ithaca, NY 14853-3201, U.S.A. **Online address:** eq25@cornell.edu

QUINSEY, Katherine M. Canadian (born Canada), b. 1955?. **Genres:** Women's Studies And Issues, Theology/Religion, Poetry, Humanities. **Career:** University of Windsor, associate professor of English, 1989, head of department. Writer. **Publications:** (Ed.) Broken Boundaries: Women & Feminism in Restoration Drama, 1996; (co-ed.) Lumen: Selected Proceedings of the Canadian Society for Eighteenth Century Studies, 1998; (co-ed.) Canadian Poetry, 2007; Tempting Grace: The Religious Imagination of Alexander Pope, forthcoming; Rhyme and Print: Pope, Poetry and the Material Text, forthcoming. Contributor to periodicals. **Address:** Department of English Language, Literature & Creative Writing, University of Windsor, 2-104 Chrysler Hall, North Windsor, ON N9B 3P4, Canada. **Online address:** kateq@uwindsor.ca

QUINSEY, Mary Beth. American (born United States), b. 1948. **Genres:** Children's Non-fiction, Medicine/Health, Sex, Young Adult Non-fiction, Reference. **Career:** Welfare eligibility examiner, 1970-72; Bates Vocational School, childbirth educator, 1974-, coordinator of childbirth program, 1987-; Oakland Alternative High School, Teen Parenting Program, teacher, 1988-93; Washington State, program manager. Writer. **Publications:** Toward a Better Beginning, 1981, 13th ed., 1996; Why Does That Man Have Such a Big Nose?, 1986; Who Shot the Stork?, 1990. **Address:** Bates Vocational School, Ruston Campus, 5219 N Shirley St., Tacoma, WA 98407-6599, U.S.A.

QUINTERO, Ruben. American (born United States), b. 1949. **Genres:** Literary Criticism And History, Humanities. **Career:** California State University, Department of English, chair and professor. Writer. **Publications:** Literate Culture: Pope's Rhetorical Art, 1992; (ed. and contrib.) A Companion to Satire: Ancient and Modern, 2007. **Address:** Department of English, California State University, 5151 State University Dr., Los Angeles, CA 90032, U.S.A. **Online address:** rquinte@calstatela.edu

QUIRK, Anne (E.). American (born United States), b. 1956?. **Genres:** Children's Fiction, Dance/Ballet. **Career:** Harper and Row, marketing staff, 1977-79, 1981-85; Philomel/Putnam, marketing staff, 1979-81; Little and Brown, marketing staff, 1986-93; freelance marketing and advertising consultant, 1993-2001; Horn Book, associate publisher, 2001-. Writer. **Publications:** Dancing with Great-Aunt Cornelia, 1997. **Address:** The Horn Book Inc., 56 Roland St., Ste. 200, Boston, MA 02129-1235, U.S.A.

QUIRK, Joe. American (born United States), b. 1966. **Genres:** Novels, History. **Career:** Writer. **Publications:** The Ultimate Rush, 1998; Sperm Are from Men, Eggs Are from Women: The Real Reason Men and Women Are Different, 2006; Exult (novel), 2009; Call to The Rescue: The Story of The Marine Mammal Center, 2009; Tools Are From Men, Talk Is From Women: Why Your Partner's Brain Is Weird, forthcoming. Contributor to periodicals. **Address:** Running Press Book Publishers, 2300 Chestnut St., Philadelphia, PA 19103, U.S.A.

QUIRK, Randolph. British/German (born Germany), b. 1920. **Genres:** Language/Linguistics, History, Reference. **Career:** University of London, University College, lecturer in English, 1947-54, professor of English language, 1960-68, Quain professor of English, 1968-81, vice-chancellor, Survey of English Usage, director; University of Durham, reader, 1954-58, professor of English language, 1958-60. Writer. **Publications:** The Concessive Relation in Old English Poetry, 1954, 1973; (with C.L. Wrenn) An Old English Grammar, 1955, 1958; (with P.G. Foote) The Saga of Gunnlaug Serpent-Tongue, 1957; (with A.H. Smith) The Teaching of English, 1958; The Use of English, 1962, 2nd ed., 1968; (with D. Crystal) Systems of Prosodic and Paralinguistic Features in English, 1964; (with J. Svartvik) Investigating Linguistic Acceptability, 1966; Essays on the English Language, 1968; (with S. Greenbaum) Elicitation Experiments in English: Linguistic Studies in Use and Attitude, 1970; (with S. Greenbaum, G. Leech and J. Svartvik) A Grammar of Contemporary English, 1972; The English Language and Images of Matter, 1972; (with S. Greenbaum) A University Grammar of English, 1973; (with S. Greenbaum) A Concise Grammar of Contemporary English, 1973; The Linguist and the English Language, 1974; (with V. Adams and D. Davy) Old English Literature, 1975; Charles Dickens and Appropriate Language, 1977; (ed. with J. Svartvik) A Corpus of English Conversation, 1980; (foreword) Growth and Structure of the English Language, 1982; Style and Communication, 1982; (co-author) A Comprehensive Grammar of the English Language, 1985; (ed. with H.G. Widdowson) English in the World, 1985; Words at Work: Lectures on Textual Structure, 1986; (with S. Greenbaum) A Student's Grammar of the English Language, 1990; (with G. Stein) English in Use, 1990; (with G. Stein and Y. Terasawa) An Introduction to Standard English, 1993; Grammatical and Lexical Variance in English, 1995. **Address:** Department of English, University of London, University College, Gower St., London, GL WC1 6BT, England.

QUIRK, William J. American (born United States), b. 1933. **Genres:** Law, Politics/Government. **Career:** City of New York, Law Department, Department of Buildings, general counsel and assistant corporation counsel, 1966-70; University of South Carolina, professor of law, 1970-; The New Republic, contributing editor, 1981-84; State Tax Notes, South Carolina correspondent, 1990-. **Publications:** (With R.R. Bridwell) Abandoned: The Betrayal of the American Middle Class since World War II, 1992; (with R.R. Bridwell) Judicial Dictatorship, 1995; Courts and Congress: America's Unwritten Constitution, 2008; Strippers and the Court-Eliminating the Unwritten Constitution from American Democracy, 2008. Contributor of articles to magazines and journals. **Address:** School of Law, University of South Carolina, Rm. 416, 701 Main St., Columbia, SC 29208, U.S.A. **Online address:** quirkwj@law.sc.edu

QUIROGA, Alejandro. British/Spanish (born Spain), b. 1972. **Genres:** Politics/Government, History. **Career:** Newcastle University, reader in Spanish history. Writer and historian. **Publications:** Los origenes del Nacionalcatolicismo José Pemartin y la Dictadura de Primo de Rivera, 2006; (with S. Balfour) The Reinvention of Spain: Nation and Identity since Democracy, 2007; Making Spaniards: Primo de Rivera and the Nationalization of the Masses, 1923-1930, 2007; (ed.) Soldados de Dios y apóstoles de la patria Las drechas españolas en la Europa de entreguerras, 2010. Contributor to books. **Address:** Newcastle University, Armstrong Bldg., Newcastle upon Tyne, TW NE1 7RU, England. **Online address:** alejandro.quiroga@ncl.ac.uk

QUIROZ, Anthony. American (born United States), b. 1958. **Genres:** History, Law, Sociology, Politics/Government. **Career:** Victoria College, adjunct instructor, 1995-96; Texas A&M University, assistant professor, professor, 1996-, Joe B. Frantz associate professor of history, Department of Humanities, chairman. Writer. **Publications:** Claiming Citizenship: Mexican Americans in Victoria, Texas, 2005. Contributor to books and periodicals. **Address:** Faculty Center, Texas A & M University, Rm. 284, 6300 Ocean Dr., Corpus Christi, TX 78412-5503, U.S.A. **Online address:** anthony.quiroz@tamucc.edu

QVORTRUP, Mads. British/Danish (born Denmark), b. 1967. **Genres:** Politics/Government, Philosophy. **Career:** IRI, research director, 1998-99; University College London, instructor, 1998-99, lecturer and senior researcher, 2008-10; Referendum Institute, senior research fellow, 1999-; Aarhus University, Department of Politcal Science, assistant professor, 1999-2001, teacher, 2001-02; London School of Economics and Political Science, lecturer and fellow, 2001-04; Robert Gordon University, research professor of political science, 2004-08, research chair of political science; University of Sydney, visiting professor, 2005; University of New South Wales, fellow; United Kingdom Defence Academy, senior lecturer, 2010-, research director; Cranfield University, Department of Management and Security, Centre for International Security and Resilience, senior lecturer of comparative politics and research director; TV2 News, analyst, 2010-11. Writer. **Publications:** A Comparative Study of Referendums: Government by the People, 2002, 2nd ed., 2005; The Political Philosophy of Jean-Jacques Rousseau: The Impossibility of Reason, 2003; Tony Blair, Host & Son, 2006; The Politics of Participation: From Athens to E-Democracy, 2007; (trans.) Michiavelli, Belfagor, 2008; The Art of Running a Little Country, Borgen, Copenhagen, 2009; Direct Democracy: Can Referendums and Citizens' Initiatives Strengthen Representative Government?, 2012; From Bullets to Ballots: Referendums on Ethno-national Issues, 2012. Contributor to periodicals. **Address:** Department of Management and Security, Cranfield University, Shrivenham Campus, Swindon, WT SN6 8LA, England. **Online address:** m.qvortrup@cranfield.ac.uk